FEDERAL RULES OF CIVIL PROCEDURE

Amendments received to May 21, 2007

2007–2008 EDUCATIONAL EDITION

THOMSON
WEST

Mat #40521389

© 2007 Thomson/West

ISBN-13: 978–0–314–17209–9

RELATED PRODUCTS IN FEDERAL LAW FROM WEST

FEDERAL PRACTICE

COURTROOM HANDBOOK ON FEDERAL EVIDENCE

Steven Goode and Olin Guy Wellborn III

FEDERAL CIVIL RULES HANDBOOK

Steven Baicker–McKee, William Janssen and John B. Corr

FEDERAL CRIMINAL RULES HANDBOOK

Laurie L. Levenson

MODERN SCIENTIFIC EVIDENCE

David L. Faigman, David H. Kaye, Michael J. Saks and Joseph Sanders

FEDERAL JURY PRACTICE AND INSTRUCTIONS

Kevin F. O'Malley, Jay E. Grenig and William C. Lee

[Also available in CD–ROM]

FEDERAL PRACTICE AND PROCEDURE

Charles Alan Wright, Arthur R. Miller, Mary Kay Kane, Edward H. Cooper, Richard L. Marcus, Kenneth W. Graham, Victor James Gold, Richard D. Freer, Patrick J. Schlitz, Vikram David Amar, Joan E. Steinman, Andrew D. Leipold, Peter J. Henning, Sarah H. Welling, Nancy J. King, Susan R. Klein, Charles H. Koch, Jr., and Michael H. Graham

[Also available in CD–ROM]

POLICE MISCONDUCT AND CIVIL RIGHTS—FEDERAL JURY PRACTICE AND INSTRUCTIONS

Stephen Yagman and Harold S. Lewis, Jr.

[Includes Instructions on Disk]

WEST'S FEDERAL ADMINISTRATIVE PRACTICE

Authored by Federal Practice Experts

WEST'S FEDERAL FORMS

Authored by Federal Practice Experts

[Also available in CD–ROM]

FEDERAL COURT OF APPEALS MANUAL

David G. Knibb

FEDERAL PRACTICE AND PROCEDURE—FEDERAL PRACTICE DESKBOOK

Charles Alan Wright and Mary Kay Kane

HANDBOOK OF FEDERAL EVIDENCE

Michael H. Graham

TREATISE ON CONSTITUTIONAL LAW

Ronald D. Rotunda and John E. Nowak

III

RELATED PRODUCTS

THE JUDGE'S EVIDENCE BENCHBOOK
Leo H. Whinery, Theodore P. Roberts, and Robert B. Smith

ADMINISTRATIVE LAW AND PRACTICE
Charles H. Koch, Jr.

FEDERAL RULES OF EVIDENCE WITH TRIAL OBJECTIONS
Charles B. Gibbons

BUSINESS AND COMMERCIAL LITIGATION IN FEDERAL COURTS
Robert L. Haig, Editor–In–Chief

NEWBERG ON CLASS ACTIONS, 3rd
Herbert Newberg and Alba Conte

HANDBOOK OF FEDERAL CIVIL DISCOVERY AND DISCLOSURE
Jay E. Grenig and Jeffrey S. Kinsler
[Includes forms on Disk]

ANNOTATED MANUAL FOR COMPLEX LITIGATION
David F. Herr

MULTIDISTRICT LITIGATION MANUAL
David F. Herr

ANNOTATED REFERENCE MANUAL ON SCIENTIFIC EVIDENCE
Michael J. Saks, David L. Faigman, David H. Kaye, and Joseph Sanders

———————

United States Code Annotated
West's Federal Practice Digest 4th
United States Code Congressional and Administrative News

———————

CRIMINAL PRACTICE

SEARCH AND SEIZURE
Wayne R. LaFave

SUBSTANTIVE CRIMINAL LAW
Wayne R. LaFave

CRIMINAL LAW DEFENSES
Paul H. Robinson

CRIMINAL PROCEDURE
Wayne R. LaFave and Jerold H. Israel

FEDERAL SENTENCING LAW AND PRACTICE
Thomas W. Hutchison, Peter B. Hoffman, Deborah Young, and Sigmund G. Popko

FEDERAL SENTENCING GUIDELINES HANDBOOK
Roger W. Haines, Jr., Frank O. Bowman III, and Jennifer C. Woll

———————

RELATED PRODUCTS

Corpus Juris Secundum
West's Federal Case News
Federal Civil Judicial Procedure and Rules
Federal Criminal Code and Rules
Federal Environmental Laws
Federal Immigration Laws and Regulations
Federal Labor Laws
Federal Sentencing Guidelines
Federal Social Security Laws, Selected Statutes and Regulations
Federal Intellectual Property Laws and Regulations
Federal Litigator
Reference Manual on Scientific Evidence, 2d

TAX PUBLICATIONS

Federal Tax Regulations
Internal Revenue Code
Internal Revenue Acts

To order any of these Federal practice tools, call your
West Representative or **1–800–328–9352**.

INTERNET ACCESS

Contact the West Editorial Department directly with your
questions and suggestions by e-mail at west.editor@thomson.com.
Visit West's home page at
west.thomson.com.

*

WESTLAW ELECTRONIC RESEARCH GUIDE

Westlaw—Expanding the Reach of Your Library

Westlaw is West's online legal research service. With Westlaw, you experience the same quality and integrity that you have come to expect from West books, plus quick, easy access to West's vast collection of statutes, case law materials, public records, and other legal resources, in addition to current news articles and business information. For the most current and comprehensive legal research, combine the strengths of West books and Westlaw.

When you research with westlaw.com you get the convenience of the Internet combined with comprehensive and accurate Westlaw content, including exclusive editorial enhancements, plus features found only in westlaw.com such as ResultsPlus™ or StatutesPlus.™

Accessing Databases Using the Westlaw Directory

The Westlaw Directory lists all databases on Westlaw and contains links to detailed information relating to the content of each database. Click **Directory** on the westlaw.com toolbar. There are several ways to access a database even when you don't know the database identifier. Browse a directory view. Scan the directory. Type all or part of a database name in the Search these Databases box. The Find a Database Wizard can help you select relevant databases for your search. You can access up to ten databases at one time for user-defined multibase searching.

Retrieving a Specific Document

To retrieve a specific document by citation or title on westlaw.com click **Find&Print** on the toolbar to display the Find a Document page. If you are unsure of the correct citation format, type the publication abbreviation, e.g., **xx st** (where xx is a state's two-letter postal abbreviation), in the Find this document by citation box and click **Go** to display a fill-in-the-blank template. To retrieve a specific case when you know one or more parties' names, click **Find a Case by Party Name**.

KeyCite®

KeyCite, the citation research service on Westlaw, makes it easy to trace the history of your case, statute, administrative decision or regulation to determine if there are recent updates, and to find other documents that cite your document. KeyCite will also find pending legislation relating to federal or state statutes. Access the powerful features of KeyCite from the westlaw.com toolbar, the **Links** tab, or KeyCite flags in a document display. KeyCite's red and yellow warning flags tell you at a glance whether your document has negative history. Depth-of-treatment stars help you focus on the most important citing references. KeyCite Alert allows you to monitor the status of your case, statute or rule, and automatically sends you updates at the frequency you specify.

ResultsPlus™

ResultsPlus is a Westlaw technology that automatically suggests additional information related to your search. The suggested materials are accessible by a set of links that appear to the right of your westlaw.com search results:

- Go directly to relevant ALR® articles and Am Jur® annotations.

- Find on-point resources by key number.
- See information from related treatises and law reviews.

StatutesPlus™

When you access a statutes database in westlaw.com you are brought to a powerful Search Center which collects, on one toolbar, the tools that are most useful for fast, efficient retrieval of statutes documents:

- Have a few key terms? Click **Statutes Index**.
- Know the common name? Click **Popular Name Table**.
- Familiar with the subject matter? Click **Table of Contents**.
- Have a citation or section number? Click **Find by Citation**.
- Interested in topical surveys providing citations across multiple state statutes? Click **50 State Surveys**.
- Or, simply search with **Natural Language** or **Terms and Connectors.**

When you access a statutes section, click on the **Links** tab for all relevant links for the current document that will also include a KeyCite section with a description of the KeyCite status flag. Depending on your document, links may also include administrative, bill text, and other sources that were previously only available by accessing and searching other databases.

Additional Information

Westlaw is available on the Web at www.westlaw.com.

For search assistance, call the West Reference Attorneys at
1–800–REF–ATTY (1–800–733–2889).

For technical assistance, call West Customer Technical Support at
1–800–WESTLAW (1–800–937–8529).

TABLE OF CONTENTS

―――――

APPENDICES

*

HISTORICAL INTRODUCTION

The Revolution and the Constitutional Role of the Supreme Court of the United States

The 13 American states that won their independence in 1783 attempted to conduct foreign relations jointly through the Continental Congress, an organization that had successfully conducted the Revolution. By 1787, the ineffectiveness of this organization was apparent. Many of the deficiencies pertained to the judicial institutions of the time. Western boundaries were disputed. The states were engaged in commercial competition, creating stress among them; merchants from other states were often victims of discrimination by local courts and local law. Merchants, especially those from foreign lands, such as England, were often unable to collect debts. This was an especially serious problem, be-cause the treaty of peace with the United Kingdom guaranteed the payment of debts by American debtors, a guarantee that the Continental Congress was impotent to perform. There was some possibility that His Majesty's Royal Navy would return to collect the debts if American courts did not.

There were other problems, the greatest being fears of larger landowners and merchants in many states that the small republics were unstable. The Revolution had been fought for the declared purpose of establishing the sovereignty of the people. Henceforth, said the Declaration of Independence, power would come up from the people, and not down from their rulers. But faith in this idea was not widely shared among persons of property, influence, and status. The fear was that the ignorance, greed, and mutual distrust of "the people" would soon cause the states to disintegrate into chaos, followed by despotism.

So, in 1787, 11 of the 13 states sent representatives to a meeting in Philadelphia to organize a new national government. The meeting was contentious, but the proposed Constitution was its product. Among the issues debated at the Constitutional Convention was whether the new government should take over the judicial function. It was early agreed that there should be a Supreme Court of the United States that would have responsibility for assuring compliance with the Constitution. An important feature of that Constitution was the division of political power; the purpose of those divisions was to prevent government "by the people" from getting out of control. "The people" were pitted against one another to assure balance. Thus, limited political powers were conferred on the national government, and the rest retained by the several states. And power within the national government was divided between two independent legislative bodies and an independent executive, each selected by a different process. A Supreme Court was clearly needed to maintain these limits of power. In this feature lay the most distinctive feature of American government, the use of law and courts to limit the powers of the other political organs.

Concurrent Jurisdiction: The Establishment of the Lower Federal Courts

Should there be lower federal courts? Some argued that the national government should take over the judicial function altogether. Others argued that the state judicial systems then in place should be retained as the lower courts to resolve private disputes between citizens. It was first decided by the Convention that there should be no lower federal courts, but then a compromise was reached, leaving to the Congress the decision whether there should be lower federal courts, yet limiting the power of Congress to confer jurisdiction on any courts that it might create. The Constitutional text as ratified by the people of the 13 states is set forth in Article III. *See Appendix B: The United States Constitution, this pamphlet.*

HISTORICAL INTRODUCTION

Ratification of the Constitution containing Article III was strongly contested in all states. One of the damaging arguments against ratification was that the power of Congress to create federal courts was a menace to the sovereignty of the people. Dire threats were heard; the federal judges would become the tool of the gentry and of the merchant class and would deny protection to the people of the farm, especially poor debtors.

To secure ratification, it was necessary for those favoring the Constitution to agree to ten amendments. These came to be known as the Bill of Rights. The Fifth, Sixth and Seventh Amendments are directed primarily at Article III and served to quiet fears of the federal judiciary. The texts of these two amendments are set forth in *Appendix B* of this pamphlet.

Among the first acts of the first Congress of the United States was the exercise in the Judiciary Act of 1789 of the power conferred by Article III to establish lower federal courts. The purpose at that time was to protect aliens (especially English creditors) and merchants engaged in interstate commerce; its major jurisdictional provision remains, with slight modification, as part of the statutory law governing the federal courts. *See Section 1332(a), Title 28, United States Code, Judiciary and Judicial Procedure (Selected Provisions), this pamphlet.*

As Article III contemplates, each state in the federal union maintains its own system of courts. These courts, unlike the federal courts, are not all courts of *limited* jurisdiction, but may be courts of *general* jurisdiction. That is, they may entertain any action of any kind that is not specifically directed by legislation to a specialized court. These courts therefore often exercise jurisdiction that is *concurrent* with the jurisdiction of the federal courts. That is to say that many actions could be brought in either a state or a federal court. A common tactical decision faced by American lawyers is whether to bring an action in a federal or a state court, or whether to remove to a federal court an action previously brought by an adversary in state court.

The Independence of the Federal and State Judiciaries

A serious problem faced in the text of the Constitution was the identity of the judges. English judges were selected from an elite social class that did not exist in most of America. Nor was there in America any tradition of a separate judicial profession of the kind that has since developed in Germany, Japan, and other countries. It was therefore clear that the federal judges appointed under Article III would be chosen from among the practicing lawyers, or perhaps occasionally from the judges of the courts of the several states. They would necessarily be persons qualified by standards more political then technocratic.

In requiring that the selection of judges be made by the President with the "advice and consent" of the Senate, the Constitution recognized that the federal judicial appointments would be politically divisive. The drafters of the Constitution knew that by subjecting political power to legal constraints they were necessarily politicizing the legal institutions that would impose those restraints. The American judiciary would in this respect be unlike any then known to the draftsmen of the Constitution.

Unsurprisingly, the first national political crisis centered on the federal judiciary. In 1800, Thomas Jefferson was elected President. Before he took office, his predecessor, President John Adams, and the outgoing Federalist Congress, created additional federal judgeships and President Adams appointed many judges who were hostile to Jefferson's political program. Jefferson seriously considered an effort to remove the opposition judges by impeachment, and one Supreme Court Justice, Samuel Chase, was impeached. Jefferson, there is no doubt, would have liked to have removed as soon as possible, the Chief Justice appointed by President Adams, who was Jefferson's cousin, John Marshall. The Chase removal failed in the Senate of the United States and the Marshall removal was never attempted. Federal judges have since been removed

only in rare instances of corruption. There is thus important meaning in the term of Article III providing that judges shall be appointed "for good behavior;" federal judicial appointments are nearly always lifetime appointments.

Especially when there is a political difference between the President and Congress, as there may often be, judicial appointments are often contested. In 1988, Congress controlled by the Democratic Party refused after a bitter contest to confirm the nomination by Republican President Ronald Reagan of Robert Bork to the Supreme Court. Nevertheless, because of the important role of the federal courts, the persons appointed as federal judges, have generally been persons of substantial professional merit who not only enjoyed some political influence in the party of the President, but who also commanded some and often much respect among lawyers where they practiced. It is rare for a person less than 40 years of age to be appointed to a federal judgeship, and many are appointed who are near the age of 60.

From the beginning, the federal courts were aware of their somewhat precarious political position. They were careful to avoid unnecessary exposure to political controversy. This was reflected in two ways. First, the phrase "case or controversy" in Article III was recognized to mean that the federal courts should perform no role other than adjudication defined rather narrowly. Second, the federal courts were scrupulous in refusing to decide any case not within the limits of their jurisdiction as defined by Congress pursuant to Article III.

State courts often play a political role in state government analogous to the role played by the federal courts in the federal constitutional scheme. Although the Supreme Court of the United States retains constitutional authority to review the actions of state courts to assure their compliance with national law, state courts are otherwise independent of any federal control or influence. No officer of the government of the United States has any influence whatever in the selection of the judges of the state courts.

Most states provide for the popular, direct election of judges for fixed terms. Many of these states employ diverse means of protecting judicial elections from some of the adverse consequences of such elective judicial politics, to assure some degree of independence of their judges from the control of those who provide campaign funds or otherwise influence the electorate. Thus, in some states, judges are assured of an opportunity to run for reelection without a named opponent, the voters choosing only to retain the judge or not. In some states, the Governor has the power of initial appointment, but is required to secure the assent of a non-political commission that is expected to appraise the "merit" of judicial candidates. Despite such efforts to moderate the influence of elective politics on the judiciary, state court judges are, even more than the federal judges, generally qualified by standards that are more political than technocratic.

Because state court judges have political responsibilities that are regarded as less consequential, decide more cases involving smaller stakes, and are usually paid less than federal judges, their offices tend to be filled by persons who, as a group, are less highly regarded by lawyers than the federal judges as a group. In rural areas, the state court judge is likely to be a local person who is politically accountable to a local electorate; particularly in such areas, the "hometown" advantage of the local litigant can be daunting to an outsider.

The Effect of Nationalization on the Dual Court System

For many years, the federal courts generally conformed their procedure to that of local state courts. That is, a federal court sitting in Virginia conformed its procedure to that of state courts of the Commonwealth of Virginia. This allowed Virginia lawyers to move comfortably from state

to federal court and back. This arrangement reflected the structure of state legal profession in America, which was highly localized, each state having its own distinctive bar.

Much of the state civil procedure was initially derived from English tradition, with substantial modifications. Many states retained the English distinction between Law and Equity; Law was the body of doctrine enforced in England by the Law Courts (*e.g.*, Court of Common Pleas or the King's Bench), while Equity was the body of doctrine en-forced in England by the Chancellor sitting in Chancery. Many states also retained the English common law forms of action; all this usually meant as a practical matter was that in an action "at Law," a plaintiff was required to correctly identify the legal theory underlying his claim at the very outset of the litigation.

Much of this anachronistic procedure was swept away by the movement for procedural law reform that first surfaced in New York in 1848. The Codes of Civil Procedure enacted in most states at that time provided for state abolition of almost all traces of English law, merging Law and Equity into a single system and abolishing the forms of action.

The American Civil War was fought from 1861 to 1865. That war had many consequences, but at least two bore directly on the judiciary. First, as a conclusion of the War, the Constitution was subjected to three additional amendments. One of these, the Fourteenth, extended the Due Process Clause, making it applicable to actions of state courts and governments as well as federal. Thereafter, the civil procedure of state courts was subject to basic minimum standards of fairness established by the Supreme Court of the United States. To a minimum degree, state procedure was federalized. Secondly, the Congress of the United States was thereafter in a position to enact legislation regulating the national economy. As part of that activity, the Congress enlarged the civil jurisdiction of the federal courts in an important way; in 1875, it enacted the provision that presently appears as Section 1331 of Title 28. See *Title 28, United States Code, Judiciary and Judicial Procedure (Selected Provisions), this pamphlet.*

This provision further enlarged the political role of the federal courts. In part, this has been a result of the Constitutional scheme to divide the political power within the government of the United States. Because it is so divided, legislative power is often exercised in a manner that expresses unclear mandates. The two houses of Congress and the President are sometimes able to agree to little more than that there is a social or economic problem requiring a federal solution; they may then leave the details of that solution to the federal courts. The antitrust laws of the United States are an excellent example of law that is left almost wholly to the federal courts to define, with almost no guidance from Congress. Other examples abound.

As a result of the growth of the federal courts' role in the national economy, the federal judicial has been steadily enlarged. In 1891, the United States Court of Appeals were established as intermediate courts of appeals to review decisions of the district courts. Since 1891, access to the Supreme Court has by stages been limited to cases that it chooses to review.

The federal courts played a significant role in the development of state law regulating the national economy. On a number of occasions that role was politically controversial. In the continuing struggle between railroads and shippers, who were usually small farmers, the federal courts were generally enforcing the rights of the railroads. In enforcing the law of patents against farmers making use of such ideas as barbed wire and windmills, the federal courts were again seen as a forum in which farmers were at a disadvantage.

The federal courts also became the place for railroads to go to secure favorable results on accident claims by workers, and where employers sometimes went to secure injunctions against strikes. Most of the practices that were seen as anti-labor were in due course constrained by Congressional legislation, as the labor unions acquired political power.

HISTORICAL INTRODUCTION

Lawyers practicing federal law became troubled by the differences in procedure in the different federal courts, each conforming generally to the practice of its local state court. The American Bar Association, established in 1879, led a campaign for national uniformity. In 1934, Congress authorized the Supreme Court of the United States to promulgate rules of "pleading and practice" that would be uniform among all the district courts of the United States. That authority is now set forth in §§ 2071–2077. *See Title 28, United States Code, Judiciary and Judicial Procedure (Selected Sections), this pamphlet.*

Such rules were promulgated in 1938 as the Federal Rules of Civil Procedure. The most notable of these rules were those bearing on discovery; private lawyers representing litigants are authorized to use the power of the court to compel adversaries and non-parties to cooperate in their efforts to secure evidence bearing on a case. Other rules have since been appended by the Court. Since 1938, the states have modified their civil procedure to conform generally to the federal practice, but significant differences remain in many.

PAUL D. CARRINGTON

*

AN OUTLINE OF THE PROCEDURE
IN A CIVIL ACTION

[Reprinted from Friedenthal, Miller, Sexton and Hershkoff, CIVIL PROCEDURE, 9th Ed., Ch. 1.B.]

Lawsuits do not begin themselves. Someone must first decide to sue someone else. If this decision is made intelligently, the person choosing to sue must have weighed several matters, among which at least three are basic.

A potential litigant obviously feels aggrieved or would not be thinking of a lawsuit. But he or she must further consider whether the grievance is one for which the law furnishes relief. There are a great many hurts a person may feel that the law will not redress. She is offended by the paint on her neighbor's house; he has worked for weeks to persuade a distributor to buy his brand of digital recorder, and sees the sale go to a competitor; she has been holding a plot of ground for speculation expecting industry to move in and the area is zoned for residential use; he slips on a spot of grease in the county courthouse but the county is immune from suit. A potential litigant often must consult an attorney before deciding whether he or she has a case.

Even if she concludes that the grievance is one for which the courts will grant relief, a potential litigant must consider the probability of winning a lawsuit. She must ask whether the person who has caused the injury can be found and brought into court; whether witnesses and documents will be available to support the claims being sued on; whether this proof will be believed; whether the potential adversary can justify its conduct or establish any defenses to the action; and whether an accurate assessment of the law can be made ahead of time.

Then, and perhaps most important of all, a potential litigant must consider whether what is won will be worth the time, the effort, and the expense it will cost, and must weigh against this the alternatives to suit, among them settlement, arbitration, self-help, and letting matters rest. What form will the relief take? Most frequently it will be restricted to a judgment for damages. If this is true, the potential litigant must decide whether the injury is one for which a monetary payment will be satisfactory. Assuming it is, will defendant be rich enough to pay? How difficult will a judgment be to collect? How expensive? Will the recovery be enough to pay the lawyer's fees and the other litigation expenses that undoubtedly will be incurred? Even in a context in which the court may grant specific relief for example, an order directing the opposing party to do something or to stop doing something will compliance by defendant be possible? Worth while? Sufficient? In the same vein, a potential litigant also must consider whether there are risks not directly tied to the suit: Will he antagonize people whose goodwill he needs? Will the action publicize an error of judgment on her part or open her private affairs to public gaze?

Only after considerable thought has resolved these and similar questions will the prospective plaintiff be ready for the steps that follow. Let us now consider those steps in the light of a relatively uncluttered hypothetical case:

Aikin, while crossing the street in front of her private home, was struck and seriously injured by an automobile driven by Beasley. On inquiry, Aikin found that the automobile was owned by Cecil and that Beasley apparently had been in Cecil's employ. Beasley was predictably without substantial assets and a judgment against him for Aikins injuries promised little material compensation. But Cecil was wealthy, and Aikin was advised that if she could establish that Beasley had indeed been working for Cecil and had been negligent, she then could recover from Cecil. Aikin decided to sue Cecil for $500,000.

OUTLINE OF A CIVIL ACTION

1. SELECTING A PROPER COURT

Aikin initially must determine in which court to bring the action. She probably will have some choice between filing her lawsuit in a state or a federal court, but her choice is not open-ended. This is because the court selected must have *jurisdiction over the subject matter* (that is, the constitution and statutes under which the court operates must have conferred upon it power to decide this type of case) and must also have *jurisdiction over the person* of Cecil (that is, Cecil must be subject or amenable to suit in the state in which the court is located so that a judgment may be entered against him).

Aikin probably will bring suit in a state court, for as we shall shortly see the subject matter jurisdiction of the federal courts is severely limited. If the court organization of Aikin's state is typical, there will be courts of *original jurisdiction* in which cases are brought and tried, and one court of *appellate jurisdiction* that sits, with rare exceptions, only to review the decisions of lower courts. (In most states there will also be a group of intermediate courts of appellate jurisdiction.) The courts of original jurisdiction probably consist of one set of courts of *general jurisdiction* and several sets of courts of *inferior jurisdiction*. The courts of general jurisdiction are organized into districts comprising for the most part several counties, although the largest or most populous counties each may constitute single districts. These district courts hear cases of many kinds and are competent to grant every kind of relief, but are usually authorized to hear claims for which the relief requested exceeds a statutorily fixed dollar amount. The courts of inferior jurisdiction will include municipal courts, whose jurisdiction resembles that of the district courts except that the claims are of smaller financial significance; justice-of-the-peace courts, which hear very minor matters; and specialized tribunals such as the traffic courts. Since Aikin's injuries are quite serious and her claim correspondingly large, she will, if she sues in a state court, bring the action in one of the district courts.

The federal government also operates a system of courts. The principal federal courts are the United States District Courts, courts of original jurisdiction of which there is at least one in every state; the thirteen United States Courts of Appeals, each of which reviews the decisions of federal district courts in the several states within its circuit (with the exception of the Courts of Appeals for the District of Columbia Circuit and the Federal Circuit); and the Supreme Court of the United States, which not only reviews the decisions of federal courts but also reviews decisions of state courts that turn on an issue of federal law.

The jurisdiction over the subject-matter of the United States District Courts extends to many, but by no means all, cases involving federal law, and also to many cases, similar to Aikin's, that do not involve federal law; the latter are cases in which there is *diversity of citizenship* (the parties are citizens of different states or one of them is a citizen of a foreign country) and the required *amount in controversy* (more than $75,000) is at stake. Diversity jurisdiction, in common with most of the federal courts' jurisdiction, is not *exclusive;* the state courts also are competent to hear these cases. But if Cecil is not a citizen of Aikin's state, Aikin may bring an action for $500,000 in a federal court. Indeed, in these circumstances, if Aikin sued Cecil in a state court in Aikin's home state Cecil could *remove* the action from the state court in which it was commenced to the federal district court in that state.[a]

It is not enough that the court selected by Aikin has jurisdiction over the subject matter, however. That court, whether state or federal, must be one in which Cecil can be required to

a. If Cecil is not a citizen of Aikin's state and Beasley is, then one of the considerations Aikin will have in deciding to join Beasley as a defendant is the effect on the availability of subject-matter jurisdiction in the federal courts. If Aikin wants to be in the federal court, she should not join Beasley; if Aikin wants to begin and stay in a state court, she should join him. In the latter case, there will not be complete diversity between plaintiff on the one side and defendants on the other.

appear so that it is appropriate for the legal system to enter a judgment again him. Traditionally, a court could enter a judgment only against a defendant who resides in the state or is physically in the state, even if temporarily. But the restrictions on a court's jurisdiction over the person have diminished in recent decades, and if Cecil is not present in Aikin's state but he directed Beasley to drive there, Aikin probably will be able to bring the action in that state because of Cecils prior contact with the state and the benefits that those contacts have brought him.

Not every court that has jurisdiction over the subject matter and jurisdiction over the person of defendant will hear a case. It also is necessary that an action be brought in a court having proper *venue.* Thus, although every court in Aikin's state could assert personal jurisdiction over Cecil if he was within its boundaries, that state's statutes typically will provide that the case should be brought in a court whose district includes the county in which either Aikin or Cecil lives. Similarly, if Aikin decides to sue in federal court based on diversity of citizenship, she must bring suit in a district that has venue as defined by federal statute (currently, the district in which Cecil resides, or in a district where a substantial part of the events giving rise to the claim occurred, or in a district where Cecil is subject to personal jurisdiction, if there is no district in which the action otherwise may be brought).

Jurisdiction over the subject matter cannot be waived by the parties. If Aikin and Cecil are both citizens of the same state, a federal court will refuse to hear the action even though both are anxious that it do so. Jurisdiction over the person and venue, on the other hand, essentially are protections for defendant, who may waive them if he wishes.

2. COMMENCING THE ACTION

Aikin must give Cecil notice of the commencement of the action by *service of process.* The process typically consists of a *summons,* which directs defendant to appear and defend under penalty of *default;* that is, unless defendant answers the summons, a judgment will be entered against him. Service of process generally is achieved by *personal service;* the summons is physically delivered to defendant or is left at his home, sometimes by plaintiff or her attorney, sometimes by a public official such as a sheriff or a United States marshal. If Cecil lives in another state, but the circumstances are such that a court in Aikin's state may assert jurisdiction over Cecil, the summons may be personally delivered to him, or some form of *substituted service,* such as sending the papers by registered mail or delivering the summons to his agent within Aikin's state, may be employed. Even if Cecil cannot be located, service in yet another form, usually by *publication* in a newspaper for a certain length of time, may be allowed, although the validity of this kind of service in the type of case Aikin is bringing against Cecil is unlikely to be upheld. The United States Supreme Court repeatedly has emphasized that service must be of a kind reasonably calculated to bring the action to defendant's notice.

3. PLEADING AND PARTIES

With the summons, Aikin usually will serve on Cecil the first of the *pleadings,* commonly called the *complaint.* This is a written statement that will contain Aikin's claim against Cecil. What should be required of such a statement? Obviously it may vary from a simple assertion that Cecil owes her $500,000, to a second-by-second narration of the accident, closely describing the scene and the conduct of each party, followed by a gruesome recital of Aikin's medical treatment and her prognosis for recovery. No procedural system insists upon either of these extremes, but systems do vary greatly in the detail required in the pleadings. The degree of detail required largely reflects the purposes that the pleadings are expected to serve. These purposes are many, but three objectives are particularly relevant and to the extent that a

procedural system regards one rather than another as crucial, we may expect to find differing amounts of detail required.

First, the system may desire the pleadings to furnish a basis for identifying and separating the legal and factual contentions involved so that the legal issues and hopefully through them the entire case may be disposed of at an early stage. Thus, suppose that Cecil's liability for Beasley's driving depends upon the degree of independence with which Beasley was working at the time of the accident. A dispute on this issue might exist on either or both of two elements. The parties might disagree as to what Beasley's duties were, and they might disagree as to whether those duties put Beasley so much under the control of Cecil that the law will impose liability on Cecil for Beasley's actions. The first disagreement would be a question of fact, and there would be no alternative to trying the suit and letting the finder of fact (usually the jury) decide the truth. But if there was agreement on that first element, a question of law would be presented by the second issue, which could be determined by the judge without a trial. The objective of which we are speaking would be fully served in such a case only if the pleadings set forth exactly what Beasley's job required him to do. It would be very inadequately served if the complaint stated only that Beasley was driving the car on Cecil's business.

Second, the pleadings may be intended to establish in advance what a party proposes to prove at trial so that his opponent will know what contentions he must prepare to meet. If this objective is regarded as very important it will not be enough for the complaint to state that Beasley was negligent, or that Aikin suffered serious bodily injuries. It must say that Beasley was speeding, or was not keeping a proper look-out, or had inadequate brakes, or describe some other act of negligence and say that Aikin suffered a concussion, or a broken neck, or fractures of three ribs, or other injuries.

Third, the pleadings may be intended to give each party only a general notice of his opponent's contentions, in which event the system would rely upon subsequent stages of the lawsuit to identify the legal and factual contentions of the parties and to enable each to prepare to meet the opponent's case. In such a case a complaint similar to that in Form 9 of the Federal Rules of Civil Procedure would be sufficient.

Obviously each of the first two objectives is desirable. It is a waste of everybody's time to try lawsuits when the underlying legal claim is inadequate to support a judgment, and it is only fair that a person called upon to defend a judicial proceeding should know what he is alleged to have done. But to achieve the first objective fully may require pleading after pleading in order to expose and sharpen the issues; if detail is insisted upon, a long time may be consumed in producing it. Moreover, a single pleading oversight may eliminate a contention necessary to one party's case that easily could have been proven, but that will be held to have been waived. To achieve the second objective through the pleadings will mean that the parties must take rigid positions as to their factual contentions at the very beginning when they do not know what they will learn about their cases by the time trial begins. Either the first or second objective, if fully pursued, requires that the parties adhere to the positions taken in the pleadings. They could not be permitted to introduce evidence in conflict with the pleadings or to change them. For to the extent that *variances* between pleading and proof or *amendments* to the pleadings are permitted, the objectives will be lost. The court frequently will find itself forced either to depart from these objectives or to tolerate cases turning on the skill of the lawyers rather than on the merits of the controversy.

The third objective, insofar as it allows the parties to use the later stages of the lawsuit to identify and flesh out the issues in the case, avoids the delays and potential injustices created by trying to decide the case based simply on the pleadings. However, simple notice pleading may be used to harass defendant when plaintiff has no real claim. More often, though, plaintiff will use

notice pleading to subject defendant to pretrial discovery (discussed more fully below), and in the process to reveal information so that plaintiff can determine whether a bona fide claim actually exists. Lawyers often refer to such use of the pleadings as a fishing expedition, or alternatively as a springboard into litigation. One way that courts have dealt with these problems is to sanction parties and lawyers who bring baseless claims.

4. THE RESPONSE

Following the service of Aikin's complaint, Cecil must respond. He may challenge the complaint by a *motion to dismiss.* This motion may challenge the court's jurisdiction over the subject matter or Cecil's person, the service of process, or venue. It also may be a *motion to dismiss for failure to state a claim or cause of action* (the older term for this motion is a *demurrer*). For the purpose of this motion, the facts alleged in the complaint are accepted as true, and the court considers whether, on this assumption, plaintiff has shown that the pleader is entitled to legal relief.

There are three general situations in which such a motion might be granted. First, the complaint may clearly show that the injury is one for which the law furnishes no redress; for example, when plaintiff simply alleges that defendant has made faces at me. Second, plaintiff may have failed to include an allegation on a necessary part of the case; for example, Aikin might have alleged the accident, her injuries, and Beasley's negligence, and have forgotten to allege that Beasley was Cecil's servant. Third, the complaint may be so general or so confused that the court finds that it does not give adequate notice of what plaintiff's claim is; this would be true, for example, of a complaint in which Aikin merely said, Cecil injured me and owes me $500,000, although complaints far more specific have fallen on this ground. Obviously, the extent to which motions to dismiss will be granted on the second and third grounds will vary with the degree of detail that the particular system requires of its pleadings. A court generally has power to allow the plaintiff an opportunity to amend her pleading to cure certain kinds of defects.

If the motion to dismiss is denied, or if none is made, Cecil must file an *answer.* In this pleading, he must admit or deny the factual allegations made by Aikin in the complaint. Moreover if Cecil wishes to rely on certain legal contentions called *affirmative defenses,* he must plead them in the answer. Thus, if he wishes to contend that Aikin was negligent in the manner in which she tried to cross the street and that this negligence was also a cause of the accident, he must in many states plead this in the answer; if the answer only denied the allegations in Aikin's complaint, Cecil may not advance at trial the contention that Aikin's negligence caused the accident.

There may be further pleadings, particularly a *reply* by Aikin. But the tendency today is to close the pleadings after the answer, and if Cecil has raised new matters in his answer, they automatically are taken as denied by Aikin. There is one major exception: if Cecil has a claim against Aikin, particularly one that arises out of the same occurrence being sued upon by Aikin, Cecil may plead this claim as a *counterclaim* as part of the answer. This is in essence a complaint by Cecil, and Aikin will have to respond to it just as Cecil had to respond to the original complaint.

The original action between Aikin and Cecil may expand in terms of the number of parties, and this frequently will occur at the pleading stage. For example, although Aikin decided not to sue Beasley, Cecil might *implead* Beasley, asking that Beasley be held liable to him for whatever amount he may be found liable to Aikin, since his liability depends upon Beasley having been at

fault. Cecil will decide whether to do this in light of a number of practical concerns, including the effect Beasley's presence will have on the Aikin v. Cecil suit.

5. OBTAINING INFORMATION PRIOR TO TRIAL

Pretrial discovery is the procedure currently designed to allow the parties to exchange information about their claims and defenses and to prepare for trial. At earlier periods, the pleadings served this purpose.

The chief method is to take *depositions* of parties and witnesses. In this procedure, the person whose deposition is to be taken is questioned by lawyers for each side through direct and cross-examination; the *deponent's* statements are taken down and transcribed. The device is useful in finding information that is relevant to the case, including unearthing leads as to other witnesses or documents; it also is useful in laying a basis for impeaching a witness who attempts to change his story at trial. The two parties almost certainly will want depositions taken of each other, as well as of Beasley; the depositions of Aikin and Cecil will be particularly important because they are treated as admissions, and can be used by their adversaries as evidence at trial. In some circumstances, even the deposition of a nonparty witness who is unavailable at trial may be used in place of live testimony.

Another device especially adapted to probing the content of an opponent's case is *written interrogatories,* which usually may be addressed only to a party to the suit. (The availability of interrogatories may be one reason why Aikin might join Beasley as a defendant with Cecil or why Cecil might implead Beasley.) These interrogatories are answered by the party with counsel's aid, and the answers will not be as spontaneous as they would be on a deposition; on the other hand, interrogatories will require him to supply some information that he does not carry in his head but can get, and may be even more valuable than the deposition in finding out what he will try to prove. Thus, information regarding Beasley's employment that Cecil cannot be expected to have in his mind may best be exposed in this way.

Other discovery devices include *the production of documents,* such as the service record of Cecil's automobile, and *requests for admissions,* which will remove uncontested issues from the case. A particularly useful device for Cecil will be a court order directing Aikin to submit to a *physical examination* by a physician of Cecil's choice to determine the real extent of Aikin's alleged injuries.

The availability of discovery, which is now common throughout the country, has had its effect on the philosophy of pleadings. This is not simply because it enables parties to prepare for trial better than pleadings ever did. Of more significance perhaps is the fact that if broad discovery is allowed, it is senseless to make parties take rigid positions with respect to the issues at the very beginning of the lawsuit before they have had the chance to utilize these very useful devices for obtaining information. In addition, the availability of discovery does much to make summary judgment, which is discussed below, a viable and fair procedure, since it enables a party to ascertain those issues on which the opposing party has no evidence, and it also gives the opponent a real chance to develop such evidence.

Amendments to the Federal Rules of Civil Procedure were promulgated in recent years that, in time, may revolutionize the way in which litigants conduct pretrial discovery. They require both parties automatically in most cases to identify individuals and provide copies of documents that the disclosing party may use to support its claims or defenses. This mandatory self-disclosure procedure theoretically should decrease considerably the amount of time and the amount of resources that the judicial system expends in overseeing the discovery process, but it is still too early to know how well they actually will work.

6. SUMMARY JUDGMENT

One of the basic difficulties with attempting to resolve cases at the pleading stage is that the allegations of the parties must be accepted as true for the purpose of ruling on a motion to dismiss. Thus, if the plaintiff tells a highly unlikely but possible story in the complaint, the court cannot dismiss the complaint even though it does not believe the allegations or think that the plaintiff will be able to prove the tale. The judge is not the decision maker and the pleading stage is not the time to resolve questions of fact.

But in some cases it will be possible to supplement the pleadings with additional documents to show that an apparent issue that is decisive of the case is spurious. This is done by a motion for *summary judgment.* This motion can be supported by demonstrating that the crucial issue will have to be resolved in the mover's favor at trial, because the opposing party will be unable to produce any admissible evidence in support of her position on the issue. For example, suppose that it is Cecil's position that prior to the accident he had fired Beasley, but that Beasley had secreted keys to Cecil's automobile and had taken Cecil's car without permission shortly before the accident. On the face of the pleadings, we have only an allegation that Beasley was Cecil's employee and a denial of that allegation; thus, the pleadings seem to present a question of credibility that cannot be resolved at this stage. Cecil now moves for summary judgment, alleging that this issue is not a genuine one; he accompanies his motion with affidavits of his own and two other witnesses that he had fired Beasley; a deposition of the garage attendant indicating that he had been instructed not to allow Beasley to have the car, and that it was taken without Cecil's knowledge; and a deposition of Beasley to the effect that he had been fired, but wanted to use the car once more for his own purposes. It is now incumbent upon Aikin to show that the issue is genuine; Aikin cannot rely simply upon her own assertion that all this is not so; after all, she has no personal knowledge of the facts. Aikin must convince the court that she has admissible evidence that Beasley still was acting as Cecil's employee in driving the car at the time of the accident. If Aikin fails to do so, judgment will be entered against her.

It should be noted that in ruling on a motion for summary judgment the judge does not decide which side is telling the truth. If Aikin presents an affidavit of a witness who claims to have been present when Cecil allegedly fired Beasley, and says that Cecil told Beasley that this was only a subterfuge and that he wanted him to continue to work for him but to pretend to steal the car, summary judgment will not be appropriate even though the judge is firmly convinced that Aikin's affiant is lying.

7. SETTING THE CASE FOR TRIAL

After discovery is completed, and if the case has not been terminated by dismissal, summary judgment, or settlement, it must be set for *trial.* Most cases will already have been disposed of prior to trial. If Aikin's law suit has not yet bee resolved, typically either party may file a *note of issue,* at which time the case will be given a number and placed on a *trial calendar.* These calendars have become extremely long in many courts, and the case may have to wait a year, three years, or more before it is called for trial, especially if a jury trial has been requested.

8. THE JURY AND ITS SELECTION

In most actions for damages, the parties have a right to have the facts tried by a *jury.* This right is assured in the federal courts by the Seventh Amendment to the Constitution, and is protected in the courts of most states by similar state constitutional provisions. If there is a right to a trial by jury, either party may assert it, but if neither wishes to do so, a judge will try

the facts as well as the law. Largely for historical reasons growing out of a division of authority in the English court structure, there are many civil actions in which neither party has a right to a jury trial; these include most cases in which plaintiff wants an order directing or prohibiting specified action by defendant rather than a judgment for damages a so-called *equitable* remedy.

If a jury has been demanded, the first order of business at trial will be to impanel the jurors. A large number of people, selected in an impartial manner from various lists, tax rolls, or street directories, will have been ordered to report to the courthouse for jury duty at a given term of court. The prospective jurors will be questioned usually by the judge but sometimes by the lawyers as to their possible biases. If one of the persons called has prior knowledge of the case or is a personal friend of one of the parties, he or she probably will be successfully *challenged for cause* and excused. But suppose Aikin is an architect and her lawyer finds that one of the jury panel has recently constructed a house and believes that he was greatly overcharged for its design and construction; this will likely not be enough to persuade the judge to excuse him, but fearing the juror may be prejudiced against her client, Aikin's lawyer will probably exercise one of the small number of *peremptory challenges* allowed for which no reason need be given. Ultimately, a panel of between six and twelve hopefully unbiased jurors will be selected.

9. THE TRIAL

After the jurors have been sworn, plaintiff's lawyer will make an *opening statement,* in which she will describe for the jury what the case is about, what contentions she will make, and how she will prove them. Defendant's lawyer also may make an opening statement at this time, but he may reserve the right to do so until he is ready to present his own case. Following the opening statement, plaintiff's lawyer calls her witnesses one by one. Each witness is first questioned by the lawyer who has called that witness this is the *direct examination;* then the lawyer for the other side has the opportunity to *cross-examine* the same witness; this may be followed by *re-direct* and *re-cross* examination, and even further stages. The judge maintains some control over the length and tenor of the examination, and in particular will see to it that the stages beyond cross-examination are not prolonged.

Just as the primary responsibility for introducing evidence is on the lawyers, so too is the responsibility for objecting to evidence that is thought to be inadmissible under the rules of evidence. Suppose that Aikin's lawyer asks: What happened while you were lying on the ground after the accident? To which Aikin replies: The driver of the car came over and said that he had been going too fast and he was sorry. Aikin's answer is objectionable because it contains *hearsay evidence;* that is, it repeats what someone else has said for the purpose of proving the truth of what was said. The judge will not raise this issue herself, however; it is up to Cecil's counsel to object, and then the judge must rule on the objection. This particular issue is not an easy one, for Aikin's answer may well come within one of the exceptions to the rule excluding hearsay evidence. This kind of issue will recur continually throughout the trial and the judge must be prepared to make instantaneous rulings if the trial is to proceed with dispatch. Small wonder that evidentiary rulings form a major source of the errors raised on appeal, but at the same time appellate courts are very reluctant to disturb the trial judge's determination. What happens if the judge rules that Aikin's answer is inadmissible? She will instruct the jury to disregard it. Can a juror who has heard such an important confession totally drive it from his or her mind?

Documents, pictures, and other tangible items may be put into evidence, but unless their admissibility has been stipulated in advance, they will be introduced through witnesses. For example, if Aikin's lawyer has had pictures taken of the accident scene and wishes to get them to the jury, she will call the photographer as a witness, have him testify that he took pictures of

the scene, and then show them to the photographer who will identify them as the pictures he took. At this point they may be formally introduced into evidence.

When plaintiff's lawyer has called all of her witnesses, and their examinations are over, plaintiff will *rest*. At this point, defendant's lawyer may ask for a *directed verdict* (now called a judgment as a matter of law in federal practice) for defendant on the ground that plaintiff has not established a prima facie case; the thrust of the motion is that plaintiff has not introduced enough evidence to permit the jury to find in her favor. If the motion is denied, defendant may rest and choose to rely on the jury's agreeing with him, but in almost all cases he will proceed to present witnesses of his own and these witnesses will be exposed to the same process of direct and cross-examination. When defendant has rested, plaintiff may present additional evidence to meet any new matter raised by defendant's witnesses. In turn, defendant, after plaintiff rests, may meet any new matter presented by plaintiff. This procedure will continue until both parties rest. Again, the trial judge will maintain considerable control to prevent the protraction of these latter stages.

When both parties have rested, either or both may move for a directed verdict. Again, this motion asks the trial judge to rule that under the evidence presented, viewed most favorably to the nonmoving party, the jury cannot find in his or her favor. If these motions are denied, the case must be submitted to the jury.

10. SUBMITTING THE CASE TO THE JURY

At this stage the judge and the lawyers will confer out of the jury's hearing with regard to the content of the judge's *instructions* or *charge* to the jury. Each lawyer may submit proposed instructions, which the trial judge will grant or deny, but the judge is under a duty to charge the jury on the basic aspects of the case in any event. If a party's lawyer has neither requested a particular instruction nor objected to the judge's charge, however, a claim that the charge was erroneous generally will not be upheld on appeal.

Ordinarily the lawyers will make their final arguments to the jury before the judge delivers the charge. The lawyers will review the evidence from their own points of view, and may suggest how the jury should weigh certain items and resolve specific issues, but it is improper for the lawyers to discuss a matter that has been excluded or has never been introduced. In other words, they are arguing, not testifying.

In the instructions the judge will summarize the facts and issues, tell the jury about the substantive law to be applied on each issue, give general information on determining the credibility of witnesses, and state who has the *burden of persuasion* on each issue of fact. The burden of persuasion in a civil case ordinarily requires that one party prove her contention on a given issue by a preponderance of the evidence. On most issues Aikin will carry this burden but on an affirmative defense such as contributory negligence the burden probably will be on Cecil. What the burden means is that if a juror is unable to resolve an issue in his mind, he should find on that issue against the party who has the burden. In the federal courts and in some states, the judge may comment on the evidence, as long as she emphasizes that her comments represent her own opinion and that the jurors should not feel bound by it; judicial comment is rare, however, and in many states it is not permitted at all.

Following the charge, the jury retires to reach its *verdict*. The verdict, the jury's decision, will be of a type chosen by the judge. There are three types, of which by far the most common is the *general verdict*. This verdict permits the jurors to determine the facts and apply the law on which they have been charged to those facts; it is simple in form in that only the conclusion as to who prevails, and the amount of the damages, if that party is a claimant, is stated. A second

type is the *general verdict with interrogatories,* which combines the form of the general verdict with several key questions that are designed to test the jury's understanding of the issues. Suppose that the accident occurred five miles away from Beasley's appointed route. Aikin's evidence is that Beasley detoured to have the vehicle's brakes fixed; Cecil's is that Beasley was going to visit his friend. The judge might charge the jury that in the former event, but not in the latter, Beasley was acting within the scope of his employment and Cecil would be liable for his negligence, and she might direct the jury, in addition to rendering a verdict for Aikin or for Cecil, to answer the question, Why did Beasley depart from his route? If the general verdict was for Aikin, but the jury's answer was that Beasley was driving to his friend's home, the judge would order judgment for Cecil, for if the answer is inconsistent with the verdict, the answer controls. The third type of verdict is the *special verdict,* in which all of the factual issues in the case are submitted to the jury as questions without instructions as to their legal effect; the judge applies the law to the jury's answers and determines which party prevails.

Traditionally, only a unanimous jury verdict has been effective. In many states, and by consent of the parties in the federal courts, a nonunanimous verdict by the jurors may stand in a civil action. If the minimum number of jurors required for a verdict are unable to reach agreement, the jury is said to be *hung,* and a new trial before a different jury is necessary.

11. POST–TRIAL MOTIONS

After the jury has returned its verdict, judgment will be entered thereon, but the losing party will have an opportunity to make certain post-trial motions. There may be a motion for a *judgment notwithstanding the verdict* (commonly called a motion for a *judgment n.o.v.,* from the Latin non obstante veredicto, but now called a renewed motion for judgment as a matter of law in federal practice); this motion raises the same question as a motion for a directed verdict. The losing party also may move for a *new trial;* the grounds for this motion are many, and may include assertions that the judge erred in admitting certain evidence, that the charge was defective, that attorneys, parties, or jurors have been guilty of misconduct, that the damages awarded are excessive, or that the jury's verdict is against the clear weight of the evidence. Should these motions fail, it is sometimes possible to reopen a judgment, even several months after the trial, on the grounds of clerical mistake, newly discovered evidence, or fraud, but the occasions on which relief is granted are very rare.

12. THE JUDGMENT AND ITS ENFORCEMENT

The *judgment* is the final determination of the lawsuit, absent an appeal. Judgment may be rendered on default when the defendant does not appear; or following the granting of a demurrer, a motion to dismiss, or a motion for summary judgment; or upon the jury's verdict, or the findings of fact and conclusions of law of the trial judge in a nonjury case. The judgment may be in the form of an award of money to plaintiff, a declaration of rights between the parties, specific recovery of property, or an order requiring or prohibiting some future activity. When defendant has prevailed, the judgment generally will not be for anything nor will it order anything; it simply will provide that plaintiff takes nothing by her complaint.

In most cases a judgment for plaintiff will not order defendant to do anything; typically it will simply state that plaintiff shall recover a sum of money from defendant. This does not necessarily mean that defendant will pay. It is up to plaintiff to collect the money. *Execution* is the common method of forcing the losing party to satisfy a money judgment, if the loser does not do so voluntarily. A *writ of execution* is issued by the court commanding an officer usually the

sheriff to seize property of the losing party and, if necessary, to sell it at public sale and use the proceeds to satisfy plaintiff's judgment.

When plaintiff's recovery takes the form of an *injunction* requiring defendant to do something or to stop doing something, the judgment (in this context typically called the *decree*) is said to operate against defendant's person (in personam). Its sanction is direct, and if defendant fails to obey, he may be held in *contempt of court* and punished by fine or imprisonment.

Costs provided by statute and certain out-of-pocket disbursements are awarded the prevailing party and included in the judgment. Usually these costs are nominal in relation to the total expense of litigation and include only such items as the clerk's fee and witnesses' mileage. In the United States, in contrast to England, attorney's fees are not recoverable as costs in ordinary litigation.

13. APPEAL

Every judicial system provides for review by an appellate court of the decisions of the trial court. Generally a party has the right to appeal any judgment to at least one higher court. When the system contains two levels of appellate courts, appeal usually lies initially to one of the intermediate courts; review at the highest level is only at the discretion of that court except in certain classes of cases. Thus, in the federal courts, district-court decisions are reviewed by the courts of appeals, but review in the United States Supreme Court must be sought in most cases by a *petition for a writ of certiorari,* which that Court may deny as a matter of discretion without reaching any conclusion as to the merits of the case. (In a few cases, a direct appeal lies from the district court to the Supreme Court.) The discretion of a higher-level appellate court generally is exercised so that only cases whose legal issues are of broad importance are taken.

The *record* on appeal will contain the pleadings, at least a portion of the *transcript of the trial* (the court reporter's verbatim record of the trial), and the orders and rulings relevant to the appeal. The parties present their contentions to the appellate court by written *briefs* and in addition, in most cases, by *oral argument.* The appellate court may review any ruling of law by the trial judge, although frequently it will limit the scope of its review by holding that particular matters were within the trial judge's discretion or that the error if any was not prejudicial, that is, it did not substantially affect the outcome of the case. There are constitutional limits to the review of a jury's verdict, but even when these limits do not apply for example, when the judge has sat without a jury an appellate court rarely will re-examine a question of fact, for a cold record does not convey the nuances of what the trier observed, notably the demeanor of the witnesses.

The appellate court has the power to *affirm, reverse,* or *modify* the judgment of the trial court. If it reverses, it may order that judgment be entered or it may *remand* the case to the trial court for a new trial or other proceedings not inconsistent with its decision. The decision of an appellate court usually is accompanied by a written *opinion,* signed by one of the judges hearing the appeal, there always being more than one judge deciding an appeal. Concurring and dissenting opinions also may be filed. The opinions of a court are designed to set forth the reasons for a decision and to furnish guidance to lower courts, lawyers, and the public. You will spend much of your time in law school and afterwards reading the opinions of appellate courts. Although trial courts frequently deliver opinions when ruling on motions or sitting without a jury, except in federal courts these usually are not published.

There is an important distinction between the *reviewability* of a particular ruling of a trial judge and its *appealability.* For example, a trial judge's ruling excluding certain evidence at trial as hearsay is reviewable; that is, when the judgment is appealed, that ruling may be assigned as

error and the appellate court will consider whether it was correct. But trial would be impossible if an appeal could be taken from every ruling. Thus, appeals lie only from judgments and from certain orders made in the course of litigation when immediate review is deemed so important that a delay in the action during appeal can be tolerated. Judicial systems differ in the extent to which *interlocutory orders* can be appealed. In the federal system, very little other than a final judgment can be taken to the courts of appeals; in some states, on the other hand, many kinds of orders can be appealed.

A good example of the contrast between the two approaches can be seen by looking at the consequences of an order denying a motion to dismiss. Suppose that Cecil moves to dismiss Aikin's complaint on the grounds that even on Aikin's view of the facts Cecil is not responsible for the conduct of Beasley, and this motion is denied. In the federal courts such an order would not be appealable, since it does not terminate the lawsuit. Indeed, the disposition of the motion means that the action will continue. In some states, however, this question could be taken immediately to a higher court for a ruling, while the other stages of the litigation wait.

The question as to which system is better is not easy to answer. One may argue in favor of the federal practice that everything should be done at one level before going to the next, that too much time is taken in waiting for appellate courts to decide these questions serially, and that no appeal may ever be necessary, since Cecil may prevail anyway. But on the other hand, if the appellate court holds at this early stage that Aikin has no claim against Cecil we will save the time necessary for discovery and trial.

One point worth noting is that the resolution of the question of the appealability of interlocutory orders has an important bearing on the procedural developments within a given system. In the case of motions to dismiss, for example, if denials are not appealable, the law on this subject will be made largely in the trial courts. The trial judge who is in doubt may tend to deny such motions rather than to grant them, and her decision generally will not be disturbed; even though the ruling theoretically is reviewable after final judgment, by that time the significance of the ruling on the pleadings may have been displaced by more substantive questions. If the denial is appealable, a tactical consideration is added and such motions will be resorted to more frequently, inasmuch as they will afford defendant an additional opportunity to delay trial and thus to wear down his opponent. With respect to other procedural rulings as in the discovery area the absence of an interlocutory appeal will strengthen the hand of the trial judge; she will in fact, if not in theory, be given a wider discretion because fewer of her rulings will come before the appellate courts and when they do they will be enmeshed in a final judgment, which will make it easy to conclude that any error was not prejudicial.

14. THE CONCLUSIVENESS OF JUDGMENTS

After the appeal and whatever further proceedings may take place, or, if no appeal is taken, when the time for appeal expires, the judgment is final. It cannot be challenged in another proceeding. It is *res judicata*, a thing decided, and now at rest. Defining the scope and effect of this finality is one of the most complex tasks in the entire law of procedure.

FEDERAL
RULES OF CIVIL PROCEDURE

FOR THE

UNITED STATES DISTRICT COURTS

Amendments received to May 21, 2007

I. SCOPE OF RULES—ONE FORM OF ACTION

Rule
1. Scope and Purpose of Rules.
2. One Form of Action.

II. COMMENCEMENT OF ACTION; SERVICE OF PROCESS, PLEADINGS, MOTIONS, AND ORDERS

3. Commencement of Action.
4. Summons.
4.1. Service of Other Process.
5. Service and Filing of Pleadings and Other Papers.
5.1. Constitutional Challenge to a Statute—Notice, Certification, and Intervention.
5.2. Privacy Protection For Filings Made with the Court.
6. Time.

III. PLEADINGS AND MOTIONS

7. Pleadings Allowed; Form of Motions.
7.1. Disclosure Statement.
8. General Rules of Pleading.

Rule

III. PLEADINGS AND MOTIONS—Cont'd

9. Pleading Special Matters.
10. Form of Pleadings.
11. Signing of Pleadings, Motions, and Other Papers; Representations to Court; Sanctions.
12. Defenses and Objections—When and How Presented—By Pleading or Motion—Motion for Judgment on Pleadings.
13. Counterclaim and Cross-Claim.
14. Third-Party Practice.
15. Amended and Supplemental Pleadings.
16. Pretrial Conferences; Scheduling; Management.

IV. PARTIES

17. Parties Plaintiff and Defendant; Capacity.
18. Joinder of Claims and Remedies.
19. Joinder of Persons Needed for Just Adjudication.
20. Permissive Joinder of Parties.
21. Misjoinder and Non-Joinder of Parties.
22. Interpleader.
23. Class Actions.
23.1. Derivative Actions by Shareholders.
23.2. Actions Relating to Unincorporated Associations.
24. Intervention.
25. Substitution of Parties.

V. DEPOSITIONS AND DISCOVERY

26. General Provisions Governing Discovery; Duty of Disclosure.
27. Depositions Before Action or Pending Appeal.
28. Persons Before Whom Depositions may be Taken.
29. Stipulations Regarding Discovery Procedure.
30. Depositions Upon Oral Examination.
31. Depositions Upon Written Questions.
32. Use of Depositions in Court Proceedings.
33. Interrogatories to Parties.
34. Production of Documents, Electronically Stored Information, and Things and Entry Upon Land for Inspection and Other Purposes.
35. Physical and Mental Examinations of Persons.
36. Requests for Admission.
37. Failure to Make Disclosure or Cooperate in Discovery; Sanctions.

VI. TRIALS

38. Jury Trial of Right.

Complete Annotation Materials, see Title 28 U.S.C.A.

RULES OF CIVIL PROCEDURE

Complete Annotation Materials, see Title 28 U.S.C.A.

RULES OF CIVIL PROCEDURE

TIME TABLE FOR LAWYERS IN FEDERAL CIVIL CASES
Amended to May 21, 2007

This Time Table, prepared by the Publisher's editorial staff as a guide to the user, indicates the time for each of the steps of a civil action as provided by the Federal Rules of Civil Procedure and the Federal Rules of Appellate Procedure. Certain steps governed by statute and by the Rules of the Supreme Court are also listed. The user should always consult the actual text of the rule or statute. Usually the periods permitted for each of these steps may be enlarged by the court in its discretion. In some cases no enlargement is permitted. Citations to supporting authority are in the form "Civ.R. ———" for the Rules of Civil Procedure; "App.R. ———" for the Rules of Appellate Procedure; "28 U.S.C.A. § ———" for statutes; and "Supreme Court Rule ———".

ADMISSIONS

Requests for admissions, service of	On any other party after the parties have conferred pursuant to Civ.R. 26(f). Civ.R. 36(a).
Response to requested admissions	Answers or objections must be served within 30 days after service of the request, or such shorter or longer time as court may allow or as parties may agree to in writing. Civ.R. 36(a).
ALTERNATE jurors	The institution of the alternate juror has been abolished. Civ.R. 47, 1991 Advisory Committee note, subd. (b).

Complete Annotation Materials, see Title 28 U.S.C.A.

ANSWER See, also, "Responsive Pleadings", this table.

 To complaint

Service within 20 days after being served with summons and complaint unless a different time is prescribed in a federal statute. Civ.R. 12(a)(1)(A).

Service within 60 days after date request is sent for waiver of service of summons or within 90 days after that date if defendant was addressed outside any judicial district of the United States unless a different time is prescribed in a federal statute. Civ.R. 12(a)(1)(B).

Service within 60 days after service upon the United States Attorney, in action against the United States or an officer or agency thereof. Civ.R. 12(a).

The time for responsive pleading is altered by service of Civ.R. 12 motions. See "Responsive Pleadings", this table.

 To cross-claim

Service within 20 days after being served with cross-claim. Civ.R. 12(a)(2).

60 days for United States. Civ.R. 12(a).

The time for responsive pleading is altered by service of Civ.R. 12(a) motions, see "Responsive Pleadings", this table.

 To third-party complaint

Service of reply within 20 days after service of answer or, if reply is ordered by a court, within 20 days after service of order. Civ.R. 12(a)(2).

60 days for United States. Civ.R. 12(a)(3).

 To notice of condemnation

Service within 20 days after service of notice. Civ.R. 71A(e).

 Removed actions

20 days after receipt of pleading, or within 20 days after service of summons, or within 5 days after filing of removal petition, whichever is longest. Civ.R. 81(c).

 Proceedings to cancel certificates of citizenship under 8 U.S.C.A. § 1451

60 days after service of petition. Civ.R. 81(a)(6).

ANSWERS (or objections) to interrogatories to party

Service within 30 days after service of the interrogatories. A shorter or longer time may be directed by the court or agreed to. Civ.R. 33(b)(3).

APPEAL
 As of right

30 days from entry of judgment or order. App.R. 4(a)(1)(A).

APPEAL

60 days in cases in which the United States or its officers, agencies are parties. App.R. 4(a)(1)(B).

60 days in cases in which the United States or its officers, agencies are parties. App.R. 4(a)(1)(B).

Entry of a judgment or order in the civil docket under Civ.R. 79(a) is entry for purposes of App.R. 4, unless Civ.R. 58(a)(1) requires a separate document, in which case entry occurs when the judgment or order is entered under Civ.R. 79(a) and either the judgment or order is set forth on a separate document, or 150 days have run from entry of the judgment or order in the civil docket. App.R. 4(a)(7)(A).

If any party files a timely motion of a type specified below, time for appeal for all parties runs from entry of order disposing of last such motion outstanding. App.R. 4(a)(4).

(1) motion for judgment under Civ.R. 50(b);
(2) Motion under Civ.R. 52(b) to amend or make additional findings of fact, whether or not granting the motion would alter the judgement;
(3) motion under Civ.R. 59 to alter or amend judgment;
(4) Motion under Civ.R. 54 for attorney's fees if time to appeal extended under Civ.R. 58.
(5) Motion under Civ.R. 59 for new trial.
(6) Motion for relief under Civ.R. 60 if motion filed no later than 10 days after entry of judgement.
App.R. 4(a)(4).

District court may extend for excusable neglect or good cause upon motion filed not later than 30 days after expiration of time prescribed by App.R. 4(a); no extension to exceed 30 days past prescribed time or 10 days from entry of order granting motion, whichever occurs later. App.R. 4(a)(5).

By other parties, within 14 days of filing of first notice of appeal, or within the time otherwise prescribed by App.R. 4(a), whichever last expires. App.R. 4(a)(3).

By permission

Petition filed with circuit clerk with proof of service within time specified by statute or rule authorizing the appeal, or if no such time is specified, within the time provided by App.R. 4(a) for filing a notice of appeal. App.R. 5(a).

Bankruptcy

If a motion for rehearing under Bankruptcy Rule 8015 is filed in a district court or in a bankruptcy appellate panel, time for appeal to court of appeals runs from entry of order disposing of motion. App.R. 6(b)(2)(A).

Class actions

Within 10 days after entry of order of district court granting or denying class action certification. Civ.R. 23(f).

RULES OF CIVIL PROCEDURE

APPEAL

Inmates
: A notice of appeal is timely filed if deposited in the institution's internal mail system on or before the last day for filing. App.R. 4(c), 25(a).

Representation statement
: Within 10 days after filing notice of appeal unless court of appeals designates another time, attorney who filed notice shall file with the circuit clerk a statement naming each party represented on appeal by that attorney. App.R. 12(b).

Entry of judgment or order, notice of
: Lack of such notice by clerk does not affect time to appeal or relieve or authorize court to relieve party for failure to appeal within time allowed, except as permitted in App.R. 4(a). Civ.R. 77(d).

Record (Appellant)
: Within 10 days after filing notice of appeal or entry of an order disposing of last timely remaining motion specified in App.R. 4(a)(4)(A), whichever is later: Appellant to place written order for transcript and file copy of order with clerk; if none to be ordered, file a certificate to that effect; unless entire transcript to be included, file a statement of issues and serve appellee a copy of order or certificate and of statement. App.R. 10(b).

Record (Appellee)
: Within 10 days after service of appellant's order or certificate and statement, appellee to file and serve on appellant a designation of additional parts of transcript to be included. Unless within 10 days after designation appellant has ordered such parts and so notified appellee, appellee may within following 10 days either order the parts or move in district court for order requiring appellant to do so. App.R. 10(b).

Record (costs)
: At time of ordering, party to make satisfactory arrangements with reporter for payment of cost of transcript. App.R. 10(b)(4).

Record (Reporter)
: If transcript cannot be completed within 30 days of receipt of order, reporter shall request extension of time from circuit clerk. App.R. 11(b).

Stay of proceedings to enforce judgment
: Effective when supersedeas bond is approved by court. Civ.R. 62(d).

: Supersedeas bond may be given at or after time of filing notice of appeal or of procuring the order allowing appeal. Civ.R. 62(d).

Briefs
: Appellant must serve and file a brief within 40 days after the record is filed. Appellee must serve and file a brief within 30 days after service of the appellant's brief. A reply brief may be filed within 14 days after service of appellee's brief and, except for good cause shown, at least 3 days before argument. A court of appeals may shorten the times allowed for briefs either by local rule for all cases or by order for a particular case. App.R. 31(a).

Transcripts
: See "RECORD", ante, this heading.

Tax Court decisions
: Review must be obtained by filing a notice of appeal with the Tax Court clerk within 90 days

Complete Annotation Materials, see Title 28 U.S.C.A.

RULES OF CIVIL PROCEDURE

APPEAL

after entry of decision. If a timely notice of appeal is filed by one party, any other party may take an appeal by filing a notice of appeal within 120 days after entry of decision by the Tax Court. If timely motion made to vacate or revise decision, time to file notice of appeal runs from entry of order disposing of motion or entry of new decision, whichever is later. App.R. 13(a).

APPEAL from magistrate judge to district judge under 28 U.S.C.A. § 636(c)(4) and Civ.R. 73(d)

 Notice of Appeal

[This Rule provided as follows, prior to its abrogation:] Filed with clerk of district court within 30 days of entry of judgment. Within 60 days if United States or officer or agency thereof is a party. Within 15 days after entry of an interlocutory decision or order. Civ.R. 74(a) [Rule 74 abrogated eff. Dec. 1, 1997].

[This Rule provided as follows, prior to its abrogation:] When timely notice is filed by a party, any other party may file notice within 14 days thereafter or within time otherwise prescribed by Civ.R. 74(a), whichever period last expires. Civ.R. 74(a) [Rule 74 abrogated eff. Dec. 1, 1997].

[This Rule provided as follows, prior to its abrogation:] Upon showing of excusable neglect, time for filing may be extended on motion filed not later than 20 days from expiration of time for filing. Civ.R. 74(a) [Rule 74 abrogated eff. Dec. 1, 1997].

Running of time for filing terminated as to all parties by timely filing of any of the following motions with the magistrate judge by any party, and the full time for appeal from judgment entered commences to run anew from entry of any of the following orders:

(1) granting or denying motion for judgment under Civ.R. 50(b);

(2) granting or denying motion under Civ.R. 52(b) to amend or make additional findings of fact;

(3) granting or denying motion under Civ.R. 59 to alter or amend judgment;

(4) denying motion for new trial under Civ.R. 59. Civ.R. 74(a) [prior to its abrogation] [Rule 74 abrogated eff. Dec. 1, 1997.]

 Joint statement of case

Parties could file in lieu of record within 10 days after filing of notice of appeal, under provisions of this rule prior to its abrogation. Civ.R. 75(b)(1) [Rule 75 abrogated eff. Dec. 1, 1997].

 Transcript

Within 10 days after filing notice of appeal appellant to make arrangements for production. Unless entire transcript is to be included, description of parts appellant intends to present must be served on the appellee and filed by the appellant within

RULES OF CIVIL PROCEDURE

APPEAL from magistrate judge to district judge under 28 U.S.C.A. § 636(c)(4) and Civ.R. 73(d)

the 10 day period. If appellee deems transcript of other parts to be necessary, designation of additional parts to be included must be served on the appellant and filed within 10 days after service of appellant's statement. Civ.R. 75(b)(2) [Rule 75 abrogated eff. Dec. 1, 1997].

Statement in lieu of transcript

If no record is available for transcription, parties must file a statement of evidence in lieu of transcript within 10 days after filing of notice of appeal. Civ.R. 75(b)(3) [Rule 75 abrogated eff. Dec. 1, 1997].

Briefs

Appellant to serve and file within 20 days after the filing of transcript, statement of case, or statement of evidence. Civ.R. 75(c)(1) [Rule 75 abrogated eff. Dec. 1, 1997].

Appellee to serve and file within 20 days after service of appellant's brief. Civ.R. 75(c)(2) [Rule 75 abrogated eff. Dec. 1, 1997].

Appellant may serve and file reply brief within 10 days after service of appellee's brief. Civ.R. 75(c)(3) [Rule 75 abrogated eff. Dec. 1, 1997].

If appellee files a cross-appeal, appellee may file a reply brief within 10 days after service of the reply brief of the appellant. Civ.R. 75(c)(4) [Rule 75 abrogated eff. Dec. 1, 1997].

Stay of judgments

Decision of district judge stayed for 10 days during which term a party may petition for rehearing. Civ.R. 76(b) [Rule 76 abrogated eff. Dec. 1, 1997].

APPEAL from magistrate judge under 28 U.S.C.A. § 636(c)(3)

Appeal to court of appeals in identical fashion as appeals from other judgments of district courts. App.R. 3.1. [Rule 3.1 abrogated eff. Dec. 1, 1998].

APPEAL to Supreme Court
Direct appeals

30 days after entry of interlocutory or final order, decree or judgment holding Act of Congress unconstitutional under circumstances provided by 28 U.S.C.A. §§ 1252, and 1253. 28 U.S.C.A. § 2101(a), as amended by Act May 24, 1949, c. 139, § 106, 63 Stat. 104. [28 U.S.C.A. § 1252 was repealed and 28 U.S.C.A. § 2101(a) was amended by Pub.L. 100–352, §§ 1, 5(b), June 27, 1988, 102 Stat. 662, 663, respectively. For effective date and applicability to cases, see section 7 of Pub.L. 100–352, set out as 28 U.S.C.A. § 1254 note.]

30 days from interlocutory judgment, order, or decree in any other direct appeal authorized by law from decision of district court. 28 U.S.C.A. § 2101(b).

60 days from final judgment, order, or decree in any other direct appeal authorized by law from decision of district court. 28 U.S.C.A. § 2101(b).

Other appeals and certiorari

90 days after entry of judgment or decree; justice of Supreme Court for good cause shown may ex-

RULES OF CIVIL PROCEDURE

APPEAL to Supreme Court	tend time for applying for writ of certiorari for period not exceeding 60 days. 28 U.S.C.A. § 2101(c).
Briefs supporting certiorari	No separate brief supporting petition for certiorari shall be filed; See Supreme Court Rule 14.2.
Brief opposing certiorari	30 days after case is placed on the docket unless time is extended by Court or a Justice or by the Clerk; See Supreme Court Rule 15.3.
Brief on merits on appeal or certiorari	By appellant or petitioner, filed within 45 days of the order granting the writ of certiorari or the order noting probable jurisdiction or postponing consideration of jurisdiction; see Supreme Court Rule 25.1.
	By appellee or respondent, filed within 35 days after the brief for the appellant or petitioner is filed; see Supreme Court Rule 25.2.
	Reply brief, if any, filed within 35 days after the brief for appellee or respondent is filed, but any reply brief must actually be received by Clerk not later than one week before the date of oral argument. See Supreme Court Rule 25.3.
Stay of mandate pending petition for certiorari	A stay of mandate pending a petition to the Supreme Court for certiorari cannot exceed 90 days unless the period is extended for good cause or unless during the period of stay, the party who obtained the stay files a petition for the writ and notifies the circuit clerk in writing in which case the stay will continue until final disposition by the Supreme Court. The court of appeals must issue the mandate immediately when a copy of the Supreme Court order denying the petition for writ of certiorari is filed. App.R. 41(d)(2).
ATTORNEY'S fees	See "Costs", this table.
BILL of particulars	Abolished. See Civ.R. 12(e), as amended in 1948. See, however, "More definite statement", this table.
CLASS actions	
Certification	At an early practicable time, when a person sues or is sued as a representative of a class, the court must determine by order whether to certify the action as a class action. Civ.R. 23(c)(1)(A).
Settlement, voluntary dismissal, or compromise	Approval by court of settlement, voluntary dismissal, or compromise that would bind class members only after hearing and on finding. Civ.R. 23(e)(1)(C).
Attorney fees	Claim for award of attorney fees and nontaxable costs must be made by motion under Civ.R. 54(d)(2) subject to Civ.R. 23(h) at a time set by the court. Notice of motion must be served on all parties and, for motions by class counsel, directed to class members in a reasonable manner. Civ.R. 23(h)(1).
CLERICAL mistakes in judgments, orders, or record	May be corrected at any time; but during pendency of appeal, may be corrected before appeal is

docketed in the appellate court, and thereafter while appeal pending may be corrected with leave of appellate court. Civ.R. 60(a).

COMPLAINT

Filing commences action—must be served with summons. Civ.R. 3.

Service of summons and complaint within 120 days after filing. Civ.R. 4(m).

COMPUTATION of time

Exclude day of the act, event or default from which designated period of time begins to run. Include last day of the period so computed unless it is a Saturday, Sunday, or legal holiday, or, when act to be done is the filing of a paper in court, a day on which weather or other conditions have made the office of the clerk of the district court inaccessible, in which event period runs until end of the next day which is not one of the aforementioned days. Civ.R. 6(a).

Intermediate Saturdays, Sundays, and legal holidays are excluded if the period is less than 11 days. Civ.R. 6(a).

Exclude day of the act, event, or default that begins the period. Include last day of the period unless it is a Saturday, Sunday, or legal holiday, or, when the act to be done is filing of paper in court, a day on which weather or other conditions have made office of clerk inaccessible. App.R. 26(a).

Intermediate Saturdays, Sundays, and legal holidays are excluded if the period is less than 11 days, unless stated in calendar days. App.R. 26(a).

Service by mail is complete upon mailing. Civ.R. 5(b).

Service by mail or by commercial carrier is complete upon mailing or delivery to the carrier. App.R. 25(c).

Service under Rule 5(b)(2)(B), (C), or (D) adds three days after the prescribed period would otherwise expire under Civ.R. 6(a). Civ.R. 6(e).

When a party is required or permitted to act within a prescribed period after service of a paper upon that party, three calendar days are added to the period unless the paper is delivered on the date of service stated in the proof of service. A paper served electronically is not treated as delivered on the day of service stated in the proof of service. App.R. 26(c).

Legal holidays are defined by Civ.R. 6(a) and App.R. 26(a)(4).

Supreme Court matters—See Supreme Court Rule 30.

RULES OF CIVIL PROCEDURE

CONDEMNATION of property
Answer to notice of condemnation — 20 days after service of notice. Civ.R. 71A(e).

CORPORATE DISCLOSURE — Nongovernmental corporate parties must file, with first appearance, pleading, motion, response, or other request addressed to the court, statement identifying a parent corporation or any publicly held corporation owning 10% or more of its stock or stating that there is no such corporation. Party must promptly file supplemental statement upon any change in the information that the statement requires. Civ.R. 7.1.

COSTS — Taxation on 1 day's notice. Motion to review taxation of costs 5 days after taxation. Civ.R. 54(d).

Failure to comply with request for waiver of service of summons and to return waiver within time allowed which must be at least 30 days from date request is sent or 60 days from that date for a defendant addressed outside any judicial district of the United States. Civ.R. 4(d).

Attorney's fees and related nontaxable expenses — Motion filed no later than 14 days after entry of judgement. Civ.R. 54(d)(2)(B).

CROSS APPEAL
Optional appeal from magistrate judge to district judge — Appellee may file reply brief within 10 days after service of reply brief of appellant. Civ.R. 75(c)(4) [Rule 75 abrogated eff. Dec. 1, 1997].

Appellate rules — Within 14 days of filing of first notice of appeal or within the time otherwise prescribed by App.R. 4(a), whichever last expires. App.R. 4(a)(3).

Inmates — Within 14 days after date when first notice of appeal was docketed by the district court. The 14 day period runs from date district court receives first notice of appeal. App.R. 4(c).

DEFAULT
Entry by clerk — No time stated. Civ.R. 55(b).

Entry by court — If party against whom default is sought has appeared, the party shall be served with written notice of application for default judgment at least 3 days prior to hearing on such application. Civ.R. 55(b).

DEFENSES and objections, presentation of
By pleading — See "Answer", this table.

By motion — Motion shall be made before pleading if further pleading is permitted. Civ.R. 12(b).

At trial — Adverse party may assert at trial any defense in law or fact to claim for relief to which such party is not required to serve responsive pleading. Civ.R. 12(b).

DEFENSES and objections, presentation of

Motion affects time for responsive pleading	Service of motion under Civ.R. 12 alters times for responsive pleading. See "Responsive Pleadings", this table.

DEMURRERS — Abolished. Civ.R. 7(c).

DEPOSITIONS — See, also, "Interrogatories", "Depositions on written questions", this table.

Notice of filing — Promptly. Civ.R. 30(f)(3) and Civ.R. 31(c).

Notice of taking

Reasonable notice to every party. Civ.R. 30(b).

Objections

As to admissibility, objection may be made at trial or hearing, but subject to Civ.R. 28(b) and 32(d)(3). Civ.R. 32(b).

As to errors or irregularities in the notice, service promptly. Civ.R. 32(d)(1).

As to disqualification of officer, objection made before deposition begins or as soon thereafter as disqualification becomes known or could be discovered. Civ.R. 32(d)(2).

As to competency of witness or competency, relevancy, or materiality of testimony—not waived by failure to make such objection before or during deposition unless the ground might have been obviated or removed if presented at that time. Civ.R. 32(d)(3)(A).

As to errors and irregularities at oral examination in manner of taking deposition, in the form of questions or answers, in the oath or affirmation, or in conduct of parties, and errors which might be obviated, removed, or cured if promptly presented—seasonable objection made at taking of deposition. Civ.R. 32(d)(3)(B).

As to form of written questions submitted under Civ.R. 31—service within time allowed for serving succeeding cross or other questions and within 5 days after service of last questions authorized. Civ.R. 32(d)(3)(C).

As to completion and return (transcription, signing, certification, sealing, etc.)—motion to suppress made with reasonable promptness after defect is or might have been ascertained. Civ.R. 32(d)(4).

Orders of protection

Subsequent to certification that movant has in good faith conferred or attempted to confer with other affected parties to resolve dispute without court action. Civ.R. 26(c).

Motion to terminate or limit examination

Any time during a deposition. Civ.R. 30(d)(3).

Perpetuate testimony pending appeal	Motion in district court upon same notice and service thereof as if action was pending in district court. Civ.R. 27(b).
Perpetuate testimony before action	Service of notice and petition 20 days before date of hearing. Civ.R. 27(a)(2).
Taking	Time specified in the notice of taking. Civ. R. 30(b)(1). Prior notice by a party to deponent and other parties to designate another method to record deponent's testimony in addition to method specified by person taking deposition. Civ.R. 30(b)(3).
Review of transcript or recording	Request by a party or deponent before completion of deposition. Deponent has 30 days after notice of availability of transcript or recording to review and to indicate changes. Civ.R. 30(e).
When taken	After parties have conferred to consider their claims, defenses and possibility of settlement and to develop a proposed discovery plan under Civ.R. 26(f). Civ.R. 26(d).

DEPOSITIONS on written questions

	See, also, "Depositions", "Interrogatories", this table.
When taken	After parties have conferred to discuss their claims, defenses and possibility of settlement and to develop a proposed discovery plan under Civ.R. 26(f). Civ.R. 26(d).
Cross questions	Service within 14 days after service of the notice and question. Court may enlarge or shorten time. Civ.R. 31(a)(4).
Redirect questions	Service within 7 days after being served with cross questions. Court may enlarge or shorten time. Civ.R. 31(a)(4).
Recross questions	Service within 7 days after service of redirect questions. Court may enlarge or shorten time. Civ.R. 31(a)(4).
Notice of filing of deposition	Promptly. Civ.R. 31(c).
Objections to form	Service within the time allowed for serving the succeeding cross or other questions and within 5 days after service of last questions authorized. Civ.R. 32(d)(3)(C).

DISCOVERY

	See, also, "Admissions", "Depositions", "Depositions on written questions", "Interrogatories", "Production of documents", this Table.
	Discovery Conference Except in exempted actions or when otherwise ordered, as soon as practicable and at least 21 days

DISCOVERY

before a scheduling conference is held or a scheduling order is due under Civ.R. 16(b), the parties must confer to consider their claims, defenses, and possibility of settlement, to make or arrange for disclosures, and to develop a proposed discovery plan. A written report outlining the plan is to be submitted to the court within 14 days after the conference. Civ.R. 26(f); See, also, Civ.R. 26(d). Without waiting for a discovery request and within 14 days after the Civ.R. 26(f) conference of parties, a party must provide information specified in Civ.R. 26(a)(1). Disclosure of expert testimony under Civ.R. 26(a)(2), in absence of court direction or stipulation, is to be made at least 90 days before trial date or date case is ready for trial or if evidence intended as rebuttal of Civ.R. 26(a)(2)(B), within 30 days after disclosure of such evidence. Civ.R. 26(a)(2)(C). All disclosures are to be promptly filed with court. Civ.R. 26(a)(4). Identification of witnesses, documents, exhibits, including summaries of other evidence, and designation of witnesses whose testimony will be by deposition with a transcript of pertinent testimony if deposition is not taken stenographically to be provided to other parties at least 30 days before trial unless otherwise directed by court. Within 14 days thereafter, unless otherwise specified by court, a party may file objections. Civ.R. 26(a)(3).

DISMISSAL for want of subject-matter jurisdiction

Any time. Civ.R. 12(h)(3).

DISMISSAL by plaintiff voluntarily without court order

Any time before service of answer or motion for summary judgment. Civ.R. 41(a)(1).

DISMISSAL of counter-claim, cross-claim or third-party claim, voluntary

Before service of responsive pleading, or if none, before introduction of evidence at trial or hearing. Civ.R. 41(c).

DISMISSAL without prejudice

Service of summons and complaint not made within 120 days after filing of complaint. Civ.R. 4(m).

DOCUMENTS, Production of

See "Production of documents", this Table.

ENLARGEMENT of time generally

Act required or allowed at or within specified time by Civil Rule, notice thereunder, or court order

Court for cause shown may (1) with or without motion or notice order period enlarged if request therefor is made before expiration of period originally prescribed or as extended by previous order, or (2) upon motion made after expiration of the specified period permit act to be done where failure to act was result of excusable neglect; but court may not extend time for taking any action under Civ.R. 50(b) and (c)(2), 52(b), 59(b), (d) and (e), and 60(b), except to extent and under conditions stated in them. Civ.R. 6(b).

Affidavits in opposition, service

Time may be extended by court. Civ.R. 6(d).

ENLARGEMENT of time
generally

Hearing of motions and defenses	May be deferred until trial. Civ.R. 12(d).
Service under Rule 5(b)(2)(B), (C), or (D)	Adds three days after which the prescribed period after service would otherwise expire under Civ.R. 6(a). Civ.R. 6(e). When a party is required or permitted to act within a prescribed period after service of a paper upon that party, three calendar days are added to the period unless the paper is delivered on the date of service stated in the proof of service. A paper served electronically is not treated as delivered on the day of service stated in the proof of service. App.R. 26(c).
Injunction—temporary restraining order	May be extended 10 days by order of court or for a longer period by consent of party against whom order is directed. Civ.R. 65(b).
Response to request for admissions	Time may be enlarged or shortened by court or as the parties may agree in writing subject to Civ.R. 29. Civ.R. 36(a).
Optional appeal from magistrate judge to district judge	Upon showing of excusable neglect, time to file notice of appeal may be extended upon motion filed not later than 20 days from expiration of time for filing. Civ.R. 74(a) [Rule 74 abrogated eff. Dec. 1, 1997].
Motion for judgment notwithstanding the verdict	No enlargement of the 10 day period except to the extent and under conditions stated in Civ.R. 50(b). Civ.R. 6(b).
Findings by the court, amendment of additional findings	No enlargement of the 10 day period except to the extent and under conditions stated in Civ.R. 52(b). Civ.R. 6(b).
Motion for new trial	No enlargement of the 10 day period except to the extent and under conditions stated in Civ.R. 59(b), (d), and (e). Civ.R. 6(b).
Motion for relief from judgment or order	No enlargement of the 1 year period except to the extent and under conditions stated in Civ.R. 60(b). Civ.R. 6(b).
Appellate rules	Court for good cause may extend time prescribed by App.Rules or by its order to perform any act or may permit act to be done after expiration of such time; but court may not extend time for filing notice of appeal, or petition for permission to appeal a notice of appeal from or a petition to enjoin, set aside, suspend, modify, enforce or otherwise review an order of an administrative agency, board, commission or officer of the United States, unless specifically authorized by law. App.R. 26(b).
Supreme Court matters	See Supreme Court Rule 30.

EXCEPTIONS for
insufficiency of pleadings Abolished. Civ.R. 7(c).

RULES OF CIVIL PROCEDURE

EXECUTION
 Stay

Automatically: No execution to issue, nor proceedings for enforcement to be taken, until expiration of 10 days after entry of judgment; exceptions—injunctions, receiverships, and patent accountings. Civ.R. 62(a).

Stay according to state law. Civ.R. 62(f).

Motion for new trial or for judgment. Civ.R. 62(b).

Stay in favor of government. Civ.R. 62(e).

Supersedeas on appeal. Civ.R. 62(d).

Stay of judgment as to multiple claims or multiple parties. Civ.R. 62(h).

Stay of judgment pending appeal from magistrate judge to district judge. Civ.R. 74(c). Stay of decision of district judge for 10 days during which time a party may petition for rehearing. Civ.R. 76(b) [Rules 74 and 76 abrogated eff. Dec. 1, 1997].

FILING papers

Complaint must be filed at commencement of action. Civ.R. 3.

Constitutional challenge to a statute. Civ.R. 5.1.

Service of summons and complaint within 120 days after filing of complaint. Civ.R. 4(m).

All papers required to be filed must be filed with clerk unless the judge permits them to be filed with the judge. Civ.R. 5(e).

Local court rules may permit or require papers to be filed by electronic means if consistent with standards of Judicial Conference of the United States. A local rule requirement of electronic filing must allow reasonable exceptions. The clerk shall not refuse for filing any paper solely because it is not presented in proper form under Rules of Civil Procedure or any local rule or practice. Civ.R. 5(e).

All papers after the complaint required to be served upon a party, together with a certificate of service, must be filed with the court within a reasonable time after service. Civ.R. 5(d).

FINDINGS
 Motion to amend

10 days after entry of judgment. Civ.R. 52(b). Exception from general rule relating to enlargement. Civ.R. 6(b).

FOREIGN law

Reasonable written notice required of party intending to raise an issue concerning the law of a foreign country. Civ.R. 44.1.

HEARING of motions

Unless local conditions make it impracticable, district court shall establish regular times and places

RULES OF CIVIL PROCEDURE

HEARING of motions

for hearing and disposition of motions requiring notice and hearing; but judge may make orders for the advancement, conduct, and hearing of actions. Civ.R. 78.

Service of notice 5 days before time specified for hearing unless otherwise provided by these rules or order of court. Civ.R. 6(d).

Hearing of certain motions and defenses before trial on application of any party unless court orders deferral until trial. Civ.R. 12(d).

HOLIDAYS

New Year's Day, Birthday of Martin Luther King, Jr., Washington's Birthday, Memorial Day, Independence Day, Labor Day, Columbus Day, Veterans' Day, Thanksgiving Day, Christmas Day, and any other day declared a holiday by the President, Congress or the state in which is located either the district court that rendered the challenged judgment or order, or the circuit clerk's principal office. Civ.R. 6(a); App.R. 26(a).

Exclusion in computation of time. Civ.R. 6(a); App.R. 26(a).

INJUNCTION (Temporary restraining order granted without notice)

Order shall be indorsed with date and hour of issuance, filed forthwith in clerk's office, and entered of record. Civ.R. 65(b).

Expiration within such time, not to exceed 10 days, as court fixes, unless within time so fixed the order is extended for like period or, with consent of party against whom order is directed, for longer period. Civ.R. 65(b).

Motion for preliminary injunction shall be set down for hearing at earliest possible time—takes precedence of all matters except older ones of same character. Civ.R. 65(b).

Motion for dissolution or modification on 2 days' notice or such shorter notice as court may prescribe; hear and determine motion as expeditiously as ends of justice require. Civ.R. 65(b).

INSTRUCTIONS

Requests

At close of evidence or at an earlier reasonable time that the court directs. After close of evidence for issues that could not reasonably have been anticipated at an earlier time for requests, and untimely requests for instructions on any issue with the court's permission. Civ.R. 51(a).

Proposed

Court must inform parties before instructing jury and before final argument, and give parties opportunity to object before instructions and arguments are delivered. Civ.R. 51(b)(1), (2).

INSTRUCTIONS

Time of

Court may instruct jury at any time after trial begins and before jury is discharged. Civ.R. 51(b)(3).

Objections

For parties informed of instructions or actions on requests before the jury is instructed and before final jury arguments, at opportunity for objection required by Civ.R. 51(b)(2). For parties not informed of instructions or actions on requests before time for objection under Civ.R. 51(b)(2), promptly after learning that instruction or request will be, or has been, given or refused. Civ.R. 51(c).

INTERROGATORIES
to parties

See, also, "Depositions", "Depositions on written questions", this table.

Service after parties have conferred pursuant to Civ.R. 26(f). Civ.R. 33(a).

Answers or objections

Service within 30 days after service of the interrogatories. A shorter or longer time may be directed by the court or agreed to. Civ.R. 33(b)(3).

INTERVENTION

Upon timely application. Civ.R. 24(a), (b).

Person desiring to intervene shall serve a motion to intervene upon the parties as provided in Civil Rule 5. Civ.R. 24(c).

JUDGMENT or order

Alter or amend judgment, motion to

Shall be filed not later than 10 days after entry of judgment. Civ.R. 59(e). Exception to general rule, relating to enlargement. Civ.R. 6(b).

Clerical mistakes

May be corrected any time; but during pendency of appeal, may be corrected before appeal is docketed in the appellate court, and thereafter while appeal pending may be corrected with leave of appellate court. Civ.R. 60(a).

Default

See "Default", this table.

Renewal of motion for judgment after trial

Not later than 10 days after entry of judgment. Exception from general rule relating to enlargement. Civ.R. 6(b).

Entry of judgment

Subject to Civ.R. 54(b), promptly by clerk without awaiting the court's direction, unless court orders otherwise, upon general verdict of jury or upon court decision that a party shall recover only a sum certain or costs or that all relief shall be denied. Promptly approved form of judgment by court, promptly entered by clerk, upon special verdict or general verdict accompanied by answers to interrogatories, or upon court decision granting other relief. Entry may not be delayed in order to tax costs or award fees. Civ.R. 58(a)(2), (c)(1).

Time of entry—Entry of a judgment or order in the civil docket under Civ.R. 79(a) is entry for purposes of these rules, unless Civ.R. 58(a)(1) re-

JUDGMENT or order

quires a separate document, in which case entry occurs when the judgment or order is entered under Civ.R. 79(a) and either the judgment or order is set forth on a separate document, or 150 days have run from entry of the judgment or order in the civil docket. Civ.R. 58(b).

Entry, notice of

Immediately upon entry, clerk shall serve notice thereof in manner provided in Civ.R. 5(b) and make note in docket of the service. Any party may in addition serve a notice of such entry in manner provided in Civ.R. 5(b) for service of papers. Civ.R. 77(d).

Lack of notice of entry by clerk does not affect time to appeal or relieve or authorize court to relieve party for failure to appeal within time allowed, except as permitted by App.R. 4(a). Civ.R. 77(d).

Offer of judgment

Service more than 10 days before trial begins. Civ.R. 68.

Acceptance, written notice of—service within 10 days after service of offer. Civ.R. 68.

On pleadings, motion for judgment

After pleadings are closed but within such time as not to delay the trial. Civ.R. 12(c).

Relief from, on grounds stated in Rule 60(b)

Motion within a reasonable time and not more than 1 year after judgment, order, or proceeding entered or taken, for following grounds: (1) mistake, inadvertence, surprise, or excusable neglect; (2) newly discovered evidence; (3) fraud, misrepresentation, or other misconduct. Civ.R. 60(b). Exception from general rule relating to enlargement. Civ.R. 60(b).

Motion within a reasonable time, for following grounds: (1) judgment void, (2) judgment satisfied, released, or discharged, (3) prior underlying judgment reversed or otherwise vacated, (4) no longer equitable that judgment have prospective application, (5) any other reason justifying relief. Civ.R. 60(b). Exception from general rule relating to enlargement. Civ.R. 6(b).

Stay

See "Execution", this table.

Summary judgment

See "Summary Judgment", this table.

JURORS

The institution of the alternate juror has been abolished. Civ.R. 47, 1991 Advisory Committee note, subd. (b).

JURY trial
Demand

Service any time after commencement of action and not later than 10 days after service of last pleading directed to the triable issue. Civ.R. 38(b).

Adverse party may serve demand for jury trial within 10 days after service of first demand or such lesser time as court fixes. Civ.R. 38(c).

JURY trial
 Removed actions

If at the time of removal all necessary pleadings have been served, demand for jury trial may be served:

By petitioner, 10 days after the petition for removal is filed;

By any other party, within 10 days after service on party of the notice of filing the petition. Civ.R. 81(c).

Demand after removal not necessary in either of two instances: (1) prior to removal, party has made express demand in accordance with state law; (2) state law does not require express demands and court does not direct otherwise. Civ.R. 81(c).

LEGAL HOLIDAY

See "Holidays", this table.

MAGISTRATE JUDGES
 Trial by consent

Consent of parties to magistrate judge's authority to be exercised within period specified by local rule. Civ.R. 73(b).

 Pretrial matters

Objections of parties to order disposing of matter not dispositive of claim or defense to be served and filed within 10 days after being served with copy of order. Civ.R. 72(a).

Clerk to forthwith mail copies to all parties of recommendation of magistrate judge for disposition of matter dispositive of claim or defense of a party or prisoner petition. Specific written objections to recommended disposition may be served and filed within 10 days after service. Response to objections may be made within 10 days after being served with copy. Civ.R. 72(b).

MAIL

Service under Rule 5(b)(2)(B), (C), or (D) adds 3 days after a prescribed period after service would otherwise expire under Civ.R. 6(a). Civ.R. 6(e).
When a party is required or permitted to act within a prescribed period after service of a paper upon that party, three calendar days are added to the period unless the paper is delivered on the date of service stated in the proof of service. A paper served electronically is not treated as delivered on the day of service stated in the proof of service. App.R. 26(c).
A brief or appendix is timely filed if on or before the last day for filing it is mailed First-Class or other class at least as expeditious, postage prepaid, or dispatched for delivery within three calendar days by a third-party commercial carrier. App.R. 25(a)(2)(B).

MASTERS
 Order appointing master

Court may enter only after master has filed affidavit disclosing whether there is ground for disqualification under 28 U.S.C. § 455 and, if ground is disclosed, after parties have consented with court's approval to waive the disqualification. Civ.R. 53(b)(3).

RULES OF CIVIL PROCEDURE

MASTERS

Amendment of order appointing	Order appointing master may be amended at any time after notice to parties, and opportunity to be heard. Civ.R. 53(b)(4).
Order of master	A master who makes an order must file the order and promptly serve a copy on each party. The clerk must enter the order on the docket. Civ.R. 53(e).
Report of master	Master must report to court as required by order of appointment. The master must file the report and promptly save a copy on each party unless the court directs otherwise. Civ.R. 53(f).
	In acting on, the court must afford an opportunity to be heard. Civ.R. 53(g)(1).
	A party may file objections or motion to adopt or modify no later than 20 days from the time the master's order, report, or recommendations are served, unless the court sets a different time. Civ.R. 53(g)(2).
Compensation of master	The court must fix the master's compensation before or after judgment on the basis and terms stated in the order of appointment but the court may set a new basis and terms after notice and opportunity to be heard. Civ.R. 53(h)(1)

MORE DEFINITE STATEMENT

Furnished	Must be furnished within 10 days after notice of order or other time fixed by court or court may strike pleading. Civ.R. 12(e).
Motion for	Must be made before responsive pleading is interposed. Civ.R. 12(e).

MOTIONS, notices, and affidavits

	See, also, specific headings, this table.
In general	A written motion, supporting affidavits, and notice of hearing thereof—service not later than 5 days before time specified for hearing unless a different time is fixed by rule or by order of court. Civ.R. 6(d).
	Opposing affidavits may be served not later than one day before hearing, unless court permits otherwise. Civ.R. 6(d).
	Pleading, written motion, or other paper not signed by attorney or party shall be stricken unless omission of signature is corrected promptly after being called to attention of attorney or party. Civ.R. 11(a).

NEW TRIAL

Motion and affidavits	Motion shall be filed not later than 10 days after entry of judgment. Civ.R. 59(b). Exception from general rule relating to enlargement. Civ.R. 6(b).

NEW TRIAL

| | If motion based on affidavits, they must be filed with motion. Civ.R. 59(c). |

Opposing affidavits — Shall be filed within 10 days of service of motion for new trial; period may be extended up to 20 days either by court for good cause shown or by parties by written stipulation. Civ.R. 59(c).

Initiative of court — Not later than 10 days after entry of judgment, court may order new trial for any reason that would justify granting one on a party's motion. Civ.R. 59(d). Exception to general rule relating to enlargement. Civ.R. 6(b).

After giving parties notice and opportunity to be heard, court may grant a timely motion for new trial, for reason not stated in the motion. Civ.R. 59(d). Exception to general rule relating to enlargement. Civ.R. 6(b).

Judgment as a matter of law — Party against whom judgment as a matter of law is rendered shall file a motion for a new trial under Civ.R. 59 no later than 10 days after entry of the judgment. Civ.R. 50(c)(2).

OBJECTIONS to orders or rulings of court

At time ruling or order of court is made or sought; if party has no opportunity to object to ruling or order at time it is made, absence of objection does not thereafter prejudice the party. Civ.R. 46.

Pretrial matters referred to magistrate judge — Objections of parties to order disposing of matter not dispositive of claim or defense to be served and filed within 10 days after being served with copy of order. Civ.R. 72(a).

Specific written objections to recommended disposition of matter dispositive of claim or defense of a party or prisoner petition may be served or filed within 10 days after service. Response to objections may be made within 10 days after being served with copy. Civ.R. 72(b).

OFFER of judgment

Must be served more than 10 days before trial. Civ.R. 68.

Acceptance must be served within 10 days after service of offer. Civ.R. 68.

ORDERS — See Judgment or order.

PARTICULARS, Bill of — Abolished. Civ.R. 12(e), as amended in 1948. See, however, "More definite statement", this table.

PLEADINGS
Amendment of — Once as matter of course before responsive pleading served or within 20 days if no response is permitted and action has not been placed on trial calendar. Civ.R. 15(a).

By leave of court or written consent of adverse parties, at any time. Civ.R. 15(a).

RULES OF CIVIL PROCEDURE

PLEADINGS

	During trial or after judgment to conform to evidence or to raise issues not raised in pleadings, but tried by express or implied consent of parties. Civ.R. 15(b).
Supplemental	Upon motion of party—court may upon reasonable notice permit service of supplemental pleading setting forth transactions, etc., which have happened since date of pleading sought to be supplemented. Civ.R. 15(d).
	Adverse party plead to supplemental pleading—if court deems advisable, it shall so order, specifying time therefor. Civ.R. 15(d)
Averments of time	Such averments are material and shall be considered like all other averments of material matter. Civ.R. 9(f).
Judgment on, motion for	After pleadings are closed but within such time as not to delay the trial. Civ.R. 12(c).
Striking of matter from	Motion made before responding to a pleading or, if no responsive pleading permitted, within 20 days after service of pleading. Civ.R. 12(f).
	On court's own initiative at any time. Civ.R. 12(f).
Signing of	
	Pleading, written motion, or other paper not signed by attorney or party shall be stricken unless omission of signature is corrected promptly after being called to attention of attorney or party. Civ.R. 11(a).
PLEAS	Abolished. Civ.R. 7(c).
PRETRIAL conferences	
	Scheduling order to issue as soon as practicable but in any event within 90 days after appearance of a defendant and within 120 days after complaint served on defendant. Civ.R. 16(b).
PROCESS	See "Summons", this Table.
PRODUCTION of documents Request for, service of	
	Without leave of court or written stipulation, request may not be served before the time specified in Civ.R. 26(d). Civ.R. 34(b).
	May accompany notice of taking deposition. Civ.R. 30(b)(5).
Response to request	
	Within 30 days after service of the request. A shorter or longer time may be directed by court or agreed to. Civ.R. 34(b).
Time of inspection	The request shall specify a reasonable time. Civ.R. 34(b).
Subpoena	See "Subpoena", this table.

RULES OF CIVIL PROCEDURE

PRODUCTION of documents

REHEARING

Petition for panel rehearing

Petitions for panel rehearings may be filed within 14 days after entry of judgement unless the time is shortened or extended by order or local rule. In all civil cases in which the United States or its agency or officer thereof is a party, the time within which any party may seek a rehearing shall be 45 days after entry of judgement unless the time is shortened or extended by order. App.R. 40(a).

Issuance of mandate

The mandate of the court must issue 7 calendar days after the time to file a petition for rehearing expires, or 7 calendar days after entry of an order denying a timely petition for panel rehearing, petition for rehearing en banc, or motion for stay of mandate, whichever is later. The court may shorten or extend the time. The timely filing of a petition for panel rehearing, petition for rehearing en banc, or motion for stay of mandate, stays the mandate until disposition of the petition or motion, unless the court orders otherwise. App.R. 41(b), (d)(1).

REMOVED actions

Answers and defenses

Within 20 days after the receipt through service or otherwise of a copy of the initial pleading setting forth the claim for relief upon which the action or proceeding is based, or within 20 days after the service of summons upon such initial pleading, then filed, or within 5 days after filing of the petition for removal, whichever period is longest. Civ.R. 81(c).

Demand for jury trial

Demand after removal not necessary in either of two instances: (1) prior to removal, party has made express demand in accordance with state law; (2) state law does not require express demands and court does not direct otherwise. Civ.R. 81(c).

Notice of removal

Within 30 days after receipt through service or otherwise of a copy of the initial pleading setting forth the claim for relief upon which the action or proceeding is based, or within 30 days after service of summons if such initial pleading has then been filed in court and is not required to be served on defendant, whichever period is shorter. 28 U.S.C.A. § 1446(b).

If the case stated by the initial pleading is not removable, a notice of removal may be filed within 30 days after receipt by the defendant, through service or otherwise, of a copy of an amended pleading, motion, order or other paper from which it may first be ascertained that the case is one which is or has become removable. 28 U.S.C.A. § 1446(b).

A case may not be removed on the basis of jurisdiction conferred by 28 U.S.C.A. § 1332 more than one year after action's commencement. 28 U.S.C.A. § 1446(b).

REPLY

See, also, "Responsive pleadings", this table.

RULES OF CIVIL PROCEDURE

REPLY

To answer or third-party answer
: Only if ordered by court. Civ.R. 7(a). Service within 20 days after service of order, unless order otherwise directs. Civ.R. 12(a).

To counterclaim
: Service within 20 days after service of answer. Civ.R. 12(a).

United States or agency or officer or employee thereof shall serve reply within 60 days after service upon U.S. attorney. Civ.R. 12(a).

Alteration of time by service of Civ.R. 12 motion
: See "Responsive pleadings", this table.

RESPONSIVE PLEADINGS

See, also, "Answer", "Reply", this table.

To amend pleading
: Within 10 days after service of amended pleading or within time remaining for response to original pleading, whichever is longer, unless court otherwise orders. Civ.R. 15(a).

To supplemental pleading
: As ordered by court. Civ.R. 15(d).

Alteration of time by service of Civ.R. 12 motion
: Service of motion permitted under Civ.R. 12 alters times for responsive pleadings as follows unless different time fixed by court:
(1) if court denies motion, service of responsive pleading within 10 days after notice of denial;
(2) if court postpones disposition until trial on merits, service of responsive pleading within 10 days after notice of postponement;
(3) if court grants motion for more definite statement, service of responsive pleading within 10 days after service of the more definite statement.

RESTRAINING order, temporary, without notice
: See "Injunction", this table.

RETURN

The court may allow a summons or proof of service to be amended. Civ.R. 4(a) & (l).

The person effecting service shall make proof thereof to the court. Civ.R. 4(l).

SANCTIONS
: Presentation to court of a pleading, written motion, or other paper is a certification under Civ.R. 11(b). If after notice and reasonable opportunity to respond, court determines that Civ.R. 11(b) was violated, sanctions may be imposed by a motion for sanctions which shall not be filed or presented to court unless, within 21 days after service of the motion, the challenged matter is not withdrawn or corrected. Civ.R. 11(c). Sanctions are inapplicable to discovery. Civ.R. 11(d).

SATURDAYS AND SUNDAYS
: Exclusion in computation of time. Civ.R. 6(a); App.R. 26(a).

STAY or supersedeas
: See "Appeal", "Execution", this table.

RULES OF CIVIL PROCEDURE

SUBPOENA

Objection

Within 14 days after service of the subpoena or before the time specified for compliance if such time is less than 14 days after service, there be served upon the party or attorney designated in the subpoena written objection to production of any or all of the designated materials or of the premises. Civ.R. 45(c)(2)(B).

Motion to compel production

If objection has been made, the party serving the subpoena may, upon notice to the person commanded to produce, move at any time for an order to compel the production, inspection, copying, testing, or sampling. Civ.R. 45(c)(2)(B).

Motion to quash

The court by which a subpoena was issued shall quash or modify the subpoena on timely motion. Civ.R. 45(c)(3)(A).

Witnesses, documentary evidence, etc.

Subpoena specifies time for attendance and giving of testimony or to produce and permit inspection, copying, testing, or sampling of designated books, documents, electronically stored information, or tangible things in the possession, custody or control of that person, or to permit inspection of premises. Civ.R. 45(a)(1)(C).

SUBSTITUTION of parties

In cases of death, incompetency, or transfer of interest—motion for substitution, together with notice of hearing, served on parties as provided in Civ.R. 5 and upon persons not parties in manner provided in Civ.R. 4 for service of a summons. Civ.R. 25(a), (b), (c).

Dismissal as to deceased party unless motion for substitution is made not later than 90 days after death is suggested upon the record. Civ.R. 25(a).

Successor of public officer substituted automatically. Order of substitution may be entered at any time. Civ.R. 25(d).

SUMMARY JUDGMENT, motion for

Claimant

May move at any time after expiration of 20 days from commencement of action or after service of motion for summary judgment by adverse party. Civ.R. 56(a).

Defending party

May move at any time. Civ.R. 56(b).

Service

Service of motion at least 10 days before time fixed for hearing. Civ.R. 56(c).

Service of opposing affidavits prior to day of hearing. Civ.R. 56(c).

SUMMONS

Served with a copy of complaint. Civ.R. 4(c)(1). If not served within 120 days after filing complaint, court may dismiss action without prejudice, direct service be effected within a specified time, or extend time for service. Civ.R. 4(m).

RULES OF CIVIL PROCEDURE

SUMMONS

The person effecting service shall make proof thereof to the court. Civ.R. 4(*l*).

Service by any nonparty at least 18, a U.S. marshal, deputy U.S. marshal, or other person or officer specially appointed. Civ.R. 4(c)(2).

SUPPLEMENTAL pleadings

See "Pleadings", this table.

SUPERSEDEAS or stay

See "Appeal", "Execution", this table.

TERM

The district courts deemed always open. Civ.R. 77(a).

Terms of court have been abolished. 28 U.S.C.A. §§ 138–141, as amended by Act of Oct. 16, 1963, Pub.L. 88–139, 77 Stat. 248.

THIRD–PARTY practice

Third-party plaintiff need not obtain leave if third-party plaintiff files third-party complaint not later than 10 days after serving the original answer. Otherwise, must obtain leave on motion upon notice to all parties to the action. Civ.R. 14(a).

VERDICT

Renewal of motion for judgment after trial

Movant may renew request for judgment as a matter of law by filing a motion no later than 10 days after the entry of judgment or — if the motion addresses a jury issue not decided by a verdict — no later than 10 days after the jury was discharged. Civ.R. 50(b).

Exception from general rule relating to enlargement. Civ.R. 6(b).

New trial where judgment as a matter of law rendered

Party against whom judgment as a matter of law is rendered shall file a motion for a new trial pursuant to Civ.R. 59 no later than 10 days after entry of the judgment. Civ.R. 50(c)(2).

EQUITY RULES REFERENCE TABLE

The Federal Rules of Civil Procedure supplant the Equity Rules since in general they cover the field now covered by the Equity Rules and the Conformity Act (former section 724 of this title).

This table shows the Equity Rules to which references are made in the notes to the Federal Rules of Civil Procedure.

Equity Rules	Federal Rules of Civil Procedure
1	77
2	77
3	79
4	77
5	77
6	78
7	4, 70
8	6, 70
9	70
10	18, 54
11	71
12	3, 4, 5, 12, 55
13	4
14	4
15	4, 45
16	6, 55
17	55
18	7, 8
19	1, 15, 61
20	12
21	11, 12
22	1
23	1, 39
24	11
25	8, 9, 10, 19
26	18, 20, 82
27	23
28	15
29	7, 12, 42, 55
30	8, 13, 82
31	7, 8, 12, 55
32	15

Equity Rules	Federal Rules of Civil Procedure
33	7, 12
34	15
35	15
36	11
37	17, 19, 20, 24
38	23
39	19
40	20
41	17
42	19, 20
43	12, 21
44	12, 21
45	25
46	43, 61
47	26
48	43
49	53
50	30, 80
51	30, 53
52	45, 53
53	53
54	26
55	30
56	40
57	40
58	26, 33, 34, 36
59	53
60	53
61	53
61½	53
62	53
63	53
64	26
65	53
66	53
67	53
68	53
69	59
70	17
70½	52
71	54
72	60, 61
73	65
74	62
75	75
76	75
77	76
78	43
79	83
80	6
81	86

ORDERS OF THE SUPREME COURT OF THE UNITED STATES ADOPTING AND AMENDING RULES

ORDER OF DECEMBER 20, 1937

It is ordered that Rules of Procedure for the District Courts of the United States be adopted pursuant to Section 2 of the Act of June 19, 1934, Chapter 651 (48 Stat. 1064), and the Chief Justice is authorized and directed to transmit the Rules as adopted to the Attorney General and to request him, as provided in that section, to report these Rules to the Congress at the beginning of the regular session in January next. MR. JUSTICE BRANDEIS states that he does not approve of the adoption of the Rules.

ORDER OF DECEMBER 28, 1939

1. That the first sentence of Rule 81(a)(6) of the Rules of Civil Procedure be amended so as to read as follows:

"(6) These rules do not apply to proceedings under the Act of September 13, 1888, c. 1015, § 13 (25 Stat. 479) as amended, U.S.C., Title 8, § 282, 8 U.S.C.A. § 282, relating to deportation of Chinese; they apply to proceedings for enforcement or review of compensation orders under the Longshoremen's and Harbor Workers' Compensation Act, Act of March 4, 1927, c. 509, §§ 18, 21 (44 Stat. 1434, 1436), U.S.C., Title 33, §§ 918, 921, 33 U.S.C.A. §§ 918, 921, except to the extent that matters of procedure are provided for in that Act".

2. **Effective Date.** That the foregoing amendment take effect on the day which is three months subsequent to the adjournment of the second regular session of the 76th Congress, but if that day is prior to September 1, 1940, then this amendment shall take effect on September 1, 1940. This amendment governs all proceedings in actions brought after it takes effect and also all further proceedings in actions then pending, except to the extent that in the opinion of the Court its application in a particular action pending when the amendment takes effect would not be feasible or would work injustice, in which event the former procedure applies.

3. That THE CHIEF JUSTICE be authorized to transmit this amendment to the Attorney General with the request that he report it to the Congress at the beginning of the regular session in January, 1940.

MR. JUSTICE BLACK does not approve of the adoption of this amendment.

ORDER OF DECEMBER 27, 1946

1. That subdivisions (a) and (b) of Rule 80 of the Rules of Civil Procedure be, and they hereby are, abrogated.

2. That Rules 6, 7, 12, 13, 14, 17, 24, 26, 27, 28, 33, 34, 36, 41, 45, 52, 54, 56, 58, 59, 60, 62, 65, 66, 68, 73, 75, 77, 79, 81, 84, and 86 of the Rules of Civil Procedure and Forms Nos. 17, 20, 22, and 25, be, and they hereby are, amended as hereinafter set forth.

[See the amendments made thereby under the respective rules and forms, post.]

3. That THE CHIEF JUSTICE be authorized to transmit these amendments to the Attorney General with the request that he report them to the Congress at the beginning of the regular session in January, 1947.

MR. JUSTICE FRANKFURTER joins in approval of the proposed amendments essentially because of his confidence in the informed judgment of the Advisory Committee on Rules of Civil Procedure.

ORDER OF DECEMBER 29, 1948

1. That the title "Rules of Civil Procedure for the District Courts of the United States" be amended to read "Rules of Civil Procedure for the United States District Courts".

2. That Rules 1, 17, 22, 24, 25, 27, 37, 45, 57, 60, 62, 65, 66, 67, 69, 72, 73, 74, 75, 76, 79, 81, 82, and 86 of the Rules of Civil Procedure and Forms Nos. 1, 19, 22, 23, and 27, be, and they hereby are, amended as hereinafter set forth.

[See the amendments made thereby under the respective rules and forms, post.]

3. That THE CHIEF JUSTICE be authorized to transmit these amendments to the Attorney General with the request that he report them to the Congress at the beginning of the regular session in January, 1949.

ORDER OF APRIL 30, 1951

1. That paragraph (7) of Rule 81(a) of the Rules of Civil Procedure, be, and it hereby is, abrogated.

2. That the Rules of Civil Procedure be, and they hereby are, amended by including therein a rule to govern condemnation cases in the United States District Courts, numbered 71A, as follows:

[See text of Rule 71A, post.]

3. Effective Date. That this Rule 71A and the amendment to Rule 81(a) will take effect on August 1, 1951. Rule 71A governs all proceedings in actions brought after it takes effect and also all further proceedings in actions then pending, except to the extent that in the opinion of the court its application in a particular action pending when the rule takes effect would not be feasible or would work injustice, in which event the former procedure applies.

4. That Forms Nos. 28 and 29 be, and they hereby are, approved and added to the Appendix of Forms to the Rules of Civil Procedure. The forms read respectively as follows:

[See text of Forms 28 and 29, post.]

5. That THE CHIEF JUSTICE be authorized to transmit these amendments to the Congress on or before May 1, 1951.

ORDER OF APRIL 17, 1961

1. That Rules 25, 54, 62 and 86 of the Rules of Civil Procedure and Forms Nos. 2 and 19, be, and they hereby are, amended as hereinafter set forth:

[See the amendments made thereby under the respective rules and forms, post.]

2. That THE CHIEF JUSTICE be authorized to transmit these amendments to Congress in accordance with the provisions of Title 28, U.S.C., Sec. 2072.

3. MR. JUSTICE BLACK does not join in approval of the Rules because he believes that it would be better for Congress to act directly by legislation on the matters treated by the Rules.

4. MR. JUSTICE DOUGLAS filed the following statement:

"Most of the proposed changes in the Rules of Civil Procedure are picayune and harmless, yet hardly worth making apart from any overall revision of the Rules. The change in Rule 25 of the Rules of Civil Procedure is, however, a major one; and it seems to me unwise. The policy that a cabinet officer under one administration pursues is often not the policy of the next administration. I would not make the contrary assumption, as does the proposed change. I think the ends served by *Snyder v. Buck*, 340 U.S. 15, 71 S.Ct. 93, 95 L.Ed. 15, are proper ones. The Rule in its present form leaves the burden on the claimant who challenges a particular government policy to re-establish that the controversy he had with a predecessor is a live one as respects the successor. The burden should rest there, not with the newcomer to office.

"The critical language in Rule 25(d) that is changed by the proposed amendment derived from 28 U.S.C. § 780 which the Revised Code dropped in 1949 because it had been incorporated in Rule 25(d). See 28 U.S.C., p. XXIX. The history of § 780 is reviewed in *Snyder v. Buck*, supra, pp. 18–19.

"Congress dealt with the matter beginning with the Act of February 8, 1899, 30 Stat. 822. The care with which it approached the problem is shown in H.R.Rep. No. 960, 55th Cong., 2d Sess., p. 2, where it is said:

" 'A mandamus proceeding against an officer is based upon the claim that he is personally refusing to perform some duty which the law requires of him in his official character, and if decided against him he is properly liable, personally, for all cost of the proceeding, but if he vacates the office before a decision, it might seem harsh to compel his successor to become a party to the suit and to the costs already accrued without having been guilty of any personal neglect of the official duty involved in the proceeding; but to provide against this seeming harshness your committee propose to amend the bill so as to give the succeeding official an opportunity to perform the official act involved in the proceeding and thereby prevent the survival of the action against himself, and if he fails to do so, he can not then complain of being mulct in costs accruing against his predecessor.'

"The provision of § 780 that the action might be continued against the successor in office on the requisite showing within the stated period was added by § 11 of the Judiciary Act of 1925. 43 Stat. 936, 941. The last word Congress spoke on the matter reflected the views in a Report submitted by Chief Justice Taft dated March 11, 1922, which explained § 11 in the following words:

" 'It will be noted that the provision is not mandatory, but leaves it to the sound discretion of the court to determine whether there is a substantial need for continuing the cause and obtaining an adjudication of the questions involved. This will tend to restrict the exercise of the right to cases which have a sound basis.' This language was repeated in the Senate Committee Print, 68th Cong., 1st Sess., of A General Review of H.R. 10479, 67th Cong., p. 16. The language so carefully tailored by Congress is now rejected by the professional group who constitute our advisors in these matters. I do not think we should allow a known and established congressional policy to be so readily abrogated.

"We said in *Snyder v. Buck*, supra, p. 20, that if Rule 25(d) is to be amended in the manner then urged and now adopted 'the amending process is available.' Where we have a matter so heavily encrusted with legislative policy, I think any change should be left to Congress.

"I, therefore, dissent from the submission to Congress of the proposed amendments to Rule 25 of the Rules of Civil Procedure under 28 U.S.C. § 2072. For under that Act the Rules submitted become effective at the expiration of a 90–day period, unless Congress takes contrary action. This machinery seems therefore, inappropriate to me for effecting such a basic change in congressional policy as the proposed Rule 25(d) achieves."

RULES OF CIVIL PROCEDURE

ORDER OF JANUARY 21, 1963

1. That the Rules of Civil Procedure be, and they hereby are, amended by including therein Forms Number 30, 31 and 32, and the amendments to Rules 4, 5, 6, 7, 12, 13, 14, 15, 24, 25, 26, 28, 30, 41, 49, 50, 52, 56, 58, 71A, 77, 79, 81, and 86 and to Forms Number 3, 4, 5, 6, 7, 8, 9, 10, 11, 12, 13, 16, 18, 21, 22–A and 22–B, as hereinafter set forth:

[See additions and amendments made thereby under the respective rules and forms, post.]

2. That THE CHIEF JUSTICE be authorized to transmit these amendments to Congress in accordance with the provisions of Title 28, U.S.C., Sec. 2072.

MR. JUSTICE BLACK and MR. JUSTICE DOUGLAS are opposed to the submission of these rules [1] to the Congress under a statute which permits them to "take effect" and to repeal "all laws in conflict with such rules" without requiring any affirmative consideration, action, or approval of the rules by Congress or by the President.[2] We believe that while some of the Rules of Civil Procedure are simply housekeeping details,[3] many determine matters so substantially affecting the rights of litigants in law suits that in practical effect they are the equivalent of new legislation which, in our judgment, the Constitution requires to be initiated in and enacted by the Congress [4] and approved by the President.[5] The Constitution, as we read it, provides that all laws shall be enacted by the House, the Senate, and the President, not by the mere failure of Congress to reject proposals of an outside agency. Even were there not this constitutional limitation, the authorizing statute itself qualifies this Court's power by imposing upon it a solemn responsibility not to submit rules that "abridge, enlarge or modify any substantive right" and by specifically charging the Court with the duty to "preserve the right to trial by jury as at common law and as declared by the Seventh Amendment to the Constitution." [6] Our chief objections to the rules relate essentially to the fact that many of their provisions do "abridge, enlarge or modify" substantive rights and do not "preserve the right to trial by jury" but actually encroach upon it.

(1)(a) Rule 50(a) is amended by making the order of a judge granting a motion for a directed verdict effective without submitting the question to the jury at all. It was pointed out in *Galloway v. United States*, 319 U.S. 372, 396, 401–407, 63 S.Ct. 1077, 87 L.Ed. 1458 (dissenting opinion), how judges have whittled away or denied the right of trial by jury through the devices of directed verdicts and judgments notwithstanding verdicts. Although the amendment here is not itself a momentous one, it gives formal sanction to the process by which the courts have been wresting from juries the power to render verdicts. Since we do not approve of this sapping of the Seventh Amendment's guarantee of a jury trial, we cannot join even this technical *coup de grace.*

(b) The proposed amendment to 50(c) in practical effect vests appellate courts with more power than they have had to grant or deny new trials. The Court in *Cone v. West Virginia Pulp & Paper Co.*, 330 U.S. 212, 217–218, 67 S.Ct. 752, 91 L.Ed. 849, and *Globe Liquor Co. v. San Roman*, 332 U.S. 571, 68 S.Ct. 246, 92 L.Ed. 177, refused to construe the federal rules then existing to allow Courts of Appeals to interfere with trial judges' discretion to grant new trials. To the extent that jury verdicts are to be set aside and new

trials granted, we believe that those who hear the evidence, the trial judges, are the ones who should primarily exercise such discretion.

(c) The proposed amendment to Rule 56(e) imposes additional burdens upon litigants to protect against summary judgments rendered without hearing evidence on the part of witnesses who are confronted by the persons against whom they testify so that these persons can subject the witnesses to cross-examination. The summary judgment procedure, while justified in some cases, is made a handy instrument to let judges rather than juries try law suits and to let those judges try cases not on evidence of witnesses subjected to cross-examination but on ex parte affidavits obtained by parties. Most trial lawyers would agree, we think, that a litigant can frequently obtain in an actual trial favorable testimony which could not have been secured by affidavits or even by depositions.

(d) If there are to be amendments, Rule 49 should be repealed. That rule authorizes judges to require juries to return "only a special verdict in the form of a special written finding upon each issue of fact" or to answer "written interrogatories upon one or more issues of fact the decision of which is necessary to a verdict" in addition to rendering the general verdict. Such devices are used to impair or wholly take away the power of a jury to render a general verdict. One of the ancient, fundamental reasons for having general jury verdicts was to preserve the right of trial by jury as an indispensable part of a free government. Many of the most famous constitutional controversies in England revolved around litigants' insistence, particularly in seditious libel cases, that a jury had the right to render a general verdict without being compelled to return a number of subsidiary findings to support its general verdict. Some English jurors had to go to jail because they insisted upon their right to render general verdicts over the repeated commands of tyrannical judges not to do so. Rule 49 is but another means utilized by courts to weaken the constitutional power of juries and to vest judges with more power to decide cases according to their own judgments. A scrutiny of the special verdict and written interrogatory cases in appellate courts will show the confusion that necessarily results from the employment of these devices and the ease with which judges can use them to take away the right to trial by jury. We believe that Rule 49 be repealed, not amplified.

(2) There is a proposal to amend Rule 41, which provides for dismissal of actions. We believe that, if the Rules are to be changed, a major amendment to this rule is required in the interest of justice. Before dismissing a plaintiff's action for failure of his lawyer to prosecute, the trial judge should be required to have notice served on the plaintiff himself. The hardship that can result from the absence of such requirement is shown by *Link v. Wabash R. Co.*, 370 U.S. 626, 82 S.Ct. 1386, 8 L.Ed.2d 734. Link's lawyer failed to appear in response to a judge's order for a pre-trial conference, and the judge dismissed the case. As pointed out in the dissent, plaintiff had been severely injured, and a fair system of justice should not have penalized him because his lawyer, through neglect or any other reason, failed to appear when ordered. It would do a defendant no injury for the court to refuse to dismiss any apparently bona fide case until the plaintiff has actually had notice that some failure of his lawyer has irked the judge.

(3) MR. JUSTICE BLACK and MR. JUSTICE DOUG-LAS object to the changes in Rule 4, which for the first time permit a Federal District Court to obtain jurisdiction over a defendant by service of process outside the state or over his property by garnishment or attachment, under the circumstances and in the manner prescribed by state law. Those changes will apparently have little effect insofar as "federal question" litigation is concerned, since 28 U.S.C. § 1391(b) requires such suits to be brought "only in the judicial district where all defendants reside...." Diversity actions, however, may be greatly increased, for the effect of proposed 4(e) is not limited to suits authorized by such statutes as the Federal Interpleader Act, 28 U.S.C. § 1335. See Advisory Committee Rept., 5–8; 28 U.S.C. § 1391(a); Fed.Rules Civ. Proc. 1. We see no justification for an increase in the number of diversity cases. We also see no reason why the extent of a Federal District Court's personal jurisdiction should depend upon the existence or nonexistence of a state "long-arm" statute. Moreover, at present a state court action commenced by attachment or garnishment can get into a District Court only if a nonresident defendant chooses to appear and remove the case, see 28 U.S.C. § 1441, and there is no good reason, absent a congressional finding, why this should be changed.

Instead of recommending changes to the present Rules, we recommend that the statute authorizing this Court to prescribe Rules of Civil Procedure, if it is to remain a law, be amended to place the responsibility upon the Judicial Conference rather than upon this Court. Since the statute was first enacted in 1934, 48 Stat. 1064, the Judicial Conference has been enlarged and improved and is now very active in its surveillance of the work of the federal courts and in recommending appropriate legislation to Congress. The present Rules produced under 28 U.S.C. § 2072 are not prepared by us but by Committees of the Judicial Conference designated by the Chief Justice, and before coming to us they are approved by the Judicial Conference pursuant to 28 U.S.C. § 331.[7] The Committees and the Conference are composed of able and distinguished members and they render a high public service. It is they, however, who do the work, not we, and the rules have only our imprimatur. The only contribution that we actually make is an occasional exercise of a veto power. If the rule-making for Federal District Courts is to continue under the present plan, we believe that the Supreme Court should not have any part in the task; rather, the statute should be amended to substitute the Judicial Conference. The Judicial Conference can participate more actively in fashioning the rules and affirmatively contribute to their content and design better than we can. Transfer of the function to the Judicial Conference would relieve us of the embarrassment of having to sit in judgment on the constitutionality of rules which we have approved and which as applied in given situations might have to be declared invalid.

1 See our earlier statements in 368 U.S. 1012–1014 and 346 U.S. 946–947.

2 28 U.S.C. § 2072 gives this Court the power to prescribe rules of practice and procedure for Federal District Courts and further provides that such rules

"shall not take effect until they have been reported to Congress by THE CHIEF JUSTICE at or after the beginning of a regular session thereof but not later than the first day of May, and until the expiration of ninety days after they have been thus reported."

"All laws in conflict with such rules shall be of no further force or effect after such rules have taken effect."

3 See 368 U.S. 1012.

4 "All legislative Powers herein granted shall be vested in a Congress of the United States, which shall consist of a Senate and House of Representatives." U.S. Const., Art. I, § 1.

5 Every Bill which shall have passed the House of Representatives and the Senate, shall, before it becomes a Law, be presented to the President of the United States;" U.S. Const., Art. I, § 7.

6 28 U.S.C. § 2072.

7 "The Conference shall also carry on a continuous study of the operation and effect of the general rules of practice and procedure now or hereafter in use as prescribed by the Supreme Court for the other courts of the United States pursuant to law. Such changes in and additions to those rules as the Conference may deem desirable to promote simplicity in procedure, fairness in administration, the just determination of litigation, and the elimination of unjustifiable expense and delay shall be recommended by the Conference from time to time to the Supreme Court for its consideration and adoption, modification or rejection, in accordance with law."

ORDER OF FEBRUARY 28, 1966

1. That the Rules of Civil Procedure for the United States District Courts be, and they hereby are, amended by including therein Rules 23.1, 23.2, 44.1 and 65.1, Supplemental Rules A, B, C, D, E and F for Certain Admiralty and Maritime Claims, and amendments to Rules 1, 4, 8, 9, 12, 13, 14, 15, 17, 18, 19, 20, 23, 24, 26, 38, 41, 42, 43, 44, 47, 53, 59, 65, 68, 73, 74, 75, 81 and 82, and to Forms 2 and 15, as hereinafter set forth:

[See added, amended and supplemental Rules and Forms, post.]

2. That the foregoing amendments and additions to the Rules of Civil Procedure shall take effect on July 1, 1966, and shall govern all proceedings in actions brought thereafter and also in all further proceedings in actions then pending, except to the extent that in the opinion of the court their application in a particular action then pending would not be feasible or would work injustice, in which event the former procedure applies.

3. That THE CHIEF JUSTICE be, and he hereby is, authorized to transmit to the Congress the foregoing amendments and additions to the Rules of Civil Procedure in accordance with the provisions of Title 28, U.S.C., §§ 2072 and 2073.

4. That: (a) subdivision (c) of Rule 6 of the Rules of Civil Procedure for the United States District Courts promulgated by this court on December 20, 1937, effective September 16, 1938; (b) Rule 2 of the Rules for Practice and Procedure under section 25 of An Act to amend and consolidate the Acts respecting copyright, approved March 4, 1909, promulgated by this court on June 1, 1909, effective July 1, 1909; and (c) the Rules of Practice in Admiralty and Maritime Cases, promulgated by this court on December 6, 1920, effective March 7, 1921, as revised, amended and supplemented, be, and they hereby are, rescinded, effective July 1, 1966.

MR. JUSTICE BLACK, dissenting.

The Amendments to the Federal Rules of Civil and Criminal Procedure today transmitted to the Congress are the work of very capable advisory committees. Those committees, not the Court, wrote the rules. Whether by this transmittal the individual members of the Court who voted to transmit the rules intended to express approval of the varied

policy decisions the rules embody I am not sure. I am reasonably certain, however, that the Court's transmittal does not carry with it a decision that the amended rules are all constitutional. For such a decision would be the equivalent of an advisory opinion which, I assume the Court would unanimously agree, we are without constitutional power to give. And I agree with my Brother DOUGLAS that some of the proposed criminal rules go to the very border line if they do not actually transgress the constitutional right of a defendant not to be compelled to be a witness against himself. This phase of the criminal rules in itself so infects the whole collection of proposals that, without mentioning other objections, I am opposed to transmittal of the proposed amendments to the criminal rules.

I am likewise opposed to transmittal of the proposed revision of the civil rules. In the first place I think the provisions of 28 U.S.C. § 2072 (1964 ed.), under which these rules are transmitted and the corresponding section, 18 U.S.C. § 3771 (1964 ed.), relating to the criminal rules, both of which provide for giving transmitted rules the effect of law as though they had been properly enacted by Congress are unconstitutional for reasons I have previously stated.[1] And in prior dissents I have stated some of the basic reasons for my objections to repeated rules revisions [2] that tend to upset established meanings and need not repeat those grounds of objection here. The confusion created by the adoption of the present rules, over my objection, has been partially dispelled by judicial interpretations of them by this Court and others. New rules and extensive amendments to present rules will mean renewed confusion resulting in new challenges and new reversals and prejudicial "pretrial" dismissals of cases before a trial on the merits for failure of lawyers to understand and comply with new rules of uncertain meaning. Despite my continuing objection to the old rules, it seems to me that since they have at least gained some degree of certainty it would be wiser to "bear those ills we have than fly to others we know not of," unless, of course, we are reasonably sure that the proposed reforms of the old rules are badly needed. But I am not. The new proposals, at least some of them, have, as I view them, objectionable possibilities that cause me to believe our judicial system could get along much better without them.

The momentum given the proposed revision of the old rules by this Court's transmittal makes it practically certain that Congress, just as has this Court, will permit the rules to take effect exactly as they were written by the Advisory Committee on Rules. Nevertheless, I am including here a memorandum I submitted to the Court expressing objections to the Committee's proposals and suggesting changes should they be transmitted. These suggestions chiefly center around rules that grant broad discretion to trial judges with reference to class suits, pretrial procedures, and dismissal of cases with prejudice. Cases coming before the federal courts over the years now filling nearly 40 volumes of Federal Rules Decisions show an accumulation of grievances by lawyers and litigants about the way many trial judges exercise their almost unlimited discretionary powers to use pretrial procedures to dismiss cases without trials. In fact, many of these cases indicate a belief of many judges and legal commentators that the cause of justice is best served in the long run not by trials on the merits but by summary dismissals based on out of court affidavits, pretrial depositions, and other pretrial techniques. My belief is that open court trials on the merits where litigants have the right to prove their case or defense best comports with due process of law.

The proposed rules revisions, instead of introducing changes designed to prevent the continued abuse of pretrial power to dismiss cases summarily without trials, move in the opposite direction. Of course, each such dismissal results in removal of one more case from our congested court dockets, but that factor should not weigh more heavily in our system of justice than assuring a full-fledged due process trial of every bona fide lawsuit brought to vindicate an honest, substantial claim. It is to protect this ancient right of a person to have his case tried rather than summarily thrown out of court that I suggested to the Court that it recommend changes in the Committee's proposals of the nature set out in the following memorandum.

"Dear Brethren:

"I have gone over all the proposed amendments carefully and while there are probably some good suggestions, it is my belief that the bad results that can come from the adoption of these amendments predominate over any good they can bring about. I particularly think that every member of the Court should examine with great care the amendments relating to class suits. It seems to me that they place too much power in the hands of the trial judges and that the rules might almost as well simply provide that 'class suits can be maintained either for or against particular groups whenever in the discretion of a judge he thinks it is wise.' The power given to the judge to dismiss such suits or to divide them up into groups at will subjects members of classes to dangers that could not follow from carefully prescribed legal standards enacted to control class suits.

"In addition, the rules as amended, in my judgment, greatly aggravate the evil of vesting judges with practically uncontrolled power to dismiss with prejudice cases brought by plaintiffs or defenses interposed by defendants. The power to dismiss a plaintiff's case or to render judgments by default against defendants can work great harm to both parties. There are many inherent urges in existence which may subconsciously incline a judge towards disposing of the cases before him without having to go through the burden of a trial. Mr. Chief Justice White, before he became Chief Justice, wrote an opinion in the case of *Hovey v. Elliott*, 167 U.S. 409 [17 S.Ct. 841, 42 L.Ed. 215], which pointed out grave constitutional questions raised by attempting to punish the parties by depriving them of the right to try their law suits or to defend against law suits brought against them by others.

"Rule 41 entitled 'Dismissal of Actions' points up the great power of judges to dismiss actions and provides an automatic method under which a dismissal must be construed as a dismissal 'with prejudice' unless the judge specifically states otherwise. For that reason I suggest to the Conference that if the Rules are accepted, including that one, the last sentence of Rule 41(b) be amended so as to provide that a simple order of dismissal by a judge instead of operating 'as an adjudication upon the merits,' as the amended rule reads, shall provide that such a dismissal 'does not operate as an adjudication upon the merits.'

"As a further guarantee against oppressive dismissals I suggest the addition of the following as subdivision (c) of Rule 41.

"'No plaintiff's case shall be dismissed or defendant's right to defend be cut off because of the neglect, misfeasance,

malfeasance, or failure of their counsel to obey any order of the court, until and unless such plaintiff or defendant shall have been personally served with notice of their counsel's delinquency, and not then unless the parties themselves do or fail to do something on their own part that can legally justify dismissal of the plaintiff's case or of the defendant's defense.'

"This proposed amendment is suggested in order to protect litigants, both plaintiffs and defendants, against being thrown out of court as a penalty for their lawyer's neglect or misconduct. The necessity for such a rule is shown, I think, by the dismissal of the plaintiff's case in *Link v. Wabash R. Co.*, 370 U.S. 626 [82 S.Ct. 1386, 8 L.Ed.2d 734]. The usual argument against this suggestion is that a party to a law suit hires his lawyer and should therefore be responsible for everything his lawyer does in the conduct of his case. This may be a good argument with reference to affluent litigants who not only know the best lawyers but are able to hire them. It is a wholly unrealistic argument, however, to make with reference to individual persons who do not know the ability of various lawyers or who are not financially able to hire those at the top of the bar and who are compelled to rely on the assumption that a lawyer licensed by the State is competent. It seems to me to be an uncivilized practice to punish clients by throwing their cases out of court because of their lawyers' conduct. It may be supportable by good, sound, formal logic but I think has no support whatever in a procedural system supposed to work as far as humanly possible to the end of obtaining equal and exact justice.

"For all the reasons stated above and in my previous objections to the transmittals of rules I dissent from the transmittals here."

[1] In a statement accompanying a previous transmittal of the civil rules, MR. JUSTICE DOUGLAS and I said:

"MR. JUSTICE BLACK and MR. JUSTICE DOUGLAS are opposed to the submission of these rules to the Congress under a statute which permits them to 'take effect' and to repeal 'all laws in conflict with such rules' without requiring any affirmative consideration, action, or approval of the rules by Congress or by the President. We believe that while some of the Rules of Civil Procedure are simply housekeeping details, many determine matters so substantially affecting the rights of litigants in lawsuits that in practical effect they are the equivalent of new legislation which, in our judgment, the Constitution requires to be initiated in and enacted by the Congress and approved by the President. The Constitution, as we read it, provides that all laws shall be enacted by the House, the Senate, and the President, not by the mere failure of Congress to reject proposals of an outside agency. * * * " (Footnotes omitted.) 374 U.S. 865–866.

[2] 346 U.S. 946, 374 U.S. 865. And see 368 U.S. 1011 and 1012.

MR. JUSTICE DOUGLAS, dissenting in part.

I reiterate today what I stated on an earlier occasion (374 U.S. 865, 869–870) (statement of Black and Douglas, JJ.), that the responsibility for promulgating Rules of the kind we send to Congress today should rest with the Judicial Conference and not the Court. It is the Judicial Conference, not the Court, which appoints the Advisory Committee on Criminal Rules which makes the actual recommendations.[1] Members of the Judicial Conference, being in large part judges of the lower courts and attorneys who are using the Rules day in and day out, are in a far better position to make a practical judgment upon their utility or inutility than we.

But since under the statute[2] the Rules go to Congress only on the initiative of the Court, I cannot be only a conduit. I think that placing our imprimatur on the amendments to the Rules entails a large degree of responsibility of judgment concerning them. Some of the criminal Rules which we forward to Congress today are very bothersome—not in the sense that they may be unwieldy or unworkable—but in the sense that they may entrench on important constitutional rights of defendants.

In my judgment, the amendments to Rule 16 dealing with discovery require further reflection. To the extent that they expand the defendant's opportunities for discovery, they accord with the views of a great many commentators who have concluded that a civilized society ought not to tolerate the conduct of a criminal prosecution as a "game."[3] But the proposed changes in the Rule go further. Rule 16(c) would permit a trial judge to condition granting the defendant discovery on the defendant's willingness to permit the prosecution to discover "scientific or medical reports, books, papers, documents, tangible objects, or copies or portions thereof" which (1) are in the defendant's possession; (2) he intends to produce at trial; and (3) are shown to be material to the preparation of the prosecution's case.[4]

The extent to which a court may compel the defendant to disclose information or evidence pertaining to his case without infringing the privilege against self-incrimination is a source of current controversy among judges, prosecutors, defense lawyers, and other legal commentators. A distinguished state court has concluded—although not without a strong dissent—that the privilege is not violated by discovery of the names of expert medical witnesses whose appearance at trial is contemplated by the defense.[5] I mean to imply no views on the point, except to note that a serious constitutional question lurks here.

The prosecution's opportunity to discover evidence in the possession of the defense is somewhat limited in the proposal with which we deal in that it is tied to the exercise by the defense of the right to discover from the prosecution. But *if* discovery, by itself, of information in the possession of the defendant would violate the privilege against self-incrimination, is it any less a violation if conditioned on the defendant's exercise of the opportunity to discover evidence? May benefits be conditioned on the abandonment of constitutional rights? See, e.g., *Sherbert v. Verner*, 374 U.S. 398, 403–406, 83 S.Ct. 1790, 1793–1795, 10 L.Ed.2d 965. To deny a defendant the opportunity to discovery—an opportunity not withheld from defendants who agree to prosecutorial discovery or from whom discovery is not sought—merely because the defendant chooses to exercise the constitutional right to refrain from self-incrimination arguably imposes a penalty upon the exercise of that fundamental privilege. It is said, however, that fairness may require disclosure by a defendant who obtains information from the prosecution.

Perhaps—but the proposed rule establishes no such standards. Its application is mechanical: if the defendant is allowed discovery, so, too, is the prosecution. No requirement is imposed, for example, that the subject matter of the material sought to be discovered by the prosecution be limited to that relating to the subject of the defendant's discovery.

The proposed addition of Rule 17.1 also suggests difficulties, perhaps of constitutional dimension. This rule would establish a pretrial conference procedure. The language of the rule and the Advisory Committee's comments suggest that under some circumstances, the conference might even

take place in the absence of the defendant! Cf. *Lewis v. United States*, 146 U.S. 370, 13 S.Ct. 136, 36 L.Ed. 1011; Fed.Rules Crim.Proc. Rule 43.

The proposed amendment to Rule 32(c)(2) states that the trial judge "may" disclose to the defendant or his counsel the contents of a presentence report on which he is relying in fixing sentence. The imposition of sentence is of critical importance to a man convicted of crime. Trial judges need presentence reports so that they may have at their disposal the fullest possible information. See *Williams v. People of State of New York*, 337 U.S. 241, 69 S.Ct. 1079, 93 L.Ed. 1337. But while the formal rules of evidence do not apply to restrict the factors which the sentencing judge may consider, fairness would, in my opinion, require that the defendant be advised of the facts—perhaps very damaging to him—on which the judge intends to rely. The presentence report may be inaccurate, a flaw which may be of constitutional dimension. Cf. *Townsend v. Burke*, 334 U.S. 736, 68 S.Ct. 1252, 92 L.Ed. 1690. It may exaggerate the gravity of the defendant's prior offenses. The investigator may have made an incomplete investigation. See Tappan, Crime, Justice and Correction 556 (1960). There may be countervailing factors not disclosed by the probation report. In many areas we can rely on the sound exercise of discretion by the trial judge; but how can a judge know whether or not the presentence report calls for a reply by the defendant? Its faults may not appear on the face of the document.

Some States require full disclosure of the report to the defense.[6] The proposed Model Penal Code takes the middle-ground and requires the sentencing judge to disclose to the defense the factual contents of the report so that there is an opportunity to reply.[7] Whatever should be the rule for the federal courts, it ought not to be one which permits a judge to impose sentence on the basis of information of which the defendant may be unaware and to which he has not been afforded an opportunity to reply.

I do not think we should approve Rule 16, 17.1, and 32(c)(2). Instead, we should refer them back to the Judicial Conference and the Advisory Committee for further consideration and reflection, where I believe they were approved only by the narrowest majority.

WILLIAM O. DOUGLAS.

[1] 28 U.S.C. § 331 (1964 ed.) which establishes the Judicial Conference of the United States, provides that the Conference shall "carry on a continuous study of the operation and effect of the general rules of practice and procedure * * * prescribed by the Supreme Court * * *." The Conference has resolved that a standing Committee on Rules of Practice and Procedure be appointed by the Chief Justice and that, in addition, five advisory committees be established to recommend to the Judicial Conference changes in the rules of practice and procedure for the federal courts. See Annual Report of the Proceedings of the Judicial Conference of the United States 6–7 (1958).

[2] 18 U.S.C. § 3771 (1964 ed.).

[3] See, e.g., Brennan, The Criminal Prosecution: Sporting Event or Quest for Truth?, 1963 Wash.U.L.Q. 279; Louisell, Criminal Discovery: Dilemma Real or Apparent?, 49 Calif.L.Rev. 56 (1961); Traynor, Ground Lost and Found in Criminal Discovery, 39 N.Y.U.L.Rev. 228 (1964).

[4] The proposed rule explicitly provides that the prosecution may not discover nonmedical documents or reports "made by the defendant, or his attorneys or agents in connection with the investigation or defense of the case, or of statements made by the defendant, or by government or defense witnesses, or by prospective government or defense witnesses, to the defendant, his agents or attorneys."

[5] *Jones v. Superior Court of Nevada County,* 58 Cal.2d 56, 22 Cal. Rptr. 879, 372 P.2d 919, 96 A.L.R.2d 1213. See Comment, 51 Calif.L.Rev. 135; Note, 76 Harv.L.Rev. 838 (1963). The case is more extensively treated in Louisell, Criminal Discovery and Self–Incrimination, 53 Calif.L.Rev. 89 (1965).

[6] E.g., Calif.Penal Code § 1203.

[7] Model Penal Code § 7.07(5) (Proposed Official Draft, 1962). The Code provides that the sources of confidential information need not be disclosed. "Less disclosure than this hardly comports with elementary fairness." Comment to § 7.07 (Tent.Draft No. 2, 1954), at 55. A discarded draft of the amendment to Fed.Rules Crim.Proc.Rule 32 would have allowed disclosure to defense counsel of the report, from which the confidential sources would be removed. A defendant not represented by counsel would be told of the "essential facts" in the report. See 8 Moore's Federal Practice ¶¶ 32.03[4], 32.09 (1965).

ORDER OF DECEMBER 4, 1967

1. That the following rules, to be known as the Federal Rules of Appellate Procedure, be, and they hereby are, prescribed, pursuant to sections 3771 and 3772 of Title 18, United States Code, and sections 2072 and 2075 of Title 28, United States Code, to govern the procedure in appeals to United States courts of appeals from the United States district courts, in the review by United States courts of appeals of decisions of the Tax Court of the United States, in proceedings in the United States courts of appeals for the review or enforcement of orders of administrative agencies, boards, commissions and officers, and in applications for writs or other relief which a United States court of appeals or judge thereof is competent to give:

[See text of Rules of Appellate Procedure, post.]

2. That the foregoing rules shall take effect on July 1, 1968, and shall govern all proceedings in appeals and petitions for review or enforcement of orders thereafter brought and in all such proceedings then pending, except to the extent that in the opinion of the court of appeals their application in a particular proceeding then pending would not be feasible or would work injustice, in which case the former procedure may be followed.

3. That Rules 6, 9, 41, 77 and 81 of the Rules of Civil Procedure for the United States District Courts be, and they hereby are, amended, effective July 1, 1968, as hereinafter set forth:

[See the amendments made thereby under the respective rules, post.]

4. That the chapter heading "IX. APPEALS", all of Rules 72, 73, 74, 75 and 76 of the Rules of Civil Procedure for the United States District Courts, and Form 27 annexed to the said rules, be, and they hereby are, abrogated, effective July 1, 1968.

[Paragraphs 5 and 6 of the order pertain to certain Rules of Criminal Procedure for the United States District Courts and to certain Forms annexed to the said rules. For text, see Pamphlet containing Federal Rules of Criminal Procedure.]

7. That THE CHIEF JUSTICE be, and he hereby is, authorized to transmit to the Congress the foregoing new rules and amendments to and abrogation of existing rules, in accordance with the provisions of Title 18, U.S.C., § 3771, and Title 28, U.S.C., §§ 2072 and 2075.

RULES OF CIVIL PROCEDURE

ORDER OF MARCH 30, 1970

1. That subdivision (a) of Rule 5, subdivision (h) of Rule 9 and Rules 26, 29, 30, 31, 32, 33, 34, 35, 36 and 37, and subdivision (d) of Rule 45, subdivision (a) of Rule 69, and Form 24 of the Rules of Civil Procedure for the United States District Courts be, and they hereby are, amended to read as follows:

[See the amendments made thereby under the respective rules and forms, post.]

2. That the foregoing amendments to the Rules of Civil Procedure shall take effect on July 1, 1970, and shall govern all proceedings in actions brought thereafter and also in all further proceedings in actions then pending, except to the extent that in the opinion of the court their application in a particular action then pending would not be feasible or would work injustice, in which event the former procedure applies.

3. That THE CHIEF JUSTICE be, and he hereby is, authorized to transmit to the Congress the foregoing amendments to the Rules of Civil Procedure in accordance with the provisions of Title 28, U.S.C. § 2072.

MR. JUSTICE BLACK and MR. JUSTICE DOUGLAS disapprove of the Amendments to the Federal Rules of Civil Procedure relating to Discovery, and dissent from the action of the Court in transmitting them to the Congress.

ORDER OF MARCH 1, 1971

1. That subdivision (a) of Rule 6, paragraph (4) of subdivision (a) of Rule 27, paragraph (6) of subdivision (b) of Rule 30, subdivision (c) of Rule 77, and paragraph (2) of subdivision (a) of Rule 81 of the Federal Rules of Civil Procedure be, and they hereby are, amended, effective July 1, 1971, to read as follows:

[See amendments made thereby under the respective rules, post.]

2. *[Certain Rules of Criminal Procedure for the United States District Courts amended].*

3. That subdivision (a) of Rule 26 and subdivision (a) of Rule 45 of the Federal Rules of Appellate Procedure be, and they hereby are, amended, effective July 1, 1971, to read as follows:

[See amendments made thereby under the respective Rules of Appellate Procedure, post.]

4. That THE CHIEF JUSTICE be, and he hereby is, authorized to transmit to the Congress the foregoing amendments to the Rules of Civil, Criminal and Appellate Procedure, in accordance with the provisions of Title 18 U.S.C. § 3771, and Title 28 U.S.C. §§ 2072 and 2075.

MR. JUSTICE BLACK and MR. JUSTICE DOUGLAS dissent.

ORDER OF NOVEMBER 20, 1972

1. That the rules hereinafter set forth, to be known as the Federal Rules of Evidence, be, and they hereby are, prescribed pursuant to Sections 3402, 3771, and 3772, Title 18, United States Code, and Sections 2072 and 2075, Title 28, United States Code, to govern procedure, in the proceedings and to the extent set forth therein, in the United States courts of appeals, the United States district courts, the District Court for the District of the Canal Zone and the district courts of Guam and the Virgin Islands, and before United States magistrates.

2. That the aforementioned Federal Rules of Evidence shall take effect on July 1, 1973, and shall be applicable to actions and proceedings brought thereafter and also to further procedure in actions and proceedings then pending, except to the extent that in the opinion of the court their application in a particular action or proceeding then pending would not be feasible or would work injustice in which event the former procedure applies.

3. That subdivision (c) of Rule 30 and Rules 43 and 44.1 of the Federal Rules of Civil Procedure be, and they hereby are, amended, effective July 1, 1973, to read as hereinafter set forth:

[See amendments made thereby under the respective rules, post.]

4. That subdivision (c) of Rule 32 of the Federal Rules of Civil Procedure be, and it hereby is, abrogated, effective July 1, 1973.

5. *[Certain Rules of Criminal Procedure for the United States District Courts amended].*

6. That THE CHIEF JUSTICE be, and he hereby is, authorized to transmit the foregoing new rules and amendments to and abrogation of existing rules to the Congress at the beginning of its next regular session, in accordance with the provisions of Title 18 U.S.C. § 3771 and Title 28 U.S.C. §§ 2072 and 2075.

ORDER OF DECEMBER 18, 1972

1. That Rule 43 of the Federal Rules of Civil Procedure, as amended by Order of this Court entered November 20, 1972, be, and it hereby is, further amended, effective July 1, 1973, to read as follows:

[See amendment made thereby under Rule 43 post.]

2. That THE CHIEF JUSTICE be, and he hereby is, authorized to transmit the foregoing amendment of Rule 43 of the Federal Rules of Civil Procedure to the Congress at the beginning of its next regular session in accordance with the provisions of Title 28, U.S.C. § 2072.

CONGRESSIONAL ACTION ON PROPOSED RULES OF EVIDENCE AND 1972 AMENDMENTS TO FEDERAL RULES OF CIVIL PROCEDURE AND FEDERAL RULES OF CRIMINAL PROCEDURE

Pub.L. 93–12, Mar. 30, 1973, 87 Stat. 9, provided: "That notwithstanding any other provisions of law, the Rules of Evidence for United States Courts and Magistrates, the Amendments to the Federal Rules of Civil Procedure, and the Amendments to the Federal Rules of Criminal Procedure, which are embraced by the orders entered by the Supreme Court of the United States on Monday, November 20, 1972, and Monday, December 18, 1972, shall have no force or effect except to the extent, and with such amendments, as they may be expressly approved by Act of Congress."

Pub.L. 93–595, § 3, Jan. 2, 1975, 88 Stat. 1959, provided that: "The Congress expressly approves the amendments to the Federal Rules of Civil Procedure, and the amendments to the Federal Rules of Criminal Procedure, which are embraced by the orders entered by the Supreme Court of the United States on November 20, 1972, and December 18,

1972, and such amendments shall take effect on the one hundred and eightieth day beginning after the date of the enactment of this Act [Jan. 2, 1975]."

ORDER OF APRIL 26, 1976

1. That the rules and forms governing proceedings in the United States District Courts under Section 2254 and Section 2255 of Title 28, United States Code, as approved by the Judicial Conference of the United States be, and they hereby are, prescribed pursuant to Section 2072 of Title 28, United States Code and Sections 3771 and 3772 of Title 18, United States Code.

2. That the aforementioned rules and forms shall take effect August 1, 1976, and shall be applicable to all proceedings then pending except to the extent that in the opinion of the court their application in a particular proceeding would not be feasible or would work injustice.

3. That THE CHIEF JUSTICE be, and he hereby is, authorized to transmit the aforementioned rules and forms governing Section 2254 and Section 2255 proceedings to the Congress in accordance with the provisions of Section 2072 of Title 28 and Sections 3771 and 3772 of Title 18, United States Code.

CONGRESSIONAL ACTION ON PROPOSED RULES AND FORMS GOVERNING PROCEEDINGS UNDER 28 U.S.C. §§ 2254 AND 2255

Pub.L. 94–349, § 2, July 8, 1976, 90 Stat. 822, provided: "That, notwithstanding the provisions of section 2072 of title 28 of the United States Code, the rules and forms governing section 2254 cases in the United States district courts and the rules and forms governing section 2255 proceedings in the United States district courts which are embraced by the order entered by the United States Supreme Court on April 26, 1976, and which were transmitted to the Congress on or about April 26, 1976, shall not take effect until thirty days after the adjournment sine die of the 94th Congress, or until and to the extent approved by Act of Congress, whichever is earlier."

Pub.L. 94–426, § 1, Sept. 28, 1976, 90 Stat. 1334, provided: "That the rules governing section 2254 cases in the United States district courts and the rules governing section 2255 proceedings for the United States district courts, as proposed by the United States Supreme Court, which were delayed by the Act entitled 'An Act to delay the effective date of certain proposed amendments to the Federal Rules of Criminal Procedure and certain other rules promulgated by the United States Supreme Court' (Public Law 94–349), are approved with the amendments set forth in section 2 of this Act and shall take effect as so amended, with respect to petitions under section 2254 and motions under section 2255 of title 28 of the United States Code filed on or after February 1, 1977."

ORDER OF APRIL 29, 1980

1. That the Federal Rules of Civil Procedure be, and they hereby are, amended by including therein amendments to Rules 4, 5, 26, 28, 30, 32, 33, 34, 37 and 45 as hereinafter set forth:

[See amendments made thereby under respective rules, post.]

2. That the foregoing amendments to the Federal Rules of Civil Procedure shall take effect on August 1, 1980, and shall govern all civil proceedings thereafter commenced and, insofar as just and practicable, all proceedings then pending.

3. That subsection (e) of Rule 37 of the Federal Rules of Civil Procedure is hereby abrogated, effective August 1, 1980.

4. That THE CHIEF JUSTICE be, and he hereby is, authorized to transmit to the Congress the foregoing amendments to the Federal Rules of Civil Procedure in accordance with the provisions of Section 2072 of Title 28, United States Code.

MR. JUSTICE POWELL, with whom MR. JUSTICE STEWART and MR. JUSTICE REHNQUIST join, filed a dissenting statement.

I dissent from the Court's adoption of the amendments to Federal Rules of Civil Procedure 26, 33, 34, and 37—the cluster of Rules authorizing and regulating discovery generally, interrogatories, production of documents, and sanctions for failure to make discovery. These amendments are not inherently objectionable. Indeed, they represent the culmination of several years' work by the Judicial Conference's distinguished and conscientious Standing Committee on Rules of Practice and Procedure and Advisory Committee on Civil Rules.[1] But the changes embodied in the amendments fall short of those needed to accomplish reforms in civil litigation that are long overdue.

The American Bar Association proposed significant and substantial reforms.[2] Although the Standing Committee initially favored most of these proposals, it ultimately rejected them in large part. The ABA now accedes to the Standing Committee's amendments because they make some improvements, but the most recent report of the ABA Section of Litigation makes clear that the "serious and widespread abuse of discovery" will remain largely uncontrolled.[3] There are wide differences of opinion within the profession as to the need for reform. The bench and the bar are familiar with the existing Rules, and it often is said that the bar has a vested interest in maintaining the status quo. I imply no criticism of the bar or the Standing Committee when I suggest that the present recommendations reflect a compromise as well as the difficulty of framing satisfactory discovery Rules. But whatever considerations may have prompted the Committee's final decision, I doubt that many judges or lawyers familiar with the proposed amendments believe they will have an appreciable effect on the acute problems associated with discovery. The Court's adoption of these inadequate changes could postpone effective reform for another decade.

When the Federal Rules first appeared in 1938, the discovery provisions properly were viewed as a constructive improvement. But experience under the discovery Rules demonstrates that "not infrequently [they have been] exploited to the disadvantage of justice." *Herbert v. Lando*, 441 U.S. 153, 179 (1979) (POWELL, J., concurring). Properly limited and controlled discovery is necessary in most civil litigation. The present Rules, however, invite discovery of such scope and duration that district judges often cannot keep the practice within reasonable bounds.[4] Even in a relatively simple case, discovery through depositions, interrogatories, and demands

RULES OF CIVIL PROCEDURE

for documents may take weeks. In complex litigation, discovery can continue for years. One must doubt whether empirical evidence would demonstrate that untrammeled discovery actually contributes to the just resolution of disputes. If there is disagreement about that, there is none whatever about the effect of discovery practices upon the average citizen's ability to afford legal remedies.

Delay and excessive expense now characterize a large percentage of all civil litigation. The problems arise in significant part, as every judge and litigator knows, from abuse of the discovery procedures available under the Rules.[5] Indeed, the National Conference on the Causes of Popular Dissatisfaction with the Administration of Justice, led by THE CHIEF JUSTICE,[6] identified "Abuse in the use of discovery [as] a major concern" within our legal system.[7] Lawyers devote an enormous number of "chargeable hours" to the practice of discovery. We may assume that discovery usually is conducted in good faith. Yet all too often discovery practices enable the party with greater financial resources to prevail by exhausting the resources of a weaker opponent. The mere threat of delay or unbearable expense denies justice to many actual or prospective litigants. Persons or businesses of comparatively limited means settle unjust claims and relinquish just claims simply because they cannot afford to litigate.[8] Litigation costs have become intolerable, and they cast a lengthening shadow over the basic fairness of our legal system.

I reiterate that I do not dissent because the modest amendments recommended by the Judicial Conference are undesirable. I simply believe that Congress' acceptance of these tinkering changes will delay for years the adoption of genuinely effective reforms. The process of change, as experience teaches, is tortuous and contentious. Favorable congressional action on these amendments will create complacency and encourage inertia. Meanwhile, the discovery Rules will continue to deny justice to those least able to bear the burdens of delay, escalating legal fees, and rising court costs.

The amendments to Rules 26, 33, 34, and 37 recommended by the Judicial Conference should be rejected, and the Conference should be directed to initiate a thorough reexamination of the discovery Rules that have become so central to the conduct of modern civil litigation.

[1] This Court's role in the rulemaking process is largely formalistic. Standing and advisory committees of the Judicial Conference make the initial studies, invite comments on their drafts, and prepare the Rules. Both the Judicial Conference and this Court necessarily rely upon the careful work of these committees. Congress should bear in mind that our approval of proposed Rules is more a certification that they are the products of proper procedures than a considered judgment on the merits of the proposals themselves. See generally 409 U.S. 1132, 1133 (1973) (DOUGLAS, J., dissenting from adoption of Federal Rules of Evidence); 383 U.S. 1032 (1966) (BLACK, J., dissenting from adoption of amendment to civil rules); 374 U.S. 865, 869–870 (1963) (statement of BLACK and DOUGLAS, JJ., upon adoption of amendments to Federal Rules of Civil Procedure).

[2] American Bar Association, Report of the Section of Litigation Special Committee for the Study of Discovery Abuse (App.Draft 1977).

[3] ABA Section of Litigation, Second Report of the Special Committee for the Study of Discovery Abuse, 5 (1980).

[4] MR. JUSTICE WHITE, writing for the Court, recently reminded the federal courts that "the discovery provisions . . . are subject to the injunction of Rule 1 that they be 'construed to secure the just, *speedy,*

and *inexpensive* determination of every action.'" *Herbert v. Lando,* 441 U.S. 153, 177 (1979).

In his most recent Annual Report on the State of the Judiciary, THE CHIEF JUSTICE declared that "[t]he responsibility for control [of pretrial process] rests on both judges and lawyers. Where existing rules and statutes permit abuse, they must be changed. Where the power lies with judges to prevent or correct abuse and misuse of the system, judges must act." Address to American Bar Association Mid–Year Meeting, 6 (Feb. 3, 1980).

[5] Writing from his wide experience as a judge, practicing lawyer, and Attorney General, Griffin B. Bell advised the Standing Committee that "the scope of discovery is far too broad and that excessive discovery has significantly contributed to the delays, complexity and high cost of civil litigation in the federal courts." Letter to The Honorable Roszel C. Thomsen, Chairman of the Committee on Rules of Practice and Procedure of the Judicial Conference, 1 (June 27, 1978).

[6] THE CHIEF JUSTICE'S keynote address to this distinguished assembly, popularly known as the Pound Conference, recognized that discovery processes "are being misused and abused." See Burger, Agenda for 2000 A.D.—A Need for Systematic Anticipation, 70 F.R.D. 83, 95–96 (1976).

[7] See Erickson, The Pound Conference Recommendations: A Blueprint for the Justice System in the Twenty-first Century, 76 F.R.D. 277, 288 (1978); ABA, Report of Pound Conference Follow-up Task Force, 74 F.R.D. 159, 171–192 (1976).

[8] "The principal function of procedural rules," as MR. JUSTICE BLACK observed in another context, "should be to serve as useful guides to help, not hinder, persons who have a legal right to bring their problems before the courts." 346 U.S. 946 (1954) (separate statement upon adoption of revised Supreme Court Rules).

ORDER OF APRIL 28, 1983

1. That the Federal Rules of Civil Procedure be, and they hereby are, amended by including therein new Rules 26(g), 53(f), 72 through 76 and new Official Forms 33 and 34, and amendments to Rules 6(b), 7(b), 11, 16, 26(a) and (b), 52(a), 53(a), (b) and (c) and 67, as hereinafter set forth:

[See additions and amendments made thereby under respective rules and forms, post.]

2. That the foregoing additions and amendments to the Federal Rules of Civil Procedure shall take effect on August 1, 1983 and shall govern all civil proceedings thereafter commenced and, insofar as just and practicable, in proceedings then pending.

3. That THE CHIEF JUSTICE be, and he hereby is, authorized to transmit to the Congress the foregoing additions to and changes in the Federal Rules of Civil Procedure in accordance with the provisions of Section 2072 of Title 28, United States Code.

ORDER OF APRIL 29, 1985

1. That the Federal Rules of Civil Procedure for the United States District Courts be, and they hereby are, amended by including therein a new Rule E(4)(f) to the Supplemental Rules for Certain Admiralty and Maritime Claims; amendments to Rules 6(a), 45(d)(2), 52(a), 71A(h) and 83; amendments to Supplemental Admiralty Rules B(1) and C(3); and amendments to Official Form 18–A, as hereinafter set forth:

[See additions and amendments made thereby under respective rules and forms, post.]

2. That the foregoing addition to and changes in the Federal Rules of Civil Procedure, the Supplemental Rules for Certain Admiralty and Maritime Claims, and the Official

Form shall take effect on August 1, 1985 and shall govern all proceedings in civil actions thereafter commenced and, insofar as just and practicable, all proceedings in civil actions then pending.

3. That THE CHIEF JUSTICE be, and he hereby is, authorized to transmit to the Congress the foregoing addition to and changes in the rules of civil procedure in accordance with the provisions of Section 2072 of Title 28, United States Code.

ORDER OF MARCH 2, 1987

1. That the Federal Rules of Civil Procedure and the Supplemental Rules for Certain Admiralty and Maritime Claims be, and they hereby are, amended by including therein amendments to Civil Rules 4, 5, 6, 8, 9, 11, 12, 13, 14, 15, 16, 17, 18, 19, 20, 22, 23, 23.1, 24, 25, 26, 27, 28, 30, 31, 32, 34, 35, 36, 37 38, 41, 43, 44, 44.1, 45, 46, 49, 50, 51, 53, 54, 55, 56, 60, 62, 63, 65, 65.1, 68, 69, 71, 71A, 73, 75, 77, 78, 81, and to the Supplemental Rules for Certain Admiralty and Maritime Claims, Rules B, C, E, and F, as hereinafter set forth:

[See amendments made thereby under respective rules, post.]

2. That the foregoing amendments to the Federal Rules of Civil Procedure and the Supplemental Rules for Certain Admiralty and Maritime Claims shall take effect on August 1, 1987.

3. That THE CHIEF JUSTICE be, and he hereby is, authorized to transmit to the Congress the foregoing amendments in accordance with the provisions of Section 2072 of Title 28, United States Code.

ORDER OF APRIL 25, 1988

1. That the Federal Rules of Civil Procedure be, and they hereby are, amended by including therein amendments to Civil Rules 17 and 71, as hereinafter set forth:

[See amendments made thereby under respective rules, post.]

2. That the foregoing amendments to the Federal Rules of Civil Procedure shall take effect on August 1, 1988.

3. That THE CHIEF JUSTICE be, and he hereby is, authorized to transmit to the Congress the foregoing amendments in accordance with the provisions of Section 2072 of Title 28, United States Code.

ORDER OF APRIL 30, 1991

1. That the Federal Rules of Civil Procedure for the United States District Courts be, and they hereby are, amended by including therein new chapter headings VIII and IX, amendments to Rules C and E of the Supplemental Rules for Certain Admiralty and Maritime Claims, new Forms 1A and 1B to the Appendix of Forms, the abrogation of Form 18A, and amendments to Civil Rules 5, 15, 24, 34, 35, 41, 44, 45, 47, 48, 50, 52, 53, 63, 72, and 77, as hereinafter set forth.

[See additions and amendments made thereby under respective rules and forms, post.]

2. That the foregoing additions to and changes in the Federal Rules of Civil Procedure, the Supplemental Rules for Certain Admiralty and Maritime Claims, and the Civil Forms shall take effect on December 1, 1991, and shall govern all proceedings in civil actions thereafter commenced and, insofar as just and practicable, all proceedings in civil actions then pending.

3. That THE CHIEF JUSTICE be, and hereby is, authorized to transmit to the Congress the foregoing addition to and changes in the Rules of Civil Procedure in accordance with the provisions of Section 2072 of Title 28, United States Code.

[Congress may postpone the proposed rule and form additions and amendments effective December 1, 1991, may decline to approve such additions and amendments, or may make changes to the additions and amendments.]

ORDER OF APRIL 22, 1993

1. That the Federal Rules of Civil Procedure for the United States District Courts be, and they hereby are, amended by including therein amendments to Civil Rules 1, 4, 5, 11, 12, 15, 16, 26, 28, 29, 30, 31, 32, 33, 34, 36, 37, 38, 50, 52, 53, 54, 58, 71A, 72, 73, 74, 75, and 76, and new Rule 4.1, and abrogation of Form 18–A, and amendments to Forms 2, 33, 34, and 34A, and new Forms 1A, 1B, and 35.

[See amendments made thereby under respective rules and forms, post.]

2. That the foregoing amendments to the Federal Rules of Civil Procedure shall take effect on December 1, 1993, and shall govern all proceedings in civil cases thereafter commenced and, insofar as just and practicable, all proceedings in civil cases then pending.

3. That THE CHIEF JUSTICE be, and he hereby is, authorized to transmit to the Congress the foregoing amendments to the Federal Rules of Civil Procedure in accordance with the provisions of Section 2072 of Title 23, United States Code.

ORDER OF APRIL 27, 1995

1. That the Federal Rules of Civil Procedure for the United States District Courts be, and they hereby are, amended by including therein amendments to Civil Rules 50, 52, 59, and 83.

[See amendments made thereby under respective rules, post.]

2. That the foregoing amendments to the Federal Rules of Civil Procedure shall take effect on December 1, 1995, and shall govern all proceedings in civil cases thereafter commenced and, insofar as just and practicable, all proceedings in civil cases then pending.

3. That THE CHIEF JUSTICE be, and hereby is, authorized to transmit to the Congress the foregoing amendments to the Federal Rules of Civil Procedure in accordance with the provisions of Section 2072 of Title 28, United States Code.

ORDER OF APRIL 23, 1996

1. That the Federal Rules of Civil Procedure for the United States District Courts be, and they hereby are, amended by including therein amendments to Civil Rules 5 and 43.

[See amendments made thereby under respective rules, post]

2. That the foregoing amendments to the Federal Rules of Civil Procedure shall take effect on December 1, 1996, and shall govern all proceedings in civil cases thereafter commenced and, insofar as just and practicable, all proceedings in civil cases then pending.

3. That THE CHIEF JUSTICE be, and hereby is, authorized to transmit to the Congress the foregoing amendments to the Federal Rules of Civil Procedure in accordance with the provisions of Section 2072 of Title 28, United States Code.

ORDER OF APRIL 11, 1997

1. That the Federal Rules of Civil Procedure for the United States District Courts be, and they hereby are, amended by including therein amendments to Civil Rules 9 and 73, and abrogation of Rules 74, 75, and 76, and amendments to Forms 33 and 34.

[See amendments made thereby under respective rules, post]

2. That the foregoing amendments to the Federal Rules of Civil Procedure shall take effect on December 1, 1997, and shall govern all proceedings in civil cases thereafter commenced and, insofar as just and practicable, all proceedings in civil cases then pending.

3. That THE CHIEF JUSTICE be, and hereby is, authorized to transmit to the Congress the foregoing amendments to the Federal Rules of Civil Procedure in accordance with the provisions of Section 2072 of Title 28, United States Code.

ORDER OF APRIL 24, 1998

1. That the Federal Rules of Civil Procedure for the United States District Courts be, and they hereby are, amended by including therein a new Civil Rule 23(f).

[See amendments made thereby under respective rules, post]

2. That the foregoing amendments to the Federal Rules of Civil Procedure shall take effect on December 1, 1998, and shall govern all proceedings in civil cases thereafter commenced and, insofar as just and practicable, all proceedings in civil cases then pending.

3. That THE CHIEF JUSTICE be, and hereby is, authorized to transmit to the Congress the foregoing amendments to the Federal Rules of Civil Procedure in accordance with the provisions of Section 2072 of Title 28, United States Code.

ORDER OF APRIL 26, 1999

1. That the Federal Rules of Civil Procedure for the United States District Courts be, and they hereby are, amended by including therein amendments to Civil Rule 6(b) and Form 2.

[See amendments made thereby under respective rules, post]

2. That the foregoing amendments to the Federal Rules of Civil Procedure shall take effect on December 1, 1999, and shall govern all proceedings in civil cases thereafter com-

menced and, insofar as just and practicable, all proceedings in civil cases then pending.

3. That THE CHIEF JUSTICE be, and hereby is, authorized to transmit to the Congress the foregoing amendments to the Federal Rules of Civil Procedure in accordance with the provisions of Section 2072 of Title 28, United States Code.

ORDER OF APRIL 17, 2000

1. That the Federal Rules of Civil Procedure for the United States District Courts be, and they hereby are, amended by including therein amendments to Civil Rules 4, 5, 12, 14, 26, 30, and 37 and to Rules B, C, and E of the Supplemental Rules for Certain Admiralty and Maritime Claims.

[See amendments made thereby under respective rules, post.]

2. That the foregoing amendments to the Federal Rules of Civil Procedure and the Supplemental Rules for Certain Admiralty and Maritime Claims shall take effect on December 1, 2000, and shall govern all proceedings in civil cases thereafter commenced and, insofar as just and practicable, all proceedings in civil cases then pending.

3. That THE CHIEF JUSTICE be, and hereby is, authorized to transmit to the Congress the foregoing amendments to the Federal Rules of Civil Procedure in accordance with the provisions of Section 2072 of Title 28, United States Code.

ORDER OF APRIL 23, 2001

1. That the Federal Rules of Civil Procedure be, and they hereby are, amended by including therein amendments to Civil Rules 5, 6, 65, 77, 81, and 82.

[See amendments made thereby under respective rules, post.]

2. That the foregoing amendments to the Federal Rules of Civil Procedure shall take effect on December 1, 2001, and shall govern in all proceedings in civil cases thereafter commenced and, insofar as just and practicable, all proceedings then pending.

3. That THE CHIEF JUSTICE be, and hereby is, authorized to transmit to the Congress the foregoing amendments to the Federal Rules of Civil Procedure in accordance with the provisions of Section 2072 of Title 28, United States Code.

4. That the Rules for Practice and Procedure under section 25 of An Act To Amend and Consolidate the Acts Respecting Copyright, approved March 4, 1909, promulgated by this Court on June 1, 1909, effective July 1, 1909, as revised, be, and they hereby are, abrogated, effective December 1, 2001.

ORDER OF APRIL 29, 2002

1. That the Federal Rules of Civil Procedure be, and they hereby are, amended by including therein amendments to Civil Rules 54, 58, and 81, and a new Rule 7.1, and Rule C of Supplemental Rules for Certain Admiralty and Maritime Claims.

[See amendments made thereby under respective rules, post.]

2. That the foregoing amendments to the Federal Rules of Civil Procedure shall take effect on December 1, 2002, and shall govern in all proceedings in civil cases thereafter commenced and, insofar as just and practicable, all proceedings then pending.

3. That the CHIEF JUSTICE be, and hereby is, authorized to transmit to the Congress the foregoing amendments to the Federal Rules of Civil Procedure in accordance with the provisions of Section 2072 of Title 28, United States Code.

ORDER OF MARCH 27, 2003

1. That the Federal Rules of Civil Procedure be, and they hereby are, amended by including therein amendments to Civil Rules 23, 51, 53, 54, and 71A.

[See amendments made thereby under respective rules and forms, post.]

2. That Forms 19, 31, and 32 in the Appendix to the Federal Rules of Civil Procedure be, and they hereby are, amended by replacing all references to "19___" with references to "20___."

3. That the foregoing amendments to the Federal Rules of Civil Procedure shall take effect on December 1, 2003, and shall govern in all proceedings in civil cases thereafter commenced and, insofar as just and practicable, all proceedings then pending.

4. That the CHIEF JUSTICE be, and hereby is, authorized to transmit to the Congress the foregoing amendments to the Federal Rules of Civil Procedure in accordance with the provisions of Section 2072 of Title 28, United States Code.

ORDER OF APRIL 25, 2005

1. That the Federal Rules of Civil Procedure be, and they hereby are, amended by including therein the amendments to Civil Rules 6, 27, and 45, and to Rules B and C of the Supplemental Rules for Certain Admiralty and Maritime Claims.

[See amendments made thereby under respective rules and forms, post.]

2. That the foregoing amendments to the Federal Rules of Civil Procedure and the Supplemental Rules for Certain Admiralty and Maritime Claims shall take effect on December 1, 2005, and shall govern in all proceedings thereafter commenced and, insofar as just and practicable, all proceedings then pending.

3. That the CHIEF JUSTICE be, and hereby is, authorized to transmit to the Congress the foregoing amendments to the Federal Rules of Civil Procedure in accordance with the provisions of Section 2072 of Title 28, United States Code.

ORDER OF APRIL 12, 2006

1. That the Federal Rules of Civil Procedure be, and they hereby are, amended by including therein the amendments to Civil Rules 5, 9, 14, 16, 24, 26, 33, 34, 37, 45, 50, and 65.1; Form 35; and new Rule 5.1.

2. That the Supplemental Rules for Admiralty or Maritime Claims and Asset Forfeiture Actions be, and they hereby are, amended by including therein the amendments to Rules A, C, and E, and new Rule G.

[See amendments made thereby under respective rules and forms, post.]

3. That the foregoing amendments to the Federal Rules of Civil Procedure and the Supplemental Rules for Admiralty or Maritime Claims and Asset Forfeiture Actions shall take effect on December 1, 2006, and shall govern in all proceedings thereafter commenced and, insofar as just and practicable, all proceedings then pending.

4. That THE CHIEF JUSTICE be, and hereby is, authorized to transmit to the Congress the foregoing amendments to the Federal Rules of Civil Procedure in accordance with the provisions of Section 2072 of Title 28, United States Code.

ORDER OF APRIL 30, 2007

1. That the Federal Rules of Civil Procedure be, and they hereby are, amended by including therein the amendments to Civil Rules 1 through 86 and new Rule 5.2.

2. That Forms 1 through 35 in the Appendix to the Federal Rules of Civil Procedure be, and they hereby are, amended to become restyled Forms 1 through 82.

[See amendments made thereby under respective rules and forms, post.]

3. That the foregoing amendments to the Federal Rules of Civil Procedure shall take effect on December 1, 2007, and shall govern in all proceedings thereafter commenced and, insofar as just and practicable, all proceedings then pending.

4. That THE CHIEF JUSTICE be, and hereby is, authorized to transmit to the Congress the foregoing amendments to the Federal Rules of Civil Procedure in accordance with the provisions of Section 2072 of Title 28, United States Code.

HISTORICAL NOTES

The original Rules of Civil Procedure for the District Courts were adopted by order of the Supreme Court on Dec. 20, 1937, transmitted to Congress by the Attorney General on Jan. 3, 1938, and became effective on Sept. 16, 1938.

The Rules have been amended Dec. 28, 1939, eff. Apr. 3, 1941; Dec. 27, 1946, eff. Mar. 19, 1948; Dec. 29, 1948, eff. Oct. 20, 1949; Apr. 30, 1951, eff. Aug. 1, 1951; Apr. 17, 1961, eff. July 19, 1961; Jan. 21, 1963, eff. July 1, 1963; Feb. 28, 1966, eff. July 1, 1966; Dec. 4, 1967, eff. July 1, 1968; Mar. 30, 1970, eff. July 1, 1970; Mar. 1, 1971, eff. July 1, 1971; Nov. 20, 1972, and Dec. 18, 1972, eff. July 1, 1975; Apr. 29, 1980, eff. Aug. 1, 1980; Oct. 21, 1980, Pub.L. 96–481, Title II, § 205(a), (b), 94 Stat. 2330; Jan. 12, 1983, Pub.L. 97–462, §§ 2–4, 96 Stat. 2527–2530, eff. Feb. 26, 1983; Apr. 28, 1983, eff. Aug. 1, 1983; Apr. 29, 1985, eff. Aug. 1, 1985; Mar. 2, 1987, eff. Aug. 1, 1987; Apr. 25, 1988, eff. Aug. 1, 1988; Nov. 18, 1988, Pub.L. 100–690, Title VII, §§ 7047(b), 7049, 7050, 102 Stat. 4401; Apr. 30, 1991, eff. Dec. 1, 1991; Apr. 22, 1993, eff. Dec. 1, 1993; Apr. 27, 1995, eff. Dec. 1, 1995; Apr. 23, 1996, eff. Dec. 1, 1996; Apr. 11, 1997, eff. Dec. 1, 1997 Apr. 24, 1998, eff. Dec. 1, 1998; Apr. 26, 1999, eff. Dec. 1, 1999; Apr. 17, 2000, eff. Dec. 1, 2000; Apr. 23, 2001, eff. Dec. 1,

2001; Apr. 29, 2002, eff. Dec. 1, 2002; Mar. 27, 2003, eff. Dec. 1, 2003; Apr. 25, 2005, eff. Dec. 1, 2005; Apr. 12, 2006, eff. Dec. 1, 2006.

I. SCOPE OF RULES—ONE FORM OF ACTION

Proposed Amendment of Heading

Effective December 1, 2007, absent contrary Congressional action, this heading is amended to read as follows:

TITLE I. SCOPE OF RULES; FORM OF ACTION

Rule 1. Scope and Purpose of Rules

These rules govern the procedure in the United States district courts in all suits of a civil nature whether cognizable as cases at law or in equity or in admiralty, with the exceptions stated in Rule 81. They shall be construed and administered to secure the just, speedy, and inexpensive determination of every action.

(As amended Dec. 29, 1948, eff. Oct. 20, 1949; Feb. 28, 1966, eff. July 1, 1966; Apr. 22, 1993, eff. Dec. 1, 1993.)

Proposed Amendment of Rule

Effective December 1, 2007, absent contrary Congressional action, this rule is amended to read as follows:

Rule 1. Scope and Purpose

These rules govern the procedure in all civil actions and proceedings in the United States district courts, except as stated in Rule 81. They should be construed and administered to secure the just, speedy, and inexpensive determination of every action and proceeding.

ADVISORY COMMITTEE NOTES

1937 Adoption

1. Rule 81 states certain limitations in the application of these rules to enumerated special proceedings.

2. The expression "district courts of the United States" appearing in the statute authorizing the Supreme Court of the United States to promulgate rules of civil procedure does not include the district courts held in the territories and insular possessions. See *Mookini et al. v. United States,* 1938, 58 S.Ct. 543, 303 U.S. 201, 82 L.Ed. 748.

3. These rules are drawn under the authority of the Act of June 19, 1934, U.S.C., Title 28, § 723b [see 2072] (Rules in actions at law; Supreme Court authorized to make), and § 723c [see 2072] (Union of equity and action at law rules; power of Supreme Court) and also other grants of rule making power to the Court. See Clark and Moore, *A New Federal Civil Procedure—I. The Background,* 44 Yale L.J. 387, 391 (1935). Under § 723b after the rules have taken effect all laws in conflict therewith are of no further force or effect. In accordance with § 723c the Court has united the general rules prescribed for cases in equity with those in

actions at law so as to secure one form of civil action and procedure for both. See Rule 2 (One Form of Action). For the former practice in equity and at law see U.S.C.A., Title 28, §§ 723 and 730 [see 2071 et seq.] (conferring power on the Supreme Court to make rules of practice in equity) and the [former] Equity Rules promulgated thereunder; U.S.C., Title 28, [former] § 724 (Conformity act); [former] Equity Rule 22 (Action at Law Erroneously Begun as Suit in Equity—Transfer); [former] Equity Rule 23 (Matters Ordinarily Determinable at Law When Arising in Suit in Equity to be Disposed of Therein); U.S.C., Title 28, [former] §§ 397 (Amendments to pleadings when case brought to wrong side of court), and 398 (Equitable defenses and equitable relief in actions at law).

4. With the second sentence compare U.S.C., Title 28, [former] §§ 777 (Defects of form; amendments), [former] 767 (Amendment of process); [former] Equity Rule 19 (Amendments Generally).

1948 Amendment

The amendment effective Oct. 20, 1949, substituted the words "United States district courts" for the words "district courts of the United States."

1966 Amendment

This is the fundamental change necessary to effect unification of the civil and admiralty procedure. Just as the 1938 rules abolished the distinction between actions at law and suits in equity, this change would abolish the distinction between civil actions and suits in admiralty. See also Rule 81.

1993 Amendments

The purpose of this revision, adding the words "and administered" to the second sentence, is to recognize the affirmative duty of the court to exercise the authority conferred by these rules to ensure that civil litigation is resolved not only fairly, but also without undue cost or delay. As officers of the court, attorneys share this responsibility with the judge to whom the case is assigned.

2007 Amendment

[Effective December 1, 2007, absent contrary Congressional action.]

The language of Rule 1 has been amended as part of the general restyling of the Civil Rules to make them more easily understood and to make style and terminology consistent throughout the rules. These changes are intended to be stylistic only.

The merger of law, equity, and admiralty practice is complete. There is no need to carry forward the phrases that initially accomplished the merger.

The former reference to "suits of a civil nature" is changed to the more modern "civil actions and proceedings." This change does not affect such questions as whether the Civil Rules apply to summary proceedings created by statute. *See SEC v. McCarthy*, 322 F.3d 650 (9th Cir. 2003); *see also New Hampshire Fire Ins. Co. v. Scanlon*, 362 U.S. 404 (1960).

The Style Project

The Civil Rules are the third set of the rules to be restyled. The restyled Rules of Appellate Procedure took effect in 1998. The restyled Rules of Criminal Procedure took effect in 2002. The restyled Rules of Civil Procedure apply the same general drafting guidelines and principles used in restyling the Appellate and Criminal Rules.

1. General Guidelines

Guidance in drafting, usage, and style was provided by Bryan Garner, *Guidelines for Drafting and Editing Court Rules*, Administrative Office of the United States Courts (1996) and Bryan Garner, *Dictionary of Modern Legal Usage* (2d ed. 1995). *See also* Joseph Kimble, *Guiding Principles for Restyling the Civil Rules*, in *Preliminary Draft of Proposed Style Revision of the Federal Rules of Civil Procedure*, at x (Feb. 2005) (available at http://www.uscourts.gov/rules/ Prelim_draft_proposed_pt1.pdf).

2. Formatting Changes

Many of the changes in the restyled Civil Rules result from using format to achieve clearer presentation. The rules are broken down into constituent parts, using progressively indented subparagraphs with headings and substituting vertical for horizontal lists. "Hanging indents" are used throughout. These formatting changes make the structure of the rules graphic and make the restyled rules easier to read and understand even when the words are not changed. Rule 14(a) illustrates the benefits of formatting changes.

3. Changes to Reduce Inconsistent, Ambiguous, Redundant, Repetitive, or Archaic Words

The restyled rules reduce the use of inconsistent terms that say the same thing in different ways. Because different words are presumed to have different meanings, such inconsistencies can result in confusion. The restyled rules reduce inconsistencies by using the same words to express the same meaning. For example, consistent expression is achieved without affecting meaning by the changes from "infant" in many rules to "minor" in all rules; from "upon motion or on its own initiative" in Rule 4(m) and variations in many other rules to "on motion or on its own"; and from "deemed" to "considered" in Rules 5(c), 12(e), and elsewhere. Some variations of expression have been carried forward when the context made that appropriate. As an example, "stipulate," "agree," and "consent" appear throughout the rules, and "written" qualifies these words in some places but not others. The number of variations has been reduced, but at times the former words were carried forward. None of the changes, when made, alters the rule's meaning.

The restyled rules minimize the use of inherently ambiguous words. For example, the word "shall" can mean "must," "may," or something else, depending on context. The potential for confusion is exacerbated by the fact that "shall" is no longer generally used in spoken or clearly written English. The restyled rules replace "shall" with "must," "may," or "should," depending on which one the context and established interpretation make correct in each rule.

The restyled rules minimize the use of redundant "intensifiers." These are expressions that attempt to add emphasis, but instead state the obvious and create negative implications for other rules. "The court in its discretion may" becomes "the court may"; "unless the order expressly directs otherwise" becomes "unless the court orders otherwise." The absence of intensifiers in the restyled rules does not change their substantive meaning. For example, the absence of the word "reasonable" to describe the written notice of foreign law required in Rule 44.1 does not mean that "unreasonable" notice is permitted.

The restyled rules also remove words and concepts that are outdated or redundant. The reference to "at law or in equity" in Rule 1 has become redundant with the merger of law and equity. Outdated words and concepts include the reference to "demurrers, pleas, and exceptions" in Rule 7(c); the reference to "mesne" process in Rule 77(c); and the reference in Rule 81(f) to a now-abolished official position.

The restyled rules remove a number of redundant cross-references. For example, Rule 8(b) states that a general denial is subject to the obligations of Rule 11, but all pleadings are subject to Rule 11. Removing such cross-references does not defeat application of the formerly cross-referenced rule.

4. Rule Numbers

The restyled rules keep the same rule numbers to minimize the effect on research. Subdivisions have been rearranged within some rules to achieve greater clarity and simplicity. The only change that moves one part of a rule to another is the transfer of former Rule 25(d)(2) to Rule 17(d). The restyled rules include a comparison chart to make it easy to identify transfers of provisions between subdivisions and redesignations of some subdivisions.

5. Other Changes

The style changes to the rules are intended to make no changes in substantive meaning. A very small number of minor technical amendments that arguably do change meaning were approved separately from the restyled rules, but become effective at the same time. An example is adding "e-mail address" to the information that must be included in pleadings. These minor changes occur in Rules 4(k), 9(h), 11(a), 14(b), 16(c)(1), 26(g)(1), 30(b), 31, 40, 71.1, and 78.

Rule 2. One Form of Action

There shall be one form of action to be known as "civil action".

Proposed Amendment of Rule

Effective December 1, 2007, absent contrary Congressional action, this rule is amended to read as follows:

Rule 2. One Form of Action

There is one form of action—the civil action.

ADVISORY COMMITTEE NOTES

1937 Adoption

1. This rule modifies U.S.C.., Title 28, [former] § 384 (Suits in equity, when not sustainable). U.S.C., Title 28, §§ 723 and 730 [sec. 2071, et seq.] (conferring power on the Supreme Court to make rules of practice in equity), are

unaffected in so far as they relate to the rule making power in admiralty. These sections, together with § 723b [sec. 2072] (Rules in actions at law; Supreme Court authorized to make) are continued in so far as they are not inconsistent with § 2072, formerly § 723c (Union of equity and action at law rules; power of Supreme Court). See Note 3 to Rule 1. U.S.C., Title 28, [former] §§ 724 (Conformity act), 397 (Amendments to pleadings when case brought to wrong side of court) and 398 (Equitable defenses and equitable relief in actions at law) are superseded.

2. Reference to actions at law or suits in equity in all statutes should now be treated as referring to the civil action prescribed in these rules.

3. This rule follows in substance the usual introductory statements to code practices which provide for a single action and mode of procedure, with abolition of forms of action and

procedural distinctions. Representative statutes are N.Y. Code 1848 (Laws 1848, ch. 379) § 62; N.Y.C.P.A. (1937) § 8; Calif.Code Civ.Proc. (Deering, 1937) § 307; 2 Minn.Stat.Ann. 1945 § 540.01; 2 Wash.Rev.Stat.Ann. (Remington, 1932) §§ 153, 255.

2007 Amendment

[Effective December 1, 2007,
absent contrary Congressional action.]

The language of Rule 2 has been amended as part of the general restyling of the Civil Rules to make them more easily understood and to make style and terminology consistent throughout the rules. These changes are intended to be stylistic only.

II. COMMENCEMENT OF ACTION; SERVICE OF PROCESS, PLEADINGS, MOTIONS, AND ORDERS

Proposed Amendment of Heading

Effective December 1, 2007, absent contrary Congressional action, this heading is amended to read as follows:

TITLE II. COMMENCING AN ACTION; SERVICE OF PROCESS, PLEADINGS, MOTIONS, AND ORDERS

Rule 3. Commencement of Action

A civil action is commenced by filing a complaint with the court.

Proposed Amendment of Rule

Effective December 1, 2007, absent contrary Congressional action, this rule is amended to read as follows:

Rule 3. *Commencing an Action*

A civil action is commenced by filing a complaint with the court.

ADVISORY COMMITTEE NOTES

1937 Adoption

1. Rule 5(e) defines what constitutes filing with the court.

2. This rule governs the commencement of all actions, including those brought by or against the United States or an officer or agency thereof, regardless of whether service is to be made personally pursuant to Rule 4(d), or otherwise pursuant to Rule 4(e).

3. With this rule compare [former] Equity Rule 12 (Issue of Subpoena—Time for Answer) and the following statutes (and other similar statutes) which provide a similar method for commencing an action:

U.S.C., Title 28:

 § 45 [former] (District courts; practice and procedure in certain cases under interstate commerce laws).

 § 762 [see 1402] (Petition in suit against United States).

 § 766 [see 2409] (Partition suits where United States is tenant in common or joint tenant).

4. This rule provides that the first step in an action is the filing of the complaint. Under Rule 4(a) this is to be followed forthwith by issuance of a summons and its delivery to an officer for service. Other rules providing for dismissal for failure to prosecute suggest a method available to attack unreasonable delay in prosecuting an action after it has been commenced. When a Federal or State statute of limitations is pleaded as a defense, a question may arise under this rule whether the mere filing of the complaint stops the running of the statute, or whether any further step is required, such as, service of the summons and complaint or their delivery to the marshal for service. The answer to this question may depend on whether it is competent for the Supreme Court, exercising the power to make rules of procedure without affecting substantive rights, to vary the operation of statutes of limitations. The requirement of rule 4(a) that the clerk shall forthwith issue the summons and deliver it to the marshal for service will reduce the chances of such a question arising.

2007 Amendments

[Effective December 1, 2007,
absent contrary Congressional action.]

The caption of Rule 3 has been amended as part of the general restyling of the Civil Rules to make them more easily understood and to make style and terminology consistent throughout the rules. These changes are intended to be stylistic only.

Rule 4. Summons

(a) Form. The summons shall be signed by the clerk, bear the seal of the court, identify the court and the parties, be directed to the defendant, and state the name and address of the plaintiff's attorney or, if unrepresented, of the plaintiff. It shall also state the time within which the defendant must appear and defend, and notify the defendant that failure to do so will result in a judgment by default against the defen-

Rule 4

dant for the relief demanded in the complaint. The court may allow a summons to be amended.

(b) Issuance. Upon or after filing the complaint, the plaintiff may present a summons to the clerk for signature and seal. If the summons is in proper form, the clerk shall sign, seal, and issue it to the plaintiff for service on the defendant. A summons, or a copy of the summons if addressed to multiple defendants, shall be issued for each defendant to be served.

(c) Service with Complaint; by Whom Made.

(1) A summons shall be served together with a copy of the complaint. The plaintiff is responsible for service of a summons and complaint within the time allowed under subdivision (m) and shall furnish the person effecting service with the necessary copies of the summons and complaint.

(2) Service may be effected by any person who is not a party and who is at least 18 years of age. At the request of the plaintiff, however, the court may direct that service be effected by a United States marshal, deputy United States marshal, or other person or officer specially appointed by the court for that purpose. Such an appointment must be made when the plaintiff is authorized to proceed in forma pauperis pursuant to 28 U.S.C. § 1915 or is authorized to proceed as a seaman under 28 U.S.C. § 1916.

(d) Waiver of Service; Duty to Save Costs of Service; Request to Waive.

(1) A defendant who waives service of a summons does not thereby waive any objection to the venue or to the jurisdiction of the court over the person of the defendant.

(2) An individual, corporation, or association that is subject to service under subdivision (e), (f), or (h) and that receives notice of an action in the manner provided in this paragraph has a duty to avoid unnecessary costs of serving the summons. To avoid costs, the plaintiff may notify such a defendant of the commencement of the action and request that the defendant waive service of a summons. The notice and request

(A) shall be in writing and shall be addressed directly to the defendant, if an individual, or else to an officer or managing or general agent (or other agent authorized by appointment or law to receive service of process) of a defendant subject to service under subdivision (h);

(B) shall be dispatched through first-class mail or other reliable means;

(C) shall be accompanied by a copy of the complaint and shall identify the court in which it has been filed;

(D) shall inform the defendant, by means of a text prescribed in an official form promulgated

pursuant to Rule 84, of the consequences of compliance and of a failure to comply with the request;

(E) shall set forth the date on which the request is sent;

(F) shall allow the defendant a reasonable time to return the waiver, which shall be at least 30 days from the date on which the request is sent, or 60 days from that date if the defendant is addressed outside any judicial district of the United States; and

(G) shall provide the defendant with an extra copy of the notice and request, as well as a prepaid means of compliance in writing.

If a defendant located within the United States fails to comply with a request for waiver made by a plaintiff located within the United States, the court shall impose the costs subsequently incurred in effecting service on the defendant unless good cause for the failure be shown.

(3) A defendant that, before being served with process, timely returns a waiver so requested is not required to serve an answer to the complaint until 60 days after the date on which the request for waiver of service was sent, or 90 days after that date if the defendant was addressed outside any judicial district of the United States.

(4) When the plaintiff files a waiver of service with the court, the action shall proceed, except as provided in paragraph (3), as if a summons and complaint had been served at the time of filing the waiver, and no proof of service shall be required.

(5) The costs to be imposed on a defendant under paragraph (2) for failure to comply with a request to waive service of a summons shall include the costs subsequently incurred in effecting service under subdivision (e), (f), or (h), together with the costs, including a reasonable attorney's fee, of any motion required to collect the costs of service.

(e) Service Upon Individuals Within a Judicial District of the United States. Unless otherwise provided by federal law, service upon an individual from whom a waiver has not been obtained and filed, other than an infant or an incompetent person, may be effected in any judicial district of the United States:

(1) pursuant to the law of the state in which the district court is located, or in which service is effected, for the service of a summons upon the defendant in an action brought in the courts of general jurisdiction of the State; or

(2) by delivering a copy of the summons and of the complaint to the individual personally or by leaving copies thereof at the individual's dwelling house or usual place of abode with some person of suitable age and discretion then residing therein or by delivering a copy of the summons and of the

complaint to an agent authorized by appointment or by law to receive service of process.

(f) Service Upon Individuals in a Foreign Country. Unless otherwise provided by federal law, service upon an individual from whom a waiver has not been obtained and filed, other than an infant or an incompetent person, may be effected in a place not within any judicial district of the United States:

(1) by any internationally agreed means reasonably calculated to give notice, such as those means authorized by the Hague Convention on the Service Abroad of Judicial and Extrajudicial Documents; or

(2) if there is no internationally agreed means of service or the applicable international agreement allows other means of service, provided that service is reasonably calculated to give notice:

(A) in the manner prescribed by the law of the foreign country for service in that country in an action in any of its courts of general jurisdiction; or

(B) as directed by the foreign authority in response to a letter rogatory or letter of request; or

(C) unless prohibited by the law of the foreign country, by

(i) delivery to the individual personally of a copy of the summons and the complaint; or

(ii) any form of mail requiring a signed receipt, to be addressed and dispatched by the clerk of the court to the party to be served; or

(3) by other means not prohibited by international agreement as may be directed by the court.

(g) Service Upon Infants and Incompetent Persons. Service upon an infant or an incompetent person in a judicial district of the United States shall be effected in the manner prescribed by the law of the state in which the service is made for the service of summons or other like process upon any such defendant in an action brought in the courts of general jurisdiction of that state. Service upon an infant or an incompetent person in a place not within any judicial district of the United States shall be effected in the manner prescribed by paragraph (2)(A) or (2)(B) of subdivision (f) or by such means as the court may direct.

(h) Service Upon Corporations and Associations. Unless otherwise provided by federal law, service upon a domestic or foreign corporation or upon a partnership or other unincorporated association that is subject to suit under a common name, and from which a waiver of service has not been obtained and filed, shall be effected:

(1) in a judicial district of the United States in the manner prescribed for individuals by subdivision (e)(1), or by delivering a copy of the summons and of the complaint to an officer, a managing or general agent, or to any other agent authorized by appointment or by law to receive service of process and, if the agent is one authorized by statute to receive service and the statute so requires, by also mailing a copy to the defendant, or

(2) in a place not within any judicial district of the United States in any manner prescribed for individuals by subdivision (f) except personal delivery as provided in paragraph (2)(C)(i) thereof.

(i) Serving the United States, Its Agencies, Corporations, Officers, or Employees.

(1) Service upon the United States shall be effected

(A) by delivering a copy of the summons and of the complaint to the United States attorney for the district in which the action is brought or to an assistant United States attorney or clerical employee designated by the United States attorney in a writing filed with the clerk of the court or by sending a copy of the summons and of the complaint by registered or certified mail addressed to the civil process clerk at the office of the United States attorney and

(B) by also sending a copy of the summons and of the complaint by registered or certified mail to the Attorney General of the United States at Washington, District of Columbia, and

(C) in any action attacking the validity of an order of an officer or agency of the United States not made a party, by also sending a copy of the summons and of the complaint by registered or certified mail to the officer or agency.

(2)(A) Service on an agency or corporation of the United States, or an officer or employee of the United States sued only in an official capacity, is effected by serving the United States in the manner prescribed by Rule 4(i)(1) and by also sending a copy of the summons and complaint by registered or certified mail to the officer, employee, agency, or corporation.

(B) Service on an officer or employee of the United States sued in an individual capacity for acts or omissions occurring in connection with the performance of duties on behalf of the United States— whether or not the officer or employee is sued also in an official capacity—is effected by serving the United States in the manner prescribed by Rule 4(i)(1) and by serving the officer or employee in the manner prescribed by Rule 4 (e), (f), or (g).

(3) The court shall allow a reasonable time to serve process under Rule 4(i) for the purpose of curing the failure to serve:

(A) all persons required to be served in an action governed by Rule 4(i)(2)(A), if the plaintiff

has served either the United States attorney or the Attorney General of the United States, or

(B) the United States in an action governed by Rule 4(i)(2)(B), if the plaintiff has served an officer or employee of the United States sued in an individual capacity.

(j) Service Upon Foreign, State, or Local Governments.

(1) Service upon a foreign state or a political subdivision, agency, or instrumentality thereof shall be effected pursuant to 28 U.S.C. § 1608.

(2) Service upon a state, municipal corporation, or other governmental organization subject to suit shall be effected by delivering a copy of the summons and of the complaint to its chief executive officer or by serving the summons and complaint in the manner prescribed by the law of that state for the service of summons or other like process upon any such defendant.

(k) Territorial Limits of Effective Service.

(1) Service of a summons or filing a waiver of service is effective to establish jurisdiction over the person of a defendant

(A) who could be subjected to the jurisdiction of a court of general jurisdiction in the state in which the district court is located, or

(B) who is a party joined under Rule 14 or Rule 19 and is served at a place within a judicial district of the United States and not more than 100 miles from the place from which the summons issues, or

(C) who is subject to the federal interpleader jurisdiction under 28 U.S.C. § 1335, or

(D) when authorized by a statute of the United States.

(2) If the exercise of jurisdiction is consistent with the Constitution and laws of the United States, serving a summons or filing a waiver of service is also effective, with respect to claims arising under federal law, to establish personal jurisdiction over the person of any defendant who is not subject to the jurisdiction of the courts of general jurisdiction of any state.

(l) Proof of Service.

If service is not waived, the person effecting service shall make proof thereof to the court. If service is made by a person other than a United States marshal or deputy United States marshal, the person shall make affidavit thereof. Proof of service in a place not within any judicial district of the United States shall, if effected under paragraph (1) of subdivision (f), be made pursuant to the applicable treaty or convention, and shall, if effected under paragraph (2) or (3) thereof, include a receipt signed by the addressee or other evidence of delivery to the addressee satisfactory to the court. Failure to make proof of service does not affect the validity of the

service. The court may allow proof of service to be amended.

(m) Time Limit for Service.

If service of the summons and complaint is not made upon a defendant within 120 days after the filing of the complaint, the court, upon motion or on its own initiative after notice to the plaintiff, shall dismiss the action without prejudice as to that defendant or direct that service be effected within a specified time; provided that if the plaintiff shows good cause for the failure, the court shall extend the time for service for an appropriate period. This subdivision does not apply to service in a foreign country pursuant to subdivision (f) or (j)(1).

(n) Seizure of Property; Service of Summons Not Feasible.

(1) If a statute of the United States so provides, the court may assert jurisdiction over property. Notice to claimants of the property shall then be sent in the manner provided by the statute or by service of a summons under this rule.

(2) Upon a showing that personal jurisdiction over a defendant cannot, in the district where the action is brought, be obtained with reasonable efforts by service of summons in any manner authorized by this rule, the court may assert jurisdiction over any of the defendant's assets found within the district by seizing the assets under the circumstances and in the manner provided by the law of the state in which the district court is located.

(As amended Jan. 21, 1963, eff. July 1, 1963; Feb. 28, 1966, eff. July 1, 1966; Apr. 29, 1980, eff. Aug. 1, 1980; Jan. 12, 1983, Pub.L. 97–462, § 2, 96 Stat. 2527; Mar. 2, 1987, eff. Aug. 1, 1987; Apr. 22, 1993, eff. Dec. 1, 1993; Apr. 17, 2000, eff. Dec. 1, 2000.)

Proposed Amendment of Rule

Effective December 1, 2007, absent contrary Congressional action, this rule is amended to read as follows:

Rule 4. Summons

(a) Contents; Amendments.

(1) *Contents. A summons must:*

(A) *name the court and the parties;*

(B) *be directed to the defendant;*

(C) *state the name and address of the plaintiff's attorney or—if unrepresented—of the plaintiff;*

(D) *state the time within which the defendant must appear and defend;*

(E) *notify the defendant that a failure to appear and defend will result in a default judgment against the defendant for the relief demanded in the complaint;*

RULES OF CIVIL PROCEDURERule 4

(F) be signed by the clerk; and

(G) bear the court's seal.

(2) Amendments. The court may permit a summons to be amended.

(b) Issuance. *On or after filing the complaint, the plaintiff may present a summons to the clerk for signature and seal. If the summons is properly completed, the clerk must sign, seal, and issue it to the plaintiff for service on the defendant. A summons—or a copy of a summons that is addressed to multiple defendants—must be issued for each defendant to be served.*

(c) Service.

(1) In General. A summons must be served with a copy of the complaint. The plaintiff is responsible for having the summons and complaint served within the time allowed by Rule 4(m) and must furnish the necessary copies to the person who makes service.

(2) By Whom. Any person who is at least 18 years old and not a party may serve a summons and complaint.

(3) By a Marshal or Someone Specially Appointed. At the plaintiff's request, the court may order that service be made by a United States marshal or deputy marshal or by a person specially appointed by the court. The court must so order if the plaintiff is authorized to proceed in forma pauperis under 28 U.S.C. § 1915 or as a seaman under 28 U.S.C. § 1916.

(d) Waiving Service.

(1) Requesting a Waiver. An individual, corporation, or association that is subject to service under Rule 4(e), (f), or (h) has a duty to avoid unnecessary expenses of serving the summons. The plaintiff may notify such a defendant that an action has been commenced and request that the defendant waive service of a summons. The notice and request must:

(A) be in writing and be addressed:

(i) to the individual defendant; or

(ii) for a defendant subject to service under Rule 4(h), to an officer, a managing or general agent, or any other agent authorized by appointment or by law to receive service of process;

(B) name the court where the complaint was filed;

(C) be accompanied by a copy of the complaint, two copies of a waiver form, and a prepaid means for returning the form;

(D) inform the defendant, using text prescribed in Form 5, of the consequences of waiving and not waiving service;

(E) state the date when the request is sent;

(F) give the defendant a reasonable time of at least 30 days after the request was sent—or at least 60 days if sent to the defendant outside any judicial district of the United States—to return the waiver; and

(G) *be sent by first-class mail or other reliable means.*

(2) Failure to Waive. If a defendant located within the United States fails, without good cause, to sign and return a waiver requested by a plaintiff located within the United States, the court must impose on the defendant:

(A) the expenses later incurred in making service; and

(B) the reasonable expenses, including attorney's fees, of any motion required to collect those service expenses.

(3) Time to Answer After a Waiver. A defendant who, before being served with process, timely returns a waiver need not serve an answer to the complaint until 60 days after the request was sent—or until 90 days after it was sent to the defendant outside any judicial district of the United States.

(4) Results of Filing a Waiver. When the plaintiff files a waiver, proof of service is not required and these rules apply as if a summons and complaint had been served at the time of filing the waiver.

(5) Jurisdiction and Venue Not Waived. Waiving service of a summons does not waive any objection to personal jurisdiction or to venue.

(e) Serving an Individual Within a Judicial District of the United States. *Unless federal law provides otherwise, an individual—other than a minor, an incompetent person, or a person whose waiver has been filed—may be served in a judicial district of the United States by:*

(1) following state law for serving a summons in an action brought in courts of general jurisdiction in the state where the district court is located or where service is made; or

(2) doing any of the following:

(A) delivering a copy of the summons and of the complaint to the individual personally;

(B) leaving a copy of each at the individual's dwelling or usual place of abode with

Complete Annotation Materials, see Title 28 U.S.C.A.
47

someone of suitable age and discretion who resides there; or

(C) delivering a copy of each to an agent authorized by appointment or by law to receive service of process.

(f) Serving an Individual in a Foreign Country. Unless federal law provides otherwise, an individual—other than a minor, an incompetent person, or a person whose waiver has been filed—may be served at a place not within any judicial district of the United States:

(1) by any internationally agreed means of service that is reasonably calculated to give notice, such as those authorized by the Hague Convention on the Service Abroad of Judicial and Extrajudicial Documents;

(2) if there is no internationally agreed means, or if an international agreement allows but does not specify other means, by a method that is reasonably calculated to give notice:

(A) as prescribed by the foreign country's law for service in that country in an action in its courts of general jurisdiction;

(B) as the foreign authority directs in response to a letter rogatory or letter of request; or

(C) unless prohibited by the foreign country's law, by:

(i) delivering a copy of the summons and of the complaint to the individual personally; or

(ii) using any form of mail that the clerk addresses and sends to the individual and that requires a signed receipt; or

(3) by other means not prohibited by international agreement, as the court orders.

(g) Serving a Minor or an Incompetent Person. A minor or an incompetent person in a judicial district of the United States must be served by following state law for serving a summons or like process on such a defendant in an action brought in the courts of general jurisdiction of the state where service is made. A minor or an incompetent person who is not within any judicial district of the United States must be served in the manner prescribed by Rule 4(f)(2)(A), (f)(2)(B), or (f)(3).

(h) Serving a Corporation, Partnership, or Association. Unless federal law provides otherwise or the defendant's waiver has been filed, a domestic or foreign corporation, or a partnership or other unincorporated association that is subject to suit under a common name, must be served:

(1) in a judicial district of the United States:

(A) in the manner prescribed by Rule 4(e)(1) for serving an individual; or

(B) by delivering a copy of the summons and of the complaint to an officer, a managing or general agent, or any other agent authorized by appointment or by law to receive service of process and—if the agent is one authorized by statute and the statute so requires—by also mailing a copy of each to the defendant; or

(2) at a place not within any judicial district of the United States, in any manner prescribed by Rule 4(f) for serving an individual, except personal delivery under (f)(2)(C)(i).

(i) Serving the United States and Its Agencies, Corporations, Officers, or Employees.

(1) United States. To serve the United States, a party must:

(A)(i) deliver a copy of the summons and of the complaint to the United States attorney for the district where the action is brought—or to an assistant United States attorney or clerical employee whom the United States attorney designates in a writing filed with the court clerk—or

(ii) send a copy of each by registered or certified mail to the civil-process clerk at the United States attorney's office;

(B) send a copy of each by registered or certified mail to the Attorney General of the United States at Washington, D.C.; and

(C) if the action challenges an order of a nonparty agency or officer of the United States, send a copy of each by registered or certified mail to the agency or officer.

(2) Agency; Corporation; Officer or Employee Sued in an Official Capacity. To serve a United States agency or corporation, or a United States officer or employee sued only in an official capacity, a party must serve the United States and also send a copy of the summons and of the complaint by registered or certified mail to the agency, corporation, officer, or employee.

(3) Officer or Employee Sued Individually. To serve a United States officer or employee sued in an individual capacity for an act or omission occurring in connection with duties performed on the United States' behalf (whether or not the officer or employee is also sued in an official capacity), a party must serve the United States and also serve the officer or employee under Rule 4(e), (f), or (g).

(4) Extending Time. The court must allow a party a reasonable time to cure its failure to:

(A) serve a person required to be served under Rule 4(i)(2), if the party has served either the United States attorney or the Attorney General of the United States; or

(B) serve the United States under Rule 4(i)(3), if the party has served the United States officer or employee.

(j) Serving a Foreign, State, or Local Government.

(1) Foreign State. A foreign state or its political subdivision, agency, or instrumentality must be served in accordance with 28 U.S.C. § 1608.

(2) State or Local Government. A state, a municipal corporation, or any other state-created governmental organization that is subject to suit must be served by:

(A) delivering a copy of the summons and of the complaint to its chief executive officer; or

(B) serving a copy of each in the manner prescribed by that state's law for serving a summons or like process on such a defendant.

(k) Territorial Limits of Effective Service.

(1) In General. Serving a summons or filing a waiver of service establishes personal jurisdiction over a defendant:

(A) who is subject to the jurisdiction of a court of general jurisdiction in the state where the district court is located;

(B) who is a party joined under Rule 14 or 19 and is served within a judicial district of the United States and not more than 100 miles from where the summons was issued;

(C) when authorized by a federal statute.

(2) Federal Claim Outside State–Court Jurisdiction. For a claim that arises under federal law, serving a summons or filing a waiver of service establishes personal jurisdiction over a defendant if:

(A) the defendant is not subject to jurisdiction in any state's courts of general jurisdiction; and

(B) exercising jurisdiction is consistent with the United States Constitution and laws.

(l) Proving Service.

(1) Affidavit Required. Unless service is waived, proof of service must be made to the court. Except for service by a United States marshal or deputy marshal, proof must be by the server's affidavit.

(2) Service Outside the United States. Service not within any judicial district of the United States must be proved as follows:

(A) if made under Rule 4(f)(1), as provided in the applicable treaty or convention; or

(B) if made under Rule 4(f)(2) or (f)(3), by a receipt signed by the addressee, or by other evidence satisfying the court that the summons and complaint were delivered to the addressee.

(3) Validity of Service; Amending Proof. Failure to prove service does not affect the validity of service. The court may permit proof of service to be amended.

(m) Time Limit for Service. If a defendant is not served within 120 days after the complaint is filed, the court—on motion or on its own after notice to the plaintiff—must dismiss the action without prejudice against that defendant or order that service be made within a specified time. But if the plaintiff shows good cause for the failure, the court must extend the time for service for an appropriate period. This subdivision (m) does not apply to service in a foreign country under Rule 4(f) or 4(j)(1).

(n) Asserting Jurisdiction over Property or Assets.

(1) Federal Law. The court may assert jurisdiction over property if authorized by a federal statute. Notice to claimants of the property must be given as provided in the statute or by serving a summons under this rule.

(2) State Law. On a showing that personal jurisdiction over a defendant cannot be obtained in the district where the action is brought by reasonable efforts to serve a summons under this rule, the court may assert jurisdiction over the defendant's assets found in the district. Jurisdiction is acquired by seizing the assets under the circumstances and in the manner provided by state law in that district.

ADVISORY COMMITTEE NOTES

1937 Adoption

Note to Subdivision (a). With the provision permitting additional summons upon request of the plaintiff, compare former Equity Rule 14 (Alias Subpoena) and the last sentence of former Equity Rule 12 (Issue of Subpoena—Time for Answer).

Note to Subdivision (b). This rule prescribes a form of summons which follows substantially the requirements stated in former Equity Rules 12 (Issue of Subpoena—Time for Answer) and 7 (Process, Mesne and Final).

U.S.C., Title 28, § 721 [now 1691] (Sealing and testing of writs) is substantially continued insofar as it applies to a summons, but its requirements as to teste of process are

superseded. U.S.C., Title 28, [former] § 722 (Teste of process, day of) is superseded.

See Rule 12(a) for a statement of the time within which the defendant is required to appear and defend.

Note to Subdivision (c). This rule does not affect U.S.C., Title 28, § 503 [see 566], as amended June 15, 1935 (Marshals; duties) and such statutes as the following insofar as they provide for service of process by a marshal, but modifies them in so far as they may imply service by a marshal only:

U.S.C., Title 15:

§ 5 (Bringing in additional parties) (Sherman Act)

§ 10 (Bringing in additional parties)

§ 25 (Restraining violations; procedure)

U.S.C., Title 28:

§ 45 [former] (Practice and procedure in certain cases under the interstate commerce laws)

Compare [former] Equity Rule 15 (Process, by Whom Served).

Note to Subdivision (d). Under this rule the complaint must always be served with the summons.

Paragraph (1). For an example of a statute providing for service upon an agent of an individual see U.S.C., Title 28, § 109 [now 1400, 1694] (Patent cases).

Paragraph (3). This enumerates the officers and agents of a corporation or of a partnership or other unincorporated association upon whom service of process may be made, and permits service of process only upon the officers, managing or general agents, or agents authorized by appointment or by law, of the corporation, partnership or unincorporated association against which the action is brought. See *Christian v. International Ass'n of Machinists,* 7 F.(2d) 481 (D.C.Ky. 1925) and *Singleton v. Order of Railway Conductors of America,* 9 F.Supp. 417 (D.C.Ill.1935). Compare *Operative Plasterers' and Cement Finishers' International Ass'n of the United States and Canada v. Case,* 93 F.(2d) 56 (App.D.C. 1937).

For a statute authorizing service upon a specified agent and requiring mailing to the defendant, see U.S.C., Title 6, § 7 (Surety companies as sureties; appointment of agents; service of process).

Paragraphs (4) and (5) provide a uniform and comprehensive method of service for all actions against the United States or an officer or agency thereof. For statutes providing for such service, see U.S.C., Title 7, §§ 217 (Proceedings for suspension of orders) 499k (Injunctions; application of injunction laws governing orders of Interstate Commerce Commission), 608c(15)(B) (Court review of ruling of Secretary of Agriculture), and 855 (making § 608c(15)(B) applicable to orders of the Secretary of Agriculture as to handlers of anti-hog-cholera serum and hog-cholera virus); U.S.C., Title 26, § 3679, (Bill in chancery to clear title to realty on which the United States has a lien for taxes); U.S.C., Title 28, former §§ 45, (District Courts; practice and procedure in certain cases under the interstate commerce laws), [former] 763 (Petition in suit against the United States; service; appearance by district attorney), 766 [now 2409] (Partition suits where United States is tenant in common or joint tenant), 902 [now 2410] (Foreclosure of mortgages or other liens on property in which the United States has an interest). These and similar statutes are modified in so far as they prescribe a different method of service or dispense with the service of a summons.

For the [former] Equity Rule on service, see [former] Equity Rule 13, Manner of Serving Subpoena.

Note to Subdivision (e). The provisions for the service of a summons or of notice or of an order in lieu of summons contained in U.S.C., Title 8, § 405 (Cancellation of certificates of citizenship fraudulently or illegally procured) (service by publication in accordance with State law); U.S.C., Title 28, § 118 [now 1655] (Absent defendants in suits to enforce liens); U.S.C., Title 35, § 72a [now 146, 291] (Jurisdiction of District Court of United States for the District of Columbia in certain equity suits where adverse parties reside elsewhere) (service by publication against parties residing in foreign countries); U.S.C., Title 38, § 445 [now 784] (Action against the United States on a veteran's contract of insurance) (parties not inhabitants of or not found within the district may be served with an order of the court, personally or by publication) and similar statutes are continued by this rule. Title 24, § 378 [now title 13, § 336] of the Code of the District of Columbia (Publication against non-resident; those absent for six months; unknown heirs or devisees; for divorce or in rem; actual service beyond District) is continued by this rule.

Note to Subdivision (f). This rule enlarges to some extent the present rule as to where service may be made. It does not, however, enlarge the jurisdiction of the district courts.

U.S.C., Title 28, §§ 113 [now 1392] (Suits in States containing more than one district) (where there are two or more defendants residing in different districts), [former] 115 (Suits of a local nature), 116 [now 1392] (Property in different districts in same state), [former] 838 (Executions run in all districts of state); U.S.C., Title 47, § 13 (Action for damages against a railroad or telegraph company whose officer or agent in control of a telegraph line refuses or fails to operate such line in a certain manner—"upon any agent of the company found in such state"); U.S.C., Title 49, § 321(c) [now 10330(b)] (Requiring designation of a process agent by interstate motor carriers and in case of failure so to do, service may be made upon any agent in the state) and similar statutes, allowing the running of process throughout a state, are substantially continued.

U.S.C., Title 15, §§ 5 (Bringing in additional parties) (Sherman Act), 25 (Restraining violations; procedure); U.S.C., Title 28, §§ 44 [now 2321] (Procedure in certain cases under interstate commerce laws; service of processes of court), 117 [now 754, 1692] (Property in different states in same circuit; jurisdiction of receiver), 839 [now 2413] (Executions; run in every State and Territory) and similar statutes, providing for the running of process beyond the territorial limits of a State, are expressly continued.

Note to Subdivision (g). With the second sentence compare [former] Equity Rule 15, (Process, by Whom Served).

Note to Subdivision (h). This rule substantially continues U.S.C., Title 28, [former] § 767 (Amendment of process).

1963 Amendment

Subdivision (b). Under amended subdivision (e) of this rule, an action may be commenced against a nonresident of the State in which the district court is held by complying with State procedures. Frequently the form of the summons

or notice required in these cases by State law differs from the Federal form of summons described in present subdivision (b) and exemplified in Form 1. To avoid confusion, the amendment of subdivision (b) states that a form of summons or notice, corresponding "as nearly as may be" to the State form, shall be employed. See also a corresponding amendment of Rule 12(a) with regard to the time to answer.

Subdivision (d)(4). This paragraph, governing service upon the United States, is amended to allow the use of certified mail as an alternative to registered mail for sending copies of the papers to the Attorney General or to a United States officer or agency. Cf. N.J. Rule 4:5–2. See also the amendment of Rule 30(f)(1).

Subdivision (d)(7). Formerly a question was raised whether this paragraph, in the context of the rule as a whole, authorized service in original Federal actions pursuant to State statutes permitting service on a State official as a means of bringing a nonresident motorist defendant into court. It was argued in *McCoy v. Siler*, 205 F.2d 498, 501–2 (3d Cir.) (concurring opinion), cert. denied, 346 U.S. 872, 74 S.Ct. 120, 98 L.Ed. 380 (1953), that the effective service in those cases occurred not when the State official was served but when notice was given to the defendant outside the State, and that subdivision (f) (Territorial limits of effective service), as then worded, did not authorize out-of-State service. This contention found little support. A considerable number of cases held the service to be good, either by fixing upon the service on the official within the State as the effective service, thus satisfying the wording of subdivision (f) as it then stood, see *Holbrook v. Cafiero*, 18 F.R.D. 218 (D.Md. 1955); *Pasternack v. Dalo*, 17 F.R.D. 420 (W.D.Pa.1955); *Super Prods. Corp. v. Parkin*, 20 F.R.D. 377 (S.D.N.Y.1957), or by reading paragraph (7) as not limited by subdivision (f). See *Giffin v. Ensign*, 234 F.2d 307 (3d Cir. 1956); 2 Moore's *Federal Practice*, ¶4.19 (2d ed. 1948); 1 Barron & Holtzoff, *Federal Practice & Procedure* § 182.1 (Wright ed. 1960); Comment, 27 U. of Chi.L.Rev. 751 (1960). See also *Olberding v. Illinois Central R.R.*, 201 F.2d 582 (6th Cir.), rev'd on other grounds, 346 U.S. 338, 74 S.Ct. 83, 98 L.Ed. 39 (1953); *Feinsinger v. Bard*, 195 F.2d 45 (7th Cir. 1952).

An important and growing class of State statutes base personal jurisdiction over nonresidents on the doing of acts or on other contacts within the State, and permit notice to be given the defendant outside the State without any requirement of service on a local State official. See, e.g., Ill.Ann. Stat., c. 110, §§ 16, 17 (Smith–Hurd 1956); Wis.Stat. § 262.06 (1959). This service, employed in original Federal actions pursuant to paragraph (7), has also been held proper. See *Farr & Co. v. Cia. Intercontinental de Nav. de Cuba*, 243 F.2d 342 (2d Cir. 1957); *Kappus v. Western Hills Oil, Inc.*, 24 F.R.D. 123 (E.D.Wis.1959); *Star v. Rogalny*, 162 F.Supp. 181 (E.D.Ill.1957). It has also been held that the clause of paragraph (7) which permits service "in the manner prescribed by the law of the state," etc., is not limited by subdivision (c) requiring that service of all process be made by certain designated persons. See *Farr & Co. v. Cia. Intercontinental de Nav. de Cuba, supra.* But *cf. Sappia v. Lauro Lines*, 130 F.Supp. 810 (S.D.N.Y.1955).

The salutary results of these cases are intended to be preserved. See paragraph (7), with a clarified reference to State law, and amended subdivisions (e) and (f).

Subdivision (e). For the general relation between subdivisions (d) and (e), see 2 Moore, supra, ¶4.32.

The amendment of the first sentence inserting the word "thereunder" supports the original intention that the "order of court" must be authorized by a specific United States statute. See 1 Barron & Holtzoff, supra, at 731. The clause added at the end of the first sentence expressly adopts the view taken by commentators that, if no manner of service is prescribed in the statute or order, the service may be made in a manner stated in Rule 4. See 2 Moore, supra, ¶4.32, at 1004; Smit, *International Aspects of Federal Civil Procedure*, 61 Colum.L.Rev. 1031, 1036–39 (1961). But see Commentary, 5 Fed. Rules Serv. 791 (1942).

Examples of the statutes to which the first sentence relates are 28 U.S.C. § 2361 (Interpleader; process and procedure); 28 U.S.C. § 1655 (Lien enforcement; absent defendants).

The second sentence, added by amendment, expressly allows resort in original Federal actions to the procedures provided by State law for effecting service on nonresident parties (as well as on domiciliaries not found within the State). See, as illustrative, the discussion under amended subdivision (d)(7) of service pursuant to State nonresident motorist statutes and other comparable State statutes. Of particular interest is the change brought about by the reference in this sentence to State procedures for commencing actions against nonresidents by attachment and the like, accompanied by notice. Although an action commenced in a State court by attachment may be removed to the Federal court if ordinary conditions for removal are satisfied, see 28 U.S.C. § 1450; *Rorick v. Devon Syndicate, Ltd.*, 307 U.S. 299, 59 S.Ct. 877, 83 L.Ed. 1303 (1939); *Clark v. Wells*, 203 U.S. 164, 27 S.Ct. 43, 51 L.Ed. 138 (1906), there has heretofore been no provision recognized by the courts for commencing an original Federal civil action by attachment. See Currie, *Attachment and Garnishment in the Federal Courts*, 59 Mich.L.Rev. 337 (1961), arguing that this result came about through historical anomaly. Rule 64, which refers to attachment, garnishment, and similar procedures under State law, furnishes only provisional remedies in actions otherwise validly commenced. See *Big Vein Coal Co. v. Read*, 229 U.S. 31, 33 S.Ct. 694, 57 L.Ed. 1053 (1913); *Davis v. Ensign–Bickford Co.*, 139 F.2d 624 (8th Cir. 1944); 7 Moore's *Federal Practice* ¶64.05 (2d ed. 1954); 3 Barron & Holtzoff, *Federal Practice & Procedure* § 1423 (Wright ed. 1958); but cf. Note, 13 So.Calif.L.Rev. 361 (1940). The amendment will now permit the institution of original Federal actions against nonresidents through the use of familiar State procedures by which property of these defendants is brought within the custody of the court and some appropriate service is made upon them.

The necessity of satisfying subject-matter jurisdictional requirements and requirements of venue will limit the practical utilization of these methods of effecting service. Within those limits, however, there appears to be no reason for denying plaintiffs means of commencing actions in Federal courts which are generally available in the State courts. See 1 Barron & Holtzoff, supra, at 374–80; Nordbye, *Comments on Proposed Amendments to Rules of Civil Procedure for the United States District Courts*, 18 F.R.D. 105, 106 (1956); Note, 34 Corn.L.Q. 103 (1948); Note, 13 So.Calif.L.Rev. 361 (1940).

If the circumstances of a particular case satisfy the applicable Federal law (first sentence of Rule 4(e), as amended)

Complete Annotation Materials, see Title 28 U.S.C.A.

and the applicable State law (second sentence), the party seeking to make the service may proceed under the Federal or the State law, at his option.

See also amended Rule 13(a), and the Advisory Committee's Note thereto.

Subdivision (f). The first sentence is amended to assure the effectiveness of service outside the territorial limits of the State in all the cases in which any of the rules authorize service beyond those boundaries. Besides the preceding provisions of Rule 4, see Rule 71A(d)(3). In addition, the new second sentence of the subdivision permits effective service within a limited area outside the State in certain special situations, namely, to bring in additional parties to a counterclaim or cross-claim (Rule 13 (h)), impleaded parties (Rule 14), and indispensable or conditionally necessary parties to a pending action (Rule 19); and to secure compliance with an order of commitment for civil contempt. In those situations effective service can be made at points not more than 100 miles distant from the courthouse in which the action is commenced, or to which it is assigned or transferred for trial.

The bringing in of parties under the 100-mile provision in the limited situations enumerated is designed to promote the objective of enabling the court to determine entire controversies. In the light of present-day facilities for communication and travel, the territorial range of the service allowed, analogous to that which applies to the service of a subpoena under Rule 45(e)(1), can hardly work hardship on the parties summoned. The provision will be especially useful in metropolitan areas spanning more than one State. Any requirements of subject-matter jurisdiction and venue will still have to be satisfied as to the parties brought in, although these requirements will be eased in some instances when the parties can be regarded as "ancillary." See *Pennsylvania R.R. v. Erie Avenue Warehouse Co.*, 5 F.R.Serv.2d 14a.62, Case 2 (3d Cir.1962); *Dery v. Wyer*, 265 F.2d 804 (2d Cir.1959); *United Artists Corp. v. Masterpiece Productions, Inc.*, 221 F.2d 213 (2d Cir.1955); *Lesnik v. Public Industrials Corp.*, 144 F.2d 968 (2d Cir.1944); *Vaughn v. Terminal Transp. Co.*, 162 F.Supp. 647 (E.D.Tenn.1957); and compare the fifth paragraph of the Advisory Committee's Note to Rule 4(e), as amended. The amendment is but a moderate extension of the territorial reach of Federal process and has ample practical justification. See 2 Moore, supra, § 4.01[13] (Supp. 1960); 1 Barron & Holtzoff, supra, § 184; Note, 51 Nw. U.L.Rev. 354 (1956). But cf. Nordbye, *Comments on Proposed Amendments to Rules of Civil Procedure for the United States District Courts*, 18 F.R.D. 105, 106 (1956).

As to the need for enlarging the territorial area in which orders of commitment for civil contempt may be served, see *Graber v. Graber*, 93 F.Supp. 281 (D.D.C.1950); *Teele Soap Mfg. Co. v. Pine Tree Products Co., Inc.*, 8 F.Supp. 546 (D.N.H.1934); *Mitchell v. Dexter*, 244 Fed. 926 (1st Cir. 1917); *In re Graves*, 29 Fed. 60 (N.D.Iowa 1886).

As to the Court's power to amend subdivisions (e) and (f) as here set forth, see *Mississippi Pub. Corp. v. Murphree*, 326 U.S. 438, 66 S.Ct. 242, 90 L.Ed. 185 (1946).

Subdivision (i). The continual increase of civil litigation having international elements makes it advisable to consolidate, amplify, and clarify the provisions governing service upon parties in foreign countries. See generally Jones, *International Judicial Assistance: Procedural Chaos and a Program for Reform*, 62 Yale L.J. 515 (1953); Longley,

Serving Process, Subpoenas and Other Documents in Foreign Territory, Proc.A.B.A., Sec.Int'l & Comp.L. 34 (1959); Smit, *International Aspects of Federal Civil Procedure*, 61 Colum.L.Rev. 1031 (1961).

As indicated in the opening lines of new subdivision (i), referring to the provisions of subdivision (e), the authority for effecting foreign service must be found in a statute of the United States or a statute or rule of court of the State in which the district court is held providing in terms or upon proper interpretation for service abroad upon persons not inhabitants of or found within the State. See the Advisory Committee's Note to amended Rule 4(d)(7) and Rule 4(e). For examples of Federal and State statutes expressly authorizing such service, see 8 U.S.C. § 1451(b); 35 U.S.C. §§ 146, 293; Me.Rev.Stat., ch. 22, § 70 (Supp.1961); Minn.Stat.Ann. § 303.13 (1947); N.Y.Veh. & Tfc.Law § 253. Several decisions have construed statutes to permit service in foreign countries, although the matter is not expressly mentioned in the statutes. See, e.g., *Chapman v. Superior Court*, 162 Cal.App.2d 421, 328 P.2d 23 (Dist.Ct.App.1958); *Sperry v. Fliegers*, 194 Misc. 438, 86 N.Y.S.2d 830 (Sup.Ct.1949); *Ewing v. Thompson*, 233 N.C. 564, 65 S.E.2d 17 (1951); *Rushing v. Bush*, 260 S.W.2d 900 (Tex.Ct.Civ.App.1953). Federal and State statutes authorizing service on nonresidents in such terms as to warrant the interpretation that service abroad is permissible include 15 U.S.C. §§ 77v(a), 78aa, 79y; 28 U.S.C. § 1655; 38 U.S.C. § 784(a); Ill.Ann.Stat., c. 110, §§ 16, 17 (Smith–Hurd 1956); Wis.Stat. § 262.06 (1959).

Under subdivisions (e) and (i), when authority to make foreign service is found in a Federal statute or statute or rule of court of a State, it is always sufficient to carry out the service in the manner indicated therein. Subdivision (i) introduces considerable further flexibility by permitting the foreign service and return thereof to be carried out in any of a number of other alternative ways that are also declared to be sufficient. Other aspects of foreign service continue to be governed by the other provisions of Rule 4. Thus, for example, subdivision (i) effects no change in the form of the summons, or the issuance of separate or additional summons, or the amendment of service.

Service of process beyond the territorial limits of the United States may involve difficulties not encountered in the case of domestic service. Service abroad may be considered by a foreign country to require the performance of judicial, and therefore, "sovereign," acts within its territory, which that country may conceive to be offensive to its policy or contrary to its law. See Jones, supra, at 537. For example, a person not qualified to serve process according to the law of the foreign country may find himself subject to sanctions if he attempts service therein. See Inter-American Juridical Committee, *Report on Uniformity of Legislation on International Cooperation in Judicial Procedures* 20 (1952). The enforcement of a judgment in the foreign country in which the service was made may be embarrassed or prevented if the service did not comport with the law of that country. See ibid.

One of the purposes of subdivision (i) is to allow accommodation to the policies and procedures of the foreign country. It is emphasized, however, that the attitudes of foreign countries vary considerably and that the question of recognition of United States judgments abroad is complex. Accordingly, if enforcement is to be sought in the country of service,

the foreign law should be examined before a choice is made among the methods of service allowed by subdivision (i).

Subdivision (i)(1). Subparagraph (a) of paragraph (1), permitting service by the method prescribed by the law of the foreign country for service on a person in that country in a civil action in any of its courts of general jurisdiction, provides an alternative that is likely to create least objection in the place of service and also is likely to enhance the possibilities of securing ultimate enforcement of the judgment abroad. See *Report on Uniformity of Legislation on International Cooperation in Judicial Procedures,* supra.

In certain foreign countries service in aid of litigation pending in other countries can lawfully be accomplished only upon request to the foreign courts, which in turn directs the service to be made. In many countries this has long been a customary way of accomplishing the service. See *In re Letters Rogatory out of First Civil Court of City of Mexico,* 261 Fed. 652 (S.D.N.Y.1919); Jones, supra, at 543; Comment, 44 Colum.L.Rev. 72 (1944); Note 58 Yale L.J. 1193 (1949). Subparagraph (B) of paragraph (1), referring to a letter rogatory, validates this method. A proviso, applicable to this subparagraph and the preceding one, requires, as a safeguard, that the service made shall be reasonably calculated to give actual notice of the proceedings to the party. See *Milliken v. Meyer,* 311 U.S. 457, 61 S.Ct. 339, 85 L.Ed. 278 (1940).

Subparagraph (C) of paragraph (1), permitting foreign service by personal delivery on individuals and corporations, partnerships, and associations, provides for a manner of service that is not only traditionally preferred, but also is most likely to lead to actual notice. Explicit provision for this manner of service was thought desirable because a number of Federal and State statutes permitting foreign service do not specifically provide for service by personal delivery abroad, see e.g., 35 U.S.C. §§ 146, 293; 46 U.S.C. § 1292; Calif.Ins.Code § 1612; N.Y.Veh. & Tfc. Law § 253, and it also may be unavailable under the law of the country in which the service is made.

Subparagraph (D) of paragraph (1), permitting service by certain types of mail, affords a manner of service that is inexpensive and expeditious, and requires a minimum of activity within the foreign country. Several statutes specifically provide for service in a foreign country by mail, e.g., Hawaii Rev.Laws §§ 230–31, 230–32 (1955); Minn.Stat.Ann. § 303.13 (1947); N.Y.Civ.Prac.Act, § 229–b; N.Y.Veh. & Tfc. Law § 253, and it has been sanctioned by the courts even in the absence of statutory provision specifying that form of service. *Zurini v. United States,* 189 F.2d 722 (8th Cir. 1951); *United States v. Cardillo,* 135 F.Supp. 798 (W.D.Pa. 1955); *Autogiro Co. v. Kay Gyroplanes, Ltd.,* 55 F.Supp. 919 (D.D.C.1944). Since the reliability of postal service may vary from country to country, service by mail is proper only when it is addressed to the party to be served and a form of mail requiring a signed receipt is used. An additional safeguard is provided by the requirement that the mailing be attended to by the clerk of the court. See also the provisions of paragraph (2) of this subdivision (i) regarding proof of service by mail.

Under the applicable law it may be necessary, when the defendant is an infant or incompetent person, to deliver the summons and complaint to a guardian, committee, or similar fiduciary. In such a case it would be advisable to make service under subparagraph (A), (B), or (E).

Subparagraph (E) of paragraph (1) adds flexibility by permitting the court by order to tailor the manner of service to fit the necessities of a particular case or the peculiar requirements of the law of the country in which the service is to be made. A similar provision appears in a number of statutes, e.g., 35 U.S.C. §§ 146, 293; 38 U.S.C. § 784(a); 46 U.S.C. § 1292.

The next-to-last sentence of paragraph (1) permits service under (C) and (E) to be made by any person who is not a party and is not less than 18 years of age or who is designated by court order or by the foreign court. Cf. Rule 45(c); N.Y.Civ.Prac.Act §§ 233, 235. This alternative increases the possibility that the plaintiff will be able to find a process server who can proceed unimpeded in the foreign country; it also may improve the changes of enforcing the judgment in the country of service. Especially is this alternative valuable when authority for the foreign service is found in a statute or rule of court that limits the group of eligible process servers to designated officials or special appointees who, because directly connected with another "sovereign," may be particularly offensive to the foreign country. See generally Smit, supra, at 1040–41. When recourse is had to subparagraph (A) or (B) the identity of the process server always will be determined by the law of the foreign country in which the service is made.

The last sentence of paragraph (1) sets forth an alternative manner for the issuance and transmission of the summons for service. After obtaining the summons from the clerk, the plaintiff must ascertain the best manner of delivering the summons and complaint to the person, court, or officer who will make the service. Thus the clerk is not burdened with the task of determining who is permitted to serve process under the law of a particular country or the appropriate governmental or nongovernmental channel for forwarding a letter rogatory. Under (D), however, the papers must always be posted by the clerk.

Subdivision (i)(2). When service is made in a foreign country, paragraph (2) permits methods for proof of service in addition to those prescribed by subdivision (g). Proof of service in accordance with the law of the foreign country is permitted because foreign process servers, unaccustomed to the form or the requirement of return of service prevalent in the United States, have on occasion been unwilling to execute the affidavit required by Rule 4(g). See Jones, supra, at 537; Longley, supra, at 35. As a corollary of the alternate manner of service in subdivision (i)(1)(E), proof of service as directed by order of the court is permitted. The special provision for proof of service by mail is intended as an additional safeguard when that method is used. On the type of evidence of delivery that may be satisfactory to a court in lieu of a signed receipt, see *Aero Associates, Inc. v. La Metropolitana,* 183 F.Supp. 357 (S.D.N.Y.1960).

1966 Amendment

The wording of Rule 4(f) is changed to accord with the amendment of Rule 13(h) referring to Rule 19 as amended.

1980 Amendment

Subdivision (a). This is a technical amendment to conform this subdivision with the amendment of subdivision (c).

Subdivision (c). The purpose of this amendment is to authorize service of process to be made by any person who is authorized to make service in actions in the courts of general jurisdiction of the state in which the district court is held or in which service is made.

There is a troublesome ambiguity in Rule 4. Rule 4(c) directs that all process is to be served by the marshal, by his deputy, or by a person specially appointed by the court. But Rule 4(d)(7) authorizes service in certain cases "in the manner prescribed by the law of the state in which the district court is held. . . ." And Rule 4(e), which authorizes service beyond the state and service in quasi in rem cases when state law permits such service, directs that "service may be made . . . under the circumstances and in the manner prescribed in the [state] statute or rule." State statutes and rules of the kind referred to in Rule 4(d)(7) and Rule 4(e) commonly designate the persons who are to make the service provided for, e.g., a sheriff or a plaintiff. When that is so, may the persons so designated by state law make service, or is service in all cases to be made by a marshal or by one specially appointed under present Rule 4(c)? The commentators have noted the ambiguity and have suggested the desirability of an amendment. See 2 Moore's *Federal Practice* ¶4.08 (1974); Wright & Miller, *Federal Practice and Procedure:* Civil § 1092 (1969). And the ambiguity has given rise to unfortunate results. See *United States for the use of Tanos v. St. Paul Mercury Ins. Co.,* 361 F.2d 838 (5th Cir. 1966); *Veeck v. Commodity Enterprises, Inc.,* 487 F.2d 423 (9th Cir.1973).

The ambiguity can be resolved by specific amendments to Rules 4(d)(7) and 4(e), but the Committee is of the view that there is no reason why Rule 4(c) should not generally authorize service of process in all cases by anyone authorized to make service in the courts of general jurisdiction of the state in which the district court is held or in which service is made. The marshal continues to be the obvious, always effective officer for service of process.

1987 Amendment

The amendments are technical. No substantive change is intended.

1993 Amendments

SPECIAL NOTE: Mindful of the constraints of the Rules Enabling Act, the Committee calls the attention of the Supreme Court and Congress to new subdivision (k)(2). Should this limited extension of service be disapproved, the Committee nevertheless recommends adoption of the balance of the rule, with subdivision (k)(1) becoming simply subdivision (k). The Committee Notes would be revised to eliminate references to subdivision (k)(2).

Purposes of Revision. The general purpose of this revision is to facilitate the service of the summons and complaint. The revised rule explicitly authorizes a means for service of the summons and complaint on any defendant. While the methods of service so authorized always provide appropriate notice to persons against whom claims are made, effective service under this rule does not assure that personal jurisdiction has been established over the defendant served.

First, the revised rule authorizes the use of any means of service provided by the law not only of the forum state, but also of the state in which a defendant is served, unless the defendant is a minor or incompetent.

Second, the revised rule clarifies and enhances the cost-saving practice of securing the assent of the defendant to dispense with actual service of the summons and complaint. This practice was introduced to the rule in 1983 by an act of Congress authorizing "service-by-mail," a procedure that effects economic service with cooperation of the defendant. Defendants that magnify costs of service by requiring expensive service not necessary to achieve full notice of an action brought against them are required to bear the wasteful costs. This provision is made available in actions against defendants who cannot be served in the districts in which the actions are brought.

Third, the revision reduces the hazard of commencing an action against the United States or its officers, agencies, and corporations. A party failing to effect service on all the offices of the United States as required by the rule is assured adequate time to cure defects in service.

Fourth, the revision calls attention to the important effect of the Hague Convention and other treaties bearing on service of documents in foreign countries and favors the use of internationally agreed means of service. In some respects, these treaties have facilitated service in foreign countries but are not fully known to the bar.

Finally, the revised rule extends the reach of federal courts to impose jurisdiction over the person of all defendant against whom federal law claims are made and who can be constitutionally subjected to the jurisdiction of the courts of the United States. The present territorial limits on the effectiveness of service to subject a defendant to the jurisdiction of the court over the defendant's person are retained for all actions in which there is a state in which personal jurisdiction can be asserted consistently with state law and the Fourteenth Amendment. A new provision enables district courts to exercise jurisdiction, if permissible under the Constitution and not precluded by statute, when a federal claim is made against a defendant not subject to the jurisdiction of any single state.

The revised rule is reorganized to make its provisions more accessible to those not familiar with all of them. Additional subdivisions in this rule allow for more captions; several overlaps among subdivisions are eliminated; and several disconnected provisions are removed, to be relocated in a new Rule 4.1.

The Caption of the Rule. Prior to this revision, Rule 4 was entitled "Process" and applied to the service of not only the summons but also other process as well, although these are not covered by the revised rule. Service of process in eminent domain proceedings is governed by Rule 71A. Service of a subpoena is governed by Rule 45, and service of papers such as orders, motions, notices, pleadings, and other documents is governed by Rule 5.

The revised rule is entitled "Summons" and applies only to that form of legal process. Unless service of the summons is waived, a summons must be served whenever a person is joined as a party against whom a claim is made. Those few provisions of the former rule which relate specifically to service of process other than a summons are relocated in Rule 4.1 in order to simplify the text of this rule.

Subdivision (a). Revised subdivision (a) contains most of the language of the former subdivision (b). The second

sentence of the former subdivision (b) has been stricken, so that the federal court summons will be the same in all cases. Few states now employ, distinctive requirements of form for a summons and the applicability of such a requirement in federal court can only serve as a trap for an unwary party or attorney. A sentence is added to this subdivision authorizing an amendment of a summons. This sentence replaces the rarely used former subdivision 4(h). See 4A Wright & Miller, Federal Practice and Procedure § 1131 (2d ed. 1987).

Subdivision (b). Revised subdivision (b) replaces the former subdivision (a). The revised text makes clear that the responsibility for filling in the summons falls on the plaintiff, not the clerk of the court. If there are multiple defendants, the plaintiff may secure issuance of a summons for each defendant, or may serve copies of a single original bearing the names of multiple defendants if the addressee of the summons is effectively identified.

Subdivision (c). Paragraph (1) of revised subdivision (c) retains language from the former subdivision (d)(1). Paragraph (2) retains language from the former subdivision (a), and adds an appropriate caution regarding the time limit for service set forth in subdivision (m).

The 1983 revision of Rule 4 relieved the marshals' offices of much of the burden of serving the summons. Subdivision (c) eliminates the requirement for service by the marshal's office in actions in which the party seeking service is the United States. The United States, like other civil litigants, is now permitted to designate any person who is 18 years of age and not a party to serve its summons.

The court remains obligated to appoint a marshal, a deputy, or some other person to effect service of a summons in two classes of cases specified by statute: actions brought in forma pauperis or by a seaman. 28 U.S.C. §§ 1915, 1916. The court also retains discretion to appoint a process server on motion of a party. If a law enforcement presence appears to be necessary or advisable to keep the peace, the court should appoint a marshal or deputy or other official person to make the service. The Department of Justice may also call upon the Marshals Service to perform services in actions brought by the United States. 28 U.S.C. § 651.

Subdivision (d). This text is new, but is substantially derived from the former subdivisions (c)(2)(C) and (D), added to the rule by Congress in 1983. The aims of the provision are to eliminate the costs of service of a summons on many parties and to foster cooperation among adversaries and counsel. The rule operates to impose upon the defendant those costs that could have been avoided if the defendant had cooperated reasonably in the manner prescribed. This device is useful in dealing with defendants who are furtive, who reside in places not easily reached by process servers, or who are outside the United States and can be served only at substantial and unnecessary expense. Illustratively, there is no useful purpose achieved by requiring a plaintiff to comply with all the formalities of service in a foreign country, including costs of translation, when suing a defendant manufacturer, fluent in English, whose products are widely distributed in the United States. See Bankston v. Toyota Motor Corp., 889 F.2d 172 (8th Cir.1989).

The former text described this process as service-by-mail. This language misled some plaintiffs into thinking that service could be effected by mail without the affirmative cooperation of the defendant. E.g., Gulley v. Mayo Foundation, 886 F.2d 161 (8th Cir.1989). It is more accurate to describe the communication sent to the defendant as a request for a waiver of formal service.

The request for waiver of service may be sent only to defendants subject to service under subdivision (e), (f), or (h). The United States is not expected to waive service for the reason that its mail receiving facilities are inadequate to assure that the notice is actually received by the correct person in the Department of Justice. The same principle is applied to agencies, corporations, and officers of the United States and to other governments and entities subject to service under subdivision (j). Moreover, there are policy reasons why governmental entities should not be confronted with the potential for bearing costs of service in cases in which they ultimately prevail. Infants or incompetent persons likewise are not called upon to waive service because, due to their presumed inability to understand the request and its consequences, they must generally be served through fiduciaries.

It was unclear whether the former rule authorized, mailing of a request for "acknowledgement of service" to defendants outside the forum state. See 1 R. Casad, Jurisdiction in Civil Actions (2d Ed.) 5–29, 30 (1991) and cases cited. But, as Professor Casad observed, there was no reason not to employ this device in an effort to obtain service outside the state, and there are many instances in which it was in fact so used, with respect both to defendants within the United States and to defendants in other countries.

The opportunity for waiver has distinct advantages to a foreign defendant. By waiving service, the defendant can reduce the costs that may ultimately be taxed against it if unsuccessful in the lawsuit, including the sometimes substantial expense of translation that may be wholly unnecessary for defendants fluent in English. Moreover, a foreign defendant that waives service is afforded substantially more time to defend against the action than if it had been formally served: under Rule 12, a defendant ordinarily has only 20 days after service in which to file its answer or raise objections by motion, but by signing a waiver it is allowed 90 days after the date the request for waiver was mailed in which to submit its defenses. Because of the additional time needed for mailing and the unreliability of some foreign mail services, a period of 60 days (rather than the 30 days required for domestic transmissions) is provided for a return of a waiver sent to a foreign country.

It is hoped that, since transmission of the notice and waiver forms is a private nonjudicial act, does not purport to effect service, and is not accompanied by any summons or directive from a court, use of the procedure will not offend foreign sovereignties, even those that have withheld their assent to formal service by mail or have objected to the "service-by-mail" provisions of the former rule. Unless the addressee consents, receipt of the request under the revised rule does not give rise to any obligation to answer the lawsuit, does not provide a basis for default judgment, and does not suspend the statute of limitations in those states where the period continues to run until service. Nor are there any adverse consequences to a foreign defendant, since the provisions for shifting the expense of service to a defendant that declines to waive service apply only if the plaintiff and defendant are both located in the United States.

With respect to a defendant located in a foreign country like the United Kingdom, which accepts documents in En-

glish, whose Central Authority acts promptly in effecting service, and whose policies discourage its residents from waiving formal service, there will be little reason for a plaintiff to send the notice and request under subdivision (d) rather than use convention methods. On the other hand, the procedure offers significant potential benefits to a plaintiff when suing a defendant that, though fluent in English, is located in a country where, as a condition to formal service under a convention, documents must be translated into another language or where formal service will be otherwise costly or time-consuming.

Paragraph (1) is explicit that a timely waiver of service of a summons does not prejudice the right of a defendant to object by means of a motion authorized by Rule 12(b)(2) to the absence of jurisdiction over the defendant's person, or to assert other defenses that may be available. The only issues eliminated are those involving the sufficiency of the summons or the sufficiency of the method by which it is served.

Paragraph (2) states what the present rule implies: the defendant has a duty to avoid costs associated with the service of a summons not needed to inform the defendant regarding the commencement of an action. The text of the rule also sets forth the requirements for a Notice and Request for Waiver sufficient to put the cost-shifting provision in place. These requirements are illustrated in Forms 1A and 1B, which replace the former Form 18–A.

Paragraph (2)(A) is explicit that a request for waiver of service by a corporate defendant must be addressed to a person qualified to receive service. The general mail rooms of large organizations cannot be required to identify the appropriate individual recipient for an institutional summons.

Paragraph (2)(B) permits the use of alternatives to the United States mails in sending the Notice and Request. While private messenger services or electronic communications may be more expensive than the mail, they may be equally reliable and on occasion more convenient to the parties. Especially with respect to transmissions to foreign countries, alternative means may be desirable, for in some countries facsimile transmission is the most efficient and economical means of communication. If electronic means such as facsimile transmission are employed, the sender should maintain a record of the transmission to assure proof of transmission if receipt is denied, but a party receiving such a transmission has a duty to cooperate and cannot avoid liability for the resulting cost of formal service if the transmission is prevented at the point of receipt.

A defendant failing to comply with a request for waiver shall be given an opportunity to show good cause for the failure, but sufficient cause should be rare. It is not a good cause for failure to waive service that the claim is unjust or that the court lacks jurisdiction. Sufficient cause not to shift the cost of service would exist, however, if the defendant did not receive the request or was insufficiently literate in English to understand it. It should be noted that the provisions for shifting the cost of service apply only if the plaintiff and the defendant are both located in the United States, and accordingly a foreign defendant need not show "good cause" for its failure to waive service.

Paragraph (3) extends the time for answer if, before being served with process, the defendant waives formal service. The extension is intended to serve as an inducement to waive service and to assure that a defendant will not gain any delay be declining to waive service and thereby causing the addi-

tional time needed to effect service. By waiving service, a defendant is not called upon to respond to the complaint until 60 days from the date the notice was sent to it—90 days if the notice was sent to a foreign country—rather than within the 20 day period from date of service specified in Rule 12.

Paragraph (4) clarifies the effective date of service when service is waived; the provision is needed to resolve an issue arising when applicable law requires service of process to toll the statute of limitations. E.g., Morse v. Elmira Country Club, 752 F.2d 35 (2d Cir.1984). Cf. Walker v. Armco Steel Corp., 446 U.S. 740 (1980).

The provisions in former subdivision (c)(2)(C)(ii) of this rule may have been misleading to some parties. Some plaintiffs, not reading the rule carefully, supposed that receipt by the defendant of the mailed complaint had the effect both of establishing the jurisdiction of the court over the defendant's person and of tolling the statute of limitations in actions in which service of the summons is required to toll the limitations period. The revised rule is clear that, if the waiver is not returned and filed, the limitations period under such a law is not tolled and the action will not otherwise proceed until formal service of process is effected.

Some state limitations laws may toll an otherwise applicable statute at the time when the defendant receives notice of the action. Nevertheless, the device of requested waiver of service is not suitable if a limitations period which is about to expire is not tolled by filing the action. Unless there is ample time, the plaintiff should proceed directly to the formal methods for service identified in subdivisions (e), (f), or (h).

The procedure of requesting waiver of service should also not be used if the time for service under subdivision (m) will expire before the date on which the waiver must be returned. While a plaintiff has been allowed additional time for service in that situation, e.g., Prather v. Raymond Constr. Co., 570 F.Supp. 278 (N.D.Ga.1983), the court could refuse a request for additional time unless the defendant appears to have evaded service pursuant to subdivision (e) or (h). It may be noted that the presumptive time limit for service under subdivision (m) does not apply to service in a foreign country.

Paragraph (5) is a cost-shifting provision retained from the former rule. The costs that may be imposed on the defendant could include, for example, the cost of the time of a process server required to make contact with a defendant residing in a guarded apartment house or residential development. The paragraph is explicit that the costs of enforcing the cost-shifting provision are themselves recoverable from a defendant who fails to return the waiver. In the absence of such a provision, the purpose of the rule would be frustrated by the cost of its enforcement, which is likely to be high in relation to the small benefit secured by the plaintiff.

Some plaintiffs may send a notice and request for waiver and, without waiting for return of the waiver, also proceed with efforts to effect formal service on the defendant. To discourage this practice, the cost-shifting provisions in paragraphs (2) and (5) are limited to costs of effecting service incurred after the time expires for the defendant to return the waiver. Moreover, by returning the waiver within the time allowed and before being served with process, a defendant receives the benefit of the longer period for responding to the complaint afforded for waivers under paragraph (3).

Subdivision (e). This subdivision replaces former subdivisions (c)(2)(C)(i) and (d)(1). It provides a means for service of summons on individuals within a judicial district of the United States. Together with subdivision (f), it provides for service on persons anywhere, subject to constitutional and statutory constraints.

Service of the summons under this subdivision does not conclusively establish the jurisdiction of the court over the person of the defendant. A defendant may assert the territorial limits of the court's reach set forth in subdivision (k), including the constitutional limitations that may be imposed by the Due Process Clause of the Fifth Amendment.

Paragraph (1) authorizes service in any judicial district in conformity with state law. This paragraph sets forth the language of former subdivision (c)(2)(C)(i), which authorized the use of the law of the state in which the district court sits, but adds as an alternative the use of the law of the state in which the service is effected.

Paragraph (2) retains the text of the former subdivision (d)(1) and authorizes the use of the familiar methods of personal or abode service or service on an authorized agent in any judicial district.

To conform to these provisions, the former subdivision (e) bearing on proceedings against parties not found within the state is stricken. Likewise stricken is the first sentence of the former subdivision (f), which had restricted the authority of the federal process server to the state in which the district court sits.

Subdivision (f). This subdivision provides for service on individuals who are in a foreign country, replacing the former subdivision (i) that was added to Rule 4 in 1963. Reflecting the pattern of Rule 4 in incorporating state law limitations on the exercise of jurisdiction over persons, the former subdivision (i) limited service outside the United States to cases in which extraterritorial service was authorized by state or federal law. The new rule eliminates the requirement of explicit authorization. On occasion, service in a foreign country was held to be improper for lack of statutory authority. E.g., Martens v. Winder, 341 F.2d 197 (9th Cir.), cert. denied, 382 U.S. 937 (1965). This authority, however, was found to exist by implication. E.g., SEC v. VTR, Inc., 39 F.R.D. 19 (S.D.N.Y.1966). Given the substantial increase in the number of international transactions and events that are the subject of litigation in federal courts, it is appropriate to infer a general legislative authority to effect service on defendants in a foreign country.

A secondary effect of this provision for foreign service of a federal summons is to facilitate the use of federal long-arm law in actions brought to enforce the federal law against defendants who cannot be served under any state law but who can be constitutionally subjected to the jurisdiction of the federal court. Such a provision is set forth in paragraph (2) of subdivision (k) of this rule, applicable only to persons not subject to the territorial jurisdiction of any particular state.

Paragraph (1) gives effect to the Hague Convention on the Service Abroad of Judicial and Extrajudicial Documents, which entered into force for the United States on February 10, 1969. See 28 U.S.C.A., Fed.R.Civ.P. 4 (Supp.1986). This Convention is an important means of dealing with problems of service in a foreign country. See generally 1 B. Ristau, International Judicial Assistance §§ 4–1–1 to 4–5–2 (1990).

Use of the Convention procedures, when available, is mandatory if documents must be transmitted abroad to effect service. See Volkswagenwerk Aktiengesellschaft v. Schlunk, 486 U.S. 694 (1988) (noting that voluntary use of these procedures may be desirable even when service could constitutionally be effected in another manner); J. Weis, The Federal Rules and the Hague Conventions: Concerns of Conformity and Comity, 50 U.Pitt.L.Rev. 903 (1989). Therefore, this paragraph provides that, when service is to be effected outside a judicial district of the United States, the methods of service appropriate under an applicable treaty shall be employed if available and if the treaty so requires.

The Hague Convention furnishes safeguards against the abridgment of rights of parties through inadequate notice. Article 15 provides for verification of actual notice or a demonstration that process was served by a method prescribed by the internal laws of the foreign state before a default judgment may be entered. Article 16 of the Convention also enables the judge to extend the time for appeal after judgment if the defendant shows a lack of adequate notice either to defend or to appeal the judgment, or has disclosed a prima facie case on the merits.

The Hague Convention does not specify a time within which a foreign country's Central Authority must effect service, but Article 15 does provide that alternate methods may be used if a Central Authority does not respond within six months. Generally, a Central Authority can be expected to respond much more quickly than that limit might permit, but there have been occasions when the signatory state was dilatory or refused to cooperate for substantive reasons. In such cases, resort may be had to the provision set forth in subdivision (f)(3).

Two minor changes in the text reflect the Hague Convention. First, the term "letter of request" has been added. Although these words are synonymous with "letter rogatory," "letter of request" is preferred in modern usage. The provision should not be interpreted to authorize use of a letter of request when there is in fact no treaty obligation on the receiving country to honor such a request from this country or when the United States does not extend diplomatic recognition to the foreign nation. Second, the passage formerly found in subdivision (i)(1)(B), "when service in either case is reasonably calculated to give actual notice," has been relocated.

Paragraph (2) provides alternative methods for use when internationally agreed methods are not intended to be exclusive, or where there is no international agreement applicable. It contains most of the language formerly set forth in subdivision (i) of the rule. Service by methods that would violate foreign law is not generally authorized. Subparagraphs (A) and (B) prescribe the more appropriate methods for conforming to local practice or using a local authority. Subparagraph (C) prescribes other methods authorized by the former rule.

Paragraph (3) authorizes the court to approve other methods of service not prohibited by international agreements. The Hague Convention, for example, authorizes special forms of service in cases of urgency if convention methods will not permit service within the time required by the circumstances. Other circumstances that might justify the use of additional methods include the failure of the foreign country's Central Authority to effect service within the six-month period provided by the Convention, or the refusal of the Central

Authority to serve a complaint seeking punitive damages or to enforce the antitrust laws of the United States. In such cases, the court may direct a special method of service not explicitly authorized by international agreement if not prohibited by the agreement. Inasmuch as our Constitution requires that reasonable notice be given, an earnest effort should be made to devise a method of communication that is consistent with due process and minimizes offense to foreign law. A court may in some instances specially authorize use of ordinary mail. Cf. Levin v. Ruby Trading Corp., 248 F.Supp. 537 (S.D.N.Y.1965).

Subdivision (g). This subdivision retains the text of former subdivision (d)(2). Provision is made for service upon an infant or incompetent person in a foreign country.

Subdivision (h). This subdivision retains the text of former subdivision (d)(3), with changes reflecting those made in subdivision (e). It also contains the provisions for service on a corporation or association in a foreign country, as formerly found in subdivision (i).

Frequent use should be made of the Notice and Request procedure set forth in subdivision (d) in actions against corporations. Care must be taken, however, to address the request to an individual officer or authorized agent of the corporation. It is not effective use of the Notice and Request procedure if the mail is sent undirected to the mail room of the organization.

Subdivision (i). This subdivision retains much of the text of former subdivisions (d)(4) and (d)(5). Paragraph (1) provides for service of a summons on the United States; it amends former subdivision (d)(4) to permit the United States attorney to be served by registered or certified mail. The rule does not authorize the use of the Notice and Request procedure of revised subdivision (d) when the United States is the defendant. To assure proper handling of mail in the United States attorney's office, the authorized mail service must be specifically addressed to the civil process clerk of the office of the United States attorney.

Paragraph (2) replaces former subdivision (d)(5). Paragraph (3) saves the plaintiff from the hazard of losing a substantive right because of failure to comply with the complex requirements of multiple service under this subdivision. That risk has proved to be more than nominal. E.g., Whale v. United States, 792 F.2d 951 (9th Cir.1986). This provision should be read in connection with the provisions of subdivision (c) of Rule 15 to preclude the loss of substantive rights against the United States or its agencies, corporations, or officers resulting from a plaintiff's failure to correctly identify and serve all the persons who should be named or served.

Subdivision (j). This subdivision retains the text of former subdivision (d)(6) without material change. The waiver-of-service provision is also inapplicable to actions against governments subject to service pursuant to this subdivision.

The revision adds a new paragraph (1) referring to the statute governing service of a summons on a foreign state and its political subdivisions, agencies, and instrumentalities, the Foreign Sovereign Immunities Act of 1976, 28 U.S.C. § 1608. The caption of the subdivision reflects that change.

Subdivision (k). This subdivision replaces the former subdivision (f), with no change in the title. Paragraph (1) retains the substance of the former rule in explicitly authorizing the exercise of personal jurisdiction over persons who can be reached under state long-arm law, the "100–mile bulge" provision added in 1963, or the federal interpleader act. Paragraph (1)(D) is new, but merely calls attention to federal legislation that may provide for nationwide or even world-wide service of process in cases arising under particular federal laws. Congress has provided for nationwide service of process and full exercise of territorial jurisdiction by all district courts with respect to specified federal actions. See 1 R. Casad, Jurisdiction in Civil Actions (2d Ed.) chap. 5 (1991).

Paragraph (2) is new. It authorizes the exercise of territorial jurisdiction over the person of any defendant against whom is made a claim arising under any federal law if that person is subject to personal jurisdiction in no state. This addition is a companion to the amendments made in revised subdivisions (e) and (f).

This paragraph corrects a gap in the enforcement of federal law. Under the former rule, a problem was presented when the defendant was a non-resident of the United States having contacts with the United States sufficient to justify the application of United States law and to satisfy federal standards of forum selection, but having insufficient contact with any single state to support jurisdiction under state long-arm legislation or meet the requirements of the Fourteenth Amendment limitation on state court territorial jurisdiction. In such cases, the defendant was shielded from the enforcement of federal law by the fortuity of a favorable limitation on the power of state courts, which was incorporated into the federal practice by the former rule. In this respect, the revision responds to the suggestion of the Supreme Court made in Omni Capital Int'l. v. Rudolf Wolff & Co., Ltd., 484 U.S. 97, 111 (1987).

There remain constitutional limitations on the exercise of territorial jurisdiction by federal courts over persons outside the United States. These restrictions arise from the Fifth Amendment rather than from the Fourteenth Amendment, which limits state-court reach and which was incorporated into federal practice by the reference to state law in the text of the former subdivision (e) that is deleted by this revision. The Fifth Amendment requires that any defendant have affiliating contacts with the United States sufficient to justify the exercise of personal jurisdiction over that party. Cf. Wells Fargo & Co. v. Wells Fargo Express Co., 556 F.2d 406, 418 (9th Cir.1977). There also may be a further Fifth Amendment constraint in that a plaintiff's forum selection might be so inconvenient to a defendant that it would be a denial of "fair play and substantial justice" required by the due process clause, even though the defendant had significant affiliating contacts with the United States. See De-James v. Magnificent Carriers, 654 F.2d 280, 286 n. 3 (3rd Cir.), cert. denied, 454 U.S. 1085 (1981). Compare World–Wide Volkswagen Corp. v. Woodson, 444 U.S. 286, 293–294 (1980); Insurance Corp. of Ireland v. Compagnie des Bauxites de Guinee, 456 U.S. 694, 702–03 (1982); Burger King Corp. v. Rudzewicz, 471 U.S. 462, 476–78 (1985); Asahi Metal Indus. v. Superior Court of Cal., Solano County, 480 U.S. 102, 108–13 (1987). See generally R. Lusardi, Nationwide Service of Process: Due Process Limitations on the Power of the Sovereign, 33 Vill.L.Rev. 1 (1988).

This provision does not affect the operation of federal venue legislation. See generally 28 U.S.C. § 1391. Nor does it affect the operation of federal law providing for the change of venue. 28 U.S.C. §§ 1404, 1406. The availability

of transfer for fairness and convenience under § 1404 should preclude most conflicts between the full exercise of territorial jurisdiction permitted by this rule and the Fifth Amendment requirement of "fair play and substantial justice."

The district court should be especially scrupulous to protect aliens who reside in a foreign country from forum selections so onerous that injustice could result. "[G]reat care and reserve should be exercised when extending our notions of personal jurisdiction into the international field." Asahi Metal Indus. v. Superior Court of Cal., Solano County, 480 U.S. 102, 115 (1987), quoting United States v. First Nat'l City Bank, 379 U.S. 378, 404 (1965) (Harlan, J., dissenting).

This narrow extension of the federal reach applies only if a claim is made against the defendant under federal law. It does not establish personal jurisdiction if the only claims are those arising under state law or the law of another country, even though there might be diversity or alienage subject matter jurisdiction as to such claims. If, however, personal jurisdiction is established under this paragraph with respect to a federal claim, then 28 U.S.C. § 1367(a) provides supplemental jurisdiction over related claims against that defendant, subject to the court's discretion to decline exercise of that jurisdiction under 28 U.S.C. § 1367(c).

Subdivision (l). This subdivision assembles in one place all the provisions of the present rule bearing on proof of service. No material change in the rule is effected. The provision that proof of service can be amended by leave of court is retained from the former subdivision (h). See generally 4A Wright & Miller, Federal Practice and Procedure § 1132 (2d ed. 1987).

Subdivision (m). This subdivision retains much of the language of the present subdivision (j).

The new subdivision explicitly provides that the court shall allow additional time if there is good cause for the plaintiff's failure to effect service in the prescribed 120 days, and authorizes the court to relieve a plaintiff of the consequences of an application of this subdivision even if there is no good cause shown. Such relief formerly was afforded in some cases, partly in reliance on Rule 6(b). Relief may be justified, for example, if the applicable statute of limitations would bar the refiled action, or if the defendant is evading service or conceals a defect in attempted service. E.g., Ditkof v. Owens–Illinois, Inc., 114 F.R.D. 104 (E.D.Mich. 1987). A specific instance of good cause is set forth in paragraph (3) of this rule, which provides for extensions if necessary to correct oversights in compliance with the requirements of multiple service in actions against the United States or its officers, agencies, and corporations. The district court should also take care to protect pro se plaintiffs from consequences of confusion or delay attending the resolution of an in forma pauperis petition. Robinson v. America's Best Contacts & Eyeglasses, 876 F.2d 596 (7th Cir. 1989).

The 1983 revision of this subdivision referred to the "party on whose behalf such service was required," rather than to the "plaintiff," a term used generically elsewhere in this rule to refer to any party initiating a claim against a person who is not a party to the action. To simplify the text, the revision returns to the usual practice in the rule of referring simply to the plaintiff even though its principles apply with equal force to defendants who may assert claims against nonparties under Rules 13(h), 14, 19, 20, or 21.

Subdivision (n). This subdivision provides for in rem and quasi-in-rem jurisdiction. Paragraph (1) incorporates any requirements of 28 U.S.C. § 1655 or similar provisions bearing on seizures or liens.

Paragraph (2) provides for other uses of quasi-in-rem jurisdiction but limits its use to exigent circumstances. Provisional remedies may be employed as a means to secure jurisdiction over the property of a defendant whose person is not within reach of the court, but occasions for the use of this provision should be rare, as where the defendant is a fugitive or assets are in imminent danger of disappearing. Until 1963, it was not possible under Rule 4 to assert jurisdiction in a federal court over the property of a defendant not personally served. The 1963 amendment to subdivision (e) authorized the use of state law procedures authorizing seizures of assets as a basis for jurisdiction. Given the liberal availability of long-arm jurisdiction, the exercise of power quasi-in-rem has become almost an anachronism. Circumstances too spare to affiliate the defendant to the forum state sufficiently to support long-arm jurisdiction over the defendant's person are also inadequate to support seizure of the defendant's assets fortuitously found within the state. Shaffer v. Heitner, 433 U.S. 186 (1977).

2000 Amendment

Paragraph (2)(B) is added to Rule 4(i) to require service on the United States when a United States officer or employee is sued in an individual capacity for acts or omissions occurring in connection with duties performed on behalf of the United States. Decided cases provide uncertain guidance on the question whether the United States must be served in such actions. See Vaccaro v. Dobre, 81 F.3d 854, 856–857 (9th Cir.1996); Armstrong v. Sears, 33 F.3d 182, 185–187 (2d Cir.1994); Ecclesiastical Order of the Ism of Am v. Chasin, 845 F.2d 113, 116 (6th Cir.1988); Light v. Wolf, 816 F.2d 746 (D.C.Cir.1987); see also Simpkins v. District of Columbia, 108 F.3d 366, 368–369 (D.C.Cir.1997). Service on the United States will help to protect the interest of the individual defendant in securing representation by the United States, and will expedite the process of determining whether the United States will provide representation. It has been understood that the individual defendant must be served as an individual defendant, a requirement that is made explicit. Invocation of the individual service provisions of subdivisions (e), (f), and (g) invokes also the waiver- of-service provisions of subdivision (d).

Paragraph 2(B) reaches service when an officer or employee of the United States is sued in an individual capacity "for acts or omissions occurring in connection with the performance of duties on behalf of the United States." This phrase has been chosen as a functional phrase that can be applied without the occasionally distracting associations of such phrases as "scope of employment," "color of office," or "arising out of the employment." Many actions are brought against individual federal officers or employees of the United States for acts or omissions that have no connection whatever to their governmental roles. There is no reason to require service on the United States in these actions. The connection to federal employment that requires service on the United States must be determined as a practical matter, considering whether the individual defendant has reasonable grounds to look to the United States for assistance and whether the

United States has reasonable grounds for demanding formal notice of the action.

An action against a former officer or employee of the United States is covered by paragraph (2)(B) in the same way as an action against a present officer or employee. Termination of the relationship between the individual defendant and the United States does not reduce the need to serve the United States.

Paragraph (3) is amended to ensure that failure to serve the United States in an action governed by paragraph 2(B) does not defeat an action. This protection is adopted because there will be cases in which the plaintiff reasonably fails to appreciate the need to serve the United States . There is no requirement, however, that the plaintiff show that the failure to serve the United States was reasonable. A reasonable time to effect service on the United States must be allowed after the failure is pointed out. An additional change ensures that if the United States or United States attorney is served in an action governed by paragraph 2(A), additional time is to be allowed even though no officer, employee, agency, or corporation of the United States was served.

GAP Report

The most important changes were made to ensure that no one would read the seemingly independent provisions of paragraphs 2(A) and 2(B) to mean that service must be made twice both on the United States and on the United States employee when the employee is sued in both official and individual capacities. The word "only" was added in subparagraph (A) and the new phrase "whether or not the officer or employee is sued also in an individual capacity" was inserted in subparagraph (B).

Minor changes were made to include "Employees" in the catch-line for subdivision (i), and to add "or employee" in paragraph 2(A). Although it may seem awkward to think of suit against an employee in an official capacity, there is no clear definition that separates "officers" from "employees" for this purpose. The published proposal to amend Rule 12(a)(3) referred to actions against an employee sued in an official capacity, and it seemed better to make the rules parallel by adding "employee" to Rule 4(i)(2)(A) than by deleting it from Rule 12(a)(3)(A).

2007 Amendment

[Effective December 1, 2007, absent contrary Congressional action.]

The language of Rule 4 has been amended as part of the general restyling of the Civil Rules to make them more easily understood and to make style and terminology consistent throughout the rules. These changes are intended to be stylistic only.

Rule 4(d)(1)(C) corrects an inadvertent error in former Rule 4(d)(2)(G). The defendant needs two copies of the waiver form, not an extra copy of the notice and request.

Rule 4(g) changes "infant" to "minor." "Infant" in the present rule means "minor." Modern word usage suggests that "minor" will better maintain the intended meaning. The same change from "infant" to "minor" is made throughout the rules. In addition, subdivision (f)(3) is added to the description of methods of service that the court may order; the addition ensures the evident intent that the court not order service by means prohibited by international agreement.

Rule 4(i)(4) corrects a misleading reference to "the plaintiff" in former Rule 4(i)(3). A party other than a plaintiff may need a reasonable time to effect service. Rule 4(i)(4) properly covers any party.

Former Rule 4(j)(2) refers to service upon an "other governmental organization subject to suit." This is changed to "any other state-created governmental organization that is subject to suit." The change entrenches the meaning indicated by the caption ("Serving a Foreign, State, or Local Government"), and the invocation of state law. It excludes any risk that this rule might be read to govern service on a federal agency, or other entities not created by state law.

The former provision describing service on interpleader claimants [former (k)(1)(C)] is deleted as redundant in light of the general provision in (k)(1)(C) recognizing personal jurisdiction authorized by a federal statute.

HISTORICAL NOTES
References in Text

Form 18–A, referred to in subsec. (c)(2)(C)(ii), was abrogated effective December 1, 1991, subject to contrary Congressional action.

Effective and Applicability Provisions

1983 Acts

Amendment by Pub.L. 97–462 effective 45 days after Jan. 12, 1983, see section 4 of Pub.L. 97–462, set out as a note under section 2071 of this title.

LEGISLATIVE STATEMENT
1983 Amendment

128 Congressional Record H 9848, Dec. 15, 1982. Mr. EDWARDS of California. Mr. Speaker, in July Mr. McClory and I brought before the House a bill to delay the effective date of proposed changes in rule 4 of the Federal Rules of Civil Procedure dealing with service of process. The Congress enacted that legislation and delayed the effective date so that we could cure certain problems in the proposed amendments to rule 4.

Since that time, Mr. McClory and I introduced a bill, H.R. 7154, that cures those problems. It was drafted in consultation with representatives of the Department of Justice, the Judicial Conference of the United States, and others.

The Department of Justice and the Judicial Conference have endorsed the bill and have urged its prompt enactment. Indeed, the Department of Justice has indicated that changes occasioned by the bill will facilitate its collection of debts owed to the Government.

I have a letter from the Office of Legislative Affairs of the Department of Justice supporting the bill that I will submit for the Record. Also, I am submitting for the Record a section-by-section analysis of the bill.

H.R. 7154 makes much needed changes in rule 4 of the Federal Rules of Civil Procedure and is supported by all interested parties. I urge my colleagues to support it.

U.S. DEPARTMENT OF JUSTICE,
OFFICE OF LEGISLATIVE AFFAIRS,

Washington, D.C., December 10, 1982.
Hon. Peter W. Rodino, Jr.

Chairman, Committee on the Judiciary House of Representatives, Washington, D.C.

Dear Mr. Chairman: This is to proffer the views of the Department of Justice on H.R. 7154, the proposed Federal Rules of Civil Procedure Amendments Act of 1982. While the agenda is extremely tight and we appreciate that fact, we do reiterate that this Department strongly endorses the enactment of H.R. 7154. We would greatly appreciate your watching for any possible way to enact this legislation expeditiously.

H.R. 7154 would amend Rule 4 of the Federal Rules of Civil Procedure to relieve effectively the United States Marshals Service of the duty of routinely serving summonses and complaints for private parties in civil actions and would thus achieve a goal this Department has long sought. Experience has shown that the Marshals Service's increasing workload and limited budget require such major relief from the burdens imposed by its role as process-server in all civil actions.

The bill would also amend Rule 4 to permit certain classes of defendants to be served by first class mail with a notice and acknowledgment of receipt form enclosed. We have previously expressed a preference for the service-by-mail provisions of the proposed amendments to Rule 4 which the Supreme Court transmitted to Congress on April 28, 1982.

The amendments proposed by the Supreme Court would permit service by registered or certified mail, return receipt requested. We had regarded the Supreme Court proposal as the more efficient because it would not require an affirmative act of signing and mailing on the part of a defendant. Moreover, the Supreme Court proposal would permit the entry of a default judgment if the record contained a returned receipt showing acceptance by the defendant or a returned envelope showing refusal of the process by the defendant and subsequent service and notice by first class mail. However, critics of that system of mail service have argued that certified mail is not an effective method of providing actual notice to defendants of claims against them because signatures may be illegible or may not match the name of the defendant, or because it may be difficult to determine whether mail has been "unclaimed" or "refused," the latter providing the sole basis for a default judgment.

As you know, in light of these criticisms the Congress enacted Public Law 97–227 (H.R. 6663) postponing the effective date of the proposed amendments to Rule 4 until October 1, 1983, so as to facilitate further review of the problem. This Department opposed the delay in the effective date, primarily because the Supreme Court's proposed amendments also contained urgently needed provisions designed to relieve the United States Marshals of the burden of serving summonses and complaints in private civil actions. In our view, these necessary relief provisions are readily separable from the issues of service by certified mail and the propriety of default judgment after service by certified mail which the Congress felt warranted additional review.

During the floor consideration of H.R. 6663 Congressman Edwards and other proponents of the delayed effective date pledged to expedite the review of the proposed amendments to Rule 4, given the need to provide prompt relief for the Marshals Service in the service of process area. In this spirit Judiciary Committee staff consulted with representatives of this Department, the Judicial Conference, and others who had voiced concern about the proposed amendments.

H.R. 7154 is the product of those consultations and accommodated the concerns of the Department in a very workable and acceptable manner.

Accordingly, we are satisfied that the provisions of H.R. 7154 merit the support of all three branches of the Federal Government and everyone else who has a stake in the fair and efficient service of process in civil actions. We urge prompt consideration of H.R. 7154 by the Committee.[1]

The Office of Management and Budget has advised that there is no objection to the submission of this report from the standpoint of the Administration's program.

Sincerely,

ROBERT A. MCCONNELL,
Assistant Attorney General

[1] In addition to amending Rule 4, we have previously recommended: (a) amendments to 28 U.S.C. § 569(b) redefining the Marshals traditional role by eliminating the statutory requirement that they serve subpoenas, as well as summonses and complaints, and; (b) amendments to 28 U.S.C. § 1921 changing the manner and level in which marshal fees are charged for serving private civil process. These legislative changes are embodied in Section 10 of S. 2567 and the Department's proposed fiscal year 1983 Appropriations Authorization bill. If, in the Committee's judgment, efforts to incorporate these suggested amendments in H.R. 7154 would in any way impede consideration of the bill during the few remaining legislative days in the 97th Congress, we would urge that they be separately considered early in the 98th Congress.

H.R. 7154—Federal Rules of Civil Procedure Amendments Act of 1982

BACKGROUND

The Federal Rules of Civil Procedure set forth the procedures to be followed in civil actions and proceedings in United States district courts. These rules are usually amended by a process established by 28 U.S.C. 2072, often referred to as the "Rules Enabling Act". The Rules Enabling Act provides that the Supreme Court can propose new rules of "practice and procedure" and amendments to existing rules by transmitting them to Congress after the start of a regular session but not later than May 1. The rules and amendments so proposed take effect 90 days after transmittal unless legislation to the contrary is enacted.[1]

On April 28, 1982, the Supreme Court transmitted to Congress several proposed amendments to the Federal Rules of Civil Procedure, the Federal Rules of Criminal Procedure (which govern criminal cases and proceedings in Federal courts), and the Rules and Forms Governing Proceedings in the United States District Courts under sections 2254 and 2255 of Title 28, United States Code (which govern habeas corpus proceedings). These amendments were to have taken effect on August 1, 1982.

The amendments to Rule 4 of the Federal Rules of Civil Procedure were intended primarily to relieve United States marshals of the burden of serving summonses and complaints in private civil actions. Appendix II, at 7 (Report of the Committee on Rules of Practice and Procedure), 16 (Advisory Committee Note). The Committee received numerous complaints that the changes not only failed to achieve that goal, but that in the process the changes saddled litigators with flawed mail service, deprived litigants of the use of

effective local procedures for service, and created a time limit for service replete with ambiguities that could only be resolved by costly litigation. See House Report No. 97–662, at 2–4 (1982).

In order to consider these criticisms, Congress enacted Public Law 97–227, postponing the effective date of the proposed amendments to Rule 4 until October 1, 1983.[2] Accordingly, in order to help shape the policy behind, and the form of, the proposed amendments, Congress must enact legislation before October 1, 1983.[3]

With that deadline and purpose in mind, consultations were held with representatives of the Judicial Conference, the Department of Justice, and others who had voiced concern about the proposed amendments. H.R. 7154 is the product of those consultations. The bill seeks to effectuate the policy of relieving the Marshals Service of the duty of routinely serving summonses and complaints. It provides a system of service by mail modeled upon a system found to be effective in California, and finally, it makes appropriate stylistic, grammatical, and other changes in Rule 4.

Need for the Legislation

1. Current Rule 4

Rule 4 of the Federal Rules of Civil Procedure relates to the issuance and service of process. Subsection (c) authorizes service of process by personnel of the Marshals Service, by a person specially appointed by the Court, or "by a person authorized to serve process in an action brought in the courts of general jurisdiction of the state in which the district court is held or in which service is made." Subsection (d) describes how a summons and complaint must be served and designates those persons who must be served in cases involving specified categories of defendants. Mail service is not directly authorized. Subsection (d)(7), however, authorizes service under the law of the state in which the district court sits upon defendants described in subsections (d)(1) (certain individuals) and (d)(3) (organizations). Thus, if state law authorizes service by mail of a summons and complaint upon an individual or organization described in subsections (d)(1) or (3), then subsection (d)(7) authorizes service by mail for United States district courts in that state.[4]

2. Reducing the Role of Marshals

The Supreme Court's proposed modifications of Rule 4 were designed to alleviate the burden on the Marshals Service of serving summonses and complaints in private civil actions. Appendix II, at 7 (Report of the Committee on Rules of Practice and Procedure), 16 (Advisory Committee Note). While the Committee received no complaints about the goal of reducing the role of the Marshals Service, the Court's proposals simply failed to achieve that goal. See House Report No. 97–662, at 2–3 (1982).

The Court's proposed Rule 4(c)(2)(B) required the Marshals Service to serve summonses and complaints "pursuant to any statutory provision expressly providing for service by a United States Marshal or his deputy." [5] One such statutory provision is 28 U.S.C. 569(b), which compels marshals to "execute *all* lawful writs, process and orders issued under authority of the United States, *including those of the courts* * * *." (emphasis added). Thus, any party could have invoked 28 U.S.C. 569(b) to utilize a marshal for service of a summons and complaint, thereby thwarting the intent of the

new subsection to limit the use of marshals. The Justice Department acknowledges that the proposed subsection did not accomplish its objectives.[6]

Had 28 U.S.C. 569(b) been inconsistent with proposed Rule 4(c)(2)(B), the latter would have nullified the former under 28 U.S.C. 2072, which provides that "All laws in conflict with such rules shall be of no further force or effect after such rules have taken effect." Since proposed Rule 4(c)(2)(B) specifically referred to statutes such as 28 U.S.C. 569(b), however, the new subsection did not conflict with 28 U.S.C. 569(b) and did not, therefore, supersede it.

H.R. 7154 cures this problem and achieves the desired reduction in the role of the Marshals Service by authorizing marshals to serve summonses and complaints "on behalf of the United States". By so doing, H.R. 7154 eliminates the loophole in the Court's proposed language and still provides for service by marshals on behalf of the Government.[7]

3. Mail Service

The Supreme Court's proposed subsection (d)(7) and (8) authorized, as an alternative to personal service, mail service of summonses and complaints on individuals and organizations described in subsection (d)(1) and (3), but only through registered or certified mail, restricted delivery. Critics of that system of mail service argued that registered and certified mail were not necessarily effective methods of providing actual notice to defendants of claims against them. This was so, they argued, because signatures may be illegible or may not match the name of the defendant, or because it may be difficult to determine whether mail has been "unclaimed" or "refused", the latter apparently providing the sole basis for a default judgment.[8]

H.R. 7154 provides for a system of service by mail similar to the system now used in California. See Cal.Civ.Pro. § 415.30 (West 1973). Service would be by ordinary mail with a notice and acknowledgment of receipt form enclosed. If the defendant returns the acknowledgment form to the sender within 20 days of mailing, the sender files the return and service is complete. If the acknowledgment is not returned within 20 days of mailing, then service must be effected through some other means provided for in the Rules.

This system of mail service avoids the notice problems created by the registered and certified mail procedures proposed by the Supreme Court. If the proper person receives the notice and returns the acknowledgment, service is complete. If the proper person does not receive the mailed form, or if the proper person receives the notice but fails to return the acknowledgment form, another method of service authorized by law is required.[9] In either instance, however, the defendant will receive actual notice of the claim. In order to encourage defendants to return the acknowledgment form, the court can order a defendant who does not return it to pay the costs of service unless the defendant can show good cause for the failure to return it.

4. The Local Option

The Court's proposed amendments to Rule 4 deleted the provision in current subsection (d)(7) that authorizes service of a summons and complaint upon individuals and organizations "in the manner prescribed by the law of the state in which the district court is held for the service of summons or

other like process upon any such defendant in an action brought in the courts of general jurisdiction of that state." The Committee received a variety of complaints about the deletion of this provision. Those in favor of preserving the local option saw no reason to forego systems of service that had been successful in achieving effective notice.[10]

H.R. 7154 carries forward the policy of the current rule and permits a party to serve a summons and complaint upon individuals and organizations described in Rule 4(d)(1) and (3) in accordance with the law of the state in which the district court sits. Thus, the bill authorizes four methods of serving a summons and complaint on such defendants: (1) service by a nonparty adult (Rule 4(c)(2)(A)); (2) service by personnel of the Marshals Service, if the party qualifies, such as because the party is proceeding in forma pauperis (Rule 4(c)(2)(B)); (3) service in any manner authorized by the law of the state in which the district court is held (Rule 4(c)(2)(C)(i)); or (4) service by regular mail with a notice and acknowledgment of receipt form enclosed (Rule 4(c)(2)(C)(ii)).[11]

5. *TIME LIMITS*

Rule 4 does not currently provide a time limit within which service must be completed. Primarily because United States marshals currently effect service of process, no time restriction has been deemed necessary, Appendix II, at 18 (Advisory Committee Note). Along with the proposed changes to subdivisions (c) and (d) to reduce the role of the Marshals Service, however, came new subdivision (j), requiring that service of a summons and complaint be made within 120 days of the filing of the complaint. If service were not accomplished within that time, proposed subdivision (j) required that the action "be dismissed as to that defendant without prejudice upon motion or upon the court's own initiative". Service by mail was deemed made for purposes of subdivision (j) "as of the date on which the process was accepted, refused, or returned as unclaimed".[12]

H.R. 7154 adopts a policy of limiting the time to effect service. It provides that if a summons and complaint have not been served within 120 days of the filing of the complaint and the plaintiff fails to show "good cause" for not completing service within that time, then the court must dismiss the action as to the unserved defendant. H.R. 7154 ensures that a plaintiff will be notified of an attempt to dismiss the action. If dismissal for failure to serve is raised by the court upon its own motion, the legislation requires that the court provide notice to the plaintiff. If dismissal is sought by someone else, Rule 5(a) of the Federal Rules of Civil Procedure requires that the motion be served upon the plaintiff.

Like proposed subsection (j), H.R. 7154 provides that a dismissal for failure to serve within 120 days shall be "without prejudice". Proposed subsection (j) was criticized by some for ambiguity because, it was argued, neither the text of subsection (j) nor the Advisory Committee Note indicated whether a dismissal without prejudice would toll a statute of limitation. *See* House Report 97–662, at 3–4 (1982). The problem would arise when a plaintiff files the complaint within the applicable statute of limitation period but does not effect service within 120 days. If the statute of limitation period expires during that period, and if the plaintiff's action is dismissed "without prejudice", can the plaintiff refile the complaint and maintain the action? The answer depends upon how the statute of limitation is tolled.[13]

If the law provides that the statute of limitation is tolled by filing and service of the complaint, then a dismissal under H.R. 7154 for failure to serve within the 120 days would, by the terms of the law controlling the tolling bar the plaintiff from later maintaining the cause of action.[14] If the law provides that the statute of limitation is tolled by filing alone, then the status of the plaintiff's cause of action turns upon the plaintiff's diligence. If the plaintiff has not been diligent, the court will dismiss the complaint for failure to serve within 120 days, and the plaintiff will be barred from later maintaining the cause of action because the statute of limitation has run. A dismissal without prejudice does not confer upon the plaintiff any rights that the plaintiff does otherwise possess and leaves a plaintiff whose action has been dismissed in the same position as if the action had never been filed.[15] If, on the other hand, the plaintiff has made reasonable efforts to effect service, then the plaintiff can move under Rule 6(b) to enlarge the time within which to serve or can oppose dismissal for failure to serve. A court would undoubtedly permit such a plaintiff additional time within which to effect service. Thus, a diligent plaintiff can preserve the cause of action. This result is consistent with the policy behind the time limit for service and with statutes of limitation, both of which are designed to encourage prompt movement of civil actions in the federal courts.

6. *CONFORMING AND CLARIFYING SUBSECTIONS (D)(4) AND (5)*

Current subsections (d)(4) and (5) prescribe which persons must be served in cases where an action is brought against the United States or an officer or agency of the United States. Under subsection (d)(4), where the United States is the named defendant, service must be made as follows: (1) personal service upon the United States attorney, an assistant United States attorney, or a designated clerical employee of the United States attorney in the district in which the action is brought; (2) registered or certified mail service to the Attorney General of the United States in Washington, D.C.; and (3) registered or certified mail service to the appropriate officer or agency if the action attacks an order of that officer or agency but does not name the officer or agency as a defendant. Under subsection (d)(5), where an officer or agency of the United States is named as a defendant, service must be made as in subsection (d)(4), except that personal service upon the officer or agency involved is required.[16]

The time limit for effecting service in H.R. 7154 would present significant difficulty to a plaintiff who has to arrange for personal service upon an officer or agency that may be thousands of miles away. There is little reason to require different types of service when the officer or agency is named as a party, and H.R. 7154 therefore conforms the manner of service under subsection (d)(5) to the manner of service under subsection (d)(4).

SECTION-BY-SECTION ANALYSIS

SECTION 1

Section 1 provides that the short title of the bill is the "Federal Rules of Civil Procedure Amendments Act of 1982".

SECTION 2

Section 2 of the bill consists of 7 numbered paragraphs, each amending a different part of Rule 4 of the Federal Rules of Civil Procedure.

Paragraph (1) deletes the requirement in present Rule 4(a) that a summons be delivered for service to the marshal or other person authorized to serve it. As amended by the legislation, Rule 4(a) provides that the summons be delivered to "the plaintiff or the plaintiff's attorney, who shall be responsible for prompt service of the summons and complaint". This change effectuates the policy proposed by the Supreme Court. See Appendix II, at — (Advisory Committee Note).

Paragraph (2) amends current Rule 4(c), which deals with the service of process. New Rule 4(c)(1) requires that all process, other than a subpoena or a summons and complaint, be served by the Marshals Service or by a person especially appointed for that purpose. Thus, the Marshals Service or persons specially appointed will continue to serve all process other than subpoenas and summonses and complaints, a policy identical to that proposed by the Supreme Court. See Appendix II, at 8 (Report of the Judicial Conference Committee on Rules of Practice and Procedure). The service of subpoenas is governed by Rule 45,[17] and the service of summonses and complaints is governed by new Rule 4(c)(2).

New Rule 4(c)(2)(A) sets forth the general rule that summonses and complaints shall be served by someone who is at least 18 years old and not a party to the action or proceeding. This is consistent with the Court's proposal. Appendix II, at 16 (Advisory Committee Note). Subparagraphs (B) and (C) of new Rule 4(c)(2) set forth exceptions to this general rule.

Subparagraph (B) sets forth 3 exceptions to the general rule. First, subparagraph (B)(i) requires the Marshals Service (or someone specially appointed by the court) to serve summonses and complaints on behalf of a party proceeding in forma pauperis or a seaman authorized to proceed under 28 U.S.C. 1916. This is identical to the Supreme Court's proposal. See Appendix II, at 3 (text of proposed rule), 16 (Advisory Committee Note). Second, subparagraph (B)(ii) requires the Marshals Service (or someone specially appointed by the court) to serve a summons and complaint when the court orders the marshals to do so in order properly to effect service in that particular action.[18] This, except for nonsubstantive changes in phrasing, is identical to the Supreme Court's proposal. See Appendix II, at 3 (text of proposed rule), 16 (Advisory Committee Note).

Subparagraph (C) of new Rule 4(c)(2) provides 2 exceptions to the general rule of service by a nonparty adult. These exceptions apply only when the summons and complaint is to be served upon persons described in Rule 4(d)(1) (certain individuals) or Rule 4(d)(3) (organizations).[19] First, subparagraph (C)(i) permits service of a summons and complaint in a manner authorized by the law of the state in which the court sits. This restates the option to follow local law currently found in Rule 4(d)(7) and would authorize service by mail if the state law so allowed. The method of mail service in that instance would, of course, be the method permitted by state law.

Second, subparagraph (C)(ii) permits service of a summons and complaint by regular mail. The sender must send to the defendant, by first-class mail, postage prepaid, a copy of the summons and complaint, together with 2 copies of a notice and acknowledgment of receipt of summons and complaint form and a postage prepaid return envelope addressed to the sender. If a copy of the notice and acknowledgment form is not received by the sender within 20 days after the date of mailing, then service must be made under Rule 4(c)(2)(A) or (B) (i.e., by a nonparty adult or, if the person qualifies,[20] by personnel of the Marshals Service or a person specially appointed by the court) in the manner prescribed by Rule 4(d)(1) or (3) (i.e., personal or substituted service).

New Rule 4(c)(2)(D) permits a court to penalize a person who avoids service by mail. It authorizes the court to order a person who does not return the notice and acknowledgment form within 20 days after mailing to pay the costs of service, unless that person can show good cause for failing to return the form. The purpose of this provision is to encourage the prompt return of the form so that the action can move forward without unnecessary delay. Fairness requires that a person who causes another additional and unnecessary expense in effecting service ought to reimburse the party who was forced to bear the additional expense.

Subparagraph (E) of Rule 4(c)(2) requires that the notice and acknowledgment form described in new Rule 4(c)(2)(C)(ii) be executed under oath or affirmation. This provision tracks the language of 28 U.S.C. 1746, which permits the use of unsworn declarations under penalty of perjury whenever an oath or affirmation is required. Statements made under penalty of perjury are subject to 18 U.S.C. 1621(2), which provides felony penalties for someone who "willfully subscribes as true any material matter which he does not believe to be true". The requirement that the form be executed under oath or affirmation is intended to encourage truthful submissions to the court, as the information contained in the form is important to the parties.[21]

New Rule 4(c)(3) authorizes the court freely to make special appointments to serve summonses and complaints under Rule 4(c)(2)(B) and all other process under Rule 4(c)(1). This carries forward the policy of present Rule 4(c).

Paragraph (3) of section 2 of the bill makes a non-substantive change in the caption of Rule 4(d) in order to reflect more accurately the provisions of Rule 4(d). Paragraph (3) also deletes a provision on service of a summons and complaint pursuant to state law. This provision is redundant in view of new Rule 4(c)(2)(C)(i).

Paragraph (4) of section 2 of the bill conforms Rule 4(d)(5) to present Rule 4(d)(4). Rule 4(d)(5) is amended to provide that service upon a named defendant agency or officer of the United States shall be made by "sending" a copy of the summons and complaint "by registered or certified mail" to the defendant.[22] Rule 4(d)(5) currently provides for service by "delivering" the copies to the defendant, but 28 U.S.C. 1391(e) authorizes delivery upon a defendant agency or officer outside of the district in which the action is brought by means of certified mail. Hence, the change is not a marked departure from current practice.

Paragraph (5) of section 2 of the bill amends the caption of Rule 4(e) in order to describe subdivision (e) more accurately.

Paragraph (6) of section 2 of the bill amends Rule 4(g), which deals with return of service. Present rule 4(g) is not changed except to provide that, if service is made pursuant to the new system of mail service (Rule 4(c)(2)(C)(ii)), the

plaintiff or the plaintiff's attorney must file the court the signed acknowledgment form returned by the person served.

Paragraph (7) of section 2 of the bill adds new subsection (j) to provide a time limitation for the service of a summons and complaint. New Rule 4(j) retains the Supreme Court's requirement that a summons and complaint be served within 120 days of the filing of the complaint. See Appendix II, at 18 (Advisory Committee Note).[23] The plaintiff must be notified of an effort or intention to dismiss the action. This notification is mandated by subsection (j) if the dismissal is being raised on the court's own initiative and will be provided pursuant to Rule 5 (which requires service of motions upon the adverse party) if the dismissal is sought by someone else.[24] The plaintiff may move under Rule 6(b) to enlarge the time period. See Appendix II, at Id. (Advisory Committee Note). If service is not made within the time period or enlarged time period, however, and if the plaintiff fails to show "good cause" for not completing service, then the court must dismiss the action as to the unserved defendant. The dismissal is "without prejudice". The term "without prejudice" means that the dismissal does not constitute an adjudication of the merits of the complaint. A dismissal "without prejudice" leaves a plaintiff whose action has been dismissed in the position in which that person would have been if the action had never been filed.

SECTION 3

Section 3 of the bill amends the Appendix of Forms at the end of the Federal Rules of Civil Procedure by adding a new form 18A, "Notice and Acknowledgment for Service by Mail". This new form is required by new Rule 4(c)(2)(C)(ii), which requires that the notice and acknowledgment form used with service by regular mail conform substantially to Form 18A.

Form 18A as set forth in section 3 of the bill is modeled upon a form used in California.[25] It contains 2 parts. The first part is a notice to the person being served that tells that person that the enclosed summons and complaint is being served pursuant to Rule 4(c)(2)(C)(ii); advises that person to sign and date the acknowledgment form and indicate the authority to receive service if the person served is not the party to the action (e.g., the person served is an officer of the organization being served); and warns that failure to return the form to the sender within 20 days may result in the court ordering the party being served to pay the expenses involved in effecting service. The notice also warns that if the complaint is not responded to within 20 days, a default judgment can be entered against the party being served. The notice is dated under penalty of perjury by the plaintiff or the plaintiff's attorney.[26]

The second part of the form contains the acknowledgment of receipt of the summons and complaint. The person served must declare on this part of the form, under penalty of perjury, the date and place of service and the person's authority to receive service.

SECTION 4

Section 4 of the bill provides that the changes in Rule 4 made by H.R. 7154 will take effect 45 days after enactment, thereby giving the bench and bar, as well as other interested persons and organizations (such as the Marshals Service), an opportunity to prepare to implement the changes made by the legislation. The delayed effective date means that ser-

vice of process issued before the effective date will be made in accordance with current Rule 4. Accordingly, all process in the hands of the Marshals Service prior to the effective date will be served by the Marshals Service under the present rule.

SECTION 5

Section 5 of the bill provides that the amendments to Rule 4 proposed by the Supreme Court (whose effective date was postponed by Public Law 97–227) shall not take effect. This is necessary because under Public Law 97–227 the proposed amendments will take effect on October 1, 1983.

[1] The drafting of the rules and amendments is actually done by a committee of the Judicial Conference of the United States. In the case of the Federal Rules of Civil Procedure, the initial draft is prepared by the Advisory Committee on Civil Rules. The Advisory Committee's draft is then reviewed by the Committee on Rules of Practice and Procedure, which must give its approval to the draft. Any draft approved by that committee is forwarded to the Judicial Conference. If the Judicial Conference approves the draft, it forwards the draft to the Supreme Court. The Judicial Conference's role in the rule-making process is defined by 28 U.S.C. 331.

For background information about how the Judicial Conference committees operate, see Wright, "Procedural Reform: Its Limitation and Its Future," 1 Ga.L.Rev. 563, 565–66 (1967) (civil rules); statement of United States District Judge Roszel C. Thomsen, Hearings on Proposed Amendments to the Federal Rules of Criminal Procedure Before the Subcommittee on Criminal Justice of the House Committee on the Judiciary, 93d Cong., 2d Sess. at 25 (1974) (criminal rules); statement of United States Circuit Judge J. Edward Lumbard, id. at 203 (criminal rules); J. Weinstein, Reform of Federal Court Rulemaking Procedure (1977); Weinstein, "Reform of Federal Rulemaking Procedures," 76 Colum.L.Rev. 905 (1976).

[2] All of the other amendments, including all of the proposed amendments to the Federal Rules of Criminal Procedure and the Rules and Forms Governing Proceedings in the United States District Courts under sections 2254 and 2255 of Title 28, United States Code, took effect on August 1, 1982, as scheduled.

[3] The President has urged Congress to act promptly. See President's Statement on Signing H.R. 6663 into Law, 18 Weekly Comp. of Pres. Doc. 982 (August 2, 1982).

[4] Where service of a summons is to be made upon a party who is neither an inhabitant of, nor found within, the state where the district court sits, subsection (e) authorizes service under a state statute or rule of court that provides for service upon such a party. This would authorize mail service if the state statute or rule of court provided for service by mail.

[5] The Court's proposal authorized service by the Marshals Service in other situations. This authority, however, was not seen as thwarting the underlying policy of limiting the use of marshals. *See* Appendix II, at 16, 17 (Advisory Committee Note).

[6] Appendix I, at 2 (letter of Assistant Attorney General Robert A. McConnell).

[7] The provisions of H.R. 7154 conflict with 28 U.S.C. 569(b) because the latter is a broader command to marshals to serve all federal court process. As a later statutory enactment, however, H.R. 7154 supersedes 28 U.S.C. 569(b), thereby achieving the goal of reducing the role of marshals.

[8] Proposed Rule 4(d)(8) provided that "Service . . . shall not be the basis for the entry of a default or a judgment by default unless the record contains a return receipt showing acceptance by the defendant or a returned envelope showing refusal of the process by the defendant." This provision reflects a desire to preclude default judgments on unclaimed mail. See Appendix II, at 7 (Report of the Committee on Rules of Practice and Procedure).

The interpretation of Rule 4(d)(8) to require a refusal of delivery in order to have a basis for a default judgment, while undoubtedly the

interpretation intended and the interpretation that reaches the fairest result, may not be the only possible interpretation. Since a default judgment can be entered for defendant's failure to respond to the complaint once defendant has been served and the time to answer the complaint has run, it can be argued that a default judgment can be obtained where the mail was unclaimed because proposed subsection (j), which authorized dismissal of a complaint not served within 120 days, provided that mail service would be deemed made "on the date on which the process was accepted, refused, or *returned as unclaimed* " (emphasis added).

9 *See* p. 15 infra.

10 Proponents of the California system of mail service, in particular, saw no reason to supplant California's proven method of mail service with a certified mail service that they believed likely to result in default judgments without actual notice to defendants. See House Report No. 97–662, at 3 (1982).

11 The parties may, of course, stipulate to service, as is frequently done now.

12 While return of the letter as unclaimed was deemed service for the purpose of determining whether the plaintiff's action could be dismissed, return of the letter as unclaimed was not service for the purpose of entry of a default judgment against the defendant. See note 8 supra.

13 The law governing the tolling of a statute of limitation depends upon the type of civil action involved. In a diversity action, state law governs tolling. *Walker v. Armco Steel Corp.,* 446 U.S. 740 (1980). In *Walker,* plaintiff had filed his complaint and thereby commenced the action under Rule 3 of the Federal Rules of Civil Procedure within the statutory period. He did not, however, serve the summons and complaint until after the statutory period had run. The Court held that state law (which required both filing and service within the statutory period) governed, barring plaintiff's action.

In the federal question action, the courts of appeals have generally held that Rule 3 governs, so that the filing of the complaint tolls a statute of limitation. *United States v. Wahl,* 538 F.2d 285 (6th Cir. 1978); *Windbrooke Dev. Co. v. Environmental Enterprises Inc. of Fla.,* 524 F.2d 461 (5th Cir. 1975); *Metropolitan Paving Co. v. International Union of Operating Engineers,* 439 F.2d 300 (10th Cir. 1971); *Moore Co. v. Sid Richardson Carbon & Gasoline Co.,* 347 F.2d 921 (8th Cir.), cert. denied, 383 U.S. 925, reh. denied, 384 U.S. 914 (1965); *Hoffman v. Halden,* 268 F.2d 280 (9th Cir. 1959). The continued validity of this line of cases, however, must be questioned in light of the *Walker* case, even though the Court in that case expressly reserved judgment about federal question actions, *see Walker v. Armco Steel Corp.,* 446 U.S. 741, 751 n.11 (1980).

14 The same result obtains even if service occurs within the 120 day period, if the service occurs after the statute of limitation has run.

15 See p. 19 infra.

16 See p. 17 infra.

17 Rule 45(c) provides that "A subpoena may be served by the marshal, by his deputy, or by any other person who is not a party and is not less than 18 years of age."

18 Some litigators have voiced concern that there may be situations in which personal service by someone other than a member of the Marshals Service may present a risk of injury to the person attempting to make the service. For example, a hostile defendant may have a history of injuring persons attempting to serve process. Federal judges undoubtedly will consider the risk of harm to private persons who would be making personal service when deciding whether to order the Marshals Service to make service under Rule 4(c)(2)(B)(iii).

19 The methods of service authorized by Rule 4(c)(2)(C) may be invoked by any person seeking to effect service. Thus, a nonparty adult who receives the summons and complaint for service under Rule 4(c)(1) may serve them personally or by mail in the manner authorized by Rule 4(c)(2)(C)(ii). Similarly, the Marshals Service may utilize the mail service authorized by Rule 4(c)(2)(C)(ii) when serving a summons and complaint under Rule 4(c)(2)(B)(i)(iii). When serving a summons and complaint under Rule 4(c)(2)(B)(ii), however, the Marshals Service must serve in the manner set forth in the court's order. If no particular manner of service is specified, then the Marshals Service may utilize Rule 4(c)(2)(C)(ii). It would not seem to be appropriate, however, for the Marshals Service to utilize Rule 4(c)(2)(C)(ii) in a situation where a previous attempt to serve by mail failed. Thus, it would not seem to be appropriate for the Marshals Service to attempt service by regular mail when serving a summons and complaint on behalf of a plaintiff who is proceeding in forma pauperis if that plaintiff previously attempted unsuccessfully to serve the defendant by mail.

20 To obtain service by personnel of the Marshals Service or someone specially appointed by the court, a plaintiff who has unsuccessfully attempted mail service under Rule 4(c)(2)(C)(ii) must meet the conditions of Rule 4(c)(2)(B)—for example, the plaintiff must be proceeding *in forma pauperis.*

21 For example, the sender must state the date of mailing on the form. If the form is not returned to the sender within 20 days of that date, then the plaintiff must serve the defendant in another manner and the defendant may be liable for the costs of such service. Thus, a defendant would suffer the consequences of a misstatement about the date of mailing.

22 See p. 12 supra.

23 The 120 day period begins to run upon the filing of each complaint. Thus, where a defendant files a cross-claim against the plaintiff, the 120 day period begins to run upon the filing of the cross-complaint, not upon the filing of the plaintiff's complaint initiating the action.

24 The person who may move to dismiss can be the putative defendant (i.e., the person named as defendant in the complaint filed with the court) or, in multi-party actions, another party to the action. (If the putative defendant moves to dismiss and the failure to effect service is due to that person's evasion of service, a court should not dismiss because the plaintiff has "good cause" for not completing service.)

25 See Cal.Civ.Pro. § 415.30 (West 1973).

26 See p. 16 supra.

TREATIES AND CONVENTIONS

CONVENTION ON THE SERVICE ABROAD OF JUDICIAL AND EXTRAJUDICIAL DOCUMENTS IN CIVIL OR COMMERCIAL MATTERS

The States signatory to the present Convention,

Desiring to create appropriate means to ensure that judicial and extrajudicial documents to be served abroad shall be brought to the notice of the addressee in sufficient time,

Desiring to improve the organisation of mutual judicial assistance for that purpose by simplifying and expediting the procedure,

Have resolved to conclude a Convention to this effect and have agreed upon the following provisions:

Article 1

The present Convention shall apply in all cases, in civil or commercial matters, where there is occasion to transmit a judicial or extrajudicial document for service abroad.

This Convention shall not apply where the address of the person to be served with the document is not known.

CHAPTER I—JUDICIAL DOCUMENTS

Article 2

Each contracting State shall designate a Central Authority which will undertake to receive requests for service coming from other contracting States and to proceed in conformity with the provisions of articles 3 to 6.

Each State shall organise the Central Authority in conformity with its own law.

Article 3

The authority or judicial officer competent under the law of the State in which the documents originate shall forward to the Central Authority of the State addressed a request conforming to the model annexed to the present Convention, without any requirement of legalisation or other equivalent formality.

The document to be served or a copy thereof shall be annexed to the request. The request and the document shall both be furnished in duplicate.

Article 4

If the Central Authority considers that the request does not comply with the provisions of the present Convention it shall promptly inform the applicant and specify its objections to the request.

Article 5

The Central Authority of the State addressed shall itself serve the document or shall arrange to have it served by an appropriate agency, either—

(a) by a method prescribed by its internal law for the service of documents in domestic actions upon persons who are within its territory, or

(b) by a particular method requested by the applicant, unless such a method is incompatible with the law of the State addressed.

Subject to sub-paragraph (b) of the first paragraph of this article, the document may always be served by delivery to an addressee who accepts it voluntarily.

If the document is to be served under the first paragraph above, the Central Authority may require the document to be written in, or translated into, the official language or one of the official languages of the State addressed.

That part of the request, in the form attached to the present Convention, which contains a summary of the document to be served, shall be served with the document.

Article 6

The Central Authority of the State addressed or any authority which it may have designated for that purpose, shall complete a certificate in the form of the model annexed to the present Convention.

The certificate shall state that the document has been served and shall include the method, the place and the date of service and the person to whom the document was delivered. If the document has not been served, the certificate shall set out the reasons which have prevented service.

The applicant may require that a certificate not completed by a Central Authority or by a judicial authority shall be countersigned by one of these authorities.

The certificate shall be forwarded directly to the applicant.

Article 7

The standard terms in the model annexed to the present Convention shall in all cases be written either in French or in English. They may also be written in the official language, or in one of the official languages, of the State in which the documents originate.

The corresponding blanks shall be completed either in the language of the State addressed or in French or in English.

Article 8

Each contracting State shall be free to effect service of judicial documents upon persons abroad, without application of any compulsion, directly through its diplomatic or consular agents.

Any State may declare that it is opposed to such service within its territory, unless the document is to be served upon a national of the State in which the documents originate.

Article 9

Each contracting State shall be free, in addition, to use consular channels to forward documents, for the purpose of service, to those authorities of another contracting State which are designated by the latter for this purpose.

Each contracting State may, if exceptional circumstances so require, use diplomatic channels for the same purpose.

Article 10

Provided the State of destination does not object, the present Convention shall not interfere with—

(a) the freedom to send judicial documents, by postal channels, directly to persons abroad,

(b) the freedom of judicial officers, officials or other competent persons of the State of origin to effect service of judicial documents directly through the judicial officers, officials or other competent persons of the State of destination,

(c) the freedom of any person interested in a judicial proceeding to effect service of judicial documents directly through the judicial officers, officials or other competent persons of the State of destination.

Article 11

The present Convention shall not prevent two or more contracting States from agreeing to permit, for the purpose of service of judicial documents, channels of transmission other than those provided for in the preceding articles and, in particular, direct communication between their respective authorities.

Article 12

The service of judicial documents coming from a contracting State shall not give rise to any payment or reimbursement of taxes or costs for the services rendered by the State addressed.

The applicant shall pay or reimburse the costs occasioned by—

(a) the employment of a judicial officer or of a person competent under the law of the State of destination,

(b) the use of a particular method of service.

Article 13

Where a request for service complies with the terms of the present Convention, the State addressed may refuse to comply therewith only if it deems that compliance would infringe its sovereignty or security.

It may not refuse to comply solely on the ground that, under its internal law, it claims exclusive jurisdiction over the subject-matter of the action or that its internal law would not permit the action upon which the application is based.

The Central Authority shall, in case of refusal, promptly inform the applicant and state the reasons for the refusal.

Article 14

Difficulties which may arise in connection with the transmission of judicial documents for service shall be settled through diplomatic channels.

Article 15

Where a writ of summons or an equivalent document had to be transmitted abroad for the purpose of service, under the provisions of the present Convention, and the defendant has not appeared, judgment shall not be given until it is established that—

(a) the document was served by a method prescribed by the internal law of the State addressed for the service of documents in domestic actions upon persons who are within its territory, or

(b) the document was actually delivered to the defendant or to his residence by another method provided for by this Convention,

and that in either of these cases the service or the delivery was effected in sufficient time to enable the defendant to defend.

Each contracting State shall be free to declare that the judge, notwithstanding the provisions of the first paragraph of this article, may give judgment even if no certificate of service or delivery has been received, if all the following conditions are fulfilled—

(a) the document was transmitted by one of the methods provided for in this Convention,

(b) a period of time of not less than six months, considered adequate by the judge in the particular case, has elapsed since the date of the transmission of the document,

(c) no certificate of any kind has been received, even though every reasonable effort has been made to obtain it through the competent authorities of the State addressed.

Notwithstanding the provisions of the preceding paragraphs the judge may order, in case of urgency, any provisional or protective measures.

Article 16

When a writ of summons or an equivalent document had to be transmitted abroad for the purpose of service, under the provisions of the present Convention, and a judgment has been entered against a defendant who has not appeared, the judge shall have the power to relieve the defendant from the effects of the expiration of the time for appeal from the judgment if the following conditions are fulfilled—

(a) the defendant, without any fault on his part, did not have knowledge of the document in sufficient time to defend, or knowledge of the judgment in sufficient time to appeal, and

(b) the defendant has disclosed a *prima facie* defense to the action on the merits.

An application for relief may be filed only within a reasonable time after the defendant has knowledge of the judgment.

Each contracting State may declare that the application will not be entertained if it is filed after the expiration of a time to be stated in the declaration, but which shall in no case be less than one year following the date of the judgment.

This article shall not apply to judgments concerning status or capacity of persons.

CHAPTER II—EXTRAJUDICIAL DOCUMENTS
Article 17

Extrajudicial documents emanating from authorities and judicial officers of a contracting State may be transmitted for the purpose of service in another contracting State by the methods and under the provisions of the present Convention.

CHAPTER III—GENERAL CLAUSES
Article 18

Each contracting State may designate other authorities in addition to the Central Authority and shall determine the extent of their competence.

The applicant shall, however, in all cases, have the right to address a request directly to the Central Authority.

Federal States shall be free to designate more than one Central Authority.

Article 19

To the extent that the internal law of a contracting State permits methods of transmission, other than those provided for in the preceding articles, of documents coming from abroad, for service within its territory, the present Convention shall not affect such provisions.

Article 20

The present Convention shall not prevent an agreement between any two or more contracting States to dispense with—

(a) the necessity for duplicate copies of transmitted documents as required by the second paragraph of article 3,

(b) the language requirements of the third paragraph of article 5 and article 7,

(c) the provisions of the fourth paragraph of article 5,

(d) the provisions of the second paragraph of article 12.

Article 21

Each contracting State shall, at the time of the deposit of its instrument of ratification or accession, or at a later date, inform the Ministry of Foreign Affairs of the Netherlands of the following—

(a) the designation of authorities, pursuant to articles 2 and 18,

(b) the designation of the authority competent to complete the certificate pursuant to article 6,

(c) the designation of the authority competent to receive documents transmitted by consular channels, pursuant to article 9.

Each contracting State shall similarly inform the Ministry, where appropriate, of—

(a) opposition to the use of methods of transmission pursuant to articles 8 and 10,

(b) declarations pursuant to the second paragraph of article 15 and the third paragraph of article 16,

(c) all modifications of the above designations, oppositions and declarations.

Article 22

Where Parties to the present Convention are also Parties to one or both of the Conventions on civil procedure signed at The Hague on 17th July 1905 [99 BFSP 990], and on 1st March 1954 [286 UNTS 265], this Convention shall replace as between them articles 1 to 7 of the earlier Conventions.

Article 23

The present Convention shall not affect the application of article 23 of the Convention on civil procedure signed at The Hague on 17th July 1905, or of article 24 of the Convention on civil procedure signed at The Hague on 1st March 1954.

These articles shall, however, apply only if methods of communication, identical to those provided for in these Conventions, are used.

Article 24

Supplementary agreements between parties to the Conventions of 1905 and 1954 shall be considered as equally applicable to the present Convention, unless the Parties have otherwise agreed.

Article 25

Without prejudice to the provisions of articles 22 and 24, the present Convention shall not derogate from Conventions containing provisions on the matters governed by this Convention to which the contracting States are, or shall become, Parties.

Article 26

The present Convention shall be open for signature by the States represented at the Tenth Session of the Hague Conference on Private International Law.

It shall be ratified, and the instruments of ratification shall be deposited with the Ministry of Foreign Affairs of the Netherlands.

Article 27

The present Convention shall enter into force on the sixtieth day after the deposit of the third instrument of ratification referred to in the second paragraph of article 26.

The Convention shall enter into force for each signatory State which ratifies subsequently on the sixtieth day after the deposit of its instrument of ratification.

Article 28

Any State not represented at the Tenth Session of the Hague Conference on Private International Law may accede to the present Convention after it has entered into force in accordance with the first paragraph of article 27. The instrument of accession shall be deposited with the Ministry of Foreign Affairs of the Netherlands.

The Convention shall enter into force for such a State in the absence of any objection from a State, which has ratified the Convention before such deposit, notified to the Ministry of Foreign Affairs of the Netherlands within a period of six months after the date on which the said Ministry has notified it of such accession.

In the absence of any such objection, the Convention shall enter into force for the acceding State on the first day of the month following the expiration of the last of the periods referred to in the preceding paragraph.

Article 29

Any State may, at the time of signature, ratification or accession, declare that the present Convention shall extend to all the territories for the international relations of which it is responsible, or to one or more of them. Such a declaration shall take effect on the date of entry into force of the Convention for the State concerned.

At any time thereafter, such extensions shall be notified to the Ministry of Foreign Affairs of the Netherlands.

The Convention shall enter into force for the territories mentioned in such an extension on the sixtieth day after the notification referred to in the preceding paragraph.

Article 30

The present Convention shall remain in force for five years from the date of its entry into force in accordance with the first paragraph of article 27, even for States which have ratified it or acceded to it subsequently.

If there has been no denunciation, it shall be renewed tacitly every five years.

Any denunciation shall be notified to the Ministry of Foreign Affairs of the Netherlands at least six months before the end of the five year period.

It may be limited to certain of the territories to which the Convention applies.

The denunciation shall have effect only as regards the State which has notified it. The Convention shall remain in force for the other contracting States.

Article 31

The Ministry of Foreign Affairs of the Netherlands shall give notice to the States referred to in article 26, and to the States which have acceded in accordance with article 28, of the following—

(a) the signatures and ratifications referred to in article 26;

(b) the date on which the present Convention enters into force in accordance with the first paragraph of article 27;

(c) the accessions referred to in article 28 and the dates on which they take effect;

(d) the extensions referred to in article 29 and the dates on which they take effect;

(e) the designations, oppositions and declarations referred to in article 21;

(f) the denunciations referred to in the third paragraph of article 30.

IN WITNESS WHEREOF the undersigned, being duly authorised thereto, have signed the present Convention.

DONE at The Hague, on the 15th day of November, 1965, in the English and French languages, both texts being equally authentic, in a single copy which shall be deposited in the archives of the Government of the Netherlands, and of which a certified copy shall be sent, through the diplomatic channel, to each of The States represented at the Tenth Session of the Hague Conference on Private International Law.

[Signatures omitted.]

Service of Documents Convention
ANNEX TO THE CONVENTION

Forms *

* These forms may be obtained from the Offices of United States Marshals.

REQUEST
FOR SERVICE ABROAD OF JUDICIAL OR EXTRAJUDICIAL DOCUMENTS

Convention on the service abroad of judicial and extrajudicial documents in civil or commercial matters, signed at The Hague, November 15, 1965.

Identity and address of the applicant	Address of receiving authority
	Identity and address of the applicant
	Address of receiving authority

The undersigned applicant has the honour to transmit—in duplicate—the documents listed below and, in conformity with article 5 of the above-mentioned Convention, requests prompt service of one copy thereof on the addressee, i.e.,
 (identity and address) .
. .

(*a*) in accordance with the provisions of sub-paragraph (*a*) of the first paragraph of article 5 of the Convention*.
(*b*) in accordance with the following particular method (sub-paragraph (*b*) of the first paragraph of article 5)*:
 .
 .
 .
(*c*) by delivery to the addressee, if he accepts it voluntarily (second paragraph of article 5)*.

The authority is requested to return or to have returned to the applicant a copy of the documents—and of the annexes*—with a certificate as provided on the reverse side.
List of documents

. .
. .
. .
. .
. .
. .
. .
Done at . ,
the .
. .
. .
Signature and/or stamp.
* Delete if inappropriate.

Reverse of the request
CERTIFICATE

The undersigned authority has the honour to certify, in conformity with article 6 of the Convention,

1) that the document has been served *
— the (date) .
— at (place, street, number) .
. .
— in one of the following methods authorised by article 5—
(*a*) in accordance with the provisions of sub-paragraph (*a*) of the first paragraph of article 5 of the Convention*.
 (*b*) in accordance with the following particular method *: .
. .
 (*c*) by delivery to the addressee, who accepted it voluntarily*.
The documents referred to in the request have been delivered to:
—(identity and description of person) .
. .
—relationship to the addressee (family, business or other) .
. .

2) that the document has not been served, by reason of the following facts*:
 .
 .
 .

In conformity with the second paragraph of article 12 of the Convention, the applicant is requested to pay or reimburse the expenses detailed in the attached statement *.
Annexes

Documents returned:
. .
. .
In appropriate cases, documents establishing the service:
. .
. .
. Signature and/or stamp.
*Delete if inappropriate.

SUMMARY OF THE DOCUMENT TO BE SERVED

Convention on the service abroad of judicial and extrajudicial documents in civil or commercial matters, signed at The Hague, the 15th of November 1965.

(article 5, fourth paragraph)

Name and address of the requesting authori-
ty:. .

. .

. .

Particulars of the parties*:
. .

. .

. .

JUDICIAL DOCUMENT **

Nature and purpose of the document:
. .

. .

Nature and purpose of the proceedings and, where appropri-
ate, the amount in dispute: .

Date and place for entering appearance**:
. .

. .

Court which has given judgment **:
. .

. .

Date of judgment **: .

Time limits stated in the document **:
. .

. .

EXTRAJUDICIAL DOCUMENT **

Nature and purpose of the document:
. .

. .

Time limits stated in the document **:
. .

. .

. .

* If appropriate, identity and address of the person interested in
the transmission of the document.

** Delete if inappropriate.

Convention on the service abroad of judicial and extrajudi-
cial documents in civil or commercial matters. Done at The
Hague November 15, 1965; entered into force for the United
States February 10, 1969. 20 UST 361; TIAS 6638; 658
UNTS 163.

Notes and Annotations to the Convention

Litigants wishing to serve a person in one of the Conven-
tion countries should request copies in duplicate of the three
forms prescribed by the Convention: the "Request", the
"Certificate" and the "Summary." These forms may be
obtained from the offices of the United States Marshals.
Upon completion of these forms, the litigants must then
transmit them, together with the documents to be served—
all in duplicate—to the local process server.

The local process server thereupon mails all these docu-
ments to the "Central Authority" abroad. After service has
been effected, one copy of the documents served and an
executed "Certificate" all be returned to the local process
server, who will transmit these documents to the litigant who
initiated the request.

—— **Annotations**

"The Effect of the Hague Convention on Service Abroad of
Judicial and Extrajudicial Documents in Civil or Commercial
Matters", 2 Cornell Int'l L.J. 125 (1969).

Julen v. Larson, 25 Cal.App.3d 325, 101 Cal. 796 (1972).

Shoei Kako Co., Ltd. v. Superior Court, 33 Cal.App.3d 808,
109 Cal. 402 (1973).

Rule 4.1. Service of Other Process

(a) Generally. Process other than a summons as
provided in Rule 4 or subpoena as provided in Rule 45
shall be served by a United States marshal, a deputy
United States marshal, or a person specially appointed
for that purpose, who shall make proof of service as
provided in Rule 4(l). The process may be served
anywhere within the territorial limits of the state in
which the district court is located, and, when author-
ized by a statute of the United States, beyond the
territorial limits of that state.

**(b) Enforcement of Orders: Commitment for
Civil Contempt.** An order of civil commitment of a
person held to be in contempt of a decree or injunc-
tion issued to enforce the laws of the United States
may be served and enforced in any district. Other
orders in civil contempt proceedings shall be served in
the state in which the court issuing the order to be
enforced is located or elsewhere within the United
States if not more than 100 miles from the place at
which the order to be enforced was issued.

(Added Apr. 22, 1993, eff. Dec. 1, 1993.)

Proposed Amendment of Rule

*Effective December 1, 2007, absent contrary Con-
gressional action, this rule is amended to read as
follows:*

Rule 4.1. Serving Other Process

*(a) In General. Process—other than a summons
under Rule 4 or a subpoena under Rule 45—must be
served by a United States marshal or deputy marshal
or by a person specially appointed for that purpose. It
may be served anywhere within the territorial limits
of the state where the district court is located and, if
authorized by a federal statute, beyond those limits.
Proof of service must be made under Rule 4(l).*

*(b) Enforcing Orders: Committing for Civil Con-
tempt. An order committing a person for civil con-
tempt of a decree or injunction issued to enforce
federal law may be served and enforced in any dis-
trict. Any other order in a civil-contempt proceeding
may be served only in the state where the issuing
court is located or elsewhere in the United States
within 100 miles from where the order was issued.*

Complete Annotation Materials, see Title 28 U.S.C.A.

1993 Adoption

This is a new rule. Its purpose is to separate those few provisions of the former Rule 4 bearing on matters other than service of a summons to allow greater textual clarity in Rule 4. Subdivision (a) contains no new language.

Subdivision (b) replaces the final clause of the penultimate sentence of the former subdivision 4(f), a clause added to the rule in 1963. The new rule provides for nationwide service of orders of civil commitment enforcing decrees of injunctions issued to compel compliance with federal law. The rule makes no change in the practice with respect to the enforcement of injunctions or decrees not involving the enforcement of federally-created rights.

Service of process is not required to notify a party of a decree or injunction, or of an order that the party show cause why that party should not be held in contempt of such an order. With respect to a party who has once been served with a summons, the service of the decree or injunction itself or of an order to show cause can be made pursuant to Rule 5. Thus, for example, an injunction may be served on a party through that person's attorney. *Chagas v. United States,* 369 F.2d 643 (5th Cir.1966). The same is true for service of an order to show cause. *Waffenschmidt v. Mackay,* 763 F.2d 711 (5th Cir.1985).

The new rule does not affect the reach of the court to impose criminal contempt sanctions. Nationwide enforcement of federal decrees and injunctions is already available with respect to criminal contempt: a federal court may effect the arrest of a criminal contemnor anywhere in the United States, 28 U.S.C. § 3041, and a contemnor when arrested may be subject to removal to the district in which punishment may be imposed. Fed.R.Crim.P. 40. Thus, the present law permits criminal contempt enforcement against a contemnor wherever that person may be found.

The effect of the revision is to provide a choice of civil or criminal contempt sanctions in those situations to which it applies. Contempt proceedings, whether civil or criminal, must be brought in the court that was allegedly defied by a contumacious act. *Ex parte Bradley,* 74 U.S. 366 (1869). This is so even if the offensive conduct or inaction occurred outside the district of the court in which the enforcement proceeding must be conducted. *E.g., McCourtney v. United States,* 291 Fed. 497 (8th Cir.), *cert. denied,* 263 U.S. 714 (1923). For this purpose, the rule as before does not distinguish between parties and other persons subject to contempt sanctions by reason of their relation or connection to parties.

2007 Amendment

*[Effective December 1, 2007,
absent contrary Congressional action.]*

The language of Rule 4.1 has been amended as part of the general restyling of the Civil Rules to make them more easily understood and to make style and terminology consistent throughout the rules. These changes are intended to be stylistic only.

Rule 5. Service and Filing of Pleadings and Other Papers

(a) Service: When required. Except as otherwise provided in these rules, every order required by its terms to be served, every pleading subsequent to the original complaint unless the court otherwise orders because of numerous defendants, every paper relating to discovery required to be served upon a party unless the court otherwise orders, every written motion other than one which may be heard ex parte, and every written notice, appearance, demand, offer of judgment, designation of record on appeal, and similar paper shall be served upon each of the parties. No service need be made on parties in default for failure to appear except that pleadings asserting new or additional claims for relief against them shall be served upon them in the manner provided for service of summons in Rule 4.

In an action begun by seizure of property, in which no person need be or is named as defendant, any service required to be made prior to the filing of an answer, claim, or appearance shall be made upon the person having custody or possession of the property at the time of its seizure.

(b) Making Service.

(1) Service under Rules 5(a) and 77(d) on a party represented by an attorney is made on the attorney unless the court orders service on the party.

(2) Service under Rule 5(a) is made by:

(A) Delivering a copy to the person served by:
(i) handing it to the person;
(ii) leaving it at the person's office with a clerk or other person in charge, or if no one is in charge leaving it in a conspicuous place in the office; or
(iii) if the person has no office or the office is closed, leaving it at the person's dwelling house or usual place of abode with someone of suitable age and discretion residing there.

(B) Mailing a copy to the last known address of the person served. Service by mail is complete on mailing.

(C) If the person served has no known address, leaving a copy with the clerk of the court.

(D) Delivering a copy by any other means, including electronic means, consented to in writing by the person served. Service by electronic means is complete on transmission; service by other consented means is complete when the person making service delivers the copy to the agency designated to make delivery. If authorized by local rule, a party may make service under this subparagraph (D) through the court's transmission facilities.

(3) Service by electronic means under Rule 5(b)(2)(D) is not effective if the party making service learns that the attempted service did not reach the person to be served.

(c) Same: Numerous Defendants. In any action in which there are unusually large numbers of defendants, the court, upon motion or of its own initiative, may order that service of the pleadings of the defendants and replies thereto need not be made as between the defendants and that any cross-claim, counterclaim, or matter constituting an avoidance or affirmative defense contained therein shall be deemed to be denied or avoided by all other parties and that the filing of any such pleading and service thereof upon the plaintiff constitutes due notice of it to the parties. A copy of every such order shall be served upon the parties in such manner and form as the court directs.

(d) Filing; Certificate of Service. All papers after the complaint required to be served upon a party, together with a certificate of service, must be filed with the court within a reasonable time after service, but disclosures under Rule 26(a)(1) or (2) and the following discovery requests and responses must not be filed until they are used in the proceeding or the court orders filing: (i) depositions, (ii) interrogatories, (iii) requests for documents or to permit entry upon land, and (iv) requests for admission.

(e) Filing with the Court Defined. The filing of papers with the court as required by these rules shall be made by filing them with the clerk of court, except that the judge may permit the papers to be filed with the judge, in which event the judge shall note thereon the filing date and forthwith transmit them to the office of the clerk. A court may by local rule permit or require papers to be filed, signed, or verified by electronic means that are consistent with technical standards, if any, that the Judicial Conference of the United States establishes. A local rule may require filing by electronic means only if reasonable exceptions are allowed. A paper filed by electronic means in compliance with a local rule constitutes a written paper for the purpose of applying these rules. The clerk shall not refuse to accept for filing any paper presented for that purpose solely because it is not presented in proper form as required by these rules or any local rules or practices.

(As amended Jan. 21, 1963, eff. July 1, 1963; Mar. 30, 1970, eff. July 1, 1970; Apr. 29, 1980, eff. Aug. 1, 1980; Mar. 2, 1987, eff. Aug. 1, 1987; Apr. 30, 1991, eff. Dec. 1, 1991; Apr. 22, 1993, eff. Dec. 1, 1993; Apr. 23, 1996, eff. Dec. 1, 1996; Apr. 17, 2000, eff. Dec. 1, 2000; Apr. 23, 2001, eff. Dec. 1, 2001; Apr. 12, 2006, eff. Dec. 1, 2006.)

Proposed Amendment of Rule

Effective December 1, 2007, absent contrary Congressional action, this rule is amended to read as follows:

Rule 5. Serving and Filing Pleadings and Other Papers

(a) Service: When Required.

(1) In General. Unless these rules provide otherwise, each of the following papers must be served on every party:

(A) an order stating that service is required;

(B) a pleading filed after the original complaint, unless the court orders otherwise under Rule 5(c) because there are numerous defendants;

(C) a discovery paper required to be served on a party, unless the court orders otherwise;

(D) a written motion, except one that may be heard ex parte; and

(E) a written notice, appearance, demand, or offer of judgment, or any similar paper.

(2) If a Party Fails to Appear. No service is required on a party who is in default for failing to appear. But a pleading that asserts a new claim for relief against such a party must be served on that party under Rule 4.

(3) Seizing Property. If an action is begun by seizing property and no person is or need be named as a defendant, any service required before the filing of an appearance, answer, or claim must be made on the person who had custody or possession of the property when it was seized.

(b) Service: How Made.

(1) Serving an Attorney. If a party is represented by an attorney, service under this rule must be made on the attorney unless the court orders service on the party.

(2) Service in General. A paper is served under this rule by:

(A) handing it to the person;

(B) leaving it:

(i) at the person's office with a clerk or other person in charge or, if no one is in charge, in a conspicuous place in the office; or

(ii) if the person has no office or the office is closed, at the person's dwelling or usual place of abode with someone of suitable age and discretion who resides there;

(C) mailing it to the person's last known address—in which event service is complete upon mailing;

(D) leaving it with the court clerk if the person has no known address;

(E) sending it by electronic means if the person consented in writing—in which event service is complete upon transmission, but is

not effective if the serving party learns that it did not reach the person to be served; or

(F) delivering it by any other means that the person consented to in writing—in which event service is complete when the person making service delivers it to the agency designated to make delivery.

(3) Using Court Facilities. If a local rule so authorizes, a party may use the court's transmission facilities to make service under Rule 5(b)(2)(E).

(c) Serving Numerous Defendants.

(1) In General. If an action involves an unusually large number of defendants, the court may, on motion or on its own, order that:

(A) defendants' pleadings and replies to them need not be served on other defendants;

(B) any crossclaim, counterclaim, avoidance, or affirmative defense in those pleadings and replies to them will be treated as denied or avoided by all other parties; and

(C) filing any such pleading and serving it on the plaintiff constitutes notice of the pleading to all parties.

(2) Notifying Parties. A copy of every such order must be served on the parties as the court directs.

(d) Filing.

(1) Required Filings; Certificate of Service. Any paper after the complaint that is required to be served—together with a certificate of service—must be filed within a reasonable time after service. But disclosures under Rule 26(a)(1) or (2) and the following discovery requests and responses must not be filed until they are used in the proceeding or the court orders filing: depositions, interrogatories, requests for documents or tangible things or to permit entry onto land, and requests for admission.

(2) How Filing Is Made—In General. A paper is filed by delivering it:

(A) to the clerk; or

(B) to a judge who agrees to accept it for filing, and who must then note the filing date on the paper and promptly send it to the clerk.

(3) Electronic Filing, Signing, or Verification. A court may, by local rule, allow papers to be filed, signed, or verified by electronic means that are consistent with any technical standards established by the Judicial Conference of the United States. A local rule may require electronic filing only if reasonable exceptions are allowed.

A paper filed electronically in compliance with a local rule is a written paper for purposes of these rules.

(4) Acceptance by the Clerk. The clerk must not refuse to file a paper solely because it is not in the form prescribed by these rules or by a local rule or practice.

ADVISORY COMMITTEE NOTES
1937 Adoption

Note to Subdivisions (a) and (b). Compare 2 Minn.Stat. (1927) §§ 9240, 9241, 9242; N.Y.C.P.A. (1937) §§ 163, 164 and N.Y.R.C.P. (1937) Rules 20, 21; 2 Wash.Rev.Stat.Ann. (Remington, 1932) §§ 244 to 249.

Note to Subdivision (d). Compare the present practice under former Equity Rule 12 (Issue of Subpoena—Time for Answer).

1963 Amendment

The words "affected thereby," stricken out by the amendment, introduced a problem of interpretation. See 1 Barron & Holtzoff, *Federal Practice & Procedure* 760–61 (Wright ed. 1960). The amendment eliminates this difficulty and promotes full exchange of information among the parties by requiring service of papers on all the parties to the action, except as otherwise provided in the rules. See also subdivision (c) of Rule 5. So, for example, a third-party defendant is required to serve his answer to the third-party complaint not only upon the defendant but also upon the plaintiff. See amended Form 22–A and the Advisory Committee's Note thereto.

As to the method of serving papers upon a party whose address is unknown, see Rule 5(b).

1970 Amendment

The amendment makes clear that all papers relating to discovery which are required to be served on any party must be served on all parties, unless the court orders otherwise. The present language expressly includes notices and demands, but it is not explicit as to answers or responses as provided in Rules 33, 34, and 36. Discovery papers may be voluminous or the parties numerous, and the court is empowered to vary the requirement if in a given case it proves needlessly onerous.

In actions begun by seizure of property, service will at times have to be made before the absent owner of the property has filed an appearance. For example, a prompt deposition may be needed in a maritime action in rem. See Rules 30(a) and 30(b)(2) and the related notes. A provision is added authorizing service on the person having custody or possession of the property at the time of its seizure.

1980 Amendment

Subdivision (d). By the terms of this rule and Rule 30(f)(1) discovery materials must be promptly filed, although it often happens that no use is made of the materials after they are filed. Because the copies required for filing are an added expense and the large volume of discovery filings presents serious problems of storage in some districts, the

Committee in 1978 first proposed that discovery materials not be filed unless on order of the court or for use in the proceedings. But such materials are sometimes of interest to those who may have no access to them except by a requirement of filing, such as members of a class, litigants similarly situated, or the public generally. Accordingly, this amendment and a change in Rule 30(f)(1) continue the requirement of filing but make it subject to an order of the court that discovery materials not be filed unless filing is requested by the court or is effected by parties who wish to use the materials in the proceeding.

1987 Amendment

The amendments are technical. No substantive change is intended.

1991 Amendment

Subdivision (d). This subdivision is amended to require that the person making service under the rule certify that service has been effected. Such a requirement has generally been imposed by local rule.

Having such information on file may be useful for many purposes, including proof of service if an issue arises concerning the effectiveness of the service. The certificate will generally specify the date as well as the manner of service, but parties employing private delivery services may sometimes be unable to specify the date of delivery. In the latter circumstance, a specification of the date of transmission of the paper to the delivery service may be sufficient for the purposes of this rule.

Subdivision (e). The words *"pleading and other"* are stricken as unnecessary. Pleadings are papers within the meaning of the rule. The revision also accommodates the development of the use of facsimile transmission for filing.

Several local district rules have directed the office of the clerk to refuse to accept for filing papers not conforming to certain requirements of form imposed by local rules or practice. This is not a suitable role for the office of the clerk, and the practice exposes litigants to the hazards of time bars; for these reasons, such rules are proscribed by this revision. The enforcement of these rules and of the local rules is a role for a judicial officer. A clerk may of course advise a party or counsel that a particular instrument is not in proper form, and may be directed to so inform the court.

1993 Amendments

This is a technical amendment, using the broader language of Rule 25 of the Federal Rules of Appellate Procedure. The district court—and the bankruptcy court by virtue of a cross-reference in Bankruptcy Rule 7005—can, by local rule, permit filing not only by facsimile transmissions but also by other electronic means, subject to standards approved by the Judicial Conference.

1996 Amendments

The present Rule 5(e) has authorized filing by facsimile or other electronic means on two conditions. The filing must be authorized by local rule. Use of this means of filing must be authorized by the Judicial Conference of the United States and must be consistent with standards established by the Judicial Conference. Attempts to develop Judicial Confer-

ence standards have demonstrated the value of several adjustments in the rule.

The most significant change discards the requirement that the Judicial Conference authorize local electronic filing rules. As before, each district may decide for itself whether it has the equipment and personnel required to establish electronic filing, but a district that wishes to establish electronic filing need no longer await Judicial Conference action.

The role of Judicial Conference standards is clarified by specifying that the standards are to govern technical matters. Technical standards can provide nationwide uniformity, enabling ready use of electronic filing without pausing to adjust for the otherwise inevitable variations among local rules. Judicial Conference adoption of technical standards should prove superior to specification in these rules. Electronic technology has advanced with great speed. The process of adopting Judicial Conference standards should prove speedier and more flexible in determining the time for the first uniform standards, in adjusting standards at appropriate intervals, and in sparing the Supreme Court and Congress the need to consider technological details. Until Judicial Conference standards are adopted, however, uniformity will occur only to the extent that local rules deliberately seek to copy other local rules.

It is anticipated that Judicial Conference standards will govern such technical specifications as data formatting, speed of transmission, means to transmit copies of supporting documents, and security of communication. Perhaps more important, standards must be established to assure proper maintenance and integrity of the record and to provide appropriate access and retrieval mechanisms. Local rules must address these issues until Judicial Conference standards are adopted.

The amended rule also makes clear the equality of filing by electronic means with written filings. An electronic filing that complies with the local rule satisfies all requirements for filing on paper, signature, or verification. An electronic filing that otherwise satisfies the requirements of 28 U.S.C. § 1746 need not be separately made in writing. Public access to electronic filings is governed by the same rules as govern written filings.

The separate reference to filing by facsimile transmission is deleted. Facsimile transmission continues to be included as an electronic means.

2000 Amendment

Subdivision (d). Rule 5(d) is amended to provide that disclosures under Rule 26(a)(1) and (2), and discovery requests and responses under Rules 30, 31, 33, 34, and 36 must not be filed until they are used in the action. "Discovery requests" includes deposition notices and "discovery responses" includes objections. The rule supersedes and invalidates local rules that forbid, permit, or require filing of these materials before they are used in the action. The former Rule 26(a)(4) requirement that disclosures under Rule 26(a)(1) and (2) be filed has been removed. Disclosures under Rule 26(a)(3), however, must be promptly filed as provided in Rule 26(a)(3). Filings in connection with Rule 35 examinations, which involve a motion proceeding when the parties do not agree, are unaffected by these amendments.

Recognizing the costs imposed on parties and courts by required filing of discovery materials that are never used in

an action, Rule 5(d) was amended in 1980 to authorize court orders that excuse filing. Since then, many districts have adopted local rules that excuse or forbid filing. In 1989 the Judicial Conference Local Rules Project concluded that these local rules were inconsistent with Rule 5(d), but urged the Advisory Committee to consider amending the rule. *Local Rules Project* at 92 (1989). The Judicial Conference of the Ninth Circuit gave the Committee similar advice in 1997. The reality of nonfiling reflected in these local rules has even been assumed in drafting the national rules. In 1993, Rule 30(f)(1) was amended to direct that the officer presiding at a deposition file it with the court or send it to the attorney who arranged for the transcript or recording. The Committee Note explained that this alternative to filing was designed for "courts which direct that depositions not be automatically filed." Rule 30(f)(1) has been amended to conform to this change in Rule 5(d).

Although this amendment is based on widespread experience with local rules, and confirms the results directed by these local rules, it is designed to supersede and invalidate local rules. There is no apparent reason to have different filing rules in different districts. Even if districts vary in present capacities to store filed materials that are not used in an action, there is little reason to continue expending court resources for this purpose. These costs and burdens would likely change as parties make increased use of audio- and videotaped depositions. Equipment to facilitate review and reproduction of such discovery materials may prove costly to acquire, maintain, and operate.

The amended rule provides that discovery materials and disclosures under Rule 26(a)(1) and (a)(2) must not be filed until they are "used in the proceeding." This phrase is meant to refer to proceedings in court. This filing requirement is not triggered by "use" of discovery materials in other discovery activities, such as depositions. In connection with proceedings in court, however, the rule is to be interpreted broadly; any use of discovery materials in court in connection with a motion, a pretrial conference under Rule 16, or otherwise, should be interpreted as use in the proceeding.

Once discovery or disclosure materials are used in the proceeding, the filing requirements of Rule 5(d) should apply to them. But because the filing requirement applies only with regard to materials that are used, only those parts of voluminous materials that are actually used need be filed. Any party would be free to file other pertinent portions of materials that are so used. *See* Fed. R. Evid. 106; *cf.* Rule 32(a)(4). If the parties are unduly sparing in their submissions, the court may order further filings. By local rule, a court could provide appropriate direction regarding the filing of discovery materials, such as depositions, that are used in proceedings.

"Shall" is replaced by "must" under the program to conform amended rules to current style conventions when there is no ambiguity.

GAP Report

The Advisory Committee recommends no changes to either the amendments to Rule 5(d) or the Committee Note as published.

2001 Amendments

Rule 5(b) is restyled.

Rule 5(b)(1) makes it clear that the provision for service on a party's attorney applies only to service made under Rules 5(a) and 77(d). Service under Rules 4, 4.1, 45(b), and 71A(d)(3)—as well as rules that invoke those rules—must be made as provided in those rules.

Subparagraphs (A), (B), and (C) of Rule 5(b)(2) carry forward the method-of-service provisions of former Rule 5(b).

Subparagraph (D) of Rule 5(b)(2) is new. It authorizes service by electronic means or any other means, but only if consent is obtained from the person served. The consent must be express, and cannot be implied from conduct. Early experience with electronic filing as authorized by Rule 5(d) is positive, supporting service by electronic means as well. Consent is required, however, because it is not yet possible to assume universal entry into the world of electronic communication. Subparagraph (D) also authorizes service by nonelectronic means. The Rule 5(b)(2)(B) provision making mail service complete on mailing is extended in subparagraph (D) to make service by electronic means complete on transmission; transmission is effected when the sender does the last act that must be performed by the sender. Service by other agencies is complete on delivery to the designated agency.

Finally, subparagraph (D) authorizes adoption of local rules providing for service through the court. Electronic case filing systems will come to include the capacity to make service by using the court's facilities to transmit all documents filed in the case. It may prove most efficient to establish an environment in which a party can file with the court, making use of the court's transmission facilities to serve the filed paper on all other parties. Transmission might be by such means as direct transmission of the paper, or by transmission of a notice of filing that includes an electronic link for direct access to the paper. Because service is under subparagraph (D), consent must be obtained from the persons served.

Consent to service under Rule 5(b)(2)(D) must be in writing, which can be provided by electronic means. Parties are encouraged to specify the scope and duration of the consent. The specification should include at least the persons to whom service should be made, the appropriate address or location for such service—such as the e-mail address or facsimile machine number, and the format to be used for attachments. A district court may establish a registry or other facility that allows advance consent to service by specified means for future actions.

Rule 6(e) is amended to allow additional time to respond when service is made under Rule 5(b)(2)(D). The additional time does not relieve a party who consents to service under Rule 5(b)(2)(D) of the responsibilities to monitor the facility designated for receiving service and to provide prompt notice of any address change.

Paragraph (3) addresses a question that may arise from a literal reading of the provision that service by electronic means is complete on transmission. Electronic communication is rapidly improving, but lawyers report continuing failures of transmission, particularly with respect to attachments. Ordinarily the risk of non-receipt falls on the person being served, who has consented to this form of service. But the risk should not extend to situations in which the person attempting service learns that the attempted service in fact did not reach the person to be served. Given actual knowledge that the attempt failed, service is not effected. The

person attempting service must either try again or show circumstances that justify dispensing with service.

Paragraph (3) does not address the similar questions that may arise when a person attempting service learns that service by means other than electronic means in fact did not reach the person to be served. Case law provides few illustrations of circumstances in which a person attempting service actually knows that the attempt failed but seeks to act as if service had been made. This negative history suggests there is no need to address these problems in Rule 5(b)(3). This silence does not imply any view on these issues, nor on the circumstances that justify various forms of judicial action even though service has not been made.

Changes Made After Publication and Comments

Rule 5(b)(2)(D) was changed to require that consent be "in writing."

Rule 5(b)(3) is new. The published proposal did not address the question of failed service in the text of the rule. Instead, the Committee Note included this statement: "As with other modes of service, however, actual notice that the transmission was not received defeats the presumption of receipt that arises from the provision that service is complete on transmission. The sender must take additional steps to effect service. Service by other agencies is complete on delivery to the designated agency." The addition of paragraph (3) was prompted by consideration of the draft Appellate Rule 25(c) that was prepared for the meeting of the Appellate Rules Advisory Committee. This draft provided: "Service by electronic means is complete on transmission, unless the party making service is notified that the paper was not received." Although Appellate Rule 25(c) is being prepared for publication and comment, while Civil Rule 5(b) has been published and otherwise is ready to recommend for adoption, it seemed desirable to achieve some parallel between the two rules.

The draft Rule 5(b)(3) submitted for consideration by the Advisory Committee covered all means of service except for leaving a copy with the clerk of the court when the person to be served has no known address. It was not limited to electronic service for fear that a provision limited to electronic service might generate unintended negative implications as to service by other means, particularly mail. This concern was strengthened by a small number of opinions that say that service by mail is effective, because complete on mailing, even when the person making service has prompt actual notice that the mail was not delivered. The Advisory Committee voted to limit Rule 5(b)(3) to service by electronic means because this means of service is relatively new, and seems likely to miscarry more frequently than service by post. It was suggested during the Advisory Committee meeting that the question of negative implication could be addressed in the Committee Note. There was little discussion of this possibility. The Committee Note submitted above includes a "no negative implications" paragraph prepared by the Reporter for consideration by the Standing Committee.

The Advisory Committee did not consider at all a question that was framed during the later meeting of the Appellate Rules Advisory Committee. As approved by the Advisory Committee, Rule 5(b)(3) defeats service by electronic means "if the party making service learns that the attempted service did not reach the person to be served." It says nothing about the time relevant to learning of the failure. The omission may seem glaring. Curing the omission, however,

requires selection of a time. As revised, proposed Appellate Rule 25(c) requires that the party making service learn of the failure within three calendar days. The Appellate Rules Advisory Committee will have the luxury of public comment and another year to consider the desirability of this short period. If Civil Rule 5(b) is to be recommended for adoption now, no such luxury is available. This issue deserves careful consideration by the Standing Committee.

Several changes are made in the Committee Note. (1) It requires that consent "be express, and cannot be implied from conduct." This addition reflects a more general concern stimulated by a reported ruling that an e-mail address on a firm's letterhead implied consent to e-mail service. (2) The paragraph discussing service through the court's facilities is expanded by describing alternative methods, including an "electronic link." (3) There is a new paragraph that states that the requirement of written consent can be satisfied by electronic means, and that suggests matters that should be addressed by the consent. (4) A paragraph is added to note the additional response time provided by amended Rule 6(e). (5) The final two paragraphs address newly added Rule 5(b)(3). The first explains the rule that electronic service is not effective if the person making service learns that it did not reach the person to be served. The second paragraph seeks to defeat any negative implications that might arise from limiting Rule 5(b)(3) to electronic service, not mail, not other means consented to such as commercial express service, and not service on another person on behalf of the person to be served.

Rule 6(e)

The Advisory Committee recommended that no change be made in Civil Rule 6(e) to reflect the provisions of Civil Rule 5(b)(2)(D) that, with the consent of the person to be served, would allow service by electronic or other means. Absent change, service by these means would not affect the time for acting in response to the paper served. Comment was requested, however, on the alternative that would allow an additional 3 days to respond. The alternative Rule 6(e) amendments are cast in a form that permits ready incorporation in the Bankruptcy Rules. Several of the comments suggest that the added three days should be provided. Electronic transmission is not always instantaneous, and may fail for any of a number of reasons. It may take three days to arrange for transmission in readable form. Providing added time to respond will not discourage people from asking for consent to electronic transmission, and may encourage people to give consent. The more who consent, the quicker will come the improvements that will make electronic service ever more attractive. Consistency with the Bankruptcy Rules will be a good thing, and the Bankruptcy Rules Advisory Committee believes the additional three days should be allowed.

2006 Amendment

Amended Rule 5(e) acknowledges that many courts have required electronic filing by means of a standing order, procedures manual, or local rule. These local practices reflect the advantages that courts and most litigants realize from electronic filing. Courts that mandate electronic filing recognize the need to make exceptions when requiring electronic filing imposes a hardship on a party. Under amended Rule 5(e), a local rule that requires electronic filing must

include reasonable exceptions, but Rule 5(e) does not define the scope of those exceptions. Experience with the local rules that have been adopted and that will emerge will aid in drafting new local rules and will facilitate gradual convergence on uniform exceptions, whether in local rules or in an amended Rule 5(e).

2007 Amendment

*[Effective December 1, 2007,
absent contrary Congressional action.]*

The language of Rule 5 has been amended as part of the general restyling of the Civil Rules to make them more easily understood and to make style and terminology consistent throughout the rules. These changes are intended to be stylistic only.

Rule 5(a)(1)(E) omits the former reference to a designation of record on appeal. Appellate Rule 10 is a self-contained provision for the record on appeal, and provides for service.

Former Rule 5(b)(2)(D) literally provided that a local rule may authorize use of the court's transmission facilities to make service by non-electronic means agreed to by the parties. That was not intended. Rule 5(b)(3) restores the intended meaning—court transmission facilities can be used only for service by electronic means.

Rule 5(d)(2)(B) provides that "a" judge may accept a paper for filing, replacing the reference in former Rule 5(e) to "the" judge. Some courts do not assign a designated judge to each case, and it may be important to have another judge accept a paper for filing even when a case is on the individual docket of a particular judge. The ministerial acts of accepting the paper, noting the time, and transmitting the paper to the court clerk do not interfere with the assigned judge's authority over the action.

Rule 5.1. Constitutional Challenge to a Statute—Notice, Certification, and Intervention

(a) Notice by a Party. A party that files a pleading, written motion, or other paper drawing into question the constitutionality of a federal or state statute must promptly:

(1) file a notice of constitutional question stating the question and identifying the paper that raises it, if:

(A) a federal statute is questioned and neither the United States nor any of its agencies, officers, or employees is a party in an official capacity, or

(B) a state statute is questioned and neither the state nor any of its agencies, officers, or employees is a party in an official capacity; and

(2) serve the notice and paper on the Attorney General of the United States if a federal statute is challenged — or on the state attorney general if a state statute is challenged — either by certified or registered mail or by sending it to an electronic address designated by the attorney general for this purpose.

(b) Certification by the Court. The court must, under 28 U.S.C. § 2403, certify to the Attorney General of the United States that there is a constitutional challenge to a federal statute, or certify to the state attorney general that there is a constitutional challenge to a state statute.

(c) Intervention; Final Decision on the Merits. Unless the court sets a later time, the attorney general may intervene within 60 days after the notice of constitutional question is filed or after the court certifies the challenge, whichever is earlier. Before the time to intervene expires, the court may reject the constitutional challenge, but may not enter a final judgment holding the statute unconstitutional.

(d) No Forfeiture. A party's failure to file and serve the notice, or the court's failure to certify, does not forfeit a constitutional claim or defense that is otherwise timely asserted.

(Added Apr. 12, 2006, eff. Dec. 1, 2006.)

Proposed Amendment of Rule

Effective December 1, 2007, absent contrary Congressional action, this rule is amended to read as follows:

Rule 5.1. Constitutional Challenge to a Statute— Notice, Certification, and Intervention

(a) Notice by a Party. A party that files a pleading, written motion, or other paper drawing into question the constitutionality of a federal or state statute must promptly:

(1) file a notice of constitutional question stating the question and identifying the paper that raises it, if:

(A) a federal statute is questioned and the parties do not include the United States, one of its agencies, or one of its officers or employees in an official capacity; or

(B) a state statute is questioned and the parties do not include the state, one of its agencies, or one of its officers or employees in an official capacity; and

(2) serve the notice and paper on the Attorney General of the United States if a federal statute is questioned—or on the state attorney general if a state statute is questioned—either by certified or registered mail or by sending it to an electronic address designated by the attorney general for this purpose.

(b) Certification by the Court. The court must, under 28 U.S.C. § 2403, certify to the appropriate attorney general that a statute has been questioned.

(c) Intervention; Final Decision on the Merits. Unless the court sets a later time, the attorney general may intervene within 60 days after the notice is

filed or after the court certifies the challenge, whichever is earlier. Before the time to intervene expires, the court may reject the constitutional challenge, but may not enter a final judgment holding the statute unconstitutional.

(d) No Forfeiture. *A party's failure to file and serve the notice, or the court's failure to certify, does not forfeit a constitutional claim or defense that is otherwise timely asserted.*

ADVISORY COMMITTEE NOTES

2006 Adoption

Rule 5.1 implements 28 U.S.C. § 2403, replacing the final three sentences of Rule 24(c). New Rule 5.1 requires a party that files a pleading, written motion, or other paper drawing in question the constitutionality of a federal or state statute to file a notice of constitutional question and serve it on the United States Attorney General or state attorney general. The party must promptly file and serve the notice of constitutional question. This notice requirement supplements the court's duty to certify a constitutional challenge to the United States Attorney General or state attorney general. The notice of constitutional question will ensure that the attorney general is notified of constitutional challenges and has an opportunity to exercise the statutory right to intervene at the earliest possible point in the litigation. The court's certification obligation remains, and is the only notice when the constitutionality of a federal or state statute is drawn in question by means other than a party's pleading, written motion, or other paper.

Moving the notice and certification provisions from Rule 24(c) to a new rule is designed to attract the parties' attention to these provisions by locating them in the vicinity of the rules that require notice by service and pleading.

Rule 5.1 goes beyond the requirements of § 2403 and the former Rule 24(c) provisions by requiring notice and certification of a constitutional challenge to any federal or state statute, not only those "affecting the public interest." It is better to assure, through notice, that the attorney general is able to determine whether to seek intervention on the ground that the act or statute affects a public interest. Rule 5.1 refers to a "federal statute," rather than the § 2403 reference to an "Act of Congress," to maintain consistency in the Civil Rules vocabulary. In Rule 5.1 "statute" means any congressional enactment that would qualify as an "Act of Congress."

Unless the court sets a later time, the 60–day period for intervention runs from the time a party files a notice of constitutional question or from the time the court certifies a constitutional challenge, whichever is earlier. Rule 5.1(a) directs that a party promptly serve the notice of constitutional question. The court may extend the 60–period [So in original. Probably should read "60-day period".] on its own or on motion. One occasion for extension may arise if the court certifies a challenge under § 2403 after a party files a notice of constitutional question. Pretrial activities may continue without interruption during the intervention period, and the court retains authority to grant interlocutory relief. The court may reject a constitutional challenge to a statute at any time. But the court may not enter a final judgment holding a statute unconstitutional before the attorney general

has responded or the intervention period has expired without response. This rule does not displace any of the statutory or rule procedures that permit dismissal of all or part of an action — including a constitutional challenge — at any time, even before service of process.

2007 Amendment

[Effective December 1, 2007, absent contrary Congressional action.]

The language of Rule 5.1 has been amended as part of the general restyling of the Civil Rules to make them more easily understood and to make style and terminology consistent throughout the rules. These changes are intended to be stylistic only.

Rule 5.2. Privacy Protection For Filings Made with the Court

(a) Redacted Filings. Unless the court orders otherwise, in an electronic or paper filing with the court that contains an individual's social-security number, taxpayer-identification number, or birth date, the name of an individual known to be a minor, or a financial-account number, a party or nonparty making the filing may include only:

(1) the last four digits of the social-security number and taxpayer-identification number;

(2) the year of the individual's birth;

(3) the minor's initials; and

(4) the last four digits of the financial-account number.

(b) Exemptions from the Redaction Requirement. The redaction requirement does not apply to the following:

(1) a financial-account number that identifies the property allegedly subject to forfeiture in a forfeiture proceeding;

(2) the record of an administrative or agency proceeding;

(3) the official record of a state-court proceeding;

(4) the record of a court or tribunal, if that record was not subject to the redaction requirement when originally filed;

(5) a filing covered by Rule 5.2(c) or (d); and

(6) a pro se filing in an action brought under 28 U.S.C. §§ 2241, 2254, or 2255.

(c) Limitations on Remote Access to Electronic Files; Social–Security Appeals and Immigration Cases. Unless the court orders otherwise, in an action for benefits under the Social Security Act, and in an action or proceeding relating to an order of removal, to relief from removal, or to immigration benefits or detention, access to an electronic file is authorized as follows:

(1) the parties and their attorneys may have remote electronic access to any part of the case file, including the administrative record;

(2) any other person may have electronic access to the full record at the courthouse, but may have remote electronic access only to:

(A) the docket maintained by the court; and

(B) an opinion, order, judgment, or other disposition of the court, but not any other part of the case file or the administrative record.

(d) Filings Made Under Seal. The court may order that a filing be made under seal without redaction. The court may later unseal the filing or order the person who made the filing to file a redacted version for the public record.

(e) Protective Orders. For good cause, the court may by order in a case:

(1) require redaction of additional information; or

(2) limit or prohibit a nonparty's remote electronic access to a document filed with the court.

(f) Option for Additional Unredacted Filing Under Seal. A person making a redacted filing may also file an unredacted copy under seal. The court must retain the unredacted copy as part of the record.

(g) Option for Filing a Reference List. A filing that contains redacted information may be filed together with a reference list that identifies each item of redacted information and specifies an appropriate identifier that uniquely corresponds to each item listed. The list must be filed under seal and may be amended as of right. Any reference in the case to a listed identifier will be construed to refer to the corresponding item of information.

(h) Waiver of Protection of Identifiers. A person waives the protection of Rule 5.2(a) as to the person's own information by filing it without redaction and not under seal.

(Added Apr. 30, 2007, eff. Dec. 1, 2007.)

Proposed Adoption of Rule

Effective December 1, 2007, absent contrary Congressional action, Rule 5.2 is adopted.

ADVISORY COMMITTEE NOTES
2007 Adoption

[Effective December 1, 2007, absent contrary Congressional action.]

The rule is adopted in compliance with section 205(c)(3) of the E–Government Act of 2002, Public Law 107–347. Section 205(c)(3) requires the Supreme Court to prescribe rules "to protect privacy and security concerns relating to electronic filing of documents and the public availability ... of documents filed electronically." The rule goes further than the E–Government Act in regulating paper filings even when they are not converted to electronic form. But the number of filings that remain in paper form is certain to diminish over

time. Most districts scan paper filings into the electronic case file, where they become available to the public in the same way as documents initially filed in electronic form. It is electronic availability, not the form of the initial filing, that raises the privacy and security concerns addressed in the E–Government Act.

The rule is derived from and implements the policy adopted by the Judicial Conference in September 2001 to address the privacy concerns resulting from public access to electronic case files. See http://www.privacy.uscourts.gov/Policy.htm. The Judicial Conference policy is that documents in case files generally should be made available electronically to the same extent they are available at the courthouse, provided that certain "personal data identifiers" are not included in the public file.

While providing for the public filing of some information, such as the last four digits of an account number, the rule does not intend to establish a presumption that this information never could or should be protected. For example, it may well be necessary in individual cases to prevent remote access by nonparties to any part of an account number or social security number. It may also be necessary to protect information not covered by the redaction requirement—such as driver's license numbers and alien registration numbers—in a particular case. In such cases, protection may be sought under subdivision (d) or (e). Moreover, the Rule does not affect the protection available under other rules, such as Civil Rules 16 and 26(c), or under other sources of protective authority.

Parties must remember that any personal information not otherwise protected by sealing or redaction will be made available over the internet. Counsel should notify clients of this fact so that an informed decision may be made on what information is to be included in a document filed with the court.

The clerk is not required to review documents filed with the court for compliance with this rule. The responsibility to redact filings rests with counsel and the party or non-party making the filing.

Subdivision (c) provides for limited public access in Social Security cases and immigration cases. Those actions are entitled to special treatment due to the prevalence of sensitive information and the volume of filings. Remote electronic access by nonparties is limited to the docket and the written dispositions of the court unless the court orders otherwise. The rule contemplates, however, that nonparties can obtain full access to the case file at the courthouse, including access through the court's public computer terminal.

Subdivision (d) reflects the interplay between redaction and filing under seal. It does not limit or expand the judicially developed rules that govern sealing. But it does reflect the possibility that redaction may provide an alternative to sealing.

Subdivision (e) provides that the court can by order in a particular case for good cause require more extensive redaction than otherwise required by the Rule. Nothing in this subdivision is intended to affect the limitations on sealing that are otherwise applicable to the court.

Subdivision (f) allows a person who makes a redacted filing to file an unredacted document under seal. This provision is derived from section 205(c)(3)(iv) of the E–Government Act.

Subdivision (g) allows the option to file a register of redacted information. This provision is derived from section 205(c)(3)(v) of the E–Government Act, as amended in 2004. In accordance with the E–Government Act, subdivision (g) refers to "redacted" information. The term "redacted" is intended to govern a filing that is prepared with abbreviated identifiers in the first instance, as well as a filing in which a personal identifier is edited after its preparation.

Subdivision (h) allows a person to waive the protections of the rule as to that person's own personal information by filing it unsealed and in unredacted form. One may wish to waive the protection if it is determined that the costs of redaction outweigh the benefits to privacy. If a person files an unredacted identifier by mistake, that person may seek relief from the court.

Trial exhibits are subject to the redaction requirements of Rule 5.2 to the extent they are filed with the court. Trial exhibits that are not initially filed with the court must be redacted in accordance with the rule if and when they are filed as part of an appeal or for other reasons.

Rule 6. Time

(a) Computation. In computing any period of time prescribed or allowed by these rules, by the local rules of any district court, by order of court, or by any applicable statute, the day of the act, event, or default from which the designated period of time begins to run shall not be included. The last day of the period so computed shall be included, unless it is a Saturday, a Sunday, or a legal holiday, or, when the act to be done is the filing of a paper in court, a day on which weather or other conditions have made the office of the clerk of the district court inaccessible, in which event the period runs until the end of the next day which is not one of the aforementioned days. When the period of time prescribed or allowed is less than 11 days, intermediate Saturdays, Sundays, and legal holidays shall be excluded in the computation. As used in this rule and in Rule 77(c), "legal holiday" includes New Year's Day, Birthday of Martin Luther King, Jr., Washington's Birthday, Memorial Day, Independence Day, Labor Day, Columbus Day, Veterans Day, Thanksgiving Day, Christmas Day, and any other day appointed as a holiday by the President or the Congress of the United States, or by the state in which the district court is held.

(b) Enlargement. When by these rules or by a notice given thereunder or by order of court an act is required or allowed to be done at or within a specified time, the court for cause shown may at any time in its discretion (1) with or without motion or notice order the period enlarged if request therefor is made before the expiration of the period originally prescribed or as extended by a previous order, or (2) upon motion made after the expiration of the specified period permit the act to be done where the failure to act was the result of excusable neglect; but it may not extend the time for taking any action under Rules 50(b) and

(c)(2), 52(b), 59(b), (d) and (e), and 60(b), except to the extent and under the conditions stated in them.

[(c) Rescinded Feb. 28, 1966, eff. July 1, 1966]

(d) For Motions—Affidavits. A written motion, other than one which may be heard ex parte, and notice of the hearing thereof shall be served not later than 5 days before the time specified for the hearing, unless a different period is fixed by these rules or by order of the court. Such an order may for cause shown be made on ex parte application. When a motion is supported by affidavit, the affidavit shall be served with the motion; and, except as otherwise provided in Rule 59(c), opposing affidavits may be served not later than 1 day before the hearing, unless the court permits them to be served at some other time.

(e) Additional Time After Certain Kinds of Service. Whenever a party must or may act within a prescribed period after service and service is made under Rule 5(b)(2)(B), (C), or (D), 3 days are added after the prescribed period would otherwise expire under subdivision (a).

(As amended Dec. 27, 1946, eff. Mar. 19, 1948; Jan. 21, 1963, eff. July 1, 1963; Feb. 28, 1966, eff. July 1, 1966; Dec. 4, 1967, eff. July 1, 1968; Mar. 1, 1971, eff. July 1, 1971; Apr. 28, 1983, eff. Aug. 1, 1983; Apr. 29, 1985, eff. Aug. 1, 1985; Mar. 2, 1987, eff. Aug. 1, 1987; Apr. 29, 1999, eff. Dec. 1, 1999; Apr. 23, 2001, eff. Dec. 1, 2001; Apr. 25, 2005, eff. Dec. 1, 2005.)

<div align="center">

Proposed Amendment of Rule

</div>

Effective December 1, 2007, absent contrary Congressional action, this rule is amended to read as follows:

Rule 6. Computing and Extending Time; Time for Motion Papers

(a) Computing Time. The following rules apply in computing any time period specified in these rules or in any local rule, court order, or statute:

(1) Day of the Event Excluded. Exclude the day of the act, event, or default that begins the period.

(2) Exclusions from Brief Periods. Exclude intermediate Saturdays, Sundays, and legal holidays when the period is less than 11 days.

(3) Last Day. Include the last day of the period unless it is a Saturday, Sunday, legal holiday, or—if the act to be done is filing a paper in court—a day on which weather or other conditions make the clerk's office inaccessible. When the last day is excluded, the period runs until the end of the next day that is not a Saturday, Sunday, legal holiday, or day when the clerk's office is inaccessible.

(4) "Legal Holiday" Defined. As used in these rules, "legal holiday" means:

(A) the day set aside by statute for observing New Year's Day, Martin Luther King Jr.'s Birthday, Washington's Birthday, Memorial Day, Independence Day, Labor Day, Columbus Day, Veterans' Day, Thanksgiving Day, or Christmas Day; and

(B) any other day declared a holiday by the President, Congress, or the state where the district court is located.

(b) Extending Time.

(1) In General. When an act may or must be done within a specified time, the court may, for good cause, extend the time:

(A) with or without motion or notice if the court acts, or if a request is made, before the original time or its extension expires; or

(B) on motion made after the time has expired if the party failed to act because of excusable neglect.

(2) Exceptions. A court must not extend the time to act under Rules 50(b) and (d), 52(b), 59(b), (d), and (e), and 60(b), except as those rules allow.

(c) Motions, Notices of Hearing, and Affidavits.

(1) In General. A written motion and notice of the hearing must be served at least 5 days before the time specified for the hearing, with the following exceptions:

(A) when the motion may be heard ex parte;

(B) when these rules set a different time; or

(C) when a court order—which a party may, for good cause, apply for ex parte—sets a different time.

(2) Supporting Affidavit. Any affidavit supporting a motion must be served with the motion. Except as Rule 59(c) provides otherwise, any opposing affidavit must be served at least 1 day before the hearing, unless the court permits service at another time.

(d) Additional Time After Certain Kinds of Service. *When a party may or must act within a specified time after service and service is made under Rule 5(b)(2)(C), (D), (E), or (F), 3 days are added after the period would otherwise expire under Rule 6(a).*

ADVISORY COMMITTEE NOTES

1937 Adoption

Note to Subdivisions (a) and (b). These are amplifications along lines common in state practices, of [former] Equity Rule 80 (Computation of Time—Sundays and Holi-

days) and of the provisions for enlargement of time found in [former] Equity Rules 8 (Enforcement of Final Decrees) and 16 (Defendant to Answer—Default—Decree Pro Confesso). See also Rule XIII, Rules and Forms in Criminal Cases, 1934, 292 U.S. 661, 666. Compare Ala.Code Ann. (Michie, 1928) § 13 and former Law Rule 8 of the Rules of the Supreme Court of the District of Columbia (1924), superseded in 1929 by Law Rule 8, Rules of the District Court of the United States for the District of Columbia (1937).

Note to Subdivision (c). This eliminates the difficulties caused by the expiration of terms of court. Such statutes as U.S.C., Title 28, [former] § 12 (Trials not discontinued by new term) are not affected. Compare Rules of the United States District Court of Minnesota, Rule 25 (Minn.Stat. (Mason, Supp.1936), p. 1089).

Note to Subdivision (d). Compare 2 Minn.Stat. (Mason, 1927) § 9246; N.Y.R.C.P. (1937) Rules 60 and 64.

1946 Amendment

Note to Subdivision (b). The purpose of the amendment is to clarify the finality of judgments. Prior to the advent of the Federal Rules of Civil Procedure, the general rule that a court loses jurisdiction to disturb its judgments, upon the expiration of the term at which they were entered, had long been the classic device which (together with the statutory limits on the time for appeal) gave finality to judgments. See note to rule 73(a). Rule 6(c) abrogates that limit on judicial power. That limit was open to many objections, one of them being inequality of operation because, under it, the time for vacating a judgment rendered early in a term was much longer than for a judgment rendered near the end of the term.

The question to be met under rule 6(b) is: how far should the desire to allow correction of judgments be allowed to postpone their finality? The rules contain a number of provisions permitting the vacation or modification of judgments on various grounds. Each of these rules contains express time limits on the motions for granting of relief. Rule 6(b) is a rule of general application giving wide discretion to the court to enlarge these time limits or revive them after they have expired, the only exceptions stated in the original rule being a prohibition against enlarging the time specified in Rule 59(b) and (d) for making motions for or granting new trials, and a prohibition against enlarging the time fixed by law for taking an appeal. It should also be noted that Rule 6(b) itself contains no limitation of time within which the court may exercise its discretion, and since the expiration of the term does not end its power, there is now no time limit on the exercise of its discretion under Rule 6(b).

Decisions of lower federal courts suggest that some of the rules containing time limits which may be set aside under Rule 6(b) are Rules 25, 50(b), 52(b), 60(b), and 73(g).

In a number of cases the effect of Rule 6(b) on the time limitations of these rules has been considered. Certainly the rule is susceptible of the interpretation that the court is given the power in its discretion to relieve a party from failure to act within the times specified in any of these other rules, with only the exceptions stated in Rule 6(b), and in some cases the rule has been so construed.

With regard to Rule 25(a) for substitution, it was held in *Anderson v. Brady*, Ky.1941, 1 F.R.D. 589, 4 Fed.Rules

Service 25a.1, Case 1, and in *Anderson v. Yungkau*, C.C.A.6, 1946, 153 F.2d 685, certiorari granted 66 S.Ct. 1025, 328 U.S. 829, 90 L.Ed. 1606, that under Rule 6(b) the court had no authority to allow substitution of parties after the expiration of the limit fixed in Rule 25(a).

As to Rules 50(b) for judgments notwithstanding the verdict and 52(b) for amendment of findings and vacation of judgment, it was recognized in *Leishman v. Associated Wholesale Electric Co.*, 1943, 63 S.Ct. 543, 318 U.S. 203, 87 L.Ed. 714, that Rule 6(b) allowed the district court to enlarge the time to make a motion for amended findings and judgment beyond the limit expressly fixed in Rule 52(b). See *Coca-Cola v. Busch*, E.D.Pa.1943, 7 Fed.Rules Service, 59b.2, Case 4. Obviously, if the time limit in Rule 52(b) could be set aside under Rule 6(b), the time limit in Rule 50(b) for granting judgment notwithstanding the verdict (and thus vacating the judgment entered "forthwith" on the verdict) likewise could be set aside.

As to Rule 59 on motions for a new trial, it has been settled that the time limits in Rule 59(b) and (d) for making motions for or granting new trial could not be set aside under Rule 6(b), because Rule 6(b) expressly refers to Rule 59, and forbids it. See *Safeway Stores, Inc. v. Coe*, App.D.C. 1943, 136 F.2d 771, 78 U.S.App.D.C. 19; *Jusino v. Morales & Tio*, C.C.A.1, 1944, 139 F.2d 946; *Coca-Cola Co. v. Busch*, E.D.Pa.1943, 7 Fed.Rules Service 59b.2, Case 4; *Peterson v. Chicago Great Western Ry. Co.*, D.Neb.1943, 3 F.R.D. 346, 7 Fed.Rules Service 59b.2, Case 1; *Leishman v. Associated Wholesale Electric Co.*, 1943, 63 S.Ct. 543, 318 U.S. 203, 87 L.Ed. 714.

As to Rule 60(b) for relief from a judgment, it was held in *Schram v. O'Connor*, Mich.1941, 5 Fed.Rules Serv. 6b.31, Case 1, 2 F.R.D. 192, s.c. 5 Fed.Rules Serv. 6b.31, Case 2, 2 F.R.D. 192, that the six-months time limit in original rule 60(b) for making a motion for relief from a judgment for surprise, mistake, or excusable neglect could be set aside under Rule 6(b). The contrary result was reached in *Wallace v. United States*, C.C.A.2, 1944, 142 F.2d 240, certiorari denied 65 S.Ct. 37, 323 U.S. 712, 89 L.Ed. 573; *Reed v. South Atlantic Steamship Co. of Del.*, Del.1942, 2 F.R.D. 475, 6 Fed.Rules Serv. 60b.31, Case 1.

As to Rule 73(g), fixing the time for docketing an appeal, it was held in *Ains-worth v. Gill Glass & Fixture Co.*, C.C.A.3, 1939, 104 F.2d 83, that under Rule 6(b) the district court, upon motion made after the expiration of the forty-day period, stated in Rule 73(g), but before the expiration of the ninety-day period therein specified, could permit the docketing of the appeal on a showing of excusable neglect. Both contrary was held in *Mutual Benefit Health & Accident Ass'n v. Snyder*, C.C.A.6, 1940, 109 F.2d 469 and in *Burke v. Canfield*, 1940, 111 F.2d 526, 72 App.D.C. 127.

The amendment of Rule 6(b) now proposed is based on the view that there should be a definite point where it can be said a judgment is final; that the right method of dealing with the problem is to list in Rule 6(b) the various other rules whose time limits may not be set aside, and then, if the time limit in any of those other rules is too short, to amend that other rule to give a longer time. The further argument is that Rule 6(c) abolished the long standing device to produce finality in judgments through expiration of the term, and since that limitation on the jurisdiction of courts to set aside their own judgments has been removed by Rule 6(c), some

other limitation must be substituted or judgments never can be said to be final.

In this connection reference is made to the established rule that if a motion for new trial is seasonably made, the mere making or pendency of the motion destroys the finality of the judgment, and even though the motion is ultimately denied, the full time for appeal starts anew from the date of denial. Also, a motion to amend the findings under Rule 52(b) has the same effect on the time for appeal. *Leishman v. Associated Wholesale Electric Co.*, 1943, 63 S.Ct. 543, 318 U.S. 203, 87 L.Ed. 714. By the same reasoning a motion for judgment under Rule 50(b), involving as it does the vacation of a judgment entered "forthwith" on the verdict (Rule 58), operates to postpone, until an order is made, the running of the time for appeal. The Committee believes that the abolition by Rule 6(c) of the old rule that a court's power over its judgments ends with the term, requires a substitute limitation, and that unless Rule 6(b) is amended to prevent enlargement of the times specified in Rules 50(b), 52(b) and 60(b), and the limitation as to Rule 59(b) and (d) is retained, no one can say when a judgment is final. This is also true with regard to proposed Rule 59(e), which authorizes a motion to alter or amend a judgment, hence that rule is also included in the enumeration in amended Rule 6(b). In consideration of the amendment, however, it should be noted that Rule 60(b) is also to be amended so as to lengthen the six-months period originally prescribed in that rule to one year.

As to Rule 25 on substitution, while finality is not involved, the limit there fixed should be controlling. That rule, as amended, gives the court power, upon showing of a reasonable excuse, to permit substitution after the expiration of the two-year period.

As to Rule 73(g), it is believed that the conflict in decisions should be resolved and not left to further litigation, and that the rule should be listed as one whose limitation may not be set aside under Rule 6(b).

As to Rule 59(c), fixing the time for serving affidavits on motion for new trial, it is believed that the court should have authority under Rule 6(b) to enlarge the time, because, once the motion for new trial is made, the judgment no longer has finality, and the extension of time for affidavits thus does not of itself disturb finality.

Other changes proposed in Rule 6(b) are merely clarifying and conforming. Thus "request" is substituted for "application" in clause (1) because an application is defined as a motion under Rule 7(b). The phrase "extend the time" is substituted for "enlarge the period" because the former is a more suitable expression and relates more clearly to both clauses (1) and (2). The final phrase in Rule 6(b), "or the period for taking an appeal as provided by law", is deleted and a reference to Rule 73(a) inserted, since it is proposed to state in that rule the time for appeal to a circuit court of appeals, which is the only appeal governed by the Federal Rules, and allows an extension of time. See Rule 72.

Subdivision (c). The purpose of this amendment is to prevent reliance upon the continued existence of a term as a source of power to disturb the finality of a judgment upon grounds other than those stated in these rules. See *Hill v. Hawes*, 1944, 64 S.Ct. 334, 320 U.S. 520, 88 L.Ed. 283; *Boaz v. Mutual Life Ins. Co. of New York*, C.C.A.8, 1944, 146 F.2d 321; *Bucy v. Nevada Construction Co.*, C.C.A.9, 1942, 125 F.2d 213.

1963 Amendment

Subdivision (a). This amendment is related to the amendment of Rule 77(c) changing the regulation of the days on which the clerk's office shall be open.

The wording of the first sentence of Rule 6(a) is clarified and the subdivision is made expressly applicable to computing periods of time set forth in local rules.

Saturday is to be treated in the same way as Sunday or a "legal holiday" in that it is not to be included when it falls on the last day of a computed period, nor counted as an intermediate day when the period is less than 7 days. "Legal holiday" is defined for purposes of this subdivision and amended Rule 77(c). Compare the definition of "holiday" in 11 U.S.C. § 1(18); also 5 U.S.C. § 86a; Executive Order No. 10358, *"Observance of Holidays,"* June 9, 1952, 17 Fed.Reg. 5269. In the light of these changes the last sentence of the present subdivision, dealing with half holidays, is eliminated.

With Saturdays and State holidays made "dies non" in certain cases by the amended subdivision, computation of the usual 5-day notice of motion or the 2-day notice to dissolve or modify a temporary restraining order may work out so as to cause embarrassing delay in urgent cases. The delay can be obviated by applying to the court to shorten the time, see Rules 6(d) and 65(b).

Subdivision (b). The prohibition against extending the time for taking action under Rule 25 (Substitution of parties) is eliminated. The only limitation of time provided for in amended Rule 25 is the 90-day period following a suggestion upon the record of the death of a party within which to make a motion to substitute the proper parties for the deceased party. See Rule 25(a)(1), as amended, and the Advisory Committee's Note thereto. It is intended that the court shall have discretion to enlarge that period.

1966 Amendment

P.L. 88–139, § 1, 77 Stat. 248, approved on October 16, 1963, amended 28 U.S.C. § 138 to read as follows: "The district court shall not hold formal terms." Thus Rule 6(c) is rendered unnecessary, and it is rescinded.

1967 Amendment

The amendment eliminates the references to Rule 73, which is to be abrogated.

1971 Amendment

The amendment adds Columbus Day to the list of legal holidays to conform the subdivision to the Act of June 28, 1968, 82 Stat. 250, which constituted Columbus Day a legal holiday effective after January 1, 1971.

The Act, which amended Title 5, U.S.C. § 6103(a), changes the day on which certain holidays are to be observed. Washington's Birthday, Memorial Day and Veterans Day are to be observed on the third Monday in February, the last Monday in May and the fourth Monday in October, respectively, rather than, as heretofore, on February 22, May 30, and November 11, respectively, Columbus Day is to be observed on the second Monday in October. New Year's Day, Independence Day, Thanksgiving Day and Christmas continue to be observed on the traditional days.

1983 Amendment

Subdivision (b). The amendment confers finality upon the judgments of magistrates by foreclosing enlargement of the time for appeal except as provided in new Rule 74(a) (20 day period for demonstration of excusable neglect).

1985 Amendment

Rule 6(a) is amended to acknowledge that weather conditions or other events may render the clerk's office inaccessible one or more days. Parties who are obliged to file something with the court during that period should not be penalized if they cannot do so. The amendment conforms to changes made in Federal Rule of Criminal Procedure 45(a), effective August 1, 1982.

The Rule also is amended to extend the exclusion of intermediate Saturdays, Sundays, and legal holidays to the computation of time periods less than 11 days. Under the current version of the Rule, parties bringing motions under rules with 10-day periods could have as few as 5 working days to prepare their motions. This hardship would be especially acute in the case of Rules 50(b) and (c)(2), 52(b), and 59(b), (d), and (e), which may not be enlarged at the discretion of the court. See Rule 6(b). If the exclusion of Saturdays, Sundays, and legal holidays will operate to cause excessive delay in urgent cases, the delay can be obviated by applying to the court to shorten the time. See Rule 6(b).

The Birthday of Martin Luther King, Jr., which becomes a legal holiday effective in 1986, has been added to the list of legal holidays enumerated in the Rule.

1987 Amendment

The amendments are technical. No substantive change is intended.

1999 Amendment

The reference to Rule 74(a) is stricken from the catalogue of time periods that cannot be extended by the district court. The change reflects the 1997 abrogation of Rule 74(a).

2001 Amendments

The additional three days provided by Rule 6(e) is extended to the means of service authorized by the new paragraph (D) added to Rule 5(b), including—with the consent of the person served—service by electronic or other means. The three-day addition is provided as well for service on a person with no known address by leaving a copy with the clerk of the court.

Changes Made After Publication and Comments

Proposed Rule 6(e) is the same as the "alternative proposal" that was published in August 1999.

2005 Amendments

Rule 6(e) is amended to remove any doubt as to the method for extending the time to respond after service by mail, leaving with the clerk of court, electronic means, or other means consented to by the party served. Three days are added after the prescribed period otherwise expires under Rule 6(a). Intermediate Saturdays, Sundays, and legal holidays are included in counting these added three days. If the third day is a Saturday, Sunday, or legal holiday, the last

day to act is the next day that is not a Saturday, Sunday, or legal holiday. The effect of invoking the day when the prescribed period would otherwise expire under Rule 6(a) can be illustrated by assuming that the thirtieth day of a thirty-day period is a Saturday. Under Rule 6(a) the period expires on the next day that is not a Sunday or legal holiday. If the following Monday is a legal holiday, under Rule 6(a) the period expires on Tuesday. Three days are then added— Wednesday, Thursday, and Friday as the third and final day to act. If the period prescribed expires on a Friday, the three added days are Saturday, Sunday, and Monday, which is the third and final day to act unless it is a legal holiday. If Monday is a legal holiday, the next day that is not a legal holiday is the third and final day to act.

Application of Rule 6(e) to a period that is less than eleven days can be illustrated by a paper that is served by mailing on a Friday. If ten days are allowed to respond, intermediate Saturdays, Sundays, and legal holidays are excluded in determining when the period expires under Rule 6(a). If there is no legal holiday, the period expires on the Friday two weeks after the paper was mailed. The three added Rule 6(e) days are Saturday, Sunday, and Monday, which is the third and final day to act unless it is a legal holiday. If Monday is a legal holiday, the next day that is not a legal holiday is the final day to act.

2007 Amendment

[Effective December 1, 2007,
absent contrary Congressional action.]

The language of Rule 6 has been amended as part of the general restyling of the Civil Rules to make them more easily understood and to make style and terminology consistent throughout the rules. These changes are intended to be stylistic only.

HISTORICAL NOTES

Effective and Applicability Provisions

1946 Amendments

Effective date of amendment to this rule, see rule 86(b).

III. PLEADINGS AND MOTIONS

Proposed Amendment of Heading

Effective December 1, 2007, absent contrary Congressional action, this heading is amended to read as follows:

TITLE III. PLEADINGS AND MOTIONS

Rule 7. Pleadings Allowed; Form of Motions

(a) Pleadings. There shall be a complaint and an answer; a reply to a counterclaim denominated as such; an answer to a cross-claim, if the answer contains a cross-claim; a third-party complaint, if a person who was not an original party is summoned under the provisions of Rule 14; and a third-party answer, if a third-party complaint is served. No other pleading shall be allowed, except that the court may order a reply to an answer or a third-party answer.

(b) Motions and Other Papers.

(1) An application to the court for an order shall be by motion which, unless made during a hearing or trial, shall be made in writing, shall state with particularity the grounds therefor, and shall set forth the relief or order sought. The requirement of writing is fulfilled if the motion is stated in a written notice of the hearing of the motion.

(2) The rules applicable to captions and other matters of form of pleadings apply to all motions and other papers provided for by these rules.

(3) All motions shall be signed in accordance with Rule 11.

(c) Demurrers, Pleas, etc., Abolished. Demurrers, pleas, and exceptions for insufficiency of a pleading shall not be used.

(As amended Dec. 27, 1946, eff. Mar. 19, 1948; Jan. 21, 1963, eff. July 1, 1963; Apr. 28, 1983, eff. Aug. 1, 1983.)

Proposed Amendment of Rule

Effective December 1, 2007, absent contrary Congressional action, this rule is amended to read as follows:

Rule 7. Pleadings Allowed; Form of Motions and Other Papers

(a) Pleadings. *Only these pleadings are allowed:*

(1) a complaint;

(2) an answer to a complaint;

(3) an answer to a counterclaim designated as a counterclaim;

(4) an answer to a crossclaim;

(5) a third-party complaint;

(6) an answer to a third-party complaint; and

(7) if the court orders one, a reply to an answer.

(b) Motions and Other Papers.

(1) In General. A request for a court order must be made by motion. The motion must:

(A) be in writing unless made during a hearing or trial;

(B) state with particularity the grounds for seeking the order; and

(C) state the relief sought.

(2) Form. The rules governing captions and other matters of form in pleadings apply to motions and other papers.

Complete Annotation Materials, see Title 28 U.S.C.A.

ADVISORY COMMITTEE NOTES
1937 Adoption

1. A provision designating pleadings and defining a motion is common in the state practice acts. See Smith-Hurd Ill.Stats. ch. 110, § 156 (Designation and order of pleadings); 2 Minn.Stat. (Mason, 1927) § 9246 (Definition of motion); and N.Y.C.P.A. (1937) § 113 (Definition of motion). Former Equity Rules 18 (Pleadings—Technical Forms Abrogated), 29 (Defenses—How Presented), and 33 (Testing Sufficiency of Defense) abolished technical forms of pleading, demurrers and pleas, and exceptions for insufficiency of an answer.

2. **Note to Subdivision (a).** This preserves the substance of [former] Equity Rule 31 (Reply—When Required—When Cause at Issue). Compare the English practice, *English Rules under the Judicature Act* (The Annual Practice, 1937) O. 23, r.r. 1, 2 (Reply to counterclaim; amended, 1933, to be subject to the rules applicable to defenses, O. 21). See O. 21, r.r. 1–14; O. 27, r. 13 (When pleadings deemed denied and put in issue). Under the codes the pleadings are generally limited. A reply is sometimes required to an affirmative defense in the answer. 1 Colo.Stat.Ann. (1935) § 66; Ore. Code Ann. (1930) §§ 1–614, 1–616. In other jurisdictions no reply is necessary to an affirmative defense in the answer, but a reply may be ordered by the court. N.C.Code Ann. (1935) § 525; 1 S.D.Comp.Laws (1929) § 2357. A reply to a counterclaim is usually required. Ark.Civ.Code (Crawford, 1934) §§ 123 to 125; Wis.Stat. (1935) §§ 263.20, 263.21. U.S.C. Title 28, [former] § 45 (District courts; practice and procedure in certain cases) is modified insofar as it may dispense with a reply to a counterclaim.

For amendment of pleadings, see Rule 15 dealing with amended and supplemental pleadings.

3. All statutes which use the words "petition", "bill of complaint", "plea", "demurrer", and other such terminology are modified in form by this rule.

1946 Amendment

Note. This amendment eliminates any question as to whether the compulsory reply, where a counterclaim is pleaded, is a reply only to the counterclaim or is a general reply to the answer containing the counterclaim. The Commentary, *Scope of Reply where Defendant Has Pleaded Counterclaim*, 1939, 1 Fed.Rules Serv. 672; *Fort Chartres and Ivy Landing Drainage and Levee District No. Five v. Thompson*, Ill.1945, 8 Fed.Rules Serv. 13.32, Case 1.

1963 Amendment

Certain redundant words are eliminated and the subdivision is modified to reflect the amendment of Rule 14(a) which in certain cases eliminates the requirement of obtaining leave to bring in a third-party defendant.

1983 Amendment

One of the reasons sanctions against improper motion practice have been employed infrequently is the lack of clarity of Rule 7. That rule has stated only generally that the pleading requirements relating to captions, signing, and other matters of form also apply to motions and other papers. The addition of Rule 7(b)(3) makes explicit the applicability of the signing requirement and the sanctions of Rule 11, which have been amplified.

2007 Amendment

[Effective December 1, 2007, absent contrary Congressional action.]

The language of Rule 7 has been amended as part of the general restyling of the Civil Rules to make them more easily understood and to make style and terminology consistent throughout the rules. These changes are intended to be stylistic only.

Former Rule 7(a) stated that "there shall be * * * an answer to a cross-claim, if the answer contains a cross-claim * * *." Former Rule 12(a)(2) provided more generally that "[a] party served with a pleading stating a cross-claim against that party shall serve an answer thereto * * *." New Rule 7(a) corrects this inconsistency by providing for an answer to a crossclaim.

For the first time, Rule 7(a)(7) expressly authorizes the court to order a reply to a counterclaim answer. A reply may be as useful in this setting as a reply to an answer, a third-party answer, or a crossclaim answer.

Former Rule 7(b)(1) stated that the writing requirement is fulfilled if the motion is stated in a written notice of hearing. This statement was deleted as redundant because a single written document can satisfy the writing requirements both for a motion and for a Rule 6(c)(1) notice.

The cross-reference to Rule 11 in former Rule 7(b)(3) is deleted as redundant. Rule 11 applies by its own terms. The force and application of Rule 11 are not diminished by the deletion.

Former Rule 7(c) is deleted because it has done its work. If a motion or pleading is described as a demurrer, plea, or exception for insufficiency, the court will treat the paper as if properly captioned.

HISTORICAL NOTES
Effective and Applicability Provisions

1946 Amendments

Effective date of amendment to this rule, see rule 86(b).

Rule 7.1. Disclosure Statement

(a) Who Must File: Nongovernmental Corporate Party. A nongovernmental corporate party to an action or proceeding in a district court must file two copies of a statement that identifies any parent corporation and any publicly held corporation that owns 10% or more of its stock or states that there is no such corporation.

(b) Time for Filing; Supplemental Filing. A party must:

(1) file the Rule 7.1(a) statement with its first appearance, pleading, petition, motion, response, or other request addressed to the court, and

(2) promptly file a supplemental statement upon any change in the information that the statement requires.

(Added Apr. 29, 2002, eff. Dec. 1, 2002.)

Proposed Amendment of Rule

Effective December 1, 2007, absent contrary Congressional action, this rule is amended to read as follows:

Rule 7.1. Disclosure Statement

(a) Who Must File; Contents. A nongovernmental corporate party must file two copies of a disclosure statement that:

(1) identifies any parent corporation and any publicly held corporation owning 10% or more of its stock; or

(2) states that there is no such corporation.

(b) Time to File; Supplemental Filing. A party must:

(1) file the disclosure statement with its first appearance, pleading, petition, motion, response, or other request addressed to the court; and

(2) promptly file a supplemental statement if any required information changes.

ADVISORY COMMITTEE NOTES
2002 Adoption

Rule 7.1 is drawn from Rule 26.1 of the Federal Rules of Appellate Procedure, with changes to adapt to the circumstances of district courts that dictate different provisions for the time of filing, number of copies, and the like. The information required by Rule 7.1(a) reflects the "financial interest" standard of Canon 3C(1)(c) of the Code of Conduct for United States Judges. This information will support properly informed disqualification decisions in situations that call for automatic disqualification under Canon 3C(1)(c). It does not cover all of the circumstances that may call for disqualification under the financial interest standard, and does not deal at all with other circumstances that may call for disqualification.

Although the disclosures required by Rule 7.1(a) may seem limited, they are calculated to reach a majority of the circumstances that are likely to call for disqualification on the basis of financial information that a judge may not know or recollect. Framing a rule that calls for more detailed disclosure will be difficult. Unnecessary disclosure requirements place a burden on the parties and on courts. Unnecessary disclosure of volumes of information may create a risk that a judge will overlook the one bit of information that might require disqualification, and also may create a risk that unnecessary disqualifications will be made rather than attempt to unravel a potentially difficult question. It has not been feasible to dictate more detailed disclosure requirements in Rule 7.1(a).

Rule 7.1 does not prohibit local rules that require disclosures in addition to those required by Rule 7.1. Developing experience with local disclosure practices and advances in electronic technology may provide a foundation for adopting more detailed disclosure requirements by future amendments of Rule 7.1.

Changes Made After Publication and Comment. The provisions that would require disclosure of additional information that may be required by the Judicial Conference have been deleted.

2007 Amendment
[Effective December 1, 2007, absent contrary Congressional action.]

The language of Rule 7.1 has been amended as part of the general restyling of the Civil Rules to make them more easily understood and to make style and terminology consistent throughout the rules. These changes are intended to be stylistic only.

Rule 8. General Rules of Pleading

(a) Claims for Relief. A pleading which sets forth a claim for relief, whether an original claim, counterclaim, cross-claim, or third-party claim, shall contain (1) a short and plain statement of the grounds upon which the court's jurisdiction depends, unless the court already has jurisdiction and the claim needs no new grounds of jurisdiction to support it, (2) a short and plain statement of the claim showing that the pleader is entitled to relief, and (3) a demand for judgment for the relief the pleader seeks. Relief in the alternative or of several different types may be demanded.

(b) Defenses; Form of Denials. A party shall state in short and plain terms the party's defenses to each claim asserted and shall admit or deny the averments upon which the adverse party relies. If a party is without knowledge or information sufficient to form a belief as to the truth of an averment, the party shall so state and this has the effect of a denial. Denials shall fairly meet the substance of the averments denied. When a pleader intends in good faith to deny only a part or a qualification of an averment, the pleader shall specify so much of it as is true and material and shall deny only the remainder. Unless the pleader intends in good faith to controvert all the averments of the preceding pleading, the pleader may make denials as specific denials of designated averments or paragraphs or may generally deny all the averments except such designated averments or paragraphs as the pleader expressly admits; but, when the pleader does so intend to controvert all its averments, including averments of the grounds upon which the court's jurisdiction depends, the pleader may do so by general denial subject to the obligations set forth in Rule 11.

(c) Affirmative Defenses. In pleading to a preceding pleading, a party shall set forth affirmatively accord and satisfaction, arbitration and award, assumption of risk, contributory negligence, discharge in bankruptcy, duress, estoppel, failure of consideration, fraud, illegality, injury by fellow servant, laches, license, payment, release, res judicata, statute of frauds, statute of limitations, waiver, and any other matter constituting an avoidance or affirmative de-

fense. When a party has mistakenly designated a defense as a counterclaim or a counterclaim as a defense, the court on terms, if justice so requires, shall treat the pleading as if there had been a proper designation.

(d) Effect of Failure to Deny. Averments in a pleading to which a responsive pleading is required, other than those as to the amount of damage, are admitted when not denied in the responsive pleading. Averments in a pleading to which no responsive pleading is required or permitted shall be taken as denied or avoided.

(e) Pleading to be Concise and Direct; Consistency.

(1) Each averment of a pleading shall be simple, concise, and direct. No technical forms of pleading or motions are required.

(2) A party may set forth two or more statements of a claim or defense alternately or hypothetically, either in one count or defense or in separate counts or defenses. When two or more statements are made in the alternative and one of them if made independently would be sufficient, the pleading is not made insufficient by the insufficiency of one or more of the alternative statements. A party may also state as many separate claims or defenses as the party has regardless of consistency and whether based on legal, equitable, or maritime grounds. All statements shall be made subject to the obligations set forth in Rule 11.

(f) Construction of Pleadings. All pleadings shall be so construed as to do substantial justice.
(As amended Feb. 28, 1966, eff. July 1, 1966; Mar. 2, 1987, eff. Aug. 1, 1987.)

Proposed Amendment of Rule

Effective December 1, 2007, absent contrary Congressional action, this rule is amended to read as follows:

Rule 8. *General Rules of Pleading*

(a) Claim for Relief. *A pleading that states a claim for relief must contain:*

(1) a short and plain statement of the grounds for the court's jurisdiction, unless the court already has jurisdiction and the claim needs no new jurisdictional support;

(2) a short and plain statement of the claim showing that the pleader is entitled to relief; and

(3) a demand for the relief sought, which may include relief in the alternative or different types of relief.

(b) Defenses; Admissions and Denials.

(1) In General. In responding to a pleading, a party must:

(A) state in short and plain terms its defenses to each claim asserted against it; and

(B) admit or deny the allegations asserted against it by an opposing party.

(2) Denials—Responding to the Substance. A denial must fairly respond to the substance of the allegation.

(3) General and Specific Denials. A party that intends in good faith to deny all the allegations of a pleading—including the jurisdictional grounds—may do so by a general denial. A party that does not intend to deny all the allegations must either specifically deny designated allegations or generally deny all except those specifically admitted.

(4) Denying Part of an Allegation. A party that intends in good faith to deny only part of an allegation must admit the part that is true and deny the rest.

(5) Lacking Knowledge or Information. A party that lacks knowledge or information sufficient to form a belief about the truth of an allegation must so state, and the statement has the effect of a denial.

(6) Effect of Failing to Deny. An allegation—other than one relating to the amount of damages—is admitted if a responsive pleading is required and the allegation is not denied. If a responsive pleading is not required, an allegation is considered denied or avoided.

(c) Affirmative Defenses.

(1) In General. In responding to a pleading, a party must affirmatively state any avoidance or affirmative defense, including:

- *accord and satisfaction;*
- *arbitration and award;*
- *assumption of risk;*
- *contributory negligence;*
- *discharge in bankruptcy;*
- *duress;*
- *estoppel;*
- *failure of consideration;*
- *fraud;*
- *illegality;*
- *injury by fellow servant;*
- *laches;*
- *license;*
- *payment;*

- *release;*
- *res judicata;*
- *statute of frauds;*
- *statute of limitations; and*
- *waiver.*

(2) Mistaken Designation. If a party mistakenly designates a defense as a counterclaim, or a counterclaim as a defense, the court must, if justice requires, treat the pleading as though it were correctly designated, and may impose terms for doing so.

(d) Pleading to Be Concise and Direct; Alternative Statements; Inconsistency.

(1) In General. Each allegation must be simple, concise, and direct. No technical form is required.

(2) Alternative Statements of a Claim or Defense. A party may set out two or more statements of a claim or defense alternatively or hypothetically, either in a single count or defense or in separate ones. If a party makes alternative statements, the pleading is sufficient if any one of them is sufficient.

(3) Inconsistent Claims or Defenses. A party may state as many separate claims or defenses as it has, regardless of consistency.

(e) Construing Pleadings. *Pleadings must be construed so as to do justice.*

ADVISORY COMMITTEE NOTES
1937 Adoption

Note to Subdivision (a). See [former] Equity Rules 25 (Bill of Complaint—Contents), and 30 (Answer—Contents—Counterclaim). Compare 2 Ind.Stat.Ann. (Burns, 1933) §§ 2–1004, 2–1015; 2 Ohio Gen.Code Ann. (Page, 1926) §§ 11305, 11314; Utah Rev.Stat.Ann. (1933) §§ 104–7–2, 104–9–1.

See Rule 19(c) for the requirement of a statement in a claim for relief of the names of persons who ought to be parties and the reason for their omission.

See Rule 23(b) for particular requirements as to the complaint in a secondary action by shareholders.

Note to Subdivision (b). 1. This rule supersedes the methods of pleading prescribed in U.S.C., Title 19, § 508 (Persons making seizures pleading general issue and proving special matter); U.S.C. Title 35, [former] §§ 40d (Proving under general issue, upon notice, that a statement in application for an extended patent is not true), 69 [now 282] (Pleading and proof in actions for infringement) and similar statutes.

2. This rule is, in part, [former] Equity Rule 30 (Answer—Contents—Counterclaim), with the matter on denials largely from the Connecticut practice. See Conn. Practice Book (1934) §§ 107, 108, and 122; Conn.Gen.Stat. (1930) §§ 5508 to 5514. Compare the English practice, *English Rules Under the Judicature Act* (The Annual Practice, 1937) O. 19, r.r. 17–20.

Note to Subdivision (c). This follows substantially *English Rules Under the Judicature Act* (The Annual Practice, 1937) O. 19, r. 15 and N.Y.C.P.A. (1937) § 242, with "surprise" omitted in this rule.

Note to Subdivision (d). The first sentence is similar to former Equity Rule 30 (Answer—Contents—Counterclaim). For the second sentence see former Equity Rule 31 (Reply—When Required—When Cause at Issue). This is similar to *English Rules Under the Judicature Act* (The Annual Practice, 1937) O. 19, r.r. 13, 18; and to the practice of the States.

Note to Subdivision (e). This rule is an elaboration upon [former] Equity Rule 30 (Answer—Contents—Counterclaim), plus a statement of the actual practice under some codes. Compare also [former] Equity Rule 18 (Pleadings—Technical Forms Abrogated). See Clark, *Code Pleading* (1928), pp. 171–4, 432–5; Hankin, *Alternative and Hypothetical Pleading* (1924), 33 Yale L.J. 365.

Note to Subdivision (f). A provision of like import is of frequent occurrence in the codes. Smith-Hurd Ill.Stats. ch. 110, § 157(3); 2 Minn.Stat. (Mason, 1927) § 9266; N.Y.C.P.A. (1937) § 275; 2 N.D.Comp.Laws Ann. (1913) § 7458.

1966 Amendment

The change here is consistent with the broad purposes of unification.

1987 Amendment

The amendments are technical. No substantive change is intended.

2007 Amendment

[Effective December 1, 2007,
absent contrary Congressional action.]

The language of Rule 8 has been amended as part of the general restyling of the Civil Rules to make them more easily understood and to make style and terminology consistent throughout the rules. These changes are intended to be stylistic only.

The former Rule 8(b) and 8(e) cross-references to Rule 11 are deleted as redundant. Rule 11 applies by its own terms. The force and application of Rule 11 are not diminished by the deletion.

Former Rule 8(b) required a pleader denying part of an averment to "specify so much of it as is true and material and * * * deny only the remainder." "[A]nd material" is deleted to avoid the implication that it is proper to deny something that the pleader believes to be true but not material.

Deletion of former Rule 8(e)(2)'s "whether based on legal, equitable, or maritime grounds" reflects the parallel deletions in Rule 1 and elsewhere. Merger is now successfully accomplished.

Rule 9. Pleading Special Matters

(a) Capacity. It is not necessary to aver the capacity of a party to sue or be sued or the authority of

a party to sue or be sued in a representative capacity or the legal existence of an organized association of persons that is made a party, except to the extent required to show the jurisdiction of the court. When a party desires to raise an issue as to the legal existence of any party or the capacity of any party to sue or be sued or the authority of a party to sue or be sued in a representative capacity, the party desiring to raise the issue shall do so by specific negative averment, which shall include such supporting particulars as are peculiarly within the pleader's knowledge.

(b) Fraud, Mistake, Condition of the Mind. In all averments of fraud or mistake, the circumstances constituting fraud or mistake shall be stated with particularity. Malice, intent, knowledge, and other condition of mind of a person may be averred generally.

(c) Conditions Precedent. In pleading the performance or occurrence of conditions precedent, it is sufficient to aver generally that all conditions precedent have been performed or have occurred. A denial of performance or occurrence shall be made specifically and with particularity.

(d) Official Document or Act. In pleading an official document or official act it is sufficient to aver that the document was issued or the act done in compliance with law.

(e) Judgment. In pleading a judgment or decision of a domestic or foreign court, judicial or quasi-judicial tribunal, or of a board or officer, it is sufficient to aver the judgment or decision without setting forth matter showing jurisdiction to render it.

(f) Time and Place. For the purpose of testing the sufficiency of a pleading, averments of time and place are material and shall be considered like all other averments of material matter.

(g) Special Damage. When items of special damage are claimed, they shall be specifically stated.

(h) Admiralty and Maritime Claims. A pleading or count setting forth a claim for relief within the admiralty and maritime jurisdiction that is also within the jurisdiction of the district court on some other ground may contain a statement identifying the claim as an admiralty or maritime claim for the purposes of Rules 14(c), 38(e), and 82, and the Supplemental Rules for Admiralty or Maritime Claims and Asset Forfeiture Actions. If the claim is cognizable only in admiralty, it is an admiralty or maritime claim for those purposes whether so identified or not. The amendment of a pleading to add or withdraw an identifying statement is governed by the principles of Rule 15. A case that includes an admiralty or maritime claim within this subdivision is an admiralty case within 28 U.S.C. § 1292(a)(3).

(As amended Feb. 28, 1966, eff. July 1, 1966; Dec. 4, 1967, eff. July 1, 1968; Mar. 30, 1970, eff. July 1, 1970; Mar. 2, 1987, eff. Aug. 1, 1987; April 11, 1997, eff. Dec. 1, 1997; Apr. 12, 2006, eff. Dec. 1, 2006.)

Proposed Amendment of Rule

Effective December 1, 2007, absent contrary Congressional action, this rule is amended to read as follows:

Rule 9. Pleading Special Matters

(a) Capacity or Authority to Sue; Legal Existence.

(1) In General. Except when required to show that the court has jurisdiction, a pleading need not allege:

(A) a party's capacity to sue or be sued;

(B) a party's authority to sue or be sued in a representative capacity; or

(C) the legal existence of an organized association of persons that is made a party.

(2) Raising Those Issues. To raise any of those issues, a party must do so by a specific denial, which must state any supporting facts that are peculiarly within the party's knowledge.

(b) Fraud or Mistake; Conditions of Mind. In alleging fraud or mistake, a party must state with particularity the circumstances constituting fraud or mistake. Malice, intent, knowledge, and other conditions of a person's mind may be alleged generally.

(c) Conditions Precedent. In pleading conditions precedent, it suffices to allege generally that all conditions precedent have occurred or been performed. But when denying that a condition precedent has occurred or been performed, a party must do so with particularity.

(d) Official Document or Act. In pleading an official document or official act, it suffices to allege that the document was legally issued or the act legally done.

(e) Judgment. In pleading a judgment or decision of a domestic or foreign court, a judicial or quasi-judicial tribunal, or a board or officer, it suffices to plead the judgment or decision without showing jurisdiction to render it.

(f) Time and Place. An allegation of time or place is material when testing the sufficiency of a pleading.

(g) Special Damages. If an item of special damage is claimed, it must be specifically stated.

(h) Admiralty or Maritime Claim.

(1) How Designated. If a claim for relief is within the admiralty or maritime jurisdiction and also within the court's subject-matter jurisdiction on some other ground, the pleading may designate the claim as an admiralty or maritime

claim for purposes of Rules 14(c), 38(e), and 82 and the Supplemental Rules for Admiralty or Maritime Claims and Asset Forfeiture Actions. A claim cognizable only in the admiralty or maritime jurisdiction is an admiralty or maritime claim for those purposes, whether or not so designated.

(2) Designation for Appeal. A case that includes an admiralty or maritime claim within this subdivision (h) is an admiralty case within 28 U.S.C. § 1292(a)(3).

ADVISORY COMMITTEE NOTES

1937 Adoption

Note to Subdivision (a). Compare [former] Equity Rule 25 (Bill of Complaint—Contents) requiring disability to be stated; Utah Rev.Stat.Ann. (1933) § 104–13–15, enumerating a number of situations where a general averment of capacity is sufficient. For provisions governing averment of incorporation, see 2 Minn.Stat. (Mason, 1927) § 9271; N.Y.R.C.P. (1937) Rule 93; 2 N.D.Comp.Laws Ann. (1913) § 7981 et seq.

Note to Subdivision (b). See *English Rules Under the Judicature Act* (The Annual Practice, 1937) O. 19, r. 22.

Note to Subdivision (c). The codes generally have this or a similar provision. See *English Rules Under the Judicature Act* (The Annual Practice, 1937) O. 19, r. 14; 2 Minn. Stat. (Mason, 1927) § 9273; N.Y.R.C.P. (1937) Rule 92; 2 N.D.Comp.Laws Ann. (1913) § 7461; 2 Wash.Rev.Stat.Ann. (Remington, 1932) § 288.

Note to Subdivision (e). The rule expands the usual code provisions on pleading a judgment by including judgments or decisions of administrative tribunals and foreign courts. Compare Ark.Civ.Code (Crawford, 1934) § 141; 2 Minn.Stat. (Mason, 1927) § 9269; N.Y.R.C.P. (1937) Rule 95; 2 Wash. Rev.Stat.Ann. (Remington, 1932) § 287.

1966 Amendment

Certain distinctive features of the admiralty practice must be preserved for what are now suits in admiralty. This raises the question: After unification, when a single form of action is established, how will the counterpart of the present suit in admiralty be identifiable? In part the question is easily answered. Some claims for relief can only be suits in admiralty, either because the admiralty jurisdiction is exclusive or because no nonmaritime ground of federal jurisdiction exists. Many claims, however, are cognizable by the district courts whether asserted in admiralty or in a civil action, assuming the existence of a nonmaritime ground of jurisdiction. Thus at present the pleader has power to determine procedural consequences by the way in which he exercises the classic privilege given by the saving-to-suitors clause (28 U.S.C. § 1333) or by equivalent statutory provisions. For example, a longshoreman's claim for personal injuries suffered by reason of the unseaworthiness of a vessel may be asserted in a suit in admiralty or, if diversity of citizenship exists, in a civil action. One of the important procedural consequences is that in the civil action either party may demand a jury trial, while in the suit in admiralty there is no right to jury trial except as provided by statute.

It is no part of the purpose of unification to inject a right to jury trial into those admiralty cases in which that right is not provided by statute. Similarly as will be more specifically noted below, there is no disposition to change the present law as to interlocutory appeals in admiralty, or as to the venue of suits in admiralty; and, of course, there is no disposition to inject into the civil practice as it now is the distinctively maritime remedies (maritime attachment and garnishment, actions in rem, possessory, petitory and partition actions and limitation of liability). The unified rules must therefore provide some device for preserving the present power of the pleader to determine whether these historically maritime procedures shall be applicable to his claim or not; the pleader must be afforded some means of designating his claim as the counterpart of the present suit in admiralty, where its character as such is not clear.

The problem is different from the similar one concerning the identification of claims that were formerly suits in equity. While that problem is not free from complexities, it is broadly true that the modern counterpart of the suit in equity is distinguishable from the former action at law by the character of the relief sought. This mode of identification is possible in only a limited category of admiralty cases. In large numbers of cases the relief sought in admiralty is simple money damages, indistinguishable from the remedy afforded by the common law. This is true, for example, in the case of the longshoreman's action for personal injuries stated above. After unification has abolished the distinction between civil actions and suits in admiralty, the complaint in such an action would be almost completely ambiguous as to the pleader's intentions regarding the procedure invoked. The allegation of diversity of citizenship might be regarded as a clue indicating an intention to proceed as at present under the saving-to-suitors clause; but this, too, would be ambiguous if there were also reference to the admiralty jurisdiction, and the pleader ought not be required to forego mention of all available jurisdictional grounds.

Other methods of solving the problem were carefully explored, but the Advisory Committee concluded that the preferable solution is to allow the pleader who now has power to determine procedural consequences by filing a suit in admiralty to exercise that power under unification, for the limited instances in which procedural differences will remain, by a simple statement in his pleading to the effect that the claim is an admiralty or maritime claim.

The choice made by the pleader in identifying or in failing to identify his claim as an admiralty or maritime claim is not an irrevocable election. The rule provides that the amendment of a pleading to add or withdraw an identifying statement is subject to the principles of Rule 15.

1968 Amendment

The amendment eliminates the reference to Rule 73 which is to be abrogated and transfers to Rule 9(h) the substance of Subsection (h) of Rule 73 which preserved the right to an interlocutory appeal in admiralty cases which is provided by 28 U.S.C. § 1292(a)(3).

1970 Amendment

The reference to Rule 26(a) is deleted, in light of the transfer of that subdivision to Rule 30(a) and the elimination

of the de bene esse procedure therefrom. See the Advisory Committee's note to Rule 30(a).

1987 Amendment

The amendment is technical. No substantive change is intended.

1997 Amendment

Section 1292(a)(3) of the Judicial Code provides for appeal from "[i]nterlocutory decrees of * * * district courts * * * determining the rights and liabilities of the parties to admiralty cases in which appeals from final decrees are allowed."

Rule 9(h) was added in 1966 with the unification of civil and admiralty procedure. Civil Rule 73(h) was amended at the same time to provide that the § 1292(a)(3) reference "to admiralty cases shall be construed to mean admiralty and maritime claims within the meaning of Rule 9(h)." This provision was transferred to Rule 9(h) when the Appellate Rules were adopted.

A single case can include both admiralty or maritime claims and nonadmiralty claims or parties. This combination reveals an ambiguity in the statement in present Rule 9(h) that an admiralty "claim" is an admiralty "case." An order "determining the rights and liabilities of the parties" within the meaning of § 1292(a)(3) may resolve only a nonadmiralty claim, or may simultaneously resolve interdependent admiralty and nonadmiralty claims. Can appeal be taken as to the nonadmiralty matter, because it is part of a case that includes an admiralty claim, or is appeal limited to the admiralty claim?

The courts of appeals have not achieved full uniformity in applying the § 1292(a)(3) requirement that an order "determin[e] the rights and liabilities of the parties." It is common to assert that the statute should be construed narrowly, under the general policy that exceptions to the final judgment rule should be construed narrowly. This policy would suggest that the ambiguity should be resolved by limiting the interlocutory appeal right to orders that determine the rights and liabilities of the parties to an admiralty claim.

A broader view is chosen by this amendment for two reasons. The statute applies to admiralty "cases," and may itself provide for appeal from an order that disposes of a nonadmiralty claim that is joined in a single case with an admiralty claim. Although a rule of court may help to clarify and implement a statutory grant of jurisdiction, the line is not always clear between permissible implementation and impermissible withdrawal of jurisdiction. In addition, so long as an order truly disposes of the rights and liabilities of the parties within the meaning of § 1292(a)(3), it may prove important to permit appeal as to the nonadmiralty claim. Disposition of the nonadmiralty claim, for example, may make it unnecessary to consider the admiralty claim and have the same effect on the case and parties as disposition of the admiralty claim. Or the admiralty and nonadmiralty claims may be interdependent. An illustration is provided by Roco Carriers, Ltd. v. M/V Nurnberg Express, 899 F.2d 1292 (2d Cir.1990). Claims for losses of ocean shipments were made against two defendants, one subject to admiralty jurisdiction and the other not. Summary judgment was granted in favor of the admiralty defendant and against the nonadmiralty defendant. The nonadmiralty defendant's appeal was accepted, with the explanation that the determination of its liability was "integrally linked with the determination of non-liability" of the admiralty defendant, and that "section 1292(a)(3) is not limited to admiralty claims; instead, it refers to admiralty cases." 899 F.2d at 1297. The advantages of permitting appeal by the nonadmiralty defendant would be particularly clear if the plaintiff had appealed the summary judgment in favor of the admiralty defendant.

It must be emphasized that this amendment does not rest on any particular assumptions as to the meaning of the § 1292(a)(3) provision that limits interlocutory appeal to orders that determine the rights and liabilities of the parties. It simply reflects the conclusion that so long as the case involves an admiralty claim and an order otherwise meets statutory requirements, the opportunity to appeal should not turn on the circumstance that the order does—or does not—dispose of an admiralty claim. No attempt is made to invoke the authority conferred by 28 U.S.C. § 1292(e) to provide by rule for appeal of an interlocutory decision that is not otherwise provided for by other subsections of § 1292.

GAP Report on Rule 9(h). No changes have been made in the published proposal.

2006 Amendment

Rule 9(h) is amended to conform to the changed title of the Supplemental Rules.

2007 Amendment

[Effective December 1, 2007,
absent contrary Congressional action.]

The language of Rule 9 has been amended as part of the general restyling of the Civil Rules to make them more easily understood and to make style and terminology consistent throughout the rules. These changes are intended to be stylistic only.

Rule 15 governs pleading amendments of its own force. The former redundant statement that Rule 15 governs an amendment that adds or withdraws a Rule 9(h) designation as an admiralty or maritime claim is deleted. The elimination of paragraph (2) means that "(3)" will be redesignated as "(2)" in Style Rule 9(h).

Rule 10. Form of Pleadings

(a) Caption; Names of Parties. Every pleading shall contain a caption setting forth the name of the court, the title of the action, the file number, and a designation as in Rule 7(a). In the complaint the title of the action shall include the names of all the parties, but in other pleadings it is sufficient to state the name of the first party on each side with an appropriate indication of other parties.

(b) Paragraphs; Separate Statements. All averments of claim or defense shall be made in numbered paragraphs, the contents of each of which shall be limited as far as practicable to a statement of a single set of circumstances; and a paragraph may be referred to by number in all succeeding pleadings. Each claim founded upon a separate transaction or occurrence and each defense other than denials shall be stated in a separate count or defense whenever a

separation facilitates the clear presentation of the matters set forth.

(c) Adoption by Reference; Exhibits. Statements in a pleading may be adopted by reference in a different part of the same pleading or in another pleading or in any motion. A copy of any written instrument which is an exhibit to a pleading is a part thereof for all purposes.

Proposed Amendment of Rule

Effective December 1, 2007, absent contrary Congressional action, this rule is amended to read as follows:

Rule 10. *Form of Pleadings*

(a) Caption; Names of Parties. Every pleading must have a caption with the court's name, a title, a file number, and a Rule 7(a) designation. The title of the complaint must name all the parties; the title of other pleadings, after naming the first party on each side, may refer generally to other parties.

(b) Paragraphs; Separate Statements. A party must state its claims or defenses in numbered paragraphs, each limited as far as practicable to a single set of circumstances. A later pleading may refer by number to a paragraph in an earlier pleading. If doing so would promote clarity, each claim founded on a separate transaction or occurrence—and each defense other than a denial—must be stated in a separate count or defense.

(c) Adoption by Reference; Exhibits. A statement in a pleading may be adopted by reference elsewhere in the same pleading or in any other pleading or motion. A copy of a written instrument that is an exhibit to a pleading is a part of the pleading for all purposes.

ADVISORY COMMITTEE NOTES

1937 Adoption

The first sentence is derived in part from the opening statement of former Equity Rule 25 (Bill of Complaint—Contents). The remainder of the rule is an expansion in conformity with usual state provisions. For numbered paragraphs and separate statements, see Conn.Gen.Stat., 1930, § 5513; Smith-Hurd Ill.Stats. ch. 110, § 157(2); N.Y.R.C.P., (1937) Rule 90. For incorporation by reference, see N.Y.R.C.P., (1937) Rule 90. For written instruments as exhibits, see Smith-Hurd Ill.Stats. ch. 110, § 160.

2007 Amendment

[Effective December 1, 2007,
absent contrary Congressional action.]

The language of Rule 10 has been amended as part of the general restyling of the Civil Rules to make them more easily understood and to make style and terminology consistent throughout the rules. These changes are intended to be stylistic only.

Rule 11. Signing of Pleadings, Motions, and Other Papers; Representations to Court; Sanctions

(a) Signature. Every pleading, written motion, and other paper shall be signed by at least one attorney of record in the attorney's individual name, or, if the party is not represented by an attorney, shall be signed by the party. Each paper shall state the signer's address and telephone number, if any. Except when otherwise specifically provided by rule or statute, pleadings need not be verified or accompanied by affidavit. An unsigned paper shall be stricken unless omission of the signature is corrected promptly after being called to the attention of the attorney or party.

(b) Representations to Court. By presenting to the court (whether by signing, filing, submitting, or later advocating) a pleading, written motion, or other paper, an attorney or unrepresented party is certifying that to the best of the person's knowledge, information, and belief, formed after an inquiry reasonable under the circumstances,—

(1) it is not being presented for any improper purpose, such as to harass or to cause unnecessary delay or needless increase in the cost of litigation;

(2) the claims, defenses, and other legal contentions therein are warranted by existing law or by a nonfrivolous argument for the extension, modification, or reversal of existing law or the establishment of new law;

(3) the allegations and other factual contentions have evidentiary support or, if specifically so identified, are likely to have evidentiary support after a reasonable opportunity for further investigation or discovery; and

(4) the denials of factual contentions are warranted on the evidence or, if specifically so identified, are reasonably based on a lack of information or belief.

(c) Sanctions. If, after notice and a reasonable opportunity to respond, the court determines that subdivision (b) has been violated, the court may, subject to the conditions stated below, impose an appropriate sanction upon the attorneys, law firms, or parties that have violated subdivision (b) or are responsible for the violation.

(1) How Initiated.

(A) By Motion. A motion for sanctions under this rule shall be made separately from other motions or requests and shall describe the specific conduct alleged to violate subdivision (b). It shall be served as provided in Rule 5, but shall not be filed with or presented to the court unless, within 21 days after service of the motion (or such other period as the court may prescribe), the

challenged paper, claim, defense, contention, allegation, or denial is not withdrawn or appropriately corrected. If warranted, the court may award to the party prevailing on the motion the reasonable expenses and attorney's fees incurred in presenting or opposing the motion. Absent exceptional circumstances, a law firm shall be held jointly responsible for violations committed by its partners, associates, and employees.

(B) On Court's Initiative. On its own initiative, the court may enter an order describing the specific conduct that appears to violate subdivision (b) and directing an attorney, law firm, or party to show cause why it has not violated subdivision (b) with respect thereto.

(2) Nature of Sanction; Limitations. A sanction imposed for violation of this rule shall be limited to what is sufficient to deter repetition of such conduct or comparable conduct by others similarly situated. Subject to the limitations in subparagraphs (A) and (B), the sanction may consist of, or include, directives of a nonmonetary nature, an order to pay a penalty into court, or, if imposed on motion and warranted for effective deterrence, an order directing payment to the movant of some or all of the reasonable attorneys' fees and other expenses incurred as a direct result of the violation.

(A) Monetary sanctions may not be awarded against a represented party for a violation of subdivision (b)(2).

(B) Monetary sanctions may not be awarded on the court's initiative unless the court issues its order to show cause before a voluntary dismissal or settlement of the claims made by or against the party which is, or whose attorneys are, to be sanctioned.

(3) Order. When imposing sanctions, the court shall describe the conduct determined to constitute a violation of this rule and explain the basis for the sanction imposed.

(d) Inapplicability to Discovery. Subdivisions (a) through (c) of this rule do not apply to disclosures and discovery requests, responses, objections, and motions that are subject to the provisions of Rules 26 through 37.

(As amended Apr. 28, 1983, eff. Aug. 1, 1983; Mar. 2, 1987, eff. Aug. 1, 1987; Apr. 22, 1993, eff. Dec. 1, 1993.)

Proposed Amendment of Rule

Effective December 1, 2007, absent contrary Congressional action, this rule is amended to read as follows:

Rule 11. Signing Pleadings, Motions, and Other Papers; Representations to the Court; Sanctions

(a) Signature. *Every pleading, written motion, and other paper must be signed by at least one attorney of record in the attorney's name—or by a party personally if the party is unrepresented. The paper must state the signer's address, e-mail address, and telephone number. Unless a rule or statute specifically states otherwise, a pleading need not be verified or accompanied by an affidavit. The court must strike an unsigned paper unless the omission is promptly corrected after being called to the attorney's or party's attention.*

(b) Representations to the Court. *By presenting to the court a pleading, written motion, or other paper—whether by signing, filing, submitting, or later advocating it—an attorney or unrepresented party certifies that to the best of the person's knowledge, information, and belief, formed after an inquiry reasonable under the circumstances:*

(1) it is not being presented for any improper purpose, such as to harass, cause unnecessary delay, or needlessly increase the cost of litigation;

(2) the claims, defenses, and other legal contentions are warranted by existing law or by a nonfrivolous argument for extending, modifying, or reversing existing law or for establishing new law;

(3) the factual contentions have evidentiary support or, if specifically so identified, will likely have evidentiary support after a reasonable opportunity for further investigation or discovery; and

(4) the denials of factual contentions are warranted on the evidence or, if specifically so identified, are reasonably based on belief or a lack of information.

(c) Sanctions.

(1) In General. If, after notice and a reasonable opportunity to respond, the court determines that Rule 11(b) has been violated, the court may impose an appropriate sanction on any attorney, law firm, or party that violated the rule or is responsible for the violation. Absent exceptional circumstances, a law firm must be held jointly responsible for a violation committed by its partner, associate, or employee.

(2) Motion for Sanctions. A motion for sanctions must be made separately from any other motion and must describe the specific conduct that allegedly violates Rule 11(b). The motion must be served under Rule 5, but it must not be filed or be presented to the court if the challenged paper, claim, defense, contention, or denial is withdrawn or appropriately corrected within 21 days after service or within another time the court sets. If warranted, the court may award to

the prevailing party the reasonable expenses, including attorney's fees, incurred for the motion.

(3) On the Court's Initiative. On its own, the court may order an attorney, law firm, or party to show cause why conduct specifically described in the order has not violated Rule 11(b).

(4) Nature of a Sanction. A sanction imposed under this rule must be limited to what suffices to deter repetition of the conduct or comparable conduct by others similarly situated. The sanction may include nonmonetary directives; an order to pay a penalty into court; or, if imposed on motion and warranted for effective deterrence, an order directing payment to the movant of part or all of the reasonable attorney's fees and other expenses directly resulting from the violation.

(5) Limitations on Monetary Sanctions. The court must not impose a monetary sanction:

 (A) against a represented party for violating Rule 11(b)(2); or

 (B) on its own, unless it issued the show-cause order under Rule 11(c)(3) before voluntary dismissal or settlement of the claims made by or against the party that is, or whose attorneys are, to be sanctioned.

(6) Requirements for an Order. An order imposing a sanction must describe the sanctioned conduct and explain the basis for the sanction.

(d) Inapplicability to Discovery. This rule does not apply to disclosures and discovery requests, responses, objections, and motions under Rules 26 through 37.

ADVISORY COMMITTEE NOTES

1937 Adoption

This is substantially the content of [former] Equity Rules 24 (Signature of Counsel) and 21 (Scandal and Impertinence) consolidated and unified. Compare former Equity Rule 36 (Officers Before Whom Pleadings Verified). Compare to similar purposes, *English Rules Under the Judicature Act* (The Annual Practice, 1937) O. 19, r. 4, and *Great Australian Gold Mining Co. v. Martin*, L.R. 5 Ch.Div. 1, 10 (1877). Subscription of pleadings is required in many codes. 2 Minn.Stat. (Mason, 1927) § 9265; N.Y.R.C.P. (1937) Rule 91; 2 N.D.Comp.Laws Ann. (1913) § 7455.

This rule expressly continues any statute which requires a pleading to be verified or accompanied by an affidavit, such as: U.S.C., Title 28:

§ 381 [former] (Preliminary injunctions and temporary restraining orders)

§ 762 [now 1402] (Suit against the United States)

U.S.C., Title 28, § 829 [now 1927] (Costs; attorney liable for, when) is unaffected by this rule.

For complaints which must be verified under these rules, see Rules 23(b) (Secondary Action by Shareholders) and 65 (Injunctions).

For abolition of former rule in equity that the averments of an answer under oath must be overcome by the testimony of two witnesses or of one witness sustained by corroborating circumstances, see 12 P.S.Pa. § 1222; for the rule in equity itself, see *Greenfield v. Blumenthal*, C.C.A.3, 1934, 69 F.2d 294.

1983 Amendment

Since its original promulgation, Rule 11 has provided for the striking of pleadings and the imposition of disciplinary sanctions to check abuses in the signing of pleadings. Its provisions have always applied to motions and other papers by virtue of incorporation by reference in Rule 7(b)(2). The amendment and the addition of Rule 7(b)(3) expressly confirms this applicability.

Experience shows that in practice Rule 11 has not been effective in deterring abuses. See 6 Wright & Miller, *Federal Practice and Procedure: Civil* § 1334 (1971). There has been considerable confusion as to (1) the circumstances that should trigger striking a pleading or motion or taking disciplinary action, (2) the standard of conduct expected of attorneys who sign pleadings and motions, and (3) the range of available and appropriate sanctions. See Rodes, Ripple & Mooney, *Sanctions Imposable for Violations of the Federal Rules of Civil Procedure* 64–65, Federal Judicial Center (1981). The new language is intended to reduce the reluctance of courts to impose sanctions, see Moore, **Federal Practice** ¶ 7.05, at 1547, by emphasizing the responsibilities of the attorney and reenforcing those obligations by the imposition of sanctions.

The amended rule attempts to deal with the problem by building upon and expanding the equitable doctrine permitting the court to award expenses, including attorney's fees, to a litigant whose opponent acts in bad faith in instituting or conducting litigation. See, e.g., *Roadway Express, Inc. v. Piper*, 447 U.S. 752 (1980); *Hall v. Cole*, 412 U.S. 1, 5 (1973). Greater attention by the district courts to pleading and motion abuses and the imposition of sanctions when appropriate, should discourage dilatory or abusive tactics and help to streamline the litigation process by lessening frivolous claims or defenses.

The expanded nature of the lawyer's certification in the fifth sentence of amended Rule 11 recognizes that the litigation process may be abused for purposes other than delay. See, e.g., *Browning Debenture Holders' Committee v. DASA Corp.*, 560 F.2d 1078 (2d Cir.1977).

The words "good ground to support" the pleading in the original rule were interpreted to have both factual and legal elements. See, e.g., *Heart Disease Research Foundation v. General Motors Corp.*, 15 Fed.R.Serv.2d 1517, 1519 (S.D.N.Y.1972). They have been replaced by a standard of conduct that is more focused.

The new language stresses the need for some prefiling inquiry into both the facts and the law to satisfy the affirmative duty imposed by the rule. The standard is one of reasonableness under the circumstances. See *Kinee v. Abraham Lincoln Fed. Sav. & Loan Ass'n*, 365 F.Supp. 975 (E.D.Pa.1973). This standard is more stringent than the original good-faith formula and thus it is expected that a

greater range of circumstances will trigger its violation. See *Nemeroff v. Abelson*, 620 F.2d 339 (2d Cir.1980).

The rule is not intended to chill an attorney's enthusiasm or creativity in pursuing factual or legal theories. The court is expected to avoid using the wisdom of hindsight and should test the signer's conduct by inquiring what was reasonable to believe at the time the pleading, motion, or other paper was submitted. Thus, what constitutes a reasonable inquiry may depend on such factors as how much time for investigation was available to the signer; whether he had to rely on a client for information as to the facts underlying the pleading, motion, or other paper; whether the pleading, motion, or other paper was based on a plausible view of the law; or whether he depended on forwarding counsel or another member of the bar.

The rule does not require a party or an attorney to disclose privileged communications or work product in order to show that the signing of the pleading, motion, or other paper is substantially justified. The provisions of Rule 26(c), including appropriate orders after *in camera* inspection by the court, remain available to protect a party claiming privilege or work product protection.

Amended Rule 11 continues to apply to anyone who signs a pleading, motion, or other paper. Although the standard is the same for unrepresented parties, who are obliged themselves to sign the pleadings, the court has sufficient discretion to take account of the special circumstances that often arise in *pro se* situations. See *Haines v. Kerner*, 404 U.S. 519 (1972).

The provision in the original rule for striking pleadings and motions as sham and false has been deleted. The passage has rarely been utilized, and decisions thereunder have tended to confuse the issue of attorney honesty with the merits of the action. See generally Risinger, *Honesty in Pleading and its Enforcement: Some "Striking" Problems with Fed.R.Civ.P. 11*, 61 Minn.L.Rev. 1 (1976). Motions under this provision generally present issues better dealt with under Rules 8, 12, or 56. See *Murchison v. Kirby*, 27 F.R.D. 14 (S.D.N.Y.1961); 5 Wright & Miller, *Federal Practice and Procedure: Civil* § 1334 (1969).

The former reference to the inclusion of scandalous or indecent matter, which is itself strong indication that an improper purpose underlies the pleading, motion, or other paper, also has been deleted as unnecessary. Such matter may be stricken under Rule 12(f) as well as dealt with under the more general language of amended Rule 11.

The text of the amended rule seeks to dispel apprehensions that efforts to obtain enforcement will be fruitless by insuring that the rule will be applied when properly invoked. The word "sanctions" in the caption, for example, stresses a deterrent orientation in dealing with improper pleadings, motions or other papers. This corresponds to the approach in imposing sanctions for discovery abuses. See *National Hockey League v. Metropolitan Hockey Club*, 427 U.S. 639 (1976) (per curiam). And the words "shall impose" in the last sentence focus the court's attention on the need to impose sanctions for pleading and motion abuses. The court, however, retains the necessary flexibility to deal appropriately with violations of the rule. It has discretion to tailor sanctions to the particular facts of the case, with which it should be well acquainted.

The references in the former text to wilfulness as a prerequisite to disciplinary action has been deleted. However, in considering the nature and severity of the sanctions to be imposed, the court should take account of the state of the attorney's or party's actual or presumed knowledge when the pleading or other paper was signed. Thus, for example, when a party is not represented by counsel, the absence of legal advice is an appropriate factor to be considered.

Courts currently appear to believe they may impose sanctions on their own motion. See *North American Trading Corp. v. Zale Corp.*, 73 F.R.D. 293 (S.D.N.Y.1979). Authority to do so has been made explicit in order to overcome the traditional reluctance of courts to intervene unless requested by one of the parties. The detection and punishment of a violation of the signing requirement, encouraged by the amended rule, is part of the court's responsibility for securing the system's effective operation.

If the duty imposed by the rule is violated, the court should have the discretion to impose sanctions on either the attorney, the party the signing attorney represents, or both, or on an unrepresented party who signed the pleading, and the new rule so provides. Although Rule 11 has been silent on the point, courts have claimed the power to impose sanctions on an attorney personally, either by imposing costs or employing the contempt technique. See 5 Wright & Miller, *Federal Practice and Procedure: Civil* § 1334 (1969); 2A Moore, *Federal Practice* ¶ 11.02, at 2104 n. 8. This power has been used infrequently. The amended rule should eliminate any doubt as to the propriety of assessing sanctions against the attorney.

Even though it is the attorney whose signature violates the rule, it may be appropriate under the circumstances of the case to impose a sanction on the client. See *Browning Debenture Holders' Committee v. DASA Corp.*, supra. This modification brings Rule 11 in line with practice under Rule 37, which allows sanctions for abuses during discovery to be imposed upon the party, the attorney, or both.

A party seeking sanctions should give notice to the court and the offending party promptly upon discovering a basis for doing so. The time when sanctions are to be imposed rests in the discretion of the trial judge. However, it is anticipated that in the case of pleadings the sanctions issue under Rule 11 normally will be determined at the end of the litigation, and in the case of motions at the time when the motion is decided or shortly thereafter. The procedure obviously must comport with due process requirements. The particular format to be followed should depend on the circumstances of the situation and the severity of the sanction under consideration. In many situations the judge's participation in the proceedings provides him with full knowledge of the relevant facts and little further inquiry will be necessary.

To assure that the efficiencies achieved through more effective operation of the pleading regimen will not be offset by the cost of satellite litigation over the imposition of sanctions, the court must to the extent possible limit the scope of sanction proceedings to the record. Thus, discovery should be conducted only by leave of the court, and then only in extraordinary circumstances.

Although the encompassing reference to "other papers" in new Rule 11 literally includes discovery papers, the certification requirement in that context is governed by proposed

new Rule 26(g). Discovery motions, however, fall within the ambit of Rule 11.

1987 Amendment

The amendments are technical. No substantive change is intended.

1993 Amendments

Purpose of revision. This revision is intended to remedy problems that have arisen in the interpretation and application of the 1983 revision of the rule. For empirical examination of experience under the 1983 rule, see, *e.g.,* New York State Bar Committee on Federal Courts, *Sanctions and Attorneys' Fees* (1987); T. Willging, *The Rule 11 Sanctioning Process* (1989); American Judicature Society, *Report of the Third Circuit Task Force on Federal Rule of Civil Procedure 11* (S. Burbank ed., 1989); E. Wiggins, T. Willging, and D. Stienstra, *Report on Rule 11* (Federal Judicial Center 1991). For book-length analyses of the case law, see G. Joseph, *Sanctions: The Federal Law of Litigation Abuse* (1989); J. Solovy, *The Federal Law of Sanctions* (1991); G. Vairo, *Rule 11 Sanctions: Case Law Perspectives and Preventive Measures* (1991).

The rule retains the principle that attorneys and pro se litigants have an obligation to the court to refrain from conduct that frustrates the aims of Rule 1. The revision broadens the scope of this obligation, but places greater constraints on the imposition of sanctions and should reduce the number of motions for sanctions presented to the court. New subdivision (d) removes from the ambit of this rule all discovery requests, responses, objections, and motions subject to the provisions of Rule 26 through 37.

Subdivision (a). Retained in this subdivision are the provisions requiring signatures on pleadings, written motions, and other papers. Unsigned papers are to be received by the Clerk, but then are to be stricken if the omission of the signature is not corrected promptly after being called to the attention of the attorney or pro se litigant. Correction can be made by signing the paper on file or by submitting a duplicate that contains the signature. A court may require by local rule that papers contain additional identifying information regarding the parties or attorneys, such as telephone numbers to facilitate facsimile transmissions, though, as for omission of a signature, the paper should not be rejected for failure to provide such information.

The sentence in the former rule relating to the effect of answers under oath is no longer needed and has been eliminated. The provision in the former rule that signing a paper constitutes a certificate that it has been read by the signer also has been eliminated as unnecessary. The obligations imposed under subdivision (b) obviously require that a pleading, written motion, or other paper be read before it is filed or submitted to the court.

Subdivisions (b) and (c). These subdivisions restate the provisions requiring attorneys and pro se litigants to conduct a reasonable inquiry into the law and facts before signing pleadings, written motions, and other documents, and prescribing sanctions for violation of these obligations. The revision in part expands the responsibilities of litigants to the court, while providing greater constraints and flexibility in dealing with infractions of the rule. The rule continues to require litigants to "stop-and-think" before initially making legal or factual contentions. It also, however, emphasizes the duty of candor by subjecting litigants to potential sanctions for insisting upon a position after it is no longer tenable and by generally providing protection against sanctions if they withdraw or correct contentions after a potential violation is called to their attention.

The rule applies only to assertions contained in papers filed with or submitted to the court. It does not cover matters arising for the first time during oral presentations to the court, when counsel may make statements that would not have been made if there had been more time for study and reflection. However, a litigant's obligations with respect to the contents of these papers are not measured solely as of the time they are filed with or submitted to the court, but include reaffirming to the court and advocating positions contained in those pleadings and motions after learning that they cease to have any merit. For example, an attorney who during a pretrial conference insists on a claim or defense should be viewed as "presenting to the court" that contention and would be subject to the obligations of subdivision (b) measured as of that time. Similarly, if after a notice of removal is filed, a party urges in federal court the allegations of a pleading filed in state court (whether as claims, defenses, or in disputes regarding removal or remand), it would be viewed as "presenting"—and hence certifying to the district court under Rule 11—those allegations.

The certification with respect to allegations and other factual contentions is revised in recognition that sometimes a litigant may have good reason to believe that a fact is true or false but may need discovery, formal or informal, from opposing parties or third persons to gather and confirm the evidentiary basis for the allegation. Tolerance of factual contentions in initial pleadings by plaintiffs or defendants when specifically identified as made on information and belief does not relieve litigants from the obligation to conduct an appropriate investigation into the facts that is reasonable under the circumstances; it is not a license to join parties, make claims, or present defenses without any factual basis or justification. Moreover, if evidentiary support is not obtained after a reasonable opportunity for further investigation or discovery, the party has a duty under the rule not to persist with that contention. Subdivision (b) does not require a formal amendment to pleadings for which evidentiary support is not obtained, but rather calls upon a litigant not thereafter to advocate such claims or defenses.

The certification is that there is (or likely will be) "evidentiary support" for the allegation, not that the party will prevail with respect to its contention regarding the fact. That summary judgment is rendered against a party does not necessarily mean, for purposes of this certification, that it had no evidentiary support for its position. On the other hand, if a party has evidence with respect to a contention that would suffice to defeat a motion for summary judgment based thereon, it would have sufficient "evidentiary support" for purposes of Rule 11.

Denials of factual contentions involve somewhat different considerations. Often, of course, a denial is premised upon the existence of evidence contradicting the alleged fact. At other times a denial is permissible because, after an appropriate investigation, a party has no information concerning the matter or, indeed, has a reasonable basis for doubting the credibility of the only evidence relevant to the matter. A party should not deny an allegation it knows to be true; but

it is not required, simply because it lacks contradictory evidence, to admit an allegation that it believes is not true.

The changes in subdivisions (b)(3) and (b)(4) will serve to equalize the burden of the rule upon plaintiffs and defendants, who under Rule 8(b) are in effect allowed to deny allegations by stating that from their initial investigation they lack sufficient information to form a belief as to the truth of the allegation. If, after further investigation or discovery, a denial is no longer warranted, the defendant should not continue to insist on that denial. While sometimes helpful, formal amendment of the pleadings to withdraw an allegation or denial is not required by subdivision (b).

Arguments for extensions, modifications, or reversals of existing law or for creation of new law do not violate subdivision (b)(2) provided they are "nonfrivolous." This establishes an objective standard, intended to eliminate any "empty-head pure-heart" justification for patently frivolous arguments. However, the extent to which a litigant has researched the issues and found some support for its theories even in minority opinions, in law review articles, or through consultation with other attorneys should certainly be taken into account in determining whether paragraph (2) has been violated. Although arguments for a change of law are not required to be specifically so identified, a contention that is so identified should be viewed with greater tolerance under the rule.

The court has available a variety of possible sanctions to impose for violations, such as striking the offending paper; issuing an admonition, reprimand, or censure; requiring participation in seminars or other educational programs; ordering a fine payable to the court; referring the matter to disciplinary authorities (or, in the case of government attorneys, to the Attorney General, Inspector General, or agency head), etc. *See Manual for Complex Litigation, Second,* § 42.3. The rule does not attempt to enumerate the factors a court should consider in deciding whether to impose a sanction or what sanctions would be appropriate in the circumstances; but, for emphasis, it does specifically note that a sanction may be nonmonetary as well as monetary. Whether the improper conduct was willful, or negligent; whether it was part of a pattern of activity, or an isolated event; whether it infected the entire pleading, or only one particular count or defense; whether the person has engaged in similar conduct in other litigation; whether it was intended to injure; what effect it had on the litigation process in time or expense; whether the responsible person is trained in the law; what amount, given the financial resources of the responsible person, is needed to deter that person from repetition in the same case; what amount is needed to deter similar activity by other litigants: all of these may in a particular case be proper considerations. The court has significant discretion in determining what sanctions, if any, should be imposed for a violation, subject to the principle that the sanctions should not be more severe than reasonably necessary to deter repetition of the conduct by the offending person or comparable conduct by similarly situated persons.

Since the purpose of Rule 11 sanctions is to deter rather than to compensate, the rule provides that, if a monetary sanction is imposed, it should ordinarily be paid into court as a penalty. However, under unusual circumstances, particularly for (b)(1) violations, deterrence may be ineffective unless the sanction not only requires the person violating the rule to make a monetary payment, but also directs that some or all of this payment be made to those injured by the violation. Accordingly, the rule authorizes the court, if requested in a motion and if so warranted, to award attorney's fees to another party. Any such award to another party, however, should not exceed the expenses and attorneys' fees for the services directly and unavoidably caused by the violation of the certification requirement. If, for example, a wholly unsupportable count were included in a multi-count complaint or counterclaim for the purpose of needlessly increasing the cost of litigation to an impecunious adversary, any award of expenses should be limited to those directly caused by inclusion of the improper count, and not those resulting from the filing of the complaint or answer itself. The award should not provide compensation for services that could have been avoided by an earlier disclosure of evidence or an earlier challenge to the groundless claims or defenses. Moreover, partial reimbursement of fees may constitute a sufficient deterrent with respect to violations by persons having modest financial resources. In cases brought under statutes providing for fees to be awarded to prevailing parties, the court should not employ cost-shifting under this rule in a manner that would be inconsistent with the standards that govern the statutory award of fees, such as stated in *Christiansburg Garment Co. v. EEOC,* 434 U.S. 412 (1978).

The sanction should be imposed on the persons—whether attorneys, law firms, or parties—who have violated the rule or who may be determined to be responsible for the violation. The person signing, filing, submitting, or advocating a document has a nondelegable responsibility to the court, and in most situations is the person to be sanctioned for a violation. Absent exceptional circumstances, a law firm is to be held also responsible when, as a result of a motion under subdivision (c)(1)(A), one of its partners, associates, or employees is determined to have violated the rule. Since such a motion may be filed only if the offending paper is not withdrawn or corrected within 21 days after service of the motion, it is appropriate that the law firm ordinarily be viewed as jointly responsible under established principles of agency. This provision is designed to remove the restrictions of the former rule. *Cf. Pavelic & LeFlore v. Marvel Entertainment Group,* 493 U.S. 120 (1989) (1983 version of Rule 11 does not permit sanctions against law firm of attorney signing groundless complaint).

The revision permits the court to consider whether other attorneys in the firm, co-counsel, other law firms, or the party itself should be held accountable for their part in causing a violation. When appropriate, the court can make an additional inquiry in order to determine whether the sanction should be imposed on such persons, firms, or parties either in addition to or, in unusual circumstances, instead of the person actually making the presentation to the court. For example, such an inquiry may be appropriate in cases involving governmental agencies or other institutional parties that frequently impose substantial restrictions on the discretion of individual attorneys employed by it.

Sanctions that involve monetary awards (such as a fine or an award of attorney's fees) may not be imposed on a represented party for causing a violation of subdivision (b)(2), involving frivolous contentions of law. Monetary responsibility for such violations is more properly placed solely on the party's attorneys. With this limitation, the rule should not

be subject to attack under the Rules Enabling Act. See *Willy v. Coastal Corp.*, —— U.S. —— (1992); *Business Guides, Inc. v. Chromatic Communications Enter. Inc.*, —— U.S. —— (1991). This restriction does not limit the court's power to impose sanctions or remedial orders that may have collateral financial consequences upon a party, such as dismissal of a claim, preclusion of a defense, or preparation of amended pleadings.

Explicit provision is made for litigants to be provided notice of the alleged violation and an opportunity to respond before sanctions are imposed. Whether the matter should be decided solely on the basis of written submissions or should be scheduled for oral argument (or, indeed, for evidentiary presentation) will depend on the circumstances. If the court imposes a sanction, it must, unless waived, indicate its reasons in a written order or on the record; the court should not ordinarily have to explain its denial of a motion for sanctions. Whether a violation has occurred and what sanctions, if any, to impose for a violation are matters committed to the discretion of the trial court; accordingly, as under current law, the standard for appellate review of these decisions will be for abuse of discretion. *See Cooter & Gell v. Hartmarx Corp.*, 496 U.S. 384 (1990) (noting, however, that an abuse would be established if the court based its ruling on an erroneous view of the law or on a clearly erroneous assessment of the evidence).

The revision leaves for resolution on a case-by-case basis, considering the particular circumstances involved, the question as to when a motion for violation of Rule 11 should be served and when, if filed, it should be decided. Ordinarily the motion should be served promptly after the inappropriate paper is filed, and, if delayed too long, may be viewed as untimely. In other circumstances, it should not be served until the other party has had a reasonable opportunity for discovery. Given the "safe harbor" provisions discussed below, a party cannot delay serving its Rule 11 motion until conclusion of the case (or judicial rejection of the offending contention).

Rule 11 motions should not be made or threatened for minor, inconsequential violations of the standards prescribed by subdivision (b). They should not be employed as a discovery device or to test the legal sufficiency or efficacy of allegations in the pleadings; other motions are available for those purposes. Nor should Rule 11 motions be prepared to emphasize the merits of a party's position, to exact an unjust settlement, to intimidate an adversary into withdrawing contentions that are fairly debatable, to increase the costs of litigation, to create a conflict of interest between attorney and client, or to seek disclosure of matters otherwise protected by the attorney-client privilege or the work-product doctrine. As under the prior rule, the court may defer its ruling (or its decision as to the identity of the persons to be sanctioned) until final resolution of the case in order to avoid immediate conflicts of interest and to reduce the disruption created if a disclosure of attorney-client communications is needed to determine whether a violation occurred or to identify the person responsible for the violation.

The rule provides that requests for sanctions must be made as a separate motion, *i.e.*, not simply included as an additional prayer for relief contained in another motion. The motion for sanctions is not, however, to be filed until at least 21 days (or such other period as the court may set) after being served. If, during this period, the alleged violation is corrected, as by withdrawing (whether formally or informally) some allegation or contention, the motion should not be filed with the court. These provisions are intended to provide a type of "safe harbor" against motions under Rule 11 in that a party will not be subject to sanctions on the basis of another party's motion unless, after receiving the motion, it refuses to withdraw that position or to acknowledge candidly that it does not currently have evidence to support a specified allegation. Under the former rule, parties were sometimes reluctant to abandon a questionable contention lest that be viewed as evidence of a violation of Rule 11; under the revision, the timely withdrawal of a contention will protect a party against a motion for sanctions.

To stress the seriousness of a motion for sanctions and to define precisely the conduct claimed to violate the rule, the revision provides that the "safe harbor" period begins to run only upon service of the motion. In most cases, however, counsel should be expected to give informal notice to the other party, whether in person or by a telephone call or letter, of a potential violation before proceeding to prepare and serve a Rule 11 motion.

As under former Rule 11, the filing of a motion for sanctions is itself subject to the requirements of the rule and can lead to sanctions. However, service of a cross motion under Rule 11 should rarely be needed since under the revision the court may award to the person who prevails on a motion under Rule 11—whether the movant or the target of the motion—reasonable expenses, including attorney's fees, incurred in presenting or opposing the motion.

The power of the court to act on its own initiative is retained, but with the condition that this be done through a show cause order. This procedure provides the person with notice and an opportunity to respond. The revision provides that a monetary sanction imposed after a court-initiated show cause order be limited to a penalty payable to the court and that it be imposed only if the show cause order is issued before any voluntary dismissal or an agreement of the parties to settle the claims made by or against the litigant. Parties settling a case should not be subsequently faced with an unexpected order from the court leading to monetary sanctions that might have affected their willingness to settle or voluntarily dismiss a case. Since show cause orders will ordinarily be issued only in situations that are akin to a contempt of court, the rule does not provide a "safe harbor" to a litigant for withdrawing a claim, defense, etc., after a show cause order has been issued on the court's own initiative. Such corrective action, however, should be taken into account in deciding what—if any—sanction to impose if, after consideration of the litigant's response, the court concludes that a violation has occurred.

Subdivision (d). Rules 26(g) and 37 establish certification standards and sanctions that apply to discovery disclosures, requests, responses, objections, and motions. It is appropriate that Rules 26 through 37, which are specially designed for the discovery process, govern such documents and conduct rather than the more general provisions of Rule 11. Subdivision (d) has been added to accomplish this result.

Rule 11 is not the exclusive source for control of improper presentations of claims, defenses, or contentions. It does not supplant statutes permitting awards of attorney's fees to prevailing parties or alter the principles governing such awards. It does not inhibit the court in punishing for contempt, in exercising its inherent powers, or in imposing

sanctions, awarding expenses, or directing remedial action authorized under other rules or under 28 U.S.C. § 1927. *See Chambers v. NASCO,* — U.S. — (1991). Chambers cautions, however, against reliance upon inherent powers if appropriate sanctions can be imposed under provisions such as Rule 11, and the procedures specified in Rule 11—notice, opportunity to respond, and findings—should ordinarily be employed when imposing a sanction under the court's inherent powers. Finally, it should be noted that Rule 11 does not preclude a party from initiating an independent action for malicious prosecution or abuse of process.

2007 Amendment

*[Effective December 1, 2007,
absent contrary Congressional action.]*

The language of Rule 11 has been amended as part of the general restyling of the Civil Rules to make them more easily understood and to make style and terminology consistent throughout the rules. These changes are intended to be stylistic only.

Providing an e-mail address is useful, but does not of itself signify consent to filing or service by e-mail.

Rule 12. Defenses and Objections—When and How Presented—By Pleading or Motion—Motion for Judgment on Pleadings

(a) When Presented.

(1) Unless a different time is prescribed in a statute of the United States, a defendant shall serve an answer

(A) within 20 days after being served with the summons and complaint, or

(B) if service of the summons has been timely waived on request under Rule 4(d), within 60 days after the date when the request for waiver was sent, or within 90 days after that date if the defendant was addressed outside any judicial district of the United States.

(2) A party served with a pleading stating a cross-claim against that party shall serve an answer thereto within 20 days after being served. The plaintiff shall serve a reply to a counterclaim in the answer within 20 days after service of the answer, or, if a reply is ordered by the court, within 20 days after service of the order, unless the order otherwise directs.

(3)(A) The United States, an agency of the United States, or an officer or employee of the United States sued in an official capacity, shall serve an answer to the complaint or cross-claim— or a reply to a counterclaim—within 60 days after the United States attorney is served with the pleading asserting the claim.

(B) An officer or employee of the United States sued in an individual capacity for acts or omissions occurring in connection with the performance of duties on behalf of the United States shall serve an answer to the complaint or cross-claim—or a reply to a counterclaim—within 60 days after service on the officer or employee, or service on the United States attorney, whichever is later.

(4) Unless a different time is fixed by court order, the service of a motion permitted under this rule alters these periods of time as follows:

(A) if the court denies the motion or postpones its disposition until the trial on the merits, the responsive pleading shall be served within 10 days after notice of the court's action; or

(B) if the court grants a motion for a more definite statement, the responsive pleading shall be served within 10 days after the service of the more definite statement.

(b) How Presented. Every defense, in law or fact, to a claim for relief in any pleading, whether a claim, counterclaim, cross-claim, or third-party claim, shall be asserted in the responsive pleading thereto if one is required, except that the following defenses may at the option of the pleader be made by motion: (1) lack of jurisdiction over the subject matter, (2) lack of jurisdiction over the person, (3) improper venue, (4) insufficiency of process, (5) insufficiency of service of process, (6) failure to state a claim upon which relief can be granted, (7) failure to join a party under Rule 19. A motion making any of these defenses shall be made before pleading if a further pleading is permitted. No defense or objection is waived by being joined with one or more other defenses or objections in a responsive pleading or motion. If a pleading sets forth a claim for relief to which the adverse party is not required to serve a responsive pleading, the adverse party may assert at the trial any defense in law or fact to that claim for relief. If, on a motion asserting the defense numbered (6) to dismiss for failure of the pleading to state a claim upon which relief can be granted, matters outside the pleading are presented to and not excluded by the court, the motion shall be treated as one for summary judgment and disposed of as provided in Rule 56, and all parties shall be given reasonable opportunity to present all material made pertinent to such a motion by Rule 56.

(c) Motion for Judgment on the Pleadings. After the pleadings are closed but within such time as not to delay the trial, any party may move for judgment on the pleadings. If, on a motion for judgment on the pleadings, matters outside the pleadings are presented to and not excluded by the court, the motion shall be treated as one for summary judgment and disposed of as provided in Rule 56, and all parties shall be given reasonable opportunity to present all material made pertinent to such a motion by Rule 56.

(d) Preliminary Hearings. The defenses specifically enumerated (1)–(7) in subdivision (b) of this rule,

whether made in a pleading or by motion, and the motion for judgment mentioned in subdivision (c) of this rule shall be heard and determined before trial on application of any party, unless the court orders that the hearing and determination thereof be deferred until the trial.

(e) Motion for More Definite Statement. If a pleading to which a responsive pleading is permitted is so vague or ambiguous that a party cannot reasonably be required to frame a responsive pleading, the party may move for a more definite statement before interposing a responsive pleading. The motion shall point out the defects complained of and the details desired. If the motion is granted and the order of the court is not obeyed within 10 days after notice of the order or within such other time as the court may fix, the court may strike the pleading to which the motion was directed or make such order as it deems just.

(f) Motion to Strike. Upon motion made by a party before responding to a pleading or, if no responsive pleading is permitted by these rules, upon motion made by a party within 20 days after the service of the pleading upon the party or upon the court's own initiative at any time, the court may order stricken from any pleading any insufficient defense or any redundant, immaterial, impertinent, or scandalous matter.

(g) Consolidation of Defenses in Motion. A party who makes a motion under this rule may join with it any other motions herein provided for and then available to the party. If a party makes a motion under this rule but omits therefrom any defense or objection then available to the party which this rule permits to be raised by motion, the party shall not thereafter make a motion based on the defense or objection so omitted, except a motion as provided in subdivision (h)(2) hereof on any of the grounds there stated.

(h) Waiver or Preservation of Certain Defenses.

(1) A defense of lack of jurisdiction over the person, improper venue, insufficiency of process, or insufficiency of service of process is waived (A) if omitted from a motion in the circumstances described in subdivision (g), or (B) if it is neither made by motion under this rule nor included in a responsive pleading or an amendment thereof permitted by Rule 15(a) to be made as a matter of course.

(2) A defense of failure to state a claim upon which relief can be granted, a defense of failure to join a party indispensable under Rule 19, and an objection of failure to state a legal defense to a claim may be made in any pleading permitted or ordered under Rule 7(a), or by motion for judgment on the pleadings, or at the trial on the merits.

(3) Whenever it appears by suggestion of the parties or otherwise that the court lacks jurisdiction of the subject matter, the court shall dism. action.

(As amended Dec. 27, 1946, eff. Mar. 19, 1948; Jan. 21, ـــ3, eff. July 1, 1963; Feb. 28, 1966, eff. July 1, 1966; Mar. 2, 1987, eff. Aug. 1, 1987; Apr. 22, 1993, eff. Dec. 1, 1993; Apr. 17, 2000, eff. Dec. 1, 2000.)

Proposed Amendment of Rule

Effective December 1, 2007, absent contrary Congressional action, this rule is amended to read as follows:

Rule 12. Defenses and Objections: When and How Presented; Motion for Judgment on the Pleadings; Consolidating Motions; Waiving Defenses; Pretrial Hearing

(a) Time to Serve a Responsive Pleading.

(1) In General. Unless another time is specified by this rule or a federal statute, the time for serving a responsive pleading is as follows:

(A) A defendant must serve an answer:

(i) within 20 days after being served with the summons and complaint; or

(ii) if it has timely waived service under Rule 4(d), within 60 days after the request for a waiver was sent, or within 90 days after it was sent to the defendant outside any judicial district of the United States.

(B) A party must serve an answer to a counterclaim or crossclaim within 20 days after being served with the pleading that states the counterclaim or crossclaim.

(C) A party must serve a reply to an answer within 20 days after being served with an order to reply, unless the order specifies a different time.

(2) United States and Its Agencies, Officers, or Employees Sued in an Official Capacity. The United States, a United States agency, or a United States officer or employee sued only in an official capacity must serve an answer to a complaint, counterclaim, or crossclaim within 60 days after service on the United States attorney.

(3) United States Officers or Employees Sued in an Individual Capacity. A United States officer or employee sued in an individual capacity for an act or omission occurring in connection with duties performed on the United States' behalf must serve an answer to a complaint, counterclaim, or crossclaim within 60 days after service on the officer or employee or service on the United States attorney, whichever is later.

(4) Effect of a Motion. Unless the court sets a different time, serving a motion under this rule alters these periods as follows:

(A) if the court denies the motion or postpones its disposition until trial, the responsive pleading must be served within 10 days after notice of the court's action; or

(B) if the court grants a motion for a more definite statement, the responsive pleading must be served within 10 days after the more definite statement is served.

(b) How to Present Defenses. *Every defense to a claim for relief in any pleading must be asserted in the responsive pleading if one is required. But a party may assert the following defenses by motion:*

(1) lack of subject-matter jurisdiction;

(2) lack of personal jurisdiction;

(3) improper venue;

(4) insufficient process;

(5) insufficient service of process;

(6) failure to state a claim upon which relief can be granted; and

(7) failure to join a party under Rule 19.

A motion asserting any of these defenses must be made before pleading if a responsive pleading is allowed. If a pleading sets out a claim for relief that does not require a responsive pleading, an opposing party may assert at trial any defense to that claim. No defense or objection is waived by joining it with one or more other defenses or objections in a responsive pleading or in a motion.

(c) Motion for Judgment on the Pleadings. *After the pleadings are closed—but early enough not to delay trial—a party may move for judgment on the pleadings.*

(d) Result of Presenting Matters Outside the Pleadings. *If, on a motion under Rule 12(b)(6) or 12(c), matters outside the pleadings are presented to and not excluded by the court, the motion must be treated as one for summary judgment under Rule 56. All parties must be given a reasonable opportunity to present all the material that is pertinent to the motion.*

(e) Motion for a More Definite Statement. *A party may move for a more definite statement of a pleading to which a responsive pleading is allowed but which is so vague or ambiguous that the party cannot reasonably prepare a response. The motion must be made before filing a responsive pleading and must point out the defects complained of and the details desired. If the court orders a more definite statement and the order is not obeyed within 10 days after notice of the order or within the time the court*

sets, the court may strike the pleading or issue any other appropriate order.

(f) Motion to Strike. *The court may strike from a pleading an insufficient defense or any redundant, immaterial, impertinent, or scandalous matter. The court may act:*

(1) on its own; or

(2) on motion made by a party either before responding to the pleading or, if a response is not allowed, within 20 days after being served with the pleading.

(g) Joining Motions.

(1) Right to Join. A motion under this rule may be joined with any other motion allowed by this rule.

(2) Limitation on Further Motions. Except as provided in Rule 12(h)(2) or (3), a party that makes a motion under this rule must not make another motion under this rule raising a defense or objection that was available to the party but omitted from its earlier motion.

(h) Waiving and Preserving Certain Defenses.

(1) When Some Are Waived. A party waives any defense listed in Rule 12(b)(2)-(5) by:

(A) omitting it from a motion in the circumstances described in Rule 12(g)(2); or

(B) failing to either:

(i) make it by motion under this rule; or

(ii) include it in a responsive pleading or in an amendment allowed by Rule 15(a)(1) as a matter of course.

(2) When to Raise Others. Failure to state a claim upon which relief can be granted, to join a person required by Rule 19(b), or to state a legal defense to a claim may be raised:

(A) in any pleading allowed or ordered under Rule 7(a);

(B) by a motion under Rule 12(c); or

(C) at trial.

(3) Lack of Subject–Matter Jurisdiction. If the court determines at any time that it lacks subject-matter jurisdiction, the court must dismiss the action.

(i) Hearing Before Trial. *If a party so moves, any defense listed in Rule 12(b)(1)–(7)—whether made in a pleading or by motion—and a motion under Rule 12(c) must be heard and decided before trial unless the court orders a deferral until trial.*

Complete Annotation Materials, see Title 28 U.S.C.A.

ADVISORY COMMITTEE NOTES
1937 Adoption

Note to Subdivision (a). 1. Compare [former] Equity Rules 12 (Issue of Subpoena—Time for Answer) and 31 (Reply—When Required—When Cause at Issue); 4 Mont. Rev.Codes Ann. (1935) §§ 9107, 9158; N.Y.C. P.A. (1937) § 263; N.Y.R.C.P. (1937) Rules 109–111.

2. U.S.C., Title 28, § 763 (now § 547) (Petition in action against United States; service; appearance by district attorney) provides that the United States as a defendant shall have 60 days within which to answer or otherwise defend. This and other statutes which provide 60 days for the United States or an officer or agency thereof to answer or otherwise defend are continued by this rule. In so far as any statutes not excepted in rule 81 provide a different time for a defendant to defend, such statutes are modified. See U.S.C., Title 28, [former] § 45 (District courts; practice and procedure in certain cases under the interstate commerce laws) (30 days).

3. Compare the last sentence of [former] Equity Rule 29 (Defenses—How Presented) and N.Y.C.P.A. (1937) § 283. See Rule 15(a) for time within which to plead to an amended pleading.

Note to Subdivisions (b) and (d). 1. See generally [former] Equity Rules 29 (Defenses—How Presented), 33 (Testing Sufficiency of Defense), 43 (Defect of Parties—Resisting Objection), and 44 (Defect of Parties—Tardy Objection); N.Y.C.P.A. (1937) §§ 277–280; N.Y.R.C.P. (1937) Rules 106–112; *English Rules Under the Judicature Act* (The Annual Practice, 1937) O. 25, r.r. 1–4; Clark, *Code Pleading*, 1928, pp. 371–381.

2. For provisions authorizing defenses to be made in the answer or reply see *English Rules Under the Judicature Act*, (The Annual Practice, 1937) O. 25, r.r. 1–4; 1 Miss.Code Ann. (1930) §§ 378, 379. Compare Equity Rule 29 (Defenses—How Presented); U.S.C.A., Title 28, [former] § 45 (District Courts; practice and procedure in certain cases under the interstate commerce laws). U.S.C., Title 28, [former] § 45, substantially continued by this rule, provides: "No replication need be filed to the answer, and objections to the sufficiency of the petition or answer as not setting forth a cause of action or defense must be taken at the final hearing or by motion to dismiss the petition based on said grounds, which motion may be made at any time before answer is filed." Compare Calif.Code Civ.Proc., (Deering, 1937) § 433; 4 Nev.Comp.Laws (Hillyer, 1929) § 8600. For provisions that the defendant may demur and answer at the same time, see Calif.Code Civ.Proc. (Deering, 1937) § 431; 4 Nev.Comp. Laws (Hillyer, 1929) § 8598.

3. [Former] Equity Rule 29 (Defenses—How Presented) abolished demurrers and provided that defenses in point of law arising on the face of the bill should be made by motion to dismiss or in the answer, with further provision that every such point of law going to the whole or material part of the cause or causes stated might be called up and disposed of before final hearing "at the discretion of the court." Likewise many state practices have abolished the demurrer, or retain it only to attack substantial and not formal defects. See 6 Tenn.Code Ann. (Williams, 1934) § 8784; Ala.Code Ann. (Michie, 1928) § 9479; 2 Mass.Gen.Laws (Ter.Ed., 1932) ch. 231, §§ 15–18; Kansas Gen.Stat.Ann. (1935) §§ 60–705, 60–706.

Note to Subdivision (c). Compare [former] Equity Rule 33 (Testing Sufficiency of Defense); N.Y.R.C.P. (1937) Rules 111 and 112.

Note to Subdivisions (e) and (f). Compare [former] Equity Rules 20 (Further and Particular Statement in Pleading May be Required) and 21 (Scandal and Impertinence); *English Rules Under the Judicature Act* (The Annual Practice, 1937) O. 19, r.r. 7, 7a, 7b, 8; 4 Mont.Rev.Codes Ann. (1935) §§ 9166, 9167; N.Y.C.P.A. (1937) § 247; N.Y.C.P.A. (1937) Rules 103, 115, 116, 117; Wyo.Rev.Stat.Ann. (Courtright, 1931) §§ 89–1033, 89–1034.

Note to Subdivision (g). Compare Rules of the District Court of the United States for the District of Columbia (1937) Equity Rule 11; N.M. Rules of Pleading, Practice and Procedure, 38 N.M.Rep. vii. [105–408] (1934); Wash.Gen. Rules of the Superior Courts, 1 Wash.Rev.Stat.Ann. (Remington, 1932) p. 160, Rule VI(e) and (f).

Note to Subdivision (h). Compare Calif.Code Civ.Proc. (Deering, 1937) § 434; 2 Minn.Stat. (Mason, 1927) § 9252; N.Y.C.P.A. (1937) §§ 278 and 279; Wash.Gen.Rules of the Superior Courts, 1 Wash.Rev.Stat.Ann. (Remington, 1932) p. 160, Rule VI(e). This rule continues U.S.C.A., Title 28, former § 80 [now 1359, 1447, 1919] (Dismissal or remand) (of action over which district court lacks jurisdiction), while U.S.C.A., Title 28, § 399 (Amendments to show diverse citizenship) is continued by Rule 15.

1946 Amendment

Note. Subdivision (a). Various minor alterations in language have been made to improve the statement of the rule. All references to bills of particulars have been stricken in accordance with changes made in subdivision (e).

Subdivision (b). The addition of defense (7), "failure to join an indispensable party", cures an omission in the rules which are silent as to the mode of raising such failure. See Commentary, *Manner of Raising Objection of Non-Joinder of Indispensable Party*, 1940, 2 Fed.Rules Serv. 658, and, 1942, 5 Fed.Rules Serv. 820. In one case, *United States v. Metropolitan Life Ins. Co.*, E.D.Pa.1941, 36 F.Supp. 399, the failure to join an indispensable party was raised under Rule 12(c).

Rule 12(b)(6), permitting a motion to dismiss for failure of the complaint to state a claim on which relief can be granted, is substantially the same as the old demurrer for failure of a pleading to state a cause of action. Some courts have held that as the rule by its terms refers to statements in the complaint, extraneous matter on affidavits, depositions or otherwise, may not be introduced in support of the motion, or to resist it. On the other hand, in many cases the district courts have permitted the introduction of such material. When these cases have reached circuit courts of appeals in situations where the extraneous material so received shows that there is no genuine issue as to any material question of fact and that on the undisputed facts as disclosed by the affidavits or depositions, one party or the other is entitled to judgment as a matter of law, the circuit courts, properly enough, have been reluctant to dispose of the case merely on the face of the pleading, and in the interest of prompt disposition of the action have made a final disposition of it. In dealing with such situations the Second Circuit has made the sound suggestion that whatever its label or original basis, the motion may be treated as a motion for summary judg-

ment and disposed of as such. *Samara v. United States,* C.C.A.2, 1942, 129 F.2d 594, certiorari denied 63 S.Ct. 258, 317 U.S. 686, 87 L.Ed. 549; *Boro Hall Corp. v. General Motors Corp.,* C.C.A.2, 1942, 124 F.2d 822, certiorari denied 63 S.Ct. 436, 317 U.S. 695, 87 L.Ed. 556. See, also, *Kithcart v. Metropolitan Life Ins. Co.,* C.C.A.8, 1945, 150 F.2d 997.

It has also been suggested that this practice could be justified on the ground that the federal rules permit "speaking" motions. The Committee entertains the view that on motion under Rule 12(b)(6) to dismiss for failure of the complaint to state a good claim, the trial court should have authority to permit the introduction of extraneous matter, such as may be offered on a motion for summary judgment, and if it does not exclude such matter the motion should then be treated as a motion for summary judgment and disposed of in the manner and on the conditions stated in Rule 56 relating to summary judgments, and, of course, in such a situation, when the case reaches the circuit court of appeals, that court should treat the motion in the same way. The Committee believes that such practice, however, should be tied to the summary judgment rule. The term "speaking motion" is not mentioned in the rules, and if there is such a thing its limitations are undefined. Where extraneous matter is received, by tying further proceedings to the summary judgment rule the courts have a definite basis in the rules for disposing of the motion.

The Committee emphasizes particularly the fact that the summary judgment rule does not permit a case to be disposed of by judgment on the merits on affidavits, which disclose a conflict on a material issue of fact, and unless this practice is tied to the summary judgment, rule, the extent to which a court, on the introduction of such extraneous matter, may resolve questions of fact on conflicting proof would be left uncertain.

The decisions dealing with this general situation may be generally grouped as follows: (1) cases dealing with the use of affidavits and other extraneous material on motions; (2) cases reversing judgments to prevent final determination on mere pleading allegations alone.

Under group (1) are: *Boro Hall Corp. v. General Motors Corp.,* C.C.A.2, 1942, 124 F.2d 822, certiorari denied 1943, 63 S.Ct. 436, 317 U.S. 695, 87 L.Ed. 556; *Gallup v. Caldwell,* C.C.A.3, 1941, 120 F.2d 90; *Central Mexico Light & Power Co. v. Munch,* C.C.A.2, 1940, 116 F.2d 85; *National Labor Relations Board v. Montgomery Ward & Co.,* 1944, 144 F.2d 528, 79 U.S.App.D.C. 200, certiorari denied 1944, 65 S.Ct. 134, 323 U.S. 774, 89 L.Ed. 619; *Urquhart v. American-La France Foamite Corp.,* 1944, 144 F.2d 542, 79 U.S.App.D.C. 219; *Samara v. United States,* C.C.A.2, 1942, 129 F.2d 594; *Cohen v. American Window Glass Co.,* C.C.A.2, 1942, 126 F.2d 111; *Sperry Products Inc. v. Association of American Railroads,* C.C.A.2, 1942, 132 F.2d 408; *Joint Council Dining Car Employees Local 370 v. Delaware, Lackawanna and Western R. Co.,* C.C.A.2, 1946, 157 F.2d 417; *Weeks v. Bareco Oil Co.,* C.C.A.7, 1941, 125 F.2d 84; *Carroll v. Morrison Hotel Corp.,* C.C.A.7, 1945, 149 F.2d 404; *Victory v. Manning,* C.C.A.3, 1942, 128 F.2d 415; *Locals No. 1470, No. 1469, and No. 1512 of International Longshoremen's Association v. Southern Pacific Co.,* C.C.A.5, 1942, 131 F.2d 605; *Lucking v. Delano,* C.C.A.6, 1942, 129 F.2d 283; *San Francisco Lodge No. 68 of International Association of Machinists v. Forrestal,* Cal.1944, 58 F.Supp. 466; *Benson v. Export Equipment Corp.,* 1945, 164 P.2d 380, 49 N.M. 356,

construing New Mexico rule identical with Rule 12(b)(6); *F. E. Myers & Bros. Co. v. Gould Pumps, Inc.,* W.D.N.Y.1946, 9 Fed.Rules Serv. 12b.33, Case 2, 5 F.R.D. 132. Cf. *Kohler v. Jacobs,* C.C.A.5, 1943, 138 F.2d 440; *Cohen v. United States,* C.C.A.8, 1942, 129 F.2d 733.

Under group (2) are: *Sparks v. England,* C.C.A.8, 1940, 113 F.2d 579; *Continental Collieries, Inc. v. Shober,* C.C.A.3, 1942, 130 F.2d 631; *Downey v. Palmer,* C.C.A.2, 1940, 114 F.2d 116; *DeLoach v. Crowley's Inc.,* C.C.A.5, 1942, 128 F.2d 378; *Leimer v. State Mutual Life Assurance Co. of Worcester, Mass.,* C.C.A.8, 1940, 108 F.2d 302; *Rossiter v. Vogel,* C.C.A.2, 1943, 134 F.2d 908, compare s.c., C.C.A.2, 1945, 148 F.2d 292; *Karl Kiefer Machine Co. v. United States Bottlers Machinery Co.,* C.C.A.7, 1940, 113 F.2d 356; *Chicago Metallic Mfg. Co. v. Edward Katzinger Co.,* C.C.A.7, 1941, 123 F.2d 518; *Louisiana Farmers' Protective Union, Inc. v. Great Atlantic & Pacific Tea Co. of America, Inc.,* C.C.A.8, 1942, 131 F.2d 419; *Publicity Bldg. Realty Corp. v. Hannegan,* C.C.A.8, 1943, 139 F.2d 583; *Dioguardi v. Durning,* C.C.A.2, 1944, 139 F.2d 774; *Package Closure Corp. v. Sealright Co., Inc.,* C.C.A.2, 1944, 141 F.2d 972; *Tahir Erk v. Glenn L. Martin Co.,* C.C.A.4, 1941, 116 F.2d 865; *Bell v. Preferred Life Assurance Society of Montgomery, Ala.,* 1943, 64 S.Ct. 5, 320 U.S. 238, 88 L.Ed. 15.

The addition at the end of subdivision (b) makes it clear that on a motion under Rule 12(b)(6) extraneous material may not be considered if the court excludes it, but that if the court does not exclude such material the motion shall be treated as a motion for summary judgment and disposed of as provided in Rule 56. It will also be observed that if a motion under Rule 12(b)(6) is thus converted into a summary judgment motion, the amendment insures that both parties shall be given a reasonable opportunity to submit affidavits and extraneous proofs to avoid taking a party by surprise through the conversion of the motion into a motion for summary judgment. In this manner and to this extent the amendment regularizes the practice above described. As the courts are already dealing with cases in this way, the effect of this amendment is really only to define the practice carefully and apply the requirements of the summary judgment rule in the disposition of the motion.

Subdivision (c). The sentence appended to subdivision (c) performs the same function and is grounded on the same reasons as the corresponding sentence added in subdivision (b).

Subdivision (d). The change here was made necessary because of the addition of defense (7) in subdivision (b).

Subdivision (e). References in this subdivision to a bill of particulars have been deleted, and the motion provided for is confined to one for more definite statement to be obtained only in cases where the movant cannot reasonably be required to frame an answer or other responsive pleading to the pleading in question. With respect to preparations for trial, the party is properly relegated to the various methods of examination and discovery provided in the rules for that purpose. *Slusher v. Jones,* E.D.Ky.1943, 7 Fed.Rules Serv. 12e.231, Case 5, 3 F.R.D. 168; *Best Foods, Inc. v. General Mills, Inc.,* D.Del.1943, 7 Fed.Rules Serv. 12e.231, Case 7, 3 F.R.D. 275; *Braden v. Callaway,* E.D.Tenn.1943, 8 Fed. Rules Serv. 12e.231, Case 1 (". . . most courts . . . conclude that the definiteness required is only such as will be sufficient for the party to prepare responsive pleadings"). Accordingly, the reference to the 20 day time limit has also

been eliminated, since the purpose of this present provision is to state a time period where the motion for a bill is made for the purpose of preparing for trial.

Rule 12(e) as originally drawn has been the subject of more judicial rulings than any other part of the rules, and has been much criticized by commentators, judges and members of the bar. See general discussion and cases cited in 1 Moore's *Federal Practice*, 1938, Cum.Supplement, § 12.07, under "Page 657"; also, Holtzoff, *New Federal Procedure and the Courts*, 1940, 35–41. And compare vote of Second Circuit Conference of Circuit and District Judges, June 1940, recommending the abolition of the bill of particulars; *Sun Valley Mfg. Co. v. Mylish*, E.D.Pa.1944, 8 Fed.Rules Serv. 12e.231, Case 6 ("Our experience . . . has demonstrated not only that 'the office of the bill of particulars is fast becoming obsolete' . . . but that in view of the adequate discovery procedure available under the Rules, motions for bills of particulars should be abolished altogether."); *Walling v. American Steamship Co.*, W.D.N.Y.1945, 4 F.R.D. 355, 8 Fed.Rules Serv. 12e.244, Case 8 (". . . the adoption of the rule was ill advised. It has led to confusion, duplication and delay.") The tendency of some courts freely to grant extended bills of particulars has served to neutralize any helpful benefits derived from rule 8, and has overlooked the intended use of the rules on depositions and discovery. The words "or to prepare for trial"—eliminated by the proposed amendment—have sometimes been seized upon as grounds for compulsory statement in the opposing pleading of all the details which the movant would have to meet at the trial. On the other hand, many courts have in effect read these words out of the rule. See *Walling v. Alabama Pipe Co.*, W.D.Mo. 1942, 3 F.R.D. 159, 6 Fed.Rules Serv. 12e.244, Case 7; *Fleming v. Mason & Dixon Lines, Inc.*, E.D.Tenn.1941, 42 F.Supp. 230; *Kellogg Co. v. National Biscuit Co.*, D.N.J. 1941, 38 F.Supp. 643; *Brown v. H. L. Green Co.*, S.D.N.Y. 1943, 7 Fed.Rules Serv. 12e.231, Case 6; *Pedersen v. Standard Accident Ins. Co.*, W.D.Mo.1945, 8 Fed.Rules Serv. 12e.231, Case 8; *Bowles v. Ohse*, D.Neb.1945, 4 F.R.D. 403, 9 Fed.Rules Serv. 12e.231, Case 1; *Klages v. Cohen*, E.D.N.Y. 1945, 9 Fed.Rules Serv. 8a.25, Case 4; *Bowles v. Lawrence*, D.Mass.1945, 8 Fed.Rules Serv. 12e.231, Case 19; *McKinney Tool & Mfg. Co. v. Hoyt*, N.D.Ohio 1945, 9 Fed.Rules Serv. 12e.235, Case 1; *Bowles v. Jack*, D.Minn.1945, 5 F.R.D. 1, 9 Fed.Rules Serv. 12e.244, Case 9. And it has been urged from the bench that the phrase be stricken, *Poole v. White*, N.D.W.Va.1941, 5 Fed.Rules Serv. 12e.231, Case 4, 2 F.R.D. 40. See also *Bowles v. Gabel*, W.D.Mo.1946, 9 Fed.Rules Serv. 12e.244, Case 10. ("The courts have never favored that portion of the rules which undertook to justify a motion of this kind for the purpose of aiding counsel in preparing his case for trial.").

Subdivision (f). This amendment affords a specific method of raising the insufficiency of a defense, a matter which has troubled some courts, although attack has been permitted in one way or another. See *Dysart v. Remington-Rand, Inc.*, D.Conn.1939, 31 F.Supp. 296; *Eastman Kodak Co. v. McAuley*, S.D.N.Y.1941, 4 Fed.Rules Serv., 12f.21, Case 8, 2 F.R.D. 21; *Schenley Distillers Corp. v. Renken*, E.D.S.C. 1940, 34 F.Supp. 678; *Yale Transport Corp. v. Yellow Truck & Coach Mfg. Co.*, S.D.N.Y.1944, 3 F.R.D. 440; *United States v. Turner Milk Co.*, N.D.Ill.1941, 4 Fed.Rules Serv. 12b.51, Case 3, 1 F.R.D. 643; *Teiger v. Stephan Oderwald, Inc.*, S.D.N.Y.1940, 31 F.Supp. 626; *Teplitsky v. Pennsylvania R. Co.*, N.D.Ill.1941, 38 F.Supp. 535; *Callagher v. Car-*

roll, E.D.N.Y.1939, 27 F.Supp. 568; *United States v. Palmer*, S.D.N.Y.1939, 28 F.Supp. 936. And see *Indemnity Ins. Co. of North America v. Pan American Airways, Inc.*, S.D.N.Y. 1944, 58 F.Supp. 338; Commentary, *Modes of Attacking Insufficient Defenses in the Answer*, 901, 1939, 1 Fed.Rules Serv. 669, 1940, 2 Fed.Rules Serv. 640.

Subdivision (g). The change in title conforms with the companion provision in subdivision (h).

The alteration of the "except" clause requires that other than provided in subdivision (h) a party who resorts to a motion to raise defenses specified in the rule, must include in one motion all that are then available to him. Under the original rule defenses which could be raised by motion were divided into two groups which could be the subjects of two successive motions.

Subdivision (h). The addition of the phrase relating to indispensable parties is one of necessity.

1963 Amendment

This amendment conforms to the amendment of Rule 4(e). See also the Advisory Committee's Note to amended Rule 4(b).

1966 Amendment

Subdivision (b)(7). The terminology of this subdivision is changed to accord with the amendment of Rule 19. See the Advisory Committee's Note to Rule 19, as amended, especially the third paragraph therein before the caption "Subdivision (c)."

Subdivision (g). Subdivision (g) has forbidden a defendant who makes a preanswer motion under this rule from making a further motion presenting any defense or objection which was available to him at the time he made the first motion and which he could have included, but did not in fact include therein. Thus if the defendant moves before answer to dismiss the complaint for failure to state a claim, he is barred from making a further motion presenting the defense of improper venue, if that defense was available to him when he made his original motion. Amended subdivision (g) is to the same effect. This required consolidation of defenses and objections in a Rule 12 motion is salutary in that it works against piecemeal consideration of a case. For exceptions to the requirement of consolidation, see the last clause of subdivision (g), referring to new subdivision (h)(2).

Subdivision (h). The question has arisen whether an omitted defense which cannot be made the basis of a second motion may nevertheless be pleaded in the answer. Subdivision (h) called for waiver of "* * * defenses and objections which he [defendant] does not present * * * by motion * * * or, if he has made no motion, in his answer * * *." If the clause "if he has made no motion," was read literally, it seemed that the omitted defense was waived and could not be pleaded in the answer. On the other hand, the clause might be read as adding nothing of substance to the preceding words; in that event it appeared that a defense was not waived by reason of being omitted from the motion and might be set up in the answer. The decisions were divided. Favoring waiver, see *Keef v. Derounian*, 6 F.R.D. 11 (N.D.Ill.1946); *Elbinger v. Precision Metal Workers Corp.*, 18 F.R.D. 467 (E.D.Wis.1956); see also *Rensing v. Turner Aviation Corp.*, 166 F.Supp. 790 (N.D.Ill.1958); *P. Beiersdorf*

& Co. v. Duke Laboratories, Inc., 10 F.R.D. 282 (S.D.N.Y. 1950); Neset v. Christensen, 92 F.Supp. 78 (E.D.N.Y.1950). Opposing waiver, see Phillips v. Baker, 121 F.2d 752 (9th Cir.1941); Crum v. Graham, 32 F.R.D. 173 (D.Mont.1963) (regretfully following the Phillips case); see also Birnbaum v. Birrell, 9 F.R.D. 72 (S.D.N.Y.1948); Johnson v. Joseph Schlitz Brewing Co., 33 F.Supp. 176 (E.D.Tenn.1940); cf. Carter v. American Bus Lines, Inc., 22 F.R.D. 323 (D.Neb. 1958).

Amended subdivision (h)(1)(A) eliminates the ambiguity and states that certain specified defenses which were available to a party when he made a preanswer motion, but which he omitted from the motion, are waived. The specified defenses are lack of jurisdiction over the person, improper venue, insufficiency of process, and insufficiency of service of process (see Rule 12(b)(2)–(5)). A party who by motion invites the court to pass upon a threshold defense should bring forward all the specified defenses he then has and thus allow the court to do a reasonably complete job. The waiver reinforces the policy of subdivision (g) forbidding successive motions.

By amended subdivision (h)(1)(B), the specified defenses, even if not waived by the operation of (A), are waived by the failure to raise them by a motion under Rule 12 or in the responsive pleading or any amendment thereto to which the party is entitled as a matter of course. The specified defenses are of such a character that they should not be delayed and brought up for the first time by means of an application to the court to amend the responsive pleading.

Since the language of the subdivisions is made clear, the party is put on fair notice of the effect of his actions and omissions and can guard himself against unintended waiver. It is to be noted that while the defenses specified in subdivision (h)(1) are subject to waiver as there provided, the more substantial defenses of failure to state a claim upon which relief can be granted, failure to join a party indispensable under Rule 19, and failure to state a legal defense to a claim (see Rule 12(b)(6), (7), (f)), as well as the defense of lack of jurisdiction over the subject matter (see Rule 12(b)(1)), are expressly preserved against waiver by amended subdivision (h)(2) and (3).

1987 Amendment

The amendments are technical. No substantive change is intended.

1993 Amendment

Subdivision (a) is divided into paragraphs for greater clarity, and paragraph (1)(B) is added to reflect amendments to Rule 4. Consistent with Rule 4(d)(3), a defendant that timely waives service is allowed 60 days from the date the request was mailed in which to respond to the complaint, with an additional 30 days afforded if the request was sent out of the country. Service is timely waived if the waiver is returned within the time specified in the request (30 days after the request was mailed, or 60 days if mailed out of the country) and before being formally served with process. Sometimes a plaintiff may attempt to serve a defendant with process while also sending the defendant a request for waiver of service; if the defendant executes the waiver of service within the time specified and before being served

with process, it should have the longer time to respond afforded by waiving service.

The date of sending the request is to be inserted by the plaintiff on the face of the request for waiver and on the waiver itself. This date is used to measure the return day for the waiver form, so that the plaintiff can know on a day certain whether formal service of process will be necessary; it is also a useful date to measure the time for answer when service is waived. The defendant who returns the waiver is given additional time for answer in order to assure that it loses nothing by waiving service of process.

2000 Amendment

Rule 12(a)(3)(B) is added to complement the addition of Rule 4(i)(2)(B). The purposes that underlie the requirement that service be made on the United States in an action that asserts individual liability of a United States officer or employee for acts occurring in connection with the performance of duties on behalf of the United States also require that the time to answer be extended to 60 days. Time is needed for the United States to determine whether to provide representation to the defendant officer or employee. If the United States provides representation, the need for an extended answer period is the same as in actions against the United States, a United States agency, or a United States officer sued in an official capacity.

An action against a former officer or employee of the United States is covered by subparagraph (3)(B) in the same way as an action against a present officer or employee. Termination of the relationship between the individual defendant and the United States does not reduce the need for additional time to answer.

GAP Report

No changes are recommended for Rule 12 as published.

2007 Amendment

[Effective December 1, 2007,
absent contrary Congressional action.]

The language of Rule 12 has been amended as part of the general restyling of the Civil Rules to make them more easily understood and to make style and terminology consistent throughout the rules. These changes are intended to be stylistic only.

Former Rule 12(a)(4)(A) referred to an order that postpones disposition of a motion "until the trial on the merits." Rule 12(a)(4) now refers to postponing disposition "until trial." The new expression avoids the ambiguity that inheres in "trial on the merits," which may become confusing when there is a separate trial of a single issue or another event different from a single all-encompassing trial.

Rule 13. Counterclaim and Cross-Claim

(a) **Compulsory Counterclaims.** A pleading shall state as a counterclaim any claim which at the time of serving the pleading the pleader has against any opposing party, if it arises out of the transaction or occurrence that is the subject matter of the opposing party's claim and does not require for its adjudication the presence of third parties of whom the court cannot acquire jurisdiction. But the pleader need not state

the claim if (1) at the time the action was commenced the claim was the subject of another pending action, or (2) the opposing party brought suit upon the claim by attachment or other process by which the court did not acquire jurisdiction to render a personal judgment on that claim, and the pleader is not stating any counterclaim under this Rule 13.

(b) Permissive Counterclaims. A pleading may state as a counterclaim any claim against an opposing party not arising out of the transaction or occurrence that is the subject matter of the opposing party's claim.

(c) Counterclaim Exceeding Opposing Claim. A counterclaim may or may not diminish or defeat the recovery sought by the opposing party. It may claim relief exceeding in amount or different in kind from that sought in the pleading of the opposing party.

(d) Counterclaim Against the United States. These rules shall not be construed to enlarge beyond the limits now fixed by law the right to assert counterclaims or to claim credits against the United States or an officer or agency thereof.

(e) Counterclaim Maturing or Acquired After Pleading. A claim which either matured or was acquired by the pleader after serving a pleading may, with the permission of the court, be presented as a counterclaim by supplemental pleading.

(f) Omitted Counterclaim. When a pleader fails to set up a counterclaim through oversight, inadvertence, or excusable neglect, or when justice requires, the pleader may by leave of court set up the counterclaim by amendment.

(g) Cross-Claim Against Co-Party. A pleading may state as a cross-claim any claim by one party against a co-party arising out of the transaction or occurrence that is the subject matter either of the original action or of a counterclaim therein or relating to any property that is the subject matter of the original action. Such cross-claim may include a claim that the party against whom it is asserted is or may be liable to the cross-claimant for all or part of a claim asserted in the action against the cross-claimant.

(h) Joinder of Additional Parties. Persons other than those made parties to the original action may be made parties to a counterclaim or cross-claim in accordance with the provisions of Rules 19 and 20.

(i) Separate Trials; Separate Judgments. If the court orders separate trials as provided in Rule 42(b), judgment on a counterclaim or cross-claim may be rendered in accordance with the terms of Rule 54(b) when the court has jurisdiction so to do, even if the claims of the opposing party have been dismissed or otherwise disposed of.

(As amended Dec. 27, 1946, eff. Mar. 19, 1948; Jan. 21, 1963, eff. July 1, 1963; Feb. 28, 1966, eff. July 1, 1966; Mar. 2, 1987, eff. Aug. 1, 1987.)

Proposed Amendment of Rule

Effective December 1, 2007, absent contrary Congressional action, this rule is amended to read as follows:

Rule 13. Counterclaim and Crossclaim

(a) Compulsory Counterclaim.

(1) In General. A pleading must state as a counterclaim any claim that—at the time of its service—the pleader has against an opposing party if the claim:

(A) arises out of the transaction or occurrence that is the subject matter of the opposing party's claim; and

(B) does not require adding another party over whom the court cannot acquire jurisdiction.

(2) Exceptions. The pleader need not state the claim if:

(A) when the action was commenced, the claim was the subject of another pending action; or

(B) the opposing party sued on its claim by attachment or other process that did not establish personal jurisdiction over the pleader on that claim, and the pleader does not assert any counterclaim under this rule.

(b) Permissive Counterclaim. A pleading may state as a counterclaim against an opposing party any claim that is not compulsory.

(c) Relief Sought in a Counterclaim. A counterclaim need not diminish or defeat the recovery sought by the opposing party. It may request relief that exceeds in amount or differs in kind from the relief sought by the opposing party.

(d) Counterclaim Against the United States. These rules do not expand the right to assert a counterclaim—or to claim a credit—against the United States or a United States officer or agency.

(e) Counterclaim Maturing or Acquired After Pleading. The court may permit a party to file a supplemental pleading asserting a counterclaim that matured or was acquired by the party after serving an earlier pleading.

(f) Omitted Counterclaim. The court may permit a party to amend a pleading to add a counterclaim if it was omitted through oversight, inadvertence, or excusable neglect or if justice so requires.

(g) Crossclaim Against a Coparty. A pleading may state as a crossclaim any claim by one party against a coparty if the claim arises out of the

Complete Annotation Materials, see Title 28 U.S.C.A.

transaction or occurrence that is the subject matter of the original action or of a counterclaim, or if the claim relates to any property that is the subject matter of the original action. The crossclaim may include a claim that the coparty is or may be liable to the cross-claimant for all or part of a claim asserted in the action against the cross-claimant.

(h) Joining Additional Parties. *Rules 19 and 20 govern the addition of a person as a party to a counterclaim or crossclaim.*

(i) Separate Trials; Separate Judgments. *If the court orders separate trials under Rule 42(b), it may enter judgment on a counterclaim or crossclaim under Rule 54(b) when it has jurisdiction to do so, even if the opposing party's claims have been dismissed or otherwise resolved.*

ADVISORY COMMITTEE NOTES

1937 Adoption

1. This is substantially [former] Equity Rule 30 (Answer—Contents—Counterclaim), broadened to include legal as well as equitable counterclaims.

2. Compare the English practice, *English Rules Under the Judicature Act* (The Annual Practice, 1937) O. 19, r.r. 2 and 3, and O. 21, r.r. 10–17; *Beddall v. Maitland*, L.R. 17 Ch.Div. 174, 181, 182 (1881).

3. Certain States have also adopted almost unrestricted provisions concerning both the subject matter of and the parties to a counterclaim. This seems to be the modern tendency. Ark.Civ.Code (Crawford, 1934) §§ 117 (as amended) and 118; N.J.Comp.Stat. (2 Cum.Supp. 1911–1924); N.Y.C.P.A. (1937) §§ 262, 266, 267 (all as amended, Laws of 1936, ch. 324), 268, 269, and 271; Wis.Stat. (1935) § 263.14(1)(c).

4. Most codes do not expressly provide for a counterclaim in the reply. Clark, *Code Pleading* (1928), p. 486. Ky.Codes (Carroll, 1932) Civ.Pract. § 98 does provide, however, for such counterclaim.

5. The provisions of this rule respecting counterclaims are subject to Rule 82 (Jurisdiction and Venue Unaffected). For a discussion of Federal jurisdiction and venue in regard to counterclaims and cross-claims, see Shulman and Jaegerman, *Some Jurisdictional Limitations in Federal Procedure* (1936), 45 Yale L.J. 393, 410 et seq.

6. This rule does not affect such statutes of the United States as U.S.C., Title 28, § 41(1) (now §§ 1332, 1345, 1359) (United States as plaintiff; civil suits at common law and in equity), relating to assigned claims in actions based on diversity of citizenship.

7. If the action proceeds to judgment without the interposition of a counterclaim as required by subdivision (a) of this rule, the counterclaim is barred. See *American Mills Co. v. American Surety Co.*, 260 U.S. 360, 43 S.Ct. 149, 67 L.Ed. 306 (1922); *Marconi Wireless Telegraph Co. v. National Electric Signalling Co.*, 206 Fed. 295 (E.D.N.Y., 1913); Hopkins, *Federal Equity Rules* (8th ed., 1933), p. 213; Simkins, *Federal Practice* (1934), p. 663.

8. For allowance of credits against the United States see U.S.C., Title 26, §§ 1672–1673 [sec. 7442] (Suits for refunds of internal revenue taxes—limitations); U.S.C., Title 28, § 774 (now § 2406) (Suits by United States against individuals; credits), [former] § 775 (Suits under postal laws; credits); U.S.C., Title 31, § 227 [now 3728] (Offsets against judgments and claims against United States).

1946 Amendment

Note. Subdivision (a). The use of the word "filing" was inadvertent. The word "serving" conforms with subdivision (e) and with usage generally throughout the rules.

The removal of the phrase "not the subject of a pending action" and the addition of the new clause at the end of the subdivision is designed to eliminate the ambiguity noted in *Prudential Insurance Co. of America v. Saxe*, App.D.C.1943, 77 U.S.App.D.C. 144, 134 F.2d 16, 33–34, cert. den., 1943, 319 U.S. 745, 63 S.Ct. 1033. The rewording of the subdivision in this respect insures against an undesirable possibility presented under the original rule whereby a party having a claim which would be the subject of a compulsory counterclaim could avoid stating it as such by bringing an independent action in another court after the commencement of the federal action but before serving his pleading in the federal action.

Subdivision (g). The amendment is to care for a situation such as where a second mortgagee is made defendant in a foreclosure proceeding and wishes to file a cross-complaint against the mortgagor in order to secure a personal judgment for the indebtedness and foreclose his lien. A claim of this sort by the second mortgagee may not necessarily arise out of the transaction or occurrence that is the subject matter of the original action under the terms of Rule 13(g).

Subdivision (h). The change clarifies the interdependence of Rules 13(i) and 54(b).

1963 Amendment

When a defendant, if he desires to defend his interest in property, is obliged to come in and litigate in a court to whose jurisdiction he could not ordinarily be subjected, fairness suggests that he should not be required to assert counterclaims, but should rather be permitted to do so at his election. If, however, he does elect to assert a counterclaim, it seems fair to require him to assert any other which is compulsory within the meaning of Rule 13(a). Clause (2), added by amendment to Rule 13(a), carries out this idea. It will apply to various cases described in Rule 4(e), as amended, where service is effected through attachment or other process by which the court does not acquire jurisdiction to render a personal judgment against the defendant. Clause (2) will also apply to actions commenced in State courts jurisdictionally grounded on attachment or the like, and removed to the Federal courts.

1966 Amendment

Rule 13(h), dealing with the joinder of additional parties to a counterclaim or cross-claim, has partaken of some of the textual difficulties of Rule 19 on necessary joinder of parties. See Advisory Committee's Note to Rule 19, as amended; cf. 3 *Moore's Federal Practice*, par. 13.39 (2d ed. 1963), and Supp. thereto; 1A Barron & Holtzoff, *Federal Practice and Procedure* § 399 (Wright ed. 1960). Rule 13(h) has also been inadequate in failing to call attention to the fact that a party pleading a counterclaim or cross-claim may join additional

persons when the conditions for permissive joinder of parties under Rule 20 are satisfied.

The amendment of Rule 13(h) supplies the latter omission by expressly referring to Rule 20, as amended, and also incorporates by direct reference the revised criteria and procedures of Rule 19, as amended. Hereafter, for the purpose of determining who must or may be joined as additional parties to a counterclaim or cross-claim, the party pleading the claim is to be regarded as a plaintiff and the additional parties as plaintiffs or defendants as the case may be, and amended Rules 19 and 20 are to be applied in the usual fashion. See also Rules 13(a) (compulsory counterclaims) and 22 (interpleader).

The amendment of Rule 13(h), like the amendment of Rule 19, does not attempt to regulate Federal jurisdiction or venue. See Rule 82. It should be noted, however, that in some situations the decisional law has recognized "ancillary" Federal jurisdiction over counterclaims and cross-claims and "ancillary" venue as to parties to these claims.

1987 Amendment

The amendments are technical. No substantive change is intended.

2007 Amendment

[Effective December 1, 2007, absent contrary Congressional action.]

The language of Rule 13 has been amended as part of the general restyling of the Civil Rules to make them more easily understood and to make style and terminology consistent throughout the rules. These changes are intended to be stylistic only.

The meaning of former Rule 13(b) is better expressed by deleting "not arising out of the transaction or occurrence that is the subject matter of the opposing party's claim." Both as a matter of intended meaning and current practice, a party may state as a permissive counterclaim a claim that does grow out of the same transaction or occurrence as an opposing party's claim even though one of the exceptions in Rule 13(a) means the claim is not a compulsory counterclaim.

Rule 14. Third-Party Practice

(a) When Defendant May Bring in Third Party. At any time after commencement of the action a defending party, as a third-party plaintiff, may cause a summons and complaint to be served upon a person not a party to the action who is or may be liable to the third-party plaintiff for all or part of the plaintiff's claim against the third-party plaintiff. The third-party plaintiff need not obtain leave to make the service if the third-party plaintiff files the third-party complaint not later than 10 days after serving the original answer. Otherwise the third-party plaintiff must obtain leave on motion upon notice to all parties to the action. The person served with the summons and third-party complaint, hereinafter called the third-party defendant, shall make any defenses to the third-party plaintiff's claim as provided in Rule 12 and any counterclaims against the third-party plaintiff and

cross-claims against other third-party defendants as provided in Rule 13. The third-party defendant may assert against the plaintiff any defenses which the third-party plaintiff has to the plaintiff's claim. The third-party defendant may also assert any claim against the plaintiff arising out of the transaction or occurrence that is the subject matter of the plaintiff's claim against the third-party plaintiff. The plaintiff may assert any claim against the third-party defendant arising out of the transaction or occurrence that is the subject matter of the plaintiff's claim against the third-party plaintiff, and the third-party defendant thereupon shall assert any defenses as provided in Rule 12 and any counterclaims and cross-claims as provided in Rule 13. Any party may move to strike the third-party claim, or for its severance or separate trial. A third-party defendant may proceed under this rule against any person not a party to the action who is or may be liable to the third-party defendant for all or part of the claim made in the action against the third-party defendant. The third-party complaint, if within the admiralty and maritime jurisdiction, may be in rem against a vessel, cargo, or other property subject to admiralty or maritime process in rem, in which case references in this rule to the summons include the warrant of arrest, and references to the third-party plaintiff or defendant include, where appropriate, a person who asserts a right under Supplemental Rule C(6)(a)(1) in the property arrested.

(b) When Plaintiff May Bring in Third Party. When a counterclaim is asserted against a plaintiff, the plaintiff may cause a third party to be brought in under circumstances which under this rule would entitle a defendant to do so.

(c) Admiralty and Maritime Claims. When a plaintiff asserts an admiralty or maritime claim within the meaning of Rule 9(h), the defendant or person who asserts a right under Supplemental Rule C(6)(a)(1), as a third-party plaintiff, may bring in a third-party defendant who may be wholly or partly liable, either to the plaintiff or to the third-party plaintiff, by way of remedy over, contribution, or otherwise on account of the same transaction, occurrence, or series of transactions or occurrences. In such a case the third-party plaintiff may also demand judgment against the third-party defendant in favor of the plaintiff, in which event the third-party defendant shall make any defenses to the claim of the plaintiff as well as to that of the third-party plaintiff in the manner provided in Rule 12 and the action shall proceed as if the plaintiff had commenced it against the third-party defendant as well as the third-party plaintiff.

(As amended Dec. 27, 1946, eff. Mar. 19, 1948; Jan. 21, 1963, eff. July 1, 1963; Feb. 28, 1966, eff. July 1, 1966; Mar. 2, 1987, eff. Aug. 1, 1987; Apr. 17, 2000, eff. Dec. 1, 2000; Apr. 12, 2006, eff. Dec. 1, 2006.)

Proposed Amendment of Rule

Effective December 1, 2007, absent contrary Congressional action, this rule is amended to read as follows:

Rule 14. Third–Party Practice

(a) When a Defending Party May Bring in a Third Party.

(1) Timing of the Summons and Complaint. A defending party may, as third-party plaintiff, serve a summons and complaint on a nonparty who is or may be liable to it for all or part of the claim against it. But the third-party plaintiff must, by motion, obtain the court's leave if it files the third-party complaint more than 10 days after serving its original answer.

(2) Third–Party Defendant's Claims and Defenses. The person served with the summons and third-party complaint—the "third-party defendant":

 (A) must assert any defense against the third-party plaintiff's claim under Rule 12;

 (B) must assert any counterclaim against the third-party plaintiff under Rule 13(a), and may assert any counterclaim against the third-party plaintiff under Rule 13(b) or any crossclaim against another third-party defendant under Rule 13(g);

 (C) may assert against the plaintiff any defense that the third-party plaintiff has to the plaintiff's claim; and

 (D) may also assert against the plaintiff any claim arising out of the transaction or occurrence that is the subject matter of the plaintiff's claim against the third-party plaintiff.

(3) Plaintiff's Claims Against a Third–Party Defendant. The plaintiff may assert against the third-party defendant any claim arising out of the transaction or occurrence that is the subject matter of the plaintiff's claim against the third-party plaintiff. The third-party defendant must then assert any defense under Rule 12 and any counterclaim under Rule 13(a), and may assert any counterclaim under Rule 13(b) or any crossclaim under Rule 13(g).

(4) Motion to Strike, Sever, or Try Separately. Any party may move to strike the third-party claim, to sever it, or to try it separately.

(5) Third–Party Defendant's Claim Against a Nonparty. A third-party defendant may proceed under this rule against a nonparty who is or may be liable to the third-party defendant for all or part of any claim against it.

(6) Third–Party Complaint In Rem. If it is within the admiralty or maritime jurisdiction, a third-party complaint may be in rem. In that event, a reference in this rule to the "summons" includes the warrant of arrest, and a reference to the defendant or third-party plaintiff includes, when appropriate, a person who asserts a right under Supplemental Rule C(6)(a)(i) in the property arrested.

(b) When a Plaintiff May Bring in a Third Party.
When a claim is asserted against a plaintiff, the plaintiff may bring in a third party if this rule would allow a defendant to do so.

(c) Admiralty or Maritime Claim.

(1) Scope of Impleader. If a plaintiff asserts an admiralty or maritime claim under Rule 9(h), the defendant or a person who asserts a right under Supplemental Rule C(6)(a)(i) may, as a third-party plaintiff, bring in a third-party defendant who may be wholly or partly liable—either to the plaintiff or to the third-party plaintiff—for remedy over, contribution, or otherwise on account of the same transaction, occurrence, or series of transactions or occurrences.

(2) Defending Against a Demand for Judgment for the Plaintiff. The third-party plaintiff may demand judgment in the plaintiff's favor against the third-party defendant. In that event, the third-party defendant must defend under Rule 12 against the plaintiff's claim as well as the third-party plaintiff's claim; and the action proceeds as if the plaintiff had sued both the third-party defendant and the third-party plaintiff.

ADVISORY COMMITTEE NOTES

1937 Adoption

Third-party impleader is in some aspects a modern innovation in law and equity although well known in admiralty. Because of its many advantages a liberal procedure with respect to it has developed in England, in the federal admiralty courts, and in some American state jurisdictions. See *English Rules Under the Judicature Act* (The Annual Practice, 1937) O. 16A, r.r. 1–13; United States Supreme Court Admiralty Rules (1920), Rule 56 (Right to Bring in Party Jointly Liable); 12 P.S.Pa. § 141; Wis.Stat. (1935) §§ 260.19, 260.20; N.Y.C.P.A. (1937) §§ 193(2), 211(a). Compare La. Code Pract. (Dart, 1932) §§ 378–388. For the practice in Texas as developed by judicial decision, see *Lottman v. Cuilla*, Tex.1926, 288 S.W. 123, 126. For a treatment of this subject see Gregory, *Legislative Loss Distribution in Negligence Actions* (1936); Shulman and Jaegerman, *Some Jurisdictional Limitations on Federal Procedure (1936)*, 45 Yale L.J. 393, 417 et seq.

Third-party impleader under the conformity act has been applied in actions at law in the Federal courts. *Lowry and Co., Inc. v. National City Bank of New York*, N.Y.1928, 28

F.2d 895; *Yellow Cab Co. of Philadelphia v. Rodgers,* C.C.A.3, 1932, 61 F.2d 729.

1946 Amendment

Note. The provisions in Rule 14(a) which relate to the impleading of a third party who is or may be liable to the plaintiff have been deleted by the proposed amendment. It has been held that under Rule 14(a) the plaintiff need not amend his complaint to state a claim against such third party if he does not wish to do so. *Satink v. Holland Township,* D.N.J.1940, 31 F.Supp. 229, noted, 1940, 88 U.Pa.L.Rev. 751; *Connelly v. Bender,* E.D.Mich.1941, 36 F.Supp. 368; *Whitmire v. Partin (Milton),* E.D.Tenn.1941, 2 F.R.D. 83, 5 Fed.Rules Serv. 14a.513, Case 2; *Crim v. Lumbermen's Mutual Casualty Co.,* D.D.C.1939, 26 F.Supp. 715; *Carbola Chemical Co., Inc. v. Trundle,* S.D.N.Y.1943, 3 F.R.D. 502, 7 Fed.Rules Serv. 14a.224, Case 1; *Roadway Express, Inc. v. Automobile Ins. Co. of Hartford, Conn., (Providence Washington Ins. Co.)* N.D.Ohio 1945, 8 Fed.Rules Serv. 14a.513, Case 3. In *Delano v. Ives,* E.D.Pa.1941, 40 F.Supp. 672, the court said: ". . . the weight of authority is to the effect that a defendant cannot compel the plaintiff, who has sued him, to sue also a third party whom he does not wish to sue, by tendering in a third party complaint the third party as an additional defendant directly liable to the plaintiff." Thus impleader here amounts to no more than a mere offer of a party to the plaintiff, and if he rejects it, the attempt is a time-consuming futility. See *Satink v. Holland Township, supra; Malkin v. Arundel Corp.,* D.Md.1941, 36 F.Supp. 948; also Koenigsberger, *Suggestions for Changes in the Federal Rules of Civil Procedure,* 1941, 4 Fed.Rules Serv. 1010. But cf. *Atlantic Coast Line R. Co. v. United States Fidelity & Guaranty Co.,* Ga.1943, 52 F.Supp. 177. Moreover, in any case where the plaintiff could not have joined the third party originally because of jurisdictional limitations such as lack of diversity of citizenship, the majority view is that any attempt by the plaintiff to amend his complaint and assert a claim against the impleaded third party would be unavailing. *Hoskie v. Prudential Ins. Co. of America, (Lorrac Real Estate Corp.),* E.D.N.Y.1941, 39 F.Supp. 305; *Johnson v. G. J. Sherrard Co., (New England Telephone & Telegraph Co.),* D.Mass.1941, 5 Fed.Rules Serv. 14a.511, Case 1, 2 F.R.D. 164; *Thompson v. Cranston,* W.D.N.Y.1942, 6 Fed.Rules Serv. 14a.511, Case 1, 2 F.R.D. 270, affirmed CCA2d, 1942, 132 F.2d 631, certiorari denied 1945, 63 S.Ct. 1028, 319 U.S. 741, 87 L.Ed. 1698; *Friend v. Middle Atlantic Transportation Co.,* C.C.A.2, 1946, 153 F.2d 778, certiorari denied 1946, 66 S.Ct. 1370, 328 U.S. 865, 90 L.Ed. 1635; *Herrington v. Jones,* E.D.La.1941, 5 Fed.Rules Serv. 14a.511, Case 2, 2 F.R.D. 108; *Banks v. Employers' Liability Assurance Corp., (Central Surety & Ins. Corp.)* W.D.Mo.1943, 7 Fed.Rules Serv. 14a.11, Case 2; *Saunders v. Baltimore & Ohio R. Co.,* S.D.W.Va.1945, 9 Fed.Rules Serv. 14a.62, Case 2; *Hull v. United States Rubber Co. (Johnson Larsen and Co.),* E.D.Mich.1945, 9 Fed.Rules Serv. 14a.62, Case 3. See also concurring opinion of Circuit Judge Minton in *People of State of Illinois for Use of Trust Co. of Chicago v. Maryland Casualty Co.,* C.C.A.7, 1942, 132 F.2d 850, 853. Contra: *Sklar v. Hayes (Singer),* E.D.Pa.1941, 4 Fed.Rules Serv. 14a.511, Case 2, 1 F.R.D. 594. Discussion of the problem will be found in Commentary, *Amendment of Plaintiff's Pleading to Assert Claim Against Third-Party Defendant,* 1942, 5 Fed.Rules Serv. 811; Commentary, *Federal Jurisdiction in*

Third-Party Practice, 1943, 6 Fed.Rules Serv. 766; Holtzoff, *Some Problems Under Federal Third-Party Practice,* 1941, 3 La.L.Rev. 408, 419–420; 1 Moore's *Federal Practice,* 1938, Cum.Supplement § 14.08. For these reasons therefore, the words "or to the plaintiff" in the first sentence of subdivision (a) have been removed by the amendment; and in conformance therewith the words "the plaintiff" in the second sentence of the subdivision, and the words "or to the third-party plaintiff" in the concluding sentence thereof have likewise been eliminated.

The third sentence of rule 14(a) has been expanded to clarify the right of the third-party defendant to assert any defenses which the third-party plaintiff may have to the plaintiff's claim. This protects the impleaded third-party defendant where the third-party plaintiff fails or neglects to assert a proper defense to the plaintiff's action. A new sentence has also been inserted giving the third-party defendant the right to assert directly against the original plaintiff any claim arising out of the transaction or occurrence that is the subject matter of the plaintiff's claim against the third-party plaintiff. This permits all claims arising out of the same transaction or occurrence to be heard and determined in the same action. See *Atlantic Coast Line R. Co. v. United States Fidelity & Guaranty Co.,* Ga.1943, 52 F.Supp. 177. Accordingly, the next to the last sentence of subdivision (a) has also been revised to make clear that the plaintiff may, if he desires, assert directly against the third-party defendant either by amendment or by a new pleading any claim he may have against him arising out of the transaction or occurrence that is the subject matter of the plaintiff's claim against the third-party plaintiff. In such a case, the third-party defendant then is entitled to assert the defenses, counter-claims and cross-claims provided in Rules 12 and 13.

The sentence reading "The third-party defendant is bound by the adjudication of the third-party plaintiff's liability to the plaintiff, as well as of his own to the plaintiff, or to the third-party plaintiff" has been stricken from Rule 14(a), not to change the law, but because the sentence states a rule of substantive law which is not within the scope of a procedural rule. It is not the purpose of the rules to state the effect of a judgment.

The elimination of the words "the third-party plaintiff, or any other party" from the second sentence of rule 14(a), together with the insertion of the new phrases therein, are not changes of substance but are merely for the purpose of clarification.

1963 Amendment

Under the amendment of the initial sentences of the subdivision, a defendant as a third-party plaintiff may freely and without leave of court bring in a third-party defendant if he files the third-party complaint not later than 10 days after he serves his original answer. When the impleader comes so early in the case, there is little value in requiring a preliminary ruling by the court on the propriety of the impleader.

After the third-party defendant is brought in, the court has discretion to strike the third-party claim if it is obviously unmeritorious and can only delay or prejudice the disposition of the plaintiff's claim, or to sever the third-party claim or accord it separate trial if confusion or prejudice would otherwise result. This discretion, applicable not merely to the cases covered by the amendment where the third-party defendant is brought in without leave, but to all impleaders

under the rule, is emphasized in the next-to-last sentence of the subdivision, added by amendment.

In dispensing with leave of court for an impleader filed not later than 10 days after serving the answer, but retaining the leave requirement for impleaders sought to be effected thereafter, the amended subdivision takes a moderate position on the lines urged by some commentators, see Note, 43 Minn.L.Rev. 115 (1958); cf. Pa.R.Civ.P. 2252–53 (60 days after service on the defendant; Minn.R.Civ.P. 14.01 (45 days). Other commentators would dispense with the requirement of leave regardless of the time when impleader is effected, and would rely on subsequent action by the court to dismiss the impleader if it would unduly delay or complicate the litigation or would be otherwise objectionable. See 1A Barron & Holtzoff, *Federal Practice & Procedure* 649–50 (Wright ed. 1960); Comment, 58 Colum.L.Rev. 532, 546 (1958); cf. N.Y.Civ.Prac.Act § 193–a; Me.R.Civ.P. 14. The amended subdivision preserves the value of a preliminary screening, through the leave procedure, of impleaders attempted after the 10-day period.

The amendment applies also when an impleader is initiated by a third-party defendant against a person who may be liable to him, as provided in the last sentence of the subdivision.

1966 Amendment

Rule 14 was modeled on Admiralty Rule 56. An important feature of Admiralty Rule 56 was that it allowed impleader not only of a person who might be liable to the defendant by way of remedy over, but also of any person who might be liable to the plaintiff. The importance of this provision was that the defendant was entitled to insist that the plaintiff proceed to judgment against the third-party defendant. In certain cases this was a valuable implementation of a substantive right. For example, in a case of ship collision where a finding of mutual fault is possible, one shipowner, if sued alone, faces the prospect of an absolute judgment for the full amount of the damage suffered by an innocent third party; but if he can implead the owner of the other vessel, and if mutual fault is found, the judgment against the original defendant will be in the first instance only for a moiety of the damages; liability for the remainder will be conditioned on the plaintiff's inability to collect from the third-party defendant.

This feature was originally incorporated in Rule 14, but was eliminated by the amendment of 1946, so that under the amended rule a third party could not be impleaded on the basis that he might be liable to the plaintiff. One of the reasons for the amendment was that the Civil Rule, unlike the Admiralty Rule, did not require the plaintiff to go to judgment against the third-party defendant. Another reason was that where jurisdiction depended on diversity of citizenship the impleader of an adversary having the same citizenship as the plaintiff was not considered possible.

Retention of the admiralty practice in those cases that will be counterparts of a suit in admiralty is clearly desirable.

1987 Amendment

The amendments are technical. No substantive change is intended.

2000 Amendment

Subdivisions (a) and (c) are amended to reflect revisions in Supplemental Rule C(6).

GAP Report

Rule B(1)(a) was modified by moving "in an in personam action" out of paragraph (a) and into the first line of subdivision (1). This change makes it clear that all paragraphs of subdivision (1) apply when attachment is sought in an in personam action. Rule B(1)(d) was modified by changing the requirement that the clerk deliver the summons and process to the person or organization authorized to serve it. The new form requires only that the summons and process be delivered, not that the clerk effect the delivery. This change conforms to present practice in some districts and will facilitate rapid service. It matches the spirit of Civil Rule 4(b), which directs the clerk to issue the summons "to the plaintiff for service on the defendant." A parallel change is made in Rule C(3)(b).

2006 Amendment

Rule 14 is amended to conform to changes in designating the paragraphs of Supplemental Rule C(6).

2007 Amendment

*[Effective December 1, 2007,
absent contrary Congressional action.]*

The language of Rule 14 has been amended as part of the general restyling of the Civil Rules to make them more easily understood and to make style and terminology consistent throughout the rules. These changes are intended to be stylistic only.

Former Rule 14 twice refers to counterclaims under Rule 13. In each case, the operation of Rule 13(a) depends on the state of the action at the time the pleading is filed. If plaintiff and third-party defendant have become opposing parties because one has made a claim for relief against the other, Rule 13(a) requires assertion of any counterclaim that grows out of the transaction or occurrence that is the subject matter of that claim. Rules 14(a)(2)(B) and (a)(3) reflect the distinction between compulsory and permissive counterclaims.

A plaintiff should be on equal footing with the defendant in making third-party claims, whether the claim against the plaintiff is asserted as a counterclaim or as another form of claim. The limit imposed by the former reference to "counterclaim" is deleted.

Rule 15. Amended and Supplemental Pleadings

(a) Amendments. A party may amend the party's pleading once as a matter of course at any time before a responsive pleading is served or, if the pleading is one to which no responsive pleading is permitted and the action has not been placed upon the trial calendar, the party may so amend it at any time within 20 days after it is served. Otherwise a party may amend the party's pleading only by leave of court or by written consent of the adverse party; and leave shall be freely given when justice so requires. A party shall plead in response to an amended pleading within the time

remaining for response to the original pleading or within 10 days after service of the amended pleading, whichever period may be the longer, unless the court otherwise orders.

(b) Amendments to Conform to the Evidence. When issues not raised by the pleadings are tried by express or implied consent of the parties, they shall be treated in all respects as if they had been raised in the pleadings. Such amendment of the pleadings as may be necessary to cause them to conform to the evidence and to raise these issues may be made upon motion of any party at any time, even after judgment; but failure so to amend does not affect the result of the trial of these issues. If evidence is objected to at the trial on the ground that it is not within the issues made by the pleadings, the court may allow the pleadings to be amended and shall do so freely when the presentation of the merits of the action will be subserved thereby and the objecting party fails to satisfy the court that the admission of such evidence would prejudice the party in maintaining the party's action or defense upon the merits. The court may grant a continuance to enable the objecting party to meet such evidence.

(c) Relation Back of Amendments. An amendment of a pleading relates back to the date of the original pleading when

(1) relation back is permitted by the law that provides the statute of limitations applicable to the action, or

(2) the claim or defense asserted in the amended pleading arose out of the conduct, transaction, or occurrence set forth or attempted to be set forth in the original pleading, or

(3) the amendment changes the party or the naming of the party against whom a claim is asserted if the foregoing provision (2) is satisfied and, within the period provided by Rule 4(m) for service of the summons and complaint, the party to be brought in by amendment (A) has received such notice of the institution of the action that the party will not be prejudiced in maintaining a defense on the merits, and (B) knew or should have known that, but for a mistake concerning the identity of the proper party, the action would have been brought against the party.

The delivery or mailing of process to the United States Attorney, or United States Attorney's designee, or the Attorney General of the United States, or an agency or officer who would have been a proper defendant if named, satisfies the requirement of subparagraphs (A) and (B) of this paragraph (3) with respect to the United States or any agency or officer thereof to be brought into the action as a defendant.

(d) Supplemental Pleadings. Upon motion of a party the court may, upon reasonable notice and upon such terms as are just, permit the party to serve a supplemental pleading setting forth transactions or occurrences or events which have happened since the date of the pleading sought to be supplemented. Permission may be granted even though the original pleading is defective in its statement of a claim for relief or defense. If the court deems it advisable that the adverse party plead to the supplemental pleading, it shall so order, specifying the time therefor.

(As amended Jan. 21, 1963, eff. July 1, 1963; Feb. 28, 1966, eff. July 1, 1966; Mar. 2, 1987, eff. Aug. 1, 1987; Apr. 30, 1991, eff. Dec. 1, 1991; Dec. 9, 1991, Pub.L. 102–198, § 11(a), 105 Stat. 1626; Apr. 22, 1993, eff. Dec. 1, 1993.)

Proposed Amendment of Rule

Effective December 1, 2007, absent contrary Congressional action, this rule is amended to read as follows:

Rule 15. Amended and Supplemental Pleadings

(a) Amendments Before Trial.

(1) Amending as a Matter of Course. A party may amend its pleading once as a matter of course:

(A) before being served with a responsive pleading; or

(B) within 20 days after serving the pleading if a responsive pleading is not allowed and the action is not yet on the trial calendar.

(2) Other Amendments. In all other cases, a party may amend its pleading only with the opposing party's written consent or the court's leave. The court should freely give leave when justice so requires.

(3) Time to Respond. Unless the court orders otherwise, any required response to an amended pleading must be made within the time remaining to respond to the original pleading or within 10 days after service of the amended pleading, whichever is later.

(b) Amendments During and After Trial.

(1) Based on an Objection at Trial. If, at trial, a party objects that evidence is not within the issues raised in the pleadings, the court may permit the pleadings to be amended. The court should freely permit an amendment when doing so will aid in presenting the merits and the objecting party fails to satisfy the court that the evidence would prejudice that party's action or defense on the merits. The court may grant a continuance to enable the objecting party to meet the evidence.

(2) For Issues Tried by Consent. When an issue not raised by the pleadings is tried by the

parties' express or implied consent, it must be treated in all respects as if raised in the pleadings. A party may move—at any time, even after judgment—to amend the pleadings to conform them to the evidence and to raise an unpleaded issue. But failure to amend does not affect the result of the trial of that issue.

(c) *Relation Back of Amendments.*

(1) When an Amendment Relates Back. An amendment to a pleading relates back to the date of the original pleading when:

(A) the law that provides the applicable statute of limitations allows relation back;

(B) the amendment asserts a claim or defense that arose out of the conduct, transaction, or occurrence set out—or attempted to be set out—in the original pleading; or

(C) the amendment changes the party or the naming of the party against whom a claim is asserted, if Rule 15(c)(1)(B) is satisfied and if, within the period provided by Rule 4(m) for serving the summons and complaint, the party to be brought in by amendment:

(i) received such notice of the action that it will not be prejudiced in defending on the merits; and

(ii) knew or should have known that the action would have been brought against it, but for a mistake concerning the proper party's identity.

(2) Notice to the United States. When the United States or a United States officer or agency is added as a defendant by amendment, the notice requirements of Rule 15(c)(1)(C)(i) and (ii) are satisfied if, during the stated period, process was delivered or mailed to the United States attorney or the United States attorney's designee, to the Attorney General of the United States, or to the officer or agency.

(d) *Supplemental Pleadings. On motion and reasonable notice, the court may, on just terms, permit a party to serve a supplemental pleading setting out any transaction, occurrence, or event that happened after the date of the pleading to be supplemented. The court may permit supplementation even though the original pleading is defective in stating a claim or defense. The court may order that the opposing party plead to the supplemental pleading within a specified time.*

ADVISORY COMMITTEE NOTES

1937 Adoption

See generally for the present federal practice, [former] Equity Rules 19 (Amendments Generally), 28 (Amendment of

Bill as of Course), 32 (Answer to Amended Bill), 34 (Supplemental Pleading), and 35 (Bills of Revivor and Supplemental Bills—Form); U.S.C. Title 28, § 399 [now 1653] (Amendments to show diverse citizenship) and [former] 777 (Defects of form; amendments). See *English Rules Under the Judicature Act* (The Annual Practice, 1937) O. 28, r. r. 1–13; O. 20, r. 4; O. 24, r. r. 1–3.

Note to Subdivision (a). The right to serve an amended pleading once as of course is common. 4 Mont.Rev.Codes Ann. (1935) § 9186; 1 Ore.Code Ann. (1930) § 1–904; 1 S.C.Code (Michie, 1932) § 493; *English Rules Under the Judicature Act* (The Annual Practice, 1937) O. 28, r. 2. Provision for amendment of pleading before trial, by leave of court, is in almost every code. If there is no statute the power of the court to grant leave is said to be inherent. Clark, *Code Pleading* (1928), pp. 498, 509.

Note to Subdivision (b). Compare [former] Equity Rule 19 (Amendments Generally) and code provisions which allow an amendment "at any time in furtherance of justice," (e.g., Ark.Civ.Code (Crawford, 1934) § 155) and which allow an amendment of pleadings to conform to the evidence, where the adverse party has not been misled and prejudiced (e.g., N.M.Stat.Ann. (Courtright, 1929) §§ 105–601, 105–602).

Note to Subdivision (c). "Relation back" is a well recognized doctrine of recent and now more frequent application. Compare Ala.Code Ann. (Michie, 1928) § 9513; Smith-Hurd Ill.Stats. ch. 110, § 170(2); 2 Wash.Rev.Stat.Ann. (Remington, 1932) § 308–3(4). See U.S.C., Title 28, § 399 [now 1653] (Amendments to show diverse citizenship) for a provision for "relation back".

Note to Subdivision (d). This is an adaptation of former Equity Rule 34 (Supplemental Pleading).

1963 Amendment

Rule 15(d) is intended to give the court broad discretion in allowing a supplemental pleading. However, some cases, opposed by other cases and criticized by the commentators, have taken the rigid and formalistic view that where the original complaint fails to state a claim upon which relief can be granted, leave to serve a supplemental complaint must be denied. See *Bonner v. Elizabeth Arden, Inc.*, 177 F.2d 703 (2d Cir. 1949); *Bowles v. Senderowitz*, 65 F.Supp. 548 (E.D.Pa.), rev'd on other grounds, 158 F.2d 435 (3d Cir. 1946), cert. denied, *Senderowitz v. Fleming*, 330 U.S. 848, 67 S.Ct. 1091, 91 L.Ed. 1292 (1947); cf. *LaSalle Nat. Bank v. 222 East Chestnut St. Corp.*, 267 F.2d 247 (7th Cir.), cert. denied, 361 U.S. 836, 80 S.Ct. 88, 4 L.Ed.2d 77 (1959). But see *Camilla Cotton Oil Co. v. Spencer Kellogg & Sons*, 257 F.2d 162 (5th Cir. 1958); *Genuth v. National Biscuit Co.*, 81 F.Supp. 213 (S.D.N.Y.1948), app. dism., 177 F.2d 962 (2d Cir. 1949); 3 Moore's *Federal Practice* ¶15.01[5] (Supp.1960); 1A Barron & Holtzoff, *Federal Practice & Procedure* 820–21 (Wright ed. 1960). Thus plaintiffs have sometimes been needlessly remitted to the difficulties of commencing a new action even though events occurring after the commencement of the original action have made clear the right to relief.

Under the amendment the court has discretion to permit a supplemental pleading despite the fact that the original pleading is defective. As in other situations where a supplemental pleading is offered, the court is to determine in the light of the particular circumstances whether filing should be permitted, and if so, upon what terms. The amendment does

not attempt to deal with such questions as the relation of the statute of limitations to supplemental pleadings, the operation of the doctrine of laches, or the availability of other defenses. All these questions are for decision in accordance with the principles applicable to supplemental pleadings generally. Cf. *Blau v. Lamb*, 191 F.Supp. 906 (S.D.N.Y.1961); *Lendonsol Amusement Corp. v. B. & Q. Assoc., Inc.*, 23 F.R.Serv. 15d.3, Case 1 (D.Mass.1957).

1966 Amendment

Rule 15(c) is amplified to state more clearly when an amendment of a pleading changing the party against whom a claim is asserted (including an amendment to correct a misnomer or misdescription of a defendant) shall "relate back" to the date of the original pleading.

The problem has arisen most acutely in certain actions by private parties against officers or agencies of the United States. Thus an individual denied social security benefits by the Secretary of Health, Education, and Welfare may secure review of the decision by bringing a civil action against that officer within sixty days. 42 U.S.C. § 405(g) (Supp. III, 1962). In several recent cases the claimants instituted timely action but mistakenly named as defendant the United States, the Department of HEW, the "Federal Security Administration" (a nonexistent agency), and a Secretary who had retired from the office nineteen days before. Discovering their mistakes, the claimants moved to amend their complaints to name the proper defendant; by this time the statutory sixty-day period had expired. The motions were denied on the ground that the amendment "would amount to the commencement of a new proceeding and would not relate back in time so as to avoid the statutory provision * * * that suit be brought within sixty days * * *" *Cohn v. Federal Security Adm.*, 199 F.Supp. 884, 885 (W.D.N.Y.1961); see also *Cunningham v. United States*, 199 F.Supp. 541 (W.D.Mo.1958); *Hall v. Department of HEW*, 199 F.Supp. 833 (S.D.Tex.1960); *Sandridge v. Folsom, Secretary of HEW*, 200 F.Supp. 25 (M.D.Tenn.1959). [The Secretary of Health, Education, and Welfare has approved certain ameliorative regulations under 42 U.S.C. § 405(g). See 29 Fed. Reg. 8209 (June 30, 1964); Jacoby, *The Effect of Recent Changes in the Law of "Nonstatutory" Judicial Review*, 53 Geo.L.J. 19, 42–43 (1964); see also *Simmons v. United States Dept. HEW*, 328 F.2d 86 (3d Cir. 1964).]

Analysis in terms of "new proceeding" is traceable to *Davis v. L. L. Cohen & Co.*, 268 U.S. 638 (1925), and *Mellon v. Arkansas Land & Lumber Co.*, 275 U.S. 460 (1928), but those cases antedate the adoption of the Rules which import different criteria for determining when an amendment is to "relate back". As lower courts have continued to rely on the *Davis* and *Mellon* cases despite the contrary intent of the Rules, clarification of Rule 15(c) is considered advisable.

Relation back is intimately connected with the policy of the statute of limitations. The policy of the statute limiting the time for suit against the Secretary of HEW would not have been offended by allowing relation back in the situations described above. For the government was put on notice of the claim within the stated period—in the particular instances, by means of the initial delivery of process to a responsible government official (see Rule 4(d)(4) and (5)). In these circumstances, characterization of the amendment as a new proceeding is not responsive to the realty [sic], but is merely question-begging; and to deny relation back is to defeat unjustly the claimant's opportunity to prove his case. See the full discussion by Byse, *Suing the "Wrong" Defendant in Judicial Review of Federal Administrative Action: Proposals for Reform*, 77 Harv.L.Rev. 40 (1963); see also Ill.Civ.P. Act § 46(4).

Much the same question arises in other types of actions against the government (see *Byse*, supra, at 45 n. 15). In actions between private parties, the problem of relation back of amendments changing defendants has generally been better handled by the courts, but incorrect criteria have sometimes been applied, leading sporadically to doubtful results. See 1A Barron & Holtzoff, *Federal Practice & Procedure* § 451 (Wright ed. 1960); 1 id. § 186 (1960); 2 id. § 543 (1961); 3 *Moore's Federal Practice*, par. 15.15 (Cum.Supp. 1962); Annot., *Change in Party After Statute of Limitations Has Run*, 8 A.L.R.2d 6 (1949). Rule 15(c) has been amplified to provide a general solution. An amendment changing the party against whom a claim is asserted relates back if the amendment satisfies the usual condition of Rule 15(c) of "arising out of the conduct * * * set forth * * * in the original pleading," and if, within the applicable limitations period, the party brought in by amendment, first, received such notice of the institution of the action—the notice need not be formal—that he would not be prejudiced in defending the action, and, second, knew or should have known that the action would have been brought against him initially had there not been a mistake concerning the identity of the proper party. Revised Rule 15(c) goes on to provide specifically in the government cases that the first and second requirements are satisfied when the government has been notified in the manner there described (see Rule 4(d)(4) and (5)). As applied to the government cases, revised Rule 15(c) further advances the objectives of the 1961 amendment of Rule 25(d) (substitution of public officers).

The relation back of amendments changing plaintiffs is not expressly treated in revised Rule 15(c) since the problem is generally easier. Again the chief consideration of policy is that of the statute of limitations, and the attitude taken in revised Rule 15(c) toward change of defendants extends by analogy to amendments changing plaintiffs. Also relevant is the amendment of Rule 17(a) (real party in interest). To avoid forfeitures of just claims, revised Rule 17(a) would provide that no action shall be dismissed on the ground that it is not prosecuted in the name of the real party in interest until a reasonable time has been allowed for correction of the defect in the manner there stated.

1987 Amendment

The amendments are technical. No substantive change is intended.

1991 Amendment

The rule has been revised to prevent parties against whom claims are made from taking unjust advantage of otherwise inconsequential pleading errors to sustain a limitations defense.

Paragraph (c)(1). This provision is new. It is intended to make it clear that the rule does not apply to preclude any relation back that may be permitted under the applicable limitations law. Generally, the applicable limitations law will be state law. If federal jurisdiction is based on the citizenship of the parties, the primary reference is the law of the

state in which the district court sits. *Walker v. Armco Steel Corp.*, 446 U.S. 740 (1980). If federal jurisdiction is based on a federal question, the reference may be to the law of the state governing relations between the parties. *E.g., Board of Regents v. Tomanio*, 446 U.S. 478 (1980). In some circumstances, the controlling limitations law may be federal law. *E.g., West v. Conrail, Inc.*, 107 S.Ct. 1538 (1987). Cf. *Burlington Northern R. Co. v. Woods*, 480 U.S. 1 (1987); *Stewart Organization v. Ricoh*, 108 S.Ct. 2239 (1988). Whatever may be the controlling body of limitations law, if that law affords a more forgiving principle of relation back than the one provided in this rule, it should be available to save the claim. Accord, *Marshall v. Mulrenin*, 508 F.2d 39 (1st cir.1974). If *Schiavone v. Fortune*, 106 S.Ct. 2379 (1986) implies the contrary, this paragraph is intended to make a material change in the rule.

Paragraph (c)(3). This paragraph has been revised to change the result in *Schiavone v. Fortune, supra*, with respect to the problem of a misnamed defendant. An intended defendant who is notified of an action within the period allowed by Rule 4(m) [subdivision (m) in Rule 4 was a proposed subdivision which was withdrawn by the Supreme Court] for service of a summons and complaint may not under the revised rule defeat the action on account of a defect in the pleading with respect to the defendant's name, provided that the requirements of clauses (A) and (B) have been met. If the notice requirement is met within the Rule 4(m) [subdivision (m) in Rule 4 was a proposed subdivision which was withdrawn by the Supreme Court] period, a complaint may be amended at any time to correct a formal defect such as a misnomer or misidentification. On the basis of the text of the former rule, the Court reached a result in *Schiavone v. Fortune* that was inconsistent with the liberal pleading practices secured by Rule 8. See Bauer, *Schiavone: An Un-Fortune-ate Illustration of the Supreme Court's Role as Interpreter of the Federal Rules of Civil Procedure*, 63 Notre Dame L.Rev. 720 (1988); Brussack, *Outrageous Fortune: The Case for Amending Rule 15(c) Again*, 61 S.Cal. L.Rev. 671 (1988); Lewis, *The Excessive History of Federal Rule 15(c) and Its Lessons for Civil Rules Revision*, 86 Mich.L.Rev. 1507 (1987).

In allowing a name-correcting amendment within the time allowed by Rule 4(m), this rule allows not only the 120 days specified in that rule, but also any additional time resulting from any extension ordered by the court pursuant to that rule, as may be granted, for example, if the defendant is a fugitive from service of the summons.

This revision, together with the revision of Rule 4(i) with respect to the failure of a plaintiff in an action against the United States to effect timely service on all the appropriate officials, is intended to produce results contrary to those reached in *Gardner v. Gartman*, 880 F.2d 797 (4th Cir. 1989), *Rys v. U.S. Postal Service*, 886 F.2d 443 (1st Cir. 1989), *Martin's Food & Liquor, Inc. v. U.S. Dept. of Agriculture*, 14 F.R.D.3d 86 (N.D.Ill.1988). *But cf. Montgomery v. United States Postal Service*, 867 F.2d 900 (5th Cir. 1989), *Warren v. Department of the Army*, 867 F.2d 1156 (8th Cir. 1989); *Miles v. Department of the Army*, 881 F.2d 777 (9th Cir. 1989), *Barsten v. Department of the Interior*, 896 F.2d 422 (9th Cir. 1990); *Brown v. Georgia Dept. of Revenue*, 881 F.2d 1018 (11th Cir. 1989).

1993 Amendments

The amendment conforms the cross reference to Rule 4 to the revision of that rule.

2007 Amendment

[Effective December 1, 2007, absent contrary Congressional action.]

The language of Rule 15 has been amended as part of the general restyling of the Civil Rules to make them more easily understood and to make style and terminology consistent throughout the rules. These changes are intended to be stylistic only.

Former Rule 15(c)(3)(A) called for notice of the "institution" of the action. Rule 15(c)(1)(C)(i) omits the reference to "institution" as potentially confusing. What counts is that the party to be brought in have notice of the existence of the action, whether or not the notice includes details as to its "institution."

HISTORICAL NOTES

Effective and Applicability Provisions

1991 Acts

Section 11(a) of Pub.L. 102–198 amended subd. (c)(3) of this rule, as transmitted to the Congress by the Supreme Court pursuant to section 2074 of title 28, United States Code, to become effective on December 1, 1991.

Rule 16. Pretrial Conferences; Scheduling; Management

(a) Pretrial Conferences; Objectives. In any action, the court may in its discretion direct the attorneys for the parties and any unrepresented parties to appear before it for a conference or conferences before trial for such purposes as

 (1) expediting the disposition of the action;

 (2) establishing early and continuing control so that the case will not be protracted because of lack of management;

 (3) discouraging wasteful pretrial activities;

 (4) improving the quality of the trial through more thorough preparation, and;

 (5) facilitating the settlement of the case.

(b) Scheduling and Planning. Except in categories of actions exempted by district court rule as inappropriate, the district judge, or a magistrate judge when authorized by district court rule, shall, after receiving the report from the parties under Rule 26(f) or after consulting with the attorneys for the parties and any unrepresented parties by a scheduling conference, telephone, mail, or other suitable means, enter a scheduling order that limits the time

 (1) to join other parties and to amend the pleadings;

 (2) to file motions; and

 (3) to complete discovery.

The scheduling order also may include

(4) modifications of the times for disclosures under Rules 26(a) and 26(e)(1) and of the extent of discovery to be permitted;

(5) provisions for disclosure or discovery of electronically stored information;

(6) any agreements the parties reach for asserting claims of privilege or of protection as trial-preparation material after production;

(7) the date or dates for conferences before trial, a final pretrial conference, and trial; and

(8) any other matters appropriate in the circumstances of the case.

The order shall issue as soon as practicable but in any event within 90 days after the appearance of a defendant and within 120 days after the complaint has been served on a defendant. A schedule shall not be modified except upon a showing of good cause and by leave of the district judge or, when authorized by local rule, by a magistrate judge.

(c) Subjects for Consideration at Pretrial Conferences. At any conference under this rule consideration may be given, and the court may take appropriate action, with respect to

(1) the formulation and simplification of the issues, including the elimination of frivolous claims or defenses;

(2) the necessity or desirability of amendments to the pleadings;

(3) the possibility of obtaining admissions of fact and of documents which will avoid unnecessary proof, stipulations regarding the authenticity of documents, and advance rulings from the court on the admissibility of evidence;

(4) the avoidance of unnecessary proof and of cumulative evidence, and limitations or restrictions on the use of testimony under Rule 702 of the Federal Rules of Evidence;

(5) the appropriateness and timing of summary adjudication under Rule 56;

(6) the control and scheduling of discovery, including orders affecting disclosures and discovery pursuant to Rule 26 and Rules 29 through 37;

(7) the identification of witnesses and documents, the need and schedule for filing and exchanging pretrial briefs, and the date or dates for further conferences and for trial;

(8) the advisability of referring matters to a magistrate judge or master;

(9) settlement and the use of special procedures to assist in resolving the dispute when authorized by statute or local rule;

(10) the form and substance of the pretrial order;

(11) the disposition of pending motions;

(12) the need for adopting special procedures for managing potentially difficult or protracted actions that may involve complex issues, multiple parties, difficult legal questions, or unusual proof problems;

(13) an order for a separate trial pursuant to Rule 42(b) with respect to a claim, counterclaim, cross-claim, or third-party claim, or with respect to any particular issue in the case;

(14) an order directing a party or parties to present evidence early in the trial with respect to a manageable issue that could, on the evidence, be the basis for a judgment as a matter of law under Rule 50(a) or a judgment on partial findings under Rule 52(c);

(15) an order establishing a reasonable limit on the time allowed for presenting evidence; and

(16) such other matters as may facilitate the just, speedy, and inexpensive disposition of the action.

At least one of the attorneys for each party participating in any conference before trial shall have authority to enter into stipulations and to make admissions regarding all matters that the participants may reasonably anticipate may be discussed. If appropriate, the court may require that a party or its representative be present or reasonably available by telephone in order to consider possible settlement of the dispute.

(d) Final Pretrial Conference. Any final pretrial conference shall be held as close to the time of trial as reasonable under the circumstances. The participants at any such conference shall formulate a plan for trial, including a program for facilitating the admission of evidence. The conference shall be attended by at least one of the attorneys who will conduct the trial for each of the parties and by any unrepresented parties.

(e) Pretrial Orders. After any conference held pursuant to this rule, an order shall be entered reciting the action taken. This order shall control the subsequent course of the action unless modified by a subsequent order. The order following a final pretrial conference shall be modified only to prevent manifest injustice.

(f) Sanctions. If a party or party's attorney fails to obey a scheduling or pretrial order, or if no appearance is made on behalf of a party at a scheduling or pretrial conference, or if a party or party's attorney is substantially unprepared to participate in the conference, or if a party or party's attorney fails to participate in good faith, the judge, upon motion or the judge's own initiative, may make such orders with regard thereto as are just, and among others any of the orders provided in Rule 37(b)(2)(B), (C), (D). In lieu of or in addition to any other sanction, the judge

shall require the party or the attorney representing the party or both to pay the reasonable expenses incurred because of any noncompliance with this rule, including attorney's fees, unless the judge finds that the noncompliance was substantially justified or that other circumstances make an award of expenses unjust.

(As amended Apr. 28, 1983, eff. Aug. 1, 1983; Mar. 2, 1987, eff. Aug. 1, 1987; Apr. 22, 1993, eff. Dec. 1, 1993; Apr. 12, 2006, eff. Dec. 1, 2006.)

Proposed Amendment of Rule

Effective December 1, 2007, absent contrary Congressional action, this rule is amended to read as follows:

Rule 16. Pretrial Conferences; Scheduling; Management

(a) Purposes of a Pretrial Conference. *In any action, the court may order the attorneys and any unrepresented parties to appear for one or more pretrial conferences for such purposes as:*

(1) expediting disposition of the action;

(2) establishing early and continuing control so that the case will not be protracted because of lack of management;

(3) discouraging wasteful pretrial activities;

(4) improving the quality of the trial through more thorough preparation; and

(5) facilitating settlement.

(b) Scheduling.

(1) Scheduling Order. Except in categories of actions exempted by local rule, the district judge—or a magistrate judge when authorized by local rule—must issue a scheduling order:

(A) after receiving the parties' report under Rule 26(f); or

(B) after consulting with the parties' attorneys and any unrepresented parties at a scheduling conference or by telephone, mail, or other means.

(2) Time to Issue. The judge must issue the scheduling order as soon as practicable, but in any event within the earlier of 120 days after any defendant has been served with the complaint or 90 days after any defendant has appeared.

(3) Contents of the Order.

(A) Required Contents. The scheduling order must limit the time to join other parties, amend the pleadings, complete discovery, and file motions.

(B) Permitted Contents. The scheduling order may:

(i) modify the timing of disclosures under Rules 26(a) and 26(e)(1);

(ii) modify the extent of discovery;

(iii) provide for disclosure or discovery of electronically stored information;

(iv) include any agreements the parties reach for asserting claims of privilege or of protection as trial-preparation material after information is produced;

(v) set dates for pretrial conferences and for trial; and

(vi) include other appropriate matters.

(4) Modifying a Schedule. A schedule may be modified only for good cause and with the judge's consent.

(c) Attendance and Matters for Consideration at a Pretrial Conference.

(1) Attendance. A represented party must authorize at least one of its attorneys to make stipulations and admissions about all matters that can reasonably be anticipated for discussion at a pretrial conference. If appropriate, the court may require that a party or its representative be present or reasonably available by other means to consider possible settlement.

(2) Matters for Consideration. At any pretrial conference, the court may consider and take appropriate action on the following matters:

(A) formulating and simplifying the issues, and eliminating frivolous claims or defenses;

(B) amending the pleadings if necessary or desirable;

(C) obtaining admissions and stipulations about facts and documents to avoid unnecessary proof, and ruling in advance on the admissibility of evidence;

(D) avoiding unnecessary proof and cumulative evidence, and limiting the use of testimony under Federal Rule of Evidence 702;

(E) determining the appropriateness and timing of summary adjudication under Rule 56;

(F) controlling and scheduling discovery, including orders affecting disclosures and discovery under Rule 26 and Rules 29 through 37;

(G) identifying witnesses and documents, scheduling the filing and exchange of any pretrial briefs, and setting dates for further conferences and for trial;

(H) referring matters to a magistrate judge or a master;

(I) settling the case and using special procedures to assist in resolving the dispute when authorized by statute or local rule;

(J) determining the form and content of the pretrial order;

(K) disposing of pending motions;

(L) adopting special procedures for managing potentially difficult or protracted actions that may involve complex issues, multiple parties, difficult legal questions, or unusual proof problems;

(M) ordering a separate trial under Rule 42(b) of a claim, counterclaim, crossclaim, third-party claim, or particular issue;

(N) ordering the presentation of evidence early in the trial on a manageable issue that might, on the evidence, be the basis for a judgment as a matter of law under Rule 50(a) or a judgment on partial findings under Rule 52(c);

(O) establishing a reasonable limit on the time allowed to present evidence; and

(P) facilitating in other ways the just, speedy, and inexpensive disposition of the action.

(d) Pretrial Orders. *After any conference under this rule, the court should issue an order reciting the action taken. This order controls the course of the action unless the court modifies it.*

(e) Final Pretrial Conference and Orders. *The court may hold a final pretrial conference to formulate a trial plan, including a plan to facilitate the admission of evidence. The conference must be held as close to the start of trial as is reasonable, and must be attended by at least one attorney who will conduct the trial for each party and by any unrepresented party. The court may modify the order issued after a final pretrial conference only to prevent manifest injustice.*

(f) Sanctions.

(1) In General. On motion or on its own, the court may issue any just orders, including those authorized by Rule 37(b)(2)(A)(ii)-(vii), if a party or its attorney:

(A) fails to appear at a scheduling or other pretrial conference;

(B) is substantially unprepared to participate—or does not participate in good faith—in the conference; or

(C) fails to obey a scheduling or other pretrial order.

(2) Imposing Fees and Costs. Instead of or in addition to any other sanction, the court must order the party, its attorney, or both to pay the reasonable expenses—including attorney's fees—incurred because of any noncompliance with this rule, unless the noncompliance was substantially justified or other circumstances make an award of expenses unjust.

ADVISORY COMMITTEE NOTES
1937 Adoption

1. Similar rules of pre-trial procedure are now in force in Boston, Cleveland, Detroit, and Los Angeles, and a rule substantially like this one has been proposed for the urban centers of New York state. For a discussion of the successful operation of pre-trial procedure in relieving the congested condition of trial calendars of the courts in such cities and for the proposed New York plan, see *A Proposal for Minimizing Calendar Delay in Jury Cases* (Dec. 1936—published by the New York Law Society); *Pre-Trial Procedure and Administration,* Third Annual Report of the Judicial Council of the State of New York (1937), pages 207–243; *Report of the Commission on the Administration of Justice in New York State* (1934), pp. (288) to (290). See also *Pre-Trial Procedure in the Wayne Circuit Court,* Detroit, Michigan, Sixth Annual Report of the Judicial Council of Michigan (1936), pp. 63 to 75; and Sunderland, *The Theory and Practice of Pre-trial Procedure* (Dec. 1937) 36 Mich.L.Rev. 215–226, 21 J.Am.Jud. Soc. 125. Compare the English procedure known as the "summons for directions", *English Rules Under the Judicature Act* (The Annual Practice, 1937) O. 38a; and a similar procedure in New Jersey, N.J.S.A. 2:27–135, 2:27–136, 2:27–160; N.J. Supreme Court Rules, 2 N.J.Misc.Rep. (1924) 1230, Rules 94, 92, 93, 95 (the last three as amended 1933, 11 N.J.Misc.Rep. (1933) 955).

2. Compare the similar procedure under Rule 56(d) (Summary Judgment—Case Not Fully Adjudicated on Motion). Rule 12(g) (Consolidation of Motions), by requiring to some extent the consolidation of motions dealing with matters preliminary to trial, is a step in the same direction. In connection with clause (5) of this rule, see Rules 53(b) (Masters; Reference) and 53(e)(3) (Master's Report; In Jury Actions).

1983 Amendment
Introduction

Rule 16 has not been amended since the Federal Rules were promulgated in 1938. In many respects, the rule has been a success. For example, there is evidence that pretrial conferences may improve the quality of justice rendered in the federal courts by sharpening the preparation and presentation of cases, tending to eliminate trial surprise, and improving, as well as facilitating, the settlement process. See 6 Wright & Miller, *Federal Practice and Procedure:* Civil § 1522 (1971). However, in other respects particularly with regard to case management, the rule has not always been as helpful as it might have been. Thus there has been a widespread feeling that amendment is necessary to encourage pretrial management that meets the needs of modern

litigation. See *Report of the National Commission for the Review of Antitrust Laws and Procedures* (1979).

Major criticism of Rule 16 has centered on the fact that its application can result in over-regulation of some cases and under-regulation of others. In simple, run-of-the-mill cases, attorneys have found pretrial requirements burdensome. It is claimed that over-administration leads to a series of mini-trials that result in a waste of an attorney's time and needless expense to a client. Pollack, *Pretrial Procedures More Effectively Handled*, 65 F.R.D. 475 (1974). This is especially likely to be true when pretrial proceedings occur long before trial. At the other end of the spectrum, the discretionary character of Rule 16 and its orientation toward a single conference late in the pretrial process has led to under-administration of complex or protracted cases. Without judicial guidance beginning shortly after institution, these cases often become mired in discovery.

Four sources of criticism of pretrial have been identified. First, conferences often are seen as a mere exchange of legalistic contentions without any real analysis of the particular case. Second, the result frequently is nothing but a formal agreement on minutiae. Third, the conferences are seen as unnecessary and time-consuming in cases that will be settled before trial. Fourth, the meetings can be ceremonial and ritualistic, having little effect on the trial and being of minimal value, particularly when the attorneys attending the sessions are not the ones who will try the case or lack authority to enter into binding stipulations. See generally *McCargo v. Hedrick*, 545 F.2d 393 (4th Cir.1976); Pollack, *Pretrial Procedures More Effectively Handled*, 65 F.R.D. 475 (1974); Rosenberg, *The Pretrial Conference and Effective Justice* 45 (1964).

There also have been difficulties with the pretrial orders that issue following Rule 16 conferences. When an order is entered far in advance of trial, some issues may not be properly formulated. Counsel naturally are cautious and often try to preserve as many options as possible. If the judge who tries the case did not conduct the conference, he could find it difficult to determine exactly what was agreed to at the conference. But any insistence on a detailed order may be too burdensome, depending on the nature or posture of the case.

Given the significant changes in federal civil litigation since 1938 that are not reflected in Rule 16, it has been extensively rewritten and expanded to meet the challenges of modern litigation. Empirical studies reveal that when a trial judge intervenes personally at an early stage to assume judicial control over a case and to schedule dates for completion by the parties of the principal pretrial steps, the case is disposed of by settlement or trial more efficiently and with less cost and delay than when the parties are left to their own devices. Flanders, *Case Management and Court Management in United States District Courts* 17, Federal Judicial Center (1977). Thus, the rule mandates a pretrial scheduling order. However, although scheduling and pretrial conferences are encouraged in appropriate cases, they are not mandated.

Discussion

Subdivision (a); Pretrial Conferences; Objectives. The amended rule makes scheduling and case management an express goal of pretrial procedure. This is done in Rule 16(a) by shifting the emphasis away from a conference focused solely on the trial and toward a process of judicial management that embraces the entire pretrial phase, especially motions and discovery. In addition, the amendment explicitly recognizes some of the objectives of pretrial conferences and the powers that many courts already have assumed. Rule 16 thus will be a more accurate reflection of actual practice.

Subdivision (b); Scheduling and Planning. The most significant change in Rule 16 is the mandatory scheduling order described in Rule 16(b), which is based in part on Wisconsin Civil Procedure Rule 802.10. The idea of scheduling orders is not new. It has been used by many federal courts. See, *e.g.*, Southern District of Indiana, Local Rule 19.

Although a mandatory scheduling order encourages the court to become involved in case management early in the litigation, it represents a degree of judicial involvement that is not warranted in many cases. Thus, subdivision (b) permits each district court to promulgate a local rule under Rule 83 exempting certain categories of cases in which the burdens of scheduling orders exceed the administrative efficiencies that would be gained. See Eastern District of Virginia, Local Rule 12(1). Logical candidates for this treatment include social security disability matters, habeas corpus petitions, forfeitures, and reviews of certain administrative actions.

A scheduling conference may be requested either by the judge, a magistrate when authorized by district court rule, or a party within 120 days after the summons and complaint are filed. If a scheduling conference is not arranged within that time and the case is not exempted by local rule, a scheduling order must be issued under Rule 16(b), after some communication with the parties, which may be by telephone or mail rather than in person. The use of the term "judge" in subdivision (b) reflects the Advisory Committee's judgment that it is preferable that this task should be handled by a district judge rather than a magistrate, except when the magistrate is acting under 28 U.S.C. § 636(c). While personal supervision by the trial judge is preferred, the rule, in recognition of the impracticality or difficulty of complying with such a requirement in some districts, authorizes a district by local rule to delegate the duties to a magistrate. In order to formulate a practicable scheduling order, the judge, or a magistrate when authorized by district court rule, and attorneys are required to develop a timetable for the matters listed in Rule 16(b)(1)–(3). As indicated in Rule 16(b)(4)–(5), the order may also deal with a wide range of other matters. The rule is phrased permissively as to clauses (4) and (5), however, because scheduling these items at an early point may not be feasible or appropriate. Even though subdivision (b) relates only to scheduling, there is no reason why some of the procedural matters listed in Rule 16(c) cannot be addressed at the same time, at least when a scheduling conference is held.

Item (1) assures that at some point both the parties and the pleadings will be fixed, by setting a time within which joinder of parties shall be completed and the pleadings amended.

Item (2) requires setting time limits for interposing various motions that otherwise might be used as stalling techniques.

Item (3) deals with the problem of procrastination and delay by attorneys in a context in which scheduling is especially important-discovery. Scheduling the completion of

discovery can serve some of the same functions as the conference described in Rule 26(f).

Item (4) refers to setting dates for conferences and for trial. Scheduling multiple pretrial conferences may well be desirable if the case is complex and the court believes that a more elaborate pretrial structure, such as that described in the *Manual for Complex Litigation*, should be employed. On the other hand, only one pretrial conference may be necessary in an uncomplicated case.

As long as the case is not exempted by local rule, the court must issue a written scheduling order even if no scheduling conference is called. The order, like pretrial orders under the former rule and those under new Rule 16(c), normally will "control the subsequent course of the action." See Rule 16(e). After consultation with the attorneys for the parties and any unrepresented parties-a formal motion is not necessary-the court may modify the schedule on a showing of good cause if it cannot reasonably be met despite the diligence of the party seeking the extension. Since the scheduling order is entered early in the litigation, this standard seems more appropriate than a "manifest injustice" or "substantial hardship" test. Otherwise, a fear that extensions will not be granted may encourage counsel to request the longest possible periods for completing pleading, joinder, and discovery. Moreover, changes in the court's calendar sometimes will oblige the judge or magistrate when authorized by district court rule to modify the scheduling order.

The district courts undoubtedly will develop several prototype scheduling orders for different types of cases. In addition, when no formal conference is held, the court may obtain scheduling information by telephone, mail, or otherwise. In many instances this will result in a scheduling order better suited to the individual case than a standard order, without taking the time that would be required by a formal conference.

Rule 16(b) assures that the judge will take some early control over the litigation, even when its character does not warrant holding a scheduling conference. Despite the fact that the process of preparing a scheduling order does not always bring the attorneys and judge together, the fixing of time limits serves

> to stimulate litigants to narrow the areas of inquiry and advocacy to those they believe are truly relevant and material. Time limits not only compress the amount of time for litigation, they should also reduce the amount of resources invested in litigation. Litigants are forced to establish discovery priorities and thus to do the most important work first.

Report of the National Commission for the Review of Antitrust Laws and Procedures 28 (1979).

Thus, except in exempted cases, the judge or a magistrate when authorized by district court rule will have taken some action in every case within 120 days after the complaint is filed that notifies the attorneys that the case will be moving toward trial. Subdivision (b) is reenforced by subdivision (f), which makes it clear that the sanctions for violating a scheduling order are the same as those for violating a pretrial order.

Subdivision (c); Subjects to be Discussed at Pretrial Conferences. This subdivision expands upon the list of things that may be discussed at a pretrial conference that appeared in original Rule 16. The intention is to encourage better planning and management of litigation. Increased judicial control during the pretrial process accelerates the processing and termination of cases. Flanders, *Case Management and Court Management in United States District Courts*, 39 Federal Judicial Center (1977). See also *Report of the National Commission for the Review of Antitrust Laws and Procedures* (1979).

The reference in Rule 16(c)(1) to "formulation" is intended to clarify and confirm the court's power to identify the litigable issues. It has been added in the hope of promoting efficiency and conserving judicial resources by identifying the real issues prior to trial, thereby saving time and expense for everyone. See generally *Meadow Gold Prods. Co. v. Wright*, 278 F.2d 867 (D.C.Cir.1960). The notion is emphasized by expressly authorizing the elimination of frivolous claims or defenses at a pretrial conference. There is no reason to require that this await a formal motion for summary judgment. Nor is there any reason for the court to wait for the parties to initiate the process called for in Rule 16(c)(1).

The timing of any attempt at issue formulation is a matter of judicial discretion. In relatively simple cases it may not be necessary or may take the form of a stipulation between counsel or a request by the court that counsel work together to draft a proposed order.

Counsel bear a substantial responsibility for assisting the court in identifying the factual issues worthy of trial. If counsel fail to identify an issue for the court, the right to have the issue tried is waived. Although an order specifying the issues is intended to be binding, it may be amended at trial to avoid manifest injustice. See Rule 16(e). However, the rule's effectiveness depends on the court employing its discretion sparingly.

Clause (6) acknowledges the widespread availability and use of magistrates. The corresponding provision in the original rule referred only to masters and limited the function of the reference to the making of "findings to be used as evidence" in a case to be tried to a jury. The new text is not limited and broadens the potential use of a magistrate to that permitted by the Magistrate's Act.

Clause (7) explicitly recognizes that it has become commonplace to discuss settlement at pretrial conferences. Since it obviously eases crowded court dockets and results in savings to the litigants and the judicial system, settlement should be facilitated at as early a stage of the litigation as possible. Although it is not the purpose of Rule 16(b)(7) to impose settlement negotiations on unwilling litigants, it is believed that providing a neutral forum for discussing the subject might foster it. See Moore's *Federal Practice* ¶ 16.17; 6 Wright & Miller, *Federal Practice and Procedure: Civil* § 1522 (1971). For instance, a judge to whom a case has been assigned may arrange, on his own motion or at a party's request, to have settlement conferences handled by another member of the court or by a magistrate. The rule does not make settlement conferences mandatory because they would be a waste of time in many cases. See Flanders, *Case Management and Court Management in the United States District Courts*, 39 Federal Judicial Center (1977). Requests for a conference from a party indicating a willingness to talk settlement normally should be honored, unless thought to be frivolous or dilatory.

A settlement conference is appropriate at any time. It may be held in conjunction with a pretrial or discovery conference, although various objectives of pretrial manage-

Complete Annotation Materials, see Title 28 U.S.C.A.

ment, such as moving the case toward trial, may not always be compatible with settlement negotiations, and thus a separate settlement conference may be desirable. See 6 Wright & Miller, *Federal Practice and Procedure: Civil* § 1522, at p. 571 (1971).

In addition to settlement, Rule 16(c)(7) refers to exploring the use of procedures other than litigation to resolve the dispute. This includes urging the litigants to employ adjudicatory techniques outside the courthouse. See, for example, the experiment described in *Green, Marks & Olson, Settling Large Case Litigation: An Alternative Approach*, 11 Loyola of L.A.L.Rev. 493 (1978).

Rule 16(c)(10) authorizes the use of special pretrial procedures to expedite the adjudication of potentially difficult or protracted cases. Some district courts obviously have done so for many years. See Rubin, *The Managed Calendar: Some Pragmatic Suggestions About Achieving the Just, Speedy and Inexpensive Determination of Civil Cases in Federal Courts*, 4 Just.Sys.J. 135 (1976). Clause 10 provides an explicit authorization for such procedures and encourages their use. No particular techniques have been described; the Committee felt that flexibility and experience are the keys to efficient management of complex cases. Extensive guidance is offered in such documents as the *Manual for Complex Litigation*.

The rule simply identifies characteristics that make a case a strong candidate for special treatment. The four mentioned are illustrative, not exhaustive, and overlap to some degree. But experience has shown that one or more of them will be present in every protracted or difficult case and it seems desirable to set them out. See Kendig, *Procedures for Management of Non-Routine Cases*, 3 Hofstra L.Rev. 701 (1975).

The last sentence of subdivision (c) is new. See Wisconsin Civil Procedure Rule 802.11(2). It has been added to meet one of the criticisms of the present practice described earlier and insure proper preconference preparation so that the meeting is more than a ceremonial or ritualistic event. The reference to "authority" is not intended to insist upon the ability to settle the litigation. Nor should the rule be read to encourage the judge conducting the conference to compel attorneys to enter into stipulations or to make admissions that they consider to be unreasonable, that touch on matters that could not normally have been anticipated to arise at the conference, or on subjects of a dimension that normally require prior consultation with and approval from the client.

Subdivision (d); Final Pretrial Conference. This provision has been added to make it clear that the time between any final pretrial conference (which in a simple case may be the **only** pretrial conference) and trial should be as short as possible to be certain that the litigants make substantial progress with the case and avoid the inefficiency of having that preparation repeated when there is a delay between the last pretrial conference and trial. An optimum time of 10 days to two weeks has been suggested by one federal judge. Rubin, *The Managed Calendar: Some Pragmatic Suggestions About Achieving the Just, Speedy and Inexpensive Determination of Civil Cases in Federal Courts*, 4 Just. Sys.J. 135, 141 (1976). The Committee, however, concluded that it would be inappropriate to fix a precise time in the rule, given the numerous variables that could bear on the matter. Thus the timing has been left to the court's discretion.

At least one of the attorneys who will conduct the trial for each party must be present at the final pretrial conference. At this late date there should be no doubt as to which attorney or attorneys this will be. Since the agreements and stipulations made at this final conference will control the trial, the presence of lawyers who will be involved in it is especially useful to assist the judge in structuring the case, and to lead to a more effective trial.

Subdivision (e); Pretrial Orders. Rule 16(e) does not substantially change the portion of the original rule dealing with pretrial orders. The purpose of an order is to guide the course of the litigation and the language of the original rule making that clear has been retained. No compelling reason has been found for major revision, especially since this portion of the rule has been interpreted and clarified by over forty years of judicial decisions with comparatively little difficulty. See 6 Wright & Miller, *Federal Practice and Procedure: Civil* §§ 1521–30 (1971). Changes in language therefore have been kept to a minimum to avoid confusion.

Since the amended rule encourages more extensive pretrial management than did the original, two or more conferences may be held in many cases. The language of Rule 16(e) recognizes this possibility and the corresponding need to issue more than one pretrial order in a single case.

Once formulated, pretrial orders should not be changed lightly; but total inflexibility is undesirable. See, *e.g., Clark v. Pennsylvania R.R. Co.*, 328 F.2d 591 (2d Cir.1964). The exact words used to describe the standard for amending the pretrial order probably are less important than the meaning given them in practice. By not imposing any limitation on the ability to modify a pretrial order, the rule reflects the reality that in any process of continuous management, what is done at one conference may have to be altered at the next. In the case of the final pretrial order, however, a more stringent standard is called for and the words "to prevent manifest injustice," which appeared in the original rule, have been retained. They have the virtue of familiarity and adequately describe the restraint the trial judge should exercise.

Many local rules make the plaintiff's attorney responsible for drafting a proposed pretrial order, either before or after the conference. Others allow the court to appoint any of the attorneys to perform the task, and others leave it to the court. See Note, *Pretrial Conference: A Critical Examination of Local Rules Adopted by Federal District Courts*, 64 Va.L.Rev. 467 (1978). Rule 16 has never addressed this matter. Since there is no consensus about which method of drafting the order works best and there is no reason to believe that nationwide uniformity is needed, the rule has been left silent on the point. See *Handbook for Effective Pretrial Procedure*, 37 F.R.D. 225 (1964).

Subdivision (f); Sanctions. Original Rule 16 did not mention the sanctions that might be imposed for failing to comply with the rule. However, courts have not hesitated to enforce it by appropriate measures. See, *e.g., Link v. Wabash R. Co.*, 370 U.S. 628 (1962) (district court's dismissal under Rule 41(b) after plaintiff's attorney failed to appear at a pretrial conference upheld); *Admiral Theatre Corp. v. Douglas Theatre*, 585 F.2d 877 (8th Cir.1978) (district court has discretion to exclude exhibits or refuse to permit the testimony of a witness not listed prior to trial in contravention of its pretrial order).

To reflect that existing practice, and to obviate dependence upon Rule 41(b) or the court's inherent power to regulate litigation, *cf. Societe Internationale Pour Participations Industrielles et Commerciales, S.A. v. Rogers,* 357 U.S. 197 (1958), Rule 16(f) expressly provides for imposing sanctions on disobedient or recalcitrant parties, their attorneys, or both in four types of situations. Rodes, Ripple & Mooney, *Sanctions Imposable for Violations of the Federal Rules of Civil Procedure* 65–67, 80–84, Federal Judicial Center (1981). Furthermore, explicit reference to sanctions reenforces the rule's intention to encourage forceful judicial management.

Rule 16(f) incorporates portions of Rule 37(b)(2), which prescribes sanctions for failing to make discovery. This should facilitate application of Rule 16(f), since courts and lawyers already are familiar with the Rule 37 standards. Among the sanctions authorized by the new subdivision are: preclusion order, striking a pleading, staying the proceeding, default judgment, contempt, and charging a party, his attorney, or both with the expenses, including attorney's fees, caused by noncompliance. The contempt sanction, however, is only available for a violation of a court order. The references in Rule 16(f) are not exhaustive.

As is true under Rule 37(b)(2), the imposition of sanctions may be sought by either the court or a party. In addition, the court has discretion to impose whichever sanction it feels is appropriate under the circumstances. Its action is reviewable under the abuse-of-discretion standard. See *National Hockey League v. Metropolitan Hockey Club, Inc.,* 427 U.S. 639 (1976).

1987 Amendment

The amendments are technical. No substantive change is intended.

1993 Amendments

Subdivision (b). One purpose of this amendment is to provide a more appropriate deadline for the initial scheduling order required by the rule. The former rule directed that the order be entered within 120 days from the filing of the complaint. This requirement has created problems because Rule 4(m) allows 120 days for service and ordinarily at least one defendant should be available to participate in the process of formulating the scheduling order. The revision provides that the order is to be entered within 90 days after the date a defendant first appears (whether by answer or by a motion under Rule 12) or, if earlier (as may occur in some actions against the United States or if service is waived under Rule 4), within 120 days after service of the complaint on a defendant. The longer time provided by the revision is not intended to encourage unnecessary delays in entering the scheduling order. Indeed, in most cases the order can and should be entered at a much earlier date. Rather, the additional time is intended to alleviate problems in multi-defendant cases and should ordinarily be adequate to enable participation by all defendants initially named in the action.

In many cases the scheduling order can and should be entered before this deadline. However, when setting a scheduling conference, the court should take into account the effect this setting will have in establishing deadlines for the parties to meet under revised Rule 26(f) and to exchange information under revised Rule 26(a)(1). While the parties are expected to stipulate to additional time for making their disclosures when warranted by the circumstances, a scheduling conference held before defendants have had time to learn much about the case may result in diminishing the value of the Rule 26(f) meeting, the parties' proposed discovery plan, and indeed the conference itself.

New paragraph (4) has been added to highlight that it will frequently be desirable for the scheduling order to include provisions relating to the timing of disclosures under Rule 26(a). While the initial disclosures required by Rule 26(a)(1) will ordinarily have been made before entry of the scheduling order, the timing and sequence for disclosure of expert testimony and of the witnesses and exhibits to be used at trial should be tailored to the circumstances of the case and is a matter that should be considered at the initial scheduling conference. Similarly, the scheduling order might contain provisions modifying the extent of discovery (*e.g.,* number and length of depositions) otherwise permitted under these rules or by a local rule.

The report from the attorneys concerning their meeting and proposed discovery plan, as required by revised Rule 26(f), should be submitted to the court before the scheduling order is entered. Their proposals, particularly regarding matters on which they agree, should be of substantial value to the court in setting the timing and limitations on discovery and should reduce the time of the court needed to conduct a meaningful conference under Rule 16(b). As under the prior rule, while a scheduling order is mandated, a scheduling conference is not. However, in view of the benefits to be derived from the litigants and a judicial officer meeting in person, a Rule 16(b) conference should, to the extent practicable, be held in all cases that will involve discovery.

This subdivision, as well as subdivision (c)(8), also is revised to reflect the new title of United States Magistrate Judges pursuant to the Judicial Improvements Act of 1990.

Subdivision (c). The primary purposes of the changes in subdivision (c) are to call attention to the opportunities for structuring of trial under Rules 42, 50, and 52 and to eliminate questions that have occasionally been raised regarding the authority of the court to make appropriate orders designed either to facilitate settlement or to provide for an efficient and economical trial. The prefatory language of this subdivision is revised to clarify the court's power to enter appropriate orders at a conference notwithstanding the objection of a party. Of course settlement is dependent upon agreement by the parties and, indeed, a conference is most effective and productive when the parties participate in a spirit of cooperation and mindful of their responsibilities under Rule 1.

Paragraph (4) is revised to clarify that in advance of trial the court may address the need for, and possible limitations on, the use of expert testimony under Rule 702 of the Federal Rules of Evidence. Even when proposed expert testimony might be admissible under the standards of Rules 403 and 702 of the evidence rules, the court may preclude or limit such testimony if the cost to the litigants—which may include the cost to adversaries of securing testimony on the same subjects by other experts—would be unduly expensive given the needs of the case and the other evidence available at trial.

Paragraph (5) is added (and the remaining paragraphs renumbered) in recognition that use of Rule 56 to avoid or reduce the scope of trial is a topic that can, and often should,

be considered at a pretrial conference. Renumbered paragraph (11) enables the court to rule on pending motions for summary adjudication that are ripe for decision at the time of the conference. Often, however, the potential use of Rule 56 is a matter that arises from discussions during a conference. The court may then call for motions to be filed.

Paragraph (6) is added to emphasize that a major objective of pretrial conferences should be to consider appropriate controls on the extent and timing of discovery. In many cases the court should also specify the times and sequence for disclosure of written reports from experts under revised Rule 26(a)(2)(B) and perhaps direct changes in the types of experts from whom written reports are required. Consideration should also be given to possible changes in the timing or form of the disclosure of trial witnesses and documents under Rule 26(a)(3).

Paragraph (9) is revised to describe more accurately the various procedures that, in addition to traditional settlement conferences, may be helpful in settling litigation. Even if a case cannot immediately be settled, the judge and attorneys can explore possible use of alternative procedures such as mini-trials, summary jury trials, mediation, neutral evaluation, and nonbinding arbitration that can lead to consensual resolution of the dispute without a full trial on the merits. The rule acknowledges the presence of statutes and local rules or plans that may authorize use of some of these procedures even when not agreed to by the parties. See 28 U.S.C. §§ 473(a)(6), 473(b)(4), 651–58; Section 104(b)(2), Pub.L. 101–650. The rule does not attempt to resolve questions as to the extent a court would be authorized to require such proceedings as an exercise of its inherent powers.

The amendment of paragraph (9) should be read in conjunction with the sentence added to the end of subdivision (c), authorizing the court to direct that, in appropriate cases, a responsible representative of the parties be present or available by telephone during a conference in order to discuss possible settlement of the case. The sentence refers to participation by a party or its representative. Whether this would be the individual party, an officer of a corporate party, a representative from an insurance carrier, or someone else would depend on the circumstances. Particularly in litigation in which governmental agencies or large amounts of money are involved, there may be no one with on-the-spot settlement authority, and the most that should be expected is access to a person who would have a major role in submitting a recommendation to the body or board with ultimate decision-making responsibility. The selection of the appropriate representative should ordinarily be left to the party and its counsel. Finally, it should be noted that the unwillingness of a party to be available, even by telephone, for a settlement conference may be a clear signal that the time and expense involved in pursuing settlement is likely to be unproductive and that personal participation by the parties should not be required.

The explicit authorization in the rule to require personal participation in the manner stated is not intended to limit the reasonable exercise of the court's inherent powers, e.g., G. Heileman Brewing Co. v. Joseph Oat Corp., 871 F.2d 648 (7th Cir.1989), or its power to require party participation under the Civil Justice Reform Act of 1990. See 28 U.S.C. § 473(b)(5) (civil justice expense and delay reduction plans adopted by district courts may include requirement that representatives "with authority to bind [parties] in settle-

ment discussions" be available during settlement conferences).

New paragraphs (13) and (14) are added to call attention to the opportunities for structuring of trial under Rule 42 and under revised Rules 50 and 52.

Paragraph (15) is also new. It supplements the power of the court to limit the extent of evidence under Rules 403 and 611(a) of the Federal Rules of Evidence, which typically would be invoked as a result of developments during trial. Limits on the length of trial established at a conference in advance of trial can provide the parties with a better opportunity to determine priorities and exercise selectivity in presenting evidence than when limits are imposed during trial. Any such limits must be reasonable under the circumstances, and ordinarily the court should impose them only after receiving appropriate submissions from the parties outlining the nature of the testimony expected to be presented through various witnesses, and the expected duration of direct and cross-examination.

2006 Amendment

The amendment to Rule 16(b) is designed to alert the court to the possible need to address the handling of discovery of electronically stored information early in the litigation if such discovery is expected to occur. Rule 26(f) is amended to direct the parties to discuss discovery of electronically stored information if such discovery is contemplated in the action. Form 35 is amended to call for a report to the court about the results of this discussion. In many instances, the court's involvement early in the litigation will help avoid difficulties that might otherwise arise.

Rule 16(b) is also amended to include among the topics that may be addressed in the scheduling order any agreements that the parties reach to facilitate discovery by minimizing the risk of waiver of privilege or work-product protection. Rule 26(f) is amended to add to the discovery plan the parties' proposal for the court to enter a case-management or other order adopting such an agreement. The parties may agree to various arrangements. For example, they may agree to initial provision of requested materials without waiver of privilege or protection to enable the party seeking production to designate the materials desired or protection for actual production, with the privilege review of only those materials to follow. Alternatively, they may agree that if privileged or protected information is inadvertently produced, the producing party may by timely notice assert the privilege or protection and obtain return of the materials without waiver. Other arrangements are possible. In most circumstances, a party who receives information under such an arrangement cannot assert that production of the information waived a claim of privilege or of protection as trial-preparation material.

An order that includes the parties' agreement may be helpful in avoiding delay and excessive cost in discovery. See Manual for Complex Litigation (4th) § 11.446. Rule 16(b)(6) recognizes the propriety of including such agreements in the court's order. The rule does not provide the court with authority to enter such a case-management or other order without party agreement, or limit the court's authority to act on motion.

2007 Amendment

*[Effective December 1, 2007,
absent contrary Congressional action.]*

The language of Rule 16 has been amended as part of the general restyling of the Civil Rules to make them more easily understood and to make style and terminology consistent throughout the rules. These changes are intended to be stylistic only.

When a party or its representative is not present, it is enough to be reasonably available by any suitable means, whether telephone or other communication device.

HISTORICAL NOTES

Change of Name

Reference to United States magistrate or to magistrate deemed to refer to United States magistrate judge pursuant to section 321 of Pub.L. 101–650, set out as a note under section 631 of this title.

IV. PARTIES

Proposed Amendment of Heading

Effective December 1, 2007, absent contrary Congressional action, this heading is amended to read as follows:

TITLE IV. PARTIES

Rule 17. Parties Plaintiff and Defendant; Capacity

(a) Real Party in Interest. Every action shall be prosecuted in the name of the real party in interest. An executor, administrator, guardian, bailee, trustee of an express trust, a party with whom or in whose name a contract has been made for the benefit of another, or a party authorized by statute may sue in that person's own name without joining the party for whose benefit the action is brought; and when a statute of the United States so provides, an action for the use or benefit of another shall be brought in the name of the United States. No action shall be dismissed on the ground that it is not prosecuted in the name of the real party in interest until a reasonable time has been allowed after objection for ratification of commencement of the action by, or joinder or substitution of, the real party in interest; and such ratification, joinder, or substitution shall have the same effect as if the action had been commenced in the name of the real party in interest.

(b) Capacity to Sue or be Sued. The capacity of an individual, other than one acting in a representative capacity, to sue or be sued shall be determined by the law of the individual's domicile. The capacity of a corporation to sue or be sued shall be determined by the law under which it was organized. In all other cases capacity to sue or be sued shall be determined by the law of the state in which the district court is held, except (1) that a partnership or other unincorporated association, which has no such capacity by the law of such state, may sue or be sued in its common name for the purpose of enforcing for or against it a substantive right existing under the Constitution or laws of the United States, and (2) that the capacity of a receiver appointed by a court of the United States to

sue or be sued in a court of the United States is governed by Title 28, U.S.C., Sections 754 and 959(a).

(c) Infants or Incompetent Persons. Whenever an infant or incompetent person has a representative, such as a general guardian, committee, conservator, or other like fiduciary, the representative may sue or defend on behalf of the infant or incompetent person. An infant or incompetent person who does not have a duly appointed representative may sue by a next friend or by a guardian ad litem. The court shall appoint a guardian ad litem for an infant or incompetent person not otherwise represented in an action or shall make such other order as it deems proper for the protection of the infant or incompetent person.

(As amended Dec. 27, 1946, eff. Mar. 19, 1948; Dec. 29, 1948, eff. Oct. 20, 1949; Feb. 28, 1966, eff. July 1, 1966; Mar. 2, 1987, eff. Aug. 1, 1987; Apr. 25, 1988, eff. Aug. 1, 1988; Nov. 18, 1988, Pub.L. 100–690, Title VII, § 7049, 102 Stat. 4401.)

Proposed Amendment of Rule

Effective December 1, 2007, absent contrary Congressional action, this rule is amended to read as follows:

Rule 17. Plaintiff and Defendant; Capacity; Public Officers

(a) Real Party in Interest.

(1) Designation in General. An action must be prosecuted in the name of the real party in interest. The following may sue in their own names without joining the person for whose benefit the action is brought:

(A) an executor;

(B) an administrator;

(C) a guardian;

(D) a bailee;

(E) a trustee of an express trust;

(F) a party with whom or in whose name a contract has been made for another's benefit; and

(G) a party authorized by statute.

(2) Action in the Name of the United States for Another's Use or Benefit. When a federal

statute so provides, an action for another's use or benefit must be brought in the name of the United States.

(3) Joinder of the Real Party in Interest. The court may not dismiss an action for failure to prosecute in the name of the real party in interest until, after an objection, a reasonable time has been allowed for the real party in interest to ratify, join, or be substituted into the action. After ratification, joinder, or substitution, the action proceeds as if it had been originally commenced by the real party in interest.

(b) Capacity to Sue or Be Sued. *Capacity to sue or be sued is determined as follows:*

(1) for an individual who is not acting in a representative capacity, by the law of the individual's domicile;

(2) for a corporation, by the law under which it was organized; and

(3) for all other parties, by the law of the state where the court is located, except that:

(A) a partnership or other unincorporated association with no such capacity under that state's law may sue or be sued in its common name to enforce a substantive right existing under the United States Constitution or laws; and

(B) 28 U.S.C. §§ 754 and 959(a) govern the capacity of a receiver appointed by a United States court to sue or be sued in a United States court.

(c) Minor or Incompetent Person.

(1) With a Representative. The following representatives may sue or defend on behalf of a minor or an incompetent person:

(A) a general guardian;

(B) a committee;

(C) a conservator; or

(D) a like fiduciary.

(2) Without a Representative. A minor or an incompetent person who does not have a duly appointed representative may sue by a next friend or by a guardian ad litem. The court must appoint a guardian ad litem—or issue another appropriate order—to protect a minor or incompetent person who is unrepresented in an action.

(d) Public Officer's Title and Name. *A public officer who sues or is sued in an official capacity may be designated by official title rather than by name, but the court may order that the officer's name be added.*

ADVISORY COMMITTEE NOTES

1937 Adoption

Note to Subdivision (a). The real party in interest provision, except for the last clause which is new, is taken verbatim from [former] Equity Rule 37 (Parties Generally—Intervention), except that the word "expressly" has been omitted. For similar provisions see N.Y.C.P.A., (1937) § 210; Wyo.Rev.Stat.Ann. (1931) §§ 89–501, 89–502, 89–503; *English Rules Under the Judicature Act* (The Annual Practice, 1937) O. 16, r. 8. See, also Equity Rule 41 (Suit to Execute Trusts of Will—Heir as Party). For examples of statutes of the United States providing particularly for an action for the use or benefit of another in the name of the United States, see U.S.C., Title 40, § 270b [see now 40 U.S.C.A. § 3133(b)] (Suit by persons furnishing labor and material for work on public building contracts * * * may sue on a payment bond, "in the name of the United States for the use of the person suing"); and U.S.C., Title 25, § 201 (Penalties under laws relating to Indians—how recovered). Compare U.S.C., Title 26, Int.Rev.Code [1939], § 3745(c) [former § 1645(c)] (Suits for penalties, fines, and forfeitures, under this title, where not otherwise provided for, to be in name of United States).

Note to Subdivision (b). For capacity see generally Clark and Moore, *New Federal Civil Procedure*—II. Pleadings and Parties, 44 Yale L.J. 1291, 1312–1317 (1935) and specifically *Coppedge v. Clinton*, 72 F.2d 531 (C.C.A.10th, 1934) (natural person); *David Lupton's Sons Co. v. Automobile Club of America*, 225 U.S. 489, 32 S.Ct. 711, 56 L.Ed. 1177, Ann.Cas.1914A, 699 (1912) (corporation); *Puerto Rico v. Russell & Co.*, 288 U.S. 476, 53 S.Ct. 447, 77 L.Ed. 903 (1933) (unincorporated assn.); *United Mine Workers of America v. Coronado Coal Co.*, 259 U.S. 344, 42 S.Ct. 570, 66 L.Ed. 975, 27 A.L.R. 762 (1922) (federal substantive right enforced against unincorporated association by suit against the association in its common name without naming all its members as parties). This rule follows the existing law as to such associations, as declared in the case last cited above. Compare *Moffat Tunnel League v. United States*, 289 U.S. 113, 53 S.Ct. 543, 77 L.Ed. 1069 (1933). See note to Rule 23, clause (1).

Note to Subdivision (c). The provision for infants and incompetent persons is substantially former Equity Rule 70 (Suits by or Against Incompetents) with slight additions. Compare the more detailed English provisions, *English Rules Under the Judicature Act* (The Annual Practice, 1937) O. 16, r.r. 16–21.

1946 Amendment

Note. The new matter [in subdivision (b)] makes clear the controlling character of Rule 66 regarding suits by or against a federal receiver in a federal court.

1948 Amendment

The amendment effective October 20, 1949, deleted the words "Rule 66" at the end of subdivision (b) and substituted the words "Title 28, U.S.C., §§ 754 and 959(a)".

1966 Amendment

The minor change in the text of the rule is designed to make it clear that the specific instances enumerated are not exceptions to, but illustrations of, the rule. These illustrations, of course, carry no negative implication to the effect that there are not other instances of recognition as the real party in interest of one whose standing as such may be in doubt. The enumeration is simply of cases in which there might be substantial doubt as to the issue but for the specific enumeration. There are other potentially arguable cases that are not excluded by the enumeration. For example, the enumeration states that the promisee in a contract for the benefit of a third party may sue as real party in interest; it does not say, because it is obvious, that the third-party beneficiary may sue (when the applicable law gives him that right.)

The rule adds to the illustrative list of real parties in interest a bailee—meaning, of course, a bailee suing on behalf of the bailor with respect to the property bailed. (When the possessor of property other than the owner sues for an invasion of the possessory interest he is the real party in interest.) The word "bailee" is added primarily to preserve the admiralty practice whereby the owner of a vessel as bailee of the cargo, or the master of the vessel as bailee of both vessel and cargo, sues for damage to either property interest or both. But there is no reason to limit such a provision to maritime situations. The owner of a warehouse in which household furniture is stored is equally entitled to sue on behalf of the numerous owners of the furniture stored. Cf. *Gulf Oil Corp. v. Gilbert*, 330 U.S. 501 (1947).

The provision that no action shall be dismissed on the ground that it is not prosecuted in the name of the real party in interest until a reasonable time has been allowed, after the objection has been raised, for ratification, substitution, etc., is added simply in the interests of justice. In its origin the rule concerning the real party in interest was permissive in purpose: it was designed to allow an assignee to sue in his own name. That having been accomplished, the modern function of the rule in its negative aspect is simply to protect the defendant against a subsequent action by the party actually entitled to recover, and to insure generally that the judgment will have its proper effect as res judicata.

This provision keeps pace with the law as it is actually developing. Modern decisions are inclined to be lenient when an honest mistake has been made in choosing the party in whose name the action is to be filed—in both maritime and nonmaritime cases. See *Levinson v. Deupree*, 345 U.S. 648 (1953); *Link Aviation, Inc. v. Downs*, 325 F.2d 613 (D.C.Cir. 1963). The provision should not be misunderstood or distorted. It is intended to prevent forfeiture when determination of the proper party to sue is difficult or when an understandable mistake has been made. It does not mean, for example, that, following an airplane crash in which all aboard were killed, an action may be filed in the name of John Doe (a fictitious person), as personal representative of Richard Roe (another fictitious person), in the hope that at a later time the attorney filing the action may substitute the real name of the real personal representative of a real victim, and have the benefit of suspension of the limitation period. It does not even mean, when an action is filed by the personal representative of John Smith, of Buffalo, in the good faith belief that he was aboard the flight, that upon discovery that Smith is alive and well, having missed the fatal flight, the representative of James Brown, of San Francisco, an actual victim, can be substituted to take advantage of the suspension of the limitation period. It is, in cases of this sort, intended to insure against forfeiture and injustice—in short, to codify in broad terms the salutary principle of *Levinson v. Deupree*, 345 U.S. 648 (1953), and *Link Aviation, Inc. v. Downs*, 325 F.2d 613 (D.C.Cir. 1963).

1987 Amendment

The amendments are technical. No substantive change is intended.

1988 Amendment

The amendment is technical. No substantive change is intended.

2007 Amendment

[Effective December 1, 2007, absent contrary Congressional action.]

The language of Rule 17 has been amended as part of the general restyling of the Civil Rules to make them more easily understood and to make style and terminology consistent throughout the rules. These changes are intended to be stylistic only.

Rule 17(d) incorporates the provisions of former Rule 25(d)(2), which fit better with Rule 17.

Rule 18. Joinder of Claims and Remedies

(a) Joinder of Claims. A party asserting a claim to relief as an original claim, counterclaim, crossclaim, or third-party claim, may join, either as independent or as alternate claims, as many claims, legal, equitable, or maritime, as the party has against an opposing party.

(b) Joinder of Remedies; Fraudulent Conveyances. Whenever a claim is one heretofore cognizable only after another claim has been prosecuted to a conclusion, the two claims may be joined in a single action; but the court shall grant relief in that action only in accordance with the relative substantive rights of the parties. In particular, a plaintiff may state a claim for money and a claim to have set aside a conveyance fraudulent as to that plaintiff, without first having obtained a judgment establishing the claim for money.

(As amended Feb. 28, 1966, eff. July 1, 1966; Mar. 2, 1987, eff. Aug. 1, 1987.)

Proposed Amendment of Rule

Effective December 1, 2007, absent contrary Congressional action, this rule is amended to read as follows:

Rule 18. Joinder of Claims

(a) In General. A party asserting a claim, counterclaim, crossclaim, or third-party claim may join, as independent or alternative claims, as many claims as it has against an opposing party.

(b) Joinder of Contingent Claims. A party may join two claims even though one of them is contingent on the disposition of the other; but the court may grant relief only in accordance with the parties' relative substantive rights. In particular, a plaintiff may state a claim for money and a claim to set aside a conveyance that is fraudulent as to that plaintiff, without first obtaining a judgment for the money.

ADVISORY COMMITTEE NOTES

1937 Adoption

Note to Subdivision (a). 1. Recent development, both in code and common law states, has been toward unlimited joinder of actions. See Ill.Rev.Stat. (1937) ch. 110, § 168; N.J.S.A. 2:27–37, as modified by N.J.Sup.Ct.Rules, Rule 21, 2 N.J.Misc. 1208 (1924); N.Y.C.P.A. (1937) § 258 as amended by Laws of 1935, ch. 339.

2. This provision for joinder of actions has been patterned upon [former] Equity Rule 26 (Joinder of Causes of Action) and broadened to include multiple parties. Compare the English practice, *English Rules Under the Judicature Act* (The Annual Practice, 1937) O. 18, r.r. 1–9 (noting rules 1 and 6). The earlier American codes set forth classes of joinder, following the now abandoned New York rule. See N.Y.C.P.A. § 258 before amended in 1935; Compare Kan. Gen.Stat.Ann. (1935) § 60–601; Wis.Stat.(1935) § 263.04 for the more liberal practice.

3. The provisions of this rule for the joinder of claims are subject to Rule 82 (Jurisdiction and Venue Unaffected). For the jurisdictional aspects of joinder of claims, see Shulman and Jaegerman, *Some Jurisdictional Limitations on Federal Procedure* (1936), 45 Yale L.J. 393, 397–410. For separate trials of joined claims, see Rule 42(b).

Note to Subdivision (b). This rule is inserted to make it clear that in a single action a party should be accorded all the relief to which he is entitled regardless of whether it is legal or equitable or both. This necessarily includes a deficiency judgment in foreclosure actions formerly provided for in [former] Equity Rule 10 (Decree for Deficiency in Foreclosures, Etc.). In respect to fraudulent conveyances the rule changes the former rule requiring a prior judgment against the owner (*Braun v. American Laundry Mach. Co.*, 56 F.2d 197 (S.D.N.Y. 1932)) to conform to the provisions of the Uniform Fraudulent Conveyance Act, §§ 9 and 10. See McLaughlin, *Application of the Uniform Fraudulent Conveyance Act*, 46 Harv.L.Rev. 404, 444 (1933).

1966 Amendment

The Rules "proceed upon the theory that no inconvenience can result from the joinder of any two or more matters in the pleadings, but only from trying two or more matters together which have little or nothing in common." Sunderland, *The New Federal Rules*, 45 W.Va.L.Q. 5, 13 (1938); see Clark, Code Pleading 58 (2d ed. 1947). Accordingly, Rule 18(a) has permitted a party to plead multiple claims of all types against an opposing party, subject to the court's power to direct an appropriate procedure for trying the claims. See Rules 42(b), 20(b), 21.

The liberal policy regarding joinder of claims in the pleadings extends to cases with multiple parties. However, the language used in the second sentence of Rule 18(a)—"if the requirements of Rules 19 [necessary joinder of parties], 20 [permissive joinder of parties], and 22 [interpleader] are satisfied"—has led some courts to infer that the rules regulating joinder of parties are intended to carry back to Rule 18(a) and to impose some special limits on joinder of claims in multiparty cases. In particular, Rule 20(a) has been read as restricting the operation of Rule 18(a) in certain situations in which a number of parties have been permissively joined in an action. In *Federal Housing Admr. v. Christianson*, 26 F.Supp. 419 (D.Conn.1939), the indorsee of two notes sued the three comakers of one note, and sought to join in the action a count on a second note which had been made by two of the three defendants. There was no doubt about the propriety of the joinder of the three parties defendant, for a right to relief was being asserted against all three defendants which arose out of a single "transaction" (the first note) and a question of fact or law "common" to all three defendants would arise in the action. See the text of Rule 20(a). The court, however, refused to allow the joinder of the count on the second note, on the ground that this right to relief, assumed to arise from a distinct transaction, did not involve a question common to all the defendants but only two of them. For analysis of the *Christianson* case and other authorities, see 2 Barron & Holtzoff, *Federal Practice & Procedure*, § 533.1 (Wright ed. 1961); 3 Moore's *Federal Practice*, par. 18.04[3] (2d ed. 1963).

If the court's view is followed, it becomes necessary to enter at the pleading stage into speculations about the exact relation between the claim sought to be joined against fewer than all the defendants properly joined in the action, and the claims asserted against all the defendants. Cf. Wright, *Joinder of Claims and Parties Under Modern Pleading Rules*, 36 Minn.L.Rev. 580, 605–06 (1952). Thus if it could be found in the Christianson situation that the claim on the second note arose out of the same transaction as the claim on the first or out of a transaction forming part of a "series," and that any question of fact or law with respect to the second note also arose with regard to the first, it would be held that the claim on the second note could be joined in the complaint. See 2 Barron & Holtzoff, supra, at 109; see also id. at 198 n. 60.4; cf. 3 Moore's *Federal Practice*, supra, at 1811. Such pleading niceties provide a basis for delaying and wasteful maneuver. It is more compatible with the design of the Rules to allow the claim to be joined in the pleading, leaving the question of possible separate trial of that claim to be later decided. See 2 Barron & Holtzoff, supra, § 533.1; Wright, supra, 36 Minn.L.Rev. at 604–11; *Developments in the Law—Multiparty Litigation in the Federal Courts*, 71 Harv. 874, 970–71 (1958); Commentary, *Relation Between Joinder of Parties and Joinder of Claims*, 5 F.R.Serv. 822 (1942). It is instructive to note that the court in the *Christianson* case, while holding that the claim on the second note could not be joined as a matter of pleading, held open the possibility that both claims would later be consolidated for trial under Rule 42(a). See 26 F.Supp. 419.

Rule 18(a) is now amended not only to overcome the *Christianson* decision and similar authority, but also to state clearly as a comprehensive proposition, that a party asserting a claim (an original claim, counterclaim, cross-claim, or third-party claim) may join as many claims as he has against an opposing party. See *Noland Co., Inc. v. Graver Tank & Mfg. Co.*, 301 F.2d 43, 49–51 (4th Cir.1962); but cf. *C. W.*

Humphrey Co. v. Security Alum. Co., 31 F.R.D. 41 (E.D.Mich.1962). This permitted joinder of claims is not affected by the fact that there are multiple parties in the action. The joinder of parties is governed by other rules operating independently.

It is emphasized that amended Rule 18(a) deals only with pleading. As already indicated, a claim properly joined as a matter of pleading need not be proceeded with together with the other claims if fairness or convenience justifies separate treatment.

Amended Rule 18(a), like the rule prior to amendment, does not purport to deal with questions of jurisdiction or venue which may arise with respect to claims properly joined as a matter of pleading. See Rule 82.

See also the amendment of Rule 20(a) and the Advisory Committee's Note thereto.

Free joinder of claims and remedies is one of the basic purposes of unification of the admiralty and civil procedure. The amendment accordingly provides for the inclusion in the rule of maritime claims as well as those which are legal and equitable in character.

1987 Amendment

The amendments are technical. No substantive change is intended.

2007 Amendment

[Effective December 1, 2007, absent contrary Congressional action.]

The language of Rule 18 has been amended as part of the general restyling of the Civil Rules to make them more easily understood and to make style and terminology consistent throughout the rules. These changes are intended to be stylistic only.

Modification of the obscure former reference to a claim "heretofore cognizable only after another claim has been prosecuted to a conclusion" avoids any uncertainty whether Rule 18(b)'s meaning is fixed by retrospective inquiry from some particular date.

Rule 19. Joinder of Persons Needed for Just Adjudication

(a) Persons to be Joined if Feasible. A person who is subject to service of process and whose joinder will not deprive the court of jurisdiction over the subject matter of the action shall be joined as a party in the action if (1) in the person's absence complete relief cannot be accorded among those already parties, or (2) the person claims an interest relating to the subject of the action and is so situated that the disposition of the action in the person's absence may (i) as a practical matter impair or impede the person's ability to protect that interest or (ii) leave any of the persons already parties subject to a substantial risk of incurring double, multiple, or otherwise inconsistent obligations by reason of the claimed interest. If the person has not been so joined, the court shall order that the person be made a party. If the person should join as a plaintiff but refuses to do so, the person may be made a defendant, or, in a proper case, an involuntary plaintiff. If the joined party objects to venue and joinder of that party would render the venue of the action improper, that party shall be dismissed from the action.

(b) Determination by Court Whenever Joinder not Feasible. If a person as described in subdivision (a)(1)–(2) hereof cannot be made a party, the court shall determine whether in equity and good conscience the action should proceed among the parties before it, or should be dismissed, the absent person being thus regarded as indispensable. The factors to be considered by the court include: first, to what extent a judgment rendered in the person's absence might be prejudicial to the person or those already parties; second, the extent to which, by protective provisions in the judgment, by the shaping of relief, or other measures, the prejudice can be lessened or avoided; third, whether a judgment rendered in the person's absence will be adequate; fourth, whether the plaintiff will have an adequate remedy if the action is dismissed for nonjoinder.

(c) Pleading Reasons for Nonjoinder. A pleading asserting a claim for relief shall state the names, if known to the pleader, of any persons as described in subdivision (a)(1)–(2) hereof who are not joined, and the reasons why they are not joined.

(d) Exception of Class Actions. This rule is subject to the provisions of Rule 23.

(As amended Feb. 28, 1966, eff. July 1, 1966; Mar. 2, 1987, eff. Aug. 1, 1987.)

Proposed Amendment of Rule

Effective December 1, 2007, absent contrary Congressional action, this rule is amended to read as follows:

Rule 19. *Required Joinder of Parties*

(a) *Persons Required to Be Joined if Feasible.*

(1) Required Party. A person who is subject to service of process and whose joinder will not deprive the court of subject-matter jurisdiction must be joined as a party if:

(A) in that person's absence, the court cannot accord complete relief among existing parties; or

(B) that person claims an interest relating to the subject of the action and is so situated that disposing of the action in the person's absence may:

(i) as a practical matter impair or impede the person's ability to protect the interest; or

(ii) leave an existing party subject to a substantial risk of incurring double, multi-

ple, or otherwise inconsistent obligations because of the interest.

(2) Joinder by Court Order. If a person has not been joined as required, the court must order that the person be made a party. A person who refuses to join as a plaintiff may be made either a defendant or, in a proper case, an involuntary plaintiff.

(3) Venue. If a joined party objects to venue and the joinder would make venue improper, the court must dismiss that party.

(b) When Joinder Is Not Feasible. *If a person who is required to be joined if feasible cannot be joined, the court must determine whether, in equity and good conscience, the action should proceed among the existing parties or should be dismissed. The factors for the court to consider include:*

(1) the extent to which a judgment rendered in the person's absence might prejudice that person or the existing parties;

(2) the extent to which any prejudice could be lessened or avoided by:

(A) protective provisions in the judgment;

(B) shaping the relief; or

(C) other measures;

(3) whether a judgment rendered in the person's absence would be adequate; and

(4) whether the plaintiff would have an adequate remedy if the action were dismissed for nonjoinder.

(c) Pleading the Reasons for Nonjoinder. *When asserting a claim for relief, a party must state:*

(1) the name, if known, of any person who is required to be joined if feasible but is not joined; and

(2) the reasons for not joining that person.

(d) Exception for Class Actions. *This rule is subject to Rule 23.*

ADVISORY COMMITTEE NOTES
1937 Adoption

Note to Subdivision (a). The first sentence with verbal differences (e.g., "united" interest for "joint" interest) is to be found in [former] Equity Rule 37 (Parties Generally—Intervention). Such compulsory joinder provisions are common. Compare Alaska Comp.Laws (1933) § 3392 (containing in same sentence a "class suit" provision); Wyo.Rev.Stat. Ann. (Courtright, 1931) § 89–515 (immediately followed by "class suit" provisions, § 89–516). See also former Equity Rule 42 (Joint and Several Demands). For example of a proper case for involuntary plaintiff, see *Independent Wireless Telegraph Co. v. Radio Corp. of America*, 269 U.S. 459, 46 S.Ct. 166, 70 L.Ed. 357 (1926).

The joinder provisions of this rule are subject to Rule 82 (Jurisdiction and Venue Unaffected).

Note to Subdivision (b). For the substance of this rule see [former] Equity Rule 39 (Absence of Persons Who Would be Proper Parties) and U.S.C., Title 28, § 111 [now § 1391] (When part of several defendants cannot be served); *Camp v. Gress*, 250 U.S. 308, 39 S.Ct. 478, 63 L.Ed. 997 (1919). See also the second and third sentences of [former] Equity Rule 37 (Parties Generally—Intervention).

Note to Subdivision (c). For the substance of this rule see the fourth subdivision of [former] Equity Rule 25 (Bill of Complaint—Contents).

1966 Amendment
General Considerations

Whenever feasible, the persons materially interested in the subject of an action—see the more detailed description of these persons in the discussion of new subdivision (a) below—should be joined as parties so that they may be heard and a complete disposition made. When this comprehensive joinder cannot be accomplished—a situation which may be encountered in Federal courts because of limitations on service of process, subject matter jurisdiction, and venue—the case should be examined pragmatically and a choice made between the alternatives of proceeding with the action in the absence of particular interested persons, and dismissing the action.

Even if the court is mistaken in its decision to proceed in the absence of an interested person, it does not by that token deprive itself of the power to adjudicate as between the parties already before it through proper service of process. But the court can make a legally binding adjudication only between the parties actually joined in the action. It is true that an adjudication between the parties before the court may on occasion adversely affect the absent person as a practical matter, or leave a party exposed to a later inconsistent recovery by the absent person. These are factors which should be considered in deciding whether the action should proceed, or should rather be dismissed; but they do not themselves negate the court's power to adjudicate as between the parties who have been joined.

Defects in the Original Rule

The foregoing propositions were well understood in the older equity practice, see Hazard, *Indispensable Party: The Historical Origin of a Procedural Phantom*, 61 Colum.L.Rev. 1254 (1961), and Rule 19 could be and often was applied in consonance with them. But experience showed that the rule was defective in its phrasing and did not point clearly to the proper basis of decision.

Textual defects.—(1) The expression "persons * * * who ought to be parties if complete relief is to be accorded between those already parties," appearing in original subdivision (b), was apparently intended as a description of the persons whom it would be desirable to join in the action, all questions of feasibility of joinder being put to one side; but it was not adequately descriptive of those persons.

(2) The word "indispensable," appearing in original subdivision (b), was apparently intended as an inclusive reference to the interested persons in whose absence it would be advisable, all factors having been considered, to dismiss the

action. Yet the sentence implied that there might be interested persons, not "indispensable," in whose absence the action ought also to be dismissed. Further, it seemed at least superficially plausible to equate the word "indispensable" with the expression "having a joint interest," appearing in subdivision (a). See *United States v. Washington Inst. of Tech., Inc.*, 138 F.2d 25, 26 (3d Cir. 1943); cf. *Chidester v. City of Newark*, 162 F.2d 598 (3d Cir. 1947). But persons holding an interest technically "joint" are not always so related to an action that it would be unwise to proceed without joining all of them, whereas persons holding an interest not technically "joint" may have this relation to an action. See Reed, *Compulsory Joinder of Parties in Civil Actions*, 55 Mich.L.Rev. 327, 356 ff., 483 (1957).

(3) The use of "indispensable" and "joint interest" in the context of original Rule 19 directed attention to the technical or abstract character of the rights or obligations of the persons whose joinder was in question, and correspondingly distracted attention from the pragmatic considerations which should be controlling.

(4) The original rule, in dealing with the feasibility of joining a person as a party to the action, besides referring to whether the person was "subject to the jurisdiction of the court as to both service of process and venue," spoke of whether the person could be made a party "without depriving the court of jurisdiction of the parties before it." The second quoted expression used "jurisdiction" in the sense of the competence of the court over the subject matter of the action, and in this sense the expression was apt. However, by a familiar confusion, the expression seems to have suggested to some that the absence from the lawsuit of a person who was "indispensable" or "who ought to be [a] part[y]" itself deprived the court of the power to adjudicate as between the parties already joined. See *Samuel Goldwyn, Inc. v. United Artists Corp.*, 113 F.2d 703, 707 (3d Cir. 1940); *McArthur v. Rosenbaum Co. of Pittsburgh*, 180 F.2d 617, 621 (3d Cir. 1949); cf. *Calcote v. Texas Pac. Coal & Oil Co.*, 157 F.2d 216 (5th Cir. 1946), cert. denied, 329 U.S. 782 (1946), noted in 56 Yale L.J. 1088 (1947); Reed, supra, 55 Mich. L.Rev. at 332–34.

Failure to point to correct basis of decision. The original rule did not state affirmatively what factors were relevant in deciding whether the action should proceed or be dismissed when joinder of interested persons was infeasible. In some instances courts did not undertake the relevant inquiry or were misled by the "jurisdiction" fallacy. In other instances there was undue preoccupation with abstract classifications of rights or obligations, as against consideration of the particular consequences of proceeding with the action and the ways by which these consequences might be ameliorated by the shaping of final relief or other precautions.

Although these difficulties cannot be said to have been general analysis of the cases showed that there was good reason for attempting to strengthen the rule. The literature also indicated how the rule should be reformed. See Reed, supra (discussion of the important case of *Shields v. Barrow*, 17 How. (58 U.S.) 130 (1854), appears at 55 Mich.L.Rev., p. 340 ff.); Hazard, supra; N.Y. Temporary Comm. on Courts, First Preliminary Report, Legis.Doc.1957, No. 6(b), pp. 28, 233; N.Y. Judicial Council, Twelfth Ann.Rep., Legis.Doc.1946, No. 17, p. 163; Joint Comm. on Michigan Procedural Revision, Final Report, Pt. III, p. 69 (1960); Note, *Indispensable Parties in the Federal Courts*, 65 Harv.L.Rev.

1050 (1952); *Developments in the Law—Multiparty Litigation in the Federal Courts*, 71 Harv.L.Rev. 874, 879 (1958); Mich.Gen.Court Rules, R. 205 (effective Jan. 1, 1963); N.Y.Civ.Prac.Law & Rules, § 1001 (effective Sept. 1, 1963).

The Amended Rule

New subdivision (a) defines the persons whose joinder in the action is desirable. Clause (1) stresses the desirability of joining those persons in whose absence the court would be obliged to grant partial or "hollow" rather than complete relief to the parties before the court. The interests that are being furthered here are not only those of the parties, but also that of the public in avoiding repeated lawsuits on the same essential subject matter. Clause (2)(i) recognizes the importance of protecting the person whose joinder is in question against the practical prejudice to him which may arise through a disposition of the action in his absence. Clause (2)(ii) recognizes the need for considering whether a party may be left, after the adjudication, in a position where a person not joined can subject him to a double or otherwise inconsistent liability. See Reed, supra, 55 Mich.L.Rev. at 330, 338; Note, supra, 65 Harv.L.Rev. at 1052–57; *Developments in the Law*, supra, 71 Harv.L.Rev. at 881–85.

The subdivision (a) definition of persons to be joined is not couched in terms of the abstract nature of their interests— "joint," "united," "separable," or the like. See N.Y. Temporary Comm. on Courts, First Preliminary Report, supra; Developments in the Law, supra, at 880. It should be noted particularly, however, that the description is not at variance with the settled authorities holding that a tortfeasor with the usual "joint-and-several" liability is merely a permissive party to an action against another with like liability. See 3 Moore's *Federal Practice* 2153 (2d ed. 1963); 2 Barron & Holtzoff, *Federal Practice & Procedure* § 513.8 (Wright ed. 1961). Joinder of these tortfeasors continues to be regulated by Rule 20; compare Rule 14 on third-party practice.

If a person as described in subdivision (a)(1)(2) is amenable to service of process and his joinder would not deprive the court of jurisdiction in the sense of competence over the action, he should be joined as a party; and if he has not been joined, the court should order him to be brought into the action. If a party joined has a valid objection to the venue and chooses to assert it, he will be dismissed from the action.

Subdivision (b).—When a person as described in subdivision (a)(1)–(2) cannot be made a party, the court is to determine whether in equity and good conscience the action should proceed among the parties already before it, or should be dismissed. That this decision is to be made in the light of pragmatic considerations has often been acknowledged by the courts. See *Roos v. Texas Co.*, 23 F.2d 171 (2d Cir. 1927), cert. denied 277 U.S. 587 (1928); *Niles-Bement-Pond Co. v. Iron Moulders' Union*, 254 U.S. 77, 80 (1920). The subdivision sets out four relevant considerations drawn from the experience revealed in the decided cases. The factors are to a certain extent overlapping, and they are not intended to exclude other considerations which may be applicable in particular situations.

The first factor brings in a consideration of what a judgment in the action would mean to the absentee. Would the absentee be adversely affected in a practical sense, and if so, would the prejudice be immediate and serious, or remote and minor? The possible collateral consequences of the judg-

ment upon the parties already joined are also to be appraised. Would any party be exposed to a fresh action by the absentee, and if so, how serious is the threat? See the elaborate discussion in Reed, supra; cf. *A. L. Smith Iron Co. v. Dickson,* 141 F.2d 3 (2d Cir. 1944); *Caldwell Mfg. Co. v. Unique Balance Co.,* 18 F.R.D. 258 (S.D.N.Y.1955).

The second factor calls attention to the measures by which prejudice may be averted or lessened. The "shaping of relief" is a familiar expedient to this end. See, e.g., the award of money damages in lieu of specific relief where the latter might affect an absentee adversely. *Ward v. Deavers,* 203 F.2d 72 (D.C.Cir.1953); *Miller & Lux, Inc. v. Nickel,* 141 F.Supp. 41 (N.D.Calif.1956). On the use of "protective provisions," see *Roos v. Texas Co.,* supra; *Atwood v. Rhode Island Hosp. Trust Co.,* 275 Fed. 513, 519 (1st Cir. 1921), cert. denied, 257 U.S. 661 (1922); cf. *Stumpf v. Fidelity Gas Co.,* 294 F.2d 886 (9th Cir. 1961); and the general statement in *National Licorice Co. v. Labor Board,* 309 U.S. 350, 363 (1940).

Sometimes the party is himself able to take measures to avoid prejudice. Thus a defendant faced with a prospect of a second suit by an absentee may be in a position to bring the latter into the action by defensive interpleader. See *Hudson v. Newell,* 172 F.2d 848, 852 mod., 176 F.2d 546 (5th Cir. 1949); *Gauss v. Kirk,* 198 F.2d 83, 86 (D.C.Cir. 1952); *Abel v. Brayton Flying Service, Inc.,* 248 F.2d 713, 716 (5th Cir. 1957) (suggestion of possibility of counter-claim under Rule 13(h)); cf. *Parker Rust-Proof Co. v. Western Union Tel. Co.,* 105 F.2d 976 (2d Cir. 1939), cert. denied, 308 U.S. 597 (1939). So also the absentee may sometimes be able to avert prejudice to himself by voluntarily appearing in the action or intervening on an ancillary basis. See *Developments in the Law,* supra, 71 Harv.L.Rev. at 882; Annot., *Intervention or Subsequent Joinder of Parties as Affecting Jurisdiction of Federal Court Based on Diversity of Citizenship,* 134 A.L.R. 335 (1941); *Johnson v. Middleton,* 175 F.2d 535 (7th Cir. 1949); *Kentucky Nat. Gas Corp. v. Duggins,* 165 F.2d 1011 (6th Cir. 1948); *McComb v. McCormack,* 159 F.2d 219 (5th Cir. 1947). The court should consider whether this, in turn, would impose undue hardship on the absentee. (For the possibility of the court's informing an absentee of the pendency of the action, see comment under subdivision (c) below.)

The third factor—whether an "adequate" judgment can be rendered in the absence of a given person—calls attention to the extent of the relief that can be accorded among the parties joined. It meshes with the other factors, especially the "shaping of relief" mentioned under the second factor. Cf. *Kroese v. General Steel Castings Corp.,* 179 F.2d 760 (3d Cir. 1949), cert. denied, 339 U.S. 983 (1950).

The fourth factor, looking to the practical effects of a dismissal, indicates that the court should consider whether there is any assurance that the plaintiff, if dismissed, could sue effectively in another forum where better joinder would be possible. See *Fitzgerald v. Haynes,* 241 F.2d 417, 420 (3d Cir. 1957); *Fouke v. Schenewerk,* 197 F.2d 234, 236 (5th Cir. 1952); cf. *Warfield v. Marks,* 190 F.2d 178 (5th Cir. 1951).

The subdivision uses the word "indispensable" only in a conclusory sense, that is, a person is "regarded as indispensable" when he cannot be made a party and, upon consideration of the factors above mentioned, it is determined that in his absence it would be preferable to dismiss the action, rather than to retain it.

A person may be added as a party at any stage of the action on motion or on the court's initiative (see Rule 21); and a motion to dismiss, on the ground that a person has not been joined and justice requires that the action should not proceed in his absence, may be made as late as the trial on the merits (see Rule 12(h)(2), as amended; cf. Rule 12(b)(7), as amended). However, when the moving party is seeking dismissal in order to protect himself against a later suit by the absent person (subdivision (a)(2)(ii)), and is not seeking vicariously to protect the absent person against a prejudicial judgment (subdivision (a)(2)(i)), his undue delay in making the motion can properly be counted against him as a reason for denying the motion. A joinder question should be decided with reasonable promptness, but decision may properly be deferred if adequate information is not available at the time. Thus the relationship of an absent person to the action, and the practical effects of an adjudication upon him and others, may not be sufficiently revealed at the pleading stage; in such a case it would be appropriate to defer decision until the action was further advanced. Cf. Rule 12(d).

The amended rule makes no special provision for the problem arising in suits against subordinate Federal officials where it has often been set up as a defense that some superior officer must be joined. Frequently this defense has been accompanied by or intermingled with defenses of sovereign community or lack of consent of the United States to suit. So far as the issue of joinder can be isolated from the rest, the new subdivision seems better adapted to handle it than the predecessor provision. See the discussion in *Johnson v. Kirkland,* 290 F.2d 440, 446–47 (5th Cir. 1961) (stressing the practical orientation of the decisions); *Shaughnessy v. Pedreiro,* 349 U.S. 48, 54 (1955). Recent legislation, P.L. 87–748, 76 Stat. 744, approved October 5, 1962, adding §§ 1361, 1391(e) to Title 28, U.S.C., vests original jurisdiction in the District Courts over actions in the nature of mandamus to compel officials of the United States to perform their legal duties, and extends the range of service of process and liberalizes venue in these actions. If, then, it is found that a particular official should be joined in the action, the legislation will make it easy to bring him in.

Subdivision (c) parallels the predecessor subdivision (c) of Rule 19. In some situations it may be desirable to advise a person who has not been joined of the fact that the action is pending, and in particular cases the court in its discretion may itself convey this information by directing a letter or other informal notice to the absentee.

Subdivision (d) repeats the exception contained in the first clause of the predecessor subdivision (a).

1987 Amendment

The amendments are technical. No substantive change is intended.

2007 Amendment

*[Effective December 1, 2007,
absent contrary Congressional action.]*

The language of Rule 19 has been amended as part of the general restyling of the Civil Rules to make them more easily understood and to make style and terminology consistent throughout the rules. These changes are intended to be stylistic only.

Former Rule 19(b) described the conclusion that an action should be dismissed for inability to join a Rule 19(a) party by carrying forward traditional terminology: "the absent person being thus regarded as indispensable." "Indispensable" was used only to express a conclusion reached by applying the tests of Rule 19(b). It has been discarded as redundant.

Rule 20.　Permissive Joinder of Parties

(a) Permissive Joinder. All persons may join in one action as plaintiffs if they assert any right to relief jointly, severally, or in the alternative in respect of or arising out of the same transaction, occurrence, or series of transactions or occurrences and if any question of law or fact common to all these persons will arise in the action. All persons (and any vessel, cargo or other property subject to admiralty process in rem) may be joined in one action as defendants if there is asserted against them jointly, severally, or in the alternative, any right to relief in respect of or arising out of the same transaction, occurrence, or series of transactions or occurrences and if any question of law or fact common to all defendants will arise in the action. A plaintiff or defendant need not be interested in obtaining or defending against all the relief demanded. Judgment may be given for one or more of the plaintiffs according to their respective rights to relief, and against one or more defendants according to their respective liabilities.

(b) Separate Trials. The court may make such orders as will prevent a party from being embarrassed, delayed, or put to expense by the inclusion of a party against whom the party asserts no claim and who asserts no claim against the party, and may order separate trials or make other orders to prevent delay or prejudice.

(As amended Feb. 28, 1966, eff. July 1, 1966; Mar. 2, 1987, eff. Aug. 1, 1987.)

Proposed Amendment of Rule

Effective December 1, 2007, absent contrary Congressional action, this rule is amended to read as follows:

Rule 20.　Permissive Joinder of Parties

(a) Persons Who May Join or Be Joined.

(1) Plaintiffs. Persons may join in one action as plaintiffs if:

(A) they assert any right to relief jointly, severally, or in the alternative with respect to or arising out of the same transaction, occurrence, or series of transactions or occurrences; and

(B) any question of law or fact common to all plaintiffs will arise in the action.

(2) Defendants. Persons—as well as a vessel, cargo, or other property subject to admiralty

process in rem—may be joined in one action as defendants if:

(A) any right to relief is asserted against them jointly, severally, or in the alternative with respect to or arising out of the same transaction, occurrence, or series of transactions or occurrences; and

(B) any question of law or fact common to all defendants will arise in the action.

(3) Extent of Relief. Neither a plaintiff nor a defendant need be interested in obtaining or defending against all the relief demanded. The court may grant judgment to one or more plaintiffs according to their rights, and against one or more defendants according to their liabilities.

(b) Protective Measures. *The court may issue orders—including an order for separate trials—to protect a party against embarrassment, delay, expense, or other prejudice that arises from including a person against whom the party asserts no claim and who asserts no claim against the party.*

ADVISORY COMMITTEE NOTES
1937 Adoption

The provisions for joinder here stated are in substance the provisions found in England, California, Illinois, New Jersey, and New York. They represent only a moderate expansion of the present federal equity practice to cover both law and equity actions.

With this rule compare also [former] Equity Rules 26 (Joinder of Causes of Action), 37 (Parties Generally—Intervention), 40 (Nominal Parties), and 42 (Joint and Several Demands).

The provisions of this rule for the joinder of parties are subject to Rule 82 (Jurisdiction and Venue Unaffected).

Note to Subdivision (a). The first sentence is derived from *English Rules Under the Judicature Act* (The Annual Practice, 1937) O. 16, r. 1. Compare Calif.Code Civ.Proc. (Deering, 1937) §§ 378, 379a; Ill.Rev.Stat. (1937) ch. 110, § 147–148; N.J.Comp.Stat. (2 Cum.Supp., 1911–1924), N.Y.C.P.A. (1937) §§ 209, 211. The second sentence is derived from *English Rules Under the Judicature Act* (The Annual Practice, 1937) O. 16, r. 4. The third sentence is derived from O. 16, r. 5, and the fourth from O. 16, r.r. 1 and 4.

Note to Subdivision (b). This is derived from *English Rules Under the Judicature Act* (The Annual Practice, 1937) O. 16, r.r. 1 and 5.

1966 Amendment

See the amendment of Rule 18(a) and the Advisory Committee's Note thereto. It has been thought that a lack of clarity in the antecedent of the word "them," as it appeared in two places in Rule 20(a), contributed to the view, taken by some courts, that this rule limited the joinder of claims in certain situations of permissive party joinder. Although the amendment of Rule 18(a) should make clear that this view is untenable, it has been considered advisable to amend Rule

20(a) to eliminate any ambiguity. See 2 Barron & Holtzoff, *Federal Practice & Procedure* 202 (Wright Ed. 1961).

A basic purpose of unification of admiralty and civil procedure is to reduce barriers to joinder; hence the reference to "any vessel," etc.

1987 Amendment

The amendments are technical. No substantive change is intended.

2007 Amendment

[Effective December 1, 2007, absent contrary Congressional action.]

The language of Rule 20 has been amended as part of the general restyling of the Civil Rules to make them more easily understood and to make style and terminology consistent throughout the rules. These changes are intended to be stylistic only.

Rule 21. Misjoinder and Non-Joinder of Parties

Misjoinder of parties is not ground for dismissal of an action. Parties may be dropped or added by order of the court on motion of any party or of its own initiative at any stage of the action and on such terms as are just. Any claim against a party may be severed and proceeded with separately.

Proposed Amendment of Rule

Effective December 1, 2007, absent contrary Congressional action, this rule is amended to read as follows:

Rule 21. Misjoinder and Nonjoinder of Parties

Misjoinder of parties is not a ground for dismissing an action. On motion or on its own, the court may at any time, on just terms, add or drop a party. The court may also sever any claim against a party.

ADVISORY COMMITTEE NOTES
1937 Adoption

See *English Rules Under the Judicature Act* (The Annual Practice, 1937) O. 16, r. 11. See also [former] Equity Rules 43 (Defect of Parties—Resisting Objection) and 44 (Defect of Parties—Tardy Objection).

For separate trials see Rules 13(i) (Counterclaims and Cross-Claims: Separate Trials; Separate Judgments), 20(b) (Permissive Joinder of Parties: Separate Trials), and 42(b) (Separate Trials, generally) and the note to the latter rule.

2007 Amendment

[Effective December 1, 2007, absent contrary Congressional action.]

The language of Rule 21 has been amended as part of the general restyling of the Civil Rules to make them more easily understood and to make style and terminology consistent throughout the rules. These changes are intended to be stylistic only.

Rule 22. Interpleader

(1) Persons having claims against the plaintiff may be joined as defendants and required to interplead when their claims are such that the plaintiff is or may be exposed to double or multiple liability. It is not ground for objection to the joinder that the claims of the several claimants or the titles on which their claims depend do not have a common origin or are not identical but are adverse to and independent of one another, or that the plaintiff avers that the plaintiff is not liable in whole or in part to any or all of the claimants. A defendant exposed to similar liability may obtain such interpleader by way of cross-claim or counterclaim. The provisions of this rule supplement and do not in any way limit the joinder of parties permitted in Rule 20.

(2) The remedy herein provided is in addition to and in no way supersedes or limits the remedy provided by Title 28, U.S.C., §§ 1335, 1397, and 2361. Actions under those provisions shall be conducted in accordance with these rules.

(As amended Dec. 29, 1948, eff. Oct. 20, 1949; Mar. 2, 1987, eff. Aug. 1, 1987.)

Proposed Amendment of Rule

Effective December 1, 2007, absent contrary Congressional action, this rule is amended to read as follows:

Rule 22. Interpleader

(a) Grounds.

(1) By a Plaintiff. Persons with claims that may expose a plaintiff to double or multiple liability may be joined as defendants and required to interplead. Joinder for interpleader is proper even though:

(A) the claims of the several claimants, or the titles on which their claims depend, lack a common origin or are adverse and independent rather than identical; or

(B) the plaintiff denies liability in whole or in part to any or all of the claimants.

(2) By a Defendant. A defendant exposed to similar liability may seek interpleader through a crossclaim or counterclaim.

(b) Relation to Other Rules and Statutes. *This rule supplements—and does not limit—the joinder of parties allowed by Rule 20. The remedy this rule provides is in addition to—and does not supersede or limit—the remedy provided by 28 U.S.C. §§ 1335, 1397, and 2361. An action under those statutes must be conducted under these rules.*

ADVISORY COMMITTEE NOTES

1937 Adoption

The first paragraph provides for interpleader relief along the newer and more liberal lines of joinder in the alternative. It avoids the confusion and restrictions that developed around actions of strict interpleader and actions in the nature of interpleader. Compare *John Hancock Mutual Life Insurance Co. v. Kegan et al.,* 22 F.Supp. 326 (D.C.Md.1938). It does not change the rules on service of process, jurisdiction, and venue, as established by judicial decision.

The second paragraph allows an action to be brought under the recent interpleader statute when applicable. By this paragraph all remedies under the statute are continued, but the manner of obtaining them is in accordance with these rules. For temporary restraining orders and preliminary injunctions under this statute, see Rule 65(e).

This rule substantially continues such statutory provisions as U.S.C., Title 38, § 445 [now 784] (Actions on claims; jurisdiction; parties; procedure; limitation; witnesses; definitions) (actions upon veterans' contracts of insurance with the United States), providing for interpleader by the United States where it acknowledges indebtedness under a contract of insurance with the United States; U.S.C., Title 49, § 97 (Interpleader of conflicting claimants) (by carrier which has issued bill of lading). See Chaffee, *The Federal Interpleader Act of 1936: I and II* (1936), 45 Yale L.J. 963, 1161.

1948 Amendment

The amendment effective October 20, 1949, substituted the reference to "Title 28, U.S.C., §§ 1335, 1397, and 2361," at the end of the first sentence of paragraph (2), for the reference to "Section 24(26) of the Judicial Code, as amended, U.S.C., Title 28, § 41(26)." The amendment also substituted the words "those provisions" in the second sentence of paragraph (2) for the words "that section."

1987 Amendment

The amendment is technical. No substantive change is intended.

2007 Amendment

[Effective December 1, 2007, absent contrary Congressional action.]

The language of Rule 22 has been amended as part of the general restyling of the Civil Rules to make them more easily understood and to make style and terminology consistent throughout the rules. These changes are intended to be stylistic only.

Rule 23. Class Actions

(a) Prerequisites to a Class Action. One or more members of a class may sue or be sued as representative parties on behalf of all only if (1) the class is so numerous that joinder of all members is impracticable, (2) there are questions of law or fact common to the class, (3) the claims or defenses of the representative parties are typical of the claims or defenses of the class, and (4) the representative parties will fairly and adequately protect the interests of the class.

(b) Class Actions Maintainable. An action may be maintained as a class action if the prerequisites of subdivision (a) are satisfied, and in addition:

(1) the prosecution of separate actions by or against individual members of the class would create a risk of

(A) inconsistent or varying adjudications with respect to individual members of the class which would establish incompatible standards of conduct for the party opposing the class, or

(B) adjudications with respect to individual members of the class which would as a practical matter be dispositive of the interests of the other members not parties to the adjudications or substantially impair or impede their ability to protect their interests; or

(2) the party opposing the class has acted or refused to act on grounds generally applicable to the class, thereby making appropriate final injunctive relief or corresponding declaratory relief with respect to the class as a whole; or

(3) the court finds that the questions of law or fact common to the members of the class predominate over any questions affecting only individual members, and that a class action is superior to other available methods for the fair and efficient adjudication of the controversy. The matters pertinent to the findings include: (A) the interest of members of the class in individually controlling the prosecution or defense of separate actions; (B) the extent and nature of any litigation concerning the controversy already commenced by or against members of the class; (C) the desirability or undesirability of concentrating the litigation of the claims in the particular forum; (D) the difficulties likely to be encountered in the management of a class action.

(c) Determining by Order Whether to Certify a Class Action; Appointing Class Counsel; Notice and Membership in Class; Judgment; Multiple Classes and Subclasses.

(1)(A) When a person sues or is sued as a representative of a class, the court must—at an early practicable time—determine by order whether to certify the action as a class action.

(B) An order certifying a class action must define the class and the class claims, issues, or defenses, and must appoint class counsel under Rule 23(g).

(C) An order under Rule 23(c)(1) may be altered or amended before final judgment.

(2)(A) For any class certified under Rule 23(b)(1) or (2), the court may direct appropriate notice to the class.

(B) For any class certified under Rule 23(b)(3), the court must direct to class members the best

notice practicable under the circumstances, including individual notice to all members who can be identified through reasonable effort. The notice must concisely and clearly state in plain, easily understood language:

- the nature of the action,
- the definition of the class certified,
- the class claims, issues, or defenses,
- that a class member may enter an appearance through counsel if the member so desires,
- that the court will exclude from the class any member who requests exclusion, stating when and how members may elect to be excluded, and
- the binding effect of a class judgment on class members under Rule 23(c)(3).

(3) The judgment in an action maintained as a class action under subdivision (b)(1) or (b)(2), whether or not favorable to the class, shall include and describe those whom the court finds to be members of the class. The judgment in an action maintained as a class action under subdivision (b)(3), whether or not favorable to the class, shall include and specify or describe those to whom the notice provided in subdivision (c)(2) was directed, and who have not requested exclusion, and whom the court finds to be members of the class.

(4) When appropriate (A) an action may be brought or maintained as a class action with respect to particular issues, or (B) a class may be divided into subclasses and each subclass treated as a class, and the provisions of this rule shall then be construed and applied accordingly.

(d) Orders in Conduct of Actions. In the conduct of actions to which this rule applies, the court may make appropriate orders: (1) determining the course of proceedings or prescribing measures to prevent undue repetition or complication in the presentation of evidence or argument; (2) requiring, for the protection of the members of the class or otherwise for the fair conduct of the action, that notice be given in such manner as the court may direct to some or all of the members of any step in the action, or of the proposed extent of the judgment, or of the opportunity of members to signify whether they consider the representation fair and adequate, to intervene and present claims or defenses, or otherwise to come into the action; (3) imposing conditions on the representative parties or on intervenors; (4) requiring that the pleadings be amended to eliminate therefrom allegations as to representation of absent persons, and that the action proceed accordingly; (5) dealing with similar procedural matters. The orders may be combined with an order under Rule 16, and may be altered or amended as may be desirable from time to time.

(e) Settlement, Voluntary Dismissal, or Compromise.

(1)(A) The court must approve any settlement, voluntary dismissal, or compromise of the claims, issues, or defenses of a certified class.

(B) The court must direct notice in a reasonable manner to all class members who would be bound by a proposed settlement, voluntary dismissal, or compromise.

(C) The court may approve a settlement, voluntary dismissal, or compromise that would bind class members only after a hearing and on finding that the settlement, voluntary dismissal, or compromise is fair, reasonable, and adequate.

(2) The parties seeking approval of a settlement, voluntary dismissal, or compromise under Rule 23(e)(1) must file a statement identifying any agreement made in connection with the proposed settlement, voluntary dismissal, or compromise.

(3) In an action previously certified as a class action under Rule 23(b)(3), the court may refuse to approve a settlement unless it affords a new opportunity to request exclusion to individual class members who had an earlier opportunity to request exclusion but did not do so.

(4)(A) Any class member may object to a proposed settlement, voluntary dismissal, or compromise that requires court approval under Rule 23(e)(1)(A).

(B) An objection made under Rule 23(e)(4)(A) may be withdrawn only with the court's approval.

(f) Appeals. A court of appeals may in its discretion permit an appeal from an order of a district court granting or denying class action certification under this rule if application is made to it within ten days after entry of the order. An appeal does not stay proceedings in the district court unless the district judge or the court of appeals so orders.

(g) Class Counsel.

(1) **Appointing Class Counsel.**

(A) Unless a statute provides otherwise, a court that certifies a class must appoint class counsel.

(B) An attorney appointed to serve as class counsel must fairly and adequately represent the interests of the class.

(C) In appointing class counsel, the court
(i) must consider:
- the work counsel has done in identifying or investigating potential claims in the action,
- counsel's experience in handling class actions, other complex litigation, and claims of the type asserted in the action,
- counsel's knowledge of the applicable law, and

● the resources counsel will commit to representing the class;

(ii) may consider any other matter pertinent to counsel's ability to fairly and adequately represent the interests of the class;

(iii) may direct potential class counsel to provide information on any subject pertinent to the appointment and to propose terms for attorney fees and nontaxable costs; and

(iv) may make further orders in connection with the appointment.

(2) Appointment Procedure.

(A) The court may designate interim counsel to act on behalf of the putative class before determining whether to certify the action as a class action.

(B) When there is one applicant for appointment as class counsel, the court may appoint that applicant only if the applicant is adequate under Rule 23(g)(1)(B) and (C). If more than one adequate applicant seeks appointment as class counsel, the court must appoint the applicant best able to represent the interests of the class.

(C) The order appointing class counsel may include provisions about the award of attorney fees or nontaxable costs under Rule 23(h).

(h) Attorney Fees Award. In an action certified as a class action, the court may award reasonable attorney fees and nontaxable costs authorized by law or by agreement of the parties as follows:

(1) Motion for Award of Attorney Fees. A claim for an award of attorney fees and nontaxable costs must be made by motion under Rule 54(d)(2), subject to the provisions of this subdivision, at a time set by the court. Notice of the motion must be served on all parties and, for motions by class counsel, directed to class members in a reasonable manner.

(2) Objections to Motion. A class member, or a party from whom payment is sought, may object to the motion.

(3) Hearing and Findings. The court may hold a hearing and must find the facts and state its conclusions of law on the motion under Rule 52(a).

(4) Reference to Special Master or Magistrate Judge. The court may refer issues related to the amount of the award to a special master or to a magistrate judge as provided in Rule 54(d)(2)(D).

(As amended Feb. 28, 1966, eff. July 1, 1966; Mar. 2, 1987, eff. Aug. 1, 1987; Apr. 24, 1998, eff. Dec. 1, 1998; Mar. 27, 2003, eff. Dec. 1, 2003.)

Proposed Amendment of Rule

Effective December 1, 2007, absent contrary Congressional action, this rule is amended to read as follows:

Rule 23. Class Actions

(a) Prerequisites. *One or more members of a class may sue or be sued as representative parties on behalf of all members only if:*

(1) the class is so numerous that joinder of all members is impracticable;

(2) there are questions of law or fact common to the class;

(3) the claims or defenses of the representative parties are typical of the claims or defenses of the class; and

(4) the representative parties will fairly and adequately protect the interests of the class.

(b) Types of Class Actions. *A class action may be maintained if Rule 23(a) is satisfied and if:*

(1) prosecuting separate actions by or against individual class members would create a risk of:

(A) inconsistent or varying adjudications with respect to individual class members that would establish incompatible standards of conduct for the party opposing the class; or

(B) adjudications with respect to individual class members that, as a practical matter, would be dispositive of the interests of the other members not parties to the individual adjudications or would substantially impair or impede their ability to protect their interests;

(2) the party opposing the class has acted or refused to act on grounds that apply generally to the class, so that final injunctive relief or corresponding declaratory relief is appropriate respecting the class as a whole; or

(3) the court finds that the questions of law or fact common to class members predominate over any questions affecting only individual members, and that a class action is superior to other available methods for fairly and efficiently adjudicating the controversy. The matters pertinent to these findings include:

(A) the class members' interests in individually controlling the prosecution or defense of separate actions;

(B) the extent and nature of any litigation concerning the controversy already begun by or against class members;

(C) the desirability or undesirability of concentrating the litigation of the claims in the particular forum; and

(D) the likely difficulties in managing a class action.

(c) Certification Order; Notice to Class Members; Judgment; Issues Classes; Subclasses.

(1) *Certification Order.*

(A) *Time to Issue.* At an early practicable time after a person sues or is sued as a class representative, the court must determine by order whether to certify the action as a class action.

(B) *Defining the Class; Appointing Class Counsel.* An order that certifies a class action must define the class and the class claims, issues, or defenses, and must appoint class counsel under Rule 23(g).

(C) *Altering or Amending the Order.* An order that grants or denies class certification may be altered or amended before final judgment.

(2) *Notice.*

(A) *For (b)(1) or (b)(2) Classes.* For any class certified under Rule 23(b) or (b)(2), the court may direct appropriate notice to the class.

(B) *For (b)(3) Classes.* For any class certified under Rule 23(b)(3), the court must direct to class members the best notice that is practicable under the circumstances, including individual notice to all members who can be identified through reasonable effort. The notice must clearly and concisely state in plain, easily understood language:

(i) the nature of the action;

(ii) the definition of the class certified;

(iii) the class claims, issues, or defenses;

(iv) that a class member may enter an appearance through an attorney if the member so desires;

(v) that the court will exclude from the class any member who requests exclusion;

(vi) the time and manner for requesting exclusion; and

(vii) the binding effect of a class judgment on members under Rule 23(c)(3).

(3) *Judgment.* Whether or not favorable to the class, the judgment in a class action must:

(A) for any class certified under Rule 23(b)(1) or (b)(2), include and describe those whom the court finds to be class members; and

(B) for any class certified under Rule 23(b)(3), include and specify or describe those to whom the Rule 23(c)(2) notice was directed, who have not requested exclusion, and whom the court finds to be class members.

(4) *Particular Issues.* When appropriate, an action may be brought or maintained as a class action with respect to particular issues.

(5) *Subclasses.* When appropriate, a class may be divided into subclasses that are each treated as a class under this rule.

(d) Conducting the Action.

(1) *In General.* In conducting an action under this rule, the court may issue orders that:

(A) determine the course of proceedings or prescribe measures to prevent undue repetition or complication in presenting evidence or argument;

(B) require—to protect class members and fairly conduct the action—giving appropriate notice to some or all class members of:

(i) any step in the action;

(ii) the proposed extent of the judgment; or

(iii) the members' opportunity to signify whether they consider the representation fair and adequate, to intervene and present claims or defenses, or to otherwise come into the action;

(C) impose conditions on the representative parties or on intervenors;

(D) require that the pleadings be amended to eliminate allegations about representation of absent persons and that the action proceed accordingly; or

(E) deal with similar procedural matters.

(2) *Combining and Amending Orders.* An order under Rule 23(d)(1) may be altered or amended from time to time and may be combined with an order under Rule 16.

(e) Settlement, Voluntary Dismissal, or Compromise. The claims, issues, or defenses of a certified class may be settled, voluntarily dismissed, or compromised only with the court's approval. The following procedures apply to a proposed settlement, voluntary dismissal, or compromise:

(1) The court must direct notice in a reasonable manner to all class members who would be bound by the proposal.

(2) If the proposal would bind class members, the court may approve it only after a hearing and on finding that it is fair, reasonable, and adequate.

(3) The parties seeking approval must file a statement identifying any agreement made in connection with the proposal.

(4) If the class action was previously certified under Rule 23(b)(3), the court may refuse to approve a settlement unless it affords a new opportunity to request exclusion to individual class members who had an earlier opportunity to request exclusion but did not do so.

(5) Any class member may object to the proposal if it requires court approval under this subdivision (e); the objection may be withdrawn only with the court's approval.

(f) Appeals. A court of appeals may permit an appeal from an order granting or denying class-action certification under this rule if a petition for permission to appeal is filed with the circuit clerk within 10 days after the order is entered. An appeal does not stay proceedings in the district court unless the district judge or the court of appeals so orders.

(g) Class Counsel.

(1) Appointing Class Counsel. Unless a statute provides otherwise, a court that certifies a class must appoint class counsel. In appointing class counsel, the court:

(A) must consider:

(i) the work counsel has done in identifying or investigating potential claims in the action;

(ii) counsel's experience in handling class actions, other complex litigation, and the types of claims asserted in the action;

(iii) counsel's knowledge of the applicable law; and

(iv) the resources that counsel will commit to representing the class;

(B) may consider any other matter pertinent to counsel's ability to fairly and adequately represent the interests of the class;

(C) may order potential class counsel to provide information on any subject pertinent to the appointment and to propose terms for attorney's fees and nontaxable costs;

(D) may include in the appointing order provisions about the award of attorney's fees or nontaxable costs under Rule 23(h); and

(E) may make further orders in connection with the appointment.

(2) Standard for Appointing Class Counsel. When one applicant seeks appointment as class counsel, the court may appoint that applicant only if the applicant is adequate under Rule

23(g)(1) and (4). If more than one adequate applicant seeks appointment, the court must appoint the applicant best able to represent the interests of the class.

(3) Interim Counsel. The court may designate interim counsel to act on behalf of a putative class before determining whether to certify the action as a class action.

(4) Duty of Class Counsel. Class counsel must fairly and adequately represent the interests of the class.

(h) Attorney's Fees and Nontaxable Costs. In a certified class action, the court may award reasonable attorney's fees and nontaxable costs that are authorized by law or by the parties' agreement. The following procedures apply:

(1) A claim for an award must be made by motion under Rule 54(d)(2), subject to the provisions of this subdivision (h), at a time the court sets. Notice of the motion must be served on all parties and, for motions by class counsel, directed to class members in a reasonable manner.

(2) A class member, or a party from whom payment is sought, may object to the motion.

(3) The court may hold a hearing and must find the facts and state its legal conclusions under Rule 52(a).

(4) The court may refer issues related to the amount of the award to a special master or a magistrate judge, as provided in Rule 54(d)(2)(D).

ADVISORY COMMITTEE NOTES

1937 Adoption

Note to Subdivision (a). This is a substantial restatement of [former] Equity Rule 38 (Representatives of Class) as that rule has been construed. It applies to all actions, whether formerly denominated legal or equitable. For a general analysis of class actions, effect of judgment, and requisites of jurisdiction see Moore, *Federal Rules of Civil Procedure: Some Problems Raised by the Preliminary Draft,* 25 Georgetown L.J. 551, 570 et seq. (1937); Moore and Cohn, *Federal Class Actions,* 32 Ill.L.Rev. 307 (1937); Moore and Cohn, *Federal Class Actions—Jurisdiction and Effect of Judgment,* 32 Ill.L.Rev. 555–567 (1938); Lesar, *Class Suits and the Federal Rules,* 22 Minn.L.Rev. 34 (1937); cf. Arnold and James, *Cases on Trials, Judgments and Appeals* (1936) 175; and see Blume, *Jurisdictional Amount in Representative Suits,* 15 Minn.L.Rev. 501 (1931).

The general test of [former] Equity Rule 38 (Representatives of Class) that the question should be "one of common or general interest to many persons constituting a class so numerous as to make it impracticable to bring them all before the court," is a common test. For states which require the two elements of a common or general interest and numerous persons, as provided for in [former] Equity

Rule 38, see Del.Ch. Rule 113; Fla.Comp.Gen.Laws Ann. (Supp., 1936) § 4918(7); Georgia Code (1933) § 37–1002, and see *English Rules Under the Judicature Act* (The Annual Practice, 1937) O. 16, r. 9. For statutory provisions providing for class actions when the question is one of common or general interest or when the parties are numerous, see Ala.Code Ann. (Michie, 1928) § 5701; 2 Ind.Stat.Ann. (Burns, 1933) § 2–220; N.Y.C.P.A. (1937) 195; Wis.Stat. (1935) § 260.12. These statutes have, however, been uniformly construed as though phrased in the conjunctive. See *Garfein v. Stiglitz*, 260 Ky. 430, 86 S.W.2d 155 (1935). The rule adopts the test of [former] Equity Rule 38, but defines what constitutes a "common or general interest". Compare with code provisions which make the action dependent upon the propriety of joinder of the parties. See Blume, *The "Common Questions" Principle in the Code Provision for Representative Suits*, 30 Mich.L.Rev. 878 (1932). For discussion of what constitutes "numerous persons" see Wheaton, *Representative Suits Involving Numerous Litigants*, 19 Corn.L.Q. 399 (1934); Note, 36 Harv.L.Rev. 89 (1922).

Clause (1), Joint, Common, or Secondary Right. This clause is illustrated in actions brought by or against representatives of an unincorporated association. See *Oster v. Brotherhood of Locomotive Firemen and Enginemen*, 271 Pa. 419, 114 Atl. 377 (1921); *Pickett v. Walsh*, 192 Mass. 572, 78 N.E. 753, 6 L.R.A., N.S., 1067 (1906); *Colt v. Hicks*, 97 Ind.App. 177, 179 N.E. 335 (1932). Compare Rule 17(b) as to when an unincorporated association has capacity to sue or be sued in its common name; *United Mine Workers of America v. Coronado Coal Co.*, 42 S.Ct. 570, 259 U.S. 344, 66 L.Ed. 975, 27 A.L.R. 762 (1922) (an unincorporated association was sued as an entity for the purpose of enforcing against it a federal substantive right); Moore, *Federal Rules of Civil Procedure: Some Problems Raised by the Preliminary Draft*, 25 Georgetown L.J. 551, 566 (for discussion of jurisdictional requisites when an unincorporated association sues or is sued in its common name and jurisdiction is founded upon diversity of citizenship). For an action brought by representatives of one group against representatives of another group for distribution of a fund held by an unincorporated association, see *Smith v. Swormstedt*, 16 How. 288, 14 L.Ed. 942 (U.S. 1853). Compare *Christopher, et al. v. Brusselback*, 1938, 58 S.Ct. 350, 302 U.S. 500, 82 L.Ed. 388.

For an action to enforce rights held in common by policyholders against the corporate issuer of the policies, see *Supreme Tribe of Ben Hur v. Cauble*, 255 U.S. 356, 41 S.Ct. 338, 65 L.Ed. 673 (1921). See also *Terry v. Little*, 101 U.S. 216, 25 L.Ed. 864 (1880); *John A. Roebling's Sons Co. v. Kinnicutt*, 248 Fed. 596 (D.C.N.Y., 1917) dealing with the right held in common by creditors to enforce the statutory liability of stockholders.

Typical of a secondary action is a suit by stockholders to enforce a corporate right. For discussion of the general nature of these actions see *Ashwander v. Tennessee Valley Authority*, 297 U.S. 288, 56 S.Ct. 466, 80 L.Ed. 688 (1936); Glenn, *The Stockholder's Suit—Corporate and Individual Grievances*, 33 Yale L.J. 580 (1924); McLaughlin, *Capacity of Plaintiff-Stockholder to Terminate a Stockholder's Suit*, 46 Yale L.J. 421 (1937). See also Subdivision (b) of this rule which deals with Shareholder's Action; Note, 15 Minn.L.Rev. 453 (1931).

Clause (2). A creditor's action for liquidation or reorganization of a corporation is illustrative of this clause. An action by a stockholder against certain named defendants as representatives of numerous claimants presents a situation converse to the creditor's action.

Clause (3). See *Everglades Drainage League v. Napoleon Broward Drainage Dist.*, 253 Fed. 246 (D.C.Fla., 1918); *Gramling v. Maxwell*, 52 F.2d 256 (D.C.N.C., 1931), approved in 30 Mich.L.Rev. 624 (1932); *Skinner v. Mitchell*, 108 Kan. 861, 197 Pac. 569 (1921); *Duke of Bedford v. Ellis* (1901) A.C. 1, for class actions when there were numerous persons and there was only a question of law or fact common to them; and see Blume, *The "Common Questions" Principle in the Code Provision for Representative Suits*, 30 Mich. L.Rev. 878 (1932).

Note to Subdivision (b). This is [former] Equity Rule 27 (Stockholder's Bill) with verbal changes. See also *Hawes v. Oakland*, 104 U.S. 450, 26 L.Ed. 827 (1882) and former Equity Rule 94, promulgated January 23, 1882, 104 U.S. IX.

Note to Subdivision (c). See McLaughlin, *Capacity of Plaintiff-Stockholder to Terminate a Stockholder's Suit*, 46 Yale L.J. 421 (1937).

Supplementary Note

Note. Subdivision (b), relating to secondary actions by shareholders, provides among other things, that in such an action the complainant "shall aver (1) that the plaintiff was a shareholder at the time of the transaction of which he complains or that his share thereafter devolved on him by operation of law * * *".

As a result of the decision in *Erie R. Co. v. Tompkins*, 1938, 304 U.S. 64, 58 S.Ct. 817 (decided April 25, 1938, after this rule was promulgated by the Supreme Court, though before it took effect) a question has arisen as to whether the provision above quoted deals with a matter of substantive right or is a matter of procedure. If it is a matter of substantive law or right, then under *Erie R. Co. v. Tompkins* clause (1) may not be validly applied in cases pending in states whose local law permits a shareholder to maintain such actions, although not a shareholder at the time of the transactions complained of. The Advisory Committee, believing the question should be settled in the courts, proposes no change in Rule 23 but thinks rather that the situation should be explained in an appropriate note.

The rule has a long history. In *Hawes v. Oakland*, 1882, 104 U.S. 450, the Court held that a shareholder could not maintain such an action unless he owned shares at the time of the transactions complained of, or unless they devolved on him by operation of law. At that time the decision in *Swift v. Tyson*, 1842, 16 Peters 1, was the law, and the federal courts considered themselves free to establish their own principles of equity jurisprudence, so the Court was not in 1882 and has not been, until *Erie R. Co. v. Tompkins* in 1938, concerned with the question whether *Hawes v. Oakland* dealt with substantive right or procedure.

Following the decision in *Hawes v. Oakland*, and at the same term, the Court, to implement its decision, adopted [former] Equity Rule 94, which contained the same provision above quoted from Rule 23 F.R.C.P. The provision in [former] Equity Rule 94 was later embodied in [former] Equity Rule 27, of which the present Rule 23 is substantially a copy.

In *City of Quincy v. Steel*, 1887, 120 U.S. 241, 245, 7 S.Ct. 520, the Court referring to *Hawes v. Oakland* said: "In order to give effect to the principles there laid down, this

Court at that term adopted Rule 94 of the rules of practice for courts of equity of the United States."

Some other cases dealing with [former] Equity Rules 94 or 27 prior to the decision in *Erie R. Co. v. Tompkins* are *Dimpfel v. Ohio & Miss. R.R.*, 1884, 3 S.Ct. 573, 110 U.S. 209, 28 L.Ed. 121; *Illinois Central R. Co. v. Adams*, 1901, 21 S.Ct. 251, 180 U.S. 28, 34, 45 L.Ed. 410; *Venner v. Great Northern Ry.*, 1908, 28 S.Ct. 328, 209 U.S. 24, 30, 52 L.Ed. 666; *Jacobson v. General Motors Corp.*, S.D.N.Y.1938, 22 F.Supp. 255, 257. These cases generally treat *Hawes v. Oakland* as establishing a "principle" of equity, or as dealing not with jurisdiction but with the "right" to maintain an action, or have said that the defense under the equity rule is analogous to the defense that the plaintiff has no "title" and results in a dismissal "for want of equity."

Those state decisions which held that a shareholder acquiring stock after the event may maintain a derivative action are founded on the view that it is a right belonging to the shareholder at the time of the transaction and which passes as a right to the subsequent purchaser. See *Pollitz v. Gould*, 1911, 202 N.Y. 11, 94 N.E. 1088.

The first case arising after the decision in *Erie R. Co. v. Tompkins*, in which this problem was involved, was *Summers v. Hearst*, S.D.N.Y.1938, 23 F.Supp. 986. It concerned [former] Equity Rule 27, as Federal Rule 23 was not then in effect. In a well considered opinion Judge Leibell reviewed the decisions and said: "The federal cases that discuss this section of [former] Rule 27 support the view that it states a principle of substantive law." He quoted *Pollitz v. Gould*, 1911, 202 N.Y. 11, 94 N.E. 1088, as saying that the United States Supreme Court "seems to have been more concerned with establishing this rule as one of practice than of substantive law" but that "whether it be regarded as establishing a principle of law or a rule of practice, this authority has been subsequently followed in the United States courts."

He then concluded that, although the federal decisions treat the equity rule as "stating a principle of substantive law", if "[former] Equity Rule 27 is to be modified or revoked in view of *Erie R. Co. v. Tompkins*, it is not the province of this Court to suggest it, much less impliedly to follow that course by disregarding the mandatory provisions of the Rule."

In *Piccard v. Sperry Corporation*, S.D.N.Y.1941, 36 F.Supp. 1006, 1009–10, affirmed without opinion, C.C.A.2d 1941, 120 F.2d 328, a shareholder, not such at the time of the transactions complained of, sought to intervene. The court held an intervenor was as much subject to Rule 23 as an original plaintiff; and that the requirement of Rule 23(b) was "a matter of practice," not substance, and applied in New York where the state law was otherwise, despite *Erie R. Co. v. Tompkins*. In *New York v. Guaranty Trust Co. of New York*, C.C.A.2, 1944, 143 F.2d 503, rev'd on other grounds, 1945, 65 S.Ct. 1464, the court said: "Restrictions on the bringing of stockholders' actions, such as those imposed by F.R.C.P. 23(b) or other state statutes are procedural," citing the *Piccard* and other cases.

Some other federal decisions since 1938 touch the question. In *Gallup v. Caldwell*, C.C.A.3, 1941, 120 F.2d 90, 95 arising in New Jersey, the point was raised but not decided, the court saying that it was not satisfied that the then New Jersey rule differed from Rule 23(b), and that "under the circumstances the proper course was to follow Rule 23(b)."

In *Mullins v. DeSoto Securities Co.*, W.D.La.1942, 45 F.Supp. 871, 878, the point was not decided, because the court found the Louisiana rule to be the same as that stated in Rule 23(b).

In *Toebelman v. Missouri-Kansas Pipe Line Co.*, D.Del. 1941, 41 F.Supp. 334, 340, the court dealt only with another part of Rule 23(b), relating to prior demands on the stockholders and did not discuss *Erie R. Co. v. Tompkins*, or its effect on the rule.

In *Perrott v. United States Banking Corp.*, D.Del.1944, 53 F.Supp. 953, it appeared that the Delaware law does not require the plaintiff to have owned shares at the time of the transaction complained of. The court sustained Rule 23(b), after discussion of the authorities, saying:

"It seems to me the rule does not go beyond procedure. * * * Simply because a particular plaintiff cannot qualify as a proper party to maintain such an action does not destroy or even whittle at the cause of action. The cause of action exists until a qualified plaintiff can get it started in a federal court."

In *Bankers Nat. Corp. v. Barr*, S.D.N.Y.1945, 9 Fed.Rules Serv. 23b.11, Case 1, the court held Rule 23(b) to be one of procedure, but that whether the plaintiff was a stockholder was a substantive question to be settled by state law.

The New York rule, as stated in *Pollitz v. Gould*, supra, has been altered by an act of the New York Legislature, Chapter 667, Laws of 1944, effective April 9, 1944, General Corporation Law, § 61, which provides that "in any action brought by a shareholder in the right of a * * * corporation, it must appear that the plaintiff was a stockholder at the time of the transaction of which he complains, or that his stock thereafter devolved upon him by operation of law." At the same time a further and separate provision was enacted, requiring under certain circumstances the giving of security for reasonable expenses and attorney's fees, to which security the corporation in whose right the action is brought and the defendants therein may have recourse. (Chapter 668, Laws of 1944, effective April 9, 1944, General Corporation Law, § 61–b.) These provisions are aimed at so-called "strike" stockholders' suits and their attendant abuses. *Shielcrawt v. Moffett*, Ct.App.1945, 294 N.Y. 180, 61 N.E.2d 435, rev'g 51 N.Y.S.2d 188, aff'g 49 N.Y.S.2d 64; *Noel Associates, Inc. v. Merrill*, Sup.Ct.1944, 184 Misc. 646, 63 N.Y.S.2d 143.

Insofar as § 61 is concerned, it has been held that the section is procedural in nature. *Klum v. Clinton Trust Co.*, Sup.Ct.1944, 183 Misc. 340, 48 N.Y.S.2d 267; *Noel Associates, Inc. v. Merrill*, supra. In the latter case the court pointed out that "The 1944 amendment to Section 61 rejected the rule laid down in the Pollitz case and substituted, in place thereof, in its precise language, the rule which has long prevailed in the Federal Courts and which is now Rule 23(b) * * *". There is, nevertheless, a difference of opinion regarding the application of the statute to pending actions. See *Klum v. Clinton Trust Co.*, supra (applicable); *Noel Associates, Inc. v. Merrill*, supra (inapplicable).

With respect to § 61–b, which may be regarded as a separate problem, *Noel Associates, Inc. v. Merrill*, supra, it has been held that even though the statute is procedural in nature—a matter not definitely decided—the Legislature evinced no intent that the provisions should apply to actions pending when it became effective. *Shielcrawt v. Moffett*, supra. As to actions instituted after the effective date of the

legislation, the constitutionality of § 61–b is in dispute. See *Wolf v. Atkinson,* Sup.Ct.1944, 182 Misc. 675, 49 N.Y.S.2d 703 (constitutional); *Citron v. Mangel Stores Corp.,* Sup.Ct. 1944, 50 N.Y.S.2d 416 (unconstitutional); Zlinkoff, *The American Investor and the Constitutionality of § 61–b of the New York General Corporation Law,* 1945, 54 Yale L.J. 352.

New Jersey also enacted a statute, similar to Chapters 667 and 668 of the New York law. See P.L.1945, Ch. 131, R.S.Cum.Supp. 14:3–15. The New Jersey provision similar to Chapter 668, § 61–b, differs, however, in that it specifically applies retroactively. It has been held that this provision is procedural and hence will not govern a pending action brought against a New Jersey corporation in the New York courts. *Shielcraut v. Moffett,* Sup.Ct.N.Y.1945, 184 Misc. 1074, 56 N.Y.S.2d 134.

See, also generally, 2 Moore's *Federal Practice,* 1938, 2250–2253, and Cum.Supplement § 23.05.

The decisions here discussed show that the question is a debatable one, and that there is respectable authority for either view, with a recent trend towards the view that Rule 23(b)(1) is procedural. There is reason to say that the question is one which should not be decided by the Supreme Court ex parte, but left to await a judicial decision in a litigated case, and that in the light of the material in this note, the only inference to be drawn from a failure to amend Rule 23(b) would be that the question is postponed to await a litigated case.

The Advisory Committee is unanimously of the opinion that this course should be followed.

If, however, the final conclusion is that the rule deals with a matter of substantive right, then the rule should be amended by adding a provision that Rule 23(b)(1) does not apply in jurisdictions where state law permits a shareholder to maintain a secondary action, although he was not a shareholder at the time of the transactions of which he complains.

1966 Amendment

Difficulties with the original rule. The categories of class actions in the original rule were defined in terms of the abstract nature of the rights involved: the so-called "true" category was defined as involving "joint, common, or secondary rights"; the "hybrid" category, as involving "several" rights related to "specific property"; the "spurious" category, as involving "several" rights affected by a common question and related to common relief. It was thought that the definitions accurately described the situations amenable to the class-suit device, and also would indicate the proper extent of the judgment in each category, which would in turn help to determine the res judicata effect of the judgment if questioned in a later action. Thus the judgments in "true" and "hybrid" class actions would extend to the class (although in somewhat different ways); the judgment in a "spurious" class action would extend only to the parties including intervenors. See Moore, *Federal Rules of Civil Procedure: Some Problems Raised by the Preliminary Draft,* 25 Geo.L.J. 551, 570–76 (1937).

In practice the terms "joint," "common," etc., which were used as the basis of the Rule 23 classification proved obscure and uncertain. See Chafee, *Some Problems of Equity* 245–46, 256–57 (1950); Kalven & Rosenfield, *The Contemporary Function of the Class Suit,* 8 U. of Chi.L.Rev. 684, 707 & n. 73 (1941); Keeffe, Levy & Donovan, *Lee Defeats Ben*

Hur, 33 Corn.L.Q. 327, 329–36 (1948); *Developments in the Law: Multiparty Litigation in the Federal Courts,* 71 Harv. L.Rev. 874, 931 (1958); Advisory Committee's Note to Rule 19, as amended. The courts had considerable difficulty with these terms. See, e.g., *Gullo v. Veterans' Coop. H. Assn.,* 13 F.R.D. 11 (D.D.C.1952); *Shipley v. Pittsburgh & L.E.R. Co.,* 70 F.Supp. 870 (W.D.Pa.1947); *Deckert v. Independence Shares Corp.,* 27 F.Supp. 763 (E.D.Pa.1939), rev'd 108 F.2d 51 (3d Cir. 1939), rev'd, 311 U.S. 282 (1940), on remand, 39 F.Supp. 592 (E.D.Pa.1941), rev'd sub nom. *Pennsylvania Co. for Ins. on Lives v. Deckert,* 123 F.2d 979 (3d Cir.1941) (see Chafee, supra, at 264–65).

Nor did the rule provide an adequate guide to the proper extent of the judgments in class actions. First, we find instances of the courts classifying actions as "true" or intimating that the judgments would be decisive for the class where these results seemed appropriate but were reached by dint of depriving the word "several" of coherent meaning. See, e.g., *System Federation No. 91 v. Reed,* 180 F.2d 991 (6th Cir.1950); *Wilson v. City of Paducah,* 100 F.Supp. 116 (W.D.Ky.1951); *Citizens Banking Co. v. Monticello State Bank,* 143 F.2d 261 (8th Cir.1944); *Redmond v. Commerce Trust Co.,* 144 F.2d 140 (8th Cir.1944), cert. denied, 323 U.S. 776 (1944); *United States v. American Optical Co.,* 97 F.Supp. 66 (N.D.Ill.1951); *National Hairdressers' & C. Assn. v. Philad Co.,* 34 F.Supp. 264 (D.Del.1940); 41 F.Supp. 701 (D.Del.1940), aff'd mem., 129 F.2d 1020 (3d Cir.1942). Second, we find cases classified by the courts as "spurious" in which, on a realistic view, it would seem fitting for the judgments to extend to the class. See, e.g., *Knapp v. Bankers Sec. Corp.,* 17 F.R.D. 245 (E.D.Pa.1954), aff'd 230 F.2d 717 (3d Cir.1956); *Giesecke v. Denver Tramway Corp.,* 81 F.Supp. 957 (D.Del.1949); *York v. Guaranty Trust Co.,* 143 F.2d 503 (2d Cir.1944), rev'd on grounds not here relevant, 326 U.S. 99 (1945) (see Chafee, supra, at 208); cf. *Webster Eisenlohr, Inc. v. Kalodner,* 145 F.2d 316, 320 (3d Cir.1944), cert. denied, 325 U.S. 867 (1945). But cf. the early decisions, *Duke of Bedford v. Ellis,* [1901] A.C. 1; *Sheffield Waterworks v. Yeomans,* L.R. 2 Ch.App. 8 (1866); *Brown v. Vermuden,* 1 Ch.Cas. 272, 22 Eng.Rep. 796 (1676).

The "spurious" action envisaged by original Rule 23 was in any event an anomaly because, although denominated a "class" action and pleaded as such, it was supposed not to adjudicate the rights or liabilities of any person not a party. It was believed to be an advantage of the "spurious" category that it would invite decisions that a member of the "class" could, like a member of the class in a "true" or "hybrid" action, intervene on an ancillary basis without being required to show an independent basis of Federal jurisdiction, and have the benefit of the date of the commencement of the action for purposes of the statute of limitations. See 3 Moore's *Federal Practice,* pars. 23.10[1], 23.12 (2d ed.1963). These results were attained in some instances but not in others. On the statute of limitations, see *Union Carbide & Carbon Corp. v. Nisley,* 300 F.2d 561 (10th Cir.1961), pet. cert. dism., 371 U.S. 801 (1963); but cf. *P. W. Husserl, Inc. v. Newman,* 25 F.R.D. 264 (S.D.N.Y.1960); *Athas v. Day,* 161 F.Supp. 916 (D.Colo.1958). On ancillary intervention, see *Amen v. Black,* 234 F.2d 12 (10th Cir.1956), cert. granted, 352 U.S. 888 (1956), dism. on stip., 355 U.S. 600 (1958); but cf. *Wagner v. Kemper,* 13 F.R.D. 128 (W.D.Mo.1952). The results, however, can hardly depend upon the mere appearance of a "spurious" category in the rule; they should turn

on more basic considerations. See discussion of subdivision (c)(1) below.

Finally, the original rule did not squarely address itself to the question of the measures that might be taken during the course of the action to assure procedural fairness, particularly giving notice to members of the class, which may in turn be related in some instances to the extension of the judgment to the class. See Chafee, supra, at 230–31; Keeffe, Levy & Donovan, supra; *Developments in the law*, supra, 71 Harv. L.Rev. at 937–38; Note, *Binding Effect of Class Actions*, 67 Harv.L.Rev. 1059, 1062–65 (1954); Note, *Federal Class Actions: A Suggested Revision of Rule 23*, 46 Colum.L.Rev. 818, 833–36 (1946); Mich.Gen.Court R. 208.4 (effective Jan. 1, 1963); Idaho R.Civ.P. 23(d); Minn.R.Civ.P. 23.04; N.Dak.R.Civ.P. 23(d).

The amended rule describes in more practical terms the occasions for maintaining class actions; provides that all class actions maintained to the end as such will result in judgments including those whom the court finds to be members of the class, whether or not the judgment is favorable to the class; and refers to the measures which can be taken to assure the fair conduct of these actions.

Subdivision (a) states the prerequisites for maintaining any class action in terms of the numerousness of the class making joinder of the members impracticable, the existence of questions common to the class, and the desired qualifications of the representative parties. See Weinstein, *Revision of Procedure: Some Problems in Class Actions*, 9 Buffalo L.Rev. 433, 458–59 (1960); 2 Barron & Holtzoff, *Federal Practice & Procedure* § 562, at 265, § 572, at 351–52 (Wright ed. 1961). These are necessary but not sufficient conditions for a class action. See, e.g., *Giordano v. Radio Corp. of Am.*, 183 F.2d 558, 560 (3d Cir.1950); *Zachman v. Erwin*, 186 F.Supp. 681 (S.D.Tex.1959); *Baim & Blank, Inc. v. Warren-Connelly Co., Inc.*, 19 F.R.D. 108 (S.D.N.Y.1956). Subdivision (b) describes the additional elements which in varying situations justify the use of a class action.

Subdivision (b)(1). The difficulties which would be likely to arise if resort were had to separate actions by or against the individual members of the class here furnish the reasons for, and the principal key to, the propriety and value of utilizing the class-action device. The considerations stated under clauses (A) and (B) are comparable to certain of the elements which define the persons whose joinder in an action is desirable as stated in Rule 19(a), as amended. See amended Rule 19(a)(2)(i) and (ii), and the Advisory Committee's Note thereto; Hazard, *Indispensable Party: The Historical Origin of a Procedural Phantom*, 61 Colum.L.Rev. 1254, 1259–60 (1961); cf. 3 Moore, supra, par. 23.08, at 3435.

Clause (A): One person may have rights against, or be under duties toward, numerous persons constituting a class, and be so positioned that conflicting or varying adjudications in lawsuits with individual members of the class might establish incompatible standards to govern his conduct. The class action device can be used effectively to obviate the actual or virtual dilemma which would thus confront the party opposing the class. The matter has been stated thus: "The felt necessity for a class action is greatest when the courts are called upon to order or sanction the alteration of the status quo in circumstances such that a large number of persons are in a position to call on a single person to alter the status quo, or to complain if it is altered, and the possibility exists that [the] actor might be called upon to act in inconsistent

ways." Louisell & Hazard, *Pleading and Procedure: State and Federal* 719 (1962); see *Supreme Tribe of Ben-Hur v. Cauble*, 255 U.S. 356, 366–67 (1921). To illustrate: Separate actions by individuals against a municipality to declare a bond issue invalid or condition or limit it, to prevent or limit the making of a particular appropriation or to compel or invalidate an assessment, might create a risk of inconsistent or varying determinations. In the same way, individual litigations of the rights and duties of riparian owners, or of landowners' rights and duties respecting a claimed nuisance, could create a possibility of incompatible adjudications. Actions by or against a class provide a ready and fair means of achieving unitary adjudication. See *Maricopa County Mun. Water Con. Dist. v. Looney*, 219 F.2d 529 (9th Cir.1955); *Rank v. Krug*, 142 F.Supp. 1, 154–59 (S.D.Calif.1956), on app., *State of California v. Rank*, 293 F.2d 340, 348 (9th Cir.1961); *Gart v. Cole*, 263 F.2d 244 (2d Cir.1959), cert. denied 359 U.S. 978 (1959); cf. *Martinez v. Maverick Cty. Water Con. & Imp. Dist.*, 219 F.2d 666 (5th Cir.1955); 3 Moore, supra, par. 23.11[2], at 3458–59.

Clause (B): This clause takes in situations where the judgment in a nonclass action by or against an individual member of the class, while not technically concluding the other members, might do so as a practical matter. The vice of an individual action would lie in the fact that the other members of the class, thus practically concluded, would have had no representation in the lawsuit. In an action by policy holders against a fraternal benefit association attacking a financial reorganization of the society, it would have hardly been practical, if indeed it would have been possible, to confine the effects of a validation of the reorganization to the individual plaintiffs. Consequently a class action was called for with adequate representation of all members of the class. See *Supreme Tribe of Ben-Hur v. Cauble*, 255 U.S. 356 (1921); *Waybright v. Columbian Mut. Life Ins. Co.*, 30 F.Supp. 885 (W.D.Tenn.1939); cf. *Smith v. Swormstedt*, 16 How. (57 U.S.) 288 (1853). For much the same reason actions by shareholders to compel the declaration of a dividend[,] the proper recognition and handling of redemption or pre-emption rights, or the like (or actions by the corporation for corresponding declarations of rights), should ordinarily be conducted as class actions, although the matter has been much obscured by the insistence that each shareholder has an individual claim. See *Knapp v. Bankers Securities Corp.*, 17 F.R.D. 245 (E.D.Pa.1954), aff'd, 230 F.2d 717 (3d Cir. 1956); *Giesecke v. Denver Tramway Corp.*, 81 F.Supp. 957 (D.Del.1949); *Zahn v. Transamerica Corp.*, 162 F.2d 36 (3d Cir.1947); *Speed v. Transamerica Corp.*, 100 F.Supp. 461 (D.Del.1951); *Sobel v. Whittier Corp.*, 95 F.Supp. 643 (E.D.Mich.1951), app. dism., 195 F.2d 361 (6th Cir.1952); *Goldberg v. Whittier Corp.*, 111 F.Supp. 382 (E.D.Mich.1953); *Dann v. Studebaker-Packard Corp.*, 288 F.2d 201 (6th Cir. 1961); *Edgerton v. Armour & Co.*, 94 F.Supp. 549 (S.D.Calif.1950); *Ames v. Mengel Co.*, 190 F.2d 344 (2d Cir.1951). (These shareholders' actions are to be distinguished from derivative actions by shareholders dealt with in new Rule 23.1). The same reasoning applies to an action which charges a breach of trust by an indenture trustee or other fiduciary similarly affecting the members of a large class of security holders or other beneficiaries, and which requires an accounting or like measures to restore the subject of the trust. See *Boesenberg v. Chicago T. & T. Co.*, 128 F.2d 245 (7th Cir.1942); *Citizens Banking Co. v. Monticello State*

Bank, 143 F.2d 261 (8th Cir.1944); *Redmond v. Commerce Trust Co.*, 144 F.2d 140 (8th Cir.1944), cert. denied, 323 U.S. 776 (1944); cf. *York v. Guaranty Trust Co.*, 143 F.2d 503 (2d Cir.1944), rev'd on grounds not here relevant, 326 U.S. 99 (1945).

In various situations an adjudication as to one or more members of the class will necessarily or probably have an adverse practical effect on the interests of other members who should therefore be represented in the lawsuit. This is plainly the case when claims are made by numerous persons against a fund insufficient to satisfy all claims. A class action by or against representative members to settle the validity of the claims as a whole, or in groups, followed by separate proof of the amount of each valid claim and proportionate distribution of the fund, meets the problem. Cf. *Dickinson v. Burnham*, 197 F.2d 973 (2d Cir.1952), cert. denied, 344 U.S. 875 (1952); 3 Moore, supra, at par. 23.09. The same reasoning applies to an action by a creditor to set aside a fraudulent conveyance by the debtor and to appropriate the property to his claim, when the debtor's assets are insufficient to pay all creditors' claims. See *Heffernan v. Bennett & Armour*, 110 Cal.App.2d 564, 243 P.2d 846 (1952); cf. *City & County of San Francisco v. Market Street Ry.*, 95 Cal.App.2d 648, 213 P.2d 780 (1950). Similar problems, however, can arise in the absence of a fund either present or potential. A negative or mandatory injunction secured by one of a numerous class may disable the opposing party from performing claimed duties toward the other members of the class or materially affect his ability to do so. An adjudication as to movie "clearances and runs" nominally affecting only one exhibitor would often have practical effects on all the exhibitors in the same territorial area. Cf. *United States v. Paramount Pictures, Inc.*, 66 F.Supp. 323, 341–46 (S.D.N.Y. 1946); 334 U.S. 131, 144–48 (1948). Assuming a sufficiently numerous class of exhibitors, a class action would be advisable. (Here representation of subclasses of exhibitors could become necessary; see subdivision (c)(3)(B).)

Subdivision (b)(2). This subdivision is intended to reach situations where a party has taken action or refused to take action with respect to a class, and final relief of an injunctive nature or of a corresponding declaratory nature, settling the legality of the behavior with respect to the class as a whole, is appropriate. Declaratory relief "corresponds" to injunctive relief when as a practical matter it affords injunctive relief or serves as a basis for later injunctive relief. The subdivision does not extend to cases in which the appropriate final relief relates exclusively or predominantly to money damages. Action or inaction is directed to a class within the meaning of this subdivision even if it has taken effect or is threatened only as to one or a few members of the class, provided it is based on grounds which have general application to the class.

Illustrative are various actions in the civil-rights field where a party is charged with discriminating unlawfully against a class, usually one whose members are incapable of specific enumeration. See *Potts v. Flax*, 313 F.2d 284 (5th Cir. 1963); *Bailey v. Patterson*, 323 F.2d 201 (5th Cir. 1963), cert. denied, 376 U.S. 910, (1964); *Brunson v. Board of Trustees of School District No. 1, Clarendon Cty., S.C.*, 311 F.2d 107 (4th Cir. 1962), cert. denied, 373 U.S. 933 (1963); *Green v. School Bd. of Roanoke, Va.*, 304 F.2d 118 (4th Cir. 1962); *Orleans Parish School Bd. v. Bush*, 242 F.2d 156 (5th Cir. 1957), cert. denied, 354 U.S. 921 (1957); *Mannings v.*

Board of Public Inst. of Hillsborough County, Fla., 277 F.2d 370 (5th Cir. 1960); *Northcross v. Board of Ed. of City of Memphis*, 302 F.2d 818 (6th Cir. 1962), cert. denied, 370 U.S. 944 (1962); *Frasier v. Board of Trustees of Univ. of N.C.*, 134 F.Supp. 589 (M.D.N.C.1955, 3-judge court), aff'd 350 U.S. 979 (1956). Subdivision (b)(2) is not limited to civil-rights cases. Thus an action looking to specific or declaratory relief could be brought by a numerous class of purchasers, say retailers of a given description, against a seller alleged to have undertaken to sell to that class at prices higher than those set for other purchasers, say retailers of another description, when the applicable law forbids such a pricing differential. So also a patentee of a machine, charged with selling or licensing the machine on condition that purchasers or licensees also purchase or obtain licenses to use an ancillary unpatented machine, could be sued on a class basis by a numerous group of purchasers or licensees, or by a numerous group of competing sellers or licensors of the unpatented machine, to test the legality of the "tying" condition.

Subdivision (b)(3). In the situations to which this subdivision relates, class-action treatment is not as clearly called for as in those described above, but it may nevertheless be convenient and desirable depending upon the particular facts. Subdivision (b)(3) encompasses those cases in which a class action would achieve economies of time, effort, and expense, and promote uniformity of decision as to persons similarly situated, without sacrificing procedural fairness or bringing about other undesirable results. Cf. Chafee, supra, at 201.

The court is required to find, as a condition of holding that a class action may be maintained under this subdivision, that the questions common to the class predominate over the questions affecting individual members. It is only where this predominance exists that economies can be achieved by means of the class-action device. In this view, a fraud perpetrated on numerous persons by the use of similar misrepresentations may be an appealing situation for a class action, and it may remain so despite the need, if liability is found, for separate determination of the damages suffered by individuals within the class. On the other hand, although having some common core, a fraud case may be unsuited for treatment as a class action if there was material variation in the representations made or in the kinds or degrees of reliance by the persons to whom they were addressed. See *Oppenheimer v. F. J. Young & Co., Inc.*, 144 F.2d 387 (2d Cir. 1944); *Miller v. National City Bank of N.Y.*, 166 F.2d 723 (2d Cir. 1948); and for like problems in other contexts, see *Hughes v. Encyclopaedia Britannica*, 199 F.2d 295 (7th Cir. 1952); *Sturgeon v. Great Lakes Steel Corp.*, 143 F.2d 819 (6th Cir. 1944). A "mass accident" resulting in injuries to numerous persons is ordinarily not appropriate for a class action because of the likelihood that significant questions, not only of damages but of liability and defenses of liability, would be present, affecting the individuals in different ways. In these circumstances an action conducted nominally as a class action would degenerate in practice into multiple lawsuits separately tried. See *Pennsylvania R.R. v. United States*, 111 F.Supp. 80 (D.N.J.1953); cf. Weinstein, supra, 9 Buffalo L.Rev. at 469. Private damage claims by numerous individuals arising out of concerted antitrust violations may or may not involve predominating common questions. See *Union Carbide & Carbon Corp. v. Nisley*, 300 F.2d 561 (10th Cir. 1961), pet. cert. dism., 371 U.S. 801 (1963); cf. *Weeks v.*

Bareco Oil Co., 125 F.2d 84 (7th Cir. 1941); *Kainz v. Anheuser-Busch, Inc.,* 194 F.2d 737 (7th Cir. 1952); *Hess v. Anderson, Clayton & Co.,* 20 F.R.D. 466 (S.D.Calif.1957).

That common questions predominate is not itself sufficient to justify a class action under subdivision (b)(3), for another method of handling the litigious situation may be available which has greater practical advantages. Thus one or more actions agreed to by the parties as test or model actions may be preferable to a class action; or it may prove feasible and preferable to consolidate actions. Cf. Weinstein, supra, 9 Buffalo L.Rev. at 438–54. Even when a number of separate actions are proceeding simultaneously, experience shows that the burdens on the parties and the courts can sometimes be reduced by arrangements for avoiding repetitious discovery or the like. Currently the Coordinating Committee on Multiple Litigation in the United States District Courts (a subcommittee of the Committee on Trial Practice and Technique of the Judicial Conference of the United States) is charged with developing methods for expediting such massive litigation. To reinforce the point that the court with the aid of the parties ought to assess the relative advantages of alternative procedures for handling the total controversy, subdivision (b)(3) requires, as a further condition of maintaining the class action, that the court shall find that that procedure is "superior" to the others in the particular circumstances.

Factors (A)–(D) are listed, non-exhaustively, as pertinent to the findings. The court is to consider the interests of individual members of the class in controlling their own litigations and carrying them on as they see fit. See *Weeks v. Bareco Oil Co.,* 125 F.2d 84, 88–90, 93–94 (7th Cir. 1941) (anti-trust action); see also *Pentland v. Dravo Corp.,* 152 F.2d 851 (3d Cir. 1945), and Chafee, supra, at 273–75, regarding policy of Fair Labor Standards Act of 1938, § 16(b), 29 U.S.C. § 216(b), prior to amendment by Portal-to-Portal Act of 1947, § 5(a). [The present provisions of 29 U.S.C. § 216(b) are not intended to be affected by Rule 23, as amended.]

In this connection the court should inform itself of any litigation actually pending by or against the individuals. The interests of individuals in conducting separate lawsuits may be so strong as to call for denial of a class action. On the other hand, these interests may be theoretic rather than practical; the class may have a high degree of cohesion and prosecution of the action through representatives would be quite unobjectionable, or the amounts at stake for individuals may be so small that separate suits would be impracticable. The burden that separate suits would impose on the party opposing the class, or upon the court calendars, may also fairly be considered. (See the discussion, under subdivision (c)(2) below, of the right of members to be excluded from the class upon their request.)

Also pertinent is the question of the desirability of concentrating the trial of the claims in the particular forum by means of a class action, in contrast to allowing the claims to be litigated separately in forums to which they would ordinarily be brought. Finally, the court should consider the problems of management which are likely to arise in the conduct of a class action.

Subdivision (c)(1). In order to give clear definition to the action, this provision requires the court to determine, as early in the proceedings as may be practicable, whether an action brought as a class action is to be so maintained. The determination depends in each case on satisfaction of the terms of subdivision (a) and the relevant provisions of subdivision (b).

An order embodying a determination can be conditional; the court may rule, for example, that a class action may be maintained only if the representation is improved through intervention of additional parties of a stated type. A determination once made can be altered or amended before the decision on the merits if, upon fuller development of the facts, the original determination appears unsound. A negative determination means that the action should be stripped of its character as a class action. See subdivision (d)(4). Although an action thus becomes a nonclass action, the court may still be receptive to interventions before the decision on the merits so that the litigation may cover as many interests as can be conveniently handled; the questions whether the intervenors in the nonclass action shall be permitted to claim "ancillary" jurisdiction or the benefit of the date of the commencement of the action for purposes of the statute of limitations are to be decided by reference to the laws governing jurisdiction and limitations as they apply in particular contexts.

Whether the court should require notice to be given to members of the class of its intention to make a determination, or of the order embodying it, is left to the court's discretion under subdivision (d)(2).

Subdivision (c)(2) makes special provision for class actions maintained under subdivision (b)(3). As noted in the discussion of the latter subdivision, the interests of the individuals in pursing their own litigations may be so strong here as to warrant denial of a class action altogether. Even when a class action is maintained under subdivision (b)(3), this individual interest is respected. Thus the court is required to direct notice to the members of the class of the right of each member to be excluded from the class upon his request. A member who does not request exclusion may, if he wishes, enter an appearance in the action through his counsel; whether or not he does so, the judgment in the action will embrace him.

The notice[,] setting forth the alternatives open to the members of the class, is to be the best practicable under the circumstances, and shall include individual notice to the members who can be identified through reasonable effort. (For further discussion of this notice, see the statement under subdivision (d)(2) below.)

Subdivision (c)(3). The judgment in a class action maintained as such to the end will embrace the class, that is, in a class action under subdivision (b)(1) or (b)(2), those found by the court to be class members; in a class action under subdivision (b)(3), those to whom the notice prescribed by subdivision (c)(2) was directed, excepting those who requested exclusion or who are ultimately found by the court not to be members of the class. The judgment has this scope whether it is favorable or unfavorable to the class. In a (b)(1) or (b)(2) action the judgment "describes" the members of the class, but need not specify the individual members; in a (b)(3) action the judgment "specifies" the individual members who have been identified and described the others.

Compare subdivision (c)(4) as to actions conducted as class actions only with respect to particular issues. Where the class-action character of the lawsuit is based solely on the existence of a "limited fund," the judgment, while extending to all claims of class members against the fund, has ordinari-

ly left unaffected the personal claims of nonappearing members against the debtor. See 3 Moore, supra, par. 23.11[4].

Hitherto, in a few actions conducted as "spurious" class actions and thus nominally designed to extend only to parties and others intervening before the determination of liability, courts have held or intimated that class members might be permitted to intervene after a decision on the merits favorable to their interests, in order to secure the benefits of the decision for themselves, although they would presumably be unaffected by an unfavorable decision. See, as to the propriety of this so-called "one-way" intervention in "spurious" actions, the conflicting views expressed in *Union Carbide & Carbon Corp. v. Nisley*, 300 F.2d 561 (10th Cir. 1961), pet. cert. dism., 371 U.S. 801 (1963); *York v. Guaranty Trust Co.*, 143 F.2d 503, 529 (2d Cir. 1944), rev'd on grounds not here relevant, 326 U.S. 99 (1945); *Pentland v. Dravo Corp.*, 152 F.2d 851, 856 (3d Cir. 1945); *Speed v. Transamerica Corp.*, 100 F.Supp. 461, 463 (D.Del.1951); *State Wholesale Grocers v. Great Atl. & Pac. Tea Co.*, 24 F.R.D. 510 (N.D.Ill.1959); *Alabama Ind. Serv. Stat. Assn. v. Shell Pet. Corp.*, 28 F.Supp. 386, 390 (N.D.Ala.1939); *Tolliver v. Cudahy Packing Co.*, 39 F.Supp. 337, 339 (E.D.Tenn.1941); Kalven & Rosenfield, supra, 8 U. of Chi.L.Rev. 684 (1941); Comment, 53 Nw.U.L.Rev. 627, 632–33 (1958); *Developments in the Law*, supra, 71 Harv.L.Rev. at 935; 2 Barron & Holtzoff, supra, § 568; but cf. *Lockwood v. Hercules Powder Co.*, 7 F.R.D. 24, 28–29 (W.D.Mo.1947); *Abram v. San Joaquin Cotton Oil Co.*, 46 F.Supp. 969, 976–77 (S.D.Calif.1942); Chafee, supra, at 280, 285; 3 Moore, supra, par. 23.12, at 3476. Under proposed subdivision (c)(3), one-way intervention is excluded; the action will have been early determined to be a class or nonclass action, and in the former case the judgment, whether or not favorable, will include the class, as above stated.

Although thus declaring that the judgment in a class action includes the class, as defined, subdivision (c)(3) does not disturb the recognized principle that the court conducting the action cannot predetermine the *res judicata* effect of the judgment; this can be tested only in a subsequent action. See Restatement, Judgments § 86, comment (h), § 116 (1942). The court, however, in framing the judgment in any suit brought as a class action, must decide what its extent or coverage shall be, and if the matter is carefully considered, questions of *res judicata* are less likely to be raised at a later time and if raised will be more satisfactorily answered. See Chafee, supra, at 294; Weinstein, supra, 9 Buffalo L.Rev. at 460.

Subdivision (c)(4). This provision recognizes that an action may be maintained as a class action as to particular issues only. For example, in a fraud or similar case the action may retain its "class" character only through the adjudication of liability to the class; the members of the class may thereafter be required to come in individually and prove the amounts of their respective claims.

Two or more classes may be represented in a single action. Where a class is found to include subclasses divergent in interest, the class may be divided correspondingly, and each subclass treated as a class.

Subdivision (d) is concerned with the fair and efficient conduct of the action and lists some types of orders which may be appropriate.

The court should consider how the proceedings are to be arranged in sequence, and what measures should be taken to simplify the proof and argument. See subdivision (d)(1).

The orders resulting from this consideration, like the others referred to in subdivision (d), may be combined with a pretrial order under Rule 16, and are subject to modification as the case proceeds.

Subdivision (d)(2) sets out a non-exhaustive list of possible occasions for orders requiring notice to the class. Such notice is not a novel conception. For example, in "limited fund" cases, members of the class have been notified to present individual claims after the basic class decision. Notice has gone to members of a class so that they might express any opposition to the representation, see *United States v. American Optical Co.*, 97 F.Supp. 66 (N.D.Ill.1951), and 1950–51 CCH Trade Cases 64573–74 (par. 62869); cf. *Weeks v. Bareco Oil Co.*, 125 F.2d 84, 94 (7th Cir. 1941), and notice may encourage interventions to improve the representation of the class. Cf. *Oppenheimer v. F. J. Young & Co.*, 144 F.2d 387 (2d Cir. 1944). Notice has been used to poll members on a proposed modification of a consent decree. See record in *Sam Fox Publishing Co. v. United States*, 366 U.S. 683 (1961).

Subdivision (d)(2) does not require notice at any stage, but rather calls attention to its availability and invokes the court's discretion. In the degree that there is cohesiveness or unity in the class and the representation is effective, the need for notice to the class will tend toward a minimum. These indicators suggest that notice under subdivision (d)(2) may be particularly useful and advisable in certain class actions maintained under subdivision (b)(3), for example, to permit members of the class to object to the representation. Indeed, under subdivision (c)(2), notice must be ordered, and is not merely discretionary, to give the members in a subdivision (b)(3) class action an opportunity to secure exclusion from the class. This mandatory notice pursuant to subdivision (c)(2), together with any discretionary notice which the court may find it advisable to give under subdivision (d)(2), is designed to fulfill requirements of due process to which the class action procedure is of course subject. See *Hansberry v. Lee*, 311 U.S. 32 (1940); *Mullane v. Central Hanover Bank & Trust Co.*, 339 U.S. 306 (1950); cf. *Dickinson v. Burnham*, 197 F.2d 973, 979 (2d Cir. 1952), and studies cited at 979 in 4; see also *All American Airways, Inc. v. Elderd*, 209 F.2d 247, 249 (2d Cir. 1954); *Gart v. Cole*, 263 F.2d 244, 248–49 (2d Cir. 1959), cert. denied, 359 U.S. 978 (1959).

Notice to members of the class, whenever employed under amended Rule 23, should be accommodated to the particular purpose but need not comply with the formalities for service of process. See Chafee, supra, at 230–31; *Brendle v. Smith*, 7 F.R.D. 119 (S.D.N.Y.1946). The fact that notice is given at one stage of the action does not mean that it must be given at subsequent stages. Notice is available fundamentally "for the protection of the members of the class or otherwise for the fair conduct of the action" and should not be used merely as a device for the undesirable solicitation of claims. See the discussion in *Cherner v. Transitron Electronic Corp.*, 201 F.Supp. 934 (D.Mass.1962); *Hormel v. United States*, 17 F.R.D. 303 (S.D.N.Y.1955).

In appropriate cases the court should notify interested government agencies of the pendency of the action or of particular steps therein.

Subdivision (d)(3) reflects the possibility of conditioning the maintenance of a class action, e.g., on the strengthening of the representation, see subdivision (c)(1) above; and rec-

ognizes that the imposition of conditions on intervenors may be required for the proper and efficient conduct of the action.

As to orders under subdivision (d)(4), see subdivision (c)(1) above.

Subdivision (e) requires approval of the court, after notice, for the dismissal or compromise of any class action.

1987 Amendment

The amendments are technical. No substantive change is intended.

1998 Amendments

Subdivision (f). This permissive interlocutory appeal provision is adopted under the power conferred by 28 U.S.C. § 1292(e). Appeal from an order granting or denying class certification is permitted in the sole discretion of the court of appeals. No other type of Rule 23 order is covered by this provision. The court of appeals is given unfettered discretion whether to permit the appeal, akin to the discretion exercised by the Supreme Court in acting on a petition for certiorari. This discretion suggests an analogy to the provision in 28 U.S.C. § 1292(b) for permissive appeal on certification by a district court. Subdivision (f), however, departs from the § 1291(b) model in two significant ways. It does not require that the district court certify the certification ruling for appeal, although the district court often can assist the parties and court of appeals by offering advice on the desirability of appeal. And it does not include the potentially limiting requirements of § 1292(b) that the district court order "involve[] a controlling question of law as to which there is substantial ground for difference of opinion and that an immediate appeal from the order may materially advance the ultimate termination of the litigation."

The courts of appeals will develop standards for granting review that reflect the changing areas of uncertainty in class litigation. The Federal Judicial Center study supports the view that many suits with class-action allegations present familiar and almost routine issues that are no more worthy of immediate appeal than many other interlocutory rulings. Yet several concerns justify expansion of present opportunities to appeal. An order denying certification may confront the plaintiff with a situation in which the only sure path to appellate review is by proceeding to final judgment on the merits of an individual claim that, standing alone, is far smaller than the costs of litigation. An order granting certification, on the other hand, may force a defendant to settle rather than incur the costs of defending a class action and run the risk of potentially ruinous liability. These concerns can be met at low cost by establishing in the court of appeals a discretionary power to grant interlocutory review in cases that show appeal-worthy certification issues.

Permission to appeal may be granted or denied on the basis of any consideration that the court of appeals finds persuasive. Permission is most likely to be granted when the certification decision turns on a novel or unsettled question of law, or when, as a practical matter, the decision on certification is likely dispositive of the litigation.

The district court, having worked through the certification decision, often will be able to provide cogent advice on the factors that bear on the decision whether to permit appeal. This advice can be particularly valuable if the certification decision is tentative. Even as to a firm certification decision, a statement of reasons bearing on the probably benefits and costs of immediate appeal can help focus the court of appeals decision, and may persuade the disappointed party that an attempt to appeal would be fruitless.

The 10–day period for seeking permission to appeal is designed to reduce the risk that attempted appeals will disrupt continuing proceedings. It is expected that the courts of appeals will act quickly in making the preliminary determination whether to permit appeal. Permission to appeal does not stay trial court proceedings. A stay should be sought first from the trial court. If the trial court refuses a stay, its action and any explanation of its views should weigh heavily with the court of appeals.

Appellate Rule 5 has been modified to establish the procedure for petitioning for leave to appeal under subdivision (f).

2003 Amendments

Subdivision (c). Subdivision (c) is amended in several respects. The requirement that the court determine whether to certify a class "as soon as practicable after commencement of an action" is replaced by requiring determination "at an early practicable time." The notice provisions are substantially revised.

Paragraph (1). Subdivision (c)(1)(A) is changed to require that the determination whether to certify a class be made "at an early practicable time." The "as soon as practicable" exaction neither reflect s prevailing practice nor captures the many valid reasons that may justify deferring the initial certification decision. See Willging, Hooper & Niemic, *Empirical Study of Class Actions in Four Federal District Courts: Final Report to the Advisory Committee on Civil Rules 26–36* (Federal Judicial Center 1996).

Time may be needed to gather information necessary to make the certification decision. Although an evaluation of the probable outcome on the merits is not properly part of the certification decision, discovery in aid of the certification decision often includes information required to identify the nature of the issues that actually will be presented at trial. In this sense it is appropriate to conduct controlled discovery into the "merits," limited to those aspects relevant to making the certification decision on an informed basis. Active judicial supervision may be required to achieve the most effective balance that expedites an informed certification determination without forcing an artificial and ultimately wasteful division between "certification discovery" and "merits discovery." A critical need is to determine how the case will be tried. An increasing number of courts require a party requesting class certification to present a "trial plan" that describes the issues likely to be presented at trial and tests whether they are susceptible of class-wide proof. See Manual For Complex Litigation Third, § 21.213, p. 44; § 30.11, p. 214; § 30.12, p. 215.

Other considerations may affect the timing of the certification decision. The party opposing the class may prefer to win dismissal or summary judgment as to the individual plaintiffs without certification and without binding the class that might have been certified. Time may be needed to explore designation of class counsel under Rule 23(g), recognizing that in many cases the need to progress toward the certification determination may require designation of interim counsel under Rule 23(g)(2)(A).

Rule 23

RULES OF CIVIL PROCEDURE

Although many circumstances may justify deferring the certification decision, active management may be necessary to ensure that the certification decision is not unjustifiably delayed.

Subdivision (c)(1)(C) reflects two amendments. The provision that a class certification "may be conditional" is deleted. A court that is not satisfied that the requirements of Rule 23 have been met should refuse certification until they have been met. The provision that permits alteration or amendment of an order granting or denying class certification is amended to set the cut-off point at final judgment rather than "the decision on the merits." This change avoids the possible ambiguity in referring to "the decision on the merits." Following a determination of liability, for example, proceedings to define the remedy may demonstrate the need to amend the class definition or subdivide the class. In this setting the final judgment concept is pragmatic. It is not the same as the concept used for appeal purposes, but it should be flexible, particularly in protracted litigation.

The authority to amend an order under Rule 23(c)(1) before final judgment does not restore the practice of "one-way intervention" that was rejected by the 1966 revision of Rule 23. A determination of liability after certification, however, may show a need to amend the class definition. Decertification may be warranted after further proceedings.

If the definition of a class certified under Rule 23(b)(3) is altered to include members who have not been afforded notice and an opportunity to request exclusion, notice—including an opportunity to request exclusion—must be directed to the new class members under Rule 23(c)(2)(B).

Paragraph (2). The first change made in Rule 23(c)(2) is to call attention to the court's authority—already established in part by Rule 23(d)(2)—to direct notice of certification to a Rule 23(b)(1) or (b)(2) class. The present rule expressly requires notice only in actions certified under Rule 23(b)(3). Members of classes certified under Rules 23(b)(1) or (b)(2) have interests that may deserve protection by notice.

The authority to direct notice to class members in a (b)(1) or (b)(2) class action should be exercised with care. For several reasons, there may be less need for notice than in a (b)(3) class action. There is no right to request exclusion from a (b)(1) or (b)(2) class. The characteristics of the class may reduce the need for formal notice. The cost of providing notice, moreover, could easily cripple actions that do not seek damages. The court may decide not to direct notice after balancing the risk that notice costs may deter the pursuit of class relief against the benefits of notice.

When the court does direct certification notice in a (b)(1) or (b)(2) class action, the discretion and flexibility established by subdivision (c)(2)(A) extend to the method of giving notice. Notice facilitates the opportunity to participate. Notice calculated to reach a significant number of class members often will protect the interests of all. Informal methods may prove effective. A simple posting in a place visited by many class members, directing attention to a source of more detailed information, may suffice. The court should consider the costs of notice in relation to the probable reach of inexpensive methods.

If a Rule 23(b)(3) class is certified in conjunction with a (b)(2) class, the (c)(2)(B) notice requirements must be satisfied as to the (b)(3) class.

The direction that class-certification notice be couched in plain, easily understood language is a reminder of the need to work unremittingly at the difficult task of communicating with class members. It is difficult to provide information about most class actions that is both accurate and easily understood by class members who are not themselves lawyers. Factual uncertainty, legal complexity, and the complication of class-action procedure raise the barriers high. The Federal Judicial Center has created illustrative clear-notice forms that provide a helpful starting point for actions similar to those described in the forms.

Subdivision (e). Subdivision (e) is amended to strengthen the process of reviewing proposed class-action settlements. Settlement may be a desirable means of resolving a class action. But court review and approval are essential to assure adequate representation of class members who have not participated in shaping the settlement.

Paragraph (1). Subdivision (e)(1)(A) expressly recognizes the power of a class representative to settle class claims, issues, or defenses.

Rule 23(e)(1)(A) resolves the ambiguity in former Rule 23(e)'s reference to dismissal or compromise of "a class action." That language could be—and at times was—read to require court approval of settlements with putative class representatives that resolved only individual claims. See Manual for Complex Litigation Third, § 30.41. The new rule requires approval only if the claims, issues, or defenses of a certified class are resolved by a settlement, voluntary dismissal, or compromise.

Subdivision (e)(1)(B) carries forward the notice requirement of present Rule 23(e) when the settlement binds the class through claim or issue preclusion; notice is not required when the settlement binds only the individual class representatives. Notice of a settlement binding on the class is required either when the settlement follows class certification or when the decisions on certification and settlement proceed simultaneously.

Reasonable settlement notice may require individual notice in the manner required by Rule 23(c)(2)(B) for certification notice to a Rule 23(b)(3) class. Individual notice is appropriate, for example, if class members are required to take action—such as filing claims—to participate in the judgment, or if the court orders a settlement opt-out opportunity under Rule 23(e)(3).

Subdivision (e)(1)(C) confirms and mandates the already common practice of holding hearings as part of the process of approving settlement, voluntary dismissal, or compromise that would bind members of a class.

Subdivision (e)(1)(C) states the standard for approving a proposed settlement that would bind class members. The settlement must be fair, reasonable, and adequate. A helpful review of many factors that may deserve consideration is provided by *In re: Prudential Ins. Co. America Sales Practice Litigation Agent Actions*, 148 F.3d 283, 316–324 (3d Cir. 1998). Further guidance can be found in the Manual for Complex Litigation.

The court must make findings that support the conclusion that the settlement is fair, reasonable, and adequate. The findings must be set out in sufficient detail to explain to class members and the appellate court the factors that bear on applying the standard.

Complete Annotation Materials, see Title 28 U.S.C.A.

148

Settlement review also may provide an occasion to review the cogency of the initial class definition. The terms of the settlement themselves, or objections, may reveal divergent interests of class members and demonstrate the need to redefine the class or to designate subclasses. Redefinition of a class certified under Rule 23(b)(3) may require notice to new class members under Rule 23(c)(2)(B). See Rule 23(c)(1)(C).

Paragraph (2). Subdivision (e)(2) requires parties seeking approval of a settlement, voluntary dismissal, or compromise under Rule 23(e)(1) to file a statement identifying any agreement made in connection with the settlement. This provision does not change the basic requirement that the parties disclose all terms of the settlement or compromise that the court must approve under Rule 23(e)(1). It aims instead at related undertakings that, although seemingly separate, may have influenced the terms of the settlement by trading away possible advantages for the class in return for advantages for others. Doubts should be resolved in favor of identification.

Further inquiry into the agreements identified by the parties should not become the occasion for discovery by the parties or objectors. The court may direct the parties to provide to the court or other parties a summary or copy of the full terms of any agreement identified by the parties. The court also may direct the parties to provide a summary or copy of any agreement not identified by the parties that the court considers relevant to its review of a proposed settlement. In exercising discretion under this rule, the court may act in steps, calling first for a summary of any agreement that may have affected the settlement and then for a complete version if the summary does not provide an adequate basis for review. A direction to disclose a summary or copy of an agreement may raise concerns of confidentiality. Some agreements may include information that merits protection against general disclosure. And the court must provide an opportunity to claim work-product or other protections.

Paragraph (3). Subdivision (e)(3) authorizes the court to refuse to approve a settlement unless the settlement affords class members a new opportunity to request exclusion from a class certified under Rule 23(b)(3) after settlement terms are known. An agreement by the parties themselves to permit class members to elect exclusion at this point by the settlement agreement may be one factor supporting approval of the settlement. Often there is an opportunity to opt out at this point because the class is certified and settlement is reached in circumstances that lead to simultaneous notice of certification and notice of settlement. In these cases, the basic opportunity to elect exclusion applies without further complication. In some cases, particularly if settlement appears imminent at the time of certification, it may be possible to achieve equivalent protection by deferring notice and the opportunity to elect exclusion until actual settlement terms are known. This approach avoids the cost and potential confusion of providing two notices and makes the single notice more meaningful. But notice should not be delayed unduly after certification in the hope of settlement.

Rule 23(e)(3) authorizes the court to refuse to approve a settlement unless the settlement affords a new opportunity to elect exclusion in a case that settles after a certification decision if the earlier opportunity to elect exclusion provided with the certification notice has expired by the time of the settlement notice. A decision to remain in the class is likely to be more carefully considered and is better informed when settlement terms are known.

The opportunity to request exclusion from a proposed settlement is limited to members of a (b)(3) class. Exclusion may be requested only by individual class members; no class member may purport to opt out other class members by way of another class action.

The decision whether to approve a settlement that does not allow a new opportunity to elect exclusion is confided to the court's discretion. The court may make this decision before directing notice to the class under Rule 23(e)(1)(B) or after the Rule 23(e)(1)(C) hearing. Many factors may influence the court's decision. Among these are changes in the information available to class members since expiration of the first opportunity to request exclusion, and the nature of the individual class members' claims.

The terms set for permitting a new opportunity to elect exclusion from the proposed settlement of a Rule 23(b)(3) class action may address concerns of potential misuse. The court might direct, for example, that class members who elect exclusion are bound by rulings on the merits made before the settlement was proposed for approval. Still other terms or conditions may be appropriate.

Paragraph (4). Subdivision (e)(4) confirms the right of class members to object to a proposed settlement, voluntary dismissal, or compromise. The right is defined in relation to a disposition that, because it would bind the class, requires court approval under subdivision (e)(1)(C).

Subdivision (e)(4)(B) requires court approval for withdrawal of objections made under subdivision (e)(4)(A). Review follows automatically if the objections are withdrawn on terms that lead to modification of the settlement with the class. Review also is required if the objector formally withdraws the objections. If the objector simply abandons pursuit of the objection, the court may inquire into the circumstances.

Approval under paragraph (4)(B) may be given or denied with little need for further inquiry if the objection and the disposition go only to a protest that the individual treatment afforded the objector under the proposed settlement is unfair because of factors that distinguish the objector from other class members. Different considerations may apply if the objector has protested that the proposed settlement is not fair, reasonable, or adequate on grounds that apply generally to a class or subclass. Such objections, which purport to represent class-wide interests, may augment the opportunity for obstruction or delay. If such objections are surrendered on terms that do not affect the class settlement or the objector's participation in the class settlement, the court often can approve withdrawal of the objections without elaborate inquiry.

Once an objector appeals, control of the proceeding lies in the court of appeals. The court of appeals may undertake review and approval of a settlement with the objector, perhaps as part of appeal settlement procedures, or may remand to the district court to take advantage of the district court's familiarity with the action and settlement.

Subdivision (g). Subdivision (g) is new. It responds to the reality that the selection and activity of class counsel are often critically important to the successful handling of a class action. Until now, courts have scrutinized proposed class counsel as well as the class representative under Rule

23(a)(4). This experience has recognized the importance of judicial evaluation of the proposed lawyer for the class, and this new subdivision builds on that experience rather than introducing an entirely new element into the class certification process. Rule 23(a)(4) will continue to call for scrutiny of the proposed class representative, while this subdivision will guide the court in assessing proposed class counsel as part of the certification decision. This subdivision recognizes the importance of class counsel, states the obligation to represent the interests of the class, and provides a framework for selection of class counsel. The procedure and standards for appointment vary depending on whether there are multiple applicants to be class counsel. The new subdivision also provides a method by which the court may make directions from the outset about the potential fee award to class counsel in the event the action is successful.

Paragraph (1) sets out the basic requirement that class counsel be appointed if a class is certified and articulates the obligation of class counsel to represent the interests of the class, as opposed to the potentially conflicting interests of individual class members. It also sets out the factors the court should consider in assessing proposed class counsel.

Paragraph (1)(A) requires that the court appoint class counsel to represent the class. Class counsel must be appointed for all classes, including each subclass that the court certifies to represent divergent interests.

Paragraph (1)(A) does not apply if "a statute provides otherwise." This recognizes that provisions of the Private Securities Litigation Reform Act of 1995, Pub. L. No. 104–67, 109 Stat. 737 (1995) (codified in various sections of 15 U.S.C.), contain directives that bear on selection of a lead plaintiff and the retention of counsel. This subdivision does not purport to supersede or to affect the interpretation of those provisions, or any similar provisions of other legislation.

Paragraph 1(B) recognizes t hat t he primary responsibility of class counsel, resulting from appointment as class counsel, is to represent the best interests of the class. The rule thus establishes the obligation of class counsel, an obligation that may be different from the customary obligations of counsel to individual clients. Appointment as class counsel means that the primary obligation of counsel is to the class rather than to any individual members of it. The class representatives do not have an unfettered right to "fire" class counsel. In the same vein, the class representatives cannot command class counsel to accept or reject a settlement proposal. To the contrary, class counsel must determine whether seeking the court's approval of a settlement would be in the best interests of the class as a whole.

Paragraph (1)(C) articulates the basic responsibility of the court to appoint class counsel who will provide the adequate representation called for by paragraph (1)(B). It identifies criteria that must be considered and invites the court to consider any other pertinent matters. Although couched in terms of the court's duty, the listing also informs counsel seeking appointment about the topics that should be addressed in an application for appointment or in the motion for class certification.

The court may direct potential class counsel to provide additional information about the topics mentioned in paragraph (1)(C) or about any other relevant topic. For example, the court may direct applicants to inform the court concerning any agreements about a prospective award of attorney fees or nontaxable costs, as such agreements may sometimes be significant in the selection of class counsel. The court might also direct that potential class counsel indicate how parallel litigation might be coordinated or consolidated with t he action before the court.

The court may also direct counsel to propose terms for a potential award of attorney fees and nontaxable costs. Attorney fee awards are an important feature of class action practice, and attention to this subject from the outset may often be a productive technique. Paragraph (2)(C) therefore authorizes the court to provide directions about attorney fees and costs when appointing class counsel. Because there will be numerous class actions in which this information is not likely to be useful, the court need not consider it in all class actions.

Some information relevant to class counsel appointment may involve matters that include adversary preparation in a way that should be shielded from disclosure to other parties. An appropriate protective order may be necessary to preserve confidentiality.

In evaluating prospective class counsel, the court should weigh all pertinent factors. No single factor should necessarily be determinative in a given case. For example, the resources counsel will commit to the case must be appropriate to its needs, but the court should be careful not to limit consideration to lawyers with the greatest resources.

If, after review of all applicants, the court concludes that none would be satisfactory class counsel, it may deny class certification, reject all applications, recommend that an application be modified, invite new applications, or make any other appropriate order regarding selection and appointment of class counsel.

Paragraph (2). This paragraph sets out the procedure that should be followed in appointing class counsel. Although it affords substantial flexibility, it provides the framework for appointment of class counsel in all class actions. For counsel who filed the action, the materials submitted in support of the motion for class certification may suffice to justify appointment so long as the information described in paragraph (g)(1)(C) is included. If there are other applicants, they ordinarily would file a formal application detailing their suitability for the position.

In a plaintiff class action the court usually would appoint as class counsel only an attorney or attorneys who have sought appointment. Different considerations may apply in defendant class actions.

The rule states that the court should appoint "class counsel." In many instances, the applicant will be an individual attorney. In other cases, however, an entire firm, or perhaps numerous attorneys who are not otherwise affiliated but are collaborating on the action will apply. No rule of thumb exists to determine when such arrangements are appropriate; the court should be alert to the need for adequate staffing of the case, but also to the risk of overstaffing or an ungainly counsel structure.

Paragraph (2)(A) authorizes the court to designate interim counsel during the pre-certification period if necessary to protect the interests of the putative class. Rule 23(c)(1)(B) directs that the order certifying the class include appointment of class counsel. Before class certification, however, it will usually be important for an attorney to take action to prepare for the certification decision. The amendment to

Rule 23(c)(1) recognizes that some discovery is often necessary for that determination. It also may be important to make or respond to motions before certification. Settlement may be discussed before certification. Ordinarily, such work is handled by the lawyer who filed the action. In some cases, however, there may be rivalry or uncertainty that makes formal designation of interim counsel appropriate. Rule 23(g)(2)(A) authorizes the court to designate interim counsel to act on behalf of the putative class before the certification decision is made. Failure to make the formal designation does not prevent the attorney who filed the action from proceeding in it. Whether or not formally designated interim counsel, an attorney who acts on behalf of the class before certification must act in the best interests of the class as a whole. For example, an attorney who negotiates a pre-certification settlement must seek a settlement that is fair, reasonable, and adequate for the class.

Rule 23(c)(1) provides that the court should decide whether to certify the class "at an early practicable time," and directs that class counsel should be appointed in the order certifying the class. In some cases, it may be appropriate for the court to allow a reasonable period after commencement of the action for filing applications to serve as class counsel. The primary ground for deferring appointment would be that there is reason to anticipate competing applications to serve as class counsel. Examples might include instances in which more than one class action has been filed, or in which other attorneys have filed individual actions on behalf of putative class members. The purpose of facilitating competing applications in such a case is to afford the best possible representation for the class. Another possible reason for deferring appointment would be that the initial applicant was found inadequate, but it seems appropriate to permit additional applications rather than deny class certification.

Paragraph (2)(B) states the basic standard the court should use in deciding whether to certify the class and appoint class counsel in the single applicant situation—that the applicant be able to provide the representation called for by paragraph (1)(B) in light of the factors identified in paragraph (1)(C).

If there are multiple adequate applicants, paragraph (2)(B) directs the court to select the class counsel best able to represent the interests of the class. This decision should also be made using the factors outlined in paragraph (1)(C), but in the multiple applicant situation the court is to go beyond scrutinizing the adequacy of counsel and make a comparison of the strengths of the various applicants. As with the decision whether to appoint the sole applicant for the position, no single factor should be dispositive in selecting class counsel in cases in which there are multiple applicants. The fact that a given attorney filed the instant action, for example, might not weigh heavily in the decision if that lawyer had not done significant work identifying or investigating claims. Depending on the nature of the case, one important consideration might be the applicant's existing attorney-client relationship with the proposed class representative.

Paragraph (2)(C) builds on the appointment process by authorizing the court to include provisions regarding attorney fees in the order appointing class counsel. Courts may find it desirable to adopt guidelines for fees or nontaxable costs, or to direct class counsel to report to the court at regular intervals on the efforts undertaken in the action, to facilitate the court's later determination of a reasonable attorney fee.

Subdivision (h). Subdivision (h) is new. Fee awards are a powerful influence on the way attorneys initiate, develop, and conclude class actions. Class action attorney fee awards have heretofore been handled, along with all other attorney fee awards, under Rule 54(d)(2), but that rule is not addressed to the particular concerns of class actions. This subdivision is designed to work in tandem with new subdivision (g) on appointment of class counsel, which may afford an opportunity for the court to provide an early framework for an eventual fee award, or for monitoring the work of class counsel during the pendency of the action.

Subdivision (h) applies to "an action certified as a class action." This includes cases in which there is a simultaneous proposal for class certification and settlement even though technically the class may not be certified unless the court approves the settlement pursuant to review under Rule 23(e). When a settlement is proposed for Rule 23(e) approval, either after certification or with a request for certification, notice to class members about class counsel's fee motion would ordinarily accompany the notice to the class about the settlement proposal itself.

This subdivision does not undertake to create new grounds for an award of attorney fees or nontaxable costs. Instead, it applies when such awards are authorized by law or by agreement of the parties. Against that background, it provides a format for all awards of attorney fees and nontaxable costs in connection with a class action, not only the award to class counsel. In some situations, there may be a basis for making an award to other counsel whose work produced a beneficial result for the class, such as attorneys who acted for the class before certification but were not appointed class counsel, or attorneys who represented objectors to a proposed settlement under Rule 23(e) or to the fee motion of class counsel. Other situations in which fee awards are authorized by law or by agreement of the parties may exist.

This subdivision authorizes an award of "reasonable" attorney fees and nontaxable costs. This is the customary term for measurement of fee awards in cases in which counsel may obtain an award of fees under the "common fund" theory that applies in many class actions, and is used in many fee-shifting statutes. Depending on the circumstances, courts have approached the determination of what is reasonable in different ways. In particular, there is some variation among courts about whether in "common fund" cases the court should use the lodestar or a percentage method of determining what fee is reasonable. The rule does not attempt to resolve the question whether the lodestar or percentage approach should be viewed as preferable.

Active judicial involvement in measuring fee awards is singularly important to the proper operation of the class-action process. Continued reliance on caselaw development of fee-award measures does not diminish the court's responsibility. In a class action, the district court must ensure that the amount and mode of payment of attorney fees are fair and proper whether the fees come from a common fund or are otherwise paid. Even in the absence of objections, the court bears this responsibility.

Courts discharging this responsibility have looked to a variety of factors. One fundamental focus is the result actually achieved for class members, a basic consideration in any case in which fees are sought on the basis of a benefit

achieved for class members. The Private Securities Litigation Reform Act of 1995 explicitly makes this factor a cap for a fee award in actions to which it applies. See 15 U.S.C. §§ 77z–1(a)(6); 78u–4(a)(6) (fee award should not exceed a "reasonable percentage of the amount of any damages and prejudgment interest actually paid to the class"). For a percentage approach to fee measurement, results achieved is the basic starting point.

In many instances, the court may need to proceed with care in assessing the value conferred on class members. Settlement regimes that provide for future payments, for example, may not result in significant actual payments to class members. In this connection, the court may need to scrutinize the manner and operation of any applicable claims procedure. In some cases, it may be appropriate to defer some portion of the fee award until actual payouts to class members are known. Settlements involving nonmonetary provisions for class members also deserve careful scrutiny to ensure that these provisions have actual value to the class. On occasion the court's Rule 23(e) review will provide a solid basis for this sort of evaluation, but in any event it is also important to assessing the fee award for the class.

At the same time, it is important to recognize that in some class actions the monetary relief obtained is not the sole determinant of an appropriate attorney fees award. Cf. *Blanchard v. Bergeron*, 489 U.S. 87, 95 (1989) (cautioning in an individual case against an "undesirable emphasis" on "the importance of the recovery of damages in civil rights litigation" that might "shortchange efforts to seek effective injunctive or declaratory relief").

Any directions or orders made by the court in connection with appointing class counsel under Rule 23(g) should weigh heavily in making a fee award under this subdivision.

Courts have also given weight to agreements among the parties regarding the fee motion, and to agreements between class counsel and others about the fees claimed by the motion. Rule 54(d)(2)(B) provides: "If directed by the court, the motion shall also disclose the terms of any agreement with respect to fees to be paid for the services for which claim is made." The agreement by a settling party not to oppose a fee application up to a certain amount, for example, is worthy of consideration, but the court remains responsible to determine a reasonable fee. "Side agreements" regarding fees provide at least perspective pertinent to an appropriate fee award.

In addition, courts may take account of the fees charged by class counsel or other attorneys for representing individual claimants or objectors in the case. In determining a fee for class counsel, the court's objective is to ensure an overall fee that is fair for counsel and equitable within the class. In some circumstances individual fee agreements between class counsel and class members might have provisions inconsistent with those goals, and the court might determine that adjustments in the class fee award were necessary as a result.

Finally, it is important to scrutinize separately the application for an award covering nontaxable costs. If costs were addressed in the order appointing class counsel, those directives should be a presumptive starting point in determining what is an appropriate award.

Paragraph (1). Any claim for an award of attorney fees must be sought by motion under Rule 54(d)(2), which invokes the provisions for timing of appeal in Rule 58 and Appellate Rule 4. Owing to the distinctive features of class action fee motions, however, the provisions of this subdivision control disposition of fee motions in class actions, while Rule 54(d)(2) applies to matters not addressed in this subdivision.

The court should direct when the fee motion must be filed. For motions by class counsel in cases subject to court review of a proposed settlement under Rule 23(e), it would be important to require the filing of at least the initial motion in time for inclusion of information about the motion in the notice to the class about the proposed settlement that is required by Rule 23(e). In cases litigated to judgment, the court might also order class counsel's motion to be filed promptly so that notice to the class under this subdivision (h) can be given.

Besides service of the motion on all parties, notice of class counsel's motion for attorney fees must be "directed to the class in a reasonable manner." Because members of the class have an interest in the arrangements for payment of class counsel whether that payment comes from the class fund or is made directly by another party, notice is required in all instances. In cases in which settlement approval is contemplated under Rule 23(e), notice of class counsel's fee motion should be combined with notice of the proposed settlement, and the provision regarding notice to the class is parallel to the requirements for notice under Rule 23(e). In adjudicated class actions, the court may calibrate the notice to avoid undue expense.

Paragraph (2). A class member and any party from whom payment is sought may object to the fee motion. Other parties—for example, nonsettling defendants—may not object because they lack a sufficient interest in the amount the court awards. The rule does not specify a time limit for making an objection. In setting the date objections are due, the court should provide sufficient time after the full fee motion is on file to enable potential objectors to examine the motion.

The court may allow an objector discovery relevant to the objections. In determining whether to allow discovery, the court should weigh the need for the information against the cost and delay that would attend discovery. See Rule 26(b)(2). One factor in determining whether to authorize discovery is the completeness of the material submitted in support of the fee motion, which depends in part on the fee measurement standard applicable to the case. If the motion provides thorough information, the burden should be on the objector to justify discovery to obtain further information.

Paragraph (3). Whether or not there are formal objections, the court must determine whether a fee award is justified and, if so, set a reasonable fee. The rule does not require a formal hearing in all cases. The form and extent of a hearing depend on the circumstances of the case. The rule does require findings and conclusions under Rule 52(a).

Paragraph (4). By incorporating Rule 54(d)(2), this provision gives the court broad authority to obtain assistance in determining the appropriate amount to award. In deciding whether to direct submission of such questions to a special master or magistrate judge, the court should give appropriate consideration to the cost and delay that such a process might entail.

2007 Amendment

[Effective December 1, 2007,
absent contrary Congressional action.]

The language of Rule 23 has been amended as part of the general restyling of the Civil Rules to make them more easily understood and to make style and terminology consistent throughout the rules. These changes are intended to be stylistic only.

Amended Rule 23(d)(2) carries forward the provisions of former Rule 23(d) that recognize two separate propositions. First, a Rule 23(d) order may be combined with a pretrial order under Rule 16. Second, the standard for amending the Rule 23(d) order continues to be the more open-ended standard for amending Rule 23(d) orders, not the more exacting standard for amending Rule 16 orders.

As part of the general restyling, intensifiers that provide emphasis but add no meaning are consistently deleted. Amended Rule 23(f) omits as redundant the explicit reference to court of appeals discretion in deciding whether to permit an interlocutory appeal. The omission does not in any way limit the unfettered discretion established by the original rule.

HISTORICAL NOTES

Amendments to Civil Rules Proposed March 27, 2003

Pub.L. 109–2, § 7, Feb. 18, 2005, 119 Stat. 13, provided that amendments to rule 23 of the Federal Rules of Civil Procedure, which are set forth in the order entered by the Supreme Court of the United States on March 27, 2003, shall take effect on the date of enactment of that Act [Feb. 18, 2005] or on December 1, 2003 (as specified in that order), whichever occurred first, see Pub.L. 109–2, § 7, set out as a note under 28 U.S.C.A. § 2074.

Rule 23.1. Derivative Actions by Shareholders

In a derivative action brought by one or more shareholders or members to enforce a right of a corporation or of an unincorporated association, the corporation or association having failed to enforce a right which may properly be asserted by it, the complaint shall be verified and shall allege (1) that the plaintiff was a shareholder or member at the time of the transaction of which the plaintiff complains or that the plaintiff's share or membership thereafter devolved on the plaintiff by operation of law, and (2) that the action is not a collusive one to confer jurisdiction on a court of the United States which it would not otherwise have. The complaint shall also allege with particularity the efforts, if any, made by the plaintiff to obtain the action the plaintiff desires from the directors or comparable authority and, if necessary, from the shareholders or members, and the reasons for the plaintiff's failure to obtain the action or for not making the effort. The derivative action may not be maintained if it appears that the plaintiff does not fairly and adequately represent the interests of the shareholders or members similarly situated in enforcing the right of the corporation or association. The action shall not be dismissed or compromised without the approval of the court, and notice of the proposed dismissal or compromise shall be given to shareholders or members in such manner as the court directs.

(Added Feb. 28, 1966, eff. July 1, 1966, and amended Mar. 2, 1987, eff. Aug. 1, 1987.)

Proposed Amendment of Rule

Effective December 1, 2007, absent contrary Congressional action, this rule is amended to read as follows:

Rule 23.1. Derivative Actions

(a) Prerequisites. *This rule applies when one or more shareholders or members of a corporation or an unincorporated association bring a derivative action to enforce a right that the corporation or association may properly assert but has failed to enforce. The derivative action may not be maintained if it appears that the plaintiff does not fairly and adequately represent the interests of shareholders or members who are similarly situated in enforcing the right of the corporation or association.*

(b) Pleading Requirements. *The complaint must be verified and must:*

(1) allege that the plaintiff was a shareholder or member at the time of the transaction complained of, or that the plaintiff's share or membership later devolved on it by operation of law;

(2) allege that the action is not a collusive one to confer jurisdiction that the court would otherwise lack; and

(3) state with particularity:

(A) any effort by the plaintiff to obtain the desired action from the directors or comparable authority and, if necessary, from the shareholders or members; and

(B) the reasons for not obtaining the action or not making the effort.

(c) Settlement, Dismissal, and Compromise. *A derivative action may be settled, voluntarily dismissed, or compromised only with the court's approval. Notice of a proposed settlement, voluntary dismissal, or compromise must be given to shareholders or members in the manner that the court orders.*

ADVISORY COMMITTEE NOTES

1966 Addition

A derivative action by a shareholder of a corporation or by a member of an unincorporated association has distinctive aspects which require the special provisions set forth in the new rule. The next-to-the-last sentence recognizes that the question of adequacy of representation may arise when the plaintiff is one of a group of shareholders or members. Cf. 3 Moore's *Federal Practice,* par. 23.08 (2d ed. 1963).

The court has inherent power to provide for the conduct of the proceedings in a derivative action, including the power to determine the course of the proceedings and require that any appropriate notice be given to shareholders or members.

1987 Amendment

The amendments are technical. No substantive change is intended.

2007 Amendment

*[Effective December 1, 2007,
absent contrary Congressional action.]*

The language of Rule 23.1 has been amended as part of the general restyling of the Civil Rules to make them more easily understood and to make style and terminology consistent throughout the rules. These changes are intended to be stylistic only.

Rule 23.2. Actions Relating to Unincorporated Associations

An action brought by or against the members of an unincorporated association as a class by naming certain members as representative parties may be maintained only if it appears that the representative parties will fairly and adequately protect the interests of the association and its members. In the conduct of the action the court may make appropriate orders corresponding with those described in Rule 23(d), and the procedure for dismissal or compromise of the action shall correspond with that provided in Rule 23(e).

(Added Feb. 28, 1966, eff. July 1, 1966.)

Proposed Amendment of Rule

Effective December 1, 2007, absent contrary Congressional action, this rule is amended to read as follows:

Rule 23.2. *Actions Relating to Unincorporated Associations*

This rule applies to an action brought by or against the members of an unincorporated association as a class by naming certain members as representative parties. The action may be maintained only if it appears that those parties will fairly and adequately protect the interests of the association and its members. In conducting the action, the court may issue any appropriate orders corresponding with those in Rule 23(d), and the procedure for settlement, voluntary dismissal, or compromise must correspond with the procedure in Rule 23(e).

ADVISORY COMMITTEE NOTES

1966 Addition

Although an action by or against representatives of the membership of an unincorporated association has often been viewed as a class action, the real or main purpose of this characterization has been to give "entity treatment" to the association when for formal reasons it cannot sue or be sued as a jural person under Rule 17(b). See Louisell & Hazard, *Pleading and Procedure: State and Federal* 718 (1962); 3 Moore's *Federal Practice*, par. 23.08 (2d ed. 1963); Story, J. in *West v. Randall*, 29 Fed.Cas. 718, 722–23, No. 17,424 (C.C.D.R.I.1820); and, for examples, *Gibbs v. Buck*, 307 U.S. 66 (1939); *Tunstall v. Brotherhood of Locomotive F. & E.*, 148 F.2d 403 (4th Cir. 1945); *Oskoian v. Canuel*, 269 F.2d 311 (1st Cir. 1959). Rule 23.2 deals separately with these actions, referring where appropriate to Rule 23.

2007 Amendment

*[Effective December 1, 2007,
absent contrary Congressional action.]*

The language of Rule 23.2 has been amended as part of the general restyling of the Civil Rules to make them more easily understood and to make style and terminology consistent throughout the rules. These changes are intended to be stylistic only.

Rule 24. Intervention

(a) Intervention of Right. Upon timely application anyone shall be permitted to intervene in an action: (1) when a statute of the United States confers an unconditional right to intervene; or (2) when the applicant claims an interest relating to the property or transaction which is the subject of the action and the applicant is so situated that the disposition of the action may as a practical matter impair or impede the applicant's ability to protect that interest, unless the applicant's interest is adequately represented by existing parties.

(b) Permissive Intervention. Upon timely application anyone may be permitted to intervene in an action: (1) when a statute of the United States confers a conditional right to intervene; or (2) when an applicant's claim or defense and the main action have a question of law or fact in common. When a party to an action relies for ground of claim or defense upon any statute or executive order administered by a federal or state governmental officer or agency or upon any regulation, order, requirement, or agreement issued or made pursuant to the statute or executive order, the officer or agency upon timely application may be permitted to intervene in the action. In exercising its discretion the court shall consider whether the intervention will unduly delay or prejudice the adjudication of the rights of the original parties.

(c) Procedure. A person desiring to intervene shall serve a motion to intervene upon the parties as provided in Rule 5. The motion shall state the grounds therefor and shall be accompanied by a pleading setting forth the claim or defense for which intervention is sought. The same procedure shall be followed when a statute of the United States gives a right to intervene.

(As amended Dec. 27, 1946, eff. Mar. 19, 1948; Dec. 29, 1948, eff. Oct. 20, 1949; Jan. 21, 1963, eff. July 1, 1963; Feb. 28, 1966, eff. July 1, 1966; Mar. 2, 1987, eff. Aug. 1, 1987; Apr. 30, 1991, eff. Dec. 1, 1991; Apr. 12, 2006, eff. Dec. 1, 2006.)

Proposed Amendment of Rule

Effective December 1, 2007, absent contrary Congressional action, this rule is amended to read as follows:

Rule 24. Intervention

(a) Intervention of Right. *On timely motion, the court must permit anyone to intervene who:*

(1) is given an unconditional right to intervene by a federal statute; or

(2) claims an interest relating to the property or transaction that is the subject of the action, and is so situated that disposing of the action may as a practical matter impair or impede the movant's ability to protect its interest, unless existing parties adequately represent that interest.

(b) Permissive Intervention.

(1) In General. On timely motion, the court may permit anyone to intervene who:

(A) is given a conditional right to intervene by a federal statute; or

(B) has a claim or defense that shares with the main action a common question of law or fact.

(2) By a Government Officer or Agency. On timely motion, the court may permit a federal or state governmental officer or agency to intervene if a party's claim or defense is based on:

(A) a statute or executive order administered by the officer or agency; or

(B) any regulation, order, requirement, or agreement issued or made under the statute or executive order.

(3) Delay or Prejudice. In exercising its discretion, the court must consider whether the intervention will unduly delay or prejudice the adjudication of the original parties' rights.

(c) Notice and Pleading Required. *A motion to intervene must be served on the parties as provided in Rule 5. The motion must state the grounds for intervention and be accompanied by a pleading that sets out the claim or defense for which intervention is sought.*

ADVISORY COMMITTEE NOTES
1937 Adoption

The right to intervene given by the following and similar statutes is preserved, but the procedure for its assertion is governed by this rule:

U.S.C., Title 28 former sections:

45a [now 2323] (Special attorneys; participation by Interstate Commerce Commission; intervention) (in certain cases under interstate commerce laws)

48 [now 2322] (Suits to be against United States; intervention by United States)

401 [now 2403] (Intervention by United States; constitutionality of Federal statute)

U.S.C., Title 40:

276a–2(b) [now 3162(a)(2)] (Bonds of contractors for public buildings or works; rights of persons furnishing labor and materials).

Compare with the last sentence of [former] Equity Rule 37 (Parties Generally—Intervention). This rule amplifies and restates the present federal practice at law and in equity. For the practice in admiralty see Admiralty Rules 34 (How Third Party May Intervene) and 42 (Claims Against Proceeds in Registry). See generally Moore and Levi, *Federal Intervention: I The Right to Intervene and Reorganization* (1936), 45 Yale L.J. 565. Under the codes two types of intervention are provided, one for the recovery of specific real or personal property (2 Ohio Gen.Code Ann. (Page, 1926) § 11263; Wyo.Rev.Stat.Ann. (Courtright, 1931) § 89–522), and the other allowing intervention generally when the applicant has an interest in the matter in litigation (1 Colo.Stat.Ann. (1935) Code Civ.Proc. § 22; La.Code Pract. (Dart, 1932) Arts. 389–394; Utah Rev.Stat.Ann. (1933) § 104–3–24). The English intervention practice is based upon various rules and decisions and falls into the two categories of absolute right and discretionary right. For the absolute right see *English Rules Under the Judicature Act* (The Annual Practice, 1937) O. 12, r. 24 (admiralty), r. 25 (land), r. 23 (probate); O. 57, r. 12 (execution); J.A. (1925) §§ 181, 182, 183(2) (divorce); *In re Metropolitan Amalgamated Estates, Ltd.,* (1912) 2 Ch. 497 (receivership); *Wilson v. Church,* 9 Ch.D. 552 (1878) (representative action). For the discretionary right see O. 16, r. 11 (non-joinder) and *Re Fowler,* 142 L.T.Jo. 94 (Ch.1916), *Vavasseur v. Krupp,* 9 Ch.D. 351 (1878) (persons out of the jurisdiction).

1946 Amendment

Note. Subdivision (a). The addition to subdivision (a)(3) covers the situation where property may be in the actual custody of some other officer or agency—such as the Secretary of the Treasury—but the control and disposition of the property is lodged in the court wherein the action is pending.

Subdivision (b). The addition in subdivision (b) permits the intervention of governmental officers or agencies in proper cases and thus avoids exclusionary constructions of the rule. For an example of the latter, see *Matter of Bender Body Co.,* Ref. Ohio 1941, 47 F.Supp. 224, holding that the Administrator of the Office of Price Administration, then acting under the authority of an Executive Order of the President, could not intervene in a bankruptcy proceeding to protest the sale of assets above ceiling prices. Compare, however, *Securities and Exchange Commission v. United States Realty & Improvement Co.,* 1940, 310 U.S. 434, 60 S.Ct. 1044, where permissive intervention of the Commission to protect the public interest in an arrangement proceeding under Chapter XI of the Bankruptcy Act was upheld. See

also dissenting opinion in *Securities and Exchange Commission v. Long Island Lighting Co.*, C.C.A.2d 1945, 148 F.2d 252, judgment vacated as moot and case remanded with direction to dismiss complaint, 1945, 325 U.S. 833, 65 S.Ct. 1085. For discussion see Commentary, *Nature of Permissive Intervention Under Rule 24b*, 1940, 3 Fed.Rules Serv. 704; Berger, *Intervention by Public Agencies in Private Litigation in the Federal Courts*, 1940, 50 Yale L.J. 65.

Regarding the construction of subdivision (b)(2), see *Allen Calculators, Inc. v. National Cash Register Co.*, 1944, 64 S.Ct. 905, 322 U.S. 137, 88 L.Ed. 1188.

1948 Amendment

The amendment effective Oct. 20, 1949, substituted the reference to "Title 28, U.S.C.A. § 2403" at the end of subdivision (c) for the reference to "the Act of August 24, 1937, c. 754, § 1."

1963 Amendment

This amendment conforms to the amendment of Rule 5(a). See the Advisory Committee's Note to that amendment.

1966 Amendment

In attempting to overcome certain difficulties which have arisen in the application of present Rule 24(a)(2) and (3), this amendment draws upon the revision of the related Rules 19 (joinder of persons needed for just adjudication) and 23 (class actions), and the reasoning underlying that revision.

Rule 24(a)(3) as amended in 1948 provided for intervention of right where the applicant established that he would be adversely affected by the distribution or disposition of property involved in an action to which he had not been made a party. Significantly, some decided cases virtually disregarded the language of this provision. Thus Professor Moore states: "The concept of a fund has been applied so loosely that it is possible for a court to find a fund in almost any in personam action." 4 Moore's *Federal Practice*, par. 24.09[3], at 55 (2d ed. 1962), and see, e.g., *Formulabs, Inc. v. Hartley Pen Co.*, 275 F.2d 52 (9th Cir.1960). This development was quite natural, for Rule 24(a)(3) was unduly restricted. If an absentee would be substantially affected in a practical sense by the determination made in an action, he should, as a general rule, be entitled to intervene, and his right to do so should not depend on whether there is a fund to be distributed or otherwise disposed of. Intervention of right is here seen to be a kind of counterpart to Rule 19(a)(2)(i) on joinder of persons needed for a just adjudication: where, upon motion of a party in an action, an absentee should be joined so that he may protect his interest which as a practical matter may be substantially impaired by the disposition of the action, he ought to have a right to intervene in the action on his own motion. See Louisell & Hazard, *Pleading and Procedure: State and Federal* 749–50 (1962).

The general purpose of original Rule 24(a)(2) was to entitle an absentee, purportedly represented by a party, to intervene in the action if he could establish with fair probability that the representation was inadequate. Thus, where an action is being prosecuted or defended by a trustee, a beneficiary of the trust should have a right to intervene if he can show that the trustee's representation of his interest probably is inadequate; similarly a member of a class should have the right to intervene in a class action if he can show

the inadequacy of the representation of his interest by the representative parties before the court.

Original Rule 24(a)(2), however, made it a condition of intervention that "the applicant is or may be bound by a judgment in the action," and this created difficulties with intervention in class actions. If the "bound" language was read literally in the sense of res judicata, it could defeat intervention in some meritorious cases. A member of a class to whom a judgment in a class action extended by its terms (see Rule 23(c)(3), as amended) might be entitled to show in a later action, when the judgment in the class action was claimed to operate as res judicata against him, that the "representative" in the class action had not in fact adequately represented him. If he could make this showing, the class-action judgment might be held not to bind him. See *Hansberry v. Lee*, 311 U.S. 32 (1940). If a class member sought to intervene in the class action proper, while it was still pending, on grounds of inadequacy of representation, he could be met with the argument: if the representation was in fact inadequate, he would not be "bound" by the judgment when it was subsequently asserted against him as res judicata, hence he was not entitled to intervene; if the representation was in fact adequate, there was no occasion or ground for intervention. See *Sam Fox Publishing Co. v. United States*, 366 U.S. 683 (1961); cf. *Sutphen Estates, Inc. v. United States*, 342 U.S. 19 (1951). This reasoning might be linguistically justified by original Rule 24(a)(2); but it could lead to poor results. Compare the discussion in *International M. & I. Corp. v. Von Clemm*, 301 F.2d 857 (2d Cir.1962); *Atlantic Refining Co. v. Standard Oil Co.*, 304 F.2d 387 (D.C.Cir. 1962). A class member who claims that his "representative" does not adequately represent him, and is able to establish that proposition with sufficient probability, should not be put to the risk of having a judgment entered in the action which by its terms extends to him, and be obliged to test the validity of the judgment as applied to his interest by a later collateral attack. Rather he should, as a general rule, be entitled to intervene in the action.

The amendment provides that an applicant is entitled to intervene in an action when his position is comparable to that of a person under Rule 19(a)(2)(i), as amended, unless his interest is already adequately represented in the action by existing parties. The Rule 19(a)(2)(i) criterion imports practical considerations, and the deletion of the "bound" language similarly frees the rule from undue preoccupation with strict considerations of res judicata.

The representation whose adequacy comes into question under the amended rule is not confined to formal representation like that provided by a trustee for his beneficiary or a representative party in a class action for a member of the class. A party to an action may provide practical representation to the absentee seeking intervention although no such formal relationship exists between them, and the adequacy of this practical representation will then have to be weighed. See *International M. & I. Crop. v. Von Clemm*, and *Atlantic Refining Co. v. Standard Oil Co.*, both supra; *Wolpe v. Poretsky*, 144 F.2d 505 (D.C.Cir.1944), cert. denied, 323 U.S. 777 (1944); cf. *Ford Motor Co. v. Bisanz Bros.*, 249 F.2d 22 (8th Cir.1957); and generally, Annot., 84 A.L.R.2d 1412 (1961).

An intervention of right under the amended rule may be subject to appropriate conditions or restrictions responsive

among other things to the requirements of efficient conduct of the proceedings.

1987 Amendment

The amendments are technical. No substantive change is intended.

1991 Amendment

Language is added to bring Rule 24(c) into conformity with the statute cited, resolving some confusion reflected in district court rules. As the text provides, counsel challenging the constitutionality of legislation in an action in which the appropriate government is not a party should call the attention of the court to its duty to notify the appropriate governmental officers. The statute imposes the burden of notification on the court, not the party making the constitutional challenge, partly in order to protect against any possible waiver of constitutional rights by parties inattentive to the need for notice. For this reason, the failure of a party to call the court's attention to the matter cannot be treated as a waiver.

2006 Amendment

New Rule 5.1 replaces the final three sentences of Rule 24(c), implementing the provisions of 28 U.S.C. § 2403. Section 2403 requires notification to the Attorney General of the United States when the constitutionality of an Act of Congress is called in question, and to the state attorney general when the constitutionality of a state statute is drawn into question.

2007 Amendment

[Effective December 1, 2007,
absent contrary Congressional action.]

The language of Rule 24 has been amended as part of the general restyling of the Civil Rules to make them more easily understood and to make style and terminology consistent throughout the rules. These changes are intended to be stylistic only.

The former rule stated that the same procedure is followed when a United States statute gives a right to intervene. This statement is deleted because it added nothing.

Rule 25. Substitution of Parties

(a) Death.

(1) If a party dies and the claim is not thereby extinguished, the court may order substitution of the proper parties. The motion for substitution may be made by any party or by the successors or representatives of the deceased party and, together with the notice of hearing, shall be served on the parties as provided in Rule 5 and upon persons not parties in the manner provided in Rule 4 for the service of a summons, and may be served in any judicial district. Unless the motion for substitution is made not later than 90 days after the death is suggested upon the record by service of a statement of the fact of the death as provided herein for the service of the motion, the action shall be dismissed as to the deceased party.

(2) In the event of the death of one or more of the plaintiffs or of one or more of the defendants in an action in which the right sought to be enforced survives only to the surviving plaintiffs or only against the surviving defendants, the action does not abate. The death shall be suggested upon the record and the action shall proceed in favor of or against the surviving parties.

(b) Incompetency. If a party becomes incompetent, the court upon motion served as provided in subdivision (a) of this rule may allow the action to be continued by or against the party's representative.

(c) Transfer of Interest. In case of any transfer of interest, the action may be continued by or against the original party, unless the court upon motion directs the person to whom the interest is transferred to be substituted in the action or joined with the original party. Service of the motion shall be made as provided in subdivision (a) of this rule.

(d) Public Officers; Death or Separation from Office.

(1) When a public officer is a party to an action in his official capacity and during its pendency dies, resigns, or otherwise ceases to hold office, the action does not abate and the officer's successor is automatically substituted as a party. Proceedings following the substitution shall be in the name of the substituted party, but any misnomer not affecting the substantial rights of the parties shall be disregarded. An order of substitution may be entered at any time, but the omission to enter such an order shall not affect the substitution.

(2) A public officer who sues or is sued in an official capacity may be described as a party by the officer's official title rather than by name; but the court may require the officer's name to be added.

(As amended Dec. 29, 1948, eff. Oct. 20, 1949; Apr. 17, 1961, eff. July 19, 1961; Jan. 21, 1963, eff. July 1, 1963; Mar. 2, 1987, eff. Aug. 1, 1987.)

Proposed Amendment of Rule

Effective December 1, 2007, absent contrary Congressional action, this rule is amended to read as follows:

Rule 25. Substitution of Parties

(a) Death.

(1) Substitution if the Claim Is Not Extinguished. If a party dies and the claim is not extinguished, the court may order substitution of the proper party. A motion for substitution may be made by any party or by the decedent's successor or representative. If the motion is not made within 90 days after service of a statement noting

the death, the action by or against the decedent must be dismissed.

(2) Continuation Among the Remaining Parties. After a party's death, if the right sought to be enforced survives only to or against the remaining parties, the action does not abate, but proceeds in favor of or against the remaining parties. The death should be noted on the record.

(3) Service. A motion to substitute, together with a notice of hearing, must be served on the parties as provided in Rule 5 and on nonparties as provided in Rule 4. A statement noting death must be served in the same manner. Service may be made in any judicial district.

(b) Incompetency. *If a party becomes incompetent, the court may, on motion, permit the action to be continued by or against the party's representative. The motion must be served as provided in Rule 25(a)(3).*

(c) Transfer of Interest. *If an interest is transferred, the action may be continued by or against the original party unless the court, on motion, orders the transferee to be substituted in the action or joined with the original party. The motion must be served as provided in Rule 25(a)(3).*

(d) Public Officers; Death or Separation from Office. *An action does not abate when a public officer who is a party in an official capacity dies, resigns, or otherwise ceases to hold office while the action is pending. The officer's successor is automatically substituted as a party. Later proceedings should be in the substituted party's name, but any misnomer not affecting the parties' substantial rights must be disregarded. The court may order substitution at any time, but the absence of such an order does not affect the substitution.*

ADVISORY COMMITTEE NOTES

1937 Adoption

Note to Subdivision (a). 1. The first paragraph of this rule is based upon [former] Equity Rule 45 (Death of Party—Revivor) and U.S.C., Title 28, former § 778 (Death of parties; substitution of executor or administrator). The *scire facias* procedure provided for in the statute cited is superseded and the writ is abolished by Rule 81(b). Paragraph two states the content of U.S.C., Title 28, former § 779 (Death of one of several plaintiffs or defendants). With these two paragraphs compare generally *English Rules Under the Judicature Act* (The Annual Practice, 1937) O. 17, r.r. 1–10.

2. This rule modifies U.S.C., Title 28, [former] §§ 778 (Death of parties; substitution of executor or administrator), 779 (Death of one of several plaintiffs or defendants), and 780 (Survival of actions, suits, or proceedings, etc.), in so far as they differ from it.

Note to Subdivisions (b) and (c). These are a combination and adaptation of N.Y.C.P.A. (1937) § 83 and Calif.Code

Civ.Proc. (1937) § 385; see also 4 Nev.Comp.Laws (Hillyer, 1929) § 8561.

Note to Subdivision (d). With the first and last sentences compare U.S.C.A., Title 28, former § 780 (Survival of actions, suits, or proceedings, etc.). With the second sentence of this subdivision compare *Ex parte La Prade*, 1933, 53 S.Ct. 682, 289 U.S. 444, 77 L.Ed. 1311.

1948 Amendment

The amendment effective October 19, 1949, inserted the words, "the Canal Zone, a territory, an insular possession," in the first sentence of subdivision (d), and, in the same sentence, after the phrase "or other governmental agency," deleted the words, "or any other officer specified in the Act of February 13, 1925, c. 229, § 11 (43 Stat. 941), formerly section 780 of this title."

1961 Amendment

Subdivision (d)(1). Present Rule 25(d) is generally considered to be unsatisfactory. 4 Moore's *Federal Practice* ¶25.01[7] (2d ed. 1950); Wright, *Amendments to the Federal Rules: The Function of a Continuing Rules Committee*, 7 Vand.L.Rev. 521, 529 (1954); *Developments in the Law—Remedies Against the United States and Its Officials*, 70 Harv.L.Rev. 827, 931–34 (1957). To require, as a condition of substituting a successor public officer as a party to a pending action, that an application be made with a showing that there is substantial need for continuing the litigation, can rarely serve any useful purpose and fosters a burdensome formality. And to prescribe a short, fixed time period for substitution which cannot be extended even by agreement, see *Snyder v. Buck*, 340 U.S. 15, 19 (1950), with the penalty of dismissal of the action, "makes a trap for unsuspecting litigants which seems unworthy of a great government." *Vibra Brush Corp. v. Schaffer*, 256 F.2d 681, 684 (2d Cir. 1958). Although courts have on occasion found means of undercutting the rule, e.g. *Acheson v. Furusho*, 212 F.2d 284 (9th Cir.1954) (substitution of defendant officer unnecessary on theory that only a declaration of status was sought), it has operated harshly in many instances, e.g. *Snyder v. Buck*, supra; *Poindexter v. Folsom*, 242 F.2d 516 (3d Cir.1957).

Under the amendment, the successor is automatically substituted as a party without an application or showing of need to continue the action. An order of substitution is not required, but may be entered at any time if a party desires or the court thinks fit.

The general term "public officer" is used in preference to the enumeration which appears in the present rule. It comprises Federal, State, and local officers.

The expression "in his official capacity" is to be interpreted in its context as part of a simple procedural rule for substitution; care should be taken not to distort its meaning by mistaken analogies to the doctrine of sovereign immunity from suit or the Eleventh Amendment. The amended rule will apply to all actions brought by public officers for the government, and to any action brought in form against a named officer, but intrinsically against the government or the office or the incumbent thereof whoever he may be from time to time during the action. Thus the amended rule will apply to actions against officers to compel performance of official duties or to obtain judicial review of their orders. It will also apply to actions to prevent officers from acting in excess of

their authority or under authority not validly conferred, cf. *Philadelphia Co. v. Stimson*, 223 U.S. 605 (1912), or from enforcing unconstitutional enactments, cf. *Ex parte Young*, 209 U.S. 123 (1908); *Ex parte La Prade*, 289 U.S. 444 (1933). In general it will apply whenever effective relief would call for corrective behavior by the one then having official status and power, rather than one who has lost that status and power through ceasing to hold office. Cf. *Land v. Dollar*, 330 U.S. 731 (1947); *Larson v. Domestic & Foreign Commerce Corp.*, 337 U.S. 682 (1949). Excluded from the operation of the amended rule will be the relatively infrequent actions which are directed to securing money judgments against the named officers enforceable against their personal assets; in these cases Rule 25(a)(1), not Rule 25(d), applies to the question of substitution. Examples are actions against officers seeking to make them pay damages out of their own pockets for defamatory utterances or other misconduct in some way related to the office, see *Barr v. Matteo*, 360 U.S. 564 (1959); *Howard v. Lyons*, 360 U.S. 593 (1959); *Gregoire v. Biddle*, 177 F.2d 579 (2d Cir.1949). cert. denied, 339 U.S. 949 (1950). Another example is the anomalous action for a tax refund against a collector of internal revenue, see *Ignelzi v. Granger*, 16 F.R.D. 517 (W.D.Pa.1955), 28 U.S.C. § 2006, 4 Moore, supra, ¶25.05, p. 531; but see 28 U.S.C. § 1346(a)(1), authorizing the bringing of such suits against the United States rather than the officer.

Automatic substitution under the amended rule, being merely a procedural device for substituting a successor for a past officeholder as a party, is distinct from and does not affect any substantive issues which may be involved in the action. Thus a defense of immunity from suit will remain in the case despite a substitution.

Where the successor does not intend to pursue the policy of his predecessor which gave rise to the lawsuit, it will be open to him, after substitution, as plaintiff to seek voluntary dismissal of the action, or as defendant to seek to have the action dismissed as moot or to take other appropriate steps to avert a judgment or decree. Contrast *Ex parte La Prade*, supra; *Allen v. Regents of the University System*, 304 U.S. 439 (1938); *McGrath v. National Assn. of Mfgrs.*, 344 U.S. 804 (1952); *Danenberg v. Cohen*, 213 F.2d 944 (7th Cir.1954).

As the present amendment of Rule 25(d)(1) eliminates a specified time period to secure substitution of public officers, the reference in Rule 6(b) (regarding enlargement of time) to Rule 25 will no longer apply to these public-officer substitutions.

As to substitution on appeal, the rules of the appellate courts should be consulted.

Subdivision (d)(2). This provision, applicable in "official capacity" cases as described above, will encourage the use of the official title without any mention of the officer individually, thereby recognizing the intrinsic character of the action and helping to eliminate concern with the problem of substitution. If for any reason it seems desirable to add the individual's name, this may be done upon motion or on the court's initiative; thereafter the procedure of amended Rule 25(d)(1) will apply if the individual named ceases to hold office.

For examples of naming the officer or title rather than the officeholder, see *Annot.*, 102 A.L.R. 943, 948–52; *Comment*, 50 Mich.L.Rev. 443, 450 (1952); cf. 26 U.S.C. § 7484. Where an action is brought by or against a board or agency with continuity of existence, it has been often decided that there is no need to name the individual members and substitution is unnecessary when the personnel changes. 4 Moore, supra, ¶25.09, p. 536. The practice encouraged by amended Rule 25(d)(2) is similar.

1963 Amendment

Present Rule 25(a)(1), together with present Rule 6(b), results in an inflexible requirement that an action be dismissed as to a deceased party if substitution is not carried out within a fixed period measured from the time of the death. The hardships and inequities of this unyielding requirement plainly appear from the cases. See, e.g., *Anderson v. Yungkau*, 329 U.S. 482, 67 S.Ct. 428, 91 L.Ed. 436 (1947); *Iovino v. Waterson*, 274 F.2d 41 (1959), cert. denied, *Carlin v. Sovino*, 362 U.S. 949, 80 S.Ct. 860, 4 L.Ed.2d 867 (1960); *Perry v. Allen*, 239 F.2d 107 (5th Cir.1956); *Starnes v. Pennsylvania R.R.*, 26 F.R.D. 625 (E.D.N.Y.), aff'd per curiam, 295 F.2d 704 (2d Cir.1961), cert. denied, 369 U.S. 813, 82 S.Ct. 688, 7 L.Ed.2d 612 (1962); *Zdanok v. Glidden Co.*, 28 F.R.D. 346 (S.D.N.Y.1961). See also 4 Moore's *Federal Practice* ¶25.01[9] (Supp.1960); 2 Barron & Holtzoff, *Federal Practice & Procedure* § 621, at 420–21 (Wright ed.1961).

The amended rule establishes a time limit for the motion to substitute based not upon the time of the death, but rather upon the time information of the death is provided by means of a suggestion of death upon the record, i.e. service of a statement of the fact of the death. Cf. Ill.Ann.Stat., c. 110, § 54(2) (Smith-Hurd 1956). The motion may not be made later than 90 days after the service of the statement unless the period is extended pursuant to Rule 6(b), as amended. See the Advisory Committee's Note to amended Rule 6(b). See also the new Official Form 30.

A motion to substitute may be made by any party or by the representative of the deceased party without awaiting the suggestion of death. Indeed, the motion will usually be so made. If a party or the representative of the deceased party desires to limit the time within which another may make the motion, he may do so by suggesting the death upon the record.

A motion to substitute made within the prescribed time will ordinarily be granted, but under the permissive language of the first sentence of the amended rule ("the court may order") it may be denied by the court in the exercise of a sound discretion if made long after the death—as can occur if the suggestion of death is not made or is delayed—and circumstances have arisen rendering it unfair to allow substitution. Cf. *Anderson v. Yungkau*, supra, 329 U.S. at 485, 486, 67 S.Ct. at 430, 431, 91 L.Ed. 436, where it was noted under the present rule that settlement and distribution of the estate of a deceased defendant might be so far advanced as to warrant denial of a motion for substitution even though made within the time limit prescribed by that rule. Accordingly, a party interested in securing substitution under the amended rule should not assume that he can rest indefinitely awaiting the suggestion of death before he makes his motion to substitute.

1987 Amendment

The amendments are technical. No substantive change is intended.

2007 Amendment

*[Effective December 1, 2007,
absent contrary Congressional action.]*

7

The language of Rule 25 has been amended as part of the general restyling of the Civil Rules to make them more easily understood and to make style and terminology consistent throughout the rules. These changes are intended to be stylistic only.

Former Rule 25(d)(2) is transferred to become Rule 17(d) because it deals with designation of a public officer, not substitution.

HISTORICAL NOTES

Effective and Applicability Provisions

1961 Amendments

Amendment adopted on Apr. 17, 1961, effective July 19, 1961, see rule 86(d).

V. DEPOSITIONS AND DISCOVERY

Proposed Amendment of Heading

Effective December 1, 2007, absent contrary Congressional action, this heading is amended to read as follows:

TITLE V. DISCLOSURES AND DISCOVERY

ADVISORY COMMITTEE'S EXPLANATORY STATEMENT CONCERNING 1970 AMENDMENTS TO DISCOVERY RULES

This statement is intended to serve as a general introduction to the amendments of Rules 26–37, concerning discovery, as well as related amendments of other rules. A separate note of customary scope is appended to amendments proposed for each rule. This statement provides a framework for the consideration of individual rule changes.

Changes in the Discovery Rules

The discovery rules, as adopted in 1938, were a striking and imaginative departure from tradition. It was expected from the outset that they would be important, but experience has shown them to play an even larger role than was initially foreseen. Although the discovery rules have been amended since 1938, the changes were relatively few and narrowly focused, made in order to remedy specific defects. The amendments now proposed reflect the first comprehensive review of the discovery rules undertaken since 1938. These amendments make substantial changes in the discovery rules. Those summarized here are among the more important changes.

Scope of Discovery. New provisions are made and existing provisions changed affecting the scope of discovery: (1) The contents of insurance policies are made discoverable (Rule 26(b)(2)). (2) A showing of good cause is no longer required for discovery of documents and things and entry upon land (Rule 34). However, a showing of need is required for discovery of "trial preparation" materials other than a party's discovery of his own statement and a witness' discovery of his own statement; and protection is afforded against disclosure in such documents of mental impressions, conclusions, opinions, or legal theories concerning the litigation. (Rule 26(b)(3)). (3) Provision is made for discovery with respect to experts retained for trial preparation, and particularly those experts who will be called to testify at trial (Rule 26(b)(4)). (4) It is provided that interrogatories and requests for admission are not objectionable simply because they relate to matters of opinion or contention, subject of course to the supervisory power of the court (Rules 33(b),

36(a)). (5) Medical examination is made available as to certain nonparties. (Rule 35(a)).

Mechanics of Discovery. A variety of changes are made in the mechanics of the discovery process, affecting the sequence and timing of discovery, the respective obligations of the parties with respect to requests, responses, and motions for court orders, and the related powers of the court to enforce discovery requests and to protect against their abusive use. A new provision eliminates the automatic grant of priority in discovery to one side (Rule 26(d)). Another provides that a party is not under a duty to supplement his responses to requests for discovery, except as specified (Rule 26(e)).

Other changes in the mechanics of discovery are designed to encourage extrajudicial discovery with a minimum of court intervention. Among these are the following: (1) The requirement that a plaintiff seek leave of court for early discovery requests is eliminated or reduced, and motions for a court order under Rule 34 are made unnecessary. Motions under Rule 35 are continued. (2) Answers and objections are to be served together and an enlargement of the time for response is provided. (3) The party seeking discovery, rather than the objecting party, is made responsible for invoking judicial determination of discovery disputes not resolved by the parties. (4) Judicial sanctions are tightened with respect to unjustified insistence upon or objection to discovery. These changes bring Rules 33, 34, and 36 substantially into line with the procedure now provided for depositions.

Failure to amend Rule 35 in the same way is based upon two considerations. First, the Columbia Survey (described below) finds that only about 5 percent of medical examinations require court motions, of which about half result in court orders. Second and of greater importance, the interest of the person to be examined in the privacy of his person was recently stressed by the Supreme Court in *Schlagenhauf v. Holder*, 379 U.S. 104 (1964). The court emphasized the trial judge's responsibility to assure that the medical examination was justified, particularly as to its scope.

Rearrangement of Rules. A limited rearrangement of the discovery rules has been made, whereby certain provisions are transferred from one rule to another. The reasons for this rearrangement are discussed below in a separate section of this statement and the details are set out in a table at the end of this statement.

Optional Procedures. In two instances, new optional procedures have been made available. A new procedure is provided to a party seeking to take the deposition of a corporation or other organization (Rule 30(b)(6)). A party

on whom interrogatories have been served requesting information derivable from his business records may under specified circumstances produce the records rather than give answers (Rule 33(c)).

Other Changes. This summary of changes is by no means exhaustive. Various changes have been made in order to improve, tighten, or clarify particular provisions, to resolve conflicts in the case law, and to improve language. All changes, whether mentioned here or not, are discussed in the appropriate note for each rule.

A Field Survey of Discovery Practice

Despite widespread acceptance of discovery as an essential part of litigation, disputes have inevitably arisen concerning the values claimed for discovery and abuses alleged to exist. Many disputes about discovery relate to particular rule provisions or court decisions and can be studied in traditional fashion with a view to specific amendment. Since discovery is in large measure extra-judicial, however, even these disputes may be enlightened by a study of discovery "in the field." And some of the larger questions concerning discovery can be pursued only by a study of its operation at the law office level and in unreported cases.

The Committee, therefore, invited the Project for Effective Justice of Columbia Law School to conduct a field survey of discovery. Funds were obtained from the Ford Foundation and the Walter E. Meyer Research Institute of Law, Inc. The survey was carried on under the direction of Prof. Maurice Rosenberg of Columbia Law School. The Project for Effective Justice has submitted a report to the Committee entitled "Field Survey of Federal Pretrial Discovery" (hereafter referred to as the Columbia Survey). The Committee is deeply grateful for the benefit of this extensive undertaking and is most appreciative of the cooperation of the Project and the funding organizations. The Committee is particularly grateful to Professor Rosenberg who not only directed the survey but has given much time in order to assist the Committee in assessing the results.

The Columbia Survey concludes, in general, that there is no empirical evidence to warrant a fundamental change in the philosophy of the discovery rules. No widespread or profound failings are disclosed in the scope or availability of discovery. The costs of discovery do not appear to be oppressive, as a general matter, either in relation to ability to pay or to the stakes of the litigation. Discovery frequently provides evidence that would not otherwise be available to the parties and thereby makes for a fairer trial or settlement. On the other hand, no positive evidence is found that discovery promotes settlement.

More specific findings of the Columbia Survey are described in other Committee notes, in relation to particular rule provisions and amendments. Those interested in more detailed information may obtain it from the Project for Effective Justice.

Rearrangement of the Discovery Rules

The present discovery rules are structured entirely in terms of individual discovery devices, except for Rule 27 which deals with perpetuation of testimony, and Rule 37 which provides sanctions to enforce discovery. Thus, Rules 26 and 28 to 32 are in terms addressed only to the taking of a deposition of a party or third person. Rules 33 to 36 then deal in succession with four additional discovery devices: Written interrogatories to parties, production for inspection of documents and things, physical or mental examination and requests for admission.

Under the rules as promulgated in 1938, therefore, each of the discovery devices was separate and self-contained. A defect of this arrangement is that there is no natural location in the discovery rules for provisions generally applicable to all discovery or to several discovery devices. From 1938 until the present, a few amendments have applied a discovery provision to several rules. For example, in 1948, the scope of deposition discovery in Rule 26(b) and the provision for protective orders in Rule 30(b) were incorporated by reference in Rules 33 and 34. The arrangement was adequate so long as there were few provisions governing discovery generally and these provisions were relatively simple.

As will be seen, however, a series of amendments are now proposed which govern most or all of the discovery devices. Proposals of a similar nature will probably be made in the future. Under these circumstances, it is very desirable, even necessary, that the discovery rules contain one rule addressing itself to discovery generally.

Rule 26 is obviously the most appropriate rule for this purpose. One of its subdivisions, Rule 26(b), in terms governs only scope of deposition discovery, but it has been expressly incorporated by reference in Rules 33 and 34 and is treated by courts as setting a general standard. By means of a transfer to Rule 26 of the provisions for protective orders now contained in Rule 30(b), and a transfer from Rule 26 of provisions addressed exclusively to depositions, Rule 26 is converted into a rule concerned with discovery generally. It becomes a convenient vehicle for the inclusion of new provisions dealing with the scope, timing, and regulation of discovery. Few additional transfers are needed. See table showing rearrangement of rules, set out following this statement.

There are, to be sure, disadvantages in transferring any provision from one rule to another. Familiarity with the present pattern, reinforced by the references made by prior court decisions and the various secondary writings about the rules, is not lightly to be sacrificed. Revision of treatises and other reference works is burdensome and costly. Moreover, many States have adopted the existing pattern as a model for their rules.

On the other hand, the amendments now proposed will in any event require revision of texts and reference works as well as reconsideration by States following the Federal model. If these amendments are to be incorporated in an understandable way, a rule with general discovery provisions is needed. As will be seen, the proposed rearrangement produces a more coherent and intelligible pattern for the discovery rules taken as a whole. The difficulties described are those encountered whenever statutes are reexamined and revised. Failure to rearrange the discovery rules now would freeze the present scheme, making future change even more difficult.

Table Showing Rearrangement of Rules

Existing Rule No.	New Rule No.
26(a)	30(a), 31(a)
26(c)	30(c)
26(d)	32(a)

Rule 26. General Provisions Governing Discovery; Duty of Disclosure

(a) Required Disclosures; Methods to Discover Additional Matter.

(1) Initial Disclosures. Except in categories of proceedings specified in Rule 26(a)(1)(E), or to the extent otherwise stipulated or directed by order, a party must, without awaiting a discovery request, provide to other parties:

(A) the name and, if known, the address and telephone number of each individual likely to have discoverable information that the disclosing party may use to support its claims or defenses, unless solely for impeachment, identifying the subjects of the information;

(B) a copy of, or a description by category and location of, all documents, electronically stored information, and tangible things that are in the possession, custody, or control of the party and that the disclosing party may use to support its claims or defenses, unless solely for impeachment;

(C) a computation of any category of damages claimed by the disclosing party, making available for inspection and copying as under Rule 34 the documents or other evidentiary material, not privileged or protected from disclosure, on which such computation is based, including materials bearing on the nature and extent of injuries suffered; and

(D) for inspection and copying as under Rule 34 any insurance agreement under which any person carrying on an insurance business may be liable to satisfy part or all of a judgment which may be entered in the action or to indemnify or reimburse for payments made to satisfy the judgment.

(E) The following categories of proceedings are exempt from initial disclosure under Rule 26(a)(1):

(i) an action for review on an administrative record;

(ii) a forfeiture action in rem arising from a federal statute;

(iii) a petition for habeas corpus or other proceeding to challenge a criminal conviction or sentence;

(iv) an action brought without counsel by a person in custody of the United States, a state, or a state subdivision;

(v) an action to enforce or quash an administrative summons or subpoena;

(vi) an action by the United States to recover benefit payments;

(vii) an action by the United States to collect on a student loan guaranteed by the United States;

(viii) a proceeding ancillary to proceedings in other courts; and

(ix) an action to enforce an arbitration award.

These disclosures must be made at or within 14 days after the Rule 26(f) conference unless a different time is set by stipulation or court order, or unless a party objects during the conference that initial disclosures are not appropriate in the circumstances of the action and states the objection in the Rule 26(f) discovery plan. In ruling on the objection, the court must determine what disclosures—if any—are to be made, and set the time for disclosure. Any party first served or otherwise joined after the Rule 26(f) conference must make these disclosures within 30 days after being served or joined unless a different time is set by stipulation or court order. A party must make its initial disclosures based on the information then reasonably available to it and is not excused from making its disclosures because it has not fully completed its investigation of the case or because it challenges the sufficiency of another party's disclosures or because another party has not made its disclosures.

(2) Disclosure of Expert Testimony.

(A) In addition to the disclosures required by paragraph (1), a party shall disclose to other parties the identity of any person who may be used at trial to present evidence under Rules 702, 703, or 705 of the Federal Rules of Evidence.

(B) Except as otherwise stipulated or directed by the court, this disclosure shall, with respect to a witness who is retained or specially employed to provide expert testimony in the case or whose duties as an employee of the party regularly involve giving expert testimony, be accompanied by a written report prepared and signed by the witness. The report shall contain a complete statement of all opinions to be expressed and the basis and reasons therefor; the data or other information considered by the witness in forming the opinions; any exhibits to be used as a summary of or support for the opinions; the qualifications of the witness, including a list of all publications authored by the witness within the preceding ten years; the compensation to be paid for the study and testimony; and a listing of any other cases in which the witness has testified as an expert at trial or by deposition within the preceding four years.

(C) These disclosures shall be made at the times and in the sequence directed by the court.

In the absence of other directions from the court or stipulation by the parties, the disclosures shall be made at least 90 days before the trial date or the date the case is to be ready for trial or, if the evidence is intended solely to contradict or rebut evidence on the same subject matter identified by another party under paragraph (2)(B), within 30 days after the disclosure made by the other party. The parties shall supplement these disclosures when required under subdivision (e)(1).

(3) Pretrial Disclosures. In addition to the disclosures required by Rule 26(a)(1) and (2), a party must provide to other parties and promptly file with the court the following information regarding the evidence that it may present at trial other than solely for impeachment:

(A) the name and, if not previously provided, the address and telephone number of each witness, separately identifying those whom the party expects to present and those whom the party may call if the need arises;

(B) the designation of those witnesses whose testimony is expected to be presented by means of a deposition and, if not taken stenographically, a transcript of the pertinent portions of the deposition testimony; and

(C) an appropriate identification of each document or other exhibit, including summaries of other evidence, separately identifying those which the party expects to offer and those which the party may offer if the need arises.

Unless otherwise directed by the court, these disclosures must be made at least 30 days before trial. Within 14 days thereafter, unless a different time is specified by the court, a party may serve and promptly file a list disclosing (i) any objections to the use under Rule 32(a) of a deposition designated by another party under Rule 26(a)(3)(B), and (ii) any objection, together with the grounds therefor, that may be made to the admissibility of materials identified under Rule 26(a)(3)(C). Objections not so disclosed, other than objections under Rules 402 and 403 of the Federal Rules of Evidence, are waived unless excused by the court for good cause.

(4) Form of Disclosures. Unless the court orders otherwise, all disclosures under Rules 26(a)(1) through (3) must be made in writing, signed, and served.

(5) Methods to Discover Additional Matter. Parties may obtain discovery by one or more of the following methods: depositions upon oral examination or written questions; written interrogatories; production of documents or things or permission to enter upon land or other property under Rule 34 or 45(a)(1)(C), for inspection and other purposes; physical and mental examinations; and requests for admission.

(b) Discovery Scope and Limits. Unless otherwise limited by order of the court in accordance with these rules, the scope of discovery is as follows:

(1) In General. Parties may obtain discovery regarding any matter, not privileged, that is relevant to the claim or defense of any party, including the existence, description, nature, custody, condition, and location of any books, documents, or other tangible things and the identity and location of persons having knowledge of any discoverable matter. For good cause, the court may order discovery of any matter relevant to the subject matter involved in the action. Relevant information need not be admissible at the trial if the discovery appears reasonably calculated to lead to the discovery of admissible evidence. All discovery is subject to the limitations imposed by Rule 26(b)(2)(i), (ii), and (iii).

(2) Limitations.

(A) By order, the court may alter the limits in these rules on the number of depositions and interrogatories or the length of depositions under Rule 30. By order or local rule, the court may also limit the number of requests under Rule 36.

(B) A party need not provide discovery of electronically stored information from sources that the party identifies as not reasonably accessible because of undue burden or cost. On motion to compel discovery or for a protective order, the party from whom discovery is sought must show that the information is not reasonably accessible because of undue burden or cost. If that showing is made, the court may nonetheless order discovery from such sources if the requesting party shows good cause, considering the limitations of Rule 26(b)(2)(C). The court may specify conditions for the discovery.

(C) The frequency or extent of use of the discovery methods otherwise permitted under these rules and by any local rule shall be limited by the court if it determines that: (i) the discovery sought is unreasonably cumulative or duplicative, or is obtainable from some other source that is more convenient, less burdensome, or less expensive; (ii) the party seeking discovery has had ample opportunity by discovery in the action to obtain the information sought; or (iii) the burden or expense of the proposed discovery outweighs its likely benefit, taking into account the needs of the case, the amount in controversy, the parties' resources, the importance of the issues at stake in the litigation, and the importance of the proposed discovery in resolving the issues. The court may act upon its own initiative after reasonable notice or pursuant to a motion under Rule 26(c).

(3) Trial Preparation: Materials. Subject to the provisions of subdivision (b)(4) of this rule, a

party may obtain discovery of documents and tangible things otherwise discoverable under subdivision (b)(1) of this rule and prepared in anticipation of litigation or for trial by or for another party or by or for that other party's representative (including the other party's attorney, consultant, surety, indemnitor, insurer, or agent) only upon a showing that the party seeking discovery has substantial need of the materials in the preparation of the party's case and that the party is unable without undue hardship to obtain the substantial equivalent of the materials by other means. In ordering discovery of such materials when the required showing has been made, the court shall protect against disclosure of the mental impressions, conclusions, opinions, or legal theories of an attorney or other representative of a party concerning the litigation. A party may obtain without the required showing a statement concerning the action or its subject matter previously made by that party. Upon request, a person not a party may obtain without the required showing a statement concerning the action or its subject matter previously made by that person. If the request is refused, the person may move for a court order. The provisions of Rule 37(a)(4) apply to the award of expenses incurred in relation to the motion. For purposes of this paragraph, a statement previously made is (A) a written statement signed or otherwise adopted or approved by the person making it, or (B) a stenographic, mechanical, electrical, or other recording, or a transcription thereof, which is a substantially verbatim recital of an oral statement by the person making it and contemporaneously recorded.

(4) Trial Preparation: Experts.

(A) A party may depose any person who has been identified as an expert whose opinions may be presented at trial. If a report from the expert is required under subdivision (a)(2)(B), the deposition shall not be conducted until after the report is provided.

(B) A party may, through interrogatories or by deposition, discover facts known or opinions held by an expert who has been retained or specially employed by another party in anticipation of litigation or preparation for trial and who is not expected to be called as a witness at trial, only as provided in Rule 35(b) or upon a showing of exceptional circumstances under which it is impracticable for the party seeking discovery to obtain facts or opinions on the same subject by other means.

(C) Unless manifest injustice would result, (i) the court shall require that the party seeking discovery pay the expert a reasonable fee for time spent in responding to discovery under this subdivision; and (ii) with respect to discovery obtained under subdivision (b)(4)(B) of this rule the court shall require the party seeking discovery to pay the other party a fair portion of the fees and expenses reasonably incurred by the latter party in obtaining facts and opinions from the expert.

(5) Claims of Privilege or Protection of Trial-Preparation Materials.

(A) Information Withheld. When a party withholds information otherwise discoverable under these rules by claiming that it is privileged or subject to protection as trial-preparation material, the party shall make the claim expressly and shall describe the nature of the documents, communications, or things not produced or disclosed in a manner that, without revealing information itself privileged or protected, will enable other parties to assess the applicability of the privilege or protection.

(B) Information Produced. If information is produced in discovery that is subject to a claim of privilege or of protection as trial-preparation material, the party making the claim may notify any party that received the information of the claim and the basis for it. After being notified, a party must promptly return, sequester, or destroy the specified information and any copies it has and may not use or disclose the information until the claim is resolved. A receiving party may promptly present the information to the court under seal for a determination of the claim. If the receiving party disclosed the information before being notified, it must take reasonable steps to retrieve it. The producing party must preserve the information until the claim is resolved.

(c) Protective Orders. Upon motion by a party or by the person from whom discovery is sought, accompanied by a certification that the movant has in good faith conferred or attempted to confer with other affected parties in an effort to resolve the dispute without court action, and for good cause shown, the court in which the action is pending or alternatively, on matters relating to a deposition, the court in the district where the deposition is to be taken may make any order which justice requires to protect a party or person from annoyance, embarrassment, oppression, or undue burden or expense, including one or more of the following:

(1) that the disclosure or discovery not be had;

(2) that the disclosure or discovery may be had only on specified terms and conditions, including a designation of the time or place;

(3) that the discovery may be had only by a method of discovery other than that selected by the party seeking discovery;

(4) that certain matters not be inquired into, or that the scope of the disclosure or discovery be limited to certain matters;

(5) that discovery be conducted with no one present except persons designated by the court;

(6) that a deposition, after being sealed, be opened only by order of the court;

(7) that a trade secret or other confidential research, development, or commercial information not be revealed or be revealed only in a designated way; and

(8) that the parties simultaneously file specified documents or information enclosed in sealed envelopes to be opened as directed by the court.

If the motion for a protective order is denied in whole or in part, the court may, on such terms and conditions as are just, order that any party or other person provide or permit discovery. The provisions of Rule 37(a)(4) apply to the award of expenses incurred in relation to the motion.

(d) Timing and Sequence of Discovery. Except in categories of proceedings exempted from initial disclosure under Rule 26(a)(1)(E), or when authorized under these rules or by order or agreement of the parties, a party may not seek discovery from any source before the parties have conferred as required by Rule 26(f). Unless the court upon motion, for the convenience of parties and witnesses and in the interests of justice, orders otherwise, methods of discovery may be used in any sequence, and the fact that a party is conducting discovery, whether by deposition or otherwise, does not operate to delay any other party's discovery.

(e) Supplementation of Disclosures and Responses. A party who has made a disclosure under subdivision (a) or responded to a request for discovery with a disclosure or response is under a duty to supplement or correct the disclosure or response to include information thereafter acquired if ordered by the court or in the following circumstances:

(1) A party is under a duty to supplement at appropriate intervals its disclosures under subdivision (a) if the party learns that in some material respect the information disclosed is incomplete or incorrect and if the additional or corrective information has not otherwise been made known to the other parties during the discovery process or in writing. With respect to testimony of an expert from whom a report is required under subdivision (a)(2)(B) the duty extends both to information contained in the report and to information provided through a deposition of the expert, and any additions or other changes to this information shall be disclosed by the time the party's disclosures under Rule 26(a)(3) are due.

(2) A party is under a duty seasonably to amend a prior response to an interrogatory, request for production, or request for admission if the party learns that the response is in some material respect incomplete or incorrect and if the additional or corrective information has not otherwise been made known to the other parties during the discovery process or in writing.

(f) Conference of Parties; Planning for Discovery. Except in categories of proceedings exempted from initial disclosure under Rule 26(a)(1)(E) or when otherwise ordered, the parties must, as soon as practicable and in any event at least 21 days before a scheduling conference is held or a scheduling order is due under Rule 16(b), confer to consider the nature and basis of their claims and defenses and the possibilities for a prompt settlement or resolution of the case, to make or arrange for the disclosures required by Rule 26(a)(1), to discuss any issues relating to preserving discoverable information, and to develop a proposed discovery plan that indicates the parties' views and proposals concerning:

(1) what changes should be made in the timing, form, or requirement for disclosures under Rule 26(a), including a statement as to when disclosures under Rule 26(a)(1) were made or will be made;

(2) the subjects on which discovery may be needed, when discovery should be completed, and whether discovery should be conducted in phases or be limited to or focused upon particular issues;

(3) any issues relating to disclosure or discovery of electronically stored information, including the form or forms in which it should be produced;

(4) any issues relating to claims of privilege or of protection as trial-preparation material, including — if the parties agree on a procedure to assert such claims after production — whether to ask the court to include their agreement in an order;

(5) what changes should be made in the limitations on discovery imposed under these rules or by local rule, and what other limitations should be imposed; and

(6) any other orders that should be entered by the court under Rule 26(c) or under Rule 16(b) and (c).

The attorneys of record and all unrepresented parties that have appeared in the case are jointly responsible for arranging the conference, for attempting in good faith to agree on the proposed discovery plan, and for submitting to the court within 14 days after the conference a written report outlining the plan. A court may order that the parties or attorneys attend the conference in person. If necessary to comply with its expedited schedule for Rule 16(b) conferences, a court may by local rule (i) require that the conference

between the parties occur fewer than 21 days before the scheduling conference is held or a scheduling order is due under Rule 16(b), and (ii) require that the written report outlining the discovery plan be filed fewer than 14 days after the conference between the parties, or excuse the parties from submitting a written report and permit them to report orally on their discovery plan at the Rule 16(b) conference.

(g) Signing of Disclosures, Discovery Requests, Responses, and Objections.

(1) Every disclosure made pursuant to subdivision (a)(1) or subdivision (a)(3) shall be signed by at least one attorney of record in the attorney's individual name, whose address shall be stated. An unrepresented party shall sign the disclosure and state the party's address. The signature of the attorney or party constitutes a certification that to the best of the signer's knowledge, information, and belief, formed after a reasonable inquiry, the disclosure is complete and correct as of the time it is made.

(2) Every discovery request, response, or objection made by a party represented by an attorney shall be signed by at least one attorney of record in the attorney's individual name, whose address shall be stated. An unrepresented party shall sign the request, response, or objection and state the party's address. The signature of the attorney or party constitutes a certification that to the best of the signer's knowledge, information, and belief, formed after a reasonable inquiry, the request, response, or objection is:

(A) consistent with these rules and warranted by existing law or a good faith argument for the extension, modification, or reversal of existing law;

(B) not interposed for any improper purpose, such as to harass or to cause unnecessary delay or needless increase in the cost of litigation; and

(C) not unreasonable or unduly burdensome or expensive, given the needs of the case, the discovery already had in the case, the amount in controversy, and the importance of the issues at stake in the litigation.

If a request, response, or objection is not signed, it shall be stricken unless it is signed promptly after the omission is called to the attention of the party making the request, response, or objection, and a party shall not be obligated to take any action with respect to it until it is signed.

(3) If without substantial justification a certification is made in violation of the rule, the court, upon motion or upon its own initiative, shall impose upon the person who made the certification, the party on whose behalf the disclosure, request, response, or objection is made, or both, an appropriate sanction, which may include an order to pay the amount of the reasonable expenses incurred because of the violation, including a reasonable attorney's fee.

(As amended Dec. 27, 1946, eff. Mar. 19, 1948; Jan. 21, 1963, eff. July 1, 1963; Feb. 28, 1966, eff. July 1, 1966; Mar. 30, 1970, eff. July 1, 1970; Apr. 29, 1980, eff. Aug. 1, 1980; Apr. 28, 1983, eff. Aug. 1, 1983; Mar. 2, 1987, eff. Aug. 1, 1987; Apr. 22, 1993, eff. Dec. 1, 1993; Apr. 17, 2000, eff. Dec. 1, 2000; Apr. 12, 2006, eff. Dec. 1, 2006.)

Proposed Amendment of Rule

Effective December 1, 2007, absent contrary Congressional action, this rule is amended to read as follows:

Rule 26. Duty to Disclose; General Provisions Governing Discovery

(a) Required Disclosures.

(1) Initial Disclosure.

(A) In General. Except as exempted by Rule 26(a)(1)(B) or as otherwise stipulated or ordered by the court, a party must, without awaiting a discovery request, provide to the other parties:

(i) the name and, if known, the address and telephone number of each individual likely to have discoverable information— along with the subjects of that information— that the disclosing party may use to support its claims or defenses, unless the use would be solely for impeachment;

(ii) a copy—or a description by category and location—of all documents, electronically stored information, and tangible things that the disclosing party has in its possession, custody, or control and may use to support its claims or defenses, unless the use would be solely for impeachment;

(iii) a computation of each category of damages claimed by the disclosing party— who must also make available for inspection and copying as under Rule 34 the documents or other evidentiary material, unless privileged or protected from disclosure, on which each computation is based, including materials bearing on the nature and extent of injuries suffered; and

(iv) for inspection and copying as under Rule 34, any insurance agreement under which an insurance business may be liable to satisfy all or part of a possible judgment in the action or to indemnify or reimburse for payments made to satisfy the judgment.

(B) Proceedings Exempt from Initial Disclosure. The following proceedings are exempt from initial disclosure:

(i) an action for review on an administrative record;

(ii) a forfeiture action in rem arising from a federal statute;

(iii) a petition for habeas corpus or any other proceeding to challenge a criminal conviction or sentence;

(iv) an action brought without an attorney by a person in the custody of the United States, a state, or a state subdivision;

(v) an action to enforce or quash an administrative summons or subpoena;

(vi) an action by the United States to recover benefit payments;

(vii) an action by the United States to collect on a student loan guaranteed by the United States;

(viii) a proceeding ancillary to a proceeding in another court; and

(ix) an action to enforce an arbitration award.

(C) Time for Initial Disclosures—In General. A party must make the initial disclosures at or within 14 days after the parties' Rule 26(f) conference unless a different time is set by stipulation or court order, or unless a party objects during the conference that initial disclosures are not appropriate in this action and states the objection in the proposed discovery plan. In ruling on the objection, the court must determine what disclosures, if any, are to be made and must set the time for disclosure.

(D) Time for Initial Disclosures—For Parties Served or Joined Later. A party that is first served or otherwise joined after the Rule 26(f) conference must make the initial disclosures within 30 days after being served or joined, unless a different time is set by stipulation or court order.

(E) Basis for Initial Disclosure; Unacceptable Excuses. A party must make its initial disclosures based on the information then reasonably available to it. A party is not excused from making its disclosures because it has not fully investigated the case or because it challenges the sufficiency of another party's disclosures or because another party has not made its disclosures.

(2) Disclosure of Expert Testimony.

(A) In General. In addition to the disclosures required by Rule 26(a)(1), a party must disclose to the other parties the identity of any

witness it may use at trial to present evidence under Federal Rule of Evidence 702, 703, or 705.

(B) Written Report. Unless otherwise stipulated or ordered by the court, this disclosure must be accompanied by a written report—prepared and signed by the witness—if the witness is one retained or specially employed to provide expert testimony in the case or one whose duties as the party's employee regularly involve giving expert testimony. The report must contain:

(i) a complete statement of all opinions the witness will express and the basis and reasons for them;

(ii) the data or other information considered by the witness in forming them;

(iii) any exhibits that will be used to summarize or support them;

(iv) the witness's qualifications, including a list of all publications authored in the previous ten years;

(v) a list of all other cases in which, during the previous four years, the witness testified as an expert at trial or by deposition; and

(vi) a statement of the compensation to be paid for the study and testimony in the case.

(C) Time to Disclose Expert Testimony. A party must make these disclosures at the times and in the sequence that the court orders. Absent a stipulation or a court order, the disclosures must be made:

(i) at least 90 days before the date set for trial or for the case to be ready for trial; or

(ii) if the evidence is intended solely to contradict or rebut evidence on the same subject matter identified by another party under Rule 26(a)(2)(B), within 30 days after the other party's disclosure.

(D) Supplementing the Disclosure. The parties must supplement these disclosures when required under Rule 26(e).

(3) Pretrial Disclosures.

(A) In General. In addition to the disclosures required by Rule 26(a)(1) and (2), a party must provide to the other parties and promptly file the following information about the evidence that it may present at trial other than solely for impeachment:

(i) the name and, if not previously provided, the address and telephone number of

each witness—separately identifying those the party expects to present and those it may call if the need arises;

(ii) the designation of those witnesses whose testimony the party expects to present by deposition and, if not taken stenographically, a transcript of the pertinent parts of the deposition; and

(iii) an identification of each document or other exhibit, including summaries of other evidence—separately identifying those items the party expects to offer and those it may offer if the need arises.

(B) *Time for Pretrial Disclosures; Objections.* Unless the court orders otherwise, these disclosures must be made at least 30 days before trial. Within 14 days after they are made, unless the court sets a different time, a party may serve and promptly file a list of the following objections: any objections to the use under Rule 32(a) of a deposition designated by another party under Rule 26(a)(3)(A)(ii); and any objection, together with the grounds for it, that may be made to the admissibility of materials identified under Rule 26(a)(3)(A)(iii). An objection not so made—except for one under Federal Rule of Evidence 402 or 403—is waived unless excused by the court for good cause.

(4) *Form of Disclosures.* Unless the court orders otherwise, all disclosures under Rule 26(a) must be in writing, signed, and served.

(b) Discovery Scope and Limits.

(1) *Scope in General.* Unless otherwise limited by court order, the scope of discovery is as follows: Parties may obtain discovery regarding any nonprivileged matter that is relevant to any party's claim or defense—including the existence, description, nature, custody, condition, and location of any documents or other tangible things and the identity and location of persons who know of any discoverable matter. For good cause, the court may order discovery of any matter relevant to the subject matter involved in the action. Relevant information need not be admissible at the trial if the discovery appears reasonably calculated to lead to the discovery of admissible evidence. All discovery is subject to the limitations imposed by Rule 26(b)(2)(C).

(2) *Limitations on Frequency and Extent.*

(A) *When Permitted.* By order, the court may alter the limits in these rules on the number of depositions and interrogatories or on the length of depositions under Rule 30. By order or local rule, the court may also limit the number of requests under Rule 36.

(B) *Specific Limitations on Electronically Stored Information.* A party need not provide discovery of electronically stored information from sources that the party identifies as not reasonably accessible because of undue burden or cost. On motion to compel discovery or for a protective order, the party from whom discovery is sought must show that the information is not reasonably accessible because of undue burden or cost. If that showing is made, the court may nonetheless order discovery from such sources if the requesting party shows good cause, considering the limitations of Rule 26(b)(2)(C). The court may specify conditions for the discovery.

(C) *When Required.* On motion or on its own, the court must limit the frequency or extent of discovery otherwise allowed by these rules or by local rule if it determines that:

(i) the discovery sought is unreasonably cumulative or duplicative, or can be obtained from some other source that is more convenient, less burdensome, or less expensive;

(ii) the party seeking discovery has had ample opportunity to obtain the information by discovery in the action; or

(iii) the burden or expense of the proposed discovery outweighs its likely benefit, considering the needs of the case, the amount in controversy, the parties' resources, the importance of the issues at stake in the action, and the importance of the discovery in resolving the issues.

(3) *Trial Preparation: Materials.*

(A) *Documents and Tangible Things.* Ordinarily, a party may not discover documents and tangible things that are prepared in anticipation of litigation or for trial by or for another party or its representative (including the other party's attorney, consultant, surety, indemnitor, insurer, or agent). But, subject to Rule 26(b)(4), those materials may be discovered if:

(i) they are otherwise discoverable under Rule 26(b)(1); and

(ii) the party shows that it has substantial need for the materials to prepare its case and cannot, without undue hardship, obtain their substantial equivalent by other means.

(B) *Protection Against Disclosure.* If the court orders discovery of those materials, it

must protect against disclosure of the mental impressions, conclusions, opinions, or legal theories of a party's attorney or other representative concerning the litigation.

(C) Previous Statement. Any party or other person may, on request and without the required showing, obtain the person's own previous statement about the action or its subject matter. If the request is refused, the person may move for a court order, and Rule 37(a)(5) applies to the award of expenses. A previous statement is either:

 (i) a written statement that the person has signed or otherwise adopted or approved; or

 (ii) a contemporaneous stenographic, mechanical, electrical, or other recording—or a transcription of it—that recites substantially verbatim the person's oral statement.

(4) Trial Preparation: Experts.

(A) Expert Who May Testify. A party may depose any person who has been identified as an expert whose opinions may be presented at trial. If Rule 26(a)(2)(B) requires a report from the expert, the deposition may be conducted only after the report is provided.

(B) Expert Employed Only for Trial Preparation. Ordinarily, a party may not, by interrogatories or deposition, discover facts known or opinions held by an expert who has been retained or specially employed by another party in anticipation of litigation or to prepare for trial and who is not expected to be called as a witness at trial. But a party may do so only:

 (i) as provided in Rule 35(b); or

 (ii) on showing exceptional circumstances under which it is impracticable for the party to obtain facts or opinions on the same subject by other means.

(C) Payment. Unless manifest injustice would result, the court must require that the party seeking discovery:

 (i) pay the expert a reasonable fee for time spent in responding to discovery under Rule 26(b)(4)(A) or (B); and

 (ii) for discovery under (B), also pay the other party a fair portion of the fees and expenses it reasonably incurred in obtaining the expert's facts and opinions.

(5) Claiming Privilege or Protecting Trial-Preparation Materials.

(A) Information Withheld. When a party withholds information otherwise discoverable by claiming that the information is privileged or subject to protection as trial-preparation material, the party must:

 (i) expressly make the claim; and

 (ii) describe the nature of the documents, communications, or tangible things not produced or disclosed—and do so in a manner that, without revealing information itself privileged or protected, will enable other parties to assess the claim.

(B) Information Produced. If information produced in discovery is subject to a claim of privilege or of protection as trial-preparation material, the party making the claim may notify any party that received the information of the claim and the basis for it. After being notified, a party must promptly return, sequester, or destroy the specified information and any copies it has; must not use or disclose the information until the claim is resolved; must take reasonable steps to retrieve the information if the party disclosed it before being notified; and may promptly present the information to the court under seal for a determination of the claim. The producing party must preserve the information until the claim is resolved.

(c) Protective Orders.

(1) In General. A party or any person from whom discovery is sought may move for a protective order in the court where the action is pending—or as an alternative on matters relating to a deposition, in the court for the district where the deposition will be taken. The motion must include a certification that the movant has in good faith conferred or attempted to confer with other affected parties in an effort to resolve the dispute without court action. The court may, for good cause, issue an order to protect a party or person from annoyance, embarrassment, oppression, or undue burden or expense, including one or more of the following:

 (A) forbidding the disclosure or discovery;

 (B) specifying terms, including time and place, for the disclosure or discovery;

 (C) prescribing a discovery method other than the one selected by the party seeking discovery;

 (D) forbidding inquiry into certain matters, or limiting the scope of disclosure or discovery to certain matters;

 (E) designating the persons who may be present while the discovery is conducted;

(F) requiring that a deposition be sealed and opened only on court order;

(G) requiring that a trade secret or other confidential research, development, or commercial information not be revealed or be revealed only in a specified way; and

(H) requiring that the parties simultaneously file specified documents or information in sealed envelopes, to be opened as the court directs.

(2) Ordering Discovery. If a motion for a protective order is wholly or partly denied, the court may, on just terms, order that any party or person provide or permit discovery.

(3) Awarding Expenses. Rule 37(a)(5) applies to the award of expenses.

(d) *Timing and Sequence of Discovery.*

(1) Timing. A party may not seek discovery from any source before the parties have conferred as required by Rule 26(f), except in a proceeding exempted from initial disclosure under Rule 26(a)(1)(B), or when authorized by these rules, by stipulation, or by court order.

(2) Sequence. Unless, on motion, the court orders otherwise for the parties' and witnesses' convenience and in the interests of justice:

(A) methods of discovery may be used in any sequence; and

(B) discovery by one party does not require any other party to delay its discovery.

(e) *Supplementing Disclosures and Responses.*

(1) In General. A party who has made a disclosure under Rule 26(a)—or who has responded to an interrogatory, request for production, or request for admission—must supplement or correct its disclosure or response:

(A) in a timely manner if the party learns that in some material respect the disclosure or response is incomplete or incorrect, and if the additional or corrective information has not otherwise been made known to the other parties during the discovery process or in writing; or

(B) as ordered by the court.

(2) Expert Witness. For an expert whose report must be disclosed under Rule 26(a)(2)(B), the party's duty to supplement extends both to information included in the report and to information given during the expert's deposition. Any additions or changes to this information must be disclosed by the time the party's pretrial disclosures under Rule 26(a)(3) are due.

(f) *Conference of the Parties; Planning for Discovery.*

(1) Conference Timing. Except in a proceeding exempted from initial disclosure under Rule 26(a)(1)(B) or when the court orders otherwise, the parties must confer as soon as practicable—and in any event at least 21 days before a scheduling conference is to be held or a scheduling order is due under Rule 16(b).

(2) Conference Content; Parties' Responsibilities. In conferring, the parties must consider the nature and basis of their claims and defenses and the possibilities for promptly settling or resolving the case; make or arrange for the disclosures required by Rule 26(a)(1); discuss any issues about preserving discoverable information; and develop a proposed discovery plan. The attorneys of record and all unrepresented parties that have appeared in the case are jointly responsible for arranging the conference, for attempting in good faith to agree on the proposed discovery plan, and for submitting to the court within 14 days after the conference a written report outlining the plan. The court may order the parties or attorneys to attend the conference in person.

(3) Discovery Plan. A discovery plan must state the parties' views and proposals on:

(A) what changes should be made in the timing, form, or requirement for disclosures under Rule 26(a), including a statement of when initial disclosures were made or will be made;

(B) the subjects on which discovery may be needed, when discovery should be completed, and whether discovery should be conducted in phases or be limited to or focused on particular issues;

(C) any issues about disclosure or discovery of electronically stored information, including the form or forms in which it should be produced;

(D) any issues about claims of privilege or of protection as trial-preparation materials, including—if the parties agree on a procedure to assert these claims after production—whether to ask the court to include their agreement in an order;

(E) what changes should be made in the limitations on discovery imposed under these rules or by local rule, and what other limitations should be imposed; and

(F) any other orders that the court should issue under Rule 26(c) or under Rule 16(b) and (c).

(4) Expedited Schedule. If necessary to comply with its expedited schedule for Rule 16(b) conferences, a court may by local rule:

(A) require the parties' conference to occur less than 21 days before the scheduling conference is held or a scheduling order is due under Rule 16(b); and

(B) require the written report outlining the discovery plan to be filed less than 14 days after the parties' conference, or excuse the parties from submitting a written report and permit them to report orally on their discovery plan at the Rule 16(b) conference.

(g) Signing Disclosures and Discovery Requests, Responses, and Objections.

(1) Signature Required; Effect of Signature. Every disclosure under Rule 26(a)(1) or (a)(3) and every discovery request, response, or objection must be signed by at least one attorney of record in the attorney's own name—or by the party personally, if unrepresented—and must state the signer's address, e-mail address, and telephone number. By signing, an attorney or party certifies that to the best of the person's knowledge, information, and belief formed after a reasonable inquiry:

(A) with respect to a disclosure, it is complete and correct as of the time it is made; and

(B) with respect to a discovery request, response, or objection, it is:

(i) consistent with these rules and warranted by existing law or by a nonfrivolous argument for extending, modifying, or reversing existing law, or for establishing new law;

(ii) not interposed for any improper purpose, such as to harass, cause unnecessary delay, or needlessly increase the cost of litigation; and

(iii) neither unreasonable nor unduly burdensome or expensive, considering the needs of the case, prior discovery in the case, the amount in controversy, and the importance of the issues at stake in the action.

(2) Failure to Sign. Other parties have no duty to act on an unsigned disclosure, request, response, or objection until it is signed, and the court must strike it unless a signature is promptly supplied after the omission is called to the attorney's or party's attention.

(3) Sanction for Improper Certification. If a certification violates this rule without substantial justification, the court, on motion or on its own, must impose an appropriate sanction on the signer, the party on whose behalf the signer was acting, or both. The sanction may include an order to pay the reasonable expenses, including attorney's fees, caused by the violation.

ADVISORY COMMITTEE NOTES

1937 Adoption

Note to Subdivision (a). This rule freely authorizes the taking of depositions under the same circumstances and by the same methods whether for the purpose of discovery or for the purpose of obtaining evidence. Many states have adopted this practice on account of its simplicity and effectiveness, safeguarding it by imposing such restrictions upon the subsequent use of the deposition at the trial or hearing as are deemed advisable. See Ark.Civ.Code (Crawford, 1934) §§ 606 to 607; Calif.Code Civ.Proc. (Deering, 1937) § 2021; 1 Colo.Stat.Ann. (1935) Code Civ.Proc. § 376; Idaho Code Ann. (1932) § 16–906; Ill.Rules of Pract.Rule 19 (Smith-Hurd Ill.Stats. c. 110, § 259.19); Smith-Hurd Ill.Stats. c. 51, § 24; 2 Ind.Stat.Ann. (Burns, 1933) §§ 2–1501, 2–1506; Ky. Codes (Carroll, 1932) Civ.Pract. § 557; 1 Mo.Rev.Stat. (1929) § 1753; 4 Mont.Rev.Codes Ann. (1935) § 10645; Neb.Comp. Stat. (1929) ch. 20, §§ 1246–7; 4 Nev.Comp.Laws (Hillyer, 1929) § 9001; 2 N.H.Pub.Laws (1926) ch. 337, § 1; N.C.Code Ann. (1935) § 1809; 2 N.D.Comp.Laws Ann. (1913) §§ 7889 to 7897; 2 Ohio Gen.Code Ann. (Page, 1926) §§ 11525–6; 1 Ore.Code Ann. (1930) Tit. 9, § 1503; 1 S.D.Comp.Laws (1929) §§ 2713–16; Vernon's Ann.Civ.Stats. Tex. arts. 3738, 3752, 3769; Utah Rev.Stat.Ann. (1933) § 104–51–7; Wash.Rules of Practice adopted by the Supreme Ct., Rule 8, 2 Wash.Rev.Stat.Ann. (Remington, 1932) § 308–8; W.Va.Code (1931) ch. 57, art. 4, § 1. Compare [former] Equity Rules 47 (Depositions—To be Taken in Exceptional Instances); 54 (Depositions Under Revised Statutes, §§ 863, 865, 866, 867—Cross Examination); 58 (Discovery—Interrogatories—Inspection and Production of Documents—Admission of Execution or Genuineness).

This and subsequent rules incorporate, modify, and broaden the provisions for depositions under U.S.C., Title 28, [former] §§ 639 (Depositions *de bene esse;* when and where taken; notice), 640 (Same; mode of taking), 641 (Same; transmission to court), 644 (Depositions under *dedimus potestatem* and *in perpetuam*), 646 (Deposition under *dedimus potestatem*; how taken). These statutes are superseded in so far as they differ from this and subsequent rules. U.S.C. Title 28, [former] § 643 (Depositions; taken in mode prescribed by State laws) is superseded by the third sentence of Subdivision (a).

While a number of states permit discovery only from parties or their agents, others either make no distinction between parties or agents of parties and ordinary witnesses, or authorize the taking of ordinary depositions, without restriction, from any persons who have knowledge of relevant facts. See Ark.Civ.Code (Crawford, 1934) §§ 606 to 607; 1 Idaho Code Ann. (1932) § 16–906; Ill.Rules of Pract., Rule 19 (Smith-Hurd Ill.Stats. c. 110, § 259.19); Smith-Hurd Ill.Stats. c. 51, § 24; 2 Ind.Stat.Ann. (Burns, 1933) § 2–1501;

Ky.Codes (Carroll, 1932) Civ.Pract. §§ 554 to 558; 2 Md. Ann.Code (Bagby, 1924) Art. 35, § 21; 2 Minn.Stat. (Mason, 1927) § 9820; Mo.St.Ann. §§ 1753, 1759, pp. 4023, 4026; Neb.Comp.Stat. (1929) ch. 20, §§ 1246–7; 2 N.H.Pub.Laws (1926) ch. 337, § 1; 2 N.D.Comp.Laws Ann. (1913) § 7897; 2 Ohio Gen.Code Ann. (Page, 1926) §§ 11525–6; 1 S.D.Comp. Laws (1929) §§ 2713–16; Vernon's Ann.Civil Stats.Tex. arts. 3738, 3752, 3769; Utah Rev.Stat.Ann. (1933) § 104–51–7; Wash.Rules of Practice adopted by Supreme Ct., Rule 8, 2 Wash.Rev.Stat.Ann. (Remington, 1932) § 308–8; W.Va.Code (1931) ch. 57, art. 4, § 1.

The more common practice in the United States is to take depositions on notice by the party desiring them, without any order from the court, and this has been followed in these rules. See Calif.Code Civ.Proc. (Deering, 1937) § 2031; 2 Fla.Comp.Gen.Laws Ann. (1927) §§ 4405–7; 1 Idaho Code Ann. (1932) § 16–902; Ill.Rules of Pract., Rule 19 (Smith-Hurd Ill.Stats. c. 110, § 259.19); Smith-Hurd Ill.Stats. c. 51, § 24; 2 Ind.Stat.Ann. (Burns, 1933) § 2–1502; Kan.Gen.Stat. Ann. (1935) § 60–2827; Ky.Codes (Carroll, 1932) Civ.Pract. § 565; 2 Minn.Stat. (Mason, 1927) § 9820; Mo.St.Ann. § 1761, p. 4029; 4 Mont.Rev.Codes Ann. (1935) § 10651; Nev.Comp.Laws (Hillyer, 1929) § 9002; N.C.Code Ann. (1935) § 1809; 2 N.D.Comp.Laws Ann. (1913) § 7895; Utah Rev.Stat.Ann. (1933) § 104–51–8.

Note to Subdivision (b). While the old chancery practice limited discovery to facts supporting the case of the party seeking it, this limitation has been largely abandoned by modern legislation. See Ala.Code Ann. (Michie, 1928) §§ 7764 to 7773; 2 Ind.Stat.Ann. (Burns, 1933) §§ 2–1028, 2–1506, 2–1728–2–1732; Iowa Code (1935) § 11185; Ky. Codes (Carroll, 1932) Civ.Pract. §§ 557, 606(8); La.Code Pract. (Dart, 1932) arts. 347–356; 2 Mass.Gen.Laws (Ter.Ed., 1932) ch. 231, §§ 61 to 67; Mo.St.Ann. §§ 1753, 1759, pp. 4023, 4026; Neb.Comp.Stat. (1929) §§ 20–1246, 20–1247; 2 N.H.Pub.Laws (1926) ch. 337, § 1; 2 Ohio Gen.Code Ann. (Page, 1926) §§ 11497, 11526; Vernon's Ann.Civ.Stats.Tex. arts. 3738, 3753, 3769; Wis.Stat. (1935) § 326.12; Ontario Consol.Rules of Pract. (1928) Rules 237–347; Quebec Code of Civ.Proc. (Curran, 1922) §§ 286 to 290.

Note to Subdivisions (d), (e), and (f). The restrictions here placed upon the use of depositions at the trial or hearing are substantially the same as those provided in U.S.C., Title 28, [former] § 641, for depositions taken, *de bene esse*, with the additional provision that any deposition may be used when the court finds the existence of exceptional circumstances. Compare English Rules Under the Judicature Act (The Annual Practice, 1937) O. 37, r. 18 (with additional provision permitting use of deposition by consent of the parties). See also [former] Equity Rule 64 (Former Depositions, Etc. May be Used Before Master); and 2 Minn. Stat. (Mason, 1927) § 9835 (Use in a subsequent action of a deposition filed in a previously dismissed action between the same parties and involving the same subject matter).

1946 Amendment

Note. Subdivision (a). The amendment eliminates the requirement of leave of court for the taking of a deposition except where a plaintiff seeks to take a deposition within 20 days after the commencement of the action. The retention of the requirement where a deposition is sought by a plaintiff within 20 days of the commencement of the action protects a defendant who has not had an opportunity to retain counsel

and inform himself as to the nature of the suit; the plaintiff, of course, needs no such protection. The present rule forbids the plaintiff to take a deposition, without leave of court, before the answer is served. Sometimes the defendant delays the serving of an answer for more than 20 days, but as 20 days are sufficient time for him to obtain a lawyer, there is no reason to forbid the plaintiff to take a deposition without leave merely because the answer has not been served. In all cases, Rule 30(a) empowers the court, for cause shown, to alter the time of the taking of a deposition, and Rule 30(b) contains provisions giving ample protection to persons who are unreasonably pressed. The modified practice here adopted is along the line of that followed in various states. See e.g., 8 Mo.Rev.Stat.Ann.1939, § 1917; 2 Burns' Ind.Stat.Ann.1933, § 2–1506.

Subdivision (b). The amendments to subdivision (b) make clear the broad scope of examination and that it may cover not only evidence for use at the trial but also inquiry into matters in themselves inadmissible as evidence but which will lead to the discovery of such evidence. The purpose of discovery is to allow a broad search for facts, the names of witnesses, or any other matters which may aid a party in the preparation or presentation of his case. *Engl v. Aetna Life Ins. Co.*, C.C.A.2, 1943, 139 F.2d 469; *Mahler v. Pennsylvania R. Co.*, E.D.N.Y.1945, 8 Fed.Rules Serv. 33.351, Case 1. In such a preliminary inquiry admissibility at trial should not be the test as to whether the information sought is within the scope of proper examination. Such a standard unnecessarily curtails the utility of discovery practice. Of course, matters entirely without bearing either as direct evidence or as leads to evidence are not within the scope of inquiry, but to the extent that the examination develops useful information, it functions successfully as an instrument of discovery, even if it produces no testimony directly admissible. *Lewis v. United Air Lines Transportation Corp.*, D.Conn.1939, 27 F.Supp. 946; *Engl v. Aetna Life Ins. Co.*, supra; *Mahler v. Pennsylvania R. Co.*, supra; *Bloomer v. Sirian Lamp Co.*, D.Del.1944, 8 Fed.Rules Serv. 26b.31, Case 3; *Rosseau v. Langley*, N.Y.1945, 9 Fed.Rules Serv. 34.41, Case 1 (Rule 26 contemplates "examinations not merely for the narrow purpose of adducing testimony which may be offered in evidence but also for the broad discovery of information which may be useful in preparation for trial."); *Olson Transportation Co. v. Socony-Vacuum Co.*, E.D.Wis. 1944, 8 Fed.Rules Serv. 34.41, Case 2 (". . . the Rules . . . permit 'fishing' for evidence as they should."); Note, 1945, 45 Col.L.Rev. 482. Thus hearsay, while inadmissible itself, may suggest testimony which properly may be proved. Under Rule 26(b) several cases, however, have erroneously limited discovery on the basis of admissibility, holding that the word "relevant" in effect meant "material and competent under the rules of evidence". *Poppino v. Jones Store Co.*, W.D.Mo.1940, 1 F.R.D. 215, 3 Fed.Rules Serv. 26b.5, Case 1; *Benevento v. A. & P. Food Stores, Inc.*, E.D.N.Y.1939, 26 F.Supp. 424. Thus it has been said that inquiry might not be made into statements or other matters which, when disclosed, amounted only to hearsay. *See Maryland for use of Montvila v. Pan-American Bus Lines, Inc.*, D.Md.1940, 1 F.R.D. 213, 3 Fed.Rules Serv. 26b.211, Case 3; *Gitto v. "Italia," Societa Anonima Di Navigazione*, E.D.N.Y.1940, 31 F.Supp. 567; *Rose Silk Mills, Inc. v. Insurance Co. of North America*, S.D.N.Y.1939, 29 F.Supp. 504; *Colpak v. Hetterick*, E.D.N.Y.1941, 40 F.Supp. 350; *Matthies v. Peter F. Connolly*

Co., E.D.N.Y.1941, 6 Fed.Rules Serv. 30a.22, Case 1, 2 F.R.D. 277; *Matter of Examination of Citizens Casualty Co. of New York*, S.D.N.Y.1942, 3 F.R.D. 171, 7 Fed.Rules Serv. 26b.211, Case 1; *United States v. Silliman*, D.C.N.J.1944, 8 Fed.Rules Serv. 26b.52, Case 1. The contrary and better view, however, has often been stated. See, e.g., *Engl v. Aetna Life Ins. Co.*, supra; *Stevenson v. Melady*, S.D.N.Y. 1940, 3 Fed.Rules Serv. 26b.31, Case 1, 1 F.R.D. 329; *Lewis v. United Air Lines Transport Corp.*, supra; *Application of Zenith Radio Corp.*, E.D.Pa.1941, 4 Fed.Rules Serv. 30b.21, Case 1, 1 F.R.D. 627; *Steingut v. Guaranty Trust Co. of New York*, S.D.N.Y.1941, 1 F.R.D. 723, 4 Fed.Rules Serv. 26b.5, Case 2; *DeSeversky v. Republic Aviation Corp.*, E.D.N.Y.1941, 2 F.R.D. 183, 5 Fed.Rules Serv. 26b.31, Case 5; *Moore v. George A. Hormel & Co.*, S.D.N.Y.1942, 6 Fed.Rules Serv. 30b.41, Case 1, 2 F.R.D. 340; *Hercules Powder Co. v. Rohm & Haas Co.*, D.Del.1943, 7 Fed.Rules Serv. 45b.311, Case 2, 3 F.R.D. 302; *Bloomer v. Sirian Lamp Co.*, supra; *Crosby Steam Gage & Valve Co. v. Manning, Maxwell & Moore, Inc.*, D.Mass.1944, 8 Fed.Rules Serv. 26b.31, Case 1; *Patterson Oil Terminals, Inc. v. Charles Kurz & Co., Inc.*, E.D.Pa.1945, 9 Fed.Rules Serv. 33.321, Case 2; *Pueblo Trading Co. v. Reclamation Dist. No. 1500*, N.D.Cal.1945, 9 Fed.Rules Serv. 33.321, Case 4, 4 F.R.D. 471. See also discussion as to the broad scope of discovery in *Hoffman v. Palmer*, C.C.A.2, 1942, 129 F.2d 976, 995–997, affirmed 63 S.Ct. 477, 318 U.S. 109, 87 L.Ed. 645; Note, 1945, 45 Col.L.Rev. 482.

1963 Amendment

This amendment conforms to the amendment of Rule 28(b). See the next-to-last paragraph of the Advisory Committee's Note to that amendment.

1966 Amendment

The requirement that the plaintiff obtain leave of court in order to serve notice of taking of a deposition within 20 days after commencement of the action gives rise to difficulties when the prospective deponent is about to become unavailable for examination. The problem is not confined to admiralty, but has been of special concern in that context because of the mobility of vessels and their personnel. When Rule 26 was adopted as Admiralty Rule 30A in 1961, the problem was alleviated by permitting depositions *de bene esse*, for which leave of court is not required. See Advisory Committee's Note to Admiralty Rule 30A (1961).

A continuing study is being made in the effort to devise a modification of the 20-day rule appropriate to both the civil and admiralty practice to the end that Rule 26(a) shall state a uniform rule applicable alike to what are now civil actions and suits in admiralty. Meanwhile, the exigencies of maritime litigation require preservation, for the time being at least, of the traditional *de bene esse* procedure for the post-unification counterpart of the present suit in admiralty. Accordingly, the amendment provides for continued availability of that procedure in admiralty and maritime claims within the meaning of Rule 9(h).

1970 Amendment

A limited rearrangement of the discovery rules is made, whereby certain rule provisions are transferred, as follows: Existing Rule 26(a) is transferred to Rules 30(a) and 31(a).

Existing Rule 26(c) is transferred to Rule 30(c). Existing Rules 26(d), (e), and (f) are transferred to Rule 32. Revisions of the transferred provisions, if any, are discussed in the notes appended to Rules 30, 31, and 32. In addition, Rule 30(b) is transferred to Rule 26(c). The purpose of this rearrangement is to establish Rule 26 as a rule governing discovery in general. (The reasons are set out in the Advisory Committee's explanatory statement.)

Subdivision (a)—Discovery Devices. This is a new subdivision listing all of the discovery devices provided in the discovery rules and establishing the relationship between the general provisions of Rule 26 and the specific rules for particular discovery devices. The provision that the frequency of use of these methods is not limited confirms existing law. It incorporates in general form a provision now found in Rule 33.

Subdivision (b)—Scope of Discovery. This subdivision is recast to cover the scope of discovery generally. It regulates the discovery obtainable through any of the discovery devices listed in Rule 26(a).

All provisions as to scope of discovery are subject to the initial qualification that the court may limit discovery in accordance with these rules. Rule 26(c) (transferred from 30(b)) confers broad powers on the courts to regulate or prevent discovery even though the materials sought are within the scope of 26(b), and these powers have always been freely exercised. For example, a party's income tax return is generally held not privileged, 2A Barron & Holtzoff, *Federal Practice and Procedure*, § 651.2 (Wright ed. 1961), and yet courts have recognized that interests in privacy may call for a measure of extra protection. E.g., *Wiesenberger v. W. E. Hutton & Co.*, 35 F.R.D. 556 (S.D.N.Y.1964). Similarly, the courts have in appropriate circumstances protected materials that are primarily of an impeaching character. These two types of materials merely illustrate the many situations, not capable of governance by precise rule, in which courts must exercise judgment. The new subsections in Rule 26(b) do not change existing law with respect to such situations.

Subdivision (b)(1)—In General. The language is changed to provide for the scope of discovery in general terms. The existing subdivision, although in terms applicable only to depositions, is incorporated by reference in existing Rules 33 and 34. Since decisions as to relevance to the subject matter of the action are made for discovery purposes well in advance of trial, a flexible treatment of relevance is required and the making of discovery, whether voluntary or under court order, is not a concession or determination of relevance for purposes of trial. Cf. 4 *Moore's Federal Practice* ¶26–16[1] (2d ed. 1966).

Subdivision (b)(2)—Insurance Policies. Both the cases and commentators are sharply in conflict on the question whether defendant's liability insurance coverage is subject to discovery in the usual situation when the insurance coverage is not itself admissible and does not bear on another issue in the case. Examples of Federal cases requiring disclosure and supporting comments: *Cook v. Welty*, 253 F.Supp. 875 (D.D.C.1966) (cases cited); *Johanek v. Aberle*, 27 F.R.D. 272 (D.Mont.1961); Williams, *Discovery of Dollar Limits in Liability Policies in Automobile Tort Cases*, 10 Ala.L.Rev. 355 (1958); Thode, *Some Reflections on the 1957 Amendments to the Texas Rules*, 37 Tex.L.Rev. 33, 40–42 (1958). Examples of Federal cases refusing disclosure and supporting com-

ments: *Bisserier v. Manning*, 207 F.Supp. 476 (D.N.J.1962); *Cooper v. Stender*, 30 F.R.D. 389 (E.D.Tenn.1962); Frank, *Discovery and Insurance, Coverage*, 1959 Ins.L.J. 281; Fournier, *Pre-trial Discovery of Insurance Coverage and Limits*, 28 Ford.L.Rev. 215 (1959).

The division in reported cases is close. State decisions based on provisions similar to the federal rules are similarly divided. See cases collected in 2A Barron & Holtzoff, *Federal Practice and Procedure* § 647.1, nn. 45.5, 45.6 (Wright ed. 1961). It appears to be difficult if not impossible to obtain appellate review of the issue. Resolution by rule amendment is indicated. The question is essentially procedural in that it bears upon preparation for trial and settlement before trial, and courts confronting the question, however they have decided it, have generally treated it as procedural and governed by the rules.

The amendment resolves this issue in favor of disclosure. Most of the decisions denying discovery, some explicitly, reason from the text of Rule 26(b) that it permits discovery only of matters which will be admissible in evidence or appear reasonably calculated to lead to such evidence; they avoid considerations of policy, regarding them as foreclosed. See *Bisserier v. Manning, supra.* Some note also that facts about a defendant's financial status are not discoverable as such, prior to judgment with execution unsatisfied, and fear that, if courts hold insurance coverage discoverable, they must extend the principle to other aspects of the defendant's financial status. The cases favoring disclosure rely heavily on the practical significance of insurance in the decisions lawyers make about settlement and trial preparation. In *Clauss v. Danker*, 264 F.Supp. 246 (S.D.N.Y.1967), the court held that the rules forbid disclosure but called for an amendment to permit it.

Disclosure of insurance coverage will enable counsel for both sides to make the same realistic appraisal of the case, so that settlement and litigation strategy are based on knowledge and not speculation. It will conduce to settlement and avoid protracted litigation in some cases, though in others it may have an opposite effect. The amendment is limited to insurance coverage, which should be distinguished from any other facts concerning defendant's financial status (1) because insurance is an asset created specifically to satisfy the claim; (2) because the insurance company ordinarily controls the litigation; (3) because information about coverage is available only from defendant or his insurer; and (4) because disclosure does not involve a significant invasion of privacy.

Disclosure is required when the insurer "may be liable" on part or all of the judgment. Thus, an insurance company must disclose even when it contests liability under the policy, and such disclosure does not constitute a waiver of its claim. It is immaterial whether the liability is to satisfy the judgment directly or merely to indemnify or reimburse another after he pays the judgment.

The provision applies only to persons "carrying on an insurance business" and thus covers insurance companies and not the ordinary business concern that enters into a contract of indemnification. *Cf.* N.Y.Ins.Law § 41. Thus, the provision makes no change in existing law on discovery of indemnity agreements other than insurance agreements by persons carrying on an insurance business. Similarly, the provision does not cover the business concern that creates a reserve fund for purposes of self-insurance.

For some purposes other than discovery, an application for insurance is treated as a part of the insurance agreement. The provision makes clear that, for discovery purposes, the application is not to be so treated. The insurance application may contain personal and financial information concerning the insured, discovery of which is beyond the purpose of this provision.

In no instance does disclosure make the facts concerning insurance coverage admissible in evidence.

Subdivision (b)(3)—Trial Preparation: Materials. Some of the most controversial and vexing problems to emerge from the discovery rules have arisen out of requests for the production of documents or things prepared in anticipation of litigation or for trial. The existing rules make no explicit provision for such materials. Yet, two verbally distinct doctrines have developed, each conferring a qualified immunity on these materials—the "good cause" requirement in Rule 34 (now generally held applicable to discovery of documents via deposition under Rule 45 and interrogatories under Rule 33) and the work-product doctrine of *Hickman v. Taylor*, 329 U.S. 495 (1947). Both demand a showing of justification before production can be had, the one of "good cause" and the other variously described in the *Hickman* case: "necessity or justification," "denial * * * would unduly prejudice the preparation of petitioner's case," or "cause hardship or injustice" 329 U.S. at 509–510.

In deciding the *Hickman* case, the Supreme Court appears to have expressed a preference in 1947 for an approach to the problem of trial preparation materials by judicial decision rather than by rule. Sufficient experience has accumulated, however, with lower court applications of the *Hickman* decision to warrant a reappraisal.

The major difficulties visible in the existing case law are (1) confusion and disagreement as to whether "good cause" is made out by a showing of relevance and lack of privilege, or requires an additional showing of necessity, (2) confusion and disagreement as to the scope of the *Hickman* work-product doctrine, particularly whether it extends beyond work actually performed by lawyers, and (3) the resulting difficulty of relating the "good cause" required by Rule 34 and the "necessity or justification" of the work-product doctrine, so that their respective roles and the distinctions between them are understood.

Basic Standard.—Since Rule 34 in terms requires a showing of "good cause" for the production of all documents and things, whether or not trial preparation is involved, courts have felt that a single formula is called for and have differed over whether a showing of relevance and lack of privilege is enough or whether more must be shown. When the facts of the cases are studied, however, a distinction emerges based upon the type of materials. With respect to documents not obtained or prepared with an eye to litigation, the decisions, while not uniform, reflect a strong and increasing tendency to relate "good cause" to a showing that the documents are relevant to the subject matter of the action. *E.g., Connecticut Mutual Life Ins. Co. v. Shields*, 17 F.R.D. 273 (S.D.N.Y. 1959), with cases cited; *Houdry Process Corp. v. Commonwealth Oil Refining Co.*, 24 F.R.D. 58 (S.D.N.Y.1955); see *Bell v. Commercial Ins. Co.*, 280 F.2d 514, 517 (3d Cir. 1960). When the party whose documents are sought shows that the request for production is unduly burdensome or oppressive, courts have denied discovery for lack of "good cause", although they might just as easily have based their decision on

the protective provisions of existing Rule 30(b) (new Rule 26(c)). *E.g., Lauer v. Tankrederi,* 39 F.R.D. 334 (E.D.Pa. 1966).

As to trial-preparation materials, however, the courts are increasingly interpreting "good cause" as requiring more than relevance. When lawyers have prepared or obtained the materials for trial, all courts require more than relevance; so much is clearly commanded by *Hickman.* But even as to the preparatory work of nonlawyers, while some courts ignore work-product and equate "good cause" with relevance, *e.g., Brown v. New York, N.H. & H.R.R.,* 17 F.R.D. 324 (S.D.N.Y.1955), the more recent trend is to read "good cause" as requiring inquiry into the importance of and need for the materials as well as into alternative sources for securing the same information. In *Guilford Nat'l Bank v. Southern Ry.,* 297 F.2d 921 (4th Cir. 1962), statements of witnesses obtained by claim agents were held not discoverable because both parties had had equal access to the witnesses at about the same time, shortly after the collision in question. The decision was based solely on Rule 34 and "good cause"; the court declined to rule on whether the statements were work-products. The court's treatment of "good cause" is quoted at length and with approval in *Schlagenhauf v. Holder,* 379 U.S. 104, 117–118 (1964). See also *Mitchell v. Bass,* 252 F.2d 513 (8th Cir. 1958); *Hauger v. Chicago, R.I. & Pac. R.R.,* 216 F.2d 501 (7th Cir. 1954); *Burke v. United States,* 32 F.R.D. 213 (E.D.N.Y.1963). While the opinions dealing with "good cause" do not often draw an explicit distinction between trial preparation materials and other materials, in fact an overwhelming proportion of the cases in which a special showing is required are cases involving trial preparation materials.

The rules are amended by eliminating the general requirement of "good cause" from Rule 34 but retaining a requirement of a special showing for trial preparation materials in this subdivision. The required showing is expressed, not in terms of "good cause" whose generality has tended to encourage confusion and controversy, but in terms of the elements of the special showing to be made: substantial need of the materials in the preparation of the case and inability without undue hardship to obtain the substantial equivalent of the materials by other means.

These changes conform to the holdings of the cases, when viewed in light of their facts. Apart from trial preparation, the fact that the materials sought are documentary does not in and of itself require a special showing beyond relevance and absence of privilege. The protective provisions are of course available, and if the party from whom production is sought raises a special issue of privacy (as with respect to income tax returns or grand jury minutes) or points to evidence primarily impeaching, or can show serious burden or expense, the court will exercise its traditional power to decide whether to issue a protective order. On the other hand, the requirement of a special showing for discovery of trial preparation materials reflects the view that each side's informal evaluation of its case should be protected, that each side should be encouraged to prepare independently, and that one side should not automatically have the benefit of the detailed preparatory work of the other side. See Field and McKusick, *Maine Civil Practice* 264 (1959).

Elimination of a "good cause" requirement from Rule 34 and the establishment of a requirement of a special showing in this subdivision will eliminate the confusion caused by

having two verbally distinct requirements of justification that the courts have been unable to distinguish clearly. Moreover, the language of the subdivision suggests the factors which the courts should consider in determining whether the requisite showing has been made. The importance of the materials sought to the party seeking them in preparation of his case and the difficulty he will have obtaining them by other means are factors noted in the *Hickman* case. The courts should also consider the likelihood that the party, even if he obtains the information by independent means, will not have the substantial equivalent of the documents the production of which he seeks.

Consideration of these factors may well lead the court to distinguish between witness statements taken by an investigator, on the one hand, and other parts of the investigative file, on the other. The court in *Southern Ry. v. Lanham,* 403 F.2d 119 (5th Cir. 1968), while it naturally addressed itself to the "good cause" requirements of Rule 34, set forth as controlling considerations the factors contained in the language of this subdivision. The analysis of the court suggests circumstances under which witness statements will be discoverable. The witness may have given a fresh and contemporaneous account in a written statement while he is available to the party seeking discovery only a substantial time thereafter. *Lanham, supra* at 127–128; *Guilford, supra* at 926. Or he may be reluctant or hostile. *Lanham, supra* at 128–129; *Brookshire v. Pennsylvania RR,* 14 F.R.D. 154 (N.D.Ohio 1953); *Diamond v. Mohawk Rubber Co.,* 33 F.R.D. 264 (D.Colo.1963). Or he may have a lapse of memory. *Tannenbaum v. Walker,* 16 F.R.D. 570 (E.D.Pa. 1954). Or he may probably be deviating from his prior statement. *Cf. Hauger v. Chicago, R.I. & Pac. RR,* 216 F.2d 501 (7th Cir. 1954). On the other hand, a much stronger showing is needed to obtain evaluative materials in an investigator's reports. *Lanham, supra* at 131–133; *Pickett v. L. R. Ryan, Inc.,* 237 F.Supp. 198 (E.D.S.C.1965).

Materials assembled in the ordinary course of business, or pursuant to public requirements unrelated to litigation, or for other nonlitigation purposes are not under the qualified immunity provided by this subdivision. *Goosman v. A. Duie Pyle, Inc.,* 320 F.2d 45 (4th Cir. 1963); *cf. United States v. New York Foreign Trade Zone Operators, Inc.,* 304 F.2d 792 (2d Cir. 1962). No change is made in the existing doctrine, noted in the *Hickman* case, that one party may discover relevant facts known or available to the other party, even though such facts are contained in a document which is not itself discoverable.

Treatment of Lawyers; Special Protection of Mental Impressions, Conclusions, Opinions, and Legal Theories Concerning the Litigation.—The courts are divided as to whether the work-product doctrine extends to the preparatory work only of lawyers. The *Hickman* case left this issue open since the statements in that case were taken by a lawyer. As to courts of appeals compare *Alltmont v. United States,* 177 F.2d 971, 976 (3d Cir. 1949), cert. denied, 339 U.S. 967 (1950) (*Hickman* applied to statements obtained by FBI agents on theory it should apply to "all statements of prospective witnesses which a party has obtained for his trial counsel's use"), with *Southern Ry. v. Campbell,* 309 F.2d 569 (5th Cir. 1962) (Statements taken by claim agents not work-product), and *Guilford Nat'l Bank v. Southern Ry.,* 297 F.2d 921 (4th Cir. 1962) (avoiding issue of work-product as to claim agents, deciding case instead under Rule 34 "good

cause"). Similarly, the district courts are divided on statements obtained by claim agents, compare, e.g., *Brown v. New York, N.H. & H.R.R.*, 17 F.R.D. 324 (S.D.N.Y.1955) with *Hanke v. Milwaukee Electric Ry. & Transp. Co.*, 7 F.R.D. 540 (E.D.Wis.1947); investigators, compare *Burke v. United States*, 32 F.R.D. 213 (E.D.N.Y.1963) with *Snyder v. United States*, 20 F.R.D. 7 (E.D.N.Y.1956); and insurers, compare *Gottlieb v. Bresler*, 24 F.R.D. 371 (D.D.C.1959) with *Burns v. Mulder*, 20 F.R.D. 605 (E.D.Pa.1957). See 4 Moore's *Federal Practice* ¶26.23[8.1] (2d ed. 1966); 2A Barron & Holtzoff, *Federal Practice and Procedure* § 652.2 (Wright ed. 1961).

A complication is introduced by the use made by courts of the "good cause" requirement of Rule 34, as described above. A court may conclude that trial preparation materials are not work-product because not the result of lawyer's work and yet hold that they are not producible because "good cause" has not been shown. *Cf. Guilford Nat'l Bank v. Southern Ry.*, 297 F.2d 921 (4th Cir. 1962), cited and described above. When the decisions on "good cause" are taken into account, the weight of authority affords protection of the preparatory work of both lawyers and nonlawyers (though not necessarily to the same extent) by requiring more than a showing of relevance to secure production.

Subdivision (b)(3) reflects the trend of the cases by requiring a special showing, not merely as to materials prepared by an attorney, but also as to materials prepared in anticipation of litigation or preparation for trial by or for a party or any representative acting on his behalf. The subdivision then goes on to protect against disclosure the mental impressions, conclusions, opinions, or legal theories concerning the litigation of an attorney or other representative of a party. The *Hickman* opinion drew special attention to the need for protecting an attorney against discovery of memoranda prepared from recollection of oral interviews. The courts have steadfastly safeguarded against disclosure of lawyers' mental impressions and legal theories, as well as mental impressions and subjective evaluations of investigators and claim-agents. In enforcing this provision of the subdivision, the courts will sometimes find it necessary to order disclosure of a document but with portions deleted.

Rules 33 and 36 have been revised in order to permit discovery calling for opinions, contentions, and admissions relating not only to fact but also to the application of law to fact. Under those rules, a party and his attorney or other representative may be required to disclose, to some extent, mental impressions, opinions, or conclusions. But documents or parts of documents containing these matters are protected against discovery by this subdivision. Even though a party may ultimately have to disclose in response to interrogatories or requests to admit, he is entitled to keep confidential documents containing such matters prepared for internal use.

Party's Right to Own Statement—An exception to the requirement of this subdivision enables a party to secure production of his own statement without any special showing. The cases are divided. Compare, *e.g., Safeway Stores, Inc. v. Reynolds*, 176 F.2d 476 (D.C. Cir.1949); *Shupe v. Pennsylvania R.R.*, 19 F.R.D. 144 (W.D.Pa.1956); with *e.g., New York Central R.R. v. Carr*, 251 F.2d 433 (4th Cir. 1957); *Belback v. Wilson Freight Forwarding Co.*, 40 F.R.D. 16 (W.D.Pa.1966).

Courts which treat a party's statement as though it were that of any witness overlook the fact that the party's state-

ment is, without more, admissible in evidence. Ordinarily, a party gives a statement without insisting on a copy because he does not yet have a lawyer and does not understand the legal consequences of his actions. Thus, the statement is given at a time when he functions at a disadvantage. Discrepancies between his trial testimony and earlier statement may result from lapse of memory or ordinary inaccuracy; a written statement produced for the first time at trial may give such discrepancies a prominence which they do not deserve. In appropriate cases the court may order a party to be deposed before his statement is produced. *E.g., Smith v. Central Linen Service Co.*, 39 F.R.D. 15 (D.Md.1966); *McCoy v. General Motors Corp.*, 33 F.R.D. 354 (W.D.Pa. 1963).

Commentators strongly support the view that a party be able to secure his statement without a showing. 4 *Moore's Federal Practice* ¶26.23[8.4] (2d ed. 1966); 2A Barron & Holtzoff, *Federal Practice and Procedure* § 652.3 (Wright ed. 1961); see also Note, *Developments in the Law—Discovery*, 74 Harv.L.Rev. 940, 1039 (1961). The following states have by statute or rule taken the same position: *Statutes:* Fla.Stat.Ann. § 92.33; Ga.Code Ann. § 38–2109(b); La.Stat. Ann.R.S. 13:3732; Mass.Gen.Laws Ann. c. 271, § 44; Minn. Stat.Ann. § 602.01; N.Y.C.P.L.R. § 3101(e); *Rules:* Mo. R.C.P. 56.01(a); N.Dak.R.C.P. 34(b); Wyo.R.C.P. 34(b); *cf.* Mich.G.C.R. 306.2.

In order to clarify and tighten the provision on statements by a party, the term "statement" is defined. The definition is adapted from 18 U.S.C. § 3500(e) (Jencks Act). The statement of a party may of course be that of plaintiff or defendant, and it may be that of an individual or of a corporation or other organization.

Witness' Right to Own Statement.—A second exception to the requirement of this subdivision permits a non-party witness to obtain a copy of his own statement without any special showing. Many, though not all, of the considerations supporting a party's right to obtain his statement apply also to the non-party witness. Insurance companies are increasingly recognizing that a witness is entitled to a copy of his statement and are modifying their regular practice accordingly.

Subdivision (b)(4)—Trial Preparation: Experts. This is a new provision dealing with discovery of information (including facts and opinions) obtained by a party from an expert retained by that party in relation to litigation or obtained by the expert and not yet transmitted to the party. The subdivision deals separately with those experts whom the party expects to call as trial witnesses and with those experts who have been retained or specially employed by the party but who are not expected to be witnesses. It should be noted that the subdivision does not address itself to the expert whose information was not acquired in preparation for trial but rather because he was an actor or viewer with respect to transactions or occurrences that are part of the subject matter of the lawsuit. Such an expert should be treated as an ordinary witness.

Subsection (b)(4)(A) deals with discovery of information obtained by or through experts who will be called as witnesses at trial. The provision is responsive to problems suggested by a relatively recent line of authorities. Many of these cases present intricate and difficult issues as to which expert testimony is likely to be determinative. Prominent

among them are food and drug, patent, and condemnation cases. See, *e.g., United States v. Nysco Laboratories, Inc.,* 26 F.R.D. 159, 162 (E.D.N.Y.1960) (food and drug); *E. I. du Pont de Nemours & Co. v. Phillips Petroleum Co.,* 24 F.R.D. 416, 421 (D.Del.1959) (patent); *Cold Metal Process Co. v. Aluminum Co. of America,* 7 F.R.D. 425 (N.D.Ohio 1947), aff'd, *Sachs v. Aluminum Co. of America,* 167 F.2d 570 (6th Cir. 1948) (same); *United States v. 50.34 Acres of Land,* 13 F.R.D. 19 (E.D.N.Y.1952) (condemnation).

In cases of this character, a prohibition against discovery of information held by expert witnesses produces in acute form the very evils that discovery has been created to prevent. Effective cross-examination of an expert witness requires advance preparation. The lawyer even with the help of his own experts frequently cannot anticipate the particular approach his adversary's expert will take or the data on which he will base his judgment on the stand. McGlothlin, *Some Practical Problems in Proof of Economic, Scientific, and Technical Facts,* 23 F.R.D. 467, 478 (1958). A California study of discovery and pretrial in condemnation cases notes that the only substitute for discovery of experts' valuation materials is "lengthy—and often fruitless—cross-examination during trial," and recommends pretrial exchange of such material. Calif.Law Rev.Comm'n, Discovery in Eminent Domain Proceedings 707–710 (Jan. 1963). Similarly, effective rebuttal requires advance knowledge of the line of testimony of the other side. If the latter is foreclosed by a rule against discovery, then the narrowing of issues and elimination of surprise which discovery normally produces are frustrated.

These considerations appear to account for the broadening of discovery against experts in the cases cited where expert testimony was central to the case. In some instances, the opinions are explicit in relating expanded discovery to improved cross-examination and rebuttal at trial. *Franks v. National Dairy Products Corp.,* 41 F.R.D. 234 (W.D.Tex. 1966); *United States v. 23.76 Acres,* 32 F.R.D. 593 (D.Md. 1963); see also an unpublished opinion of Judge Hincks, quoted in *United States v. 48 Jars, etc.,* 23 F.R.D. 192, 198 (D.D.C.1958). On the other hand, the need for a new provision is shown by the many cases in which discovery of expert trial witnesses is needed for effective cross-examination and rebuttal, and yet courts apply the traditional doctrine and refuse disclosure. *E.g., United States v. Certain Parcels of Land,* 25 F.R.D. 192 (N.D.Cal.1959); *United States v. Certain Acres,* 18 F.R.D. 98 (M.D.Ga.1955).

Although the trial problems flowing from lack of discovery of expert witnesses are most acute and noteworthy when the case turns largely on experts, the same problems are encountered when a single expert testifies. Thus, subdivision (b)(4)(A) draws no line between complex and simple cases, or between cases with many experts and those with but one. It establishes by rule substantially the procedure adopted by decision of the court in *Knighton v. Villian & Fassio,* 39 F.R.D. 11 (D.Md.1965). For a full analysis of the problem and strong recommendations to the same effect, see Friedenthal, *Discovery and Use of an Adverse Party's Expert Information,* 14 Stan.L.Rev. 455, 485–488 (1962); Long, *Discovery and Experts under the Federal Rules of Civil Procedure,* 38 F.R.D. 111 (1965).

Past judicial restrictions on discovery of an adversary's expert, particularly as to his opinions, reflect the fear that one side will benefit unduly from the other's better prepara-

tion. The procedure established in subsection (b)(4)(A) holds the risk to a minimum. Discovery is limited to trial witnesses, and may be obtained only at a time when the parties know who their expert witnesses will be. A party must as a practical matter prepare his own case in advance of that time, for he can hardly hope to build his case out of his opponent's experts.

Subdivision (b)(4)(A) provides for discovery of an expert who is to testify at the trial. A party can require one who intends to use the expert to state the substance of the testimony that the expert is expected to give. The court may order further discovery, and it has ample power to regulate its timing and scope and to prevent abuse. Ordinarily, the order for further discovery shall compensate the expert for his time, and may compensate the party who intends to use the expert for past expenses reasonably incurred in obtaining facts or opinions from the expert. Those provisions are likely to discourage abusive practices.

Subdivision (b)(4)(B) deals with an expert who has been retained or specially employed by the party in anticipation of litigation or preparation for trial (thus excluding an expert who is simply a general employee of the party not specially employed on the case), but who is not expected to be called as a witness. Under its provisions, a party may discover facts known or opinions held by such an expert only on a showing of exceptional circumstances under which it is impracticable for the party seeking discovery to obtain facts or opinions on the same subject by other means.

Subdivision (b)(4)(B) is concerned only with experts retained or specially consulted in relation to trial preparation. Thus the subdivision precludes discovery against experts who were informally consulted in preparation for trial, but not retained or specially employed. As an ancillary procedure, a party may on a proper showing require the other party to name experts retained or specially employed, but not those informally consulted.

These new provisions of subdivision (b)(4) repudiate the few decisions that have held an expert's information privileged simply because of his status as an expert, *e.g., American Oil Co. v. Pennsylvania Petroleum Products Co.,* 23 F.R.D. 680, 685–686 (D.R.I.1959). See *Louisell, Modern California Discovery* 315–316 (1963). They also reject as ill-considered the decisions which have sought to bring expert information within the work-product doctrine. See *United States v. McKay,* 372 F.2d 174, 176–177 (5th Cir. 1967). The provisions adopt a form of the more recently developed doctrine of "unfairness". See *e.g., United States v. 23.76 Acres of Land,* 32 F.R.D. 593, 597 (D.Md.1963); Louisell, *supra,* at 317–318; 4 *Moore's Federal Practice* 26.24 (2d ed. 1966).

Under subdivision (b)(4)(C), the court is directed or authorized to issue protective orders, including an order that the expert be paid a reasonable fee for time spent in responding to discovery, and that the party whose expert is made subject to discovery be paid a fair portion of the fees and expenses that the party incurred in obtaining information from the expert. The court may issue the latter order as a condition of discovery, or it may delay the order until after discovery is completed. These provisions for fees and expenses meet the objection that it is unfair to permit one side to obtain without cost the benefit of an expert's work for which the other side has paid, often a substantial sum. E.g., *Lewis v. United Air Lines Transp. Corp.,* 32 F.Supp. 21

(W.D.Pa.1940); *Walsh v. Reynolds Metal Co.*, 15 F.R.D. 376 (D.N.J.1954). On the other hand, a party may not obtain discovery simply by offering to pay fees and expenses. Cf. *Boynton v. R. J. Reynolds Tobacco Co.*, 36 F.Supp. 593 (D.Mass.1941).

In instances of discovery under subdivision (b)(4)(B), the court is directed to award fees and expenses to the other party, since the information is of direct value to the discovering party's preparation of his case. In ordering discovery under (b)(4)(A)(ii), the court has discretion whether to award fees and expenses to the other party; its decision should depend upon whether the discovering party is simply learning about the other party's case or is going beyond this to develop his own case. Even in cases where the court is directed to issue a protective order, it may decline to do so if it finds that manifest injustice would result. Thus, the court can protect, when necessary and appropriate, the interests of an indigent party.

Subdivision (c)—Protective Orders. The provisions of existing Rule 30(b) are transferred to this subdivision (c), as part of the rearrangement of Rule 26. The language has been changed to give it application to discovery generally. The subdivision recognizes the power of the court in the district where a deposition is being taken to make protective orders. Such power is needed when the deposition is being taken far from the court where the action is pending. The court in the district where the deposition is being taken may, and frequently will, remit the deponent or party to the court where the action is pending.

In addition, drafting changes are made to carry out and clarify the sense of the rule. Insertions are made to avoid any possible implication that a protective order does not extend to "time" as well as to "place" or may not safeguard against "undue burden or expense."

The new reference to trade secrets and other confidential commercial information reflects existing law. The courts have not given trade secrets automatic and complete immunity against disclosure, but have in each case weighed their claim to privacy against the need for disclosure. Frequently, they have been afforded a limited protection. See, *e.g.*, *Covey Oil Co. v. Continental Oil Co.*, 340 F.2d 993 (10th Cir. 1965); *Julius M. Ames Co. v. Bostitch, Inc.*, 235 F.Supp. 856 (S.D.N.Y.1964).

The subdivision contains new matter relating to sanctions. When a motion for a protective order is made and the court is disposed to deny it, the court may go a step further and issue an order to provide or permit discovery. This will bring the sanctions of Rule 37(b) directly into play. Since the court has heard the contentions of all interested persons, an affirmative order is justified. See *Rosenberg, Sanctions to Effectuate Pretrial Discovery*, 58 Col.L.Rev. 480, 492–493 (1958). In addition, the court may require the payment of expenses incurred in relation to the motion.

Subdivision (d)—Sequence and Priority. This new provision is concerned with the sequence in which parties may proceed with discovery and with related problems of timing. The principal effects of the new provision are first, to eliminate any fixed priority in the sequence of discovery, and second, to make clear and explicit the court's power to establish priority by an order issued in a particular case.

A priority rule developed by some courts, which confers priority on the party who first serves notice of taking a deposition, is unsatisfactory in several important respects:

First, this priority rule permits a party to establish a priority running to all depositions as to which he has given earlier notice. Since he can on a given day serve notice of taking many depositions he is in a position to delay his adversary's taking of depositions for an inordinate time. Some courts have ruled that deposition priority also permits a party to delay his answers to interrogatories and production of documents. *E.g.*, *E. I. du Pont de Nemours & Co. v. Phillips Petroleum Co.*, 23 F.R.D. 237 (D.Del.1959); *but cf. Sturdevant v. Sears, Roebuck & Co.*, 32 F.R.D. 426 (W.D.Mo. 1963).

Second, since notice is the key to priority, if both parties wish to take depositions first a race results. See *Caldwell-Clements, Inc. v. McGraw-Hill Pub. Co.*, 11 F.R.D. 156 (S.D.N.Y.1951) (description of tactics used by parties). But the existing rules on notice of deposition create a race with runners starting from different positions. The plaintiff may not give notice without leave of court until 20 days after commencement of the action, whereas the defendant may serve notice at any time after commencement. Thus, a careful and prompt defendant can almost always secure priority. This advantage of defendants is fortuitous, because the purpose of requiring plaintiff to wait 20 days is to afford defendant an opportunity to obtain counsel, not to confer priority.

Third, although courts have ordered a change in the normal sequence of discovery on a number of occasions, *e.g.*, *Kaeppler v. James H. Matthews & Co.*, 200 F.Supp. 229 (E.D.Pa.1961); *Park & Tilford Distillers Corp. v. Distillers Co.*, 19 F.R.D. 169 (S.D.N.Y.1956), and have at all times avowed discretion to vary the usual priority, most commentators are agreed that courts in fact grant relief only for "the most obviously compelling reasons." 2A Barron & Holtzoff, *Federal Practice and Procedure* 44–47 (Wright ed. 1961); see also Younger, *Priority of Pretrial Examination in the Federal Courts—A Comment*, 34 N.Y.U.L.Rev. 1271 (1959); Freund, *The Pleading and Pretrial of an Antitrust Claim*, 46 Corn.L.Q. 555, 564 (1964). Discontent with the fairness of actual practice has been evinced by other observers. Comments, 59 Yale L.J. 117, 134–136 (1949); Yudkin, *Some Refinements in Federal Discovery Procedure*, 11 Fed.B.J. 289, 296–297 (1951); *Developments in the Law-Discovery*, 74 Harv.L.Rev. 940, 954–958 (1961).

Despite these difficulties, some courts have adhered to the priority rule, presumably because it provides a test which is easily understood and applied by the parties without much court intervention. It thus permits deposition discovery to function extrajudicially, which the rules provide for and the courts desire. For these same reasons, courts are reluctant to make numerous exceptions to the rule.

The Columbia Survey makes clear that the problem of priority does not affect litigants generally. It found that most litigants do not move quickly to obtain discovery. In over half of the cases, both parties waited at least 50 days. During the first 20 days after commencement of the action— the period when defendant might assure his priority by noticing depositions—16 percent of the defendants acted to obtain discovery. A race could not have occurred in more than 16 percent of the cases and it undoubtedly occurred in fewer. On the other hand, five times as many defendants as

plaintiffs served notice of deposition during the first 19 days. To the same effect, see Comment, *Tactical Use and Abuse of Depositions Under the Federal Rules*, 59 Yale L.J. 117, 134 (1949).

These findings do not mean, however, that the priority rule is satisfactory or that a problem of priority does not exist. The court decisions show that parties do battle on this issue and carry their disputes to court. The statistics show that these court cases are not typical. By the same token, they reveal that more extensive exercise of judicial discretion to vary the priority will not bring a flood of litigation, and that a change in the priority rule will in fact affect only a small fraction of the cases.

It is contended by some that there is no need to alter the existing priority practice. In support, it is urged that there is no evidence that injustices in fact result from present practice and that, in any event, the courts can and do promulgate local rules, as in New York, to deal with local situations and issue orders to avoid possible injustice in particular cases.

Subdivision (d) is based on the contrary view that the rule of priority based on notice is unsatisfactory and unfair in its operation. Subdivision (d) follows an approach adapted from Civil Rule 4 of the District Court for the Southern District of New York. That rule provides that starting 40 days after commencement of the action, unless otherwise ordered by the court, the fact that one party is taking a deposition shall not prevent another party from doing so "concurrently." In practice, the depositions are not usually taken simultaneously; rather, the parties work out arrangements for alternation in the taking of depositions. One party may take a complete deposition and then the other, or, if the depositions are extensive, one party deposes for a set time, and then the other. See *Caldwell-Clements, Inc. v. McCraw-Hill Pub. Co.*, 11 F.R.D. 156 (S.D.N.Y.1951).

In principle, one party's initiation of discovery should not wait upon the other's completion, unless delay is dictated by special considerations. Clearly the principle is feasible with respect to all methods of discovery other than depositions. And the experience of the Southern District of New York shows that the principle can be applied to depositions as well. The courts have not had an increase in motion business on this matter. Once it is clear to lawyers that they bargain on an equal footing, they are usually able to arrange for an orderly succession of depositions without judicial intervention. Professor Moore has called attention to Civil Rule 4 and suggested that it may usefully be extended to other areas. 4 *Moore's Federal Practice* 1154 (2d ed. 1966).

The court may upon motion and by order grant priority in a particular case. But a local court rule purporting to confer priority in certain classes of cases would be inconsistent with this subdivision and thus void.

Subdivision (e)—Supplementation of Responses. The rules do not now state whether interrogatories (and questions at deposition as well as requests for inspection and admissions) impose a "continuing burden" on the responding party to supplement his answers if he obtains new information. The issue is acute when new information renders substantially incomplete or inaccurate an answer which was complete and accurate when made. It is essential that the rules provide an answer to this question. The parties can adjust to a rule either way, once they know what it is. See 4 *Moore's Federal Practice* ¶33.25[4] (2d ed. 1966).

Arguments can be made both ways. Imposition of a continuing burden reduces the proliferation of additional sets of interrogatories. Some courts have adopted local rules establishing such a burden. *E.g.*, E.D.Pa.R. 20(f), quoted in *Taggart v. Vermont Transp. Co.*, 32 F.R.D. 587 (E.D.Pa. 1963); D.Me.R. 15(c). Others have imposed the burden by decision. *E.g., Chenault v. Nebraska Farm Products, Inc.*, 9 F.R.D. 529, 533 (D.Nebr.1949). On the other hand, there are serious objections to the burden, especially in protracted cases. Although the party signs the answers, it is his lawyer who understands their significance and bears the responsibility to bring answers up to date. In a complex case all sorts of information reaches the party, who little understands its bearing on answers previously given to interrogatories. In practice, therefore, the lawyer under a continuing burden must periodically recheck all interrogatories and canvass all new information. But a full set of new answers may no longer be needed by the interrogating party. Some issues will have been dropped from the case, some questions are now seen as unimportant, and other questions must in any event be reformulated. See *Novick v. Pennsylvania R.R.*, 18 F.R.D. 296, 298 (W.D.Pa.1955).

Subdivision (e) provides that a party is not under a continuing burden except as expressly provided. Cf. Note, 68 Harv.L.Rev. 673, 677 (1955). An exception is made as to the identity of persons having knowledge of discoverable matters, because of the obvious importance to each side of knowing all witnesses and because information about witnesses routinely comes to each lawyer's attention. Many of the decisions on the issue of a continuing burden have in fact concerned the identity of witnesses. An exception is also made as to expert trial witnesses in order to carry out the provisions of Rule 26(b)(4). See *Diversified Products Corp. v. Sports Center Co.*, 42 F.R.D. 3 (D.Md.1967).

Another exception is made for the situation in which a party, or more frequently his lawyer, obtains actual knowledge that a prior response is incorrect. This exception does not impose a duty to check the accuracy of prior responses, but it prevents knowing concealment by a party or attorney. Finally, a duty to supplement may be imposed by order of the court in a particular case (including an order resulting from a pretrial conference) or by agreement of the parties. A party may of course make a new discovery request which requires supplementation of prior responses.

The duty will normally be enforced, in those limited instances where it is imposed, through sanctions imposed by the trial court, including exclusion of evidence, continuance, or other action, as the court may deem appropriate.

1980 Amendment

Subdivision (f). This subdivision is new. There has been widespread criticism of abuse of discovery. The Committee has considered a number of proposals to eliminate abuse, including a change in Rule 26(b)(1) with respect to the scope of discovery and a change in Rule 33(a) to limit the number of questions that can be asked by interrogatories to parties.

The Committee believes that abuse of discovery, while very serious in certain cases, is not so general as to require such basic changes in the rules that govern discovery in all cases. A very recent study of discovery in selected metropolitan districts tends to support its belief. P. Connolly, E.

Holleman, & M. Kuhlman, *Judicial Controls and the Civil Litigative Process: Discovery* (Federal Judicial Center, 1978). In the judgment of the Committee abuse can best be prevented by intervention by the court as soon as abuse is threatened.

To this end this subdivision provides that counsel who has attempted without success to effect with opposing counsel a reasonable program or plan for discovery is entitled to the assistance of the court.

It is not contemplated that requests for discovery conferences will be made routinely. A relatively narrow discovery dispute should be resolved by resort to Rules 26(c) or 37(a), and if it appears that a request for a conference is in fact grounded in such a dispute, the court may refer counsel to those rules. If the court is persuaded that a request is frivolous or vexatious, it can strike it. See Rules 11 and 7(b)(2).

A number of courts routinely consider discovery matters in preliminary pretrial conferences held shortly after the pleadings are closed. This subdivision does not interfere with such a practice. It authorizes the court to combine a discovery conference with a pretrial conference under Rule 16 if a pretrial conference is held sufficiently early to prevent or curb abuse.

1983 Amendment

Excessive discovery and evasion or resistance to reasonable discovery requests pose significant problems. Recent studies have made some attempt to determine the sources and extent of the difficulties. See Brazil, *Civil Discovery: Lawyers' Views of its Effectiveness, Principal Problems and Abuses*, American Bar Foundation (1980); Connolly, Holleman & Kuhlman, *Judicial Controls and the Civil Litigative Process: Discovery*, Federal Judicial Center (1978); Ellington, *A Study of Sanctions for Discovery Abuse*, Department of Justice (1979); Schroeder & Frank, *The Proposed Changes in the Discovery Rules*, 1978 Ariz.St.L.J. 475.

The purpose of discovery is to provide a mechanism for making relevant information available to the litigants. "Mutual knowledge of all the relevant facts gathered by both parties is essential to proper litigation." *Hickman v. Taylor*, 329 U.S. 495, 507 (1947). Thus the spirit of the rules is violated when advocates attempt to use discovery tools as tactical weapons rather than to expose the facts and illuminate the issues by overuse of discovery or unnecessary use of defensive weapons or evasive responses. All of this results in excessively costly and time-consuming activities that are disproportionate to the nature of the case, the amount involved, or the issues or values at stake.

Given our adversary tradition and the current discovery rules, it is not surprising that there are many opportunities, if not incentives, for attorneys to engage in discovery that, although authorized by the broad, permissive terms of the rules, nevertheless results in delay. See Brazil, *The Adversary Character of Civil Discovery: A Critique and Proposals for Change*, 31 Vand.L.Rev. 1259 (1978). As a result, it has been said that the rules have "not infrequently [been] exploited to the disadvantage of justice." *Herbert v. Lando*, 441 U.S. 153, 179 (1979) (Powell, J., concurring). These practices impose costs on an already overburdened system and impede the fundamental goal of the "just, speedy, and inexpensive determination of every action." Fed.R.Civ.P. 1.

Subdivision (a); Discovery Methods. The deletion of the last sentence of Rule 26(a)(1), which provided that unless the court ordered otherwise under Rule 26(c) "the frequency of use" of the various discovery methods was not to be limited, is an attempt to address the problem of duplicative, redundant, and excessive discovery and to reduce it. The amendment, in conjunction with the changes in Rule 26(b)(1), is designed to encourage district judges to identify instances of needless discovery and to limit the use of the various discovery devices accordingly. The question may be raised by one of the parties, typically on a motion for a protective order, or by the court on its own initiative. It is entirely appropriate to consider a limitation on the frequency of use of discovery at a discovery conference under Rule 26(f) or at any other pretrial conference authorized by these rules. In considering the discovery needs of a particular case, the court should consider the factors described in Rule 26(b)(1).

Subdivision (b); Discovery Scope and Limits. Rule 26(b)(1) has been amended to add a sentence to deal with the problem of over-discovery. The objective is to guard against redundant or disproportionate discovery by giving the court authority to reduce the amount of discovery that may be directed to matters that are otherwise proper subjects of inquiry. The new sentence is intended to encourage judges to be more aggressive in identifying and discouraging discovery overuse. The grounds mentioned in the amended rule for limiting discovery reflect the existing practice of many courts in issuing protective orders under Rule 26(c). See, e.g., *Carlson Cos. v. Sperry & Hutchinson Co.*, 374 F.Supp. 1080 (D.Minn.1974); *Dolgow v. Anderson*, 53 F.R.D. 661 (E.D.N.Y.1971); *Mitchell v. American Tobacco Co.*, 33 F.R.D. 262 (M.D.Pa.1963); *Welty v. Clute*, 1 F.R.D. 446 (W.D.N.Y.1941). On the whole, however, district judges have been reluctant to limit the use of the discovery devices. See, e.g., *Apco Oil Co. v. Certified Transp., Inc.*, 46 F.R.D. 428 (W.D.Mo.1969). See generally 8 Wright & Miller, *Federal Practice and Procedure: Civil* §§ 2036, 2037, 2039, 2040 (1970).

The first element of the standard, Rule 26(b)(1)(i), is designed to minimize redundancy in discovery and encourage attorneys to be sensitive to the comparative costs of different methods of securing information. Subdivision (b)(1)(ii) also seeks to reduce repetitiveness and to oblige lawyers to think through their discovery activities in advance so that full utilization is made of each deposition, document request, or set of interrogatories. The elements of Rule 26(b)(1)(iii) address the problem of discovery that is disproportionate to the individual lawsuit as measured by such matters as its nature and complexity, the importance of the issues at stake in a case seeking damages, the limitations on a financially weak litigant to withstand extensive opposition to a discovery program or to respond to discovery requests, and the significance of the substantive issues, as measured in philosophic, social, or institutional terms. Thus the rule recognizes that many cases in public policy spheres, such as employment practices, free speech, and other matters, may have importance far beyond the monetary amount involved. The court must apply the standards in an even-handed manner that will prevent use of discovery to wage a war of attrition or as a device to coerce a party, whether financially weak or affluent.

The rule contemplates greater judicial involvement in the discovery process and thus acknowledges the reality that it cannot always operate on a self-regulating basis. See Con-

nolly, Holleman & Kuhlman, *Judicial Controls and the Civil Litigative Process: Discovery* 77, Federal Judicial Center (1978). In an appropriate case the court could restrict the number of depositions, interrogatories, or the scope of a production request. But the court must be careful not to deprive a party of discovery that is reasonably necessary to afford a fair opportunity to develop and prepare the case.

The court may act on motion, or its own initiative. It is entirely appropriate to resort to the amended rule in conjunction with a discovery conference under Rule 26(f) or one of the other pretrial conferences authorized by the rules.

Subdivision (g); Signing of Discovery Requests, Responses, and Objections. Rule 26(g) imposes an affirmative duty to engage in pretrial discovery in a responsible manner that is consistent with the spirit and purposes of Rules 26 through 37. In addition, Rule 26(g) is designed to curb discovery abuse by explicitly encouraging the imposition of sanctions. The subdivision provides a deterrent to both excessive discovery and evasion by imposing a certification requirement that obliges each attorney to stop and think about the legitimacy of a discovery request, a response thereto, or an objection. The term "response" includes answers to interrogatories and to requests to admit as well as responses to production requests.

If primary responsibility for conducting discovery is to continue to rest with the litigants, they must be obliged to act responsibly and avoid abuse. With this in mind, Rule 26(g), which parallels the amendments to Rule 11, requires an attorney or unrepresented party to sign each discovery request, response, or objection. Motions relating to discovery are governed by Rule 11. However, since a discovery request, response, or objection usually deals with more specific subject matter than motions or papers, the elements that must be certified in connection with the former are spelled out more completely. The signature is a certification of the elements set forth in Rule 26(g).

Although the certification duty requires the lawyer to pause and consider the reasonableness of his request, response, or objection, it is not meant to discourage or restrict necessary and legitimate discovery. The rule simply requires that the attorney make a reasonable inquiry into the factual basis of his response, request, or objection.

The duty to make a "reasonable inquiry" is satisfied if the investigation undertaken by the attorney and the conclusions drawn therefrom are reasonable under the circumstances. It is an objective standard similar to the one imposed by Rule 11. See the Advisory Committee Note to Rule 11. See also *Kinee v. Abraham Lincoln Fed. Sav. & Loan Ass'n*, 365 F.Supp. 975 (E.D.Pa.1973). In making the inquiry, the attorney may rely on assertions by the client and on communications with other counsel in the case as long as that reliance is appropriate under the circumstances. Ultimately, what is reasonable is a matter for the court to decide on the totality of the circumstances.

Rule 26(g) does not require the signing attorney to certify the truthfulness of the client's factual responses to a discovery request. Rather, the signature certifies that the lawyer has made a reasonable effort to assure that the client has provided all the information and documents available to him that are responsive to the discovery demand. Thus, the lawyer's certification under Rule 26(g) should be distinguished from other signature requirements in the rules, such as those in Rules 30(e) and 33.

Nor does the rule require a party or an attorney to disclose privileged communications or work product in order to show that a discovery request, response, or objection is substantially justified. The provisions of Rule 26(c), including appropriate orders after *in camera* inspection by the court, remain available to protect a party claiming privilege or work product protection.

The signing requirement means that every discovery request, response, or objection should be grounded on a theory that is reasonable under the precedents or a good faith belief as to what should be the law. This standard is heavily dependent on the circumstances of each case. The certification speaks as of the time it is made. The duty to supplement discovery responses continues to be governed by Rule 26(e).

Concern about discovery abuse has led to widespread recognition that there is a need for more aggressive judicial control and supervision. *ACF Industries, Inc. v. EEOC*, 439 U.S. 1081 (1979) (certiorari denied) (Powell, J., dissenting). Sanctions to deter discovery abuse would be more effective if they were diligently applied "not merely to penalize those whose conduct may be deemed to warrant such a sanction, but to deter those who might be tempted to such conduct in the absence of such a deterrent." *National Hockey League v. Metropolitan Hockey Club*, 427 U.S. 639, 643 (1976). See also Note, *The Emerging Deterrence Orientation in the Imposition of Discovery Sanctions*, 91 Harv.L.Rev. 1033 (1978). Thus the premise of Rule 26(g) is that imposing sanctions on attorneys who fail to meet the rule's standards will significantly reduce abuse by imposing disadvantages therefor.

Because of the asserted reluctance to impose sanctions on attorneys who abuse the discovery rules, see Brazil, *Civil Discovery: Lawyers' Views of its Effectiveness, Principal Problems and Abuses*, American Bar Foundation (1980); Ellington, *A Study of Sanctions for Discovery Abuse*, Department of Justice (1979), Rule 26(g) makes explicit the authority judges now have to impose appropriate sanctions and requires them to use it. This authority derives from Rule 37, 28 U.S.C. § 1927, and the court's inherent power. See *Roadway Express, Inc. v. Piper*, 447 U.S. 752 (1980); *Martin v. Bell Helicopter Co.*, 85 F.R.D. 654, 661–62 (D.Col. 1980); Note, *Sanctions Imposed by Courts on Attorneys Who Abuse the Judicial Process*, 44 U.Chi.L.Rev. 619 (1977). The new rule mandates that sanctions be imposed on attorneys who fail to meet the standards established in the first portion of Rule 26(g). The nature of the sanction is a matter of judicial discretion to be exercised in light of the particular circumstances. The court may take into account any failure by the party seeking sanctions to invoke protection under Rule 26(c) at an early stage in the litigation.

The sanctioning process must comport with due process requirements. The kind of notice and hearing required will depend on the facts of the case and the severity of the sanction being considered. To prevent the proliferation of the sanction procedure and to avoid multiple hearings, discovery in any sanction proceeding normally should be permitted only when it is clearly required by the interests of justice. In most cases the court will be aware of the circumstances and only a brief hearing should be necessary.

Complete Annotation Materials, see Title 28 U.S.C.A.

1987 Amendment

The amendments are technical. No substantive change is intended.

1993 Amendments

Subdivision (a). Through the addition of paragraphs (1)–(4), this subdivision imposes on parties a duty to disclose, without awaiting formal discovery requests, certain basic information that is needed in most cases to prepare for trial or make an informed decision about settlement. The rule requires all parties (1) early in the case to exchange information regarding potential witnesses, documentary evidence, damages, and insurance, (2) at an appropriate time during the discovery period to identify expert witnesses and provide a detailed written statement of the testimony that may be offered at trial through specially retained experts, and (3) as the trial date approaches to identify the particular evidence that may be offered at trial. The enumeration in Rule 26(a) of items to be disclosed does not prevent a court from requiring by order or local rule that the parties disclose additional information without a discovery request. Nor are parties precluded from using traditional discovery methods to obtain further information regarding these matters, as for example asking an expert during a deposition about testimony given in other litigation beyond the four-year period specified in Rule 26(a)(2)(B).

A major purpose of the revision is to accelerate the exchange of basic information about the case and to eliminate the paper work involved in requesting such information, and the rule should be applied in a manner to achieve those objectives. The concepts of imposing a duty of disclosure were set forth in Brazil, *The Adversary Character of Civil Discovery: A Critique and Proposals for Change,* 31 *Vand. L.Rev.* 1348 (1978), and Schwarzer, *The Federal Rules, the Adversary Process, and Discovery Reform,* 50 *U.Pitt.L.Rev. 703, 721–23 (1989).*

The rule is based upon the experience of district courts that have required disclosure of some of this information through local rules, court-approved standard interrogatories, and standing orders. Most have required pretrial disclosure of the kind of information described in Rule 26(a)(3). Many have required written reports from experts containing information like that specified in Rule 26(a)(2)(B). While far more limited, the experience of the few state and federal courts that have required pre-discovery exchange of core information such as is contemplated in Rule 26(a)(1) indicates that savings in time and expense can be achieved, particularly if the litigants meet and discuss the issues in the case as a predicate for this exchange and if a judge supports the process, as by using the results to guide further proceedings in the case. Courts in Canada and the United Kingdom have for many years required disclosure of certain information without awaiting a request from an adversary.

Paragraph (1). As the functional equivalent of court-ordered interrogatories, this paragraph requires early disclosure, without need for any request, of four types of information that have been customarily secured early in litigation through formal discovery. The introductory clause permits the court, by local rule, to exempt all or particular types of cases from these disclosure requirement *[sic]* or to modify the nature of the information to be disclosed. It is expected that courts would, for example, exempt cases like Social Security reviews and government collection cases in which discovery would not be appropriate or would be unlikely. By order the court may eliminate or modify the disclosure requirements in a particular case, and similarly the parties, unless precluded by order or local rule, can stipulate to elimination or modification of the requirements for that case. The disclosure obligations specified in paragraph (1) will not be appropriate for all cases, and it is expected that changes in these obligations will be made by the court or parties when the circumstances warrant.

Authorization of these local variations is, in large measure, included in order to accommodate the Civil Justice Reform Act of 1990, which implicitly directs districts to experiment during the study period with differing procedures to reduce the time and expense of civil litigation. The civil justice delay and expense reduction plans adopted by the courts under the Act differ as to the type, form, and timing of disclosures required. Section 105(c)(1) of the Act calls for a report by the Judicial Conference to Congress by December 31, 1995, comparing experience in twenty of these courts; and section 105(c)(2)(B) contemplates that some changes in the Rules may then be needed. While these studies may indicate the desirability of further changes in Rule 26(a)(1), these changes probably could not become effective before December 1998 at the earliest. In the meantime, the present revision puts in place a series of disclosure obligations that, unless a court acts affirmatively to impose other requirements or indeed to reject all such requirements for the present, are designed to eliminate certain discovery, help focus the discovery that is needed, and facilitate preparation for trial or settlement.

Subparagraph (A) requires identification of all persons who, based on the investigation conducted thus far, are likely to have discoverable information relevant to the factual disputes between the parties. All persons with such information should be disclosed, whether or not their testimony will be supportive of the position of the disclosing party. As officers of the court, counsel are expected to disclose the identity of those persons who may be used by them as witnesses or who, if their potential testimony were known, might reasonably be expected to be deposed or called as a witness by any of the other parties. Indicating briefly the general topics on which such persons have information should not be burdensome, and will assist other parties in deciding which depositions will actually be needed.

Subparagraph (B) is included as a substitute for the inquiries routinely made about the existence and location of documents and other tangible things in the possession, custody, or control of the disclosing party. Although, unlike subdivision (a)(3)(C), an itemized listing of each exhibit is not required, the disclosure should describe and categorize, to the extent identified during the initial investigation, the nature and location of potentially relevant documents and records, including computerized data and other electronically-recorded information, sufficiently to enable opposing parties (1) to make an informed decision concerning which documents might need to be examined, at least initially, and (2) to frame their document requests in a manner likely to avoid squabbles resulting from the wording of the requests. As with potential witnesses, the requirement for disclosure of documents applies to all potentially relevant items then known to the party, whether or not supportive of its contentions in the case.

Unlike subparagraphs (C) and (D), subparagraph (B) does not require production of any documents. Of course, in cases involving few documents a disclosing party may prefer to provide copies of the documents rather than describe them, and the rule is written to afford this option to the disclosing party. If, as will be more typical, only the description is provided, the other parties are expected to obtain the documents desired by proceeding under Rule 34 or through informal requests. The disclosing party does not, by describing documents under subparagraph (B), waive its right to object to production on the basis of privilege or work product protection, or to assert that the documents are not sufficiently relevant to justify the burden or expense of production.

The initial disclosure requirements of subparagraphs (A) and (B) are limited to identification of potential evidence "relevant to disputed facts alleged with particularity in the pleadings." There is no need for a party to identify potential evidence with respect to allegations that are admitted. Broad, vague, and conclusory allegations sometimes tolerated in notice pleading—for example, the assertion that a product with many component parts is defective in some unspecified manner—should not impose upon responding parties the obligation at that point to search for and identify all persons possibly involved in, or all documents affecting, the design, manufacture, and assembly of the product. The greater the specificity and clarity of the allegations in the pleadings, the more complete should be the listing of potential witnesses and types of documentary evidence. Although paragraphs (1)(A) and (1)(B) by their terms refer to the factual disputes defined in the pleadings, the rule contemplates that these issues would be informally refined and clarified during the meeting of the parties under subdivision (f) and that the disclosure obligations would be adjusted in the light of these discussions. The disclosure requirements should, in short, be applied with common sense in light of the principles of Rule 1, keeping in mind the salutary purposes that the rule is intended to accomplish. The litigants should not indulge in gamesmanship with respect to the disclosure obligations.

Subparagraph (C) imposes a burden of disclosure that includes the functional equivalent of a standing Request for Production under Rule 34. A party claiming damages or other monetary relief must, in addition to disclosing the calculation of such damages, make available the supporting documents for inspection and copying as if a request for such materials had been made under Rule 34. This obligation applies only with respect to documents then reasonably available to it and not privileged or protected as work product. Likewise, a party would not be expected to provide a calculation of damages which, as in many patent infringement actions, depends on information in the possession of another party or person.

Subparagraph (D) replaces subdivision (b)(2) of Rule 26, and provides that liability insurance policies be made available for inspection and copying. The last two sentences of that subdivision have been omitted as unnecessary, not to signify any change of law. The disclosure of insurance information does not thereby render such information admissible in evidence. See Rule 411, Federal Rules of Evidence. Nor does subparagraph (D) require disclosure of applications for insurance, though in particular cases such information may be discoverable in accordance with revised subdivision (a)(5).

Unless the court directs a different time, the disclosures required by subdivision (a)(1) are to be made at or within 10 days after the meeting of the parties under subdivision (f). One of the purposes of this meeting is to refine the factual disputes with respect to which disclosures should be made under paragraphs (1)(A) and (1)(B), particularly if an answer has not been filed by a defendant, or, indeed, to afford the parties an opportunity to modify by stipulation the timing or scope of these obligations. The time of this meeting is generally left to the parties provided it is held at least 14 days before a scheduling conference is held or before a scheduling order is due under Rule 16(b). In cases in which no scheduling conference is held, this will mean that the meeting must ordinarily be held within 75 days after a defendant has first appeared in the case and hence that the initial disclosures would be due no later than 85 days after the first appearance of a defendant.

Before making its disclosures, a party has the obligation under subdivision (g)(1) to make a reasonable inquiry into the facts of the case. The rule does not demand an exhaustive investigation at this stage of the case, but one that is reasonable under the circumstances, focusing on the facts that are alleged with particularity in the pleadings. The type of investigation that can be expected at this point will vary based upon such factors as the number and complexity of the issues; the location, nature, number, and availability of potentially relevant witnesses and documents; the extent of past working relationships between the attorney and the client, particularly in handling related or similar litigation; and of course how long the party has to conduct an investigation, either before or after filing of the case. As provided in the last sentence of subdivision (a)(1), a party is not excused from the duty of disclosure merely because its investigation is incomplete. The party should make its initial disclosures based on the pleadings and the information then reasonably available to it. As its investigation continues and as the issues in the pleadings are clarified, it should supplement its disclosures as required by subdivision (e)(1). A party is not relieved from its obligation of disclosure merely because another party has not made its disclosures or has made an inadequate disclosure.

It will often be desirable, particularly if the claims made in the complaint are broadly stated, for the parties to have their Rule 26(f) meeting early in the case, perhaps before a defendant has answered the complaint or had time to conduct other than a cursory investigation. In such circumstances, in order to facilitate more meaningful and useful initial disclosures, they can and should stipulate to a period of more than 10 days after the meeting in which to make these disclosures, at least for defendants who had no advance notice of the potential litigation. A stipulation at an early meeting affording such a defendant at least 60 days after receiving the complaint in which to make its disclosures under subdivision (a)(1)—a period that is two weeks longer than the time formerly specified for responding to interrogatories served with a complaint—should be adequate and appropriate in most cases.

Paragraph (2). This paragraph imposes an additional duty to disclose information regarding expert testimony sufficiently in advance of trial that opposing parties have a reasonable opportunity to prepare for effective cross examination and perhaps arrange for expert testimony from other witnesses. Normally the court should prescribe a time for

these disclosures in a scheduling order under Rule 16(b), and in most cases the party with the burden of proof on an issue should disclose its expert testimony on that issue before other parties are required to make their disclosures with respect to that issue. In the absence of such a direction, the disclosures are to be made by all parties at least 90 days before the trial date or the date by which the case is to be ready for trial, except that an additional 30 days is allowed (unless the court specifies another time) for disclosure of expert testimony to be used solely to contradict or rebut the testimony that may be presented by another party's expert. For a discussion of procedures that have been used to enhance the reliability of expert testimony, see M. Graham, *Expert Witness Testimony and the Federal Rules of Evidence: Insuring Adequate Assurance of Trustworthiness,* 1986 U.Ill.L.Rev. 90.

Paragraph (2)(B) requires that persons retained or specially employed to provide expert testimony, or whose duties as an employee of the party regularly involve the giving of expert testimony, must prepare a detailed and complete written report, stating the testimony the witness is expected to present during direct examination, together with the reasons therefor. The information disclosed under the former rule in answering interrogatories about the "substance" of expert testimony was frequently so sketchy and vague that it rarely dispensed with the need to depose the expert and often was even of little help in preparing for a deposition of the witness. Revised Rule 37(c)(1) provides an incentive for full disclosure; namely, that a party will not ordinarily be permitted to use on direct examination any expert testimony not so disclosed. Rule 26(a)(2)(B) does not preclude counsel from providing assistance to experts in preparing the reports, and indeed, with experts such as automobile mechanics, this assistance may be needed. Nevertheless, the report, which is intended to set forth the substance of the direct examination, should be written in a manner that reflects the testimony to be given by the witness and it must be signed by the witness.

The report is to disclose the data and other information considered by the expert and any exhibits or charts that summarize or support the expert's opinions. Given this obligation of disclosure, litigants should no longer be able to argue that materials furnished to their experts to be used in forming their opinions—whether or not ultimately relied upon by the expert—are privileged or otherwise protected from disclosure when such persons are testifying or being deposed.

Revised subdivision (b)(4)(A) authorizes the deposition of expert witnesses. Since depositions of experts required to prepare a written report may be taken only after the report has been served, the length of the deposition of such experts should be reduced, and in many cases the report may eliminate the need for a deposition. Revised subdivision (e)(1) requires disclosure of any material changes made in the opinions of an expert from whom a report is required, whether the changes are in the written report or in testimony given at a deposition.

For convenience, this rule and revised Rule 30 continue to use the term "expert" to refer to those persons who will testify under Rule 702 of the Federal Rules of Evidence with respect to scientific, technical, and other specialized matters. The requirement of a written report in paragraph (2)(B), however, applies only to those experts who are retained or specially employed to provide such testimony in the case or whose duties as an employee of a party regularly involve the giving of such testimony. A treating physician, for example, can be deposed or called to testify at trial without any requirement for a written report. By local rule, order, or written stipulation, the requirement of a written report may be waived for particular experts or imposed upon additional persons who will provide opinions under Rule 702.

Paragraph (3). This paragraph imposes an additional duty to disclose, without any request, information customarily needed in final preparation for trial. These disclosures are to be made in accordance with schedules adopted by the court under Rule 16(b) or by special order. If no such schedule is directed by the court, the disclosures are to be made at least 30 days before commencement of the trial. By its terms, rule 26(a)(3) does not require disclosure of evidence to be used solely for impeachment purposes; however, disclosure of such evidence—as well as other items relating to conduct of trial—may be required by local rule or a pretrial order.

Subparagraph (A) requires the parties to designate the persons whose testimony they may present as substantive evidence at trial, whether in person or by deposition. Those who will probably be called as witnesses should be listed separately from those who are not likely to be called but who are being listed in order to preserve the right to do so if needed because of developments during trial. Revised Rule 37(c)(1) provides that only persons so listed may be used at trial to present substantive evidence. This restriction does not apply unless the omission was "without substantial justification" and hence would not bar an unlisted witness if the need for such testimony is based upon developments during trial that could not reasonably have been anticipated—*e.g.,* a change of testimony.

Listing a witness does not obligate the party to secure the attendance of the person at trial, but should preclude the party from objecting if the person is called to testify by another party who did not list the person as a witness.

Subparagraph (B) requires the party to indicate which of these potential witnesses will be presented by deposition at trial. A party expecting to use at trial a deposition not recorded by stenographic means is required by revised Rule 32 to provide the court with a transcript of the pertinent portions of such depositions. This rule requires that copies of the transcript of a nonstenographic deposition be provided to other parties in advance of trial for verification, an obvious concern since counsel often utilize their own personnel to prepare transcripts from audio or video tapes. By order or local rule, the court may require that parties designate the particular portions of stenographic depositions to be used at trial.

Subparagraph (C) requires disclosure of exhibits, including summaries (whether to be offered in lieu of other documentary evidence or to be used as an aid in understanding such evidence), that may be offered as substantive evidence. The rule requires a separate listing of each such exhibit, though it should permit voluminous items of a similar or standardized character to be described by meaningful categories. For example, unless the court has otherwise directed, a series of vouchers might be shown collectively as a single exhibit with their starting and ending dates. As with witnesses, the exhibits that will probably be offered are to be listed separately from those which are unlikely to be offered but which

are listed in order to preserve the right to do so if needed because of developments during trial. Under revised Rule 37(c)(1) the court can permit use of unlisted documents the need for which could not reasonably have been anticipated in advance of trial.

Upon receipt of these final pretrial disclosures, other parties have 14 days (unless a different time is specified by the court) to disclose any objections they wish to preserve to the usability of the deposition testimony or to the admissibility of the documentary evidence (other than under Rules 402 and 403 of the Federal Rules of Evidence). Similar provisions have become commonplace either in pretrial orders or by local rules, and significantly expedite the presentation of evidence at trial, as well as eliminate the need to have available witnesses to provide "foundation" testimony for most items of documentary evidence. The listing of a potential objection does not constitute the making of that objection or require the court to rule on the objection; rather, it preserves the right of the party to make the objection when and as appropriate during trial. The court may, however, elect to treat the listing as a motion "in limine" and rule upon the objections in advance of trial to the extent appropriate.

The time specified in the rule for the final pretrial disclosures is relatively close to the trial date. The objective is to eliminate the time and expense in making these disclosures of evidence and objections in those cases that settle shortly before trial, while affording a reasonable time for final preparation for trial in those cases that do not settle. In many cases, it will be desirable for the court in a scheduling or pretrial order to set an earlier time for disclosures of evidence and provide more time for disclosing potential objections.

Paragraph (4). This paragraph prescribes the form of disclosures. A signed written statement is required, reminding the parties and counsel of the solemnity of the obligations imposed; and the signature on the initial or pretrial disclosure is a certification under subdivision (g)(1) that it is complete and correct as of the time when made. Consistent with Rule 5(d), these disclosures are to be filed with the court unless otherwise directed. It is anticipated that many courts will direct that expert reports required under paragraph (2)(B) not be filed until needed in connection with a motion or for trial.

Paragraph (5). This paragraph is revised to take note of the availability of revised Rule 45 for inspection from nonparties of documents and premises without the need for a deposition.

Subdivision (b). This subdivision is revised in several respects. First, former paragraph (1) is subdivided into two paragraphs for ease of reference and to avoid renumbering of paragraphs (3) and (4). Textual changes are then made in new paragraph (2) to enable the court to keep tighter rein on the extent of discovery. The information explosion of recent decades has greatly increased both the potential cost of wide-ranging discovery and the potential for discovery to be used as an instrument for delay or oppression. Amendments to Rules 30, 31, and 33 place presumptive limits on the number of depositions and interrogatories, subject to leave of court to pursue additional discovery. The revisions in Rule 26(b)(2) are intended to provide the court with broader discretion to impose additional restrictions on the scope and extent of discovery and to authorize courts that develop case tracking systems based on the complexity of cases to increase or

decrease by local rule the presumptive number of depositions and interrogatories allowed in particular types or classifications of cases. The revision also dispels any doubt as to the power of the court to impose limitations on the length of depositions under Rule 30 or on the number of requests for admission under Rule 36.

Second, former paragraph (2), relating to insurance, has been relocated as part of the required initial disclosures under subdivision (a)(1)(D), and revised to provide for disclosure of the policy itself.

Third, paragraph (4)(A) is revised to provide that experts who are expected to be witnesses will be subject to deposition prior to trial, conforming the norm stated in the rule to the actual practice followed in most courts, in which depositions of experts have become standard. Concerns regarding the expense of such depositions should be mitigated by the fact that the expert's fees for the deposition will ordinarily be borne by the party taking the deposition. The requirement under subdivision (a)(2)(B) of a complete and detailed report of the expected testimony of certain forensic experts may, moreover, eliminate the need for some such depositions or at least reduce the length of the depositions. Accordingly, the deposition of an expert required by subdivision (a)(2)(B) to provide a written report may be taken only after the report has been served.

Paragraph (4)(C), bearing on compensation of experts, is revised to take account of the changes in paragraph (4)(A).

Paragraph (5) is a new provision. A party must notify other parties if it is withholding materials otherwise subject to disclosure under the rule or pursuant to a discovery request because it is asserting a claim of privilege or work product protection. To withhold materials without such notice is contrary to the rule, subjects the party to sanctions under Rule 37(b)(2), and may be viewed as a waiver of the privilege or protection.

The party must also provide sufficient information to enable other parties to evaluate the applicability of the claimed privilege or protection. Although the person from whom the discovery is sought decides whether to claim a privilege or protection, the court ultimately decides whether, if this claim is challenged, the privilege or protection applies. Providing information pertinent to the applicability of the privilege or protection should reduce the need for in camera examination of the documents.

The rule does not attempt to define for each case what information must be provided when a party asserts a claim of privilege or work product protection. Details concerning time, persons, general subject matter, etc., may be appropriate if only a few items are withheld, but may be unduly burdensome when voluminous documents are claimed to be privileged or protected, particularly if the items can be described by categories. A party can seek relief through a protective order under subdivision (c) if compliance with the requirement for providing this information would be an unreasonable burden. In rare circumstances some of the pertinent information affecting applicability of the claim, such as the identity of the client, may itself be privileged; the rule provides that such information need not be disclosed.

The obligation to provide pertinent information concerning withheld privileged materials applies only to items "otherwise discoverable." If a broad discovery request is made—for example, for all documents of a particular type during a

twenty year period—and the responding party believes in good faith that production of documents for more than the past three years would be unduly burdensome, it should make its objection to the breadth of the request and, with respect to the documents generated in that three year period, produce the unprivileged documents and describe those withheld under the claim of privilege. If the court later rules that documents for a seven year period are properly discoverable, the documents for the additional four years should then be either produced (if not privileged) or described (if claimed to be privileged).

Subdivision (c). The revision requires that before filing a motion for a protective order the movant must confer—either in person or by telephone—with the other affected parties in a good faith effort to resolve the discovery dispute without the need for court intervention. If the movant is unable to get opposing parties even to discuss the matter, the efforts in attempting to arrange such a conference should be indicated in the certificate.

Subdivision (d). This subdivision is revised to provide that formal discovery—as distinguished from interviews of potential witnesses and other informal discovery—not commence until the parties have met and conferred as required by subdivision (f). Discovery can begin earlier if authorized under Rule 30(a)(2)(C) (deposition of person about to leave the country) or by local rule, order, or stipulation. This will be appropriate in some cases, such as those involving requests for a preliminary injunction or motions challenging personal jurisdiction. If a local rule exempts any types of cases in which discovery may be needed from the requirement of a meeting under Rule 26(f), it should specify when discovery may commence in those cases.

The meeting of counsel is to take place as soon as practicable and in any event at least 14 days before the date of the scheduling conference under Rule 16(b) or the date a scheduling order is due under Rule 16(b). The court can assure that discovery is not unduly delayed either by entering a special order or by setting the case for a scheduling conference.

Subdivision (e). This subdivision is revised to provide that the requirement for supplementation applies to all disclosures required by subdivisions (a)(1)–(3). Like the former rule, the duty, while imposed on a "party," applies whether the corrective information is learned by the client or by the attorney. Supplementations need not be made as each new item of information is learned but should be made at appropriate intervals during the discovery period, and with special promptness as the trial date approaches. It may be useful for the scheduling order to specify the time or times when supplementations should be made.

The revision also clarifies that the obligation to supplement responses to formal discovery requests applies to interrogatories, requests for production, and requests for admissions, but not ordinarily to deposition testimony. However, with respect to experts from whom a written report is required under subdivision (a)(2)(B), changes in the opinions expressed by the expert whether in the report or at a subsequent deposition are subject to a duty of supplemental disclosure under subdivision (e)(1).

The obligation to supplement disclosures and discovery responses applies whenever a party learns that its prior disclosures or responses are in some material respect incomplete or incorrect. There is, however, no obligation to provide supplemental or corrective information that has been otherwise made known to the parties in writing or during the discovery process, as when a witness not previously disclosed is identified during the taking of a deposition or when an expert during a deposition corrects information contained in an earlier report.

Subdivision (f). This subdivision was added in 1980 to provide a party threatened with abusive discovery with a special means for obtaining judicial intervention other than through discrete motions under Rules 26(c) and 37(a). The amendment envisioned a two-step process: first, the parties would attempt to frame a mutually agreeable plan; second, the court would hold a "discovery conference" and then enter an order establishing a schedule and limitations for the conduct of discovery. It was contemplated that the procedure, an elective one triggered on request of a party, would be used in special cases rather than as a routine matter. As expected, the device has been used only sparingly in most courts, and judicial controls over the discovery process have ordinarily been imposed through scheduling orders under Rule 16(b) or through rulings on discovery motions.

The provisions relating to a conference with the court are removed from subdivision (f). This change does not signal any lessening of the importance of judicial supervision. Indeed, there is a greater need for early judicial involvement to consider the scope and timing of the disclosure requirements of Rule 26(a) and the presumptive limits on discovery imposed under these rules or by local rules. Rather, the change is made because the provisions addressing the use of conferences with the court to control discovery are more properly included in Rule 16, which is being revised to highlight the court's powers regarding the discovery process.

The desirability of some judicial control of discovery can hardly be doubted. Rule 16, as revised, requires that the court set a time for completion of discovery and authorizes various other orders affecting the scope, timing, and extent of discovery and disclosures. Before entering such orders, the court should consider the views of the parties, preferably by means of a conference, but at the least through written submissions. Moreover, it is desirable that the parties' proposals regarding discovery be developed through a process where they meet in person, informally explore the nature and basis of the issues, and discuss how discovery can be conducted most efficiently and economically.

As noted above, former subdivision (f) envisioned the development of proposed discovery plans as an optional procedure to be used in relatively few cases. The revised rule directs that in all cases not exempted by local rule or special order the litigants must meet in person and plan for discovery. Following this meeting, the parties submit to the court their proposals for a discovery plan and can begin formal discovery. Their report will assist the court in seeing that the timing and scope of disclosures under revised Rule 26(a) and the limitations on the extent of discovery under these rules and local rules are tailored to the circumstances of the particular case.

To assure that the court has the litigants' proposals before deciding on a scheduling order and that the commencement of discovery is not delayed unduly, the rule provides that the meeting of the parties take place as soon as practicable and in any event at least 14 days before a scheduling conference is held or before a scheduling order is due under Rule 16(b).

(Rule 16(b) requires that a scheduling order be entered within 90 days after the first appearance of a defendant or, if earlier, within 120 days after the complaint has been served on any defendant.) The obligation to participate in the planning process is imposed on all parties that have appeared in the case, including defendants who, because of a pending Rule 12 motion, may not have yet filed an answer in the case. Each such party should attend the meeting, either through one of its attorneys or in person if unrepresented. If more parties are joined or appear after the initial meeting, an additional meeting may be desirable.

Subdivision (f) describes certain matters that should be accomplished at the meeting and included in the proposed discovery plan. This listing does not exclude consideration of other subjects, such as the time when any dispositive motions should be filed and when the case should be ready for trial.

The parties are directed under subdivision (a)(1) to make the disclosures required by that subdivision at or within 10 days after this meeting. In many cases the parties should use the meeting to exchange, discuss, and clarify their respective disclosures. In other cases, it may be more useful if the disclosures are delayed until after the parties have discussed at the meeting the claims and defenses in order to define the issues with respect to which the initial disclosures should be made. As discussed in the Notes to subdivision (a)(1), the parties may also need to consider whether a stipulation extending this 10–day period would be appropriate, as when a defendant would otherwise have less than 60 days after being served in which to make its initial disclosure. The parties should also discuss at the meeting what additional information, although not subject to the disclosure requirements, can be made available informally without the necessity for formal discovery requests.

The report is to be submitted to the court within 10 days after the meeting and should not be difficult to prepare. In most cases counsel should be able to agree that one of them will be responsible for its preparation and submission to the court. Form 35 has been added in the Appendix to the Rules, both to illustrate the type of report that is contemplated and to serve as a checklist for the meeting.

The litigants are expected to attempt in good faith to agree on the contents of the proposed discovery plan. If they cannot agree on all aspects of the plan, their report to the court should indicate the competing proposals of the parties on those items, as well as the matters on which they agree. Unfortunately, there may be cases in which, because of disagreements about time or place or for other reasons, the meeting is not attended by all parties or, indeed, no meeting takes place. In such situations, the report—or reports—should describe the circumstances and the court may need to consider sanctions under Rule 37(g).

By local rule or special order, the court can exempt particular cases or types of cases from the meet-and-confer requirement of subdivision (f). In general this should include any types of cases which are exempted by local rule from the requirement for a scheduling order under Rule 16(b), such as cases in which there will be no discovery (*e.g.*, bankruptcy appeals and reviews of social security determinations). In addition, the court may want to exempt cases in which discovery is rarely needed (*e.g.*, government collection cases and proceedings to enforce administrative summonses) or in which a meeting of the parties might be impracticable (*e.g.*, actions by unrepresented prisoners). Note that if a court exempts from the requirements for a meeting any types of cases in which discovery may be needed, it should indicate when discovery may commence in those cases.

Subdivision (g). Paragraph (1) is added to require signatures on disclosures, a requirement that parallels the provisions of paragraph (2) with respect to discovery requests, responses, and objections. The provisions of paragraph (3) have been modified to be consistent with Rules 37(a)(4) and 37(c)(1); in combination, these rules establish sanctions for violation of the rules regarding disclosures and discovery matters. Amended Rule 11 no longer applies to such violations.

2000 Amendment

Purposes of amendments. The Rule 26(a)(1) initial disclosure provisions are amended to establish a nationally uniform practice. The scope of the disclosure obligation is narrowed to cover only information that the disclosing party may use to support its position. In addition, the rule exempts specified categories of proceedings from initial disclosure, and permits a party who contends that disclosure is not appropriate in the circumstances of the case to present its objections to the court, which must then determine whether disclosure should be made. Related changes are made in Rules 26(d) and (f).

The initial disclosure requirements added by the 1993 amendments permitted local rules directing that disclosure would not be required or altering its operation. The inclusion of the "opt out" provision reflected the strong opposition to initial disclosure felt in some districts, and permitted experimentation with differing disclosure rules in those districts that were favorable to disclosure. The local option also recognized that—partly in response to the first publication in 1991 of a proposed disclosure rule—many districts had adopted a variety of disclosure programs under the aegis of the Civil Justice Reform Act. It was hoped that developing experience under a variety of disclosure systems would support eventual refinement of a uniform national disclosure practice. In addition, there was hope that local experience could identify categories of actions in which disclosure is not useful.

A striking array of local regimes in fact emerged for disclosure and related features introduced in 1993. *See* D. Stienstra, *Implementation of Disclosure in United States District Courts, With Specific Attention to Courts' Responses to Selected Amendments to Federal Rule of Civil Procedure 26* (Federal Judicial Center, March 30, 1998) (describing and categorizing local regimes). In its final report to Congress on the CJRA experience, the Judicial Conference recommended reexamination of the need for national uniformity, particularly in regard to initial disclosure. Judicial Conference, *Alternative Proposals for Reduction of Cost and Delay: Assessment of Principles, Guidelines and Techniques*, 175 F.R.D. 62, 98 (1997).

At the Committee's request, the Federal Judicial Center undertook a survey in 1997 to develop information on current disclosure and discovery practices. *See* T. Willging, J. Shapard, D. Stienstra & D. Miletich, *Discovery and Disclosure Practice, Problems, and Proposals for Change* (Federal Judicial Center, 1997). In addition, the Committee convened two conferences on discovery involving lawyers from around the country and received reports and recommendations on possible discovery amendments from a number of bar groups.

Papers and other proceedings from the second conference are published in 39 Boston Col. L. Rev. 517–840 (1998).

The Committee has discerned widespread support for national uniformity. Many lawyers have experienced difficulty in coping with divergent disclosure and other practices as they move from one district to another. Lawyers surveyed by the Federal Judicial Center ranked adoption of a uniform national disclosure rule second among proposed rule changes (behind increased availability of judges to resolve discovery disputes) as a means to reduce litigation expenses without interfering with fair outcomes. *Discovery and Disclosure Practice, supra,* at 44–45. National uniformity is also a central purpose of the Rules Enabling Act of 1934, as amended, 28 U.S.C. §§ 2072–2077.

These amendments restore national uniformity to disclosure practice. Uniformity is also restored to other aspects of discovery by deleting most of the provisions authorizing local rules that vary the number of permitted discovery events or the length of depositions. Local rule options are also deleted from Rules 26(d) and (f).

Subdivision (a)(1). The amendments remove the authority to alter or opt out of the national disclosure requirements by local rule, invalidating not only formal local rules but also informal "standing" orders of an individual judge or court that purport to create exemptions from—or limit or expand—the disclosure provided under the national rule. *See* Rule 83. Case-specific orders remain proper, however, and are expressly required if a party objects that initial disclosure is not appropriate in the circumstances of the action. Specified categories of proceedings are excluded from initial disclosure under subdivision (a)(1)(E). In addition, the parties can stipulate to forgo disclosure, as was true before. But even in a case excluded by subdivision (a)(1)(E) or in which the parties stipulate to bypass disclosure, the court can order exchange of similar information in managing the action under Rule 16.

The initial disclosure obligation of subdivisions (a)(1)(A) and (B) has been narrowed to identification of witnesses and documents that the disclosing party may use to support its claims or defenses. "Use" includes any use at a pretrial conference, to support a motion, or at trial. The disclosure obligation is also triggered by intended use in discovery, apart from use to respond to a discovery request; use of a document to question a witness during a deposition is a common example. The disclosure obligation attaches both to witnesses and documents a party intends to use and also to witnesses and to documents the party intends to use if—in the language of Rule 26(a)(3)—"the need arises."

A party is no longer obligated to disclose witnesses or documents, whether favorable or unfavorable, that it does not intend to use. The obligation to disclose information the party may use connects directly to the exclusion sanction of Rule 37(c)(1). Because the disclosure obligation is limited to material that the party may use, it is no longer tied to particularized allegations in the pleadings. Subdivision (e)(1), which is unchanged, requires supplementation if information later acquired would have been subject to the disclosure requirement. As case preparation continues, a party must supplement its disclosures when it determines that it may use a witness or document that it did not previously intend to use.

The disclosure obligation applies to "claims and defenses," and therefore requires a party to disclose information it may use to support its denial or rebuttal of the allegations, claim, or defense of another party. It thereby bolsters the requirements of Rule 11(b)(4), which authorizes denials "warranted on the evidence," and disclosure should include the identity of any witness or document that the disclosing party may use to support such denials.

Subdivision (a)(3) presently excuses pretrial disclosure of information solely for impeachment. Impeachment information is similarly excluded from the initial disclosure requirement.

Subdivisions (a)(1)(C) and (D) are not changed. Should a case be exempted from initial disclosure by Rule 26(a)(1)(E) or by agreement or order, the insurance information described by subparagraph (D) should be subject to discovery, as it would have been under the principles of former Rule 26(b)(2), which was added in 1970 and deleted in 1993 as redundant in light of the new initial disclosure obligation.

New subdivision (a)(1)(E) excludes eight specified categories of proceedings from initial disclosure. The objective of this listing is to identify cases in which there is likely to be little or no discovery, or in which initial disclosure appears unlikely to contribute to the effective development of the case. The list was developed after a review of the categories excluded by local rules in various districts from the operation of Rule 16(b) and the conference requirements of subdivision (f). Subdivision (a)(1)(E) refers to categories of "proceedings" rather than categories of "actions" because some might not properly be labeled " actions." Case designations made by the parties or the clerk's office at the time of filing do not control application of the exemptions. The descriptions in the rule are generic and are intended to be administered by the parties—and, when needed, the courts—with the flexibility needed to adapt to gradual evolution in the types of proceedings that fall within these general categories. The exclusion of an action for review on an administrative record, for example, is intended to reach a proceeding that is framed as an " appeal" based solely on an administrative record. The exclusion should not apply to a proceeding in a form that commonly permits admission of new evidence to supplement the record. Item (vii), excluding a proceeding ancillary to proceedings in other courts, does not refer to bankruptcy proceedings; application of the Civil Rules to bankruptcy proceedings is determined by the Bankruptcy Rules.

Subdivision (a)(1)(E) is likely to exempt a substantial proportion of the cases in most districts from the initial disclosure requirement. Based on 1996 and 1997 case filing statistics, Federal Judicial Center staff estimate that, nationwide, these categories total approximately one-third of all civil filings.

The categories of proceedings listed in subdivision (a)(1)(E) are also exempted from the subdivision (f) conference requirement and from the subdivision (d) moratorium on discovery. Although there is no restriction on commencement of discovery in these cases, it is not expected that this opportunity will often lead to abuse since there is likely to be little or no discovery in most such cases. Should a defendant need more time to respond to discovery requests filed at the beginning of an exempted action, it can seek relief by motion under Rule 26(c) if the plaintiff is unwilling to defer the due date by agreement.

Subdivision (a)(1)(E)'s enumeration of exempt categories is exclusive. Although a case-specific order can alter or excuse

initial disclosure, local rules or "standing" orders that purport to create general exemptions are invalid. *See* Rule 83.

The time for initial disclosure is extended to 14 days after the subdivision (f) conference unless the court orders otherwise. This change is integrated with corresponding changes requiring that the subdivision (f) conference be held 21 days before the Rule 16(b) scheduling conference or scheduling order, and that the report on the subdivision (f) conference be submitted to the court 14 days after the meeting. These changes provide a more orderly opportunity for the parties to review the disclosures, and for the court to consider the report. In many instances, the subdivision (f) conference and the effective preparation of the case would benefit from disclosure before the conference, and earlier disclosure is encouraged.

The presumptive disclosure date does not apply if a party objects to initial disclosure during the subdivision (f) conference and states its objection in the subdivision (f) discovery plan. The right to object to initial disclosure is not intended to afford parties an opportunity to "opt out" of disclosure unilaterally. It does provide an opportunity for an objecting party to present to the court its position that disclosure would be "inappropriate in the circumstances of the action." Making the objection permits the objecting party to present the question to the judge before any party is required to make disclosure. The court must then rule on the objection and determine what disclosures—if any—should be made. Ordinarily, this determination would be included in the Rule 16(b) scheduling order, but the court could handle the matter in a different fashion. Even when circumstances warrant suspending some disclosure obligations, others—such as the damages and insurance information called for by subdivisions (a)(1)(C) and (D)—may continue to be appropriate.

The presumptive disclosure date is also inapplicable to a party who is "first served or otherwise joined" after the subdivision (f) conference. This phrase refers to the date of service of a claim on a party in a defensive posture (such as a defendant or third-party defendant), and the date of joinder of a party added as a claimant or an intervenor. Absent court order or stipulation, a new party has 30 days in which to make its initial disclosures. But it is expected that later-added parties will ordinarily be treated the same as the original parties when the original parties have stipulated to forgo initial disclosure, or the court has ordered disclosure in a modified form.

Subdivision (a)(3). The amendment to Rule 5(d) forbids filing disclosures under subdivisions (a)(1) and (a)(2) until they are used in the proceeding, and this change is reflected in an amendment to subdivision (a)(4) . Disclosures under subdivision (a)(3), however, may be important to the court in connection with the final pretrial conference or otherwise in preparing for trial. The requirement that objections to certain matters be filed points up the court's need to be provided with these materials. Accordingly, the requirement that subdivision (a)(3) materials be filed has been moved from subdivision (a)(4) to subdivision (a)(3), and it has also been made clear that they—and any objections—should be filed "promptly."

Subdivision (a)(4). The filing requirement has been removed from this subdivision. Rule 5(d) has been amended to provide that disclosures under subdivisions (a)(1) and (a)(2) must not be filed until used in the proceeding. Subdivision (a)(3) has been amended to require that the disclosures it

directs, and objections to them, be filed promptly. Subdivision (a)(4) continues to require that all disclosures under subdivisions (a)(1), (a)(2), and (a)(3) be in writing, signed, and served.

"Shall" is replaced by "must" under the program to conform amended rules to current style conventions when there is no ambiguity.

GAP Report

The Advisory Committee recommends that the amendments to Rules 26(a)(1)(A) and (B) be changed so that initial disclosure applies to information the disclosing party "may use to support" its claims or defenses. It also recommends changes in the Committee Note to explain that disclosure requirement. In addition, it recommends inclusion in the Note of further explanatory matter regarding the exclusion from initial disclosure provided in new Rule 26(a)(1)(E) for actions for review on an administrative record and the impact of these exclusions on bankruptcy proceedings. Minor wording improvements in the Note are also proposed.

Subdivision (b)(1). In 1978, the Committee published for comment a proposed amendment, suggested by the Section of Litigation of the American Bar Association, to refine the scope of discovery by deleting the "subject matter" language. This proposal was withdrawn, and the Committee has since then made other changes in the discovery rules to address concerns about overbroad discovery. Concerns about costs and delay of discovery have persisted nonetheless, and other bar groups have repeatedly renewed similar proposals for amendment to this subdivision to delete the "subject matter" language. Nearly one-third of the lawyers surveyed in 1997 by the Federal Judicial Center endorsed narrowing the scope of discovery as a means of reducing litigation expense without interfering with fair case resolutions. *Discovery and Disclosure Practice, supra,* at 44–45 (1997). The Committee has heard that in some instances, particularly cases involving large quantities of discovery, parties seek to justify discovery requests that sweep far beyond the claims and defenses of the parties on the ground that they nevertheless have a bearing on the "subject matter" involved in the action.

The amendments proposed for subdivision (b)(1) include one element of these earlier proposals but also differ from these proposals in significant ways. The similarity is that the amendments describe the scope of party- controlled discovery in terms of matter relevant to the claim or defense of any party. The court, however, retains authority to order discovery of any matter relevant to the subject matter involved in the action for good cause. The amendment is designed to involve the court more actively in regulating the breadth of sweeping or contentious discovery. The Committee has been informed repeatedly by lawyers that involvement of the court in managing discovery is an important method of controlling problems of inappropriately broad discovery. Increasing the availability of judicial officers to resolve discovery disputes and increasing court management of discovery were both strongly endorsed by the attorneys surveyed by the Federal Judicial Center. *See Discovery and Disclosure Practice, supra,* at 44. Under the amended provisions, if there is an objection that discovery goes beyond material relevant to the parties' claims or defenses, the court would become involved to determine whether the discovery is relevant to the claims or defenses and, if not, whether good cause exists for authorizing it so long as it is relevant to the subject matter of the

action. The good-cause standard warranting broader discovery is meant to be flexible.

The Committee intends that the parties and the court focus on the actual claims and defenses involved in the action. The dividing line between information relevant to the claims and defenses and that relevant only to the subject matter of the action cannot be defined with precision. A variety of types of information not directly pertinent to the incident in suit could be relevant to the claims or defenses raised in a given action. For example, other incidents of the same type, or involving the same product, could be properly discoverable under the revised standard. Information about organizational arrangements or filing systems of a party could be discoverable if likely to yield or lead to the discovery of admissible information. Similarly, information that could be used to impeach a likely witness, although not otherwise relevant to the claims or defenses, might be properly discoverable. In each instance, the determination whether such information is discoverable because it is relevant to the claims or defenses depends on the circumstances of the pending action.

The rule change signals to the court that it has the authority to confine discovery to the claims and defenses asserted in the pleadings, and signals to the parties that they have no entitlement to discovery to develop new claims or defenses that are not already identified in the pleadings. In general, it is hoped that reasonable lawyers can cooperate to manage discovery without the need for judicial intervention. When judicial intervention is invoked, the actual scope of discovery should be determined according to the reasonable needs of the action. The court may permit broader discovery in a particular case depending on the circumstances of the case, the nature of the claims and defenses, and the scope of the discovery requested.

The amendments also modify the provision regarding discovery of information not admissible in evidence. As added in 1946, this sentence was designed to make clear that otherwise relevant material could not be withheld because it was hearsay or otherwise inadmissible. The Committee was concerned that the "reasonably calculated to lead to the discovery of admissible evidence" standard set forth in this sentence might swallow any other limitation on the scope of discovery. Accordingly, this sentence has been amended to clarify that information must be relevant to be discoverable, even though inadmissible, and that discovery of such material is permitted if reasonably calculated to lead to the discovery of admissible evidence. As used here, "relevant" means within the scope of discovery as defined in this subdivision, and it would include information relevant to the subject matter involved in the action if the court has ordered discovery to that limit based on a showing of good cause.

Finally, a sentence has been added calling attention to the limitations of subdivision (b)(2)(i), (ii), and (iii). These limitations apply to discovery that is otherwise within the scope of subdivision (b)(1). The Committee has been told repeatedly that courts have not implemented these limitations with the vigor that was contemplated. *See 8 Federal Practice & Procedure § 2008.1 at 121.* This otherwise redundant cross-reference has been added to emphasize the need for active judicial use of subdivision (b)(2) to control excessive discovery. *Cf. Crawford-El v. Britton*, 118 S. Ct. 1584, 1597 (1998) (quoting Rule 26(b)(2)(iii) and stating that "Rule 26 vests the trial judge with broad discretion to tailor discovery narrowly").

GAP Report

The Advisory Committee recommends changing the rule to authorize the court to expand discovery to any "matter"—not "information"—relevant to the subject matter involved in the action. In addition, it recommends additional clarifying material in the Committee Note about the impact of the change on some commonly disputed discovery topics, the relationship between cost-bearing under Rule 26(b)(2) and expansion of the scope of discovery on a showing of good cause, and the meaning of "relevant" in the revision to the last sentence of current subdivision (b)(1). In addition, some minor clarifications of language changes have been proposed for the Committee Note .

Subdivision (b)(2). Rules 30, 31, and 33 establish presumptive national limits on the numbers of depositions and interrogatories. New Rule 30(d)(2) establishes a presumptive limit on the length of depositions. Subdivision (b)(2) is amended to remove the previous permission for local rules that establish different presumptive limits on these discovery activities. There is no reason to believe that unique circumstances justify varying these nationally-applicable presumptive limits in certain districts. The limits can be modified by court order or agreement in an individual action, but "standing" orders imposing different presumptive limits are not authorized. Because there is no national rule limiting the number of Rule 36 requests for admissions, the rule continues to authorize local rules that impose numerical limits on them. This change is not intended to interfere with differentiated case management in districts that use this technique by case-specific order as part of their Rule 16 process.

Subdivision (d). The amendments remove the prior authority to exempt cases by local rule from the moratorium on discovery before the subdivision (f) conference, but the categories of proceedings exempted from initial disclosure under subdivision (a)(1)(E) are excluded from subdivision (d). The parties may agree to disregard the moratorium where it applies, and the court may so order in a case, but "standing" orders altering the moratorium are not authorized.

Subdivision (f). As in subdivision (d), the amendments remove the prior authority to exempt cases by local rule from the conference requirement. The Committee has been informed that the addition of the conference was one of the most successful changes made in the 1993 amendments, and it therefore has determined to apply the conference requirement nationwide. The categories of proceedings exempted from initial disclosure under subdivision (a)(1)(E) are exempted from the conference requirement for the reasons that warrant exclusion from initial disclosure. The court may order that the conference need not occur in a case where otherwise required, or that it occur in a case otherwise exempted by subdivision (a)(1)(E). "Standing" orders altering the conference requirement for categories of cases are not authorized.

The rule is amended to require only a "conference" of the parties, rather than a "meeting." There are important benefits to face-to-face discussion of the topics to be covered in the conference, and those benefits may be lost if other means of conferring were routinely used when face-to- face meetings would not impose burdens. Nevertheless, geographic conditions in some districts may exact costs far out of proportion to these benefits. The amendment allows the court by case-specific order to require a face-to- face meeting, but "standing" orders so requiring are not authorized.

Complete Annotation Materials, see Title 28 U.S.C.A.

As noted concerning the amendments to subdivision (a)(1), the time for the conference has been changed to at least 21 days before the Rule 16 scheduling conference, and the time for the report is changed to no more than 14 days after the Rule 26(f) conference. This should ensure that the court will have the report well in advance of the scheduling conference or the entry of the scheduling order.

Since Rule 16 was amended in 1983 to mandate some case management activities in all courts, it has included deadlines for Completing these tasks to ensure that all courts do so within a reasonable time. Rule 26(f) was fit into this scheme when it was adopted in 1993. It was never intended, however, that the national requirements that certain activities be completed by a certain time should delay case management in districts that move much faster than the national rules direct, and the rule is therefore amended to permit such a court to adopt a local rule that shortens the period specified for the completion of these tasks.

"Shall" is replaced by "must," "does," or an active verb under the program to conform amended rules to current style conventions when there is no ambiguity.

GAP Report

The Advisory Committee recommends adding a sentence to the published amendments to Rule 26(f) authorizing local rules shortening the time between the attorney conference and the court's action under Rule 16(b), and addition to the Committee Note of explanatory material about this change to the rule. This addition can be made without republication in response to public comments.

2006 Amendment

Subdivision (a). Rule 26(a)(1)(B) is amended to parallel Rule 34(a) by recognizing that a party must disclose electronically stored information as well as documents that it may use to support its claims or defenses. The term "electronically stored information" has the same broad meaning in Rule 26(a)(1) as in Rule 34(a). This amendment is consistent with the 1993 addition of Rule 26(a)(1)(B). The term "data compilations" is deleted as unnecessary because it is a subset of both documents and electronically stored information.

[Subdivision (a)(1)(E).] Civil forfeiture actions are added to the list of exemptions from Rule 26(a)(1) disclosure requirements. These actions are governed by new Supplemental Rule G. Disclosure is not likely to be useful.

Subdivision (b)(2). The amendment to Rule 26(b)(2) is designed to address issues raised by difficulties in locating, retrieving, and providing discovery of some electronically stored information. Electronic storage systems often make it easier to locate and retrieve information. These advantages are properly taken into account in determining the reasonable scope of discovery in a particular case. But some sources of electronically stored information can be accessed only with substantial burden and cost. In a particular case, these burdens and costs may make the information on such sources not reasonably accessible.

It is not possible to define in a rule the different types of technological features that may affect the burdens and costs of accessing electronically stored information. Information systems are designed to provide ready access to information used in regular ongoing activities. They also may be designed so as to provide ready access to information that is not regularly used. But a system may retain information on sources that are accessible only by incurring substantial burdens or costs. Subparagraph (B) is added to regulate discovery from such sources.

Under this rule, a responding party should produce electronically stored information that is relevant, not privileged, and reasonably accessible, subject to the (b)(2)(C) limitations that apply to all discovery. The responding party must also identify, by category or type, the sources containing potentially responsive information that it is neither searching nor producing. The identification should, to the extent possible, provide enough detail to enable the requesting party to evaluate the burdens and costs of providing the discovery and the likelihood of finding responsive information on the identified sources.

A party's identification of sources of electronically stored information as not reasonably accessible does not relieve the party of its common-law or statutory duties to preserve evidence. Whether a responding party is required to preserve unsearched sources of potentially responsive information that it believes are not reasonably accessible depends on the circumstances of each case. It is often useful for the parties to discuss this issue early in discovery.

The volume of — and the ability to search — much electronically stored information means that in many cases the responding party will be able to produce information from reasonably accessible sources that will fully satisfy the parties' discovery needs. In many circumstances the requesting party should obtain and evaluate the information from such sources before insisting that the responding party search and produce information contained on sources that are not reasonably accessible. If the requesting party continues to seek discovery of information from sources identified as not reasonably accessible, the parties should discuss the burdens and costs of accessing and retrieving the information, the needs that may establish good cause for requiring all or part of the requested discovery even if the information sought is not reasonably accessible, and conditions on obtaining and producing the information that may be appropriate.

If the parties cannot agree whether, or on what terms, sources identified as not reasonably accessible should be searched and discoverable information produced, the issue may be raised either by a motion to compel discovery or by a motion for a protective order. The parties must confer before bringing either motion. If the parties do not resolve the issue and the court must decide, the responding party must show that the identified sources of information are not reasonably accessible because of undue burden or cost. The requesting party may need discovery to test this assertion. Such discovery might take the form of requiring the responding party to conduct a sampling of information contained on the sources identified as not reasonably accessible; allowing some form of inspection of such sources; or taking depositions of witnesses knowledgeable about the responding party's information systems.

Once it is shown that a source of electronically stored information is not reasonably accessible, the requesting party may still obtain discovery by showing good cause, considering the limitations of Rule 26(b)(2)(C) that balance the costs and potential benefits of discovery. The decision whether to require a responding party to search for and produce information that is not reasonably accessible depends not only on the burdens and costs of doing so, but also on whether those

burdens and costs can be justified in the circumstances of the case. Appropriate considerations may include: (1) the specificity of the discovery request; (2) the quantity of information available from other and more easily accessed sources; (3) the failure to produce relevant information that seems likely to have existed but is no longer available on more easily accessed sources; (4) the likelihood of finding relevant, responsive information that cannot be obtained from other, more easily accessed sources; (5) predictions as to the importance and usefulness of the further information; (6) the importance of the issues at stake in the litigation; and (7) the parties' resources.

The responding party has the burden as to one aspect of the inquiry — whether the identified sources are not reasonably accessible in light of the burdens and costs required to search for, retrieve, and produce whatever responsive information may be found. The requesting party has the burden of showing that its need for the discovery outweighs the burdens and costs of locating, retrieving, and producing the information. In some cases, the court will be able to determine whether the identified sources are not reasonably accessible and whether the requesting party has shown good cause for some or all of the discovery, consistent with the limitations of Rule 26(b)(2)(C), through a single proceeding or presentation. The good-cause determination, however, may be complicated because the court and parties may know little about what information the sources identified as not reasonably accessible might contain, whether it is relevant, or how valuable it may be to the litigation. In such cases, the parties may need some focused discovery, which may include sampling of the sources, to learn more about what burdens and costs are involved in accessing the information, what the information consists of, and how valuable it is for the litigation in light of information that can be obtained by exhausting other opportunities for discovery.

The good-cause inquiry and consideration of the Rule 26(b)(2)(C) limitations are coupled with the authority to set conditions for discovery. The conditions may take the form of limits on the amount, type, or sources of information required to be accessed and produced. The conditions may also include payment by the requesting party of part or all of the reasonable costs of obtaining information from sources that are not reasonably accessible. A requesting party's willingness to share or bear the access costs may be weighed by the court in determining whether there is good cause. But the producing party's burdens in reviewing the information for relevance and privilege may weigh against permitting the requested discovery.

The limitations of Rule 26(b)(2)(C) continue to apply to all discovery of electronically stored information, including that stored on reasonably accessible electronic sources.

Subdivision (b)(5). The Committee has repeatedly been advised that the risk of privilege waiver, and the work necessary to avoid it, add to the costs and delay of discovery. When the review is of electronically stored information, the risk of waiver, and the time and effort required to avoid it, can increase substantially because of the volume of electronically stored information and the difficulty in ensuring that all information to be produced has in fact been reviewed. Rule 26(b)(5)(A) provides a procedure for a party that has withheld information on the basis of privilege or protection as trial-preparation material to make the claim so that the requesting party can decide whether to contest the claim and

the court can resolve the dispute. Rule 26(b)(5)(B) is added to provide a procedure for a party to assert a claim of privilege or trial-preparation material protection after information is produced in discovery in the action and, if the claim is contested, permit any party that received the information to present the matter to the court for resolution.

Rule 26(b)(5)(B) does not address whether the privilege or protection that is asserted after production was waived by the production. The courts have developed principles to determine whether, and under what circumstances, waiver results from inadvertent production of privileged or protected information. Rule 26(b)(5)(B) provides a procedure for presenting and addressing these issues. Rule 26(b)(5)(B) works in tandem with Rule 26(f), which is amended to direct the parties to discuss privilege issues in preparing their discovery plan, and which, with amended Rule 16(b), allows the parties to ask the court to include in an order any agreements the parties reach regarding issues of privilege or trial-preparation material protection. Agreements reached under Rule 26(f)(4) and orders including such agreements entered under Rule 16(b)(6) may be considered when a court determines whether a waiver has occurred. Such agreements and orders ordinarily control if they adopt procedures different from those in Rule 26(b)(5)(B).

A party asserting a claim of privilege or protection after production must give notice to the receiving party. That notice should be in writing unless the circumstances preclude it. Such circumstances could include the assertion of the claim during a deposition. The notice should be as specific as possible in identifying the information and stating the basis for the claim. Because the receiving party must decide whether to challenge the claim and may sequester the information and submit it to the court for a ruling on whether the claimed privilege or protection applies and whether it has been waived, the notice should be sufficiently detailed so as to enable the receiving party and the court to understand the basis for the claim and to determine whether waiver has occurred. Courts will continue to examine whether a claim of privilege or protection was made at a reasonable time when delay is part of the waiver determination under the governing law.

After receiving notice, each party that received the information must promptly return, sequester, or destroy the information and any copies it has. The option of sequestering or destroying the information is included in part because the receiving party may have incorporated the information in protected trial-preparation materials. No receiving party may use or disclose the information pending resolution of the privilege claim. The receiving party may present to the court the questions whether the information is privileged or protected as trial-preparation material, and whether the privilege or protection has been waived. If it does so, it must provide the court with the grounds for the privilege or protection specified in the producing party's notice, and serve all parties. In presenting the question, the party may use the content of the information only to the extent permitted by the applicable law of privilege, protection for trial-preparation material, and professional responsibility.

If a party disclosed the information to nonparties before receiving notice of a claim of privilege or protection as trial-preparation material, it must take reasonable steps to retrieve the information and to return it, sequester it until claim is resolved, or destroy it.

Whether the information is returned or not, the producing party must preserve the information pending the court's ruling on whether the claim of privilege or of protection is properly asserted and whether it was waived. As with claims made under Rule 26(b)(5)(A), there may be no ruling if the other parties do not contest the claim.

Subdivision (f). Rule 26(f) is amended to direct the parties to discuss discovery of electronically stored information during their discovery-planning conference. The rule focuses on "issues relating to disclosure or discovery of electronically stored information"; the discussion is not required in cases not involving electronic discovery, and the amendment imposes no additional requirements in those cases. When the parties do anticipate disclosure or discovery of electronically stored information, discussion at the outset may avoid later difficulties or ease their resolution.

When a case involves discovery of electronically stored information, the issues to be addressed during the Rule 26(f) conference depend on the nature and extent of the contemplated discovery and of the parties' information systems. It may be important for the parties to discuss those systems, and accordingly important for counsel to become familiar with those systems before the conference. With that information, the parties can develop a discovery plan that takes into account the capabilities of their computer systems. In appropriate cases identification of, and early discovery from, individuals with special knowledge of a party's computer systems may be helpful.

The particular issues regarding electronically stored information that deserve attention during the discovery planning stage depend on the specifics of the given case. *See Manual for Complex Litigation* (4th) § 40.25(2) (listing topics for discussion in a proposed order regarding meet-and-confer sessions). For example, the parties may specify the topics for such discovery and the time period for which discovery will be sought. They may identify the various sources of such information within a party's control that should be searched for electronically stored information. They may discuss whether the information is reasonably accessible to the party that has it, including the burden or cost of retrieving and reviewing the information. *See* Rule 26(b)(2)(B). Rule 26(f)(3) explicitly directs the parties to discuss the form or forms in which electronically stored information might be produced. The parties may be able to reach agreement on the forms of production, making discovery more efficient. Rule 34(b) is amended to permit a requesting party to specify the form or forms in which it wants electronically stored information produced. If the requesting party does not specify a form, Rule 34(b) directs the responding party to state the forms it intends to use in the production. Early discussion of the forms of production may facilitate the application of Rule 34(b) by allowing the parties to determine what forms of production will meet both parties' needs. Early identification of disputes over the forms of production may help avoid the expense and delay of searches or productions using inappropriate forms.

Rule 26(f) is also amended to direct the parties to discuss any issues regarding preservation of discoverable information during their conference as they develop a discovery plan. This provision applies to all sorts of discoverable information, but can be particularly important with regard to electronically stored information. The volume and dynamic nature of electronically stored information may complicate preserva-

tion obligations. The ordinary operation of computers involves both the automatic creation and the automatic deletion or overwriting of certain information. Failure to address preservation issues early in the litigation increases uncertainty and raises a risk of disputes.

The parties' discussion should pay particular attention to the balance between the competing needs to preserve relevant evidence and to continue routine operations critical to ongoing activities. Complete or broad cessation of a party's routine computer operations could paralyze the party's activities. *Cf. Manual for Complex Litigation* (4th) § 11.422 ("A blanket preservation order may be prohibitively expensive and unduly burdensome for parties dependent on computer systems for their day-to-day operations.") The parties should take account of these considerations in their discussions, with the goal of agreeing on reasonable preservation steps.

The requirement that the parties discuss preservation does not imply that courts should routinely enter preservation orders. A preservation order entered over objections should be narrowly tailored. Ex parte preservation orders should issue only in exceptional circumstances.

Rule 26(f) is also amended to provide that the parties should discuss any issues relating to assertions of privilege or of protection as trial-preparation materials, including whether the parties can facilitate discovery by agreeing on procedures for asserting claims of privilege or protection after production and whether to ask the court to enter an order that includes any agreement the parties reach. The Committee has repeatedly been advised about the discovery difficulties that can result from efforts to guard against waiver of privilege and work-product protection. Frequently parties find it necessary to spend large amounts of time reviewing materials requested through discovery to avoid waiving privilege. These efforts are necessary because materials subject to a claim of privilege or protection are often difficult to identify. A failure to withhold even one such item may result in an argument that there has been a waiver of privilege as to all other privileged materials on that subject matter. Efforts to avoid the risk of waiver can impose substantial costs on the party producing the material and the time required for the privilege review can substantially delay access for the party seeking discovery.

These problems often become more acute when discovery of electronically stored information is sought. The volume of such data, and the informality that attends use of e-mail and some other types of electronically stored information, may make privilege determinations more difficult, and privilege review correspondingly more expensive and time consuming. Other aspects of electronically stored information pose particular difficulties for privilege review. For example, production may be sought of information automatically included in electronic files but not apparent to the creator or to readers. Computer programs may retain draft language, editorial comments, and other deleted matter (sometimes referred to as "embedded data" or "embedded edits") in an electronic file but not make them apparent to the reader. Information describing the history, tracking, or management of an electronic file (sometimes called "metadata") is usually not apparent to the reader viewing a hard copy or a screen image. Whether this information should be produced may be among the topics discussed in the Rule 26(f) conference. If it is, it may need to be reviewed to ensure that no privileged infor-

mation is included, further complicating the task of privilege review.

Parties may attempt to minimize these costs and delays by agreeing to protocols that minimize the risk of waiver. They may agree that the responding party will provide certain requested materials for initial examination without waiving any privilege or protection — sometimes known as a "quick peek." The requesting party then designates the documents it wishes to have actually produced. This designation is the Rule 34 request. The responding party then responds in the usual course, screening only those documents actually requested for formal production and asserting privilege claims as provided in Rule 26(b)(5)(A). On other occasions, parties enter agreements — sometimes called "clawback agreements"— that production without intent to waive privilege or protection should not be a waiver so long as the responding party identifies the documents mistakenly produced, and that the documents should be returned under those circumstances. Other voluntary arrangements may be appropriate depending on the circumstances of each litigation. In most circumstances, a party who receives information under such an arrangement cannot assert that production of the information waived a claim of privilege or of protection as trial-preparation material.

Although these agreements may not be appropriate for all cases, in certain cases they can facilitate prompt and economical discovery by reducing delay before the discovering party obtains access to documents, and by reducing the cost and burden of review by the producing party. A case-management or other order including such agreements may further facilitate the discovery process. Form 35 is amended to include a report to the court about any agreement regarding protections against inadvertent forfeiture or waiver of privilege or protection that the parties have reached, and Rule 16(b) is amended to recognize that the court may include such an agreement in a case-management or other order. If the parties agree to entry of such an order, their proposal should be included in the report to the court.

Rule 26(b)(5)(B) is added to establish a parallel procedure to assert privilege or protection as trial-preparation material after production, leaving the question of waiver to later determination by the court.

2007 Amendment

*[Effective December 1, 2007,
absent contrary Congressional action.]*

The language of Rule 26 has been amended as part of the general restyling of the Civil Rules to make them more easily understood and to make style and terminology consistent throughout the rules. These changes are intended to be stylistic only.

Former Rule 26(a)(5) served as an index of the discovery methods provided by later rules. It was deleted as redundant. Deletion does not affect the right to pursue discovery in addition to disclosure.

Former Rule 26(b)(1) began with a general statement of the scope of discovery that appeared to function as a preface to each of the five numbered paragraphs that followed. This preface has been shifted to the text of paragraph (1) because it does not accurately reflect the limits embodied in paragraphs (2), (3), or (4), and because paragraph (5) does not address the scope of discovery.

The reference to discovery of "books" in former Rule 26(b)(1) was deleted to achieve consistent expression throughout the discovery rules. Books remain a proper subject of discovery.

Amended Rule 26(b)(3) states that a party may obtain a copy of the party's own previous statement "on request." Former Rule 26(b)(3) expressly made the request procedure available to a nonparty witness, but did not describe the procedure to be used by a party. This apparent gap is closed by adopting the request procedure, which ensures that a party need not invoke Rule 34 to obtain a copy of the party's own statement.

Rule 26(e) stated the duty to supplement or correct a disclosure or discovery response "to include information thereafter acquired." This apparent limit is not reflected in practice; parties recognize the duty to supplement or correct by providing information that was not originally provided although it was available at the time of the initial disclosure or response. These words are deleted to reflect the actual meaning of the present rule.

Former Rule 26(e) used different phrases to describe the time to supplement or correct a disclosure or discovery response. Disclosures were to be supplemented "at appropriate intervals." A prior discovery response must be "seasonably * * * amend[ed]." The fine distinction between these phrases has not been observed in practice. Amended Rule 26(e)(1)(A) uses the same phrase for disclosures and discovery responses. The party must supplement or correct "in a timely manner."

Former Rule 26(g)(1) did not call for striking an unsigned disclosure. The omission was an obvious drafting oversight. Amended Rule 26(g)(2) includes disclosures in the list of matters that the court must strike unless a signature is provided "promptly * * * after being called to the attorney's or party's attention."

Former Rule 26(b)(2)(A) referred to a "good faith" argument to extend existing law. Amended Rule 26(b)(1)(B)(i) changes this reference to a "nonfrivolous" argument to achieve consistency with Rule 11(b)(2).

As with the Rule 11 signature on a pleading, written motion, or other paper, disclosure and discovery signatures should include not only a postal address but also a telephone number and electronic-mail address. A signer who lacks one or more of those addresses need not supply a nonexistent item.

Rule 11(b)(2) recognizes that it is legitimate to argue for establishing new law. An argument to establish new law is equally legitimate in conducting discovery.

Rule 27. Depositions Before Action or Pending Appeal

(a) Before Action.

(1) Petition. A person who desires to perpetuate testimony regarding any matter that may be cognizable in any court of the United States may file a verified petition in the United States district court in the district of the residence of any expected adverse party. The petition shall be entitled in the name of the petitioner and shall show: 1, that the petitioner expects to be a party to an action cogniza-

ble in a court of the United States but is presently unable to bring it or cause it to be brought, 2, the subject matter of the expected action and the petitioner's interest therein, 3, the facts which the petitioner desires to establish by the proposed testimony and the reasons for desiring to perpetuate it, 4, the names or a description of the persons the petitioner expects will be adverse parties and their addresses so far as known, and 5, the names and addresses of the persons to be examined and the substance of the testimony which the petitioner expects to elicit from each, and shall ask for an order authorizing the petitioner to take the depositions of the persons to be examined named in the petition, for the purpose of perpetuating their testimony.

(2) Notice and Service. At least 20 days before the hearing date, the petitioner must serve each expected adverse party with a copy of the petition and a notice stating the time and place of the hearing. The notice may be served either inside or outside the district or state in the manner provided in Rule 4. If that service cannot be made with due diligence on an expected adverse party, the court may order service by publication or otherwise. The court must appoint an attorney to represent persons not served in the manner provided by Rule 4 and to cross-examine the deponent if an unserved person is not otherwise represented. Rule 17(c) applies if any expected adverse party is a minor or is incompetent.

(3) Order and Examination. If the court is satisfied that the perpetuation of the testimony may prevent a failure or delay of justice, it shall make an order designating or describing the persons whose depositions may be taken and specifying the subject matter of the examination and whether the depositions shall be taken upon oral examination or written interrogatories. The depositions may then be taken in accordance with these rules; and the court may make orders of the character provided for by Rules 34 and 35. For the purpose of applying these rules to depositions for perpetuating testimony, each reference therein to the court in which the action is pending shall be deemed to refer to the court in which the petition for such deposition was filed.

(4) Use of Deposition. If a deposition to perpetuate testimony is taken under these rules or if, although not so taken, it would be admissible in evidence in the courts of the state in which it is taken, it may be used in any action involving the same subject matter subsequently brought in a United States district court, in accordance with the provisions of Rule 32(a).

(b) Pending Appeal. If an appeal has been taken from a judgment of a district court or before the

taking of an appeal if the time therefor has not expired, the district court in which the judgment was rendered may allow the taking of the depositions of witnesses to perpetuate their testimony for use in the event of further proceedings in the district court. In such case the party who desires to perpetuate the testimony may make a motion in the district court for leave to take the depositions, upon the same notice and service thereof as if the action was pending in the district court. The motion shall show (1) the names and addresses of persons to be examined and the substance of the testimony which the party expects to elicit from each; (2) the reasons for perpetuating their testimony. If the court finds that the perpetuation of the testimony is proper to avoid a failure or delay of justice, it may make an order allowing the depositions to be taken and may make orders of the character provided for by Rules 34 and 35, and thereupon the depositions may be taken and used in the same manner and under the same conditions as are prescribed in these rules for depositions taken in actions pending in the district court.

(c) Perpetuation by Action. This rule does not limit the power of a court to entertain an action to perpetuate testimony.
(As amended Dec. 27, 1946, eff. Mar. 19, 1948; Dec. 29, 1948, eff. Oct. 20, 1949; Mar. 1, 1971, eff. July 1, 1971; Mar. 2, 1987, eff. Aug. 1, 1987; Apr. 25, 2005, eff. Dec. 1, 2005.)

Proposed Amendment of Rule

Effective December 1, 2007, absent contrary Congressional action, this rule is amended to read as follows:

Rule 27. *Depositions to Perpetuate Testimony*

(a) *Before an Action Is Filed.*

(1) Petition. A person who wants to perpetuate testimony about any matter cognizable in a United States court may file a verified petition in the district court for the district where any expected adverse party resides. The petition must ask for an order authorizing the petitioner to depose the named persons in order to perpetuate their testimony. The petition must be titled in the petitioner's name and must show:

(A) that the petitioner expects to be a party to an action cognizable in a United States court but cannot presently bring it or cause it to be brought;

(B) the subject matter of the expected action and the petitioner's interest;

(C) the facts that the petitioner wants to establish by the proposed testimony and the reasons to perpetuate it;

(D) the names or a description of the persons whom the petitioner expects to be adverse

parties and their addresses, so far as known; and

(E) the name, address, and expected substance of the testimony of each deponent.

(2) *Notice and Service.* At least 20 days before the hearing date, the petitioner must serve each expected adverse party with a copy of the petition and a notice stating the time and place of the hearing. The notice may be served either inside or outside the district or state in the manner provided in Rule 4. If that service cannot be made with reasonable diligence on an expected adverse party, the court may order service by publication or otherwise. The court must appoint an attorney to represent persons not served in the manner provided in Rule 4 and to cross-examine the deponent if an unserved person is not otherwise represented. If any expected adverse party is a minor or is incompetent, Rule 17(c) applies.

(3) *Order and Examination.* If satisfied that perpetuating the testimony may prevent a failure or delay of justice, the court must issue an order that designates or describes the persons whose depositions may be taken, specifies the subject matter of the examinations, and states whether the depositions will be taken orally or by written interrogatories. The depositions may then be taken under these rules, and the court may issue orders like those authorized by Rules 34 and 35. A reference in these rules to the court where an action is pending means, for purposes of this rule, the court where the petition for the deposition was filed.

(4) *Using the Deposition.* A deposition to perpetuate testimony may be used under Rule 32(a) in any later-filed district-court action involving the same subject matter if the deposition either was taken under these rules or, although not so taken, would be admissible in evidence in the courts of the state where it was taken.

(b) Pending Appeal.

(1) *In General.* The court where a judgment has been rendered may, if an appeal has been taken or may still be taken, permit a party to depose witnesses to perpetuate their testimony for use in the event of further proceedings in that court.

(2) *Motion.* The party who wants to perpetuate testimony may move for leave to take the depositions, on the same notice and service as if the action were pending in the district court. The motion must show:

(A) the name, address, and expected substance of the testimony of each deponent; and

(B) the reasons for perpetuating the testimony.

(3) *Court Order.* If the court finds that perpetuating the testimony may prevent a failure or delay of justice, the court may permit the depositions to be taken and may issue orders like those authorized by Rules 34 and 35. The depositions may be taken and used as any other deposition taken in a pending district-court action.

(c) Perpetuation by an Action. This rule does not limit a court's power to entertain an action to perpetuate testimony.

ADVISORY COMMITTEE NOTES

1937 Adoption

Note to Subdivision (a). This rule offers a simple method of perpetuating testimony in cases where it is usually allowed under equity practice or under modern statutes. See *Arizona v. California*, 1934, 54 S.Ct. 735, 292 U.S. 341, 78 L.Ed. 1298; *Todd Engineering Dry Dock and Repair Co. v. United States*, C.C.A.5, 1929, 32 F.2d 734; *Hall v. Stout*, 4 Del.Ch. 269 (1871). For comparable state statutes see Ark.Civ.Code (Crawford, 1934) §§ 666 to 670; Calif.Code Civ.Proc. (Deering, 1937) 2083–2089; Smith-Hurd Ill.Stats. c. 51, §§ 39 to 46; Iowa Code (1935) §§ 11400 to 11407; 2 Mass.Gen.Laws (Ter.Ed., 1932) ch. 233, §§ 46 to 63; N.Y.C.P.A. (1937) § 295; Ohio Gen.Code Ann. (Throckmorton, 1936) §§ 12216 to 12222; Va.Code Ann. (Michie, 1936) § 6235; Wis.Stat. (1935) §§ 326.27 to 326.29. The appointment of an attorney to represent absent parties or parties not personally notified, or a guardian ad litem to represent minors and incompetents, is provided for in several of the above statutes.

Note to Subdivision (b). This follows the practice approved in *Richter v. Union Trust Co.*, 1885, 5 S.Ct. 1162, 115 U.S. 55, 29 L.Ed. 345, by extending the right to perpetuate testimony to cases pending an appeal.

Note to Subdivision (c). This preserves the right to employ a separate action to perpetuate testimony under U.S.C., Title 28, [former] § 644 (Depositions under *dedimus potestatem* and *in perpetuam*) as an alternate method.

1946 Amendment

Note. Since the second sentence in subdivision (a)(3) refers only to depositions, it is arguable that Rules 34 and 35 are inapplicable in proceedings to perpetuate testimony. The new matter [in subdivisions (a)(3) and (b)] clarifies. A conforming change is also made in subdivision (b).

1948 Amendment

The amendment effective October 1949, substituted the words "United States district court" in subdivision (a)(1) and (4) for "district court of the United States."

1971 Amendment

The reference intended in this subdivision is to the rule governing the use of depositions in court proceedings. For-

merly Rule 26(d), that rule is now Rule 32(a). The subdivision is amended accordingly.

1987 Amendment

The amendments are technical. No substantive change is intended.

2005 Amendment

The outdated cross-reference to former Rule 4(d) is corrected to incorporate all Rule 4 methods of service. Former Rule 4(d) has been allocated to many different subdivisions of Rule 4. Former Rule 4(d) did not cover all categories of defendants or modes of service, and present Rule 4 reaches further than all of former Rule 4. But there is no reason to distinguish between the different categories of defendants and modes of service encompassed by Rule 4. Rule 4 service provides effective notice. Notice by such means should be provided to any expected adverse party that comes within Rule 4.

Other changes are made to conform Rule 27(a)(2) to current style conventions.

2007 Amendment

*[Effective December 1, 2007,
absent contrary Congressional action.]*

The language of Rule 27 has been amended as part of the general restyling of the Civil Rules to make them more easily understood and to make style and terminology consistent throughout the rules. These changes are intended to be stylistic only.

HISTORICAL NOTES

References in Text

"Rule 4(d)", referred to in subd. (a)(2), is Rule 4(d) prior to amendment by Supreme Court of the United States order dated Apr. 22, 1993, which failed to make conforming amendments to subd. (a)(2) of this rule. Rule 4(d) does not relate to manner of service which is provided for in Rule 4(e)(2) and (g) to (j).

Rule 28. Persons Before Whom Depositions may be Taken

(a) Within the United States. Within the United States or within a territory or insular possession subject to the jurisdiction of the United States, depositions shall be taken before an officer authorized to administer oaths by the laws of the United States or of the place where the examination is held, or before a person appointed by the court in which the action is pending. A person so appointed has power to administer oaths and take testimony. The term officer as used in Rules 30, 31 and 32 includes a person appointed by the court or designated by the parties under Rule 29.

(b) In Foreign Countries. Depositions may be taken in a foreign country (1) pursuant to any applicable treaty or convention, or (2) pursuant to a letter of request (whether or not captioned a letter rogatory), or (3) on notice before a person authorized to adminis-

ter oaths in the place where the examination is held, either by the law thereof or by the law of the United States, or (4) before a person commissioned by the court, and a person so commissioned shall have the power by virtue of the commission to administer any necessary oath and take testimony. A commission or a letter of request shall be issued on application and notice and on terms that are just and appropriate. It is not requisite to the issuance of a commission or a letter of request that the taking of the deposition in any other manner is impracticable or inconvenient; and both a commission and a letter of request may be issued in proper cases. A notice or commission may designate the person before whom the deposition is to be taken either by name or descriptive title. A letter of request may be addressed "To the Appropriate Authority in [here name the country]." When a letter of request or any other device is used pursuant to any applicable treaty or convention, it shall be captioned in the form prescribed by that treaty or convention. Evidence obtained in response to a letter of request need not be excluded merely because it is not a verbatim transcript, because the testimony was not taken under oath, or because of any similar departure from the requirements for depositions taken within the United States under these rules.

(c) Disqualification for Interest. No deposition shall be taken before a person who is a relative or employee or attorney or counsel of any of the parties, or is a relative or employee of such attorney or counsel, or is financially interested in the action.

(As amended Dec. 27, 1946, eff. Mar. 19, 1948; Jan. 21, 1963, eff. July 1, 1963; Apr. 29, 1980, eff. Aug. 1, 1980; Mar. 2, 1987, eff. Aug. 1, 1987; Apr. 22, 1993, eff. Dec. 1, 1993.)

Proposed Amendment of Rule

Effective December 1, 2007, absent contrary Congressional action, this rule is amended to read as follows:

Rule 28. Persons Before Whom Depositions May be Taken

(a) Within the United States.

(1) In General. Within the United States or a territory or insular possession subject to United States jurisdiction, a deposition must be taken before:

(A) an officer authorized to administer oaths either by federal law or by the law in the place of examination; or

(B) a person appointed by the court where the action is pending to administer oaths and take testimony.

(2) Definition of "Officer". The term "officer" in Rules 30, 31, and 32 includes a person ap-

pointed by the court under this rule or designated by the parties under Rule 29(a).

(b) In a Foreign Country.

(1) In General. A deposition may be taken in a foreign country:

(A) under an applicable treaty or convention;

(B) under a letter of request, whether or not captioned a "letter rogatory";

(C) on notice, before a person authorized to administer oaths either by federal law or by the law in the place of examination; or

(D) before a person commissioned by the court to administer any necessary oath and take testimony.

(2) Issuing a Letter of Request or a Commission. A letter of request, a commission, or both may be issued:

(A) on appropriate terms after an application and notice of it; and

(B) without a showing that taking the deposition in another manner is impracticable or inconvenient.

(3) Form of a Request, Notice, or Commission. When a letter of request or any other device is used according to a treaty or convention, it must be captioned in the form prescribed by that treaty or convention. A letter of request may be addressed "To the Appropriate Authority in [name of country]." A deposition notice or a commission must designate by name or descriptive title the person before whom the deposition is to be taken.

(4) Letter of Request—Admitting Evidence. Evidence obtained in response to a letter of request need not be excluded merely because it is not a verbatim transcript, because the testimony was not taken under oath, or because of any similar departure from the requirements for depositions taken within the United States.

(c) Disqualification. A deposition must not be taken before a person who is any party's relative, employee, or attorney; who is related to or employed by any party's attorney; or who is financially interested in the action.

ADVISORY COMMITTEE NOTES

1937 Adoption

In effect this rule is substantially the same as U.S.C., Title 28, [former] § 639 (Depositions *de bene esse*; when and where taken; notice). U.S.C., Title 28, [former] § 642 (Depositions, acknowledgments, and affidavits taken by notaries public) does not conflict with subdivision (a).

1946 Amendments

Note. The added language [in subdivision (a)] provides for the situation, occasionally arising, when depositions must be taken in an isolated place where there is no one readily available who has the power to administer oaths and take testimony according to the terms of the rule as originally stated. In addition, the amendment affords a more convenient method of securing depositions in the case where state lines intervene between the location of various witnesses otherwise rather closely grouped. The amendment insures that the person appointed shall have adequate power to perform his duties. It has been held that a person authorized to act in the premises, as, for example, a master, may take testimony outside the district of his appointment. *Consolidated Fastener Co. v. Columbian Button & Fastener Co.*, C.C.N.D.N.Y.1898, 85 Fed. 54; *Mathieson Alkali Works v. Arnold, Hoffman & Co.*, C.C.A.1, 1929, 31 F.2d 1.

1963 Amendments

The amendment of clause (1) is designed to facilitate depositions in foreign countries by enlarging the class of persons before whom the depositions may be taken on notice. The class is no longer confined, as at present, to a secretary of embassy or legation, consul general, consul, vice consul, or consular agent of the United States. In a country that regards the taking of testimony by a foreign official in aid of litigation pending in a court of another country as an infringement upon its sovereignty, it will be expedient to notice depositions before officers of the country in which the examination is taken. See generally *Symposium, Letters Rogatory* (Grossman ed. 1956); Doyle, *Taking Evidence by Deposition and Letters Rogatory and Obtaining Documents in Foreign Territory*, Proc.A.B.A., Sec.Int'l & Comp.L. 37 (1959); Heilpern, *Procuring Evidence Abroad*, 14 Tul.L.Rev. 29 (1939); Jones, *International Judicial Assistance: Procedural Chaos and a Program for Reform*, 62 Yale L.J. 515, 526–29 (1953); Smit, *International Aspects of Federal Civil Procedure*, 61 Colum.L.Rev. 1031, 1056–58 (1961).

Clause (2) of amended subdivision (b), like the corresponding provision of subdivision (a) dealing with depositions taken in the United States, makes it clear that the appointment of a person by commission in itself confers power upon him to administer any necessary oath.

It has been held that a letter rogatory will not be issued unless the use of a notice or commission is shown to be impossible or impractical. See, e.g., *United States v. Matles*, 154 F.Supp. 574 (E.D.N.Y.1957); *The Edmund Fanning*, 89 F.Supp. 282 (E.D.N.Y.1950); *Branyan v. Koninklijke Luchtvaart Maatschappij*, 13 F.R.D. 425 (S.D.N.Y.1953). See also *Ali Akber Kiachif v. Philco International Corp.*, 10 F.R.D. 277 (S.D.N.Y.1950). The intent of the fourth sentence of the amended subdivision is to overcome this judicial antipathy and to permit a sound choice between depositions under a letter rogatory and on notice or by commission in the light of all the circumstances. In a case in which the foreign country will compel a witness to attend or testify in aid of a letter rogatory but not in aid of a commission, a letter rogatory may be preferred on the ground that it is less expensive to execute, even if there is plainly no need for compulsive process. A letter rogatory may also be preferred when it cannot be demonstrated that a witness will be recalcitrant or

when the witness states that he is willing to testify voluntarily, but the contingency exists that he will change his mind at the last moment. In the latter case, it may be advisable to issue both a commission and a letter rogatory, the latter to be executed if the former fails. The choice between a letter rogatory and a commission may be conditioned by other factors, including the nature and extent of the assistance that the foreign country will give to the execution of either.

In executing a letter rogatory the courts of other countries may be expected to follow their customary procedure for taking testimony. See *United States v. Paraffin Wax*, 2255 Bags, 23 F.R.D. 289 (E.D.N.Y.1959). In many noncommon-law countries the judge questions the witness, sometimes without first administering an oath, the attorneys put any supplemental questions either to the witness or through the judge, and the judge dictates a summary of the testimony, which the witness acknowledges as correct. See *Jones, supra,* at 530–32; *Doyle, supra,* at 39–41. The last sentence of the amended subdivision provides, contrary to the implications of some authority, that evidence recorded in such a fashion need not be excluded on that account. See *The Mandu*, 11 F.Supp. 845 (E.D.N.Y.1935). But *cf. Nelson v. United States*, 17 Fed.Cas. 1340 (No. 10,116) (C.C.D.Pa. 1816); *Winthrop v. Union Ins. Co.*, 30 Fed.Cas. 376 (No. 17901) (C.C.D.Pa.1807). The specific reference to the lack of an oath or a verbatim transcript is intended to be illustrative. Whether or to what degree the value or weight of the evidence may be affected by the method of taking or recording the testimony is left for determination according to the circumstances of the particular case, *cf. Uebersee Finanz-Korporation, A.G. v. Brownell*, 121 F.Supp. 420 (D.D.C. 1954); *Danisch v. Guardian Life Ins. Co.*, 19 F.R.D. 235 (S.D.N.Y.1956); the testimony may indeed be so devoid of substance or probative value as to warrant its exclusion altogether.

Some foreign countries are hostile to allowing a deposition to be taken in their country, especially by notice or commission, or to lending assistance in the taking of a deposition. Thus compliance with the terms of amended subdivision (b) may not in all cases ensure completion of a deposition abroad. Examination of the law and policy of the particular foreign country in advance of attempting a deposition is therefore advisable. See 4 *Moore's Federal Practice* ¶¶28.05–28.08 (2d ed. 1950).

1980 Amendments

The amendments are clarifying.

1987 Amendments

The amendment is technical. No substantive change is intended.

1993 Amendments

This revision is intended to make effective use of the Hague Convention on the Taking of Evidence Abroad in Civil or Commercial Matters, and of any similar treaties that the United States may enter into in the future which provide procedures for taking depositions abroad. The party taking the deposition is ordinarily obliged to conform to an applicable treaty or convention if an effective deposition can be taken by such internationally approved means, even though a verbatim transcript is not available or testimony cannot be

taken under oath. For a discussion of the impact of such treaties upon the discovery process, and of the application of principles of comity upon discovery in countries not signatories to a convention, see *Société Nationale Industrielle Aérospatiale v. United States District Court*, 482 U.S. 522 (1987).

The term "letter of request" has been substituted in the rule for the term "letter rogatory" because it is the primary method provided by the Hague Convention. A letter rogatory is essentially a form of letter of request. There are several other minor changes that are designed merely to carry out the intent of the other alterations.

2007 Amendment

[Effective December 1, 2007, absent contrary Congressional action.]

The language of Rule 28 has been amended as part of the general restyling of the Civil Rules to make them more easily understood and to make style and terminology consistent throughout the rules. These changes are intended to be stylistic only.

HISTORICAL NOTES

Treaties and Conventions; Taking of Evidence Abroad in Civil or Commercial Matters; Observance On and After Oct. 7, 1972, by United States and Citizens and Persons Subject to Jurisdiction of United States

For text of Convention, see provisions set out as a note under section 1781 of this title.

Rule 29. Stipulations Regarding Discovery Procedure

Unless otherwise directed by the court, the parties may by written stipulation (1) provide that depositions may be taken before any person, at any time or place, upon any notice, and in any manner and when so taken may be used like other depositions, and (2) modify other procedures governing or limitations placed upon discovery, except that stipulations extending the time provided in Rules 33, 34, and 36 for responses to discovery may, if they would interfere with any time set for completion of discovery, for hearing of a motion, or for trial, be made only with the approval of the court.

(As amended Mar. 30, 1970, eff. July 1, 1970; Apr. 22, 1993, eff. Dec. 1, 1993.)

Proposed Amendment of Rule

Effective December 1, 2007, absent contrary Congressional action, this rule is amended to read as follows:

Rule 29. *Stipulations About Discovery Procedure*

Unless the court orders otherwise, the parties may stipulate that:

(a) a deposition may be taken before any person, at any time or place, on any notice, and in the manner specified—in which event it may be used in the same way as any other deposition; and

(b) other procedures governing or limiting discovery be modified—but a stipulation extending the time for any form of discovery must have court approval if it would interfere with the time set for completing discovery, for hearing a motion, or for trial.

ADVISORY COMMITTEE NOTES

1970 Amendment

There is no provision for stipulations varying the procedures by which methods of discovery other than depositions are governed. It is common practice for parties to agree on such variations, and the amendment recognizes such agreements and provides a formal mechanism in the rules for giving them effect. Any stipulation varying the procedures may be superseded by court order, and stipulations extending the time for response to discovery under Rules 33, 34, and 36 require court approval.

1993 Amendments

This rule is revised to give greater opportunity for litigants to agree upon modifications to the procedures governing discovery or to limitations upon discovery. Counsel are encouraged to agree on less expensive and time-consuming methods to obtain information, as through voluntary exchange of documents, use of interviews in lieu of depositions, etc. Likewise, when more depositions or interrogatories are needed than allowed under these rules or when more time is needed to complete a deposition than allowed under a local rule, they can, by agreeing to the additional discovery, eliminate the need for a special motion addressed to the court.

Under the revised rule, the litigants ordinarily are not required to obtain the court's approval of these stipulations. By order or local rule, the court can, however, direct that its approval be obtained for particular types of stipulations; and, in any event, approval must be obtained if a stipulation to extend the 30–day period for responding to interrogatories, requests for production, or requests for admissions would interfere with dates set by the court for completing discovery, for hearing of a motion, or for trial.

2007 Amendment

[Effective December 1, 2007, absent contrary Congressional action.]

The language of Rule 29 has been amended as part of the general restyling of the Civil Rules to make them more easily understood and to make style and terminology consistent throughout the rules. These changes are intended to be stylistic only.

Rule 30. Depositions Upon Oral Examination

(a) When Depositions May Be Taken; When Leave Required.

(1) A party may take the testimony of any person, including a party, by deposition upon oral examination without leave of court except as provided in paragraph (2). The attendance of witnesses may be compelled by subpoena as provided in Rule 45.

(2) A party must obtain leave of court, which shall be granted to the extent consistent with the principles stated in Rule 26(b)(2), if the person to be examined is confined in prison or if, without the written stipulation of the parties,

(A) a proposed deposition would result in more than ten depositions being taken under this rule or Rule 31 by the plaintiffs, or by the defendants, or by third-party defendants;

(B) the person to be examined already has been deposed in the case; or

(C) a party seeks to take a deposition before the time specified in Rule 26(d) unless the notice contains a certification, with supporting facts, that the person to be examined is expected to leave the United States and be unavailable for examination in this country unless deposed before that time.

(b) Notice of Examination: General Requirements; Method of Recording; Production of Documents and Things; Deposition of Organization; Deposition by Telephone.

(1) A party desiring to take the deposition of any person upon oral examination shall give reasonable notice in writing to every other party to the action. The notice shall state the time and place for taking the deposition and the name and address of each person to be examined, if known, and, if the name is not known, a general description sufficient to identify the person or the particular class or group to which the person belongs. If a subpoena duces tecum is to be served on the person to be examined, the designation of the materials to be produced as set forth in the subpoena shall be attached to, or included in, the notice.

(2) The party taking the deposition shall state in the notice the method by which the testimony shall be recorded. Unless the court orders otherwise, it may be recorded by sound, sound-and-visual, or stenographic means, and the party taking the deposition shall bear the cost of the recording. Any party may arrange for a transcription to be made from the recording of a deposition taken by non-stenographic means.

(3) With prior notice to the deponent and other parties, any party may designate another method to record the deponent's testimony in addition to the method specified by the person taking the deposition. The additional record or transcript shall be made at that party's expense unless the court otherwise orders.

(4) Unless otherwise agreed by the parties, a deposition shall be conducted before an officer appointed or designated under Rule 28 and shall begin with a statement on the record by the officer that includes (A) the officer's name and business ad-

dress; (B) the date, time, and place of the deposition; (C) the name of the deponent; (D) the administration of the oath or affirmation to the deponent; and (E) an identification of all persons present. If the deposition is recorded other than stenographically, the officer shall repeat items (A) through (C) at the beginning of each unit of recorded tape or other recording medium. The appearance or demeanor of deponents or attorneys shall not be distorted through camera or sound-recording techniques. At the end of the deposition, the officer shall state on the record that the deposition is complete and shall set forth any stipulations made by counsel concerning the custody of the transcript or recording and the exhibits, or concerning other pertinent matters.

(5) The notice to a party deponent may be accompanied by a request made in compliance with Rule 34 for the production of documents and tangible things at the taking of the deposition. The procedure of Rule 34 shall apply to the request.

(6) A party may in the party's notice and in a subpoena name as the deponent a public or private corporation or a partnership or association or governmental agency and describe with reasonable particularity the matters on which examination is requested. In that event, the organization so named shall designate one or more officers, directors, or managing agents, or other persons who consent to testify on its behalf, and may set forth, for each person designated, the matters on which the person will testify. A subpoena shall advise a non-party organization of its duty to make such a designation. The persons so designated shall testify as to matters known or reasonably available to the organization. This subdivision (b)(6) does not preclude taking a deposition by any other procedure authorized in these rules.

(7) The parties may stipulate in writing or the court may upon motion order that a deposition be taken by telephone or other remote electronic means. For the purposes of this rule and Rules 28(a), 37(a)(1), and 37(b)(1), a deposition taken by such means is taken in the district and at the place where the deponent is to answer questions.

(c) Examination and Cross–Examination; Record of Examination; Oath; Objections.

Examination and cross-examination of witnesses may proceed as permitted at the trial under the provisions of the Federal Rules of Evidence except Rules 103 and 615. The officer before whom the deposition is to be taken shall put the witness on oath or affirmation and shall personally, or by someone acting under the officer's direction and in the officer's presence, record the testimony of the witness. The testimony shall be taken stenographi-

cally or recorded by any other method authorized by subdivision (b)(2) of this rule. All objections made at the time of the examination to the qualifications of the officer taking the deposition, to the manner of taking it, to the evidence presented, to the conduct of any party, or to any other aspect of the proceedings shall be noted by the officer upon the record of the deposition; but the examination shall proceed, with the testimony being taken subject to the objections. In lieu of participating in the oral examination, parties may serve written questions in a sealed envelope on the party taking the deposition and the party taking the deposition shall transmit them to the officer, who shall propound them to the witness and record the answers verbatim.

(d) Schedule and Duration; Motion to Terminate or Limit Examination.

(1) Any objection during a deposition must be stated concisely and in a non-argumentative and non-suggestive manner. A person may instruct a deponent not to answer only when necessary to preserve a privilege, to enforce a limitation directed by the court, or to present a motion under Rule 30(d) (4).

(2) Unless otherwise authorized by the court or stipulated by the parties, a deposition is limited to one day of seven hours. The court must allow additional time consistent with Rule 26(b)(2) if needed for a fair examination of the deponent or if the deponent or another person , or other circumstance, impedes or delays the examination.

(3) If the court finds that any impediment, delay, or other conduct has frustrated the fair examination of the deponent, it may impose upon the persons responsible an appropriate sanction, including the reasonable costs and attorney's fees incurred by any parties as a result thereof.

(4) At any time during a deposition, on motion of a party or of the deponent and upon a showing that the examination is being conducted in bad faith or in such manner as unreasonably to annoy, embarrass, or oppress the deponent or party, the court in which the action is pending or the court in the district where the deposition is being taken may order the officer conducting the examination to cease forthwith from taking the deposition, or may limit the scope and manner of the taking of the deposition as provided in Rule 26(c). If the order made terminates the examination, it may be resumed thereafter only upon the order of the court in which the action is pending. Upon demand of the objecting party or deponent, the taking of the deposition must be suspended for the time necessary to make a motion for an order. The provisions of Rule

37(a)(4) apply to the award of expenses incurred in relation to the motion.

(e) Review by Witness; Changes; Signing.

If requested by the deponent or a party before completion of the deposition, the deponent shall have 30 days after being notified by the officer that the transcript or recording is available in which to review the transcript or recording and, if there are changes in form or substance, to sign a statement reciting such changes and the reasons given by the deponent for making them. The officer shall indicate in the certificate prescribed by subdivision (f)(1) whether any review was requested and, if so, shall append any changes made by the deponent during the period allowed.

(f) Certification and Delivery by Officer; Exhibits; Copies.

(1) The officer must certify that the witness was duly sworn by the officer and that the deposition is a true record of the testimony given by the witness. This certificate must be in writing and accompany the record of the deposition. Unless otherwise ordered by the court, the officer must securely seal the deposition in an envelope or package indorsed with the title of the action and marked "Deposition of [here insert name of witness]" and must promptly send it to the attorney who arranged for the transcript or recording, who must store it under conditions that will protect it against loss, destruction, tampering, or deterioration. Documents and things produced for inspection during the examination of the witness must, upon the request of a party, be marked for identification and annexed to the deposition and may be inspected and copied by any party, except that if the person producing the materials desires to retain them the person may (A) offer copies to be marked for identification and annexed to the deposition and to serve thereafter as originals if the person affords to all parties fair opportunity to verify the copies by comparison with the originals, or (B) offer the originals to be marked for identification, after giving to each party an opportunity to inspect and copy them, in which event the materials may then be used in the same manner as if annexed to the deposition. Any party may move for an order that the original be annexed to and returned with the deposition to the court, pending final disposition of the case.

(2) Unless otherwise ordered by the court or agreed by the parties, the officer shall retain stenographic notes of any deposition taken stenographically or a copy of the recording of any deposition taken by another method. Upon payment of reasonable charges therefor, the officer shall furnish a copy of the transcript or other recording of the deposition to any party or to the deponent.

(3) The party taking the deposition shall give prompt notice of its filing to all other parties.

(g) Failure to Attend or to Serve Subpoena; Expenses.

(1) If the party giving the notice of the taking of a deposition fails to attend and proceed therewith and another party attends in person or by attorney pursuant to the notice, the court may order the party giving the notice to pay to such other party the reasonable expenses incurred by that party and that party's attorney in attending, including reasonable attorney's fees.

(2) If the party giving the notice of the taking of a deposition of a witness fails to serve a subpoena upon the witness and the witness because of such failure does not attend, and if another party attends in person or by attorney because that party expects the deposition of that witness to be taken, the court may order the party giving the notice to pay to such other party the reasonable expenses incurred by that party and that party's attorney in attending, including reasonable attorney's fees.

(As amended Jan. 21, 1963, eff. July 1, 1963; Mar. 30, 1970, eff. July 1, 1970; Mar. 1, 1971, eff. July 1, 1971; Nov. 20, 1972, eff. July 1, 1975; Apr. 29, 1980, eff. Aug. 1, 1980; Mar. 2, 1987, eff. Aug. 1, 1987; Apr. 22, 1993, eff. Dec. 1, 1993; Apr. 17, 2000, eff. Dec. 1, 2000.)

Proposed Amendment of Rule

Effective December 1, 2007, absent contrary Congressional action, this rule is amended to read as follows:

Rule 30. Depositions by Oral Examination

(a) When a Deposition May Be Taken.

(1) Without Leave. A party may, by oral questions, depose any person, including a party, without leave of court except as provided in Rule 30(a)(2). The deponent's attendance may be compelled by subpoena under Rule 45.

(2) With Leave. A party must obtain leave of court, and the court must grant leave to the extent consistent with Rule 26(b)(2):

(A) if the parties have not stipulated to the deposition and:

(i) the deposition would result in more than 10 depositions being taken under this rule or Rule 31 by the plaintiffs, or by the defendants, or by the third-party defendants;

(ii) the deponent has already been deposed in the case; or

(iii) the party seeks to take the deposition before the time specified in Rule 26(d), unless the party certifies in the notice, with

supporting facts, that the deponent is expected to leave the United States and be unavailable for examination in this country after that time; or

(B) if the deponent is confined in prison.

(b) Notice of the Deposition; Other Formal Requirements.

(1) Notice in General. A party who wants to depose a person by oral questions must give reasonable written notice to every other party. The notice must state the time and place of the deposition and, if known, the deponent's name and address. If the name is unknown, the notice must provide a general description sufficient to identify the person or the particular class or group to which the person belongs.

(2) Producing Documents. If a subpoena duces tecum is to be served on the deponent, the materials designated for production, as set out in the subpoena, must be listed in the notice or in an attachment. The notice to a party deponent may be accompanied by a request under Rule 34 to produce documents and tangible things at the deposition.

(3) Method of Recording.

(A) Method Stated in the Notice. The party who notices the deposition must state in the notice the method for recording the testimony. Unless the court orders otherwise, testimony may be recorded by audio, audiovisual, or stenographic means. The noticing party bears the recording costs. Any party may arrange to transcribe a deposition.

(B) Additional Method. With prior notice to the deponent and other parties, any party may designate another method for recording the testimony in addition to that specified in the original notice. That party bears the expense of the additional record or transcript unless the court orders otherwise.

(4) By Remote Means. The parties may stipulate—or the court may on motion order—that a deposition be taken by telephone or other remote means. For the purpose of this rule and Rules 28(a), 37(a)(2), and 37(b)(1), the deposition takes place where the deponent answers the questions.

(5) Officer's Duties.

(A) Before the Deposition. Unless the parties stipulate otherwise, a deposition must be conducted before an officer appointed or designated under Rule 28. The officer must begin the deposition with an on-the-record statement that includes:

(i) the officer's name and business address;

(ii) the date, time, and place of the deposition;

(iii) the deponent's name;

(iv) the officer's administration of the oath or affirmation to the deponent; and

(v) the identity of all persons present.

(B) Conducting the Deposition; Avoiding Distortion. If the deposition is recorded nonstenographically, the officer must repeat the items in Rule 30(b)(5)(A)(i)-(iii) at the beginning of each unit of the recording medium. The deponent's and attorneys' appearance or demeanor must not be distorted through recording techniques.

(C) After the Deposition. At the end of a deposition, the officer must state on the record that the deposition is complete and must set out any stipulations made by the attorneys about custody of the transcript or recording and of the exhibits, or about any other pertinent matters.

(6) Notice or Subpoena Directed to an Organization. In its notice or subpoena, a party may name as the deponent a public or private corporation, a partnership, an association, a governmental agency, or other entity and must describe with reasonable particularity the matters for examination. The named organization must then designate one or more officers, directors, or managing agents, or designate other persons who consent to testify on its behalf; and it may set out the matters on which each person designated will testify. A subpoena must advise a nonparty organization of its duty to make this designation. The persons designated must testify about information known or reasonably available to the organization. This paragraph (6) does not preclude a deposition by any other procedure allowed by these rules.

(c) Examination and Cross–Examination; Record of the Examination; Objections; Written Questions.

(1) Examination and Cross–Examination. The examination and cross-examination of a deponent proceed as they would at trial under the Federal Rules of Evidence, except Rules 103 and 615. After putting the deponent under oath or affirmation, the officer must record the testimony by the method designated under Rule 30(b)(3)(A). The testimony must be recorded by the officer personally or by a person acting in the presence and under the direction of the officer.

(2) Objections. An objection at the time of the examination—whether to evidence, to a party's conduct, to the officer's qualifications, to the manner of taking the deposition, or to any other aspect of the deposition—must be noted on the record, but the examination still proceeds; the testimony is taken subject to any objection. An objection must be stated concisely in a nonargumentative and nonsuggestive manner. A person may instruct a deponent not to answer only when necessary to preserve a privilege, to enforce a limitation ordered by the court, or to present a motion under Rule 30(d)(3).

(3) Participating Through Written Questions. Instead of participating in the oral examination, a party may serve written questions in a sealed envelope on the party noticing the deposition, who must deliver them to the officer. The officer must ask the deponent those questions and record the answers verbatim.

(d) Duration; Sanction; Motion to Terminate or Limit.

(1) Duration. Unless otherwise stipulated or ordered by the court, a deposition is limited to 1 day of 7 hours. The court must allow additional time consistent with Rule 26(b)(2) if needed to fairly examine the deponent or if the deponent, another person, or any other circumstance impedes or delays the examination.

(2) Sanction. The court may impose an appropriate sanction—including the reasonable expenses and attorney's fees incurred by any party—on a person who impedes, delays, or frustrates the fair examination of the deponent.

(3) Motion to Terminate or Limit.

(A) Grounds. At any time during a deposition, the deponent or a party may move to terminate or limit it on the ground that it is being conducted in bad faith or in a manner that unreasonably annoys, embarrasses, or oppresses the deponent or party. The motion may be filed in the court where the action is pending or the deposition is being taken. If the objecting deponent or party so demands, the deposition must be suspended for the time necessary to obtain an order.

(B) Order. The court may order that the deposition be terminated or may limit its scope and manner as provided in Rule 26(c). If terminated, the deposition may be resumed only by order of the court where the action is pending.

(C) Award of Expenses. Rule 37(a)(5) applies to the award of expenses.

(e) Review by the Witness; Changes.

(1) Review; Statement of Changes. On request by the deponent or a party before the deposition is completed, the deponent must be allowed 30 days after being notified by the officer that the transcript or recording is available in which:

(A) to review the transcript or recording; and

(B) if there are changes in form or substance, to sign a statement listing the changes and the reasons for making them.

(2) Changes Indicated in the Officer's Certificate. The officer must note in the certificate prescribed by Rule 30(f)(1) whether a review was requested and, if so, must attach any changes the deponent makes during the 30–day period.

(f) Certification and Delivery; Exhibits; Copies of the Transcript or Recording; Filing.

(1) Certification and Delivery. The officer must certify in writing that the witness was duly sworn and that the deposition accurately records the witness's testimony. The certificate must accompany the record of the deposition. Unless the court orders otherwise, the officer must seal the deposition in an envelope or package bearing the title of the action and marked "Deposition of [witness's name]" and must promptly send it to the attorney who arranged for the transcript or recording. The attorney must store it under conditions that will protect it against loss, destruction, tampering, or deterioration.

(2) Documents and Tangible Things.

(A) Originals and Copies. Documents and tangible things produced for inspection during a deposition must, on a party's request, be marked for identification and attached to the deposition. Any party may inspect and copy them. But if the person who produced them wants to keep the originals, the person may:

(i) offer copies to be marked, attached to the deposition, and then used as originals—after giving all parties a fair opportunity to verify the copies by comparing them with the originals; or

(ii) give all parties a fair opportunity to inspect and copy the originals after they are marked—in which event the originals may be used as if attached to the deposition.

(B) Order Regarding the Originals. Any party may move for an order that the originals be attached to the deposition pending final disposition of the case.

(3) Copies of the Transcript or Recording. Unless otherwise stipulated or ordered by the court, the officer must retain the stenographic notes of a deposition taken stenographically or a copy of the recording of a deposition taken by another method. When paid reasonable charges, the officer must furnish a copy of the transcript or recording to any party or the deponent.

(4) Notice of Filing. A party who files the deposition must promptly notify all other parties of the filing.

***(g) Failure to Attend a Deposition or Serve a Subpoena; Expenses.** A party who, expecting a deposition to be taken, attends in person or by an attorney may recover reasonable expenses for attending, including attorney's fees, if the noticing party failed to:*

(1) attend and proceed with the deposition; or

(2) serve a subpoena on a nonparty deponent, who consequently did not attend.

ADVISORY COMMITTEE NOTES

1937 Adoption

Note to Subdivision (a). This is in accordance with common practice. See U.S.C., Title 28, [former] § 639 (Depositions *de bene esse*; when and where taken; notice), the relevant provisions of which are incorporated in this rule; West's Ann.Code Civ.Proc. § 2031; and statutes cited in respect to notice in the Note to Rule 26(a). The provision for enlarging or shortening the time of notice has been added to give flexibility to the rule.

Note to Subdivisions (b) and (d). These are introduced as a safeguard for the protection of parties and deponents on account of the unlimited right of discovery given by Rule 26.

Note to Subdivisions (c) and (e). These follow the general plan of [former] Equity Rule 51 (Evidence Taken Before Examiners, Etc.) and U.S.C., Title 28, [former] §§ 640 (Depositions *de bene esse*; mode of taking), and [former] 641 (Same; transmission to court), but are more specific. They also permit the deponent to require the officer to make changes in the deposition if the deponent is not satisfied with it. See also [former] Equity Rule 50 (Stenographer—Appointment—Fees.)

Note to Subdivision (f). Compare [former] Equity Rule 55 (Depositions Deemed Published When Filed.)

Note to Subdivision (g). This is similar to 2 Minn.Stat. (Mason, 1927) § 9833, but is more extensive.

1963 Amendments

This amendment corresponds to the change in Rule 4(d)(4). See Advisory Committee's Note to that amendment.

1970 Amendments

Subdivision (a). This subdivision contains the provisions of existing Rule 26(a), transferred here as part of the rearrangement relating to Rule 26. Existing Rule 30(a) is transferred to 30(b). Changes in language have been made to conform to the new arrangement.

This subdivision is further revised in regard to the requirement of leave of court for taking a deposition. The present procedure, requiring a plaintiff to obtain leave of court if he serves notice of taking a deposition within 20 days after commencement of the action, is changed in several respects. First, leave is required by reference to the time the deposition is to be taken rather than the date of serving notice of taking. Second, the 20-day period is extended to 30 days and runs from the service of summons and complaint on any defendant, rather than the commencement of the action. *Cf.* Ill.S.Ct.R. 19–1 S–H Ill.Ann.Stat. § 101.19–1. Third, leave is not required beyond the time that defendant initiates discovery, thus showing that he has retained counsel. As under the present practice, a party not afforded a reasonable opportunity to appear at a deposition, because he has not yet been served with process, is protected against use of the deposition at trial against him. See Rule 32(a), transferred from 26(d). Moreover, he can later redepose the witness if he so desires.

The purpose of requiring the plaintiff to obtain leave of court is, as stated by the Advisory Committee that proposed the present language of Rule 26(a), to protect "a defendant who has not had an opportunity to retain counsel and inform himself as to the nature of the suit." Note to 1948 amendment of Rule 26(a), quoted in 3A Barron & Holtzoff, *Federal Practice and Procedure* 455–456 (Wright ed. 1958). In order to assure defendant of this opportunity, the period is lengthened to 30 days. This protection, however, is relevant to the time of taking the deposition, not to the time that notice is served. Similarly, the protective period should run from the service of process rather than the filing of the complaint with the court. As stated in the note to Rule 26(d), the courts have used the service of notice as a convenient reference point for assigning priority in taking depositions, but with the elimination of priority in new Rule 26(d) the reference point is no longer needed. The new procedure is consistent in principle with the provisions of Rules 33, 34, and 36 as revised.

Plaintiff is excused from obtaining leave even during the initial 30-day period if he gives the special notice provided in subdivision (b)(2). The required notice must state that the person to be examined is about to go out of the district where the action is pending and more than 100 miles from the place of trial, or out of the United States, or on a voyage to sea, and will be unavailable for examination unless deposed within the 30-day period. These events occur most often in maritime litigation, when seamen are transferred from one port to another or are about to go to sea. Yet, there are analogous situations in nonmaritime litigation, and although the maritime problems are more common, a rule limited to claims in the admiralty and maritime jurisdiction is not justified.

In the recent unification of the civil and admiralty rules, this problem was temporarily met through addition in Rule 26(a) of a provision that depositions *de bene esse* may continue to be taken as to admiralty and maritime claims within the meaning of Rule 9(h). It was recognized at the time that "a uniform rule applicable alike to what are now civil actions and suits in admiralty" was clearly preferable, but the de bene esse procedure was adopted "for the time being at least." See Advisory Committee's Note in Report of the Judicial Conference: Proposed Amendments to Rules of Civil Procedure 43–44 (1966).

The changes in Rule 30(a) and the new Rule 30(b)(2) provide a formula applicable to ordinary civil as well as maritime claims. They replace the provision for depositions *de bene esse.* They authorize an early deposition without leave of court where the witness is about to depart and, unless his deposition is promptly taken, (1) it will be impossible or very difficult to depose him before trial or (2) his deposition can later be taken but only with substantially increased effort and expense. *Cf. S.S. Hai Chang,* 1966 A.M.C. 2239 (S.D.N.Y.1966), in which the deposing party is required to prepay expenses and counsel fees of the other party's lawyer when the action is pending in New York and depositions are to be taken on the West Coast. Defendant is protected by a provision that the deposition cannot be used against him if he was unable through exercise of diligence to obtain counsel to represent him.

The distance of 100 miles from place of trial is derived from the *de bene esse* provision and also conforms to the reach of a subpoena of the trial court, as provided in Rule 45(e). See also S.D.N.Y. Civ.R. 5(a). Some parts of the *de bene esse* provision are omitted from Rule 30(b)(2). Modern deposition practice adequately covers the witness who lives more than 100 miles away from place of trial. If a witness is aged or infirm, leave of court can be obtained.

Subdivision (b). Existing Rule 30(b) on protective orders has been transferred to Rule 26(c), and existing Rule 30(a) relating to the notice of taking deposition has been transferred to this subdivision. Because new material has been added, subsection numbers have been inserted.

Subdivision (b)(1). If a subpoena duces tecum is to be served, a copy thereof or a designation of the materials to be produced must accompany the notice. Each party is thereby enabled to prepare for the deposition more effectively.

Subdivision (b)(2). This subdivision is discussed in the note to subdivision (a), to which it relates.

Subdivision (b)(3). This provision is derived from existing Rule 30(a), with a minor change of language.

Subdivision (b)(4). In order to facilitate less expensive procedures, provision is made for the recording of testimony by other than stenographic means—*e.g.,* by mechanical, electronic, or photographic means. Because these methods give rise to problems of accuracy and trustworthiness, the party taking the deposition is required to apply for a court order. The order is to specify how the testimony is to be recorded, preserved, and filed, and it may contain whatever additional safeguards the court deems necessary.

Subdivision (b)(5). A provision is added to enable a party, through service of notice, to require another party to produce documents or things at the taking of his deposition. This may now be done as to a nonparty deponent through use of a subpoena duces tecum as authorized by Rule 45, but some courts have held that documents may be secured from a party only under Rule 34. See 2A Barron & Holtzoff, *Federal Practice and Procedure* § 644.1 n. 83.2, § 792 n. 16 (Wright ed. 1961). With the elimination of "good cause" from Rule 34, the reason for this restrictive doctrine has disappeared. *Cf.* N.Y.C.P.L.R. § 3111.

Whether production of documents or things should be obtained directly under Rule 34 or at the deposition under this rule will depend on the nature and volume of the documents or things. Both methods are made available. When the documents are few and simple, and closely related

to the oral examination, ability to proceed via this rule will facilitate discovery. If the discovering party insists on examining many and complex documents at the taking of the deposition, thereby causing undue burdens on others, the latter may, under Rules 26(c) or 30(d), apply for a court order that the examining party proceed via Rule 34 alone.

Subdivision (b)(6). A new provision is added, whereby a party may name a corporation, partnership, association, or governmental agency as the deponent and designate the matters on which he requests examination, and the organization shall then name one or more of its officers, directors, or managing agents, or other persons consenting to appear and testify on its behalf with respect to matters known or reasonably available to the organization. *Cf.* Alberta Sup.Ct.R. 255. The organization may designate persons other than officers, directors, and managing agents, but only with their consent. Thus, an employee or agent who has an independent or conflicting interest in the litigation—for example, in a personal injury case—can refuse to testify on behalf of the organization.

This procedure supplements the existing practice whereby the examining party designates the corporate official to be deposed. Thus, if the examining party believes that certain officials who have not testified pursuant to this subdivision have added information, he may depose them. On the other hand, a court's decision whether to issue a protective order may take account of the availability and use made of the procedures provided in this subdivision.

The new procedure should be viewed as an added facility for discovery, one which may be advantageous to both sides as well as an improvement in the deposition process. It will reduce the difficulties now encountered in determining, prior to the taking of a deposition, whether a particular employee or agent is a "managing agent." See Note, *Discovery Against Corporations Under the Federal Rules,* 47 Iowa L.Rev. 1006–1016 (1962). It will curb the "bandying" by which officers or managing agents of a corporation are deposed in turn but each disclaims knowledge of facts that are clearly known to persons in the organization and thereby to it. *Cf. Haney v. Woodward & Lothrop, Inc.,* 330 F.2d 940, 944 (4th Cir. 1964). The provision should also assist organizations which find that an unnecessarily large number of their officers and agents are being deposed by a party uncertain of who in the organization has knowledge. Some courts have held that under the existing rules a corporation should not be burdened with choosing which person is to appear for it. E.g., *United States v. Gahagan Dredging Corp.,* 24 F.R.D. 328, 329 (S.D.N.Y.1958). This burden is not essentially different from that of answering interrogatories under Rule 33, and is in any case lighter than that of an examining party ignorant of who in the corporation has knowledge.

Subdivision (c). A new sentence is inserted at the beginning, representing the transfer of existing Rule 26(c) to this subdivision. Another addition conforms to the new provision in subdivision (b)(4).

The present rule provides that transcription shall be carried out unless all parties waive it. In view of the many depositions taken from which nothing useful is discovered, the revised language provides that transcription is to be performed if any party requests it. The fact of the request is relevant to the exercise of the court's discretion in determining who shall pay for transcription.

Parties choosing to serve written questions rather than participate personally in an oral deposition are directed to serve their questions on the party taking the deposition, since the officer is often not identified in advance. Confidentiality is preserved, since the questions may be served in a sealed envelope.

Subdivision (d). The assessment of expenses incurred in relation to motions made under this subdivision (d) is made subject to the provisions of Rule 37(a). The standards for assessment of expenses are more fully set out in Rule 37(a), and these standards should apply to the essentially similar motions of this subdivision.

Subdivision (e). The provision relating to the refusal of a witness to sign his deposition is tightened through insertion of a 30-day time period.

Subdivision (f)(1). A provision is added which codifies in a flexible way the procedure for handling exhibits related to the deposition and at the same time assures each party that he may inspect and copy documents and things produced by a nonparty witness in response to a subpoena duces tecum. As a general rule and in the absence of agreement to the contrary or order of the court, exhibits produced without objection are to be annexed to and returned with the deposition, but a witness may substitute copies for purposes of marking and he may obtain return of the exhibits. The right of the parties to inspect exhibits for identification and to make copies is assured. *Cf.* N.Y.C.P.L.R. § 3116(c).

1971 Amendments

The subdivision permits a party to name a corporation or other form of organization as a deponent in the notice of examination and to describe in the notice the matters about which discovery is desired. The organization is then obliged to designate natural persons to testify on its behalf. The amendment clarifies the procedure to be followed if a party desires to examine a non-party organization through persons designated by the organization. Under the rules, a subpoena rather than a notice of examination is served on a non-party to compel attendance at the taking of a deposition. The amendment provides that a subpoena may name a non-party organization as the deponent and may indicate the matters about which discovery is desired. In that event, the non-party organization must respond by designating natural persons, who are then obliged to testify as to matters known or reasonably available to the organization. To insure that a non-party organization that is not represented by counsel has knowledge of its duty to designate, the amendment directs the party seeking discovery to advise of the duty in the body of the subpoena.

1972 Amendments

Subdivision (c). Existing Rule 43(b), which is to be abrogated, deals with the use of leading questions, the calling, interrogation, impeachment, and scope of cross-examination of adverse parties, officers, etc. These topics are dealt with in many places in the Rules of Evidence. Moreover, many pertinent topics included in the Rules of Evidence are not mentioned in Rule 43(b), e.g. privilege. A reference to the Rules of Evidence generally is therefore made in subdivision (c) of Rule 30.

1980 Amendments

Subdivision (b)(4). It has been proposed that electronic recording of depositions be authorized as a matter of course, subject to the right of a party to seek an order that a deposition be recorded by stenographic means. The Committee is not satisfied that a case has been made for a reversal of present practice. The amendment is made to encourage parties to agree to the use of electronic recording of depositions so that conflicting claims with respect to the potential of electronic recording for reducing costs of depositions can be appraised in the light of greater experience. The provision that the parties may stipulate that depositions may be recorded by other than stenographic means seems implicit in Rule 29. The amendment makes it explicit. The provision that the stipulation or order shall designate the person before whom the deposition is to be taken is added to encourage the naming of the recording technician as that person, eliminating the necessity of the presence of one whose only function is to administer the oath. See Rules 28(a) and 29.

Subdivision (b)(7). Depositions by telephone are now authorized by Rule 29 upon stipulation of the parties. The amendment authorizes that method by order of the court. The final sentence is added to make it clear that when a deposition is taken by telephone it is taken in the district and at the place where the witness is to answer the questions rather than that where the questions are propounded.

Subdivision (f)(1). For the reasons set out in the Note following the amendment of Rule 5(d), the court may wish to permit the parties to retain depositions unless they are to be used in the action. The amendment of the first paragraph permits the court to so order.

The amendment of the second paragraph is clarifying. The purpose of the paragraph is to permit a person who produces materials at a deposition to offer copies for marking and annexation to the deposition. Such copies are a "substitute" for the originals, which are not to be marked and which can thereafter be used or even disposed of by the person who produces them. In the light of that purpose, the former language of the paragraph had been justly termed "opaque." Wright & Miller, *Federal Practice and Procedure: Civil* § 2114.

1987 Amendments

The amendments are technical. No substantive change is intended.

1993 Amendments

Subdivision (a). Paragraph (1) retains the first and third sentences from the former subdivision (a) without significant modification. The second and fourth sentences are relocated.

Paragraph (2) collects all provisions bearing on requirements of leave of court to take a deposition.

Paragraph (2)(A) is new. It provides a limit on the number of depositions the parties may take, absent leave of court or stipulation with the other parties. One aim of this revision is to assure judicial review under the standards stated in Rule 26(b)(2) before any side will be allowed to take more than ten depositions in a case without agreement of the other parties. A second objective is to emphasize that

counsel have a professional obligation to develop a mutual cost-effective plan for discovery in the case. Leave to take additional depositions should be granted when consistent with the principles of Rule 26(b)(2), and in some cases the ten-per-side limit should be reduced in accordance with those same principles. Consideration should ordinarily be given at the planning meeting of the parties under Rule 26(f) and at the time of a scheduling conference under Rule 16(b) as to enlargements or reductions in the number of depositions, eliminating the need for special motions.

A deposition under Rule 30(b)(6) should, for purposes of this limit, be treated as a single deposition even though more than one person may be designated to testify.

In multi-party cases, the parties on any side are expected to confer and agree as to which depositions are most needed, given the presumptive limit on the number of depositions they can take without leave of court. If these disputes cannot be amicably resolved, the court can be requested to resolve the dispute or permit additional depositions.

Paragraph (2)(B) is new. It requires leave of court if any witness is to be deposed in the action more than once. This requirement does not apply when a deposition is temporarily recessed for convenience of counsel or the deponent or to enable additional materials to be gathered before resuming the deposition. If significant travel costs would be incurred to resume the deposition, the parties should consider the feasibility of conducting the balance of the examination by telephonic means.

Paragraph (2)(C) revises the second sentence of the former subdivision (a) as to when depositions may be taken. Consistent with the changes made in Rule 26(d), providing that formal discovery ordinarily not commence until after the litigants have met and conferred as directed in revised Rule 26(f), the rule requires leave of court or agreement of the parties if a deposition is to be taken before that time (except when a witness is about to leave the country).

Subdivision (b). The primary change in subdivision (b) is that parties will be authorized to record deposition testimony by nonstenographic means without first having to obtain permission of the court or agreement from other counsel.

Former subdivision (b)(2) is partly relocated in subdivision (a)(2)(C) of this rule. The latter two sentences of the first paragraph are deleted, in part because they are redundant to Rule 26(g) and in part because Rule 11 no longer applies to discovery requests. The second paragraph of the former subdivision (b)(2), relating to use of depositions at trial where a party was unable to obtain counsel in time for an accelerated deposition, is relocated in Rule 32.

New paragraph (2) confers on the party taking the deposition the choice of the method of recording, without the need to obtain prior court approval for one taken other than stenographically. A party choosing to record a deposition only by videotape or audiotape should understand that a transcript will be required by Rule 26(a)(3)(B) and Rule 32(c) if the deposition is later to be offered as evidence at trial or on a dispositive motion under Rule 56. Objections to the nonstenographic recording of a deposition, when warranted by the circumstances, can be presented to the court under Rule 26(c).

Paragraph (3) provides that other parties may arrange, at their own expense, for the recording of a deposition by a means (stenographic, visual, or sound) in addition to the method designated by the person noticing the deposition. The former provisions of this paragraph, relating to the court's power to change the date of a deposition, have been eliminated as redundant in view of Rule 26(c)(2).

Revised paragraph (4) requires that all depositions be recorded by an officer designated or appointed under Rule 28 and contains special provisions designed to provide basic safeguards to assure the utility and integrity of recordings taken other than stenographically.

Paragraph (7) is revised to authorize the taking of a deposition not only by telephone but also by other remote electronic means, such as satellite television, when agreed to by the parties or authorized by the court.

Subdivision (c). Minor changes are made in this subdivision to reflect those made in subdivision (b) and to complement the new provisions of subdivision (d)(1), aimed at reducing the number of interruptions during depositions.

In addition, the revision addresses a recurring problem as to whether other potential deponents can attend a deposition. Courts have disagreed, some holding that witnesses should be excluded through invocation of Rule 615 of the evidence rules, and others holding that witnesses may attend unless excluded by an order under Rule 26(c)(5). The revision provides that other witnesses are not automatically excluded from a deposition simply by the request of a party. Exclusion, however, can be ordered under Rule 26(c)(5) when appropriate; and, if exclusion is ordered, consideration should be given as to whether the excluded witnesses likewise should be precluded from reading, or being otherwise informed about, the testimony given in the earlier depositions. The revision addresses only the matter of attendance by potential deponents, and does not attempt to resolve issues concerning attendance by others, such as members of the public or press.

Subdivision (d). The first sentence of new paragraph (1) provides that any objections during a deposition must be made concisely and in a non-argumentative and non-suggestive manner. Depositions frequently have been unduly prolonged, if not unfairly frustrated, by lengthy objections and colloquy, often suggesting how the deponent should respond. While objections may, under the revised rule, be made during a deposition, they ordinarily should be limited to those that under Rule 32(d)(3) might be waived if not made at that time, i.e., objections on grounds that might be immediately obviated, removed, or cured, such as to the form of a question or the responsiveness of an answer. Under Rule 32(b), other objections can, even without the so-called "usual stipulation" preserving objections, be raised for the first time at trial and therefore should be kept to a minimum during a deposition.

Directions to a deponent not to answer a question can be even more disruptive than objections. The second sentence of new paragraph (1) prohibits such directions except in the three circumstances indicated: to claim a privilege or protection against disclosure (e.g., as work product), to enforce a court directive limiting the scope or length of permissible discovery, or to suspend a deposition to enable presentation of a motion under paragraph (3).

Paragraph (2) is added to this subdivision to dispel any doubts regarding the power of the court by order or local rule to establish limits on the length of depositions. The rule also explicitly authorizes the court to impose the cost result-

ing from obstructive tactics that unreasonably prolong a deposition on the person engaged in such obstruction. This sanction may be imposed on a non-party witness as well as a party or attorney, but is otherwise congruent with Rule 26(g).

It is anticipated that limits on the length of depositions prescribed by local rules would be presumptive only, subject to modification by the court or by agreement of the parties. Such modifications typically should be discussed by the parties in their meeting under Rule 26(f) and included in the scheduling order required by Rule 16(b). Additional time, moreover, should be allowed under the revised rule when justified under the principles stated in Rule 26(b)(2). To reduce the number of special motions, local rules should ordinarily permit—and indeed encourage—the parties to agree to additional time, as when, during the taking of a deposition, it becomes clear that some additional examination is needed.

Paragraph (3) authorizes appropriate sanctions not only when a deposition is unreasonably prolonged, but also when an attorney engages in other practices that improperly frustrate the fair examination of the deponent, such as making improper objections or giving directions not to answer prohibited by paragraph (1). In general, counsel should not engage in any conduct during a deposition that would not be allowed in the presence of a judicial officer. The making of an excessive number of unnecessary objections may itself constitute sanctionable conduct, as may the refusal of an attorney to agree with other counsel on a fair apportionment of the time allowed for examination of a deponent or a refusal to agree to a reasonable request for some additional time to complete a deposition, when that is permitted by the local rule or order.

Subdivision (e). Various changes are made in this subdivision to reduce problems sometimes encountered when depositions are taken stenographically. Reporters frequently have difficulties obtaining signatures—and the return of depositions—from deponents. Under the revision pre-filing review by the deponent is required only if requested before the deposition is completed. If review is requested, the deponent will be allowed 30 days to review the transcript or recording and to indicate any changes in form or substance. Signature of the deponent will be required only if review is requested and changes are made.

Subdivision (f). Minor changes are made in this subdivision to reflect those made in subdivision (b). In courts which direct that depositions not be automatically filed, the reporter can transmit the transcript or recording to the attorney taking the deposition (or ordering the transcript or record), who then becomes custodian for the court of the original record of the deposition. Pursuant to subdivision (f)(2), as under the prior rule, any other party is entitled to secure a copy of the deposition from the officer designated to take the deposition; accordingly, unless ordered or agreed, the officer must retain a copy of the recording or the stenographic notes.

2000 Amendment

Subdivision (d). Paragraph (1) has been amended to clarify the terms regarding behavior during depositions. The references to objections " to evidence" and limitations "on evidence" have been removed to avoid disputes about what is "evidence" and whether an objection is to, or a limitation is on, discovery instead. It is intended that the rule apply to any objection to a question or other issue arising during a deposition, and to any limitation imposed by the court in connection with a deposition, which might relate to duration or other matters.

The current rule places limitations on instructions that a witness not answer only when the instruction is made by a "party." Similar limitations should apply with regard to anyone who might purport to instruct a witness not to answer a question. Accordingly, the rule is amended to apply the limitation to instructions by any person. The amendment is not intended to confer new authority on nonparties to instruct witnesses to refuse to answer deposition questions. The amendment makes it clear that, whatever the legitimacy of giving such instructions, the nonparty is subject to the same limitations as parties.

Paragraph (2) imposes a presumptive durational limitation of one day of seven hours for any deposition. The Committee has been informed that overlong depositions can result in undue costs and delays in some circumstances. This limitation contemplates that there will be reasonable breaks during the day for lunch and other reasons, and that the only time to be counted is the time occupied by the actual deposition. For purposes of this durational limit, the deposition of each person designated under Rule 30(b)(6) should be considered a separate deposition. The presumptive duration may be extended, or otherwise altered, by agreement. Absent agreement, a court order is needed. The party seeking a court order to extend the examination, or otherwise alter the limitations, is expected to show good cause to justify such an order.

Parties considering extending the time for a deposition—and courts asked to order an extension—might consider a variety of factors. For example, if the witness needs an interpreter, that may prolong the examination. If the examination will cover events occurring over a long period of time, that may justify allowing additional time. In cases in which the witness will be questioned about numerous or lengthy documents, it is often desirable for the interrogating party to send copies of the documents to the witness sufficiently in advance of the deposition so that the witness can become familiar with them. Should the witness nevertheless not read the documents in advance, thereby prolonging the deposition, a court could consider that a reason for extending the time limit. If the examination reveals that documents have been requested but not produced, that may justify further examination once production has occurred. In multi-party cases, the need for each party to examine the witness may warrant additional time, although duplicative questioning should be avoided and parties with similar interests should strive to designate one lawyer to question about areas of common interest. Similarly, should the lawyer for the witness want to examine the witness, that may require additional time. Finally, with regard to expert witnesses, there may more often be a need for additional time—even after the submission of the report required by Rule 26(a)(2)—for full exploration of the theories upon which the witness relies.

It is expected that in most instances the parties and the witness will make reasonable accommodations to avoid the need for resort to the court. The limitation is phrased in terms of a single day on the assumption that ordinarily a single day would be preferable to a deposition extending over

multiple days; if alternative arrangements would better suit the parties, they may agree to them. It is also assumed that there will be reasonable breaks during the day. Preoccupation with timing is to be avoided.

The rule directs the court to allow additional time where consistent with Rule 26(b)(2) if needed for a fair examination of the deponent. In addition, if the deponent or another person impedes or delays the examination, the court must authorize extra time. The amendment makes clear that additional time should also be allowed where the examination is impeded by an "other circumstance," which might include a power outage, a health emergency, or other event.

In keeping with the amendment to Rule 26(b)(2), the provision added in 1993 granting authority to adopt a local rule limiting the time permitted for depositions has been removed. The court may enter a case-specific order directing shorter depositions for all depositions in a case or with regard to a specific witness. The court may also order that a deposition be taken for limited periods on several days.

Paragraph (3) includes sanctions provisions formerly included in paragraph (2). It authorizes the court to impose an appropriate sanction on any person responsible for an impediment that frustrated the fair examination of the deponent. This could include the deponent, any party, or any other person involved in the deposition. If the impediment or delay results from an "other circumstance" under paragraph (2), ordinarily no sanction would be appropriate.

Former paragraph (3) has been renumbered (4) but is otherwise unchanged .

Subdivision (f)(1): This subdivision is amended because Rule 5(d) has been amended to direct that discovery materials, including depositions, ordinarily should not be filed. The rule already has provisions directing that the lawyer who arranged for the transcript or recording preserve the deposition. Rule 5(d) provides that, once the deposition is used in the proceeding, the attorney must file it with the court.

"Shall" is replaced by "must" or "may" under the program to conform amended rules to current style conventions when there is no ambiguity.

GAP Report

The Advisory Committee recommends deleting the requirement in the published proposed amendments that the deponent consent to extending a deposition beyond one day, and adding an amendment to Rule 30(f)(1) to conform to the published amendment to Rule 5(d) regarding filing of depositions. It also recommends conforming the Committee Note with regard to the deponent veto, and adding material to the Note to provide direction on computation of the durational limitation on depositions, to provide examples of situations in which the parties might agree—or the court order—that a deposition be extended, and to make clear that no new authority to instruct a witness is conferred by the amendment. One minor wording improvement in the Note is also suggested.

2007 Amendment

*[Effective December 1, 2007,
absent contrary Congressional action.]*

The language of Rule 30 has been amended as part of the general restyling of the Civil Rules to make them more easily understood and to make style and terminology consistent

throughout the rules. These changes are intended to be stylistic only.

The right to arrange a deposition transcription should be open to any party, regardless of the means of recording and regardless of who noticed the deposition.

"[O]ther entity" is added to the list of organizations that may be named as deponent. The purpose is to ensure that the deposition process can be used to reach information known or reasonably available to an organization no matter what abstract fictive concept is used to describe the organization. Nothing is gained by wrangling over the place to fit into current rule language such entities as limited liability companies, limited partnerships, business trusts, more exotic common-law creations, or forms developed in other countries.

HISTORICAL NOTES

Effective Date of Amendment Proposed November 20, 1972

Amendment of this rule embraced by the order entered by the Supreme Court of the United States on November 20, 1972, effective on the 180th day beginning after January 2, 1975, see section 3 of Pub.L. 93–595, Jan. 2, 1975, 88 Stat. 1959, set out as a note under section 2071 of Title 28.

Rule 31. Depositions Upon Written Questions
(a) Serving Questions; Notice.

(1) A party may take the testimony of any person, including a party, by deposition upon written questions without leave of court except as provided in paragraph (2). The attendance of witnesses may be compelled by the use of subpoena as provided in Rule 45.

(2) A party must obtain leave of court, which shall be granted to the extent consistent with the principles stated in Rule 26(b)(2), if the person to be examined is confined in prison or if, without the written stipulation of the parties.

(A) a proposed deposition would result in more than ten depositions being taken under this rule or Rule 30 by the plaintiffs, or by the defendants, or by third-party defendants;

(B) the person to be examined has already been deposed in the case; or

(C) a party seeks to take a deposition before the time specified in Rule 26(d).

(3) A party desiring to take a deposition upon written questions shall serve them upon every other party with a notice stating (1) the name and address of the person who is to answer them, if known, and if the name is not known, a general description sufficient to identify the person or the particular class or group to which the person belongs, and (2) the name or descriptive title and address of the officer before whom the deposition is to be taken. A deposition upon written questions may be taken of a public or private corporation or a partnership or association or governmental agency in accordance with the provisions of Rule 30(b)(6).

(4) Within 14 days after the notice and written questions are served, a party may serve cross questions upon all other parties. Within 7 days after being served with cross questions, a party may serve redirect questions upon all other parties. Within 7 days after being served with redirect questions, a party may serve recross questions upon all other parties. The court may for cause shown enlarge or shorten the time.

(b) Officer to Take Responses and Prepare Record. A copy of the notice and copies of all questions served shall be delivered by the party taking the deposition to the officer designated in the notice, who shall proceed promptly, in the manner provided by Rule 30(c), (e), and (f), to take the testimony of the witness in response to the questions and to prepare, certify, and file or mail the deposition, attaching thereto the copy of the notice and the questions received by the officer.

(c) Notice of Filing. When the deposition is filed the party taking it shall promptly give notice thereof to all other parties.

(As amended Mar. 30, 1970, eff. July 1, 1970; Mar. 2, 1987, eff. Aug. 1, 1987; Apr. 22, 1993, eff. Dec. 1, 1993.)

Proposed Amendment of Rule

Effective December 1, 2007, absent contrary Congressional action, this rule is amended to read as follows:

Rule 31. Depositions by Written Questions

(a) When a Deposition May Be Taken.

(1) Without Leave. A party may, by written questions, depose any person, including a party, without leave of court except as provided in Rule 31(a)(2). The deponent's attendance may be compelled by subpoena under Rule 45.

(2) With Leave. A party must obtain leave of court, and the court must grant leave to the extent consistent with Rule 26(b)(2):

(A) if the parties have not stipulated to the deposition and:

(i) the deposition would result in more than 10 depositions being taken under this rule or Rule 30 by the plaintiffs, or by the defendants, or by the third-party defendants;

(ii) the deponent has already been deposed in the case; or

(iii) the party seeks to take a deposition before the time specified in Rule 26(d); or

(B) if the deponent is confined in prison.

(3) Service; Required Notice. A party who wants to depose a person by written questions must serve them on every other party, with a notice stating, if known, the deponent's name and address. If the name is unknown, the notice must provide a general description sufficient to identify the person or the particular class or group to which the person belongs. The notice must also state the name or descriptive title and the address of the officer before whom the deposition will be taken.

(4) Questions Directed to an Organization. A public or private corporation, a partnership, an association, or a governmental agency may be deposed by written questions in accordance with Rule 30(b)(6).

(5) Questions from Other Parties. Any questions to the deponent from other parties must be served on all parties as follows: cross-questions, within 14 days after being served with the notice and direct questions; redirect questions, within 7 days after being served with cross-questions; and recross-questions, within 7 days after being served with redirect questions. The court may, for good cause, extend or shorten these times.

(b) Delivery to the Officer; Officer's Duties. *The party who noticed the deposition must deliver to the officer a copy of all the questions served and of the notice. The officer must promptly proceed in the manner provided in Rule 30(c), (e), and (f) to:*

(1) take the deponent's testimony in response to the questions;

(2) prepare and certify the deposition; and

(3) send it to the party, attaching a copy of the questions and of the notice.

(c) Notice of Completion or Filing.

(1) Completion. The party who noticed the deposition must notify all other parties when it is completed.

(2) Filing. A party who files the deposition must promptly notify all other parties of the filing.

ADVISORY COMMITTEE NOTES

1937 Adoption

This rule is in accordance with common practice. In most of the states listed in the Note to Rule 26(a), provisions similar to this rule will be found in the statutes which in their respective statutory compilations follow those cited in the Note to Rule 26(a).

1970 Amendment

Confusion is created by the use of the same terminology to describe both the taking of a deposition upon "written interrogatories" pursuant to this rule and the serving of "written interrogatories" upon parties pursuant to Rule 33. The distinction between these two modes of discovery will be

more readily and clearly grasped through substitution of the word "questions" for "interrogatories" throughout this rule.

Subdivision (a). A new paragraph is inserted at the beginning of this subdivision to conform to the rearrangement of provisions in Rules 26(a), 30(a), and 30(b).

The revised subdivision permits designation of the deponent by general description or by class or group. This conforms to the practice for depositions on oral examination.

The new procedure provided in Rule 30(b)(6) for taking the deposition of a corporation or other organization through persons designated by the organization is incorporated by reference.

The service of all questions, including cross, redirect, and recross, is to be made on all parties. This will inform the parties and enable them to participate fully in the procedure.

The time allowed for service of cross, redirect, and recross questions has been extended. Experience with the existing time limits shows them to be unrealistically short. No special restriction is placed on the time for serving the notice of taking the deposition and the first set of questions. Since no party is required to serve cross questions less than 30 days after the notice and questions are served, the defendant has sufficient time to obtain counsel. The court may for cause shown enlarge or shorten the time.

Subdivision (d). Since new Rule 26(c) provides for protective orders with respect to all discovery, and expressly provides that the court may order that one discovery device be used in place of another, subdivision (d) is eliminated as unnecessary.

1987 Amendment

The amendments are technical. No substantive change is intended.

1993 Amendments

Subdivision (a). The first paragraph of subdivision (a) is divided into two subparagraphs, with provisions comparable to those made in the revision of Rule 30. Changes are made in the former third paragraph, numbered in the revision as paragraph (4), to reduce the total time for developing cross-examination, redirect, and recross questions from 50 days to 28 days.

2007 Amendment

*[Effective December 1, 2007,
absent contrary Congressional action.]*

The language of Rule 31 has been amended as part of the general restyling of the Civil Rules to make them more easily understood and to make style and terminology consistent throughout the rules. These changes are intended to be stylistic only.

The party who noticed a deposition on written questions must notify all other parties when the deposition is completed, so that they may make use of the deposition. A deposition is completed when it is recorded and the deponent has either waived or exercised the right of review under Rule 30(e)(1).

Rule 32. Use of Depositions in Court Proceedings

(a) Use of Depositions. At the trial or upon the hearing of a motion or an interlocutory proceeding, any part or all of a deposition, so far as admissible under the rules of evidence applied as though the witness were then present and testifying, may be used against any party who was present or represented at the taking of the deposition or who had reasonable notice thereof, in accordance with any of the following provisions:

(1) Any deposition may be used by any party for the purpose of contradicting or impeaching the testimony of deponent as a witness, or for any other purpose permitted by the Federal Rules of Evidence.

(2) The deposition of a party or of anyone who at the time of taking the deposition was an officer, director, or managing agent, or a person designated under Rule 30(b)(6) or 31(a) to testify on behalf of a public or private corporation, partnership or association or governmental agency which is a party may be used by an adverse party for any purpose.

(3) The deposition of a witness, whether or not a party, may be used by any party for any purpose if the court finds:

(A) that the witness is dead; or

(B) that the witness is at a greater distance than 100 miles from the place of trial or hearing, or is out of the United States, unless it appears that the absence of the witness was procured by the party offering the deposition; or

(C) that the witness is unable to attend or testify because of age, illness, infirmity, or imprisonment; or

(D) that the party offering the deposition has been unable to procure the attendance of the witness by subpoena; or

(E) upon application and notice, that such exceptional circumstances exist as to make it desirable, in the interest of justice and with due regard to the importance of presenting the testimony of witnesses orally in open court, to allow the deposition to be used.

A deposition taken without leave of court pursuant to a notice under Rule 30(a)(2)(C) shall not be used against a party who demonstrates that, when served with the notice, it was unable through the exercise of diligence to obtain counsel to represent it at the taking of the deposition; nor shall a deposition be used against a party who, having received less than 11 days notice of a deposition, has promptly upon receiving such notice filed a motion for a protective order under Rule 26(c)(2) requesting that the deposition not be held or be held at a different time or

place and such motion is pending at the time the deposition is held.

(4) If only part of a deposition is offered in evidence by a party, an adverse party may require the offeror to introduce any other part which ought in fairness to be considered with the part introduced, and any party may introduce any other parts.

Substitution of parties pursuant to Rule 25 does not affect the right to use depositions previously taken; and, when an action has been brought in any court of the United States or of any State and another action involving the same subject matter is afterward brought between the same parties or their representatives or successors in interest, all depositions lawfully taken and duly filed in the former action may be used in the latter as if originally taken therefor. A deposition previously taken may also be used as permitted by the Federal Rules of Evidence.

(b) Objections to Admissibility. Subject to the provisions of Rule 28(b) and subdivision (d)(3) of this rule, objection may be made at the trial or hearing to receiving in evidence any deposition or part thereof for any reason which would require the exclusion of the evidence if the witness were then present and testifying.

(c) Form of Presentation. Except as otherwise directed by the court, a party offering deposition testimony pursuant to this rule may offer it in stenographic or nonstenographic form, but, if in nonstenographic form, the party shall also provide the court with a transcript of the portions so offered. On request of any party in a case tried before a jury, deposition testimony offered other than for impeachment purposes shall be presented in nonstenographic form, if available, unless the court for good cause orders otherwise.

(d) Effect of Errors and Irregularities in Depositions.

(1) **As to Notice.** All errors and irregularities in the notice for taking a deposition are waived unless written objection is promptly served upon the party giving the notice.

(2) **As to Disqualification of Officer.** Objection to taking a deposition because of disqualification of the officer before whom it is to be taken is waived unless made before the taking of the deposition begins or as soon thereafter as the disqualification becomes known or could be discovered with reasonable diligence.

(3) **As to Taking of Deposition.**

(A) Objections to the competency of a witness or to the competency, relevancy, or materiality of testimony are not waived by failure to make them before or during the taking of the deposition, unless the ground of the objection is one which might have been obviated or removed if presented at that time.

(B) Errors and irregularities occurring at the oral examination in the manner of taking the deposition, in the form of the questions or answers, in the oath or affirmation, or in the conduct of parties, and errors of any kind which might be obviated, removed, or cured if promptly presented, are waived unless seasonable objection thereto is made at the taking of the deposition.

(C) Objections to the form of written questions submitted under Rule 31 are waived unless served in writing upon the party propounding them within the time allowed for serving the succeeding cross or other questions and within 5 days after service of the last questions authorized.

(4) **As to Completion and Return of Deposition.** Errors and irregularities in the manner in which the testimony is transcribed or the deposition is prepared, signed, certified, sealed, indorsed, transmitted, filed, or otherwise dealt with by the officer under Rules 30 and 31 are waived unless a motion to suppress the deposition or some part thereof is made with reasonable promptness after such defect is, or with due diligence might have been, ascertained.

(As amended Mar. 30, 1970, eff. July 1, 1970; Nov. 20, 1972, eff. July 1, 1975; Apr. 29, 1980, eff. Aug. 1, 1980; Mar. 2, 1987, eff. Aug. 1, 1987; Apr. 22, 1993, eff. Dec. 1, 1993.)

Proposed Amendment of Rule

Effective December 1, 2007, absent contrary Congressional action, this rule is amended to read as follows:

Rule 32. Using Depositions in Court Proceedings

(a) Using Depositions.

(1) In General. At a hearing or trial, all or part of a deposition may be used against a party on these conditions:

(A) the party was present or represented at the taking of the deposition or had reasonable notice of it;

(B) it is used to the extent it would be admissible under the Federal Rules of Evidence if the deponent were present and testifying; and

(C) the use is allowed by Rule 32(a)(2) through (8).

(2) Impeachment and Other Uses. Any party may use a deposition to contradict or impeach the testimony given by the deponent as a witness,

or for any other purpose allowed by the Federal Rules of Evidence.

(3) Deposition of Party, Agent, or Designee. An adverse party may use for any purpose the deposition of a party or anyone who, when deposed, was the party's officer, director, managing agent, or designee under Rule 30(b)(6) or 31(a)(4).

(4) Unavailable Witness. A party may use for any purpose the deposition of a witness, whether or not a party, if the court finds:

 (A) that the witness is dead;

 (B) that the witness is more than 100 miles from the place of hearing or trial or is outside the United States, unless it appears that the witness's absence was procured by the party offering the deposition;

 (C) that the witness cannot attend or testify because of age, illness, infirmity, or imprisonment;

 (D) that the party offering the deposition could not procure the witness's attendance by subpoena; or

 (E) on motion and notice, that exceptional circumstances make it desirable—in the interest of justice and with due regard to the importance of live testimony in open court—to permit the deposition to be used.

(5) Limitations on Use.

 (A) Deposition Taken on Short Notice. A deposition must not be used against a party who, having received less than 11 days' notice of the deposition, promptly moved for a protective order under Rule 26(c)(1)(B) requesting that it not be taken or be taken at a different time or place—and this motion was still pending when the deposition was taken.

 (B) Unavailable Deponent; Party Could Not Obtain an Attorney. A deposition taken without leave of court under the unavailability provision of Rule 30(a)(2)(A)(iii) must not be used against a party who shows that, when served with the notice, it could not, despite diligent efforts, obtain an attorney to represent it at the deposition.

(6) Using Part of a Deposition. If a party offers in evidence only part of a deposition, an adverse party may require the offeror to introduce other parts that in fairness should be considered with the part introduced, and any party may itself introduce any other parts.

(7) Substituting a Party. Substituting a party under Rule 25 does not affect the right to use a deposition previously taken.

(8) Deposition Taken in an Earlier Action. A deposition lawfully taken and, if required, filed in any federal- or state-court action may be used in a later action involving the same subject matter between the same parties, or their representatives or successors in interest, to the same extent as if taken in the later action. A deposition previously taken may also be used as allowed by the Federal Rules of Evidence.

(b) Objections to Admissibility. Subject to Rules 28(b) and 32(d)(3), an objection may be made at a hearing or trial to the admission of any deposition testimony that would be inadmissible if the witness were present and testifying.

(c) Form of Presentation. Unless the court orders otherwise, a party must provide a transcript of any deposition testimony the party offers, but may provide the court with the testimony in nontranscript form as well. On any party's request, deposition testimony offered in a jury trial for any purpose other than impeachment must be presented in nontranscript form, if available, unless the court for good cause orders otherwise.

(d) Waiver of Objections.

(1) To the Notice. An objection to an error or irregularity in a deposition notice is waived unless promptly served in writing on the party giving the notice.

(2) To the Officer's Qualification. An objection based on disqualification of the officer before whom a deposition is to be taken is waived if not made:

 (A) before the deposition begins; or

 (B) promptly after the basis for disqualification becomes known or, with reasonable diligence, could have been known.

(3) To the Taking of the Deposition.

 (A) Objection to Competence, Relevance, or Materiality. An objection to a deponent's competence—or to the competence, relevance, or materiality of testimony—is not waived by a failure to make the objection before or during the deposition, unless the ground for it might have been corrected at that time.

 (B) Objection to an Error or Irregularity. An objection to an error or irregularity at an oral examination is waived if:

 (i) it relates to the manner of taking the deposition, the form of a question or answer, the oath or affirmation, a party's conduct, or

other matters that might have been corrected at that time; and

 (ii) it is not timely made during the deposition.

(C) Objection to a Written Question. An objection to the form of a written question under Rule 31 is waived if not served in writing on the party submitting the question within the time for serving responsive questions or, if the question is a recross-question, within 5 days after being served with it.

(4) To Completing and Returning the Deposition. An objection to how the officer transcribed the testimony—or prepared, signed, certified, sealed, endorsed, sent, or otherwise dealt with the deposition—is waived unless a motion to suppress is made promptly after the error or irregularity becomes known or, with reasonable diligence, could have been known.

ADVISORY COMMITTEE NOTES

1937 Adoption

This rule is in accordance with common practice. In most of the states listed in the note to rule 26, provisions similar to this rule will be found in the statutes which in their respective statutory compilations follow those cited in the Note to Rule 26.

1970 Amendment

As part of the rearrangement of the discovery rules, existing subdivisions (d), (e), and (f) of Rule 26 are transferred to Rule 32 as new subdivisions (a), (b), and (c). The provisions of Rule 32 are retained as subdivision (d) of Rule 32 with appropriate changes in the lettering and numbering of subheadings. The new rule is given a suitable new title. A beneficial byproduct of the rearrangement is that provisions which are naturally related to one another are placed in one rule.

A change is made in new Rule 32(a), whereby it is made clear that the rules of evidence are to be applied to depositions offered at trial as though the deponent were then present and testifying at trial. This eliminates the possibility of certain technical hearsay objections which are based, not on the contents of deponent's testimony, but on his absence from court. The language of present Rule 26(d) does not appear to authorize these technical objections, but it is not entirely clear. Note present Rule 26(e), transferred to Rule 32(b); see 2A Barron & Holtzoff, *Federal Practice and Procedure* 164–166 (Wright ed. 1961).

An addition in Rule 32(a)(2) provides for use of a deposition of a person designated by a corporation or other organization, which is a party, to testify on its behalf. This complements the new procedure for taking the deposition of a corporation or other organization provided in Rules 30(b)(6) and 31(a). The addition is appropriate, since the deposition is in substance and effect that of the corporation or other organization which is a party.

A change is made in the standard under which a party offering part of a deposition in evidence may be required to introduce additional parts of the deposition. The new standard is contained in a proposal made by the Advisory Committee on Rules of Evidence. See Rule 1–07 and accompanying Note, *Preliminary Draft of Proposed Rules of Evidence for the United States District Courts and Magistrates* 21–22 (March, 1969).

References to other rules are changed to conform to the rearrangement, and minor verbal changes have been made for clarification. The time for objecting to written questions served under Rule 31 is slightly extended.

1972 Amendment

Subdivision (c). The concept of "making a person one's own witness" appears to have had significance principally in two respects: impeachment and waiver of incompetency. Neither retains any vitality under the Rules of Evidence. The old prohibition against impeaching one's own witness is eliminated by Evidence Rule 607. The lack of recognition in the Rules of Evidence of state rules of incompetency in the Dead Man's area renders it unnecessary to consider aspects of waiver arising from calling the incompetent party-witness. Subdivision (c) is deleted because it appears to be no longer necessary in the light of the Rules of Evidence.

1980 Amendment

Subdivision (a)(1). Rule 801(d) of the Federal Rules of Evidence permits a prior inconsistent statement of a witness in a deposition to be used as substantive evidence. And Rule 801(d)(2) makes the statement of an agent or servant admissible against the principal under the circumstances described in the Rule. The language of the present subdivision is, therefore, too narrow.

Subdivision (a)(4). The requirement that a prior action must have been dismissed before depositions taken for use in it can be used in a subsequent action was doubtless an oversight, and the courts have ignored it. See Wright & Miller, *Federal Practice and Procedure: Civil* § 2150. The final sentence is added to reflect the fact that the Federal Rules of Evidence permit a broader use of depositions previously taken under certain circumstances. For example, Rule 804(b)(1) of the Federal Rules of Evidence provides that if a witness is unavailable, as that term is defined by the rule, his deposition in any earlier proceeding can be used against a party to the prior proceeding who had an opportunity and similar motive to develop the testimony of the witness.

1987 Amendment

The amendment is technical. No substantive change is intended.

1993 Amendments

Subdivision (a). The last sentence of revised subdivision (a) not only includes the substance of the provisions formerly contained in the second paragraph of Rule 30(b)(2), but adds a provision to deal with the situation when a party, receiving minimal notice of a proposed deposition, is unable to obtain a court ruling on its motion for a protective order seeking to delay or change the place of the deposition. Ordinarily a party does not obtain protection merely by the filing of a motion for a protective order under Rule 26(c); any protec-

tion is dependent upon the court's ruling. Under the revision, a party receiving less than 11 days notice of a deposition can, provided its motion for a protective order is filed promptly, be spared the risks resulting from nonattendance at the deposition held before its motion is ruled upon. Although the revision of Rule 32(a) covers only the risk that the deposition could be used against the non-appearing movant, it should also follow that, when the proposed deponent is the movant, the deponent would have "just cause" for failing to appear for purposes of Rule 37(d)(1). Inclusion of this provision is not intended to signify that 11 days' notice is the minimum advance notice for all depositions or that greater than 10 days should necessarily be deemed sufficient in all situations.

Subdivision (c). This new subdivision, inserted at the location of a subdivision previously abrogated, is included in view of the increased opportunities for video-recording and audio-recording of depositions under revised Rule 30(b). Under this rule a party may offer deposition testimony in any of the forms authorized under Rule 30(b) but, if offering it in a nonstenographic form, must provide the court with a transcript of the portions so offered. On request of any party in a jury trial, deposition testimony offered other than for impeachment purposes is to be presented in a nonstenographic form if available, unless the court directs otherwise. Note that under Rule 26(a)(3)(B) a party expecting to use nonstenographic deposition testimony as substantive evidence is required to provide other parties with a transcript in advance of trial.

2007 Amendment

*[Effective December 1, 2007,
absent contrary Congressional action.]*

The language of Rule 32 has been amended as part of the general restyling of the Civil Rules to make them more easily understood and to make style and terminology consistent throughout the rules. These changes are intended to be stylistic only.

Former Rule 32(a) applied "[a]t the trial or upon the hearing of a motion or an interlocutory proceeding." The amended rule describes the same events as "a hearing or trial."

The final paragraph of former Rule 32(a) allowed use in a later action of a deposition "lawfully taken and duly filed in the former action." Because of the 2000 amendment of Rule 5(d), many depositions are not filed. Amended Rule 32(a)(8) reflects this change by excluding use of an unfiled deposition only if filing was required in the former action.

HISTORICAL NOTES

References in Text

The Federal Rules of Evidence, referred to in subd. (a)(1), (4), are set out in this title.

Effective Date of Amendment Proposed November 20, 1972

Amendment of this rule embraced by the order entered by the Supreme Court of the United States on November 20, 1972, effective on the 180th day beginning after January 2, 1975, see section 3 of Pub.L. 93–595, Jan. 2, 1975, 88 Stat. 1959, set out as a note under section 2071 of Title 28.

Rule 33. Interrogatories to Parties

(a) Availability. Without leave of court or written stipulation, any party may serve upon any other party written interrogatories, not exceeding 25 in number including all discrete subparts, to be answered by the party served or, if the party served is a public or private corporation or a partnership or association or governmental agency, by any officer or agent, who shall furnish such information as is available to the party. Leave to serve additional interrogatories shall be granted to the extent consistent with the principles of Rule 26(b)(2). Without leave of court or written stipulation, interrogatories may not be served before the time specified in Rule 26(d).

(b) Answers and Objections.

(1) Each interrogatory shall be answered separately and fully in writing under oath, unless it is objected to, in which event the objecting party shall state the reasons for objection and shall answer to the extent the interrogatory is not objectionable.

(2) The answers are to be signed by the person making them, and the objections signed by the attorney making them.

(3) The party upon whom the interrogatories have been served shall serve a copy of the answers, and objections if any, within 30 days after the service of the interrogatories. A shorter or longer time may be directed by the court or, in the absence of such an order, agreed to in writing by the parties subject to Rule 29.

(4) All grounds for an objection to an interrogatory shall be stated with specificity. Any ground not stated in a timely objection is waived unless the party's failure to object is excused by the court for good cause shown.

(5) The party submitting the interrogatories may move for an order under Rule 37(a) with respect to any objection to or other failure to answer an interrogatory.

(c) Scope; Use at Trial. Interrogatories may relate to any matters which can be inquired into under Rule 26(b)(1), and the answers may be used to the extent permitted by the rules of evidence.

An interrogatory otherwise proper is not necessarily objectionable merely because an answer to the interrogatory involves an opinion or contention that relates to fact or the application of law to fact, but the court may order that such an interrogatory need not be answered until after designated discovery has been completed or until a pre-trial conference or other later time.

(d) Option to Produce Business Records. Where the answer to an interrogatory may be derived or ascertained from the business records, including elec-

tronically stored information, of the party upon whom the interrogatory has been served or from an examination, audit or inspection of such business records, including a compilation, abstract or summary thereof, and the burden of deriving or ascertaining the answer is substantially the same for the party serving the interrogatory as for the party served, it is a sufficient answer to such interrogatory to specify the records from which the answer may be derived or ascertained and to afford to the party serving the interrogatory reasonable opportunity to examine, audit or inspect such records and to make copies, compilations, abstracts, or summaries. A specification shall be in sufficient detail to permit the interrogating party to locate and to identify, as readily as can the party served, the records from which the answer may be ascertained.

(As amended Dec. 27, 1946, eff. Mar. 19, 1948; Mar. 30, 1970, eff. July 1, 1970; Apr. 29, 1980, eff. Aug. 1, 1980; Apr. 22, 1993, eff. Dec. 1, 1993; Apr. 12, 2006, eff. Dec. 1, 2006.)

Proposed Amendment of Rule

Effective December 1, 2007, absent contrary Congressional action, this rule is amended to read as follows:

Rule 33. *Interrogatories to Parties*

(a) In General.

(1) Number. Unless otherwise stipulated or ordered by the court, a party may serve on any other party no more than 25 written interrogatories, including all discrete subparts. Leave to serve additional interrogatories may be granted to the extent consistent with Rule 26(b)(2).

(2) Scope. An interrogatory may relate to any matter that may be inquired into under Rule 26(b). An interrogatory is not objectionable merely because it asks for an opinion or contention that relates to fact or the application of law to fact, but the court may order that the interrogatory need not be answered until designated discovery is complete, or until a pretrial conference or some other time.

(b) Answers and Objections.

(1) Responding Party. The interrogatories must be answered:

(A) by the party to whom they are directed; or

(B) if that party is a public or private corporation, a partnership, an association, or a governmental agency, by any officer or agent, who must furnish the information available to the party.

(2) Time to Respond. The responding party must serve its answers and any objections within

30 days after being served with the interrogatories. A shorter or longer time may be stipulated to under Rule 29 or be ordered by the court.

(3) Answering Each Interrogatory. Each interrogatory must, to the extent it is not objected to, be answered separately and fully in writing under oath.

(4) Objections. The grounds for objecting to an interrogatory must be stated with specificity. Any ground not stated in a timely objection is waived unless the court, for good cause, excuses the failure.

(5) Signature. The person who makes the answers must sign them, and the attorney who objects must sign any objections.

(c) Use. An answer to an interrogatory may be used to the extent allowed by the Federal Rules of Evidence.

(d) Option to Produce Business Records. If the answer to an interrogatory may be determined by examining, auditing, compiling, abstracting, or summarizing a party's business records (including electronically stored information), and if the burden of deriving or ascertaining the answer will be substantially the same for either party, the responding party may answer by:

(1) specifying the records that must be reviewed, in sufficient detail to enable the interrogating party to locate and identify them as readily as the responding party could; and

(2) giving the interrogating party a reasonable opportunity to examine and audit the records and to make copies, compilations, abstracts, or summaries.

ADVISORY COMMITTEE NOTES

1937 Adoption

This rule restates the substance of [former] Equity Rule 58 (Discovery—Interrogatories—Inspection and Production of Documents—Admission of Execution or Genuineness), with modifications to conform to these rules.

1946 Amendment

Note. The added second sentence in the first paragraph of Rule 33 conforms with a similar change in Rule 26(a) and will avoid litigation as to when the interrogatories may be served. Original Rule 33 does not state the times at which parties may serve written interrogatories upon each other. It has been the accepted view, however, that the times were the same in Rule 33 as those stated in Rule 26(a). *United States v. American Solvents & Chemical Corp. of California,* D.Del.1939, 30 F.Supp. 107; *Sheldon v. Great Lakes Transit Corp.,* W.D.N.Y.1942, 2 F.R.D. 272, 5 Fed.Rules Serv. 33.11, Case 3; *Musher Foundation, Inc., v. Alba Trading Co.,* S.D.N.Y.1941, 42 F.Supp. 281; 2 *Moore's Federal Practice,* 1938, 2621. The time within which leave of court must be

secured by a plaintiff has been fixed at 10 days, in view of the fact that a defendant has 10 days within which to make objections in any case, which should give him ample time to engage counsel and prepare.

Further in the first paragraph of Rule 33, the word "service" is substituted for "delivery" in conformance with the use of the word "serve" elsewhere in the rule and generally throughout the rules. See also Note to Rule 13(a) herein. The portion of the rule dealing with practice on objections has been revised so as to afford a clearer statement of the procedure. The addition of the words "to interrogatories to which objection is made" insures that only the answers to the objectionable interrogatories may be deferred, and that the answers to interrogatories not objectionable shall be forthcoming within the time prescribed in the rule. Under the original wording, answers to all interrogatories may be withheld until objections, sometimes to but a few interrogatories, are determined. The amendment expedites the procedure of the rule and serves to eliminate the strike value of objections to minor interrogatories. The elimination of the last sentence of the original rule is in line with the policy stated subsequently in this note.

The added second paragraph in Rule 33 contributes clarity and specificity as to the use and scope of interrogatories to the parties. The field of inquiry will be as broad as the scope of examination under Rule 26(b). There is no reason why interrogatories should be more limited than depositions, particularly when the former represent an inexpensive means of securing useful information. See *Hoffman v. Wilson Line, Inc.*, E.D.Pa.1946, 9 Fed.Rules Serv. 33.514, Case 2; *Brewster v. Technicolor, Inc.*, N.Y.1941, 2 F.R.D. 186, 5 Fed.Rules Serv. 33.319, Case 3; *Kingsway Press, Inc. v. Farrell Publishing Corp.*, S.D.N.Y.1939, 30 F.Supp. 775. Under present Rule 33 some courts have unnecessarily restricted the breadth of inquiry on various grounds. See *Auer v. Hershey Creamery Co.*, D.N.J.1939, 2 Fed.Rules Serv. 33.31, Case 2, 1 F.R.D. 14; *Tudor v. Leslie*, D.Mass.1940, 1 F.R.D. 448, 4 Fed.Rules Serv. 33.324, Case 1. Other courts have read into the rule the requirement that interrogation should be directed only towards "important facts", and have tended to fix a more or less arbitrary limit as to the number of interrogatories which could be asked in any case. See *Knox v. Alter*, W.D.Pa.1942, 2 F.R.D. 337, 6 Fed.Rules Serv. 33.352, Case 1; *Byers Theaters, Inc. v. Murphy*, W.D.Va.1940, 3 Fed.Rules Serv. 33.31, Case 3, 1 F.R.D. 286; *Coca-Cola Co. v. Dixi-Cola Laboratories, Inc.*, D.Md.1939, 30 F.Supp. 275. See also comment on these restrictions in Holtzoff, *Instruments of Discovery under Federal Rules of Civil Procedure*, 1942, 41 Mich.L.Rev. 205, 216–217. Under amended Rule 33, the party interrogated is given the right to invoke such protective orders under Rule 30(b) as are appropriate to the situation. At the same time, it is provided that the number of or number of sets of interrogatories to be served may not be limited arbitrarily or as a general policy to any particular number, but that a limit may be fixed only as justice requires to avoid annoyance, expense, embarrassment or oppression in individual cases. The party interrogated, therefore, must show the necessity for limitation on that basis. It will be noted that in accord with this change the last sentence of the present rule, restricting the sets of interrogatories to be served, has been stricken. In *J. Schoeneman, Inc. v. Brauer*, W.D.Mo.1940, 1 F.R.D. 292, 3 Fed.Rules Serv. 33.31, Case 2, the court said: "Rule 33 * * * has been interpreted * * * as being just as broad in its implications as in the case

of depositions * * * It makes no difference therefore, how many interrogatories are propounded. If the inquiries are pertinent the opposing party cannot complain." To the same effect, see *Canuso v. City of Niagara Falls*, W.D.N.Y.1945, 8 Fed.Rules Serv. 33.352, Case 1; *Hoffman v. Wilson Line, Inc.*, supra.

By virtue of express language in the added second paragraph of Rule 33, as amended, any uncertainty as to the use of the answers to interrogatories is removed. The omission of a provision on this score in the original rule has caused some difficulty. See, e.g., *Bailey v. New England Mutual Life Ins. Co.*, S.D.Cal.1940, 1 F.R.D. 494, 4 Fed.Rules Serv. 33.46, Case 1.

The second sentence of the second paragraph in Rule 33, as amended, concerns the situation where a party wishes to serve interrogatories on a party after having taken his deposition, or vice versa. It has been held that an oral examination of a party, after the submission to him and answer of interrogatories, would be permitted. *Howard v. State Marine Corp.*, S.D.N.Y.1940, 4 Fed.Rules Serv. 33.62, Case 1, 1 F.R.D. 499; *Stevens v. Minder Construction Co.*, S.D.N.Y.1943, 3 F.R.D. 498, 7 Fed.Rules Serv. 30b.31, Case 2. But objections have been sustained to interrogatories served after the oral deposition of a party had been taken. *McNally v. Simons*, S.D.N.Y.1940, 3 Fed.Rules Serv. 33.61, Case 1, 1 F.R.D. 254; *Currier v. Currier*, S.D.N.Y.1942, 3 F.R.D. 21, 6 Fed.Rules Serv. 33.61, Case 1. Rule 33, as amended, permits either interrogatories after a deposition or a deposition after interrogatories. It may be quite desirable or necessary to elicit additional information by the inexpensive method of interrogatories where a deposition has already been taken. The party to be interrogated, however, may seek a protective order from the court under Rule 30(b) where the additional deposition or interrogation works a hardship or injustice on the party from whom it is sought.

1970 Amendment

Subdivision (a). The mechanics of the operation of Rule 33 are substantially revised by the proposed amendment, with a view to reducing court intervention. There is general agreement that interrogatories spawn a greater percentage of objections and motions than any other discovery device. The Columbia Survey shows that, although half of the litigants resorted to depositions and about one-third used interrogatories, about 65 percent of the objections were made with respect to interrogatories and 26 percent related to depositions. See also Speck, *The Use of Discovery in United States District Courts*, 60 Yale L.J. 1132, 1144, 1151 (1951); Note, 36 Minn.L.Rev. 364, 379 (1952).

The procedures now provided in Rule 33 seem calculated to encourage objections and court motions. The time periods now allowed for responding to interrogatories—15 days for answers and 10 days for objections—are too short. The Columbia Survey shows that tardy response to interrogatories is common, virtually expected. The same was reported in Speck, *supra*, 60 Yale L.J. 1132, 1144. The time pressures tend to encourage objections as a means of gaining time to answer.

The time for objections is even shorter than for answers, and the party runs the risk that if he fails to object in time he may have waived his objections. E.g., *Cleminshaw v. Beech Aircraft Corp.*, 21 F.R.D. 300 (D.Del.1957); See 4

Moore's Federal Practice, ¶33.27 (2d ed. 1966); 2A Barron & Holtzoff, *Federal Practice and Procedure* 372–373 (Wright ed. 1961). It often seems easier to object than to seek an extension of time. Unlike Rules 30(d) and 37(a), Rule 33 imposes no sanction of expenses on a party whose objections are clearly unjustified.

Rule 33 assures that the objections will lead directly to court, through its requirement that they be served with a notice of hearing. Although this procedure does not preclude an out-of-court resolution of the dispute, the procedure tends to discourage informal negotiations. If answers are served and they are thought inadequate, the interrogating party may move under Rule 37(a) for an order compelling adequate answers. There is no assurance that the hearing on objections and that on inadequate answers will be heard together.

The amendment improves the procedure of Rule 33 in the following respects:

(1) The time allowed for response is increased to 30 days and this time period applies to both answers and objections, but a defendant need not respond in less than 45 days after service of the summons and complaint upon him. As is true under existing law, the responding party who believes that some parts or all of the interrogatories are objectionable may choose to seek a protective order under new Rule 26(c) or may serve objections under this rule. Unless he applies for a protective order, he is required to serve answers or objections in response to the interrogatories, subject to the sanctions provided in Rule 37(d). Answers and objections are served together, so that a response to each interrogatory is encouraged, and any failure to respond is easily noted.

(2) In view of the enlarged time permitted for response, it is no longer necessary to require leave of court for service of interrogatories. The purpose of this requirement—that defendant have time to obtain counsel before a response must be made—is adequately fulfilled by the requirement that interrogatories be served upon a party with or after service of the summons and complaint upon him.

Some would urge that the plaintiff nevertheless not be permitted to serve interrogatories with the complaint. They fear that a routine practice might be invited, whereby form interrogatories would accompany most complaints. More fundamentally, they feel that, since very general complaints are permitted in present-day pleading, it is fair that the defendant have a right to take the lead in serving interrogatories. (These views apply also to Rule 36.) The amendment of Rule 33 rejects these views, in favor of allowing both parties to go forward with discovery, each free to obtain the information he needs respecting the case.

(3) If objections are made, the burden is on the interrogating party to move under Rule 37(a) for a court order compelling answers, in the course of which the court will pass on the objections. The change in the burden of going forward does not alter the existing obligation of an objecting party to justify his objections. *E.g., Pressley v. Bochlke,* 33 F.R.D. 316 (W.D.N.C. 1963). If the discovering party asserts that an answer is incomplete or evasive, again he may look to Rule 37(a) for relief, and he should add this assertion to his motion to overrule objections. There is no requirement that the parties consult informally concerning their differences, but the new procedure should encourage consultation, and the court may by local rule require it.

The proposed changes are similar in approach to those adopted by California in 1961. See Calif.Code Civ.Proc. § 2030(a). The experience of the Los Angeles Superior Court is informally reported as showing that the California amendment resulted in a significant reduction in court motions concerning interrogatories. Rhode Island takes a similar approach. See R. 33, *R.I.R. Civ.Proc. Official Draft,* p. 74 (Boston Law Book Co.).

A change is made in subdivision (a) which is not related to the sequence of procedures. The restriction to "adverse" parties is eliminated. The courts have generally construed this restriction as precluding interrogatories unless an issue between the parties is disclosed by the pleadings—even though the parties may have conflicting interests. E.g., *Mozeika v. Kaufman Construction Co.,* 25 F.R.D. 233 (E.D.Pa.1960) (plaintiff and third-party defendant); *Biddle v. Hutchinson,* 24 F.R.D. 256 (M.D.Pa.1959) (codefendants). The resulting distinctions have often been highly technical. In *Schlagenhauf v. Holder,* 379 U.S. 104 (1964), the Supreme Court rejected a contention that examination under Rule 35 could be had only against an "opposing" party, as not in keeping "with the aims of a liberal, nontechnical application of the Federal Rules." 379 U.S. at 116. Eliminating the requirement of "adverse" parties from Rule 33 brings it into line with all other discovery rules.

A second change in subdivision (a) is the addition of the term "governmental agency" to the listing of organizations whose answers are to be made by any officer or agent of the organization. This does not involve any change in existing law. Compare the similar listing in Rule 30(b)(6).

The duty of a party to supplement his answers to interrogatories is governed by a new provision in Rule 26(e).

Subdivision (b). There are numerous and conflicting decisions on the question whether and to what extent interrogatories are limited to matters "of fact," or may elicit opinions, contentions, and legal conclusions. Compare, e.g., *Payer, Hewitt & Co. v. Bellanca Corp.,* 26 F.R.D. 219 (D.Del.1960) (opinions bad); *Zinsky v. New York Central R.R.,* 36 F.R.D. 680 (N.D.Ohio 1964) (factual opinion or contention good, but legal theory bad); *United States v. Carter Products, Inc.,* 28 F.R.D. 373 (S.D.N.Y.1961) (factual contentions and legal theories bad) with *Taylor v. Sound Steamship Lines, Inc.,* 100 F.Supp. 388 (D.Conn.1951) (opinions good); *Bynum v. United States,* 36 F.R.D. 14 (E.D.La.1964) (contentions as to facts constituting negligence good). For lists of the many conflicting authorities, see 4 *Moore's Federal Practice* ¶33.17 (2d ed. 1966); 2A Barron & Holtzoff, *Federal Practice and Procedure* § 768 (Wright ed. 1961).

Rule 33 is amended to provide that an interrogatory is not objectionable merely because it calls for an opinion or contention that relates to fact or the application of law to fact. Efforts to draw sharp lines between facts and opinions have invariably been unsuccessful, and the clear trend of the cases is to permit "factual" opinions. As to requests for opinions or contentions that call for the application of law to fact, they can be most useful in narrowing and sharpening the issues, which is a major purpose of discovery. See *Diversified Products Corp. v. Sports Center Co.,* 42 F.R.D. 3 (D.Md. 1967); Moore, *supra;* Field & McKusick, *Maine Civil Practice* § 26.18 (1959). On the other hand, under the new language interrogatories may not extend to issues of "pure law," *i.e.,* legal issues unrelated to the facts of the case. *Cf.*

United States v. Maryland & Va. Milk Producers Assn., Inc., 22 F.R.D. 300 (D.D.C.1958).

Since interrogatories involving mixed questions of law and fact may create disputes between the parties which are best resolved after much or all of the other discovery has been completed, the court is expressly authorized to defer an answer. Likewise, the court may delay determination until pretrial conference, if it believes that the dispute is best resolved in the presence of the judge.

The principal question raised with respect to the cases permitting such interrogatories is whether they reintroduce undesirable aspects of the prior pleading practice, whereby parties were chained to misconceived contentions or theories, and ultimate determination on the merits was frustrated. See James, *The Revival of Bills of Particulars under the Federal Rules,* 71 Harv.L.Rev. 1473 (1958). But there are few if any instances in the recorded cases demonstrating that such frustration has occurred. The general rule governing the use of answers to interrogatories is that under ordinary circumstances they do not limit proof. See, *e.g., McElroy v. United Air Lines, Inc.,* 21 F.R.D. 100 (W.D.Mo.1967); *Pressley v. Boehlke,* 33 F.R.D. 316, 317 (W.D.N.C.1963). Although in exceptional circumstances reliance on an answer may cause such prejudice that the court will hold the answering party bound to his answer, *e.g., Zielinski v. Philadelphia Piers, Inc.,* 139 F.Supp. 408 (E.D.Pa.1956), the interrogating party will ordinarily not be entitled to rely on the unchanging character of the answers he receives and cannot base prejudice on such reliance. The rule does not affect the power of a court to permit withdrawal or amendment of answers to interrogatories.

The use of answers to interrogatories at trial is made subject to the rules of evidence. The provisions governing use of depositions, to which Rule 33 presently refers, are not entirely apposite to answers to interrogatories, since deposition practice contemplates that all parties will ordinarily participate through cross-examination. See 4 *Moore's Federal Practice* ¶33.29[1] (2d ed. 1966).

Certain provisions are deleted from subdivision (b) because they are fully covered by new Rule 26(c) providing for protective orders and Rules 26(a) and 26(d). The language of the subdivision is thus simplified without any change of substance.

Subdivision (c). This is a new subdivision, adapted from Calif.Code Civ.Proc. § 2030(c), relating especially to interrogatories which require a party to engage in burdensome or expensive research into his own business records in order to give an answer. The subdivision gives the party an option to make the records available and place the burden of research of the party who seeks the information. "This provision, without undermining the liberal scope of interrogatory discovery, places the burden of discovery upon its potential benefittee," Louisell, *Modern California Discovery,* 124–125 (1963), and alleviates a problem which in the past has troubled Federal courts. See Speck, *The Use of Discovery in United States District Courts,* 60 Yale L.J. 1132, 1142–1144 (1951). The interrogating party is protected against abusive use of this provision through the requirement that the burden of ascertaining the answer be substantially the same for both sides. A respondent may not impose on an interrogating party a mass of records as to which research is feasible only for one familiar with the records. At the same time, the respondent unable to invoke this subdivision does not on that account lose the protection available to him under new Rule 26(c) against oppressive or unduly burdensome or expensive interrogatories. And even when the respondent successfully invokes the subdivision, the court is not deprived of its usual power, in appropriate cases, to require that the interrogating party reimburse the respondent for the expense of assembling his records and making them intelligible.

1980 Amendment

Subdivision (c). The Committee is advised that parties upon whom interrogatories are served have occasionally responded by directing the interrogating party to a mass of business records or by offering to make all of their records available, justifying the response by the option provided by this subdivision. Such practices are an abuse of the option. A party who is permitted by the terms of this subdivision to offer records for inspection in lieu of answering an interrogatory should offer them in a manner than permits the same direct and economical access that is available to the party. If the information sought exists in the form of compilations, abstracts or summaries then available to the responding party, those should be made available to the interrogating party. The final sentence is added to make it clear that a responding party has the duty to specify, by category and location, the records from which answers to interrogatories can be derived.

1993 Amendments

Purpose of Revision. The purpose of this revision is to reduce the frequency and increase the efficiency of interrogatory practice. The revision is based on experience with local rules. For ease of reference, subdivision (a) is divided into two subdivisions and the remaining subdivisions renumbered.

Subdivision (a). Revision of this subdivision limits interrogatory practice. Because Rule 26(a)(1)–(3) requires disclosure of much of the information previously obtained by this form of discovery, there should be less occasion to use it. Experience in over half of the district courts has confirmed that limitations on the number of interrogatories are useful and manageable. Moreover, because the device can be costly and may be used as a means of harassment, it is desirable to subject its use to the control of the court consistent with the principles stated in Rule 26(b)(2), particularly in multi-party cases where it has not been unusual for the same interrogatory to be propounded to a party by more than one of its adversaries.

Each party is allowed to serve 25 interrogatories upon any other party, but must secure leave of court (or a stipulation from the opposing party) to serve a larger number. Parties cannot evade this presumptive limitation through the device of joining as "subparts" questions that seek information about discrete separate subjects. However, a question asking about communications of a particular type should be treated as a single interrogatory even though it requests that the time, place, persons present, and contents be stated separately for each such communication.

As with the number of depositions authorized by Rule 30, leave to serve additional interrogatories is to be allowed when consistent with Rule 26(b)(2). The aim is not to prevent needed discovery, but to provide judicial scrutiny before parties make potentially excessive use of this discovery device. In many cases it will be appropriate for the

court to permit a larger number of interrogatories in the scheduling order entered under Rule 16(b).

Unless leave of court is obtained, interrogatories may not be served prior to the meeting of the parties under Rule 26(f).

When a case with outstanding interrogatories exceeding the number permitted by this rule is removed to federal court, the interrogating party must seek leave allowing the additional interrogatories, specify which twenty-five are to be answered, or resubmit interrogatories that comply with the rule. Moreover, under Rule 26(d), the time for response would be measured from the date of the parties' meeting under Rule 26(f). See Rule 81(c), providing that these rules govern procedures after removal.

Subdivision (b). A separate subdivision is made of the former second paragraph of subdivision (a). Language is added to paragraph (1) of this subdivision to emphasize the duty of the responding party to provide full answers to the extent not objectionable. If, for example, an interrogatory seeking information about numerous facilities or products is deemed objectionable, but an interrogatory seeking information about a lesser number of facilities or products would not have been objectionable, the interrogatory should be answered with respect to the latter even though an objection is raised as to the balance of the facilities or products. Similarly, the fact that additional time may be needed to respond to some questions (or to some aspects of questions) should not justify a delay in responding to those questions (or other aspects of questions) that can be answered within the prescribed time.

Paragraph (4) is added to make clear that objections must be specifically justified, and that unstated or untimely grounds for objection ordinarily are waived. Note also the provisions of revised Rule 26(b)(5), which require a responding party to indicate when it is withholding information under a claim of privilege or as trial preparation materials.

These provisions should be read in light of Rule 26(g), authorizing the court to impose sanctions on a party and attorney making an unfounded objection to an interrogatory.

Subdivisions (c) and (d). The provisions of former subdivisions (b) and (c) are renumbered.

2006 Amendment

Rule 33(d) is amended to parallel Rule 34(a) by recognizing the importance of electronically stored information. The term "electronically stored information" has the same broad meaning in Rule 33(d) as in Rule 34(a). Much business information is stored only in electronic form; the Rule 33(d) option should be available with respect to such records as well.

Special difficulties may arise in using electronically stored information, either due to its form or because it is dependent on a particular computer system. Rule 33(d) allows a responding party to substitute access to documents or electronically stored information for an answer only if the burden of deriving the answer will be substantially the same for either party. Rule 33(d) states that a party electing to respond to an interrogatory by providing electronically stored information must ensure that the interrogating party can locate and identify it "as readily as can the party served," and that the responding party must give the interrogating party a "reasonable opportunity to examine, audit, or inspect" the infor-

mation. Depending on the circumstances, satisfying these provisions with regard to electronically stored information may require the responding party to provide some combination of technical support, information on application software, or other assistance. The key question is whether such support enables the interrogating party to derive or ascertain the answer from the electronically stored information as readily as the responding party. A party that wishes to invoke Rule 33(d) by specifying electronically stored information may be required to provide direct access to its electronic information system, but only if that is necessary to afford the requesting party an adequate opportunity to derive or ascertain the answer to the interrogatory. In that situation, the responding party's need to protect sensitive interests of confidentiality or privacy may mean that it must derive or ascertain and provide the answer itself rather than invoke Rule 33(d).

2007 Amendment

[Effective December 1, 2007,
absent contrary Congressional action.]

The language of Rule 33 has been amended as part of the general restyling of the Civil Rules to make them more easily understood and to make style and terminology consistent throughout the rules. These changes are intended to be stylistic only.

The final sentence of former Rule 33(a) was a redundant cross-reference to the discovery moratorium provisions of Rule 26(d). Rule 26(d) is now familiar, obviating any need to carry forward the redundant cross-reference.

Former Rule 33(b)(5) was a redundant reminder of Rule 37(a) procedure and is omitted as no longer useful.

Former Rule 33(c) stated that an interrogatory "is not necessarily objectionable merely because an answer * * * involves an opinion or contention * * *." "[I]s not necessarily" seemed to imply that the interrogatory might be objectionable merely for this reason. This implication has been ignored in practice. Opinion and contention interrogatories are used routinely. Amended Rule 33(a)(2) embodies the current meaning of Rule 33 by omitting "necessarily."

Rule 34. Production of Documents, Electronically Stored Information, and Things and Entry Upon Land for Inspection and Other Purposes

(a) Scope. Any party may serve on any other party a request (1) to produce and permit the party making the request, or someone acting on the requestor's behalf, to inspect, copy, test, or sample any designated documents or electronically stored information — including writings, drawings, graphs, charts, photographs, sound recordings, images, and other data or data compilations stored in any medium from which information can be obtained — translated, if necessary, by the respondent into reasonably usable form, or to inspect, copy, test, or sample any designated tangible things which constitute or contain matters within the scope of Rule 26(b) and which are in the possession, custody or control of the party upon whom

the request is served; or (2) to permit entry upon designated land or other property in the possession or control of the party upon whom the request is served for the purpose of inspection and measuring, surveying, photographing, testing, or sampling the property or any designated object or operation thereon, within the scope of Rule 26(b).

(b) Procedure. The request shall set forth, either by individual item or by category, the items to be inspected, and describe each with reasonable particularity. The request shall specify a reasonable time, place, and manner of making the inspection and performing the related acts. The request may specify the form or forms in which electronically stored information is to be produced. Without leave of court or written stipulation, a request may not be served before the time specified in Rule 26(d).

The party upon whom the request is served shall serve a written response within 30 days after the service of the request. A shorter or longer time may be directed by the court or, in the absence of such an order, agreed to in writing by the parties, subject to Rule 29. The response shall state, with respect to each item or category, that inspection and related activities will be permitted as requested, unless the request is objected to, including an objection to the requested form or forms for producing electronically stored information, stating the reasons for the objection. If objection is made to part of an item or category, the part shall be specified and inspection permitted of the remaining parts. If objection is made to the requested form or forms for producing electronically stored information — or if no form was specified in the request — the responding party must state the form or forms it intends to use. The party submitting the request may move for an order under Rule 37(a) with respect to any objection to or other failure to respond to the request or any part thereof, or any failure to permit inspection as requested.

Unless the parties otherwise agree, or the court otherwise orders:

 (i) a party who produces documents for inspection shall produce them as they are kept in the usual course of business or shall organize and label them to correspond with the categories in the request;

 (ii) if a request does not specify the form or forms for producing electronically stored information, a responding party must produce the information in a form or forms in which it is ordinarily maintained or in a form or forms that are reasonably usable; and

 (iii) a party need not produce the same electronically stored information in more than one form.

(c) Persons Not Parties. A person not a party to the action may be compelled to produce documents

and things or to submit to an inspection as provided in Rule 45.

(As amended Dec. 27, 1946, effective March 19, 1948; Mar. 30, 1970, eff. July 1, 1970; Apr. 29, 1980, eff. Aug. 1, 1980; Mar. 2, 1987, eff. Aug. 1, 1987; Apr. 30, 1991, eff. Dec. 1, 1991; Apr. 22, 1993, eff. Dec. 1, 1993; Apr. 12, 2006, eff. Dec. 1, 2006.)

Proposed Amendment of Rule

Effective December 1, 2007, absent contrary Congressional action, this rule is amended to read as follows:

Rule 34. Producing Documents, Electronically Stored Information, and Tangible Things, or Entering onto Land, for Inspection and Other Purposes

(a) In General. *A party may serve on any other party a request within the scope of Rule 26(b):*

 (1) to produce and permit the requesting party or its representative to inspect, copy, test, or sample the following items in the responding party's possession, custody, or control:

 (A) any designated documents or electronically stored information—including writings, drawings, graphs, charts, photographs, sound recordings, images, and other data or data compilations—stored in any medium from which information can be obtained either directly or, if necessary, after translation by the responding party into a reasonably usable form; or

 (B) any designated tangible things; or

 (2) to permit entry onto designated land or other property possessed or controlled by the responding party, so that the requesting party may inspect, measure, survey, photograph, test, or sample the property or any designated object or operation on it.

(b) Procedure.

 (1) Contents of the Request. The request:

 (A) must describe with reasonable particularity each item or category of items to be inspected;

 (B) must specify a reasonable time, place, and manner for the inspection and for performing the related acts; and

 (C) may specify the form or forms in which electronically stored information is to be produced.

 (2) Responses and Objections.

 (A) Time to Respond. The party to whom the request is directed must respond in writing

within 30 days after being served. A shorter or longer time may be stipulated to under Rule 29 or be ordered by the court.

(B) Responding to Each Item. For each item or category, the response must either state that inspection and related activities will be permitted as requested or state an objection to the request, including the reasons.

(C) Objections. An objection to part of a request must specify the part and permit inspection of the rest.

(D) Responding to a Request for Production of Electronically Stored Information. The response may state an objection to a requested form for producing electronically stored information. If the responding party objects to a requested form—or if no form was specified in the request—the party must state the form or forms it intends to use.

(E) Producing the Documents or Electronically Stored Information. Unless otherwise stipulated or ordered by the court, these procedures apply to producing documents or electronically stored information:

(i) A party must produce documents as they are kept in the usual course of business or must organize and label them to correspond to the categories in the request;

(ii) If a request does not specify a form for producing electronically stored information, a party must produce it in a form or forms in which it is ordinarily maintained or in a reasonably usable form or forms; and

(iii) A party need not produce the same electronically stored information in more than one form.

*(c) **Nonparties.** As provided in Rule 45, a nonparty may be compelled to produce documents and tangible things or to permit an inspection.*

ADVISORY COMMITTEE NOTES

1937 Adoption

In England orders are made for the inspection of documents, *English Rules Under the Judicature Act (The Annual Practice,* 1937) O. 31, r.r. 14, et seq., or for the inspection of tangible property or for entry upon land, O. 50, r. 3. Michigan provides for inspection of damaged property when such damage is the ground of the action. Mich.Court Rules Ann. (Searl, 1933) Rule 41, § 2.

Practically all states have statutes authorizing the court to order parties in possession or control of documents to permit other parties to inspect and copy them before trial. See Ragland, *Discovery Before Trial* (1932) Appendix, p. 267, setting out the statutes.

Compare [former] Equity Rule 58 (Discovery—Interrogatories—Inspection and Production of Documents—Admission of Execution or Genuineness) (fifth paragraph).

1946 Amendment

Note. The changes in clauses (1) and (2) correlate the scope of inquiry permitted under Rule 34 with that provided in Rule 26(b), and thus remove any ambiguity created by the former differences in language. As stated in *Olson Transportation Co. v. Socony-Vacuum Oil Co.,* E.D.Wis.1944, 8 Fed.Rules Serv. 34.41, Case 2, "* * * Rule 34 is a direct and simple method of discovery." At the same time the addition of the words following the term "parties" makes certain that the person in whose custody, possession, or control the evidence reposes may have the benefit of the applicable protective orders stated in Rule 30(b). This change should be considered in the light of the proposed expansion of Rule 30(b).

An objection has been made that the word "designated" in Rule 34 has been construed with undue strictness in some district court cases so as to require great and impracticable specificity in the description of documents, papers, books, etc., sought to be inspected. The Committee, however, believes that no amendment is needed, and that the proper meaning of "designated" as requiring specificity has already been delineated by the Supreme Court. *See Brown v. United States,* 1928, 48 S.Ct. 288, 276 U.S. 134, 143, 72 L.Ed. 500 ("The subpoena * * * specifies * * * with reasonable particularity the subjects to which the documents called for related."); *Consolidated Rendering Co. v. Vermont,* 1908, 28 S.Ct. 178, 207 U.S. 541, 543–544, 52 L.Ed. 327 ("We see no reason why all such books, papers and correspondence which related to the subject of inquiry, and were described with reasonable detail, should not be called for and the company directed to produce them. Otherwise, the State would be compelled to designate each particular paper which it desired, which presupposes an accurate knowledge of such papers, which the tribunal desiring the papers would probably rarely, if ever, have.").

1970 Amendment

Rule 34 is revised to accomplish the following major changes in the existing rule: (1) to eliminate the requirement of good cause; (2) to have the rule operate extrajudicially; (3) to include testing and sampling as well as inspecting or photographing tangible things; and (4) to make clear that the rule does not preclude an independent action for analogous discovery against persons not parties.

Subdivision (a). Good cause is eliminated because it has furnished an uncertain and erratic protection to the parties from whom production is sought and is now rendered unnecessary by virtue of the more specific provisions added to Rule 26(b) relating to materials assembled in preparation for trial and to experts retained or consulted by parties.

The good cause requirement was originally inserted in Rule 34 as a general protective provision in the absence of experience with the specific problems that would arise thereunder. As the note to Rule 26(b)(3) on trial preparation materials makes clear, good cause has been applied differently to varying classes of documents, though not without confusion. It has often been said in court opinions that good cause requires a consideration of need for the materials and

of alternative means of obtaining them, i.e., something more than relevance and lack of privilege. But the overwhelming proportion of the cases in which the formula of good cause has been applied to require a special showing are those involving trial preparation. In practice, the courts have not treated documents as having a special immunity to discovery simply because of their being documents. Protection may be afforded to claims of privacy or secrecy or of undue burden or expense under what is now Rule 26(c) (previously Rule 30(b)). To be sure, an appraisal of "undue" burden inevitably entails consideration of the needs of the party seeking discovery. With special provisions added to govern trial preparation materials and experts, there is no longer any occasion to retain the requirement of good cause.

The revision of Rule 34 to have it operate extrajudicially, rather than by court order, is to a large extent a reflection of existing law office practice. The Columbia Survey shows that of the litigants seeking inspection of documents or things, only about 25 percent filed motions for court orders. This minor fraction nevertheless accounted for a significant number of motions. About half of these motions were uncontested and in almost all instances the party seeking production ultimately prevailed. Although an extrajudicial procedure will not drastically alter existing practice under Rule 34—it will conform to it in most cases—it has the potential of saving court time in a substantial though proportionately small number of cases tried annually.

The inclusion of testing and sampling of tangible things and objects or operations on land reflects a need frequently encountered by parties in preparation for trial. If the operation of a particular machine is the basis of a claim for negligent injury, it will often be necessary to test its operating parts or to sample and test the products it is producing. Cf. Mich.Gen.Ct.R. 310.1(1) (1963) (testing authorized).

The inclusive description of "documents" is revised to accord with changing technology. It makes clear that Rule 34 applies to electronics data compilations from which information can be obtained only with the use of detection devices, and that when the data can as a practical matter be made usable by the discovering party only through respondent's devices, respondent may be required to use his devices to translate the data into usable form. In many instances, this means that respondent will have to supply a print-out of computer data. The burden thus placed on respondent will vary from case to case, and the courts have ample power under Rule 26(c) to protect respondent against undue burden or expense, either by restricting discovery or requiring that the discovering party pay costs. Similarly, if the discovering party needs to check the electronic source itself, the court may protect respondent with respect to preservation of his records, confidentiality of nondiscoverable matters, and costs.

Subdivision (b). The procedure provided in Rule 34 is essentially the same as that in Rule 33, as amended, and the discussion in the note appended to that rule is relevant to Rule 34 as well. Problems peculiar to Rule 34 relate to the specific arrangements that must be worked out for inspection and related acts of copying, photographing, testing, or sampling. The rule provides that a request for inspection shall set forth the items to be inspected either by item or category, describing each with reasonable particularity, and shall specify a reasonable time, place, and manner of making the inspection.

Subdivision (c). Rule 34 as revised continues to apply only to parties. Comments from the bar make clear that in the preparation of cases for trial it is occasionally necessary to enter land or inspect large tangible things in the possession of a person not a party, and that some courts have dismissed independent actions in the nature of bills in equity for such discovery on the ground that Rule 34 is preemptive. While an ideal solution to this problem is to provide for discovery against persons not parties in Rule 34, both the jurisdictional and procedural problems are very complex. For the present, this subdivision makes clear that Rule 34 does not preclude independent actions for discovery against persons not parties.

1980 Amendment

Subdivision (b). The Committee is advised that, "It is apparently not rare for parties deliberately to mix critical documents with others in the hope of obscuring significance." *Report of the Special Committee for the Study of Discovery Abuse, Section of Litigation of the American Bar Association* (1977) 22. The sentence added by this subdivision follows the recommendation of the *Report*.

1987 Amendment

The amendment is technical. No substantive change is intended.

1991 Amendment

This amendment reflects the change effected by revision of Rule 45 to provide for subpoenas to compel non-parties to produce documents and things and to submit to inspections of premises. The deletion of the text of the former paragraph is not intended to preclude an independent action for production of documents or things or for permission to enter upon land, but such actions may no longer be necessary in light of this revision.

1993 Amendments

The rule is revised to reflect the change made by Rule 26(d), preventing a party from seeking formal discovery prior to the meeting of the parties required by Rule 26(f). Also, like a change made in Rule 33, the rule is modified to make clear that, if a request for production is objectionable only in part, production should be afforded with respect to the unobjectionable portions.

When a case with outstanding requests for production is removed to federal court, the time for response would be measured from the date of the parties' meeting. See Rule 81(c), providing that these rules govern procedures after removal.

2006 Amendment

Subdivision (a). As originally adopted, Rule 34 focused on discovery of "documents" and "things." In 1970, Rule 34(a) was amended to include discovery of data compilations, anticipating that the use of computerized information would increase. Since then, the growth in electronically stored information and in the variety of systems for creating and storing such information has been dramatic. Lawyers and judges interpreted the term "documents" to include electronically stored information because it was obviously improper

to allow a party to evade discovery obligations on the basis that the label had not kept pace with changes in information technology. But it has become increasingly difficult to say that all forms of electronically stored information, many dynamic in nature, fit within the traditional concept of a "document." Electronically stored information may exist in dynamic databases and other forms far different from fixed expression on paper. Rule 34(a) is amended to confirm that discovery of electronically stored information stands on equal footing with discovery of paper documents. The change clarifies that Rule 34 applies to information that is fixed in a tangible form and to information that is stored in a medium from which it can be retrieved and examined. At the same time, a Rule 34 request for production of "documents" should be understood to encompass, and the response should include, electronically stored information unless discovery in the action has clearly distinguished between electronically stored information and "documents."

Discoverable information often exists in both paper and electronic form, and the same or similar information might exist in both. The items listed in Rule 34(a) show different ways in which information may be recorded or stored. Images, for example, might be hard-copy documents or electronically stored information. The wide variety of computer systems currently in use, and the rapidity of technological change, counsel against a limiting or precise definition of electronically stored information. Rule 34(a)(1) is expansive and includes any type of information that is stored electronically. A common example often sought in discovery is electronic communications, such as e-mail. The rule covers — either as documents or as electronically stored information — information "stored in any medium," to encompass future developments in computer technology. Rule 34(a)(1) is intended to be broad enough to cover all current types of computer-based information, and flexible enough to encompass future changes and developments.

References elsewhere in the rules to "electronically stored information" should be understood to invoke this expansive approach. A companion change is made to Rule 33(d), making it explicit that parties choosing to respond to an interrogatory by permitting access to responsive records may do so by providing access to electronically stored information. More generally, the term used in Rule 34(a)(1) appears in a number of other amendments, such as those to Rules 26(a)(1), 26(b)(2), 26(b)(5)(B), 26(f), 34(b), 37(f), and 45. In each of these rules, electronically stored information has the same broad meaning it has under Rule 34(a)(1). References to "documents" appear in discovery rules that are not amended, including Rules 30(f), 36(a), and 37(c)(2). These references should be interpreted to include electronically stored information as circumstances warrant.

The term "electronically stored information" is broad, but whether material that falls within this term should be produced, and in what form, are separate questions that must be addressed under Rules 26(b), 26(c), and 34(b).

The Rule 34(a) requirement that, if necessary, a party producing electronically stored information translate it into reasonably usable form does not address the issue of translating from one human language to another. *See In re Puerto Rico Elect. Power Auth.*, 687 F.2d 501, 504–510 (1st Cir. 1989).

Rule 34(a)(1) is also amended to make clear that parties may request an opportunity to test or sample materials sought under the rule in addition to inspecting and copying them. That opportunity may be important for both electronically stored information and hard-copy materials. The current rule is not clear that such testing or sampling is authorized; the amendment expressly permits it. As with any other form of discovery, issues of burden and intrusiveness raised by requests to test or sample can be addressed under Rules 26(b)(2) and 26(c). Inspection or testing of certain types of electronically stored information or of a responding party's electronic information system may raise issues of confidentiality or privacy. The addition of testing and sampling to Rule 34(a) with regard to documents and electronically stored information is not meant to create a routine right of direct access to a party's electronic information system, although such access might be justified in some circumstances. Courts should guard against undue intrusiveness resulting from inspecting or testing such systems.

Rule 34(a)(1) is further amended to make clear that tangible things must — like documents and land sought to be examined — be designated in the request.

Subdivision (b). Rule 34(b) provides that a party must produce documents as they are kept in the usual course of business or must organize and label them to correspond with the categories in the discovery request. The production of electronically stored information should be subject to comparable requirements to protect against deliberate or inadvertent production in ways that raise unnecessary obstacles for the requesting party. Rule 34(b) is amended to ensure similar protection for electronically stored information.

The amendment to Rule 34(b) permits the requesting party to designate the form or forms in which it wants electronically stored information produced. The form of production is more important to the exchange of electronically stored information than of hard-copy materials, although a party might specify hard copy as the requested form. Specification of the desired form or forms may facilitate the orderly, efficient, and cost-effective discovery of electronically stored information. The rule recognizes that different forms of production may be appropriate for different types of electronically stored information. Using current technology, for example, a party might be called upon to produce word processing documents, e-mail messages, electronic spreadsheets, different image or sound files, and material from databases. Requiring that such diverse types of electronically stored information all be produced in the same form could prove impossible, and even if possible could increase the cost and burdens of producing and using the information. The rule therefore provides that the requesting party may ask for different forms of production for different types of electronically stored information.

The rule does not require that the requesting party choose a form or forms of production. The requesting party may not have a preference. In some cases, the requesting party may not know what form the producing party uses to maintain its electronically stored information, although Rule 26(f)(3) is amended to call for discussion of the form of production in the parties' prediscovery conference.

The responding party also is involved in determining the form of production. In the written response to the production request that Rule 34 requires, the responding party must state the form it intends to use for producing electronically stored information if the requesting party does not

specify a form or if the responding party objects to a form that the requesting party specifies. Stating the intended form before the production occurs may permit the parties to identify and seek to resolve disputes before the expense and work of the production occurs. A party that responds to a discovery request by simply producing electronically stored information in a form of its choice, without identifying that form in advance of the production in the response required by Rule 34(b), runs a risk that the requesting party can show that the produced form is not reasonably usable and that it is entitled to production of some or all of the information in an additional form. Additional time might be required to permit a responding party to assess the appropriate form or forms of production.

If the requesting party is not satisfied with the form stated by the responding party, or if the responding party has objected to the form specified by the requesting party, the parties must meet and confer under Rule 37(a)(2)(B) in an effort to resolve the matter before the requesting party can file a motion to compel. If they cannot agree and the court resolves the dispute, the court is not limited to the forms initially chosen by the requesting party, stated by the responding party, or specified in this rule for situations in which there is no court order or party agreement.

If the form of production is not specified by party agreement or court order, the responding party must produce electronically stored information either in a form or forms in which it is ordinarily maintained or in a form or forms that are reasonably usable. Rule 34(a) requires that, if necessary, a responding party "translate" information it produces into a "reasonably usable" form. Under some circumstances, the responding party may need to provide some reasonable amount of technical support, information on application software, or other reasonable assistance to enable the requesting party to use the information. The rule does not require a party to produce electronically stored information in the form it which it is ordinarily maintained, as long as it is produced in a reasonably usable form. But the option to produce in a reasonably usable form does not mean that a responding party is free to convert electronically stored information from the form in which it is ordinarily maintained to a different form that makes it more difficult or burdensome for the requesting party to use the information efficiently in the litigation. If the responding party ordinarily maintains the information it is producing in a way that makes it searchable by electronic means, the information should not be produced in a form that removes or significantly degrades this feature.

Some electronically stored information may be ordinarily maintained in a form that is not reasonably usable by any party. One example is "legacy" data that can be used only by superseded systems. The questions whether a producing party should be required to convert such information to a more usable form, or should be required to produce it at all, should be addressed under Rule 26(b)(2)(B).

Whether or not the requesting party specified the form of production, Rule 34(b) provides that the same electronically stored information ordinarily need be produced in only one form.

2007 Amendment

*[Effective December 1, 2007,
absent contrary Congressional action.]*

The language of Rule 34 has been amended as part of the general restyling of the Civil Rules to make them more easily understood and to make style and terminology consistent throughout the rules. These changes are intended to be stylistic only.

The final sentence in the first paragraph of former Rule 34(b) was a redundant cross-reference to the discovery moratorium provisions of Rule 26(d). Rule 26(d) is now familiar, obviating any need to carry forward the redundant cross-reference.

The redundant reminder of Rule 37(a) procedure in the second paragraph of former Rule 34(b) is omitted as no longer useful.

Rule 35. Physical and Mental Examinations of Persons

(a) Order for Examination. When the mental or physical condition (including the blood group) of a party or of a person in the custody or under the legal control of a party, is in controversy, the court in which the action is pending may order the party to submit to a physical or mental examination by a suitably licensed or certified examiner or to produce for examination the person in the party's custody or legal control. The order may be made only on motion for good cause shown and upon notice to the person to be examined and to all parties and shall specify the time, place, manner, conditions, and scope of the examination and the person or persons by whom it is to be made.

(b) Report of Examiner.

(1) If requested by the party against whom an order is made under Rule 35(a) or the person examined, the party causing the examination to be made shall deliver to the requesting party a copy of the detailed written report of the examiner setting out the examiner's findings, including results of all tests made, diagnoses and conclusions, together with like reports of all earlier examinations of the same condition. After delivery the party causing the examination shall be entitled upon request to receive from the party against whom the order is made a like report of any examination, previously or thereafter made, of the same condition, unless, in the case of a report of examination of a person not a party, the party shows that the party is unable to obtain it. The court on motion may make an order against a party requiring delivery of a report on such terms as are just, and if an examiner fails or refuses to make a report the court may exclude the examiner's testimony if offered at trial.

(2) By requesting and obtaining a report of the examination so ordered or by taking the deposition of the examiner, the party examined waives any privilege the party may have in that action or any other involving the same controversy, regarding the testimony of every other person who has examined

or may thereafter examine the party in respect of the same mental or physical condition.

(3) This subdivision applies to examinations made by agreement of the parties, unless the agreement expressly provides otherwise. This subdivision does not preclude discovery of a report of an examiner or the taking of a deposition of the examiner in accordance with the provisions of any other rule.

(As amended Mar. 30, 1970, eff. July 1, 1970; Mar. 2, 1987, eff. Aug. 1, 1987; Nov. 18, 1988, Pub.L. 100–690, Title VII, § 7047(b), 102 Stat. 4401; Apr. 30, 1991, eff. Dec. 1, 1991.)

Proposed Amendment of Rule

Effective December 1, 2007, absent contrary Congressional action, this rule is amended to read as follows:

Rule 35. Physical and Mental Examinations

(a) Order for an Examination.

(1) In General. The court where the action is pending may order a party whose mental or physical condition—including blood group—is in controversy to submit to a physical or mental examination by a suitably licensed or certified examiner. The court has the same authority to order a party to produce for examination a person who is in its custody or under its legal control.

(2) Motion and Notice; Contents of the Order. The order:

(A) may be made only on motion for good cause and on notice to all parties and the person to be examined; and

(B) must specify the time, place, manner, conditions, and scope of the examination, as well as the person or persons who will perform it.

(b) Examiner's Report.

(1) Request by the Party or Person Examined. The party who moved for the examination must, on request, deliver to the requester a copy of the examiner's report, together with like reports of all earlier examinations of the same condition. The request may be made by the party against whom the examination order was issued or by the person examined.

(2) Contents. The examiner's report must be in writing and must set out in detail the examiner's findings, including diagnoses, conclusions, and the results of any tests.

(3) Request by the Moving Party. After delivering the reports, the party who moved for the examination may request—and is entitled to receive—from the party against whom the examination order was issued like reports of all earlier or later examinations of the same condition. But those reports need not be delivered by the party with custody or control of the person examined if the party shows that it could not obtain them.

(4) Waiver of Privilege. By requesting and obtaining the examiner's report, or by deposing the examiner, the party examined waives any privilege it may have—in that action or any other action involving the same controversy—concerning testimony about all examinations of the same condition.

(5) Failure to Deliver a Report. The court on motion may order—on just terms—that a party deliver the report of an examination. If the report is not provided, the court may exclude the examiner's testimony at trial.

(6) Scope. This subdivision (b) applies also to an examination made by the parties' agreement, unless the agreement states otherwise. This subdivision does not preclude obtaining an examiner's report or deposing an examiner under other rules.

ADVISORY COMMITTEE NOTES

1937 Adoption

Physical examination of parties before trial is authorized by statute or rule in a number of states. See Ariz.Rev. Code Ann. (Struckmeyer, 1928) § 4468; Mich. Court Rules Ann. (Searl, 1933) Rule 41, § 2; 2 N.J.Comp.Stat. (1910); N.Y.C.P.A. (1937) § 306; 1 S.D.Comp.Laws (1929) § 2716A; 3 Wash.Rev.Stat.Ann. (Remington, 1932) § 1230–1.

Mental examination of parties is authorized in Iowa. Iowa Code (1935) ch. 491–F1. See McCash, *The Evolution of the Doctrine of Discovery and Its Present Status in Iowa,* 20 Ia.L.Rev. 68 (1934).

The constitutionality of legislation providing for physical examination of parties was sustained in *Lyon v. Manhattan Railway Co.,* 1894, 37 N.E. 113, 142 N.Y. 298, and *McGovern v. Hope,* 1899, 42 A. 830, 63 N.J.L. 76. In *Union Pacific Ry. Co. v. Botsford,* 1891, 11 S.Ct. 1000, 141 U.S. 250, 35 L.Ed. 734, it was held that the court could not order the physical examination of a party in the absence of statutory authority. But in *Camden and Suburban Ry. Co. v. Stetson,* 1900, 20 S.Ct. 617, 177 U.S. 172, 44 L.Ed. 721 where there was statutory authority for such examination, derived from a state statute made operative by the conformity act, the practice was sustained. Such authority is now found in the present rule made operative by the Act of June 19, 1934, c. 651, U.S.C., Title 28, § 2072, formerly §§ 723b (Rules in actions at law; Supreme Court authorized to make) and 723c (Union of equity and action at law rules; power of Supreme Court).

1970 Amendment

Subdivision (a). Rule 35(a) has hitherto provided only for an order requiring a party to submit to an examination. It is desirable to extend the rule to provide for an order against the party for examination of a person in his custody

or under his legal control. As appears from the provisions of amended Rule 37(b)(2) and the comment under that rule, an order to "produce" the third person imposes only an obligation to use good faith efforts to produce the person.

The amendment will settle beyond doubt that a parent or guardian suing to recover for injuries to a minor may be ordered to produce the minor for examination. Further, the amendment expressly includes blood examination within the kinds of examinations that can be ordered under the rule. See *Beach v. Beach*, 114 F.2d 479 (D.C. Cir. 1940). Provisions similar to the amendment have been adopted in at least 10 States: Calif. Code Civ.Proc. § 2032; Ida.R.Civ.P. 35; Ill. S–H Ann. c. 110A, § 215; Md.R.P. 420; Mich.Gen.Ct.R. 311; Minn.R.Civ.P. 35; Mo.Vern.Ann.R.Civ.p. 60.01; N.Dak.R.Civ.P. 35; N.Y.C.P.L. § 3121; Wyo.R.Civ.P. 35.

The amendment makes no change in the requirements of Rule 35 that, before a court order may issue, the relevant physical or mental condition must be shown to be "in controversy" and "good cause" must be shown for the examination. Thus, the amendment has no effect on the recent decision of the Supreme Court in *Schlagenhauf v. Holder*, 379 U.S. 104 (1964), stressing the importance of these requirements and applying them to the facts of the case. The amendment makes no reference to employees of a party. Provisions relating to employees in the State statutes and rules cited above appear to have been virtually unused.

Subdivision (b)(1). This subdivision is amended to correct an imbalance in Rule 35(b)(1) as heretofore written. Under that text, a party causing a Rule 35(a) examination to be made is required to furnish to the party examined, on request, a copy of the examining physician's report. If he delivers this copy, he is in turn entitled to receive from the party examined reports of all examinations of the same condition previously or later made. But the rule has not in terms entitled the examined party to receive from the party causing the Rule 35(a) examination any reports of earlier examinations of the same condition to which the latter may have access. The amendment cures this defect. See La. Stat.Ann., Civ.Proc. art 1495 (1960); Utah R.Civ.P. 35(c).

The amendment specifies that the written report of the examining physician includes results of all tests made, such as results of X-rays and cardiograms. It also embodies changes required by the broadening of Rule 35(a) to take in persons who are not parties.

Subdivision (b)(3). This new subdivision removes any possible doubt that reports of examination may be obtained although no order for examination has been made under Rule 35(a). Examinations are very frequently made by agreement, and sometimes before the party examined has an attorney. The courts have uniformly ordered that reports be supplied, see 4 *Moore's Federal Practice* ¶35.06, n. 1 (2d ed. 1966); 2A Barron & Holtzoff, *Federal Practice and Procedure* § 823, n. 22 (Wright ed. 1961), and it appears best to fill the technical gap in the present rule.

The subdivision also makes clear that reports of examining physicians are discoverable not only under Rule 35(b), but under other rules as well. To be sure, if the report is privileged, then discovery is not permissible under any rule other than Rule 35(b) and it is permissible under Rule 35(b) only if the party requests a copy of the report of examination made by the other party's doctor. *Sher v. De Haven*, 199 F.2d 777 (D.C. Cir. 1952), *cert. denied* 345 U.S. 936 (1953). But if the report is unprivileged and is subject to discovery

under the provisions of rules other than Rule 35(b)—such as Rules 34 or 26(b)(3) or (4)—discovery should not depend upon whether the person examined demands a copy of the report. Although a few cases have suggested the contrary, *e.g., Galloway v. National Dairy Products Corp.*, 24 F.R.D. 362 (E.D.Pa.1959), the better considered district court decisions hold that Rule 35(b) is not preemptive. *E.g., Leszynski v. Russ*, 29 F.R.D. 10, 12 (D.Md.1961) and cases cited. The question was recently given full consideration in *Buffington v. Wood*, 351 F.2d 292 (3d Cir. 1965), holding that Rule 35(b) is not preemptive.

1987 Amendment

The amendments are technical. No substantive change is intended.

1991 Amendment

The revision authorizes the court to require physical or mental examinations conducted by any person who is suitably licensed or certified.

The rule was revised in 1988 by Congressional enactment to authorize mental examinations by licensed clinical psychologists. This revision extends that amendment to include other certified or licensed professionals, such as dentists or occupational therapists, who are not physicians or clinical psychologists, but who may be well-qualified to give valuable testimony about the physical or mental condition that is the subject of dispute.

The requirement that the examiner be *suitably* licensed or certified is a new requirement. The court is thus expressly authorized to assess the credentials of the examiner to assure that no person is subjected to a court-ordered examination by an examiner whose testimony would be of such limited value that it would be unjust to require the person to undergo the invasion of privacy associated with the examination. This authority is not wholly new, for under the former rule, the court retained discretion to refuse to order an examination, or to restrict an examination. 8 WRIGHT & MILLER, FEDERAL PRACTICE & PROCEDURE § 2234 (1986 Supp.). The revision is intended to encourage the exercise of this discretion, especially with respect to examinations by persons having narrow qualifications.

The court's responsibility to determine the suitability of the examiner's qualifications applies even to a proposed examination by a physician. If the proposed examination and testimony calls for an expertise that the proposed examiner does not have, it should not be ordered, even if the proposed examiner is a physician. The rule does not, however, require that the license or certificate be conferred by the jurisdiction in which the examination is conducted.

2007 Amendment

[Effective December 1, 2007, absent contrary Congressional action.]

The language of Rule 35 has been amended as part of the general restyling of the Civil Rules to make them more easily understood and to make style and terminology consistent throughout the rules. These changes are intended to be stylistic only.

Rule 36. Requests for Admission

(a) Request for Admission. A party may serve upon any other party a written request for the admission, for purposes of the pending action only, of the truth of any matters within the scope of Rule 26(b)(1) set forth in the request that relate to statements or opinions of fact or of the application of law to fact, including the genuineness of any documents described in the request. Copies of documents shall be served with the request unless they have been or are otherwise furnished or made available for inspection and copying. Without leave of court or written stipulation, requests for admission may not be served before the time specified in Rule 26(d).

Each matter of which an admission is requested shall be separately set forth. The matter is admitted unless, within 30 days after service of the request, or within such shorter or longer time as the court may allow or as the parties may agree to in writing, subject to Rule 29, the party to whom the request is directed serves upon the party requesting the admission a written answer or objection addressed to the matter, signed by the party or by the party's attorney. If objection is made, the reasons therefor shall be stated. The answer shall specifically deny the matter or set forth in detail the reasons why the answering party cannot truthfully admit or deny the matter. A denial shall fairly meet the substance of the requested admission, and when good faith requires that a party qualify an answer or deny only a part of the matter of which an admission is requested, the party shall specify so much of it as is true and qualify or deny the remainder. An answering party may not give lack of information or knowledge as a reason for failure to admit or deny unless the party states that the party has made reasonable inquiry and that the information known or readily obtainable by the party is insufficient to enable the party to admit or deny. A party who considers that a matter of which an admission has been requested presents a genuine issue for trial may not, on that ground alone, object to the request; the party may, subject to the provisions of Rule 37(c), deny the matter or set forth reasons why the party cannot admit or deny it.

The party who has requested the admissions may move to determine the sufficiency of the answers or objections. Unless the court determines that an objection is justified, it shall order that an answer be served. If the court determines that an answer does not comply with the requirements of this rule, it may order either that the matter is admitted or that an amended answer be served. The court may, in lieu of these orders, determine that final disposition of the request be made at a pre-trial conference or at a designated time prior to trial. The provisions of Rule 37(a)(4) apply to the award of expenses incurred in relation to the motion.

(b) Effect of Admission. Any matter admitted under this rule is conclusively established unless the court on motion permits withdrawal or amendment of the admission. Subject to the provision of Rule 16 governing amendment of a pre-trial order, the court may permit withdrawal or amendment when the presentation of the merits of the action will be subserved thereby and the party who obtained the admission fails to satisfy the court that withdrawal or amendment will prejudice that party in maintaining the action or defense on the merits. Any admission made by a party under this rule is for the purpose of the pending action only and is not an admission for any other purpose nor may it be used against the party in any other proceeding.

(As amended Dec. 27, 1946, effective Mar. 19, 1948; Mar. 30, 1970, eff. July 1, 1970; Mar. 2, 1987, eff. Aug. 1, 1987; Apr. 22, 1993, eff. Dec. 1, 1993.)

Proposed Amendment of Rule

Effective December 1, 2007, absent contrary Congressional action, this rule is amended to read as follows:

Rule 36. Requests for Admission

(a) Scope and Procedure.

(1) Scope. A party may serve on any other party a written request to admit, for purposes of the pending action only, the truth of any matters within the scope of Rule 26(b)(1) relating to:

(A) facts, the application of law to fact, or opinions about either; and

(B) the genuineness of any described documents.

(2) Form; Copy of a Document. Each matter must be separately stated. A request to admit the genuineness of a document must be accompanied by a copy of the document unless it is, or has been, otherwise furnished or made available for inspection and copying.

(3) Time to Respond; Effect of Not Responding. A matter is admitted unless, within 30 days after being served, the party to whom the request is directed serves on the requesting party a written answer or objection addressed to the matter and signed by the party or its attorney. A shorter or longer time for responding may be stipulated to under Rule 29 or be ordered by the court.

(4) Answer. If a matter is not admitted, the answer must specifically deny it or state in detail why the answering party cannot truthfully admit or deny it. A denial must fairly respond to the substance of the matter; and when good faith requires that a party qualify an answer or deny only a part of a matter, the answer must specify

the part admitted and qualify or deny the rest. The answering party may assert lack of knowledge or information as a reason for failing to admit or deny only if the party states that it has made reasonable inquiry and that the information it knows or can readily obtain is insufficient to enable it to admit or deny.

(5) Objections. The grounds for objecting to a request must be stated. A party must not object solely on the ground that the request presents a genuine issue for trial.

(6) Motion Regarding the Sufficiency of an Answer or Objection. The requesting party may move to determine the sufficiency of an answer or objection. Unless the court finds an objection justified, it must order that an answer be served. On finding that an answer does not comply with this rule, the court may order either that the matter is admitted or that an amended answer be served. The court may defer its final decision until a pretrial conference or a specified time before trial. Rule 37(a)(5) applies to an award of expenses.

(b) Effect of an Admission; Withdrawing or Amending It. *A matter admitted under this rule is conclusively established unless the court, on motion, permits the admission to be withdrawn or amended. Subject to Rule 16(e), the court may permit withdrawal or amendment if it would promote the presentation of the merits of the action and if the court is not persuaded that it would prejudice the requesting party in maintaining or defending the action on the merits. An admission under this rule is not an admission for any other purpose and cannot be used against the party in any other proceeding.*

ADVISORY COMMITTEE NOTES

1937 Adoption

Compare similar rules: [Former] Equity Rule 58 (last paragraph, which provides for the admission of the execution and genuineness of documents); *English Rules Under the Judicature Act* (The Annual Practice, 1937) O. 32; Ill.Rev. Stat. (1937) ch. 110, § 182 and Rule 18 (Ill.Rev.Stat. (1937) ch. 110, § 259.18); 2 Mass.Gen.Laws (Ter.Ed., 1932) ch. 231, § 69; Mich. Court Rules Ann. (Searl, 1933) Rule 42; N.J. Comp.Stat. (2 Cum.Supp. 1911–1924); N.Y.C.P.A. (1937) §§ 322, 323; Wis.Stat. (1935) § 327.22.

1946 Amendment

Note. The first change in the first sentence of Rule 36(a) and the addition of the new second sentence, specifying when requests for admissions may be served, bring Rule 36 in line with amended Rules 26(a) and 33. There is no reason why these rules should not be treated alike. Other provisions of Rule 36(a) give the party whose admissions are requested adequate protection.

The second change in the first sentence of the rule [subdivision (a)] removes any uncertainty as to whether a party can be called upon to admit matters of fact other than those set forth in relevant documents described in and exhibited with the request. In *Smyth v. Kaufman*, C.C.A.2, 1940, 114 F.2d 40, it was held that the word "therein", now stricken from the rule [said subdivision] referred to the request and that a matter of fact not related to any document could be presented to the other party for admission or denial. The rule of this case is now clearly stated.

The substitution of the word "served" for "delivered" in the third sentence of the amended rule [said subdivision] is in conformance with the use of the word "serve" elsewhere in the rule and generally throughout the rules. See also Notes to Rules 13(a) and 33 herein. The substitution [in said subdivision] of "shorter or longer" for "further" will enable a court to designate a lesser period than 10 days for answer. This conforms with a similar provision already contained in Rule 33.

The addition of clause (1) [in said subdivision] specifies the method by which a party may challenge the propriety of a request to admit. There has been considerable difference of judicial opinion as to the correct method, if any, available to secure relief from an allegedly improper request. See Commentary, *Methods of Objecting to Notice to Admit*, 1942, 5 Fed.Rules Serv. 835; *International Carbonic Engineering Co. v. Natural Carbonic Products, Inc.*, S.D.Cal.1944, 57 F.Supp. 248. The changes in clause (1) are merely of a clarifying and conforming nature.

The first of the added last two sentences [in said subdivision] prevents an objection to a part of a request from holding up the answer, if any, to the remainder. See similar proposed change in Rule 33. The last sentence strengthens the rule by making the denial accurately reflect the party's position. It is taken, with necessary changes, from Rule 8(b).

1970 Amendment

Rule 36 serves two vital purposes, both of which are designed to reduce trial time. Admissions are sought, first to facilitate proof with respect to issues that cannot be eliminated from the case, and secondly, to narrow the issues by eliminating those that can be. The changes made in the rule are designed to serve these purposes more effectively. Certain disagreements in the courts about the proper scope of the rule are resolved. In addition, the procedural operation of the rule is brought into line with other discovery procedures, and the binding effect of an admission is clarified. See generally Finman, *The Request for Admissions in Federal Civil Procedure*, 71 Yale L.J. 371 (1962).

Subdivision (a). As revised, the subdivision provides that a request may be made to admit any matters within the scope of Rule 26(b) that relate to statements or opinions of fact or of the application of law to fact. It thereby eliminates the requirement that the matters be "of fact." This change resolves conflicts in the court decisions as to whether a request to admit matters of "opinion" and matters involving "mixed law and fact" is proper under the rule. As to "opinion," compare, *e.g., Jackson Buff Corp. v. Marcelle*, 20 F.R.D. 139 (E.D.N.Y.1957); *California v. The S. S. Jules Fribourg*, 19 F.R.D. 432 (N.D.Calif.1955), with *e.g., Photon, Inc. v. Harris Intertype, Inc.*, 28 F.R.D. 327 (D.Mass.1961); *Hise v. Lockwood Grader Corp.*, 153 F.Supp. 276

(D.Nebr.1957). As to "mixed law and fact" the majority of courts sustain objections, *e.g., Minnesota Mining and Mfg. Co. v. Norton Co.,* 36 F.R.D. 1 (N.D.Ohio 1964), but *McSparran v. Hanigan,* 225 F.Supp. 628 (E.D.Pa.1963) is to the contrary.

Not only is it difficult as a practical matter to separate "fact" from "opinion," see 4 *Moore's Federal Practice* ¶36.04 (2d ed. 1966); cf. 2A Barron & Holtzoff, *Federal Practice and Procedure* 317 (Wright ed. 1961), but an admission on a matter of opinion may facilitate proof or narrow the issues or both. An admission of a matter involving the application of law to fact may, in a given case, even more clearly narrow the issues. For example, an admission that an employee acted in the scope of his employment may remove a major issue from the trial. In *McSparran v. Hanigan, supra,* plaintiff admitted that "the premises on which said accident occurred, were occupied or under the control" of one of the defendants, 225 F.Supp. at 636. This admission, involving law as well as fact, removed one of the issues from the lawsuit and thereby reduced the proof required at trial. The amended provision does not authorize requests for admissions of law unrelated to the facts of the case.

Requests for admission involving the application of law to fact may create disputes between the parties which are best resolved in the presence of the judge after much or all of the other discovery has been completed. Power is therefore expressly conferred upon the court to defer decision until a pretrial conference is held or until a designated time prior to trial. On the other hand, the court should not automatically defer decision; in many instances, the importance of the admission lies in enabling the requesting party to avoid the burdensome accumulation of proof prior to the pretrial conference.

Courts have also divided on whether an answering party may properly object to request for admission as to matters which that party regards as "in dispute." Compare, *e.g., Syracuse Broadcasting Corp. v. Newhouse,* 271 F.2d 910, 917 (2d Cir. 1959); *Driver v. Gindy Mfg. Corp.,* 24 F.R.D. 473 (E.D.Pa.1959); with, *e.g., McGonigle v. Baxter,* 27 F.R.D. 504 (E.D.Pa.1961); *United States v. Ehbauer,* 13 F.R.D. 462 (W.D.Mo.1952). The proper response in such cases is an answer. The very purpose of the request is to ascertain whether the answering party is prepared to admit or regards the matter as presenting a genuine issue for trial. In his answer, the party may deny, or he may give as his reason for inability to admit or deny the existence of a genuine issue. The party runs no risk of sanctions if the matter is genuinely in issue, since Rule 37(c) provides a sanction of costs only when there are no good reasons for a failure to admit.

On the other hand, requests to admit may be so voluminous and so framed that the answering party finds the task of identifying what is in dispute and what is not unduly burdensome. If so, the responding party may obtain a protective order under Rule 26(c). Some of the decisions sustaining objections on "disputability" grounds could have been justified by the burdensome character of the requests. See, *e.g., Syracuse Broadcasting Corp. v. Newhouse, supra.*

Another sharp split of authority exists on the question whether a party may base his answer on lack of information or knowledge without seeking out additional information. One line of cases has held that a party may answer on the basis of such knowledge as he has at the time he answers. *E.g., Jackson Buff Corp. v. Marcelle,* 20 F.R.D. 139

(E.D.N.Y.1957); *Sladek v. General Motors Corp.,* 16 F.R.D. 104 (S.D.Iowa 1954). A larger group of cases, supported by commentators, has taken the view that if the responding party lacks knowledge, he must inform himself in reasonable fashion. *E.g., Hise v. Lockwood Grader Corp.,* 153 F.Supp. 276 (D.Nebr. 1957); *E. H. Tate Co. v. Jiffy Enterprises, Inc.,* 16 F.R.D. 571 (E.D.Pa.1954); Finman, *supra,* 71 Yale L.J. 371, 404–409; 4 *Moore's Federal Practice* ¶36.04 (2d ed. 1966); 2A Barron & Holtzoff, *Federal Practice and Procedure* 509 (Wright ed. 1961).

The rule as revised adopts the majority view, as in keeping with a basic principle of the discovery rules that a reasonable burden may be imposed on the parties when its discharge will facilitate preparation for trial and ease the trial process. It has been argued against this view that one side should not have the burden of "proving" the other side's case. The revised rule requires only that the answering party make reasonable inquiry and secure such knowledge and information as are readily obtainable by him. In most instances, the investigation will be necessary either to his own case or to preparation for rebuttal. Even when it is not, the information may be close enough at hand to be "readily obtainable." Rule 36 requires only that the party state that he has taken these steps. The sanction for failure of a party to inform himself before he answers lies in the award of costs after trial, as provided in Rule 37(c).

The requirement that the answer to a request for admission be sworn is deleted, in favor of a provision that the answer be signed by the party or by his attorney. The provisions of Rule 36 make it clear that admissions function very much as pleadings do. Thus, when a party admits in part and denies in part, his admission is for purposes of the pending action only and may not be used against him in any other proceeding. The broadening of the rule to encompass mixed questions of law and fact reinforces this feature. Rule 36 does not lack a sanction for false answers; Rule 37(c) furnishes an appropriate deterrent.

The existing language describing the available grounds for objection to a request for admission is eliminated as neither necessary nor helpful. The statement that objection may be made to any request which is "improper" adds nothing to the provisions that the party serve an answer or objection addressed to each matter and that he state his reasons for any objection. None of the other discovery rules sets forth grounds for objection, except so far as all are subject to the general provisions of Rule 26.

Changes are made in the sequence of procedures in Rule 36 so that they conform to the new procedures in Rules 33 and 34. The major changes are as follows:

(1) The normal time for response to a request for admissions is lengthened from 10 to 30 days, conforming more closely to prevailing practice. A defendant need not respond, however, in less than 45 days after service of the summons and complaint upon him. The court may lengthen or shorten the time when special situations require it.

(2) The present requirement that the plaintiff wait 10 days to serve requests without leave of court is eliminated. The revised provision accords with those in Rules 33 and 34.

(3) The requirement that the objecting party move automatically for a hearing on his objection is eliminated, and the burden is on the requesting party to move for an order. The change in the burden of going forward does not modify

present law on burden of persuasion. The award of expenses incurred in relation to the motion is made subject to the comprehensive provisions of Rule 37(a)(4).

(4) A problem peculiar to Rule 36 arises if the responding party serves answers that are not in conformity with the requirements of the rule—for example, a denial is not "specific," or the explanation of inability to admit or deny is not "in detail." Rule 36 now makes no provision for court scrutiny of such answers before trial, and it seems to contemplate that defective answers bring about admissions just as effectively as if no answer had been served. Some cases have so held. *E.g., Southern Ry. Co. v. Crosby,* 201 F.2d 878 (4th Cir. 1953); *United States v. Laney,* 96 F.Supp. 482 (E.D.S.C.1951).

Giving a defective answer the automatic effect of an admission may cause unfair surprise. A responding party who purported to deny or to be unable to admit or deny will for the first time at trial confront the contention that he has made a binding admission. Since it is not always easy to know whether a denial is "specific" or an explanation is "in detail," neither party can know how the court will rule at trial and whether proof must be prepared. Some courts, therefore, have entertained motions to rule on defective answers. They have at times ordered that amended answers be served, when the defects were technical, and at other times have declared that the matter was admitted. *E.g., Woods v. Stewart,* 171 F.2d 544 (5th Cir. 1948); *SEC v. Kaye, Real & Co.,* 122 F.Supp. 639 (S.D.N.Y.1954); *Sieb's Hatcheries, Inc. v. Lindley,* 13 F.R.D. 113 (W.D.Ark.1952). The rule as revised conforms to the latter practice.

Subdivision (b). The rule does not how indicate the extent to which a party is bound by his admission. Some courts view admissions as the equivalent of sworn testimony. *E.g., Ark–Tenn Distributing Corp. v. Breidt,* 209 F.2d 359 (3d Cir. 1954); *United States v. Lemons,* 125 F.Supp. 686 (W.D.Ark.1954); 4 *Moore's Federal Practice* ¶36.08 (2d ed. 1966 Supp.). At least in some jurisdictions a party may rebut his own testimony, *e.g., Alamo v. Del Rosario,* 98 F.2d 328 (D.C.Cir.1938), and by analogy an admission made pursuant to Rule 36 may likewise be thought rebuttable. The courts in *Ark–Tenn* and *Lemons, supra,* reasoned in this way, although the results reached may be supported on different grounds. In *McSparran v. Hanigan,* 225 F.Supp. 628, 636–637 (E.D.Pa.1963), the court held that an admission is conclusively binding, though noting the confusion created by prior decisions.

The new provisions give an admission a conclusively binding effect, for purposes only of the pending action, unless the admission is withdrawn or amended. In form and substance a Rule 36 admission is comparable to an admission in pleadings or a stipulation drafted by counsel for use at trial, rather than to an evidentiary admission of a party. Louisell, *Modern California Discovery* § 8.07 (1963); 2A Barron & Holtzoff, *Federal Practice and Procedure* § 838 (Wright ed. 1961). Unless the party securing an admission can depend on its binding effect, he cannot safely avoid the expense of preparing to prove the very matters on which he has secured the admission, and the purpose of the rule is defeated. Field v. McKusick, *Maine Civil Practice* § 36.4 (1959); Finman, *supra,* 71 Yale L.J. 371, 418–426; Comment, 56 Nw.U.L.Rev. 679, 682–683 (1961).

Provision is made for withdrawal or amendment of an admission. This provision emphasizes the importance of

having the action resolved on the merits, while at the same time assuring each party that justified reliance on an admission in preparation for trial will not operate to his prejudice. *Cf. Moosman v. Joseph P. Blitz, Inc.,* 358 F.2d 686 (2d Cir. 1966).

1987 Amendment

The amendments are technical. No substantive change is intended.

1993 Amendments

The rule is revised to reflect the change made by Rule 26(d), preventing a party from seeking formal discovery until after the meeting of the parties required by Rule 26(f).

2007 Amendment

[Effective December 1, 2007, absent contrary Congressional action.]

The language of Rule 36 has been amended as part of the general restyling of the Civil Rules to make them more easily understood and to make style and terminology consistent throughout the rules. These changes are intended to be stylistic only.

The final sentence of the first paragraph of former Rule 36(a) was a redundant cross-reference to the discovery moratorium provisions of Rule 26(d). Rule 26(d) is now familiar, obviating any need to carry forward the redundant cross-reference. The redundant reminder of Rule 37(c) in the second paragraph was likewise omitted.

Rule 37. Failure to Make Disclosure or Cooperate in Discovery; Sanctions

(a) Motion For Order Compelling Disclosure or Discovery. A party, upon reasonable notice to other parties and all persons affected thereby, may apply for an order compelling disclosure or discovery as follows:

(1) Appropriate Court. An application for an order to a party shall be made to the court in which the action is pending. An application for an order to a person who is not a party shall be made to the court in the district where the discovery is being, or is to be, taken.

(2) Motion.

(A) If a party fails to make a disclosure required by Rule 26(a), any other party may move to compel disclosure and for appropriate sanctions. The motion must include a certification that the movant has in good faith conferred or attempted to confer with the party not making the disclosure in an effort to secure the disclosure without court action.

(B) If a deponent fails to answer a question propounded or submitted under Rules 30 or 31, or a corporation or other entity fails to make a designation under Rule 30(b)(6) or 31(a), or a party fails to answer an interrogatory submitted

under Rule 33, or if a party, in response to a request for inspection submitted under Rule 34, fails to respond that inspection will be permitted as requested or fails to permit inspection as requested, the discovering party may move for an order compelling an answer, or a designation, or an order compelling inspection in accordance with the request. The motion must include a certification that the movant has in good faith conferred or attempted to confer with the person or party failing to make the discovery in an effort to secure the information or material without court action. When taking a deposition on oral examination, the proponent of the question may complete or adjourn the examination before applying for an order.

(3) Evasive or Incomplete Disclosure, Answer, or Response. For purposes of this subdivision an evasive or incomplete disclosure, answer, or response is to be treated as a failure to disclose, answer, or respond.

(4) Expenses and Sanctions.

(A) If the motion is granted or if the disclosure or requested discovery is provided after the motion was filed, the court shall, after affording an opportunity to be heard, require the party or deponent whose conduct necessitated the motion or the party or attorney advising such conduct or both of them to pay to the moving party the reasonable expenses incurred in making the motion, including attorney's fees, unless the court finds that the motion was filed without the movant's first making a good faith effort to obtain the disclosure or discovery without court action, or that the opposing party's nondisclosure, response, or objection was substantially justified, or that other circumstances make an award of expenses unjust.

(B) If the motion is denied, the court may enter any protective order authorized under Rule 26(c) and shall, after affording an opportunity to be heard, require the moving party or the attorney filing the motion or both of them to pay to the party or deponent who opposed the motion the reasonable expenses incurred in opposing the motion, including attorney's fees, unless the court finds that the making of the motion was substantially justified or that other circumstances make an award of expenses unjust.

(C) If the motion is granted in part and denied in part, the court may enter any protective order authorized under Rule 26(c) and may, after affording an opportunity to be heard, apportion the reasonable expenses incurred in relation to the motion among the parties and persons in a just manner.

(b) Failure to Comply With Order.

(1) Sanctions by Court in District Where Deposition is Taken. If a deponent fails to be sworn or to answer a question after being directed to do so by the court in the district in which the deposition is being taken, the failure may be considered a contempt of that court.

(2) Sanctions by Court in Which Action is Pending. If a party or an officer, director, or managing agent of a party or a person designated under Rule 30(b)(6) or 31(a) to testify on behalf of a party fails to obey an order to provide or permit discovery, including an order made under subdivision (a) of this rule or Rule 35, or if a party fails to obey an order entered under Rule 26(f), the court in which the action is pending may make such orders in regard to the failure as are just, and among others the following:

(A) An order that the matters regarding which the order was made or any other designated facts shall be taken to be established for the purposes of the action in accordance with the claim of the party obtaining the order;

(B) An order refusing to allow the disobedient party to support or oppose designated claims or defenses, or prohibiting that party from introducing designated matters in evidence;

(C) An order striking out pleadings or parts thereof, or staying further proceedings until the order is obeyed, or dismissing the action or proceeding or any part thereof, or rendering a judgment by default against the disobedient party;

(D) In lieu of any of the foregoing orders or in addition thereto, an order treating as a contempt of court the failure to obey any orders except an order to submit to a physical or mental examination;

(E) Where a party has failed to comply with an order under Rule 35(a) requiring that party to produce another for examination, such orders as are listed in paragraphs (A), (B), and (C) of this subdivision, unless the party failing to comply shows that that party is unable to produce such person for examination.

In lieu of any of the foregoing orders or in addition thereto, the court shall require the party failing to obey the order or the attorney advising that party or both to pay the reasonable expenses, including attorney's fees, caused by the failure, unless the court finds that the failure was substantially justified or that other circumstances make an award of expenses unjust.

(c) Failure to Disclose; False or Misleading Disclosure; Refusal to Admit.

(1) A party that without substantial justification fails to disclose information required by Rule 26(a) or 26(e)(1), or to amend a prior response to discov-

ery as required by Rule 26(e)(2), is not, unless such failure is harmless, permitted to use as evidence at a trial, at a hearing, or on a motion any witness or information not so disclosed. In addition to or in lieu of this sanction, the court, on motion and after affording an opportunity to be heard, may impose other appropriate sanctions. In addition to requiring payment of reasonable expenses, including attorney's fees, caused by the failure, these sanctions may include any of the actions authorized under Rule 37(b)(2)(A), (B), and (C) and may include informing the jury of the failure to make the disclosure.

(2) If a party fails to admit the genuineness of any document or the truth of any matter as requested under Rule 36, and if the party requesting the admissions thereafter proves the genuineness of the document or the truth of the matter, the requesting party may apply to the court for an order requiring the other party to pay the reasonable expenses incurred in making that proof, including reasonable attorney's fees. The court shall make the order unless it finds that (A) the request was held objectionable pursuant to Rule 36(a), or (B) the admission sought was of no substantial importance, or (C) the party failing to admit had reasonable ground to believe that the party might prevail on the matter, or (D) there was other good reason for the failure to admit.

(d) Failure of Party to Attend at Own Deposition or Serve Answers to Interrogatories or Respond to Request for Inspection. If a party or an officer, director, or managing agent of a party or a person designated under Rule 30(b)(6) or 31(a) to testify on behalf of a party fails (1) to appear before the officer who is to take the deposition, after being served with a proper notice, or (2) to serve answers or objections to interrogatories submitted under Rule 33, after proper service of the interrogatories, or (3) to serve a written response to a request for inspection submitted under Rule 34, after proper service of the request, the court in which the action is pending on motion may make such orders in regard to the failure as are just, and among others it may take any action authorized under subparagraphs (A), (B), and (C) of subdivision (b)(2) of this rule. Any motion specifying a failure under clause (2) or (3) of this subdivision shall include a certification that the movant has in good faith conferred or attempted to confer with the party failing to answer or respond in an effort to obtain such answer or response without court action. In lieu of any order or in addition thereto, the court shall require the party failing to act or the attorney advising that party or both to pay the reasonable expenses, including attorney's fees, caused by the failure unless the court finds that the failure was

substantially justified or that other circumstances make an award of expenses unjust.

The failure to act described in this subdivision may not be excused on the ground that the discovery sought is objectionable unless the party failing to act has a pending motion for a protective order as provided by Rule 26(c).

(e) [Abrogated]

(f) Electronically Stored Information. Absent exceptional circumstances, a court may not impose sanctions under these rules on a party for failing to provide electronically stored information lost as a result of the routine, good-faith operation of an electronic information system.

(g) Failure to Participate in the Framing of a Discovery Plan. If a party or a party's attorney fails to participate in good faith in the development and submission of a proposed discovery plan as required by Rule 26(f), the court may, after opportunity for hearing, require such party or attorney to pay to any other party the reasonable expenses, including attorney's fees, caused by the failure.

(As amended Dec. 29, 1948, eff. Oct. 20, 1949; Mar. 30, 1970, eff. July 1, 1970; Apr. 29, 1980, eff. Aug. 1, 1980; Pub.L. 96–481, Title II, § 205(a), Oct. 21, 1980, 94 Stat. 2330; Mar. 2, 1987, eff. Aug. 1, 1987; Apr. 22, 1993, eff. Dec. 1, 1993; Apr. 17, 2000, eff. Dec. 1, 2000; Apr. 12, 2006, eff. Dec. 1, 2006.)

Proposed Amendment of Rule

Effective December 1, 2007, absent contrary Congressional action, this rule is amended to read as follows:

Rule 37. Failure to Make Disclosures or to Cooperate in Discovery; Sanctions

(a) Motion for an Order Compelling Disclosure or Discovery.

(1) In General. On notice to other parties and all affected persons, a party may move for an order compelling disclosure or discovery. The motion must include a certification that the movant has in good faith conferred or attempted to confer with the person or party failing to make disclosure or discovery in an effort to obtain it without court action.

(2) Appropriate Court. A motion for an order to a party must be made in the court where the action is pending. A motion for an order to a nonparty must be made in the court where the discovery is or will be taken.

(3) Specific Motions.

(A) To Compel Disclosure. If a party fails to make a disclosure required by Rule 26(a), any other party may move to compel disclosure and for appropriate sanctions.

(B) To Compel a Discovery Response. A party seeking discovery may move for an order compelling an answer, designation, production, or inspection. This motion may be made if:

> *(i) a deponent fails to answer a question asked under Rule 30 or 31;*
>
> *(ii) a corporation or other entity fails to make a designation under Rule 30(b)(6) or 31(a)(4);*
>
> *(iii) a party fails to answer an interrogatory submitted under Rule 33; or*
>
> *(iv) a party fails to respond that inspection will be permitted—or fails to permit inspection—as requested under Rule 34.*

(C) Related to a Deposition. When taking an oral deposition, the party asking a question may complete or adjourn the examination before moving for an order.

(4) Evasive or Incomplete Disclosure, Answer, or Response. For purposes of this subdivision (a), an evasive or incomplete disclosure, answer, or response must be treated as a failure to disclose, answer, or respond.

(5) Payment of Expenses; Protective Orders.

(A) If the Motion Is Granted (or Disclosure or Discovery Is Provided After Filing). If the motion is granted—or if the disclosure or requested discovery is provided after the motion was filed—the court must, after giving an opportunity to be heard, require the party or deponent whose conduct necessitated the motion, the party or attorney advising that conduct, or both to pay the movant's reasonable expenses incurred in making the motion, including attorney's fees. But the court must not order this payment if:

> *(i) the movant filed the motion before attempting in good faith to obtain the disclosure or discovery without court action;*
>
> *(ii) the opposing party's nondisclosure, response, or objection was substantially justified; or*
>
> *(iii) other circumstances make an award of expenses unjust.*

(B) If the Motion Is Denied. If the motion is denied, the court may issue any protective order authorized under Rule 26(c) and must, after giving an opportunity to be heard, require the movant, the attorney filing the motion, or both to pay the party or deponent who opposed the motion its reasonable expenses incurred in opposing the motion, including

attorney's fees. But the court must not order this payment if the motion was substantially justified or other circumstances make an award of expenses unjust.

(C) If the Motion Is Granted in Part and Denied in Part. If the motion is granted in part and denied in part, the court may issue any protective order authorized under Rule 26(c) and may, after giving an opportunity to be heard, apportion the reasonable expenses for the motion.

(b) Failure to Comply with a Court Order.

(1) Sanctions in the District Where the Deposition Is Taken. If the court where the discovery is taken orders a deponent to be sworn or to answer a question and the deponent fails to obey, the failure may be treated as contempt of court.

(2) Sanctions in the District Where the Action Is Pending.

(A) For Not Obeying a Discovery Order. If a party or a party's officer, director, or managing agent—or a witness designated under Rule 30(b)(6) or 31(a)(4)—fails to obey an order to provide or permit discovery, including an order under Rule 26(f), 35, or 37(a), the court where the action is pending may issue further just orders. They may include the following:

> *(i) directing that the matters embraced in the order or other designated facts be taken as established for purposes of the action, as the prevailing party claims;*
>
> *(ii) prohibiting the disobedient party from supporting or opposing designated claims or defenses, or from introducing designated matters in evidence;*
>
> *(iii) striking pleadings in whole or in part;*
>
> *(iv) staying further proceedings until the order is obeyed;*
>
> *(v) dismissing the action or proceeding in whole or in part;*
>
> *(vi) rendering a default judgment against the disobedient party; or*
>
> *(vii) treating as contempt of court the failure to obey any order except an order to submit to a physical or mental examination.*

(B) For Not Producing a Person for Examination. If a party fails to comply with an order under Rule 35(a) requiring it to produce another person for examination, the court may issue any of the orders listed in Rule

37(b)(2)(A)(i)–(vi), unless the disobedient party shows that it cannot produce the other person.

(C) Payment of Expenses. Instead of or in addition to the orders above, the court must order the disobedient party, the attorney advising that party, or both to pay the reasonable expenses, including attorney's fees, caused by the failure, unless the failure was substantially justified or other circumstances make an award of expenses unjust.

(c) Failure to Disclose, to Supplement an Earlier Response, or to Admit.

(1) Failure to Disclose or Supplement. If a party fails to provide information or identify a witness as required by Rule 26(a) or (e), the party is not allowed to use that information or witness to supply evidence on a motion, at a hearing, or at a trial, unless the failure was substantially justified or is harmless. In addition to or instead of this sanction, the court, on motion and after giving an opportunity to be heard:

(A) may order payment of the reasonable expenses, including attorney's fees, caused by the failure;

(B) may inform the jury of the party's failure; and

(C) may impose other appropriate sanctions, including any of the orders listed in Rule 37(b)(2)(A)(i)–(vi).

(2) Failure to Admit. If a party fails to admit what is requested under Rule 36 and if the requesting party later proves a document to be genuine or the matter true, the requesting party may move that the party who failed to admit pay the reasonable expenses, including attorney's fees, incurred in making that proof. The court must so order unless:

(A) the request was held objectionable under Rule 36(a);

(B) the admission sought was of no substantial importance;

(C) the party failing to admit had a reasonable ground to believe that it might prevail on the matter; or

(D) there was other good reason for the failure to admit.

(d) Party's Failure to Attend Its Own Deposition, Serve Answers to Interrogatories, or Respond to a Request for Inspection.

(1) In General.

(A) Motion; Grounds for Sanctions. The court where the action is pending may, on motion, order sanctions if:

(i) a party or a party's officer, director, or managing agent—or a person designated under Rule 30(b)(6) or 31(a)(4)—fails, after being served with proper notice, to appear for that person's deposition; or

(ii) a party, after being properly served with interrogatories under Rule 33 or a request for inspection under Rule 34, fails to serve its answers, objections, or written response.

(B) Certification. A motion for sanctions for failing to answer or respond must include a certification that the movant has in good faith conferred or attempted to confer with the party failing to act in an effort to obtain the answer or response without court action.

(2) Unacceptable Excuse for Failing to Act. A failure described in Rule 37(d)(1)(A) is not excused on the ground that the discovery sought was objectionable, unless the party failing to act has a pending motion for a protective order under Rule 26(c).

(3) Types of Sanctions. Sanctions may include any of the orders listed in Rule 37(b)(2)(A)(i)–(vi). Instead of or in addition to these sanctions, the court must require the party failing to act, the attorney advising that party, or both to pay the reasonable expenses, including attorney's fees, caused by the failure, unless the failure was substantially justified or other circumstances make an award of expenses unjust.

(e) Failure to Provide Electronically Stored Information. *Absent exceptional circumstances, a court may not impose sanctions under these rules on a party for failing to provide electronically stored information lost as a result of the routine, good-faith operation of an electronic information system.*

(f) Failure to Participate in Framing a Discovery Plan. *If a party or its attorney fails to participate in good faith in developing and submitting a proposed discovery plan as required by Rule 26(f), the court may, after giving an opportunity to be heard, require that party or attorney to pay to any other party the reasonable expenses, including attorney's fees, caused by the failure.*

ADVISORY COMMITTEE NOTES

1937 Adoption

The provisions of this rule authorizing orders establishing facts or excluding evidence or striking pleadings, or authorizing judgments of dismissal or default, for refusal to answer questions or permit inspection or otherwise make discovery,

are in accord with *Hammond Packing Co. v. Arkansas,* 1909, 29 S.Ct. 370, 212 U.S. 322, 53 L.Ed. 530, 15 Ann.Cas. 645, which distinguishes between the justifiable use of such measures as a means of compelling the production of evidence, and their unjustifiable use, as in *Hovey v. Elliott,* 1897, 17 S.Ct. 841, 167 U.S. 409, 42 L.Ed. 215, for the mere purpose of punishing for contempt.

1948 Amendment

The amendment effective October 1949, substituted the reference to "Title 28, U.S.C., § 1783" in subdivision (e) for the reference to "the Act of July 3, 1926, c. 762, § 1 (44 Stat. 835), U.S.C., Title 28, § 711."

1970 Amendment

Rule 37 provides generally for sanctions against parties or persons unjustifiably resisting discovery. Experience has brought to light a number of defects in the language of the rule as well as instances in which it is not serving the purposes for which it was designed. See Rosenberg, *Sanctions to Effectuate Pretrial Discovery,* 58 Col.L.Rev. 480 (1958). In addition, changes being made in other discovery rules require conforming amendments to Rule 37.

Rule 37 sometimes refers to a "failure" to afford discovery and at other times to a "refusal" to do so. Taking note of this dual terminology, courts have imported into "refusal" a requirement of "wilfullness." See *Roth v. Paramount Pictures Corp.,* 8 F.R.D. 31 (W.D.Pa.1948); *Campbell v. Johnson,* 101 F.Supp. 705, 707 (S.D.N.Y.1951). In *Societe Internationale v. Rogers,* 357 U.S. 197 (1958), the Supreme Court concluded that the rather random use of these two terms in Rule 37 showed no design to use them with consistently distinctive meanings, that "refused" in Rule 37(b)(2) meant simply a failure to comply, and that wilfullness was relevant only to the selection of sanctions, if any, to be imposed. Nevertheless, after the decision in *Societe,* the court in *Hinson v. Michigan Mutual Liability Co.,* 275 F.2d 537 (5th Cir. 1960) once again ruled that "refusal" required wilfullness. Substitution of "failure" for "refusal" throughout Rule 37 should eliminate this confusion and bring the rule into harmony with the *Societe Internationale* decision. See Rosenberg, *supra,* 58 Col.L.Rev. 480, 489–490 (1958).

Subdivision (a). Rule 37(a) provides relief to a party seeking discovery against one who, with or without stated objections, fails to afford the discovery sought. It has always fully served this function in relation to depositions, but the amendments being made to Rules 33 and 34 give Rule 37(a) added scope and importance. Under existing Rule 33, a party objecting to interrogatories must make a motion for court hearing on his objections. The changes now made in Rules 33 and 37(a) make it clear that the interrogating party must move to compel answers, and the motion is provided for in Rule 37(a). Existing Rule 34, since it requires a court order prior to production of documents or things or permission to enter on land, has no relation to Rule 37(a). Amendments of Rules 34 and 37(a) create a procedure similar to that provided for Rule 33.

Subdivision (a)(1). This is a new provision making clear to which court a party may apply for an order compelling discovery. Existing Rule 37(a) refers only to the court in which the deposition is being taken; nevertheless, it has been held that the court where the action is pending has "inherent power" to compel a party deponent to answer. *Lincoln Laboratories, Inc. v. Savage Laboratories, Inc.,* 27 F.R.D. 476 (D.Del.1961). In relation to Rule 33 interrogatories and Rule 34 requests for inspection, the court where the action is pending is the appropriate enforcing tribunal. The new provision eliminates the need to resort to inherent power by spelling out the respective roles of the court where the action is pending and the court where the deposition is taken. In some instances, two courts are available to a party seeking to compel answers from a party deponent. The party seeking discovery may choose the court to which he will apply, but the court has power to remit the party to the other court as a more appropriate forum.

Subdivision (a)(2). This subdivision contains the substance of existing provisions of Rule 37(a) authorizing motions to compel answers to questions put at depositions and to interrogatories. New provisions authorize motions for orders compelling designation under Rules 30(b)(6) and 31(a) and compelling inspection in accordance with a request made under Rule 34. If the court denies a motion, in whole or part, it may accompany the denial with issuance of a protective order. Compare the converse provision in Rule 26(c).

Subdivision (a)(3). This new provision makes clear that an evasive or incomplete answer is to be considered, for purposes of subdivision (a), a failure to answer. The courts have consistently held that they have the power to compel adequate answers. *E.g., Cone Mills Corp. v. Joseph Bancroft & Sons Co.,* 33 F.R.D. 318 (D.Del.1963). This power is recognized and incorporated into the rule.

Subdivision (a)(4). This subdivision amends the provisions for award of expenses, including reasonable attorney's fees, to the prevailing party or person when a motion is made for an order compelling discovery. At present, an award of expenses is made only if the losing party or person is found to have acted without substantial justification. The change requires that expenses be awarded unless the conduct of the losing party or person is found to have been substantially justified. The test of "substantial justification" remains, but the change in language is intended to encourage judges to be more alert to abuses occurring in the discovery process.

On many occasions, to be sure, the dispute over discovery between the parties is genuine, though ultimately resolved one way or the other by the court. In such cases, the losing party is substantially justified in carrying the matter to court. But the rules should deter the abuse implicit in carrying or forcing a discovery dispute to court when no genuine dispute exists. And the potential or actual imposition of expenses is virtually the sole formal sanction in the rules to deter a party from pressing to a court hearing frivolous requests for or objections to discovery.

The present provision of Rule 37(a) that the court shall require payment if it finds that the defeated party acted without "substantial justification" may appear adequate, but in fact it has been little used. Only a handful of reported cases include an award of expenses, and the Columbia Survey found that in only one instance out of about 50 motions decided under Rule 37(a) did the court award expenses. It appears that the courts do not utilize the most important available sanction to deter abusive resort to the judiciary.

The proposed change provides in effect that expenses should ordinarily be awarded unless a court finds that the losing party acted justifiably in carrying his point to court.

At the same time, a necessary flexibility is maintained, since the court retains the power to find that other circumstances make an award of expenses unjust—as where the prevailing party also acted unjustifiably. The amendment does not significantly narrow the discretion of the court, but rather presses the court to address itself to abusive practices. The present provision that expenses may be imposed upon either the party or his attorney or both is unchanged. But it is not contemplated that expenses will be imposed upon the attorney merely because the party is indigent.

Subdivision (b). This subdivision deals with sanctions for failure to comply with a court order. The present captions for subsections (1) and (2) entitled, "Contempt" and "Other Consequences," respectively, are confusing. One of the consequences listed in (2) is the arrest of the party, representing the exercise of the contempt power. The contents of the subsections show that the first authorizes the sanction of contempt (and no other) by the court in which the deposition is taken, whereas the second subsection authorizes a variety of sanctions, including contempt, which may be imposed by the court in which the action is pending. The captions of the subsections are changed to reflect their contents.

The scope of Rule 37(b)(2) is broadened by extending it to include any order "to provide or permit discovery," including orders issued under Rules 37(a) and 35. Various rules authorize orders for discovery—e.g., Rule 35(b)(1), Rule 26(c) as revised, Rule 37(d). See Rosenberg, *supra*, 58 Col.L.Rev. 480, 484–486. Rule 37(b)(2) should provide comprehensively for enforcement of all these orders. *Cf. Societe Internationale v. Rogers*, 357 U.S. 197, 207 (1958). On the other hand, the reference to Rule 34 is deleted to conform to the changed procedure in that rule.

A new subsection (E) provides that sanctions which have been available against a party for failure to comply with an order under Rule 35(a) to submit to examination will now be available against him for his failure to comply with a Rule 35(a) order to produce a third person for examination, unless he shows that he is unable to produce the person. In this context, "unable" means in effect "unable in good faith." See *Societe Internationale v. Rogers*, 357 U.S. 197 (1958).

Subdivision (b)(2) is amplified to provide for payment of reasonable expenses caused by the failure to obey the order. Although Rules 37(b)(2) and 37(d) have been silent as to award of expenses, courts have nevertheless ordered them on occasion. *E.g., United Sheeplined Clothing Co. v. Arctic Fur Cap Corp.*, 165 F.Supp. 193 (S.D.N.Y.1958); *Austin Theatre, Inc. v. Warner Bros. Pictures, Inc.*, 22 F.R.D. 302 (S.D.N.Y. 1958). The provision places the burden on the disobedient party to avoid expenses by showing that his failure is justified or that special circumstances make an award of expenses unjust. Allocating the burden in this way conforms to the changed provisions as to expenses in Rule 37(a), and is particularly appropriate when a court order is disobeyed.

An added reference to directors of a party is similar to a change made in subdivision (d) and is explained in the note to that subdivision. The added reference to persons designated by a party under Rules 30(b)(6) or 31(a) to testify on behalf of the party carries out the new procedure in those rules for taking a deposition of a corporation or other organization.

Subdivision (c). Rule 37(c) provides a sanction for the enforcement of Rule 36 dealing with requests for admission. Rule 36 provides the mechanism whereby a party may obtain

from another party in appropriate instances either (1) an admission, or (2) a sworn and specific denial or (3) a sworn statement "setting forth in detail the reasons why he cannot truthfully admit or deny." If the party obtains the second or third of these responses, in proper form, Rule 36 does not provide for a pretrial hearing on whether the response is warranted by the evidence thus far accumulated. Instead, Rule 37(c) is intended to provide posttrial relief in the form of a requirement that the party improperly refusing the admission pay the expenses of the other side in making the necessary proof at trial.

Rule 37(c), as now written, addresses itself in terms only to the sworn denial and is silent with respect to the statement of reasons for an inability to admit or deny. There is no apparent basis for this distinction, since the sanction provided in Rule 37(c) should deter all unjustified failures to admit. This omission in the rule has caused confused and diverse treatment in the courts. One court has held that if a party give inadequate reasons, he should be treated before trial as having denied the request, so that Rule 37(c) may apply. *Bertha Bldg. Corp. v. National Theatres Corp.*, 15 F.R.D. 339 (E.D.N.Y.1954). Another has held that the party should be treated as having admitted the request. *Heng Hsin Co. v. Stern, Morgenthau & Co.*, 20 Fed.Rules Serv. 36a.52, Case 1 (S.D.N.Y. Dec. 10, 1954). Still another has ordered a new response, without indicating what the outcome should be if the new response were inadequate. *United States Plywood Corp. v. Hudson Lumber Co.*, 127 F.Supp. 489, 497–498 (S.D.N.Y.1954). See generally Finman, *The Request for Admissions in Federal Civil Procedure*, 71 Yale L.J. 371, 426–430 (1962). The amendment eliminates this defect in Rule 37(c) by bringing within its scope all failures to admit.

Additional provisions in Rule 37(c) protect a party from having to pay expenses if the request for admission was held objectionable under Rule 36(a) or if the party failing to admit had reasonable ground to believe that he might prevail on the matter. The latter provision emphasizes that the true test under Rule 37(c) is not whether a party prevailed at trial but whether he acted reasonably in believing that he might prevail.

Subdivision (d). The scope of subdivision (d) is broadened to include responses to requests for inspection under Rule 34, thereby conforming to the new procedures of Rule 34.

Two related changes are made in subdivision (d): the permissible sanctions are broadened to include such orders "as are just"; and the requirement that the failure to appear or respond be "wilful" is eliminated. Although Rule 37(d) in terms provides for only three sanctions, all rather severe, the courts have interpreted it as permitting softer sanctions than those which it sets forth. *E.g., Gill v. Stolow*, 240 F.2d 669 (2d Cir.1957); *Saltzman v. Birrell*, 156 F.Supp. 538 (S.D.N.Y.1957); 2A Barron & Holtzoff, *Federal Practice and Procedure* 554–557 (Wright ed. 1961). The rule is changed to provide the greater flexibility as to sanctions which the cases show is needed.

The resulting flexibility as to sanctions eliminates any need to retain the requirement that the failure to appear or respond be "wilful." The concept of "wilful failure" is at best subtle and difficult, and the cases do not supply a bright line. Many courts have imposed sanctions without referring to wilfullness. *E.g., Milewski v. Schneider Transportation Co.*,

238 F.2d 397 (6th Cir.1956); *Dictograph Products, Inc. v. Kentworth Corp.*, 7 F.R.D. 543 (W.D.Ky.1947). In addition, in view of the possibility of light sanctions, even a negligent failure should come within Rule 37(d). If default is caused by counsel's ignorance of Federal practice, cf. *Dunn v. Pa. R.R.*, 96 F.Supp. 597 (N.D.Ohio 1951), or by his preoccupation with another aspect of the case, cf. *Maurer–Neuer, Inc. v. United Packinghouse Workers*, 26 F.R.D. 139 (D.Kans.1960), dismissal of the action and default judgment are not justified, but the imposition of expenses and fees may well be. "Wilfullness" continues to play a role, along with various other factors, in the choice of sanctions. Thus, the scheme conforms to Rule 37(b) as construed by the Supreme Court in *Societe Internationale v. Rogers*, 357 U.S. 197, 208 (1958).

A provision is added to make clear that a party may not properly remain completely silent even when he regards a notice to take his deposition or a set of interrogatories or requests to inspect as improper and objectionable. If he desires not to appear or not to respond, he must apply for a protective order. The cases are divided on whether a protective order must be sought. Compare *Collins v. Wayland*, 139 F.2d 677 (9th Cir. 1944), *cert. den.* 322 U.S. 744; *Bourgeois v. El Paso Natural Gas Co.*, 20 F.R.D. 358 (S.D.N.Y. 1957); *Loosley v. Stone*, 15 F.R.D. 373 (S.D.Ill.1954), with *Scarlatos v. Kulukundis*, 21 F.R.D. 185 (S.D.N.Y.1957); *Ross v. True Temper Corp.*, 11 F.R.D. 307 (N.D.Ohio 1951). Compare also Rosenberg, *supra*, 58 Col.L.Rev. 480, 496 (1958) with 2A Barron & Holtzoff, *Federal Practice and Procedure* 530–531 (Wright ed. 1961). The party from whom discovery is sought is afforded, through Rule 26(c), a fair and effective procedure whereby he can challenge the request made. At the same time, the total noncompliance with which Rule 37(d) is concerned may impose severe inconvenience or hardship on the discovering party and substantially delay the discovery process. Cf. 2B Barron & Holtzoff, *Federal Practice and Procedure* 306–307 (Wright ed. 1961) (response to a subpoena).

The failure of an officer or managing agent of a party to make discovery as required by present Rule 37(d) is treated as the failure of the party. The rule as revised provides similar treatment for a director of a party. There is slight warrant for the present distinction between officers and managing agents on the one hand and directors on the other. Although the legal power over a director to compel his making discovery may not be as great as over officers or managing agents, *Campbell v. General Motors Corp.*, 13 F.R.D. 331 (S.D.N.Y.1952), the practical differences are negligible. That a director's interests are normally aligned with those of his corporation is shown by the provisions of old Rule 26(d)(2), transferred to 32(a)(2) (deposition of director of party may be used at trial by an adverse party for any purpose) and of Rule 43(b) (director of party may be treated at trial as a hostile witness on direct examination by any adverse party). Moreover, in those rare instances when a corporation is unable through good faith efforts to compel a director to make discovery, it is unlikely that the court will impose sanctions. Cf. *Societe Internationale v. Rogers*, 357 U.S. 197 (1958).

Subdivision (e). The change in the caption conforms to the language of 28 U.S.C. § 1783, as amended in 1964.

Subdivision (f). Until recently, costs of a civil action could be awarded against the United States only when

expressly provided by Act of Congress, and such provision was rarely made. See H.R.Rep.No. 1535, 89th Cong., 2d Sess., 2–3 (1966). To avoid any conflict with this doctrine, Rule 37(f) has provided that expenses and attorney's fees may not be imposed upon the United States under Rule 37. See 2A Barron & Holtzoff, *Federal Practice and Procedure* 857 (Wright ed. 1961).

A major change in the law was made in 1966, 80 Stat. 308, 28 U.S.C. § 2412 (1966), whereby a judgment for costs may ordinarily be awarded to the prevailing party in any civil action brought by or against the United States. Costs are not to include the fees and expenses of attorneys. In light of this legislative development, Rule 37(f) is amended to permit the award of expenses and fees against the United States under Rule 37, but only to the extent permitted by statute. The amendment brings Rule 37(f) into line with present and future statutory provisions.

1980 Amendment

Subdivision (b)(2). New Rule 26(f) provides that if a discovery conference is held, at its close the court shall enter an order respecting the subsequent conduct of discovery. The amendment provides that the sanctions available for violation of other court orders respecting discovery are available for violation of the discovery conference order.

Subdivision (e). Subdivision (e) is stricken. Title 28, U.S.C. § 1783 no longer refers to sanctions. The subdivision otherwise duplicates Rule 45(e)(2).

Subdivision (g). New Rule 26(f) imposes a duty on parties to participate in good faith in the framing of a discovery plan by agreement upon the request of any party. This subdivision authorizes the court to award to parties who participate in good faith in an attempt to frame a discovery plan the expenses incurred in the attempt if any party or his attorney fails to participate in good faith and thereby causes additional expense.

Failure of United States to Participate in Good Faith in Discovery. Rule 37 authorizes the court to direct that parties or attorneys who fail to participate in good faith in the discovery process pay the expenses, including attorneys' fees, incurred by other parties as a result of that failure. Since attorneys' fees cannot ordinarily be awarded against the United States (28 U.S.C. § 2412), there is often no practical remedy for the misconduct of its officers and attorneys. However, in the case of a government attorney who fails to participate in good faith in discovery, nothing prevents a court in an appropriate case from giving written notification of that fact to the Attorney General of the United States and other appropriate heads of offices or agencies thereof.

1987 Amendment

The amendments are technical. No substantive change is intended.

1993 Amendments

Subdivision (a). This subdivision is revised to reflect the revision of Rule 26(a), requiring disclosure of matters without a discovery request.

Pursuant to new subdivision (a)(2)(A), a party dissatisfied with the disclosure made by an opposing party may under

this rule move for an order to compel disclosure. In providing for such a motion, the revised rule parallels the provisions of the former rule dealing with failures to answer particular interrogatories. Such a motion may be needed when the information to be disclosed might be helpful to the party seeking the disclosure but not to the party required to make the disclosure. If the party required to make the disclosure would need the material to support its own contentions, the more effective enforcement of the disclosure requirement will be to exclude the evidence not disclosed, as provided in subdivision (c)(1) of this revised rule.

Language is included in the new paragraph and added to the subparagraph (B) that requires litigants to seek to resolve discovery disputes by informal means before filing a motion with the court. This requirement is based on successful experience with similar local rules of court promulgated pursuant to Rule 83.

The last sentence of paragraph (2) is moved into paragraph (4).

Under revised paragraph (3), evasive or incomplete disclosures and responses to interrogatories and production requests are treated as failures to disclose or respond. Interrogatories and requests for production should not be read or interpreted in an artificially restrictive or hypertechnical manner to avoid disclosure of information fairly covered by the discovery request, and to do so is subject to appropriate sanctions under subdivision (a).

Revised paragraph (4) is divided into three subparagraphs for ease of reference, and in each the phrase "after opportunity for hearing" is changed to "after affording an opportunity to be heard" to make clear that the court can consider such questions on written submissions as well as on oral hearings.

Subparagraph (A) is revised to cover the situation where information that should have been produced without a motion to compel is produced after the motion is filed but before it is brought on for hearing. The rule also is revised to provide that a party should not be awarded its expenses for filing a motion that could have been avoided by conferring with opposing counsel.

Subparagraph (C) is revised to include the provision that formerly was contained in subdivision (a)(2) and to include the same requirement of an opportunity to be heard that is specified in subparagraphs (A) and (B).

Subdivision (c). The revision provides a self-executing sanction for failure to make a disclosure required by Rule 26(a), without need for a motion under subdivision (a)(2)(A).

Paragraph (1) prevents a party from using as evidence any witnesses or information that, without substantial justification, has not been disclosed as required by Rules 26(a) and 26(e)(1). This automatic sanction provides a strong inducement for disclosure of material that the disclosing party would expect to use as evidence, whether at a trial, at a hearing, or on a motion, such as one under Rule 56. As disclosure of evidence offered solely for impeachment purposes is not required under these rules, this preclusion sanction likewise does not apply to that evidence.

Limiting the automatic sanction to violations "without substantial justification," coupled with the exception for violations that are "harmless," is needed to avoid unduly harsh penalties in a variety of situations: *e.g.*, the inadvertent omission from a Rule 26(a)(1)(A) disclosure of the name of a potential witness known to all parties; the failure to list as a trial witness a person so listed by another party; or the lack of knowledge of a pro se litigant of the requirement to make disclosures. In the latter situation, however, exclusion would be proper if the requirement for disclosure had been called to the litigant's attention by either the court or another party.

Preclusion of evidence is not an effective incentive to compel disclosure of information that, being supportive of the position of the opposing party, might advantageously be concealed by the disclosing party. However, the rule provides the court with a wide range of other sanctions—such as declaring specified facts to be established, preventing contradictory evidence, or, like spoliation of evidence, allowing the jury to be informed of the fact of nondisclosure—that, though not self-executing, can be imposed when found to be warranted after a hearing. The failure to identify a witness or document in a disclosure statement would be admissible under the Federal Rules of Evidence under the same principles that allow a party's interrogatory answers to be offered against it.

Subdivision (d). This subdivision is revised to require that, where a party fails to file any response to interrogatories or a Rule 34 request, the discovering party should informally seek to obtain such responses before filing a motion for sanctions.

The last sentence of this subdivision is revised to clarify that it is the pendency of a motion for protective order that may be urged as an excuse for a violation of subdivision (d). If a party's motion has been denied, the party cannot argue that its subsequent failure to comply would be justified. In this connection, it should be noted that the filing of a motion under Rule 26(c) is not self-executing—the relief authorized under that rule depends on obtaining the court's order to that effect.

Subdivision (g). This subdivision is modified to conform to the revision of Rule 26(f).

2000 Amendment

Subdivision (c)(1). When this subdivision was added in 1993 to direct exclusion of materials not disclosed as required, the duty to supplement discovery responses pursuant to Rule 26(e)(2) was omitted. In the face of this omission, courts may rely on inherent power to sanction for failure to supplement as required by Rule 26(e)(2), *see 8 Federal Practice & Procedure* § 2050 at 607–09, but that is an uncertain and unregulated ground for imposing sanctions. There is no obvious occasion for a Rule 37(a) motion in connection with failure to supplement, and ordinarily only Rule 37(c)(1) exists as rule-based authority for sanctions if this supplementation obligation is violated.

The amendment explicitly adds failure to comply with Rule 26(e)(2) as a ground for sanctions under Rule 37(c)(1), including exclusion of withheld materials. The rule provides that this sanction power only applies when the failure to supplement was "without substantial justification." Even if the failure was not substantially justified, a party should be allowed to use the material that was not disclosed if the lack of earlier notice was harmless.

"Shall" is replaced by "is" under the program to conform amended rules to current style conventions when there is no ambiguity.

GAP Report

The Advisory Committee recommends that the published amendment proposal be modified to state that the exclusion sanction can apply to failure "to amend a prior response to discovery as required by Rule 26(e)(2)." In addition, one minor phrasing change is recommended for the Committee Note.

2006 Amendment

Subdivision (f). Subdivision (f) is new. It focuses on a distinctive feature of computer operations, the routine alteration and deletion of information that attends ordinary use. Many steps essential to computer operation may alter or destroy information, for reasons that have nothing to do with how that information might relate to litigation. As a result, the ordinary operation of computer systems creates a risk that a party may lose potentially discoverable information without culpable conduct on its part. Under Rule 37(f), absent exceptional circumstances, sanctions cannot be imposed for loss of electronically stored information resulting from the routine, good-faith operation of an electronic information system.

Rule 37(f) applies only to information lost due to the "routine operation of an electronic information system" — the ways in which such systems are generally designed, programmed, and implemented to meet the party's technical and business needs. The "routine operation" of computer systems includes the alteration and overwriting of information, often without the operator's specific direction or awareness, a feature with no direct counterpart in hard-copy documents. Such features are essential to the operation of electronic information systems.

Rule 37(f) applies to information lost due to the routine operation of an information system only if the operation was in good faith. Good faith in the routine operation of an information system may involve a party's intervention to modify or suspend certain features of that routine operation to prevent the loss of information, if that information is subject to a preservation obligation. A preservation obligation may arise from many sources, including common law, statutes, regulations, or a court order in the case. The good faith requirement of Rule 37(f) means that a party is not permitted to exploit the routine operation of an information system to thwart discovery obligations by allowing that operation to continue in order to destroy specific stored information that it is required to preserve. When a party is under a duty to preserve information because of pending or reasonably anticipated litigation, intervention in the routine operation of an information system is one aspect of what is often called a "litigation hold." Among the factors that bear on a party's good faith in the routine operation of an information system are the steps the party took to comply with a court order in the case or party agreement requiring preservation of specific electronically stored information.

Whether good faith would call for steps to prevent the loss of information on sources that the party believes are not reasonably accessible under Rule 26(b)(2) depends on the circumstances of each case. One factor is whether the party reasonably believes that the information on such sources is likely to be discoverable and not available from reasonably accessible sources.

The protection provided by Rule 37(f) applies only to sanctions "under these rules." It does not affect other sources of authority to impose sanctions or rules of professional responsibility.

This rule restricts the imposition of "sanctions." It does not prevent a court from making the kinds of adjustments frequently used in managing discovery if a party is unable to provide relevant responsive information. For example, a court could order the responding party to produce an additional witness for deposition, respond to additional interrogatories, or make similar attempts to provide substitutes or alternatives for some or all of the lost information.

2007 Amendment

*[Effective December 1, 2007,
absent contrary Congressional action.]*

The language of Rule 37 has been amended as part of the general restyling of the Civil Rules to make them more easily understood and to make style and terminology consistent throughout the rules. These changes are intended to be stylistic only.

HISTORICAL NOTES

Effective and Applicability Provisions

1980 Acts

Amendment by Pub.L. 96–481 effective Oct. 1, 1981, and applicable to adversary adjudication defined in section 504(b)(1)(C) of Title 5, and to civil actions and adversary adjudications described in section 2412 of Title 28, Judiciary and Judicial Procedure, which are pending on, or commenced on or after Oct. 1, 1981, see section 208 of Pub.L. 96–481, set out as an Effective Date note under section 504 of Title 5, Government Organization and Employees.

VI. TRIALS

Proposed Amendment of Heading

Effective December 1, 2007, absent contrary Congressional action, this heading is amended to read as follows:

TITLE VI. TRIALS

Rule 38. Jury Trial of Right

(a) Right Preserved. The right of trial by jury as declared by the Seventh Amendment to the Constitution or as given by a statute of the United States shall be preserved to the parties inviolate.

(b) Demand. Any party may demand a trial by jury of any issue triable of right by a jury by (1) serving upon the other parties a demand therefor in writing at any time after the commencement of the action and not later than 10 days after the service of the last pleading directed to such issue, and (2) filing

the demand as required by Rule 5(d). Such demand may be indorsed upon a pleading of the party.

(c) Same: Specification of Issues. In the demand a party may specify the issues which the party wishes so tried; otherwise the party shall be deemed to have demanded trial by jury for all the issues so triable. If the party has demanded trial by jury for only some of the issues, any other party within 10 days after service of the demand or such lesser time as the court may order, may serve a demand for trial by jury of any other or all of the issues of fact in the action.

(d) Waiver. The failure of a party to serve and file a demand as required by this rule constitutes a waiver by the party of trial by jury. A demand for trial by jury made as herein provided may not be withdrawn without the consent of the parties.

(e) Admiralty and Maritime Claims. These rules shall not be construed to create a right to trial by jury of the issues in an admiralty or maritime claim within the meaning of Rule 9(h).

(As amended Feb. 28, 1966, eff. July 1, 1966; Mar. 2, 1987, eff. Aug. 1, 1987; Apr. 22, 1993, eff. Dec. 1, 1993.)

Proposed Amendment of Rule

Effective December 1, 2007, absent contrary Congressional action, this rule is amended to read as follows:

Rule 38. Right to a Jury Trial; Demand

(a) Right Preserved. *The right of trial by jury as declared by the Seventh Amendment to the Constitution—or as provided by a federal statute—is preserved to the parties inviolate.*

(b) Demand. *On any issue triable of right by a jury, a party may demand a jury trial by:*

(1) serving the other parties with a written demand—which may be included in a pleading—no later than 10 days after the last pleading directed to the issue is served; and

(2) filing the demand in accordance with Rule 5(d).

(c) Specifying Issues. *In its demand, a party may specify the issues that it wishes to have tried by a jury; otherwise, it is considered to have demanded a jury trial on all the issues so triable. If the party has demanded a jury trial on only some issues, any other party may—within 10 days after being served with the demand or within a shorter time ordered by the court—serve a demand for a jury trial on any other or all factual issues triable by jury.*

(d) Waiver; Withdrawal. *A party waives a jury trial unless its demand is properly served and filed. A proper demand may be withdrawn only if the parties consent.*

(e) Admiralty and Maritime Claims. *These rules do not create a right to a jury trial on issues in a claim that is an admiralty or maritime claim under Rule 9(h).*

ADVISORY COMMITTEE NOTES

1937 Adoption

This rule provides for the preservation of the constitutional right of trial by jury as directed in the enabling act (act of June 19, 1934, 48 Stat. 1064, U.S.C., Title 28, § 723c [sec. 2072]), and it and the next rule make definite provision for claim and waiver of jury trial, following the method used in many American states and in England and the British Dominions. Thus the claim must be made at once on initial pleading or appearance under Ill.Rev.Stat. (1937) ch. 110, § 188; 6 Tenn.Code Ann. (Williams, 1934) § 8734; compare Wyo.Rev.Stat.Ann. (1931) § 89–1320 (with answer or reply); within 10 days after the pleadings are completed or the case is at issue under 2 Conn.Gen.Stat. (1930) § 5624; Hawaii Rev.Laws (1935) § 4101; 2 Mass.Gen.Laws (Ter.Ed.1932) ch. 231, § 60; 3 Mich.Comp.Laws (1929) § 14263; Mich. Court Rules Ann. (Searl, 1933) Rule 33 (15 days); England (until 1933) O. 36, r.r. 2 and 6; and Ontario Jud. Act (1927) § 57(1) (4 days, or, where prior notice of trial, 2 days from such notice); or at a definite time varying under different codes, from 10 days before notice of trial to 10 days after notice, or, as in many, when the case is called for assignment, Ariz.Rev. Code Ann. (Struckmeyer, 1928) § 3802; Calif. Code Civ.Proc. (Deering, 1937) § 631, par. 4; Iowa Code (1935) § 10724; 4 Nev.Comp.Laws (Hillyer, 1929) § 8782; N.M. Stat.Ann. (Courtright, 1929) § 105–814; N.Y.C.P.A. (1937) § 426, subdivision 5 (applying to New York, Bronx, Richmond, Kings, and Queens Counties); R.I. Pub. Laws (1929), ch. 1327, amending R.I. Gen.Laws (1923) ch. 337, § 6; Utah Rev.Stat. Ann. (1933) § 104–23–6; 2 Wash.Rev.Stat.Ann. (Remington, 1932) § 316; England (4 days after notice of trial), Administration of Justice Act (1933) § 6 and amended rule under the Judicature Act (The Annual Practice, 1937), O. 36, r. 1; Australia High Court Procedure Act (1921) § 12, Rules, O. 33, r. 2; Alberta Rules of Ct. (1914) 172, 183, 184; British Columbia Sup.Ct.Rules (1925) O. 36, r.r. 2, 6, 11, and 16; New Brunswick Jud. Act (1927) O. 36, r.r. 2 and 5. See James, Trial by Jury and the New Federal Rules of Procedure (1936), 45 Yale L.J. 1022.

Rule 81(c) provides for claim for jury trial in removed actions.

The right to trial by jury as declared in U.S.C., Title 28, § 770 (Trial of issues of fact; by jury; exceptions), and similar statutes, is unaffected by this rule. This rule modifies U.S.C., Title 28, [former] § 773 (Trial of issues of fact; by court).

1966 Amendments

See Note to Rule 9(h), supra.

1987 Amendments

The amendments are technical. No substantive change is intended.

1993 Amendments

Language requiring the filing of a jury demand as provided in subdivision (d) is added to subdivision (b) to eliminate an apparent ambiguity between the two subdivisions. For proper scheduling of cases, it is important that jury demands not only be served on other parties, but also be filed with the court.

2007 Amendment

[Effective December 1, 2007, absent contrary Congressional action.]

The language of Rule 38 has been amended as part of the general restyling of the Civil Rules to make them more easily understood and to make style and terminology consistent throughout the rules. These changes are intended to be stylistic only.

Rule 39. Trial by Jury or by the Court

(a) By Jury. When trial by jury has been demanded as provided in Rule 38, the action shall be designated upon the docket as a jury action. The trial of all issues so demanded shall be by jury, unless (1) the parties or their attorneys of record, by written stipulation filed with the court or by an oral stipulation made in open court and entered in the record, consent to trial by the court sitting without a jury or (2) the court upon motion or of its own initiative finds that a right of trial by jury of some or all of those issues does not exist under the Constitution or statutes of the United States.

(b) By the Court. Issues not demanded for trial by jury as provided in Rule 38 shall be tried by the court; but, notwithstanding the failure of a party to demand a jury in an action in which such a demand might have been made of right, the court in its discretion upon motion may order a trial by a jury of any or all issues.

(c) Advisory Jury and Trial by Consent. In all actions not triable of right by a jury the court upon motion or of its own initiative may try any issue with an advisory jury or, except in actions against the United States when a statute of the United States provides for trial without a jury, the court, with the consent of both parties, may order a trial with a jury whose verdict has the same effect as if trial by jury had been a matter of right.

Proposed Amendment of Rule

Effective December 1, 2007, absent contrary Congressional action, this rule is amended to read as follows:

Rule 39. Trial by Jury or by the Court

(a) When a Demand Is Made. When a jury trial has been demanded under Rule 38, the action must be designated on the docket as a jury action. The trial on all issues so demanded must be by jury unless:

(1) the parties or their attorneys file a stipulation to a nonjury trial or so stipulate on the record; or

(2) the court, on motion or on its own, finds that on some or all of those issues there is no federal right to a jury trial.

(b) When No Demand Is Made. Issues on which a jury trial is not properly demanded are to be tried by the court. But the court may, on motion, order a jury trial on any issue for which a jury might have been demanded.

(c) Advisory Jury; Jury Trial by Consent. In an action not triable of right by a jury, the court, on motion or on its own:

(1) may try any issue with an advisory jury; or

(2) may, with the parties' consent, try any issue by a jury whose verdict has the same effect as if a jury trial had been a matter of right, unless the action is against the United States and a federal statute provides for a nonjury trial.

ADVISORY COMMITTEE NOTES

1937 Adoption

The provisions for express waiver of jury trial found in U.S.C., Title 28, [former] § 773 (Trial of issues of fact; by court) are incorporated in this rule. See Rule 38, however, which extends the provisions for waiver of jury. U.S.C., Title 28, [former] § 772 (Trial of issues of fact; in equity in patent causes) is unaffected by this rule. When certain of the issues are to be tried by jury and others by the court, the court may determine the sequence in which such issues shall be tried. *See Liberty Oil Co. v. Condon Nat. Bank*, 260 U.S. 235, 43 S.Ct. 118, 67 L.Ed. 232 (1922).

A discretionary power in the courts to send issues of fact to the jury is common in state procedure. Compare Calif. Code Civ.Proc. (Deering, 1937) § 592; 1 Colo.Stat.Ann. (1935) Code Civ.Proc., ch. 12, § 191; Conn.Gen.Stat. (1930) § 5625; 2 Minn.Stat. (Mason, 1927) § 9288; 4 Mont.Rev. Codes Ann. (1935) § 9327; N.Y.C.P.A. (1937) § 430; 2 Ohio Gen.Code Ann. (Page, 1926) § 11380; 1 Okla.Stat.Ann. (Harlow, 1931) § 351 [12 Okl.St.Ann. § 557]; Utah Rev.Stat.Ann. (1933) § 104–23–5; 2 Wash.Rev.Stat.Ann. (Remington, 1932) § 315; Wis.Stat. (1935) § 270.07. See [former] Equity Rule 23 (Matters Ordinarily Determinable at Law When Arising in Suit in Equity to be Disposed of Therein) and U.S.C., Title 28 [former] § 772 (Trial of issues of fact; in equity in patent causes); *Colleton Merc. Mfg. Co. v. Savannah River Lumber Co.*, C.C.A.4, 1922, 280 F. 358; *Fed. Res. Bk. of San Francisco v. Idaho Grimm Alfalfa Seed Growers' Ass'n*, C.C.A.9, 1925, 8 F.2d 922, certiorari denied 46 S.Ct. 347, 270 U.S. 646, 70 L.Ed. 778 (1926); *Watt v. Starke*, 1879, 101 U.S. 247, 25 L.Ed. 826.

2007 Amendment

[Effective December 1, 2007, absent contrary Congressional action.]

The language of Rule 39 has been amended as part of the general restyling of the Civil Rules to make them more easily understood and to make style and terminology consistent throughout the rules. These changes are intended to be stylistic only.

Rule 40. Assignment of Cases for Trial

The district courts shall provide by rule for the placing of actions upon the trial calendar (1) without request of the parties or (2) upon request of a party and notice to the other parties or (3) in such other manner as the courts deem expedient. Precedence shall be given to actions entitled thereto by any statute of the United States.

Proposed Amendment of Rule

Effective December 1, 2007, absent contrary Congressional action, this rule is amended to read as follows:

Rule 40. Scheduling Cases for Trial

Each court must provide by rule for scheduling trials. The court must give priority to actions entitled to priority by a federal statute.

ADVISORY COMMITTEE NOTES

1937 Adoption

U.S.C., Title 28, [former] § 769 (Notice of case for trial) is modified. See former Equity Rule 56 (On Expiration of Time for Depositions, Case Goes on Trial Calendar). See also [former] Equity Rule 57 (Continuances).

For examples of statutes giving precedence, see U.S.C., Title 28, § 47 (now §§ 1253, 2101, 2325) (Injunctions as to orders of Interstate Commerce Commission); § 380 (now §§ 1253, 2101, 2284) (Injunctions; alleged unconstitutionality of state statutes); § 380a (now §§ 1253, 2101, 2284) (Same; Constitutionality of federal statute); [former] § 768 (Priority of cases where a state is party); Title 15, § 28 (Antitrust laws; suits against monopolies expedited); Title 22, § 240 (Petition for restoration of property seized as munitions of war, etc.); and Title 49, [former] § 44 (Proceedings in equity under interstate commerce laws; expedition of suits).

2007 Amendment

[Effective December 1, 2007, absent contrary Congressional action.]

The language of Rule 40 has been amended as part of the general restyling of the Civil Rules to make them more easily understood and to make style and terminology consistent throughout the rules. These changes are intended to be stylistic only.

The best methods for scheduling trials depend on local conditions. It is useful to ensure that each district adopts an explicit rule for scheduling trials. It is not useful to limit or dictate the provisions of local rules.

Rule 41. Dismissal of Actions

(a) Voluntary Dismissal: Effect Thereof.

(1) By Plaintiff; by Stipulation. Subject to the provisions of Rule 23(e), of Rule 66, and of any statute of the United States, an action may be dismissed by the plaintiff without order of court (i) by filing a notice of dismissal at any time before service by the adverse party of an answer or of a motion for summary judgment, whichever first occurs, or (ii) by filing a stipulation of dismissal signed by all parties who have appeared in the action. Unless otherwise stated in the notice of dismissal or stipulation, the dismissal is without prejudice, except that a notice of dismissal operates as an adjudication upon the merits when filed by a plaintiff who has once dismissed in any court of the United States or of any state an action based on or including the same claim.

(2) By Order of Court. Except as provided in paragraph (1) of this subdivision of this rule, an action shall not be dismissed at the plaintiff's instance save upon order of the court and upon such terms and conditions as the court deems proper. If a counterclaim has been pleaded by a defendant prior to the service upon the defendant of the plaintiff's motion to dismiss, the action shall not be dismissed against the defendant's objection unless the counterclaim can remain pending for independent adjudication by the court. Unless otherwise specified in the order, a dismissal under this paragraph is without prejudice.

(b) Involuntary Dismissal: Effect Thereof. For failure of the plaintiff to prosecute or to comply with these rules or any order of court, a defendant may move for dismissal of an action or of any claim against the defendant. Unless the court in its order for dismissal otherwise specifies, a dismissal under this subdivision and any dismissal not provided for in this rule, other than a dismissal for lack of jurisdiction, for improper venue, or for failure to join a party under Rule 19, operates as an adjudication upon the merits.

(c) Dismissal of Counterclaim, Cross-Claim, or Third-Party Claim. The provisions of this rule apply to the dismissal of any counterclaim, cross-claim, or third-party claim. A voluntary dismissal by the claimant alone pursuant to paragraph (1) of subdivision (a) of this rule shall be made before a responsive pleading is served or, if there is none, before the introduction of evidence at the trial or hearing.

(d) Costs of Previously-Dismissed Action. If a plaintiff who has once dismissed an action in any court commences an action based upon or including the same claim against the same defendant, the court may make such order for the payment of costs of the action previously dismissed as it may deem proper and may stay the proceedings in the action until the plaintiff has complied with the order.

(As amended Dec. 27, 1946, eff. Mar. 19, 1948; Jan. 21, 1963, eff. July 1, 1963; Feb. 28, 1966, eff. July 1, 1966; Dec. 4, 1967, eff. July 1, 1968; Mar. 2, 1987, eff. Aug. 1, 1987; Apr. 30, 1991, eff. Dec. 1, 1991.)

Proposed Amendment of Rule

Effective December 1, 2007, absent contrary Congressional action, this rule is amended to read as follows:

Rule 41. Dismissal of Actions

(a) Voluntary Dismissal.

(1) By the Plaintiff.

(A) Without a Court Order. Subject to Rules 23(e), 23.1(c), 23.2, and 66 and any applicable federal statute, the plaintiff may dismiss an action without a court order by filing:

(i) a notice of dismissal before the opposing party serves either an answer or a motion for summary judgment; or

(ii) a stipulation of dismissal signed by all parties who have appeared.

(B) Effect. Unless the notice or stipulation states otherwise, the dismissal is without prejudice. But if the plaintiff previously dismissed any federal- or state-court action based on or including the same claim, a notice of dismissal operates as an adjudication on the merits.

(2) By Court Order; Effect. Except as provided in Rule 41(a)(1), an action may be dismissed at the plaintiff's request only by court order, on terms that the court considers proper. If a defendant has pleaded a counterclaim before being served with the plaintiff's motion to dismiss, the action may be dismissed over the defendant's objection only if the counterclaim can remain pending for independent adjudication. Unless the order states otherwise, a dismissal under this paragraph (2) is without prejudice.

(b) Involuntary Dismissal; Effect. *If the plaintiff fails to prosecute or to comply with these rules or a court order, a defendant may move to dismiss the action or any claim against it. Unless the dismissal order states otherwise, a dismissal under this subdivision (b) and any dismissal not under this rule—except one for lack of jurisdiction, improper venue, or failure to join a party under Rule 19—operates as an adjudication on the merits.*

(c) Dismissing a Counterclaim, Crossclaim, or Third-Party Claim. *This rule applies to a dismissal of any counterclaim, crossclaim, or third-party claim. A claimant's voluntary dismissal under Rule 41(a)(1)(A)(i) must be made:*

(1) before a responsive pleading is served; or

(2) if there is no responsive pleading, before evidence is introduced at a hearing or trial.

(d) Costs of a Previously Dismissed Action. *If a plaintiff who previously dismissed an action in any court files an action based on or including the same claim against the same defendant, the court:*

(1) may order the plaintiff to pay all or part of the costs of that previous action; and

(2) may stay the proceedings until the plaintiff has complied.

ADVISORY COMMITTEE NOTES

1937 Adoption

Note to Subdivision (a). Compare Ill.Rev.Stat. (1937) c. 110, § 176, and *English Rules Under the Judicature Act* (The Annual Practice, 1937) O. 26.

Provisions regarding dismissal in such statutes as U.S.C., Title 8, § 164 [see 1329] (Jurisdiction of district courts in immigration cases) and U.S.C., Title 31, § 232 [now 3730] (Liability of persons making false claims against United States; suits) are preserved by paragraph (1).

Note to Subdivision (b). This provides for the equivalent of a nonsuit on motion by the defendant after the completion of the presentation of evidence by the plaintiff. Also, for actions tried without a jury, it provides the equivalent of the directed verdict practice for jury actions which is regulated by Rule 50.

1946 Amendment

Note. Subdivision (a). The insertion of the reference to Rule 66 correlates Rule 41(a)(1) with the express provisions concerning dismissal set forth in amended Rule 66 on receivers.

The change in Rule 41(a)(1)(i) gives the service of a motion for summary judgment by the adverse party the same effect in preventing unlimited dismissal as was originally given only to the service of an answer. The omission of reference to a motion for summary judgment in the original rule was subject to criticism. 3 *Moore's Federal Practice*, 1938, 3037–3038, n. 12. A motion for summary judgment may be forthcoming prior to answer, and if well taken will eliminate the necessity for an answer. Since such a motion may require even more research and preparation than the answer itself, there is good reason why the service of the motion, like that of the answer, should prevent a voluntary dismissal by the adversary without court approval.

The word "generally" has been stricken from Rule 41(a)(1)(ii) in order to avoid confusion and to conform with the elimination of the necessity for special appearance by original Rule 12(b).

Subdivision (b). In some cases tried without a jury, where at the close of plaintiff's evidence the defendant moves for dismissal under Rule 41(b) on the ground that plaintiff's evidence is insufficient for recovery, the plaintiff's own evidence may be conflicting or present questions of credibility. In ruling on the defendant's motion, questions arise as to the function of the judge in evaluating the testimony and whether findings should be made if the motion is sustained. Three circuits hold that as the judge is the trier of the facts in such

Rule 41

RULES OF CIVIL PROCEDURE

a situation his function is not the same as on a motion to direct a verdict, where the jury is the trier of the facts, and that the judge in deciding such a motion in a non-jury case may pass on conflicts of evidence and credibility, and if he performs that function of evaluating the testimony and grants the motion on the merits, findings are required. *Young v. United States,* C.C.A.9, 1940, 111 F.2d 823; *Gary Theatre Co. v. Columbia Pictures Corporation,* C.C.A.7, 1941, 120 F.2d 891; *Bach v. Friden Calculating Machine Co., Inc.,* C.C.A.6, 1945, 148 F.2d 407. Cf. *Mateas v. Fred Harvey, a Corporation,* C.C.A.9, 1945, 146 F.2d 989. The Third Circuit has held that on such a motion the function of the court is the same as on a motion to direct in a jury case, and that the court should only decide whether there is evidence which would support a judgment for the plaintiff, and therefore, findings are not required by Rule 52. *Federal Deposit Insurance Corp. v. Mason,* C.C.A.3, 1940, 115 F.2d 548; *Schad v. Twentieth Century-Fox Film Corp.,* C.C.A.3, 1943, 136 F.2d 991. The added sentence in Rule 41(b) incorporates the view of the Sixth, Seventh and Ninth Circuits. See also 3 *Moore's Federal Practice,* 1938, Cum.Supplement § 41.03, under "Page 3045"; Commentary, *The Motion to Dismiss in Non-Jury Cases,* 1946, 9 Fed.Rules Serv., Comm.Pg. 41b.14.

1963 Amendment

Under the present text of the second sentence of this subdivision, the motion for dismissal at the close of the plaintiff's evidence may be made in a case tried to a jury as well as in a case tried without a jury. But, when made in a jury-tried case, this motion overlaps the motion for a directed verdict under Rule 50(a), which is also available in the same situation. It has been held that the standard to be applied in deciding the Rule 41(b) motion at the close of the plaintiff's evidence in a jury-tried case is the same as that used upon a motion for a directed verdict made at the same stage; and, just as the court need not make findings pursuant to Rule 52(a) when it directs a verdict, so in a jury-tried case it may omit these findings in granting the Rule 41(b) motion. See generally *O'Brien v. Westinghouse Electric Corp.,* 293 F.2d 1, 5–10 (3d Cir. 1961).

As indicated by the discussion in the *O'Brien* case, the overlap has caused confusion. Accordingly, the second and third sentences of Rule 41(b) are amended to provide that the motion for dismissal at the close of the plaintiff's evidence shall apply only to nonjury cases (including cases tried with an advisory jury). Hereafter the correct motion in jury-tried cases will be the motion for a directed verdict. This involves no change of substance. It should be noted that the court upon a motion for a directed verdict may in appropriate circumstances deny that motion and grant instead a new trial, or a voluntary dismissal without prejudice under Rule 41(a)(2). See 6 *Moore's Federal Practice* ¶59.08[5] (2d ed. 1954); *cf. Cone v. West Virginia Pulp & Paper Co.,* 330 U.S. 212, 217, 67 S.Ct. 752, 91 L.Ed. 849 (1947).

The first sentence of Rule 41(b), providing for dismissal for failure to prosecute or to comply with the Rules or any order of court, and the general provisions of the last sentence remain applicable in jury as well as nonjury cases.

The amendment of the last sentence of Rule 41(b) indicates that a dismissal for lack of an indispensable party does not operate as an adjudication on the merits. Such a dismissal does not bar a new action, for it is based merely "on a plaintiff's failure to comply with a precondition requisite to the Court's going forward to determine the merits of his substantive claim." See *Costello v. United States,* 365 U.S. 265, 284–288, 81 S.Ct. 534, 5 L.Ed.2d 551 & n. 5 (1961); *Mallow v. Hinde,* 12 Wheat. (25 U.S.) 193, 6 L.Ed. 599 (1827); Clark, *Code Pleading* 602 (2d ed. 1947); *Restatement of Judgments* § 49, comm. a, b (1942). This amendment corrects an omission from the rule and is consistent with an earlier amendment, effective in 1948, adding "the defense of failure to join an indispensable party" to clause (1) of Rule 12(h).

1966 Amendment

The terminology is changed to accord with the amendment of Rule 19. See that amended rule and the Advisory Committee's Note thereto.

1968 Amendment

The amendment corrects an inadvertent error in the reference to amended Rule 23.

1987 Amendment

The amendment is technical. No substantive change is intended.

1991 Amendment

Language is deleted that authorized the use of this rule as a means of terminating a non-jury action on the merits when the plaintiff has failed to carry a burden of proof in presenting the plaintiff's case. The device is replaced by the new provisions of Rule 52(c), which authorize entry of judgment against the defendant as well as the plaintiff, and earlier than the close of the case of the party against whom judgment is rendered. A motion to dismiss under Rule 41 on the ground that a plaintiff's evidence is legally insufficient should now be treated as a motion for judgment on partial findings as provided in Rule 52(c).

2007 Amendment

[Effective December 1, 2007, absent contrary Congressional action.]

The language of Rule 41 has been amended as part of the general restyling of the Civil Rules to make them more easily understood and to make style and terminology consistent throughout the rules. These changes are intended to be stylistic only.

When Rule 23 was amended in 1966, Rules 23.1 and 23.2 were separated from Rule 23. Rule 41(a)(1) was not then amended to reflect the Rule 23 changes. In 1968 Rule 41(a)(1) was amended to correct the cross-reference to what had become Rule 23(e), but Rules 23.1 and 23.2 were inadvertently overlooked. Rules 23.1 and 23.2 are now added to the list of exceptions in Rule 41(a)(1)(A). This change does not affect established meaning. Rule 23.2 explicitly incorporates Rule 23(e), and thus was already absorbed directly into the exceptions in Rule 41(a)(1). Rule 23.1 requires court approval of a compromise or dismissal in language parallel to Rule 23(e) and thus supersedes the apparent right to dismiss by notice of dismissal.

Complete Annotation Materials, see Title 28 U.S.C.A.

246

Rule 42. Consolidation; Separate Trials

(a) Consolidation. When actions involving a common question of law or fact are pending before the court, it may order a joint hearing or trial of any or all the matters in issue in the actions; it may order all the actions consolidated; and it may make such orders concerning proceedings therein as may tend to avoid unnecessary costs or delay.

(b) Separate Trials. The court, in furtherance of convenience or to avoid prejudice, or when separate trials will be conducive to expedition and economy, may order a separate trial of any claim, cross-claim, counterclaim, or third-party claim, or of any separate issue or of any number of claims, cross-claims, counterclaims, third-party claims, or issues, always preserving inviolate the right of trial by jury as declared by the Seventh Amendment to the Constitution or as given by a statute of the United States.
(As amended Feb. 28, 1966, eff. July 1, 1966.)

Proposed Amendment of Rule

Effective December 1, 2007, absent contrary Congressional action, this rule is amended to read as follows:

Rule 42. Consolidation; Separate Trials

(a) Consolidation. *If actions before the court involve a common question of law or fact, the court may:*

(1) join for hearing or trial any or all matters at issue in the actions;

(2) consolidate the actions; or

(3) issue any other orders to avoid unnecessary cost or delay.

(b) Separate Trials. *For convenience, to avoid prejudice, or to expedite and economize, the court may order a separate trial of one or more separate issues, claims, crossclaims, counterclaims, or third-party claims. When ordering a separate trial, the court must preserve any federal right to a jury trial.*

ADVISORY COMMITTEE NOTES

1937 Adoption

Subdivision (a) is based upon U.S.C., Title 28, [former] § 734 (Orders to save costs; consolidation of causes of like nature) but in so far as the statute differs from this rule, it is modified.

For comparable statutes dealing with consolidation see Ark.Dig.Stat. (Crawford & Moses, 1921) § 1081; Calif.Code Civ.Proc. (Deering, 1937) § 1048; N.M.Stat.Ann. (Courtright, 1929) § 105–828; N.Y.C.P.A. (1937) §§ 96, 96a, and 97; American Judicature Society, Bulletin XIV, (1919) Art. 26.

For severance or separate trials see Calif.Code Civ.Proc. (Deering, 1937) § 1048; N.Y.C.P.A. (1937) § 96; American Judicature Society, Bulletin XIV (1919) Art. 3, § 2 and Art. 10, § 10. See also the third sentence of Equity Rule 29

(Defenses—How Presented) providing for discretionary separate hearing and disposition before trial of pleas in bar or abatement, and see also Rule 12(d) of these rules for preliminary hearings of defenses and objections.

For the entry of separate judgments, see Rule 54(b) (Judgment at Various Stages).

1966 Amendment

In certain suits in admiralty separation for trial of the issues of liability and damages (or of the extent of liability other than damages, such as salvage and general average) has been conducive to expedition and economy, especially because of the statutory right to interlocutory appeal in admiralty cases (which is of course preserved by these Rules). While separation of issues for trial is not to be routinely ordered, it is important that it be encouraged where experience has demonstrated its worth. Cf. Weinstein, *Routine Bifurcation of Negligence Trials*, 14 Vand. L.Rev. 831 (1961).

In cases (including some cases within the admiralty and maritime jurisdiction) in which the parties have a constitutional or statutory right of trial by jury, separation of issues may give rise to problems. See *e.g.*, *United Air Lines, Inc. v. Wiener*, 286 F.2d 302 (9th Cir.1961). Accordingly, the proposed change in Rule 42 reiterates the mandate of Rule 38 respecting preservation of the right to jury trial.

2007 Amendment

[Effective December 1, 2007, absent contrary Congressional action.]

The language of Rule 42 has been amended as part of the general restyling of the Civil Rules to make them more easily understood and to make style and terminology consistent throughout the rules. These changes are intended to be stylistic only.

Rule 43. Taking of Testimony

(a) Form. In every trial, the testimony of witnesses shall be taken in open court, unless a federal law, these rules, the Federal Rules of Evidence, or other rules adopted by the Supreme Court provide otherwise. The court may, for good cause shown in compelling circumstances and upon appropriate safeguards, permit presentation of testimony in open court by contemporaneous transmission from a different location.

[(b), (c) Abrogated]

(d) Affirmation in Lieu of Oath. Whenever under these rules an oath is required to be taken, a solemn affirmation may be accepted in lieu thereof.

(e) Evidence on Motions. When a motion is based on facts not appearing of record the court may hear the matter on affidavits presented by the respective parties, but the court may direct that the matter be heard wholly or partly on oral testimony or deposition.

(f) Interpreters. The court may appoint an interpreter of its own selection and may fix the interpret-

er's reasonable compensation. The compensation shall be paid out of funds provided by law or by one or more of the parties as the court may direct, and may be taxed ultimately as costs, in the discretion of the court.

(As amended Feb. 28, 1966, eff. July 1, 1966; Nov. 20, 1972, and Dec. 18, 1972, eff. July 1, 1975; Mar. 2, 1987, eff. Aug. 1, 1987; Apr. 23, 1996, eff. Dec. 1, 1996.)

Proposed Amendment of Rule

Effective December 1, 2007, absent contrary Congressional action, this rule is amended to read as follows:

Rule 43. Taking Testimony

(a) In Open Court. *At trial, the witnesses' testimony must be taken in open court unless a federal statute, the Federal Rules of Evidence, these rules, or other rules adopted by the Supreme Court provide otherwise. For good cause in compelling circumstances and with appropriate safeguards, the court may permit testimony in open court by contemporaneous transmission from a different location.*

(b) Affirmation Instead of an Oath. *When these rules require an oath, a solemn affirmation suffices.*

(c) Evidence on a Motion. *When a motion relies on facts outside the record, the court may hear the matter on affidavits or may hear it wholly or partly on oral testimony or on depositions.*

(d) Interpreter. *The court may appoint an interpreter of its choosing; fix reasonable compensation to be paid from funds provided by law or by one or more parties; and tax the compensation as costs.*

ADVISORY COMMITTEE NOTES

1937 Adoption

Note to Subdivision (a). The first sentence is a restatement of the substance of U.S.C., Title 28, § 635 (Proof in common-law actions), [former] § 637 (see §§ 2072, 2073) (Proof in equity and admiralty), and [former] Equity Rule 46 (Trial—Testimony Usually Taken in Open Court—Rulings on Objections to Evidence). This rule abolishes in patent and trademark actions, the practice under [former] Equity Rule 48 of setting forth in affidavits the testimony in chief of expert witnesses whose testimony is directed to matters of opinion. The second and third sentences on admissibility of evidence and Subdivision (b) on contradiction and cross-examination modify U.S.C., Title 28, § 725 (now 1652) (Laws of states as rules of decision) insofar as that statute has been construed to prescribe conformity to state rules of evidence. Compare Callahan and Ferguson, *Evidence and the New Federal Rules of Civil Procedure*, 45 Yale L.J. 622 (1936), and *Same: 2*, 47 Yale L.J. 195 (1937). The last sentence modifies to the extent indicated U.S.C., Title 28, [former] § 631 (Competency of witnesses governed by State laws).

Note to Subdivision (b). See 4 *Wigmore on Evidence* (2d ed., 1923) § 1885 et seq.

Note to Subdivision (c). See [former] Equity Rule 46 (Trial—Testimony Usually Taken in Open Court-Rulings on

Objections to Evidence). With the last sentence compare *Dowagiac v. Lochren*, 143 Fed. 211 (C.C.A. 8th, 1906). See also *Blease v. Garlington*, 92 U.S. 1, 23 L.Ed. 521 (1876); *Nelson v. United States*, 201 U.S. 92, 114, 26 S.Ct. 358, 50 L.Ed. 673 (1906); *Unkle v. Wills*, 281 Fed. 29 (C.C.A. 8th, 1922).

See Rule 61 for harmless error in either the admission or exclusion of evidence.

Note to Subdivision (d). See [former] Equity Rule 78 (Affirmation in Lieu of Oath) and U.S.C., Title 1, § 1 (Words importing singular number, masculine gender, etc.; extended application), providing for affirmation in lieu of oath.

Supplementary Note on Advisory Committee Regarding Rules 43 and 44

Note. These rules have been criticized and suggested improvements offered by commentators. 1 *Wigmore on Evidence*, 3d ed. 1940, 200–204; Green, *The Admissibility of Evidence Under the Federal Rules*, 1941, 55 Harv.L.Rev. 197. Cases indicate, however, that the rule is working better than these commentators had expected. *Boerner v. United States*, C.C.A.2d, 1941, 117 F.2d 387, cert. den., 1941, 313 U.S. 587, 61 S.Ct. 1120; *Mosson v. Liberty Fast Freight Co.*, C.C.A.2d, 1942, 124 F.2d, 448; *Hartford Accident & Indemnity Co. v. Olivier*, C.C.A. 5th, 1941, 123 F.2d 709; *Anzano v. Metropolitan Life Ins. Co. of New York*, C.C.A.3d, 1941, 118 F.2d 430; *Franzen v. E. I. DuPont De Nemours & Co.*, C.C.A.3d, 1944, 146 F.2d 837; *Fakouri v. Cadais*, C.C.A. 5th, 1945, 147 F.2d 667; *In re C. & P. Co.*, S.D.Cal.1945, 63 F.Supp. 400, 408. But cf. *United States v. Aluminum Co. of America*, S.D.N.Y.1938, 1 Fed.Rules Serv. 43a.3, Case 1; Note, 1946, 46 Col.L.Rev. 267. While consideration of a comprehensive and detailed set of rules of evidence seems very desirable, it has not been feasible for the Committee so far to undertake this important task. Such consideration should include the adaptability to federal practice of all or parts of the proposed Code of Evidence of the American Law Institute. See Armstrong, *Proposed Amendments to Federal Rules of Civil Procedure*, 4 F.R.D. 124, 137–138.

1966 Amendment

Note to Subdivision (f). This new subdivision [subdivision (f)] authorizes the court to appoint interpreters (including interpreters for the deaf), to provide for their compensation, and to tax the compensation as costs. Compare proposed subdivision (b) of Rule 28 of the Federal Rules of Criminal Procedure.

1972 Amendment

Rule 43, entitled Evidence, has heretofore served as the basic rule of evidence for civil cases in federal courts. Its very general provisions are superseded by the detailed provisions of the new Rules of Evidence. The original title and many of the provisions of the rule are, therefore, no longer appropriate.

Subdivision (a). The provision for taking testimony in open court is not duplicated in the Rules of Evidence and is retained. Those dealing with admissibility of evidence and competency of witnesses, however, are no longer needed or appropriate since those topics are covered at large in the Rules of Evidence. They are accordingly deleted. The

language is broadened, however, to take account of acts of Congress dealing with the taking of testimony, as well as of the Rules of Evidence and any other rules adopted by the Supreme Court.

Subdivision (b). The subdivision is no longer needed or appropriate since the matters with which it deals are treated in the Rules of Evidence. The use of leading questions, both generally and in the interrogation of an adverse party or witness identified with him, is the subject of Evidence Rule 611(c). Who may impeach is treated in Evidence Rule 601 [sic; probably means 607], and scope of cross-examination is covered in Evidence Rule 611(b). The subdivision is accordingly deleted.

Subdivision (c). Offers of proof and making a record of excluded evidence are treated in Evidence Rule 103. The subdivision is no longer needed or appropriate and is deleted.

1987 Amendment

The amendment is technical. No substantive change is intended.

1996 Amendment

Rule 43(a) is revised to conform to the style conventions adopted for simplifying the present Civil Rules. The only intended changes of meaning are described below.

The requirement that testimony be taken "orally" is deleted. The deletion makes it clear that testimony of a witness may be given in open court by other means if the witness is not able to communicate orally. Writing or sign language are common examples. The development of advanced technology may enable testimony to be given by other means. A witness unable to sign or write by hand may be able to communicate through a computer or similar device.

Contemporaneous transmission of testimony from a different location is permitted only on showing good cause in compelling circumstances. The importance of presenting live testimony in court cannot be forgotten. The very ceremony of trial and the presence of the factfinder may exert a powerful force for truthtelling. The opportunity to judge the demeanor of a witness face-to-face is accorded great value in our tradition. Transmission cannot be justified merely by showing that it is inconvenient for the witness to attend the trial.

The most persuasive showings of good cause and compelling circumstances are likely to arise when a witness is unable to attend trial for unexpected reasons, such as accident or illness, but remains able to testify from a different place. Contemporaneous transmission may be better than an attempt to reschedule the trial, particularly if there is a risk that other—and perhaps more important—witnesses might not be available at a later time.

Other possible justifications for remote transmission must be approached cautiously. Ordinarily depositions, including video depositions, provide a superior means of securing the testimony of a witness who is beyond the reach of a trial subpoena, or of resolving difficulties in scheduling a trial that can be attended by all witnesses. Deposition procedures ensure the opportunity of all parties to be represented while the witness is testifying. An unforeseen need for the testimony of a remote witness that arises during trial, however, may establish good cause and compelling circumstances. Justification is particularly likely if the need arises from the interjection of new issues during trial or from the unexpected inability to present testimony as planned from a different witness.

Good cause and compelling circumstances may be established with relative ease if all parties agree that testimony should be presented by transmission. The court is not bound by a stipulation, however, and can insist on live testimony. Rejection of the parties' agreement will be influenced, among other factors, by the apparent importance of the testimony in the full context of the trial.

A party who could reasonably foresee the circumstances offered to justify transmission of testimony will have special difficulty in showing good cause and the compelling nature of the circumstances. Notice of a desire to transmit testimony from a different location should be given as soon as the reasons are known, to enable other parties to arrange a deposition, or to secure an advance ruling on transmission so as to know whether to prepare to be present with the witness while testifying.

No attempt is made to specify the means of transmission that may be used. Audio transmission without video images may be sufficient in some circumstances, particularly as to less important testimony. Video transmission ordinarily should be preferred when the cost is reasonable in relation to the matters in dispute, the means of the parties, and the circumstances that justify transmission. Transmission that merely produces the equivalent of a written statement ordinarily should not be used.

Safeguards must be adopted that ensure accurate identification of the witness and that protect against influence by persons present with the witness. Accurate transmission likewise must be assured.

Other safeguards should be employed to ensure that advance notice is given to all parties of foreseeable circumstances that may lead the proponent to offer testimony by transmission. Advance notice is important to protect the opportunity to argue for attendance of the witness at trial. Advance notice also ensures an opportunity to depose the witness, perhaps by video record, as a means of supplementing transmitted testimony.

2007 Amendment

*[Effective December 1, 2007,
absent contrary Congressional action.]*

The language of Rule 43 has been amended as part of the general restyling of the Civil Rules to make them more easily understood and to make style and terminology consistent throughout the rules. These changes are intended to be stylistic only.

HISTORICAL NOTES

References in Text

The Federal Rules of Evidence, referred to in subd. (a), are set out in this title.

Effective Date of Amendments Proposed November 20, 1972, and December 18, 1972

Amendments of this rule embraced by orders entered by the Supreme Court of the United States on November 20, 1972, and December 18, 1972, effective on the 180th day beginning after January 2, 1975, see section 3 of Pub.L.

93–595, Jan. 2, 1975, 88 Stat. 1959, set out as a note under section 2071 of Title 28.

Rule 44. Proof of Official Record

(a) Authentication.

(1) **Domestic.** An official record kept within the United States, or any state, district, or commonwealth, or within a territory subject to the administrative or judicial jurisdiction of the United States, or an entry therein, when admissible for any purpose, may be evidenced by an official publication thereof or by a copy attested by the officer having the legal custody of the record, or by the officer's deputy, and accompanied by a certificate that such officer has the custody. The certificate may be made by a judge of a court of record of the district or political subdivision in which the record is kept, authenticated by the seal of the court, or may be made by any public officer having a seal of office and having official duties in the district or political subdivision in which the record is kept, authenticated by the seal of the officer's office.

(2) **Foreign.** A foreign official record, or an entry therein, when admissible for any purpose, may be evidenced by an official publication thereof; or a copy thereof, attested by a person authorized to make the attestation, and accompanied by a final certification as to the genuineness of the signature and official position (i) of the attesting person, or (ii) of any foreign official whose certificate of genuineness of signature and official position relates to the attestation or is in a chain of certificates of genuineness of signature and official position relating to the attestation. A final certification may be made by a secretary of embassy or legation, consul general, vice consul, or consular agent of the United States, or a diplomatic or consular official of the foreign country assigned or accredited to the United States. If reasonable opportunity has been given to all parties to investigate the authenticity and accuracy of the documents, the court may, for good cause shown, (i) admit an attested copy without final certification or (ii) permit the foreign official record to be evidenced by an attested summary with or without a final certification. The final certification is unnecessary if the record and the attestation are certified as provided in a treaty or convention to which the United States and the foreign country in which the official record is located are parties.

(b) Lack of Record. A written statement that after diligent search no record or entry of a specified tenor is found to exist in the records designated by the statement, authenticated as provided in subdivision (a)(1) of this rule in the case of a domestic record, or complying with the requirements of subdivision (a)(2) of this rule for a summary in the case of a foreign record, is admissible as evidence that the records contain no such record or entry.

(c) Other Proof. This rule does not prevent the proof of official records or of entry or lack of entry therein by any other method authorized by law.

(As amended Feb. 28, 1966, eff. July 1, 1966; Mar. 2, 1987, eff. Aug. 1, 1987; Apr. 30, 1991, eff. Dec. 1, 1991.)

Proposed Amendment of Rule

Effective December 1, 2007, absent contrary Congressional action, this rule is amended to read as follows:

Rule 44. *Proving an Official Record*

(a) Means of Proving.

(1) Domestic Record. Each of the following evidences an official record—or an entry in it—that is otherwise admissible and is kept within the United States, any state, district, or commonwealth, or any territory subject to the administrative or judicial jurisdiction of the United States:

(A) an official publication of the record; or

(B) a copy attested by the officer with legal custody of the record—or by the officer's deputy—and accompanied by a certificate that the officer has custody. The certificate must be made under seal:

(i) by a judge of a court of record in the district or political subdivision where the record is kept; or

(ii) by any public officer with a seal of office and with official duties in the district or political subdivision where the record is kept.

(2) Foreign Record.

(A) In General. Each of the following evidences a foreign official record—or an entry in it—that is otherwise admissible:

(i) an official publication of the record; or

(ii) the record—or a copy—that is attested by an authorized person and is accompanied either by a final certification of genuineness or by a certification under a treaty or convention to which the United States and the country where the record is located are parties.

(B) Final Certification of Genuineness. A final certification must certify the genuineness of the signature and official position of the attester or of any foreign official whose certificate of genuineness relates to the attestation or is in a chain of certificates of genuineness relating to the attestation. A final certification

may be made by a secretary of a United States embassy or legation; by a consul general, vice consul, or consular agent of the United States; or by a diplomatic or consular official of the foreign country assigned or accredited to the United States.

 (C) Other Means of Proof. If all parties have had a reasonable opportunity to investigate a foreign record's authenticity and accuracy, the court may, for good cause, either:

 (i) admit an attested copy without final certification; or

 (ii) permit the record to be evidenced by an attested summary with or without a final certification.

 (b) *Lack of a Record.* A written statement that a diligent search of designated records revealed no record or entry of a specified tenor is admissible as evidence that the records contain no such record or entry. For domestic records, the statement must be authenticated under Rule 44(a)(1). For foreign records, the statement must comply with (a)(2)(C)(ii).

 (c) *Other Proof.* A party may prove an official record—or an entry or lack of an entry in it—by any other method authorized by law.

ADVISORY COMMITTEE NOTES

1937 Adoption

 This rule provides a simple and uniform method of proving public records, and entry or lack of entry therein, in all cases including those specifically provided for by statutes of the United States. Such statutes are not superseded, however, and proof may also be made according to their provisions whenever they differ from this rule. Some of those statutes are:

U.S.C., Title 28 [former sections]:

 § 661[now 1733] (Copies of department or corporation records and papers; admissibility; seal)

 § 662[now 1733] (Same; in office of General Counsel of the Treasury)

 § 663[now 1733] (Instruments and papers of Comptroller of Currency; admissibility)

 § 664[now 1733] (Organization certificates of national banks; admissibility)

 § 665[now 1733] (Transcripts from books of Treasury in suits against delinquents; admissibility)

 § 666[now 1733] (Same; certificate by Secretary or Assistant Secretary)

 § 670[now 1743] (Admissibility of copies of statements of demands by Post Office Department)

 § 671[now 1733] (Admissibility of copies of post office records and statement of accounts)

 § 672[former] (Admissibility of copies of records in General Land Office)

 § 673[now 1744] (Admissibility of copies of records, and so forth, of Patent Office)

 § 674[now 1745] (Copies of foreign letters patent as prima facie evidence)

 § 675[former] (Copies of specifications and drawings of patents admissible)

 § 676[now 1736] (Extracts from Journals of Congress admissible when injunction of secrecy removed)

 § 677[now 1740] (Copies of records in offices of United States consuls admissible)

 § 678[former] (Books and papers in certain district courts)

 § 679[former] (Records in clerks' offices, western district of North Carolina)

 § 680[former] (Records in clerks' offices of former district of California)

 § 681[now 1734] (Original records lost or destroyed; certified copy admissible)

 § 682[now 1734] (Same; when certified copy not obtainable)

 § 685[now 1735] (Same; certified copy of official papers)

 § 687[now 1738] (Authentication of legislative acts; proof of judicial proceedings of State)

 § 688[now 1739] (Proofs of records in offices not pertaining to courts)

 § 689[now 1742] (Copies of foreign records relating to land titles)

 § 695[now 1732] (Writings and records made in regular course of business; admissibility)

 § 695e[now 1741] (Foreign documents on record in public offices; certification)

U.S.C., Title 1:

 § 30[now 112] (Statutes at large; contents; admissibility in evidence)

 § 30a[now 113] ("Little and Brown's" edition of laws and treaties competent evidence of Acts of Congress)

 § 54[now 204] (Codes and supplements as establishing prima facie the laws of United States and District of Columbia, etc.)

 § 55[now 208] (Copies of supplements to Code of Laws of United States and of District of Columbia Code and supplements; conclusive evidence of original)

U.S.C., Title 5:

 § 490[former] (Records of Department of Interior; authenticated copies as evidence)

U.S.C., Title 6:

 § 7[now Title 31, § 9306] (Surety Companies as sureties; appointment of agents; service of process)

U.S.C., Title 8:

 § 9a[see 1435(c)] (Citizenship of children of persons naturalized under certain laws; repatriation of native-born women married to aliens prior to September 22, 1922; copies of proceedings)

 § 356[see 1443] (Regulations for execution of naturalization laws; certified copies of papers as evidence)

 § 399b(d)[see 1443] (Certifications of naturalization records; authorization; admissibility as evidence)

U.S.C., Title 11:

 § 44(d), (e), (f), (g)[former] (Bankruptcy court proceedings and orders as evidence)

 § 204[former] (Extensions extended, etc.; evidence of confirmation)

§ 207(j)[former] (Corporate reorganizations; certified copy of decree as evidence)

U.S.C., Title 15:

§ 127 (Trade-mark records in Patent Office; copies as evidence)

U.S.C., Title 20:

§ 52 (Smithsonian Institution; evidence of title to site and buildings)

U.S.C., Title 25:

§ 6 (Bureau of Indian Affairs; seal; authenticated and certified documents; evidence)

U.S.C., Title 31:

§ 46[now 704] (Laws governing General Accounting Office; copies of books, records, etc., thereof as evidence)

U.S.C., Title 38:

§ 11g[see 202] (Seal of Veterans' Administration; authentication of copies of records)

U.S.C., Title 40:

§ 238 [former 44 U.S.C.A. § 300h] (National Archives; seal; reproduction of archives; fee; admissibility in evidence of reproductions)

§ 270c [see now 40 U.S.C.A. § 3133(a)] (Bonds of contractors for public works; right of person furnishing labor or material to copy of bond)

U.S.C., Title 43:

§§ 57–59 (Copies of land surveys, etc., in certain states and districts admissible as evidence)

§ 83 (General Land Office registers and receivers; transcripts of records as evidence)

U.S.C., Title 46:

§ 823 (Records of Maritime Commission; copies; publication of reports; evidence)

U.S.C., Title 47:

§ 154(m) (Federal Communications Commission; copies of reports and decisions as evidence)

§ 412 (Documents filed with Federal Communications Commission as public records; prima facie evidence; confidential records)

U.S.C., Title 49:

§ 14(3)[now 10310] (Interstate Commerce Commission reports and decisions; printing and distribution of copies)

§ 16(13)[now 10303(b)] (Copies of schedules, tariffs, etc. filed with Interstate Commerce Commission as evidence)

§ 19a(i)[now 10785(c)] (Valuation of property of carriers by Interstate Commerce Commission; final published valuations as evidence)

Supplementary Note of Advisory Committee Regarding Rules 43 and 44.

For supplementary note of Advisory Committee on this rule, see note under Rule 43.

1966 Amendment

Note to Subdivision (a)(1). These provisions on proof of official records kept within the United States are similar in substance to those heretofore appearing in Rule 44. There is a more exact description of the geographical areas covered. An official record kept in one of the areas enumerated qualifies for proof under subdivision (a)(1) even though it is not a United States official record. For example, an official record kept in one of these areas by a government in exile falls within subdivision (a)(1). It also falls within subdivision (a)(2) which may be availed of alternatively. Cf. *Banco de Espana v. Federal Reserve Bank*, 114 F.2d 438 (2d Cir. 1940).

Note to Subdivision (a)(2). Foreign official records may be proved, as heretofore, by means of official publications thereof. See *United States v. Aluminum Co. of America*, 1 F.R.D. 71 (S.D.N.Y.1939). Under this rule, a document that, on its face, appears to be an official publication, is admissible, unless a party opposing its admission into evidence shows that it lacks that character.

The rest of subdivision (a)(2) aims to provide greater clarity, efficiency, and flexibility in the procedure for authenticating copies of foreign official records.

The reference to attestation by "the officer having the legal custody of the record," hitherto appearing in Rule 44, has been found inappropriate for official records kept in foreign countries where the assumed relation between custody and the authority to attest does not obtain. See 2B Barron & Holtzoff, Federal Practice & Procedure § 992 (Wright ed. 1961). Accordingly it is provided that an attested copy may be obtained from any person authorized by the law of the foreign country to make the attestation without regard to whether he is charged with responsibility for maintaining the record or keeping it in his custody.

Under Rule 44 a United States foreign service officer has been called on to certify to the authority of the foreign official attesting the copy as well as the genuineness of his signature and his official position. See Schlesinger, *Comparative Law 57* (2d ed. 1959); Smit. *International Aspects of Federal Civil Procedure*, 61 Colum.L.Rev. 1031, 1063 (1961); 22 C.F.R. § 92.41(a), (e) (1958). This has created practical difficulties. For example, the question of the authority of the foreign officer might raise issues of foreign law which were beyond the knowledge of the United States officer. The difficulties are met under the amended rule by eliminating the element of the authority of the attesting foreign official from the scope of the certifying process, and by specifically permitting use of the chain-certificate method. Under this method, it is sufficient if the original attestation purports to have been issued by an authorized person and is accompanied by a certificate of another foreign official whose certificate may in turn be followed by that of a foreign official of higher rank. The process continues until a foreign official is reached as to whom the United States foreign service official (or a diplomatic or consular officer of the foreign country assigned or accredited to the United States) has adequate information upon which to base a "final certification." See *New York Life Ins. Co. v. Aronson*, 38 F.Supp. 687 (W.D.Pa.1941); 22 C.F.R. § 92.37 (1958).

The final certification (a term used in contradistinction to the certificates prepared by the foreign officials in a chain) relates to the incumbency and genuineness of signature of the foreign official who attested the copy of the record or, where the chain-certificate method is used, of a foreign official whose certificate appears in the chain, whether that certificate is the last in the chain or not. A final certification may be prepared on the basis of material on file in the consulate or any other satisfactory information.

Although the amended rule will generally facilitate proof of foreign official records, it is recognized that in some situations it may be difficult or even impossible to satisfy the basic requirements of the rule. There may be no United States consul in a particular foreign country; the foreign officials may not cooperate, peculiarities may exist or arise hereafter in the law or practice of a foreign country. See *United States v. Grabina*, 119 F.2d 863 (2d Cir. 1941); and, generally, Jones, *International Judicial Assistance: Procedural Chaos and a Program for Reform*, 62 Yale L.J. 515, 548–49 (1953). Therefore the final sentence of subdivision (a)(2) provides the court with discretion to admit an attested copy of a record without a final certification, or an attested summary of a record with or without a final certification. See Rep. of Comm. on Comparative Civ.Proc. & Prac., Proc. A.B.A., Sec. Int'l & Comp.L. 123, 130–31 (1952); Model Code of Evidence §§ 517, 519 (1942). This relaxation should be permitted only when it is shown that the party has been unable to satisfy the basic requirements of the amended rule despite his reasonable efforts. Moreover it is specially provided that the parties must be given a reasonable opportunity in these cases to examine into the authenticity and accuracy of the copy or summary.

Note to Subdivision (b). This provision relating to proof of lack of record is accommodated to the changes made in subdivision (a).

Note to Subdivision (c). The amendment insures that international agreements of the United States are unaffected by the rule. Several consular conventions contain provisions for reception of copies or summaries of foreign official records. See, e.g., Consular Conv. with Italy, May 8, 1878, art. X, 20 Stat. 725, T.S. No. 178 (Dept. State 1878). See also 28 U.S.C. §§ 1740–42, 1745; *Fakouri v. Cadais*, 149 F.2d 321 (5th Cir.1945), cert. denied 326 U.S. 742 (1945); 5 *Moore's Federal Practice*, par. 44.05 (2d ed. 1951).

1987 Amendment

The amendments are technical. No substantive change is intended.

1991 Amendment

The amendment to paragraph (a)(1) strikes the references to specific territories, two of which are no longer subject to the jurisdiction of the United States, and adds a generic term to describe governments having a relationship with the United States such that their official records should be treated as domestic records.

The amendment to paragraph (a)(2) adds a sentence to dispense with the final certification by diplomatic officers when the United States and the foreign country where the record is located are parties to a treaty or convention that abolishes or displaces the requirement. In that event the treaty or convention is to be followed. This changes the former procedure for authenticating foreign official records only with respect to records from countries that are parties to the Hague Convention Abolishing the Requirement of Legalization for Foreign Public Documents. Moreover, it does not affect the former practice of attesting the records, but only changes the method of certifying the attestation.

The Hague Public Documents Convention provides that the requirement of a final certification is abolished and replaced with a model *apostille*, which is to be issued by officials of the country where the records are located. See Hague Public Documents Convention, Arts. 2–4. The *apostille* certifies the signature, official position, and seal of the attesting officer. The authority who issues the *apostille* must maintain a register or card index showing the serial number of the *apostille* and other relevant information recorded on it. A foreign court can then check the serial number and information on the *apostille* with the issuing authority in order to guard against the use of fraudulent *apostilles*. This system provides a reliable method for maintaining the integrity of the authentication process, and the *apostille* can be accorded greater weight than the normal authentication procedure because foreign officials are more likely to know the precise capacity under their law of the attesting officer than would an American official. See generally Comment, *The United States and the Hague Convention Abolishing the Requirement of Legalization for Foreign Public Documents*, 11 HARV. INT'L L.J. 476, 482, 488 (1970).

2007 Amendment

*[Effective December 1, 2007,
absent contrary Congressional action.]*

The language of Rule 44 has been amended as part of the general restyling of the Civil Rules to make them more easily understood and to make style and terminology consistent throughout the rules. These changes are intended to be stylistic only.

TREATIES AND CONVENTIONS

CONVENTION ABOLISHING THE REQUIREMENT OF LEGALISATION FOR FOREIGN PUBLIC DOCUMENTS

The States signatory to the present Convention,

Desiring to abolish the requirement of diplomatic or consular legalisation for foreign public documents,

Have resolved to conclude a Convention to this effect and have agreed upon the following provisions:

ARTICLE 1

The present Convention shall apply to public documents which have been executed in the territory of one contracting State and which have to be produced in the territory of another contracting State.

For the purposes of the present Convention, the following are deemed to be public documents:

(a) Documents emanating from an authority or an official connected with the courts or tribunals of the State, including those emanating from a public prosecutor, a clerk of a court or a process server ("huissier de justice");

(b) Administrative documents;

(c) Notarial acts;

(d) Official certificates which are placed on documents signed by persons in their private capacity, such as official certificates recording the registration of a document or the fact that it was in existence on a certain date and official and notarial authentications of signatures.

However, the present Convention shall not apply:

(a) To documents executed by diplomatic or consular agents;

(b) To administrative documents dealing directly with commercial or customs operations.

ARTICLE 2

Each contracting State shall exempt from legalisation documents to which the present Convention applies and which have to be produced in its territory. For the purposes of the present Convention, legalisation means only the formality by which the diplomatic or consular agents of the country in which the document has to be produced certify the authenticity of the signature, the capacity in which the person signing the document has acted and, where appropriate, the identity of the seal or stamp which it bears.

ARTICLE 3

The only formality that may be required in order to certify the authenticity of the signature, the capacity in which the person signing the document has acted and, where appropriate, the identity of the seal or stamp which it bears, is the addition of the certificate described in Article 4, issued by the competent authority of the State from which the document emanates.

However, the formality mentioned in the preceding paragraph cannot be required when either the laws, regulations, or practice in force in the State where the document is produced or an agreement between two or more contracting States have abolished or simplified it, or exempt the document itself from legalisation.

ARTICLE 4

The certificate referred to in the first paragraph of Article 3 shall be placed on the document itself or on an "allonge"; it shall be in the form of the model annexed to the present Convention.

It may, however, be drawn up in the official language of the authority which issues it. The standard terms appearing therein may be in a second language also. The title "Apostille (Convention de La Haye du 5 octobre 1961)" shall be in the French language.

ARTICLE 5

The certificate shall be issued at the request of the person who has signed the document or of any bearer.

When properly filled in, it will certify the authenticity of the signature, the capacity in which the person signing the document has acted and, where appropriate, the identity of the seal or stamp which the document bears.

The signature, seal and stamp on the certificate are exempt from all certification.

ARTICLE 6

Each contracting State shall designate by reference to their official function, the authorities who are competent to issue the certificate referred to in the first paragraph of Article 3.

It shall give notice of such designation to the Ministry of Foreign Affairs of the Netherlands at the time it deposits its instrument of ratification or of accession or its declaration of extension. It shall also give notice of any change in the designated authorities.

ARTICLE 7

Each of the authorities designated in accordance with Article 6 shall keep a register or card index in which it shall record the certificates issued, specifying:

(a) The number and date of the certificate,

(b) The name of the person signing the public document and the capacity in which he has acted, or in the case of unsigned documents, the name of the authority which has affixed the seal or stamp.

At the request of any interested person, the authority which has issued the certificate shall verify whether the particulars in the certificate correspond with those in the register or card index.

ARTICLE 8

When a treaty, convention or agreement between two or more contracting States contains provisions which subject the certification of a signature, seal or stamp to certain formalities, the present Convention will only override such provisions if those formalities are more rigorous than the formality referred to in Articles 3 and 4.

ARTICLE 9

Each contracting State shall take the necessary steps to prevent the performance of legalisations by its diplomatic or consular agents in cases where the present Convention provides for exemption.

ARTICLE 10

The present Convention shall be open for signature by the States represented at the Ninth session of the Hague Conference on Private International Law and Iceland, Ireland, Liechtenstein and Turkey.

It shall be ratified, and the instruments of ratification shall be deposited with the Ministry of Foreign Affairs of the Netherlands.

ARTICLE 11

The present Convention shall enter into force on the sixtieth day after the deposit of the third instrument of ratification referred to in the second paragraph of Article 10.

The Convention shall enter into force for each signatory State which ratifies subsequently on the sixtieth day after the deposit of its instrument of ratification.

ARTICLE 12

Any State not referred to in Article 10 may accede to the present Convention after it has entered into force in accordance with the first paragraph of Article 11. The instrument of accession shall be deposited with the Ministry of Foreign Affairs of the Netherlands.

Such accession shall have effect only as regards the relations between the acceding State and those contracting States which have not raised an objection to its accession in the six months after the receipt of the notification referred to in sub-paragraph (d) of Article 15. Any such objection shall be notified to the Ministry of Foreign Affairs of the Netherlands.

The Convention shall enter into force as between the acceding State and the States which have raised no objection

to its accession on the sixtieth day after the expiry of the period of six months mentioned in the preceding paragraph.

ARTICLE 13

Any State may, at the time of signature, ratification or accession, declare that the present Convention shall extend to all the territories for the international relations of which it is responsible, or to one or more of them. Such a declaration shall take effect on the date of entry into force of the Convention for the State concerned.

At any time thereafter, such extension shall be notified to the Ministry of Foreign Affairs of the Netherlands.

When the declaration of extension is made by a State which has signed and ratified, the Convention shall enter into force for the territories concerned in accordance with Article 11. When the declaration of extension is made by a State which has acceded, the Convention shall enter into force for the territories concerned in accordance with Article 12.

ARTICLE 14

The present Convention shall remain in force for five years from the date of its entry into force in accordance with the first paragraph of Article 11, even for States which have ratified it or acceded to it subsequently.

If there has been no denunciation, the Convention shall be renewed tacitly every five years.

Any denunciation shall be notified to the Ministry of Foreign Affairs of the Netherlands at least six months before the end of the five year period.

It may be limited to certain of the territories to which the Convention applies.

The denunciation will only have effect as regards the State which has notified it. The Convention shall remain in force for the other contracting States.

ARTICLE 15

The Ministry of Foreign Affairs of the Netherlands shall give notice to the States referred to in Article 10, and to the States which have acceded in accordance with Article 12, of the following:

(a) The notifications referred to in the second paragraph of Article 6;

(b) The signatures and ratifications referred to in Article 10;

(c) The date on which the present Convention enters into force in accordance with the first paragraph of Article 11;

(d) The accessions and objections referred to in Article 12 and the date on which such accessions take effect;

(e) The extensions referred to in Article 13 and the date on which they take effect;

(f) The denunciations referred to in the third paragraph of Article 14.

In witness whereof the undersigned, being duly authorised thereto, have signed the present Convention.

Done at The Hague the 5th October 1961, in French and in English, the French text prevailing in case of divergence between the two texts, in a single copy which shall be deposited in the archives of the Government of the Netherlands, and of which a certified copy shall be sent, through the diplomatic channel, to each of the States represented at the Ninth session of the Hague Conference on Private International Law and also to Iceland, Ireland, Liechtenstein and Turkey.

[Signatures omitted.]

ANNEX TO THE CONVENTION
Model of certificate

The certificate will be in the form of a square with sides at least 9 centimetres long

APOSTILLE
(Convention de La Haye du 5 octobre 1961)

1. Country:
This public document
2. has been signed by .
3. acting in the capacity of .
4. bears the seal/stamp of .

Certified
5. at 6. the
7. by .
8. N°
9. Seal/stamp: 10. Signature:
. .

Convention abolishing the requirement of legalization for foreign public documents, with annex. Done at The Hague October 5, 1961; entered into force for the United States October 15, 1981. (TIAS 10072; 527 UNTS 189).

Rule 44.1. Determination of Foreign Law

A party who intends to raise an issue concerning the law of a foreign country shall give notice by pleadings or other reasonable written notice. The court, in determining foreign law, may consider any relevant material or source, including testimony, whether or not submitted by a party or admissible under the Federal Rules of Evidence. The court's determination shall be treated as a ruling on a question of law.

(Added Feb. 28, 1966, eff. July 1, 1966, and amended Nov. 20, 1972, eff. July 1, 1975; Mar. 2, 1987, eff. Aug. 1, 1987.)

Proposed Amendment of Rule

Effective December 1, 2007, absent contrary Congressional action, this rule is amended to read as follows:

Rule 44.1. *Determining Foreign Law*

A party who intends to raise an issue about a foreign country's law must give notice by a pleading or other writing. In determining foreign law, the court may consider any relevant material or source, including testimony, whether or not submitted by a party or admissible under the Federal Rules of Evi-

dence. The court's determination must be treated as a ruling on a question of law.

ADVISORY COMMITTEE NOTES

1966 Adoption

Rule 44.1 is added by amendment to furnish Federal courts with a uniform and effective procedure for raising and determining an issue concerning the law of a foreign country.

To avoid unfair surprise, the *first sentence* of the new rule requires that a party who intends to raise an issue of foreign law shall give notice thereof. The uncertainty under Rule 8(a) about whether foreign law must be pleaded—compare *Siegelman v. Cunard White Star, Ltd.*, 221 F.2d 189 (2d Cir.1955), and *Pedersen v. United States*, 191 F.Supp. 95 (D. Guam 1961), with *Harrison v. United Fruit Co.*, 143 F.Supp. 598 (S.D.N.Y.1956)—is eliminated by the provision that the notice shall be "written" and "reasonable." It may, but need not be, incorporated in the pleadings. In some situations the pertinence of foreign law is apparent from the outset; accordingly the necessary investigation of that law will have been accomplished by the party at the pleading stage, and the notice can be given conveniently in the pleadings. In other situations the pertinence of foreign law may remain doubtful until the case is further developed. A requirement that notice of foreign law be given only through the medium of the pleadings would tend in the latter instances to force the party to engage in a peculiarly burdensome type of investigation which might turn out to be unnecessary; and correspondingly the adversary would be forced into a possible wasteful investigation. The liberal provisions for amendment of the pleadings afford help if the pleadings are used as the medium of giving notice of the foreign law; but it seems best to permit a written notice to be given outside of and later than the pleadings, provided the notice is reasonable.

The new rule does not attempt to set any definite limit on the party's time for giving the notice of an issue of foreign law; in some cases the issue may not become apparent until the trial and notice then given may still be reasonable. The stage which the case had reached at the time of the notice, the reason proffered by the party for his failure to give earlier notice, and the importance to the case as a whole of the issue of foreign law sought to be raised, are among the factors which the court should consider in deciding a question of the reasonableness of a notice. If notice is given by one party it need not be repeated by any other and serves as a basis for presentation of material on the foreign law by all parties.

The *second sentence* of the new rule describes the materials to which the court may resort in determining an issue of foreign law. Heretofore the district courts, applying Rule 43(a), have looked in certain cases to State law to find the rules of evidence by which the content of foreign-country law is to be established. The State laws vary; some embody procedures which are inefficient, time consuming and expensive. See, generally, Nussbaum, *Proving the Law of Foreign Countries*, 3 Am. J. Comp. L. 60 (1954). In all events the ordinary rules of evidence are often inapposite to the problem of determining foreign law and have in the past prevented examination of material which could have provided a proper basis for the determination. The new rule permits consideration by the court of any relevant material, including testimony, without regard to its admissibility under Rule 43.

Cf. N.Y. Civ. Prac. Law & Rules, R. 4511 (effective Sept. 1, 1963); 2 Va. Code Ann. tit. 8, § 8–273; 2 W. Va. Code Ann. § 5711.

In further recognition of the peculiar nature of the issue of foreign law, the new rule provides that in determining this law the court is not limited by material presented by the parties; it may engage in its own research and consider any relevant material thus found. The court may at its disposal better foreign law materials than counsel have presented, or may wish to reexamine and amplify material that has been presented by counsel in partisan fashion or in insufficient detail. On the other hand, the court is free to insist on a complete presentation by counsel.

There is no requirement that the court give formal notice to the parties of its intention to engage in its own research on an issue of foreign law which has been raised by them, or of its intention to raise and determine independently an issue not raised by them. Ordinarily the court should inform the parties of material it has found diverging substantially from the material which they have presented; and in general the court should give the parties an opportunity to analyze and counter new points upon which it proposes to rely. See Schlesinger, *Comparative Law* 142 (2d ed. 1959); Wyzanski, *A Trial Judge's Freedom and Responsibility*, 65 Harv. L.Rev. 1281, 1296 (1952); cf. *Siegelman v. Cunard White Star, Ltd.*, supra, 221 F.2d at 197. To require, however, that the court give formal notice from time to time as it proceeds with its study of the foreign law would add an element of undesirable rigidity to the procedure for determining issues of foreign law.

The new rule refrains from imposing an obligation on the court to take "judicial notice" of foreign law because this would put an extreme burden on the court in many cases; and it avoids use of the concept of "judicial notice" in any form because of the uncertain meaning of that concept as applied to foreign law. See, e.g., Stern, *Foreign Law in the Courts: Judicial Notice and Proof*, 45 Calif.L.Rev. 23, 43 (1957). Rather the rule provides flexible procedures for presenting and utilizing material on issues of foreign law by which a sound result can be achieved with fairness to the parties.

Under the *third sentence*, the court's determination of an issue of foreign law is to be treated as a ruling on a question of "law," not "fact," so that appellate review will not be narrowly confined by the "clearly erroneous" standard of Rule 52(a). Cf. *Uniform Judicial Notice of Foreign Law Act* § 3; Note, 72 Harv.L.Rev. 318 (1958).

The new rule parallels Article IV of the Uniform Interstate and International Procedure Act, approved by the Commissioners on Uniform State Laws in 1962, except that § 4.03 of Article IV states that "[t]he court, not the jury" shall determine foreign law. The new rule does not address itself to this problem, since the Rules refrain from allocating functions as between the court and the jury. See Rule 38(a). It has long been thought, however, that the jury is not the appropriate body to determine issues of foreign law. See, e.g., Story, *Conflict of Laws*, § 638 (1st ed. 1834, 8th ed. 1883); 1 Greenleaf, *Evidence*, § 486 (1st ed. 1842, 16th ed. 1899); 4 Wigmore, *Evidence* § 2558 (1st ed. 1905); 9 id. § 2558 (3d ed. 1940). The majority of the States have committed such issues to determination by the court. See Article 5 of the Uniform Judicial Notice of Foreign Law Act, adopted by twenty-six states, 9A U.L.A. 318 (1957)

(Suppl.1961, at 134); N.Y.Civ.Prac.Law & Rules, R. 4511 (effective Sept. 1, 1963); Wigmore, loc. cit. And Federal courts that have considered the problem in recent years have reached the same conclusion without reliance on statute. See *Jansson v. Swedish American Line*, 185 F.2d 212, 216 (1st Cir.1950); *Bank of Nova Scotia v. San Miguel*, 196 F.2d 950, 957, n. 6 (1st Cir.1952); *Liechti v. Roche*, 198 F.2d 174 (5th Cir.1952); *Daniel Lumber Co. v. Empresas Hondurenas, S.A.*, 215 F.2d 465 (5th Cir.1954).

1972 Amendment

Since the purpose of the provision is to free the judge, in determining foreign law, from any restrictions imposed by evidence rules, a general reference to the Rules of Evidence is appropriate and is made.

1987 Amendment

The amendment is technical. No substantive change is intended.

2007 Amendment

[Effective December 1, 2007, absent contrary Congressional action.]

The language of Rule 44.1 has been amended as part of the general restyling of the Civil Rules to make them more easily understood and to make style and terminology consistent throughout the rules. These changes are intended to be stylistic only.

HISTORICAL NOTES

References in Text

The Federal Rules of Evidence, referred to in text, are set out in this title.

Effective Date of Amendment Proposed November 20, 1972

Amendment of this rule embraced by the order entered by the Supreme Court of the United States on November 20, 1972, effective on the 180th day beginning after January 2, 1975, see section 3 of Pub.L. 93–595, Jan. 2, 1975, 88 Stat. 1959, set out as a note under section 2071 of Title 28.

Rule 45. Subpoena

(a) Form; Issuance.

(1) Every subpoena shall

(A) state the name of the court from which it is issued; and

(B) state the title of the action, the name of the court in which it is pending, and its civil action number; and

(C) command each person to whom it is directed to attend and give testimony or to produce and permit inspection, copying, testing, or sampling of designated books, documents, electronically stored information, or tangible things in the possession, custody or control of that person, or to permit inspection of premises, at a time and place therein specified; and

(D) set forth the text of subdivisions (c) and (d) of this rule.

A command to produce evidence or to permit inspection, copying, testing, or sampling may be joined with a command to appear at trial or hearing or at deposition, or may be issued separately. A subpoena may specify the form or forms in which electronically stored information is to be produced.

(2) A subpoena must issue as follows:

(A) for attendance at a trial or hearing, from the court for the district where the trial or hearing is to be held;

(B) for attendance at a deposition, from the court for the district where the deposition is to be taken, stating the method for recording the testimony; and

(C) for production, inspection, copying, testing, or sampling, if separate from a subpoena commanding a person's attendance, from the court for the district where the production or inspection is to be made.

(3) The clerk shall issue a subpoena, signed but otherwise in blank, to a party requesting it, who shall complete it before service. An attorney as officer of the court may also issue and sign a subpoena on behalf of

(A) a court in which the attorney is authorized to practice; or

(B) a court for a district in which a deposition or production is compelled by the subpoena, if the deposition or production pertains to an action pending in a court in which the attorney is authorized to practice.

(b) Service.

(1) A subpoena may be served by any person who is not a party and is not less than 18 years of age. Service of a subpoena upon a person named therein shall be made by delivering a copy thereof to such person and, if the person's attendance is commanded, by tendering to that person the fees for one day's attendance and the mileage allowed by law. When the subpoena is issued on behalf of the United States or an officer or agency thereof, fees and mileage need not be tendered. Prior notice of any commanded production of documents and things or inspection of premises before trial shall be served on each party in the manner prescribed by Rule 5(b).

(2) Subject to the provisions of clause (ii) of subparagraph (c)(3)(A) of this rule, a subpoena may be served at any place within the district of the court by which it is issued, or at any place without the district that is within 100 miles of the place of the deposition, hearing, trial, production, inspection, copying, testing, or sampling specified in the subpoena or at any place within the state where a state

statute or rule of court permits service of a subpoena issued by a state court of general jurisdiction sitting in the place of the deposition, hearing, trial, production, inspection, copying, testing, or sampling specified in the subpoena. When a statute of the United States provides therefor, the court upon proper application and cause shown may authorize the service of a subpoena at any other place. A subpoena directed to a witness in a foreign country who is a national or resident of the United States shall issue under the circumstances and in the manner and be served as provided in Title 28, U. S.C. § 1783.

(3) Proof of service when necessary shall be made by filing with the clerk of the court by which the subpoena is issued a statement of the date and manner of service and of the names of the persons served, certified by the person who made the service.

(c) Protection of Persons Subject to Subpoenas.

(1) A party or an attorney responsible for the issuance and service of a subpoena shall take reasonable steps to avoid imposing undue burden or expense on a person subject to that subpoena. The court on behalf of which the subpoena was issued shall enforce this duty and impose upon the party or attorney in breach of this duty an appropriate sanction, which may include, but is not limited to, lost earnings and a reasonable attorney's fee.

(2)(A) A person commanded to produce and permit inspection, copying, testing, or sampling of designated electronically stored information, books, papers, documents or tangible things, or inspection of premises need not appear in person at the place of production or inspection unless commanded to appear for deposition, hearing or trial.

(B) Subject to paragraph (d)(2) of this rule, a person commanded to produce and permit inspection, copying, testing, or sampling may, within 14 days after service of the subpoena or before the time specified for compliance if such time is less than 14 days after service, serve upon the party or attorney designated in the subpoena written objection to producing any or all of the designated materials or inspection of the premises — or to producing electronically stored information in the form or forms requested. If objection is made, the party serving the subpoena shall not be entitled to inspect, copy, test, or sample the materials or inspect the premises except pursuant to an order of the court by which the subpoena was issued. If objection has been made, the party serving the subpoena may, upon notice to the person commanded to produce, move at any time for an order to compel the production, inspection, copying, testing, or sampling. Such an order to compel shall protect any person who is not a party or an officer of a party from significant expense resulting from the inspection, copying, testing, or sampling commanded.

(3)(A) On timely motion, the court by which a subpoena was issued shall quash or modify the subpoena if it

(i) fails to allow reasonable time for compliance;

(ii) requires a person who is not a party or an officer of a party to travel to a place more than 100 miles from the place where that person resides, is employed or regularly transacts business in person, except that, subject to the provisions of clause (c)(3)(B)(iii) of this rule, such a person may in order to attend trial be commanded to travel from any such place within the state in which the trial is held;

(iii) requires disclosure of privileged or other protected matter and no exception or waiver applies; or

(iv) subjects a person to undue burden.

(B) If a subpoena

(i) requires disclosure of a trade secret or other confidential research, development, or commercial information, or

(ii) requires disclosure of an unretained expert's opinion or information not describing specific events or occurrences in dispute and resulting from the expert's study made not at the request of any party, or

(iii) requires a person who is not a party or an officer of a party to incur substantial expense to travel more than 100 miles to attend trial, the court may, to protect a person subject to or affected by the subpoena, quash or modify the subpoena or, if the party in whose behalf the subpoena is issued shows a substantial need for the testimony or material that cannot be otherwise met without undue hardship and assures that the person to whom the subpoena is addressed will be reasonably compensated, the court may order appearance or production only upon specified conditions.

(d) Duties in Responding to Subpoena.

(1)(A) A person responding to a subpoena to produce documents shall produce them as they are kept in the usual course of business or shall organize and label them to correspond with the categories in the demand.

(B) If a subpoena does not specify the form or forms for producing electronically stored information, a person responding to a subpoena must produce the information in a form or forms in which the person ordinarily maintains it or in a form or forms that are reasonably usable.

(C) A person responding to a subpoena need not produce the same electronically stored information in more than one form.

(D) A person responding to a subpoena need not provide discovery of electronically stored information from sources that the person identifies as not reasonably accessible because of undue burden or cost. On motion to compel discovery or to quash, the person from whom discovery is sought must show that the information sought is not reasonably accessible because of undue burden or cost. If that showing is made, the court may nonetheless order discovery from such sources if the requesting party shows good cause, considering the limitations of Rule 26(b)(2)(C). The court may specify conditions for the discovery.

(2)(A) When information subject to a subpoena is withheld on a claim that it is privileged or subject to protection as trial-preparation materials, the claim shall be made expressly and shall be supported by a description of the nature of the documents, communications, or things not produced that is sufficient to enable the demanding party to contest the claim.

(B) If information is produced in response to a subpoena that is subject to a claim of privilege or of protection as trial-preparation material, the person making the claim may notify any party that received the information of the claim and the basis for it. After being notified, a party must promptly return, sequester, or destroy the specified information and any copies it has and may not use or disclose the information until the claim is resolved. A receiving party may promptly present the information to the court under seal for a determination of the claim. If the receiving party disclosed the information before being notified, it must take reasonable steps to retrieve it. The person who produced the information must preserve the information until the claim is resolved.

(e) Contempt. Failure of any person without adequate excuse to obey a subpoena served upon that person may be deemed a contempt of the court from which the subpoena issued. An adequate cause for failure to obey exists when a subpoena purports to require a nonparty to attend or produce at a place not within the limits provided by clause (ii) of subparagraph (c)(3)(A).

(As amended Dec. 27, 1946, eff. Mar. 19, 1948; Dec. 29, 1948, eff. Oct. 20, 1949; Mar. 30, 1970, eff. July 1, 1970; Apr. 29, 1980, eff. Aug. 1, 1980; Apr. 29, 1985, eff. Aug. 1, 1985; Mar. 2, 1987, eff. Aug. 1, 1987; Apr. 30, 1991, eff. Dec. 1, 1991; Apr. 25, 2005, eff. Dec. 1, 2005; Apr. 12, 2006, eff. Dec. 1, 2006.)

Proposed Amendment of Rule

Effective December 1, 2007, absent contrary Congressional action, this rule is amended to read as follows:

Rule 45. Subpoena

(a) In General.

(1) Form and Contents.

(A) Requirements—In General. Every subpoena must:

(i) state the court from which it issued;

(ii) state the title of the action, the court in which it is pending, and its civil-action number;

(iii) command each person to whom it is directed to do the following at a specified time and place: attend and testify; produce designated documents, electronically stored information, or tangible things in that person's possession, custody, or control; or permit the inspection of premises; and

(iv) set out the text of Rule 45(c) and (d).

(B) Command to Attend a Deposition—Notice of the Recording Method. A subpoena commanding attendance at a deposition must state the method for recording the testimony.

(C) Combining or Separating a Command to Produce or to Permit Inspection; Specifying the Form for Electronically Stored Information. A command to produce documents, electronically stored information, or tangible things or to permit the inspection of premises may be included in a subpoena commanding attendance at a deposition, hearing, or trial, or may be set out in a separate subpoena. A subpoena may specify the form or forms in which electronically stored information is to be produced.

(D) Command to Produce; Included Obligations. A command in a subpoena to produce documents, electronically stored information, or tangible things requires the responding party to permit inspection, copying, testing, or sampling of the materials.

(2) Issued from Which Court. A subpoena must issue as follows:

(A) for attendance at a hearing or trial, from the court for the district where the hearing or trial is to be held;

(B) for attendance at a deposition, from the court for the district where the deposition is to be taken; and

(C) for production or inspection, if separate from a subpoena commanding a person's at-

tendance, from the court for the district where the production or inspection is to be made.

(3) Issued by Whom. The clerk must issue a subpoena, signed but otherwise in blank, to a party who requests it. That party must complete it before service. An attorney also may issue and sign a subpoena as an officer of:

(A) a court in which the attorney is authorized to practice; or

(B) a court for a district where a deposition is to be taken or production is to be made, if the attorney is authorized to practice in the court where the action is pending.

(b) Service.

(1) By Whom; Tendering Fees; Serving a Copy of Certain Subpoenas. Any person who is at least 18 years old and not a party may serve a subpoena. Serving a subpoena requires delivering a copy to the named person and, if the subpoena requires that person's attendance, tendering the fees for 1 day's attendance and the mileage allowed by law. Fees and mileage need not be tendered when the subpoena issues on behalf of the United States or any of its officers or agencies. If the subpoena commands the production of documents, electronically stored information, or tangible things or the inspection of premises before trial, then before it is served, a notice must be served on each party.

(2) Service in the United States. Subject to Rule 45(c)(3)(A)(ii), a subpoena may be served at any place:

(A) within the district of the issuing court;

(B) outside that district but within 100 miles of the place specified for the deposition, hearing, trial, production, or inspection;

(C) within the state of the issuing court if a state statute or court rule allows service at that place of a subpoena issued by a state court of general jurisdiction sitting in the place specified for the deposition, hearing, trial, production, or inspection; or

(D) that the court authorizes on motion and for good cause, if a federal statute so provides.

(3) Service in a Foreign Country. 28 U.S.C. § 1783 governs issuing and serving a subpoena directed to a United States national or resident who is in a foreign country.

(4) Proof of Service. Proving service, when necessary, requires filing with the issuing court a statement showing the date and manner of service and the names of the persons served. The statement must be certified by the server.

(c) Protecting a Person Subject to a Subpoena.

(1) Avoiding Undue Burden or Expense; Sanctions. A party or attorney responsible for issuing and serving a subpoena must take reasonable steps to avoid imposing undue burden or expense on a person subject to the subpoena. The issuing court must enforce this duty and impose an appropriate sanction—which may include lost earnings and reasonable attorney's fees—on a party or attorney who fails to comply.

(2) Command to Produce Materials or Permit Inspection.

(A) *Appearance Not Required.* A person commanded to produce documents, electronically stored information, or tangible things, or to permit the inspection of premises, need not appear in person at the place of production or inspection unless also commanded to appear for a deposition, hearing, or trial.

(B) *Objections.* A person commanded to produce documents or tangible things or to permit inspection may serve on the party or attorney designated in the subpoena a written objection to inspecting, copying, testing or sampling any or all of the materials or to inspecting the premises—or to producing electronically stored information in the form or forms requested. The objection must be served before the earlier of the time specified for compliance or 14 days after the subpoena is served. If an objection is made, the following rules apply:

(i) At any time, on notice to the commanded person, the serving party may move the issuing court for an order compelling production or inspection.

(ii) These acts may be required only as directed in the order, and the order must protect a person who is neither a party nor a party's officer from significant expense resulting from compliance.

(3) Quashing or Modifying a Subpoena.

(A) *When Required.* On timely motion, the issuing court must quash or modify a subpoena that:

(i) fails to allow a reasonable time to comply;

(ii) requires a person who is neither a party nor a party's officer to travel more than 100 miles from where that person resides, is employed, or regularly transacts business in person—except that, subject to Rule 45(c)(3)(B)(iii), the person may be commanded to attend a trial by traveling from

any such place within the state where the trial is held;

(iii) requires disclosure of privileged or other protected matter, if no exception or waiver applies; or

(iv) subjects a person to undue burden.

(B) When Permitted. To protect a person subject to or affected by a subpoena, the issuing court may, on motion, quash or modify the subpoena if it requires:

(i) disclosing a trade secret or other confidential research, development, or commercial information;

(ii) disclosing an unretained expert's opinion or information that does not describe specific occurrences in dispute and results from the expert's study that was not requested by a party; or

(iii) a person who is neither a party nor a party's officer to incur substantial expense to travel more than 100 miles to attend trial.

(C) Specifying Conditions as an Alternative. In the circumstances described in Rule 45(c)(3)(B), the court may, instead of quashing or modifying a subpoena, order appearance or production under specified conditions if the serving party:

(i) shows a substantial need for the testimony or material that cannot be otherwise met without undue hardship; and

(ii) ensures that the subpoenaed person will be reasonably compensated.

(d) Duties in Responding to a Subpoena.

(1) Producing Documents or Electronically Stored Information. These procedures apply to producing documents or electronically stored information:

(A) Documents. A person responding to a subpoena to produce documents must produce them as they are kept in the ordinary course of business or must organize and label them to correspond to the categories in the demand.

(B) Form for Producing Electronically Stored Information Not Specified. If a subpoena does not specify a form for producing electronically stored information, the person responding must produce it in a form or forms in which it is ordinarily maintained or in a reasonably usable form or forms.

(C) Electronically Stored Information Produced in Only One Form. The person respond-

ing need not produce the same electronically stored information in more than one form.

(D) Inaccessible Electronically Stored Information. The person responding need not provide discovery of electronically stored information from sources that the person identifies as not reasonably accessible because of undue burden or cost. On motion to compel discovery or for a protective order, the person responding must show that the information is not reasonably accessible because of undue burden or cost. If that showing is made, the court may nonetheless order discovery from such sources if the requesting party shows good cause, considering the limitations of Rule 26(b)(2)(C). The court may specify conditions for the discovery.

(2) Claiming Privilege or Protection.

(A) Information Withheld. A person withholding subpoenaed information under a claim that it is privileged or subject to protection as trial-preparation material must:

(i) expressly make the claim; and

(ii) describe the nature of the withheld documents, communications, or tangible things in a manner that, without revealing information itself privileged or protected, will enable the parties to assess the claim.

(B) Information Produced. If information produced in response to a subpoena is subject to a claim of privilege or of protection as trial-preparation material, the person making the claim may notify any party that received the information of the claim and the basis for it. After being notified, a party must promptly return, sequester, or destroy the specified information and any copies it has; must not use or disclose the information until the claim is resolved; must take reasonable steps to retrieve the information if the party disclosed it before being notified; and may promptly present the information to the court under seal for a determination of the claim. The person who produced the information must preserve the information until the claim is resolved.

(e) Contempt. The issuing court may hold in contempt a person who, having been served, fails without adequate excuse to obey the subpoena. A nonparty's failure to obey must be excused if the subpoena purports to require the nonparty to attend or produce at a place outside the limits of Rule 45(c)(3)(A)(ii).

ADVISORY COMMITTEE NOTES
1937 Adoption

This rule applies to subpoenas ad testificandum and duces tecum issued by the district courts for attendance at a

hearing or a trial, or to take depositions. It does not apply to the enforcement of subpoenas issued by administrative officers and commissions pursuant to statutory authority. The enforcement of such subpoenas by the district courts is regulated by appropriate statutes. Many of these statutes do not place any territorial limits on the validity of subpoenas so issued, but provide that they may be served anywhere within the United States. Among such statutes are the following:

U.S.C., Title 7, §§ 222 and 511n (Secretary of Agriculture)

U.S.C., Title 15, § 49 (Federal Trade Commission)

U.S.C., Title 15, §§ 77v(b), 78u(c), 79r(d) (Securities and Exchange Commission)

U.S.C., Title 16, §§ 797(g) and 825f (Federal Power Commission)

U.S.C., Title 19, § 1333(b) (Tariff Commission)

U.S.C., Title 22, §§ 268, 270d and 270e (International Commissions, etc.)

U.S.C., Title 26, §§ 614, 619(b) [see 7456] (Board of Tax Appeals)

U.S.C., Title 26, § 1523(a) [see 7608] (Internal Revenue Officers)

U.S.C., Title 29, § 161 (Labor Relations Board)

U.S.C., Title 33, § 506 (Secretary of Army)

U.S.C., Title 35, §§ 54 to 56 [now 24] (Patent Office proceedings)

U.S.C., Title 38, [former] § 133 (Veterans' Administration)

U.S.C., Title 41, § 39 (Secretary of Labor)

U.S.C., Title 45, § 157 Third. (h) (Board of Arbitration under Railway Labor Act)

U.S.C., Title 45, § 222(b) (Investigation Commission under Railroad Retirement Act of 1935)

U.S.C., Title 46, § 1124(b) (Maritime Commission)

U.S.C., Title 47, § 409(c) and (d) (Federal Communications Commission)

U.S.C., Title 49, § 12(2) and (3) [now 10321] (Interstate Commerce Commission)

U.S.C., Title 49, § 173a [see 1484] (Secretary of Commerce)

Note to Subdivisions (a) and (b). These simplify the form of subpoena as provided in U.S.C., Title 28, [former] § 655 (Witnesses; subpoena; form; attendance under); and broaden U.S.C, Title 28, [former] § 636 (Production for books and writings) to include all actions, and to extend to any person. With the provision for relief from an oppressive or unreasonable subpoena duces tecum, compare N.Y.C.P.A. (1937) § 411.

Note to Subdivision (c). This provides for the simple and convenient method of service permitted under many state codes; e.g., N.Y.C.P.A. (1937) §§ 220, 404, J.Ct.Act, § 191; 3 Wash.Rev.Stat.Ann. (Remington, 1932) § 1218. Compare former Equity Rule 15 (Process, by Whom Served).

For statutes governing fees and mileage of witnesses see:

U.S.C., Title 28 former sections:

600a[now 1871] (Per diem; mileage)

600c[now 1821, 1823] (Amount per diem and mileage for witnesses; subsistence)

600d[former] (Fees and mileage in certain states)

601[former] (Witnesses' fees; enumeration)

602[now 1824] (Fees and mileage of jurors and witnesses)

603[see Title 5, §§ 5515, 5537] (No officer of court to have witness fees)

Note to Subdivision (d). The method provided in paragraph (1) for the authorization of the issuance of subpoenas has been employed in some districts. See *Henning v. Boyle*, S.D.N.Y.1901, 112 F. 397. The requirement of an order for the issuance of a subpoena duces tecum is in accordance with U.S.C., Title 28, [former] § 647 (Deposition under dedimus potestatem; subpoena duces tecum). The provisions of paragraph (2) are in accordance with common practice. See U.S.C., Title 28, former § 648 (Deposition under dedimus potestatem; witnesses, when required to attend); N.Y.C.P.A. (1937) § 300; 1 N.J.Rev.Stat. (1937) 2:27–174.

Note to Subdivision (e). The first paragraph continues the substance of U.S.C., Title 28, [former] § 654 (Witnesses; subpoenas; may run into another district). Compare U.S.C., Title 11, [former] § 69 (Referees in bankruptcy; contempts before) (production of books and writings) which is not affected by this rule. For examples of statutes which allow the court, upon proper application and cause shown, to authorize the clerk of the court to issue a subpoena for a witness who lives in another district and at a greater distance than 100 miles from the place of the hearing or trial, see:

U.S.C., Title 15:

§ 23 (Suits by United States; subpoenas for witnesses) (under antitrust laws).

U.S.C., Title 38:

§ 445[now 784] (Actions on claims; jurisdiction; parties; procedure; limitation; witnesses; definitions) (Veterans' insurance contracts).

The second paragraph continues the present procedure applicable to certain witnesses who are in foreign countries. See U.S.C., Title 28, §§ 711 [now 1783] (Letters rogatory to take testimony of witness, addressed to court of foreign country; failure of witness to appear; subpoena) and 713 [now 1783] (Service of Subpoena on witness in foreign country).

Note to Subdivision (f). Compare [former] Equity Rule 52 (Attendance of Witnesses Before Commissioner, Master, or Examiner).

1946 Amendment

Note to Subdivision (b). The added words, "or tangible things" in subdivision (b) merely make the rule for the subpoena duces tecum at the trial conform to that of subdivision (d) for the subpoena at the taking of depositions. The insertion of the words "or modify" in clause (1) affords desirable flexibility.

Subdivision (d). The added last sentence of amended subdivision (d)(1) properly gives the subpoena for documents or tangible things the same scope as provided in Rule 26(b), thus promoting uniformity. The requirement in the last sentence of original Rule 45(d)(1)—to the effect that leave of court should be obtained for the issuance of such a subpoena—has been omitted. This requirement is unnecessary and oppressive on both counsel and court, and it had been criticized by district judges. There is no satisfactory reason

for a differentiation between a subpoena for the production of documentary evidence by a witness at a trial (Rule 45(a)) and for the production of the same evidence at the taking of a deposition. Under this amendment, the person subpoenaed may obtain the protection afforded by any of the orders permitted under Rule 30(b) or Rule 45(b). See *Application of Zenith Radio Corp.*, E.D.Pa.1941, 4 F.Rules Serv. 30b.21. Case 1, 1 F.R.D. 627; *Fox v. House*, Okla.1939, 29 F.Supp. 673; *United States of America for the Use of Tilo Roofing Co., Inc. v. J. Slotnik Co.*, Conn.1944, 3 F.R.D. 408.

The changes in subdivisions (d)(2) give the court the same power in the case of residents of the district as is conferred in the case of non-residents, and permit the court to fix a place for attendance which may be more convenient and accessible for the parties than that specified in the rule.

1948 Amendment

The amendment effective October 1949, substituted the reference to "Title 28, U.S.C., § 1783" at the end of subdivision (e)(2) for the reference to "the Act of July 3, 1926, c. 762, §§ 1, 3 (44 Stat. 835), U.S.C., Title 28, § 713."

1970 Amendment

At present, when a subpoena duces tecum is issued to a deponent, he is required to produce the listed materials at the deposition, but is under no clear compulsion to permit their inspection and copying. This results in confusion and uncertainty before the time the deposition is taken, with no mechanism provided whereby the court can resolve the matter. Rule 45(d)(1), as revised, makes clear that the subpoena authorizes inspection and copying of the materials produced. The deponent is afforded full protection since he can object, thereby forcing the party serving the subpoena to obtain a court order if he wishes to inspect and copy. The procedure is thus analogous to that provided in Rule 34.

The changed references to other rules conform to changes made in those rules. The deletion of words in the clause describing the proper scope of the subpoena conforms to a change made in the language of Rule 34. The reference to Rule 26(b) is unchanged but encompasses new matter in that subdivision. The changes make it clear that the scope of discovery through a subpoena is the same as that applicable to Rule 34 and the other discovery rules.

1980 Amendment

Subdivision (d)(1). The amendment defines the term "proof of service" as used in the first sentence of the present subdivision. For want of a definition, the district court clerks have been obliged to fashion their own, with results that vary from district to district. All that seems required is a simple certification on a copy of the notice to take a deposition that the notice has been served on every other party to the action. That is the proof of service required by Rule 25(d) of both the Federal Rules of Appellate Procedure and the Supreme Court Rules.

Subdivision (e)(1). The amendment makes the reach of a subpoena of a district court at least as extensive as that of the state courts of general jurisdiction in the state in which the district court is held. Under the present rule the reach of a district court subpoena is often greater, since it extends throughout the district. No reason appears why it should be less, as it sometimes is because of the accident of district

lines. Restrictions upon the reach of subpoenas are imposed to prevent undue inconvenience to witnesses. State statutes and rules of court are quite likely to reflect the varying degrees of difficulty and expense attendant upon local travel.

1985 Amendment

Present Rule 45(d)(2) has two sentences setting forth the territorial scope of deposition subpoenas. The first sentence is directed to depositions taken in the judicial district in which the deponent resides; the second sentence addresses situations in which the deponent is not a resident of the district in which the deposition is to take place. The Rule, as currently constituted, creates anomalous situations that often cause logistical problems in conducting litigation.

The first sentence of the present Rule states that a deponent may be required to attend only in the *county* wherein that person resides or is employed or transacts business in person, that is, where the person lives or works. Under this provision a deponent can be compelled, without court order, to travel from one end of that person's home county to the other, no matter how far that may be. The second sentence of the Rule is somewhat more flexible, stating that someone who does not reside in the district in which the deposition is to be taken can be required to attend in the county where the person is served with the subpoena, *or* within 40 miles from the place of service.

Under today's conditions there is no sound reason for distinguishing between residents of the district or county in which a deposition is to be taken and nonresidents, and the Rule is amended to provide that any person may be subpoenaed to attend a deposition within a specified radius from that person's residence, place of business, or where the person was served. The 40-mile radius has been increased to 100 miles.

1987 Amendment

The amendments are technical. No substantive change is intended.

1991 Amendment

Purposes of Revision. The purposes of this revision are (1) to clarify and enlarge the protections afforded persons who are required to assist the court by giving information or evidence; (2) to facilitate access outside the deposition procedure provided by Rule 30 to documents and other information in the possession of persons who are not parties; (3) to facilitate service of subpoenas for depositions or productions of evidence at places distant from the district in which an action is proceeding; (4) to enable the court to compel a witness found within the state in which the court sits to attend trial; (5) to clarify the organization of the text of the rule.

Subdivision (a). This subdivision is amended in seven significant respects.

First, Paragraph (a)(3) modifies the requirement that a subpoena be issued by the clerk of court. Provision is made for the issuance of subpoenas by attorneys as officers of the court. This revision perhaps culminates an evolution. Subpoenas were long issued by specific order of the court. As this became a burden to the court, general orders were made authorizing clerks to issue subpoenas on request. Since

Complete Annotation Materials, see Title 28 U.S.C.A.

1948, they have been issued in blank by the clerk of any federal court to any lawyer, the clerk serving as stationer to the bar. In allowing counsel to issue the subpoena, the rule is merely a recognition of present reality.

Although the subpoena is in a sense the command of the attorney who completes the form, defiance of a subpoena is nevertheless an act in defiance of a court order and exposes the defiant witness to contempt sanctions. In *ICC v. Brimson*, 154 U.S. 447 (1894), the Court upheld a statute directing federal courts to issue subpoenas to compel testimony before the ICC. In *CAB v. Hermann*, 353 U.S. 322 (1957), the Court approved as established practice the issuance of administrative subpoenas as a matter of absolute agency right. And in *NLRB v. Warren Co.*, 350 U.S. 107 (1955), the Court held that the lower court had no discretion to withhold sanctions against a contemnor who violated such subpoenas. The 1948 revision of Rule 45 put the attorney in a position similar to that of the administrative agency, as a public officer entitled to use the court's contempt power to investigate facts in dispute. Two courts of appeals have touched on the issue and have described lawyer-issued subpoenas as mandates of the court. *Waste Conversion, Inc. v. Rollins Environmental Services (NJ), Inc.*, 893 F.2d 605 (3d cir., 1990); *Fisher v. Marubent Cotton Corp.*, 526 F.2d 1338, 1340 (8th cir., 1975). Cf. *Young v. United States ex rel Vuitton et Fils S.A.*, 481 U.S. 787, 821 (1987) (Scalia, J., concurring). This revision makes the rule explicit that the attorney acts as an officer of the court in issuing and signing subpoenas.

Necessarily accompanying the evolution of this power of the lawyer as officer of the court is the development of increased responsibility and liability for the misuse of this power. The latter development is reflected in the provisions of subdivision (c) of this rule, and also in the requirement imposed by paragraph (3) of this subdivision that the attorney issuing a subpoena must sign it.

Second, Paragraph (a)(3) authorizes attorneys in distant districts to serve as officers authorized to issue commands in the name of the court. Any attorney permitted to represent a client in a federal court, even one admitted pro haec vice, has the same authority as a clerk to issue a subpoena from any federal court for the district in which the subpoena is served and enforced. In authorizing attorneys to issue subpoenas from distant courts, the amended rule effectively authorizes service of a subpoena anywhere in the United States by an attorney representing any party. This change is intended to ease the administrative burdens of inter-district law practice. The former rule resulted in delay and expense caused by the need to secure forms from clerks' offices some distance from the place at which the action proceeds. This change does not enlarge the burden on the witness.

Pursuant to Paragraph (a)(2), a subpoena for a deposition must still issue from the court in which the deposition or production would be compelled. Accordingly, a motion to quash such a subpoena if it overbears the limits of the subpoena power must, as under the previous rule, be presented to the court for the district in which the deposition would occur. Likewise, the court in whose name the subpoena is issued is responsible for its enforcement.

Third, in order to relieve attorneys of the need to secure an appropriate seal to affix to a subpoena issued as an officer of a distant court, the requirement that a subpoena be under seal is abolished by the provisions of Paragraph (a)(1).

Fourth, Paragraph (a)(1) authorizes the issuance of a subpoena to compel a non-party to produce evidence independent of any deposition. This revision spares the necessity of a deposition of the custodian of evidentiary material required to be produced. A party seeking additional production from a person subject to such a subpoena may serve an additional subpoena requiring additional production at the same time and place.

Fifth, Paragraph (a)(2) makes clear that the person subject to the subpoena is required to produce materials in that person's control whether or not the materials are located within the district or within the territory within which the subpoena can be served. The non-party witness is subject to the same scope of discovery under this rule as that person would be as a party to whom a request is addressed pursuant to Rule 34.

Sixth, Paragraph (a)(1) requires that the subpoena include a statement of the rights and duties of witnesses by setting forth in full the text of the new subdivisions (c) and (d).

Seventh, the revised rule authorizes the issuance of a subpoena to compel the inspection of premises in the possession of a non-party. Rule 34 has authorized such inspections of premises in the possession of a party as discovery compelled under Rule 37, but prior practice required an independent proceeding to secure such relief ancillary to the federal proceeding when the premises were not in the possession of a party. Practice in some states has long authorized such use of a subpoena for this purpose without apparent adverse consequence.

Subdivision (b). Paragraph (b)(1) retains the text of the former subdivision (c) with minor changes.

The reference to the United States marshal and deputy marshal is deleted because of the infrequency of the use of these officers for this purpose. Inasmuch as these officers meet the age requirement, they may still be used if available.

A provision requiring service of prior notice pursuant to Rule 5 of compulsory pretrial production or inspection has been added to paragraph (b)(1). The purpose of such notice is to afford other parties an opportunity to object to the production or inspection, or to serve a demand for additional documents or things. Such additional notice is not needed with respect to a deposition because of the requirement of notice imposed by Rule 30 or 31. But when production or inspection is sought independently of a deposition, other parties may need notice in order to monitor the discovery and in order to pursue access to any information that may or should be produced.

Paragraph (b)(2) retains language formerly set forth in subdivision (e) and extends its application to subpoenas for depositions or production.

Paragraph (b)(3) retains language formerly set forth in paragraph (d)(1) and extends its applications to subpoenas for trial or hearing or production.

Subdivision (c). This provision is new and states the rights of witnesses. It is not intended to diminish rights conferred by Rules 26–37 or any other authority.

Paragraph (c)(1) gives specific application to the principle stated in Rule 26(g) and specifies liability for earnings lost by a non-party witness as a result of a misuse of the subpoena. No change in existing law is thereby effected. Abuse of a subpoena is an actionable tort, *Board of Ed. v. Farmingdale*

Classroom Teach. Ass'n, 38 N.Y.2d 397, 380 N.Y.S.2d 635, 343 N.E.2d 278 (1975), and the duty of the attorney to the non-party is also embodied in Model Rule of Professional Conduct 4.4. The liability of the attorney is correlative to the expanded power of the attorney to issue subpoenas. The liability may include the cost of fees to collect attorneys' fees owed as a result of a breach of this duty.

Paragraph (c)(2) retains language from the former subdivision (b) and paragraph (d)(1). The 10–day period for response to a subpoena is extended to 14 days to avoid the complex calculations associated with short time periods under Rule 6 and to allow a bit more time for such objections to be made.

A non-party required to produce documents or materials is protected against significant expense resulting from involuntary assistance to the court. This provision applies, for example, to a non-party required to provide a list of class members. The court is not required to fix the costs in advance of production, although this will often be the most satisfactory accommodation to protect the party seeking discovery from excessive costs. In some instances, it may be preferable to leave uncertain costs to be determined after the materials have been produced, provided that the risk of uncertainty is fully disclosed to the discovering party. See, *e.g., United States v. Columbia Broadcasting Systems, Inc.,* 666 F.2d 364 (9th Cir.1982).

Paragraph (c)(3) explicitly authorizes the quashing of a subpoena as a means of protecting a witness from misuse of the subpoena power. It replaces and enlarges on the former subdivision (b) of this rule and tracks the provisions of Rule 26(c). While largely repetitious, this rule is addressed to the witness who may read it on the subpoena, where it is required to be printed by the revised paragraph (a)(1) of this rule.

Subparagraph (c)(3)(A) identifies those circumstances in which a subpoena must be quashed or modified. It restates the former provisions with respect to the limits of mandatory travel that are set forth in the former paragraphs (d)(2) and (e)(1), with one important change. Under the revised rule, a federal court can compel a witness to come from any place in the state to attend trial, whether or not the local state law so provides. This extension is subject to the qualification provided in the next paragraph, which authorizes the court to condition enforcement of a subpoena compelling a non-party witness to bear substantial expense to attend trial. The traveling non-party witness may be entitled to reasonable compensation for the time and effort entailed.

Clause (c)(3)(A)(iv) requires the court to protect all persons from undue burden imposed by the use of the subpoena power. Illustratively, it might be unduly burdensome to compel an adversary to attend trial as a witness if the adversary is known to have no personal knowledge of matters in dispute, especially so if the adversary would be required to incur substantial travel burdens.

Subparagraph (c)(3)(B) identifies circumstances in which a subpoena should be quashed unless the party serving the subpoena shows a substantial need and the court can devise an appropriate accommodation to protect the interests of the witness. An additional circumstance in which such action is required is a request for costly production of documents; that situation is expressly governed by subparagraph (b)(2)(B)[1].

Clause (c)(3)(B)(i) authorizes the court to quash, modify, or condition a subpoena to protect the person subject to or affected by the subpoena from unnecessary or unduly harmful disclosures of confidential information. It corresponds to Rule 26(c)(7).

Clause (c)(3)(B)(ii) provides appropriate protection for the intellectual property of the non-party witness; it does not apply to the expert retained by a party, whose information is subject to the provisions of Rule 26(b)(4). A growing problem has been the use of subpoenas to compel the giving of evidence and information by unretained experts. Experts are not exempt from the duty to give evidence, even if they cannot be compelled to prepare themselves to give effective testimony, *e.g., Carter–Wallace, Inc. v. Otte,* 474 F.2d 529 (2d Cir.1972), but compulsion to give evidence may threaten the intellectual property of experts denied the opportunity to bargain for the value of their services. See generally Maurer, *Compelling the Expert Witness: Fairness and Utility Under the Federal Rules of Civil Procedure,* 19 GA.L.REV. 71 (1984); Note, *Discovery and Testimony of Unretained Experts,* 1987 DUKE L.J. 140. Arguably the compulsion to testify can be regarded as a "taking" of intellectual property. The rule establishes the right of such persons to withhold their expertise, at least unless the party seeking it makes the kind of showing required for a conditional denial of a motion to quash as provided in the final sentence of subparagraph (c)(3)(B); that requirement is the same as that necessary to secure work product under Rule 26(b)(3) and gives assurance of reasonable compensation. The Rule thus approves the accommodation of competing interests exemplified in *United States v. Columbia Broadcasting Systems Inc.,* 666 F.2d 364 (9th Cir.1982). See also *Wright v. Jeep Corporation,* 547 F.Supp. 871 (E.D.Mich.1982).

As stated in *Kaufman v. Edelstein,* 539 F.2d 811, 822 (2d Cir.1976), the district court's discretion in these matters should be informed by "the degree to which the expert is being called because of his knowledge of facts relevant to the case rather than in order to give opinion testimony; the difference between testifying to a previously formed or expressed opinion and forming a new one; the possibility that, for other reasons, the witness is a unique expert; the extent to which the calling party is able to show the unlikelihood that any comparable witness will willingly testify; and the degree to which the witness is able to show that he has been oppressed by having continually to testify...."

Clause (c)(3)(B)(iii) protects non-party witnesses who may be burdened with the duty to travel in order to provide testimony at trial. The provision requires the court to condition a subpoena requiring travel of more than 100 miles on reasonable compensation.

Subdivision (d). This provision is new. Paragraph (d)(1) extends to non-parties the duty imposed on parties by the last paragraph of Rule 34(b), which was added in 1980.

Paragraph (d)(2) is new and corresponds to the new Rule 26(b)(5) [paragraph (5) in Rule 26(b) was a proposed paragraph which was withdrawn by the Supreme Court]. Its purpose is to provide a party whose discovery is constrained by a claim of privilege or work product protection with information sufficient to evaluate such a claim and to resist if it seems unjustified. The person claiming a privilege or protection cannot decide the limits of that party's own entitlement.

A party receiving a discovery request who asserts a privilege or protection but fails to disclose that claim is at risk of waiving the privilege or protection. A person claiming a privilege or protection who fails to provide adequate information about the privilege or protection claim to the party seeking the information is subject to an order to show cause why the person should not be held in contempt under subdivision (e). Motions for such orders and responses to motions are subject to the sanctions provisions of Rules 7 and 11.

A person served a subpoena that is too broad may be faced with a burdensome task to provide full information regarding all that person's claims to privilege or work product protection. Such a person is entitled to protection that may be secured through an objection made pursuant to paragraph (c)(2).

Subdivision (e). This provision retains most of the language of the former subdivision (f).

"Adequate cause" for a failure to obey a subpoena remains undefined. In at least some circumstances, a non-party might be guilty of contempt for refusing to obey a subpoena even though the subpoena manifestly overreaches the appropriate limits of the subpoena power. *E.g., Walker v. City of Birmingham,* 388 U.S. 307 (1967). But, because the command of the subpoena is not in fact one uttered by a judicial officer, contempt should be very sparingly applied when the non-party witness has been overborne by a party or attorney. The language added to subdivision (f) is intended to assure that result where a non-party has been commanded, on the signature of an attorney, to travel greater distances than can be compelled pursuant to this rule.

1 So in original. Probably should be "subparagraph (c)(2)(B)".

2005 Amendments

This amendment closes a small gap in regard to notifying witnesses of the manner for recording a deposition. A deposition subpoena must state the method for recording the testimony.

Rule 30(b)(2) directs that the party noticing a deposition state in the notice the manner for recording the testimony, but the notice need not be served on the deponent. The deponent learns of the recording method only if the deponent is a party or is informed by a party. Rule 30(b)(3) permits another party to designate an additional method of recording with prior notice to the deponent and the other parties. The deponent thus has notice of the recording method when an additional method is designated. This amendment completes the notice provisions to ensure that a nonparty deponent has notice of the recording method when the recording method is described only in the deposition notice.

A subpoenaed witness does not have a right to refuse to proceed with a deposition due to objections to the manner of recording. But under rare circumstances, a nonparty witness might have a ground for seeking a protective order under Rule 26(c) with regard to the manner of recording or the use of the deposition if recorded in a certain manner. Should such a witness not learn of the manner of recording until the deposition begins, undesirable delay or complication might result. Advance notice of the recording method affords an opportunity to raise such protective issues.

Other changes are made to conform Rule 45(a)(2) to current style conventions.

2006 Amendments

Rule 45 is amended to conform the provisions for subpoenas to changes in other discovery rules, largely related to discovery of electronically stored information. Rule 34 is amended to provide in greater detail for the production of electronically stored information. Rule 45(a)(1)(C) is amended to recognize that electronically stored information, as defined in Rule 34(a), can also be sought by subpoena. Like Rule 34(b), Rule 45(a)(1) is amended to provide that the subpoena can designate a form or forms for production of electronic data. Rule 45(c)(2) is amended, like Rule 34(b), to authorize the person served with a subpoena to object to the requested form or forms. In addition, as under Rule 34(b), Rule 45(d)(1)(B) is amended to provide that if the subpoena does not specify the form or forms for electronically stored information, the person served with the subpoena must produce electronically stored information in a form or forms in which it is usually maintained or in a form or forms that are reasonably usable. Rule 45(d)(1)(C) is added to provide that the person producing electronically stored information should not have to produce the same information in more than one form unless so ordered by the court for good cause.

As with discovery of electronically stored information from parties, complying with a subpoena for such information may impose burdens on the responding person. Rule 45(c) provides protection against undue impositions on nonparties. For example, Rule 45(c)(1) directs that a party serving a subpoena "shall take reasonable steps to avoid imposing undue burden or expense on a person subject to the subpoena," and Rule 45(c)(2)(B) permits the person served with the subpoena to object to it and directs that an order requiring compliance "shall protect a person who is neither a party nor a party's officer from significant expense resulting from" compliance. Rule 45(d)(1)(D) is added to provide that the responding person need not provide discovery of electronically stored information from sources the party identifies as not reasonably accessible, unless the court orders such discovery for good cause, considering the limitations of Rule 26(b)(2)(C), on terms that protect a nonparty against significant expense. A parallel provision is added to Rule 26(b)(2).

Rule 45(a)(1)(B) is also amended, as is Rule 34(a), to provide that a subpoena is available to permit testing and sampling as well as inspection and copying. As in Rule 34, this change recognizes that on occasion the opportunity to perform testing or sampling may be important, both for documents and for electronically stored information. Because testing or sampling may present particular issues of burden or intrusion for the person served with the subpoena, however, the protective provisions of Rule 45(c) should be enforced with vigilance when such demands are made. Inspection or testing of certain types of electronically stored information or of a person's electronic information system may raise issues of confidentiality or privacy. The addition of sampling and testing to Rule 45(a) with regard to documents and electronically stored information is not meant to create a routine right of direct access to a person's electronic information system, although such access might be justified in some circumstances. Courts should guard against undue intrusiveness resulting from inspecting or testing such systems.

Rule 45(d)(2) is amended, as is Rule 26(b)(5), to add a procedure for assertion of privilege or of protection as trial-

preparation materials after production. The receiving party may submit the information to the court for resolution of the privilege claim, as under Rule 26(b)(5)(B).

Other minor amendments are made to conform the rule to the changes described above.

2007 Amendment

*[Effective December 1, 2007,
absent contrary Congressional action.]*

The language of Rule 45 has been amended as part of the general restyling of the Civil Rules to make them more easily understood and to make style and terminology consistent throughout the rules. These changes are intended to be stylistic only.

The reference to discovery of "books" in former Rule 45(a)(1)(C) was deleted to achieve consistent expression throughout the discovery rules. Books remain a proper subject of discovery.

Former Rule 45(b)(1) required "prior notice" to each party of any commanded production of documents and things or inspection of premises. Courts have agreed that notice must be given "prior" to the return date, and have tended to converge on an interpretation that requires notice to the parties before the subpoena is served on the person commanded to produce or permit inspection. That interpretation is adopted in amended Rule 45(b)(1) to give clear notice of general present practice.

The language of former Rule 45(d)(2) addressing the manner of asserting privilege is replaced by adopting the wording of Rule 26(b)(5). The same meaning is better expressed in the same words.

HISTORICAL NOTES

Treaties and Conventions; Taking of Evidence Abroad in Civil or Commercial Matters; Observance On and After Oct. 7, 1972, by United States and Citizens and Persons Subject to Jurisdiction of United States

For text of Convention, see provisions set out as a note under section 1781 of this title.

Rule 46. Exceptions Unnecessary

Formal exceptions to rulings or orders of the court are unnecessary; but for all purposes for which an exception has heretofore been necessary it is sufficient that a party, at the time the ruling or order of the court is made or sought, makes known to the court the action which the party desires the court to take or the party's objection to the action of the court and the grounds therefor; and, if a party has no opportunity to object to a ruling or order at the time it is made, the absence of an objection does not thereafter prejudice the party.
(As amended Mar. 2, 1987, eff. Aug. 1, 1987.)

Proposed Amendment of Rule

Effective December 1, 2007, absent contrary Congressional action, this rule is amended to read as follows:

Rule 46. Objecting to a Ruling or Order

A formal exception to a ruling or order is unnecessary. When the ruling or order is requested or made, a party need only state the action that it wants the court to take or objects to, along with the grounds for the request or objection. Failing to object does not prejudice a party who had no opportunity to do so when the ruling or order was made.

ADVISORY COMMITTEE NOTES

1937 Adoption

Abolition of formal exceptions is often provided by statute. See Ill.Rev.Stat. (1937), ch. 110, § 204; Neb.Comp.Stat. (1929) § 20–1139; N.M.Stat.Ann. (Courtright, 1929) § 105–830; 2 N.D.Comp.Laws Ann. (1913) § 7653; Ohio Code Ann. (Throckmorton, 1936) § 11560; 1 S.D.Comp.Laws (1929) § 2542; Utah Rev.Stat.Ann. (1933) §§ 104–39–2, 104–24–18; Va.Rules of Court, Rule 22, 163 Va. v. xii (1935); Wis.Stat. (1935) § 270.39. Compare N.Y.C.P.A. (1937) §§ 583, 445, and 446, all as amended by L.1936, ch. 915. Rule 51 deals with objections to the court's instructions to the jury.

U.S.C., Title 28, [former] § 776 (Bill of exceptions; authentication; signing of by judge) and [former] § 875 (Review of findings in cases tried without a jury) are superseded insofar as they provide for formal exceptions, and a bill of exceptions.

1987 Amendment

The amendments are technical. No substantive change is intended.

2007 Amendments

*[Effective December 1, 2007,
absent contrary Congressional action.]*

The language of Rule 46 has been amended as part of the general restyling of the Civil Rules to make them more easily understood and to make style and terminology consistent throughout the rules. These changes are intended to be stylistic only.

Rule 47. Selection of Jurors

(a) Examination of Jurors. The court may permit the parties or their attorneys to conduct the examination of prospective jurors or may itself conduct the examination. In the latter event, the court shall permit the parties or their attorneys to supplement the examination by such further inquiry as it deems proper or shall itself submit to the prospective jurors such additional questions of the parties or their attorneys as it deems proper.

(b) Peremptory Challenges. The court shall allow the number of peremptory challenges provided by 28 U.S.C. § 1870.

(c) Excuse. The court may for good cause excuse a juror from service during trial or deliberation.
(As amended Feb. 28, 1966, eff. July 1, 1966; Apr. 30, 1991, eff. Dec. 1, 1991.)

Proposed Amendment of Rule

Effective December 1, 2007, absent contrary Congressional action, this rule is amended to read as follows:

Rule 47. Selecting Jurors

(a) Examining Jurors. *The court may permit the parties or their attorneys to examine prospective jurors or may itself do so. If the court examines the jurors, it must permit the parties or their attorneys to make any further inquiry it considers proper, or must itself ask any of their additional questions it considers proper.*

(b) Peremptory Challenges. *The court must allow the number of peremptory challenges provided by 28 U.S.C. § 1870.*

(c) Excusing a Juror. *During trial or deliberation, the court may excuse a juror for good cause.*

ADVISORY COMMITTEE NOTES

1937 Adoption

Note to Subdivision (a). This permits a practice found very useful by Federal trial judges. For an example of a state practice in which the examination by the court is supplemented by further inquiry by counsel, see Rule 27 of the Code of Rules for the District Courts of Minnesota, 186 Minn. xxxiii (1932), 3 Minn.Stat. (Mason, Supp.1936) Appendix 4, p. 1062.

Note to Subdivision (b). The provision for an alternate juror is one often found in modern state codes. See N.C.Code (1935) § 2330(a); Ohio Gen.Code Ann. (Page, Supp.1926–1935) § 11419–47; Pa.Stat.Ann. (Purdon, Supp. 1936) Title 17, § 1153; compare U.S.C., Title 28, [former] § 417a (Alternate jurors in criminal trials); 1 N.J.Rev.Stat. (1937) 2:91A–1, 2:91A–2, 2:91A–3.

Provisions for qualifying, drawing, and challenging of jurors are found in U.S.C., Title 28:

- § 411 [now 1861] (Qualifications and exemptions)
- § 412 [now 1864] (Manner of drawing)
- § 413 [now 1865] (Apportioned in district)
- § 415 [see 1862] (Not disqualified because of race or color)
- § 416 [now 1867] (Venire; service and return)
- § 417 [now 1866] (Talesmen for petit jurors)
- § 418 [now 1866] (Special juries)
- § 423 [now 1869] (Jurors not to serve more than once a year)
- § 424 [now 1870] (Challenges)

and D.C.Code (1930) Title 18, §§ 341 to 360 (Juries and Jury Commission) and Title 6, § 366 (Peremptory challenges).

1966 Amendment

The revision of this subdivision brings it into line with the amendment of Rule 24(c) of this Federal Rules of Criminal Procedure. That rule previously allowed four alternate jurors, as contrasted with the two allowed in civil cases, and the amendments increase the number to a maximum of six in all cases. The Advisory Committee's Note to amended Criminal Rule 24(c) points to experience demonstrating that four alternates may not be enough in some lengthy criminal trials; and the same may be said of civil trials. The Note adds:

"The words 'or are found to be' are added to the second sentence to make clear that an alternate juror may be called in the situation where it is first discovered during the trial that a juror was unable or disqualified to perform his duties at the time he was sworn."

1991 Amendment

Subdivision (b). The former provision for alternate jurors is stricken and the institution of the alternate juror abolished.

The former rule reflected the long-standing assumption that a jury would consist of exactly twelve members. It provided for additional jurors to be used as substitutes for jurors who are for any reason excused or disqualified from service after the commencement of the trial. Additional jurors were traditionally designated at the outset of the trial, and excused at the close of the evidence if they had not been promoted to full service on account of the elimination of one of the original jurors.

The use of alternate jurors has been a source of dissatisfaction with the jury system because of the burden it places on alternates who are required to listen to the evidence but denied the satisfaction of participating in its evaluation.

Subdivision (c). This provision makes it clear that the court may in appropriate circumstances excuse a juror during the jury deliberations without causing a mistrial. Sickness, family emergency or juror misconduct that might occasion a mistrial are examples of appropriate grounds for excusing a juror. It is not grounds for the dismissal of a juror that the juror refuses to join with fellow jurors in reaching a unanimous verdict.

2007 Amendments

[Effective December 1, 2007, absent contrary Congressional action.]

The language of Rule 47 has been amended as part of the general restyling of the Civil Rules to make them more easily understood and to make style and terminology consistent throughout the rules. These changes are intended to be stylistic only.

Rule 48. Number of Jurors—Participation in Verdict

The court shall seat a jury of not fewer than six and not more than twelve members and all jurors shall participate in the verdict unless excused from service by the court pursuant to Rule 47(c). Unless the parties otherwise stipulate, (1) the verdict shall be unanimous and (2) no verdict shall be taken from a jury reduced in size to fewer than six members. (As amended Apr. 30, 1991, eff. Dec. 1, 1991.)

Proposed Amendment of Rule

Effective December 1, 2007, absent contrary Congressional action, this rule is amended to read as follows:

Rule 48. *Number of Jurors; Verdict*

A jury must initially have at least 6 and no more than 12 members, and each juror must participate in the verdict unless excused under Rule 47(c). Unless the parties stipulate otherwise, the verdict must be unanimous and be returned by a jury of at least 6 members.

ADVISORY COMMITTEE NOTES
1937 Adoption

For provisions in state codes, compare Utah Rev.Stat.Ann. (1933) § 48–0–5 (In civil cases parties may agree in open court on lesser number of jurors); 2 Wash.Rev.Stat.Ann. (Remington, 1932) § 323 (Parties may consent to any number of jurors not less than three).

1991 Amendment

The former rule was rendered obsolete by the adoption in many districts of local rules establishing six as the standard size for a civil jury.

It appears that the minimum size of a jury consistent with the Seventh Amendment is six. *Cf. Ballew v. Georgia*, 435 U.S. 223 (1978) (holding that a conviction based on a jury of less than six is a denial of due process of law). If the parties agree to trial before a smaller jury, a verdict can be taken, but the parties should not other than in exceptional circumstances be encouraged to waive the right to a jury of six, not only because of the constitutional stature of the right, but also because smaller juries are more erratic and less effective in serving to distribute responsibility for the exercise of judicial power.

Because the institution of the alternate juror has been abolished by the proposed revision of Rule 47, it will ordinarily be prudent and necessary, in order to provide for sickness or disability among jurors, to seat more than six jurors. The use of jurors in excess of six increases the representativeness of the jury and harms no interest of a party. *Ray v. Parkside Surgery Center*, 13 F.R.Serv. 585 (6th Cir.1989).

If the court takes the precaution of seating a jury larger than six, an illness occurring during the deliberation period will not result in a mistrial, as it did formerly, because all seated jurors will participate in the verdict and a sufficient number will remain to render a unanimous verdict of six or more.

In exceptional circumstances, as where a jury suffers depletions during trial and deliberation that are greater than can reasonably be expected, the parties may agree to be bound by a verdict rendered by fewer than six jurors. The court should not, however, rely upon the availability of such an agreement, for the use of juries smaller than six is problematic for reasons fully explained in *Ballew v. Georgia*, supra.

2007 Amendments

[Effective December 1, 2007, absent contrary Congressional action.]

The language of Rule 48 has been amended as part of the general restyling of the Civil Rules to make them more easily understood and to make style and terminology consistent throughout the rules. These changes are intended to be stylistic only.

Rule 49. Special Verdicts and Interrogatories

(a) Special Verdicts. The court may require a jury to return only a special verdict in the form of a special written finding upon each issue of fact. In that event the court may submit to the jury written questions susceptible of categorical or other brief answer or may submit written forms of the several special findings which might properly be made under the pleadings and evidence; or it may use such other method of submitting the issues and requiring the written findings thereon as it deems most appropriate. The court shall give to the jury such explanation and instruction concerning the matter thus submitted as may be necessary to enable the jury to make its findings upon each issue. If in so doing the court omits any issue of fact raised by the pleadings or by the evidence, each party waives the right to a trial by jury of the issue so omitted unless before the jury retires the party demands its submission to the jury. As to an issue omitted without such demand the court may make a finding; or, if it fails to do so, it shall be deemed to have made a finding in accord with the judgment on the special verdict.

(b) General Verdict Accompanied by Answer to Interrogatories. The court may submit to the jury, together with appropriate forms for a general verdict, written interrogatories upon one or more issues of fact the decision of which is necessary to a verdict. The court shall give such explanation or instruction as may be necessary to enable the jury both to make answers to the interrogatories and to render a general verdict, and the court shall direct the jury both to make written answers and to render a general verdict. When the general verdict and the answers are harmonious, the appropriate judgment upon the verdict and answers shall be entered pursuant to Rule 58. When the answers are consistent with each other but one or more is inconsistent with the general verdict, judgment may be entered pursuant to Rule 58 in accordance with the answers, notwithstanding the general verdict, or the court may return the jury for further consideration of its answers and verdict or may order a new trial. When the answers are inconsistent with each other and one or more is likewise inconsistent with the general verdict, judgment shall not be entered, but the court shall return the jury for further consideration of its answers and verdict or shall order a new trial.

(As amended Jan. 21, 1963, eff. July 1, 1963; Mar. 2, 1987, eff. Aug. 1, 1987.)

Proposed Amendment of Rule

Effective December 1, 2007, absent contrary Congressional action, this rule is amended to read as follows:

Rule 49. Special Verdict; General Verdict and Questions

(a) Special Verdict.

(1) In General. The court may require a jury to return only a special verdict in the form of a special written finding on each issue of fact. The court may do so by:

(A) submitting written questions susceptible of a categorical or other brief answer;

(B) submitting written forms of the special findings that might properly be made under the pleadings and evidence; or

(C) using any other method that the court considers appropriate.

(2) Instructions. The court must give the instructions and explanations necessary to enable the jury to make its findings on each submitted issue.

(3) Issues Not Submitted. A party waives the right to a jury trial on any issue of fact raised by the pleadings or evidence but not submitted to the jury unless, before the jury retires, the party demands its submission to the jury. If the party does not demand submission, the court may make a finding on the issue. If the court makes no finding, it is considered to have made a finding consistent with its judgment on the special verdict.

(b) General Verdict with Answers to Written Questions.

(1) In General. The court may submit to the jury forms for a general verdict, together with written questions on one or more issues of fact that the jury must decide. The court must give the instructions and explanations necessary to enable the jury to render a general verdict and answer the questions in writing, and must direct the jury to do both.

(2) Verdict and Answers Consistent. When the general verdict and the answers are consistent, the court must approve, for entry under Rule 58, an appropriate judgment on the verdict and answers.

(3) Answers Inconsistent with the Verdict. When the answers are consistent with each other but one or more is inconsistent with the general verdict, the court may:

(A) approve, for entry under Rule 58, an appropriate judgment according to the answers, notwithstanding the general verdict;

(B) direct the jury to further consider its answers and verdict; or

(C) order a new trial.

(4) Answers Inconsistent with Each Other and the Verdict. When the answers are inconsistent with each other and one or more is also inconsistent with the general verdict, judgment must not be entered; instead, the court must direct the jury to further consider its answers and verdict, or must order a new trial.

ADVISORY COMMITTEE NOTES

1937 Adoption

The Federal courts are not bound to follow state statutes authorizing or requiring the court to ask a jury to find a special verdict or to answer interrogatories. *Victor American Fuel Co. v. Peccarich*, 209 Fed. 568 (C.C.A.8th, 1913), cert. den. 232 U.S. 727, 34 S.Ct. 603, 58 L.Ed. 817 (1914); *Spokane and I.E.R. Co. v. Campbell*, 217 Fed. 518 (C.C.A.9th, 1914), affd. 241 U.S. 497, 36 S.Ct. 683, 60 L.Ed. 1125 (1916); Simkins, *Federal Practice* (1934) § 186. The power of a territory to adopt by statute the practice under Subdivision (b) has been sustained. *Walker v. New Mexico and Southern Pacific R.R.*, 165 U.S. 593, 17 S.Ct. 421, 41 L.Ed. 837 (1897); *Southwestern Brewery and Ice Co. v. Schmidt*, 226 U.S. 162, 33 S.Ct. 68, 57 L.Ed. 170 (1912).

Compare Wis.Stat. (1935) §§ 270.27, 270.28 and 270.30; Green, *A New Development in Jury Trial* (1927), 13 A.B.A.J. 715; Morgan, *A Brief History of Special Verdicts and Special Interrogatories*, 1923, 32 Yale L.J. 575.

The provisions of U.S.C., Title 28, [former] § 400(3) (now §§ 2201, 2202) (Declaratory judgments authorized; procedure) permitting the submission of issues of fact to a jury are covered by this rule.

1963 Amendment

This amendment conforms to the amendment of Rule 58. See the Advisory Committee's Note to Rule 58, as amended.

1987 Amendment

The amendments are technical. No substantive change is intended.

2007 Amendments

[Effective December 1, 2007, absent contrary Congressional action.]

The language of Rule 49 has been amended as part of the general restyling of the Civil Rules to make them more easily understood and to make style and terminology consistent throughout the rules. These changes are intended to be stylistic only.

Rule 50. Judgment as a Matter of Law in Jury Trials; Alternative Motion for New Trial; Conditional Rulings

(a) Judgment as a Matter of Law.

(1) In General. If a party has been fully heard on an issue during a jury trial and the court finds that a reasonable jury would not have a legally

sufficient evidentiary basis to find for the party on that issue, the court may:

(A) resolve the issue against the party; and

(B) grant a motion for judgment as a matter of law against the party on a claim or defense that, under the controlling law, can be maintained or defeated only with a favorable finding on that issue.

(2) **Motion.** A motion for judgment as a matter of law may be made at any time before the case is submitted to the jury. The motion must specify the judgment sought and the law and facts that entitle the movant to the judgment.

(b) **Renewing the Motion After Trial; Alternative Motion for a New Trial.** If the court does not grant a motion for judgment as a matter of law made under subdivision (a), the court is considered to have submitted the action to the jury subject to the court's later deciding the legal questions raised by the motion. The movant may renew its request for judgment as a matter of law by filing a motion no later than 10 days after the entry of judgment or — if the motion addresses a jury issue not decided by a verdict — no later than 10 days after the jury was discharged. The movant may alternatively request a new trial or join a motion for a new trial under Rule 59.

In ruling on a renewed motion, the court may:

(1) if a verdict was returned:

(A) allow the judgment to stand,

(B) order a new trial, or

(C) direct entry of judgment as a matter of law; or

(2) if no verdict was returned:

(A) order a new trial, or

(B) direct entry of judgment as a matter of law.

(c) **Granting Renewed Motion for Judgment as a Matter of Law; Conditional Rulings; New Trial Motion**

(1) If the renewed motion for judgment as a matter of law is granted, the court shall also rule on the motion for a new trial, if any, by determining whether it should be granted if the judgment is thereafter vacated or reversed, and shall specify the grounds for granting or denying the motion for the new trial. If the motion for a new trial is thus conditionally granted, the order thereon does not affect the finality of the judgment. In case the motion for a new trial has been conditionally granted and the judgment is reversed on appeal, the new trial shall proceed unless the appellate court has otherwise ordered. In case the motion for a new trial has been conditionally denied, the appellee on appeal may assert error in that denial; and if the judgment is reversed on appeal, subsequent pro-

ceedings shall be in accordance with the order of the appellate court.

(2) Any motion for a new trial under Rule 59 by a party against whom judgment as a matter of law is rendered shall be filed no later than 10 days after entry of the judgment.

(d) **Same: Denial of Motion for Judgment as a Matter of Law.** If the motion for judgment as a matter of law is denied, the party who prevailed on that motion may, as appellee, assert grounds entitling the party to a new trial in the event the appellate court concludes that the trial court erred in denying the motion for judgment. If the appellate court reverses the judgment, nothing in this rule precludes it from determining that the appellee is entitled to a new trial, or from directing the trial court to determine whether a new trial shall be granted.

(As amended Jan. 21, 1963, eff. July 1, 1963; Mar. 2, 1987, eff. Aug. 1, 1987; Apr. 30, 1991, eff. Dec. 1, 1991; Apr. 22, 1993, eff. Dec. 1, 1993; Apr. 27, 1995, eff. Dec. 1, 1995; Apr. 12, 2006, Dec. 1, 2006.)

Proposed Amendment of Rule

Effective December 1, 2007, absent contrary Congressional action, this rule is amended to read as follows:

Rule 50. Judgment as a Matter of Law in a Jury Trial; Related Motion for a New Trial; Conditional Ruling

(a) Judgment as a Matter of Law.

(1) In General. If a party has been fully heard on an issue during a jury trial and the court finds that a reasonable jury would not have a legally sufficient evidentiary basis to find for the party on that issue, the court may:

(A) resolve the issue against the party; and

(B) grant a motion for judgment as a matter of law against the party on a claim or defense that, under the controlling law, can be maintained or defeated only with a favorable finding on that issue.

(2) Motion. A motion for judgment as a matter of law may be made at any time before the case is submitted to the jury. The motion must specify the judgment sought and the law and facts that entitle the movant to the judgment.

(b) Renewing the Motion After Trial; Alternative Motion for a New Trial. If the court does not grant a motion for judgment as a matter of law made under Rule 50(a), the court is considered to have submitted the action to the jury subject to the court's later deciding the legal questions raised by the motion. No later than 10 days after the entry of judgment—or if the motion addresses a jury issue not decided by a

verdict, no later than 10 days after the jury was discharged—the movant may file a renewed motion for judgment as a matter of law and may include an alternative or joint request for a new trial under Rule 59. In ruling on the renewed motion, the court may:

(1) allow judgment on the verdict, if the jury returned a verdict;

(2) order a new trial; or

(3) direct the entry of judgment as a matter of law.

(c) Granting the Renewed Motion; Conditional Ruling on a Motion for a New Trial.

(1) In General. If the court grants a renewed motion for judgment as a matter of law, it must also conditionally rule on any motion for a new trial by determining whether a new trial should be granted if the judgment is later vacated or reversed. The court must state the grounds for conditionally granting or denying the motion for a new trial.

(2) Effect of a Conditional Ruling. Conditionally granting the motion for a new trial does not affect the judgment's finality; if the judgment is reversed, the new trial must proceed unless the appellate court orders otherwise. If the motion for a new trial is conditionally denied, the appellee may assert error in that denial; if the judgment is reversed, the case must proceed as the appellate court orders.

(d) Time for a Losing Party's New–Trial Motion. *Any motion for a new trial under Rule 59 by a party against whom judgment as a matter of law is rendered must be filed no later than 10 days after the entry of the judgment.*

(e) Denying the Motion for Judgment as a Matter of Law; Reversal on Appeal. *If the court denies the motion for judgment as a matter of law, the prevailing party may, as appellee, assert grounds entitling it to a new trial should the appellate court conclude that the trial court erred in denying the motion. If the appellate court reverses the judgment, it may order a new trial, direct the trial court to determine whether a new trial should be granted, or direct the entry of judgment.*

ADVISORY COMMITTEE NOTES

1937 Adoption

Note to Subdivision (a). The present federal rule is changed to the extent that the formality of an express reservation of rights against waiver is no longer necessary. See *Sampliner v. Motion Picture Patents Co.*, 41 S.Ct. 79, 254 U.S. 233, 65 L.Ed. 240 (1920); *Union Indemnity Co. v. United States*, 74 F.2d 645 (C.C.A. 6th, 1935). The requirement that specific grounds for the motion for a directed

verdict must be stated settles a conflict in the federal cases. See Simkins, *Federal Practice* (1934) § 189.

Note to Subdivision (b). For comparable state practice upheld under the conformity act, see *Baltimore and Carolina Line v. Redman*, 55 S.Ct. 890, 295 U.S. 654, 79 L.Ed. 1636 (1935); compare *Slocum v. New York Life Ins. Co.*, 33 S.Ct. 523, 228 U.S. 364, 57 L.Ed. 879, Ann.Cas.1914D, 1029 (1913).

See *Northern Ry. Co. v. Page*, 47 S.Ct. 491, 274 U.S. 65, 71 L.Ed. 929 (1927), following the Massachusetts practice of alternative verdicts, explained in Thorndike, *Trial by Jury in United States Courts*, 26 Harv.L.Rev. 732 (1913). See also Thayer, *Judicial Administration*, 63 U. of Pa.L.Rev. 585, 600–601, and note 32 (1915); Scott, *Trial by Jury and the Reform of Civil Procedure*, 31 Harv.L.Rev. 669, 685 (1918); Comment, 34 Mich.L.Rev. 93, 98 (1935).

1963 Amendment

Subdivision (a). The practice, after the court has granted a motion for a directed verdict, of requiring the jury to express assent to a verdict they did not reach by their own deliberations serves no useful purpose and may give offense to the members of the jury. See 2B Barron & Holtzoff, *Federal Practice & Procedure* § 1072, at 367 (Wright ed. 1961); Blume, *Origin and Development of the Directed Verdict*, 48 Mich.L.Rev. 555, 582–85, 589–90 (1950). The final sentence of the subdivision, added by amendment, provides that the court's order granting a motion for a directed verdict is effective in itself, and that no action need be taken by the foreman or other members of the jury. See Ariz. R.Civ.P. 50(c); cf. Fed.R.Crim.P. 29(a). No change is intended in the standard to be applied in deciding the motion. To assure this interpretation, and in the interest of simplicity, the traditional term, "directed verdict," is retained.

Subdivision (b). A motion for judgment notwithstanding the verdict will not lie unless it was preceded by a motion for a directed verdict made at the close of all the evidence.

The amendment of the second sentence of this subdivision sets the time limit for making the motion for judgment n.o.v. at 10 days after the entry of judgment, rather than 10 days after the reception of the verdict. Thus the time provision is made consistent with that contained in Rule 59(b) (time for motion for new trial) and Rule 52(b) (time for motion to amend findings by the court).

Subdivision (c) deals with the situation where a party joins a motion for a new trial with his motion for judgment n.o.v., or prays for a new trial in the alternative, and the motion for judgment n.o.v. is granted. The procedure to be followed in making rulings on the motion for the new trial, and the consequences of the rulings thereon, were partly set out in *Montgomery Ward & Co. v. Duncan*, 311 U.S. 243, 253, 61 S.Ct. 189, 85 L.Ed. 147 (1940), and have been further elaborated in later cases. See *Cone v. West Virginia Pulp & Paper Co.*, 330 U.S. 212, 67 S.Ct. 752, 91 L.Ed. 849 (1947); *Globe Liquor Co., Inc. v. San Roman*, 332 U.S. 571, 68 S.Ct. 246, 92 L.Ed. 177 (1948); *Fountain v. Filson*, 336 U.S. 681, 69 S.Ct. 754, 93 L.Ed. 971 (1949); *Johnson v. New York, N.H. & H.R.R. Co.*, 344 U.S. 48, 73 S.Ct. 125, 97 L.Ed. 77 (1952). However, courts as well as counsel have often misunderstood the procedure, and it will be helpful to summarize the proper practice in the text of the rule. The amendments

do not alter the effects of a jury verdict or the scope of appellate review.

In the situation mentioned, subdivision (c)(1) requires that the court make a "conditional" ruling on the new-trial motion, i.e., a ruling which goes on the assumption that the motion for judgment n.o.v. was erroneously granted and will be reversed or vacated; and the court is required to state its grounds for the conditional ruling. Subdivision (c)(1) then spells out the consequences of a reversal of the judgment in the light of the conditional ruling on the new-trial motion.

If the motion for new trial has been conditionally granted, and the judgment is reversed, "the new trial shall proceed unless the appellate court has otherwise ordered." The party against whom the judgment n.o.v. was entered below may, as appellant, besides seeking to overthrow that judgment, also attack the conditional grant of the new trial. And the appellate court, if it reverses the judgment n.o.v., may in an appropriate case also reverse the conditional grant of the new trial and direct that judgment be entered on the verdict. See *Bailey v. Slentz,* 189 F.2d 406 (10th Cir. 1951); *Moist Cold Refrigerator Co. v. Lou Johnson Co.,* 249 F.2d 246 (9th Cir. 1957), cert. denied, 356 U.S. 968, 78 S.Ct. 1008, 2 L.Ed.2d 1074 (1958); *Peters v. Smith,* 221 F.2d 721 (3d Cir. 1955); *Dailey v. Timmer,* 292 F.2d 824 (3d Cir. 1961), explaining *Lind v. Schenley Industries, Inc.,* 278 F.2d 79 (3d Cir.), cert. denied, 364 U.S. 835, 81 S.Ct. 58, 5 L.Ed.2d 60 (1960); *Cox v. Pennsylvania R.R.,* 120 A.2d 214 (D.C.Mun. Ct.App.1956); 3 Barron & Holtzoff, *Federal Practice & Procedure* § 1302.1 at 346–47 (Wright ed. 1958); 6 *Moore's Federal Practice* ¶59.16 at 3915 n. 8a (2d ed. 1954).

If the motion for a new trial has been conditionally denied, and the judgment is reversed, "subsequent proceedings shall be in accordance with the order of the appellate court." The party in whose favor judgment n.o.v. was entered below may, as appellee, besides seeking to uphold that judgment, also urge on the appellate court that the trial court committed error in conditionally denying the new trial. The appellee may assert this error in his brief, without taking a cross-appeal. *Cf. Patterson v. Pennsylvania R.R.,* 238 F.2d 645, 650 (6th Cir. 1956); *Hughes v. St. Louis Nat. L. Baseball Club, Inc.,* 359 Mo. 993, 997, 224 S.W.2d 989, 992 (1949). If the appellate court concludes that the judgment cannot stand, but accepts the appellee's contention that there was error in the conditional denial of the new trial, it may order a new trial in lieu of directing the entry of judgment upon the verdict.

Subdivision (c)(2), which also deals with the situation where the trial court has granted the motion for judgment n.o.v., states that the verdict-winner may apply to the trial court for a new trial pursuant to Rule 59 after the judgment n.o.v. has been entered against him. In arguing to the trial court in opposition to the motion for judgment n.o.v., the verdict-winner may, and often will, contend that he is entitled, at the least, to a new trial, and the court has a range of discretion to grant a new trial or (where plaintiff won the verdict) to order a dismissal of the action without prejudice instead of granting judgment n.o.v. See *Cone v. West Virginia Pulp & Paper Co.,* supra, 330 U.S. at 217, 218, 67 S.Ct. at 755, 756, 91 L.Ed. 849. Subdivision (c)(2) is a reminder that the verdict-winner is entitled, even after entry of judgment n.o.v. against him, to move for a new trial in the usual course. If in these circumstances the motion is granted, the judgment is superseded.

In some unusual circumstances, however, the grant of the new-trial motion may be only conditional, and the judgment will not be superseded. See the situation in *Tribble v. Bruin,* 279 F.2d 424 (4th Cir. 1960) (upon a verdict for plaintiff, defendant moves for and obtains judgment n.o.v.; plaintiff moves for a new trial on the ground of inadequate damages; trial court might properly have granted plaintiff's motion, conditional upon reversal of the judgment n.o.v.).

Even if the verdict-winner makes no motion for a new trial, he is entitled upon his appeal from the judgment n.o.v. not only to urge that that judgment should be reversed and judgment entered upon the verdict, but that errors were committed during the trial which at the least entitle him to a new trial.

Subdivision (d) deals with the situation where judgment has been entered on the jury verdict, the motion for judgment n.o.v. and any motion for a new trial having been denied by the trial court. The verdict-winner, as appellee, besides seeking to uphold the judgment may urge upon the appellate court that in case the trial court is found to have erred in entering judgment on the verdict, there are grounds for granting him a new trial instead of directing the entry of judgment for his opponent. In appropriate cases the appellate court is not precluded from itself directing that a new trial be had. See *Weade v. Dichmann, Wright & Pugh, Inc.,* 337 U.S. 801, 69 S.Ct. 1326, 93 L.Ed. 1704 (1949). Nor is it precluded in proper cases from remanding the case for a determination by the trial court as to whether a new trial should be granted. The latter course is advisable where the grounds urged are suitable for the exercise of trial court discretion.

Subdivision (d) does not attempt a regulation of all aspects of the procedure where the motion for judgment n.o.v. and any accompanying motion for a new trial are denied, since the problems have not been fully canvassed in the decisions and the procedure is in some respects still in a formative stage. It is, however, designed to give guidance on certain important features of the practice.

1987 Amendment

The amendments are technical. No substantive change is intended.

1991 Amendment

Subdivision (a). The revision of this subdivision aims to facilitate the exercise by the court of its responsibility to assure the fidelity of its judgment to the controlling law, a responsibility imposed by the Due Process Clause of the Fifth Amendment. *Cf. Galloway v. United States,* 319 U.S. 372 (1943).

The revision abandons the familiar terminology of *direction of verdict* for several reasons. The term is misleading as a description of the relationship between judge and jury. It is also freighted with anachronisms some of which are the subject of the text of former subdivision (a) of this rule that is deleted in this revision. Thus, it should not be necessary to state in the text of this rule that a motion made pursuant to it is not a waiver of the right to jury trial, and only the antiquities of directed verdict practice suggest that it might have been. The term "judgment as a matter of law" is an almost equally familiar term and appears in the text of

Rule 56; its use in Rule 50 calls attention to the relationship between the two rules. Finally, the change enables the rule to refer to preverdict and post-verdict motions with a terminology that does not conceal the common identity of two motions made at different times in the proceeding.

If a motion is denominated a motion for directed verdict or for judgment notwithstanding the verdict, the party's error is merely formal. Such a motion should be treated as a motion for judgment as a matter of law in accordance with this rule.

Paragraph (a)(1) articulates the standard for the granting of a motion for judgment as a matter of law. It effects no change in the existing standard. That existing standard was not expressed in the former rule, but was articulated in long-standing case law. *See generally* Cooper, *Directions for Directed Verdicts: A Compass for Federal Courts*, 55 MINN.L.REV. 903 (1971). The expressed standard makes clear that action taken under the rule is a performance of the court's duty to assure enforcement of the controlling law and is not an intrusion on any responsibility for factual determinations conferred on the jury by the Seventh Amendment or any other provision of federal law. Because this standard is also used as a reference point for entry of summary judgment under 56(a), it serves to link the two related provisions.

The revision authorizes the court to perform its duty to enter judgment as a matter of law at any time during the trial, as soon as it is apparent that either party is unable to carry a burden of proof that is essential to that party's case. Thus, the second sentence of paragraph (a)(1) authorizes the court to consider a motion for judgment as a matter of law as soon as a party has completed a presentation on a fact essential to that party's case. Such early action is appropriate when economy and expedition will be served. In no event, however, should the court enter judgment against a party who has not been apprised of the materiality of the dispositive fact and been afforded an opportunity to present any available evidence bearing on that fact. In order further to facilitate the exercise of the authority provided by this rule, Rule 16 is also revised to encourage the court to schedule an order of trial that proceeds first with a presentation on an issue that is likely to be dispositive, if such an issue is identified in the course of pretrial. Such scheduling can be appropriate where the court is uncertain whether favorable action should be taken under Rule 56. Thus, the revision affords the court the alternative of denying a motion for summary judgment while scheduling a separate trial of the issue under Rule 42(b) or scheduling the trial to begin with a presentation on that essential fact which the opposing party seems unlikely to be able to maintain.

Paragraph (a)(2) retains the requirement that a motion for judgment be made prior to the close of the trial, subject to renewal after a jury verdict has been rendered. The purpose of this requirement is to assure the responding party an opportunity to cure any deficiency in that party's proof that may have been overlooked until called to the party's attention by a late motion for judgment. Cf. *Farley Transp. Co. v. Santa Fe Trail Transp. Co.*, 786 F.2d 1342 (9th Cir.1986) ("If the moving party is then permitted to make a later attack on the evidence through a motion for judgment notwithstanding the verdict or an appeal, the opposing party may be prejudiced by having lost the opportunity to present additional evidence before the case was submitted to the jury"); *Benson v. Allphin*, 786 F.2d 268 (7th Cir.1986) ("the motion for directed verdict at the close of all the evidence

provides the nonmovant an opportunity to do what he can to remedy the deficiencies in his case . . .); *McLaughlin v. The Fellows Gear Shaper Co.*, 4 F.R.Serv.3d 607 (3d Cir.1986) (per Adams, J., dissenting: "This Rule serves important practical purposes in ensuring that neither party is precluded from presenting the most persuasive case possible and in preventing unfair surprise after a matter has been submitted to the jury"). At one time, this requirement was held to be of constitutional stature, being compelled by the Seventh Amendment. Cf. *Slocum v. New York Insurance Co.*, 228 U.S. 364 (1913). But cf. *Baltimore & Carolina Line v. Redman*, 295 U.S. 654 (1935).

The second sentence of paragraph (a)(2) does impose a requirement that the moving party articulate the basis on which a judgment as a matter of law might be rendered. The articulation is necessary to achieve the purpose of the requirement that the motion be made before the case is submitted to the jury, so that the responding party may seek to correct any overlooked deficiencies in the proof. The revision thus alters the result in cases in which courts have used various techniques to avoid the requirement that a motion for a directed verdict be made as a predicate to a motion for judgment notwithstanding the verdict. E.g., *Benson v. Allphin*, 788 F.2d 268 (7th Cir.1986) ("this circuit has allowed something less than a formal motion for directed verdict to preserve a party's right to move for judgment notwithstanding the verdict"). *See generally* 9 WRIGHT & MILLER, FEDERAL PRACTICE AND PROCEDURE § 2537 (1971 and Supp.). The information required with the motion may be supplied by explicit reference to materials and argument previously supplied to the court.

This subdivision deals only with the entry of judgment and not with the resolution of particular factual issues as a matter of law. The court may, as before, properly refuse to instruct a jury to decide an issue if a reasonable jury could on the evidence presented decide that issue in only one way.

Subdivision (b). This provision retains the concept of the former rule that the post-verdict motion is a renewal of an earlier motion made at the close of the evidence. One purpose of this concept was to avoid any question arising under the Seventh Amendment. *Montgomery Ward & Co. v. Duncan*, 311 U.S. 243 (1940). It remains useful as a means of defining the appropriate issue posed by the post-verdict motion. A post-trial motion for judgment can be granted only on grounds advanced in the pre-verdict motion. E.g., *Kutner Buick, Inc. v. American Motors Corp.*, 848 F.2d 614 (3d Cir.1989).

Often it appears to the court or to the moving party that a motion for judgment as a matter of law made at the close of the evidence should be reserved for a post-verdict decision. This is so because a jury verdict for the moving party moots the issue and because a preverdict ruling gambles that a reversal may result in a new trial that might have been avoided. For these reasons, the court may often wisely decline to rule on a motion for judgment as a matter of law made at the close of the evidence, and it is not inappropriate for the moving party to suggest such a postponement of the ruling until after the verdict has been rendered.

In ruling on such a motion, the court should disregard any jury determination for which there is no legally sufficient evidentiary basis enabling a reasonable jury to make it. The court may then decide such issues as a matter of law and enter judgment if all other material issues have been decided

by the jury on the basis of legally sufficient evidence, or by the court as a matter of law.

The revised rule is intended for use in this manner with Rule 49. Thus, the court may combine facts established as a matter of law either before trial under Rule 56 or at trial on the basis of the evidence presented with other facts determined by the jury under instructions provided under Rule 49 to support a proper judgment under this rule.

This provision also retains the former requirement that a post-trial motion under the rule must be made within 10 days after entry of a contrary judgment. The renewed motion must be served and filed as provided by Rule 5. A purpose of this requirement is to meet the requirements of F.R.App.P. 4(a)(4).

Subdivision (c). Revision of this subdivision conforms the language to the change in diction set forth in subdivision (a) of this revised rule.

Subdivision (d). Revision of this subdivision conforms the language to that of the previous subdivisions.

1993 Amendments

This technical amendment corrects an ambiguity in the text of the 1991 revision of the rule, which, as indicated in the Notes, was not intended to change the existing standards under which "directed verdicts" could be granted. This amendment makes clear that judgments as a matter of law in jury trials may be entered against both plaintiffs and defendants and with respect to issues or defenses that may not be wholly dispositive of a claim or defense.

1995 Amendments

The only change, other than stylistic, intended by this revision is to prescribe a uniform explicit time for filing of post-judgment motions under this rule—no later than 10 days after entry of the judgment. Previously, there was an inconsistency in the wording of Rules 50, 52, and 59 with respect to whether certain post-judgment motions had to be filed, or merely served, during that period. This inconsistency caused special problems when motions for a new trial were joined with other post-judgment motions. These motions affect the finality of the judgment, a matter often of importance to third persons as well as the parties and the court. The Committee believes that each of these rules should be revised to require filing before end of the 10–day period. Filing is an event that can be determined with certainty from court records. The phrase "no later than" is used—rather than "within"—to include post-judgment motions that sometimes are filed before actual entry of the judgment by the clerk. It should be noted that under Rule 6(a) Saturdays, Sundays, and legal holidays are excluded in measuring the 10–day period, and that under Rule 5 the motions when filed are to contain a certificate of service on other parties.

2006 Amendment

The language of Rule 50(a) has been amended as part of the general restyling of the Civil Rules to make them more easily understood and to make style and terminology consistent throughout the rules. These changes are intended to be stylistic only.

Rule 50(b) is amended to permit renewal of any Rule 50(a) motion for judgment as a matter of law, deleting the requirement that a motion be made at the close of all the evidence. Because the Rule 50(b) motion is only a renewal of the preverdict motion, it can be granted only on grounds advanced in the preverdict motion. The earlier motion informs the opposing party of the challenge to the sufficiency of the evidence and affords a clear opportunity to provide additional evidence that may be available. The earlier motion also alerts the court to the opportunity to simplify the trial by resolving some issues, or even all issues, without submission to the jury. This fulfillment of the functional needs that underlie present Rule 50(b) also satisfies the Seventh Amendment. Automatic reservation of the legal questions raised by the motion conforms to the decision in *Baltimore & Carolina Line v. Redman*, 297 U.S. 654 (1935).

This change responds to many decisions that have begun to move away from requiring a motion for judgment as a matter of law at the literal close of all the evidence. Although the requirement has been clearly established for several decades, lawyers continue to overlook it. The courts are slowly working away from the formal requirement. The amendment establishes the functional approach that courts have been unable to reach under the present rule and makes practice more consistent and predictable.

Many judges expressly invite motions at the close of all the evidence. The amendment is not intended to discourage this useful practice.

Finally, an explicit time limit is added for making a posttrial motion when the trial ends without a verdict or with a verdict that does not dispose of all issues suitable for resolution by verdict. The motion must be made no later than 10 days after the jury was discharged.

2007 Amendments

[Effective December 1, 2007,
absent contrary Congressional action.]

The language of Rule 50 has been amended as part of the general restyling of the Civil Rules to make them more easily understood and to make style and terminology consistent throughout the rules. These changes are intended to be stylistic only.

Former Rule 50(b) stated that the court reserves ruling on a motion for judgment as a matter of law made at the close of all the evidence "[i]f, for any reason, the court does not grant" the motion. The words "for any reason" reflected the proposition that the reservation is automatic and inescapable. The ruling is reserved even if the court explicitly denies the motion. The same result follows under the amended rule. If the motion is not granted, the ruling is reserved.

Amended Rule 50(e) identifies the appellate court's authority to direct the entry of judgment. This authority was not described in former Rule 50(d), but was recognized in *Weisgram v. Marley Co.*, 528 U.S. 440 (2000), and in *Neely v. Martin K. Eby Construction Company*, 386 U.S. 317 (1967). When Rule 50(d) was drafted in 1963, the Committee Note stated that "[s]ubdivision (d) does not attempt a regulation of all aspects of the procedure where the motion for judgment n.o.v. and any accompanying motion for a new trial are denied * * *." Express recognition of the authority to direct entry of judgment does not otherwise supersede this caution.

Rule 51. Instructions to Jury; Objections; Preserving a Claim of Error

(a) Requests.

(1) A party may, at the close of the evidence or at an earlier reasonable time that the court directs, file and furnish to every other party written requests that the court instruct the jury on the law as set forth in the requests.

(2) After the close of the evidence, a party may:

(A) file requests for instructions on issues that could not reasonably have been anticipated at an earlier time for requests set under Rule 51(a)(1), and

(B) with the court's permission file untimely requests for instructions on any issue.

(b) Instructions. The court:

(1) must inform the parties of its proposed instructions and proposed action on the requests before instructing the jury and before final jury arguments;

(2) must give the parties an opportunity to object on the record and out of the jury's hearing to the proposed instructions and actions on requests before the instructions and arguments are delivered; and

(3) may instruct the jury at any time after trial begins and before the jury is discharged.

(c) Objections.

(1) A party who objects to an instruction or the failure to give an instruction must do so on the record, stating distinctly the matter objected to and the grounds of the objection.

(2) An objection is timely if:

(A) a party that has been informed of an instruction or action on a request before the jury is instructed and before final jury arguments, as provided by Rule 51(b)(1), objects at the opportunity for objection required by Rule 51(b)(2); or

(B) a party that has not been informed of an instruction or action on a request before the time for objection provided under Rule 51(b)(2) objects promptly after learning that the instruction or request will be, or has been, given or refused.

(d) Assigning Error; Plain Error.

(1) A party may assign as error:

(A) an error in an instruction actually given if that party made a proper objection under Rule 51(c), or

(B) a failure to give an instruction if that party made a proper request under Rule 51(a), and—unless the court made a definitive ruling on the record rejecting the request—also made a proper objection under Rule 51(c).

(2) A court may consider a plain error in the instructions affecting substantial rights that has not been preserved as required by Rule 51(d)(1)(A) or (B).

(As amended Mar. 2, 1987, eff. Aug. 1, 1987; Mar. 27, 2003, eff. Dec. 1, 2003.)

Proposed Amendment of Rule

Effective December 1, 2007, absent contrary Congressional action, this rule is amended to read as follows:

Rule 51. *Instructions to the Jury; Objections; Preserving a Claim of Error*

(a) *Requests.*

(1) Before or at the Close of the Evidence. At the close of the evidence or at any earlier reasonable time that the court orders, a party may file and furnish to every other party written requests for the jury instructions it wants the court to give.

(2) After the Close of the Evidence. After the close of the evidence, a party may:

(A) file requests for instructions on issues that could not reasonably have been anticipated by an earlier time that the court set for requests; and

(B) with the court's permission, file untimely requests for instructions on any issue.

(b) *Instructions. The court:*

(1) must inform the parties of its proposed instructions and proposed action on the requests before instructing the jury and before final jury arguments;

(2) must give the parties an opportunity to object on the record and out of the jury's hearing before the instructions and arguments are delivered; and

(3) may instruct the jury at any time before the jury is discharged.

(c) *Objections.*

(1) How to Make. A party who objects to an instruction or the failure to give an instruction must do so on the record, stating distinctly the matter objected to and the grounds for the objection.

(2) When to Make. An objection is timely if:

(A) a party objects at the opportunity provided under Rule 51(b)(2); or

(B) a party was not informed of an instruction or action on a request before that opportunity to object, and the party objects promptly

after learning that the instruction or request will be, or has been, given or refused.

(d) Assigning Error; Plain Error.

(1) Assigning Error. A party may assign as error:

 (A) an error in an instruction actually given, if that party properly objected; or

 (B) a failure to give an instruction, if that party properly requested it and—unless the court rejected the request in a definitive ruling on the record—also properly objected.

(2) Plain Error. A court may consider a plain error in the instructions that has not been preserved as required by Rule 51(d)(1) if the error affects substantial rights.

ADVISORY COMMITTEE NOTES

1937 Adoption

Supreme Court Rule 8 requires exceptions to the charge of the court to the jury which shall distinctly state the several matters of law in the charge to which exception is taken. Similar provisions appear in the rules of the various Circuit Courts of Appeals.

1987 Amendment

Although Rule 51 in its present form specifies that the court shall instruct the jury only after the arguments of the parties are completed, in some districts (typically those in states where the practice is otherwise) it is common for the parties to stipulate to instruction before the arguments. The purpose of the amendment is to give the court discretion to instruct the jury either before or after argument. Thus, the rule as revised will permit resort to the long-standing federal practice or to an alternative procedure, which has been praised because it gives counsel the opportunity to explain the instructions, argue their application to the facts and thereby give the jury the maximum assistance in determining the issues and arriving at a good verdict on the law and the evidence. As an ancillary benefit, this approach aids counsel by supplying a natural outline so that arguments may be directed to the essential fact issues which the jury must decide. See generally Raymond, *Merits and Demerits of the Missouri System of Instructing Juries*, 5 St. Louis U.L.J. 317 (1959). Moreover, if the court instructs before an argument, counsel then know the precise words the court has chosen and need not speculate as to the words the court will later use in its instructions. Finally, by instructing ahead of argument the court has the attention of the jurors when they are fresh and can give their full attention to the court's instructions. It is more difficult to hold the attention of jurors after lengthy arguments.

2003 Amendments

Rule 51 is revised to capture many of the interpretations that have emerged in practice. The revisions in text will make uniform the conclusions reached by a majority of decisions on each point. Additions also are made to cover

some practices that cannot now be anchored in the text of Rule 51.

Scope. Rule 51 governs instructions to the trial jury on the law that governs the verdict. A variety of other instructions cannot practicably be brought within Rule 51. Among these instructions are preliminary instructions to a venire, and cautionary or limiting instructions delivered in immediate response to events at trial.

Requests. Subdivision (a) governs requests. Apart from the plain error doctrine recognized in subdivision (d)(2), a court is not obliged to instruct the jury on issues raised by the evidence unless a party requests an instruction. The revised rule recognizes the court's authority to direct that requests be submitted before trial.

The close-of-the-evidence deadline may come before trial is completed on all potential issues. Trial may be formally bifurcated or may be sequenced in some less formal manner. The close of the evidence is measured by the occurrence of two events: completion of all intended evidence on an identified phase of the trial and impending submission to the jury with instructions.

The risk in directing a pretrial request deadline is that trial evidence may raise new issues or reshape issues the parties thought they had understood. Courts need not insist on pretrial requests in all cases. Even if the request time is set before trial or early in the trial, subdivision (a)(2)(A) permits requests after the close of the evidence to address issues that could not reasonably have been anticipated at the earlier time for requests set by the court.

Subdivision (a)(2)(B) expressly recognizes the court's discretion to act on an untimely request. The most important consideration in exercising the discretion confirmed by subdivision (a)(2)(B) is the importance of the issue to the case—the closer the issue lies to the "plain error" that would be recognized under subdivision (d)(2), the better the reason to give an instruction. The cogency of the reason for failing to make a timely request also should be considered. To be considered under subdivision (a)(2)(B) a request should be made before final instructions and before final jury arguments. What is a "final" instruction and argument depends on the sequence of submitting the case to the jury. If separate portions of the case are submitted to the jury in sequence, the final arguments and final instructions are those made on submitting to the jury the portion of the case addressed by the arguments and instructions.

Instructions. Subdivision (b)(1) requires the court to inform the parties, before instructing the jury and before final jury arguments related to the instruction, of the proposed instructions as well as the proposed action on instruction requests. The time limit is addressed to final jury arguments to reflect the practice that allows interim argument s during trial in complex cases; it may not be feasible to develop final instructions before such interim arguments. It is enough that counsel know of the intended instructions before making final arguments addressed to the issue. If the trial is sequenced or bifurcated, the final arguments addressed to an issue may occur before the close of the entire trial.

Subdivision (b)(2) complements subdivision (b)(1) by carrying forward the opportunity to object established by present Rule 51. It makes explicit the opportunity to object on the record, ensuring a clear memorial of the objection.

Subdivision (b)(3) reflects common practice by authorizing instructions at any time after trial begins and before the jury is discharged.

Objections. Subdivision (c) states the right to object to an instruction or the failure to give an instruction. It carries forward the formula of present Rule 51 requiring that the objection state distinctly the matter objected to and the grounds of the objection, and makes explicit the requirement that the objection be made on the record. The provisions on the time to object make clear that it is timely to object promptly after learning of an instruction or action on a request when the court has not provided advance information as required by subdivision (b)(1). The need to repeat a request by way of objection is continued by new subdivision (d)(1)(B) except where the court made a definitive ruling on the record.

Preserving a claim of error and plain error. Many cases hold that a proper request for a jury instruction is not alone enough to preserve the right to appeal failure to give the instruction. The request must be renewed by objection. This doctrine is appropriate when the court may not have sufficiently focused on the request, or may believe that the request has been granted in substance although in different words. But this doctrine may also prove a trap for the unwary who fail to add an objection after the court has made it clear that the request has been considered and rejected on the merits. Subdivision (d)(1)(B) establishes authority to review the failure to grant a timely request, despite a failure to add an objection, when the court has made a definitive ruling on the record rejecting the request.

Many circuits have recognized that an error not preserved under Rule 51 may be reviewed in exceptional circumstances. The language adopted to capture these decisions in subdivision (d)(2) is borrowed from Criminal Rule 52. Although the language is the same, the context of civil litigation often differs from the context of criminal prosecution; actual application of the plain-error standard takes account of the differences. The Supreme Court has summarized application of Criminal Rule 52 as involving four elements: (1) there must be an error; (2) the error must be plain; (3) the error must affect substantial rights; and (4) the error must seriously affect the fairness, integrity, or public reputation of judicial proceedings. Johnson v. U.S., 520 U.S. 461, 466–467, 469–470 (1997). (The Johnson case quoted the fourth element from its decision in a civil action, U.S. v. Atkinson, 297 U.S. 157, 160 (1936): "In exceptional circumstances, especially in criminal cases, appellate courts, in the public interest, may, of their own motion, notice errors to which no exception has been taken, if the errors are obvious, or if they otherwise substantially affect the fairness, integrity, or public reputation of judicial proceedings.")

The court's duty to give correct jury instructions in a civil action is shaped by at least four factors.

The factor most directly implied by a "plain" error rule is the obviousness of the mistake. The importance of the error is a second major factor. The costs of correcting an error reflect a third factor that is affected by a variety of circumstances. In a case that seems close to the fundamental error line, account also may be taken of the impact a verdict may have on nonparties.

2007 Amendments

*[Effective December 1, 2007,
absent contrary Congressional action.]*

The language of Rule 51 has been amended as part of the general restyling of the Civil Rules to make them more easily understood and to make style and terminology consistent throughout the rules. These changes are intended to be stylistic only.

Rule 52. Findings by the Court; Judgment on Partial Findings

(a) Effect. In all actions tried upon the facts without a jury or with an advisory jury, the court shall find the facts specially and state separately its conclusions of law thereon, and judgment shall be entered pursuant to Rule 58; and in granting or refusing interlocutory injunctions the court shall similarly set forth the findings of fact and conclusions of law which constitute the grounds of its action. Requests for findings are not necessary for purposes of review. Findings of fact, whether based on oral or documentary evidence, shall not be set aside unless clearly erroneous, and due regard shall be given to the opportunity of the trial court to judge of the credibility of the witnesses. The findings of a master, to the extent that the court adopts them, shall be considered as the findings of the court. It will be sufficient if the findings of fact and conclusions of law are stated orally and recorded in open court following the close of the evidence or appear in an opinion or memorandum of decision filed by the court. Findings of fact and conclusions of law are unnecessary on decisions of motions under Rule 12 or 56 or any other motion except as provided in subdivision (c) of this rule.

(b) Amendment. On a party's motion filed no later than 10 days after entry of judgment, the court may amend its findings—or make additional findings—and may amend the judgment accordingly. The motion may accompany a motion for a new trial under Rule 59. When findings of fact are made in actions tried without a jury, the sufficiency of the evidence supporting the findings may be later questioned whether or not in the district court the party raising the question objected to the findings, moved to amend them, or moved for partial findings.

(c) Judgment on Partial Findings. If during a trial without a jury a party has been fully heard on an issue and the court finds against the party on that issue, the court may enter judgment as a matter of law against that party with respect to a claim or defense that cannot under the controlling law be maintained or defeated without a favorable finding on that issue, or the court may decline to render any judgment until the close of all the evidence. Such a judgment shall be supported by findings of fact and conclusions of law as required by subdivision (a) of this rule.

(As amended Dec. 27, 1946, eff. Mar. 19, 1948; Jan. 21, 1963, eff. July 1, 1963; Apr. 28, 1983, eff. Aug. 1, 1983; Apr. 29, 1985, eff. Aug. 1, 1985; Apr. 30, 1991, eff. Dec. 1, 1991; Apr. 22, 1993, eff. Dec. 1, 1993; Apr. 27, 1995, eff. Dec. 1, 1995.)

Proposed Amendment of Rule

Effective December 1, 2007, absent contrary Congressional action, this rule is amended to read as follows:

Rule 52. Findings and Conclusions by the Court; Judgment on Partial Findings

(a) Findings and Conclusions.

(1) In General. In an action tried on the facts without a jury or with an advisory jury, the court must find the facts specially and state its conclusions of law separately. The findings and conclusions may be stated on the record after the close of the evidence or may appear in an opinion or a memorandum of decision filed by the court. Judgment must be entered under Rule 58.

(2) For an Interlocutory Injunction. In granting or refusing an interlocutory injunction, the court must similarly state the findings and conclusions that support its action.

(3) For a Motion. The court is not required to state findings or conclusions when ruling on a motion under Rule 12 or 56 or, unless these rules provide otherwise, on any other motion.

(4) Effect of a Master's Findings. A master's findings, to the extent adopted by the court, must be considered the court's findings.

(5) Questioning the Evidentiary Support. A party may later question the sufficiency of the evidence supporting the findings, whether or not the party requested findings, objected to them, moved to amend them, or moved for partial findings.

(6) Setting Aside the Findings. Findings of fact, whether based on oral or other evidence, must not be set aside unless clearly erroneous, and the reviewing court must give due regard to the trial court's opportunity to judge the witnesses' credibility.

(b) Amended or Additional Findings. *On a party's motion filed no later than 10 days after the entry of judgment, the court may amend its findings—or make additional findings—and may amend the judgment accordingly. The motion may accompany a motion for a new trial under Rule 59.*

(c) Judgment on Partial Findings. *If a party has been fully heard on an issue during a nonjury trial and the court finds against the party on that issue, the court may enter judgment against the party on a claim or defense that, under the controlling law, can*

be maintained or defeated only with a favorable finding on that issue. The court may, however, decline to render any judgment until the close of the evidence. A judgment on partial findings must be supported by findings of fact and conclusions of law as required by Rule 52(a).

ADVISORY COMMITTEE NOTES

1937 Adoption

See [former] Equity Rule 70½, as amended Nov. 25, 1935, (Findings of Fact and Conclusions of Law) and U.S.C., Title 28, [former] § 764 (Opinion, findings, and conclusions in action against United States) which are substantially continued in this rule. The provisions of U.S.C., Title 28, [former] §§ 773 (Trial of issues of fact; by court) and [former] 875 (Review in cases tried without a jury) are superseded in so far as they provide a different method of finding facts and a different method of appellate review. The rule stated in the third sentence of Subdivision (a) accords with the decisions on the scope of the review in modern federal equity practice. It is applicable to all classes of findings in cases tried without a jury whether the finding is of a fact concerning which there was conflict of testimony, or of a fact deduced or inferred from uncontradicted testimony. See *Silver King Coalition Mines Co. v. Silver King Consolidated Mining Co.*, C.C.A.8, 1913, 204 F. 166, certiorari denied 33 S.Ct. 1051, 229 U.S. 624, 57 L.Ed. 1356; *Warren v. Keep*, 1894, 15 S.Ct. 83, 155 U.S. 265, 39 L.Ed. 144; *Furrer v. Ferris*, 1892, 12 S.Ct. 821, 145 U.S. 132, 36 L.Ed. 649; *Tilghman v. Proctor*, 1888, 8 S.Ct. 894, 125 U.S. 136, 149, 31 L.Ed. 664; *Kimberly v. Arms*, 1889, 9 S.Ct. 355, 129 U.S. 512, 524, 32 L.Ed. 764. Compare *Kaeser & Blair Inc. v. Merchants' Ass'n*, C.C.A.6, 1933, 64 F.2d 575, 576; *Dunn v. Trefry*, C.C.A.1, 1919, 260 F. 147.

In the following states findings of fact are required in all cases tried without a jury (waiver by the parties being permitted as indicated at the end of the listing): Arkansas, Civ.Code (Crawford, 1934) § 364; California, Code Civ.Proc. (Deering, 1937) §§ 632, 634; Colorado, 1 Stat.Ann. (1935) Code Civ.Proc. §§ 232, 291 (in actions before referees or for possession of and damages to land); Connecticut, Gen.Stats. §§ 5660, 5664; Idaho, 1 Code Ann. (1932) §§ 7–302 through 7–305; Massachusetts (equity cases), 2 Gen.Laws (Ter.Ed., 1932) ch. 214, § 23; Minnesota, 2 Stat. (Mason, 1927) § 9311; Nevada, 4 Comp.Laws (Hillyer, 1929) §§ 8783–8784; New Jersey, Sup.Ct.Rule 113, 2 N.J.Misc. 1197, 1239 (1924); New Mexico, Stat.Ann. (Courtright, 1929) §§ 105–813; North Carolina, Code (1935) § 569; North Dakota, 2 Comp.Laws Ann. (1913) § 7641; Oregon, 2 Code Ann. (1930) §§ 2–502; South Carolina, Code (Michie, 1932) § 649; South Dakota, 1 Comp. Laws (1929) §§ 2525–2526; Utah, Rev.Stat.Ann. (1933) §§ 104–26–2, 104–26–3; Vermont (where jury trial waived), Pub.Laws (1933) § 2069; Washington, 2 Rev.Stat.Ann. (Remington, 1932) § 367; Wisconsin, Stat. (1935) § 270.33. The parties may waive this requirement for findings in California, Idaho, North Dakota, Nevada, New Mexico, Utah, and South Dakota.

In the following states the review of findings of fact in all non-jury cases, including jury waived cases, is assimilated to the equity review: Alabama, Code Ann. (Michie, 1928) §§ 9498, 8599; California, Code Civ.Proc. (Derring, 1937) § 956a; but see 20 Calif.Law Rev. 171 (1932); Colorado,

Johnson v. Kountze, 1895, 43 P. 445, 21 Colo. 486, semble; Illinois, *Baker v. Hinricks,* 1934, 194 N.E. 284, 359 Ill. 138; *Weininger v. Metropolitan Fire Ins. Co.,* 1935, 195 N.E. 420, 359 Ill. 584, 98 A.L.R. 169; Minnesota, *State Bank of Gibbon v. Walter,* 1926, 208 N.W. 423, 167 Minn. 37; *Waldron v. Page,* 1934, 253 N.W. 894, 191 Minn. 302; New Jersey N.J.S.A. 2:27–241, 2:27–363, as interpreted in *Bussy v. Hatch,* 1920, 111 A. 546, 95 N.J.L. 56; New York, *York Mortgage Corporation v. Clotar Const. Corp.,* 1930, 172 N.E. 265, 254 N.Y. 128; North Dakota, Comp.Laws Ann. (1913) § 7846, as amended by N.D.Laws 1933, c. 208; *Milnor Holding Co. v. Holt,* 1933, 248 N.W. 315, 63 N.D. 362, 370; Oklahoma, *Wichita Mining and Improvement Co. v. Hale,* 1908, 94 P. 530, 20 Okl. 159; South Dakota, *Randall v. Burk Township,* 4 S.D. 337, 57 N.W. 4 (1893); Texas, *Custard v. Flowers,* 1929, 14 S.W.2d 109; Utah, Rev.Stat.Ann. (1933) § 104–41–5; Vermont, *Roberge v. Troy,* 1933, 163 A. 770, 105 Vt. 134; Washington, 2 Rev.Stat.Ann. (Remington, 1932) §§ 309–316; *McCullough v. Puget Sound Realty Associates,* 1913, 136 Pac. 1146, 76 Wash. 700, but see *Cornwall v. Anderson,* 1915, 148 P. 1, 85 Wash. 369; West Virginia, *Kinsey v. Carr,* 1906, 55 S.E. 1004, 60 W.Va. 449, semble; Wisconsin, Stat. (1935) § 251.09; *Campbell v. Sutliff,* 1927, 214 N.W. 374, 193 Wis. 370; *Gessler v. Erwin Co.,* 1924, 193 N.W. 303, 182 Wis. 315.

For examples of an assimilation of the review of findings of fact in cases tried without a jury to the review at law as made in several states, see Clark and Stone, *Review of Findings of Fact,* 4 U. of Chi.L.Rev. 190, 215 (1937).

1946 Amendment

Note to Subdivision (a). The amended rule makes clear that the requirement for findings of fact and conclusions of law thereon applies in a case with an advisory jury. This removes an ambiguity in the rule as originally stated, but carries into effect what has been considered its intent. 3 *Moore's Federal Practice,* 1938, 3119. *Hurwitz v. Hurwitz,* 1943, 136 F.2d 796, 78 U.S.App.D.C. 66.

The two sentences added at the end of Rule 52(a) eliminate certain difficulties which have arisen concerning findings and conclusions. The first of the two sentences permits findings of fact and conclusions of law to appear in an opinion or memorandum of decision. See, e.g., *United States v. One 1941 Ford Sedan,* S.D.Tex.1946, 65 F.Supp. 84. Under original Rule 52(a) some courts have expressed the view that findings and conclusions could not be incorporated in an opinion. *Detective Comics, Inc. v. Bruns Publications,* S.D.N.Y.1939, 28 F.Supp. 399; *Pennsylvania Co. for Insurance on Lives & Granting Annuities v. Cincinnati & L.E.R. Co.,* S.D.Ohio 1941, 43 F.Supp. 5; *United States v. Aluminum Co. of America,* S.D.N.Y.1941, 2 F.R.D. 224, 5 Fed. Rules Serv. 52a.11, Case 3; see also s.c., 44 F.Supp. 97. But, to the contrary, see *Wellman v. United States,* D.Mass.1938, 25 F.Supp. 868; *Cook v. United States,* D.Mass.1939, 26 F.Supp. 253; *Proctor v. White,* D.Mass.1939, 28 F.Supp. 161; *Green Valley Creamery, Inc. v. United States,* C.C.A.1, 1939, 108 F.2d 342. See also *Matton Oil Transfer Corp. v. The Dynamic,* C.C.A.2, 1941, 123 F.2d 999; *Carter Coal Co. v. Litz,* C.C.A.4, 1944, 140 F.2d 934; *Woodruff v. Heiser,* C.C.A.10, 1945, 150 F.2d 869; *Coca Cola Co. v. Busch,* Pa.1943, 7 Fed. Rules Serv. 59b.2, Case 4; Oglebay, *Some Developments in Bankruptcy Law,* 1944, 18 J. of Nat'l Ass'n of Ref. 68, 69. Findings of fact aid in the process of

judgment and in defining for future cases the precise limitations of the issues and the determination thereon. Thus they not only aid the appellate court on review, *Hurwitz v. Hurwitz,* App.D.C.1943, 136 F.2d 796, 78 U.S.App.D.C. 66, but they are an important factor in the proper application of the doctrines of res judicata and estoppel by judgment. Nordbye, *Improvements in Statement of Findings of Fact and Conclusions of Law,* 1 F.R.D. 25, 26–27; *United States v. Forness,* C.C.A.2, 1942, 125 F.2d 928, certiorari denied 1942, 62 S.Ct. 1293, 316 U.S. 694, 86 L.Ed. 1764. These findings should represent the judge's own determination and not the long, often argumentative statements of successful counsel. *United States v. Forness,* supra; *United States v. Crescent Amusement Co.,* 1944, 1945, 65 S.Ct. 254, 323 U.S. 173, 89 L.Ed. 160. Consequently, they should be a part of the judge's opinion and decision, either stated therein or stated separately. *Matton Oil Transfer Corp. v. The Dynamic,* supra. But the judge need only make brief, definite, pertinent findings and conclusions upon the contested matters; there is no necessity for over-elaboration of detail or particularization of facts. *United States v. Forness,* supra; *United States v. Crescent Amusement Co.,* supra. See also *Petterson Lighterage & Towing Corp. v. New York Central R. Co.,* C.C.A.2, 1942, 126 F.2d 992; *Brown Paper Mill Co., Inc. v. Irwin,* C.C.A.8, 1943, 134 F.2d 337; *Allen Bradley Co. v. Local Union No. 3, I.B.E.W.,* C.C.A.2, 1944, 145 F.2d 215, reversed on other grounds 65 S.Ct. 1533, 325 U.S. 797; *Young v. Murphy,* Ohio 1946, 9 Fed.Rules Serv. 52a.11, Case 2.

The last sentence of Rule 52(a) as amended will remove any doubt that findings and conclusions are unnecessary upon decision of a motion, particularly one under Rule 12 or Rule 56, except as provided in amended Rule 41(b). As so holding, see *Thomas v. Peyser,* App.D.C.1941, 118 F.2d 369; *Schad v. Twentieth Century-Fox Corp.,* C.C.A.3, 1943, 136 F.2d 991; *Prudential Ins. Co. of America v. Goldstein,* N.Y.1942, 43 F.Supp. 767; *Somers Coal Co. v. United States,* N.D.Ohio 1942, 2 F.R.D. 532, 6 Fed.Rules Serv. 52a.1, Case 1; *Pen-Ken Oil & Gas Corp. v. Warfield Natural Gas Co.,* E.D.Ky.1942, 2 F.R.D. 355, 5 Fed. Rules Serv. 52a.1, Case 3; also Commentary, *Necessity of Findings of Fact,* 1941, 4 Fed. Rules Serv. 936.

1963 Amendment

This amendment conforms to the amendment of Rule 58. See the Advisory Committee's Note to Rule 58, as amended.

1983 Amendment

Rule 52(a) has been amended to revise its penultimate sentence to provide explicitly that the district judge may make the findings of fact and conclusions of law required in nonjury cases orally. Nothing in the prior text of the rule forbids this practice, which is widely utilized by district judges. See Christensen, *A Modest Proposal for Immeasurable Improvement,* 64 A.B.A.J. 693 (1978). The objective is to lighten the burden on the trial court in preparing findings in nonjury cases. In addition, the amendment should reduce the number of published district court opinions that embrace written findings.

1985 Amendment

Rule 52(a) has been amended (1) to avoid continued confusion and conflicts among the circuits as to the standard of appellate review of findings of fact by the court, (2) to eliminate the disparity between the standard of review as literally stated in Rule 52(a) and the practice of some courts of appeals, and (3) to promote nationwide uniformity. See Note, *Rule 52(a): Appellate Review of Findings of Fact Based on Documentary or Undisputed Evidence*, 49 Va. L.Rev. 506, 536 (1963).

Some courts of appeal have stated that when a trial court's findings do not rest on demeanor evidence and evaluation of a witness' credibility, there is no reason to defer to the trial court's findings and the appellate court more readily can find them to be clearly erroneous. See, e.g., *Marcum v. United States*, 621 F.2d 142, 144–45 (5th Cir.1980). Others go further, holding that appellate review may be had without application of the "clearly erroneous" test since the appellate court is in as good a position as the trial court to review a purely documentary record. See, *e.g., Atari, Inc. v. North American Philips Consumer Electronics Corp.*, 672 F.2d 607, 614 (7th Cir.), cert. denied, 459 U.S. 880 (1982); *Lydle v. United States*, 635 F.2d 763, 765 n. 1 (6th Cir.1981); *Swanson v. Baker Indus., Inc.*, 615 F.2d 479, 483 (8th Cir.1980); *Taylor v. Lombard*, 606 F.2d 371, 372 (2d Cir.1979), cert. denied, 445 U.S. 946 (1980); *Jack Kahn Music Co. v. Baldwin Piano & Organ Co.*, 604 F.2d 755, 758 (2d Cir.1979); *John R. Thompson Co. v. United States*, 477 F.2d 164, 167 (7th Cir.1973).

A third group has adopted the view that the "clearly erroneous" rule applies in all nonjury cases even when findings are based solely on documentary evidence or on inferences from undisputed facts. See, *e.g., Maxwell v. Sumner*, 673 F.2d 1031, 1036 (9th Cir.), *cert. denied*, 459 U.S. 976 (1982); *United States v. Texas Education Agency*, 647 F.2d 504, 506–07 (5th Cir.1981), *cert. denied*, 454 U.S. 1143 (1982); *Constructora Maza, Inc. v. Banco de Ponce*, 616 F.2d 573, 576 (1st Cir.1980); *In re Sierra Trading Corp.*, 482 F.2d 333, 337 (10th Cir.1973); *Case v. Morrisette*, 475 F.2d 1300, 1306–07 (D.C.Cir.1973).

The commentators also disagree as to the proper interpretation of the Rule. *Compare* Wright, *The Doubtful Omniscience of Appellate Courts*, 41 Minn.L.Rev. 751, 769–70 (1957) (language and intent of Rule support view that "clearly erroneous" test should apply to all forms of evidence), *and* 9 C. Wright & A. Miller, *Federal Practice and Procedure: Civil § 2587*, at 740 (1971) (language of the Rule is clear), *with* 5A J. Moore, *Federal Practice* ¶ 52.04, 2687–88 (2d ed. 1982) (Rule as written supports broader review of findings based on non-demeanor testimony).

The Supreme Court has not clearly resolved the issue. See, *Bose Corp. v. Consumers Union of United States, Inc.*, 466 U.S. 485, 104 S.Ct. 1949, 1958 (1984); *Pullman Standard v. Swint*, 456 U.S. 273, 293 (1982); *United States v. General Motors Corp.*, 384 U.S. 127, 141 n. 16 (1966); *United States v. United States Gypsum Co.*, 333 U.S. 364, 394–96 (1948).

The principal argument advanced in favor of a more searching appellate review of findings by the district court based solely on documentary evidence is that the rationale of Rule 52(a) does not apply when the findings do not rest on the trial court's assessment of credibility of the witnesses but on an evaluation of documentary proof and the drawing of inferences from it, thus eliminating the need for any special deference to the trial court's findings. These considerations are outweighed by the public interest in the stability and judicial economy that would be promoted by recognizing that the trial court, not the appellate tribunal, should be the finder of the facts. To permit courts of appeals to share more actively in the fact-finding function would tend to undermine the legitimacy of the district courts in the eyes of litigants, multiply appeals by encouraging appellate retrial of some factual issues, and needlessly reallocate judicial authority.

1991 Amendment

Subdivision (c) is added. It parallels the revised Rule 50(a), but is applicable to non-jury trials. It authorizes the court to enter judgment at any time that it can appropriately make a dispositive finding of fact on the evidence.

The new subdivision replaces part of Rule 41(b), which formerly authorized a dismissal at the close of the plaintiff's case if the plaintiff had failed to carry an essential burden of proof. Accordingly, the reference to Rule 41 formerly made in subdivision (a) of this rule is deleted.

As under the former Rule 41(b), the court retains discretion to enter no judgment prior to the close of the evidence.

Judgment entered under this rule differs from a summary judgment under Rule 56 in the nature of the evaluation made by the court. A judgment on partial findings is made after the court has heard all the evidence bearing on the crucial issue of fact, and the finding is reversible only if the appellate court finds it to be "clearly erroneous." A summary judgment, in contrast, is made on the basis of facts established on account of the absence of contrary evidence or presumptions; such establishments of fact are rulings on questions of law as provided in Rule 56(a) and are not shielded by the "clear error" standard of review.

1993 Amendments

This technical amendment corrects an ambiguity in the text of the 1991 revision of the rule, similar to the revision being made to Rule 50. This amendment makes clear that judgments as a matter of law in nonjury trials may be entered against both plaintiffs and defendants and with respect to issues or defenses that may not be wholly dispositive of a claim or defense.

1995 Amendments

The only change, other than stylistic, intended by this revision is to require that any motion to amend or add findings after a nonjury trial must be filed no later than 10 days after entry of the judgment. Previously, there was an inconsistency in the wording of Rules 50, 52, and 59 with respect to whether certain post-judgment motions had to be filed, or merely served, during that period. This inconsistency caused special problems when motions for a new trial were joined with other post-judgment motions. These motions affect the finality of the judgment, a matter often of importance to third persons as well as the parties and the court. The Committee believes that each of these rules should be revised to require filing before end of the 10–day period. Filing is an event that can be determined with certainty from court records. The phrase "no later than" is used—rather than "within"—to include post-judgment mo-

tions that sometimes are filed before actual entry of the judgment by the clerk. It should be noted that under Rule 6(a) Saturdays, Sundays, and legal holidays are excluded in measuring the 10–day period, and that under Rule 5 the motions when filed are to contain a certificate of service on other parties.

2007 Amendments

[Effective December 1, 2007, absent contrary Congressional action.]

The language of Rule 52 has been amended as part of the general restyling of the Civil Rules to make them more easily understood and to make style and terminology consistent throughout the rules. These changes are intended to be stylistic only.

Former Rule 52(a) said that findings are unnecessary on decisions of motions "except as provided in subdivision (c) of this rule." Amended Rule 52(a)(3) says that findings are unnecessary "unless these rules provide otherwise." This change reflects provisions in other rules that require Rule 52 findings on deciding motions. Rules 23(e), 23(h), and 54(d)(2)(C) are examples.

Amended Rule 52(a)(5) includes provisions that appeared in former Rule 52(a) and 52(b). Rule 52(a) provided that requests for findings are not necessary for purposes of review. It applied both in an action tried on the facts without a jury and also in granting or refusing an interlocutory injunction. Rule 52(b), applicable to findings "made in actions tried without a jury," provided that the sufficiency of the evidence might be "later questioned whether or not in the district court the party raising the question objected to the findings, moved to amend them, or moved for partial findings." Former Rule 52(b) did not explicitly apply to decisions granting or refusing an interlocutory injunction. Amended Rule 52(a)(5) makes explicit the application of this part of former Rule 52(b) to interlocutory injunction decisions.

Former Rule 52(c) provided for judgment on partial findings, and referred to it as "judgment as a matter of law." Amended Rule 52(c) refers only to "judgment," to avoid any confusion with a Rule 50 judgment as a matter of law in a jury case. The standards that govern judgment as a matter of law in a jury case have no bearing on a decision under Rule 52(c).

Rule 53. Masters

(a) Appointment.

(1) Unless a statute provides otherwise, a court may appoint a master only to:

 (A) perform duties consented to by the parties;

 (B) hold trial proceedings and make or recommend findings of fact on issues to be decided by the court without a jury if appointment is warranted by

 (i) some exceptional condition, or

 (ii) the need to perform an accounting or resolve a difficult computation of damages; or

 (C) address pretrial and post-trial matters that cannot be addressed effectively and timely by an available district judge or magistrate judge of the district.

(2) A master must not have a relationship to the parties, counsel, action, or court that would require disqualification of a judge under 28 U.S.C. § 455 unless the parties consent with the court's approval to appointment of a particular person after disclosure of any potential grounds for disqualification.

(3) In appointing a master, the court must consider the fairness of imposing the likely expenses on the parties and must protect against unreasonable expense or delay.

(b) Order Appointing Master.

(1) **Notice.** The court must give the parties notice and an opportunity to be heard before appointing a master. A party may suggest candidates for appointment.

(2) **Contents.** The order appointing a master must direct the master to proceed with all reasonable diligence and must state:

 (A) the master's duties, including any investigation or enforcement duties, and any limits on the master's authority under Rule 53(c);

 (B) the circumstances—if any—in which the master may communicate ex parte with the court or a party;

 (C) the nature of the materials to be preserved and filed as the record of the master's activities;

 (D) the time limits, method of filing the record, other procedures, and standards for reviewing the master's orders, findings, and recommendations; and

 (E) the basis, terms, and procedure for fixing the master's compensation under Rule 53(h).

(3) **Entry of Order.** The court may enter the order appointing a master only after the master has filed an affidavit disclosing whether there is any ground for disqualification under 28 U.S.C. § 455 and, if a ground for disqualification is disclosed, after the parties have consented with the court's approval to waive the disqualification.

(4) **Amendment.** The order appointing a master may be amended at any time after notice to the parties, and an opportunity to be heard.

(c) Master's Authority.
Unless the appointing order expressly directs otherwise, a master has authority to regulate all proceedings and take all appropriate measures to perform fairly and efficiently the assigned duties. The master may by order impose upon a party any noncontempt sanction provided by Rule 37 or 45, and may recommend a contempt sanction against a party and sanctions against a nonparty.

(d) Evidentiary Hearings.
Unless the appointing order expressly directs otherwise, a master conducting an evidentiary hearing may exercise the power of the appointing court to compel, take, and record evidence.

(e) Master's Orders. A master who makes an order must file the order and promptly serve a copy on each party. The clerk must enter the order on the docket.

(f) Master's Reports. A master must report to the court as required by the order of appointment. The master must file the report and promptly serve a copy of the report on each party unless the court directs otherwise.

(g) Action on Master's Order, Report, or Recommendations.

(1) Action. In acting on a master's order, report, or recommendations, the court must afford an opportunity to be heard and may receive evidence, and may: adopt or affirm; modify; wholly or partly reject or reverse; or resubmit to the master with instructions.

(2) Time To Object or Move. A party may file objections to—or a motion to adopt or modify—the master's order, report, or recommendations no later than 20 days from the time the master's order, report, or recommendations are served, unless the court sets a different time.

(3) Fact Findings. The court must decide de novo all objections to findings of fact made or recommended by a master unless the parties stipulate with the court's consent that:

(A) the master's findings will be reviewed for clear error, or

(B) the findings of a master appointed under Rule 53(a)(1)(A) or (C) will be final.

(4) Legal Conclusions. The court must decide de novo all objections to conclusions of law made or recommended by a master.

(5) Procedural Matters. Unless the order of appointment establishes a different standard of review, the court may set aside a master's ruling on a procedural matter only for an abuse of discretion.

(h) Compensation.

(1) Fixing Compensation. The court must fix the master's compensation before or after judgment on the basis and terms stated in the order of appointment, but the court may set a new basis and terms after notice and an opportunity to be heard.

(2) Payment. The compensation fixed under Rule 53(h)(1) must be paid either:

(A) by a party or parties; or

(B) from a fund or subject matter of the action within the court's control.

(3) Allocation. The court must allocate payment of the master's compensation among the parties after considering the nature and amount of the controversy, the means of the parties, and the extent to which any party is more responsible than other parties for the reference to a master. An interim allocation may be amended to reflect a decision on the merits.

(i) Appointment of Magistrate Judge. A magistrate judge is subject to this rule only when the order referring a matter to the magistrate judge expressly provides that the reference is made under this rule. (As amended Feb. 28, 1966, eff. July 1, 1966; Apr. 28, 1983, eff. Aug. 1, 1983; Mar. 2, 1987, eff. Aug. 1, 1987; Apr. 30, 1991, eff. Dec. 1, 1991; Apr. 22, 1993, eff. Dec. 1, 1993; Mar. 27, 2003, eff. Dec. 1, 2003.)

Proposed Amendment of Rule

Effective December 1, 2007, absent contrary Congressional action, this rule is amended to read as follows:

Rule 53. Masters

(a) Appointment.

(1) Scope. Unless a statute provides otherwise, a court may appoint a master only to:

(A) perform duties consented to by the parties;

(B) hold trial proceedings and make or recommend findings of fact on issues to be decided without a jury if appointment is warranted by:

(i) some exceptional condition; or

(ii) the need to perform an accounting or resolve a difficult computation of damages; or

(C) address pretrial and posttrial matters that cannot be effectively and timely addressed by an available district judge or magistrate judge of the district.

(2) Disqualification. A master must not have a relationship to the parties, attorneys, action, or court that would require disqualification of a judge under 28 U.S.C. § 455, unless the parties, with the court's approval, consent to the appointment after the master discloses any potential grounds for disqualification.

(3) Possible Expense or Delay. In appointing a master, the court must consider the fairness of imposing the likely expenses on the parties and must protect against unreasonable expense or delay.

(b) Order Appointing a Master.

(1) Notice. Before appointing a master, the court must give the parties notice and an opportunity to be heard. Any party may suggest candidates for appointment.

(2) Contents. The appointing order must direct the master to proceed with all reasonable diligence and must state:

(A) the master's duties, including any investigation or enforcement duties, and any limits on the master's authority under Rule 53(c);

(B) the circumstances, if any, in which the master may communicate ex parte with the court or a party;

(C) the nature of the materials to be preserved and filed as the record of the master's activities;

(D) the time limits, method of filing the record, other procedures, and standards for reviewing the master's orders, findings, and recommendations; and

(E) the basis, terms, and procedure for fixing the master's compensation under Rule 53(g).

(3) *Issuing.* The court may issue the order only after:

(A) the master files an affidavit disclosing whether there is any ground for disqualification under 28 U.S.C. § 455; and

(B) if a ground is disclosed, the parties, with the court's approval, waive the disqualification.

(4) *Amending.* The order may be amended at any time after notice to the parties and an opportunity to be heard.

(c) Master's Authority.

(1) *In General.* Unless the appointing order directs otherwise, a master may:

(A) regulate all proceedings;

(B) take all appropriate measures to perform the assigned duties fairly and efficiently; and

(C) if conducting an evidentiary hearing, exercise the appointing court's power to compel, take, and record evidence.

(2) *Sanctions.* The master may by order impose on a party any noncontempt sanction provided by Rule 37 or 45, and may recommend a contempt sanction against a party and sanctions against a nonparty.

(d) Master's Orders. A master who issues an order must file it and promptly serve a copy on each party. The clerk must enter the order on the docket.

(e) Master's Reports. A master must report to the court as required by the appointing order. The master must file the report and promptly serve a copy on each party, unless the court orders otherwise.

(f) Action on the Master's Order, Report, or Recommendations.

(1) *Opportunity for a Hearing; Action in General.* In acting on a master's order, report, or recommendations, the court must give the parties notice and an opportunity to be heard; may receive evidence; and may adopt or affirm, modify, wholly or partly reject or reverse, or resubmit to the master with instructions.

(2) *Time to Object or Move to Adopt or Modify.* A party may file objections to—or a motion to adopt or modify—the master's order, report, or recommendations no later than 20 days after a copy is served, unless the court sets a different time.

(3) *Reviewing Factual Findings.* The court must decide de novo all objections to findings of fact made or recommended by a master, unless the parties, with the court's approval, stipulate that:

(A) the findings will be reviewed for clear error; or

(B) the findings of a master appointed under Rule 53(a)(1)(A) or (C) will be final.

(4) *Reviewing Legal Conclusions.* The court must decide de novo all objections to conclusions of law made or recommended by a master.

(5) *Reviewing Procedural Matters.* Unless the appointing order establishes a different standard of review, the court may set aside a master's ruling on a procedural matter only for an abuse of discretion.

(g) Compensation.

(1) *Fixing Compensation.* Before or after judgment, the court must fix the master's compensation on the basis and terms stated in the appointing order, but the court may set a new basis and terms after giving notice and an opportunity to be heard.

(2) *Payment.* The compensation must be paid either:

(A) by a party or parties; or

(B) from a fund or subject matter of the action within the court's control.

(3) *Allocating Payment.* The court must allocate payment among the parties after considering the nature and amount of the controversy, the parties' means, and the extent to which any party is more responsible than other parties for the reference to a master. An interim allocation may be amended to reflect a decision on the merits.

(h) Appointing a Magistrate Judge. A magistrate judge is subject to this rule only when the order

referring a matter to the magistrate judge states that the reference is made under this rule.

ADVISORY COMMITTEE NOTES

1937 Adoption

Note to Subdivision (a). This is a modification of former Equity Rule 68 (Appointment and Compensation of Masters).

Note to Subdivision (b). This is substantially the first sentence of [former] Equity Rule 59 (Reference to Master—Exceptional, Not Usual) extended to actions formerly legal. See *Ex parte Peterson*, 1920, 40 S.Ct. 543, 253 U.S. 300, 64 L.Ed. 919.

Note to Subdivision (c). This is [former] Equity Rules 62 (Powers of Master) and 65 (Claimants Before Master Examinable by Him) with slight modifications. Compare [former] Equity Rules 49 (Evidence Taken Before Examiners, Etc.) and 51 (Evidence Taken Before Examiners, Etc.).

Note to Subdivision (d). **(1)** This is substantially a combination of the second sentence of [former] Equity Rule 59 (Reference to Master—Exceptional, Not Usual) and [former] Equity Rule 60 (Proceedings Before Master). Compare [former] Equity Rule 53 (Notice of Taking Testimony Before Examiner, Etc.).

(2) This is substantially [former] Equity Rule 52 (Attendance of Witnesses Before Commissioner, Master, or Examiner).

(3) This is substantially [former] Equity Rule 63 (Form of Accounts Before Master).

Note to Subdivision (e). This contains the substance of [former] Equity Rules 61 (Master's Report—Documents Identified but not Set Forth), 61½ (Master's Report—Presumption as to Correctness—Review), and 66 (Return of Master's Report—Exceptions—Hearing), with modifications as to the form and effect of the report and for inclusion of reports by auditors, referees, and examiners, and references in actions formerly legal. Compare [former] Equity Rules 49 (Evidence Taken Before Examiners, Etc.) and 67 (Costs on Exceptions to Master's Report). See *Camden v. Stuart*, 144 U.S. 104, 12 S.Ct. 585, 36 L.Ed. 363 (1892); *Ex parte Peterson*, 253 U.S. 300, 40 S.Ct. 543, 64 L.Ed. 919 (1920).

1966 Amendment

These changes are designed to preserve the admiralty practice whereby difficult computations are referred to a commissioner or assessor, especially after an interlocutory judgment determining liability. As to separation of issues for trial see Rule 42(b).

1983 Amendment

Subdivision (a). The creation of full-time magistrates, who serve at government expense and have no nonjudicial duties competing for their time, eliminates the need to appoint standing masters. Thus the prior provision in Rule 53(a) authorizing the appointment of standing masters is deleted. Additionally, the definition of "master" in subdivision (a) now eliminates the superseded office of commissioner.

The term "special master" is retained in Rule 53 in order to maintain conformity with 28 U.S.C. § 636(b)(2), authorizing a judge to designate a magistrate "to serve as a special master pursuant to the applicable provisions of this title and the Federal Rules of Civil Procedure for the United States District Courts." Obviously, when a magistrate serves as a special master, the provisions for compensation of masters are inapplicable, and the amendment to subdivision (a) so provides.

Although the existence of magistrates may make the appointment of outside masters unnecessary in many instances, see, e.g., *Gautreaux v. Chicago Housing Authority*, 384 F.Supp. 37 (N.D.Ill.1974), mandamus denied *sub nom., Chicago Housing Authority v. Austin*, 511 F.2d 82 (7th Cir. 1975); *Avco Corp. v. American Tel. & Tel. Co.*, 68 F.R.D. 532 (S.D.Ohio 1975), such masters may prove useful when some special expertise is desired or when a magistrate is unavailable for lengthy and detailed supervision of a case.

Subdivision (b). The provisions of 28 U.S.C. § 636(b)(2) not only permit magistrates to serve as masters under Rule 53(b) but also eliminate the exceptional condition requirement of Rule 53(b) when the reference is made with the consent of the parties. The amendment to subdivision (b) brings Rule 53 into harmony with the statute by exempting magistrates, appointed with the consent of the parties, from the general requirement that some exceptional condition requires the reference. It should be noted that subdivision (b) does not address the question, raised in recent decisional law and commentary, as to whether the exceptional condition requirement is applicable when *private masters* who are not magistrates are appointed with the consent of the parties. See Silberman, *Masters and Magistrates Part II: The American Analogue*, 50 N.Y.U.L.Rev. 1297, 1354 (1975).

Subdivision (c). The amendment recognizes the abrogation of Federal Rule 43(c) by the Federal Rules of Evidence.

Subdivision (f). The new subdivision responds to confusion flowing from the dual authority for references of pretrial matters to magistrates. Such references can be made, with or without the consent of the parties, pursuant to Rule 53 or under 28 U.S.C. § 636(b)(1)(A) and (b)(1)(B). There are a number of distinctions between references made under the statute and under the rule. For example, under the statute nondispositive pretrial matters may be referred to a magistrate, without consent, for final determination with reconsideration by the district judge if the magistrate's order is clearly erroneous or contrary to law. Under the rule, however, the appointment of a master, without consent of the parties, to supervise discovery would require some exceptional condition (Rule 53(b)) and would subject the proceedings to the report procedures of Rule 53(e). If an order of reference does not clearly articulate the source of the court's authority the resulting proceedings could be subject to attack on grounds of the magistrate's noncompliance with the provisions of Rule 53. This subdivision therefore establishes a presumption that the limitations of Rule 53 are not applicable unless the reference is specifically made subject to Rule 53.

A magistrate serving as a special master under 28 U.S.C. § 636(b)(2) is governed by the provisions of Rule 53, with the exceptional condition requirement lifted in the case of a consensual reference.

1987 Amendment

The amendments are technical. No substantive change is intended.

1991 Amendment

The purpose of the revision is to expedite proceedings before a master. The former rule required only a filing of the master's report, with the clerk then notifying the parties of the filing. To receive a copy, a party would then be required to secure it from the clerk. By transmitting directly to the parties, the master can save some efforts of counsel. Some local rules have previously required such action by the master.

1993 Amendments

This revision is made to conform the rule to changes made by the Judicial Improvements Act of 1990.

2003 Amendments

Rule 53 is revised extensively to reflect changing practices in using masters. From the beginning in 1938, Rule 53 focused primarily on special masters who perform trial functions. Since then, however, courts have gained experience with masters appointed to perform a variety of pretrial and post-trial functions. See Willging, Hooper, Leary, Miletich, Reagan, & Shapard, *Special Masters' Incidence and Activity* (Federal Judicial Center 2000). This revised Rule 53 recognizes that in appropriate circumstances masters may properly be appointed to perform these functions and regulates such appointments. Rule 53 continues to address trial masters as well, but permits appointment of a trial master in an action to be tried to a jury only if the parties consent. The new rule clarifies the provisions that govern the appointment and function of masters for all purposes. Rule 53(g) also changes the standard of review for findings of fact made or recommended by a master. The core of the original Rule 53 remains, including its prescription that appointment of a master must be the exception and not the rule.

Special masters are appointed in many circumstances outside the Civil Rules. Rule 53 applies only to proceedings that Rule 1 brings within its reach.

Subdivision (a)(1)

District judges bear primary responsibility for the work of their courts. A master should be appointed only in limited circumstances. Subdivision (a)(1) describes three different standards, relating to appointments by consent of the parties, appointments for trial duties, and appointments for pretrial or post-trial duties.

Consent Masters. Subparagraph (a)(1)(A) authorizes appointment of a master with the parties' consent. Party consent does not require that the court make the appointment; the court retains unfettered discretion to refuse appointment.

Trial Masters. Use of masters for the core functions of trial has been progressively limited. These limits are reflected in the provisions of subparagraph (a)(1)(B) that restrict appointments to exercise trial functions. The Supreme Court gave clear direction to this trend in *La Buy v. Howes Leather Co.*, 352 U.S. 249 (1957); earlier roots are sketched in *Los Angeles Brush Mfg. Corp. v. James*, 272 U.S. 701 (1927). As to nonjury trials, this trend has developed through elaboration of the "exceptional condition" requirement in present Rule 53(b). This phrase is retained, and will continue to have the same force as it has developed. Although the provision that a reference "shall be the exception and not the rule" is deleted, its meaning is embraced for this setting by the exceptional condition requirement.

Subparagraph (a)(1)(B)(ii) carries forward the approach of present Rule 53(b), which exempts from the "exceptional condition" requirement "matters of account and of difficult computation of damages." This approach is justified only as to essentially ministerial determinations that require mastery of much detailed information but that do not require extensive determinations of credibility. Evaluations of witness credibility should only be assigned to a trial master when justified by an exceptional condition.

The use of a trial master without party consent is abolished as to matters to be decided by a jury unless a statute provides for this practice.

Abolition of the direct power to appoint a trial master as t o issues to be decided by a jury leaves the way free to appoint a trial master with the consent of all parties. A trial master should be appointed in a jury case, with consent of the parties and concurrence of the court, only if the parties waive jury trial with respect to the issues submitted to the master or if the master's findings are to be submitted to the jury as evidence in the manner provided by former Rule 53(e)(3). In no circumstance may a master be appointed to preside at a jury trial.

The central function of a trial master is to preside over an evidentiary hearing on the merits of the claims or defenses in the action. This function distinguishes the trial master from most functions of pretrial and post-trial masters. If any master is to be used for such matters as a preliminary injunction hearing or a determination of complex damages issues, for example, the master should be a trial master. The line, however, is not distinct. A pretrial master might well conduct an evidentiary hearing on a discovery dispute, and a post-trial master might conduct evidentiary hearings on questions of compliance.

Rule 53 has long provided authority to report the evidence without recommendations in nonjury trials. This authority is omitted from Rule 53(a)(1)(B). In some circumstances a master may be appointed under Rule 53(a)(1)(A) or (C) to take evidence and report without recommendations.

For nonjury cases, a master also may be appointed to assist the court in discharging trial duties other than conducting an evidentiary hearing.

Pretrial and Post–Trial Masters. Subparagraph (a)(1)(C) authorizes appointment of a master to address pretrial or post-trial matters. Appointment is limited to matters that cannot be addressed effectively and in a timely fashion by an available district judge or magistrate judge of the district. A master's pretrial or post-trial duties may include matters that could be addressed by a judge, such as reviewing discovery documents for privilege, or duties that might not be suitable for a judge. Some forms of settlement negotiations, investigations, or administration of an organization are familiar examples of duties that a judge might not feel free to undertake.

Magistrate Judges. Particular attention should be paid to the prospect that a magistrate judge may be available for special assignments. United States magistrate judges are authorized by statute to perform many pretrial functions in civil actions. 28 U.S.C. § 636(b)(1). Ordinarily a district judge who delegates these functions should refer them to a magistrate judge acting as magistrate judge.

There is statutory authority to appoint a magistrate judge as special master. 28 U.S.C. § 636(b)(2). In special circumstances, or when expressly authorized by a statute other than § 636(b)(2), it may be appropriate to appoint a magistrate judge as a master when needed to perform functions outside those listed in § 636(b)(1). There is no apparent reason to appoint a magistrate judge to perform as master duties that could be performed in the role of magistrate judge. Party consent is required for trial before a magistrate judge, moreover, and this requirement should not be undercut by resort to Rule 53 unless specifically authorized by statute; see 42 U.S.C. § 2000e–5(f)(5).

Pretrial Masters. The appointment of masters to participate in pretrial proceedings has developed extensively over the last two decades as some district courts have felt the need for additional help in managing complex litigation. This practice is not well regulated by present Rule 53, which focuses on masters as trial participants. Rule 53 is amended to confirm the authority to appoint—and to regulate the use of—pretrial masters.

A pretrial master should be appointed only when the need is clear. Direct judicial performance of judicial functions may be particularly important in cases that involve important public issues or many parties. At the extreme, a broad delegation of pretrial responsibility as well as a delegation of trial responsibilities can run afoul of Article III.

A master also may be appointed to address matters that blur the divide between pretrial and trial functions. The court's responsibility to interpret patent claims as a matter of law, for example, may be greatly assisted by appointing a master who has expert knowledge of the field in which the patent operates. Review of the master's findings will be de novo under Rule 53(g)(4), but the advantages of initial determination by a master may make the process more effective and timely than disposition by the judge acting alone. Determination of foreign law may present comparable difficulties. The decision whether to appoint a master to address such matters is governed by subdivision (a)(1)(C), not the trial-master provisions of subdivision (a)(1)(B).

Post–Trial Masters. Courts have come to rely on masters to assist in framing and enforcing complex decrees. Present Rule 53 does not directly address this practice. Amended Rule 53 authorizes appointment of post-trial masters for these and similar purposes. The constraint of subdivision (a)(1)(C) limits this practice to cases in which the master's duties cannot be performed effectively and in a timely fashion by an available district judge or magistrate judge of the district.

Reliance on a master is appropriate when a complex decree requires complex policing, particularly when a party has proved resistant or intransigent. This practice has been recognized by the Supreme Court, see *Local 28, Sheet Metal Workers' Internat. Assn. v. EEOC,* 478 U.S. 421, 481–482 (1986). The master's role in enforcement may extend to investigation in ways that are quite unlike the traditional role of judicial officers in an adversary system.

Expert Witness Overlap. This rule does not address the difficulties that arise when a single person is appointed to perform overlapping roles as master and as court-appointed expert witness under Evidence Rule 706. Whatever combination of functions is involved, the Rule 53(a)(1)(B) limit that confines trial masters to issues to be decided by the court does not apply to a person who also is appointed as an expert witness under Evidence Rule 706.

Subdivision (a)(2) and (3)

Masters are subject to the Code of Conduct for United States Judges, with exceptions spelled out in the Code. Special care must be taken to ensure that there is no actual or apparent conflict of interest involving a master. The standard of disqualification is established by 28 U.S.C. § 455. The affidavit required by Rule 53(b)(3) provides an important source of information about possible grounds for disqualification, but careful inquiry should be made at the time of making the initial appointment. The disqualification standards established by § 455 are strict. Because a master is not a public judicial officer, it may be appropriate to permit the parties to consent to appointment of a particular person as master in circumstances that would require disqualification of a judge. The judge must be careful to ensure that no party feels any pressure to consent, but with such assurances—and with the judge's own determination that there is no troubling conflict of interests or disquieting appearance of impropriety—consent may justify an otherwise barred appointment.

One potential disqualification issue is peculiar to the master's role. It may happen that a master who is an attorney represents a client whose litigation is assigned to the judge who appointed the attorney as master. Other parties to the litigation may fear that the attorney-master will gain special respect from the judge. A flat prohibition on appearance before the appointing judge during the time of service as master, however, might in some circumstances unduly limit the opportunity to make a desirable appointment. These matters may be regulated to some extent by state rules of professional responsibility. The question of present conflicts, and the possibility of future conflicts, can be considered at the time of appointment. Depending on the circumstances, the judge may consider it appropriate to impose a non-appearance condition on the lawyer-master, and perhaps on the master's firm as well.

Subdivision (b)

The order appointing a pretrial master is vitally important in informing the master and the parties about the nature and extent of the master's duties and authority. Care must be taken to make the order as precise as possible. The parties must be given notice and opportunity to be heard on the question whether a master should be appointed and on the terms of the appointment. To the extent possible, the notice should describe the master's proposed duties, time to complete the duties, standards of review, and compensation. Often it will be useful to engage the parties in the process of identifying the master, inviting nominations, and reviewing potential candidates. Party involvement may be particularly useful if a pretrial master is expected to promote settlement.

The hearing requirement of Rule 53(b)(1) can be satisfied by an opportunity to make written submissions unless the circumstances require live testimony.

Rule 53(b)(2) requires precise designation of the master's duties and authority. Clear identification of any investigating or enforcement duties is particularly important. Clear delineation of topics for any reports or recommendations is also an important part of this process. And it is important to protect against delay by establishing a time schedule for performing the assigned duties. Early designation of the

procedure for fixing the master's compensation also may provide useful guidance to the parties.

Ex parte communications between a master and the court present troubling questions. Ordinarily the order should prohibit such communications, assuring that the parties know where authority is lodged at each step of the proceedings. Prohibiting ex parte communications between master and court also can enhance the role of a settlement master by assuring the parties that settlement can be fostered by confidential revelations that will not be shared with the court. Yet there may be circumstances in which the master's role is enhanced by the opportunity for ex parte communications with the court. A master assigned to help coordinate multiple proceedings, for example, may benefit from off-the-record exchanges with the court about logistical matters. The rule does not directly regulate these matters. It requires only that the court exercise its discretion and address the topic in the order of appointment.

Similarly difficult questions surround ex part e communications between a master and the parties. Ex parte communications may be essential in seeking to advance settlement. Ex parte communications also may prove useful in other settings, as with in camera review of documents to resolve privilege questions. In most settings, however, ex parte communications with the parties should be discouraged or prohibited. The rule requires that the court address the topic in the order of appointment.

Subdivision (b)(2)(C) provides that the appointment order must state the nature of the materials to be preserved and filed as the record of the master's activities, and (b)(2)(D) requires that the order state the method of filing the record. It is not feasible to prescribe the nature of the record without regard to the nature of the master's duties. The records appropriate to discovery duties may be different from those appropriate to encouraging settlement, investigating possible violations of a complex decree, or making recommendations for trial findings. A basic requirement, however, is that the master must make and file a complete record of the evidence considered in making or recommending findings of fact on the basis of evidence. The order of appointment should routinely include this requirement unless the nature of the appointment precludes any prospect that the master will make or recommend evidence-based findings of fact. In some circumstances it may be appropriate for a party to file materials directly with the court as provided by Rule 5(e), but in many circumstances filing with the court may be inappropriate. Confidentiality is important with respect to many materials that may properly be considered by a master. Materials in the record can be transmitted to the court, and filed, in connection with review of a master's order, report, or recommendations under subdivisions (f) and (g). Independently of review proceedings, the court may direct filing of any materials that it wishes to make part of the public record.

The provision in subdivision (b)(2)(D) that the order must state the standards for reviewing the master's orders, findings, or recommendations is a reminder of the provisions of subdivision (g)(3) that recognize stipulations for review less searching than the presumptive requirement of de novo decision by the court. Subdivision (b)(2)(D) does not authorize the court to supersede the limits of subdivision (g)(3).

In setting the procedure for fixing the master's compensation, it is useful at the outset to establish specific guidelines

to control total expense. The court has power under subdivision (h) to change the basis and terms for determining compensation after notice to the parties.

Subdivision (b)(3) permits entry of the order appointing a master only after the master has filed an affidavit disclosing whether there is any ground for disqualification under 28 U.S.C. § 455. If the affidavit discloses a possible ground for disqualification, the order can enter only if the court determines that there is no ground for disqualification or if the parties, knowing of the ground for disqualification, consent with the court's approval to waive the disqualification.

The provision in Rule 53(b)(4) for amending the order of appointment is as import ant as the provisions for the initial order. Anything that could be done in the initial order can be done by amendment. The hearing requirement can be satisfied by an opportunity to make written submissions unless the circumstances require live testimony.

Subdivision (c)

Subdivision (c) is a simplification of the provisions scattered throughout present Rule 53. It is intended to provide the broad and flexible authority necessary to discharge the master's responsibilities. The most important delineation of a master's authority and duties is provided by the Rule 53(b) appointing order.

Subdivision (d)

The subdivision (d) provisions for evidentiary hearings are reduced from the extensive provisions in current Rule 53. This simplification of the rule is not intended to diminish the authority that may be delegated to a master. Reliance is placed on the broad and general terms of subdivision (c).

Subdivision (e)

Subdivision (e) provides that a master's order must be filed and entered on the docket. It must be promptly served on the parties, a task ordinarily accomplished by mailing or other means as permitted by Rule 5(b). In some circumstances it may be appropriate to have the clerk's office assist the master in mailing the order to the parties.

Subdivision (f)

Subdivision (f) restates some of the provisions of present Rule 53(e)(1). The report is the master's primary means of communication with the court. The materials to be provided to support review of the report will depend on the nature of the report. The master should provide all portions of the record preserved under Rule 53(b)(2)(C) that the master deems relevant to the report. The parties may designate additional materials from the record, and may seek permission to supplement the record with evidence. The court may direct that additional materials from the record be provided and filed. Given the wide array of tasks that may be assigned to a pretrial master, there may be circumstances that justify sealing a report or review record against public access—a report on continuing or failed settlement efforts is the most likely example. A post-trial master may be assigned duties in formulating a decree that deserve similar protection. Such circumstances may even justify denying access to the report or review materials by the parties, although this step should be taken only for the most compelling reasons. Sealing is much less likely to be appropriate with respect to a trial master's report.

Before formally making an order, report, or recommendations, a master may find it helpful to circulate a draft to the

parties for review and comment. The usefulness of this practice depends on the nature of the master's proposed action.

Subdivision (g)

The provisions of subdivision (g)(1), describing the court's powers to afford a hearing, take evidence, and act on a master's order, report, or recommendations are drawn from present Rule 53(e)(2), but are not limited, as present Rule 53(e)(2) is limited, to the report of a trial master in a nonjury action. The requirement that the court must afford an opportunity to be heard can be satisfied by taking written submissions when the court acts on the report without taking live testimony.

The subdivision (g)(2) time limits for objecting to—or seeking adoption or modification of—a master's order, report, or recommendations, are important. They are not jurisdictional. Although a court may properly refuse to entertain untimely review proceedings, the court may excuse the failure to seek timely review. The basic time period is lengthened to 20 days because the present 10–day period may be too short to permit thorough study and response to a complex report dealing with complex litigation. If no party asks the court to act on a master's report, the court is free to adopt the master's action or to disregard it at any relevant point in the proceedings.

Subdivision (g)(3) establishes the standards of review for a master's findings of fact or recommended findings of fact. The court must decide de novo all objections to findings of fact made or recommended by the master unless the parties stipulate, with the court's consent, that the findings will be reviewed for clear error or—with respect to a master appointed on the parties' consent or appointed to address pretrial or post-trial matters—that the findings will be final. Clear-error review is more likely to be appropriate with respect to findings that do not go to the merits of the underlying claims or defenses, such as findings of fact bearing on a privilege objection to a discovery request. Even if no objection is made, the court is free to decide the facts de novo; to review for clear error if an earlier approved stipulation provided clear-error review; or to withdraw its consent to a stipulation for clear-error review or finality, and then to decide de novo. If the court withdraws its consent to a stipulation for finality or clear-error review, it may reopen the opportunity to object.

Under Rule 53(g)(4), the court must decide de novo all objections to conclusions of law made or recommended by a master. As with findings of fact, the court also may decide conclusions of law de novo when no objection is made.

Apart from factual and legal questions, masters often make determinations that, when made by a trial court, would be treated as matters of procedural discretion. The court may set a standard for review of such matters in the order of appointment, and may amend the order to establish the standard. If no standard is set by the original or amended order appointing the master, review of procedural matters is for abuse of discretion. The subordinate role of the master means that the trial court's review for abuse of discretion

may be more searching than the review that an appellate court makes of a trial court.

If a master makes a recommendation on any matter that does not fall within Rule 53(g)(3), (4), or (5), the court may act on the recommendation under Rule 53(g)(1).

Subdivision (h)

The need to pay compensation is a substantial reason for care in appointing private persons as masters.

Payment of the master's fees must be allocated among the parties and any property or subject-matter within the court's control. The amount in controversy and the means of the parties may provide some guidance in making the allocation. The nature of the dispute also may be important—parties pursuing matters of public interest, for example, may deserve special protection. A party whose unreasonable behavior has occasioned the need to appoint a master, on the other hand, may properly be charged all or a major portion of the master's fees. It may be proper to revise an interim allocation after decision on the merits. The revision need not await a decision that is final for purposes of appeal, but may be made to reflect disposition of a substantial portion of the case.

The basis and terms for fixing compensation should be stated in the order of appointment. The court retains power to alter the initial basis and terms, after notice and an opportunity to be heard, but should protect the parties against unfair surprise.

The provision of former Rule 53(a) that the "provision for compensation shall not apply when a United States Magistrate Judge is designated to serve as a master" is deleted as unnecessary. Other provisions of law preclude compensation.

Subdivision (i)

Rule 53(i) carries forward unchanged former Rule 53(f).

2007 Amendments

[Effective December 1, 2007,
absent contrary Congressional action.]

The language of Rule 53 has been amended as part of the general restyling of the Civil Rules to make them more easily understood and to make style and terminology consistent throughout the rules. These changes are intended to be stylistic only.

HISTORICAL NOTES

References in Text

The Federal Rules of Evidence, referred to in subd. (d), are set out in this title.

Change of Name

United States magistrate appointed under section 631 of Title 28, Judiciary and Judicial Procedure, to be known as United States magistrate judge after Dec. 1, 1990, with any reference to United States magistrate or magistrate in Title 28, in any other Federal statute, etc., deemed a reference to United States magistrate judge appointed under section 631 of Title 28, see section 321 of Pub.L. 101–650, set out as a note under section 631 of Title 28.

VII. JUDGMENT

Proposed Amendment of Heading

Effective December 1, 2007, absent contrary Congressional action, this heading is amended to read as follows:

TITLE VII. JUDGMENT

Rule 54. Judgments; Costs

(a) Definition; Form. "Judgment" as used in these rules includes a decree and any order from which an appeal lies. A judgment shall not contain a recital of pleadings, the report of a master, or the record of prior proceedings.

(b) Judgment Upon Multiple Claims or Involving Multiple Parties. When more than one claim for relief is presented in an action, whether as a claim, counterclaim, cross-claim, or third-party claim, or when multiple parties are involved, the court may direct the entry of a final judgment as to one or more but fewer than all of the claims or parties only upon an express determination that there is no just reason for delay and upon an express direction for the entry of judgment. In the absence of such determination and direction, any order or other form of decision, however designated, which adjudicates fewer than all the claims or the rights and liabilities of fewer than all the parties shall not terminate the action as to any of the claims or parties, and the order or other form of decision is subject to revision at any time before the entry of judgment adjudicating all the claims and the rights and liabilities of all the parties.

(c) Demand for Judgment. A judgment by default shall not be different in kind from or exceed in amount that prayed for in the demand for judgment. Except as to a party against whom a judgment is entered by default, every final judgment shall grant the relief to which the party in whose favor it is rendered is entitled, even if the party has not demanded such relief in the party's pleadings.

(d) Costs; Attorneys' Fees.

(1) Costs Other than Attorneys' Fees. Except when express provision therefor is made either in a statute of the United States or in these rules, costs other than attorneys' fees shall be allowed as of course to the prevailing party unless the court otherwise directs; but costs against the United States, its officers, and agencies shall be imposed only to the extent permitted by law. Such costs may be taxed by the clerk on one day's notice. On motion served within 5 days thereafter, the action of the clerk may be reviewed by the court.

(2) Attorneys' Fees.

(A) Claims for attorneys' fees and related non-taxable expenses shall be made by motion unless the substantive law governing the action provides for the recovery of such fees as an element of damages to be proved at trial.

(B) Unless otherwise provided by statute or order of the court, the motion must be filed no later than 14 days after entry of judgment; must specify the judgment and the statute, rule, or other grounds entitling the moving party to the award; and must state the amount or provide a fair estimate of the amount sought. If directed by the court, the motion shall also disclose the terms of any agreement with respect to fees to be paid for the services for which claim is made.

(C) On request of a party or class member, the court shall afford an opportunity for adversary submissions with respect to the motion in accordance with Rule 43(e) or Rule 78. The court may determine issues of liability for fees before receiving submissions bearing on issues of evaluation of services for which liability is imposed by the court. The court shall find the facts and state its conclusions of law as provided in Rule 52(a).

(D) By local rule the court may establish special procedures by which issues relating to such fees may be resolved without extensive evidentiary hearings. In addition, the court may refer issues relating to the value of services to a special master under Rule 53 without regard to the provisions of Rule 53(a)(1) and may refer a motion for attorneys' fees to a magistrate judge under Rule 72(b) as if it were a dispositive pretrial matter.

(E) The provisions of subparagraphs (A) through (D) do not apply to claims for fees and expenses as sanctions for violations of these rules or under 28 U.S.C. § 1927.

(As amended Dec. 27, 1946, eff. Mar. 19, 1948; Apr. 17, 1961, eff. July 19, 1961; Mar. 2, 1987, eff. Aug. 1, 1987; Apr. 22, 1993, eff. Dec. 1, 1993; Apr. 29, 2002, eff. Dec. 1, 2002; Mar. 27, 2003, eff. Dec. 1, 2003.)

Proposed Amendment of Rule

Effective December 1, 2007, absent contrary Congressional action, this rule is amended to read as follows:

Rule 54. Judgment; Costs

(a) Definition; Form. *"Judgment" as used in these rules includes a decree and any order from which an appeal lies. A judgment should not include recitals of pleadings, a master's report, or a record of prior proceedings.*

(b) Judgment on Multiple Claims or Involving Multiple Parties. *When an action presents more*

than one claim for relief—whether as a claim, counterclaim, crossclaim, or third-party claim—or when multiple parties are involved, the court may direct entry of a final judgment as to one or more, but fewer than all, claims or parties only if the court expressly determines that there is no just reason for delay. Otherwise, any order or other decision, however designated, that adjudicates fewer than all the claims or the rights and liabilities of fewer than all the parties does not end the action as to any of the claims or parties and may be revised at any time before the entry of a judgment adjudicating all the claims and all the parties' rights and liabilities.

(c) Demand for Judgment; Relief to Be Granted. A default judgment must not differ in kind from, or exceed in amount, what is demanded in the pleadings. Every other final judgment should grant the relief to which each party is entitled, even if the party has not demanded that relief in its pleadings.

(d) Costs; Attorney's Fees.

(1) Costs Other Than Attorney's Fees. Unless a federal statute, these rules, or a court order provides otherwise, costs—other than attorney's fees—should be allowed to the prevailing party. But costs against the United States, its officers, and its agencies may be imposed only to the extent allowed by law. The clerk may tax costs on 1 day's notice. On motion served within the next 5 days, the court may review the clerk's action.

(2) Attorney's Fees.

(A) Claim to Be by Motion. A claim for attorney's fees and related nontaxable expenses must be made by motion unless the substantive law requires those fees to be proved at trial as an element of damages.

(B) Timing and Contents of the Motion. Unless a statute or a court order provides otherwise, the motion must:

(i) be filed no later than 14 days after the entry of judgment;

(ii) specify the judgment and the statute, rule, or other grounds entitling the movant to the award;

(iii) state the amount sought or provide a fair estimate of it; and

(iv) disclose, if the court so orders, the terms of any agreement about fees for the services for which the claim is made.

(C) Proceedings. Subject to Rule 23(h), the court must, on a party's request, give an opportunity for adversary submissions on the motion in accordance with Rule 43(c) or 78. The court may decide issues of liability for fees before receiving submissions on the value of

services. The court must find the facts and state its conclusions of law as provided in Rule 52(a).

(D) Special Procedures by Local Rule; Reference to a Master or a Magistrate Judge. By local rule, the court may establish special procedures to resolve fee-related issues without extensive evidentiary hearings. Also, the court may refer issues concerning the value of services to a special master under Rule 53 without regard to the limitations of Rule 53(a)(1), and may refer a motion for attorney's fees to a magistrate judge under Rule 72(b) as if it were a dispositive pretrial matter.

(E) Exceptions. Subparagraphs (A)–(D) do not apply to claims for fees and expenses as sanctions for violating these rules or as sanctions under 28 U.S.C. § 1927.

ADVISORY COMMITTEE NOTES

1937 Adoption

Note to Subdivision (a). The second sentence is derived substantially from [former] Equity Rule 71 (Form of Decree).

Note to Subdivision (b). This provides for the separate judgment of equity and code practice. See Wis.Stat. (1935) § 270.54; Compare N.Y.C.P.A. (1937) § 476.

Note to Subdivision (c). For the limitation on default contained in the first sentence, see 2 N.D.Comp.Laws Ann. (1913) § 7680; N.Y.C.P.A. (1937) § 479. Compare *English Rules Under the Judicature Act* (The Annual Practice, 1937) O. 13, r.r. 3–12. The remainder is a usual code provision. It makes clear that a judgment should give the relief to which a party is entitled, regardless of whether it is legal or equitable or both. This necessarily includes the deficiency judgment in foreclosure cases formerly provided for by Equity Rule 10 (Decree for Deficiency in Foreclosures, Etc.).

Note to Subdivision (d). For the present rule in common law actions, see *Ex parte Peterson*, 253 U.S. 300, 40 S.Ct. 543, 64 L.Ed. 919 (1920); Payne, *Costs in Common Law Actions in the Federal Courts* (1935), 21 Va.L.Rev. 397.

The provisions as to costs in actions in forma pauperis contained in U.S.C., Title 28, former §§ 832–836 [now 1915] are unaffected by this rule. Other sections of U.S.C., Title 28, which are unaffected by this rule are: [former] §§ 815 (Costs; plaintiff not entitled to, when), 821 [now 1928] (Costs; infringement of patent; disclaimer), 825 (Costs; several actions), 829 [now 1927] (Costs; attorney liable for, when), and 830 [now 1920] (Costs; bill of; taxation).

The provisions of the following and similar statutes as to costs against the United States and its officers and agencies are specifically continued:

U.S.C., Title 15, §§ 77v(a), 78aa, 79y (Securities and Exchange Commission)

U.S.C., Title 16, § 825p (Federal Power Commission)

U.S.C., Title 26, [former] §§ 3679(d) and 3745(d) (Internal revenue actions)

off

U.S.C., Title 26, [former] § 3770(b)(2) (Reimbursement of costs of recovery against revenue officers)

U.S.C., Title 28, [former] § 817 (Internal revenue actions)

U.S.C., Title 28, § 836 [now 1915] (United States—actions in *forma pauperis*)

U.S.C., Title 28, § 842 [now 2006] (Actions against revenue officers)

U.S.C., Title 28, § 870 [now 2408] (United States—in certain cases)

U.S.C., Title 28, [former] § 906 (United States—foreclosure actions)

U.S.C., Title 47, § 401 (Communications Commission)

The provisions of the following and similar statutes as to costs are unaffected:

U.S.C., Title 7, § 210(f) (Actions for damages based on an order of the Secretary of Agriculture under Stockyards Act)

U.S.C., Title 7, § 499g(c) (Appeals from reparations orders of Secretary of Agriculture under Perishable Commodities Act)

U.S.C., Title 8, [former] § 45 (Action against district attorneys in certain cases)

U.S.C., Title 15, § 15 (Actions for injuries due to violation of antitrust laws)

U.S.C., Title 15, § 72 (Actions for violation of law forbidding importation or sale of articles at less than market value or wholesale prices)

U.S.C., Title 15, § 77k (Actions by persons acquiring securities registered with untrue statements under Securities Act of 1933)

U.S.C., Title 15, § 78i(e) (Certain actions under the Securities Exchange Act of 1934)

U.S.C., Title 15, § 78r (Similar to 78i(e))

U.S.C., Title 15, § 96 (Infringement of trade-mark—damages)

U.S.C., Title 15, § 99 (Infringement of trade-mark—injunctions)

U.S.C., Title 15, § 124 (Infringement of trade-mark—damages)

U.S.C., Title 19, § 274 (Certain actions under customs law)

U.S.C., Title 30, § 32 (Action to determine right to possession of mineral lands in certain cases)

U.S.C., Title 31, §§ 232 [now 3730] and 234 [former] (Action for making false claims upon United States)

U.S.C., Title 33, § 926 (Actions under Harbor Workers' Compensation Act)

U.S.C., Title 35, § 67 [now 281, 284] (Infringement of patent—damages)

U.S.C., Title 35, § 69 [now 282] (Infringement of patent—pleading and proof)

U.S.C., Title 35, § 71 [now 288] (Infringement of patent—when specification too broad)

U.S.C., Title 45, § 153p (Actions for non-compliance with an order of National R.R. Adjustment Board for payment of money)

U.S.C., Title 46, [former] § 38 (Action for penalty for failure to register vessel)

U.S.C., Title 46, § 829 (Action based on non-compliance with an order of Maritime Commission for payment of money)

U.S.C., Title 46, § 941 (Certain actions under Ship Mortgage Act)

U.S.C., Title 46, § 1227 (Actions for damages for violation of certain provisions of the Merchant Marine Act, 1936)

U.S.C., Title 47, § 206 (Actions for certain violations of Communications Act of 1934)

U.S.C., Title 49, § 16(2) [now 11705] (Action based on non-compliance with an order of I.C.C. for payment of money)

1946 Amendment

Note. The historic rule in the federal courts has always prohibited piecemeal disposal of litigation and permitted appeals only from final judgments except in those special instances covered by statute. *Hohorst v. Hamburg—American Packet Co.*, 1893, 13 S.Ct. 590, 148 U.S. 262, 37 L.Ed. 443; *Rexford v. Brunswick-Balke-Collender Co.*, 1913, 33 S.Ct. 515, 228 U.S. 339, 57 L.Ed. 864; *Collins v. Miller*, 1920, 40 S.Ct. 347, 252 U.S. 364, 64 L.Ed. 616. Rule 54(b) was originally adopted in view of the wide scope and possible content of the newly created "civil action" in order to avoid the possible injustice of a delay in judgment of a distinctly separate claim to await adjudication of the entire case. It was not designed to overturn the settled federal rule stated above, which, indeed, has more recently been reiterated in *Catlin v. United States*, 1945, 65 S.Ct. 631, 324 U.S. 229, 89 L.Ed. 911. See also *United States v. Florian*, 1941, 61 S.Ct. 713, 312 U.S. 656, 85 L.Ed. 1105; *Reeves v. Beardall*, 1942, 62 S.Ct. 1085, 316 U.S. 283, 86 L.Ed. 1478.

Unfortunately, this was not always understood, and some confusion ensued. Hence situations arose where district courts made a piecemeal disposition of an action and entered what the parties thought amounted to a judgment, although a trial remained to be had on other claims similar or identical with those disposed of. In the interim the parties did not know their ultimate rights, and accordingly took an appeal, thus putting the finality of the partial judgment in question. While most appellate courts have reached a result generally in accord with the intent of the rule, yet there have been divergent precedents and division of views which have served to render the issues more clouded to the parties appellant. It hardly seems a case where multiplicity of precedents will tend to remove the problem from debate. The problem is presented and discussed in the following cases: *Atwater v. North American Coal Corp.*, C.C.A.2, 1940, 111 F.2d 125; *Rosenblum v. Dingfelder*, C.C.A.2, 1940, 111 F.2d 406; *Audi-Vision, Inc. v. RCA Mfg. Co., Inc.*, C.C.A.2, 1943, 136 F.2d 621; *Zalkind v. Scheinman*, C.C.A.2, 1943, 139 F.2d 895; *Oppenheimer v. F. J. Young & Co., Inc.*, C.C.A.2, 1944, 144 F.2d 387; *Libbey-Owens-Ford Glass Co. v. Sylvania Industrial Corp.*, C.C.A.2, 1946, 154 F.2d 814, certiorari denied 1946, 66 S.Ct. 1353, 328 U.S. 859, 90 L.Ed. 1630; *Zarati Steamship Co. v. Park Bridge Corp.*, C.C.A.2, 1946, 154 F.2d 377; *Baltimore and Ohio R. Co. v. United Fuel Gas Co.*, C.C.A.4, 1946, 154 F.2d 545; *Jefferson Electric Co. v. Sola Electric Co.*, C.C.A.7, 1941, 122 F.2d 124; *Leonard v. Sony-Vacuum Oil Co.*, C.C.A.7, 1942, 130 F.2d 535; *Markham v. Kasper*, C.C.A.7, 1945, 152 F.2d 270; *Hanney v. Franklin Fire Ins. Co. of Philadelphia*, C.C.A.9, 1944, 142 F.2d 864; *Toomey v. Toomey*, App.D.C.1945, 149 F.2d 19, 80 U.S.App. D.C. 77.

In view of the difficulty thus disclosed, the Advisory Committee in its two preliminary drafts of proposed amendments

attempted to redefine the original rule with particular stress upon the interlocutory nature of partial judgments which did not adjudicate all claims arising out of a single transaction or occurrence. This attempt appeared to meet with almost universal approval from those of the profession commenting upon it, although there were, of course, helpful suggestions for additional changes in language or clarification of detail. But cf. Circuit Judge Frank's dissenting opinion in *Libbey-Owens-Ford Glass Co. v. Sylvania Industrial Corp.*, supra, n. 21 of the dissenting opinion. The Committee, however, became convinced on careful study of its own proposals that the seeds of ambiguity still remained, and that it had not completely solved the problem of piecemeal appeals. After extended consideration, it concluded that a retention of the older federal rule was desirable, and that this rule needed only the exercise of a discretionary power to afford a remedy in the infrequent harsh case to provide a simple, definite, workable rule. This is afforded by amended Rule 54(b). It re-establishes an ancient policy with clarity and precision. For the possibility of staying execution where not all claims are disposed of under Rule 54(b), see amended Rule 62(h).

1961 Amendment

This rule permitting appeal, upon the trial court's determination of "no just reason for delay," from a judgment upon one or more but less than all the claims in an action, has generally been given a sympathetic construction by the courts and its validity is settled. *Reeves v. Beardall*, 316 U.S. 283 (1942); *Sears, Roebuck & Co. v. Mackey*, 351 U.S. 427 (1956); *Cold Metal Process Co. v. United Engineering & Foundry Co.*, 351 U.S. 445 (1956).

A serious difficulty has, however, arisen because the rule speaks of claims but nowhere mentions parties. A line of cases has developed in the circuits consistently holding the rule to be inapplicable to the dismissal, even with the requisite trial court determination, of one or more but less than all defendants jointly charged in an action, i.e. charged with various forms of concerted or related wrongdoing or related liability. See *Mull v. Ackerman*, 279 F.2d 25 (2d Cir. 1960); *Richards v. Smith*, 276 F.2d 652 (5th Cir. 1960); *Hardy v. Bankers Life & Cas. Co.*, 222 F.2d 827 (7th Cir. 1955); *Steiner v. 20th Century-Fox Film Corp.*, 220 F.2d 105 (9th Cir. 1955). For purposes of Rule 54(b) it was arguable that there were as many "claims" as there were parties defendant and that the rule in its present text applied where less than all of the parties were dismissed, cf. *United Artists Corp. v. Masterpiece Productions, Inc.*, 221 F.2d 213, 215 (2d Cir. 1955); *Bowling Machines, Inc. v. First Nat. Bank*, 283 F.2d 39 (1st Cir. 1960); but the Courts of Appeals are now committed to an opposite view.

The danger of hardship through delay of appeal until the whole action is concluded may be at least as serious in the multiple-parties situations as in multiple-claims cases, see *Pabellon v. Grace Line, Inc.*, 191 F.2d 169, 179 (2d Cir. 1951), cert. denied, 342 U.S. 893 (1951), and courts and commentators have urged that Rule 54(b) be changed to take in the former. See *Reagan v. Traders & General Ins. Co.*, 255 F.2d 845 (5th Cir. 1958); *Meadows v. Greyhound Corp.*, 235 F.2d 233 (5th Cir. 1956); *Steiner v. 20th Century-Fox Film Corp.*, supra; 6 Moore's Federal Practice ¶54.34[2] (2d ed. 1953); 3 Barron & Holtzoff, *Federal Practice & Procedure* § 1193.2 (Wright ed. 1958); *Developments in the Law—Multiparty Litigation*, 71 Harv.L.Rev. 874, 981 (1958); Note,

62 Yale L.J. 263, 271 (1953); Ill.Ann.Stat. ch. 110, § 50(2) (Smith-Hurd 1956). The amendment accomplishes this purpose by referring explicitly to parties.

There has been some recent indication that interlocutory appeal under the provisions of 28 U.S.C. § 1292(b), added in 1958, may now be available for the multiple-parties cases here considered. See *Jaftex Corp. v. Randolph Mills, Inc.*, 282 F.2d 508 (2d Cir. 1960). The Rule 54(b) procedure seems preferable for those cases, and § 1292(b) should be held inapplicable to them when the rule is enlarged as here proposed. See *Luckenbach Steamship Co., Inc., v. H. Muehlstein & Co., Inc.*, 280 F.2d 755, 757 (2d Cir. 1960); 1 Barron & Holtzoff, supra, § 58.1, p. 321 (Wright ed. 1960).

1987 Amendment

The amendment is technical. No substantive change is intended.

1993 Amendments

Subdivision (d). This revision adds paragraph (2) to this subdivision to provide for a frequently recurring form of litigation not initially contemplated by the rules—disputes over the amount of attorneys' fees to be awarded in the large number of actions in which prevailing parties may be entitled to such awards or in which the court must determine the fees to be paid from a common fund. This revision seeks to harmonize and clarify procedures that have been developed through case law and local rules.

Paragraph (1). Former subdivision (d), providing for taxation of costs by the clerk, is renumbered as paragraph (1) and revised to exclude applications for attorneys' fees.

Paragraph (2). This new paragraph establishes a procedure for presenting claims for attorneys' fees, whether or not denominated as "costs." It applies also to requests for reimbursement of expenses, not taxable as costs, when recoverable under governing law incident to the award of fees. *Cf. West Virginia Univ. Hosp. v. Casey*, —— U.S. —— (1991), holding, prior to the Civil Rights Act of 1991, that expert witness fees were not recoverable under 42 U.S.C. § 1988. As noted in subparagraph (A), it does not, however, apply to fees recoverable as an element of damages, as when sought under the terms of a contract; such damages typically are to be claimed in a pleading and may involve issues to be resolved by a jury. Nor, as provided in subparagraph (E), does it apply to awards of fees as sanctions authorized or mandated under these rules or under 28 U.S.C. § 1927.

Subparagraph (B) provides a deadline for motions for attorneys' fees—14 days after final judgment unless the court or a statute specifies some other time. One purpose of this provision is to assure that the opposing party is informed of the claim before the time for appeal has elapsed. Prior law did not prescribe any specific time limit on claims for attorneys' fees. White v. New Hampshire Dep't of Employment Sec., 455 U.S. 445 (1982). In many nonjury cases the court will want to consider attorneys' fee issues immediately after rendering its judgment on the merits of the case. Note that the time for making claims is specifically stated in some legislation, such as the Equal Access to Justice Act, 28 U.S.C. § 2412(d)(1)(B) (30–day filing period).

Prompt filing affords an opportunity for the court to resolve fee disputes shortly after trial, while the services

performed are freshly in mind. It also enables the court in appropriate circumstances to make its ruling on a fee request in time for any appellate review of a dispute over fees to proceed at the same time as review on the merits of the case.

Filing a motion for fees under this subdivision does not affect the finality or the appealability of a judgment, though revised Rule 58 provides a mechanism by which prior to appeal the court can suspend the finality to resolve a motion for fees. If an appeal on the merits of the case is taken, the court may rule on the claim for fees, may defer its ruling on the motion, or may deny the motion without prejudice, directing under subdivision (d)(2)(B) a new period for filing after the appeal has been resolved. A notice of appeal does not extend the time for filing a fee claim based on the initial judgment, but the court under subdivision (d)(2)(B) may effectively extend the period by permitting claims to be filed after resolution of the appeal. A new period for filing will automatically begin if a new judgment is entered following a reversal or remand by the appellate court or the granting of a motion under Rule 59.

The rule does not require that the motion be supported at the time of filing with the evidentiary material bearing on the fees. This material must of course be submitted in due course, according to such schedule as the court may direct in light of the circumstances of the case. What is required is the filing of a motion sufficient to alert the adversary and the court that there is a claim for fees, and the amount of such fees (or a fair estimate).

If directed by the court, the moving party is also required to disclose any fee agreement, including those between attorney and client, between attorneys sharing a fee to be awarded, and between adversaries made in partial settlement of a dispute where the settlement must be implemented by court action as may be required by Rules 23(e) and 23.1 or other like provisions. With respect to the fee arrangements requiring court approval, the court may also by local rule require disclosure immediately after such arrangements are agreed to. *E.g.,* Rule 5 of United States District Court for the Eastern District of New York; *cf. In re "Agent Orange" Product Liability Litigation (MDL 381),* 611 F.Supp. 1452, 1464 (E.D.N.Y.1985).

In the settlement of class actions resulting in a common fund from which fees will be sought, courts frequently have required that claims for fees be presented in advance of hearings to consider approval of the proposed settlement. The rule does not affect this practice, as it permits the court to require submissions of fee claims in advance of entry of judgment.

Subparagraph (C) assures the parties of an opportunity to make an appropriate presentation with respect to issues involving the evaluation of legal services. In some cases, an evidentiary hearing may be needed, but this is not required in every case. The amount of time to be allowed for the preparation of submissions both in support of and in opposition to awards should be tailored to the particular case.

The court is explicitly authorized to make a determination of the liability for fees before receiving submissions by the parties bearing on the amount of an award. This option may be appropriate in actions in which the liability issue is doubtful and the evaluation issues are numerous and complex.

The court may order disclosure of additional information, such as that bearing on prevailing local rates or on the appropriateness of particular services for which compensation is sought.

On rare occasion, the court may determine that discovery under Rules 26–37 would be useful to the parties. *Compare* Rules Governing Section 2254 Cases in the U.S. District Courts, Rule 6. *See* Note, *Determining the Reasonableness of Attorneys' Fees—the Discoverability of Billing Records,* 64 *B.U.L.Rev.* 241 (1984). In complex fee disputes, the court may use case management techniques to limit the scope of the dispute or to facilitate the settlement of fee award disputes.

Fee awards should be made in the form of a separate judgment under Rule 58 since such awards are subject to review in the court of appeals. To facilitate review, the paragraph provides that the court set forth its findings and conclusions as under Rule 52(a), though in most cases this explanation could be quite brief.

Subparagraph (D) explicitly authorizes the court to establish procedures facilitating the efficient and fair resolution of fee claims. A local rule, for example, might call for matters to be presented through affidavits, or might provide for issuance of proposed findings by the court, which would be treated as accepted by the parties unless objected to within a specified time. A court might also consider establishing a schedule reflecting customary fees or factors affecting fees within the community, as implicitly suggested by Justice O'Connor in *Pennsylvania v. Delaware Valley Citizens' Council,* 483 U.S. 711, 733 (1987) (O'Connor, J., concurring) (how particular markets compensate for contingency). *Cf. Thompson v. Kennickell,* 710 F.Supp. 1 (D.D.C.1989) (use of findings in other cases to promote consistency). The parties, of course, should be permitted to show that in the circumstances of the case such a schedule should not be applied or that different hourly rates would be appropriate.

The rule also explicitly permits, without need for a local rule, the court to refer issues regarding the amount of a fee award in a particular case to a master under Rule 53. The district judge may designate a magistrate judge to act as a master for this purpose or may refer a motion for attorneys' fees to a magistrate judge for proposed findings and recommendations under Rule 72(b). This authorization eliminates any controversy as to whether such references are permitted under Rule 53(b) as "matters of account and of difficult computation of damages" and whether motions for attorneys' fees can be treated as the equivalent of a dispositive pretrial matter that can be referred to a magistrate judge. For consistency and efficiency, all such matters might be referred to the same magistrate judge.

Subparagraph (E) excludes from this rule the award of fees as sanctions under these rules or under 28 U.S.C. § 1927.

2002 Amendments

Subdivision (d)(2)(C) is amended to delete the requirement that judgment on a motion for attorney fees be set forth in a separate document. This change complements the amendment of Rule 58(a)(1), which deletes the separate document requirement for an order disposing of a motion for attorney fees under Rule 54. These changes are made to support amendment of Rule 4 of the Federal Rules of Appellate

Procedure. It continues to be important that a district court make clear its meaning when it intends an order to be the final disposition of a motion for attorney fees.

The requirement in subdivision (d)(2)(B) that a motion for attorney fees be not only filed but also served no later than 14 days after entry of judgment is changed to require filing only, to establish a parallel with Rules 50, 52, and 59. Service continues to be required under Rule 5(a).

2003 Amendments

Rule 54(d)(2)(D) is revised to reflect amendments to Rule 53.

2007 Amendments

[Effective December 1, 2007,
absent contrary Congressional action.]

The language of Rule 54 has been amended as part of the general restyling of the Civil Rules to make them more easily understood and to make style and terminology consistent throughout the rules. These changes are intended to be stylistic only.

The words "or class member" have been removed from Rule 54(d)(2)(C) because Rule 23(h)(2) now addresses objections by class members to attorney-fee motions. Rule 54(d)(2)(C) is amended to recognize that Rule 23(h) now controls those aspects of attorney-fee motions in class actions to which it is addressed.

HISTORICAL NOTES

Effective and Applicability Provisions

1961 Amendments

Amendment adopted on Apr. 17, 1961, effective July 19, 1961, see Rule 86(d).

Rule 55. Default

(a) Entry. When a party against whom a judgment for affirmative relief is sought has failed to plead or otherwise defend as provided by these rules and that fact is made to appear by affidavit or otherwise, the clerk shall enter the party's default.

(b) Judgment. Judgment by default may be entered as follows:

(1) By the Clerk. When the plaintiff's claim against a defendant is for a sum certain or for a sum which can by computation be made certain, the clerk upon request of the plaintiff and upon affidavit of the amount due shall enter judgment for that amount and costs against the defendant, if the defendant has been defaulted for failure to appear and is not an infant or incompetent person.

(2) By the Court. In all other cases the party entitled to a judgment by default shall apply to the court therefor; but no judgment by default shall be entered against an infant or incompetent person unless represented in the action by a general guardian, committee, conservator, or other such representative who has appeared therein. If the party

against whom judgment by default is sought has appeared in the action, the party (or, if appearing by representative, the party's representative) shall be served with written notice of the application for judgment at least 3 days prior to the hearing on such application. If, in order to enable the court to enter judgment or to carry it into effect, it is necessary to take an account or to determine the amount of damages or to establish the truth of any averment by evidence or to make an investigation of any other matter, the court may conduct such hearings or order such references as it deems necessary and proper and shall accord a right of trial by jury to the parties when and as required by any statute of the United States.

(c) Setting Aside Default. For good cause shown the court may set aside an entry of default and, if a judgment by default has been entered, may likewise set it aside in accordance with Rule 60(b).

(d) Plaintiffs, Counterclaimants, Cross-Claimants. The provisions of this rule apply whether the party entitled to the judgment by default is a plaintiff, a third-party plaintiff, or a party who has pleaded a cross-claim or counterclaim. In all cases a judgment by default is subject to the limitations of Rule 54(c).

(e) Judgment Against the United States. No judgment by default shall be entered against the United States or an officer or agency thereof unless the claimant establishes a claim or right to relief by evidence satisfactory to the court.
(As amended Mar. 2, 1987, eff. Aug. 1, 1987.)

Proposed Amendment of Rule

Effective December 1, 2007, absent contrary Congressional action, this rule is amended to read as follows:

Rule 55. Default; Default Judgment

(a) Entering a Default. *When a party against whom a judgment for affirmative relief is sought has failed to plead or otherwise defend, and that failure is shown by affidavit or otherwise, the clerk must enter the party's default.*

(b) Entering a Default Judgment.

(1) By the Clerk. If the plaintiff's claim is for a sum certain or a sum that can be made certain by computation, the clerk—on the plaintiff's request, with an affidavit showing the amount due—must enter judgment for that amount and costs against a defendant who has been defaulted for not appearing and who is neither a minor nor an incompetent person.

(2) By the Court. In all other cases, the party must apply to the court for a default judgment. A default judgment may be entered against a minor or incompetent person only if represented by

a general guardian, conservator, or other like fiduciary who has appeared. If the party against whom a default judgment is sought has appeared personally or by a representative, that party or its representative must be served with written notice of the application at least 3 days before the hearing. The court may conduct hearings or make referrals—preserving any federal statutory right to a jury trial—when, to enter or effectuate judgment, it needs to:

(A) conduct an accounting;

(B) determine the amount of damages;

(C) establish the truth of any allegation by evidence; or

(D) investigate any other matter.

(c) Setting Aside a Default or a Default Judgment. *The court may set aside an entry of default for good cause, and it may set aside a default judgment under Rule 60(b).*

(d) Judgment Against the United States. *A default judgment may be entered against the United States, its officers, or its agencies only if the claimant establishes a claim or right to relief by evidence that satisfies the court.*

ADVISORY COMMITTEE NOTES
1937 Adoption

This represents the joining of the equity decree *pro confesso* (former Equity Rules 12 (Issue of Subpoena—Time for Answer), 16 (Defendant to Answer—Default—Decree *Pro Confesso*), 17 (Decree *Pro Confesso* to be Followed by Final Decree—Setting Aside Default), 29 (Defenses—How Presented), 31 (Reply—When Required—When Cause at Issue)) and the judgment by default now governed by U.S.C., Title 28, [former] § 724 (Conformity act). For dismissal of an action for failure to comply with these rules or any order of the court, see Rule 41(b).

Note to Subdivision (a). The provision for the entry of default comes from the Massachusetts practice, 2 Mass.Gen. Laws (Ter.Ed., 1932) ch. 231, § 57. For affidavit of default, see 2 Minn.Stat. (Mason, 1927) § 9256.

Note to Subdivision (b). The provision in paragraph (1) for the entry of judgment by the clerk when plaintiff claims a sum certain is found in the N.Y.C.P.A. (1937) § 485, in Calif.Code Civ.Proc. (Deering, 1937) § 585(1), and in Conn.Practice Book (1934) § 47. For provisions similar to paragraph (2), compare Calif.Code, *supra*, § 585(2); N.Y.C.P.A. (1937) § 490; 2 Minn.Stat. (Mason, 1927) § 9256(3); 2 Wash.Rev.Stat.Ann. (Remington, 1932) § 411(2). U.S.C., Title 28, § 1874, formerly § 785 (Action to recover forfeiture in bond) and similar statutes are preserved by the last clause of paragraph (2).

Note to Subdivision (e). This restates substantially the last clause of U.S.C., Title 28, [former] § 763 (Action against the United States under the Tucker Act). As this rule governs in all actions against the United States, U.S.C., Title 28, [former] § 45 (Practice and procedure in certain cases

under the interstate commerce laws) and similar statutes are modified insofar as they contain anything inconsistent therewith.

Supplementary Note

Note. The operation of Rule 55(b) (Judgment) is directly affected by the Soldiers' and Sailors' Civil Relief Act of 1940, 50 U.S.C. Appendix, § 501 et seq. Section 200 of the Act [50 U.S.C. Appendix, § 520] imposes specific requirements which must be fulfilled before a default judgment can be entered, e.g., *Ledwith v. Storkan,* D.Neb.1942, 6 Fed.Rules Serv. 60b.24, Case 2, 2 F.R.D. 539, and also provides for the vacation of a judgment in certain circumstances. See discussion in Commentary, Effect of Conscription Legislation on the Federal Rules, 1940, 3 Fed.Rules Serv. 725; 3 *Moore's Federal Practice*, 1938, Cum.Supplement § 55.02.

1987 Amendment

The amendments are technical. No substantive change is intended.

2007 Amendments

[Effective December 1, 2007, absent contrary Congressional action.]

The language of Rule 55 has been amended as part of the general restyling of the Civil Rules to make them more easily understood and to make style and terminology consistent throughout the rules. These changes are intended to be stylistic only.

Former Rule 55(a) directed the clerk to enter a default when a party failed to plead or otherwise defend "as provided by these rules." The implication from the reference to defending "as provided by these rules" seemed to be that the clerk should enter a default even if a party did something showing an intent to defend, but that act was not specifically described by the rules. Courts in fact have rejected that implication. Acts that show an intent to defend have frequently prevented a default even though not connected to any particular rule. "[A]s provided by these rules" is deleted to reflect Rule 55(a)'s actual meaning.

Amended Rule 55 omits former Rule 55(d), which included two provisions. The first recognized that Rule 55 applies to described claimants. The list was incomplete and unnecessary. Rule 55(a) applies Rule 55 to any party against whom a judgment for affirmative relief is requested. The second provision was a redundant reminder that Rule 54(c) limits the relief available by default judgment.

Rule 56. Summary Judgment

(a) For Claimant. A party seeking to recover upon a claim, counterclaim, or cross-claim or to obtain a declaratory judgment may, at any time after the expiration of 20 days from the commencement of the action or after service of a motion for summary judgment by the adverse party, move with or without supporting affidavits for a summary judgment in the party's favor upon all or any part thereof.

(b) For Defending Party. A party against whom a claim, counterclaim, or cross-claim is asserted or a declaratory judgment is sought may, at any time,

move with or without supporting affidavits for a summary judgment in the party's favor as to all or any part thereof.

(c) Motion and Proceedings Thereon. The motion shall be served at least 10 days before the time fixed for the hearing. The adverse party prior to the day of hearing may serve opposing affidavits. The judgment sought shall be rendered forthwith if the pleadings, depositions, answers to interrogatories, and admissions on file, together with the affidavits, if any, show that there is no genuine issue as to any material fact and that the moving party is entitled to a judgment as a matter of law. A summary judgment, interlocutory in character, may be rendered on the issue of liability alone although there is a genuine issue as to the amount of damages.

(d) Case Not Fully Adjudicated on Motion. If on motion under this rule judgment is not rendered upon the whole case or for all the relief asked and a trial is necessary, the court at the hearing of the motion, by examining the pleadings and the evidence before it and by interrogating counsel, shall if practicable ascertain what material facts exist without substantial controversy and what material facts are actually and in good faith controverted. It shall thereupon make an order specifying the facts that appear without substantial controversy, including the extent to which the amount of damages or other relief is not in controversy, and directing such further proceedings in the action as are just. Upon the trial of the action the facts so specified shall be deemed established, and the trial shall be conducted accordingly.

(e) Form of Affidavits; Further Testimony; Defense Required. Supporting and opposing affidavits shall be made on personal knowledge, shall set forth such facts as would be admissible in evidence, and shall show affirmatively that the affiant is competent to testify to the matters stated therein. Sworn or certified copies of all papers or parts thereof referred to in an affidavit shall be attached thereto or served therewith. The court may permit affidavits to be supplemented or opposed by depositions, answers to interrogatories, or further affidavits. When a motion for summary judgment is made and supported as provided in this rule, an adverse party may not rest upon the mere allegations or denials of the adverse party's pleading, but the adverse party's response, by affidavits or as otherwise provided in this rule, must set forth specific facts showing that there is a genuine issue for trial. If the adverse party does not so respond, summary judgment, if appropriate, shall be entered against the adverse party.

(f) When Affidavits are Unavailable. Should it appear from the affidavits of a party opposing the motion that the party cannot for reasons stated present by affidavit facts essential to justify the party's opposition, the court may refuse the application for judgment or may order a continuance to permit affidavits to be obtained or depositions to be taken or discovery to be had or may make such other order as is just.

(g) Affidavits Made in Bad Faith. Should it appear to the satisfaction of the court at any time that any of the affidavits presented pursuant to this rule are presented in bad faith or solely for the purpose of delay, the court shall forthwith order the party employing them to pay to the other party the amount of the reasonable expenses which the filing of the affidavits caused the other party to incur, including reasonable attorney's fees, and any offending party or attorney may be adjudged guilty of contempt.

(As amended Dec. 27, 1946, eff. Mar. 19, 1948; Jan. 21, 1963, eff. July 1, 1963; Mar. 2, 1987, eff. Aug. 1, 1987.)

Proposed Amendment of Rule

Effective December 1, 2007, absent contrary Congressional action, this rule is amended to read as follows:

Rule 56. Summary Judgment

(a) By a Claiming Party. A party claiming relief may move, with or without supporting affidavits, for summary judgment on all or part of the claim. The motion may be filed at any time after:

(1) 20 days have passed from commencement of the action; or

(2) the opposing party serves a motion for summary judgment.

(b) By a Defending Party. A party against whom relief is sought may move at any time, with or without supporting affidavits, for summary judgment on all or part of the claim.

(c) Serving the Motion; Proceedings. The motion must be served at least 10 days before the day set for the hearing. An opposing party may serve opposing affidavits before the hearing day. The judgment sought should be rendered if the pleadings, the discovery and disclosure materials on file, and any affidavits show that there is no genuine issue as to any material fact and that the movant is entitled to judgment as a matter of law.

(d) Case Not Fully Adjudicated on the Motion.

(1) Establishing Facts. If summary judgment is not rendered on the whole action, the court should, to the extent practicable, determine what material facts are not genuinely at issue. The court should so determine by examining the pleadings and evidence before it and by interrogating the attorneys. It should then issue an order specifying what facts—including items of damages or other relief—are not genuinely at

issue. The facts so specified must be treated as established in the action.

(2) Establishing Liability. An interlocutory summary judgment may be rendered on liability alone, even if there is a genuine issue on the amount of damages.

(e) Affidavits; Further Testimony.

(1) In General. A supporting or opposing affidavit must be made on personal knowledge, set out facts that would be admissible in evidence, and show that the affiant is competent to testify on the matters stated. If a paper or part of a paper is referred to in an affidavit, a sworn or certified copy must be attached to or served with the affidavit. The court may permit an affidavit to be supplemented or opposed by depositions, answers to interrogatories, or additional affidavits.

(2) Opposing Party's Obligation to Respond. When a motion for summary judgment is properly made and supported, an opposing party may not rely merely on allegations or denials in its own pleading; rather, its response must—by affidavits or as otherwise provided in this rule—set out specific facts showing a genuine issue for trial. If the opposing party does not so respond, summary judgment should, if appropriate, be entered against that party.

(f) When Affidavits Are Unavailable. *If a party opposing the motion shows by affidavit that, for specified reasons, it cannot present facts essential to justify its opposition, the court may:*

(1) deny the motion;

(2) order a continuance to enable affidavits to be obtained, depositions to be taken, or other discovery to be undertaken; or

(3) issue any other just order.

(g) Affidavit Submitted in Bad Faith. *If satisfied that an affidavit under this rule is submitted in bad faith or solely for delay, the court must order the submitting party to pay the other party the reasonable expenses, including attorney's fees, it incurred as a result. An offending party or attorney may also be held in contempt.*

ADVISORY COMMITTEE NOTES

1937 Adoption

This rule is applicable to all actions, including those against the United States or an officer or agency thereof.

Summary judgment procedure is a method for promptly disposing of actions in which there is no genuine issue as to any material fact. It has been extensively used in England for more than 50 years and has been adopted in a number of American states. New York, for example, has made great use of it. During the first nine years after its adoption there, the records of New York county alone show 5,600 applications for summary judgments. Report of the Commission on the Administration of Justice in New York State (1934), p. 383. See also *Third Annual Report of the Judicial Council of the State of New York* (1937), p. 30.

In England it was first employed only in cases of liquidated claims, but there has been a steady enlargement of the scope of the remedy until it is now used in actions to recover land or chattels and in all other actions at law, for liquidated or unliquidated claims, except for a few designated torts and breach of promise of marriage. *English Rules Under the Judicature Act* (The Annual Practice, 1937) O. 3, r. 6; Orders 14, 14A, and 15; see also O. 32, r. 6, authorizing an application for judgment at any time upon admissions. In Michigan (3 Comp.Laws (1929) § 14260) and Illinois (Smith-Hurd Ill.Stats. c. 110, §§ 181, 259.15, 259.16), it is not limited to liquidated demands. New York (N.Y.R.C.P. (1937) Rule 113; see also Rule 107) has brought so many classes of actions under the operation of the rule that the Commission on Administration of Justice in New York State (1934) recommend that all restrictions be removed and that the remedy be available "in any action" (p. 287). For the history and nature of the summary judgment procedure and citations of state statutes, see Clark and Samenow, *The Summary Judgment* (1929), 38 Yale L.J. 423.

Note to Subdivision (d). See Rule 16 (Pre-Trial Procedure; Formulating Issues) and the Note thereto.

Note to Subdivisions (e) and (f). These are similar to rules in Michigan. Mich.Court Rules Ann. (Searl, 1933) Rule 30.

1946 Amendment

Note to Subdivision (a). The amendment allows a claimant to move for a summary judgment at any time after the expiration of 20 days from the commencement of the action or after service of a motion for summary judgment by the adverse party. This will normally operate to permit an earlier motion by the claimant than under the original rule, where the phrase "at any time after the pleading in answer thereto has been served" operates to prevent a claimant from moving for summary judgment, even in a case clearly proper for its exercise, until a formal answer has been filed. Thus in *Peoples Bank v. Federal Reserve Bank of San Francisco*, N.D.Cal.1944, 58 F.Supp. 25, the plaintiff's countermotion for a summary judgment was stricken as premature, because the defendant had not filed an answer. Since Rule 12(a) allows at least 20 days for an answer, that time plus the 10 days required in Rule 56(c) means that under original Rule 56(a) a minimum period of 30 days necessarily has to elapse in every case before the claimant can be heard on his right to a summary judgment. An extension of time by the court or the service of preliminary motions of any kind will prolong that period even further. In many cases this merely represents unnecessary delay. See *United States v. Adler's Creamery, Inc.*, C.C.A.2, 1939, 107 F.2d 987. The changes are in the interest of more expeditious litigation. The 20-day period, as provided, gives the defendant an opportunity to secure counsel and determine a course of action. But in a case where the defendant himself makes a motion for summary judgment within that time, there is no reason to restrict the plaintiff and the amended rule so provides.

Subdivision (c). The amendment of Rule 56(c), by the addition of the final sentence, resolves a doubt expressed in *Sartor v. Arkansas Natural Gas Corp.*, 1944, 64 S.Ct. 724, 321 U.S. 620, 88 L.Ed. 967. See also Commentary, Summary Judgment as to Damages, 1944, 7 Fed.Rules Serv. 974; *Madeirense Do Brasil S/A v. Stulman-Emrick Lumber Co.*, C.C.A.2d, 1945, 147 F.2d 399, certiorari denied 1945, 65 S.Ct. 1201, 325 U.S. 861, 89 L.Ed. 1982. It makes clear that although the question of recovery depends on the amount of damages, the summary judgment rule is applicable and summary judgment may be granted in a proper case. If the case is not fully adjudicated it may be dealt with as provided in subdivision (d) of Rule 56, and the right to summary recovery determined by a preliminary order, interlocutory in character, and the precise amount of recovery left for trial.

Subdivision (d). Rule 54(a) defines "judgment" as including a decree and "any order from which an appeal lies." Subdivision (d) of Rule 56 indicates clearly, however, that a partial summary "judgment" is not a final judgment, and, therefore, that it is not appealable, unless in the particular case some statute allows an appeal from the interlocutory order involved. The partial summary judgment is merely a pretrial adjudication that certain issues shall be deemed established for the trial of the case. This adjudication is more nearly akin to the preliminary order under Rule 16, and likewise serves the purpose of speeding up litigation by eliminating before trial matters wherein there is no genuine issue of fact. See *Leonard v. Socony-Vacuum Oil Co.*, C.C.A.7, 1942, 130 F.2d 535; *Biggins v. Oltmer Iron Works*, C.C.A.7, 1946, 154 F.2d 214; 3 *Moore's Federal Practice*, 1938, 3190–3192. Since interlocutory appeals are not allowed, except where specifically provided by statute, see 3 Moore, op. cit. supra, 3155–3156, this interpretation is in line with that policy, *Leonard v. Socony-Vacuum Oil Co.*, supra. See also *Audi Vision Inc. v. RCA Mfg. Co.*, C.C.A.2, 1943, 136 F.2d 621; *Toomey v. Toomey*, 1945, 149 F.2d 19, 80 U.S.App.D.C. 77; *Biggins v. Oltmer Iron Works*, supra; *Catlin v. United States*, 1945, 65 S.Ct. 631, 324 U.S. 229, 89 L.Ed. 911.

1963 Amendment

Subdivision (c). By the amendment "answers to interrogatories" are included among the materials which may be considered on motion for summary judgment. The phrase was inadvertently omitted from the rule, see 3 Barron & Holtzoff, *Federal Practice & Procedure* 159–60 (Wright ed. 1958), and the courts have generally reached by interpretation the result which will hereafter be required by the text of the amended rule. See Annot., 74 A.L.R.2d 984 (1960).

Subdivision (e). The words "answers to interrogatories" are added in the third sentence of this subdivision to conform to the amendment of subdivision (c).

The last two sentences are added to overcome a line of cases, chiefly in the Third Circuit, which has impaired the utility of the summary judgment device. A typical case is as follows: A party supports his motion for summary judgment by affidavits or other evidentiary matter sufficient to show that there is no genuine issue as to a material fact. The adverse party, in opposing the motion, does not produce any evidentiary matter, or produces some but not enough to establish that there is a genuine issue for trial. Instead, the adverse party rests on averments of his pleadings which on their face present an issue. In this situation Third Circuit

cases have taken the view that summary judgment must be denied, at least if the averments are "well-pleaded," and not suppositious, conclusory, or ultimate. See *Frederick Hart & Co., Inc. v. Recordgraph Corp.*, 169 F.2d 580 (3d Cir. 1948); *United States ex rel. Kolton v. Halpern*, 260 F.2d 590 (3d Cir. 1958); *United States ex rel. Nobles v. Ivey Bros. Constr. Co., Inc.*, 191 F.Supp. 383 (D.Del.1961); *Jamison v. Pennsylvania Salt Mfg. Co.*, 22 F.R.D. 238 (W.D.Pa.1958); *Bunny Bear, Inc. v. Dennis Mitchell Industries*, 139 F.Supp. 542 (E.D.Pa.1956); *Levy v. Equitable Life Assur. Society*, 18 F.R.D. 164 (E.D.Pa.1955).

The very mission of the summary judgment procedure is to pierce the pleadings and to assess the proof in order to see whether there is a genuine need for trial. The Third Circuit doctrine, which permits the pleadings themselves to stand in the way of granting an otherwise justified summary judgment, is incompatible with the basic purpose of the rule. See 6 *Moore's Federal Practice* 2069 (2d ed. 1953); 3 Barron & Holtzoff, supra, § 1235.1.

It is hoped that the amendment will contribute to the more effective utilization of the salutary device of summary judgment.

The amendment is not intended to derogate from the solemnity of the pleadings. Rather it recognizes that, despite the best efforts of counsel to make his pleadings accurate, they may be overwhelmingly contradicted by the proof available to his adversary.

Nor is the amendment designed to affect the ordinary standards applicable to the summary judgment motion. So, for example: Where an issue as to a material fact cannot be resolved without observation of the demeanor of witnesses in order to evaluate their credibility, summary judgment is not appropriate. Where the evidentiary matter in support of the motion does not establish the absence of a genuine issue, summary judgment must be denied even if no opposing evidentiary matter is presented. And summary judgment may be inappropriate where the party opposing it shows under subdivision (f) that he cannot at the time present facts essential to justify his opposition.

1987 Amendment

The amendments are technical. No substantive change is intended.

2007 Amendments

[Effective December 1, 2007, absent contrary Congressional action.]

The language of Rule 56 has been amended as part of the general restyling of the Civil Rules to make them more easily understood and to make style and terminology consistent throughout the rules. These changes are intended to be stylistic only.

Former Rule 56(a) and (b) referred to summary-judgment motions on or against a claim, counterclaim, or crossclaim, or to obtain a declaratory judgment. The list was incomplete. Rule 56 applies to third-party claimants, intervenors, claimants in interpleader, and others. Amended Rule 56(a) and (b) carry forward the present meaning by referring to a party claiming relief and a party against whom relief is sought.

Former Rule 56(c), (d), and (e) stated circumstances in which summary judgment "shall be rendered," the court

"shall if practicable" ascertain facts existing without substantial controversy, and "if appropriate, shall" enter summary judgment. In each place "shall" is changed to "should." It is established that although there is no discretion to enter summary judgment when there is a genuine issue as to any material fact, there is discretion to deny summary judgment when it appears that there is no genuine issue as to any material fact. *Kennedy v. Silas Mason Co.*, 334 U.S. 249, 256–257 (1948). Many lower court decisions are gathered in 10A Wright, Miller & Kane, Federal Practice & Procedure: Civil 3d, § 2728. "Should" in amended Rule 56(c) recognizes that courts will seldom exercise the discretion to deny summary judgment when there is no genuine issue as to any material fact. Similarly sparing exercise of this discretion is appropriate under Rule 56(e)(2). Rule 56(d)(1), on the other hand, reflects the more open-ended discretion to decide whether it is practicable to determine what material facts are not genuinely at issue.

Former Rule 56(d) used a variety of different phrases to express the Rule 56(c) standard for summary judgment— that there is no genuine issue as to any material fact. Amended Rule 56(d) adopts terms directly parallel to Rule 56(c).

Rule 57. Declaratory Judgments

The procedure for obtaining a declaratory judgment pursuant to Title 28, U.S.C., § 2201, shall be in accordance with these rules, and the right to trial by jury may be demanded under the circumstances and in the manner provided in Rules 38 and 39. The existence of another adequate remedy does not preclude a judgment for declaratory relief in cases where it is appropriate. The court may order a speedy hearing of an action for a declaratory judgment and may advance it on the calendar.

(As amended Dec. 29, 1948, eff. Oct. 20, 1949.)

Proposed Amendment of Rule

Effective December 1, 2007, absent contrary Congressional action, this rule is amended to read as follows:

Rule 57. Declaratory Judgment

These rules govern the procedure for obtaining a declaratory judgment under 28 U.S.C. § 2201. Rules 38 and 39 govern a demand for a jury trial. The existence of another adequate remedy does not preclude a declaratory judgment that is otherwise appropriate. The court may order a speedy hearing of a declaratory-judgment action.

ADVISORY COMMITTEE NOTES

1937 Adoption

The fact that a declaratory judgment may be granted "whether or not further relief is or could be prayed" indicates that declaratory relief is alternative or cumulative and not exclusive or extraordinary. A declaratory judgment is appropriate when it will "terminate the controversy" giving rise on undisputed or relatively undisputed facts, it operates frequently as a summary proceeding, justifying docketing the case for early hearing as on a motion, as provided for in California (Code Civ.Proc. (Deering, 1937) § 1062a), Michigan (3 Comp.Laws (1929) § 13904), and Kentucky (Codes (Carroll, 1932) Civ.Pract. § 639a–3).

The "controversy" must necessarily be "of a justiciable nature, thus excluding an advisory decree upon a hypothetical state of facts." *Ashwander v. Tennessee Valley Authority*, 1936, 56 S.Ct. 466, 473, 297 U.S. 288, 80 L.Ed. 688. The existence or non-existence of any right, duty, power, liability, privilege, disability, or immunity or of any fact upon which such legal relations depend, or of a status, may be declared. The petitioner must have a practical interest in the declaration sought and all parties having an interest therein or adversely affected must be made parties or be cited. A declaration may not be rendered if a special statutory proceeding has been provided for the adjudication of some special type of case, but general ordinary or extraordinary legal remedies, whether regulated by statute or not, are not deemed special statutory proceedings.

When declaratory relief will not be effective in settling the controversy, the court may decline to grant it. But the fact that another remedy would be equally effective affords no ground for declining declaratory relief. The demand for relief shall state with precision the declaratory judgment relief, cumulatively or in the alternative; but when coercive relief only is sought but is deemed ungrantable, or inappropriate, the court may *sua sponte*, if it serves a useful purpose, grant instead a declaration of rights. *Hasselbring v. Koepke*, 1933, 248 N.W. 869, 263 Mich. 466, 93 A.L.R. 1170. Written instruments, including ordinances and statutes, may be construed before or after breach at the petition of a properly interested party, process being served on the private parties or public officials interested. In other respects the Uniform Declaratory Judgment Act affords a guide to the scope and function of the Federal act. Compare *Aetna Life Insurance Co. v. Haworth*, 1937, 57 S.Ct. 461, 300 U.S. 227, 81 L.Ed. 617, 108 A.L.R. 1000; *Nashville, Chattanooga & St. Louis Ry. v. Wallace*, 1933, 53 S.Ct. 345, 288 U.S. 249, 77 L.Ed. 730, 87 A.L.R. 1191; *Gully, Tax Collector v. Interstate Natural Gas Co.*, 82 F.2d 145 (C.C.A.5, 1936); *Ohio Casualty Ins. Co. v. Plummer*, Tex.1935, 13 F.Supp. 169; Borchard, Declaratory Judgments (1934), *passim*.

1948 Amendment

The amendment effective October 1949, substituted the reference to "Title 28, U.S.C., § 2201" in the first sentence for the reference to "Section 274(d) of the Judicial Code, as amended, U.S.C., Title 28, § 400".

2007 Amendments

[Effective December 1, 2007, absent contrary Congressional action.]

The language of Rule 57 has been amended as part of the general restyling of the Civil Rules to make them more easily understood and to make style and terminology consistent throughout the rules. These changes are intended to be stylistic only.

Rule 58. Entry of Judgment

(a) Separate Document.

(1) Every judgment and amended judgment must be set forth on a separate document, but a separate document is not required for an order disposing of a motion:

 (A) for judgment under Rule 50(b);

 (B) to amend or make additional findings of fact under Rule 52(b);

 (C) for attorney fees under Rule 54;

 (D) for a new trial, or to alter or amend the judgment, under Rule 59; or

 (E) for relief under Rule 60.

(2) Subject to Rule 54(b):

 (A) unless the court orders otherwise, the clerk must, without awaiting the court's direction, promptly prepare, sign, and enter the judgment when:

 (i) the jury returns a general verdict,

 (ii) the court awards only costs or a sum certain, or

 (iii) the court denies all relief;

 (B) the court must promptly approve the form of the judgment, which the clerk must promptly enter, when:

 (i) the jury returns a special verdict or a general verdict accompanied by interrogatories, or

 (ii) the court grants other relief not described in Rule 58(a)(2).

(b) Time of Entry. Judgment is entered for purposes of these rules:

(1) if Rule 58(a)(1) does not require a separate document, when it is entered in the civil docket under Rule 79(a), and

(2) if Rule 58(a)(1) requires a separate document, when it is entered in the civil docket under Rule 79(a) and when the earlier of these events occurs:

 (A) when it is set forth on a separate document, or

 (B) when 150 days have run from entry in the civil docket under Rule 79(a).

(c) Cost or Fee Awards.

(1) Entry of judgment may not be delayed, nor the time for appeal extended, in order to tax costs or award fees, except as provided in Rule 58(c)(2).

(2) When a timely motion for attorney fees is made under Rule 54(d)(2), the court may act before a notice of appeal has been filed and has become effective to order that the motion have the same effect under Federal Rule of Appellate Procedure 4(a)(4) as a timely motion under Rule 59.

(d) Request for Entry. A party may request that judgment be set forth on a separate document as required by Rule 58(a)(1).

(As amended Dec. 27, 1946, eff. Mar. 19, 1948; Jan. 21, 1963, eff. July 1, 1963; Apr. 22, 1993, eff. Dec. 1, 1993; Apr. 29, 2002, eff. Dec. 1, 2002.)

Proposed Amendment of Rule

Effective December 1, 2007, absent contrary Congressional action, this rule is amended to read as follows:

Rule 58. Entering Judgment

(a) Separate Document. Every judgment and amended judgment must be set out in a separate document, but a separate document is not required for an order disposing of a motion:

 (1) for judgment under Rule 50(b);

 (2) to amend or make additional findings under Rule 52(b);

 (3) for attorney's fees under Rule 54;

 (4) for a new trial, or to alter or amend the judgment, under Rule 59; or

 (5) for relief under Rule 60.

(b) Entering Judgment.

 (1) Without the Court's Direction. Subject to Rule 54(b) and unless the court orders otherwise, the clerk must, without awaiting the court's direction, promptly prepare, sign, and enter the judgment when:

 (A) the jury returns a general verdict;

 (B) the court awards only costs or a sum certain; or

 (C) the court denies all relief.

 (2) Court's Approval Required. Subject to Rule 54(b), the court must promptly approve the form of the judgment, which the clerk must promptly enter, when:

 (A) the jury returns a special verdict or a general verdict with answers to written questions; or

 (B) the court grants other relief not described in this subdivision (b).

(c) Time of Entry. For purposes of these rules, judgment is entered at the following times:

 (1) if a separate document is not required, when the judgment is entered in the civil docket under Rule 79(a); or

 (2) if a separate document is required, when the judgment is entered in the civil docket under Rule 79(a) and the earlier of these events occurs:

 (A) it is set out in a separate document; or

 (B) 150 days have run from the entry in the civil docket.

(d) Request for Entry. *A party may request that judgment be set out in a separate document as required by Rule 58(a).*

(e) Cost or Fee Awards. *Ordinarily, the entry of judgment may not be delayed, nor the time for appeal extended, in order to tax costs or award fees. But if a timely motion for attorney's fees is made under Rule 54(d)(2), the court may act before a notice of appeal has been filed and become effective to order that the motion have the same effect under Federal Rule of Appellate Procedure 4(a)(4) as a timely motion under Rule 59.*

ADVISORY COMMITTEE NOTES
1937 Adoption

See Wis.Stat. (1935) § 270.31 (judgment entered forthwith on verdict of jury unless otherwise ordered), § 270.65 (where trial is by the court, entered by direction of the court), § 270.63 (entered by clerk on judgment on admitted claim for money). Compare 1 Idaho Code Ann. (1932) § 7–1101, and 4 Mont.Rev.Codes Ann. (1935) § 9403, which provide that judgment in jury cases be entered by clerk within 24 hours after verdict unless court otherwise directs. Conn.Practice Book (1934), § 200, provides that all judgments shall be entered within one week after rendition. In some States such as Washington, 2 Rev.Stat.Ann. (Remington, 1932), § 431, in jury cases the judgment is entered two days after the return of verdict to give time for making motion for new trial; § 435 (*ibid.*), provides that all judgments shall be entered by the clerk, subject to the court's direction.

1946 Amendment

Note. The reference to Rule 54(b) is made necessary by the amendment of that rule.

Two changes have been made in Rule 58 in order to clarify the practice. The substitution of the more inclusive phrase "all relief be denied" for the words "there be no recovery", makes it clear that the clerk shall enter the judgment forthwith in the situations specified without awaiting the filing of a formal judgment approved by the court. The phrase "all relief be denied" covers cases such as the denial of a bankrupt's discharge and similar situations where the relief sought is refused but there is literally no denial of a "recovery".

The addition of the last sentence in the rule emphasizes that judgments are to be entered promptly by the clerk without waiting for the taxing of costs. Certain district court rules, for example, Civil Rule 22 of the Southern District of New York—until its annulment Oct. 1, 1945, for conflict with this rule—and the like rule of the Eastern District of New York, are expressly in conflict with this provision, although the federal law is of long standing and well settled. *Fowler v. Hamill*, 1891, 11 S.Ct. 663, 139 U.S. 549, 35 L.Ed. 266; *Craig v. The Hartford*, C.C.Cal.1856, Fed.Cas. No. 3,333; *Tuttle v. Claflin*, C.C.A.2, 1895, 60 F. 7, certiorari denied 1897; 17 S.Ct. 992, 166 U.S. 721, 41 L.Ed. 1188; *Prescott & A.C. Ry. Co. v. Atchison, T. & S.F.R. Co.*, C.C.A.2, 1897, 84 F. 213; *Stallo v. Wagner*, C.C.A.2, 1917, 245 F. 636, 639–40; *Brown v. Parker*, C.C.A.8, 1899, 97 F. 446; *Allis-Chalmers v. United States*, C.C.A.7, 1908, 162 F. 679. And this applies

even though state law is to the contrary. *United States v. Nordbye*, C.C.A.8, 1935, 75 F.2d 744, certiorari denied 56 S.Ct. 103, 296 U.S. 572, 80 L.Ed. 404. Inasmuch as it has been held that failure of the clerk thus to enter judgment is a "misprision" "not to be excused", *The Washington*, C.C.A.2, 1926, 16 F.2d 206, such a district court rule may have serious consequences for a district court clerk. Rules of this sort also provide for delay in entry of the judgment contrary to Rule 58. See *Commissioner of Internal Revenue v. Bedford's Estate*, 1945, 65 S.Ct. 1157, 325 U.S. 283, 91 L.Ed. 1611.

1963 Amendment

Under the present rule a distinction has sometimes been made between judgments on general jury verdicts, on the one hand, and, on the other, judgments upon decisions of the court that a party shall recover only money or costs or that all relief shall be denied. In the first situation, it is clear that the clerk should enter the judgment without awaiting a direction by the court unless the court otherwise orders. In the second situation it was intended that the clerk should similarly enter the judgment forthwith upon the court's decision; but because of the separate listing in the rule, and the use of the phrase "upon receipt . . . of the direction," the rule has sometimes been interpreted as requiring the clerk to await a separate direction of the court. All these judgments are usually uncomplicated, and should be handled in the same way. The amended rule accordingly deals with them as a single group in clause (1) (substituting the expression "only a sum certain" for the present expression "only money"), and requires the clerk to prepare, sign and enter them forthwith, without awaiting court direction, unless the court makes a contrary order. (The clerk's duty is ministerial and may be performed by a deputy clerk in the name of the clerk. See 28 U.S.C. § 956; cf. *Gilbertson v. United States*, 168 Fed. 672 (7th Cir. 1909).) The more complicated judgments described in clause (2) must be approved by the court before they are entered.

Rule 58 is designed to encourage all reasonable speed in formulating and entering the judgment when the case has been decided. Participation by the attorneys through the submission of forms of judgment involves needless expenditure of time and effort and promotes delay, except in special cases where counsel's assistance can be of real value. See *Matteson v. United States*, 240 F.2d 517, 518–19 (2d Cir. 1956). Accordingly, the amended rule provides that attorneys shall not submit forms of judgment unless directed to do so by the court. This applies to the judgments mentioned in clause (2) as well as clause (1).

Hitherto some difficulty has arisen, chiefly where the court has written an opinion or memorandum containing some apparently directive or dispositive words, e.g., "the plaintiff's motion [for summary judgment] is granted," see *United States v. F. & M. Schaefer Brewing Co.*, 356 U.S. 227, 229, 78 S.Ct. 674, 2 L.Ed.2d 721 (1958). Clerks on occasion have viewed these opinions or memoranda as being in themselves a sufficient basis for entering judgment in the civil docket as provided by Rule 79(a). However, where the opinion or memorandum has not contained all the elements of a judgment, or where the judge has later signed a formal judgment, it has become a matter of doubt whether the purported entry of judgment was effective, starting the time running

for post-verdict motions and for the purpose of appeal. See id.; and compare *Blanchard v. Commonwealth Oil Co.*, 294 F.2d 834 (5th Cir. 1961); *United States v. Higginson*, 238 F.2d 439 (1st Cir. 1956); *Danzig v. Virgin Isle Hotel, Inc.*, 278 F.2d 580 (3d Cir. 1960); *Sears v. Austin*, 282 F.2d 340 (9th Cir. 1960), with *Matteson v. United States*, supra; *Erstling v. Southern Bell Tel. & Tel. Co.*, 255 F.2d 93 (5th Cir. 1958); *Barta v. Oglala Sioux Tribe*, 259 F.2d 553 (8th Cir. 1958) cert. denied, 358 U.S. 932, 79 S.Ct. 320, 3 L.Ed.2d 304 (1959); *Beacon Fed. S. & L. Assn. v. Federal Home L. Bank Bd.*, 266 F.2d 246 (7th Cir.), cert. denied, 361 U.S. 823, 80 S.Ct. 70, 4 L.Ed.2d 67 (1959); *Ram v. Paramount Film D. Corp.*, 278 F.2d 191 (4th Cir. 1960).

The amended rule eliminates these uncertainties by requiring that there be a judgment set out on a separate document—distinct from any opinion or memorandum—which provides the basis for the entry of judgment. That judgment shall be on separate documents is also indicated in Rule 79(b); and see General Rule 10 of the U.S. District Courts for the Eastern and Southern Districts of New York; *Ram v. Paramount Film D. Corp.*, supra, at 194.

See the amendment of Rule 79(a) and the new specimen forms of judgment, Forms 31 and 32.

See also Rule 55(b)(1) and (2) covering the subject of judgments by default.

1993 Amendments

Ordinarily the pendency or post-judgment filing of a claim for attorney's fees will not affect the time for appeal from the underlying judgment. See Budinich v. Becton Dickinson & Co., 486 U.S. 196 (1988). Particularly if the claim for fees involves substantial issues or is likely to be affected by the appellate decision, the district court may prefer to defer consideration of the claim for fees until after the appeal is resolved. However, in many cases it may be more efficient to decide fee questions before an appeal is taken so that appeals relating to the fee award can be heard at the same time as appeals relating to the merits of the case. This revision permits, but does not require, the court to delay the finality of the judgment for appellate purposes under revised Fed.R.App.P. 4(a) until the fee dispute is decided. To accomplish this result requires entry of an order by the district court before the time a notice of appeal becomes effective for appellate purposes. If the order is entered, the motion for attorney's fees is treated in the same manner as a timely motion under Rule 59.

2002 Amendments

Rule 58 has provided that a judgment is effective only when set forth on a separate document and entered as provided in Rule 79(a). This simple separate document requirement has been ignored in many cases. The result of failure to enter judgment on a separate document is that the time for making motions under Rules 50, 52, 54(d)(2)(B), 59, and some motions under Rule 60, never begins to run. The time to appeal under Appellate Rule 4(a) also does not begin to run. There have been few visible problems with respect to Rule 50, 52, 54(d)(2)(B), 59, or 60 motions, but there have been many and horridly confused problems under Appellate Rule 4(a). These amendments are designed to work in conjunction with Appellate Rule 4(a) to ensure that appeal time does not linger on indefinitely, and to maintain the inte-

gration of the time periods set for Rules 50, 52, 54(d)(2)(B), 59, and 60 with Appellate Rule 4(a).

Rule 58(a) preserves the core of the present separate document requirement, both for the initial judgment and for any amended judgment. No attempt is made to sort through the confusion that some courts have found in addressing the elements of a separate document. It is easy to prepare a separate document that recites the terms of the judgment without offering additional explanation or citation of authority. Forms 31 and 32 provide examples.

Rule 58 is amended, however, to address a problem that arises under Appellate Rule 4(a). Some courts treat such orders as those that deny a motion for new trial as a "judgment," so that appeal time does not start to run until the order is entered on a separate document. Without attempting to address the question whether such orders are appealable, and thus judgments as defined by Rule 54(a), the amendment provides that entry on a separate document is not required for an order disposing of the motions listed in Appellate Rule 4(a). The enumeration of motions drawn from the Appellate Rule 4(a) list is generalized by omitting details that are important for appeal time purposes but that would unnecessarily complicate the separate document requirement. As one example, it is not required that any of the enumerated motions be timely. Many of the enumerated motions are frequently made before judgment is entered. The exemption of the order disposing of the motion does not excuse the obligation to set forth the judgment itself on a separate document. And if disposition of the motion results in an amended judgment, the amended judgment must be set forth on a separate document.

Rule 58(b) discards the attempt to define the time when a judgment becomes "effective." Taken in conjunction with the Rule 54(a) definition of a judgment to include "any order from which an appeal lies," the former Rule 58 definition of effectiveness could cause strange difficulties in implementing pretrial orders that are appealable under interlocutory appeal provisions or under expansive theories of finality. Rule 58(b) replaces the definition of effectiveness with a new provision that defines the time when judgment is entered. If judgment is promptly set forth on a separate document, as should be done when required by Rule 58(a)(1), the new provision will not change the effect of Rule 58. But in the cases in which court and clerk fail to comply with this simple requirement, the motion time periods set by Rules 50, 52, 54, 59, and 60 begin to run after expiration of 150 days from entry of the judgment in the civil docket as required by Rule 79(a).

A companion amendment of Appellate Rule 4(a)(7) integrates these changes with the time to appeal.

The new all-purpose definition of the entry of judgment must be applied with common sense to other questions that may turn on the time when judgment is entered. If the 150–day provision in Rule 58(b)(2)(B)—designed to integrate the time for post-judgment motions with appeal time—serves no purpose, or would defeat the purpose of another rule, it should be disregarded. In theory, for example, the separate document requirement continues to apply to an interlocutory order that is appealable as a final decision under collateral-order doctrine. Appealability under collateral-order doctrine should not be complicated by failure to enter the order as a judgment on a separate document—there is little reason to force trial judges to speculate about the potential appealabili-

ty of every order, and there is no means to ensure that the trial judge will always reach the same conclusion as the court of appeals. Appeal time should start to run when the collateral order is entered without regard to creation of a separate document and without awaiting expiration of the 150 days provided by Rule 58(b)(2). Drastic surgery on Rules 54(a) and 58 would be required to address this and related issues, however, and it is better to leave this conundrum to the pragmatic disregard that seems its present fate. The present amendments do not seem to make matters worse, apart from one false appearance. If a pretrial order is set forth on a separate document that meets the requirements of Rule 58(b), the time to move for reconsideration seems to begin to run, perhaps years before final judgment. And even if there is no separate document, the time to move for reconsideration seems to begin 150 days after entry in the civil docket. This apparent problem is resolved by Rule 54(b), which expressly permits revision of all orders not made final under Rule 54(b) "at any time before the entry of judgment adjudicating all the claims and the rights and liabilities of all the parties."

New Rule 58(d) replaces the provision that attorneys shall not submit forms of judgment except on direction of the court. This provision was added to Rule 58 to avoid the delays that were frequently encountered by the former practice of directing the attorneys for the prevailing party to prepare a form of judgment, and also to avoid the occasionally inept drafting that resulted from attorney-prepared judgments. See 11 Wright, Miller & Kane, Federal Practice & Procedure: Civil 2d, § 2786. The express direction in Rule 58(a)(2) for prompt action by the clerk, and by the court if court action is required, addresses this concern. The new provision allowing any party to move for entry of judgment on a separate document will protect all needs for prompt commencement of the periods for motions, appeals, and execution or other enforcement.

Changes Made After Publication and Comment Minor style changes were made. The definition of the time of entering judgment in Rule 58(b) was extended to reach all Civil Rules, not only the Rules described in the published version—Rules 50, 52, 54(d)(2)(B), 59, 60, and 62. And the time of entry was extended from 60 days to 150 days after entry in the civil docket without a required separate document.

2007 Amendments

[Effective December 1, 2007, absent contrary Congressional action.]

The language of Rule 58 has been amended as part of the general restyling of the Civil Rules to make them more easily understood and to make style and terminology consistent throughout the rules. These changes are intended to be stylistic only.

Rule 59. New Trials; Amendment of Judgments

(a) Grounds. A new trial may be granted to all or any of the parties and on all or part of the issues (1) in an action in which there has been a trial by jury, for any of the reasons for which new trials have heretofore been granted in actions at law in the courts of the United States; and (2) in an action tried without a jury, for any of the reasons for which rehearings have heretofore been granted in suits in equity in the courts of the United States. On a motion for a new trial in an action tried without a jury, the court may open the judgment if one has been entered, take additional testimony, amend findings of fact and conclusions of law or make new findings and conclusions, and direct the entry of a new judgment.

(b) Time for Motion. Any motion for a new trial shall be filed no later than 10 days after entry of the judgment.

(c) Time for Serving Affidavits. When a motion for new trial is based on affidavits, they shall be filed with the motion. The opposing party has 10 days after service to file opposing affidavits, but that period may be extended for up to 20 days, either by the court for good cause or by the parties' written stipulation. The court may permit reply affidavits.

(d) On Court's Initiative; Notice; Specifying Grounds. No later than 10 days after entry of judgment the court, on its own, may order a new trial for any reason that would justify granting one on a party's motion. After giving the parties notice and an opportunity to be heard, the court may grant a timely motion for a new trial for a reason not stated in the motion. When granting a new trial on its own initiative or for a reason not stated in a motion, the court shall specify the grounds in its order.

(e) Motion to Alter or Amend Judgment. Any motion to alter or amend a judgment shall be filed no later than 10 days after entry of the judgment.
(As amended Dec. 27, 1946, eff. Mar. 19, 1948; Feb. 28, 1966, eff. July 1, 1966; Apr. 27, 1995, eff. Dec. 1, 1995.)

Proposed Amendment of Rule

Effective December 1, 2007, absent contrary Congressional action, this rule is amended to read as follows:

Rule 59. New Trial; Altering or Amending a Judgment

(a) In General.

(1) Grounds for New Trial. The court may, on motion, grant a new trial on all or some of the issues—and to any party—as follows:

(A) after a jury trial, for any reason for which a new trial has heretofore been granted in an action at law in federal court; or

(B) after a nonjury trial, for any reason for which a rehearing has heretofore been granted in a suit in equity in federal court.

(2) Further Action After a Nonjury Trial. After a nonjury trial, the court may, on motion for a new trial, open the judgment if one has been

*entered, take additional testimony, amend find-
ings of fact and conclusions of law or make new
ones, and direct the entry of a new judgment.*

(b) Time to File a Motion for a New Trial. *A
motion for a new trial must be filed no later than 10
days after the entry of judgment.*

(c) Time to Serve Affidavits. *When a motion for a
new trial is based on affidavits, they must be filed
with the motion. The opposing party has 10 days after
being served to file opposing affidavits; but that peri-
od may be extended for up to 20 days, either by the
court for good cause or by the parties' stipulation.
The court may permit reply affidavits.*

**(d) New Trial on the Court's Initiative or for
Reasons Not in the Motion.** *No later than 10 days
after the entry of judgment, the court, on its own,
may order a new trial for any reason that would
justify granting one on a party's motion. After giving
the parties notice and an opportunity to be heard, the
court may grant a timely motion for a new trial for a
reason not stated in the motion. In either event, the
court must specify the reasons in its order.*

(e) Motion to Alter or Amend a Judgment. *A
motion to alter or amend a judgment must be filed no
later than 10 days after the entry of the judgment.*

ADVISORY COMMITTEE NOTES

1937 Adoption

This rule represents an amalgamation of the petition for
rehearing of [former] Equity Rule 69 (Petition for Rehear-
ing) and the motion for new trial of 28 U.S.C., § 2111,
formerly § 391 (New trials; harmless error), made in the
light of the experience and provision of the code States.
Compare Calif.Code Civ.Proc., Deering, 1937, §§ 656 to 663a,
28 U.S.C., § 2111, formerly § 391 (New trials; harmless
error) is thus substantially continued in this rule. U.S.C.,
Title 28, [former] § 840 (Executions; stay on conditions) is
modified insofar as it contains time provisions inconsistent
with Subdivision (b). For the effect of the motion for new
trial upon the time for taking an appeal see *Morse v. United
States*, 1926, 46 S.Ct. 241, 270 U.S. 151, 70 L.Ed. 518; *Aspen
Mining and Smelting Co. v. Billings*, 1893, 14 S.Ct. 4, 150
U.S. 31, 37 L.Ed. 986.

For partial new trials which are permissible under Subdivi-
sion (a), see *Gasoline Products Co., Inc. v. Champlin Refin-
ing Co.*, 1931, 51 S.Ct. 513, 283 U.S. 494, 75 L.Ed. 1188;
Schuerholz v. Roach, C.C.A.4, 1932, 58 F.2d 32; *Simmons v.
Fish*, 1912, 97 N.E. 102, 210 Mass. 563, Ann.Cas.1912D, 588
(sustaining and recommending the practice and citing federal
cases and cases in accord from about sixteen States and
contra from three States). The procedure in several States
provides specifically for partial new trials. Ariz.Rev.Code
Ann., Struckmeyer, 1928, § 3852; Calif.Code Civ.Proc.,
Deering, 1937, §§ 657, 662; Smith-Hurd Ill.Stats., 1937, c.
110, § 216 (Par. (f)); Md.Ann.Code, Bagby, 1924, Art. 5,
§§ 25, 26; Mich.Court Rules Ann., Searl, 1933, Rule 47, § 2;
Miss.Sup.Ct.Rule 12, 161 Miss. 903, 905, 1931; N.J.Sup.Ct.
Rules 131, 132, 147, 2 N.J.Misc. 1197, 1246–1251, 1255, 1924;

2 N.D.Comp.Laws Ann., 1913, § 7844, as amended by
N.D.Laws 1927, ch. 214.

1946 Amendment

Note. Subdivision (b). With the time for appeal to a
circuit court of appeals reduced in general to 30 days by the
proposed amendment of Rule 73(a), the utility of the original
"except" clause, which permits a motion for a new trial on
the ground of newly discovered evidence to be made before
the expiration of the time for appeal, would have been
seriously restricted. It was thought advisable, therefore, to
take care of this matter in another way. By amendment of
Rule 60(b), newly discovered evidence is made the basis for
relief from a judgment, and the maximum time limit has been
extended to one year. Accordingly the amendment of Rule
59(b) eliminates the "except" clause and its specific treatment
of newly discovered evidence as a ground for a motion for
new trial. This ground remains, however, as a basis for a
motion for new trial served not later than 10 days after the
entry of judgment. See also Rule 60(b).

As to the effect of a motion under subdivision (b) upon the
running of appeal time, see amended Rule 73(a) and Note.

Note to Subdivision (e). This subdivision has been added
to care for a situation such as that arising in *Boaz v. Mutual
Life Ins. Co. of New York*, C.C.A.8, 1944, 146 F.2d 321, and
makes clear that the district court possesses the power
asserted in that case to alter or amend a judgment after its
entry. The subdivision deals only with alteration or amend-
ment of the original judgment in a case and does not relate
to a judgment upon motion as provided in Rule 50(b). As to
the effect of a motion under subdivision (e) upon the running
of appeal time, see amended Rule 73(a) and Note.

The title of Rule 59 has been expanded to indicate the
inclusion of this subdivision.

1966 Amendment

By narrow interpretation of Rule 59(b) and (d), it has been
held that the trial court is without power to grant a motion
for a new trial, timely served, by an order made more than
10 days after the entry of judgment, based upon a ground
not stated in the motion but perceived and relied on by the
trial court sua sponte. *Freid v. McGrath*, 133 F.2d 350
(D.C.Cir. 1942); *National Farmers Union Auto. & Cas. Co.
v. Wood*, 207 F.2d 659 (10th Cir. 1953); *Bailey v. Slentz*, 189
F.2d 406 (10th Cir. 1951); *Marshall's U.S. Auto Supply, Inc.
v. Cashman*, 111 F.2d 140 (10th Cir. 1940), cert. denied, 311
U.S. 667 (1940); but see *Steinberg v. Indemnity Ins. Co.*, 36
F.R.D. 253 (E.D.La.1964).

The result is undesirable. Just as the court has power
under Rule 59(d) to grant a new trial of its own initiative
within the 10 days, so it should have power, when an effective
new trial motion has been made and is pending, to decide it
on grounds thought meritorious by the court although not
advanced in the motion. The second sentence added by
amendment to Rule 59(d) confirms the court's power in the
latter situation, with provision that the parties be afforded a
hearing before the power is exercised. See 6 *Moore's Feder-
al Practice*, par. 59.09[2] (2d ed. 1953).

In considering whether a given ground has or has not been
advanced in the motion made by the party, it should be borne
in mind that the particularity called for in stating the
grounds for a new trial motion is the same as that required

for all motions by Rule 7(b)(1). The latter rule does not require ritualistic detail but rather a fair indication to court and counsel of the substance of the grounds relied on. See *Lebeck v. William A. Jarvis Co.*, 250 F.2d 285 (3d Cir. 1957); *Tsai v. Rosenthal*, 297 F.2d 614 (8th Cir. 1961); *General Motors Corp. v. Perry*, 303 F.2d 544 (7th Cir. 1962); cf. *Grimm v. California Spray-Chemical Corp.*, 264 F.2d 145 (9th Cir. 1959); *Cooper v. Midwest Feed Products Co.*, 271 F.2d 177 (8th Cir. 1959).

1995 Amendments

The only change, other than stylistic, intended by this revision is to add explicit time limits for filing motions for a new trial, motions to alter or amend a judgment, and affidavits opposing a new trial motion. Previously, there was an inconsistency in the wording of Rules 50, 52, and 59 with respect to whether certain post-judgment motions had to be filed, or merely served, during the prescribed period. This inconsistency caused special problems when motions for a new trial were joined with other post-judgment motions. These motions affect the finality of the judgment, a matter often of importance to third persons as well as the parties and the court. The Committee believes that each of these rules should be revised to require filing before end of the 10–day period. Filing is an event that can be determined with certainty from court records. The phrase "no later than" is used—rather than "within"—to include post-judgment motions that sometimes are filed before actual entry of the judgment by the clerk. It should be noted that under Rule 5 the motions when filed are to contain a certificate of service on other parties. It also should be noted that under Rule 6(a) Saturdays, Sundays, and legal holidays are excluded in measuring the 10–day period, but that Bankruptcy Rule 9006(a) excludes intermediate Saturdays, Sundays, and legal holidays only in computing periods less than 8 days.

2007 Amendments

*[Effective December 1, 2007,
absent contrary Congressional action.]*

The language of Rule 59 has been amended as part of the general restyling of the Civil Rules to make them more easily understood and to make style and terminology consistent throughout the rules. These changes are intended to be stylistic only.

Rule 60. Relief From Judgment or Order

(a) Clerical Mistakes. Clerical mistakes in judgments, orders or other parts of the record and errors therein arising from oversight or omission may be corrected by the court at any time of its own initiative or on the motion of any party and after such notice, if any, as the court orders. During the pendency of an appeal, such mistakes may be so corrected before the appeal is docketed in the appellate court, and thereafter while the appeal is pending may be so corrected with leave of the appellate court.

(b) Mistakes; Inadvertence; Excusable Neglect; Newly Discovered Evidence; Fraud, Etc. On motion and upon such terms as are just, the court may relieve a party or a party's legal representative from a final judgment, order, or proceeding for the following reasons: (1) mistake, inadvertence, surprise, or excusable neglect; (2) newly discovered evidence which by due diligence could not have been discovered in time to move for a new trial under Rule 59(b); (3) fraud (whether heretofore denominated intrinsic or extrinsic), misrepresentation, or other misconduct of an adverse party; (4) the judgment is void; (5) the judgment has been satisfied, released, or discharged, or a prior judgment upon which it is based has been reversed or otherwise vacated, or it is no longer equitable that the judgment should have prospective application; or (6) any other reason justifying relief from the operation of the judgment. The motion shall be made within a reasonable time, and for reasons (1), (2), and (3) not more than one year after the judgment, order, or proceeding was entered or taken. A motion under this subdivision (b) does not affect the finality of a judgment or suspend its operation. This rule does not limit the power of a court to entertain an independent action to relieve a party from a judgment, order, or proceeding, or to grant relief to a defendant not actually personally notified as provided in Title 28, U.S.C., § 1655, or to set aside a judgment for fraud upon the court. Writs of coram nobis, coram vobis, audita querela, and bills of review and bills in the nature of a bill of review, are abolished, and the procedure for obtaining any relief from a judgment shall be by motion as prescribed in these rules or by an independent action.

(As amended Dec. 27, 1946, eff. Mar. 19, 1948; Dec. 29, 1948, eff. Oct. 20, 1949; Mar. 2, 1987, eff. Aug. 1, 1987.)

Proposed Amendment of Rule

Effective December 1, 2007, absent contrary Congressional action, this rule is amended to read as follows:

Rule 60. Relief from a Judgment or Order

(a) Corrections Based on Clerical Mistakes; Oversights and Omissions. *The court may correct a clerical mistake or a mistake arising from oversight or omission whenever one is found in a judgment, order, or other part of the record. The court may do so on motion or on its own, with or without notice. But after an appeal has been docketed in the appellate court and while it is pending, such a mistake may be corrected only with the appellate court's leave.*

(b) Grounds for Relief from a Final Judgment, Order, or Proceeding. *On motion and just terms, the court may relieve a party or its legal representative from a final judgment, order, or proceeding for the following reasons:*

(1) mistake, inadvertence, surprise, or excusable neglect;

(2) newly discovered evidence that, with reasonable diligence, could not have been discovered in time to move for a new trial under Rule 59(b);

(3) fraud (whether previously called intrinsic or extrinsic), misrepresentation, or misconduct by an opposing party;

(4) the judgment is void;

(5) the judgment has been satisfied, released or discharged; it is based on an earlier judgment that has been reversed or vacated; or applying it prospectively is no longer equitable; or

(6) any other reason that justifies relief.

(c) Timing and Effect of the Motion.

(1) Timing. A motion under Rule 60(b) must be made within a reasonable time—and for reasons (1), (2), and (3) no more than a year after the entry of the judgment or order or the date of the proceeding.

(2) Effect on Finality. The motion does not affect the judgment's finality or suspend its operation.

(d) Other Powers to Grant Relief. *This rule does not limit a court's power to:*

(1) entertain an independent action to relieve a party from a judgment, order, or proceeding;

(2) grant relief under 28 U.S.C. § 1655 to a defendant who was not personally notified of the action; or

(3) set aside a judgment for fraud on the court.

(e) Bills and Writs Abolished. *The following are abolished: bills of review, bills in the nature of bills of review, and writs of coram nobis, coram vobis, and audita querela.*

ADVISORY COMMITTEE NOTES

1937 Adoption

Note to Subdivision (a). See [former] Equity Rule 72 (Correction of Clerical Mistakes in Orders and Decrees); Mich.Court Rules Ann. (Searl, 1933) Rule 48, § 3; 2 Wash. Rev.Stat.Ann. (Remington, 1932) § 464(3); Wyo.Rev.Stat. Ann. (Courtright, 1931) § 89–2301(3). For an example of a very liberal provision for the correction of clerical errors and for amendment after judgment, see Va.Code Ann. (Michie, 1936) §§ 6329, 6333.

Note to Subdivision (b). Application to the court under this subdivision does not extend the time for taking an appeal, as distinguished from the motion for new trial. This section is based upon Calif.Code Civ.Proc. (Deering, 1937) § 473. See also N.Y.C.P.A. (1937) § 108; 2 Minn.Stat. (Mason, 1927) § 9283.

For the independent action to relieve against mistake, etc., see Dobie, *Federal Procedure*, pages 760 to 765, compare 639; and Simkins, *Federal Practice*, ch. CXXI (pp. 820 to 830) and ch. CXXII (pp. 831 to 834), compare § 214.

1946 Amendment

Note. Subdivision (a). The amendment incorporates the view expressed in *Perlman v. 322 West Seventy-Second Street, Co., Inc.,* C.C.A.2d, 1942, 127 F.2d 716; 3 *Moore's Federal Practice,* 1938, 3276, and further permits correction after docketing, with leave of the appellate court. Some courts have thought that upon the taking of an appeal the district court lost its power to act. See *Schram v. Safety Investment Co.,* E.D.Mich.1942, 45 F.Supp. 636; also *Miller v. United States,* C.C.A.7th, 1940, 114 F.2d 267.

Subdivision (b). When promulgated, the rules contained a number of provisions, including those found in Rule 60(b), describing the practice by a motion to obtain relief from judgments, and these rules, coupled with the reservation in Rule 60(b) of the right to entertain a new action to relieve a party from a judgment, were generally supposed to cover the field. Since the rules have been in force, decisions have been rendered that the use of bills of review, coram nobis, or audita querela, to obtain relief from final judgments is still proper, and that various remedies of this kind still exist although they are not mentioned in the rules and the practice is not prescribed in the rules. It is obvious that the rules should be complete in this respect and define the practice with respect to any existing rights or remedies to obtain relief from final judgments. For extended discussion of the old common law writs and equitable remedies, the interpretation of Rule 60, and proposals for change, see Moore and Rogers, *Federal Relief from Civil Judgments,* 1946, 55 Yale L.J. 623. See also 3 *Moore's Federal Practice,* 1938, 3254 et seq.; Commentary, *Effect of Rule 60b on Other Methods of Relief From Judgment,* 1941, 4 Fed.Rules Serv. 942, 945; *Wallace v. United States,* C.C.A.2d, 1944, 142 F.2d 240, certiorari denied 65 S.Ct. 37, 323 U.S. 712, 89 L.Ed. 573.

The reconstruction of Rule 60(b) has for one of its purposes a clarification of this situation. Two types of procedure to obtain relief from judgments are specified in the rules as it is proposed to amend them. One procedure is by motion in the court and in the action in which the judgment was rendered. The other procedure is by a new or independent action to obtain relief from a judgment, which action may or may not be begun in the court which rendered the judgment. Various rules, such as the one dealing with a motion for new trial and for amendment of judgments, Rule 59, one for amended findings, Rule 52, and one for judgment notwithstanding the verdict, Rule 50(b), and including the provisions of Rule 60(b) as amended, prescribe the various types of cases in which the practice by motion is permitted. In each case there is a limit upon the time within which resort to a motion is permitted, and this time limit may not be enlarged under Rule 6(b). If the right to make a motion is lost by the expiration of the time limits fixed in these rules, the only other procedural remedy is by a new or independent action to set aside a judgment upon those principles which have heretofore been applied in such an action. Where the independent action is resorted to, the limitations of time are those of laches or statutes of limitations. The Committee has endeavored to ascertain all the remedies and types of relief heretofore available by coram nobis, coram vobis, audita querela, bill of review, or bill in the nature of a bill of review. See Moore and Rogers, *Federal Relief from Civil Judgments,* 1946, 55 Yale L.J. 623, 659 to 682. It endeav-

ored then to amend the rules to permit, either by motion or by independent action, the granting of various kinds of relief from judgments which were permitted in the federal courts prior to the adoption of these rules, and the amendment concludes with a provision abolishing the use of bills of review and the other common law writs referred to, and requiring the practice to be by motion or by independent action.

To illustrate the operation of the amendment, it will be noted that under Rule 59(b) as it now stands, without amendment, a motion for new trial on the ground of newly discovered evidence is permitted within ten days after the entry of the judgment, or after that time upon leave of the court. It is proposed to amend Rule 59(b) by providing that under that rule a motion for new trial shall be served not later than ten days after the entry of the judgment, whatever the ground be for the motion, whether error by the court or newly discovered evidence. On the other hand, one of the purposes of the bill of review in equity was to afford relief on the ground of newly discovered evidence long after the entry of the judgment. Therefore, to permit relief by a motion similar to that heretofore obtained on bill of review, Rule 60(b) as amended permits an application for relief to be made by motion, on the ground of newly discovered evidence, within one year after judgment. Such a motion under Rule 60(b) does not affect the finality of the judgment, but a motion under Rule 59, made within 10 days, does affect finality and the running of the time for appeal.

If these various amendments, including principally those to Rule 60(b), accomplish the purpose for which they are intended, the federal rules will deal with the practice in every sort of case in which relief from final judgments is asked, and prescribe the practice. With reference to the question whether, as the rules now exist, relief by coram nobis, bills of review, and so forth, is permissible, the generally accepted view is that the remedies are still available, although the precise relief obtained in a particular case by use of these ancillary remedies is shrouded in ancient lore and mystery. See *Wallace v. United States*, C.C.A.2d, 1944, 142 F.2d 240, certiorari denied 65 S.Ct. 37, 323 U.S. 712, 89 L.Ed. 573; *Fraser v. Doing*, App.D.C.1942, 130 F.2d 617; *Jones v. Watts*, C.C.A.5th, 1944, 142 F.2d 575; *Preveden v. Hahn*, S.D.N.Y.1941, 36 F.Supp. 952; *Cavallo v. Agwilines, Inc.*, S.D.N.Y.1942, 6 Fed.Rules Serv. 60b.31, Case 2, 2 F.R.D. 526; *McGinn v. United States*, D.C.Mass.1942, 6 Fed.Rules Serv. 60b.51, Case 3, 2 F.R.D. 562; *City of Shattuck, Oklahoma ex rel. Versluis v. Oliver*, W.D.Okl.1945, 8 Fed.Rules Serv. 60b.31, Case 3; Moore and Rogers, *Federal Relief from Civil Judgments*, 1946, 55 Yale L.J. 623, 631 to 653; 3 *Moore's Federal Practice*, 1938, 3254 et seq.; Commentary, *Effect of Rule 60b on Other Methods of Relief From Judgment*, op. cit. supra. Cf. *Norris v. Camp*, C.C.A.10th, 1944, 144 F.2d 1; *Reed v. South Atlantic Steamship Co. of Delaware*, D.Del.1942, 2 F.R.D. 475, 6 Fed.Rules Serv. 60b.31, Case 1; *Laughlin v. Berens*, D.D.C.1945, 8 Fed.Rules Serv. 60b.51, Case 1, 73 W.L.R. 209.

The transposition of the words "the court" and the addition of the word "and" at the beginning of the first sentence are merely verbal changes. The addition of the qualifying word "final" emphasizes the character of the judgments, orders or proceedings from which Rule 60(b) affords relief; and hence interlocutory judgments are not brought within the restrictions of the rule, but rather they are left subject to the complete power of the court rendering them to afford such relief from them as justice requires.

The qualifying pronoun "his" has been eliminated on the basis that it is too restrictive, and that the subdivision should include the mistake or neglect of others which may be just as material and call just as much for supervisory jurisdiction as where the judgment is taken against the party through *his* mistake, inadvertence, etc.

Fraud, whether intrinsic or extrinsic, misrepresentation, or other misconduct of an adverse party are express grounds for relief by motion under amended subdivision (b). There is no sound reason for their exclusion. The incorporation of fraud and the like within the scope of the rule also removes confusion as to the proper procedure. It has been held that relief from a judgment obtained by extrinsic fraud could be secured by motion within a "reasonable time," which might be after the time stated in the rule had run. *Fiske v. Buder*, C.C.A.8th, 1942, 125 F.2d 841; see also inferentially *Bucy v. Nevada Construction Co.*, C.C.A.9th, 1942, 125 F.2d 213. On the other hand, it has been suggested that in view of the fact that fraud was omitted from original Rule 60(b) as a ground for relief, an independent action was the only proper remedy. Commentary, *Effect of Rule 60b on Other Methods of Relief From Judgment*, 1941, 4 Fed.Rules Serv. 942, 945. The amendment settles this problem by making fraud an express ground for relief by motion; and under the saving clause, fraud may be urged as a basis for relief by independent action insofar as established doctrine permits. See Moore and Rogers, *Federal Relief from Civil Judgments*, 1946, 55 Yale L.J. 623, 653 to 659; 3 Moore's Federal Practice, 1938, 3267 et seq. And the rule expressly does not limit the power of the court, when fraud has been perpetrated upon it, to give relief under the saving clause. As an illustration of this situation, see *Hazel-Atlas Glass Co. v. Hartford Empire Co.*, 1944, 64 S.Ct. 997, 322 U.S. 238, 88 L.Ed. 1250.

The time limit for relief by motion in the court and in the action in which the judgment was rendered has been enlarged from six months to one year.

It should be noted that Rule 60(b) does not assume to define the substantive law as to the grounds for vacating judgments, but merely prescribes the practice in proceedings to obtain relief. It should also be noted that under § 200(4) of the Soldiers' and Sailors' Civil Relief Act of 1940, § 501 et seq. [§ 520(4)] of the Appendix to Title 50, a judgment rendered in any action or proceeding governed by the section may be vacated under certain specified circumstances upon proper application to the court.

1948 Amendment

The amendment effective October, 1949 substituted the reference to "Title 28, U.S.C. § 1655," in the next to the last sentence of subdivision (b), for the reference to "Section 57 of the Judicial Code, U.S.C., Title 28, § 118".

1987 Amendment

The amendment is technical. No substantive change is intended.

2007 Amendments

[Effective December 1, 2007, absent contrary Congressional action.]

The language of Rule 60 has been amended as part of the general restyling of the Civil Rules to make them more easily understood and to make style and terminology consistent throughout the rules. These changes are intended to be stylistic only.

The final sentence of former Rule 60(b) said that the procedure for obtaining any relief from a judgment was by motion as prescribed in the Civil Rules or by an independent action. That provision is deleted as unnecessary. Relief continues to be available only as provided in the Civil Rules or by independent action.

Rule 61. Harmless Error

No error in either the admission or the exclusion of evidence and no error or defect in any ruling or order or in anything done or omitted by the court or by any of the parties is ground for granting a new trial or for setting aside a verdict or for vacating, modifying, or otherwise disturbing a judgment or order, unless refusal to take such action appears to the court inconsistent with substantial justice. The court at every stage of the proceeding must disregard any error or defect in the proceeding which does not affect the substantial rights of the parties.

Proposed Amendment of Rule

Effective December 1, 2007, absent contrary Congressional action, this rule is amended to read as follows:

Rule 61. Harmless Error

Unless justice requires otherwise, no error in admitting or excluding evidence—or any other error by the court or a party—is ground for granting a new trial, for setting aside a verdict, or for vacating, modifying, or otherwise disturbing a judgment or order. At every stage of the proceeding, the court must disregard all errors and defects that do not affect any party's substantial rights.

ADVISORY COMMITTEE NOTES
1937 Adoption

A combination of U.S.C., Title 28, § 2111, [former] § 391 (New trials; harmless error) and [former] § 777 (Defects of form; amendments) with modifications. See *McCandless v. United States,* 1936, 56 S.Ct. 764, 298 U.S. 342, 80 L.Ed. 1205. Compare [former] Equity Rule 72 (Correction of Clerical Mistakes in Orders and Decrees); and last sentence of [former] Equity Rule 46 (Trial—Testimony Usually Taken in Open Court—Rulings on Objections to Evidence). For the last sentence see the last sentence of [former] Equity Rule 19 (Amendments Generally).

2007 Amendments

[Effective December 1, 2007, absent contrary Congressional action.]

The language of Rule 61 has been amended as part of the general restyling of the Civil Rules to make them more easily understood and to make style and terminology consistent throughout the rules. These changes are intended to be stylistic only.

Rule 62. Stay of Proceedings to Enforce a Judgment

(a) Automatic Stay; Exceptions—Injunctions, Receiverships, and Patent Accountings. Except as stated herein, no execution shall issue upon a judgment nor shall proceedings be taken for its enforcement until the expiration of 10 days after its entry. Unless otherwise ordered by the court, an interlocutory or final judgment in an action for an injunction or in a receivership action, or a judgment or order directing an accounting in an action for infringement of letters patent, shall not be stayed during the period after its entry and until an appeal is taken or during the pendency of an appeal. The provisions of subdivision (c) of this rule govern the suspending, modifying, restoring, or granting of an injunction during the pendency of an appeal.

(b) Stay on Motion for New Trial or for Judgment. In its discretion and on such conditions for the security of the adverse party as are proper, the court may stay the execution of or any proceedings to enforce a judgment pending the disposition of a motion for a new trial or to alter or amend a judgment made pursuant to Rule 59, or of a motion for relief from a judgment or order made pursuant to Rule 60, or of a motion for judgment in accordance with a motion for a directed verdict made pursuant to Rule 50, or of a motion for amendment to the findings or for additional findings made pursuant to Rule 52(b).

(c) Injunction Pending Appeal. When an appeal is taken from an interlocutory or final judgment granting, dissolving, or denying an injunction, the court in its discretion may suspend, modify, restore, or grant an injunction during the pendency of the appeal upon such terms as to bond or otherwise as it considers proper for the security of the rights of the adverse party. If the judgment appealed from is rendered by a district court of three judges specially constituted pursuant to a statute of the United States, no such order shall be made except (1) by such court sitting in open court or (2) by the assent of all the judges of such court evidenced by their signatures to the order.

(d) Stay Upon Appeal. When an appeal is taken the appellant by giving a supersedeas bond may obtain a stay subject to the exceptions contained in subdivision (a) of this rule. The bond may be given at or after the time of filing the notice of appeal or of procuring the order allowing the appeal, as the case may be. The stay is effective when the supersedeas bond is approved by the court.

(e) Stay in Favor of the United States or Agency Thereof. When an appeal is taken by the United States or an officer or agency thereof or by direction

of any department of the Government of the United States and the operation or enforcement of the judgment is stayed, no bond, obligation, or other security shall be required from the appellant.

(f) Stay According to State Law. In any state in which a judgment is a lien upon the property of the judgment debtor and in which the judgment debtor is entitled to a stay of execution, a judgment debtor is entitled, in the district court held therein, to such stay as would be accorded the judgment debtor had the action been maintained in the courts of that state.

(g) Power of Appellate Court Not Limited. The provisions in this rule do not limit any power of an appellate court or of a judge or justice thereof to stay proceedings during the pendency of an appeal or to suspend, modify, restore, or grant an injunction during the pendency of an appeal or to make any order appropriate to preserve the status quo or the effectiveness of the judgment subsequently to be entered.

(h) Stay of Judgment as to Multiple Claims or Multiple Parties. When a court has ordered a final judgment under the conditions stated in Rule 54(b), the court may stay enforcement of that judgment until the entering of a subsequent judgment or judgments and may prescribe such conditions as are necessary to secure the benefit thereof to the party in whose favor the judgment is entered.

(As amended Dec. 27, 1946, eff. Mar. 19, 1948; Dec. 29, 1948, eff. Oct. 20, 1949; Apr. 17, 1961, eff. July 19, 1961; Mar. 2, 1987, eff. Aug. 1, 1987.)

Proposed Amendment of Rule

Effective December 1, 2007, absent contrary Congressional action, this rule is amended to read as follows:

Rule 62. Stay of Proceedings to Enforce a Judgment

(a) Automatic Stay; Exceptions for Injunctions, Receiverships, and Patent Accountings. *Except as stated in this rule, no execution may issue on a judgment, nor may proceedings be taken to enforce it, until 10 days have passed after its entry. But unless the court orders otherwise, the following are not stayed after being entered, even if an appeal is taken:*

(1) an interlocutory or final judgment in an action for an injunction or a receivership; or

(2) a judgment or order that directs an accounting in an action for patent infringement.

(b) Stay Pending the Disposition of a Motion. *On appropriate terms for the opposing party's security, the court may stay the execution of a judgment—or any proceedings to enforce it—pending disposition of any of the following motions:*

(1) under Rule 50, for judgment as a matter of law;

(2) under Rule 52(b), to amend the findings or for additional findings;

(3) under Rule 59, for a new trial or to alter or amend a judgment; or

(4) under Rule 60, for relief from a judgment or order.

(c) Injunction Pending an Appeal. *While an appeal is pending from an interlocutory order or final judgment that grants, dissolves, or denies an injunction, the court may suspend, modify, restore, or grant an injunction on terms for bond or other terms that secure the opposing party's rights. If the judgment appealed from is rendered by a statutory three-judge district court, the order must be made either:*

(1) by that court sitting in open session; or

(2) by the assent of all its judges, as evidenced by their signatures.

(d) Stay with Bond on Appeal. *If an appeal is taken, the appellant may obtain a stay by supersedeas bond, except in an action described in Rule 62(a)(1) or (2). The bond may be given upon or after filing the notice of appeal or after obtaining the order allowing the appeal. The stay takes effect when the court approves the bond.*

(e) Stay Without Bond on an Appeal by the United States, Its Officers, or Its Agencies. *The court must not require a bond, obligation, or other security from the appellant when granting a stay on an appeal by the United States, its officers, or its agencies or on an appeal directed by a department of the federal government.*

(f) Stay in Favor of a Judgment Debtor Under State Law. *If a judgment is a lien on the judgment debtor's property under the law of the state where the court is located, the judgment debtor is entitled to the same stay of execution the state court would give.*

(g) Appellate Court's Power Not Limited. *This rule does not limit the power of the appellate court or one of its judges or justices:*

(1) to stay proceedings—or suspend, modify, restore, or grant an injunction—while an appeal is pending; or

(2) to issue an order to preserve the status quo or the effectiveness of the judgment to be entered.

(h) Stay with Multiple Claims or Parties. *A court may stay the enforcement of a final judgment entered under Rule 54(b) until it enters a later judgment or judgments, and may prescribe terms necessary to secure the benefit of the stayed judgment for the party in whose favor it was entered.*

Complete Annotation Materials, see Title 28 U.S.C.A.

ADVISORY COMMITTEE NOTES

1937 Adoption

Note to Subdivision (a). The first sentence states the substance of the last sentence of U.S.C., Title 28, [former] § 874 (Supersedeas). The remainder of the subdivision states the substance of the last clause of U.S.C., Title 28, § 1292, [formerly] § 227 (Appeals in proceedings for injunctions; receivers; and admiralty), and of §§ 1292, 2107, [formerly] § 227a (Appeals in suits in equity for infringement of letters patent for inventions; stay of proceedings for accounting), but extended to include final as well as interlocutory judgments.

Note to Subdivision (b). This modifies U.S.C., Title 28, [former] § 840 (Executions; stay on conditions).

Note to Subdivision (c). Compare [former] Equity Rule 74 (Injunction Pending Appeal); and *Cumberland Telephone and Telegraph Co. v. Louisiana Public Service Commission,* 1922, 43 S.Ct. 75, 260 U.S. 212, 67 L.Ed. 217. See Simkins, Federal Practice (1934), § 916, in regard to the effect of appeal on injunctions and the giving of bonds. See U.S.C., [former] Title 6 (Official and Penal Bonds) for bonds by surety companies. For statutes providing for a specially constituted district court of three judges, see:

U.S.C., Title 7:

§ 217 (Proceedings for suspension of orders of Secretary of Agriculture under Stockyards Act)—by reference.

§ 499k (Injunctions; application of injunction laws governing orders of Interstate Commerce Commission to orders of Secretary of Agriculture under Perishable Commodities Act)—by reference.

U.S.C., Title 15:

§ 28 (Antitrust laws; suits against monopolies expedited)

U.S.C., Title 28, former:

§ 47 [now 2325 (repealed)] (Injunctions as to orders of Interstate Commerce Commission, etc.)

§ 380 [now 2284] (Injunctions; alleged unconstitutionality of State statutes)

§ 380a [now 2284] (Same; constitutionality of federal statute)

U.S.C., Title 49:

§ 44 [former] (Suits in equity under interstate commerce laws; expedition of suits)

Note to Subdivision (d). This modifies U.S.C., Title 28, [former] § 874 (Supersedeas). See Rule 36(2), Rules of the Supreme Court of the United States, which governs supersedeas bonds on direct appeals to the Supreme Court, and Rule 73(d), of these rules, which governs supersedeas bonds on appeals to a circuit court of appeals. The provisions governing supersedeas bonds in both kinds of appeals are substantially the same.

Note to Subdivision (e). This states the substance of U.S.C., Title 28, § 2408, formerly § 870 (Bond; not required of the United States).

Note to Subdivision (f). This states the substance of U.S.C., Title 28, [former] § 841 (Executions; stay of one term) with appropriate modification to conform to the provisions of Rule 6(c) as to terms of court.

1946 Amendment

Note. Subdivision (a). [This subdivision not amended]. Sections 203 and 204 of the Soldiers' and Sailors' Civil Relief Act of 1940, 50 U.S.C., Appendix, § 501 et seq. [§§ 523, 524], provide under certain circumstances for the issuance and continuance of a stay of execution of any judgment or order entered against a person in military service. See *Bowsman v. Peterson,* D.Neb.1942, 45 F.Supp. 741. Section 201 of the Act [50 U.S.C. App. § 521] permits under certain circumstances the issuance of a stay of any action or proceeding at any stage thereof, where either the plaintiff or defendant is a person in military service. See also note to Rule 64 herein.

Subdivision (b). This change was necessary because of the proposed addition to Rule 59 of subdivision (e).

Subdivision (h). In proposing to revise Rule 54(b), the Committee thought it advisable to include a separate provision in Rule 62 for stay of enforcement of a final judgment in cases involving multiple claims.

1948 Amendment

The amendment effective October 1949 deleted at the end of subdivision (g) the following language which originally appeared after the word "entered": "and these rules do not supersede the provisions of Section 210 of the Judicial Code, as amended, U.S.C., Title 28, [former] § 47a, or of other statutes of the United States to the effect that stays pending appeals to the Supreme Court may be granted only by that court or a justice thereof."

1961 Amendment

The amendment adopted Apr. 17, 1961, effective July 19, 1961, eliminated words "on some but not all of the claims presented in the action" which followed "final judgment".

1987 Amendment

The amendment is technical. No substantive change is intended.

2007 Amendments

*[Effective December 1, 2007,
absent contrary Congressional action.]*

The language of Rule 62 has been amended as part of the general restyling of the Civil Rules to make them more easily understood and to make style and terminology consistent throughout the rules. These changes are intended to be stylistic only.

The final sentence of former Rule 62(a) referred to Rule 62(c). It is deleted as an unnecessary. Rule 62(c) governs of its own force.

Rule 63. Inability of a Judge to Proceed

If a trial or hearing has been commenced and the judge is unable to proceed, any other judge may proceed with it upon certifying familiarity with the record and determining that the proceedings in the case may be completed without prejudice to the parties. In a hearing or trial without a jury, the succes-

sor judge shall at the request of a party recall any witness whose testimony is material and disputed and who is available to testify again without undue burden. The successor judge may also recall any other witness.

(As amended Mar. 2, 1987, eff. Aug. 1, 1987; Apr. 30, 1991, eff. Dec. 1, 1991.)

Proposed Amendment of Rule

Effective December 1, 2007, absent contrary Congressional action, this rule is amended to read as follows:

Rule 63. Judge's Inability to Proceed

If a judge conducting a hearing or trial is unable to proceed, any other judge may proceed upon certifying familiarity with the record and determining that the case may be completed without prejudice to the parties. In a hearing or a nonjury trial, the successor judge must, at a party's request, recall any witness whose testimony is material and disputed and who is available to testify again without undue burden. The successor judge may also recall any other witness.

ADVISORY COMMITTEE NOTES

1937 Adoption

This rule adapts and extends the provisions of U.S.C., Title 28, [former] § 776 (Bill of exceptions; authentication; signing of by judge) to include all duties to be performed by the judge after verdict or judgment. The statute is therefore superseded.

1987 Amendment

The amendments are technical. No substantive change is intended.

1991 Amendment

The revision substantially displaces the former rule. The former rule was limited to the disability of the judge, and made no provision for disqualification or possible other reasons for the withdrawal of the judge during proceedings. In making provision for other circumstances, the revision is not intended to encourage judges to discontinue participation in a trial for any but compelling reasons. Cf. *United States v. Lane*, 708 F.2d 1394, 1395–1397 (9th Cir.1983). Manifestly, a substitution should not be made for the personal convenience of the court, and the reasons for a substitution should be stated on the record.

The former rule made no provision for the withdrawal of the judge during the trial, but was limited to disqualification after trial. Several courts concluded that the text of the former rule prohibited substitution of a new judge prior to the points described in the rule, thus requiring a new trial,

whether or not a fair disposition was within reach of a substitute judge. *E.g., Whalen v. Ford Motor Credit Co.,* 684 F.2d 272 (4th Cir.1982, en banc) *cert. denied,* 459 U.S. 910 (1982) (jury trial); *Arrow–Hart, Inc. v. Philip Carey Co.,* 552 F.2d 711 (6th Cir.1977) (non-jury trial). *See generally* Comment, *The Case of the Dead Judge: Fed.R.Civ.P. 63: Whalen v. Ford Motor Credit Co.,* 67 MINN.L.REV. 827 (1983).

The increasing length of federal trials has made it likely that the number of trials interrupted by the disability of the judge will increase. An efficient mechanism for completing these cases without unfairness is needed to prevent unnecessary expense and delay. To avoid the injustice that may result if the substitute judge proceeds despite unfamiliarity with the action, the new Rule provides, in language similar to Federal Rule of Criminal Procedure 25(a), that the successor judge must certify familiarity with the record and determine that the case may be completed before that judge without prejudice to the parties. This will necessarily require that there be available a transcript or a videotape of the proceedings prior to substitution. If there has been a long but incomplete jury trial, the prompt availability of the transcript or videotape is crucial to the effective use of this rule, for the jury cannot long be held while an extensive transcript is prepared without prejudice to one or all parties.

The revised text authorizes the substitute judge to make a finding of fact at a bench trial based on evidence heard by a different judge. This may be appropriate in limited circumstances. First, if a witness has become unavailable, the testimony recorded at trial can be considered by the successor judge pursuant to F.R.Ev. 804, being equivalent to a recorded deposition available for use at trial pursuant to Rule 32. For this purpose, a witness who is no longer subject to a subpoena to compel testimony at trial is unavailable. Secondly, the successor judge may determine that particular testimony is not material or is not disputed, and so need not be reheard. The propriety of proceeding in this manner may be marginally affected by the availability of a videotape record; a judge who has reviewed a trial on videotape may be entitled to greater confidence in his or her ability to proceed.

The court would, however, risk error to determine the credibility of a witness not seen or heard who is available to be recalled. Cf. *Anderson v. City of Bessemer City NC,* 470 U.S. 564, 575 (1985); *Marshall v. Jerrico Inc.,* 446 U.S. 238, 242 (1980). See also *United States v. Radatz,* 447 U.S. 667 (1980).

2007 Amendments

[Effective December 1, 2007, absent contrary Congressional action.]

The language of Rule 63 has been amended as part of the general restyling of the Civil Rules to make them more easily understood and to make style and terminology consistent throughout the rules. These changes are intended to be stylistic only.

VIII. PROVISIONAL AND FINAL REMEDIES

Proposed Amendment of Heading

Effective December 1, 2007, absent contrary Congressional action, this heading is amended to read as follows:

TITLE VIII. PROVISIONAL AND FINAL REMEDIES

ADVISORY COMMITTEE NOTES
1991 Amendment

The purpose of the revision is to divide this chapter of the Rules into two. No substantive change is effected.

Rule 64. Seizure of Person or Property

At the commencement of and during the course of an action, all remedies providing for seizure of person or property for the purpose of securing satisfaction of the judgment ultimately to be entered in the action are available under the circumstances and in the manner provided by the law of the state in which the district court is held, existing at the time the remedy is sought, subject to the following qualifications: (1) any existing statute of the United States governs to the extent to which it is applicable; (2) the action in which any of the foregoing remedies is used shall be commenced and prosecuted or, if removed from a state court, shall be prosecuted after removal, pursuant to these rules. The remedies thus available include arrest, attachment, garnishment, replevin, sequestration, and other corresponding or equivalent remedies, however designated and regardless of whether by state procedure the remedy is ancillary to an action or must be obtained by an independent action.

Proposed Amendment of Rule

Effective December 1, 2007, absent contrary Congressional action, this rule is amended to read as follows:

Rule 64. Seizing a Person or Property

(a) Remedies Under State Law—In General. *At the commencement of and throughout an action, every remedy is available that, under the law of the state where the court is located, provides for seizing a person or property to secure satisfaction of the potential judgment. But a federal statute governs to the extent it applies.*

(b) Specific Kinds of Remedies. *The remedies available under this rule include the following—however designated and regardless of whether state procedure requires an independent action:*

- *arrest;*
- *attachment;*
- *garnishment;*
- *replevin;*
- *sequestration; and*
- *other corresponding or equivalent remedies.*

ADVISORY COMMITTEE NOTES
1937 Adoption

This rule adopts the existing Federal law, except that it specifies the applicable State law to be that of the time when the remedy is sought. Under U.S.C., Title 28, [former] § 726 (Attachments as provided by State laws) the plaintiff was entitled to remedies by attachment or other process which were on June 1, 1872, provided by the applicable State law, and the district courts might, from time to time, by general rules, adopt such State laws as might be in force. This statute is superseded as are district court rules which are rendered unnecessary by the rule.

Lis pendens. No rule concerning lis pendens is stated, for this would appear to be a matter of substantive law affecting State laws of property. It has been held that in the absence of a State statute expressly providing for the recordation of notice of the pendency of Federal actions, the commencement of a Federal action is notice to all persons affected. *King v. Davis*, 137 F. 198 (W.D.Va., 1903). It has been held, however, that when a state statute does so provide expressly, its provisions are binding. *United States v. Calcasieu Timber Co.*, 236 F. 196 (C.C.A.5th, 1916).

For statutes of the United States on attachment, see, e.g.: U.S.C., Title 28 former:

§ 737 [now 2710] (Attachment in postal suits)

§ 738 [now 2711] (Attachment; application for warrant)

§ 739 [now 2712] (Attachment; issue of warrant)

§ 740 [now 2713] (Attachment; trial of ownership of property)

§ 741 [now 2714] (Attachment; investment of proceeds of attached property)

§ 742 [now 2715] (Attachment; publication of attachment)

§ 743 [now 2716] (Attachment; personal notice of attachment)

§ 744 [now 2717] (Attachment; discharge; bond)

§ 745 [former] (Attachment; accrued rights not affected)

§ 746 (Attachments dissolved in conformity with State laws)

For statutes of the United States on garnishment, see, e.g.: U.S.C., Title 28, former:

§ 748 [now 2405] (Garnishees in suits by United States against a corporation)

§ 749 [now 2405] (Same; issue tendered on denial of indebtedness)

§ 750 [now 2405] (Same; garnishee failing to appear)

For statutes of the United States on arrest, see, e.g.:

U.S.C., Title 28 former:

§ 376 [now 1651] (Writs of ne exeat)

§ 755 [former] (Special bail in suits for duties and penalties)

§ 756 [former] (Defendant giving bail in one district and committed in another)

§ 757 [former] (Defendant giving bail in one district and committed in another; defendant held until judgment in first suit)

§ 758 [former] (Bail and affidavits; taking by commissioners)

§ 759 [former] (Calling of bail in Kentucky)

§ 760 [former] (Clerks may take bail de bene esse)

§ 843 [now 2007] (Imprisonment for debt)

§ 844 [now 2007] (Imprisonment for debt; discharge according to State laws)

§ 845 [now 2007] (Imprisonment for debt; jail limits)

For statutes of the United States on replevin, see, e.g.:

U.S.C., Title 28:

§ 2463, formerly § 747 (Replevy of property taken under revenue laws).

Supplementary Note

Note. Sections 203 and 204 of the Soldiers' and Sailors' Civil Relief Act of 1940, 50 U.S.C.Appendix, § 501 et seq. [§§ 523 and 524], provide under certain circumstances for the issuance and continuance of a stay of the execution of any judgment entered against a person in military service, or the vacation or stay of any attachment or garnishment directed against such person's property, money, or debts in the hands of another. See also Note to Rule 62 herein.

2007 Amendments

[Effective December 1, 2007,
absent contrary Congressional action.]

The language of Rule 64 has been amended as part of the general restyling of the Civil Rules to make them more easily understood and to make style and terminology consistent throughout the rules. These changes are intended to be stylistic only.

Former Rule 64 stated that the Civil Rules govern an action in which any remedy available under Rule 64(a) is used. The Rules were said to govern from the time the action is commenced if filed in federal court, and from the time of removal if removed from state court. These provisions are deleted as redundant. Rule 1 establishes that the Civil Rules apply to all actions in a district court, and Rule 81(c)(1) adds reassurance that the Civil Rules apply to a removed action "after it is removed."

Rule 65. Injunctions

(a) Preliminary Injunction.

(1) *Notice.* No preliminary injunction shall be issued without notice to the adverse party.

(2) *Consolidation of Hearing With Trial on Merits.* Before or after the commencement of the hearing of an application for a preliminary injunction, the court may order the trial of the action on the merits to be advanced and consolidated with the hearing of the application. Even when this consolidation is not ordered, any evidence received upon an application for a preliminary injunction which would be admissible upon the trial on the merits becomes part of the record on the trial and need not be repeated upon the trial. This subdivision (a)(2) shall be so construed and applied as to save to the parties any rights they may have to trial by jury.

(b) Temporary Restraining Order; Notice; Hearing; Duration. A temporary restraining order may be granted without written or oral notice to the adverse party or that party's attorney only if (1) it clearly appears from specific facts shown by affidavit or by the verified complaint that immediate and irreparable injury, loss, or damage will result to the applicant before the adverse party or that party's attorney can be heard in opposition, and (2) the applicant's attorney certifies to the court in writing the efforts, if any, which have been made to give the notice and the reasons supporting the claim that notice should not be required. Every temporary restraining order granted without notice shall be indorsed with the date and hour of issuance; shall be filed forthwith in the clerk's office and entered of record; shall define the injury and state why it is irreparable and why the order was granted without notice; and shall expire by its terms within such time after entry, not to exceed 10 days, as the court fixes, unless within the time so fixed the order, for good cause shown, is extended for a like period or unless the party against whom the order is directed consents that it may be extended for a longer period. The reasons for the extension shall be entered of record. In case a temporary restraining order is granted without notice, the motion for a preliminary injunction shall be set down for hearing at the earliest possible time and takes precedence of all matters except older matters of the same character; and when the motion comes on for hearing the party who obtained the temporary restraining order shall proceed with the application for a preliminary injunction and, if the party does not do so, the court shall dissolve the temporary restraining order. On 2 days' notice to the party who obtained the temporary restraining order without notice or on such shorter notice to that party as the court may prescribe, the adverse party may appear and move its dissolution or modification and in that event the court shall proceed to hear and determine such motion as expeditiously as the ends of justice require.

(c) Security. No restraining order or preliminary injunction shall issue except upon the giving of security by the applicant, in such sum as the court deems proper, for the payment of such costs and damages as may be incurred or suffered by any party who is found to have been wrongfully enjoined or restrained.

No such security shall be required of the United States or of an officer or agency thereof.

The provisions of Rule 65.1 apply to a surety upon a bond or undertaking under this rule.

(d) Form and Scope of Injunction or Restraining Order. Every order granting an injunction and every restraining order shall set forth the reasons for its issuance; shall be specific in terms; shall describe in reasonable detail, and not by reference to the complaint or other document, the act or acts sought to be restrained; and is binding only upon the parties to the action, their officers, agents, servants, employees, and attorneys, and upon those persons in active concert or participation with them who receive actual notice of the order by personal service or otherwise.

(e) Employer and Employee; Interpleader; Constitutional Cases. These rules do not modify any statute of the United States relating to temporary restraining orders and preliminary injunctions in actions affecting employer and employee; or the provisions of Title 28, U.S.C., § 2361, relating to preliminary injunctions in actions of interpleader or in the nature of interpleader; or Title 28, U.S.C., § 2284, relating to actions required by Act of Congress to be heard and determined by a district court of three judges.

(f) Copyright Impoundment. This rule applies to copyright impoundment proceedings.

(As amended Dec. 27, 1946, eff. Mar. 19, 1948; Dec. 29, 1948, eff. Oct. 20, 1949; Feb. 28, 1966, eff. July 1, 1966; Mar. 2, 1987, eff. Aug. 1, 1987; Apr. 23, 2001, eff. Dec. 1, 2001.)

Proposed Amendment of Rule

Effective December 1, 2007, absent contrary Congressional action, this rule is amended to read as follows:

Rule 65. *Injunctions and Restraining Orders*

(a) *Preliminary Injunction.*

(1) Notice. The court may issue a preliminary injunction only on notice to the adverse party.

(2) Consolidating the Hearing with the Trial on the Merits. Before or after beginning the hearing on a motion for a preliminary injunction, the court may advance the trial on the merits and consolidate it with the hearing. Even when consolidation is not ordered, evidence that is received on the motion and that would be admissible at trial becomes part of the trial record and need not be repeated at trial. But the court must preserve any party's right to a jury trial.

(b) *Temporary Restraining Order.*

(1) Issuing Without Notice. The court may issue a temporary restraining order without

written or oral notice to the adverse party or its attorney only if:

(A) specific facts in an affidavit or a verified complaint clearly show that immediate and irreparable injury, loss, or damage will result to the movant before the adverse party can be heard in opposition; and

(B) the movant's attorney certifies in writing any efforts made to give notice and the reasons why it should not be required.

(2) Contents; Expiration. Every temporary restraining order issued without notice must state the date and hour it was issued; describe the injury and state why it is irreparable; state why the order was issued without notice; and be promptly filed in the clerk's office and entered in the record. The order expires at the time after entry—not to exceed 10 days—that the court sets, unless before that time the court, for good cause, extends it for a like period or the adverse party consents to a longer extension. The reasons for an extension must be entered in the record.

(3) Expediting the Preliminary–Injunction Hearing. If the order is issued without notice, the motion for a preliminary injunction must be set for hearing at the earliest possible time, taking precedence over all other matters except hearings on older matters of the same character. At the hearing, the party who obtained the order must proceed with the motion; if the party does not, the court must dissolve the order.

(4) Motion to Dissolve. On 2 days' notice to the party who obtained the order without notice—or on shorter notice set by the court—the adverse party may appear and move to dissolve or modify the order. The court must then hear and decide the motion as promptly as justice requires.

(c) *Security.* The court may issue a preliminary injunction or a temporary restraining order only if the movant gives security in an amount that the court considers proper to pay the costs and damages sustained by any party found to have been wrongfully enjoined or restrained. The United States, its officers, and its agencies are not required to give security.

(d) *Contents and Scope of Every Injunction and Restraining Order.*

(1) Contents. Every order granting an injunction and every restraining order must:

(A) state the reasons why it issued;

(B) state its terms specifically; and

(C) describe in reasonable detail—and not by referring to the complaint or other document—the act or acts restrained or required.

(2) Persons Bound. The order binds only the following who receive actual notice of it by personal service or otherwise:

 (A) the parties;

 (B) the parties' officers, agents, servants, employees, and attorneys; and

 (C) other persons who are in active concert or participation with anyone described in Rule 65(d)(2)(A) or (B).

(e) Other Laws Not Modified. *These rules do not modify the following:*

 (1) any federal statute relating to temporary restraining orders or preliminary injunctions in actions affecting employer and employee;

 (2) 28 U.S.C. § 2361, which relates to preliminary injunctions in actions of interpleader or in the nature of interpleader; or

 (3) 28 U.S.C. § 2284, which relates to actions that must be heard and decided by a three-judge district court.

(f) Copyright Impoundment. *This rule applies to copyright-impoundment proceedings.*

ADVISORY COMMITTEE NOTES

1937 Adoption

Note to Subdivisions (a) and (b). These are taken from U.S.C., Title 28, [former] § 381 (Injunctions; preliminary injunctions and temporary restraining orders).

Note to Subdivision (c). Except for the last sentence, this is substantially U.S.C., Title 28, [former] § 382 (Injunctions; security on issuance of). The last sentence continues the following and similar statutes which expressly except the United States or an officer or agency thereof from such security requirements: U.S.C. Title 15, §§ 77t(b), 78u(e), and 79r(f) (Securities and Exchange Commission). It also excepts the United States or an officer or agency thereof from such security requirements in any action in which a restraining order or interlocutory judgment of injunction issues in its favor whether there is an express statutory exception from such security requirements or not.

See U.S.C., [former] Title 6 (Official and Penal Bonds) for bonds by surety companies.

Note to Subdivision (d). This is substantially U.S.C., Title 28, [former] § 383 (Injunctions; requisites of order; binding effect).

Note to Subdivision (e). The words "relating to temporary restraining orders and preliminary injunctions in actions affecting employer and employee" are words of description and not of limitation.

Compare [former] Equity Rule 73 (Preliminary Injunctions and Temporary Restraining Orders) which is substantially equivalent to the statutes.

For other statutes dealing with injunctions which are continued, see e.g.:
U.S.C., Title 28 former:

§ 46 [now 2324] (Suits to enjoin orders of Interstate Commerce Commission to be against United States)

§ 47 [now 2325] (Injunctions as to orders of Interstate Commerce Commission; appeal to Supreme Court; time for taking)

§ 378 [former] (Injunctions; when granted)

§ 379 [now 2283] (Injunctions; stay in State courts)

§ 380 [now 1253, 2101, 2281, 2284] (Injunctions; alleged unconstitutionality of State statutes; appeal to Supreme Court)

§ 380a [now 1253, 2101, 2281, 2284] (Injunctions; constitutionality of Federal statute; application for hearing; appeal to Supreme Court)

U.S.C., Title 7:

§ 216 (Court proceedings to enforce orders; injunction)

§ 217 (Proceedings for suspension of orders)

U.S.C., Title 15:

§ 4 (Jurisdiction of courts; duty of district attorney; procedure)

§ 25 (Restraining violations; procedure)

§ 26 (Injunctive relief for private parties; exceptions)

§ 77t(b) (Injunctions and prosecution of offenses)

1946 Amendment

Note. It has been held that in actions on preliminary injunction bonds the district court has discretion to grant relief in the same proceeding or to require the institution of a new action on the bond. *Russell v. Farley,* 1881, 105 U.S. 433, 466. It is believed, however, that in all cases the litigant should have a right to proceed on the bond in the same proceeding, in the manner provided in Rule 73(f) for a similar situation. The paragraph added to Rule 65(c) insures this result and is in the interest of efficiency. There is no reason why Rules 65(c) and 73(f) should operate differently. Compare § 50, sub. n of the Bankruptcy Act, 11 U.S.C. § 78, sub. n, under which actions on all bonds furnished pursuant to the Act may be proceeded upon summarily in the bankruptcy court. See 2 *Collier on Bankruptcy,* 14th ed. by Moore and Oglebay, 1853–1854.

1948 Amendment

The amendment effective October 1949, changed subdivision (e) in the following respects: in the first clause the amendment substituted the words "any statute of the United States" for the words "the Act of October 15, 1914, c. 323, §§ 1 and 20 (38 Stat. 730), U.S.C., Title 29, §§ 52 and 53, or the Act of March 23, 1932, c. 90 (47 Stat. 70), U.S.C., Title 29, c. 6"; in the second clause of subdivision (e) the amendment substituted the reference to "Title 28, U.S.C., § 2361" for the reference to "Section 24(26) of the Judicial Code as amended, U.S.C., Title 28, § 41(26)"; and the third clause was amended to read "Title 28, U.S.C., § 2284," etc., as at present, instead of "the Act of August 24, 1937, c. 754, § 3, relating to actions to enjoin the enforcement of acts of Congress."

1966 Amendment

Subdivision (a)(2). This new subdivision provides express authority for consolidating the hearing of an application for a preliminary injunction with the trial on the merits. The authority can be exercised with particular profit when it appears that a substantial part of the evidence offered on the

application will be relevant to the merits and will be presented in such form as to qualify for admission on the trial proper. Repetition of evidence is thereby avoided. The fact that the proceedings have been consolidated should cause no delay in the disposition of the application for the preliminary injunction, for the evidence will be directed in the first instance to that relief, and the preliminary injunction, if justified by the proof, may be issued in the course of the consolidated proceedings. Furthermore, to consolidate the proceedings will tend to expedite the final disposition of the action. It is believed that consolidation can be usefully availed of in many cases.

The subdivision further provides that even when consolidation is not ordered, evidence received in connection with an application for a preliminary injunction which would be admissible on the trial on the merits forms part of the trial record. This evidence need not be repeated on the trial. On the other hand, repetition is not altogether prohibited. That would be impractical and unwise. For example, a witness testifying comprehensively on the trial who has previously testified upon the application for a preliminary injunction might sometimes be hamstrung in telling his story if he could not go over some part of his prior testimony to connect it with his present testimony. So also, some repetition of testimony may be called for where the trial is conducted by a judge who did not hear the application for the preliminary injunction. In general, however, repetition can be avoided with an increase of efficiency in the conduct of the case and without any distortion of the presentation of evidence by the parties.

Since an application for a preliminary injunction may be made in an action in which, with respect to all or part of the merits, there is a right to trial by jury, it is appropriate to add the caution appearing in the last sentence of the subdivision. In such a case the jury will have to hear all the evidence bearing on its verdict, even if some part of the evidence has already been heard by the judge alone on the application for the preliminary injunction.

The subdivision is believed to reflect the substance of the best current practice and introduces no novel conception.

Subdivision (b). In view of the possibly drastic consequences of a temporary restraining order, the opposition should be heard, if feasible, before the order is granted. Many judges have properly insisted that, when time does not permit of formal notice of the application to the adverse party, some expedient, such as telephonic notice to the attorney for the adverse party, be resorted to if this can reasonably be done. On occasion, however, temporary restraining orders have been issued without any notice when it was feasible for some fair, although informal, notice to be given. See the emphatic criticisms in *Pennsylvania Rd. Co. v. Transport Workers Union*, 278 F.2d 693, 694 (3d Cir. 1960); *Arvida Corp. v. Sugarman*, 259 F.2d 428, 429 (2d Cir. 1958); *Lummus Co. v. Commonwealth Oil Ref. Co., Inc.*, 297 F.2d 80, 83 (2d Cir. 1961), cert. denied, 368 U.S. 986 (1962).

Heretofore the first sentence of subdivision (b), in referring to a notice "served" on the "adverse party" on which a "hearing" could be held, perhaps invited the interpretation that the order might be granted without notice if the circumstances did not permit of a formal hearing on the basis of a formal notice. The subdivision is amended to make it plain that informal notice, which may be communicated to the

attorney rather than the adverse party, is to be preferred to no notice at all.

Before notice can be dispensed with, the applicant's counsel must give his certificate as to any efforts made to give notice and the reasons why notice should not be required. This certificate is in addition to the requirement of an affidavit or verified complaint setting forth the facts as to the irreparable injury which would result before the opposition could be heard.

The amended subdivision continues to recognize that a temporary restraining order may be issued without any notice when the circumstances warrant.

Subdivision (c). Original Rules 65 and 73 contained substantially identical provisions for summary proceedings against sureties on bonds required or permitted by the rules. There was fragmentary coverage of the same subject in the Admiralty Rules. Clearly, a single comprehensive rule is required, and is incorporated as Rule 65.1.

1987 Amendment

The amendments are technical. No substantive change is intended.

2001 Amendments

New subdivision (f) is added in conjunction with abrogation of the antiquated Copyright Rules of Practice adopted for proceedings under the 1909 Copyright Act. Courts have naturally turned to Rule 65 in response to the apparent inconsistency of the former Copyright Rules with the discretionary impoundment procedure adopted in 1976, 17 U.S.C. § 503(a). Rule 65 procedures also have assuaged well-founded doubts whether the Copyright Rules satisfy more contemporary requirements of due process. See, e.g., *Religious Technology Center v. Netcom On–Line Communications Servs., Inc.*, 923 F.Supp. 1231, 1260–1265 (N.D.Cal.1995); *Paramount Pictures Corp. v. Doe*, 821 F.Supp. 82 (E.D.N.Y. 1993); *WPOW, Inc. v. MRLJ Enterprises*, 584 F.Supp. 132 (D.D.C.1984).

A common question has arisen from the experience that notice of a proposed impoundment may enable an infringer to defeat the court's capacity to grant effective relief. Impoundment may be ordered on an ex parte basis under subdivision (b) if the applicant makes a strong showing of the reasons why notice is likely to defeat effective relief. Such no-notice procedures are authorized in trademark infringement proceedings, see 15 U.S.C. § 1116(d), and courts have provided clear illustrations of the kinds of showings that support ex parte relief. See *Matter of Vuitton et Fils S.A.*, 606 F.2d 1 (2d Cir.1979); *Vuitton v. White*, 945 F.2d 569 (3d Cir.1991). In applying the tests for no-notice relief, the court should ask whether impoundment is necessary, or whether adequate protection can be had by a less intrusive form of no-notice relief shaped as a temporary restraining order.

This new subdivision (f) does not limit use of trademark procedures in cases that combine trademark and copyright claims. Some observers believe that trademark procedures should be adopted for all copyright cases, a proposal better considered by Congressional processes than by rulemaking processes.

2007 Amendments

[Effective December 1, 2007, absent contrary Congressional action.]

The language of Rule 65 has been amended as part of the general restyling of the Civil Rules to make them more easily understood and to make style and terminology consistent throughout the rules. These changes are intended to be stylistic only.

The final sentence of former Rule 65(c) referred to Rule 65.1. It is deleted as unnecessary. Rule 65.1 governs of its own force.

Rule 65(d)(2) clarifies two ambiguities in former Rule 65(d). The former rule was adapted from former 28 U.S.C. § 363, but omitted a comma that made clear the common doctrine that a party must have actual notice of an injunction in order to be bound by it. Amended Rule 65(d) restores the meaning of the earlier statute, and also makes clear the proposition that an injunction can be enforced against a person who acts in concert with a party's officer, agent, servant, employee, or attorney.

Rule 65.1. Security: Proceedings Against Sureties

Whenever these rules, including the Supplemental Rules for Admiralty or Maritime Claims and Asset Forfeiture Actions, require or permit the giving of security by a party, and security is given in the form of a bond or stipulation or other undertaking with one or more sureties, each surety submits to the jurisdiction of the court and irrevocably appoints the clerk of the court as the surety's agent upon whom any papers affecting the surety's liability on the bond or undertaking may be served. The surety's liability may be enforced on motion without the necessity of an independent action. The motion and such notice of the motion as the court prescribes may be served on the clerk of the court, who shall forthwith mail copies to the sureties if their addresses are known.

(Added Feb. 28, 1966, eff. July 1, 1966, and amended Mar. 2, 1987, eff. Aug. 1, 1987; Apr. 12, 2006, eff. Dec. 1, 2006.)

Proposed Amendment of Rule

Effective December 1, 2007, absent contrary Congressional action, this rule is amended to read as follows:

Rule 65.1. Proceedings Against a Surety

Whenever these rules (including the Supplemental Rules for Admiralty or Maritime Claims and Asset Forfeiture Actions) require or allow a party to give security, and security is given through a bond or other undertaking with one or more sureties, each surety submits to the court's jurisdiction and irrevocably appoints the court clerk as its agent for receiving service of any papers that affect its liability on the bond or undertaking. The surety's liability may be enforced on motion without an independent action. The motion and any notice that the court orders may be served on the court clerk, who must promptly mail

a copy of each to every surety whose address is known.

ADVISORY COMMITTEE NOTES

1966 Addition

See Note to Rule 65.

1987 Amendment

The amendments are technical. No substantive change is intended.

2006 Amendment

Rule 65.1 is amended to conform to the changed title of the Supplemental Rules.

2007 Amendments

[Effective December 1, 2007, absent contrary Congressional action.]

The language of Rule 65.1 has been amended as part of the general restyling of the Civil Rules to make them more easily understood and to make style and terminology consistent throughout the rules. These changes are intended to be stylistic only.

Rule 66. Receivers Appointed by Federal Courts

An action wherein a receiver has been appointed shall not be dismissed except by order of the court. The practice in the administration of estates by receivers or by other similar officers appointed by the court shall be in accordance with the practice heretofore followed in the courts of the United States or as provided in rules promulgated by the district courts. In all other respects the action in which the appointment of a receiver is sought or which is brought by or against a receiver is governed by these rules.

(As amended Dec. 27, 1946, eff. Mar. 19, 1948; Dec. 29, 1948, eff. Oct. 20, 1949.)

Proposed Amendment of Rule

Effective December 1, 2007, absent contrary Congressional action, this rule is amended to read as follows:

Rule 66. Receivers

These rules govern an action in which the appointment of a receiver is sought or a receiver sues or is sued. But the practice in administering an estate by a receiver or a similar court-appointed officer must accord with the historical practice in federal courts or with a local rule. An action in which a receiver has been appointed may be dismissed only by court order.

ADVISORY COMMITTEE NOTES

1946 Amendment

Note. The title of Rule 66 has been expanded to make clear the subject of the rule, i.e., federal equity receivers.

The first sentence added to Rule 66 prevents a dismissal by any party, after a federal equity receiver has been appointed, except upon leave of court. A party should not be permitted to oust the court and its officer without the consent of that court. See Civil Rule 31(e), Eastern District of Washington.

The second sentence added at the beginning of the rule deals with suits by or against a federal equity receiver. The first clause thereof eliminates the formal ceremony of an ancillary appointment before suit can be brought by a receiver, and is in accord with the more modern state practice, and with more expeditious and less expensive judicial administration. 2 *Moore's Federal Practice*, 1938, 2088–2091. For the rule necessitating ancillary appointment, see *Sterrett v. Second Nat. Bank*, 1918, 39 S.Ct. 27, 248 U.S. 73, 63 L.Ed. 135; *Kelley v. Queeney*, W.D.N.Y.1941, 41 F.Supp. 1015; see also *McCandless v. Furlaud*, 1934, 55 S.Ct. 42, 293 U.S. 67, 79 L.Ed. 202. This rule has been extensively criticized. First, *Extraterritorial Powers of Receivers*, 1932, 27 Ill.L.Rev. 271; Rose, *Extraterritorial Actions by Receivers*, 1933, 17 Minn. L.Rev. 704; Laughlin, *The Extraterritorial Powers of Receivers*, 1932, 45 Harv.L.Rev. 429; Clark and Moore, *A New Federal Civil Procedure—II, Pleadings and Parties*, 1935, 44 Yale L.J. 1291, 1312–1315; Note, 1932, 30 Mich.L.Rev. 1322. See also comment in *Bicknell v. Lloyd-Smith*, C.C.A.2d, 1940, 109 F.2d 527, certiorari denied 61 S.Ct. 15, 311 U.S. 650, 85 L.Ed. 416. The second clause of the sentence merely incorporates the well-known and general rule that, absent statutory authorization, a federal receiver cannot be sued without leave of the court which appointed him, applied in the federal courts since *Barton v. Barbour*, 1881, 104 U.S. 126. See also 1 *Clark on Receivers*, 2d ed., § 549. Under [§ 959 of this title, formerly] 28 U.S.C. § 125 leave of court is unnecessary when a receiver is sued "in respect of any act or transaction of his in carrying on the business" connected with the receivership property, but such suit is subject to the general equity jurisdiction of the court in which the receiver was appointed, so far as justice necessitates.

Capacity of a state court receiver to sue or be sued in Federal court is governed by Rule 17(b).

The last sentence added to Rule 66 assures the application of the rules in all matters except actual administration of the receivership estate itself. Since this implicitly carries with it the applicability of those rules relating to appellate procedure, the express reference thereto contained in Rule 66 has been stricken as superfluous. Under Rule 81(a)(1) the rules do not apply to bankruptcy proceedings except as they may be made applicable by order of the Supreme Court. Rule 66 is applicable to what is commonly known as a federal "chancery" or "equity" receiver, or similar type of court officer. It is not designed to regulate or affect receivers in bankruptcy, which are governed by the Bankruptcy Act and the General Orders. Since the Federal Rules are applicable in bankruptcy by virtue of General Orders in Bankruptcy 36 and 37 [see Appendix II following Rules of Bankruptcy Procedure, Title 11] only to the extent that they are not inconsistent with the Bankruptcy Act or the General Orders, Rule 66 is not applicable to bankruptcy receivers. See 1 *Collier on Bankruptcy*, 14th ed. by Moore and Oglebay, ¶¶2.23–2.36.

1948 Amendment

The amendment effective October 1949 deleted a sentence which formerly appeared immediately following the first sentence and which read as follows: "A receiver shall have the capacity to sue in any district court without ancillary appointment; but actions against a receiver may not be commenced without leave of the court appointing him except when authorized by a statute of the United States."

2007 Amendments

[Effective December 1, 2007, absent contrary Congressional action.]

The language of Rule 66 has been amended as part of the general restyling of the Civil Rules to make them more easily understood and to make style and terminology consistent throughout the rules. These changes are intended to be stylistic only.

Rule 67. Deposit in Court

In an action in which any part of the relief sought is a judgment for a sum of money or the disposition of a sum of money or the disposition of any other thing capable of delivery, a party, upon notice to every other party, and by leave of court, may deposit with the court all or any part of such sum or thing, whether or not that party claims all or any part of the sum or thing. The party making the deposit shall serve the order permitting deposit on the clerk of the court. Money paid into court under this rule shall be deposited and withdrawn in accordance with the provisions of Title 28, U.S.C., §§ 2041, and 2042; the Act of June 26, 1934, c. 756, § 23, as amended (48 Stat. 1236, 58 Stat. 845), U.S.C., Title 31, § 725v; or any like statute. The fund shall be deposited in an interest-bearing account or invested in an interest-bearing instrument approved by the court.

(As amended Dec. 29, 1948, eff. Oct. 20, 1949; Apr. 28, 1983, eff. Aug. 1, 1983.)

Proposed Amendment of Rule

Effective December 1, 2007, absent contrary Congressional action, this rule is amended to read as follows:

Rule 67. Deposit into Court

*(a) **Depositing Property.** If any part of the relief sought is a money judgment or the disposition of a sum of money or some other deliverable thing, a party—on notice to every other party and by leave of court—may deposit with the court all or part of the money or thing, whether or not that party claims any of it. The depositing party must deliver to the clerk a copy of the order permitting deposit.*

*(b) **Investing and Withdrawing Funds.** Money paid into court under this rule must be deposited and withdrawn in accordance with 28 U.S.C. §§ 2041 and 2042 and any like statute. The money must be depos-*

Rule 67 RULES OF CIVIL PROCEDURE

ited in an interest-bearing account or invested in a court-approved, interest-bearing instrument.

ADVISORY COMMITTEE NOTES

1937 Adoption

This rule provides for deposit in court generally, continuing similar special provisions contained in such statutes as U.S.C., Title 28, [§§ 1335, 1397, 2361, formerly] § 41(26) (Original jurisdiction of bills of interpleader, and of bills in the nature of interpleader). See generally *Howard v. United States,* 1902, 22 S.Ct. 543, 184 U.S. 676, 46 L.Ed. 754; United States Supreme Court Admiralty Rules (1920), Rules 37 (Bringing Funds into Court), 41 (Funds in Court Registry), and 42 (Claims Against Proceeds in Registry). With the first sentence, compare *English Rules Under the Judicature Act* (The Annual Practice, 1937) O. 22, r. 1(1).

1948 Amendment

The amendment effective October 1949 substituted the reference to "Title 28, U.S.C.A., §§ 2041, and 2042" for the reference to "Sections 995 and 996, Revised Statutes, as amended, U.S.C.A., Title 28, §§ 851, 852." The amendment also added the words "as amended" following the citation of the Act of June 26, 1934, c. 756, § 23, and, in the parenthetical citation immediately following, added the reference to "58 Stat. 845".

1983 Amendment

Rule 67 has been amended in three ways. The first change is the addition of the clause in the first sentence. Some courts have construed the present rule to permit deposit only when the party making it claims no interest in the fund or thing deposited. E.g., *Blasin-Stern v. Beech-Nut Life Savers Corp.,* 429 F.Supp. 533 (D. Puerto Rico 1975); *Dinkins v. General Aniline & Film Corp.,* 214 F.Supp. 281 (S.D.N.Y.1963). However, there are situations in which a litigant may wish to be relieved of responsibility for a sum or thing, but continue to claim an interest in all or part of it. In these cases the deposit-in-court procedure should be available; in addition to the advantages to the party making the deposit, the procedure gives other litigants assurance that any judgment will be collectable. The amendment is intended to accomplish that.

The second change is the addition of a requirement that the order of deposit be served on the clerk of the court in which the sum or thing is to be deposited. This is simply to assure that the clerk knows what is being deposited and what his responsibilities are with respect to the deposit. The latter point is particularly important since the rule as amended contemplates that deposits will be placed in interest-bearing accounts; the clerk must know what treatment has been ordered for the particular deposit.

The third change is to require that any money be deposited in an interest-bearing account or instrument approved by the court.

2007 Amendments

[Effective December 1, 2007, absent contrary Congressional action.]

The language of Rule 67 has been amended as part of the general restyling of the Civil Rules to make them more easily understood and to make style and terminology consistent throughout the rules. These changes are intended to be stylistic only.

HISTORICAL NOTES

References in Text

The Act of June 26, 1934, c. 756, § 23, as amended (48 Stat. 1236, 58 Stat. 845), 31 U.S.C. § 725v, referred to in text, was repealed by Pub.L. 97–258, § 5(b), Sept. 13, 1982, 96 Stat. 1074, the first section of which enacted Title 31, Money and Finance. Insofar as not superseded by sections 2041 and 2042 of Title 28, Judiciary and Judicial Procedure, the Act of June 26, 1934, § 23, as amended (31 U.S.C. 725v) was reenacted as sections 572a and 2043 of Title 28 by Pub.L. 97–258, § 2(g)(3), (4).

Rule 68. Offer of Judgment

At any time more than 10 days before the trial begins, a party defending against a claim may serve upon the adverse party an offer to allow judgment to be taken against the defending party for the money or property or to the effect specified in the offer, with costs then accrued. If within 10 days after the service of the offer the adverse party serves written notice that the offer is accepted, either party may then file the offer and notice of acceptance together with proof of service thereof and thereupon the clerk shall enter judgment. An offer not accepted shall be deemed withdrawn and evidence thereof is not admissible except in a proceeding to determine costs. If the judgment finally obtained by the offeree is not more favorable than the offer, the offeree must pay the costs incurred after the making of the offer. The fact that an offer is made but not accepted does not preclude a subsequent offer. When the liability of one party to another has been determined by verdict or order or judgment, but the amount or extent of the liability remains to be determined by further proceedings, the party adjudged liable may make an offer of judgment, which shall have the same effect as an offer made before trial if it is served within a reasonable time not less than 10 days prior to the commencement of hearings to determine the amount or extent of liability.

(As amended Dec. 27, 1946, eff. Mar. 19, 1948; Feb. 28, 1966, eff. July 1, 1966; Mar. 2, 1987, eff. Aug. 1, 1987.)

Proposed Amendment of Rule

Effective December 1, 2007, absent contrary Congressional action, this rule is amended to read as follows:

Rule 68. Offer of Judgment

(a) Making an Offer; Judgment on an Accepted Offer. *More than 10 days before the trial begins, a party defending against a claim may serve on an opposing party an offer to allow judgment on specified terms, with the costs then accrued. If, within 10*

Complete Annotation Materials, see Title 28 U.S.C.A.

320

days after being served, the opposing party serves written notice accepting the offer, either party may then file the offer and notice of acceptance, plus proof of service. The clerk must then enter judgment.

***(b) Unaccepted Offer.** An unaccepted offer is considered withdrawn, but it does not preclude a later offer. Evidence of an unaccepted offer is not admissible except in a proceeding to determine costs.*

***(c) Offer After Liability Is Determined.** When one party's liability to another has been determined but the extent of liability remains to be determined by further proceedings, the party held liable may make an offer of judgment. It must be served within a reasonable time—but at least 10 days—before a hearing to determine the extent of liability.*

***(d) Paying Costs After an Unaccepted Offer.** If the judgment that the offeree finally obtains is not more favorable than the unaccepted offer, the offeree must pay the costs incurred after the offer was made.*

ADVISORY COMMITTEE NOTES

1937 Adoption

See 2 Minn.Stat. (Mason, 1927) § 9323; 4 Mont.Rev.Codes Ann. (1935) § 9770; N.Y.C.P.A. (1937) § 177.

For the recovery of costs against the United States, see Rule 54(d).

1946 Amendment

Note. The third sentence of Rule 68 has been altered to make clear that evidence of an unaccepted offer is admissible in a proceeding to determine the costs of the action but is not otherwise admissible.

The two sentences substituted for the deleted last sentence of the rule assure a party the right to make a second offer where the situation permits—as, for example, where a prior offer was not accepted but the plaintiff's judgment is nullified and a new trial ordered, whereupon the defendant desires to make a second offer. It is implicit, however, that as long as the case continues—whether there be a first, second or third trial—and the defendant makes no further offer, his first and only offer will operate to save him the costs from the time of that offer if the plaintiff ultimately obtains a judgment less than the sum offered. In the case of successive offers not accepted, the offeror is saved the costs incurred after the making of the offer which was equal to or greater than the judgment ultimately obtained. These provisions should serve to encourage settlements and avoid protracted litigation.

The phrase "before the trial begins", in the first sentence of the rule, has been construed in *Cover v. Chicago Eye Shield Co.,* C.C.A.7th, 1943, 136 F.2d 374, certiorari denied 64 S.Ct. 53, 320 U.S. 749, 88 L.Ed. 445.

1966 Amendment

This logical extension of the concept of offer of judgment is suggested by the common admiralty practice of determining liability before the amount of liability is determined.

1987 Amendment

The amendments are technical. No substantive change is intended.

2007 Amendments

[Effective December 1, 2007, absent contrary Congressional action.]

The language of Rule 68 has been amended as part of the general restyling of the Civil Rules to make them more easily understood and to make style and terminology consistent throughout the rules. These changes are intended to be stylistic only.

Rule 69. Execution

(a) In General. Process to enforce a judgment for the payment of money shall be a writ of execution, unless the court directs otherwise. The procedure on execution, in proceedings supplementary to and in aid of a judgment, and in proceedings on and in aid of execution shall be in accordance with the practice and procedure of the state in which the district court is held, existing at the time the remedy is sought, except that any statute of the United States governs to the extent that it is applicable. In aid of the judgment or execution, the judgment creditor or a successor in interest when that interest appears of record, may obtain discovery from any person, including the judgment debtor, in the manner provided in these rules or in the manner provided by the practice of the state in which the district court is held.

(b) Against Certain Public Officers. When a judgment has been entered against a collector or other officer of revenue under the circumstances stated in Title 28, U.S.C., § 2006, or against an officer of Congress in an action mentioned in the Act of March 3, 1875, ch. 130, § 8 (18 Stat. 401), U.S.C., Title 2, § 118, and when the court has given the certificate of probable cause for the officer's act as provided in those statutes, execution shall not issue against the officer or the officer's property but the final judgment shall be satisfied as provided in such statutes.

(As amended Dec. 29, 1948, eff. Oct. 20, 1949; Mar. 30, 1970, eff. July 1, 1970; Mar. 2, 1987, eff. Aug. 1, 1987.)

Proposed Amendment of Rule

Effective December 1, 2007, absent contrary Congressional action, this rule is amended to read as follows:

Rule 69. Execution

(a) In General.

(1) Money Judgment; Applicable Procedure. A money judgment is enforced by a writ of execution, unless the court directs otherwise. The procedure on execution—and in proceedings supplementary to and in aid of judgment or execution—must accord with the procedure of the

state where the court is located, but a federal statute governs to the extent it applies.

(2) Obtaining Discovery. In aid of the judgment or execution, the judgment creditor or a successor in interest whose interest appears of record may obtain discovery from any person— including the judgment debtor—as provided in these rules or by the procedure of the state where the court is located.

(b) Against Certain Public Officers. *When a judgment has been entered against a revenue officer in the circumstances stated in 28 U.S.C. § 2006, or against an officer of Congress in the circumstances stated in 2 U.S.C. § 118, the judgment must be satisfied as those statutes provide.*

ADVISORY COMMITTEE NOTES

1937 Adoption

Note to Subdivision (a). This follows in substance U.S.C. Title 28, [former] §§ 727 (Executions as provided by State laws) and [former 729] [now Title 42, § 1988] (Proceedings in vindication of civil rights), except that, as in the similar case of attachments (see note to Rule 64), the rule specifies the applicable state law to be that of the time when the remedy is sought, and thus renders unnecessary, as well as supersedeas, local district court rules.

Statutes of the United States on execution, when applicable, govern under this rule. Among these are:

U.S.C., Title 12:

§ 91 (Transfers by bank and other acts in contemplation of insolvency)

§ 632 (Jurisdiction of United States district courts in cases arising out of foreign banking jurisdiction where Federal reserve bank a party)

U.S.C., Title 19:

§ 199 (Judgments for customs duties, how payable)

U.S.C., Title 26 [I.R.C.1939]:

§ 1610(a) [former] (Surrender of property subject to distraint)

U.S.C., Title 28 former:

§ 122 [now 1656] (Creation of new district or transfer of territory; lien)

§ 350 [now 2101] (Time for making application for appeal or certiorari; stay pending application for certiorari)

§ 489 [now 547] (District Attorneys; reports to Department of Justice)

§ 574 [now 1921] (Marshals, fees enumerated)

§ 786 [former] (Judgments for duties; collected in coin)

§ 811 [now 1961] (Interest on judgments)

§ 838 [former] (Executions; run in all districts of State)

§ 839 [now 2413] (Executions; run in every State and Territory)

§ 840 [former] (Executions; stay on conditions), as modified by Rule 62(b)

§ 841 [former] (Executions; stay of one term), as modified by Rule 62(f)

§ 842 [now 2006] (Executions; against officers of revenue in cases of probable cause), as incorporated in Subdivision (b) of this rule

§ 843 [now 2007] (Imprisonment for debt)

§ 844 [now 2007] (Imprisonment for debt; discharge according to State laws)

§ 845 [now 2007] (Imprisonment for debt; jail limits)

§ 846 [now 2005] (Fieri Facias; appraisal of goods; appraisers)

§ 847 [now 2001] (Sales; real property under order or decree)

§ 848 [now 2004] (Sales; personal property under order or decree)

§ 849 [now 2002] (Sales; necessity of notice)

§ 850 [now 2003] (Sales; death of marshall after levy or after sale)

§ 869 [former] (Bond in former error and on appeal), as incorporated in Rule 73(c)

§ 874 [former] (Supersedeas), as modified by Rules 62(d) and 73(d)

U.S.C., Title 31:

§ 195 [now 3715] (Purchase on execution)

U.S.C., Title 33:

§ 918 (Collection of defaulted payments)

U.S.C., Title 49:

§ 74(g) [former] (Causes of action arising out of Federal control of railroads; execution and other process)

Special statutes of the United States on exemption from execution are also continued. Among these are:

U.S.C., Title 2:

§ 118 (Actions against officers of Congress for official acts)

U.S.C., Title 5 former:

§ 729 [see 8346, 8470] (Federal employees retirement annuities not subject to assignment, execution, levy or other legal process)

U.S.C., Title 10 former:

§ 610 [now 3690, 8690] (Exemption of enlisted men from arrest on civil process)

U.S.C., Title 22 former:

§ 21(h) [see 4060] (Foreign service retirement and disability system; establishment; rules and regulations; annuities; nonassignable; exemption from legal process)

U.S.C., Title 33:

§ 916 (Assignment and exemption from claims of creditors) (Longshoremen's and Harborworkers' Compensation Act)

U.S.C., Title 38 former:

§ 54 [see 3101] (Attachment, levy or seizure of moneys due pensioners prohibited)

§ 393 [former] (Army and Navy Medal of Honor Roll; pensions additional to other pensions; liability to attachment, etc.) Compare [former] Title 34, § 365(c) (Medal of Honor Roll; special pension to persons enrolled)

§ 618 [see 3101] (Benefits exempt from seizure under process and taxation; no deductions for indebtedness to United States)

U.S.C., Title 43:

§ 175 (Exemption from execution of homestead land)

U.S.C., Title 48 former:

§ 1371*o* (Panama canal and railroad retirement annuities, exemption from execution and so forth.)

Supplementary Note

Note. With respect to the provisions of the Soldiers' and Sailors' Civil Relief Act of 1940, 50 U.S.C. Appendix, § 501 et seq., see notes to Rules 62 and 64 herein.

1948 Amendment

The amendment effective October 1949, substituted the citation of "Title 28, U.S.C., § 2006" in subdivision (b) in place of the citation to "Section 989, Revised Statutes, U.S.C., Title 28, § 842".

1970 Amendment

The amendment assures that, in aid of execution on a judgment, all discovery procedures provided in the rules are available and not just discovery via the taking of a deposition. Under the present language, one court had held that Rule 34 discovery is unavailable to the judgment creditor. *M. Lowenstein & Sons, Inc. v. American Underwear Mfg. Co.*, 11 F.R.D. 172 (E.D.Pa.1951). Notwithstanding the language, and relying heavily on legislative history referring to Rule 33, the Fifth Circuit has held that a judgment creditor may invoke Rule 33 interrogatories. *United States v. McWhirter*, 376 F.2d 102 (5th Cir. 1967). But the court's reasoning does not extend to discovery except as provided in Rules 26–33. One commentator suggests that the existing language might properly be stretched to all discovery, 7 *Moore's Federal Practice* ¶69.05[1] (2d ed. 1966), but another believes that a rules amendment is needed. 3 Barron & Holtzoff, *Federal Practice and Procedure* 1484 (Wright ed. 1958). Both commentators and the court in *McWhirter* are clear that, as a matter of policy, Rule 69 should authorize the use of all discovery devices provided in the rules.

1987 Amendment

The amendments are technical. No substantive change is intended.

2007 Amendments

[Effective December 1, 2007, absent contrary Congressional action.]

The language of Rule 69 has been amended as part of the general restyling of the Civil Rules to make them more easily understood and to make style and terminology consistent throughout the rules. These changes are intended to be stylistic only.

Amended Rule 69(b) incorporates directly the provisions of 2 U.S.C. § 118 and 28 U.S.C. § 2006, deleting the incomplete statement in former Rule 69(b) of the circumstances in which execution does not issue against an officer.

Rule 70. Judgment for Specific Acts; Vesting Title

If a judgment directs a party to execute a conveyance of land or to deliver deeds or other documents or to perform any other specific act and the party fails to comply within the time specified, the court may direct the act to be done at the cost of the disobedient party by some other person appointed by the court and the act when so done has like effect as if done by the party. On application of the party entitled to performance, the clerk shall issue a writ of attachment or sequestration against the property of the disobedient party to compel obedience to the judgment. The court may also in proper cases adjudge the party in contempt. If real or personal property is within the district, the court in lieu of directing a conveyance thereof may enter a judgment divesting the title of any party and vesting it in others and such judgment has the effect of a conveyance executed in due form of law. When any order or judgment is for the delivery of possession, the party in whose favor it is entered is entitled to a writ of execution or assistance upon application to the clerk.

Proposed Amendment of Rule

Effective December 1, 2007, absent contrary Congressional action, this rule is amended to read as follows:

Rule 70. Enforcing a Judgment for a Specific Act

(a) Party's Failure to Act; Ordering Another to Act. *If a judgment requires a party to convey land, to deliver a deed or other document, or to perform any other specific act and the party fails to comply within the time specified, the court may order the act to be done—at the disobedient party's expense—by another person appointed by the court. When done, the act has the same effect as if done by the party.*

(b) Vesting Title. *If the real or personal property is within the district, the court—instead of ordering a conveyance—may enter a judgment divesting any party's title and vesting it in others. That judgment has the effect of a legally executed conveyance.*

(c) Obtaining a Writ of Attachment or Sequestration. *On application by a party entitled to performance of an act, the clerk must issue a writ of attachment or sequestration against the disobedient party's property to compel obedience.*

(d) Obtaining a Writ of Execution or Assistance. *On application by a party who obtains a judgment or order for possession, the clerk must issue a writ of execution or assistance.*

(e) Holding in Contempt. *The court may also hold the disobedient party in contempt.*

ADVISORY COMMITTEE NOTES

1937 Adoption

Compare [former] Equity Rules 7 (Process, Mesne and Final), 8 (Enforcement of Final Decrees), and 9 (Writ of Assistance). To avoid possible confusion, both old and new denominations for attachment (sequestration) and execution (assistance) are used in this rule. Compare with the provi-

sion in this rule that the judgment may itself vest title, 6 Tenn.Ann.Code (Williams, 1934), § 10594; 2 Conn.Gen.Stat. (1930), § 5455; N.M.Stat.Ann. (Courtright, 1929), § 117–117; 2 Ohio Gen.Code Ann. (Page, 1926), § 11590; and England, Supreme Court of Judicature Act (1925), § 47.

2007 Amendments

*[Effective December 1, 2007,
absent contrary Congressional action.]*

The language of Rule 70 has been amended as part of the general restyling of the Civil Rules to make them more easily understood and to make style and terminology consistent throughout the rules. These changes are intended to be stylistic only.

Rule 71. Process in Behalf of and Against Persons not Parties

When an order is made in favor of a person who is not a party to the action, that person may enforce obedience to the order by the same process as if a party; and, when obedience to an order may be lawfully enforced against a person who is not a party, that person is liable to the same process for enforcing obedience to the order as if a party.
(As amended Mar. 2, 1987, eff. Aug. 1, 1987.)

Proposed Amendment of Rule

Effective December 1, 2007, absent contrary Congressional action, this rule is amended to read as follows:

Rule 71. Enforcing Relief for or Against a Nonparty

When an order grants relief for a nonparty or may be enforced against a nonparty, the procedure for enforcing the order is the same as for a party.

ADVISORY COMMITTEE NOTES

1937 Adoption

Compare [former] Equity Rule 11 (Process in Behalf of and Against Persons Not Parties). Compare also *Terrell v. Allison*, 1875, 21 Wall. 289, 22 L.Ed. 634; *Farmers' Loan and Trust Co. v. Chicago and A. Ry. Co.*, C.C.Ind.1890, 44 F. 653; *Robert Findlay Mfg. Co. v. Hygrade Lighting Fixture Corp.*, E.D.N.Y.1923, 288 F. 80; *Thompson v. Smith*, C.C.Minn.1870, Fed.Cas. No. 13,977.

1987 Amendment

The amendments are technical. No substantive change is intended.

2007 Amendments

*[Effective December 1, 2007,
absent contrary Congressional action.]*

The language of Rule 71 has been amended as part of the general restyling of the Civil Rules to make them more easily understood and to make style and terminology consistent throughout the rules. These changes are intended to be stylistic only.

IX. SPECIAL PROCEEDINGS [1]

[1] Another Title IX which was set out post has been abrogated.

Proposed Amendment of Heading

Effective December 1, 2007, absent contrary Congressional action, this heading is amended to read as follows:

TITLE IX. SPECIAL PROCEEDINGS

ADVISORY COMMITTEE NOTES

1991 Addition

This chapter heading is to be inserted between Rule 71 and Rule 71A.

Rule 71A. Condemnation of Property

(a) Applicability of Other Rules. The Rules of Civil Procedure for the United States District Courts govern the procedure for the condemnation of real and personal property under the power of eminent domain, except as otherwise provided in this rule.

(b) Joinder of Properties. The plaintiff may join in the same action one or more separate pieces of property, whether in the same or different ownership and whether or not sought for the same use.

(c) Complaint.

(1) Caption. The complaint shall contain a caption as provided in Rule 10(a), except that the plaintiff shall name as defendants the property, designated generally by kind, quantity, and location, and at least one of the owners of some part of or interest in the property.

(2) Contents. The complaint shall contain a short and plain statement of the authority for the taking, the use for which the property is to be taken, a description of the property sufficient for its identification, the interests to be acquired, and as to each separate piece of property a designation of the defendants who have been joined as owners thereof or of some interest therein. Upon the commencement of the action, the plaintiff need join as defendants only the persons having or claiming an interest in the property whose names are then known, but prior to any hearing involving the compensation to be paid for a piece of property, the plaintiff shall add as defendants all persons having or claiming an interest in that property whose names can be ascertained by a reasonably diligent search of the rec-

ords, considering the character and value of the property involved and the interests to be acquired, and also those whose names have otherwise been learned. All others may be made defendants under the designation "Unknown Owners." Process shall be served as provided in subdivision (d) of this rule upon all defendants, whether named as defendants at the time of the commencement of the action or subsequently added, and a defendant may answer as provided in subdivision (e) of this rule. The court meanwhile may order such distribution of a deposit as the facts warrant.

(3) Filing. In addition to filing the complaint with the court, the plaintiff shall furnish to the clerk at least one copy thereof for the use of the defendants and additional copies at the request of the clerk or of a defendant.

(d) Process.

(1) Notice; Delivery. Upon the filing of the complaint the plaintiff shall forthwith deliver to the clerk joint or several notices directed to the defendants named or designated in the complaint. Additional notices directed to defendants subsequently added shall be so delivered. The delivery of the notice and its service have the same effect as the delivery and service of the summons under Rule 4.

(2) Same; Form. Each notice shall state the court, the title of the action, the name of the defendant to whom it is directed, that the action is to condemn property, a description of the defendant's property sufficient for its identification, the interest to be taken, the authority for the taking, the uses for which the property is to be taken, that the defendant may serve upon the plaintiff's attorney an answer within 20 days after service of the notice, and that the failure so to serve an answer constitutes a consent to the taking and to the authority of the court to proceed to hear the action and to fix the compensation. The notice shall conclude with the name of the plaintiff's attorney and an address within the district in which action is brought where the attorney may be served. The notice need contain a description of no other property than that to be taken from the defendants to whom it is directed.

(3) Service of Notice.

(A) Personal Service. Personal service of the notice (but without copies of the complaint) shall be made in accordance with Rule 4 upon a defendant whose residence is known and who resides within the United States or a territory subject to the administrative or judicial jurisdiction of the United States.

(B) Service by Publication. Upon the filing of a certificate of the plaintiff's attorney stating that the attorney believes a defendant cannot be personally served, because after diligent inquiry within the state in which the complaint is filed the defendant's place of residence cannot be ascertained by the plaintiff or, if ascertained, that it is beyond the territorial limits of personal service as provided in this rule, service of the notice shall be made on this defendant by publication in a newspaper published in the county where the property is located, or if there is no such newspaper, then in a newspaper having a general circulation where the property is located, once a week for not less than three successive weeks. Prior to the last publication, a copy of the notice shall also be mailed to a defendant who cannot be personally served as provided in this rule but whose place of residence is then known. Unknown owners may be served by publication in like manner by a notice addressed to "Unknown Owners."

Service by publication is complete upon the date of the last publication. Proof of publication and mailing shall be made by certificate of the plaintiff's attorney, to which shall be attached a printed copy of the published notice with the name and dates of the newspaper marked thereon.

(4) Return; Amendment. Proof of service of the notice shall be made and amendment of the notice or proof of its service allowed in the manner provided for the return and amendment of the summons under Rule 4.

(e) Appearance or Answer. If a defendant has no objection or defense to the taking of the defendant's property, the defendant may serve a notice of appearance designating the property in which the defendant claims to be interested. Thereafter, the defendant shall receive notice of all proceedings affecting it. If a defendant has any objection or defense to the taking of the property, the defendant shall serve an answer within 20 days after the service of notice upon the defendant. The answer shall identify the property in which the defendant claims to have an interest, state the nature and extent of the interest claimed, and state all the defendant's objections and defenses to the taking of the property. A defendant waives all defenses and objections not so presented, but at the trial of the issue of just compensation, whether or not the defendant has previously appeared or answered, the defendant may present evidence as to the amount of the compensation to be paid for the property, and the defendant may share in the distribution of the award. No other pleading or motion asserting any additional defense or objection shall be allowed.

(f) Amendment of Pleadings. Without leave of court, the plaintiff may amend the complaint at any time before the trial of the issue of compensation and as many times as desired, but no amendment shall be made which will result in a dismissal forbidden by

subdivision (i) of this rule. The plaintiff need not serve a copy of an amendment, but shall serve notice of the filing, as provided in Rule 5(b), upon any party affected thereby who has appeared and, in the manner provided in subdivision (d) of this rule, upon any party affected thereby who has not appeared. The plaintiff shall furnish to the clerk of the court for the use of the defendants at least one copy of each amendment and shall furnish additional copies on the request of the clerk or of a defendant. Within the time allowed by subdivision (e) of this rule a defendant may serve an answer to the amended pleading, in the form and manner and with the same effect as there provided.

(g) Substitution of Parties. If a defendant dies or becomes incompetent or transfers an interest after the defendant's joinder, the court may order substitution of the proper party upon motion and notice of hearing. If the motion and notice of hearing are to be served upon a person not already a party, service shall be made as provided in subdivision (d)(3) of this rule.

(h) Trial. If the action involves the exercise of the power of eminent domain under the law of the United States, any tribunal specially constituted by an Act of Congress governing the case for the trial of the issue of just compensation shall be the tribunal for the determination of that issue; but if there is no such specially constituted tribunal any party may have a trial by jury of the issue of just compensation by filing a demand therefor within the time allowed for answer or within such further time as the court may fix, unless the court in its discretion orders that, because of the character, location, or quantity of the property to be condemned, or for other reasons in the interest of justice, the issue of compensation shall be determined by a commission of three persons appointed by it.

In the event that a commission is appointed the court may direct that not more than two additional persons serve as alternate commissioners to hear the case and replace commissioners who, prior to the time when a decision is filed, are found by the court to be unable or disqualified to perform their duties. An alternate who does not replace a regular commissioner shall be discharged after the commission renders its final decision. Before appointing the members of the commission and alternates the court shall advise the parties of the identity and qualifications of each prospective commissioner and alternate and may permit the parties to examine each such designee. The parties shall not be permitted or required by the court to suggest nominees. Each party shall have the right to object for valid cause to the appointment of any person as a commissioner or alternate. If a commission is appointed it shall have the authority of a master provided in Rule 53(c) and proceedings before it shall be governed by the provisions of Rule 53(d). Its action and report shall be determined by a majori-

ty and its findings and report shall have the effect, and be dealt with by the court in accordance with the practice, prescribed in Rule 53(e), (f), and (g). Trial of all issues shall otherwise be by the court.

(i) Dismissal of Action.

(1) As of Right. If no hearing has begun to determine the compensation to be paid for a piece of property and the plaintiff has not acquired the title or a lesser interest in or taken possession, the plaintiff may dismiss the action as to that property, without an order of the court, by filing a notice of dismissal setting forth a brief description of the property as to which the action is dismissed.

(2) By Stipulation. Before the entry of any judgment vesting the plaintiff with title or a lesser interest in or possession of property, the action may be dismissed in whole or in part, without an order of the court, as to any property by filing a stipulation of dismissal by the plaintiff and the defendant affected thereby; and, if the parties so stipulate, the court may vacate any judgment that has been entered.

(3) By Order of the Court. At any time before compensation for a piece of property has been determined and paid and after motion and hearing, the court may dismiss the action as to that property, except that it shall not dismiss the action as to any part of the property of which the plaintiff has taken possession or in which the plaintiff has taken title or a lesser interest, but shall award just compensation for the possession, title or lesser interest so taken. The court at any time may drop a defendant unnecessarily or improperly joined.

(4) Effect. Except as otherwise provided in the notice, or stipulation of dismissal, or order of the court, any dismissal is without prejudice.

(j) Deposit and its Distribution. The plaintiff shall deposit with the court any money required by law as a condition to the exercise of the power of eminent domain; and, although not so required, may make a deposit when permitted by statute. In such cases the court and attorneys shall expedite the proceedings for the distribution of the money so deposited and for the ascertainment and payment of just compensation. If the compensation finally awarded to any defendant exceeds the amount which has been paid to that defendant on distribution of the deposit, the court shall enter judgment against the plaintiff and in favor of that defendant for the deficiency. If the compensation finally awarded to any defendant is less than the amount which has been paid to that defendant, the court shall enter judgment against that defendant and in favor of the plaintiff for the overpayment.

(k) Condemnation Under a State's Power of Eminent Domain. The practice as herein prescribed governs in actions involving the exercise of the power of eminent domain under the law of a state, provided that if the state law makes provision for trial of any issue by jury, or for trial of the issue of compensation by jury or commission or both, that provision shall be followed.

(*l*) Costs. Costs are not subject to Rule 54(d).

(Added Apr. 30, 1951, eff. Aug. 1, 1951, and amended Jan. 21, 1963, eff. July 1, 1963; Apr. 29, 1985, eff. Aug. 1, 1985; Mar. 2, 1987, eff. Aug. 1, 1987; Apr. 25, 1988, eff. Aug. 1, 1988; Nov. 18, 1988, Pub.L. 100–690, Title VII, § 7050, 102 Stat. 4401; Apr. 22, 1993, eff. Dec. 1, 1993; Mar. 27, 2003, eff. Dec. 1, 2003.)

Proposed Redesignation and Amendment of Rule

Effective December 1, 2007, absent contrary Congressional action, this Rule 71A is redesignated Rule 71.1 and is amended to read as follows:

Rule 71.1. Condemning Real or Personal Property

(a) Applicability of Other Rules. *These rules govern proceedings to condemn real and personal property by eminent domain, except as this rule provides otherwise.*

(b) Joinder of Properties. *The plaintiff may join separate pieces of property in a single action, no matter whether they are owned by the same persons or sought for the same use.*

(c) Complaint.

(1) Caption. The complaint must contain a caption as provided in Rule 10(a). The plaintiff must, however, name as defendants both the property—designated generally by kind, quantity, and location—and at least one owner of some part of or interest in the property.

(2) Contents. The complaint must contain a short and plain statement of the following:

(A) the authority for the taking;

(B) the uses for which the property is to be taken;

(C) a description sufficient to identify the property;

(D) the interests to be acquired; and

(E) for each piece of property, a designation of each defendant who has been joined as an owner or owner of an interest in it.

(3) Parties. When the action commences, the plaintiff need join as defendants only those persons who have or claim an interest in the property and whose names are then known. But before any hearing on compensation, the plaintiff must add as defendants all those persons who have or claim an interest and whose names have become known or can be found by a reasonably diligent search of the records, considering both the property's character and value and the interests to be acquired. All others may be made defendants under the designation "Unknown Owners."

(4) Procedure. Notice must be served on all defendants as provided in Rule 71.1(d), whether they were named as defendants when the action commenced or were added later. A defendant may answer as provided in Rule 71.1(e). The court, meanwhile, may order any distribution of a deposit that the facts warrant.

(5) Filing; Additional Copies. In addition to filing the complaint, the plaintiff must give the clerk at least one copy for the defendants' use and additional copies at the request of the clerk or a defendant.

(d) Process.

(1) Delivering Notice to the Clerk. On filing a complaint, the plaintiff must promptly deliver to the clerk joint or several notices directed to the named defendants. When adding defendants, the plaintiff must deliver to the clerk additional notices directed to the new defendants.

(2) Contents of the Notice.

(A) Main Contents. Each notice must name the court, the title of the action, and the defendant to whom it is directed. It must describe the property sufficiently to identify it, but need not describe any property other than that to be taken from the named defendant. The notice must also state:

(i) that the action is to condemn property;

(ii) the interest to be taken;

(iii) the authority for the taking;

(iv) the uses for which the property is to be taken;

(v) that the defendant may serve an answer on the plaintiff's attorney within 20 days after being served with the notice;

(vi) that the failure to so serve an answer constitutes consent to the taking and to the court's authority to proceed with the action and fix the compensation; and

(vii) that a defendant who does not serve an answer may file a notice of appearance.

(B) Conclusion. The notice must conclude with the name, telephone number, and e-mail address of the plaintiff's attorney and an address within the district in which the action is brought where the attorney may be served.

Complete Annotation Materials, see Title 28 U.S.C.A.

(3) Serving the Notice.

(A) Personal Service. When a defendant whose address is known resides within the United States or a territory subject to the administrative or judicial jurisdiction of the United States, personal service of the notice (without a copy of the complaint) must be made in accordance with Rule 4.

(B) Service by Publication.

(i) A defendant may be served by publication only when the plaintiff's attorney files a certificate stating that the attorney believes the defendant cannot be personally served, because after diligent inquiry within the state where the complaint is filed, the defendant's place of residence is still unknown or, if known, that it is beyond the territorial limits of personal service. Service is then made by publishing the notice—once a week for at least three successive weeks—in a newspaper published in the county where the property is located or, if there is no such newspaper, in a newspaper with general circulation where the property is located. Before the last publication, a copy of the notice must also be mailed to every defendant who cannot be personally served but whose place of residence is then known. Unknown owners may be served by publication in the same manner by a notice addressed to "Unknown Owners."

(ii) Service by publication is complete on the date of the last publication. The plaintiff's attorney must prove publication and mailing by a certificate, attach a printed copy of the published notice, and mark on the copy the newspaper's name and the dates of publication.

(4) Effect of Delivery and Service. Delivering the notice to the clerk and serving it have the same effect as serving a summons under Rule 4.

(5) Proof of Service; Amending the Proof or Notice. Rule 4(l) governs proof of service. The court may permit the proof or the notice to be amended.

(e) Appearance or Answer.

(1) Notice of Appearance. A defendant that has no objection or defense to the taking of its property may serve a notice of appearance designating the property in which it claims an interest. The defendant must then be given notice of all later proceedings affecting the defendant.

(2) Answer. A defendant that has an objection or defense to the taking must serve an answer

within 20 days after being served with the notice. The answer must:

(A) identify the property in which the defendant claims an interest;

(B) state the nature and extent of the interest; and

(C) state all the defendant's objections and defenses to the taking.

(3) Waiver of Other Objections and Defenses; Evidence on Compensation. A defendant waives all objections and defenses not stated in its answer. No other pleading or motion asserting an additional objection or defense is allowed. But at the trial on compensation, a defendant—whether or not it has previously appeared or answered— may present evidence on the amount of compensation to be paid and may share in the award.

(f) Amending Pleadings. *Without leave of court, the plaintiff may—as often as it wants—amend the complaint at any time before the trial on compensation. But no amendment may be made if it would result in a dismissal inconsistent with Rule 71.1(i)(1) or (2). The plaintiff need not serve a copy of an amendment, but must serve notice of the filing, as provided in Rule 5(b), on every affected party who has appeared and, as provided in Rule 71.1(d), on every affected party who has not appeared. In addition, the plaintiff must give the clerk at least one copy of each amendment for the defendants' use, and additional copies at the request of the clerk or a defendant. A defendant may appear or answer in the time and manner and with the same effect as provided in Rule 71.1(e).*

(g) Substituting Parties. *If a defendant dies, becomes incompetent, or transfers an interest after being joined, the court may, on motion and notice of hearing, order that the proper party be substituted. Service of the motion and notice on a nonparty must be made as provided in Rule 71.1(d)(3).*

(h) Trial of the Issues.

(1) Issues Other Than Compensation; Compensation. In an action involving eminent domain under federal law, the court tries all issues, including compensation, except when compensation must be determined:

(A) by any tribunal specially constituted by a federal statute to determine compensation; or

(B) if there is no such tribunal, by a jury when a party demands one within the time to answer or within any additional time the court sets, unless the court appoints a commission.

(2) Appointing a Commission; Commission's Powers and Report.

(A) Reasons for Appointing. If a party has demanded a jury, the court may instead appoint a three-person commission to determine compensation because of the character, location, or quantity of the property to be condemned or for other just reasons.

(B) Alternate Commissioners. The court may appoint up to two additional persons to serve as alternate commissioners to hear the case and replace commissioners who, before a decision is filed, the court finds unable or disqualified to perform their duties. Once the commission renders its final decision, the court must discharge any alternate who has not replaced a commissioner.

(C) Examining the Prospective Commissioners. Before making its appointments, the court must advise the parties of the identity and qualifications of each prospective commissioner and alternate, and may permit the parties to examine them. The parties may not suggest appointees, but for good cause may object to a prospective commissioner or alternate.

(D) Commission's Powers and Report. A commission has the powers of a master under Rule 53(c). Its action and report are determined by a majority. Rule 53(d), (e), and (f) apply to its action and report.

(i) Dismissal of the Action or a Defendant.

(1) Dismissing the Action.

(A) By the Plaintiff. If no compensation hearing on a piece of property has begun, and if the plaintiff has not acquired title or a lesser interest or taken possession, the plaintiff may, without a court order, dismiss the action as to that property by filing a notice of dismissal briefly describing the property.

(B) By Stipulation. Before a judgment is entered vesting the plaintiff with title or a lesser interest in or possession of property, the plaintiff and affected defendants may, without a court order, dismiss the action in whole or in part by filing a stipulation of dismissal. And if the parties so stipulate, the court may vacate a judgment already entered.

(C) By Court Order. At any time before compensation has been determined and paid, the court may, after a motion and hearing, dismiss the action as to a piece of property. But if the plaintiff has already taken title, a lesser interest, or possession as to any part of it, the court must award compensation for the title, lesser interest, or possession taken.

(2) Dismissing a Defendant. The court may at any time dismiss a defendant who was unnecessarily or improperly joined.

(3) Effect. A dismissal is without prejudice unless otherwise stated in the notice, stipulation, or court order.

(j) Deposit and Its Distribution.

(1) Deposit. The plaintiff must deposit with the court any money required by law as a condition to the exercise of eminent domain and may make a deposit when allowed by statute.

(2) Distribution; Adjusting Distribution. After a deposit, the court and attorneys must expedite the proceedings so as to distribute the deposit and to determine and pay compensation. If the compensation finally awarded to a defendant exceeds the amount distributed to that defendant, the court must enter judgment against the plaintiff for the deficiency. If the compensation awarded to a defendant is less than the amount distributed to that defendant, the court must enter judgment against that defendant for the overpayment.

(k) Condemnation Under a State's Power of Eminent Domain. This rule governs an action involving eminent domain under state law. But if state law provides for trying an issue by jury—or for trying the issue of compensation by jury or commission or both—that law governs.

(l) Costs. Costs are not subject to Rule 54(d).

ADVISORY COMMITTEE NOTES

1951 Addition

Supplementary Report

The Court will remember that at its conference on December 2, 1948, the discussion was confined to subdivision (h) of the rule (* * *), the particular question being whether the tribunal to award compensation should be a commission or a jury in cases where the Congress has not made specific provision on the subject. The Advisory Committee was agreed from the outset that a rule should not be promulgated which would overturn the decision of the Congress as to the kind of tribunal to fix compensation, provided that the system established by Congress was found to be working well. We found two instances where the Congress had specified the kind of tribunal to fix compensation. One case was the District of Columbia ([former] §§ 361 to 386 of Title 40 [now D.C. Code, Title 16, § 1301 et seq.]) where a rather unique system exists under which the court is required in all cases to order the selection of a "jury" of five from among not less than twenty names drawn from "the special box provided by law." They must have the usual qualifications of jurors and in addition must be freeholders of the District and not in the service of the United States or the District. That system has been in effect for many years, and our inquiry revealed that it works well under the conditions prevailing in the

District, and is satisfactory to the courts of the District, the legal profession and to property owners.

The other instance is that of the Tennessee Valley Authority, where the act of Congress (section 831x of Title 16) provides that compensation is fixed by three disinterested commissioners appointed by the court, whose award goes before the District Court for confirmation or modification. The Advisory Committee made a thorough inquiry into the practical operation of the TVA commission system. We obtained from counsel for the TVA the results of their experience, which afforded convincing proof that the commission system is preferable under the conditions affecting TVA and that the jury system would not work satisfactorily. We then, under date of February 6, 1947, wrote every Federal judge who had ever sat in a TVA condemnation case, asking his views as to whether the commission system is satisfactory and whether a jury system should be preferred. Of 21 responses from the judges 17 approved the commission system and opposed the substitution of a jury system for the TVA. Many of the judges went further and opposed the use of juries in any condemnation cases. Three of the judges preferred the jury system, and one dealt only with the TVA provision for a three judge district court. The Advisory Committee has not considered abolition of the three judge requirement of the TVA Act, because it seemed to raise a question of jurisdiction, which cannot be altered by rule. Nevertheless the Department of Justice continued its advocacy of the jury system for its asserted expedition and economy; and others favored a uniform procedure. In consequence of these divided counsels the Advisory Committee was itself divided, but in its May 1948 Report to the Court recommended the following rule as approved by a majority (* * *):

(h) Trial. If the action involves the exercise of the power of eminent domain under the law of the United States, any tribunal especially constituted by an Act of Congress governing the case for the trial of the issue of just compensation shall be the tribunal for the determination of that issue; but if there is no such specially constituted tribunal any party may have a trial by jury of the issue of just compensation by filing a demand therefor within the time allowed for answer or within such further time as the court may fix. Trial of all issues shall otherwise be by the court.

The effect of this was to preserve the existing systems in the District of Columbia and in TVA cases, but to provide for a jury to fix compensation in all other cases.

Before the Court's conference of December 2, 1948, the Chief Justice informed the Committee that the Court was particularly interested in the views expressed by Judge John Paul, Judge of the United States District Court for the Western District of Virginia, in a letter from him to the chairman of the Advisory Committee, dated February 13, 1947. Copies of all the letters from judges who had sat in TVA cases had been made available to the Court, and this letter from Judge Paul is one of them. Judge Paul strongly opposed jury trials and recommended the commission system in large projects like the TVA, and his views seemed to have impressed the Court and to have been the occasion for the conference.

The reasons which convinced the Advisory Committee that the use of commissioners instead of juries is desirable in TVA cases were these:

1. The TVA condemns large areas of land of similar kind, involving many owners. Uniformity in awards is essential. The commission system tends to prevent discrimination and provide for uniformity in compensation. The jury system tends to lack of uniformity. Once a reasonable and uniform standard of values for the area has been settled by a commission, litigation ends and settlements result.

2. Where large areas are involved many small landowners reside at great distances from the place where a court sits. It is a great hardship on humble people to have to travel long distances to attend a jury trial. A commission may travel around and receive the evidence of the owner near his home.

3. It is impracticable to take juries long distances to view the premises.

4. If the cases are tried by juries the burden on the time of the courts is excessive.

These considerations are the very ones Judge Paul stressed in his letter. He pointed out that they applied not only to the TVA but to other large governmental projects, such as flood control, hydroelectric power, reclamation, national forests, and others. So when the representatives of the Advisory Committee appeared at the Court's conference December 2, 1948, they found it difficult to justify the proposed provision in subdivision (h) of the rule that a jury should be used to fix compensation in all cases where Congress had not specified the tribunal. If our reasons for preserving the TVA system were sound, provision for a jury in similar projects of like magnitude seemed unsound.

Aware of the apparent inconsistency between the acceptance of the TVA system and the provision for a jury in all other cases, the members of the Committee attending the conference of December 2, 1948, then suggested that in the other cases the choice of jury or commission be left to the discretion of the District Court, going back to a suggestion previously made by Committee members and reported at page 15 of the Preliminary Draft of June 1947. They called the attention of the Court to the fact that the entire Advisory Committee had not been consulted about this suggestion and proposed that the draft be returned to the Committee for further consideration, and that was done.

The proposal we now make for subdivision (h) is as follows:

(h) Trial. If the action involves the exercise of the power of eminent domain under the law of the United States, any tribunal specially constituted by an Act of Congress governing the case for the trial of the issue of just compensation shall be the tribunal for the determination of that issue; but if there is no such specially constituted tribunal any party may have a trial by jury of the issue of just compensation by filing a demand therefor within the time allowed for answer or within such further time as the court may fix, unless the court in its discretion orders that, because of the character, location, or quantity of the property to be condemned, or for other reasons in the interest of justice, the issue of compensation shall be determined by a commission of three persons appointed by it. If a commission is appointed it shall have the powers of a master provided in subdivision (c) of Rule 53 and proceedings before it shall be governed by the provisions of paragraphs (1) and (2) of subdivision (d) of Rule 53. Its action and report shall be determined by a majority and its findings and report shall have the effect, and be dealt with

by the court in accordance with the practice, prescribed in paragraph (2) of subdivision (e) of Rule 53. Trial of all issues shall otherwise be by the court.

In the 1948 draft the Committee had been almost evenly divided as between jury or commission and that made it easy for us to agree on the present draft. It would be difficult to state in a rule the various conditions to control the District Court in its choice and we have merely stated generally the matters which should be considered by the District Court.

The rule as now drafted seems to meet Judge Paul's objection. In large projects like the TVA the court may decide to use a commission. In a great number of cases involving only sites for buildings or other small areas, where use of a jury is appropriate, a jury may be chosen. The District Court's discretion may also be influenced by local preference or habit, and the preference of the Department of Justice and the reasons for its preference will doubtless be given weight. The Committee is convinced that there are some types of cases in which use of a commission is preferable and others in which a jury may be appropriately used, and that it would be a mistake to provide that the same kind of tribunal should be used in all cases. We think the available evidence clearly leads to that conclusion.

When this suggestion was made at the conference of December 2, 1948, representatives of the Department of Justice opposed it, expressing opposition to the use of a commission in any case. Their principal ground for opposition to commissions was then based on the assertion that the commission system is too expensive because courts allow commissioners too large compensation. The obvious answer to that is that the compensation of commissioners ought to be fixed or limited by law, as was done in the TVA Act, and the agency dealing with appropriations—either the Administrative Office or some other interested department of the government—should correct that evil, if evil there be, by obtaining such legislation. Authority to promulgate rules of procedure does not include power to fix compensation of government employees. The Advisory Committee is not convinced that even without such legislation the commission system is more expensive than the jury system. The expense of jury trials includes not only the per diem and mileage of the jurors impaneled for a case but like items for the entire venire. In computing cost of jury trials, the salaries of court officials, judges, clerks, marshals and deputies must be considered. No figures have been given to the Committee to establish that the cost of the commission system is the greater.

We earnestly recommend the rule as now drafted for promulgation by the Court, in the public interest.

The Advisory Committee have given more time to this rule, including time required for conferences with the Department of Justice to hear statements of its representatives, than has been required by any other rule. The rule may not be perfect but if faults develop in practice they may be promptly cured. Certainly the present conformity system is atrocious.

Under state practices, just compensation is normally determined by one of three methods: by commissioners; by commissioners with a right of appeal to and trial de novo before a jury; and by a jury, without a commission. A trial to the court or to the court including a master are, however, other methods that are occasionally used. Approximately 5 states use only commissioners; 23 states use commissioners with a trial de novo before a jury; and 18 states use only the jury. This classification is advisedly stated in approximate terms, since the same state may utilize diverse methods, depending upon different types of condemnations or upon the locality of the property, and since the methods used in a few states do not permit of a categorical classification. To reject the proposed rule and leave the situation as it is would not satisfy the views of the Department of Justice. The Department and the Advisory Committee agree that the use of a commission, with appeal to a jury, is a wasteful system.

The Department of Justice has a voluminous "Manual on Federal Eminent Domain," the 1940 edition of which has 948 pages with an appendix of 73 more pages. The title page informs us the preparation of the manual was begun during the incumbency of Attorney General Cummings, was continued under Attorney General Murphy, and completed during the incumbency of Attorney General Jackson. The preface contains the following statement:

It should also be mentioned that the research incorporated in the manual would be of invaluable assistance in the drafting of a new uniform code, or rules of court, for federal condemnation proceedings, which are now greatly confused, not only by the existence of over seventy federal statutes governing condemnations for different purposes—statutes which sometimes conflict with one another—but also by the countless problems occasioned by the requirements of conformity to state law. Progress of the work has already demonstrated that the need for such reform exists.

It is not surprising that more than once Attorneys General have asked the Advisory Committee to prepare a federal rule and rescue the government from this morass.

The Department of Justice has twice tried and failed to persuade the Congress to provide that juries shall be used in all condemnation cases. The debates in Congress show that part of the opposition to the Department of Justice's bills came from representatives opposed to jury trials in all cases, and in part from a preference for the conformity system. Our present proposal opens the door for district judges to yield to local preferences on the subject. It does much for the Department's points of view. It is a great improvement over the present so-called conformity system. It does away with the wasteful "double" system prevailing in 23 states where awards by commissions are followed by jury trials.

Aside from the question as to the choice of a tribunal to award compensation, the proposed rule would afford a simple and improved procedure.

We turn now to an itemized explanation of the other changes we have made in the 1948 draft. Some of these result from recent amendments to the Judicial Code. Others result from a reconsideration by the Advisory Committee of provisions which we thought could be improved.

1. In the amended Judicial Code, the district courts are designated as "United States District Courts" instead of "District Courts of the United States," and a corresponding change has been made in the rule.

2. After the 1948 draft was referred back to the committee, the provision in subdivision (c)(2), relating to naming defendants, * * * which provided that the plaintiff shall add as defendants all persons having or claiming an interest in that property whose names can be ascertained by a search of the records to the extent commonly made by competent searchers of title in the vicinity "in light of

the type and value of the property involved," the phrase in quotation marks was changed to read "in the light of the character and value of the property involved and the interests to be acquired."

The Department of Justice made a counter proposal * * * that there be substituted the words "reasonably diligent search of the records, considering the type." When the American Bar Association thereafter considered the draft, it approved the Advisory Committee's draft of this subdivision, but said that it had no objection to the Department's suggestion. Thereafter, in an effort to eliminate controversy, the Advisory Committee accepted the Department's suggestion as to (c)(2), using the word "character" instead of the word "type."

The Department of Justice also suggested that in subdivision (d)(3)(ii) relating to service by publication, the search for a defendant's residence as a preliminary to publication be limited to the state in which the complaint is filed. Here again the American Bar Association's report expressed the view that the Department's suggestion was unobjectionable and the Advisory Committee thereupon adopted it.

3. Subdivision (k) of the 1948 draft is as follows:

(k) Condemnation Under a State's Power of Eminent Domain. If the action involves the exercise of the power of eminent domain under the law of a state, the practice herein prescribed may be altered to the extent necessary to observe and enforce any condition affecting the substantial rights of a litigant attached by the state law to the exercise of the state's power of eminent domain.

Occasionally condemnation cases under a state's power of eminent domain reach a United States District Court because of diversity of citizenship. Such cases are rare, but provision should be made for them.

The 1948 draft of (k) required a district court to decide whether a provision of state law specifying the tribunal to award compensation is or is not a "condition" attached to the exercise of the state's power. On reconsideration we concluded that it would be wise to redraft (k) so as to avoid that troublesome question. As to conditions in state laws which affect the substantial rights of a litigant, the district courts would be bound to give them effect without any rule on the subject. Accordingly we present two alternative revisions. One suggestion supported by a majority of the Advisory Committee is as follows:

(k) Condemnation Under a State's Power of Eminent Domain. The practice herein prescribed governs in actions involving the exercise of the power of eminent domain under the law of a state, provided that if the state law makes provision for trial of any issue by jury, or for trial of the issue of compensation by jury or commission or both, that provision shall be followed.

The other is as follows:

(k) Condemnation Under a State's Power of Eminent Domain. The practice herein prescribed governs in actions involving the exercise of the power of eminent domain under the law of a state, provided that if the state law gives a right to a trial by jury such a trial shall in any case be allowed to the party demanding it within the time permitted by these rules, and in that event no hearing before a commission shall be had.

The first proposal accepts the state law as to the tribunals to fix compensation, and in that respect leaves the parties in precisely the same situation as if the case were pending in a state court, including the use of a commission with appeal to a jury, if the state law so provides. It has the effect of avoiding any question as to whether the decisions in *Erie R. Co. v. Tompkins* and later cases have application to a situation of this kind.

The second proposal gives the parties a right to a jury trial if that is provided for by state law, but prevents the use of both commission and jury. Those members of the Committee who favor the second proposal do so because of the obvious objections to the double trial, with a commission and appeal to a jury. As the decisions in *Erie R. Co. v. Tompkins* and later cases may have a bearing on this point, and the Committee is divided, we think both proposals should be placed before the Court.

4. The provision * * * of the 1948 draft * * * prescribing the effective date of the rule was drafted before the recent amendment of the Judicial Code on that subject. On May 10, 1950, the President approved an act which amended section 2072 of Title 28, United States Code, to read as follows:

Such rules shall not take effect until they have been reported to Congress by the Chief Justice at or after the beginning of a regular session thereof but not later than the first day of May, and until the expiration of ninety days after they have been thus reported.

To conform to the statute now in force, we suggest a provision as follows:

Effective Date. This Rule 71A and the amendment to Rule 81(a) will take effect on August 1, 1951. Rule 71A governs all proceedings in actions brought after it takes effect and also all further proceedings in actions then pending, except to the extent that in the opinion of the court its application in a particular action pending when the rule takes effect would not be feasible or would work injustice, in which event the former procedure applies.

If the rule is not reported to Congress by May 1, 1951, this provision must be altered.

[Par. 3 of Supreme Court Order adopted Apr. 30, 1951, setting out this rule and providing for the abrogation of par. (7) of Rule 81(a), and providing for the Effective Date, as stated herein, was transmitted to Congress on May 1, 1951 by the Chief Justice of the United States (House Document No. 121, May 1, 1951, 82nd Cong., 1st Sess.), in conformity with § 2072 of this title. As no action was taken by Congress within the 90-day period required by that section, this rule and the abrogation of par. (7) of Rule 81(a) took effect on Aug. 1, 1951, as provided in said order.]

5. We call attention to the fact that the proposed rule does not contain a provision for the procedure to be followed in order to exercise the right of the United States to take immediate possession or title, when the condemnation proceeding is begun. There are several statutes conferring such a right which are cited in the original notes to the May 1948 draft * * *. The existence of this right is taken into account in the rule. In subdivision (c)(2), * * * it is stated: "Upon the commencement of the action, the plaintiff need join as defendants only the persons having or claiming an interest in the property whose names are then known." That is to enable the United States to exercise the right to immediate title or possession without the delay involved in ascertaining the names

of all interested parties. The right is also taken into account in the provision relating to dismissal (paragraph (i), subdivisions (1), (2), and (3), * * *); also in paragraph (j) relating to deposits and their distribution.

The Advisory Committee considered whether the procedure for exercising the right should be specified in the rule and decided against it, as the procedure now being followed seems to be giving no trouble, and to draft a rule to fit all the statutes on the subject might create confusion.

The American Bar Association has taken an active interest in a rule for condemnation cases. In 1944 its House of Delegates adopted a resolution which among other things resolved:

That before adoption by the Supreme Court of the United States of any redraft of the proposed rule, time and opportunity should be afforded to the bar to consider and make recommendations concerning any such redraft.

Accordingly, in 1950 the revised draft was submitted to the American Bar Association and its section of real property, probate and trust law appointed a committee to consider it. That committee was supplied with copies of the written statement from the Department of Justice giving the reasons relied on by the Department for preferring a rule to use juries in all cases. The Advisory Committee's report was approved at a meeting of the section of real property law, and by the House of Delegates at the annual meeting of September 1950. The American Bar Association report gave particular attention to the question whether juries or commissions should be used to fix compensation, approved the Advisory Committee's solution appearing in their latest draft designed to allow use of commissions in projects comparable to the TVA, and rejected the proposal for use of juries in all cases.

In November 1950 a committee of the Federal Bar Association, the chairman of which was a Special Assistant to the Attorney General, made a report which reflected the attitude of the Department of Justice on the condemnation rule.

Aside from subdivision (h) about the tribunal to award compensation the final draft of the condemnation rule here presented has the approval of the American Bar Association and, we understand, the Department of Justice, and we do not know of any opposition to it. Subdivision (h) has the unanimous approval of the Advisory Committee and has been approved by the American Bar Association. The use of commissions in TVA cases, and, by fair inference, in cases comparable to the TVA, is supported by 17 out of 20 judges who up to 1947 had sat in TVA cases. The legal staff of the TVA has vigorously objected to the substitution of juries for commissions in TVA cases. We regret to report that the Department of Justice still asks that subdivision (h) be altered to provide for jury trials in an cases where Congress has not specified the tribunal. We understand that the Department approves the proposal that the system prevailing in 23 states for the "double" trial, by commission with appeal to and trial de novo before a jury, should be abolished, and also asks that on demand a jury should be substituted for a commission, in those states where use of a commission alone is now required. The Advisory Committee has no evidence that commissions do not operate satisfactorily in the case of projects comparable to the TVA.

Original Report

General Statement. 1. Background. When the Advisory Committee was formulating its recommendations to the Court concerning rules of procedure, which subsequently became the Federal Rules of 1938, the Committee concluded at an early stage not to fix the procedure in condemnation cases. This is a matter principally involving the exercise of the federal power of eminent domain, as very few condemnation cases involving the state's power reach the United States District Courts. The Committee's reasons at that time were that inasmuch as condemnation proceedings by the United States are governed by statutes of the United States, prescribing different procedure for various agencies and departments of the government, or, in the absence of such statutes, by local state practice under the Conformity Act (former § 258 of Title 40), it would be extremely difficult to draft a uniform rule satisfactory to the various agencies and departments of the government and to private parties; and that there was no general demand for a uniform rule. The Committee continued in that belief until shortly before the preparation of the April 1937 Draft of the Rules, when the officials of the Department of Justice having to do with condemnation cases urgently requested the Committee to propose rules on this subject. The Committee undertook the task and drafted a Condemnation Rule which appeared for the first time as Rule 74 of the April 1937 Draft. After the publication and distribution of this initial draft many objections were urged against it by counsel for various governmental agencies, whose procedure in condemnation cases was prescribed by federal statutes. Some of these agencies wanted to be excepted in whole or in part from the operation of the uniform rule proposed in April 1937. And the Department of Justice changed its position and stated that it preferred to have government condemnations conducted by local attorneys familiar with the state practice, which was applied under the Conformity Act where the Acts of Congress do not prescribe the practice; that it preferred to work under the Conformity Act without a uniform rule of procedure. The profession generally showed little interest in the proposed uniform rule. For these reasons the Advisory Committee in its Final Report to the Court in November 1937 proposed that all of Rule 74 be stricken and that the Federal Rules be made applicable only to appeals in condemnation cases. See note to Rule 74 of the Final Report.

Some of six or seven years later when the Advisory Committee was considering the subject of amendments to the Federal Rules both government officials and the profession generally urged the adoption of some uniform procedure. This demand grew out of the volume of condemnation proceedings instituted during the war, and the general feeling of dissatisfaction with the diverse condemnation procedures that were applicable in the federal courts. A strongly held belief was that both the sovereign's power to condemn and the property owner's right to compensation could be promoted by a simplified rule. As a consequence the Committee proposed a Rule 71A on the subject of condemnation in its Preliminary Draft of May 1944. In the Second Preliminary Draft of May 1945 this earlier proposed Rule 71A was, however, omitted. The Committee did not then feel that it had sufficient time to prepare a revised draft satisfactorily to it which would meet legitimate objections made to the draft of May 1944. To avoid unduly delaying the proposed amendments to existing rules the Committee concluded to proceed

in the regular way with the preparation of the amendments to these rules and deal with the question of a condemnation rule as an independent matter. As a consequence it made no recommendations to the Court on condemnation in its Final Report of Proposed Amendments of June 1946; and the amendments which the Court adopted in December 1946 did not deal with condemnation. After concluding its task relative to amendments, the Committee returned to a consideration of eminent domain, its proposed Rule 71A of May 1944, the suggestions and criticisms that had been presented in the interim, and in June 1947 prepared and distributed to the profession another draft of a proposed condemnation rule. This draft contained several alternative provisions, specifically called attention to and asked for opinion relative to these matters, and in particular as to the constitution of the tribunal to award compensation. The present draft was based on the June 1947 formulation, in light of the advice of the profession on both matters of substance and form.

2. Statutory Provisions. The need for a uniform condemnation rule in the federal courts arises from the fact that by various statutes Congress has prescribed diverse procedures for certain condemnation proceedings, and, in the absence of such statutes, has prescribed conformity to local state practice under former § 258 of Title 40. This general conformity adds to the diversity of procedure since in the United States there are multifarious methods of procedure in existence. Thus in 1931 it was said that there were 269 different methods of judicial procedure in different classes of condemnation cases and 56 methods of nonjudicial or administrative procedure. First Report of Judicial Council of Michigan, 1931, § 46, pp. 55 to 56. These numbers have not decreased. Consequently, the general requirement of conformity to state practice and procedure, particularly where the condemnor is the United States, leads to expense, delay and uncertainty. In advocacy of a uniform federal rule, see Armstrong, *Proposed Amendments to Federal Rules for Civil Procedure,* 1944, 4 F.R.D. 124, 134; id., *Report of the Advisory Committee on Federal Rules of Civil Procedure Recommending Amendments,* 1946, 5 F.R.D. 339, 357.

There are a great variety of Acts of Congress authorizing the exercise of the power of eminent domain by the United States and its officers and agencies. These statutes for the most part do not specify the exact procedure to be followed, but where procedure is prescribed, it is by no means uniform.

The following are instances of Acts which merely authorize the exercise of the power without specific declaration as to the procedure:

U.S.C., Title 16:

§ 404c–11 (Mammoth Cave National Park; acquisition of lands, interests in lands or other property for park by the Secretary of the Interior).

§ 426d (Stones River National Park; acquisition of land for parks by the Secretary of the Army).

§ 450aa (George Washington Carver National Monument; acquisition of land by the Secretary of the Interior).

§ 517 (National forest reservation; title to lands to be acquired by the Secretary of Agriculture).

U.S.C., Title 42:

§§ 1805(b)(5), 1813(b) [now §§ 2061 and 2112, and §§ 2221 to 2224, respectively, of Title 42] (Atomic Energy Act).

The following are instances of Acts which authorized condemnation and declare that the procedure is to conform what that of similar actions in state courts:

U.S.C., Title 16:

§ 423k (Richmond National Battlefield Park; acquisition of lands by the Secretary of the Interior).

§ 814 (Exercise by water power licensee of power of eminent domain).

U.S.C., Title 24:

§ 78 [Repealed] (Condemnation of land for the former National Home for Disabled Volunteer Soldiers).

U.S.C., Title 33:

§ 591 (Condemnation of lands and materials for river and harbor improvement by the Secretary of the Army).

U.S.C., Title 40:

§ 257 [now § 3113] (Condemnation of realty for sites for public building and for other public uses by the Secretary of the Treasury authorized).

§ 258 [Omitted as superseded by this rule] (Same procedure).

U.S.C., Title 50:

§ 171 [Repealed and is now covered by § 2663 of Title 10] (Acquisition of land by the Secretary of the Army for national defense).

§ 172 [Repealed and is now covered by §§ 2664 and 2665 of Title 10] (Acquisition of property by the Secretary of the Army, etc., for production of lumber).

§ 632 App. [Omitted as terminated by § 645 of the Appendix to Title 50] (Second War Powers Act, 1942; acquisition of real property for war purposes by the Secretary of Army, the Secretary of the Navy and others).

The following are Acts in which a more or less complete code of procedure is set forth in connection with the taking:

U.S.C., Title 16:

§ 831x (Condemnation by Tennessee Valley Authority).

U.S.C., Title 40:

§ 361–386 [Repealed] [now D.C.Code, Title 16, § 1301 et seq.] (Acquisition of lands in District of Columbia for use of United States; condemnation).

3. Adjustment of Rule to Statutory Provisions. While it was apparent that the principle of uniformity should be the basis for a rule to replace the multiple diverse procedures set out above, there remained a serious question as to whether an exception could properly be made relative to the method of determining compensation. Where Congress had provided for conformity to state law the following were the general methods in use: an initial determination by commissioners, with appeal to a judge; an initial award, likewise made by commissioners, but with the appeal to a jury; and determination by a jury without a previous award by commissioners. In two situations Congress had specified the tribunal to determine the issue of compensation: condemnation by the Tennessee Valley Authority; and condemnation in the District of Columbia. Under the TVA procedure the initial determination of value is by three disinterested commissioners, appointed by the court, from a locality other than the one in which the land lies. Either party may except to the award of the commission; in that case the exceptions are to be heard by three district judges (unless the parties stipulate for a lesser number), with a right of appeal to the circuit court of appeals. The TVA is a regional agency. It is faced

with the necessity of acquiring a very substantial acreage within a relatively small area, and charged with the task of carrying on within the Tennessee Valley and in cooperation with the local people a permanent program involving navigation and flood control, electric power, soil conservation, and general regional development. The success of this program is partially dependent upon the good will and cooperation of the people of the Tennessee Valley, and this in turn partially depends upon the land acquisition program. Disproportionate awards among landowners would create dissatisfaction and ill will. To secure uniformity in treatment Congress provided the rather unique procedure of the three-judge court to review de novo the initial award of the commissioners. This procedure has worked to the satisfaction of the property owners and the TVA. A full statement of the TVA position and experience is set forth in Preliminary Draft of Proposed Rule to Govern Condemnation Cases (June, 1947) 15–19. A large majority of the district judges with experience under this procedure approve it, subject to some objection to the requirement for a three-judge district court to review commissioners' awards. A statutory three-judge requirement is, however, jurisdictional and must be strictly followed. *Stratton v. St. Louis, Southwestern Ry. Co.*, 1930, 51 S.Ct. 8, 282 U.S. 10, 75 L.Ed. 135; *Ayrshire Collieries Corp. v. United States*, 1947, 67 S.Ct. 1168, 331 U.S. 132, 91 L.Ed. 1391. Hence except insofar as the TVA statute itself authorizes the parties to stipulate for a court of less than three judges, the requirement must be followed, and would seem to be beyond alteration by court rule even if change were thought desirable. Accordingly the TVA procedure is retained for the determination of compensation in TVA condemnation cases. It was also thought desirable to retain the specific method Congress had prescribed for the District of Columbia, which is a so-called jury of five appointed by the court. This is a local matter and the specific treatment accorded by Congress has given local satisfaction.

Aside from the foregoing limited exceptions dealing with the TVA and the District of Columbia, the question was whether a uniform method for determining compensation should be a commission with appeal to a district judge, or a commission with appeal to a jury, or a jury without a commission. Experience with the commission on a nation-wide basis, and in particular with the utilization of a commission followed by an appeal to a jury, has been that the commission is time consuming and expensive. Furthermore, it is largely a futile procedure where it is preparatory to jury trial. Since in the bulk of states a land owner is entitled eventually to a jury trial, since the jury is a traditional tribunal for the determination of questions of value, and since experience with juries has proved satisfactory to both government and land owner, the right to jury trial is adopted as the general rule. Condemnation involving the TVA and the District of Columbia are the two exceptions. See Note to Subdivision (h), infra.

Note to Subdivision (a). As originally promulgated the Federal Rules governed appeals in condemnation proceedings but were not otherwise applicable. Rule 81(a)(7). Pre-appeal procedure, in the main, conformed to state procedure. See statutes and discussion, supra. The purpose of Rule 71A is to provide a uniform procedure for condemnation in the federal district courts, including the District of Columbia. To achieve this purpose Rule 71A prescribes such specialized procedure as is required by condemnation proceedings, otherwise it utilizes the general framework of the Federal Rules

where specific detail is unnecessary. The adoption of Rule 71A, of course, renders paragraph (7) of Rule 81(a) unnecessary.

The promulgation of a rule for condemnation procedure is within the rulemaking power. The Enabling Act [Act of June 19, 1934, c. 651, §§ 1, 2 (48 Stat. 1064), former §§ 723b, 723c, now § 2072, of this title] gives the Supreme Court "the power to prescribe, by general rules * * * the forms of process, writs, pleadings, and motions, and the practice and procedure in civil actions at law." Such rules, however, must not abridge, enlarge, or modify substantive rights. In *Kohl v. United States*, 1875, 91 U.S. 367, 23 L.Ed. 449, a proceeding instituted by the United States to appropriate land for a postoffice site under a statute enacted for such purpose, the Supreme Court held that "a proceeding to take land in virtue of the government's eminent domain, and determining the compensation to be made for it, is * * * a suit at common law, when initiated in a court." See, also, *Madisonville Traction Co. v. Saint Bernard Mining Co.*, 1905, 25 S.Ct. 251, 196 U.S. 239, 49 L.Ed. 462, infra, under subdivision (k). And the Conformity Act [former § 258 of Title 40], which is superseded by Rule 71A, deals only with "practice, pleadings, forms and proceedings and not with matters of substantive laws." *United States v. 243.22 Acres of Land in Village of Farmingdale, Town of Babylon, Suffolk County, N.Y.*, D.C.N.Y.1942, 43 F.Supp. 561, affirmed 129 F.2d 678, certiorari denied 63 S.Ct. 441, 317 U.S. 698, 87 L.Ed. 558.

Rule 71A affords a uniform procedure for all cases of condemnation invoking the national power of eminent domain, and, to the extent stated in subdivision (k), for cases invoking a state's power of eminent domain; and supplants all statutes prescribing a different procedure. While the almost exclusive utility of the rule is for the condemnation of real property, it also applies to the condemnation of personal property, either as an incident to real property or as the sole object of the proceeding, when permitted or required by statute. See former § 438j [now § 5001] of Title 38 (World War Veterans' Relief Act); former §§ 1805, 1811, and 1813 of Title 42 (Atomic Energy Act); former § 79 [now § 100] of Title 50 (Nitrates Act); former §§ 161 to 165 and § 166, of Title 50 (Helium Gas Act). Requisitioning of personal property with the right in the owner to sue the United States, where the compensation cannot be agreed upon (see former § 1813 [now §§ 2221 to 2224] of Title 42, for example) will continue to be the normal method of acquiring personal property and Rule 71A in no way interferes with or restricts any such right. Only where the law requires or permits the formal procedure of condemnation to be utilized will the rule have any applicability to the acquisition of personal property.

Rule 71A is not intended to and does not supersede the Act of February 26, 1931, c. 307, §§ 1 to 5 (46 Stat. 1421), §§ 258a to 258e of Title 40, which is a supplementary condemnation statute, permissive in its nature and designed to permit the prompt acquisition of title by the United States, pending the condemnation proceeding, upon a deposit in court. See *United States v. 76,800 Acres, More or Less, of Land, in Bryan and Liberty Counties, Ga.*, D.C.Ga.1942, 44 F.Supp. 653; *United States v. 17,280 Acres of Land, More or Less, Situated in Saunders County, Neb.*, D.C.Neb.1942, 47 F.Supp. 267. The same is true insofar as the following or any other statutes authorize the acquisition of title or the taking of immediate possession:

U.S.C., Title 33:

§ 594 (When immediate possession of land may be taken; for a work of river and harbor improvements.)

U.S.C., Title 42:

§ 1813(b) [now §§ 2221 to 2224 of Title 42] (When immediate possession may be taken under Atomic Energy Act).

U.S.C., Title 50:

§ 171 [Repealed and is now covered by § 2663 of Title 10] (Acquisition of land by the Secretary of the Army for national defense).

§ 632 App. [Omitted as terminated by § 645 of the Appendix to Title 50] (Second War Powers Act, 1942; acquisition of real property for war purposes by the Secretary of the Army, the Secretary of the Navy, and others).

Note to Subdivision (b). This subdivision provides for broad joinder in accordance with the tenor of other rules such as Rule 18. To require separate condemnation proceedings for each piece of property separately owned would be unduly burdensome and would serve no useful purpose. And a restriction that only properties may be joined which are to be acquired for the same public use would also cause difficulty. For example, a unified project to widen a street, construct a bridge across a navigable river, and for the construction of approaches to the level of the bridge on both sides of the river might involve acquiring property for different public uses. Yet it is eminently desirable that the plaintiff may in one proceeding condemn all the property interests and rights necessary to carry out this project. Rule 21 which allows the court to sever and proceed separately with any claim against a party, and Rule 42(b) giving the court broad discretion to order separate trials give adequate protection to all defendants in condemnation proceedings.

Note to Subdivision (c). Since a condemnation proceeding is in rem and since a great many property owners are often involved, paragraph (1) requires the property to be named and only one of the owners. In other respects and caption will contain the name of the court, the title of the action, file number, and a designation of the pleading as a complaint in accordance with Rule 10(a).

Since the general standards of pleading are stated in other rules, paragraph (2) prescribes only the necessary detail for condemnation proceedings. Certain statutes allow the United States to acquire title or possession immediately upon commencement of an action. See the Act of February 26, 1931, c. 307, §§ 1 to 5 (46 Stat. 1421), §§ 258a to 258e of Title 40; and § 594 of Title 33, former § 1813(b) of Title 42, former § 171 of Title 50, former § 632 of the Appendix to Title 50, supra. To carry out the purpose of such statutes and to aid the condemnor in instituting the action even where title is not acquired at the outset, the plaintiff is initially required to join as defendants only the persons having or claiming an interest in the property whose names are then known. This is no way prejudices the property owner, who must eventually be joined as a defendant, served with process, and allowed to answer before there can be any hearing involving the compensation to be paid for his piece of property. The rule requires the plaintiff to name all persons having or claiming an interest in the property of whom the plaintiff has learned and, more importantly, those appearing of record. By charging the plaintiff with the necessity to make "a search of the records of the extent commonly made by competent searches of title in the vicinity in light of the type and value of the property involved" both the plaintiff and property owner are protected. Where a short term interest in property of little value is involved, as a two or three year easement over a vacant land for purposes of ingress and egress to other property, a search of the records covering a long period of time is not required. Where on the other hand fee simple title in valuable property is being condemned the search must necessarily cover a much longer period of time and be commensurate with the interests involved. But even here the search is related to the type made by competent title searchers in the vicinity. A search that extends back to the original patent may be feasible in some midwestern and western states and be proper under certain circumstances. In the Atlantic seaboard states such a search is normally not feasible nor desirable. There is a common sense business accommodation of what title searchers can and should do. For state statutes requiring persons appearing as owners or otherwise interested in the property to be named as defendants, see 3 Colo.Stat.Ann., 1935, c. 61, § 2; Ill.Ann.Stat. (Smith-Hurd) c. 47, § 2; 1 Iowa Code, 1946, § 472.3; Kans.Stat.Ann., 1935, § 26–101; 2 Mass.Laws Ann., 1932, c. 80A, § 4; 7 Mich.Stat.Ann., 1936, § 8.2; 2 Minn.Stat., Mason 1927, § 6541; 20 N.J.Stat.Ann., 1939, § 1–2; 3 Wash.Revised Stat., Remington, 1932, Title 6, § 891. For state provisions allowing persons whose names are not known to be designated under the descriptive term of "unknown owner", see Hawaii Revised Laws, 1945, c. 8, § 310 ("such [unknown] defendant may be joined in the petition under a fictitious name."); Ill.Ann.Stat. (Smith-Hurd) c. 47, § 2 ("Persons interested, whose names are unknown, may be made parties defendant by the description of the unknown owners; * * *"); Maryland Code Ann., 1939, Art. 33A, § 1 ("In case any owner or owners is or are not known, he or they may be described in such petition as the unknown owner or owners, or the unknown heir or heirs of a deceased owner."); 2 Mass.Laws Ann., 1932, c. 80A, § 4 ("Persons not in being, unascertained or unknown who may have an interest in any of such land shall be made parties respondent by such description as seems appropriate, * * *"); New Mex.Stat.Ann., 1941, § 25–901 ("the owners * * * shall be parties defendant, by name, if the names are known, and by description of the unknown owners of the land therein described, if their names are unknown."); Utah Code Ann., 1943, § 104–61–7 ("The names of all owners and claimants of the property, if known, or a statement that they are unknown, who must be styled defendants").

The last sentence of paragraph (2) enables the court to expedite the distribution of a deposit, in whole or in part, as soon as pertinent facts of ownership, value and the like are established. See also subdivision (j).

The signing of the complaint is governed by Rule 11.

Note to Subdivision (d). In lieu of a summons, which is the initial process in other civil actions under Rule 4(a), subdivision (d) provides for a notice which is to contain sufficient information so that the defendant in effect obtains the plaintiff's statement of his claim against the defendant to whom the notice is directed. Since the plaintiff's attorney is an officer of the court and to prevent unduly burdening the clerk of the court, paragraph (1) of subdivision (d) provides that plaintiff's attorney shall prepare and deliver a notice or notices to the clerk. Flexibility is provided by the provision for joint or several notices, and for additional notices.

Where there are only a few defendants it may be convenient to prepare but one notice directed to all the defendants. In other cases where there are many defendants it will be more convenient to prepare two or more notices; but in any event a notice must be directed to each named defendant. Paragraph (2) provides that the notice is to be signed by the plaintiff's attorney. Since the notice is to be delivered to the clerk, the issuance of the notice will appear of record in the court. The clerk should forthwith deliver the notice or notices for service to the marshal or to a person specially appointed to serve the notice. Rule 4(a). The form of the notice is such that, in addition to informing the defendant of the plaintiff's statement of claim, it tells the defendant precisely what his rights are. Failure on the part of the defendant to serve an answer constitutes a consent to the taking and to the authority of the court to proceed to fix compensation therefor, but it does not preclude the defendant from presenting evidence as to the amount of compensation due him or in sharing the award of distribution. See subdivision (e); Form 28.

While under Rule 4(f) the territorial limits of a summons are normally the territorial limits of the state in which the district court is held, the territorial limits for personal service of a notice under Rule 71A(d)(3) are those of the nation. This extension of process is here proper since the aim of the condemnation proceeding is not to enforce any personal liability and the property owner is helped, not imposed upon, by the best type of service possible. If personal service cannot be made either because the defendant's whereabouts cannot be ascertained, or, if ascertained, the defendant cannot be personally served, as where he resides in a foreign country such as Canada or Mexico, then service by publication is proper. The provisions for this type of service are set forth in the rule and are in no way governed by § 118 [now § 1655] of this title.

Note to Subdivision (e). Departing from the scheme of Rule 12, subdivision (e) requires all defenses and objections to be presented in an answer and does not authorize a preliminary motion. There is little need for the latter in condemnation proceedings. The general standard of pleading is governed by other rules, particularly Rule 8, and this subdivision (e) merely prescribes what matters the answer should set forth. Merely by appearing in the action a defendant can receive notice of all proceedings affecting him. And without the necessity of answering a defendant may present evidence as to the amount of compensation due him, and he may share in the distribution of the award. See also subdivision (d)(2); Form 28.

Note to Subdivision (f). Due to the number of persons who may be interested in the property to be condemned, there is a likelihood that the plaintiff will need to amend his complaint, perhaps many times, to add new parties or state new issues. This subdivision recognizes that fact and does not burden the court with applications by the plaintiff for leave to amend. At the same time all defendants are adequately protected; and their need to amend the answer is adequately protected by Rule 15, which is applicable by virtue of subdivision (a) of this Rule 71A.

Note to Subdivision (g). A condemnation action is a proceeding in rem. Commencement of the action as against a defendant by virtue of his joinder pursuant to subdivision (c)(2) is the point of cut-off and there is no mandatory requirement for substitution because of a subsequent change

of interest, although the court is given ample power to require substitution. Rule 25 is inconsistent with subdivision (g) and hence inapplicable. Accordingly, the time periods of Rule 25 do not govern to require dismissal nor to prevent substitution.

Note to Subdivision (h). This subdivision prescribes the method for determining the issue of just compensation in cases involving the federal power of eminent domain. The method of jury trial provided by subdivision (h) will normally apply in cases involving the state power by virtue of subdivision (k).

Congress has specially constituted a tribunal for the trial of the issue of just compensation in two instances: condemnation under the Tennessee Valley Authority Act; and condemnation in the District of Columbia. These tribunals are retained for reasons set forth in the General Statement: 3. Adjustment of Rule to Statutory Provisions, supra. Subdivision (h) also has prospective application so that if Congress should create another special tribunal, that tribunal will determine the issue of just compensation. Subject to these exceptions the general method of trial of that issue is to be by jury if any party demands it, otherwise that issue, as well as all other issues, are to be tried by the court.

As to the TVA procedure that is continued, § 831x of Title 16 requires that three commissioners be appointed to fix the compensation; that exceptions to their award are to be heard by three district judges (unless the parties stipulate for a lesser number) and that the district judges try the question de novo; that an appeal to the circuit court of appeals may be taken within 30 days from the filing of the decision of the district judges; and that the circuit court of appeals shall on the record fix compensation "without regard to the awards of findings theretofore made by the commissioners or the district judges." The mode of fixing compensation in the District of Columbia, which is also continued, is prescribed in former §§ 361 to 386 of Title 40. Under former § 371 the court is required in all cases to order the selection of a jury of five from among not less than 20 names, drawn "from the special box provided by law." They must have the usual qualifications of jurors and in addition must be freeholders of the District, and not in the service of the United States or the District. A special oath is administered to the chosen jurors. The trial proceeds in the ordinary way, except that the jury is allowed to separate after they have begun to consider their verdict.

There is no constitutional right to jury trial in a condemnation proceeding. *Bauman v. Ross,* 1897, 17 S.Ct. 966, 167 U.S. 548, 42 L.Ed. 270. See, also, Hines, *Does the Seventh Amendment to the Constitution of the United States Require Jury Trials in all Condemnation Proceedings?,* 1925, 11 Va.L.Rev. 505; Blair, *Federal Condemnation Proceedings and the Seventh Amendment,* 1927, 41 Harv.L.Rev. 29; 3 *Moore's Federal Practice,* 1938, 3007. Prior to Rule 71A, jury trial in federal condemnation proceedings was, however, enjoyed under the general conformity statute, former § 258 of Title 40, in states which provided for jury trial. See generally, 2 Lewis, *Eminent Domain,* 3d ed. 1909, §§ 509, 510; 3 Moore, op. cit. supra. Since the general conformity statute is superseded by Rule 71A, see supra under subdivision (a), and since it was believed that the rule to be substituted should likewise give a right to jury trial, subdivision (h) establishes that method as the general one for determining the issue of just compensation.

Note to Subdivision (i). Both the right of the plaintiff to dismiss by filing a notice of dismissal and the right of the court to permit a dismissal are circumscribed to the extent that where the plaintiff has acquired the title or a lesser interest or possession, viz., any property interest for which just compensation should be paid, the action may not be dismissed, without the defendant's consent, and the property owner remitted to another court, such as the Court of Claims, to recover just compensation for the property right taken. Circuity of action is thus prevented without increasing the liability of the plaintiff to pay just compensation for any interest that is taken. Freedom of dismissal is accorded, where both the condemnor and condemnee agree, up to the time of the entry of judgment vesting plaintiff with title. And power is given to the court, where the parties agree, to vacate the judgment and thus revest title in the property owner. In line with Rule 21, the court may at any time drop a defendant who has been unnecessarily or improperly joined as where it develops that he has no interest.

Note to Subdivision (j). Whatever the substantive law is concerning the necessity of making a deposit will continue to govern. For statutory provisions concerning deposit in court in condemnation proceedings by the United States, see § 258a of [former] Title 40; § 594 of Title 33; acquisition of title and possession statutes referred to in note to subdivision (a), supra. If the plaintiff is invoking the state's power of eminent domain the necessity of deposit will be governed by the state law. For discussion of such law, see 1 Nichols, Eminent Domain, 2d ed. 1917, §§ 209 to 216. For discussion of the function of deposit and the power of the court to enter judgment in cases both of deficiency and overpayment, see *United States v. Miller*, 1943, 63 S.Ct. 276, 317 U.S. 369, 87 L.Ed. 336, 147 A.L.R. 55, rehearing denied 63 S.Ct. 557, 318 U.S. 798, 87 L.Ed. 1162 (judgment in favor of plaintiff for overpayment ordered).

The court is to make distribution of the deposit as promptly as the facts of the case warrant. See also subdivision (c)(2).

Note to Subdivision (k). While the overwhelming number of cases that will be brought in the federal courts under this rule will be actions involving the federal power of eminent domain, a small percentage of cases may be instituted in the federal court or removed thereto on the basis of diversity or alienage which will involve the power of eminent domain under the law of a state. See *Boom Co. v. Patterson*, 1878, 98 U.S. 403, 25 L.Ed. 206; *Searl v. School District No. 2*, 1888, 8 S.Ct. 460, 124 U.S. 197, 31 L.Ed. 415; *Madisonville Traction Co. v. Saint Bernard Mining Co.*, 1905, 25 S.Ct. 251, 196 U.S. 239, 49 L.Ed. 462. In the Madisonville case, and in cases cited therein, it has been held that condemnation actions brought by state corporations in the exercise of a power delegated by the state might be governed by procedure prescribed by the laws of the United States, whether the cases were begun in or removed to the federal court. See, also, *Franzen v. Chicago, M. & St. P. Ry. Co.*, C.C.A.7th, 1921, 278 F. 370, 372.

Any condition affecting the substantial right of a litigant attached by state law is to be observed and enforced, such as making a deposit in court where the power of eminent domain is conditioned upon so doing. (See also subdivision (j). Subject to this qualification, subdivision (k) provides that in cases involving the state power of eminent domain, the practice prescribed by other subdivisions of Rule 71A shall govern.

Note to Subdivision (l). Since the condemnor will normally be the prevailing party and since he should not recover his costs against the property owner, Rule 54(d), which provides generally that costs shall go to the prevailing party, is made inapplicable. Without attempting to state what the rule on costs is, the effect of subdivision (l) is that costs shall be awarded in accordance with the law that has developed in condemnation cases. This has been summarized as follows: "Costs of condemnation proceedings are not assessable against the condemnee, unless by stipulation he agrees to assume some or all of them. Such normal expenses of the proceeding as bills for publication of notice, commissioners' fees, the cost of transporting commissioners and jurors to take a view, fees for attorneys to represent defendants who have failed to answer, and witness' fees, are properly charged to the government, though not taxed as costs. Similarly, if it is necessary that a conveyance be executed by a commissioner, the United States pay his fees and those for recording the deed. However, the distribution of the award is a matter in which the United States has no legal interest. Expenses incurred in ascertaining the identity of distributees and deciding between conflicting claimants are properly chargeable against the award, not against the United States, although United States attorneys are expected to aid the court in such matters as amici curiae." Lands Division Manual 861. For other discussion and citation, see *Grand River Dam Authority v. Jarvis*, C.C.A.10th, 1942, 124 F.2d 914. Costs may not be taxed against the United States except to the extent permitted by law. *United States v. 125.71 Acres of Land in Loyalhanna Tp., Westmoreland County, Pa.*, D.C.Pa.1944, 54 F.Supp. 193; Lands Division Manual 859. Even if it were thought desirable to allow the property owner's costs to be taxed against the United States, this is a matter for legislation and not court rule.

1963 Amendment

This amendment conforms to the amendment of Rule 4(f).

1985 Amendment

Rule 71A(h) provides that except when Congress has provided otherwise, the issue of just compensation in a condemnation case may be tried by a jury if one of the parties so demands, unless the court in its discretion orders the issue determined by a commission of three persons. In 1980, the Comptroller General of the United States in a Report to Congress recommended that use of the commission procedure should be encouraged in order to improve and expedite the trial of condemnation cases. The Report noted that long delays were being caused in many districts by such factors as crowded dockets, the precedence given criminal cases, the low priority accorded condemnation matters, and the high turnover of Assistant United States Attorneys. The Report concluded that revising Rule 71A to make the use of the commission procedure more attractive might alleviate the situation.

Accordingly, Rule 71A(h) is being amended in a number of respects designed to assure the quality and utility of a Rule 71A commission. First, the amended Rule will give the court discretion to appoint, in addition to the three members of a commission, up to two additional persons as alternate com-

missioners who would hear the case and be available, at any time up to the filing of the decision by the three-member commission, to replace any commissioner who becomes unable or disqualified to continue. The discretion to appoint alternate commissioners can be particularly useful in protracted cases, avoiding expensive retrials that have been required in some cases because of the death or disability of a commissioner. Prior to replacing a commissioner an alternate would not be present at, or participate in, the commission's deliberations.

Second, the amended Rule requires the court, before appointment, to advise the parties of the identity and qualifications of each prospective commissioner and alternate. The court then may authorize the examination of prospective appointees by the parties and each party has the right to challenge for cause. The objective is to insure that unbiased and competent commissioners are appointed.

The amended Rule does not prescribe a qualification standard for appointment to a commission, although it is understood that only persons possessing background and ability to appraise real estate valuation testimony and to award fair and just compensation on the basis thereof would be appointed. In most situations the chairperson should be a lawyer and all members should have some background qualifying them to weigh proof of value in the real estate field and, when possible, in the particular real estate market embracing the land in question.

The amended Rule should give litigants greater confidence in the commission procedure by affording them certain rights to participate in the appointment of commission members that are roughly comparable to the practice with regard to jury selection. This is accomplished by giving the court permission to allow the parties to examine prospective commissioners and by recognizing the right of each party to object to the appointment of any person for cause.

1987 Amendment

The amendments are technical. No substantive change is intended.

1988 Amendment

The amendment is technical. No substantive change is intended.

1993 Amendments

The references to the subdivisions of Rule 4 are deleted in light of the revision of that rule.

2003 Amendments

The references to specific subdivisions of Rule 53 are deleted or revised to reflect amendments of Rule 53.

2007 Amendments

*[Effective December 1, 2007,
absent contrary Congressional action.]*

The language of Rule 71A has been amended as part of the general restyling of the Civil Rules to make them more easily understood and to make style and terminology consistent throughout the rules. These changes are intended to be stylistic only.

Former Rule 71A has been redesignated as Rule 71.1 to conform to the designations used for all other rules added with the original numbering system.

Rule 71.1(e) allows a defendant to appear without answering. Former form 28 (now form 60) includes information about this right in the Rule 71.1(d)(2) notice. It is useful to confirm this practice in the rule.

The information that identifies the attorney is changed to include telephone number and electronic-mail address, in line with similar amendments to Rules 11(a) and 26(g)(1).

Rule 72. Magistrate Judges; Pretrial Orders

(a) Nondispositive Matters. A magistrate judge to whom a pretrial matter not dispositive of a claim or defense of a party is referred to hear and determine shall promptly conduct such proceedings as are required and when appropriate enter into the record a written order setting forth the disposition of the matter. Within 10 days after being served with a copy of the magistrate judge's order, a party may serve and file objections to the order; a party may not thereafter assign as error a defect in the magistrate judge's order to which objection was not timely made. The district judge to whom the case is assigned shall consider such objections and shall modify or set aside any portion of the magistrate judge's order found to be clearly erroneous or contrary to law.

(b) Dispositive Motions and Prisoner Petitions. A magistrate judge assigned without consent of the parties to hear a pretrial matter dispositive of a claim or defense of a party or a prisoner petition challenging the conditions of confinement shall promptly conduct such proceedings as are required. A record shall be made of all evidentiary proceedings before the magistrate judge, and a record may be made of such other proceedings as the magistrate judge deems necessary. The magistrate judge shall enter into the record a recommendation for disposition of the matter, including proposed findings of fact when appropriate. The clerk shall forthwith mail copies to all parties.

A party objecting to the recommended disposition of the matter shall promptly arrange for the transcription of the record, or portions of it as all parties may agree upon or the magistrate judge deems sufficient, unless the district judge otherwise directs. Within 10 days after being served with a copy of the recommended disposition, a party may serve and file specific, written objections to the proposed findings and recommendations. A party may respond to another party's objections within 10 days after being served with a copy thereof. The district judge to whom the case is assigned shall make a de novo determination upon the record, or after additional evidence, of any portion of the magistrate judge's disposition to which specific written objection has been made in accordance with this rule. The district judge may accept, reject, or modify the recommended decision, receive further

evidence, or recommit the matter to the magistrate judge with instructions.

(Added Apr. 28, 1983, eff. Aug. 1, 1983, and amended Apr. 30, 1991, eff. Dec. 1, 1991; Apr. 22, 1993, eff. Dec. 1, 1993.)

Proposed Amendment of Rule

Effective December 1, 2007, absent contrary Congressional action, this rule is amended to read as follows:

Rule 72. Magistrate Judges: Pretrial Order

(a) Nondispositive Matters. *When a pretrial matter not dispositive of a party's claim or defense is referred to a magistrate judge to hear and decide, the magistrate judge must promptly conduct the required proceedings and, when appropriate, issue a written order stating the decision. A party may serve and file objections to the order within 10 days after being served with a copy. A party may not assign as error a defect in the order not timely objected to. The district judge in the case must consider timely objections and modify or set aside any part of the order that is clearly erroneous or is contrary to law.*

(b) Dispositive Motions and Prisoner Petitions.

(1) Findings and Recommendations. A magistrate judge must promptly conduct the required proceedings when assigned, without the parties' consent, to hear a pretrial matter dispositive of a claim or defense or a prisoner petition challenging the conditions of confinement. A record must be made of all evidentiary proceedings and may, at the magistrate judge's discretion, be made of any other proceedings. The magistrate judge must enter a recommended disposition, including, if appropriate, proposed findings of fact. The clerk must promptly mail a copy to each party.

(2) Objections. Within 10 days after being served with a copy of the recommended disposition, a party may serve and file specific written objections to the proposed findings and recommendations. A party may respond to another party's objections within 10 days after being served with a copy. Unless the district judge orders otherwise, the objecting party must promptly arrange for transcribing the record, or whatever portions of it the parties agree to or the magistrate judge considers sufficient.

(3) Resolving Objections. The district judge must determine de novo any part of the magistrate judge's disposition that has been properly objected to. The district judge may accept, reject, or modify the recommended disposition; receive further evidence; or return the matter to the magistrate judge with instructions.

ADVISORY COMMITTEE NOTES
1983 Addition

Subdivision (a). This subdivision addresses court-ordered referrals of nondispositive matters under 28 U.S.C. § 636(b)(1)(A). The rule calls for a written order of the magistrate's disposition to preserve the record and facilitate review. An oral order read into the record by the magistrate will satisfy this requirement.

No specific procedures or timetables for raising objections to the magistrate's rulings on nondispositive matters are set forth in the Magistrates Act. The rule fixes a 10-day period in order to avoid uncertainty and provide uniformity that will eliminate the confusion that might arise if different periods were prescribed by local rule in different districts. It also is contemplated that a party who is successful before the magistrate will be afforded an opportunity to respond to objections raised to the magistrate's ruling.

The last sentence of subdivision (a) specifies that reconsideration of a magistrate's order, as provided for in the Magistrates Act, shall be by the district judge to whom the case is assigned. This rule does not restrict experimentation by the district courts under 28 U.S.C. § 636(b)(3) involving references of matters other than pretrial matters, such as appointment of counsel, taking of default judgments, and acceptance of jury verdicts when the judge is unavailable.

Subdivision (b). This subdivision governs court-ordered referrals of dispositive pretrial matters and prisoner petitions challenging conditions of confinement, pursuant to statutory authorization in 28 U.S.C. § 636(b)(1)(B). This rule does not extend to habeas corpus petitions, which are covered by the specific rules relating to proceedings under Sections 2254 and 2255 of Title 28.

This rule implements the statutory procedures for making objections to the magistrate's proposed findings and recommendations. The 10–day period, as specified in the statute, is subject to Rule 6(e) which provides for an additional 3–day period when service is made by mail. Although no specific provision appears in the Magistrates Act, the rule specifies a 10–day period for a party to respond to objections to the magistrate's recommendation.

Implementing the statutory requirements, the rule requires the district judge to whom the case is assigned to make a de novo determination of those portions of the report, findings, or recommendations to which timely objection is made. The term "de novo" signifies that the magistrate's findings are not protected by the clearly erroneous doctrine, but does not indicate that a second evidentiary hearing is required. See *United States v. Raddatz*, 417 [447] U.S. 667 (1980). See also Silberman, *Masters and Magistrates Part II: The American Analogue*, 50 N.Y.U. L.Rev. 1297, 1367 (1975). When no timely objection is filed, the court need only satisfy itself that there is no clear error on the face of the record in order to accept the recommendation. See *Campbell v. United States Dist. Court*, 501 F.2d 196, 206 (9th Cir.1974), cert. denied, 419 U.S. 879, quoted in House Report No. 94–1609, 94th Cong.2d Sess. (1976) at 3. Compare *Park Motor Mart, Inc. v. Ford Motor Co.*, 616 F.2d 603 (1st Cir.1980). Failure to make timely objection to the magistrate's report prior to its adoption by the district judge may constitute a waiver of appellate review of the district judge's order. *See United States v. Walters*, 638 F.2d 947 (6th Cir.1981).

1991 Amendment

This amendment is intended to eliminate a discrepancy in measuring the 10 days for serving and filing objections to a magistrate's action under subdivisions (a) and (b) of this Rule. The rule as promulgated in 1983 required objections to the magistrate's handling of nondispositive matters to be served and filed within 10 days of entry of the order, but required objections to dispositive motions to be made within 10 days of being served with a copy of the recommended disposition. Subdivision (a) is here amended to conform to subdivision (b) to avoid any confusion or technical defaults, particularly in connection with magistrate orders that rule on both dispositive and nondispositive matters.

The amendment is also intended to assure that objections to magistrate's orders that are not timely made shall not be considered. *Compare* Rule 51.

1993 Amendments

This revision is made to conform the rule to changes made by the Judicial Improvements Act of 1990.

2007 Amendments

[Effective December 1, 2007, absent contrary Congressional action.]

The language of Rule 72 has been amended as part of the general restyling of the Civil Rules to make them more easily understood and to make style and terminology consistent throughout the rules. These changes are intended to be stylistic only.

HISTORICAL NOTES

Change of Name

Reference to United States magistrate or to magistrate deemed to refer to United States magistrate judge pursuant to section 321 of Pub.L. 101–650, set out as a note under section 631 of this title.

Rule 73. Magistrate Judges; Trial by Consent and Appeal Options

(a) Powers; Procedure. When specially designated to exercise such jurisdiction by local rule or order of the district court and when all parties consent thereto, a magistrate judge may exercise the authority provided by Title 28, U.S.C. § 636(c) and may conduct any or all proceedings, including a jury or nonjury trial, in a civil case. A record of the proceedings shall be made in accordance with the requirements of Title 28, U.S.C. § 636(c)(5).

(b) Consent. When a magistrate judge has been designated to exercise civil trial jurisdiction, the clerk shall give written notice to the parties of their opportunity to consent to the exercise by a magistrate judge of civil jurisdiction over the case, as authorized by Title 28, U.S.C. § 636(c). If, within the period specified by local rule, the parties agree to a magistrate judge's exercise of such authority, they shall execute and file a joint form of consent or separate forms of consent setting forth such election.

A district judge, magistrate judge, or other court official may again advise the parties of the availability of the magistrate judge, but, in so doing, shall also advise the parties that they are free to withhold consent without adverse substantive consequences. A district judge or magistrate judge shall not be informed of a party's response to the clerk's notification, unless all parties have consented to the referral of the matter to a magistrate judge.

The district judge, for good cause shown on the judge's own initiative, or under extraordinary circumstances shown by a party, may vacate a reference of a civil matter to a magistrate judge under this subdivision.

(c) Appeal. In accordance with Title 28, U.S.C. § 636(c)(3), appeal from a judgment entered upon direction of a magistrate judge in proceedings under this rule will lie to the court of appeals as it would from a judgment of the district court.

[(d) Optional Appeal Route.] (Abrogated, April 11, 1997, eff. Dec. 1, 1997)

(Added Apr. 28, 1983, eff. Aug. 1, 1983, and amended Mar. 2, 1987, eff. Aug. 1, 1987; Apr. 22, 1993, eff. Dec. 1, 1993; Apr. 11, 1997, eff. Dec. 1, 1997.)

Proposed Amendment of Rule

Effective December 1, 2007, absent contrary Congressional action, this rule is amended to read as follows:

Rule 73. Magistrate Judges: Trial by Consent; Appeal

(a) Trial by Consent. When authorized under 28 U.S.C. § 636(c), a magistrate judge may, if all parties consent, conduct a civil action or proceeding, including a jury or nonjury trial. A record must be made in accordance with 28 U.S.C. § 636(c)(5).

(b) Consent Procedure.

(1) In General. When a magistrate judge has been designated to conduct civil actions or proceedings, the clerk must give the parties written notice of their opportunity to consent under 28 U.S.C. § 636(c). To signify their consent, the parties must jointly or separately file a statement consenting to the referral. A district judge or magistrate judge may be informed of a party's response to the clerk's notice only if all parties have consented to the referral.

(2) Reminding the Parties About Consenting. A district judge, magistrate judge, or other court official may remind the parties of the magistrate judge's availability, but must also advise them that they are free to withhold consent without adverse substantive consequences.

(3) Vacating a Referral. On its own for good cause—or when a party shows extraordinary cir-

cumstances—the district judge may vacate a referral to a magistrate judge under this rule.

(c) Appealing a Judgment. *In accordance with 28 U.S.C. § 636(c)(3), an appeal from a judgment entered at a magistrate judge's direction may be taken to the court of appeals as would any other appeal from a district-court judgment.*

ADVISORY COMMITTEE NOTES
1983 Addition

Subdivision (a). This subdivision implements the broad authority of the 1979 amendments to the Magistrates Act, 28 U.S.C. § 636(c), which permit a magistrate to sit in lieu of a district judge and exercise civil jurisdiction over a case, when the parties consent. See McCabe, *The Federal Magistrate Act of 1979*, 16 Harv.J.Legis. 343, 364–79 (1979). In order to exercise this jurisdiction, a magistrate must be specially designated under 28 U.S.C. § 636(c)(1) by the district court or courts he serves. The only exception to a magistrate's exercise of civil jurisdiction, which includes the power to conduct jury and nonjury trials and decide dispositive motions, is the contempt power. A hearing on contempt is to be conducted by the district judge upon certification of the facts and an order to show cause by the magistrate. See 28 U.S.C. § 639(e). In view of 28 U.S.C. § 636(c)(1) and this rule, it is unnecessary to amend Rule 58 to provide that the decision of a magistrate is a "decision by the court" for the purposes of that rule and a "final decision of the district court" for purposes of 28 U.S.C. § 1291 governing appeals.

Subdivision (b). This subdivision implements the blind consent provision of 28 U.S.C. § 636(c)(2) and is designed to ensure that neither the judge nor the magistrate attempts to induce a party to consent to reference of a civil matter under this rule to a magistrate. See House Rep. No. 96–444, 96th Cong. 1st Sess. 8 (1979).

The rule opts for a uniform approach in implementing the consent provision by directing the clerk to notify the parties of their opportunity to elect to proceed before a magistrate and by requiring the execution and filing of a consent form or forms setting forth the election. However, flexibility at the local level is preserved in that local rules will determine how notice shall be communicated to the parties, and local rules will specify the time period within which an election must be made.

The last paragraph of subdivision (b) reiterates the provision in 28 U.S.C. § 636(c)(6) for vacating a reference to the magistrate.

Subdivision (c). Under 28 U.S.C. § 636(c)(3), the normal route of appeal from the judgment of a magistrate—the only route that will be available unless the parties otherwise agree in advance—is an appeal by the aggrieved party "directly to the appropriate United States court of appeals from the judgment of the magistrate in the same manner as an appeal from any other judgment of a district court." The quoted statutory language indicates Congress' intent that the same procedures and standards of appealability that govern appeals from district court judgments govern appeals from magistrates' judgments.

Subdivision (d). 28 U.S.C. § 636(c)(4) offers parties who consent to the exercise of civil jurisdiction by a magistrate an alternative appeal route to that provided in subdivision (c) of

this rule. This optional appellate route was provided by Congress in recognition of the fact that not all civil cases warrant the same appellate treatment. In cases where the amount in controversy is not great and there are no difficult questions of law to be resolved, the parties may desire to avoid the expense and delay of appeal to the court of appeals by electing an appeal to the district judge. See McCabe, *The Federal Magistrate Act of 1979*, 16 Harv.J.Legis. 343, 388 (1979). This subdivision provides that the parties may elect the optional appeal route at the time of reference to a magistrate. To this end, the notice by the clerk under subdivision (b) of this rule shall explain the appeal option and the corollary restriction on review by the court of appeals. This approach will avoid later claims of lack of consent to the avenue of appeal. The choice of the alternative appeal route to the judge of the district court should be made by the parties in their forms of consent. Special appellate rules to govern appeals from a magistrate to a district judge appear in new Rules 74 through 76.

1987 Amendment

The amendment is technical. No substantive change is intended.

1993 Amendments

This revision is made to conform the rule to changes made by the Judicial Improvements Act of 1990. The Act requires that, when being reminded of the availability of a magistrate judge, the parties be advised that withholding of consent will have no "adverse substantive consequences." They may, however, be advised if the withholding of consent will have the adverse procedural consequence of a potential delay in trial.

1997 Amendments

The Federal Courts Improvement Act of 1996 repealed the former provisions of 28 U.S.C. § 636(c)(4) and (5) that enabled parties that had agreed to trial before a magistrate judge to agree also that appeal should be taken to the district court. Rule 73 is amended to conform to this change. Rules 74, 75, and 76 are abrogated for the same reason. The portions of Form 33 and Form 34 that referred to appeals to the district court also are deleted.

2007 Amendments

[Effective December 1, 2007, absent contrary Congressional action.]

The language of Rule 73 has been amended as part of the general restyling of the Civil Rules to make them more easily understood and to make style and terminology consistent throughout the rules. These changes are intended to be stylistic only.

HISTORICAL NOTES
Change of Name

Reference to United States magistrate or to magistrate deemed to refer to United States magistrate judge pursuant to section 321 of Pub.L. 101–650, set out as a note under section 631 of this title.

[Rule 74. Method of Appeal From Magistrate Judge to District Judge Under Title 28, U.S.C. § 636(c)(4) and Rule 73(d)] (Abrogated April 11, 1997, eff. Dec. 1, 1997)

ADVISORY COMMITTEE NOTES
1997 Amendment

Rule 74 is abrogated for the reasons described in the Note to Rule 73.

2007 Amendment

[Effective December 1, 2007, absent contrary Congressional action.]

Rule 74 was abrogated in 1997 to reflect repeal of the statute providing for appeal from a magistrate judge's judgment to the district court. The rule number is reserved for possible future use.

[Rule 75. Proceedings on Appeal From Magistrate Judge to District Judge Under Rule 73(d)] (Abrogated April 11, 1997, eff. Dec. 1, 1997)

ADVISORY COMMITTEE NOTES
1997 Amendment

Rule 75 is abrogated for the reasons described in the Note to Rule 73.

2007 Amendment

[Effective December 1, 2007, absent contrary Congressional action.]

Rule 75 was abrogated in 1997 to reflect repeal of the statute providing for appeal from a magistrate judge's judgment to the district court. The rule number is reserved for possible future use.

[Rule 76. Judgment of the District Judge on the Appeal Under Rule 73(d) and Costs] (Abrogated April 11, 1997, eff. Dec. 1, 1997)

ADVISORY COMMITTEE NOTES
1997 Amendment

Rule 76 is abrogated for the reasons described in the Note to Rule 73.

2007 Amendment

[Effective December 1, 2007, absent contrary Congressional action.]

Rule 76 was abrogated in 1997 to reflect repeal of the statute providing for appeal from a magistrate judge's judgment to the district court. The rule number is reserved for possible future use.

[IX. APPEALS [1] (Abrogated)]

[1] Another Title IX is set out ante.

HISTORICAL NOTES
Prior Provisions

The heading "IX. APPEALS" and Rules 72 to 76, formerly constituting the provisions of IX, were abrogated Dec. 4, 1967, effective July 1, 1968. Former Rules 72 to 76 were the civil rules relating to appeals, the provisions of which, except for Rule 73(h), were transferred to and covered by the Federal Rules of Appellate Procedure and (in the case of Rule 72) the Rules of the Supreme Court. The substance of Rule 73(h) was transferred to Rule 9(h) of these Rules.

X. DISTRICT COURTS AND CLERKS

Proposed Amendment of Heading

Effective December 1, 2007, absent contrary Congressional action, this heading is amended to read as follows:

TITLE X. DISTRICT COURTS AND CLERKS: CONDUCTING BUSINESS; ISSUING ORDERS

Rule 77. District Courts and Clerks

(a) District Courts Always Open. The district courts shall be deemed always open for the purpose of filing any pleading or other proper paper, of issuing and returning mesne and final process, and of making and directing all interlocutory motions, orders, and rules.

(b) Trials and Hearings; Orders in Chambers. All trials upon the merits shall be conducted in open court and so far as convenient in a regular court room. All other acts or proceedings may be done or conducted by a judge in chambers, without the attendance of the clerk or other court officials and at any place either within or without the district; but no hearing, other than one ex parte, shall be conducted outside the district without the consent of all parties affected thereby.

(c) Clerk's Office and Orders by Clerk. The clerk's office with the clerk or a deputy in attendance shall be open during business hours on all days except Saturdays, Sundays, and legal holidays, but a district court may provide by local rule or order that its clerk's office shall be open for specified hours on Saturdays or particular legal holidays other than New Year's Day, Birthday of Martin Luther King, Jr., Washington's Birthday, Memorial Day, Independence

Day, Labor Day, Columbus Day, Veterans Day, Thanksgiving Day, and Christmas Day. All motions and applications in the clerk's office for issuing mesne process, for issuing final process to enforce and execute judgments, for entering defaults or judgments by default, and for other proceedings which do not require allowance or order of the court are grantable of course by the clerk; but the clerk's action may be suspended or altered or rescinded by the court upon cause shown.

(d) Notice of Orders or Judgments. Immediately upon the entry of an order or judgment the clerk shall serve a notice of the entry in the manner provided for in Rule 5(b) upon each party who is not in default for failure to appear, and shall make a note in the docket of the service. Any party may in addition serve a notice of such entry in the manner provided in Rule 5(b) for the service of papers. Lack of notice of the entry by the clerk does not affect the time to appeal or relieve or authorize the court to relieve a party for failure to appeal within the time allowed, except as permitted in Rule 4(a) of the Federal Rules of Appellate Procedure.

(As amended Dec. 27, 1946, eff. Mar. 19, 1948; Jan. 21, 1963, eff. July 1, 1963; Dec. 4, 1967, eff. July 1, 1968; Mar. 1, 1971, eff. July 1, 1971; Mar. 2, 1987, eff. Aug. 1, 1987; Apr. 30, 1991, eff. Dec. 1, 1991; Apr. 23, 2001, eff. Dec. 1, 2001.)

Proposed Amendment of Rule

Effective December 1, 2007, absent contrary Congressional action, this rule is amended to read as follows:

Rule 77. Conducting Business; Clerk's Authority; Notice of an Order or Judgment

(a) When Court Is Open. *Every district court is considered always open for filing any paper, issuing and returning process, making a motion, or entering an order.*

(b) Place for Trial and Other Proceedings. *Every trial on the merits must be conducted in open court and, so far as convenient, in a regular courtroom. Any other act or proceeding may be done or conducted by a judge in chambers, without the attendance of the clerk or other court official, and anywhere inside or outside the district. But no hearing—other than one ex parte—may be conducted outside the district unless all the affected parties consent.*

(c) Clerk's Office Hours; Clerk's Orders.

(1) Hours. The clerk's office—with a clerk or deputy on duty—must be open during business hours every day except Saturdays, Sundays, and legal holidays. But a court may, by local rule or order, require that the office be open for specified hours on Saturday or a particular legal holiday other than one listed in Rule 6(a)(4)(A).

(2) Orders. Subject to the court's power to suspend, alter, or rescind the clerk's action for good cause, the clerk may:

 (A) issue process;

 (B) enter a default;

 (C) enter a default judgment under Rule 55(b)(1); and

 (D) act on any other matter that does not require the court's action.

(d) Serving Notice of an Order or Judgment.

(1) Service. Immediately after entering an order or judgment, the clerk must serve notice of the entry, as provided in Rule 5(b), on each party who is not in default for failing to appear. The clerk must record the service on the docket. A party also may serve notice of the entry as provided in Rule 5(b).

(2) Time to Appeal Not Affected by Lack of Notice. Lack of notice of the entry does not affect the time for appeal or relieve—or authorize the court to relieve—a party for failing to appeal within the time allowed, except as allowed by Federal Rule of Appellate Procedure (4)(a).

ADVISORY COMMITTEE NOTES

1937 Adoption

This rule states the substance of U.S.C., Title 28, § 452, formerly § 13 (Courts open as courts of admiralty and equity). Compare [former] Equity Rules 1 (District Court Always Open For Certain Purposes—Orders at Chambers), 2 (Clerk's Office Always Open, Except, Etc.), 4 (Notice of Orders), and 5 (Motions Grantable of Course by Clerk).

1946 Amendment

Note. Rule 77(d) has been amended to avoid such situations as the one arising in *Hill v. Hawes,* 1944, 64 S.Ct. 334, 320 U.S. 520, 88 L.Ed. 283. In that case, an action instituted in the District Court for the District of Columbia, the clerk failed to give notice of the entry of a judgment for defendant as required by Rule 77(d). The time for taking an appeal then was 20 days under Rule 10 of the Court of Appeals (later enlarged by amendment to thirty days), and due to lack of notice of the entry of judgment the plaintiff failed to file his notice of appeal within the prescribed time. On this basis the trial court vacated the original judgment and then re-entered it, whereupon notice of appeal was filed. The Court of Appeals dismissed the appeal as taken too late. The Supreme Court, however, held that although rule 77(d) did not purport to attach any consequence to the clerk's failure to give notice as specified, the terms of the rule were such that the appellant was entitled to rely on it, and the trial court in such a case, in the exercise of a sound discretion, could vacate the former judgment and enter a new one, so that the appeal would be within the allowed time.

Because of Rule 6(c), which abolished the old rule that the expiration of the term ends a court's power over its judgment, the effect of the decision in *Hill v. Hawes* is to give the

district court power, in its discretion and without time limit, and long after the term may have expired, to vacate a judgment and reenter it for the purpose of reviving the right of appeal. This seriously affects the finality of judgments. See also proposed Rule 6(c) and Note; proposed Rule 60(b) and Note; and proposed Rule 73(a) and Note.

Rule 77(d) as amended makes it clear that notification by the clerk of the entry of a judgment has nothing to do with the starting of the time for appeal; that time starts to run from the date of entry of judgment and not from the date of notice of the entry. Notification by the clerk is merely for the convenience of litigants. And lack of such notification in itself has no effect upon the time for appeal; but in considering an application for extension of time for appeal as provided in Rule 73(a), the court may take into account, as one of the factors affecting its decision, whether the clerk failed to give notice as provided in Rule 77(d) or the party failed to receive the clerk's notice. It need not, however, extend the time for appeal merely because the clerk's notice was not sent or received. It would, therefore, be entirely unsafe for a party to rely on absence of notice from the clerk of the entry of a judgment, or to rely on the adverse party's failure to serve notice of the entry of a judgment. Any party may, of course, serve timely notice of the entry of a judgment upon the adverse party and thus preclude a successful application, under Rule 73(a), for the extension of the time for appeal.

1963 Amendment

Subdivision (c). The amendment authorizes closing of the clerk's office on Saturday as far as civil business is concerned. However, a district court may require its clerk's office to remain open for specified hours on Saturdays or "legal holidays" other than those enumerated ("Legal holiday" is defined in Rule 6(a), as amended.) The clerk's offices of many district courts have customarily remained open on some of the days appointed as holidays by State law. This practice could be continued by local rule or order.

Subdivision (d). This amendment conforms to the amendment of Rule 5(a). See the Advisory Committee's Note to that amendment.

1968 Amendment

The provisions of Rule 73(a) are incorporated in Rule 4(a) of the Federal Rules of Appellate Procedure.

1971 Amendment

The amendment adds Columbus Day to the list of legal holidays. See the Note accompanying the amendment of Rule 6(a).

1987 Amendment

The amendments are technical. No substantive change is intended. The Birthday of Martin Luther King, Jr. is added to the list of national holidays in Rule 77.

1991 Amendment

This revision is a companion to the concurrent amendment to Rule 4 of the Federal Rules of Appellate Procedure. The purpose of the revisions is to permit district courts to ease strict sanctions now imposed on appellants whose notices of appeal are filed late because of their failure to receive notice of entry of a judgment. See, e.g. *Tucker v. Commonwealth Land Title Ins. Co.*, 800 F.2d 1054 (11th Cir.1986); *Ashby Enterprises, Ltd. v. Weitzman, Dym & Associates*, 780 F.2d 1043 (D.C.Cir.1986); *In re OPM Leasing Services, Inc.*, 769 F.2d 911 (2d Cir.1985); *Spika v. Village of Lombard, Ill.*, 763 F.2d 282 (7th Cir.1985); *Hall v. Community Mental Health Center of Beaver County*, 772 F.2d 42 (3d Cir.1985); *Wilson v. Atwood v. Stark*, 725 F.2d 255 (5th Cir. en banc), cert. dismissed, 105 S.Ct. 17 (1984); *Case v. BASF Wyandotte*, 727 F.2d 1034 (Fed.Cir.1984), cert. denied, 105 S.Ct. 386 (1984); *Hensley v. Chesapeake & Ohio R.R. Co.*, 651 F.2d 226 (4th Cir.1981); *Buckeye Cellulose Corp. v. Electric Construction Co.*, 569 F.2d 1036 (8th Cir.1978).

Failure to receive notice may have increased in frequency with the growth in the caseload in the clerks' offices. The present strict rule imposes a duty on counsel to maintain contact with the court while a case is under submission. Such contact is more difficult to maintain if counsel is outside the district, as is increasingly common, and can be a burden to the court as well as counsel.

The effect of the revisions is to place a burden on prevailing parties who desire certainty that the time for appeal is running. Such parties can take the initiative to assure that their adversaries receive effective notice. An appropriate procedure for such notice is provided in Rule 5.

The revised rule lightens the responsibility but not the workload of the clerk's offices, for the duty of that office to give notice of entry of judgment must be maintained.

2001 Amendments

Rule 77(d) is amended to reflect changes in Rule 5(b). A few courts have experimented with serving Rule 77(d) notices by electronic means on parties who consent to this procedure. The success of these experiments warrants express authorization. Because service is made in the manner provided in Rule 5(b), party consent is required for service by electronic or other means described in Rule 5(b)(2)(D). The same provision is made for a party who wishes to ensure actual communication of the Rule 77(d) notice by also serving notice.

Changes Made After Publication and Comments

Rule 77(d) was amended to correct an oversight in the published version. The clerk is to note "service," not "mailing," on the docket.

2007 Amendments

*[Effective December 1, 2007,
absent contrary Congressional action.]*

The language of Rule 77 has been amended as part of the general restyling of the Civil Rules to make them more easily understood and to make style and terminology consistent throughout the rules. These changes are intended to be stylistic only.

HISTORICAL NOTES

References in Text

The Federal Rules of Appellate Procedure, referred to in subd. (d), are set out in Title 28, U.S.C.A., Federal Rules of Appellate Procedure.

Rule 78. Motion Day

Unless local conditions make it impracticable, each district court shall establish regular times and places, at intervals sufficiently frequent for the prompt dispatch of business, at which motions requiring notice and hearing may be heard and disposed of; but the judge at any time or place and on such notice, if any, as the judge considers reasonable may make orders for the advancement, conduct, and hearing of actions.

To expedite its business, the court may make provision by rule or order for the submission and determination of motions without oral hearing upon brief written statements of reasons in support and opposition.

(As amended Mar. 2, 1987, eff. Aug. 1, 1987.)

Proposed Amendment of Rule

Effective December 1, 2007, absent contrary Congressional action, this rule is amended to read as follows:

Rule 78. Hearing Motions; Submission on Briefs

(a) Providing a Regular Schedule for Oral Hearings. *A court may establish regular times and places for oral hearings on motions.*

(b) Providing for Submission on Briefs. *By rule or order, the court may provide for submitting and determining motions on briefs, without oral hearings.*

ADVISORY COMMITTEE NOTES

1937 Adoption

Compare [former] Equity Rule 6 (Motion Day) with the first paragraph of this rule. The second paragraph authorizes a procedure found helpful for the expedition of business in some of the Federal and State courts. See Rule 43(e) of these rules dealing with evidence on motions. Compare *Civil Practice Rules of the Municipal Court of Chicago* (1935), Rules 269, 270, 271.

1987 Amendment

The amendment is technical. No substantive change is intended.

2007 Amendments

[Effective December 1, 2007, absent contrary Congressional action.]

The language of Rule 78 has been amended as part of the general restyling of the Civil Rules to make them more easily understood and to make style and terminology consistent throughout the rules. These changes are intended to be stylistic only.

Rule 16 has superseded any need for the provision in former Rule 78 for orders for the advancement, conduct, and hearing of actions.

Rule 79. Books and Records Kept by the Clerk and Entries Therein

(a) Civil Docket. The clerk shall keep a book known as "civil docket" of such form and style as may be prescribed by the Director of the Administrative Office of the United States Courts with the approval of the Judicial Conference of the United States, and shall enter therein each civil action to which these rules are made applicable. Actions shall be assigned consecutive file numbers. The file number of each action shall be noted on the folio of the docket whereon the first entry of the action is made. All papers filed with the clerk, all process issued and returns made thereon, all appearances, orders, verdicts, and judgments shall be entered chronologically in the civil docket on the folio assigned to the action and shall be marked with its file number. These entries shall be brief but shall show the nature of each paper filed or writ issued and the substance of each order or judgment of the court and of the returns showing execution of process. The entry of an order or judgment shall show the date the entry is made. When in an action trial by jury has been properly demanded or ordered the clerk shall enter the word "jury" on the folio assigned to that action.

(b) Civil Judgments and Orders. The clerk shall keep, in such form and manner as the Director of the Administrative Office of the United States Courts with the approval of the Judicial Conference of the United States may prescribe, a correct copy of every final judgment or appealable order, or order affecting title to or lien upon real or personal property, and any other order which the court may direct to be kept.

(c) Indices; Calendars. Suitable indices of the civil docket and of every civil judgment and order referred to in subdivision (b) of this rule shall be kept by the clerk under the direction of the court. There shall be prepared under the direction of the court calendars of all actions ready for trial, which shall distinguish "jury actions" from "court actions."

(d) Other Books and Records of the Clerk. The clerk shall also keep such other books and records as may be required from time to time by the Director of the Administrative Office of the United States Courts with the approval of the Judicial Conference of the United States.

(As amended Dec. 27, 1946, eff. Mar. 19, 1948; Dec. 29, 1948, eff. Oct. 20, 1949; Jan. 21, 1963, eff. July 1, 1963.)

Proposed Amendment of Rule

Effective December 1, 2007, absent contrary Congressional action, this rule is amended to read as follows:

Rule 79. Records Kept by the Clerk

(a) Civil Docket.

(1) In General. The clerk must keep a record known as the "civil docket" in the form and manner prescribed by the Director of the Administrative Office of the United States Courts with the approval of the Judicial Conference of the United States. The clerk must enter each civil action in the docket. Actions must be assigned consecutive file numbers, which must be noted in the docket where the first entry of the action is made.

(2) Items to be Entered. The following items must be marked with the file number and entered chronologically in the docket:

 (A) papers filed with the clerk;

 (B) process issued, and proofs of service or other returns showing execution; and

 (C) appearances, orders, verdicts, and judgments.

(3) Contents of Entries; Jury Trial Demanded. Each entry must briefly show the nature of the paper filed or writ issued, the substance of each proof of service or other return, and the substance and date of entry of each order and judgment. When a jury trial has been properly demanded or ordered, the clerk must enter the word "jury" in the docket.

(b) Civil Judgments and Orders. The clerk must keep a copy of every final judgment and appealable order; of every order affecting title to or a lien on real or personal property; and of any other order that the court directs to be kept. The clerk must keep these in the form and manner prescribed by the Director of the Administrative Office of the United States Courts with the approval of the Judicial Conference of the United States.

(c) Indexes; Calendars. Under the court's direction, the clerk must:

 (1) keep indexes of the docket and of the judgments and orders described in Rule 79(b); and

 (2) prepare calendars of all actions ready for trial, distinguishing jury trials from nonjury trials.

(d) Other Records. The clerk must keep any other records required by the Director of the Administrative Office of the United States Courts with the approval of the Judicial Conference of the United States.

ADVISORY COMMITTEE NOTES

1937 Adoption

Compare [former] Equity Rule 3 (Books Kept by Clerk and Entries Therein). In connection with this rule, see also the following statutes of the United States:
U.S.C., Title 5 former:

§ 301 [See Title 28, § 526] (Officials for investigation of official acts, records and accounts of marshals, attorneys, clerks of courts, United States commissioners, referees and trustees)

§ 318 [former] (Accounts of district attorneys)

U.S.C., Title 28 former:

 § 556 [former] (Clerks of district courts; books open to inspection)

 § 567 [now 751] (Same; accounts)

 § 568 [now 751] (Same; reports and accounts of moneys received; dockets)

 § 813 [former] (Indices of judgment debtors to be kept by clerks)

And see "Instructions to United States Attorneys, Marshals, Clerks and Commissioners" issued by the Attorney General of the United States.

1946 Amendment

Note. Subdivision (a). The amendment substitutes the Director of the Administrative Office of the United States Courts, acting subject to the approval of the Judicial Conference of Senior Circuit Judges, in the place of the Attorney General as a consequence of and in accordance with the provisions of the act establishing the Administrative Office and transferring functions thereto. Act of August 7, 1939, c. 501, §§ 1 to 7, 53 Stat. 1223, 28 U.S.C.A. §§ 601 to 610, formerly §§ 444 to 450.

Subdivision (b). The change in this subdivision does not alter the nature of the judgments and orders to be recorded in permanent form but it does away with the express requirement that they be recorded in a book. This merely gives latitude for the preservation of court records in other than book form, if that shall seem advisable, and permits with the approval of the Judicial Conference the adoption of such modern, space-saving methods as microphotography. See *Proposed Improvements in the Administration of the Offices of Clerks of United States District Courts,* prepared by the Bureau of the Budget, 1941, 38–42. See also Rule 55, Federal Rules of Criminal Procedure.

Subdivision (c). The words "Separate and" have been deleted as unduly rigid. There is no sufficient reason for requiring that the indices in all cases be separate; on the contrary, the requirement frequently increases the labor of persons searching the records as well as the labor of the clerk's force preparing them. The matter should be left to administrative discretion.

The other changes in the subdivision merely conform with those made in subdivision (b) of the rule.

Subdivision (d). Subdivision (d) is a new provision enabling the Administrative Office, with the approval of the Judicial Conference, to carry out any improvements in clerical procedure with respect to books and records which may be deemed advisable. See report cited in Note to subdivision (b), supra.

1948 Amendment

The amendment effective October 1949, substituted the name, "Judicial Conference of the United States," for "Judicial Conference of Senior Circuit Judges," in the first sentence of subdivision (a), and in subdivisions (b) and (d).

1963 Amendment

The terminology is clarified without any change of the prescribed practice. See amended Rule 58, and the Advisory Committee's Note thereto.

2007 Amendments

[Effective December 1, 2007, absent contrary Congressional action.]

The language of Rule 79 has been amended as part of the general restyling of the Civil Rules to make them more easily understood and to make style and terminology consistent throughout the rules. These changes are intended to be stylistic only.

Rule 80. Stenographer; Stenographic Report or Transcript as Evidence

[(a) Abrogated (Dec. 27, 1946, eff. Mar. 19, 1948)].

[(b) Abrogated (Dec. 27, 1946, eff. Mar. 19, 1948)].

(c) Stenographic Report or Transcript as Evidence. Whenever the testimony of a witness at a trial or hearing which was stenographically reported is admissible in evidence at a later trial, it may be proved by the transcript thereof duly certified by the person who reported the testimony.
(As amended Dec. 27, 1946, eff. Mar. 19, 1948.)

Proposed Amendment of Rule

Effective December 1, 2007, absent contrary Congressional action, this rule is amended to read as follows:

Rule 80. Stenographic Transcript as Evidence

If stenographically reported testimony at a hearing or trial is admissible in evidence at a later trial, the testimony may be proved by a transcript certified by the person who reported it.

ADVISORY COMMITTEE NOTES

1937 Adoption

Note to Subdivision (a). This follows substantially [former] Equity Rule 50 (Stenographer— Appointment— Fees). [This subdivision was abrogated. See amendment note of Advisory Committee below.]

Note to Subdivision (b). See *Reports of Conferences of Senior Circuit Judges with the Chief Justice of the United States* (1936), 22 A.B.A.J. 818, 819; (1937), 24 A.B.A.J. 75, 77. [This subdivision was abrogated. See amendment note of Advisory Committee below.]

Note to Subdivision (c). Compare Iowa Code (1935) § 11353.

1946 Amendment

Note. Subdivisions (a) and (b) of Rule 80 have been abrogated because of Public Law 222, 78th Cong., c. 3, 2d Sess., approved Jan. 20, 1944, 28 U.S.C. §§ 550, 604, 753, 1915, 1920, formerly § 9a, providing for the appointment of official stenographers for each district court, prescribing their duties, providing for the furnishing of transcripts, the taxation of the fees therefor as costs, and other related matters. This statute has now been implemented by Congressional appropriation available for the fiscal year beginning July 1, 1945.

Subdivision (c) of Rule 80 (Stenographic Report or Transcript as Evidence) has been retained unchanged.

2007 Amendments

[Effective December 1, 2007, absent contrary Congressional action.]

The language of Rule 80 has been amended as part of the general restyling of the Civil Rules to make them more easily understood and to make style and terminology consistent throughout the rules. These changes are intended to be stylistic only.

XI. GENERAL PROVISIONS

Proposed Amendment of Heading

Effective December 1, 2007, absent contrary Congressional action, this heading is amended to read as follows:

TITLE XI. GENERAL PROVISIONS

Rule 81. Applicability in General

(a) To What Proceedings Applicable.

(1) These rules do not apply to prize proceedings in admiralty governed by Title 10, U.S.C., §§ 7651–7681. They do apply to proceedings in bankruptcy to the extent provided by the Federal Rules of Bankruptcy Procedure.

(2) These rules are applicable to proceedings for admission to citizenship, habeas corpus, and quo warranto, to the extent that the practice in such proceedings is not set forth in statutes of the United States, the Rules Governing Section 2254 Cases, or the Rules Governing Section 2255 Proceedings, and has heretofore conformed to the practice in civil actions.

(3) In proceedings under Title 9, U.S.C., relating to arbitration, or under the Act of May 20, 1926, ch. 347, § 9 (44 Stat. 585), U.S.C., Title 45, § 159, relating to boards of arbitration of railway labor disputes, these rules apply only to the extent that matters of procedure are not provided for in those statutes. These rules apply to proceedings to compel the giving of testimony or production of documents in accordance with a subpoena issued by an officer or agency of the United States under any statute of the United States except as otherwise provided by statute or by rules of the district court or by order of the court in the proceedings.

(4) These rules do not alter the method prescribed by the Act of February 18, 1922, ch. 57, § 2 (42 Stat. 388), U.S.C., Title 7, § 292; or by the Act of June 10, 1930, ch. 436, § 7 (46 Stat. 534), as amended, U.S.C., Title 7, § 499g(c), for instituting proceedings in the United States district courts to review orders of the Secretary of Agriculture; or prescribed by the Act of June 25, 1934, ch. 742, § 2 (48 Stat. 1214), U.S.C., Title 15, § 522, for instituting proceedings to review orders of the Secretary of the Interior; or prescribed by the Act of February 22, 1935, ch. 18, § 5 (49 Stat. 31), U.S.C., Title 15, § 715d(c), as extended, for instituting proceedings to review orders of petroleum control boards; but the conduct of such proceedings in the district courts shall be made to conform to these rules so far as applicable.

(5) These rules do not alter the practice in the United States district courts prescribed in the Act of July 5, 1935, ch. 372, §§ 9 and 10 (49 Stat. 453), as amended, U.S.C., Title 29, §§ 159 and 160, for beginning and conducting proceedings to enforce orders of the National Labor Relations Board; and in respects not covered by those statutes, the practice in the district courts shall conform to these rules so far as applicable.

(6) These rules apply to proceedings for enforcement or review of compensation orders under the Longshoremen's and Harbor Workers' Compensation Act, Act of March 4, 1927, c. 509, §§ 18, 21 (44 Stat. 1434, 1436), as amended, U.S.C., Title 33, §§ 918, 921, except to the extent that matters of procedure are provided for in that Act. The provisions for service by publication and for answer in proceedings to cancel certificates of citizenship under the Act of June 27, 1952, c. 477, Title III, c. 2, § 340 (66 Stat. 260), U.S.C., Title 8, § 1451, remain in effect.

[(7) Abrogated, effective Aug. 1, 1951. (Supreme Court Order, Apr. 30, 1951.)]

(b) Scire Facias and Mandamus. The writs of scire facias and mandamus are abolished. Relief heretofore available by mandamus or scire facias may be obtained by appropriate action or by appropriate motion under the practice prescribed in these rules.

(c) Removed Actions. These rules apply to civil actions removed to the United States district courts from the state courts and govern procedure after removal. Repleading is not necessary unless the court so orders. In a removed action in which the defendant has not answered, the defendant shall answer or present the other defenses or objections available under these rules within 20 days after the receipt through service or otherwise of a copy of the initial pleading setting forth the claim for relief upon which the action or proceeding is based, or within 20 days after the service of summons upon such initial pleading, then filed, or within 5 days after the filing of the petition for removal, whichever period is longest. If at the time of removal all necessary pleadings have been served, a party entitled to trial by jury under Rule 38 shall be accorded it, if the party's demand therefor is served within 10 days after the petition for removal is filed if the party is the petitioner, or if not the petitioner within 10 days after service on the party of the notice of filing the petition. A party who, prior to removal, has made an express demand for trial by jury in accordance with state law, need not make a demand after removal. If state law applicable in the court from which the case is removed does not require the parties to make express demands in order to claim trial by jury, they need not make demands after removal unless the court directs that they do so within a specified time if they desire to claim trial by jury. The court may make this direction on its own motion and shall do so as a matter of course at the request of any party. The failure of a party to make demand as directed constitutes a waiver by that party of trial by jury.

[(d) Abrogated, effective Oct. 20, 1949. (Supreme Court Order, Dec. 29, 1948)].

(e) Law Applicable. Whenever in these rules the law of the state in which the district court is held is made applicable, the law applied in the District of Columbia governs proceedings in the United States District Court for the District of Columbia. When the word "state" is used, it includes, if appropriate, the District of Columbia. When the term "statute of the United States" is used, it includes, so far as concerns proceedings in the United States District Court for the District of Columbia, any Act of Congress locally applicable to and in force in the District of Columbia. When the law of a state is referred to, the word "law" includes the statutes of that state and the state judicial decisions construing them.

(f) References to Officer of the United States. Under any rule in which reference is made to an officer or agency of the United States, the term "officer" includes a district director of internal revenue, a former district director or collector of internal revenue, or the personal representative of a deceased district director or collector of internal revenue.

(As amended Dec. 28, 1939, eff. Apr. 3, 1941; Dec. 27, 1946, eff. Mar. 19, 1948; Dec. 29, 1948, eff. Oct. 20, 1949; Apr. 30, 1951, eff. Aug. 1, 1951; Jan. 21, 1963, eff. July 1, 1963; Feb. 28, 1966, eff. July 1, 1966; Dec. 4, 1967, eff. July 1, 1968; Mar. 1, 1971, eff. July 1, 1971; Mar. 2, 1987, eff. Aug. 1, 1987; Apr. 23, 2001, eff. Dec. 1, 2001; Apr. 29, 2002, eff. Dec. 1, 2002.)

Proposed Amendment of Rule

Effective December 1, 2007, absent contrary Congressional action, this rule is amended to read as follows:

Rule 81. Applicability of the Rules in General; Removed Actions

(a) Applicability to Particular Proceedings.

(1) Prize Proceedings. These rules do not apply to prize proceedings in admiralty governed by 10 U.S.C. §§ 7651–7681.

(2) Bankruptcy. These rules apply to bankruptcy proceedings to the extent provided by the Federal Rules of Bankruptcy Procedure.

(3) Citizenship. These rules apply to proceedings for admission to citizenship to the extent that the practice in those proceedings is not specified in federal statutes and has previously conformed to the practice in civil actions. The provisions of 8 U.S.C. § 1451 for service by publication and for answer apply in proceedings to cancel citizenship certificates.

(4) Special Writs. These rules apply to proceedings for habeas corpus and for quo warranto to the extent that the practice in those proceedings:

(A) is not specified in a federal statute, the Rules Governing Section 2254 Cases, or the Rules Governing Section 2255 Cases; and

(B) has previously conformed to the practice in civil actions.

(5) Proceedings Involving a Subpoena. These rules apply to proceedings to compel testimony or the production of documents through a subpoena issued by a United States officer or agency under a federal statute, except as otherwise provided by statute, by local rule, or by court order in the proceedings.

(6) Other Proceedings. These rules, to the extent applicable, govern proceedings under the following laws, except as these laws provide other procedures:

(A) 7 U.S.C. §§ 292, 499g(c), for reviewing an order of the Secretary of Agriculture;

(B) 9 U.S.C., relating to arbitration;

(C) 15 U.S.C. § 522, for reviewing an order of the Secretary of the Interior;

(D) 15 U.S.C. § 715d(c), for reviewing an order denying a certificate of clearance;

(E) 29 U.S.C. §§ 159, 160, for enforcing an order of the National Labor Relations Board;

(F) 33 U.S.C. §§ 918, 921, for enforcing or reviewing a compensation order under the Longshore and Harbor Workers' Compensation Act; and

(G) 45 U.S.C. § 159, for reviewing an arbitration award in a railway-labor dispute.

(b) Scire Facias and Mandamus.
The writs of scire facias and mandamus are abolished. Relief previously available through them may be obtained by appropriate action or motion under these rules.

(c) Removed Actions.

(1) Applicability. These rules apply to a civil action after it is removed from a state court.

(2) Further Pleading. After removal, repleading is unnecessary unless the court orders it. A defendant who did not answer before removal must answer or present other defenses or objections under these rules within the longest of these periods:

(A) 20 days after receiving—through service or otherwise—a copy of the initial pleading stating the claim for relief;

(B) 20 days after being served with the summons for an initial pleading on file at the time of service; or

(C) 5 days after the notice of removal is filed.

(3) Demand for a Jury Trial.

(A) As Affected by State Law. A party who, before removal, expressly demanded a jury trial in accordance with state law need not renew the demand after removal. If the state law did not require an express demand for a jury trial, a party need not make one after removal unless the court orders the parties to do so within a specified time. The court must so order at a party's request and may so order on its own. A party who fails to make a demand when so ordered waives a jury trial.

(B) Under Rule 38. If all necessary pleadings have been served at the time of removal, a party entitled to a jury trial under Rule 38 must be given one if the party serves a demand within 10 days after:

(i) it files a notice of removal; or

(ii) it is served with a notice of removal filed by another party.

(d) Law Applicable.

(1) State Law. When these rules refer to state law, the term "law" includes the state's statutes and the state's judicial decisions.

(2) District of Columbia. The term "state" includes, where appropriate, the District of Columbia. When these rules provide for state law to apply, in the District Court for the District of Columbia:

(A) the law applied in the District governs; and

(B) the term "federal statute" includes any Act of Congress that applies locally to the District.

ADVISORY COMMITTEE NOTES
1937 Adoption

Note to Subdivision (a). Paragraph (1): Compare the enabling act, Act of June 19, 1934, U.S.C., Title 28, § 2072, formerly § 723b (Rules in actions at law; Supreme Court authorized to make) and § 2072, formerly § 723c (Union of equity and action at law rules; power of Supreme Court). For the application of these rules in bankruptcy and copyright proceedings, see Orders xxxvi and xxxvii in Bankruptcy and Rule 1 of Rules of Practice and Procedure under § 25 of the copyright act, Act of March 4, 1909, U.S.C., Title 17, former § 25 [see 412, 501 et seq.] (Infringement and rules of procedure).

For examples of statutes which are preserved by paragraph (2) see: U.S.C., Title 8, [former] ch. 9 (Naturalization); Title 28, former ch. 14 [now 153] (Habeas corpus); Title 28, former §§ 377a to 377c [now D.C.Code, Title 16 § 3501 et seq.] (Quo warranto); and such forfeiture statutes as U.S.C., Title 7, former § 116 (Misbranded seeds, confiscation), and Title 21, § 334(b), formerly § 14 (Pure Food and Drug Act—condemnation of adulterated or misbranded Food; procedure). See also *443 Cans of Frozen Eggs Product v. U.S.,* 1912, 33 S.Ct. 50, 226 U.S. 172, 57 L.Ed. 174.

For examples of statutes which under paragraph (7) will continue to govern procedure in condemnation cases, see U.S.C. [former] Title 40, [former] § 258 (Condemnation of realty for sites for public building, etc., procedure); U.S.C., Title 16, § 831x (Condemnation by Tennessee Valley Authority); U.S.C., [former] Title 40, § 120 (Acquisition of lands for public use in District of Columbia); [former] Title 40, ch. 7 [now D.C.Code, Title 16, § 1301 et seq.] (Acquisition of lands in District of Columbia for use of United States; condemnation).

Note to Subdivision (b). Some statutes which will be affected by this subdivision are;

U.S.C., Title 7:
- § 222 (Federal Trade Commission powers adopted for enforcement of Stockyards Act) (By reference to Title 15, § 49)

U.S.C., Title 15:
- § 49 (Enforcement of Federal Trade Commission orders and antitrust laws)
- § 77t(c) (Enforcement of Securities and Exchange Commission orders and Securities Act of 1933)
- § 78u(f) (Same; Securities Exchange Act of 1934)
- § 79r(g) (Same; Public Utility Holding Company Act of 1935)

U.S.C., Title 16:
- § 820 (Proceedings in equity for revocation or to prevent violations of license of Federal Power Commission licensee)
- § 825m(b) (Mandamus to compel compliance with Federal Water Power Act, etc.)

U.S.C., Title 19:

§ 1333(c) (Mandamus to compel compliance with orders of Tariff Commission, etc.)

U.S.C., Title 28, former:
- § 377 [now 1651] (Power to issue writs)
- § 572 [now 1923] (Fees, attorneys, solicitors and proctors)
- § 778 [former] (Death of parties; substitution of executor or administrator). Compare Rule 25(a) (Substitution of parties; death), and the note thereto.

U.S.C., Title 33:
- § 495 (Removal of bridges over navigable waters)

U.S.C., Title 45:
- § 88 (Mandamus against Union Pacific Railroad Company)
- § 153(p) (Mandamus to enforce orders of Adjustment Board under Railway Labor Act)
- § 185 (Same; National Air Transport Adjustment Board) (By reference to § 153)

U.S.C., Title 47:
- § 11 (Powers of Federal Communications Commission)
- § 401(a) (Enforcement of Federal Communications Act and orders of Commission)
- § 406 (Same; Compelling furnishing of facilities; mandamus)

U.S.C., Title 49:
- § 19a(*l*) [now 11703] (Mandamus to compel compliance with Interstate Commerce Act)
- § 20(9) [now 11703] (Jurisdiction to compel compliance with interstate commerce laws by mandamus)

For comparable provisions in state practice see Smith-Hurd Ill.Stats.c. 110, § 179 (1937); Calif.Code Civ.Proc. (Deering, 1937) § 802.

Note to Subdivision (c). Such statutes as the following dealing with the removal of actions are substantially continued and made subject to these rules:

U.S.C., Title 28 former:
- § 71 [now 1441, 1445, 1447] (Removal of suits from state courts)
- § 72 [now 1446, 1447] (Same; procedure)
- § 73 [former] (Same; suits under grants of land from different states)
- § 74 [now 1443, 1446, 1447] (Same; causes against persons denied civil rights)
- § 75 [now 1446] (Same; petitioner in actual custody of state court)
- § 76 [now 1442, 1446, 1447] (Same; suits and prosecutions against revenue officers)
- § 77 [now 1442] (Same; suits by aliens)
- § 78 [now 1449] (Same; copies of records refused by clerk of state court)
- § 79 [now 1450] (Same; previous attachment bonds or orders)
- § 80 [now 1359, 1447, 1919] (Same; dismissal or remand)
- § 81 [now 1447] (Same; proceedings in suits removed)
- § 82 [former] (Same; record; filing and return)
- § 83 [now 1447, 1448] (Service of process after removal)

U.S.C., Title 28, §§ 1446, 1447, formerly § 72, supra, however, is modified by shortening the time for pleading in removed actions.

Note to Subdivision (e). The last sentence of this subdivision modifies U.S.C., Title 28, § 1652, formerly § 725 (Laws of States as rules of decision) in so far as that statute has been construed to govern matters of procedure and to exclude state judicial decisions relative thereto.

1946 Amendment

Note to Subdivision (a). Despite certain dicta to the contrary, *Lynn v. United States*, C.C.A.5th, 1940, 110 F.2d 586; *Mount Tivy Winery, Inc. v. Lewis*, N.D.Cal.1942, 42 F.Supp. 636, it is manifest that the rules apply to actions against the United States under the Tucker Act [28 U.S.C., §§ 41(20), 250, 251, 254, 257, 258, 287, 289, 292, 761–765 [now 791, 1346, 1401, 1402, 1491, 1493, 1496, 1501, 1503, 2071, 2072, 2411, 2412, 2501, 2506, 2509, 2510]]. See United States to use of *Foster Wheeler Corp. v. American Surety Co. of New York*, E.D.N.Y.1939, 25 F.Supp. 700; *Boerner v. United States*, E.D.N.Y.1939, 26 F.Supp. 769; *United States v. Gallagher*, C.C.A.9th, 1945, 151 F.2d 556. Rules 1 and 81 provide that the rules shall apply to all suits of a civil nature, whether cognizable as cases at law or in equity except those specifically excepted; and the character of the various proceedings excepted by express statement in Rule 81, as well as the language of the rules generally, shows that the term "civil action" [Rule 2] includes actions against the United States. Moreover, the rules in many places expressly make provision for the situation wherein the United States is a party as either plaintiff or defendant. See Rules 4(d)(4), 12(a), 13(d), 25(d), 37(f), 39(c), 45(c), 54(d), 55(e), 62(e), and 65(c). In *United States v. Sherwood*, 1941, 61 S.Ct. 767, 312 U.S. 584, 85 L.Ed. 1058, the Solicitor General expressly conceded in his brief for the United States that the rules apply to Tucker Act cases. The Solicitor General stated: "The Government, of course, recognizes that the Federal Rules of Civil Procedure apply to cases brought under the Tucker Act." (Brief for the United States, p. 31.) Regarding *Lynn v. United States*, supra, the Solicitor General said: "In *Lynn v. United States* . . . the Circuit Court of Appeals for the Fifth Circuit went beyond the Government's contention there, and held that an action under the Tucker Act is neither an action at law nor a suit in equity and, seemingly, that the Federal Rules of Civil Procedure are, therefore, inapplicable. We think the suggestion is erroneous. Rules 4(d), 12(a), 39(c), and 55(e) expressly contemplate suits against the United States, and nothing in the enabling Act (48 Stat. 1064, 28 U.S.C. §§ 723b, 723c [see 2072]) suggests that the Rules are inapplicable to Tucker Act proceedings, which in terms are to accord with court rules and their subsequent modifications (Sec. 4, Act of March 3, 1887, 24 Stat. 505, 28 U.S.C. § 761 [see 2071, 2072])." (Brief for the United States, p. 31, n. 17.)

United States v. Sherwood, supra, emphasizes, however, that the application of the rules in Tucker Act cases affects only matters of procedure and does not operate to extend jurisdiction. See also Rule 82. In the Sherwood case, the New York Supreme Court, acting under § 795 of the New York Civil Practice Act, made an order, authorizing Sherwood, as a judgment creditor, to maintain a suit under the Tucker Act to recover damages from the United States for breach of its contract with the judgment debtor, Kaiser, for construction of a post office building. Sherwood brought suit against the United States and Kaiser in the District Court for the Eastern District of New York. The question before the United States Supreme Court was whether a United States District Court had jurisdiction to entertain a suit against the United States wherein private parties were joined as parties defendant. It was contended that either the Federal Rules of Civil Procedure or the Tucker Act, or both, embodied the consent of the United States to be sued in litigations in which issues between the plaintiff and third persons were to be adjudicated. Regarding the effect of the Federal Rules, the Court declared that nothing in the rules, so far as they may be applicable in Tucker Act cases, authorized the maintenance of any suit against the United States to which it had not otherwise consented. The matter involved was not one of procedure but of jurisdiction, the limits of which were marked by the consent of the United States to be sued. The jurisdiction thus limited is unaffected by the Federal Rules of Civil Procedure.

Subdivision (a)(2). The added sentence makes it clear that the rules have not superseded the requirements of U.S.C., Title 28, § 2253, formerly § 466. *Schenk v. Plummer*, C.C.A.9, 1940, 113 F.2d 726.

For correct application of the rules in proceedings for forfeiture of property for violation of a statute of the United States, such as under U.S.C., Title 22, § 405 (seizure of war materials intended for unlawful export) or U.S.C., Title 21, § 334(b) (Federal Food, Drug, and Cosmetic Act; formerly Title 21, U.S.C. § 14, Pure Food and Drug Act), see *Reynal v. United States*, C.C.A.5, 1945, 153 F.2d 929; *United States v. 108 Boxes of Cheddar Cheese*, S.D.Iowa 1943, 3 F.R.D. 40.

Subdivision (a)(3). The added sentence makes it clear that the rules apply to appeals from proceedings to enforce administrative subpoenas. See *Perkins v. Endicott Johnson Corp.*, C.C.A.2d 1942, 128 F.2d 208, affirmed on other grounds 63 S.Ct. 339, 317 U.S. 501, 87 L.Ed. 424; *Walling v. News Printing Inc.*, C.C.A.3, 1945, 148 F.2d 57; *McCrone v. United States*, 1939, 59 S.Ct. 685, 307 U.S. 61, 83 L.Ed. 1108. And, although the provision allows full recognition of the fact that the rigid application of the rules in the proceedings themselves may conflict with the summary determination desired, *Goodyear Tire & Rubber Co. v. National Relations Board*, C.C.A.6, 1941, 122 F.2d 450; *Cudahy Packing Co. v. National Labor Relations Board*, C.C.A.10, 1941, 117 F.2d 692, it is drawn so as to permit application of any of the rules in the proceedings whenever the district court deems them helpful. See, e.g., *Peoples Natural Gas Co. v. Federal Power Commission*, App.D.C.1942, 127 F.2d 153, certiorari denied 62 S.Ct. 1298, 316 U.S. 700, 86 L.Ed. 1769; *Martin v. Chandis Securities Co.*, C.C.A.9th, 1942, 128 F.2d 731. Compare the application of the rules in summary proceedings in bankruptcy under General Order 37. See 1 *Collier on Bankruptcy*, 14th ed. by Moore and Oglebay, 326–327; 2 Collier, op.cit.supra, 1401–1402; 3 Collier, op.cit.supra, 228–231; 4 Collier, op.cit.supra, 1199–1202.

Subdivision (a)(6). Section 405 of U.S.C., Title 8 originally referred to in the last sentence of paragraph (6), has been repealed and § 738 [now 1451], U.S.C., Title 8, has been enacted in its stead. The last sentence of paragraph (6) has, therefore, been amended in accordance with this change. The sentence has also been amended so as to refer directly to the statute regarding the provision of time for answer, thus avoiding any confusion attendant upon a change in the statute.

That portion of subdivision (a)(6) making the rules applicable to proceedings for enforcement or review of compensa-

tion orders under the Longshoremen's and Harbor Workers' Compensation Act [33 U.S.C. § 901 et seq.] was added by an amendment made pursuant to order of the Court, December 28, 1939, effective three months subsequent to the adjournment of the 76th Congress, January 3, 1941.

Subdivision (c). The change in subdivision (c) effects more speedy trials in removed actions. In some states many of the courts have only two terms a year. A case, if filed 20 days before a term, is returnable to that term, but if filed less than 20 days before a term, is returnable to the following term, which convenes six months later. Hence, under the original wording of Rule 81(c), where a case is filed less than 20 days before the term and is removed within a few days but before answer, it is possible for the defendant to delay interposing his answer or presenting his defenses by motion for six months or more. The rule as amended prevents this result.

Subdivision (f). The use of the phrase "the United States or an officer or agency thereof" in the rules (as e.g., in Rule 12(a) and amended Rule 73(a)) could raise the question of whether "officer" includes a collector of internal revenue, a former collector, or the personal representative of a deceased collector, against whom suits for tax refunds are frequently instituted. Difficulty might ensue for the reason that a suit against a collector or his representative has been held to be a personal action. *Sage v. United States*, 1919, 39 S.Ct. 415, 250 U.S. 33, 63 L.Ed. 828; *Smietanka v. Indiana Steel Co.*, 1921, 42 S.Ct. 1, 257 U.S. 1, 66 L.Ed. 99; *United States v. Nunnally Investment Co.*, 1942, 62 S.Ct. 1064, 316 U.S. 258, 86 L.Ed. 1455. The addition of subdivision (f) to Rule 81 dispels any doubts on the matter and avoids further litigation.

1948 Amendment

The amendment effective October 1949, substituted the words "United States District Court" for the words "District Court of the United States" in the last sentence of subdivision (a)(1) and in the first and third sentences of subdivision (e). The amendment substituted the words "United States district courts" in lieu of "district courts of the United States" in subdivision (a)(4) and (5) and in the first sentence of subdivision (c).

The amendment effective October 20, 1949, also made the following changes:

In subdivision (a)(1), the reference to "Title 17, U.S.C." was substituted for the reference to "the Act of March 4, 1909, c. 320, § 25 (35 Stat. 1081), as amended, U.S.C., Title 17, § 25."

In subdivision (a)(2), the reference to "Title 28, U.S.C., § 2253" was substituted for "U.S.C., Title 28, § 466."

In subdivision (a)(3), the reference in the first sentence to "Title 9, U.S.C.," was substituted for "the Act of February 12, 1925, c. 213 (43 Stat. 883), U.S.C., Title 9".

In subdivision (a)(5), the words "as amended" were inserted after the parenthetical citation of "(49 Stat. 453)," and after the citations of "Title 29, §§ 159 and 160," former references to subdivisions "(e), (g), and (i)" were deleted.

In subdivision (a)(6), after the words "These rules" at the beginning of the first sentence, the following words were deleted: "do not apply to proceedings under the Act of September 13, 1888, c. 1015, § 13 (25 Stat. 479), as amended, U.S.C., Title 8, [former] § 282, relating to deportation of

Chinese; they". Also in the first sentence, after the parenthetical citation of "(44 Stat. 1434, 1436)," the words "as amended" were added. In the last sentence, the words "October 14, 1940, c. 876, § 338 (54 Stat. 1158)" were inserted in lieu of the words "June 29, 1906, c. 3592, § 15 (34 Stat. 601), as amended."

In subdivision (c), the word "all" originally appearing in the first sentence between the words "govern" and "procedure" was deleted. In the third sentence, the portion beginning with the words "20 days after the receipt" and including all the remainder of that sentence was substituted for the following language: "the time allowed for answer by the law of the state or within 5 days after the filing of the transcript of the record in the district court of the United States, whichever period is longer, but in any event within 20 days after the filing of the transcript". In the fourth or last sentence, after the words at the beginning of the sentence, "If at the time of removal all necessary pleadings have been," the word "served" was inserted in lieu of the word "filed," and the concluding words of the sentence, "petition for removal is filed if he is the petitioner," together with the final clause immediately following, were substituted for the words "record of the action is filed in the district court of the United States."

1963 Amendment

Subdivision (a)(4). This change reflects the transfer of functions from the Secretary of Commerce to the Secretary of the Interior made by 1939 Reorganization Plan No. II, § 4(e), 53 Stat. 1433.

Subdivision (a)(6). The proper current reference is to the 1952 statute superseding the 1940 statute.

Subdivision (c). Most of the cases have held that a party who has made a proper express demand for jury trial in the State court is not required to renew the demand after removal of the action. *Zakoscielny v. Waterman Steamship Corp.*, 16 F.R.D. 314 (D.Md.1954); *Talley v. American Bakeries Co.*, 15 F.R.D. 391 (E.D.Tenn.1954); *Rehrer v. Service Trucking Co.*, 15 F.R.D. 113 (D.Del.1953); 5 *Moore's Federal Practice* ¶38.39[3] (2d ed. 1951); 1 Barron & Holtzoff, *Federal Practice & Procedure* § 132 (Wright ed. 1960). But there is some authority to the contrary. *Petsel v. Chicago, B. & Q.R. Co.*, 101 F.Supp. 1006 (S.D.Iowa 1951); *Nelson v. American Nat. Bank & Trust Co.*, 9 F.R.D. 680 (E.D.Tenn. 1950). The amendment adopts the preponderant view.

In order still further to avoid unintended waivers of jury trial, the amendment provides that where by State law applicable in the court from which the case is removed a party is entitled to jury trial without making an express demand, he need not make a demand after removal. However, the district court for calendar or other purposes may on its own motion direct the parties to state whether they demand a jury, and the court must make such a direction upon the request of any party. Under the amendment a district court may find it convenient to establish a routine practice of giving these directions to the parties in appropriate cases.

Subdivision (f). The amendment recognizes the change of nomenclature made by Treasury Dept. Order 150–26(2), 18 Fed.Reg. 3499 (1953).

As to a special problem arising under Rule 25 (Substitution of parties) in actions for refund of taxes, see the Advisory Committee's Note to the amendment of Rule 25(d), effective July 19, 1961; and 4 *Moore's Federal Practice* ¶25.09 at 531 (2d ed. 1950).

1966 Amendment

See Note to Rule 1, supra.

Statutory proceedings to forfeit property for violation of the laws of the United States, formerly governed by the admiralty rules, will be governed by the unified and supplemental rules. See Supplemental Rule A.

Upon the recommendation of the judges of the United States District Court for the District of Columbia, the Federal Rules of Civil Procedure are made applicable to probate proceedings in that court. The exception with regard to adoption proceedings is removed because the court no longer has jurisdiction of those matters; and the words "mental health" are substituted for "lunacy" to conform to the current characterization in the District.

The purpose of the amendment to paragraph (3) is to permit the deletion from Rule 73(a) of the clause "unless a shorter time is provided by law." The 10 day period fixed for an appeal under 45 U.S.C. § 159 is the only instance of a shorter time provided for appeals in civil cases. Apart from the unsettling effect of the clause, it is eliminated because its retention would preserve the 15 day period heretofore allowed by 28 U.S.C. § 2107 for appeals from interlocutory decrees in admiralty, it being one of the purposes of the amendment to make the time for appeals in civil and admiralty cases uniform under the unified rules. See Advisory Committee's Note to subdivision (a) of Rule 73.

1968 Amendment

The amendments eliminate inappropriate references to appellate procedure.

1971 Amendment

Title 28, U.S.C., § 2243 now requires that the custodian of a person detained must respond to an application for a writ of habeas corpus "within three days unless for good cause additional time, not exceeding twenty days, is allowed." The amendment increases to forty days the additional time that the district court may allow in habeas corpus proceedings involving persons in custody pursuant to a judgment of a state court. The substantial increase in the number of such proceedings in recent years has placed a considerable burden on state authorities. Twenty days has proved in practice too short a time in which to prepare and file the return in many such cases. Allowance of additional time should, of course, be granted only for good cause.

While the time allowed in such a case for the return of the writ may not exceed forty days, this does not mean that the state must necessarily be limited to that period of time to provide for the federal court the transcript of the proceedings of a state trial or plenary hearing if the transcript must be prepared after the habeas corpus proceeding has begun in the federal court.

1987 Amendment

The amendments are technical. No substantive change is intended.

2001 Amendments

Former Copyright Rule 1 made the Civil Rules applicable to copyright proceedings except to the extent the Civil Rules were inconsistent with Copyright Rules. Abrogation of the Copyright Rules leaves the Civil Rules fully applicable to copyright proceedings. Rule 81(a)(1) is amended to reflect this change.

The District of Columbia Court Reform and Criminal Procedure Act of 1970, Pub.L. 91–358, 84 Stat. 473, transferred mental health proceedings formerly held in the United States District Court for the District of Columbia to local District of Columbia courts. The provision that the Civil Rules do not apply to these proceedings is deleted as superfluous.

The reference to incorporation of the Civil Rules in the Federal Rules of Bankruptcy Procedure has been restyled.

Changes Made After Publication and Comments

The Committee Note was amended to correct the inadvertent omission of a negative. As revised, it correctly reflects the language that is stricken from the rule.

2002 Amendments

This amendment brings Rule 81(a)(2) into accord with the Rules Governing § 2254 and § 2255 proceedings. In its present form, Rule 81(a)(2) includes return-time provisions that are inconsistent with the provisions in the Rules Governing §§ 2254 and 2255. The inconsistency should be eliminated, and it is better that the time provisions continue to be set out in the other rules without duplication in Rule 81. Rule 81 also directs that the writ be directed to the person having custody of the person detained. Similar directions exist in the § 2254 and § 2255 rules, providing additional detail for applicants subject to future custody. There is no need for partial duplication in Rule 81.

The provision that the civil rules apply to the extent that practice is not set forth in the § 2254 and § 2255 rules dovetails with the provisions in Rule 11 of the § 2254 rules and Rule 12 of the § 2255 rules.

Changes Made After Publication and Comment The only change since publication is deletion of an inadvertent reference to § 2241 proceedings.

2007 Amendments

[Effective December 1, 2007, absent contrary Congressional action.]

The language of Rule 81 has been amended as part of the general restyling of the Civil Rules to make them more easily understood and to make style and terminology consistent throughout the rules. These changes are intended to be stylistic only.

Rule 81(c) has been revised to reflect the amendment of 28 U.S.C. § 1446(a) that changed the procedure for removal fiom a petition for removal to a notice of removal.

Former Rule 81(e), drafted before the decision in *Erie R.R. v. Tompkins*, 304 U.S. 64 (1938), defined state law to include "the statutes of that state and the state judicial

decisions construing them." The *Erie* decision reinterpreted the Rules of Decision Act, now 28 U.S.C. § 1652, recognizing that the "laws" of the states include the common law established by judicial decisions. Long-established practice reflects this understanding, looking to state common law as well as statutes and court rules when a Civil Rule directs use of state law. Amended Rule 81(d)(1) adheres to this practice, including all state judicial decisions, not only those that construe state statutes.

Former Rule 81(f) is deleted. The office of district director of internal revenue was abolished by restructuring under the Internal Revenue Service Restructuring and Reform Act of 1998, Pub.L. 105–206, July 22, 1998, 26 U.S.C. § 1 Note.

HISTORICAL NOTES

Effective Date of Abrogation

Abrogation of par. (7) of subdivision (a) of this rule as effective Aug. 1, 1951, see Effective Date note incorporated within the Supplementary Report set out under the heading 1951 Addition in the Advisory Committee Notes appearing under Rule 71A of these rules.

Pending Actions

For applicability of Supreme Court amendments to pending cases, see Orders of the Supreme Court of the United States Adopting and Amending Rules set out preceding Rule 1 of these rules.

Rule 82.　Jurisdiction and Venue Unaffected

These rules shall not be construed to extend or limit the jurisdiction of the United States district courts or the venue of actions therein. An admiralty or maritime claim within the meaning of Rule 9(h) shall not be treated as a civil action for the purposes of Title 28, U.S.C., §§ 1391–1392.

(As amended Dec. 29, 1948, eff. Oct. 20, 1949; Feb. 28, 1966, eff. July 1, 1966; Apr. 23, 2001, eff. Dec. 1, 2001.)

Proposed Amendment of Rule

Effective December 1, 2007, absent contrary Congressional action, this rule is amended to read as follows:

Rule 82.　*Jurisdiction and Venue Unaffected*

These rules do not extend or limit the jurisdiction of the district courts or the venue of actions in those courts. An admiralty or maritime claim under Rule 9(h) is not a civil action for purposes of 28 U.S.C. §§ 1391–1392.

ADVISORY COMMITTEE NOTES

1937 Adoption

These rules grant extensive power of joining claims and counterclaims in one action, but, as this rule states, such grant does not extend federal jurisdiction. The rule is declaratory of existing practice under the [former] Federal Equity Rules with regard to such provisions as [former] Equity Rule 26 on Joinder of Causes of Action and [former] Equity Rule 30 on Counterclaims. Compare Shulman and

Jaegerman, *Some Jurisdictional Limitations on Federal Procedure*, 45 Yale L.J. 393 (1936).

1948 Amendment

The amendment effective October 1949, substituted the words "United States district courts" for "district courts of the United States."

1966 Amendment

Title 28, U.S.C., § 1391(b) provides: "A civil action wherein jurisdiction is not founded solely on diversity of citizenship may be brought only in the judicial district where all defendants reside, except as otherwise provided by law." This provision cannot appropriately be applied to what were formerly suits in admiralty. The rationale of decisions holding it inapplicable rests largely on the use of the term "civil action": i.e., a suit in admiralty is not a "civil action" within the statute. By virtue of the amendment to Rule 1, the provisions of Rule 2 convert suits in admiralty into civil actions. The added sentence is necessary to avoid an undesirable change in existing law with respect to venue.

2001 Amendments

The final sentence of Rule 82 is amended to delete the reference to 28 U.S.C. § 1393, which has been repealed.

Style Comment

The recommendation that the change be made without publication carries with it a recommendation that style changes not be made. Styling would carry considerable risks. The first sentence of Rule 82, for example, states that the Civil Rules do not "extend or limit the jurisdiction of the United States district courts." That sentence is a flat lie if "jurisdiction" includes personal or quasi-in rem jurisdiction. The styling project on this rule requires publication and comment.

2007 Amendments

[Effective December 1, 2007, absent contrary Congressional action.]

The language of Rule 82 has been amended as part of the general restyling of the Civil Rules to make them more easily understood and to make style and terminology consistent throughout the rules. These changes are intended to be stylistic only.

Rule 83.　Rules by District Courts; Judge's Directives

(a) Local Rules

(1) Each district court, acting by a majority of its district judges, may, after giving appropriate public notice and an opportunity for comment, make and amend rules governing its practice. A local rule shall be consistent with—but not duplicative of— Acts of Congress and rules adopted under 28 U.S.C. §§ 2072 and 2075, and shall conform to any uniform numbering system prescribed by the Judicial Conference of the United States. A local rule takes effect on the date specified by the district court and remains in effect unless amended by the court or

abrogated by the judicial council of the circuit. Copies of rules and amendments shall, upon their promulgation, be furnished to the judicial council and the Administrative Office of the United States Courts and be made available to the public.

(2) A local rule imposing a requirement of form shall not be enforced in a manner that causes a party to lose rights because of a nonwillful failure to comply with the requirement.

(b) Procedures When There is No Controlling Law. A judge may regulate practice in any manner consistent with federal law, rules adopted under 28 U.S.C. §§ 2072 and 2075, and local rules of the district. No sanction or other disadvantage may be imposed for noncompliance with any requirement not in federal law, federal rules, or the local district rules unless the alleged violator has been furnished in the particular case with actual notice of the requirement. (As amended Apr. 29, 1985, eff. Aug. 1, 1985; Apr. 27, 1995, eff. Dec. 1, 1995.)

Proposed Amendment of Rule

Effective December 1, 2007, absent contrary Congressional action, this rule is amended to read as follows:

Rule 83. Rules by District Courts; Judge's Directives

(a) Local Rules.

(1) In General. After giving public notice and an opportunity for comment, a district court, acting by a majority of its district judges, may adopt and amend rules governing its practice. A local rule must be consistent with—but not duplicate—federal statutes and rules adopted under 28 U.S.C. §§ 2072 and 2075, and must conform to any uniform numbering system prescribed by the Judicial Conference of the United States. A local rule takes effect on the date specified by the district court and remains in effect unless amended by the court or abrogated by the judicial council of the circuit. Copies of rules and amendments must, on their adoption, be furnished to the judicial council and the Administrative Office of the United States Courts and be made available to the public.

(2) Requirement of Form. A local rule imposing a requirement of form must not be enforced in a way that causes a party to lose any right because of a nonwillful failure to comply.

(b) Procedure When There Is No Controlling Law. *A judge may regulate practice in any manner consistent with federal law, rules adopted under 28 U.S.C. §§ 2072 and 2075, and the district's local rules. No sanction or other disadvantage may be imposed for noncompliance with any requirement not in feder-*

al law, federal rules, or the local rules unless the alleged violator has been furnished in the particular case with actual notice of the requirement.

ADVISORY COMMITTEE NOTES

1937 Adoption

This rule substantially continues U.S.C., Title 28, § 2071, formerly § 731 (Rules of practice in district courts) with the additional requirement that copies of such rules and amendments be furnished to the Supreme Court of the United States. See [former] Equity Rule 79 (Additional Rules by District Court). With the last sentence compare United States Supreme Court Admiralty Rules, 1920, Rule 44 (Right of Trial Courts to Make Rules of Practice) (originally promulgated in 1842).

1985 Amendment

Rule 83, which has not been amended since the Federal Rules were promulgated in 1938, permits each district to adopt local rules not inconsistent with the Federal Rules by a majority of the judges. The only other requirement is that copies be furnished to the Supreme Court.

The widespread adoption of local rules and the modest procedural prerequisites for their promulgation have led many commentators to question the soundness of the process as well as the validity of some rules. See 12 C. Wright & A. Miller, *Federal Practice and Procedure: Civil* § 3152, at 217 (1973); Caballero, *Is There an Over-Exercise of Local Rule-Making Powers by the United States District Courts?*, 24 Fed.Bar News 325 (1977). Although the desirability of local rules for promoting uniform practice within a district is widely accepted, several commentators also have suggested reforms to increase the quality, simplicity, and uniformity of the local rules. See Note, *Rule 83 and the Local Federal Rules*, 67 Colum.L.Rev. 1251 (1967), and Comment, *The Local Rules of Civil Procedure in the Federal District Courts—A Survey*, 1966 Duke L.J. 1011.

The amended Rule attempts, without impairing the procedural validity of existing local rules, to enhance the local rulemaking process by requiring appropriate public notice of proposed rules and an opportunity to comment on them. Although some district courts apparently consult the local bar before promulgating rules, many do not, which has led to criticism of a process that has district judges consulting only with each other. See 12 C. Wright & A. Miller, *supra*, § 3152, at 217; Blair, *The New Local Rules for Federal Practice in Iowa*, 23 Drake L.Rev. 517 (1974). The new language subjects local rulemaking to scrutiny similar to that accompanying the Federal Rules, administrative rulemaking, and legislation. It attempts to assure that the expert advice of practitioners and scholars is made available to the district court before local rules are promulgated. See Weinstein, *Reform of Court Rule-Making Procedures* 84–87, 127–37, 151 (1977).

The amended Rule does not detail the procedure for giving notice and an opportunity to be heard since conditions vary from district to district. Thus, there is no explicit requirement for a public hearing, although a district may consider that procedure appropriate in all or some rulemaking situations. See generally, Weinstein, *supra*, at 117–37, 151. The new Rule does not foreclose any other form of consultation. For example, it can be accomplished through the mechanism

of an "Advisory Committee" similar to that employed by the Supreme Court in connection with the Federal Rules themselves.

The amended Rule provides that a local rule will take effect upon the date specified by the district court and will remain in effect unless amended by the district court or abrogated by the judicial council. The effectiveness of a local rule should not be deferred until approved by the judicial council because that might unduly delay promulgation of a local rule that should become effective immediately, especially since some councils do not meet frequently. Similarly, it was thought that to delay a local rule's effectiveness for a fixed period of time would be arbitrary and that to require the judicial council to abrogate a local rule within a specified time would be inconsistent with its power under 28 U.S.C. § 332 (1976) to nullify a local rule at any time. The expectation is that the judicial council will examine all local rules, including those currently in effect, with an eye toward determining whether they are valid and consistent with the Federal Rules, promote inter-district uniformity and efficiency, and do not undermine the basic objectives of the Federal Rules.

The amended Rule requires copies of local rules to be sent upon their promulgation to the judicial council and the Administrative Office of the United States Courts rather than to the Supreme Court. The Supreme Court was the appropriate filing place in 1938, when Rule 83 originally was promulgated, but the establishment of the Administrative Office makes it a more logical place to develop a centralized file of local rules. This procedure is consistent with both the Criminal and the Appellate Rules. See Fed.R.Crim.P. 57(a); Fed.R.App.P. 47. The Administrative Office also will be able to provide improved utilization of the file because of its recent development of a Local Rules Index.

The practice pursued by some judges of issuing standing orders has been controversial, particularly among members of the practicing bar. The last sentence in Rule 83 has been amended to make certain that standing orders are not inconsistent with the Federal Rules or any local district court rules. Beyond that, it is hoped that each district will adopt procedures, perhaps by local rule, for promulgating and reviewing single-judge standing orders.

1995 Amendments

Subdivision (a). This rule is amended to reflect the requirement that local rules be consistent not only with the national rules but also with Acts of Congress. The amendment also states that local rules should not repeat Acts of Congress or national rules.

The amendment also requires that the numbering of local rules conform with any uniform numbering system that may be prescribed by the Judicial Conference. Lack of uniform numbering might create unnecessary traps for counsel and litigants. A uniform numbering system would make it easier for an increasingly national bar and for litigants to locate a local rule that applies to a particular procedural issue.

Paragraph (2) is new. Its aim is to protect against loss of rights in the enforcement of local rules relating to matters of form. For example, a party should not be deprived of a right to a jury trial because its attorney, unaware of—or forgetting—a local rule directing that jury demands be noted in the caption of the case, includes a jury demand only in the body of the pleading. The proscription of paragraph (2) is narrowly drawn—covering only violations attributable to nonwillful failure to comply and only those involving local rules directed to matters of form. It does not limit the court's power to impose substantive penalties upon a party if it or its attorney contumaciously or willfully violates a local rule, even one involving merely a matter of form. Nor does it affect the court's power to enforce local rules that involve more than mere matters of form—for example, a local rule requiring parties to identify evidentiary matters relied upon to support or oppose motions for summary judgment.

Subdivision (b). This rule provides flexibility to the court in regulating practice when there is no controlling law. Specifically, it permits the court to regulate practice in any manner consistent with Acts of Congress, with rules adopted under 28 U.S.C. §§ 2072 and 2075, and with the district local rules.

This rule recognizes that courts rely on multiple directives to control practice. Some courts regulate practice through the published Federal Rules and the local rules of the court. Some courts also have used internal operating procedures, standing orders, and other internal directives. Although such directives continue to be authorized, they can lead to problems. Counsel or litigants may be unaware of various directives. In addition, the sheer volume of directives may impose an unreasonable barrier. For example, it may be difficult to obtain copies of the directives. Finally, counsel or litigants may be unfairly sanctioned for failing to comply with a directive. For these reasons, the amendment to this rule disapproves imposing any sanction or other disadvantage on a person for noncompliance with such an internal directive, unless the alleged violator has been furnished actual notice of the requirement in a particular case.

There should be no adverse consequence to a party or attorney for violating special requirements relating to practice before a particular court unless the party or attorney has actual notice of those requirements. Furnishing litigants with a copy outlining the judge's practices—or attaching instructions to a notice setting a case for conference or trial—would suffice to give actual notice, as would an order in a case specifically adopting by reference a judge's standing order and indicating how copies can be obtained.

2007 Amendments

*[Effective December 1, 2007,
absent contrary Congressional action.]*

The language of Rule 83 has been amended as part of the general restyling of the Civil Rules to make them more easily understood and to make style and terminology consistent throughout the rules. These changes are intended to be stylistic only.

HISTORICAL NOTES

Change of Name

Reference to United States magistrate or to magistrate deemed to refer to United States magistrate judge pursuant to section 321 of Pub.L. 101–650, set out as a note under section 631 of this title.

Rule 84. Forms

The forms contained in the Appendix of Forms are sufficient under the rules and are intended to indicate the simplicity and brevity of statement which the rules contemplate.

(As amended Dec. 27, 1946, eff. Mar. 19, 1948.)

Proposed Amendment of Rule

Effective December 1, 2007, absent contrary Congressional action, this rule is amended to read as follows:

Rule 84. Forms

The forms in the Appendix suffice under these rules and illustrate the simplicity and brevity that these rules contemplate.

ADVISORY COMMITTEE NOTES

1937 Adoption

In accordance with the practice found useful in many codes, provision is here made for a limited number of official forms which may serve as guides in pleading. Compare 2 Mass.Gen.Laws (Ter.Ed., 1932) ch. 231, § 147, Forms 1–47; *English Annual Practice* (1937) Appendix A to M, inclusive; *Conn.Practice Book* (1934) Rules, 47–68, pp. 123 to 427.

1946 Amendment

Note. The amendment serves to emphasize that the forms contained in the Appendix of Forms are sufficient to withstand attack under the rules under which they are drawn, and that the practitioner using them may rely on them to that extent. The circuit courts of appeals generally have upheld the use of the forms as promoting desirable simplicity and brevity of statement. *Sierocinski v. E. I. DuPont DeNemours & Co.*, C.C.A.3, 1939, 103 F.2d 843; *Swift & Co. v. Young*, C.C.A.4, 1939, 107 F.2d 170; *Sparks v. England*, C.C.A.8, 1940, 113 F.2d 579; *Ramsouer v. Midland Valley R. Co.*, C.C.A.8, 1943, 135 F.2d 101. And the forms as a whole have met with widespread approval in the courts. See cases cited in 1 Moore's Federal Practice, 1938, Cum. Supplement § 8.07, under "Page 554"; see also Commentary, The Official Forms, 1941, 4 Fed.Rules Serv. 954. In Cook, "Facts" and "Statements of Fact", 1937, 4 U.Chi.L.Rev. 233, 245–246, it is said with reference to what is now Rule 84: ". . . pleaders in the federal courts are not to be left to guess as to the meaning of [the] language" in Rule 8(a) regarding the form of the complaint. "All of which is as it should be. In no other way can useless litigation be avoided." Ibid. The amended rule will operate to discourage isolated results such as those found in *Washburn v. Moorman Mfg. Co.*, S.D.Cal. 1938, 25 F.Supp. 546; *Employers Mutual Liability Ins. Co. of Wisconsin v. Blue Line Transfer Co.*, W.D.Mo.1941, 2 F.R.D. 121, 5 Fed.Rules Serv. 12e.235, Case 2.

2007 Amendments

[Effective December 1, 2007, absent contrary Congressional action.]

The language of Rule 84 has been amended as part of the general restyling of the Civil Rules to make them more easily understood and to make style and terminology consistent throughout the rules. These changes are intended to be stylistic only.

Rule 85. Title

These rules may be known and cited as the Federal Rules of Civil Procedure.

Proposed Amendment of Rule

Effective December 1, 2007, absent contrary Congressional action, this rule is amended to read as follows:

Rule 85. Title

These rules may be cited as the Federal Rules of Civil Procedure.

ADVISORY COMMITTEE NOTES

2007 Amendments

[Effective December 1, 2007, absent contrary Congressional action.]

The language of Rule 85 has been amended as part of the general restyling of the Civil Rules to make them more easily understood and to make style and terminology consistent throughout the rules. These changes are intended to be stylistic only.

Rule 86. Effective Date

(a) [Effective Date of Original Rules].[1] These rules will take effect on the day which is 3 months subsequent to the adjournment of the second regular session of the 75th Congress, but if that day is prior to September 1, 1938, then these rules will take effect on September 1, 1938. They govern all proceedings in actions brought after they take effect and also all further proceedings in actions then pending, except to the extent that in the opinion of the court their application in a particular action pending when the rules take effect would not be feasible or would work injustice, in which event the former procedure applies.

(b) Effective Date of Amendments. The amendments adopted by the Supreme Court on December 27, 1946, and transmitted to the Attorney General on January 2, 1947, shall take effect on the day which is three months subsequent to the adjournment of the first regular session of the 80th Congress, but, if that day is prior to September 1, 1947, then these amendments shall take effect on September 1, 1947. They govern all proceedings in actions brought after they take effect and also all further proceedings in actions then pending, except to the extent that in the opinion of the court their application in a particular action pending when the amendments take effect would not be feasible or would work injustice, in which event the former procedure applies.

(c) Effective Date of Amendments. The amendments adopted by the Supreme Court on December 29, 1948, and transmitted to the Attorney General on

December 31, 1948, shall take effect on the day following the adjournment of the first regular session of the 81st Congress.

(d) Effective Date of Amendments. The amendments adopted by the Supreme Court on April 17, 1961, and transmitted to the Congress on April 18, 1961, shall take effect on July 19, 1961. They govern all proceedings in actions brought after they take effect and also all further proceedings in actions then pending, except to the extent that in the opinion of the court their application in a particular action pending when the amendments take effect would not be feasible or would work injustice, in which event the former procedure applies.

(e) Effective Date of Amendments. The amendments adopted by the Supreme Court on January 21, 1963, and transmitted to the Congress on January 21, 1963, shall take effect on July 1, 1963. They govern all proceedings in actions brought after they take effect and also all further proceedings in actions then pending, except to the extent that in the opinion of the court their application in a particular action pending when the amendments take effect would not be feasible or would work injustice, in which event the former procedure applies.

(As amended Dec. 27, 1946, eff. Mar. 19, 1948; Dec. 29, 1948, eff. Oct. 20, 1949; Apr. 17, 1961, eff. July 19, 1961; Jan. 21 and Mar. 18, 1963, eff. July 1, 1963.)

1 Subdivision heading supplied editorially.

Proposed Amendment of Rule

Effective December 1, 2007, absent contrary Congressional action, this rule is amended to read as follows:

Rule 86. Effective Dates

(a) In General. These rules and any amendments take effect at the time specified by the Supreme Court, subject to 28 U.S.C. § 2074. They govern:

(1) proceedings in an action commenced after their effective date; and

(2) proceedings after that date in an action then pending unless:

(A) the Supreme Court specifies otherwise; or

(B) the court determines that applying them in a particular action would be infeasible or work an injustice.

(b) December 1, 2007 Amendments. If any provision in Rules 1–5.1, 6–73, or 77–86 conflicts with another law, priority in time for the purpose of 28 U.S.C. § 2072(b) is not affected by the amendments taking effect on December 1, 2007.

ADVISORY COMMITTEE NOTES

1937 Adoption

See former Equity Rule 81 (These Rules Effective February 1, 1913—Old Rules Abrogated).

2007 Amendments

[Effective December 1, 2007, absent contrary Congressional action.]

The language of Rule 86 has been amended as part of the general restyling of the Civil Rules to make them more easily understood and to make style and terminology consistent throughout the rules. These changes are intended to be stylistic only.

The subdivisions that provided a list of the effective dates of the original Civil Rules and amendments made up to 1963 are deleted as no longer useful.

Rule 86(b) is added to clarify the relationship of amendments taking effect on December 1, 2007, to other laws for the purpose of applying the "supersession" clause in 28 U.S.C. § 2072(b). Section 2072(b) provides that a law in conflict with an Enabling Act Rule "shall be of no further force or effect after such rule[] ha[s] taken effect." The amendments that take effect on December 1, 2007, result from the general restyling of the Civil Rules and from a small number of technical revisions adopted on a parallel track. None of these amendments is intended to affect resolution of any conflict that might arise between a rule and another law. Rule 86(b) makes this intent explicit. Any conflict that arises should be resolved by looking to the date the specific conflicting rule provision first became effective.

HISTORICAL NOTES

Effective and Applicability Provisions

1948 Amendments

The first regular session of the 81st Congress adjourned sine die on Oct. 19, 1949, therefore the amendments to Rules 1, 17, 22, 24, 25, 27, 37, 45, 57, 60, 65, 66, 67, 69, 72–76, 79, 81, 82, and 86 and to forms 1, 19, 22, 23, and 27 became effective on Oct. 20, 1949, following the adjournment as provided for in subsection (c) of this rule.

1946 Amendments

The first regular session of the 80th Congress adjourned sine die on Friday, Dec. 19, 1947, therefore the amendments to Rules 6, 7, 12, 13, 14, 17, 24, 26, 27, 28, 33, 34, 36, 41, 45, 52, 54, 56, 58, 59, 60, 62, 65, 66, 68, 73, 75, 77, 79, 80, 81, 84, and 86, became effective Mar. 19, 1948 as provided for in subsection (b) of this rule.

Effective Date of 1970 Amendments; Transmission to Congress

Sections 2 and 3 of the Order of the Supreme Court, dated Mar. 30, 1970, provided:

"2. That the foregoing amendments to the Rules of Civil Procedure shall take effect on July 1, 1970, and shall govern all proceedings in actions brought thereafter and also in all further proceedings in actions then pending, except to the extent that in the opinion of the court their application in a particular action then pending would not be feasible or would work injustice, in which event the former procedure applies.

"3. That the Chief Justice be, and he hereby is, authorized to transmit to the Congress the foregoing amendments to the Rules of Civil Procedure in accordance with the provisions of Title 28, U.S.C. § 2072."

Effective Date of 1966 Amendment; Transmission to Congress; Rescission

Sections 2 to 4 of the Order of the Supreme Court, dated Feb. 28, 1966, 383 U.S. 1031, provided:

"2. That the foregoing amendments and additions to the Rules of Civil Procedure shall take effect on July 1, 1966, and shall govern all proceedings in actions brought thereafter and also in all further proceedings in actions then pending, except to the extent that in the opinion of the court their application in a particular action then pending would not be feasible or would work injustice, in which event the former procedure applies.

"3. That the Chief Justice be, and he hereby is, authorized to transmit to the Congress the foregoing amendments and additions to the Rules of Civil Procedure in accordance with the provisions of Title 28, U.S.C., §§ 2072 and 2073.

"4. That: (a) subdivision (c) of Rule 6 of the Rules of Civil Procedure for the United States District Courts promulgated by this court on December 20, 1937, effective September 16, 1938; (b) Rule 2 of the Rules for Practice and Procedure under section 25 of An Act To amend and consolidate the Acts respecting copyright, approved March 4, 1909, promulgated by this court on June 1, 1909, effective July 1, 1909; and (c) the Rules of Practice in Admiralty and Maritime Cases, promulgated by this court on December 6, 1920, effective March 7, 1921, as revised, amended and supplemented, be, and they hereby are, rescinded, effective July 1, 1966."

APPENDIX OF FORMS

(See Rule 84)

Amendment of Forms

Forms 1 to 35 effective until December 1, 2007.

For forms effective December 1, 2007, absent contrary Congressional action, see Forms 1 to 82 following this Appendix of Forms.

INTRODUCTORY STATEMENT

1. The following forms are intended for illustration only. They are limited in number. No attempt is made to furnish a manual of forms. Each form assumes the action to be brought in the Southern District of New York. If the district in which an action is brought has divisions, the division should be indicated in the caption.

2. Except where otherwise indicated each pleading, motion, and other paper should have a caption similar to that of the summons, with the designation of the particular paper substituted for the word "Summons." In the caption of the summons and in the caption of the complaint all parties must be named but in other pleadings and papers, it is sufficient to state the name of the first party on either side, with an appropriate indication of other parties. See Rules 4(b), 7(b)(2), and 10(a).

3. In Form 3 and the forms following, the words, "Allegation of jurisdiction," are used to indicate the appropriate allegation in Form 2.

4. Each pleading, motion, and other paper is to be signed in his individual name by at least one attorney of record (Rule 11). The attorney's name is to be followed by his address as indicated in Form 3. In forms following Form 3 the signature and address are not indicated.

5. If a party is not represented by an attorney, the signature and address of the party are required in place of those of the attorney.

Form 1. Summons

Form effective until December 1, 2007.

United States District Court for the
Southern District of New York

Civil Action, File Number _____

A. B., Plaintiff)
 v.) *Summons*
C. D., Defendant)

To the above-named Defendant:

You are hereby summoned and required to serve upon _____, plaintiff's attorney, whose address is _____, an answer to the complaint which is herewith served upon you, within 20 [1] days after service of this summons upon you, exclusive of the day of service. If you fail to do so, judgment by default will be taken against you for the relief demanded in the complaint.

 Clerk of Court.

[Seal of the U.S. District Court]

Dated _____

(This summons is issued pursuant to Rule 4 of the Federal Rules of Civil Procedure)

(As amended Dec. 29, 1948, eff. Oct. 20, 1949.)

[1] If the United States or an officer or agency there of is a defendant, the time to be inserted as to it is 60 days.

Amendment of Forms

Form effective until December 1, 2007. For forms effective December 1, 2007, absent contrary Congres-

sional action, see Forms 1 to 82 following this Appendix of Forms.

Form 1A. Notice of Lawsuit and Request for Waiver of Service of Summons

Form effective until December 1, 2007.

TO: (A)

[as (B) of (C)]

A lawsuit has been commenced against you (or the entity on whose behalf you are addressed). A copy of the complaint is attached to this notice. It has been filed in the United States District Court for the (D) and has been assigned docket number (E).

This is not a formal summons or notification from the court, but rather my request that you sign and return the enclosed waiver of service in order to save the cost of serving you with a judicial summons and an additional copy of the complaint. The cost of service will be avoided if I receive a signed copy of the waiver within (F) days after the date designated below as the date on which this Notice and Request is sent. I enclose a stamped and addressed envelope (or other means of cost-free return) for your use. An extra copy of the waiver is also attached for your records.

If you comply with this request and return the signed waiver, it will be filed with the court and no summons will be served on you. The action will then proceed as if you had been served on the date the waiver is filed, except that you will not be obligated to answer the complaint before 60 days from the date designated below as the date on which this notice is sent (or before 90 days from that date if your address is not in any judicial district of the United States).

If you do not return the signed waiver within the time indicated, I will take appropriate steps to effect formal service in a manner authorized by the Federal Rules of Civil Procedure and will then, to the extent authorized by those Rules, ask the court to require you (or the party on whose behalf you are addressed) to pay the full costs of such service. In that connection, please read the statement concerning the duty of parties to waive the service of the summons, which is set forth on the reverse side (or at the foot) of the waiver form.

I affirm that this request is being sent to you on behalf of the plaintiff, this ___ day of _____, _____.

Signature of Plaintiff's Attorney
or Unrepresented Plaintiff

Notes:

A—Name of individual defendant (or name of officer or agent of corporate defendant)

B—Title, or other relationship of individual to corporate defendant

C—Name of corporate defendants, if any

D—District

E—Docket number of action

F—Addresses must be given at least 30 days (60 days if located in foreign country) in which to return waiver

(Added Apr. 22, 1993, eff. Dec. 1, 1993.)

Amendment of Forms

Form effective until December 1, 2007. For forms effective December 1, 2007, absent contrary Congressional action, see Forms 1 to 82 following this Appendix of Forms.

ADVISORY COMMITTEE NOTES

1993 Adoption

Forms 1A and 1B reflect the revision of Rule 4. They replace Form 18–A.

HISTORICAL NOTES

Effective and Applicability Provisions of Enactment and Abrogation

1991 Acts

Amendments by Supreme Court Order dated Apr. 30, 1991, adding Form 1A "Notice of Lawsuit and Request for Waiver of Service of Summons" and Form 1B "Waiver of Service of Summons" became effective Dec. 1, 1991. Pub.L. 102–198, § 11(b), Dec. 9, 1991, 105 Stat. 1626, set out as a note under section 2074 of Title 28, Judiciary and Judicial Procedure, provided that, effective Dec. 9, 1991, Forms 1A and 1B are not to be effective.

Form 1B. Waiver of Service of Summons

Form effective until December 1, 2007.

TO: (name of plaintiff's attorney or unrepresented plaintiff)

I acknowledge receipt of your request that I waive service of a summons in the action of (caption of action), which is case number (docket number) in the United States District Court for the (district). I have also received a copy of the complaint in the action, two copies of this instrument, and a means by which I can return the signed waiver to you without cost to me.

I agree to save the cost of service of a summons and an additional copy of the complaint in this lawsuit by not requiring that I (or the entity on whose behalf I am acting) be served with judicial process in the manner provided by Rule 4.

I (or the entity on whose behalf I am acting) will retain all defenses or objections to the lawsuit or to the jurisdiction or venue of the court except for objections based on a defect in the summons or in the service of the summons.

I understand that a judgment may be entered against me (or the party on whose behalf I am acting) if an answer or motion under Rule 12 is not served upon you within 60 days after (date request was sent),

or within 90 days after that date if the request was sent outside the United States.

Date	Signature

Printed/typed name: _____

 [as _____]

 [of _____]

To be printed on reverse side of the waiver form or set forth at the foot of the form:

Duty to Avoid Unnecessary Costs of Service of Summons

Rule 4 of the Federal Rules of Civil Procedure requires certain parties to cooperate in saving unnecessary costs of service of the summons and complaint. A defendant located in the United States who, after being notified of an action and asked by a plaintiff located in the United States to waive service of a summons, fails to do so will be required to bear the cost of such service unless good cause be shown for its failure to sign and return the waiver.

It is not good cause for a failure to waive service that a party believes that the complaint is unfounded, or that the action has been brought in an improper place or in a court that lacks jurisdiction over the subject matter of the action or over its person or property. A party who waives service of the summons retains all defenses and objections (except any relating to the summons or to the service of the summons), and may later object to the jurisdiction of the court or to the place where the action has been brought.

A defendant who waives service must within the time specified on the waiver form serve on the plaintiff's attorney (or unrepresented plaintiff) a response to the complaint and must also file a signed copy of the response with the court. If the answer or motion is not served within this time, a default judgment may be taken against that defendant. By waiving service, a defendant is allowed more time to answer than if the summons had been actually served when the request for waiver of service was received.

(Added Apr. 22, 1993, eff. Dec. 1, 1993.)

Amendment of Forms

Form effective until December 1, 2007. For forms effective December 1, 2007, absent contrary Congressional action, see Forms 1 to 82 following this Appendix of Forms.

ADVISORY COMMITTEE NOTES

1993 Adoption

Forms 1A and 1B reflect the revision of Rule 4. They replace Form 18–A.

HISTORICAL NOTES

Effective and Applicability Provisions of Enactment and Abrogation

1991 Acts

Amendments by Supreme Court Order dated Apr. 30, 1991, adding Form 1A "Notice of Lawsuit and Request for Waiver of Service of Summons" and Form 1B "Waiver of Service of Summons" became effective Dec. 1, 1991. Pub.L. 102–198, § 11(b), Dec. 9, 1991, 105 Stat. 1626, set out as a note under section 2074 of Title 28, Judiciary and Judicial Procedure, provided that, effective Dec. 9, 1991, Forms 1A and 1B are not to be effective.

Congressional Action Contrary to Supreme Court Enactment of Form

Enactment of Form 1–B, relating to waiver of service of summons, as transmitted to Congress by the Supreme Court pursuant to section 2074 of this title, which was to take effect Dec. 1, 1991, was nullified by Congress, see section 11 of Pub.L. 102–198, set out as a note under section 2074 of this title.

Form 2. Allegation of Jurisdiction

Form effective until December 1, 2007.

(a) Jurisdiction founded on diversity of citizenship and amount.

Plaintiff is a [citizen of the State of Connecticut][1] [corporation incorporated under the laws of the State of Connecticut having its principal place of business in the State of Connecticut] and defendant is a corporation incorporated under the laws of the State of New York having its principal place of business in a State other than the State of Connecticut. The matter in controversy exceeds, exclusive of interest and costs, the sum specified by 28 U.S.C. § 1332.

(b) Jurisdiction founded on the existence of a Federal question.

The action arises under [the Constitution of the United States, Article ___, Section ___]; [the ___ Amendment to the Constitution of the United States, Section ___]; [the Act of ___, ___ Stat. ___; U.S.C., Title ___, § ___]; [the Treaty of the United States (here describe the treaty)][2] as hereinafter more fully appears.

(c) Jurisdiction founded on the existence of a question arising under particular statutes.

The action arises under the Act of ___, ___ Stat. ___; U.S.C., Title ___, § ___, as hereinafter more fully appears.

(d) Jurisdiction founded on the admiralty or maritime character of the claim.

This is a case of admiralty and maritime jurisdiction, as hereinafter more fully appears. [If the pleader wishes to invoke the distinctively maritime procedures referred to in Rule 9(h), add the following or its substantial equivalent: This is an admiral-

ty or maritime claim within the meaning of Rule 9(h).]

1 Form for natural person.

2 Use the appropriate phrase or phrases. The general allegation of the existence of a Federal question is ineffective unless the matters constituting the claim for relief as set forth in the complaint raise a Federal question.

NOTES

1. Diversity of citizenship. U.S.C., Title 28, § 1332 (Diversity of citizenship; amount in controversy; costs) as amended by PL 85–554, 72 Stat. 415, July 25, 1958, states in subsection (c) that "For the purposes of this section and section 1441 of this title [removable actions], a corporation shall be deemed a citizen of any State by which it has been incorporated and of the State where it has its principal place of business." Thus if the defendant corporation in Form 2(a) had its principal place of business in Connecticut, diversity of citizenship would not exist. An allegation regarding the principal place of business of each corporate party must be made in addition to an allegation regarding its place of incorporation.

2. Jurisdictional amount. U.S.C., Title 28, § 1331 (Federal question; amount in controversy; costs) and § 1332 (Diversity of citizenship; amount in controversy; costs), as amended by PL 85–554, 72 Stat. 415, July 25, 1958, require that the amount in controversy, exclusive of interest and costs, be in excess of $10,000. The allegation as to the amount in controversy may be omitted in any case where by law no jurisdictional amount is required. See, for example, U.S.C., Title 28, § 1338 (Patents, copyrights, trade-marks, and unfair competition), § 1343 (Civil rights and elective franchise).

3. Pleading venue. Since improper venue is a matter of defense, it is not necessary for plaintiff to include allegations showing the venue to be proper. See 1 *Moore's Federal Practice*, par. 0.140[1–4] (2d ed. 1959).

(As amended Apr. 17, 1961, eff. July 19, 1961; Feb. 28, 1966, eff. July 1, 1966; Apr. 22, 1993, eff. Dec. 1, 1993; Apr. 29, 1999, eff. Dec. 1, 1999.)

Amendment of Forms

Form effective until December 1, 2007. For forms effective December 1, 2007, absent contrary Congressional action, see Forms 1 to 82 following this Appendix of Forms.

ADVISORY COMMITTEE NOTES

1966 Amendment

Since the Civil Rules have not heretofore been applicable to proceedings in Admiralty (Rule 81(a)(1)), Form 2 naturally has not contained a provision for invoking the admiralty jurisdiction. The form has never purported to be comprehensive, as making provision for all possible grounds of jurisdiction; but a provision for invoking the admiralty jurisdiction is particularly appropriate as an incident of unification.

Certain distinctive features of the admiralty practice must be preserved in unification, just as certain distinctive characteristics of equity were preserved in the merger of law and equity in 1938. Rule 9(h) provides the device whereby, after unification, with its abolition of the distinction between civil actions and suits in admiralty, the pleader may indicate his choice of the distinctively maritime procedures, and designates those features that are preserved. This form illustrates an appropriate way in which the pleader may invoke those procedures. Use of this device is not necessary if the claim is cognizable only by virtue of the admiralty and maritime jurisdiction, nor if the claim is within the exclusive admiralty jurisdiction of the district court.

Omission of a statement such as this from the pleading indicates the pleader's choice that the action proceed as a conventional civil action, if this is jurisdictionally possible, without the distinctive maritime remedies and procedures. It should be remembered, however, that Rule 9(h) provides that a pleading may be amended to add or withdraw such an identifying statement subject to the principles stated in Rule 15.

1993 Amendments

This form is revised to reflect amendments to 28 U.S.C. §§ 1331 and 1332 providing jurisdiction for federal questions without regard to the amount in controversy and raising the amount required to be in controversy in diversity cases to fifty thousand dollars.

HISTORICAL NOTES

Effective and Applicability Provisions

1961 Amendments

Amendment adopted on Apr. 17, 1961, effective July 19, 1961, see Rule 86(d).

Form 3. Complaint on a Promissory Note

Form effective until December 1, 2007.

1. Allegation of jurisdiction.

2. Defendant on or about June 1, 1935, executed and delivered to plaintiff a promissory note [in the following words and figures: (here set out the note verbatim)]; [a copy of which is hereto annexed as Exhibit A]; [whereby defendant promised to pay to plaintiff or order [1] on June 1, 1936 the sum of _____ dollars with interest thereon at the rate of six percent. per annum].

3. Defendant owes to plaintiff the amount of said note and interest.

Wherefore plaintiff demands judgment against defendant for the sum of _____ dollars, interest, and costs.

Signed: _____
Attorney for Plaintiff.
Address: _____

NOTES

1. The pleader may use the material in one of the three sets of brackets. His choice will depend upon whether he desires to plead the document verbatim, or by exhibit, or according to its legal effect.

2. Under the rules free joinder of claims is permitted. See rules 8(e) and 18. Consequently the claims set forth in each and all of the following forms may be joined with this complaint or with each other. Ordinarily each claim should be stated in a separate division of the complaint, and the divisions should be designated as counts successively numbered. In particular the rules permit alternative and inconsistent pleading. See Form 10.

(As amended Jan. 21, 1963, eff. July 1, 1963.)

¹ So in original.

Amendment of Forms

Form effective until December 1, 2007. For forms effective December 1, 2007, absent contrary Congressional action, see Forms 1 to 82 following this Appendix of Forms.

ADVISORY COMMITTEE NOTES

1963 Amendment

At various places, these Forms [Forms 3, 4, 5, 6, 7, 8, 9, 10, 11, 12, 13, 18, 21] allege or refer to damages of "ten thousand dollars, interest, and costs," or the like. The Forms were written at a time when the jurisdictional amount in ordinary "diversity" and "Federal question" cases was an amount in excess of $3,000, exclusive of interest and costs, so the illustrative amounts set out in the Forms were adequate for jurisdictional purposes. However, U.S.C. Title 28, § 1331 (Federal question; amount in controversy; costs) and § 1332 (Diversity of citizenship; amount in controversy; costs), as amended by Pub.L. 85–554, 72 Stat. 415, July 25, 1958, now require that the amount in controversy, exclusive of interest and costs, be in excess of $10,000. Accordingly the Forms are misleading. They are amended at appropriate places by deleting the stated dollar amount and substituting a blank, to be properly filled in by the pleader.

Form 4. Complaint on an Account

Form effective until December 1, 2007.

1. Allegation of jurisdiction.

2. Defendant owes plaintiff _____ dollars according to the account hereto annexed as Exhibit A.

Wherefore (etc. as in Form 3).

(As amended Jan. 21, 1963, eff. July 1, 1963.)

Amendment of Forms

Form effective until December 1, 2007. For forms effective December 1, 2007, absent contrary Congressional action, see Forms 1 to 82 following this Appendix of Forms.

ADVISORY COMMITTEE NOTES

1963 Amendment

This form was amended in 1963 by deleting the stated dollar amount and substituting a blank, to be properly filled in by the pleader. See Note of Advisory Committee under Form 3.

Form 5. Complaint for Goods Sold and Delivered

Form effective until December 1, 2007.

1. Allegation of jurisdiction.

2. Defendant owes plaintiff _____ dollars for goods sold and delivered by plaintiff to defendant between June 1, 1936 and December 1, 1936.

Wherefore (etc. as in Form 3).

NOTE

This form may be used where the action is for an agreed price or for the reasonable value of the goods.

(As amended Jan. 21, 1963, eff. July 1, 1963.)

Amendment of Forms

Form effective until December 1, 2007. For forms effective December 1, 2007, absent contrary Congressional action, see Forms 1 to 82 following this Appendix of Forms.

ADVISORY COMMITTEE NOTES

1963 Amendment

This form was amended in 1963 by deleting the stated dollar amount and substituting a blank, to be properly filled in by the pleader. See Note of Advisory Committee under Form 3.

Form 6. Complaint for Money Lent

Form effective until December 1, 2007.

1. Allegation of jurisdiction.

2. Defendant owes plaintiff _____ dollars for money lent by plaintiff to defendant on June 1, 1936.

Wherefore (etc. as in Form 3).

(As amended Jan. 21, 1963, eff. July 1, 1963.)

Amendment of Forms

Form effective until December 1, 2007. For forms effective December 1, 2007, absent contrary Congressional action, see Forms 1 to 82 following this Appendix of Forms.

ADVISORY COMMITTEE NOTES

1963 Amendment

This form was amended in 1963 by deleting the stated dollar amount and substituting a blank, to be properly filled in by the pleader. See Note of Advisory Committee under Form 3.

Form 7. Complaint for Money Paid by Mistake

Form effective until December 1, 2007.

1. Allegation of jurisdiction.

2. Defendant owes plaintiff _____ dollars for money paid by plaintiff to defendant by mistake on June 1, 1936, under the following circumstances: [here state the circumstances with particularity—see Rule 9(b)].

Wherefore (etc. as in Form 3).

(As amended Jan. 21, 1963, eff. July 1, 1963.)

Amendment of Forms

Form effective until December 1, 2007. For forms effective December 1, 2007, absent contrary Congressional action, see Forms 1 to 82 following this Appendix of Forms.

ADVISORY COMMITTEE NOTES

1963 Amendment

This form was amended in 1963 by deleting the stated dollar amount and substituting a blank, to be properly filled in by the pleader. See Note of Advisory Committee under Form 3.

Form 8. Complaint for Money Had and Received

Form effective until December 1, 2007.

1. Allegation of jurisdiction.

2. Defendant owes plaintiff _____ dollars for money had and received from one G. H. on June 1, 1936, to be paid by defendant to plaintiff.

Wherefore (etc. as in Form 3).

(As amended Jan. 21, 1963, eff. July 1, 1963.)

Amendment of Forms

Form effective until December 1, 2007. For forms effective December 1, 2007, absent contrary Congressional action, see Forms 1 to 82 following this Appendix of Forms.

ADVISORY COMMITTEE NOTES

1963 Amendment

This form was amended in 1963 by deleting the stated dollar amount and substituting a blank, to be properly filled in by the pleader. See Note of Advisory Committee under Form 3.

Form 9. Complaint for Negligence

Form effective until December 1, 2007.

1. Allegation of jurisdiction.

2. On June 1, 1936, in a public highway called Boylston Street in Boston, Massachusetts, defendant negligently drove a motor vehicle against plaintiff who was then crossing said highway.

3. As a result plaintiff was thrown down and had his leg broken and was otherwise injured, was prevented from transacting his business, suffered great pain of body and mind, and incurred expenses for medical attention and hospitalization in the sum of one thousand dollars.

Wherefore plaintiff demands judgment against defendant in the sum of _____ dollars and costs.

NOTE

Since contributory negligence is an affirmative defense, the complaint need contain no allegation of due care of plaintiff.

(As amended Jan. 21, 1963, eff. July 1, 1963.)

Amendment of Forms

Form effective until December 1, 2007. For forms effective December 1, 2007, absent contrary Congressional action, see Forms 1 to 82 following this Appendix of Forms.

ADVISORY COMMITTEE NOTES

1963 Amendment

This form was amended in 1963 by deleting the stated dollar amount and substituting a blank, to be properly filled in by the pleader. See Note of Advisory Committee under Form 3.

Form 10. Complaint for Negligence Where Plaintiff is Unable to Determine Definitely Whether the Person Responsible is C. D. or E. F. or Whether Both are Responsible and Where his Evidence may Justify a Finding of Wilfulness or of Recklessness or of Negligence

Form effective until December 1, 2007.

A. B., Plaintiff)
 v.) *Complaint*
C. D. and E. F., Defendants)

1. Allegation of jurisdiction.

2. On June 1, 1936, in a public highway called Boylston Street in Boston, Massachusetts, defendant C. D. or defendant E. F., or both defendants C. D. and E. F. wilfully or recklessly or negligently drove or caused to be driven a motor vehicle against plaintiff who was then crossing said highway.

3. As a result plaintiff was thrown down and had his leg broken and was otherwise injured, was prevented from transacting his business, suffered great pain of body and mind, and incurred expenses for medical attention and hospitalization in the sum of one thousand dollars.

Wherefore plaintiff demands judgment against C. D. or against E. F. or against both in the sum of _____ dollars and costs.

(As amended Jan. 21, 1963, eff. July 1, 1963.)

Amendment of Forms

Form effective until December 1, 2007. For forms effective December 1, 2007, absent contrary Congressional action, see Forms 1 to 82 following this Appendix of Forms.

ADVISORY COMMITTEE NOTES

1963 Amendment

This form was amended in 1963 by deleting the stated dollar amount and substituting a blank, to be properly filled

in by the pleader. See Note of Advisory Committee under Form 3.

Form 11. Complaint for Conversion

Form effective until December 1, 2007.

1. Allegation of jurisdiction.

2. On or about December 1, 1936, defendant converted to his own use ten bonds of the _____ Company (here insert brief identification as by number and issue) of the value of _____ dollars, the property of plaintiff.

Wherefore plaintiff demands judgment against defendant in the sum of _____ dollars, interest, and costs.

(As amended Jan. 21, 1963, eff. July 1, 1963.)

Amendment of Forms

Form effective until December 1, 2007. For forms effective December 1, 2007, absent contrary Congressional action, see Forms 1 to 82 following this Appendix of Forms.

ADVISORY COMMITTEE NOTES

1963 Amendment

This form was amended in 1963 by deleting the stated dollar amount and substituting a blank, to be properly filled in by the pleader. See Note of Advisory Committee under Form 3.

Form 12. Complaint for Specific Performance of Contract to Convey Land

Form effective until December 1, 2007.

1. Allegation of jurisdiction.

2. On or about December 1, 1936, plaintiff and defendant entered into an agreement in writing a copy of which is hereto annexed as Exhibit A.

3. In accord with the provisions of said agreement plaintiff tendered to defendant the purchase price and requested a conveyance of the land, but defendant refused to accept the tender and refused to make the conveyance.

4. Plaintiff now offers to pay the purchase price.

Wherefore plaintiff demands (1) that defendant be required specifically to perform said agreement, (2) damages in the sum of one thousand dollars, and (3) that if specific performance is not granted plaintiff have judgment against defendant in the sum of _____ dollars.

NOTE

Here, as in Form 3, plaintiff may set forth the contract verbatim in the complaint or plead it, as indicated, by exhibit, or plead it according to its legal effect. Furthermore, plaintiff may seek legal or equitable relief or both even though this was impossible under the system in operation before these rules.

(As amended Jan. 21, 1963, eff. July 1, 1963.)

Amendment of Forms

Form effective until December 1, 2007. For forms effective December 1, 2007, absent contrary Congressional action, see Forms 1 to 82 following this Appendix of Forms.

ADVISORY COMMITTEE NOTES

1963 Amendment

This form was amended in 1963 by deleting the stated dollar amount and substituting a blank, to be properly filled in by the pleader. See Note of Advisory Committee under Form 3.

Form 13. Complaint on Claim for Debt and to Set Aside Fraudulent Conveyance Under Rule 18(b)

Form effective until December 1, 2007.

A. B., Plaintiff)
 v.) *Complaint*
C. D. and E. F., Defendants)

1. Allegation of jurisdiction.

2. Defendant C. D. on or about _____ executed and delivered to plaintiff a promissory note [in the following words and figures: (here set out the note verbatim)]; [a copy of which is hereto annexed as Exhibit A]; [whereby defendant C. D. promised to pay to plaintiff or order [1] on _____ the sum of five thousand dollars with interest thereon at the rate of _____ percent. per annum].

3. Defendant C. D. owes to plaintiff the amount of said note and interest.

4. Defendant C. D. on or about _____ conveyed all his property, real and personal [or specify and describe] to defendant E. F. for the purpose of defrauding plaintiff and hindering and delaying the collection of the indebtedness evidenced by the note above referred to.

Wherefore plaintiff demands:

(1) That plaintiff have judgment against defendant C. D. for _____ dollars and interest; (2) that the aforesaid conveyance to defendant E. F. be declared void and the judgment herein be declared a lien on said property; (3) that plaintiff have judgment against the defendants for costs.

(As amended Jan. 21, 1963, eff. July 1, 1963.)

[1] So in original.

Amendment of Forms

Form effective until December 1, 2007. For forms effective December 1, 2007, absent contrary Congressional action, see Forms 1 to 82 following this Appendix of Forms.

1963 Amendment

This form was amended in 1963 by deleting the stated dollar amount and substituting a blank, to be properly filled in by the pleader. See Note of Advisory Committee under Form 3.

Form 14. Complaint for Negligence Under Federal Employer's Liability Act

Form effective until December 1, 2007.

1. Allegation of jurisdiction.

2. During all the times herein mentioned defendant owned and operated in interstate commerce a railroad which passed through a tunnel located at _____ and known as Tunnel No. ___.

3. On or about June 1, 1936, defendant was repairing and enlarging the tunnel in order to protect interstate trains and passengers and freight from injury and in order to make the tunnel more conveniently usable for interstate commerce.

4. In the course of thus repairing and enlarging the tunnel on said day defendant employed plaintiff as one of its workmen, and negligently put plaintiff to work in a portion of the tunnel which defendant had left unprotected and unsupported.

5. By reason of defendant's negligence in thus putting plaintiff to work in that portion of the tunnel, plaintiff was, while so working pursuant to defendant's orders, struck and crushed by a rock, which fell from the unsupported portion of the tunnel, and was (here describe plaintiff's injuries).

6. Prior to these injuries, plaintiff was a strong, able-bodied man, capable of earning and actually earning _____ dollars per day. By these injuries he has been made incapable of any gainful activity, has suffered great physical and mental pain, and has incurred expense in the amount of _____ dollars for medicine, medical attendance, and hospitalization.

Wherefore plaintiff demands judgment against defendant in the sum of _____ dollars and costs.

Amendment of Forms

Form effective until December 1, 2007. For forms effective December 1, 2007, absent contrary Congressional action, see Forms 1 to 82 following this Appendix of Forms.

Form 15. Complaint for Damages Under Merchant Marine Act

Form effective until December 1, 2007.

1. Allegation of jurisdiction. [If the pleader wishes to invoke the distinctively maritime procedures referred to in Rule 9(h), add the following or its substantial equivalent: This is an admiralty or maritime claim within the meaning of Rule 9(h).]

2. During all the times herein mentioned defendant was the owner of the steamship _____ and used it in the transportation of freight for hire by water in interstate and foreign commerce.

3. During the first part of (month and year) at _____ plaintiff entered the employ of defendant as an able seaman on said steamship under seamen's articles of customary form for a voyage from _____ ports to the Orient and return at a wage of _____ dollars per month and found, which is equal to a wage of _____ dollars per month as a shore worker.

4. On June 1, 1936, said steamship was about ___ days out of the port of _____ and was being navigated by the master and crew on the return voyage to _____ ports. (Here describe weather conditions and the condition of the ship and state as in an ordinary complaint for personal injuries the negligent conduct of defendant.)

5. By reason of defendant's negligence in thus (brief statement of defendant's negligent conduct) and the unseaworthiness of said steamship, plaintiff was (here describe plaintiff's injuries).

6. Prior to these injuries, plaintiff was a strong, able-bodied man, capable of earning and actually earning _____ dollars per day. By these injuries he has been made incapable of any gainful activity; has suffered great physical and mental pain, and has incurred expense in the amount of _____ dollars for medicine, medical attendance, and hospitalization.

Wherefore plaintiff demands judgment against defendant in the sum of _____ dollars and costs.
(As amended Feb. 28, 1966, eff. July 1, 1966.)

Amendment of Forms

Form effective until December 1, 2007. For forms effective December 1, 2007, absent contrary Congressional action, see Forms 1 to 82 following this Appendix of Forms.

1966 Amendment

See Advisory Committee's Note to Form 2.

Form 16. Complaint for Infringement of Patent

Form effective until December 1, 2007.

1. Allegation of jurisdiction.

2. On May 16, 1934, United States Letters Patent No. ___ were duly and legally issued to plaintiff for an invention in an electric motor; and since that date plaintiff has been and still is the owner of those Letters Patent.

3. Defendant has for a long time past been and still is infringing those Letters Patent by making, selling, and using electric motors embodying the pat-

ented invention, and will continue to do so unless enjoined by this court.

4. Plaintiff has placed the required statutory notice on all electric motors manufactured and sold by him under said Letters Patent, and has given written notice to defendant of his said infringement.

Wherefore plaintiff demands a preliminary and final injunction against continued infringement, an accounting for damages, and an assessment of interest and costs against defendant.

(As amended Jan. 21, 1963, eff. July 1, 1963.)

Amendment of Forms

Form effective until December 1, 2007. For forms effective December 1, 2007, absent contrary Congressional action, see Forms 1 to 82 following this Appendix of Forms.

ADVISORY COMMITTEE NOTES
1963 Amendment

The prayer for relief is amended to reflect the language of the present patent statute, Title 35, U.S.C., § 284 (Damages).

Form 17. Complaint for Infringement of Copyright and Unfair Competition

Form effective until December 1, 2007.

1. Allegation of jurisdiction.

2. Prior to March, 1936, plaintiff, who then was and ever since has been a citizen of the United States, created and wrote an original book, entitled ____.

3. This book contains a large amount of material wholly original with plaintiff and is copyrightable subject matter under the laws of the United States.

4. Between March 2, 1936, and March 10, 1936, plaintiff complied in all respects with the Act of (give citation) and all other laws governing copyright, and secured the exclusive rights and privileges in and to the copyright of said book, and received from the Register of Copyrights a certificate of registration, dated and identified as follows: "March 10, 1936, Class ___, No. ___."

5. Since March 10, 1936, said book has been published by plaintiff and all copies of it made by plaintiff or under his authority or license have been printed, bound, and published in strict conformity with the provisions of the Act of ____ and all other laws governing copyright.

6. Since March 10, 1936, plaintiff has been and still is the sole proprietor of all rights, title, and interest in and to the copyright in said book.

7. After March 10, 1936, defendant infringed said copyright by publishing and placing upon the market a book entitled ____, which was copied largely from plaintiff's copyrighted book, entitled ____.

8. A copy of plaintiff's copyrighted book is hereto attached as "Exhibit 1"; and a copy of defendant's infringing book is hereto attached as "Exhibit 2."

9. Plaintiff has notified defendant that defendant has infringed the copyright of plaintiff, and defendant has continued to infringe the copyright.

10. After March 10, 1936, and continuously since about ____, defendant has been publishing, selling and otherwise marketing the book entitled ____, and has thereby been engaging in unfair trade practices and unfair competition against plaintiff to plaintiff's irreparable damage.

Wherefore plaintiff demands:

(1) That defendant, his agents, and servants be enjoined during the pendency of this action and permanently from infringing said copyright of said plaintiff in any manner, and from publishing, selling, marketing or otherwise disposing of any copies of the book entitled ____.

(2) That defendant be required to pay to plaintiff such damages as plaintiff has sustained in consequence of defendant's infringement of said copyright and said unfair trade practices and unfair competition and to account for

(a) all gains, profits and advantages derived by defendant by said trade practices and unfair competition and

(b) all gains, profits, and advantages derived by defendant by his infringement of plaintiff's copyright or such damages as to the court shall appear proper within the provisions of the copyright statutes, but not less than two hundred and fifty dollars.

(3) That defendant be required to deliver up to be impounded during the pendency of this action all copies of said book entitled ____ in his possession or under his control and to deliver up for destruction all infringing copies and all plates, molds, and other matter for making such infringing copies.

(4) That defendant pay to plaintiff the costs of this action and reasonable attorney's fees to be allowed to the plaintiff by the court.

(5) That plaintiff have such other and further relief as is just.

(As amended Dec. 27, 1946, eff. Mar. 19, 1948.)

Amendment of Forms

Form effective until December 1, 2007. For forms effective December 1, 2007, absent contrary Congressional action, see Forms 1 to 82 following this Appendix of Forms.

ADVISORY COMMITTEE NOTES
1946 Amendment

This form, as set out, incorporates amendments made at the same time certain rules of the Federal Rules of Civil Procedure were amended. See Rule 86(b) of such rules.

Form 18. Complaint for Interpleader and Declaratory Relief

Form effective until December 1, 2007.

1. Allegation of jurisdiction.

2. On or about June 1, 1935, plaintiff issued to G. H. a policy of life insurance whereby plaintiff promised to pay to K. L. as beneficiary the sum of _____ dollars upon the death of G. H. The policy required the payment by G. H. of a stipulated premium on June 1, 1936, and annually thereafter as a condition precedent to its continuance in force.

3. No part of the premium due June 1, 1936, was ever paid and the policy ceased to have any force or effect on July 1, 1936.

4. Thereafter, on September 1, 1936, G. H. and K. L. died as the result of a collision between a locomotive and the automobile in which G. H. and K. L. were riding.

5. Defendant C. D. is the duly appointed and acting executor of the will of G. H.; defendant E. F. is the duly appointed and acting executor of the will of K. L.; defendant X. Y. claims to have been duly designated as beneficiary of said policy in place of K. L.

6. Each of defendants, C. D., E. F., and X. Y. is claiming that the above-mentioned policy was in full force and effect at the time of the death of G. H.; each of them is claiming to be the only person entitled to receive payment of the amount of the policy and has made demand for payment thereof.

7. By reason of these conflicting claims of the defendants, plaintiff is in great doubt as to which defendant is entitled to be paid the amount of the policy, if it was in force at the death of G. H.

Wherefore plaintiff demands that the court adjudge:

(1) That none of the defendants is entitled to recover from plaintiff the amount of said policy or any part thereof.

(2) That each of the defendants be restrained from instituting any action against plaintiff for the recovery of the amount of said policy or any part thereof.

(3) That, if the court shall determine that said policy was in force at the death of G. H., the defendants be required to interplead and settle between themselves their rights to the money due under said policy, and that plaintiff be discharged from all liability in the premises except to the person whom the court shall adjudge entitled to the amount of said policy.

(4) That plaintiff recover its costs.

(As amended Jan. 21, 1963, eff. July 1, 1963.)

Amendment of Forms

Form effective until December 1, 2007. For forms effective December 1, 2007, absent contrary Congressional action, see Forms 1 to 82 following this Appendix of Forms.

ADVISORY COMMITTEE NOTES
1963 Amendment

This form was amended in 1963 by deleting the stated dollar amount and substituting a blank, to be properly filled in by the pleader. See Note of Advisory Committee under Form 3.

Form 18–A. [Abrogated]
ADVISORY COMMITTEE NOTES

This form is superseded by Forms 1A and 1B in view of the revision of Rule 4.

HISTORICAL NOTES
Effective Date of Abrogation

Abrogation effective Dec. 1, 1993, absent contrary Congressional action.

Form 19. Motion to Dismiss, Presenting Defenses of Failure to State a Claim, of Lack of Service of Process, of Improper Venue, and of Lack of Jurisdiction Under Rule 12(b)

Form effective until December 1, 2007.

The defendant moves the court as follows:

1. To dismiss the action because the complaint fails to state a claim against defendant upon which relief can be granted.

2. To dismiss the action or in lieu thereof to quash the return of service of summons on the grounds (a) that the defendant is a corporation organized under the laws of Delaware and was not and is not subject to service of process within the Southern District of New York, and (b) that the defendant has not been properly served with process in this action, all of which more clearly appears in the affidavits of M. N. and X. Y. hereto annexed as Exhibit A and Exhibit B respectively.

3. To dismiss the action on the ground that it is in the wrong district because (a) the jurisdiction of this court is invoked solely on the ground that the action arises under the Constitution and laws of the United States and (b) the defendant is a corporation incorporated under the laws of the State of Delaware and is not licensed to do or doing business in the Southern District of New York, all of which more clearly appears in the affidavits of K. L. and V. W. hereto annexed as Exhibits C and D, respectively.

4. To dismiss the action on the ground that the court lacks jurisdiction because the amount actually in

controversy is less than ten thousand dollars exclusive of interest and costs.

Signed: _____
Attorney for Defendant.
Address: _____

Notice of Motion

To: _____
Attorney for Plaintiff.

Please take notice, that the undersigned will bring the above motion on for hearing before this Court at Room ___, United States Court House, Foley Square, City of New York, on the ___ day of _____, 20___, at 10 o'clock in the forenoon of that day or as soon thereafter as counsel can be heard.

Signed: _____
Attorney for Defendant.
Address: _____

NOTES

1. The above motion and notice of motion may be combined and denominated Notice of Motion. See Rule 7(b).

2. As to paragraph 3, see U.S.C., Title 28, § 1391 (Venue generally), subsections (b) and (c).

3. As to paragraph 4, see U.S.C., Title 28, § 1331 (Federal question; amount in controversy; costs), as amended by P.L. 85–554, 72 Stat. 415, July 25, 1958, requiring that the amount in controversy, exclusive of interest and costs, be in excess of $10,000. [Editor's note: This Note reflects U.S.C., Title 28, § 1331, prior to the 1976 and 1980 amendments eliminating the $10,000 jurisdictional amount. See U.S.C., Title 28, § 1332.]

(As amended Dec. 29, 1948, eff. Oct. 20, 1949; Apr. 17, 1961, eff. July 19, 1961; Mar. 27, 2003, eff. Dec. 1, 2003.)

Amendment of Forms

Form effective until December 1, 2007. For forms effective December 1, 2007, absent contrary Congressional action, see Forms 1 to 82 following this Appendix of Forms.

Form 20. Answer Presenting Defenses Under Rule 12(b)

Form effective until December 1, 2007.

First Defense

The complaint fails to state a claim against defendant upon which relief can be granted.

Second Defense

If defendant is indebted to plaintiffs for the goods mentioned in the complaint, he is indebted to them jointly with G. H. G. H. is alive; is a citizen of the State of New York and a resident of this district, is subject to the jurisdiction of this court, as to both service of process and venue; can be made a party without depriving this court of jurisdiction of the present parties, and has not been made a party.

Third Defense

Defendant admits the allegation contained in paragraphs 1 and 4 of the complaint; alleges that he is without knowledge or information sufficient to form a belief as to the truth of the allegations contained in paragraph 2 of the complaint; and denies each and every other allegation contained in the complaint.

Fourth Defense

The right of action set forth in the complaint did not accrue within six years next before the commencement of this action.

Counterclaim

(Here set forth any claim as a counterclaim in the manner in which a claim is pleaded in a complaint. No statement of the grounds on which the court's jurisdiction depends need be made unless the counterclaim requires independent grounds of jurisdiction.)

Cross-Claim Against Defendant M. N.

(Here set forth the claim constituting a cross-claim against defendant M. N. in the manner in which a claim is pleaded in a complaint. The statement of grounds upon which the court's jurisdiction depends need not be made unless the cross-claim requires independent grounds of jurisdiction.)

NOTE

The above form contains examples of certain defenses provided for in Rule 12(b). The first defense challenges the legal sufficiency of the complaint. It is a substitute for a general demurrer or a motion to dismiss.

The second defense embodies the old plea in abatement; the decision thereon, however, may well provide under Rules 19 and 21 for the citing in of the party rather than an abatement of the action.

The third defense is an answer on the merits.

The fourth defense is one of the affirmative defenses provided for in Rule 8(c).

The answer also includes a counterclaim and a cross-claim.

Amendment of Forms

Form effective until December 1, 2007. For forms effective December 1, 2007, absent contrary Congressional action, see Forms 1 to 82 following this Appendix of Forms.

ADVISORY COMMITTEE NOTES

1946 Amendment

The explanatory note incorporates revisions made by the Advisory Committee at the same time amendments to certain rules of the Federal Rules of Civil Procedure were made. See also Rule 12(b) as amended.

Form 21. Answer to Complaint Set Forth in Form 8, With Counterclaim for Interpleader

Form effective until December 1, 2007.

Defense

Defendant admits the allegations stated in paragraph 1 of the complaint; and denies the allegations stated in paragraph 2 to the extent set forth in the counterclaim herein.

Counterclaim for Interpleader

1. Defendant received the sum of _____ dollars as a deposit from E. F.

2. Plaintiff has demanded the payment of such deposit to him by virtue of an assignment of it which he claims to have received from E. F.

3. E. F. has notified the defendant that he claims such deposit, that the purported assignment is not valid, and that he holds the defendant responsible for the deposit.

Wherefore defendant demands:

(1) That the court order E. F. to be made a party defendant to respond to the complaint and to this counterclaim.[1]

(2) That the court order the plaintiff and E. F. to interplead their respective claims.

(3) That the court adjudge whether the plaintiff or E. F. is entitled to the sum of money.

(4) That the court discharge defendant from all liability in the premises except to the person it shall adjudge entitled to the sum of money.

(5) That the court award to the defendant its costs and attorney's fees.

(As amended Jan. 21, 1963, eff. July 1, 1963.)

[1] Rule 13(h) provides for the court ordering parties to a counterclaim, but who are not parties to the original action, to be brought in as defendants.

Amendment of Forms

Form effective until December 1, 2007. For forms effective December 1, 2007, absent contrary Congressional action, see Forms 1 to 82 following this Appendix of Forms.

ADVISORY COMMITTEE NOTES
1963 Amendment

This form was amended in 1963 by deleting the stated dollar amount and substituting a blank, to be properly filled in by the pleader. See Note of Advisory Committee under Form 3.

[Form 22. Eliminated, eff. July 1, 1963]
HISTORICAL NOTES

Codifications

Form 22 for motion to bring in third-party defendant, setting out as an exhibit summons and third-party complaint, and for notice of motion, was superseded by Forms 22–A and 22–B, setting out summons and complaint against third-party defendant, and motion to bring in third-party defendant, effective July 1, 1963. See Advisory Committee notes under Forms 22–A and 22–B.

Form 22–A. Summons and Complaint Against Third-Party Defendant

Form effective until December 1, 2007.

United States District Court for the
Southern District of New York

Civil Action, File Number ____

A. B., Plaintiff)
v.)
C. D., Defendant and)
Third–Party Plaintiff) *Summons*
v.)
E. F., Third-Party Defendant)

To the above-named Third-Party Defendant:

You are hereby summoned and required to serve upon _____, plaintiff's attorney whose address is _____, and upon _____, who is attorney for C. D., defendant and third-party plaintiff, and whose address is _____, an answer to the third-party complaint which is herewith served upon you within 20 days after the service of this summons upon you exclusive of the day of service. If you fail to do so, judgment by default will be taken against you for the relief demanded in the third-party complaint. There is also served upon you herewith a copy of the complaint of the plaintiff which you may but are not required to answer.

_____,
Clerk of Court.

[Seal of District Court]

Dated _____

United States District Court for the
Southern District of New York

Civil Action, File Number ____

A. B., Plaintiff)
v.)
C. D., Defendant and)
Third–Party Plaintiff) *Third-Party Complaint*
v.)
E. F., Third-Party Defendant)

1. Plaintiff A. B. has filed against defendant C. D. a complaint, a copy of which is hereto attached as "Exhibit A."

2. (Here state the grounds upon which C. D. is entitled to recover from E. F., all or part of what A. B. may recover from C. D. The statement should be framed as in an original complaint.)

Wherefore C. D. demands judgment against third-party defendant E. F. for all sums[1] that may be adjudged against defendant C. D. in favor of plaintiff A. B.

Signed: _____

Attorney for C. D.,
Third-Party Plaintiff

Address: _____

(Added Jan. 21, 1963, eff. July 1, 1963.)

[1] Make appropriate change where C. D. is entitled to only partial recovery-over against E. F.

Amendment of Forms

Form effective until December 1, 2007. For forms effective December 1, 2007, absent contrary Congressional action, see Forms 1 to 82 following this Appendix of Forms.

ADVISORY COMMITTEE NOTES

1963 Adoption

Under the amendment of Rule 14(a), a defendant who files a third-party complaint not later than 10 days after serving his original answer need not obtain leave of court to bring in the third-party defendant by service under Rule 4. Form 22-A is intended for use in these cases.

The changes in the form of summons reflect an earlier amendment of Rule 14(a), effective in 1948, making it permissive, rather than mandatory, for the third-party defendant to answer the plaintiff's complaint. See *Cooper v. D/S A/S Progress*, 188 F.Supp. 578 (E.D.Pa.1960); 1A Barron & Holtzoff, *Federal Practice & Procedure* 696 (Wright ed. 1960).

Under the amendment of Rule 5(a) requiring, with certain exceptions, that papers be served upon all the parties to the action, the third-party defendant, even if he makes no answer to the plaintiff's complaint, is obliged to serve upon the plaintiff a copy of his answer to the third-party complaint. Similarly, the defendant is obliged to serve upon the plaintiff a copy of the summons and complaint against the third-party defendant.

Form 22-B. Motion to Bring in Third-Party Defendant

Form effective until December 1, 2007.

Defendant moves for leave, as third-party plaintiff, to cause to be served upon E. F. a summons and third-party complaint, copies of which are hereto attached as Exhibit X.

Signed: _____,

Attorney for Defendant C. D.

Address: _____

Notice of Motion

(Contents the same as in Form 19. The notice should be addressed to all parties to the action.)

Exhibit X

(Contents the same as in Form 22-A.)

(Added Jan. 21, 1963, eff. July 1, 1963.)

Amendment of Forms

Form effective until December 1, 2007. For forms effective December 1, 2007, absent contrary Congressional action, see Forms 1 to 82 following this Appendix of Forms.

ADVISORY COMMITTEE NOTES

1963 Adoption

Form 22-B is intended for use when, under amended Rule 14(a), leave of court is required to bring in a third-party defendant.

Form 23. Motion to Intervene as a Defendant Under Rule 24

Form effective until December 1, 2007.

(Based upon the complaint, Form 16)

United States District Court for the
Southern District of New York

Civil Action, File Number ___

A. B., plaintiff)
v.) *Motion to intervene*
) *as a defendant*
C. D., defendant)
E. F., applicant)
for intervention)

E. F. moves for leave to intervene as a defendant in this action, in order to assert the defenses set forth in his proposed answer, of which a copy is hereto attached, on the ground that he is the manufacturer and vendor to the defendant, as well as to others, of the articles alleged in the complaint to be an infringement of plaintiff's patent, and as such has a defense to plaintiff's claim presenting both questions of law and of fact which are common to the main action.[1]

Signed: _____,

Attorney for E. F.,
Applicant for Intervention.

Address: _____

Notice of Motion

(Contents the same as in Form 19)

United States District Court for the
Southern District of New York

Civil Action, File Number ___

A. B., plaintiff)
v.) *Intervener's Answer*
C. D., defendant)
E. F., intervener)

First Defense

Intervener admits the allegations stated in paragraphs 1 and 4 of the complaint; denies the allegations in paragraph 3, and denies the allegations in paragraph 2 in so far as they assert the legality of the issuance of the Letters Patent to plaintiff.

Second Defense

Plaintiff is not the first inventor of the articles covered by the Letters Patent specified in his complaint, since articles substantially identical in character were previously patented in Letters Patent granted to intervener on January 5, 1920.

Signed: _____,
Attorney for E. F.,
Intervener.

Address: _____

(As amended Dec. 29, 1948, eff. Oct. 20, 1949.)

1 For other grounds of intervention, either of right or in the discretion of the court, see Rule 24(a) and (b).

Amendment of Forms

Form effective until December 1, 2007. For forms effective December 1, 2007, absent contrary Congressional action, see Forms 1 to 82 following this Appendix of Forms.

Form 24. Request for Production of Documents, etc., Under Rule 34

Form effective until December 1, 2007.

Plaintiff A. B. requests defendant C. D. to respond within _____ days to the following requests:

(1) That defendant produce and permit plaintiff to inspect and to copy each of the following documents:

(Here list the documents either individually or by category and describe each of them.)

(Here state the time, place, and manner of making the inspection and performance of any related acts.)

(2) That defendant produce and permit plaintiff to inspect and to copy, test, or sample each of the following objects:

(Here list the objects either individually or by category and describe each of them.)

(Here state the time, place, and manner of making the inspection and performance of any related acts.)

(3) That defendant permit plaintiff to enter (here describe property to be entered) and to inspect and to photograph, test or sample (here describe the portion of the real property and the objects to be inspected).

(Here state the time, place, and manner of making the inspection and performance of any related acts.)

Signed: _____,
Attorney for Plaintiff.
Address: _____

(As amended Mar. 30, 1970, eff. July 1, 1970.)

Amendment of Forms

Form effective until December 1, 2007. For forms effective December 1, 2007, absent contrary Congressional action, see Forms 1 to 82 following this Appendix of Forms.

ADVISORY COMMITTEE NOTES

1970 Amendment

Form 24 is revised to accord with the changes made in Rule 34.

Form 25. Request for Admission Under Rule 36

Form effective until December 1, 2007.

Plaintiff A. B. requests defendant C. D. within ____ days after service of this request to make the following admissions for the purpose of this action only and subject to all pertinent objections to admissibility which may be interposed at the trial:

1. That each of the following documents, exhibited with this request, is genuine.

(Here list the documents and describe each document.)

2. That each of the following statements is true.

(Here list the statements.)

Signed: _____,
Attorney for Plaintiff.
Address: _____

(As amended Dec. 27, 1946, eff. Mar. 19, 1948.)

Amendment of Forms

Form effective until December 1, 2007. For forms effective December 1, 2007, absent contrary Congressional action, see Forms 1 to 82 following this Appendix of Forms.

Form 26. Allegation of Reason for Omitting Party

Form effective until December 1, 2007.

When it is necessary, under Rule 19(c), for the pleader to set forth in his pleading the names of persons who ought to be made parties, but who are not so made, there should be an allegation such as the one set out below:

John Doe named in this complaint is not made a party to this action [because he is not subject to the jurisdiction of this court]; [because he cannot be made a party to this action without depriving this court of jurisdiction].

Amendment of Forms

Form effective until December 1, 2007. For forms effective December 1, 2007, absent contrary Congres-

Form 26

RULES OF CIVIL PROCEDURE

sional action, see Forms 1 to 82 following this Appendix of Forms.

Form 27. [Abrogated. Dec. 4, 1967, eff. July 1, 1968]

ADVISORY COMMITTEE NOTES

1967 Amendment

The form of notice of appeal is transferred to the Federal Rules of Appellate Procedure as Form 1.

Form 28. Notice: Condemnation

Form effective until December 1, 2007.

United States District Court for the
Southern District of New York

Civil Action, File Number ____

United States of America, plaintiff)
v.)
1,000 Acres of Land in [here insert a)
general location as "City of ____") *Notice*
or "County of ____"], John Doe et)
al., and Unknown Owners, Defendants)

To (here insert the names of the defendants to whom the notice is directed):

You are hereby notified that a complaint in condemnation has heretofore been filed in the office of the clerk of the United States District Court for the Southern District of New York, in the United States Court House in New York City, New York, for the taking (here state the interest to be acquired, as "an estate in fee simple") for use (here state briefly the use, "as a site for a post-office building") of the following described property in which you have or claim an interest.

(Here insert brief description of the property in which the defendants, to whom the notice is directed, have or claim an interest.)

The authority for the taking is (here state briefly, as "the Act of ____, ____ Stat. ____, U.S.C., Title ____, § ____".) [1]

You are further notified that if you desire to present any objection or defense to the taking of your property you are required to serve your answer on the plaintiff's attorney at the address herein designated within twenty days after _____. [2]

Your answer shall identify the property in which you claim to have an interest, state the nature and extent of the interest you claim, and state all of your objections and defenses to the taking of your property. All defenses and objections not so presented are waived. And in case of your failure so to answer the complaint, judgment of condemnation of that part of the above-described property in which you have or claim an interest will be rendered.

But without answering, you may serve on the plaintiff's attorney a notice of appearance designating the property in which you claim to be interested. Thereafter you will receive notice of all proceedings affecting it. At the trial of the issue of just compensation, whether or not you have previously appeared or answered, you may present evidence as to the amount of the compensation to be paid for your property, and you may share in the distribution of the award.

United States Attorney.
Address _____

(Here state an address within the district where the United States Attorney may be served as "United States Court House, New York, N.Y.".)

Dated _____

(Added May 1, 1951, eff. Aug. 1, 1951.)

[1] And where appropriate add a citation to any applicable Executive Order.

[2] Here insert the words "personal service of this notice upon you," if personal service is to be made pursuant to subdivision (d)(3)(i) of this rule [Rule 71A]; or, insert the date of the last publication of notice, if service by publication is to be made pursuant to subdivision (d)(3)(ii) of this rule.

Amendment of Forms

Form effective until December 1, 2007. For forms effective December 1, 2007, absent contrary Congressional action, see Forms 1 to 82 following this Appendix of Forms.

Form 29. Complaint: Condemnation

Form effective until December 1, 2007.

United States District Court for the
Southern District of New York

Civil Action, File Number ____

United States of America, Plaintiff)
v.)
1,000 Acres of Land in [here insert a) *Complaint*
general location as "City of ____")
or "County of ____"], John Doe, et)
al., and Unknown Owners, Defendants)

1. This is an action of a civil nature brought by the United States of America for the taking of property under the power of eminent domain and for the ascertainment and award of just compensation to the owners and parties in interest.[1]

2. The authority for the taking is (here state briefly, as "the Act of ____, ____ Stat. ____, U.S.C., Title ____, § ____").[2]

3. The use for which the property is to be taken is (here state briefly the use, "as a site for a post-office building").

4. The interest to be acquired in the property is (here state the interest as "an estate in fee simple").

Complete Annotation Materials, see Title 28 U.S.C.A.

5. The property so to be taken is (here set forth a description of the property sufficient for its identification) or (described in Exhibit A hereto attached and made a part hereof).

6. The persons known to the plaintiff to have or claim an interest in the property [3] are:

(Here set forth the names of such persons and the interests claimed.) [4]

7. In addition to the persons named, there are or may be others who have or may claim some interest in the property to be taken, whose names are unknown to the plaintiff and on diligent inquiry have not been ascertained. They are made parties to the action under the designation "Unknown Owners."

Wherefore the plaintiff demands judgment that the property be condemned and that just compensation for the taking be ascertained and awarded and for such other relief as may be lawful and proper.

United States Attorney.
Address _____

(Here state an address within the district where the United States Attorney may be served, as "United States Court House, New York, N.Y.".)

(Added May 1, 1951, eff. Aug. 1, 1951.)

[1] If the plaintiff is not the United States, but is, for example, a corporation invoking the power of eminent domain delegated to it by the state, then this paragraph 1 of the complaint should be appropriately modified and should be preceded by a paragraph appropriately alleging federal jurisdiction for the action, such as diversity. See Form 2.

[2] And where appropriate add a citation to any applicable Executive Order.

[3] At the commencement of the action the plaintiff need name as defendants only the persons having or claiming an interest in the property whose names are then known, but prior to any hearing involving the compensation to be paid for a particular piece of property the plaintiff must add as defendants all persons having or claiming an interest in that property whose names can be ascertained by an appropriate search of the records and also those whose names have otherwise been learned. See Rule 71A(c)(2).

[4] The plaintiff should designate, as to each separate piece of property, the defendants who have been joined as owners thereof or of some interest therein. See Rule 71A(c)(2).

Amendment of Forms

Form effective until December 1, 2007. For forms effective December 1, 2007, absent contrary Congressional action, see Forms 1 to 82 following this Appendix of Forms.

Form 30. Suggestion of Death Upon the Record Under Rule 25(a)(1)

Form effective until December 1, 2007.

A. B. [describe as a party, or as executor, administrator, or other representative or successor of C. D., the deceased party] suggests upon the record, pursu-

ant to Rule 25(a)(1), the death of C. D. [describe as party] during the pendency of this action.

(Added Jan. 21, 1963, eff. July 1, 1963.)

Amendment of Forms

Form effective until December 1, 2007. For forms effective December 1, 2007, absent contrary Congressional action, see Forms 1 to 82 following this Appendix of Forms.

Form 31. Judgment on Jury Verdict

Form effective until December 1, 2007.

United States District Court for the
Southern District of New York

Civil Action, File Number ___

A. B., Plaintiff)	
v.)	*Judgment*
C. D., Defendant)	

This action came on for trial before the Court and a jury, Honorable John Marshall, District Judge, presiding, and the issues having been duly tried and the jury having duly rendered its verdict,

It is Ordered and Adjudged

[that the plaintiff A. B. recover of the defendant C. D. the sum of _____, with interest thereon at the rate of _____ percent as provided by law, and his costs of action.]

[that the plaintiff take nothing, that the action be dismissed on the merits, and that the defendant C. D. recover of the plaintiff A. B. his costs of action.]

Dated at New York, New York, this ___ day of _____, 20___.

Clerk of Court.

NOTE

1. This Form is illustrative of the judgment to be entered upon the general verdict of a jury. It deals with the cases where there is a general jury verdict awarding the plaintiff money damages or finding for the defendant, but is adaptable to other situations of jury verdicts.

2. The clerk, unless the court otherwise orders, is required forthwith to prepare, sign, and enter the judgment upon a general jury verdict without awaiting any direction by the court. The form of the judgment upon a special verdict or a general verdict accompanied by answers to interrogatories shall be promptly approved by the court, and the clerk shall thereupon enter it. See Rule 58, as amended.

3. The Rules contemplate a simple judgment promptly entered. See Rule 54(a). Every judgment shall be set forth on a separate document. See Rule 58, as amended.

4. Attorneys are not to submit forms of judgment unless directed in exceptional cases to do so by the court. See Rule 58, as amended.

(Added Jan. 21, 1963, eff. July 1, 1963, and amended Mar. 27, 2003, eff. Dec. 1, 2003.)

Amendment of Forms

Form effective until December 1, 2007. For forms effective December 1, 2007, absent contrary Congressional action, see Forms 1 to 82 following this Appendix of Forms.

Form 32. Judgment on Decision by the Court

Form effective until December 1, 2007.

United States District Court for the
Southern District of New York

Civil Action, File Number ____

A. B., Plaintiff)
 v.) *Judgment*
C. D., Defendant)

This action came on for [trial] [hearing] before the Court, Honorable John Marshall, District Judge, presiding, and the issues having been duly [tried] [heard] and a decision having been duly rendered,

It is Ordered and Adjudged

[that the plaintiff A. B. recover of the defendant C. D. the sum of ____, with interest thereon at the rate of ____ percent as provided by law, and his costs of action.]

[that the plaintiff take nothing, that the action be dismissed on the merits, and that the defendant C. D. recover of the plaintiff A. B. his costs of action.]

Dated at New York, New York, this ____ day of ____, 20__.

_____,
 Clerk of Court.

NOTES

1. This Form is illustrative of the judgment to be entered upon a decision of the court. It deals with the cases of decisions by the court awarding a party only money damages or costs, but is adaptable to other decisions by the court.

2. The clerk, unless the court otherwise orders, is required forthwith, without awaiting any direction by the court, to prepare, sign, and enter the judgment upon a decision by the court that a party shall recover only a sum certain or costs or that all relief shall be denied. The form of the judgment upon a decision by the court granting other relief shall be promptly approved by the court, and the clerk shall thereupon enter it. See Rule 58, as amended.

3. See also paragraphs 3–4 of the Explanatory Note to Form 31.

(Added Jan. 21, 1963, eff. July 1, 1963, and amended Mar. 27, 2003, eff. Dec. 1, 2003.)

Amendment of Forms

Form effective until December 1, 2007. For forms effective December 1, 2007, absent contrary Congres-

sional action, see Forms 1 to 82 following this Appendix of Forms.

Form 33. Notice of Availability of Magistrate Judge to Exercise Jurisdiction

Form effective until December 1, 2007.

In accordance with the provisions of Title 28, U.S.C. § 636(c), you are hereby notified that a United States magistrate judge of this district court is available to exercise the court's jurisdiction and to conduct any or all proceedings in this case including a jury or nonjury trial, and entry of a final judgment. Exercise of this jurisdiction by a magistrate judge is, however, permitted only if all parties voluntarily consent.

You may, without adverse substantive consequences, withhold your consent, but this will prevent the court's jurisdiction from being exercised by a magistrate judge. If any party withholds consent, the identity of the parties consenting or withholding consent will not be communicated to any magistrate judge or to the district judge to whom the case has been assigned.

An appeal from a judgment entered by a magistrate judge may be taken directly to the United States court of appeals for this judicial circuit in the same manner as an appeal from any other judgment of a district court.

Copies of the Form for the "Consent to Jurisdiction by a United States Magistrate Judge" are available from the clerk of the court.

(Added Apr. 28, 1983, eff. Aug. 1, 1983, and amended Apr. 22, 1993, eff. Dec. 1, 1993; April 11, 1997, eff. Dec. 1, 1997.)

Amendment of Forms

Form effective until December 1, 2007. For forms effective December 1, 2007, absent contrary Congressional action, see Forms 1 to 82 following this Appendix of Forms.

ADVISORY COMMITTEE NOTES

1993 Amendments

This form, together with Form 34, is revised in light of the Judicial Improvements Act of 1990. Section 308 modified 28 U.S.C. § 636(c)(2) to enhance the potential of parties consenting to trial before a magistrate judge. While the exercise of jurisdiction by a magistrate judge remains dependent on the voluntary consent of the parties, the statute provides that the parties should be advised, and may be reminded, of the availability of this option and eliminates the proscription against judicial suggestions of the potential benefits of referral provided the parties are also advised that they "are free to withhold consent without adverse substantive consequences." The parties may be advised if the withholding of consent will result in a potential delay in trial.

HISTORICAL NOTES

Change of Name

United States magistrate appointed under section 631 of Title 28, Judiciary and Judicial Procedure, to be known as United States magistrate judge after Dec. 1, 1990, with any reference to United States magistrate or magistrate in Title 28, in any other Federal statute, etc., deemed a reference to United States magistrate judge appointed under section 631 of Title 28, see section 321 of Pub.L. 101–650, set out as a note under section 631 of Title 28.

Form 34. Consent to Exercise of Jurisdiction by a United States Magistrate Judge

Form effective until December 1, 2007.

UNITED STATES DISTRICT COURT

_____ DISTRICT OF _____

)	
Plaintiff,)	
)	
vs.)	Docket No. _____
)	
Defendant.)	

CONSENT TO JURISDICTION BY A UNITED STATES MAGISTRATE JUDGE

In accordance with the provisions of Title 28, U.S.C. § 636(c), the undersigned party or parties to the above-captioned civil matter hereby voluntarily consent to have a United States magistrate judge conduct any and all further proceedings in the case, including trial, and order the entry of a final judgment.

_____ _____
Date Signature

Note: Return this form to the Clerk of the Court if you consent to jurisdiction by a magistrate judge. Do not send a copy of this form to any district judge or magistrate judge.

(Added Apr. 28, 1983, eff. Aug. 1, 1983, and amended Apr. 22, 1993, eff. Dec. 1, 1993; April 11, 1997, eff. Dec. 1, 1997.)

Amendment of Forms

Form effective until December 1, 2007. For forms effective December 1, 2007, absent contrary Congressional action, see Forms 1 to 82 following this Appendix of Forms.

HISTORICAL NOTES

Change of Name

United States magistrate appointed under section 631 of Title 28, Judiciary and Judicial Procedure, to be known as United States magistrate judge after Dec. 1, 1990, with any reference to United States magistrate or magistrate in Title 28, in any other Federal statute, etc., deemed a reference to United States magistrate judge appointed under section 631 of Title 28, see section 321 of Pub.L. 101–650, set out as a note under section 631 of Title 28.

Form 34A. Order of Reference

Form effective until December 1, 2007.

UNITED STATES DISTRICT COURT

_____ DISTRICT OF _____

)	
Plaintiff,)	
)	
vs.)	Docket No. _____
)	
Defendant.)	

ORDER OF REFERENCE

IT IS HEREBY ORDERED that the above-captioned matter be referred to United States Magistrate Judge for all further proceedings and entry of judgment in accordance with Title 28, U.S.C. § 636(c) and the consent of the parties.

U.S. District Judge

(Added Apr. 22, 1993, eff. Dec. 1, 1993.)

Amendment of Forms

Form effective until December 1, 2007. For forms effective December 1, 2007, absent contrary Congressional action, see Forms 1 to 82 following this Appendix of Forms.

Form 35. Report of Parties' Planning Meeting

Form effective until December 1, 2007.

[Caption and Names of Parties]

1. Pursuant to Fed.R.Civ.P. 26(f), a meeting was held on (date) at (place) and was attended by:

(name) for plaintiff(s)

(name) for defendant(s) (party name)

(name) for defendant(s) (party name)

2. Pre–Discovery Disclosures. The parties [have exchanged] [will exchange by (date)] the information required by [Fed.R.Civ.P. 26(a)(1)] [local rule ___].

3. Discovery Plan. The parties jointly propose to the court the following discovery plan: [Use separate paragraphs or subparagraphs as necessary if parties disagree.]

Discovery will be needed on the following subjects: (brief description of subjects on which discovery will be needed)

Disclosure or discovery of electronically stored information should be handled as follows: (brief description of parties' proposals)

The parties have agreed to an order regarding claims of privilege or of protection as trial-preparation material asserted after production, as follows: (brief description of provisions of proposed order).

All discovery commenced in time to be completed by _____ (date) _____. [Discovery on _____ (issue for early discovery) _____ to be completed by _____ (date) _____.]

Maximum of ___ interrogatories by each party to any other party. [Responses due ___ days after service.]

Maximum of ___ requests for admission by each party to any other party. [Responses due ___ days after service.]

Maximum of ___ depositions by plaintiff(s) and ___ by defendant(s).

Each deposition [other than of _____] limited to maximum of ___ hours unless extended by agreement of parties.

Reports from retained experts under Rule 26(a)(2) due:

 from plaintiff(s) by (date)

 from defendant(s) by (date)

Supplementations under Rule 26(e) due (time(s) or interval(s)).

4. Other Items. [Use separate paragraphs or subparagraphs as necessary if parties disagree.]

The parties [request] [do not request] a conference with the court before entry of the scheduling order.

The parties request a pretrial conference in (month and year).

Plaintiff(s) should be allowed until (date) to join additional parties and until (date) to amend the pleadings.

Defendant(s) should be allowed until (date) to join additional parties and until (date) to amend the pleadings.

All potentially dispositive motions should be filed by (date).

Settlement [is likely] [is unlikely] [cannot be evaluated prior to (date)] [may be enhanced by use of the following alternative dispute resolution procedure: [_____].

Final lists of witnesses and exhibits under Rule 26(a)(3) should be due

 from plaintiff(s) by (date)

 from defendant(s) by (date)

Parties should have ___ days after service of final lists of witnesses and exhibits to list objections under Rule 26(a)(3).

The case should be ready for trial by (date) [and at this time is expected to take approximately (length of time)].

[Other matters.]

Date: _____

(Added Apr. 22, 1993, eff. Dec. 1, 1993, and amended Apr. 12, 2006, eff. Dec. 1, 2006)

Amendment of Forms

Form effective until December 1, 2007. For forms effective December 1, 2007, absent contrary Congressional action, see Forms 1 to 82 following this Appendix of Forms.

ADVISORY COMMITTEE NOTES

1993 Adoption

This form illustrates the type of report the parties are expected to submit to the court under revised Rule 26(f) and may be useful as a checklist of items to be discussed at the meeting.

PROPOSED APPENDIX OF FORMS

Form 1. Caption

Form effective December 1, 2007, absent contrary Congressional action.

A B, Plaintiff)
)
v.)
)
C D, Defendant)
)
v.)
)
E F, Third–Party Defendant)
(Use if needed.))

(Name of Document)

(Added Apr. 30, 2007, eff. Dec. 1, 2007.)

Form 2. Date, Signature, Address, E–Mail Address, and Telephone Number

Form effective December 1, 2007, absent contrary Congressional action.

(Use at the conclusion of pleadings and other papers that require a signature.)

Date _____

(Signature of the attorney or unrepresented party)

(Printed name)

(Address)

(E-mail address)

(Telephone number)

(Added Apr. 30, 2007, eff. Dec. 1, 2007.)

(Use on every summons, complaint, answer, motion, or other document.)

United States District Court
for the
_____ District of _____

Civil Action No. _____

Form 3. Summons

Form effective December 1, 2007, absent contrary Congressional action.

(Caption—See Form 1.)

To *name the defendant*:

A lawsuit has been filed against you.

Within 20 days after service of this summons on you (not counting the day you received it), you must serve on the plaintiff an answer to the attached complaint or a motion under Rule 12 of the Federal Rules of Civil Procedure. The answer or motion must be served on the plaintiff's attorney, _____, whose address is _____. If you fail to do so, judgment by default will be entered against you for the relief demanded in the complaint. You also must file your answer or motion with the court.

Date _____

Clerk of Court

(Court Seal)

(Use 60 days if the defendant is the United States or a United States agency, or is an officer or employee of the United States allowed 60 days by Rule 12(a)(3).)

(Added Apr. 30, 2007, eff. Dec. 1, 2007.)

Form effective December 1, 2007, absent contrary Congressional action. For forms effective until December 1, 2007, see Forms 1 to 35 preceding this Appendix of Forms.

Form 4. Summons on a Third–Party Complaint

Form effective December 1, 2007, absent contrary Congressional action.

(Caption—See Form 1.)

To *name the third-party defendant*:

A lawsuit has been filed against defendant _____, who as third-party plaintiff is making this claim against you to pay part or all of what [he] may owe to the plaintiff _____.

Within 20 days after service of this summons on you (not counting the day you received it), you must serve on the plaintiff and on the defendant an answer to the attached third-party complaint or a motion under Rule 12 of the Federal Rules of Civil Procedure. The answer or motion must be served on the defendant's attorney, _____ , whose address is, _____ , and also on the plaintiff's attorney, _____ , whose address is, _____. If you fail to do so, judgment by default will be entered against you for the relief demanded in the third-party complaint. You also must file the answer or motion with the court and serve it on any other parties.

A copy of the plaintiff's complaint is also attached. You may—but are not required to—respond to it.

Date _____

Clerk of Court

(Court Seal)

(Added Apr. 30, 2007, eff. Dec. 1, 2007.)

Amendment of Forms

Form effective December 1, 2007, absent contrary Congressional action. For forms effective until December 1, 2007, see Forms 1 to 35 preceding this Appendix of Forms.

Form 5. Notice of a Lawsuit and Request to Waive Service of a Summons

Form effective December 1, 2007, absent contrary Congressional action.

(Caption—See Form 1.)

To *(name the defendant—or if the defendant is a corporation, partnership, or association name an officer or agent authorized to receive service)*:

Why are you getting this?

A lawsuit has been filed against you, or the entity you represent, in this court under the number shown above. A copy of the complaint is attached.

This is not a summons, or an official notice from the court. It is a request that, to avoid expenses, you waive formal service of a summons by signing and returning the enclosed waiver. To avoid these expenses, you must return the signed waiver within *(give at least 30 days or at least 60 days if the defendant is outside any judicial district of the United States)* from the date shown below, which is the date this notice was sent. Two copies of the waiver form are enclosed, along with a stamped, self-addressed envelope or other prepaid means for returning one copy. You may keep the other copy.

What happens next?

If you return the signed waiver, I will file it with the court. The action will then proceed as if you had been served on the date the waiver is filed, but no summons will be served on you and you will have 60 days from the date this notice is sent (see the date below) to answer the complaint (or 90 days if this notice is sent to you outside any judicial district of the United States).

If you do not return the signed waiver within the time indicated, I will arrange to have the summons and complaint served on you. And I will ask the court to require you, or the entity you represent, to pay the expenses of making service.

Please read the enclosed statement about the duty to avoid unnecessary expenses.

I certify that this request is being sent to you on the date below.

(Date and sign—See Form 2.)

(Added Apr. 30, 2007, eff. Dec. 1, 2007.)

Amendment of Forms

Form effective December 1, 2007, absent contrary Congressional action. For forms effective until December 1, 2007, see Forms 1 to 35 preceding this Appendix of Forms.

Form 6. Waiver of the Service of Summons

Form effective December 1, 2007, absent contrary Congressional action.

(Caption—See Form 1.)

To *name the plaintiff's attorney or the unrepresented plaintiff*:

I have received your request to waive service of a summons in this action along with a copy of the complaint, two copies of this waiver form, and a prepaid means of returning one signed copy of the form to you.

I, or the entity I represent, agree to save the expense of serving a summons and complaint in this case.

I understand that I, or the entity I represent, will keep all defenses or objections to the lawsuit, the court's jurisdiction, and the venue of the action, but that I waive any objections to the absence of a summons or of service.

I also understand that I, or the entity I represent, must file and serve an answer or a motion under Rule 12 within 60 days from _____, the date when this request was sent (or 90 days if it was sent outside the United States). If I fail to do so, a default judgment will be entered against me or the entity I represent.

(Date and sign—See Form 2.)

(Attach the following to Form 6.)

Duty to Avoid Unnecessary Expenses of Serving a Summons

Rule 4 of the Federal Rules of Civil Procedure requires certain defendants to cooperate in saving unnecessary expenses of serving a summons and complaint. A defendant who is located in the United States and who fails to return a signed waiver of service requested by a plaintiff located in the United States will be required to pay the expenses of service, unless the defendant shows good cause for the failure.

"Good cause" does *not* include a belief that the lawsuit is groundless, or that it has been brought in an improper venue, or that the court has no jurisdiction over this matter or over the defendant or the defendant's property.

If the waiver is signed and returned, you can still make these and all other defenses and objections, but you cannot object to the absence of a summons or of service.

If you waive service, then you must, within the time specified on the waiver form, serve an answer or a motion under Rule 12 on the plaintiff and file a copy with the court. By signing and returning the waiver form, you are allowed more time to respond than if a summons had been served.

(Added Apr. 30, 2007, eff. Dec. 1, 2007.)

Amendment of Forms

Form effective December 1, 2007, absent contrary Congressional action. For forms effective until December 1, 2007, see Forms 1 to 35 preceding this Appendix of Forms.

Form 7. Statement of Jurisdiction

Form effective December 1, 2007, absent contrary Congressional action.

a. (*For diversity-of-citizenship jurisdiction.*) The plaintiff is [a citizen of *Michigan*] [a corporation incorporated under the laws of *Michigan* with its principal place of business in *Michigan*]. The defendant is [a citizen of *New York*] [a corporation incorporated under the laws of *New York* with its principal place of business in *New York*]. The amount in controversy, without interest and costs, exceeds the sum or value specified by 28 U.S.C. § 1332.

b. (*For federal-question jurisdiction.*) This action arises under [the United States Constitution, *specify the article or amendment and the section*] [a United States treaty *specify*] [a federal statute, ___ U.S.C. § ___].

c. (*For a claim in the admiralty or maritime jurisdiction.*) This is a case of admiralty or maritime jurisdiction. (*To invoke admiralty status under Rule 9(h) use the following:* This is an admiralty or maritime claim within the meaning of Rule 9(h).)

(Added Apr. 30, 2007, eff. Dec. 1, 2007.)

Amendment of Forms

Form effective December 1, 2007, absent contrary Congressional action. For forms effective until December 1, 2007, see Forms 1 to 35 preceding this Appendix of Forms.

Form 8. Statement of Reasons for Omitting a Party

Form effective December 1, 2007, absent contrary Congressional action.

(*If a person who ought to be made a party under Rule 19(a) is not named, include this statement in accordance with Rule 19(c).*)

This complaint does not join as a party *name* who [is not subject to this court's personal jurisdiction] [cannot be made a party without depriving this court of subject-matter jurisdiction] because *state the reason.*

(Added Apr. 30, 2007, eff. Dec. 1, 2007.)

Amendment of Forms

Form effective December 1, 2007, absent contrary Congressional action. For forms effective until December 1, 2007, see Forms 1 to 35 preceding this Appendix of Forms.

Form 9. Statement Noting a Party's Death

Form effective December 1, 2007, absent contrary Congressional action.

(Caption—See Form 1.)

In accordance with Rule 25(a) *name the person,* who is [a party to this action] [a representative of or successor to the deceased party] notes the death during the pendency of this action of *name,* [*describe as party* in this action].

(Date and sign—See Form 2.)
(Added Apr. 30, 2007, eff. Dec. 1, 2007.)

Amendment of Forms

Form effective December 1, 2007, absent contrary Congressional action. For forms effective until December 1, 2007, see Forms 1 to 35 preceding this Appendix of Forms.

Form 10. Complaint to Recover a Sum Certain

Form effective December 1, 2007, absent contrary Congressional action.

(Caption—See Form 1.)

1. (Statement of Jurisdiction—See Form 7.)

(Use one or more of the following as appropriate and include a demand for judgment.)

(a) On a Promissory Note

2. On *date,* the defendant executed and delivered a note promising to pay the plaintiff on *date* the sum of $_____ with interest at the rate of ___ percent. A copy of the note [is attached as Exhibit A] [is summarized as follows: _____.]

3. The defendant has not paid the amount owed.

(b) On an Account

2. The defendant owes the plaintiff $_____ according to the account set out in Exhibit A.

(c) For Goods Sold and Delivered

2. The defendant owes the plaintiff $_____ for goods sold and delivered by the plaintiff to the defendant from *date* to *date.*

(d) For Money Lent

2. The defendant owes the plaintiff $_____ for money lent by the plaintiff to the defendant on *date.*

(e) For Money Paid by Mistake

2. The defendant owes the plaintiff $_____ for money paid by mistake to the defendant on *date* under these circumstances: *describe with particularity in accordance with Rule 9(b).*

(f) For Money Had and Received

2. The defendant owes the plaintiff $_____ for money that was received from *name* on *date* to be paid by the defendant to the plaintiff.

Demand for Judgment

Therefore, the plaintiff demands judgment against the defendant for $_____, plus interest and costs.

(Date and sign—See Form 2.)
(Added Apr. 30, 2007, eff. Dec. 1, 2007.)

Amendment of Forms

Form effective December 1, 2007, absent contrary Congressional action. For forms effective until De-

cember 1, 2007, see Forms 1 to 35 preceding this Appendix of Forms.

Form 11. Complaint for Negligence

Form effective December 1, 2007, absent contrary Congressional action.

(Caption—See Form 1.)

1. (Statement of Jurisdiction—See Form 7.)

2. On *date*, at *place*, the defendant negligently drove a motor vehicle against the plaintiff.

3. As a result, the plaintiff was physically injured, lost wages or income, suffered physical and mental pain, and incurred medical expenses of $_____.

Therefore, the plaintiff demands judgment against the defendant for $_____, plus costs.

(Date and sign—See Form 2).
(Added Apr. 30, 2007, eff. Dec. 1, 2007.)

Amendment of Forms

Form effective December 1, 2007, absent contrary Congressional action. For forms effective until December 1, 2007, see Forms 1 to 35 preceding this Appendix of Forms.

Form 12. Complaint for Negligence when the Plaintiff Does Not Know Who is Responsible

Form effective December 1, 2007, absent contrary Congressional action.

(Caption—See Form 1.)

1. (Statement of Jurisdiction—See Form 7.)

2. On *date*, at *place*, defendant *name* or defendant *name* or both of them willfully or recklessly or negligently drove, or caused to be driven, a motor vehicle against the plaintiff.

3. As a result, the plaintiff was physically injured, lost wages or income, suffered mental and physical pain, and incurred medical expenses of $_____.

Therefore, the plaintiff demands judgment against one or both defendants for $_____, plus costs.

(Date and sign—See Form 2.)
(Added Apr. 30, 2007, eff. Dec. 1, 2007.)

Amendment of Forms

Form effective December 1, 2007, absent contrary Congressional action. For forms effective until December 1, 2007, see Forms 1 to 35 preceding this Appendix of Forms.

Form 13. Complaint for Negligence Under the Federal Employers' Liability Act

Form effective December 1, 2007, absent contrary Congressional action.

(Caption—See Form 1.)

1. (Statement of Jurisdiction—See Form 7.)

2. At the times below, the defendant owned and operated in interstate commerce a railroad line that passed through a tunnel located at _____.

3. On *date*, the plaintiff was working to repair and enlarge the tunnel to make it convenient and safe for use in interstate commerce.

4. During this work, the defendant, as the employer, negligently put the plaintiff to work in a section of the tunnel that the defendant had left unprotected and unsupported.

5. The defendant's negligence caused the plaintiff to be injured by a rock that fell from an unsupported portion of the tunnel.

6. As a result, the plaintiff was physically injured, lost wages or income, suffered mental and physical pain, and incurred medical expenses of $_____.

Therefore, the plaintiff demands judgment against the defendant for $_____, and costs.

(Date and sign—See Form 2.)

(Added Apr. 30, 2007, eff. Dec. 1, 2007.)

Amendment of Forms

Form effective December 1, 2007, absent contrary Congressional action. For forms effective until December 1, 2007, see Forms 1 to 35 preceding this Appendix of Forms.

Form 14. Complaint for Damages Under the Merchant Marine Act

Form effective December 1, 2007, absent contrary Congressional action.

(Caption—See Form 1.)

1. (Statement of Jurisdiction—See Form 7.)

2. At the times below, the defendant owned and operated the vessel *name* and used it to transport cargo for hire by water in interstate and foreign commerce.

3. On *date*, at *place*, the defendant hired the plaintiff under seamen's articles of customary form for a voyage from _____ to _____ and return at a wage of $_____ a month and found, which is equal to a shore worker's wage of $_____ a month.

4. On *date*, the vessel was at sea on the return voyage. (*Describe the weather and the condition of the vessel.*)

5. (*Describe as in Form 11 the defendant's negligent conduct.*)

6. As a result of the defendant's negligent conduct and the unseaworthiness of the vessel, the plaintiff was physically injured, has been incapable of any gainful activity, suffered mental and physical pain, and has incurred medical expenses of $_____.

Therefore, the plaintiff demands judgment against the defendant for $_____, plus costs.

(Date and sign—See Form 2.)

(Added Apr. 30, 2007, eff. Dec. 1, 2007.)

Amendment of Forms

Form effective December 1, 2007, absent contrary Congressional action. For forms effective until December 1, 2007, see Forms 1 to 35 preceding this Appendix of Forms.

Form 15. Complaint for the Conversion of Property

Form effective December 1, 2007, absent contrary Congressional action.

(Caption—See Form 1.)

1. (Statement of Jurisdiction—See Form 7.)

2. On *date*, at *place*, the defendant converted to the defendant's own use property owned by the plaintiff. The property converted consists of *describe*.

3. The property is worth $_____.

Therefore, the plaintiff demands judgment against the defendant for $_____, plus costs.

(Date and sign—See Form 2.)

(Added Apr. 30, 2007, eff. Dec. 1, 2007.)

Amendment of Forms

Form effective December 1, 2007, absent contrary Congressional action. For forms effective until December 1, 2007, see Forms 1 to 35 preceding this Appendix of Forms.

Form 16. Third–Party Complaint

Form effective December 1, 2007, absent contrary Congressional action.

(Caption—See Form 1.)

1. Plaintiff *name* has filed against defendant *name* a complaint, a copy of which is attached.

2. (*State grounds entitling defendant's name to recover from third-party defendant's name for (all or an identified share) of any judgment for plaintiff's name against defendant's name.*)

Therefore, the defendant demands judgment against *third-party defendant's name* for *all or an*

identified share of sums that may be adjudged against the defendant in the plaintiff's favor.

(Date and sign—See Form 2.)

(Added Apr. 30, 2007, eff. Dec. 1, 2007.)

Amendment of Forms

Form effective December 1, 2007, absent contrary Congressional action. For forms effective until December 1, 2007, see Forms 1 to 35 preceding this Appendix of Forms.

Form 17. Complaint for Specific Performance of a Contract to Convey Land

Form effective December 1, 2007, absent contrary Congressional action.

(Caption—See Form 1.)

1. (Statement of Jurisdiction—See Form 7.)
2. On *date*, the parties agreed to the contract [attached as Exhibit A][summarize the contract].
3. As agreed, the plaintiff tendered the purchase price and requested a conveyance of the land, but the defendant refused to accept the money or make a conveyance.
4. The plaintiff now offers to pay the purchase price.

Therefore, the plaintiff demands that:

 (a) the defendant be required to specifically perform the agreement and pay damages of $_____, plus interest and costs, or

 (b) if specific performance is not ordered, the defendant be required to pay damages of $_____, plus interest and costs.

(Date and sign—See Form 2.)

(Added Apr. 30, 2007, eff. Dec. 1, 2007.)

Amendment of Forms

Form effective December 1, 2007, absent contrary Congressional action. For forms effective until December 1, 2007, see Forms 1 to 35 preceding this Appendix of Forms.

Form 18. Complaint for Patent Infringement

Form effective December 1, 2007, absent contrary Congressional action.

(Caption—See Form 1.)

1. (Statement of Jurisdiction—See Form 7.)
2. On *date*, United States Letters Patent No. _____ were issued to the plaintiff for an invention in an *electric motor*. The plaintiff owned the patent throughout the period of the defendant's infringing acts and still owns the patent.
3. The defendant has infringed and is still infringing the Letters Patent by making, selling, and using *electric motors* that embody the patented

invention, and the defendant will continue to do so unless enjoined by this court.

4. The plaintiff has complied with the statutory requirement of placing a notice of the Letters Patent on all *electric motors* it manufactures and sells and has given the defendant written notice of the infringement.

Therefore, the plaintiff demands:

 (a) a preliminary and final injunction against the continuing infringement;

 (b) an accounting for damages; and

 (c) interest and costs.

(Date and sign—See Form 2.)

(Added Apr. 30, 2007, eff. Dec. 1, 2007.)

Amendment of Forms

Form effective December 1, 2007, absent contrary Congressional action. For forms effective until December 1, 2007, see Forms 1 to 35 preceding this Appendix of Forms.

Form 19. Complaint for Copyright Infringement and Unfair Competition

Form effective December 1, 2007, absent contrary Congressional action.

(Caption—See Form 1.)

1. (Statement of Jurisdiction—See Form 7.)
2. Before *date*, the plaintiff, a United States citizen, wrote a book entitled _____.
3. The book is an original work that may be copyrighted under United States law. A copy of the book is attached as Exhibit A.
4. Between *date* and *date*, the plaintiff applied to the copyright office and received a certificate of registration dated _____ and identified as *date, class, number*.
5. Since *date*, the plaintiff has either published or licensed for publication all copies of the book in compliance with the copyright laws and has remained the sole owner of the copyright.
6. After the copyright was issued, the defendant infringed the copyright by publishing and selling a book entitled _____, which was copied largely from the plaintiff's book. A copy of the defendant's book is attached as Exhibit B.
7. The plaintiff has notified the defendant in writing of the infringement.
8. The defendant continues to infringe the copyright by continuing to publish and sell the infringing book in violation of the copyright, and further has engaged in unfair trade practices and unfair competition in connection with its publication and sale of the infringing book, thus causing irreparable damage.

Therefore, the plaintiff demands that:

 (a) until this case is decided the defendant and the defendant's agents be enjoined from disposing of any copies of the defendant's book by sale or otherwise;

 (b) the defendant account for and pay as damages to the plaintiff all profits and advantages gained from unfair trade practices and unfair competition in selling the defendant's book, and all profits and advantages gained from infringing the plaintiff's copyright (but no less than the statutory minimum);

 (c) the defendant deliver for impoundment all copies of the book in the defendant's possession or control and deliver for destruction all infringing copies and all plates, molds, and other materials for making infringing copies;

 (d) the defendant pay the plaintiff interest, costs, and reasonable attorney's fees; and

 (e) the plaintiff be awarded any other just relief.

(Date and sign—See Form 2.)

(Added Apr. 30, 2007, eff. Dec. 1, 2007.)

Amendment of Forms

Form effective December 1, 2007, absent contrary Congressional action. For forms effective until December 1, 2007, see Forms 1 to 35 preceding this Appendix of Forms.

Form 20. Complaint for Interpleader and Declaratory Relief

Form effective December 1, 2007, absent contrary Congressional action.

(Caption—See Form 1.)

1. (Statement of Jurisdiction—See Form 7.)

2. On *date*, the plaintiff issued a life insurance policy on the life of *name* with *name* as the named beneficiary.

3. As a condition for keeping the policy in force, the policy required payment of a premium during the first year and then annually.

4. The premium due on *date* was never paid, and the policy lapsed after that date.

5. On *date* , after the policy had lapsed, both the insured and the named beneficiary died in an automobile collision.

6. Defendant *name* claims to be the beneficiary in place of *name* and has filed a claim to be paid the policy's full amount.

7. The other two defendants are representatives of the deceased persons' estates. Each defendant has filed a claim on behalf of each estate to receive payment of the policy's full amount.

8. If the policy was in force at the time of death, the plaintiff is in doubt about who should be paid.

Therefore, the plaintiff demands that:

 (a) each defendant be restrained from commencing any action against the plaintiff on the policy;

 (b) a judgment be entered that no defendant is entitled to the proceeds of the policy or any part of it, but if the court determines that the policy was in effect at the time of the insured's death, that the defendants be required to interplead and settle among themselves their rights to the proceeds, and that the plaintiff be discharged from all liability except to the defendant determined to be entitled to the proceeds; and

 (c) the plaintiff recover its costs.

(Date and sign—See Form 2.)

(Added Apr. 30, 2007, eff. Dec. 1, 2007.)

Amendment of Forms

Form effective December 1, 2007, absent contrary Congressional action. For forms effective until December 1, 2007, see Forms 1 to 35 preceding this Appendix of Forms.

Form 21. Complaint on a Claim for a Debt and to Set Aside a Fraudulent Conveyance Under Rule 18(b)

Form effective December 1, 2007, absent contrary Congressional action.

(Caption—See Form 1.)

1. (Statement of Jurisdiction—See Form 7.)

2. On *date*, defendant *name* signed a note promising to pay to the plaintiff on *date* the sum of $_____ with interest at the rate of ___ percent. [The pleader may, but need not, attach a copy or plead the note verbatim.]

3. Defendant *name* owes the plaintiff the amount of the note and interest.

4. On *date*, defendant *name* conveyed all defendant's real and personal property *if less than all, describe it fully* to defendant *name* for the purpose of defrauding the plaintiff and hindering or delaying the collection of the debt.

Therefore, the plaintiff demands that:

 (a) judgment for $_____, plus costs, be entered against defendant(s) *name(s)*; and

 (b) the conveyance to defendant *name* be declared void and any judgment granted be made a lien on the property.

(Date and sign—See Form 2.)

(Added Apr. 30, 2007, eff. Dec. 1, 2007.)

Amendment of Forms

Form effective December 1, 2007, absent contrary Congressional action. For forms effective until December 1, 2007, see Forms 1 to 35 preceding this Appendix of Forms.

Form 30. Answer Presenting Defenses Under Rule 12(b)

Form effective December 1, 2007, absent contrary Congressional action.

(Caption—See Form 1.)

Responding to Allegations in the Complaint

1. Defendant admits the allegations in paragraphs _____.

2. Defendant lacks knowledge or information sufficient to form a belief about the truth of the allegations in paragraphs _____.

3. Defendant admits *identify part of the allegation* in paragraph _____ and denies or lacks knowledge or information sufficient to form a belief about the truth of the rest of the paragraph.

Failure to State a Claim

4. The complaint fails to state a claim upon which relief can be granted.

Failure to Join a Required Party

5. If there is a debt, it is owed jointly by the defendant and *name* who is a citizen of _____. This person can be made a party without depriving this court of jurisdiction over the existing parties.

Affirmative Defense–Statute of Limitations

6. The plaintiff's claim is barred by the statute of limitations because it arose more than _____ years before this action was commenced.

Counterclaim

7. *(Set forth any counterclaim in the same way a claim is pleaded in a complaint. Include a further statement of jurisdiction if needed.)*

Crossclaim

8. *(Set forth a crossclaim against a coparty in the same way a claim is pleaded in a complaint. Include a further statement of jurisdiction if needed.)*

(Date and sign—See Form 2.)

(Added Apr. 30, 2007, eff. Dec. 1, 2007.)

Amendment of Forms

Form effective December 1, 2007, absent contrary Congressional action. For forms effective until December 1, 2007, see Forms 1 to 35 preceding this Appendix of Forms.

Form 31. Answer to a Complaint for Money Had and Received With a Counterclaim for Interpleader

Form effective December 1, 2007, absent contrary Congressional action.

(Caption—See Form 1.)

Response to the Allegations in the Complaint

(See Form 30.)

Counterclaim for Interpleader

1. The defendant received from *name* a deposit of $_____.

2. The plaintiff demands payment of the deposit because of a purported assignment from *name*, who has notified the defendant that the assignment is not valid and who continues to hold the defendant responsible for the deposit.

Therefore, the defendant demands that:

 (a) *name* be made a party to this action;

 (b) the plaintiff and *name* be required to interplead their respective claims;

 (c) the court decide whether the plaintiff or *name* or either of them is entitled to the deposit and discharge the defendant of any liability except to the person entitled to the deposit; and

 (d) the defendant recover costs and attorney's fees.

(Date and sign—See Form 2.)

(Added Apr. 30, 2007, eff. Dec. 1, 2007.)

Amendment of Forms

Form effective December 1, 2007, absent contrary Congressional action. For forms effective until December 1, 2007, see Forms 1 to 35 preceding this Appendix of Forms.

Form 40. Motion to Dismiss Under Rule 12(b) for Lack of Jurisdiction, Improper Venue, Insufficient Service of Process, or Failure to State a Claim

Form effective December 1, 2007, absent contrary Congressional action.

(Caption—See Form 1.)

The defendant moves to dismiss the action because:

1. the amount in controversy is less than the sum or value specified by 28 U.S.C. § 1332;

2. the defendant is not subject to the personal jurisdiction of this court;

3. venue is improper (this defendant does not reside in this district and no part of the events or omissions giving rise to the claim occurred in the district);

4. the defendant has not been properly served, as shown by the attached affidavits of _____; or

5. the complaint fails to state a claim upon which relief can be granted.

(Date and sign—See Form 2.)

(Added Apr. 30, 2007, eff. Dec. 1, 2007.)

Amendment of Forms

Form effective December 1, 2007, absent contrary Congressional action. For forms effective until December 1, 2007, see Forms 1 to 35 preceding this Appendix of Forms.

Form 41. Motion to Bring in a Third–Party Defendant

Form effective December 1, 2007, absent contrary Congressional action.

(Caption—See Form 1.)

The defendant, as third-party plaintiff, moves for leave to serve on *name* a summons and third-party complaint, copies of which are attached.

(Date and sign—See Form 2.)

(Added Apr. 30, 2007, eff. Dec. 1, 2007.)

Amendment of Forms

Form effective December 1, 2007, absent contrary Congressional action. For forms effective until December 1, 2007, see Forms 1 to 35 preceding this Appendix of Forms.

Form 42. Motion to Intervene as a Defendant Under Rule 24

Form effective December 1, 2007, absent contrary Congressional action.

(Caption—See Form 1.)

1. *name* moves for leave to intervene as a defendant in this action and to file the attached answer.

(State grounds under Rule 24(a) or (b).)

2. The plaintiff alleges patent infringement. We manufacture and sell to the defendant the articles involved, and we have a defense to the plaintiff's claim.

3. Our defense presents questions of law and fact that are common to this action.

(Date and sign—See Form 2.)

[An Intervener's Answer must be attached. See Form 30.]

(Added Apr. 30, 2007, eff. Dec. 1, 2007.)

Amendment of Forms

Form effective December 1, 2007, absent contrary Congressional action. For forms effective until December 1, 2007, see Forms 1 to 35 preceding this Appendix of Forms.

Form 50. Request to Produce Documents and Tangible Things, or to Enter onto Land Under Rule 34

Form effective December 1, 2007, absent contrary Congressional action.

(Caption—See Form 1.)

The plaintiff *name* requests that the defendant *name* respond within ____ days to the following requests:

1. To produce and permit the plaintiff to inspect and copy and to test or sample the following documents, including electronically stored information:

(Describe each document and the electronically stored information, either individually or by category.)

(State the time, place, and manner of the inspection and any related acts.)

2. To produce and permit the plaintiff to inspect and copy—and to test or sample—the following tangible things:

(Describe each thing, either individually or by category.)

(State the time, place, and manner of the inspection and any related acts.)

3. To permit the plaintiff to enter onto the following land to inspect, photograph, test, or sample the property or an object or operation on the property.

(Describe the property and each object or operation.)

(State the time and manner of the inspection and any related acts.)

(Date and sign—See Form 2.)

(Added Apr. 30, 2007, eff. Dec. 1, 2007.)

Amendment of Forms

Form effective December 1, 2007, absent contrary Congressional action. For forms effective until December 1, 2007, see Forms 1 to 35 preceding this Appendix of Forms.

Form 51. Request for Admissions Under Rule 36

Form effective December 1, 2007, absent contrary Congressional action.

(Caption—See Form 1.)

The plaintiff *name* asks the defendant *name* to respond within 30 days to these requests by admitting, for purposes of this action only and subject to objections to admissibility at trial:

1. The genuineness of the following documents, copies of which [are attached] [are or have been furnished or made available for inspection and copying].

(*List each document.*)

2. The truth of each of the following statements:

(*List each statement.*)

(Date and sign—See Form 2.)

(Added Apr. 30, 2007, eff. Dec. 1, 2007.)

Amendment of Forms

Form effective December 1, 2007, absent contrary Congressional action. For forms effective until December 1, 2007, see Forms 1 to 35 preceding this Appendix of Forms.

Form 52. Report of the Parties' Planning Meeting

Form effective December 1, 2007, absent contrary Congressional action.

(Caption—See Form 1.)

1. The following persons participated in a Rule 26(f) conference on *date* by *state the method of conferring*:

(*e.g., name* representing the plaintiff.)

2. Initial Disclosures. The parties [have completed] [will complete by *date*] the initial disclosures required by Rule 26(a)(1).

3. Discovery Plan. The parties propose this discovery plan:

(*Use separate paragraphs or subparagraphs if the parties disagree.*)

(a) Discovery will be needed on these subjects: (*describe.*)

(b) (Dates for commencing and completing discovery, including discovery to be commenced or completed before other discovery.)

(c) (Maximum number of interrogatories by each party to another party, along with the dates the answers are due.)

(d) (Maximum number of requests for admission, along with the dates responses are due.)

(e) (Maximum number of depositions by each party.)

(f) (Limits on the length of depositions, in hours.)

(g) (Dates for exchanging reports of expert witnesses.)

(h) (Dates for supplementations under Rule 26(e).)

4. Other Items:

(a) (A date if the parties ask to meet with the court before a scheduling order.)

(b) (Requested dates for pretrial conferences.)

(c) (Final dates for the plaintiff to amend pleadings or to join parties.)

(d) (Final dates for the defendant to amend pleadings or to join parties.)

(e) (Final dates to file dispositive motions.)

(f) (State the prospects for settlement.)

(g) (Identify any alternative dispute resolution procedure that may enhance settlement prospects.)

(h) (Final dates for submitting Rule 26(a)(3) witness lists, designations of witnesses whose testimony will be presented by deposition, and exhibit lists.)

(i) (Final dates to file objections under Rule 26(a)(3).)

(j) (Suggested trial date and estimate of trial length.)

(k) (Other matters.)

(Date and sign—see Form 2.)

(Added Apr. 30, 2007, eff. Dec. 1, 2007.)

Amendment of Forms

Form effective December 1, 2007, absent contrary Congressional action. For forms effective until December 1, 2007, see Forms 1 to 35 preceding this Appendix of Forms.

Form 60. Notice of Condemnation

Form effective December 1, 2007, absent contrary Congressional action.

(Caption—See Form 1.)

To *name the defendant*.

1. A complaint in condemnation has been filed in the United States District Court for the _____District of _____, to take property to use for *purpose*. The interest to be taken is *describe*. The court is located in the United States courthouse at this address: _____.

2. The property to be taken is described below. You have or claim an interest in it.

(*Describe the property.*)

3. The authority for taking this property is *cite*.

4. If you want to object or present any defense to the taking you must serve an answer on the plaintiff's attorney within 20 days [after being served with this notice][from (insert the date of the last publication of notice)]. Send your answer to this address: _____.

5. Your answer must identify the property in which you claim an interest, state the nature and extent of that interest, and state all your objections and defenses to the taking. Objections and defenses not presented are waived.

6. If you fail to answer you consent to the taking and the court will enter a judgment that takes your described property interest.

7. Instead of answering, you may serve on the plaintiff's attorney a notice of appearance that designates the property in which you claim an interest. After you do that, you will receive a notice of any proceedings that affect you. Whether or not you have previously appeared or answered, you may present evidence at a trial to determine compensation for the property and share in the overall award.

<p align="center">(Date and sign—See Form 2.)</p>

(Added Apr. 30, 2007, eff. Dec. 1, 2007.)

<p align="center">**Amendment of Forms**</p>

Form effective December 1, 2007, absent contrary Congressional action. For forms effective until December 1, 2007, see Forms 1 to 35 preceding this Appendix of Forms.

Form 61. **Complaint for Condemnation**

Form effective December 1, 2007, absent contrary Congressional action.

(Caption—See Form 1; name as defendants the property and at least one owner.)

1. (Statement of Jurisdiction—See Form 7.)

2. This is an action to take property under the power of eminent domain and to determine just compensation to be paid to the owners and parties in interest.

3. The authority for the taking is _____.

4. The property is to be used for _____.

5. The property to be taken is (*describe in enough detail for identification—or attach the description and state "is described in Exhibit A, attached."*)

6. The interest to be acquired is _____.

7. The persons known to the plaintiff to have or claim an interest in the property are: _____. (*For each person include the interest claimed.*)

8. There may be other persons who have or claim an interest in the property and whose names could not be found after a reasonably diligent search. They are made parties under the designation "Unknown Owners."

Therefore, the plaintiff demands judgment:

(a) condemning the property;

(b) determining and awarding just compensation; and

(c) granting any other lawful and proper relief.

<p align="center">(Date and sign—See Form 2.)</p>

(Added Apr. 30, 2007, eff. Dec. 1, 2007.)

<p align="center">**Amendment of Forms**</p>

Form effective December 1, 2007, absent contrary Congressional action. For forms effective until December 1, 2007, see Forms 1 to 35 preceding this Appendix of Forms.

Form 70. **Judgment on a Jury Verdict**

Form effective December 1, 2007, absent contrary Congressional action.

<p align="center">(Caption—See Form 1.)</p>

This action was tried by a jury with Judge _____ presiding, and the jury has rendered a verdict.

It is ordered that:

[the plaintiff *name* recover from the defendant *name* the amount of $_____ with interest at the rate of ___%, along with costs.]

[the plaintiff recover nothing, the action be dismissed on the merits, and the defendant *name* recover costs from the plaintiff *name*.]

Date _____

<p align="center">Clerk of Court</p>

(Added Apr. 30, 2007, eff. Dec. 1, 2007.)

<p align="center">**Amendment of Forms**</p>

Form effective December 1, 2007, absent contrary Congressional action. For forms effective until December 1, 2007, see Forms 1 to 35 preceding this Appendix of Forms.

Form 71. **Judgment by the Court Without a Jury**

Form effective December 1, 2007, absent contrary Congressional action.

<p align="center">(Caption—See Form 1.)</p>

This action was tried by Judge _____ without a jury and the following decision was reached:

It is ordered that [the plaintiff *name* recover from the defendant *name* the amount of $_____, with prejudgment interest at the rate of ___%, post-

judgment interest at the rate of ___%, along with costs.] [the plaintiff recover nothing, the action be dismissed on the merits, and the defendant *name* recover costs from the plaintiff *name*.]

Date_____

Clerk of Court

(Added Apr. 30, 2007, eff. Dec. 1, 2007.)

Amendment of Forms

Form effective December 1, 2007, absent contrary Congressional action. For forms effective until December 1, 2007, see Forms 1 to 35 preceding this Appendix of Forms.

Form 80. Notice of a Magistrate Judge's Availability

Form effective December 1, 2007, absent contrary Congressional action.

1. A magistrate judge is available under title 28 U.S.C. § 636(c) to conduct the proceedings in this case, including a jury or nonjury trial and the entry of final judgment. But a magistrate judge can be assigned only if all parties voluntarily consent.

2. You may withhold your consent without adverse substantive consequences. The identity of any party consenting or withholding consent will not be disclosed to the judge to whom the case is assigned or to any magistrate judge.

3. If a magistrate judge does hear your case, you may appeal directly to a United States court of appeals as you would if a district judge heard it.

A form called *Consent to an Assignment to a United States Magistrate Judge* is available from the court clerk's office.

(Added Apr. 30, 2007, eff. Dec. 1, 2007.)

Amendment of Forms

Form effective December 1, 2007, absent contrary Congressional action. For forms effective until December 1, 2007, see Forms 1 to 35 preceding this Appendix of Forms.

Form 81. Consent to an Assignment to a Magistrate Judge

Form effective December 1, 2007, absent contrary Congressional action.

(Caption—See Form 1.)

I voluntarily consent to have a United States magistrate judge conduct all further proceedings in this case, including a trial, and order the entry of final judgment. (Return this form to the court clerk—not to a judge or magistrate judge.)

Date_____

Signature of the Party

(Added Apr. 30, 2007, eff. Dec. 1, 2007.)

Amendment of Forms

Form effective December 1, 2007, absent contrary Congressional action. For forms effective until December 1, 2007, see Forms 1 to 35 preceding this Appendix of Forms.

Form 82. Order of Assignment to a Magistrate Judge

Form effective December 1, 2007, absent contrary Congressional action.

(Caption—See Form 1.)

With the parties' consent it is ordered that this case be assigned to United States Magistrate Judge _____ of this district to conduct all proceedings and enter final judgment in accordance with 28 U.S.C. § 636(c).

Date _____

United States District Judge

(Added Apr. 30, 2007, eff. Dec. 1, 2007.)

Amendment of Forms

Form effective December 1, 2007, absent contrary Congressional action. For forms effective until December 1, 2007, see Forms 1 to 35 preceding this Appendix of Forms.

SUPPLEMENTAL RULES FOR ADMIRALTY OR MARITIME CLAIMS AND ASSET FORFEITURE ACTIONS

ADVISORY COMMITTEE NOTES

1966 Adoption

The amendments to the Federal Rules of Civil Procedure to unify the civil and admiralty procedure, together with the Supplemental Rules for Certain Admiralty and Maritime Claims, completely superseded the Admiralty Rules, effective July 1, 1966. Accordingly, the latter were rescinded.

1985 Amendment

Since their promulgation in 1966, the Supplemental Rules for Certain Admiralty and Maritime Claims have preserved the special procedures of arrest and attachment unique to admiralty law. In recent years, however, these Rules have been challenged as violating the principles of procedural due process enunciated in the United States Supreme Court's decision in *Sniadach v. Family Finance Corp.*, 395 U.S. 337 (1969), and later developed in *Fuentes v. Shevin*, 407 U.S. 67 (1972); *Mitchell v. W.T. Grant Co.*, 416 U.S. 600 (1974); and *North Georgia Finishing, Inc. v. Di–Chem, Inc.*, 419 U.S. 601 (1975). These Supreme Court decisions provide five basic criteria for a constitutional seizure of property: (1) effective notice to persons having interests in the property seized, (2) judicial review prior to attachment, (3) avoidance of conclusory allegations in the complaint, (4) security posted by the plaintiff to protect the owner of the property under attachment, and (5) a meaningful and timely hearing after attachment.

Several commentators have found the Supplemental Rules lacking on some or all five grounds. *E.g.*, Batiza & Partridge, *The Constitutional Challenge to Maritime Seizures*, 26 Loy.L.Rev. 203 (1980); Morse, *The Conflict Between the Supreme Court Admiralty Rules and Sniadach–Fuentes: A Collision Course?*, 3 Fla.St.U.L.Rev. 1 (1975). The federal courts have varied in their disposition of challenges to the Supplemental Rules. The Fourth and Fifth Circuits have affirmed the constitutionality of Rule C. *Amstar Corp. v. S/S Alexandros T.*, 664 F.2d 904 (4th Cir.1981); *Merchants National Bank of Mobile v. The Dredge General G.L. Gillespie*, 663 F.2d 1338 (5th Cir.1981), *cert. dismissed*, 456 U.S. 966 (1982). However, a district court in the Ninth Circuit found Rule C unconstitutional. *Alyeska Pipeline Service Co. v. The Vessel Bay Ridge*, 509 F.Supp. 1115 (D. Alaska 1981), *appeal dismissed*, 703 F.2d 381 (9th Cir.1983). Rule B(1) has received similar inconsistent treatment. The Ninth and Eleventh Circuits have upheld its constitutionality. *Polar Shipping, Ltd. v. Oriental Shipping Corp.*, 680 F.2d 627 (9th Cir.1982); *Schiffahartsgesellschaft Leonhardt & Co. v. A. Bottacchi S.A. de Navegacion*, 732 F.2d 1543 (11th Cir.1984). On the other hand, a Washington district court has found it to be constitutionally deficient. *Grand Bahama Petroleum Co. v. Canadian Transportation Agencies, Ltd.*, 450 F.Supp. 447 (W.D. Wash. 1978). The constitutionality of both rules was questioned in *Techem Chem Co. v. M/T Choyo Maru*, 416 F.Supp. 960 (D. Md. 1976). Thus, there is uncertainty as to whether the current rules prescribe constitutionally sound procedures for guidance of courts and counsel. See general-ly Note, *Due Process in Admiralty Arrest and Attachment*, 56 Tex.L.Rev. 1091 (1978).

Due to the controversy and uncertainty that have surrounded the Supplemental Rules, local admiralty bars and the Maritime Law Association of the United States have sought to strengthen the constitutionality of maritime arrest and attachment by encouraging promulgation of local admiralty rules providing for prompt post-seizure hearings. Some districts also adopted rules calling for judicial scrutiny of applications for arrest or attachment. Nonetheless, the result has been a lack of uniformity and continued concern over the constitutionality of the existing practice. The amendments that follow are intended to provide rules that meet the requirements prescribed by the Supreme Court and to develop uniformity in the admiralty practice.

Rule A. Scope of Rules

(1) These Supplemental Rules apply to:

(A) the procedure in admiralty and maritime claims within the meaning of Rule 9(h) with respect to the following remedies:

(i) maritime attachment and garnishment,

(ii) actions in rem,

(iii) possessory, petitory, and partition actions, and

(iv) actions for exoneration from or limitation of liability;

(B) forfeiture actions in rem arising from a federal statute; and

(C) the procedure in statutory condemnation proceedings analogous to maritime actions in rem, whether within the admiralty and maritime jurisdiction or not. Except as otherwise provided, references in these Supplemental Rules to actions in rem include such analogous statutory condemnation proceedings.

(2) The Federal Rules of Civil Procedure also apply to the foregoing proceedings except to the extent that they are inconsistent with these Supplemental Rules. (Added Feb. 28, 1966, eff. July 1, 1966, and amended Apr. 12, 2006, eff. Dec. 1, 2006)

ADVISORY COMMITTEE NOTES

1966 Adoption

Certain distinctively maritime remedies must be preserved in unified rules. The commencement of an action by attachment or garnishment has heretofore been practically unknown in federal jurisprudence except in admiralty, although the amendment of Rule 4(e) effective July 1, 1963, makes available that procedure in accordance with state law. The maritime proceeding in rem is unique, except as it has been emulated by statute, and is closely related to the substantive maritime law relating to liens. Arrest of the vessel or other

maritime property is an historic remedy in controversies over title or right to possession, and in disputes among co-owners over the vessel's employment. The statutory right to limit liability is limited to owners of vessels, and has its own complexities. While the unified federal rules are generally applicable to these distinctive proceedings, certain special rules dealing with them are needed.

Arrest of the person and imprisonment for debt are not included because there remedies are not peculiarly maritime. The practice is not uniform but conforms to state law. See 2 Benedict § 286 [Note: reference is to the 6th Edition of Benedict on Admiralty and not to the current 7th Edition]; 28 U.S.C., § 2007; FRCP 64, 69. The relevant provisions of Admiralty Rules 2, 3, and 4 are unnecessary or obsolete.

No attempt is here made to compile a complete and self-contained code governing these distinctively maritime remedies. The more limited objective is to carry forward the relevant provisions of the former Rules of Practice for Admiralty and Maritime Cases, modernized and revised to some extent but still in the context of history and precedent. Accordingly, these Rules are not to be construed as limiting or impairing the traditional power of a district court, exercising the admiralty and maritime jurisdiction, to adapt its procedures and its remedies in the individual case, consistently with these rules, to secure the just, speedy, and inexpensive determination of every action. (See *Swift & Co., Packers v. Compania Columbiana Del Caribe, S/A,* 339 U.S. 684, (1950); Rule 1). In addition, of course, the district courts retain the power to make local rules not inconsistent with these rules. See Rule 83; cf. Admiralty Rule 44.

2006 Amendment

Rule A is amended to reflect the adoption of Rule G to govern procedure in civil forfeiture actions. Rule G(1) contemplates application of other Supplemental Rules to the extent that Rule G does not address an issue. One example is the Rule E(4)(c) provision for arresting intangible property.

Rule B. In Personam Actions: Attachment and Garnishment

(1) When Available; Complaint, Affidavit, Judicial Authorization, and Process. In an in personam action:

(a) If a defendant is not found within the district when a verified complaint praying for attachment and the affidavit required by Rule B(1)(b) are filed, a verified complaint may contain a prayer for process to attach the defendant's tangible or intangible personal property—up to the amount sued for—in the hands of garnishees named in the process.

(b) The plaintiff or the plaintiff's attorney must sign and file with the complaint an affidavit stating that, to the affiant's knowledge, or on information and belief, the defendant cannot be found within the district. The court must review the complaint and affidavit and, if the conditions of this Rule B appear to exist, enter an order so stating and authorizing process of attachment and garnishment. The clerk may issue supplemental process enforcing the court's order upon application without further court order.

(c) If the plaintiff or the plaintiff's attorney certifies that exigent circumstances make court review impracticable, the clerk must issue the summons and process of attachment and garnishment. The plaintiff has the burden in any post-attachment hearing under Rule E(4)(f) to show that exigent circumstances existed.

(d)(i) If the property is a vessel or tangible property on board a vessel, the summons, process, and any supplemental process must be delivered to the marshal for service.

(ii) If the property is other tangible or intangible property, the summons, process, and any supplemental process must be delivered to a person or organization authorized to serve it, who may be (A) a marshal; (B) someone under contract with the United States; (C) someone specially appointed by the court for that purpose; or, (D) in an action brought by the United States, any officer or employee of the United States.

(e) The plaintiff may invoke state-law remedies under Rule 64 for seizure of person or property for the purpose of securing satisfaction of the judgment.

(2) Notice to Defendant. No default judgment may be entered except upon proof—which may be by affidavit—that:

(a) the complaint, summons, and process of attachment or garnishment have been served on the defendant in a manner authorized by Rule 4;

(b) the plaintiff or the garnishee has mailed to the defendant the complaint, summons, and process of attachment or garnishment, using any form of mail requiring a return receipt; or

(c) the plaintiff or the garnishee has tried diligently to give notice of the action to the defendant but could not do so.

(3) Answer.

(a) By Garnishee. The garnishee shall serve an answer, together with answers to any interrogatories served with the complaint, within 20 days after service of process upon the garnishee. Interrogatories to the garnishee may be served with the complaint without leave of court. If the garnishee refuses or neglects to answer on oath as to the debts, credits, or effects of the defendant in the garnishee's hands, or any interrogatories concerning such debts, credits, and effects that may be propounded by the plaintiff, the court may award compulsory process against the garnishee. If the garnishee admits any debts, credits, or effects, they shall be held in the garnishee's hands or paid into

the registry of the court, and shall be held in either case subject to the further order of the court.

(b) By Defendant. The defendant shall serve an answer within 30 days after process has been executed, whether by attachment of property or service on the garnishee.

(Added Feb. 28, 1966, eff. July 1, 1966, and amended Apr. 29, 1985, eff. Aug. 1, 1985; Mar. 2, 1987, eff. Aug. 1, 1987; Apr. 17, 2000, eff. Dec. 1, 2000; Apr. 25, 2005, eff. Dec. 1, 2005.)

ADVISORY COMMITTEE NOTES

1966 Adoption

Subdivision (1)

This preserves the traditional maritime remedy of attachment and garnishment, and carries forward the relevant substance of Admiralty Rule 2. In addition, or in the alternative, provision is made for the use of similar state remedies made available by the amendment of Rule 4(e) effective July 1, 1963. On the effect of appearance to defend against attachment see Rule E(8).

The rule follows closely the language of Admiralty Rule 2. No change is made with respect to the property subject to attachment. No change is made in the condition that makes the remedy available. The rules have never defined the clause, "if the defendant shall not be found within the district," and no definition is attempted here. The subject seems one best left for the time being to development on a case-by-case basis. The proposal does shift from the marshal (on whom it now rests in theory) to the plaintiff the burden of establishing that the defendant cannot be found in the district.

A change in the context of the practice is brought about by Rule 4(f), which will enable summons to be served throughout the state instead of, as heretofore, only within the district. The Advisory Committee considered whether the rule on attachment and garnishment should be correspondingly changed to permit those remedies only when the defendant cannot be found within the state and concluded that the remedy should not be so limited.

The effect is to enlarge the class of cases in which the plaintiff may proceed by attachment or garnishment although jurisdiction of the person of the defendant may be independently obtained. This is possible at the present time where, for example, a corporate defendant has appointed an agent within the district to accept service of process but is not carrying on activities there sufficient to subject it to jurisdiction. (*Seawind Compania, S.A. v. Crescent Line, Inc.,* 320 F.2d 580 (2d Cir.1963)), or where, though the foreign corporation's activities in the district are sufficient to subject it personally to the jurisdiction, there is in the district no officer on whom process can be served (*United States v. Cia. Naviera Continental, S.A.,* 178 F.Supp. 561, (S.D.N.Y.1959)).

Process of attachment or garnishment will be limited to the district. See Rule E(3)(a).

Subdivision (2)

The former Admiralty Rules did not provide for notice to the defendant in attachment and garnishment proceedings. None is required by the principles of due process, since it is assumed that the garnishee or custodian of the property attached will either notify the defendant or be deprived of the right to plead the judgment as a defense in an action against him by the defendant. *Harris v. Balk,* 198 U.S. 215 (1905); *Pennoyer v. Neff,* 95 U.S. 714 (1878). Modern conceptions of fairness, however, dictate that actual notice be given to persons known to claim an interest in the property that is the subject of the action where that is reasonably practicable. In attachment and garnishment proceedings the persons whose interests will be affected by the judgment are identified by the complaint. No substantial burden is imposed on the plaintiff by a simple requirement that he notify the defendant of the action by mail.

In the usual case the defendant is notified of the pendency of the proceedings by the garnishee or otherwise, and appears to claim the property and to make his answer. Hence notice by mail is not routinely required in all cases, but only in those in which the defendant has not appeared prior to the time when a default judgment is demanded. The rule therefore provides only that no default judgment shall be entered except upon proof of notice, or of inability to give notice despite diligent efforts to do so. Thus the burden of giving notice is further minimized.

In some cases the plaintiff may prefer to give notice by serving process in the usual way instead of simply by mail. (Rule 4(d).) In particular, if the defendant is in a foreign country the plaintiff may wish to utilize the modes of notice recently provided to facilitate compliance with foreign laws and procedures (Rule 4(i)). The rule provides for these alternatives.

The rule does not provide for notice by publication because there is no problem concerning unknown claimants, and publication has little utility in proportion to its expense where the identity of the defendant is known.

Subdivision (3)

Subdivision (a) incorporates the substance of Admiralty Rule 36.

The Admiralty Rules were silent as to when the garnishee and the defendant were to answer. See also 2 Benedict ch. XXIV [Reference is to the 6th Edition of Benedict on Admiralty and not to the current 7th Edition].

The rule proceeds on the assumption that uniform and definite periods of time for responsive pleadings should be substituted for return days (see the discussion under Rule C(6), below). Twenty days seems sufficient time for the garnishee to answer (cf. FRCP 12(a)), and an additional 10 days should suffice for the defendant. When allowance is made for the time required for notice to reach the defendant this gives the defendant in attachment and garnishment approximately the same time that defendants have to answer when personally served.

1985 Amendment

Rule B(1) has been amended to provide for judicial scrutiny before the issuance of any attachment or garnishment process. Its purpose is to eliminate doubts as to whether the Rule is consistent with the principles of procedural due process enunciated by the Supreme Court in *Sniadach v. Family Finance Corp.,* 395 U.S. 337 (1969); and later developed in *Fuentes v. Shevin,* 407 U.S. 67 (1972); *Mitchell v. W.T. Grant Co.,* 416 U.S. 600 (1974); and *North Georgia Finishing, Inc. v. Di-Chem, Inc.,* 419 U.S. 601 (1975). Such doubts were raised in *Grand Bahama Petroleum Co. v.*

Canadian Transportation Agencies, Ltd., 450 F.Supp. 447 (W.D.Wash.1978); and Schiffahartsgesellschaft Leonhardt & Co. v. A. Bottacchi S.A. de Navegacion, 552 F.Supp. 771 (S.D.Ga.1982), which was reversed, 732 F.2d 1543 (11th Cir. 1984). But compare Polar Shipping Ltd. v. Oriental Shipping Corp., 680 F.2d 627 (9th Cir.1982), in which a majority of the panel upheld the constitutionality of Rule B because of the unique commercial context in which it is invoked. The practice described in Rule B(1) has been adopted in some districts by local rule. E.g., N.D. Calif. Local Rule 603.3; W.D.Wash. Local Admiralty Rule 15(d).

The rule envisions that the order will issue when the plaintiff makes a prima facie showing that he has a maritime claim against the defendant in the amount sued for and the defendant is not present in the district. A simple order with conclusory findings is contemplated. The reference to review by the "court" is broad enough to embrace review by a magistrate as well as by a district judge.

The new provision recognizes that in some situations, such as when the judge is unavailable and the ship is about to depart from the jurisdiction, it will be impracticable, if not impossible, to secure the judicial review contemplated by Rule B(1). When "exigent circumstances" exist, the rule enables the plaintiff to secure the issuance of the summons and process of attachment and garnishment, subject to a later showing that the necessary circumstances actually existed. This provision is intended to provide a safety valve without undermining the requirement of preattachment scrutiny. Thus, every effort to secure judicial review, including conducting a hearing by telephone, should be pursued before resorting to the exigent-circumstances procedure.

Rule B(1) also has been amended so that the garnishee shall be named in the "process" rather than in the "complaint." This should solve the problem presented in Filia Compania Naviera, S.A. v. Petroship, S.A., 1983 A.M.C. 1 (S.D.N.Y.1982), and eliminate any need for an additional judicial review of the complaint and affidavit when a garnishee is added.

1987 Amendment

The amendments are technical. No substantive change is intended.

2000 Amendment

Rule B(1) is amended in two ways, and style changes have been made.

The service provisions of Rule C(3) are adopted in paragraph (d), providing alternatives to service by a marshal if the property to be seized is not a vessel or tangible property on board a vessel.

The provision that allows the plaintiff to invoke state attachment and garnishment remedies is amended to reflect the 1993 amendments of Civil Rule 4. Former Civil Rule 4(e), incorporated in Rule B(1), allowed general use of state quasi-in-rem jurisdiction if the defendant was not an inhabitant of, or found within, the state. Rule 4(e) was replaced in 1993 by Rule 4(n)(2), which permits use of state law to seize a defendant's assets only if personal jurisdiction over the defendant cannot be obtained in the district where the action is brought. Little purpose would be served by incorporating Rule 4(n)(2) in Rule B, since maritime attachment and garnishment are available whenever the defendant is not found

within the district, a concept that allows attachment or garnishment even in some circumstances in which personal jurisdiction also can be asserted. In order to protect against any possibility that elimination of the reference to state quasi-in-rem jurisdiction remedies might seem to defeat continued use of state security devices, paragraph (e) expressly incorporates Civil Rule 64. Because Rule 64 looks only to security, not jurisdiction, the former reference to Rule E(8) is deleted as no longer relevant.

Rule B(2)(a) is amended to reflect the 1993 redistribution of the service provisions once found in Civil Rule 4(d) and (i). These provisions are now found in many different subdivisions of Rule 4. The new reference simply incorporates Rule 4, without designating the new subdivisions, because the function of Rule B(2) is simply to describe the methods of notice that suffice to support a default judgment. Style changes also have been made.

2005 Amendments

Rule B(1) is amended to incorporate the decisions in Heidmar, Inc. v. Anomina Ravennate Di Armamento Sp.A. of Ravenna, 132 F.3d 264, 267–268 (5th Cir. 1998), and Navieros InterAmericanos, S.A. v. M/V Vasilia Express, 120 F.3d 304, 314–315 (1st Cir. 1997). The time for determining whether a defendant is "found" in the district is set at the time of filing the verified complaint that prays for attachment and the affidavit required by Rule B(1)(b). As provided by Rule B(1)(b), the affidavit must be filed with the complaint. A defendant cannot defeat the security purpose of attachment by appointing an agent for service of process after the complaint and affidavit are filed. The complaint praying for attachment need not be the initial complaint. So long as the defendant is not found in the district, the prayer for attachment may be made in an amended complaint; the affidavit that the defendant cannot be found must be filed with the amended complaint.

Rule C. In Rem Actions: Special Provisions

(1) When Available. An action in rem may be brought:

(a) To enforce any maritime lien;

(b) Whenever a statute of the United States provides for a maritime action in rem or a proceeding analogous thereto.

Except as otherwise provided by law a party who may proceed in rem may also, or in the alternative, proceed in personam against any person who may be liable.

Statutory provisions exempting vessels or other property owned or possessed by or operated by or for the United States from arrest or seizure are not affected by this rule. When a statute so provides, an action against the United States or an instrumentality thereof may proceed on in rem principles.

(2) Complaint. In an action in rem the complaint must:

(a) be verified;

(b) describe with reasonable particularity the property that is the subject of the action; and

(c) state that the property is within the district or will be within the district while the action is pending.

(3) Judicial Authorization and Process.

(a) Arrest Warrant.

(i) The court must review the complaint and any supporting papers. If the conditions for an in rem action appear to exist, the court must issue an order directing the clerk to issue a warrant for the arrest of the vessel or other property that is the subject of the action.

(ii) If the plaintiff or the plaintiff's attorney certifies that exigent circumstances make court review impracticable, the clerk must promptly issue a summons and a warrant for the arrest of the vessel or other property that is the subject of the action. The plaintiff has the burden in any post-arrest hearing under Rule E(4)(f) to show that exigent circumstances existed.

(b) Service.

(i) If the property that is the subject of the action is a vessel or tangible property on board a vessel, the warrant and any supplemental process must be delivered to the marshal for service.

(ii) If the property that is the subject of the action is other property, tangible or intangible, the warrant and any supplemental process must be delivered to a person or organization authorized to enforce it, who may be: (A) a marshal; (B) someone under contract with the United States; (C) someone specially appointed by the court for that purpose; or, (D) in an action brought by the United States, any officer or employee of the United States.

(c) Deposit in Court. If the property that is the subject of the action consists in whole or in part of freight, the proceeds of property sold, or other intangible property, the clerk must issue—in addition to the warrant—a summons directing any person controlling the property to show cause why it should not be deposited in court to abide the judgment.

(d) Supplemental Process. The clerk may upon application issue supplemental process to enforce the court's order without further court order.

(4) Notice. No notice other than execution of process is required when the property that is the subject of the action has been released under Rule E(5). If the property is not released within 10 days after execution, the plaintiff must promptly—or within the time that the court allows—give public notice of the action and arrest in a newspaper designated by court order and having general circulation in the district, but publication may be terminated if the property is released before publication is completed. The notice must specify the time under Rule C(6) to file a statement of interest in or right against the seized property and to answer. This rule does not affect the notice requirements in an action to foreclose a preferred ship mortgage under 46 U.S.C. §§ 31301 et seq., as amended.

(5) Ancillary Process. In any action in rem in which process has been served as provided by this rule, if any part of the property that is the subject of the action has not been brought within the control of the court because it has been removed or sold, or because it is intangible property in the hands of a person who has not been served with process, the court may, on motion, order any person having possession or control of such property or its proceeds to show cause why it should not be delivered into the custody of the marshal or other person or organization having a warrant for the arrest of the property, or paid into court to abide the judgment; and, after hearing, the court may enter such judgment as law and justice may require.

(6) Responsive Pleading; Interrogatories.

(a) Maritime Arrests and Other Proceedings.

(i) a [1] person who asserts a right of possession or any ownership interest in the property that is the subject of the action must file a verified statement of right or interest:

(A) within 10 days after the execution of process, or

(B) within the time that the court allows;

(ii) the statement of right or interest must describe the interest in the property that supports the person's demand for its restitution or right to defend the action;

(iii) an agent, bailee, or attorney must state the authority to file a statement of right or interest on behalf of another; and

(iv) a person who asserts a right of possession or any ownership interest must serve an answer within 20 days after filing the statement of interest or right.

(b) Interrogatories. Interrogatories may be served with the complaint in an in rem action without leave of court. Answers to the interrogatories must be served with the answer to the complaint.

(Added Feb. 28, 1966, eff. July 1, 1966, and amended Apr. 29, 1985, eff. Aug. 1, 1985; Mar. 2, 1987, eff. Aug. 1, 1987; Apr. 30, 1991, eff. Dec. 1, 1991; Apr. 17, 2000, eff. Dec. 1, 2000; Apr. 29, 2002, eff. Dec. 1, 2002; Apr. 25, 2005, eff. Dec. 1, 2005; Apr. 12, 2006, eff. Dec. 1, 2006.)

[1] Text begins so in original.

Subdivision (1).

This rule is designed not only to preserve the proceeding in rem as it now exists in admiralty cases, but to preserve the substance of Admiralty Rules 13–18. The general reference to enforcement of any maritime lien is believed to state the existing law, and is an improvement over the enumeration in the former Admiralty Rules, which is repetitious and incomplete (e.g., there was no reference to general average). The reference to any maritime lien is intended to include liens created by state law which are enforceable in admiralty.

The main concern of Admiralty Rules 13–18 was with the question whether certain actions might be brought in rem or also, or in the alternative, in personam. Essentially, therefore, these rules deal with questions of substantive law, for in general an action in rem may be brought to enforce any maritime lien, and no action in personam may be brought when the substantive law imposes no personal liability.

These rules may be summarized as follows:

1. Cases in which the plaintiff may proceed in rem and/or in personam:
 a. Suits for seamen's wages;
 b. Suits by materialmen for supplies, repairs, etc.;
 c. Suits for pilotage;
 d. Suits for collision damages;
 e. Suits founded on mere maritime hypothecation;
 f. Suits for salvage.
2. Cases in which the plaintiff may proceed only in personam:
 a. Suits for assault and beating.
3. Cases in which the plaintiff may proceed only in rem:
 a. Suits on bottomry bonds.

The coverage is incomplete, since the rules omit mention of many cases in which the plaintiff may proceed in rem or in personam. This revision proceeds on the principle that it is preferable to make a general statement as to the availability of the remedies, leaving out conclusions on matters of substantive law. Clearly it is not necessary to enumerate the cases listed under Item 1, above, nor to try to complete the list.

The rule eliminates the provision of Admiralty Rule 15 that actions for assault and beating may be brought only in personam. A preliminary study fails to disclose any reason for the rule. It is subject to so many exceptions that it is calculated to deceive rather than to inform. A seaman may sue in rem when he has been beaten by a fellow member of the crew so vicious as to render the vessel unseaworthy, *The Rolph*, 293 Fed. 269, aff'd 299 Fed. 52 (9th Cir. 1923), or where the theory of the action is that a beating by the master is a breach of the obligation under the shipping articles to treat the seaman with proper kindness, *The David Evans*, 187 Fed. 775 (D.Hawaii 1911); and a passenger may sue in rem on the theory that the assault is a breach of the contract of passage, *The Western States*, 159 Fed. 354 (2d Cir. 1908). To say that an action for money damages may be brought only in personam seems equivalent to saying that a maritime lien shall not exist; and that, in turn, seems equivalent to announcing a rule of substantive law rather than a rule of procedure. Dropping the rule will leave it to the courts to determine whether a lien exists as a matter of substantive law.

The specific reference to bottomry bonds is omitted because, as a matter of hornbook substantive law, there is no personal liability on such bonds.

Subdivision (2).

This incorporates the substance of Admiralty Rules 21 and 22.

Subdivision (3).

Derived from Admiralty Rules 10 and 37. The provision that the warrant is to be issued by the clerk is new, but is assumed to state existing law.

There is remarkably little authority bearing on Rule 37, although the subject would seem to be an important one. The rule appears on its face to have provided for a sort of ancillary process, and this may well be the case when tangible property, such as a vessel, is arrested, and intangible property such as freight is incidentally involved. It can easily happen, however, that the only property against which the action may be brought is intangible, as where the owner of a vessel under charter has a lien on subfreights. See 2 Benedict § 299 and cases cited. [Reference is to the 6th Edition of Benedict on Admiralty and not to the current 7th Edition]. In such cases it would seem that the order to the person holding the fund is equivalent to original process, taking the place of the warrant for arrest. That being so, it would also seem that (1) there should be some provision for notice, comparable to that given when tangible property is arrested, and (2) it should not be necessary, as Rule 37 provided, to petition the court for issuance of the process, but that it should issue as of course. Accordingly the substance of Rule 37 is included in the rule covering ordinary process, and notice will be required by Rule C(4). Presumably the rules omit any requirement of notice in these cases because the holder of the funds (e.g., the cargo owner) would be required on general principles (cf. *Harris v. Balk*, 198 U.S. 215 (1905)) to notify his obligee (e.g., the charterer); but in actions in rem such notice seems plainly inadequate because there may be adverse claims to the fund (e.g., there may be liens against the subfreights for seamen's wages, etc.). Compare Admiralty Rule 9.

Subdivision (4).

This carries forward the notice provision of Admiralty Rule 10, with one modification. Notice by publication is too expensive and ineffective a formality to be routinely required. When, as usually happens, the vessel or other property is released on bond or otherwise there is no point in publishing notice; the vessel is freed from the claim of the plaintiff and no other interest in the vessel can be affected by the proceedings. If, however, the vessel is not released, general notice is required in order that all persons, including unknown claimants, may appear and be heard, and in order that the judgment in rem shall be binding on all the world.

Subdivision (5).

This incorporates the substance of Admiralty Rule 9.

There are remarkably few cases dealing directly with the rule. In The *George Prescott*, 10 Fed.Cas. 222 (No. 5,339) (E.D.N.Y.1865), the master and crew of a vessel libeled her for wages, and other lienors also filed libels. One of the lienors suggested to the court that prior to the arrest of the vessel the master had removed the sails, and asked that he be ordered to produce them. He admitted removing the

sails and selling them, justifying on the ground that he held a mortgage on the vessel. He was ordered to pay the proceeds into court. Cf. *United States v. The Zarko*, 187 F.Supp. 371 (S.D.Cal.1960), where an armature belonging to a vessel subject to a preferred ship mortgage was in possession of a repairman claiming a lien.

It is evident that, though the rule has had a limited career in the reported cases, it is a potentially important one. It is also evident that the rule is framed in terms narrower than the principle that supports it. There is no apparent reason for limiting it to ships and their appurtenances (2 Benedict § 299) [Reference is to the 6th Edition of Benedict on Admiralty and not to the current 7th Edition]. Also, the reference to "third parties" in the existing rule seems unfortunate. In *The George Prescott*, the person who removed and sold the sails was a plaintiff in the action, and relief against him was just as necessary as if he had been a stranger.

Another situation in which process of this kind would seem to be useful is that in which the principal property that is the subject of the action is a vessel, but her pending freight is incidentally involved. The warrant of arrest, and notice of its service, should be all that is required by way of original process and notice; ancillary process without notice should suffice as to the incidental intangibles.

The distinction between Admiralty Rules 9 and 37 is not at once apparent, but seems to be this: Where the action was against property that could not be seized by the marshal because it was intangible, the original process was required to be similar to that issued against a garnishee, and general notice was required (though not provided for by the present rule; cf. Advisory Committee's Note to Rule C(3)). Under Admiralty Rule 9 property had been arrested and general notice had been given, but some of the property had been removed or for some other reason could not be arrested. Here no further notice was necessary.

The rule also makes provision for this kind of situation: The proceeding is against a vessel's pending freight only; summons has been served on the person supposedly holding the funds, and general notice has been given; it develops that another person holds all or part of the funds. Ancillary process should be available here without further notice. Subdivision (6).

Adherence to the practice of return days seems unsatisfactory. The practice varies significantly from district to district. A uniform rule should be provided so that any claimant or defendant can readily determine when he is required to file or serve a claim or answer.

A virtue of the return-day practice is that it requires claimants to come forward and identify themselves at an early stage of the proceedings—before they could fairly be required to answer. The draft is designed to preserve this feature of the present practice by requiring early filing of the claim. The time schedule contemplated in the draft is closely comparable to the present practice in the Southern District of New York, where the claimant has a minimum of 8 days to claim and three weeks thereafter to answer.

This rule also incorporates the substance of Admiralty Rule 25. The present rule's emphasis on "the true and bona fide owner" is omitted, since anyone having the right to possession can claim (2 Benedict § 324) [Reference is to the 6th Edition of Benedict on Admiralty and not to the current 7th Edition].

1985 Amendment

Rule C(3) has been amended to provide for judicial scrutiny before the issuance of any warrant of arrest. Its purpose is to eliminate any doubt as to the rule's constitutionality under the *Sniadach* line of cases. *Sniadach v. Family Finance Corp.*, 395 U.S. 337 (1969); *Fuentes v. Shevin*, 407 U.S. 67 (1972); *Mitchell v. W.T. Grant Co.*, 416 U.S. 600 (1974); and *North Georgia Finishing, Inc. v. Di-Chem, Inc.*, 419 U.S. 601 (1975). This was thought desirable even though both the Fourth and the Fifth Circuits have upheld the existing rule. *Amstar Corp. v. S/S Alexandros T.*, 664 F.2d 904 (4th Cir.1981); *Merchants National Bank of Mobile v. The Dredge General G.L. Gillespie*, 663 F.2d 1338 (5th Cir.1981), *cert. dismissed*, 456 U.S. 966 (1982). A contrary view was taken by Judge Tate in the *Merchants National Bank* case and by the district court in *Alyeska Pipeline Service Co. v. The Vessel Bay Ridge*, 509 F.Supp. 1115 (D.Alaska 1981), *appeal dismissed*, 703 F.2d 381 (9th Cir. 1983).

The rule envisions that the order will issue upon a prima facie showing that the plaintiff has an action in rem against the defendant in the amount sued for and that the property is within the district. A simple order with conclusory findings is contemplated. The reference to review by the "court" is broad enough to embrace a magistrate as well as a district judge.

The new provision recognizes that in some situations, such as when a judge is unavailable and the vessel is about to depart from the jurisdiction, it will be impracticable, if not impossible, to secure the judicial review contemplated by Rule C(3). When "exigent circumstances" exist, the rule enables the plaintiff to secure the issuance of the summons and warrant of arrest, subject to a later showing that the necessary circumstances actually existed. This provision is intended to provide a safety valve without undermining the requirement of pre-arrest scrutiny. Thus, every effort to secure judicial review, including conducting a hearing by telephone, should be pursued before invoking the exigent-circumstances procedure.

The foregoing requirements for prior court review or proof of exigent circumstances do not apply to actions by the United States for forfeitures for federal statutory violations. In such actions a prompt hearing is not constitutionally required, *United States v. Eight Thousand Eight Hundred and Fifty Dollars*, 103 S.Ct. 2005 (1983); *Calero-Toledo v. Pearson Yacht Leasing Co.*, 416 U.S. 663 (1974), and could prejudice the government in its prosecution of the claimants as defendants in parallel criminal proceedings since the forfeiture hearing could be misused by the defendants to obtain by way of civil discovery information to which they would not otherwise be entitled and subject the government and the courts to the unnecessary burden and expense of two hearings rather than one.

1987 Amendment

The amendments are technical. No substantive change is intended.

1991 Amendment

These amendments are designed to conform the rule to Fed.R.Civ.P. 4, as amended. As with recent amendments to Rule 4, it is intended to relieve the Marshals Service of the burden of using its limited personnel and facilities for execution of process in routine circumstances. Doing so may involve a contractual arrangement with a person or organization retained by the government to perform these services, or the use of other government officers and employees, or the special appointment by the court of persons available to perform suitably.

The seizure of a vessel, with or without cargo, remains a task assigned to the Marshal. Successful arrest of a vessel frequently requires the enforcement presence of an armed government official and the cooperation of the United States Coast Guard and other governmental authorities. If the marshal is called upon to seize the vessel, it is expected that the same officer will also be responsible for the seizure of any property on board the vessel at the time of seizure that is to be the object of arrest or attachment.

2000 Amendment

Style changes have been made throughout the revised portions of Rule C. Several changes of meaning have been made as well.

Subdivision 2. In rem jurisdiction originally extended only to property within the judicial district. Since 1986, Congress has enacted a number of jurisdictional and venue statutes for forfeiture and criminal matters that in some circumstances permit a court to exercise authority over property outside the district. 28 U.S.C. § 1355(b)(1) allows a forfeiture action in the district where an act or omission giving rise to forfeiture occurred, or in any other district where venue is established by § 1395 or by any other statute. Section 1355(b)(2) allows an action to be brought as provided in (b)(1) or in the United States District Court for the District of Columbia when the forfeiture property is located in a foreign country or has been seized by authority of a foreign government. Section 1355(d) allows a court with jurisdiction under § 1355(b) to cause service in any other district of process required to bring the forfeiture property before the court. Section 1395 establishes venue of a civil proceeding for forfeiture in the district where the forfeiture accrues or the defendant is found; in any district where the property is found; in any district into which the property is brought, if the property initially is outside any judicial district; or in any district where the vessel is arrested if the proceeding is an admiralty proceeding to forfeit a vessel. Section 1395(e) deals with a vessel or cargo entering a port of entry closed by the President, and transportation to or from a state or section declared to be in insurrection. 18 U.S.C. § 981(h) creates expanded jurisdiction and venue over property located elsewhere that is related to a criminal prosecution pending in the district. These amendments, and related amendments of Rule E(3), bring these Rules into step with the new statutes. No change is made as to admiralty and maritime proceedings that do not involve a forfeiture governed by one of the new statutes.

Subdivision (2) has been separated into lettered paragraphs to facilitate understanding.

Subdivision (3). Subdivision (3) has been rearranged and divided into lettered paragraphs to facilitate understanding.

Paragraph (b)(i) is amended to make it clear that any supplemental process addressed to a vessel or tangible property on board a vessel, as well as the original warrant, is to be served by the marshal.

Subdivision (4). Subdivision (4) has required that public notice state the time for filing an answer, but has not required that the notice set out the earlier time for filing a statement of interest or claim. The amendment requires that both times be stated.

A new provision is added, allowing termination of publication if the property is released more than 10 days after execution but before publication is completed. Termination will save money, and also will reduce the risk of confusion as to the status of the property.

Subdivision (6). Subdivision (6) has applied a single set of undifferentiated provisions to civil forfeiture proceedings and to in rem admiralty proceedings. Because some differences in procedure are desirable, these proceedings are separated by adopting a new paragraph (a) for civil forfeiture proceedings and recasting the present rule as paragraph (b) for in rem admiralty proceedings. The provision for interrogatories and answers is carried forward as paragraph (c). Although this established procedure for serving interrogatories with the complaint departs from the general provisions of Civil Rule 26(d), the special needs of expedition that often arise in admiralty justify continuing the practice.

Both paragraphs (a) and (b) require a statement of interest or right rather than the "claim" formerly required. The new wording permits parallel drafting, and facilitates cross-references in other rules. The substantive nature of the statement remains the same as the former claim. The requirements of (a) and (b) are, however, different in some respects.

In a forfeiture proceeding governed by paragraph (a), a statement must be filed by a person who asserts an interest in or a right against the property involved. This category includes every right against the property, such as a lien, whether or not it establishes ownership or a right to possession. In determining who has an interest in or a right against property, courts may continue to rely on precedents that have developed the meaning of "claims" or "claimants" for the purpose of civil forfeiture proceedings.

In an admiralty and maritime proceeding governed by paragraph (b), a statement is filed only by a person claiming a right of possession or ownership. Other claims against the property are advanced by intervention under Civil Rule 24, as it may be supplemented by local admiralty rules. The reference to ownership includes every interest that qualifies as ownership under domestic or foreign law. If an ownership interest is asserted, it makes no difference whether its character is legal, equitable, or something else.

Paragraph (a) provides more time than paragraph (b) for filing a statement. Admiralty and maritime in rem proceedings often present special needs for prompt action that do not commonly arise in forfeiture proceedings .

Paragraphs (a) and (b) do not limit the right to make a restricted appearance under Rule E(8).

2002 Amendments

Rule C(3) is amended to reflect the provisions of 18 U.S.C. § 985, enacted by the Civil Asset Forfeiture Reform Act of 2000, 114 Stat. 202, 214–215. Section 985 provides, subject to

enumerated exceptions, that real property that is the subject of a civil forfeiture action is not to be seized until an order of forfeiture is entered. A civil forfeiture action is initiated by filing a complaint, posting notice, and serving notice on the property owner. The summons and arrest procedure is no longer appropriate.

Rule C(6)(a)(i)(A) is amended to adopt the provision enacted by 18 U.S.C. § 983(a)(4)(A), shortly before Rule C(6)(a)(i)(A) took effect, that sets the time for filing a verified statement as 30 days rather than 20 days, and that sets the first alternative event for measuring the 30 days as the date of service of the Government's complaint.

Rule C(6)(a)(iii) is amended to give notice of the provision enacted by 18 U.S.C. § 983(a)(4)(B) that requires that the answer in a forfeiture proceeding be filed within 20 days. Without this notice, unwary litigants might rely on the provision of Rule 5(d) that allows a reasonable time for filing after service.

Rule C(6)(b)(iv) is amended to change the requirement that an answer be filed within 20 days to a requirement that it be served within 20 days. Service is the ordinary requirement, as in Rule 12(a). Rule 5(d) requires filing within a reasonable time after service.

Changes Made After Publication and Comment No changes have been made since publication.

2005 Amendments

Rule C(6)(b)(i)(A) is amended to delete the reference to a time 10 days after completed publication under Rule C(4). This change corrects an oversight in the amendments made in 2000. Rule C(4) requires publication of notice only if the property that is the subject of the action is not released within 10 days after execution of process. Execution of process will always be earlier than publication.

2006 Amendment

Rule C is amended to reflect the adoption of Rule G to govern procedure in civil forfeiture actions.

HISTORICAL NOTES

References in Text

The Act of June 5, 1920, c. 250, § 30, referred to in subd. (4), is section 30 of Act June 5, 1920, c. 250, 41 Stat. 988, as amended, known as the "Ship Mortgage Act, 1920", which was classified generally to chapter 25 (section 911 et seq.) of the Appendix to Title 46, Shipping, prior to the repeal of that chapter by Pub.L. 100–710, Title I, § 106(b)(2), Nov. 23, 1988, 102 Stat. 4752. Successor provisions were enacted by Pub.L. 100–710, Title I, § 102(c), Nov. 23, 1988, 102 Stat. 4738, and are set out in chapters 301 (section 30101 et seq.) and 313 (section 31301 seq.) of Subtitle III of Title 46, Shipping (other chapters in that Subtitle being reserved for future legislation). For complete classification of former provisions of Act June 5, 1920, c. 250, § 30, 41 Stat. 988, as amended, see Disposition Table preceding the first section of revised Title 46, Shipping.

Rule D. Possessory, Petitory, and Partition Actions

In all actions for possession, partition, and to try title maintainable according to the course of the admiralty practice with respect to a vessel, in all actions so maintainable with respect to the possession of cargo or other maritime property, and in all actions by one or more part owners against the others to obtain security for the return of the vessel from any voyage undertaken without their consent, or by one or more part owners against the others to obtain possession of the vessel for any voyage on giving security for its safe return, the process shall be by a warrant of arrest of the vessel, cargo, or other property, and by notice in the manner provided by Rule B(2) to the adverse party or parties.

(Added Feb. 28, 1966, eff. July 1, 1966.)

ADVISORY COMMITTEE NOTES

1966 Adoption

This carries forward the substance of Admiralty Rule 19.

Rule 19 provided the remedy of arrest in controversies involving title and possession in general. See *The Tilton,* 23 Fed.Cas.1277 (No. 14,054) (C.C.D.Mass.1830). In addition it provided that remedy in controversies between co-owners respecting the employment of a vessel. It did not deal comprehensively with controversies between co-owners, omitting the remedy of partition. Presumably the omission is traceable to the fact that, when the rules were originally promulgated, concepts of substantive law (sometimes stated as concepts of jurisdiction) denied the remedy of partition except where the parties in disagreement were the owners of equal shares. See *The Steamboat Orleans,* 36 U.S. (11 Pet.) 175 (1837). The Supreme Court has now removed any doubt as to the jurisdiction of the district courts to partition a vessel, and has held in addition that no fixed principle of federal admiralty law limits the remedy to the case of equal shares. *Madruga v. Superior Court,* 346 U.S. 556 (1954). It is therefore appropriate to include a reference to partition in the rule.

Rule E. Actions in Rem and Quasi in Rem: General Provisions

(1) Applicability. Except as otherwise provided, this rule applies to actions in personam with process of maritime attachment and garnishment, actions in rem, and petitory, possessory, and partition actions, supplementing Rules B, C, and D.

(2) Complaint; Security.

(a) *Complaint.* In actions to which this rule is applicable the complaint shall state the circumstances from which the claim arises with such particularity that the defendant or claimant will be able, without moving for a more definite statement, to commence an investigation of the facts and to frame a responsive pleading.

(b) *Security for Costs.* Subject to the provisions of Rule 54(d) and of relevant statutes, the court may, on the filing of the complaint or on the appearance of any defendant, claimant, or any other party, or at any later time, require the plaintiff, defendant,

claimant, or other party to give security, or additional security, in such sum as the court shall direct to pay all costs and expenses that shall be awarded against the party by any interlocutory order or by the final judgment, or on appeal by any appellate court.

(3) Process.

(a) In admiralty and maritime proceedings process in rem or of maritime attachment and garnishment may be served only within the district.

(b) Issuance and Delivery. Issuance and delivery of process in rem, or of maritime attachment and garnishment, shall be held in abeyance if the plaintiff so requests.

(4) Execution of Process; Marshal's Return; Custody of Property; Procedures for Release.

(a) *In General.* Upon issuance and delivery of the process, or, in the case of summons with process of attachment and garnishment, when it appears that the defendant cannot be found within the district, the marshal or other person or organization having a warrant shall forthwith execute the process in accordance with this subdivision (4), making due and prompt return.

(b) *Tangible Property.* If tangible property is to be attached or arrested, the marshal or other person or organization having the warrant shall take it into the marshal's possession for safe custody. If the character or situation of the property is such that the taking of actual possession is impracticable, the marshal or other person executing the process shall affix a copy thereof to the property in a conspicuous place and leave a copy of the complaint and process with the person having possession or the person's agent. In furtherance of the marshal's custody of any vessel the marshal is authorized to make a written request to the collector of customs not to grant clearance to such vessel until notified by the marshal or deputy marshal or by the clerk that the vessel has been released in accordance with these rules.

(c) *Intangible Property.* If intangible property is to be attached or arrested the marshal or other person or organization having the warrant shall execute the process by leaving with the garnishee or other obligor a copy of the complaint and process requiring the garnishee or other obligor to answer as provided in Rules B(3)(a) and C(6); or the marshal may accept for payment into the registry of the court the amount owed to the extent of the amount claimed by the plaintiff with interest and costs, in which event the garnishee or other obligor shall not be required to answer unless alias process shall be served.

(d) *Directions With Respect to Property in Custody.* The marshal or other person or organization having the warrant may at any time apply to the court for directions with respect to property that has been attached or arrested, and shall give notice of such application to any or all of the parties as the court may direct.

(e) *Expenses of Seizing and Keeping Property; Deposit.* These rules do not alter the provisions of Title 28, U.S.C., § 1921, as amended, relative to the expenses of seizing and keeping property attached or arrested and to the requirement of deposits to cover such expenses.

(f) *Procedure for Release From Arrest or Attachment.* Whenever property is arrested or attached, any person claiming an interest in it shall be entitled to a prompt hearing at which the plaintiff shall be required to show why the arrest or attachment should not be vacated or other relief granted consistent with these rules. This subdivision shall have no application to suits for seamen's wages when process is issued upon a certification of sufficient cause filed pursuant to Title 46, U.S.C. §§ 603 and 604 or to actions by the United States for forfeitures for violation of any statute of the United States.

(5) Release of Property.

(a) Special Bond. Whenever process of maritime attachment and garnishment or process in rem is issued the execution of such process shall be stayed, or the property released, on the giving of security, to be approved by the court or clerk, or by stipulation of the parties, conditioned to answer the judgment of the court or of any appellate court. The parties may stipulate the amount and nature of such security. In the event of the inability or refusal of the parties so to stipulate the court shall fix the principal sum of the bond or stipulation at an amount sufficient to cover the amount of the plaintiff's claim fairly stated with accrued interest and costs; but the principal sum shall in no event exceed (i) twice the amount of the plaintiff's claim or (ii) the value of the property on due appraisement, whichever is smaller. The bond or stipulation shall be conditioned for the payment of the principal sum and interest thereon at 6 per cent per annum.

(b) *General Bond.* The owner of any vessel may file a general bond or stipulation, with sufficient surety, to be approved by the court, conditioned to answer the judgment of such court in all or any actions that may be brought thereafter in such court in which the vessel is attached or arrested. Thereupon the execution of all such process against such vessel shall be stayed so long as the amount secured by such bond or stipulation is at least double the aggregate amount claimed by plaintiffs

in all actions begun and pending in which such vessel has been attached or arrested. Judgments and remedies may be had on such bond or stipulation as if a special bond or stipulation had been filed in each of such actions. The district court may make necessary orders to carry this rule into effect, particularly as to the giving of proper notice of any action against or attachment of a vessel for which a general bond has been filed. Such bond or stipulation shall be indorsed by the clerk with a minute of the actions wherein process is so stayed. Further security may be required by the court at any time.

If a special bond or stipulation is given in a particular case, the liability on the general bond or stipulation shall cease as to that case.

(c) *Release by Consent or Stipulation; Order of Court or Clerk; Costs.* Any vessel, cargo, or other property in the custody of the marshal or other person or organization having the warrant may be released forthwith upon the marshal's acceptance and approval of a stipulation, bond, or other security, signed by the party on whose behalf the property is detained or the party's attorney and expressly authorizing such release, if all costs and charges of the court and its officers shall have first been paid. Otherwise no property in the custody of the marshal, other person or organization having the warrant, or other officer of the court shall be released without an order of the court; but such order may be entered as of course by the clerk, upon the giving of approved security as provided by law and these rules, or upon the dismissal or discontinuance of the action; but the marshal or other person or organization having the warrant shall not deliver any property so released until the costs and charges of the officers of the court shall first have been paid.

(d) *Possessory, Petitory, and Partition Actions.* The foregoing provisions of this subdivision (5) do not apply to petitory, possessory, and partition actions. In such cases the property arrested shall be released only by order of the court, on such terms and conditions and on the giving of such security as the court may require.

(6) Reduction or Impairment of Security. Whenever security is taken the court may, on motion and hearing, for good cause shown, reduce the amount of security given; and if the surety shall be or become insufficient, new or additional sureties may be required on motion and hearing.

(7) Security on Counterclaim.

(a) When a person who has given security for damages in the original action asserts a counterclaim that arises from the transaction or occurrence that is the subject of the original action, a plaintiff for whose benefit the security has been given must give security for damages demanded in the counterclaim unless the court for cause shown, directs otherwise. Proceedings on the original claim must be stayed until this security is given unless the court directs otherwise.

(b) The plaintiff is required to give security under Rule E(7)(a) when the United States or its corporate instrumentality counterclaims and would have been required to give security to respond in damages if a private party but is relieved by law from giving security.

(8) Restricted Appearance. An appearance to defend against an admiralty and maritime claim with respect to which there has issued process in rem, or process of attachment and garnishment, may be expressly restricted to the defense of such claim, and in that event is not an appearance for the purposes of any other claim with respect to which such process is not available or has not been served.

(9) Disposition of Property; Sales.

(a) Interlocutory Sales; Delivery.

(i) On application of a party, the marshal, or other person having custody of the property, the court may order all or part of the property sold—with the sales proceeds, or as much of them as will satisfy the judgment, paid into court to await further orders of the court—if:

(A) the attached or arrested property is perishable, or liable to deterioration, decay, or injury by being detained in custody pending the action;

(B) the expense of keeping the property is excessive or disproportionate; or

(C) there is an unreasonable delay in securing release of the property.

(ii) In the circumstances described in Rule E(9)(a)(i), the court, on motion by a defendant or a person filing a statement of interest or right under Rule C(6), may order that the property, rather than being sold, be delivered to the movant upon giving security under these rules.

(b) Sales; Proceeds. All sales of property shall be made by the marshal or a deputy marshal, or by other person or organization having the warrant, or by any other person assigned by the court where the marshal or other person or organization having the warrant is a party in interest; and the proceeds of sale shall be forthwith paid into the registry of the court to be disposed of according to law.

[(c) Redesignated (b)]

(10) Preservation of Property. When the owner or another person remains in possession of property attached or arrested under the provisions of Rule E(4)(b) that permit execution of process without taking actual possession, the court, on a party's motion or

on its own, may enter any order necessary to preserve the property and to prevent its removal.
(Added Feb. 28, 1966, eff. July 1, 1966, and amended Apr. 29, 1985, eff. Aug. 1, 1985; Mar. 2, 1987, eff. Aug. 1, 1987; Apr. 30, 1991, eff. Dec. 1, 1991; Apr. 17, 2000, eff. Dec. 1, 2000; Apr. 12, 2006, eff. Dec. 1, 2006.)

ADVISORY COMMITTEE NOTES
1966 Adoption

Subdivisions (1), (2).

Adapted from Admiralty Rule 24. The rule is based on the assumption that there is no more need for security for costs in maritime personal actions than in civil cases generally, but that there is reason to retain the requirement for actions in which property is seized. As to proceedings for limitation of liability see Rule F(1).

Subdivision (3).

The Advisory Committee has concluded for practical reasons that process requiring seizure of property should continue to be served only within the geographical limits of the district. Compare Rule B(1), continuing the condition that process of attachment and garnishment may be served only if the defendant is not found within the district.

The provisions of Admiralty Rule 1 concerning the persons by whom process is to be served will be superseded by FRCP 4(c).

Subdivision (4).

This rule is intended to preserve the provisions of Admiralty Rules 10 and 36 relating to execution of process, custody of property seized by the marshal, and the marshal's return. It is also designed to make express provision for matters not heretofore covered.

The provision relating to clearance in subdivision (b) is suggested by Admiralty Rule 44 of the District of Maryland.

Subdivision (d) is suggested by English Rule 12, Order 75.

28 U.S.C., § 1921 as amended in 1962 contains detailed provisions relating to the expenses of seizing and preserving property attached or arrested.

Subdivision (5).

In addition to Admiralty Rule 11 (see Rule E(9)), the release of property seized on process of attachment or in rem was dealt with by Admiralty Rules 5, 6, 12, and 57, and 28 U.S.C., § 2464 (formerly Rev.Stat. § 941). The rule consolidates these provisions and makes them uniformly applicable to attachment and garnishment and actions in rem.

The rule restates the substance of Admiralty Rule 5. Admiralty Rule 12 dealt only with ships arrested on in rem process. Since the same ground appears to be covered more generally by 28 U.S.C., § 2464, the subject matter of Rule 12 is omitted. The substance of Admiralty Rule 57 is retained. 28 U.S.C., § 2464 is incorporated with changes of terminology, and with a substantial change as to the amount of the bond. See 2 Benedict 395 n. 1a [Reference is to the 6th Edition of Benedict on Admiralty and not to the current 7th Edition.] *The Lotosland*, 2 F.Supp. 42 (S.D.N.Y.1933). The provision for general bond is enlarged to include the contingency of attachment as well as arrest of the vessel.

Subdivision (6).

Adapted from Admiralty Rule 8.

Subdivision (7).

Derived from Admiralty Rule 50.

Title 46, U.S.C., § 783 extends the principle of Rule 50 to the Government when sued under the Public Vessels Act, presumably on the theory that the credit of the Government is the equivalent of the best security. The rule adopts this principle and extends it to all cases in which the Government is defendant although the Suits in Admiralty Act contains no parallel provisions.

Subdivision (8).

Under the liberal joinder provisions of unified rules the plaintiff will be enabled to join with maritime actions in rem, or maritime actions in personam with process of attachment and garnishment, claims with respect to which such process is not available, including nonmaritime claims. Unification should not, however, have the result that, in order to defend against an admiralty and maritime claim with respect to which process in rem or quasi in rem has been served, the claimant or defendant must subject himself personally to the jurisdiction of the court with reference to other claims with respect to which such process is not available or has not been served, especially when such other claims are nonmaritime. So far as attachment and garnishment are concerned this principle holds true whether process is issued according to admiralty tradition and the Supplemental Rules or according to Rule 4(e) as incorporated by Rule B(1).

A similar problem may arise with respect to civil actions other than admiralty and maritime claims within the meaning of Rule 9(h). That is to say, in an ordinary civil action, whether maritime or not, there may be joined in one action claims with respect to which process of attachment and garnishment is available under state law and Rule 4(e) and claims with respect to which such process is not available or has not been served. The general Rules of Civil Procedure do not specify whether an appearance in such cases to defend the claim with respect to which process of attachment and garnishment has issued is an appearance for the purposes of the other claims. In that context the question has been considered best left to case-by-case development. Where admiralty and maritime claims within the meaning of Rule 9(h) are concerned, however, it seems important to include a specific provision to avoid an unfortunate and unintended effect of unification. No inferences whatever as to the effect of such an appearance in an ordinary civil action should be drawn from the specific provision here and the absence of such a provision in the general Rules.

Subdivision (9).

Adapted from Admiralty Rules 11, 12, and 40. Subdivision (a) is necessary because of various provisions as to disposition of property in forfeiture proceedings. In addition to particular statutes, note the provisions of 28 U.S.C., §§ 2461–65.

The provision of Admiralty Rule 12 relating to unreasonable delay was limited to ships but should have broader application. See 2 Benedict 404 [Reference is to the 6th Edition of Benedict on Admiralty and not to the current 7th Edition]. Similarly, both Rules 11 and 12 were limited to actions in rem, but should equally apply to attached property.

1985 Amendment

Rule E(4)(f) makes available the type of prompt post-seizure hearing in proceedings under Supplemental Rules B

and C that the Supreme Court has called for in a number of cases arising in other contexts. See *North Georgia Finishing, Inc. v. Di-Chem, Inc.,* 419 U.S. 601 (1975); *Mitchell v. W.T. Grant Co.,* 416 U.S. 600 (1974). Although post-attachment and post-arrest hearings always have been available on motion, an explicit statement emphasizing promptness and elaborating the procedure has been lacking in the Supplemental Rules. Rule E(4)(f) is designed to satisfy the constitutional requirement of due process by guaranteeing to the shipowner a prompt post-seizure hearing at which he can attack the complaint, the arrest, the security demanded, or any other alleged deficiency in the proceedings. The amendment also is intended to eliminate the previously disparate treatment under local rules of defendants whose property has been seized pursuant to Supplemental Rules B and C.

The new Rule E(4)(f) is based on a proposal by the Maritime Law Association of the United States and on local admiralty rules in the Eastern, Northern, and Southern Districts of New York. E.D.N.Y. Local Rule 13; N.D.N.Y. Local Rule 13; S.D.N.Y. Local Rule 12. Similar provisions have been adopted by other maritime districts. E.g., N.D.Calif. Local Rule 603.4; W.D.La. Local Admiralty Rule 21. Rule E(4)(f) will provide uniformity in practice and reduce constitutional uncertainties.

Rule E(4)(f) is triggered by the defendant or any other person with an interest in the property seized. Upon an oral or written application similar to that used in seeking a temporary restraining order, see Rule 65(b), the court is required to hold a hearing as promptly as possible to determine whether to allow the arrest or attachment to stand. The plaintiff has the burden of showing why the seizure should not be vacated. The hearing also may determine the amount of security to be granted or the propriety of imposing counter-security to protect the defendant from an improper seizure.

The foregoing requirements for prior court review or proof of exigent circumstances do not apply to actions by the United States for forfeitures for federal statutory violations. In such actions a prompt hearing is not constitutionally required, *United States v. Eight Thousand Eight Hundred and Fifty Dollars,* 103 S.Ct. 2005 (1983); *Calero-Toledo v. Pearson Yacht Leasing Co.,* 416 U.S. 663 (1974), and could prejudice the government in its prosecution of the claimants as defendants in parallel criminal proceedings since the forfeiture hearing could be misused by the defendants to obtain by way of civil discovery information to which they would not otherwise be entitled and subject the government and the courts to the unnecessary burden and expense of two hearings rather than one.

1987 Amendment

The amendments are technical. No substantive change is intended.

1991 Amendment

These amendments are designed to conform this rule to Fed.R.Civ.P. 4, as amended. They are intended to relieve the Marshals Service of the burden of using its limited personnel and facilities for execution of process in routine circumstances. Doing so may involve a contractual arrangement with a person or organization retained by the government to perform these services, or the use of other government officers and employees, or the special appointment by the court of persons available to perform suitably.

2000 Amendment

Style changes have been made throughout the revised portions of Rule E. Several changes of meaning have been made as well.

Subdivision (3). Subdivision (3) is amended to reflect the distinction drawn in Rule C(2)(c) and (d). Service in an admiralty or maritime proceeding still must be made within the district, as reflected in Rule C(2)(c), while service in forfeiture proceedings may be made outside the district when authorized by statute, as reflected in Rule C(2)(d).

Subdivision (7). Subdivision (7)(a) is amended to make it clear that a plaintiff need give security to meet a counterclaim only when the counterclaim is asserted by a person who has given security to respond in damages in the original action.

Subdivision (8). Subdivision (8) is amended to reflect the change in Rule B(1)(e) that deletes the former provision incorporating state quasi-in-rem jurisdiction. A restricted appearance is not appropriate when state law is invoked only for security under Civil Rule 64, not as a basis of quasi-in-rem jurisdiction. But if state law allows a special, limited, or restricted appearance as an incident of the remedy adopted from state law, the state practice applies through Rule 64 "in the manner provided by" state law.

Subdivision (9). Subdivision 9(b)(ii) is amended to reflect the change in Rule C(6) that substitutes a statement of interest or right for a claim.

Subdivision (10). Subdivision 10 is new. It makes clear the authority of the court to preserve and to prevent removal of attached or arrested property that remains in the possession of the owner or other person under Rule E(4)(b).

2006 Amendment

Rule E is amended to reflect the adoption of Rule G to govern procedure in civil forfeiture actions.

HISTORICAL NOTES

References in Text

Sections 603 and 604 of Title 46, referred to in subd. (4)(f), were repealed by Pub.L. 98–89, § 4(b), Aug. 26, 1983, 97 Stat. 600, section 1 of which enacted Title 46, Shipping.

Rule F. Limitation of Liability

(1) Time for Filing Complaint; Security. Not later than six months after receipt of a claim in writing, any vessel owner may file a complaint in the appropriate district court, as provided in subdivision (9) of this rule, for limitation of liability pursuant to statute. The owner (a) shall deposit with the court, for the benefit of claimants, a sum equal to the amount or value of the owner's interest in the vessel and pending freight, or approved security therefor, and in addition such sums, or approved security therefor, as the court may from time to time fix as necessary to carry out the provisions of the statutes as amended; or (b) at the owner's option shall transfer to

a trustee to be appointed by the court, for the benefit of claimants, the owner's interest in the vessel and pending freight, together with such sums, or approved security therefor, as the court may from time to time fix as necessary to carry out the provisions of the statutes as amended. The plaintiff shall also give security for costs and, if the plaintiff elects to give security, for interest at the rate of 6 percent per annum from the date of the security.

(2) Complaint. The complaint shall set forth the facts on the basis of which the right to limit liability is asserted and all facts necessary to enable the court to determine the amount to which the owner's liability shall be limited. The complaint may demand exoneration from as well as limitation of liability. It shall state the voyage if any, on which the demands sought to be limited arose, with the date and place of its termination; the amount of all demands including all unsatisfied liens or claims of lien, in contract or in tort or otherwise, arising on that voyage, so far as known to the plaintiff, and what actions and proceedings, if any, are pending thereon; whether the vessel was damaged, lost, or abandoned, and, if so, when and where; the value of the vessel at the close of the voyage or, in case of wreck, the value of her wreckage, strippings, or proceeds, if any, and where and in whose possession they are; and the amount of any pending freight recovered or recoverable. If the plaintiff elects to transfer the plaintiff's interest in the vessel to a trustee, the complaint must further show any prior paramount liens thereon, and what voyages or trips, if any, she has made since the voyage or trip on which the claims sought to be limited arose, and any existing liens arising upon any such subsequent voyage or trip, with the amounts and causes thereof, and the names and addresses of the lienors, so far as known; and whether the vessel sustained any injury upon or by reason of such subsequent voyage or trip.

(3) Claims Against Owner; Injunction. Upon compliance by the owner with the requirements of subdivision (1) of this rule all claims and proceedings against the owner or the owner's property with respect to the matter in question shall cease. On application of the plaintiff the court shall enjoin the further prosecution of any action or proceeding against the plaintiff or the plaintiff's property with respect to any claim subject to limitation in the action.

(4) Notice to Claimants. Upon the owner's compliance with subdivision (1) of this rule the court shall issue a notice to all persons asserting claims with respect to which the complaint seeks limitation, admonishing them to file their respective claims with the clerk of the court and to serve on the attorneys for the plaintiff a copy thereof on or before a date to be named in the notice. The date so fixed shall not be less than 30 days after issuance of the notice. For cause shown, the court may enlarge the time within which claims may be filed. The notice shall be published in such newspaper or newspapers as the court may direct once a week for four successive weeks prior to the date fixed for the filing of claims. The plaintiff not later than the day of second publication shall also mail a copy of the notice to every person known to have made any claim against the vessel or the plaintiff arising out of the voyage or trip on which the claims sought to be limited arose. In cases involving death a copy of such notice shall be mailed to the decedent at the decedent's last known address, and also to any person who shall be known to have made any claim on account of such death.

(5) Claims and Answer. Claims shall be filed and served on or before the date specified in the notice provided for in subdivision (4) of this rule. Each claim shall specify the facts upon which the claimant relies in support of the claim, the items thereof, and the dates on which the same accrued. If a claimant desires to contest either the right to exoneration from or the right to limitation of liability the claimant shall file and serve an answer to the complaint unless the claim has included an answer.

(6) Information to be Given Claimants. Within 30 days after the date specified in the notice for filing claims, or within such time as the court thereafter may allow, the plaintiff shall mail to the attorney for each claimant (or if the claimant has no attorney to the claimant) a list setting forth (a) the name of each claimant, (b) the name and address of the claimant's attorney (if the claimant is known to have one), (c) the nature of the claim, i.e., whether property loss, property damage, death, personal injury etc., and (d) the amount thereof.

(7) Insufficiency of Fund or Security. Any claimant may by motion demand that the funds deposited in court or the security given by the plaintiff be increased on the ground that they are less than the value of the plaintiff's interest in the vessel and pending freight. Thereupon the court shall cause due appraisement to be made of the value of the plaintiff's interest in the vessel and pending freight; and if the court finds that the deposit or security is either insufficient or excessive it shall order its increase or reduction. In like manner any claimant may demand that the deposit or security be increased on the ground that it is insufficient to carry out the provisions of the statutes relating to claims in respect of loss of life or bodily injury; and, after notice and hearing, the court may similarly order that the deposit or security be increased or reduced.

(8) Objections to Claims: Distribution of Fund. Any interested party may question or controvert any claim without filing an objection thereto. Upon determination of liability the fund deposited or secured, or the proceeds of the vessel and pending freight, shall

be divided pro rata, subject to all relevant provisions of law, among the several claimants in proportion to the amounts of their respective claims, duly proved, saving, however, to all parties any priority to which they may be legally entitled.

(9) Venue; Transfer. The complaint shall be filed in any district in which the vessel has been attached or arrested to answer for any claim with respect to which the plaintiff seeks to limit liability; or, if the vessel has not been attached or arrested, then in any district in which the owner has been sued with respect to any such claim. When the vessel has not been attached or arrested to answer the matters aforesaid, and suit has not been commenced against the owner, the proceedings may be had in the district in which the vessel may be, but if the vessel is not within any district and no suit has been commenced in any district, then the complaint may be filed in any district. For the convenience of parties and witnesses, in the interest of justice, the court may transfer the action to any district; if venue is wrongly laid the court shall dismiss or, if it be in the interest of justice, transfer the action to any district in which it could have been brought. If the vessel shall have been sold, the proceeds shall represent the vessel for the purposes of these rules.

(Added Feb. 28, 1966, eff. July 1, 1966, and amended Mar. 2, 1987, eff. Aug. 1, 1987.)

ADVISORY COMMITTEE NOTES
1966 Adoption

Subdivision (1).

The amendments of 1936 to the Limitation Act superseded to some extent the provisions of Admiralty Rule 51, especially with respect to the time of filing the complaint and with respect to security. The rule here incorporates in substance the 1936 amendment of the Act (46 U.S.C., § 185) with a slight modification to make it clear that the complaint may be filed at any time not later than six months after a claim has been lodged with the owner.

Subdivision (2).

Derived from Admiralty Rules 51 and 53.

Subdivision (3).

This is derived from the last sentence of 46 U.S.C. § 185 and the last paragraph of Admiralty Rule 51.

Subdivision (4).

Derived from Admiralty Rule 51.

Subdivision (5).

Derived from Admiralty Rules 52 and 53.

Subdivision (6).

Derived from Admiralty Rule 52.

Subdivision (7).

Derived from Admiralty Rule 52 and 46 U.S.C., § 185.

Subdivision (8).

Derived from Admiralty Rule 52.

Subdivision (9).

Derived from Admiralty Rule 54. The provision for transfer is revised to conform closely to the language of 28 U.S.C.

§§ 1404(a) and 1406(a), though it retains the existing rule's provision for transfer to any district for convenience. The revision also makes clear what has been doubted: that the court may transfer if venue is wrongly laid.

1987 Amendment

The amendments are technical. No substantive change is intended.

Rule G. Forfeiture Actions In Rem

(1) Scope. This rule governs a forfeiture action in rem arising from a federal statute. To the extent that this rule does not address an issue, Supplemental Rules C and E and the Federal Rules of Civil Procedure also apply.

(2) Complaint. The complaint must:

(a) be verified;

(b) state the grounds for subject-matter jurisdiction, in rem jurisdiction over the defendant property, and venue;

(c) describe the property with reasonable particularity;

(d) if the property is tangible, state its location when any seizure occurred and — if different — its location when the action is filed;

(e) identify the statute under which the forfeiture action is brought; and

(f) state sufficiently detailed facts to support a reasonable belief that the government will be able to meet its burden of proof at trial.

(3) Judicial Authorization and Process.

(a) Real Property. If the defendant is real property, the government must proceed under 18 U.S.C. § 985.

(b) Other Property; Arrest Warrant. If the defendant is not real property:

(i) the clerk must issue a warrant to arrest the property if it is in the government's possession, custody, or control;

(ii) the court—on finding probable cause—must issue a warrant to arrest the property if it is not in the government's possession, custody, or control and is not subject to a judicial restraining order; and

(iii) a warrant is not necessary if the property is subject to a judicial restraining order.

(c) Execution of Process.

(i) The warrant and any supplemental process must be delivered to a person or organization authorized to execute it, who may be: (A) a marshal or any other United States officer or employee; (B) someone under contract with the United States; or (C) someone specially appointed by the court for that purpose.

(ii) The authorized person or organization must execute the warrant and any supplemental process on property in the United States as soon as practicable unless:

(A) the property is in the government's possession, custody, or control; or

(B) the court orders a different time when the complaint is under seal, the action is stayed before the warrant and supplemental process are executed, or the court finds other good cause.

(iii) The warrant and any supplemental process may be executed within the district or, when authorized by statute, outside the district.

(iv) If executing a warrant on property outside the United States is required, the warrant may be transmitted to an appropriate authority for serving process where the property is located.

(4) Notice.

(a) Notice by Publication.

(i) When Publication Is Required. A judgment of forfeiture may be entered only if the government has published notice of the action within a reasonable time after filing the complaint or at a time the court orders. But notice need not be published if:

(A) the defendant property is worth less than $1,000 and direct notice is sent under Rule G(4)(b) to every person the government can reasonably identify as a potential claimant; or

(B) the court finds that the cost of publication exceeds the property's value and that other means of notice would satisfy due process.

(ii) Content of the Notice. Unless the court orders otherwise, the notice must:

(A) describe the property with reasonable particularity;

(B) state the times under Rule G(5) to file a claim and to answer; and

(C) name the government attorney to be served with the claim and answer.

(iii) Frequency of Publication. Published notice must appear:

(A) once a week for three consecutive weeks; or

(B) only once if, before the action was filed, notice of nonjudicial forfeiture of the same property was published on an official internet government forfeiture site for at least 30 consecutive days, or in a newspaper of general circulation for three consecutive weeks in a district where publication is authorized under Rule G(4)(a)(iv).

(iv) Means of Publication. The government should select from the following options a means of publication reasonably calculated to notify potential claimants of the action:

(A) if the property is in the United States, publication in a newspaper generally circulated in the district where the action is filed, where the property was seized, or where property that was not seized is located;

(B) if the property is outside the United States, publication in a newspaper generally circulated in a district where the action is filed, in a newspaper generally circulated in the country where the property is located, or in legal notices published and generally circulated in the country where the property is located; or

(C) instead of (A) or (B), posting a notice on an official internet government forfeiture site for at least 30 consecutive days.

(b) Notice to Known Potential Claimants.

(i) Direct Notice Required. The government must send notice of the action and a copy of the complaint to any person who reasonably appears to be a potential claimant on the facts known to the government before the end of the time for filing a claim under Rule G(5)(a)(ii)(B).

(ii) Content of the Notice. The notice must state:

(A) the date when the notice is sent;

(B) a deadline for filing a claim, at least 35 days after the notice is sent;

(C) that an answer or a motion under Rule 12 must be filed no later than 20 days after filing the claim; and

(D) the name of the government attorney to be served with the claim and answer.

(iii) Sending Notice.

(A) The notice must be sent by means reasonably calculated to reach the potential claimant.

(B) Notice may be sent to the potential claimant or to the attorney representing the potential claimant with respect to the seizure of the property or in a related investigation, administrative forfeiture proceeding, or criminal case.

(C) Notice sent to a potential claimant who is incarcerated must be sent to the place of incarceration.

(D) Notice to a person arrested in connection with an offense giving rise to the forfeiture who is not incarcerated when notice is sent may be sent to the address that person last gave to the agency that arrested or released the person.

(E) Notice to a person from whom the property was seized who is not incarcerated when notice is sent may be sent to the last address that person gave to the agency that seized the property.

(iv) When Notice Is Sent. Notice by the following means is sent on the date when it is placed in the mail, delivered to a commercial carrier, or sent by electronic mail.

(v) Actual Notice. A potential claimant who had actual notice of a forfeiture action may not oppose or seek relief from forfeiture because of the government's failure to send the required notice.

(5) Responsive Pleadings.

(a) Filing a Claim.

(i) A person who asserts an interest in the defendant property may contest the forfeiture by filing a claim in the court where the action is pending. The claim must:

(A) identify the specific property claimed;

(B) identify the claimant and state the claimant's interest in the property;

(C) be signed by the claimant under penalty of perjury; and

(D) be served on the government attorney designated under Rule G(4)(a)(ii)(C) or (b)(ii)(D).

(ii) Unless the court for good cause sets a different time, the claim must be filed:

(A) by the time stated in a direct notice sent under Rule G(4)(b);

(B) if notice was published but direct notice was not sent to the claimant or the claimant's attorney, no later than 30 days after final publication of newspaper notice or legal notice under Rule G(4)(a) or no later than 60 days after the first day of publication on an official internet government forfeiture site; or

(C) if notice was not published and direct notice was not sent to the claimant or the claimant's attorney:

(1) if the property was in the government's possession, custody, or control when the complaint was filed, no later than 60 days after the filing, not counting any time when the complaint was under seal or when the action was stayed before execution of a warrant issued under Rule G(3)(b); or

(2) if the property was not in the government's possession, custody, or control when the complaint was filed, no later than 60 days after the government complied with 18 U.S.C. § 985(c) as to real property, or 60 days after process was executed on the property under Rule G(3).

(iii) A claim filed by a person asserting an interest as a bailee must identify the bailor, and if filed on the bailor's behalf must state the authority to do so.

(b) Answer. A claimant must serve and file an answer to the complaint or a motion under Rule 12 within 20 days after filing the claim. A claimant waives an objection to in rem jurisdiction or to venue if the objection is not made by motion or stated in the answer.

(6) Special Interrogatories.

(a) Time and Scope. The government may serve special interrogatories limited to the claimant's identity and relationship to the defendant property without the court's leave at any time after the claim is filed and before discovery is closed. But if the claimant serves a motion to dismiss the action, the government must serve the interrogatories within 20 days after the motion is served.

(b) Answers or Objections. Answers or objections to these interrogatories must be served within 20 days after the interrogatories are served.

(c) Government's Response Deferred. The government need not respond to a claimant's motion to dismiss the action under Rule G(8)(b) until 20 days after the claimant has answered these interrogatories.

(7) Preserving, Preventing Criminal Use, and Disposing of Property; Sales.

(a) Preserving and Preventing Criminal Use of Property. When the government does not have actual possession of the defendant property the court, on motion or on its own, may enter any order necessary to preserve the property, to prevent its removal or encumbrance, or to prevent its use in a criminal offense.

(b) Interlocutory Sale or Delivery.

(i) Order to Sell. On motion by a party or a person having custody of the property, the court may order all or part of the property sold if:

(A) the property is perishable or at risk of deterioration, decay, or injury by being detained in custody pending the action;

(B) the expense of keeping the property is excessive or is disproportionate to its fair market value;

(C) the property is subject to a mortgage or to taxes on which the owner is in default; or

(D) the court finds other good cause.

(ii) Who Makes the Sale. A sale must be made by a United States agency that has authority to sell the property, by the agency's contractor, or by any person the court designates.

(iii) Sale Procedures. The sale is governed by 28 U.S.C. §§ 2001, 2002, and 2004, unless all parties, with the court's approval, agree to the sale, aspects of the sale, or different procedures.

(iv) Sale Proceeds. Sale proceeds are a substitute res subject to forfeiture in place of the

property that was sold. The proceeds must be held in an interest-bearing account maintained by the United States pending the conclusion of the forfeiture action.

(v) Delivery on a Claimant's Motion. The court may order that the property be delivered to the claimant pending the conclusion of the action if the claimant shows circumstances that would permit sale under Rule G(7)(b)(i) and gives security under these rules.

(c) Disposing of Forfeited Property. Upon entry of a forfeiture judgment, the property or proceeds from selling the property must be disposed of as provided by law.

(8) Motions.

(a) Motion To Suppress Use of the Property as Evidence. If the defendant property was seized, a party with standing to contest the lawfulness of the seizure may move to suppress use of the property as evidence. Suppression does not affect forfeiture of the property based on independently derived evidence.

(b) Motion To Dismiss the Action.

(i) A claimant who establishes standing to contest forfeiture may move to dismiss the action under Rule 12(b).

(ii) In an action governed by 18 U.S.C. § 983(a)(3)(D) the complaint may not be dismissed on the ground that the government did not have adequate evidence at the time the complaint was filed to establish the forfeitability of the property. The sufficiency of the complaint is governed by Rule G(2).

(c) Motion To Strike a Claim or Answer.

(i) At any time before trial, the government may move to strike a claim or answer:

(A) for failing to comply with Rule G(5) or (6), or

(B) because the claimant lacks standing.

(ii) The motion:

(A) must be decided before any motion by the claimant to dismiss the action; and

(B) may be presented as a motion for judgment on the pleadings or as a motion to determine after a hearing or by summary judgment whether the claimant can carry the burden of establishing standing by a preponderance of the evidence.

(d) Petition To Release Property.

(i) If a United States agency or an agency's contractor holds property for judicial or nonjudicial forfeiture under a statute governed by 18 U.S.C. § 983(f), a person who has filed a claim to the property may petition for its release under § 983(f).

(ii) If a petition for release is filed before a judicial forfeiture action is filed against the property, the petition may be filed either in the district where the property was seized or in the district where a warrant to seize the property issued. If a judicial forfeiture action against the property is later filed in another district — or if the government shows that the action will be filed in another district — the petition may be transferred to that district under 28 U.S.C. § 1404.

(e) Excessive Fines. A claimant may seek to mitigate a forfeiture under the Excessive Fines Clause of the Eighth Amendment by motion for summary judgment or by motion made after entry of a forfeiture judgment if:

(i) the claimant has pleaded the defense under Rule 8; and

(ii) the parties have had the opportunity to conduct civil discovery on the defense.

(9) Trial. Trial is to the court unless any party demands trial by jury under Rule 38.
(Added Apr. 12, 2006, eff. Dec. 1, 2006.)

ADVISORY COMMITTEE NOTES
2006 Adoption

Rule G is added to bring together the central procedures that govern civil forfeiture actions. Civil forfeiture actions are in rem proceedings, as are many admiralty proceedings. As the number of civil forfeiture actions has increased, however, reasons have appeared to create sharper distinctions within the framework of the Supplemental Rules. Civil forfeiture practice will benefit from distinctive provisions that express and focus developments in statutory, constitutional, and decisional law. Admiralty practice will be freed from the pressures that arise when the needs of civil forfeiture proceedings counsel interpretations of common rules that may not be suitable for admiralty proceedings.

Rule G generally applies to actions governed by the Civil Asset Forfeiture Reform Act of 2000 (CAFRA) and also to actions excluded from it. The rule refers to some specific CAFRA provisions; if these statutes are amended, the rule should be adapted to the new provisions during the period required to amend the rule.

Rule G is not completely self-contained. Subdivision (1) recognizes the need to rely at times on other Supplemental Rules and the place of the Supplemental Rules within the basic framework of the Civil Rules.

Supplemental Rules A, C, and E are amended to reflect the adoption of Rule G.

Subdivision (1).

Rule G is designed to include the distinctive procedures that govern a civil forfeiture action. Some details, however, are better supplied by relying on Rules C and E. Subdivision (1) incorporates those rules for issues not addressed by Rule G. This general incorporation is at times made explicit — subdivision (7)(b)(v), for example, invokes the security provisions of Rule E. But Rules C and E are not to be invoked to create conflicts with Rule G. They are to be used only when Rule G, fairly construed, does not address the issue.

The Civil Rules continue to provide the procedural framework within which Rule G and the other Supplemental Rules operate. Both Rule G(1) and Rule A state this basic proposition. Rule G, for example, does not address pleadings amendments. Civil Rule 15 applies, in light of the circumstances of a forfeiture action.

Subdivision (2).

Rule E(2)(a) requires that the complaint in an admiralty action "state the circumstances from which the claim arises with such particularity that the defendant or claimant will be able, without moving for a more definite statement, to commence an investigation of the facts and to frame a responsive pleading." Application of this standard to civil forfeiture actions has evolved to the standard stated in subdivision (2)(f). The complaint must state sufficiently detailed facts to support a reasonable belief that the government will be able to meet its burden of proof at trial. *See U. S. v. Mondragon*, 313 F.3d 862 (4th Cir. 2002). Subdivision (2)(f) carries this forfeiture case law forward without change.

Subdivision (3).

Subdivision (3) governs in rem process in a civil forfeiture action.

Paragraph (a). Paragraph (a) reflects the provisions of 18 U.S.C. § 985.

Paragraph (b). Paragraph (b) addresses arrest warrants when the defendant is not real property. Subparagraph (i) directs the clerk to issue a warrant if the property is in the government's possession, custody, or control. If the property is not in the government's possession, custody, or control and is not subject to a restraining order, subparagraph (ii) provides that a warrant issues only if the court finds probable cause to arrest the property. This provision departs from former Rule C(3)(a)(i), which authorized issuance of summons and warrant by the clerk without a probable-cause finding. The probable-cause finding better protects the interests of persons interested in the property. Subparagraph (iii) recognizes that a warrant is not necessary if the property is subject to a judicial restraining order. The government remains free, however, to seek a warrant if it anticipates that the restraining order may be modified or vacated.

Paragraph (c). Subparagraph (ii) requires that the warrant and any supplemental process be served as soon as practicable unless the property is already in the government's possession, custody, or control. But it authorizes the court to order a different time. The authority to order a different time recognizes that the government may have secured orders sealing the complaint in a civil forfeiture action or have won a stay after filing. The seal or stay may be ordered for reasons, such as protection of an ongoing criminal investigation, that would be defeated by prompt service of the warrant. Subparagraph (ii) does not reflect any independent ground for ordering a seal or stay, but merely reflects the consequences for execution when sealing or a stay is ordered. A court also may order a different time for service if good cause is shown for reasons unrelated to a seal or stay. Subparagraph (iv) reflects the uncertainty surrounding service of an arrest warrant on property not in the United States. It is not possible to identify in the rule the appropriate authority for serving process in all other countries. Transmission of the warrant to an appropriate authority, moreover, does not ensure that the warrant will be executed. The rule requires only that the warrant be transmitted to an appropriate authority.

Subdivision (4).

Paragraph (a). Paragraph (a) reflects the traditional practice of publishing notice of an in rem action.

Subparagraph (i) recognizes two exceptions to the general publication requirement. Publication is not required if the defendant property is worth less than $1,000 and direct notice is sent to all reasonably identifiable potential claimants as required by subdivision (4)(b). Publication also is not required if the cost would exceed the property's value and the court finds that other means of notice would satisfy due process. Publication on a government-established internet forfeiture site, as contemplated by subparagraph (iv), would be at a low marginal publication cost, which would likely be the cost to compare to the property value.

Subparagraph (iv) states the basic criterion for selecting the means and method of publication. The purpose is to adopt a means reasonably calculated to reach potential claimants. The government should choose from among these means a method that is reasonably likely to reach potential claimants at a cost reasonable in the circumstances.

If the property is in the United States and newspaper notice is chosen, publication may be where the action is filed, where the property was seized, or — if the property was not seized — where the property is located. Choice among these places is influenced by the probable location of potential claimants.

If the property is not in the United States, account must be taken of the sensitivities that surround publication of legal notices in other countries. A foreign country may forbid local publication. If potential claimants are likely to be in the United States, publication in the district where the action is filed may be the best choice. If potential claimants are likely to be located abroad, the better choice may be publication by means generally circulated in the country where the property is located.

Newspaper publication is not a particularly effective means of notice for most potential claimants. Its traditional use is best defended by want of affordable alternatives. Paragraph (iv)(C) contemplates a government-created internet forfeiture site that would provide a single easily identified means of notice. Such a site could allow much more direct access to notice as to any specific property than publication provides.

Paragraph (b). Paragraph (b) is entirely new. For the first time, Rule G expressly recognizes the due process obligation to send notice to any person who reasonably appears to be a potential claimant.

Subparagraph (i) states the obligation to send notice. Many potential claimants will be known to the government because they have filed claims during the administrative forfeiture stage. Notice must be sent, however, no matter what source of information makes it reasonably appear that a person is a potential claimant. The duty to send notice terminates when the time for filing a claim expires.

Notice of the action does not require formal service of summons in the manner required by Rule 4 to initiate a personal action. The process that begins an in rem forfeiture action is addressed by subdivision (3). This process commonly gives notice to potential claimants. Publication of notice is required in addition to this process. Due process requirements have moved beyond these traditional means of

notice, but are satisfied by practical means that are reasonably calculated to accomplish actual notice.

Subparagraph (ii)(B) directs that the notice state a deadline for filing a claim that is at least 35 days after the notice is sent. This provision applies both in actions that fall within 18 U.S.C. § 983(a)(4)(A) and in other actions. Section 983(a)(4)(A) states that a claim should be filed no later than 30 days after service of the complaint. The variation introduced by subparagraph (ii)(B) reflects the procedure of § 983(a)(2)(B) for nonjudicial forfeiture proceedings. The nonjudicial procedure requires that a claim be filed "not later than the deadline set forth in a personal notice letter (which may be not earlier than 35 days after the date the letter is sent) * * *." This procedure is as suitable in a civil forfeiture action as in a nonjudicial forfeiture proceeding. Thirty–five days after notice is sent ordinarily will extend the claim time by no more than a brief period; a claimant anxious to expedite proceedings can file the claim before the deadline; and the government has flexibility to set a still longer period when circumstances make that desirable.

Subparagraph (iii) begins by stating the basic requirement that notice must be sent by means reasonably calculated to reach the potential claimant. No attempt is made to list the various means that may be reasonable in different circumstances. It may be reasonable, for example, to rely on means that have already been established for communication with a particular potential claimant. The government's interest in choosing a means likely to accomplish actual notice is bolstered by its desire to avoid post-forfeiture challenges based on arguments that a different method would have been more likely to accomplish actual notice. Flexible rule language accommodates the rapid evolution of communications technology.

Notice may be directed to a potential claimant through counsel, but only to counsel already representing the claimant with respect to the seizure of the property, or in a related investigation, administrative forfeiture proceeding, or criminal case.

Subparagraph (iii)(C) reflects the basic proposition that notice to a potential claimant who is incarcerated must be sent to the place of incarceration. Notice directed to some other place, such as a pre-incarceration residence, is less likely to reach the potential claimant. This provision does not address due process questions that may arise if a particular prison has deficient procedures for delivering notice to prisoners. *See Dusenbery v. U.S.*, 534 U.S. 161 (2002).

Items (D) and (E) of subparagraph (iii) authorize the government to rely on an address given by a person who is not incarcerated. The address may have been given to the agency that arrested or released the person, or to the agency that seized the property. The government is not obliged to undertake an independent investigation to verify the address.

Subparagraph (iv) identifies the date on which notice is considered to be sent for some common means, without addressing the circumstances for choosing among the identified means or other means. The date of sending should be determined by analogy for means not listed. Facsimile transmission, for example, is sent upon transmission. Notice by personal delivery is sent on delivery.

Subparagraph (v), finally, reflects the purpose to effect actual notice by providing that a potential claimant who had actual notice of a forfeiture proceeding cannot oppose or seek relief from forfeiture because the government failed to comply with subdivision (4)(b).

Subdivision (5).

Paragraph (a). Paragraph (a) establishes that the first step of contesting a civil forfeiture action is to file a claim. A claim is required by 18 U.S.C. § 983(a)(4)(A) for actions covered by § 983. Paragraph (a) applies this procedure as well to actions not covered by § 983. "Claim" is used to describe this first pleading because of the statutory references to claim and claimant. It functions in the same way as the statement of interest prescribed for an admiralty proceeding by Rule C(6), and is not related to the distinctive meaning of "claim" in admiralty practice.

If the claimant states its interest in the property to be as bailee, the bailor must be identified. A bailee who files a claim on behalf of a bailor must state the bailee's authority to do so.

The claim must be signed under penalty of perjury by the person making it. An artificial body that can act only through an agent may authorize an agent to sign for it. Excusable inability of counsel to obtain an appropriate signature may be grounds for an extension of time to file the claim.

Paragraph (a)(ii) sets the time for filing a claim. Item (C) applies in the relatively rare circumstance in which notice is not published and the government did not send direct notice to the claimant because it did not know of the claimant or did not have an address for the claimant.

Paragraph (b). Under 18 U.S.C. § 983(a)(4)(B), which governs many forfeiture proceedings, a person who asserts an interest by filing a claim "shall file an answer to the Government's complaint for forfeiture not later than 20 days after the date of the filing of the claim." Paragraph (b) recognizes that this statute works within the general procedures established by Civil Rule 12. Rule 12(a)(4) suspends the time to answer when a Rule 12 motion is served within the time allowed to answer. Continued application of this rule to proceedings governed by § 983(a)(4)(B) serves all of the purposes advanced by Rule 12(a)(4), *see U. S. v. $8,221,877.16*, 330 F.3d 141 (3d Cir. 2003); permits a uniform procedure for all civil forfeiture actions; and recognizes that a motion under Rule 12 can be made only after a claim is filed that provides background for the motion.

Failure to present an objection to in rem jurisdiction or to venue by timely motion or answer waives the objection. Waiver of such objections is familiar. An answer may be amended to assert an objection initially omitted. But Civil Rule 15 should be applied to an amendment that for the first time raises an objection to in rem jurisdiction by analogy to the personal jurisdiction objection provision in Civil Rule 12(h)(1)(B). The amendment should be permitted only if it is permitted as a matter of course under Rule 15(a).

A claimant's motion to dismiss the action is further governed by subdivisions (6)(c), (8)(b), and (8)(c).

Subdivision (6).

Subdivision (6) illustrates the adaptation of an admiralty procedure to the different needs of civil forfeiture. Rule C(6) permits interrogatories to be served with the complaint in an in rem action without limiting the subjects of inquiry. Civil forfeiture practice does not require such an extensive departure from ordinary civil practice. It remains useful, however, to permit the government to file limited interroga-

tories at any time after a claim is filed to gather information that bears on the claimant's standing. Subdivisions (8)(b) and (c) allow a claimant to move to dismiss only if the claimant has standing, and recognize the government's right to move to dismiss a claim for lack of standing. Subdivision (6) interrogatories are integrated with these provisions in that the interrogatories are limited to the claimant's identity and relationship to the defendant property. If the claimant asserts a relationship to the property as bailee, the interrogatories can inquire into the bailor's interest in the property and the bailee's relationship to the bailor. The claimant can accelerate the time to serve subdivision (6) interrogatories by serving a motion to dismiss — the interrogatories must be served within 20 days after the motion is served. Integration is further accomplished by deferring the government's obligation to respond to a motion to dismiss until 20 days after the claimant moving to dismiss has answered the interrogatories.

Special interrogatories served under Rule G(6) do not count against the presumptive 25–interrogatory limit established by Rule 33(a). Rule 33 procedure otherwise applies to these interrogatories.

Subdivision (6) supersedes the discovery "moratorium" of Rule 26(d) and the broader interrogatories permitted for admiralty proceedings by Rule C(6).

Subdivision (7).

Paragraph (a). Paragraph (a) is adapted from Rule E(9)(b). It provides for preservation orders when the government does not have actual possession of the defendant property. It also goes beyond Rule E(9) by recognizing the need to prevent use of the defendant property in ongoing criminal offenses.

Paragraph (b). Paragraph (b)(i)(C) recognizes the authority, already exercised in some cases, to order sale of property subject to a defaulted mortgage or to defaulted taxes. The authority is narrowly confined to mortgages and tax liens; other lien interests may be addressed, if at all, only through the general good-cause provision. The court must carefully weigh the competing interests in each case.

Paragraph (b)(i)(D) establishes authority to order sale for good cause. Good cause may be shown when the property is subject to diminution in value. Care should be taken before ordering sale to avoid diminished value.

Paragraph (b)(iii) recognizes that if the court approves, the interests of all parties may be served by their agreement to sale, aspects of the sale, or sale procedures that depart from governing statutory procedures.

Paragraph (c) draws from Rule E(9)(a), (b), and (c). Disposition of the proceeds as provided by law may require resolution of disputed issues. A mortgagee's claim to the property or sale proceeds, for example, may be disputed on the ground that the mortgage is not genuine. An undisputed lien claim, on the other hand, may be recognized by payment after an interlocutory sale.

Subdivision (8).

Subdivision (8) addresses a number of issues that are unique to civil forfeiture actions.

Paragraph (a). Standing to suppress use of seized property as evidence is governed by principles distinct from the principles that govern claim standing. A claimant with standing to contest forfeiture may not have standing to seek suppression. Rule G does not of itself create a basis of suppression standing that does not otherwise exist.

Paragraph (b). Paragraph (b)(i) is one element of the system that integrates the procedures for determining a claimant's standing to claim and for deciding a claimant's motion to dismiss the action. Under paragraph (c)(ii), a motion to dismiss the action cannot be addressed until the court has decided any government motion to strike the claim or answer. This procedure is reflected in the (b)(i) reminder that a motion to dismiss the forfeiture action may be made only by a claimant who establishes claim standing. The government, moreover, need not respond to a claimant's motion to dismiss until 20 days after the claimant has answered any subdivision (6) interrogatories.

Paragraph (b)(ii) mirrors 18 U.S.C. § 983(a)(3)(D). It applies only to an action independently governed by § 983(a)(3)(D), implying nothing as to actions outside § 983(a)(3)(D). The adequacy of the complaint is measured against the pleading requirements of subdivision (2), not against the quality of the evidence available to the government when the complaint was filed.

Paragraph (c). As noted with paragraph (b), paragraph (c) governs the procedure for determining whether a claimant has standing. It does not address the principles that govern claim standing.

Paragraph (c)(i)(A) provides that the government may move to strike a claim or answer for failure to comply with the pleading requirements of subdivision (5) or to answer subdivision (6) interrogatories. As with other pleadings, the court should strike a claim or answer only if satisfied that an opportunity should not be afforded to cure the defects under Rule 15. Not every failure to respond to subdivision (6) interrogatories warrants an order striking the claim. But the special role that subdivision (6) plays in the scheme for determining claim standing may justify a somewhat more demanding approach than the general approach to discovery sanctions under Rule 37.

Paragraph (c)(ii) directs that a motion to strike a claim or answer be decided before any motion by the claimant to dismiss the action. A claimant who lacks standing is not entitled to challenge the forfeiture on the merits.

Paragraph (c)(ii) further identifies three procedures for addressing claim standing. If a claim fails on its face to show facts that support claim standing, the claim can be dismissed by judgment on the pleadings. If the claim shows facts that would support claim standing, those facts can be tested by a motion for summary judgment. If material facts are disputed, precluding a grant of summary judgment, the court may hold an evidentiary hearing. The evidentiary hearing is held by the court without a jury. The claimant has the burden to establish claim standing at a hearing; procedure on a government summary judgment motion reflects this allocation of the burden.

Paragraph (d). The hardship release provisions of 18 U.S.C. § 983(f) do not apply to a civil forfeiture action exempted from § 983 by § 983(i).

Paragraph (d)(ii) reflects the venue provisions of 18 U.S.C. § 983(f)(3)(A) as a guide to practitioners. In addition, it makes clear the status of a civil forfeiture action as a "civil action" eligible for transfer under 28 U.S.C. § 1404. A transfer decision must be made on the circumstances of the particular proceeding. The district where the forfeiture

action is filed has the advantage of bringing all related proceedings together, avoiding the waste that flows from consideration of different parts of the same forfeiture proceeding in the court where the warrant issued or the court where the property was seized. Transfer to that court would serve consolidation, the purpose that underlies nationwide enforcement of a seizure warrant. But there may be offsetting advantages in retaining the petition where it was filed. The claimant may not be able to litigate, effectively or at all, in a distant court. Issues relevant to the petition may be better litigated where the property was seized or where the warrant issued. One element, for example, is whether the claimant has sufficient ties to the community to provide assurance that the property will be available at the time of trial. Another is whether continued government possession would prevent the claimant from working. Determining whether seizure of the claimant's automobile prevents work may turn on assessing the realities of local public transit facilities.

Paragraph (e). The Excessive Fines Clause of the Eighth Amendment forbids an excessive forfeiture. *U.S. v. Bajakajian*, 524 U.S. 321 (1998). 18 U.S.C. § 983(g) provides a "petition" "to determine whether the forfeiture was constitutionally excessive" based on finding "that the forfeiture is grossly disproportional to the offense." Paragraph (e) describes the procedure for § 983(g) mitigation petitions and adopts the same procedure for forfeiture actions that fall outside § 983(g). The procedure is by motion, either for summary judgment or for mitigation after a forfeiture judgment is entered. The claimant must give notice of this defense by pleading, but failure to raise the defense in the initial answer may be cured by amendment under Rule 15. The issues that bear on mitigation often are separate from the issues that determine forfeiture. For that reason it may be convenient to resolve the issue by summary judgment before trial on the forfeiture issues. Often, however, it will be more convenient to determine first whether the property is to be forfeited. Whichever time is chosen to address mitigation, the parties must have had the opportunity to conduct civil discovery on the defense. The extent and timing of discovery are governed by the ordinary rules.

Subdivision (9).

Subdivision (9) serves as a reminder of the need to demand jury trial under Rule 38. It does not expand the right to jury trial. *See U.S. v. One Parcel of Property Located at 32 Medley Lane*, 2005 WL 465241 (D.Conn.2005), ruling that the court, not the jury, determines whether a forfeiture is constitutionally excessive.

RULES OF PROCEDURE OF THE JUDICIAL PANEL ON MULTIDISTRICT LITIGATION

I. GENERAL RULES/RULES FOR MULTIDISTRICT LITIGATION UNDER 28 U.S.C. § 1407

Rule 1.1. Definitions

As used in these Rules "Panel" means the members of the Judicial Panel on Multidistrict Litigation appointed by the Chief Justice of the United States pursuant to Section 1407, Title 28, United States Code.

"Clerk of the Panel" means the official appointed by the Panel to act as Clerk of the Panel and shall include those deputized by the Clerk of the Panel to perform or assist in the performance of the duties of the Clerk of the Panel.

"Chairman" means the Chairman of the Judicial Panel on Multidistrict Litigation appointed by the Chief Justice of the United States pursuant to Section 1407, or the member of the Panel designated by the Panel to act as Chairman in the absence or inability of the appointed Chairman.

A "tag-along action" refers to a civil action pending in a district court and involving common questions of fact with actions previously transferred under Section 1407.

(Added May 3, 1993, eff. July 1, 1993, and amended Sept. 1, 1998, eff. Nov. 2, 1998; Apr. 2, 2001, eff. Apr. 2, 2001.)

Rule 1.2. Practice

Where not fixed by statute or rule, the practice shall be that heretofore customarily followed by the Panel.

(Added May 3, 1993, eff. July 1, 1993, and amended Sept. 1, 1998, eff. Nov. 2, 1998; Apr. 2, 2001, eff. Apr. 2, 2001.)

Rule 1.3. Failure to Comply with Rules

The Clerk of the Panel may, when a paper submitted for filing is not in compliance with the provisions of these Rules, advise counsel of the deficiencies and a date for full compliance. If full compliance is not accomplished within the established time, the non-complying paper shall nonetheless be filed by the Clerk of the Panel but it may be stricken by order of the Chairman of the Panel.

(Added May 3, 1993, eff. July 1, 1993, and amended Sept. 1, 1998, eff. Nov. 2, 1998; Apr. 2, 2001, eff. Apr. 2, 2001.)

Rule 1.4. Admission to Practice Before the Panel and Representation in Transferred Actions

Every member in good standing of the Bar of any district court of the United States is entitled without condition to practice before the Judicial Panel on

Multidistrict Litigation. Any attorney of record in any action transferred under Section 1407 may continue to represent his or her client in any district court of the United States to which such action is transferred. Parties to any action transferred under Section 1407 are not required to obtain local counsel in the district to which such action is transferred.

(Added May 3, 1993, eff. July 1, 1993, and amended Sept. 1, 1998, eff. Nov. 2, 1998; Apr. 2, 2001, eff. Apr. 2, 2001.)

Rule 1.5. Effect of the Pendency of an Action Before the Panel

The pendency of a motion, order to show cause, conditional transfer order or conditional remand order before the Panel concerning transfer or remand of an action pursuant to 28 U.S.C. § 1407 does not affect or suspend orders and pretrial proceedings in the district court in which the action is pending and does not in any way limit the pretrial jurisdiction of that court. A transfer or remand pursuant to 28 U.S.C. § 1407 shall be effective when the transfer or remand order is filed in the office of the clerk of the district court of the transferee district.

(Added May 3, 1993, eff. July 1, 1993, and amended Sept. 1, 1998, eff. Nov. 2, 1998; Apr. 2, 2001, eff. Apr. 2, 2001.)

Rule 1.6. Transfer of Files

(a) Upon receipt of a certified copy of a transfer order from the clerk of the transferee district court, the clerk of the transferor district court shall forward to the clerk of the transferee district court the complete original file and a certified copy of the docket sheet for each transferred action.

(b) If an appeal is pending, or a notice of appeal has been filed, or leave to appeal has been sought under 28 U.S.C. § 1292(b) or a petition for an extraordinary writ is pending, in any action included in an order of transfer under 28 U.S.C. § 1407, and the original file or parts thereof have been forwarded to the court of appeals, the clerk of the transferor district court shall notify the clerk of the court of appeals of the order of transfer and secure the original file long enough to prepare and transmit to the clerk of the transferee district court a certified copy of all papers contained in the original file and a certified copy of the docket sheet.

(c) If the transfer order provides for the separation and simultaneous remand of any claim, cross-claim, counterclaim, or third-party claim, the clerk of the transferor district court shall retain the original file and shall prepare and transmit to the clerk of the transferee district court a certified copy of the docket sheet and copies of all papers except those relating exclusively to separated and remanded claims.

(d) Upon receipt of an order to remand from the Clerk of the Panel, the transferee district court shall

prepare and send to the clerk of the transferor district court the following:

(i) a certified copy of the individual docket sheet for each action being remanded;

(ii) a certified copy of the master docket sheet, if applicable;

(iii) the entire file for each action being remanded, as originally received from the transferor district court and augmented as set out in this rule;

(iv) a certified copy of the final pretrial order, if applicable; and

(v) a "record on remand" to be composed of those parts of the files and records produced during coordinated or consolidated pretrial proceedings which have been stipulated to or designated by counsel as being necessary for any or all proceedings to be conducted following remand. It shall be the responsibility of counsel originally preparing or filing any document to be included in the "record on remand" to furnish on request sufficient copies to the clerk of the transferee district court.

(e) The Clerk of the Panel shall be notified when any files have been transmitted pursuant to this Rule.

(Added May 3, 1993, eff. July 1, 1993, and amended Sept. 1, 1998, eff. Nov. 2, 1998; Apr. 2, 2001, eff. Apr. 2, 2001.)

Rule 5.1. Keeping Records and Files

(a) The records and files of the Panel shall be kept by the Clerk of the Panel at the offices of the Panel. Records and files may be temporarily or permanently removed to such places at such times as the Panel or the Chairman of the Panel shall direct. The Clerk of the Panel may charge fees, as prescribed by the Judicial Conference of the United States, for duplicating records and files. Records and files may be transferred whenever appropriate to the Federal Records Center.

(b) In order to assist the Panel in carrying out its functions, the Clerk of the Panel shall obtain the complaints and docket sheets in all actions under consideration for transfer under 28 U.S.C. § 1407 from the clerk of each district court wherein such actions are pending. The Clerk of the Panel shall similarly obtain any other pleadings and orders that could affect the Panel's decision under 28 U.S.C. § 1407.

(Added May 3, 1993, eff. July 1, 1993, and amended Sept. 1, 1998, eff. Nov. 2, 1998; Apr. 2, 2001, eff. Apr. 2, 2001.)

Rule 5.11. Place of Filing of Papers

All papers for consideration by the Panel shall be submitted for filing to the Clerk of the Panel by mailing or delivering to:

Clerk of the Panel
Judicial Panel on Multidistrict Litigation
Thurgood Marshall Federal Judiciary Building
One Columbus Circle, N.E., Room G–255, North Lobby
Washington, D.C. 20002–8004

No papers shall be left with or mailed to a Judge of the Panel.

(Added May 3, 1993, eff. July 1, 1993, and amended Sept. 1, 1998, eff. Nov. 2, 1998; Apr. 2, 2001, eff. Apr. 2, 2001.)

Rule 5.12. Manner of Filing of Papers

(a) An original of the following papers shall be submitted for filing to the Clerk of the Panel: a proof of service pursuant to Rule 5.2(a) and (b) of these Rules, a notice of appearance pursuant to Rule 5.2(c) and (d) of these Rules, a corporate disclosure statement pursuant to Rule 5.3 of these Rules, a status notice pursuant to Rules 7.2(f), 7.3(e) and 7.4(b) of these Rules, a notice of opposition pursuant to Rules 7.4(c) and 7.6(f)(ii) of these Rules, a notice of related action pursuant to Rules 7.2(i), 7.3(a) and 7.5(e) of these Rules, an application for extension of time pursuant to Rule 6.2 of these Rules, or a notice of presentation or waiver of oral argument pursuant to Rule 16.1(d) of these Rules. An original and ~~eleven~~four copies [1] of all other papers shall be submitted for filing to the Clerk of the Panel. The Clerk of the Panel may require that additional copies also be submitted for filing.

(b) When papers are submitted for filing, the Clerk of the Panel shall endorse thereon the date for filing.

(c) Copies of motions for transfer of an action or actions pursuant to 28 U.S.C. § 1407 shall be filed in each district court in which an action is pending that will be affected by the motion. Copies of a motion for remand pursuant to 28 U.S.C. § 1407 shall be filed in the Section 1407 transferee district court in which any action affected by the motion is pending.

(d) Papers requiring only an original may be faxed to the Panel office with prior approval of the Clerk of the Panel. No papers requiring multiple copies shall be accepted via fax.

(Added May 3, 1993, eff. July 1, 1993, and amended Sept. 1, 1998, eff. Nov. 2, 1998; Apr. 2, 2001, eff. Apr. 2, 2001.)

[1] An order issued by the Judicial Panel on Multidistrict Litigation filed April 19, 2005, entitled "Order Partially Suspending Panel Rule 5.12(a), Manner of Filing Papers" provided that, "IT IS HEREBY ORDERED that, because the Panel is utilizing filed papers and electronic distribution of those papers, Panel Rule 5.12(a), Manner of Filing Papers, R.P.J.P.M.L., 199 F.R.D. 425, 429 (2001), is partially suspended insofar as papers submitted for filing requiring an original and eleven copies shall be reduced to four copies along with an original."

Rule 5.13. Filing of Papers: Computer Generated Disk Required

(a) Whenever an original paper and eleven copies is required to be submitted for filing to the Clerk of the Panel pursuant to Rule 5.12(a) of these Rules, and where a party is represented by counsel, one copy of that paper must also be submitted on a computer readable disk and shall be filed at the time the party's paper is filed. The disk shall contain the entire paper exclusive of computer non-generated exhibits. The label of the disk shall include i) "MDL #___," ii) an abbreviated version of the MDL descriptive title, or other appropriate descriptive title, if not yet designated by the Panel, iii) the identity of the type of paper being filed (i.e. motion, response, reply, etc.), iv) the name of the counsel who signed the paper, and v) the first named represented party on the paper.

(b) The paper must be on a 3 1/2 inch disk in WordPerfect for Windows format.

(c) One copy of the disk may be served on each party separately represented by counsel. If a party chooses to serve a copy of the disk, the proof of service, as required by Rule 5.2 of these Rules, must indicate service of the paper in both paper and electronic format.

(d) A party may be relieved from the requirements of this Rule by submitting a written application for a waiver, in a timely manner in advance of submission of the paper, certifying that compliance with the Rule would impose undue hardship, that the text of the paper is not available on disk, or that other unusual circumstances preclude compliance with this Rule. The requirements of this Rule shall not apply to parties appearing pro se. Papers embraced by this Rule and submitted by counsel after June 1, 2000 without a computer disk copy or Panel-approved waiver of the requirements of this Rule shall be governed by Rule 1.3 of these Rules.

(Added May 22, 2000, eff. June 1, 2000, and amended Apr. 2, 2001, eff. Apr. 2, 2001.)

Rule 5.2. Service of Papers Filed

(a) All papers filed with the Clerk of the Panel shall be accompanied by proof of previous or simultaneous service on all other parties in all actions involved in the litigation. Service and proof of service shall be made as provided in Rules 5 and 6 of the Federal Rules of Civil Procedure. The proof of service shall indicate the name and complete address of each person served and shall indicate the party represented by each. If a party is not represented by counsel, the proof of service shall indicate the name of the party and the party's last known address. The proof of service shall indicate why any person named as a party in a constituent complaint was not served with the Section 1407 pleading. The original proof of ser-

vice shall be filed with the Clerk of the Panel and copies thereof shall be sent to each person included within the proof of service. After the "Panel Service List" described in subsection (d) of this Rule has been received from the Clerk of the Panel, the "Panel Service List" shall be utilized for service of responses to motions and all other filings. In such instances, the "Panel Service List" shall be attached to the proof of service and shall be supplemented in the proof of service in the event of the presence of additional parties or subsequent corrections relating to any party, counsel or address already on the "Panel Service List."

(b) The proof of service pertaining to motions for transfer of actions pursuant to 28 U.S.C. § 1407 shall certify that copies of the motions have been mailed or otherwise delivered for filing to the clerk of each district court in which an action is pending that will be affected by the motion. The proof of service pertaining to a motion for remand pursuant to 28 U.S.C. § 1407 shall certify that a copy of the motion has been mailed or otherwise delivered for filing to the clerk of the Section 1407 transferee district court in which any action affected by the motion is pending.

(c) Within eleven days of filing of a motion to transfer, an order to show cause or a conditional transfer order, each party or designated attorney shall notify the Clerk of the Panel, in writing, of the name and address of the attorney designated to receive service of all pleadings, notices, orders and other papers relating to practice before the Judicial Panel on Multidistrict Litigation. Only one attorney shall be designated for each party. Any party not represented by counsel shall be served by mailing such pleadings to the party's last known address. Requests for an extension of time to file the designation of attorney shall not be granted except in extraordinary circumstances.

(d) In order to facilitate compliance with subsection (a) of this Rule, the Clerk of the Panel shall prepare and serve on all counsel and parties not represented by counsel, a "Panel Service List" containing the names and addresses of the designated attorneys and the party or parties they represent in the actions under consideration by the Panel and the names and addresses of the parties not represented by counsel in the actions under consideration by the Panel. After the "Panel Service List" has been received from the Clerk of the Panel, notice of subsequent corrections relating to any party, counsel or address on the "Panel Service List" shall be served on all other parties in all actions involved in the litigation.

(e) If following transfer of any group of multidistrict litigation, the transferee district court appoints liaison counsel, this Rule shall be satisfied by serving each party in each affected action and all liaison counsel. Liaison counsel designated by the transferee district court shall receive copies of all Panel orders concerning their particular litigation and shall be responsible for distribution to the parties for whom he or she serves as liaison counsel.

(Added May 3, 1993, eff. July 1, 1993, and amended Sept. 1, 1998, eff. Nov. 2, 1998; Apr. 2, 2001, eff. Apr. 2, 2001.)

Rule 5.3. Corporate Disclosure Statement

(a) Any nongovernmental corporate party to a matter before the Panel shall file a statement identifying all its parent corporations and listing any publicly held company that owns 10% or more of the party's stock.

(b) A party shall file the corporate disclosure statement within eleven days of the filing of a motion to transfer or remand, an order to show cause, or a motion to vacate a conditional transfer order or a conditional remand order.

(c) Once a corporate disclosure statement by a party has been filed in an MDL docket pursuant to subsection (b) of this Rule, such a party is required to update the statement to reflect any change in the information therein i) until the matter before the Panel is decided, and ii) within eleven days of the filing of any subsequent motion to transfer or remand, order to show cause, or motion to vacate a conditional transfer order or a conditional remand order in that docket.

(Added Apr. 2, 2001, eff. Apr. 2, 2001.)

Rule 6.2. Applications for Extensions of Time

Any application for an extension of time to file a pleading or perform an act required by these Rules must be in writing, must request a specific number of additional days and may be acted upon by the Clerk of the Panel. Such an application will be evaluated in relation to the impact on the Panel's calendar as well as on the basis of the reasons set forth in support of the application. Any party aggrieved by the Clerk of the Panel's action on such application may submit its objections to the Panel for consideration. Absent exceptional circumstances, no extensions of time shall be granted to file a notice of opposition to either a conditional transfer order or a conditional remand order. All applications for extensions of time shall be filed and served in conformity with Rules 5.12, 5.2 and 7.1 of these Rules.

(Added May 3, 1993, eff. July 1, 1993, and amended Sept. 1, 1998, eff. Nov. 2, 1998; Apr. 2, 2001, eff. Apr. 2, 2001.)

Rule 7.1. Form of Papers Filed

(a) Averments in any motion seeking action by the Panel shall be made in numbered paragraphs, each of which shall be limited, as far as practicable, to a statement of a single factual averment.

(b) Responses to averments in motions shall be made in numbered paragraphs, each of which shall correspond to the number of the paragraph of the motion to which the responsive paragraph is directed. Each responsive paragraph shall admit or deny wholly or in part the averment of the motion, and shall contain the respondent's version of the subject matter when the averment or the motion is not wholly admitted.

(c) Each pleading filed shall be:

(i) flat and unfolded;

(ii) plainly written, typed in double space, printed or prepared by means of a duplicating process, without erasures or interlineations which materially deface it;

(iii) on opaque, unglazed, white paper (not onionskin);

(iv) approximately 8–1/2 x 11 inches in size; and

(v) fastened at the top-left corner without side binding or front or back covers.

(d) The heading on the first page of each pleading shall commence not less than three inches from the top of the page. Each pleading shall bear the heading "Before the Judicial Panel on Multidistrict Litigation," the identification "MDL Docket No.____" and the descriptive title designated by the Panel for the litigation involved. If the Panel has not yet designated a title, an appropriate descriptive title shall be used.

(e) The final page of each pleading shall contain the name, address and telephone number of the attorney or party in active charge of the case. Each attorney shall also include the name of each party represented.

(f) Except with the approval of the Panel, each brief submitted for filing with the Panel shall be limited to twenty pages, exclusive of exhibits. Absent exceptional circumstances, motions to exceed page limits shall not be granted.

(g) Exhibits exceeding a cumulative total of 50 pages shall be fastened separately from the accompanying pleading.

(h) Proposed Panel orders shall not be submitted with papers for filing.
(Added May 3, 1993, eff. July 1, 1993, and amended Sept. 1, 1998, eff. Nov. 2, 1998; Apr. 2, 2001, eff. Apr. 2, 2001.)

Rule 7.2. **Motion Practice**

(a) All requests for action by the Panel under 28 U.S.C. § 1407 shall be made by written motion. Every motion shall be accompanied by:

(i) a brief in support thereof in which the background of the litigation and factual and legal contentions of the movant shall be concisely stated in separate portions of the brief with citation of applicable authorities; and

(ii) a schedule giving

(A) the complete name of each action involved, listing the full name of each party included as such on the district court's docket sheet, not shortened by the use of references such as "et al." or "etc.";

(B) the district court and division in which each action is pending;

(C) the civil action number of each action; and

(D) the name of the judge assigned each action, if known.

(b) The Clerk of the Panel shall notify recipients of a motion of the filing date, caption, MDL docket number, briefing schedule and pertinent Panel policies.

(c) Within twenty days after filing of a motion, all other parties shall file a response thereto. Failure of a party to respond to a motion shall be treated as that party's acquiescence to the action requested in the motion.

(d) The movant may, within five days after the lapse of the time period for filing responsive briefs, file a single brief in reply to any opposition.

(e) Motions, their accompaniments, responses, and replies shall also be governed by Rules 5.12, 5.2 and 7.1 of these Rules.

(f) With respect to any action that is the subject of Panel consideration, counsel shall promptly notify the Clerk of the Panel of any development that would partially or completely moot the matter before the Panel.

(g) A joinder in a motion shall not add any action to the previous motion.

(h) Once a motion is filed, any other pleading that purports to be a "motion" in the docket shall be filed by the Clerk of the Panel as a response unless the "motion" adds an action. The Clerk of the Panel, upon designating such a pleading as a motion, shall acknowledge that designation by the distribution of a briefing schedule to all parties in the docket. Response time resulting from an additional motion shall ordinarily be extended only to those parties directly affected by the additional motion. An accelerated briefing schedule for the additional motion may be set by the Clerk of the Panel to conform with the hearing session schedule established by the Chairman.

(i) Any party or counsel in a new group of actions under consideration by the Panel for transfer under Section 1407 shall promptly notify the Clerk of the Panel of any potential tag-along action in which that party is also named or in which that counsel appears.
(Added May 3, 1993, eff. July 1, 1993, and amended Sept. 1, 1998, eff. Nov. 2, 1998; Apr. 2, 2001, eff. Apr. 2, 2001.)

Rule 7.3. Show Cause Orders

(a) When transfer of multidistrict litigation is being considered on the initiative of the Panel pursuant to 28 U.S.C. § 1407(c)(i), an order shall be filed by the Clerk of the Panel directing the parties to show cause why the action or actions should not be transferred for coordinated or consolidated pretrial proceedings. Any party or counsel in such actions shall promptly notify the Clerk of the Panel of any other federal district court actions related to the litigation encompassed by the show cause order. Such notification shall be made for additional actions pending at the time of the issuance of the show cause order and whenever new actions are filed.

(b) Any party may file a response to the show cause order within twenty days of the filing of said order unless otherwise provided for in the order. Failure of a party to respond to a show cause order shall be treated as that party's acquiescence to the Panel action contemplated in the order.

(c) Within five days after the lapse of the time period for filing a response, any party may file a reply limited to new matters.

(d) Responses and replies shall be filed and served in conformity with Rules 5.12, 5.2 and 7.1 of these Rules.

(e) With respect to any action that is the subject of Panel consideration, counsel shall promptly notify the Clerk of the Panel of any development that would partially or completely moot the matter before the Panel.
(Added May 3, 1993, eff. July 1, 1993, and amended Sept. 1, 1998, eff. Nov. 2, 1998; Apr. 2, 2001, eff. Apr. 2, 2001.)

Rule 7.4. Conditional Transfer Orders for "Tag–Along Actions"

(a) Upon learning of the pendency of a potential "tag-along action," as defined in Rule 1.1 of these Rules, an order may be entered by the Clerk of the Panel transferring that action to the previously designated transferee district court on the basis of the prior hearing session(s) and for the reasons expressed in previous opinions and orders of the Panel in the litigation. The Clerk of the Panel shall serve this order on each party to the litigation but, in order to afford all parties the opportunity to oppose transfer, shall not send the order to the clerk of the transferee district court for fifteen days from the entry thereof.

(b) Parties to an action subject to a conditional transfer order shall notify the Clerk of the Panel within the fifteen-day period if that action is no longer pending in its transferor district court.

(c) Any party opposing the transfer shall file a notice of opposition with the Clerk of the Panel within the fifteen-day period. If a notice of opposition is received by the Clerk of the Panel within this fifteen-day period, the Clerk of the Panel shall not transmit said order to the clerk of the transferee district court until further order of the Panel. The Clerk of the Panel shall notify the parties of the briefing schedule.

(d) Within fifteen days of the filing of its notice of opposition, the party opposing transfer shall file a motion to vacate the conditional transfer order and brief in support thereof. The Chairman of the Panel shall set the motion for the next appropriate hearing session of the Panel. Failure to file and serve a motion and brief shall be treated as withdrawal of the opposition and the Clerk of the Panel shall forthwith transmit the order to the clerk of the transferee district court.

(e) Conditional transfer orders do not become effective unless and until they are filed with the clerk of the transferee district court.

(f) Notices of opposition and motions to vacate such orders of the Panel and responses thereto shall be governed by Rules 5.12, 5.2, 7.1 and 7.2 of these Rules.
(Added May 3, 1993, eff. July 1, 1993, and amended Sept. 1, 1998, eff. Nov. 2, 1998; Apr. 2, 2001, eff. Apr. 2, 2001.)

Rule 7.5. Miscellaneous Provisions Concerning "Tag–Along Actions"

(a) Potential "tag-along actions" filed in the transferee district require no action on the part of the Panel and requests for assignment of such actions to the Section 1407 transferee judge should be made in accordance with local rules for the assignment of related actions.

(b) Upon learning of the pendency of a potential "tag-along action" and having reasonable anticipation of opposition to transfer of that action, the Panel may direct the Clerk of the Panel to file a show cause order, in accordance with Rule 7.3 of these Rules, instead of a conditional transfer order.

(c) Failure to serve one or more of the defendants in a potential "tag-along action" with the complaint and summons as required by Rule 4 of the Federal Rules of Civil Procedure does not preclude transfer of such action under Section 1407. Such failure, however, may be submitted by such a defendant as a basis for opposing the proposed transfer if prejudice can be shown. The inability of the Clerk of the Panel to serve a conditional transfer order on all plaintiffs or defendants or their counsel shall not render the transfer of the action void but can be submitted by such a party as a basis for moving to remand as to such party if prejudice can be shown.

(d) A civil action apparently involving common questions of fact with actions under consideration by the Panel for transfer under Section 1407, which was either not included in a motion under Rule 7.2 of these

Rules, or was included in such a motion that was filed too late to be included in the initial hearing session, will ordinarily be treated by the Panel as a potential "tag-along action."

(e) Any party or counsel in actions previously transferred under Section 1407 or under consideration by the Panel for transfer under Section 1407 shall promptly notify the Clerk of the Panel of any potential "tag-along actions" in which that party is also named or in which that counsel appears.

(Added May 3, 1993, eff. July 1, 1993, and amended Sept. 1, 1998, eff. Nov. 2, 1998; Apr. 2, 2001, eff. Apr. 2, 2001.)

Rule 7.6. Termination and Remand

In the absence of unusual circumstances—

(a) Actions terminated in the transferee district court by valid judgment, including but not limited to summary judgment, judgment of dismissal and judgment upon stipulation, shall not be remanded by the Panel and shall be dismissed by the transferee district court. The clerk of the transferee district court shall send a copy of the order terminating the action to the Clerk of the Panel but shall retain the original files and records unless otherwise directed by the transferee judge or by the Panel.

(b) Each action transferred only for coordinated or consolidated pretrial proceedings that has not been terminated in the transferee district court shall be remanded by the Panel to the transferor district for trial. Actions that were originally filed in the transferee district require no action by the Panel to be reassigned to another judge in the transferee district at the conclusion of the coordinated or consolidated pretrial proceedings affecting those actions.

(c) The Panel shall consider remand of each transferred action or any separable claim, cross-claim, counterclaim or third-party claim at or before the conclusion of coordinated or consolidated pretrial proceedings on

 (i) motion of any party,

 (ii) suggestion of the transferee district court, or

 (iii) the Panel's own initiative, by entry of an order to show cause, a conditional remand order or other appropriate order.

(d) The Panel is reluctant to order remand absent a suggestion of remand from the transferee district court. If remand is sought by motion of a party, the motion shall be accompanied by:

 (i) an affidavit reciting

 (A) whether the movant has requested a suggestion of remand from the transferee district court, how the court responded to any request, and, if no such request was made, why;

 (B) whether all common discovery and other pretrial proceedings have been completed in the action sought to be remanded, and if not, what remains to be done; and

 (C) whether all orders of the transferee district court have been satisfactorily complied with, and if not, what remains to be done; and

 (ii) a copy of the transferee district court's final pretrial order, where such order has been entered.

Motions to remand and responses thereto shall be governed by Rules 5.12, 5.2, 7.1 and 7.2 of these Rules.

(e) When an order to show cause why an action or actions should not be remanded is entered pursuant to subsection (c), paragraph (iii) of this Rule, any party may file a response within twenty days of the filing of said order unless otherwise provided for in the order. Within five days of filing of a party's response, any party may file a reply brief limited to new matters. Failure of a party to respond to a show cause order regarding remand shall be treated as that party's acquiescence to the remand. Responses and replies shall be filed and served in conformity with Rules 5.12, 5.2 and 7.1 of these Rules.

(f) Conditional Remand Orders.

 (i) When the Panel has been advised by the transferee district judge, or otherwise has reason to believe, that pretrial proceedings in the litigation assigned to the transferee district judge are concluded or that remand of an action or actions is otherwise appropriate, an order may be entered by the Clerk of the Panel remanding the action or actions to the transferor district court. The Clerk of the Panel shall serve this order on each party to the litigation but, in order to afford all parties the opportunity to oppose remand, shall not send the order to the clerk of the transferee district court for fifteen days from the entry thereof.

 (ii) Any party opposing the remand shall file a notice of opposition with the Clerk of the Panel within the fifteen-day period. If a notice of opposition is received by the Clerk of the Panel within this fifteen-day period, the Clerk of the Panel shall not transmit said order to the clerk of the transferee district court until further order of the Panel. The Clerk of the Panel shall notify the parties of the briefing schedule.

 (iii) Within fifteen days of the filing of its notice of opposition, the party opposing remand shall file a motion to vacate the conditional remand order and brief in support thereof. The Chairman of the Panel shall set the motion for the next appropriate hearing session of the Panel. Failure to file and serve a motion and brief shall be treated as a withdrawal of the opposition and the Clerk of the Panel shall forthwith transmit the order to the clerk of the transferee district court.

(iv) Conditional remand orders do not become effective unless and until they are filed with the clerk of the transferee district court.

(v) Notices of opposition and motions to vacate such orders of the Panel and responses thereto shall be governed by Rules 5.12, 5.2, 7.1 and 7.2 of these Rules.

(g) Upon receipt of an order to remand from the Clerk of the Panel, the parties shall furnish forthwith to the transferee district clerk a stipulation or designation of the contents of the record or part thereof to be remanded and furnish the transferee district clerk all necessary copies of any pleading or other matter filed so as to enable the transferee district clerk to comply with the order of remand.

(Added May 3, 1993, eff. July 1, 1993, and amended Sept. 1, 1998, eff. Nov. 2, 1998; Apr. 2, 2001, eff. Apr. 2, 2001.)

Rule 16.1. Hearing Sessions and Oral Argument

(a) Hearing sessions of the Panel for the presentation of oral argument and consideration of matters taken under submission without oral argument shall be held as ordered by the Panel. The Panel shall convene whenever and wherever desirable or necessary in the judgment of the Chairman. The Chairman shall determine which matters shall be considered at each hearing session and the Clerk of the Panel shall give notice to counsel for all parties involved in the litigation to be so considered of the time, place and subject matter of such hearing session.

(b) Each party filing a motion or a response to a motion or order of the Panel under Rules 7.2, 7.3, 7.4 or 7.6 of these Rules may file simultaneously therewith a separate statement limited to one page setting forth reasons why oral argument should, or need not, be heard. Such statements shall be captioned "Reasons Why Oral Argument Should [Need Not] Be Heard," and shall be filed and served in conformity with Rules 5.12 and 5.2 of these Rules.

(c) No transfer or remand determination regarding any action pending in the district court shall be made by the Panel when any party timely opposes such transfer or remand unless a hearing session has been held for the presentation of oral argument except that the Panel may dispense with oral argument if it determines that:

(i) the dispositive issue(s) have been authoritatively decided; or

(ii) the facts and legal arguments are adequately presented in the briefs and record, and the decisional process would not be significantly aided by oral argument.

Unless otherwise ordered by the Panel, all other matters before the Panel, such as a motion for reconsideration, shall be considered and determined upon the basis of the papers filed.

(d) In those matters in which oral argument is not scheduled by the Panel, counsel shall be promptly advised. If oral argument is scheduled in a matter the Clerk of the Panel may require counsel for all parties who wish to make or to waive oral argument to file and serve notice to that effect within a stated time in conformity with Rules 5.12 and 5.2 of these Rules. Failure to do so shall be deemed a waiver of oral argument by that party. If oral argument is scheduled but not attended by a party, the matter shall not be rescheduled and that party's position shall be treated as submitted for decision by the Panel on the basis of the papers filed.

(e) Except for leave of the Panel on a showing of good cause, only those parties to actions scheduled for oral argument who have filed a motion or written response to a motion or order shall be permitted to appear before the Panel and present oral argument.

(f) Counsel for those supporting transfer or remand under Section 1407 and counsel for those opposing such transfer or remand are to confer separately prior to the oral argument for the purpose of organizing their arguments and selecting representatives to present all views without duplication.

(g) Unless otherwise ordered by the Panel, a maximum of twenty minutes shall be allotted for oral argument in each matter. The time shall be divided equally among those with varying viewpoints. Counsel for the moving party or parties shall generally be heard first.

(h) So far as practicable and consistent with the purposes of Section 1407, the offering of oral testimony before the Panel shall be avoided. Accordingly, oral testimony shall not be received except upon notice, motion and order of the Panel expressly providing for it.

(i) After an action or group of actions has been set for a hearing session, consideration of such action(s) may be continued only by order of the Panel on good cause shown.

(Added May 3, 1998, eff. July 1, 1993, and amended Sept. 1, 1998, eff. Nov. 2, 1998; Apr. 2, 2001, eff. Apr. 2, 2001.)

II. RULES FOR MULTICIRCUIT PETITIONS FOR REVIEW UNDER 28 U.S.C. § 2112(a)(3)

Rule 17.1. **Random Selection**

(a) Upon filing a notice of multicircuit petitions for review, the Clerk of the Panel or designated deputy shall randomly select a circuit court of appeals from a drum containing an entry for each circuit wherein a constituent petition for review is pending. Multiple petitions for review pending in a single circuit shall be allotted only a single entry in the drum. This random selection shall be witnessed by the Clerk of the Panel or a designated deputy other than the random selector. Thereafter, an order on behalf of the Panel shall be issued, signed by the random selector and the witness,

(i) consolidating the petitions for review in the court of appeals for the circuit that was randomly selected; and

(ii) designating that circuit as the one in which the record is to be filed pursuant to Rules 16 and 17 of the Federal Rules of Appellate Procedure.

(b) A consolidation of petitions for review shall be effective when the Panel's consolidation order is filed at the offices of the Panel by the Clerk of the Panel.
(Added May 3, 1993, eff. July 1, 1993, and amended Sept. 1, 1998, eff. Nov. 2, 1998; Apr. 2, 2001, eff. Apr. 2, 2001.)

Rule 25.1. **Filing of Notices**

(a) An original of a notice of multicircuit petitions for review pursuant to 28 U.S.C. § 2112(a)(3) shall be submitted for filing to the Clerk of the Panel by the affected agency, board, commission or officer. The term "agency" as used in Section II of these Rules shall include agency, board, commission or officer.

(b) All notices of multicircuit petitions for review submitted by the affected agency for filing with the Clerk of the Panel shall embrace exclusively petitions for review filed in the courts of appeals within ten days after issuance of an agency order and received by the affected agency from the petitioners within that ten-day period.

(c) When a notice of multicircuit petitions for review is submitted for filing to the Clerk of the Panel, the Clerk of the Panel shall file the notice and endorse thereon the date of filing.

(d) Copies of notices of multicircuit petitions for review shall be filed by the affected agency with the clerk of each circuit court of appeals in which a petition for review is pending that is included in the notice.
(Added May 3, 1993, eff. July 1, 1993, and amended Sept. 1, 1998, eff. Nov. 2, 1998; Apr. 2, 2001, eff. Apr. 2, 2001.)

Rule 25.2. **Accompaniments to Notices**

(a) All notices of multicircuit petitions for review shall be accompanied by:

(i) a copy of each involved petition for review as the petition for review is defined in 28 U.S.C. § 2112(a)(2); and

(ii) a schedule giving

(A) the date of the relevant agency order;

(B) the case name of each petition for review involved;

(C) the circuit court of appeals in which each petition for review is pending;

(D) the appellate docket number of each petition for review;

(E) the date of filing by the court of appeals of each petition for review; and

(F) the date of receipt by the agency of each petition for review.

(b) The schedule in Subsection (a)(ii) of this Rule shall also be governed by Rules 25.1, 25.3 and 25.4(a) of these Rules.
(Added May 3, 1993, eff. July 1, 1993, and amended Sept. 1, 1998, eff. Nov. 2, 1998; Apr. 2, 2001, eff. Apr. 2, 2001.)

Rule 25.3. **Service of Notices**

(a) All notices of multicircuit petitions for review shall be accompanied by proof of service by the affected agency on all other parties in all petitions for review included in the notice. Service and proof of service shall be made as provided in Rule 25 of the Federal Rules of Appellate Procedure. The proof of service shall state the name and address of each person served and shall indicate the party represented by each. If a party is not represented by counsel, the proof of service shall indicate the name of the party and his or her last known address. The original proof of service shall be submitted by the affected agency for filing with the Clerk of the Panel and copies thereof shall be sent by the affected agency to each person included within the proof of service.

(b) The proof of service pertaining to notices of multicircuit petitions for review shall certify that copies of the notices have been mailed or otherwise delivered by the affected agency for filing to the clerk of each circuit court of appeals in which a petition for review is pending that is included in the notice.
(Added May 3, 1993, eff. July 1, 1993, and amended Sept. 1, 1998, eff. Nov. 2, 1998; Apr. 2, 2001, eff. Apr. 2, 2001.)

Rule 25.4. **Form of Notices**

(a) Each notice of multicircuit petitions for review shall be

(i) flat and unfolded;

(ii) plainly written, typed in double space, printed or prepared by means of a duplicating process, without erasures or interlineations which materially deface it;

(iii) on opaque, unglazed white paper (not onionskin);

(iv) approximately 8–1/2 x 11 inches in size; and

(v) fastened at the top-left corner without side binding or front or back covers.

(b) The heading on the first page of each notice of multicircuit petitions for review shall commence not less that three inches from the top of the page. Each notice shall bear the heading "Notice to the Judicial Panel on Multidistrict Litigation of Multicircuit Petitions for Review," followed by a brief caption identifying the involved agency, the relevant agency order, and the date of the order.

(c) The final page of each notice of multicircuit petitions for review shall contain the name, address and telephone number of the individual or individuals who submitted the notice on behalf of the agency.

(Added May 3, 1993, eff. July 1, 1993, and amended Sept. 1, 1998, eff. Nov. 2, 1998; Apr. 2, 2001, eff. Apr. 2, 2001.)

Rule 25.5. Service of Panel Consolidation Order

(a) The Clerk of the Panel shall serve the Panel's consolidation order on the affected agency through the individual or individuals, as identified in Rule 25.4(c) of these Rules, who submitted the notice of multicircuit petitions for review on behalf of the agency.

(b) That individual or individuals, or anyone else designated by the agency, shall promptly serve the Panel's consolidation order on all other parties in all petitions for review included in the Panel's consolidation order, and shall promptly submit a proof of that service to the Clerk of the Panel. Service and proof of that service shall also be governed by Rule 25.3 of these Rules.

(c) The Clerk of the Panel shall serve the Panel's consolidation order on the clerks of all circuit courts of appeals that were among the candidates for the Panel's random selection.

(Added May 3, 1993, eff. July 1, 1993, and amended Sept. 1, 1998, eff. Nov. 2, 1998; Apr. 2, 2001, eff. Apr. 2, 2001.)

RULES GOVERNING SECTION 2254 CASES IN THE UNITED STATES DISTRICT COURTS

Rule

APPENDIX OF FORMS

ORDERS OF THE SUPREME COURT OF THE UNITED STATES ADOPTING AND AMENDING RULES GOVERNING SECTION 2254 PROCEEDINGS IN THE UNITED STATES DISTRICT COURTS

ORDER OF APRIL 26, 1976

1. That the rules and forms governing proceedings in the United States District Courts under Section 2254 and Section 2255 of Title 28, United States Code, as approved by the Judicial Conference of the United States be, and they hereby are, prescribed pursuant to Section 2072 of Title 28, United States Code and Sections 3771 and 3772 of Title 18, United States Code.

2. That the aforementioned rules and forms shall take effect August 1, 1976, and shall be applicable to all proceedings then pending except to the extent that in the opinion of the court their application in a particular proceeding would not be feasible or would work injustice.

3. That THE CHIEF JUSTICE be, and he hereby is, authorized to transmit the aforementioned rules and forms governing Section 2254 and Section 2255 proceedings to the Congress in accordance with the provisions of Section 2072 of Title 28 and Sections 3771 and 3772 of Title 18, United States Code.

CONGRESSIONAL ACTION ON PROPOSED RULES AND FORMS GOVERNING PROCEEDING UNDER 28 U.S.C. §§ 2254 AND 2255

Pub.L. 94–349, § 2, July 8, 1976, 90 Stat. 822, provided: "That, notwithstanding the provisions of section 2072 of title 28 of the United States Code, the rules and forms governing section 2254 cases in the United States district courts and the rules and forms governing section 2255 proceedings in the United States district courts which are embraced by the order entered by the United States Supreme Court on April 26, 1976, and which were transmitted to the Congress on or about April 26, 1976, shall not take effect until thirty days after the adjournment sine die of the 94th Congress, or until and to the extent approved by Act of Congress, whichever is earlier."

Pub.L. 94–426, § 1, Sept. 28, 1976, 90 Stat. 1334, provided: "That the rules governing section 2254 cases in the United States district courts and the rules governing section 2255 proceedings for the United States Supreme Court, which were delayed by the Act entitled 'An Act to delay the effective date of certain proposed amendments to the Federal Rules of Criminal Procedure and certain other rules promulgated by the United States Supreme Court' (Public Law 94–349), are approved with the amendments set forth in section 2 of this Act and shall take effect as so amended, with respect to petitions under section 2254 and motions under section 2255 of title 28 of the United States Code filed on or after February 1, 1977."

ORDER OF APRIL 30, 1979

1. That Rule 10 of the Rules Governing Proceedings in the United States District Courts on application under Section 2254 of Title 28, United States Code, be, and hereby is, amended to read as follows:

[See amendment made thereby under Rule 10, post.]

2. That Rules 10 and 11 of the Rules Governing Proceedings in the United States District Courts on a motion under Section 2255 of Title 28, United States Code, be, and they hereby are, amended to read as follows:

[See amendments made hereby under Rules 10 and 11 set out following section 2255.]

3. That the foregoing amendments to the Rules Governing Proceedings in the United States District Courts under Section 2254 and Section 2255 of Title 28, United States Code, shall take effect on August 1, 1979, and shall be applicable to all proceedings then pending except to the extent that in the opinion of the court their application in a particular proceeding would not be feasible or would work injustice.

4. That THE CHIEF JUSTICE be, and he hereby is, authorized to transmit the aforementioned amendments to the Rules Governing Section 2254 and Section 2255 Proceedings to the Congress in accordance with the provisions of Section 2072 of Title 28, United States Code, and Sections 3771 and 3772 of Title 18, United States Code.

ORDER OF APRIL 28, 1982

1. That the rules and forms governing proceedings in the United States district courts under Section 2254 and Section

2255 of Title 28, United States Code, be, and they hereby are, amended by including therein an amendment to Rule 2(c) of the rules for Section 2254 cases, an amendment to Rule 2(b) of the rules for Section 2255 proceedings, and amendments to the model forms for use in applications under Section 2254 and motions under Section 2255, as hereinafter set forth:

[See amendments made thereby under respective rules and forms post and following section 2255.]

2. That the aforementioned amendments shall take effect August 1, 1982, and shall be applicable to all proceedings thereafter commenced and, insofar as just and practicable, all proceedings then pending.

3. That THE CHIEF JUSTICE be, and he hereby is, authorized to transmit the aforementioned amendments to the Congress in accordance with Section 2072 of Title 28 and Sections 3771 and 3772 of Title 18, United States Code.

ORDER OF APRIL 26, 2004

1. That the Federal Rules of Criminal Procedure be, and they hereby are, amended by including therein an amendment to Criminal Rule 35.

2. That the rules and forms governing cases in the United States District Courts under Section 2254 and Section 2255 of Title 28, United States Code, be, and they hereby are, amended by including therein amendments to Rules 1 through 11 of the Rules Governing Section 2254 Cases in the United States District Courts, Rules 1 through 12 of the Rules Governing Section 2255 Cases in the United States District Courts, and forms for use in applications under Section 2254 and motions under Section 2255.

[See amendments made thereby under respective rules, post.]

3. That the foregoing amendments to the Federal Rules of Criminal Procedure, the Rules Governing Section 2254 Cases in the United States District Courts, and the Rules Governing Section 2255 Cases in the United States District Courts shall take effect on December 1, 2004, and shall govern in all proceedings thereafter commenced and, insofar as just and practicable, all proceedings then pending.

4. That the CHIEF JUSTICE be, and hereby is, authorized to transmit to the Congress the foregoing amendments to the Federal Rules of Criminal Procedure, the Rules Governing Section 2254 Cases in the United States District Courts, and the Rules Governing Section 2255 Cases in the United States District Courts in accordance with the provisions of Section 2072 of Title 28, United States Code.

HISTORICAL NOTES

Effective Date of Rules; 1976 Act

Rules governing section 2254 cases, and the amendments thereto by Pub.L. 94–426, Sept. 28, 1976, 90 Stat. 1334, effective with respect to petitions under section 2254 of this title and motions under section 2255 of this title filed on or after Feb. 1, 1977, see section 1 of Pub.L. 94–426, set out as a note under section 2254 of this title.

Rule 1. Scope

(a) Cases Involving a Petition under 28 U.S.C. § 2254. These rules govern a petition for a writ of habeas corpus filed in a United States district court under 28 U.S.C. § 2254 by:

(1) a person in custody under a state-court judgment who seeks a determination that the custody violates the Constitution, laws, or treaties of the United States; and

(2) a person in custody under a state-court or federal-court judgment who seeks a determination that future custody under a state-court judgment would violate the Constitution, laws, or treaties of the United States.

(b) Other Cases. The district court may apply any or all of these rules to a habeas corpus petition not covered by Rule 1(a).

(As amended Apr. 26, 2004, eff. Dec. 1, 2004.)

ADVISORY COMMITTEE NOTES

1976 Adoption

Rule 1 provides that the habeas corpus rules are applicable to petitions by persons in custody pursuant to a judgment of a state court. See *Preiser v. Rodriguez,* 411 U.S. 475, 484 (1973). Whether the rules ought to apply to other situations (*e.g.*, person in active military service, *Glazier v. Hackel,* 440 F.2d 592 (9th Cir. 1971); or a reservist called to active duty but not reported, *Hammond v. Lenfest,* 398 F.2d 705 (2d Cir. 1968)) is left to the discretion of the court.

The basic scope of habeas corpus is prescribed by statute. 28 U.S.C. § 2241(c) provides that the "writ of habeas corpus shall not extend to a prisoner unless * * * (h)e is *in custody* in violation of the Constitution." 28 U.S.C. § 2254 deals specifically with state custody, providing that habeas corpus shall apply only "in behalf of a person in custody pursuant to a judgment of a state court * * *."

In *Preiser v. Rodriguez, supra,* the court said: "It is clear . . . that the essence of habeas corpus is an attack by a person in custody upon the legality of that custody, and that the traditional function of the writ is to secure release from illegal custody." 411 U.S. at 484.

Initially the Supreme Court held that habeas corpus was appropriate only in those situations in which petitioner's claim would, if upheld, result in an immediate release from present custody. *McNally v. Hill,* 293 U.S. 131 (1934). This was changed in *Peyton v. Rowe,* 391 U.S. 54 (1968), in which the court held that habeas corpus was a proper way to attack a consecutive sentence to be served in the future, expressing the view that consecutive sentences resulted in present custody under both judgments, not merely the one imposing the first sentence. This view was expanded in *Carafas v. LaVallee,* 391 U.S. 234 (1968), to recognize the propriety of habeas corpus in a case in which petitioner was in custody when the petition had been originally filed but had since been unconditionally released from custody.

See also *Preiser v. Rodriguez,* 411 U.S. at 486 et seq.

Since *Carafas,* custody has been construed more liberally by the courts so as to make a § 2255 motion or habeas corpus petition proper in more situations. "In custody" now

includes a person who is: on parole, *Jones v. Cunningham,* 371 U.S. 236 (1963); at large on his own recognizance but subject to several conditions pending execution of his sentence, *Hensley v. Municipal Court,* 411 U.S. 345 (1973); or released on bail after conviction pending final disposition of his case, *Lefkowitz v. Newsome,* 95 S.Ct. 886 (1975). See also *United States v. Re,* 372 F.2d 641 (2d Cir.), cert. denied, 388 U.S. 912 (1967) (on probation); *Walker v. North Carolina,* 262 F.Supp. 102 (W.D.N.C.1966), aff'd per curiam, 372 F.2d 129 (4th Cir.), cert. denied, 388 U.S. 917 (1967) (recipient of a conditionally suspended sentence); *Burris v. Ryan,* 397 F.2d 553 (7th Cir. 1968); *Marden v. Purdy,* 409 F.2d 784 (5th Cir. 1969) (free on bail); *United States ex rel. Smith v. Dibella,* 314 F.Supp. 446 (D.Conn.1970) (release on own recognizance); *Choung v. California,* 320 F.Supp. 625 (E.D.Cal.1970) (federal stay of state court sentence); *United States ex rel. Meadows v. New York,* 426 F.2d 1176 (2d Cir. 1970), cert. denied, 401 U.S. 941 (1971) (subject to parole detainer warrant); *Capler v. City of Greenville,* 422 F.2d 299 (5th Cir. 1970) (released on appeal bond); *Glover v. North Carolina,* 301 F.Supp. 364 (E.D.N.C.1969) (sentence served, but as convicted felon disqualified from engaging in several activities).

The courts are not unanimous in dealing with the above situations, and the boundaries of custody remain somewhat unclear. In *Morgan v. Thomas,* 321 F.Supp. 565 (S.D.Miss. 1970), the court noted:

It is axiomatic that actual physical custody or restraint is not required to confer habeas jurisdiction. Rather, the term is synonymous with restraint of liberty. The real question is how much restraint of one's liberty is necessary before the right to apply for the writ comes into play. * * *

It is clear however, that something more than moral restraint is necessary to make a case for habeas corpus.

321 F.Supp. at 573

Hammond v. Lenfest, 398 F.2d 705 (2d Cir. 1968), reviewed prior "custody" doctrine and reaffirmed a generalized flexible approach to the issue. In speaking about 28 U.S.C. § 2241, the first section in the habeas corpus statutes, the court said:

While the language of the Act indicates that a writ of habeas corpus is appropriate only when a petitioner is "in custody" * * * the Act "does not attempt to mark the boundaries of 'custody' nor in any way other than by use of that word attempt to limit the situations in which the writ can be used." * * * And, recent Supreme Court decisions have made clear that "[i]t [habeas corpus] is not now and never has been a static, narrow, formalistic remedy; its scope has grown to achieve its grand purpose—the protection of individuals against erosion of their right to be free from wrongful restraints upon their liberty." * * * "[B]esides physical imprisonment, there are other restraints on a man's liberty, restraints not shared by the public generally, which have been thought sufficient in the English-speaking world to support the issuance of habeas corpus."

398 F.2d at 710–711

There is, as of now, no final list of the situations which are appropriate for habeas corpus relief. It is not the intent of these rules or notes to define or limit "custody."

It is, however, the view of the Advisory Committee that claims of improper conditions of custody or confinement (not related to the propriety of the custody itself), can better be handled by other means such as 42 U.S.C. § 1983 and other related statutes. In *Wilwording v. Swanson,* 404 U.S. 249 (1971), the court treated a habeas corpus petition by a state prisoner challenging the conditions of confinement as a claim for relief under 42 U.S.C. § 1983, the Civil Rights Act. Compare *Johnson v. Avery,* 393 U.S. 483 (1969).

The distinction between duration of confinement and conditions of confinement may be difficult to draw. Compare *Preiser v. Rodriguez,* 411 U.S. 475 (1973), with *Clutchette v. Procunier,* 497 F.2d 809 (9th Cir. 1974), modified, 510 F.2d 613 (1975).

2004 Amendments

The language of Rule 1 has been amended as part of general restyling of the rules to make them more easily understood and to make style and terminology consistent throughout the rules. These changes are intended to be stylistic and no substantive change is intended.

Rule 2. The Petition

(a) Current Custody; Naming the Respondent. If the petitioner is currently in custody under a state-court judgment, the petition must name as respondent the state officer who has custody.

(b) Future Custody; Naming the Respondents and Specifying the Judgment. If the petitioner is not yet in custody—but may be subject to future custody—under the state-court judgment being contested, the petition must name as respondents both the officer who has current custody and the attorney general of the state where the judgment was entered. The petition must ask for relief from the state-court judgment being contested.

(c) Form. The petition must:

(1) specify all the grounds for relief available to the petitioner;

(2) state the facts supporting each ground;

(3) state the relief requested;

(4) be printed, typewritten, or legibly handwritten; and

(5) be signed under penalty of perjury by the petitioner or by a person authorized to sign it for the petitioner under 28 U.S.C. § 2242.

(d) Standard Form. The petition must substantially follow either the form appended to these rules or a form prescribed by a local district-court rule. The clerk must make forms available to petitioners without charge.

(e) Separate Petitions for Judgments of Separate Courts. A petitioner who seeks relief from judgments of more than one state court must file a separate petition covering the judgment or judgments of each court.

(As amended Pub.L. 94–426, § 2(1), (2), Sept. 28, 1976, 90 Stat. 1334; Apr. 28, 1982, eff. Aug. 1, 1982; Apr. 26, 2004, eff. Dec. 1, 2004.)

ADVISORY COMMITTEE NOTES
1976 Adoption

Rule 2 describes the requirements of the actual petition, including matters relating to its form, contents, scope, and sufficiency. The rule provides more specific guidance for a petitioner and the court than 28 U.S.C. § 2242, after which it is patterned.

Subdivision (a) provides that an applicant challenging a state judgment, pursuant to which he is presently in custody, must make his application in the form of a petition for a writ of habeas corpus. It also requires that the state officer having custody of the applicant be named as respondent. This is consistent with 28 U.S.C. § 2242, which says in part, [Application for a writ of habeas corpus] shall allege * * * the name of the person who has custody over [the applicant] * * *." The proper person to be served in the usual case is either the warden of the institution in which the petitioner is incarcerated (*Sanders v. Bennett*, 148 F.2d 19 (D.C.Cir. 1945)) or the chief officer in charge of state penal institutions.

Subdivision (b) prescribes the procedure to be used for a petition challenging a judgment under which the petitioner will be subject to custody in the future. In this event the relief sought will usually not be released from present custody, but rather for a declaration that the judgment being attacked is invalid. Subdivision (b) thus provides for a prayer for "appropriate relief." It is also provided that the attorney general of the state of the judgment as well as the state officer having actual custody of the petitioner shall be named as respondents. This is appropriate because no one will have custody of the petitioner in the state of the judgment being attacked, and the habeas corpus action will usually be defended by the attorney general. The attorney general is in the best position to inform the court as to who the proper party respondent is. If it is not the attorney general, he can move for a substitution of party.

Since the concept of "custody" requisite to the consideration of a petition for habeas corpus has been enlarged significantly in recent years, it may be worthwhile to spell out the various situations which might arise and who should be named as respondent(s) for each situation.

(1) The applicant is in jail, prison, or other actual physical restraint due to the state action he is attacking. The named respondent shall be the state officer who has official custody of the petitioner (for example, the warden of the prison).

(2) The applicant is on probation or parole due to the state judgment he is attacking. The named respondents shall be the particular probation or parole officer responsible for supervising the applicant, and the official in charge of the parole or probation agency, or the state correctional agency, as appropriate.

(3) The applicant is in custody in any other manner differing from (1) and (2) above due to the effects of the state action he seeks relief from. The named respondent should be the attorney general of the state wherein such action was taken.

(4) The applicant is in jail, prison, or other actual physical restraint but is attacking a state action which will cause him to be kept in custody in the future rather than the government action under which he is presently confined. The named respondents shall be the state or federal officer who has official custody of him at the time the petition is filed and the attorney general of the state whose action subjects the petitioner to future custody.

(5) The applicant is in custody, although not physically restrained, and is attacking a state action which will result in his future custody rather than the government action out of which his present custody arises. The named respondent(s) shall be the attorney general of the state whose action subjects the petitioner to future custody, as well as the government officer who has present official custody of the petitioner if there is such an officer and his identity is ascertainable.

In any of the above situations the judge may require or allow the petitioner to join an additional or different party as a respondent if to do so would serve the ends of justice.

As seen in rule 1 and paragraphs (4) and (5) above, these rules contemplate that a petitioner currently in federal custody will be permitted to apply for habeas relief from a state restraint which is to go into effect in the future. There has been disagreement in the courts as to whether they have jurisdiction of the habeas application under these circumstances (compare *Piper v. United States*, 306 F.Supp. 1259 (D.Conn.1969), with *United States ex rel. Meadows v. New York*, 426 F.2d 1176 (2d Cir. 1970), cert. denied, 401 U.S. 941 (1971)). This rule seeks to make clear that they do have such jurisdiction.

Subdivision (c) provides that unless a district court requires otherwise by local rule, the petition must be in the form annexed to these rules. Having a standard prescribed form has several advantages. In the past, petitions have frequently contained mere conclusions of law, unsupported by any facts. Since it is the relationship of the facts to the claim asserted that is important, these petitions were obviously deficient. In addition, lengthy and often illegible petitions, arranged in no logical order, were submitted to judges who have had to spend hours deciphering them. For example, in *Passic v. Michigan*, 98 F.Supp. 1015, 1016 (E.D.Mich. 1951), the court dismissed a petition for habeas corpus, describing it as "two thousand pages of irrational, prolix and redundant pleadings * * *."

Administrative convenience, of benefit to both the court and the petitioner, results from the use of a prescribed form. Judge Hubert L. Will briefly described the experience with the use of a standard form in the Northern District of Illinois:

Our own experience, though somewhat limited, has been quite satisfactory. * * *

In addition, [petitions] almost always contain the necessary basic information * * *. Very rarely do we get the kind of hybrid federal-state habeas corpus petition with civil rights allegations thrown in which were not uncommon in the past. * * * [W]hen a real constitutional issue is raised it is quickly apparent * * *.

33 F.R.D. 363, 384

Approximately 65 to 70% of all districts have adopted forms or local rules which require answers to essentially the same questions as contained in the standard form annexed to

these rules. All courts using forms have indicated the petitions are time-saving and more legible. The form is particularly helpful in getting information about whether there has been an exhaustion of state remedies or, at least, where that information can be obtained.

The requirement of a standard form benefits the petitioner as well. His assertions are more readily apparent, and a meritorious claim is more likely to be properly raised and supported. The inclusion in the form of the ten most frequently raised grounds in habeas corpus petitions is intended to encourage the applicant to raise all his asserted grounds in one petition. It may better enable him to recognize if an issue he seeks to raise is cognizable under habeas corpus and hopefully inform him of those issues as to which he must first exhaust his state remedies.

Some commentators have suggested that the use of forms is of little help because the questions usually are too general, amounting to little more than a restatement of the statute. They contend the blanks permit a prisoner to fill in the same ambiguous answers he would have offered without the aid of a form. See Comment, Developments in the Law—Federal Habeas Corpus, 83 Harv.L.Rev. 1038, 1177–1178 (1970). Certainly, as long as the statute requires factual pleading, the adequacy of a petition will continue to be affected largely by the petitioner's intelligence and the legal advice available to him. On balance, however, the use of forms has contributed enough to warrant mandating their use.

Giving the petitioner a list of often—raised grounds may, it is said, encourage perjury. See Comment, Developments in the Law—Federal Habeas Corpus, 83 Harv.L.Rev. 1038, 1178 (1970). Most inmates are aware of, or have access to, some common constitutional grounds for relief. Thus, the risk of perjury is not likely to be substantially increased and the benefit of the list for some inmates seems sufficient to outweigh any slight risk that perjury will increase. There is a penalty for perjury, and this would seem the most appropriate way to try to discourage it.

Legal assistance is increasingly available to inmates either through paraprofessional programs involving law students or special programs staffed by members of the bar. See Jacob and Sharma, Justice After Trial: Prisoners' Need for Legal Services in the Criminal-Correctional Process, 18 Kan.L.Rev. 493 (1970). In these situations, the prescribed form can be filled out more competently, and it does serve to ensure a degree of uniformity in the manner in which habeas corpus claims are presented.

Subdivision (c) directs the clerk of the district court to make available to applicants upon request, without charge, blank petitions in the prescribed form.

Subdivision (c) also requires that all available grounds for relief be presented in the petition, including those grounds of which, by the exercise of reasonable diligence, the petitioner should be aware. This is reinforced by rule 9(b), which allows dismissal of a second petition which fails to allege new grounds or, if new grounds are alleged, the judge finds an inexcusable failure to assert the ground in the prior petition.

Both subdivision (c) and the annexed form require a legibly handwritten or typewritten petition. As required by 28 U.S.C. § 2242, the petition must be signed and sworn to by the petitioner (or someone acting in his behalf).

Subdivision (d) provides that a single petition may assert a claim only against the judgment or judgments of a single state court (*i.e.*, a court of the same county or judicial district or circuit). This permits, but does not require, an attack in a single petition on judgments based upon separate indictments or on separate counts even though sentences were imposed on separate days by the same court. A claim against a judgment of a court of a different political subdivision must be raised by means of a separate petition.

Subdivision (e) allows the clerk to return an insufficient petition to the petitioner, and it must be returned if the clerk is so directed by a judge of the court. Any failure to comply with the requirements of rule 2 or 3 are grounds for insufficiency. In situations where there may be arguable noncompliance with another rule, such as rule 9, the judge, not the clerk, must make the decision. If the petition is returned it must be accompanied by a statement of the reason for its return. No petitioner should be left to speculate as to why or in what manner his petition failed to conform to these rules.

Subdivision (e) also provides that the clerk shall retain one copy of the insufficient petition. If the prisoner files another petition, the clerk will be in a better position to determine the sufficiency of the new petition. If the new petition is insufficient, comparison with the prior petition may indicate whether the prisoner has failed to understand the clerk's prior explanation for its insufficiency, so that the clerk can make another, hopefully successful, attempt at transmitting this information to the petitioner. If the petitioner insists that the original petition was in compliance with the rules, a copy of the original petition is available for the consideration of the judge. It is probably better practice to make a photocopy of a petition which can be corrected by the petitioner, thus saving the petitioner the task of completing an additional copy.

1982 Amendment

Subdivision (c). The amendment takes into account 28 U.S.C. § 1746, enacted after adoption of the § 2254 rules. Section 1746 provides that in lieu of an affidavit an unsworn statement may be given under penalty of perjury in substantially the following form if executed within the United States, its territories, possessions or commonwealths: "I declare (or certify, verify, or state) under penalty of perjury that the foregoing is true and correct. Executed on (date). (Signature)." The statute is "intended to encompass prisoner litigation," and the statutory alternative is especially appropriate in such cases because a notary might not be readily available. *Carter v. Clark*, 616 F.2d 228 (5th Cir. 1980). The § 2254 forms have been revised accordingly.

2004 Amendments

The language of Rule 2 has been amended as part of general restyling of the rules to make them more easily understood and to make style and terminology consistent throughout the rules. These changes are intended to be stylistic and no substantive change is intended, except as described below.

Revised Rule 2(c)(5) has been amended by removing the requirement that the petition be signed personally by the petitioner. As reflected in 28 U.S.C. § 2242, an application for habeas corpus relief may be filed by the person who is seeking relief, or by someone acting on behalf of that person. *See, e.g., Whitmore v. Arkansas*, 495 U.S. 149 (1990) (discus-

sion of requisites for "next friend" standing in petition for habeas corpus). Thus, under the, amended rule the petition may be signed by petitioner personally or by someone acting on behalf of the petitioner, assuming that the person is authorized to do so, for example, an attorney for the petitioner. The Committee envisions that the courts will apply third-party, or "next-friend," standing analysis in deciding whether the signer was actually authorized to sign the petition on behalf of the petitioner.

The language in new Rule 2(d) has been changed to reflect that a petitioner must substantially follow the standard form, which is appended to the rules, or a form provided by the court. The current rule, Rule 2(c), seems to indicate a preference for the standard "national" form. Under the amended rule, there is no stated preference. The Committee understood that current practice in some courts is that if the petitioner first files a petition using the national form, the courts may then ask the petitioner to supplement it with the local form.

Current Rule 2(e), which provided for returning an insufficient petition, has been deleted. The Committee believed that the approach in Federal Rule of Civil Procedure 5(e) was more appropriate for dealing with petitions that do not conform to the form requirements of the rule. That Rule provides that the clerk may not refuse to accept a filing solely for the reason that it fails to comply with these rules or local rules. Before the adoption of a one-year statute of limitations in the Antiterrorism and Effective Death Penalty Act of 1996, 110 Stat. 1214, the petitioner suffered no penalty, other than delay, if the petition was deemed insufficient. Now that a one-year statute of limitations applies to petitions filed under § 2254, see 28 U.S.C. § 2244(d)(1), the court's dismissal of a petition because it is not in proper form may pose a significant penalty for a petitioner, who may not be able to file another petition within the one-year limitations period. Now, under revised Rule 3(b), the clerk is required to file a petition, even though it may otherwise fail to comply with the provisions in revised Rule 2(c). The Committee believed that the better procedure was to accept the defective petition and require the petitioner to submit a corrected petition that conforms to Rule 2(c).

Rule 3. Filing the Petition; Inmate Filing

(a) **Where to File; Copies; Filing Fee.** An original and two copies of the petition must be filed with the clerk and must be accompanied by:

(1) the applicable filing fee, or

(2) a motion for leave to proceed in forma pauperis, the affidavit required by 28 U.S.C. § 1915, and a certificate from the warden or other appropriate officer of the place of confinement showing the amount of money or securities that the petitioner has in any account in the institution.

(b) **Filing.** The clerk must file the petition and enter it on the docket.

(c) **Time to File.** The time for filing a petition is governed by 28 U.S.C. § 2244(d).

(d) **Inmate Filing.** A paper filed by an inmate confined in an institution is timely if deposited in the institution's internal mailing system on or before the last day for filing. If an institution has a system designed for legal mail, the inmate must use that system to receive the benefit of this rule. Timely filing may be shown by a declaration in compliance with 28 U.S.C. § 1746 or by a notarized statement, either of which must set forth the date of deposit and state that first-class postage has been prepaid.

(As amended Apr. 26, 2004, eff. Dec. 1, 2004.)

ADVISORY COMMITTEE NOTES

1976 Adoption

Rule 3 sets out the procedures to be followed by the petitioner and the court in filing the petition. Some of its provisions are currently dealt with by local rule or practice, while others are innovations. Subdivision (a) specifies the petitioner's responsibilities. It requires that the petition, which must be accompanied by two conformed copies thereof, be filed in the office of the clerk of the district court. The petition must be accompanied by the filing fee prescribed by law (presently $5; see 28 U.S.C. § 1914(a)), unless leave to prosecute the petition in forma pauperis is applied for and granted. In the event the petitioner desires to prosecute the petition in forma pauperis, he must file the affidavit required by 28 U.S.C. § 1915, together with a certificate showing the amount of funds in his institutional account.

Requiring that the petition be filed in the office of the clerk of the district court provides an efficient and uniform system of filing habeas corpus petitions.

Subdivision (b) requires the clerk to file the petition. If the filing fee accompanies the petition, it may be filed immediately, and, if not, it is contemplated that prompt attention will be given to the request to proceed in forma pauperis. The court may delegate the issuance of the order to the clerk in those cases in which it is clear from the petition that there is full compliance with the requirements to proceed in forma pauperis.

Requiring the copies of the petition to be filed with the clerk will have an impact not only upon administrative matters, but upon more basic problems as well. In districts with more than one judge, a petitioner under present circumstances may send a petition to more than one judge. If no central filing system exists for each district, two judges may independently take different action on the same petition. Even if the action taken is consistent, there may be needless duplication of effort.

The requirement of an additional two copies of the form of the petition is a current practice in many courts. An efficient filing system requires one copy for use by the court (central file), one for the respondent (under 3(b), the respondent receives a copy of the petition whether an answer is required or not), and one for petitioner's counsel, if appointed. Since rule 2 provides that blank copies of the petition in the prescribed form are to be furnished to the applicant free of charge, there should be no undue burden created by this requirement.

Attached to copies of the petition supplied in accordance with rule 2 is an affidavit form for the use of petitioners desiring to proceed in forma pauperis. The form requires information concerning the petitioner's financial resources.

In forma pauperis cases, the petition must also be accompanied by a certificate indicating the amount of funds in the petitioner's institution account. Usually the certificate will be from the warden. If the petitioner is on probation or parole, the court might want to require a certificate from the supervising officer. Petitions by persons on probation or parole are not numerous enough, however, to justify making special provision for this situation in the text of the rule.

The certificate will verify the amount of funds credited to the petitioner in an institution account. The district court may by local rule require that any amount credited to the petitioner, in excess of a stated maximum, must be used for the payment of the filing fee. Since prosecuting an action in forma pauperis is a privilege (see *Smart v. Heinze*, 347 F.2d 114, 116 (9th Cir. 1965), it is not to be granted when the petitioner has sufficient resources.

Subdivision (b) details the clerk's duties with regard to filing the petition. If the petition does not appear on its face to comply with the requirements of rules 2 and 3, it may be returned in accordance with rule 2(e). If it appears to comply, it must be filed and entered on the docket in the clerk's office. However, under this subdivision the respondent is not required to answer or otherwise move with respect to the petition unless so ordered by the court.

2004 Amendments

The language of Rule 3 has been amended as part of general restyling of the rules to make them more easily understood and to make style and terminology consistent throughout the rules. These changes are intended to be stylistic and no substantive change is intended except as described below.

The last sentence of current Rule 3(b), dealing with an answer being filed by the respondent, has been moved to revised Rule 5(a).

Revised Rule 3(b) is new and is intended to parallel Federal Rule of Civil Procedure 5(e), which provides that the clerk may not refuse to accept a filing solely for the reason that it fails to comply with these rules or local rules. Before the adoption of a one-year statute of limitations in the Antiterrorism and Effective Death Penalty Act of 1996, 110 Stat. 1214, the petitioner suffered no penalty, other than delay, if the petition was deemed insufficient. That Act, however, added a one-year statute of limitations to petitions filed under § 2254, *see* 28 U.S.C. § 2244(d)(1). Thus, a court's dismissal of a defective petition may pose a significant penalty for a petitioner who may not be able to file a corrected petition within the one-year limitations period. The Committee believed that the better procedure was to accept the defective petition and require the petitioner to submit a corrected petition that conforms to Rule 2. Thus, revised Rule 3(b) requires the clerk to file a petition, even though it may otherwise fail to comply with Rule 2. The rule, however, is not limited to those instances where the petition is defective only in form; the clerk would also be required, for example, to file the petition even though it lacked the requisite filing fee or an *in forma pauperis* form.

Revised Rule 3(c), which sets out a specific reference to 28 U.S.C. § 2244(d), is new and has been added to put petitioners on notice that a one-year statute of limitations applies to petitions filed under these Rules. Although the rule does not address the issue, every circuit that has addressed the issue has taken the position that equitable tolling of the statute of limitations is available in appropriate circumstances. *See, e.g., Smith v. McGinnis*, 208 F.3d 13, 17–18 (2d Cir. 2000); *Miller v. New Jersey State Department of Corrections*, 145 F.3d 616, 618–19 (3d Cir. 1998); *Harris v. Hutchinson*, 209 F.3d 325, 330 (4th Cir. 2000). The Supreme Court has not addressed the question directly. *See Duncan v. Walker*, 533 U.S. 167, 181 (2001) ("We . . . have no occasion to address the question that Justice Stevens raises concerning the availability of equitable tolling.").

Rule 3(d) is new and provides guidance on determining whether a petition from an inmate is considered to have been filed in a timely fashion. The new provision parallels Federal Rule of Appellate Procedure 25(a)(2)(C).

Rule 4. Preliminary Review; Serving the Petition and Order

The clerk must promptly forward the petition to a judge under the court's assignment procedure, and the judge must promptly examine it. If it plainly appears from the petition and any attached exhibits that the petitioner is not entitled to relief in the district court, the judge must dismiss the petition and direct the clerk to notify the petitioner. If the petition is not dismissed, the judge must order the respondent to file an answer, motion, or other response within a fixed time, or to take other action the judge may order. In every case, the clerk must serve a copy of the petition and any order on the respondent and on the attorney general or other appropriate officer of the state involved.
(As amended Apr. 26, 2004, eff. Dec. 1, 2004.)

ADVISORY COMMITTEE NOTES
1976 Adoption

Rule 4 outlines the options available to the court after the petition is properly filed. The petition must be promptly presented to and examined by the judge to whom it is assigned. If it plainly appears from the face of the petition and any exhibits attached thereto that the petitioner is not entitled to relief in the district court, the judge must enter an order summarily dismissing the petition and cause the petitioner to be notified. If summary dismissal is not ordered, the judge must order the respondent to file an answer or to otherwise plead to the petition within a time period to be fixed in the order.

28 U.S.C. § 2243 requires that the writ shall be awarded, or an order to show cause issued, "unless it appears from the application that the applicant or person detained is not entitled thereto." Such consideration may properly encompass any exhibits attached to the petition, including, but not limited to, transcripts, sentencing records, and copies of state court opinions. The judge may order any of these items for his consideration if they are not yet included with the petition. See 28 U.S.C. § 753(f) which authorizes payment for transcripts in habeas corpus cases.

It has been suggested that an answer should be required in every habeas proceeding, taking into account the usual petitioner's lack of legal expertise and the important functions served by the return. See Developments in the Law—

Federal Habeas Corpus, 83 Harv.L.Rev. 1038, 1178 (1970). However, under § 2243 it is the duty of the court to screen out frivolous applications and eliminate the burden that would be placed on the respondent by ordering an unnecessary answer. *Allen v. Perini*, 424 F.2d 134, 141 (6th Cir. 1970). In addition, "notice" pleading is not sufficient, for the petition is expected to state facts that point to a "real possibility of constitutional error." See *Aubut v. State of Maine*, 431 F.2d 688, 689 (1st Cir. 1970).

In the event an answer is ordered under rule 4, the court is accorded greater flexibility than under § 2243 in determining within what time period an answer must be made. Under § 2243, the respondent must make a return within three days after being so ordered, with additional time of up to forty days allowed under the Federal Rules of Civil Procedure, Rule 81(a)(2), for good cause. In view of the widespread state of work overload in prosecutors' offices (see, *e.g.*, *Allen*, 424 F.2d at 141), additional time is granted in some jurisdictions as a matter of course. Rule 4, which contains no fixed time requirement, gives the court the discretion to take into account various factors such as the respondent's workload and the availability of transcripts before determining a time within which an answer must be made.

Rule 4 authorizes the judge to "take such other action as the judge deems appropriate." This is designed to afford the judge flexibility in a case where either dismissal or an order to answer may be inappropriate. For example, the judge may want to authorize the respondent to make a motion to dismiss based upon information furnished by respondent, which may show that petitioner's claims have already been decided on the merits in a federal court; that petitioner has failed to exhaust state remedies; that the petitioner is not in custody within the meaning of 28 U.S.C. § 2254; or that a decision in the matter is pending in state court. In these situations, a dismissal may be called for on procedural grounds, which may avoid burdening the respondent with the necessity of filing an answer on the substantive merits of the petition. In other situations, the judge may want to consider a motion from respondent to make the petition more certain. Or the judge may want to dismiss some allegations in the petition, requiring the respondent to answer only those claims which appear to have some arguable merit.

Rule 4 requires that a copy of the petition and any order be served by certified mail on the respondent and the attorney general of the state involved. See 28 U.S.C. § 2252. Presently, the respondent often does not receive a copy of the petition unless the court directs an answer under 28 U.S.C. § 2243. Although the attorney general is served, he is not required to answer if it is more appropriate for some other agency to do so. Although the rule does not specifically so provide, it is assumed that copies of the court orders to respondent will be mailed to petitioner by the court.

2004 Amendments

The language of Rule 4 has been amended as part of general restyling of the rules to make them more easily understood and to make style and terminology consistent throughout the rules. These changes are intended to be stylistic and no substantive change is intended, except as described below.

The amended rule reflects that the response to a habeas petition may be a motion.

The requirement that in every case the clerk must serve a copy of the petition on the respondent by certified mail has been deleted. In addition, the current requirement that the petition be sent to the Attorney General of the state has been modified to reflect practice in some jurisdictions that the appropriate state official may be someone other than the Attorney General, for example, the officer in charge of a local confinement facility. This comports with a similar provision in 28 U.S.C. § 2252, which addresses notice of habeas corpus proceedings to the state's attorney general or other appropriate officer of the state.

Rule 5. The Answer and the Reply

(a) When Required. The respondent is not required to answer the petition unless a judge so orders.

(b) Contents: Addressing the Allegations; Stating a Bar. The answer must address the allegations in the petition. In addition, it must state whether any claim in the petition is barred by a failure to exhaust state remedies, a procedural bar, non-retroactivity, or a statute of limitations.

(c) Contents: Transcripts. The answer must also indicate what transcripts (of pretrial, trial, sentencing, or post-conviction proceedings) are available, when they can be furnished, and what proceedings have been recorded but not transcribed. The respondent must attach to the answer parts of the transcript that the respondent considers relevant. The judge may order that the respondent furnish other parts of existing transcripts or that parts of untranscribed recordings be transcribed and furnished. If a transcript cannot be obtained, the respondent may submit a narrative summary of the evidence.

(d) Contents: Briefs on Appeal and Opinions. The respondent must also file with the answer a copy of:

> **(1)** any brief that the petitioner submitted in an appellate court contesting the conviction or sentence, or contesting an adverse judgment or order in a post-conviction proceeding;

> **(2)** any brief that the prosecution submitted in an appellate court relating to the conviction or sentence; and

> **(3)** the opinions and dispositive orders of the appellate court relating to the conviction or the sentence.

(e) Reply. The petitioner may submit a reply to the respondent's answer or other pleading within a time fixed by the judge.

(As amended Apr. 26, 2004, eff. Dec. 1, 2004.)

ADVISORY COMMITTEE NOTES
1976 Adoption

Rule 5 details the contents of the "answer". (This is a change in terminology from "return," which is still used

below when referring to prior practice.) The answer plays
an obviously important role in a habeas proceeding:

The return serves several important functions: it permits
the court and the parties to uncover quickly the disputed
issues; it may reveal to the petitioner's attorney grounds
for release that the petitioner did not know; and it may
demonstrate that the petitioner's claim is wholly without
merit.

Developments in the Law—Federal Habeas Corpus, 83
Harv.L.Rev. 1083, 1178 (1970).

The answer must respond to the allegations of the petition.
While some districts require this by local rule (see, *e.g.*,
E.D.N.C.R. 17(B)), under 28 U.S.C. § 2243 little specificity
is demanded. As a result, courts occasionally receive an-
swers which contain only a statement certifying the true
cause of detention, or a series of delaying motions such as
motions to dismiss. The requirement of the proposed rule
that the "answer shall respond to the allegations of the
petition" is intended to ensure that a responsive pleading will
be filed and thus the functions of the answer fully served.

The answer must also state whether the petitioner has
exhausted his state remedies. This is a prerequisite to
eligibility for the writ under 28 U.S.C. § 2254(b) and applies
to every ground the petitioner raises. Most form petitions
now in use contain questions requiring information relevant
to whether the petitioner has exhausted his remedies. How-
ever, the exhaustion requirement is often not understood by
the unrepresented petitioner. The attorney general has both
the legal expertise and access to the record and thus is in a
much better position to inform the court on the matter of
exhaustion of state remedies. An alleged failure to exhaust
state remedies as to any ground in the petition may be raised
by a motion by the attorney general, thus avoiding the
necessity of a formal answer as to that ground.

The rule requires the answer to indicate what transcripts
are available, when they can be furnished, and also what
proceedings have been recorded and not transcribed. This
will serve to inform the court and petitioner as to what
factual allegations can be checked against the actual tran-
scripts. The transcripts include pretrial transcripts relating,
for example, to pretrial motions to suppress; transcripts of
the trial or guilty plea proceeding; and transcripts of any
post-conviction proceedings which may have taken place.
The respondent is required to furnish those portions of the
transcripts which he believes relevant. The court may order
the furnishing of additional portions of the transcripts upon
the request of petitioner or upon the court's own motion.

Where transcripts are unavailable, the rule provides that a
narrative summary of the evidence may be submitted.

Rule 5 (and the general procedure set up by this entire set
of rules) does not contemplate a traverse to the answer,
except under special circumstances. See advisory committee
note to rule 9. Therefore, the old common law assumption of
verity of the allegations of a return until impeached, as
codified in 28 U.S.C. § 2248, is no longer applicable. The
meaning of the section, with its exception to the assumption
"to the extent that the judge finds from the evidence that
they (the allegations) are not true," has given attorneys and
courts a great deal of difficulty. It seems that when the
petition and return pose an issue of fact, no traverse is
required; *Stewart v. Overholser*, 186 F.2d 339 (D.C.Cir.
1950).

We read § 2248 of the Judicial Code as not requiring a
traverse when a factual issue has been clearly framed by
the petition and the return or answer. This section pro-
vides that the allegations of a return or answer to an order
to show cause shall be accepted as true if not traversed,
except to the extent the judge finds from the evidence that
they are not true. This contemplates that where the
petition and return or answer do present an issue of fact
material to the legality of detention, evidence is required
to resolve that issue despite the absence of a traverse.
This reference to evidence assumes a hearing on issues
raised by the allegations of the petition and the return or
answer to the order to show cause.

186 F.2d at 342, n. 5

In actual practice, the traverse tends to be a mere pro forma
refutation of the return, serving little if any expository
function. In the interests of a more streamlined and man-
ageable habeas corpus procedure, it is not required except in
those instances where it will serve a truly useful purpose.
Also, under rule 11 the court is given the discretion to
incorporate Federal Rules of Civil Procedure when appropri-
ate, so civil rule 15(a) may be used to allow the petitioner to
amend his petition when the court feels this is called for by
the contents of the answer.

Rule 5 does not indicate who the answer is to be served
upon, but it necessarily implies that it will be mailed to the
petitioner (or to his attorney if he has one). The number of
copies of the answer required is left to the court's discretion.
Although the rule requires only a copy of petitioner's brief on
appeal, respondent is free also to file a copy of respondent's
brief. In practice, courts have found it helpful to have a copy
of respondent's brief.

2004 Amendments

The language of Rule 5 has been amended as part of
general restyling of the rules to make them more easily
understood and to make style and terminology consistent
throughout the rules. These changes are intended to be
stylistic and no substantive change is intended, except as
described below.

Revised Rule 5(a), which provides that the respondent is
not required to file an answer to the petition, unless a judge
so orders, is taken from current Rule 3(b). The revised rule
does not address the practice in some districts, where the
respondent files a pre-answer motion to dismiss the petition.
But revised Rule 4 permits that practice and reflects the
view that if the court does not dismiss the petition, it may
require (or permit) the respondent to file a motion.

Rule 5(b) has been amended to require that the answer
address not only failure to exhaust state remedies, but also
procedural bars, non-retroactivity, and any statute of limita-
tions. Although the latter three matters are not addressed in
the current rule, the Committee intends no substantive
change with the additional new language. *See, e.g.,* 28 U.S.C.
§ 2254(b)(3). Instead, the Committee believes that the explic-
it mention of those issues in the rule conforms to current
case law and statutory provisions. *See, e.g.,* 28 U.S.C.
§ 2244(d)(1).

Revised Rule 5(d) includes new material. First, Rule
5(d)(2), requires a respondent—assuming an answer is
filed—to provide the court with a copy of any brief submitted

by the prosecution to the appellate court. And Rule 5(d)(3) now provides that the respondent also file copies of any opinions and dispositive orders of the appellate court concerning the conviction or sentence. These provisions are intended to ensure that the court is provided with additional information that may assist it in resolving the issues raised, or not raised, in the petition.

Finally, revised Rule 5(e) adopts the practice in some jurisdictions of giving the petitioner an opportunity to file a reply to the respondent's answer. Rather than using terms such as "traverse," *see* 28 U.S.C. § 2248, to identify the petitioner's response to the answer, the rule uses the more general term "reply." The Rule prescribes that the court set the time for such responses and in lieu of setting specific time limits in each case, the court may decide to include such time limits in its local rules.

Rule 6. Discovery

(a) Leave of Court Required. A judge may, for good cause, authorize a party to conduct discovery under the Federal Rules of Civil Procedure and may limit the extent of discovery. If necessary for effective discovery, the judge must appoint an attorney for a petitioner who qualifies to have counsel appointed under 18 U.S.C. § 3006A.

(b) Requesting Discovery. A party requesting discovery must provide reasons for the request. The request must also include any proposed interrogatories and requests for admission, and must specify any requested documents.

(c) Deposition Expenses. If the respondent is granted leave to take a deposition, the judge may require the respondent to pay the travel expenses, subsistence expenses, and fees of the petitioner's attorney to attend the deposition.

(As amended Apr. 26, 2004, eff. Dec. 1, 2004.)

ADVISORY COMMITTEE NOTES

1976 Adoption

This rule prescribes the procedures governing discovery in habeas corpus cases. Subdivision (a) provides that any party may utilize the processes of discovery available under the Federal Rules of Civil Procedure (rules 26–37) if, and to the extent that, the judge allows. It also provides for the appointment of counsel for a petitioner who qualifies for this when counsel is necessary for effective utilization of discovery procedures permitted by the judge.

Subdivision (a) is consistent with *Harris v. Nelson*, 394 U.S. 286 (1969). In that case the court noted,

[I]t is clear that there was no intention to extend to habeas corpus, as a matter of right, the broad discovery provisions * * * of the new [Federal Rules of Civil Procedure].

394 U.S. at 295

However, citing the lack of methods for securing information in habeas proceedings, the court pointed to an alternative.

Clearly, in these circumstances * * * the courts may fashion appropriate modes of procedure, by analogy to existing rules or otherwise in conformity with judicial usage. * * * Their authority is expressly confirmed in the All Writs Act, 28 U.S.C. § 1651.

394 U.S. at 299

The court concluded that the issue of discovery in habeas corpus cases could best be dealt with as part of an effort to provide general rules of practice for habeas corpus cases:

In fact, it is our view that the rulemaking machinery should be invoked to formulate rules of practice with respect to federal habeas corpus and § 2255 proceedings, on a comprehensive basis and not merely one confined to discovery. The problems presented by these proceedings are materially different from those dealt with in the Federal Rules of Civil Procedure and the Federal Rules of Criminal Procedure, and reliance upon usage and the opaque language of Civil Rule 81(a)(2) is transparently inadequate. In our view the results of a meticulous formulation and adoption of special rules for federal habeas corpus and § 2255 proceedings would promise much benefit.

394 U.S. at 301 n. 7

Discovery may, in appropriate cases, aid in developing facts necessary to decide whether to order an evidentiary hearing or to grant the writ following an evidentiary hearing:

We are award that confinement sometimes induces fantasy which has its basis in the paranoia of prison rather than in fact. But where specific allegations before the court show reason to believe that the petitioner may, if the facts are fully developed, be able to demonstrate that he is confined illegally and is therefore entitled to relief, it is the duty of the court to provide the necessary facilities and procedures for an adequate inquiry. Obviously, in exercising this power, the court may utilize familiar procedures, as appropriate, whether these are found in the civil or criminal rules or elsewhere in the "usages and principles."

Granting discovery is left to the discretion of the court, discretion to be exercised where there is a showing of good cause why discovery should be allowed. Several commentators have suggested that at least some discovery should be permitted without leave of court. It is argued that the courts will be burdened with weighing the propriety of requests to which the discovered party has no objection. Additionally, the availability of protective orders under Fed. R.Civ.R., Rules 30(b) and 31(d) will provide the necessary safeguards. See Developments in the Law—Federal Habeas Corpus, 83 Harv.L.Rev. 1038, 1186–87 (1970); Civil Discovery in Habeas Corpus, 67 Colum.L.Rev. 1296, 1310 (1967).

Nonetheless, it is felt the requirement of prior court approval of all discovery is necessary to prevent abuse, so this requirement is specifically mandated in the rule.

While requests for discovery in habeas proceedings normally follow the granting of an evidentiary hearing, there may be instances in which discovery would be appropriate beforehand. Such an approach was advocated in *Wagner v. United States*, 418 F.2d 618, 621 (9th Cir.1969), where the opinion stated the trial court could permit interrogatories, provide for deposing witnesses, and "take such other pre-hearing steps as may be appropriate." While this was an action under § 2255, the reasoning would apply equally well to petitions by state prisoners. Such pre-hearing discovery

may show an evidentiary hearing to be unnecessary, as when there are "no disputed issues of law or fact." 83 Harv.L.Rev. 1038, 1181 (1970). The court in Harris alluded to such a possibility when it said "the court may * * * authorize such proceedings with respect to development, *before or in conjunction with the hearing* of the facts * * *." [emphasis added] 394 U.S. at 300. Such pre-hearing discovery, like all discovery under rule 6, requires leave of court. In addition, the provisions in rule 7 for the use of an expanded record may eliminate much of the need for this type of discovery. While probably not as frequently sought or granted as discovery in conjunction with a hearing, it may nonetheless serve a valuable function.

In order to make pre-hearing discovery meaningful, subdivision (a) provides that the judge should appoint counsel for a petitioner who is without counsel and qualifies for appointment when this is necessary for the proper utilization of discovery procedures. Rule 8 provides for the appointment of counsel at the evidentiary hearing stage (see rule 8(b) and advisory committee note), but this would not assist the petitioner who seeks to utilize discovery to stave off dismissal of his petition (see rule 9 and advisory committee note) or to demonstrate that an evidentiary hearing is necessary. Thus, if the judge grants a petitioner's request for discovery prior to making a decision as to the necessity for an evidentiary hearing, he should determine whether counsel is necessary for the effective utilization of such discovery and, if so, appoint counsel for the petitioner if the petitioner qualifies for such appointment.

This rule contains very little specificity as to what types and methods of discovery should be made available to the parties in a habeas proceeding, or how, once made available, these discovery procedures should be administered. The purpose of this rule is to get some experience in how discovery would work in actual practice by letting district court judges fashion their own rules in the context of individual cases. When the results of such experience are available it would be desirable to consider whether further, more specific codification should take place.

Subdivision (b) provides for judicial consideration of all matters subject to discovery. A statement of the interrogatories, or requests for admission sought to be answered, and a list of any documents sought to be produced, must accompany a request for discovery. This is to advise the judge of the necessity for discovery and enable him to make certain that the inquiry is relevant and appropriately narrow.

Subdivision (c) refers to the situation where the respondent is granted leave to take the deposition of the petitioner or any other person. In such a case the judge may direct the respondent to pay the expenses and fees of counsel for the petitioner to attend the taking of the deposition, as a condition granting the respondent such leave. While the judge is not required to impose this condition subdivision (c) will give the court the means to do so. Such a provision affords some protection to the indigent petitioner who may be prejudiced by his inability to have counsel, often court-appointed, present at the taking of a deposition. It is recognized that under 18 U.S.C. § 3006A(g), court-appointed counsel in a § 2254 proceeding is entitled to receive up to $250 and reimbursement for expenses reasonably incurred. (Compare Fed.R.Crim.P. 15(c).) Typically, however, this does not adequately reimburse counsel if he must attend the taking of depositions or be involved in other pre-hearing

proceedings. Subdivision (c) is intended to provide additional funds, if necessary, to be paid by the state government (respondent) to petitioner's counsel.

Although the rule does not specifically so provide, it is assumed that a petitioner who qualifies for the appointment of counsel under 18 U.S.C. § 3006A(g) and is granted leave to take a deposition will be allowed witness costs. This will include recording and transcription of the witness's statement. Such costs are payable pursuant to 28 U.S.C. § 1825. See Opinion of Comptroller General, February 28, 1974.

Subdivision (c) specifically recognizes the right of the respondent to take the deposition of the petitioner. Although the petitioner could not be called to testify against his will in a criminal trial, it is felt the nature of the habeas proceeding, along with the safeguards accorded by the Fifth Amendment and the presence of counsel, justify this provision. See 83 Harv.L.Rev. 1038, 1183–84 (1970).

2004 Amendments

The language of Rule 6 has been amended as part of general restyling of the rules to make them more easily understood and to make style and terminology consistent throughout the rules. These changes are intended to be stylistic and no substantive change is intended.

Although current Rule 6(b) contains no requirement that the parties provide reasons for the requested discovery, the revised rule does so and also includes a requirement that the request be accompanied by any proposed interrogatories and requests for admission, and must specify any requested documents. The Committee believes that the revised rule makes explicit what has been implicit in current practice.

Rule 7. Expanding the Record

(a) **In General.** If the petition is not dismissed, the judge may direct the parties to expand the record by submitting additional materials relating to the petition. The judge may require that these materials be authenticated.

(b) **Types of Materials.** The materials that may be required include letters predating the filing of the petition, documents, exhibits, and answers under oath to written interrogatories propounded by the judge. Affidavits may also be submitted and considered as part of the record.

(c) **Review by the Opposing Party.** The judge must give the party against whom the additional materials are offered an opportunity to admit or deny their correctness.

(As amended Apr. 26, 2004, eff. Dec. 1, 2004.)

ADVISORY COMMITTEE NOTES

1976 Adoption

This rule provides that the judge may direct that the record be expanded. The purpose is to enable the judge to dispose of some habeas petitions not dismissed on the pleadings, without the time and expense required for an evidentiary hearing. An expanded record may also be helpful when an evidentiary hearing is ordered.

The record may be expanded to include additional material relevant to the merits of the petition. While most petitions are dismissed either summarily or after a response has been made, of those that remain, by far the majority require an evidentiary hearing. In the fiscal year ending June 30, 1970, for example, of 8,423 § 2254 cases terminated, 8,231 required court action. Of these, 7,812 were dismissed before a prehearing conference and 469 merited further court action (*e.g.*, expansion of the record, prehearing conference, or an evidentiary hearing). Of the remaining 469 cases, 403 required an evidentiary hearing, often time-consuming, costly, and, at least occasionally, unnecessary. See Director of the Administrative Office of the United States Courts, Annual Report, 245a–245c (table C4) (1970). In some instances these hearings were necessitated by slight omissions in the state record which might have been cured by the use of an expanded record.

Authorizing expansion of the record will, hopefully, eliminate some unnecessary hearings. The value of this approach was articulated in *Raines v. United States*, 423 F.2d 526, 529–530 (4th Cir. 1970):

> Unless it is clear from the pleadings and the files and records that the prisoner is entitled to no relief, the statute makes a hearing mandatory. We think there is a permissible intermediate step that may avoid the necessity for an expensive and time consuming evidentiary hearing in every Section 2255 case. It may instead be perfectly appropriate, depending upon the nature of the allegations, for the district court to proceed by requiring that the record be expanded to include letters, documentary evidence, and, in an appropriate case, even affidavits. *United States v. Carlino*, 400 F.2d 56 (2nd Cir. 1968); *Mirra v. United States*, 379 F.2d 782 (2nd Cir. 1967); *Accardi v. United States*, 379 F.2d 312 (2nd Cir. 1967). When the issue is one of credibility, resolution on the basis of affidavits can rarely be conclusive, but that is not to say they may not be helpful.

In *Harris v. Nelson*, 394 U.S. 286, 300 (1969), the court said:

> At any time in the proceedings * * * *either on [the court's] own motion* or upon cause shown by the petitioner, it may issue such writs and take or authorize such proceedings * * * *before* or in conjunction with the hearing of the facts * * *. [emphasis added]

Subdivision (b) specifies the materials which may be added to the record. These include, without limitation, letters predating the filing of the petition in the district court, documents, exhibits, and answers under oath directed to written interrogatories propounded by the judge. Under this subdivision affidavits may be submitted and considered part of the record. Subdivision (b) is consistent with 28 U.S.C. §§ 2246 and 2247 and the decision in *Raines* with regard to types of material that may be considered upon application for a writ of habeas corpus. See *United States v. Carlino*, 400 F.2d 56, 58 (2d Cir. 1968), and *Machibroda v. United States*, 368 U.S. 487 (1962).

Under subdivision (c) all materials proposed to be included in the record must be submitted to the party against whom they are to be offered.

Under subdivision (d) the judge can require authentication if he believes it desirable to do so.

2004 Amendments

The language of Rule 7 has been amended as part of general restyling of the rules to make them more easily understood and to make style and terminology consistent throughout the rules. These changes are intended to be stylistic and no substantive change is intended, except as noted below.

Revised Rule 7(a) is not intended to restrict the court's authority to expand the record through means other than requiring the parties themselves to provide the information. Further, the rule has been changed to remove the reference to the "merits" of the petition in the recognition that a court may wish to expand the record in order to assist it in deciding an issue other than the merits of the petition.

The language in current Rule 7(d), which deals with authentication of materials in the expanded record, has been moved to revised Rule 7(a).

Rule 8. Evidentiary Hearing

(a) Determining Whether to Hold a Hearing. If the petition is not dismissed, the judge must review the answer, any transcripts and records of state-court proceedings, and any materials submitted under Rule 7 to determine whether an evidentiary hearing is warranted.

(b) Reference to a Magistrate Judge. A judge may, under 28 U.S.C. § 636(b), refer the petition to a magistrate judge to conduct hearings and to file proposed findings of fact and recommendations for disposition. When they are filed, the clerk must promptly serve copies of the proposed findings and recommendations on all parties. Within 10 days after being served, a party may file objections as provided by local court rule. The judge must determine *de novo* any proposed finding or recommendation to which objection is made. The judge may accept, reject, or modify any proposed finding or recommendation.

(c) Appointing Counsel; Time of Hearing. If an evidentiary hearing is warranted, the judge must appoint an attorney to represent a petitioner who qualifies to have counsel appointed under 18 U.S.C. § 3006A. The judge must conduct the hearing as soon as practicable after giving the attorneys adequate time to investigate and prepare. These rules do not limit the appointment of counsel under § 3006A at any stage of the proceeding.

(As amended Pub.L. 94–426, § 2(5), Sept. 28, 1976, 90 Stat. 1334; Pub.L. 94–577, § 2(a)(1), (b)(1), Oct. 21, 1976, 90 Stat. 2730, 2731; Apr. 26, 2004, eff. Dec. 1, 2004.)

ADVISORY COMMITTEE NOTES

1976 Adoption

This rule outlines the procedure to be followed by the court immediately prior to and after the determination of whether to hold an evidentiary hearing.

The provisions are applicable if the petition has not been dismissed at a previous stage in the proceeding [including a summary dismissal under Rule 4; a dismissal pursuant to a

motion by the respondent; a dismissal after the answer and petition are considered; or a dismissal after consideration of the pleadings and an expanded record].

If dismissal has not been ordered, the court must determine whether an evidentiary hearing is required. This determination is to be made upon a review of the answer, the transcript and record of state court proceedings, and if there is one, the expanded record. As the United States Supreme Court noted in *Townsend v. Sam*, 372 U.S. 293, 319 (1963):

> Ordinarily [the complete state-court] record—including the transcript of testimony (or if unavailable some adequate substitute, such as a narrative record), the pleadings, court opinions, and other pertinent documents—is indispensable to determining whether the habeas applicant received a full and fair state-court evidentiary hearing resulting in reliable findings.

Subdivision (a) contemplates that all of these materials, if available, will be taken into account. This is especially important in view of the standard set down in *Townsend* for determining *when* a hearing in the federal habeas proceeding is mandatory.

> The appropriate standard * * * is this: Where the facts are in dispute, the federal court in habeas corpus must hold an evidentiary hearing if the habeas applicant did not receive a full and fair evidentiary hearing in a state court, either at the time of the trial or in a collateral proceeding.

372 U.S. at 312

The circumstances under with a federal hearing is mandatory are now specified in 28 U.S.C. § 2254(d). The 1966 amendment clearly places the burden on the petitioner, when there has already been a state hearing, to show that it was not a fair or adequate hearing for one or more of the specifically enumerated reasons, in order to force a federal evidentiary hearing. Since the function of an evidentiary hearing is to try issues of fact (372 U.S. at 309), such a hearing is unnecessary when only issues of law are raised. See, *e.g.*, *Yeaman v. United States*, 326 F.2d 293 (9th Cir. 1963).

In situations in which an evidentiary hearing is not mandatory, the judge may nonetheless decide that an evidentiary hearing is desirable:

> The purpose of the test is to indicate the situations in which the holding of an evidentiary hearing is mandatory. In all other cases where the material facts are in dispute, the holding of such a hearing is in the discretion of the district judge.

372 U.S. at 318

If the judge decides that an evidentiary hearing is neither required nor desirable, he shall make such a disposition of the petition "as justice shall require." Most habeas petitions are dismissed before the prehearing conference stage (see Director of the Administrative Office of the United States Courts, Annual Report 245–245c (table C4) (1970)) and of those not dismissed, the majority raise factual issues that necessitate an evidentiary hearing. If no hearing is required, most petitions are dismissed, but in unusual cases the court may grant the relief sought without a hearing. This includes immediate release from custody or nullification of a judgment under which the sentence is to be served in the future.

Subdivision (b) provides that a magistrate, when so empowered by rule of the district court, may recommend to the district judge that an evidentiary hearing be held or that the petition be dismissed, provided he gives the district judge a sufficiently detailed description of the facts so that the judge may decide whether or not to hold an evidentiary hearing. This provision is not inconsistent with the holding in *Wingo v. Wedding*, 418 U.S. 461 (1974), that the Federal Magistrates Act did not change the requirement of the habeas corpus statute that federal judges personally conduct habeas evidentiary hearings, and that consequently a local district court rule was invalid insofar as it authorized a magistrate to hold such hearings. 28 U.S.C. § 636(b) provides that a district court may by rule authorize any magistrate to perform certain additional duties, including preliminary review of applications for posttrial relief made by individuals convicted of criminal offenses, and submission of a report and recommendations to facilitate the decision of the district judge having jurisdiction over the case as to whether there should be a hearing.

As noted in *Wingo*, review "by Magistrates of applications for post-trial relief is thus limited to review for the purpose of proposing, not holding, evidentiary hearings."

Utilization of the magistrate as specified in subdivision (b) will aid in the expeditious and fair handling of habeas petitions.

> A qualified, experienced magistrate will, it is hoped, acquire an expertise in examining these [postconviction review] applications and summarizing their important contents for the district judge, thereby facilitating his decisions. Law clerks are presently charged with this responsibility by many judges, but judges have noted that the normal 1-year clerkship does not afford law clerks the time or experience necessary to attain real efficiency in handling such applications.

S.Rep. No. 371, 90th Cong., 1st Sess., 26 (1967).

Under subdivision (c) there are two provisions that differ from the procedure set forth in 28 U.S.C. § 2243. These are the appointment of counsel and standard for determining how soon the hearing will be held.

If an evidentiary hearing is required the judge must appoint counsel for a petitioner who qualified [sic] for appointment under the Criminal Justice Act. Currently, the appointment of counsel is not recognized as a right at any stage of a habeas proceeding. See, *e.g.*, *United States ex rel. Marshall v. Wilkins*, 338 F.2d 404 (2d Cir. 1964). Some district courts have, however, by local rule, required that counsel must be provided for indigent petitioners in cases requiring a hearing. See, *e.g.*, D.N.M.R. 21(f), E.D.N.Y.R. 26(d). Appointment of counsel at this stage is mandatory under subdivision (c). This requirement will not limit the authority of the court to provide counsel at an earlier stage if it is thought desirable to do so as is done in some courts under current practice. At the evidentiary hearing stage, however, an indigent petitioner's access to counsel should not depend on local practice and, for this reason, the furnishing of counsel is made mandatory.

Counsel can perform a valuable function benefiting both the court and the petitioner. The issues raised can be more clearly identified if both sides have the benefit of trained legal personnel. The presence of counsel at the prehearing conference may help to expedite the evidentiary hearing or

make it unnecessary, and counsel will be able to make better use of available prehearing discovery procedures. Compare ABA Project on Standards for Criminal Justice, Standards Relating to Post-Conviction Remedies § 4.4, p. 66 (Approved Draft 1968). At a hearing, the petitioner's claims are more likely to be effectively and properly presented by counsel.

Under 18 U.S.C. § 3006A(g), payment is allowed counsel up to $250, plus reimbursement for expenses reasonably incurred. The standards of indigency under this section are less strict than those regarding eligibility to prosecute a petition in forma pauperis, and thus many who cannot qualify to proceed under 28 U.S.C. § 1915 will be entitled to the benefits of counsel under 18 U.S.C. § 3006A(g). Under Rule 6(c), the court may order the respondent to reimburse counsel from state funds for fees and expenses incurred as the result of the utilization of discovery procedures by the respondent.

Subdivision (c) provides that the hearing shall be conducted as promptly as possible, taking into account "the need of counsel for both parties for adequate time for investigation and preparation." This differs from the language of 28 U.S.C. § 2243, which requires that the day for the hearing be set "not more than five days after the return unless for good cause additional time is allowed." This time limit fails to take into account the function that may be served by a prehearing conference and the time required to prepare adequately for an evidentiary hearing. Although "additional time" is often allowed under § 2243, subdivision (c) provides more flexibility to take account of the complexity of the case, the availability of important materials, the workload of the attorney general, and the time required by appointed counsel to prepare.

While the rule does not make specific provision for a prehearing conference, the omission is not intended to cast doubt upon the value of such a conference:

The conference may limit the questions to be resolved, identify areas of agreement and dispute, and explore evidentiary problems that may be expected to arise. * * * [S]uch conferences may also disclose that a hearing is unnecessary * * *.

ABA Project on Standards for Criminal Justice, Standards Relating to Post-Conviction Remedies § 4.6, commentary pp. 74–75. (Approved Draft, 1968.)

See also Developments in the Law—Federal Habeas Corpus, 83 Harv.L.Rev. 1038, 1188 (1970).

The rule does not contain a specific provision on the subpoenaing of witnesses. It is left to local practice to determine the method for doing this. The implementation of 28 U.S.C. § 1825 on the payment of witness fees is dealt with in an opinion of the Comptroller General, February 28, 1974.

2004 Amendments

The language of Rule 8 has been amended as part of general restyling of the rules to make them more easily understood and to make style and terminology consistent throughout the rules. These changes are intended to be stylistic and no substantive change is intended.

Rule 8(a) is not intended to supersede the restrictions on evidentiary hearings contained in 28 U.S.C. § 2254(e)(2).

The requirement in current Rule 8(b)(2) that a copy of the magistrate judge's findings must be promptly mailed to all parties has been changed in revised Rule 8(b) to require that

copies of those findings be served on all parties. As used in this rule, "service" means service consistent with Federal Rule of Civil Procedure 5(b), which allows mailing the copies.

HISTORICAL NOTES

Effective and Applicability Provisions

1976 Acts

Section 2(c) of Pub.L. 94–577 provided that: "The amendments made by this section [amending subdivs. (b) and (c) of this rule and Rule 8(b), (c) of the Rules Governing Proceedings Under Section 2255 of this title] shall take effect with respect to petitions under section 2254 and motions under section 2255 of title 28 of the United States Code filed on or after February 1, 1977."

Rule 9. Second or Successive Petitions

Before presenting a second or successive petition, the petitioner must obtain an order from the appropriate court of appeals authorizing the district court to consider the petition as required by 28 U.S.C. § 2244(b)(3) and (4).

(As amended Pub.L. 94–426, § 2(7), (8), Sept. 28, 1976, 90 Stat. 1335; Apr. 26, 2004, eff. Dec. 1, 2004.)

ADVISORY COMMITTEE NOTES

1976 Adoption

This rule is intended to minimize abuse of the writ of habeas corpus by limiting the right to assert stale claims and to file multiple petitions. Subdivision (a) deals with the delayed petition. Subdivision (b) deals with the second or successive petition.

Subdivision (a) provides that a petition attacking the judgment of a state court may be dismissed on the grounds of delay if the petitioner knew or should have known of the existence of the grounds he is presently asserting in the petition and the delay has resulted in the state being prejudiced in its ability to respond to the petition. If the delay is more than five years after the judgment of conviction, prejudice is presumed, although this presumption is rebuttable by the petitioner. Otherwise, the state has the burden of showing such prejudice.

The assertion of stale claims is a problem which is not likely to decrease in frequency. Following the decisions in *Jones v. Cunningham*, 371 U.S. 236 (1963), and *Benson v. California*, 328 F.2d 159 (9th Cir. 1964), the concept of custody expanded greatly, lengthening the time period during which a habeas corpus petition may be filed. The petitioner who is not unconditionally discharged may be on parole or probation for many years. He may at some date, perhaps ten or fifteen years after conviction, decide to challenge the state court judgment. The grounds most often troublesome to the courts are ineffective counsel, denial of right of appeal, plea of guilty unlawfully induced, use of a coerced confession, and illegally constituted jury. The latter four grounds are often interlocked with the allegation of ineffective counsel. When they are asserted after the passage of many years, both the attorney for the defendant and the state have difficulty in ascertaining what the facts are. It often develops that the defense attorney has little or no recollection as to what took place and that many of the

participants in the trial are dead or their whereabouts unknown. The court reporter's notes may have been lost or destroyed, thus eliminating any exact record of what transpired. If the case was decided on a guilty plea, even if the record is intact, it may not satisfactorily reveal the extent of the defense attorney's efforts in behalf of the petitioner. As a consequence, there is obvious difficulty in investigating petitioner's allegations.

The interest of both the petitioner and the government can best be served if claims are raised while the evidence is still fresh. The American Bar Association has recognized the interest of the state in protecting itself against stale claims by limiting the right to raise such claims after completion of service of a sentence imposed pursuant to a challenged judgment. See ABA Standards Relating to Post-Conviction Remedies § 2.4(c), p. 45 (Approved Draft, 1968). Subdivision (a) is not limited to those who have completed their sentence. Its reach is broader, extending to all instances where delay by the petitioner has prejudiced the state, subject to the qualifications and conditions contained in the subdivision.

In *McMann v. Richardson*, 397 U.S. 759 (1970), the court made reference to the issue of the stale claim:

> What is at stake in this phase of the case is not the integrity of the state convictions obtained on guilty pleas, *but whether, years later*, defendants must be permitted to withdraw their pleas, which were perfectly valid when made, and be given another choice between admitting their guilt and putting the State to its proof. [Emphasis added.]

397 U.S. at 773

The court refused to allow this, intimating its dislike of collateral attacks on sentences long since imposed which disrupt the state's interest in finality of convictions which were constitutionally valid when obtained.

Subdivision (a) is not a statute of limitations. Rather, the limitation is based on the equitable doctrine of laches. "Laches is such delay in enforcing one's rights as works disadvantage to another." 30A C.J.S. Equity § 112, p. 19. Also, the language of the subdivision, "a petition *may* be dismissed" [emphasis added], is permissive rather than mandatory. This clearly allows the court which is considering the petition to use discretion in assessing the equities of the particular situation.

The use of a flexible rule analogous to laches to bar the assertion of stale claims is suggested in ABA Standards Relating to Post-Conviction Remedies § 2.4, commentary at 48 (Approved Draft, 1968). Additionally, in *Fay v. Noia*, 372 U.S. 391 (1963), the Supreme Court noted:

> Furthermore, habeas corpus has traditionally been regarded as governed by equitable principles. *United States ex rel. Smith v. Baldi*, 344 U.S. 561, 573 (dissenting opinion). Among them is the principle that a suitor's conduct in relation to the matter at hand may disentitle him to the relief he seeks.

372 U.S. at 438

Finally, the doctrine of laches has been applied with reference to another postconviction remedy, the writ of coram nobis. See 24 C.J.S. Criminal Law § 1606(25), p. 779.

The standard used for determining if the petitioner shall be barred from asserting his claim is consistent with that used in laches provisions generally. The petitioner is held to a standard of reasonable diligence. Any inference or presumption arising by reason of the failure to attack collaterally a conviction may be disregarded where (1) there has been a change of law or fact (new evidence) or (2) where the court, in the interest of justice, feels that the collateral attack should be entertained and the prisoner makes a proper showing as to why he has not asserted a particular ground for relief.

Subdivision (a) establishes the presumption that the passage of more than five years from the time of the judgment of conviction to the time of filing a habeas petition is prejudicial to the state. "Presumption" has the meaning given it by Fed.R.Evid. 301. The prisoner has "the burden of going forward with evidence to rebut or meet the presumption" that the state has not been prejudiced by the passage of a substantial period of time. This does not impose too heavy a burden on the petitioner. He usually knows what persons are important to the issue of whether the state has been prejudiced. Rule 6 can be used by the court to allow petitioner liberal discovery to learn whether witnesses have died or whether other circumstances prejudicial to the state have occurred. Even if the petitioner should fail to overcome the presumption of prejudice to the state, he is not automatically barred from asserting his claim. As discussed previously, he may proceed if he neither knew nor, by the exercise of reasonable diligence, could have known of the grounds for relief.

The presumption of prejudice does not come into play if the time lag is not more than five years.

The time limitation should have a positive effect in encouraging petitioners who have knowledge of it to assert all their claims as soon after conviction as possible. The implementation of this rule can be substantially furthered by the development of greater legal resources for prisoners. See ABA Standards Relating to Post-Conviction Remedies § 3.1, pp. 49–50 (Approved Draft, 1968).

Subdivision (a) does not constitute an abridgement or modification of a substantive right under 28 U.S.C. § 2072. There are safeguards for the hardship case. The rule provides a flexible standard for determining when a petition will be barred.

Subdivision (b) deals with the problem of successive habeas petitions. It provides that the judge may dismiss a second or successive petition (1) if it fails to allege new or different grounds for relief or (2) if new or different grounds for relief are alleged and the judge finds the failure of the petitioner to assert those grounds in a prior petition is inexcusable.

In *Sanders v. United States*, 373 U.S. 1 (1963), the court, in dealing with the problem of successive applications, stated:

> Controlling weight *may* be given to denial of a prior application for federal habeas corpus or § 2255 relief only if (1) the same ground presented in the subsequent application was determined adversely to the applicant on the prior application, (2) the prior determination was on the merits, and (3) the ends of justice would not be served by reaching the merits of the subsequent application. [Emphasis added.]

373 U.S. at 15

The requirement is that the prior determination of the same ground has been on the merits. This requirement is in

Complete Annotation Materials, see Title 28 U.S.C.A.

28 U.S.C. § 2244(b) and has been reiterated in many cases since *Sanders.* See *Gains v. Allgood,* 391 F.2d 692 (5th Cir. 1968); *Hutchinson v. Craven,* 415 F.2d 278 (9th Cir. 1969); *Brown v. Peyton,* 435 F.2d 1352 (4th Cir. 1970).

With reference to a successive application asserting a new ground or one not previously decided on the merits, the court in *Sanders* noted:

> In either case, full consideration of the merits of the new application can be avoided only if there has been an abuse of the writ * * * and this the Government has the burden of pleading. * * *
>
> Thus, for example, if a prisoner deliberately withholds one of two grounds for federal collateral relief at the time of filing his first application, * * * he may be deemed to have waived his right to a hearing on a second application presenting the withheld ground.

373 U.S. at 17–18

Subdivision (b) has incorporated this principle and requires that the judge find petitioner's failure to have asserted the new grounds in the prior petition to be inexcusable.

Sanders, 18 [sic] U.S.C. § 2244, and subdivision (b) make it clear that the court has discretion to entertain a successive application.

The burden is on the government to plead abuse of the writ. See *Sanders v. United States,* 373 U.S. 1, 10 (1963); *Dixon v. Jacobs,* 427 F.2d 589, 596 (D.C.Cir.1970); cf. *Johnson v. Copinger,* 420 F.2d 395 (4th Cir. 1969). Once the government has done this, the petitioner has the burden of proving that he has not abused the writ. In *Price v. Johnston,* 334 U.S. 266, 292 (1948), the court said:

> [I]f the Government chooses * * * to claim that the prisoner has abused the writ of *habeas corpus,* it rests with the Government to make that claim with clarity and particularity in its return to the order to show cause. That is not an intolerable burden. The Government is usually well acquainted with the facts that are necessary to make such a claim. Once a particular abuse has been alleged, the prisoner has the burden of answering that allegation and of proving that he has not abused the writ.

Subdivision (b) is consistent with the important and well established purpose of habeas corpus. It does not eliminate a remedy to which the petitioner is rightfully entitled. However, in *Sanders,* the court pointed out:

> Nothing in the traditions of habeas corpus requires the federal courts to tolerate needless piecemeal litigation, or to entertain collateral proceedings whose only purpose is to vex, harass, or delay.

373 U.S. at 18

There are instances in which petitioner's failure to assert a ground in a prior petition is excusable. A retroactive change in the law and newly discovered evidence are examples. In rare instances, the court may feel a need to entertain a petition alleging grounds that have already been decided on the merits. *Sanders,* 373 U.S. at 1, 16. However, abusive use of the writ should be discouraged, and instances of abuse are frequent enough to require a means of dealing with them. For example, a successive application, already decided on the merits, may be submitted in the hope of getting before a different judge in multijudge courts. A known ground may be deliberately withheld in the hope of getting two or more

hearings or in the hope that delay will result in witnesses and records being lost. There are instances in which a petitioner will have three or four petitions pending at the same time in the same court. There are many hundreds of cases where the application is at least the second one by the petitioner. This subdivision is aimed at screening out the abusive petitions from this large volume, so that the more meritorious petitions can get quicker and fuller consideration.

The form petition, supplied in accordance with Rule 2(c), encourages the petitioner to raise all of his available grounds in one petition. It sets out the most common grounds asserted so that these may be brought to his attention.

Some commentators contend that the problem of abuse of the writ of habeas corpus is greatly overstated:

> Most prisoners, of course, are interested in being released as soon as possible; only rarely will one inexcusably neglect to raise all available issues in his first federal application. The purpose of the "abuse" bar is apparently to deter repetitious applications from those few bored or vindictive prisoners * * *.

83 Harv.L.Rev. at 1153–1154

See also ABA Standards Relating to Post-Conviction Remedies § 6.2, commentary at 92 (Approved Draft, 1968), which states: "The occasional, highly litigious prisoner stands out as the rarest exception." While no recent systematic study of repetitious applications exists, there is no reason to believe that the problem has decreased in significance in relation to the total number of § 2254 petitions filed. That number has increased from 584 in 1949 to 12,088 in 1971. See Director of the Administrative Office of the United States Courts, Annual Report, table 16 (1971). It is appropriate that action be taken by rule to allow the courts to deal with this problem, whatever its specific magnitude. The bar set up by subdivision (b) is not one of rigid application, but rather is within the discretion of the courts on a case-by-case basis.

If it appears to the court after examining the petition and answer (where appropriate) that there is a high probability that the petition will be barred under either subdivision of Rule 9, the court ought to afford petitioner an opportunity to explain his apparent abuse. One way of doing this is by the use of the form annexed hereto. The use of a form will ensure a full airing of the issue so that the court is in a better position to decide whether the petition should be barred. This conforms with *Johnson v. Copinger,* 420 F.2d 395 (4th Cir. 1969), where the court stated:

> [T]he petitioner is obligated to present facts demonstrating that his earlier failure to raise his claims is excusable and does not amount to an abuse of the writ. However, it is inherent in this obligation placed upon the petitioner that he must be given an opportunity to make his explanation, if he has one. If he is not afforded such an opportunity, the requirement that he satisfy the court that he has not abused the writ is meaningless. Nor do we think that a procedure which allows the imposition of a forfeiture for abuse of the writ, without allowing the petitioner an opportunity to be heard on the issue, comports with the minimum requirements of fairness.

420 F.2d at 399

Use of the recommended form will contribute to an orderly handling of habeas petitions and will contribute to the ability

of the court to distinguish the excusable from the inexcusable delay or failure to assert a ground for relief in a prior petition.

2004 Amendments

The language of Rule 9 has been amended as part of general restyling of the rules to make them more easily understood and to make style and terminology consistent throughout the rules. These changes are intended to be stylistic and no substantive change is intended, except as noted below.

First, current Rule 9(a) has been deleted as unnecessary in light of the applicable one-year statute of limitations for § 2254 petitions, added as part of the Antiterrorism and Effective Death Penalty Act of 1996, 28 U.S.C. § 2244(d).

Second, current Rule 9(b), now Rule 9, has been changed to also reflect provisions in the Antiterrorism and Effective Death Penalty Act of 1996, 28 U.S.C. § 2244(b)(3) and (4), which now require a petitioner to obtain approval from the appropriate court of appeals before filing a second or successive petition.

Finally, the title of Rule 9 has been changed to reflect the fact that the only topic now addressed in the rules is that of second or successive petitions.

Rule 10. Powers of a Magistrate Judge

A magistrate judge may perform the duties of a district judge under these rules, as authorized under 28 U.S.C. § 636.
(As amended Pub.L. 94–426, § 2(11), Sept. 28, 1976, 90 Stat. 1335; Apr. 30, 1979, eff. Aug. 1, 1979; Apr. 26, 2004, eff. Dec. 1, 2004.)

ADVISORY COMMITTEE NOTES

1976 Adoption

Under this rule the duties imposed upon the judge of the district court by rules 2, 3, 4, 6, and 7 may be performed by a magistrate if and to the extent he is empowered to do so by a rule of the district court. However, when such duties involve the making of an order under rule 4 disposing of the petition, that order must be made by the court. The magistrate in such instances must submit to the court his report as to the facts and his recommendation with respect to the order.

The Federal Magistrates Act allows magistrates, when empowered by local rule, to perform certain functions in proceedings for post-trial relief. See 28 U.S.C. § 636(b)(3). The performance of such functions, when authorized, is intended to "afford some degree of relief to district judges and their law clerks, who are presently burdened with burgeoning numbers of habeas corpus petitions and applications under 28 U.S.C. § 2255." Committee on the Judiciary, The Federal Magistrates Act, S.Rep. No. 371, 90th Cong., 1st sess., 26 (1967).

Under 28 U.S.C. § 636(b), any district court,
> by the concurrence of a majority of all the judges of such district court, may establish rules pursuant to which any full-time United States magistrate * * * may be assigned within the territorial jurisdiction of such court such additional duties as are not inconsistent with the Constitution and laws of the United States.

The proposed rule recognizes the limitations imposed by 28 U.S.C. § 636(b) upon the powers of magistrates to act in federal postconviction proceedings. These limitations are: (1) that the magistrate may act only pursuant to a rule passed by the majority of the judges in the district court in which the magistrate serves, and (2) that the duties performed by the magistrate pursuant to such rule be consistent with the Constitution and laws of the United States.

It has been suggested magistrates be empowered by law to hold hearings and make final decisions in habeas proceedings. See Proposed Reformation of Federal Habeas Corpus Procedure: Use of Federal Magistrates, 54 Iowa L.Rev. 1147, 1158 (1969). However, the Federal Magistrates Act does not authorize such use of magistrates. *Wingo v. Wedding,* 418 U.S. 461 (1974). See advisory committee note to Rule 8. While the use of magistrates can help alleviate the strain imposed on the district courts by the large number of unmeritorious habeas petitions, neither 28 U.S.C. § 636(b) nor this rule contemplate the abdication by the court of its decision-making responsibility. See also Developments in the Law—Federal Habeas Corpus, 83 Harv.L.Rev. 1038, 1188 (1970).

Where a full-time magistrate is not available, the duties contemplated by this rule may be assigned to a part-time magistrate.

2004 Amendments

The language of Rule 10 has been amended as part of general restyling of the rules to make them more easily understood and to make style and terminology consistent throughout the rules. These changes are intended to be stylistic and no substantive change is intended.

HISTORICAL NOTES

Change of Name

United States magistrate appointed under section 631 of Title 28, Judiciary and Judicial Procedure, to be known as United States magistrate judge after Dec. 1, 1990, with any reference to United States magistrate or magistrate in Title 28, in any other Federal statute, etc., deemed a reference to United States magistrate judge appointed under section 631 of Title 28, see section 321 of Pub.L. 101–650, set out as a note under section 631 of Title 28.

Rule 11. Applicability of the Federal Rules of Civil Procedure

The Federal Rules of Civil Procedure, to the extent that they are not inconsistent with any statutory provisions or these rules, may be applied to a proceeding under these rules.
(As amended Apr. 26, 2004, eff. Dec. 1, 2004.)

ADVISORY COMMITTEE NOTES

1976 Adoption

Habeas corpus proceedings are characterized as civil in nature. See, *e.g., Fisher v. Baker,* 203 U.S. 174, 181 (1906). However, under Fed.R.Civ.P. 81(a)(2), the applicability of the civil rules to habeas corpus actions has been limited, although the various courts which have considered this problem have had difficulty in setting out the boundaries of this limitation.

See *Harris v. Nelson*, 394 U.S. 286 (1969) at 289, footnote 1. Rule 11 is intended to conform with the Supreme Court's approach in the *Harris* case. There the court was dealing with the petitioner's contention that Civil Rule 33 granting the right to discovery via written interrogatories is wholly applicable to habeas corpus proceedings. The court held:

> We agree with the Ninth Circuit that Rule 33 of the Federal Rules of Civil Procedure is not applicable to habeas corpus proceedings and that 28 U.S.C. § 2246 does not authorize interrogatories except in limited circumstances not applicable to this case; but we conclude that, in appropriate circumstances, a district court, confronted by a petition for habeas corpus which establishes a prima facie case for relief, may use or authorize the use of suitable discovery procedures, including interrogatories, reasonably fashioned to elicit facts necessary to help the court to "dispose of the matter as law and justice require" 28 U.S.C. § 2243.

394 U.S. at 290

The court then went on to consider the contention that the "conformity" provision of Rule 81(a)(2) should be rigidly applied so that the civil rules would be applicable only to the extent that habeas corpus practice had conformed to the practice in civil actions at the time of the adoption of the Federal Rules of Civil Procedure on September 16, 1938. The court said:

> Although there is little direct evidence, relevant to the present problem, of the purpose of the "conformity" provision of Rule 81(a)(2), the concern of the draftsmen, as a general matter, seems to have been to provide for the continuing applicability of the "civil" rules in their new form to those areas of practice in habeas corpus and other enumerated proceedings in which the "specified" proceedings had theretofore utilized the modes of civil practice. Otherwise, those proceedings were to be considered outside of the scope of the rules without prejudice, of course, to the use of particular rules by analogy or otherwise, where appropriate.

394 U.S. at 294

The court then reiterated its commitment to judicial discretion in formulating rules and procedures for habeas corpus proceedings by stating:

> [T]he habeas corpus jurisdiction and the duty to exercise it being present, the courts may fashion appropriate modes of procedure, by analogy to existing rules or otherwise in conformity with judicial usage.

Where their duties require it, this is the inescapable obligation of the courts. Their authority is expressly confirmed in the All Writs Act, 28 U.S.C. § 1651.

394 U.S. at 299

Rule 6 of these proposed rules deals specifically with the issue of discovery in habeas actions in a manner consistent with *Harris*. Rule 11 extends this approach to allow the court considering the petition to use any of the rules of civil procedure (unless inconsistent with these rules of habeas corpus) when in its discretion the court decides they are appropriate under the circumstances of the particular case. The court does not have to rigidly apply rules which would be inconsistent or inequitable in the overall framework of habeas corpus. Rule 11 merely recognizes and affirms their discretionary power to use their judgment in promoting the ends of justice.

Rule 11 permits application of the civil rules only when it would be appropriate to do so. Illustrative of an inappropriate application is that rejected by the Supreme Court in *Pitchess v. Davis*, 95 S.Ct. 1748 (1975), holding that Fed. R.Civ.P. 60(b) should not be applied in a habeas case when it would have the effect of altering the statutory exhaustion requirement of 28 U.S.C. § 2254.

2004 Amendments

The language of Rule 11 has been amended as part of general restyling of the rules to make them more easily understood and to make style and terminology consistent throughout the rules. These changes are intended to be stylistic and no substantive change is intended.

APPENDIX OF FORMS

**Petition for Relief From a Conviction or Sentence
By a Person in State Custody**
**(Petition Under 28 U.S.C. § 2254 for a Writ of
Habeas Corpus)**
Instructions

1. To use this form, you must be a person who is currently serving a sentence under a judgment against you in a state court. You are asking for relief from the conviction or the sentence. This form is your petition for relief.

2. You may also use this form to challenge a state judgment that imposed a sentence to be served in the future, but you must fill in the name of the state where the judgment was entered. If you want to challenge a <u>federal</u> judgment that imposed a sentence to be served in the future, you should file a motion under 28 U.S.C. § 2255 in the federal court that entered the judgment.

3. Make sure the form is typed or neatly written.

4. You must tell the truth and sign the form. If you make a false statement of a material fact, you may be prosecuted for perjury.

5. Answer all the questions. You do not need to cite law. You may submit additional pages if necessary. If you do not fill out the form properly, you will be asked to submit additional or correct information. If you want to submit a brief or arguments, you must submit them in a separate memorandum.

6. You must pay a fee of $5. If the fee is paid, your petition will be filed. If you cannot pay the fee, you may ask to proceed *in forma pauperis* (as a poor person). To do that, you must fill out the last page of this form. Also, you must submit a certificate signed by an officer at the institution where you are confined showing the amount of money that the institution is holding for you. If your account exceeds $____, you must pay the filing fee.

7. In this petition, you may challenge the judgment entered by only one court. If you want to challenge a judgment entered by a different court (either in the same state or in different states), you must file a separate petition.

8. When you have completed the form, send the original and two copies to the Clerk of the United States District Court at this address:

 Clerk, United States District Court for _____
 Address
 City, State Zip Code

9. **<u>CAUTION</u>: You must include in this petition <u>all</u> the grounds for relief from the conviction or sentence that you challenge. And you must state the facts that support each ground. If you fail to set forth all the grounds in this petition, you may be barred from presenting additional grounds at a later date.**

10. **<u>CAPITAL CASES</u>: If you are under a sentence of death, you are entitled to the assistance of counsel and should request the appointment of counsel.**

PETITION UNDER 28 U.S.C. § 2254 FOR WRIT OF HABEAS CORPUS BY A PERSON IN STATE CUSTODY

United States District Court District _____

Name (under which you were convicted): _____ Docket or Case No.: _____

Place of Confinement: _____ Prisoner No.: _____

Petitioner
(include the name under which you were convicted)

Respondent
(authorized person having custody of petitioner)

v.

The Attorney General of the State of _____

PETITION

1. (a) Name and location of court that entered the judgment of conviction you are challenging: _____

 (b) Criminal docket or case number (if you know): ___

2. (a) Date of the judgment of conviction (if you know): _____

 (b) Date of sentencing: _____

3. Length of sentence: _____

4. In this case, were you convicted on more than one count or of more than one crime? Yes ☐ No ☐

5. Identify all crimes of which you were convicted and sentenced in this case: _____

6. (a) What was your plea? (Check one)
 - (1) Not guilty ☐
 - (2) Guilty ☐
 - (3) Nolo contendere (no contest) ☐
 - (4) Insanity plea ☐

 (b) If you entered a guilty plea to one count or charge and a not guilty plea to another count or charge, what did you plead guilty to and what did you plead not guilty to? _____

 (c) If you went to trial, what kind of trial did you have? (Check one)
 Jury ☐ Judge only ☐

7. Did you testify at a pretrial hearing, trial, or a post-trial hearing?
 Yes ☐ No ☐

8. Did you appeal from the judgment of conviction?
 Yes ☐ No ☐

9. If you did appeal, answer the following:
 (a) Name of court: _____
 (b) Docket or case number (if you know): _____

(c) Result: _____
(d) Date of result (if you know): _____
(e) Citation to the case (if you know): _____
(f) Grounds raised: _____

(g) Did you seek further review by a higher state court? Yes ☐ No ☐
 If yes, answer the following:
 (1) Name of court: _____
 (2) Docket or case number (if you know): _____
 (3) Result: _____
 (4) Date of result (if you know): _____
 (5) Citation to the case (if you know): _____
 (6) Grounds raised: _____

(h) Did you file a petition for certiorari in the United States Supreme Court?
 Yes ☐ No ☐
 If yes, answer the following:
 (1) Docket or case number (if you know): _____
 (2) Result: _____

 (3) Date of result (if you know): _____
 (4) Citation to the case (if you know): _____

10. Other than the direct appeals listed above, have you previously filed any other petitions, applications, or motions concerning this judgment of conviction in any state court?
 Yes ☐ No ☐

11. If your answer to Question 10 was "Yes," give the following information:
 (a) (1) Name of court: _____
 (2) Docket or case number (if you know): _____
 (3) Date of filing (if you know): _____
 (4) Nature of the proceeding: _____
 (5) Grounds raised: _____

 (6) Did you receive a hearing where evidence was given on your petition, application, or motion?
 Yes ☐ No ☐
 (7) Result: _____
 (8) Date of result (if you know): _____

 (b) If you filed any second petition, application, or motion, give the same information:
 (1) Name of court: _____
 (2) Docket or case number (if you know): _____
 (3) Date of filing (if you know): _____
 (4) Nature of the proceeding: _____

(5) Grounds raised: _____

(6) Did you receive a hearing where evidence was given on your petition, application, or motion?
Yes ☐ No ☐
(7) Result: _____
(8) Date of result (if you know): _____

(c) If you filed any third petition, application, or motion, give the same information:
(1) Name of court: _____
(2) Docket or case number (if you know): _____
(3) Date of filing (if you know): _____
(4) Nature of the proceeding: _____
(5) Grounds raised: _____

(6) Did you receive a hearing where evidence was given on your petition, application, or motion?
Yes ☐ No ☐
(7) Result: _____
(8) Date of result (if you know):

(d) Did you appeal to the highest state court having jurisdiction over the action taken on your petition, application, or motion?
(1) First petition: Yes ☐ No ☐
(2) Second petition: Yes ☐ No ☐
(3) Third petition: Yes ☐ No ☐

(e) If you did not appeal to the highest state court having jurisdiction, explain why you did not: ___

12. For this petition, state every ground on which you claim that you are being held in violation of the Constitution, laws, or treaties of the United States. Attach additional pages if you have more than four grounds. State the facts supporting each ground.

CAUTION: To proceed in the federal court, you must ordinarily first exhaust (use up) your available state-court remedies on each ground on which you request action by the federal court. Also, if you fail to set forth all the grounds in this petition, you may be barred from presenting additional grounds at a later date.

GROUND ONE: _____

(a) Supporting facts (Do not argue or cite law. Just state the specific facts that support your claim.): _____

(b) If you did not exhaust your state remedies on Ground One, explain why: _____

(c) **Direct Appeal of Ground One:**
(1) If you appealed from the judgment of conviction, did you raise this issue?
Yes ☐ No ☐
(2) If you did not raise this issue in your direct appeal, explain why: _____

(d) **Post-Conviction Proceedings:**
(1) Did you raise this issue through a post-conviction motion or petition for habeas corpus in a state trial court?
Yes ☐ No ☐
(2) If your answer to Question (d)(1) is "Yes," state:
Type of motion or petition: _____
Name and location of the court where the motion or petition was filed: _____

Docket or case number (if you know): _____
Date of the court's decision: _____
Result (attach a copy of the court's opinion or order, if available): _____

(3) Did you receive a hearing on your motion or petition?
Yes ☐ No ☐
(4) Did you appeal from the denial of your motion or petition?
Yes ☐ No ☐
(5) If your answer to Question (d)(4) is "Yes," did you raise this issue in the appeal?
Yes ☐ No ☐
(6) If your answer to Question (d)(4) is "Yes," state:
Name and location of the court where the appeal was filed: _____

Docket or case number (if you know): _____
Date of the court's decision: _____
Result (attach a copy of the court's opinion or order, if available): _____

(7) If your answer to Question (d)(4) or Question (d)(5) is "No," explain why you did not raise this issue: ___

(e) **Other Remedies:** Describe any other procedures (such as habeas corpus, administrative remedies, etc.) that you have used to exhaust your state remedies on Ground One: _____

GROUND TWO: _____

(a) Supporting facts (Do not argue or cite law. Just state the specific facts that support your claim.): _____

(b) If you did not exhaust your state remedies on Ground Two, explain why: _____

(c) **Direct Appeal of Ground Two:**
(1) If you appealed from the judgment of conviction, did you raise this issue?
Yes ☐ No ☐
(2) If you did not raise this issue in your direct appeal, explain why: _____

(d) **Post-Conviction Proceedings:**
(1) Did you raise this issue through a post-conviction motion or petition for habeas corpus in a state trial court?
Yes ☐ No ☐
(2) If your answer to Question (d)(1) is "Yes," state:
Type of motion or petition: _____
Name and location of the court where the motion or petition was filed: _____

Docket or case number (if you know):_____
Date of the court's decision: _____
Result (attach a copy of the court's opinion or order, if available): _____

(3) Did you receive a hearing on your motion or petition?
Yes ☐ No ☐
(4) Did you appeal from the denial of your motion or petition?
Yes ☐ No ☐
(5) If your answer to Question (d)(4) is "Yes," did you raise this issue in the appeal?
Yes ☐ No ☐
(6) If your answer to Question (d)(4) is "Yes," state:
Name and location of the court where the appeal was filed: _____

Docket or case number (if you know): _____
Date of the court's decision: _____
Result (attach a copy of the court's opinion or order, if available): _____

(7) If your answer to Question (d)(4) or Question (d)(5) is "No," explain why you did not raise this issue: _____

(e) **Other Remedies:** Describe any other procedures (such as habeas corpus, administrative remedies, etc.) that you have used to exhaust your state remedies on Ground Two: _____

GROUND THREE: _____

(a) Supporting facts (Do not argue or cite law. Just state the specific facts that support your claim.): _____

(b) If you did not exhaust your state remedies on Ground Three, explain why: _____

(c) **Direct Appeal of Ground Three:**
(1) If you appealed from the judgment of conviction, did you raise this issue?
Yes ☐ No ☐
(2) If you did not raise this issue in your direct appeal, explain why: _____

(d) **Post-Conviction Proceedings:**
(1) Did you raise this issue through a post-conviction motion or petition for habeas corpus in a state trial court?
Yes ☐ No ☐
(2) If your answer to Question (d)(1) is "Yes," state:
Type of motion or petition: _____
Name and location of the court where the motion or petition was filed: _____

Docket or case number (if you know):_____
Date of the court's decision: _____
Result (attach a copy of the court's opinion or order, if available): _____

(3) Did you receive a hearing on your motion or petition?
Yes ☐ No ☐
(4) Did you appeal from the denial of your motion or petition?
Yes ☐ No ☐
(5) If your answer to Question (d)(4) is "Yes," did you raise this issue in the appeal?
Yes ☐ No ☐
(6) If your answer to Question (d)(4) is "Yes," state:
Name and location of the court where the appeal was filed: _____

Docket or case number (if you know): _____
Date of the court's decision: _____

Result (attach a copy of the court's opinion or order, if available): _____

(7) If your answer to Question (d)(4) or Question (d)(5) is "No," explain why you did not raise this issue: ____

(e) **Other Remedies:** Describe any other procedures (such as habeas corpus, administrative remedies, etc.) that you have used to exhaust your state remedies on Ground Three: _____

GROUND FOUR: _____

(a) Supporting facts (Do not argue or cite law. Just state the specific facts that support your claim.): _____

(b) If you did not exhaust your state remedies on Ground Four, explain why: _____

(c) **Direct Appeal of Ground Four:**
(1) If you appealed from the judgment of conviction, did you raise this issue?
Yes ☐ No ☐
(2) If you did not raise this issue in your direct appeal, explain why:

(d) **Post-Conviction Proceedings:**
(1) Did you raise this issue through a post-conviction motion or petition for habeas corpus in a state trial court?
Yes ☐ No ☐
(2) If your answer to Question (d)(1) is "Yes," state:
Type of motion or petition: _____
Name and location of the court where the motion or petition was filed: _____
Docket or case number (if you know): _____
Date of the court's decision: _____
Result (attach a copy of the court's opinion or order, if available): _____

(3) Did you receive a hearing on your motion or petition?
Yes ☐ No ☐
(4) Did you appeal from the denial of your motion or petition?
Yes ☐ No ☐
(5) If your answer to Question (d)(4) is "Yes," did you raise this issue in the appeal?
Yes ☐ No ☐
(6) If your answer to Question (d)(4) is "Yes," state:

Name and location of the court where the appeal was filed: _____

Docket or case number (if you know): _____
Date of the court's decision: _____
Result (attach a copy of the court's opinion or order, if available): _____

(7) If your answer to Question (d)(4) or Question (d)(5) is "No," explain why you did not raise this issue: ____

(e) **Other Remedies:** Describe any other procedures (such as habeas corpus, administrative remedies, etc.) that you have used to exhaust your state remedies on Ground Four:

13. Please answer these additional questions about the petition you are filing:
(a) Have all grounds for relief that you have raised in this petition been presented to the highest state court having jurisdiction? Yes ☐ No ☐
If your answer is "No," state which grounds have not been so presented and give your reason(s) for not presenting them: _____

(b) Is there any ground in this petition that has not been presented in some state or federal court? If so, which ground or grounds have not been presented, and state your reasons for not presenting them: ____

14. Have you previously filed any type of petition, application, or motion in a federal court regarding the conviction that you challenge in this petition? Yes ☐ No ☐
If "Yes," state the name and location of the court, the docket or case number, the type of proceeding, the issues raised, the date of the court's decision, and the result for each petition, application, or motion filed. Attach a copy of any court opinion or order, if available.

15. Do you have any petition or appeal now pending (filed and not decided yet) in any court, either state or federal, for the judgment you are challenging? Yes ☐ No ☐
If "Yes," state the name and location of the court, the docket or case number, the type of proceeding, and the issues raised. _____

16. Give the name and address, if you know, of each attorney who represented you in the following stages of the judgment you are challenging:
(a) At preliminary hearing: _____

(b) At arraignment and plea: _____

(c) At trial: _____

(d) At sentencing: _____

(e) On appeal: _____

(f) In any post-conviction proceeding: _____

(g) On appeal from any ruling against you in a post-conviction proceeding: _____

17. Do you have any future sentence to serve after you complete the sentence for the judgment that you are challenging? Yes ☐ No ☐
(a) If so, give name and location of court that imposed the other sentence you will serve in the future: _____

(b) Give the date the other sentence was imposed: ___

(c) Give the length of the other sentence: _____

(d) Have you filed, or do you plan to file, any petition that challenges the judgment or sentence to be served in the future? Yes ☐ No ☐

18. TIMELINESS OF PETITION: If your judgment of conviction became final over one year ago, you must explain why the one-year statute of limitations as contained in 28 U.S.C. § 2244(d) does not bar your petition.*

* The Antiterrorism and Effective Death Penalty Act of 1996 ("AEDPA") as contained in 28 U.S.C. § 2244(d) provides in part that:

(1) A one-year period of limitation shall apply to an application for a writ of habeas corpus by a person in custody pursuant to the judgment of a State court. The limitation period shall run from the latest of—
(A) the date on which the judgment became final by the conclusion of direct review or the expiration of the time for seeking such review;
(B) the date on which the impediment to filing an application created by State action in violation of the Constitution or laws of the United States is removed, if the applicant was prevented from filing by such state action;
(C) the date on which the constitutional right asserted was initially recognized by the Supreme Court, if the right has been newly recognized by the Supreme Court and made retroactively applicable to cases on collateral review; or
(D) the date on which the factual predicate of the claim or claims presented could have been discovered through the exercise of due diligence.
(2) The time during which a properly filed application for State post-conviction or other collateral review with respect to the pertinent judgment or claim is pending shall not be counted toward any period of limitation under this subsection.

Therefore, petitioner asks that the Court grant the following relief: _____

or any other relief to which petitioner may be entitled.

Signature of Attorney (if any)

I declare (or certify, verify, or state) under penalty of perjury that the foregoing is true and correct and that this Petition for Writ of Habeas Corpus was placed in the prison mailing system on _____
_____(month, date, year).

Executed (signed) on (date).

Signature of Petitioner

If the person signing is not petitioner, state relationship to petitioner and explain why petitioner is not signing this petition. _____

IN FORMA PAUPERIS DECLARATION

[Insert appropriate court]

HABEAS CORPUS

(Petitioner)

v.

(Respondent(s))

DECLARATION IN
SUPPORT
OF REQUEST
TO PROCEED
*IN FORMA
PAUPERIS*

I, _____, declare that I am the petitioner in the above entitled case; that in support of my motion to proceed without being required to prepay fees, costs or give security therefor, I state that because of my poverty I am unable to pay the costs of said proceeding or to give security therefor; that I believe I am entitled to relief.

1. Are you presently employed? Yes ☐ No ☐
 a. If the answer is "yes," state the amount of your salary or wages per month, and give the name and address of your employer.

 b. If the answer is "no," state the date of last employment and the amount of the salary and wages per month which you received.

2. Have you received within the past twelve months any money from any of the following sources?
 a. Business, profession or form of self-employment? Yes ☐ No ☐
 b. Rent payments, interest or dividends? Yes ☐ No ☐
 c. Pensions, annuities or life insurance payments? Yes ☐ No ☐
 d. Gifts or inheritances? Yes ☐ No ☐
 e. Any other sources? Yes ☐ No ☐
 If the answer to any of the above is "yes," describe each source of money and state the amount received from each during the past twelve months.

3. Do you own cash, or do you have money in a checking or savings account?
 Yes ☐ No ☐ (Include any funds in prison accounts.)
 If the answer is "yes," state the total value of the items owned.

4. Do you own any real estate, stocks, bonds, notes, automobiles, or other valuable property (excluding ordinary household furnishings and clothing)?
 Yes ☐ No ☐
 If the answer is "yes," describe the property and state its approximate value.

5. List the persons who are dependent upon you for support, state your relationship to those persons, and indicate how much you contribute toward their support.

I declare (or certify, verify, or state) under penalty of perjury that the foregoing is true and correct. Executed on _____.

(date)

Signature of Petitioner

CERTIFICATE

I hereby certify that the petitioner herein has the sum of $_____ on account to his credit at the _____ institution where he is confined. I further certify that petitioner

likewise has the following securities to his credit according to the records of said _____ institution:

Authorized Officer of Institution

(As amended Apr. 28, 1982, eff. Aug. 1, 1982; Apr. 26, 2004, eff. Dec. 1, 2004.)

RULES GOVERNING SECTION 2255 PROCEEDINGS FOR THE UNITED STATES DISTRICT COURTS

Effective February 1, 1977
Amendments received to May 21, 2007

Rule
1. Scope.
2. The Motion.
3. Filing the Motion; Inmate Filing.
4. Preliminary Review.
5. The Answer and the Reply.
6. Discovery.
7. Expanding the Record.
8. Evidentiary Hearing.
9. Second or Successive Motions.
10. Powers of a Magistrate Judge.
11. Time to Appeal.
12. Applicability of the Federal Rules of Civil Procedure and the Federal Rules of Criminal Procedure.

APPENDIX OF FORMS

Forms. Motion to Vacate, Set Aside, or Correct a Sentence By a Person in Federal Custody
(Motion Under 28 U.S.C. § 2255)

ORDERS OF THE SUPREME COURT OF THE UNITED STATES ADOPTING AND AMENDING RULES GOVERNING SECTION 2255 PROCEEDINGS

ORDER OF APRIL 26, 1976

1. That the rules and forms governing proceedings in the United States District Courts under Section 2254 and Section 2255 of Title 28, United States Code, as approved by the Judicial Conference of the United States be, and they hereby are, prescribed pursuant to Section 2072 of Title 28, United States Code and Sections 3771 and 3772 of Title 18, United States Code.

2. That the aforementioned rules and forms shall take effect August 1, 1976, and shall be applicable to all proceedings then pending except to the extent that in the opinion of the court their application in a particular proceeding would not be feasible or would work injustice.

3. That THE CHIEF JUSTICE be, and he hereby is, authorized to transmit the aforementioned rules and forms governing Section 2254 and Section 2255 proceedings to the Congress in accordance with the provisions of Section 2072 of Title 28 and Sections 3771 and 3772 of Title 18, United States Code.

CONGRESSIONAL ACTION ON PROPOSED RULES AND FORMS GOVERNING PROCEEDING UNDER 28 U.S.C. §§ 2254 AND 2255

Pub.L. 94–349, § 2, July 8, 1976, 90 Stat. 822, provided: "That, notwithstanding the provisions of section 2072 of title 28 of the United States Code, the rules and forms governing section 2254 cases in the United States district courts and the rules and forms governing section 2255 proceedings in the United States district courts which are embraced by the order entered by the United States Supreme Court on April 26, 1976, and which were transmitted to the Congress on or about April 26, 1976, shall not take effect until thirty days after the adjournment sine die of the 94th Congress, or until and to the extent approved by Act of Congress, whichever is earlier."

Pub.L. 94–426, § 1, Sept. 28, 1976, 90 Stat. 1334, provided: "That the rules governing section 2254 cases in the United States district courts and the rules governing section 2255 proceedings for the United States district courts, as proposed by the United States Supreme Court, which were delayed by the Act entitled 'An Act to delay the effective date of certain proposed amendments to the Federal Rules of Criminal Procedure and certain other rules promulgated by the United States Supreme Court' (Public Law 94–349), are approved with the amendments set forth in section 2 of this Act and shall take effect as so amended, with respect to petitions under section 2254 and motions under section 2255 of title 28 of the United States Code filed on or after February 1, 1977."

ORDER OF APRIL 30, 1979

1. That Rule 10 of the Rules Governing Proceedings in the United States District Courts on application under Section 2254 of Title 28, United States Code, be, and hereby is, amended to read as follows:

[See amendment made thereby under Rule 10 set out following section 2254.]

2. That Rules 10 and 11 of the Rules Governing Proceedings in the United States District Courts on a motion under Section 2255 of Title 28, United States Code, be, and they hereby are, amended to read as follows:

[See amendments made thereby under the respective rules, post.]

3. That the foregoing amendments to the Rules Governing Proceedings in the United States District Courts under Section 2254 and Section 2255 of Title 28, United States Code, shall take effect on August 1, 1979, and shall be applicable to all proceedings then pending except to the extent that in the opinion of the court their application in a particular proceeding would not be feasible or would work injustice.

4. That THE CHIEF JUSTICE be, and he hereby is, authorized to transmit the aforementioned amendments to the Rules Governing Section 2254 and Section 2255 Proceedings to the Congress in accordance with the provisions of Section 2072 of Title 28, United States Code, and Sections 3771 and 3772 of Title 18, United States Code.

ORDER OF APRIL 28, 1982

1. That the rules and forms governing proceedings in the United States district courts under Section 2254 and Section 2255 of Title 28, United States Code, be, and they hereby are, amended by including therein an amendment to Rule 2(c) of the rules for Section 2254 cases, an amendment to Rule 2(b) of the rules for Section 2255 proceedings, and amendments to the model forms for use in applications under Section 2254 and motions under Section 2255, as hereinafter set forth:

[See amendments made thereby under respective rules and forms post and following section 2254.]

2. That the aforementioned amendments shall take effect August 1, 1982, and shall be applicable to all proceedings thereafter commenced and, insofar as just and practicable, all proceedings then pending.

3. That THE CHIEF JUSTICE be, and he hereby is, authorized to transmit the aforementioned amendments to the Congress in accordance with Section 2072 of Title 28 and Sections 3771 and 3772 of Title 18, United States Code.

ORDER OF APRIL 22, 1993

1. That the Federal Rules of Criminal Procedure for the United States District Courts be, and they hereby are, amended by including therein amendments to Criminal Rules 1, 3, 4, 5, 5.1, 6, 9, 12, 16, 17, 26.2, 32, 32.1, 40, 41, 44, 46, 49, 50, 54, 55, 57, and 58, and new Rule 26.3, and an amendment to Rule 8 of the Rules Governing Section 2255 Proceedings.

[See amendments made thereby under the respective rules set out in the Federal Criminal Code and Rules and under Rule 8, post.]

2. That the foregoing amendments to the Federal Rules of Criminal Procedure shall take effect on December 1, 1993, and shall govern all proceedings in criminal cases thereafter commenced and, insofar as just and practicable, all proceedings in criminal cases then pending.

3. That THE CHIEF JUSTICE be, and he hereby is, authorized to transmit to the Congress the foregoing amendments to the Federal Rules of Criminal Procedure in accordance with the provisions of Section 2072 of Title 28, United States Code.

ORDER OF APRIL 26, 2004

1. That the Federal Rules of Criminal Procedure be, and they hereby are, amended by including therein an amendment to Criminal Rule 35.

2. That the rules and forms governing cases in the United States District Courts under Section 2254 and Section 2255 of Title 28, United States Code, be, and they hereby are, amended by including therein amendments to Rules 1 through 11 of the Rules Governing Section 2254 Cases in the United States District Courts, Rules 1 through 12 of the Rules Governing Section 2255 Cases in the United States District Courts, and forms for use in applications under Section 2254 and motions under Section 2255.

[See amendments made thereby under respective rules, post.]

3. That the foregoing amendments to the Federal Rules of Criminal Procedure, the Rules Governing Section 2254 Cases in the United States District Courts, and the Rules Governing Section 2255 Cases in the United States District Courts shall take effect on December 1, 2004, and shall govern in all proceedings thereafter commenced and, insofar as just and practicable, all proceedings then pending.

4. That the CHIEF JUSTICE be, and hereby is, authorized to transmit to the Congress the foregoing amendments to the Federal Rules of Criminal Procedure, the Rules Governing Section 2254 Cases in the United States District Courts, and the Rules Governing Section 2255 Cases in the United States District Courts in accordance with the provisions of Section 2072 of Title 28, United States Code.

HISTORICAL NOTES

Effective Date of Rules; 1976 Act

Rules, and the amendments thereto by Pub.L. 94–426, Sept. 28, 1976, 90 Stat. 1334, effective with respect to petitions under section 2254 of this title and motions under section 2255 of this title filed on or after Feb. 1, 1977, see section 1 of Pub.L. 94–426, set out as a note under section 2255 of this title.

Rule 1. Scope

These rules govern a motion filed in a United States district court under 28 U.S.C. § 2255 by:

(a) a person in custody under a judgment of that court who seeks a determination that:

 (1) the judgment violates the Constitution or laws of the United States;

 (2) the court lacked jurisdiction to enter the judgment;

 (3) the sentence exceeded the maximum allowed by law; or

 (4) the judgment or sentence is otherwise subject to collateral review; and

(b) a person in custody under a judgment of a state court or another federal court, and subject to future custody under a judgment of the district court, who seeks a determination that:

 (1) future custody under a judgment of the district court would violate the Constitution or laws of the United States;

 (2) the district court lacked jurisdiction to enter the judgment;

 (3) the district court's sentence exceeded the maximum allowed by law; or

 (4) the district court's judgment or sentence is otherwise subject to collateral review.

(As amended Apr. 26, 2004, eff. Dec. 1, 2004.)

ADVISORY COMMITTEE NOTES
1976 Adoption

The basic scope of this postconviction remedy is prescribed by 28 U.S.C. § 2255. Under these rules the person seeking relief from federal custody files a motion to vacate, set aside, or correct sentence, rather than a petition for habeas corpus. This is consistent with the terminology used in section 2255 and indicates the difference between this remedy and federal habeas for a state prisoner. Also, habeas corpus is available to the person in federal custody if his "remedy by motion is inadequate or ineffective to test the legality of his detention."

Whereas sections 2241–2254 (dealing with federal habeas corpus for those in state custody) speak of the district court judge "issuing the writ" as the operative remedy, section 2255 provides that, if the judge finds the movant's assertions to be meritorious, he "shall discharge the prisoner or resentence him or grant a new trial or correct the sentence as may appear appropriate." This is possible because a motion under § 2255 is a further step in the movant's criminal case and not a separate civil action, as appears from the legislative history of section 2 of S. 20, 80th Congress, the provisions of which were incorporated by the same Congress in title 28 U.S.C. as § 2255. In reporting S. 20 favorably the Senate Judiciary Committee said (Sen.Rep. 1526, 80th Cong.2d Sess., p. 2):

The two main advantages of such motion remedy over the present habeas corpus are as follows:

First, habeas corpus is a separate civil action and not a further step in the criminal case in which petitioner is sentenced (Ex parte *Tom Tong*, 108 U.S. 556, 559 (1883)). It is not a determination of guilt or innocence of the charge upon which petitioner was sentenced. Where a prisoner sustains his right to discharge in habeas corpus, it is usually because some right—such as lack of counsel—has been denied which reflects no determination of his guilt or innocence but affects solely the fairness of his earlier criminal trial. Even under the broad power in the statute "to dispose of the party as law and justice require" (28 U.S.C.A., sec. 461), the court or judge is by no means in the same advantageous position in habeas corpus to do justice as would be so if the matter were determined in the criminal proceeding (see *Medley*, petitioner, 134 U.S. 160, 174 (1890)). For instance, the judge (by habeas corpus) cannot grant a new trial in the criminal case. Since the motion remedy is in the criminal proceeding, this section 2 affords the opportunity and expressly gives the broad powers to set aside the judgment and to "discharge the prisoner or resentence him or grant a new trial or correct the sentence as may appear appropriate."

The fact that a motion under § 2255 is a further step in the movant's criminal case rather than a separate civil action has significance at several points in these rules. See, *e.g.*, advisory committee note to Rule 3 (re no filing fee), advisory committee note to Rule 4 (re availability of files, etc., relating to the judgment), advisory committee note to Rule 6 (re availability of discovery under criminal procedure rules), advisory committee note to Rule 11 (re no extension of time for appeal), and advisory committee note to Rule 12 (re applicability of federal criminal rules). However, the fact that Congress has characterized the motion as a further step in the criminal proceedings does *not* mean that proceedings upon such a motion are of necessity governed by the legal principles which are applicable at a criminal trial regarding such matters as counsel, presence, confrontation, self-incrimination, and burden of proof.

The challenge of decisions such as the revocation of probation or parole are not appropriately dealt with under 28 U.S.C. § 2255, which is a continuation of the original criminal action. Other remedies, such as habeas corpus, are available in such situations.

Although Rule 1 indicates that these rules apply to a motion for a determination that the judgment was imposed "in violation of the . . . laws of the United States," the language of 28 U.S.C. § 2255, it is not the intent of these rules to define or limit what is encompassed within that phrase. See *Davis v. United States*, 417 U.S. 333 (1974), holding that it is not true "that every asserted error of law can be raised on a § 2255 motion," and that the appropriate inquiry is "whether the claimed error of law was 'a fundamental defect which inherently results in a complete miscarriage of justice,' and whether '[i]t . . . present[s] exceptional circumstances where the need for the remedy afforded by the writ of habeas corpus is apparent.' "

For a discussion of the "custody" requirement and the intended limited scope of this remedy, see advisory committee note to § 2254 Rule 1.

2004 Amendments

The language of Rule 1 has been amended as part of general restyling of the rules to make them more easily understood and to make style and terminology consistent throughout the rules. These changes are intended to be stylistic and no substantive change is intended.

Rule 2. The Motion

(a) Applying for Relief. The application must be in the form of a motion to vacate, set aside, or correct the sentence.

(b) Form. The motion must:

(1) specify all the grounds for relief available to the moving party;

(2) state the facts supporting each ground;

(3) state the relief requested;

(4) be printed, typewritten, or legibly handwritten; and

(5) be signed under penalty of perjury by the movant or by a person authorized to sign it for the movant.

(c) Standard Form. The motion must substantially follow either the form appended to these rules or a form prescribed by a local district-court rule. The clerk must make forms available to moving parties without charge.

(d) Separate Motions for Separate Judgments. A moving party who seeks relief from more than one judgment must file a separate motion covering each judgment.

(As amended Pub.L. 94–426, § 2(3), (4), Sept. 28, 1976, 90 Stat. 1334; Apr. 28, 1982, eff. Aug. 1, 1982; Apr. 26, 2004, eff. Dec. 1, 2004.)

ADVISORY COMMITTEE NOTES

1976 Adoption

Under these rules the application for relief is in the form of a motion rather than a petition (see Rule 1 and advisory committee note). Therefore, there is no requirement that the movant name a respondent. This is consistent with 28 U.S.C. § 2255. The United States Attorney for the district in which the judgment under attack was entered is the proper party to oppose the motion since the federal government is the movant's adversary of record.

If the movant is attacking a federal judgment which will subject him to future custody, he must be in present custody (see Rule 1 and advisory committee note) as the result of a state or federal governmental action. He need not alter the nature of the motion by trying to include the government officer who presently has official custody of him as a pseudo-respondent, or third-party plaintiff, or other fabrication. The court hearing his motion attacking the future custody can exercise jurisdiction over those having him in present custody without the use of artificial pleading devices.

There is presently a split among the courts as to whether a person currently in state custody may use a § 2255 motion to obtain relief from a federal judgment under which he will be subjected to custody in the future. Negative, see *Newton v. United States*, 329 F.Supp. 90 (S.D. Texas 1971); affirmative, see *Desmond v. The United States Board of Parole*, 397 F.2d 386 (1st Cir.1968), *cert. denied*, 393 U.S. 919 (1968); and *Paalino v. United States*, 314 F.Supp. 875 (C.D.Cal.1970). It is intended that these rules settle the matter in favor of the prisoner's being able to file a § 2255 motion for relief under those circumstances. The proper district in which to file such a motion is the one in which is situated the court which rendered the sentence under attack.

Under Rule 35, Federal Rules of Criminal Procedure, the court may correct an illegal sentence or a sentence imposed in an illegal manner, or may reduce the sentence. This remedy should be used, rather than a motion under these § 2255 rules, whenever applicable, but there is some overlap between the two proceedings which has caused the courts difficulty.

The movant should not be barred from an appropriate remedy because he has misstyled his motion. See *United States v. Morgan*, 346 U.S. 502, 505 (1954). The court should construe it as whichever one is proper under the circumstances and decide it on its merits. For a § 2255 motion construed as a Rule 35 motion, see *Heflin v. United States*, 358 U.S. 415 (1959); and *United States v. Coke*, 404 F.2d 836 (2d Cir.1968). For writ of error coram nobis treated as a Rule 35 motion, see *Hawkins v. United States*, 324 F.Supp. 223 (E.D. Texas, Tyler Division 1971). For a Rule 35 motion treated as a § 2255 motion, see *Moss v. United States*, 263 F.2d 615 (5th Cir.1959); *Jones v. United States*, 400 F.2d 892 (8th Cir.1968), *cert. denied* 394 U.S. 991 (1969); and *United States v. Brown*, 413 F.2d 878 (9th Cir.1969), *cert. denied*, 397 U.S. 947 (1970).

One area of difference between § 2255 and Rule 35 motions is that for the latter there is no requirement that the movant be "in custody." *Heflin v. United States*, 358 U.S. 415, 418, 422 (1959); *Duggins v. United States*, 240 F.2d 479, 483 (6th Cir.1957). Compare with Rule 1 and advisory committee note for § 2255 motions. The importance of this distinction has decreased since *Peyton v. Rowe*, 391 U.S. 54

(1968), but it might still make a difference in particular situations.

A Rule 35 motion is used to attack the sentence imposed, not the basis for the sentence. The court in *Gilinsky v. United States*, 335 F.2d 914, 916 (9th Cir.1964), stated, "a Rule 35 motion presupposes a valid conviction. * * * [C]ollateral attack on errors allegedly committed at trial is not permissible under Rule 35." By illustration the court noted at page 917: "a Rule 35 proceeding contemplates the correction of a sentence of a court having jurisdiction. * * * [J]urisdictional defects * * * involve a collateral attack, they must ordinarily be presented under 28 U.S.C. § 2255." In *United States v. Semet*, 295 F.Supp. 1084 (E.D.Okla.1968), the prisoner moved under Rule 35 and § 2255 to invalidate the sentence he was serving on the grounds of his failure to understand the charge to which he pleaded guilty. The court said:

> As regards Defendant's Motion under Rule 35, said Motion must be denied as its [sic] presupposes a valid conviction of the offense with which he was charged and may be used only to attack the sentence. It may not be used to examine errors occurring prior to the imposition of sentence.

295 F.Supp. at 1085

See also: *Moss v. United States*, 263 F.2d at 616; *Duggins v. United States*, 240 F.2d at 484; *Migdal v. United States*, 298 F.2d 513, 514 (9th Cir.1961); *Jones v. United States*, 400 F.2d at 894; *United States v. Coke*, 404 F.2d at 847; and *United States v. Brown*, 413 F.2d at 879.

A major difficulty in deciding whether Rule 35 or § 2255 is the proper remedy is the uncertainty as to what is meant by an "illegal sentence." The Supreme Court dealt with this issue in *Hill v. United States*, 368 U.S. 424 (1962). The prisoner brought a § 2255 motion to vacate sentence on the ground that he had not been given a Fed.R.Crim.P. 32(a) opportunity to make a statement in his own behalf at the time of sentencing. The majority held this was not an error subject to collateral attack under § 2255. The five-member majority considered the motion as one brought pursuant to Rule 35, but denied relief, stating:

> [T]he narrow function of Rule 35 is to permit correction at any time of an illegal *sentence*, not to re-examine errors occurring at the trial or other proceedings prior to the imposition of sentence. The sentence in this case was not illegal. The punishment meted out was not in excess of that prescribed by the relevant statutes, multiple terms were not imposed for the same offense, nor were the terms of the sentence itself legally or constitutionally invalid in any other respect.

368 U.S. at 430

The four dissenters felt the majority definition of "illegal" was too narrow.

> [Rule 35] provides for the correction of an "illegal sentence" without regard to the reasons why that sentence is illegal and contains not a single word to support the Court's conclusion that only a sentence illegal by reason of the punishment it imposes is "illegal" within the meaning of the Rule. I would have thought that a sentence imposed in an illegal manner—whether the amount or form of the punishment meted out constitutes an additional

violation of law or not—would be recognized as an "illegal sentence" under any normal reading of the English language.

368 U.S. at 431–432

The 1966 amendment of Rule 35 added language permitting correction of a sentence imposed in an "illegal manner." However, there is a 120-day time limit on a motion to do this, and the added language does not clarify the intent of the rule or its relation to § 2255.

The courts have been flexible in considering motions under circumstances in which relief might appear to be precluded by *Hill v. United States.* In *Peterson v. United States,* 432 F.2d 545 (8th Cir.1970), the court was confronted with a motion for reduction of sentence by a prisoner claiming to have received a harsher sentence than his codefendants because he stood trial rather than plead guilty. He alleged that this violated his constitutional right to a jury trial. The court ruled that, even though it was past the 120-day time period for a motion to reduce sentence, the claim was still cognizable under Rule 35 as a motion to correct an illegal sentence.

The courts have made even greater use of § 2255 in these types of situations. In *United States v. Lewis,* 392 F.2d 440 (4th Cir.1968), the prisoner moved under § 2255 and Rule 35 for relief from a sentence he claimed was the result of the judge's misunderstanding of the relevant sentencing law. The court held that he could not get relief under Rule 35 because it was past the 120 days for correction of a sentence imposed in an illegal manner and under *Hill v. United States* it was not an illegal sentence. However, § 2255 was applicable because of its "otherwise subject to collateral attack" language. The flaw was not a mere trial error relating to the finding of guilt, but a rare and unusual error which amounted to "exceptional circumstances" embraced in § 2255's words "collateral attack." See 368 U.S. at 444 for discussion of other cases allowing use of § 2255 to attack the sentence itself in similar circumstances, especially where the judge has sentenced out of a misapprehension of the law.

In *United States v. McCarthy,* 433 F.2d 591, 592 (1st Cir.1970), the court allowed a prisoner who was past the time limit for a proper Rule 35 motion to use § 2255 to attack the sentence which he received upon a plea of guilty on the ground that it was induced by an unfulfilled promise of the prosecutor to recommend leniency. The court specifically noted that under § 2255 this was a proper collateral attack on the sentence and there was no need to attack the conviction as well.

The court in *United States v. Malcolm,* 432 F.2d 809, 814, 818 (2d Cir.1970), allowed a prisoner to challenge his sentence under § 2255 without attacking the conviction. It held Rule 35 inapplicable because the sentence was not illegal on its face, but the manner in which the sentence was imposed raised a question of the denial of due process in the sentencing itself which was cognizable under § 2255.

The flexible approach taken by the courts in the above cases seems to be the reasonable way to handle these situations in which Rule 35 and § 2255 appear to overlap. For a further discussion of this problem, see C. Wright, Federal Practice and Procedure: Criminal §§ 581–587 (1969, Supp. 1975).

See the advisory committee note to Rule 2 of the § 2254 rules for further discussion of the purposes and intent of Rule 2 of these § 2255 rules.

1982 Amendment

Subdivision (b). The amendment takes into account 28 U.S.C. § 1746, enacted after adoption of the § 2255 rules. Section 1746 provides that in lieu of an affidavit an unsworn statement may be given under penalty of perjury in substantially the following form if executed within the United States, its territories, possessions or commonwealths: "I declare (or certify, verify, or state) under penalty of perjury that the foregoing is true and correct. Executed on (date). (Signature)." The statute is "intended to encompass prisoner litigation," and the statutory alternative is especially appropriate in such cases because a notary might not be readily available. *Carter v. Clark,* 616 F.2d 228 (5th Cir.1980). The § 2255 forms have been revised accordingly.

2004 Amendments

The language of Rule 2 has been amended as part of general restyling of the rules to make them more easily understood and to make style and terminology consistent throughout the rules. These changes are intended to be stylistic and no substantive change is intended, except as described below.

Revised Rule 2(b)(5) has been amended by removing the requirement that the motion be signed personally by the moving party. Thus, under the amended rule the motion may be signed by movant personally or by someone acting on behalf of the movant, assuming that the person is authorized to do so, for example, an attorney for the movant. The Committee envisions that the courts would apply third-party, or "next-friend," standing analysis in deciding whether the signer was actually authorized to sign the motion on behalf of the movant. *See generally Whitmore v. Arkansas,* 495 U.S. 149 (1990) (discussion of requisites for "next friend" standing in habeas petitions). *See also* 28 U.S.C. § 2242 (application for state habeas corpus relief may be filed by the person who is seeking relief, or by someone acting on behalf of that person).

The language in new Rule 2(c) has been changed to reflect that a moving party must substantially follow the standard form, which is appended to the rules, or a form provided by the court. The current rule, Rule 2(c), seems to indicate a preference for the standard "national" form. Under the amended rule, there is no stated preference. The Committee understood that the current practice in some courts is that if the moving party first files a motion using the national form, that courts may ask the moving party to supplement it with the local form.

Current Rule 2(d), which provided for returning an insufficient motion has been deleted. The Committee believed that the approach in Federal Rule of Civil Procedure 5(e) was more appropriate for dealing with motions that do not conform to the form requirements of the rule. That Rule provides that the clerk may not refuse to accept a filing solely for the reason that it fails to comply with these rules or local rules. Before the adoption of a one-year statute of limitations in the Antiterrorism and Effective Death Penalty Act of 1996, 110 Stat. 1214, the moving party suffered no penalty, other than delay, if the motion was deemed insufficient. Now

that a one-year statute of limitations applies to motions filed under § 2255, *see* 28 U.S.C. § 2244(d) (1), the court's dismissal of a motion because it is not in proper form may pose a significant penalty for a moving party, who may not be able to file another motion within the one-year limitations period. Now, under revised Rule 3(b), the clerk is required to file a motion, even though it may otherwise fail to comply with the provisions in revised Rule 2(b). The Committee believed that the better procedure was to accept the defective motion and require the moving party to submit a corrected motion that conforms to Rule 2(b).

Rule 3. Filing the Motion; Inmate Filing

(a) Where to File; Copies. An original and two copies of the motion must be filed with the clerk.

(b) Filing and Service. The clerk must file the motion and enter it on the criminal docket of the case in which the challenged judgment was entered. The clerk must then deliver or serve a copy of the motion on the United States attorney in that district, together with a notice of its filing.

(c) Time to File. The time for filing a motion is governed by 28 U.S.C. § 2255 para. 6.

(d) Inmate Filing. A paper filed by an inmate confined in an institution is timely if deposited in the institution's internal mailing system on or before the last day for filing. If an institution has a system designed for legal mail, the inmate must use that system to receive the benefit of this rule. Timely filing may be shown by a declaration in compliance with 28 U.S.C. § 1746 or by a notarized statement, either of which must set forth the date of deposit and state that first-class postage has been prepaid.
(As amended Apr. 26, 2004, eff. Dec. 1, 2004.)

ADVISORY COMMITTEE NOTES

1976 Adoption

There is no filing fee required of a movant under these rules. This is a change from the practice of charging $15 and is done to recognize specifically the nature of a § 2255 motion as being a continuation of the criminal case whose judgment is under attack.

The long-standing practice of requiring a $15 filing fee has followed from 28 U.S.C. § 1914(a) whereby "parties instituting any civil action * * * pay a filing fee of $15, except that on an application for a writ of habeas corpus the filing fee shall be $5." This has been held to apply to a proceeding under § 2255 despite the rationale that such a proceeding is a motion and thus a continuation of the criminal action. (See note to Rule 1.)

A motion under Section 2255 is a civil action and the clerk has no choice but to charge a $15.00 filing fee unless by leave of court it is filed in forma pauperis.

McCune v. United States, 406 F.2d 417, 419 (6th Cir.1969).

Although the motion has been considered to be a new civil action in the nature of habeas corpus for filing purposes, the reduced fee for habeas has been held not applicable. The Tenth Circuit considered the specific issue in *Martin v.*

United States, 273 F.2d 775 (10th Cir.1960), cert. denied, 365 U.S. 853 (1961), holding that the reduced fee was exclusive to habeas petitions.

Counsel for Martin insists that, if a docket fee must be paid, the amount is $5 rather than $15 and bases his contention on the exception contained in 28 U.S.C. § 1914 that in habeas corpus the fee is $5. This reads into § 1914 language which is not there. While an application under § 2255 may afford the same relief as that previously obtainable by habeas corpus, it is not a petition for a writ of habeas corpus. A change in § 1914 must come from Congress.

273 F.2d at 778

Although for most situations § 2255 is intended to provide to the federal prisoner a remedy equivalent to habeas corpus as used by state prisoners, there is a major distinction between the two. Calling a § 2255 request for relief a motion rather than a petition militates toward charging no new filing fee, not an increased one. In the absence of convincing evidence to the contrary, there is no reason to suppose that Congress did not mean what it said in making a § 2255 action a motion. Therefore, as in other motions filed in a criminal action, there is no requirement of a filing fee. It is appropriate that the present situation of docketing a § 2255 motion as a new action and charging a $15 filing fee be remedied by rule when the whole question of § 2255 motions is thoroughly thought through and organized.

Even though there is no need to have a forma pauperis affidavit to proceed with the action since there is no requirement of a fee for filing the motion the affidavit remains attached to the form to be supplied potential movants. Most such movants are indigent, and this is a convenient way of getting this into the official record so that the judge may appoint counsel, order the government to pay witness fees, allow docketing of an appeal, and grant any other rights to which an indigent is entitled in the course of a § 2255 motion, when appropriate to the particular situation, without the need for an indigency petition and adjudication at such later point in the proceeding. This should result in a streamlining of the process to allow quicker disposition of these motions.

For further discussion of this rule, see the advisory committee note to Rule 3 of the § 2254 rules.

2004 Amendments

The language of Rule 3 has been amended as part of general restyling of the rules to make them more easily understood and to make style and terminology consistent throughout the rules. These changes are intended to be stylistic and no substantive change is intended, except as indicated below.

Revised Rule 3(b) is new and is intended to parallel Federal Rule of Civil Procedure 5(e), which provides that the clerk may not refuse to accept a filing solely for the reason that it fails to comply with these rules or local rules. Before the adoption of a one-year statute of limitations in the Antiterrorism and Effective Death Penalty Act of 1996, 110 Stat. 1214, the moving party suffered no penalty, other than delay, if the petition was deemed insufficient. That Act, however, added a one-year statute of limitations to motions filed under § 2255, *see* 28 U.S.C. § 2244(d)(1). Thus, a court's

dismissal of a defective motion may pose a significant penalty for a moving party who may not be able to file a corrected motion within the one-year limitation period. The Committee believed that the better procedure was to accept the defective motion and require the moving party to submit a corrected motion that conforms to Rule 2. Thus, revised Rule 3(b) requires the clerk to file a motion, even though it may otherwise fail to comply with Rule 2.

Revised Rule 3(c), which sets out a specific reference to 28 U.S.C. § 2255, paragraph 6, is new and has been added to put moving parties on notice that a one-year statute of limitations applies to motions filed under these Rules. Although the rule does not address the issue, every circuit that has addressed the issue has taken the position that equitable tolling of the statute of limitations is available in appropriate circumstances. *See, e.g., Dunlap v. United States,* 250 F.3d 1001, 1004–07 (6th Cir. 2001); *Moore v. United States,* 173 F.3d 1131, 1133–35 (8th Cir. 1999); *Sandvik v. United States,* 177 F.3d 1269, 1270–72 (11th Cir. 1999). The Supreme Court has not addressed the question directly. *See Duncan v. Walker,* 533 U.S. 167, 181 (2001) ("We . . . have no occasion to address the question that Justice Stevens raises concerning the availability of equitable tolling.").

Rule 3(d) is new and provides guidance on determining whether a motion from an inmate is considered to have been filed in a timely fashion. The new provision parallels Federal Rule of Appellate Procedure 25(a)(2)(C).

Rule 4. Preliminary Review

(a) Referral to a Judge. The clerk must promptly forward the motion to the judge who conducted the trial and imposed sentence or, if the judge who imposed sentence was not the trial judge, to the judge who conducted the proceedings being challenged. If the appropriate judge is not available, the clerk must forward the motion to a judge under the court's assignment procedure.

(b) Initial Consideration by the Judge. The judge who receives the motion must promptly examine it. If it plainly appears from the motion, any attached exhibits, and the record of prior proceedings that the moving party is not entitled to relief, the judge must dismiss the motion and direct the clerk to notify the moving party. If the motion is not dismissed, the judge must order the United States attorney to file an answer, motion, or other response within a fixed time, or to take other action the judge may order.

(As amended Apr. 26, 2004, eff. Dec. 1, 2004.)

ADVISORY COMMITTEE NOTES

1976 Adoption

Rule 4 outlines the procedure for assigning the motion to a specific judge of the district court and the options available to the judge and the government after the motion is properly filed.

The long-standing majority practice in assigning motions made pursuant to § 2255 has been for the trial judge to determine the merits of the motion. In cases where the § 2255 motion is directed against the sentence, the merits have traditionally been decided by the judge who imposed sentence. The reasoning for this was first noted in *Carvell v. United States,* 173 F.2d 348–349 (4th Cir.1949):

> Complaint is made that the judge who tried the case passed upon the motion. Not only was there no impropriety in this, but it is highly desirable in such cases that the motions be passed on by the judge who is familiar with the facts and circumstances surrounding the trial, and is consequently not likely to be misled by false allegations as to what occurred.

This case, and its reasoning, has been almost unanimously endorsed by other courts dealing with the issue.

Commentators have been critical of having the motion decided by the trial judge. See Developments in the Law—Federal Habeas Corpus, 83 Harv.L.Rev. 1038, 1206–1208 (1970).

> [T]he trial judge may have become so involved with the decision that it will be difficult for him to review it objectively. Nothing in the legislative history suggests that "court" refers to a specific judge, and the procedural advantages of section 2255 are available whether or not the trial judge presides at the hearing.

> The theory that Congress intended the trial judge to preside at a section 2255 hearing apparently originated in *Carvell v. United States,* 173 F.2d 348 (4th Cir.1949) (per curiam), where the panel of judges included Chief Judge Parker of the Fourth Circuit, chairman of the Judicial Conference committee which drafted section 2255. But the legislative history does not indicate that Congress wanted the trial judge to preside. Indeed the advantages of section 2255 can all be achieved if the case is heard in the sentencing district, regardless of which judge hears it. According to the Senate committee report the purpose of the bill was to make the proceeding a part of the criminal action so the court could resentence the applicant, or grant him a new trial. (A judge presiding over a habeas corpus action does not have these powers.) In addition, Congress did not want the cases heard in the district of confinement because that tended to concentrate the burden on a few districts, and made it difficult for witnesses and records to be produced.

83 Harv.L.Rev. at 1207–1208

The Court of Appeals for the First Circuit has held that a judge other than the trial judge should rule on the 2255 motion. See *Halliday v. United States,* 380 F.2d 270 (1st Cir.1967).

There is a procedure by which the movant can have a judge other than the trial judge decide his motion in courts adhering to the majority rule. He can file an affidavit alleging bias in order to disqualify the trial judge. And there are circumstances in which the trial judge will, on his own, disqualify himself. See, *e.g., Webster v. United States,* 330 F.Supp. 1080 (1972). However, there has been some questioning of the effectiveness of this procedure. See Developments in the Law—Federal Habeas Corpus, 83 Harv.L.Rev. 1038, 1200–1207 (1970).

Subdivision (a) adopts the majority rule and provides that the trial judge, or sentencing judge if different and appropriate for the particular motion, will decide the motion made pursuant to these rules, recognizing that, under some circumstances, he may want to disqualify himself. A movant is not without remedy if he feels this is unfair to him. He can file

an affidavit of bias. And there is the right to appellate review if the trial judge refuses to grant his motion. Because the trial judge is thoroughly familiar with the case, there is obvious administrative advantage in giving him the first opportunity to decide whether there are grounds for granting the motion.

Since the motion is part of the criminal action in which was entered the judgment to which it is directed, the files, records, transcripts, and correspondence relating to that judgment are automatically available to the judge in his consideration of the motion. He no longer need order them incorporated for that purpose.

Rule 4 has its basis in § 2255 (rather than 28 U.S.C. § 2243 in the corresponding habeas corpus rule) which does not have a specific time limitation as to when the answer must be made. Also, under § 2255, the United States Attorney for the district is the party served with the notice and a copy of the motion and required to answer (when appropriate). Subdivision (b) continues this practice since there is no respondent involved in the motion (unlike habeas) and the United States Attorney, as prosecutor in the case in question, is the most appropriate one to defend the judgment and oppose the motion.

The judge has discretion to require an answer or other appropriate response from the United States Attorney. See advisory committee note to Rule 4 of the § 2254 rules.

2004 Amendments

The language of Rule 4 has been amended as part of general restyling of the rules to make them more easily understood and to make style and terminology consistent throughout the rules. These changes are intended to be stylistic and no substantive change is intended.

The amended rule reflects that the response to a Section 2255 motion may be a motion to dismiss or some other response.

Rule 5. The Answer and the Reply

(a) **When Required.** The respondent is not required to answer the motion unless a judge so orders.

(b) **Contents.** The answer must address the allegations in the motion. In addition, it must state whether the moving party has used any other federal remedies, including any prior post-conviction motions under these rules or any previous rules, and whether the moving party received an evidentiary hearing.

(c) **Records of Prior Proceedings.** If the answer refers to briefs or transcripts of the prior proceedings that are not available in the court's records, the judge must order the government to furnish them within a reasonable time that will not unduly delay the proceedings.

(d) **Reply.** The moving party may submit a reply to the respondent's answer or other pleading within a time fixed by the judge.

(As amended Apr. 26, 2004, eff. Dec. 1, 2004.)

ADVISORY COMMITTEE NOTES

1976 Adoption

Unlike the habeas corpus statutes (see 28 U.S.C. §§ 2243, 2248) § 2255 does not specifically call for a return or answer by the United States Attorney or set any time limits as to when one must be submitted. The general practice, however, if the motion is not summarily dismissed, is for the government to file an answer to the motion as well as counter-affidavits, when appropriate. Rule 4 provides for an answer to the motion by the United States Attorney, and Rule 5 indicates what its contents should be.

There is no requirement that the movant exhaust his remedies prior to seeking relief under § 2255. However, the courts have held that such a motion is inappropriate if the movant is simultaneously appealing the decision.

We are of the view that there is no jurisdictional bar to the District Court's entertaining a Section 2255 motion during the pendency of a direct appeal but that the orderly administration of criminal law precludes considering such a motion absent extraordinary circumstances.

Womack v. United States, 395 F.2d 630, 631 (D.C.Cir.1968)

Also see *Masters v. Eide*, 353 F.2d 517 (8th Cir.1965). The answer may thus cut short consideration of the motion if it discloses the taking of an appeal which was omitted from the form motion filed by the movant.

There is nothing in § 2255 which corresponds to the § 2248 requirement of a traverse to the answer. Numerous cases have held that the government's answer and affidavits are not conclusive against the movant, and if they raise disputed issues of fact a hearing must be held. *Machibroda v. United States*, 368 U.S. 487, 494, 495 (1962); *United States v. Salerno*, 290 F.2d 105, 106 (2d Cir.1961); *Romero v. United States*, 327 F.2d 711, 712 (5th Cir.1964); *Scott v. United States*, 349 F.2d 641, 642, 643 (6th Cir.1965); *Schiebelhut v. United States*, 357 F.2d 743, 745 (6th Cir.1966); and *Del Piano v. United States*, 362 F.2d 931, 932, 933 (3d Cir.1966). None of these cases make any mention of a traverse by the movant to the government's answer. As under Rule 5 of the § 2254 rules, there is no intention here that such a traverse be required, except under special circumstances. See advisory committee note to Rule 9.

Subdivision (b) provides for the government to supplement its answers with appropriate copies of transcripts or briefs if for some reason the judge does not already have them under his control. This is because the government will in all probability have easier access to such papers than the movant, and it will conserve the court's time to have the government produce them rather than the movant, who would in most instances have to apply in forma pauperis for the government to supply them for him anyway.

For further discussion, see the advisory committee note to Rule 5 of the § 2254 rules.

2004 Amendments

The language of Rule 5 has been amended as part of general restyling of the rules to make them more easily understood and to make style and terminology consistent throughout the rules. These changes are intended to be stylistic and no substantive change is intended.

Revised Rule 5(a), which provides that the respondent is not required to file an answer to the motion, unless a judge so orders, is taken from current Rule 3(b). The revised rule does not address the practice in some districts, where the respondent files a pre-answer motion to dismiss the motion. But revised Rule 4(b) contemplates that practice and has been changed to reflect the view that if the court does not dismiss the motion, it may require (or permit) the respondent to file a motion.

Finally, revised Rule 5(d) adopts the practice in some jurisdictions giving the movant an opportunity to file a reply to the respondent's answer. Rather than using terms such as "traverse," *see* 28 U.S.C. § 2248, to identify the movant's response to the answer, the rule uses the more general term " reply." The Rule prescribes that the court set the time for such responses, and in lieu of setting specific time limits in each case, the court may decide to include such time limits in its local rules.

Rule 6. Discovery

(a) **Leave of Court Required.** A judge may, for good cause, authorize a party to conduct discovery under the Federal Rules of Criminal Procedure or Civil Procedure, or in accordance with the practices and principles of law. If necessary for effective discovery, the judge must appoint an attorney for a moving party who qualifies to have counsel appointed under 18 U.S.C. § 3006A.

(b) **Requesting Discovery.** A party requesting discovery must provide reasons for the request. The request must also include any proposed interrogatories and requests for admission, and must specify any requested documents.

(c) **Deposition Expenses.** If the government is granted leave to take a deposition, the judge may require the government to pay the travel expenses, subsistence expenses, and fees of the moving party's attorney to attend the deposition.
(As amended Apr. 26, 2004, eff. Dec. 1, 2004.)

ADVISORY COMMITTEE NOTES
1976 Adoption

This rule differs from the corresponding discovery rule under the § 2254 rules in that it includes the processes of discovery available under the Federal Rules of Criminal Procedure as well as the civil. This is because of the nature of a § 2255 motion as a continuing part of the criminal proceeding (see advisory committee note to Rule 1) as well as a remedy analogous to habeas corpus by state prisoners.

See the advisory committee note to rule 6 of the § 2254 rules. The discussion there is fully applicable to discovery under these rules for § 2255 motions.

2004 Amendments

The language of Rule 6 has been amended as part of general restyling of the rules to make them more easily understood and to make style and terminology consistent throughout the rules. These changes are intended to be stylistic and no substantive change is intended, except as indicated below.

Although current Rule 6(b) contains no requirement that the parties provide reasons for the requested discovery, the revised rule does so and also includes a requirement that the request be accompanied by any proposed interrogatories and requests for admission, and must specify any requested documents. The Committee believes that the revised rule makes explicit what has been implicit in current practice.

Rule 7. Expanding the Record

(a) **In General.** If the motion is not dismissed, the judge may direct the parties to expand the record by submitting additional materials relating to the motion. The judge may require that these materials be authenticated.

(b) **Types of Materials.** The materials that may be required include letters predating the filing of the motion, documents, exhibits, and answers under oath to written interrogatories propounded by the judge. Affidavits also may be submitted and considered as part of the record.

(c) **Review by the Opposing Party.** The judge must give the party against whom the additional materials are offered an opportunity to admit or deny their correctness.
(As amended Apr. 26, 2004, eff. Dec. 1, 2004.)

ADVISORY COMMITTEE NOTES
1976 Adoption

It is less likely that the court will feel the need to expand the record in a § 2255 proceeding than in a habeas corpus proceeding, because the trial (or sentencing) judge is the one hearing the motion (see Rule 4) and should already have a complete file on the case in his possession. However, Rule 7 provides a convenient method for supplementing his file if the case warrants it.

See the advisory committee note to Rule 7 of the § 2254 rules for a full discussion of reasons and procedures for expanding the record.

2004 Amendments

The language of Rule 7 has been amended as part of general restyling of the rules to make them more easily understood and to make style and terminology consistent throughout the rules. These changes are intended to be stylistic and no substantive change is intended.

Revised Rule 7(a) is not intended to restrict the court's authority to expand the record through means other than requiring the parties themselves to provide the information.

The language in current Rule 7(d), which deals with authentication of materials in the expanded record, has been moved to revised Rule 7(a).

Rule 8. Evidentiary Hearing

(a) **Determining Whether to Hold a Hearing.** If the motion is not dismissed, the judge must review the answer, any transcripts and records of prior proceed-

ings, and any materials submitted under Rule 7 to determine whether an evidentiary hearing is warranted.

(b) Reference to a Magistrate Judge. A judge may, under 28 U.S.C. § 636(b), refer the motion to a magistrate judge to conduct hearings and to file proposed findings of fact and recommendations for disposition. When they are filed, the clerk must promptly serve copies of the proposed findings and recommendations on all parties. Within 10 days after being served, a party may file objections as provided by local court rule. The judge must determine *de novo* any proposed finding or recommendation to which objection is made. The judge may accept, reject, or modify any proposed finding or recommendation.

(c) Appointing Counsel; Time of Hearing. If an evidentiary hearing is warranted, the judge must appoint an attorney to represent a moving party who qualifies to have counsel appointed under 18 U.S.C. § 3006A. The judge must conduct the hearing as soon as practicable after giving the attorneys adequate time to investigate and prepare. These rules do not limit the appointment of counsel under § 3006A at any stage of the proceeding.

(d) Producing a Statement. Federal Rule of Criminal Procedure 26.2(a)–(d) and (f) applies at a hearing under this rule. If a party does not comply with a Rule 26.2(a) order to produce a witness's statement, the court must not consider that witness's testimony.

(As amended Pub.L. 94–426, § 2(6), Sept. 28, 1976, 90 Stat. 1335; Pub.L. 94–577, § 2(a) (2), (b) (2), Oct. 21, 1976, 90 Stat. 2730, 2731; Apr. 22, 1993, eff. Dec. 1, 1993; Apr. 26, 2004, eff. Dec. 1, 2004.)

ADVISORY COMMITTEE NOTES

1976 Adoption

The standards for § 2255 hearings are essentially the same as for evidentiary hearings under a habeas petition, except that the previous federal fact-finding proceeding is in issue rather than the state's. Also § 2255 does not set specific time limits for holding the hearing, as does § 2243 for a habeas action. With these minor differences in mind, see the advisory committee note to Rule 8 of § 2254 rules, which is applicable to Rule 8 of these § 2255 rules.

1993 Amendment

The amendment to Rule 8 is one of a series of parallel amendments to Federal Rules of Criminal Procedure 32, 32.1, and 46 which extend the scope of Rule 26.2 (Production of Witness Statements) to proceedings other than the trial itself. The amendments are grounded on the compelling need for accurate and credible information in making decisions concerning the defendant's liberty. *See* the Advisory Committee Note to Rule 26.2(g). A few courts have recognized the authority of a judicial officer to order production of prior statements by a witness at a Section 2255 hearing, see, e.g., *United States v. White*, 342 F.2d 379, 382, n. 4 (4th Cir.1959). The amendment to Rule 8 grants explicit authori-

ty to do so. The amendment is not intended to require production of a witness's statement before the witness actually presents oral testimony.

2004 Amendments

The language of Rule 8 has been amended as part of general restyling of the rules to make them more easily understood and to make style and terminology consistent throughout the rules. These changes are intended to be stylistic and no substantive change is intended, except as described below.

The requirement in current Rule 8(b)(2) that a copy of the magistrate judge's findings must be promptly mailed to all parties has been changed in revised Rule 8(b) to require that copies of those findings be served on all parties. As used in this rule, "service" means service consistent with Federal Rule of Civil Procedure 5(b), which allows mailing the copies.

HISTORICAL NOTES

Effective and Applicability Provisions

1976 Acts

Amendments made by Pub.L. 94–577 effective with respect to motions under section 2255 of this title filed on or after Feb. 1, 1977, see section 2(c) of Pub.L. 94–577, set out as a note under Rule 8 of the Rules Governing Cases Under Section 2254 of this title.

Rule 9. Second or Successive Motions

Before presenting a second or successive motion, the moving party must obtain an order from the appropriate court of appeals authorizing the district court to consider the motion, as required by 28 U.S.C. § 2255, para. 8.

(As amended Pub.L. 94–426, § 2(9), (10), Sept. 28, 1976, 90 Stat. 1335; Apr. 26, 2004, eff. Dec. 1, 2004.)

ADVISORY COMMITTEE NOTES

1976 Adoption

Unlike the statutory provisions on habeas corpus (28 U.S.C. §§ 2241–2254), § 2255 specifically provides that "a motion for such relief may be made *at any time*." [Emphasis added.] Subdivision (a) provides that delayed motions may be barred from consideration if the government has been prejudiced in its ability to respond to the motion by the delay and the movant's failure to seek relief earlier is not excusable within the terms of the rule. Case law, dealing with this issue, is in conflict.

Some courts have held that the literal language of § 2255 precludes any possible time bar to a motion brought under it. In *Heflin v. United States*, 358 U.S. 415 (1959), the concurring opinion noted:

The statute [28 U.S.C. § 2255] further provides: "A motion * * * may be made at any time." This * * * simply means that, as in habeas corpus, there is no statute of limitations, no *res judicata*, and that the doctrine of laches is inapplicable.

358 U.S. at 420

McKinney v. United States, 208 F.2d 844 (D.C.Cir.1953) reversed the district court's dismissal of a § 2255 motion for being too late, the court stating:

McKinney's present application for relief comes late in the day: he has served some fifteen years in prison. But tardiness is irrelevant where a constitutional issue is raised and where the prisoner is still confined.

208 F.2d at 846, 847

In accord, see; *Juelich v. United States*, 300 F.2d 381, 383 (5th Cir.1962); *Conners v. United States*, 431 F.2d 1207, 1208 (9th Cir.1970); *Sturrup v. United States*, 218 F.Supp. 279, 281 (E.D.N.Car.1963); and *Banks v. United States*, 319 F.Supp. 649, 652 (S.D.N.Y.1970).

It has also been held that delay in filing a § 2255 motion does not bar the movant because of lack of reasonable diligence in pressing the claim.

The statute [28 U.S.C. § 2255], when it states that the motion may be made at any time, excludes the addition of a showing of diligence in delayed filings. A number of courts have considered contentions similar to those made here and have concluded that there are no time limitations. This result excludes the requirement of diligence which is in reality a time limitation.

Haier v. United States, 334 F.2d 441, 442 (10th Cir.1964)

Other courts have recognized that delay may have a negative effect on the movant. In *Raines v. United States*, 423 F.2d 526 (4th Cir.1970), the court stated:

[B]oth petitioners' silence for extended periods, one for 28 months and the other for nine years, serves to render their allegations less believable. "Although a delay in filing a section 2255 motion is not a controlling element * * * it may merit some consideration * * * ."

423 F.2d at 531

In *Aiken v. United States*, 191 F.Supp. 43, 50 (M.D.N.Car. 1961), aff'd 296 F.2d 604 (4th Cir.1961), the court said: "While motions under 28 U.S.C. § 2255 may be made at any time, the lapse of time affects the good faith and credibility of the moving party." For similar conclusions, see: *Parker v. United States*, 358 F.2d 50, 54 n. 4 (7th Cir.1965), cert. denied, 386 U.S. 916 (1967); *Le Clair v. United States*, 241 F.Supp. 819, 824 (N.D.Ind.1965); *Malone v. United States*, 299 F.2d 254, 256 (6th Cir.1962), cert. denied, 371 U.S. 863 (1962); *Howell v. United States*, 442 F.2d 265, 274 (7th Cir.1971); and *United States v. Wiggins*, 184 F.Supp. 673, 676 (D.C.Cir.1960).

There have been holdings by some courts that a delay in filing a § 2255 motion operates to increase the burden of proof which the movant must meet to obtain relief. The reasons for this, as expressed in *United States v. Bostic*, 206 F.Supp. 855 (D.C.Cir.1962), are equitable in nature.

Obviously, the burden of proof on a motion to vacate a sentence under 28 U.S.C. § 2255 is on the moving party. . . . The burden is particularly heavy if the issue is one of fact and a long time has elapsed since the trial of the case. While neither the statute of limitations nor laches can bar the assertion of a constitutional right, nevertheless, the passage of time may make it impracticable to

retry a case if the motion is granted and a new trial is ordered. No doubt, at times such a motion is a product of an afterthought. Long delay may raise a question of good faith.

206 F.Supp. at 856–857

See also *United States v. Wiggins*, 184 F.Supp. at 676.

A requirement that the movant display reasonable diligence in filing a § 2255 motion has been adopted by some courts dealing with delayed motions. The court in *United States v. Moore*, 166 F.2d 102 (7th Cir.1948), cert. denied, 334 U.S. 849 (1948), did this, again for equitable reasons.

[W]e agree with the District Court that the petitioner has too long slept upon his rights. * * * [A]pparently there is no limitation of time within which * * * a motion to vacate may be filed, except that an applicant must show reasonable diligence in presenting his claim. * * *

The reasons which support the rule requiring diligence seem obvious. * * * Law enforcement officials change, witnesses die, memories grow dim. The prosecuting tribunal is put to a disadvantage if an unexpected retrial should be necessary after long passage of time.

166 F.2d at 105

In accord see *Desmond v. United States*, 333 F.2d 378, 381 (1st Cir.1964), on remand, 345 F.2d 225 (1st Cir.1965).

One of the major arguments advanced by the courts which would penalize a movant who waits an unduly long time before filing a § 2255 motion is that such delay is highly prejudicial to the prosecution. In *Desmond v. United States*, writing of a § 2255 motion alleging denial of effective appeal because of deception by movant's own counsel, the court said:

[A]pplications for relief such as this must be made promptly. It will not do for a prisoner to wait until government witnesses have become unavailable as by death, serious illness or absence from the country, or until the memory of available government witnesses has faded. It will not even do for a prisoner to wait any longer than is reasonably necessary to prepare appropriate moving papers, however inartistic, after discovery of the deception practiced upon him by his attorney.

333 F.2d at 381

In a similar vein are *United States v. Moore* and *United States v. Bostic*, supra, and *United States v. Wiggins*, 184 F.Supp. at 676.

Subdivision (a) provides a flexible, equitable time limitation based on laches to prevent movants from withholding their claims so as to prejudice the government both in meeting the allegations of the motion and in any possible retrial. It includes a reasonable diligence requirement for ascertaining possible grounds for relief. If the delay is found to be excusable, or nonprejudicial to the government, the time bar is inoperative.

Subdivision (b) is consistent with the language of § 2255 and relevant case law.

The annexed form is intended to serve the same purpose as the comparable one included in the § 2254 rules.

For further discussion applicable to this rule, see the advisory committee note to Rule 9 of the § 2254 rules.

2004 Amendments

The language of Rule 9 has been amended as part of general restyling of the rules to make them more easily understood and to make style and terminology consistent throughout the rules. These changes are intended to be stylistic and no substantive change is intended, except as indicated below.

First, current Rule 9(a) has been deleted as unnecessary in light of the applicable one-year statute of limitations for § 2255 motions, added as part of the Antiterrorism and Effective Death Penalty Act of 1996, 28 U.S.C. § 2255, para. 6.

Second, the remainder of revised Rule 9 reflects provisions in the Antiterrorism and Effective Death Penalty Act of 1996, 28 U.S.C. § 2255, para. 8, which now require a moving party to obtain approval from the appropriate court of appeals before filing a second or successive motion.

Finally, the title of the rule has been changed to reflect the fact that the revised version addresses only the topic of second or successive motions.

Rule 10. Powers of a Magistrate Judge

A magistrate judge may perform the duties of a district judge under these rules, as authorized by 28 U.S.C. § 636.

(As amended Pub.L. 94–426, § 2(12), Sept. 28, 1976, 90 Stat. 1335; Apr. 30, 1979, eff. Aug. 1, 1979; Apr. 26, 2004, eff. Dec. 1, 2004.)

ADVISORY COMMITTEE NOTES

1976 Adoption

See the advisory committee note to Rule 10 of the § 2254 rules for a discussion fully applicable here as well.

1979 Amendment

This amendment conforms the rule to 18 U.S.C. § 636. See Advisory Committee Note to Rule 10 of the Rules Governing Section 2254 Cases in the United States District Courts.

2004 Amendments

The language of Rule 10 has been amended as part of general restyling of the rules to make them more easily understood and to make style and terminology consistent throughout the rules. These changes are intended to be stylistic and no substantive change is intended.

HISTORICAL NOTES

Change of Name

United States magistrate appointed under section 631 of Title 28, Judiciary and Judicial Procedure, to be known as United States magistrate judge after Dec. 1, 1990, with any reference to United States magistrate or magistrate in Title 28, in any other Federal statute, etc., deemed a reference to United States magistrate judge appointed under section 631 of Title 28, see section 321 of Pub.L. 101–650, set out as a note under section 631 of Title 28.

Rule 11. Time to Appeal

Federal Rule of Appellate Procedure 4(a) governs the time to appeal an order entered under these rules. These rules do not extend the time to appeal the original judgment of conviction.

(As amended Apr. 30, 1979, eff. Aug. 1, 1979; Apr. 26, 2004, eff. Dec. 1, 2004.)

ADVISORY COMMITTEE NOTES

1976 Adoption

Rule 11 is intended to make clear that, although a § 2255 action is a continuation of the criminal case, the bringing of a § 2255 action does not extend the time.

1979 Amendment

Prior to the promulgation of the Rules Governing Section 2255 Proceedings, the courts consistently held that the time for appeal in a section 2255 case is as provided in Fed. R.App.P. 4(a), that is, 60 days when the government is a party, rather than as provided in appellate rule 4(b), which says that the time is 10 days in criminal cases. This result has often been explained on the ground that rule 4(a) has to do with civil cases and that "proceedings under section 2255 are civil in nature." E.g., *Rothman v. United States*, 508 F.2d 648 (3d Cir.1975). Because the new section 2255 rules are based upon the premise "that a motion under § 2255 is a further step in the movant's criminal case rather than a separate civil action," see Advisory Committee Note to Rule 1, the question has arisen whether the new rules have the effect of shortening the time for appeal to that provided in appellate rule 4(b). A sentence has been added to Rule 11 in order to make it clear that this is not the case.

Even though section 2255 proceedings are a further step in the criminal case, the added sentence correctly states current law. In *United States v. Hayman*, 342 U.S. 205 (1952), the Supreme Court noted that such appeals "are governed by the civil rules applicable to appeals from final judgments in habeas corpus actions." In support, the Court cited *Mercado v. United States*, 183 F.2d 486 (1st Cir.1950), a case rejecting the argument that because § 2255 proceedings are criminal in nature the time for appeal is only 10 days. The *Mercado* court concluded that the situation was governed by that part of 28 U.S.C. § 2255 which reads: "An appeal may be taken to the court of appeals from the order entered on the motion as from a final judgment on application for a writ of habeas corpus." Thus, because appellate rule 4(a) is applicable in habeas cases, it likewise governs in § 2255 cases even though they are criminal in nature.

2004 Amendments

The language of Rule 11 has been amended as part of general restyling of the rules to make them more easily understood and to make style and terminology consistent throughout the rules. These changes are intended to be stylistic and no substantive change is intended.

Rule 12. Applicability of the Federal Rules of Civil Procedure and the Federal Rules of Criminal Procedure

The Federal Rules of Civil Procedure and the Federal Rules of Criminal Procedure, to the extent that

they are not inconsistent with any statutory provisions or these rules, may be applied to a proceeding under these rules.

(As amended Apr. 26, 2004, eff. Dec. 1, 2004.)

ADVISORY COMMITTEE NOTES

1976 Adoption

This rule differs from rule 11 of the § 2254 rules in that it includes the Federal Rules of Criminal Procedure as well as the civil. This is because of the nature of a § 2255 motion as a continuing part of the criminal proceeding (see advisory committee note to Rule 1) as well as a remedy analogous to habeas corpus by state prisoners.

Since § 2255 has been considered analogous to habeas as respects the restrictions in Fed.R.Civ.P. 81(a) (2) (see *Sullivan v. United States*, 198 F.Supp. 624 (S.D.N.Y.1961)), Rule

12 is needed. For discussion, see the advisory committee note to Rule 11 of the § 2254 rules.

2004 Amendments

The language of Rule 12 has been amended as part of general restyling of the rules to make them more easily understood and to make style and terminology consistent throughout the rules. These changes are intended to be stylistic and no substantive change is intended.

HISTORICAL NOTES

References in Text

The Federal Rules of Criminal Procedure, referred to in text, are set out in Title 18, Crimes and Criminal Procedure.

The Federal Rules of Civil Procedure, referred to in text, are set out in this title.

APPENDIX OF FORMS

Motion to Vacate, Set Aside, or Correct a Sentence By a Person in Federal Custody
(Motion Under 28 U.S.C. § 2255)

Instructions

1. To use this form, you must be a person who is serving a sentence under a judgment against you in a federal court. You are asking for relief from the conviction or the sentence. This form is your motion for relief.

2. You must file the form in the United States district court that entered the judgment that you are challenging. If you want to challenge a federal judgment that imposed a sentence to be served in the future, you should file the motion in the federal court that entered that judgment.

3. Make sure the form is typed or neatly written.

4. You must tell the truth and sign the form. If you make a false statement of a material fact, you may be prosecuted for perjury.

5. Answer all the questions. You do not need to cite law. You may submit additional pages if necessary. If you do not fill out the form properly, you will be asked to submit additional or correct information. If you want to submit a brief or arguments, you must submit them in a separate memorandum.

6. If you cannot pay for the costs of this motion (such as costs for an attorney or transcripts), you may ask to proceed *in forma pauperis* (as a poor person). To do that, you must fill out the last page of this form. Also, you must submit a certificate signed by an officer at the institution where you are confined showing the amount of money that the institution is holding for you.

7. In this motion, you may challenge the judgment entered by only one court. If you want to challenge a judgment entered by a different judge or division (either in the same district or in a different district), you must file a separate motion.

8. When you have completed the form, send the original and two copies to the Clerk of the United States District Court at this address:

 Clerk, United States District Court for

 Address
 City, State Zip Code

9. **CAUTION: You must include in this motion all the grounds for relief from the conviction or sentence that you challenge. And you must state the facts that support each ground. If you fail to set forth all the grounds in this motion, you may be barred from presenting additional grounds at a later date.**

10. **CAPITAL CASES: If you are under a sentence of death, you are entitled to the assistance of counsel and should request the appointment of counsel.**

MOTION UNDER 28 U.S.C. § 2255 TO VACATE, SET ASIDE, OR CORRECT SENTENCE BY A PERSON IN FEDERAL CUSTODY

United States District Court District _____

Name (under which you were Docket or Case No.:
convicted):

Place of Confinement: Prisoner No.:

UNITED STATES OF Movant (include name under
AMERICA which convicted)

v.

MOTION

1. (a) Name and location of court that entered the judgment of conviction you are challenging: _____

 (b) Criminal docket or case number (if you know): ___

2. (a) Date of the judgment of conviction (if you know):

 (b) Date of sentencing: _____

3. Length of sentence: _____

4. Nature of crime (all counts): _____

5. (a) What was your plea? (Check one)
 (1) Not guilty ☐ (2) Guilty ☐
 (3) Nolo contendere (no contest) ☐
 (b) If you entered a guilty plea to one count or indictment, and a not guilty plea to another count or indictment, what did you plead guilty to and what did you plead not guilty to? _____

6. If you went to trial, what kind of trial did you have? (Check one) Jury ☐ Judge only ☐

7. Did you testify at a pretrial hearing, trial, or post-trial hearing? Yes ☐ No ☐

8. Did you appeal from the judgment of conviction? Yes ☐ No ☐

9. If you did appeal, answer the following:
 (a) Name of court: _____
 (b) Docket or case number (if you know): _____
 (c) Result: _____
 (d) Date of result (if you know): _____
 (e) Citation to the case (if you know): _____
 (f) Grounds raised: _____

 (g) Did you file a petition for certiorari in the United States Supreme Court?
 Yes ☐ No ☐
 If "Yes," answer the following:
 (1) Docket or case number (if you know):_____
 (2) Result:_____

 (3) Date of result (if you know): _____
 (4) Citation to the case (if you know): _____
 (5) Grounds raised: _____

10. Other than the direct appeals listed above, have you previously filed any other motions, petitions, or applications concerning this judgment of conviction in any court?
 Yes ☐ No ☐

11. If your answer to Question 10 was "Yes," give the following information:
 (a) (1) Name of court: _____
 (2) Docket or case number (if you know): _____
 (3) Date of filing (if you know): _____
 (4) Nature of the proceeding: _____
 (5) Grounds raised: _____

 (6) Did you receive a hearing where evidence was given on your motion, petition, or application?
 Yes ☐ No ☐
 (7) Result: _____
 (8) Date of result (if you know): _____
 (b) If you filed any second motion, petition, or application, give the same information:
 (1) Name of court: _____
 (2) Docket or case number (if you know): _____
 (3) Date of filing (if you know):_____
 (4) Nature of the proceeding: _____
 (5) Grounds raised: _____

 (6) Did you receive a hearing where evidence was given on your motion, petition, or application?
 Yes ☐ No ☐
 (7) Result: _____
 (8) Date of result (if you know): _____
 (c) Did you appeal to a federal appellate court having jurisdiction over the action taken on your motion, petition, or application?
 (1) First petition: Yes ☐ No ☐
 (2) Second petition: Yes ☐ No ☐
 (d) If you did not appeal from the action on any motion, petition, or application, explain briefly why

you did not: _____

12. For this motion, state every ground on which you claim that you are being held in violation of the Constitution, laws, or treaties of the United States. Attach additional pages if you have more than four grounds. State the facts supporting each ground.

GROUND ONE: _____

(a) Supporting facts (Do not argue or cite law. Just state the specific facts that support your claim.): _____

(b) **Direct Appeal of Ground One:**
(1) If you appealed from the judgment of conviction, did you raise this issue?
Yes ☐ No ☐
(2) If you did not raise this issue in your direct appeal, explain why: _____

(c) **Post-Conviction Proceedings:**
(1) Did you raise this issue in any post-conviction motion, petition, or application?
Yes ☐ No ☐
(2) If your answer to Question (c)(1) is "Yes," state:
Type of motion or petition: _____
Name and location of the court where the motion or petition was filed: _____

Docket or case number (if you know): _____
Date of the court's decision: _____
Result (attach a copy of the court's opinion or order, if available): _____

(3) Did you receive a hearing on your motion, petition, or application?
Yes ☐ No ☐
(4) Did you appeal from the denial of your motion, petition, or application?
Yes ☐ No ☐
(5) If your answer to Question (c)(4) is "Yes," did you raise this issue in the appeal?
Yes ☐ No ☐
(6) If your answer to Question (c)(4) is "Yes," state:
Name and location of the court where the appeal was filed: _____

Docket or case number (if you know): _____
Date of the court's decision: _____
Result (attach a copy of the court's opinion or order, if available): _____

(7) If your answer to Question (c)(4) or Question (c)(5) is "No," explain why you did not appeal or raise this issue: _____

GROUND TWO: _____

(a) Supporting facts (Do not argue or cite law. Just state the specific facts that support your claim.): _____

(b) **Direct Appeal of Ground Two:**
(1) If you appealed from the judgment of conviction, did you raise this issue?
Yes ☐ No ☐
(2) If you did not raise this issue in your direct appeal, explain why: _____

(c) **Post-Conviction Proceedings:**
(1) Did you raise this issue in any post-conviction motion, petition, or application?
Yes ☐ No ☐
(2) If your answer to Question (c)(1) is "Yes," state:
Type of motion or petition: _____
Name and location of the court where the motion or petition was filed: _____

Docket or case number (if you know): _____
Date of the court's decision: _____
Result (attach a copy of the court's opinion or order, if available): _____

(3) Did you receive a hearing on your motion, petition, or application?
Yes ☐ No ☐
(4) Did you appeal from the denial of your motion, petition, or application?
Yes ☐ No ☐
(5) If your answer to Question (c)(4) is "Yes," did you raise this issue in the appeal?
Yes ☐ No ☐
(6) If your answer to Question (c)(4) is "Yes," state:
Name and location of the court where the appeal was filed: _____

Docket or case number (if you know): _____
Date of the court's decision: _____
Result (attach a copy of the court's opinion or order, if available): _____

(7) If your answer to Question (c)(4) or Question (c)(5) is "No," explain why you did not appeal or raise this issue: _____

GROUND THREE: _____

(a) Supporting facts (Do not argue or cite law. Just state the specific facts that support your claim.): _____

(b) **Direct Appeal of Ground Three:**
(1) If you appealed from the judgment of conviction, did you raise this issue?
Yes ☐ No ☐
(2) If you did not raise this issue in your direct appeal, explain why: _____

(c) **Post-Conviction Proceedings:**
(1) Did you raise this issue in any post-conviction motion, petition, or application?
Yes ☐ No ☐
(2) If your answer to Question (c)(1) is "Yes," state:
Type of motion or petition: _____
Name and location of the court where the motion or petition was filed: _____

Docket or case number (if you know): _____
Date of the court's decision: _____
Result (attach a copy of the court's opinion or order, if available): _____

(3) Did you receive a hearing on your motion, petition, or application?
Yes ☐ No ☐
(4) Did you appeal from the denial of your motion, petition, or application?
Yes ☐ No ☐
(5) If your answer to Question (c)(4) is "Yes," did you raise this issue in the appeal?
Yes ☐ No ☐
(6) If your answer to Question (c)(4) is "Yes," state:
Name and location of the court where the appeal was filed: _____

Docket or case number (if you know): _____
Date of the court's decision: _____
Result (attach a copy of the court's opinion or order, if available): _____

(7) If your answer to Question (c)(4) or Question (c)(5) is "No," explain why you did not appeal or raise this issue: _____

GROUND FOUR: _____

(a) Supporting facts (Do not argue or cite law. Just state the specific facts that support your claim.):

(b) **Direct Appeal of Ground Four:**
(1) If you appealed from the judgment of conviction, did you raise this issue?
Yes ☐ No ☐
(2) If you did not raise this issue in your direct appeal, explain why: _____

(c) **Post-Conviction Proceedings:**
(1) Did you raise this issue in any post-conviction motion, petition, or application?
Yes ☐ No ☐
(2) If your answer to Question (c)(1) is "Yes," state:
Type of motion or petition: _____
Name and location of the court where the motion or petition was filed: _____
Docket or case number (if you know): _____
Date of the court's decision: _____
Result (attach a copy of the court's opinion or order, if available): _____

(3) Did you receive a hearing on your motion, petition, or application?
Yes ☐ No ☐
(4) Did you appeal from the denial of your motion, petition, or application?
Yes ☐ No ☐
(5) If your answer to Question (c)(4) is "Yes," did you raise this issue in the appeal?
Yes ☐ No ☐
(6) If your answer to Question (c)(4) is "Yes," state:
Name and location of the court where the appeal was filed: _____

Docket or case number (if you know): _____
Date of the court's decision: _____
Result (attach a copy of the court's opinion or order, if available): _____

(7) If your answer to Question (c)(4) or Question (c)(5) is "No," explain why you did not appeal or raise this issue: _____

13. Is there any ground in this motion that you have <u>not</u> previously presented in some federal court? If so, which ground or grounds have not been presented, and state your reasons for not presenting them: _____

MOTION ATTACKING SENTENCE

14. Do you have any motion, petition, or appeal <u>now pending</u> (filed and not decided yet) in any court for the judgment you are challenging? Yes ☐ No ☐
If "Yes," state the name and location of the court, the docket or case number, the type of proceeding, and the issues raised. _____

15. Give the name and address, if known, of each attorney who represented you in the following stages of the judgment you are challenging:
(a) At preliminary hearing: _____

(b) At arraignment and plea: _____

(c) At trial: _____

(d) At sentencing: _____

(e) On appeal: _____

(f) In any post-conviction proceeding: _____

(g) On appeal from any ruling against you in a post-conviction proceeding: _____

16. Were you sentenced on more than one count of an indictment, or on more than one indictment, in the same court and at the same time? Yes ☐ No ☐
17. Do you have any future sentence to serve after you complete the sentence for the judgment that you are challenging? Yes ☐ No ☐
(a) If so, give name and location of court that imposed the other sentence you will serve in the future: _____

(b) Give the date the other sentence was imposed: _____
(c) Give the length of the other sentence: _____
(d) Have you filed, or do you plan to file, any motion, petition, or application that challenges the judgment or sentence to be served in the future? Yes ☐ No ☐
18. TIMELINESS OF MOTION: If your judgment of conviction became final over one year ago, you must explain why the one-year statute of limitations as contained in 28 U.S.C. § 2255 does not bar your motion.*

* The Antiterrorism and Effective Death Penalty Act of 1996 ("AEDPA") as contained in 28 U.S.C. § 2255, paragraph 6, provides in part that:

A one-year period of limitation shall apply to a motion under this section. The limitation period shall run from the latest of—
(1) the date on which the judgment of conviction became final;
(2) the date on which the impediment to making a motion created by governmental action in violation of the Constitution or laws of the United States is removed, if the movant was prevented from making such a motion by such governmental action;
(3) the date on which the right asserted was initially recognized by the Supreme Court, if that right has been newly recognized by the Supreme Court and made retroactively applicable to cases on collateral review; or
(4) the date on which the facts supporting the claim or claims presented could have been discovered through the exercise of due diligence.

Therefore, movant asks that the Court grant the following relief: _____

or any other relief to which movant may be entitled.

Signature of Attorney (if any)

I declare (or certify, verify, or state) under penalty of perjury that the foregoing is true and correct and that this Motion Under 28 U.S.C. § 2255 was placed in the prison mailing system on _____
_____ (month, date, year).

Executed (signed) on _____
_____ (date).

Signature of Movant

If the person signing is not movant, state relationship to movant and explain why movant is not signing this motion.

IN FORMA PAUPERIS DECLARATION

[INSERT APPROPRIATE COURT]

<table>
<tr><td>United States</td><td>DECLARATION IN SUPPORT</td></tr>
<tr><td>v.</td><td>OF REQUEST</td></tr>
</table>

United States

v.

(Movant)

DECLARATION IN
SUPPORT
OF REQUEST
TO PROCEED
*IN FORMA
PAUPERIS*

I, _____, declare that I am the movant in the above entitled case; that in support of my motion to proceed without being required to prepay fees, costs or give security therefor, I state that because of my poverty, I am unable to pay the costs of said proceeding or to give security therefor; that I believe I am entitled to relief.

1. Are you presently employed? Yes ☐ No ☐
 a. If the answer is "yes," state the amount of your salary or wages per month, and give the name and address of your employer.

 b. If the answer is "no," state the date of last employment and the amount of the salary and wages per month which you received.

2. Have you received within the past twelve months any money from any of the following sources?
 a. Business, profession or form of self-employment? Yes ☐ No ☐
 b. Rent payments, interest or dividends? Yes ☐ No ☐
 c. Pensions, annuities or life insurance payments? Yes ☐ No ☐
 d. Gifts or inheritances? Yes ☐ No ☐
 e. Any other sources? Yes ☐ No ☐
 If the answer to any of the above is "yes," describe each source of money and state the amount received from each during the past twelve months.

3. Do you own any cash, or do you have money in a checking or savings account?
 Yes ☐ No ☐ (Include any funds in prison accounts)
 If the answer is "yes," state the total value of the items owned.

4. Do you own real estate, stocks, bonds, notes, automobiles, or other valuable property (excluding ordinary household furnishings and clothing)?
 Yes ☐ No ☐
 If the answer is "yes," describe the property and state its approximate value.

5. List the persons who are dependent upon you for support, state your relationship to those persons, and indicate how much you contribute toward their support.

I declare (or certify, verify, or state) under penalty of perjury that the foregoing is true and correct. Executed on _____.
 (date)

 Signature of Movant

CERTIFICATE

I hereby certify that the movant herein has the sum of $_____ on account to his credit at the _____ institution where he is confined. I further certify that movant likewise has the following securities to his credit according to the records of said _____ institution:

MOTION ATTACKING SENTENCE

Authorized Officer of Institution

(As amended Apr. 28, 1982, eff. Aug. 1, 1982; Apr. 26, 2004, eff. Dec. 1, 2004.)

FEDERAL RULES OF APPELLATE PROCEDURE

Amendments received to May 21, 2007

Complete Annotation Materials, see Title 28 U.S.C.A.

RULES OF APPELLATE PROCEDURE

ORDERS OF THE SUPREME COURT OF THE UNITED STATES ADOPTING AND AMENDING RULES

ORDER OF DECEMBER 4, 1967

ORDERED:

1. That the following rules, to be known as the Federal Rules of Appellate Procedure, be, and they hereby are, prescribed, pursuant to sections 3771 and 3772 of Title 18, United States Code, and sections 2072 and 2075 of Title 28, United States Code, to govern the procedure in appeals to United States courts of appeals from the United States district courts, in the review by United States courts of appeals of decisions of the Tax Court of the United States, in proceedings in the United States courts of appeals for the review or enforcement of orders of administrative agencies, boards, commissions and officers, and in applications for writs or other relief which a United States court of appeals or judge thereof is competent to give:

[See text of Rules of Appellate Procedure, post]

2. That the foregoing rules shall take effect on July 1, 1968, and shall govern all proceedings in appeals and petitions for review or enforcement of orders thereafter brought and in all such proceedings then pending, except to the extent that in the opinion of the court of appeals their application in a particular proceeding then pending would not be feasible or would work injustice, in which case the former procedure may be followed.

3. That Rules 6, 9, 41, 77 and 81 of the Rules of Civil Procedure for the United States District Courts be, and they hereby are, amended, effective July 1, 1968, as hereinafter set forth:

[See amendments made thereby under the Rules of Civil Procedure, ante]

4. That the chapter heading "IX. APPEALS", all of Rules 72, 73, 74, 75 and 76 of the Rules of Civil Procedure for the United States District Courts, and Form 27 annexed to the said rules, be, and they hereby are, abrogated, effective July 1, 1968.

5. That Rules 45, 49, 56 and 57 of the Rules of Criminal Procedure for the United States District Courts be, and they hereby are, amended, effective July 1, 1968, as hereinafter set forth:

[For text of amendments, see pamphlet containing Federal Rules of Criminal Procedure]

6. That the chapter heading "VIII. APPEAL", all of Rules 37 and 39, and subdivisions (b) and (c) of Rule 38, of the Rules of Criminal Procedure for the United States District Courts, and Forms 26 and 27 annexed to the said rules, be, and they hereby are, abrogated, effective July 1, 1968.

7. That the Chief Justice be, and he hereby is, authorized to transmit to the Congress the foregoing new rules and amendments to and abrogation of existing rules, in accordance with the provisions of Title 18, U.S.C., § 3771, and Title 28, U.S.C., §§ 2072 and 2075.

ORDER OF MARCH 30, 1970

1. That subdivisions (a) and (c) of Rule 30 and subdivision (a) of Rule 31 of the Federal Rules of Appellate Procedure be, and they hereby are, amended as follows:

[See the amendments made thereby under the respective rules, post]

2. That the foregoing amendments to the Federal Rules of Appellate Procedure shall take effect on July 1, 1970, and shall govern all proceedings in actions brought thereafter and also in all further proceedings in actions then pending, except to the extent that in the opinion of the court their application in a particular action then pending would not be feasible or would work injustice, in which event the former procedure applies.

3. That the Chief Justice be, and he hereby is, authorized to transmit to the Congress the foregoing amendments to existing rules, in accordance with the provisions of Title 18, U.S.C., § 3772, and Title 28, U.S.C., §§ 2072 and 2075.

ORDER OF MARCH 1, 1971

1. That subdivision (a) of Rule 6, paragraph (4) of subdivision (a) of Rule 27, paragraph (6) of subdivision (b) of Rule 30, subdivision (c) of Rule 77, and paragraph (2) of subdivision (a) of Rule 81 of the Federal Rules of Civil Procedure be, and hereby are, amended, effective July 1, 1971, to read as follows:

[See amendments made thereby under the Rules of Civil Procedure, ante]

2. That subdivision (a) of Rule 45 and all of Rule 56 of the Federal Rules of Criminal Procedure be, and they hereby are, amended, effective July 1, 1971, to read as follows:

[For text of amendments, see pamphlet containing Federal Rules of Criminal Procedure]

3. That subdivision (a) of Rule 26 and subdivision (a) of Rule 45 of the Federal Rules of Appellate Procedure be, and they hereby are, amended, effective July 1, 1971, to read as follows:

[See amendments made thereby under the respective rules, post]

4. That THE CHIEF JUSTICE be, and he hereby is, authorized to transmit to the Congress the foregoing amendments to the Rules of Civil, Criminal and Appellate Procedure, in accordance with the provisions of Title 18, U.S.C., § 3771, and Title 28, U.S.C., §§ 2072 and 2075.

MR. JUSTICE BLACK and MR. JUSTICE DOUGLAS dissent.

ORDER OF APRIL 24, 1972

1. That Rules 1, 3, 4(b) & (c), 5, 5.1, 6(b), 7(c), 9(b), (c) & (d), 17(a) & (g), 31(e), 32(b), 38(a), 40, 41, 44, 46, 50, 54 and 55 of the Federal Rules of Criminal Procedure be, and they hereby are, amended effective October 1, 1972, to read as follows:

[For text of amendments, see pamphlet containing Federal Rules of Criminal Procedure]

2. That Rule 9(c) of the Federal Rules of Appellate Procedure be, and hereby is amended, effective October 1, 1972, to read as follows:

RULES OF APPELLATE PROCEDURE

*[See amendments made thereby under
the respective rules, post]*

3. That THE CHIEF JUSTICE be, and he hereby is, authorized to transmit to the Congress the foregoing amendments to Rules of Criminal and Appellate Procedure, in accordance with the provisions of Title 18, U.S.Code, §§ 3771 and 3772.

MR. JUSTICE DOUGLAS dissented to adoption of Rule 50(b) of the Federal Rules of Criminal Procedure.

ORDER OF APRIL 30, 1979

1. That the Federal Rules of Appellate Procedure be, and they hereby are, amended by including therein amendments to Rules 1(a), 3(c), (d) and (e), 4(a), 5(d), 6(d), 7, 10(b), 11(a), (b), (c) and (d), 12, 13(a), 24(b), 27(b), 28(g) and (j), 34(a) and (b), 35(b) and (c), 39(c) and (d), and 40 as hereinafter set forth:

*[See amendments made thereby under
the respective rules, post]*

2. That the foregoing amendments to the Federal Rules of Appellate Procedure shall take effect on August 1, 1979, and shall govern all appellate proceedings thereafter commenced and, insofar as just and practicable, all proceedings then pending.

3. That THE CHIEF JUSTICE be, and he hereby is, authorized to transmit to the Congress the foregoing amendments to the Federal Rules of Appellate Procedure in accordance with the provisions of Section 3772 of Title 18, United States Code, and Sections 2072 and 2075 of Title 28, United States Code.

ORDER OF MARCH 10, 1986

1. That the Federal Rules of Appellate Procedure be, and they hereby are, amended by including therein new Appellate Rules 3.1, 5.1 and 15.1 and amendments to Appellate Rules 3(d), 8(b), 10(b) and (c), 11(b), 12(a), 19, 23(b) and (c), 24(a), 25(a) and (b), 26(a) and (c), 28(c) and (j), 30(a), (b) and (c), 31(a) and (c), 34(a) and (e), 39(c) and (d), 43(a) and (c), 45(a), (b), and (d), and 46(a) and (b), as hereinafter set forth:

*[See amendments made thereby under
the respective rules, post]*

2. That the foregoing additions to and changes in the Federal Rules of Appellate Procedure, shall take effect on July 1, 1986 and shall govern all proceedings in appellate actions thereafter commenced and, insofar as just and practicable, all proceedings in appellate actions then pending.

3. That THE CHIEF JUSTICE be, and he hereby is, authorized to transmit to the Congress the foregoing additions to and changes in the rules of appellate procedure in accordance with the provisions of Section 3772 of Title 18 and Section 2072 of Title 28, United States Code.

ORDER OF APRIL 25, 1989

1. That the Federal Rules of Appellate Procedure be, and they hereby are, amended by including therein amendments to Appellate Rules 1(a), 3(a), 26(a), 27(a), 28(g) and new Rules 6 and 26.1, and a new Form 5 as hereinafter set forth:

*[See amendments made thereby under
the respective rules, post]*

2. That the foregoing additions to and changes in the Federal Rules of Appellate Procedure, shall take effect on December 1, 1989 and shall govern all proceedings in appellate actions thereafter commenced and, insofar as just and practicable, all proceedings in appellate actions then pending.

3. That THE CHIEF JUSTICE be, and he hereby is, authorized to transmit to the Congress the foregoing additions to and changes in the rules of appellate procedure in accordance with the provisions of Section 2072 of Title 28, United States Code.

ORDER OF APRIL 30, 1991

1. That the Federal Rules of Appellate Procedure be, and they hereby are, amended by including therein amendments to Appellate Rules 4(a), 6, 10(c), 25(a), 26(a), 26.1, 28(a), (b), and (h), 30(b), and 34(d).

*[See amendments made thereby under
the respective rules, post]*

2. That the foregoing amendments to the Federal Rules of Appellate Procedure shall take effect on December 1, 1991, and shall govern all proceedings in appellate cases thereafter commenced and, insofar as just and practicable, all proceedings in appellate cases then pending.

3. That THE CHIEF JUSTICE be, and he hereby is, authorized to transmit to the Congress the foregoing amendments to the Federal Rules of Appellate Procedure in accordance with the provisions of Section 2072 of Title 28, United States Code.

ORDER OF APRIL 22, 1993

1. That the Federal Rules of Appellate Procedure be, and they hereby are, amended by including therein amendments to Appellate Rules 3, 3.1, 4, 5.1, 6, 10, 12, 15, 25, 28, and 34, and to Forms 1, 2, and 3.

*[See amendments made thereby under the
respective rules and forms, post.]*

2. That the foregoing amendments to the Federal Rules of Appellate Procedure shall take effect on December 1, 1993, and shall govern all proceedings in appellate cases thereafter commenced and, insofar as just and practicable, all proceedings in appellate cases then pending.

3. That THE CHIEF JUSTICE be, and he hereby is, authorized to transmit to the Congress the foregoing amendments to the Federal Rules of Appellate Procedure in accordance with the provisions of Section 2072 of Title 28, United States Code.

ORDER OF APRIL 29, 1994

1. That the Federal Rules of Appellate Procedure be, and they hereby are, amended by including therein amendments to Appellate Rules 1, 3, 5, 5.1, 9, 13, 21, 25, 26.1, 27, 28, 30, 31, 33, 35, 38, 40, 41, and 48.

*[See amendments made hereby under
respective rules, post]*

2. That the foregoing amendments to the Federal Rules of Appellate Procedure shall take effect on December 1, 1994, and shall govern all proceedings in appellate cases

thereafter commenced and, insofar as just and practicable, all proceedings in appellate cases then pending.

3. That THE CHIEF JUSTICE be, and he hereby is, authorized to transmit to the Congress the foregoing amendments to the Federal Rules of Appellate Procedure in accordance with the provisions of Section 2072 of Title 28, United States Code.

ORDER OF APRIL 27, 1995

1. That the Federal Rules of Appellate Procedure be, and they hereby are, amended by including therein amendments to Appellate Rules 4, 8, 10, and 47.

[See amendments made thereby under the respective rules, post.]

2. That the foregoing amendments to the Federal Rules of Appellate Procedure shall take effect on December 1, 1995, and shall govern all proceedings in appellate cases thereafter commenced and, insofar as just and practicable, all proceedings in appellate cases then pending.

3. That THE CHIEF JUSTICE be, and he hereby is, authorized to transmit to the Congress the foregoing amendments to the Federal Rules of Appellate Procedure in accordance with the provisions of Section 2072 of Title 28, United States Code.

ORDER OF APRIL 23, 1996

1. That the Federal Rules of Appellate Procedure be, and they hereby are, amended by including therein amendments to Appellate Rules 21, 25, and 26.

[See amendments made thereby under respective rules, post]

2. That the foregoing amendments to the Federal Rules of Appellate Procedure shall take effect on December 1, 1996, and shall govern all proceedings in appellate cases thereafter commenced and, insofar as just and practicable, all proceedings in appellate cases then pending.

3. That THE CHIEF JUSTICE be, and hereby is, authorized to transmit to the Congress the foregoing amendments to the Federal Rules of Appellate Procedure in accordance with the provisions of Section 2072 of Title 28, United States Code.

ORDER OF APRIL 24, 1998

1. That the Federal Rules of Appellate Procedure be, and they hereby are, amended by including therein amendments to Appellate Rules 1–48 and to Form 4.

[See amendments made thereby under respective rules, post]

2. That the foregoing amendments to the Federal Rules of Appellate Procedure shall take effect on December 1, 1998, and shall govern in all proceedings thereafter commenced and, insofar as just and practicable, all proceedings then pending.

3. That THE CHIEF JUSTICE be, and hereby is, authorized to transmit to the Congress the foregoing amendments to the Federal Rules of Appellate Procedure in accordance with the provisions of Section 2072 of Title 28, United States Code.

ORDER OF APRIL 29, 2002

1. That the Federal Rules of Appellate Procedure be, and they hereby are, amended by including therein amendments to Appellate Rules 1, 4, 5, 21, 24, 25, 26, 26.1, 27, 28, 31, 32, 36, 41, 44, and 45 and new Form 6.

[See amendments made thereby under respective rules and forms, post]

2. That the foregoing amendments to the Federal Rules of Appellate Procedure shall take effect on December 1, 2002, and shall govern in all proceedings in appellate cases thereafter commenced and, insofar as just and practicable, all proceedings then pending.

3. That THE CHIEF JUSTICE be, and hereby is, authorized to transmit to the Congress the foregoing amendments to the Federal Rules of Appellate Procedure in accordance with the provisions of Section 2072 of Title 28, United States Code.

ORDER OF MARCH 27, 2003

1. That Forms 1, 2, 3, and 5 in the Appendix to the Federal Rules of Appellate Procedure be, and they hereby are, amended by replacing all references to "19___" with references to "20___."

[See amendments made thereby under respective forms, post]

2. That the foregoing amendments to the forms in the Appendix to the Federal Rules of Appellate Procedure shall take effect on December 1, 2003, and shall govern in all proceedings in appellate cases thereafter commenced and, insofar as just and practicable, all proceedings then pending.

3. That THE CHIEF JUSTICE be, and hereby is, authorized to transmit to the Congress the foregoing amendments to the Federal Rules of Appellate Procedure in accordance with the provisions of Section 2072 of Title 28, United States Code.

ORDER OF APRIL 25, 2005

1. That the Federal Rules of Appellate Procedure be, and they hereby are, amended by including therein amendments to Appellate Rules 4, 26, 27, 28, 32, 34, 35, 45, and new Rule 28.1.

[See amendments made thereby under respective rules, post]

2. That the foregoing amendments to the Federal Rules of Appellate Procedure shall take effect on December 1, 2005, and shall govern in all proceedings thereafter commenced and, insofar as just and practicable, all proceedings then pending.

3. That THE CHIEF JUSTICE be, and hereby is, authorized to transmit to the Congress the foregoing amendments to the Federal Rules of Appellate Procedure in accordance with the provisions of Section 2072 of Title 28, United States Code.

ORDER OF APRIL 12, 2006

1. That the Federal Rules of Appellate Procedure be, and they hereby are, amended by including therein an amendment to Appellate Rule 25 and a new Rule 32.1.

[See amendments made thereby under respective rules, post]

2. That the foregoing amendment and new rule shall take effect on December 1, 2006, and shall govern in all proceedings thereafter commenced and, insofar as just and practicable, all proceedings then pending.

3. That the CHIEF JUSTICE be, and hereby is, authorized to transmit to the Congress the foregoing amendments to the Federal Rules of Appellate Procedure in accordance with the provisions of Section 2072 of Title 28, United States Code.

ORDER OF APRIL 30, 2007

1. That the Federal Rules of Appellate Procedure be, and they hereby are, amended by including therein an amendment to Appellate Rule 25.

[See amendments made thereby under respective rules, post]

2. That the foregoing amendment to the Federal Rules of Appellate Procedure shall take effect on December 1, 2007, and shall govern in all proceedings thereafter commenced and, insofar as just and practicable, all proceedings then pending.

3. That the CHIEF JUSTICE be, and hereby is, authorized to transmit to the Congress the foregoing amendment to the Federal Rules of Appellate Procedure in accordance with the provisions of Section 2072 of Title 28, United States Code.

HISTORICAL NOTES

Effective and Applicability Provisions; Application; Transmission to Congress

The Federal Rules of Appellate Procedure were adopted by order of the Supreme Court on Dec. 4, 1967, transmitted to Congress by the Chief Justice on Jan. 15, 1968, and became effective on July 1, 1968.

The Rules have been amended Mar. 30, 1970, eff. July 1, 1970; Mar. 1, 1971, eff. July 1, 1971; Apr. 24, 1972, eff. Oct. 1, 1972; Apr. 30, 1979, eff. Aug. 1, 1979; Oct. 12, 1984, Pub.L. 98–473, Title II, § 210, 98 Stat. 1987; Mar. 10, 1986, eff. July 1, 1986; Nov. 18, 1988, Pub.L. 100–690, Title VII, § 7111, 102 Stat. 4419; Apr. 25, 1989, eff. Dec. 1, 1989; Apr. 30, 1991, eff. Dec. 1, 1991; Apr. 22, 1993, eff. Dec. 1, 1993; Apr. 29, 1994, eff. Dec. 1, 1994; Apr. 27, 1995, eff. Dec. 1, 1995; Apr. 23, 1996, eff. Dec. 1, 1996; Apr. 24, 1998, eff. Dec. 1, 1998; Apr. 29, 2002, eff. Dec. 1, 2002; Mar. 27, 2003, eff. Dec. 1, 2003; Apr. 25, 2005, eff. Dec. 1, 2005; Apr. 12, 2006, eff. Dec. 1, 2006.

TITLE I. APPLICABILITY OF RULES

Rule 1. Scope of Rules; Title

(a) Scope of Rules.

(1) These rules govern procedure in the United States courts of appeals.

(2) When these rules provide for filing a motion or other document in the district court, the procedure must comply with the practice of the district court.

(b) [Abrogated]

(c) Title. These rules are to be known as the Federal Rules of Appellate Procedure.

(As amended Apr. 30, 1979, eff. Aug. 1, 1979; Apr. 25, 1989, eff. Dec. 1, 1989; Apr. 29, 1994, eff. Dec. 1, 1994; Apr. 24, 1998, eff. Dec. 1, 1998; Apr. 29, 2002, eff. Dec. 1, 2002.)

1967 Adoption

These rules are drawn under the authority of 28 U.S.C. § 2072 as amended by the Act of November 6, 1966, 80 Stat. 1323 (1 U.S.Code Cong. & Ad.News, p. 1546 (1966)) (Rules of Civil Procedure); 28 U.S.C. § 2075 (Bankruptcy Rules); and 18 U.S.C. §§ 3771 [§ 3771 of Title 18, Crimes and Criminal Procedure] (Procedure to and including verdict) and 3772 [§ 3772 of Title 18] (Procedure after verdict). Those statutes combine to give to the Supreme Court power to make rules of practice and procedure for all cases within the jurisdiction of the courts of appeals. By the terms of the statutes, after the rules have taken effect all laws in conflict with them are of no further force or effect. Practice and procedure in the eleven courts of appeals are now regulated by rules promulgated by each court under the authority of 28 U.S.C. § 2071. Rule 47 expressly authorizes the courts of appeals to make rules of practice not inconsistent with these rules.

As indicated by the titles under which they are found, the following rules are of special application: Rules 3 through 12 apply to appeals from judgments and orders of the district courts; Rules 13 and 14 apply to appeals from decisions of the Tax Court (Rule 13 establishes an appeal as the mode of review of decisions of the Tax Court in place of the present petition for review); Rules 15 through 20 apply to proceedings for review or enforcement of orders of administrative agencies, boards, commissions and officers. Rules 22 through 24 regulate habeas corpus proceedings and appeals in forma pauperis. All other rules apply to all proceedings in the courts of appeals.

1979 Amendment

The Federal Rules of Appellate Procedure were designed as an integrated set of rules to be followed in appeals to the courts of appeals, covering all steps in the appellate process, whether they take place in the district court or in the court of appeals, and with their adoption Rules 72 to 76 of the F.R.C.P. [rules 72 to 76, Federal Rules of Civil Procedure] were abrogated. In some instances, however, the F.R.A.P. provide that a motion or application for relief may, or must, be made in the district court. See Rules 4(a), 10(b) and 24. The proposed amendment would make it clear that when this is so the motion or application is to be made in the form and manner prescribed by the F.R.C.P. or F.R.Cr.P. [Federal Rules Criminal Procedure] and local rules relating to the form and presentation of motions and is not governed by

Rule 27 of the F.R.A.P. See Rule 7(b) of the F.R.C.P. [rule 7(b), Federal Rules of Civil Procedure] and Rule 47 of the F.R.Cr.P. [rule 47, Federal Rules of Criminal Procedure].

1989 Amendment

The amendment is technical. No substantive change is intended.

1994 Amendment

Subdivision (c). A new subdivision is added to the rule. The text of new subdivision (c) has been moved from Rule 48 to Rule 1 to allow the addition of new rules at the end of the existing set of appellate rules without burying the title provision among other rules. In a similar fashion the Bankruptcy Rules combine the provisions governing the scope of the rules and the title in the first rule.

1998 Amendments

The language and organization of the rule are amended to make the rule more easily understood. In addition to changes made to improve the understanding, the Advisory Committee has changed language to make style and terminology consistent throughout the appellate rules. These changes are intended to be stylistic only. The Advisory Committee recommends deleting the language in subdivision (a) that describes the different types of proceedings that may be brought in a court of appeals. The Advisory Committee believes that the language is unnecessary and that it s omission does not work any substantive change.

2002 Amendments

Subdivision (b). Two recent enactments make it likely that, in the future, one or more of the Federal Rules of Appellate Procedure ("FRAP") will extend or limit the jurisdiction of the courts of appeals. In 1990, Congress amended the Rules Enabling Act to give the Supreme Court authority to use the federal rules of practice and procedure to define when a ruling of a district court is final for purposes of 28 U.S.C. § 1291. See 28 U.S.C. § 2072(c). In 1992, Congress amended 28 U.S.C. § 1292 to give the Supreme Court authority to use the federal rules of practice and procedure to provide for appeals of interlocutory decisions that are not already authorized by 28 U.S.C. § 1292. See 28 U.S.C. § 1292(e). Both § 1291 and § 1292 are unquestionably jurisdictional statutes, and thus, as soon as FRAP is amended to define finality for purposes of the former or to authorize interlocutory appeals not provided for by the latter, FRAP will "extend or limit the jurisdiction of the courts of appeals," and subdivision (b) will become obsolete. For that reason, subdivision (b) has been abrogated.

Changes Made After Publication and Comments No changes were made to the text of the proposed amendment or to the Committee Note.

HISTORICAL NOTES

Pending Actions

Amendments of Supreme Court to Federal Rules of Appellate Procedure effective December 1, 1993, applicable, insofar as just and practicable, in all proceedings then pending, pursuant to the Order of April 22, 1993.

Rule 2. Suspension of Rules

On its own or a party's motion, a court of appeals may—to expedite its decision or for other good cause—suspend any provision of these rules in a particular case and order proceedings as it directs, except as otherwise provided in Rule 26(b).
(As amended Apr. 24, 1998, eff. Dec. 1, 1998.)

ADVISORY COMMITTEE NOTES

1967 Adoption

The primary purpose of this rule is to make clear the power of the courts of appeals to expedite the determination of cases of pressing concern to the public or to the litigants by prescribing a time schedule other than that provided by the rules. The rule also contains a general authorization to the courts to relieve litigants of the consequences of default where manifest injustice would otherwise result. Rule 26(b) prohibits a court of appeals from extending the time for taking appeal or seeking review.

1998 Amendments

The language of the rule is amended to make the rule more easily understood. In addition to changes made to improve the understanding, the Advisory Committee has changed the language to make style and terminology consistent throughout the appellate rules. These changes are intended to by stylistic only.

TITLE II. APPEAL FROM A JUDGMENT OR ORDER OF A DISTRICT COURT

Rule 3. Appeal as of Right—How Taken

(a) Filing the Notice of Appeal.

(1) An appeal permitted by law as of right from a district court to a court of appeals may be taken only by filing a notice of appeal with the district clerk within the time allowed by Rule 4. At the time of filing, the appellant must furnish the clerk with enough copies of the notice to enable the clerk to comply with Rule 3(d).

(2) An appellant's failure to take any step other than the timely filing of a notice of appeal does not affect the validity of the appeal, but is ground only for the court of appeals to act as it considers appropriate, including dismissing the appeal.

(3) An appeal from a judgment by a magistrate judge in a civil case is taken in the same way as an appeal from any other district court judgment.

(4) An appeal by permission under 28 U.S.C. § 1292(b) or an appeal in a bankruptcy case may be taken only in the manner prescribed by Rules 5 and 6, respectively.

(b) Joint or Consolidated Appeals.

(1) When two or more parties are entitled to appeal from a district-court judgment or order, and their interests make joinder practicable, they may file a joint notice of appeal. They may then proceed on appeal as a single appellant.

(2) When the parties have filed separate timely notices of appeal, the appeals may be joined or consolidated by the court of appeals.

(c) Contents of the Notice of Appeal.

(1) The notice of appeal must:

(A) specify the party or parties taking the appeal by naming each one in the caption or body of the notice, but an attorney representing more than one party may describe those parties with such terms as "all plaintiffs," "the defendants," "the plaintiffs A, B, et al.," or "all defendants except X";

(B) designate the judgment, order, or part thereof being appealed; and

(C) name the court to which the appeal is taken.

(2) A pro se notice of appeal is considered filed on behalf of the signer and the signer's spouse and minor children (if they are parties), unless the notice clearly indicates otherwise.

(3) In a class action, whether or not the class has been certified, the notice of appeal is sufficient if it names one person qualified to bring the appeal as representative of the class.

(4) An appeal must not be dismissed for informality of form or title of the notice of appeal, or for failure to name a party whose intent to appeal is otherwise clear from the notice.

(5) Form 1 in the Appendix of Forms is a suggested form of a notice of appeal.

(d) Serving the Notice of Appeal.

(1) The district clerk must serve notice of the filing of a notice of appeal by mailing a copy to each party's counsel of record—excluding the appellant's—or, if a party is proceeding pro se, to the party's last known address. When a defendant in a criminal case appeals, the clerk must also serve a copy of the notice of appeal on the defendant, either by personal service or by mail addressed to the defendant. The clerk must promptly send a copy of the notice of appeal and of the docket entries—and any later docket entries—to the clerk of the court of appeals named in the notice. The district clerk must note, on each copy, the date when the notice of appeal was filed.

(2) If an inmate confined in an institution files a notice of appeal in the manner provided by Rule 4(c), the district clerk must also note the date when the clerk docketed the notice.

(3) The district clerk's failure to serve notice does not affect the validity of the appeal. The clerk must note on the docket the names of the parties to whom the clerk mails copies, with the date of mailing. Service is sufficient despite the death of a party or the party's counsel.

(e) Payment of Fees. Upon filing a notice of appeal, the appellant must pay the district clerk all required fees. The district clerk receives the appellate docket fee on behalf of the court of appeals. (As amended Apr. 30, 1979, eff. Aug. 1, 1979; Mar. 10, 1986, eff. July 1, 1986; Apr. 25, 1989, eff. Dec. 1, 1989; Apr. 22, 1993, eff. Dec. 1, 1993; Apr. 29, 1994, eff. Dec. 1, 1994; Apr. 24, 1998, eff. Dec. 1, 1998.)

ADVISORY COMMITTEE NOTES

1967 Adoption

General Note. Rule 3 and Rule 4 combine to require that a notice of appeal be filed with the clerk of the district court within the time prescribed for taking an appeal. Because the timely filing of a notice of appeal is "mandatory and jurisdictional," *United States v. Robinson*, 361 U.S. 220, 224, 80 S.Ct. 282, 4 L.Ed.2d 259 (1960), compliance with the provisions of those rules is of the utmost importance. But the proposed rules merely restate, in modified form, provisions now found in the civil and criminal rules (FRCP 5(e), 73 [Rules 5(e) and 73, Federal Rules of Civil Procedure]; FRCrP 37 [rule 37, Federal Rules of Criminal Procedure], and decisions under the present rules which dispense with literal compliance in cases in which it cannot fairly be exacted should control interpretation of these rules. Illustrative decisions are: *Fallen v. United States*, 378 U.S. 139, 84 S.Ct. 1689, 12 L.Ed.2d 760 (1964) (notice of appeal by a prisoner, in the form of a letter delivered, well within the time fixed for appeal, to prison authorities for mailing to the clerk of the district court held timely filed notwithstanding that it was received by the clerk after expiration of the time for appeal; the appellant "did all he could" to effect timely filing); *Richey v. Wilkins*, 335 F.2d 1 (2d Cir. 1964) (notice filed in the court of appeals by a prisoner without assistance of counsel held sufficient; *Halfen v. United States*, 324 F.2d 52 (10th Cir. 1963) (notice mailed to district judge in time to have been received by him in normal course held sufficient); *Riffle v. United States*, 299 F.2d 802 (5th Cir. 1962) (letter of prisoner to judge of court of appeals held sufficient). Earlier cases evidencing "a liberal view of papers filed by indigent and incarcerated defendants" are listed in *Coppedge v. United States*, 369 U.S. 438, 442, n. 5, 82 S.Ct. 917, 8 L.Ed.2d 21 (1962).

Subdivision (a). The substance of this subdivision is derived from FRCP 73(a) [rule 73(a), Federal Rules of Civil Procedure] and FRCrP 37(a)(1) [rule 37(a)(1), Federal Rules of Criminal Procedure]. The proposed rule follows those rules in requiring nothing other than the filing of a notice of appeal in the district court for the perfection of the appeal. The petition for allowance (except for appeals governed by Rules 5 and 6), citations, assignments of error, summons and severance—all specifically abolished by earlier modern

rules—are assumed to be sufficiently obsolete as no longer to require pointed abolition.

Subdivision (b). The first sentence is derived from FRCP 74 [rule 74, Federal Rules of Civil Procedure]. The second sentence is added to encourage consolidation of appeals whenever feasible.

Subdivision (c). This subdivision is identical with corresponding provisions in FRCP 73(b) [rule 73(b), Federal Rules of Civil Procedure] and FRCrP 37(a)(1) [rule 37(a)(1), Federal Rules of Criminal Procedure].

Subdivision (d). This subdivision is derived from FRCP 73(b) [rule 73(b), Federal Rules of Civil Procedure] and FRCrP 37(a)(1) [rule 37(a)(1), Federal Rules of Criminal Procedure]. The duty of the clerk to forward a copy of the notice of appeal and of the docket entries to the court of appeals in a criminal case is extended to habeas corpus and 28 U.S.C. § 2255 proceedings.

1979 Amendments

Subdivision (c). The proposed amendment would add the last sentence. Because of the fact that the timely filing of the notice of appeal has been characterized as jurisdictional (see, e.g., Brainerd v. Real (C.A. 7th, 1974) 498 F.2d 901, in which the filing of a notice of appeal one day late was fatal), it is important that the right to appeal not be lost by mistakes of mere form. In a number of decided cases it has been held that so long as the function of notice is met by the filing of a paper indicating an intention to appeal, the substance of the rule has been complied with. See, e.g., Cobb v. Lewis (C.A. 5th, 1974), 488 F.2d 41; *Holley v. Capps* (C.A. 5th, 1972) 468 F.2d 1366. The proposed amendment would give recognition to this practice.

When a notice of appeal is filed, the clerk should ascertain whether any judgment designated therein has been entered in compliance with Rules 58 and 79(a) of the F.R.C.P. [rules 58 and 79(a), Federal Rules of Civil Procedure]. See Note to Rule 4(a)(6), *infra*.

Subdivision (d). The proposed amendment would extend to civil cases the present provision applicable to criminal cases, habeas corpus cases, and proceedings under 28 U.S.C. § 2255, requiring the clerk of the district court to transmit to the clerk of the court of appeals a copy of the notice of appeal and of the docket entries, which should include reference to compliance with the requirements for payment of fees. See Note to (e), *infra*.

This requirement is the initial step in proposed changes in the rules to place in the court of appeals an increased practical control over the early steps in the appeal.

Subdivision (e). Proposed new Rule 3(e) represents the second step in shifting to the court of appeals the control of the early stages of an appeal. See Note to Rule 3(d) above. Under the present rules the payment of the fee prescribed by 28 U.S.C. 1917 is not covered. Under the statute, however, this fee is paid to the clerk of the district court at the time the notice of appeal is filed. Under present Rule 12, the "docket fee" fixed by the Judicial Conference of the United States under 28 U.S.C. § 1913 must be paid to the clerk of the court of appeals within the time fixed for transmission of the record, ". . . and the clerk shall thereupon enter the appeal upon the docket."

Under the proposed new Rule 3(e) both fees would be paid to the clerk of the district court at the time the notice of appeal is filed, the clerk of the district court receiving the docket fee on behalf of the court of appeals.

In view of the provision in Rule 3(a) that "[f]ailure of an appellant to take any step other than the timely filing of a notice of appeal does not affect the validity of the appeal, but is ground only for such action as the court of appeals deems appropriate, which may include dismissal of the appeal," the case law indicates that the failure to prepay the statutory filing fee does not constitute a jurisdictional defect. See *Parissi v. Telechron*, 349 U.S. 46 (1955); *Gould v. Members of N.J. Division of Water Policy & Supply*, 555 F.2d 340 (3d Cir. 1977). Similarly, under present Rule 3(e), failure to pay the docket fee within the time prescribed may be excused by the court of appeals. See, e.g., *Walker v. Mathews*, 546 F.2d 814 (9th Cir. 1976). Proposed new Rule 3(e) adopts the view of these cases, requiring that both fees be paid at the time the notice of appeal is filed, but subject to the provisions of Rule 26(b) preserving the authority of the court of appeals to permit late payment.

1986 Amendments

The amendments to Rule 3(d) are technical. No substantive change is intended.

1989 Amendments

The amendment is technical. No substantive change is intended.

1993 Amendments

Note to subdivision (c). The amendment is intended to reduce the amount of satellite litigation spawned by the Supreme Court's decision in Torres v. Oakland Scavenger Co., 487 U.S. 312 (1988). In Torres the Supreme Court held that the language in Rule 3(c) requiring a notice of appeal to "specify the party or parties taking the appeal" is a jurisdictional requirement and that naming the first named party and adding "et al.," without any further specificity is insufficient to identify the appellants. Since the Torres decision, there has been a great deal of litigation regarding whether a notice of appeal that contains some indication of the appellants' identities but does not name the appellants is sufficiently specific.

The amendment states a general rule that specifying the parties should be done by naming them. Naming an appellant in an otherwise timely and proper notice of appeal ensures that the appellant has perfected an appeal. However, in order to prevent the loss of a right to appeal through inadvertent omission of a party's name or continued use of such terms as "et al.," which are sufficient in all district court filings after the complaint, the amendment allows an attorney representing more than one party the flexibility to indicate which parties are appealing without naming them individually. The test established by the rule for determining whether such designations are sufficient is whether it is objectively clear that a party intended to appeal. A notice of appeal filed by a party proceeding pro se is filed on behalf of the party signing the notice and the signer's spouse and minor children, if they are parties, unless the notice clearly indicates a contrary intent.

In class actions, naming each member of a class as an appellant may be extraordinarily burdensome or even impos-

sible. In class actions if class certification has been denied, named plaintiffs may appeal the order denying the class certification on their own behalf and on behalf of putative class members, *United States Parole Comm'n v. Geraghty,* 445 U.S. 388 (1980); or if the named plaintiffs choose not to appeal the order denying the class certification, putative class members may appeal, *United Airlines, Inc. v. Mc-Donald,* 432 U.S. 385 (1977). If no class has been certified, naming each of the putative class members as an appellant would often be impossible. Therefore the amendment provides that in class actions, whether or not the class has been certified, it is sufficient for the notice to name one person qualified to bring the appeal as a representative of the class.

Finally, the rule makes it clear that dismissal of an appeal should not occur when it is otherwise clear from the notice that the party intended to appeal. If a court determines it is objectively clear that a party intended to appeal, there are neither administrative concerns nor fairness concerns that should prevent the appeal from going forward.

Note to subdivision (d). The amendment requires the district court clerk to send to the clerk of the court of appeals a copy of every docket entry in a case after the filing of a notice of appeal. This amendment accompanies the amendment to Rule 4(a)(4), which provides that when one of the posttrial motions enumerated in Rule 4(a)(4) is filed, a notice of appeal filed before the disposition of the motion becomes effective upon disposition of the motion. The court of appeals needs to be advised that the filing of a posttrial motion has suspended a notice of appeal. The court of appeals also needs to know when the district court has ruled on the motion. Sending copies of all docket entries after the filing of a notice of appeal should provide the courts of appeals with the necessary information.

1994 Amendments

Subdivision (a). The amendment requires a party filing a notice of appeal to provide the court with sufficient copies of the notice for service on all other parties.

1998 Amendments

The language and organization of the rule are amended to make the rule more easily understood. In addition to changes made to improve the understanding, the Advisory Committee has changed language to make style and terminology consistent throughout the appellate rules. These changes are generally intended to by stylistic only; in this rule, however, substantive changes are made in subdivisions (a), (b), and (d).

Subdivision (a). The provision in paragraph (a)(3) is transferred from former Rule 3.1(b). The Federal Courts Improvement Act of 1996, Pub.L. No. 104–317, repealed paragraphs (4) and (5) of 28 U.S.C. § 636(c). That statutory change made the continued separate existence of Rule 3.1 unnecessary. New paragraph (a)(3) of this rule simply makes it clear that an appeal from a judgment by a magistrate judge is taken in identical fashion to any other appeal from a district-court judgment.

Subdivision (b). A joint appeal is authorized only when two or more persons may appeal from a single judgment or order. A joint appeal is treated as a single appeal and the joint appellants file a single brief. Under existing Rule 3(b) parties decide whether to join their appeals. They may do so

by filing a joint notice of appeal or by joining their appeals after filing separate notices of appeal.

In consolidated appeals the separate appeals do not merge into one. The parties do not proceed as a single appellant. Under existing Rule 3(b) it is unclear whether appeals may be consolidated without court order if the parties stipulate to consolidation. The language resolves that ambiguity by requiring court action.

The language also requires court action to join appeals after separate notices of appeal have been filed.

Subdivision (d). Paragraph (d)(2) has been amended to require that when an inmate files a notice of appeal by depositing the notice in the institution's internal mail system, the clerk must note the docketing date—rather than the receipt date—on the notice of appeal before serving copies of it. This change conforms to a change in Rule 4(c). Rule 4(c) is amended to provide that when an inmate files the first notice of appeal in a civil case by depositing the notice in an institution's internal mail system, the time for filing a cross-appeal runs from the date the district court dockets the inmate's notice of appeal. Existing Rule 4(c) says that in such a case the time for filing a cross-appeal runs from the date the district court receives the inmate's notice of appeal. A court may "receive" a paper when its mail is delivered to it even if the mail is not processed for a day or two, making the date of receipt uncertain. "Docketing" is an easily identified event. The change is made to eliminate the uncertainty.

[Rule 3.1. Abrogated Apr. 24, 1998, eff. Dec. 1, 1998]

ADVISORY COMMITTEE NOTES

1998 Amendments

The Federal Courts Improvement Act of 1996, Pub.L. No. 104–317, repealed paragraphs (4) and (5) of 28 U.S.C. § 636(c). That statutory change means that when parties consent to trial before a magistrate judge, appeal lies directly, and as a matter of right, to the court of appeals under § 636(c)(3). The parties may not choose to appeal first to a district judge and thereafter seek discretionary review in the court of appeals.

As a result of the statutory amendments, subdivision (a) of Rule 3.1 is no longer necessary. Since Rule 3.1 existed primarily because of the provisions in subdivision (a), subdivision (b) has been moved to Rule 3(a)(3) and Rule 3.1 has been abrogated.

HISTORICAL NOTES

The abrogated rule provided that: "When the parties consent to a trial before a magistrate judge under 28 U.S.C. § 636(c)(1), any appeal from the judgment must be heard by the court of appeals in accordance with 28 U.S.C. § 636(c)(3), unless the parties consent to an appeal on the record to a district judge and thereafter, by petition only, to the court of appeals, in accordance with 28 U.S.C. § 636(c)(4). An appeal under 28 U.S.C. § 636(c)(3) must be taken in identical fashion as an appeal from any other judgment of the district court."

Rule 4. Appeal as of Right—When Taken
(a) Appeal in a Civil Case.

(1) Time for Filing a Notice of Appeal.

(A) In a civil case, except as provided in Rules 4(a)(1)(B), 4(a)(4), and 4(c), the notice of appeal required by Rule 3 must be filed with the district clerk within 30 days after the judgment or order appealed from is entered.

(B) When the United States or its officer or agency is a party, the notice of appeal may be filed by any party within 60 days after the judgment or order appealed from is entered.

(C) An appeal from an order granting or denying an application for a writ of error coram nobis is an appeal in a civil case for purposes of Rule 4(a).

(2) Filing Before Entry of Judgment. A notice of appeal filed after the court announces a decision or order—but before the entry of the judgment or order—is treated as filed on the date of and after the entry.

(3) Multiple Appeals. If one party timely files a notice of appeal, any other party may file a notice of appeal within 14 days after the date when the first notice was filed, or within the time otherwise prescribed by this Rule 4(a), whichever period ends later.

(4) Effect of a Motion on a Notice of Appeal.

(A) If a party timely files in the district court any of the following motions under the Federal Rules of Civil Procedure, the time to file an appeal runs for all parties from the entry of the order disposing of the last such remaining motion:

(i) for judgment under Rule 50(b);

(ii) to amend or make additional factual findings under Rule 52(b), whether or not granting the motion would alter the judgment;

(iii) for attorney's fees under Rule 54 if the district court extends the time to appeal under Rule 58;

(iv) to alter or amend the judgment under Rule 59;

(v) for a new trial under Rule 59; or

(vi) for relief under Rule 60 if the motion is filed no later than 10 days after the judgment is entered.

(B)(i) If a party files a notice of appeal after the court announces or enters a judgment—but before it disposes of any motion listed in Rule 4(a)(4)(A)—the notice becomes effective to appeal a judgment or order, in whole or in part, when the order disposing of the last such remaining motion is entered.

(ii) A party intending to challenge an order disposing of any motion listed in Rule 4(a)(4)(A), or a judgment altered or amended upon such a motion, must file a notice of appeal, or an amended notice of appeal—in compliance with Rule 3(c)—within the time prescribed by this Rule measured from the entry of the order disposing of the last such remaining motion.

(iii) No additional fee is required to file an amended notice.

(5) Motion for Extension of Time.

(A) The district court may extend the time to file a notice of appeal if:

(i) a party so moves no later than 30 days after the time prescribed by this Rule 4(a) expires; and

(ii) regardless of whether its motion is filed before or during the 30 days after the time prescribed by this Rule 4(a) expires, that party shows excusable neglect or good cause.

(B) A motion filed before the expiration of the time prescribed in Rule 4(a)(1) or (3) may be ex parte unless the court requires otherwise. If the motion is filed after the expiration of the prescribed time, notice must be given to the other parties in accordance with local rules.

(C) No extension under this Rule 4(a)(5) may exceed 30 days after the prescribed time or 10 days after the date when the order granting the motion is entered, whichever is later.

(6) Reopening the Time to File an Appeal. The district court may reopen the time to file an appeal for a period of 14 days after the date when its order to reopen is entered, but only if all the following conditions are satisfied:

(A) the court finds that the moving party did not receive notice under Federal Rule of Civil Procedure 77(d) of the entry of the judgment or order sought to be appealed within 21 days after entry;

(B) the motion is filed within 180 days after the judgment or order is entered or within 7 days after the moving party receives notice under Federal Rule of Civil Procedure 77(d) of the entry, whichever is earlier; and

(C) the court finds that no party would be prejudiced.

(7) Entry Defined.

(A) A judgment or order is entered for purposes of this Rule 4(a):

(i) if Federal Rule of Civil Procedure 58(a)(1) does not require a separate document, when the judgment or order is entered in the civil docket under Federal Rule of Civil Procedure 79(a); or

(ii) if Federal Rule of Civil Procedure 58(a)(1) requires a separate document, when the judgment or order is entered in the civil docket under Federal Rule of Civil Procedure 79(a) and when the earlier of these events occurs:

- the judgment or order is set forth on a separate document, or

- 150 days have run from entry of the judgment or order in the civil docket under Federal Rule of Civil Procedure 79(a).

(B) A failure to set forth a judgment or order on a separate document when required by Federal Rule of Civil Procedure 58(a)(1) does not affect the validity of an appeal from that judgment or order.

(b) Appeal in a Criminal Case.

(1) Time for Filing a Notice of Appeal.

(A) In a criminal case, a defendant's notice of appeal must be filed in the district court within 10 days after the later of:

(i) the entry of either the judgment or the order being appealed; or

(ii) the filing of the government's notice of appeal.

(B) When the government is entitled to appeal, its notice of appeal must be filed in the district court within 30 days after the later of:

(i) the entry of the judgment or order being appealed; or

(ii) the filing of a notice of appeal by any defendant.

(2) Filing Before Entry of Judgment. A notice of appeal filed after the court announces a decision, sentence, or order—but before the entry of the judgment or order—is treated as filed on the date of and after the entry.

(3) Effect of a Motion on a Notice of Appeal.

(A) If a defendant timely makes any of the following motions under the Federal Rules of Criminal Procedure, the notice of appeal from a judgment of conviction must be filed within 10 days after the entry of the order disposing of the last such remaining motion, or within 10 days after the entry of the judgment of conviction, whichever period ends later. This provision applies to a timely motion:

(i) for judgment of acquittal under Rule 29;

(ii) for a new trial under Rule 33, but if based on newly discovered evidence, only if the motion is made no later than 10 days after the entry of the judgment; or

(iii) for arrest of judgment under Rule 34.

(B) A notice of appeal filed after the court announces a decision, sentence, or order—but before it disposes of any of the motions referred to in Rule 4(b)(3)(A)—becomes effective upon the later of the following:

(i) the entry of the order disposing of the last such remaining motion; or

(ii) the entry of the judgment of conviction.

(C) A valid notice of appeal is effective—without amendment—to appeal from an order disposing of any of the motions referred to in Rule 4(b)(3)(A).

(4) Motion for Extension of Time. Upon a finding of excusable neglect or good cause, the district court may—before or after the time has expired, with or without motion and notice—extend the time to file a notice of appeal for a period not to exceed 30 days from the expiration of the time otherwise prescribed by this Rule 4(b).

(5) Jurisdiction. The filing of a notice of appeal under this Rule 4(b) does not divest a district court of jurisdiction to correct a sentence under Federal Rule of Criminal Procedure 35(a), nor does the filing of a motion under 35(a) affect the validity of a notice of appeal filed before entry of the order disposing of the motion. The filing of a motion under Federal Rule of Criminal Procedure 35(a) does not suspend the time for filing a notice of appeal from a judgment of conviction.

(6) Entry Defined. A judgment or order is entered for purposes of this Rule 4(b) when it is entered on the criminal docket.

(c) Appeal by an Inmate Confined in an Institution.

(1) If an inmate confined in an institution files a notice of appeal in either a civil or a criminal case, the notice is timely if it is deposited in the institution's internal mail system on or before the last day for filing. If an institution has a system designed for legal mail, the inmate must use that system to receive the benefit of this rule. Timely filing may be shown by a declaration in compliance with 28 U.S.C. § 1746 or by a notarized statement, either of which must set forth the date of deposit and state that first-class postage has been prepaid.

(2) If an inmate files the first notice of appeal in a civil case under this Rule 4(c), the 14–day period provided in Rule 4(a)(3) for another party to file a notice of appeal runs from the date when the district court dockets the first notice.

(3) When a defendant in a criminal case files a notice of appeal under this Rule 4(c), the 30–day period for the government to file its notice of appeal runs from the entry of the judgment or order appealed from or from the district court's docketing of the defendant's notice of appeal, whichever is later.

(d) Mistaken Filing in the Court of Appeals. If a notice of appeal in either a civil or a criminal case is mistakenly filed in the court of appeals, the clerk of that court must note on the notice the date when it was received and send it to the district clerk. The

notice is then considered filed in the district court on the date so noted.

(As amended Apr. 30, 1979, eff. Aug. 1, 1979; Nov. 18, 1988, Pub.L. 100–690, Title VII, § 7111, 102 Stat. 4419; Apr. 30, 1991, eff. Dec. 1, 1991; Apr. 22, 1993, eff. Dec. 1, 1993; Apr. 27, 1995, eff. Dec. 1, 1995; Apr. 24, 1998, eff. Dec. 1, 1998; Apr. 29, 2002, eff. Dec. 1, 2002; Apr. 25, 2005, eff. Dec. 1, 2005.)

ADVISORY COMMITTEE NOTES

1967 Adoption

Subdivision (a). This subdivision is derived from FRCP 73(a) [rule 73(a), Federal Rules of Civil Procedure, this title] without any change of substance. The requirement that a request for an extension of time for filing the notice of appeal made after expiration of the time be made by motion and on notice codifies the result reached under the present provisions of FRCP 73(a) and 6(b) [rules 73(a) and 6(b), Federal Rules of Civil Procedure]. *North Umberland Mining Co. v. Standard Accident Ins. Co.*, 193 F.2d 951 (9th Cir., 1952); *Cohen v. Plateau Natural Gas Co.*, 303 F.2d 273 (10th Cir., 1962); *Plant Economy, Inc. v. Mirror Insulation Co.*, 308 F.2d 275 (3d Cir., 1962).

Since this subdivision governs appeals in all civil cases, it supersedes the provisions of § 25 of the Bankruptcy Act (11 U.S.C. § 48). Except in cases to which the United States or an officer or agency thereof is a party, the change is a minor one, since a successful litigant in a bankruptcy proceeding may, under § 25, oblige an aggrieved party to appeal within 30 days after entry of judgment—the time fixed by this subdivision in cases involving private parties only—by serving him with notice of entry on the day thereof, and by the terms of § 25 and aggrieved party must in any event appeal within 40 days after entry of judgment. No reason appears why the time for appeal in bankruptcy should not be the same as that in civil cases generally. Furthermore, § 25 is a potential trap for the uninitiated. The time for appeal which it provides is not applicable to all appeals which may fairly be termed appeals in bankruptcy. Section 25 governs only those cause referred to in § 24 as "proceedings in bankruptcy" and "controversies arising in proceedings in bankruptcy." *Lowenstein v. Reikes*, 54 F.2d 481 (2d Cir., 1931), cert. den., 285 U.S. 539, 52 S.Ct. 311, 76 L.Ed. 932 (1932). The distinction between such cases and other cases which arise out of bankruptcy is often difficult to determine. See 2 Moore's Collier on Bankruptcy ¶24.12 through ¶24.36 (1962). As a result it is not always clear whether an appeal is governed by § 25 or by FRCP 73(a) [rule 73(a), Federal Rules of Civil Procedure, this title], which is applicable to such appeals in bankruptcy as are not governed by § 25.

In view of the unification of the civil and admiralty procedure accomplished by the amendments of the Federal Rules of Civil Procedure effective July 1, 1966, this subdivision governs appeals in those civil actions which involve admiralty or maritime claims and which prior to that date were known as suits in admiralty.

The only other change possibly effected by this subdivision is in the time for appeal from a decision of a district court on a petition for impeachment of an award of a board of arbitration under the Act of May 20, 1926, c. 347, § 9 (44 Stat. 585), 45 U.S.C. § 159. The act provides that a notice of appeal from such a decision shall be filed within 10 days of the decision. This singular provision was apparently repealed by the enactment in 1948 of 28 U.S.C. § 2107, which fixed 30 days from the date of entry of judgment as the time for appeal in all actions a civil nature except actions in admiralty or bankruptcy matters or those in which the United States is a party. But it was not expressly repealed, and its status is in doubt. See 7 Moore's Federal Practice ¶73.09[2] (1966). The doubt should be resolved, and no reason appears why appeals in such cases should not be taken within the time provided for civil cases generally.

Subdivision (b). This subdivision is derived from FRCrP 37(a)(2) [rule 37(a)(2), Federal Rules of Criminal Procedure] without change of substance.

1979 Amendment

Subdivision (a)(1). The words "(including a civil action which involves an admiralty or maritime claim and a proceeding in bankruptcy or a controversy arising therein)," which appear in the present rule are struck out as unnecessary and perhaps misleading in suggesting that there may be other categories that are not either civil or criminal within the meaning of Rule 4(a) and (b).

The phrases "within 30 days of such entry" and "within 60 days of such entry" have been changed to read "after" instead of "or." The change is for clarity only, since the word "of" in the present rule appears to be used to mean "after." Since the proposed amended rule deals directly with the premature filing of a notice of appeal, it was thought useful to emphasize the fact that except as provided, the period during which a notice of appeal may be filed is the 30 days, or 60 days as the case may be, following the entry of the judgment or order appealed from. See Notes to Rule 4(a)(2) and (4), below.

Subdivision (a)(2). The proposed amendment to Rule 4(a)(2) would extend to civil cases the provisions of Rule 4(b), dealing with criminal cases, designed to avoid the loss of the right to appeal by filing the notice of appeal prematurely. Despite the absence of such a provision in Rule 4(a) the courts of appeals quite generally have held premature appeals effective. See, e.g., *Matter of Grand Jury Empanelled Jan. 21, 1975*, 541 F.2d 373 (3d Cir. 1976); *Hodge v. Hodge*, 507 F.2d 87 (3d Cir. 1976); *Song Jook Suh v. Rosenberg*, 437 F.2d 1098 (9th Cir. 1971); *Ruby v. Secretary of the Navy*, 365 F.2d 385 (9th Cir. 1966); *Firchau v. Diamond Nat'l Corp.*, 345 F.2d 269 (9th Cir. 1965).

The proposed amended rule would recognize this practice but make an exception in cases in which a post trial motion has destroyed the finality of the judgment. See Note to Rule 4(a)(4) below.

Subdivision (a)(4). The proposed amendment would make it clear that after the filing of the specified post trial motions, a notice of appeal should await disposition of the motion. Since the proposed amendments to Rules 3, 10, and 12 contemplate that immediately upon the filing of the notice of appeal the fees will be paid and the case docketed in the court of appeals, and the steps toward its disposition set in motion, it would be undesirable to proceed with the appeal while the district court has before it a motion the granting of which would vacate or alter the judgment appealed from. See, e.g., *Keith v. Newcourt*, 530 F.2d 826 (8th Cir. 1976). Under the present rule, since docketing may not take place until the record is transmitted, premature filing is much less

likely to involve waste effort. See, e.g. *Stockes v. Peyton's Inc.*, 508 F.2d 1287 (5th Cir. 1975). Further, since a notice of appeal filed before the disposition of a post trial motion, even if it were treated as valid for purposes of jurisdiction, would not embrace objections to the denial of the motion, it is obviously preferable to postpone the notice of appeal until after the motion is disposed of.

The present rule, since it provides for the "termination" of the "running" of the appeal time, is ambiguous in its application to a notice of appeal filed prior to a post trial motion filed within the 10 day limit. The amendment would make it clear that in such circumstances the appellant should not proceed with the appeal during pendency of the motion but should file a new notice of appeal after the motion is disposed of.

Subdivision (a)(5). Under the present rule it is provided that upon a showing of excusable neglect the district court at any time may extend the time for the filing of a notice of appeal for a period not to exceed 30 days from the expiration of the time otherwise prescribed by the rule, but that if the application is made after the original time has run, the order may be made only on motion with such notice as the court deems appropriate.

A literal reading of this provision would require that the extension be ordered and the notice of appeal filed within the 30 day period, but despite the surface clarity of the rule, it has produced considerable confusion. See the discussion by Judge Friendly in In re Orbitek, 520 F.2d 358 (2d Cir. 1975). The proposed amendment would make it clear that a motion to extend the time must be filed no later than 30 days after the expiration of the original appeal time, and that if the motion is timely filed the district court may act upon the motion at a later date, and may extend the time not in excess of 10 days measured from the date on which the order granting the motion is entered.

Under the present rule there is a possible implication that prior to the time the initial appeal time has run, the district court may extend the time on the basis of an informal application. The amendment would require that the application must be made by motion, though the motion may be made *ex parte*. After the expiration of the initial time a motion for the extension of the time must be made in compliance with the F.R.C.P. [Federal Rules of Civil Procedure] and local rules of the district court. See Note to proposed amended Rule 1, *supra*. And see Rules 6(d), 7(b) of the F.R.C.P. [rules 6(d) and 7(b), Federal Rules of Civil Procedure].

The proposed amended rule expands to some extent the standard for the grant of an extension of time. The present rule requires a "showing of excusable neglect." While this was an appropriate standard in cases in which the motion is made after the time for filing the notice of appeal has run, and remains so, it has never fit exactly the situation in which the appellant seeks an extension before the expiration of the initial time. In such a case "good cause," which is the standard that is applied in the granting of other extensions of time under Rule 26(b) seems to be more appropriate.

Subdivision (a)(6). The proposed amendment would call attention to the requirement of Rule 58 of the F.R.C.P. [Federal Rules of Civil Procedure] that the judgment constitute a separate document. See *United States v. Indrelunas*, 411 U.S. 216 (1973). When a notice of appeal is filed, the clerk should ascertain whether any judgment designated

therein has been entered in compliance with Rules 58 and 79(a) and if not, so advise all parties and the district judge. While the requirement of Rule 58 is not jurisdictional, (see *Bankers Trust Co. v. Mallis*, 431 U.S. 928 (1977)), compliance is important since the time for the filing of a notice of appeal by other parties is measured by the time at which the judgment is properly entered.

1991 Amendment

The amendment provides a limited opportunity for relief in circumstances where the notice of entry of a judgment or order, required to be mailed by the clerk of the district court pursuant to Rule 77(d) of the Federal Rules of Civil Procedure, is either not received by a party or is received so late as to impair the opportunity to file a timely notice of appeal. The amendment adds a new subdivision (6) allowing a district court to reopen for a brief period the time for appeal upon a finding that notice of entry of a judgment or order was not received from the clerk or a party within 21 days of its entry and that no party would be prejudiced. By "prejudice" the Committee means some adverse consequence other than the cost of having to oppose the appeal and encounter the risk of reversal, consequences that are present in every appeal. Prejudice might arise, for example, if the appellee had taken some action in reliance on the expiration of the normal time period for filing a notice of appeal.

Reopening may be ordered only upon a motion filed within 180 days of the entry of a judgment or order or within 7 days of receipt of notice of such entry, whichever is earlier. This provision establishes an outer time limit of 180 days for a party who fails to receive timely notice of entry of a judgment to seek additional time to appeal and enables any winning party to shorten the 180-day period by sending (and establishing proof of receipt of) its own notice of entry of a judgment, as authorized by Fed.R.Civ.P. 77(d). Winning parties are encouraged to send their own notice in order to lessen the chance that a judge will accept a claim of non-receipt in the face of evidence that notices were sent by both the clerk and the winning party. Receipt of a winning party's notice will shorten only the time for reopening the time for appeal under this subdivision, leaving the normal time periods for appeal unaffected.

If the motion is granted, the district court may reopen the time for filing a notice of appeal only for a period of 14 days from the date of entry of the order reopening the time for appeal.

Transmittal Note: Upon transmittal of this rule to Congress, the Advisory Committee recommends that the attention of Congress be called to the fact that language in the fourth paragraph of 28 U.S.C. § 2107 might appropriately be revised in light of this proposed rule.

1993 Amendment

Note to Paragraph (a)(1). The amendment is intended to alert readers to the fact that paragraph (a)(4) extends the time for filing an appeal when certain posttrial motions are filed. The Committee hopes that awareness of the provisions of paragraph (a)(4) will prevent the filing of a notice of appeal when a posttrial tolling motion is pending.

Note to Paragraph (a)(2). The amendment treats a notice of appeal filed after the announcement of a decision or order, but before its formal entry, as if the notice had been filed after entry. The amendment deletes the language that made paragraph (a)(2) inapplicable to a notice of appeal filed after announcement of the disposition of a posttrial motion enumerated in paragraph (a)(4) but before the entry of the order, see *Acosta v. Louisiana Dep't of Health & Human Resources*, 478 U.S. 251 (1986) (per curiam); *Alerte v. McGinnis*, 898 F.2d 69 (7th Cir.1990). Because the amendment of paragraph (a)(4) recognizes all notices of appeal filed after announcement or entry of judgment—even those that are filed while the posttrial motions enumerated in paragraph (a)(4) are pending—the amendment of this paragraph is consistent with the amendment of paragraph (a)(4).

Note to Paragraph (a)(3). The amendment is technical in nature; no substantive change is intended.

Note to Paragraph (a)(4). The 1979 amendment of this paragraph created a trap for an unsuspecting litigant who files a notice of appeal before a posttrial motion, or while a posttrial motion is pending. The 1979 amendment requires a party to file a new notice of appeal after the motion's disposition. Unless a new notice is filed, the court of appeals lacks jurisdiction to hear the appeal. *Griggs v. Provident Consumer Discount Co.*, 459 U.S. 56 (1982). Many litigants, especially pro se litigants, fail to file the second notice of appeal, and several courts have expressed dissatisfaction with the rule. See, e.g., *Averhart v. Arrendondo*, 773 F.2d 919 (7th Cir.1985); *Harcon Barge Co. v. D & G Boat Rentals, Inc.*, 746 F.2d 278 (5th Cir.1984), cert. denied, 479 U.S. 930 (1986).

The amendment provides that a notice of appeal filed before the disposition of a specified posttrial motion will become effective upon disposition of the motion. A notice filed before the filing of one of the specified motions or after the filing of a motion but before disposition of the motion is, in effect, suspended until the motion is disposed of, whereupon, the previously filed notice effectively places jurisdiction in the court of appeals.

Because a notice of appeal will ripen into an effective appeal upon disposition of a posttrial motion, in some instances there will be an appeal from a judgment that has been altered substantially because the motion was granted in whole or in part. Many such appeals will be dismissed for want of prosecution when the appellant fails to meet the briefing schedule. But, the appellee may also move to strike the appeal. When responding to such a motion, the appellant would have an opportunity to state that, even though some relief sought in a posttrial motion was granted, the appellant still plans to pursue the appeal. Because the appellant's response would provide the appellee with sufficient notice of the appellant's intentions, the Committee does not believe that an additional notice of appeal is needed.

The amendment provides that a notice of appeal filed before the disposition of a posttrial tolling motion is sufficient to bring the underlying case, as well as any orders specified in the original notice, to the court of appeals. If the judgment is altered upon disposition of a posttrial motion, however, and if a party wishes to appeal from the disposition of the motion, the party must amend the notice to so indicate. When a party files an amended notice, no additional fees are required because the notice is an amendment of the original and not a new notice of appeal.

Paragraph (a)(4) is also amended to include, among motions that extend the time for filing a notice of appeal, a Rule 60 motion that is served within 10 days after entry of judgment. This eliminates the difficulty of determining whether a posttrial motion made within 10 days after entry of a judgment is a Rule 59(e) motion, which tolls the time for filing an appeal, or a Rule 60 motion, which historically has not tolled the time. The amendment comports with the practice in several circuits of treating all motions to alter or amend judgments that are made within 10 days after entry of judgment as Rule 59(e) motions for purposes of Rule 4(a)(4). See, e.g., *Finch v. City of Vernon*, 845 F.2d 256 (11th Cir.1988); *Rados v. Celotex Corp.*, 809 F.2d 170 (2d Cir.1986); *Skagerberg v. Oklahoma*, 797 F.2d 881 (10th Cir. 1986). To conform to a recent Supreme Court decision, however—*Budinich v. Becton Dickinson and Co.*, 486 U.S. 196 (1988)—the amendment excludes motions for attorney's fees from the class of motions that extend the filing time unless a district court, acting under Rule 58, enters an order extending the time for appeal. This amendment is to be read in conjunction with the amendment of Fed.R.Civ.P. 58.

Note to subdivision (b). The amendment grammatically restructures the portion of this subdivision that lists the types of motions that toll the time for filing an appeal. This restructuring is intended to make the rule easier to read. No substantive change is intended other than to add a motion for judgment of acquittal under Criminal Rule 29 to the list of tolling motions. Such a motion is the equivalent of a Fed.R.Civ.P. 50(b) motion for judgment notwithstanding the verdict, which tolls the running of time for an appeal in a civil case.

The proposed amendment also eliminates an ambiguity from the third sentence of this subdivision. Prior to this amendment, the third sentence provided that if one of the specified motions was filed, the time for filing an appeal would run from the entry of an order denying the motion. That sentence, like the parallel provision in Rule 4(a)(4), was intended to toll the running of time for appeal if one of the posttrial motions is timely filed. In a criminal case, however, the time for filing the motions runs not from entry of judgment (as it does in civil cases), but from the verdict or finding of guilt. Thus, in a criminal case, a posttrial motion may be disposed of more than 10 days before sentence is imposed, i.e. before the entry of judgment. *United States v. Hashagen*, 816 F.2d 899, 902 n. 5 (3d Cir.1987). To make it clear that a notice of appeal need not be filed before entry of judgment, the amendment states that an appeal may be taken within 10 days after the entry of an order disposing of the motion, or within 10 days after the entry of judgment, whichever is later. The amendment also changes the language in the third sentence providing that an appeal may be taken within 10 days after the entry of an order *denying* the motion; the amendment says instead that an appeal may be taken within 10 days after the entry of an order *disposing* of the last such motion outstanding. (Emphasis added) The change recognizes that there may be multiple posttrial motions filed and that, although one or more motions may be granted in whole or in part, a defendant may still wish to pursue an appeal.

The amendment also states that a notice of appeal filed before the disposition of any of the posttrial tolling motions becomes effective upon disposition of the motions. In most circuits this language simply restates the current practice.

See *United States v. Cortes*, 895 F.2d 1245 (9th Cir.), cert. denied, 495 U.S. 939 (1990). Two circuits, however, have questioned that practice in light of the language of the rule, see *United States v. Gargano*, 826 F.2d 610 (7th Cir.1987), and *United States v. Jones*, 669 F.2d 559 (8th Cir.1982), and the Committee wishes to clarify the rule. The amendment is consistent with the proposed amendment of Rule 4(a)(4).

Subdivision (b) is further amended in light of new Fed. R.Crim.P. 35(c), which authorizes a sentencing court to correct any arithmetical, technical, or other clear errors in sentencing within 7 days after imposing the sentence. The Committee believes that a sentencing court should be able to act under Criminal Rule 35(c) even if a notice of appeal has already been filed; and that a notice of appeal should not be affected by the filing of a Rule 35(c) motion or by correction of a sentence under Rule 35(c).

Note to subdivision (c). In *Houston v. Lack*, 487 U.S. 266 (1988), the Supreme Court held that a *pro se* prisoner's notice of appeal is "filed" at the moment of delivery to prison authorities for forwarding to the district court. The amendment reflects that decision. The language of the amendment is similar to that in Supreme Court Rule 29.2.

Permitting an inmate to file a notice of appeal by depositing it in an institutional mail system requires adjustment of the rules governing the filing of cross-appeals. In a civil case, the time for filing a cross-appeal ordinarily runs from the date when the first notice of appeal is filed. If an inmate's notice of appeal is filed by depositing it in an institution's mail system, it is possible that the notice of appeal will not arrive in the district court until several days after the "filing" date and perhaps even after the time for filing a cross-appeal has expired. To avoid that problem, subdivision (c) provides that in a civil case when an institutionalized person files a notice of appeal by depositing it in the institution's mail system, the time for filing a cross-appeal runs from the district court's receipt of the notice. The amendment makes a parallel change regarding the time for the government to appeal in a criminal case.

1995 Amendment

Subdivision (a). Fed.R.Civ.P. 50, 52, and 59 were previously inconsistent with respect to whether certain post-judgment motions had to be filed or merely served no later than 10 days after entry of judgment. As a consequence Rule 4(a)(4) spoke of making or serving such motions rather than filing them. Civil Rules 50, 52, and 59, are being revised to require filing before the end of the 10-day period. As a consequence, this rule is being amended to provide that 'filing' must occur within the 10 day period in order to affect the finality of the judgment and extend the period for filing a notice of appeal.

The Civil Rules require the filing of postjudgment motions 'no later than 10 days after entry of judgment'—rather than 'within' 10 days—to include postjudgment motions that are filed before actual entry of the judgment by the clerk. This rule is amended, therefore, to use the same terminology.

The rule is further amended to clarify the fact that a party who wants to obtain review of an alteration or amendment of a judgment must file a notice of appeal or amend a previously filed notice to indicate intent to appeal from the altered judgment.

1998 Amendments

The language and organization of the rule are amended to make the rule more easily understood. In addition to changes made to improve the understanding the Advisory Committee has changed language to make style and terminology consistent throughout the appellate rules. These changes are intended to be stylistic only; in this rule, however, substantive changes are made in paragraphs (a)(6) and (b)(4), and in subdivision (c).

Subdivision (a), paragraph (1). Although the Advisory Committee does not intend to make any substantive changes in this paragraph, cross-references to Rules 4(a)(1)(B) and (4)(c) have been added to subparagraph (a)(1)(A).

Subdivision (a), paragraph (4). Item (iv) in subparagraph (A) of Rule 4(a)(4) provides that filing a motion for relief under Fed.R.Civ.P. 60 will extend the time for filing a notice of appeal if the Rule 60 motion is filed no later than 10 days after judgment is entered. Again, the Advisory Committee does not intend to make any substantive change in this paragraph. But because Fed.R.Civ.P. 6(a) and Fed.R.App.P. 26(a) have different methods for computing time, one might be uncertain whether the 10-day period referred to in Rule 4(a)(4) is computed using Civil Rule 6(a) or Appellate Rule 26(a). Because the Rule 60 motion is filed in the district court, and because Fed.R.App.P. 1(a)(2) says that when the appellate rules provide for filing a motion in the district court, "the procedure must comply with the practice of the district court," the rule provides that the 10-day period is computed using Fed.R.Civ.P. 6(a)

Subdivision (a), paragraph (6). Paragraph (6) permits a district court to reopen the time for appeal if a party has not received notice of the entry of judgment and no party would be prejudiced by the reopening. Before reopening the time for appeal, the existing rule requires the district court to find that the moving party was entitled to notice of the entry of judgment and did not receive it "from the clerk or any party within 21 days of its entry." The Advisory Committee makes a substantive change. The finding must be that the movant did not receive notice "from the district court or any party within 21 days after entry." This change broadens the type of notice that can preclude reopening the time for appeal. The existing rule provides that only notice from a party or from the clerk bars reopening. The new language precludes reopening if the movant has received notice from "the court."

Subdivision (b). Two substantive changes are made in what will be paragraph (b)(4). The current rule permits an extension of time to file a notice of appeal if there is a "showing of excusable neglect." First, the rule is amended to permit a court to extend the time for "good cause" as well as for excusable neglect. Rule 4(a) permits extensions for both reasons in civil cases and the Advisory Committee believes that "good cause" should be sufficient in criminal cases as well. The amendment does not limit extensions for good cause to instances in which the motion for extension of time is filed before the original time has expired. The rule gives the district court discretion to grant extensions for good cause whenever the court believes it appropriate to do so provided that the extended period does not exceed 30 days after the expiration of the time otherwise prescribed by Rule 4(b). Second, paragraph (b)(4) is amended to require only a "finding" of excusable neglect or good cause and not a "showing" of them. Because the rule authorizes the court to

provide an extension without a motion, a "showing" is obviously not required; a "finding" is sufficient.

Subdivision (c). Substantive amendments are made in this subdivision. The current rule provides that if an inmate confined in an institution files a notice of appeal by depositing it in the institution's internal mail system, the notice is timely filed if deposited on or before the last day for filing. Some institutions have special internal mail systems for handling legal mail; such systems often record the date of deposit of mail by an inmate, the date of delivery of mail to an inmate, etc. The Advisory Committee amends the rule to require an inmate to use the system designed for legal mail, if there is one, in order to receive the benefit of this subdivision.

When an inmate uses the filing method authorized by subdivision (c), the current rule provides that the time for other parties to appeal begins to run from the date the district court "receives" the inmate's notice of appeal. The rule is amended so that the time for other parties begins to run when the district court "dockets" the inmates appeal. A court may "receive" a paper when its mail is delivered to it even if the mail is not processed for a day or two, making the date of receipt uncertain. "Docketing" is an easily identified event. The change eliminates uncertainty. Paragraph (c)(3) is further amended to make it clear that the time for the government to file its appeal runs from the later of the entry of the judgment or order appealed from or the district court's docketing of a defendant's notice filed under this paragraph (c).

2002 Amendments

Subdivision (a)(1)(C). The federal courts of appeals have reached conflicting conclusions about whether an appeal from an order granting or denying an application for a writ of error *coram nobis* is governed by the time limitations of Rule 4(a) (which apply in civil cases) or by the time limitations of Rule 4(b) (which apply in criminal cases). *Compare United States v. Craig*, 907 F.2d 653, 655–57, *amended* 919 F.2d 57 (7th Cir. 1990); *United States v. Cooper*, 876 F.2d 1192, 1193–94 (5th Cir. 1989); and *United States v. Keogh*, 391 F.2d 138, 140 (2d Cir. 1968) (applying the time limitations of Rule 4(a)); *with Yasui v. United States*, 772 F.2d 1496, 1498–99 (9th Cir. 1985); and *United States v. Mills*, 430 F.2d 526, 527–28 (8th Cir. 1970) (applying the time limitations of Rule 4(b)). A new part (C) has been added to Rule 4(a)(1) to resolve this conflict by providing that the time limitations of Rule 4(a) will apply.

Subsequent to the enactment of Fed. R. Civ. P. 60(b) and 28 U.S.C. § 2255, the Supreme Court has recognized the continued availability of a writ of error *coram nobis* in at least one narrow circumstance. In 1954, the Court permitted a litigant who had been convicted of a crime, served his full sentence, and been released from prison, but who was continuing to suffer a legal disability on account of the conviction, to seek a writ of error *coram nobis* to set aside the conviction. *United States v. Morgan*, 346 U.S. 502 (1954). As the Court recognized, in the *Morgan* situation an application for a writ of error *coram nobis* "is of the same general character as [a motion] under 28 U.S.C. § 2255." *Id.* at 506 n.4. Thus, it seems appropriate that the time limitations of Rule 4(a), which apply when a district court grants or denies relief under 28 U.S.C. § 2255, should also apply when a district court grants or denies a writ of error *coram nobis*. In

addition, the strong public interest in the speedy resolution of criminal appeals that is reflected in the shortened deadlines of Rule 4(b) is not present in the *Morgan* situation, as the party seeking the writ of error *coram nobis* has already served his or her full sentence.

Notwithstanding *Morgan*, it is not clear whether the Supreme Court continues to believe that the writ of error *coram nobis* is available in federal court. In civil cases, the writ has been expressly abolished by Fed. R. Civ. P. 60(b). In criminal cases, the Supreme Court has recently stated that it has become " 'difficult to conceive of a situation' " in which the writ " 'would be necessary or appropriate.' " *Carlisle v. United States*, 517 U.S. 416, 429 (1996) (quoting *United States v. Smith*, 331 U.S. 469, 475 n.4 (1947)). The amendment to Rule 4(a)(1) is not intended to express any view on this issue; rather, it is merely meant to specify time limitations for appeals.

Rule 4(a)(1)(C) applies only to motions that are in substance, and not merely in form, applications for writs of error *coram nobis*. Litigants may bring and label as applications for a writ of error *coram nobis* what are in reality motions for a new trial under Fed. R. Crim. P. 33 or motions for correction or reduction of a sentence under Fed. R. Crim. P. 35. In such cases, the time limitations of Rule 4(b), and not those of Rule 4(a), should be enforced.

Changes Made After Publication and Comments No changes were made to the text of the proposed amendment or to the Committee Note.

Subdivision (a)(4)(A)(vi). Rule 4(a)(4)(A)(vi) has been amended to remove a parenthetical that directed that the 10–day deadline be "computed using Federal Rule of Civil Procedure 6(a)." That parenthetical has become superfluous because Rule 26(a)(2) has been amended to require that all deadlines under 11 days be calculated as they are under Fed. R. Civ. P. 6(a).

Changes Made After Publication and Comments No changes were made to the text of the proposed amendment or to the Committee Note.

Subdivision (a)(5)(A)(ii). Rule 4(a)(5)(A) permits the district court to extend the time to file a notice of appeal if two conditions are met. First, the party seeking the extension must file its motion no later than 30 days after the expiration of the time originally prescribed by Rule 4(a). Second, the party seeking the extension must show either excusable neglect or good cause. The text of Rule 4(a)(5)(A) does not distinguish between motions filed prior to the expiration of the original deadline and those filed after the expiration of the original deadline. Regardless of whether the motion is filed before or during the 30 days after the original deadline expires, the district court may grant an extension if a party shows either excusable neglect or good cause.

Despite the text of Rule 4(a)(5)(A), most of the courts of appeals have held that the good cause standard applies only to motions brought prior to the expiration of the original deadline and that the excusable neglect standard applies only to motions brought during the 30 days following the expiration of the original deadline. *See Pontarelli v. Stone*, 930 F.2d 104, 109–10 (1st Cir. 1991) (collecting cases from the Second, Fifth, Sixth, Seventh, Eighth, Ninth, and Eleventh Circuits). These courts have relied heavily upon the Advisory Committee Note to the 1979 amendment to Rule 4(a)(5). But the Advisory Committee Note refers to a draft of the 1979

amendment that was ultimately rejected. The rejected draft directed that the good cause standard apply only to motions filed prior to the expiration of the original deadline. Rule 4(a)(5), as actually amended, did not. *See* 16A CHARLES ALAN WRIGHT, ET AL., FEDERAL PRACTICE AND PROCEDURE § 3950.3, at 148–49 (2d ed. 1996).

The failure of the courts of appeals to apply Rule 4(a)(5)(A) as written has also created tension between that rule and Rule 4(b)(4). As amended in 1998, Rule 4(b)(4) permits the district court to extend the time for filing a notice of appeal in a *criminal* case for an additional 30 days upon a finding of excusable neglect or good cause. Both Rule 4(b)(4) and the Advisory Committee Note to the 1998 amendment make it clear that an extension can be granted for either excusable neglect or good cause, regardless of whether a motion for an extension is filed before or during the 30 days following the expiration of the original deadline.

Rule 4(a)(5)(A)(ii) has been amended to correct this misunderstanding and to bring the rule in harmony in this respect with Rule 4(b)(4). A motion for an extension filed prior to the expiration of the original deadline may be granted if the movant shows either excusable neglect or good cause. Likewise, a motion for an extension filed during the 30 days following the expiration of the original deadline may be granted if the movant shows either excusable neglect or good cause.

The good cause and excusable neglect standards have "different domains." *Lorenzen v. Employees Retirement Plan*, 896 F.2d 228, 232 (7th Cir. 1990). They are not interchangeable, and one is not inclusive of the other. The excusable neglect standard applies in situations in which there is fault; in such situations, the need for an extension is usually occasioned by something within the control of the movant. The good cause standard applies in situations in which there is no fault—excusable or otherwise. In such situations, the need for an extension is usually occasioned by something that is not within the control of the movant.

Thus, the good cause standard can apply to motions brought during the 30 days following the expiration of the original deadline. If, for example, the Postal Service fails to deliver a notice of appeal, a movant might have good cause to seek a post-expiration extension. It may be unfair to make such a movant prove that its "neglect" was excusable, given that the movant may not have been neglectful at all. Similarly, the excusable neglect standard can apply to motions brought prior to the expiration of the original deadline. For example, a movant may bring a pre-expiration motion for an extension of time when an error committed by the movant makes it unlikely that the movant will be able to meet the original deadline.

Changes Made After Publication and Comments No changes were made to the text of the proposed amendment. The stylistic changes to the Committee Note suggested by Judge Newman were adopted. In addition, two paragraphs were added at the end of the Committee Note to clarify the difference between the good cause and excusable neglect standards.

Subdivision (a)(7). Several circuit splits have arisen out of uncertainties about how Rule 4(a)(7)'s definition of when a judgment or order is "entered" interacts with the requirement in Fed. R. Civ. P. 58 that, to be "effective," a judgment must be set forth on a separate document. Rule 4(a)(7) and Fed. R. Civ. P. 58 have been amended to resolve those splits.

1. The first circuit split addressed by the amendments to Rule 4(a)(7) and Fed. R. Civ. P. 58 concerns the extent to which orders that dispose of post-judgment motions must be set forth on separate documents. Under Rule 4(a)(4)(A), the filing of certain post-judgment motions tolls the time to appeal the underlying judgment until the "entry" of the order disposing of the last such remaining motion. Courts have disagreed about whether such an order must be set forth on a separate document before it is treated as "entered." This disagreement reflects a broader dispute among courts about whether Rule 4(a)(7) independently imposes a separate document requirement (a requirement that is distinct from the separate document requirement that is imposed by the Federal Rules of Civil Procedure ("FRCP")) or whether Rule 4(a)(7) instead incorporates the separate document requirement as it exists in the FRCP. Further complicating the matter, courts in the former "camp" disagree among themselves about the scope of the separate document requirement that they interpret Rule 4(a)(7) as imposing, and courts in the latter "camp" disagree among themselves about the scope of the separate document requirement imposed by the FRCP.

Rule 4(a)(7) has been amended to make clear that it simply incorporates the separate document requirement as it exists in Fed. R. Civ. P. 58. If Fed. R. Civ. P. 58 does not require that a judgment or order be set forth on a separate document, then neither does Rule 4(a)(7); the judgment or order will be deemed entered for purposes of Rule 4(a) when it is entered in the civil docket. If Fed. R. Civ. P. 58 requires that a judgment or order be set forth on a separate document, then so does Rule 4(a)(7); the judgment or order will not be deemed entered for purposes of Rule 4(a) until it is so set forth and entered in the civil docket (with one important exception, described below).

In conjunction with the amendment to Rule 4(a)(7), Fed. R. Civ. P. 58 has been amended to provide that orders disposing of the postjudgment motions listed in new Fed. R. Civ. P. 58(a)(1) (which postjudgment motions include, but are not limited to, the post-judgment motions that can toll the time to appeal under Rule 4(a)(4)(A)) do not have to be set forth on separate documents. *See* Fed. R. Civ. P. 58(a)(1). Thus, such orders are entered for purposes of Rule 4(a) when they are entered in the civil docket pursuant to Fed. R. Civ. P. 79(a). *See* Rule 4(a)(7)(A)(1).

2. The second circuit split addressed by the amendments to Rule 4(a)(7) and Fed. R. Civ. P. 58 concerns the following question: When a judgment or order is required to be set forth on a separate document under Fed. R. Civ. P. 58 but is not, does the time to appeal the judgment or order—or the time to bring post-judgment motions, such as a motion for a new trial under Fed. R. Civ. P. 59—ever begin to run? According to every circuit except the First Circuit, the answer is "no." The First Circuit alone holds that parties will be deemed to have waived their right to have a judgment or order entered on a separate document three months after the judgment or order is entered in the civil docket. *See Fiore v. Washington County Community Mental Health Ctr.*, 960 F.2d 229, 236 (1st Cir. 1992) (en banc). Other circuits have rejected this cap as contrary to the relevant rules. *See, e.g., United States v. Haynes*, 158 F.3d 1327, 1331 (D.C. Cir. 1998); *Hammack v. Baroid Corp.*, 142 F.3d 266, 269–70 (5th Cir. 1998); *Rubin v. Schottenstein, Zox & Dunn*, 110 F.3d

1247, 1253 n.4 (6th Cir. 1997), *vacated on other grounds*, 143 F.3d 263 (6th Cir. 1998) (en banc). However, no court has questioned the wisdom of imposing such a cap as a matter of policy.

Both Rule 4(a)(7)(A) and Fed. R. Civ. P. 58 have been amended to impose such a cap. Under the amendments, a judgment or order is generally treated as entered when it is entered in the civil docket pursuant to Fed. R. Civ. P. 79(a). There is one exception: When Fed. R. Civ. P. 58(a)(1) requires the judgment or order to be set forth on a separate document, that judgment or order is not treated as entered until it is set forth on a separate document (in addition to being entered in the civil docket) or until the expiration of 150 days after its entry in the civil docket, whichever occurs first. This cap will ensure that parties will not be given forever to appeal (or to bring a postjudgment motion) when a court fails to set forth a judgment or order on a separate document in violation of Fed. R. Civ. P. 58(a)(1).

3. The third circuit split—this split addressed only by the amendment to Rule 4(a)(7)—concerns whether the appellant may waive the separate document requirement over the objection of the appellee. In *Bankers Trust Co. v. Mallis*, 435 U.S. 381, 387 (1978) (per curiam), the Supreme Court held that the "parties to an appeal may waive the separate-judgment requirement of Rule 58." Specifically, the Supreme Court held that when a district court enters an order and "clearly evidence[s] its intent that the ... order ... represent[s] the final decision in the case," the order is a "final decision" for purposes of 28 U.S.C. § 1291, even if the order has not been set forth on a separate document for purposes of Fed. R. Civ. P. 58. *Id.* Thus, the parties can choose to appeal without waiting for the order to be set forth on a separate document.

Courts have disagreed about whether the consent of all parties is necessary to waive the separate document requirement. Some circuits permit appellees to object to attempted *Mallis* waivers and to force appellants to return to the trial court, request that judgment be set forth on a separate document, and appeal a second time. *See, e.g., Selletti v. Carey*, 173 F.3d 104, 109–10 (2d Cir. 1999); *Williams v. Borg*, 139 F.3d 737, 739–40 (9th Cir. 1998); *Silver Star Enters., Inc. v. M/V Saramacca*, 19 F.3d 1008, 1013 (5th Cir. 1994). Other courts disagree and permit *Mallis* waivers even if the appellee objects. *See, e.g., Haynes*, 158 F.3d at 1331; *Miller v. Artistic Cleaners*, 153 F.3d 781, 783–84 (7th Cir. 1998); *Alvord-Polk, Inc. v. F. Schumacher & Co.*, 37 F.3d 996, 1006 n.8 (3d Cir. 1994).

New Rule 4(a)(7)(B) is intended both to codify the Supreme Court's holding in *Mallis* and to make clear that the decision whether to waive the requirement that the judgment or order be set forth on a separate document is the appellant's alone. It is, after all, the appellant who needs a clear signal as to when the time to file a notice of appeal has begun to run. If the appellant chooses to bring an appeal without waiting for the judgment or order to be set forth on a separate document, then there is no reason why the appellee should be able to object. All that would result from honoring the appellee's objection would be delay.

4. The final circuit split addressed by the amendment to Rule 4(a)(7) concerns the question whether an appellant who chooses to waive the separate document requirement must appeal within 30 days (60 days if the government is a party) from the entry in the civil docket of the judgment or order

that should have been set forth on a separate document but was not. In *Townsend v. Lucas*, 745 F.2d 933 (5th Cir. 1984), the district court dismissed a 28 U.S.C. § 2254 action on May 6, 1983, but failed to set forth the judgment on a separate document. The plaintiff appealed on January 10, 1984. The Fifth Circuit dismissed the appeal, reasoning that, if the plaintiff waived the separate document requirement, then his appeal would be from the May 6 order, and if his appeal was from the May 6 order, then it was untimely under Rule 4(a)(1). The Fifth Circuit stressed that the plaintiff could return to the district court, move that the judgment be set forth on a separate document, and appeal from that judgment within 30 days. *Id.* at 934. Several other cases have embraced the *Townsend* approach. *See, e.g., Armstrong v. Ahitow*, 36 F.3d 574, 575 (7th Cir. 1994) (per curiam); *Hughes v. Halifax County Sch. Bd.*, 823 F.2d 832, 835–36 (4th Cir. 1987); *Harris v. McCarthy*, 790 F.2d 753, 756 n.1 (9th Cir. 1986).

Those cases are in the distinct minority. There are numerous cases in which courts have heard appeals that were not filed within 30 days (60 days if the government was a party) from the judgment or order that should have been set forth on a separate document but was not. *See, e.g., Haynes*, 158 F.3d at 1330–31; *Clough v. Rush*, 959 F.2d 182, 186 (10th Cir. 1992); *McCalden v. California Library Ass'n*, 955 F.2d 1214, 1218–19 (9th Cir. 1990). In the view of these courts, the remand in *Townsend* was "precisely the purposeless spinning of wheels abjured by the Court in the [*Mallis*] case." 15B CHARLES ALAN WRIGHT ET AL., FEDERAL PRACTICE AND PROCEDURE § 3915, at 259 n.8 (3d ed. 1992).

The Committee agrees with the majority of courts that have rejected the *Townsend* approach. In drafting new Rule 4(a)(7)(B), the Committee has been careful to avoid phrases such as "otherwise timely appeal" that might imply an endorsement of *Townsend*.

Changes Made After Publication and Comments No changes were made to the text of proposed Rule 4(a)(7)(B) or to the third or fourth numbered sections of the Committee Note, except that, in several places, references to a judgment being "entered" on a separate document were changed to references to a judgment being "set forth" on a separate document. This was to maintain stylistic consistency. The appellate rules and the civil rules consistently refer to "entering" judgments on the civil docket and to "setting forth" judgments on separate documents.

Two major changes were made to the text of proposed Rule 4(a)(7)(A)—one substantive and one stylistic. The substantive change was to increase the "cap" from 60 days to 150 days. The Appellate Rules Committee and the Civil Rules Committee had to balance two concerns that are implicated whenever a court fails to enter its final decision on a separate document. On the one hand, potential appellants need a clear signal that the time to appeal has begun to run, so that they do not unknowingly forfeit their rights. On the other hand, the time to appeal cannot be allowed to run forever. A party who receives no notice whatsoever of a judgment has only 180 days to move to reopen the time to appeal from that judgment. *See* Rule 4(a)(6)(A). It hardly seems fair to give a party who *does* receive notice of a judgment an unlimited amount of time to appeal, merely because that judgment was not set forth on a separate piece of paper. Potential appellees and the judicial system need *some* limit on the time within which appeals can be brought.

The 150–day cap properly balances these two concerns. When an order is not set forth on a separate document, what signals litigants that the order is final and appealable is a lack of further activity from the court. A 60–day period of inactivity is not sufficiently rare to signal to litigants that the court has entered its last order. By contrast, 150 days of inactivity is much less common and thus more clearly signals to litigants that the court is done with their case.

The major stylistic change to Rule 4(a)(7) requires some explanation. In the published draft, proposed Rule 4(a)(7)(A) provided that "[a] judgment or order is entered for purposes of this Rule 4(a) when it is entered for purposes of Rule 58(b) of the Federal Rules of Civil Procedure." In other words, Rule 4(a)(7)(A) told readers to look to FRCP 58(b) to ascertain when a judgment is entered for purposes of starting the running of the time to appeal. Sending appellate lawyers to the civil rules to discover when time began to run for purposes of the appellate rules was itself somewhat awkward, but it was made more confusing by the fact that, when readers went to proposed FRCP 58(b), they found this introductory clause: "Judgment is entered for purposes of Rules 50, 52, 54(d)(2)(B), 59, 60, and 62 when. . . . "

This introductory clause was confusing for both appellate lawyers and trial lawyers. It was confusing for appellate lawyers because Rule 4(a)(7) informed them that FRCP 58(b) would tell them when the time begins to run for purposes of the *appellate* rules, but when they got to FRCP 58(b) they found a rule that, by its terms, dictated only when the time begins to run for purposes of certain *civil* rules. The introductory clause was confusing for trial lawyers because FRCP 58(b) described when judgment is entered for some purposes under the civil rules, but then was completely silent about when judgment is entered for other purposes.

To avoid this confusion, the Civil Rules Committee, on the recommendation of the Appellate Rules Committee, changed the introductory clause in FRCP 58(b) to read simply: "Judgment is entered for purposes of *these Rules* when. . . . " In addition, Rule 4(a)(7)(A) was redrafted [1] so that the triggering events for the running of the time to appeal (entry in the civil docket, and being set forth on a separate document or passage of 150 days) were incorporated directly into Rule 4(a)(7), rather than indirectly through a reference to FRCP 58(b). This eliminates the need for appellate lawyers to examine Rule 58(b) and any chance that Rule 58(b)'s introductory clause (even as modified) might confuse them.

We do not believe that republication of Rule 4(a)(7) or FRCP 58 is necessary. In *substance*, rewritten Rule 4(a)(7)(A) and FRCP 58(b) operate identically to the published versions, except that the 60–day cap has been replaced with a 150–day cap—a change that was suggested by some of the commentators and that makes the cap more forgiving.

1. A redraft of Rule 4(a)(7) was faxed to members of the Appellate Rules Committee two weeks after our meeting in New Orleans. The Committee consented to the redraft without objection.

Subdivision (b)(5). Federal Rule of Criminal Procedure 35(a) permits a district court, acting within 7 days after the imposition of sentence, to correct an erroneous sentence in a criminal case. Some courts have held that the filing of a motion for correction of a sentence suspends the time for filing a notice of appeal from the judgment of conviction. *See, e.g., United States v. Carmouche,* 138 F.3d 1014, 1016 (5th Cir. 1998) (per curiam); *United States v. Morillo,* 8 F.3d 864, 869 (1st Cir. 1993). Those courts establish conflicting timeta-

bles for appealing a judgment of conviction after the filing of a motion to correct a sentence. In the First Circuit, the time to appeal is suspended only for the period provided by Fed. R. Crim. P. 35(a) for the district court to correct a sentence; the time to appeal begins to run again once 7 days have passed after sentencing, even if the motion is still pending. By contrast, in the Fifth Circuit, the time to appeal does not begin to run again until the district court actually issues an order disposing of the motion.

Rule 4(b)(5) has been amended to eliminate the inconsistency concerning the effect of a motion to correct a sentence on the time for filing a notice of appeal. The amended rule makes clear that the time to appeal continues to run, even if a motion to correct a sentence is filed. The amendment is consistent with Rule 4(b)(3)(A), which lists the motions that toll the time to appeal, and notably omits any mention of a Fed. R. Crim. P. 35(a) motion. The amendment also should promote certainty and minimize the likelihood of confusion concerning the time to appeal a judgment of conviction.

If a district court corrects a sentence pursuant to Fed. R. Crim. P. 35(a), the time for filing a notice of appeal of the corrected sentence under Rule 4(b)(1) would begin to run when the court enters a new judgment reflecting the corrected sentence.

Changes Made After Publication and Comments The reference to Federal Rule of Criminal Procedure 35(c) was changed to Rule 35(a) to reflect the pending amendment of Rule 35. The proposed amendment to Criminal Rule 35, if approved, will take effect at the same time that the proposed amendment to Appellate Rule 4 will take effect, if approved.

2005 Amendments

Rule 4(a)(6) has permitted a district court to reopen the time to appeal a judgment or order upon finding that four conditions were satisfied. First, the district court had to find that the appellant did not receive notice of the entry of the judgment or order from the district court or any party within 21 days after the judgment or order was entered. Second, the district court had to find that the appellant moved to reopen the time to appeal within 7 days after the appellant received notice of the entry of the judgment or order. Third, the district court had to find that the appellant moved to reopen the time to appeal within 180 days after the judgment or order was entered. Finally, the district court had to find that no party would be prejudiced by the reopening of the time to appeal.

Rule 4(a)(6) has been amended to specify more clearly what type of "notice" of the entry of a judgment or order precludes a party from later moving to reopen the time to appeal. In addition, Rule 4(a)(6) has been amended to address confusion about what type of "notice" triggers the 7-day period to bring a motion to reopen. Finally, Rule 4(a)(6) has been reorganized to set forth more logically the conditions that must be met before a district court may reopen the time to appeal.

Subdivision (a)(6)(A). Former subdivision (a)(6)(B) has been redesignated as subdivision (a)(6)(A), and one substantive change has been made. As amended, the subdivision will preclude a party from moving to reopen the time to appeal a judgment or order only if the party receives (within 21 days) formal notice of the entry of that judgment or order under

Civil Rule 77(d). No other type of notice will preclude a party.

The reasons for this change take some explanation. Prior to 1998, former subdivision (a)(6)(B) permitted a district court to reopen the time to appeal if it found "that a party entitled to notice of the entry of a judgment or order did not receive such notice from the clerk or any party within 21 days of its entry." The rule was clear that the "notice" to which it referred was the notice required under Civil Rule 77(d), which must be served by the clerk pursuant to Civil Rule 5(b) and may also be served by a party pursuant to that same rule. In other words, prior to 1998, former subdivision (a)(6)(B) was clear that, if a party did not receive formal notice of the entry of a judgment or order under Civil Rule 77(d), that party could later move to reopen the time to appeal (assuming that the other requirements of subdivision (a)(6) were met).

In 1998, former subdivision (a)(6)(B) was amended to change the description of the type of notice that would preclude a party from moving to reopen. As a result of the amendment, former subdivision (a)(6)(B) no longer referred to the failure of the moving party to receive "*such* notice"— that is, the notice required by Civil Rule 77(d)—but instead referred to the failure of the moving party to receive "*the* notice." And former subdivision (a)(6)(B) no longer referred to the failure of the moving party to receive notice from "the *clerk* or any party," both of whom are explicitly mentioned in Civil Rule 77(d). Rather, former subdivision (a)(6)(B) referred to the failure of the moving party to receive notice from "the *district court* or any party."

The 1998 amendment meant, then, that the type of notice that precluded a party from moving to reopen the time to appeal was no longer limited to Civil Rule 77(d) notice. Under the 1998 amendment, *some* type of notice, in addition to Civil Rule 77(d) notice, precluded a party. But the text of the amended rule did not make clear what type of notice qualified. This was an invitation for litigation, confusion, and possible circuit splits.

To avoid such problems, former subdivision (a)(6)(B)—new subdivision (a)(6)(A)—has been amended to restore its pre–1998 simplicity. Under new subdivision (a)(6)(A), if the court finds that the moving party was not notified under Civil Rule 77(d) of the entry of the judgment or order that the party seeks to appeal within 21 days after that judgment or order was entered, then the court is authorized to reopen the time to appeal (if all of the other requirements of subdivision (a)(6) are met). Because Civil Rule 77(d) requires that notice of the entry of a judgment or order be formally served under Civil Rule 5(b), any notice that is not so served will not operate to preclude the reopening of the time to appeal under new subdivision (a)(6)(A).

Subdivision (a)(6)(B). Former subdivision (a)(6)(A) required a party to move to reopen the time to appeal "within 7 days after the moving party receives notice of the entry [of the judgment or order sought to be appealed]." Former subdivision (a)(6)(A) has been redesignated as subdivision (a)(6)(B), and one important substantive change has been made: The subdivision now makes clear that only formal notice of the entry of a judgment or order under Civil Rule 77(d) will trigger the 7–day period to move to reopen the time to appeal.

The circuits have been split over what type of "notice" is sufficient to trigger the 7–day period. The majority of cir-

cuits that addressed the question held that only *written* notice was sufficient, although nothing in the text of the rule suggested such a limitation. *See, e.g., Bass v. United States Dep't of Agric.*, 211 F.3d 959, 963 (5th Cir. 2000). By contrast, the Ninth Circuit held that while former subdivision (a)(6)(A) did not require written notice, "the quality of the communication [had to] rise to the functional equivalent of written notice." *Nguyen v. Southwest Leasing & Rental, Inc.*, 282 F.3d 1061, 1066 (9th Cir. 2002). Other circuits suggested in dicta that former subdivision (a)(6)(A) required only "actual notice," which, presumably, could have included oral notice that was not "the functional equivalent of written notice." *See, e.g., Lowry v. McDonnell Douglas Corp.*, 211 F.3d 457, 464 (8th Cir. 2000). And still other circuits read into former subdivision (a)(6)(A) restrictions that appeared only in former subdivision (a)(6)(B) (such as the requirement that notice be received "from the district court or any party," *see Benavides v. Bureau of Prisons*, 79 F.3d 1211, 1214 (D.C. Cir. 1996)) or that appeared in neither former subdivision (a)(6)(A) nor former subdivision (a)(6)(B) (such as the requirement that notice be served in the manner prescribed by Civil Rule 5, *see Ryan v. First Unum Life Ins. Co.*, 174 F.3d 302, 304–05 (2d Cir. 1999)).

Former subdivision (a)(6)(A)—new subdivision (a)(6)(B)—has been amended to resolve this circuit split by providing that only formal notice of the entry of a judgment or order under Civil Rule 77(d) will trigger the 7–day period. Using Civil Rule 77(d) notice as the trigger has two advantages: First, because Civil Rule 77(d) is clear and familiar, circuit splits are unlikely to develop over its meaning. Second, because Civil Rule 77(d) notice must be served under Civil Rule 5(b), establishing whether and when such notice was provided should generally not be difficult.

Using Civil Rule 77(d) notice to trigger the 7–day period will not unduly delay appellate proceedings. Rule 4(a)(6) applies to only a small number of cases—cases in which a party was not notified of a judgment or order by either the clerk or another party within 21 days after entry. Even with respect to those cases, an appeal cannot be brought more than 180 days after entry, no matter what the circumstances. In addition, Civil Rule 77(d) permits parties to serve notice of the entry of a judgment or order. The winning party can prevent Rule 4(a)(6) from even coming into play simply by serving notice of entry within 21 days. Failing that, the winning party can always trigger the 7–day deadline to move to reopen by serving belated notice.

Rule 5. Appeal by Permission

(a) Petition for Permission to Appeal.

(1) To request permission to appeal when an appeal is within the court of appeals' discretion, a party must file a petition for permission to appeal. The petition must be filed with the circuit clerk with proof of service on all other parties to the district-court action.

(2) The petition must be filed within the time specified by the statute or rule authorizing the appeal or, if no such time is specified, within the time provided by Rule 4(a) for filing a notice of appeal.

(3) If a party cannot petition for appeal unless the district court first enters an order granting permission to do so or stating that the necessary conditions are met, the district court may amend its order, either on its own or in response to a party's motion, to include the required permission or statement. In that event, the time to petition runs from entry of the amended order.

(b) Contents of the Petition; Answer or Cross–Petition; Oral Argument.

(1) The petition must include the following:

(A) the facts necessary to understand the question presented;

(B) the question itself;

(C) the relief sought;

(D) the reasons why the appeal should be allowed and is authorized by a statute or rule; and

(E) an attached copy of:

(i) the order, decree, or judgment complained of and any related opinion or memorandum, and

(ii) any order stating the district court's permission to appeal or finding that the necessary conditions are met.

(2) A party may file an answer in opposition or a cross-petition within 7 days after the petition is served.

(3) The petition and answer will be submitted without oral argument unless the court of appeals orders otherwise.

(c) Form of Papers; Number of Copies. All papers must conform to Rule 32(c)(2). Except by the court's permission, a paper must not exceed 20 pages, exclusive of the disclosure statement, the proof of service, and the accompanying documents required by Rule 5(b)(1)(E). An original and 3 copies must be filed unless the court requires a different number by local rule or by order in a particular case.

(d) Grant of Permission; Fees; Cost Bond; Filing the Record.

(1) Within 10 days after the entry of the order granting permission to appeal, the appellant must:

(A) pay the district clerk all required fees; and

(B) file a cost bond if required under Rule 7.

(2) A notice of appeal need not be filed. The date when the order granting permission to appeal is entered serves as the date of the notice of appeal for calculating time under these rules.

(3) The district clerk must notify the circuit clerk once the petitioner has paid the fees. Upon receiving this notice, the circuit clerk must enter the appeal on the docket. The record must be forwarded and filed in accordance with Rules 11 and 12(c).

(As amended Apr. 30, 1979, eff. Aug. 1, 1979; Apr. 29, 1994, eff. Dec. 1, 1994; Apr. 24, 1998, eff. Dec. 1, 1998; Apr. 29, 2002, eff. Dec. 1, 2002.)

ADVISORY COMMITTEE NOTES

1967 Adoption

This rule is derived in the main from Third Circuit Rule 11(2), which is similar to the rule governing appeals under 28 U.S.C. § 1292(b) in a majority of the circuits. The second sentence of subdivision (a) resolves a conflict over the question of whether the district court can amend an order by supplying the statement required by § 1292(b) at any time after entry of the order, with the result that the time fixed by the statute commences to run on the date of entry of the order as amended. Compare *Milbert v. Bison Laboratories*, 260 F.2d 431 (3d Cir., 1958) with *Sperry Rand Corporation v. Bell Telephone Laboratories*, 272 F.2d 29 (2d Cir., 1959), *Hadjipateras v. Pacifica, S.A.*, 290 F.2d 697 (5th Cir., 1961) and *Houston Fearless Corporation v. Teter*, 313 F.2d 91 (10th Cir., 1962). The view taken by the Second, Fifth and Tenth Circuits seems theoretically and practically sound, and the rule adopts it. Although a majority of the circuits now require the filing of a notice of appeal following the grant of permission to appeal, filing of the notice serves no function other than to provide a time from which the time for transmitting the record and docketing the appeal begins to run.

1979 Amendment

The proposed amendment [to subdivision (d)] adapts to the practice in appeals from interlocutory orders under 28 U.S.C. § 1292(b) the provisions of proposed Rule 3(e) above, requiring payment of all fees in the district court upon the filing of the notice of appeal. See Note to proposed amended Rule 3(e), *supra*.

1994 Amendments

Subdivision (c). The amendment makes it clear that a court may require a different number of copies either by rule or by order in an individual case. The number of copies of any document that a court of appeals needs varies depending upon the way in which the court conducts business. The internal operation of the courts of appeals necessarily varies from circuit to circuit because of differences in the number of judges, the geographic area included within the circuit, and other such factors. Uniformity could be achieved only by setting the number of copies artificially high so that parties in all circuits file enough copies to satisfy the needs of the court requiring the greatest number. Rather than do that, the Committee decided to make it clear that local rules may require a greater or lesser number of copies and that, if the circumstances of a particular case indicate the need for a different number of copies in that case, the court may so order.

1998 Amendments

In 1992 Congress added subsection (e) to 28 U.S.C. § 1292. Subsection (e) says that the Supreme Court has power to prescribe rules that "provide for an appeal of an interlocutory decision to the courts of appeals that is not otherwise provided for" in section 1292. The amendment of Rule 5 was prompted by the possibility of new rules authorizing addi-

tional interlocutory appeals. Rather than add a separate rule governing each such appeal, the Committee believes it is preferable to amend Rule 5 so that it will govern all such appeals.

In addition the Federal Courts Improvement Act of 12996, Pub.L. 104–317, abolished appeals by permission under 28 U.S.C. § 636(c)(5), making Rule 5.1 obsolete.

This new Rule 5 is intended to govern all discretionary appeals from district-court orders, judgments, or decrees. At this time that includes interlocutory appeals under 28 U.S.C. § 1292(b), (c)(1), (d)(1) & (2). If additional interlocutory appeals are authorized under § 1292(e), the new Rule is intended to govern them if the appeals are discretionary.

Subdivision (a). Paragraph (a)(1) says that when granting an appeal is within a court of appeals' discretion, a party may file a petition for permission to appeal. The time for filing provision states only that the petition must be filed within the time provided in the statute or rule authorizing the appeal or, if no such time is specified, within the time provided by Rule 4(a) for filing a notice of appeal.

Section 1292(b), (c), and (d) provide that the petition must be filed within 10 days after entry of the order containing the statement prescribed in the statute. Existing Rule 5(a) provides that if a district court amends an order to contain the prescribed statement, the petition must be filed within 10 days after entry of the amended order. The new rule similarly says that if a party cannot petition without the district court's permission or statement that necessary circumstances are present, the district court may amend its order to include such a statement and the time to petition runs from entry of the amended order.

The provision that the Rule 4(a) time for filing a notice of appeal should apply if the statute or rule is silent about the filing time was drawn from existing Rule 5.1

Subdivision (b). The changes made in the provisions in paragraph (b)(1) are intended only to broaden them sufficiently to make them appropriate for all discretionary appeals.

In paragraph (b)(2) a uniform time—7 days—is established for filing an answer in opposition or cross-petition. Seven days is the time for responding under existing Rule 5 and is an appropriate length of time when dealing with an interlocutory appeal. Although existing Rule 5.1 provides 14 days for responding, the Committee does not believe that the longer response time is necessary.

Subdivision (c). Subdivision (c) is substantively unchanged.

Subdivision (d). Paragraph (d)(2) is amended to state that "the date when the order granting permission to appeal is entered serves as the date of the notice of appeal" for purposes of calculating time under the rules. That language simply clarifies existing practice.

2002 Amendments

Subdivision (c). A petition for permission to appeal, a cross-petition for permission to appeal, and an answer to a petition or cross-petition for permission to appeal are all "other papers" for purposes of Rule 32(c)(2), and all of the requirements of Rule 32(a) apply to those papers, except as provided in Rule 32(c)(2). During the 1998 restyling of the Federal Rules of Appellate Procedure, Rule 5(c) was inadver-

tently changed to suggest that only the requirements of Rule 32(a)(1) apply to such papers. Rule 5(c) has been amended to correct that error.

Rule 5(c) has been further amended to limit the length of papers filed under Rule 5.

Changes Made After Publication and Comments No changes were made to the text of the proposed amendment or to the Committee Note.

[Rule 5.1. Appeal by Leave Under 28 U.S.C. § 636(c)(5)] (Abrogated Apr. 24, 1998, eff. Dec. 1, 1998)

ADVISORY COMMITTEE NOTES
1998 Amendments

The Federal Courts Improvement Act of 1996, Pub.L. No. 104–317, abolished appeals by permission under 28 U.S.C. § 636(c)(5), making Rule 5.1 obsolete. Rule 5.1 is, therefore, abrogated.

HISTORICAL NOTES

The abrogated rule provided that:

"(a) Petition for Leave to Appeal; Answer or Cross Petition. An appeal from a district court judgment, entered after an appeal under 28 U.S.C. § 636(c)(4) to a district judge from a judgment entered upon direction of a magistrate judge in a civil case, may be sought by filing a petition for leave to appeal. An appeal on petition for leave to appeal is not a matter of right, but its allowance is a matter of sound judicial discretion. The petition shall be filed with the clerk of the court of appeals within the time provided by Rule 4(a) for filing a notice of appeal, with proof of service on all parties to the action in the district court. A notice of appeal need not be filed. Within 14 days after service of the petition, a party may file an answer in opposition or a cross petition.

"(b) Content of Petition; Answer. The petition for leave to appeal shall contain a statement of the facts necessary to an understanding of the questions to be presented by the appeal; a statement of those questions and of the relief sought; a statement of the reasons why in the opinion of the petitioner the appeal should be allowed; and a copy of the order, decree or judgment complained of and any opinion or memorandum relating thereto. The petition and answer shall be submitted to a panel of judges of the court of appeals without oral argument unless otherwise ordered.

"(c) Form of Papers; Number of Copies. All papers may be typewritten. An original and three copies must be filed unless the court requires the filing of a different number by local rule or by order in a particular case.

"(d) Allowance of the Appeal; Fees; Cost Bond; Filing of Record. Within 10 days after the entry of an order granting the appeal, the appellant shall (1) pay to the clerk of the district court the fees established by statute and the docket fee prescribed by the Judicial Conference of the United States and (2) file a bond for costs if required pursuant to Rule 7. The clerk of the district court shall notify the clerk of the court of appeals of the payment of the fees. Upon receipt of such notice, the clerk of the court of appeals shall enter the appeal upon the docket. The record shall be transmitted and filed in accordance with Rules 11 and 12(b)."

Rule 6. Appeal in a Bankruptcy Case From a Final Judgment, Order, or Decree of a District Court or Bankruptcy Appellate Panel

(a) Appeal From a Judgment, Order, or Decree of a District Court Exercising Original Jurisdiction in a Bankruptcy Case. An appeal to a court of appeals from a final judgment, order, or decree of a district court exercising jurisdiction under 28 U.S.C. § 1334 is taken as any other civil appeal under these rules.

(b) Appeal From a Judgment, Order, or Decree of a District Court or Bankruptcy Appellate Panel Exercising Appellate Jurisdiction in a Bankruptcy Case.

(1) **Applicability of Other Rules.** These rules apply to an appeal to a court of appeals under 28 U.S.C. § 158(d) from a final judgment, order, or decree of a district court or bankruptcy appellate panel exercising appellate jurisdiction under 28 U.S.C. § 158(a) or (b). But there are 3 exceptions:

(A) Rules 4(a)(4), 4(b), 9, 10, 11, 12(b), 13–20, 22–23, and 24(b) do not apply;

(B) the reference in Rule 3(c) to 'Form 1 in the Appendix of Forms' must be read as a reference to Form 5; and

(C) when the appeal is from a bankruptcy appellate panel, the term 'district court,' as used in any applicable rule, means 'appellate panel.'

(2) **Additional Rules.** In addition to the rules made applicable by Rule 6(b)(1), the following rules apply:

(A) **Motion for rehearing.**

(i) If a timely motion for rehearing under Bankruptcy Rule 8015 is filed, the time to appeal for all parties runs from the entry of the order disposing of the motion. A notice of appeal filed after the district court or bankruptcy appellate panel announces or enters a judgment, order, or decree—but before disposition of the motion for rehearing—becomes effective when the order disposing of the motion for rehearing is entered.

(ii) Appellate review of the order disposing of the motion requires the party, in compliance with Rules 3(c) and 6(b)(1)(B), to amend a previously filed notice of appeal. A party intending to challenge an altered or amended judgment, order, or decree must file a notice of appeal or amended notice of appeal within the time prescribed by Rule 4—excluding Rules 4(a)(4) and 4(b)—measured from the entry of the order disposing of the motion.

(iii) No additional fee is required to file an amended notice.

(B) **The record on appeal.**

(i) Within 10 days after filing the notice of appeal, the appellant must file with the clerk possessing the record assembled in accordance with Bankruptcy Rule 8006—and serve on the appellee—a statement of the issues to be presented on appeal and a designation of the record to be certified and sent to the circuit clerk.

(ii) An appellee who believes that other parts of the record are necessary must, within 10 days after being served with the appellant's designation, file with the clerk and serve on the appellant a designation of additional parts to be included.

(iii) The record on appeal consists of:

● the redesignated record as provided above;

● the proceedings in the district court or bankruptcy appellate panel; and

● a certified copy of the docket entries prepared by the clerk under Rule 3(d).

(C) **Forwarding the record.**

(i) When the record is complete, the district clerk or bankruptcy appellate panel clerk must number the documents constituting the record and send them promptly to the circuit clerk together with a list of the documents correspondingly numbered and reasonably identified. Unless directed to do so by a party or the circuit clerk, the clerk will not send to the court of appeals documents of unusual bulk or weight, physical exhibits other than documents, or other parts of the record designated for omission by local rule of the court of appeals. If the exhibits are unusually bulky or heavy, a party must arrange with the clerks in advance for their transportation and receipt.

(ii) All parties must do whatever else is necessary to enable the clerk to assemble and forward the record. The court of appeals may provide by rule or order that a certified copy of the docket entries be sent in place of the redesignated record, but any party may request at any time during the pendency of the appeal that the redesignated record be sent.

(D) **Filing the record.** Upon receiving the record—or a certified copy of the docket entries sent in place of the redesignated record—the circuit clerk must file it and immediately notify all parties of the filing date.

(Added Apr. 25, 1989, eff. Dec. 1, 1989, and amended Apr. 30, 1991, eff. Dec. 1, 1991; Apr. 22, 1993, eff. Dec. 1, 1993; Apr. 24, 1998, eff. Dec. 1, 1998.)

1989 Addition

A new Rule 6 is proposed. The Bankruptcy Reform Act of 1978, Pub.L. No. 95–598, 92 Stat. 2549, the Supreme Court

decision in *Northern Pipeline Construction Co. v. Marathon Pipe Line Co.*, 458 U.S. 50 (1982), and the Bankruptcy Amendments and Federal Judgeship Act of 1984, Pub.L. No. 98–353, 98 Stat. 333, have made the existing Rule 6 obsolete.

Subdivision (a). Subdivision (a) provides that when a district court exercises original jurisdiction in a bankruptcy matter, rather than referring it to a bankruptcy judge for a final determination, the appeal should be taken in identical fashion as appeals from district court decisions in other civil actions. A district court exercises original jurisdiction and this subdivision applies when the district court enters a final order or judgment upon consideration of a bankruptcy judge's proposed findings of fact and conclusions of law in a non-core proceeding pursuant to 28 U.S.C. § 157(c)(1) or when a district court withdraws a proceeding pursuant to 28 U.S.C. § 157(d). This subdivision is included to avoid uncertainty arising from the question of whether a bankruptcy case is a civil case. The rules refer at various points to the procedure "in a civil case", *see,* e.g. Rule 4(a)(1). Subdivision (a) makes it clear that such rules apply to an appeal from a district court bankruptcy decision.

Subdivision (b). Subdivision (b) governs appeals that follow intermediate review of a bankruptcy judge's decision by a district court or a bankruptcy appellate panel.

Subdivision (b)(1). Subdivision (b)(1) provides for the general applicability of the Federal Rules of Appellate Procedure, with specified exceptions, to appeals covered by subdivision (b) and makes necessary word adjustments.

Subdivision (b)(2). Paragraph (i) provides that the time for filing a notice of appeal shall begin to run anew from the entry of an order denying a rehearing or from the entry of a subsequent judgment. The Committee deliberately omitted from the rule any provision governing the validity of a notice of appeal filed prior to the entry of an order denying a rehearing; the Committee intended to leave undisturbed the current state of the law on that issue. Paragraph (ii) calls for a redesignation of the appellate record assembled in the bankruptcy court pursuant to Rule 8006 of the Rules of Bankruptcy Procedure. After an intermediate appeal, a party may well narrow the focus of its efforts on the second appeal and a redesignation of the record may eliminate unnecessary material. The proceedings during the first appeal are included to cover the possibility that independent error in the intermediate appeal, for example failure to follow appropriate procedures, may be assigned in the court of appeals. Paragraph (iii) provides for the transmission of the record and tracks the appropriate subsections of Rule 11. Paragraph (iv) provides for the filing of the record and notices to the parties. Paragraph (ii) and Paragraph (iv) both refer to "a certified copy of the docket entries". The "docket entries" referred to are the docket entries in the district court or the bankruptcy appellate panel, not the entire docket in the bankruptcy court.

1993 Amendments

Note to Subparagraph (b)(2)(i). The amendment accompanies concurrent changes to Rule 4(a)(4). Although Rule 6 never included language such as that being changed in Rule 4(a)(4), language that made a notice of appeal void if it was filed before, or during the pendency of, certain posttrial motions, courts have found that a notice of appeal is premature if it is filed before the court disposes of a motion for rehearing. See, e.g., *In re X–Cel, Inc.*, 823 F.2d 192 (7th

Cir.1987); *In re Shah*, 859 F.2d 1463 (10th Cir.1988). The Committee wants to achieve the same result here as in Rule 4, the elimination of a procedural trap.

1998 Amendments

The language and organization of the rule are amended to make the rule more easily understood. In addition to changes made to improve the understanding, the Advisory Committee has changed language to make style and terminology consistent throughout the appellate rules. These changes are intended to be stylistic only.

Subdivision (b). Language is added to Rule 6(b)(2)(A)(ii) to conform with the corresponding provision in Rule 4(a)(4). The new language is clarifying rather than substantive. The existing rule states that a party intending to challenge an alteration or amendment of a judgment must file an amended notice of appeal. Of course, if a party has not previously filed a notice of appeal, the party would simply file a notice of appeal not an amended one. The new language states that the party must file "a notice of appeal or amended notice of appeal."

Rule 7. Bond for Costs on Appeal in a Civil Case

In a civil case, the district court may require an appellant to file a bond or provide other security in any form and amount necessary to ensure payment of costs on appeal. Rule 8(b) applies to a surety on a bond given under this rule.

(As amended Apr. 30, 1979, eff. Aug. 1, 1979; Apr. 24, 1998, eff. Dec. 1, 1998.)

ADVISORY COMMITTEE NOTES

1967 Adoption

This rule is derived from FRCP 73(c) [rule 73(c), Federal Rules of Civil Procedure, this title] without change in substance.

1979 Amendment

The amendment would eliminate the provision of the present rule that requires the appellant to file a $250 bond for costs on appeal at the time of filing his notice of appeal. The $250 provision was carried forward in the F.R.App.P. [these rules] from former Rule 73(c) of the F.R.Civ.P. [rule 73(c), Federal Rules of Civil Procedure], and the $250 figure has remained unchanged since the adoption of that rule in 1937. Today it bears no relationship to actual costs. The amended rule would leave the question of the need for a bond for costs and its amount in the discretion of the court.

1998 Amendments

The language of the rule is amended to make the rule more easily understood. In addition to changes made to improve the understanding, the Advisory Committee has changed language to make style and terminology consistent throughout the appellate rules. These changes are intended to be stylistic only.

Rule 8. Stay or Injunction Pending Appeal

(a) Motion for Stay.

(1) Initial Motion in the District Court. A party must ordinarily move first in the district court for the following relief:

 (A) a stay of the judgment or order of a district court pending appeal;

 (B) approval of a supersedeas bond; or

 (C) an order suspending, modifying, restoring, or granting an injunction while an appeal is pending.

(2) Motion in the Court of Appeals; Conditions on Relief. A motion for the relief mentioned in Rule 8(a)(1) may be made to the court of appeals or to one of its judges.

 (A) The motion must:

 (i) show that moving first in the district court would be impracticable; or

 (ii) state that, a motion having been made, the district court denied the motion or failed to afford the relief requested and state any reasons given by the district court for its action.

 (B) The motion must also include:

 (i) the reasons for granting the relief requested and the facts relied on;

 (ii) originals or copies of affidavits or other sworn statements supporting facts subject to dispute; and

 (iii) relevant parts of the record.

 (C) The moving party must give reasonable notice of the motion to all parties.

 (D) A motion under this Rule 8(a)(2) must be filed with the circuit clerk and normally will be considered by a panel of the court. But in an exceptional case in which time requirements make that procedure impracticable, the motion may be made to and considered by a single judge.

 (E) The court may condition relief on a party's filing a bond or other appropriate security in the district court.

(b) Proceeding Against a Surety.
If a party gives security in the form of a bond or stipulation or other undertaking with one or more sureties, each surety submits to the jurisdiction of the district court and irrevocably appoints the district clerk as the surety's agent on whom any papers affecting the surety's liability on the bond or undertaking may be served. On motion, a surety's liability may be enforced in the district court without the necessity of an independent action. The motion and any notice that the district court prescribes may be served on the district clerk, who must promptly mail a copy to each surety whose address is known.

(c) Stay in a Criminal Case.
Rule 38 of the Federal Rules of Criminal Procedure governs a stay in a criminal case.

(As amended Mar. 10, 1986, eff. July 1, 1986; Apr. 27, 1995, eff. Dec. 1, 1995; Apr. 24, 1998, eff. Dec. 1, 1998.)

ADVISORY COMMITTEE NOTES

1967 Adoption

Subdivision (a). While the power of a court of appeals to stay proceedings in the district court during the pendency of an appeal is not explicitly conferred by statute, it exists by virtue of the all writs statute, 28 U.S.C. § 1651. *Eastern Greyhound Lines v. Fusco,* 310 F.2d 632 (6th Cir., 1962); *United States v. Lynd,* 301 F.2d 818 (5th Cir., 1962); *Public Utilities Commission of Dist. of Col. v. Capital Transit Co.,* 94 U.S.App.D.C. 140, 214 F.2d 242 (1954). And the Supreme Court has termed the power "inherent" (*In re McKenzie,* 180 U.S. 536, 551, 21 S.Ct. 468, 45 L.Ed. 657 (1901)) and "part of its (the court of appeals') traditional equipment for the administration of justice." (*Scripps-Howard Radio v. F.C.C.,* 316 U.S. 4, 9–10, 62 S.Ct. 875, 86 L.Ed. 1229 (1942)). The power of a single judge of the court of appeals to grant a stay pending appeal was recognized in *In re McKenzie, supra. Alexander v. United States,* 173 F.2d 865 (9th Cir., 1949) held that a single judge could not stay the judgment of a district court, but it noted the absence of a rule of court authorizing the practice. FRCP 62(g) [rule 62(g), Federal Rules of Civil Procedure] adverts to the grant of a stay by a single judge of the appellate court. The requirement that application be first made to the district court is the case law rule. *Cumberland Tel. & Tel. Co. v. Louisiana Public Service Commission,* 260 U.S. 212, 219, 43 S.Ct. 75, 67 L.Ed. 217 (1922); *United States v. El-O-Pathic Pharmacy,* 192 F.2d 62 (9th Cir., 1951); *United States v. Hansell,* 109 F.2d 613 (2d Cir., 1940). The requirement is explicitly stated in FRCrP 38(c) [rule 38(c), Federal Rules of Criminal Procedure] and in the rules of the First, Third, Fourth and Tenth Circuits. See also Supreme Court Rules 18 and 27.

The statement of the requirement in the proposed rule would work a minor change in present practice. FRCP 73(e) [rule 73(e), Federal Rules of Civil Procedure] requires that if a bond for costs on appeal or a supersedeas bond is offered after the appeal is docketed, leave to file the bond must be obtained from the court of appeals. There appears to be no reason why matters relating to supersedeas and cost bonds should not be initially presented to the district court whenever they arise prior to the disposition of the appeal. The requirement of FRCP 73(e) appears to be a concession of the view that once an appeal is perfected, the district court loses all power over its judgment. See *In re Federal Facilities Realty Trust,* 227 F.2d 651 (7th Cir., 1955) and cases cited at 654–655. No reason appears why all questions related to supersedeas or the bond for costs on appeal should not be presented in the first instance to the district court in the ordinary case.

Subdivision (b). The provisions respecting a surety upon a bond or other undertaking are based upon FRCP 65.1 [rule 65.1, Federal Rules of Civil Procedure].

1986 Amendment

The amendments to Rule 8(b) are technical. No substantive change is intended.

1995 Amendment

Subdivision (c). The amendment conforms subdivision (c) to previous amendments to Fed.R.Crim.P. 38. This amendment strikes the reference to subdivision (a) of Fed. R.Crim.P. 38 so that Fed.R.App.P. 8(c) refers instead to all of Criminal Rule 38. When Rule 8(c) was adopted Fed. R.Crim.P. 38(a) included the procedures for obtaining a stay of execution when the sentence in question was death, imprisonment, a fine, or probation. Criminal Rule 38 was later amended and now addresses those topics in separate subdivisions. Subdivision 38(a) now addresses only stays of death sentences. The proper cross reference is to all of Criminal Rule 38.

1998 Amendments

The language and organization of the rule are amended to make the rule more easily understood. In addition to changes made to improve the understanding, the Advisory Committee has changed language to make style and terminology consistent throughout the appellate rules. These changes are intended to by stylistic only.

Rule 9. Release in a Criminal Case

(a) Release Before Judgment of Conviction.

(1) The district court must state in writing, or orally on the record, the reasons for an order regarding the release or detention of a defendant in a criminal case. A party appealing from the order must file with the court of appeals a copy of the district court's order and the court's statement of reasons as soon as practicable after filing the notice of appeal. An appellant who questions the factual basis for the district court's order must file a transcript of the release proceedings or an explanation of why a transcript was not obtained.

(2) After reasonable notice to the appellee, the court of appeals must promptly determine the appeal on the basis of the papers, affidavits, and parts of the record that the parties present or the court requires. Unless the court so orders, briefs need not be filed.

(3) The court of appeals or one of its judges may order the defendant's release pending the disposition of the appeal.

(b) Release After Judgment of Conviction.
A party entitled to do so may obtain review of a district-court order regarding release after a judgment of conviction by filing a notice of appeal from that order in the district court, or by filing a motion in the court of appeals if the party has already filed a notice of appeal from the judgment of conviction. Both the order and the review are subject to Rule 9(a). The papers filed by the party seeking review must include a copy of the judgment of conviction.

(c) Criteria for Release.
The court must make its decision regarding release in accordance with the applicable provisions of 18 U.S.C. §§ 3142, 3143, and 3145(c).

(As amended Apr. 24, 1972, eff. Oct. 1, 1972; Oct. 12, 1984, Pub.L. 98–473, Title II, § 210, 98 Stat. 1987; Apr. 29, 1994, eff. Dec. 1, 1994; Apr. 24, 1998, eff. Dec. 1, 1998.)

ADVISORY COMMITTEE NOTES

1967 Adoption

Subdivision (a). The appealability of release orders entered prior to a judgment of conviction is determined by the provisions of 18 U.S.C. § 3147, as qualified by 18 U.S.C. § 3148, and by the rule announced in *Stack v. Boyle*, 342 U.S. 1, 72 S.Ct. 1, 96 L.Ed. 3 (1951), holding certain orders respecting release appealable as final orders under 28 U.S.C. § 1291. The language of the rule, "(a)n appeal authorized by law from an order refusing or imposing conditions of release," is intentionally broader than that used in 18 U.S.C. § 3147 in describing orders made appealable by that section. The summary procedure ordained by the rule is intended to apply to all appeals from orders respecting release, and it would appear that at least some orders not made appealable by 18 U.S.C. § 3147 are nevertheless appealable under the *Stack v. Boyle* rationale. See, for example, *United States v. Foster*, 278 F.2d 567 (2d Cir., 1960), holding appealable an order refusing to extend bail limits. Note also the provisions of 18 U.S.C. § 3148, which after withdrawing from persons charged with an offense punishable by death and from those who have been convicted of an offense the right of appeal granted by 18 U.S.C. § 3147, expressly preserves "other rights to judicial review of conditions of release or orders of detention."

The purpose of the subdivision is to insure the expeditious determination of appeals respecting release orders, an expedition commanded by 18 U.S.C. § 3147 and by the Court in *Stack v. Boyle*, supra. It permits such appeals to be heard on an informal record without the necessity of briefs and on reasonable notice. Equally important to the just and speedy disposition of these appeals is the requirement that the district court state the reasons for its decision. See *Jones v. United States*, 358 F.2d 543 (D.C.Cir., 1966); *Rhodes v. United States*, 275 F.2d 78 (4th Cir., 1960); *United States v. Williams*, 253 F.2d 144 (7th Cir., 1958).

Subdivision (b). This subdivision regulates procedure for review of an order respecting release at a time when the jurisdiction of the court of appeals has already attached by virtue of an appeal from the judgment of conviction. Notwithstanding the fact that jurisdiction has passed to the court of appeals, both 18 U.S.C. § 3148 and FRCrP 38(c) [rule 38(c), Federal Rules of Criminal Procedure] contemplate that the initial determination of whether a convicted defendant is to be released pending the appeal is to be made by the district court. But at this point there is obviously no need for a separate appeal from the order of the district court respecting release. The court of appeals or a judge thereof has power to effect release on motion as an incident to the pending appeal. See FRCrP 38(c) and 46(a)(2) [rules 38(c) and 46(a)(2), Federal Rules of Criminal Procedure]. But the motion is functionally identical with the appeal regulated by subdivision (a) and requires the same speedy determination if relief is to be effective. Hence the similarity of the procedure outlined in the two subdivisions.

1972 Amendment

Subdivision (c) is intended to bring the rule into conformity with 18 U.S.C. § 3148 and to allocate to the defendant the burden of establishing that he will not flee and that he poses no danger to pay other person or to the community. The burden is placed upon the defendant in the view that the fact of his conviction justifies retention in custody in situations where doubt exists as to whether he can be safely released pending disposition of his appeal. Release pending appeal may also be denied if "it appears that an appeal is frivolous or taken for delay." 18 U.S.C. § 3148. The burden of establishing the existence of these criteria remains with the government.

1994 Amendments

Rule 9 has been entirely rewritten. The basic structure of the rule has been retained. Subdivision (a) governs appeals from bail decisions made before the judgment of conviction is entered at the time of sentencing. Subdivision (b) governs review of bail decisions made after sentencing and pending appeal.

Subdivision (a). The subdivision applies to appeals from "an order regarding release or detention" of a criminal defendant before judgment of conviction, *i.e.*, before sentencing. *See* Fed. R. Crim. P. 32. The old rule applied only to a defendant's appeal from an order "refusing or imposing conditions of release." The new broader language is needed because the government is now permitted to appeal bail decisions in certain circumstances. 18 U.S.C. §§ 3145 and 3731. For the same reason, the rule now requires a district court to state reasons for its decision in all instances, not only when it refuses release or imposes conditions on release.

The rule requires a party appealing from a district court's decision to supply the court of appeals with a copy of the district court's order and its statement of reasons. In addition, an appellant who questions the factual basis for the district court's decision must file a transcript of the release proceedings, if possible. The rule also permits a court to require additional papers. A court must act promptly to decide these appeals; lack of pertinent information can cause delays. The old rule left the determination of what should be filed entirely within the party's, discretion; it stated that the court of appeals would hear the appeal "upon such papers, affidavits, and portions of the record as the parties shall present."

Subdivision (b). This subdivision applies to review of a district court's decision regarding release made after judgment of conviction. As in subdivision (a), the language has been changed to accommodate the government's ability to seek review.

The word "review" is used in this subdivision, rather than "appeal" because review may be obtained, in some instances, upon motion. Review may be obtained by motion if the party has already filed a notice of appeal from the judgment of conviction. If the party desiring review of the release decision has not filed such a notice of appeal, review may be obtained only by filing a notice of appeal from the order regarding release.

The requirements of subdivision (a) apply to both the order and the review. That is, the district court must state its reasons for the order. The party seeking review must supply the court of appeals with the same information re-quired by subdivision (a). In addition, the party seeking review must also supply the court with information about the conviction and the sentence.

Subdivision (c). This subdivision has been amended to include references to the correct statutory provisions.

1998 Amendments

The language and organization of the rule are amended to make the rule more easily understood. In addition to changes made to improve the understanding, the Advisory Committee has changed language to make style and terminology consistent throughout the appellate rules. These changes are intended to by stylistic only.

Rule 10. The Record on Appeal

(a) Composition of the Record on Appeal. The following items constitute the record on appeal:

(1) the original papers and exhibits filed in the district court;

(2) the transcript of proceedings, if any; and

(3) a certified copy of the docket entries prepared by the district clerk.

(b) The Transcript of Proceedings.

(1) Appellant's Duty to Order. Within 10 days after filing the notice of appeal or entry of an order disposing of the last timely remaining motion of a type specified in Rule 4(a)(4)(A), whichever is later, the appellant must do either of the following:

(A) order from the reporter a transcript of such parts of the proceedings not already on file as the appellant considers necessary, subject to a local rule of the court of appeals and with the following qualifications:

(i) the order must be in writing;

(ii) if the cost of the transcript is to be paid by the United States under the Criminal Justice Act, the order must so state; and

(iii) the appellant must, within the same period, file a copy of the order with the district clerk; or

(B) file a certificate stating that no transcript will be ordered.

(2) Unsupported Finding or Conclusion. If the appellant intends to urge on appeal that a finding or conclusion is unsupported by the evidence or is contrary to the evidence, the appellant must include in the record a transcript of all evidence relevant to that finding or conclusion.

(3) Partial Transcript. Unless the entire transcript is ordered:

(A) the appellant must—within the 10 days provided in Rule 10(b)(1)—file a statement of the issues that the appellant intends to present on the appeal and must serve on the appellee a copy of both the order or certificate and the statement;

(B) if the appellee considers it necessary to have a transcript of other parts of the proceedings, the appellee must, within 10 days after the service of the order or certificate and the statement of the issues, file and serve on the appellant a designation of additional parts to be ordered; and

(C) unless within 10 days after service of that designation the appellant has ordered all such parts, and has so notified the appellee, the appellee may within the following 10 days either order the parts or move in the district court for an order requiring the appellant to do so.

(4) Payment. At the time of ordering, a party must make satisfactory arrangements with the reporter for paying the cost of the transcript.

(c) Statement of the Evidence When the Proceedings Were Not Recorded or When a Transcript Is Unavailable. If the transcript of a hearing or trial is unavailable, the appellant may prepare a statement of the evidence or proceedings from the best available means, including the appellant's recollection. The statement must be served on the appellee, who may serve objections or proposed amendments within 10 days after being served. The statement and any objections or proposed amendments must then be submitted to the district court for settlement and approval. As settled and approved, the statement must be included by the district clerk in the record on appeal.

(d) Agreed Statement as the Record on Appeal. In place of the record on appeal as defined in Rule 10(a), the parties may prepare, sign, and submit to the district court a statement of the case showing how the issues presented by the appeal arose and were decided in the district court. The statement must set forth only those facts averred and proved or sought to be proved that are essential to the court's resolution of the issues. If the statement is truthful, it—together with any additions that the district court may consider necessary to a full presentation of the issues on appeal—must be approved by the district court and must then be certified to the court of appeals as the record on appeal. The district clerk must then send it to the circuit clerk within the time provided by Rule 11. A copy of the agreed statement may be filed in place of the appendix required by Rule 30.

(e) Correction or Modification of the Record.

(1) If any difference arises about whether the record truly discloses what occurred in the district court, the difference must be submitted to and settled by that court and the record conformed accordingly.

(2) If anything material to either party is omitted from or misstated in the record by error or accident, the omission or misstatement may be correct-

ed and a supplemental record may be certified and forwarded:

(A) on stipulation of the parties;

(B) by the district court before or after the record has been forwarded; or

(C) by the court of appeals.

(3) All other questions as to the form and content of the record must be presented to the court of appeals.

(As amended Apr. 30, 1979, eff. Aug. 1, 1979; Mar. 10, 1986, eff. July 1, 1986; Apr. 30, 1991, eff. Dec. 1, 1991; Apr. 22, 1993, eff. Dec. 1, 1993; Apr. 27, 1995, eff. Dec. 1, 1995; Apr. 24, 1998, eff. Dec. 1, 1998.)

ADVISORY COMMITTEE NOTES

1967 Adoption

This rule is derived from FRCP 75(a), (b), (c) and (d) and FRCP 76 [rule 75(a), (b), (c) and (d) and rule 76, Federal Rules of Civil Procedure], without change in substance.

1979 Amendment

The proposed amendments to Rule 10(b) would require the appellant to place with the reporter a written order for the transcript of proceedings and file a copy with the clerk, and to indicate on the order if the transcript is to be provided under the Criminal Justice Act. If the appellant does not plan to order a transcript of any of the proceedings, he must file a certificate to that effect. These requirements make the appellant's steps in readying the appeal a matter of record and give the district court notice of requests for transcripts at the expense of the United States under the Criminal Justice Act. They are also the third step in giving the court of appeals some control over the production and transmission of the record. See Note to Rules 3(d)(e) above and Rule 11 below.

In the event the appellant orders no transcript, or orders a transcript of less than all the proceedings, the procedure under the proposed amended rule remains substantially as before. The appellant must serve on the appellee a copy of his order or in the event no order is placed, of the certificate to that effect, and a statement of the issues he intends to present on appeal, and the appellee may thereupon designate additional parts of the transcript to be included, and upon appellant's refusal to order the additional parts, may either order them himself or seek an order requiring the appellant to order them. The only change proposed in this procedure is to place a 10 day time limit on motions to require the appellant to order the additional portions.

Rule 10(b) is made subject to local rules of the courts of appeals in recognition of the practice in some circuits in some classes of cases, e.g., appeals by indigents in criminal cases after a short trial, of ordering immediate preparation of a complete transcript, thus making compliance with the rule unnecessary.

1986 Amendment

The amendments to Rules 10(b) and (c) are technical. No substantive change is intended.

1993 Amendment

The amendment is technical and no substantive change is intended.

1995 Amendment

Subdivision (b)(1). The amendment conforms this rule to amendments made in Rule 4(a)(4) in 1993. The amendments to Rule 4(a)(4) provide that certain postjudgment motions have the effect of suspending a filed notice of appeal until the disposition of the last of such motions. The purpose of this amendment is to suspend the 10–day period for ordering a transcript if a timely postjudgment motion is made and a notice of appeal is suspended under Rule 4(a)(4). The 10–day period set forth in the first sentence of this rule begins to run when the order disposing of the last of such postjudgment motions outstanding is entered.

1998 Amendments

The language and organization of the rule are amended to make the rule more easily understood. In addition to changes made to improve the understanding, the Advisory Committee has changed language to make style and terminology consistent throughout the appellate rules. These changes are intended to by stylistic only.

HISTORICAL NOTES

References in Text

The Criminal Justice Act, referred to in subd. (b)(1), probably means the Criminal Justice Act of 1964, Pub.L. 88–455, Aug. 20, 1964, 78 Stat. 552, which is classified to § 3006A of Title 18, Crimes and Criminal Procedure.

Rule 11. Forwarding the Record

(a) Appellant's Duty. An appellant filing a notice of appeal must comply with Rule 10(b) and must do whatever else is necessary to enable the clerk to assemble and forward the record. If there are multiple appeals from a judgment or order, the clerk must forward a single record.

(b) Duties of Reporter and District Clerk.

(1) Reporter's Duty to Prepare and File a Transcript. The reporter must prepare and file a transcript as follows:

(A) Upon receiving an order for a transcript, the reporter must enter at the foot of the order the date of its receipt and the expected completion date and send a copy, so endorsed, to the circuit clerk.

(B) If the transcript cannot be completed within 30 days of the reporter's receipt of the order, the reporter may request the circuit clerk to grant additional time to complete it. The clerk must note on the docket the action taken and notify the parties.

(C) When a transcript is complete, the reporter must file it with the district clerk and notify the circuit clerk of the filing.

(D) If the reporter fails to file the transcript on time, the circuit clerk must notify the district judge and do whatever else the court of appeals directs.

(2) District Clerk's Duty to Forward. When the record is complete, the district clerk must number the documents constituting the record and send them promptly to the circuit clerk together with a list of the documents correspondingly numbered and reasonably identified. Unless directed to do so by a party or the circuit clerk, the district clerk will not send to the court of appeals documents of unusual bulk or weight, physical exhibits other than documents, or other parts of the record designated for omission by local rule of the court of appeals. If the exhibits are unusually bulky or heavy, a party must arrange with the clerks in advance for their transportation and receipt.

(c) Retaining the Record Temporarily in the District Court for Use in Preparing the Appeal. The parties may stipulate, or the district court on motion may order, that the district clerk retain the record temporarily for the parties to use in preparing the papers on appeal. In that event the district clerk must certify to the circuit clerk that the record on appeal is complete. Upon receipt of the appellee's brief, or earlier if the court orders or the parties agree, the appellant must request the district clerk to forward the record.

(d) [Abrogated.]

(e) Retaining the Record by Court Order.

(1) The court of appeals may, by order or local rule, provide that a certified copy of the docket entries be forwarded instead of the entire record. But a party may at any time during the appeal request that designated parts of the record be forwarded.

(2) The district court may order the record or some part of it retained if the court needs it while the appeal is pending, subject, however, to call by the court of appeals.

(3) If part or all of the record is ordered retained, the district clerk must send to the court of appeals a copy of the order and the docket entries together with the parts of the original record allowed by the district court and copies of any parts of the record designated by the parties.

(f) Retaining Parts of the Record in the District Court by Stipulation of the Parties. The parties may agree by written stipulation filed in the district court that designated parts of the record be retained in the district court subject to call by the court of appeals or request by a party. The parts of the record so designated remain a part of the record on appeal.

(g) Record for a Preliminary Motion in the Court of Appeals. If, before the record is forwarded, a party makes any of the following motions in the court of appeals:

- for dismissal;
- for release;
- for a stay pending appeal;
- for additional security on the bond on appeal or on a supersedeas bond; or
- for any other intermediate order—

the district clerk must send the court of appeals any parts of the record designated by any party.

(As amended Apr. 30, 1979, eff. Aug. 1, 1979; Mar. 10, 1986, eff. July 1, 1986; Apr. 24, 1998, eff. Dec. 1, 1998.)

ADVISORY COMMITTEE NOTES

1967 Adoption

Subdivisions (a) and (b). These subdivisions are derived from FRCP 73(g) and FRCP 75(e) [rules 73(g) and 75(e), Federal Rules of Civil Procedure]. FRCP 75(e) presently directs the clerk of the district court to transmit the record within the time allowed or fixed for its filing, which, under the provisions of FRCP 73(g) is within 40 days from the date of filing the notice of appeal, unless an extension is obtained from the district court. The precise time at which the record must be transmitted thus depends upon the time required for delivery of the record from the district court to the court of appeals, since, to permit its timely filing, it must reach the court of appeals before expiration of the 40-day period or an extension thereof. Subdivision (a) of this rule provides that the record is to be transmitted within the 40-day period, or any extension thereof; subdivision (b) provides that transmission is effected when the clerk of the district court mails or otherwise forwards the record to the clerk of the court of appeals; Rule 12(b) directs the clerk of the court of appeals to file the record upon its receipt following timely docketing and transmittal. It can thus be determined with certainty precisely when the clerk of the district court must forward the record to the clerk of the court of appeals in order to effect timely filing: the final day of the 40-day period or of any extension thereof.

Subdivision (c). This subdivision is derived from FRCP 75(e) [rule 75(e), Federal Rules of Civil Procedure] without change of substance.

Subdivision (d). This subdivision is derived from FRCP 73(g) [rule 73(g), Federal Rules of Civil Procedure] and FRCrP 39(c) [rule 39(c), Federal Rules of Criminal Procedure]. Under present rules the district court is empowered to extend the time for filing the record and docketing the appeal. Since under the proposed rule timely transmission now insures timely filing (see note to subdivisions (a) and (b) above) the power of the district court is expressed in terms of its power to extend the time for transmitting the record. Restriction of that power to a period of 90 days after the filing of the notice of appeal represents a change in the rule with respect to appeals in criminal cases. FRCrP 39(c) now permits the district court to extend the time for filing and docketing without restriction. No good reason appears for a difference between the civil and criminal rule in this regard,

and subdivision (d) limits the power of the district court to extend the time for transmitting the record in all cases to 90 days from the date of filing the notice of appeal, just as its power is now limited with respect to docketing and filing in civil cases. Subdivision (d) makes explicit the power of the court of appeals to permit the record to be filed at any time. See *Pyramid Motor Freight Corporation v. Ispass*, 330 U.S. 695, 67 S.Ct. 954, 91 L.Ed. 1184 (1947).

Subdivisions (e), (f) and (g). These subdivisions are derived from FRCP 75(f) [rule 75(f), Federal Rules of Civil Procedure], (a) and (g), respectively, without change of substance.

1979 Amendment

Under present Rule 11(a) it is provided that the record shall be transmitted to the court of appeals within 40 days after the filing of the notice of appeal. Under present Rule 11(d) the district court, on request made during the initial time or any extension thereof, and cause shown, may extend the time for the transmission of the record to a point not more than 90 days after the filing of the first notice of appeal. If the district court is without authority to grant a request to extend the time, or denies a request for extension, the appellant may make a motion for extension of time in the court of appeals. Thus the duty to see that the record is transmitted is placed on the appellant. Aside from ordering the transcript within the time prescribed the appellant has no control over the time at which the record is transmitted, since all steps beyond this point are in the hands of the reporter and the clerk. The proposed amendments recognize this fact and place the duty directly on the reporter and the clerk. After receiving the written order for the transcript (See Note to Rule 10(b) above), the reporter must acknowledge its receipt, indicate when he expects to have it completed, and mail the order so endorsed to the clerk of the court of appeals. Requests for extensions of time must be made by the reporter to the clerk of the court of appeals and action on such requests is entered on the docket. Thus from the point at which the transcript is ordered the clerk of the court of appeals is made aware of any delays. If the transcript is not filed on time, the clerk of the court of appeals will notify the district judge.

Present Rule 11(b) provides that the record shall be transmitted when it is "complete for the purposes of the appeal." The proposed amended rule continues this requirement. The record is complete for the purposes of the appeal when it contains the original papers on file in the clerk's office, all necessary exhibits, and the transcript, if one is to be included. Cf. present Rule 11(c). The original papers will be in the custody of the clerk of the district court at the time the notice of appeal is filed. See Rule 5(e) of the F.R.C.P. [rule 5(e), Federal Rules of Civil Procedure]. The custody of exhibits is often the subject of local rules. Some of them require that documentary exhibits must be deposited with the clerk. See Local Rule 13 of the Eastern District of Virginia. Others leave exhibits with counsel, subject to order of the court. See Local Rule 33 of the Northern District of Illinois. If under local rules the custody of exhibits is left with counsel, the district court should make adequate provision for their preservation during the time during which an appeal may be taken, the prompt deposit with the clerk of such as under Rule 11(b) are to be transmitted to the court of appeals, and the availability of others in

the event that the court of appeals should require their transmission. Cf. Local Rule 11 of the Second Circuit [rule 11, U.S.Ct. of App. 2d Cir.].

Usually the record will be complete with the filing of the transcript. While the proposed amendment requires transmission "forthwith" when the record is complete, it was not designed to preclude a local requirement by the court of appeals that the original papers and exhibits be transmitted when complete without awaiting the filing of the transcript.

The proposed amendments continue the provision in the present rule that documents of unusual bulk or weight and physical exhibits other than documents shall not be transmitted without direction by the parties or by the court of appeals, and the requirement that the parties make special arrangements for transmission and receipt of exhibits of unusual bulk or weight. In addition, they give recognition to local rules that make transmission of other record items subject to order of the court of appeals. See Local Rule 4 of the Seventh Circuit [rule 4, U.S.Ct. of App. 7th Cir., this title].

1986 Amendment

The amendments to Rule 11(b) are technical. No substantive change is intended.

1998 Amendments

The language and organization of the rule are amended to make the rule more easily understood. In addition to changes made to improve the understanding, the Advisory Committee has changed language to make style and terminology consistent throughout the appellate rules. These changes are intended to be stylistic only.

Rule 12. Docketing the Appeal; Filing a Representation Statement; Filing the Record

(a) Docketing the Appeal. Upon receiving the copy of the notice of appeal and the docket entries from the district clerk under Rule 3(d), the circuit clerk must docket the appeal under the title of the district-court action and must identify the appellant, adding the appellant's name if necessary.

(b) Filing a Representation Statement. Unless the court of appeals designates another time, the attorney who filed the notice of appeal must, within 10 days after filing the notice, file a statement with the circuit clerk naming the parties that the attorney represents on appeal.

(c) Filing the Record, Partial Record, or Certificate. Upon receiving the record, partial record, or district clerk's certificate as provided in Rule 11, the circuit clerk must file it and immediately notify all parties of the filing date.

(As amended Apr. 30, 1979, eff. Aug. 1, 1979; Mar. 10, 1986, eff. July 1, 1986; Apr. 22, 1993, eff. Dec. 1, 1993; Apr. 24, 1998, eff. Dec. 1, 1998.)

ADVISORY COMMITTEE NOTES
1967 Adoption

Subdivision (a). All that is involved in the docketing of an appeal is the payment of the docket fee. In practice, after the clerk of the court of appeals receives the record from the clerk of the district court he notifies the appellant of its receipt and requests payment of the fee. Upon receipt of the fee, the clerk enters the appeal upon the docket and files the record. The appellant is allowed to pay the fee at any time within the time allowed or fixed for transmission of the record and thereby to discharge his responsibility for docketing. The final sentence is added in the interest of facilitating future reference and citation and location of cases in indexes. Compare 3d Cir.Rule 10(2) [rule 10(2), U.S.Ct. of App. 3d Cir.]; 4th Cir.Rule 9(8) [rule 9(8), U.S.Ct. of App. 4th Cir.]; 6th Cir.Rule 14(1) [rule 14(1), U.S.Ct. of App. 6th Cir.].

Subdivision (c). The rules of the circuits generally permit the appellee to move for dismissal in the event the appellant fails to effect timely filing of the record. See 1st Cir.Rule 21(3) [rule 21(3), U.S.Ct. of App. 1st Cir.]; 3d Cir.Rule 21(4) [rule 21(4), U.S.Ct. of App. 3d Cir.]; 5th Cir.Rule 16(1) [rule 16(1), U.S.Ct. of App. 5th Cir.]; 8th Cir.Rule 7(d) [rule 7(d), U.S.Ct. of App. 8th Cir.].

1979 Amendments

Subdivision (a). Under present Rule 12(a) the appellant must pay the docket fee within the time fixed for the transmission of the record, and upon timely payment of the fee, the appeal is docketed. The proposed amendment takes the docketing out of the hands of the appellant. The fee is paid at the time the notice of appeal is filed and the appeal is entered on the docket upon receipt of a copy of the notice of appeal and of the docket entries, which are sent to the court of appeals under the provisions of Rule 3(d). This is designed to give the court of appeals control of its docket at the earliest possible time so that within the limits of its facilities and personnel it can screen cases for appropriately different treatment, expedite the proceedings through prehearing conferences or otherwise, and in general plan more effectively for the prompt disposition of cases.

Subdivision (b). The proposed amendment conforms the provision to the changes in Rule 11.

1986 Amendments

The amendment to Rule 12(a) is technical. No substantive change is intended.

1993 Amendments

Note to new subdivision (b). This amendment is a companion to the amendment of Rule 3(c). The Rule 3(c) amendment allows an attorney who represents more than one party on appeal to "specify" the appellants by general description rather than by naming them individually. The requirement added here is that whenever an attorney files a notice of appeal, the attorney must soon thereafter file a statement indicating all parties represented on the appeal by that attorney. Although the notice of appeal is the jurisdictional document and it must clearly indicate who is bringing the appeal, the representation statement will be helpful especially to the court of appeals in identifying the individual appellants.

The rule allows a court of appeals to require the filing of the representation statement at some time other than specified in the rule so that if a court of appeals requires a

docketing statement or appearance form the representation statement may be combined with it.

1998 Amendments

The language of the rule are amended to make the rule more easily understood. In addition to changes made to

improve the understanding, the Advisory Committee has changed language to make style and terminology consistent throughout the appellate rules. These changes are intended to by stylistic only.

TITLE III. REVIEW OF A DECISION OF THE UNITED STATES TAX COURT

Rule 13. Review of a Decision of the Tax Court

(a) How Obtained; Time for Filing Notice of Appeal.

(1) Review of a decision of the United States Tax Court is commenced by filing a notice of appeal with the Tax Court clerk within 90 days after the entry of the Tax Court's decision. At the time of filing, the appellant must furnish the clerk with enough copies of the notice to enable the clerk to comply with Rule 3(d). If one party files a timely notice of appeal, any other party may file a notice of appeal within 120 days after the Tax Court's decision is entered.

(2) If, under Tax Court rules, a party makes a timely motion to vacate or revise the Tax Court's decision, the time to file a notice of appeal runs from the entry of the order disposing of the motion or from the entry of a new decision, whichever is later.

(b) Notice of Appeal; How Filed. The notice of appeal may be filed either at the Tax Court clerk's office in the District of Columbia or by mail addressed to the clerk. If sent by mail the notice is considered filed on the postmark date, subject to § 7502 of the Internal Revenue Code, as amended, and the applicable regulations.

(c) Contents of the Notice of Appeal; Service; Effect of Filing and Service. Rule 3 prescribes the contents of a notice of appeal, the manner of service, and the effect of its filing and service. Form 2 in the Appendix of Forms is a suggested form of a notice of appeal.

(d) The Record on Appeal; Forwarding; Filing.

(1) An appeal from the Tax Court is governed by the parts of Rules 10, 11, and 12 regarding the record on appeal from a district court, the time and manner of forwarding and filing, and the docketing in the court of appeals. References in those rules and in Rule 3 to the district court and district clerk are to be read as referring to the Tax Court and its clerk.

(2) If an appeal from a Tax Court decision is taken to more than one court of appeals, the original record must be sent to the court named in the first notice of appeal filed. In an appeal to any

other court of appeals, the appellant must apply to that other court to make provision for the record.

(As amended Apr. 30, 1979, eff. Aug. 1, 1979; Apr. 29, 1994, eff. Dec. 1, 1994; Apr. 24, 1998, eff. Dec. 1, 1998.)

ADVISORY COMMITTEE NOTES

1967 Adoption

Subdivision (a). This subdivision effects two changes in practice respecting review of Tax Court decisions: (1) § 7483 of the Internal Revenue Code, 68A Stat. 891, 26 U.S.C. § 7483, provides that review of a Tax Court decision may be obtained by filing a petition for review. The subdivision provides for review by the filing of the simple and familiar notice of appeal used to obtain review of district court judgments; (2) § 7483, supra, requires that a petition for review be filed within 3 months after a decision is rendered, and provides that if a petition is so filed by one party, any other party may file a petition for review within 4 months after the decision is rendered. In the interest of fixing the time for review with precision, the proposed rule substitutes "90 days" and "120 days" for the statutory "3 months" and "4 months", respectively. The power of the Court to regulate these details of practice is clear. Title 28 U.S.C. § 2072, as amended by the Act of November 6, 1966, 80 Stat. 1323 (1 U.S.Code Cong. & Ad. News, p. 1546 (1966)), authorizes the Court to regulate ". . . practice and procedure in proceedings for the review by the courts of appeals of decisions of the Tax Court of the United States. . . ."

The second paragraph states the settled teaching of the case law. See *Robert Louis Stevenson Apartments, Inc. v. C.I.R.*, 337 F.2d 681, 10 A.L.R.3d 112 (8th Cir., 1964); *Denholm & McKay Co. v. C.I.R.*, 132 F.2d 243 (1st Cir., 1942); *Helvering v. Continental Oil Co.*, 63 App.D.C. 5, 68 F.2d 750 (1934); *Burnet v. Lexington Ice & Coal Co.*, 62 F.2d 906 (4th Cir.1933); *Griffiths v. C.I.R.*, 50 F.2d 782 (7th Cir., 1931).

Subdivision (b). The subdivision incorporates the statutory provision (Title 26, U.S.C., § 7502) that timely mailing is to be treated as timely filing. The statute contains special provisions respecting other than ordinary mailing. If the notice of appeal is sent by registered mail, registration is deemed prima facie evidence that the notice was delivered to the clerk of the Tax Court, and the date of registration is deemed the postmark date. If the notice of appeal is sent by certified mail, the effect of certification with respect to prima facie evidence of delivery and the postmark date depends upon regulations of the Secretary of the Treasury. The effect of a postmark made other than by the United States Post Office likewise depends upon regulations of the Secre-

tary. Current regulations are found in 26 CFR § 301.7502–1.

1979 Amendments

The proposed amendment reflects the change in the title of the Tax Court to "United States Tax Court." See 26 U.S.C. § 7441.

1994 Amendments

Subdivision (a). The amendment requires a party filing a notice of appeal to provide the court with sufficient copies of the notice for service on all other parties.

1998 Amendments

The language and organization of the rule are amended to make the rule more easily understood. In addition to changes made to improve the understanding, the Advisory Committee has changed language to make style and terminology consistent throughout the appellate rules. These changes are intended to by stylistic only.

Rule 14. Applicability of Other Rules to the Review of a Tax Court Decision

All provisions of these rules, except Rules 4–9, 15–20, and 22–23, apply to the review of a Tax Court decision.

(As amended Apr. 24, 1998, eff. Dec. 1, 1998.)

ADVISORY COMMITTEE NOTES

1967 Adoption

The proposed rule continues the present uniform practice of the circuits of regulating review of decisions of the Tax Court by the general rules applicable to appeals from judgments of the district courts.

1998 Amendments

The language of the rule are amended to make the rule more easily understood. In addition to changes made to improve the understanding, the Advisory Committee has changed language to make style and terminology consistent throughout the appellate rules. These changes are intended to by stylistic only.

TITLE IV. REVIEW OR ENFORCEMENT OF AN ORDER OF AN ADMINISTRATIVE AGENCY, BOARD, COMMISSION, OR OFFICER

Rule 15. Review or Enforcement of an Agency Order—How Obtained; Intervention

(a) Petition for Review; Joint Petition.

(1) Review of an agency order is commenced by filing, within the time prescribed by law, a petition for review with the clerk of a court of appeals authorized to review the agency order. If their interests make joinder practicable, two or more persons may join in a petition to the same court to review the same order.

(2) The petition must:

(A) name each party seeking review either in the caption or the body of the petition—using such terms as 'et al.,' 'petitioners,' or 'respondents' does not effectively name the parties;

(B) name the agency as a respondent (even though not named in the petition, the United States is a respondent if required by statute); and

(C) specify the order or part thereof to be reviewed.

(3) Form 3 in the Appendix of Forms is a suggested form of a petition for review.

(4) In this rule 'agency' includes an agency, board, commission, or officer; 'petition for review' includes a petition to enjoin, suspend, modify, or otherwise review, or a notice of appeal, whichever form is indicated by the applicable statute.

(b) Application or Cross–Application to Enforce an Order; Answer; Default.

(1) An application to enforce an agency order must be filed with the clerk of a court of appeals authorized to enforce the order. If a petition is filed to review an agency order that the court may enforce, a party opposing the petition may file a cross-application for enforcement.

(2) Within 20 days after the application for enforcement is filed, the respondent must serve on the applicant an answer to the application and file it with the clerk. If the respondent fails to answer in time, the court will enter judgment for the relief requested.

(3) The application must contain a concise statement of the proceedings in which the order was entered, the facts upon which venue is based, and the relief requested.

(c) Service of the Petition or Application. The circuit clerk must serve a copy of the petition for review, or an application or cross-application to enforce an agency order, on each respondent as prescribed by Rule 3(d), unless a different manner of service is prescribed by statute. At the time of filing, the petitioner must:

(1) serve, or have served, a copy on each party admitted to participate in the agency proceedings, except for the respondents;

(2) file with the clerk a list of those so served; and

(3) give the clerk enough copies of the petition or application to serve each respondent.

(d) Intervention. Unless a statute provides another method, a person who wants to intervene in a proceeding under this rule must file a motion for leave to intervene with the circuit clerk and serve a copy on all parties. The motion—or other notice of intervention authorized by statute—must be filed within 30 days after the petition for review is filed and must contain a concise statement of the interest of the moving party and the grounds for intervention.

(e) Payment of Fees. When filing any separate or joint petition for review in a court of appeals, the petitioner must pay the circuit clerk all required fees. (As amended Apr. 22, 1993, eff. Dec. 1, 1993; Apr. 24, 1998, eff. Dec. 1, 1998.)

ADVISORY COMMITTEE NOTES

1967 Adoption

General Note. The power of the Supreme Court to prescribe rules of practice and procedure for the judicial review or enforcement of orders of administrative agencies, boards, commissions, and officers is conferred by 28 U.S.C. § 2072, as amended by the Act of November 6, 1966, § 1, 80 Stat. 1323 (1 U.S.Code Cong. & Ad. News, p. 1546 (1966). Section 11 of the Hobbs Administrative Orders Review Act of 1950, 64 Stat. 1132, reenacted as 28 U.S.C. § 2352 (28 U.S.C.A. § 2352 (Supp.1966)), repealed by the Act of November 6, 1966, § 4, supra, directed the courts of appeals to adopt and promulgate, subject to approval by the Judicial Conference rules governing practice and procedure in proceedings to review the orders of boards, commissions and officers whose orders were made reviewable in the courts of appeals by the Act. Thereafter, the Judicial Conference approved a uniform rule, and that rule, with minor variations, is now in effect in all circuits. Third Circuit Rule 18 [rule 18, U.S.Ct. of App. 3rd Cir.] is a typical circuit rule, and for convenience it is referred to as the uniform rule in the notes which accompany rules under this Title.

Subdivision (a). The uniform rule (see General Note above) requires that the petition for review contain "a concise statement, in barest outline, of the nature of the proceedings as to which relief is sought, the facts upon which venue is based, the grounds upon which relief is sought, and the relief prayed." That language is derived from § 4 of the Hobbs Administrative Orders Review Act of 1950, 64 Stat. 1130, reenacted as 28 U.S.C. § 2344 (28 U.S.C.A. § 2344 (Supp. 1966)). A few other statutes also prescribe the content of the petition, but the great majority are silent on the point. The proposed rule supersedes 28 U.S.C. § 2344 and other statutory provisions prescribing the form of the petition for review and permits review to be initiated by the filing of a simple petition similar in form to the notice of appeal used in appeals from judgments of district courts. The more elaborate form of petition for review now required is rarely useful either to the litigants or to the courts. There is no effective, reasonable way of obliging petitioners to come to the real issues before those issues are formulated in the briefs. Other provisions of this subdivision are derived from §§ 1 and 2 of the uniform rule.

Subdivision (b). This subdivision is derived from §§ 3, 4 and 5 of the uniform rule.

Subdivision (c). This subdivision is derived from § 1 of the uniform rule.

Subdivision (d). This subdivision is based upon § 6 of the uniform rule. Statutes occasionally permit intervention by the filing of a notice of intention to intervene. The uniform rule does not fix a time limit for intervention, and the only time limits fixed by statute are the 30–day periods found in the Communications Act Amendments, 1952, § 402(e), 66 Stat. 719, 47 U.S.C. § 402(e), and the Sugar Act of 1948, § 205(d), 61 Stat. 927, 7 U.S.C. § 1115(d).

1993 Amendments

Subdivision (a). The amendment is a companion to the amendment of Rule 3(c). Both Rule 3(c) and Rule 15(a) state that a notice of appeal or petition for review must name the parties seeking appellate review. Rule 3(c), however, provides an attorney who represents more than one party on appeal the flexibility to describe the parties in general terms rather than naming them individually. Rule 15(a) does not allow that flexibility; each petitioner must be named. A petition for review of an agency decision is the first filing in any court and, therefore, is analogous to a complaint in which all parties must be named.

Subdivision (e). The amendment adds subdivision (e). Subdivision (e) parallels Rule 3(e) that requires the payment of fees when filing a notice of appeal. The omission of such a requirement from Rule 15 is an apparent oversight. Five circuits have local rules requiring the payment of such fees, see, e.g., Fifth Cir.Loc.R. 15.1, and Fed.Cir.Loc.R. 15(a)(2).

1998 Amendments

The language and organization of the rule are amended to make the rule more easily understood. In addition to changes made to improve the understanding, the Advisory Committee has changed language to make style and terminology consistent throughout the appellate rules. These changes are intended to by stylistic only.

Rule 15.1. Briefs and Oral Argument in a National Labor Relations Board Proceeding

In either an enforcement or a review proceeding, a party adverse to the National Labor Relations Board proceeds first on briefing and at oral argument, unless the court orders otherwise. (Added Mar. 10, 1986, eff. July 1, 1986, and amended Apr. 24, 1998, eff. Dec. 1, 1998.)

ADVISORY COMMITTEE NOTES

1986 Addition

This rule simply confirms the existing practice in most circuits.

1998 Amendments

The language of the rule are amended to make the rule more easily understood. In addition to changes made to improve the understanding, the Advisory Committee has

changed language to make style and terminology consistent throughout the appellate rules. These changes are intended to by stylistic only.

Rule 16. The Record on Review or Enforcement

(a) Composition of the Record. The record on review or enforcement of an agency order consists of:

(1) the order involved;

(2) any findings or report on which it is based; and

(3) the pleadings, evidence, and other parts of the proceedings before the agency.

(b) Omissions From or Misstatements in the Record. The parties may at any time, by stipulation, supply any omission from the record or correct a misstatement, or the court may so direct. If necessary, the court may direct that a supplemental record be prepared and filed.

(As amended Apr. 24, 1998, eff. Dec. 1, 1998.)

ADVISORY COMMITTEE NOTES
1967 Adoption

Subdivision (a) is based upon 28 U.S.C § 2112(b). There is no distinction between the record compiled in the agency proceeding and the record on review; they are one and the same. The record in agency cases is thus the same as that in appeals from the district court—the original papers, transcripts and exhibits in the proceeding below. Subdivision (b) is based upon § 8 of the uniform rule (see General Note following Rule 15).

1998 Amendments

The language and organization of the rule are amended to make the rule more easily understood. In addition to changes made to improve the understanding, the Advisory Committee has changed language to make style and terminology consistent throughout the appellate rules. These changes are intended to by stylistic only.

Rule 17. Filing the Record

(a) Agency to File; Time for Filing; Notice of Filing. The agency must file the record with the circuit clerk within 40 days after being served with a petition for review, unless the statute authorizing review provides otherwise, or within 40 days after it files an application for enforcement unless the respondent fails to answer or the court orders otherwise. The court may shorten or extend the time to file the record. The clerk must notify all parties of the date when the record is filed.

(b) Filing—What Constitutes.

(1) The agency must file:

(A) the original or a certified copy of the entire record or parts designated by the parties; or

(B) a certified list adequately describing all documents, transcripts of testimony, exhibits, and other material constituting the record, or describing those parts designated by the parties.

(2) The parties may stipulate in writing that no record or certified list be filed. The date when the stipulation is filed with the circuit clerk is treated as the date when the record is filed.

(3) The agency must retain any portion of the record not filed with the clerk. All parts of the record retained by the agency are a part of the record on review for all purposes and, if the court or a party so requests, must be sent to the court regardless of any prior stipulation.

(As amended Apr. 24, 1998, eff. Dec. 1, 1998.)

ADVISORY COMMITTEE NOTES
1967 Adoption

Subdivision (a). This subdivision is based upon § 7 of the uniform rule (see General Note following Rule 15). That rule does not prescribe a time for filing the record in enforcement cases. Forty days are allowed in order to avoid useless preparation of the record or certified list in cases where the application for enforcement is not contested.

Subdivision (b). This subdivision is based upon 28 U.S.C. § 2112 and § 7 of the uniform rule. It permits the agency to file either the record itself or a certified list of its contents. It also permits the parties to stipulate against transmission of designated parts of the record without the fear that an inadvertent stipulation may "diminish" the record. Finally, the parties may, in cases where consultation of the record is unnecessary, stipulate that neither the record nor a certified list of its contents be filed.

1998 Amendments

The language and organization of the rule are amended to make the rule more easily understood. In addition to changes made to improve the understanding, the Advisory Committee has changed language to make style and terminology consistent throughout the appellate rules. These changes are intended to by stylistic only; a substantive change is made, however, in subdivision (b).

Subdivision (b). The current rule provides that when a court of appeals is asked to review or enforce an agency order, the agency must file either "the entire record or such parts thereof as the parties may designate by stipulation filed with the agency" or a certified list describing the documents, transcripts, exhibits, and other material constituting the record. If the agency is not filing a certified list, the current rule requires the agency to file the entire record unless the parties file a "stipulation" designating only parts of the record. Such a "stipulation" presumably requires agreement of the parties as to the parts to be filed. The amended language in subparagraph (b)(1)(A) permits the filing of less than the entire record even when the parties do not agree as to which parts should be filed. Each party can designate the parts that it wants filed; the agency can then forward the parts designated by each party. In contrast, paragraph (b)(2) continues to require stipulation, that is

agreement of the parties, that the agency need not file either the record or a certified list.

Rule 18. Stay Pending Review

(a) Motion for a Stay.

(1) **Initial Motion Before the Agency.** A petitioner must ordinarily move first before the agency for a stay pending review of its decision or order.

(2) **Motion in the Court of Appeals.** A motion for a stay may be made to the court of appeals or one of its judges.

(A) The motion must:

(i) show that moving first before the agency would be impracticable; or

(ii) state that, a motion having been made, the agency denied the motion or failed to afford the relief requested and state any reasons given by the agency for its action.

(B) The motion must also include:

(i) the reasons for granting the relief requested and the facts relied on;

(ii) originals or copies of affidavits or other sworn statements supporting facts subject to dispute; and

(iii) relevant parts of the record.

(C) The moving party must give reasonable notice of the motion to all parties.

(D) The motion must be filed with the circuit clerk and normally will be considered by a panel of the court. But in an exceptional case in which time requirements make that procedure impracticable, the motion may be made to and considered by a single judge.

(b) Bond. The court may condition relief on the filing of a bond or other appropriate security.

(As amended Apr. 24, 1998, eff. Dec. 1, 1998.)

ADVISORY COMMITTEE NOTES

1967 Adoption

While this rule has no counterpart in present rules regulating review of agency proceedings, it merely assimilates the procedure for obtaining stays in agency proceedings with that for obtaining stays in appeals from the district courts. The same considerations which justify the requirement of an initial application to the district court for a stay pending appeal support the requirement of an initial application to the agency pending review. See Note accompanying Rule 8. Title 5, U.S.C. § 705 (5 U.S.C.A. § 705 (1966 Pamphlet)), confers general authority on both agencies and reviewing courts to stay agency action pending review. Many of the statutes authorizing review of agency action by the courts of appeals deal with the question of stays, and at least one, the Act of June 15, 1936, 49 Stat. 1499 (7 U.S.C. § 10a), prohibits a stay pending review. The proposed rule in nowise affects such statutory provisions respecting stays. By its terms, it simply indicates the procedure to be followed when a stay is sought.

1998 Amendments

The language and organization of the rule are amended to make the rule more easily understood. In addition to changes made to improve the understanding, the Advisory Committee has changed language to make style and terminology consistent throughout the appellate rules. These changes are intended to by stylistic only.

Rule 19. Settlement of a Judgment Enforcing an Agency Order in Part

When the court files an opinion directing entry of judgment enforcing the agency's order in part, the agency must within 14 days file with the clerk and serve on each other party a proposed judgment conforming to the opinion. A party who disagrees with the agency's proposed judgment must within 7 days file with the clerk and serve the agency with a proposed judgment that the party believes conforms to the opinion. The court will settle the judgment and direct entry without further hearing or argument. (As amended Mar. 10, 1986, eff. July 1, 1986; Apr. 24, 1998, eff. Dec. 1, 1998.)

ADVISORY COMMITTEE NOTES

1967 Adoption

This is § 12 of the uniform rule (see General Note following Rule 15) with changes in phraseology.

1986 Amendment

The deletion of the words "in whole or" is designed to eliminate delay in the issuance of a judgment when the court of appeals has either enforced completely the order of an agency or denied completely such enforcement. In such a clear-cut situation, it serves no useful purpose to delay the issuance of the judgment until a proposed judgment is submitted by the agency and reviewed by the respondent. This change conforms the Rule to the existing practice in most circuits. Other amendments are technical and no substantive change is intended.

1998 Amendments

The language of the rule are amended to make the rule more easily understood. In addition to changes made to improve the understanding, the Advisory Committee has changed language to make style and terminology consistent throughout the appellate rules. These changes are intended to by stylistic only.

Rule 20. Applicability of Rules to the Review or Enforcement of an Agency Order

All provisions of these rules, except Rules 3–14 and 22–23, apply to the review or enforcement of an agency order. In these rules, 'appellant' includes a petitioner or applicant, and 'appellee' includes a respondent.

(As amended Apr. 24, 1998, eff. Dec. 1, 1998.)

ADVISORY COMMITTEE NOTES

1967 Adoption

The proposed rule continues the present uniform practice of the circuits of regulating agency review or enforcement proceedings by the general rules applicable to appeals from judgments of the district courts.

1998 Amendments

The language of the rule are amended to make the rule more easily understood. In addition to changes made to improve the understanding, the Advisory Committee has changed language to make style and terminology consistent throughout the appellate rules. These changes are intended to by stylistic only.

TITLE V. EXTRAORDINARY WRITS

Rule 21. Writs of Mandamus and Prohibition, and Other Extraordinary Writs

(a) Mandamus or Prohibition to a Court: Petition, Filing, Service, and Docketing.

(1) A party petitioning for a writ of mandamus or prohibition directed to a court must file a petition with the circuit clerk with proof of service on all parties to the proceeding in the trial court. The party must also provide a copy to the trial-court judge. All parties to the proceeding in the trial court other than the petitioner are respondents for all purposes.

(2)(A) The petition must be titled 'In re [name of petitioner].'

(B) The petition must state:

 (i) the relief sought;

 (ii) the issues presented;

 (iii) the facts necessary to understand the issue presented by the petition; and

 (iv) the reasons why the writ should issue.

(C) The petition must include a copy of any order or opinion or parts of the record that may be essential to understand the matters set forth in the petition.

(3) Upon receiving the prescribed docket fee, the clerk must docket the petition and submit it to the court.

(b) Denial; Order Directing Answer; Briefs; Precedence.

(1) The court may deny the petition without an answer. Otherwise, it must order the respondent, if any, to answer within a fixed time.

(2) The clerk must serve the order to respond on all persons directed to respond.

(3) Two or more respondents may answer jointly.

(4) The court of appeals may invite or order the trial-court judge to address the petition or may invite an amicus curiae to do so. The trial-court judge may request permission to address the petition but may not do so unless invited or ordered to do so by the court of appeals.

(5) If briefing or oral argument is required, the clerk must advise the parties, and when appropriate, the trial-court judge or amicus curiae.

(6) The proceeding must be given preference over ordinary civil cases.

(7) The circuit clerk must send a copy of the final disposition to the trial-court judge.

(c) Other Extraordinary Writs. An application for an extraordinary writ other than one provided for in Rule 21(a) must be made by filing a petition with the circuit clerk with proof of service on the respondents. Proceedings on the application must conform, so far as is practicable, to the procedures prescribed in Rule 21(a) and (b).

(d) Form of Papers; Number of Copies. All papers must conform to Rule 32(c)(2). Except by the court's permission, a paper must not exceed 30 pages, exclusive of the disclosure statement, the proof of service, and the accompanying documents required by Rule 21(a)(2)(C). An original and 3 copies must be filed unless the court requires the filing of a different number by local rule or by order in a particular case. (As amended Apr. 29, 1994, eff. Dec. 1, 1994; Apr. 23, 1996, eff. Dec. 1, 1996; Apr. 24, 1998, eff. Dec. 1, 1998; Apr. 29, 2002, eff. Dec. 1, 2002.)

ADVISORY COMMITTEE NOTES

1967 Adoption

The authority of courts of appeals to issue extraordinary writs is derived from 28 U.S.C. § 1651. Subdivisions (a) and (b) regulate in detail the procedure surrounding the writs most commonly sought—mandamus or prohibition directed to a judge or judges. Those subdivisions are based upon Supreme Court Rule 31, with certain changes which reflect the uniform practice among the circuits (Seventh Circuit Rule 19 is a typical circuit rule). Subdivision (c) sets out a very general procedure to be followed in applications for the variety of other writs which may be issued under the authority of 28 U.S.C. § 1651.

1994 Amendments

Subdivision (d). The amendment makes it clear that a court may require a different number of copies either by rule or by order in an individual case. The number of copies of any document that a court of appeals needs varies depending upon the way in which the court conducts business. The internal operation of the courts of appeals necessarily varies from circuit to circuit because of differences in the number of

judges, the geographic area included within the circuit, and other such factors. Uniformity could be achieved only by setting the number of copies artificially high so that parties in all circuits file enough copies to satisfy the needs of the courts requiring the greatest number. Rather than do that, the Committee decided to make it clear that local rules may require a greater or lesser number of copies and that, if the circumstances of a particular case indicate the need for a different number of copies in that case, the court may so order.

1996 Amendments

In most instances, a writ of mandamus or prohibition is not actually directed to a judge in any more personal way than is an order reversing a court's judgment. Most often a petition for a writ of mandamus seeks review of the intrinsic merits of a judge's action and is in reality an adversary proceeding between the parties. See, *e.g., Walker v. Columbia Broadcasting System, Inc.,* 443 F.2d 33 (7th Cir.1971). In order to change the tone of the rule and of mandamus proceedings generally, the rule is amended so that the judge is not treated as a respondent. The caption and subdivision (a) are amended by deleting the reference to the writs as being "directed to a judge or judges."

Subdivision (a). Subdivision (a) applies to writs of mandamus or prohibition directed to a court, but it is amended so that a petition for a writ of mandamus or prohibition does not bear the name of the judge. The amendments to subdivision (a) speak, however, about mandamus or prohibition "directed to a court." This language is inserted to distinguish subdivision (a) from subdivision (c). Subdivision (c) governs all other extraordinary writs, including a writ of mandamus or prohibition directed to an administrative agency rather than to a court and a writ of habeas corpus.

The amendments require the petitioner to provide a copy of the petition to the trial court judge. This will alert the judge to the filing of the petition. This is necessary because the trial court judge is not treated as a respondent and, as a result, is not served. A companion amendment is made in subdivision (b). It requires the circuit clerk to send a copy of the disposition of the petition to the trial court judge.

Subdivision (b). The amendment provides that even if relief is requested of a particular judge, although the judge may request permission to respond, the judge may not do so unless the court invites or orders a response.

The court of appeals ordinarily will be adequately informed not only by the opinions or statements made by the trial court judge contemporaneously with the entry of the challenged order but also by the arguments made on behalf of the party opposing the relief. The latter does not create an attorney-client relationship between the party's attorney and the judge whose action is challenged, nor does it give rise to any right to compensation from the judge.

If the court of appeals desires to hear from the trial court judge, however, the court may invite or order the judge to respond. In some instances, especially those involving court administration or the failure of a judge to act, it may be that no one other than the judge can provide a thorough explanation of the matters at issue. Because it is ordinarily undesirable to place the trial court judge, even temporarily, in an adversarial posture with a litigant, the rule permits a court of appeals to invite an *amicus curiae* to provide a response to the petition. In those instances in which the respondent does not oppose issuance of the writ or does not have sufficient perspective on the issue to provide an adequate response, participation of an *amicus* may avoid the need for the trial judge to participate.

Subdivision (c). The changes are stylistic only. No substantive changes are intended.

1998 Amendments

The language and organization of the rule are amended to make the rule more easily understood. In addition to changes made to improve the understanding, the Advisory Committee has changed language to make style and terminology consistent throughout the appellate rules. These changes are intended to by stylistic only.

2002 Amendments

Subdivision (d). A petition for a writ of mandamus or prohibition, an application for another extraordinary writ, and an answer to such a petition or application are all "other papers" for purposes of Rule 32(c)(2), and all of the requirements of Rule 32(a) apply to those papers, except as provided in Rule 32(c)(2). During the 1998 restyling of the Federal Rules of Appellate Procedure, Rule 21(d) was inadvertently changed to suggest that only the requirements of Rule 32(a)(1) apply to such papers. Rule 21(d) has been amended to correct that error.

Rule 21(d) has been further amended to limit the length of papers filed under Rule 21.

Changes Made After Publication and Comments No changes were made to the text of the proposed amendment or to the Committee Note, except that the page limit was increased from 20 pages to 30 pages. The Committee was persuaded by some commentators that petitions for extraordinary writs closely resemble principal briefs on the merits and should be allotted more than 20 pages.

TITLE VI. HABEAS CORPUS; PROCEEDINGS IN FORMA PAUPERIS

Rule 22. **Habeas Corpus and Section 2255 Proceedings**

(a) Application for the Original Writ. An application for a writ of habeas corpus must be made to the appropriate district court. If made to a circuit judge, the application must be transferred to the appropriate district court. If a district court denies an application made or transferred to it, renewal of the application before a circuit judge is not permitted. The applicant may, under 28 U.S.C. § 2253, appeal to the court of appeals from the district court's order denying the application.

(b) Certificate of Appealability.

(1) In a habeas corpus proceeding in which the detention complained of arises from process issued

by a state court, or in a 28 U.S.C. § 2255 proceeding, the applicant cannot take an appeal unless a circuit justice or a circuit or district judge issues a certificate of appealability under 28 U.S.C. § 2253(c). If an applicant files a notice of appeal, the district judge who rendered the judgment must either issue a certificate of appealability or state why a certificate should not issue. The district clerk must send the certificate or statement to the court of appeals with the notice of appeal and the file of the district-court proceedings. If the district judge has denied the certificate, the applicant may request a circuit judge to issue the certificate.

(2) A request addressed to the court of appeals may be considered by a circuit judge or judges, as the court prescribes. If no express request for a certificate is filed, the notice of appeal constitutes a request addressed to the judges of the court of appeals.

(3) A certificate of appealability is not required when a state or its representative or the United States or its representative appeals.

(As amended Pub.L. 104–132, Title I, § 103, Apr. 24, 1996, 110 Stat. 1218; Apr. 24, 1998, eff. Dec. 1, 1998.)

ADVISORY COMMITTEE NOTES

1967 Adoption

Subdivision (a). Title 28 U.S.C. § 2241(a) authorizes circuit judges to issue the writ of habeas corpus. Section 2241(b) [§ 2241(b) of this title], however, authorizes a circuit judge to decline to entertain an application and to transfer it to the appropriate district court, and this is the usual practice. The first two sentences merely make present practice explicit. Title 28 U.S.C. § 2253 seems clearly to contemplate that once an application is presented to a district judge and is denied by him, the remedy is an appeal from the order of denial. But the language of 28 U.S.C. § 2241 seems to authorize a second original application to a circuit judge following a denial by a district judge. *In re Gersing*, 79 U.S.App.D. 245, 145 F.2d 481 (D.C.Cir., 1944) and *Chapman v. Teets*, 241 F.2d 186 (9th Cir., 1957) acknowledge the availability of such a procedure. But the procedure is ordinarily a waste of time for all involved, and the final sentence attempts to discourage it.

A court of appeals has no jurisdiction as a court to grant an original writ of habeas corpus, and courts of appeals have dismissed applications addressed to them. *Loum v. Alvis*, 263 F.2d 836 (6th Cir., 1959); *In re Berry*, 221 F.2d 798 (9th Cir., 1955); *Posey v. Dowd*, 134 F.2d 613 (7th Cir., 1943). The fairer and more expeditious practice is for the court of appeals to regard an application addressed to it as being addressed to one of its members, and to transfer the application to the appropriate district court in accordance with the provisions of this rule. Perhaps such a disposition is required by the rationale of *In re Burwell*, 350 U.S. 521, 76 S.Ct. 539, 100 L.Ed. 666 (1956).

Subdivision (b). Title 28 U.S.C. § 2253 provides that an appeal may not be taken in a habeas corpus proceeding where confinement is under a judgment of a state court

unless the judge who rendered the order in the habeas corpus proceeding, or a circuit justice or judge, issues a certificate of probable cause. In the interest of insuring that the matter of the certificate will not be overlooked and that, if the certificate is denied, the reasons for denial in the first instance will be available on any subsequent application, the proposed rule requires the district judge to issue the certificate or to state reasons for its denial.

While 28 U.S.C. § 2253 does not authorize the court of appeals as a court to grant a certificate of probable cause, *In re Burwell*, 350 U.S. 521, 76 S.Ct. 539, 100 L.Ed. 666 (1956) makes it clear that a court of appeals may not decline to consider a request for the certificate addressed to it as a court but must regard the request as made to the judges thereof. The fourth sentence incorporates the Burwell rule.

Although 28 U.S.C. § 2253 appears to require a certificate of probable cause even when an appeal is taken by a state or its representative, the legislative history strongly suggests that the intention of Congress was to require a certificate only in the case in which an appeal is taken by an applicant for the writ. See *United States ex rel. Tillery v. Cavell*, 294 F.2d 12 (3d Cir., 1960). Four of the five circuits which have ruled on the point have so interpreted § 2253. *United States ex rel. Tillery v. Cavell*, supra; *Buder v. Bell*, 306 F.2d 71 (6th Cir., 1962); *United States ex rel. Calhoun v. Pate*, 341 F.2d 885 (7th Cir., 1965); *State of Texas v. Graves*, 352 F.2d 514 (5th Cir., 1965). Cf. *United States ex rel. Carrol v. LaVallee*, 342 F.2d 641 (2d Cir., 1965). The final sentence makes it clear that a certificate of probable cause is not required of a state or its representative.

1998 Amendments

The language and organization of the rule are amended to make the rule more easily understood. In addition to changes made to improve the understanding, the Advisory Committee has changed language to make style and terminology consistent throughout the appellate rules. These changes are intended to by stylistic only; in this rule, however, substantive changes are made in paragraphs (b)(1) and (b)(3).

Subdivision (b), paragraph (1). Two substantive changes are made in this paragraph. First, the paragraph is made applicable to 28 U.S.C. § 2255 proceedings. This brings the rule into conformity with 28 U.S.C. § 2253 as amended by the Anti-Terrorism and Effective Death Penalty Act of 1996, Pub.L. No. 104–132. Second, the rule states that a certificate of appealability may be issued by a "circuit justice or a circuit or district judge." That language adds a reference to the circuit justice which also brings the rule into conformity with section 2253. The language continues to state that in addition to the circuit justice, both a circuit and a district judge may issue a certificate of appealability. The language of section 2253 is ambiguous; it states that a certificate of appealability may be issued by "a circuit justice or judge." Since the enactment of the Anti–Terrorism and Effective Death Penalty Act, three circuits have held that both district and circuit judges, as well as the circuit justice, may issue a certificate of appealability. *Else v. Johnson*, 104 F.3d 82 (5th Cir. 1997); *Lyons v. Ohio Adult Parole Authority*, 105 F.3d 1063 (6th Cir. 1997); and *Hunter v. United States*, 101 F.3d 1565 (11th Cir. 1996). The approach taken by the rule is consistent with those decisions.

Subdivision (b), paragraph (3). The Anti-Terrorism and Effective Death Penalty Act of 1996, Pub.L. No. 104–132,

amended 28 U.S.C. § 2253 to make it applicable to § 2255 proceedings. Accordingly, paragraph (3) is amended to provide that when the United States or its representative appeals, a certificate of appealability is not required.

Rule 23. Custody or Release of a Prisoner in a Habeas Corpus Proceeding

(a) Transfer of Custody Pending Review. Pending review of a decision in a habeas corpus proceeding commenced before a court, justice, or judge of the United States for the release of a prisoner, the person having custody of the prisoner must not transfer custody to another unless a transfer is directed in accordance with this rule. When, upon application, a custodian shows the need for a transfer, the court, justice, or judge rendering the decision under review may authorize the transfer and substitute the successor custodian as a party.

(b) Detention or Release Pending Review of Decision Not to Release. While a decision not to release a prisoner is under review, the court or judge rendering the decision, or the court of appeals, or the Supreme Court, or a judge or justice of either court, may order that the prisoner be:

(1) detained in the custody from which release is sought;

(2) detained in other appropriate custody; or

(3) released on personal recognizance, with or without surety.

(c) Release Pending Review of Decision Ordering Release. While a decision ordering the release of a prisoner is under review, the prisoner must—unless the court or judge rendering the decision, or the court of appeals, or the Supreme Court, or a judge or justice of either court orders otherwise—be released on personal recognizance, with or without surety.

(d) Modification of the Initial Order on Custody. An initial order governing the prisoner's custody or release, including any recognizance or surety, continues in effect pending review unless for special reasons shown to the court of appeals or the Supreme Court, or to a judge or justice of either court, the order is modified or an independent order regarding custody, release, or surety is issued.

(As amended Mar. 10, 1986, eff. July 1, 1986; Apr. 24, 1998, eff. Dec. 1, 1998.)

ADVISORY COMMITTEE NOTES

1967 Adoption

The rule is the same as Supreme Court Rule 49 as amended on June 12, 1967, effective October 2, 1967.

1986 Amendment

The amendments to Rules 23(b) and (c) are technical. No substantive change is intended.

1998 Amendments

The language and organization of the rule are amended to make the rule more easily understood. In addition to changes made to improve the understanding, the Advisory Committee has changed language to make style and terminology consistent throughout the appellate rules. These changes are intended to by stylistic only.

Subdivision (d). The current rule states that the initial order governing custody or release "shall govern review" in the court of appeals. The amended language says that the initial order generally "continues in effect" pending review.

When Rule 23 was adopted it used the same language as Supreme Court Rule 49, which then governed custody of prisoners in habeas corpus proceedings. The "shall govern review" language was drawn from the Supreme Court Rule. The Supreme Court has since amended its rule, now Rule 36, to say that the initial order "shall continue in effect" unless for reasons shown it is modified or a new order is entered. Rule 23 is amended to similarly state that the initial order "continues in effect." The new language is clearer. It removes the possible implication that the initial order created law of the case, a strange notion to attach to an order regarding custody or release.

Rule 24. Proceeding in Forma Pauperis

(a) Leave to Proceed in Forma Pauperis.

(1) Motion in the District Court. Except as stated in Rule 24(a)(3), a party to a district-court action who desires to appeal in forma pauperis must file a motion in the district court. The party must attach an affidavit that:

(A) shows in the detail prescribed by Form 4 of the Appendix of Forms the party's inability to pay or to give security for fees and costs;

(B) claims an entitlement to redress; and

(C) states the issues that the party intends to present on appeal.

(2) Action on the Motion. If the district court grants the motion, the party may proceed on appeal without prepaying or giving security for fees and costs, unless a statute provides otherwise. If the district court denies the motion, it must state its reasons in writing.

(3) Prior Approval. A party who was permitted to proceed in forma pauperis in the district-court action, or who was determined to be financially unable to obtain an adequate defense in a criminal case, may proceed on appeal in forma pauperis without further authorization, unless:

(A) the district court—before or after the notice of appeal is filed—certifies that the appeal is not taken in good faith or finds that the party is not otherwise entitled to proceed in forma pauperis and states in writing its reasons for the certification or finding; or

(B) a statute provides otherwise.

(4) Notice of District Court's Denial. The district clerk must immediately notify the parties and the court of appeals when the district court does any of the following:

(A) denies a motion to proceed on appeal in forma pauperis;

(B) certifies that the appeal is not taken in good faith; or

(C) finds that the party is not otherwise entitled to proceed in forma pauperis.

(5) Motion in the Court of Appeals. A party may file a motion to proceed on appeal in forma pauperis in the court of appeals within 30 days after service of the notice prescribed in Rule 24(a)(4). The motion must include a copy of the affidavit filed in the district court and the district court's statement of reasons for its action. If no affidavit was filed in the district court, the party must include the affidavit prescribed by Rule 24(a)(1).

(b) Leave to Proceed in Forma Pauperis on Appeal or Review of an Administrative–Agency Proceeding. When an appeal or review of a proceeding before an administrative agency, board, commission, or officer (including for the purpose of this rule the United States Tax Court) proceeds directly in a court of appeals, a party may file in the court of appeals a motion for leave to proceed on appeal in forma pauperis with an affidavit prescribed by Rule 24(a)(1).

(c) Leave to Use Original Record. A party allowed to proceed on appeal in forma pauperis may request that the appeal be heard on the original record without reproducing any part.

(As amended Apr. 30, 1979, eff. Aug. 1, 1979; Mar. 10, 1986, eff. July 1, 1986; Apr. 24, 1998, eff. Dec. 1, 1998; Apr. 29, 2002, eff. Dec. 1, 2002.)

ADVISORY COMMITTEE NOTES

1967 Adoption

Subdivision (a). Authority to allow prosecution of an appeal in forma pauperis is vested in "[a]ny court of the United States" by 28 U.S.C. § 1915(a). The second paragraph of § 1915(a) seems to contemplate initial application to the district court for permission to proceed in forma pauperis, and although the circuit rules are generally silent on the question, the case law requires initial application to the district court. *Hayes v. United States*, 258 F.2d 400 (5th Cir., 1958), cert. den. 358 U.S. 856, 79 S.Ct. 87, 3 L.Ed.2d 89 (1958); *Elkins v. United States*, 250 F.2d 145 (9th Cir., 1957) see 364 U.S. 206, 80 S.Ct. 1437, 4 L.Ed.2d 1669 (1960); *United States v. Farley*, 238 F.2d 575 (2d Cir., 1956) see 354 U.S. 521, 77 S.Ct. 1371, 1 L.Ed.2d 1529 (1957). D.C.Cir. Rule 41(a) requires initial application to the district court. The content of the affidavit follows the language of the statute; the requirement of a statement of the issues comprehends the statutory requirement of a statement of "the nature of the . . . appeal. . . ." The second sentence is in accord with the decision in *McGann v. United States*, 362 U.S. 309, 80 S.Ct. 725, 4 L.Ed.2d 734 (1960). The requirement contained in the third sentence has no counterpart in

present circuit rules, but it has been imposed by decision in at least two circuits. *Ragan v. Cox*, 305 F.2d 58 (10th Cir., 1962); *United States ex rel. Breedlove v. Dowd*, 269 F.2d 693 (7th Cir., 1959).

The second paragraph permits one whose indigency has been previously determined by the district court to proceed on appeal in forma pauperis without the necessity of a redetermination of indigency, while reserving to the district court its statutory authority to certify that the appeal is not taken in good faith, 28 U.S.C. § 1915(a), and permitting an inquiry into whether the circumstances of the party who was originally entitled to proceed in forma pauperis have changed during the course of the litigation. Cf. Sixth Circuit Rule 26 [rule 26, U.S.Ct. of App. 6th Cir.].

The final paragraph establishes a subsequent motion in the court of appeals, rather than an appeal from the order of denial or from the certification of lack of good faith, as the proper procedure for calling in question the correctness of the action of the district court. The simple and expeditious motion procedure seems clearly preferable to an appeal. This paragraph applies only to applications for leave to appeal in forma pauperis. The order of a district court refusing leave to initiate an action in the district court in forma pauperis is reviewable on appeal. See *Roberts v. United States District Court*, 339 U.S. 844, 70 S.Ct. 954, 94 L.Ed. 1326 (1950).

Subdivision (b). Authority to allow prosecution in forma pauperis is vested only in a "court of the United States" (see Note to subdivision (a), above). Thus in proceedings brought directly in a court of appeals to review decisions of agencies or of the Tax Court, authority to proceed in forma pauperis should be sought in the court of appeals. If initial review of agency action is had in a district court, an application to appeal to a court of appeals in forma pauperis from the judgment of the district court is governed by the provisions of subdivision (a).

1979 Amendment

The proposed amendment reflects the change in the title of the Tax Court to "United States Tax Court." See 26 U.S.C. § 7441.

1986 Amendment

The amendments to Rule 24(a) are technical. No substantive change is intended.

1998 Amendments

The language and organization of the rule are amended to make the rule more easily understood. In addition to changes made to improve the understanding, the Advisory Committee has changed language to make style and terminology consistent throughout the appellate rules. These changes are intended to by stylistic only. The Advisory Committee deletes the language in subdivision (c) authorizing a party proceeding in forma pauperis to file papers in typewritten form because the authorization is unnecessary. The rules permit all parties to file typewritten documents.

Subdivision (a)(2). Section 804 of the Prison Litigation Reform Act of 1995 ("PLRA") amended 28 U.S.C. § 1915 to require that prisoners who bring civil actions or appeals from civil actions must "pay the full amount of a filing fee." 28 U.S.C. § 1915(b)(1). Prisoners who are unable to pay the full amount of the filing fee at the time that their actions or appeals are filed are generally required to pay part of the fee and then to pay the remainder of the fee in installments. 28 U.S.C. § 1915(b). By contrast, Rule 24(a)(2) has provided that, after the district court grants a litigant's motion to proceed on appeal in forma pauperis, the litigant may proceed "without prepaying or giving security for fees and costs." Thus, the PLRA and Rule 24(a)(2) appear to be in conflict.

Rule 24(a)(2) has been amended to resolve this conflict. Recognizing that future legislation regarding prisoner litigation is likely, the Committee has not attempted to incorporate into Rule 24 all of the requirements of the current version of 28 U.S.C. § 1915. Rather, the Committee has amended Rule 24(a)(2) to clarify that the rule is not meant to conflict with anything required by the PLRA or any other statute.

Subdivision (a)(3). Rule 24(a)(3) has also been amended to eliminate an apparent conflict with the PLRA. Rule 24(a)(3) has provided that a party who was permitted to proceed in forma pauperis in the district court may continue to proceed in forma pauperis in the court of appeals without further authorization, subject to certain conditions. The PLRA, by contrast, provides that a prisoner who was permitted to proceed in forma pauperis in the district court and who wishes to continue to proceed in forma pauperis on appeal may not do so "automatically," but must seek permission. *See, e.g., Morgan v. Haro,* 112 F.3d 788, 789 (5th Cir. 1997) ("A prisoner who seeks to proceed IFP on appeal must obtain leave to so proceed despite proceeding IFP in the district court.").

Rule 24(a)(3) has been amended to resolve this conflict. Again, recognizing that future legislation regarding prisoner litigation is likely, the Committee has not attempted to incorporate into Rule 24 all of the requirements of the current version of 28 U.S.C. § 1915. Rather, the Committee has amended Rule 24(a)(3) to clarify that the rule is not meant to conflict with anything required by the PLRA or any other statute.

Changes Made After Publication and Comments No changes were made to the text of the proposed amendment or to the Committee Note, except that "a statute provides otherwise" was substituted in place of "the law requires otherwise" in the text of the rule and conforming changes (as well as a couple of minor stylistic changes) were made to the Committee Note.

TITLE VII. GENERAL PROVISIONS

Rule 25. Filing and Service

(a) Filing.

(1) Filing with the Clerk. A paper required or permitted to be filed in a court of appeals must be filed with the clerk.

(2) Filing: Method and Timeliness.

(A) In general. Filing may be accomplished by mail addressed to the clerk, but filing is not timely unless the clerk receives the papers within the time fixed for filing.

(B) A brief or appendix. A brief or appendix is timely filed, however, if on or before the last day for filing, it is:

(i) mailed to the clerk by First–Class Mail, or other class of mail that is at least as expeditious, postage prepaid; or

(ii) dispatched to a third-party commercial carrier for delivery to the clerk within 3 calendar days.

(C) Inmate filing. A paper filed by an inmate confined in an institution is timely if deposited in the institution's internal mailing system on or before the last day for filing. If an institution has a system designed for legal mail, the inmate must use that system to receive the benefit of this rule. Timely filing may be shown by a declaration in compliance with 28 U.S.C. § 1746 or by a notarized statement, either of which must set forth the date of deposit and state that first-class postage has been prepaid.

(D) Electronic filing. A court of appeals may by local rule permit or require papers to be filed, signed, or verified by electronic means that are consistent with technical standards, if any, that the Judicial Conference of the United States establishes. A local rule may require filing by electronic means only if reasonable exceptions are allowed. A paper filed by electronic means in compliance with a local rule constitutes a written paper for the purpose of applying these rules.

(3) Filing a Motion with a Judge. If a motion requests relief that may be granted by a single judge, the judge may permit the motion to be filed with the judge; the judge must note the filing date on the motion and give it to the clerk.

(4) Clerk's Refusal of Documents. The clerk must not refuse to accept for filing any paper presented for that purpose solely because it is not presented in proper form as required by these rules or by any local rule or practice.

(b) Service of All Papers Required. Unless a rule requires service by the clerk, a party must, at or before the time of filing a paper, serve a copy on the other parties to the appeal or review. Service on a party represented by counsel must be made on the party's counsel.

(c) Manner of Service.

(1) Service may be any of the following:

(A) personal, including delivery to a responsible person at the office of counsel;

(B) by mail;

(C) by third-party commercial carrier for delivery within 3 calendar days; or

(D) by electronic means, if the party being served consents in writing.

(2) If authorized by local rule, a party may use the court's transmission equipment to make electronic service under Rule 25(c)(1)(D).

(3) When reasonable considering such factors as the immediacy of the relief sought, distance, and cost, service on a party must be by a manner at least as expeditious as the manner used to file the paper with the court.

(4) Service by mail or by commercial carrier is complete on mailing or delivery to the carrier. Service by electronic means is complete on transmission, unless the party making service is notified that the paper was not received by the party served.

(d) Proof of Service.

(1) A paper presented for filing must contain either of the following:

(A) an acknowledgment of service by the person served; or

(B) proof of service consisting of a statement by the person who made service certifying:

(i) the date and manner of service;

(ii) the names of the persons served; and

(iii) their mail or electronic addresses, facsimile numbers, or the addresses of the places of delivery, as appropriate for the manner of service.

(2) When a brief or appendix is filed by mailing or dispatch in accordance with Rule 25(a)(2)(B), the proof of service must also state the date and manner by which the document was mailed or dispatched to the clerk.

(3) Proof of service may appear on or be affixed to the papers filed.

(e) Number of Copies. When these rules require the filing or furnishing of a number of copies, a court may require a different number by local rule or by order in a particular case.

(As amended Mar. 10, 1986, eff. July 1, 1986; Apr. 30, 1991, eff. Dec. 1, 1991; Apr. 22, 1993, eff. Dec. 1, 1993; Apr. 29, 1994, eff. Dec. 1, 1994; Apr. 23, 1996, eff. Dec. 1, 1996; Apr. 24, 1998, eff. Dec. 1, 1998; Apr. 29, 2002, eff. Dec. 1, 2002: Apr. 12, 2006, eff. Dec. 1, 2006.)

Proposed Addition of Subdivision (a)(5)

Effective December 1, 2007, absent contrary Congressional action, subdivision (a)(5) of this rule is added to read as follows:

(5) Privacy Protection. *An appeal in a case whose privacy protection was governed by Federal Rule of Bankruptcy Procedure 9037, Federal Rule of Civil Procedure 5.2, or Federal Rule of Criminal Procedure 49.1 is governed by the same rule on appeal. In all other proceedings, privacy protection is governed by Federal Rule of Civil Procedure 5.2, except that Federal Rule of Criminal Procedure 49.1 governs when an extraordinary writ is sought in a criminal case.*

ADVISORY COMMITTEE NOTES

1967 Adoption

The rule that filing is not timely unless the papers filed are received within the time allowed is the familiar one. *Ward v. Atlantic Coast Line R.R. Co.*, 265 F.2d 75 (5th Cir., 1959), rev'd on other grounds 362 U.S. 396, 80 S.Ct. 789, 4 L.Ed.2d 820 (1960); *Kahler-Ellis Co. v. Ohio Turnpike Commission*, 225 F.2d 922 (6th Cir., 1955). An exception is made in the case of briefs and appendices in order to afford the parties the maximum time for their preparation. By the terms of the exception, air mail delivery must be used whenever it is the most expeditious manner of delivery.

A majority of the circuits now require service of all papers filed with the clerk. The usual provision in present rules is for service on "adverse" parties. In view of the extreme simplicity of service by mail, there seems to be no reason why a party who files a paper should not be required to serve all parties to the proceeding in the court of appeals, whether or not they may be deemed adverse. The common requirement of proof of service is retained, but the rule permits it to be made by simple certification, which may be endorsed on the copy which is filed.

1986 Amendment

The amendments to Rules 25(a) and (b) are technical. No substantive change is intended.

1991 Amendment

Subdivision (a). The amendment permits, but does not require, courts of appeals to adopt local rules that allow filing of papers by electronic means. However, courts of appeals cannot adopt such local rules until the Judicial Conference of the United States authorizes filing by facsimile or other electronic means.

1993 Amendment

The amendment accompanies new subdivision (c) of Rule 4 and extends the holding in *Houston v. Lack*, 487 U.S. 266 (1988), to all papers filed in the courts of appeals by persons confined in institutions.

1994 Amendment

Subdivision (a). Several circuits have local rules that authorize the office of the clerk to refuse to accept for filing papers that are not in the form required by these rules or by local rules. This is not a suitable role for the office of the clerk and the practice exposes litigants to the hazards of time

bars; for these reasons, such rules are proscribed by this rule. This provision is similar to Fed.R.Civ.P. 5(e) and Fed.R.Bankr.P. 5005.

The Committee wishes to make it clear that the provision prohibiting a clerk from refusing a document does not mean that a clerk's office may no longer screen documents to determine whether they comply with the rules. A court may delegate to the clerk authority to inform a party about any noncompliance with the rules and, if the party is willing to correct the document, to determine a date by which the corrected document must be resubmitted. If a party refuses to take the steps recommended by the clerk or if in the clerk's judgment the party fails to correct the noncompliance, the clerk must refer the matter to the court for a ruling.

Subdivision (d). Two changes have been made in this subdivision. Subdivision (d) provides that a paper presented for filing must contain proof of service.

The last sentence of subdivision (d) has been deleted as unnecessary. That sentence stated that a clerk could permit papers to be filed without the acknowledgment or proof of service but must require that it be filed promptly thereafter. In light of the change made in subdivision (a) which states that a clerk may not refuse to accept for filing a document because it is not in the proper form, there is no further need for a provision stating that a clerk may accept a paper lacking a proof of service. The clerk must accept such a paper. That portion of the deleted sentence stating that the clerk must require that proof of service be filed promptly after the filing of the document if the proof is not filed concurrently with the document is also unnecessary.

The second amendment requires that the certificate of service must state the addresses to which the papers were mailed or at which they were delivered. The Federal Circuit has a similar local rule, Fed.Cir.R. 25.

Subdivision (e). Subdivision (e) is a new subdivision. It makes it clear that whenever these rules require a party to file or furnish a number of copies a court may require a different number of copies either by rule or by order in an individual case. The number of copies of any document that a court of appeals needs varies depending upon the way in which the court conducts business. The internal operation of the courts of appeals necessarily varies from circuit to circuit because of differences in the number of judges, the geographic area included within the circuit, and other such factors. Uniformity could be achieved only by setting the number of copies artificially high so that parties in all circuits file enough copies to satisfy the needs of the court requiring the greatest number. Rather than do that, the Committee decided to make it clear that local rules may require a greater or lesser number of copies and that, if the circumstances of a particular case indicate the need for a different number of copies in that case, the court may so order.

A party must consult local rules to determine whether the court requires a different number than that specified in these national rules. The Committee believes it would be helpful if each circuit either: 1) included a chart at the beginning of its local rules showing the number of copies of each document required to be filed with the court along with citation to the controlling rule; or 2) made available such a chart to each party upon commencement of an appeal; or both. If a party fails to file the required number of copies, the failure does not create a jurisdictional defect. Rule 3(a) states: "Failure of an appellant to take any step other than the timely filing of a notice of appeal does not affect the validity of the appeal, but is ground only for such action as the court of appeals deems appropriate...."

1996 Amendments

Subdivision (a). The amendment deletes the language requiring a party to use "the most expeditious form of delivery by mail, except special delivery" in order to file a brief using the mailbox rule. That language was adopted before the Postal Service offered Express Mail and other expedited delivery services. The amendment makes it clear that it is sufficient to use First–Class Mail. Other equally or more expeditious classes of mail service, such as Express Mail, also may be used. In addition, the amendment permits the use of commercial carriers. The use of private, overnight courier services has become commonplace in law practice. Expedited services offered by commercial carriers often provide faster delivery than First–Class Mail; therefore, there should be no objection to the use of commercial carriers as long as they are reliable. In order to make use of the mailbox rule when using a commercial carrier, the amendment requires that the filer employ a carrier who undertakes to deliver the document in no more than three calendar days. The three-calendar-day period coordinates with the three-day extension provided by Rule 26(c).

Subdivision (c). The amendment permits service by commercial carrier if the carrier is to deliver the paper to the party being served within three days of the carrier's receipt of the paper. The amendment also expresses a desire that when reasonable, service on a party be accomplished by a manner as expeditious as the manner used to file the paper with the court. When a brief or motion is filed with the court by hand delivering the paper to the clerk's office, or by overnight courier, the copies should be served on the other parties by an equally expeditious manner—meaning either by personal service, if distance permits, or by overnight courier, if mail delivery to the party is not ordinarily accomplished overnight. The reasonableness standard is included so that if a paper is hand delivered to the clerk's office for filing but the other parties must be served in a different city, state, or region, personal service on them ordinarily will not be expected. If use of an equally expeditious manner of service is not reasonable, use of the next most expeditious manner may be. For example, if the paper is filed by hand delivery to the clerk's office but the other parties reside in distant cities, service on them need not be personal but in most instances should be by overnight courier. Even that may not be required, however, if the number of parties that must be served would make the use of overnight service too costly. A factor that bears upon the reasonableness of serving parties expeditiously is the immediacy of the relief requested.

Subdivision (d). The amendment adds a requirement that when a brief or appendix is filed by mail or commercial carrier, the certificate of service state the date and manner by which the document was mailed or dispatched to the clerk. Including that information in the certificate of service avoids the necessity for a separate certificate concerning the date and manner of filing.

1998 Amendments

The language and organization of the rule are amended to make the rule more easily understood. In addition to changes made to improve the understanding, the Advisory Committee has changed language to make style and terminology consistent throughout the appellate rules. These changes are intended to by stylistic only; a substantive amendment is made, however, in subdivision (a).

Subdivision (a). The substantive amendment in this subdivision is in subparagraph (a)(2)(C) and is a companion to an amendment in Rule 4(c). Currently Rule 25(a)(2(C) provides that if an inmate confined in an institution files a document by depositing it in the institution's internal mail system, the document is timely filed if deposited on or before the last day for filing. Some institutions have special internal mail systems for handling legal mail; such systems often record the date of deposit of mail by an inmate, the date of delivery of mail to an inmate, etc. The Advisory Committee amends the rule to require an inmate to use the system designed for legal mail, if there is one, in order to receive the benefit of this subparagraph

2002 Amendments

Rule 25(a)(2)(D) presently authorizes the courts of appeals to permit papers to be *filed* by electronic means. Rule 25 has been amended in several respects to permit papers also to be *served* electronically. In addition, Rule 25(c) has been reorganized and subdivided to make it easier to understand.

Subdivision (c)(1)(D). New subdivision (c)(1)(D) has been added to permit service to be made electronically, such as by e-mail or fax. No party may be served electronically, either by the clerk or by another party, unless the party has consented in writing to such service.

A court of appeals may not, by local rule, forbid the use of electronic service on a party that has consented to its use. At the same time, courts have considerable discretion to use local rules to regulate electronic service. Difficult and presently unforeseeable questions are likely to arise as electronic service becomes more common. Courts have the flexibility to use their local rules to address those questions. For example, courts may use local rules to set forth specific procedures that a party must follow before the party will be deemed to have given written consent to electronic service.

Parties also have the flexibility to define the terms of their consent; a party's consent to electronic service does not have to be "all-or-nothing." For example, a party may consent to service by facsimile transmission, but not by electronic mail; or a party may consent to electronic service only if "courtesy" copies of all transmissions are mailed within 24 hours; or a party may consent to electronic service of only documents that were created with Corel WordPerfect.

Subdivision (c)(2). The courts of appeals are authorized under Rule 25(a)(2)(D) to permit papers to be filed electronically. Technological advances may someday make it possible for a court to forward an electronically filed paper to all parties automatically or semi-automatically. When such court-facilitated service becomes possible, courts may decide to permit parties to use the courts' transmission facilities to serve electronically filed papers on other parties who have consented to such service. Court personnel would use the court's computer system to forward the papers, but the papers would be considered served by the filing parties, just as papers that are carried from one address to another by the United States Postal Service are considered served by the sending parties. New subdivision (c)(2) has been added so that the courts of appeals may use local rules to authorize such use of their transmission facilities, as well as to address the many questions that court-facilitated electronic service is likely to raise.

Subdivision (c)(4). The second sentence of new subdivision (c)(4) has been added to provide that electronic service is complete upon transmission. Transmission occurs when the sender performs the last act that he or she must perform to transmit a paper electronically; typically, it occurs when the sender hits the "send" or "transmit" button on an electronic mail program. There is one exception to the rule that electronic service is complete upon transmission: If the sender is notified—by the sender's e-mail program or otherwise—that the paper was not received, service is not complete, and the sender must take additional steps to effect service. A paper has been "received" by the party on which it has been served as long as the party has the ability to retrieve it. A party cannot defeat service by choosing not to access electronic mail on its server.

Changes Made After Publication and Comments No changes were made to the text of the proposed amendment. A paragraph was added to the Committee Note to clarify that consent to electronic service is not an "all-or-nothing" matter.

Subdivision (d)(1)(B)(iii). Subdivision (d)(1)(B)(iii) has been amended to require that, when a paper is served electronically, the proof of service of that paper must include the electronic address or facsimile number to which the paper was transmitted.

Changes Made After Publication and Comments The text of the proposed amendment was changed to refer to "electronic" addresses (instead of to "e-mail" addresses), to include "facsimile numbers," and to add the concluding phrase "as appropriate for the manner of service." Conforming changes were made to the Committee Note.

2006 Amendment

Subdivision (a)(2)(D). Amended Rule 25(a)(2)(D) acknowledges that many courts have required electronic filing by means of a standing order, procedures manual, or local rule. These local practices reflect the advantages that courts and most litigants realize from electronic filing. Courts that mandate electronic filing recognize the need to make exceptions when requiring electronic filing imposes a hardship on a party. Under Rule 25(a)(2)(D), a local rule that requires electronic filing must include reasonable exceptions, but Rule 25(a)(2)(D) does not define the scope of those exceptions. Experience with the local rules that have been adopted and that will emerge will aid in drafting new local rules and will facilitate gradual convergence on uniform exceptions, whether in local rules or in an amended Rule 25(a)(2)(D).

A local rule may require that both electronic and "hard" copies of a paper be filed. Nothing in the last sentence of Rule 25(a)(2)(D) is meant to imply otherwise.

2007 Amendments

[Effective December 1, 2007, absent contrary Congressional action.]

Subdivision (a)(5). Section 205(c)(3)(A)(i) of the E–Government Act of 2002 (Public Law 107–347, as amended by Public Law 108–281) requires that the rules of practice and procedure be amended "to protect privacy and security concerns relating to electronic filing of documents and the public availability ... of documents filed electronically." In response to that directive, the Federal Rules of Bankruptcy, Civil, and Criminal Procedure have been amended, not merely to address the privacy and security concerns raised by documents that are filed electronically, but also to address similar concerns raised by documents that are filed in paper form. *See* Fed. R. Bankr. P. 9037; Fed. R. Civ. P. 5.2; and Fed. R. Crim. P. 49.1.

Appellate Rule 25(a)(5) requires that, in cases that arise on appeal from a district court, bankruptcy appellate panel, or bankruptcy court, the privacy rule that applied to the case below will continue to apply to the case on appeal. With one exception, all other cases—such as cases involving the review or enforcement of an agency order, the review of a decision of the tax court, or the consideration of a petition for an extraordinary writ—will be governed by Civil Rule 5.2. The only exception is when an extraordinary writ is sought in a criminal case—that is, a case in which the related trial-court proceeding is governed by Criminal Rule 49.1. In such a case, Criminal Rule 49.1 will govern in the court of appeals as well.

Rule 26. Computing and Extending Time

(a) Computing Time. The following rules apply in computing any period of time specified in these rules or in any local rule, court order, or applicable statute:

(1) Exclude the day of the act, event, or default that begins the period.

(2) Exclude intermediate Saturdays, Sundays, and legal holidays when the period is less than 11 days, unless stated in calendar days.

(3) Include the last day of the period unless it is a Saturday, Sunday, legal holiday, or—if the act to be done is filing a paper in court—a day on which the weather or other conditions make the clerk's office inaccessible.

(4) As used in this rule, "legal holiday" means New Year's Day, Martin Luther King, Jr.'s Birthday, Washington's Birthday, Memorial Day, Independence Day, Labor Day, Columbus Day, Veterans' Day, Thanksgiving Day, Christmas Day, and any other day declared a holiday by the President, Congress, or the state in which is located either the district court that rendered the challenged judgment or order, or the circuit clerk's principal office.

(b) Extending Time. For good cause, the court may extend the time prescribed by these rules or by its order to perform any act, or may permit an act to be done after that time expires. But the court may not extend the time to file:

(1) a notice of appeal (except as authorized in Rule 4) or a petition for permission to appeal; or

(2) a notice of appeal from or a petition to enjoin, set aside, suspend, modify, enforce, or otherwise review an order of an administrative agency, board, commission, or officer of the United States, unless specifically authorized by law.

(c) Additional Time after Service. When a party is required or permitted to act within a prescribed period after a paper is served on that party, 3 calendar days are added to the prescribed period unless the paper is delivered on the date of service stated in the proof of service. For purposes of this Rule 26(c), a paper that is served electronically is not treated as delivered on the date of service stated in the proof of service.

(As amended Mar. 1, 1971, eff. July 1, 1971; Mar. 10, 1986, eff. July 1, 1986; Apr. 25, 1989, eff. Dec. 1, 1989; Apr. 30, 1991, eff. Dec. 1, 1991; Apr. 23, 1996, eff. Dec. 1, 1996; Apr. 24, 1998, eff. Dec. 1, 1998; Apr. 29, 2002, eff. Dec. 1, 2002; Apr. 25, 2005, eff. Dec. 1, 2005.)

ADVISORY COMMITTEE NOTES
1967 Adoption

The provisions of this rule are based upon FRCP 6(a), (b) and (e) [rule 6(a), (b) and (e), Federal Rules of Civil Procedure]. See also Supreme Court Rule 34 and FRCrP 45 [rule 45, Federal Rules of Criminal Procedure]. Unlike FRCP 6(b), this rule, read with Rule 27, requires that every request for enlargement of time be made by motion, with proof of service on all parties. This is the simplest, most convenient way of keeping all parties advised of developments. By the terms of Rule 27(b) a motion for enlargement of time under Rule 26(b) may be entertained and acted upon immediately, subject to the right of any party to seek reconsideration. Thus the requirement of motion and notice will not delay the granting of relief of a kind which a court is inclined to grant as of course. Specifically, if a court is of the view that an extension of time sought before expiration of the period originally prescribed or as extended by a previous order ought to be granted in effect ex parte, as FRCP 6(b) permits, it may grant motions seeking such relief without delay.

1971 Amendments

The amendment adds Columbus Day to the list of legal holidays to conform the subdivision to the Act of June 28, 1968, 82 Stat. 250, which constituted Columbus Day a legal holiday effective after January 1, 1971.

The Act, which amended Title 5, U.S.C. § 6103(a), changes the day on which certain holidays are to be observed. Washington's Birthday, Memorial Day and Veterans Day are to be observed on the third Monday in February, the last Monday in May and the fourth Monday in October, respectively, rather than, as heretofore, on February 22, May 30, and November 11, respectively. Columbus Day is to be observed on the second Monday in October. New Year's Day, Independence Day, Thanksgiving Day and Christmas continue to be observed on the traditional days.

1986 Amendments

The Birthday of Martin Luther King, Jr. is added to the list of national holidays in Rule 26(a). The amendment to Rule 26(c) is technical. No substantive change is intended.

1989 Amendments

The proposed amendment brings Rule 26(a) into conformity with the provisions of Rule 6(a) of the Rules of Civil Procedure, Rule 45(a) of the Rules of Criminal Procedure, and Rule 9006(a) of the Rules of Bankruptcy Procedure which allow additional time for filing whenever a clerk's office is inaccessible on the last day for filing due to weather or other conditions.

1996 Amendments

The amendment is a companion to the proposed amendments to Rule 25 that permit service on a party by commercial carrier. The amendments to subdivision (c) of this rule make the three-day extension applicable not only when service is accomplished by mail, but whenever delivery to the party being served occurs later than the date of service stated in the proof of service. When service is by mail or commercial carrier, the proof of service recites the date of mailing or delivery to the commercial carrier. If the party being served receives the paper on a later date, the three-day extension applies. If the party being served receives the paper on the same date as the date of service recited in the proof of service, the three-day extension is not available.

The amendment also states that the three-day extension is three calendar days. Rule 26(a) states that when a period prescribed or allowed by the rules is less than seven days, intermediate Saturdays, Sundays, and legal holidays do not count. Whether the three-day extension in Rule 26(c) is such a period, meaning that three-days could actually be five or even six days, is unclear. The D.C. Circuit recently held that the parallel three-day extension provided in the Civil Rules is not such a period and that weekends and legal holidays do count. *CNPq v. Inter-Trade, 50 F.3d 56 (D.C.Cir.1995).* The Committee believes that is the right result and that the issue should be resolved. Providing that the extension is three calendar days means that if a period would otherwise end on Thursday but the three-day extension applies, the paper must be filed on Monday. Friday, Saturday, and Sunday are the extension days. Because the last day of the period as extended is Sunday, the paper must be filed the next day, Monday.

1998 Amendments

The language and organization of the rule are amended to make the rule more easily understood. In addition to changes made to improve the understanding, the Advisory Committee has changed language to make style and terminology consistent throughout the appellate rules. These changes are intended to by stylistic only; two substantive changes are made, however, in subdivision (a).

Subdivision (a). First, the amendments make the computation method prescribed in this rule applicable to any time period imposed by a local rule. This means that if a local rule establishing a time limit is permitted, the national rule will govern the computation of that period.

Second, paragraph (a)(2) includes language clarifying that whenever the rules establish a time period in "calendar days," weekends and legal holidays are counted.

2002 Amendments

Subdivision (a)(2). The Federal Rules of Civil Procedure and the Federal Rules of Criminal Procedure compute time differently than the Federal Rules of Appellate Procedure. Fed. R. Civ. P. 6(a) and Fed. R. Crim. P. 45(a) provide that, in computing any period of time, "[w]hen the period of time prescribed or allowed is less than 11 days, intermediate Saturdays, Sundays, and legal holidays shall be excluded in the computation." By contrast, Rule 26(a)(2) provides that, in computing any period of time, a litigant should "[e]xclude intermediate Saturdays, Sundays, and legal holidays when the period is less than 7 days, unless stated in calendar days." Thus, deadlines of 7, 8, 9, and 10 days are calculated differently under the rules of civil and criminal procedure than they are under the rules of appellate procedure. This creates a trap for unwary litigants. No good reason for this discrepancy is apparent, and thus Rule 26(a)(2) has been amended so that, under all three sets of rules, intermediate Saturdays, Sundays, and legal holidays will be excluded when computing deadlines under 11 days but will be counted when computing deadlines of 11 days and over.

Changes Made After Publication and Comments No changes were made to the text of the proposed amendment or to the Committee Note.

Subdivision (c). Rule 26(c) has been amended to provide that when a paper is served on a party by electronic means, and that party is required or permitted to respond to that paper within a prescribed period, 3 calendar days are added to the prescribed period. Electronic service is usually instantaneous, but sometimes it is not, because of technical problems. Also, if a paper is electronically transmitted to a party on a Friday evening, the party may not realize that he or she has been served until two or three days later. Finally, extending the "3–day rule" to electronic service will encourage parties to consent to such service under Rule 25(c).

Changes Made After Publication and Comments No changes were made to the text of the proposed amendment or to the Committee Note.

2005 Amendments

Subdivision (a)(4). Rule 26(a)(4) has been amended to refer to the third Monday in February as "Washington's Birthday." A federal statute officially designates the holiday as "Washington's Birthday," reflecting the desire of Congress specially to honor the first president of the United States. *See* 5 U.S.C. § 6103(a). During the 1998 restyling of the Federal Rules of Appellate Procedure, references to "Washington's Birthday" were mistakenly changed to "Presidents' Day." The amendment corrects that error.

Rule 26.1. Corporate Disclosure Statement

(a) Who Must File. Any nongovernmental corporate party to a proceeding in a court of appeals must file a statement that identifies any parent corporation and any publicly held corporation that owns 10% or more of its stock or states that there is no such corporation.

(b) Time for Filing; Supplemental Filing. A party must file the Rule 26.1(a) statement with the principal brief or upon filing a motion, response, petition, or

answer in the court of appeals, whichever occurs first, unless a local rule requires earlier filing. Even if the statement has already been filed, the party's principal brief must include the statement before the table of contents. A party must supplement its statement whenever the information that must be disclosed under Rule 26.1(a) changes.

(c) Number of Copies. If the Rule 26.1(a) statement is filed before the principal brief, or if a supplemental statement is filed, the party must file an original and 3 copies unless the court requires a different number by local rule or by order in a particular case.

(Added Apr. 25, 1989, eff. Dec. 1, 1989, and amended Apr. 30, 1991, eff. Dec. 1, 1991; Apr. 29, 1994, eff. Dec. 1, 1994; Apr. 24, 1998, eff. Dec. 1, 1998; Apr. 29, 2002, eff. Dec. 1, 2002.)

ADVISORY COMMITTEE NOTES

1989 Addition

The purpose of this rule is to assist judges in making a determination of whether they have any interests in any of a party's related corporate entities that would disqualify the judges from hearing the appeal. The committee believes that this rule represents minimum disclosure requirements. If a Court of Appeals wishes to require additional information, a court is free to do so by local rule. However, the committee requests the courts to consider the desirability of uniformity and the burden that varying circuit rules creates on attorneys who practice in many circuits.

1994 Amendment

The amendment requires a party to file three copies of the disclosure statement whenever the statement is filed before the party's principle brief. Because the statement is included in each copy of the party's brief, there is no need to require the filing of additional copies at that time. A court of appeals may require the filing of a different number of copies by local rule or by order in a particular case.

1998 Amendments

The language and organization of the rule are amended to make the rule more easily understood. In addition to changes made to improve the understanding, the Advisory Committee has changed language to make style and terminology consistent throughout the appellate rules. These changes are intended to by stylistic only; a substantive change is made, however, in subdivision (a).

Subdivision (a). The amendment deletes the requirement that a corporate party identify subsidiaries and affiliates that have issued shares to the public. Although several circuit rules require identification of such entities, the Committee believes that such disclosure is unnecessary.

A disclosure statement assists a judge in ascertaining whether or not the judge has an interest that should cause the judge to recuse himself or herself from the case. Given that purpose, disclosure of entities that would not be adversely affected by a decision in the case is unnecessary.

Disclosure of a party's parent corporation is necessary because a judgment against a subsidiary can negatively impact the parent. A judge who owns stock in the parent corporation, therefore, has an interest in litigation involving the subsidiary. The rule requires disclosure of all of a party's parent corporations meaning grandparent and great grandparent corporations as well. For example, if a party is a closely held corporation, the majority shareholder of which is a corporation formed by a publicly traded corporation for the purpose of acquiring and holding the shares of the party, the publicly traded grandparent corporation should be disclosed. Conversely, disclosure of a party's subsidiaries or affiliated corporations is ordinarily unnecessary. For example, if a party is a part owner of a corporation in which a judge owns stock, the possibility is quite remote that the judge might be biased by the fact that the judge and the litigant are co-owners of a corporation.

The amendment, however, adds a requirement that the party lists all its stockholders that are publicly held companies owning 10% or more of the stock of the party. A judgment against a corporate party can adversely affect the value of the company's stock and, therefore, persons owning stock in the party have an interest in the outcome of the litigation. A judge owning stock in a corporate party ordinarily recuses himself or herself. The new requirement takes the analysis one step further and assumes that if a judge owns stock in a publicly held corporation which in turn owns 10% or more of the stock in the party, the judge may have sufficient interest in the litigation to require recusal. The 10% threshold ensures that the corporation in which the judge may own stock is itself sufficiently invested in the party that a judgment adverse to the party could have an adverse impact upon the investing corporation in which the judge may own stock. This requirement is modeled on the Seventh Circuit's disclosure requirement.

Subdivision (b). The language requiring inclusion of the disclosure statement in a party's principal brief is moved to this subdivision because it deals with the time for filing the statement.

2002 Amendments

Subdivision (a). Rule 26.1(a) requires nongovernmental corporate parties to file a "corporate disclosure statement." In that statement, a nongovernmental corporate party is required to identify all of its parent corporations and all publicly held corporations that own 10% or more of its stock. The corporate disclosure statement is intended to assist judges in determining whether they must recuse themselves by reason of "a financial interest in the subject matter in controversy." Code of Judicial Conduct, Canon 3C(1)(c) (1972).

Rule 26.1(a) has been amended to require that nongovernmental corporate parties who have not been required to file a corporate disclosure statement—that is, nongovernmental corporate parties who do not have any parent corporations and at least 10% of whose stock is not owned by any publicly held corporation—inform the court of that fact. At present, when a corporate disclosure statement is not filed, courts do not know whether it has not been filed because there was nothing to report or because of ignorance of Rule 26.1.

Subdivision (b). Rule 26.1(b) has been amended to require parties to file supplemental disclosure statements whenever there is a change in the information that Rule 26.1(a) requires the parties to disclose. For example, if a publicly held corporation acquires 10% or more of a party's stock after the

party has filed its disclosure statement, the party should file a supplemental statement identifying that publicly held corporation.

Subdivision (c). Rule 26.1(c) has been amended to provide that a party who is required to file a supplemental disclosure statement must file an original and 3 copies, unless a local rule or an order entered in a particular case provides otherwise.

Changes Made After Publication and Comments The Committee is submitting two versions of proposed Rule 26.1 for the consideration of the Standing Committee.

The first version—"Alternative One"—is the same as the version that was published, except that the rule has been amended to refer to "any information that may be *publicly designated* by the Judicial Conference" instead of to "any information that may be *required* by the Judicial Conference." At its April meeting, the Committee gave unconditional approval to all of "Alternative One," except the Judicial Conference provisions. The Committee conditioned its approval of the Judicial Conference provisions on the Standing Committee's assuring itself that lawyers would have ready access to any standards promulgated by the Judicial Conference and that the Judicial Conference provisions were consistent with the Rules Enabling Act.

The second version—"Alternative Two"—is the same as the version that was published, except that the Judicial Conference provisions have been eliminated. The Civil Rules Committee met several days after the Appellate Rules Committee and joined the Bankruptcy Rules Committee in disapproving the Judicial Conference provisions. Given the decreasing likelihood that the Judicial Conference provisions will be approved by the Standing Committee, I asked Prof. Schiltz to draft, and the Appellate Rules Committee to approve, a version of Rule 26.1 that omitted those provisions. "Alternative Two" was circulated to and approved by the Committee in late April.

I should note that, at its April meeting, the Appellate Rules Committee discussed the financial disclosure provision that was approved by the Bankruptcy Rules Committee. That provision defines the scope of the financial disclosure obligation much differently than the provisions approved by the Appellate, Civil, and Criminal Rules Committees, which are based on existing Rule 26.1. For example, the bankruptcy provision requires disclosure when a party "directly or indirectly" owns 10 percent or more of "any class" of a publicly *or* privately held corporation's "equity interests." Members of the Appellate Rules Committee expressed several concerns about the provision approved by the Bankruptcy Rules Committee, objecting both to its substance and to its ambiguity.

Rule 27. Motions

(a) In General.

(1) Application for Relief. An application for an order or other relief is made by motion unless these rules prescribe another form. A motion must be in writing unless the court permits otherwise.

(2) Contents of a Motion.

(A) Grounds and relief sought. A motion must state with particularity the grounds for the

motion, the relief sought, and the legal argument necessary to support it.

(B) Accompanying documents.

(i) Any affidavit or other paper necessary to support a motion must be served and filed with the motion.

(ii) An affidavit must contain only factual information, not legal argument.

(iii) A motion seeking substantive relief must include a copy of the trial court's opinion or agency's decision as a separate exhibit.

(C) Documents barred or not required.

(i) A separate brief supporting or responding to a motion must not be filed.

(ii) A notice of motion is not required.

(iii) A proposed order is not required.

(3) Response.

(A) Time to file. Any party may file a response to a motion; Rule 27(a)(2) governs its contents. The response must be filed within 8 days after service of the motion unless the court shortens or extends the time. A motion authorized by Rules 8, 9, 18, or 41 may be granted before the 8–day period runs only if the court gives reasonable notice to the parties that it intends to act sooner.

(B) Request for affirmative relief. A response may include a motion for affirmative relief. The time to respond to the new motion, and to reply to that response, are governed by Rule 27(a)(3)(A) and (a)(4). The title of the response must alert the court to the request for relief.

(4) Reply to Response. Any reply to a response must be filed within 5 days after service of the response. A reply must not present matters that do not relate to the response.

(b) Disposition of a Motion for a Procedural Order. The court may act on a motion for a procedural order—including a motion under Rule 26(b)—at any time without awaiting a response, and may, by rule or by order in a particular case, authorize its clerk to act on specified types of procedural motions. A party adversely affected by the court's, or the clerk's, action may file a motion to reconsider, vacate, or modify that action. Timely opposition filed after the motion is granted in whole or in part does not constitute a request to reconsider, vacate, or modify the disposition; a motion requesting that relief must be filed.

(c) Power of a Single Judge to Entertain a Motion. A circuit judge may act alone on any motion, but may not dismiss or otherwise determine an appeal or other proceeding. A court of appeals may provide by rule or by order in a particular case that only the court may act on any motion or class of motions. The court may review the action of a single judge.

(d) Form of Papers; Page Limits; and Number of Copies.

(1) Format.

(A) Reproduction. A motion, response, or reply may be reproduced by any process that yields a clear black image on light paper. The paper must be opaque and unglazed. Only one side of the paper may be used.

(B) Cover. A cover is not required, but there must be a caption that includes the case number, the name of the court, the title of the case, and a brief descriptive title indicating the purpose of the motion and identifying the party or parties for whom it is filed. If a cover is used, it must be white.

(C) Binding. The document must be bound in any manner that is secure, does not obscure the text, and permits the document to lie reasonably flat when open.

(D) Paper size, line spacing, and margins. The document must be on 8½ by 11 inch paper. The text must be double-spaced, but quotations more than two lines long may be indented and single-spaced. Headings and footnotes may be single-spaced. Margins must be at least one inch on all four sides. Page numbers may be placed in the margins, but no text may appear there.

(E) Typeface and type styles. The document must comply with the typeface requirements of Rule 32(a)(5) and the type-style requirements of Rule 32(a)(6).

(2) Page Limits. A motion or a response to a motion must not exceed 20 pages, exclusive of the corporate disclosure statement and accompanying documents authorized by Rule 27(a)(2)(B), unless the court permits or directs otherwise. A reply to a response must not exceed 10 pages.

(3) Number of Copies. An original and 3 copies must be filed unless the court requires a different number by local rule or by order in a particular case.

(e) Oral Argument. A motion will be decided without oral argument unless the court orders otherwise.

(As amended Apr. 30, 1979, eff. Aug. 1, 1979; Apr. 25, 1989, eff. Dec. 1, 1989; Apr. 29, 1994, eff. Dec. 1, 1994; Apr. 24, 1998, eff. Dec. 1, 1998; Apr. 29, 2002, eff. Dec. 1, 2002; Apr. 25, 2005, eff. Dec. 1, 2005.)

ADVISORY COMMITTEE NOTES
1967 Adoption

Subdivisions (a) and (b). Many motions seek relief of a sort which is ordinarily unopposed or which is granted as of course. The provision of subdivision (a) which permits any party to file a response in opposition to a motion within 7 days after its service upon him assumes that the motion is one of substance which ought not to be acted upon without affording affected parties an opportunity to reply. A motion to dismiss or otherwise determine an appeal is clearly such a motion. Motions authorized by Rules 8, 9, 18 and 41 are likewise motions of substance; but in the nature of the relief sought, to afford an adversary an automatic delay of at least 7 days is undesirable, thus such motions may be acted upon after notice which is reasonable under the circumstances.

The term "motions for procedural orders" is used in subdivision (b) to describe motions which do not substantially affect the rights of the parties or the ultimate disposition of the appeal. To prevent delay in the disposition of such motions, subdivision (b) provides that they may be acted upon immediately without awaiting a response, subject to the right of any party who is adversely affected by the action to seek reconsideration.

Subdivision (c). Within the general consideration of procedure on motions is the problem of the power of a single circuit judge. Certain powers are granted to a single judge of a court of appeals by statute. Thus, under 28 U.S.C. § 2101(f) a single judge may stay execution and enforcement of a judgment to enable a party aggrieved to obtain certiorari; under 28 U.S.C. § 2251 a judge before whom a habeas corpus proceeding involving a person detained by state authority is pending may stay any proceeding against the person; under 28 U.S.C. § 2253 a single judge may issue a certificate of probably cause. In addition, certain of these rules expressly grant power to a single judge. See Rules 8, 9 and 18.

This subdivision empowers a single circuit judge to act upon virtually all requests for intermediate relief which may be made during the course of an appeal or other proceeding. By its terms he may entertain and act upon any motion other than a motion to dismiss or otherwise determine an appeal or other proceeding. But the relief sought must be "relief which under these rules may properly be sought by motion."

Examples of the power conferred on a single judge by this subdivision are: to extend the time for transmitting the record or docketing the appeal (Rules 11 and 12); to permit intervention in agency cases (Rule 15), or substitution in any case (Rule 43); to permit an appeal in forma pauperis (Rule 24); to enlarge any time period fixed by the rules other than that for initiating a proceeding in the court of appeals (Rule 26(b)); to permit the filing of a brief by amicus curiae (Rule 29); to authorize the filing of a deferred appendix (Rule 30(c)), or dispense with the requirement of an appendix in a specific case (Rule 30(f)), or permit carbon copies of briefs or appendices to be used (Rule 32(a)); to permit the filing of additional briefs (Rule 28(c)), or the filing of briefs of extraordinary length (Rule 28(g)); to postpone oral argument (Rule 34(a)), or grant additional time therefor (Rule 34(b)).

Certain rules require that application for the relief or orders which they authorize be made by petition. Since relief under those rules may not properly be sought by motion, a single judge may not entertain requests for such relief. Thus a single judge may not act upon requests for permission to appeal (see Rules 5 and 6); or for mandamus or other extraordinary writs (see Rule 21), other than for stays or injunctions *pendente lite*, authority to grant which is "expressly conferred by these rules" on a single judge under certain circumstances (see Rules 8 and 18); or upon petitions for rehearing (see Rule 40).

A court of appeals may by order or rule abridge the power of a single judge if it is of the view that a motion or a class of motions should be disposed of by a panel. Exercise of any power granted a single judge is discretionary with the judge. The final sentence in this subdivision makes the disposition of any matter by a single judge subject to review by the court.

1979 Amendment

The proposed amendment would give sanction to local rules in a number of circuits permitting the clerk to dispose of specified types of procedural motions.

1989 Amendment

The amendment is technical. No substantive change is intended.

1994 Amendments

Subdivision (d). The amendment makes it clear that a court may require a different number of copies either by rule or by order in an individual case. The number of copies of any document that a court of appeals needs varies depending upon the way in which the court conducts business. The internal operation of the courts of appeals necessarily varies from circuit to circuit because of differences in the number of judges, the geographic area included within the circuit, and other such factors. Uniformity could be achieved only by setting the number of copies artificially high so that parties in all circuits file enough copies to satisfy the needs of the court requiring the greatest number. Rather than do that, the Committee decided to make it clear that local rules may require a greater or lesser number of copies and that, if the circumstances of a particular case indicate the need for a different number of copies in that case, the court may so order.

1998 Amendments

In addition to amending Rule 27 to conform to uniform drafting standards, several substantive amendments are made. The Advisory Committee had been working on substantive amendments to Rule 27 just prior to completion of this larger project.

Subdivision (a). Paragraph (1) retains the language of the existing rule indicating that an application for an order or other relief is made by filing a motion unless another form is required by some other provision in the rules.

Paragraph (1) also states that a motion must be in writing unless the court permits otherwise. The writing requirement has been implicit in the rule; the Advisory Committee decided to make it explicit. There are, however, instances in which a court may permit oral motions. Perhaps the most common such instance would be a motion made during oral argument in the presence of opposing counsel; for example, a request for permission to submit a supplemental brief on an issue raised by the court for the first time at oral argument. Rather than limit oral motions to those made during oral argument or, conversely, assume the propriety of making even extremely complex motions orally during argument, the Advisory Committee decided that it is better to leave the determination of the propriety of an oral motion to the court's discretion. The provision does not disturb the practice

in those circuits that permit certain procedural motions, such as a motion for extension of time for filing a brief, to be made by telephone and ruled upon by the clerk.

Paragraph (2) outlines the contents of a motion. It begins with the general requirement from the current rule that a motion must state with particularity the grounds supporting it and the relief requested. It adds a requirement that all legal arguments should be presented in the body of the motion; a separate brief or memorandum supporting or responding to a motion must not be filed. The Supreme Court uses this single document approach. Sup. Ct. R. 21.1. In furtherance of the requirement that all legal argument must be contained in the body of the motion, paragraph (2) also states that an affidavit that is attached to a motion should contain only factual information and not legal argument.

Paragraph (2) further states that whenever a motion requests substantive relief, a copy of the trial court's opinion or agency's decision must be attached.

Although it is common to present a district court with a proposed order along with the motion requesting relief, that is not the practice in the courts of appeals. A proposed order is not required and is not expected or desired. Nor is a notice of motion required.

Paragraph (3) retains the provisions of the current rule concerning the filing of a response to a motion except that the time for responding has been expanded to 10 days rather than 7 days. Because the time periods in the rule apply to a substantive motion as well as a procedural motion, the longer time period may help reduce the number of motions for extension of time, or at least provide a more realistic time frame within which to make and dispose of such a motion.

A party filing a response in opposition to a motion may also request affirmative relief. It is the Advisory Committee's judgment that it is permissible to combine the response and the new motion in the same document. Indeed, because there may be substantial overlap of arguments in the response and in the request for affirmative relief, a combined document may be preferable. If a request for relief is combined with a response, the caption of the document must alert the court to the request for relief. The time for a response to such a new request and for reply to that response are governed by the general rules regulating responses and replies.

Paragraph (4) is new. Two circuits currently have rules authorizing a reply. As a general matter, a reply should not reargue propositions presented in the motion or present matters that do not relate to the response. Sometimes matters relevant to the motion arise after the motion is filed; treatment of such matters in the reply is appropriate even though strictly speaking it may not relate to the response.

Subdivision (b). The material in this subdivision remains substantively unchanged except to clarify that one may file a motion for reconsideration, etc. of a disposition by either the court or the clerk. A new sentence is added indicating that if a motion is granted in whole or in part before the filing of timely opposition to the motion, the filing of the opposition is not treated as a request for reconsideration, etc., A party wishing to have the court reconsider, vacate, or modify the disposition must file a new motion that addresses the order granting the motion.

Although the rule does not require a court to do so, it would be helpful if, whenever a motion is disposed of before

receipt of any response from the opposing party, the ruling indicates that it was issued without awaiting a response. Such a statement will aid the opposing party in deciding whether to request reconsideration. The opposing party may have mailed a response about the time of the ruling and be uncertain whether the court has considered it.

Subdivision (c). The changes in this subdivision are stylistic only. No substantive changes are intended.

Subdivision (d). This subdivision has been substantially revised.

The format requirements have been moved from Rule 32(b) to paragraph (1) of this subdivision. No cover is required, but a caption is needed as well as a descriptive title indicating the purpose of the motion and identifying the party or parties for whom it is filed. Spiral binding or secure stapling at the upper left-hand corner satisfies the binding requirement. But they are not intended to be the exclusive methods of binding.

Paragraph (2) establishes page limits; twenty pages for a motion or a response, and ten pages for a reply. Three circuits have established page limits by local rule. This rule does not establish special page limits for those instances in which a party combines a response to a motion with a new request for affirmative relief. Because a combined document most often will be used when there is substantial overlap in the argument in opposition to the motion and in the argument for the affirmative relief, twenty pages may be sufficient in most instances. If it is not, the party may request additional pages. If ten pages is insufficient for the original movant to both reply to the response, and respond to the new request for affirmative relief, two separate documents may be used or a request for additional pages may be made.

The changes in paragraph (4) are stylistic only. No substantive changes are intended.

Subdivision (e). This new provision makes it clear that there is no right to oral argument on a motion. Seven circuits have local rules stating that oral argument of motions will not be held unless the court orders it.

2002 Amendments

Subdivision (a)(3)(A). Subdivision (a)(3)(A) presently requires that a response to a motion be filed within 10 days after service of the motion. Intermediate Saturdays, Sundays, and legal holidays are counted in computing that 10–day deadline, which means that, except when the 10–day deadline ends on a weekend or legal holiday, parties generally must respond to motions within 10 actual days.

Fed. R. App. P. 26(a)(2) has been amended to provide that, in computing any period of time, a litigant should "[e]xclude intermediate Saturdays, Sundays, and legal holidays when the period is less than 11 days, unless stated in calendar days." This change in the method of computing deadlines means that 10–day deadlines (such as that in subdivision (a)(3)(A)) have been lengthened as a practical matter. Under the new computation method, parties would never have less than 14 actual days to respond to motions, and legal holidays could extend that period to as much as 18 days.

Permitting parties to take two weeks or more to respond to motions would introduce significant and unwarranted delay into appellate proceedings. For that reason, the 10–day deadline in subdivision (a)(3)(A) has been reduced to 8 days. This change will, as a practical matter, ensure that every

party will have at least 10 actual days—but, in the absence of a legal holiday, no more than 12 actual days—to respond to motions. The court continues to have discretion to shorten or extend that time in appropriate cases.

Changes Made After Publication and Comments In response to the objections of commentators, the time to respond to a motion was increased from the proposed 7 days to 8 days. No other changes were made to the text of the proposed amendment or to the Committee Note.

Subdivision (a)(4). Subdivision (a)(4) presently requires that a reply to a response to a motion be filed within 7 days after service of the response. Intermediate Saturdays, Sundays, and legal holidays are counted in computing that 7–day deadline, which means that, except when the 7–day deadline ends on a weekend or legal holiday, parties generally must reply to responses to motions within one week.

Fed. R. App. P. 26(a)(2) has been amended to provide that, in computing any period of time, a litigant should "[e]xclude intermediate Saturdays, Sundays, and legal holidays when the period is less than 11 days, unless stated in calendar days." This change in the method of computing deadlines means that 7–day deadlines (such as that in subdivision (a)(4)) have been lengthened as a practical matter. Under the new computation method, parties would never have less than 9 actual days to reply to responses to motions, and legal holidays could extend that period to as much as 13 days.

Permitting parties to take 9 or more days to reply to a response to a motion would introduce significant and unwarranted delay into appellate proceedings. For that reason, the 7–day deadline in subdivision (a)(4) has been reduced to 5 days. This change will, as a practical matter, ensure that every party will have 7 actual days to file replies to responses to motions (in the absence of a legal holiday).

Changes Made After Publication and Comments No changes were made to the text of the proposed amendment or to the Committee Note.

Subdivision (d)(1)(B). A cover is not required on motions, responses to motions, or replies to responses to motions. However, Rule 27(d)(1)(B) has been amended to provide that if a cover is nevertheless used on such a paper, the cover must be white. The amendment is intended to promote uniformity in federal appellate practice.

Changes Made After Publication and Comments No changes were made to the text of the proposed amendment or to the Committee Note.

2005 Amendments

Subdivision (d)(1)(E). A new subdivision (E) has been added to Rule 27(d)(1) to provide that a motion, a response to a motion, and a reply to a response to a motion must comply with the typeface requirements of Rule 32(a)(5) and the type-style requirements of Rule 32(a)(6). The purpose of the amendment is to promote uniformity in federal appellate practice and to prevent the abuses that might occur if no restrictions were placed on the size of typeface used in motion papers.

Rule 28. Briefs

(a) Appellant's Brief. The appellant's brief must contain, under appropriate headings and in the order indicated:

(1) a corporate disclosure statement if required by Rule 26.1;

(2) a table of contents, with page references;

(3) a table of authorities—cases (alphabetically arranged), statutes, and other authorities—with references to the pages of the brief where they are cited;

(4) a jurisdictional statement, including:

 (A) the basis for the district court's or agency's subject-matter jurisdiction, with citations to applicable statutory provisions and stating relevant facts establishing jurisdiction;

 (B) the basis for the court of appeals' jurisdiction, with citations to applicable statutory provisions and stating relevant facts establishing jurisdiction;

 (C) the filing dates establishing the timeliness of the appeal or petition for review; and

 (D) an assertion that the appeal is from a final order or judgment that disposes of all parties' claims, or information establishing the court of appeals' jurisdiction on some other basis;

(5) a statement of the issues presented for review;

(6) a statement of the case briefly indicating the nature of the case, the course of proceedings, and the disposition below;

(7) a statement of facts relevant to the issues submitted for review with appropriate references to the record (see Rule 28(e));

(8) a summary of the argument, which must contain a succinct, clear, and accurate statement of the arguments made in the body of the brief, and which must not merely repeat the argument headings;

(9) the argument, which must contain:

 (A) appellant's contentions and the reasons for them, with citations to the authorities and parts of the record on which the appellant relies; and

 (B) for each issue, a concise statement of the applicable standard of review (which may appear in the discussion of the issue or under a separate heading placed before the discussion of the issues);

(10) a short conclusion stating the precise relief sought; and

(11) the certificate of compliance, if required by Rule 32(a)(7).

(b) Appellee's Brief. The appellee's brief must conform to the requirements of Rule 28(a)(1)–(9) and (11), except that none of the following need appear unless the appellee is dissatisfied with the appellant's statement:

(1) the jurisdictional statement;

(2) the statement of the issues;

(3) the statement of the case;

(4) the statement of the facts; and

(5) the statement of the standard of review.

(c) Reply Brief. The appellant may file a brief in reply to the appellee's brief. Unless the court permits, no further briefs may be filed. A reply brief must contain a table of contents, with page references, and a table of authorities—cases (alphabetically arranged), statutes, and other authorities—with references to the pages of the reply brief where they are cited.

(d) References to Parties. In briefs and at oral argument, counsel should minimize use of the terms "appellant" and "appellee." To make briefs clear, counsel should use the parties' actual names or the designations used in the lower court or agency proceeding, or such descriptive terms as "the employee," "the injured person," "the taxpayer," "the ship," "the stevedore."

(e) References to the Record. References to the parts of the record contained in the appendix filed with the appellant's brief must be to the pages of the appendix. If the appendix is prepared after the briefs are filed, a party referring to the record must follow one of the methods detailed in Rule 30(c). If the original record is used under Rule 30(f) and is not consecutively paginated, or if the brief refers to an unreproduced part of the record, any reference must be to the page of the original document. For example:

- Answer p. 7;

- Motion for Judgment p. 2;

- Transcript p. 231.

Only clear abbreviations may be used. A party referring to evidence whose admissibility is in controversy must cite the pages of the appendix or of the transcript at which the evidence was identified, offered, and received or rejected.

(f) Reproduction of Statutes, Rules, Regulations, etc. If the court's determination of the issues presented requires the study of statutes, rules, regulations, etc., the relevant parts must be set out in the brief or in an addendum at the end, or may be supplied to the court in pamphlet form.

(g) [Reserved]

(h) [Deleted]

(i) Briefs in a Case Involving Multiple Appellants or Appellees. In a case involving more than one appellant or appellee, including consolidated cases, any number of appellants or appellees may join in a brief, and any party may adopt by reference a part of another's brief. Parties may also join in reply briefs.

(j) Citation of Supplemental Authorities. If pertinent and significant authorities come to a party's attention after the party's brief has been filed—or after oral argument but before decision—a party may promptly advise the circuit clerk by letter, with a copy to all other parties, setting forth the citations. The letter must state the reasons for the supplemental citations, referring either to the page of the brief or to a point argued orally. The body of the letter must not exceed 350 words. Any response must be made promptly and must be similarly limited.

(As amended Apr. 30, 1979, eff. Aug. 1, 1979; Mar. 10, 1986, eff. July 1, 1986; Apr. 25, 1989, eff. Dec. 1, 1989; Apr. 30, 1991, eff. Dec. 1, 1991; Apr. 22, 1993, eff. Dec. 1, 1993; Apr. 29, 1994, eff. Dec. 1, 1994; Apr. 24, 1998, eff. Dec. 1, 1998; Apr. 29, 2002, eff. Dec. 1, 2002; Apr. 25, 2005, eff. Dec. 1, 2005.)

ADVISORY COMMITTEE NOTES

1967 Adoption

This rule is based upon Supreme Court Rule 40. For variations in present circuit rules on briefs see 2d Cir. Rule 17 [rule 17, U.S.Ct. of App. 2d Cir.], 3d Cir. Rule 24 [rule 24, U.S.Ct. of App. 3d Cir.], 5th Cir. Rule 24 [rule 24, U.S.Ct. of App. 5th Cir.], and 7th Cir. Rule 17 [rule 17, U.S.Ct. of App. 7th Cir.]. All circuits now limit the number of pages of briefs, a majority limiting the brief to 50 pages of standard typographic printing. Fifty pages of standard typographic printing is the approximate equivalent of 70 pages of typewritten text, given the page sizes required by Rule 32 and the requirement set out there that text produced by a method other than standard typographic must be double spaced.

1979 Amendments

Subdivision (g). The proposed amendment eliminates the distinction appearing in the present rule between the permissible length in pages of printed and typewritten briefs, investigation of the matter having disclosed that the number of words on the printed page is little if any larger than the number on a page typed in standard elite type.

The provision is made subject to local rule to permit the court of appeals to require that typewritten briefs be typed in larger type and permit a correspondingly larger number of pages.

Subdivision (j). Proposed new Rule 28(j) makes provision for calling the court's attention to authorities that come to the party's attention after the brief has been filed. It is patterned after the practice under local rule in some of the circuits.

1986 Amendments

While Rule 28(g) can be read as requiring that tables of authorities be included in a reply brief, such tables are often not included. Their absence impedes efficient use of the reply brief to ascertain the appellant's response to a particular argument of the appellee or to the appellee's use of a particular authority. The amendment to Rule 28(c) is intended to make it clear that such tables are required in reply briefs.

The amendment to Rule 28(j) is technical. No substantive change is intended.

1989 Amendments

The amendment provides that the corporate disclosure statement required by new Rule 26.1 shall be treated similarly to tables of contents and tables of citations and shall not be counted for purposes of the number of pages allowed in a brief.

1991 Amendments

Subdivision (a). The amendment adds a new subparagraph (2) that requires an appellant to include a specific jurisdictional statement in the appellant's brief to aid the court of appeals in determining whether it has both federal subject matter and appellate jurisdiction.

Subdivision (b). The amendment requires the appellee to include a jurisdictional statement in the appellee's brief except that the appellee need not include the statement if the appellee is satisfied with the appellant's jurisdictional statement.

Subdivision (h). The amendment provides that when more than one party appeals from a judgment or order, the party filing the first appeal is normally treated as the appellant for purposes of this rule and Rules 30 and 31. The party who first files an appeal usually is the principal appellant and should be treated as such. Parties who file a notice of appeal after the first notice often bring protective appeals and they should be treated as cross appellants. Local rules in the Fourth and Federal Circuits now take that approach. If notices of appeal are filed on the same day, the rule follows the old approach of treating the plaintiff below as the appellant. For purposes of this rule, in criminal cases "the plaintiff" means the United States. In those instances where the designations provided by the rule are inappropriate, they may be altered by agreement of the parties or by an order of the court.

1993 Amendments

Note to paragraph (a)(5). The amendment requires an appellant's brief to state the standard of review applicable to each issue on appeal. Five circuits currently require these statements. Experience in those circuits indicates that requiring a statement of the standard of review generally results in arguments that are properly shaped in light of the standard.

1994 Amendments

Subdivision (a). The amendment adds a requirement that an appellant's brief contain a summary of the argument. A number of circuits have local rules requiring a summary and the courts report that they find the summary useful. See, D.C. Cir.R. 11(a)(5); 5th Cir.R. 28.2.2; 8th Cir.R. 28A(i)(6); 11th Cir.R. 28–2(i); and Fed. Cir.R. 28.

Subdivision (b). The amendment adds a requirement that an appellee's brief contain a summary of the argument.

Subdivision (g). The amendment adds proof of service to the list of items in a brief that do not count for purposes of the page limitation. The concurrent amendment to Rule 25(d) requires a certificate of service to list the addresses to which a paper was mailed or at which it was delivered.

When a number of parties must be served, the listing of addresses may run to several pages and those pages should not count for purposes of the page limitation.

1998 Amendments

The language and organization of the rule are amended to make the rule more easily understood. In addition to changes made to improve the understanding, the Advisory Committee has changed language to make style and terminology consistent throughout the appellate rules. These changes are intended to by stylistic only.

Several substantive changes are made in this rule, however. Most of them are necessary to confirm Rule 28 with changes recommended in Rule 32.

Subdivision (a). The current rule requires a brief to include a statement of the case which includes a description of the nature of the case, the course of proceedings, the disposition of the case—all of which might be described as the procedural history—as well as a statement of the facts. The amendments separate this into two statements; one procedural, called the statement of the case; and one factual, called the statement of the facts. The Advisory Committee believes that the separation will be helpful to the judges. The table of contents and table of authorities have also been separated into two distinct items.

An additional amendment of subdivision (a) is made to conform it with an amendment being made to Rule 32. Rule 32(a)(7) generally requires a brief to include a certificate of compliance with type-volume limitations contained in that rule. (No certificate is required if a brief does not exceed 30 pages, or 15 pages for a reply brief.) Rule 28(a) is amended to include that certificate in the list of items that must be included in a brief whenever it is required by Rule 32.

Subdivision (g). The amendments delete subdivision (g) that limited a principal brief to 50 pages and a reply brief to 25 pages. The length limitations have been moved to Rule 32. Rule 32 deals generally with the format for a brief or appendix.

Subdivision (h). The amendment requires an appellee's brief to comply with Rule 28(a)(1) through (11) with regard to a cross-appeal. The addition of separate paragraphs requiring a corporate disclosure statement, table of authorities, statement of facts, and certificate of compliance increased the relevant paragraphs of subdivision (a) from (7) to (11). The other changes are stylistic; no substantive changes are intended.

2002 Amendments

Subdivision (j). In the past, Rule 28(j) has required parties to describe supplemental authorities "without argument." Enforcement of this restriction has been lax, in part because of the difficulty of distinguishing "state[ment] . . . [of] the reasons for the supplemental citations," which is required, from "argument" about the supplemental citations, which is forbidden.

As amended, Rule 28(j) continues to require parties to state the reasons for supplemental citations, with reference to the part of a brief or oral argument to which the supplemental citations pertain. But Rule 28(j) no longer forbids "argument." Rather, Rule 28(j) permits parties to decide for themselves what they wish to say about supplemental authorities. The only restriction upon parties is that the body of a Rule 28(j) letter—that is, the part of the letter that begins with the first word after the salutation and ends with the last word before the complimentary close—cannot exceed 350 words. All words found in footnotes will count toward the 350-word limit.

Changes Made After Publication and Comments No changes were made to the text of the proposed amendment or to the Committee Note, except that the word limit was increased from 250 to 350 in response to the complaint of some commentators that parties would have difficulty bringing multiple supplemental authorities to the attention of the court in one 250-word letter.

2005 Amendments

Subdivision (c). Subdivision (c) has been amended to delete a sentence that authorized an appellee who had cross-appealed to file a brief in reply to the appellant's response. All rules regarding briefing in cases involving cross-appeals have been consolidated into new Rule 28.1.

Subdivision (h). Subdivision (h)—regarding briefing in cases involving cross-appeals—has been deleted. All rules regarding such briefing have been consolidated into new Rule 28.1.

Rule 28.1. Cross–Appeals

(a) Applicability. This rule applies to a case in which a cross-appeal is filed. Rules 28(a)-(c), 31(a)(1), 32(a)(2), and 32(a)(7)(A)-(B) do not apply to such a case, except as otherwise provided in this rule.

(b) Designation of Appellant. The party who files a notice of appeal first is the appellant for the purposes of this rule and Rules 30 and 34. If notices are filed on the same day, the plaintiff in the proceeding below is the appellant. These designations may be modified by the parties' agreement or by court order.

(c) Briefs. In a case involving a cross-appeal:

(1) Appellant's Principal Brief. The appellant must file a principal brief in the appeal. That brief must comply with Rule 28(a).

(2) Appellee's Principal and Response Brief. The appellee must file a principal brief in the cross-appeal and must, in the same brief, respond to the principal brief in the appeal. That appellee's brief must comply with Rule 28(a), except that the brief need not include a statement of the case or a statement of the facts unless the appellee is dissatisfied with the appellant's statement.

(3) Appellant's Response and Reply Brief. The appellant must file a brief that responds to the principal brief in the cross-appeal and may, in the same brief, reply to the response in the appeal. That brief must comply with Rule 28(a)(2)–(9) and (11), except that none of the following need appear unless the appellant is dissatisfied with the appellee's statement in the cross-appeal:

(A) the jurisdictional statement;

(B) the statement of the issues;

(C) the statement of the case;

(D) the statement of the facts; and

(E) the statement of the standard of review.

(4) Appellee's Reply Brief. The appellee may file a brief in reply to the response in the cross-appeal. That brief must comply with Rule 28(a)(2)–(3) and (11) and must be limited to the issues presented by the cross-appeal.

(5) No Further Briefs. Unless the court permits, no further briefs may be filed in a case involving a cross-appeal.

(d) Cover. Except for filings by unrepresented parties, the cover of the appellant's principal brief must be blue; the appellee's principal and response brief, red; the appellant's response and reply brief, yellow; the appellee's reply brief, gray; an intervenor's or amicus curiae's brief, green; and any supplemental brief, tan. The front cover of a brief must contain the information required by Rule 32(a)(2).

(e) Length.

(1) Page Limitation. Unless it complies with Rule 28.1(e)(2) and (3), the appellant's principal brief must not exceed 30 pages; the appellee's principal and response brief, 35 pages; the appellant's response and reply brief, 30 pages; and the appellee's reply brief, 15 pages.

(2) Type-Volume Limitation.

(A) The appellant's principal brief or the appellant's response and reply brief is acceptable if:

(i) it contains no more than 14,000 words; or

(ii) it uses a monospaced face and contains no more than 1,300 lines of text.

(B) The appellee's principal and response brief is acceptable if:

(i) it contains no more than 16,500 words; or

(ii) it uses a monospaced face and contains no more than 1,500 lines of text.

(C) The appellee's reply brief is acceptable if it contains no more than half of the type volume specified in Rule 28.1(e)(2)(A).

(3) Certificate of Compliance. A brief submitted under Rule 28.1(e)(2) must comply with Rule 32(a)(7)(C).

(f) Time to Serve and File a Brief. Briefs must be served and filed as follows:

(1) the appellant's principal brief, within 40 days after the record is filed;

(2) the appellee's principal and response brief, within 30 days after the appellant's principal brief is served;

(3) the appellant's response and reply brief, within 30 days after the appellee's principal and response brief is served; and

(4) the appellee's reply brief, within 14 days after the appellant's response and reply brief is served, but at least 3 days before argument unless the court, for good cause, allows a later filing.

(As added April 25, 2005, eff. Dec. 1, 2005.)

ADVISORY COMMITTEE NOTES

2005 Adoption

The Federal Rules of Appellate Procedure have said very little about briefing in cases involving cross-appeals. This vacuum has frustrated judges, attorneys, and parties who have sought guidance in the rules. More importantly, this vacuum has been filled by conflicting local rules regarding such matters as the number and length of briefs, the colors of the covers of briefs, and the deadlines for serving and filing briefs. These local rules have created a hardship for attorneys who practice in more than one circuit.

New Rule 28.1 provides a comprehensive set of rules governing briefing in cases involving cross-appeals. The few existing provisions regarding briefing in such cases have been moved into new Rule 28.1, and several new provisions have been added to fill the gaps in the existing rules. The new provisions reflect the practices of the large majority of circuits and, to a significant extent, the new provisions have been patterned after the requirements imposed by Rules 28, 31, and 32 on briefs filed in cases that do not involve cross-appeals.

Subdivision (a). Subdivision (a) makes clear that, in a case involving a cross-appeal, briefing is governed by new Rule 28.1, and not by Rules 28(a), 28(b), 28(c), 31(a)(1), 32(a)(2), 32(a)(7)(A), and 32(a)(7)(B), except to the extent that Rule 28.1 specifically incorporates those rules by reference.

Subdivision (b). Subdivision (b) defines who is the "appellant" and who is the "appellee" in a case involving a cross-appeal. Subdivision (b) is taken directly from former Rule 28(h), except that subdivision (b) refers to a party being designated as an appellant "for the purposes of this rule and Rules 30 and 34," whereas former Rule 28(h) also referred to Rule 31. Because the matter addressed by Rule 31(a)(1)—the time to serve and file briefs—is now addressed directly in new Rule 28.1(f), the cross-reference to Rule 31 is no longer necessary. In Rule 31 and in all rules other than Rules 28.1, 30, and 34, references to an "appellant" refer both to the appellant in an appeal and to the cross-appellant in a cross-appeal, and references to an "appellee" refer both to the appellee in an appeal and to the cross-appellee in a cross-appeal. Cf. Rule 31(c).

Subdivision (c). Subdivision (c) provides for the filing of four briefs in a case involving a cross-appeal. This reflects the practice of every circuit except the Seventh. *See* 7th Cir. R. 28(d)(1)(a).

The first brief is the "appellant's principal brief." That brief—like the appellant's principal brief in a case that does not involve a cross-appeal—must comply with Rule 28(a).

The second brief is the "appellee's principal and response brief." Because this brief serves as the appellee's principal brief on the merits of the cross-appeal, as well as the appellee's response brief on the merits of the appeal, it must also comply with Rule 28(a), with the limited exceptions noted in the text of the rule.

The third brief is the "appellant's response and reply brief." Like a response brief in a case that does not involve a cross-appeal—that is, a response brief that does not also serve as a principal brief on the merits of a cross-appeal—the appellant's response and reply brief must comply with Rule 28(a)(2)-(9) and (11), with the exceptions noted in the text of the rule. *See* Rule 28(b). The one difference between the appellant's response and reply brief, on the one hand, and a response brief filed in a case that does not involve a cross-appeal, on the other, is that the latter must include a corporate disclosure statement. *See* Rule 28(a)(1) and (b). An appellant filing a response and reply brief in a case involving a cross-appeal has already filed a corporate disclosure statement with its principal brief on the merits of the appeal.

The fourth brief is the "appellee's reply brief." Like a reply brief in a case that does not involve a cross-appeal, it must comply with Rule 28(c), which essentially restates the requirements of Rule 28(a)(2)–(3) and (11). (Rather than restating the requirements of Rule 28(a)(2)-(3) and (11), as Rule 28(c) does, Rule 28.1(c)(4) includes a direct cross-reference.) The appellee's reply brief must also be limited to the issues presented by the cross-appeal.

Subdivision (d). Subdivision (d) specifies the colors of the covers on briefs filed in a case involving a cross-appeal. It is patterned after Rule 32(a)(2), which does not specifically refer to cross-appeals.

Subdivision (e). Subdivision (e) sets forth limits on the length of the briefs filed in a case involving a cross-appeal. It is patterned after Rule 32(a)(7), which does not specifically refer to cross-appeals. Subdivision (e) permits the appellee's principal and response brief to be longer than a typical principal brief on the merits because this brief serves not only as the principal brief on the merits of the cross-appeal, but also as the response brief on the merits of the appeal. Likewise, subdivision (e) permits the appellant's response and reply brief to be longer than a typical reply brief because this brief serves not only as the reply brief in the appeal, but also as the response brief in the cross-appeal. For purposes of determining the maximum length of an amicus curiae's brief filed in a case involving a cross-appeal, Rule 29(d)'s reference to "the maximum length authorized by these rules for a party's principal brief" should be understood to refer to subdivision (e)'s limitations on the length of an appellant's principal brief.

Subdivision (f). Subdivision (f) provides deadlines for serving and filing briefs in a cross-appeal. It is patterned after Rule 31(a)(1), which does not specifically refer to cross-appeals.

Rule 29. Brief of an Amicus Curiae

(a) When Permitted. The United States or its officer or agency, or a State, Territory, Commonwealth, or the District of Columbia may file an amicus-curiae brief without the consent of the parties or leave of court. Any other amicus curiae may file a brief only by leave of court or if the brief states that all parties have consented to its filing.

(b) Motion for Leave to File. The motion must be accompanied by the proposed brief and state:

(1) the movant's interest; and

(2) the reason why an amicus brief is desirable and why the matters asserted are relevant to the disposition of the case.

(c) Contents and Form. An amicus brief must comply with Rule 32. In addition to the requirements of Rule 32, the cover must identify the party or parties supported and indicate whether the brief supports affirmance or reversal. If an amicus curiae is a corporation, the brief must include a disclosure statement like that required of parties by Rule 26.1. An amicus brief need not comply with Rule 28, but must include the following:

(1) a table of contents, with page references;

(2) a table of authorities—cases (alphabetically arranged), statutes and other authorities—with references to the pages of the brief where they are cited;

(3) a concise statement of the identity of the amicus curiae, its interest in the case, and the source of its authority to file;

(4) an argument, which may be preceded by a summary and which need not include a statement of the applicable standard of review; and

(5) a certificate of compliance, if required by Rule 32(a)(7).

(d) Length. Except by the court's permission, an amicus brief may be no more than one-half the maximum length authorized by these rules for a party's principal brief. If the court grants a party permission to file a longer brief, that extension does not affect the length of an amicus brief.

(e) Time for Filing. An amicus curiae must file its brief, accompanied by a motion for filing when necessary, no later than 7 days after the principal brief of the party being supported is filed. An amicus curiae that does not support either party must file its brief no later than 7 days after the appellant's or petitioner's principal brief is filed. A court may grant leave for later filing, specifying the time within which an opposing party may answer.

(f) Reply Brief. Except by the court's permission, an amicus curiae may not file a reply brief.

(g) Oral Argument. An amicus curiae may participate in oral argument only with the court's permission.

(As amended Apr. 24, 1998, eff. Dec. 1, 1998.)

ADVISORY COMMITTEE NOTES

1967 Adoption

Only five circuits presently regulate the filing of the brief of an amicus curiae. See D.C.Cir. Rule 18(j) [rule 18(j), U.S.Ct. of App.Dist. of Col.Cir., this title]; 1st Cir. Rule 23(10) [rule 23(10), U.S.Ct. of App. 1st Cir.]; 6th Cir. Rule 17(4) [rule 17(4), U.S.Ct. of App. 6th Cir.]; 9th Cir. Rule 18(9) [rule 18(9), U.S.Ct. of App. 9th Cir.]; 10th Cir. Rule 20

[rule 20, U.S.Ct. of App. 10th Cir.]. This rule follows the practice of a majority of circuits in requiring leave of court to file an amicus brief except under the circumstances stated therein. Compare Supreme Court Rule 42.

1998 Amendments

The language and organization of the rule are amended to make the rule more easily understood. In addition to changes made to improve the understanding, the Advisory Committee has changed language to make style and terminology consistent through the appellate rules. These changes are intended to be stylistic only.

Several substantive changes are made in this rule, however.

Subdivision (a). The major change in this subpart is that when a brief is filed with the consent of all parties, it is no longer necessary to obtain the parties' written consent and to file the consents with the brief. It is sufficient to obtain the parties' oral consent and to state in the brief that all parties have consented. It is sometimes difficult to obtain all the written consents by the filing deadline and it is not unusual for counsel to represent that parties have consented; for example, in a motion for extension of time to file a brief it is not unusual for the movant to state that the other parties have been consulted and they do not object to the extension. If a party's consent has been misrepresented, the party will be able to take action before the court considers the amicus brief.

The District of Columbia is added to the list of entities allowed to file an amicus brief without consent of all parties. The other changes in this material are stylistic.

Subdivision (b). The provision in the former rule, granting permission to conditionally file the brief with the motion, is changed to one requiring that the brief accompany the motion. Sup. Ct. R. 37.4 requires that the proposed brief be presented with the motion.

The former rule only required the motion to identify the applicant's interest and to generally state the reasons why an amicus brief is desirable. The amended rule additionally requires that the motion state the relevance of the matters asserted to the disposition of the case. As Sup. Ct. R. 37.1 states:

> An *amicus curiae* brief which brings relevant matter to the attention of the Court that has not already been brought to its attention by the parties is of considerable help to the Court. An *amicus curiae* brief which does not serve this purpose simply burdens the staff and facilities of the Court and its filing is not favored.

Because the relevance of the matters asserted by an amicus is ordinarily the most compelling reason for granting leave to file, the Committee believes that it is helpful to explicitly require such a showing.

Subdivision (c). The provisions in this subdivision are entirely new. Previously there was confusion as to whether an amicus brief must include all of the items listed in Rule 28. Out of caution practitioners in some circuits included all those items. Ordinarily that is unnecessary.

The requirement that the cover identify the party supported and indicate whether the amicus supports affirmance or reversal is an administrative aid.

Paragraph (c)(3) requires an amicus to state the source of its authority to file. The amicus simply must identify which of the provisions in Rule 29(a) provides the basis for the amicus to file its brief.

Subdivision (d). This new provision imposes a shorter page limit for an amicus brief than for a party's brief. This is appropriate for two reasons. First, an amicus may omit certain items that must be included in a party's brief. Second, an amicus brief is supplemental. It need not address all issues or all facets of a case. It should treat only matter not adequately addressed by a party.

Subdivision (e). The time limit for filing is changed. An amicus brief must be filed no later than 7 days after the principal brief of the party being supported is filed. Occasionally, an amicus supports neither party; in such instances, the amendment provides that the amicus brief must be filed no later than 7 days after the appellant's or petitioner's principal brief is filed. Note that in both instances the 7–day period runs from when a brief is filed. The passive voice—"is filed"—is used deliberately. A party or amicus can send its brief to a court for filing and, under Rule 25, the brief is timely if mailed within the filing period. Although the brief is timely if mailed within the filing period, it is not "filed" until the court receives it and file stamps it. "Filing" is done by the court, not by the party. It may be necessary for an amicus to contact the court to ascertain the filing date.

The 7–day stagger was adopted because it is long enough to permit an amicus to review the completed brief of the party being supported and avoid repetitious argument. A 7–day period also is short enough that no adjustment need be made in the opposing party's briefing schedule. The opposing party will have sufficient time to review arguments made by the amicus and address them in the party's responsive pleading. The timetable for filing the parties' briefs is unaffected by this change.

A court may grant permission to file an amicus brief in a context in which the party does not file a "principal brief"; for example, an amicus may be permitted to file in support of a party's petition for rehearing. In such instances the court will establish the filing time for the amicus.

The former rule's statement that a court may, for cause shown, grant leave for later filing is unnecessary. Rule 26(b) grants general authority to enlarge the time prescribed in these rules for good cause shown. This new rule, however, states that when a court grants permission for later filing, the court must specify the period within which an opposing party may answer the arguments of the amicus.

Subdivision (f). This subdivision generally prohibits the filing of a reply brief by an amicus curiae. Sup. Ct. R. 37 and local rules of the D.C., Ninth, and Federal Circuits state that an amicus may not file a reply brief. The role of an amicus should not require the use of a reply brief.

Subdivision (g). The language of this subdivision stating that an amicus will be granted permission to participate in oral argument "only for extraordinary reasons" has been deleted. The change is made to reflect more accurately the current practice in which it is not unusual for a court to permit an amicus to argue when a party is willing to share its argument time with the amicus. The Committee does not intend, however, to suggest that in other instances an amicus will be permitted to argue absent extraordinary circumstances.

Rule 30. Appendix to the Briefs

(a) Appellant's Responsibility.

(1) Contents of the Appendix. The appellant must prepare and file an appendix to the briefs containing:

(A) the relevant docket entries in the proceeding below;

(B) the relevant portions of the pleadings, charge, findings, or opinion;

(C) the judgment, order, or decision in question; and

(D) other parts of the record to which the parties wish to direct the court's attention.

(2) Excluded Material. Memoranda of law in the district court should not be included in the appendix unless they have independent relevance. Parts of the record may be relied on by the court or the parties even though not included in the appendix.

(3) Time to File; Number of Copies. Unless filing is deferred under Rule 30(c), the appellant must file 10 copies of the appendix with the brief and must serve one copy on counsel for each party separately represented. An unrepresented party proceeding in forma pauperis must file 4 legible copies with the clerk, and one copy must be served on counsel for each separately represented party. The court may by local rule or by order in a particular case require the filing or service of a different number.

(b) All Parties' Responsibilities.

(1) Determining the Contents of the Appendix. The parties are encouraged to agree on the contents of the appendix. In the absence of an agreement, the appellant must, within 10 days after the record is filed, serve on the appellee a designation of the parts of the record the appellant intends to include in the appendix and a statement of the issues the appellant intends to present for review. The appellee may, within 10 days after receiving the designation, serve on the appellant a designation of additional parts to which it wishes to direct the court's attention. The appellant must include the designated parts in the appendix. The parties must not engage in unnecessary designation of parts of the record, because the entire record is available to the court. This paragraph applies also to a cross-appellant and a cross-appellee.

(2) Costs of Appendix. Unless the parties agree otherwise, the appellant must pay the cost of the appendix. If the appellant considers parts of the record designated by the appellee to be unnecessary, the appellant may advise the appellee, who must then advance the cost of including those parts. The cost of the appendix is a taxable cost. But if any party causes unnecessary parts of the record to be included in the appendix, the court may impose the cost of those parts on that party. Each circuit must, by local rule, provide for sanctions against attorneys who unreasonably and vexatiously increase litigation costs by including unnecessary material in the appendix.

(c) Deferred Appendix.

(1) Deferral Until After Briefs Are Filed. The court may provide by rule for classes of cases or by order in a particular case that preparation of the appendix may be deferred until after the briefs have been filed and that the appendix may be filed 21 days after the appellee's brief is served. Even though the filing of the appendix may be deferred, Rule 30(b) applies; except that a party must designate the parts of the record it wants included in the appendix when it serves its brief, and need not include a statement of the issues presented.

(2) References to the Record.

(A) If the deferred appendix is used, the parties may cite in their briefs the pertinent pages of the record. When the appendix is prepared, the record pages cited in the briefs must be indicated by inserting record page numbers, in brackets, at places in the appendix where those pages of the record appear.

(B) A party who wants to refer directly to pages of the appendix may serve and file copies of the brief within the time required by Rule 31(a), containing appropriate references to pertinent pages of the record. In that event, within 14 days after the appendix is filed, the party must serve and file copies of the brief, containing references to the pages of the appendix in place of or in addition to the references to the pertinent pages of the record. Except for the correction of typographical errors, no other changes may be made to the brief.

(d) Format of the Appendix. The appendix must begin with a table of contents identifying the page at which each part begins. The relevant docket entries must follow the table of contents. Other parts of the record must follow chronologically. When pages from the transcript of proceedings are placed in the appendix, the transcript page numbers must be shown in brackets immediately before the included pages. Omissions in the text of papers or of the transcript must be indicated by asterisks. Immaterial formal matters (captions, subscriptions, acknowledgments, etc.) should be omitted.

(e) Reproduction of Exhibits. Exhibits designated for inclusion in the appendix may be reproduced in a separate volume, or volumes, suitably indexed. Four copies must be filed with the appendix, and one copy must be served on counsel for each separately

represented party. If a transcript of a proceeding before an administrative agency, board, commission, or officer was used in a district-court action and has been designated for inclusion in the appendix, the transcript must be placed in the appendix as an exhibit.

(f) Appeal on the Original Record Without an Appendix. The court may, either by rule for all cases or classes of cases or by order in a particular case, dispense with the appendix and permit an appeal to proceed on the original record with any copies of the record, or relevant parts, that the court may order the parties to file.

(As amended Mar. 30, 1970, eff. July 1, 1970; Mar. 10, 1986, eff. July 1, 1986; Apr. 30, 1991, eff. Dec. 1, 1991; Apr. 29, 1994, eff. Dec. 1, 1994; Apr. 24, 1998. eff. Dec. 1, 1998.)

ADVISORY COMMITTEE NOTES
1967 Adoption

Subdivision (a). Only two circuits presently require a printed record (5th Cir. Rule 23(a) [rule 23(a), U.S.Ct. of App. 5th Cir.]; 8th Cir. Rule 10 [rule 10, U.S.Ct. of App. 8th Cir.] (in civil appeals only)), and the rules and practice in those circuits combine to make the difference between a printed record and the appendix, which is now used in eight circuits and in the Supreme Court in lieu of the printed record, largely nominal. The essential characteristics of the appendix method are: (1) the entire record may not be reproduced; (2) instead, the parties are to set out in an appendix to the briefs those parts of the record which in their judgment the judges must consult in order to determine the issues presented by the appeal; (3) the appendix is not the record but merely a selection therefrom for the convenience of the judges of the court of appeals; the record is the actual trial court record, and the record itself is always available to supply inadvertent omissions from the appendix. These essentials are incorporated, either by rule or by practice, in the circuits that continue to require the printed record rather than the appendix. See 5th Cir. Rule 23(a)(9) [23(a)(9), U.S.Ct. of App. 5th Cir.] and 8th Cir. Rule 10(a)–(d) [rule 10(a)–(d), U.S.Ct. of App. 8th Cir.].

Subdivision (b). Under the practice in six of the eight circuits which now use the appendix method, unless the parties agree to use a single appendix, the appellant files with his brief an appendix containing the parts of the record which he deems it essential that the court read in order to determine the questions presented. If the appellee deems additional parts of the record necessary he must include such parts as an appendix to his brief. The proposed rule differs from that practice. By the new rule a single appendix is to be filed. It is to be prepared by the appellant, who must include therein those parts which he deems essential and those which the appellee designates as essential.

Under the practice by which each party files his own appendix the resulting reproduction of essential parts of the record is often fragmentary; it is not infrequently necessary to piece several appendices together to arrive at a usable reproduction. Too, there seems to be a tendency on the part of some appellants to reproduce less than what is necessary for a determination of the issues presented (see *Moran Towing Corp. v. M. A. Gammino Construction Co.*, 363 F.2d 108 (1st Cir. 1966); *Walters v. Shari Music Publishing Corp.*, 298 F.2d 206 (2d Cir. 1962) and cases cited therein; *Morrison v. Texas Co.*, 289 F.2d 382 (7th Cir. 1961) and cases cited therein), a tendency which is doubtless encouraged by the requirement in present rules that the appellee reproduce in his separately prepared appendix such necessary parts of the record as are not included by the appellant.

Under the proposed rule responsibility for the preparation of the appendix is placed on the appellant. If the appellee feels that the appellant has omitted essential portions of the record, he may require the appellant to include such portions in the appendix. The appellant is protected against a demand that he reproduce parts which he considers unnecessary by the provisions entitling him to require the appellee to advance the costs of reproducing such parts and authorizing denial of costs for matter unnecessarily reproduced.

Subdivision (c). This subdivision permits the appellant to elect to defer the production of the appendix to the briefs until the briefs of both sides are written, and authorizes a court of appeals to require such deferred filing by rule or order. The advantage of this method of preparing the appendix is that it permits the parties to determine what parts of the record need to be reproduced in the light of the issues actually presented by the briefs. Often neither side is in a position to say precisely what is needed until the briefs are completed. Once the argument on both sides is known, it should be possible to confine the matter reproduced in the appendix to that which is essential to a determination of the appeal or review. This method of preparing the appendix is presently in use in the Tenth Circuit (Rule 17) [rule 17, U.S.Ct. of App. 10th Cir.] and in other circuits in review of agency proceedings, and it has proven its value in reducing the volume required to be reproduced. When the record is long, use of this method is likely to result in substantial economy to the parties.

Subdivision (e). The purpose of this subdivision is to reduce the cost of reproducing exhibits. While subdivision (a) requires that 10 copies of the appendix be filed, unless the court requires a lesser number, subdivision (e) permits exhibits necessary for the determination of an appeal to be bound separately, and requires only 4 copies of such a separate volume or volumes to be filed and a single copy to be served on counsel.

Subdivision (f). The subdivision authorizes a court of appeals to dispense with the appendix method of reproducing parts of the record and to hear appeals on the original record and such copies of it as the court may require.

Since 1962 the Ninth Circuit has permitted all appeals to be heard on the original record and a very limited number of copies. Under the practice as adopted in 1962, any party to an appeal could elect to have the appeal heard on the original record and two copies thereof rather than on the printed record theretofore required. The resulting substantial saving of printing costs led to the election of the new practice in virtually all cases, and by 1967 the use of printed records had ceased. By a recent amendment, the Ninth Circuit has abolished the printed record altogether. Its rules now provide that all appeals are to be heard on the original record, and it has reduced the number of copies required to two sets of copies of the transmitted original papers (excluding copies of exhibits, which need not be filed unless specifically ordered). See 9 Cir. Rule 10 [rule 10 U.S.Ct. of App. 9th Cir.],

as amended June 2, 1967, effective September 1, 1967. The Eighth Circuit permits appeals in criminal cases and in habeas corpus and 28 U.S.C. § 2255 proceedings to be heard on the original record and two copies thereof. See 8 Cir. Rule 8(i)–(j) [rule 8(i)–(j), U.S.Ct. of App. 8th Cir.]. The Tenth Circuit permits appeals in all cases to be heard on the original record and four copies thereof whenever the record consists of two hundred pages or less. See 10 Cir. Rule 17(a) [rule 17(a), U.S.Ct. of App. 10th Cir.]. This subdivision expressly authorizes the continuation of the practices in the Eighth, Ninth and Tenth Circuits.

The judges of the Court of Appeals for the Ninth Circuit have expressed complete satisfaction with the practice there in use and have suggested that attention be called to the advantages which it offers in terms of reducing cost.

1970 Amendments

Subdivision (a). The amendment of subdivision (a) is related to the amendment of Rule 31(a), which authorizes a court of appeals to shorten the time for filing briefs. By virtue of this amendment, if the time for filing the brief of the appellant is shortened the time for filing the appendix is likewise shortened.

Subdivision (c). As originally written, subdivision (c) permitted the appellant to elect to defer filing of the appendix until 21 days after service of the brief of the appellee. As amended, subdivision (c) requires that an order of court be obtained before filing of the appendix can be deferred, unless a court permits deferred filing by local rule. The amendment should not cause use of the deferred appendix to be viewed with disfavor. In cases involving lengthy records, permission to defer filing of the appendix should be freely granted as an inducement to the parties to include in the appendix only matter that the briefs show to be necessary for consideration by the judges. But the Committee is advised that appellants have elected to defer filing of the appendix in cases involving brief records merely to obtain the 21 day delay. The subdivision is amended to prevent that practice.

1986 Amendments

Subdivision (a). During its study of the separate appendix [see Report of the Advisory Committee on the Federal Appellate Rules on the Operation of Rule 30, FRD (1985)], the Advisory Committee found that this document was frequently encumbered with memoranda submitted to the trial court. *United States v. Noall*, 587 F.2d 123, 125 n. 1 (2nd Cir.1978). See generally *Drewett v. Aetna Cas. & Sur. Co.*, 539 F.2d 496, 500 (5th Cir.1976); *Volkswagenwerk Aktiengesellschaft v. Church*, 413 F.2d 1126, 1128 (9th Cir.1969). Inclusion of such material makes the appendix more bulky and therefore less useful to the appellate panel. It also can increase significantly the costs of litigation.

There are occasions when such trial court memoranda have independent relevance in the appellate litigation. For instance, there may be a dispute as to whether a particular point was raised or whether a concession was made in the district court. In such circumstances, it is appropriate to include pertinent sections of such memoranda in the appendix.

Subdivision (b). The amendment to subdivision (b) is designed to require the circuits, by local rule, to establish a procedural mechanism for the imposition of sanctions against those attorneys who conduct appellate litigation in bad faith. Both 28 U.S.C. § 1927 and the inherent power of the court authorize such sanctions. See *Brennan v. Local 357, International Brotherhood of Teamsters*, 709 F.2d 611 (9th Cir. 1983). See generally *Roadway Express, Inc. v. Piper*, 447 U.S. 752 (1980). While considerations of uniformity are important and doubtless will be taken into account by the judges of the respective circuits, the Advisory Committee believes that, at this time, the circuits need the flexibility to tailor their approach to the conditions of local practice. The local rule shall provide for notice and opportunity to respond before the imposition of any sanction.

Technical amendments also are made to subdivisions (a), (b) and (c) which are not intended to be substantive changes.

1991 Amendments

Subdivision (b). The amendment requires a cross appellant to serve the appellant with a statement of the issues that the cross appellant intends to pursue on appeal. No later than ten days after the record is filed, the appellant and cross appellant must serve each other with a statement of the issues each intends to present for review and with a designation of the parts of the record that each wants included in the appendix. Within the next ten days, both the appellee and the cross appellee may designate additional materials for inclusion in the appendix. The appellant must then include in the appendix the parts thus designated for both the appeal and any cross appeals. The Committee expects that simultaneous compliance with this subdivision by an appellant and a cross appellant will be feasible in most cases. If a cross appellant cannot fairly be expected to comply until receipt of the appellant's statement of issues, relief may be sought by motion in the court of appeals.

1994 Amendments

Subdivision (a). The only substantive change is to allow a court to require the filing of a greater number of copies of an appendix as well as a lesser number.

1998 Amendments

The language and organization of the new rule are amended to make the rule more easily understood. In addition to changes made to improve the understanding, the Advisory Committee has changed language to make style and terminology consistent throughout the appellate Rules. These changes are intended to be stylistic only.

Subdivision (a). Paragraph (a)(3) is amended so that it is consistent with Rule 31(b). An unrepresented party proceeding in forma pauperis is only required to file 4 copies of the appendix rather than 10.

Subdivision (c). When a deferred appendix is used, a brief must make reference to the original record rather than to the appendix because it does not exist when the briefs are prepared. Unless a party later files an amended brief with direct references to the pages of the appendix (as provided in subparagraph (c)(2)(B)), the material in the appendix must indicate the pages of the original record from which it was drawn so that a reader of the brief can make meaningful use of the appendix. The instructions in the current rule for cross-referencing the appendix materials to the original rec-

ord are unclear. The language in paragraph (c)(2) has been amended to try to clarify the procedure.

Subdivision (d). In recognition of the fact that use of a typeset appendix is exceedingly rare in the courts of appeals, the last sentence—permitting a question and answer (as from a transcript) to be in a single paragraph—has been omitted.

HISTORICAL NOTES
Taxation of Fees in Appeals in Which Requirement of Appendix is Dispensed With

See item (6) in the Judicial Conference Schedule of Fees note under 28 U.S.C.A. § 1913.

Rule 31. Serving and Filing Briefs
(a) Time to Serve and File a Brief.

(1) The appellant must serve and file a brief within 40 days after the record is filed. The appellee must serve and file a brief within 30 days after the appellant's brief is served. The appellant may serve and file a reply brief within 14 days after service of the appellee's brief but a reply brief must be filed at least 3 days before argument, unless the court, for good cause, allows a later filing.

(2) A court of appeals that routinely considers cases on the merits promptly after the briefs are filed may shorten the time to serve and file briefs, either by local rule or by order in a particular case.

(b) Number of Copies. Twenty-five copies of each brief must be filed with the clerk and 2 copies must be served on each unrepresented party and on counsel for each separately represented party. An unrepresented party proceeding in forma pauperis must file 4 legible copies with the clerk, and one copy must be served on each unrepresented party and on counsel for each separately represented party. The court may by local rule or by order in a particular case require the filing or service of a different number.

(c) Consequence of Failure to File. If an appellant fails to file a brief within the time provided by this rule, or within an extended time, an appellee may move to dismiss the appeal. An appellee who fails to file a brief will not be heard at oral argument unless the court grants permission.

(As amended Mar. 30, 1970, eff. July 1, 1970; Mar. 10, 1986, eff. July 1, 1986; Apr. 29, 1994, eff. Dec. 1, 1994; Apr. 24, 1998, eff. Dec. 1, 1998; Apr. 29, 2002, eff. Dec. 1, 2002.)

ADVISORY COMMITTEE NOTES
1967 Adoption

A majority of the circuits now require the brief of the appellant to be filed within 30 days from the date on which the record is filed. But in those circuits an exchange of designations is unnecessary in the preparation of the appendix. The appellant files with his brief an appendix containing the parts of the record which he deems essential. If the appellee considers other parts essential, he includes those

parts in his own appendix. Since the proposed rule requires the appellant to file with his brief an appendix containing necessary parts of the record as designated by both parties, the rule allows the appellant 40 days in order to provide time for the exchange of designations respecting the content of the appendix (see Rule 30(b)).

1970 Amendment

The time prescribed by Rule 31(a) for preparing briefs—40 days to the appellant, 30 days to the appellee—is well within the time that must ordinarily elapse in most circuits before an appeal can be reached for consideration. In those circuits, the time prescribed by the Rule should not be disturbed. But if a court of appeals maintains a current calendar, that is, if an appeal can be heard as soon as the briefs have been filed, or if the practice of the court permits the submission of appeals for preliminary consideration as soon as the briefs have been filed, the court should be free to prescribe shorter periods in the interest of expediting decision.

1986 Amendment

The amendments to Rules 31(a) and (c) are technical. No substantive change is intended.

1994 Amendments

Subdivision (b). The amendment allows a court of appeals to require the filing of a greater, as well as a lesser, number of copies of briefs. The amendment also allows the required number to be prescribed by local rule as well as by order in a particular case.

1998 Amendments

The language and organization of the rule are amended to make the rule more easily understood. In addition to changes made to improve the understanding, the advisory committee has changed language to make style and terminology consistent throughout the appellate rules. These changes are intended to by stylistic only; a substantive change is made, however, in subdivision (b).

Subdivision (a). Paragraph (a)(2) explicitly authorizes a court of appeals to shorten a briefing schedule if the court routinely considers cases on the merits promptly after the briefs are filed. Extensions of the briefing schedule, by order, are permitted under the general provisions of Rule 26(b).

Subdivision (b). The current rules says that a party who is permitted to file "typewritten ribbon and carbon copies of the brief" need only file and original and three copies of the brief. The quoted language, in conjunction with current rule 24(c), means that a party allowed to proceed in forma pauperis need not file 25 copies of the brief. Two changes are made in this subdivision. First, it is anachronistic to refer to a party who is allowed to file a typewritten brief as if that would distinguish the party from all other parties; any party is permitted to file a typewritten brief. The amended rule states directly that it applies to a party to proceed in forma pauperis. Second, the amended rule does not generally permit parties who are represented by counsel to file the lesser number of brief. Inexpensive methods of copying are generally available. Unless it would impose hardship, in which case

a motion to file a lesser number should be filed, a represented party must file the usual number of briefs.

2002 Amendments

Subdivision (b). In requiring that two copies of each brief "must be served on counsel for each separately represented party," Rule 31(b) may be read to imply that copies of briefs need not be served on unrepresented parties. The Rule has been amended to clarify that briefs must be served on all parties, including those who are not represented by counsel.

Changes Made After Publication and Comments No changes were made to the text of the proposed amendment or to the Committee Note.

Rule 32. Form of Briefs, Appendices, and Other Papers

(a) Form of a Brief.

(1) Reproduction.

(A) A brief may be reproduced by any process that yields a clear black image on light paper. The paper must be opaque and unglazed. Only one side of the paper may be used.

(B) Text must be reproduced with a clarity that equals or exceeds the output of a laser printer.

(C) Photographs, illustrations, and tables may be reproduced by any method that results in a good copy of the original; a glossy finish is acceptable if the original is glossy.

(2) Cover. Except for filings by unrepresented parties, the cover of the appellant's brief must be blue; the appellee's, red; an intervenor's or amicus curiae's, green; any reply brief, gray; and any supplemental brief, tan. The front cover of a brief must contain:

(A) the number of the case centered at the top;

(B) the name of the court;

(C) the title of the case (see Rule 12(a));

(D) the nature of the proceeding (e.g., Appeal, Petition for Review) and the name of the court, agency, or board below;

(E) the title of the brief, identifying the party or parties for whom the brief is filed; and

(F) the name, office address, and telephone number of counsel representing the party for whom the brief is filed.

(3) Binding. The brief must be bound in any manner that is secure, does not obscure the text, and permits the brief to lie reasonably flat when open.

(4) Paper Size, Line Spacing, and Margins. The brief must be on 8½ by 11 inch paper. The text must be double-spaced, but quotations more than two lines long may be indented and single-spaced. Headings and footnotes may be single-spaced. Margins must be at least one inch on all four sides.

Page numbers may be placed in the margins, but no text may appear there.

(5) Typeface. Either a proportionally spaced or a monospaced face may be used.

(A) A proportionally spaced face must include serifs, but sans-serif type may be used in headings and captions. A proportionally spaced face must be 14–point or larger.

(B) A monospaced face may not contain more than 10½ characters per inch.

(6) Type Styles. A brief must be set in a plain, roman style, although italics or boldface may be used for emphasis. Case names must be italicized or underlined.

(7) Length.

(A) Page limitation. A principal brief may not exceed 30 pages, or a reply brief 15 pages, unless it complies with Rule 32(a)(7)(B) and (C).

(B) Type-volume limitation.

(i) A principal brief is acceptable if:

- it contains no more than 14,000 words;

or

- it uses a monospaced face and contains no more than 1,300 lines of text.

(ii) A reply brief is acceptable if it contains no more than half of the type volume specified in Rule 32(a)(7)(B)(i).

(iii) Headings, footnotes, and quotations count toward the word and line limitations. The corporate disclosure statement, table of contents, table of citations, statement with respect to oral argument, any addendum containing statutes, rules or regulations, and any certificates of counsel do not count toward the limitation.

(C) Certificate of compliance.

(i) A brief submitted under Rules 28.1(e)(2) or 32(a)(7)(B) must include a certificate by the attorney, or an unrepresented party, that the brief complies with the type-volume limitation. The person preparing the certificate may rely on the word or line count of the word-processing system used to prepare the brief. The certificate must state either:

- the number of words in the brief; or

- the number of lines of monospaced type in the brief.

(ii) Form 6 in the Appendix of Forms is a suggested form of a certificate of compliance. Use of Form 6 must be regarded as sufficient to meet the requirements of Rules 28.1(e)(3) and 32(a)(7)(C)(i).

(b) Form of an Appendix. An appendix must comply with Rule 32(a)(1), (2), (3), and (4), with the following exceptions:

(1) The cover of a separately bound appendix must be white.

(2) An appendix may include a legible photocopy of any document found in the record or of a printed judicial or agency decision.

(3) When necessary to facilitate inclusion of odd-sized documents such as technical drawings, an appendix may be a size other than 8½ by 11 inches, and need not lie reasonably flat when opened.

(c) Form of Other Papers.

(1) **Motion.** The form of a motion is governed by Rule 27(d).

(2) **Other Papers.** Any other paper, including a petition for panel rehearing and a petition for hearing or rehearing en banc, and any response to such a petition, must be reproduced in the manner prescribed by Rule 32(a), with the following exceptions:

(A) A cover is not necessary if the caption and signature page of the paper together contain the information required by Rule 32(a)(2). If a cover is used, it must be white.

(B) Rule 32(a)(7) does not apply.

(d) Signature. Every brief, motion, or other paper filed with the court must be signed by the party filing the paper or, if the party is represented, by one of the party's attorneys.

(e) Local Variation. Every court of appeals must accept documents that comply with the form requirements of this rule. By local rule or order in a particular case a court of appeals may accept documents that do not meet all of the form requirements of this rule. (As amended Apr. 24, 1998, eff. Dec. 1, 1998; Apr. 29, 2002, eff. Dec. 1, 2002; Apr. 25, 2005, eff. Dec. 1, 2005.)

ADVISORY COMMITTEE NOTES

1967 Adoption

Only two methods of printing are now generally recognized by the circuits—standard typographic printing and the offset duplicating process (multilith). A third, mimeographing, is permitted in the Fifth Circuit. The District of Columbia, Ninth, and Tenth Circuits permit records to be reproduced by copying processes. The Committee feels that recent and impending advances in the arts of duplicating and copying warrant experimentation with less costly forms of reproduction than those now generally authorized. The proposed rule permits, in effect, the use of any process other than the carbon copy process which produces a clean, readable page. What constitutes such is left in first instance to the parties and ultimately to the court to determine. The final sentence of the first paragraph of subdivision (a) is added to allow the use of multilith, mimeograph, or other forms of copies of the reporter's original transcript whenever such are available.

1998 Amendments

In addition to amending Rule 32 to conform to uniform drafting standards, several substantive amendments are made. The Advisory Committee had been working on substantive amendments to Rule 32 for some time prior to completion of this larger project.

Subdivision (a). Form of a Brief.

Paragraph (a)(1). Reproduction.

The rule permits the use of "light" paper, not just "white" paper. Cream and buff colored paper, including recycled paper, are acceptable. The rule permits printing on only one side of the paper. Although some argue that paper could be saved by allowing double-sided printing, others argue that in order to preserve legibility a heavier weight paper would be needed, resulting in little, if any, paper saving. In addition, the blank sides of a brief are commonly used by judges and their clerks for making notes about the case.

Because photocopying is inexpensive and widely available and because use of carbon paper is now very rare, all references to the use of carbon copies have been deleted.

The rule requires that the text be reproduced with a clarity that equals or exceeds the output of a laser printer. That means that the method used must have a print resolution of 300 dots per inch (dpi) or more. This will ensure the legibility of the brief. A brief produced by a typewriter or a daisy wheel printer, as well as one produced by a laser printer, has a print resolution of 300 dpi or more. But a brief produced by a dot-matrix printer, fax machine, or portable printer that uses head or dye to transfer methods does not. Some ink jet printers are 300 dpi or more, but some are 216 dpi and would not be sufficient.

Photographs, illustrations, and tables may be reproduced by any method that results in a good copy.

Paragraph (a)(2). Cover.

The rule requires that the number of the case be centered at the top of the front cover of a brief. This will aid in identification of the brief. The idea was drawn from a local rule. The rule also requires that the title of the brief identify the party or parties on whose behalf the brief is filed. When there are multiple appellants or appellees, the information is necessary to the court. If, however, the brief is filed on behalf of all appellants or appellees, it may so indicate. Further, it may be possible to identify the class of parties on whose behalf the brief is filed. Otherwise, it may be necessary to name each party. The rule also requires that attorneys' telephone numbers appear on the front cover of a brief or appendix.

Paragraph (a)(3). Binding.

The rule requires a brief to be bound in any manner that is secure, does not obscure the text, and that permits the brief to lie reasonable flat when open. Many judges and most court employees do much of their work at computer keyboards and a brief that lies flat when open is significantly more convenient. One circuit already has such a requirement and another states a preference for it. While a spiral binding would comply with this requirement, it is not intended to be the exclusive method of binding. Stapling a brief at the upper left-hand corner also satisfies this requirement as long as it is sufficiently secure.

Paragraph (a)(4). Paper Size, Line Spacing, and Margins.

The provisions for pamphlet-size briefs are deleted because their use is so rare. If a circuit wishes to authorize their use, it has authority to do so under subdivision (d) of this rule.

Paragraph (a)(5). Typeface.

This paragraph and the next one, governing type style, are new. The existing rule simply states that a brief produced by the standard typographic process must be printed in at least 11 point type, or if produced in any other manner, the lines of text must be double spaced. Today few briefs are produced by commercial printers or by typewriters; most are produced on and printed by computer. The availability of computer fonts in a variety of sizes and styles has given rise to local rules limiting type styles. The Advisory Committee believes that some standards are needed both to ensure that all litigants have an equal opportunity to present their material and to ensure that the briefs are easily legible.

With regard to typeface there are two options; proportionally-spaced typeface or monospaced typeface.

A proportionally-spaced typeface gives a different amount of horizontal space to characters depending upon the width of the character. A capital "M" is given more horizontal space than a lower case "i". The rule requires that a proportionally-spaced typeface have serifs. Serifs are small horizontal or vertical strokes at the ends of the lines that make up the letters and numbers. Studies have shown that long passages of serif type are easier to read and comprehend than long passages of sans-serif type. The rule accordingly limits the principal sections of submissions to serif type although sans-serif type may be used in headings and captions. This is the same approach magazines, newspapers, and commercial printers take. Look at a professionally printed brief; you will find sans–serif type confined to captions, if it is used at all. The next line shows two characters enlarged for detail. The first has serifs, the second does not.

Y Y *

[* For original representation of characters, see House Document 105–269 of the 105th Congress, 2d Session dated May 11, 1998 entitled "Amendments to the Federal Rules of Appellate Procedure (Executive Communication No. 9072)."]

So that the type is easily legible, the rule requires a minimum type size of 14 points for proportionally-spaced typeface.

A monospaced typeface is one in which all characters have the same advance width. That means that each character is given the same horizontal space on the line. A wide letter such as a capital "M" and a narrow letter such as a lower case "i" are given the same space. Most typewriters produce mono-spaced type, and most computers also can do so using fonts with names such as "Courier."

This sentence is in a proportionally spaced font; as you can see, the m and i have different widths. *

[* For original representation of characters, see House Document 105–269 of the 105th Congress, 2d Session dated May 11, 1998 entitled "Amendments to the Federal Rules of Appellate Procedure (Executive Communication No. 9072)."]

This sentence is in a monospaced font; as you can see, the m and i have the same width. *

[* For original representation of characters, see House Document 105–269 of the 105th Congress, 2d Session dated May 11, 1998 entitled "Amendments to the Federal Rules of Appellate Procedure (Executive Communication No. 9072)."]

The rule requires use of a monospaced typeface that produces no more than 10 ½ characters per inch. A standard typewriter with pica type produces a monospaced typeface with 10 characters per inch (cpi). That is the ideal monospaced typeface. The rule permits up to 10 ½ cpi because some computer software programs contain monospaced fonts that purport to produce 10 cpi but that in fact produce slightly more than 10 cpi. In order to avoid the need to reprint a brief produced in good faith reliance upon such a program, the rule permits a bit of leeway. A monospaced typeface with no more than 10 cpi is preferred.

Paragraph (a)(6). Type Styles.

The rule requires use of plain roman, that is not italic or script, type. Italics and boldface may be used for emphasis. Italicizing case names is preferred but underlining may be used.

Paragraph (a)(7). Type-Volume Limitation.

Subparagraph (a)(7)(A) contains a safe-harbor provision. A principal brief that does not exceed 30 pages complies with the type-volume limitation without further question or certification. A reply brief that does not exceed 15 pages is similarly treated. The current limit is 50 pages but that limit was established when most briefs were produced on typewriters. The widespread use of personal computers has made a multitude of printing options available to practitioners. Use of a proportional typeface alone can greatly increase the amount of material per page as compared with use of a monospaced typeface. Even though the rule requires use of 14–point proportional type, there is great variation in the x-height of different 14–point typefaces. Selection of a typeface with a small x-height increases the amount of text per page. Computers also make possible fine gradations in spacing between lines and tight tracking between letters and words. All of this, and more, have made the 50–page limit virtually meaningless. Establishing a safe-harbor of 50 pages would permit a person who makes use of the multitude of printing "tricks" available with most personal computers to file a brief far longer than the "old" 50–page brief. Therefore, as to those briefs not subject to any other volume control than a page limit, a 30–page limit is imposed.

The limits in subparagraph (B) approximate the current 50–page limit and compliance with them is easy even for a person without a personal computer. The aim of these provisions is to create a level playing field. The rule gives every party an equal opportunity to make arguments, without permitting those with the best in-house typesetting an opportunity to expand their submissions.

The length can be determined either by counting words or lines. That is, the length of a brief is determined not by the number of pages but by the number or words or lines in the brief. This gives every party the same opportunity to present an argument without regard to the typeface used and eliminates any incentive to use footnotes or typographical "tricks" to squeeze more material onto a page.

The word counting method can be used with any typeface.

A monospaced brief can meet the volume limitation by using the word or a line count. If the line counting method is used, the number of lines may not exceed 1,300—26 lines per page in a 50–page brief. The number of lines is easily counted manually. Line counting is not sufficient if a proportionally spaced typeface is used, because the amount of material per line can vary widely.

A brief using the type-volume limitations in subparagraph (B) must include a certificate by the attorney, or party

proceeding pro se, that the brief complies with the limitation. The rule permits the person preparing the certification to rely upon the word or line count of the word-processing system used to prepare the brief.

Currently, Rule 28(g) governs the length of a brief. Rule 28(g) begins with the words "[e]xcept by permission of the court," signaling that a party may file a motion to exceed the limits established in the rule. The absence of similar language in Rule 32 does not mean that the Advisory Committee intends to prohibit motions to deviate from the requirements of the rule. The Advisory Committee does not believe that any such language is needed to authorize such a motion.

Subdivision (b). Form of an Appendix.

The provisions governing the form of a brief generally apply to an appendix. The rule recognizes, however, that an appendix is usually produced by photocopying existing documents. The rule requires that the photocopies be legible.

The rule permits inclusion not only of documents from the record but also copies of a printed judicial or agency decision. If a decision that is part of the record in the case has been published, it is helpful to provide a copy of the published decision in place of a copy of the decision from the record.

Subdivision (c). Form of Other Papers.

The old rule required a petition for rehearing to be produced in the same manner as a brief or appendix. The new rule also requires that a petition for rehearing en banc and a response to either a petition for panel rehearing or a petition for rehearing en banc be prepared in the same manner. But the length limitations of paragraph (a)(7) do not apply to those documents and a cover is not required if all the formation needed by the court to properly identify the document and the parties is included in the caption or signature page.

Existing subdivision (b) states that other papers may be produced in like manner, or "they may be typewritten upon opaque, unglazed paper 8 ½ by 11 inches in size." The quoted language is deleted but that method of preparing documents is not eliminated because (a)(5)(b) permits use of standard pica type. The only change is that the new rule now specifies margins for typewritten documents.

Subdivision (d). Local Variation.

A brief that complies with the national rule should be acceptable in every court. Local rules may move in one direction only; they may authorize noncompliance with certain of the national norms. For example, a court that wishes to do so may authorize printing of briefs on both sides of the paper, or the use of smaller type size or sans-serif proportional type. A local rules may not, however, impose requirements that are not in the national rule.

2002 Amendments

Subdivision (a)(2). On occasion, a court may permit or order the parties to file supplemental briefs addressing an issue that was not addressed—or adequately addressed—in the principal briefs. Rule 32(a)(2) has been amended to require that tan covers be used on such supplemental briefs. The amendment is intended to promote uniformity in federal appellate practice. At present, the local rules of the circuit courts conflict. *See, e.g.,* D.C. Cir. R. 28(g) (requiring yellow covers on supplemental briefs); 11th Cir. R. 32, I.O.P. 1 (requiring white covers on supplemental briefs).

Changes Made After Publication and Comments No changes were made to the text of the proposed amendment or to the Committee Note.

Subdivision (a)(7)(C). If the principal brief of a party exceeds 30 pages, or if the reply brief of a party exceeds 15 pages, Rule 32(a)(7)(C) provides that the party or the party's attorney must certify that the brief complies with the type-volume limitation of Rule 32(a)(7)(B). Rule 32(a)(7)(C) has been amended to refer to Form 6 (which has been added to the Appendix of Forms) and to provide that a party or attorney who uses Form 6 has complied with Rule 32(a)(7)(C). No court may provide to the contrary, in its local rules or otherwise.

Form 6 requests not only the information mandated by Rule 32(a)(7)(C), but also information that will assist courts in enforcing the typeface requirements of Rule 32(a)(5) and the type style requirements of Rule 32(a)(6). Parties and attorneys are not required to use Form 6, but they are encouraged to do so.

Subdivision (c)(2)(A). Under Rule 32(c)(2)(A), a cover is not required on a petition for panel rehearing, petition for hearing or rehearing en banc, answer to a petition for panel rehearing, response to a petition for hearing or rehearing en banc, or any other paper. Rule 32(d) makes it clear that no court can require that a cover be used on any of these papers. However, nothing prohibits a court from providing in its local rules that if a cover on one of these papers is "voluntarily" used, it must be a particular color. Several circuits have adopted such local rules. *See, e.g.,* Fed. Cir. R. 35(c) (requiring yellow covers on petitions for hearing or rehearing en banc and brown covers on responses to such petitions); Fed. Cir. R. 40(a) (requiring yellow covers on petitions for panel rehearing and brown covers on answers to such petitions); 7th Cir. R. 28 (requiring blue covers on petitions for rehearing filed by appellants or answers to such petitions, and requiring red covers on petitions for rehearing filed by appellees or answers to such petitions); 9th Cir. R. 40–1 (requiring blue covers on petitions for panel rehearing filed by appellants and red covers on answers to such petitions, and requiring red covers on petitions for panel rehearing filed by appellees and blue covers on answers to such petitions); 11th Cir. R. 35–6 (requiring white covers on petitions for hearing or rehearing en banc).

These conflicting local rules create a hardship for counsel who practice in more than one circuit. For that reason, Rule 32(c)(2)(A) has been amended to provide that if a party chooses to use a cover on a paper that is not required to have one, that cover must be white. The amendment is intended to preempt all local rulemaking on the subject of cover colors and thereby promote uniformity in federal appellate practice.

Changes Made After Publication and Comments No changes were made to the text of the proposed amendment or to the Committee Note.

Subdivisions (d) and (e). Former subdivision (d) has been redesignated as subdivision (e), and a new subdivision (d) has been added. The new subdivision (d) requires that every brief, motion, or other paper filed with the court be signed by the attorney or unrepresented party who files it, much as Fed. R. Civ. P. 11(a) imposes a signature requirement on papers filed in district court. Only the original copy of every paper must be signed. An appendix filed with the court does not have to be signed at all.

By requiring a signature, subdivision (d) ensures that a readily identifiable attorney or party takes responsibility for every paper. The courts of appeals already have authority to sanction attorneys and parties who file papers that contain misleading or frivolous assertions, *see, e.g.,* 28 U.S.C. § 1912, Fed. R. App. P. 38 & 46(b)(1)(B), and thus subdivision (d) has not been amended to incorporate provisions similar to those found in Fed. R. Civ. P. 11(b) and 11(c).

Changes Made After Publication and Comments No changes were made to the text of the proposed amendment. A line was added to the Committee Note to clarify that only the original copy of a paper needs to be signed.

2005 Amendments

Subdivision (a)(7)(C). Rule 32(a)(7)(C) has been amended to add cross-references to new Rule 28.1, which governs briefs filed in cases involving cross-appeals. Rule 28.1(e)(2) prescribes type-volume limitations that apply to such briefs, and Rule 28.1(e)(3) requires parties to certify compliance with those type-volume limitations under Rule 32(a)(7)(C).

Rule 32.1. Citing Judicial Dispositions

(a) Citation Permitted. A court may not prohibit or restrict the citation of federal judicial opinions, orders, judgments, or other written dispositions that have been:

 (i) designated as "unpublished," "not for publication," "non-precedential," "not precedent," or the like; and

 (ii) issued on or after January 1, 2007.

(b) Copies Required. If a party cites a federal judicial opinion, order, judgment, or other written disposition that is not available in a publicly accessible electronic database, the party must file and serve a copy of that opinion, order, judgment, or disposition with the brief or other paper in which it is cited. (Added Apr. 12, 2006, eff. Dec. 1, 2006.)

ADVISORY COMMITTEE NOTES

2006 Adoption

Rule 32.1 is a new rule addressing the citation of judicial opinions, orders, judgments, or other written dispositions that have been designated by a federal court as "unpublished," "not for publication," "non-precedential," "not precedent," or the like. This Committee Note will refer to these dispositions collectively as "unpublished" opinions.

Rule 32.1 is extremely limited. It does not require any court to issue an unpublished opinion or forbid any court from doing so. It does not dictate the circumstances under which a court may choose to designate an opinion as "unpublished" or specify the procedure that a court must follow in making that determination. It says nothing about what effect a court must give to one of its unpublished opinions or to the unpublished opinions of another court. Rule 32.1 addresses only the *citation* of federal judicial dispositions that have been *designated* as "unpublished" or "non-precedential" — whether or not those dispositions have been published in some way or are precedential in some sense.

Subdivision (a). Every court of appeals has allowed unpublished opinions to be cited in some circumstances, such as to support a contention of issue preclusion or claim preclusion. But the circuits have differed dramatically with respect to the restrictions that they have placed on the citation of unpublished opinions for their persuasive value. Some circuits have freely permitted such citation, others have discouraged it but permitted it in limited circumstances, and still others have forbidden it altogether.

Rule 32.1(a) is intended to replace these inconsistent standards with one uniform rule. Under Rule 32.1(a), a court of appeals may not prohibit a party from citing an unpublished opinion of a federal court for its persuasive value or for any other reason. In addition, under Rule 32.1(a), a court may not place any restriction on the citation of such opinions. For example, a court may not instruct parties that the citation of unpublished opinions is discouraged, nor may a court forbid parties to cite unpublished opinions when a published opinion addresses the same issue.

Rule 32.1(a) applies only to unpublished opinions issued on or after January 1, 2007. The citation of unpublished opinions issued before January 1, 2007, will continue to be governed by the local rules of the circuits.

Subdivision (b). Under Rule 32.1(b), a party who cites an opinion of a federal court must provide a copy of that opinion to the court of appeals and to the other parties, unless that opinion is available in a publicly accessible electronic database — such as a commercial database maintained by a legal research service or a database maintained by a court. A party who is required under Rule 32.1(b) to provide a copy of an opinion must file and serve the copy with the brief or other paper in which the opinion is cited. Rule 32.1(b) applies to all unpublished opinions, regardless of when they were issued.

Rule 33. Appeal Conferences

The court may direct the attorneys—and, when appropriate, the parties—to participate in one or more conferences to address any matter that may aid in disposing of the proceedings, including simplifying the issues and discussing settlement. A judge or other person designated by the court may preside over the conference, which may be conducted in person or by telephone. Before a settlement conference, the attorneys must consult with their clients and obtain as much authority as feasible to settle the case. The court may, as a result of the conference, enter an order controlling the course of the proceedings or implementing any settlement agreement. (As amended Apr. 29, 1994, eff. Dec. 1, 1994; Apr. 24, 1998, eff. Dec. 1, 1998.)

ADVISORY COMMITTEE NOTES

1967 Adoption

The uniform rule for review or enforcement of orders of administrative agencies, boards, commissions or officers (see the general note following Rule 15) authorizes a prehearing conference in agency review proceedings. The same considerations which make a prehearing conference desirable in such proceedings may be present in certain cases on appeal

from the district courts. The proposed rule is based upon subdivision 11 of the present uniform rule for review of agency orders.

1994 Amendment

Rule 33 has been entirely rewritten. The new rule makes several changes.

The caption of the rule has been changed from "Prehearing Conference" to "Appeal Conferences" to reflect the fact that occasionally a conference is held after oral argument.

The rule permits the court to require the parties to attend the conference in appropriate cases. The Committee does not contemplate that attendance of the parties will become routine, but in certain instances the parties' presence can be useful. The language of the rule is broad enough to allow a court to determine that an executive or an employee (other than the general counsel) of a corporation or government agency with authority regarding the matter at issue, constitutes "the party."

The rule includes the possibility of settlement among the possible conference topics.

The rule recognizes that conferences are often held by telephone.

The rule allows a judge or other person designated by the court to preside over a conference. A number of local rules permit persons other than judges to preside over conferences. 1st Cir. R. 47.5; 6th Cir. R. 18; 8th Cir. R. 33A; 9th Cir. R. 33–1; and 10th Cir. R. 33.

The rule requires an attorney to consult with his or her client before a settlement conference and obtain as much authority as feasible to settle the case. An attorney can never settle a case without his or her client's consent. Certain entities, especially government entities, have particular difficulty obtaining authority to settle a case. The rule requires counsel to obtain only as much authority "as feasible."

1998 Amendments

The language of the rule is amended to make the rule more easily understood. In addition to changes made to improve the understanding, the Advisory Committee has changed language to make style and terminology consistent throughout the appellate rules. These changes are intended to be stylistic only.

Rule 34. Oral Argument

(a) **In General.**

(1) **Party's Statement.** Any party may file, or a court may require by local rule, a statement explaining why oral argument should, or need not, be permitted.

(2) **Standards.** Oral argument must be allowed in every case unless a panel of three judges who have examined the briefs and record unanimously agrees that oral argument is unnecessary for any of the following reasons:

(A) the appeal is frivolous;

(B) the dispositive issue or issues have been authoritatively decided; or

(C) the facts and legal arguments are adequately presented in the briefs and record, and the decisional process would not be significantly aided by oral argument.

(b) **Notice of Argument; Postponement.** The clerk must advise all parties whether oral argument will be scheduled, and, if so, the date, time, and place for it, and the time allowed for each side. A motion to postpone the argument or to allow longer argument must be filed reasonably in advance of the hearing date.

(c) **Order and Contents of Argument.** The appellant opens and concludes the argument. Counsel must not read at length from briefs, records, or authorities.

(d) **Cross-Appeals and Separate Appeals.** If there is a cross-appeal, Rule 28.1(b) determines which party is the appellant and which is the appellee for purposes of oral argument. Unless the court directs otherwise, a cross-appeal or separate appeal must be argued when the initial appeal is argued. Separate parties should avoid duplicative argument.

(e) **Nonappearance of a Party.** If the appellee fails to appear for argument, the court must hear appellant's argument. If the appellant fails to appear for argument, the court may hear the appellee's argument. If neither party appears, the case will be decided on the briefs, unless the court orders otherwise.

(f) **Submission on Briefs.** The parties may agree to submit a case for decision on the briefs, but the court may direct that the case be argued.

(g) **Use of Physical Exhibits at Argument; Removal.** Counsel intending to use physical exhibits other than documents at the argument must arrange to place them in the courtroom on the day of the argument before the court convenes. After the argument, counsel must remove the exhibits from the courtroom, unless the court directs otherwise. The clerk may destroy or dispose of the exhibits if counsel does not reclaim them within a reasonable time after the clerk gives notice to remove them.

(As amended Apr. 30, 1979, eff. Aug. 1, 1979; Mar. 10, 1986, eff. July 1, 1986; Apr. 30, 1991, eff. Dec. 1, 1991; Apr. 22, 1993, eff. Dec. 1, 1993; Apr. 24, 1998, eff. Dec. 1, 1998; Apr. 25, 2005, eff. Dec. 1, 2005.)

ADVISORY COMMITTEE NOTES

1967 Adoption

A majority of circuits now limit oral argument to thirty minutes for each side, with the provision that additional time may be made available upon request. The Committee is of the view that thirty minutes to each side is sufficient in most cases, but that where additional time is necessary it should be freely granted on a proper showing of cause therefor. It further feels that the matter of time should be left ultimately

to each court of appeals, subject to the spirit of the rule that a reasonable time should be allowed for argument. The term "side" is used to indicate that the time allowed by the rule is afforded to opposing interests rather than to individual parties. Thus if multiple appellants or appellees have a common interest, they constitute only a single side. If counsel for multiple parties who constitute a single side feel that additional time is necessary, they may request it. In other particulars this rule follows the usual practice among the circuits. See 3d Cir. Rule 31 [rule 31, U.S.Ct. of App.3rd Cir.]; 6th Cir. Rule 20 [rule 20, U.S.Ct. of App.6th Cir.]; 10th Cir. Rule 23 [rule 23, U.S.Ct. of App.10th Cir.].

1979 Amendment

The proposed amendment, patterned after the recommendations in the Report of the Commission on Revision of the Federal Court Appellate System, *Structure and Internal Procedures: Recommendations for Change*, 1975, created by Public Law 489 of the 92nd Cong.2nd Sess., 86 Stat. 807, sets forth general principles and minimum standards to be observed in formulating any local rule.

1986 Amendment

The amendments to Rules 34(a) and (e) are technical. No substantive change is intended.

1991 Amendment

Subdivision (d). The amendment of subdivision (d) conforms this rule with the amendment of Rule 28(h).

1993 Amendment

Subdivision (c). The amendment deletes the requirement that the opening argument must include a fair statement of the case. The Committee proposed the change because in some circuits the court does not want appellants to give such statements. In those circuits, the rule is not followed and is misleading. Nevertheless, the Committee does not want the deletion of the requirement to indicate disapproval of the practice. Those circuits that desire a statement of the case may continue the practice.

1998 Amendments

The language of the rule is amended to make the rule more easily understood. In addition to changes made to improve the understanding, the Advisory Committee has changed language to make style and terminology consistent throughout the appellate rules. These changes are intended to be stylistic only. Substantive changes are made in subdivision (a).

Subdivision (a). Currently subdivision (a) says that oral argument must be permitted unless, applying a local rule, a panel of three judges unanimously agrees that oral argument is not necessary. Rule 34 then outlines the criteria to be used to determine whether oral argument is needed and requires any local rule to "conform substantially" to the "minimum standard[s]" established in the national rule. The amendments omit the local rule requirement and make the criteria applicable by force of the national rule. The local rule is an unnecessary instrument.

Paragraph (a)(2) states that one reason for deciding that oral argument is unnecessary is that the dispositive issue has been authoritatively decided. the amended language no longer states that the issue must have been "recently" decided. The Advisory Committee does not intend any substantive change, but thinks that the use of "recently" may be misleading.

Subdivision (d). A cross–reference to Rule 28(h) has been substituted for a reiteration of the provisions of Rule 28(h).

2005 Amendments

Subdivision (d). A cross-reference in subdivision (d) has been changed to reflect the fact that, as part of an effort to collect within one rule all provisions regarding briefing in cases involving cross-appeals, former Rule 28(h) has been abrogated and its contents moved to new Rule 28.1(b).

Rule 35. En Banc Determination

(a) When Hearing or Rehearing En Banc May Be Ordered. A majority of the circuit judges who are in regular active service and who are not disqualified may order that an appeal or other proceeding be heard or reheard by the court of appeals en banc. An en banc hearing or rehearing is not favored and ordinarily will not be ordered unless:

(1) en banc consideration is necessary to secure or maintain uniformity of the court's decisions; or

(2) the proceeding involves a question of exceptional importance.

(b) Petition for Hearing or Rehearing En Banc. A party may petition for a hearing or rehearing en banc.

(1) The petition must begin with a statement that either:

(A) the panel decision conflicts with a decision of the United States Supreme Court or of the court to which the petition is addressed (with citation to the conflicting case or cases) and consideration by the full court is therefore necessary to secure and maintain uniformity of the court's decisions; or

(B) the proceeding involves one or more questions of exceptional importance, each of which must be concisely stated; for example, a petition may assert that a proceeding presents a question of exceptional importance if it involves an issue on which the panel decision conflicts with the authoritative decisions of other United States Courts of Appeals that have addressed the issue.

(2) Except by the court's permission, a petition for an en banc hearing or rehearing must not exceed 15 pages, excluding material not counted under Rule 32.

(3) For purposes of the page limit in Rule 35(b)(2), if a party files both a petition for panel rehearing and a petition for rehearing en banc, they are considered a single document even if they are

filed separately, unless separate filing is required by local rule.

(c) Time for Petition for Hearing or Rehearing En Banc. A petition that an appeal be heard initially en banc must be filed by the date when the appellee's brief is due. A petition for a rehearing en banc must be filed within the time prescribed by Rule 40 for filing a petition for rehearing.

(d) Number of Copies. The number of copies to be filed must be prescribed by local rule and may be altered by order in a particular case.

(e) Response. No response may be filed to a petition for an en banc consideration unless the court orders a response.

(f) Call for a Vote. A vote need not be taken to determine whether the case will be heard or reheard en banc unless a judge calls for a vote.

(As amended Apr. 30, 1979, eff. Aug. 1, 1979; Apr. 29, 1994, eff. Dec. 1, 1994; Apr. 24, 1998, eff. Dec. 1, 1998; Apr. 25, 2005, eff. Dec. 1, 2005.)

ADVISORY COMMITTEE NOTES

1967 Adoption

Statutory authority for in banc hearings is found in 28 U.S.C. § 46(c). The proposed rule is responsive to the Supreme Court's view in *Western Pacific Ry. Corp. v. Western Pacific Ry. Co.*, 345 U.S. 247, 73 S.Ct. 656, 97 L.Ed. 986 (1953), that litigants should be free to suggest that a particular case is appropriate for consideration by all the judges of a court of appeals. The rule is addressed to the procedure whereby a party may suggest the appropriateness of convening the court in banc. It does not affect the power of a court of appeals to initiate in banc hearings *sua sponte*.

The provision that a vote will not be taken as a result of the suggestion of the party unless requested by a judge of the court in regular active service or by a judge who was a member of the panel that rendered a decision sought to be reheard is intended to make it clear that a suggestion of a party as such does not require any action by the court. See *Western Pacific Ry. Corp. v. Western Pacific Ry. Co.*, supra, 345 U.S. at 262, 73 S.Ct. 656. The rule merely authorizes a suggestion, imposes a time limit on suggestions for rehearings in banc, and provides that suggestions will be directed to the judges of the court in regular active service.

In practice, the suggestion of a party that a case be reheard in banc is frequently contained in a petition for rehearing, commonly styled "petition for rehearing in banc." Such a petition is in fact merely a petition for a rehearing, with a suggestion that the case be reheard in banc. Since no response to the suggestion, as distinguished from the petition for rehearing, is required, the panel which heard the case may quite properly dispose of the petition without reference to the suggestion. In such a case the fact that no response has been made to the suggestion does not affect the finality of the judgment or the issuance of the mandate, and the final sentence of the rule expressly so provides.

1979 Amendment

Under the present rule there is no specific provision for a response to a suggestion that an appeal be heard in banc. This has led to some uncertainty as to whether such a response may be filed. The proposed amendment would resolve this uncertainty.

While the present rule provides a time limit for suggestions for rehearing in banc, it does not deal with the timing of a request that the appeal be heard in banc initially. The proposed amendment fills this gap as well, providing that the suggestion must be made by the date of which the appellee's brief is filed.

Provision is made for circulating the suggestions to members of the panel despite the fact that senior judges on the panel would not be entitled to vote on whether a suggestion will be granted.

1994 Amendment

Subdivision (d). Subdivision (d) is added; it authorizes the courts of appeals to prescribe the number of copies of suggestions for hearing or rehearing in banc that must be filed. Because the number of copies needed depends directly upon the number of judges in the circuit, local rules are the best vehicle for setting the required number of copies.

1998 Amendments

The language and organization of the rule are amended to make the rule more easily understood. In addition to changes made to improve the understanding, the Advisory Committee has changed language to make style and terminology consistent throughout the appellate rules. These changes are intended to be stylistic only.

Several substantive changes are made to this rule, however.

One of the purposes of the substantive amendments is to treat a request for a rehearing en banc like a petition for panel rehearing so that a request for a rehearing en banc will suspend the finality of the court of appeals' judgment and delay the running of the period for filing a petition for writ of certiorari. Companion amendments are made to Rule 41.

Subdivision (a). The title of this subdivision is changed from "When hearing or rehearing in banc *will* be ordered" to "When Hearing or Rehearing En Banc *May* Be Ordered." The change emphasizes the discretion a court has with regard to granting an en banc review.

Subdivision (b). The term "petition" for rehearing en banc is substituted for the term "suggestion" for rehearing en banc. The terminology change reflects the Committee's intent to treat similarly a petition for panel rehearing and a request for a rehearing en banc. The terminology change also delays the running of the time for filing a petition for a writ of certiorari because Sur. Ct. R. 13.3 says:

if a petition for rehearing is timely filed in the lower court by any party, the time to file the petition for a writ of certiorari for all parties...runs from the date of the denial of the petition for rehearing or, if the petition for rehearing is granted, the subsequent entry of judgment.

The amendments also require each petition for en banc consideration to begin with a statement concisely demonstrating that the case meets the usual criteria for en banc consideration. It is the Committee's hope that requiring such

a statement will cause the drafter of a petition to focus on the narrow grounds that support en banc consideration and to realize that a petition should not be filed unless the case meets those rigid standards.

Intercircuit conflict is cited as one reason for asserting that a proceeding involves a question of "exceptional importance." Intercircuit conflicts create problems. When the circuits construe the same federal law differently, parties' rights and duties depend upon where a case is litigated. Given the increase in the number of cases decided by the federal courts and the limitation on the number of cases the Supreme Court can hear, conflicts between the circuits may remain unresolved by the Supreme Court for an extended period of time. The existence of an intercircuit conflict often generates additional litigation in the other circuits as well as in the circuits that are already in conflict. Although an en banc proceeding will not necessarily prevent intercircuit conflicts, an en banc proceeding provides a safeguard against unnecessary intercircuit conflicts.

Some circuits have had rules or internal operating procedures that recognize a conflict with another circuit as a legitimate basis for granting a rehearing en banc. An intercircuit conflict may present a question of "exceptional importance" because of the costs that intercircuit conflicts impose on the system as a whole, in addition to the significance of the issues involved. It is not, however, the Committee's intent to make the granting of a hearing or rehearing en banc mandatory whenever there is an intercircuit conflict.

The amendment states that "a petition may assert that a proceeding presents a question of exceptional importance if it involves an issue on which the panel decision conflicts with the authoritative decisions of every other United States Court of Appeals that has addressed the issue." That language contemplates two situations in which a rehearing en banc may be appropriate. The first is when a panel decision creates a conflict. A panel decision creates a conflict when it conflicts with the decisions of all other circuits that have considered the issue. If a panel decision simply joins one side of an already existing conflict, a rehearing en banc may not be as important because it cannot avoid the conflict. The Second situation that may be a strong candidate for a rehearing en banc is one in which the circuit persists in a conflict created by a pre-existing decision of the same circuit and no other circuits have joined on that side of the conflict. The amendment states that the conflict must be with an "authoritative" decision of another circuit. "Authoritative" is used rather than "published" because in some circuits unpublished opinions may be treated as authoritative.

Counsel are reminded that their duty is fully discharged without filing a petition for rehearing en banc unless the case meets the rigid standards of subdivision (a) of this rule and even then the granting of a petition is entirely within the court's discretion.

Paragraph (2) of this subdivision establishes a maximum length for a petition. Fifteen pages is the length currently used in several circuits. Each request for en banc consideration must be studied by every active judge of the court and is a serious call on limited judicial resources. The extraordinary nature of the issue or the threat to uniformity of the court's decision can be established in most cases in less than fifteen pages. A court may shorten the maximum length on a case by case basis but the rule does not permit a circuit to shorten the length by local rule. The Committee has retained

page limits rather than using word or line counts similar to those in amended Rule 32 because there has not been a serious enough problem to justify importing the word and line–count and typeface requirement that are applicable to briefs into other contexts.

Paragraph (3), although similar to (2), is separate because it deals with those instances in which a party files both a petition for rehearing en banc under this rule and a petition for panel rehearing under Rule 40.

To improve the clarity of the rule, the material dealing with filing a response to a petition and with voting on a petition have been moved to new subdivisions (e) and (f).

Subdivision (c). Two changes are made in this subdivision. First, the sentence stating that a request for a rehearing en banc does not affect the finality of the judgment or stay the issuance of the mandate is deleted. Second, the language permitting a party to include a request for rehearing en banc in a petition for panel rehearing is deleted. The Committee believes that those circuits that want to require two separate documents should have the option to do so.

Subdivision (e). This is a new subdivision. The substance of the subdivision, however, was drawn from former subdivision (b). The only changes are stylistic; no substantive changes are intended.

Subdivision (f). This is a new subdivision. The substance of the subdivision, however, was drawn from former subdivision (b).

Because of the discretionary nature of the en banc procedure, the filing of a suggestion for rehearing en banc has not required a vote; a vote is taken only when requested by a judge. It is not the Committee's intent to change the discretionary nature of the procedure or to require a vote on a petition for rehearing en banc. The rule continues, therefore, to provide that a court is not obligated to vote on such petitions. It is necessary, however, that each court develop a procedure for disposing of such petitions because they will suspend the finality of the court's judgment and toll the time for filing a petition for certiorari.

Former subdivision (b) contained language directing the clerk to distribute a "suggestion" to certain judges and indicating which judges may call for a vote. New subdivision (f) does not address those issues because they deal with internal court procedures.

2005 Amendments

Subdivision (a). Two national standards—28 U.S.C. § 46(c) and Rule 35(a)—provide that a hearing or rehearing en banc may be ordered by "a majority of the circuit judges who are in regular active service." Although these standards apply to all of the courts of appeals, the circuits are deeply divided over the interpretation of this language when one or more active judges are disqualified.

The Supreme Court has never addressed this issue. In *Shenker v. Baltimore & Ohio R.R. Co.*, 374 U.S. 1 (1963), the Court rejected a petitioner's claim that his rights under § 46(c) had been violated when the Third Circuit refused to rehear his case en banc. The Third Circuit had 8 active judges at the time; 4 voted in favor of rehearing the case, 2 against, and 2 abstained. No judge was disqualified. The Supreme Court ruled against the petitioner, holding, in essence, that § 46(c) did not provide a cause of action, but

instead simply gave litigants "the right to know the administrative machinery that will be followed and the right to suggest that the *en banc* procedure be set in motion in his case." *Id.* at 5. *Shenker* did stress that a court of appeals has broad discretion in establishing internal procedures to handle requests for rehearings—or, as *Shenker* put it, " 'to devise its own administrative machinery to provide the *means* whereby a majority may order such a hearing.' " *Id.* (quoting *Western Pac. R.R. Corp. v. Western Pac. R.R. Co.*, 345 U.S. 247, 250 (1953) (emphasis added)). But *Shenker* did not address what is meant by "a majority" in § 46(c) (or Rule 35(a), which did not yet exist)—and *Shenker* certainly did not suggest that the phrase should have different meanings in different circuits.

In interpreting that phrase, 7 of the courts of appeals follow the "absolute majority" approach. *See* Marie Leary, Defining the "Majority" Vote Requirement in Federal Rule of Appellate Procedure 35(a) for Rehearings En Banc in the United States Courts of Appeals 8 tbl.1 (Federal Judicial Center 2002). Under this approach, disqualified judges are counted in the base in calculating whether a majority of judges have voted to hear a case en banc. Thus, in a circuit with 12 active judges, 7 must vote to hear a case en banc. If 5 of the 12 active judges are disqualified, all 7 non-disqualified judges must vote to hear the case en banc. The votes of 6 of the 7 non-disqualified judges are not enough, as 6 is not a majority of 12.

Six of the courts of appeals follow the "case majority" approach. *Id.* Under this approach, disqualified judges are not counted in the base in calculating whether a majority of judges have voted to hear a case en banc. Thus, in a case in which 5 of a circuit's 12 active judges are disqualified, only 4 judges (a majority of the 7 non-disqualified judges) must vote to hear a case en banc. (The First and Third Circuits explicitly qualify the case majority approach by providing that a case cannot be heard en banc unless a majority of all active judges—disqualified and non-disqualified—are eligible to participate.)

Rule 35(a) has been amended to adopt the case majority approach as a uniform national interpretation of § 46(c). The federal rules of practice and procedure exist to "maintain consistency," which Congress has equated with "promot[ing] the interest of justice." 28 U.S.C. § 2073(b). The courts of appeals should not follow two inconsistent approaches in deciding whether sufficient votes exist to hear a case en banc, especially when there is a governing statute and governing rule that apply to all circuits and that use identical terms, and especially when there is nothing about the local conditions of each circuit that justifies conflicting approaches.

The case majority approach represents the better interpretation of the phrase "the circuit judges . . . in regular active service" in the first sentence of § 46(c). The second sentence of § 46(c)—which defines which judges are eligible to participate in a case being heard or reheard en banc—uses the similar expression "all circuit judges in regular active service." It is clear that "all circuit judges in regular active service" in the second sentence does not include disqualified judges, as disqualified judges clearly cannot participate in a case being heard or reheard en banc. Therefore, assuming that two nearly identical phrases appearing in adjacent sentences in a statute should be interpreted in the same way, the best reading of "the circuit judges . . . in regular active

service" in the first sentence of § 46(c) is that it, too, does not include disqualified judges.

This interpretation of § 46(c) is bolstered by the fact that the case majority approach has at least two major advantages over the absolute majority approach:

First, under the absolute majority approach, a disqualified judge is, as a practical matter, counted as voting against hearing a case en banc. This defeats the purpose of recusal. To the extent possible, the disqualification of a judge should not result in the equivalent of a vote for or against hearing a case en banc.

Second, the absolute majority approach can leave the en banc court helpless to overturn a panel decision with which almost all of the circuit's active judges disagree. For example, in a case in which 5 of a circuit's 12 active judges are disqualified, the case cannot be heard en banc even if 6 of the 7 non-disqualified judges strongly disagree with the panel opinion. This permits one active judge—perhaps sitting on a panel with a visiting judge—effectively to control circuit precedent, even over the objection of all of his or her colleagues. *See Gulf Power Co. v. FCC*, 226 F.3d 1220, 1222–23 (11th Cir. 2000) (Carnes, J., concerning the denial of reh'g en banc), *rev'd sub nom. National Cable & Telecomm. Ass'n, Inc. v. Gulf Power Co.*, 534 U.S. 327 (2002). Even though the en banc court may, in a future case, be able to correct an erroneous legal interpretation, the en banc court will never be able to correct the injustice inflicted by the panel on the parties to the case. Moreover, it may take many years before sufficient non-disqualified judges can be mustered to overturn the panel's erroneous legal interpretation. In the meantime, the lower courts of the circuit must apply—and the citizens of the circuit must conform their behavior to—an interpretation of the law that almost all of the circuit's active judges believe is incorrect.

The amendment to Rule 35(a) is not meant to alter or affect the quorum requirement of 28 U.S.C. § 46(d). In particular, the amendment is not intended to foreclose the possibility that § 46(d) might be read to require that more than half of all circuit judges in regular active service be eligible to participate in order for the court to hear or rehear a case en banc.

Rule 36. Entry of Judgment; Notice

(a) Entry. A judgment is entered when it is noted on the docket. The clerk must prepare, sign, and enter the judgment:

 (1) after receiving the court's opinion—but if settlement of the judgment's form is required, after final settlement; or

 (2) if a judgment is rendered without an opinion, as the court instructs.

(b) Notice. On the date when judgment is entered, the clerk must serve on all parties a copy of the opinion—or the judgment, if no opinion was written—and a notice of the date when the judgment was entered.

(As amended Apr. 24, 1998, eff. Dec. 1, 1998; Apr. 29, 2002, eff. Dec. 1, 2002.)

ADVISORY COMMITTEE NOTES
1967 Adoption

This is the typical rule. See 1st Cir. Rule 29 [rule 29, U.S.Ct. of App. 1st Cir.]; 3d Cir. Rule 32 [rule 32, U.S.Ct. of App. 3rd Cir.]; 6th Cir. Rule 21 [rule 21, U.S.Ct. of App. 6th Cir.]. At present, uncertainty exists as to the date of entry of judgment when the opinion directs subsequent settlement of the precise terms of the judgment, a common practice in cases involving enforcement of agency orders. See Stern and Gressman, Supreme Court Practice, p. 203 (3d Ed., 1962). The principle of finality suggests that in such cases entry of judgment should be delayed until approval of the judgment in final form.

1998 Amendments

The language and organization of the rule are amended to make the rule more easily understood. In addition to changes made to improve the understanding, the Advisory Committee has changed language to make style and terminology consistent throughout the appellate rules. These changes are intended to be stylistic only.

2002 Amendments

Subdivision (b). Subdivision (b) has been amended so that the clerk may use electronic means to serve a copy of the opinion or judgment or to serve notice of the date when judgment was entered upon parties who have consented to such service.

Changes Made After Publication and Comments No changes were made to the text of the proposed amendment or to the Committee Note.

Rule 37. Interest on Judgment

(a) When the Court Affirms. Unless the law provides otherwise, if a money judgment in a civil case is affirmed, whatever interest is allowed by law is payable from the date when the district court's judgment was entered.

(b) When the Court Reverses. If the court modifies or reverses a judgment with a direction that a money judgment be entered in the district court, the mandate must contain instructions about the allowance of interest.

(As amended Apr. 24, 1998, eff. Dec. 1, 1998.)

ADVISORY COMMITTEE NOTES
1967 Adoption

The first sentence makes it clear that if a money judgment is affirmed in the court of appeals, the interest which attaches to money judgments by force of law (see 28 U.S.C. § 1961 and § 2411) upon their initial entry is payable as if no appeal had been taken, whether or not the mandate makes mention of interest. There has been some confusion on this point. *See Blair v. Durham,* 139 F.2d 260 (6th Cir., 1943) and cases cited therein.

In reversing or modifying the judgment of the district court, the court of appeals may direct the entry of a money judgment, as, for example, when the court of appeals reverses a judgment notwithstanding the verdict and directs entry of judgment on the verdict. In such a case the question may arise as to whether interest is to run from the date of entry of the judgment directed by the court of appeals or from the date on which the judgment would have been entered in the district court except for the erroneous ruling corrected on appeal. In *Briggs v. Pennsylvania R. Co.,* 334 U.S. 304, 68 S.Ct. 1039, 92 L.Ed. 1403 (1948), the Court held that where the mandate of the court of appeals directed entry of judgment upon a verdict but made no mention of interest from the date of the verdict to the date of the entry of the judgment directed by the mandate, the district court was powerless to add such interest. The second sentence of the proposed rule is a reminder to the court, the clerk and counsel of the *Briggs* rule. Since the rule directs that the matter of interest be disposed of by the mandate, in cases where interest is simply overlooked, a party who conceives himself entitled to interest from a date other than the date of entry of judgment in accordance with the mandate should be entitled to seek recall of the mandate for determination of the question.

1998 Amendments

The language and organization of the rule are amended to make the rule more easily understood. In addition to changes made to improve the understanding, the Advisory Committee has changed language to make style and terminology consistent throughout the appellate rules. These changes are intended to be stylistic only.

Rule 38. Frivolous Appeal—Damages and Costs

If a court of appeals determines that an appeal is frivolous, it may, after a separately filed motion or notice from the court and reasonable opportunity to respond, award just damages and single or double costs to the appellee.

(As amended Apr. 29, 1994, eff. Dec. 1, 1994; Apr. 24, 1998, eff. Dec. 1, 1998.)

ADVISORY COMMITTEE NOTES
1967 Adoption

Compare 28 U.S.C. § 1912. While both the statute and the usual rule on the subject by courts of appeals (Fourth Circuit Rule 20 [rule 20, U.S.Ct. of App. 4th Cir.] is a typical rule) speak of "damages for delay," the courts of appeals quite properly allow damages, attorney's fees and other expenses incurred by an appellee if the appeal is frivolous without requiring a showing that the appeal resulted in delay. See *Dunscombe v. Sayle,* 340 F.2d 311 (5th Cir., 1965), cert. den., 382 U.S. 814, 86 S.Ct. 32, 15 L.Ed.2d 62 (1965); *Lowe v. Willacy,* 239 F.2d 179 (9th Cir., 1956); *Griffin Wellpoint Corp. v. Munro-Langstroth, Inc.,* 269 F.2d 64 (1st Cir., 1959); *Ginsburg v. Stern,* 295 F.2d 698 (3d Cir., 1961). The subjects of interest and damages are separately regulated, contrary to the present practice of combining the two (see Fourth Circuit Rule 20) to make it clear that the awards are distinct and independent. Interest is provided for by law; damages are awarded by the court in its discretion in the case of a frivolous appeal as a matter of justice to the appellee and as a penalty against the appellant.

1994 Amendments

The amendment requires that before a court of appeals may impose sanctions, the person to be sanctioned must have notice and an opportunity to respond. The amendment reflects the basic principle enunciated in the Supreme Court's opinion in *Roadway Express, Inc. v. Piper*, 447 U.S. 752, 767 (1980), that notice and opportunity to respond must precede the imposition of sanctions. A separately filed motion requesting sanctions constitutes notice. A statement inserted in a party's brief that the party moves for sanctions is not sufficient notice. Requests in briefs for sanctions have become so commonplace that it is unrealistic to expect careful responses to such requests without any indication that the court is actually contemplating such measures. Only a motion, the purpose of which is to request sanctions, is sufficient. If there is no such motion filed, notice must come from the court. The form of notice from the court and of the opportunity for comment purposely are left to the court's discretion.

1998 Amendments

Only the caption of this rule has been amended. The changes are intended to be stylistic only.

Rule 39. Costs

(a) Against Whom Assessed. The following rules apply unless the law provides or the court orders otherwise:

(1) if an appeal is dismissed, costs are taxed against the appellant, unless the parties agree otherwise;

(2) if a judgment is affirmed, costs are taxed against the appellant;

(3) if a judgment is reversed, costs are taxed against the appellee;

(4) if a judgment is affirmed in part, reversed in part, modified, or vacated, costs are taxed only as the court orders.

(b) Costs For and Against the United States. Costs for or against the United States, its agency, or officer will be assessed under Rule 39(a) only if authorized by law.

(c) Costs of Copies. Each court of appeals must, by local rule, fix the maximum rate for taxing the cost of producing necessary copies of a brief or appendix, or copies of records authorized by Rule 30(f). The rate must not exceed that generally charged for such work in the area where the clerk's office is located and should encourage economical methods of copying.

(d) Bill of Costs: Objections; Insertion in Mandate.

(1) A party who wants costs taxed must—within 14 days after entry of judgment—file with the circuit clerk, with proof of service, an itemized and verified bill of costs.

(2) Objections must be filed within 10 days after service of the bill of costs, unless the court extends the time.

(3) The clerk must prepare and certify an itemized statement of costs for insertion in the mandate, but issuance of the mandate must not be delayed for taxing costs. If the mandate issues before costs are finally determined, the district clerk must—upon the circuit clerk's request—add the statement of costs, or any amendment of it, to the mandate.

(e) Costs on Appeal Taxable in the District Court. The following costs on appeal are taxable in the district court for the benefit of the party entitled to costs under this rule:

(1) the preparation and transmission of the record;

(2) the reporter's transcript, if needed to determine the appeal;

(3) premiums paid for a supersedeas bond or other bond to preserve rights pending appeal; and

(4) the fee for filing the notice of appeal.

(As amended Apr. 30, 1979, eff. Aug. 1, 1979; Mar. 10, 1986, eff. July 1, 1986; Apr. 24, 1998, eff. Dec. 1, 1998.)

ADVISORY COMMITTEE NOTES

1967 Adoption

Subdivision (a). Statutory authorization for taxation of costs is found in 28 U.S.C. § 1920. The provisions of this subdivision follow the usual practice in the circuits. A few statutes contain specific provisions in derogation of these general provisions. (See 28 U.S.C. § 1928, which forbids the award of costs to a successful plaintiff in a patent infringement action under the circumstances described by the statute). These statutes are controlling in cases to which they apply.

Subdivision (b). The rules of the courts of appeals at present commonly deny costs to the United States except as allowance may be directed by statute. Those rules were promulgated at a time when the United States was generally invulnerable to an award of costs against it, and they appear to be based on the view that if the United States is not subject to costs if it loses, it ought not be entitled to recover costs if it wins.

The number of cases affected by such rules has been greatly reduced by the Act of July 18, 1966, 80 Stat. 308 (1 U.S.Code Cong. & Ad.News, p. 349 (1966), 89th Cong., 2d Sess., which amended 28 U.S.C. § 2412, the former general bar to the award of costs against the United States. Section 2412 as amended generally places the United States on the same footing as private parties with respect to the award of costs in civil cases. But the United States continues to enjoy immunity from costs in certain cases. By its terms amended § 2412 authorizes an award of costs against the United States only in civil actions, and it excepts from its general authorization of an award of costs against the United States cases which are "otherwise specifically provided (for) by statute." Furthermore, the Act of July 18, 1966, *supra*, provides that the amendments of § 2412 which it effects shall

apply only to actions filed subsequent to the date of its enactment. The second clause continues in effect, for these and all other cases in which the United States enjoys immunity from costs, the presently prevailing rule that the United States may recover costs as the prevailing party only if it would have suffered them as the losing party.

Subdivision (c). While only five circuits (D.C.Cir. Rule 20(d) [rule 20(d), U.S.Ct. of App. Dist. of Col.]; 1st Cir. Rule 31(4) [rule 31(4), U.S.Ct. of App. 1st Cir.]; 3d Cir. Rule 35(4) [rule 35(4), U.S.Ct. of App. 3rd Cir.]; 4th Cir. Rule 21(4) [rule 21(4) U.S.Ct. of App. 4th Cir.]; 9th Cir. Rule 25 [rule 25, U.S.Ct. of App.9th Cir.], as amended June 2, 1967) presently tax the cost of printing briefs, the proposed rule makes the cost taxable in keeping with the principle of this rule that all cost items expended in the prosecution of a proceeding should be borne by the unsuccessful party.

Subdivision (e). The costs described in this subdivision are costs of the appeal and, as such, are within the undertaking of the appeal bond. They are made taxable in the district court for general convenience. Taxation of the cost of the reporter's transcript is specifically authorized by 28 U.S.C. § 1920, but in the absence of a rule some district courts have held themselves without authority to tax the cost (*Perlman v. Feldmann*, 116 F.Supp. 102 (D. Conn., 1953); *Firtag v. Gendleman*, 152 F.Supp. 226 (D.D.C., 1957); *Todd Atlantic Shipyards Corp. v. The Southport*, 100 F.Supp. 763 (E.D.S.C., 1951). Provision for taxation of the cost of premiums paid for supersedeas bonds is common in the local rules of district courts and the practice is established in the Second, Seventh, and Ninth Circuits. *Berner v. British Commonwealth Pacific Air Lines, Ltd.*, 362 F.2d 799 (2d Cir. 1966); *Land Oberoesterreich v. Gude*, 93 F.2d 292 (2d Cir., 1937); *In re Northern Ind. Oil Co.*, 192 F.2d 139 (7th Cir., 1951); *Lunn v. F. W. Woolworth*, 210 F.2d 159 (9th Cir., 1954).

1979 Amendment

Subdivision (c). The proposed amendment would permit variations among the circuits in regulating the maximum rates taxable as costs for printing or otherwise reproducing briefs, appendices, and copies of records authorized by Rule 30(f). The present rule has had a different effect in different circuits depending upon the size of the circuit, the location of the clerk's office, and the location of other cities. As a consequence there was a growing sense that strict adherence to the rule produces some unfairness in some of the circuits and the matter should be made subject to local rule.

Subdivision (d). The present rule makes no provision for objections to a bill of costs. The proposed amendment would allow 10 days for such objections. Cf. Rule 54(d) of the F.R.C.P. [rule 54(d), Federal Rules of Civil Procedure]. It provides further that the mandate shall not be delayed for taxation of costs.

1986 Amendment

The amendment to subdivision (c) is intended to increase the degree of control exercised by the courts of appeals over rates for printing and copying recoverable as costs. It further requires the courts of appeals to encourage cost-consciousness by requiring that, in fixing the rate, the court consider the most economical methods of printing and copying.

The amendment to subdivision (d) is technical. No substantive change is intended.

1998 Amendments

The language and organization of the rule are amended to make the rule more easily understood. In addition to changes made to improve the understanding, the Advisory Committee has changed language to make style and terminology consistent throughout the appellate rules. These changes are intended to be stylistic only. All references to the cost of "printing" have been deleted from subdivision (c) because commercial printing is so rarely used for preparation of documents filed with a court of appeals.

Rule 40. Petition for Panel Rehearing

(a) Time to File; Contents; Answer; Action by the Court if Granted.

(1) Time. Unless the time is shortened or extended by order or local rule, a petition for panel rehearing may be filed within 14 days after entry of judgment. But in a civil case, if the United States or its officer or agency is a party, the time within which any party may seek rehearing is 45 days after entry of judgment, unless an order shortens or extends the time.

(2) Contents. The petition must state with particularity each point of law or fact that the petitioner believes the court has overlooked or misapprehended and must argue in support of the petition. Oral argument is not permitted.

(3) Answer. Unless the court requests, no answer to a petition for panel rehearing is permitted. But ordinarily rehearing will not be granted in the absence of such a request.

(4) Action by the Court. If a petition for panel rehearing is granted, the court may do any of the following:

 (A) make a final disposition of the case without reargument;

 (B) restore the case to the calendar for reargument or resubmission; or

 (C) issue any other appropriate order.

(b) Form of Petition; Length. The petition must comply in form with Rule 32. Copies must be served and filed as Rule 31 prescribes. Unless the court permits or a local rule provides otherwise, a petition for panel rehearing must not exceed 15 pages.
(As amended Apr. 30, 1979, eff. Aug. 1, 1979; Apr. 29, 1994, eff. Dec. 1, 1994; Apr. 24, 1998, eff. Dec. 1, 1998.)

ADVISORY COMMITTEE NOTES

1967 Adoption

This is the usual rule among the circuits, except that the express prohibition against filing a reply to the petition is found only in the rules of the Fourth, Sixth and Eighth Circuits (it is also contained in Supreme Court Rule 58(3)

[rule 58(3), U.S.Sup.Ct.Rules). It is included to save time and expense to the party victorious on appeal. In the very rare instances in which a reply is useful, the court will ask for it.

1979 Amendment

Subdivision (a). The Standing Committee added to the first sentence of Rule 40(a) the words "or by local rule," to conform to current practice in the circuits. The Standing Committee believes the change noncontroversial.

Subdivision (b). The proposed amendment would eliminate the distinction drawn in the present rule between printed briefs and those duplicated from typewritten pages in fixing their maximum length. See Note to Rule 28. Since petitions for rehearing must be prepared in a short time, making typographic printing less likely, the maximum number of pages is fixed at 15, the figure used in the present rule for petitions duplicated by means other than typographic printing.

1994 Amendment

Subdivision (a). The amendment lengthens the time for filing a petition for rehearing from 14 to 45 days in civil cases involving the United States or its agencies or officers. It has no effect upon the time for filing in criminal cases. The amendment makes nation-wide the current practice in the District of Columbia and the Tenth Circuits, *see* D.C. Cir. R. 15 (a), 10th Cir. R. 40.3. This amendment, analogous to the provision in Rule 4(a) extending the time for filing a notice of appeal in cases involving the United States, recognizes that the Solicitor General needs time to conduct a thorough review of the merits of a case before requesting a rehearing. In a case in which a court of appeals believes it necessary to restrict the time for filing a rehearing petition, the amendment provides that the court may do so by order. Although the first sentence of Rule 40 permits a court of appeals to shorten or lengthen the usual 14 day filing period by order or by local rule, the sentence governing appeals in civil cases involving the United States purposely limits a court's power to alter the 45 day period to orders in specific cases. If a court of appeals could adopt a local rule shortening the time for filing a petition for rehearing in all cases involving the United States, the purpose of the amendment would be defeated.

1998 Amendments

The language and organization of the rule are amended to make the rule more easily understood. In addition to changes made to improve the understanding, the Advisory Committee has changed language to make style and terminology consistent throughout the appellate rules. These changes are intended to be stylistic only.

Rule 41. Mandate: Contents; Issuance and Effective Date; Stay

(a) Contents. Unless the court directs that a formal mandate issue, the mandate consists of a certified copy of the judgment, a copy of the court's opinion, if any, and any direction about costs.

(b) When Issued. The court's mandate must issue 7 calendar days after the time to file a petition for rehearing expires, or 7 calendar days after entry of an order denying a timely petition for panel rehearing, petition for rehearing en banc, or motion for stay of mandate, whichever is later. The court may shorten or extend the time.

(c) Effective Date. The mandate is effective when issued.

(d) Staying the Mandate.

(1) On Petition for Rehearing or Motion. The timely filing of a petition for panel rehearing, petition for rehearing en banc, or motion for stay of mandate, stays the mandate until disposition of the petition or motion, unless the court orders otherwise.

(2) Pending Petition for Certiorari.

(A) A party may move to stay the mandate pending the filing of a petition for a writ of certiorari in the Supreme Court. The motion must be served on all parties and must show that the certiorari petition would present a substantial question and that there is good cause for a stay.

(B) The stay must not exceed 90 days, unless the period is extended for good cause or unless the party who obtained the stay files a petition for the writ and so notifies the circuit clerk in writing within the period of the stay. In that case, the stay continues until the Supreme Court's final disposition.

(C) The court may require a bond or other security as a condition to granting or continuing a stay of the mandate.

(D) The court of appeals must issue the mandate immediately when a copy of a Supreme Court order denying the petition for writ of certiorari is filed.

(As amended Apr. 29, 1994, eff. Dec. 1, 1994; Apr. 24, 1998, eff. Dec. 1, 1998; Apr. 29, 2002, eff. Dec. 1, 2002.)

ADVISORY COMMITTEE NOTES
1967 Adoption

The proposed rule follows the rule or practice in a majority of circuits by which copies of the opinion and the judgment serve in lieu of a formal mandate in the ordinary case. Compare Supreme Court Rule 59. Although 28 U.S.C. § 2101(c) permits a writ of certiorari to be filed within 90 days after entry of judgment, seven of the eight circuits which now regulate the matter of stays pending application for certiorari limit the initial stay of the mandate to the 30-day period provided in the proposed rule. Compare D.C.Cir. Rule 27(e) [rule 27(e), U.S.Ct. of App. Dist. of Col.].

1994 Amendment

Subdivision (a). The amendment conforms Rule 41(a) to the amendment made to Rule 40(a). The amendment keys the time for issuance of the mandate to the expiration of the

time for filing a petition for rehearing, unless such a petition is filed in which case the mandate issues 7 days after the entry of the order denying the petition. Because the amendment to Rule 40(a) lengthens the time for filing a petition for rehearing in civil cases involving the United States from 14 to 45 days, the rule requiring the mandate to issue 21 days after the entry of judgment would cause the mandate to issue while the government is still considering requesting a rehearing. Therefore, the amendment generally requires the mandate to issue 7 days after the expiration of the time for filing a petition for rehearing.

Subdivision (b). The amendment requires a party who files a motion requesting a stay of mandate to file, at the same time, proof of service on all other parties. The old rule required the party to give notice to the other parties; the amendment merely requires the party to provide the court with evidence of having done so.

The amendment also states that the motion must show that a petition for certiorari would present a substantial question and that there is good cause for a stay. The amendment is intended to alert the parties to the fact that a stay of mandate is not granted automatically and to the type of showing that needs to be made. The Supreme Court has established conditions that must be met before it will stay a mandate. *See* Robert L. Stern et al., Supreme Court Practice § 17.19 (6th ed. 1986).

1998 Amendments

The language and organization of the rule are amended to make the rule more easily understood. In addition to changes made to improve the understanding, the Advisory Committee has changed language to make style and terminology consistent throughout the appellate rules. These changes are intended to be stylistic only.

Several substantive changes are made in this rule, however.

Subdivision (b). The existing rule provides that the mandate issues 7 days after the time to file a petition for panel rehearing expires unless such a petition for rehearing en banc or motion for stay of mandate is filed, the mandate does not issue until 7 days after entry of an order denying the last of all such requests. If a petition for rehearing or a petition for rehearing en banc is granted, the court enters a new judgment after the rehearing and the mandate issues within the normal time after entry of that judgment.

Subdivision (c). Subdivision (c) is new. It provides that the mandate is effective when the court issues it. A court of appeals' judgment or order is not final until issuance of the mandate; at that time the parties' obligations become fixed. This amendment is intended to make it clear that the mandate is effective upon issuance and that its effectiveness is not delayed until receipt of the mandate by the trial court or agency, or until the trial court or agency acts upon it. This amendment is consistent with the current understanding. Unless the court orders that the mandate issue earlier than provided in the rule, the parties can easily calculate the anticipated date of issuance and verify issuance of the mandate, the entry of the order on the docket alerts the parties to that fact.

Subdivision (d). Amended paragraph (1) provides that the filing of a petition for panel rehearing, a petition for rehearing en banc or a motion for a stay of mandate pending petition to the Supreme Court for a writ of certiorari stays the issuance of the mandate until the court disposes of the petition or motion. The provision that a petition for rehearing en banc stays the mandate is a companion to the amendment of Rule 35 that deletes the language stating that a request for a rehearing en banc does not affect the finality of the judgment or stay the issuance of the mandate. The Committee's objective is to treat a request for a rehearing en banc like a petition for panel rehearing so that a request for a rehearing en banc will suspend the finality of the court of appeals' judgment and delay the running of the period for filing a petition for writ of certiorari. Because the filing of a petition for rehearing en banc will stay the mandate, a court of appeals will need to take final action on the petition but the procedure for doing so is left to local practice.

Paragraph (1) also provides that the filing of a motion for a stay of mandate pending petition to the Supreme Court for a writ of certiorari stays the mandate until the court disposes of the motion. If the court denies the motion, the court must issue the mandate 7 days after entering the order denying the motion. If the court grants the motion, the mandate is stayed according to the terms of the order granting the stay. Delaying issuance of the mandate eliminates the need to recall the mandate if the motion for a stay is granted. If, however, the court believes that it would be inappropriate to delay issuance of the mandate until disposition of the motion for a stay, the court may order that the mandate issue immediately.

Paragraph (2). The amendment changes the maximum period for a stay of mandate, absent the court of appeals granting an extension for cause, to 90 days. The presumptive 30–day period was adopted when a party had to file a petition for a writ of certiorari in criminal cases within 30 days after entry of judgment. Supreme Court Rule 13.1 now provides that a party has 90 days after entry of judgment by a court of appeals to file a petition for a writ of certiorari whether the case is civil or criminal.

The amendment does not require a court of appeals to grant a stay of mandate that is coextensive with the period granted for filing a petition for a writ of certiorari. The granting of a stay and the length of the stay remain within the discretion of the court of appeals. The amendment means only that a 90–day stay may be granted without a need to show cause for a stay longer than 30 days.

Subparagraph (C) is not new; it has been moved from the end of the rule to this position.

2002 Amendments

Subdivision (b). Subdivision (b) directs that the mandate of a court must issue 7 days after the time to file a petition for rehearing expires or 7 days after the court denies a timely petition for panel rehearing, petition for rehearing en banc, or motion for stay of mandate, whichever is later. Intermediate Saturdays, Sundays, and legal holidays are counted in computing that 7–day deadline, which means that, except when the 7–day deadline ends on a weekend or legal holiday, the mandate issues exactly one week after the triggering event.

Fed. R. App. P. 26(a)(2) has been amended to provide that, in computing any period of time, one should "[e]xclude intermediate Saturdays, Sundays, and legal holidays when the period is less than 11 days, unless stated in calendar

days." This change in the method of computing deadlines means that 7–day deadlines (such as that in subdivision (b)) have been lengthened as a practical matter. Under the new computation method, a mandate would never issue sooner than 9 actual days after a triggering event, and legal holidays could extend that period to as much as 13 days.

Delaying mandates for 9 or more days would introduce significant and unwarranted delay into appellate proceedings. For that reason, subdivision (b) has been amended to require that mandates issue 7 *calendar* days after a triggering event.

Changes Made After Publication and Comments No changes were made to the text of the proposed amendment or to the Committee Note.

Rule 42. Voluntary Dismissal

(a) Dismissal in the District Court. Before an appeal has been docketed by the circuit clerk, the district court may dismiss the appeal on the filing of a stipulation signed by all parties or on the appellant's motion with notice to all parties.

(b) Dismissal in the Court of Appeals. The circuit clerk may dismiss a docketed appeal if the parties file a signed dismissal agreement specifying how costs are to be paid and pay any fees that are due. But no mandate or other process may issue without a court order. An appeal may be dismissed on the appellant's motion on terms agreed to by the parties or fixed by the court.

(As amended Apr. 24, 1998, eff. Dec. 1, 1998.)

ADVISORY COMMITTEE NOTES
1967 Adoption

Subdivision (a). This subdivision is derived from FRCP 73(a) [rule 73(a), Federal Rules of Civil Procedure] without change of substance.

Subdivision (b). The first sentence is a common provision in present circuit rules. The second sentence is added. Compare Supreme Court Rule 60.

1998 Amendments

The language of the rule is amended to make the rule more easily understood. In addition to changes made to improve the understanding, the Advisory Committee has changed language to make style and terminology consistent throughout the appellate rules. These changes are intended to be stylistic only.

Rule 43. Substitution of Parties

(a) Death of a Party.

(1) After Notice of Appeal Is Filed. If a party dies after a notice of appeal has been filed or while a proceeding is pending in the court of appeals, the decedent's personal representative may be substituted as a party on motion filed with the circuit clerk by the representative or by any party. A party's motion must be served on the representative in accordance with Rule 25. If the decedent has no

representative, any party may suggest the death on the record, and the court of appeals may then direct appropriate proceedings.

(2) Before Notice of Appeal Is Filed—Potential Appellant. If a party entitled to appeal dies before filing a notice of appeal, the decedent's personal representative—or, if there is no personal representative, the decedent's attorney of record— may file a notice of appeal within the time prescribed by these rules. After the notice of appeal is filed, substitution must be in accordance with Rule 43(a)(1).

(3) Before Notice of Appeal Is Filed—Potential Appellee. If a party against whom an appeal may be taken dies after entry of a judgment or order in the district court, but before a notice of appeal is filed, an appellant may proceed as if the death had not occurred. After the notice of appeal is filed, substitution must be in accordance with Rule 43(a)(1).

(b) Substitution for a Reason Other Than Death. If a party needs to be substituted for any reason other than death, the procedure prescribed in Rule 43(a) applies.

(c) Public Officer: Identification; Substitution.

(1) Identification of Party. A public officer who is a party to an appeal or other proceeding in an official capacity may be described as a party by the public officer's official title rather than by name. But the court may require the public officer's name to be added.

(2) Automatic Substitution of Officeholder. When a public officer who is a party to an appeal or other proceeding in an official capacity dies, resigns, or otherwise ceases to hold office, the action does not abate. The public officer's successor is automatically substituted as a party. Proceedings following the substitution are to be in the name of the substituted party, but any misnomer that does not affect the substantial rights of the parties may be disregarded. An order of substitution may be entered at any time, but failure to enter an order does not affect the substitution.

(As amended Mar. 10, 1986, eff. July 1, 1986; Apr. 24, 1998, eff. Dec. 1, 1998.)

ADVISORY COMMITTEE NOTES
1967 Adoption

Subdivision (a). The first three sentences describe a procedure similar to the rule on substitution in civil actions in the district court. See FRCP 25(a) [rule 25(a), Federal Rules of Civil Procedure]. The fourth sentence expressly authorizes an appeal to be taken against one who has died after the entry of judgment. Compare FRCP 73(b) [rule 73(b), Federal Rules of Civil Procedure], which impliedly authorizes such an appeal.

The sixth sentence authorizes an attorney of record for the deceased to take an appeal on behalf of successors in interest if the deceased has no representative. At present, if a party entitled to appeal dies before the notice of appeal is filed, the appeal can presumably be taken only by his legal representative and must be taken within the time ordinarily prescribed. 13 Cyclopedia of Federal Procedure (3d Ed.) § 63.21. The states commonly make special provision for the even of the death of a party entitled to appeal, usually by extending the time otherwise prescribed. Rules of Civil Procedure for Superior Courts of Arizona, Rule 73(t), 16 A.R.S.; New Jersey Rev.Rules 1:3–3; New York Civil Practice Law and Rules, § 1022; Wisconsin Statutes Ann. 274.01(2). The Provision in the proposed rule is derived from California Code of Civil Procedure, § 941.

Subdivision (c). This subdivision is derived from FRCP 25(d) [rule 25(d), Federal Rules of Civil Procedure] and Supreme Court Rule 48, with appropriate changes.

1986 Amendment

The amendments to Rules 43(a) and (c) are technical. No substantive change is intended.

1998 Amendments

The language and organization of the rule are amended to make the rule more easily understood. In addition to changes made to improve the understanding, the Advisory Committee has changed language to make style and terminology consistent throughout the appellate rules. These changes are intended to be stylistic only.

Rule 44. Case Involving a Constitutional Question When the United States or the Relevant State is Not a Party

(a) Constitutional Challenge to Federal Statute. If a party questions the constitutionality of an Act of Congress in a proceeding in which the United States or its agency, officer, or employee is not a party in an official capacity, the questioning party must give written notice to the circuit clerk immediately upon the filing of the record or as soon as the question is raised in the court of appeals. The clerk must then certify that fact to the Attorney General.

(b) Constitutional Challenge to State Statute. If a party questions the constitutionality of a statute of a State in a proceeding in which that State or its agency, officer, or employee is not a party in an official capacity, the questioning party must give written notice to the circuit clerk immediately upon the filing of the record or as soon as the question is raised in the court of appeals. The clerk must then certify that fact to the attorney general of the State.

(As amended Apr. 24, 1998, eff. Dec. 1, 1998; Apr. 29, 2002, eff. Dec. 1, 2002.)

ADVISORY COMMITTEE NOTES
1967 Adoption

This rule is now found in the rules of a majority of the circuits. It is in response to the Act of August 24, 1937 (28

U.S.C. § 2403), which requires all courts of the United States to advise the Attorney General of the existence of an action or proceeding of the kind described in the rule.

1998 Amendments

The language of the rule is amended to make the rule more easily understood. In addition to changes made to improve the understanding, the Advisory Committee has changed language to make style and terminology consistent throughout the appellate rules. These changes are intended to be stylistic only.

2002 Amendments

Rule 44 requires that a party who "questions the constitutionality of an Act of Congress" in a proceeding in which the United States is not a party must provide written notice of that challenge to the clerk. Rule 44 is designed to implement 28 U.S.C. § 2403(a), which states that:

> In any action, suit or proceeding in a court of the United States to which the United States or any agency, officer or employee thereof is not a party, wherein the constitutionality of any Act of Congress affecting the public interest is drawn in question, the court shall certify such fact to the Attorney General, and shall permit the United States to intervene . . . for argument on the question of constitutionality.

The subsequent section of the statute—§ 2403(*b*)—contains virtually identical language imposing upon the courts the duty to notify the attorney general of a *state* of a constitutional challenge to any statute of that state. But § 2403(b), unlike § 2403(a), was not implemented in Rule 44.

Rule 44 has been amended to correct this omission. The text of former Rule 44 regarding constitutional challenges to federal statutes now appears as Rule 44(a), while new language regarding constitutional challenges to state statutes now appears as Rule 44(b).

Changes Made After Publication and Comments No changes were made to the text of the proposed amendment or to the Committee Note.

Rule 45. Clerk's Duties

(a) General Provisions.

(1) Qualifications. The circuit clerk must take the oath and post any bond required by law. Neither the clerk nor any deputy clerk may practice as an attorney or counselor in any court while in office.

(2) When Court Is Open. The court of appeals is always open for filing any paper, issuing and returning process, making a motion, and entering an order. The clerk's office with the clerk or a deputy in attendance must be open during business hours on all days except Saturdays, Sundays, and legal holidays. A court may provide by local rule or by order that the clerk's office be open for specified hours on Saturdays or on legal holidays other than New Year's Day, Martin Luther King, Jr.'s Birthday, Washington's Birthday, Memorial Day, Inde-

pendence Day, Labor Day, Columbus Day, Veterans' Day, Thanksgiving Day, and Christmas Day.

(b) Records.

(1) The Docket. The circuit clerk must maintain a docket and an index of all docketed cases in the manner prescribed by the Director of the Administrative Office of the United States Courts. The clerk must record all papers filed with the clerk and all process, orders, and judgments.

(2) Calendar. Under the court's direction, the clerk must prepare a calendar of cases awaiting argument. In placing cases on the calendar for argument, the clerk must give preference to appeals in criminal cases and to other proceedings and appeals entitled to preference by law.

(3) Other Records. The clerk must keep other books and records required by the Director of the Administrative Office of the United States Courts, with the approval of the Judicial Conference of the United States, or by the court.

(c) Notice of an Order or Judgment. Upon the entry of an order or judgment, the circuit clerk must immediately serve a notice of entry on each party, with a copy of any opinion, and must note the date of service on the docket. Service on a party represented by counsel must be made on counsel.

(d) Custody of Records and Papers. The circuit clerk has custody of the court's records and papers. Unless the court orders or instructs otherwise, the clerk must not permit an original record or paper to be taken from the clerk's office. Upon disposition of the case, original papers constituting the record on appeal or review must be returned to the court or agency from which they were received. The clerk must preserve a copy of any brief, appendix, or other paper that has been filed.

(As amended Mar. 1, 1971, eff. July 1, 1971; Mar. 10, 1986, eff. July 1, 1986; Apr. 24, 1998, eff. Dec. 1, 1998; Apr. 29, 2002, eff. Dec. 1, 2002; Apr. 25, 2005, eff. Dec. 1, 2005.)

ADVISORY COMMITTEE NOTES

1967 Adoption

The duties imposed upon clerks of the courts of appeals by this rule are those imposed by rule or practice in a majority of the circuits. The second sentence of subdivision (a) authorizing the closing of the clerk's office on Saturday and nonnational legal holidays follows a similar provision respecting the district court clerk's office found in FRCP 77(c) [rule 77(c), Federal Rules of Civil Procedure] and in FRCrP 56 [rule 56, Federal Rules of Criminal Procedure].

1971 Amendment

The amendment adds Columbus Day to the list of legal holidays. See the Note accompanying the amendment of Rule 26(a).

1986 Amendment

The amendment to Rule 45(b) permits the courts of appeals to maintain computerized dockets. The Committee believes that the Administrative Office of the United States Courts ought to have maximum flexibility in prescribing the format of this docket in order to ensure a smooth transition from manual to automated systems and subsequent adaptation to technological improvements.

The amendments to Rules 45(a) and (d) are technical. No substantive change is intended. The Birthday of Martin Luther King, Jr. has been added to the list of national holidays.

1998 Amendments

The language and organization of the rule are amended to make the rule more easily understood. In addition to changes made to improve the understanding, the Advisory Committee has changed language to make style and terminology consistent throughout the appellate rules. These changes are intended to be stylistic only.

2002 Amendments

Subdivision (c). Subdivision (c) has been amended so that the clerk may use electronic means to serve notice of entry of an order or judgment upon parties who have consented to such service.

Changes Made After Publication and Comments No changes were made to the text of the proposed amendment or to the Committee Note.

2005 Amendments

Subdivision (a)(2). Rule 45(a)(2) has been amended to refer to the third Monday in February as "Washington's Birthday." A federal statute officially designates the holiday as "Washington's Birthday," reflecting the desire of Congress specially to honor the first president of the United States. *See* 5 U.S.C. § 6103(a). During the 1998 restyling of the Federal Rules of Appellate Procedure, references to "Washington's Birthday" were mistakenly changed to "Presidents' Day." The amendment corrects that error.

Rule 46. Attorneys

(a) Admission to the Bar.

(1) Eligibility. An attorney is eligible for admission to the bar of a court of appeals if that attorney is of good moral and professional character and is admitted to practice before the Supreme Court of the United States, the highest court of a state, another United States court of appeals, or a United States district court (including the district courts for Guam, the Northern Mariana Islands, and the Virgin Islands).

(2) Application. An applicant must file an application for admission, on a form approved by the court that contains the applicant's personal statement showing eligibility for membership. The applicant must subscribe to the following oath or affirmation:

"I, _____, do solemnly swear [or affirm] that I will conduct myself as an attorney and counselor of this court, uprightly and according to law; and that I will support the Constitution of the United States."

(3) Admission Procedures. On written or oral motion of a member of the court's bar, the court will act on the application. An applicant may be admitted by oral motion in open court. But, unless the court orders otherwise, an applicant need not appear before the court to be admitted. Upon admission, an applicant must pay the clerk the fee prescribed by local rule or court order.

(b) Suspension or Disbarment.

(1) Standard. A member of the court's bar is subject to suspension or disbarment by the court if the member:

(A) has been suspended or disbarred from practice in any other court; or

(B) is guilty of conduct unbecoming a member of the court's bar.

(2) Procedure. The member must be given an opportunity to show good cause, within the time prescribed by the court, why the member should not be suspended or disbarred.

(3) Order. The court must enter an appropriate order after the member responds and a hearing is held, if requested, or after the time prescribed for a response expires, if no response is made.

(c) Discipline. A court of appeals may discipline an attorney who practices before it for conduct unbecoming a member of the bar or for failure to comply with any court rule. First, however, the court must afford the attorney reasonable notice, an opportunity to show cause to the contrary, and, if requested, a hearing.

(As amended Mar. 10, 1986, eff. July 1, 1986; Apr. 24, 1998, eff. Dec. 1, 1998.)

ADVISORY COMMITTEE NOTES

1967 Adoption

Subdivision (a). The basic requirement of membership in the bar of the Supreme Court, or of the highest court of a state, or in another court of appeals or a district court is found, with minor variations, in the rules of ten circuits. The only other requirement in those circuits is that the applicant be of good moral and professional character. In the District of Columbia Circuit applicants other than members of the District of Columbia District bar or the Supreme Court bar must claim membership in the bar of the highest court of a state, territory or possession for three years prior to application for admission (D.C.Cir. Rule 7 [rule 7, U.S.Ct. of App. Dist. of Col.]). Members of the District of Columbia District bar and the Supreme Court bar again excepted, applicants for admission to the District of Columbia Circuit bar must meet precisely defined prelaw and law school study require-

ments (D.C.Cir. Rule 7½ [rule 7½, U.S.Ct. of App.Dist. of Col.]).

A few circuits now require that application for admission be made by oral motion by a sponsor member in open court. The proposed rule permits both the application and the motion by the sponsor member to be in writing, and permits action on the motion without the appearance of the applicant or the sponsor, unless the court otherwise orders.

Subdivision (b). The provision respecting suspension or disbarment is uniform. Third Circuit Rule 8(3) [rule 8(3), U.S.Ct. of App. 3rd Cir.] is typical.

Subdivision (c). At present only Fourth Circuit Rule 36 [rule 36, U.S.Ct. of App. 4th Cir.] contains an equivalent provision. The purpose of this provision is to make explicit the power of a court of appeals to impose sanctions less serious than suspension or disbarment for the breach of rules. It also affords some measure of control over attorneys who are not members of the bar of the court. Several circuits permit a non-member attorney to file briefs and motions, membership being required only at the time of oral argument. And several circuits permit argument pro hac vice by non-member attorneys.

1986 Amendments

The amendments to Rules 46(a) and (b) are technical. No substantive change is intended.

1998 Amendments

The language and organization of the rule are amended to make the rule more easily understood. In addition to changes made to improve the understanding, the Advisory Committee has changed language to make style and terminology consistent throughout the appellate rules. These changes are intended to be stylistic only.

HISTORICAL NOTES
Termination of United States District Court for the District of the Canal Zone

For termination of the United States District Court for the District of the Canal Zone at end of the "transition period", being the 30–month period beginning Oct. 1, 1979, and ending midnight Mar. 31, 1982, see Paragraph 5 of Article XI of the Panama Canal Treaty of 1977 and sections 3831 and 3841 to 3843 of Title 22, Foreign Relations and Intercourse.

Rule 47. Local Rules by Courts of Appeals
(a) Local Rules.

(1) Each court of appeals acting by a majority of its judges in regular active service may, after giving appropriate public notice and opportunity for comment, make and amend rules governing its practice. A generally applicable direction to parties or lawyers regarding practice before a court must be in a local rule rather than an internal operating procedure or standing order. A local rule must be consistent with—but not duplicative of—Acts of Congress and rules adopted under 28 U.S.C. § 2072 and must conform to any uniform numbering system prescribed by the Judicial Conference of the

United States. Each circuit clerk must send the Administrative Office of the United States Courts a copy of each local rule and internal operating procedure when it is promulgated or amended.

(2) A local rule imposing a requirement of form must not be enforced in a manner that causes a party to lose rights because of a nonwillful failure to comply with the requirement.

(b) Procedure When There Is No Controlling Law. A court of appeals may regulate practice in a particular case in any manner consistent with federal law, these rules, and local rules of the circuit. No sanction or other disadvantage may be imposed for noncompliance with any requirement not in federal law, federal rules, or the local circuit rules unless the alleged violator has been furnished in the particular case with actual notice of the requirement.

(As amended Apr. 27, 1995, eff. Dec. 1, 1995; Apr. 24, 1998, eff. Dec. 1, 1998.)

ADVISORY COMMITTEE NOTES

1967 Adoption

This rule continues the authority now vested in individual courts of appeals by 28 U.S.C. § 2071 to make rules consistent with rules of practice and procedure promulgated by the Supreme Court.

1995 Amendments

Subdivision (a). This rule is amended to require that a generally applicable direction regarding practice before a court of appeals must be in a local rule rather than an internal operating procedure or some other general directive. It is the intent of this rule that a local rule may not bar any practice that these rules explicitly or implicitly permit. Subdivision (b) allows a court of appeals to regulate practice in an individual case by entry of an order in the case. The amendment also reflects the requirement that local rules be consistent not only with the national rules but also with Acts of Congress. The amendment also states that local rules should not repeat national rules and Acts of Congress.

The amendment also requires that the numbering of local rules conform with any uniform numbering system that may be prescribed by the Judicial Conference. Lack of uniform numbering might create unnecessary traps for counsel and litigants. A uniform numbering system would make it easier for an increasingly national bar and for litigants to locate a local rule that applies to a particular procedural issue.

Paragraph (2) is new. Its aim is to protect against loss of rights in the enforcement of local rules relating to matters of form. The proscription of paragraph (2) is narrowly drawn—covering only violations that are not willful and only those involving local rules directed to matters of form. It does not limit the court's power to impose substantive penalties upon a party if it or its attorney stubbornly or repeatedly violates a local rule, even one involving merely a matter of form. Nor does it affect the court's power to enforce local rules that involve more than mere matters of form.

Subdivision (b). This rule provides flexibility to the court in regulating practice in a particular case when there is no controlling law. Specifically, it permits the court to regulate practice in any manner consistent with Acts of Congress, with rules adopted under 28 U.S.C. § 2072, and with the circuit's local rules.

The amendment to this rule disapproves imposing any sanction or other disadvantage on a person for noncompliance with such a directive, unless the alleged violator has been furnished in a particular case with actual notice of the requirement. There should be no adverse consequence to a party or attorney for violating special requirements relating to practice before a particular court unless the party or attorney has actual notice of those requirements.

1998 Amendments

The language of the rule is amended to make the rule more easily understood. In addition to changes made to improve the understanding, the Advisory Committee has changed language to make style and terminology consistent throughout the appellate rules. These changes are intended to be stylistic only.

Rule 48. Masters

(a) Appointment; Powers. A court of appeals may appoint a special master to hold hearings, if necessary, and to recommend factual findings and disposition in matters ancillary to proceedings in the court. Unless the order referring a matter to a master specifies or limits the master's powers, those powers include, but are not limited to, the following:

(1) regulating all aspects of a hearing;

(2) taking all appropriate action for the efficient performance of the master's duties under the order;

(3) requiring the production of evidence on all matters embraced in the reference; and

(4) administering oaths and examining witnesses and parties.

(b) Compensation. If the master is not a judge or court employee, the court must determine the master's compensation and whether the cost is to be charged to any party.

(As amended Apr. 29, 1994, eff. Dec. 1, 1994; Apr. 24, 1998, eff. Dec. 1, 1998.)

ADVISORY COMMITTEE NOTES

1994 Amendments

The text of the existing Rule 48 concerning the title was moved to Rule 1.

This new Rule 48 authorizes a court of appeals to appoint a special master to make recommendations concerning ancillary matters. The courts of appeals have long used masters in contempt proceedings where the issue is compliance with an enforcement order. See *Polish National Alliance v. NLRB*, 159 F.2d 38 (7th Cir. 1946); *NLRB v. Arcade-Sunshine Co.*, 132 F.2d 8 (D.C. Cir. 1942); *NLRB v. Remington Rand, Inc.*, 130 F.2d 919 (2d Cir. 1942). There are other instances when the question before a court of appeals

requires a factual determination. An application for fees or eligibility for Criminal Justice Act status on appeal are examples.

Ordinarily when a factual issue is unresolved, a court of appeals remands the case to the district court or agency that originally heard the case. It is not the Committee's intent to alter that practice. However, when factual issues arise in the first instance in the court of appeals, such as fees for representation on appeal, it would be useful to have authority to refer such determinations to a master for a recommendation.

1998 Amendments

The language and organization of the rule are amended to make the rule more easily understood. In addition to changes made to improve the understanding, the Advisory Committee has changed language to make style and terminology consistent throughout the appellate rules. These changes are intended to be stylistic only.

APPENDIX OF FORMS

Form 1. Notice of Appeal to a Court of Appeals From a Judgment or Order of a District Court

United States District Court for the _____
District of _____
File Number _____

A.B., Plaintiff)
)
v.) *Notice of Appeal*
)
C.D., Defendant)

Notice is hereby given that [____ (here name all parties taking the appeal)____, (plaintiffs) (defendants) in the above named case,[1]] hereby appeal to the United States Court of Appeals for the _____ Circuit (from the final judgment) (from an order (describing it)) entered in this action on the _____ day of _____, 20__.

(s) _____
Attorney for [_____]
[Address:_____]

(As amended Apr. 22, 1993, eff. Dec. 1, 1993; Mar. 27, 2003, eff. Dec. 1, 2003.)

[1] See Rule 3(c) for permissible ways of identifying appellants.

Form 2. Notice of Appeal to a Court of Appeals From a Decision of the United States Tax Court

UNITED STATES TAX COURT

Washington, D.C.

A.B., Petitioner)
)
v.) Docket No. _____
)
Commissioner of Internal)
Revenue, Respondent)

Notice of Appeal

Notice is hereby given that [____ here name all parties taking the appeal [1]____], hereby appeals to the United States Court of Appeals for the _____ Circuit from (that part of) the decision of this court entered in the above captioned proceeding on the _____ day of _____, 20__ (relating to _____).

(s) _____
Counsel for [_____]
[Address:_____]

(As amended Apr. 22, 1993, eff. Dec. 1, 1993; Mar. 27, 2003, eff. Dec. 1, 2003.)

[1] See Rule 3(c) for permissible ways of identifying appellants.

Form 3. Petition for Review of Order of an Agency, Board, Commission or Officer

United States Court of Appeals
for the _____ Circuit

A.B., Petitioner)
)
v.) Petition for Review
XYZ Commission, Respondent)

[____ (here name all parties bringing the petition[1]) ____] hereby petitions the court for review of the Order of the XYZ Commission (describe the order) entered on _____, 20__.

[(s)] _____
Attorney for Petitioners
Address:_____

(As amended Apr. 22, 1993, eff. Dec. 1, 1993; Mar. 27, 2003, eff. Dec. 1, 2003.)

[1] See Rule 15.

Form 4. Affidavit Accompanying Motion for Permission to Appeal In Forma Pauperis

**United States District Court
for the
_____ District of _____**

A.B., Plaintiff
v. Case No. _____
C.D., Defendant

Affidavit in Support of Motion	**Instructions**
I swear or affirm under penalty of perjury that, because of my poverty, I cannot prepay the docket fees of my appeal or post a bond for them. I believe I am entitled to redress. I swear or affirm under penalty of perjury under United States laws that my answers on this form are true and correct. (28 U.S.C. § 1746; 18 U.S.C. § 1621.)	Complete all questions in this application and then sign it. Do not leave any blanks: if the answer to a question is "0," "none," or "not applicable (N/A)," write in that response. If you need more space to answer a question or to explain your answer, attach a separate sheet of paper identified with your name, your case's docket number, and the question number.

Signed: _____ Date: _____

My issues on appeal are:

1. For both you and your spouse estimate the average amount of money received from each of the following sources during the past 12 months. Adjust any amount that was

received weekly, biweekly, quarterly, semiannually, or annually to show the monthly rate. Use gross amounts, that is, amounts before any deductions for taxes or otherwise.

Income source	Average monthly amount during the past 12 months		Amount expected next month	
Income source	Average monthly amount during the past 12 months		Amount expected next month	
	You	Spouse	You	Spouse
Employment	$____	$____	$____	$____
Self-employment	$____	$____	$____	$____
Income from real property (such as rental income)	$____	$____	$____	$____
Interest and dividends	$____	$____	$____	$____
Gifts	$____	$____	$____	$____
Alimony	$____	$____	$____	$____
Child support	$____	$____	$____	$____
Retirement (such as social security, pensions, annuities, insurance)	$____	$____	$____	$____
Disability (such as social security, insurance payments)	$____	$____	$____	$____
Unemployment payments	$____	$____	$____	$____
Public-assistance (such as welfare)	$____	$____	$____	$____
Other (specify): _	$____	$____	$____	$____
Total monthly income:	$____	$____	$____	$____

2. List your employment history, most recent employer first. (Gross monthly pay is before taxes or other deductions.)

Employer	Address	Dates of employment	Gross monthly pay
_____	_____	_____	_____
_____	_____	_____	_____
_____	_____	_____	_____

3. List your spouse's employment history, most recent employer first. (Gross monthly pay is before taxes or other deductions.)

Employer	Address	Dates of employment	Gross monthly pay
_____	_____	_____	_____
_____	_____	_____	_____
_____	_____	_____	_____

4. How much cash do you and your spouse have?
$_____
Below, state any money you or your spouse have in bank accounts or in any other financial institution.

Financial institution	Type of account	Amount you have	Amount your spouse has
_____	_____	$____	$____
_____	_____	$____	$____
_____	_____	$____	$____

If you are a prisoner, you must attach a statement certified by the appropriate institutional officer showing all receipts, expenditures, and balances during the last six months in your institutional accounts. If you have multiple accounts, perhaps because you have been in multiple institutions, attach one certified statement of each account.

5. List the assets, and their values, which you own or your spouse owns. Do not list clothing and ordinary household furnishings.

Home (Value)	Other real estate (Value)	Motor vehicle #1 (Value)
_____	_____	Make & year: ____
_____	_____	Model: ____
_____	_____	Registration #: ____

Motor vehicle #2 (Value)	Other assets (Value)	Other assets (Value)
Make & year: ____	____	____
Model: ____	____	____
Registration #: ____	____	____

6. State every person, business, or organization owing you or your spouse money, and the amount owed.

Person owing you or your spouse money	Amount owed to you	Amount owed to your spouse
_____	_____	_____
_____	_____	_____
_____	_____	_____

7. State the persons who rely on you or your spouse for support.

Name	Relationship	Age
_____	_____	____
_____	_____	____
_____	_____	____

8. Estimate the average monthly expenses of you and your family. Show separately the amounts paid by your spouse. Adjust any payments that are made weekly, biweekly, quarterly, semiannually, or annually to show the monthly rate.

	You	Your Spouse
Rent or home-mortgage payment (include lot rented for mobile home)	$____	$____
Are real-estate taxes included? ☐ Yes ☐ No		
Is property insurance included? ☐ Yes ☐ No		
Utilities (electricity, heating fuel, water, sewer, and Telephone)	$____	$____
Home maintenance (repairs and upkeep)	$____	$____

Food	$_____	$_____
Clothing	$_____	$_____
Laundry and dry-cleaning	$_____	$_____
Medical and dental expenses	$_____	$_____
Transportation (not including motor vehicle payments)	$_____	$_____
Recreation, entertainment, newspapers, magazines, etc.	$_____	$_____
Insurance (not deducted from wages or included in Mortgage payments)	$_____	$_____
Homeowner's or renter's	$_____	$_____
Life	$_____	$_____
Health	$_____	$_____
Motor Vehicle	$_____	$_____
Other: _____	$_____	$_____
Taxes (not deducted from wages or included in Mortgage payments) (specify): _____	$_____	$_____
Installment payments	$_____	$_____
Motor Vehicle	$_____	$_____
Credit card (name): _____	$_____	$_____
Department store (name): __	$_____	$_____
Other: _____	$_____	$_____
Alimony, maintenance, and support paid to others	$_____	$_____
Regular expenses for operation of business, profession, or farm (attach detailed statement)	$_____	$_____
Other (specify): ____	$_____	$_____
Total monthly expenses:	$_____	$_____

9. Do you expect any major changes to your monthly income or expenses or in your assets or liabilities during the next 12 months?

☐ Yes ☐ No If yes, describe on an attached sheet.

10. Have you paid—or will you be paying—an attorney any money for services in connection with this case, including the completion of this form? Yes No
If yes, how much? $_____
If yes, state the attorney's name, address, and telephone number:

11. Have you paid—or will you be paying—anyone other than an attorney (such as a paralegal or a typist) any money for services in connection with this case, including the completion of this form?
☐ Yes ☐ No
If yes, how much? $_____
If yes, state the person's name, address, and telephone number:

12. Provide any other information that will help explain why you cannot pay the docket fees for your appeal.

13. State the address of your legal residence.

Your daytime phone number: ___ _____
Your age: _____ Your years of schooling: _____
Your social-security number: _____

(As amended Apr. 24, 1998, eff. Dec. 1, 1998.)

Form 5. Notice of Appeal to a Court of Appeals from a Judgment or Order of a District Court or a Bankruptcy Appellate Panel

United States District Court for the
 District of

In re)
)
.....................,)
Debtor)
) File No..........
.....................,)
Plaintiff)
)
v.)
)
.....................,)
Defendant)

Notice of Appeal to
United States Court of Appeals
 for the Circuit
........................., the plaintiff [or defendant or other party] appeals to the United States Court of Appeals for the Circuit from the final judgment [or order or decree] of the district court for the district of
[or bankruptcy appellate panel of the circuit], entered in this case on, 20.... [here describe the judgment, order, or decree]
 The parties to the judgment [or order or decree] appealed from and the names and addresses of their respective attorneys are as follows:

 Dated
 Signed
 Attorney for Appellant

Address:

...............................

(Added Apr. 25, 1989, eff. Dec. 1, 1989; Mar. 27, 2003, eff. Dec. 1, 2003.)

Form 6. Certificate of Compliance with Rule 32(a)

Certificate of Compliance With Type-Volume
Limitation, Typeface Requirements, and
Type Style Requirements

1. This brief complies with the type-volume limitation of Fed. R. App. P. 32(a)(7)(B) because:

☐ this brief contains [*state the number of*] words, excluding the parts of the brief exempted by Fed. R. App. P. 32(a)(7)(B)(iii), *or*

☐ this brief uses a monospaced typeface and contains [*state the number of*] lines of text, excluding the parts of the brief exempted by Fed. R. App. P. 32(a)(7)(B)(iii).

2. This brief complies with the typeface requirements of Fed. R. App. P. 32(a)(5) and the type style requirements of Fed. R. App. P. 32(a)(6) because:

☐ this brief has been prepared in a proportionally spaced typeface using [*state name and version of word processing program*] in [*state font size and name of type style*], or

☐ this brief has been prepared in a monospaced typeface using [*state name and version of word processing program*] with [*state number of characters per inch and name of type style*].

(s)_____

Attorney for _____

Dated: _____

(Added Apr. 29, 2002, eff. Dec. 1, 2002.)

ADVISORY COMMITTEE NOTES
2002 Adoption

Changes Made After Publication and Comments No changes were made to the text of the proposed amendment or to the Committee Note.

RULES
OF THE
SUPREME COURT
OF
THE UNITED STATES

Adopted January 11, 1999
Effective May 3, 1999

Amendments received to May 21, 2007

TABLE OF CORRESPONDING SUPREME COURT RULES

This table shows corresponding relationship between the rules effective July 1, 1925, the rules effective July 1, 1928, the rules effective Feb. 27, 1939, the rules effective July 1,

1954, the rules effective Oct. 2, 1967, the rules effective July 1, 1970, and the rules effective June 30, 1980.

1925	1928	1939	1954	1967	1970	1980
1	1	1	1	1	1	1
2	2	2	5, 6, 8	5, 6, 8	5, 6, 8	5, 6, 8
		3	7	7	7	7
3	4	4	2	2	2	2
		5	9	9	9	9
4	5					
5	6	6	9, 59	9, 59	9, 59	9, 52
6	7	7	16, 20, 24, 35, 44	16, 20, 24, 35, 44	16, 20, 24, 35, 44	16, 18, 22, 23, 28
7	8	8				
8	9	9				
9	10	10	12	12	12	13
10	11	11	13, 14	13, 14	13, 14	12, 14
	12	12	15, 16	15, 16	15, 16	15, 16
11	13	13	17, 26, 36	17, 26, 36	17, 26, 36	30
12	14	14	37	37	37	31
13	15	15				
14	16	16				
15	17	17	32	32	32	
16	18	18	38	38	38	32
17	19	19	48	48	48	40
18	20	20	35, 43	35, 43	35, 43	37, 42
19	21	21				
20	22	22				
21	23	23				
22	24	24				
23	25	25	45	45	45	38
24	26	26	39	39	39	33
25	27	27	40 to 42	40 to 42	40 to 42	34 to 36
26	28	28	44	44	44	38
27	29	29	55	55	55	48
28	30	30	56	56	56	49
	31	31				
29	32	32	52, 57	52, 57	52, 57	45, 50
30	33	33	58	58	58	51
31	34	34	25, 59	25, 59	25, 59	23, 52
32	35	35	60	60	60	53
33	36	36	18	18	18	44
34	37	37	28	28	28	24
35	38	38	19, 21 to 24, 27, 36	19, 21 to 24, 27, 36	19, 21 to 24, 27, 36	17, 19 to 22, 30, 44
		38½	11, 22	11, 22	11, 22	11, 20
36	39	39	20	20	20	18
37	40	40	28	28	28	24
38	41	41	19	19	19	17
39	42	42	19	19	19	17
40	43	43	25	25	25	23
41	44	44				
42	45	45	49	49	49	41
	46	46				
	46½	47				
		48	46	46	46	10, 19
43	47	49	4	4	4	4
44	48	50	3	3	3	3
45	49	51	61	62	62	55
			62	61	61	54

PART I. THE COURT

Rule 1. Clerk

1. The Clerk receives documents for filing with the Court and has authority to reject any submitted filing that does not comply with these Rules.

2. The Clerk maintains the Court's records and will not permit any of them to be removed from the Court building except as authorized by the Court. Any document filed with the Clerk and made a part of the Court's records may not thereafter be withdrawn from the official Court files. After the conclusion of proceedings in this Court, original records and documents transmitted to this Court by any other court will be returned to the court from which they were received.

3. Unless the Court or the Chief Justice orders otherwise, the Clerk's office is open from 9 a.m. to 5 p.m., Monday through Friday, except on federal legal holidays listed in 5 U.S.C. § 6103.

Rule 2. Library

1. The Court's library is available for use by appropriate personnel of this Court, members of the Bar

of this Court, Members of Congress and their legal staffs, and attorneys for the United States and for federal departments and agencies.

2. The library's hours are governed by regulations made by the Librarian with the approval of the Chief Justice or the Court.

3. Library books may not be removed from the Court building, except by a Justice or a member of a Justice's staff.

Rule 3. Term

The Court holds a continuous annual Term commencing on the first Monday in October and ending on the day before the first Monday in October of the following year. See 28 U.S.C. § 2. At the end of each Term, all cases pending on the docket are continued to the next Term.

Rule 4. Sessions and Quorum

1. Open sessions of the Court are held beginning at 10 a.m. on the first Monday in October of each year, and thereafter as announced by the Court. Unless it orders otherwise, the Court sits to hear arguments from 10 a.m. until noon and from 1 p.m. until 3 p.m.

2. Six Members of the Court constitute a quorum. See 28 U.S.C. § 1. In the absence of a quorum on any day appointed for holding a session of the Court, the Justices attending—or if no Justice is present, the Clerk or a Deputy Clerk—may announce that the Court will not meet until there is a quorum.

3. When appropriate, the Court will direct the Clerk or the Marshal to announce recesses.

PART II. ATTORNEYS AND COUNSELORS

Rule 5. Admission to the Bar

1. To qualify for admission to the Bar of this Court, an applicant must have been admitted to practice in the highest court of a State, Commonwealth, Territory or Possession, or the District of Columbia for a period of at least three years immediately before the date of application; must not have been the subject of any adverse disciplinary action pronounced or in effect during that 3–year period; and must appear to the Court to be of good moral and professional character.

2. Each applicant shall file with the Clerk (1) a certificate from the presiding judge, clerk, or other authorized official of that court evidencing the applicant's admission to practice there and the applicant's current good standing, and (2) a completely executed copy of the form approved by this Court and furnished by the Clerk containing (a) the applicant's personal statement, and (b) the statement of two sponsors endorsing the correctness of the applicant's statement, stating that the applicant possesses all the qualifications required for admission, and affirming that the applicant is of good moral and professional character. Both sponsors must be members of the Bar of this Court who personally know, but are not related to, the applicant.

3. If the documents submitted demonstrate that the applicant possesses the necessary qualifications, and if the applicant has signed the oath or affirmation and paid the required fee, the Clerk will notify the applicant of acceptance by the Court as a member of the Bar and issue a certificate of admission. An applicant who so wishes may be admitted in open court on oral motion by a member of the Bar of this Court, provided that all other requirements for admission have been satisfied.

4. Each applicant shall sign the following oath or affirmation: I,, do solemnly swear (or affirm) that as an attorney and as a counselor of this Court, I will conduct myself uprightly and according to law, and that I will support the Constitution of the United States.

5. The fee for admission to the Bar and a certificate bearing the seal of the Court is $100, payable to the United States Supreme Court. The Marshal will deposit such fees in a separate fund to be disbursed by the Marshal at the direction of the Chief Justice for the costs of admissions, for the benefit of the Court and its Bar, and for related purposes.

6. The fee for a duplicate certificate of admission to the Bar bearing the seal of the Court is $15, and the fee for a certificate of good standing is $10, payable to the United States Supreme Court. The proceeds will be maintained by the Marshal as provided in paragraph 5 of this Rule.

(As amended Jan. 11, 1999, eff. May 3, 1999.)

Rule 6. Argument *Pro Hac Vice*

1. An attorney not admitted to practice in the highest court of a State, Commonwealth, Territory or Possession, or the District of Columbia for the requisite three years, but otherwise eligible for admission to practice in this Court under Rule 5.1, may be permitted to argue *pro hac vice*.

2. An attorney qualified to practice in the courts of a foreign state may be permitted to argue *pro hac vice*.

3. Oral argument *pro hac vice* is allowed only on motion of the counsel of record for the party on whose

behalf leave is requested. The motion shall state concisely the qualifications of the attorney who is to argue *pro hac vice*. It shall be filed with the Clerk, in the form required by Rule 21, no later than the date on which the respondent's or appellee's brief on the merits is due to be filed, and it shall be accompanied by proof of service as required by Rule 29.

Rule 7. Prohibition Against Practice

No employee of this Court shall practice as an attorney or counselor in any court or before any agency of government while employed by the Court; nor shall any person after leaving such employment participate in any professional capacity in any case pending before this Court or in any case being considered for filing in this Court, until two years have elapsed after separation; nor shall a former employee ever participate in any professional capacity in any case that was pending in this Court during the employee's tenure.

Rule 8. Disbarment and Disciplinary Action

1. Whenever a member of the Bar of this Court has been disbarred or suspended from practice in any court of record, or has engaged in conduct unbecoming a member of the Bar of this Court, the Court will enter an order suspending that member from practice before this Court and affording the member an opportunity to show cause, within 40 days, why a disbarment order should not be entered. Upon response, or if no response is timely filed, the Court will enter an appropriate order.

2. After reasonable notice and an opportunity to show cause why disciplinary action should not be taken, and after a hearing if material facts are in dispute, the Court may take any appropriate disciplinary action against any attorney who is admitted to practice before it for conduct unbecoming a member of the Bar or for failure to comply with these Rules or any Rule or order of the Court.

Rule 9. Appearance of Counsel

1. An attorney seeking to file a document in this Court in a representative capacity must first be admitted to practice before this Court as provided in Rule 5, except that admission to the Bar of this Court is not required for an attorney appointed under the Criminal Justice Act of 1964, see 18 U.S.C. § 3006A(d)(6), or under any other applicable federal statute. The attorney whose name, address, and telephone number appear on the cover of a document presented for filing is considered counsel of record, and a separate notice of appearance need not be filed. If the name of more than one attorney is shown on the cover of the document, the attorney who is counsel of record shall be clearly identified.

2. An attorney representing a party who will not be filing a document shall enter a separate notice of appearance as counsel of record indicating the name of the party represented. A separate notice of appearance shall also be entered whenever an attorney is substituted as counsel of record in a particular case.

PART III. JURISDICTION ON WRIT OF CERTIORARI

Rule 10. Considerations Governing Review on Certiorari

Review on a writ of certiorari is not a matter of right, but of judicial discretion. A petition for a writ of certiorari will be granted only for compelling reasons. The following, although neither controlling nor fully measuring the Court's discretion, indicate the character of the reasons the Court considers:

(a) a United States court of appeals has entered a decision in conflict with the decision of another United States court of appeals on the same important matter; has decided an important federal question in a way that conflicts with a decision by a state court of last resort; or has so far departed from the accepted and usual course of judicial proceedings, or sanctioned such a departure by a lower court, as to call for an exercise of this Court's supervisory power;

(b) a state court of last resort has decided an important federal question in a way that conflicts

with the decision of another state court of last resort or of a United States court of appeals;

(c) a state court or a United States court of appeals has decided an important question of federal law that has not been, but should be, settled by this Court, or has decided an important federal question in a way that conflicts with relevant decisions of this Court.

A petition for a writ of certiorari is rarely granted when the asserted error consists of erroneous factual findings or the misapplication of a properly stated rule of law.

Rule 11. Certiorari to a United States Court of Appeals Before Judgment

A petition for a writ of certiorari to review a case pending in a United States court of appeals, before judgment is entered in that court, will be granted only upon a showing that the case is of such imperative public importance as to justify deviation from normal

appellate practice and to require immediate determination in this Court. See 28 U.S.C. § 2101(e).

Rule 12. Review on Certiorari: How Sought; Parties

1. Except as provided in paragraph 2 of this Rule, the petitioner shall file 40 copies of a petition for a writ of certiorari, prepared as required by Rule 33.1, and shall pay the Rule 38(a) docket fee.

2. A petitioner proceeding *in forma pauperis* under Rule 39 shall file an original and 10 copies of a petition for a writ of certiorari prepared as required by Rule 33.2, together with an original and 10 copies of the motion for leave to proceed *in forma pauperis*. A copy of the motion shall precede and be attached to each copy of the petition. An inmate confined in an institution, if proceeding *in forma pauperis* and not represented by counsel, need file only an original petition and motion.

3. Whether prepared under Rule 33.1 or Rule 33.2, the petition shall comply in all respects with Rule 14 and shall be submitted with proof of service as required by Rule 29. The case then will be placed on the docket. It is the petitioner's duty to notify all respondents promptly, on a form supplied by the Clerk, of the date of filing, the date the case was placed on the docket, and the docket number of the case. The notice shall be served as required by Rule 29.

4. Parties interested jointly, severally, or otherwise in a judgment may petition separately for a writ of certiorari; or any two or more may join in a petition. A party not shown on the petition as joined therein at the time the petition is filed may not later join in that petition. When two or more judgments are sought to be reviewed on a writ of certiorari to the same court and involve identical or closely related questions, a single petition for a writ of certiorari covering all the judgments suffices. A petition for a writ of certiorari may not be joined with any other pleading, except that any motion for leave to proceed *in forma pauperis* shall be attached.

5. No more than 30 days after a case has been placed on the docket, a respondent seeking to file a conditional cross-petition (*i.e.,* a cross-petition that otherwise would be untimely) shall file, with proof of service as required by Rule 29, 40 copies of the cross-petition prepared as required by Rule 33.1, except that a cross-petitioner proceeding *in forma pauperis* under Rule 39 shall comply with Rule 12.2. The cross-petition shall comply in all respects with this Rule and Rule 14, except that material already reproduced in the appendix to the opening petition need not be reproduced again. A cross-petitioning respondent shall pay the Rule 38(a) docket fee or submit a motion for leave to proceed *in forma pauperis*. The cover of

the cross-petition shall indicate clearly that it is a conditional cross-petition. The cross-petition then will be placed on the docket, subject to the provisions of Rule 13.4. It is the cross-petitioner's duty to notify all cross-respondents promptly, on a form supplied by the Clerk, of the date of filing, the date the cross-petition was placed on the docket, and the docket number of the cross-petition. The notice shall be served as required by Rule 29. A cross-petition for a writ of certiorari may not be joined with any other pleading, except that any motion for leave to proceed *in forma pauperis* shall be attached. The time to file a conditional cross-petition will not be extended.

6. All parties to the proceeding in the court whose judgment is sought to be reviewed are deemed parties entitled to file documents in this Court, unless the petitioner notifies the Clerk of this Court in writing of the petitioner's belief that one or more of the parties below have no interest in the outcome of the petition. A copy of such notice shall be served as required by Rule 29 on all parties to the proceeding below. A party noted as no longer interested may remain a party by notifying the Clerk promptly, with service on the other parties, of an intention to remain a party. All parties other than the petitioner are considered respondents, but any respondent who supports the position of a petitioner shall meet the petitioner's time schedule for filing documents, except that a response supporting the petition shall be filed within 20 days after the case is placed on the docket, and that time will not be extended. Parties who file no document will not qualify for any relief from this Court.

7. The clerk of the court having possession of the record shall keep it until notified by the Clerk of this Court to certify and transmit it. In any document filed with this Court, a party may cite or quote from the record, even if it has not been transmitted to this Court. When requested by the Clerk of this Court to certify and transmit the record, or any part of it, the clerk of the court having possession of the record shall number the documents to be certified and shall transmit therewith a numbered list specifically identifying each document transmitted. If the record, or stipulated portions, have been printed for the use of the court below, that printed record, plus the proceedings in the court below, may be certified as the record unless one of the parties or the Clerk of this Court requests otherwise. The record may consist of certified copies, but if the lower court is of the view that original documents of any kind should be seen by this Court, that court may provide by order for the transport, safekeeping, and return of such originals.

Rule 13. Review on Certiorari: Time for Petitioning

1. Unless otherwise provided by law, a petition for a writ of certiorari to review a judgment in any case,

civil or criminal, entered by a state court of last resort or a United States court of appeals (including the United States Court of Appeals for the Armed Forces) is timely when it is filed with the Clerk of this Court within 90 days after entry of the judgment. A petition for a writ of certiorari seeking review of a judgment of a lower state court that is subject to discretionary review by the state court of last resort is timely when it is filed with the Clerk within 90 days after entry of the order denying discretionary review.

2. The Clerk will not file any petition for a writ of certiorari that is jurisdictionally out of time. See, *e.g.*, 28 U.S.C. § 2101(c).

3. The time to file a petition for a writ of certiorari runs from the date of entry of the judgment or order sought to be reviewed, and not from the issuance date of the mandate (or its equivalent under local practice). But if a petition for rehearing is timely filed in the lower court by any party, or if the lower court appropriately entertains an untimely petition for rehearing or *sua sponte* considers rehearing, the time to file the petition for a writ of certiorari for all parties (whether or not they requested rehearing or joined in the petition for rehearing) runs from the date of the denial of rehearing or, if rehearing is granted, the subsequent entry of judgment.

4. A cross-petition for a writ of certiorari is timely when it is filed with the Clerk as provided in paragraphs 1, 3, and 5 of this Rule, or in Rule 12.5. However, a conditional cross-petition (which except for Rule 12.5 would be untimely) will not be granted unless another party's timely petition for a writ of certiorari is granted.

5. For good cause, a Justice may extend the time to file a petition for a writ of certiorari for a period not exceeding 60 days. An application to extend the time to file shall set out the basis for jurisdiction in this Court, identify the judgment sought to be reviewed, include a copy of the opinion and any order respecting rehearing, and set out specific reasons why an extension of time is justified. The application must be filed with the Clerk at least 10 days before the date the petition is due, except in extraordinary circumstances. For the time and manner of presenting the application, see Rules 21, 22, 30, and 33.2. An application to extend the time to file a petition for a writ of certiorari is not favored.

(As amended Jan. 11, 1999, eff. May 3, 1999; Jan. 27, 2003, eff. May 1, 2003; Mar. 14, 2005, eff. May 2, 2005.)

Rule 14. Content of a Petition for a Writ of Certiorari

1. A petition for a writ of certiorari shall contain, in the order indicated:

(a) The questions presented for review, expressed concisely in relation to the circumstances of the case, without unnecessary detail. The questions should be short and should not be argumentative or repetitive. If the petitioner or respondent is under a death sentence that may be affected by the disposition of the petition, the notation "capital case" shall precede the questions presented. The questions shall be set out on the first page following the cover, and no other information may appear on that page. The statement of any question presented is deemed to comprise every subsidiary question fairly included therein. Only the questions set out in the petition, or fairly included therein, will be considered by the Court.

(b) A list of all parties to the proceeding in the court whose judgment is sought to be reviewed (unless the caption of the case contains the names of all the parties), and a corporate disclosure statement as required by Rule 29.6.

(c) If the petition exceeds five pages, a table of contents and a table of cited authorities.

(d) Citations of the official and unofficial reports of the opinions and orders entered in the case by courts or administrative agencies.

(e) A concise statement of the basis for jurisdiction in this Court, showing:

(i) the date the judgment or order sought to be reviewed was entered (and, if applicable, a statement that the petition is filed under this Court's Rule 11);

(ii) the date of any order respecting rehearing, and the date and terms of any order granting an extension of time to file the petition for a writ of certiorari;

(iii) express reliance on Rule 12.5, when a cross-petition for a writ of certiorari is filed under that Rule, and the date of docketing of the petition for a writ of certiorari in connection with which the cross-petition is filed;

(iv) the statutory provision believed to confer on this Court jurisdiction to review on a writ of certiorari the judgment or order in question; and

(v) if applicable, a statement that the notifications required by Rule 29.4(b) or (c) have been made.

(f) The constitutional provisions, treaties, statutes, ordinances, and regulations involved in the case, set out verbatim with appropriate citation. If the provisions involved are lengthy, their citation alone suffices at this point, and their pertinent text shall be set out in the appendix referred to in subparagraph 1(i).

(g) A concise statement of the case setting out the facts material to consideration of the questions presented, and also containing the following:

(i) If review of a state-court judgment is sought, specification of the stage in the proceedings, both in the court of first instance and in the appellate courts, when the federal questions sought to be reviewed were raised; the method or manner of raising them and the way in which they were passed on by those courts; and pertinent quotations of specific portions of the record or summary thereof, with specific reference to the places in the record where the matter appears (*e.g.*, court opinion, ruling on exception, portion of court's charge and exception thereto, assignment of error), so as to show that the federal question was timely and properly raised and that this Court has jurisdiction to review the judgment on a writ of certiorari. When the portions of the record relied on under this subparagraph are voluminous, they shall be included in the appendix referred to in subparagraph 1(i).

(ii) If review of a judgment of a United States court of appeals is sought, the basis for federal jurisdiction in the court of first instance.

(h) A direct and concise argument amplifying the reasons relied on for allowance of the writ. See Rule 10.

(i) An appendix containing, in the order indicated:

(i) the opinions, orders, findings of fact, and conclusions of law, whether written or orally given and transcribed, entered in conjunction with the judgment sought to be reviewed;

(ii) any other relevant opinions, orders, findings of fact, and conclusions of law entered in the case by courts or administrative agencies, and, if reference thereto is necessary to ascertain the grounds of the judgment, of those in companion cases (each document shall include the caption showing the name of the issuing court or agency, the title and number of the case, and the date of entry);

(iii) any order on rehearing, including the caption showing the name of the issuing court, the title and number of the case, and the date of entry;

(iv) the judgment sought to be reviewed if the date of its entry is different from the date of the opinion or order required in sub-subparagraph (i) of this subparagraph;

(v) material required by subparagraphs 1(f) or 1(g)(i); and

(vi) any other material the petitioner believes essential to understand the petition.

If the material required by this subparagraph is voluminous, it may be presented in a separate volume or volumes with appropriate covers.

2. All contentions in support of a petition for a writ of certiorari shall be set out in the body of the petition, as provided in subparagraph 1(h) of this

Rule. No separate brief in support of a petition for a writ of certiorari may be filed, and the Clerk will not file any petition for a writ of certiorari to which any supporting brief is annexed or appended.

3. A petition for a writ of certiorari should be stated briefly and in plain terms and may not exceed the page limitations specified in Rule 33.

4. The failure of a petitioner to present with accuracy, brevity, and clarity whatever is essential to ready and adequate understanding of the points requiring consideration is sufficient reason for the Court to deny a petition.

5. If the Clerk determines that a petition submitted timely and in good faith is in a form that does not comply with this Rule or with Rule 33 or Rule 34, the Clerk will return it with a letter indicating the deficiency. A corrected petition received no more than 60 days after the date of the Clerk's letter will be deemed timely.

Rule 15. Briefs in Opposition; Reply Briefs; Supplemental Briefs

1. A brief in opposition to a petition for a writ of certiorari may be filed by the respondent in any case, but is not mandatory except in a capital case, see Rule 14.1(a), or when ordered by the Court.

2. A brief in opposition should be stated briefly and in plain terms and may not exceed the page limitations specified in Rule 33. In addition to presenting other arguments for denying the petition, the brief in opposition should address any perceived misstatement of fact or law in the petition that bears on what issues properly would be before the Court if certiorari were granted. Counsel are admonished that they have an obligation to the Court to point out in the brief in opposition, and not later, any perceived misstatement made in the petition. Any objection to consideration of a question presented based on what occurred in the proceedings below, if the objection does not go to jurisdiction, may be deemed waived unless called to the Court's attention in the brief in opposition.

3. Any brief in opposition shall be filed within 30 days after the case is placed on the docket, unless the time is extended by the Court or a Justice, or by the Clerk under Rule 30.4. Forty copies shall be filed, except that a respondent proceeding *in forma pauperis* under Rule 39, including an inmate of an institution, shall file the number of copies required for a petition by such a person under Rule 12.2, together with a motion for leave to proceed *in forma pauperis*, a copy of which shall precede and be attached to each copy of the brief in opposition. If the petitioner is proceeding *in forma pauperis*, the respondent may file an original and 10 copies of a brief in opposition prepared as required by Rule 33.2. Whether prepared under Rule

33.1 or Rule 33.2, the brief in opposition shall comply with the requirements of Rule 24 governing a respondent's brief, except that no summary of the argument is required. A brief in opposition may not be joined with any other pleading, except that any motion for leave to proceed *in forma pauperis* shall be attached. The brief in opposition shall be served as required by Rule 29.

4. No motion by a respondent to dismiss a petition for a writ of certiorari may be filed. Any objections to the jurisdiction of the Court to grant a petition for a writ of certiorari shall be included in the brief in opposition.

5. The Clerk will distribute the petition to the Court for its consideration upon receiving an express waiver of the right to file a brief in opposition, or, if no waiver or brief in opposition is filed, upon the expiration of the time allowed for filing. If a brief in opposition is timely filed, the Clerk will distribute the petition, brief in opposition, and any reply brief to the Court for its consideration no less than 10 days after the brief in opposition is filed.

6. Any petitioner may file a reply brief addressed to new points raised in the brief in opposition, but distribution and consideration by the Court under paragraph 5 of this Rule will not be deferred pending its receipt. Forty copies shall be filed, except that a petitioner proceeding *in forma pauperis* under Rule 39, including an inmate of an institution, shall file the number of copies required for a petition by such a person under Rule 12.2. The reply brief shall be served as required by Rule 29.

7. If a cross-petition for a writ of certiorari has been docketed, distribution of both petitions will be deferred until the cross-petition is due for distribution under this Rule.

8. Any party may file a supplemental brief at any time while a petition for a writ of certiorari is pending, calling attention to new cases, new legislation, or other intervening matter not available at the time of the party's last filing. A supplemental brief shall be restricted to new matter and shall follow, insofar as applicable, the form for a brief in opposition prescribed by this Rule. Forty copies shall be filed, except that a party proceeding *in forma pauperis* under Rule 39, including an inmate of an institution, shall file the number of copies required for a petition by such a person under Rule 12.2. The supplemental brief shall be served as required by Rule 29.

Rule 16. Disposition of a Petition for a Writ of Certiorari

1. After considering the documents distributed under Rule 15, the Court will enter an appropriate order. The order may be a summary disposition on the merits.

2. Whenever the Court grants a petition for a writ of certiorari, the Clerk will prepare, sign, and enter an order to that effect and will notify forthwith counsel of record and the court whose judgment is to be reviewed. The case then will be scheduled for briefing and oral argument. If the record has not previously been filed in this Court, the Clerk will request the clerk of the court having possession of the record to certify and transmit it. A formal writ will not issue unless specially directed.

3. Whenever the Court denies a petition for a writ of certiorari, the Clerk will prepare, sign, and enter an order to that effect and will notify forthwith counsel of record and the court whose judgment was sought to be reviewed. The order of denial will not be suspended pending disposition of a petition for rehearing except by order of the Court or a Justice.

PART IV. OTHER JURISDICTION

Rule 17. Procedure in an Original Action

1. This Rule applies only to an action invoking the Court's original jurisdiction under Article III of the Constitution of the United States. See also 28 U.S.C. § 1251 and U.S. Const., Amdt. 11. A petition for an extraordinary writ in aid of the Court's appellate jurisdiction shall be filed as provided in Rule 20.

2. The form of pleadings and motions prescribed by the Federal Rules of Civil Procedure is followed. In other respects, those Rules and the Federal Rules of Evidence may be taken as guides.

3. The initial pleading shall be preceded by a motion for leave to file, and may be accompanied by a brief in support of the motion. Forty copies of each document shall be filed, with proof of service. Service

shall be as required by Rule 29, except that when an adverse party is a State, service shall be made on both the Governor and the Attorney General of that State.

4. The case will be placed on the docket when the motion for leave to file and the initial pleading are filed with the Clerk. The Rule 38(a) docket fee shall be paid at that time.

5. No more than 60 days after receiving the motion for leave to file and the initial pleading, an adverse party shall file 40 copies of any brief in opposition to the motion, with proof of service as required by Rule 29. The Clerk will distribute the filed documents to the Court for its consideration upon receiving an express waiver of the right to file

a brief in opposition, or, if no waiver or brief is filed, upon the expiration of the time allowed for filing. If a brief in opposition is timely filed, the Clerk will distribute the filed documents to the Court for its consideration no less than 10 days after the brief in opposition is filed. A reply brief may be filed, but consideration of the case will not be deferred pending its receipt. The Court thereafter may grant or deny the motion, set it for oral argument, direct that additional documents be filed, or require that other proceedings be conducted.

6. A summons issued out of this Court shall be served on the defendant 60 days before the return day specified therein. If the defendant does not respond by the return day, the plaintiff may proceed *ex parte*.

7. Process against a State issued out of this Court shall be served on both the Governor and the Attorney General of that State.

Rule 18. Appeal from a United States District Court

1. When a direct appeal from a decision of a United States district court is authorized by law, the appeal is commenced by filing a notice of appeal with the clerk of the district court within the time provided by law after entry of the judgment sought to be reviewed. The time to file may not be extended. The notice of appeal shall specify the parties taking the appeal, designate the judgment, or part thereof, appealed from and the date of its entry, and specify the statute or statutes under which the appeal is taken. A copy of the notice of appeal shall be served on all parties to the proceeding as required by Rule 29, and proof of service shall be filed in the district court together with the notice of appeal.

2. All parties to the proceeding in the district court are deemed parties entitled to file documents in this Court, but a party having no interest in the outcome of the appeal may so notify the Clerk of this Court and shall serve a copy of the notice on all other parties. Parties interested jointly, severally, or otherwise in the judgment may appeal separately, or any two or more may join in an appeal. When two or more judgments involving identical or closely related questions are sought to be reviewed on appeal from the same court, a notice of appeal for each judgment shall be filed with the clerk of the district court, but a single jurisdictional statement covering all the judgments suffices. Parties who file no document will not qualify for any relief from this Court.

3. No more than 60 days after filing the notice of appeal in the district court, the appellant shall file 40 copies of a jurisdictional statement and shall pay the Rule 38 docket fee, except that an appellant proceeding *in forma pauperis* under Rule 39, including an inmate of an institution, shall file the number of copies required for a petition by such a person under Rule 12.2, together with a motion for leave to proceed *in forma pauperis*, a copy of which shall precede and be attached to each copy of the jurisdictional statement. The jurisdictional statement shall follow, insofar as applicable, the form for a petition for a writ of certiorari prescribed by Rule 14, and shall be served as required by Rule 29. The case will then be placed on the docket. It is the appellant's duty to notify all appellees promptly, on a form supplied by the Clerk, of the date of filing, the date the case was placed on the docket, and the docket number of the case. The notice shall be served as required by Rule 29. The appendix shall include a copy of the notice of appeal showing the date it was filed in the district court. For good cause, a Justice may extend the time to file a jurisdictional statement for a period not exceeding 60 days. An application to extend the time to file a jurisdictional statement shall set out the basis for jurisdiction in this Court; identify the judgment sought to be reviewed; include a copy of the opinion, any order respecting rehearing, and the notice of appeal; and set out specific reasons why an extension of time is justified. For the time and manner of presenting the application, see Rules 21, 22, and 30. An application to extend the time to file a jurisdictional statement is not favored.

4. No more than 30 days after a case has been placed on the docket, an appellee seeking to file a conditional cross-appeal (*i.e.*, a cross-appeal that otherwise would be untimely) shall file, with proof of service as required by Rule 29, a jurisdictional statement that complies in all respects (including number of copies filed) with paragraph 3 of this Rule, except that material already reproduced in the appendix to the opening jurisdictional statement need not be reproduced again. A cross-appealing appellee shall pay the Rule 38 docket fee or submit a motion for leave to proceed *in forma pauperis*. The cover of the cross-appeal shall indicate clearly that it is a conditional cross-appeal. The cross-appeal then will be placed on the docket. It is the cross-appellant's duty to notify all cross-appellees promptly, on a form supplied by the Clerk, of the date of filing, the date the cross-appeal was placed on the docket, and the docket number of the cross-appeal. The notice shall be served as required by Rule 29. A cross-appeal may not be joined with any other pleading, except that any motion for leave to proceed *in forma pauperis* shall be attached. The time to file a cross-appeal will not be extended.

5. After a notice of appeal has been filed in the district court, but before the case is placed on this Court's docket, the parties may dismiss the appeal by stipulation filed in the district court, or the district court may dismiss the appeal on the appellant's motion, with notice to all parties. If a notice of appeal

has been filed, but the case has not been placed on this Court's docket within the time prescribed for docketing, the district court may dismiss the appeal on the appellee's motion, with notice to all parties, and may make any just order with respect to costs. If the district court has denied the appellee's motion to dismiss the appeal, the appellee may move this Court to docket and dismiss the appeal by filing an original and 10 copies of a motion presented in conformity with Rules 21 and 33.2. The motion shall be accompanied by proof of service as required by Rule 29, and by a certificate from the clerk of the district court, certifying that a notice of appeal was filed and that the appellee's motion to dismiss was denied. The appellant may not thereafter file a jurisdictional statement without special leave of the Court, and the Court may allow costs against the appellant.

6. Within 30 days after the case is placed on this Court's docket, the appellee may file a motion to dismiss, to affirm, or in the alternative to affirm or dismiss. Forty copies of the motion shall be filed, except that an appellee proceeding *in forma pauperis* under Rule 39, including an inmate of an institution, shall file the number of copies required for a petition by such a person under Rule 12.2, together with a motion for leave to proceed *in forma pauperis*, a copy of which shall precede and be attached to each copy of the motion to dismiss, to affirm, or in the alternative to affirm or dismiss. The motion shall follow, insofar as applicable, the form for a brief in opposition prescribed by Rule 15, and shall comply in all respects with Rule 21.

7. The Clerk will distribute the jurisdictional statement to the Court for its consideration upon receiving an express waiver of the right to file a motion to dismiss or to affirm or, if no waiver or motion is filed, upon the expiration of the time allowed for filing. If a motion to dismiss or to affirm is timely filed, the Clerk will distribute the jurisdictional statement, motion, and any brief opposing the motion to the Court for its consideration no less than 10 days after the motion is filed.

8. Any appellant may file a brief opposing a motion to dismiss or to affirm, but distribution and consideration by the Court under paragraph 7 of this Rule will not be deferred pending its receipt. Forty copies shall be filed, except that an appellant proceeding *in forma pauperis* under Rule 39, including an inmate of an institution, shall file the number of copies required for a petition by such a person under Rule 12.2. The brief shall be served as required by Rule 29.

9. If a cross-appeal has been docketed, distribution of both jurisdictional statements will be deferred until the cross-appeal is due for distribution under this Rule.

10. Any party may file a supplemental brief at any time while a jurisdictional statement is pending, calling attention to new cases, new legislation, or other intervening matter not available at the time of the party's last filing. A supplemental brief shall be restricted to new matter and shall follow, insofar as applicable, the form for a brief in opposition prescribed by Rule 15. Forty copies shall be filed, except that a party proceeding *in forma pauperis* under Rule 39, including an inmate of an institution, shall file the number of copies required for a petition by such a person under Rule 12.2. The supplemental brief shall be served as required by Rule 29.

11. The clerk of the district court shall retain possession of the record until notified by the Clerk of this Court to certify and transmit it. See Rule 12.7.

12. After considering the documents distributed under this Rule, the Court may dispose summarily of the appeal on the merits, note probable jurisdiction, or postpone consideration of jurisdiction until a hearing of the case on the merits. If not disposed of summarily, the case stands for briefing and oral argument on the merits. If consideration of jurisdiction is postponed, counsel, at the outset of their briefs and at oral argument, shall address the question of jurisdiction. If the record has not previously been filed in this Court, the Clerk of this Court will request the clerk of the court in possession of the record to certify and transmit it.

13. If the Clerk determines that a jurisdictional statement submitted timely and in good faith is in a form that does not comply with this Rule or with Rule 33 or Rule 34, the Clerk will return it with a letter indicating the deficiency. If a corrected jurisdictional statement is received no more than 60 days after the date of the Clerk's letter, its filing will be deemed timely.

Rule 19. Procedure on a Certified Question

1. A United States court of appeals may certify to this Court a question or proposition of law on which it seeks instruction for the proper decision of a case. The certificate shall contain a statement of the nature of the case and the facts on which the question or proposition of law arises. Only questions or propositions of law may be certified, and they shall be stated separately and with precision. The certificate shall be prepared as required by Rule 33.2 and shall be signed by the clerk of the court of appeals.

2. When a question is certified by a United States court of appeals, this Court, on its own motion or that of a party, may consider and decide the entire matter in controversy. See 28 U.S.C. § 1254(2).

3. When a question is certified, the Clerk will notify the parties and docket the case. Counsel shall

then enter their appearances. After docketing, the Clerk will submit the certificate to the Court for a preliminary examination to determine whether the case should be briefed, set for argument, or dismissed. No brief may be filed until the preliminary examination of the certificate is completed.

4. If the Court orders the case briefed or set for argument, the parties will be notified and permitted to file briefs. The Clerk of this Court then will request the clerk of the court in possession of the record to certify and transmit it. Any portion of the record to which the parties wish to direct the Court's particular attention should be printed in a joint appendix, prepared in conformity with Rule 26 by the appellant or petitioner in the court of appeals, but the fact that any part of the record has not been printed does not prevent the parties or the Court from relying on it.

5. A brief on the merits in a case involving a certified question shall comply with Rules 24, 25, and 33.1, except that the brief for the party who is the appellant or petitioner below shall be filed within 45 days of the order requiring briefs or setting the case for argument.

Rule 20. Procedure on a Petition for an Extraordinary Writ

1. Issuance by the Court of an extraordinary writ authorized by 28 U.S.C. § 1651(a) is not a matter of right, but of discretion sparingly exercised. To justify the granting of any such writ, the petition must show that the writ will be in aid of the Court's appellate jurisdiction, that exceptional circumstances warrant the exercise of the Court's discretionary powers, and that adequate relief cannot be obtained in any other form or from any other court.

2. A petition seeking a writ authorized by 28 U.S.C. § 1651(a), § 2241, or § 2254(a) shall be prepared in all respects as required by Rules 33 and 34. The petition shall be captioned "*In re* [name of petitioner]" and shall follow, insofar as applicable, the form of a petition for a writ of certiorari prescribed by Rule 14. All contentions in support of the petition shall be included in the petition. The case will be placed on the docket when 40 copies of the petition are filed with the Clerk and the docket fee is paid, except that a petitioner proceeding *in forma pauperis* under Rule 39, including an inmate of an institution, shall file the number of copies required for a petition by such a person under Rule 12.2, together with a motion for leave to proceed *in forma pauperis*, a copy of which shall precede and be attached to each copy of the petition. The petition shall be served as required by Rule 29 (subject to subparagraph 4(b) of this Rule).

3. (a) A petition seeking a writ of prohibition, a writ of mandamus, or both in the alternative shall state the name and office or function of every person against whom relief is sought and shall set out with particularity why the relief sought is not available in any other court. A copy of the judgment with respect to which the writ is sought, including any related opinion, shall be appended to the petition together with any other document essential to understanding the petition.

(b) The petition shall be served on every party to the proceeding with respect to which relief is sought. Within 30 days after the petition is placed on the docket, a party shall file 40 copies of any brief or briefs in opposition thereto, which shall comply fully with Rule 15. If a party named as a respondent does not wish to respond to the petition, that party may so advise the Clerk and all other parties by letter. All persons served are deemed respondents for all purposes in the proceedings in this Court.

4. (a) A petition seeking a writ of habeas corpus shall comply with the requirements of 28 U.S.C. §§ 2241 and 2242, and in particular with the provision in the last paragraph of § 2242, which requires a statement of the "reasons for not making application to the district court of the district in which the applicant is held." If the relief sought is from the judgment of a state court, the petition shall set out specifically how and where the petitioner has exhausted available remedies in the state courts or otherwise comes within the provisions of 28 U.S.C. § 2254(b). To justify the granting of a writ of habeas corpus, the petitioner must show that exceptional circumstances warrant the exercise of the Court's discretionary powers, and that adequate relief cannot be obtained in any other form or from any other court. This writ is rarely granted.

(b) Habeas corpus proceedings, except in capital cases, are *ex parte*, unless the Court requires the respondent to show cause why the petition for a writ of habeas corpus should not be granted. A response, if ordered, or in a capital case, shall comply fully with Rule 15. Neither the denial of the petition, without more, nor an order of transfer to a district court under the authority of 28 U.S.C. § 2241(b), is an adjudication on the merits, and therefore does not preclude further application to another court for the relief sought.

5. The Clerk will distribute the documents to the Court for its consideration when a brief in opposition under subparagraph 3(b) of this Rule has been filed, when a response under subparagraph 4(b) has been ordered and filed, when the time to file has expired, or when the right to file has been expressly waived.

6. If the Court orders the case set for argument, the Clerk will notify the parties whether additional briefs are required, when they shall be filed, and, if the case involves a petition for a common-law writ of

certiorari, that the parties shall prepare a joint appendix in accordance with Rule 26.

PART V. MOTIONS AND APPLICATIONS

Rule 21. Motions to the Court

1. Every motion to the Court shall clearly state its purpose and the facts on which it is based and may present legal argument in support thereof. No separate brief may be filed. A motion should be concise and shall comply with any applicable page limits. Rule 22 governs an application addressed to a single Justice.

2. (a) A motion in any action within the Court's original jurisdiction shall comply with Rule 17.3.

(b) A motion to dismiss as moot (or a suggestion of mootness), a motion for leave to file a brief as *amicus curiae*, and any motion the granting of which would dispose of the entire case or would affect the final judgment to be entered (other than a motion to docket and dismiss under Rule 18.5 or a motion for voluntary dismissal under Rule 46) shall be prepared as required by Rule 33.1, and 40 copies shall be filed, except that a movant proceeding *in forma pauperis* under Rule 39, including an inmate of an institution, shall file a motion prepared as required by Rule 33.2, and shall file the number of copies required for a petition by such a person under Rule 12.2. The motion shall be served as required by Rule 29.

(c) Any other motion to the Court shall be prepared as required by Rule 33.2; the moving party shall file an original and 10 copies. The Court subsequently may order the moving party to prepare the motion as required by Rule 33.1; in that event, the party shall file 40 copies.

3. A motion to the Court shall be filed with the Clerk and shall be accompanied by proof of service as required by Rule 29. No motion may be presented in open Court, other than a motion for admission to the Bar, except when the proceeding to which it refers is being argued. Oral argument on a motion will not be permitted unless the Court so directs.

4. Any response to a motion shall be filed as promptly as possible considering the nature of the relief sought and any asserted need for emergency action, and, in any event, within 10 days of receipt, unless the Court or a Justice, or the Clerk under Rule 30.4, orders otherwise. A response to a motion prepared as required by Rule 33.1, except a response to a motion for leave to file an *amicus curiae* brief (see Rule 37.5), shall be prepared in the same manner if time permits. In an appropriate case, the Court may act on a motion without waiting for a response.

Rule 22. Applications to Individual Justices

1. An application addressed to an individual Justice shall be filed with the Clerk, who will transmit it promptly to the Justice concerned if an individual Justice has authority to grant the sought relief.

2. The original and two copies of any application addressed to an individual Justice shall be prepared as required by Rule 33.2, and shall be accompanied by proof of service as required by Rule 29.

3. An application shall be addressed to the Justice allotted to the Circuit from which the case arises. When the Circuit Justice is unavailable for any reason, the application addressed to that Justice will be distributed to the Justice then available who is next junior to the Circuit Justice; the turn of the Chief Justice follows that of the most junior Justice.

4. A Justice denying an application will note the denial thereon. Thereafter, unless action thereon is restricted by law to the Circuit Justice or is untimely under Rule 30.2, the party making an application, except in the case of an application for an extension of time, may renew it to any other Justice, subject to the provisions of this Rule. Except when the denial is without prejudice, a renewed application is not favored. Renewed application is made by a letter to the Clerk, designating the Justice to whom the application is to be directed, and accompanied by 10 copies of the original application and proof of service as required by Rule 29.

5. A Justice to whom an application for a stay or for bail is submitted may refer it to the Court for determination.

6. The Clerk will advise all parties concerned, by appropriately speedy means, of the disposition made of an application.

Rule 23. Stays

1. A stay may be granted by a Justice as permitted by law.

2. A party to a judgment sought to be reviewed may present to a Justice an application to stay the enforcement of that judgment. See 28 U.S.C. § 2101(f).

3. An application for a stay shall set out with particularity why the relief sought is not available from any other court or judge. Except in the most extraordinary circumstances, an application for a stay will not be entertained unless the relief requested was first sought in the appropriate court or courts below

or from a judge or judges thereof. An application for a stay shall identify the judgment sought to be reviewed and have appended thereto a copy of the order and opinion, if any, and a copy of the order, if any, of the court or judge below denying the relief sought, and shall set out specific reasons why a stay is justified. The form and content of an application for a stay are governed by Rules 22 and 33.2.

4. A judge, court, or Justice granting an application for a stay pending review by this Court may condition the stay on the filing of a supersedeas bond having an approved surety or sureties. The bond will be conditioned on the satisfaction of the judgment in full, together with any costs, interest, and damages for delay that may be awarded. If a part of the judgment sought to be reviewed has already been satisfied, or is otherwise secured, the bond may be conditioned on the satisfaction of the part of the judgment not otherwise secured or satisfied, together with costs, interest, and damages.

PART VI. BRIEFS ON THE MERITS AND ORAL ARGUMENT

Rule 24. Briefs on the Merits: In General

1. A brief on the merits for a petitioner or an appellant shall comply in all respects with Rules 33.1 and 34 and shall contain in the order here indicated:

(a) The questions presented for review under Rule 14.1(a). The questions shall be set out on the first page following the cover, and no other information may appear on that page. The phrasing of the questions presented need not be identical with that in the petition for a writ of certiorari or the jurisdictional statement, but the brief may not raise additional questions or change the substance of the questions already presented in those documents. At its option, however, the Court may consider a plain error not among the questions presented but evident from the record and otherwise within its jurisdiction to decide.

(b) A list of all parties to the proceeding in the court whose judgment is under review (unless the caption of the case in this Court contains the names of all parties). Any amended corporate disclosure statement as required by Rule 29.6 shall be placed here.

(c) If the brief exceeds five pages, a table of contents and a table of cited authorities.

(d) Citations of the official and unofficial reports of the opinions and orders entered in the case by courts and administrative agencies.

(e) A concise statement of the basis for jurisdiction in this Court, including the statutory provisions and time factors on which jurisdiction rests.

(f) The constitutional provisions, treaties, statutes, ordinances, and regulations involved in the case, set out verbatim with appropriate citation. If the provisions involved are lengthy, their citation alone suffices at this point, and their pertinent text, if not already set out in the petition for a writ of certiorari, jurisdictional statement, or an appendix to either document, shall be set out in an appendix to the brief.

(g) A concise statement of the case, setting out the facts material to the consideration of the questions presented, with appropriate references to the joint appendix, e.g., App. 12, or to the record, e.g., Record 12.

(h) A summary of the argument, suitably paragraphed. The summary should be a clear and concise condensation of the argument made in the body of the brief; mere repetition of the headings under which the argument is arranged is not sufficient.

(i) The argument, exhibiting clearly the points of fact and of law presented and citing the authorities and statutes relied on.

(j) A conclusion specifying with particularity the relief the party seeks.

2. A brief on the merits for a respondent or an appellee shall conform to the foregoing requirements, except that items required by subparagraphs 1(a), (b), (d), (e), (f), and (g) of this Rule need not be included unless the respondent or appellee is dissatisfied with their presentation by the opposing party.

3. A brief on the merits may not exceed the page limitations specified in Rule 33.1(g). An appendix to a brief may include only relevant material, and counsel are cautioned not to include in an appendix arguments or citations that properly belong in the body of the brief.

4. A reply brief shall conform to those portions of this Rule applicable to the brief for a respondent or an appellee, but, if appropriately divided by topical headings, need not contain a summary of the argument.

5. A reference to the joint appendix or to the record set out in any brief shall indicate the appropriate page number. If the reference is to an exhibit, the page numbers at which the exhibit appears, at which it was offered in evidence, and at which it was ruled on by the judge shall be indicated, e.g., Pl.Exh. 14, Record 199, 2134.

6. A brief shall be concise, logically arranged with proper headings, and free of irrelevant, immaterial, or scandalous matter. The Court may disregard or strike a brief that does not comply with this paragraph.

Rule 25. Briefs on the Merits: Number of Copies and Time to File

1. The petitioner or appellant shall file 40 copies of the brief on the merits within 45 days of the order granting the writ of certiorari, noting probable jurisdiction, or postponing consideration of jurisdiction. Any respondent or appellee who supports the petitioner or appellant shall meet the petitioner's or appellant's time schedule for filing documents.

2. The respondent or appellee shall file 40 copies of the brief on the merits within 35 days after the brief for the petitioner or appellant is filed.

3. The petitioner or appellant shall file 40 copies of the reply brief, if any, within 35 days after the brief for the respondent or appellee is filed, but any reply brief must actually be received by the Clerk not later than one week before the date of oral argument. Any respondent or appellee supporting the petitioner or appellant may file a reply brief.

4. The time periods stated in paragraphs 1 and 2 of this Rule may be extended as provided in Rule 30. An application to extend the time to file a brief on the merits is not favored. If a case is advanced for hearing, the time to file briefs on the merits may be abridged as circumstances require pursuant to an order of the Court on its own motion or that of a party.

5. A party wishing to present late authorities, newly enacted legislation, or other intervening matter that was not available in time to be included in a brief may file 40 copies of a supplemental brief, restricted to such new matter and otherwise presented in conformity with these Rules, up to the time the case is called for oral argument or by leave of the Court thereafter.

6. After a case has been argued or submitted, the Clerk will not file any brief, except that of a party filed by leave of the Court.

7. The Clerk will not file any brief that is not accompanied by proof of service as required by Rule 29.

(As amended Jan. 11, 1999, eff. May 3, 1999; Jan. 27, 2003, eff. May 1, 2003.)

Rule 26. Joint Appendix

1. Unless the Clerk has allowed the parties to use the deferred method described in paragraph 4 of this Rule, the petitioner or appellant, within 45 days after entry of the order granting the writ of certiorari, noting probable jurisdiction, or postponing consideration of jurisdiction, shall file 40 copies of a joint appendix, prepared as required by Rule 33.1. The joint appendix shall contain: (1) the relevant docket entries in all the courts below; (2) any relevant pleadings, jury instructions, findings, conclusions, or opinions; (3) the judgment, order, or decision under review; and (4) any other parts of the record that the parties particularly wish to bring to the Court's attention. Any of the foregoing items already reproduced in a petition for a writ of certiorari, jurisdictional statement, brief in opposition to a petition for a writ of certiorari, motion to dismiss or affirm, or any appendix to the foregoing, that was prepared as required by Rule 33.1, need not be reproduced again in the joint appendix. The petitioner or appellant shall serve three copies of the joint appendix on each of the other parties to the proceeding as required by Rule 29.

2. The parties are encouraged to agree on the contents of the joint appendix. In the absence of agreement, the petitioner or appellant, within 10 days after entry of the order granting the writ of certiorari, noting probable jurisdiction, or postponing consideration of jurisdiction, shall serve on the respondent or appellee a designation of parts of the record to be included in the joint appendix. Within 10 days after receiving the designation, a respondent or appellee who considers the parts of the record so designated insufficient shall serve on the petitioner or appellant a designation of additional parts to be included in the joint appendix, and the petitioner or appellant shall include the parts so designated. If the Court has permitted the respondent or appellee to proceed *in forma pauperis*, the petitioner or appellant may seek by motion to be excused from printing portions of the record the petitioner or appellant considers unnecessary. In making these designations, counsel should include only those materials the Court should examine; unnecessary designations should be avoided. The record is on file with the Clerk and available to the Justices, and counsel may refer in briefs and in oral argument to relevant portions of the record not included in the joint appendix.

3. When the joint appendix is filed, the petitioner or appellant immediately shall file with the Clerk a statement of the cost of printing 50 copies and shall serve a copy of the statement on each of the other parties as required by Rule 29. Unless the parties agree otherwise, the cost of producing the joint appendix shall be paid initially by the petitioner or appellant; but a petitioner or appellant who considers that parts of the record designated by the respondent or appellee are unnecessary for the determination of the issues presented may so advise the respondent or appellee, who then shall advance the cost of printing the additional parts, unless the Court or a Justice otherwise fixes the initial allocation of the costs. The

cost of printing the joint appendix is taxed as a cost in the case, but if a party unnecessarily causes matter to be included in the joint appendix or prints excessive copies, the Court may impose these costs on that party.

4. **(a)** On the parties' request, the Clerk may allow preparation of the joint appendix to be deferred until after the briefs have been filed. In that event, the petitioner or appellant shall file the joint appendix no more than 14 days after receiving the brief for the respondent or appellee. The provisions of paragraphs 1, 2, and 3 of this Rule shall be followed, except that the designations referred to therein shall be made by each party when that party's brief is served. Deferral of the joint appendix is not favored.

(b) If the deferred method is used, the briefs on the merits may refer to the pages of the record. In that event, the joint appendix shall include in brackets on each page thereof the page number of the record where that material may be found. A party wishing to refer directly to the pages of the joint appendix may serve and file copies of its brief prepared as required by Rule 33.2 within the time provided by Rule 25, with appropriate references to the pages of the record. In that event, within 10 days after the joint appendix is filed, copies of the brief prepared as required by Rule 33.1 containing references to the pages of the joint appendix in place of, or in addition to, the initial references to the pages of the record, shall be served and filed. No other change may be made in the brief as initially served and filed, except that typographical errors may be corrected.

5. The joint appendix shall be prefaced by a table of contents showing the parts of the record that it contains, in the order in which the parts are set out, with references to the pages of the joint appendix at which each part begins. The relevant docket entries shall be set out after the table of contents, followed by the other parts of the record in chronological order. When testimony contained in the reporter's transcript of proceedings is set out in the joint appendix, the page of the transcript at which the testimony appears shall be indicated in brackets immediately before the statement that is set out. Omissions in the transcript or in any other document printed in the joint appendix shall be indicated by asterisks. Immaterial formal matters (*e.g.*, captions, subscriptions, acknowledgments) shall be omitted. A question and its answer may be contained in a single paragraph.

6. Exhibits designated for inclusion in the joint appendix may be contained in a separate volume or volumes suitably indexed. The transcript of a proceeding before an administrative agency, board, commission, or officer used in an action in a district court or court of appeals is regarded as an exhibit for the purposes of this paragraph.

7. The Court, on its own motion or that of a party, may dispense with the requirement of a joint appendix and may permit a case to be heard on the original record (with such copies of the record, or relevant parts thereof, as the Court may require) or on the appendix used in the court below, if it conforms to the requirements of this Rule.

8. For good cause, the time limits specified in this Rule may be shortened or extended by the Court or a Justice, or by the Clerk under Rule 30.4.

Rule 27. Calendar

1. From time to time, the Clerk will prepare a calendar of cases ready for argument. A case ordinarily will not be called for argument less than two weeks after the brief on the merits for the respondent or appellee is due.

2. The Clerk will advise counsel when they are required to appear for oral argument and will publish a hearing list in advance of each argument session for the convenience of counsel and the information of the public.

3. The Court, on its own motion or that of a party, may order that two or more cases involving the same or related questions be argued together as one case or on such other terms as the Court may prescribe.

Rule 28. Oral Argument

1. Oral argument should emphasize and clarify the written arguments in the briefs on the merits. Counsel should assume that all Justices have read the briefs before oral argument. Oral argument read from a prepared text is not favored.

2. The petitioner or appellant shall open and may conclude the argument. A cross-writ of certiorari or cross-appeal will be argued with the initial writ of certiorari or appeal as one case in the time allowed for that one case, and the Court will advise the parties who shall open and close.

3. Unless the Court directs otherwise, each side is allowed one-half hour for argument. Counsel is not required to use all the allotted time. Any request for additional time to argue shall be presented by motion under Rule 21 no more than 15 days after the petitioner's or appellant's brief on the merits is filed, and shall set out specifically and concisely why the case cannot be presented within the half-hour limitation. Additional time is rarely accorded.

4. Only one attorney will be heard for each side, except by leave of the Court on motion filed no more than 15 days after the respondent's or appellee's brief on the merits is filed. Any request for divided argument shall be presented by motion under Rule 21 and

shall set out specifically and concisely why more than one attorney should be allowed to argue. Divided argument is not favored.

5. Regardless of the number of counsel participating in oral argument, counsel making the opening argument shall present the case fairly and completely and not reserve points of substance for rebuttal.

6. Oral argument will not be allowed on behalf of any party for whom a brief has not been filed.

7. By leave of the Court, and subject to paragraph 4 of this Rule, counsel for an *amicus curiae* whose brief has been filed as provided in Rule 37 may argue orally on the side of a party, with the consent of that party. In the absence of consent, counsel for an *amicus curiae* may seek leave of the Court to argue orally by a motion setting out specifically and concisely why oral argument would provide assistance to the Court not otherwise available. Such a motion will be granted only in the most extraordinary circumstances.

PART VII. PRACTICE AND PROCEDURE

Rule 29. Filing and Service of Documents; Special Notifications; Corporate Listing

1. Any document required or permitted to be presented to the Court or to a Justice shall be filed with the Clerk.

2. A document is timely filed if it is received by the Clerk within the time specified for filing; or if it is sent to the Clerk through the United States Postal Service by first-class mail (including express or priority mail), postage prepaid, and bears a postmark, other than a commercial postage meter label, showing that the document was mailed on or before the last day for filing; or if it is delivered on or before the last day for filing to a third-party commercial carrier for delivery to the Clerk within 3 calendar days. If submitted by an inmate confined in an institution, a document is timely filed if it is deposited in the institution's internal mail system on or before the last day for filing and is accompanied by a notarized statement or declaration in compliance with 28 U.S.C. § 1746 setting out the date of deposit and stating that first-class postage has been prepaid. If the postmark is missing or not legible, or if the third-party commercial carrier does not provide the date the document was received by the carrier, the Clerk will require the person who sent the document to submit a notarized statement or declaration in compliance with 28 U.S.C. § 1746 setting out the details of the filing and stating that the filing took place on a particular date within the permitted time.

3. Any document required by these Rules to be served may be served personally, by mail, or by third-party commercial carrier for delivery within 3 calendar days on each party to the proceeding at or before the time of filing. If the document has been prepared as required by Rule 33.1, three copies shall be served on each other party separately represented in the proceeding. If the document has been prepared as required by Rule 33.2, service of a single copy on each other separately represented party suffices. If personal service is made, it shall consist of delivery at the office of the counsel of record, either to counsel or to

an employee therein. If service is by mail or third-party commercial carrier, it shall consist of depositing the document with the United States Postal Service, with no less than first-class postage prepaid, or delivery to the carrier for delivery within 3 calendar days, addressed to counsel of record at the proper address. When a party is not represented by counsel, service shall be made on the party, personally, by mail, or by commercial carrier. Ordinarily, service on a party must be by a manner at least as expeditious as the manner used to file the document with the Court.

4. **(a)** If the United States or any federal department, office, agency, officer, or employee is a party to be served, service shall be made on the Solicitor General of the United States, Room 5614, Department of Justice, 950 Pennsylvania Ave., N.W., Washington, DC 20530-0001. When an agency of the United States that is a party is authorized by law to appear before this Court on its own behalf, or when an officer or employee of the United States is a party, the agency, officer, or employee shall be served in addition to the Solicitor General.

(b) In any proceeding in this Court in which the constitutionality of an Act of Congress is drawn into question, and neither the United States nor any federal department, office, agency, officer, or employee is a party, the initial document filed in this Court shall recite that 28 U.S.C. § 2403(a) may apply and shall be served on the Solicitor General of the United States, Room 5614, Department of Justice, 950 Pennsylvania Ave., N.W., Washington, DC 20530-0001. In such a proceeding from any court of the United States, as defined by 28 U.S.C. § 451, the initial document also shall state whether that court, pursuant to 28 U.S.C. § 2403(a), certified to the Attorney General the fact that the constitutionality of an Act of Congress was drawn into question. See Rule 14.1(e)(v).

(c) In any proceeding in this Court in which the constitutionality of any statute of a State is drawn into question, and neither the State nor any agency, officer, or employee thereof is a party, the initial document filed in this Court shall recite that 28 U.S.C.

§ 2403(b) may apply and shall be served on the Attorney General of that State. In such a proceeding from any court of the United States, as defined by 28 U.S.C. § 451, the initial document also shall state whether that court, pursuant to 28 U.S.C. § 2403(b), certified to the State Attorney General the fact that the constitutionality of a statute of that State was drawn into question. See Rule 14.1(e)(v).

5. Proof of service, when required by these Rules, shall accompany the document when it is presented to the Clerk for filing and shall be separate from it. Proof of service shall contain, or be accompanied by, a statement that all parties required to be served have been served, together with a list of the names, addresses, and telephone numbers of counsel indicating the name of the party or parties each counsel represents. It is not necessary that service on each party required to be served be made in the same manner or evidenced by the same proof. Proof of service may consist of any one of the following:

(a) an acknowledgment of service, signed by counsel of record for the party served, and bearing the address and telephone number of such counsel;

(b) a certificate of service, reciting the facts and circumstances of service in compliance with the appropriate paragraph or paragraphs of this Rule, and signed by a member of the Bar of this Court representing the party on whose behalf service is made or by an attorney appointed to represent that party under the Criminal Justice Act of 1964, see 18 U.S.C. § 3006A(d)(6), or under any other applicable federal statute; or

(c) a notarized affidavit or declaration in compliance with 28 U.S.C. § 1746, reciting the facts and circumstances of service in accordance with the appropriate paragraph or paragraphs of this Rule, whenever service is made by any person not a member of the Bar of this Court and not an attorney appointed to represent a party under the Criminal Justice Act of 1964, see 18 U.S.C. § 3006A(d)(6), or under any other applicable federal statute.

6. Every document, except a joint appendix or *amicus curiae* brief, filed by or on behalf of a nongovernmental corporation shall contain a corporate disclosure statement identifying the parent corporations and listing any publicly held company that owns 10% or more of the corporation's stock. If there is no parent or publicly held company owning 10% or more of the corporation's stock, a notation to this effect shall be included in the document. If a statement has been included in a document filed earlier in the case, reference may be made to the earlier document (except when the earlier statement appeared in a document prepared under Rule 33.2), and only amendments to the statement to make it current need be included in the document being filed.

(As amended Jan. 11, 1999, eff. May 3, 1999; Jan. 27, 2003, eff. May 1, 2003.)

Rule 30. Computation and Extension of Time

1. In the computation of any period of time prescribed or allowed by these Rules, by order of the Court, or by an applicable statute, the day of the act, event, or default from which the designated period begins to run is not included. The last day of the period shall be included, unless it is a Saturday, Sunday, federal legal holiday listed in 5 U.S.C. § 6103, or day on which the Court building is closed by order of the Court or the Chief Justice, in which event the period shall extend until the end of the next day that is not a Saturday, Sunday, federal legal holiday, or day on which the Court building is closed.

2. Whenever a Justice or the Clerk is empowered by law or these Rules to extend the time to file any document, an application seeking an extension shall be filed within the period sought to be extended. An application to extend the time to file a petition for a writ of certiorari or to file a jurisdictional statement must be filed at least 10 days before the specified final filing date as computed under these Rules; if filed less than 10 days before the final filing date, such application will not be granted except in the most extraordinary circumstances.

3. An application to extend the time to file a petition for a writ of certiorari, to file a jurisdictional statement, to file a reply brief on the merits, or to file a petition for rehearing shall be made to an individual Justice and presented and served on all other parties as provided by Rule 22. Once denied, such an application may not be renewed.

4. An application to extend the time to file any document or paper other than those specified in paragraph 3 of this Rule may be presented in the form of a letter to the Clerk setting out specific reasons why an extension of time is justified. The letter shall be served on all other parties as required by Rule 29. The application may be acted on by the Clerk in the first instance, and any party aggrieved by the Clerk's action may request that the application be submitted to a Justice or to the Court. The Clerk will report action under this paragraph to the Court as instructed.

(As amended Jan. 27, 2003, eff. May 1, 2003.)

Rule 31. Translations

Whenever any record to be transmitted to this Court contains material written in a foreign language without a translation made under the authority of the lower court, or admitted to be correct, the clerk of the court transmitting the record shall advise the Clerk of this Court immediately so that this Court may order

that a translation be supplied and, if necessary, printed as part of the joint appendix.

Rule 32. Models, Diagrams, Exhibits, and Lodgings

1. Models, diagrams, and exhibits of material forming part of the evidence taken in a case and brought to this Court for its inspection shall be placed in the custody of the Clerk at least two weeks before the case is to be heard or submitted.

2. All models, diagrams, exhibits, and other items placed in the custody of the Clerk shall be removed by the parties no more than 40 days after the case is decided. If this is not done, the Clerk will notify counsel to remove the articles forthwith. If they are not removed within a reasonable time thereafter, the Clerk will destroy them or dispose of them in any other appropriate way.

3. Any party or *amicus curiae* desiring to lodge non-record material with the Clerk must set out in a letter, served on all parties, a description of the material proposed for lodging and the reasons why the non-record material may properly be considered by the Court. The material proposed for lodging may not be submitted until and unless requested by the Clerk. (As amended Jan. 11, 1999, eff. May 3, 1999; Jan. 27, 2003, eff. May 1, 2003.)

Rule 33. Document Preparation: Booklet Format; 8½- by 11-inch Paper Format

1. **Booklet Format:** (a) Except for a document expressly permitted by these Rules to be submitted on 8½- by 11-inch paper, see, e.g., Rules 21, 22, and 39, every document filed with the Court shall be prepared in a 6⅛- by 9¼-inch booklet format using a standard typesetting process (e.g., hot metal, photocomposition, or computer typesetting) to produce text printed in typographic (as opposed to typewriter) characters. The process used must produce a clear, black image on white paper. The text must be reproduced with a clarity that equals or exceeds the output of a laser printer.

(b) The text of every booklet-format document, including any appendix thereto, shall be typeset in Roman 11-point or larger type with 2-point or more leading between lines. The typeface should be similar to that used in current volumes of the United States Reports. Increasing the amount of text by using condensed or thinner typefaces, or by reducing the space between letters, is strictly prohibited. Type size and face shall be consistent throughout. Quotations in excess of 50 words shall be indented. The typeface of footnotes shall be 9-point or larger with 2-point or more leading between lines. The text of the document must appear on both sides of the page.

(c) Every booklet-format document shall be produced on paper that is opaque, unglazed, and not less than 60 pounds in weight, and shall have margins of at least three-fourths of an inch on all sides. The text field, including footnotes, may not exceed 4⅛ by 7⅛ inches. The document shall be bound firmly in at least two places along the left margin (saddle stitch or perfect binding preferred) so as to permit easy opening, and no part of the text should be obscured by the binding. Spiral, plastic, metal, or string bindings may not be used. Copies of patent documents, except opinions, may be duplicated in such size as is necessary in a separate appendix.

(d) Every booklet-format document shall comply with the page limits shown on the chart in subparagraph 1(g) of this Rule. The page limits do not include the questions presented, the list of parties and the corporate disclosure statement, the table of contents, the table of cited authorities, or any appendix. Verbatim quotations required under Rule 14.1(f), if set out in the text of a brief rather than in the appendix, are also excluded. For good cause, the Court or a Justice may grant leave to file a document in excess of the page limits, but application for such leave is not favored. An application to exceed page limits shall comply with Rule 22 and must be received by the Clerk at least 15 days before the filing date of the document in question, except in the most extraordinary circumstances.

(e) Every booklet-format document shall have a suitable cover consisting of 65-pound weight paper in the color indicated on the chart in subparagraph 1(g) of this Rule. If a separate appendix to any document is filed, the color of its cover shall be the same as that of the cover of the document it supports. The Clerk will furnish a color chart upon request. Counsel shall ensure that there is adequate contrast between the printing and the color of the cover. A document filed by the United States, or by any other federal party represented by the Solicitor General, shall have a gray cover. A joint appendix, answer to a bill of complaint, motion for leave to intervene, and any other document not listed in subparagraph 1(g) of this Rule shall have a tan cover.

(f) Forty copies of a booklet-format document shall be filed.

(g) Page limits and cover colors for booklet-format documents are as follows:

Type of Document	Page Limits	Color of Cover
(i) Petition for a Writ of Certiorari (Rule 14); Motion for Leave to File a Bill of Complaint and Brief in Support (Rule 17.3); Jurisdictional Statement (Rule 18.3); Peti-		

Type of Document	Page Limits	Color of Cover
tion for an Extraordinary Writ (Rule 20.2)	30	white
(ii) Brief in Opposition (Rule 15.3); Brief in Opposition to Motion for Leave to File an Original Action (Rule 17.5); Motion to Dismiss or Affirm (Rule 18.6); Brief in Opposition to Mandamus or Prohibition (Rule 20.3(b)); Response to a Petition for Habeas Corpus (Rule 20.4)	30	orange
(iii) Reply to Brief in Opposition (Rules 15.6 and 17.5); Brief Opposing a Motion to Dismiss or Affirm (Rule 18.8)	10	tan
(iv) Supplemental Brief (Rules 15.8, 17, 18.10, and 25.5)	10	tan
(v) Brief on the Merits for Petitioner or Appellant (Rule 24); Exceptions by Plaintiff to Report of Special Master (Rule 17)	50	light blue
(vi) Brief on the Merits for Respondent or Appellee (Rule 24.2); Brief on the Merits for Respondent or Appellee Supporting Petitioner or Appellant (Rule 12.6); Exceptions by Party Other Than Plaintiff to Report of Special Master (Rule 17)	50	light red
(vii) Reply Brief on the Merits (Rule 24.4)	20	yellow
(viii) Reply to Plaintiff's Exceptions to Report of Special Master (Rule 17)	50	orange
(ix) Reply to Exceptions by Party Other Than Plaintiff to Report of Special Master (Rule 17)	50	yellow
(x) Brief for an Amicus Curiae at the Petition Stage (Rule 37.2)	20	cream
(xi) Brief for an Amicus Curiae in Support of the Plaintiff, Petitioner, or Appellant, or in Support of Neither Party, on the Merits or in an Original Action at the Exceptions Stage (Rule 37.3)	30	light green
(xii) Brief for an Amicus Curiae in Support of the Defendant, Respondent, or Appellee, on the Merits or in an Original Action at the Exceptions Stage (Rule 37.3)	30	dark green
(xiii) Petition for Rehearing (Rule 44)	10	tan

2. **8½– by 11–Inch Paper Format: (a)** The text of every document, including any appendix thereto, ex-

pressly permitted by these Rules to be presented to the Court on 8½– by 11–inch paper shall appear double spaced, except for indented quotations, which shall be single spaced, on opaque, unglazed, white paper. The document shall be stapled or bound at the upper left-hand corner. Copies, if required, shall be produced on the same type of paper and shall be legible. The original of any such document (except a motion to dismiss or affirm under Rule 18.6) shall be signed by the party proceeding pro se or by counsel of record who must be a member of the Bar of this Court or an attorney appointed under the Criminal Justice Act of 1964, see 18 U.S.C. § 3006A(d)(6), or under any other applicable federal statute. Subparagraph 1(g) of this Rule does not apply to documents prepared under this paragraph.

(b) Page limits for documents presented on 8½– by 11–inch paper are: 40 pages for a petition for a writ of certiorari, jurisdictional statement, petition for an extraordinary writ, brief in opposition, or motion to dismiss or affirm; and 15 pages for a reply to a brief in opposition, brief opposing a motion to dismiss or affirm, supplemental brief, or petition for rehearing. The page exclusions specified in subparagraph 1(d) of this Rule apply.
(As amended Jan. 11, 1999, eff. May 3, 1999.)

Rule 34. Document Preparation: General Requirements

Every document, whether prepared under Rule 33.1 or Rule 33.2, shall comply with the following provisions:

1. Each document shall bear on its cover, in the order indicated, from the top of the page:

(a) the docket number of the case or, if there is none, a space for one;

(b) the name of this Court;

(c) the caption of the case as appropriate in this Court;

(d) the nature of the proceeding and the name of the court from which the action is brought (*e.g.*, "On Petition for Writ of Certiorari to the United States Court of Appeals for the Fifth Circuit"; or, for a merits brief, "On Writ of Certiorari to the United States Court of Appeals for the Fifth Circuit");

(e) the title of the document (*e.g.*, "Petition for Writ of Certiorari," "Brief for Respondent," "Joint Appendix");

(f) the name of the attorney who is counsel of record for the party concerned (who must be a member of the Bar of this Court except as provided in Rule 33.2), and on whom service is to be made, with a notation directly thereunder identifying the attorney as counsel of record and setting out counsel's office address and telephone number. Only

one counsel of record may be noted on a single document. The names of other members of the Bar of this Court or of the bar of the highest court of a State acting as counsel, and, if desired, their addresses, may be added, but counsel of record shall be clearly identified. Names of persons other than attorneys admitted to a state bar may not be listed, unless the party is appearing *pro se*, in which case the party's name, address, and telephone number shall appear. The foregoing shall be displayed in an appropriate typographic manner and, except for the identification of counsel, may not be set in type smaller than standard 11–point, if the document is prepared as required by Rule 33.1.

2. Every document exceeding five pages (other than a joint appendix), whether prepared under Rule 33.1 or Rule 33.2, shall contain a table of contents and a table of cited authorities (*i.e.*, cases alphabetically arranged, constitutional provisions, statutes, treatises, and other materials) with references to the pages in the document where such authorities are cited.

3. The body of every document shall bear at its close the name of counsel of record and such other counsel, identified on the cover of the document in conformity with subparagraph 1(g) of this Rule, as may be desired.

(As amended Jan. 11, 1999, eff. May 3, 1999.)

Rule 35. Death, Substitution, and Revivor; Public Officers

1. If a party dies after the filing of a petition for a writ of certiorari to this Court, or after the filing of a notice of appeal, the authorized representative of the deceased party may appear and, on motion, be substituted as a party. If the representative does not voluntarily become a party, any other party may suggest the death on the record and, on motion, seek an order requiring the representative to become a party within a designated time. If the representative then fails to become a party, the party so moving, if a respondent or appellee, is entitled to have the petition for a writ of certiorari or the appeal dismissed, and if a petitioner or appellant, is entitled to proceed as in any other case of nonappearance by a respondent or appellee. If the substitution of a representative of the deceased is not made within six months after the death of the party, the case shall abate.

2. Whenever a case cannot be revived in the court whose judgment is sought to be reviewed, because the deceased party's authorized representative is not subject to that court's jurisdiction, proceedings will be conducted as this Court may direct.

3. When a public officer who is a party to a proceeding in this Court in an official capacity dies, resigns, or otherwise ceases to hold office, the action does not abate and any successor in office is automati-

cally substituted as a party. The parties shall notify the Clerk in writing of any such successions. Proceedings following the substitution shall be in the name of the substituted party, but any misnomer not affecting substantial rights of the parties will be disregarded.

4. A public officer who is a party to a proceeding in this Court in an official capacity may be described as a party by the officer's official title rather than by name, but the Court may require the name to be added.

(As amended Jan. 11, 1999, eff. May 3, 1999.)

Rule 36. Custody of Prisoners in Habeas Corpus Proceedings

1. Pending review in this Court of a decision in a habeas corpus proceeding commenced before a court, Justice, or judge of the United States, the person having custody of the prisoner may not transfer custody to another person unless the transfer is authorized under this Rule.

2. Upon application by a custodian, the court, Justice, or judge who entered the decision under review may authorize transfer and the substitution of a successor custodian as a party.

3. (a) Pending review of a decision failing or refusing to release a prisoner, the prisoner may be detained in the custody from which release is sought or in other appropriate custody or may be enlarged on personal recognizance or bail, as may appear appropriate to the court, Justice, or judge who entered the decision, or to the court of appeals, this Court, or a judge or Justice of either court.

(b) Pending review of a decision ordering release, the prisoner shall be enlarged on personal recognizance or bail, unless the court, Justice, or judge who entered the decision, or the court of appeals, this Court, or a judge or Justice of either court, orders otherwise.

4. An initial order respecting the custody or enlargement of the prisoner, and any recognizance or surety taken, shall continue in effect pending review in the court of appeals and in this Court unless for reasons shown to the court of appeals, this Court, or a judge or Justice of either court, the order is modified or an independent order respecting custody, enlargement, or surety is entered.

Rule 37. Brief for an Amicus Curiae

1. An *amicus curiae* brief that brings to the attention of the Court relevant matter not already brought to its attention by the parties may be of considerable help to the Court. An *amicus curiae* brief that does not serve this purpose burdens the Court, and its filing is not favored.

2. **(a)** An *amicus curiae* brief submitted before the Court's consideration of a petition for a writ of certiorari, motion for leave to file a bill of complaint, jurisdictional statement, or petition for an extraordinary writ, may be filed if accompanied by the written consent of all parties, or if the Court grants leave to file under subparagraph 2(b) of this Rule. The brief shall be submitted within the time allowed for filing a brief in opposition or for filing a motion to dismiss or affirm. The *amicus curiae* brief shall specify whether consent was granted, and its cover shall identify the party supported.

(b) When a party to the case has withheld consent, a motion for leave to file an *amicus curiae* brief before the Court's consideration of a petition for a writ of certiorari, motion for leave to file a bill of complaint, jurisdictional statement, or petition for an extraordinary writ may be presented to the Court. The motion, prepared as required by Rule 33.1 and as one document with the brief sought to be filed, shall be submitted within the time allowed for filing an *amicus curiae* brief, and shall indicate the party or parties who have withheld consent and state the nature of the movant's interest. Such a motion is not favored.

3. **(a)** An *amicus curiae* brief in a case before the Court for oral argument may be filed if accompanied by the written consent of all parties, or if the Court grants leave to file under subparagraph 3(b) of this Rule. The brief shall be submitted within the time allowed for filing the brief for the party supported, or if in support of neither party, within the time allowed for filing the petitioner's or appellant's brief. The *amicus curiae* brief shall specify whether consent was granted, and its cover shall identify the party supported or indicate whether it suggests affirmance or reversal. The Clerk will not file a reply brief for an *amicus curiae*, or a brief for an *amicus curiae* in support of, or in opposition to, a petition for rehearing.

(b) When a party to a case before the Court for oral argument has withheld consent, a motion for leave to file an *amicus curiae* brief may be presented to the Court. The motion, prepared as required by Rule 33.1 and as one document with the brief sought to be filed, shall be submitted within the time allowed for filing an *amicus curiae* brief, and shall indicate the party or parties who have withheld consent and state the nature of the movant's interest.

4. No motion for leave to file an *amicus curiae* brief is necessary if the brief is presented on behalf of the United States by the Solicitor General; on behalf of any agency of the United States allowed by law to appear before this Court when submitted by the agency's authorized legal representative; on behalf of a State, Commonwealth, Territory, or Possession when submitted by its Attorney General; or on behalf of a

city, county, town, or similar entity when submitted by its authorized law officer.

5. A brief or motion filed under this Rule shall be accompanied by proof of service as required by Rule 29, and shall comply with the applicable provisions of Rules 21, 24, and 33.1 (except that it suffices to set out in the brief the interest of the *amicus curiae*, the summary of the argument, the argument, and the conclusion). A motion for leave to file may not exceed five pages. A party served with the motion may file an objection thereto, stating concisely the reasons for withholding consent; the objection shall be prepared as required by Rule 33.2.

6. Except for briefs presented on behalf of *amicus curiae* listed in Rule 37.4, a brief filed under this Rule shall indicate whether counsel for a party authored the brief in whole or in part and shall identify every person or entity, other than the *amicus curiae*, its members, or its counsel, who made a monetary contribution to the preparation or submission of the brief. The disclosure shall be made in the first footnote on the first page of text.

Rule 38. Fees

Under 28 U.S.C. § 1911, the fees charged by the Clerk are:

(a) for docketing a case on a petition for a writ of certiorari or on appeal or for docketing any other proceeding, except a certified question or a motion to docket and dismiss an appeal under Rule 18.5, $300;

(b) for filing a petition for rehearing or a motion for leave to file a petition for rehearing, $200;

(c) for reproducing and certifying any record or paper, $1 per page; and for comparing with the original thereof any photographic reproduction of any record or paper, when furnished by the person requesting its certification, $.50 per page;

(d) for a certificate bearing the seal of the Court, $10; and

(e) for a check paid to the Court, Clerk, or Marshal that is returned for lack of funds, $35.

Rule 39. Proceedings *In Forma Pauperis*

1. A party seeking to proceed *in forma pauperis* shall file a motion for leave to do so, together with the party's notarized affidavit or declaration (in compliance with 28 U.S.C. § 1746) in the form prescribed by the Federal Rules of Appellate Procedure, Form 4. The motion shall state whether leave to proceed *in forma pauperis* was sought in any other court and, if so, whether leave was granted. If the United States district court or the United States court of appeals has appointed counsel under the Criminal Justice Act of 1964, 18 U.S.C. § 3006A, or under any other applicable federal statute, no affidavit or declaration is re-

quired, but the motion shall cite the statute under which counsel was appointed.

2. If leave to proceed *in forma pauperis* is sought for the purpose of filing a document, the motion, and an affidavit or declaration if required, shall be filed together with that document and shall comply in every respect with Rule 21. As provided in that Rule, it suffices to file an original and 10 copies, unless the party is an inmate confined in an institution and is not represented by counsel, in which case the original, alone, suffices. A copy of the motion, and affidavit or declaration if required, shall precede and be attached to each copy of the accompanying document.

3. Except when these Rules expressly provide that a document shall be prepared as required by Rule 33.1, every document presented by a party proceeding under this Rule shall be prepared as required by Rule 33.2 (unless such preparation is impossible). Every document shall be legible. While making due allowance for any case presented under this Rule by a person appearing *pro se*, the Clerk will not file any document if it does not comply with the substance of these Rules or is jurisdictionally out of time.

4. When the documents required by paragraphs 1 and 2 of this Rule are presented to the Clerk, accompanied by proof of service as required by Rule 29, they will be placed on the docket without the payment of a docket fee or any other fee.

5. The respondent or appellee in a case filed *in forma pauperis* shall respond in the same manner and within the same time as in any other case of the same nature, except that the filing of an original and 10 copies of a response prepared as required by Rule 33.2, with proof of service as required by Rule 29, suffices. The respondent or appellee may challenge the grounds for the motion for leave to proceed *in forma pauperis* in a separate document or in the response itself.

6. Whenever the Court appoints counsel for an indigent party in a case set for oral argument, the briefs on the merits submitted by that counsel, unless otherwise requested, shall be prepared under the Clerk's supervision. The Clerk also will reimburse appointed counsel for any necessary travel expenses to Washington, D.C., and return in connection with the argument.

7. In a case in which certiorari has been granted, probable jurisdiction noted, or consideration of jurisdiction postponed, this Court may appoint counsel to represent a party financially unable to afford an attorney to the extent authorized by the Criminal Justice Act of 1964, 18 U.S.C. § 3006A, or by any other applicable federal statute.

8. If satisfied that a petition for a writ of certiorari, jurisdictional statement, or petition for an extraordinary writ is frivolous or malicious, the Court may deny leave to proceed *in forma pauperis*.

(As amended Jan. 27, 2003, eff. May 1, 2003.)

Rule 40. Veterans, Seamen, and Military Cases

1. A veteran suing to establish reemployment rights under any provision of law exempting veterans from the payment of fees or court costs, may file a motion for leave to proceed on papers prepared as required by Rule 33.2. The motion shall ask leave to proceed as a veteran and be accompanied by an affidavit or declaration setting out the moving party's veteran status. A copy of the motion shall precede and be attached to each copy of the petition for a writ of certiorari or other substantive document filed by the veteran.

2. A seaman suing under 28 U.S.C. § 1916 may proceed without prepayment of fees or costs or furnishing security therefor, but is not entitled to proceed under Rule 33.2, except as authorized by the Court on separate motion under Rule 39.

3. An accused person petitioning for a writ of certiorari to review a decision of the United States Court of Appeals for the Armed Forces under 28 U.S.C. § 1259 may proceed without prepayment of fees or costs or furnishing security therefor and without filing an affidavit of indigency, but is not entitled to proceed on papers prepared as required by Rule 33.2, except as authorized by the Court on separate motion under Rule 39.

PART VIII. DISPOSITION OF CASES

Rule 41. Opinions of the Court

Opinions of the Court will be released by the Clerk immediately upon their announcement from the bench, or as the Court otherwise directs. Thereafter, the Clerk will cause the opinions to be issued in slip form, and the Reporter of Decisions will prepare them for publication in the preliminary prints and bound volumes of the United States Reports.

Rule 42. Interest and Damages

1. If a judgment for money in a civil case is affirmed, any interest allowed by law is payable from the date the judgment under review was entered. If a judgment is modified or reversed with a direction that a judgment for money be entered below, the mandate will contain instructions with respect to the allowance of interest. Interest in cases arising in a state court

is allowed at the same rate that similar judgments bear interest in the courts of the State in which judgment is directed to be entered. Interest in cases arising in a court of the United States is allowed at the interest rate authorized by law.

2. When a petition for a writ of certiorari, an appeal, or an application for other relief is frivolous, the Court may award the respondent or appellee just damages, and single or double costs under Rule 43. Damages or costs may be awarded against the petitioner, appellant, or applicant, against the party's counsel, or against both party and counsel.

Rule 43. Costs

1. If the Court affirms a judgment, the petitioner or appellant shall pay costs unless the Court otherwise orders.

2. If the Court reverses or vacates a judgment, the respondent or appellee shall pay costs unless the Court otherwise orders.

3. The Clerk's fees and the cost of printing the joint appendix are the only taxable items in this Court. The cost of the transcript of the record from the court below is also a taxable item, but shall be taxable in that court as costs in the case. The expenses of printing briefs, motions, petitions, or jurisdictional statements are not taxable.

4. In a case involving a certified question, costs are equally divided unless the Court otherwise orders, except that if the Court decides the whole matter in controversy, as permitted by Rule 19.2, costs are allowed as provided in paragraphs 1 and 2 of this Rule.

5. To the extent permitted by 28 U.S.C. § 2412, costs under this Rule are allowed for or against the United States or an officer or agent thereof, unless expressly waived or unless the Court otherwise orders.

6. When costs are allowed in this Court, the Clerk will insert an itemization of the costs in the body of the mandate or judgment sent to the court below. The prevailing side may not submit a bill of costs.

7. In extraordinary circumstances the Court may adjudge double costs.

Rule 44. Rehearing

1. Any petition for the rehearing of any judgment or decision of the Court on the merits shall be filed within 25 days after entry of the judgment or decision, unless the Court or a Justice shortens or extends the time. The petitioner shall file 40 copies of the rehearing petition and shall pay the filing fee prescribed by Rule 38(b), except that a petitioner proceeding *in forma pauperis* under Rule 39, including an inmate of an institution, shall file the number of copies required

for a petition by such a person under Rule 12.2. The petition shall state its grounds briefly and distinctly and shall be served as required by Rule 29. The petition shall be presented together with certification of counsel (or of a party unrepresented by counsel) that it is presented in good faith and not for delay; one copy of the certificate shall bear the signature of counsel (or of a party unrepresented by counsel). A copy of the certificate shall follow and be attached to each copy of the petition. A petition for rehearing is not subject to oral argument and will not be granted except by a majority of the Court, at the instance of a Justice who concurred in the judgment or decision.

2. Any petition for the rehearing of an order denying a petition for a writ of certiorari or extraordinary writ shall be filed within 25 days after the date of the order of denial and shall comply with all the form and filing requirements of paragraph 1 of this Rule, including the payment of the filing fee if required, but its grounds shall be limited to intervening circumstances of a substantial or controlling effect or to other substantial grounds not previously presented. The petition shall be presented together with certification of counsel (or of a party unrepresented by counsel) that it is restricted to the grounds specified in this paragraph and that it is presented in good faith and not for delay; one copy of the certificate shall bear the signature of counsel (or of a party unrepresented by counsel). The certificate shall be bound with each copy of the petition. The Clerk will not file a petition without a certificate. The petition is not subject to oral argument.

3. The Clerk will not file any response to a petition for rehearing unless the Court requests a response. In the absence of extraordinary circumstances, the Court will not grant a petition for rehearing without first requesting a response.

4. The Clerk will not file consecutive petitions and petitions that are out of time under this Rule.

5. The Clerk will not file any brief for an *amicus curiae* in support of, or in opposition to, a petition for rehearing.

6. If the Clerk determines that a petition for rehearing submitted timely and in good faith is in a form that does not comply with this Rule or with Rule 33 or Rule 34, the Clerk will return it with a letter indicating the deficiency. A corrected petition for rehearing received no more than 15 days after the date of the Clerk's letter will be deemed timely.

(As amended Jan. 11, 1999, eff. May 3, 1999; Jan. 27, 2003, eff. May 1, 2003.)

Rule 45. Process; Mandates

1. All process of this Court issues in the name of the President of the United States.

2. In a case on review from a state court, the mandate issues 25 days after entry of the judgment, unless the Court or a Justice shortens or extends the time, or unless the parties stipulate that it issue sooner. The filing of a petition for rehearing stays the mandate until disposition of the petition, unless the Court orders otherwise. If the petition is denied, the mandate issues forthwith.

3. In a case on review from any court of the United States, as defined by 28 U.S.C. § 451, a formal mandate does not issue unless specially directed; instead, the Clerk of this Court will send the clerk of the lower court a copy of the opinion or order of this Court and a certified copy of the judgment. The certified copy of the judgment, prepared and signed by this Court's Clerk, will provide for costs if any are awarded. In all other respects, the provisions of paragraph 2 of this Rule apply.

Rule 46. Dismissing Cases

1. At any stage of the proceedings, whenever all parties file with the Clerk an agreement in writing that a case be dismissed, specifying the terms for payment of costs, and pay to the Clerk any fees then due, the Clerk, without further reference to the Court, will enter an order of dismissal.

2. (a) A petitioner or appellant may file a motion to dismiss the case, with proof of service as required by Rule 29, tendering to the Clerk any fees due and costs payable. No more than 15 days after service thereof, an adverse party may file an objection, limited to the amount of damages and costs in this Court alleged to be payable or to showing that the moving party does not represent all petitioners or appellants. The Clerk will not file any objection not so limited.

(b) When the objection asserts that the moving party does not represent all the petitioners or appellants, the party moving for dismissal may file a reply within 10 days, after which time the matter will be submitted to the Court for its determination.

(c) If no objection is filed—or if upon objection going only to the amount of damages and costs in this Court, the party moving for dismissal tenders the additional damages and costs in full within 10 days of the demand therefor—the Clerk, without further reference to the Court, will enter an order of dismissal. If, after objection as to the amount of damages and costs in this Court, the moving party does not respond by a tender within 10 days, the Clerk will report the matter to the Court for its determination.

3. No mandate or other process will issue on a dismissal under this Rule without an order of the Court.

PART IX. DEFINITIONS AND EFFECTIVE DATE

Rule 47. Reference to "State Court" and "State Law"

The term "state court," when used in these Rules, includes the District of Columbia Court of Appeals, the Supreme Court of the Commonwealth of Puerto Rico, the courts of the Northern Mariana Islands, and the local courts of Guam. References in these Rules to the statutes of a State include the statutes of the District of Columbia, the Commonwealth of Puerto Rico, the Commonwealth of the Northern Mariana Islands, and the Territory of Guam.

(As amended Mar. 14, 2005, eff. May 2, 2005.)

Rule 48. Effective Date of Rules

1. These Rules, adopted January 27, 2003, will be effective May 1, 2003.

2. The Rules govern all proceedings after their effective date except to the extent that, in the opinion of the Court, their application to a pending matter would not be feasible or would work an injustice, in which event the former procedure applies.

TITLE 28

JUDICIARY AND JUDICIAL PROCEDURE

CONSTITUTIONAL PROVISIONS

The Constitution of the United States, Article 3, § 1, provides that: "The judicial Power of the United States, shall be vested in one supreme Court, and in such inferior Courts as the Congress may from time to time ordain and establish. The Judges, both of the supreme and inferior Courts, shall hold their Offices during good Behaviour, and shall, at stated Times, receive for their Services, a Compensation, which shall not be diminished during their Continuance in Office."

Article 2, § 2, authorizes the President of the United States to nominate and, by and with the advice and consent of the senate, to appoint judges of the supreme court, and all other officers of the United States, whose appointments are not "herein" otherwise provided for, and which shall be established by law.

Section 2 of Article 3 provides as follows: "The judicial Power shall extend to all Cases, in Law and Equity, arising under this Constitution, the Laws of the United States, and Treaties made, or which shall be made, under their Authority;—to all Cases affecting Ambassadors, other public Ministers and Consuls;—to all Cases of admiralty and maritime Jurisdiction;—to Controversies to which the United States shall be a Party;—to Controversies between two or more States;—between a State and Citizens of another State;—between Citizens of different

States,—between Citizens of the same State claiming Lands under Grants of different States, and between a State, or the Citizens thereof, and foreign States, Citizens or Subjects.

"In all Cases affecting Ambassadors, other public Ministers and Consuls, and those in which a State shall be Party, the supreme Court shall have original Jurisdiction. In all the other Cases before mentioned, the supreme Court shall have appellate Jurisdiction, both as to Law and Fact, with such Exceptions, and under such Regulations as the Congress shall make."

Section 8 of Article 1 authorizes the Congress "To constitute Tribunals inferior to the Supreme Court".

Amendment 7 provides that: "In Suits at common law, where the value in controversy shall exceed twenty dollars, the right of trial by jury shall be preserved, and no fact tried by a jury, shall be otherwise reexamined in any Court of the United States, than according to the rules of the common law."

Under Amendment 11, the "Judicial power of the United States shall not be construed to extend to any suit in law or equity, commenced or prosecuted against one of the United States by Citizens of another State, or by Citizens or Subjects of any Foreign State."

HISTORICAL AND STATUTORY NOTES

Effective and Applicability Provisions

Section 38 of Act June 25, 1948, c. 646, 62 Stat. 992, provided that: "The provisions of this Act shall take effect on Sept. 1, 1948."

Separability of Provisions

Section 34 of Act June 25, 1948, c. 646, 62 Stat. 991, provided that: "If any part of Title 28, Judiciary and Judicial Procedure, as set out in section 1 of this Act, shall be held invalid, the remainder shall not be affected thereby."

Enactment into Law; Citation

Section 1 of Act June 25, 1948, c. 646, 62 Stat. 869, provided in part: "That title 28 of the United States Code, entitled 'Judicial Code and Judiciary' is hereby revised, codified, and enacted into law, and may be cited as 'Title 28, United States Code, section ___.'"

Miscellaneous Provisions

Sections 2 to 32 of Act June 25, 1948, c. 646, 62 Stat. 985 to 991 contained certain executing provisions and conforming amendments to sections in other titles of the United States Code. For text of sections 2 to 32, see "Act June 25, 1948, c. 646, §§ 2 to 39, 62 Stat. 985 to 991," set out following the last section of Title 28.

Section 35 of Act June 25, 1948, c. 646, 62 Stat. 991, was not classified to the United States Code. For text of section 35, see "Act June 25, 1948, c. 646, §§ 2 to 39, 62 Stat. 985 to 991" set out following the last section of Title 28.

Sections 36 and 37 of Act June 25, 1948, c. 646, 62 Stat. 991, 992, contained certain executing provisions and conforming amendments to sections in other titles of the United States Code. For text of sections 36 and 37, see "Act June 25, 1948, c. 646, §§ 2 to 39, 62 Stat. 985 to 991", set out following the last section of Title 28.

Legislative Construction

Section 33 of Act June 25, 1948, c. 646, 62 Stat. 991, provided that: "No inference of a legislative construction is to be drawn by reason of the chapter in Title 28, Judiciary and Judicial Procedure, as set out in section 1 of this Act, in which any section is placed, nor by reason of the catchlines used in such title."

Repeals; Rights and Liabilities Saved

Section 39 of Act June 25, 1948, c. 646, 62 Stat. 992, repealed the sections or parts thereof of the Revised Statutes of the United States, Statutes at Large, or the Revised Statutes of the District of Columbia covering provisions codified in this title, but saved any rights or liabilities then existing under said sections or parts thereof.

Writs of Error

Act Jan. 31, 1928, c. 14, § 1, 45 Stat. 54 [section 861a of former Title 28, Judicial Code and Judiciary], provided that: "The writ of error in cases, civil and criminal, is abolished. All relief which heretofore [Jan. 31, 1928] could be obtained by writ of error shall hereafter be obtainable by appeal." This provision was omitted from the 1948 Revised Judicial Code as obsolete, and repealed by Act June 25, 1948, c. 646, § 39, 62 Stat. 992.

R.S. § 1012 as affected by Act Mar. 3, 1911, c. 231, § 291, 36 Stat. 1167 [Section 880 of former Title 28, Judicial Code and Judiciary], provided that appeals from district courts shall be subject to the same rules, regulations, and restrictions as are or may be prescribed in law in cases of writs of error. This provision was repealed by Act June 25, 1948, c. 646, § 39, 62 Stat. 992. Section 2 of Act Jan. 31, 1928, c. 14, 45 Stat. 54, as amended Apr. 26, 1928, c. 440, 45 Stat. 466; June 25, 1948, c. 646, § 23, 62 Stat. 990 [section 861b of former Title 28, Judicial Code and Judiciary], provided that: "All Acts of Congress referring to writs of error shall be construed as amended to the extent necessary to substitute appeal for writ of error."

Title 28 as Continuation of Existing Law; Change of Name of Circuit Courts of Appeals

Section 2(b) of Act June 25, 1948, c. 646, 62 Stat. 985, provided that: "The provisions of Title 28, Judiciary and Judicial Procedure, of the United States Code, set out in section 1 of this Act, with respect to the organization of each of the several courts therein provided for and of the Administrative Office of the United States Courts, shall be construed as continuations of existing law, and the tenure of the judges, officers, and employees thereof and of the United States attorneys and marshals and their deputies and assistants, in office on the effective date of this Act [Sept. 1, 1948], shall not be affected by its enactment, but each of them shall continue to serve in the same capacity under the appropriate provisions of title 28, as set out in section 1 of this Act, pursuant to his prior appointment: Provided, however, That each circuit court of appeals shall, as in said title 28 set out, hereafter be known as a United States court of appeals. No loss of rights, interruption of jurisdiction, or prejudice to matters pending in any of such courts on the effective date of this Act shall result from its enactment."

PART I—ORGANIZATION OF COURTS

HISTORICAL AND STATUTORY NOTES

Codifications

Analysis of chapters comprising Part I was amended by Pub.L. 95–598, Title II, § 201(b), Nov. 6, 1978, 92 Stat. 2660, effective June 28, 1984, pursuant to Pub.L. 95–598, Title IV, § 402(b), Nov. 6, 1978, 92 Stat. 2682, as amended by Pub.L. 98–249, § 1(a), Mar. 31, 1984, 98 Stat. 116; Pub.L. 98–271, § 1(a), Apr. 30, 1984, 98 Stat. 163; Pub.L. 98–299, § 1(a), May 25, 1984, 98 Stat. 214; Pub.L. 98–325, § 1(a), June 20, 1984, 98 Stat. 268, by adding:

Section 402(b) of Pub.L. 95–598 was amended by section 113 of Pub.L. 98–353, Title I, July 10, 1984, 98 Stat. 343, by substituting "shall not be effective" for "shall take effect on June 28, 1984", thereby eliminating the amendment by section 201(b) of Pub.L. 95–598, effective June 27, 1984, pursuant to section 122(c) of Pub.L. 98–353, set out as an Effective Date note under section 151 of the title.

Section 121(a) of Pub.L. 98–353 directed that section 402(b) of Pub.L. 95–598 be amended by substituting "the date of enactment of the Bankruptcy Amendments and Federal Judgeship Act of 1984 [i.e. July 10, 1984]" for "June 28, 1984". This amendment was not executed in view of the prior amendment to section 402(b) of Pub.L. 95–598 by section 113 of Pub.L. 98–353.

Change of Name

References to United States Claims Court deemed to refer to United States Court of Federal Claims and references to Claims Court deemed to refer to Court of Federal Claims, see section 902(b) of Pub.L. 102–572, set out as a note under section 171 of Title 28, Judiciary and Judicial Procedure.

CHAPTER 1—SUPREME COURT

§ 1. Number of justices; quorum

The Supreme Court of the United States shall consist of a Chief Justice of the United States and eight associate justices, any six of whom shall constitute a quorum.

(June 25, 1948, c. 646, 62 Stat. 869.)

HISTORICAL AND STATUTORY NOTES

Short Title

2005 Amendments

Pub.L. 109–63, § 1, Sept. 9, 2005, 119 Stat. 1993, provided that: "This Act [amending 28 U.S.C.A. §§ 48, 141, 152, and 636] may be cited as the 'Federal Judiciary Emergency Special Sessions Act of 2005'."

Pub.L. 109–8, Title XII, § 1223(a), April 20, 2005, 119 Stat. 196, provided that: "This section [amending 28 U.S.C.A. § 152 and enacting provisions set out as notes under 28 U.S.C.A. § 152] may be cited as the 'Bankruptcy Judgeship Act of 2005'."

Pub.L. 109–2, § 1(a), Feb. 18, 2005, 119 Stat. 4, provided that: "This Act [enacting 28 U.S.C.A. § 1453 and chapter 114 of this title, 28 U.S.C.A. § 1711 et seq., amending 28

U.S.C.A. §§ 1332, 1335, and 1603, and enacting provisions set out as notes under 28 U.S.C.A. §§ 1332, 1711, 2071, and 2074] may be cited as the 'Class Action Fairness Act of 2005'."

2002 Amendments

Pub.L. 107–273, Div. C, Title I, § 11020(a), Nov. 2, 2002, 116 Stat. 1826, provided that: "This section [enacting 28 U.S.C.A. §§ 1369, 1697, and 1785, amending 28 U.S.C.A. §§ 1391 and 1441, and enacting provisions set out as a note under 28 U.S.C.A. § 1369] may be cited as the 'Multiparty, Multiforum Trial Jurisdiction Act of 2002'."

Pub.L. 107–273, Div. C, Title I, § 11041, Nov. 2, 2002, 116 Stat. 1848, provided that: "This subtitle [Pub.L. 107–273, Div. C, Title I, Subtitle C, §§ 11041 to 11044, Nov. 2, 2002, 116 Stat. 1848, enacting chapter 16 of this title (28 U.S.C.A. § 351 et seq.), amending 28 U.S.C.A. §§ 331, 332, 372, 375, and 604, and 38 U.S.C.A. § 7253, and enacting provisions set out as a note under 28 U.S.C.A. § 351] may be cited as the 'Judicial Improvements Act of 2002'."

2000 Amendments

Pub.L. 106–518, § 1(a), Nov. 13, 2000, 114 Stat. 2410, provided that: "This Act [enacting sections 179 and 613 of this title and provisions set out as notes under sections 613, 996 and 1931 of this title, amending sections 117, 175, 332, 371, 376, 604, 611, 612, 627, 631, 636, 797, 996, 1865, 1930, and 2671 of this title, sections 3102 and 5551 of Title 5, section 1228 of Title 11, sections 3006A and 3401 of Title 18, and section 13n of Title 40, and provisions set out as notes under sections 471, 581, and 1931 of this title, and repealing 2520 of

this title] may be cited as the 'Federal Courts Improvement Act of 2000'."

1998 Amendments

Pub.L. 105–315, § 1, Oct. 30, 1998, 112 Stat. 2993, provided that: "This Act [amending sections 651 to 658 of this title, enacting a provision set out as a note under section 651 of this title, and amending a provision set out as a note under section 652 of this title] may be cited as the 'Alternative Dispute Resolution Act of 1998'."

1996 Amendments

Pub.L. 104–317, § 1(a), Oct. 19, 1996, 110 Stat. 3847, provided that: "This Act [enacting sections 258 and 1932 of this title, amending sections 112, 125, 134, 253, 331, 332, 371, 376, 601, 621, 627, 636, 753, 954, 1332, 1404, 1406, 1442, 1446, 1827, 1914, 1931, 1963, and 2511 of this title, sections 3154, 3401, and 3603 of Title 18, Crimes and Criminal Procedure, sections 1983 and 1988 of Title 42, The Public Health and Welfare, and sections 719, 743, 745, 1104, and 1105 of Title 45, Railroads, enacting provisions set out as notes under sections 258, 1332, 1404, 1827, 1914, 1931, and 2412 of this title and section 719 of Title 45, and amending provisions set out as notes under sections 133, 152, 471, and 1913 of this title] may be cited as the 'Federal Courts Improvement Act of 1996'."

1994 Amendments

Pub.L. 103–420, § 1, Oct. 25, 1994, 108 Stat. 4343, provided that: "This Act [amending section 612 of this title, amending provisions set out as notes under sections 471 and 651 of this title, and repealing a provision set out as a note under section 651 of this title] may be cited as the 'Judicial Amendments Act of 1994'."

Pub.L. 103–383, § 1, Oct. 20, 1994, 108 Stat. 4063 provided that: "This Act [enacting section 1738B of this title and a provision set out as a note under section 1738B of this title] may be cited as the 'Full Faith and Credit for Child Support Orders Act'."

Pub.L. 103–270, § 1, June 30, 1994, 108 Stat. 732, provided that: "This Act [amending sections 591 through 596 and 599 of this title and enacting provisions set out as notes under section 591 of this title and section 113 of Title 3, The President] may be cited as the 'Independent Counsel Reauthorization Act of 1994'."

1992 Amendments

Pub.L. 102–572, § 1, Oct. 29, 1992, 106 Stat. 4506, provided that: "This Act [Pub.L. 102–572, Oct. 29, 1992, 106 Stat. 4506, for classifications to which see Tables] may be cited as the 'Federal Courts Administration Act of 1992'."

Pub.L. 102–572, Title IX, § 901, Oct. 29, 1992, 106 Stat. 4516, provided that: "This title [Title IX of Pub.L. 102–572, Oct. 29, 1992, 106 Stat. 4516, for classifications to which see Tables] may be cited as the 'Court of Federal Claims Technical and Procedural Improvements Act of 1992'."

Pub.L. 102–559, § 1, Oct. 28, 1992, 106 Stat. 4227, provided that: "This Act [enacting chapter 178 of this title and provisions set out as a note under section 3701 of this title] may be cited as the 'Professional and Amateur Sports Protection Act'."

Pub.L. 102–417, § 1, Oct. 14, 1992, 106 Stat. 2138, provided that: "This Act [amending section 1821 of this title and enacting provisions set out as a note under section 1821 of this title] may be cited as the 'Incarcerated Witness Fees Act of 1991'."

Pub.L. 102–361, § 1, Aug. 26, 1992, 106 Stat. 965, provided that: "This Act [amending section 152 of this title and enacting provisions set out as a note under section 152 of this title] may be cited as the 'Bankruptcy Judgeship Act of 1992'."

1990 Amendments

Pub.L. 101–650, § 1, Dec. 1, 1990, 104 Stat. 5089, provided: "That this Act [enacting sections 178, 471 to 482, 1367, and 1658 of this title, section 8440b of Title 5, Government Organization and Employees, sections 106A and 120 of Title 17, Copyrights, and section 404c of Title 47, Telegraphs, Telephones, and Radiotelegraphs, amending sections 44, 108, 112, 122, 133, 152, 332, 333, 372, 375, 376, 377, 453, 601, 602, 604, 631, 636, 995, 996, 1334, 1391, 1441, 1452, 1499, 1605, 1610, 1821, 1871, 2072, and 2077 of this title, sections 8331, 8334, 8336, 8339, and 8402 of Title 5, section 104 of Appendix 6 to Title 5, section 502 of Appendix 7 to Title 5, section 305 of Title 11, Bankruptcy, and sections 101, 102, 106, 107, 109, 113, 301, 411, 412, 501, and 506 of Title 17, enacting provisions set out as notes under sections 1, 44, 133, 331, 332, 372, 376, 471, 620, 631, 1367, and 1658 of this title, section 8331 of Title 5, section 307 of Title 11, sections 101, 106A, 109, and 205 of Title 17, and sections 3006A and 3551 of Title 18, Crimes and Criminal Procedure, and amending provisions set out as notes under sections 533 and 581 of this title] may be cited as the 'Judicial Improvements Act of 1990'."

Pub.L. 101–650, Title I, § 101, Dec. 1, 1990, 104 Stat. 5089, provided that: "This title [enacting section 471 to 482 of this title and provisions set out as notes under section 471 of this title] may be cited as the 'Civil Justice Reform Act of 1990'."

Pub.L. 101–650, Title II, § 201, Dec. 1, 1990, 104 Stat. 5098, provided that: "This title [amending sections 44 and 133 of this title and enacting provisions set out as notes under sections 44, 133, and 331 of this title] may be cited as the 'Federal Judgeship Act of 1990'."

Pub.L. 101–650, Title III, § 301, Dec. 1, 1990, 104 Stat. 5104, provided that: "This title [enacting sections 178, 1367, and 1658 of this title and section 8440b of Title 5, Government Organization and Employees, amending sections 108, 112, 122, 133, 152, 158, 332, 333, 375, 376, 377, 601, 602, 604, 631, 636, 995, 996, 1334, 1391, 1441, 1452, 1499, 1605, 1610, 1821, 1871, and 2072 of this title, sections 8331, 8334, 8336, 8339, and 8402 of Title 5, section 502 of Appendix 7 to Title 5, and section 305 of Title 11, Bankruptcy, enacting provisions set out as notes under sections 376, 620, 631, 1367, and 1658 of this title, sections 8331 of Title 5, section 307 of Title 11, and sections 3006A and 3551 of Title 18, Crimes and Criminal Procedure, and amending provisions set out as notes under sections 533 and 581 of this title] may be cited as the 'Federal Courts Study Committee Implementation Act of 1990'."

Pub.L. 101–650, Title IV, § 401, Dec. 1, 1990, 104 Stat. 5122, provided that: "This title [amending sections 332, 372, 453, and 2077 of this title and section 104 of Appendix 6 to Title 5, Government Organization and Employees, and enacting provisions set out as notes under sections 332 and 372 of this title] may be cited as the 'Judicial Discipline and Removal Reform Act of 1990'."

Pub.L. 101–647, Title XXXVI, § 3601, Nov. 29, 1990, 104 Stat. 4933, provided that: "This title [enacting section 2044

and chapter 176 (section 3001 et seq.) of this title, amending sections 550, 1962, 1963 and 2410 of this title, section 523 of Title 11, Bankruptcy, and sections 3142 and 3552 of Title 18, Crimes and Criminal Procedure, and enacting provisions set out as a note under section 3001 of this title] may be cited as the 'Federal Debt Collection Procedures Act of 1990'."

1988 Amendments

Pub. L. 100–702, § 1, Nov. 19, 1988, 102 Stat. 4642, provided that: "This Act [enacting chapter 44 (§§ 651 to 658) and sections 297, 1878, and 2072 to 2074 of this title, 5 U.S.C.A. § 5584, and 9 U.S.C.A. § 15, amending sections 89, 153, 156, 172, 331, 332, 371, 372, 376, 455, 462, 604, 611, 620, 623, 624, 626, 627, 629, 631, 634, 636, 712, 752, 794, 1292, 1295, 1332, 1338, 1391, 1400, 1441, 1446, 1447, 1498, 1827, 1863, 1864, 1865, 1866, 1869, 1963, 2071, 2072, 2077, and 2520 of this title, 5 U.S.C.A. § 5108, 16 U.S.C.A. § 460n–8, 17 U.S.C.A. § 912, 18 U.S.C.A. § 3402, and 42 U.S.C.A. §§ 10702, 10704, 10705, 10706, and 10708, repealing chapter 44 (§§ 651 to 658) and sections 1393, 1963A, 2072, and 2076 of this title, 18 U.S.C.A. §§ 3771 and 3772, and enacting provisions set out as notes under sections 1, 89, 153, 331, 371, 376, 611, 626, 651, 652, 1292, 1332, 1391, 1393, 1827, 1963, 2071, and 2520 of this title and 5 U.S.C.A. § 5584] may be cited as the 'Judicial Improvements and Access to Justice Act'."

Pub. L. 100–702, Title VII, § 701, Nov. 19, 1988, 102 Stat. 4654, provided that: "This title [amending section 1827(a) to (e), (g) to (k) of this title and enacting provisions set out as notes under section 1827 of this title] may be cited as the 'Court Interpreter Amendments Act of 1988'."

Pub. L. 100–694, § 1, Nov. 18, 1988, 102 Stat. 4563, provided that: "This Act [enacting 16 U.S.C.A. § 831c–2, amending sections 2671, 2674, and 2679(b), (d) of this title, and enacting provisions set out as notes under sections 2671 and 2679 of this title] may be cited as the 'Federal Employees Liability Reform and Tort Compensation Act of 1988'."

Pub. L. 100–659, § 1, Nov. 15, 1988, 102 Stat. 3910, provided that: "This Act [which enacted section 377 of this title and section 8440a of Title 5, Government Organization and Employees, amended sections 155, 375, 376, 604, 631, and 636 of this title and sections 8334 and 8402 of Title 5 and enacted provisions set out as notes under sections 376 and 377 of this title] may be cited as the 'Retirement and Survivors' Annuities for Bankruptcy Judges and Magistrates Act of 1988'."

1987 Amendments

Pub.L. 100–191, § 1, Dec. 15, 1987, 101 Stat. 1293, provided that: "This Act [enacting section 599 of this title, amending sections 49 and 591 to 598 of this title, sections 203 and 205 of the Ethics in Government Act of 1978, set out in Appendix 4 to Title 5, Government Organization and Employees, and section 202 of Title 18, Crimes and Criminal Procedure, and enacting provisions set out as a note under section 591 of this title and amending provisions set out as a note under section 591 of this title] may be cited as the 'Independent Counsel Reauthorization Act of 1987'."

1986 Amendments

Pub.L. 99–657, § 1, Nov. 14, 1986, 100 Stat. 3670, provided that: "This Act [amending sections 90 and 121 of this title, and enacting provisions set out as a note under section 121 of this title] may be cited as the 'Judicial Housekeeping Act of 1986'."

Pub.L. 99–570, Title I, § 1151, Oct. 27, 1986, 100 Stat. 3207–12, provided that: "This subtitle [subtitle b

(§§ 1151–1153) of Title 1 of amending section 524 of this title, section 1963 of Title 18, Crimes and Criminal Procedure, section 1613a of Title 19, Customs Duties, and section 853 of Title 21, Food and Drugs, and repealing section 1613b of Title 19] may be cited as the 'Department of Justice Assets Forfeiture Fund Amendments Act of 1986'."

Pub.L. 99–363, § 1, July 11, 1986, 100 Stat. 770, provided that: "This Act [amending section 994 of this title] may be cited as the 'Sentencing Guidelines Act of 1986'."

Pub.L. 99–336, § 1, June 19, 1986, 100 Stat. 633, provided that: "This Act [amending sections 376, 620, 1441, 1914, and 2342 of this title, section 288d of Title 2, The Congress, and sections 8706, 8714a, 8714b, and 8714c of Title 5, Government Organization and Employees, and enacting provisions set out as notes under sections 376, 620, 1441, 1914, and 2342 of this title and section 8706 of Title 5] may be cited as the 'Judicial Improvements Act of 1985'."

1984 Amendments

Pub.L. 98–620, Title IV, § 404, Nov. 8, 1984, 98 Stat. 3361, provided that: "This subtitle [subtitle B (sections 404 to 411) of Title IV of Pub.L. 98–620, which amended sections 85, 90, 93, 112, 124, and 126 of this title and enacted provisions set out as notes under sections 85, 90, 93 and 124 of this title] may be cited as the 'Federal District Court Organization Act of 1984'."

Pub.L. 98–620, Title IV, preceding § 412, Nov. 8, 1984, 98 Stat. 3362, provided that: "This subtitle [subtitle C (sections 412 to 416) of Title IV of Pub.L. 98–620, enacting section 798 of this title, amending section 1292 of this title, section 1071 of Title 15, Commerce and Trade, section 1337 of Title 19, Customs Duties, and sections 142 to 144 of Title 35, Patents, and enacting provisions set out as notes under section 713 of this title and section 142 of Title 35] may be cited as the 'Technical Amendments to the Federal Courts Improvement Act of 1982'."

For short title of Pub.L. 98–353, July 10, 1984, 98 Stat. 333 as the "Bankruptcy Amendments and Federal Judgeship Act of 1984", see Short Title of 1984 Amendments note set out under section 151 of this title.

1983 Amendments

Pub.L. 97–409, § 1, Jan. 3, 1983, 96 Stat. 2039, provided: "That this Act [amending sections 49, 591 to 598 of this title and amending provisions set out as a note under section 591 of this title] may be cited as the 'Ethics in Government Act Amendments of 1982'."

1982 Amendments

For provisions authorizing the citation of sections 2–6 of Pub.L. 97–394 as the Indian Claims Limitation Act of 1982, see section 1 of Pub.L. 97–394, as amended, set out as a note under section 2415 of this title.

Pub.L. 97–292, § 1, Oct. 12, 1982, 96 Stat. 1259, provided: "That this Act [amending section 534 of this title] may be cited as the 'Missing Children Act'."

Pub.L. 97–164, § 1, Apr. 2, 1982, 96 Stat. 25, provided: "That this Act [enacting sections 176, 177, 462, 463, 714, 715, 1295, 1296, 1631, 2077, and 2522 of this title, amending sections 41, 44, 45, 46, 48, 136, 160, 171 to 175, 256, 291, 292, 293, 331, 372, 451, 456, 460, 518, 520, 605, 610, 713, 753, 791, 794 to 797, 957, 1291, 1292, 1294, 1336, 1346, 1398, 1402, 1406, 1491, 1492, 1494 to 1503, 1505, 1507, 1926, 1961, 2342, 2411, 2501 to 2517, 2519, 2520, and 2645 of this title, section 308

and rule 1101 in the Appendix to this title, section 356 of Title 2, The Congress, sections 7703, 8332, 8334, 8715, and 8912 of Title 5, Government Organization and Employees, section 2461 of Title 7, Agriculture, section 2273 of Title 10, Armed Forces, sections 714b, 1071, 1121, and 2210 of Title 15, Commerce and Trade, section 831s of Title 16, Conservation, sections 204, 3006A, and 6001 of Title 18, Crimes and Criminal Procedure, sections 1337, 1516, 1516a, 1528, and 2395 of Title 19, Customs Duties, sections 1642b and 2356 of Title 22, Foreign Relations and Intercourse, sections 70v–3, 119, 475a, 652, 1401, and 1402 of Title 25, Indians, sections 6110, 7422, 7428, 7456, and 7482 of Title 26, Internal Revenue Code, section 193a of Title 30, Mineral Lands and Mining, sections 72 and 724a of Title 31, Money and Finance, sections 1321 and 1479 of Title 33, Navigation and Navigable Waters, sections 141 to 146, 183, and 282 of Title 35, Patents, section 330 of Title 40, Public Buildings, Property, and Works, sections 113, 114, 607, and 609 of Title 41, Public Contracts, sections 2182, 2221, 2223, and 2475 of Title 42, The Public Health and Welfare, sections 713, 906, and 1103 of Title 44, Public Printing and Documents, section 87 of Title 45, Railroads, and sections 42, 1213, 1215, 1216, 1218, 1218a, 1224, and 1984 of the Appendix to Title 50, War and National Defense, repealing sections 142, 211 to 216, 415, 792, 831 to 834, 1255, 1256, 1504, 1506, 1541 to 1546, 1584, 2110, 2353, 2518, and 2601–2604 of this title, and enacting provisions set out as notes under sections 44, 45, 171, and 753 of this title, section 7456 of Title 26, and section 3006A of Title 18] may be cited as the 'Federal Courts Improvement Act of 1982'."

1980 Amendments

Pub.L. 96–486, § 1, Dec. 1, 1980, 94 Stat. 2369, provided: "That this Act [amending section 1331 of this title and section 2072 of Title 15, Commerce and Trade, and enacting provisions set out as a note under section 1331 of this title] may be cited as the 'Federal Question Jurisdictional Amendments Act of 1980'."

Pub.L. 96–462, § 1, Oct. 15, 1980, 94 Stat. 2053, provided that: "This Act [amending sections 84, 95, 105, 113, and 124 of this title, and enacting provisions set out as notes under sections 84, 95, 105, and 113 of this title] may be cited as the 'Federal District Court Organization Act of 1980'."

Pub.L. 96–458, § 1, Oct. 15, 1980, 94 Stat. 2035, provided that: "This Act [amending sections 331, 332, 372, and 604 of this title, and enacting provisions set out as notes under section 331 of this title] may be cited as the 'Judicial Councils Reform and Judicial Conduct and Disability Act of 1980'."

Pub.L. 96–452, § 1, Oct. 14, 1980, 94 Stat. 1994, provided: "That this Act [amending sections 41, 44 and 48 of this title, and enacting provisions set out as notes under section 41 of this title] may be cited as the 'Fifth Circuit Court of Appeals Reorganization Act of 1980'."

Pub.L. 96–417, § 1, Oct. 10, 1980, 94 Stat. 1727, provided: "That this Act [which enacted sections 1546, 1581 to 1585, 1876, 1963A, 2603, 2604, and 2631 to 2647 of this title and section 2395 of Title 19, Customs Duties; amended sections 251 to 255, 257, 292, 293, 372, 451, 456, 518, 569, 605, 610, 751, 871 to 873, 1337, 1340, 1352, 1355, 1356, 1491, 1541, 1543, 1862, 1919, 2414, 2601, and 2602 of this title and section 308 of Pub.L. 95–521 in the Appendix of this title, section 791 of Title 16, Conservation, section 6001 of Title 18, Crimes and Criminal Procedure, sections 1305, 1337, 1502, 1503, 1514 to 1516a, 1528, 1592, 1604, and 1641 of Title 19, Customs Duties, section 7443 of Title 26, Internal Revenue Code, and section

906 of Title 44, Public Printing and Documents; repealed sections 405a and 2322 of Title 19, Customs Duties; omitted former sections 1581, 1582, and 2631 to 2639 of this title; and enacted provisions set out as notes under section 251 of this title] may be cited as the 'Customs Courts Act of 1980'."

1979 Amendments

For short title of Pub.L. 96–82, as the "Federal Magistrate Act of 1979", see section 1 of Pub.L. 96–82, set out as a note under section 631 of this title.

1978 Amendments

For short title of Pub.L. 95–572 as the "Jury System Improvements Act of 1978", see section 1 of Pub.L. 95–572, set out as a note under section 1861 of this title.

Pub.L. 95–539, § 1, Oct. 28, 1978, 92 Stat. 2040, provided: "That this Act [enacting sections 1827 and 1828 of this title, amending sections 602 to 604 and 1920 of this title, enacting provisions set out as notes under section 602 of this title, and repealing a provision set out as a note under section 602 of this title] may be cited as the 'Court Interpreters Act'."

Pub.L. 95–408, § 1, Oct. 2, 1978, 92 Stat. 883, provided that: "This Act [amending sections 89, 93, 97, 98, 104, 112, 114, 133 of this title and enacting provisions set out as a note under section 89 of this title] may be cited as the 'Federal District Court Organization Act of 1978'."

1976 Amendments

Pub.L. 94–583, § 1, Oct. 21, 1976, 90 Stat. 2891, provided: "That this Act [enacting sections 1330 and 1602 to 1611 of this title, amending sections 1332, 1391, and 1441 of this title, and enacting provisions set out as notes under section 1602 of this title] may be cited as the 'Foreign Sovereign Immunities Act of 1976'."

Pub.L. 94–554, § 1, Oct. 19, 1976, 90 Stat. 2603, provided: "That this Act [amending this section, and enacting provisions set out as notes under section 376 of this title] may be cited as the 'Judicial Survivors' Annuities Reform Act'."

1970 Amendments

Pub.L. 91–271, Title I, § 101, June 2, 1970, 84 Stat. 274, provided that: "This title [enacting sections 256 and 257 of this title, amending sections 253 to 255, 1541, 1582, 2601, 2602, and 2631 to 2639 of this title, repealing sections 1583 and 2640 to 2642 of this title, and enacting provisions set out as notes under sections 1 and 256 of this title] may be cited as 'The Customs Courts Act of 1970'."

1966 Amendments

Pub.L. 89–504, Title II, § 201, July 18, 1966, 80 Stat. 293, provided that: "This title [enacting provisions set out as notes under sections 603, 604, and 753 of this title] may be cited as the 'Federal Judicial Salary Act of 1966'."

1964 Acts

Pub.L. 88–426, Title IV, § 401, Aug. 14, 1964, 78 Stat. 433, provided that: "This title [amending this section and sections 44, 135, 173, 213, 252, 603 and 792 of this title, section 867 of Title 10, Armed Forces, section 68 of former Title 11, Bankruptcy, and section 7443 of Title 26, Internal Revenue Code, and enacting provisions set out as notes under sections 603, 604 and 753 of this title] may be cited as the 'Federal Judicial Salary Act of 1964'."

Gifts to the United States Supreme Court

Pub.L. 108–356, § 3, Oct. 21, 2004, 118 Stat. 1416, provided that: "The Chief Justice or his designee is authorized to accept, hold, administer, and utilize gifts and bequests of personal property pertaining to the history of the United States Supreme Court or its justices, but gifts or bequests of money shall be covered into the Treasury."

§ 2. Terms of court

The Supreme Court shall hold at the seat of government a term of court commencing on the first Monday in October of each year and may hold such adjourned or special terms as may be necessary.

(June 25, 1948, c. 646, 62 Stat. 869.)

§ 3. Vacancy in office of Chief Justice; disability

Whenever the Chief Justice is unable to perform the duties of his office or the office is vacant, his powers and duties shall devolve upon the associate justice next in precedence who is able to act, until such disability is removed or another Chief Justice is appointed and duly qualified.

(June 25, 1948, c. 646, 62 Stat. 869.)

§ 4. Precedence of associate justices

Associate justices shall have precedence according to the seniority of their commissions. Justices whose commissions bear the same date shall have precedence according to seniority in age.

(June 25, 1948, c. 646, 62 Stat. 869.)

§ 5. Salaries of justices

The Chief Justice and each associate justice shall each receive a salary at annual rates determined under section 225 of the Federal Salary Act of 1967 (2 U.S.C. 351–361), as adjusted by section 461 of this title.

(June 25, 1948, c. 646, 62 Stat. 870; Mar. 2, 1955, c. 9, § 1(a), 69 Stat. 9; Aug. 14, 1964, Pub.L. 88–426, Title IV, § 403(a), 78 Stat. 434; Aug. 9, 1975, Pub.L. 94–82, Title II, § 205(b) (1), 89 Stat. 422.)

HISTORICAL AND STATUTORY NOTES

References in Text

Section 225 of the Federal Salary Act of 1967, referred to in text, is section 225 of Pub.L. 90–206, Dec. 16, 1967, 81 Stat. 642, as amended, which is classified to chapter 11 (section 351 et seq.) of Title 2, The Congress.

Effective and Applicability Provisions

1964 Acts

Amendment by Pub.L. 88–426 effective on the first day of the first pay period which begins on or after July 1, 1964, except to the extent provided in section 501(c) of Pub.L. 88–426, see section 501 of Pub.L. 88–426.

1955 Acts

Amendment by Act Mar. 2, 1955, effective Mar. 1, 1955, see section 5 of Act Mar. 2, 1955, set out as a note under section 31 of Title 2, The Congress.

Increase in Salaries

2006—Ex. Ord. No. 13393, Dec. 22, 2005, 70 F.R. 76655, set out as a note under 5 U.S.C.A. § 5332, adjusted the rates of basic pay or salaries for certain Judicial offices and positions, effective on the first day of the first applicable pay period beginning on or after Jan. 1, 2006. See Schedule of Judicial Salaries, set out as Schedule 7 of that Executive Order, set out in a note under 5 U.S.C.A. § 5332. Schedule 7 is also set out as follows:

SCHEDULE 7—JUDICIAL SALARIES

(Effective on the first day of the first applicable pay period beginning on or after January 1, 2006)

Chief Justice of the United States $212,100
Associate Justices of the Supreme Court 203,000
Circuit Judges . 175,100
District Judges . 165,200
Judges of the Court of International Trade 165,200

2005—Salaries of the Chief Justice and Associate Justices increased to $208,100, and $199,200 per annum, respectively, effective on the first day of the first applicable pay period beginning on or after Jan. 1, 2005, by Ex. Ord. No. 13368, Dec. 30, 2004, 70 F.R. 1147, formerly set out as a note under 5 U.S.C.A. § 5332.

2004—Salaries of the Chief Justice and Associate Justices increased to $203,000, and $194,300 per annum, respectively, effective on the first day of the first applicable pay period beginning on or after Jan. 1, 2004, see Ex. Ord. No. 13332, Mar. 3, 2004, 69 F.R. 10891, which superseded Ex. Ord. No. 13322, Dec. 30, 2003, 69 F.R. 231, formerly set out as a note under 5 U.S.C.A. § 5332.

2004—Salaries of the Chief Justice and Associate Justices increased to $203,000, and $194,300 per annum, respectively, effective on the first day of the first applicable pay period beginning on or after Jan. 1, 2004, by Ex. Ord. No. 13322, Dec. 30, 2003, 69 F.R. 231, which was superseded by Ex. Ord. No. 13332, Mar. 3, 2004, 69 F.R. 10891, formerly set out as a note under 5 U.S.C.A. § 5332.

2003—Salaries of the Chief Justice and Associate Justices increased to $198,600, and $190,100 per annum, respectively, effective on the first day of the first applicable pay period beginning on or after Jan. 1, 2003, by Ex. Ord. No. 13282, Dec. 31, 2002, 68 F.R. 1133, as amended by Ex. Ord. No. 13291, Mar. 21, 2003, 68 F.R. 2003, formerly set out as a note under 5 U.S.C.A. § 5332.

2002—Salaries of the Chief Justice and Associate Justices increased to $192,600, and $184,400 per annum, respectively, effective on the first day of the first applicable pay period beginning on or after Jan. 1, 2002, by Ex. Ord. No. 13249, Dec. 28, 2001, 67 F.R. 639, set out as a note under 5 U.S.C.A. § 5332.

2001—Salaries of the Chief Justice and Associate Justices increased to $186,300, and $178,300 per annum, respectively, effective on the first day of the first applicable pay period beginning on or after Jan. 1, 2001, by Ex. Ord. No. 13182,

Dec. 23, 2000, 65 F.R. 82879, set out as a note under section 5332 of Title 5, Government Organization and Employees.

2000—Salaries of the Chief Justice and Associate Justices increased to $181,400, and $173,600 per annum, respectively, effective on the first day of the first applicable pay period beginning on or after Jan. 1, 2000, by Ex. Ord. No. 13144, Dec. 21, 1999, 64 F.R. 72237, formerly set out as a note under section 5332 of Title 5, Government Organization and Employees.

1999—Salaries of the Chief Justice and Associate Justices continued at $175,400, and $167,900 per annum, respectively, effective on the first day of the first applicable pay period beginning on or after Jan. 1, 1999, by Ex. Ord. No. 13106, Dec. 7, 1998, 63 F.R. 68151, formerly set out as a note under section 5332 of Title 5, Government Organization and Employees.

1998—Salaries of the Chief Justice and Associate Justices increased to $175,400, and $167,900 per annum, respectively, effective on the first day of the first applicable pay period beginning on or after Jan. 1, 1998, by Ex. Ord. No. 13071, Dec. 29, 1997, 62 F.R. 68521, formerly set out as a note under section 5332 of Title 5, Government Organization and Employees.

1997—Salaries of the Chief Justice and Associate Justices continued at $171,500, and $164,100 per annum, respectively, effective on the first day of the first applicable pay period beginning on or after Jan. 1, 1997, by Ex. Ord. No. 13033, Dec. 27, 1996, 61 F.R. 68987, formerly set out as a note under section 5332 of Title 5, Government Organization and Employees.

1996—Salaries of the Chief Justice and Associate Justices continued at $171,500, and $164,100 per annum, respectively, effective on the first day of the first applicable pay period beginning on or after Jan. 1, 1996, by Ex. Ord. No. 12984, Dec. 28, 1995, 61 F.R. 237, formerly set out as a note under section 5332 of Title 5, Government Organization and Employees.

1995—Salaries of the Chief Justice and Associate Justices continued at $171,500, and $164,100 per annum, respectively, effective on the first day of the first applicable pay period beginning on or after Jan. 1, 1995, by Ex. Ord. No. 12944, Dec. 28, 1994, 60 F.R. 309, formerly set out as a note under section 5332 of Title 5, Government Organization and Employees.

1993—Salaries of the Chief Justice and Associate Justices increased to $171,500, and $164,100 per annum, respectively, effective on the first day of the first applicable pay period beginning on or after Jan. 1, 1993, by Ex. Ord. No. 12826, Dec. 30, 1992, 56 F.R. 62909, formerly set out as a note under section 5332 of Title 5, Government Organization and Employees.

1992—Salaries of the Chief Justice and Associate Justices increased to $166,200, and $159,000 per annum, respectively, effective on the first day of the first applicable pay period beginning on or after Jan. 1, 1992, by Ex. Ord. No. 12786, Dec. 26, 1991, 56 F.R. 67453, formerly set out as a note under section 5332 of Title 5.

1991—Salaries of the Chief Justice and Associate Justices increased to $160,600, and $153,600 per annum, respectively, effective on the first day of the first applicable pay period beginning on or after Jan. 1, 1991, by Ex. Ord. No. 12736,

Dec. 12, 1990, 55 F.R. 51385, formerly set out as a note under section 5332 of Title 5.

1990—Salaries of Chief Justice and Associate Justices continued respectively at $115,000 and $110,000 per annum, and increased to $124,000 and $118,600, respectively, effective on first day of first pay period beginning on or after Jan. 31, 1990, by Ex. Ord. No. 12698, Dec. 23, 1989, 54 F.R. 53473, formerly set out as a note under section 5332 of Title 5.

1989—Salaries of Chief Justice and Associate Justices increased in the amount of 25 percent of their respective rates (as last in effect before the increase), effective Jan. 1, 1991, see Pub.L. 101–194, Title VII, § 703(a)(3), Nov. 30, 1989, 103 Stat. 1768, set out as a note under section 5318 of Title 5.

Salaries of Chief Justice and Associate Justices continued respectively at $115,000 and $110,000 per annum by Ex. Ord. No. 12663, Jan. 6, 1989, 54 F.R. 791, formerly set out as a note under section 5332 of Title 5.

1988—Salaries of the Chief Justice and Associate Justices continued at $115,000 and $110,000, respectively, effective on the first day of the first applicable pay period beginning on or after Jan. 1, 1988, by Ex. Ord. No. 12622, Dec. 31, 1987, 53 F.R. 222, formerly set out as a note under section 5332 of Title 5.

1987—Salaries of Chief Justice and Associate Justices increased respectively to $115,000 and $110,000 per annum, on recommendation of the President of the United States, see note set out under section 358 of Title 2, The Congress.

Salaries of the Chief Justice and Associate Justices increased to $111,700 and $107,200, respectively, as required by section 406 of the Judiciary Appropriation Act, 1987, as incorporated in section 101(b) of Pub.L. 99–500 and section 101(b) of Pub.L. 99–591, effective on the first day of the first applicable pay period beginning on or after Jan. 1, 1987, by Ex. Ord. No. 12578, Dec. 31, 1986, 52 F.R. 505, formerly set out as a note under section 5332 of Title 5.

1985—Salaries of the Chief Justice and Associate Justices increased to $108,400 and $104,100, respectively, effective on the first day of the first day period beginning on or after Jan. 1, 1985, by Ex. Ord. No. 12496, Dec. 28, 1984, 50 F.R. 211, as amended by Ex. Ord. No. 12540, Dec. 30, 1985, 51 F.R. 577, formerly set out as a note under section 5332 of Title 5, Government Organization and Employees. Prior to its amendment by Ex. Ord. No. 12540, schedule 7 of Ex. Ord. No. 12496 had contained a footnote directing that, pursuant to section 140 of Pub.L. 97–92, set out as a note under section 461 of this title, funds were not available to pay any such salary after Dec. 15, 1981, at a rate exceeding the rate on that date, which was $96,800 for the Chief Justice and $93,000 for the Associate Justices.

See also section 2207 of Pub.L. 98–369, set out as a note under section 461 of this title, which provided for overall percentage adjustment increases in certain rates of pay under the General Schedule.

1984—Salaries of the Chief Justice and Associate Justices increased to $104,700 and $100,600, respectively, effective on the first day of the first pay period beginning on or after Jan. 1, 1984, by Ex. Ord.No. 12456, Dec. 30, 1983, 49 F.R. 347, as amended Ex. Ord. No. 12477, May 23, 1984, 49 F.R. 22041; Ex. Ord. No. 12487, Sept. 14, 1984, 49 F.R. 36493, formerly set out as a note under section 5332 of Title 5.

1982—Salaries of the Chief Justice and Associate Justices increased to $100,700, and $96,700, respectively, effective on the first day of the first pay period beginning on or after Oct. 1, 1982, by Ex. Ord. No. 12387, Oct. 8, 1982, 47 F.R. 44981, formerly set out as a note under section 5332 of Title 5, Government Organization and Employees. Ex. Ord. No. 12387 further provided that pursuant to section 140 of Pub.L. 97–92, funds are not available to pay a salary at a rate which exceeds the rate in effect on Dec. 15, 1981, which was $96,800 for the Chief Justice and $93,000 for the Associate Justices.

Maximum rates payable after Dec. 17, 1982, increased from $96,800 and $93,000 to $100,700 and $96,700, respectively, see Pub.L. 97–377, Title I, § 129(b)–(d), Dec. 21, 1982, 96 Stat. 1941, set out as a note under section 5318 of Title 5.

Limitations on use of funds for fiscal year ending Sept. 30, 1983, appropriated by any Act to pay the salary or pay of any individual in legislative, executive, or judicial branch in position equal to or above level V of the Executive Schedule, see section 101(e) of Pub.L. 97–276, as amended, set out as a note under section 5318 of Title 5.

1981—Salaries of the Chief Justice and Associate Justices increased to $96,800 and $93,000 respectively, effective on the first day of the first pay period beginning on or after Oct. 1, 1981, by Ex. Ord. No. 12330, Oct. 15, 1981, 46 F.R. 50921, formerly set out as a note under section 5332 of Title 5.

Limitations on use of funds for fiscal year ending Sept. 30, 1982, appropriated by any Act to pay the salary or pay of any individual in legislative, executive, or judicial branch in position equal to or above level V of the Executive Schedule, see sections 101(g) and 141 of Pub.L. 97–92, set out as a note under section 5318 of Title 5.

1980—Salaries of the Chief Justice and Associate Justices increased to $92,400 and $88,700, respectively, effective on the first day of the first pay period beginning on or after Oct. 1, 1980, by Ex. Ord. No. 12248, Oct. 16, 1980, 45 F.R. 69199, formerly set out as a note under section 5332 of Title 5. Ex. Ord. No. 12248 further provided that pursuant to Pub.L. 96–369 funds are not available to pay a salary at a rate which exceeds the rate in effect on Sept. 30, 1980, which was $79,125 for the Chief Justice and $75,960 for the Associate Justices.

Limitations on use of funds for fiscal year ending Sept. 30, 1981, appropriated by any Act to pay the salary or pay of any individual in legislative, executive, or judicial branch in position equal to or above level V of the Executive Schedule, see section 101(c) of Pub.L. 96–536, as amended, set out as a note under section 5318 of Title 5.

1979—Salaries of the Chief Justice and Associate Justices increased to $84,700 and $81,300, respectively, effective on the first day of the first applicable pay period beginning on or after Oct. 1, 1979, by Ex. Ord. No. 12165, Oct. 9, 1979, 44 F.R. 58671, as amended by Ex. Ord. No. 12200, Mar. 12, 1980, 45 F.R. 16443, formerly set out as a note under section 5332 of Title 5. Ex. Ord. No. 12165 further provided that pursuant to Pub.L. 96–86 funds appropriated for fiscal year 1980 may not be used to pay a salary at a rate which exceeds an increase of 5.5 percent over the applicable rate payable for such position or office in effect on Sept. 30, 1978, which was $79,125 for the Chief Justice and $75,960 for the Associate Justices.

Applicability to funds appropriated by any Act for fiscal year ending Sept. 30, 1980, of limitation of section 304 of Pub.L. 95–391 on use of funds to pay the salary or pay of any individual in legislative, executive, or judicial branch in position equal to or above level V of the Executive Schedule, see section 101(c) of Pub.L. 96–86, set out as a note under section 5318 of Title 5.

1978—Salaries of the Chief Justice and Associate Justices increased to $79,100 and $76,000, respectively, effective on the first day of the first pay period beginning on or after Oct. 1, 1978, by Ex. Ord. No. 12087, Oct. 7, 1978, 43 F.R. 46823, formerly set out as a note under section 5332 of Title 5. Ex. Ord. No. 12087, further provided that pursuant to the Legislative Branch Appropriation Act, 1979 [Pub.L. 95–391, Title III, § 304, Sept. 30, 1978, 92 Stat. 788, set out as a note under section 5318 of Title 5], funds are not available to pay a salary at a rate which exceeds the rate in effect on Sept. 30, 1978, which was $75,000 for the Chief Justice and $72,000 for the Associate Justices.

1977—Salaries of the Chief Justice and Associate Justices increased respectively to $75,000 and $72,000 per annum, upon recommendation of the President of the United States, see note set out under section 358 of Title 2, The Congress.

1976—Salaries of the Chief Justice and Associate Justices increased to $68,800 and $66,000, respectively, effective on the first day of the first pay period beginning on or after Oct. 1, 1976, by Ex. Ord. No. 11941, Oct. 1, 1976, 41 F.R. 43889, formerly set out as a note under section 5332 of Title 5, Government Organization and Employees. Ex. Ord. No. 11941, further provided that pursuant to the Legislative Branch Appropriation Act, 1977, funds are not available to pay a salary at a rate which exceeds the rate in effect on Sept. 30, 1976, which was $65,600 for the Chief Justice and $63,000 for the Associate Justices.

1975—Salaries of the Chief Justice and Associate Justices increased to $65,600 and $63,000, respectively, effective on the first day of the first pay period beginning on or after Oct. 1, 1975, by Ex. Ord. No. 11883, Oct. 6, 1975, 40 F.R. 47091, formerly set out as a note under section 5332 of Title 5.

1969—Salaries of the Chief Justice and Associate Justices increased respectively from $40,000 and $39,500 to $62,500 and $60,000 per annum, commencing February 14, 1969, upon recommendation of the President of the United States, see note set out under section 358 of Title 2, The Congress.

1946—The salary of the Chief Justice was increased from $20,500 to $25,500 a year, and the salaries of the associate justices were increased from $20,000 to $25,000 per year, by Act July 31, 1946, c. 704, § 1, 60 Stat. 716.

1925—Salary of the Chief Justice was increased from $15,000 for year to $20,500 per year, and the salaries of the associate justices were increased from $14,500 per year to $20,000 per year, by Act Dec. 13, 1926, c. 6, § 1, 44 Stat. 919.

1911—Salary of the Chief Justice was set at $15,000 a year and the salaries of the associate justices were set at $14,500 a year by the Judicial Code of 1911, Act Mar. 3, 1911, c. 231, § 1, 36 Stat. 1152.

§ 6. Records of former court of appeals

The records and proceedings of the court of appeals, appointed previous to the adoption of the Constitution, shall be kept until deposited with the National Archives of the United States in the office of the

clerk of the Supreme Court, who shall furnish copies thereof to any person requiring and paying for them, in the manner provided by law for giving copies of the records and proceedings of the Supreme Court. Such copies shall have the same faith and credit as proceedings of the Supreme Court.

(June 25, 1948, c. 646, 62 Stat. 870; Oct. 25, 1951, c. 562, § 4(7), 65 Stat. 640.)

CHAPTER 3—COURTS OF APPEALS

§ 41. Number and composition of circuits

The thirteen judicial circuits of the United States are constituted as follows:

Circuits	Composition
District of Columbia	District of Columbia.
First	Maine, Massachusetts, New Hampshire, Puerto Rico, Rhode Island.
Second	Connecticut, New York, Vermont.
Third	Delaware, New Jersey, Pennsylvania, Virgin Islands.
Fourth	Maryland, North Carolina, South Carolina, Virginia, West Virginia.
Fifth	District of the Canal Zone, Louisiana, Mississippi, Texas.
Sixth	Kentucky, Michigan, Ohio, Tennessee.
Seventh	Illinois, Indiana, Wisconsin.
Eighth	Arkansas, Iowa, Minnesota, Missouri, Nebraska, North Dakota, South Dakota.
Ninth	Alaska, Arizona, California, Idaho, Montana, Nevada, Oregon, Washington, Guam, Hawaii.
Tenth	Colorado, Kansas, New Mexico, Oklahoma, Utah, Wyoming.
Eleventh	Alabama, Florida, Georgia.
Federal	All Federal judicial districts.

(June 25, 1948, c. 646, 62 Stat. 870; Oct. 31, 1951, c. 655, § 34, 65 Stat. 723; Oct. 14, 1980, Pub.L. 96–452, § 2, 94 Stat. 1994; Apr. 2, 1982, Pub.L. 97–164, Title I, § 101, 96 Stat. 25.)

HISTORICAL AND STATUTORY NOTES

Effective and Applicability Provisions

1982 Acts

Amendment by Pub.L. 97–164 effective Oct. 1, 1982, see section 402 of Pub.L. 97–164, set out as a note under section 171 of this title.

1980 Acts

Section 12 of Pub.L. 96–452 provided that: "This Act [see Short Title of 1980 Amendments note set out under section 1 of this title] and the amendments made by this Act [amending sections 41, 44, and 48 of this title, and enacting provisions set out as notes under this section] shall take effect on October 1, 1981."

Administrative Action by Fifth Circuit Court of Appeals; Termination of Court

Section 11 of Pub.L. 96–452 provided that: "The court of appeals for the fifth circuit as constituted on the day before the effective date of this Act [Oct. 1, 1981] may take such administrative action as may be required to carry out this Act [see Short Title of 1980 Amendments note set out under section 1 of this title]. Such court shall cease to exist for administrative purposes on July 1, 1984."

Appeals Court Administrative Units

Pub.L. 95–486, § 6, Oct. 20, 1978, 92 Stat. 1633, provided that: "Any court of appeals having more than 15 active judges may constitute itself into administrative units complete with such facilities and staff as may be prescribed by the Administrative Office of the United States Courts, and may perform its en banc function by such number of members of its en banc courts as may be prescribed by rule of the court of appeals."

Assignment of Judges and Procedure For Administration of Pending Cases With Regard to Reorganization of the Fifth Circuit Court of Appeals

Sections 5 to 10 of Pub.L. 96–452 provided that:

"Sec. 5. Each circuit judge in regular active service of the former fifth circuit whose official station on the day before the effective date of this Act [Oct. 1, 1981]—

"(1) is in Louisiana, Mississippi, or Texas is assigned as a circuit judge of the new fifth circuit; and

"(2) is in Alabama, Florida, or Georgia is assigned as a circuit judge of the new eleventh circuit.

"Sec. 6. Each judge who is a senior judge of the former fifth circuit on the day before the effective date of this Act [Oct. 1, 1981] may elect to be assigned to the new fifth circuit or to the eleventh circuit and shall notify the Director of the Administrative Office of the United States Courts of such election.

"Sec. 7. The seniority of each judge—

"(1) who is assigned under section 5 of this Act; or

"(2) who elects to be assigned under section 6 of this Act;

shall run from the date of commission of such judge as a judge of the former fifth circuit.

"Sec. 8. The eleventh circuit is authorized to hold terms or sessions of court at New Orleans, Louisiana, until such time as adequate facilities for such court are provided in Atlanta, Georgia.

"Sec. 9. The provisions of the following paragraphs of this section apply to any case in which, on the day before the effective date of this Act [Oct. 1, 1981], an appeal or other proceeding has been filed with the former fifth circuit:

"(1) If the matter has been submitted for decision, further proceedings in respect of the matter shall be had in the same manner and with the same effect as if this Act [see Short Title of 1980 Amendments note under section 1 of this title] had not been enacted.

"(2) If the matter has not been submitted for decision, the appeal or proceeding, together with the original papers, printed records, and record entries duly certified, shall, by appropriate orders, be transferred to the court to which it would have gone had this Act [see Short Title of 1980 Amendments note under section 1 of this title] been in full force and effect at the time such appeal was taken or other proceeding commenced, and further proceedings in respect of the case shall be had in the same manner and with the same effect as if the appeal or other proceeding had been filed in such court.

"(3) A petition for rehearing or a petition for rehearing en banc in a matter decided before the effective date of this Act [Oct. 1, 1981], or submitted before the effective date of this Act and decided on or after the effective date as provided in paragraph (1) of this section, shall be treated in the same manner and with the same effect as though this Act [see Short Title of 1980 Amendments note under section 1 of this title] had not been enacted. If a petition for rehearing en banc is granted, the matter shall be reheard by a court comprised as though this Act [see Short Title of 1980 Amendments note under section 1 of this title] had not been enacted.

"Sec. 10. As used in sections 5, 6, 7, 8, and 9 of this Act, the term—

"(1) 'former fifth circuit' means the fifth judicial circuit of the United States as in existence on the day before the effective date of this Act [Oct. 1, 1981];

"(2) the term 'new fifth circuit' means the fifth judicial circuit of the United States established by the amendment made by section 2(2) of this Act [amending this section]; and

"(3) the term 'eleventh circuit' means the eleventh judicial circuit of the United States established by the amendment made by section 2(3) of this Act [amending this section]."

Commission on Revision of the Federal Appellate System

Pub.L. 92–489, Oct. 13, 1972, 86 Stat. 807, as amended by Pub.L. 93–420, Sept. 19, 1974, 88 Stat. 1153, provided for the establishment, membership, travel expenses, personnel, experts and consultants, administrative and research services, cooperation of other governmental agencies, and appropriations of not to exceed $606,000 of a Commission on Revision of the Federal Court Appellate System which Commission

was to study the geographical division of the judicial circuits and the structure and internal procedures of the appellate court system and to report to the President, Congress, and the Chief Justice its recommendations for changes in the geographical boundaries of the circuits to expedite disposition of judicial business and for changes in the appellate court structure to expedite disposition of the appellate court structure to expedite disposition of the appellate courts caseload in a manner consistent with fundamental concepts of fairness and due process. The Commission was to cease existence ninety days after submission of its final report, which report was submitted June 20, 1975.

Commission on Structural Alternatives for the Federal Courts of Appeals

Pub.L. 105–119, Title III, § 305, Nov. 26, 1997, 111 Stat. 2491, provided that:

"(a) Commission on Structural Alternatives for the Federal Courts of Appeal.—

"(1) Establishment and functions of commission.—

"(A) Establishment.—There is established a Commission on Structural Alternatives for the Federal Courts of Appeals (hereinafter referred to as the 'Commission').

"(B) Functions.—The functions of the Commission shall be to—

"(i) study the present division of the United States into the several judicial circuits;

"(ii) study the structure and alignment of the Federal Court of Appeals system, with particular reference to the Ninth Circuit; and

"(iii) report to the President and the Congress its recommendations for such changes in circuit boundaries or structure as may be appropriate for the expeditious and effective disposition of the caseload of the Federal Courts of Appeals, consistent with fundamental concepts of fairness and due process.

"(2) Membership.—

"(A) Composition.—The Commission shall be composed of five members who shall be appointed by the Chief Justice of the United States.

"(B) Appointment.—The members of the Commission shall be appointed within 30 days after the date of enactment of this Act.

"(C) Vacancy.—Any vacancy in the Commission shall be filled in the same manner as the original appointment.

"(D) Chair.—The Commission shall elect a chair and vice chair from among its members.

"(E) Quorum.—Three members of the Commission shall constitute a quorum, but two may conduct hearings.

"(3) Compensation.—

"(A) In general.—Members of the Commission who are officers, or full-time employees, of the United States shall receive no additional compensation for their services, but shall be reimbursed for travel, subsistence, and other necessary expenses incurred in the performance of duties vested in the Commission, but not in excess of the maximum amounts authorized under section 456 of title 28, United States Code.

"**(B) Private members.**—Members of the Commission from private life shall receive $200 for each day (including travel time) during which the member is engaged in the actual performance of duties, but not in excess of the maximum amounts authorized under section 456 of title 28, United States Code.

"**(4) Personnel.**—

"**(A) Executive Director.**—The Commission may appoint an Executive Director who shall receive compensation at a rate not exceeding the rate prescribed for level V of the Executive Schedule under section 5316 of title 5, United States Code.

"**(B) Staff.**—The Executive Director, with the approval of the Commission, may appoint and fix the compensation of such additional personnel as the Executive Director determines necessary, without regard to the provisions of title 5, United States Code, governing appointments in the competitive service or the provisions of chapter 51 [section 5101 et seq. of Title 5] and subchapter III of chapter 53 of such title [section 5331 et seq. of Title 5] relating to classification and General Schedule pay rates. Compensation under this paragraph shall not exceed the annual maximum rate of basic pay for a position above GS–15 of the General Schedule under section 5108 of title 5, United States Code.

"**(C) Experts and consultants.**—The Executive Director may procure personal services of experts and consultants as authorized by section 3109 of title 5, United States Code, at rates not to exceed the highest level payable under the General Schedule pay rates under section 5332 of title 5, United States Code.

"**(D) Services.**—The Administrative Office of the United States Courts shall provide administrative services, including financial and budgeting services, to the Commission on a reimbursable basis. The Federal Judicial Center shall provide necessary research services to the Commission on a reimbursable basis.

"**(5) Information.**—The Commission is authorized to request from any department, agency, or independent instrumentality of the Government any information and assistance the Commission determines necessary to carry out its functions under this section. Each such department, agency, and independent instrumentality is authorized to provide such information and assistance to the extent permitted by law when requested by the chair of the Commission.

"**(6) Report.**—The Commission shall conduct the studies required in this section during the 10–month period beginning on the date on which a quorum of the Commission has been appointed. Not later than 2 months following the completion of such 10–month period, the Commission shall submit its report to the President and the Congress. The Commission shall terminate 90 days after the date of the submission of its report.

"**(b) Authorization of appropriations.**—There are authorized to be appropriated to the Commission such sums, not to exceed $900,000, as may be necessary to carry out the purposes of this section. Such sums as are appropriated shall remain available until expended."

Continuation of Organization of Court

Section 2(b) of Act June 25, 1948, c. 646, 62 Stat. 985, provided in part that the provisions of this title as set out in section 1 of said Act of June 25, 1948, with respect to the organization of each of the several courts therein provided, shall be construed as a continuation of existing law, and the tenure of the judges, officers, and employees in office on Sept. 1, 1948, and of the United States attorneys and marshals and their deputies and assistants in office on that date, shall not be affected by its enactment but each of them shall continue to serve in the same capacity under the appropriate provisions of this title, pursuant to his prior appointment.

Northern Mariana Islands

Pub.L. 95–157, § 1(a), Nov. 8, 1977, 91 Stat. 1265, provided that the Northern Mariana Islands be part of the same judicial circuit as Guam, i.e., the Ninth Circuit. See section 1694(a) of Title 48, Territories and Insular Possessions.

Puerto Rico

The name of the island of "Porto Rico" was changed to "Puerto Rico" by Act May 17, 1932, c. 190, 47 Stat. 158.

Tenth Judicial Circuit

Act Feb. 28, 1929, c. 363, § 1, 45 Stat. 1346, divided the eight judicial circuit and created the tenth judicial circuit. Prior to such division the eighth judicial circuit included, in addition, the states now constituting the tenth judicial circuit.

Termination of United States District Court for the District of the Canal Zone

For termination of the United States District Court for the District of the Canal Zone at end of the "transition period", being the 30–month period beginning Oct. 1, 1979, and ending midnight Mar. 31, 1982, see Paragraph 5 of Article XI of the Panama Canal Treaty of 1977 and sections 3831 and 3841 to 3843 of Title 22, Foreign Relations and Intercourse.

§ 42. Allotment of Supreme Court justices to circuits

The Chief Justice of the United States and the associate justices of the Supreme Court shall from time to time be allotted as circuit justices among the circuits by order of the Supreme Court. The Chief Justice may make such allotments in vacation.

A justice may be assigned to more than one circuit, and two or more justices may be assigned to the same circuit.

(June 25, 1948, c. 646, 62 Stat. 870.)

§ 43. Creation and composition of courts

(a) There shall be in each circuit a court of appeals, which shall be a court of record, known as the United States Court of Appeals for the circuit.

(b) Each court of appeals shall consist of the circuit judges of the circuit in regular active service. The circuit justice and justices or judges designated or assigned shall be competent to sit as judges of the court.

(June 25, 1948, c. 646, 62 Stat. 870; Nov. 13, 1963, Pub.L. 88–176, § 1(a), 77 Stat. 331.)

HISTORICAL AND STATUTORY NOTES

Change of Name of Court

Section 2(b) of Act June 25, 1948, c. 646, 62 Stat. 869, provided in part that each circuit court of appeals should, after Sept. 1, 1948, be known as a United States Court of Appeals, but that the enactment of said Act June 25, 1948 should in no way entail any loss of rights, interruption of jurisdiction, or prejudice to matters pending in any such courts on Sept. 1, 1948.

§ 44. Appointment, tenure, residence and salary of circuit judges

(a) The President shall appoint, by and with the advice and consent of the Senate, circuit judges for the several circuits as follows:

Circuits	Number of Judges
District of Columbia	12
First	6
Second	13
Third	14
Fourth	15
Fifth	17
Sixth	16
Seventh	11
Eighth	11
Ninth	28
Tenth	12
Eleventh	12
Federal	12.

(b) Circuit judges shall hold office during good behavior.

(c) Except in the District of Columbia, each circuit judge shall be a resident of the circuit for which appointed at the time of his appointment and thereafter while in active service. While in active service, each circuit judge of the Federal judicial circuit appointed after the effective date of the Federal Courts Improvement Act of 1982, and the chief judge of the Federal judicial circuit, whenever appointed, shall reside within fifty miles of the District of Columbia. In each circuit (other than the Federal judicial circuit) there shall be at least one circuit judge in regular active service appointed from the residents of each state [1] in that circuit.

(d) Each circuit judge shall receive a salary at an annual rate determined under section 225 of the Federal Salary Act of 1967 (2 U.S.C. 351–361), as adjusted by section 461 of this title.

(June 25, 1948, c. 646, 62 Stat. 871; Aug. 3, 1949, c. 387, § 1, 63 Stat. 493; Feb. 10, 1954, c. 6, § 1, 68 Stat. 8; Mar. 2, 1955, c. 9, § 1(b), 69 Stat. 10; May 19, 1961, Pub.L. 87–36, § 1(b), 75 Stat. 80; Aug. 14, 1964, Pub.L. 88–426, Title IV, § 403(b), 78 Stat. 434; Mar. 18, 1966, Pub.L. 89–372, § 1(b), 80 Stat. 75; June 18, 1968, Pub.L. 90–347, § 3, 82 Stat. 184; Aug. 9, 1975, Pub.L. 94–82, Title II, § 205(b) (2), 89 Stat. 422; Oct. 20, 1978, Pub.L. 95–486, § 3(b), 92 Stat. 1632; Oct. 14, 1980, Pub.L. 96–452, § 3, 94 Stat. 1994; Apr. 2, 1982, Pub.L. 97–164, Title I, § 102, 96 Stat. 25; July 10, 1984, Pub.L.

98–353, Title II, § 201(b), 98 Stat. 346; Dec. 1, 1990, Pub.L. 101–650, Title II, § 202(b), 104 Stat. 5099; Dec. 9, 1991, Pub.L. 102–198, § 10(c), 105 Stat. 1626; Nov. 26, 1997, Pub.L. 105–119, Title III, § 307, 111 Stat. 2493.)

1 So in original. Probably should be capitalized.

HISTORICAL AND STATUTORY NOTES

References in Text

The effective date of the Federal Courts Improvement Act of 1982, referred to in subsec. (c), is Oct. 1, 1982. See Effective and Applicability Provisions of 1982 Amendments note set out under section 171 of this title.

Section 225 of the Federal Salary Act of 1967, referred to in subsec. (d), is section 225 of Pub.L. 90–206, Dec. 16, 1967, 81 Stat. 642, as amended, which is classified to chapter 11 (section 351 et seq.) of Title 2, The Congress.

Effective and Applicability Provisions

1990 Acts

Section 206 of Title II of Pub.L. 101–650 provided that: "This title [amending this section and section 133 of this title and enacting provisions set out as notes under this section and sections 133 and 331 of this title] shall take effect on the date of the enactment of this title [Dec. 1, 1990]."

1982 Acts

Amendment by Pub.L. 97–164 effective Oct. 1, 1982, see section 402 of Pub.L. 97–164, set out as a note under section 171 of this title.

1980 Acts

Amendment by Pub.L. 96–452 effective Oct. 1, 1981, see section 12 of Pub.L. 96–452, set out as a note under section 41 of this title.

1964 Acts

Amendment by Pub.L. 88–426 effective on the first day of the first pay period which begins on or after July 1, 1964, except to the extent provided in section 501(c) of Pub.L. 88–426, see section 501 of Pub.L. 88–426.

1955 Acts

Amendment by Act Mar. 2, 1955, effective Mar. 1, 1955, see section 5 of Act Mar. 2, 1955, set out as a note under section 31 of Title 2, The Congress.

Additional Judges

Since 1925, the appointment of additional judges was authorized by the following acts:

Second circuit. Act May 31, 1938, c. 290, § 1, 52 Stat. 584.

Third circuit. Act Aug. 3, 1949, c. 387, § 1, 63 Stat. 493; Act Dec. 7, 1944, c. 521, § 1, 58 Stat. 796; Act June 10, 1930, c. 438, 46 Stat. 538; Act June 24, 1936, c. 735, § 1, 49 Stat. 1903, repealed by Act May 31, 1938, c. 290, § 3, 52 Stat. 585.

Fifth circuit. Act Dec. 14, 1942, c. 731, 56 Stat. 1050; Act May 31, 1938, c. 290, § 1, 52 Stat. 584; Act June 10, 1930, c. 437, 46 Stat. 538.

Sixth circuit. Act May 24, 1940, c. 209, § 1, 54 Stat. 219; Act May 31, 1938, c. 290, § 1, 52 Stat. 584.

Seventh circuit. Act Aug. 3, 1949, c. 387, § 1, 63 Stat. 493; Act May 31, 1938, c. 290, § 1, 52 Stat. 584.

Eighth circuit. Act May 24, 1940, c. 209, § 1, 54 Stat. 219; Act Mar. 3, 1925, c. 437, 43 Stat. 1116.

Ninth circuit. Act Apr. 14, 1937, c. 80, 50 Stat. 64; Act Aug. 2, 1935, c. 425, § 1, 49 Stat. 508; Act June 16, 1933, c. 102, 48, Stat. 310 (removing limitation on filling of vacancy); Act Mar. 1, 1929, c. 413, 45 Stat. 1414.

Tenth circuit. Act Aug. 3, 1949, c. 387, § 1, 63 Stat. 493.

District of Columbia Court of Appeals. Act Aug. 3, 1949, c. 387, § 1, 63 Stat. 493; Act May 31, 1938, c. 290, § 2, 52 Stat. 584; Act June 19, 1930, c. 538, 46 Stat. 785.

Act Feb. 28, 1929, c. 363, § 2, 45 Stat. 1346, 1347 provided that "There shall be in the sixth, seventh, and tenth circuits, respectively, four circuit judges; and in the second and eighth circuits, respectively, five circuit judges; and in each of the other circuits three circuit judges, to be appointed by the President by and with the advice and consent of the Senate."

Another part of section 1 of Act Feb. 10, 1954, which amended subsec. (a) of this section, provided for the appointment by the President, by and with the advice and consent of the Senate, of the additional judges for the Fifth and Ninth Circuits, provided for in such amendment.

Section 1(a) of Pub.L. 87–36 provided that: "The President shall appoint, by and with the advice and consent of the Senate, three additional circuit judges for the second circuit, one additional circuit judge for the third circuit, two additional circuit judges for the fourth circuit, two additional circuit judges for the fifth circuit, one additional circuit judge for the seventh circuit, and one additional circuit judge for the tenth circuit."

Section 1(a) of Pub.L. 89–372 provided that: "The President shall appoint, by and with the advice and consent of the Senate, two additional circuit judges for the fourth circuit, two additional circuit judges for the sixth circuit, one additional circuit judge for the seventh circuit, and one additional circuit judge for the eighth circuit."

Section 1(c) of Pub.L. 89–372, as amended by Pub.L. 90–347, § 2, June 18, 1968, 82 Stat. 183, provided that: "The President shall appoint, by and with the advice and consent of the Senate, four additional circuit judges for the fifth circuit." The second sentence of section 1(c) of Pub.L. 89–372 which provided that the first four vacancies occurring in the office of circuit judge in the fifth circuit shall not be filled was deleted by section 2 of Pub.L. 90–347, which also made those judgeships permanent and further provided that the present incumbents of such judgeships shall henceforth hold their offices under this section.

Section 1 of Pub.L. 90–347 provided: "That the President shall appoint, by and with the advice and consent of the Senate, one additional circuit judge for the third circuit, two additional circuit judges for the fifth circuit, one additional circuit judge for the sixth circuit, four additional circuit judges for the ninth circuit, and one additional circuit judge for the tenth circuit."

Section 3(a) of Pub.L. 95–486 provided that: "The President shall appoint, by and with the advice and consent of the Senate, one additional circuit judgeship for the first circuit, two additional circuit judgeships for the second circuit, one additional circuit judgeship for the third circuit, three additional circuit judgeships for the fourth circuit, eleven additional circuit judgeships for the fifth circuit, two additional circuit judgeships for the sixth circuit, one additional circuit judgeship for the seventh circuit, one additional circuit judgeship for the eighth circuit, ten additional circuit judgeships for the ninth circuit, one additional circuit judgeship for the tenth circuit, and two additional circuit judgeships for the District of Columbia."

Section 201(a) of Pub.L. 98–353 provided that:

"(1) Subject to the provisions of paragraph (2), the President shall appoint, by and with the advice and consent of the Senate, two additional circuit judges for the first circuit court of appeals, two additional circuit judges for the second circuit court of appeals, two additional circuit judges for the third circuit court of appeals, one additional circuit judge for the fourth circuit court of appeals, two additional circuit judges for the fifth circuit court of appeals, four additional circuit judges for the sixth circuit court of appeals, two additional circuit judges for the seventh circuit court of appeals, one additional circuit judge for the eighth circuit court of appeals, five additional circuit judges for the ninth circuit court of appeals, two additional circuit judges for the tenth circuit court of appeals, and one additional circuit judge for the District of Columbia circuit court of appeals.

"(2) The President shall appoint, by and with the advice and consent of the Senate, no more than 11 of such judges prior to January 21, 1985."

Section 202(a) of Pub.L. 101–650 provided that: "The President shall appoint, by and with the advice and consent of the Senate—

"(1) 2 additional circuit judges for the third circuit court of appeals;

"(2) 4 additional circuit judges for the fourth circuit court of appeals;

"(3) 1 additional circuit judge for the fifth circuit court of appeals;

"(4) 1 additional circuit judge for the sixth circuit court of appeals;

"(5) 1 additional circuit judge for the eighth circuit court of appeals; and

"(6) 2 additional circuit judges for the tenth circuit court of appeals."

Congressional Statement Regarding Appointment of Judges of United States Court of Appeals for the Federal Circuit and United States Claims Court

Section 168 of Pub.L. 97–164 provided that: "The Congress—

"(1) takes notice of the fact that the quality of the Federal judiciary is determined by the competence and experience of its judges; and

"(2) suggests that the President, in nominating individuals to judgeships on the United States Court of Appeals for the Federal Circuit and the United States Claims Court [now the United States Court of Federal Claims], select from a broad range of qualified individuals."

Continued Service of Judges of Court of Claims and Court of Customs and Patent Appeals as Judges of Court of Appeals for the Federal Circuit

Section 165 of Pub.L. 97–164 provided that: "The judges of the United States Court of Claims and of the United States Court of Customs and Patent Appeals in regular active service on the effective date of this Act [Oct. 1, 1982] shall continue in office as judges of the United States Court of Appeals for the Federal Circuit. Senior judges of the

United States Court of Claims and of the United States Court of Customs and Patent Appeals on the effective date of this Act [Oct. 1, 1982] shall continue in office as senior judges of the United States Court of Appeals for the Federal Circuit."

Increase in Salaries

2006—Ex. Ord. No. 13393, Dec. 22, 2005, 70 F.R. 76655, set out as a note under 5 U.S.C.A. § 5332, adjusted the rates of basic pay or salaries for certain Judicial offices and positions, effective on the first day of the first applicable pay period beginning on or after Jan. 1, 2006. See Schedule of Judicial Salaries, set out as Schedule 7 of that Executive Order, set out in a note under 5 U.S.C.A. § 5332 and also set out in a note under 28 U.S.C.A. § 5.

2005—Salaries of the circuit judges increased to $171,800 per annum, respectively, effective on the first day of the first applicable pay period beginning on or after Jan. 1, 2005, by Ex. Ord. No. 13368, Dec. 30, 2004, 70 F.R. 1147, formerly set out as a note under 5 U.S.C.A. § 5332.

2004—Salaries of the circuit judges increased to $167,600 per annum, respectively, effective on the first day of the first applicable pay period beginning on or after Jan. 1, 2004, see Ex. Ord. No. 13332, Mar. 3, 2004, 69 F.R. 10891, which superseded Ex. Ord. No. 13322, Dec. 30, 2003, 69 F.R. 231, formerly set out as a note under 5 U.S.C.A. § 5332.

2004—Salaries of the circuit judges increased to $167,600 per annum, respectively, effective on the first day of the first applicable pay period beginning on or after Jan. 1, 2004, by Ex. Ord. No. 13322, Dec. 30, 2003, 69 F.R. 231, which was superseded by Ex. Ord. No. 13332, Mar. 3, 2004, 69 F.R. 10891, formerly set out as a note under 5 U.S.C.A. § 5332.

2003—Salaries of the circuit judges increased to $164,000 per annum, respectively, effective on the first day of the first applicable pay period beginning on or after Jan. 1, 2003, by Ex. Ord. No. 13282, Dec. 31, 2002, 68 F.R. 1133, as amended by Ex. Ord. No. 13291, Mar. 21, 2003, 68 F.R. 2003, formerly set out as a note under 5 U.S.C.A. § 5332.

2002—Salaries of circuit judges increased to $159,100 per annum, effective on the first day of the first applicable pay period beginning on or after Jan. 1, 2002, by Ex. Ord. No. 13249, Dec. 28, 2001, 67 F.R. 639, set out as a note under 5 U.S.C.A. § 5332.

2001—Salaries of circuit judges increased to $153,900, effective on the first day of the first applicable pay period beginning on or after Jan. 1, 2001, by Ex. Ord. No. 13182, Dec. 23, 2000, 65 F.R. 82879, set out as a note under section 5332 of Title 5, Government Organization and Employees.

2000—Salaries of circuit judges increased to $149,900, effective on the first day of the first applicable pay period beginning on or after Jan. 1, 2000, by Ex. Ord. No. 13144, Dec. 21, 1999, 64 F.R. 72237, formerly set out as a note under section 5332 of Title 5, Government Organization and Employees.

1999—Salaries of circuit judges continued at $145,000, effective on the first day of the first applicable pay period beginning on or after Jan. 1, 1999, by Ex. Ord. No. 13106, Dec. 7, 1998, 63 F.R. 68151, formerly set out as a note under section 5332 of Title 5, Government Organization and Employees.

1998—Salaries of circuit judges increased to $145,000, effective on the first day of the first applicable pay period

beginning on or after Jan. 1, 1998, by Ex. Ord. No. 13071, Dec. 29, 1997, 62 F.R. 68521, formerly set out as a note under section 5332 of Title 5, Government Organization and Employees.

1997—Salaries of circuit judges continued at $141,700, effective on the first day of the first applicable pay period beginning on or after Jan. 1, 1997, by Ex. Ord. No. 13033, Dec. 27, 1996, 61 F.R. 68987, formerly set out as a note under section 5332 of Title 5, Government Organization and Employees.

1996—Salaries of circuit judges continued at $141,700, effective on the first day of the first applicable pay period beginning on or after Jan. 1, 1996, by Ex. Ord. No. 12984, Dec. 28, 1995, 61 F.R. 237, formerly set out as a note under section 5332 of Title 5, Government Organization and Employees.

1995—Salaries of circuit judges continued at $141,700, effective on the first day of the first applicable pay period beginning on or after Jan. 1, 1995, by Ex. Ord. No. 12944, Dec. 28, 1994, 60 F.R. 309, formerly set out as a note under section 5332 of Title 5, Government Organization and Employees.

1993—Salaries of circuit judges increased to $141,700, effective on the first day of the first applicable pay period beginning on or after Jan. 1, 1993, by Ex. Ord. No. 12826, Dec. 30, 1992, 57 F.R. 62909, formerly set out as a note under section 5332 of Title 5, Government Organization and Employees.

1992—Salaries of circuit judges increased to $137,300, effective on the first day of the first applicable pay period beginning on or after Jan. 1, 1992, by Ex. Ord. No. 12786, Dec. 26, 1991, 56 F.R. 67453, formerly set out as a note under section 5332 of Title 5.

1991—Salaries of circuit judges increased to $132,700, effective on the first day of the first applicable pay period beginning on or after Jan. 1, 1991, by Ex. Ord. No. 12736, Dec. 12, 1990, 55 F.R. 51385, formerly set out as a note under section 5332 of Title 5.

1990—Salaries of circuit judges continued at $95,000 per annum, and increased to $102,500, effective on first day of first pay period beginning on or after Jan. 31, 1990, by Ex. Ord. No. 12698, Dec. 23, 1989, 54 F.R. 53473, formerly set out as a note under section 5332 of Title 5.

1989—Salaries of circuit judges increased in the amount of 25 percent of their rates (as last in effect before the increase), effective Jan. 1, 1991, see Pub.L. 101–194, Title VII, § 703(a)(3), Nov. 30, 1989, 103 Stat. 1768, set out as a note under section 5318 of Title 5.

Salaries of circuit judges continued at $95,000 per annum, effective on the first day of the first applicable pay period beginning on or after Jan. 1, 1989, by Ex. Ord. No. 12663, Jan. 6, 1989, 54 F.R. 791, formerly set out as a note under section 5332 of Title 5.

1988—Salaries of circuit judges continued at $95,000 per annum, effective on the first day of the first applicable pay period beginning on or after Jan. 1, 1988, by Ex. Ord. No. 12622, Dec. 31, 1987, 53 F.R. 222, formerly set out as a note under section 5332 of Title 5.

1987—Salaries of circuit judges increased to $95,000 per annum, on recommendation of the President of the United

States, see note set out under section 358 of Title 2, The Congress.

Salaries of circuit judges increased to $85,700, as required by section 406 of the Judiciary Appropriation Act, 1987, as incorporated in section 101(b) of Pub.L. 99–500 and section 101(b) of Pub.L. 99–591, effective on the first day of the first applicable pay period beginning on or after Jan. 1, 1987, by Ex. Ord. No. 12578, Dec. 31, 1986, 52 F.R. 505, formerly set out as a note under section 5332 of Title 5.

1985—Salaries of circuit judges increased to $83,200 effective on the first day of the first pay period beginning on or after Jan. 1, 1985, by Ex. Ord. No. 12496, Dec. 28, 1984, 50 F.R. 211, as amended by Ex. Ord. No. 12540, Dec. 30, 1985, 51 F.R. 577, formerly set out as a note under section 5332 of Title 5, Government Organization and Employees. Prior to its amendment by Ex. Ord. No. 12540. schedule 7 of Ex. Ord. 12496 had contained a footnote directing that, pursuant to section 140 of Pub.L. 97–92, set out as a note under section 461 of this title, funds were not available to pay a salary at a rate which exceeded the rate in effect on Dec. 15, 1981, which was $74,300.

See also section 2207 of Pub.L. 98–369, set out as a note under section 461 of this title, which provided for overall percentage adjustment increases in certain rates of pay under the General Schedule.

1984—Salaries of circuit judges increased to $80,400 effective on the first day of the first pay period beginning on or after Jan. 1, 1984, by Ex. Ord. No. 12456, Dec. 30, 1983, 49 F.R. 347, as amended Ex. Ord. No. 12477, May 23, 1984, 49 F.R. 22041; Ex. Ord. No. 12487, Sept. 14, 1984, 49 F.R. 36493, formerly set out as a note under section 5332 of Title 5.

1982—Salaries of circuit judges increased to $77,300 effective on the first day of the first pay period beginning on or after Oct. 1, 1982, by Ex. Ord. No. 12387, Oct. 8, 1982, 47 F.R. 44981, formerly set out as a note under section 5332 of Title 5, Government Organization and Employees. Ex. Ord. No. 12387 further provided that pursuant to section 140 of Pub.L. 97–92 funds are not available to pay a salary at a rate which exceeds the rate in effect on Dec. 15, 1981, which was $74,300.

Maximum rate payable after Dec. 17, 1982, increased from $74,300 to $77,300, see Pub.L. 97–377, Title I, § 129(b)–(d), Dec. 21, 1982, 96 Stat. 1914, set out as a note under section 5318 of Title 5.

Limitations on use of funds for fiscal year ending Sept. 30, 1983, appropriated by any Act to pay the salary or pay of any individual in legislative, executive, or judicial branch in position equal to or above level V of the Executive Schedule, see section 101(e) of Pub.L. 97–276, as amended, set out as a note under section 5318 of Title 5.

1981—Salaries of circuit judges increased to $74,300 effective on the first day of the first pay period beginning on or after Oct. 1, 1981, by Ex. Ord. No. 12330, Oct. 15, 1981, 46 F.R. 50921, formerly set out as a note under section 5332 of Title 5.

Limitations on use of funds for fiscal year ending Sept. 30, 1982, appropriated by any Act to pay the salary or pay of any individual in legislative, executive, or judicial branch in position equal to or above level V of the Executive Schedule, see sections 101(g) and 141 of Pub.L. 97–92, set out as a note under section 5318 of Title 5.

1980—Salaries of circuit judges increased to $70,900 effective on the first day of the first pay period beginning on or after Oct. 1, 1980, by Ex. Ord. No. 12248, Oct. 16, 1980, 45 F.R. 69199, formerly set out as a note under section 5332 of Title 5. Ex. Ord. No. 12248 further provided that pursuant to Pub.L. 96–369 funds are not available to pay a salary at a rate which exceeds the rate in effect on Sept. 30, 1980, which was $60,662.50.

Limitations on use of funds for fiscal year ending Sept. 30, 1981, appropriated by any Act to pay the salary or pay of any individual in legislative, executive, or judicial branch in position equal to or above level V of the Executive Schedule, see section 101(c) of Pub.L. 96–536, as amended, set out as a note under section 5318 of Title 5.

1979—Salaries of circuit judges increased to $65,000 effective on the first day of the first applicable pay period beginning on or after Oct. 1, 1979, by Ex. Ord. No. 12165, Oct. 9, 1979, 44 F.R. 58671, as amended by Ex. Ord. No. 12200, Mar. 12, 1980, 45 F.R. 16443, formerly set out as a note under section 5332 of Title 5. Ex. Ord. No. 12165 further provided that pursuant to Pub.L. 96–86 funds appropriated for fiscal year 1980 may not be used to pay a salary at a rate which exceeds an increase of 5.5 percent over the applicable rate payable for such position or office in effect on Sept. 30, 1978, which was $60,662.50 for circuit judges.

Applicability to funds appropriated by any Act for fiscal year ending Sept. 30, 1980, of limitation of section 304 of Pub.L. 95–391 on use of funds to pay the salary or pay of any individual in legislative, executive, or judicial branch in position equal to or above level V of the Executive Schedule, see section 101 of Pub.L. 96–86, set out as a note under section 5318 of Title 5.

1978—Salaries of circuit judges increased to $60,700 effective on the first day of the first pay period beginning on or after Oct. 1, 1978, by Ex. Ord. No. 12087, Oct. 7, 1978, 43 F.R. 46823, formerly set out as a note under section 5332 of Title 5. Ex. Ord. No. 12087 further provided that pursuant to the Legislative Branch Appropriation Act, 1979 [Pub.L. 95–391, Title III, § 304, Sept. 30, 1978, 92 Stat. 788, set out as a note under section 5318 of Title 5], funds are not available to pay a salary at a rate which exceeds the rate in effect on Sept. 30, 1978, which was $57,500.

1977—Salaries of circuit judges increased to $57,500 per annum, upon recommendation of the President of the United States, see note set out under section 358 of Title 2, The Congress.

1976—Salaries of circuit judges increased to $46,800 effective on the first day of the first pay period beginning on or after Oct. 1, 1976, by Ex. Ord. No. 11941, Oct. 1, 1976, 41 F.R. 43889, formerly set out as a note under section 5332 of Title 5, Government Organization and Employees. Ex. Ord. No. 11941 further provided that pursuant to the Legislative Branch Appropriation Act, 1977, funds are not available to pay a salary at a rate which exceeds the rate in effect on Sept. 30, 1976, which was $44,600.

1975—Salaries of circuit judges increased to $44,600 effective on the first day of the first pay period beginning on or after Oct. 1, 1975, by Ex. Ord. No. 11883, Oct. 6, 1975, 40 F.R. 47091, formerly set out as a note under section 5332 of Title 5.

1969—Salary of circuit judges increased from $33,000 to $42,500 per annum, commencing February 14, 1969, upon recommendation of the President of the United States, see note set out under section 358 of Title 2, The Congress.

1946—The salaries of the circuit judges were increased from $12,500 to $17,500 a year by Act July 31, 1946, c. 704, § 1, 60 Stat. 716.

1926—Salaries of the circuit judges were increased from $8,500 to $12,500 a year by Act Dec. 13, 1926, c. 6, § 1, 44 Stat. 919.

1919—Salaries of the circuit judges were increased from $7,000 to $8,500 a year by Act Feb. 25, 1919, c. 29, § 1, 40 Stat. 1156.

1911—Salaries of circuit court judges had been set at $7,000 a year by the Judicial Code of 1911, Act Mar. 3, 1911, c. 231, § 118, 36 Stat. 1131.

Nomination to Federal Judgeship on Nondiscriminatory Basis

Section 211 of Pub.L. 98–353 provided that: "It is the sense of the Congress that the President, in selecting individuals for nomination to the Federal judgeships created by this Act [see Short Title of 1984 Amendments note set out under section 151 of this title], shall give due consideration to qualified individuals without regard to race, color, sex, religion, or national origin."

§ 45. Chief judges; precedence of judges

(a)(1) The chief judge of the circuit shall be the circuit judge in regular active service who is senior in commission of those judges who—

(A) are sixty-four years of age or under;

(B) have served for one year or more as a circuit judge; and

(C) have not served previously as chief judge.

(2)(A) In any case in which no circuit judge meets the qualifications of paragraph (1), the youngest circuit judge in regular active service who is sixty-five years of age or over and who has served as circuit judge for one year or more shall act as the chief judge.

(B) In any case under subparagraph (A) in which there is no circuit judge in regular active service who has served as a circuit judge for one year or more, the circuit judge in regular active service who is senior in commission and who has not served previously as chief judge shall act as the chief judge.

(3)(A) Except as provided in subparagraph (C), the chief judge of the circuit appointed under paragraph (1) shall serve for a term of seven years and shall serve after expiration of such term until another judge is eligible under paragraph (1) to serve as chief judge of the circuit.

(B) Except as provided in subparagraph (C), a circuit judge acting as chief judge under subparagraph (A) or (B) of paragraph (2) shall serve until a judge has been appointed who meets the qualifications under paragraph (1).

(C) No circuit judge may serve or act as chief judge of the circuit after attaining the age of seventy years unless no other circuit judge is qualified to serve as chief judge of the circuit under paragraph (1) or is qualified to act as chief judge under paragraph (2).

(b) The chief judge shall have precedence and preside at any session of the court which he attends. Other circuit judges of the court in regular active service shall have precedence and preside according to the seniority of their commissions. Judges whose commissions bear the same date shall have precedence according to seniority in age. The circuit justice, however, shall have precedence over all the circuit judges and shall preside at any session which he attends.

(c) If the chief judge desires to be relieved of his duties as chief judge while retaining his active status as circuit judge, he may so certify to the Chief Justice of the United States, and thereafter the chief judge of the circuit shall be such other circuit judge who is qualified to serve or act as chief judge under subsection (a).

(d) If a chief judge is temporarily unable to perform his duties as such, they shall be performed by the circuit judge in active service, present in the circuit and able and qualified to act, who is next in precedence.

(June 25, 1948, c. 646, 62 Stat. 871; Oct. 31, 1951, c. 655, § 35, 65 Stat. 723; Aug. 6, 1958, Pub.L. 85–593, § 1, 72 Stat. 497; Apr. 2, 1982, Pub.L. 97–164, Title II, §§ 201, 204, 96 Stat. 51, 53.)

HISTORICAL AND STATUTORY NOTES
Effective and Applicability Provisions

1982 Acts

Amendment by Pub.L. 97–164 effective Oct. 1, 1982, see section 402 of Pub.L. 97–164, set out as a note under section 171 of this title.

1958 Acts

Section 3 of Pub.L. 85–593, as amended by Pub.L. 95–486, § 4, Oct. 20, 1978, 92 Stat. 1632, provided that: "The amendments to sections 45 and 136 of title 28 of the United States Code [this section and section 136 of this title] made by this Act shall take effect at the expiration of one year from the date of enactment of this Act [Aug. 6, 1958]."

Savings Provisions

Section 203 of part A of Title II of Pub.L. 97–164 provided that:

"(a) The amendments to section 45 of title 28, United States Code [this section], and to section 136 of such title [section 136 of this title], made by sections 201 and 202 of this Act, shall not apply to or affect any person serving as chief judge on the effective date of this Act [Oct. 1, 1982].

"(b) The provisions of section 45(a) of title 28, United States Code [subsec. (a) of this section], as in effect on the

day before the effective date of this Act [Oct. 1, 1982], shall apply to the chief judge of a circuit serving on such effective date. The provisions of section 136(a) of title 28, United States Code [section 136(a) of this title], as in effect on the day before the effective date of this part [Oct. 1, 1982], shall apply to the chief judge of a district court serving on such effective date."

Appointment of Chief Judge of Court of Appeals for the Federal Circuit

Section 166 of Pub.L. 97–164 provided that: "Notwithstanding the provisions of section 45(a) of title 28, United States Code [subsec. (a) of this section], the first chief judge of the United States Court of Appeals for the Federal Circuit shall be the Chief Judge of the United States Court of Claims or the Chief Judge of the United States Court of Customs and Patent Appeals, whoever has served longer as chief judge of his court. Notwithstanding section 45 of title 28, United States Code [this section], whichever of the two chief judges does not become the first chief judge of the United States Court of Appeals for the Federal Circuit under the preceding sentence shall, while in active service, have precedence and be deemed senior in commission over all the circuit judges of the United States Court of Appeals for the Federal Circuit (other than the first chief judge of that circuit). When the person who first serves as chief judge of the United States Court of Appeals for the Federal Circuit vacates that position, the position shall be filled in accordance with section 45(a) of title 28, United States Code [subsec. (a) of this section], as modified by the preceding sentence of this section."

Chief Judge of Court of Appeals for District of Columbia

Section 2(a) of Act June 25, 1948, provided in part that the Chief Justice of the Court of Appeals for the District of Columbia in office on Sept. 1, 1948, shall thereafter be known as the Chief Judge.

§ 46. Assignment of judges; panels; hearings; quorum

(a) Circuit judges shall sit on the court and its panels in such order and at such times as the court directs.

(b) In each circuit the court may authorize the hearing and determination of cases and controversies by separate panels, each consisting of three judges, at least a majority of whom shall be judges of that court, unless such judges cannot sit because recused or disqualified, or unless the chief judge of that court certifies that there is an emergency including, but not limited to, the unavailability of a judge of the court because of illness. Such panels shall sit at the times and places and hear the cases and controversies assigned as the court directs. The United States Court of Appeals for the Federal Circuit shall determine by rule a procedure for the rotation of judges from panel to panel to ensure that all of the judges sit on a representative cross section of the cases heard and, notwithstanding the first sentence of this subsection, may determine by rule the number of judges, not less than three, who constitute a panel.

(c) Cases and controversies shall be heard and determined by a court or panel of not more than three judges (except that the United States Court of Appeals for the Federal Circuit may sit in panels of more than three judges if its rules so provide), unless a hearing or rehearing before the court in banc is ordered by a majority of the circuit judges of the circuit who are in regular active service. A court in banc shall consist of all circuit judges in regular active service, or such number of judges as may be prescribed in accordance with section 6 of Public Law 95–486 (92 Stat. 1633), except that any senior circuit judge of the circuit shall be eligible (1) to participate, at his election and upon designation and assignment pursuant to section 294(c) of this title and the rules of the circuit, as a member of an in banc court reviewing a decision of a panel of which such judge was a member, or (2) to continue to participate in the decision of a case or controversy that was heard or reheard by the court in banc at a time when such judge was in regular active service.

(d) A majority of the number of judges authorized to constitute a court or panel thereof, as provided in paragraph (c), shall constitute a quorum.

(June 25, 1948, c. 646, 62 Stat. 871; Nov. 13, 1963, Pub.L. 88–176, § 1(b), 77 Stat. 331; Oct. 20, 1978, Pub.L. 95–486, § 5(a), (b), 92 Stat. 1633; Apr. 2, 1982, Pub.L. 97–164, Title I, § 103, Title II, § 205, 96 Stat. 25, 53; Aug. 6, 1996, Pub.L. 104–175, § 1, 110 Stat. 1556.)

CHIEF CIRCUIT JUDGE (FIFTH CIRCUIT): ORDER DECLARING AN EMERGENCY UNDER 28 U.S.C. § 46(b)

This court is authorized 17 judges in active service. Today the number of active judges is 14. One of the vacancies has been in existence for two and one-half years. Two nominations have been sent to the Senate for its advice and consent and are pending. In addition, one active judge was recently injured seriously in an automobile accident and will be unavailable to perform his judicial duties for an indefinite period of time needed for his recuperation and rehabilitation. Effectively this places the court's strength at 13 active judges.

As of June 30, 1999, the court's workload is nearly at its historical record, with some 8,325 new filings and 5,430 pending actions.

During the last nine years, the court's filings have increased 65%, but the court has resisted an increase in the number of authorized judgeships, believing that efficiency and economy would thereby be promoted. The result has been an extremely heavy per judge workload even when operating with a full complement of judges. We have now reached the point where we are so far below our authorized strength that the timeliness and quality of our work will be jeopardized if we are unable to enlist the aid of visiting judges in greater numbers.

In sum, the three judicial vacancies, the injury to an active judge and the sustained high level of case filings have created a judicial emergency in the court. Until such time as

the injured judge can return to his judicial duties and until the President has nominated and the Congress has advised and consented to the appointment of the number of judges in regular active service provided by law, a judicial emergency exists. This emergency prevents the routine empaneling of three-judge panels consisting of judges at least a majority of whom are judges of this court.

During the continuation of this declared emergency, the hearing and determination of cases and controversies may be conducted by panels of three judges selected without regard to the qualification in 28 U.S.C. § 46(b) that a majority of each panel be composed of judges of this court.

Signed this 28th day of September, 1999.

CAROLYN DINEEN KING
CHIEF JUDGE

Filed: Sept. 28, 1999

CHIEF CIRCUIT JUDGE (FOURTH CIRCUIT): ORDER REGARDING PERFORMANCE OF JUDICIAL DUTIES

Pursuant to the authority set forth in 28 U.S.C. § 46(c) and 28 U.S.C. § 294(c), all senior circuit judges in this circuit are hereby assigned to perform all judicial duties in any case, or in the decision of any matter, such as a motion or any other procedural or administrative matter, which has been properly assigned to them, whether in the ordinary course of business or otherwise. Any senior circuit judge who undertakes the performance of any official duties pursuant to this designation consents to participate (except upon absence from duty station or the like) in the consideration of the same until terminated, including, but not exclusively, participation in in banc consideration of the matter.

ENTERED this 31st day of March, 1993.

SAM J. ERVIN, III
CHIEF CIRCUIT JUDGE

HISTORICAL AND STATUTORY NOTES

References in Text

Section 6 of Public Law 95–486 (92 Stat. 1633), referred to in subsec. (c), is section 6 of Pub.L. 95–486, Oct. 20, 1978, 92 Stat. 1633, which is set out as an Appeals Court Administrative Units note under section 41 of this title.

Effective and Applicability Provisions

1982 Acts

Amendment by Pub.L. 97–164 effective Oct. 1, 1982, see section 402 of Pub.L. 97–164, set out as a note under section 171 of this title.

§ 47. Disqualification of trial judge to hear appeal

No judge shall hear or determine an appeal from the decision of a case or issue tried by him.

(June 25, 1948, c. 646, 62 Stat. 872.)

§ 48. Terms of court

(a) The courts of appeals shall hold regular sessions at the places listed below, and at such other places within the respective circuit as each court may designate by rule.

Circuits	Places
District of Columbia	Washington.
First	Boston.
Second	New York.
Third	Philadelphia.
Fourth	Richmond, Asheville.
Fifth	New Orleans, Fort Worth, Jackson.
Sixth	Cincinnati.
Seventh	Chicago.
Eighth	St. Louis, Kansas City, Omaha, St. Paul.
Ninth	San Francisco, Los Angeles, Portland, Seattle.
Tenth	Denver, Wichita, Oklahoma City.
Eleventh	Atlanta, Jacksonville, Montgomery.
Federal	District of Columbia, and in any other place listed above as the court by rule directs.

(b) Each court of appeals may hold special sessions at any place within its circuit as the nature of the business may require, and upon such notice as the court orders. The court may transact any business at a special session which it might transact at a regular session.

(c) Any court of appeals may pretermit any regular session of court at any place for insufficient business or other good cause.

(d) The times and places of the sessions of the Court of Appeals for the Federal Circuit shall be prescribed with a view to securing reasonable opportunity to citizens to appear before the court with as little inconvenience and expense to citizens as is practicable.

(e) Each court of appeals may hold special sessions at any place within the United States outside the circuit as the nature of the business may require and upon such notice as the court orders, upon a finding by either the chief judge of the court of appeals (or, if the chief judge is unavailable, the most senior available active judge of the court of appeals) or the judicial council of the circuit that, because of emergency conditions, no location within the circuit is reasonably available where such special sessions could be held. The court may transact any business at a special session outside the circuit which it might transact at a regular session.

(f) If a court of appeals issues an order exercising its authority under subsection (e), the court—

(1) through the Administrative Office of the United States Courts, shall—

(A) send notice of such order, including the reasons for the issuance of such order, to the Committee on the Judiciary of the Senate and the Committee on the Judiciary of the House of Representatives; and

(B) not later than 180 days after the expiration of such court order submit a brief report to the Committee on the Judiciary of the Senate and the Committee on the Judiciary of the House of Representatives describing the impact of such order, including—

(i) the reasons for the issuance of such order;

(ii) the duration of such order;

(iii) the impact of such order on litigants; and

(iv) the costs to the judiciary resulting from such order; and

(2) shall provide reasonable notice to the United States Marshals Service before the commencement of any special session held pursuant to such order.

(June 25, 1948, c. 646, 62 Stat. 872; Oct. 31, 1951, c. 655, § 36, 65 Stat. 723; Oct. 14, 1980, Pub.L. 96–452, § 4, 94 Stat. 1994; Apr. 2, 1982, Pub.L. 97–164, Title I, § 104, 96 Stat. 26; Oct. 29, 1992, Pub.L. 102–572, Title V, § 501, 106 Stat. 4512; Sept. 9, 2005, Pub.L. 109–63, § 2(a), 119 Stat. 1993.)

HISTORICAL AND STATUTORY NOTES

Effective and Applicability Provisions

1992 Acts

Amendment by Pub.L. 102–572 effective Jan. 1, 1993, see section 1101(a) of Pub.L. 102–572, set out as a note under section 905 of Title 2, The Congress.

1982 Acts

Amendment by Pub.L. 97–164 effective Oct. 1, 1982, see section 402 of Pub.L. 97–164, set out as a note under section 171 of this title.

1980 Acts

Amendment by Pub.L. 96–452 effective Oct. 1, 1981, see section 12 of Pub.L. 96–452, set out as a note under section 41 of this title.

Survey of Judicial Business in Alaska

Section 23(a) of Pub.L. 86–70, June 25, 1959, 73 Stat. 147, provided that: "The Judicial Conference of the United States, with the assistance of the Administrative Office of the United States Courts, shall conduct a study, including a field survey, of the Federal judicial business arising in the State of Alaska with a view toward directing the United States Court of Appeals for the Ninth Circuit to hold such terms of court in Anchorage or such other Alaskan cities as may be necessary for the prompt and efficient administration of justice."

§ 49. Assignment of judges to division to appoint independent counsels

(a) Beginning with the two-year period commencing on the date of the enactment of this section, three judges or justices shall be assigned for each successive two-year period to a division of the United States Court of Appeals for the District of Columbia to be the division of the court for the purpose of appointing independent counsels. The Clerk of the United States Court of Appeals for the District of Columbia Circuit shall serve as the clerk of such division of the court and shall provide such services as are needed by such division of the court.

(b) Except as provided under subsection (f) of this section, assignment to such division of the court shall not be a bar to other judicial assignments during the term of such division.

(c) In assigning judges or justices to sit on such division of the court, priority shall be given to senior circuit judges and retired justices.

(d) The Chief Justice of the United States shall designate and assign three circuit court judges or justices, one of whom shall be a judge of the United States Court of Appeals for the District of Columbia, to such division of the court. Not more than one judge or justice or senior or retired judge or justice may be named to such division from a particular court.

(e) Any vacancy in such division of the court shall be filled only for the remainder of the two-year period in which such vacancy occurs and in the same manner as initial assignments to such division were made.

(f) Except as otherwise provided in chapter 40 of this title, no member of such division of the court who participated in a function conferred on the division under chapter 40 of this title involving an independent counsel shall be eligible to participate in any judicial proceeding concerning a matter which involves such independent counsel while such independent counsel is serving in that office or which involves the exercise of such independent counsel's official duties, regardless of whether such independent counsel is still serving in that office.

(Added Pub.L. 95–521, Title VI, § 602(a), Oct. 26, 1978, 92 Stat. 1873, and amended Pub.L. 97–409, § 2(b)(1), Jan. 3, 1983, 96 Stat. 2039; Pub.L. 99–554, Title I, § 144(g)(3), Oct. 27, 1986, 100 Stat. 3097; Pub.L. 100–191, §§ 4, 5(a), Dec. 15, 1987, 101 Stat. 1307.)

HISTORICAL AND STATUTORY NOTES

References in Text

The date of the enactment of this section, referred to in subsec. (a), means Oct. 26, 1978, the date on which Pub.L. 95–521 was approved.

Effective and Applicability Provisions

1987 Acts

Amendment by Pub.L. 100–191 effective on Dec. 15, 1987, see section 6 of Pub.L. 100–191, set out as a note under section 591 of this title.

1986 Acts

Amendment by Pub.L. 99–554 effective 30 days after Oct. 27, 1986, see section 302(a) of Pub.L. 99–554, as amended, set out as a note under section 581 of this title.

1978 Acts

Section effective Oct. 26, 1978, see section 604 of Pub.L. 95–521, set out as a note under section 591 of this title.

Appointment of Regulatory Independent Counsel

Division of the court described in this section authorized to appoint as independent counsel any individual who, on June 30, 1994, is serving as a regulatory independent counsel under parts 600 and 603 of title 28, Code of Federal Regulations, notwithstanding the restriction in section 593(b)(2) of this title, see section 7(h) of Pub.L. 103–270, set out as an Effective Date of 1994 Acts note under section 591 of this title.

CHAPTER 5—DISTRICT COURTS

HISTORICAL AND STATUTORY NOTES

Short Title

1978 Amendments

For short title of Pub.L. 95–408, Oct. 2, 1978, 92 Stat. 883, as "Federal District Court Organization Act of 1978", see note set out under section 1 of this title.

§ 81. Alabama

Alabama is divided into three judicial districts to be known as the Northern, Middle, and Southern Districts of Alabama.

Northern District

(a) The Northern District comprises seven divisions.

(1) The Northwestern Division comprises the counties of Colbert, Franklin, and Lauderdale.

Court for the Northwestern Division shall be held at Florence.

(2) The Northeastern Division comprises the counties of Cullman, Jackson, Lawrence, Limestone, Madison, and Morgan.

Court for the Northeastern Division shall be held at Huntsville and Decatur.

(3) The Southern Division comprises the counties of Blount, Jefferson, and Shelby.

Court for the Southern Division shall be held at Birmingham.

(4) The Eastern Division comprises the counties of Calhoun, Clay, Cleburne, and Talladega.

Court for the Eastern Division shall be held at Anniston.

(5) The Western Division comprises the counties of Bibb, Greene, Pickens, Sumter, and Tuscaloosa.

Court for the Western Division shall be held at Tuscaloosa.

(6) The Middle Division comprises the counties of Cherokee, De Kalb, Etowah, Marshall, and Saint Clair.

Court for the Middle Division shall be held at Gadsden.

(7) The Jasper Division comprises the counties of Fayette, Lamar, Marion, Walker, and Winston.

Court for the Jasper Division shall be held at Jasper.

Middle District

(b) The Middle District comprises three divisions.

(1) The Northern Division comprises the counties of Autauga, Barbour, Bullock, Butler, Chilton, Coosa, Covington, Crenshaw, Elmore, Lowndes, Montgomery, and Pike.

Court for the Northern Division shall be held at Montgomery.

(2) The Southern Division comprises the counties of Coffee, Dale, Geneva, Henry, and Houston.

Court for the Southern Division shall be held at Dothan.

(3) The Eastern Division comprises the counties of Chambers, Lee, Macon, Randolph, Russell, and Tallapoosa.

Court for the Eastern Division shall be held at Opelika.

Southern District

(c) The Southern District comprises two divisions.

(1) The Northern Division comprises the counties of Dallas, Hale, Marengo, Perry, and Wilcox.

Court for the Northern Division shall be held at Selma.

(2) The Southern Division comprises the counties of Baldwin, Choctaw, Clarke, Conecuh, Escambia, Mobile, Monroe, and Washington.

Court for the Southern Division shall be held at Mobile.

(June 25, 1948, c. 646, 62 Stat. 873; May 19, 1961, Pub.L. 87–36, § 3(a), 75 Stat. 83.)

§ 81A. Alaska

Alaska constitutes one judicial district.

Court shall be held at Anchorage, Fairbanks, Juneau, Ketchikan, and Nome.

(Added Pub.L. 85–508, § 12(b), July 7, 1958, 72 Stat. 348, and amended Pub.L. 86–70, § 23(b), June 25, 1959, 73 Stat. 147.)

HISTORICAL AND STATUTORY NOTES

Effective and Applicability Provisions

1958 Acts

Section 12 of Pub.L. 85–508 provided in part that this section, and the amendments to sections 133, 333, 373, 376, 460, 610, 753, 1252, 1291, 1292, 1294, 1346, 1963, 2072, 2201 and 2410 of this title, former section 341b of Title 5, Government Organization and Employees, and sections 3241, 3401, 3771 and 3772 of Title 18, Crimes and Criminal Procedure, shall be effective upon the admission of Alaska into the Union. Admission as a State was accomplished Jan. 3, 1959 upon issuance of Proc. No. 3269, Jan. 3, 1959, 24 F.R. 81, 73 Stat. c16, as required by sections 1 and 8(c) of Pub.L. 85–508. See notes set out preceding section 21 of Title 48, Territories and Insular Possessions.

Appeals

Section 14 of Pub.L. 85–508 provided that: "All appeals taken from the District Court for the Territory of Alaska to the Supreme Court of the United States or the United States Court of Appeals for the Ninth Circuit, previous to the admission of Alaska as a State, shall be prosecuted to final determination as though this Act had not been passed. All cases in which final judgment has been rendered in such district court, and in which appeals might be had except for the admission of such State, may still be sued out, taken, and prosecuted to the Supreme Court of the United States or the United States Court of Appeals for the Ninth Circuit under the provisions of then existing law, and there held and determined in like manner; and in either case, the Supreme Court of the United States, or the United States Court of Appeals, in the event of reversal, shall remand the said cause to either the State supreme court or other final appellate court of said State, or the United States district court for said district, as the case may require: *Provided*, That the time allowed by existing law for appeals from the district court for said Territory shall not be enlarged thereby."

Continuation of Suits

Section 13 of Pub.L. 85–508 provided that: "No writ, action, indictment, cause, or proceeding pending in the District Court for the Territory of Alaska on the date when said Territory shall become a State, and no case pending in an appellate court upon appeal from the District Court for the Territory of Alaska at the time said Territory shall become a State, shall abate by the admission of the State of Alaska into the Union, but the same shall be transferred and proceeded with as hereinafter provided.

"All civil causes of action and all criminal offenses which shall have arisen or been committed prior to the admission of said State, but as to which no suit, action, or prosecution shall be pending at the date of such admission, shall be subject to prosecution in the appropriate State courts or in the United States District Court for the District of Alaska in like manner, to the same extent, and with like right of

appellate review, as if said State had been created and said courts had been established prior to the accrual of said causes of action or the commission of such offenses; and such of said criminal offenses as shall have been committed against the laws of the Territory shall be tried and punished by the appropriate courts of said State, and such as shall have been committed against the laws of the United States shall be tried and punished in the United States District Court for the District of Alaska."

Pending Cases

Section 17 of Pub.L. 85–508 provided that: "All cases pending in the District Court for the Territory of Alaska at the time said Territory becomes a State not transferred to the United States District Court for the District of Alaska shall be proceeded with and determined by the courts created by said State with the right to prosecute appeals to the appellate courts created by said State, and also with the same right to prosecute appeals or writs of certiorari from the final determination in said causes made by the court of last resort created by such State to the Supreme Court of the United States, as now provided by law for appeals and writs of certiorari from the court of last resort of a State to the Supreme Court of the United States."

Schedule of Fees, Mileage, or Other Compensation

Section 23(c) of Pub.L. 86–70, June 25, 1959, 73 Stat. 147, provided that: "Such authority as has been exercised by the Attorney General heretofore, with regard to the Federal court system in Alaska, pursuant to section 30 of the Act of June 6, 1900 (48 U.S.C. 25) [omitted], shall continue to be exercised by him after the court created by section 12(b) of the Act of July 7, 1958 (72 Stat. 339, 348) [this section], providing for the admission of the State of Alaska into the Union, is established."

Succession of Courts

Section 16 of Pub.L. 85–508 provided that: "Jurisdiction of all cases pending or determined in the District Court for the Territory of Alaska not transferred to the United States District Court for the District of Alaska shall devolve upon and be exercised by the courts of original jurisdiction created by said State, which shall be deemed to be the successor of the District Court for the Territory of Alaska with respect to cases not so transferred and, as such, shall take and retain custody of all records, dockets, journals, and files of such court pertaining to such cases. The files and papers in all cases so transferred to the United States district court, together with a transcript of all book entries to complete the record in such particular cases so transferred, shall be in like manner transferred to said district court."

Termination of Jurisdiction of District Court for the Territory of Alaska

Section 18 of Pub.L. 85–508 provided that: "The provisions of the preceding sections with respect to the termination of the jurisdiction of the District Court for the Territory of Alaska, the continuation of suits, the succession of courts, and the satisfaction of rights of litigants in suits before such courts, shall not be effective until three years after the effective date of this Act [see section 8(b) of Pub.L. 85–508, set out as a note preceding section 21 of Title 48, Territories and Insular Possessions] unless the President, by Executive order, shall sooner proclaim that the United States District

Court for the District of Alaska, established in accordance with the provisions of this Act, is prepared to assume the functions imposed upon it. During such period of three years or until such Executive order is issued, the United States District Court for the Territory of Alaska shall continue to function as heretofore. The tenure of the judges, the United States attorneys, marshals, and other officers of the United States District Court for the Territory of Alaska shall terminate at such time as that court shall cease to function as provided in this section."

Based on Title 28, U.S.C., 1940 ed., § 216, and District of Columbia Code, 1940 ed., § 11–205 (Acts Feb. 9, 1893, c. 74, § 6, 27 Stat. 435; July 30, 1894, c. 172, § 2, 28 Stat. 161; Mar. 3, 1901, c. 854, § 225, 31 Stat. 1225; Mar. 3, 1911, c. 231, § 120, 36 Stat. 1132).

The provision in section 11–205 of the District of Columbia Code, 1940 ed., that a justice of the district court while on the bench of the Court of Appeals in the District of Columbia shall not sit in review of judgment, order, or decree rendered by him below, was consolidated with a similar provision of section 216 of Title 28 U.S.C., 1940 ed. The consolidation simplifies the language without change of substance.

Transfer of Cases

Section 15 of Pub.L. 85–508 provided that: "All causes pending or determined in the District Court for the Territory of Alaska at the time of the admission of Alaska as a State which are of such nature as to be within the jurisdiction of a district court of the United States shall be transferred to the United States District Court for the District of Alaska for final disposition and enforcement in the same manner as is now provided by law with reference to the judgments and decrees in existing United States district courts. All other causes pending or determined in the District Court for the Territory of Alaska at the time of the admission of Alaska as a State shall be transferred to the appropriate State court of Alaska. All final judgments and decrees rendered upon such transferred cases in the United States District Court for the District of Alaska may be reviewed by the Supreme Court of the United States or by the United States Court of Appeals for the Ninth Circuit in the same manner as is now provided by law with reference to the judgments and decrees in existing United States district courts."

§ 82. Arizona

Arizona constitutes one judicial district.

Court shall be held at Globe, Phoenix, Prescott, and Tucson.

(June 25, 1948, c. 646, 62 Stat. 874.)

§ 83. Arkansas

Arkansas is divided into two judicial districts to be known as the Eastern and Western Districts of Arkansas.

Eastern District

(a) The Eastern District comprises five divisions.

(1) The Eastern Division comprises the counties of Cross, Lee, Monroe, Phillips, Saint Francis, and Woodruff.

Court for the Eastern Division shall be held at Helena.

(2) The Western Division comprises the counties of Conway, Faulkner, Lonoke, Perry, Pope, Prairie, Pulaski, Saline, Van Buren, White, and Yell.

Court for the Western Division shall be held at Little Rock.

(3) The Pine Bluff Division comprises the counties of Arkansas, Chicot, Cleveland, Dallas, Desha, Drew, Grant, Jefferson, and Lincoln.

Court for the Pine Bluff Division shall be held at Pine Bluff.

(4) The Northern Division comprises the counties of Cleburne, Fulton, Independence, Izard, Jackson, Sharp, and Stone.

Court for the Northern Division shall be held at Batesville.

(5) The Jonesboro Division comprises the counties of Clay, Craighead, Crittenden, Greene, Lawrence, Mississippi, Poinsett, and Randolph.

Court for the Jonesboro Division shall be held at Jonesboro.

Western District

(b) The Western District comprises six divisions.

(1) The Texarkana Division comprises the counties of Hempstead, Howard, Lafayette, Little River, Miller, Nevada, and Sevier.

Court for the Texarkana Division shall be held at Texarkana, and may be held anywhere within the Federal courthouse in Texarkana that is located astride the State line between Texas and Arkansas.

(2) The El Dorado Division comprises the counties of Ashley, Bradley, Calhoun, Columbia, Ouachita, and Union.

Court for the El Dorado Division shall be held at El Dorado.

(3) The Fort Smith Division comprises the counties of Crawford, Franklin, Johnson, Logan, Polk, Scott, and Sebastian.

Court for the Fort Smith Division shall be held at Fort Smith.

(4) The Harrison Division comprises the counties of Baxter, Boone, Carroll, Marion, Newton, and Searcy.

Court for the Harrison Division shall be held at Harrison.

(5) The Fayetteville Division comprises the counties of Benton, Madison, and Washington.

Court for the Fayetteville Division shall be held at Fayetteville.

(6) The Hot Springs Division comprises the counties of Clark, Garland, Hot Springs, Montgomery, and Pike.

Court for the Hot Springs Division shall be held at Hot Springs.

(June 25, 1948, c. 646, 62 Stat. 874; May 19, 1961, Pub.L. 87–36, § 5, 75 Stat. 84; Dec. 10, 2004, Pub.L. 108–455, § 3, 118 Stat. 3628.)

§ 84. California

California is divided into four judicial districts to be known as the Northern, Eastern, Central, and Southern Districts of California.

Northern District

(a) The Northern District comprises the counties of Alameda, Contra Costa, Del Norte, Humboldt, Lake, Marin, Mendocino, Monterey, Napa, San Benito, Santa Clara, Santa Cruz, San Francisco, San Mateo, and Sonoma.

Court for the Northern District shall be held at Eureka, Oakland, San Francisco, and San Jose.

Eastern District

(b) The Eastern District comprises the counties of Alpine, Amador, Butte, Calaveras, Colusa, El Dorado, Fresno, Glenn, Inyo, Kern, Kings, Lassen, Madera, Mariposa, Merced, Modoc, Mono, Nevada, Placer, Plumas, Sacramento, San Joaquin, Shasta, Sierra, Siskiyou, Solano, Stanislaus, Sutter, Tehama, Trinity, Tulare, Tuolumne, Yolo, and Yuba.

Court for the Eastern District shall be held at Fresno, Redding, and Sacramento.

Central District

(c) The Central District comprises 3 divisions.

(1) The Eastern Division comprises the counties of Riverside and San Bernardino.

Court for the Eastern Division shall be held at a suitable site in the city of Riverside, the city of San Bernardino, or not more than 5 miles from the boundary of either such city.

(2) The Western Division comprises the counties of Los Angeles, San Luis Obispo, Santa Barbara, and Ventura.

Court for the Western Division shall be held at Los Angeles.

(3) The Southern Division comprises Orange County.

Court for the Southern Division shall be held at Santa Ana.

Southern District

(d) The Southern District comprises the counties of Imperial and San Diego.

Court for the Southern District shall be held at San Diego.

(June 25, 1948, c. 646, 62 Stat. 875; Mar. 18, 1966, Pub.L. 89–372, § 3(a), 80 Stat. 75; Oct. 15, 1980, Pub.L. 96–462, § 2, 94 Stat. 2053; Aug. 26, 1992, Pub.L. 102–357, § 2, 106 Stat. 958.)

HISTORICAL AND STATUTORY NOTES

Effective and Applicability Provisions

1992 Acts

Section 3 of Pub.L. 102–357 provided that:

"**(a)** In general

"This Act and the amendments made by this Act [amending this section and enacting provisions set out as a note under this section] shall take effect 6 months after the date of the enactment of this Act [Aug. 26, 1992].

"**(b)** Pending cases not affected

"This Act and the amendments made by this Act [amending this section and enacting provisions set out as a note under this section] shall not affect any action commenced before the effective date of this Act and pending in the United States District Court for the Central District of California on such date.

"**(c)** Juries not affected

"This Act and the amendments made by this Act [amending this section and enacting provisions set out as a note under this section] shall not affect the composition, or preclude the service, of any grand or petit jury summoned, empaneled, or actually serving in the Central Judicial District of California on the effective date of this Act."

1980 Acts

Section 7 of Pub.L. 96–462 provided that:

"**(a)** This Act and the amendments made by this Act [amending sections 84, 95, 105, 113, and 124 of this title and enacting provisions set out as notes under sections 95, 105, and 113 of this title] shall take effect on October 1, 1981.

"**(b)** Nothing in this Act shall affect the composition or preclude the service of any grand or petit juror summoned, empaneled, or actually serving in any judicial district on the effective date of this Act [Oct. 1, 1981]."

1966 Acts

Section 3(i) of Pub.L. 89–372 provided that: "The provisions of this section [amending this section and enacting provisions set out as a note under this section and section 133 of this title] shall become effective six months after the date of enactment of this Act [March 18, 1966]."

Congressional Findings Concerning Creation of Three Divisions in Central District

Section 1 of Pub.L. 102–357 provided that:

"The Congress makes the following findings:

"**(1)** The Federal Government has the responsibility to provide quality services which are readily accessible to the people it serves.

"**(2)** The court facilities in the Central Judicial District of California are presently inadequate, and current and projected growth exacerbates the problem.

"**(3)** The population demographics of southern California have changed dramatically over the last decade, as the center of population shifts inland. Between 1980 and 1990,

the population of Riverside County increased 76.5 percent, and San Bernardino County's population increased 58.5 percent, to a combined population of 2,600,000.

"**(4)** In the next 15 years, the population in Riverside and San Bernardino Counties is expected to increase again by 70 percent, and 67 percent, respectively. By the year 2005, Riverside and San Bernardino Counties will have 4,400,000 residents.

"**(5)** As a result of the population growth, the freeways connecting the Pacific coast and the inland areas are tremendously overburdened, and Federal offices along the coast are no longer accessible to the residents of Riverside and San Bernardino Counties.

"**(6)** The creation of 3 divisions in the Central Judicial District of California is urgently needed to provide for the delivery of judicial services to all areas and all residents of the Central Judicial District of California."

Creation of Eastern and Central Districts: Transfer of District Judges; Transfer and Appointment of United States Attorneys and United States Marshals

Section 3(b) to (g) of Pub.L. 89–372 provided that:

"**(b)** The two district judges for the northern district of California holding office on the day before the effective date of this section [see Effective and Applicability Provisions of 1966 Acts note under this section] and whose official station is Sacramento shall, on and after such date, be district judges for the eastern district of California. All other district judges for the northern district of California holding office on the day before the effective date of this section shall, on and after such date, be district judges for the northern district of California.

"**(c)** The district judge for the southern district of California, residing in the northern division thereof and holding office on the day before the effective date of this section [see Effective and Applicability Provisions of 1966 Acts note under this section], shall, on and after such date, be a district judge for the eastern district of California. The two district judges for the southern district of California holding office on the day before the effective date of this section, and whose official station is San Diego shall, on and after such date, be the district judges for the southern district of California. All other district judges for the southern district of California holding office on the day before the effective date of this section shall, on and after such date, be district judges for the central district of California.

"**(d)** Nothing in this Act [amending sections 44, 84, and 133 of this title and enacting provisions set out as notes under sections 44, 84, and 133 of this title] shall in any manner affect the tenure of office of the United States attorney and the United States marshal for the northern district of California who are in office on the effective date of this section [see Effective and Applicability Provisions of 1966 Amendments note under this section], and who shall be during the remainder of their present terms of office the United States attorney and marshal for such district as constituted by this Act.

"**(e)** Nothing in this Act [amending sections 44, 84, and 133 of this title and enacting provisions set out as notes under sections 44, 84, and 133 of this title] shall in any manner affect the tenure of office of the United States attorney and the United States marshal for the southern district of California who are in office on the effective date of

this section, and who shall be during the remainder of their present terms of office the United States attorney and marshal for the central district of California.

"(f) The President shall appoint, by and with the advice and consent of the Senate, a United States attorney and a United States marshal for the southern district of California.

"(g) The President shall appoint, by and with the advice and consent of the Senate, a United States attorney and a United States marshal for the eastern district of California."

Study of Judicial Business in Central District, California and Eastern District, New York and Recommendations for Creation of New Judicial Districts

Pub.L. 95–573, § 5, Nov. 2, 1978, 92 Stat. 2458, required the Director of the Administrative Office of the United States Courts to conduct a study of the judicial business of the Central District of California and the Eastern District of New York, within one year of Nov. 2, 1978, and to make recommendations to Congress with respect to the need for creation of new judicial districts.

§ 85. Colorado

Colorado constitutes one judicial district.

Court shall be held at Boulder, Colorado Springs, Colorado Springs,[1] Denver, Durango, Grand Junction, Montrose, Pueblo, and Sterling.

(June 25, 1948, c. 646, 62 Stat. 875; Nov. 8, 1984, Pub.L. 98–620, Title IV, § 409, 98 Stat. 3362; Dec. 10, 2004, Pub.L. 108–455, § 5, 118 Stat. 3629; Dec. 23, 2004, Pub.L. 108–482, Title III, § 301, 118 Stat. 3918.)

[1] So in original. Pub.L. 108–455, § 5 and Pub.L. 108–482, § 301 both added "Colorado Springs," after "Boulder,".

HISTORICAL AND STATUTORY NOTES
Effective and Applicability Provisions

1984 Acts

Section 411 of Pub.L. 98–620 provided that:

"(a) The amendments made by this subtitle [amending sections 85, 90, 93, 112, 124 and 126 of this title and enacting provisions set out as notes under sections 1, 90, 93, and 124 of this title] shall take effect on January 1, 1985.

"(b) The amendments made by this subtitle shall not affect the composition, or preclude the service, of any grand or petit jury summoned, impaneled, or actually serving on the effective date of this subtitle [Jan. 1, 1985]."

§ 86. Connecticut

Connecticut constitutes one judicial district.

Court shall be held at Bridgeport, Hartford, New Haven, New London, and Waterbury.

(June 25, 1948, c. 646, 62 Stat. 875; May 19, 1961, Pub.L. 87–36, § 3(b), 75 Stat. 83; Sept. 7, 1966, Pub.L. 89–558, 80 Stat. 705.)

§ 87. Delaware

Delaware constitutes one judicial district.

Court shall be held at Wilmington.

(June 25, 1948, c. 646, 62 Stat. 875.)

§ 88. District of Columbia

The District of Columbia constitutes one judicial district.

Court shall be held at Washington.

(June 25, 1948, c. 646, 62 Stat. 875.)

§ 89. Florida

Florida is divided into three judicial districts to be known as the Northern, Middle, and Southern Districts of Florida.

Northern District

(a) The Northern District comprises the counties of Alachua, Bay, Calhoun, Dixie, Escambia, Franklin, Gadsden, Gilchrist, Gulf, Holmes, Jackson, Jefferson, Lafayette, Leon, Levy, Liberty, Madison, Okaloosa, Santa Rosa, Taylor, Wakulla, Walton, and Washington.

Court for the Northern District shall be held at Gainesville, Marianna, Panama City, Pensacola, and Tallahassee.

Middle District

(b) The Middle District comprises the counties of Baker, Bradford, Brevard, Charlotte, Citrus, Clay, Collier, Columbia, De Soto, Duval, Flagler, Glades, Hamilton, Hardee, Hendry, Hernando, Hillsborough, Lake, Lee, Manatee, Marion, Nassau, Orange, Osceola, Pasco, Pinellas, Polk, Putnam, St. Johns, Sarasota, Seminole, Sumter, Suwannee, Union, and Volusia.

Court for the Middle District shall be held at Fernandina, Fort Myers, Jacksonville, Live Oak, Ocala, Orlando, Saint Petersburg, and Tampa.

Southern District

(c) The Southern District comprises the counties of Broward, Dade, Highlands, Indian River, Martin, Monroe, Okeechobee, Palm Beach, and Saint Lucie.

Court for the Southern District shall be held at Fort Lauderdale, Fort Pierce, Key West, Miami, and West Palm Beach.

(June 25, 1948, c. 646, 62 Stat. 876; July 17, 1952, c. 929, 66 Stat. 757; May 19, 1961, Pub.L. 87–36, § 3(f), 75 Stat. 83; July 30, 1962, Pub.L. 87–562, § 1, 76 Stat. 247; June 2, 1970, Pub.L. 91–272, § 10, 84 Stat. 298; Oct. 2, 1978, Pub.L. 95–408, § 4(a), 92 Stat. 884; Nov. 19, 1988, Pub.L. 100–702, Title X, § 1021(a), 102 Stat. 4672.)

HISTORICAL AND STATUTORY NOTES
Effective and Applicability Provisions

1988 Acts

Section 1021(b), (c) of Pub. L. 100–702 provided that:

"(b) **Effective Date.**—(1) The amendments made by this section [amending subsecs. (b) and (c) of this section] shall take effect 90 days after the date of enactment of this title [Nov. 19, 1988].

"(2) The amendments made by subsection (a) [amending subsecs. (b) and (c) of this section] shall apply to any action commenced in the United States District Court for the Middle District of Florida, or in the United States District Court for the Southern District of Florida, on or after the effective date of this title [probably should be effective date of this section], and shall not affect any action pending in either such court on such effective date.

"(c) Juries.—The amendments made by this section [amending subsecs. (b) and (c) of this section] shall not affect the composition, or preclude the service, of any grand or petit jury summoned, empaneled, or actually serving on the effective date of this title [probably should be effective date of this section]."

1978 Acts

Section 5 of Pub.L. 95–408 provided that:

"(a) The amendments made by this Act [amending sections 89, 93, 97, 98, 104, 112, 114, and 133 of this title and enacting provisions set out as a note under section 81 of this title] shall take effect 180 days after the date of enactment of this Act [Oct. 2, 1978].

"(b) Nothing in this Act [amending sections 89, 93, 97, 98, 104, 112, 114, and 133 of this title and enacting provisions set out as a note under section 81 of this title] shall affect the composition or preclude the service of any grand or petit juror summoned, empaneled, or actually serving in any judicial district on the effective date of this Act."

1962 Acts

Section 5 of Pub.L. 87–562 provided that: "This Act [amending this section and section 133 of this title, and enacting provisions set out as notes under this section and section 142 of this title] shall become effective ninety days after the date of enactment [July 30, 1962]."

District Judges, United States Attorneys, and United States Marshals; Designations; Tenure; Appointments

Section 2 of Pub.L. 87–562 provided that:

"(a) The district judge appointed September 26, 1950, the district judge appointed August 13, 1955, and the district judge appointed March 8, 1961, all for the Southern District of Florida, shall hereafter be designated as district judges for the Middle District of Florida.

"(b) The district judge for the Northern and Southern Districts of Florida shall hereafter be designated as the district judge for the Northern, Middle, and Southern Districts of Florida.

"(c) Nothing in this Act [amending this section and section 133 of this title, and enacting provisions set out as notes under this section and section 142 of this title] shall in any manner affect the tenure of office of the United States Attorney and the United States Marshal for the Northern District of Florida who are in office at the time of the enactment of this Act [July 30, 1962], and who shall be during the remainder of their present terms of office the United States Attorney and Marshal for such district as constituted by this Act.

"(d) Nothing in this Act [amending this section and section 133 of this title, and enacting provisions set out as notes under this section and section 142 of this title] shall in any manner affect the tenure of office of the United States Attorney and the United States Marshal for the Southern District of Florida who are in office at the time of the

enactment of this Act [July 30, 1962], and who shall be during the remainder of their present terms of office the United States Attorney and Marshal for the Middle District of Florida as constituted by this Act.

"(e) The President is authorized to appoint, by and with the advice and consent of the Senate, a United States Attorney and a United States Marshal for the Southern District of Florida."

Elimination of District Judgeship for Northern, Middle, and Southern Districts of Florida

District judgeship for northern, middle, and southern districts changed to district judgeship for middle district only, see section (b) of Pub.L. 89–372, set out as a note under section 133 of this title.

§ 90. Georgia

Georgia is divided into three judicial districts to be known as the Northern, Middle, and Southern Districts of Georgia.

Northern District

(a) The Northern District comprises four divisions.

(1) The Gainesville Division comprises the counties of Banks, Barrow, Dawson, Fannin, Forsyth, Gilmer, Habersham, Hall, Jackson, Lumpkin, Pickens, Rabun, Stephens, Towns, Union, and White.

Court for the Gainesville Division shall be held at Gainesville.

(2) The Atlanta Division comprises the counties of Cherokee, Clayton, Cobb, De Kalb, Douglas, Fulton, Gwinnett, Henry, Newton, and Rockdale.

Court for the Atlanta Division shall be held at Atlanta.

(3) The Rome Division comprises the counties of Bartow, Catoosa, Chattooga, Dade, Floyd, Gordon, Murray, Paulding, Polk, Walker, and Whitfield.

Court for the Rome Division shall be held at Rome.

(4) The Newnan Division comprises the counties of Carroll, Coweta, Fayette, Haralson, Heard, Meriwether, Pike, Spalding, and Troup.

Court for the Newnan Division shall be held at Newnan.

Middle District

(b) The Middle District comprises seven divisions.

(1) The Athens Division comprises the counties of Clarke, Elbert, Franklin, Greene, Hart, Madison, Morgan, Oconee, Oglethorpe, and Walton.

Court for the Athens Division shall be held at Athens.

(2) The Macon Division comprises the counties of Baldwin, Bibb, Bleckley, Butts, Crawford, Hancock, Houston, Jasper, Jones, Lamar, Monroe,

Peach, Pulaski, Putnam, Twiggs, Upson, Washington, and Wilkinson.

Court for the Macon Division shall be held at Macon.

(3) The Columbus Division comprises the counties of Chattahoochee, Clay, Harris, Marion, Muscogee, Quitman, Randolph, Stewart, Talbot, and Taylor.

Court for the Columbus Division shall be held at Columbus.

(4) The Americus Division comprises the counties of Ben Hill, Crisp, Dooly, Lee, Macon, Schley, Sumter, Terrell, Webster, and Wilcox.

Court for the Americus Division shall be held at Americus.

(5) The Albany Division comprises the counties of Baker, Calhoun, Dougherty, Early, Miller, Mitchell, Turner, and Worth.

Court for the Albany Division shall be held at Albany.

(6) The Valdosta Division comprises the counties of Berrien, Clinch, Cook, Echols, Irwin, Lanier, Lowndes, and Tift.

Court for the Valdosta Division shall be held at Valdosta.

(7) The Thomasville Division comprises the counties of Brooks, Colquitt, Decatur, Grady, Seminole, and Thomas.

Court for the Thomasville Division shall be held at Thomasville.

Southern District

(c) The Southern District comprises six divisions.

(1) The Augusta Division comprises the counties of Burke, Columbia, Glascock, Jefferson, Lincoln, McDuffie, Richmond, Taliaferro, Warren, and Wilkes.

Court for the Augusta Division shall be held at Augusta.

(2) The Dublin Division comprises the counties of Dodge, Johnson, Laurens, Montgomery, Telfair, Treutlen, and Wheeler.

Court for the Dublin Division shall be held at Dublin.

(3) The Savannah Division comprises the counties of Bryan, Chatham, Effingham, and Liberty.

Court for the Savannah Division shall be held at Savannah.

(4) The Waycross Division comprises the counties of Atkinson, Bacon, Brantley, Charlton, Coffee, Pierce, and Ware.

Court for the Waycross Division shall be held at Waycross.

(5) The Brunswick Division comprises the counties of Appling, Camden, Glynn, Jeff Davis, Long, McIntosh, and Wayne.

Court for the Brunswick Division shall be held at Brunswick.

(6) The Statesboro Division comprises the counties of Bulloch, Candler, Emanuel, Evans, Jenkins, Screven, Tattnall, and Toombs.

Court for the Statesboro Division shall be held at Statesboro.

(June 25, 1948, c. 646, 62 Stat. 876; Aug. 16, 1949, c. 444, 63 Stat. 610; Oct. 31, 1951, c. 655, § 36a, 65 Stat. 723; Nov. 8, 1984, Pub.L. 98–620, Title IV, § 408(a)–(c), 98 Stat. 3362; Nov. 14, 1986, Pub.L. 99–657, § 3, 100 Stat. 3670.)

HISTORICAL AND STATUTORY NOTES

Effective and Applicability Provisions

1986 Acts

Amendment by Pub.L. 99–657 effective 90 days after Nov. 14, 1986, and not to affect any action commenced before and pending on such effective date, or to affect the composition, or preclude the service, of any grand or petit jury summoned, empaneled, or actually serving on such date, see section 4 of Pub.L. 99–657, set out as a note under section 121 of this title.

1984 Acts

Section 408(d) of Pub.L. 98–620 provided that: "The amendments made by this section [amending subsecs. (a) and (c) of this section] shall apply to any action commenced in the United States District Court for the Northern District of Georgia on or after the effective date of this subtitle [Jan. 1, 1985], and shall not affect any action pending in such court on such effective date."

Amendment by Pub.L. 98–620 effective Jan. 1, 1985, and not to affect the composition, or preclude the service, of any grand or petit jury summoned, impaneled, or actually serving on that date, see section 411 of Pub.L. 98–620, set out as a note under section 85 of this title.

§ 91. Hawaii

Hawaii constitutes one judicial district which includes the Midway Islands, Wake Island, Johnston Island, Sand Island, Kingman Reef, Palmyra Island, Baker Island, Howland Island, Jarvis Island, Canton Island, and Enderbury Island: *Provided*, That the inclusion of Canton and Enderbury Islands in such judicial district shall in no way be construed to be prejudicial to the claims of the United Kingdom to said Islands in accordance with the agreement of April 6, 1939, between the Governments of the United States and of the United Kingdom to set up a regime for their use in common.

Court shall be held at Honolulu.

(June 25, 1948, c. 646, 62 Stat. 877; May 24, 1949, c. 139, § 64a, 63 Stat. 99; Mar. 18, 1959, Pub.L. 86–3, § 14(i), 73 Stat. 11; July 12, 1960, Pub.L. 86–624, § 19, 74 Stat. 416.)

HISTORICAL AND STATUTORY NOTES

Effective and Applicability Provisions

1959 Acts

Section 14 of Pub.L. 86–3 provided that the amendments of sections 91, 373, 1252, 1293, and 1294 of this title, sections 3771 and 3772 of Title 18, Crimes and Criminal Procedure, and section 644a of Title 48, Territories and Insular Possessions, the repeal of sections 536, 539, 634, 634a, and 645 of title 48, and notes set out under sections 371 and 373 of this title, are effective on admission of the State of Hawaii into the Union. See Admission of Hawaii as State note under this section.

Admission of Hawaii as State

Admission of Hawaii into the Union was accomplished Aug. 21, 1959, upon issuance of Proc. No. 3309, Aug. 21, 1959, 25 F.R. 6868, 73 Stat. c74, as required by sections 1 and 7(c) of Pub.L. 86–3, Mar. 18, 1959, 73 Stat. 4, set out as notes preceding section 491 of Title 48, Territories and Insular Possessions.

Appeals

Section 13 of Pub.L. 86–3 provided that: "Parties shall have the same rights of appeal from and appellate review of final decisions of the United States District Court for the District of Hawaii or the Supreme Court of the Territory of Hawaii in any case finally decided prior to admission of said State into the Union, whether or not an appeal therefrom shall have been perfected prior to such admission, and the United States Court of Appeals for the Ninth Circuit and the Supreme Court of the United States shall have the same jurisdiction therein, as by law provided prior to admission of said State into the Union, and any mandate issued subsequent to the admission of said State shall be to the United States District Court for the District of Hawaii or a court of the State, as may be appropriate. Parties shall have the same rights of appeal from and appellate review of all orders, judgments, and decrees of the United States District Court for the District of Hawaii and of the Supreme Court of the State of Hawaii as successor to the Supreme Court of the Territory of Hawaii, in any case pending at the time of admission of said State into the Union, and the United States Court of Appeals for the Ninth Circuit and the Supreme Court of the United States shall have the same jurisdiction therein, as by law provided in any case arising subsequent to the admission of said State into the Union."

Canton and Enderbury Islands; Sovereignty of Kiribati

By a treaty of friendship, TIAS 10777, which entered into force Sept. 23, 1983, the United States recognized the sovereignty of Kiribati over Canton Island and Enderbury Island.

Continuation of Suits

Section 12 of Pub.L. 86–3 provided that: "No writ, action, indictment, cause, or proceeding pending in any court of the Territory of Hawaii or in the United States District Court for the District of Hawaii shall abate by reason of the admission of said State into the Union, but the same shall be transferred to and proceeded with in such appropriate State courts as shall be established under the constitution of said State, or shall continue in the United States District Court for the District of Hawaii, as the nature of the case may require. And no writ, action, indictment, cause or proceeding shall abate by reason of any change in the courts, but

shall be proceeded with in the State or United States courts according to the laws thereof, respectively. And the appropriate State courts shall be the successors of the courts of the Territory as to all cases arising within the limits embraced within the jurisdiction of such courts, respectively, with full power to proceed with the same, and award mesne or final process therein, and all the files, records, indictments, and proceedings relating to any such writ, action, indictment, cause or proceeding shall be transferred to such appropriate State courts and the same shall be proceeded with therein in due course of law.

"All civil causes of action and all criminal offenses which shall have arisen or been committed prior to the admission of said State, but as to which no writ, action, indictment or proceeding shall be pending at the date of such admission, shall be subject to prosecution in the appropriate State courts or in the United States District Court for the District of Hawaii in like manner, to the same extent, and with like right of appellate review, as if said State had been created and said State courts had been established prior to the accrual of such causes of action or the commission of such offenses. The admission of said State shall effect no change in the substantive or criminal law governing such causes of action and criminal offenses which shall have arisen or been committed; and such of said criminal offenses as shall have been committed against the laws of the Territory shall be tried and punished by the appropriate courts of said State, and such as shall have been committed against the laws of the United States shall be tried and punished in the United States District Court for the District of Hawaii."

Court of the United States; District Judges

Section 9(a) of Pub.L. 86–3 provided that: "The United States District Court for the District of Hawaii established by and existing under title 28 of the United States Code shall thenceforth be a court of the United States with judicial power derived from article III, section 1, of the Constitution of the United States: *Provided, however,* That the terms of office of the district judges for the district of Hawaii then in office shall terminate upon the effective date of this section and the President, pursuant to sections 133 and 134 of title 28, United States Code, as amended by this Act, shall appoint, by and with the advice and consent of the Senate, two district judges for the said district who shall hold office during good behavior."

Section 9 of Pub.L. 86–3 provided in part that subsec. (a) of that section shall be effective upon the admission of the State of Hawaii into the Union.

Extension of Jurisdiction of United States District Court for District of Hawaii and of Civil and Criminal Laws to Midway, Wake, Johnson, Sand, etc., Islands

The jurisdiction of the United States District Court for the District of Hawaii and the laws of the United States relating to civil acts or offenses consummated or committed on the high seas on board a vessel belonging to the United States were extended to the Midway Islands, Wake, Johnson, Sand, etc., Islands by section 644a of Title 48, Territories and Insular Possessions.

§ 92. Idaho

Idaho, exclusive of Yellowstone National Park, constitutes one judicial district.

Court shall be held at Boise, Coeur d'Alene, Moscow, and Pocatello.

(June 25, 1948, c. 646, 62 Stat. 877; June 2, 1970, Pub.L. 91–272, § 5, 84 Stat. 297.)

§ 93. Illinois

Illinois is divided into three judicial districts to be known as the Northern, Central, and Southern Districts of Illinois.

Northern District

(a) The Northern District comprises two divisions.

(1) The Eastern Division comprises the counties of Cook, Du Page, Grundy, Kane, Kendall, Lake, La Salle, and Will.

Court for the Eastern Division shall be held at Chicago and Wheaton.

(2) The Western Division comprises the counties of Boone, Carroll, De Kalb, Jo Daviess, Lee, McHenry, Ogle, Stephenson, Whiteside, and Winnebago.

Court for the Western Division shall be held at Freeport and Rockford.

Central District

(b) The Central District comprises the counties of Adams, Brown, Bureau, Cass, Champaign, Christian, Coles, De Witt, Douglas, Edgar, Ford, Fulton, Greene, Hancock, Henderson, Henry, Iroquois, Kankakee, Knox, Livingston, Logan, McDonough, McLean, Macoupin, Macon, Marshall, Mason, Menard, Mercer, Montgomery, Morgan, Moultrie, Peoria, Piatt, Pike, Putnam, Rock Island, Sangamon, Schuyler, Scott, Shelby, Stark, Tazewell, Vermilion, Warren, and Woodford.

Court for the Central District shall be held at Champaign/Urbana, Danville, Peoria, Quincy, Rock Island, and Springfield.

Southern District

(c) The Southern District comprises the counties of Alexander, Bond, Calhoun, Clark, Clay, Clinton, Crawford, Cumberland, Edwards, Effingham, Fayette, Franklin, Gallatin, Hamilton, Hardin, Jackson, Jasper, Jefferson, Jersey, Johnson, Lawrence, Madison, Marion, Massac, Monroe, Perry, Pope, Pulaski, Randolph, Richland, St. Clair, Saline, Union, Wabash, Washington, Wayne, White, and Williamson.

Court for the Southern District shall be held at Alton, Benton, Cairo, and East Saint Louis.

(June 25, 1948, c. 646, 62 Stat. 878; Aug. 10, 1950, c. 675, § 1, 64 Stat. 438; May 19, 1961, Pub.L. 87–36, § 3(c), 75 Stat. 83; June 2, 1970, Pub.L. 91–272, § 8, 84 Stat. 297; Oct. 2, 1978, Pub.L. 95–408, § 4(b) (1), 92 Stat. 884; Nov. 2, 1978, Pub.L. 95–573, § 1, 92 Stat. 2458; Nov. 8, 1984, Pub.L. 98–620, Title

IV, § 406(a), (c), 98 Stat. 3361; Dec. 6, 1999, Pub.L. 106–130, § 2, 113 Stat. 1677.)

HISTORICAL AND STATUTORY NOTES

Effective and Applicability Provisions

1984 Acts

Section 406(b) of Pub.L. 98–620 provided that: "The amendments made by subsection (a) of this section [amending subsec. (a) of this section] shall apply to any action commenced in the United States District Court for the Northern District of Illinois on or after the effective date of this subtitle [Jan. 1, 1985], and shall not affect any action pending in such court on such effective date."

Amendment by Pub.L. 98–620 effective Jan. 1, 1985, and not to affect the composition, or preclude the service, of any grand or petit jury summoned, impaneled, or actually serving on that date, see section 411 of Pub.L. 98–620, set out as a note under section 85 of this title.

1978 Acts

Section 6 of Pub.L. 95–573, as amended by Pub.L. 96–4, § 2, Mar. 30, 1979, 93 Stat. 7, provided that:

"(a) Except as provided in subsection (b) of this section, the provisions of this Act [amending sections 93, 99, 112 and 118 of this title and enacting provisions set out as a note under section 84 of this title] shall take effect 180 days after the date of enactment of this Act [Nov. 2, 1978].

"(b)(1) The provisions of section 5 of this Act [set out as a note under section 84 of this title] shall take effect on the date of enactment of this Act [Nov. 2, 1978].

"(2) The provisions of the first section of this Act [amending this section] shall take effect on March 31, 1979.

"(c) Nothing in this Act [amending sections 93, 99, 112, and 118 of this title and enacting provisions set out as a note under section 84 of this title] shall affect the composition or preclude the service of any grand or petit juror summoned, empaneled, or actually serving in any judicial district on the effective date of this Act."

Amendment by Pub.L. 95–408 effective 180 days after Oct. 2, 1978, such amendment not to affect the composition or preclude the service of any grand or petit juror summoned, empaneled, or actually serving in any judicial district on the effective date of this Act, see section 5 of Pub.L. 95–408, set out as a note under section 89 of this title.

District Judges, United States Attorneys, Assistant United States Attorneys, and United States Marshals For Central and Southern Districts; Designation; Tenure; Appointment; Grand Jury

Pub.L. 95–408, § 4(b)(2)–(4), as added Pub.L. 96–4, § 1, Mar. 30, 1979, 93 Stat. 6, provided that:

"(2) The district judge for the Eastern District of Illinois in office on the effective date of this Act [180 days after Oct. 2, 1978] who is senior in commission shall, on and after the effective date of this Act, be a district judge for the Southern District of Illinois. The remaining district judge for the Eastern District of Illinois who is in office on the effective date of this Act and the district judges for the Southern District of Illinois who are in office on the effective date of this Act shall, on and after the effective date of this Act, be district judges for the Central District of Illinois. The President shall appoint, by and with the advice and consent

of the Senate, a second district judge for the Southern District of Illinois.

"(3) This section does not in any manner affect the tenure of the United States attorney, the assistant United States attorneys, or the United States marshal for the Eastern District of Illinois or for the Southern District of Illinois who are in office on the effective date of this Act [180 days after Oct. 2, 1978]. The United States attorney, the assistant United States attorneys, and the United States marshal for the Eastern District and for the Southern District of Illinois shall, on the effective date of this Act, become the United States attorney, the assistant United States attorneys, and the United States marshal for the Southern District and for the Central District of Illinois, respectively.

"(4) Notwithstanding section 3240 of title 18, United States Code [section 3240 of Title 18, Crimes and Criminal Procedure], any grand jury impaneled on or after the effective date of this Act [180 days after Oct. 2, 1978] by a district court for the Central District or the Southern District of Illinois may inquire into and return indictments charging offenses against the criminal laws of the United States alleged to have been committed anywhere within the territory of the respective judicial districts as such districts were constituted before or after the effective date of this Act."

§ 94. Indiana

Indiana is divided into two judicial districts to be known as the Northern and Southern Districts of Indiana.

Northern District

(a) The Northern District comprises three divisions.

(1) The Fort Wayne Division comprises the counties of Adams, Allen, Blackford, De Kalb, Grant, Huntington, Jay, Lagrange, Noble, Steuben, Wells, and Whitley.

Court for the Fort Wayne Division shall be held at Fort Wayne.

(2) The South Bend Division comprises the counties of Cass, Elkhart, Fulton, Kosciusko, La Porte, Marshall, Miami, Pulaski, St. Joseph, Starke, and Wabash.

Court for the South Bend Division shall be held at South Bend.

(3) The Hammond Division comprises the counties of Benton, Carroll, Jasper, Lake, Newton, Porter, Tippecanoe, Warren, and White.

Court for the Hammond Division shall be held at Hammond and Lafayette.

Southern District

(b) The Southern District comprises four divisions.

(1) The Indianapolis Division comprises the counties of Bartholomew, Boone, Brown, Clinton, Decatur, Delaware, Fayette, Fountain, Franklin, Hamilton, Hancock, Hendricks, Henry, Howard, Johnson, Madison, Marion, Monroe, Montgomery, Morgan, Randolph, Rush, Shelby, Tipton, Union, and Wayne.

Court for the Indianapolis Division shall be held at Indianapolis and Richmond.

(2) The Terre Haute Division comprises the counties of Clay, Greene, Knox, Owen, Parke, Putnam, Sullivan, Vermilion, and Vigo.

Court for the Terre Haute Division shall be held at Terre Haute.

(3) The Evansville Division comprises the counties of Davies, Dubois, Gibson, Martin, Perry, Pike, Posey, Spencer, Vanderburgh, and Warrick.

Court for the Evansville Division shall be held at Evansville.

(4) The New Albany Division comprises the counties of Clark, Crawford, Dearborn, Floyd, Harrison, Jackson, Jefferson, Jennings, Lawrence, Ohio, Orange, Ripley, Scott, Switzerland, and Washington.

Court for the New Albany Division shall be held at New Albany.

(June 25, 1948, c. 646, 62 Stat. 878; Feb. 10, 1954, c. 6, § 2(b)(7), 68 Stat. 11; June 2, 1970, Pub.L. 91–272, § 9, 84 Stat. 298.)

§ 95. Iowa

Iowa is divided into two judicial districts to be known as the Northern and Southern Districts of Iowa.

Northern District

(a) The Northern District comprises four divisions.

(1) The Cedar Rapids Division comprises the counties of Benton, Cedar, Grundy, Hardin, Iowa, Jones, Linn, and Tama.

Court for the Cedar Rapids Division shall be held at Cedar Rapids.

(2) The Eastern Division comprises the counties of Allamakee, Black Hawk, Bremer, Buchanan, Chickasaw, Clayton, Delaware, Dubuque, Fayette, Floyd, Howard, Jackson, Mitchell, and Winneshiek.

Court for the Eastern Division shall be held at Dubuque and Waterloo.

(3) The Western Division comprises the counties of Buena Vista, Cherokee, Clay, Crawford, Dickinson, Ida, Lyon, Monona, O'Brien, Osceola, Plymouth, Sac, Sioux, and Woodbury.

Court for the Western Division shall be held at Sioux City.

(4) The Central Division comprises the counties of Butler, Calhoun, Carroll, Cerro Gordo, Emmet, Franklin, Hamilton, Hancock, Humboldt, Kossuth, Palo Alto, Pocahontas, Webster, Winnebago, Worth, and Wright.

Court for the Central Division shall be held at Fort Dodge and Mason City.

Southern District

(b) The Southern District comprises six divisions.

(1) The Central Division comprises the counties of Boone, Dallas, Greene, Guthrie, Jasper, Madison, Marion, Marshall, Polk, Poweshiek, Story, and Warren.

Court for the Central Division shall be held at Des Moines.

(2) The Eastern Division comprises the counties of Des Moines, Henry, Lee, Louisa, and Van Buren.

Court for the Eastern Division shall be held at Keokuk.

(3) The Western Division comprises the counties of Audubon, Cass, Fremont, Harrison, Mills, Montgomery, Page, Pottawattamie, and Shelby.

Court for the Western Division shall be held at Council Bluffs.

(4) The Southern Division comprises the counties of Adair, Adams, Clarke, Decatur, Lucas, Ringgold, Taylor, Union, and Wayne.

Court for the Southern Division shall be held at Creston.

(5) The Davenport Division comprises the counties of Clinton, Johnson, Muscatine, Scott, and Washington.

Court for the Davenport Division shall be held at Davenport.

(6) The Ottumwa Division comprises the counties of Appanoose, Davis, Jefferson, Keokuk, Mahaska, Monroe, and Wapello.

Court for the Ottumwa Division shall be held at Ottumwa.

(June 25, 1948, c. 646, 62 Stat. 879; Oct. 15, 1980, Pub.L. 96–462, § 3(a), 94 Stat. 2053.)

HISTORICAL AND STATUTORY NOTES

Effective and Applicability Provisions

1980 Acts

Amendment by Pub.L. 96–462 effective Oct. 1, 1981, but not to affect the composition or preclude the service of any grand or petit juror summoned, empaneled, or actually serving in any judicial district on Oct. 1, 1981, see section 7 of Pub.L. 96–462, set out as a note under section 84 of this title.

Section 3(b) of Pub.L. 96–462 provided that: "The amendments made by subsection (a) [amending subsec. (b)(3), (4) of this section] shall not apply to any action commenced before the effective date of such amendments [Oct. 1, 1981] and pending in the United States District Court for the Southern District of Iowa on such date."

Holding Court for the Southern District of Iowa

Pub.L. 107–273, Div. C, Title I, § 11029, Nov. 2, 2002, 116 Stat. 1836, as amended Pub.L. 108–455, § 1, Dec. 10, 2004,

118 Stat. 3628, provided that: "Notwithstanding any other provision of law, during the period beginning on January 1, 2003, through July 1, 2006, the United States District Court for the Southern District of Iowa may—

"(1) with the consent of the parties in any case filed in the Eastern Division or the Davenport Division of the Southern District of Iowa, hold court on that case in Rock Island, Illinois; and

"(2) summon jurors from the Southern District of Iowa to serve in any case described under paragraph (1)."

§ 96. Kansas

Kansas constitutes one judicial district.

Court shall be held at Kansas City, Lawrence, Leavenworth, Salina, Topeka, Hutchinson, Wichita, Dodge City, and Fort Scott.

(June 25, 1948, c. 646, 62 Stat. 880; Aug. 27, 1949, c. 516, 63 Stat. 666; Oct. 27, 1986, Pub.L. 99–554, Title I, § 141, 100 Stat. 3096.)

HISTORICAL AND STATUTORY NOTES

Effective and Applicability Provisions

1986 Acts

Amendment by Pub.L. 99–554 effective 30 days after Oct. 27, 1986, see section 302(a) of Pub.L. 99–554, set out as a note under section 581 of this title.

§ 97. Kentucky

Kentucky is divided into two judicial districts to be known as the Eastern and Western Districts of Kentucky.

Eastern District

(a) The Eastern District comprises the counties of Anderson, Bath, Bell, Boone, Bourbon, Boyd, Boyle, Bracken, Breathitt, Campbell, Carroll, Carter, Clark, Clay, Elliott, Estill, Fayette, Fleming, Floyd, Franklin, Gallatin, Garrard, Grant, Greenup, Harlan, Harrison, Henry, Jackson, Jessamine, Johnson, Kenton, Knott, Knox, Laurel, Lawrence, Lee, Leslie, Letcher, Lewis, Lincoln, McCreary, Madison, Magoffin, Martin, Mason, Menifee, Mercer, Montgomery, Morgan, Nicholas, Owen, Owsley, Pendleton, Perry, Pike, Powell, Pulaski, Robertson, Rockcastle, Rowan, Scott, Shelby, Trimble, Wayne, Whitley, Wolfe, and Woodford.

Court for the Eastern District shall be held at Ashland, Catlettsburg, Covington, Frankfort, Jackson, Lexington, London, Pikeville, and Richmond.

Western District

(b) The Western District comprises the counties of Adair, Allen, Ballard, Barren, Breckenridge, Bullitt, Butler, Caldwell, Calloway, Carlisle, Casey, Christian, Clinton, Crittenden, Cumberland, Daviess, Edmonson, Fulton, Graves, Grayson, Green, Hancock, Hardin, Hart, Henderson, Hickman, Hopkins, Jefferson, Larue, Livingston, Logan, Lyon, McCracken, McLean,

Marion, Marshall, Meade, Metcalfe, Monroe, Muhlenberg, Nelson, Ohio, Oldham, Russell, Simpson, Spencer, Taylor, Todd, Trigg, Union, Warren, Washington, and Webster.

Court for the Western District shall be held at Bowling Green, Louisville, Owensboro, and Paducah.

(June 25, 1948, c. 646, 62 Stat. 880; Oct. 2, 1978, Pub.L. 95–408, § 2(a), 92 Stat. 883.)

HISTORICAL AND STATUTORY NOTES

Effective and Applicability Provisions

1978 Acts

Amendment by Pub.L. 95–408 effective 180 days after Oct. 2, 1978, such amendment not to affect the composition or preclude the service of any grand or petit juror summoned, empaneled, or actually serving in any judicial district on the effective date of this Act, see section 5 of Pub.L. 95–408, set out as a note under section 89 of this title.

§ 98. Louisiana

Louisiana is divided into three judicial districts to be known as the Eastern, Middle, and Western Districts of Louisiana.

Eastern District

(a) The Eastern District comprises the parishes of Assumption, Jefferson, Lafourche, Orleans, Plaquemines, Saint Bernard, Saint Charles, Saint James, Saint John the Baptist, Saint Tammany, Tangipahoa, Terrebonne, and Washington.

Court for the Eastern District shall be held at New Orleans, and Houma.

Middle District

(b) The Middle District comprises the parishes of Ascension, East Baton Rouge, East Feliciana, Iberville, Livingston, Pointe Coupee, Saint Helena, West Baton Rouge, and West Feliciana.

Court for the Middle District shall be held at Baton Rouge.

Western District

(c) The Western District comprises the parishes of Acadia, Allen, Avoyelles, Beauregard, Bienville, Bossier, Caddo, Calcasieu, Caldwell, Cameron, Catahoula, Claiborne, Concordia, Jefferson Davis, De Soto, East Carroll, Evangeline, Franklin, Grant, Iberia, Jackson, Lafayette, La Salle, Lincoln, Madison, Morehouse, Natchitoches, Ouachita, Rapides, Red River, Richland, Sabine, Saint Landry, Saint Martin, Saint Mary, Tensas, Union, Vermilion, Vernon, Webster, West Carroll, and Winn.

Court for the Western District shall be held at Alexandria, Lafayette, Lake Charles, Monroe, Opelousas, and Shreveport.

(June 25, 1948, c. 646, 62 Stat. 881; May 19, 1961, Pub.L. 87–36, § 4, 75 Stat. 83; Dec. 18, 1971, Pub.L. 92–208, § 3(a), 85 Stat. 741; Oct. 2, 1978, Pub.L. 95–408, § 3(a), 92 Stat. 883; July 10, 1984, Pub.L. 98–353, Title II, § 203(b), 98 Stat. 350.)

HISTORICAL AND STATUTORY NOTES

Effective and Applicability Provisions

1978 Acts

Amendment by Pub.L. 95–408 effective 180 days after Oct. 2, 1978, such amendment not to affect the composition or preclude the service of any grand or petit juror summoned, empaneled, or actually serving in any judicial district on the effective date of this Act, see section 5 of Pub.L. 95–408, set out as a note under section 89 of this title.

1971 Acts

Section 3(f) of Pub.L. 92–208 provided that: "The provisions of this section [amending this section and sections 133 and 134 of this title and enacting provisions set out as a note under this section] shall become effective one hundred and twenty days after the date of enactment of this Act [Dec. 18, 1971]."

District Judge, United States Attorney, and United States Marshal For Middle District; Designation; Tenure; Appointment

Section 3(b), (c) of Pub.L. 92–208 provided that:

"(b) The district judge for the Eastern District of Louisiana holding office on the day immediately prior to the effective date of this section [see Effective and Applicability Provisions of 1971 Amendments note under this section], and whose official station on such date is Baton Rouge, shall, on and after such date, be the district judge for the Middle District of Louisiana. All other district judges for the Eastern District of Louisiana holding office on the day immediately prior to the effective date of this section shall be district judges for the Eastern District of Louisiana as constituted by this section.

"(c)(1) Nothing in this section [amending this section and sections 133 and 134 of this title] shall in any manner affect the tenure of office of the United States attorney and the United States marshal for the Eastern District of Louisiana who are in office on the effective date of this section [see Effective and Applicability Provisions of 1971 Amendments note under this section], and who shall be during the remainder of their present terms of office the United States attorney and marshal for the Eastern District of Louisiana as constituted by this section.

"(2) The President shall appoint, by and with the advice and consent of the Senate, a United States attorney and marshal for the Middle District of Louisiana."

§ 99. Maine

Maine constitutes one judicial district.

Court shall be held at Bangor and Portland.

(June 25, 1948, c. 646, 62 Stat. 881; Nov. 2, 1978, Pub.L. 95–573, § 2, 92 Stat. 2458.)

HISTORICAL AND STATUTORY NOTES

Effective and Applicability Provisions

1978 Acts

Amendment by Pub.L. 95–573 effective 180 days after Nov. 2, 1978, except as otherwise provided, except that nothing in this Act shall affect the composition or preclude the service of any grand or petit juror summoned, empaneled, or actually serving in any judicial district on such effective date, see section 6 of Pub.L. 95–573, set out as a note under section 93 of this title.

§ 100. Maryland

Maryland constitutes one judicial district comprising two divisions.

(1) The Northern Division comprises the counties of Allegany, Anne Arundel, Baltimore, Caroline, Carroll, Cecil, Dorchester, Frederick, Garrett, Harford, Howard, Kent, Queen Anne's, Somerset, Talbot, Washington, Wicomico, and Worcester, and the City of Baltimore.

Court for the Northern Division shall be held at Baltimore, Cumberland, and Denton.

(2) The Southern Division comprises the counties of Calvert, Charles, Montgomery, Prince George's, and St. Mary's.

Court for the Southern Division shall be held at a suitable site in Montgomery or Prince George's County not more than five miles from the boundary of Montgomery and Prince George's Counties.

(June 25, 1948, c. 646, 62 Stat. 882; Dec. 14, 1970, Pub.L. 91–546, § 4, 84 Stat. 1412; Oct. 14, 1988, Pub.L. 100–487, § 1, 102 Stat. 2431.)

HISTORICAL AND STATUTORY NOTES

Effective and Applicability Provisions

1988 Acts

Section 2 of Pub.L. 100–487 provided that:

"(a) **In General.**—This Act [Pub.L. 100–487] and the amendments made by this Act [amending this section] shall take effect 180 days after the date of the enactment of this Act [Oct. 14, 1988].

"(b) **Pending Cases Not Affected.**—This Act [Pub.L. 100–487] and the amendments made by this Act [amending this section] shall not affect any action commenced before the effective date of this Act [180 days after Oct. 14, 1988] and pending in the United States District Court for the District of Maryland on such date.

"(c) **Juries Not Affected.**—This Act [Pub.L. 100–487] and the amendments made by this Act [amending this section] shall not affect the composition, or preclude the service, of any grand or petit jury summoned, empaneled, or actually serving in the Judicial District of Maryland on the effective date of this Act [180 days after Oct. 14, 1988]."

§ 101. Massachusetts

Massachusetts constitutes one judicial district.

Court shall be held at Boston, New Bedford, Springfield, and Worcester.

(June 25, 1948, c. 646, 62 Stat. 882.)

§ 102. Michigan

Michigan is divided into two judicial districts to be known as the Eastern and Western Districts of Michigan.

Eastern District

(a) The Eastern District comprises two divisions.

(1) The Southern Division comprises the counties of Genesee, Jackson, Lapeer, Lenawee, Livingston, Macomb, Monroe, Oakland, Saint Clair, Sanilac, Shiawassee, Washtenaw, and Wayne.

Court for the Southern Division shall be held at Ann Arbor, Detroit, Flint, and Port Huron.

(2) The Northern Division comprises the counties of Alcona, Alpena, Arenac, Bay, Cheboygan, Clare, Crawford, Gladwin, Gratiot, Huron, Iosco, Isabella, Midland, Montmorency, Ogemaw, Oscoda, Otsego, Presque Isle, Roscommon, Saginaw, and Tuscola.

Court for the Northern Division shall be held at Bay City.

Western District

(b) The Western District comprises two divisions.

(1) The Southern Division comprises the counties of Allegan, Antrim, Barry, Benzie, Berrien, Branch, Calhoun, Cass, Charlevoix, Clinton, Eaton, Emmet, Grand Traverse, Hillsdale, Ingham, Ionia, Kalamazoo, Kalkaska, Kent, Lake, Leelanau, Manistee, Mason, Mecosta, Missaukee, Montcalm, Muskegon, Newaygo, Oceana, Osceola, Ottawa, Saint Joseph, Van Buren, and Wexford.

Court for the Southern Division shall be held at Grand Rapids, Kalamazoo, Lansing, and Traverse City.

(2) The Northern Division comprises the counties of Alger, Baraga, Chippewa, Delta, Dickinson, Gogebic, Houghton, Iron, Keweenaw, Luce, Mackinac, Marquette, Menominee, Ontonagon, and Schoolcraft.

Court for the Northern Division shall be held at Marquette and Sault Sainte Marie.

(June 25, 1948, c. 646, 62 Stat. 882; Feb. 10, 1954, c. 6, § 2(b)(8), 68 Stat. 11; May 19, 1961, Pub.L. 87–36, § 3(d), 75 Stat. 83; Oct. 6, 1964, Pub.L. 88–627, 78 Stat. 1003; June 2, 1970, Pub.L. 91–272, § 11, 84 Stat. 298.)

§ 103. Minnesota

Minnesota constitutes one judicial district comprising six divisions.

(1) The First Division comprises the counties of Dodge, Fillmore, Houston, Mower, Olmsted, Steele, Wabasha, and Winona.

Court for the First Division shall be held at Winona.

(2) The Second Division comprises the counties of Blue Earth, Brown, Cottonwood, Faribault, Freeborn, Jackson, Lac qui Parle, Le Sueur, Lincoln, Lyon, Martin, Murray, Nicollet, Nobles, Pipestone, Redwood, Rock, Sibley, Waseca, Watonwan, and Yellow Medicine.

Court for the Second Division shall be held at Mankato.

(3) The Third Division comprises the counties of Chisago, Dakota, Goodhue, Ramsey, Rice, Scott, and Washington.

Court for the Third Division shall be held at Saint Paul.

(4) The Fourth Division comprises the counties of Anoka, Carver, Chippewa, Hennepin, Isanti, Kandiyohi, McLeod, Meeker, Renville, Sherburne, Swift, and Wright.

Court for the Fourth Division shall be held at Minneapolis.

(5) The Fifth Division comprises the counties of Aitkin, Benton, Carlton, Cass, Cook, Crow Wing, Itasca, Kanabec, Koochiching, Lake, Mille Lacs, Morrison, Pine, and Saint Louis.

Court for the Fifth Division shall be held at Duluth.

(6) The Sixth Division comprises the counties of Becker, Beltrami, Big Stone, Clay, Clearwater, Douglas, Grant, Hubbard, Kittson, Lake of the Woods, Mahnomen, Marshall, Norman, Otter Tail, Pennington, Polk, Pope, Red Lake, Roseau, Stearns, Stevens, Todd, Traverse, Wadena, and Wilkin.

Court for the Sixth Division shall be held at Fergus Falls.

(June 25, 1948, c. 646, 62 Stat. 882.)

§ 104. Mississippi

Mississippi is divided into two judicial districts to be known as the northern and southern districts of Mississippi.

Northern District

(a) The northern district comprises four divisions.

(1) Eastern division comprises the counties of Alcorn, Attala, Chickasaw, Choctaw, Clay, Itawamba, Lee, Lowndes, Monroe, Oktibbeha, Prentiss, Tishomingo, and Winston.

Court for the eastern division shall be held at Aberdeen, Ackerman, and Corinth.

(2) The Western Division comprises the counties of Benton, Calhoun, Grenada, Lafayette, Marshall, Montgomery, Pontotoc, Tippah, Union, Webster, and Yalobusha.

Court for the western division shall be held at Oxford.

(3) The Delta Division comprises the counties of Bolivar, Coahoma, De Soto, Panola, Quitman, Tallahatchie, Tate, and Tunica.

Court for the Delta Division shall be held at Clarksdale and Cleveland.

(4) The Greenville Division comprises the counties of Carroll, Humphreys, Leflore, Sunflower, and Washington.

Court for the Greenville Division shall be held at Greenville.

Southern District

(b) The southern district comprises five divisions.

(1) The Jackson Division comprises the counties of Amite, Copiah, Franklin, Hinds, Holmes, Leake, Lincoln, Madison, Pike, Rankin, Scott, Simpson, and Smith.

Court for the Jackson Division shall be held at Jackson.

(2) The Eastern Division comprises the counties of Clarke, Jasper, Kemper, Lauderdale, Neshoba, Newton, Noxubee, and Wayne.

Court for the Eastern Division shall be held at Meridian.

(3) The western division comprises the counties of Adams, Claiborne, Issaquena, Jefferson, Sharkey, Warren, Wilkinson, and Yazoo.

Court for the western division shall be held at Natchez and Vicksburg.

(4) The southern division comprises the counties of George, Hancock, Harrison, Jackson, Pearl River, and Stone.

Court for the southern division shall be held at Biloxi and Gulfport.

(5) The Hattiesburg division comprises the counties of Covington, Forrest, Greene, Jefferson Davis, Jones, Lamar, Lawrence, Marion, Perry, and Walthall.

Court for the Hattiesburg division shall be held at Hattiesburg.

(June 25, 1948, c. 646, 62 Stat. 883; Aug. 7, 1950, c. 601, 64 Stat. 415; Sept. 27, 1967, Pub.L. 90–92, 81 Stat. 229; Dec. 14, 1970, Pub.L. 91–546, §§ 2, 3, 84 Stat. 1412; Oct. 2, 1978, Pub.L. 95–408, § 2(b), 92 Stat. 883; Dec. 6, 1999, Pub.L. 106–130, § 1, 113 Stat. 1677; Dec. 10, 2004, Pub.L. 108–455, § 2, 118 Stat. 3628.)

HISTORICAL AND STATUTORY NOTES

Effective and Applicability Provisions

1978 Acts

Amendment by Pub.L. 95–408 effective 180 days after Oct. 2, 1978, such amendment not to affect the composition or preclude the service of any grand or petit juror summoned, empaneled, or actually serving in any judicial district on the

effective date of this Act, see section 5 of Pub.L. 95–408, set out as a note under section 89 of this title.

§ 105. Missouri

Missouri is divided into two judicial districts to be known as the Eastern and Western Districts of Missouri.

Eastern District

(a) The Eastern District comprises three divisions.

(1) The Eastern Division comprises the counties of Crawford, Dent, Franklin, Gasconade, Iron, Jefferson, Lincoln, Maries, Phelps, Saint Charles, Saint Francois, Saint Genevieve, Saint Louis, Warren, and Washington, and the city of Saint Louis.

Court for the Eastern Division shall be held at Saint Louis.

(2) The Northern Division comprises the counties of Adair, Audrain, Chariton, Clark, Knox, Lewis, Linn, Macon, Marion, Monroe, Montgomery, Pike, Ralls, Randolph, Schuyler, Scotland, and Shelby.

Court for the Northern Division shall be held at Hannibal.

(3) The Southeastern Division comprises the counties of Bollinger, Butler, Cape Girardeau, Carter, Dunklin, Madison, Mississippi, New Madrid, Pemiscot, Perry, Reynolds, Ripley, Scott, Shannon, Stoddard, and Wayne.

Court for the Southeastern Division shall be held at Cape Girardeau.

Western District

(b) The Western District comprises five divisions.

(1) The Western Division comprises the counties of Bates, Carroll, Cass, Clay, Henry, Jackson, Johnson, Lafayette, Ray, Saint Clair, and Saline.

Court for the Western Division shall be held at Kansas City.

(2) The Southwestern Division comprises the counties of Barton, Barry, Jasper, Lawrence, McDonald, Newton, Stone, and Vernon.

Court for the Southwestern Division shall be held at Joplin.

(3) The Saint Joseph Division comprises the counties of Andrew, Atchison, Buchanan, Caldwell, Clinton, Daviess, De Kalb, Gentry, Grundy, Harrison, Holt, Livingston, Mercer, Nodaway, Platte, Putnam, Sullivan, and Worth.

Court for the Saint Joseph Division shall be held at Saint Joseph.

(4) The Central Division comprises the counties of Benton, Boone, Callaway, Camden, Cole, Cooper, Hickory, Howard, Miller, Moniteau, Morgan, Osage, and Pettis.

Court for the Central Division shall be held at Jefferson City.

(5) The Southern Division comprises the counties of Cedar, Christian, Dade, Dallas, Douglas, Greene, Howell, Laclede, Oregon, Ozark, Polk, Pulaski, Taney, Texas, Webster, and Wright.

Court for the Southern Division shall be held at Springfield.

(June 25, 1948, c. 646, 62 Stat. 884; May 31, 1962, Pub.L. 87–461, 76 Stat. 85; Oct. 15, 1980, Pub.L. 96–462, § 4(a), 94 Stat. 2053.)

HISTORICAL AND STATUTORY NOTES

Effective and Applicability Provisions

1980 Acts

Amendment by Pub.L. 96–462 effective Oct. 1, 1981 with that amendment not to affect the composition or preclude the service of any grand or petit juror summoned, empaneled, or actually serving in any judicial district on Oct. 1, 1981, see section 7 of Pub.L. 96–462, set out as a note under section 84 of this title.

Section 4(b) of Pub.L. 96–462 provided that: "The amendments made by subsection (a) [amending subsec. (a)(1), (2) of this section] shall not apply to any action commenced before the effective date of such amendments [Oct. 1, 1981] and pending in the United States District Court for the Eastern District of Missouri on such date."

§ 106. Montana

Montana, exclusive of Yellowstone National Park, constitutes one judicial district.

Court shall be held at Billings, Butte, Glasgow, Great Falls, Havre, Helena, Kalispell, Lewistown, Livingston, Miles City, and Missoula.

(June 25, 1948, c. 646, 62 Stat. 884.)

§ 107. Nebraska

Nebraska constitutes one judicial district.

Court shall be held at Lincoln, North Platte, and Omaha.

(June 25, 1948, c. 646, 62 Stat. 884; Aug. 9, 1955, c. 627, § 1, 69 Stat. 546.)

HISTORICAL AND STATUTORY NOTES

Effective and Applicability Provisions

1955 Acts

Section 2 of Act Aug. 9, 1955, provided that: "The amendment made by the first section of this Act [amending this section] shall take effect on September 1, 1955."

§ 108. Nevada

Nevada constitutes one judicial district.

Court shall be held at Carson City, Elko, Las Vegas, Reno, Ely, and Lovelock.

(June 25, 1948, c. 646, 62 Stat. 885; Dec. 1, 1990, Pub.L. 101–650, Title III, § 324(a)(1), 104 Stat. 5120.)

§ 109. New Hampshire

New Hampshire constitutes one judicial district.

Court shall be held at Concord and Littleton.
(June 25, 1948, c. 646, 62 Stat. 885.)

§ 110. New Jersey

New Jersey constitutes one judicial district.

Court shall be held at Camden, Newark and Trenton.
(June 25, 1948, c. 646, 62 Stat. 885.)

§ 111. New Mexico

New Mexico constitutes one judicial district.

Court shall be held at Albuquerque, Las Cruces, Las Vegas, Roswell, Santa Fe, and Silver City.
(June 25, 1948, c. 646, 62 Stat. 885.)

§ 112. New York

New York is divided into four judicial districts to be known as the Northern, Southern, Eastern, and Western Districts of New York.

Northern District

(a) The Northern District comprises the counties of Albany, Broome, Cayuga, Chenango, Clinton, Columbia, Cortland, Delaware, Essex, Franklin, Fulton, Greene, Hamilton, Herkimer, Jefferson, Lewis, Madison, Montgomery, Oneida, Onondaga, Oswego, Otsego, Rensselaer, Saint Lawrence, Saratoga, Schenectady, Schoharie, Tioga, Tompkins, Ulster, Warren, and Washington.

Court for the Northern District shall be held at Albany, Auburn, Binghamton, Malone, Plattsburgh,[1] Syracuse, Utica, Watertown, and Plattsburgh.[1]

Southern District

(b) The Southern District comprises the counties of Bronx, Dutchess, New York, Orange, Putnam, Rockland, Sullivan, and Westchester and concurrently with the Eastern District, the waters within the Eastern District.

Court for the Southern District shall be held at New York, White Plains, and in the Middletown-Wallkill area of Orange County or such nearby location as may be deemed appropriate.

Eastern District

(c) The Eastern District comprises the counties of Kings, Nassau, Queens, Richmond, and Suffolk and concurrently with the Southern District, the waters within the counties of Bronx and New York.

Court for the Eastern District shall be held at Brooklyn, Hauppauge, Hempstead (including the village of Uniondale), and Central Islip.

Western District

(d) The Western District comprises the counties of Allegany, Cattaraugus, Chautauqua, Chemung, Erie, Genesee, Livingston, Monroe, Niagara, Ontario, Orleans, Schuyler, Seneca, Steuben, Wayne, Wyoming, and Yates.

Court for the Western District shall be held at Buffalo, Canandaigua, Elmira, Jamestown, and Rochester.

(June 25, 1948, c. 646, 62 Stat. 885; Dec. 18, 1967, Pub.L. 90–217, 81 Stat. 662; Dec. 14, 1970, Pub.L. 91–546, § 1, 84 Stat. 1412; Apr. 28, 1978, Pub.L. 95–271, § 1, 92 Stat. 221; Oct. 2, 1978, Pub.L. 95–408, § 4(c), 92 Stat. 885; Nov. 2, 1978, Pub.L. 95–573, § 3, 92 Stat. 2458; Nov. 8, 1984, Pub.L. 98–620, Title IV, § 405, 98 Stat. 3361; Dec. 1, 1990, Pub.L. 101–650, Title III, § 324(a)(2), 104 Stat. 5120; Oct. 19, 1996, Pub.L. 104–317, Title VI, § 609, 110 Stat. 3860; Nov. 29, 1999, Pub.L. 106–113, Div. B, § 1000(a)(1) [Title III, § 306], 113 Stat. 1535, 1501A–37; Dec. 10, 2004, Pub.L. 108–455, § 4, 118 Stat. 3628; Dec. 23, 2004, Pub.L. 108–482, Title III, § 302, 118 Stat. 3918.)

[1] So in original. Pub.L. 108–455, § 4 and Pub.L. 108–482, § 302 both inserted a reference to Plattsburgh in this paragraph.

HISTORICAL AND STATUTORY NOTES
Effective and Applicability Provisions
1984 Acts

Amendment by Pub.L. 98–620 to take effect on Jan. 1, 1985, and not to affect the composition, or preclude the service, of any grand or petit jury summoned, impaneled, or actually serving on that date, see section 411 of Pub.L. 98–620, set out as a note under section 85 of this title.

1978 Acts

Amendment by Pub.L. 95–573 effective 180 days after Nov. 2, 1978, except as otherwise provided, except that nothing in this Act shall affect the composition or preclude the service of any grand or petit juror summoned, empaneled, or actually serving in any judicial district on such effective date, see section 6 of Pub.L. 95–573, set out as a note under section 93 of this title.

Amendment by Pub.L. 95–408 effective 180 days after Oct. 2, 1978, such amendment not to affect the composition or preclude the service of any grand or petit juror summoned, empaneled, or actually serving in any judicial district on the effective date of this Act, see section 5 of Pub.L. 95–408, set out as a note under section 89 of this title.

Pretermission of Regular Session of Court at Hempstead and Holding of Special Session at Westbury; Procedures Applicable, Appropriations, Etc.

Pub.L. 95–271, §§ 2 to 5, Apr. 28, 1978, 92 Stat. 221, provided that:

"Sec. 2. The United States District Court for the Eastern District of New York, by order made anywhere within its district, may pretermit the regular session of court at Hempstead until Federal quarters and accommodations are avail-

able and ready for occupancy, except that for the entire period and such pretermission, a special session of the court shall be held at Westbury. Pretermission may be ordered without regard to the provisions of section 140(a) of title 28, United States Code [section 140(a) of this title].

"Sec. 3. Notwithstanding the provisions of section 142 of title 28, United States Code [section 142 of this title], the Administrator of General Services, at the request of the Director of the Administrative Office of the United States Courts, shall continue to provide existing quarters and accommodations at Westbury for the duration of the special session held pursuant to section 2 of this Act. Appropriations to the judicial branch of Government shall be available to the Director to make necessary disbursements for such quarters and accommodations, and to pay user charges as required by section 210 of the Federal Property and Administrative Services Act of 1949, as amended (40 U.S.C. 490) [see now 40 U.S.C.A. § 581 et seq.], at rates otherwise authorized by law.

"Sec. 4. Notwithstanding the provisions of section 456 of title 28, United States Code [section 456 of this title], any judge, and any officer or employee of the judicial branch, whose official station is, on the day before the date of enactment of this Act [Apr. 28, 1978], Westbury, may maintain that official station for the duration of the special session held pursuant to section 2 of this Act.

"Sec. 5. The Director of the Administrative Office of the United States Courts may pay travel and transportation expenses in accordance with subchapter II, chapter 57 of title 5, United States Code [section 5721 et seq. of Title 5, Government Organization and Employees], to any officer or employee of the judicial branch whose official station changes as a consequence of this Act [amending subsec. (c) of this section] and who relocates his residence incident to such change of official station."

§ 113. North Carolina

North Carolina is divided into three judicial districts to be known as the Eastern, Middle, and Western Districts of North Carolina.

Eastern District

(a) The Eastern District comprises the counties of Beaufort, Bertie, Bladen, Brunswick, Camden, Carteret, Chowan, Columbus, Craven, Cumberland, Currituck, Dare, Duplin, Edgecombe, Franklin, Gates, Granville, Greene, Halifax, Harnett, Hertford, Hyde, Johnston, Jones, Lenoir, Martin, Nash, New Hanover, Northampton, Onslow, Pamlico, Pasquotank, Pender, Perquimans, Pitt, Robeson, Sampson, Tyrrell, Vance, Wake, Warren, Washington, Wayne, and Wilson and that portion of Durham County encompassing the Federal Correctional Institution, Butner, North Carolina.

Court for the Eastern District shall be held at Elizabeth City, Fayetteville, Greenville, New Bern, Raleigh, Wilmington, and Wilson.

Middle District

(b) The Middle District comprises the counties of Alamance, Cabarrus, Caswell, Chatham, Davidson, Davie, Durham (excluding that portion of Durham County encompassing the Federal Correctional Institution, Butner, North Carolina), Forsythe, Guilford, Hoke, Lee, Montgomery, Moore, Orange, Person, Randolph, Richmond, Rockingham, Rowan, Scotland, Stanly, Stokes, Surry, and Yadkin.

Court for the Middle District shall be held at Durham, Greensboro, and Winston-Salem.

Western District

(c) The Western District comprises the counties of Alexander, Alleghany, Anson, Ashe, Avery, Buncombe, Burke, Caldwell, Catawba, Cherokee, Clay, Cleveland, Gaston, Graham, Haywood, Henderson, Iredell, Jackson, Lincoln, McDowell, Macon, Madison, Mecklenburg, Mitchell, Polk, Rutherford, Swain, Transylvania, Union, Watauga, Wilkes, and Yancey.

Court for the Western District shall be held at Asheville, Bryson City, Charlotte, Shelby, and Statesville.

(June 25, 1948, c. 646, 62 Stat. 886; Nov. 2, 1965, Pub.L. 89–319, 79 Stat. 1186; Oct. 15, 1980, Pub.L. 96–462, § 5(a)–(c), 94 Stat. 2053, 2054; Apr. 21, 1992, Pub.L. 102–272, 106 Stat. 112.)

HISTORICAL AND STATUTORY NOTES
Effective and Applicability Provisions
1980 Acts

Amendment by Pub.L. 96–462 effective Oct. 1, 1981, with that amendment not to affect the composition or preclude the service of any grand or petit juror summoned, empaneled, or actually serving in any judicial district on Oct. 1, 1981, see section 7 of Pub.L. 96–462, set out as a note under section 84 of this title.

Section 5(d) of Pub.L. 96–462 provided that: "The amendments made by this section [amending this section] shall not apply to any action commenced before the effective date of such amendments [Oct. 1, 1981] and pending in any judicial district of North Carolina on such date."

§ 114. North Dakota

North Dakota constitutes one judicial district comprising four divisions.

(1) The Southwestern Division comprises the counties of Adams, Billings, Bowman, Burleigh, Dunn, Emmons, Golden Valley, Grant, Hettinger, Kidder, Logan, McIntosh, McLean, Mercer, Morton, Oliver, Sioux, Slope, and Stark.

Court for the Southwestern Division shall be held at Bismarck.

(2) The Southeastern Division comprises the counties of Barnes, Cass, Dickey, Eddy, Foster, Griggs, La Moure, Ransom, Richland, Sargent, Steele, and Stutsman.

Court for the Southeastern Division shall be held at Fargo.

(3) The Northeastern Division comprises the counties of Benson, Cavalier, Grand Forks, Nelson, Pembina, Ramsey, Rolette, Towner, Traill, and Walsh.

Court for the Northeastern Division shall be held at Grand Forks.

(4) The Northwestern Division comprises the counties of Bottineau, Burke, Divide, McHenry, McKenzie, Mountrail, Pierce, Renville, Sheridan, Ward, Wells, and Williams.

Court for the Northwestern Division shall be held at Minot.

(June 25, 1948, c. 646, 62 Stat. 886; Oct. 2, 1978, Pub.L. 95–408, § 3(b), 92 Stat. 883.)

HISTORICAL AND STATUTORY NOTES

Effective and Applicability Provisions

1978 Acts

Amendment by Pub.L. 95–408 effective 180 days after Oct. 2, 1978, such amendment not to affect the composition or preclude the service of any grand or petit juror summoned, empaneled, or actually serving in any judicial district on the effective date of this Act, see section 5 of Pub.L. 95–408, set out as a note under section 89 of this title.

§ 115. Ohio

Ohio is divided into two judicial districts to be known as the Northern and Southern Districts of Ohio.

Northern District

(a) The Northern District comprises two divisions.

(1) The Eastern Division comprises the counties of Ashland, Ashtabula, Carroll, Columbiana, Crawford, Cuyahoga, Geauga, Holmes, Lake, Lorain, Mahoning, Medina, Portage, Richland, Stark, Summit, Trumbull, Tuscarawas, and Wayne.

Court for the Eastern Division shall be held at Cleveland, Youngstown, and Akron.

(2) The Western Division comprises the counties of Allen, Auglaize, Defiance, Erie, Fulton, Hancock, Hardin, Henry, Huron, Lucas, Marion, Mercer, Ottawa, Paulding, Putnam, Sandusky, Seneca, Van Wert, Williams, Woods, and Wyandot.

Court for the Western Division shall be held at Lima and Toledo.

Southern District

(b) The Southern District comprises two divisions.

(1) The Western Division comprises the counties of Adams, Brown, Butler, Champaign, Clark, Clermont, Clinton, Darke, Greene, Hamilton, Highland, Lawrence, Miami, Montgomery, Preble, Scioto, Shelby, and Warren.

Court for the Western Division shall be held at Cincinnati and Dayton.

(2) The Eastern Division comprises the counties of Athens, Belmont, Coshocton, Delaware, Fairfield, Fayette, Franklin, Gallia, Guernsey, Harrison, Hocking, Jackson, Jefferson, Knox, Licking, Logan, Madison, Meigs, Monroe, Morgan, Morrow, Muskingum, Noble, Perry, Pickaway, Pike, Ross, Union, Vinton, and Washington.

Court for the Eastern Division shall be held at Columbus, St. Clairsville, and Steubenville.

(June 25, 1948, c. 646, 62 Stat. 887; Feb. 10, 1954, c. 6, § 2(b)(9), 68 Stat. 11; Nov. 2, 2002, Pub.L. 107–273, Div. C, Title I, § 11021, 116 Stat. 1829.)

§ 116. Oklahoma

Oklahoma is divided into three judicial districts to be known as the Northern, Eastern, and Western Districts of Oklahoma.

Northern District

(a) The Northern District comprises the counties of Craig, Creek, Delaware, Mayes, Nowata, Osage, Ottawa, Pawnee, Rogers, Tulsa, and Washington.

Court for the Northern District shall be held at Bartlesville, Miami, Pawhuska, Tulsa, and Vinita.

Eastern District

(b) The Eastern District comprises the counties of Adair, Atoka, Bryan, Carter, Cherokee, Choctaw, Coal, Haskell, Hughes, Johnston, Latimer, Le Flore, Love, McCurtain, McIntosh, Marshall, Murray, Muskogee, Okfuskee, Okmulgee, Pittsburg, Pontotoc, Pushmataha, Seminole, Sequoyah, and Wagoner.

Court for the Eastern District shall be held at Ada, Ardmore, Durant, Hugo, Muskogee, Okmulgee, Poteau, and S. McAlester.

Western District

(c) The Western District comprises the counties of Alfalfa, Beaver, Beckham, Blaine, Caddo, Canadian, Cimarron, Cleveland, Comanche, Cotton, Custer, Dewey, Ellis, Garfield, Garvin, Grady, Grant, Greer, Harmon, Harper, Jackson, Jefferson, Kay, Kingfisher, Kiowa, Lincoln, Logan, McClain, Major, Noble, Oklahoma, Payne, Pottawatomie, Roger Mills, Stephens, Texas, Tillman, Washita, Woods, and Woodward.

Court for the Western District shall be held at Chickasha, Enid, Guthrie, Lawton, Mangum, Oklahoma City, Pauls Valley, Ponca City, Shawnee, and Woodward.

(June 25, 1948, c. 646, 62 Stat. 887; Aug. 4, 1966, Pub.L. 89–526, § 1, 80 Stat. 335.)

HISTORICAL AND STATUTORY NOTES

Effective and Applicability Provisions

1966 Acts

Section 2 of Pub.L. 89–526 provided that: "The amendments made by this Act [to subsecs. (b) and (c) of this section] shall take effect on the sixtieth day after the date of enactment of this Act [Aug. 4, 1966]."

§ 117. Oregon

Oregon constitutes one judicial district.

Court shall be held at Coquille, Eugene or Springfield, Klamath Falls, Medford, Pendleton, and Portland.

(June 25, 1948, c. 646, 62 Stat. 888; Aug. 3, 1950, c. 514, 64 Stat. 393; June 2, 1970, Pub.L. 91–272, § 7, 84 Stat. 297; Nov. 13, 2000, Pub.L. 106–518, Title V, § 502, 114 Stat. 2422.)

§ 118. Pennsylvania

Pennsylvania is divided into three judicial districts to be known as the Eastern, Middle, and Western Districts of Pennsylvania.

Eastern District

(a) The Eastern District comprises the counties of Berks, Bucks, Chester, Delaware, Lancaster, Lehigh, Montgomery, Northampton, and Philadelphia.

Court for the Eastern District shall be held at Allentown, Easton, Lancaster, Reading, and Philadelphia.

Middle District

(b) The Middle District comprises the counties of Adams, Bradford, Cameron, Carbon, Centre, Clinton, Columbia, Cumberland, Dauphin, Franklin, Fulton, Huntingdon, Juniata, Lackawanna, Lebanon, Luzerne, Lycoming, Mifflin, Monroe, Montour, Northumberland, Perry, Pike, Potter, Schuylkill, Snyder, Sullivan, Susquehanna, Tioga, Union, Wayne, Wyoming, and York.

Court for the Middle District shall be held at Harrisburg, Lewisburg, Scranton, Wilkes-Barre, and Williamsport.

Western District

(c) The Western District comprises the counties of Allegheny, Armstrong, Beaver, Bedford, Blair, Butler, Cambria, Clarion, Clearfield, Crawford, Elk, Erie, Fayette, Forest, Greene, Indiana, Jefferson, Lawrence, McKean, Mercer, Somerset, Venango, Warren, Washington, and Westmoreland.

Court for the Western District shall be held at Erie, Johnstown, and Pittsburgh.

(June 25, 1948, c. 646, 62 Stat. 888; June 2, 1970, Pub.L. 91–272, § 6, 84 Stat. 297; Nov. 2, 1978, Pub.L. 95–573, § 4, 92 Stat. 2458; Oct. 6, 1992, Pub.L. 102–396, Title IX, § 9161, 106 Stat. 1947; Oct. 21, 1998, Pub.L. 105–277, Div. A, § 101(b) [Title VI, § 624(a)], 112 Stat. 2681–116.)

HISTORICAL AND STATUTORY NOTES

Effective and Applicability Provisions

1998 Acts

Pub.L. 105–277, Div. A, § 101(b) [Title VI, § 624(b)], Oct. 21, 1998, 112 Stat. 2681–116, provided that: "**(b)(1)** This section and the amendments made by this section [amending this section] shall take effect 180 days after the date of the enactment of this Act [Oct. 21, 1998].

"**(2)** This section and the amendments made by this section [amending this section] shall not affect any action commenced before the effective date of this section [Oct. 21, 1998] and pending on such date in the United States District Court for the Eastern District of Pennsylvania.

"**(3)** This section and the amendments made by this section [amending this section] shall not affect the composition, or preclude the service, of any grand or petit jury summoned, impaneled, or actually serving on the effective date of this section [Oct. 21, 1998]."

1978 Acts

Amendment by Pub.L. 95–573 effective 180 days after Nov. 2, 1978, except as otherwise provided, except that nothing in this Act shall affect the composition or preclude the service of any grand or petit juror summoned, empaneled, or actually serving in any judicial district on such effective date, see section 6 of Pub.L. 95–573, set out as a note under section 93 of this title.

§ 119. Puerto Rico

Puerto Rico constitutes one judicial district.

Court shall be held at Mayaguez, Ponce, and San Juan.

(June 25, 1948, c. 646, 62 Stat. 889.)

§ 120. Rhode Island

Rhode Island constitutes one judicial district.

Court shall be held at Providence.

(June 25, 1948, c. 646, 62 Stat. 889.)

§ 121. South Carolina

South Carolina constitutes one judicial district comprising eleven divisions.

(1) The Charleston Division comprises the counties of Berkeley, Charleston, Clarendon, Colleton, Dorchester, and Georgetown.

Court for the Charleston Division shall be held at Charleston.

(2) The Columbia Division comprises the counties of Kershaw, Lee, Lexington, Richland, and Sumter.

Court for the Columbia Division shall be held at Columbia.

(3) The Florence Division comprises the counties of Chesterfield, Darlington, Dillon, Florence, Horry, Marion, Marlboro, and Williamsburg.

Court for the Florence Division shall be held at Florence.

(4) The Aiken Division comprises the counties of Aiken, Allendale, and Barnwell.

Court for the Aiken Division shall be held at Aiken.

(5) The Orangeburg Division comprises the counties of Bamberg, Calhoun, and Orangeburg.

Court for the Orangeburg Division shall be held at Orangeburg.

(6) The Greenville Division comprises the counties of Greenville and Laurens.

Court for the Greenville Division shall be held at Greenville.

(7) The Rock Hill Division comprises the counties of Chester, Fairfield, Lancaster, and York.

Court for the Rock Hill Division shall be held at Rock Hill.

(8) The Greenwood Division comprises the counties of Abbeville, Edgefield, Greenwood, McCormick, Newberry, and Saluda.

Court for the Greenwood Division shall be held at Greenwood.

(9) The Anderson Division comprises the counties of Anderson, Oconee, and Pickens.

Court for the Anderson Division shall be held at Anderson.

(10) The Spartanburg Division comprises the counties of Cherokee, Spartanburg, and Union.

Court for the Spartanburg Division shall be held at Spartanburg.

(11) The Beaufort Division comprises the counties of Beaufort, Hampton, and Jasper.

Court for the Beaufort Division shall be held at Beaufort.

(June 25, 1948, c. 646, 62 Stat. 889; Oct. 7, 1965, Pub.L. 89–242, § 1(a), 79 Stat. 951; Nov. 14, 1986, Pub.L. 99–657, § 2, 100 Stat. 3670; Oct. 28, 1991, Pub.L. 102–140, Title III, § 304, 105 Stat. 810.)

HISTORICAL AND STATUTORY NOTES

Effective and Applicability Provisions

1986 Acts

Section 4 of Pub.L. 99–657 provided that:

"**(a) Effective date.**—(1) The amendments made by sections 2 and 3 [amending this section and section 90 of this title, respectively] take effect 90 days after the date of the enactment of this Act [Nov. 14, 1986].

"**(2)** The amendment made by section 4 [enacting this note] takes effect on the date of the enactment of this Act [Nov. 14, 1986].

"**(b) Pending actions.**—The amendments made by this Act [amending this section and section 90 of this title, and enacting provisions set out as a note under section 1 of this title] shall not affect any action commenced before the effective date of such amendments and pending on such date.

"**(c) Juries.**—The amendments made by this Act [amending this section and section 90 of this title, and enacting provisions set out as a note under section 1 of this title] shall not affect the composition, or preclude the service, of any grand or petit jury summoned, empaneled, or actually serving on the effective date of such amendments."

1965 Acts

Section 6 of Pub.L. 89–242 provided that: "The provisions of this Act [amending this section and section 133 of this title and enacting provisions set out as notes under this section] shall become effective on the first day of the month following the date of enactment of this Act [Oct. 7, 1965]."

Consolidation of South Carolina Into a Single Judicial District

Sections 2 to 5 of Pub.L. 89–242 provided that:

"**Sec. 2. [Continuity of Judicial Business; Clerk of Court; Records].** In compliance with section 132 of title 28 of the United States Code [section 132 of this title] the District Courts for the Eastern and Western Districts of South Carolina are hereby consolidated into, and shall henceforth constitute, a single District Court for the District of South Carolina. No loss or interruption of the jurisdiction of the consolidated District Court for the District of South Carolina over cases and controversies heretofore decided by or now pending in the District Courts for the Eastern and Western Districts of South Carolina shall result from such consolidation and prosecutions for offenses committed within the Eastern and Western Districts of South Carolina prior to the effective date of this Act [Nov. 1, 1965] shall be commenced and proceeded with the same as if such consolidation had not occurred. For the purpose of the trial of such offenses, the District Courts for the Eastern and Western Districts of South Carolina are continued in existence and the judges of the District Court for the District of South Carolina shall sit as judges in such courts according to assignment made by the chief judge of the United States District Court for the District of South Carolina or the chief judge of the United States Court of Appeals for the Fourth Circuit. The District Court for the District of South Carolina shall appoint a clerk who shall supersede the clerks of the District Courts for the Eastern and Western Districts of South Carolina and who shall maintain his office at Columbia until the court otherwise directs pursuant to sections 457 and 751(c) of title 28 of the United States Code [sections 457 and 751(c) of this title]. The presently existing records of the District Courts for the Eastern and Western Districts of South Carolina shall be placed in his custody.

"**Sec. 3. [United States Attorney].** When the term of office of either the United States attorney for the Eastern District of South Carolina or the United States attorney for the Western District of South Carolina, holding office on the date of enactment of this Act, has expired, the President is authorized to appoint a United States attorney for the District of South Carolina as provided by section 501 of title 28 of the United States Code [section 501 of this title]. Until the United States attorney for the District of South Carolina has been appointed as herein authorized and has qualified, the United States attorney for the Eastern District of South Carolina holding office on the date of enactment of this Act [Oct. 7, 1965] shall continue to serve as a United States attorney and to perform the duties of such office in the Charleston, Columbia, Orangeburg, Florence, and Aiken divi-

sions of the District of South Carolina, and the United States attorney for the Western District of South Carolina holding office on the date of enactment of this Act [Oct. 7, 1965] shall continue to serve as a United States attorney and to perform the duties of such office in the Greenville, Rock Hill, Greenwood, Spartanburg, and Anderson divisions of the District of South Carolina. In the event a vacancy, other than a vacancy resulting from expiration of term, arises in either of such offices prior to the appointment as herein authorized and qualification, of a United States attorney for the District of South Carolina the incumbent of the other such office shall also perform the duties of the office in which the vacancy occurs until such appointment and qualification.

"Sec. 4. [**United States Marshal**]. When the term of office of either the United States marshal for the Eastern District of South Carolina or the United States marshal for the Western District of South Carolina, holding office on the date of enactment of this Act [Oct. 7, 1965], has expired, the President is authorized to appoint a United States marshal for the District of South Carolina as provided by section 541(a) of title 28 of the United States Code [section 541(a) of this title]. Until the United States marshal for the District of South Carolina has been appointed as herein authorized and has qualified, the United States marshal for the Eastern District of South Carolina holding office on the date of enactment of this Act [Oct. 7, 1965] shall continue to serve as a United States marshal and to perform the duties of such office in the Charleston, Columbia, Orangeburg, Florence, and Aiken divisions of the District of South Carolina, and the United States marshal for the Western District of South Carolina holding office on the date of enactment of this Act [Oct. 7, 1965] shall continue to serve as a United States marshal and to perform the duties of such office in the Greenville, Rock Hill, Greenwood, Spartanburg, and Anderson divisions of the District of South Carolina. In the event a vacancy, other than a vacancy resulting from expiration of term, arises in either of such offices prior to the appointment as herein authorized and qualification of a United States marshal for the District of South Carolina the incumbent of the other such office shall also perform the duties of the office in which the vacancy occurs until such appointment and qualification.

"Sec. 5. [**Other Court Personnel**]. All deputy clerks, clerical assistants, and other employees of the clerks, all court reporters, all probation officers and their clerical assistants, all referees in bankruptcy and their clerical assistants, all United States commissioners and all other presently serving officers and employees of the United States District Courts for the Eastern and Western Districts of South Carolina shall henceforth be officers or employees, as the case may be, of the United States District Court for the District of South Carolina and shall hold their offices or employment under and perform their duties for that court. All presently serving assistant United States attorneys and clerical assistants of the United States attorneys and all presently serving deputy marshals and clerical assistants of the United States marshals appointed for the Eastern or Western District of South Carolina shall henceforth hold their offices or employment for the District of South Carolina."

§ 122. South Dakota

South Dakota constitutes one judicial district comprising four divisions.

(1) The Northern Division comprises the counties of Brown, Campbell, Clark, Codington, Corson, Day, Deuel, Edmonds, Grant, Hamlin, McPherson, Marshall, Roberts, Spink, and Walworth.

Court for the Northern Division shall be held at Aberdeen.

(2) The Southern Division comprises the counties of Aurora, Beadle, Bon Homme, Brookings, Brule, Charles Mix, Clay, Davison, Douglas, Hanson, Hutchinson, Kingsbury, Lake, Lincoln, McCook, Miner, Minnehaha, Moody, Sanborn, Turner, Union, and Yankton.

Court for the Southern Division shall be held at Sioux Falls.

(3) The central division comprises the counties of Buffalo, Dewey, Faulk, Gregory, Haakon, Hand, Hughes, Hyde, Jerauld, Jones, Lyman, Mellette, Potter, Stanley, Sully, Todd, Tripp, and Ziebach.

Court for the Central Division shall be held at Pierre.

(4) The Western Division comprises the counties of Bennett, Butte, Custer, Fall River, Harding, Jackson, Lawrence, Meade, Pennington, Perkins, and Shannon.

Court for the Western Division shall be held at Deadwood and Rapid City.

(June 25, 1948, c. 646, 62 Stat. 889; Oct. 10, 1966, Pub.L. 89–638, 80 Stat. 883; Aug. 10, 1972, Pub.L. 92–376, 86 Stat. 529; Dec. 1, 1990, Pub.L. 101–650, Title III, § 324(b), 104 Stat. 5120.)

§ 123. Tennessee

Tennessee is divided into three judicial districts to be known as the Eastern, Middle, and Western Districts of Tennessee.

Eastern District

(a) The Eastern District comprises four divisions.

(1) The Northern Division comprises the counties of Anderson, Blount, Campbell, Claiborne, Grainger, Jefferson, Knox, Loudon, Monroe, Morgan, Roane, Scott, Sevier, and Union.

Court for the Northern Division shall be held at Knoxville.

(2) The Northeastern Division comprises the counties of Carter, Cocke, Greene, Hamblen, Hancock, Hawkins, Johnson, Sullivan, Unicoi, and Washington.

Court for the Northeastern Division shall be held at Greenville.

(3) The Southern Division comprises the counties of Bledsoe, Bradley, Hamilton, McMinn, Marion, Meigs, Polk, Rhea, and Sequatchie.

Court for the Southern Division shall be held at Chattanooga.

(4) The Winchester Division comprises the counties of Bedford, Coffee, Franklin, Grundy, Lincoln, Moore, Van Buren, and Warren.

Court for the Winchester Division shall be held at Winchester.

Middle District

(b) The Middle District comprises three divisions.

(1) The Nashville Division comprises the counties of Cannon, Cheatham, Davidson, Dickson, Houston, Humphreys, Montgomery, Robertson, Rutherford, Stewart, Sumner, Trousdale, Williamson, and Wilson.

Court for the Nashville Division shall be held at Nashville.

(2) The Northeastern Division comprises the counties of Clay, Cumberland, De Kalb, Fentress, Jackson, Macon, Overton, Pickett, Putnam, Smith, and White.

Court for the Northeastern Division shall be held at Cookeville.

(3) The Columbia Division comprises the counties of Giles, Hickman, Lawrence, Lewis, Marshall, Maury, and Wayne.

Court for the Columbia Division shall be held at Columbia.

Western District

(c) The Western District comprises two divisions.

(1) The Eastern Division comprises the counties of Benton, Carroll, Chester, Crockett, Decatur, Gibson, Hardeman, Hardin, Haywood, Henderson, Henry, Lake, McNairy, Madison, Obion, Perry, and Weakley.

The Eastern Division also includes the waters of Tennessee River to low-water mark on the eastern shore wherever such river forms the boundary between the western and middle districts from the north line of Alabama north to the point in Henry County, Tennessee, where the south boundary of Kentucky strikes the east bank of the river.

Court for the Eastern Division shall be held at Jackson.

(2) The Western Division comprises the counties of Dyer, Fayette, Lauderdale, Shelby, and Tipton.

Court for the Western Division shall be held at Memphis and Dyersburg.

The district judge for the Eastern District in office on November 27, 1940, shall hold court in the Northern and Northeastern Divisions. The other judge of that district shall hold the terms of court in the Southern and Winchester Divisions. Each may appoint and remove all officers and employees of the court whose official headquarters are located in the divisions within which he holds court and whose appointments are vested by law in a district judge or chief judge of a district.

(June 25, 1948, c. 646, 62 Stat. 890; May 19, 1961, Pub.L. 87-36, § 3(e), 75 Stat. 83; July 11, 1961, Pub.L. 87-86, 75 Stat. 203; June 2, 1970, Pub.L. 91-272, § 12, 84 Stat. 298.)

HISTORICAL AND STATUTORY NOTES

Codifications

Section 3(e) of Pub.L. 87-36 provided that "The second sentence of section 123(c)(2), title 18, United States Code, is amended to read as follows:". Pub.L. 87-86 corrected such reference to "title 18" to "title 28."

§ 124. Texas

Texas is divided into four judicial districts to be known as the Northern, Southern, Eastern, and Western Districts of Texas.

Northern District

(a) The Northern District comprises seven divisions.

(1) The Dallas Division comprises the counties of Dallas, Ellis, Hunt, Johnson, Kaufman, Navarro, and Rockwall.

Court for the Dallas Division shall be held at Dallas.

(2) The Fort Worth Division comprises the counties of Comanche, Erath, Hood, Jack, Palo Pinto, Parker, Tarrant, and Wise.

Court for the Fort Worth Division shall be held at Fort Worth.

(3) The Abilene Division comprises the counties of Callahan, Eastland, Fisher, Haskell, Howard, Jones, Mitchell, Nolan, Shackleford, Stephens, Stonewall, Taylor, and Throckmorton.

Court for the Abilene Division shall be held at Abilene.

(4) The San Angelo Division comprises the counties of Brown, Coke, Coleman, Concho, Crockett, Glasscock, Irion, Menard, Mills, Reagan, Runnels, Schleicher, Sterling, Sutton, and Tom Green.

Court for the San Angelo Division shall be held at San Angelo.

(5) The Amarillo Division comprises the counties of Armstrong, Brisco, Carson, Castro, Childress, Collingsworth, Dallam, Deaf Smith, Donley, Gray, Hall, Hansford, Hartley, Hemphill, Hutchinson, Lipscomb, Moore, Ochiltree, Oldham, Parmer, Potter, Randall, Roberts, Sherman, Swisher, and Wheeler.

Court for the Amarillo Division shall be held at Amarillo.

(6) The Wichita Falls Division comprises the counties of Archer, Baylor, Clay, Cottle, Foard, Hardeman, King, Knox, Montague, Wichita, Wilbarger, and Young.

Court for the Wichita Falls Division shall be held at Wichita Falls.

(7) The Lubbock Division comprises the counties of Bailey, Borden, Cochran, Crosby, Dawson, Dickens, Floyd, Gaines, Garza, Hale, Hockley, Kent, Lamb, Lubbock, Lynn, Motley, Scurry, Terry, and Yoakum.

Court for the Lubbock Division shall be held at Lubbock.

Southern District

(b) The Southern District comprises seven divisions.

(1) The Galveston Division comprises the counties of Brazoria, Chambers, Galveston, and Matagorda.

Court for the Galveston Division shall be held at Galveston.

(2) The Houston Division comprises the counties of Austin, Brazos, Colorado, Fayette, Fort Bend, Grimes, Harris, Madison, Montgomery, San Jacinto, Walker, Waller, and Wharton.

Court for the Houston Division shall be held at Houston.

(3) The Laredo Division comprises the counties of Jim Hogg, La Salle, McMullen, Webb, and Zapata.

Court for the Laredo Division shall be held at Laredo.

(4) The Brownsville Division comprises the counties of Cameron and Willacy.

Court for the Brownsville Division shall be held at Brownsville.

(5) The Victoria Division comprises the counties of Calhoun, DeWitt, Goliad, Jackson, Lavaca, Refugio, and Victoria.

Court for the Victoria Division shall be held at Victoria.

(6) The Corpus Christi Division comprises the counties of Aransas, Bee, Brooks, Duval, Jim Wells, Kenedy, Kleberg, Live Oak, Nueces, and San Patricio.

Court for the Corpus Christi Division shall be held at Corpus Christi.

(7) The McAllen Division comprises the counties of Hidalgo and Starr.

Court for the McAllen Division shall be held at McAllen.

Eastern District

(c) The Eastern District comprises seven divisions.

(1) The Tyler Division comprises the counties of Anderson, Cherokee, Gregg, Henderson, Panola, Rains, Rusk, Smith, Van Zandt, and Wood.

Court for Tyler Division will be held at Tyler.

(2) The Beaumont Division comprises the counties of Hardin, Jasper, Jefferson, Liberty, Newton, and Orange.

Court for the Beaumont Division is to be held at Beaumont.

(3) The Sherman Division comprises the counties of Collin, Cook, Delta, Denton, Fannin, Grayson, Hopkins, and Lamar.

Court for the Sherman Division shall be held at Sherman and Plano.

(4) The Marshall Division comprises the counties of Camp, Cass, Harrison, Marion, Morris, and Upshur.

Court for the Marshall Division shall be held at Marshall.

(5) The Texarkana Division comprises the counties of Bowie, Franklin, Red River, and Titus.

Court for the Texarkana Division shall be held at Texarkana, and may be held anywhere within the Federal courthouse in Texarkana that is located astride the State line between Texas and Arkansas.

(6) The Lufkin Division comprises the counties of Angelina, Houston, Nacogdoches, Polk, Sabine, San Augustine, Shelby, Trinity, and Tyler.

Court for the Lufkin Division shall be held at Lufkin.

Western District

(d) The Western District comprises seven divisions.

(1) The Austin Division comprises the counties of Bastrop, Blanco, Burleson, Burnet, Caldwell, Gillespie, Hays, Kimble, Lampasas, Lee, Llano, Mason, McCulloch, San Saba, Travis, Washington, and Williamson.

Court for the Austin Division shall be held at Austin.

(2) The Waco Division comprises the counties of Bell, Bosque, Coryell, Falls, Freestone, Hamilton, Hill, Leon, Limestone, McLennan, Milam, Robertson, and Somervell.

Court for the Waco Division shall be held at Waco.

(3) The El Paso Division comprises the county of El Paso.

Court for the El Paso Division shall be held at El Paso.

(4) The San Antonio Division comprises the counties of Atascosa, Bandera, Bexar, Comal, Dimmit, Frio, Gonzales, Guadalupe, Karnes, Kendall, Kerr, Medina, Real, and Wilson.

Court for the San Antonio Division shall be held at San Antonio.

(5) The Del Rio Division comprises the counties of Edwards, Kinney, Maverick, Terrell, Uvalde, Val Verde, and Zavalla.

Court for the Del Rio Division shall be held at Del Rio.

(6) The Pecos Division comprises the counties of Brewster, Culberson, Jeff Davis, Hudspeth, Loving, Pecos, Presidio, Reeves, Ward, and Winkler.

Court for the Pecos Division shall be held at Pecos.

(7) The Midland-Odessa Division comprises the counties of Andrews, Crane, Ector, Martin, Midland, and Upton.

Court for the Midland-Odessa Division shall be held at Midland. Court may be held, in the discretion of the court, in Odessa, when courtroom facilities are made available at no expense to the Government.

(June 25, 1948, c. 646, 62 Stat. 891; Feb. 10, 1954, c. 6, § 2(b)(9)(a), (b), 68 Stat. 11; Sept. 4, 1957, Pub.L. 85–298, §§ 1, 2, 71 Stat. 618; Oct. 4, 1961, Pub.L. 87–352, 75 Stat. 772; Mar. 11, 1964, Pub.L. 88–282, 78 Stat. 163; Aug. 30, 1964, Pub.L. 88–512, 78 Stat. 695; Dec. 18, 1967, Pub.L. 90–216, 81 Stat. 661; Oct. 15, 1980, Pub.L. 96–462, § 6, 94 Stat. 2054; Nov. 8, 1984, Pub.L. 98–620, Title IV, § 407(a), 98 Stat. 3362; Dec. 3, 2003, Pub.L. 108–157, § 1(a), 117 Stat. 1947; Dec. 10, 2004, Pub.L. 108–455, § 3, 118 Stat. 3628.)

HISTORICAL AND STATUTORY NOTES

Effective and Applicability Provisions

2003 Acts

Pub.L. 108–157, § 1(b), Dec. 3, 2003, 117 Stat. 1947, provided that:

"(1) In general.—This section and the amendments made by this section [amending this section] shall take effect on the date of the enactment of this Act [Dec. 3, 2003].

"(2) Pending cases not affected.—This section and the amendments made by this section [amending this section] shall not affect any action commenced before the effective date of this section and pending in the United States District Court for the Eastern District of Texas on such date.

"(3) Juries not affected.—This section and the amendments made by this section [amending this section] shall not affect the composition, or preclude the service, of any grand or petit jury summoned, impaneled, or actually serving in the Eastern Judicial District of Texas on the effective date of this section."

1984 Acts

Section 407(b) of Pub.L. 98–620 provided that: "The amendments made by subsection (a) of this section [amending subsec. (b) of this section] shall apply to any action commenced in the United States District Court for the Southern District of Texas on or after the effective date of

this subtitle [Jan. 1, 1985], and shall not affect any action pending in such court on such effective date."

Amendment by Pub.L. 98–620 to take effect Jan. 1, 1985, and not to affect the composition, or preclude the service, of any grand or petit jury summoned, impaneled, or actually serving on that date, see section 411 of Pub.L. 98–620, set out as a note under section 85 of this title.

1980 Acts

Amendment by Pub.L. 96–462 effective Oct. 1, 1981, with that amendment not to affect the composition or preclude the service of any grand or petit juror summoned, empaneled, or actually serving in any judicial district on Oct. 1, 1981, see section 7 of Pub.L. 96–462, set out as a note under section 84 of this title.

§ 125. Utah

Utah constitutes one judicial district comprising two divisions.

(1) The Northern Division comprises the counties of Box Elder, Cache, Davis, Morgan, Rich, and Weber.

Court for the Northern Division shall be held at Salt Lake City and Ogden.

(2) The Central Division comprises the counties of Beaver, Carbon, Daggett, Duchesne, Emery, Garfield, Grand, Iron, Juab, Kane, Millard, Piute, Salt Lake, San Juan, Sanpete, Sevier, Summit, Tooele, Uintah, Utah, Wasatch, Washington, and Wayne.

Court for the Central Division shall be held at Salt Lake City, Provo, and St. George.

(June 25, 1948, c. 646, 62 Stat. 893; Oct. 19, 1996, Pub.L. 104–317, Title VI, § 606, 110 Stat. 3859.)

§ 126. Vermont

Vermont constitutes one judicial district.

Court shall be held at Bennington, Brattleboro, Burlington, Montpelier, Rutland, Saint Johnsbury, and Windsor.

(June 25, 1948, c. 646, 62 Stat. 893; May 28, 1964, Pub.L. 88–312, 78 Stat. 201; Nov. 8, 1984, Pub.L. 98–620, Title IV, § 410, 98 Stat. 3362.)

HISTORICAL AND STATUTORY NOTES

Effective and Applicability Provisions

1984 Acts

Amendment by Pub.L. 98–620 to take effect on Jan. 1, 1985, and not to affect the composition, or preclude the service, of any grand or petit jury summoned, impaneled, or actually serving on that date, see section 411 of Pub.L. 98–620, set out as a note under section 85 of this title.

§ 127. Virginia

Virginia is divided into two judicial districts, to be known as the Eastern and Western Districts of Virginia.

Eastern District

(a) The Eastern District comprises the counties of Accomac, Amelia, Arlington, Brunswick, Caroline, Charles City, Chesterfield, Dinwiddie, Elizabeth City, Essex, Fairfax, Fauquier, Gloucester, Goochland, Greensville, Hanover, Henrico, Isle of Wight, James City, King and Queen, King George, King William, Lancaster, Loudoun, Lunenburg, Mathews, Mecklenburg, Middlesex, Nansemond, New Kent, Norfolk, Northampton, Northumberland, Nottoway, Powhatan, Prince Edward, Prince George, Prince William, Princess Anne, Richmond, Southampton, Spotsylvania, Stafford, Surry, Sussex, Warwick, Westmoreland, and York.

Court for the Eastern District shall be held at Alexandria, Newport News, Norfolk, and Richmond.

Western District

(b) The Western District comprises the counties of Albemarle, Alleghany, Amherst, Appomattox, Augusta, Bath, Bedford, Bland, Botetourt, Buchanan, Buckingham, Campbell, Carroll, Charlotte, Clarke, Craig, Culpeper, Cumberland, Dickenson, Floyd, Fluvanna, Franklin, Frederick, Giles, Grayson, Greene, Halifax, Henry, Highland, Lee, Louisa, Madison, Montgomery, Nelson, Orange, Page, Patrick, Pittsylvania, Pulaski, Rappahannock, Roanoke, Rockbridge, Rockingham, Russell, Scott, Shenandoah, Smyth, Tazewell, Warren, Washington, Wise, and Wythe.

Court for the Western District shall be held at Abingdon, Big Stone Gap, Charlottesville, Danville, Harrisonburg, Lynchburg, and Roanoke.

(c) Cities and incorporated towns are included in that district in which are included the counties within the exterior boundaries of which such cities and incorporated towns are geographically located or out of the territory of which they have been incorporated.

(June 25, 1948, c. 646, 62 Stat. 893; July 5, 1968, Pub.L. 90–383, 82 Stat. 292; Dec. 10, 1991, Pub.L. 102–200, § 1, 105 Stat. 1630.)

HISTORICAL AND STATUTORY NOTES

Effective and Applicability Provisions

1991 Acts

Section 2 of Pub.L 102–200 provided that:

"(a) **Pending Actions.**—The amendments made by section 1 [amending subsecs. (a) and (b) of this section] shall not apply to any action commenced before the date of the enactment of this Act [Dec. 10, 1991] and pending in the United States District Court for the Eastern District of Virginia on such date.

"(b) **Juries.**—The amendments made by section 1 [amending subsecs. (a) and (b) of this section] shall not affect the composition, or preclude the service, of any grand or petit jury summoned, empaneled, or actually serving in the Eastern or Western District of Virginia on the date of the enactment of this Act [Dec. 10, 1991]."

§ 128. Washington

Washington is divided into two judicial districts to be known as the Eastern and Western Districts of Washington.

Eastern District

(a) The Eastern District comprises the counties of Adams, Asotin, Benton, Chelan, Columbia, Douglas, Ferry, Franklin, Garfield, Grant, Kittitas, Klickitat, Lincoln, Okanogan, Pend Oreille, Spokane, Stevens, Walla Walla, Whitman, and Yakima.

Court for the Eastern District shall be held at Spokane, Yakima, Walla Walla, and Richland.

Western District

(b) The Western District comprises the counties of Clallam, Clark, Cowlitz, Grays Harbor, Island, Jefferson, King, Kitsap, Lewis, Mason, Pacific, Pierce, San Juan, Skagit, Skamania, Snohomish, Thurston, Wahkiakum, and Whatcom.

Court for the Western District shall be held at Bellingham, Seattle, and Tacoma.

(June 25, 1948, c. 646, 62 Stat. 894; Sept. 25, 1962, Pub.L. 87–699, 76 Stat. 598; June 2, 1970, Pub.L. 91–272, § 4, 84 Stat. 297.)

§ 129. West Virginia

West Virginia is divided into two judicial districts to be known as the Northern and Southern Districts of West Virginia.

Northern District

(a) The Northern District comprises the counties of Barbour, Berkeley, Braxton, Brooke, Calhoun, Doddridge, Gilmer, Grant, Hampshire, Hancock, Hardy, Harrison, Jefferson, Lewis, Marion, Marshall, Mineral, Monongalia, Morgan, Ohio, Pendleton, Pleasants, Pocahontas, Preston, Randolph, Ritchie, Taylor, Tucker, Tyler, Upshur, Webster, and Wetzel.

Court for the Northern District shall be held at Clarksburg, Elkins, Fairmont, Martinsburg, and Wheeling.

Southern District

(b) The Southern District comprises the counties of Boone, Cabell, Clay, Fayette, Greenbrier, Jackson, Kanawha, Lincoln, Logan, McDowell, Mason, Mercer, Mingo, Monroe, Nicholas, Putnam, Raleigh, Roane, Summers, Wayne, Wirt, Wood, and Wyoming.

Court for the Southern District shall be held at Beckley, Bluefield, Charleston, Huntington, Lewisburg, and Parkersburg.

(June 25, 1948, c. 646, 62 Stat. 894; Jan. 14, 1983, Pub.L. 97–471, § 1, 96 Stat. 2601.)

§ 130. Wisconsin

Wisconsin is divided into two judicial districts to be known as the Eastern and Western districts of Wisconsin.

Eastern District

(a) The Eastern District comprises the counties of Brown, Calumet, Dodge, Door, Florence, Fond du Lac, Forest, Green Lake, Kenosha, Kewaunee, Langlade, Manitowoc, Marinette, Marquette, Menominee, Milwaukee, Oconto, Outagamie, Ozaukee, Racine, Shawano, Sheboygan, Walworth, Washington, Waukesha, Waupaca, Waushara, and Winnebago.

Court for the Eastern District shall be held at Green Bay, Milwaukee, and Oshkosh.

Western District

(b) The Western District comprises the counties of Adams, Ashland, Barron, Bayfield, Buffalo, Burnett, Chippewa, Clark, Columbia, Crawford, Dane, Douglas, Dunn, Eau Claire, Grant, Green, Iowa, Iron, Jackson, Jefferson, Juneau, La Crosse, Lafayette, Lincoln, Marathon, Monroe, Oneida, Pepin, Pierce, Polk, Portage, Price, Richland, Rock, Rusk, Saint Croix, Sauk, Sawyer, Taylor, Trempealeau, Vernon, Vilas, Washburn, and Wood.

Court for the Western District shall be held at Eau Claire, La Crosse, Madison, Superior, and Wausau.

(June 25, 1948, c. 646, 62 Stat. 894; Aug. 6, 1962, Pub.L. 87–573, 76 Stat. 307.)

HISTORICAL AND STATUTORY NOTES

Designation of Judge to Hold Court, Eastern District

Pub.L. 106–553, § 1(a)(2) [Title III, § 305(c)], Dec. 21, 2000, 114 Stat. 2762, 2762A–85, provided that: "The chief judge of the eastern district of Wisconsin shall designate 1 judge who shall hold court for such district in Green Bay, Wisconsin."

§ 131. Wyoming

Wyoming and those portions of Yellowstone National Park situated in Montana and Idaho constitute one judicial district.

Court shall be held at Casper, Cheyenne, Evanston, Lander, Jackson, and Sheridan.

(June 25, 1948, c. 646, 62 Stat. 895; July 10, 1984, Pub.L. 98–353, Title II, § 203(a), 98 Stat. 350.)

§ 132. Creation and composition of district courts

(a) There shall be in each judicial district a district court which shall be a court of record known as the United States District Court for the district.

(b) Each district court shall consist of the district judge or judges for the district in regular active service. Justices or judges designated or assigned shall be competent to sit as judges of the court.

(c) Except as otherwise provided by law, or rule or order of court, the judicial power of a district court with respect to any action, suit or proceeding may be exercised by a single judge, who may preside alone and hold a regular or special session of court at the same time other sessions are held by other judges.

(June 25, 1948, c. 646, 62 Stat. 895; Nov. 13, 1963, Pub.L. 88–176, § 2, 77 Stat. 331.)

HISTORICAL AND STATUTORY NOTES

Continuation of Organization of Court

Section 2(b) of Act June 25, 1948, provided in part that the provisions of this title as set out in section 1 of said Act June 25, 1948, with respect to the organization of the court, shall be construed as a continuation of existing law, and the tenure of the judges, officers, and employees thereof, and of the United States attorneys and marshals and their deputies and assistants, in office on Sept. 1, 1948, shall not be affected by its enactment but each of them shall continue to serve in the same capacity under the appropriate provisions of this title pursuant to his prior appointment.

§ 133. Appointment and number of district judges

(a) The President shall appoint, by and with the advice and consent of the Senate, district judges for the several judicial districts, as follows:

DISTRICTS	JUDGES
Alabama:	
Northern	7
Middle	3
Southern	3
Alaska	3
Arizona	12
Arkansas:	
Eastern	5
Western	3
California:	
Northern	14
Eastern	6
Central	27
Southern	13
Colorado	7
Connecticut	8
Delaware	4
District of Columbia	15
Florida:	
Northern	4

DISTRICTS	JUDGES
Middle	15
Southern	17
Georgia:	
Northern	11
Middle	4
Southern	3
Hawaii	3
Idaho	2
Illinois:	
Northern	22
Central	4
Southern	4
Indiana:	
Northern	5
Southern	5
Iowa:	
Northern	2
Southern	3
Kansas	5
Kentucky:	
Eastern	5
Western	4
Eastern and Western	1
Louisiana:	
Eastern	12
Middle	3
Western	7
Maine	3
Maryland	10
Massachusetts	13
Michigan:	
Eastern	15
Western	4
Minnesota	7
Mississippi:	
Northern	3
Southern	6
Missouri:	
Eastern	6
Western	5
Eastern and Western	2
Montana	3
Nebraska	3
Nevada	7
New Hampshire	3
New Jersey	17
New Mexico	6
New York:	
Northern	5

DISTRICTS	JUDGES
Southern	28
Eastern	15
Western	4
North Carolina:	
Eastern	4
Middle	4
Western	4
North Dakota	2
Ohio:	
Northern	11
Southern	8
Oklahoma:	
Northern	3
Eastern	1
Western	6
Northern, Eastern, and Western	1
Oregon	6
Pennsylvania:	
Eastern	22
Middle	6
Western	10
Puerto Rico	7
Rhode Island	3
South Carolina	10
South Dakota	3
Tennessee:	
Eastern	5
Middle	4
Western	5
Texas:	
Northern	12
Southern	19
Eastern	7
Western	13
Utah	5
Vermont	2
Virginia:	
Eastern	11
Western	4
Washington:	
Eastern	4
Western	7
West Virginia:	
Northern	3
Southern	5
Wisconsin:	
Eastern	5
Western	2
Wyoming	3.

(b)(1) In any case in which a judge of the United States (other than a senior judge) assumes the duties of a full-time office of Federal judicial administration, the President shall appoint, by and with the advice and consent of the Senate, an additional judge for the court on which such judge serves. If the judge who assumes the duties of such full-time office leaves that office and resumes the duties as an active judge of the court, then the President shall not appoint a judge to

fill the first vacancy which occurs thereafter in that court.

(2) For purposes of paragraph (1), the term "office of Federal judicial administration" means a position as Director of the Federal Judicial Center, Director of the Administrative Office of the United States Courts, or administrative assistant to the Chief Justice.

(June 25, 1948, c. 646, 62 Stat. 895; Aug. 3, 1949, c. 387, § 2(a), 63 Stat. 493; Aug. 14, 1950, c. 708, 64 Stat. 443; Aug. 29, 1950, c. 819, § 1, 64 Stat. 562; Sept. 5, 1950, c. 848, § 1, 64 Stat. 578; Feb. 10, 1954, c. 6, § 2(a)(3), 68 Stat. 9; Sept. 7, 1957, Pub.L. 85–310, 71 Stat. 631; July 7, 1958, Pub.L. 85–508, § 12(c), 72 Stat. 348; Mar. 18, 1959, Pub.L. 86–3, § 9(b), 73 Stat. 8; May 19, 1961, Pub.L. 87–36, § 2(d), 75 Stat. 81; July 30, 1962, Pub.L. 87–562, § 3, 76 Stat. 248; Oct. 7, 1965, Pub.L. 89–242, § 1(c), 79 Stat. 951; Mar. 18, 1966, Pub.L. 89–372, § 4, 80 Stat. 77; June 2, 1970, Pub.L. 91–272, § 1(d), 84 Stat. 295; Dec. 18, 1971, Pub.L. 92–208, § 3(d), 85 Stat. 742; Oct. 2, 1978, Pub.L. 95–408, § 4(b)(2), 92 Stat. 883; Oct. 20, 1978, Pub.L. 95–486, § 1(c), 92 Stat. 1630; Jan. 14, 1983, Pub.L. 97–471, § 3, 96 Stat. 2601; July 10, 1984, Pub.L. 98–353, Title II, § 202(e), 98 Stat. 348; Dec. 1, 1990, Pub.L. 101–650, Title II, § 203(d), Title III, § 303, 104 Stat. 5101, 5105; Oct. 6, 1997, Pub.L. 105–53, § 4, 111 Stat. 1174; Nov. 29, 1999, Pub.L. 106–113, Div. B, § 1000(a)(1) [Title III, § 309(b)], 113 Stat. 1535, 1501A–37; Dec. 21, 2000, Pub.L. 106–553, § 1(a)(2) [Title III, § 305(b)], 114 Stat. 2762, 2762A–85; Nov. 2, 2002, Pub.L. 107–273, Div. A, Title III, § 312(a)(2), (b)(2), 116 Stat. 1787, 1788.)

HISTORICAL AND STATUTORY NOTES

Codifications

Section 4(b)(2) of Pub.L. 95–408, set out in the credit of this section, was stricken by Pub.L. 96–4, § 1, Mar. 30, 1979, 93 Stat. 6, and replaced by section 4(b)(2) to (4) of Pub.L. 95–408, as added by Pub.L. 96–4, § 1, Mar. 30, 1979, 93 Stat. 6, which provisions are now set out as a note under section 93 of this title.

Effective and Applicability Provisions

2002 Acts

Pub.L. 107–273, Div. A, Title III, § 312(a)(3), Nov. 2, 2002, 116 Stat. 1787, provided that: "This subsection [amending subsec. (a) of this section and enacting provisions set out as a note under this section] shall take effect on July 15, 2003."

Pub.L. 107–273, Div. A, Title III, § 312(b)(3), Nov. 2, 2002, 116 Stat. 1788, provided that: "With respect to the central or southern district of Illinois, the northern district of New York, or the eastern district of Virginia, this subsection [amending subsec. (a) of this section and enacting provisions set out as notes under this section] shall take effect on the earlier of—

"(A) the date on which the first vacancy in the office of district judge occurs in such district; or

"(B) July 15, 2003."

1990 Acts

Amendment by section 203(d) of Pub.L. 101–650 effective Dec. 1, 1990, see section 206 of Pub.L. 101–650, set out as a note under section 44 of this title.

1978 Acts

Section 7 of Pub.L. 95–486 provided that:

"(a) The first section and section 2 of this Act [amending this section and enacting provisions set out as notes under this section] shall take effect immediately upon the President's promulgation and publication of standards and guidelines for the selection, on the basis of merit, of nominees for United States district court judgeships authorized by this Act [amending this section, sections 44, 46, 1337, and 1445 of this title, section 5108 of Title 5, Government Organization and Employees, enacting provisions set out as notes under this section and sections 41 and 44 of this title, and amending provisions set out as a note under section 45 of this title].

"(b) The President may waive such standards and guidelines with respect to any nomination by notifying the Senate of the reasons for such waiver.

"(c) Following the promulgation and publication of such standards and guidelines, no nomination or appointment to a United States district court judgeship may be invalidated on the basis of the President's failure to comply with this section or with any standards or guidelines promulgated under this section.

"(d) This Act, other than the first section and section 2 [amending this section and enacting provisions set out as notes under this section], shall take effect on the date of enactment of this Act [Oct. 20, 1978]."

Section 11 of Pub.L. 95–486 provided that: "Notwithstanding any other provision of this Act [amending this section, sections 44, 46, 1337 and 1445 of this title, section 5108 of Title 5, Government Organization and Employees, enacting provisions set out as notes under this section, sections 41, 44 of this title, and amending provisions set out as notes under section 45 of this title], the first section and section 2 [amending this section and enacting provisions set out as notes under this section] shall not take effect before November 1, 1978."

Amendment by Pub.L. 95–408 effective 180 days after Oct. 2, 1978, such amendment not to affect the composition or preclude the service of any grand or petit juror summoned, empaneled, or actually serving in any judicial district on the effective date of this Act, see section 5 of Pub.L. 95–408, set out as a note under section 89 of this title.

1971 Acts

Amendment by Pub.L. 92–208 effective one hundred and twenty days after Dec. 18, 1971, see section 3(f) of Pub.L. 92–208, set out as a note under section 98 of this title.

1965 Acts

Amendment by Pub.L. 89–242 effective on the first day of the month following the date of enactment of Pub.L. 89–242, see section 6 of Pub.L. 89–242, set out as a note under section 121 of this title.

1962 Acts

Amendment by Pub.L. 87–562 effective 90 days after July 30, 1962, see section 5 of Pub.L. 87–562, set out as a note under section 89 of this title.

1959 Acts

Section 9 of Pub.L. 86–3 provided in part that the amendment of this section and section 134(a) of this title shall be effective upon the admission of the State of Hawaii into the Union. Admission of Hawaii into the Union was accomplished Aug. 21, 1959, upon issuance of Proc. No. 3309, Aug. 21, 1959, 25 F.R. 6868, 73 Stat. c74, as required by sections 1

and 7(c) of Pub.L. 86–3, Mar. 18, 1959, 73 Stat. 4, set out as notes preceding section 491 of Title 48, Territories and Insular Possessions.

1958 Acts

Amendment by Pub.L. 85–508 effective Jan. 3, 1959, upon admission of Alaska into the Union pursuant to Proc. No. 3269, Jan. 3, 1959, 24 F.R. 81, 73 Stat. c16, as required by sections 1 and 8(c) of Pub.L. 85–508, see notes set out under section 81A of this title and preceding section 21 of Title 48, Territories and Insular Possessions.

Conversion of Temporary Judgeships to Permanent Judgeships

Pub.L. 107–273, Div. A, Title III, § 312(b)(1), Nov. 2, 2002, 116 Stat. 1787, provided that: "The existing district judgeships for the central district and the southern district of Illinois, the northern district of New York, and the eastern district of Virginia authorized by section 203(c) (3), (4), (9), and (12) of the Judicial Improvements Act of 1990 (Public Law 101–650, 28 U.S.C. 133 note) shall be authorized under section 133 of title 28, United States Code [this section], and the incumbents in such offices shall hold the offices under section 133 of title 28, United States Code [this section] (as amended by this section)."

Temporary Judgeships

Pub.L. 107–273, Div. A, Title III, § 312(c), Nov. 2, 2002, 116 Stat. 1788, provided that:

"**(1) In general.**—The President shall appoint, by and with the advice and consent of the Senate—

"**(A)** 1 additional district judge for the northern district of Alabama;

"**(B)** 1 additional judge for the district of Arizona;

"**(C)** 1 additional judge for the central district of California;

"**(D)** 1 additional judge for the southern district of Florida;

"**(E)** 1 additional district judge for the district of New Mexico;

"**(F)** 1 additional district judge for the western district of North Carolina; and

"**(G)** 1 additional district judge for the eastern district of Texas.

"**(2) Vacancies not filled.**—The first vacancy in the office of district judge in each of the offices of district judge authorized by this subsection [this note], occurring 10 years or more after the confirmation date of the judge named to fill the temporary district judgeship created in the applicable district by this subsection [this note], shall not be filled.

"**(3) Effective date.**—This subsection [this note] shall take effect on July 15, 2003."

Additional Federal Judgeships

Pub.L. 109–115, Div. A, Title IV, § 406, Nov. 30, 2005, 119 Stat. 2470, provided that: "The existing judgeship for the eastern district of Missouri authorized by section 203(c) of the Judicial Improvements Act of 1990 (Public Law 101–650, 104 Stat. 5089) as amended by Public Law 105–53 [set out in a note under this heading], as of the effective date of this Act [Nov. 30, 2005, the effective date of the Transportation, Treasury, Housing and Urban Development, the Judiciary, and Independent Agencies Appropriations Act, 2006, Pub.L.

109–115, Div. A, 119 Stat. 2396, which enacted this note], shall be extended. The first vacancy in the office of district judge in this district occurring 20 years or more after the confirmation date of the judge named to fill the temporary judgeship created by section 203(c) shall not be filled."

Pub.L. 107–273, Div. A, Title III, § 312(a)(1), Nov. 2, 2002, 116 Stat. 1786, provided that: "The President shall appoint, by and with the advice and consent of the Senate—

"**(A)** 5 additional district judges for the southern district of California;

"**(B)** 1 additional district judge for the western district of North Carolina; and

"**(C)** 2 additional district judges for the western district of Texas."

[Pub.L. 107–273, Div. A, Title III, § 312(a)(3), Nov. 2, 2002, 116 Stat. 1787, provided that: "This subsection [amending subsec. (a) of this section and enacting provisions set out as a note under this section] shall take effect on July 15, 2003."]

Pub.L. 106–553, § 1(a)(2) [Title III, § 305(a)], Dec. 21, 2000, 114 Stat. 2762, 2762a–84, provided that:

"**(a) In general**—The President shall appoint, by and with the advice and consent of the Senate—

"**(1)** 1 additional district judge for the district of Arizona;

"**(2)** 1 additional district judge for the southern district of Florida;

"**(3)** 1 additional district judge for the eastern district of Kentucky;

"**(4)** 1 additional district judge for the district of Nevada;

"**(5)** 1 additional district judge for the district of New Mexico;

"**(6)** 1 additional district judge for the district of South Carolina;

"**(7)** 1 additional district judge for the southern district of Texas;

"**(8)** 1 additional district judge for the western district of Texas;

"**(9)** 1 additional district judge for the eastern district of Virginia; and

"**(10)** 1 additional district judge for the eastern district of Wisconsin."

Pub.L. 106–113, Div. B, § 1000(a)(1) [Title III, § 309(a)], Nov. 29, 1999, 113 Stat. 1535, 1501A–37, provided that:

"(a) The President shall appoint, by and with the advice and consent of the Senate—

"**(1)** three additional district judges for the district of Arizona;

"**(2)** four additional district judges for the middle district of Florida; and

"**(3)** two additional district judges for the district of Nevada."

Section 203(a) to (c) of Title II of Pub.L. 101–650, as amended Pub.L. 104–60, Nov. 28, 1995, 109 Stat. 635; Pub.L. 104–317, Title III, § 304, Oct. 19, 1996, 110 Stat. 3852; Pub.L. 105–53, § 3, Oct. 6, 1997, 111 Stat. 1173; Pub.L. 107–273, Div. A, Title III, § 312(d)(1), Nov. 2, 2002, 116 Stat. 1788; Pub.L. 109–289, Div. B, Title II, § 21056, as added Pub.L. 110–5, § 2, Feb. 15, 2007, 121 Stat. 55, provided that:

"(a) **In general.**—The President shall appoint, by and with the advice and consent of the Senate—

"(1) 1 additional district judge for the western district of Arkansas;

"(2) 2 additional district judges for the northern district of California;

"(3) 5 additional district judges for the central district of California;

"(4) 1 additional district judge for the southern district of California;

"(5) 2 additional district judges for the district of Connecticut;

"(6) 2 additional district judges for the middle district of Florida;

"(7) 1 additional district judge for the northern district of Florida;

"(8) 1 additional district judge for the southern district of Florida;

"(9) 1 additional district judge for the middle district of Georgia;

"(10) 1 additional district judge for the northern district of Illinois;

"(11) 1 additional district judge for the southern district of Iowa;

"(12) 1 additional district judge for the western district of Louisiana;

"(13) 1 additional district judge for the district of Maine;

"(14) 1 additional district judge for the district of Massachusetts;

"(15) 1 additional district judge for the southern district of Mississippi;

"(16) 1 additional district judge for the eastern district of Missouri;

"(17) 1 additional district judge for the district of New Hampshire;

"(18) 3 additional district judges for the district of New Jersey;

"(19) 1 additional district judge for the district of New Mexico;

"(20) 1 additional district judge for the southern district of New York;

"(21) 3 additional district judges for the eastern district of New York;

"(22) 1 additional district judge for the middle district of North Carolina;

"(23) 1 additional district judge for the southern district of Ohio;

"(24) 1 additional district judge for the northern district of Oklahoma;

"(25) 1 additional district judge for the western district of Oklahoma;

"(26) 1 additional district judge for the district of Oregon;

"(27) 3 additional district judges for the eastern district of Pennsylvania;

"(28) 1 additional district judge for the middle district of Pennsylvania;

"(29) 1 additional district judge for the district of South Carolina;

"(30) 1 additional district judge for the eastern district of Tennessee;

"(31) 1 additional district judge for the western district of Tennessee;

"(32) 1 additional district judge for the middle district of Tennessee;

"(33) 2 additional district judges for the northern district of Texas;

"(34) 1 additional district judge for the eastern district of Texas;

"(35) 5 additional district judges for the southern district of Texas;

"(36) 3 additional district judges for the western district of Texas;

"(37) 1 additional district judge for the district of Utah;

"(38) 1 additional district judge for the eastern district of Washington;

"(39) 1 additional district judge for the northern district of West Virginia;

"(40) 1 additional district judge for the southern district of West Virginia; and

"(41) 1 additional district judge for the district of Wyoming.

"(b) **Existing judgeships.**—(1) The existing district judgeships for the western district of Arkansas, the northern district of Illinois, the northern district of Indiana, the district of Massachusetts, the western district of New York, the eastern district of North Carolina, the northern district of Ohio, and the western district of Washington authorized by section 202(b) of the Bankruptcy Amendments and Federal Judgeship Act of 1984 (Public Law 98–353, 98 Stat. 347–348) [set out as a note under this section] shall, as of the effective date of this title [Dec. 1, 1990], be authorized under section 133 of title 28, United States Code [this section], and the incumbents in those offices shall hold the office under section 133 of title 28, United States Code [this section], as amended by this title.

"(2)(A) The existing 2 district judgeships for the eastern and western districts of Arkansas (provided by section 133 of title 28, United States Code [this section], as in effect on the day before the effective date of this title [Dec. 1, 1990]) shall be district judgeships for the eastern district of Arkansas only, and the incumbents of such judgeships shall hold the offices under section 133 of title 28, United States Code [this section], as amended by this title.

"(B) The existing district judgeship for the northern and southern districts of Iowa (provided by section 133 of title 28, United States Code [this section], as in effect on the day before the effective date of this title [Dec. 1, 1990]) shall be a district judgeship for the northern district of Iowa only, and the incumbent of such judgeship shall hold the office under section 133 of title 28, United States Code [this section], as amended by this title.

"(C) The existing district judgeship for the northern, eastern, and western districts of Oklahoma (provided by section 133 of title 28, United States Code [this section], as in effect on the day before the effective date of this title [Dec. 1, 1990]) and the occupant of which has his or her official duty station at Oklahoma City on the date of the enactment of this title [Dec. 1, 1990], shall be a district judgeship for the western district of Oklahoma only, and the incumbent of such

judgeship shall hold the office under section 133 of title 28, United States Code [this section], as amended by this title.

"**(c) Temporary judgeships.**—The President shall appoint, by and with the advice and consent of the Senate—

"**(1)** 1 additional district judge for the eastern district of California;

"**(2)** 1 additional district judge for the district of Hawaii;

"**(3)** 1 additional district judge for the central district of Illinois;

"**(4)** 1 additional district judge for the southern district of Illinois;

"**(5)** 1 additional district judge for the district of Kansas;

"**(6)** 1 additional district judge for the western district of Michigan;

"**(7)** 1 additional district judge for the eastern district of Missouri;

"**(8)** 1 additional district judge for the district of Nebraska;

"**(9)** 1 additional district judge for the northern district of New York;

"**(10)** 1 additional district judge for the northern district of Ohio;

"**(11)** 1 additional district judge for the eastern district of Pennsylvania; and

"**(12)** 1 additional district judge for the eastern district of Virginia.

"[**(13)** Redesignated (12)]

Except with respect to the district of Kansas, the western district of Michigan, the eastern district of Pennsylvania, and the northern district of Ohio, the first vacancy in the office of district judge in each of the judicial districts named in this subsection [this note], occurring 10 years or more after the confirmation date of the judge named to fill the temporary judgeship created by this subsection, shall not be filled. The first vacancy in the office of district judge in the district of Kansas occurring 16 years or more after the confirmation date of the judge named to fill the temporary judgeship created for such district under this subsection [this note], shall not be filled. The first vacancy in the office of district judge in the western district of Michigan, occurring after December 1, 1995, shall not be filled. The first vacancy in the office of district judge in the eastern district of Pennsylvania, occurring 5 years or more after the confirmation date of the judge named to fill the temporary judgeship created for such district under this subsection, shall not be filled. The first vacancy in the office of district judge in the northern district of Ohio occurring 15 years or more after the confirmation date of the judge named to fill the temporary judgeship created under this subsection [this note] shall not be filled. For districts named in this subsection [this note] for which multiple judgeships are created by this Act, the last of those judgeships filled shall be the judgeships created under this section."

[Pub.L. 107–273, Div. A, Title III, § 312(d)(2), Nov. 2, 2002, 116 Stat. 1788, provided that: "The amendments made by this subsection [amending this note] shall take effect on the date of enactment of this Act [Nov. 2, 2002]."]

Section 202(a) to (d) of Pub.L. 98–353 provided that:

"**(a)** Subject to the provisions of subsection (c), the President shall appoint, by and with the advice and consent of the Senate, one additional district judge for the southern district of Alabama, one additional district judge for the district of Alaska, five additional district judges for the central district of California, one additional district judge for the district of Colorado, one additional district judge for the district of Connecticut, one additional district judge for the district of Delaware, three additional district judges for the southern district of Florida, one additional district judge for the middle district of Georgia, one additional district judge for the district of Hawaii, four additional district judges for the northern district of Illinois, one additional district judge for the southern district of Illinois, one additional district judge for the western district of Kentucky, one additional district judge for the western district of Louisiana, one additional district judge for the district of Maryland, one additional district judge for the district of Massachusetts, two additional district judges for the eastern district of Michigan, one additional district judge for the district of Minnesota, one additional district judge for the northern district of Mississippi, two additional district judges for the southern district of Mississippi, one additional district judge for the eastern district of Missouri, one additional district judge for the district of Montana, one additional district judge for the district of Nevada, three additional district judges for the district of New Jersey, one additional district judge for the northern district of New York, two additional district judges for the eastern district of New York, one additional district judge for the southern district of Ohio, one additional district judge for the western district of Oklahoma, one additional district judge for the district of Rhode Island, one additional district judge for the eastern district of Tennessee, one additional district judge for the western district of Tennessee, one additional district judge for the northern district of Texas, two additional district judges for the eastern district of Texas, one additional district judge for the western district of Texas, one additional district judge for the district of Utah, one additional district judge for the eastern district of Virginia, one additional district judge for the eastern district of Washington, one additional district judge for the western district of Washington, and one additional district judge for the district of Wyoming.

"**(b)** Subject to the provisions of subsection (c) the President shall appoint, by and with the advice and consent of the Senate, one additional district judge for the western district of Arkansas, one additional district judge for the northern district of Illinois, one additional district judge for the northern district of Indiana, one additional district judge for the district of Massachusetts, one additional district judge for the western district of New York, one additional district judge for the eastern district of North Carolina, one additional district judge for the northern district of Ohio, and one additional district judge for the western district of Washington. The first vacancy in each of the offices of district judge authorized by this subsection, occurring five years or more after the effective date of this Act [probably means July 10, 1984], shall not be filled.

"**(c)** For the judgeships created in subsections (a) and (b), the President shall appoint, by and with the advice and consent of the Senate, no more than twenty-nine of such judges prior to January 21, 1985.

"**(d)** The existing district judgeship for the district of Minnesota and the existing district judgeship for the northern district of Ohio, heretofore authorized by section 2 of the Act of October 20, 1978 (Public Law 95–486, 92 Stat. 1631)

[set out as a note under this section], shall, as of the effective date of this Act [probably means July 10, 1984], be authorized under section 133 of title 28, United States Code [this section], and the incumbents of those offices shall henceforth hold their offices under section 133 [this section], as amended by this Act [Pub.L. 98–353]."

Section 1(a) of Pub.L. 95–486 provided that: "The President shall appoint, by and with the advice and consent of the Senate, three additional district judges for the northern district of Alabama, one additional district judge for the middle district of Alabama, three additional district judges for the district of Arizona, two additional district judges for the eastern district of Arkansas, one additional district judge for the northern district of California, three additional district judges for the eastern district of California, one additional district judge for the central district of California, two additional district judges for the southern district of California, two additional district judges for the district of Colorado, one additional district judge for the district of Connecticut, one additional district judge for the northern district of Florida, three additional district judges for the middle district of Florida, five additional district judges for the southern district of Florida, five additional district judges for the northern district of Georgia, one additional district judge for the southern district of Georgia, three additional district judges for the northern district of Illinois, one additional district judge for the central district of Illinois, one additional district judge for the northern district of Indiana, one additional district judge for the southern district of Indiana, one additional district judge for the southern district of Iowa, one additional district judge for the district of Kansas, two additional district judges for the eastern district of Kentucky, four additional judges for the eastern district of Louisiana, one additional district judge for the middle district of Louisiana, one additional district judge for the western district of Louisiana, one additional district judge for the district of Maine, two additional district judges for the district of Maryland, four additional district judges for the district of Massachusetts, three additional district judges for the eastern district of Michigan, two additional district judges for the western district of Michigan, one additional district judge for the district of Minnesota, one additional district judge for the eastern district of Missouri, two additional district judges for the western district of Missouri, one additional district judge for the district of Nevada, one additional district judge for the district of New Hampshire, two additional district judges for the district of New Jersey, one additional district judge for the district of New Mexico, one additional district judge for the northern district of New York, one additional district judge for the eastern district of New York, one additional district judge for the eastern district of North Carolina, one additional district judge for the middle district of North Carolina, one additional district judge for the western district of North Carolina, one additional district judge for the northern district of Ohio, one additional district judge for the southern district of Ohio, one additional district judge for the western district of Oklahoma, one additional district judge for the northern district of Oklahoma, two additional district judges for the district of Oregon, two additional district judges for the middle district of Pennsylvania, four additional district judges for the district of Puerto Rico, three additional district judges for the district of South Carolina, one additional district judge for the district of South Dakota, one additional district judge for the middle district of Tennessee,

three additional district judges for the northern district of Texas, one additional district judge for the eastern district of Texas, five additional district judges for the southern district of Texas, one additional district judge for the western district of Texas, one additional district judge for the district of Utah, two additional district judges for the eastern district of Virginia, two additional district judges for the western district of Virginia, one additional district judge for the eastern district of Washington, one additional district judge for the western district of Washington, one additional district judge for the southern district of West Virginia, one additional district judge for the eastern district of Wisconsin, and one additional district judge for the western district of Wisconsin."

Section 2 of Pub.L. 95–486 provided that: "The President shall appoint, by and with the advice and consent of the Senate, one additional district judge for the eastern district of Kentucky, one additional district judge for the district of Minnesota, one additional district judge for the northern district of Ohio, and one additional district judge for the southern district of West Virginia. The first vacancy in the office of district judge in the judicial districts named in this section occurring five years or more after the effective date of this Act [Oct. 20, 1978] shall not be filled."

Section 1(a) of Pub.L. 91–272 provided that: "The President shall appoint, by and with the advice and consent of the Senate, one additional district judge for the northern district of Alabama, one additional district judge for the middle district of Alabama, one additional district judge for the district of Arizona, two additional district judges for the northern district of California, three additional district judges for the central district of California, three additional district judges for the southern district of California, one additional district judge for the district of Colorado, one additional district judge for the middle district of Florida, two additional district judges for the southern district of Florida, three additional district judges for the northern district of Georgia, one additional district judge for the southern district of Georgia, two additional district judges for the northern district of Illinois, one additional district judge for the eastern district of Kentucky, one additional district judge for the western district of Kentucky, two additional district judges for the eastern district of Louisiana, one additional district judge for the western district of Louisiana, two additional district judges for the district of Maryland, two additional district judges for the eastern district of Michigan, one additional district judge for the eastern district of Missouri, one additional district judge for the district of Nebraska, one additional district judge for the district of New Jersey, one additional district judge for the district of New Mexico, one additional district judge for the eastern district of New York, three additional district judges for the southern district of New York, one additional district judge for the northern district of Ohio, one additional district judge for the southern district of Ohio, six additional district judges for the eastern district of Pennsylvania, two additional district judges for the western district of Pennsylvania, one additional district judge for the district of Puerto Rico, one additional district judge for the district of South Carolina, one additional district judge for the western district of Tennessee, one additional district judge for the northern district of Texas, one additional district judge for the eastern district of Texas, one additional district judge for the south-

ern district of Texas, one additional district judge for the western district of Texas, one additional district judge for the eastern district of Virginia, and one additional district judge for the southern district of West Virginia."

Section 2(a) of Pub.L. 89–372 provided that: "The President shall appoint, by and with the advice and consent of the Senate, one district judge for the middle and southern districts of Alabama, one additional district judge for the district of Arizona, one additional district judge for the northern district of Florida, one additional district judge for the middle district of Florida, two additional district judges for the southern district of Florida, one additional district judge for the northern district of Illinois, one additional district judge for the southern district of Indiana, four additional district judges for the eastern district of Louisiana, one additional district judge for the district of Maryland, one additional district judge for the northern district of Mississippi, one additional district judge for the southern district of Mississippi, one additional district judge for the western district of New York, one additional district judge for the northern district of Ohio, one additional district judge for the southern district of Ohio, one additional district judge for the district of Rhode Island, two additional district judges for the southern district of Texas, one additional district judge for the western district of Texas, two additional district judges for the eastern district of Virginia, and one additional district judge for the district of Vermont."

Section 2(a) of Pub.L. 87–36 provided that: "The President shall appoint, by and with the advice and consent of the Senate, one additional district judge for the northern district of Alabama, one additional district judge for the district of Alaska, one additional district judge for the district of Arizona, one additional district judge for the eastern and western districts of Arkansas, two additional district judges for the northern district of California, two additional district judges for the southern district of California, one additional district judge for the district of Colorado, two additional district judges for the district of Connecticut, two additional district judges for the southern district of Florida, one additional district judge for the northern district of Georgia, two additional district judges for the northern district of Illinois, one additional district judge for the northern district of Indiana, one additional district judge for the southern district of Indiana, one additional district judge for the northern and southern districts of Iowa, one additional district judge for the district of Kansas, two additional district judges for the eastern district of Louisiana, one additional district judge for the western district of Louisiana, two additional district judges for the district of Maryland, one additional district judge for the district of Massachusetts, two additional district judges for the eastern district of Michigan, one additional district judge for the southern district of Mississippi, one additional district judge for the western district of Missouri, one additional district judge for the district of Nevada, one additional district judge for the district of New Jersey, two additional district judges for the eastern district of New York, six additional district judges for the southern district of New York, one additional district judge for the eastern district of North Carolina, one additional district judge for the middle district of North Carolina, one additional district judge for the western district of North Carolina, one additional district judge for the northern district of Ohio, one additional district judge for the northern, eastern, and western districts of Oklahoma, three additional

district judges for the eastern district of Pennsylvania, one additional district judge for the middle district of Pennsylvania, two additional district judges for the western district of Pennsylvania, one additional district judge for the district of Puerto Rico, one additional district judge for the eastern and western districts of South Carolina, one additional district judge for the eastern district of Tennessee, one additional district judge for the middle district of Tennessee, one additional district judge for the western district of Tennessee, two additional district judges for the northern district of Texas, one additional district judge for the southern district of Texas, one additional district judge for the western district of Texas, and one additional district judge for the eastern and western districts of Washington."

Subsec. (a)(1) of section 2 of Act Feb. 10, 1954, subsec. (a)(3) of which section amended the table in this section, provided for the appointment by the President, by and with the advice and consent of the Senate, of the additional judges for the districts for which additional permanent judgeships were provided in such amendment.

Alabama.—Section 1(b) of Pub.L. 91–272 provided that: "The existing district judgeship for the middle and southern districts of Alabama, heretofore provided for by section 133 of title 28 of the United States Code [this section], shall hereafter be a district judgeship for the southern district of Alabama only, and the present incumbent of such judgeship shall henceforth hold his office under such section 133, as amended by subsection (d) of this section."

California.—Section 3(h) of Pub.L. 89–372 provided that: "The President shall appoint, by and with the advice and consent of the Senate, three additional district judges for the central district of California, and two additional district judges for the northern district of California."

Delaware.—Act July 24, 1946, c. 602, 60 Stat. 654, which authorized the appointment of an additional judge for the district of Delaware was repealed by section 2 of Act Sept. 5, 1950, cited to text, which by section 1 of said Act Sept. 5, 1950, made the additional judgeship permanent. However, said section 2 also provided that the repeal in no way affected the tenure of the present incumbent.

Florida.—Section 2(b) of Pub.L. 89–372 provided that: "The existing district judgeship for the northern, middle and southern districts of Florida heretofore provided for by section 133 of title 28, United States Code [this section], shall hereafter be a district judgeship for the middle district of Florida only, and the present incumbent of such judgeship shall henceforth hold his office under section 133, as amended by this Act."

Georgia.—Act Mar. 29, 1949, c. 37, 63 Stat. 16, which authorized the appointment of an additional judge for the middle district, was repealed by section 2(b) of Pub.L. 87–36, which made the judgeship permanent and also provided that the incumbent of the judgeship created by Act Mar. 29, 1949, should henceforth hold his office under this section, as amended by Pub.L. 87–36, section 2(d).

Kansas.—Section 5(a) of Pub.L. 89–372, Mar. 18, 1966, 80 Stat. 78, which authorized the appointment of an additional district judge for the eastern district of Kansas and which provided that the first vacancy which occurred in the office of district judge in such district not be filled was repealed by section 1(c) of Pub.L. 91–272, June 2, 1970, 84 Stat. 294, which provided, in part, that such judgeship be a permanent

judgeship and that the present incumbent henceforth hold his office under section 133 of title 28, United States Code [this section], as amended by section 1(d) of Pub.L. 91–272.

Missouri.—In connection with the permanent additional judgeship for the Eastern and Western Districts of Missouri, added by section 2(a), (2), (3) of Act Feb. 10, 1954, which previously had been authorized on a temporary basis by Act Dec. 24, 1942, c. 827, 56 Stat. 1083, section 2(b)(10) of Act Feb. 10, 1954, provided: "The present incumbent of the judgeship created by the Act entitled 'An Act to provide for the appointment of an additional district judge for the eastern and western districts of Missouri', approved December 24, 1942 (56 Stat. 1983), shall henceforth hold such office under section 133 of title 28 of the United States Code [this section] as amended by this Act."

Nevada.—Section 2(b)(2) of Act Feb. 10, 1954, provided: "The President shall appoint, by and with the advice and consent of the Senate, one additional district judge for the district of Nevada. The first vacancy occurring in the office of district judge in said district shall not be filled."

New Jersey.—Section 2(a) of Pub.L. 91–272 provided that: "The President shall appoint, by and with the advice and consent of the Senate, one additional district judge for the district of New Jersey. The first vacancy occurring in the office of district judge in that district shall not be filled."

New Mexico.—Act Feb. 10, 1954, c. 6, § 2(b)(1), 68 Stat. 10, which authorized the appointment of an additional judge for the district, was repealed by section 2(b) of Pub.L. 87–36, which made the judgeship permanent and also provided that the incumbent of the judgeship created by Act Feb. 10, 1954, should henceforth hold his office under this section, as amended by Pub.L. 87–36, § 2(d).

North Carolina.—Section 2(c) of Pub.L. 91–272 provided that: "The President shall appoint, by and with the advice and consent of the Senate, one additional district judge for the eastern district of North Carolina. The first vacancy occurring in the office of district judge in that district shall not be filled."

Ohio.—Act May 1, 1941, c. 83, 55 Stat. 148, which provided for the appointment of an additional judge for the northern district was repealed by Act Aug. 3, 1949, c. 387, § 2(e), 63 Stat. 495, which also provided that the incumbent of the judgeship created by said Act May 1, 1941, shall henceforth hold his office under this section, as amended by Act Aug. 3, 1949, § 2(a).

Section 2(e)(1), (2) of Pub.L. 87–36 provided that:

"(1) The President shall appoint, by and with the advice and consent of the Senate, one additional district judge for the southern district of Ohio. The first vacancy occurring in the office of district judge in said district shall not be filled.

"(2) The President shall appoint, by and with the advice and consent of the Senate, one additional district judge for the northern district of Ohio. The first vacancy occurring in the office of district judge in said district shall not be filled."

Oklahoma.—Act May 24, 1940, c. 209, § 2(a), 54 Stat. 219, providing for additional judgeships was amended by Act Aug. 3, 1949, c. 387, 63 Stat. 495, to strike out "western district of Oklahoma", and to make the incumbent of the judgeship created by said Act May 24, 1940, henceforth hold his office under this section, as amended by Act Aug. 3, 1949, § 2(a).

Pennsylvania.—Section 2(b) of Pub.L. 91–272 provided that: "The President shall appoint, by and with the advice

and consent of the Senate, one additional district judge for the middle district of Pennsylvania. The first vacancy occurring in the office of district judge in that district shall not be filled."

Section 5(b) of Pub.L. 89–372, Mar. 18, 1966, 80 Stat. 78, as amended by Pub.L. 90–90, Sept. 23, 1967, 81 Stat. 228, which authorized the appointment of three additional district judges for the eastern district of Pennsylvania and which provided that the second, third, and fourth vacancies occurring after Mar. 18, 1966, in the office of district judge in such district not be filled was repealed by section 1(c) of Pub.L. 91–272, June 2, 1970, 84 Stat. 294, which provided, in part, that such judgeships be permanent judgeships and that the present incumbents henceforth hold their offices under section 133 of title 28, United States Code [this section], as amended by section 1(d) of Pub.L. 91–272.

Act Feb. 10, 1954, c. 6, § 2(b)(5), 68 Stat. 10, which authorized the appointment of an additional judge for the western district, was repealed by section 2(b) of Pub.L. 87–36, which made the judgeship permanent and also provided that the incumbent of the judgeship created by Act Feb. 10, 1954, should henceforth hold his office under this section, as amended by Pub.L. 87–36, section 2(d).

Section 2 of Act July 24, 1946, c. 600, 60 Stat. 654, as amended by section 6 of Act Feb. 10, 1954, c. 6, 68 Stat. 14, provided: "The President is authorized to appoint, by and with the advice and consent of the Senate, one additional United States district judge, who shall be an additional district judge for the eastern, middle, and western districts of Pennsylvania. The judge so appointed shall at the time of his appointment be a resident and a citizen of the State of Pennsylvania: *Provided*, That when a vacancy occurs in said office it shall not be filled: *Provided further*, That unless the President shall submit a nomination to the Senate to fill the office hereby created within ninety days after the effective date of this Act [July 24, 1946], then in that event this Act shall be of no force and effect. If a vacancy arises in the office of district judge for the middle district of Pennsylvania while the judge appointed pursuant to this section is holding the office created by this section, such judge shall thereafter be a district judge for the middle district of Pennsylvania."

Section 2(c) of Act Aug. 3, 1949, c. 387, 63 Stat. 495, which provided for an additional temporary judgeship for the western district of Pennsylvania was repealed by section 2 of Act Aug. 29, 1950, which by section 1 of said Act Aug. 29, 1950 made the additional judgeship permanent. However, said section 2 also provided that the repeal in no way affected the tenure of the present incumbent.

South Carolina.—Section 1(b) of Pub.L. 89–242 provided that: "The existing district judgeships for the Eastern District of South Carolina, the Western District of South Carolina, and the Eastern and Western Districts of South Carolina heretofore provided for by section 133 of title 28 of the United States Code [this section] shall hereafter be district judgeships for the District of South Carolina and the present incumbents of such judgeships shall henceforth hold their offices under section 133, as amended by this Act."

South Dakota.—Pub.L. 85–310 provided: "The President is authorized to appoint, by and with the advice and consent of the Senate an additional district judge for the district of South Dakota as authorized by paragraph (3) of section 2(b)

of the Act of February 10, 1954 [set out as a note under this section]."

Section 2(b)(3) of Act Feb. 10, 1954, as amended by Pub.L. 85–310, Sept. 7, 1957, 71 Stat. 631, provided: "The President shall appoint, by and with the advice and consent of the Senate, one additional district judge for the district of South Dakota."

Tennessee.—Section 2(b)(4) of Act Feb. 10, 1954, provided: "The President shall appoint, by and with the advice and consent of the Senate, one additional district judge for the middle district of Tennessee. The first vacancy occurring in the office of district judge in said district shall not be filled."

Texas.—In connection with the permanent additional judgeship for the Southern District of Texas, added by section 2(a)(2), (3) of Act Feb. 10, 1954, which previously had been authorized on a temporary basis, section 2(b)(11) of Act Feb. 10, 1954, provided: "The present incumbent of the judgeship for the southern district of Texas created by section 2(d) of the Act entitled 'An Act to provide for the appointment of additional circuit and district judges, and for other purposes', approved August 3, 1949 (63 Stat. 495), shall henceforth hold such office under section 133 of title 28 of the United States Code [this section], as amended by this Act, and section 2(d) of the said Act approved August 3, 1949, is repealed."

Utah.—Act Feb. 10, 1954, c. 6, § 2(b)(6), 68 Stat. 11, which authorized the appointment of an additional judge for the district, was repealed by section 2(b) of Pub.L. 87–36, which made the judgeship permanent and also provided that the incumbent of the judgeship created by Act Feb. 10, 1954, should henceforth hold his office under this section, as amended by Pub.L. 87–36, § 2(d).

Virgin Islands.—Section 3(a) of Pub.L. 91–272 provided that: "The President shall appoint, by and with the advice and consent of the Senate, one additional judge for the District Court of the Virgin Islands, who shall hold office for the term of eight years and until his successor is chosen and qualified, unless sooner removed by the President for cause."

Washington.—Section 1(b) of Pub.L. 95–486 provided that: "The existing district judgeship for the eastern and western districts of Washington, heretofore provided for by section 133 of title 28 of the United States Code [this section], shall hereafter be a district judgeship for the western district of Washington only, and the present incumbent of such judgeship shall henceforth hold his office under section 133 [this section], as amended by this Act [Pub.L. 95–486]."

Section 2(c) of Pub.L. 87–36 provided that: "The existing district judgeship for the eastern and western districts of Washington, heretofore provided for by section 133 of title 28 of the United States Code [this section], shall hereafter be a district judgeship for the western district of Washington only, and the present incumbent of such judgeship shall henceforth hold his office under section 133 [this section], as amended by this Act [Pub.L. 87–36]."

West Virginia.—Section 2 of Pub.L. 97–471 provided that:

"**(a)** The existing district judgeship for the Southern District of West Virginia, authorized by section 2 of the Act entitled 'An Act to provide for the appointment of additional district and circuit judges and for other purposes', approved October 20, 1978 [Pub.L. 95–486] (92 Stat. 1632; 28 U.S.C. 133 note), shall, as of the date of enactment of this Act [Jan.

14, 1983], be authorized under section 133 of title 28 of the United States Code [this section] as a district judgeship for the Northern District of West Virginia, and the incumbent of that office shall henceforth hold office under section 133, as amended by this Act.

"**(b)** The existing district judgeship for the Northern and Southern Districts of West Virginia shall be authorized as the district judgeship for the Southern District."

In connection with the permanent additional judgeship for the Northern and Southern Districts of West Virginia, added by section 2(a)(2), (3) of Act Feb. 10, 1954, which previously had been authorized on a temporary basis by Act June 22, 1936, C. 695, 49 Stat. 1805, section (b)(12) of Act Feb. 10, 1954, provided: "The present incumbent of the judgeship created by the Act entitled 'An Act to provide for the appointment of an additional district judge for the northern and southern districts of West Virginia', approved June 22, 1936 (49 Stat. 1805), shall henceforth hold such office under section 133 of title 28 of the United States Code [this section], as amended by this Act."

Wisconsin.—Section 5(c) of Pub.L. 89–372, Mar. 18, 1966, 80 Stat. 78, which authorized the appointment of an additional district judge for the district of Wisconsin and which provided that the first vacancy occurring in the office of district judge in such district not be filled was repealed by section 1(c) of Pub.L. 91–272, June 2, 1970, 84 Stat. 294, which provided, in part, that such judgeship be a permanent judgeship and that the present incumbent henceforth hold his office under section 133 of title 28, United States Code [this section], as amended by section 1(d) of Pub.L. 91–272.

Nomination of Women and Blacks to Federal Judgeships

Section 8 of Pub.L. 95–486 provided that: "The Congress—

"**(1)** takes notice of the fact that only 1 percent of Federal judges are women and only 4 percent are blacks; and

"**(2)** suggests that the President, in selecting individuals for nomination to the Federal judgeships created by this Act [amending this section, sections 44, 46, 1337, and 1445 of this title, section 5108 of Title 5, Government Organization and Employees, enacting provisions set out as notes under this section, sections 41, 44 of this title, and amending provisions set out as notes under section 45 of this title], give due consideration to qualified individuals regardless of race, color, sex, religion, or national origin."

Residence of Additional Judge for Kansas

Section 2(b)(2) Act Aug. 3, 1949, provided that: "The judge first appointed for the district of Kansas under the authority contained in subsection (a) [amending this section] shall reside at Wichita."

§ 134. Tenure and residence of district judges

(a) The district judges shall hold office during good behavior.

(b) Each district judge, except in the District of Columbia, the Southern District of New York, and the Eastern District of New York, shall reside in the district or one of the districts for which he is appointed. Each district judge of the Southern District of New York and the Eastern District of New York may

reside within 20 miles of the district to which he or she is appointed.

(c) If the public interest and the nature of the business of a district court require that a district judge should maintain his abode at or near a particular place for holding court in the district or within a particular part of the district the judicial council of the circuit may so declare and may make an appropriate order. If the district judges of such a district are unable to agree as to which of them shall maintain his abode at or near the place or within the area specified in such an order the judicial council of the circuit may decide which of them shall do so.

(June 25, 1948, c. 646, 62 Stat. 896; Aug. 3, 1949, c. 387, § 2(b)(1), 63 Stat. 495; Feb. 10, 1954, c. 6, § 2(b)(13)(a), 68 Stat. 12; Mar. 18, 1959, Pub.L. 86–3, § 9(c), 73 Stat. 8; May 19, 1961, Pub.L. 87–36, § 2(e)(3), 75 Stat. 83; Sept. 12, 1966, Pub.L. 89–571, § 1, 80 Stat. 764; Dec. 18, 1971, Pub.L. 92–208, § 3(e), 85 Stat. 742; Oct. 19, 1996, Pub.L. 104–317, Title VI, § 607, 110 Stat. 3860.)

HISTORICAL AND STATUTORY NOTES

Effective and Applicability Provisions

1971 Acts

Amendment by Pub.L. 92–208 effective one hundred and twenty days after Dec. 18, 1971, see section 3(f) of Pub.L. 92–208, set out as a note under section 98 of this title.

1959 Acts

Amendment by Pub.L. 86–3 effective upon the admission of Hawaii into the Union, see note set out under Section 133 of this title. Admission of Hawaii into the Union was accomplished Aug. 21, 1959 upon issuance of Proc. No. 3309, Aug. 21, 1959, 25 F.R. 6868, 73 Stat. c74, as required by Sections 1 and 7(c) of Pub.L. 86–3, Mar. 18, 1959, 73 Stat. 4, set out as notes preceding Section 491 of Title 48, Territories and Insular Possessions.

Applicability of Orders under 1954 Amendment

Section 2(b)(13)(b) of Act Feb. 10, 1954, provided: "Orders made by the judicial councils of the circuits under the second sentence of subsection (c) of section 134 of title 28 [this section], as amended by this section, determining that a specified district judge shall maintain his abode at or near a place or within an area which the council has theretofore designated for the abode of a district judge under the first sentence of such subsection, shall be applicable only to district judges appointed after the enactment of this Act [Feb. 10, 1954]."

Tenure and Salary Rights of Judges in Puerto Rico in Office on September 12, 1966

Section 4 of Pub.L. 89–571 provided that: "The amendments made by this section to sections 134 [this section] and 373 of title 28, United States Code [section 373 of this title], shall not affect the tenure of office or right to continue to receive salary after resignation, retirement, or failure of reappointment of any district judge for the district of Puerto Rico who is in office on the date of enactment of this Act [Sept. 12, 1966]."

§ 135. Salaries of district judges

Each judge of a district court of the United States shall receive a salary at an annual rate determined under section 225 of the Federal Salary Act of 1967 (2 U.S.C. 351–361), as adjusted by section 461 of this title.

(June 25, 1948, c. 646, 62 Stat. 897; Mar. 2, 1955, c. 9, § 1(c), 69 Stat. 10; Aug. 14, 1964, Pub.L. 88–426, Title IV, § 403(c), 78 Stat. 434; Aug. 9, 1975, Pub.L. 94–82, Title II, § 205(b)(3), 89 Stat. 422.)

HISTORICAL AND STATUTORY NOTES

References in Text

Section 225 of the Federal Salary Act of 1967, referred to in text, is section 225 of Pub.L. 90–206, Dec. 16, 1967, 81 Stat. 642, as amended, which is classified to Chapter 11 (section 351 et seq.) of Title 2, The Congress.

Effective and Applicability Provisions

1964 Acts

Amendment by Pub.L. 88–426 effective on the first day of the first pay period which begins on or after July 1, 1964, except to the extent provided in section 501(c) of Pub.L. 88–426, see section 501 of Pub.L. 88–426.

1955 Acts

Amendment by Act Mar. 2, 1955, effective Mar. 1, 1955, see section 5 of Act Mar. 2, 1955, set out as a note under section 31 of Title 2, The Congress.

Increase in Salaries

2006—Ex. Ord. No. 13393, Dec. 22, 2005, 70 F.R. 76655, set out as a note under 5 U.S.C.A. § 5332, adjusted the rates of basic pay or salaries for certain Judicial offices and positions, effective on the first day of the first applicable pay period beginning on or after Jan. 1, 2006. See Schedule of Judicial Salaries, set out as Schedule 7 of that Executive Order, set out in a note under 5 U.S.C.A. § 5332 and also set out in a note under 28 U.S.C.A. § 5.

2005—Salaries of the district judges increased to $162,100 per annum, respectively, effective on the first day of the first applicable pay period beginning on or after Jan. 1, 2005, by Ex. Ord. No. 13368, Dec. 30, 2004, 70 F.R. 1147, formerly set out as a note under 5 U.S.C.A. § 5332.

2004—Salaries of the district judges increased to $158,100 per annum, respectively, effective on the first day of the first applicable pay period beginning on or after Jan. 1, 2004, see Ex. Ord. No. 13332, Mar. 3, 2004, 69 F.R. 10891, which superseded Ex. Ord. No. 13322, Dec. 30, 2003, 69 F.R. 231, formerly set out as a note under 5 U.S.C.A. § 5332.

2004—Salaries of the district judges increased to $158,100 per annum, respectively, effective on the first day of the first applicable pay period beginning on or after Jan. 1, 2004, by Ex. Ord. No. 13322, Dec. 30, 2003, 69 F.R. 231, which was superseded by Ex. Ord. No. 13332, Mar. 3, 2004, 69 F.R. 10891, formerly set out as a note under 5 U.S.C.A. § 5332.

2003—Salaries of the district judges increased to $154,700 per annum, respectively, effective on the first day of the first applicable pay period beginning on or after Jan. 1, 2003, by Ex. Ord. No. 13282, Dec. 31, 2002, 68 F.R. 1133, as amended by Ex. Ord. No. 13291, Mar. 21, 2003, 68 F.R. 2003, formerly set out as a note under 5 U.S.C.A. § 5332.

2002—Salaries of district judges increased to $150,000 per annum, effective on the first day of the first applicable pay period beginning on or after Jan. 1, 2002, by Ex. Ord. No. 13249, Dec. 28, 2001, 67 F.R. 639, set out as a note under 5 U.S.C.A. § 5332.

2001—Salaries of district judges increased to $145,100, effective on the first day of the first applicable pay period beginning on or after Jan. 1, 2001, by Ex. Ord. No. 13182, Dec. 23, 2000, 65 F.R. 82879, set out as a note under section 5332 of Title 5, Government Organization and Employees.

2000—Salaries of district judges increased to $141,300, effective on the first day of the first applicable pay period beginning on or after Jan. 1, 2000, by Ex. Ord. No. 13144, Dec. 21, 1999, 64 F.R. 72237, formerly set out as a note under section 5332 of Title 5, Government Organization and Employees.

1999—Salaries of district judges continued at $136,700, effective on the first day of the first applicable pay period beginning on or after Jan. 1, 1999, by Ex. Ord. No. 13106, Dec. 7, 1998, 63 F.R. 68151, formerly set out as a note under section 5332 of Title 5, Government Organization and Employees.

1998—Salaries of district judges increased to $136,700, effective on the first day of the first applicable pay period beginning on or after Jan. 1, 1998, by Ex. Ord. No. 13071, Dec. 29, 1997, 62 F.R. 68521, formerly set out as a note under section 5332 of Title 5, Government Organization and Employees.

1997—Salaries of district judges continued at $133,600 effective on the first day of the first applicable pay period beginning on or after Jan. 1, 1997, by Ex. Ord. No. 13033, Dec. 27, 1996, 61 F.R. 68987, formerly set out as a note under section 5332 of Title 5, Government Organization and Employees.

1996—Salaries of district judges continued at $133,600 effective on the first day of the first applicable pay period beginning on or after Jan. 1, 1996, by Ex. Ord. No. 12984, Dec. 28, 1995, 61 F.R. 237, formerly set out as a note under section 5332 of Title 5, Government Organization and Employees.

1995—Salaries of district judges continued at $133,600 effective on the first day of the first applicable pay period beginning on or after Jan. 1, 1995, by Ex. Ord. No. 12944, Dec. 28, 1994, 60 F.R. 309, formerly set out as a note under section 5332 of Title 5, Government Organization and Employees.

1993—Salaries of district judges increased to $133,600 effective on the first day of the first applicable pay period beginning on or after Jan. 1, 1993, by Ex. Ord. No. 12826, Dec. 30, 1992, 57 F.R. 62909, formerly set out as a note under section 5332 of Title 5, Government Organization and Employees.

1992—Salaries of district judges increased to $129,500 per annum, effective on the first day of the first applicable pay period beginning on or after Jan. 1, 1992, by Ex. Ord. No. 12786, Dec. 26, 1991, 56 F.R. 67453, formerly set out as a note under section 5332 of Title 5.

1991—Salaries of district judges increased to $125,100 per annum, effective on the first day of the first applicable pay period beginning on or after Jan. 1, 1991, by Ex. Ord. No. 12736, Dec. 12, 1990, 55 F.R. 51385, formerly set out as a note under section 5332 of Title 5.

1990—Salaries of district judges continued at $89,500 per annum, and increased to $96,600, effective on first day of first pay period beginning on or after Jan. 31, 1990, by Ex. Ord. No. 12698, Dec. 23, 1989, 54 F.R. 53473, formerly set out as a note under section 5332 of Title 5.

1989—Salaries of district judges increased in the amount of 25 percent of their rates (as last in effect before the increase), effective Jan. 1, 1991, see Pub.L. 101–194, Title VII, § 703(a)(3), Nov. 30, 1989, 103 Stat. 1768, set out as a note under section 5318 of Title 5.

Salaries of district judges continued at $89,500 per annum, effective on the first day of the first applicable pay period beginning on or after Jan. 1, 1989, by Ex. Ord. No. 12663, Jan. 6, 1989, 54 F.R. 791, formerly set out as a note under section 5332 of Title 5.

1988—Salaries of district judges continued at $89,500 per annum, effective on the first day of the first applicable pay period beginning on or after Jan. 1, 1988, by Ex. Ord. No. 12622, Dec. 31, 1987, 53 F.R. 222, formerly set out as a note under section 5332 of Title 5.

1987—Salaries of district judges increased to $89,500 per annum, on recommendation of the President of the United States, see note set out under section 358 of Title 2, The Congress.

Salaries of district judges increased to $81,100, as required by section 406 of the Judiciary Appropriation Act, 1987, as incorporated in section 101(b) of Pub.L. 99–500 and section 101(b) of Pub.L. 99–591, effective on the first day of the first applicable pay period beginning on or after Jan. 1, 1987, by Ex. Ord. No. 12578, Dec. 31, 1986, 52 F.R. 505, formerly set out as a note under section 5332 of Title 5.

1985—Salaries of district judges increased to $78,700 effective on the first day of the first pay period beginning on or after Jan. 1, 1985, by Ex. Ord. No. 12496, Dec. 28, 1984, 50 F.R. 211, as amended by Ex. Ord. No. 12540, Dec. 30, 1985, 51 F.R. 577, formerly set out as a note under section 5332 of Title 5, Government Organization and Employees. Prior to its amendment by Ex. Ord. No. 12540, schedule 7 of Ex. Ord. No. 12496 had contained a footnote directing that, pursuant to section 140 of Pub.L. 97–92, set out as a note under section 461 of this title, funds were not available to pay a salary at a rate which exceeded the rate in effect on Dec. 15, 1981, which was $70,300.

See also section 2207 of Pub.L. 98–369, set out as a note under section 461 of this title, which provided for overall percentage adjustment increases in certain rates of pay under the General Schedule.

1984—Salaries of district judges increased to $76,000 effective on the first day of the first pay period beginning on or after Jan. 1, 1984, by Ex. Ord. No. 12456, Dec. 30, 1983, 49 F.R. 347, as amended Ex. Ord.No. 12477, May 23, 1984, 49 F.R. 22041; Ex. Ord. No. 12487, Sept. 14, 1984, 49 F.R. 36493, formerly set out as a note under section 5332 of Title 5.

1982—Salaries of district judges increased to $73,100 effective on the first day of the first pay period beginning on or after Oct. 1, 1982, by Ex. Ord. No. 12387, Oct. 8, 1982, 47 F.R. 44981, formerly set out as a note under section 5332 of Title 5, Government Organization and Employees. Ex. Ord. No. 12387 further provided that pursuant to section 140 of Pub.L. 97–92 funds are not available to pay a salary at a rate

which exceeds the rate in effect on Dec. 15, 1981, which was $70,300.

Maximum rate payable after Dec. 17, 1982, increased from $70,300 to $73,100, see Pub.L. 97–377, Title I, § 129(b)–(d), Dec. 21, 1982, 96 Stat. 1914, set out as a note under section 5318 of Title 5.

Limitations on use of funds for fiscal year ending Sept. 30, 1983, appropriated by any Act to pay the salary or pay of any individual in legislative, executive, or judicial branch in position equal to or above level V of the Executive Schedule, see section 101(e) of Pub.L. 97–276, as amended, set out as a note under section 5318 of Title 5.

1981—Salaries of district judges increased to $70,300 effective on the first day of the first pay period beginning on or after Oct. 1, 1981, by Ex. Ord. No. 12330, Oct. 15, 1981, 46 F.R. 50921, formerly set out as a note under section 5332 of Title 5.

Limitations on use of funds for fiscal year ending Sept. 30, 1982, appropriated by any Act to pay the salary or pay of any individual in legislative, executive, or judicial branch in position equal to or above level V of the Executive Schedule, see sections 101(g) and 141 of Pub.L. 97–92, set out as a note under section 5318 of Title 5.

1980—Salaries of district judges increased to $67,100 effective on the first day of the first pay period beginning on or after Oct. 1, 1980, by Ex. Ord. No. 12248, Oct. 16, 1980, 45 F.R. 69199, formerly set out as a note under section 5332 of Title 5. Ex. Ord. No. 12248 further provided that pursuant to Pub.L. 96–369 funds are not available to pay a salary at a rate which exceeds the rate in effect on Sept. 30, 1980, which was $57,497.50.

Limitations on use of funds for fiscal year ending Sept. 30, 1981, appropriated by any Act to pay the salary or pay of any individual in legislative, executive, or judicial branch in position equal to or above level V of the Executive Schedule, see section 101(c) of Pub.L. 96–536, as amended, set out as a note under section 5318 of Title 5.

1979—Salaries of district judges increased to $61,500 effective on the first day of the first applicable pay period beginning on or after Oct. 1, 1979, by Ex. Ord. No. 12165, Oct. 9, 1979, 44 F.R. 58671, as amended by Ex. Ord. No. 12200, Mar. 12, 1980, 45 F.R. 16443, formerly set out as a note under section 5332 of Title 5. Ex. Ord. No. 12165 further provided that pursuant to Pub.L. 96–86 funds appropriated for fiscal year 1980 may not be used to pay a salary at a rate which exceeds an increase of 5.5 percent over the applicable rate payable for such position or office in effect on Sept. 30, 1978, which was $57,497.50 for district judges.

Applicability to funds appropriated by any Act for fiscal year ending Sept. 30, 1980, of limitation of section 304 of Pub.L. 95–391 on use of funds to pay the salary or pay of any individual in legislative, executive, or judicial branch in position equal to or above level V of the Executive Schedule, see section 101 of Pub.L. 96–86, set out as a note under section 5318 of Title 5.

1978—Salaries of district judges increased to $57,500 effective on the first day of the first pay period beginning on or after Oct. 1, 1978, by Ex. Ord. No. 12087, Oct. 7, 1978, 43 F.R. 46823, formerly set out as a note under section 5332 of Title 5. Ex. Ord. No. 12087, further provided that pursuant to the Legislative Branch Appropriation Act, 1979 [Pub.L. 95–391, Title III, § 304, Sept. 30, 1978, 92 Stat. 788, set out as a note under section 5318 of Title 5], funds are not available to pay a salary at a rate which exceeds the rate in effect on Sept. 30, 1978, which was $54,500.

1977—Salaries of district judges increased to $54,500 per annum, upon recommendation of the President of the United States, see note set out under section 358 of Title 2, The Congress.

1976—Salaries of district judges increased to $44,000 effective on the first day of the first pay period beginning on or after Oct. 1, 1976, by Ex. Ord. No. 11941, Oct. 1, 1976, 41 F.R. 43889, formerly set out as a note under section 5332 of Title 5, Government Organization and Employees. Ex. Ord. No. 11941, further provided that pursuant to the Legislative Branch Appropriation Act, 1977, funds are not available to pay a salary at a rate which exceeds the rate in effect on Sept. 30, 1976, which was $42,000.

1975—Salaries of district judges increased to $42,000 effective on the first day of the first pay period beginning on or after Oct. 1, 1975, by Ex. Ord. No. 11883, Oct. 6, 1975, 40 F.R. 47091, formerly set out as a note under section 5332 of Title 5.

1969—Salary of judge increased from $30,000 to $40,000 per annum, commencing February 14, 1969, upon recommendation of the President of the United States, see note set out under section 358 of Title 2, The Congress.

1946—The salary of the chief judge of District Court for the District of Columbia was increased from $10,500 to $15,500 a year, and the salaries of all other district court judges were increased from $10,000 to $15,000 by Act July 31, 1946, c. 704, § 1, 60 Stat. 716.

1926—Salary of the chief judge of the District Court of the District of Columbia was increased from $7,500 to $10,500 a year, and the salaries of all other district court judges was increased from $7,500 to $10,000 a year by Act Dec. 13, 1926, c. 6, § 1, 44 Stat. 919.

1919—Salaries of district court judges were increased from $6,000 to $7,500 a year by Act Feb. 25, 1919, c. 29, § 1, 40 Stat. 1156.

Salaries of the chief justice and associate justices of the Supreme Court of the District of Columbia, the forerunner of the District Court for the District of Columbia, were set at $5,000 by Act Mar. 3, 1901, c. 854, § 1, 30 Stat. 1199, and increased to $7,500 a year by Act Feb. 25, 1919, c. 29, § 1, 40 Stat. 1156.

1911—Salaries of district court judges had been set at $6,000 a year by the Judicial Code of 1911, Act Mar. 3, 1911, c. 231, § 1, 36 Stat. 1087.

§ 136. Chief judges; precedence of district judges

(a)(1) In any district having more than one district judge, the chief judge of the district shall be the district judge in regular active service who is senior in commission of those judges who—

(A) are sixty-four years of age or under;

(B) have served for one year or more as a district judge; and

(C) have not served previously as chief judge.

(2)(A) In any case in which no district judge meets the qualifications of paragraph (1), the youngest district judge in regular active service who is sixty-five years of age or over and who has served as district judge for one year or more shall act as the chief judge.

(B) In any case under subparagraph (A) in which there is no district judge in regular active service who has served as a district judge for one year or more, the district judge in regular active service who is senior in commission and who has not served previously as chief judge shall act as the chief judge.

(3)(A) Except as provided in subparagraph (C), the chief judge of the district appointed under paragraph (1) shall serve for a term of seven years and shall serve after expiration of such term until another judge is eligible under paragraph (1) to serve as chief judge of the district.

(B) Except as provided in subparagraph (C), a district judge acting as chief judge under subparagraph (A) or (B) of paragraph (2) shall serve until a judge has been appointed who meets the qualifications under paragraph (1).

(C) No district judge may serve or act as chief judge of the district after attaining the age of seventy years unless no other district judge is qualified to serve as chief judge of the district under paragraph (1) or is qualified to act as chief judge under paragraph (2).

(b) The chief judge shall have precedence and preside at any session which he attends.

Other district judges shall have precedence and preside according to the seniority of their commissions. Judges whose commissions bear the same date shall have precedence according to seniority in age.

(c) A judge whose commission extends over more than one district shall be junior to all district judges except in the district in which he resided at the time he entered upon the duties of his office.

(d) If the chief judge desires to be relieved of his duties as chief judge while retaining his active status as district judge, he may so certify to the Chief Justice of the United States, and thereafter, the chief judge of the district shall be such other district judge who is qualified to serve or act as chief judge under subsection (a).

(e) If a chief judge is temporarily unable to perform his duties as such, they shall be performed by the district judge in active service, present in the district and able and qualified to act, who is next in precedence.

(June 25, 1948, c. 646, 62 Stat. 897; Oct. 31, 1951, c. 655, § 37, 65 Stat. 723; Aug. 6, 1958, Pub.L. 85–593, § 2, 72 Stat. 497; Apr. 2, 1982, Pub.L. 97–164, Title II, § 202, 96 Stat. 52.)

HISTORICAL AND STATUTORY NOTES

Effective and Applicability Provisions

1982 Acts

Amendment by Pub.L. 97–164 effective Oct. 1, 1982, see section 402 of Pub.L. 97–164, set out as a note under section 171 of this title.

1958 Acts

Section 3 of Pub.L. 85–593 provided in part that the amendment to this section by Pub.L. 85–593 shall take effect at the expiration of one year from Aug. 6, 1958, see section 3 of Pub.L. 85–593, as amended, set out as a note under section 45 of this title.

Savings Provisions

Amendment of this section by Pub.L. 97–164 not to apply or affect any person serving as chief judge on the effective date of Pub.L. 97–164 [Oct. 1, 1982], and the provisions of subsec. (a) of this section as in effect on the day before the effective date of part A of Title II of Pub.L. 97–164 [Oct. 1, 1982] to apply to the chief judge of a district court serving on Oct. 1, 1982, see section 203 of Pub.L. 97–164, set out as a note under section 45 of this title.

Chief Justice of District Court for the District of Columbia to be known as Chief Judge

Section 2(a) of Act June 25, 1948, provided in part that the Chief Justice of the District Court for the District of Columbia in office on Sept. 1, 1948, shall thereafter be known as the Chief Judge.

§ 137. Division of business among district judges

The business of a court having more than one judge shall be divided among the judges as provided by the rules and orders of the court.

The chief judge of the district court shall be responsible for the observance of such rules and orders, and shall divide the business and assign the cases so far as such rules and orders do not otherwise prescribe.

If the district judges in any district are unable to agree upon the adoption of rules or orders for that purpose the judicial council of the circuit shall make the necessary orders.

(June 25, 1948, c. 646, 62 Stat. 897.)

§ 138. Terms abolished

The district court shall not hold formal terms.

(June 25, 1948, c. 646, 62 Stat. 897; Oct. 16, 1963, Pub.L. 88–139, § 1, 77 Stat. 248.)

§ 139. Times for holding regular sessions

The times for commencing regular sessions of the district court for transacting judicial business at the places fixed by this chapter shall be determined by the rules or orders of the court. Such rules or orders may provide that at one or more of such places the court shall be in continuous session for such purposes on all business days throughout the year. At other places a session of the court shall continue for such

purposes until terminated by order of final adjournment or by commencement of the next regular session at the same place.

(June 25, 1948, c. 646, 62 Stat. 897; Oct. 16, 1963, Pub.L. 88–139, § 1, 77 Stat. 248.)

§ 140. Adjournment

(a) Any district court may, by order made anywhere within its district, adjourn or, with the consent of the judicial council of the circuit, pretermit any regular session of court for insufficient business or other good cause.

(b) If the judge of a district court is unable to attend and unable to make an order of adjournment, the clerk may adjourn the court to the next regular session or to any earlier day which he may determine.

(June 25, 1948, c. 646, 62 Stat. 897; Oct. 16, 1963, Pub.L. 88–139, § 1, 77 Stat. 248.)

§ 141. Special sessions; places; notice

(a)(1) Special sessions of the district court may be held at such places in the district as the nature of the business may require, and upon such notice as the court orders.

(2) Any business may be transacted at a special session which might be transacted at a regular session.

(b)(1) Special sessions of the district court may be held at such places within the United States outside the district as the nature of the business may require and upon such notice as the court orders, upon a finding by either the chief judge of the district court (or, if the chief judge is unavailable, the most senior available active judge of the district court) or the judicial council of the circuit that, because of emergency conditions, no location within the district is reasonably available where such special sessions could be held.

(2) Pursuant to this subsection, any business which may be transacted at a regular session of a district court may be transacted at a special session conducted outside the district, except that a criminal trial may not be conducted at a special session outside the State in which the crime has been committed unless the defendant consents to such a criminal trial.

(3) Notwithstanding any other provision of law, in any case in which special sessions are conducted pursuant to this section, the district court may summon jurors—

 (A) in civil proceedings, from any part of the district in which the court ordinarily conducts business or the district in which it is holding a special session; and

 (B) in criminal trials, from any part of the district in which the crime has been committed and, if the defendant so consents, from any district in

which the court is conducting business pursuant to this section.

(4) If a district court issues an order exercising its authority under paragraph (1), the court—

 (A) through the Administrative Office of the United States Courts, shall—

 (i) send notice of such order, including the reasons for the issuance of such order, to the Committee on the Judiciary of the Senate and the Committee on the Judiciary of the House of Representatives; and

 (ii) not later than 180 days after the expiration of such court order submit a brief report to the Committee on the Judiciary of the Senate and the Committee on the Judiciary of the House of Representatives describing the impact of such order, including—

 (I) the reasons for the issuance of such order;

 (II) the duration of such order;

 (III) the impact of such order on litigants; and

 (IV) the costs to the judiciary resulting from such order; and

 (B) shall provide reasonable notice to the United States Marshals Service before the commencement of any special session held pursuant to such order.

(5) If a district court issues an order exercising its authority under paragraph (1), the court shall direct the United States marshal of the district where the court is meeting to furnish transportation and subsistence to the same extent as that provided in sections 4282 and 4285 of title 18.

(June 25, 1948, c. 646, 62 Stat. 897; Oct. 16, 1963, Pub.L. 88–139, § 1, 77 Stat. 248; Sept. 9, 2005, Pub.L. 109–63, § 2(b), 119 Stat. 1994; Jan. 5, 2006, Pub.L. 109–162, Title XI, § 1198(a), 119 Stat. 3132.)

[§ 142. Repealed. Pub.L. 97–164, Title I, § 115(c)(3), Apr. 2, 1982, 96 Stat. 32]

HISTORICAL AND STATUTORY NOTES

Section, Acts June 25, 1948, c. 646, 62 Stat. 898; Oct. 9, 1962, Pub.L. 87–764, 76 Stat. 762; Nov. 19, 1977, Pub.L. 95–196, 91 Stat. 1420, related to the providing of accommodations at places for holding court. See section 462 of this title.

Effective Date of Repeal

Repeal effective Oct. 1, 1982, see section 402 of Pub.L. 97–164, set out as an Effective Date of 1982 Amendment note under section 171 of this title.

Waiver of Limitations and Restrictions

The limitations and restrictions contained in this section prior to its repeal were waived with respect to the holding of court at certain places by the following Acts:

Pub. L. 87-833, Oct. 15, 1962, 76 Stat. 959, related to Akron, Ohio.

Pub. L. 87-699, Sept. 25, 1962, 76 Stat. 598, related to Richland, Washington.

Pub. L. 87-562, §4, July 30, 1962, 76 Stat. 248, related to Fort Meyers, Saint Petersburg, Fort Pierce, and West Palm Beach, Florida.

Pub. L. 87-560, July 27, 1962, 76 Stat. 247, related to Marshall, Texas.

Pub. L. 87-559, July 27, 1962, 76 Stat. 246, related to Decatur, Alabama.

Pub. L. 87-553, July 27, 1962, 76 Stat. 222, related to Winchester, Tennessee.

Pub. L. 87-551, July 27, 1962, 76 Stat. 221, related to Bridgeport, Connecticut.

Pub. L. 87-337, Oct. 3, 1961, 75 Stat. 750, related to Lafayette, Louisiana.

Pub. L. 87-36, §3(g), May 19, 1961, 75 Stat. 83, related to Kalamazoo, Michigan; Fayetteville, North Carolina; and Dyersburg, Tennessee.

Pub. L. 86-366, Sept. 22, 1959, 73 Stat. 647, related to Durant, Oklahoma.

Act July 20, 1956, c. 657, 70 Stat. 594, related to Bryson City, North Carolina.

Act Sept. 23, 1950, c. 1006, 64 Stat. 982, related to Klamath Falls, Oregon.

Act Aug. 21, 1950, c. 767, 64 Stat. 469, related to Newnan, Georgia.

Act Aug. 10, 1950, c. 675, § 2, 64 Stat. 438, related to Rock Island, Illinois.

Act Oct. 26, 1949, c. 744, 63 Stat. 923, related to Thomasville, Georgia.

Act Oct. 26, 1949, c. 740, 63 Stat. 921, related to Brunswick, Georgia.

§ 143. Vacant judgeship as affecting proceedings

When the office of a district judge becomes vacant, all pending process, pleadings and proceedings shall, when necessary, be continued by the clerk until a judge is appointed or designated to hold such court. (June 25, 1948, c. 646, 62 Stat. 898.)

§ 144. Bias or prejudice of judge

Whenever a party to any proceeding in a district court makes and files a timely and sufficient affidavit that the judge before whom the matter is pending has a personal bias or prejudice either against him or in favor of any adverse party, such judge shall proceed no further therein, but another judge shall be assigned to hear such proceeding.

The affidavit shall state the facts and the reasons for the belief that bias or prejudice exists, and shall be filed not less than ten days before the beginning of the term at which the proceeding is to be heard, or good cause shall be shown for failure to file it within such time. A party may file only one such affidavit in any case. It shall be accompanied by a certificate of counsel of record stating that it is made in good faith. (June 25, 1948, c. 646, 62 Stat. 898; May 24, 1949, c. 139, § 65, 63 Stat. 99.)

CHAPTER 6—BANKRUPTCY JUDGES

[1] So in original. Does not conform to section catchline.

HISTORICAL AND STATUTORY NOTES

Codifications

Chapter heading and section analysis of chapter 6, as added by Pub.L. 95–598, Title II, § 201(a), Nov. 6, 1978, 92 Stat. 2657, and amended Pub.L. 97–164, Title I, § 110(d), Apr. 2, 1982, 96 Stat. 29, effective June 28, 1984, pursuant to Pub.L. 95–598, Title IV, § 402(b), Nov. 6, 1978, 92 Stat. 2682, as amended by Pub.L. 98–249, § 1(a), Mar. 31, 1984, 98 Stat. 116; Pub.L. 98–271, § 1(a), Apr. 30, 1984, 98 Stat. 163; Pub.L. 98–299, § 1(a), May 25, 1984, 98 Stat. 214; Pub.L. 98–325, § 1(a), June 20, 1984, 98 Stat. 268, set out as a note preceding section 101 of Title 11, Bankruptcy, read as follows:

CHAPTER 6—BANKRUPTCY COURTS

Section 402(b) of Pub.L. 95–598 was amended by section 113 of Pub.L. 98–353 by substituting "shall not be effective" for "shall take effect on June 28, 1984", thereby eliminating the addition of the chapter heading and section analysis of chapter 6 by section 201(a) of Pub.L. 95–598, effective June 27, 1984, pursuant to section 122(c) of Pub.L. 98–353, set out as an Effective and Applicability Provisions note under section 151 of this title.

Section 121(a) of Pub.L. 98–353 directed that section 402(b) of Pub.L. 95–598 be amended by substituting "the date of enactment of the Bankruptcy Amendments and Federal Judgeship Act of 1984 [i.e. July 10, 1984]" for "June 28, 1984". This amendment was not executed in view of the prior amendment to section 402(b) of Pub.L. 95–598 by section 113 of Pub.L. 98–353.

Effective and Applicability Provisions

2005 Acts

Amendments by Pub.L. 109–8, Title VI, § 601, effective 18 months after Apr. 20, 2005, see Pub.L. 109–8, § 601(c), set out as a note under 28 U.S.C.A. § 159.

Except as otherwise provided, amendments by Pub.L. 109–8 effective 180 days after April 20, 2005, and inapplicable with respect to cases commenced under Title 11 before the effective date, see Pub.L. 109–8, § 1501, set out as a note under 11 U.S.C.A. § 101.

Courts During Transition

Pub.L. 95–598, Title IV, § 404, Nov. 6, 1978, 92 Stat. 2683, as amended by Pub.L. 98–249, § 1(b), Mar. 31, 1984, 98 Stat. 116; Pub.L. 98–271, § 1(b), Apr. 30, 1984, 98 Stat. 163; Pub.L. 98–299, § 1(b), May 25, 1984, 98 Stat. 214; Pub.L. 98–325, § 1(b), June 20, 1984, 98 Stat. 268; Pub.L. 98–353, Title I, § 121(b), July 10, 1984, 98 Stat. 345, which provided that, for purposes of Pub.L. 95–598, which enacted Title 11, Bankruptcy, and the amendments made by Pub.L. 95–598, the courts of bankruptcy as defined under section 1(10) of former Title 11, created by section 11(a) of former Title 11, and existing on Sept. 30, 1979, continue to be courts of bankruptcy during the transition period beginning Oct. 1, 1979, and ending June 27, 1984, made provision for extension of the term of office of referees in bankruptcy serving on Nov. 6, 1978, and for such a referee to have the title of United States bankruptcy judge, established for each State a merit screening committee to pass on qualifications of such a referee and determine if the term of such referee should be extended, and set forth the rules and provisions applicable to United States bankruptcy judges during the transition period, was repealed by Pub.L. 98–353, Title I, § 114, 122(a), July 10, 1984, 98 Stat. 343, 346, eff. July 10, 1984.

[Section 121(b) of Pub.L. 98–353 purported to amend section 404 of Pub.L. 95–598 by substituting "the day before the date of enactment of the Bankruptcy Amendments and Federal Judgeship Act of 1984 [i.e. July 9, 1984]" for "June 27, 1984" each place it appeared. This amendment was not executed as the probable intent of Congress in view of the repeal of section 404 of Pub.L. 95–598 by section 114 of Pub.L. 98–353.]

Extension and Termination of Term of Office of Bankruptcy Judge Serving on June 27, 1984

Section 121(e) of Pub.L. 98–353 provided that: "The term of office of any bankruptcy judge who was serving on June 27, 1984, is extended to and shall expire at the end of the day of enactment of this Act [July 10, 1984]."

[Section 121(e) of Pub.L. 98–353 effective June 27, 1984, see section 122(c) of Pub.L. 98–353, set out as an Effective and Applicability Provisions note under section 151 of this title.]

For prior extensions of the term of office of bankruptcy judges see:

Pub.L. 98–325, § 2, June 20, 1984, 98 Stat. 268.

Pub.L. 98–299, § 2, May 25, 1984, 98 Stat. 214.

Pub.L. 98–271, § 2, Apr. 30, 1984, 98 Stat. 163.

Pub.L. 98–249, § 2, Mar. 31, 1984, 98 Stat. 116.

Judicial Administration During Transition

Pub.L. 95–598, Title IV, § 407, Nov. 6, 1978, 92 Stat. 2686, which provided that the Director of the Administrative Office of the United States Courts appoint a committee of not fewer than seven United States bankruptcy judges to advise the Director with respect to matters arising during the transition period, or that are relevant to the purposes of the transition period, and directed that during the transition period, the chief judge of each circuit summon at least one bankruptcy judge from each judicial district within the circuit to the judicial conference of such circuit called and held under section 332 of this title, was repealed by Pub.L. 98–353, Title I, §§ 114, 122(a), July 10, 1984, 98 Stat. 343, 346, eff. July 10, 1984.

Transition Study

Pub.L. 95–598, Title IV, § 406, Nov. 6, 1978, 92 Stat. 2686, as amended by Pub.L. 98–249, § 1(c), Mar. 31, 1984, 98 Stat. 116; Pub.L. 98–271, § 1(c), Apr. 30, 1984, 98 Stat. 163; Pub.L. 98–299, § 1(c), May 25, 1984, 98 Stat. 214; Pub.L. 98–325, § 1(c), June 20, 1984, 98 Stat. 268; Pub.L. 98–353, Title I, § 121(c), July 10, 1984, 98 Stat. 346, which provided that during the transition period, Oct. 1, 1979 to June 27, 1984, the Director of the Administrative Office of the United States Courts make continuing studies and surveys in the judicial districts to determine the number of bankruptcy judges needed after June 27, 1984, to provide for the expeditious and effective administration of justice, their regular places of offices, and the places where the court will be held, and that the Director report to the judicial councils of the circuits and the Judicial Conference of the United States his recommendations, the judicial councils advise the Conference stating their recommendations, and the Conference advise the Congress and the President, before Jan. 3, 1983, the number of bankruptcy judges needed after June 27, 1984, and the locations at which they were to serve, was repealed by Pub.L. 98–353, Title I, §§ 114, 122(a), July 10, 1984, 98 Stat. 343, 346 eff. July 10, 1984.

[Section 121(c) of Pub.L. 98–353 purported to amend section 406 of Pub.L. 95–598 by substituting "the day before the date of enactment of the Bankruptcy Amendments and Federal Judgeship Act of 1984 [i.e. July 9, 1984]" for "June 27, 1984" each place it appeared. This amendment was not executed as the probable intent of Congress in view of the repeal of section 406 of Pub.L. 95–598 by section 114 of Pub.L. 98–353.]

§ 151. Designation of bankruptcy courts

In each judicial district, the bankruptcy judges in regular active service shall constitute a unit of the district court to be known as the bankruptcy court for that district. Each bankruptcy judge, as a judicial officer of the district court, may exercise the authority conferred under this chapter with respect to any action, suit, or proceeding and may preside alone and hold a regular or special session of the court, except

as otherwise provided by law or by rule or order of the district court.

(Added Pub.L. 98–353, Title I, § 104(a), July 10, 1984, 98 Stat. 336.)

HISTORICAL AND STATUTORY NOTES

Codifications

This section as added by Pub.L. 95–598, Title II, § 201(a), Nov. 6, 1978, 92 Stat. 2657, effective June 28, 1984, pursuant to Pub.L. 95–598, Title IV, § 402(b), Nov. 6, 1978, 92 Stat. 2682, as amended by Pub.L. 98–249, § 1(a), Mar. 31, 1984, 98 Stat. 116; Pub.L. 98–271, § 1(a), Apr. 30, 1984, 98 Stat. 163; Pub.L. 98–299, § 1(a), May 25, 1984, 98 Stat. 214; Pub.L. 98–325, § 1(a), June 20, 1984, 98 Stat. 268, set out as a note preceding section 101 of Title 11, Bankruptcy, read as follows:

§ 151. Creation and composition of bankruptcy courts

(a) There shall be in each judicial district, as an adjunct to the district court for such district, a bankruptcy court which shall be a court of record known as the United States Bankruptcy Court for the district.

(b) Each bankruptcy court shall consist of the bankruptcy judge or judges for the district in regular active service. Justices or judges designated and assigned shall be competent to sit as judges of the bankruptcy court.

(c) Except as otherwise provided by law, or rule or order of court, the judicial power of a bankruptcy court with respect to any action, suit or proceeding may be exercised by a single bankruptcy judge, who may preside alone and hold a regular or special session of court at the same time other sessions are held by other bankruptcy judges.

Section 402(b) of Pub.L. 95–598 was amended by section 113 of Pub.L. 98–353 by substituting "shall not be effective" for "shall take effect on June 28, 1984", thereby eliminating the addition of section 151 by section 201(a) of Pub.L. 95–598, effective June 27, 1984, pursuant to section 122(c) of Pub.L. 98–353, set out as an Effective and Applicability Provisions note under this section.

Section 121(a) of Pub.L. 98–353 directed that section 402(b) of Pub.L. 95–598 be amended by substituting "the date of enactment of the Bankruptcy Amendments and Federal Judgeship Act of 1984 [i.e. July 10, 1984]" for "June 28, 1984". This amendment was not executed in view of the prior amendment to section 402(b) of Pub.L. 95–598 by section 113 of Pub.L. 98–353.

Effective and Applicability Provisions

1984 Acts

Section 122 of Title I of Pub.L. 98–353 provided that:

"(a) Except as otherwise provided in this section, this title and the amendments made by this title [Title I of Pub.L. 98–353, enacting this chapter, and sections 1408 to 1412 and 1452 of this title, amending sections 372, 634, 957, 1334, 1360, and 1930 of this title, sections 8331, 8334, 8336, 8339, 8341, and 8344 of Title 5, Government Organization and Employees, and section 105 of Title 11, Bankruptcy, enacting provisions set out as notes preceding section 151 of this title and under sections 151, 152, 153, 634, and 1334 of this title and section 8331 of Title 5, amending provisions set out as notes preceding sections 151 and 1471 of this title and section 101 of Title 11, and repealing provisions set out as notes preced-

ing this section and section 1471 of this title] shall take effect on the date of the enactment of this Act [July 10, 1984].

"(b) Section 1334(c)(2) of title 28, United States Code [section 1334(c)(2) of this title], and section 1411(a) of title 28, United States Code, as added by this Act [section 1411(a) of this title], shall not apply with respect to cases under title 11 of the United States Code [Title 11] that are pending on the date of enactment of this Act [July 10, 1984], or to proceedings arising in or related to such cases.

"(c) Sections 108(b) [enacting provisions set out as a note under section 634 of this title], 113 [amending section 402(b) of Pub.L. 95–598, set out as a note preceding section 101 of Title 11], and 121(e) [enacting provisions set out as a note preceding section 151 of this title] shall take effect on June 27, 1984."

Separability of Provisions

Section 119 of Pub.L. 98–353 provided that: "If any provision of this Act [see Short Title of 1984 Amendments note set out under this section] or the application thereof to any person or circumstance is held invalid, the remainder of this Act, or the application of that provision to persons or circumstances other than those as to which it is held invalid, is not affected thereby."

Short Title

1984 Amendments

Section 1 of Pub.L. 98–353 provided: That this Act [enacting this chapter and sections 1408 to 1412 and 1452 of this title and sections 557, 558, 559, and 1113 of Title 11, Bankruptcy, amending sections 44, 98, 131, 133, 371, 372, 634, 957, 1334, 1360, and 1930 of this title, sections 8331, 8334, 8336, 8339, 8341, 8344, 8701, 8706, 8714a, and 8714b of Title 5, Government Organization and Employees, and sections 101, 102, 103, 105, 108, 109, 303, 321, 322, 326, 327, 328, 329, 330, 342, 343, 345, 346, 349, 350, 361, 362, 363, 365, 366, 501, 502, 503, 505, 506, 507, 509, 510, 521, 522, 523, 524, 525, 541, 542, 543, 544, 545, 546, 547, 548, 549, 550, 552, 553, 554, 555, 702, 703, 704, 707, 723, 724, 725, 726, 727, 728, 741, 745, 752, 761, 763, 764, 765, 766, 901, 902, 903, 921, 922, 927, 943, 945, 1102, 1103, 1105, 1106, 1107, 1108, 1112, 1121, 1123, 1124, 1125, 1126, 1127, 1129, 1141, 1142, 1144, 1145, 1146, 1166, 1168, 1169, 1170, 1171, 1173, 1301, 1302, 1304, 1307, 1322, 1324, 1325, 1326, 1328, 1329, 15103, and 151302 of Title 11, Bankruptcy Rules 2002 and 3001, Title 11, and Bankruptcy Form No. 1, Title 11, enacting provisions set out as notes preceding section 151 of this title and under sections 44, 133, 151, 152, 153, 371, 634, 1334, and 2075 of this title, sections 8331 and 8706 of Title 5, and preceding section 101 and sections 101, 365, and 1113 of Title 11, amending provisions set out as notes preceding sections 151, 581 and 1471 of this title and section 101 of Title 11, and repealing provisions set out as notes preceding this section and section 1471 of this title] may be cited as the 'Bankruptcy Amendments and Federal Judgeship Act of 1984'."

§ 152. Appointment of bankruptcy judges

(a)(1) Each bankruptcy judge to be appointed for a judicial district, as provided in paragraph (2), shall be appointed by the court of appeals of the United States for the circuit in which such district is located. Such appointments shall be made after considering the recommendations of the Judicial Conference submit-

ted pursuant to subsection (b). Each bankruptcy judge shall be appointed for a term of fourteen years, subject to the provisions of subsection (e). However, upon the expiration of the term, a bankruptcy judge may, with the approval of the judicial council of the circuit, continue to perform the duties of the office until the earlier of the date which is 180 days after the expiration of the term or the date of the appointment of a successor. Bankruptcy judges shall serve as judicial officers of the United States district court established under Article III of the Constitution.

(2) The bankruptcy judges appointed pursuant to this section shall be appointed for the several judicial districts as follows:

Districts	Judges
Alabama:	
Northern	5
Middle	2
Southern	2
Alaska	2
Arizona	7
Arkansas:	
Eastern and Western	3
California:	
Northern	9
Eastern	6
Central	21
Southern	4
Colorado	5
Connecticut	3
Delaware	1
District of Columbia	1
Florida:	
Northern	1
Middle	8
Southern	5
Georgia:	
Northern	8
Middle	3
Southern	2
Hawaii	1
Idaho	2
Illinois:	
Northern	10
Central	3
Southern	1
Indiana:	
Northern	3
Southern	4
Iowa:	
Northern	2
Southern	2
Kansas	4
Kentucky:	
Eastern	2
Western	3

Districts	Judges
Louisiana:	
Eastern	2
Middle	1
Western	3
Maine	2
Maryland	4
Massachusetts	5
Michigan:	
Eastern	4
Western	3
Minnesota	4
Mississippi:	
Northern	1
Southern	2
Missouri:	
Eastern	3
Western	3
Montana	1
Nebraska	2
Nevada	3
New Hampshire	1
New Jersey	8
New Mexico	2
New York:	
Northern	2
Southern	9
Eastern	6
Western	3
North Carolina:	
Eastern	2
Middle	2
Western	2
North Dakota	1
Ohio:	
Northern	8
Southern	7
Oklahoma:	
Northern	2
Eastern	1
Western	3
Oregon	5
Pennsylvania:	
Eastern	5
Middle	2
Western	4
Puerto Rico	2
Rhode Island	1
South Carolina	2
South Dakota	2
Tennessee:	
Eastern	3
Middle	3
Western	4
Texas:	
Northern	6
Eastern	2
Southern	6
Western	4

Districts	Judges
Utah	3
Vermont	1
Virginia:	
Eastern	5
Western	3
Washington:	
Eastern	2
Western	5
West Virginia:	
Northern	1
Southern	1
Wisconsin:	
Eastern	4
Western	2
Wyoming	1

(3) Whenever a majority of the judges of any court of appeals cannot agree upon the appointment of a bankruptcy judge, the chief judge of such court shall make such appointment.

(4) The judges of the district courts for the territories shall serve as the bankruptcy judges for such courts. The United States court of appeals for the circuit within which such a territorial district court is located may appoint bankruptcy judges under this chapter for such district if authorized to do so by the Congress of the United States under this section.

(b)(1) The Judicial Conference of the United States shall, from time to time, and after considering the recommendations submitted by the Director of the Administrative Office of the United States Courts after such Director has consulted with the judicial council of the circuit involved, determine the official duty stations of bankruptcy judges and places of holding court.

(2) The Judicial Conference shall, from time to time, submit recommendations to the Congress regarding the number of bankruptcy judges needed and the districts in which such judges are needed.

(3) Not later than December 31, 1994, and not later than the end of each 2–year period thereafter, the Judicial Conference of the United States shall conduct a comprehensive review of all judicial districts to assess the continuing need for the bankruptcy judges authorized by this section, and shall report to the Congress its findings and any recommendations for the elimination of any authorized position which can be eliminated when a vacancy exists by reason of resignation, retirement, removal, or death.

(c)(1) Each bankruptcy judge may hold court at such places within the judicial district, in addition to the official duty station of such judge, as the business of the court may require.

(2)(A) Bankruptcy judges may hold court at such places within the United States outside the judicial district as the nature of the business of the court may require, and upon such notice as the court orders, upon a finding by either the chief judge of the bankruptcy court (or, if the chief judge is unavailable, the most senior available bankruptcy judge) or by the judicial council of the circuit that, because of emergency conditions, no location within the district is reasonably available where the bankruptcy judges could hold court.

(B) Bankruptcy judges may transact any business at special sessions of court held outside the district pursuant to this paragraph that might be transacted at a regular session.

(C) If a bankruptcy court issues an order exercising its authority under subparagraph (A), the court—

(i) through the Administrative Office of the United States Courts, shall—

(I) send notice of such order, including the reasons for the issuance of such order, to the Committee on the Judiciary of the Senate and the Committee on the Judiciary of the House of Representatives; and

(II) not later than 180 days after the expiration of such court order submit a brief report to the Committee on the Judiciary of the Senate and the Committee on the Judiciary of the House of Representatives describing the impact of such order, including—

(aa) the reasons for the issuance of such order;

(bb) the duration of such order;

(cc) the impact of such order on litigants; and

(dd) the costs to the judiciary resulting from such order; and

(ii) shall provide reasonable notice to the United States Marshals Service before the commencement of any special session held pursuant to such order.

(d) With the approval of the Judicial Conference and of each of the judicial councils involved, a bankruptcy judge may be designated to serve in any district adjacent to or near the district for which such bankruptcy judge was appointed.

(e) A bankruptcy judge may be removed during the term for which such bankruptcy judge is appointed, only for incompetence, misconduct, neglect of duty, or physical or mental disability and only by the judicial council of the circuit in which the judge's official duty station is located. Removal may not occur unless a majority of all of the judges of such council concur in the order of removal. Before any order of removal may be entered, a full specification of charges shall be furnished to such bankruptcy judge who shall be accorded an opportunity to be heard on such charges.
(Added Pub.L. 98–353, Title I, § 104(a), July 10, 1984, 98 Stat. 336, and amended Pub.L. 99–554, Title I, § 101, Oct. 27,

1986, 100 Stat. 3088; Pub.L. 100–587, Nov. 3, 1988, 102 Stat. 2982; Pub.L. 101–650, Title III, § 304, Dec. 1, 1990, 104 Stat. 5105; Pub.L. 102–361, §§ 2, 4, Aug. 26, 1992, 106 Stat. 965, 966; Pub.L. 109–8, Title XII, § 1223(d), Apr. 20, 2005, 119 Stat. 198; Pub.L. 109–63, § 2(c), Sept. 9, 2005, 119 Stat. 1994.)

HISTORICAL AND STATUTORY NOTES

Codifications

This section as added by Pub.L. 95–598, Title II, § 201(a), Nov. 6, 1978, 92 Stat. 2657, effective June 28, 1984, pursuant to Pub.L. 95–598, Title IV, § 402(b), Nov. 6, 1978, 92 Stat. 2682, as amended by Pub.L. 98–249, § 1(a), Mar. 31, 1984, 98 Stat. 116; Pub.L. 98–271, § 1(a), Apr. 30, 1984, 98 Stat. 163; Pub.L. 98–299, § 1(a), May 25, 1984, 98 Stat. 214; Pub.L. 98–325, § 1(a), June 20, 1984, 98 Stat. 268, set out as a note preceding section 101 of Title 11, Bankruptcy, read as follows:

"§ 152. Appointment of bankruptcy judges

"The President shall appoint, by and with the advice and consent of the Senate, bankruptcy judges for the several judicial districts. In each instance, the President shall give due consideration to the recommended nominee or nominees of the Judicial Council of the Circuit within which an appointment is to be made."

Section 402(b) of Pub.L. 95–598 was amended by section 113 of Pub.L. 98–353 by substituting "shall not be effective" for "shall take effect on June 28, 1984", thereby eliminating the addition of section 152 by section 201(a) of Pub.L. 95–598, effective June 27, 1984, pursuant to section 122(c) of Pub.L. 98–353, set out as an Effective and Applicability Provisions note under 28 U.S.C.A. § 151.

Section 121(a) of Pub.L. 98–353 directed that section 402(b) of Pub.L. 95–598 be amended by substituting "the date of enactment of the Bankruptcy Amendments and Federal Judgeship Act of 1984 [i.e. July 10, 1984]" for "June 28, 1984". This amendment was not executed in view of the prior amendment to section 402(b) of Pub.L. 95–598 by section 113 of Pub.L. 98–353.

Effective and Applicability Provisions

2005 Acts

Pub.L. 109–8, Title XII, § 1223(e), Apr. 20, 2005, 119 Stat. 198, provided that: "The amendments made by this section [amending this section and enacting provisions set out as notes under this section and 28 U.S.C.A. § 1] shall take effect on the date of the enactment of this Act [Apr. 20, 2005]."

Except as otherwise provided, amendments by Pub.L. 109–8 effective 180 days after April 20, 2005, and inapplicable with respect to cases commenced under Title 11 before the effective date, see Pub.L. 109–8, § 1501, set out as a note under 11 U.S.C.A. § 101.

1986 Acts

Amendment by Pub.L. 99–554 effective on Oct. 27, 1986, see section 302(b) of Pub.L. 99–554, set out as a note under section 581 of this title.

1984 Acts

Section effective July 10, 1984, see section 122(a) of Pub.L. 98–353, set out as a note under section 151 of this title.

Termination of Reporting Requirements

For termination of reporting provisions of subsec. (b)(2) of this section, effective May 15, 2000, see Pub.L. 104–66, § 3003, as amended, set out as a note under 31 U.S.C.A. § 1113, and the 16th item on page 12 of House Document No. 103–7.

Temporary Judgeships: Appointments, Vacancies, and Extensions

Pub.L. 109–8, Title XII, § 1223(b), (c), Apr. 20, 2005, 119 Stat. 196, 198, provided that:

"(1) **Appointments.**—The following bankruptcy judges shall be appointed in the manner prescribed in section 152(a)(1) of title 28, United States Code, for the appointment of bankruptcy judges provided for in section 152(a)(2) of such title:

"**(A)** One additional bankruptcy judge for the eastern district of California.

"**(B)** Three additional bankruptcy judges for the central district of California.

"**(C)** Four additional bankruptcy judges for the district of Delaware.

"**(D)** Two additional bankruptcy judges for the southern district of Florida.

"**(E)** One additional bankruptcy judge for the southern district of Georgia.

"**(F)** Three additional bankruptcy judges for the district of Maryland.

"**(G)** One additional bankruptcy judge for the eastern district of Michigan.

"**(H)** One additional bankruptcy judge for the southern district of Mississippi.

"**(I)** One additional bankruptcy judge for the district of New Jersey.

"**(J)** One additional bankruptcy judge for the eastern district of New York.

"**(K)** One additional bankruptcy judge for the northern district of New York.

"**(L)** One additional bankruptcy judge for the southern district of New York.

"**(M)** One additional bankruptcy judge for the eastern district of North Carolina.

"**(N)** One additional bankruptcy judge for the eastern district of Pennsylvania.

"**(O)** One additional bankruptcy judge for the middle district of Pennsylvania.

"**(P)** One additional bankruptcy judge for the district of Puerto Rico.

"**(Q)** One additional bankruptcy judge for the western district of Tennessee.

"**(R)** One additional bankruptcy judge for the eastern district of Virginia.

"**(S)** One additional bankruptcy judge for the district of South Carolina.

"**(T)** One additional bankruptcy judge for the district of Nevada.

"(2) **Vacancies.**—

"**(A) Districts with single appointments.**—Except as provided in subparagraphs (B), (C), (D), and (E), the first vacancy occurring in the office of bankruptcy judge in each of the judicial districts set forth in paragraph (1)—

"(i) occurring 5 years or more after the appointment date of the bankruptcy judge appointed under paragraph (1) to such office; and

"(ii) resulting from the death, retirement, resignation, or removal of a bankruptcy judge;

shall not be filled.

"(B) **Central district of California.**—The 1st, 2d, and 3d vacancies in the office of bankruptcy judge in the central district of California—

"(i) occurring 5 years or more after the respective 1st, 2d, and 3d appointment dates of the bankruptcy judges appointed under paragraph (1)(B); and

"(ii) resulting from the death, retirement, resignation, or removal of a bankruptcy judge;

shall not be filled.

"(C) **District of Delaware.**—The 1st, 2d, 3d, and 4th vacancies in the office of bankruptcy judge in the district of Delaware—

"(i) occurring 5 years or more after the respective 1st, 2d, 3d, and 4th appointment dates of the bankruptcy judges appointed under paragraph (1)(F); and

"(ii) resulting from the death, retirement, resignation, or removal of a bankruptcy judge;

shall not be filled.

"(D) **Southern district of Florida.**—The 1st and 2d vacancies in the office of bankruptcy judge in the southern district of Florida—

"(i) occurring 5 years or more after the respective 1st and 2d appointment dates of the bankruptcy judges appointed under paragraph (1)(D); and

"(ii) resulting from the death, retirement, resignation, or removal of a bankruptcy judge;

shall not be filled.

"(E) **District of Maryland.**—The 1st, 2d, and 3d vacancies in the office of bankruptcy judge in the district of Maryland—

"(i) occurring 5 years or more after the respective 1st, 2d, and 3d appointment dates of the bankruptcy judges appointed under paragraph (1)(F); and

"(ii) resulting from the death, retirement, resignation, or removal of a bankruptcy judge;

shall not be filled.

"(c) **Extensions.**—

"(1) **In general.**—The temporary office of bankruptcy judges authorized for the northern district of Alabama, the district of Delaware, the district of Puerto Rico, and the eastern district of Tennessee under paragraphs (1), (3), (7), and (9) of section 3(a) of the Bankruptcy Judgeship Act of 1992 (28 U.S.C. 152 note) are extended until the first vacancy occurring in the office of a bankruptcy judge in the applicable district resulting from the death, retirement, resignation, or removal of a bankruptcy judge and occurring 5 years after the date of the enactment of this Act [April 20, 2005].

"(2) **Applicability of other provisions.**—All other provisions of section 3 of the Bankruptcy Judgeship Act of 1992 (28 U.S.C. 152 note) remain applicable to the temporary office of bankruptcy judges referred to in this subsection."

[Amendments by Pub.L. 109–8, § 1223, effective Apr. 20, 2005, see Pub.L. 109–8, § 1223(e), set out as a note under this section.]

Temporary Appointment of Additional Judges

Section 3 of Pub.L. 102–361, as amended Pub.L. 104–317, Title III, § 307, Oct. 19, 1996, 110 Stat. 3852, provided that:

"(a) **Appointments.**—The following bankruptcy judges shall be appointed in the manner prescribed in section 152(a)(1) of title 28, United States Code [subsec. (a)(1) of this section]:

"(1) 1 additional bankruptcy judge for the northern district of Alabama.

"(2) 1 additional bankruptcy judge for the district of Colorado.

"(3) 1 additional bankruptcy judge for the district of Delaware.

"(4) 1 additional bankruptcy judge for the southern district of Illinois.

"(5) 1 additional bankruptcy judge for the district of New Hampshire.

"(6) 1 additional bankruptcy judge for the middle district of North Carolina.

"(7) 1 additional bankruptcy judge for the district of Puerto Rico.

"(8) 1 additional bankruptcy judge for the district of South Carolina.

"(9) 1 additional bankruptcy judge for the eastern district of Tennessee.

"(10) 1 additional bankruptcy judge for the western district of Texas.

"(b) **Vacancies.**—The first vacancy in the office of bankruptcy judge in each of the judicial districts set forth in subsection (a), resulting from the death, retirement, resignation, or removal of a bankruptcy judge, and occurring 5 years or more after the appointment date of the judge named to fill the temporary judgeship position shall not be filled. In the case of a vacancy resulting from the expiration of the term of a bankruptcy judge not described in the preceding sentence, that judge shall be eligible for reappointment as a bankruptcy judge in that district."

Appointment to Fill Vacancies; Nominations; Qualifications

Section 120 of Pub.L. 98–353, as amended Pub.L. 99–554, Title I, § 102, Oct. 22, 1986, 100 Stat. 3089; Pub.L. 104–317, Title III, § 303, Oct. 19, 1996, 110 Stat. 3852, provided that:

"(a)(1) Whenever a court of appeals is authorized to fill a vacancy that occurs on a bankruptcy court of the United States, such court of appeals shall appoint to fill that vacancy a person whose character, experience, ability, and impartiality such person to serve in the Federal judiciary.

"(2) It is the sense of the Congress that the courts of appeals should consider for appointment under section 152 of title 28, United States Code [this section], to the first vacancy which arises after the date of the enactment of this Act [July 10, 1984] in the office of each bankruptcy judge, the bankruptcy judge who holds such office immediately before such vacancy arises, if such bankruptcy judge requests to be considered for such appointment.

"(3) When filling vacancies, the court of appeals may consider reappointing incumbent bankruptcy judges under

procedures prescribed by regulations issued by the Judicial Conference of the United States.

"(b) The judicial council of the circuit involved shall assist the court of appeals by evaluating potential nominees and by recommending to such court for consideration for appointment to each vacancy on the bankruptcy court persons who are qualified to be bankruptcy judges under regulations prescribed by the Judicial Conference of the United States. In the case of the first vacancy which arises after the date of the enactment of this Act [July 10, 1984] in the office of each bankruptcy judge, such potential nominees shall include the bankruptcy judge who holds such office immediately before such vacancy arises, if such bankruptcy judge requests to be considered for such appointment and the judicial council determines that such judge is qualified under subsection (c) of this section to continue to serve. Such potential nominees shall receive consideration equal to that given all other potential nominees for such position. All incumbent nominees seeking reappointment thereafter may be considered for such reappointment, pursuant to a majority vote of the judges of the appointing court of appeals, under procedures authorized under subsection (a)(3).

"(c) Before transmitting to the court of appeals the names of the persons the judicial council for the circuit deems best qualified to fill any existing vacancy, the judicial council shall have determined that—

"(1) public notice of such vacancy has been given and an effort has been made, in the case of each such vacancy, to identify qualified candidates, without regard to race, color, sex, religion, or national origin,

"(2) such persons are members in good standing of at least one State bar, the District of Columbia bar, or the bar of the Commonwealth of Puerto Rico, and members in good standing of every other bar of which they are members,

"(3) such persons possess, and have a reputation for, integrity and good character,

"(4) such persons are of sound physical and mental health,

"(5) such persons possess and have demonstrated commitment to equal justice under law,

"(6) such persons possess and have demonstrated outstanding legal ability and competence, as evidenced by substantial legal experience, ability to deal with complex legal problems, aptitude for legal scholarship and writing, and familiarity with courts and court processes, and

"(7) such persons [sic] demeanor, character, and personality indicate that they would exhibit judicial temperament if appointed to the position of United States bankruptcy judge."

Extension and Termination of Term of Office of Bankruptcy Judge and Part-Time Bankruptcy Judge Serving on July 10, 1984; Practice of Law by Part-Time Bankruptcy Judge

Section 106 of Pub.L. 98–353 provided that:

"(a) Notwithstanding section 152 of title 28, United States Code, as added by this Act [this section], the term of office of a bankruptcy judge who is serving on the date of enactment of this Act [July 10, 1984] is extended to and expires four years after the date such bankruptcy judge was last appointed to such office or on October 1, 1986, whichever is later.

"(b)(1) Notwithstanding section 153(a) of title 28, United States Code, as added by this Act [section 153(a) of this title], and notwithstanding subsection (a) of this section, a bankruptcy judge serving on a part-time basis on the date of enactment of this Act [July 10, 1984] may continue to serve on such basis for a period not to exceed two years from the date of enactment of this Act [July 10, 1984].

"(2) Notwithstanding the provisions of section 153(b) of title 28, United States Code [section 153(b) of this title], a bankruptcy judge serving on a part-time basis may engage in the practice of law but may not engage in any other practice, business, occupation, or employment inconsistent with the expeditious, proper, and impartial performance of such bankruptcy judge's duties as a judicial officer. The Judicial Conference of the United States may promulgate appropriate rules and regulations to implement this paragraph."

Extension and Termination of Term of Office of Part-Time Bankruptcy Judge Serving on July 2, 1986, In District of Oregon, Western District of Michigan, and Eastern District of Oklahoma

Pub.L. 99–349, Title I, July 2, 1986, 100 Stat. 718, provided that: "Notwithstanding the provisions of section 106(b)(1) of the Bankruptcy Amendments and Federal Judgeship Act of 1984 [section 106(b)(1) of Pub.L. 98–353, set out as a note under this section], a bankruptcy judge serving on a part-time basis on the date of enactment of this Act [July 2, 1986] may continue to serve as a part-time judge for such district until December 31, 1986, or until such time as a full-time bankruptcy judge for such district is appointed, whichever is earlier: *Provided,* That these provisions shall apply only to part-time bankruptcy judges serving in the district of Oregon, the western district of Michigan, and the eastern district of Oklahoma."

§ 153. Salaries; character of service

(a) Each bankruptcy judge shall serve on a full-time basis and shall receive as full compensation for his services, a salary at an annual rate that is equal to 92 percent of the salary of a judge of the district court of the United States as determined pursuant to section 135, to be paid at such times as the Judicial Conference of the United States determines.

(b) A bankruptcy judge may not engage in the practice of law and may not engage in any other practice, business, occupation, or employment inconsistent with the expeditious, proper, and impartial performance of such bankruptcy judge's duties as a judicial officer. The Conference may promulgate appropriate rules and regulations to implement this subsection.

(c) Each individual appointed under this chapter shall take the oath or affirmation prescribed by section 453 of this title before performing the duties of the office of bankruptcy judge.

(d) A bankruptcy judge appointed under this chapter shall be exempt from the provisions of subchapter I of chapter 63 of title 5.

(Added Pub.L. 98–353, Title I, § 104(a), July 10, 1984, 98 Stat. 338, and amended Pub.L. 100–202, § 101(a) [Title IV,

§ 408(a)], Dec. 22, 1987, 101 Stat. 1329–26; Pub.L. 100–702, Title X, § 1003(a)(1), Nov. 19, 1988, 102 Stat. 4665.)

HISTORICAL AND STATUTORY NOTES

Codifications

This section as added by Pub.L. 95–598, Title II, § 201(a), Nov. 6, 1978, 92 Stat. 2657, effective June 28, 1984, pursuant to Pub.L. 95–598, Title IV, § 402(b), Nov. 6, 1978, 92 Stat. 2682, as amended by Pub.L. 98–249, § 1(a), Mar. 31, 1984, 98 Stat. 116; Pub.L. 98–271, § 1(a), Apr. 30, 1984, 98 Stat. 163; Pub.L. 98–299, § 1(a), May 25, 1984, 98 Stat. 214; Pub.L. 98–325, § 1(a), June 20, 1984, 98 Stat. 268, set out as a note preceding section 101 of Title 11, Bankruptcy, read as follows:

§ 153. Tenure and residence of bankruptcy judges

(a) Each bankruptcy judge shall hold office for a term of 14 years, but may continue to perform the duties of his office until his successor takes office, unless such office has been eliminated.

(b) Removal of a bankruptcy judge during the term for which he is appointed shall be only for incompetency, misconduct, neglect of duty, or physical or mental disability. Removal shall be by the judicial council of the circuit or circuits in which the bankruptcy judge serves, but removal may not occur unless a majority of all the judges of such circuit council or councils concur in the order of removal. Before any order of removal may be entered, a full specification of the charges shall be furnished to the bankruptcy judge, and he shall be accorded an opportunity to be heard on the charges. Any cause for removal of any bankruptcy judge coming to the knowledge of the Director of the Administrative Office of the United States Courts shall be reported by him to the chief judge of the circuit or circuits in which he serves, and a copy of the report shall at the same time be transmitted to the circuit council or councils and to the bankruptcy judge.

(c) Each bankruptcy judge shall reside in the district or one of the districts for which he is appointed, or within 20 miles of his official station.

(d) If the public interest and the nature of the business of a bankruptcy court require that a bankruptcy judge should maintain his abode at or near a particular part of the district the judicial council of the circuit may so declare and may make an appropriate order. If the bankruptcy judges of such a district are unable to agree as to which of them shall maintain his abode at or near the place or within the area specified in such an order the judicial council of the circuit may decide which of them shall do so.

Section 402(b) of Pub.L. 95–598 was amended by section 113 of Pub.L. 98–353 by substituting "shall not be effective" for "shall take effect on June 28, 1984", thereby eliminating the addition of section 153 by section 201(a) of Pub.L. 95–598, effective June 27, 1984, pursuant to section 122(c) of Pub.L. 98–353, set out as an Effective Date note under section 151 of this title.

Section 121(a) of Pub.L. 98–353 directed that section 402(b) of Pub.L. 95–598 be amended by substituting "the date of enactment of the Bankruptcy Amendments and Federal Judgeship Act of 1984 [i.e. July 10, 1984]" for "June 28, 1984". This amendment was not executed in view of the prior amendment to section 402(b) of Pub.L. 95–598 by section 113 of Pub.L. 98–353.

Effective and Applicability Provisions

1987 Acts

Section 101(a) [Title IV, § 408(d)] of Pub.L. 100–202 provided that: "This section [amending this section, section 634 of this title, and section 356 of Title 2, The Congress] shall become effective October 1, 1988, and any salary affected by the provisions of this section shall be adjusted at the beginning of the first applicable pay period commencing on or after such date of enactment [probably should read "such date", meaning Oct. 1, 1988]."

1984 Acts

Section effective July 10, 1984, see section 122(a) of Pub.L. 98–353, set out as a note under section 151 of this title.

Continuation of Salaries of Bankruptcy Judges in Effect on June 27, 1984

Section 105(a) of Pub.L. 98–353 provided that: "The salary of a bankruptcy judge in effect on June 27, 1984, shall remain in effect until changed as a result of a determination or adjustment made pursuant to section 153(a) of title 28, United States Code, as added by this Act [subsec. (a) of this section]."

Increase in Salaries

1988—Salaries of bankruptcy judges continued at $72,500 per annum by Ex. Ord. No. 12622, Dec. 31, 1987, 53 F.R. 222, formerly set out as a note under section 5332 of Title 5, Government Organization and Employees.

1987—Salaries of bankruptcy judges increased to $72,500 per annum, on recommendation of the President of the United States, see note set out under section 358 of Title 2, The Congress.

Salaries of bankruptcy judges increased to $70,500 effective on the first day of the first pay period beginning on or after January 1, 1987, by Ex. Ord. No. 12578, Dec. 31, 1986, 52 F.R. 505, formerly set out as a note under section 5332 of Title 5.

1985—Salaries of bankruptcy judges increased to $68,400 effective on the first day of the first pay period beginning on or after Jan. 1, 1985, by Ex. Ord. No. 12496, Dec. 28, 1984, 50 F.R. 211, as amended by Ex. Ord. No. 12540, Dec. 30, 1985, 51 F.R. 577, formerly set out as a note under section 5332 of Title 5.

1984—Salaries of bankruptcy judges (full-time) and bankruptcy judges (part-time) (maximum rate) increased to $66,100 and $33,100, respectively, effective on the first day of the first pay period beginning on or after Jan. 1, 1984, by Ex. Ord. No. 12456, Dec. 30, 1983, 49 F.R. 347, as amended Ex. Ord. No. 12477, May 23, 1984, 49 F.R. 22041; Ex. Ord. No. 12487, Sept. 14, 1984, 49 F.R. 36493, formerly set out as a note under section 5332 of Title 5.

1982—Salaries of bankruptcy judges and referees in bankruptcy (full-time), or referees in bankruptcy (part-time) (maximum rate) increased to $63,600 and $31,800, respectively, effective on the first day of the first pay period beginning on or after Oct. 1, 1982, by Ex. Ord. No. 12387, Oct. 8, 1982, 47 F.R. 44981, formerly set out as a note under section 5332 of Title 5, Government Organization and Employees. Ex. Ord. No. 12387 further provided that pursuant to section 101(e) of Pub.L. 97–276 funds are not available to pay a salary at a rate which exceeds the rate in effect on Sept. 30,

1982, which was $58,500 for bankruptcy judges and referees in bankruptcy (full-time), and $30,600 for referees in bankruptcy (part-time) (maximum rate).

Maximum rate payable to bankruptcy judges after Dec. 17, 1982, increased from $58,500 to $63,600, see Pub.L. 97–377, Title I, § 129(b)–(d), Dec. 21, 1982, 96 Stat. 1914, set out as a note under section 5318 of Title 5.

1981—Salaries of bankruptcy judges and referees in bankruptcy (full-time), or referees in bankruptcy (part-time) (maximum rate) increased to $61,200 and $30,600, respectively, effective on the first day of the first pay period beginning on or after Oct. 1, 1981, by Ex. Ord. No. 12330, Oct. 15, 1981, 46 F.R. 50921, formerly set out as a note under section 5332 of Title 5. Ex. Ord. No. 12330 further provided that pursuant to section 101(c) of Pub.L. 97–51 funds are not available to pay a salary at a rate which exceeds the rate in effect on Sept. 30, 1981, which was $51,167.50 for bankruptcy judges and referees in bankruptcy (full-time), and $25,583.75 for referees in bankruptcy (part-time) (maximum rate).

1980—Salaries of bankruptcy judges and referees in bankruptcy (full-time), or referees in bankruptcy (part-time) (maximum rate) increased to $58,400 and $29,200, respectively, effective on the first day of the first pay period beginning on or after Oct. 1, 1980, by Ex. Ord. No. 12248, Oct. 16, 1980, 45 F.R. 69199, formerly set out as a note under section 5332 of Title 5. Ex. Ord. No. 12248 further provided that pursuant to section 101(c) of Pub.L. 96–369 funds are not available to pay a salary which exceeds the rate in effect on Sept. 30, 1980, which was $51,167.50 for bankruptcy judges and referees in bankruptcy (full-time), and $25,583.75 for referees in bankruptcy (part-time) (maximum rate).

For limitations on use of funds for period Oct. 1, 1980 through June 5, 1981, appropriated by any Act to pay the salary or pay of any individual in legislative, executive, or judicial branch in position equal to or above level V of the Executive Schedule, see section 101(c) of Pub.L. 96–369 and section 101(c) of Pub.L. 96–536, set out as notes under section 5318 of Title 5.

1979—Salaries of bankruptcy judges increased to $53,500 effective on the first day of the first applicable pay period beginning on or after Oct. 1, 1979, by Ex. Ord. No. 12165, Oct. 9, 1979, 44 F.R. 58671, as amended by Ex. Ord. No. 12200, Mar. 12, 1980, 45 F.R. 16443, formerly set out as a note under section 5332 of Title 5. Ex. Ord. No. 12165 further provided that pursuant to Pub.L. 96–86 funds appropriated for fiscal year 1980 may not be used to pay a salary at a rate which exceeds an increase of 5.5 percent over the applicable rate payable for such position or office in effect on Sept. 30, 1978, which was $51,167.50 for bankruptcy judges.

Part–Time Bankruptcy Judges

For provision that notwithstanding subsecs. (a) and (b) of this section, a bankruptcy judge serving on a part-time basis on July 10, 1984, may continue to serve on such basis for two years from such date, and may engage in the practice of law, see section 106 of Pub.L. 98–353, set out as a note under section 152 of this title.

Transition Provisions

Section 1003(b) of Pub.L. 100–702 provided that:

"(1) If an individual who is exempted from the Leave Act by operation of amendments under this section [amending this section and sections 156, 631, 634, 712, 752, and 794 of this title] and who was previously subject to the provisions of subchapter I of chapter 63 of title 5, United States Code [section 6301 et seq. of Title 5, Government Organization and Employees], without a break in service, again becomes subject to this subchapter on completion of his service as an exempted officer, the unused annual leave and sick leave standing to his credit when he was exempted from this subchapter is deemed to have remained to his credit.

"(2) In computing an annuity under section 8339 of title 5, United States Code [section 8339 of Title 5], the total service of a person specified in paragraph (1) of this subsection who retired on an immediate annuity or dies leaving a survivor or survivors entitled to an annuity includes, without regard to the limitations imposed by subsection (f) of section 8339 of title 5, United States Code [section 8339(f) of Title 5], the days of unused sick leave standing to his credit when he was exempted from subchapter I of chapter 63 of title 5, United States Code [section 6301 et seq. of Title 5], except that these days will not be counted in determining average pay or annuity eligibility."

§ 154. Division of businesses; chief judge

(a) Each bankruptcy court for a district having more than one bankruptcy judge shall by majority vote promulgate rules for the division of business among the bankruptcy judges to the extent that the division of business is not otherwise provided for by the rules of the district court.

(b) In each district court having more than one bankruptcy judge the district court shall designate one judge to serve as chief judge of such bankruptcy court. Whenever a majority of the judges of such district court cannot agree upon the designation as chief judge, the chief judge of such district court shall make such designation. The chief judge of the bankruptcy court shall ensure that the rules of the bankruptcy court and of the district court are observed and that the business of the bankruptcy court is handled effectively and expeditiously.

(Added Pub.L. 98–353, Title I, § 104(a), July 10, 1984, 98 Stat. 339.)

HISTORICAL AND STATUTORY NOTES

Codifications

This section as added by Pub.L. 95–598, Title II, § 201(a), Nov. 6, 1978, 92 Stat. 2657, effective June 28, 1984, pursuant to Pub.L. 95–598, Title IV, § 402(b), Nov. 6, 1978, 92 Stat. 2682, as amended by Pub.L. 98–249, § 1(a), Mar. 31, 1984, 98 Stat. 116; Pub.L. 98–271, § 1(a), Apr. 30, 1984, 98 Stat. 163; Pub.L. 98–299, § 1(a), May 25, 1984, 98 Stat. 214; Pub.L. 98–325, § 1(a), June 20, 1984, 98 Stat. 268, set out as a note preceding section 101 of Title 11, Bankruptcy, read as follows:

§ 154. Salaries of bankruptcy judges

Each judge of a bankruptcy court shall receive a salary at an annual rate of $50,000, subject to adjustment under section 225 of the Federal Salary Act of 1967 (2 U.S.C. 351–361), and section 461 of this title.

Section 402(b) of Pub.L. 95–598 was amended by section 113 of Pub.L. 98–353 by substituting "shall not be effective" for "shall take effect on June 28, 1984", thereby eliminating the addition of section 154 by section 201(a) of Pub.L. 95–598, effective June 27, 1984, pursuant to section 122(c) of Pub.L. 98–353, set out as an Effective Date note under section 151 of this title.

Section 121(a) of Pub.L. 98–353 directed that section 402(b) of Pub.L. 95–598 be amended by substituting "the date of enactment of the Bankruptcy Amendments and Federal Judgeship Act of 1984 [i.e. July 10, 1984]" for "June 28, 1984". This amendment was not executed in view of the prior amendment to section 402(b) of Pub.L. 95–598 by section 113 of Pub.L. 98–353.

Effective and Applicability Provisions

1984 Acts

Section effective July 10, 1984, see section 122(a) of Pub.L. 98–353, set out as a note under section 151 of this title.

§ 155. Temporary transfer of bankruptcy judges

(a) A bankruptcy judge may be transferred to serve temporarily as a bankruptcy judge in any judicial district other than the judicial district for which such bankruptcy judge was appointed upon the approval of the judicial council of each of the circuits involved.

(b) A bankruptcy judge who has retired may, upon consent, be recalled to serve as a bankruptcy judge in any judicial district by the judicial council of the circuit within which such district is located. Upon recall, a bankruptcy judge may receive a salary for such service in accordance with regulations promulgated by the Judicial Conference of the United States, subject to the restrictions on the payment of an annuity in section 377 of this title or in subchapter III of chapter 83, and chapter 84, of title 5 which are applicable to such judge.

(Added Pub.L. 98–353, Title I, § 104(a), July 10, 1984, 98 Stat. 339, and amended Pub.L. 99–651, Title II, § 202(a), Nov. 14, 1986, 100 Stat. 3648; Pub.L. 100–659, § 4(a), Nov. 15, 1988, 102 Stat. 3918.)

HISTORICAL AND STATUTORY NOTES

Codifications

This section as added by Pub.L. 95–598, Title II, § 201(a), Nov. 6, 1978, 92 Stat. 2658, effective June 28, 1984, pursuant to Pub.L. 95–598, Title IV, § 402(b), Nov. 6, 1978, 92 Stat. 2682, as amended by Pub.L. 98–249, § 1(a), Mar. 31, 1984, 98 Stat. 116; Pub.L. 98–271, § 1(a), Apr. 30, 1984, 98 Stat. 163; Pub.L. 98–299, § 1(a), May 25, 1984, 98 Stat. 214; Pub.L. 98–325, § 1(a), June 20, 1984, 98 Stat. 268, set out as a note preceding section 101 of Title 11, Bankruptcy, read as follows:

§ 155. Chief judge; precedence of bankruptcy judges

(a) In each district having more than one judge the bankruptcy judge in regular active service who is senior in commission and under seventy years of age shall be the chief judge of the bankruptcy court. If all the bankruptcy judges

in regular active service are 70 years of age or older the youngest shall act as chief judge until a judge has been appointed and qualified who is under 70 years of age, but a judge may not act as chief judge until he has served as a bankruptcy judge for one year.

(b) The chief judge shall have precedence and preside at any session which he attends.

Other bankruptcy judges shall have precedence and preside according to the seniority of their commissions. Judges whose commissions bear the same date shall have precedence according to seniority in age.

(c) A judge whose commission extends over more than one district shall be junior to all bankruptcy judges except in the district in which he resided at the time he entered upon the duties of his office.

(d) If a chief judge desires to be relieved of his duties as chief judge while retaining his active status as a bankruptcy judge, he may so certify to the chief judge of the court of appeals for the circuit in which the bankruptcy judge serves, and thereafter the bankruptcy judge in active service next in precedence and willing to serve shall be designated by the chief judge of the court of appeals as the chief judge of the bankruptcy court.

(e) If a chief judge is temporarily unable to perform his duties as such, they shall be performed by the bankruptcy judge in active service, present in the district and able and qualified to act, who is next in precedence.

(f) Service as a referee in bankruptcy or as a bankruptcy judge under the Bankruptcy Act shall be taken into account in the determination of seniority of commission under this section.

Section 402(b) of Pub.L. 95–598 was amended by section 113 of Pub.L. 98–353 by substituting "shall not be effective" for "shall take effect on June 28, 1984", thereby eliminating the addition of section 155 by section 201(a) of Pub.L. 95–598, effective June 27, 1984, pursuant to section 122(c) of Pub.L. 98–353, set out as an Effective Date note under section 151 of this title.

Section 121(a) of Pub.L. 98–353 directed that section 402(b) of Pub.L. 95–598 be amended by substituting "the date of enactment of the Bankruptcy Amendments and Federal Judgeship Act of 1984 [i.e. July 10, 1984]" for "June 28, 1984". This amendment was not executed in view of the prior amendment to section 402(b) of Pub.L. 95–598 by section 113 of Pub.L. 98–353.

Effective and Applicability Provisions

1988 Acts

Amendment to this section by Pub.L. 100–659 to take effect on Nov. 15, 1988, and shall apply to bankruptcy judges and magistrates who retire on or after Nov. 15, 1988, with special election provisions for bankruptcy judges, etc., who left office on or after July 31, 1987, and before Nov. 15, 1988, see section 9 of Pub.L. 100–659, set out as a note under section 377 of this title.

1986 Acts

Section 203 of Title II of Pub.L. 99–651 provided that: "This title and the amendments made by this title [enacting section 375 of this title, and amending sections 155, 374, 631, 633, 636, and 797 of this title] take effect on January 1, 1987."

1984 Acts

Section effective July 10, 1984, see section 122(a) of Pub.L. 98–353, set out as a note under section 151 of this title.

§ 156. Staff; expenses

(a) Each bankruptcy judge may appoint a secretary, a law clerk, and such additional assistants as the Director of the Administrative Office of the United States Courts determines to be necessary. A law clerk appointed under this section shall be exempt from the provisions of subchapter I of chapter 63 of title 5, unless specifically included by the appointing judge or by local rule of court.

(b) Upon certification to the judicial council of the circuit involved and to the Director of the Administrative Office of the United States Courts that the number of cases and proceedings pending within the jurisdiction under section 1334 of this title within a judicial district so warrants, the bankruptcy judges for such district may appoint an individual to serve as clerk of such bankruptcy court. The clerk may appoint, with the approval of such bankruptcy judges, and in such number as may be approved by the Director, necessary deputies, and may remove such deputies with the approval of such bankruptcy judges.

(c) Any court may utilize facilities or services, either on or off the court's premises, which pertain to the provision of notices, dockets, calendars, and other administrative information to parties in cases filed under the provisions of title 11, United States Code, where the costs of such facilities or services are paid for out of the assets of the estate and are not charged to the United States. The utilization of such facilities or services shall be subject to such conditions and limitations as the pertinent circuit council may prescribe.

(d) No office of the bankruptcy clerk of court may be consolidated with the district clerk of court office without the prior approval of the Judicial Conference and the Congress.

(e) In a judicial district where a bankruptcy clerk has been appointed pursuant to subsection (b), the bankruptcy clerk shall be the official custodian of the records and dockets of the bankruptcy court.

(f) For purposes of financial accountability in a district where a bankruptcy clerk has been certified, such clerk shall be accountable for and pay into the Treasury all fees, costs, and other monies collected by such clerk except uncollected fees not required by an Act of Congress to be prepaid. Such clerk shall make returns thereof to the Director of the Administrative Office of the United States Courts and the Director of the Executive Office For United States Trustees, under regulations prescribed by such Directors.

(Added Pub.L. 98–353, Title I, § 104(a), July 10, 1984, 98 Stat. 339, and amended Pub.L. 99–554, Title I, §§ 103, 142, 144(a), Oct. 27, 1986, 100 Stat. 3090, 3096; Pub.L. 100–702, Title X, § 1003(a)(3), Nov. 19, 1988, 102 Stat. 4665.)

HISTORICAL AND STATUTORY NOTES

Codifications

This section as added by Pub.L. 95–598, Title II, § 201(a), Nov. 6, 1978, 92 Stat. 2659, effective June 28, 1984, pursuant to Pub.L. 95–598, Title IV, § 402(b), Nov. 6, 1978, 92 Stat. 2682, as amended by Pub.L. 98–249, § 1(a), Mar. 31, 1984, 98 Stat. 116; Pub.L. 98–271, § 1(a), Apr. 30, 1984, 98 Stat. 163; Pub.L. 98–299, § 1(a), May 25, 1984, 98 Stat. 214; Pub.L. 98–325, § 1(a), June 20, 1984, 98 Stat. 268, set out as a note preceding section 101 of Title 11, Bankruptcy, read as follows:

§ 156. **Division of business among bankruptcy judges**

The business of a bankruptcy court having more than one judge shall be divided among the judges as provided by the rules and orders of the court.

The chief judge of the bankruptcy court shall be responsible for the observance of such rules and orders, and shall divide the business and assign the cases so far as such rules and orders do not otherwise prescribe.

If the bankruptcy judges in any district are unable to agree upon the adoption of rules or orders for that purpose the judicial council of the circuit shall make the necessary orders.

Section 402(b) of Pub.L. 95–598 was amended by section 113 of Pub.L. 98–353 by substituting "shall not be effective" for "shall take effect on June 28, 1984", thereby eliminating the addition of section 156 by section 201(a) of Pub.L. 95–598, effective June 27, 1984, pursuant to section 122(c) of Pub.L. 98–353, set out as an Effective Date note under section 151 of this title.

Section 121(a) of Pub.L. 98–353 directed that section 402(b) of Pub.L. 95–598 be amended by substituting "the date of enactment of the Bankruptcy Amendments and Federal Judgeship Act of 1984 [i.e. July 10, 1984]" for "June 28, 1984". This amendment was not executed in view of the prior amendment to section 402(b) of Pub.L. 95–598 by section 113 of Pub.L. 98–353.

Effective and Applicability Provisions

1986 Acts

Amendment of subsec. (d) by section 103 of Pub.L. 99–554 effective on Oct. 27, 1986, see section 302(b) of Pub.L. 99–554, set out as a note under section 581 of this title.

Enactment of subsecs. (e) and (f) by sections 142 and 144(a) of Pub.L. 99–554 effective 30 days after Oct. 27, 1986, except as otherwise provided for, see section 302(a) of Pub.L. 99–554, set out as a note under section 581 of this title.

1984 Acts

Section effective July 10, 1984, see section 122(a) of Pub.L. 98–353, set out as a note under section 151 of this title.

§ 157. Procedures

(a) Each district court may provide that any or all cases under title 11 and any or all proceedings arising under title 11 or arising in or related to a case under title 11 shall be referred to the bankruptcy judges for the district.

(b)(1) Bankruptcy judges may hear and determine all cases under title 11 and all core proceedings aris-

ing under title 11, or arising in a case under title 11, referred under subsection (a) of this section, and may enter appropriate orders and judgments, subject to review under section 158 of this title.

(2) Core proceedings include, but are not limited to—

 (A) matters concerning the administration of the estate;

 (B) allowance or disallowance of claims against the estate or exemptions from property of the estate, and estimation of claims or interests for the purposes of confirming a plan under chapter 11, 12, or 13 of title 11 but not the liquidation or estimation of contingent or unliquidated personal injury tort or wrongful death claims against the estate for purposes of distribution in a case under title 11;

 (C) counterclaims by the estate against persons filing claims against the estate;

 (D) orders in respect to obtaining credit;

 (E) orders to turn over property of the estate;

 (F) proceedings to determine, avoid, or recover preferences;

 (G) motions to terminate, annul, or modify the automatic stay;

 (H) proceedings to determine, avoid, or recover fraudulent conveyances;

 (I) determinations as to the dischargeability of particular debts;

 (J) objections to discharges;

 (K) determinations of the validity, extent, or priority of liens;

 (L) confirmations of plans;

 (M) orders approving the use or lease of property, including the use of cash collateral;

 (N) orders approving the sale of property other than property resulting from claims brought by the estate against persons who have not filed claims against the estate;

 (O) other proceedings affecting the liquidation of the assets of the estate or the adjustment of the debtor-creditor or the equity security holder relationship, except personal injury tort or wrongful death claims; and

 (P) recognition of foreign proceedings and other matters under chapter 15 of title 11.

(3) The bankruptcy judge shall determine, on the judge's own motion or on timely motion of a party, whether a proceeding is a core proceeding under this subsection or is a proceeding that is otherwise related to a case under title 11. A determination that a proceeding is not a core proceeding shall not be made solely on the basis that its resolution may be affected by State law.

(4) Non-core proceedings under section 157(b)(2)(B) of title 28, United States Code, shall not be subject to the mandatory abstention provisions of section 1334(c)(2).

(5) The district court shall order that personal injury tort and wrongful death claims shall be tried in the district court in which the bankruptcy case is pending, or in the district court in the district in which the claim arose, as determined by the district court in which the bankruptcy case is pending.

(c)(1) A bankruptcy judge may hear a proceeding that is not a core proceeding but that is otherwise related to a case under title 11. In such proceeding, the bankruptcy judge shall submit proposed findings of fact and conclusions of law to the district court, and any final order or judgment shall be entered by the district judge after considering the bankruptcy judge's proposed findings and conclusions and after reviewing de novo those matters to which any party has timely and specifically objected.

(2) Notwithstanding the provisions of paragraph (1) of this subsection, the district court, with the consent of all the parties to the proceeding, may refer a proceeding related to a case under title 11 to a bankruptcy judge to hear and determine and to enter appropriate orders and judgments, subject to review under section 158 of this title.

(d) The district court may withdraw, in whole or in part, any case or proceeding referred under this section, on its own motion or on timely motion of any party, for cause shown. The district court shall, on timely motion of a party, so withdraw a proceeding if the court determines that resolution of the proceeding requires consideration of both title 11 and other laws of the United States regulating organizations or activities affecting interstate commerce.

(e) If the right to a jury trial applies in a proceeding that may be heard under this section by a bankruptcy judge, the bankruptcy judge may conduct the jury trial if specially designated to exercise such jurisdiction by the district court and with the express consent of all the parties.

(Added Pub.L. 98–353, Title I, § 104(a), July 10, 1984, 98 Stat. 340, and amended Pub.L. 99–554, Title I, §§ 143, 144(b), Oct. 27, 1986, 100 Stat. 3096; Pub.L. 103–394, Title I, § 112, Oct. 22, 1994, 108 Stat. 4117; Pub.L. 109–8, Title VIII, § 802(c)(1), Apr. 20, 2005, 119 Stat. 145.)

HISTORICAL AND STATUTORY NOTES

References in Text

 Chapter 11, 12, or 13 of title 11, referred to in subsec. (b)(2)(B), is 11 U.S.C.A. § 1101 et seq., 11 U.S.C.A. § 1201 et seq., or 11 U.S.C.A. § 1301 et seq., respectively.

Chapter 15 of title 11, referred to in subsec. (b)(2)(P), is 11 U.S.C.A. § 1501 et seq.

Codifications

This section as added by Pub.L. 95–598, Title II, § 201(a), Nov. 6, 1978, 92 Stat. 2659, effective June 28, 1984, pursuant to Pub.L. 95–598, Title IV, § 402(b), Nov. 6, 1978, 92 Stat. 2682, as amended by Pub.L. 98–249, § 1(a), Mar. 31, 1984, 98 Stat. 116; Pub.L. 98–271, § 1(a), Apr. 30, 1984, 98 Stat. 163; Pub.L. 98–299, § 1(a), May 25, 1984, 98 Stat. 214; Pub.L. 98–325, § 1(a), June 20, 1984, 98 Stat. 268, set out as a note preceding section 101 of Title 11, Bankruptcy, read as follows:

"§ 157. Times of holding court

"**(a)** The bankruptcy court at each designated location shall be deemed to be in continuous session on all business days throughout the year.

"**(b)** Each bankruptcy court may establish by local rule or order schedules of court sessions at designated places of holding court other than the headquarters office of the court. Such schedules may be pretermitted by order of the court.

"**(c)** Bankruptcy court may be held at any place within the territory served, in any case, on order of the bankruptcy court, for the convenience of the parties, on such notice as the bankruptcy court orders."

Section 402(b) of Pub.L. 95–598 was amended by section 113 of Pub.L. 98–353 by substituting "shall not be effective" for "shall take effect on June 28, 1984", thereby eliminating the addition of section 157 by section 201(a) of Pub.L. 95–598, effective June 27, 1984, pursuant to section 122(c) of Pub.L. 98–353, set out as an Effective Date note under section 151 of this title.

Section 121(a) of Pub.L. 98–353 directed that section 402(b) of Pub.L. 95–598 be amended by substituting "the date of enactment of the Bankruptcy Amendments and Federal Judgeship Act of 1984 [i.e. July 10, 1984]" for "June 28, 1984". This amendment was not executed in view of the prior amendment to section 402(b) of Pub.L. 95–598 by section 113 of Pub.L. 98–353.

Effective and Applicability Provisions

2005 Acts

Except as otherwise provided, amendments by Pub.L. 109–8 effective 180 days after April 20, 2005, and inapplicable with respect to cases commenced under Title 11 before the effective date, see Pub.L. 109–8, § 1501, set out as a note under 11 U.S.C.A. § 101.

1994 Acts

Amendment by Pub.L. 103–394 effective on Oct. 22, 1994, and not to apply with respect to cases commenced under Title 11 of the United States Code before Oct. 22, 1994, see section 702 of Pub.L. 103–394, set out as a note under section 101 of Title 11, Bankruptcy.

1986 Acts

Amendment by Pub.L. 99–554 effective 30 days after Oct. 27, 1986, except as otherwise provided for, see section 302(a) of Pub.L. 99–554, set out as a note under section 581 of this title.

1984 Acts

Section effective July 10, 1984, see section 122(a) of Pub.L. 98–353, set out as a note under section 151 of this title.

Separability of Provisions

If any provision of or amendment made by Pub.L. 103–394 or the application of such provision or amendment to any person or circumstance is held to be unconstitutional, the remaining provisions of and amendments made by Pub.L. 103–394 and the application of such provisions and amendments to any person or circumstance shall not be affected thereby, see section 701 of Pub.L. 103–394, set out as a note under section 101 of Title 11, Bankruptcy.

§ 158. Appeals

(a) The district courts of the United States shall have jurisdiction to hear appeals [1]

 (1) from final judgments, orders, and decrees;

 (2) from interlocutory orders and decrees issued under section 1121(d) of title 11 increasing or reducing the time periods referred to in section 1121 of such title; and

 (3) with leave of the court, from other interlocutory orders and decrees;

and, with leave of the court, from interlocutory orders and decrees, of bankruptcy judges entered in cases and proceedings referred to the bankruptcy judges under section 157 of this title. An appeal under this subsection shall be taken only to the district court for the judicial district in which the bankruptcy judge is serving.

(b)(1) The judicial council of a circuit shall establish a bankruptcy appellate panel service composed of bankruptcy judges of the districts in the circuit who are appointed by the judicial council in accordance with paragraph (3), to hear and determine, with the consent of all the parties, appeals under subsection (a) unless the judicial council finds that—

 (A) there are insufficient judicial resources available in the circuit; or

 (B) establishment of such service would result in undue delay or increased cost to parties in cases under title 11.

Not later than 90 days after making the finding, the judicial council shall submit to the Judicial Conference of the United States a report containing the factual basis of such finding.

(2)(A) A judicial council may reconsider, at any time, the finding described in paragraph (1).

(B) On the request of a majority of the district judges in a circuit for which a bankruptcy appellate panel service is established under paragraph (1), made after the expiration of the 1–year period beginning on the date such service is established, the judicial council of the circuit shall determine whether a circumstance specified in subparagraph (A) or (B) of such paragraph exists.

(C) On its own motion, after the expiration of the 3–year period beginning on the date a bankruptcy

appellate panel service is established under paragraph (1), the judicial council of the circuit may determine whether a circumstance specified in subparagraph (A) or (B) of such paragraph exists.

(D) If the judicial council finds that either of such circumstances exists, the judicial council may provide for the completion of the appeals then pending before such service and the orderly termination of such service.

(3) Bankruptcy judges appointed under paragraph (1) shall be appointed and may be reappointed under such paragraph.

(4) If authorized by the Judicial Conference of the United States, the judicial councils of 2 or more circuits may establish a joint bankruptcy appellate panel comprised of bankruptcy judges from the districts within the circuits for which such panel is established, to hear and determine, upon the consent of all the parties, appeals under subsection (a) of this section.

(5) An appeal to be heard under this subsection shall be heard by a panel of 3 members of the bankruptcy appellate panel service, except that a member of such service may not hear an appeal originating in the district for which such member is appointed or designated under section 152 of this title.

(6) Appeals may not be heard under this subsection by a panel of the bankruptcy appellate panel service unless the district judges for the district in which the appeals occur, by majority vote, have authorized such service to hear and determine appeals originating in such district.

(c)(1) Subject to subsections (b) and (d)(2), each appeal under subsection (a) shall be heard by a 3–judge panel of the bankruptcy appellate panel service established under subsection (b)(1) unless—

(A) the appellant elects at the time of filing the appeal; or

(B) any other party elects, not later than 30 days after service of notice of the appeal;

to have such appeal heard by the district court.

(2) An appeal under subsections (a) and (b) of this section shall be taken in the same manner as appeals in civil proceedings generally are taken to the courts of appeals from the district courts and in the time provided by Rule 8002 of the Bankruptcy Rules.

(d)(1) The courts of appeals shall have jurisdiction of appeals from all final decisions, judgments, orders, and decrees entered under subsections (a) and (b) of this section.

(2)(A) The appropriate court of appeals shall have jurisdiction of appeals described in the first sentence of subsection (a) if the bankruptcy court, the district court, or the bankruptcy appellate panel involved,

acting on its own motion or on the request of a party to the judgment, order, or decree described in such first sentence, or all the appellants and appellees (if any) acting jointly, certify that—

(i) the judgment, order, or decree involves a question of law as to which there is no controlling decision of the court of appeals for the circuit or of the Supreme Court of the United States, or involves a matter of public importance;

(ii) the judgment, order, or decree involves a question of law requiring resolution of conflicting decisions; or

(iii) an immediate appeal from the judgment, order, or decree may materially advance the progress of the case or proceeding in which the appeal is taken;

and if the court of appeals authorizes the direct appeal of the judgment, order, or decree.

(B) If the bankruptcy court, the district court, or the bankruptcy appellate panel—

(i) on its own motion or on the request of a party, determines that a circumstance specified in clause (i), (ii), or (iii) of subparagraph (A) exists; or

(ii) receives a request made by a majority of the appellants and a majority of appellees (if any) to make the certification described in subparagraph (A);

then the bankruptcy court, the district court, or the bankruptcy appellate panel shall make the certification described in subparagraph (A).

(C) The parties may supplement the certification with a short statement of the basis for the certification.

(D) An appeal under this paragraph does not stay any proceeding of the bankruptcy court, the district court, or the bankruptcy appellate panel from which the appeal is taken, unless the respective bankruptcy court, district court, or bankruptcy appellate panel, or the court of appeals in which the appeal in pending, issues a stay of such proceeding pending the appeal.

(E) Any request under subparagraph (B) for certification shall be made not later than 60 days after the entry of the judgment, order, or decree.

(Added Pub.L. 98–353, Title I, § 104(a), July 10, 1984, 98 Stat. 341, and amended Pub.L. 101–650, Title III, § 305, Dec. 1, 1990, 104 Stat. 5105; Pub.L. 103–394, Title I, §§ 102, 104(c), (d), Oct. 22, 1994, 108 Stat. 4108–4110; Pub.L. 109–8, Title XII, § 1233(a), Apr. 20, 2005, 119 Stat. 202.)

1 So in original.

HISTORICAL AND STATUTORY NOTES

Codifications

Amendment by section 102 of Pub.L. 103–394, which directed amendment of subsec. (a) by striking "from" the first place it appeared and all that followed through "decrees,"

and making a substitution for such language, was executed by striking through "decrees," the first place it appeared, as the probable intent of Congress.

This section (section 158) and section 159 as added by Pub.L. 95–598, Title II, § 201(a), Nov. 6, 1978, 92 Stat. 2659, and section 160, as added by Pub.L. 95–598, Title II, § 201(a), Nov. 6, 1978, 92 Stat. 2659, and amended Pub.L. 97–164, Title I, § 110(d), Apr. 2, 1982, 96 Stat. 29, effective June 28, 1984, pursuant to Pub.L. 95–598, Title IV, § 402(b), Nov. 6, 1978, 92 Stat. 2682, as amended by Pub.L. 98–249, § 1(a), Mar. 31, 1984, 98 Stat. 116; Pub.L. 98–271, § 1(a), Apr. 30, 1984, 98 Stat. 163; Pub.L. 98–299, § 1(a), May 25, 1984, 98 Stat. 214; Pub.L. 98–325, § 1(a), June 20, 1984, 98 Stat. 268, set out as a note preceding section 101 of Title II, Bankruptcy, read as follows:

"**§ 158. Accommodations at places for holding court**

"Court shall be held only at places where Federal quarters and accommodations are available, or suitable quarters and accommodations are furnished without cost to the United States. The foregoing restrictions shall not, however, preclude the Administrator of General Services, at the request of the Director of the Administrative Office of the United States Courts, from providing such court quarters and accommodations as the Administrator determines can appropriately be made available at places where court is authorized by law to be held, but only if such court quarters and accommodations have been approved as necessary by the judicial council of the appropriate circuit.

"**§ 159. Vacant judgeship as affecting proceedings**

"When the office of a bankruptcy judge becomes vacant, all pending process, pleadings and proceedings shall, when necessary, be continued by the clerk until a judge is appointed or designated to hold such court.

"**§ 160. Appellate panels**

"**(a)** If the circuit council of a circuit orders application of this section to a district within such circuit, the chief judge of each circuit shall designate panels of three bankruptcy judges to hear appeals from judgments, orders, and decrees of the bankruptcy court of the United States for such district. Except as provided in section 293(b) of this title, a panel shall be composed only of bankruptcy judges for districts located in the circuit in which the appeal arises. The chief judge shall designate a sufficient number of such panels so that appeals may be heard and disposed of expeditiously.

"**(b)** A panel designated under subsection (a) of this section may not hear an appeal from a judgment, order, or decree entered by a member of the panel.

"**(c)** When hearing an appeal, a panel designated under subsection (a) of this section shall sit at a place convenient to the parties to the appeal."

Section 402(b) of Pub.L. 95–598 was amended by section 113 of Pub.L. 98–353 by substituting "shall not be effective" for "shall take effect on June 28, 1984", thereby eliminating the additions of sections 158 to 160 by section 201(a) of Pub.L. 95–598, effective June 27, 1984, pursuant to section 122(c) of Pub.L. 98–353, set out as an Effective Date note under section 151 of this title.

Section 121(a) of Pub.L. 98–353 directed that section 402(b) of Pub.L. 95–598 be amended by substituting "the date of enactment of the Bankruptcy Amendments and Federal Judgeship Act of 1984 [i.e. July 10, 1984]" for "June 28,

1984". This amendment was not executed in view of the prior amendment to section 402(b) of Pub.L. 95–598 by section 113 of Pub.L. 98–353.

Effective and Applicability Provisions

2005 Acts

Except as otherwise provided, amendments by Pub.L. 109–8 effective 180 days after April 20, 2005, and inapplicable with respect to cases commenced under Title 11 before the effective date, see Pub.L. 109–8, § 1501, set out as a note under 11 U.S.C.A. § 101.

1994 Acts

Amendments by Pub.L. 103–394 effective on Oct. 22, 1994, and not to apply with respect to cases commenced under Title 11 of the United States Code before Oct. 22, 1994, see section 702 of Pub.L. 103–394, set out as a note under 11 U.S.C.A. § 101.

1984 Acts

Section effective July 10, 1984, see section 122(a) of Pub.L. 98–353, set out as a note under 28 U.S.C.A. § 151.

Separability of Provisions

If any provision of or amendment made by Pub.L. 103–394 or the application of such provision or amendment to any person or circumstance is held to be unconstitutional, the remaining provisions of and amendments made by Pub.L. 103–394 and the application of such provisions and amendments to any person or circumstance shall not be affected thereby, see section 701 of Pub.L. 103–394, set out as a note under 11 U.S.C.A. § 101.

Procedural Rules

Pub.L. 109–8, Title XII, § 1233(b), Apr. 20, 2005, 119 Stat. 203, provided that:

"**(1) Temporary application.**—A provision of this subsection shall apply to appeals under section 158(d)(2) of title 28, United States Code, until a rule of practice and procedure relating to such provision and such appeals is promulgated or amended under chapter 131 of such title [28 U.S.C.A. § 2071 et seq.].

"**(2) Certification.**—A district court, a bankruptcy court, or a bankruptcy appellate panel may make a certification under section 158(d)(2) of title 28, United States Code, only with respect to matters pending in the respective bankruptcy court, district court, or bankruptcy appellate panel.

"**(3) Procedure.**—Subject to any other provision of this subsection, an appeal authorized by the court of appeals under section 158(d)(2)(A) of title 28, United States Code, shall be taken in the manner prescribed in subdivisions (a)(1), (b), (c), and (d) of rule 5 of the Federal Rules of Appellate Procedure. For purposes of subdivision (a)(1) of rule 5—

"**(A)** a reference in such subdivision to a district court shall be deemed to include a reference to a bankruptcy court and a bankruptcy appellate panel, as appropriate; and

"**(B)** a reference in such subdivision to the parties requesting permission to appeal to be served with the petition shall be deemed to include a reference to the parties to the judgment, order, or decree from which the appeal is taken.

"**(4) Filing of petition with attachment.**—A petition requesting permission to appeal, that is based on a certification

made under subparagraph (A) or (B) of section 158(d)(2) shall—

"**(A)** be filed with the circuit clerk not later than 10 days after the certification is entered on the docket of the bankruptcy court, the district court, or the bankruptcy appellate panel from which the appeal is taken; and

"**(B)** have attached a copy of such certification.

"**(5) References in rule 5.**—For purposes of rule 5 of the Federal Rules of Appellate Procedure—

"**(A)** a reference in such rule to a district court shall be deemed to include a reference to a bankruptcy court and to a bankruptcy appellate panel; and

"**(B)** a reference in such rule to a district clerk shall be deemed to include a reference to a clerk of a bankruptcy court and to a clerk of a bankruptcy appellate panel.

"**(6) Application of rules.**—The Federal Rules of Appellate Procedure [set out in Title 28, Judiciary and Judicial Procedure] shall apply in the courts of appeals with respect to appeals authorized under section 158(d)(2)(A), to the extent relevant and as if such appeals were taken from final judgments, orders, or decrees of the district courts or bankruptcy appellate panels exercising appellate jurisdiction under subsection (a) or (b) of section 158 of title 28, United States Code."

[Except as otherwise provided, amendments by Pub.L. 109–8 effective 180 days after April 20, 2005, and inapplicable with respect to cases commenced under Title 11 before the effective date, see Pub.L. 109–8, § 1501, set out as a note under 11 U.S.C.A. § 101.]

§ 159. Bankruptcy statistics

(a) The clerk of the district court, or the clerk of the bankruptcy court if one is certified pursuant to section 156(b) of this title, shall collect statistics regarding debtors who are individuals with primarily consumer debts seeking relief under chapters 7, 11, and 13 of title 11. Those statistics shall be in a standardized format prescribed by the Director of the Administrative Office of the United States Courts (referred to in this section as the "Director").

(b) The Director shall—

(1) compile the statistics referred to in subsection (a);

(2) make the statistics available to the public; and

(3) not later than July 1, 2008, and annually thereafter, prepare, and submit to Congress a report concerning the information collected under subsection (a) that contains an analysis of the information.

(c) The compilation required under subsection (b) shall—

(1) be itemized, by chapter, with respect to title 11;

(2) be presented in the aggregate and for each district; and

(3) include information concerning—

(A) the total assets and total liabilities of the debtors described in subsection (a), and in each category of assets and liabilities, as reported in the schedules prescribed pursuant to section 2075 of this title and filed by debtors;

(B) the current monthly income, average income, and average expenses of debtors as reported on the schedules and statements that each such debtor files under sections 521 and 1322 of title 11;

(C) the aggregate amount of debt discharged in cases filed during the reporting period, determined as the difference between the total amount of debt and obligations of a debtor reported on the schedules and the amount of such debt reported in categories which are predominantly nondischargeable;

(D) the average period of time between the date of the filing of the petition and the closing of the case for cases closed during the reporting period;

(E) for cases closed during the reporting period—

(i) the number of cases in which a reaffirmation agreement was filed; and

(ii)(I) the total number of reaffirmation agreements filed;

(II) of those cases in which a reaffirmation agreement was filed, the number of cases in which the debtor was not represented by an attorney; and

(III) of those cases in which a reaffirmation agreement was filed, the number of cases in which the reaffirmation agreement was approved by the court;

(F) with respect to cases filed under chapter 13 of title 11, for the reporting period—

(i)(I) the number of cases in which a final order was entered determining the value of property securing a claim in an amount less than the amount of the claim; and

(II) the number of final orders entered determining the value of property securing a claim;

(ii) the number of cases dismissed, the number of cases dismissed for failure to make payments under the plan, the number of cases refiled after dismissal, and the number of cases in which the plan was completed, separately itemized with respect to the number of modifications made before completion of the plan, if any; and

(iii) the number of cases in which the debtor filed another case during the 6–year period preceding the filing;

(G) the number of cases in which creditors were fined for misconduct and any amount of

punitive damages awarded by the court for creditor misconduct; and

 (H) the number of cases in which sanctions under rule 9011 of the Federal Rules of Bankruptcy Procedure were imposed against debtor's attorney or damages awarded under such Rule.

(Added Pub.L. 109–8, Title VI, § 601(a), Apr. 20, 2005, 119 Stat. 119.)

HISTORICAL AND STATUTORY NOTES

References in Text

Chapters 7 and 11 of title 11, referred to in subsec. (a), are 11 U.S.C.A. § 701 et seq. and 11 U.S.C.A. § 1101 et seq., respectively.

Chapter 13 of title 11, referred to in subsecs. (a) and (c)(3)(F), is 11 U.S.C.A. § 1301 et seq.

The Federal Rules of Bankruptcy Procedure, referred to in subsec. (c)(3)(H), are set out in Title 11.

Effective and Applicability Provisions

2005 Acts

Pub.L. 109–8, Title VI, § 601(c), Apr. 20, 2005, 119 Stat. 120, provided that: "The amendments made by this section [enacting this section] shall take effect 18 months after the date of enactment of this Act [April 20, 2005]."

Except as otherwise provided, amendments by Pub.L. 109–8 effective 180 days after April 20, 2005, and inapplicable with respect to cases commenced under Title 11 before the effective date, see Pub.L. 109–8, § 1501, set out as a note under 11 U.S.C.A. § 101.

[CHAPTER 9—REPEALED]

[§§ 211 to 216. Repealed. Pub.L. 97–164, Title I, § 106, Apr. 2, 1982, 96 Stat. 28]

HISTORICAL AND STATUTORY NOTES

Section 211, Acts June 25, 1948, c. 646, 62 Stat. 899; Aug. 25, 1958, Pub.L. 85–755, § 1, 72 Stat. 848, provided for the creation of the United States Court of Customs and Patent Appeals under article III of the United States Constitution and for the appointment of a chief judge and four associate judges for that court.

Section 212, Act June 25, 1948, c. 646, 62 Stat. 899, provided for the order of precedence of the chief judge and associate judges of the Court of Customs and Patent Appeals.

Section 213, Acts June 25, 1948, c. 646, 62 Stat. 899; Mar. 2, 1955, c. 9, § 1(e), 69 Stat. 10; Aug. 14, 1964, Pub.L. 88–426, Title IV, § 403(e), 78 Stat. 434; Aug. 9, 1975, Pub.L. 94–82, Title II, § 205(b) (5), 89 Stat. 422, provided for the tenure and salaries of the judges of the Court of Customs and Patent Appeals.

Section 214, Act June 25, 1948, c. 646, 62 Stat. 899, authorized the Court of Customs and Patent Appeals to hold court at such times and places as it might fix by rule.

Section 215, Act June 25, 1948, c. 646, 62 Stat. 899, provided that three judges of the Court of Customs and

Patent Appeals constituted a quorum and that the concurrence of three judges was necessary to any decision.

Section 216, Act June 25, 1948, c. 646, 62 Stat. 899, provided for the filing of written opinions by the Court of Customs and Patent Appeals on appeals from decisions of the Patent Office and the recording of those opinions in the Patent Office.

Effective Date of Repeal

Repeal effective Oct. 1, 1982, see section 402 of Pub.L. 97–164, set out as a note under section 171 of this title.

Transfer of Matters and Petitions Pending in United States Court of Customs and Patent Appeals on October 1, 1982

For provisions that any matter pending before the United States Court of Customs and Patent Appeals on Oct. 1, 1982, and any petition for rehearing, reconsideration, alteration, modification, or other change in any decision of the United States Court of Customs and Patent Appeals rendered prior to Oct. 1, 1982, that has not been determined on that date or that is filed after that date, be determined by the United States Court of Appeals for the Federal Circuit, see section 403(b), (c) of Pub.L. 97–164, set out as a note under section 171 of this title.

CHAPTER 13—ASSIGNMENT OF JUDGES TO OTHER COURTS

§ 291. Circuit judges

 (a) The Chief Justice of the United States may, in the public interest, designate and assign temporarily any circuit judge to act as circuit judge in another circuit upon request by the chief judge or circuit justice of such circuit.

 (b) The chief judge of a circuit or the circuit justice may, in the public interest, designate and assign temporarily any circuit judge within the circuit, including a judge designated and assigned to temporary duty

therein, to hold a district court in any district within the circuit.

(June 25, 1948, c. 646, 62 Stat. 900; July 28, 1953, c. 253, § 2, 67 Stat. 226; Sept. 3, 1954, c. 1263, § 39(b), 68 Stat. 1240; July 9, 1956, c. 517, § 1(a), 70 Stat. 497; Aug. 25, 1958, Pub.L. 85–755, § 2, 72 Stat. 848; Nov. 6, 1978, Pub.L. 95–598, Title II, § 202, 92 Stat. 2660; Apr. 2, 1982, Pub.L. 97–164, Title I, § 108, 96 Stat. 28; Oct. 29, 1992, Pub.L. 102–572, Title I, § 104, 106 Stat. 4507.)

HISTORICAL AND STATUTORY NOTES

Codifications

Subsec. (c) of this section was amended by Pub.L. 95–598, Title II, § 202, Nov. 6, 1978, 92 Stat. 2660, effective June 28, 1984, pursuant to Pub.L. 95–598, Title IV, § 402(b), Nov. 6, 1978, 92 Stat. 2682, as amended by Pub.L. 98–249, § 1(a), Mar. 31, 1984, 98 Stat. 116; Pub.L. 98–271, § 1(a), Apr. 30, 1984, 98 Stat. 163; Pub.L. 98–299, § 1(a), May 25, 1984, 98 Stat. 214; Pub.L. 98–325, § 1(a), June 20, 1984, 98 Stat. 268, set out as a note preceding section 101 of Title 11, Bankruptcy, by adding "or bankruptcy" after "to hold a district".

Section 402(b) of Pub.L. 95–598 was amended by section 113 of Pub.L. 98–353, Title I, July 10, 1984, 98 Stat. 343, by substituting "shall not be effective" for "shall take effect on June 28, 1984", thereby eliminating the amendment by section 202 of Pub.L. 95–598, effective June 27, 1984, pursuant to section 122(c) of Pub.L. 98–353, set out as an Effective Date note under section 151 of this title.

Section 121(a) of Pub.L. 98–353 directed that section 402(b) of Pub.L. 95–598 be amended by substituting "the date of enactment of the Bankruptcy Amendments and Federal Judgeship Act of 1984 [i.e. July 10, 1984]" for "June 28, 1984". This amendment was not executed in view of the prior amendment to section 402(b) of Pub.L. 95–598 by section 113 of Pub.L. 98–353.

Effective and Applicability Provisions

1992 Acts

Amendment by Pub.L. 102–572 effective Jan. 1, 1993, see section 1101(a) of Pub.L. 102–572, set out as a note under section 905 of Title 2, The Congress.

1982 Acts

Amendment by Pub.L. 97–164 effective Oct. 1, 1982, see section 402 of Pub.L. 97–164, set out as a note under section 171 of this title.

Jurisdiction of United States Court of Customs and Patent Appeals

Section 7 of Pub.L. 85–755 provided that: "Nothing contained in this Act [amending sections 211 and 291 to 295 of this title] shall be construed in any way to limit or alter the jurisdiction heretofore conferred upon the United States Court of Customs and Patent Appeals [now United States Court of Appeals for the Federal Circuit] by any provision of law."

§ 292. District judges

(a) The chief judge of a circuit may designate and assign one or more district judges within the circuit to sit upon the court of appeals or a division thereof whenever the business of that court so requires. Such designations or assignments shall be in conformity

with the rules or orders of the court of appeals of the circuit.

(b) The chief judge of a circuit may, in the public interest, designate and assign temporarily any district judge of the circuit to hold a district court in any district within the circuit.

(c) The chief judge of the United States Court of Appeals for the District of Columbia Circuit may, upon presentation of a certificate of necessity by the chief judge of the Superior Court of the District of Columbia pursuant to section 11–908(c) of the District of Columbia Code, designate and assign temporarily any district judge of the circuit to serve as a judge of such Superior Court, if such assignment (1) is approved by the Attorney General of the United States following a determination by him to the effect that such assignment is necessary to meet the ends of justice, and (2) is approved by the chief judge of the United States District Court for the District of Columbia.

(d) The Chief Justice of the United States may designate and assign temporarily a district judge of one circuit for service in another circuit, either in a district court or court of appeals, upon presentation of a certificate of necessity by the chief judge or circuit justice of the circuit wherein the need arises.

(e) The Chief Justice of the United States may designate and assign temporarily any district judge to serve as a judge of the Court of International Trade upon presentation to him of a certificate of necessity by the chief judge of the court.

(June 25, 1948, c. 646, 62 Stat. 901; July 28, 1953, c. 253, § 3, 67 Stat. 226; Sept. 3, 1954, c. 1263, § 39(c), 68 Stat. 1240; July 9, 1956, c. 517, § 1(b), 70 Stat. 497; July 14, 1956, c. 589, § 2, 70 Stat. 532; Aug. 25, 1958, Pub.L. 85–755, § 3, 72 Stat. 848; July 29, 1970, Pub.L. 91–358, Title I, § 172(e), 84 Stat. 591; Nov. 6, 1978, Pub.L. 95–598, Title II, §§ 203, 204, 92 Stat. 2660; Oct. 10, 1980, Pub.L. 96–417, Title V, § 501(7), 94 Stat. 1742; Apr. 2, 1982, Pub.L. 97–164, Title I, § 109, 96 Stat. 28.)

HISTORICAL AND STATUTORY NOTES

Codifications

This section was amended by Pub.L. 95–598, Title II, §§ 203, 204, Nov. 6, 1978, 92 Stat. 2660, effective June 28, 1984, pursuant to Pub.L. 95–598, Title IV, § 402(b), Nov. 6, 1978, 92 Stat. 2682, as amended by Pub.L. 98–249, § 1(a), Mar. 31, 1984, 98 Stat. 116; Pub.L. 98–271, § 1(a), Apr. 30, 1984, 98 Stat. 163; Pub.L. 98–299, § 1(a), May 25, 1984, 98 Stat. 214; Pub.L. 98–325, § 1(a), June 20, 1984, 98 Stat. 268, set out as a note preceding section 101 of Title II, Bankruptcy, in subsec. (b) by substituting "a district court or a bankruptcy court" for "a district court" and in subsec. (d) by substituting "in a bankruptcy court, district court, or court of appeals" for "either in a district court or court of appeals".

Section 402(b) of Pub.L. 95–598 was amended by section 113 of Pub.L. 98–353, Title I, July 10, 1984, 98 Stat. 343, by substituting "shall not be effective" for "shall take effect on

June 28, 1984", thereby eliminating the amendments by sections 203 and 204 of Pub.L. 95–598, effective June 27, 1984, pursuant to section 122(c) of Pub.L. 98–353, set out as an Effective Date note under section 151 of this title.

Section 121(a) of Pub.L. 98–353 directed that section 402(b) of Pub.L. 95–598 be amended by substituting "the date of enactment of the Bankruptcy Amendments and Federal Judgeship Act of 1984 [i.e. July 10, 1984]" for "June 28, 1984". This amendment was not executed in view of the prior amendment to section 402(b) of Pub.L. 95–598 by section 113 of Pub.L. 98–353.

Effective and Applicability Provisions

1982 Acts

Amendment by Pub.L. 97–164 effective Oct. 1, 1982, see section 402 of Pub.L. 97–164, set out as a note under section 171 of this title.

1980 Acts

Amendment by Pub.L. 96–417 effective on Nov. 1, 1980, and applicable with respect to civil actions pending on or commenced on or after such date, see section 701(a) of Pub.L. 96–417, as amended, set out as a note under section 251 of this title.

1970 Acts

Amendment by Pub.L. 91–358 effective the first day of the seventh calendar month which begins after July 29, 1970, see section 199(a) of Pub.L. 91–358, set out as a note under section 1257 of this title.

Jurisdiction of United States Court of Customs and Patent Appeals

Amendment by Pub.L. 85–755 not limiting or altering the jurisdiction of the United States Court of Customs and Patent Appeals [now United States Court of Appeals for the Federal Circuit], see section 7 of Pub.L. 85–755, set out as a note under section 291 of this title.

Limitation or Alteration of Jurisdiction

Amendment by Act July 14, 1956, not to be construed as limiting or altering the jurisdiction heretofore conferred upon the Customs Court [now the United States Court of International Trade], see section 4 of Act July 14, 1956, set out as a note under section 251 of this title.

§ 293. Judges of the Court of International Trade

(a)[1] The Chief Justice of the United States may designate and assign temporarily any judge of the Court of International Trade to perform judicial duties in any circuit, either in a court of appeals or district court, upon presentation of a certificate of necessity by the chief judge or circuit justice of the circuit in which the need arises.

(June 25, 1948, c. 646, 62 Stat. 901; July 14, 1956, c. 589, § 3(a), 70 Stat. 532; Aug. 25, 1958, Pub.L. 85–755, § 4, 72 Stat. 848; Nov. 6, 1978, Pub.L. 95–598, Title II, § 205, 92 Stat. 2660; Oct. 10, 1980, Pub.L. 96–417, Title I, § 102, Title V, § 501(8), 94 Stat. 1727, 1742; Apr. 2, 1982, Pub.L. 97–164, Title I, § 110(a), (b), 96 Stat. 29.)

1 There is no subsec. (b).

HISTORICAL AND STATUTORY NOTES

Codifications

This section was amended by Pub.L. 95–598, Title II, § 205, Nov. 6, 1978, 92 Stat. 2660; Pub.L. 97–164, Title I, § 110(a)(3), Apr. 2, 1982, 96 Stat. 29, effective June 28, 1984, pursuant to Pub.L. 95–598, Title IV, § 402(b), Nov. 6, 1978, 92 Stat. 2682, as amended by Pub.L. 98–249, § 1(a), Mar. 31, 1984, 98 Stat. 116; Pub.L. 98–271, § 1(a), Apr. 30, 1984, 98 Stat. 163; Pub.L. 98–299, § 1(a), May 25, 1984, 98 Stat. 214; Pub.L. 98–325, § 1(a), June 20, 1984, 98 Stat. 268, set out as a note preceding section 101 of Title II, Bankruptcy, by adding a subsec. (b) to read as follows:

(b)(1) The Chief Justice of the United States may designate and assign temporarily a bankruptcy judge of one circuit for service in a bankruptcy court in another circuit upon presentation of a certificate of necessity by the chief judge or circuit justice of the circuit wherein the need arises.

(2) The chief judge of a circuit may, in the public interest, designate and assign temporarily a bankruptcy judge of the circuit to hold a bankruptcy court in any district within the circuit.

Section 402(b) of Pub.L. 95–598 was amended by section 113 of Pub.L. 98–353, Title I, July 10, 1984, 98 Stat. 343, by substituting "shall not be effective" for "shall take effect on June 28, 1984," thereby eliminating the amendment by section 205 of Pub.L. 95–598, effective June 27, 1984, pursuant to section 122(c) of Pub.L. 98–353, set out as an Effective Date note under section 151 of this title.

Section 121(a) of Pub.L. 98–353 directed that section 402(b) of Pub.L. 95–598 be amended by substituting "the date of enactment of the Bankruptcy Amendments and Federal Judgeship Act of 1984 [i.e. July 10, 1984]" for "June 28, 1984". This amendment was not executed in view of the prior amendment to section 402(b) of Pub.L. 95–598 by section 113 of Pub.L. 98–353.

Effective and Applicability Provisions

1982 Acts

Amendment by Pub.L. 97–164 effective Oct. 1, 1982, see section 402 of Pub.L. 97–164, set out as a note under section 171 of this title.

1980 Acts

Amendment by Pub.L. 96–417 effective on Nov. 1, 1980, and applicable with respect to civil actions pending on or commenced on or after such date, see section 701(a) of Pub.L. 96–417, as amended, set out as a note under section 251 of this title.

Jurisdiction of United States Court of Customs and Patent Appeals

Amendment by Pub.L. 85–755 not limiting or altering the jurisdiction of the United States Court of Customs and Patent Appeals [now United States Court of Appeals for the Federal Circuit], see section 7 of Pub.L. 85–755, set out as a note under section 291 of this title.

Limitation or Alteration of Jurisdiction

Amendment by Act July 14, 1956, not to be construed as limiting or altering the jurisdiction heretofore conferred upon the Customs Court [now United States Court of International Trade], see section 4 of Act July 14, 1956, set out as a note under section 251 of this title.

§ 294. Assignment of retired Justices or judges to active duty

(a) Any retired Chief Justice of the United States or Associate Justice of the Supreme Court may be designated and assigned by the Chief Justice of the United States to perform such judicial duties in any circuit, including those of a circuit justice, as he is willing to undertake.

(b) Any judge of the United States who has retired from regular active service under section 371(b) or 372(a) of this title shall be known and designated as a senior judge and may continue to perform such judicial duties as he is willing and able to undertake, when designated and assigned as provided in subsections (c) and (d).

(c) Any retired circuit or district judge may be designated and assigned by the chief judge or judicial council of his circuit to perform such judicial duties within the circuit as he is willing and able to undertake. Any other retired judge of the United States may be designated and assigned by the chief judge of his court to perform such judicial duties in such court as he is willing and able to undertake.

(d) The Chief Justice of the United States shall maintain a roster of retired judges of the United States who are willing and able to undertake special judicial duties from time to time outside their own circuit, in the case of a retired circuit or district judge, or in a court other than their own, in the case of other retired judges, which roster shall be known as the roster of senior judges. Any such retired judge of the United States may be designated and assigned by the Chief Justice to perform such judicial duties as he is willing and able to undertake in a court outside his own circuit, in the case of a retired circuit or district judge, or in a court other than his own, in the case of any other retired judge of the United States. Such designation and assignment to a court of appeals or district court shall be made upon the presentation of a certificate of necessity by the chief judge or circuit justice of the circuit wherein the need arises and to any other court of the United States upon the presentation of a certificate of necessity by the chief judge of such court. No such designation or assignment shall be made to the Supreme Court.

(e) No retired Justice or judge shall perform judicial duties except when designated and assigned.

(June 25, 1948, c. 646, 62 Stat. 901; July 9, 1956, c. 517, § 1(c), 70 Stat. 497; Aug. 29, 1957, Pub.L. 85–219, 71 Stat. 495; Aug. 25, 1958, Pub.L. 85–755, § 5, 72 Stat. 849; Nov. 6, 1978, Pub.L. 95–598, Title II, § 206, 92 Stat. 2660.)

HISTORICAL AND STATUTORY NOTES

Codifications

This section was amended by Pub.L. 95–598, Title II, § 206, Nov. 6, 1978, 92 Stat. 2660, effective June 28, 1984, pursuant to Pub.L. 95–598, Title IV, § 402(b), Nov. 6, 1978,

92 Stat. 2682, as amended by Pub.L. 98–249, § 1(a), Mar. 31, 1984, 98 Stat. 116; Pub.L. 98–271, § 1(a), Apr. 30, 1984, 98 Stat. 163; Pub.L. 98–299, § 1(a), May 25, 1984, 98 Stat. 214; Pub.L. 98–325, § 1(a), June 20, 1984, 98 Stat. 268, set out as a note preceding section 101 of Title II, Bankruptcy, in subsec. (c) by deleting "or district" and inserting "district or bankruptcy judge" and in subsec. (d) by striking out "or district judge" and inserting in lieu thereof ", district judge or bankruptcy judge".

Section 402(b) of Pub.L. 95–598 was amended by section 113 of Pub.L. 98–353, Title I, July 10, 1984, 98 Stat. 343, by substituting "shall not be effective" for "shall take effect on June 28, 1984", thereby eliminating the amendment by section 206 of Pub.L. 95–598, effective June 27, 1984, pursuant to section 122(c) of Pub.L. 98–353, set out as an Effective Date note under section 151 of this title.

Section 121(a) of Pub.L. 98–353 directed that section 402(b) of Pub.L. 95–598 be amended by substituting "the date of enactment of the Bankruptcy Amendments and Federal Judgeship Act of 1984 [i.e. July 10, 1984]" for "June 28, 1984". This amendment was not executed in view of the prior amendment to section 402(b) of Pub.L. 95–598 by section 113 of Pub.L. 98–353.

Jurisdiction of United States Court of Customs and Patent Appeals

Amendment by Pub.L. 85–755 not limiting or altering the jurisdiction of the United States Court of Customs and Patent Appeals [now United States Court of Appeals for the Federal Circuit], see section 7 of Pub.L. 85–755, set out as a note under section 291 of this title.

§ 295. Conditions upon designation and assignment

No designation and assignment of a circuit or district judge in active service shall be made without the consent of the chief judge or judicial council of the circuit from which the judge is to be designated and assigned. No designation and assignment of a judge of any other court of the United States in active service shall be made without the consent of the chief judge of such court.

All designations and assignments of justices and judges shall be filed with the clerks and entered on the minutes of the courts from and to which made.

The Chief Justice of the United States, a circuit justice or a chief judge of a circuit may make new designation and assignments in accordance with the provisions of this chapter and may revoke those previously made by him.

(June 25, 1948, c. 646, 62 Stat. 901; Sept. 3, 1954, c. 1263, § 39(d), 68 Stat. 1240; July 14, 1956, c. 589, § 3(b), 70 Stat. 532; Aug. 25, 1958, Pub.L. 85–755, § 6, 72 Stat. 850; Nov. 6, 1978, Pub.L. 95–598, Title II, § 207, 92 Stat. 2660.)

HISTORICAL AND STATUTORY NOTES

Codifications

This section was amended by Pub.L. 95–598, Title II, § 207, Nov. 6, 1978, 92 Stat. 2660, effective June 28, 1984, pursuant to Pub.L. 95–598, Title IV, § 402(b), Nov. 6, 1978,

92 Stat. 2682, as amended by Pub.L. 98–249, § 1(a), Mar. 31, 1984, 98 Stat. 116; Pub.L. 98–271, § 1(a), Apr. 30, 1984, 98 Stat. 163; Pub.L. 98–299, § 1(a), May 25, 1984, 98 Stat. 214; Pub.L. 98–325, § 1(a), June 20, 1984, 98 Stat. 268, set out as a note preceding section 101 of Title II, Bankruptcy, by substituting "circuit, district, or bankruptcy judge" for "circuit or district judge".

Section 402(b) of Pub.L. 95–598 was amended by section 113 of Pub.L. 98–353, Title I, July 10, 1984, 98 Stat. 343, by substituting "shall not be effective" for "shall take effect on June 28, 1984", thereby eliminating the amendment by section 207 of Pub.L. 95–598, effective June 27, 1984, pursuant to section 122(c) of Pub.L. 98–353, set out as an Effective Date note under section 151 of this title.

Section 121(a) of Pub.L. 98–353 directed that section 402(b) of Pub.L. 95–598 be amended by substituting "the date of enactment of the Bankruptcy Amendments and Federal Judgeship Act of 1984 [i.e. July 10, 1984]" for "June 28, 1984". This amendment was not executed in view of the prior amendment to section 402(b) of Pub.L. 95–598 by section 113 of Pub.L. 98–353.

Jurisdiction of United States Court of Customs and Patent Appeals

Amendment by Pub.L. 85–755 not limiting or altering the jurisdiction of the United States Court of Customs and Patent Appeals [now United States Court of Appeals for the Federal Circuit], see section 7 of Pub.L. 85–755, set out as a note under section 291 of this title.

Limitation or Alteration of Jurisdiction

Amendment by Act July 14, 1956, not to be construed as limiting or altering the jurisdiction heretofore conferred upon the Customs Court [now United States Court of International Trade], see section 4 of Act July 14, 1956, set out as a note under section 251 of this title.

§ 296. Powers upon designation and assignment

A justice or judge shall discharge, during the period of his designation and assignment, all judicial duties for which he is designated and assigned. He may be required to perform any duty which might be required of a judge of the court or district or circuit to which he is designated and assigned.

Such justice or judge shall have all the powers of a judge of the court, circuit or district to which he is designated and assigned, except the power to appoint any person to a statutory position or to designate permanently a depository of funds or a newspaper for publication of legal notices.

A justice or judge who has sat by designation and assignment in another district or circuit may, notwithstanding his absence from such district or circuit or the expiration of the period of his designation and assignment, decide or join in the decision and final disposition of all matters submitted to him during such period and in the consideration and disposition of applications for rehearing or further proceedings in such matters.

(June 25, 1948, c. 646, 62 Stat. 901.)

§ 297. Assignment of judges to courts of the freely associated compact states

(a) The Chief Justice or the chief judge of the United States Court of Appeals for the Ninth Circuit may assign any circuit or district judge of the Ninth Circuit, with the consent of the judge so assigned, to serve temporarily as a judge of any duly constituted court of the freely associated compact states whenever an official duly authorized by the laws of the respective compact state requests such assignment and such assignment is necessary for the proper dispatch of the business of the respective court.

(b) The Congress consents to the acceptance and retention by any judge so authorized of reimbursement from the countries referred to in subsection (a) of all necessary travel expenses, including transportation, and of subsistence, or of a reasonable per diem allowance in lieu of subsistence. The judge shall report to the Administrative Office of the United States Courts any amount received pursuant to this subsection.

(Added Pub.L. 100–702, Title X, § 1022(1), Nov. 19, 1988, 102 Stat. 4672.)

CHAPTER 15—CONFERENCES AND COUNCILS OF JUDGES

§ 331. Judicial Conference of the United States

The Chief Justice of the United States shall summon annually the chief judge of each judicial circuit, the chief judge of the Court of International Trade, and a district judge from each judicial circuit to a conference at such time and place in the United States as he may designate. He shall preside at such conference which shall be known as the Judicial Conference of the United States. Special sessions of the Conference may be called by the Chief Justice at such times and places as he may designate.

The district judge to be summoned from each judicial circuit shall be chosen by the circuit and district judges of the circuit and shall serve as a member of the Judicial Conference of the United States for a term of not less than 3 successive years nor more than 5 successive years, as established by majority vote of

all circuit and district judges of the circuit. A district judge serving as a member of the Judicial Conference may be either a judge in regular active service or a judge retired from regular active service under section 371(b) of this title.

If the chief judge of any circuit, the chief judge of the Court of International Trade, or the district judge chosen by the judges of the circuit is unable to attend, the Chief Justice may summon any other circuit or district judge from such circuit or any other judge of the Court of International Trade, as the case may be. Every judge summoned shall attend and, unless excused by the Chief Justice, shall remain throughout the sessions of the conference and advise as to the needs of his circuit or court and as to any matters in respect of which the administration of justice in the courts of the United States may be improved.

The Conference shall make a comprehensive survey of the condition of business in the courts of the United States and prepare plans for assignment of judges to or from circuits or districts where necessary. It shall also submit suggestions and recommendations to the various courts to promote uniformity of management procedures and the expeditious conduct of court business. The Conference is authorized to exercise the authority provided in chapter 16 of this title as the Conference, or through a standing committee. If the Conference elects to establish a standing committee, it shall be appointed by the Chief Justice and all petitions for review shall be reviewed by that committee. The Conference or the standing committee may hold hearings, take sworn testimony, issue subpoenas and subpoenas duces tecum, and make necessary and appropriate orders in the exercise of its authority. Subpoenas and subpoenas duces tecum shall be issued by the clerk of the Supreme Court or by the clerk of any court of appeals, at the direction of the Chief Justice or his designee and under the seal of the court, and shall be served in the manner provided in rule 45(c) of the Federal Rules of Civil Procedure for subpoenas and subpoenas duces tecum issued on behalf of the United States or an officer or any agency thereof. The Conference may also prescribe and modify rules for the exercise of the authority provided in chapter 16 of this title. All judicial officers and employees of the United States shall promptly carry into effect all orders of the Judicial Conference or the standing committee established pursuant to this section.

The Conference shall also carry on a continuous study of the operation and effect of the general rules of practice and procedure now or hereafter in use as prescribed by the Supreme Court for the other courts of the United States pursuant to law. Such changes in and additions to those rules as the Conference may deem desirable to promote simplicity in procedure, fairness in administration, the just determination of litigation, and the elimination of unjustified expense and delay shall be recommended by the Conference from time to time to the Supreme Court for its consideration and adoption, modification or rejection, in accordance with law.

The Judicial Conference shall review rules prescribed under section 2071 of this title by the courts, other than the Supreme Court and the district courts, for consistency with Federal law. The Judicial Conference may modify or abrogate any such rule so reviewed found inconsistent in the course of such a review.

The Attorney General shall, upon request of the Chief Justice, report to such Conference on matters relating to the business of the several courts of the United States, with particular reference to cases to which the United States is a party.

The Chief Justice shall submit to Congress an annual report of the proceedings of the Judicial Conference and its recommendations for legislation.
(June 25, 1948, c. 646, 62 Stat. 902; July 9, 1956, c. 517, § 1(d), 70 Stat. 497; Aug. 28, 1957, Pub.L. 85–202, 71 Stat. 476; July 11, 1958, Pub.L. 85–513, 72 Stat. 356; Sept. 19, 1961, Pub.L. 87–253, §§ 1, 2, 75 Stat. 521; Nov. 6, 1978, Pub.L. 95–598, Title II, § 208, 92 Stat. 2660; Oct. 15, 1980, Pub.L. 96–458, § 4, 94 Stat. 2040; Apr. 2, 1982, Pub.L. 97–164, Title I, § 111, 96 Stat. 29; Oct. 14, 1986, Pub.L. 99–466, § 1, 100 Stat. 1190; Nov. 19, 1988, Pub.L. 100–702, Title IV, § 402(b), 102 Stat. 4650; Oct. 19, 1996, Pub.L. 104–317, Title VI, § 601(a), 110 Stat. 3857; Nov. 2, 2002, Pub.L. 107–273, Div. C, Title I, § 110403(b), 116 Stat. 1855.)

HISTORICAL AND STATUTORY NOTES

References in Text

Rule 45(c) of the Federal Rules of Civil Procedure, referred to in fourth undesignated paragraph, means rule 45(c), Federal Rules of Civil Procedure, set out in this title.

Codifications

The first three paragraphs of this section were amended by Pub.L. 95–598, Title II, § 208, Nov. 6, 1978, 92 Stat. 2660, effective June 28, 1984, pursuant to Pub.L. 95–598, Title IV, § 402(b), Nov. 6, 1978, 92 Stat. 2682, as amended by Pub.L. 98–249, § 1(a), Mar. 31, 1984, 98 Stat. 116; Pub.L. 98–271, § 1(a), Apr. 30, 1984, 98 Stat. 163; Pub.L. 98–299, § 1(a), May 25, 1984, 98 Stat. 214; Pub.L. 98–325, § 1(a), June 20, 1984, 98 Stat. 268, set out as a note preceding section 101 of Title II, Bankruptcy, to read as follows:

"The Chief Justice of the United States shall summon annually the chief judge of each judicial circuit, a district judge for each judicial circuit, and two bankruptcy judges to a conference at such time and place in the United States as he may designate. He shall preside at such conference which shall be known as the Judicial Conference of the United States. Special sessions of the conference may be called by the Chief Justice at such times and places as he may designate.

"The district judge to be summoned from each judicial circuit shall be chosen by the circuit and district judges of the circuit at the annual judicial conference of the circuit held

pursuant to section 333 of this title and shall serve as a member of the conference for three successive years, except that in the year following the enactment of this amended section the circuit and district judges of the first, fourth, seventh, and tenth circuits shall choose a district judge to serve for one year, the circuit and district judges in the second, fifth, and eighth circuits shall choose a district judge to serve for two years and the circuit and district judges in the third, sixth, ninth, and District of Columbia circuits shall choose a district judge to serve for three years. The bankruptcy judges to be summoned shall be chosen at large by all the bankruptcy judges. Each bankruptcy judge chosen shall serve as a member of the conference for three successive years, except that in the year following the effective date of this sentence the bankruptcy judges shall choose one bankruptcy judge to serve for two years.

"If the chief judge of any circuit or the district judge chosen by the judges of the circuit or a bankruptcy judge chosen by the bankruptcy judges is unable to attend, the Chief Justice may summon any other circuit or district judge from such circuit or any other bankruptcy judge. Every judge summoned shall attend and, unless excused by the Chief Justice, shall remain throughout the sessions of the conference and advise as to the needs of his circuit or court and as to any matters in respect of which the administration of justice in the courts of the United States may be improved."

Section 402(b) of Pub.L. 95–598 was amended by section 113 of Pub.L. 98–353, Title I, July 10, 1984, 98 Stat. 343, by substituting "shall not be effective" for "shall take effect on June 28, 1984", thereby eliminating the amendment by section 208 of Pub.L. 95–598, effective June 27, 1984, pursuant to section 122(c) of Pub.L. 98–353, set out as an Effective and Applicability Provisions note under 28 U.S.C.A. § 151.

Section 121(a) of Pub.L. 98–353 directed that section 402(b) of Pub.L. 95–598 be amended by substituting "the date of enactment of the Bankruptcy Amendments and Federal Judgeship Act of 1984 [i.e. July 10, 1984]" for "June 28, 1984". This amendment was not executed in view of the prior amendment to section 402(b) of Pub.L. 95–598 by section 113 of Pub.L. 98–353.

Effective and Applicability Provisions

1988 Acts

Amendment by Pub.L. 100–702 effective Dec. 1, 1988, see section 407 of Pub.L. 100–702, set out as a note under section 2071 of this title.

1986 Acts

Section 4 of Pub.L. 99–466 provided that: "This Act and the amendments made by this Act [enacting section 335 of this title, amending this section and section 569 of this title, repealing former section 872 of this title, and redesignating section 873 of this title as 872] shall take effect 60 days after the date of the enactment of this Act [Oct. 14, 1986]."

1982 Acts

Amendment by Pub.L. 97–164 effective Oct. 1, 1982, see section 402 of Pub.L. 97–164, set out as a note under section 171 of this title.

1980 Acts

Section 7 of Pub.L. 96–458 provided that: "This Act [amending this section and sections 332, 372 and 604 of this title, and enacting provisions set out as notes under this

section and section 1 of this title] shall become effective on October 1, 1981".

Termination of Reporting Requirements

For termination, effective May 15, 2000, of provisions in this section relating to requirement that the Chief Justice submit to Congress an annual report of proceedings of the Judicial Conference and recommendations for legislation, see Pub.L. 104–66, § 3003, as amended, set out as a note under 31 U.S.C.A. § 1113 and page 13 of House Document No. 103–7.

Deposit and Use of Fees for Processing Violations Through Central Violations Bureau Cases

Pub.L. 108–447, Div. B, Title III, § 308, Dec. 8, 2004, 118 Stat. 2895, as amended Pub.L. 109–13, Div. A, Title VI, § 6066, May 11, 2005, 119 Stat. 299, provided that: "For fiscal year 2005 and hereafter, such fees as shall be collected for the processing of violations through the Central Violations Bureau cases as prescribed by the Judicial Conference of the United States shall be deposited as offsetting receipts to the fund established under 28 U.S.C. 1931 and shall remain available to the Judiciary until expended to reimburse any appropriation for the amount paid out of such appropriation for expenses of the Courts of Appeals, District Courts, and Other Judicial Services and the Administrative Offices of the United States Courts."

Authorization of Appropriations

Section 6 of Pub.L. 96–458 provided that: "There are authorized to be appropriated such sums as may be necessary to carry out the provisions of this Act [amending this section and sections 332, 372 and 604 of this title, and enacting provisions set out as notes under this section and section 1 of this title]."

Federal Courts Study Committee

Pub.L. 100–702, Title I, Nov. 19, 1988, 102 Stat. 4644, provided that:

"Sec. 101. Short title.

"This title may be cited as the 'Federal Courts Study Act'.

"Sec. 102. Establishment and purposes.

"(a) Establishment.—There is hereby established within the Judicial Conference of the United States, a Federal Courts Study Committee on the future of the Federal judiciary (hereafter referred to as the 'Committee').

"(b) Purposes.—The purposes of the Committee are to—

"(1) examine problems and issues currently facing the courts of the United States;

"(2) develop a long-range plan for the future of the Federal judiciary, including assessments involving—

"(A) alternative methods of dispute resolution;

"(B) the structure and administration of the Federal court system;

"(C) methods of resolving intracircuit and intercircuit conflicts in the courts of appeals; and

"(D) the types of disputes resolved by the Federal courts; and

"(3) report to the Judicial Conference of the United States, the President, the Congress, the Conference of Chief Justices, and the State Justice Institute on the revisions, if any, in the laws of the United States which the

Committee, based on its study and evaluation, deems advisable.

"Sec. 103. Membership of the Committee.

"(a) **Appointments.**—The Committee shall be composed of fifteen members to be appointed by the Chief Justice of the United States, within ten days after the effective date of this title [Jan. 1, 1989].

"(b) **Selection.**—The membership of the Committee shall be selected in such a manner as to be representative of the various interests, needs and concerns which may be affected by the jurisdiction of the Federal courts. The Chief Justice shall designate one of the members of the Committee to serve as Chairman.

"(c) **Term of Office.**—The Committee members shall serve at the pleasure of the Chief Justice.

"(d) **Rules of Procedure.**—Rules of procedure shall be promulgated by vote of a majority of the Committee.

"Sec. 104. Powers of the Committee.

"(a) **Hearings.**—The Committee or, on the authorization of the Committee, any subcommittee thereof may, for the purpose of carrying out its functions and duties, hold such hearings and sit and act at such times and places, as the Committee or any such subcommittee may deem advisable.

"(b) **Information and assistance.**—The Administrative Office of the United States Courts, the Federal Judicial Center, and each department, agency, and instrumentality of the executive branch of the Government, including the National Institute of Justice and independent agencies, shall furnish to the Committee, upon request made by the Chairman, such information and assistance as the Committee may reasonably deem necessary to carry out its functions under this title [Title I of Pub.L. 100–702], consistent with other applicable provisions of law governing the release of such information.

"(c) **Personnel.**—(1) Subject to such rules and regulations as may be adopted by the Committee, the Director of the Administrative Office shall furnish to the Committee necessary staff and technical assistance in response to needs specified.

"(2) [Amendment of section 5108(c)(1) of Title 5, Government Organization and Employees.]

"(d) **Advisory Panels.**—The Committee is authorized, for the purpose of carrying out its functions and duties pursuant to the provisions of this title [Title I of Pub.L. 100–702], to establish advisory panels consisting of Committee members or members of the public. Such panels shall be established to provide expertise and assistance in specific areas, as the Committee deems necessary.

"Sec. 105. Functions and duties.

"The Committee shall—

"(1) make a complete study of the courts of the United States and of the several States and transmit a report to the President, the Chief Justice of the United States, the Congress, the Judicial Conference of the United States, the Conference of Chief Justices, and the State Justice Institute on such study, within fifteen months after the effective date of this title [Jan. 1. 1989];

"(2) recommend revisions to be made to laws of the United States as the Committee, on the basis of such study, deems advisable;

"(3) develop a long-range plan for the judicial system; and

"(4) make such other recommendations and conclusions it deems advisable.

"Sec. 106. Compensation of members.

"(a) **Employees of the Government.**—A member of the Committee who is an officer or full-time employee of the United States shall receive no additional compensation for his or her services, but shall be reimbursed for travel, subsistence, and other necessary expenses incurred in the performance of duties vested in the Committee, not to exceed the maximum amounts authorized under section 456 of title 28 [section 456 of this title].

"(b) **Private Sector.**—A member of the Committee who is from the private sector shall receive $200 per diem for each day (including travel time) during which he or she is engaged in the actual performance of duties vested in the Committee, plus reimbursement for travel, subsistence, and other necessary expenses incurred in the performance of such duties, not to exceed the maximum amounts authorized under section 456 of title 28 [section 456 of this title].

"Sec. 107. Expiration of the Committee.

"The Committee shall cease to exist on the date 60 days after it transmits the report pursuant to section 105.

"Sec. 108. Authorization of appropriations.

"To carry out the purposes of this title [Title I of Pub.L. 100–702] there are authorized to be appropriated $300,000 for each of the fiscal years 1989 and 1990.

"Sec. 109. Effective date.

"This title [Title I of Pub.L. 100–702] shall become effective on January 1, 1989."

Policies, Procedures, and Methodologies Used in Recommendation For Creation of Additional Federal Judgeships; Study by General Accounting Office [now Government Accountability Office] and Report to Congress

Pub.L. 101–650, Title II, § 205, Dec. 1, 1990, 104 Stat. 5103, provided that:

"(a) **In general.**—The Comptroller General of the United States shall review the policies, procedures, and methodologies used by the Judicial Conference of the United States in recommending to the Congress the creation of additional Federal judgeships. In conducting such review the Comptroller General shall, at a minimum, determine the extent to which such policies, procedures, and methodologies—

"(1) provide an accurate measure of the workload of existing judges;

"(2) are applied consistently to the various circuit courts of appeals and district courts; and

"(3) provide an accurate indicator of the need for additional judgeships.

"(b) **Report to Congress.**—The Comptroller General shall, not later than 18 months after the date of the enactment of this Act [Dec. 1, 1990], report the results of the review conducted under subsection (a) to the Committees on the Judiciary of the House of Representatives and the Senate. The report shall include such recommendations as the Comptroller General considers appropriate for revisions of the policies, procedures, and methodologies used by the Judicial Conference that were reviewed in the report."

§ 332. Judicial councils of circuits

(a)(1) The chief judge of each judicial circuit shall call, at least twice in each year and at such places as he or she may designate, a meeting of the judicial council of the circuit, consisting of the chief judge of the circuit, who shall preside, and an equal number of circuit judges and district judges of the circuit, as such number is determined by majority vote of all such judges of the circuit in regular active service.

(2) Members of the council shall serve for terms established by a majority vote of all judges of the circuit in regular active service.

(3) Except for the chief judge of the circuit, either judges in regular active service or judges retired from regular active service under section 371(b) of this title may serve as members of the council. Service as a member of a judicial council by a judge retired from regular active service under section 371(b) may not be considered for meeting the requirements of section 371(f)(1) (A), (B), or (C).

(4) No more than one district judge from any one district shall serve simultaneously on the council, unless at least one district judge from each district within the circuit is already serving as a member of the council.

(5) In the event of the death, resignation, retirement under section 371(a) or 372(a) of this title, or disability of a member of the council, a replacement member shall be designated to serve the remainder of the unexpired term by the chief judge of the circuit.

(6) Each member of the council shall attend each council meeting unless excused by the chief judge of the circuit.

(b) The council shall be known as the Judicial Council of the circuit.

(c) The chief judge shall submit to the council the semiannual reports of the Director of the Administrative Office of the United States Courts. The council shall take such action thereon as may be necessary.

(d)(1) Each judicial council shall make all necessary and appropriate orders for the effective and expeditious administration of justice within its circuit. Any general order relating to practice and procedure shall be made or amended only after giving appropriate public notice and an opportunity for comment. Any such order so relating shall take effect upon the date specified by such judicial council. Copies of such orders so relating shall be furnished to the Judicial Conference and the Administrative Office of the United States Courts and be made available to the public. Each council is authorized to hold hearings, to take sworn testimony, and to issue subpoenas and subpoenas duces tecum. Subpoenas and subpoenas duces tecum shall be issued by the clerk of the court of appeals, at the direction of the chief judge of the

circuit or his designee and under the seal of the court, and shall be served in the manner provided in rule 45(c) of the Federal Rules of Civil Procedure for subpoenas and subpoenas duces tecum issued on behalf of the United States or an officer or agency thereof.

(2) All judicial officers and employees of the circuit shall promptly carry into effect all orders of the judicial council. In the case of failure to comply with an order made under this subsection or a subpoena issued under chapter 16 of this title, a judicial council or a special committee appointed under section 353 of this title may institute a contempt proceeding in any district court in which the judicial officer or employee of the circuit who fails to comply with the order made under this subsection shall be ordered to show cause before the court why he or she should not be held in contempt of court.

(3) Unless an impediment to the administration of justice is involved, regular business of the courts need not be referred to the council.

(4) Each judicial council shall periodically review the rules which are prescribed under section 2071 of this title by district courts within its circuit for consistency with rules prescribed under section 2072 of this title. Each council may modify or abrogate any such rule found inconsistent in the course of such a review.

(e) The judicial council of each circuit may appoint a circuit executive. In appointing a circuit executive, the judicial council shall take into account experience in administrative and executive positions, familiarity with court procedures, and special training. The circuit executive shall exercise such administrative powers and perform such duties as may be delegated to him by the circuit council. The duties delegated to the circuit executive of each circuit may include but need not be limited to:

(1) Exercising administrative control of all nonjudicial activities of the court of appeals of the circuit in which he is appointed.

(2) Administering the personnel system of the court of appeals of the circuit.

(3) Administering the budget of the court of appeals of the circuit.

(4) Maintaining a modern accounting system.

(5) Establishing and maintaining property control records and undertaking a space management program.

(6) Conducting studies relating to the business and administration of the courts within the circuit and preparing appropriate recommendations and reports to the chief judge, the circuit council, and the Judicial Conference.

(7) Collecting, compiling, and analyzing statistical data with a view to the preparation and presentation of reports based on such data as may be directed by the chief judge, the circuit council, and the Administrative Office of the United States Courts.

(8) Representing the circuit as its liaison to the courts of the various States in which the circuit is located, the marshal's office, State and local bar associations, civic groups, news media, and other private and public groups having a reasonable interest in the administration of the circuit.

(9) Arranging and attending meetings of the judges of the circuit and of the circuit council, including preparing the agenda and serving as secretary in all such meetings.

(10) Preparing an annual report to the circuit and to the Administrative Office of the United States Courts for the preceding calendar year, including recommendations for more expeditious disposition of the business of the circuit.

All duties delegated to the circuit executive shall be subject to the general supervision of the chief judge of the circuit.

(f)(1) Each circuit executive shall be paid at a salary to be established by the Judicial Conference of the United States not to exceed the annual rate of level IV of the Executive Schedule pay rates under section 5315 of title 5.

(2) The circuit executive shall serve at the pleasure of the judicial council of the circuit.

(3) The circuit executive may appoint, with the approval of the council, necessary employees in such number as may be approved by the Director of the Administrative Office of the United States Courts.

(4) The circuit executive and his staff shall be deemed to be officers and employees of the judicial branch of the United States Government within the meaning of subchapter III of chapter 83 (relating to civil service retirement), chapter 87 (relating to Federal employees' life insurance program), and chapter 89 (relating to Federal employees' health benefits program) of title 5, United States Code.

(g) No later than January 31 of each year, each judicial council shall submit a report to the Administrative Office of the United States Courts on the number and nature of orders entered under this section during the preceding calendar year that relate to judicial misconduct or disability.

(h)(1) The United States Court of Appeals for the Federal Circuit may appoint a circuit executive, who shall serve at the pleasure of the court. In appointing a circuit executive, the court shall take into account experience in administrative and executive positions, familiarity with court procedures, and special training.

The circuit executive shall exercise such administrative powers and perform such duties as may be delegated by the court. The duties delegated to the circuit executive may include the duties specified in subsection (e) of this section, insofar as such duties are applicable to the Court of Appeals for the Federal Circuit.

(2) The circuit executive shall be paid the salary for circuit executives established under subsection (f) of this section.

(3) The circuit executive may appoint, with the approval of the court, necessary employees in such number as may be approved by the Director of the Administrative Office of the United States Courts.

(4) The circuit executive and staff shall be deemed to be officers and employees of the United States within the meaning of the statutes specified in subsection (f)(4).

(5) The court may appoint either a circuit executive under this subsection or a clerk under section 711 of this title, but not both, or may appoint a combined circuit executive/clerk who shall be paid the salary of a circuit executive.

(June 25, 1948, c. 646, 62 Stat. 902; Nov. 13, 1963, Pub.L. 88–176, § 3, 77 Stat. 331; Jan. 5, 1971, Pub.L. 91–647, 84 Stat. 1907; Nov. 6, 1978, Pub.L. 95–598, Title II, § 209, 92 Stat. 2661; Oct. 15, 1980, Pub.L. 96–458, § 2(a) to (d)(1), 94 Stat. 2035, 2036; Oct. 1, 1988, Pub.L. 100–459, Title IV, § 407, 102 Stat. 2213; Nov. 19, 1988, Pub.L. 100–702, Title IV, § 403(a)(2), (b), Title X, §§ 1018, 1020(a)(1), 102 Stat. 4651, 4670, 4671; Dec. 1, 1990, Pub.L. 101–650, Title III, §§ 323, 325(b)(1), Title IV, § 403, 104 Stat. 5120, 5121, 5124; Dec. 9, 1991, Pub.L. 102–198, § 1, 105 Stat. 1623; Oct. 19, 1996, Pub.L. 104–317, Title II, § 208, 110 Stat. 3851; Nov. 13, 2000, Pub.L. 106–518, Title II, § 205, Title III, § 306, 114 Stat. 2414, 2418; Dec. 21, 2000, Pub.L. 106–553, § 1(a)(2) [Title III, § 306], 114 Stat. 2762, 2762A–85; Nov. 2, 2002, Pub.L. 107–273, Div. C, Title I, § 11043(c), 116 Stat. 1855.)

HISTORICAL AND STATUTORY NOTES

References in Text

Section 371(f) of this title, referred to in subsec. (a)(3), was redesignated section 28 U.S.C.A. §371(e) Pub.L. 106–398, § 1 [Div. A, Title VI, Sec. 654(a)(1)(B)], Oct. 30, 2000, 114 Stat. 1654, 1654A–165.

Rule 45(c) of the Federal Rules of Civil Procedure, referred to in subsec. (d)(1), is rule 45(c) of the Federal Rules of Civil Procedure, set out in this title.

Codifications

Subsec. (d) of this section was amended by Pub.L. 95–598, Title II, § 209, Nov. 6, 1978, 92 Stat. 2661, effective June 28, 1984, pursuant to Pub.L. 95–598, Title IV, § 402(b), Nov. 6, 1978, 92 Stat. 2682, as amended by Pub.L. 98–249, § 1(a), Mar. 31, 1984, 98 Stat. 116; Pub.L. 98–271, § 1(a), Apr. 30, 1984, 98 Stat. 163; Pub.L. 98–299, § 1(a), May 25, 1984, 98 Stat. 214; Pub.L. 98–325, § 1(a), June 20, 1984, 98 Stat. 268, set out as a note preceding section 101 of Title 11, Bankrupt-

cy, by inserting "and bankruptcy judges" following "The district judges".

Section 402(b) of Pub.L. 95–598 was amended by section 113 of Pub.L. 98–353, Title I, July 10, 1984, 98 Stat. 343, by substituting "shall not be effective" for "shall take effect on June 28, 1984", thereby eliminating the amendment by section 209 of Pub.L. 95–598, effective June 27, 1984, pursuant to section 122(c) of Pub.L. 98–353, set out as an Effective Date note under section 151 of this title.

Section 121(a) of Pub.L. 98–353 directed that section 402(b) of Pub.L. 95–598 be amended by substituting "the date of enactment of the Bankruptcy Amendments and Federal Judgeship Act of 1984 [i.e. July 10, 1984]" for "June 28, 1984". This amendment was not executed in view of the prior amendment to section 402(b) of Pub.L. 95–598 by section 113 of Pub.L. 98–353.

Effective and Applicability Provisions

1990 Acts

Section 407 of Pub.L. 101–650 provided that: "The amendments made by this subtitle [subtitle I of Title IV of Pub.L. 101–650, amending this section and sections 372, 453, and 2077 of this title and section 104 of Appendix 6 to Title 5, Government Organization and Employees] shall take effect 90 days after the date of the enactment of this Act [Dec. 1, 1990]."

1988 Acts

Amendment of subsec. (d)(1) and enactment of subsec. (d)(4) by Pub.L. 100–702 effective Dec. 1, 1988, see section 407 of Pub.L. 100–702, set out as a note under section 2071 of this title.

1980 Acts

Amendment by Pub.L. 96–458 effective Oct. 1, 1981, see section 7 of Pub.L. 96–458, set out as a note under section 331 of this title.

§ 333. Judicial conferences of circuits

The chief judge of each circuit may summon biennially, and may summon annually, the circuit, district, and bankruptcy judges of the circuit, in active service, to a conference at a time and place that he designates, for the purpose of considering the business of the courts and advising means of improving the administration of justice within such circuit. He may preside at such conference, which shall be known as the Judicial Conference of the circuit. The judges of the District Court of Guam, the District Court of the Virgin Islands, and the District Court of the Northern Mariana Islands may also be summoned biennially, and may be summoned annually, to the conferences of their respective circuits.

Every judge summoned may attend.

The court of appeals for each circuit shall provide by its rules for representation and active participation at such conference by members of the bar of such circuit.

(June 25, 1948, c. 646, 62 Stat. 903; Dec. 29, 1950, c. 1185, 64 Stat. 1128; Oct. 31, 1951, c. 655, § 38, 65 Stat. 723; July 7, 1958, Pub.L. 85–508, § 12(e), 72 Stat. 348; Nov. 6, 1978,

Pub.L. 95–598, Title II, § 210, 92 Stat. 2661; Dec. 1, 1990, Pub.L. 101–650, Title III, § 320, 104 Stat. 5117; Apr. 26, 1996, Pub.L. 104–134, Title I, § 101[(a)][Title III, § 305], 110 Stat. 1321–36; renumbered Title I May 2, 1996, Pub.L. 104–140, § 1(a), 110 Stat. 1327.)

HISTORICAL AND STATUTORY NOTES
Effective and Applicability Provisions

1978 Acts

Amendment by Pub.L. 95–598 effective Oct. 1, 1979, see section 402(c) of Pub.L. 95–598, as amended, set out as an Effective Date note preceding section 101 of Title 11, Bankruptcy.

1958 Acts

Amendment by Pub.L. 85–508 effective Jan. 3, 1959, upon admission of Alaska into the Union pursuant to Proc. No. 3269, Jan. 31, 1959, 24 F.R. 81, 73 Stat. c16, as required by sections 1 and 8(c) of Pub.L. 85–508, see notes set out under section 81A of this title and preceding section 21 of Title 48, Territories and Insular Possessions.

Termination of United States District Court for the District of the Canal Zone

For termination of the United States District Court for the District of the Canal Zone at end of the "transition period", being the 30–month period beginning Oct. 1, 1979, and ending midnight Mar. 31, 1982, see Paragraph 5 of Article XI of the Panama Canal Treaty of 1977 and sections 3831 and 3841 to 3843 of Title 22, Foreign Relations and Intercourse.

§ 334. Institutes and joint councils on sentencing

(a) In the interest of uniformity in sentencing procedures, there is hereby authorized to be established under the auspices of the Judicial Conference of the United States, institutes and joint councils on sentencing. The Attorney General and/or the chief judge of each circuit may at any time request, through the Director of the Administrative Office of the United States Courts, the Judicial Conference to convene such institutes and joint councils for the purpose of studying, discussing, and formulating the objectives, policies, standards, and criteria for sentencing those convicted of crimes and offenses in the courts of the United States. The agenda of the institutes and joint councils may include but shall not be limited to: (1) The development of standards for the content and utilization of presentence reports; (2) the establishment of factors to be used in selecting cases for special study and observation in prescribed diagnostic clinics; (3) the determination of the importance of psychiatric, emotional, sociological and physiological factors involved in crime and their bearing upon sentences; (4) the discussion of special sentencing problems in unusual cases such as treason, violation of public trust, subversion, or involving abnormal sex behavior, addiction to drugs or alcohol, and mental or physical handicaps; (5) the formulation of sentencing principles and criteria which will assist in promoting

the equitable administration of the criminal laws of the United States.

(b) After the Judicial Conference has approved the time, place, participants, agenda, and other arrangements for such institutes and joint councils, the chief judge of each circuit is authorized to invite the attendance of district judges under conditions which he thinks proper and which will not unduly delay the work of the courts.

(c) The Attorney General is authorized to select and direct the attendance at such institutes and meetings of United States attorneys and other officials of the Department of Justice and may invite the participation of other interested Federal officers. He may also invite specialists in sentencing methods, criminologists, psychiatrists, penologists, and others to participate in the proceedings.

(d) The expenses of attendance of judges shall be paid from applicable appropriations for the judiciary of the United States. The expenses connected with the preparation of the plans and agenda for the conference and for the travel and other expenses incident to the attendance of officials and other participants invited by the Attorney General shall be paid from applicable appropriations of the Department of Justice.

(Added Pub.L. 85–752, § 1, Aug. 25, 1958, 72 Stat. 845.)

HISTORICAL AND STATUTORY NOTES

Sentencing Procedures

Section 7 of Pub.L. 85–752 provided that: "This Act [adding this section and sections 4208 and 4209 of Title 18, Crimes and Criminal Procedure, and provisions set out as a note under section 4208 of Title 18] does not apply to any offense for which there is provided a mandatory penalty."

§ 335. Judicial Conference of the Court of International Trade

(a) The chief judge of the Court of International Trade is authorized to summon annually the judges of such court to a judicial conference, at a time and place that such chief judge designates, for the purpose of considering the business of such court and improvements in the administration of justice in such court.

(b) The Court of International Trade shall provide by its rules for representation and active participation at such conference by members of the bar.

(Added Pub.L. 99–466, § 2(a), Oct. 14, 1986, 100 Stat. 1190.)

HISTORICAL AND STATUTORY NOTES

Effective and Applicability Provisions

1986 Acts

Section effective 60 days after Oct. 14, 1986, see section 4 of Pub.L. 99–466, set out as a note under section 331 of this title.

CHAPTER 17—RESIGNATION AND RETIREMENT OF JUSTICES AND JUDGES

Sec.
371. Retirement on salary; retirement in senior status.
372. Retirement for disability; substitute judge on failure to retire.
373. Judges in Territories and Possessions.[1]
374. Residence of retired judges; official station.
375. Recall of certain judges and magistrate judges.
376. Annuities for survivors of certain judicial officials of the United States.
377. Retirement of bankruptcy judges and magistrates.

[1] Section catchline amended by Pub.L. 99–396 without corresponding amendment of analysis.

HISTORICAL AND STATUTORY NOTES

Change of Name

"United States magistrate judge" substituted for "United States magistrate" in item 375 pursuant to section 321 of Pub.L. 101–650, set out as a note under 28 U.S.C.A. § 631.

§ 371. Retirement on salary; retirement in senior status

(a) Any justice or judge of the United States appointed to hold office during good behavior may retire from the office after attaining the age and meeting the service requirements, whether continuous or otherwise, of subsection (c) and shall, during the remainder of his lifetime, receive an annuity equal to the salary he was receiving at the time he retired.

(b)(1) Any justice or judge of the United States appointed to hold office during good behavior may retain the office but retire from regular active service after attaining the age and meeting the service requirements, whether continuous or otherwise, of subsection (c) of this section and shall, during the remainder of his or her lifetime, continue to receive the salary of the office if he or she meets the requirements of subsection (e).

(2) In a case in which a justice or judge who retires under paragraph (1) does not meet the requirements of subsection (e), the justice or judge shall continue to receive the salary that he or she was receiving when he or she was last in active service or, if a certification under subsection (e) was made for such justice or judge, when such a certification was last in effect. The salary of such justice or judge shall be adjusted under section 461 of this title.

(c) The age and service requirements for retirement under this section are as follows:

Attained Age:	Years of Service:
65	15

Attained Age:	Years of Service:
66	14
67	13
68	12
69	11
70	10

(d) The President shall appoint, by and with the advice and consent of the Senate, a successor to a justice or judge who retires under this section.

(e)(1) In order to continue receiving the salary of the office under subsection (b), a justice must be certified in each calendar year by the Chief Justice, and a judge must be certified by the chief judge of the circuit in which the judge sits, as having met the requirements set forth in at least one of the following subparagraphs:

(A) The justice or judge must have carried in the preceding calendar year a caseload involving courtroom participation which is equal to or greater than the amount of work involving courtroom participation which an average judge in active service would perform in three months. In the instance of a justice or judge who has sat on both district courts and courts of appeals, the caseload of appellate work and trial work shall be determined separately and the results of those determinations added together for purposes of this paragraph.

(B) The justice or judge performed in the preceding calendar year substantial judicial duties not involving courtroom participation under subparagraph (A), including settlement efforts, motion decisions, writing opinions in cases that have not been orally argued, and administrative duties for the court to which the justice or judge is assigned. Any certification under this subparagraph shall include a statement describing in detail the nature and amount of work and certifying that the work done is equal to or greater than the work described in this subparagraph which an average judge in active service would perform in three months.

(C) The justice or judge has, in the preceding calendar year, performed work described in subparagraphs (A) and (B) in an amount which, when calculated in accordance with such subparagraphs, in the aggregate equals at least 3 months work.

(D) The justice or judge has, in the preceding calendar year, performed substantial administrative duties directly related to the operation of the courts, or has performed substantial duties for a Federal or State governmental entity. A certification under this subparagraph shall specify that the work done is equal to the full-time work of an employee of the judicial branch. In any year in which a justice or judge performs work described under this subpara-

graph for less than the full year, one-half of such work may be aggregated with work described under subparagraph (A), (B), or (C) of this paragraph for the purpose of the justice or judge satisfying the requirements of such subparagraph.

(E) The justice or judge was unable in the preceding calendar year to perform judicial or administrative work to the extent required by any of subparagraphs (A) through (D) because of a temporary or permanent disability. A certification under this subparagraph shall be made to a justice who certifies in writing his or her disability to the Chief Justice, and to a judge who certifies in writing his or her disability to the chief judge of the circuit in which the judge sits. A justice or judge who is certified under this subparagraph as having a permanent disability shall be deemed to have met the requirements of this subsection for each calendar year thereafter.

(2) Determinations of work performed under subparagraphs (A), (B), (C), and (D) of paragraph (1) shall be made pursuant to rules promulgated by the Judicial Conference of the United States. In promulgating such criteria, the Judicial Conference shall take into account existing standards promulgated by the Conference for allocation of space and staff for senior judges.

(3) If in any year a justice or judge who retires under subsection (b) does not receive a certification under this subsection (except as provided in paragraph (1)(E)), he or she may thereafter receive a certification for that year by satisfying the requirements of subparagraph (A), (B), (C), or (D) of paragraph (1) of this subsection in a subsequent year and attributing a sufficient part of the work performed in such subsequent year to the earlier year so that the work so attributed, when added to the work performed during such earlier year, satisfies the requirements for certification for that year. However, a justice or judge may not receive credit for the same work for purposes of certification for more than 1 year.

(4) In the case of any justice or judge who retires under subsection (b) during a calendar year, there shall be included in the determination under this subsection of work performed during that calendar year all work performed by that justice or judge (as described in subparagraphs (A), (B), (C), and (D) of paragraph (1)) during that calendar year before such retirement.

(June 25, 1948, c. 646, 62 Stat. 903; Oct. 31, 1951, c. 655, § 39, 65 Stat. 724; Feb. 10, 1954, c. 6, § 4(a), 68 Stat. 12; July 10, 1984, Pub.L. 98–353, Title II, § 204(a), 98 Stat. 350; Nov. 19, 1988, Pub.L. 100–702, Title X, § 1005(a), 102 Stat. 4666; Nov. 30, 1989, Pub.L. 101–194, Title VII, § 705(a), 103 Stat. 1770; Oct. 19, 1996, Pub.L. 104–317, Title III, § 301, 110 Stat. 3851; Oct. 30, 2000, Pub.L. 106–398, § 1 [Div. A,

Title VI, § 654(a)], 114 Stat. 1654, 1654A–165; Nov. 13, 2000, Pub.L. 106–518, Title III, § 303, 114 Stat. 2417.)

HISTORICAL AND STATUTORY NOTES

Codifications

Pub.L. 106–518, § 303, purported to amend subsec. (e) by inserting ", except such pay as is deductible from the retired or retainer pay as a result of participation in any survivor's benefits plan in connection with the retired pay,". The amendment could not be executed, because, retroactively effective Oct. 1, 1999, former subsec. (e) was struck out by Pub.L. 106–398 [Div. A, Title VI, § 654(a)(1)] which also redesignated former subsec. (f) as subsec. (e).

Effective and Applicability Provisions

2000 Acts

Amendment to subsecs. (b), (e) and (f) by Pub.L. 106–398, § 1 [Div. A, Title VI, § 654(a)] retroactively effective Oct. 1, 1999; see Pub.L. 106–398, § 1 [Div. A, Title VI, § 654(c)], set out as a note under section 180 of this title.

1989 Acts

Section 705(b) of Pub.L. 101–194 provided that:

"(1) **In general.**—The amendments made by subsection (a) [amending this section] shall first apply with respect to work performed on or after January 1, 1990, by a justice or judge of the United States who has retired under section 371(b) of title 28, United States Code [subsec. (b) of this section].

"(2) **Calendar year 1990.**—In the case certifications required by section 371(f) of title 28, United States Code [subsec. (f) of this section], for calendar year 1990—

"(A) such certifications shall be based on the 10-month period beginning on January 1, 1990, and ending on October 31, 1990, and shall be completed not later than December 15, 1990;

"(B) determinations of work performed under section 371(f) of title 28, United States Code [subsec. (f) of this section], shall be made pro rata on the basis of such 10-month period; and

"(C) such certifications shall be deemed to be certifications made in calendar year 1991."

1988 Acts

Section 1005(b) of Pub.L. 100–702 provided that: "The amendment made by this section [enacting subsec. (e) of this section] shall apply to a justice or judge who retires, or has retired, from the judicial office or from regular active service (into senior status) as such justice or judge of the United States on or after the effective date of section 5532(c) of title 5 [effective 90 days after Oct. 13, 1978 (see Effective Date of 1978 Amendment note under section 5532 of Title 5, Government Organization and Employees)], and to whom section 5532(c) would otherwise be applicable."

1984 Acts

Section 204(c) of Pub.L. 98–353 provided that: "The amendments made by this section [amending this section] shall apply with respect to any justice or judge of the United States appointed to hold office during good behavior who retires on or after the date of enactment of this Act [July 10, 1984]."

Computation of Judicial Service, District of Alaska

Pub.L. 89–70, July 8, 1965, 79 Stat. 213, provided: "That, notwithstanding any other provision of law, any service as a judge of the District Court for the Territory of Alaska shall be included in computing under sections 371 and 372 of title 28, United States Code [this section and section 372 of this title], the aggregate years of judicial service of a United States district judge for the district of Alaska."

Judicial Service in Hawaii Included Within Computation of Aggregate Years of Judicial Service

Pub.L. 86–3, § 14(d), Mar. 18, 1959, 73 Stat. 10, provided in part: "That service as a judge of the District Court for the Territory of Hawaii or as a judge of the United States District Court for the District of Hawaii or as a justice of the Supreme Court of the Territory of Hawaii or as a judge of the circuit courts of the Territory of Hawaii shall be included in computing under section 371, 372, or 373 of title 28, United States Code [this section, section 372, or section 373 of this title], the aggregate years of judicial service of any person who is in office as a district judge for the District of Hawaii on the date of enactment of this Act [Mar. 18, 1959]."

§ 372. Retirement for disability; substitute judge on failure to retire

(a) Any justice or judge of the United States appointed to hold office during good behavior who becomes permanently disabled from performing his duties may retire from regular active service, and the President shall, by and with the advice and consent of the Senate, appoint a successor.

Any justice or judge of the United States desiring to retire under this section shall certify to the President his disability in writing.

Whenever an associate justice of the Supreme Court, a chief judge of a circuit or the chief judge of the Court of International Trade, desires to retire under this section, he shall furnish to the President a certificate of disability signed by the Chief Justice of the United States.

A circuit or district judge, desiring to retire under this section, shall furnish to the President a certificate of disability signed by the chief judge of his circuit.

A judge of the Court of International Trade desiring to retire under this section, shall furnish to the President a certificate of disability signed by the chief judge of his court.

Each justice or judge retiring under this section after serving ten years continuously or otherwise shall, during the remainder of his lifetime, receive the salary of the office. A justice or judge retiring under this section who has served less than ten years in all shall, during the remainder of his lifetime, receive one-half the salary of the office.

(b) Whenever any judge of the United States appointed to hold office during good behavior who is eligible to retire under this section does not do so and a certificate of his disability signed by a majority of

the members of the Judicial Council of his circuit in the case of a circuit or district judge, or by the Chief Justice of the United States in the case of the Chief Judge of the Court of International Trade, or by the chief judge of his court in the case of a judge of the Court of International Trade, is presented to the President and the President finds that such judge is unable to discharge efficiently all the duties of his office by reason of permanent mental or physical disability and that the appointment of an additional judge is necessary for the efficient dispatch of business, the President may make such appointment by and with the advice and consent of the Senate. Whenever any such additional judge is appointed, the vacancy subsequently caused by the death, resignation, or retirement of the disabled judge shall not be filled. Any judge whose disability causes the appointment of an additional judge shall, for purpose of precedence, service as chief judge, or temporary performance of the duties of that office, be treated as junior in commission to the other judges of the circuit, district, or court.

[(c) Repealed. Pub.L. 107–273, Div. C, Title I, § 11043(a)(1)(B), Nov. 2, 2002, 116 Stat. 1855]

(June 25, 1948, c. 646, 62 Stat. 903; May 24, 1949, c. 139, § 67, 63 Stat. 99; Feb. 10, 1954, c. 6, § 4(a), 68 Stat. 12; Sept. 2, 1957, Pub.L. 85–261, 71 Stat. 586; Oct. 10, 1980, Pub.L. 96–417, Title V, § 501(9), 94 Stat. 1742; Oct. 15, 1980, Pub.L. 96–458, § 3(a), (b), 94 Stat. 2036, 2040; Apr. 2, 1982, Pub.L. 97–164, Title I, § 112, 96 Stat. 29; July 10, 1984, Pub.L. 98–353, Title I, § 107, 98 Stat. 342; Nov. 19, 1988, Pub.L. 100–702, Title IV, § 403(c), 102 Stat. 4651; Dec. 1, 1990, Pub.L. 101–650, Title III, § 321, Title IV, § 402, 104 Stat. 5117, 5122; Oct. 29, 1992, Pub.L. 102–572, Title IX, § 902(b)(1), 106 Stat. 4516; Nov. 2, 2002, Pub.L. 107–273, Div. C, Title I, § 11043(a)(1), 116 Stat. 1855.)

HISTORICAL AND STATUTORY NOTES

Effective and Applicability Provisions

1992 Acts

Amendment by Pub.L. 102–572 effective Oct. 29, 1992, see section 911 of Pub.L. 102–572, set out as a note under section 171 of this title.

1990 Acts

Amendment by section 402 of Pub.L. 101–650 effective 90 days after Dec. 1, 1990, see section 407 of Pub.L. 101–650, set out as a note under section 332 of this title.

1988 Acts

Amendment by Pub.L. 100–702 effective Dec. 1, 1988, see section 407 of Pub.L. 100–702, set out as a note under section 2071 of this title.

1984 Acts

Amendment by Pub.L. 98–353 effective July 10, 1984, see section 122(a) of Pub.L. 98–353, set out as a note under section 151 of this title.

1982 Acts

Amendment by Pub.L. 97–164 effective Oct. 1, 1982, see section 402 of Pub.L. 97–164, set out as a note under section 171 of this title.

1980 Acts

Amendment by Pub.L. 96–458 effective Oct. 1, 1981, see section 7 of Pub.L. 96–458, set out as a note under section 331 of this title.

Amendment by Pub.L. 96–417 effective on Nov. 1, 1980, and applicable with respect to civil actions pending on or commenced on or after such date, see section 701(a) of Pub.L. 96–417, as amended, set out as a note under section 251 of this title.

Change of Name

References to United States Claims Court deemed to refer to United States Court of Federal Claims and references to Claims Court deemed to refer to Court of Federal Claims, see section 902(b) of Pub.L. 102–572, set out as a note under section 171 of Title 28, Judiciary and Judicial Procedure.

"United States magistrate judge" substituted for "United States magistrate" in text pursuant to section 321 of Pub.L. 101–650, set out as a note under 28 U.S.C.A. § 631.

Transfer of Functions

Any reference in any provision of law enacted before Jan. 4, 1995, to a function, duty, or authority of the Clerk of the House of Representatives treated as referring, with respect to that function, duty, or authority, to the officer of the House of Representatives exercising that function, duty, or authority, as determined by the Committee on House Oversight of the House of Representatives, see section 2(1) of Pub.L. 104–14, set out as a note preceding section 21 of Title 2, The Congress.

Computation of Judicial Service, District of Alaska

Inclusion of service as judge of the District Court for the Territory of Alaska in the computation of years of judicial service for judges of the United States District Court for the District of Alaska, see Pub.L. 89–70, July 8, 1965, 79 Stat. 213, set out as a note under section 371 of this title.

Extension of Time For Report by National Commission on Judicial Discipline and Removal

Pub.L. 102–368, Title I, Sept. 23, 1992, 106 Stat. 1118, provided in part that: "Notwithstanding the requirement of section 415 of Public Law 101–650 [set out as a note under this section] to submit the report mandated by said section not later than one year after the date of the Commission's first meeting, the National Commission on Judicial Discipline and Removal shall submit to each House of Congress, the Chief Justice of the United States, and the President, the report mandated in said section no later than August 1, 1993."

Judicial Service in Hawaii

Certain judicial service in Hawaii as included within computation of aggregate years of judicial service, see section 14(d) of Pub.L. 86–3, Mar. 18, 1959, 73 Stat. 10, set out as a note under section 371 of this title.

National Commission on Judicial Discipline and Removal

Subtitle II (sections 408 to 418) of Title IV of Pub.L. 101–650, as amended Pub.L. 102–198, § 8(a),(b)(2), Dec. 9, 1991, 105 Stat. 1625, 1626, provided that:

"Sec. 408. Short Title.

"This subtitle [subtitle II of Title IV of Pub.L. 101–650] may be cited as the 'National Commission on Judicial Discipline and Removal Act'.

"Sec. 409. Establishment.

"There is hereby established a commission to be known as the 'National Commission on Judicial Discipline and Removal' (hereinafter in this subtitle referred to as the 'Commission').

"Sec. 410. Duties of Commission.

"The duties of the Commission are—

"(1) to investigate and study the problems and issues involved in the tenure (including discipline and removal) of an article III judge;

"(2) to evaluate the advisability of proposing alternatives to current arrangements with respect to such problems and issues, including alternatives for discipline or removal of judges that would require amendment to the Constitution; and

"(3) to prepare and submit to the Congress, the Chief Justice of the United States, and the President a report in accordance with section 415.

"Sec. 411. Membership.

"(a) Number and appointment.—The Commission shall be composed of 13 members as follows:

"(1) Three appointed by the President pro tempore of the Senate.

"(2) Three appointed by the Speaker of the House of Representatives.

"(3) Three appointed by the Chief Justice of the United States.

"(4) Three appointed by the President.

"(5) One appointed by the Conference of Chief Justices of the States of the United States.

"(b) Term.—Members of the Commission shall be appointed for the life of the Commission.

"(c) Quorum.—Six members of the Commission shall constitute a quorum, but a lesser number may conduct meetings.

"(d) Chairman.—The members of the Commission shall select one of the members to be the Chairman.

"(e) Vacancy.—A vacancy on the Commission resulting from the death or resignation of a member shall not affect its powers and shall be filled in the same manner in which the original appointment was made.

"(f) Continuation of membership.—If any member of the Commission who was appointed to the Commission as a Member of Congress or as an officer or employee of a government leaves that office, or if any member of the Commission who was appointed from persons who are not officers or employees of a government becomes an officer or employee of a government, the member may continue as a member of the Commission for not longer than the 90–day period beginning on the date the member leaves that office or becomes such an officer or employee, as the case may be.

"Sec. 412. Compensation of the Commission.

"(a) Pay.—(1) Except as provided in paragraph (2), each member of the Commission who is not otherwise employed by the United States Government shall be entitled to receive the daily equivalent of the annual rate of basic pay payable for GS–18 of the General Schedule under section 5332 of title 5, United States Code [section 5332 of Title 5, Government Organization and Employees], for each day (including travel time) during which he or she is engaged in the actual performance of duties as a member of the Commission.

"(2) A member of the Commission who is an officer or employee of the United States Government shall serve without additional compensation.

"(b) Travel.—All members of the Commission shall be reimbursed for travel, subsistence, and other necessary expenses incurred by them in the performance of their duties.

"Sec. 413. Director and staff of Commission; experts and consultants.

"(a) Director.—The Commission shall, without regard to section 5311(b) of title 5, United States Code [section 5311(b) of Title 5], have a Director who shall be appointed by the Chairman and who shall be paid at a rate not to exceed the rate of basic pay payable for level V of the Executive Schedule under section 5316 of such title [section 5316 of Title 5].

"(b) Staff.—The Chairman of the Commission may appoint and fix the pay of such additional personnel as the Chairman finds necessary to enable the Commission to carry out its duties. Such personnel may be appointed without regard to the provisions of title 5, United States Code [Title 5], governing appointments in the competitive service, and may be paid without regard to the provisions of chapter 51 and subchapter III of chapter 53 of such title [section 5101 et seq. and section 5331 et seq. of Title 5] relating to classification and General Schedule pay rates, except that the annual rate of pay for any individual so appointed may not exceed a rate equal to the annual rate of basic pay payable for GS–18 of the General Schedule under section 5332 of such title [section 5332 of Title 5].

"(c) Experts and consultants.—The Commission may procure temporary and intermittent services of experts and consultants under section 3109(b) of title 5, United States Code [section 3109(b) of Title 5].

"Sec. 414. Powers of Commission.

"(a) Hearings and sessions.—The Commission or, on authorization of the Commission, a member of the Commission may, for the purpose of carrying out this subtitle, hold such hearings, sit and act at such times and places, take such testimony, and receive such evidence, as the Commission considers appropriate. The Commission may administer oaths or affirmations to witnesses appearing before it.

"(b) Obtaining official data.—The Commission may secure directly from any department, agency, or entity within the executive or judicial branch of the Federal Government information necessary to enable it to carry out this subtitle. Upon request of the Chairman of the Commission, the head of such department or agency shall furnish such information to the Commission.

"(c) Facilities and support services.—The Administrator of General Services shall provide to the Commission on a reimbursable basis such facilities and support services as the Commission may request. Upon request of the Commission, the head of any Federal agency is authorized to make any of the facilities and services of such agency available to the Commission to assist the Commission in carrying out its duties under this subtitle.

"(d) Expenditures and contracts.—The Commission or, on authorization of the Commission, a member of the Commission may make expenditures and enter into contracts for

the procurement of such supplies, services, and property as the Commission or member considers appropriate for the purposes of carrying out the duties of the Commission. Such expenditures and contracts may be made only to such extent or in such amounts as are provided in appropriation Acts.

"**(e) Mails.**—The Commission may use the United States mails in the same manner and under the same conditions as other departments and agencies of the United States.

"**(f) Gifts.**—The Commission may accept, use, and dispose of gifts or donations of services or property.

"**Sec. 415. Report.**

"The Commission shall submit to each House of Congress, the Chief Justice of the United States, and the President a report not later than one year after the date of its first meeting. The report shall contain a detailed statement of the findings and conclusions of the Commission, together with its recommendations for such legislative or administrative action as it considers appropriate.

"**Sec. 416. Termination.**

"The Commission shall cease to exist on the date 30 days after the date it submits its report to the President and the Congress under section 415.

"**Sec. 417. Authorization of appropriations.**

"There is authorized to be appropriated the sum of $750,000 to carry out the provisions of this subtitle.

"**Sec. 418. Effective date.**

"This subtitle shall take effect on the date of the enactment of this Act [Dec. 1, 1990]."

[References in laws to the rates of pay for GS–16, 17, or 18, or to maximum rates of pay under the General Schedule, to be considered references to rates payable under specified sections of Title 5, Government Organization and Employees, see section 529 [Title I, § 101(c)(1)] of Pub.L. 101–509, set out in a note under section 5376 of Title 5.]

[For provisions extending the time for submission by the National Commission on Judicial Discipline and Removal of the report required by section 415 of Pub.L. 101–650, see Pub.L. 102–368, Title 1, Sept. 23, 1992, 106 Stat. 1118, set out as a note under this section.]

[For termination, effective May 15, 2000, of reporting provisions pertaining to the findings and conclusions of the Commission of Pub.L. 101–650, § 415 set out above, see Pub.L. 104–66, § 3003, as amended, set out as a note under 31 U.S.C.A. § 1113, and the 4th item on page 181 of House Document No. 103–7.]

§ 373. Judges in territories and possessions

(a) Any judge of the District Court of Guam, the District Court of the Northern Mariana Islands, or the District Court of the Virgin Islands who retires from office after attaining the age and meeting the service requirements whether continuous or otherwise, of subsection (b) shall, during the remainder of his lifetime, receive an annuity equal to the salary he is receiving at the time he retires.

(b) The age and service requirements for retirement under subsection (a) of this section are as follows:

Attained Age:	Years of Service:
65	15
66	14
67	13
68	12
69	11
70	10

(c)(1) Any judge or former judge who is receiving an annuity pursuant to this section may elect to become a senior judge of the court upon which he served before retiring.

(2) The chief judge of a judicial circuit may recall any such senior judge, with the judge's consent, to perform, for the court from which he retired, such judicial duties for such periods of time as the chief judge may specify.

(3) Any act or failure to act by a senior judge performing judicial duties pursuant to recall under paragraph (2) of this subsection shall have the same force and effect as if it were an act or failure to act of a judge on active duty; but such senior judge shall not be counted as a judge of the court on which he is serving as a recalled annuitant for purposes of the number of judgeships authorized for that court.

(4) Any senior judge performing judicial duties pursuant to recall under paragraph (2) of this subsection shall be paid, while performing such duties, the same compensation (in lieu of the annuity payable under subsection (a) of this section) and the same allowances for travel and other expenses as a judge on active duty with the court being served.

(5) Any senior judge performing judicial duties pursuant to recall under paragraph (2) of this subsection shall at all times be governed by the code of judicial conduct for United States judges approved by the Judicial Conference of the United States.

(d) Any judge who elects to become a senior judge under subsection (c) of this section and who thereafter—

(1) accepts civil office or employment under the Government of the United States (other than the performance of judicial duties pursuant to recall under subsection (c) of this section);

(2) engages in the practice of law; or

(3) materially violates the code of judicial conduct for United States judges,

shall cease to be a senior judge and to be eligible for recall pursuant to subsection (c) of this section.

(e) Any judge of the District Court of Guam, the District Court of the Northern Mariana Islands, or the District Court of the Virgin Islands who is removed by the President of the United States upon the sole ground of mental or physical disability, or who is

not reappointed (as judge of such court), shall be entitled, upon attaining the age of sixty-five years or upon relinquishing office if he is then beyond the age of sixty-five years, (1) if his judicial service, continuous or otherwise, aggregates fifteen years or more, to receive during the remainder of his life an annuity equal to the salary he received when he left office, or (2) if his judicial service, continuous or otherwise, aggregated less than fifteen years but not less than ten years, to receive during the remainder of his life an annuity equal to that proportion of such salary which the aggregate number of his years of his judicial service bears to fifteen.

(f) Service at any time as a judge of the courts referred to in subsection (a) or of any other court of the United States, as defined by section 451 of this title, shall be included in the computation of aggregate years of judicial service for purposes of this section.

(g) Any retired judge who is entitled to receive an annuity under subsection (a) shall be entitled to a cost of living adjustment in the amount payable to him computed as specified in section 8340(b) of title 5, except that in no case may the annuity payable to such retired judge, as increased under this subsection, exceed 95 per centum of the salary of a United States district judge in regular active service.

(June 25, 1948, c. 646, 62 Stat. 904; Oct. 31, 1951, c. 655, § 40, 65 Stat. 724; Feb. 10, 1954, c. 6, § 5, 68 Stat. 13; July 7, 1958, Pub.L. 85–508, § 12(d), 72 Stat. 348; Mar. 18, 1959, Pub.L. 86–3, § 14(d), 73 Stat. 10; Sept. 12, 1966, Pub.L. 89–571, § 2, 80 Stat. 764; Oct. 11, 1976, Pub.L. 94–470, 90 Stat. 2052; Aug. 27, 1986, Pub.L. 99–396, § 21(a), 100 Stat. 844.)

HISTORICAL AND STATUTORY NOTES

Effective and Applicability Provisions

1986 Acts

Section 21(c) of Pub.L. 99–396 provided that: "The amendments made by this section [amending this section and section 376 of this title] shall not affect the amount payable to a judge who retired in accordance with the provisions of section 373 of title 28, United States Code [this section], in effect on the day before the date of enactment of this Act [Aug. 27, 1986]."

1959 Acts

Amendment by Pub.L. 86–3 effective upon the admission of the State of Hawaii into the Union, see note set out under section 91 of this title. Admission of Hawaii into the Union was accomplished Aug. 21, 1959 upon issuance of Proc. No. 3309, Aug. 21, 1959, 25 F.R. 6868, 73 Stat. c74, as required by sections 1 and 7(c) of Pub.L. 86–3, Mar. 18, 1959, 73 Stat. 4, set out as notes preceding 491 of Title 48, Territories and Insular Possessions.

1958 Acts

Amendment by Pub.L. 85–508 effective Jan. 3, 1959 upon admission of Alaska into the Union pursuant to Proc. No. 3269, Jan. 5, 1959, 24 F.R. 81, 73 Stat. c16, as required by sections 1 and 8(c) of Pub.L. 85–508, see notes set out under section 81A of this title and preceding section 21 of Title 48, Territories and Insular Possessions.

Election, Recall, Status, Compensation, Conduct, and Termination of Senior Judges

Pub.L. 98–454, Title X, § 1002, Oct. 5, 1984, 98 Stat. 1745, provided that:

"(a) Any judge or former judge who is receiving, or will upon attaining the age of sixty-five years be entitled to receive, payments pursuant to section 373 of title 28, United States Code[,] [this section] may elect to become a senior judge of the court on which he served while on active duty.

"(b) The chief judge of a judicial circuit may recall any such senior judge of his circuit, with the judge's consent, to perform in the District Court of Guam, the District Court of the Virgin Islands, or the District Court for the Northern Mariana Islands such judicial duties and for such periods of time as the chief judge may specify.

"(c) Any act or failure to act by a senior judge performing judicial duties pursuant to this section shall have the same force and effect as if it were the act or failure to act of a judge on active duty; but such senior judge shall not be counted as a judge of the court on which he is serving for purposes of the number of judgeships authorized for that court.

"(d) Any senior judge shall be paid, while performing duties pursuant to this section, the same compensation (in lieu of payments pursuant to section 373 of title 28, United States Code) [this section] and the same allowances for travel and other expenses as a judge in active service.

"(e) Senior judges under subsection (a) of this section shall at all times be governed by the code of judicial conduct for the United States judges, approved by the Judicial Conference of the United States.

"(f) Any person who has elected to be a senior judge under subsection (a) of this section and who thereafter—

"(1) accepts civil office or employment under the Government of the United States (other than the performance of judicial duties pursuant to subsection (b) of this section);

"(2) engages in the practice of law; or

"(3) materially violated the code of judicial conduct for the United States judges,

shall cease to be a senior judge and to be eligible for recall pursuant to subsection (b) of this section."

Judicial Service in Hawaii

Certain judicial service in Hawaii as included within computation of aggregate years of judicial service, see section 14(d) of Pub.L. 86–3, set out as a note under section 371 of this title.

Preservation of Rights of Retired Judges of the District Court for the District of Hawaii and Justices of the Supreme Court of the Territory of Hawaii

Section 14(d) of Pub.L. 86–3 provided in part: "That the amendments made by this subsection shall not affect the rights of any judge or justice who may have retired before the effective date of this subsection". See Effective and Applicability Provisions of 1959 Amendments note set out under this section.

Preservation of Rights of Retired Judges of the District Court for the Territory of Alaska

Section 12(d) of Pub.L. 85–508 provided in part: "That the amendment made by this subsection [amending this section] shall not affect the rights of any judge who may have retired before it takes effect". See Effective and Applicability Provisions of 1958 Amendments note set out under this section.

Tenure and Salary Rights of Judges in Puerto Rico in Office on September 12, 1966

Amendment by Pub.L. 89–571 not to affect tenure of office or right to continue to receive salary after resignation, retirement, or failure of reappointment of any district judge for the district of Puerto Rico in office on September 12, 1966, see section 4 of Pub.L. 89–571, set out as a note under section 134 of this title.

§ 374. Residence of retired judges; official station

Retired judges of the United States are not subject to restrictions as to residence. The place where a retired judge maintains the actual abode in which he customarily lives shall be deemed to be his official station for the purposes of section 456 of this title. The place where a judge or magistrate judge recalled under section 155, 375, 636, or 797 of this title maintains the actual abode in which the judge or magistrate judge customarily lives shall be deemed to be the official station of such judge or magistrate judge for purposes of section 604(a)(7) of this title.

(June 25, 1948, c. 646, 62 Stat. 904; Sept. 21, 1959, Pub.L. 86–312, § 1, 73 Stat. 587; Nov. 14, 1986, Pub.L. 99–651, Title II, § 202(b), 100 Stat. 3648; Dec. 1, 1990, Pub.L. 101–650, Title III, § 321, 104 Stat. 5117.)

HISTORICAL AND STATUTORY NOTES

Effective and Applicability Provisions

1986 Acts

Amendment by Pub.L. 99–651 effective Jan. 1, 1987, see section 203 of Pub.L. 99–651, set out as a note under section 155 of this title.

Change of Name

"United States magistrate judge" substituted for "United States magistrate" in text pursuant to section 321 of Pub.L. 101–650, set out as a note under 28 U.S.C.A. § 631.

§ 375. Recall of certain judges and magistrate judges

(a)(1) A bankruptcy judge or a United States magistrate judge appointed under chapter 43 of this title, who has retired under the provisions of section 377 of this title or under the applicable provisions of title 5 upon attaining the age and years of service requirements established in section 371(c) of this title, may agree to be recalled to serve under this section for a period of five years as a bankruptcy judge or magistrate judge, as the case may be, upon certification that substantial service is expected to be performed by such retired judge or magistrate judge during such

5–year period. With the agreement of the judge or magistrate judge involved, a certification under this subsection may be renewed for successive 5–year periods.

(2) For purposes of paragraph (1) of this subsection, a certification may be made, in the case of a bankruptcy judge or a United States magistrate,[1] by the judicial council of the circuit in which the official duty station of the judge or magistrate at the time of retirement was located.

(3) For purposes of this section, the term "bankruptcy judge" means a bankruptcy judge appointed under chapter 6 of this title or serving as a bankruptcy judge on March 31, 1984.

(b) A judge or magistrate judge recalled under this section may exercise all of the powers and duties of the office of judge or magistrate judge held at the time of retirement, including the ability to serve in any other judicial district to the extent applicable, but may not engage in the practice of law or engage in any other business, occupation, or employment inconsistent with the expeditious, proper, and impartial performance of duties as a judicial officer.

(c) During the 5–year period in which a certification under subsection (a) is in effect, the judge or magistrate judge involved shall receive, in addition to the annuity provided under the provisions of section 377 of this title or under the applicable provisions of title 5, an amount equal to the difference between that annuity and the current salary of the office to which the judge or magistrate judge is recalled. The annuity of a bankruptcy judge or magistrate judge who completes that 5–year period of service, whose certification is not renewed, and who retired under section 377 of this title shall be equal to the salary in effect, at the end of that 5–year period, for the office from which he or she retired.

(d) A certification under subsection (a) may be terminated in accordance with chapter 16 of this title, and such a certification shall be terminated upon the death of the recalled judge or magistrate judge involved.

(e) Except as provided in subsection (b), nothing in this section shall affect the right of judges or magistrate judges who retire under the provisions of chapter 83 or chapter 84 of title 5 to serve as reemployed annuitants in accordance with the provisions of title 5. A judge or magistrate judge to whom this section applies may be recalled under section 155, 636(h), or 797 of this title, as the case may be, other than during a 5–year period in which a certification under subsection (a) is in effect with respect to that judge or magistrate judge.

(f) For purposes of determining the years of service requirements in order to be eligible for recall

under this section, any service as a bankruptcy judge or a United States magistrate judge, and any prior service as a referee in bankruptcy or a United States commissioner, may be credited.

(g) Except as provided in subsection (c), a judge or magistrate judge recalled under this section who retired under the applicable provisions of title 5 shall be considered to be a reemployed annuitant under chapter 83 or chapter 84, as the case may be, of title 5.

(h) The Judicial Conference of the United States may promulgate regulations to implement this section.
(Added Pub.L. 99–651, Title II, § 201(b)(1), Nov. 14, 1986, 100 Stat. 3647, and amended Pub.L. 100–659, § 4(b), Nov. 15, 1988, 102 Stat. 3918; Pub.L. 101–650, Title III, §§ 321, 325(b)(2), Dec. 1, 1990, 104 Stat. 5117, 5121; Pub.L. 102–572, Title IX, § 904(a), Oct. 29, 1992, 106 Stat. 4517; Pub.L. 107–273, Div. C, Title I, § 11043(d), Nov. 2, 2002, 116 Stat. 1855.)

1 So in original. Probably should be "United States magistrate judge."

HISTORICAL AND STATUTORY NOTES

Effective and Applicability Provisions

1992 Acts

Amendment by Title IX of Pub.L. 102–572 effective Oct. 29, 1992, see section 911 of Pub.L. 102–572, set out as a note under section 171 of Title 28, Judiciary and Judicial Procedure.

1988 Acts

Amendment to this section by Pub.L. 100–659 to take effect on Nov. 15, 1988, and shall apply to bankruptcy judges and magistrates who retire on or after Nov. 15, 1988, with special election provisions for bankruptcy judges, etc., who left office on or after July 31, 1987, and before Nov. 15, 1988, see section 9 of Pub.L. 100–659, set out as a note under section 377 of this title.

1986 Acts

Section effective Jan. 1, 1987, see section 203 of Pub.L. 99–651, set out as an Effective and Applicability Provisions of 1986 Amendments note under section 155 of this title.

Change of Name

References to United States Claims Court deemed to refer to United States Court of Federal Claims and references to Claims Court deemed to refer to Court of Federal Claims, see section 902(b) of Pub.L. 102–572, set out as a note under section 171 of Title 28, Judiciary and Judicial Procedure.

"United States magistrate judge" substituted for "United States magistrate" in text pursuant to section 321 of Pub.L. 101–650, set out as a note under 28 U.S.C.A. § 631.

Prior Provisions

A prior section 375, added Aug. 28, 1954, c. 1053, § 1, 68 Stat. 918, and amended Aug. 3, 1956, c. 944, § 1(b), 70 Stat. 1021; Aug. 22, 1972, Pub.L. 92–397, § 1, 86 Stat. 579, which provided for annuities to widows of justices, was repealed by Pub.L. 96–504, § 5, Dec. 5, 1980, 94 Stat. 2742.

§ 376. Annuities for survivors of certain judicial officials of the United States

(a) For the purposes of this section—

(1) "judicial official" means:

(A) a Justice or judge of the United States, as defined by section 451 of this title;

(B) a judge of the District Court of Guam, the District Court of the Northern Mariana Islands, or the District Court of the Virgin Islands;

(C) a Director of the Administrative Office of the United States Courts, after he or she has filed a waiver under subsection (a) of section 611 of this title;

(D) a Director of the Federal Judicial Center, after he or she has filed a waiver under subsection (a) of section 627 of this title;

(E) an administrative assistant to the Chief Justice of the United States, after he or she has filed a waiver in accordance with both subsection (a) of section 677 and subsection (a) of section 611 of this title;

(F) a full-time bankruptcy judge or a full-time United States magistrate judge; or

(G) a judge of the United States Court of Federal Claims;

who notifies the Director of the Administrative Office of the United States Courts in writing of his or her intention to come within the purview of this section within six months after (i) the date upon which he or she takes office, (ii) the date upon which he or she marries, (iii) January 1, 1977, (iv) October 1, 1986, (v) the date of the enactment of the Retirement and Survivors' Annuities for Bankruptcy Judges and Magistrates Act of 1988, in the case of a full-time bankruptcy judge or United States magistrate judge in active service on that date, (vi) the date of the enactment of the Federal Courts Study Committee Implementation Act of 1990, in the case of a full-time judge of the Court of Federal Claims in active service on that date, or (vii) the date of the enactment of the Federal Courts Administration Act of 1992;

(2) "retirement salary" means:

(A) in the case of a Justice or judge of the United States, as defined by section 451 of this title, salary paid (i) after retirement from regular active service under subsection (b) of section 371 or subsection (a) of section 372 of this title, or (ii) after retirement from office by resignation on salary under subsection (a) of section 371 of this title;

(B) in the case of a judge of the District Court of Guam, the District Court of the Northern Mariana Islands, or the District Court of the Virgin Islands, (i) an annuity paid under subsection (a) of section 373 of this title or (ii) compen-

sation paid under paragraph (4) of subsection (c) of section 373 of this title;

(C) in the case of a Director of the Administrative Office of the United States Courts, an annuity paid under subsection (b) or (c) of section 611 of this title;

(D) in the case of a Director of the Federal Judicial Center, an annuity paid under subsection (b) or (c) of section 627 of this title;

(E) in the case of an administrative assistant to the Chief Justice of the United States, an annuity paid in accordance with both subsection (a) of section 677 and subsection (a) of section 611 of this title;

(F) in the case of a bankruptcy judge or United States magistrate judge, an annuity paid under section 377 of this title; and

(G) in the case of a judge of the United States Court of Federal Claims, an annuity paid under section 178 of this title;

(3) "widow" means the surviving wife of a "judicial official", who:

(A) has been married to him for at least one year on the day of his death; or

(B) is the mother of issue by that marriage;

(4) "widower" means the surviving husband of a "judicial official", who:

(A) has been married to her for at least one year on the day of her death; or

(B) is the father of issue by that marriage;

(5) "child" means:

(A) an unmarried child under eighteen years of age, including (i) an adopted child and (ii) a stepchild or recognized natural child who lived with the judicial official in a regular parent-child relationship;

(B) such unmarried child between eighteen and twenty-two years of age who is a student regularly pursuing a full-time course of study or training in residence in a high school, trade school, technical or vocational institute, junior college, college, university, or comparable educational institution. A child whose twenty-second birthday occurs before July 1, or after August 31, of a calendar year, and while he or she is regularly pursuing such a course of study or training, is deemed to have become twenty-two years of age on the first day of July immediately following that birthday. A child who is a student is deemed not to have ceased being a student during an interim period between school years, if that interim period lasts no longer than five consecutive months and if that child shows, to the satisfaction of the Director of the Administrative Office of the United States Courts, that he or she has a bona fide intention of continuing to pursue a course of study or training in the same or a different school

during the school semester, or other period into which the school year is divided, immediately following that interim period; or

(C) such unmarried child, regardless of age, who is incapable of self-support because of a mental or physical disability incurred either (i) before age eighteen, or (ii) in the case of a child who is receiving an annuity as a full-time student under paragraph (5)(B) of this subsection, before the termination of that annuity;

(6) "former spouse" means a former spouse of a judicial official if the former spouse was married to such judicial official for at least 9 months; and

(7) "assassinated" and "assassination" mean the killing of a judicial official described in paragraph (1)(A), (B), (F), or (G) of this subsection that is motivated by the performance by that judicial official of his or her official duties.

(b)(1) Every judicial official who files a written notification of his or her intention to come within the purview of this section, in accordance with paragraph (1) of subsection (a) of this section, shall be deemed thereby to consent and agree to having deducted and withheld from his or her salary a sum equal to 2.2 percent of that salary, and a sum equal to 3.5 percent of his or her retirement salary. The deduction from any retirement salary—

(A) of a justice or judge of the United States retired from regular active service under section 371(b) or section 372(a) of this title,

(B) of a judge of the United States Court of Federal Claims retired under section 178 of this title, or

(C) of a judicial official on recall under section 155(b), 373(c)(4), 375, or 636(h) of this title,

shall be an amount equal to 2.2 percent of retirement salary.

(2) A judicial official who is not entitled to receive an immediate retirement salary upon leaving office but who is eligible to receive a deferred retirement salary on a later date shall file, within 90 days before leaving office, a written notification of his or her intention to remain within the purview of this section under such conditions and procedures as may be determined by the Director of the Administrative Office of the United States Courts. Every judicial official who files a written notification in accordance with this paragraph shall be deemed to consent to contribute, during the period before such a judicial official begins to receive his or her retirement salary, a sum equal to 3.5 percent of the deferred retirement salary which that judicial official is entitled to receive. Any judicial official who fails to file a written notification under this paragraph shall be deemed to have

revoked his or her election under subsection (a) of this section.

(3) The amounts deducted and withheld from the salary of each judicial official under paragraphs (1) and (2) of this subsection shall, in accordance with such procedures as may be prescribed by the Comptroller General of the United States, be covered into the Treasury of the United States and credited to the "Judicial Survivors' Annuities Fund" established by section 3 of the Judicial Survivors' Annuities Reform Act. Such fund shall be used for the payment of annuities, refunds, and allowances as provided by this section. Payment of such salary less such deductions (and any deductions made under section 178 or 377 of this title or under subchapter III of chapter 83, or chapter 84, of title 5) shall be a full and complete discharge and acquittance of all claims and demands whatsoever for all services rendered by such judicial official during the period covered by such payment, except the rights to those benefits to which such judicial official, or his or her survivors, shall be entitled under the provisions of this section (and under section 178 or 377 of this title or under subchapter III of chapter 83, or chapter 84, of title 5).

(c)(1) There shall also be deposited to the credit of the Judicial Survivors' Annuities Fund, in accordance with such procedures as the Comptroller General of the United States may prescribe, amounts required to reduce to zero the unfunded liability of the Judicial Survivors' Annuities Fund: *Provided*, That such amounts shall not exceed the equivalent of 9 percent of salary or retirement salary. Such deposits shall, subject to appropriations Acts, be taken from the fund used to pay the compensation of the judicial official, and shall immediately become an integrated part of the Judicial Survivors' Annuities Fund for any use required under this section.

(2) For purposes of paragraph (1), the term "unfunded liability" means the estimated excess, determined on an annual basis in accordance with the provisions of section 9503 of title 31, United States Code, of the present value of all benefits payable from the Judicial Survivors' Annuities Fund, over the sum of—

(A) the present value of deductions to be withheld from the future basic pay of judicial officials; plus

(B) the balance in the Fund as of the date the unfunded liability is determined.

In making any determination under this paragraph, the Comptroller General shall use the applicable information contained in the reports filed pursuant to section 9503 of title 31, United States Code, with respect to the judicial survivors' annuities plan established by this section.

(3) There are authorized to be appropriated such sums as may be necessary to carry out this subsection.

(d) Each judicial official shall deposit, with interest at 4 percent per annum to December 31, 1947, and at 3 percent per annum thereafter, compounded on December 31 of each year, to the credit of the "Judicial Survivors' Annuities Fund":

(1) a sum equal to 3.5 percent of that salary, including "retirement salary", which he or she has received for serving in any of the offices designated in paragraph (1) of subsection (a) of this section prior to the date upon which he or she filed notice of an intention to come within the purview of this section with the Director of the Administrative Office of the United States Courts; and

(2) a sum equal to 3.5 percent of the basic salary, pay, or compensation which he or she has received for serving as a Senator, Representative, Delegate, or Resident Commissioner in Congress, or for serving as an "employee", as that term is defined in subsection (1) of section 8331 of title 5, prior to assuming the responsibilities of any of the offices designated in paragraph (1) of subsection (a) of this section.

The interest otherwise required by this subsection shall not be required for any period during which a judicial official was separated from all such service and was not receiving any retirement salary.

Each such judicial official may elect to make such deposits in installments, during the continuance of his or her service in those offices designated in paragraph (1) of subsection (a) of this section, in such amounts and under such conditions as may be determined in each instance by the Director of the Administrative Office of the United States Courts: *Provided*, That, in each instance in which a judicial official does elect to make such deposits in installments, the Director shall require (i) that the first installment payment made shall be in an amount no smaller than that amount necessary to cover at least the last eighteen months of prior creditable civilian service, and (ii) that at least one additional installment payment shall be made every eighteen months thereafter until the total of all such deposits have been made.

Notwithstanding the failure of any such judicial official to make all such deposits or installment payments, credit shall be allowed for the service rendered, but the annuity of that judicial official's widow or widower shall be reduced by an amount equal to 10 percent of the amount of such deposits, computed as of the date of the death of such judicial official, unless such widow or widower shall elect to eliminate such service entirely from credit under subsection (k) of this section: *Provided*, That no deposit shall be required from any such judicial official for any honor-

able active duty service in the Army, Navy, Air Force, Marine Corps, or Coast Guard of the United States, or for any other creditable service rendered prior to August 1, 1920.

(e) The amounts deducted and withheld in accordance with subsection (b) of this section, and the amounts deposited in accordance with subsection (d) of this section, shall be credited to individual accounts in the name of each judicial official from whom such amounts are received, for credit to the "Judicial Survivors' Annuities Fund".

(f) The Secretary of the Treasury shall invest, from time to time, in interest bearing securities of the United States or Federal farm loan bonds, those portions of the "Judicial Survivors' Annuities Fund" which in his judgment may not be immediately required for the payment of annuities, refunds, and allowances as provided in this section. The income derived from such investments shall constitute a part of such fund for the purposes of paying annuities and carrying out the provisions of subsections (g), (h), (m), (o), (p), and (q) of this section.

(g) If any judicial official leaves office and is ineligible to receive a retirement salary or leaves office and is entitled to a deferred retirement salary but fails to make an election under subsection (b)(2) of this section, all amounts credited to his or her account established under subsection (e), together with interest at 4 percent per annum to December 31, 1947, and at 3 percent per annum thereafter, compounded on December 31 of each year, to the date of his or her relinquishment of office, minus a sum equal to 2.2 percent of salary for service while deductions were withheld under subsection (b) or for which a deposit was made by the judicial official under subsection (d), shall be returned to that judicial official in a lump-sum payment within a reasonable period of time following the date of his or her relinquishment of office. For the purposes of this section, a "reasonable period of time" shall be presumed to be no longer than 1 year following the date upon which such judicial official relinquishes his or her office.

(h) Annuities payable under this section shall be paid only in accordance with the following provisions:

(1) In any case in which a judicial official dies while in office, while receiving retirement salary, or after filing an election and otherwise complying with the conditions under subsection (b)(2) of this section (A) after having completed at least eighteen months of creditable civilian service, as computed in accordance with subsection (k) of this section, for the last eighteen months of which the salary deductions provided by subsection (b) of this section or, in lieu thereof, the deposits required by subsection (d) of this section have actually been made, or (B) if the death of such judicial official was by assassination, before having satisfied the requirements of clause (A) if, for the period of such service, the deductions provided by subsection (b) or, in lieu thereof, the deposits required by subsection (d) have actually been made—

(i) if such judicial official is survived by a widow or widower, but not by a child, there shall be paid to such widow or widower an annuity, beginning on the day on which such judicial official died, in an amount computed as provided in subsection (*l*) of this section; or

(ii) if such judicial official is survived by a widow or widower and a child or children, there shall be paid to such widow or widower an annuity, beginning on the day on which such judicial official died, in an amount computed as provided in subsection (*l*) of this section, and there shall also be paid to or on behalf of each such child an immediate annuity equal to:

(I) 10 percent of the average annual salary determined under subsection (*l*)(1) of this section; or

(II) 20 percent of such average annual salary, divided by the number of children;

whichever is smallest; or

(iii) if such judicial official leaves no surviving widow or widower, but does leave a surviving child or children, there shall be paid to or on behalf of each such child an immediate annuity equal to:

(I) the amount of the annuity to which the judicial official's widow or widower would have been entitled under clause (i) of this paragraph, had such widow or widower survived the judicial official, divided by the number of children; or

(II) 20 percent of the average annual salary determined under subsection (*l*)(1) of this section; or

(III) 40 percent of such average annual salary amount, divided by the number of children;

whichever is smallest.

(2) An annuity payable to a widow or widower under clause (i) or (ii) of paragraph (1) of this subsection shall be terminated upon his or her death or remarriage before attaining age 55.

(3) An annuity payable to a child under this subsection shall terminate:

(A) if such child is receiving an annuity based upon his or her status under paragraph (5)(A) of subsection (a) of this section, on the last day of the month during which he or she becomes eighteen years of age;

(B) if such child is receiving an annuity based upon his or her status under paragraph (5)(B) of subsection (a) of this section, either (i) on the first

day of July immediately following his or her twenty-second birthday or (ii) on the last day of the month during which he or she ceases to be a full-time student in accordance with paragraph (5)(B) of subsection (a) of this section, whichever occurs first: *Provided,* That if such child is rendered incapable of self-support because of a mental or physical disability incurred while receiving that annuity, that annuity shall not terminate, but shall continue without interruption and shall be deemed to have become, as of the date of disability, an annuity based upon his or her status under clause (ii) of paragraph (5)(C) of subsection (a) of this section;

 (C) if such child is receiving an annuity based upon his or her status under paragraph (5)(C) of subsection (a) of this section, on the last day of the month during which he or she ceases to be incapable of self-support because of mental or physical disability; or

 (D) on the last day of the month during which such child dies or marries.

 (4) An annuity payable to a child or children under paragraph (1)(ii) of this subsection shall be recomputed and paid as provided in paragraph (1)(iii) of this subsection upon the death, but not upon the remarriage, of the widow or widower who is receiving an annuity under paragraph (1)(ii) of this subsection.

 (5) In any case in which the annuity of a child is terminated, the annuity of each remaining child which is based upon the service of the same judicial official shall be recomputed and paid as though the child whose annuity has been terminated had not survived that judicial official.

 (6) In the case of the survivor or survivors of a judicial official to whom paragraph (1)(B) applies, there shall be deducted from the annuities otherwise payable under this section an amount equal to the amount of salary deductions that would have been made if such deductions had been made for 18 months prior to the judicial official's death.

(i)(1) All questions of dependency and disability arising under this section shall be determined by the Director of the Administrative Office of the United States Courts, subject to review only by the Judicial Conference of the United States, and the decision of the Judicial Conference of the United States shall be final and conclusive. The Director may order or direct at any time such medical or other examinations as he deems necessary to determine the facts relative to the nature and degree of disability of any child who is an annuitant, or an applicant for an annuity, under this section, and may suspend or deny any such annuity for failure to submit to any such examination.

 (2) The Director of the Administrative Office of the United States Courts shall determine whether the killing of a judicial official was an assassination, subject to review only by the Judicial Conference of the United States. The head of any Federal agency that investigates the killing of a judicial official shall provide information to the Director that would assist the Director in making such determination.

 (j) In any case in which a payment under this section is to be made to a minor, or to a person mentally incompetent or under other legal disability, as determined by a court of competent jurisdiction, such payment may be made to the person who is constituted guardian or other fiduciary of such claimant by the laws of the State of residence of such claimant, or to any other person who is otherwise legally vested with the care of the claimant or of the claimant's estate, and need not be made directly to such claimant. The Director of the Administrative Office of the United States Courts may, at his or her discretion, determine whether such payment is made directly to such claimant or to such guardian, fiduciary, or other person legally vested with the care of such claimant or the claimant's estate. Where no guardian or other fiduciary of such minor or such person under legal disability has been appointed under the laws of the State of residence of such claimant, the Director of the Administrative Office of the United States Courts shall determine the person who is otherwise legally vested with the care of the claimant or of the claimant's estate.

 (k) The years of service rendered by a judicial official which may be creditable in calculating the amount of an annuity for such judicial official's widow or widower under subsection (*l*) of this section shall include—

 (1) those years during which such judicial official served in any of the offices designated in paragraph (1) of subsection (a) of this section, including in the case of a Justice or judge of the United States those years during which he or she continued to hold office following retirement from regular active service under section 371 or subsection (a) of section 372 of this title;

 (2) those years during which such judicial official served as a Senator, Representative, Delegate, or Resident Commissioner in Congress, prior to assuming the responsibilities of any of the offices designated in paragraph (1) of subsection (a) of this section;

 (3) those years during which such judicial official honorably served on active duty in the Army, Navy, Air Force, Marine Corps, or Coast Guard of the United States, prior to assuming the responsibilities of any of the offices designated in paragraph (1) of subsection (a) of this section: *Provided,* That those

years of such military service for which credit has been allowed for the purposes of retirement or retired pay under any other provision of law shall not be included as allowable years of such service under this section;

(4) those years during which such judicial official served as an "employee", as that term is defined in subsection (1) of section 8331 of title 5, prior to assuming the responsibilities of any of the offices designated in paragraph (1) of subsection (a) of this section,[1] and

(5) those years during which such judicial official had deductions withheld from his or her retirement salary in accordance with subsection (b)(1) or (2) of this section.

For the purposes of this subsection the term "years" shall mean full years and twelfth parts thereof, excluding from the aggregate any fractional part of a month which numbers less than fifteen full days and including, as one full month, any fractional part of a month which numbers fifteen full days or more. Nothing in this subsection shall be interpreted as waiving or canceling that reduction in the annuity of a widow or widower which is required by subsection (d) of this section due to the failure of a judicial official to make those deposits required by subsection (d) of this section.

(*l*) The annuity of a widow or widower of a judicial official shall be an amount equal to the sum of—

(1) 1.5 percent of the average annual salary, including retirement salary, which such judicial official received for serving in any of the offices designated in paragraph (1) of subsection (a) of this section (i) during those three years of such service, or during those three years while receiving a retirement salary, in which his or her annual salary or retirement salary was greatest, or (ii) if such judicial official has so served less than three years, then during the total period of such service prior to his or her death, multiplied by the total of:

(A) the number of years of creditable service tabulated in accordance with paragraph (1) of subsection (k) of this section; plus

(B) the number of years of creditable service tabulated in accordance with paragraph (2) of subsection (k) of this section; plus

(C) the number of years of creditable service tabulated in accordance with paragraph (3) of subsection (k) of this section; plus

(D) the number of years during which the judicial official had deductions withheld from his or her retirement salary under subsection (b)(1) or (2) of this section; plus

(E) the number of years up to, but not exceeding, fifteen of creditable service tabulated in ac-

cordance with paragraph (4) of subsection (k) of this section,

plus:

(2) three-fourths of 1 percent of such average annual salary, multiplied by the number of years of any prior creditable service, as tabulated in accordance with subsection (k) of this section, not applied under paragraph (1) of this subsection;

except that such annuity shall not exceed an amount equal to 50 percent of such average annual salary, nor be less than an amount equal to 25 percent of such average annual salary. Any annuity determined in accordance with the provisions of this subsection shall be reduced to the extent required by subsection (d) of this section, and by the amount of any annuity payable to a former spouse under subsection (t).

(m) Each time that an increase is made under section 8340(b) of title 5 in annuities paid under subchapter III of chapter 83 of such title, each annuity payable from the Judicial Survivors' Annuities Fund shall be increased at the same time by the same percentage by which annuities are increased under that section.

(n) Each annuity authorized under this section shall accrue monthly and shall be due and payable in monthly installments on the first business day of the month following the month or other period for which the annuity shall have accrued. No annuity authorized under this section shall be assignable, either in law or in equity, except as provided in subsections (s) and (t), or subject to execution, levy, attachment, garnishment, or other legal process.

(o)(1) In any case in which a judicial official dies while in office, while receiving retirement salary, or after filing an election and otherwise complying with the conditions under subsection (b)(2) of this section, and;

(A) subject to paragraph (2) of this subsection, before having completed eighteen months of civilian service, computed in accordance with subsection (k) of this section, during which the salary deductions provided by subsection (b) of this section or the deposit required by subsection (d) of this section have actually been made; or

(B) after having completed eighteen months of civilian service, computed in accordance with subsection (k) of this section, during which all such deductions or deposits have been made, but without a survivor or survivors who are entitled to receive the annuity benefits provided by subsection (h) or (t) of this section; or

(C) the rights of all persons entitled to receive the annuity benefits provided by subsection (h) or (t) of this section terminate before a valid claim therefor has been established;

the total amount credited to the individual account of that judicial official, established under subsection (e) of this section, with interest at 4 percent per annum to December 31, 1947, and at 3 percent per annum thereafter, compounded on December 31, of each year, to the date of that judicial official's death, shall be paid, upon the establishment of a valid claim therefor, to the person or persons surviving at the date title to the payment arises, in the following order of precedence:

First, to the beneficiary or beneficiaries whom that judicial official may have designated in a writing received by the Administrative Office of the United States Courts prior to his or her death;

Second, if there be no such beneficiary, to the widow or widower of such judicial official;

Third, if none of the above, to the child or children of such judicial official and the descendants of any deceased children by representation;

Fourth, if none of the above, to the parents of such judicial official or the survivor of them;

Fifth, if none of the above, to the duly appointed executor, executrix, administrator, or administratrix of the estate of such judicial official;

Sixth, if none of the above, to such other next of kin of such judicial official, as may be determined by the Director of the Administrative Office of the United States Courts to be entitled to such payment, under the laws of the domicile of such judicial official, at the time of his or her death.

Such payment shall be a bar to recovery by any other person. For the purposes of this subsection only, a determination that an individual is a widow, widower, or child of a judicial official may be made by the Director of the Administrative Office of the United States Courts without regard to the definitions of those terms contained in paragraphs (3), (4), and (5) of subsection (a) of this section.

(2) In cases in which a judicial official dies as a result of assassination and leaves a survivor or survivors who are entitled to receive the annuity benefits provided by subsection (h) or (t) of this section, paragraph (1)(A) of this subsection shall not apply.

(p) In any case in which all the annuities which are authorized by this section and based upon the service of a given official terminate before the aggregate amount of annuity payments received by the annuitant or annuitants equals the total amount credited to the individual account of such judicial official, established under subsection (e) of this section with interest at 4 percent per annum to December 31, 1947, and at 3 percent per annum thereafter, compounded on December 31, of each year, to the date of that judicial official's death, the difference between such total amount, with such interest, and such aggregate amount shall be paid, upon establishment of a valid claim therefor, in the order of precedence prescribed in subsection (o) of this section.

(q) Any accrued annuity benefits remaining unpaid upon the termination of an annuity, other than by the death of an annuitant, shall be paid to that annuitant. Any accrued annuity benefits remaining unpaid upon the death of an annuitant shall be paid, upon the establishment of a valid claim therefor, in the following order of precedence:

First, to the duly appointed executor, executrix, administrator, or administratrix of the estate of such annuitant;

Second, if there is no such executor, executrix, administrator, or administratrix, payments shall be made, after the expiration of sixty days from the date of death of such annuitant, to such individual or individuals as may appear, in the judgment of the Director of the Administrative Office of the United States Courts, to be legally entitled thereto, and such payment shall be a bar to recovery by any other individual.

(r) Nothing contained in this section shall be interpreted to prevent a widow or widower eligible for an annuity under this section from simultaneously receiving such an annuity while also receiving any other annuity to which such widow or widower may also be entitled under any other law without regard to this section: *Provided*, That service used in the computation of the annuity conferred by this section shall not also be credited in computing any such other annuity.

(s) A judicial official who has a former spouse may elect, under procedures prescribed by the Director of the Administrative Office of the United States Courts, to provide a survivor annuity for such former spouse under subsection (t). An election under this subsection shall be made at the time of retirement, or, if later, within 2 years after the date on which the marriage of the former spouse to the judicial official is dissolved. An election under this subsection—

(1) shall not be effective to the extent that it—

(A) conflicts with—

(i) any court order or decree referred to in subsection (t)(1), which was issued before the date of such election, or

(ii) any agreement referred to in such subsection which was entered into before such date; or

(B) would cause the total of survivor annuities payable under subsections (h) and (t) based on the service of the judicial official to exceed 55 percent of the average annual salary (as such term is used in subsection (*l*)) of such official; and

(2) shall not be effective, in the case of a judicial official who is then married, unless it is made with the spouse's written consent.

The Director of the Administrative Office of the United States Courts shall provide by regulation that paragraph (2) of this subsection may be waived if the judicial official establishes to the satisfaction of the Director that the spouse's whereabouts cannot be determined, or that, due to exceptional circumstances, requiring the judicial official to seek the spouse's consent would otherwise be inappropriate.

(t)(1) Subject to paragraphs (2) through (4) of this subsection, a former spouse of a deceased judicial official is entitled to a survivor annuity under this section if and to the extent expressly provided for in an election under subsection (s), or in the terms of any decree of divorce or annulment or any court order or court-approved property settlement agreement incident to such decree.

(2) The annuity payable to a former spouse under this subsection may not exceed the difference between—

(A) the maximum amount that would be payable as an annuity to a widow or widower under subsection (l), determined without taking into account any reduction of such annuity caused by payment of an annuity to a former spouse; and

(B) the amount of any annuity payable under this subsection to any other former spouse of the judicial official, based on an election previously made under subsection (s), or a court order previously issued.

(3) The commencement and termination of an annuity payable under this subsection shall be governed by the terms of the applicable order, decree, agreement, or election, as the case may be, except that any such annuity—

(A) shall not commence before—

(i) the day after the judicial official dies, or

(ii) the first day of the second month beginning after the date on which the Director of the Administrative Office of the United States Courts receives written notice of the order, decree, agreement, or election, as the case may be, together with such additional information or documentation as the Director may prescribe,

whichever is later, and

(B) shall terminate no later than the last day of the month before the former spouse remarries before becoming 55 years of age or dies.

(4) For purposes of this section, a modification in a decree, order, agreement, or election referred to in paragraph (1) of this subsection shall not be effective—

(A) if such modification is made after the retirement of the judicial official concerned, and

(B) to the extent that such modification involves an annuity under this subsection.

(u) In the case of a judicial official who is assassinated, an annuity shall be paid under this section notwithstanding a survivor's eligibility for or receipt of benefits under chapter 81 of title 5, except that the annuity for which a surviving spouse is eligible under this section shall be reduced to the extent that the total benefits paid under this section and chapter 81 of title 5 for any year would exceed the current salary for that year of the office of the judicial official.

(v) Subject to the terms of a decree, court order, or agreement described in subsection (t)(1), if any judicial official ceases to be married after making the election under subsection (a), he or she may revoke such election in writing by notifying the Director of the Administrative Office of the United States Courts. The judicial official shall also notify any spouse or former spouse of the application for revocation in accordance with such requirements as the Director of the Administrative Office of the United States Courts shall by regulation prescribe. The Director may provide under such regulations that the notification requirement may be waived with respect to a spouse or former spouse if the judicial official establishes to the satisfaction of the Director that the whereabouts of such spouse or former spouse cannot be determined.

(w) The Comptroller General of the United States shall, at the end of each 3–fiscal year period, determine whether the contributions by judicial officials under subsection (b) during that 3–year period accounted for 50 percent of the costs of the Judicial Survivors' Annuities Fund and if not, then what adjustments in the contribution rates under subsection (b) should be made to achieve that 50 percent figure. The Comptroller General shall report the results of each determination under this subsection to the Congress.

(Added Aug. 3, 1956, c. 944, § 2, 70 Stat. 1021, and amended July 7, 1958, Pub.L. 85–508, § 12(n), 72 Stat. 348; Dec. 20, 1967, Pub.L. 90–219, Title II, § 202, 81 Stat. 668; Aug. 8, 1968, Pub.L. 90–466, § 1(a), 82 Stat. 662; Aug. 22, 1972, Pub.L. 92–397, §§ 2, 3(c), 86 Stat. 579, 580; Oct. 19, 1976, Pub.L. 94–554, § 2, 90 Stat. 2603; Nov. 6, 1978, Pub.L. 95–598, Title II, § 211, 92 Stat. 2661; June 19, 1986, Pub.L. 99–336, § 2(a), (d)(1) to (3), (e), 100 Stat. 633, 635 to 637; Aug. 27, 1986, Pub.L. 99–396, § 21(b), 100 Stat. 846; Nov. 15, 1988, Pub.L. 100–659, § 3(a), 102 Stat. 3917; Nov. 19, 1988, Pub.L. 100–702, Title X, § 1017(a), 102 Stat. 4670; Dec. 1, 1990, Pub.L. 101–650, Title III, §§ 306(b), 321, 322(a) to (f), (g)[(h)], 104 Stat. 5109, 5117 to 5120; Oct. 29, 1992, Pub.L. 102–572, Title II, § 201(a) to (i), Title IX, § 902(b), 106 Stat. 4508 to 4510, 4516; Oct. 19, 1996, Pub.L. 104–317, Title III, §§ 302, 308, 110 Stat. 3851, 3853; Nov. 13, 2000, Pub.L. 106–518, Title III, § 312(b), 114 Stat. 2421.)

1 So in original. Probably should be a semicolon.

HISTORICAL AND STATUTORY NOTES

References in Text

The date of the enactment of the Retirement and Survivors' Annuities for Bankruptcy Judges and Magistrates Act of 1988, referred to in subsec. (a)(1)(v), is the date of the enactment of Pub.L. 100–659 (which amended this section), which was approved Nov. 15, 1988.

The date of the enactment of the Federal Courts Study Committee Implementation Act of 1990, referred to in subsec. (a)(1)(vi), is the date of enactment of Title III of Pub.L. 101–650, which was approved Dec. 1, 1990.

The date of the enactment of the Federal Courts Administration Act of 1992, referred to in subsec. (a)(1)(vii), means the date of enactment of Pub.L. 102–572, which was approved Oct. 29, 1992.

Section 3 of the Judicial Survivors' Annuities Reform Act, referred to in subsec. (b)(3), is section 3 of Pub.L. 94–554, which is set out as a note under this section.

Codifications

Amendments by section 312(b) of Pub.L. 106–518, were executed to subsec. (a) as the probable intent of Congress, despite directory language purporting to amend paragraphs (1)(D) and (2)(D) of section 376 of title 28, leaving out the subsec. (a) identifier from the directory language.

Subsec. (a)(2)(A) of this section was amended by Pub.L. 95–598, Title II, § 211, Nov. 6, 1978, 92 Stat. 2668, effective June 28, 1984, pursuant to Pub.L. 95–598, Title IV, § 402(b), Nov. 6, 1978, 92 Stat. 2682, as amended by Pub.L. 98–249, § 1(a), Mar. 31, 1984, 98 Stat. 116; Pub.L. 98–271, § 1(a), Apr. 30, 1984, 98 Stat. 163; Pub.L. 98–299, § 1(a), May 25, 1984, 98 Stat. 214; Pub.L. 98–325, § 1(a), June 20, 1984, 98 Stat. 268, set out as a note preceding section 101 of Title 11, Bankruptcy, by inserting ", or (iii) in the case of a bankruptcy judge, after retirement under section 337 of this title" following "(ii) after retirement from office by resignation on salary under subsection (a) of section 371 of this title".

Section 402(b) of Pub.L. 95–598 was amended by section 113 of Pub.L. 98–353, Title I, July 10, 1984, 98 Stat. 343, by substituting "shall not be effective" for "shall take effect on June 28, 1984", thereby eliminating the amendment by section 211 of Pub.L. 95–598, effective June 27, 1984, pursuant to section 122(c) of Pub.L. 98–353, set out as an Effective Date note under section 151 of this title.

Section 121(a) of Pub.L. 98–353 directed that section 402(b) of Pub.L. 95–598 be amended by substituting "the date of enactment of the Bankruptcy Amendments and Federal Judgeship Act of 1984 [i.e. July 10, 1984]" for "June 28, 1984". This amendment was not executed in view of the prior amendment to section 402(b) of Pub.L. 95–598 by section 113 of Pub.L. 98–353.

Effective and Applicability Provisions

1992 Acts

Section 202 of Pub.L. 102–572 provided that: "This title [Title II of Pub.L. 102–572, Oct. 29, 1992, 106 Stat. 4508] and the amendments made by this title [amending this section and enacting provisions set out as notes under this section] shall take effect on the date of the enactment of this Act [Oct. 29, 1992]."

Amendment by section 902(b) of Pub.L. 102–572 effective Oct. 29, 1992, see section 911 of Pub.L. 102–572, set out as a note under section 171 of this title.

1988 Acts

Section 1017(c) of Title X of Pub.L. 100–702 provided that: "The amendment made by subsection (a) [enacting subsec. (m) and deleting former subsec. (m) of this section] shall apply with respect to increases in annuities which are made under section 8340(b) of title 5, United States Code [section 8340(b) of Title 5, Government Organization and Employees], on or after the date of enactment of this title [Nov. 19, 1988]."

Amendment to this section by Pub.L. 100–659 to take effect on Nov. 15, 1988, and shall apply to bankruptcy judges and magistrates who retire on or after Nov. 15, 1988, with special election provisions for bankruptcy judges, etc., who left office on or after July 31, 1987, and before Nov. 15, 1988, see section 9 of Pub.L. 100–659, set out as a note under section 377 of this title.

1986 Acts

Amendment by Pub.L. 99–396 not to affect the amount payable to a judge who retired in accordance with the provisions of section 373 of this title in effect on the day before Aug. 27, 1986, see section 21(c) of Pub.L. 99–396, set out as a note under section 373 of this title.

Section 2(f) of Pub.L. 99–336 provided that: "This section [amending this section and enacting provisions set out as notes under this section] shall take effect on October 1, 1986."

1976 Acts

Section 8 of Pub.L. 94–554 provided: "That this Act [amending this section and enacting provisions set out as notes under this section] shall become effective on the first day of the third month following the month in which it is enacted [Jan. 1, 1977], or on October 1, 1976, whichever occurs last."

1958 Acts

Amendment by Pub.L. 85–508 effective Jan. 3, 1959 upon admission of Alaska into the Union pursuant to Proc. No. 3269, Jan. 5, 1959, 24 F.R. 81, 73 Stat. c16, as required by sections 1 and 8(c) of Pub.L. 85–508, see notes set out under section 81A of this title and preceding section 21 of Title 48, Territories and Insular Possessions.

Change of Name

References to United States Claims Court deemed to refer to United States Court of Federal Claims and references to Claims Court deemed to refer to Court of Federal Claims, see section 902(b) of Pub.L. 102–572, set out as a note under section 171 of Title 28, Judiciary and Judicial Procedure.

"United States magistrate judge" substituted for "United States magistrate" in text pursuant to section 321 of Pub.L. 101–650, set out as a note under 28 U.S.C.A. § 631.

Transfer of Functions

For transfer of authorities, functions, personnel, and assets of the Coast Guard, including the authorities and functions of the Secretary of Transportation relating thereto, to the Department of Homeland Security, and for treatment of related references, see 6 U.S.C.A. §§ 468(b), 551(d), 552(d) and 557, and the Department of Homeland Security Reorga-

nization Plan of November 25, 2002, as modified, set out as a note under 6 U.S.C.A. § 542.

Savings Provisions

Section 6 of Pub.L. 94–554 provided: "That the benefits conferred by this Act shall, on the date upon which this Act becomes effective [see Effective and Applicability Provisions of 1976 Amendments note under this section], immediately become available to any individual then receiving an annuity under section 2 of the Act of August 3, 1956 (70 Stat. 1021) [which enacted this section], as amended: *Provided*, That although the rights of any judicial official electing to come within the purview of section 376 of title 28, United States Code [this section], on or after the date upon which this Act becomes effective, shall be determined exclusively under the provisions of that section as amended by this Act, nothing in this Act shall be interpreted to cancel, abrogate, or diminish any rights to which an individual or his or her survivors may be entitled by virtue of that individuals [sic] having contributed to the judicial survivors annuity fund established by section 2 of the Act of August 3, 1956 (70 Stat. 1021) [which enacted this section], as amended, before the date upon which this Act becomes effective."

Effective and Applicability Provisions of 1990 Amendments; Transition Provisions

Amendment by section 306(b) of Pub.L. 101–650 applicable to judges of, and senior judges in active service with, the United States Court of Federal Claims on or after Dec. 1, 1990, see section 306(f) of Pub.L. 101–650, set out as a note under section 8331 of Title 5, Government Organization and Employees.

Section 322(g) of Pub.L. 101–650 provided that:

"(1) **Effective date.**—Subject to paragraph (2), the amendments made by this Act [probably means section 322 of Pub.L. 101–650, amending this section] shall apply to all judicial officials assassinated on or after May 28, 1979.

"(2) **Rules for retroactive application.**—(A) In the case of a judicial official who was assassinated on or after May 28, 1979, and before the date of the enactment of this Act [Dec. 1, 1990], if the salary deductions provided by subsection (b) of section 376 of title 28, United States Code [subsec. (b) of this section], or the deposits required by subsection (d) of such section [subsec. (d) of this section], have been withdrawn pursuant to subsection (*o*) of such section [subsec. (*o*) of this section], there shall be deducted from the annuities otherwise payable to the survivor or survivors of such judicial official, and the payment authorized by subparagraph (C) of this paragraph, an amount equal to the amount so withdrawn, with interest on the amount withdrawn at 3 percent per annum compounded on December 31 of each year.

"(B) In the case of the survivor or survivors of a judicial official to whom this paragraph applies who had less than 18 months of service before being assassinated, there shall be deducted from the annuities otherwise payable to the survivor or survivors of such judicial official, and the payment authorized by subparagraph (C) of this paragraph, an amount equal to the amount of salary deductions that would have been made if such deductions [had] been made for 18 months before the judicial official's death, plus interest as described in subparagraph (A).

"(C) Subject to subparagraphs (A) and (B), the survivor or survivors of a judicial official to whom this paragraph applies shall be entitled to the payment of annuities they would have received under section 376 of title 28, United States Code [this section], for the period beginning on the date such judicial official was assassinated and ending the date of the enactment of this Act [Dec. 1, 1990]. The Secretary of the Treasury shall pay into the Judicial Survivors' Annuities fund, out of any money in the Treasury not otherwise appropriated, the amount of the annuities to which the survivor or survivors are entitled under this subparagraph.

"(3) **Definition.**—For purposes of this subsection, the term—

"(A) 'assassinated' has the meaning given that term in section 376(a)(7) of title 28, United States Code [subsec. (a) of this section], as added by this section; and

"(B) 'judicial official' has the meaning given that term in section 376(a)(1)(A) and (B) of title 28, United States Code [subsec. (a)(1)(A) and (B) of this section]."

Retroactive Effect of 1967 Amendments

The provisions of section 611(a) of this title, the first paragraph of section 611(b) of this title, and subsec. (s) of this section, as added by Pub.L. 90–219, applicable to a Director or former Director of the Administrative Office of the United States Courts who was first appointed prior to Dec. 20, 1967 if at the time such Director or former Director left or leaves such office he had, or shall have, attained the age of sixty-five years and completed fifteen years of service as Director of the Administrative Office of the United States Courts and if, on or before the expiration of six months following Dec. 20, 1967, he makes the election referred to in section 611(a) of this title or subsec. (s) of this section, or both, as the case may be, see section 205(b) of Pub.L. 90–219, set out as a note under section 611 of this title.

Annuity Payment to Surviving Spouses of Judges Who Died Before October 19, 1976

Pub.L. 96–504, § 3, Dec. 5, 1980, 94 Stat. 2741, provided that:

"(a) As of the first pay period beginning after the effective date of this Act [see note set out under section 8344 of Title 5, Government Organization and Employees], a surviving spouse, other than a surviving spouse who has remarried, of any Justice of the United States (as defined by section 451 of title 28, United States Code) [section 451 of this title], who died before October 19, 1976, shall be paid an annuity in accordance with the provisions of section 376 of title 28, United States Code [this section], at a rate of $20,000 per year as if such Justice had elected to come within the provisions of, and having made the full deposit required by, section 376(d) of title 28, United States Code [subsec. (d) of this section].

"(b) Notwithstanding the provisions of section 376(h) of title 28, United States Code [subsec. (h) of this section], such annuity shall be payable as provided in section 376(m) of title 28, United States Code [subsec. (m) of this section], until the date of the death of any such spouse."

Appropriations

Section 5 of Act Aug. 3, 1956, c. 944, 70 Stat. 1026, provided that: "Funds necessary to carry out the provisions of this Act [enacting this section and provisions set out as notes hereunder, and amending sections 375, 604(a)(7), and

605 of this title] may be appropriated out of any money in the Treasury not otherwise appropriated."

Audit by General Accounting Office [now Government Accountability Office]

Section 201(*l*) of Pub.L. 102–572 provided that: "The Comptroller General shall—

"(1) conduct an audit of the judicial survivors annuities program under section 376 of title 28, United States Code [this section], for the 3–year period beginning on the date of the enactment of this Act [Oct. 29, 1992]; and

"(2) report to the Congress, not later than 60 days after the end of that 3–year period, on the results of such audit, comparing such program to other survivors annuities programs within the Federal Government."

Compensation for Actuarial Deficiency in the Annuities Fund

Section 4 of Pub.L. 94–554 provided: "That on the date upon which this Act becomes effective [see Effective and Applicability Provisions of 1976 Amendments note under this section] the Secretary of the Treasury shall ascertain from the Director of the Administrative Office of the United States Courts the amount of the actuarial deficiency in the fund transferred by section 3 of this Act [see Judicial Survivors' Annuities Fund note under this section] on the date of that fund's transfer and, at the earliest time thereafter at which appropriated funds in that amount shall become available, the Secretary shall deposit such funds, in a single payment, into the Judicial Survivors' Annuities Fund established by section 3 of this Act. Such funds as are necessary to carry out this section are hereby authorized to be appropriated."

Covered Beneficiaries under Pub.L. 99–336

Section 2(b) of Pub.L. 99–336 provided that: "The benefits conferred by section 376 of title 28, United States Code [this section], by reason of the amendments made by this section [amending this section] shall apply only to individuals who become eligible for annuities under such section on or after the effective date of this section [Oct. 1, 1986], except that—

"(1) such annuities shall be computed in accordance with the provisions of section 376 of title 28, United States Code, as amended by this section [this section], notwithstanding contributions or deposits made in accordance with applicable law at lower rates; and

"(2) no additional liability shall be created with respect to deposits made in accordance with applicable law before the effective date of this section [October 1, 1986], or after such effective date pursuant to an agreement entered into before such effective date."

Credit for Contributions Prior to 1992 Amendment at Higher Rate

Section 201(j) of Pub.L. 102–572 provided that: "Notwithstanding any other provision of law, the contribution under section 376(b)(1) or (2) of title 28, United States Code (as amended by this section) [subsec. (b)(1) or (2) of this section], of any judicial official who is within the purview of such section 376 on the effective date of this title [Oct. 29, 1992] shall be reduced by 0.5 percent for a period of time equal to the number of years of service for which the judicial official has made contributions or deposits before the enactment of this Act [probably means date of enactment of Pub.L. 102–572, which was approved Oct. 29, 1992] to the credit of

the Judicial Survivors' Annuities Fund or for 18 months, whichever is less, if such contributions or deposits were never returned to the judicial official. For purposes of this subsection, the term 'years' shall mean full years and twelfth parts thereof."

Increase for Existing Annuitants

Section 1017(b) of Pub.L. 100–702 provided that: "Each annuity payable from the Judicial Survivors' Annuities Fund under section 376 of title 28, United States Code [this section], on the date of the enactment of this title [Nov. 19, 1988] shall be increased by 10 percent, effective on such date of enactment [Nov. 19, 1988]."

Increases in Widows' Annuities Paid under Section 2 of Act August 3, 1956

Section 5 of Pub.L. 94–554 provided: "That on the date upon which this Act becomes effective [see Effective and Applicability Provisions of 1976 Amendments note under this section] each annuity then being paid to a widow from the judicial survivors annuity fund established by section 2 of the Act of August 3, 1956 (70 Stat. 1021) [which enacted this section], as amended, shall be increased by an amount equal to one-fifth of 1 percent of the amount of such annuity multiplied by the number of months which have passed since the commencement of that annuity. For the purposes of this section, any fractional part of a month which numbers less than fifteen full days shall be excluded from the computation of the number of months and any fractional part of a month which numbers fifteen full days or more shall be included in the computation as one full month. Such funds as are necessary to carry out this section are authorized to be appropriated and, upon appropriation, shall be deposited by the Secretary of the Treasury, in a single payment, to credit of the Judicial Survivors' Annuities Fund established by section 3 of this Act [see Judicial Survivors' Annuities Fund note under this section]."

Judge Taking Office on August 8, 1968

Section 1(b) of Pub.L. 90–466 provided that: "For the purpose of the amendment made by subsection (a) [to subsec. (a) of this section], a judge who is in office on the date of enactment of this Act [Aug. 8, 1968] shall be deemed to have taken office on that date [Aug. 8, 1968]."

Judicial Survivors' Annuities Fund

Section 3 of Pub.L. 94–554 provided: "That on the date upon which this Act becomes effective [see Effective and Applicability Provisions of 1976 Amendments note under this section] there shall be established on the books of the Treasury a fund which shall be known as 'The Judicial Survivors' Annuities Fund,' and all money credited to the judicial survivors annuity fund established by section 2 of the Act of August 3, 1956 (70 Stat. 1021) [which enacted this section], as amended, shall be transferred to the credit of the Judicial Survivors' Annuities Fund established by this section."

Judicial Survivors' Annuity Fund; Authorization of Appropriations

Pub.L. 96–504, § 4, Dec. 5, 1980, 94 Stat. 2742, required the Secretary of the Treasury in consultation with the Director of the Administrative Office of the United States Courts to determine as of Dec. 5, 1980, and deposit as soon

as possible thereafter, the amount necessary to offset any actuarial deficiency in the Judicial Survivors Annuities Fund.

Payment of Retirement Salary Pursuant to Court Decree of Divorce, Etc.

Section 2(d)(4) of Pub.L. 99–336 provided that: "Payments of retirement salary as defined in section 376(a)(2) of title 28, United States Code [subsec. (a)(2) of this section], which would otherwise be made to the judicial official upon whose service the retirement salary is based, shall be paid (in whole or in part) to another person if and to the extent expressly provided for in the terms of any court decree of divorce, annulment, or legal separation, or the terms of any court order or court-approved property settlement agreement incident to any court decree of divorce, annulment, or legal separation. Any payment under this paragraph to a person bars recovery by any other person. This paragraph shall apply only to payments made after the date of receipt by the Director of the Administrative Office of [the] United States Courts of written notice of such decree, order, or agreement, and such additional information and documentation as the Director may prescribe. As used in this paragraph, 'court' means any court of any State or the District of Columbia."

Preservation of Rights of Judges of the District Court for the Territory of Alaska

Section 12(n) of Pub.L. 85–508 provided in part that the amendment of subsec. (q) of this section by Pub.L. 85–508 shall not affect the rights under this section of any present or former judge of the District Court for the Territory of Alaska or his survivors.

Prior Death of Judge

Section 7 of Act Aug. 3, 1956, c. 944, 70 Stat. 1021, provided that: "In the case of a living widow of a judge of the United States as defined in section 451 of title 28, United States Code, who died prior to the date of enactment of this Act [Aug. 3, 1956], an annuity shall be paid as provided in section 376 of title 28, United States Code, as added by section 2 of this Act [this section], as if such judge had died on such date and had elected to bring himself within the purview of such section 376 [this section], but had not made the deposit provided for by subsection (c) of the said section: *Provided*, (a) That such widow has not remarried; and (b) that the amount of such annuity and the reduction therein because of such deposit not having been made shall be computed on the basis of the actual length of judicial and other allowable service of such judge: *And provided further*, That notwithstanding the provisions of subsection (g) of such section 376 [this section] such annuity shall be payable even though such judge had not rendered five years of civilian service prior to his death. In the case of a judge of the United States as defined in section 451 of title 28, United States Code, who dies within 6 months after the date of enactment of this Act [August 3, 1956] after having rendered at least 5 years of civilian service computed as prescribed in subsection (o) of section 376 of title 28, United States Code, as added by section 2 of this Act, but without having made an election as provided in such section 376 [this section] to bring himself within the purview of that section, an annuity shall be paid to his widow and surviving dependent children as provided in such section 376 [this section] as if such judge had elected on the day of his death to bring himself within the purview of such section 376 [this section] but had not made

the deposit provided for by subsection (c) of the said section. An annuity shall be payable under this section computed on the basis of the actual length of judicial and other allowable service of the judge and subject to the reduction required by subsection (c) of such section 376 even though no deposit has been made, as required by subsection (g) of such section 376 [this section], with respect to any of such service."

Redeposit of Contributions Prior to 1992 Amendment

Section 201(k) of Pub.L. 102–572 provided that: "Any judicial official as defined in section 376(a)(1) of title 28, United States Code [subsec. (a)(1) of this section], who makes an election under section 376(b) of title 28, United States Code [subsec. (b) of this section], may make a redeposit, as required by section 7 of Public Law 94–554 [set out as a note under this section] and section 2(c)(2) of Public Law 99–336 [set out as a note under this section], to the credit of the Judicial Survivors' Annuities Fund in installments, in such amounts and under such conditions as may be determined in each instance by the Director of the Administrative Office of the United States Courts. If a judicial official elects to make a redeposit in installments—

"(1) the Director shall require that the first installment payment made shall be in an amount no smaller than the last 18 months of salary deductions or deposits previously returned to that judicial official in a lump-sum payment; and

"(2) the election under section 376(b) of title 28, United States Code [subsec. (b) of this section], shall be effective upon payment of the first such installment."

Resigned, Removed, and Retired Judges

Section 6 of Act Aug. 3, 1956, c. 944, 70 Stat. 1021, provided that: "A judge who resigned prior to the date of enactment of this Act [Aug. 3, 1956] and who on that date is receiving salary under section 371(a) of title 28, United States Code, or who resigned, was removed or failed of reappointment prior to the date of enactment of this Act [Aug. 3, 1956] and who on that date is receiving salary under section 373 of title 28, United States Code, shall be considered a judge within the meaning of section 376 of title 28, United States Code, as added by section 2 of this Act [this section], and as such shall be entitled within six months after the date of enactment of this Act [Aug. 3, 1956] to make the election authorized by and to receive the benefits of that section. A judge who retired from regular active service under section 260 of the Judicial Code of 1911 or the Act of August 5, 1939, chapter 433, and who is living on the date of enactment of this Act shall be deemed for the purposes of this Act to have retired from regular active service under section 371(b) or 372(a), as the case may be, of title 28, United States Code."

Revocation of Election to Participate in Annuities Program

Section 2(c) of Pub.L. 99–336 provided that:

"(1) Within 180 days after the effective date of this section [Oct. 1, 1986], any judicial official who, before such effective date, made an election under section 376 of title 28, United States Code [this section], to come within the purview of that section, shall be entitled to revoke that election. Such revocation shall constitute a complete withdrawal from the judicial survivors' annuities program provided for in such section 376 [this section]. No such revocation shall be effective unless it is submitted in writing to the Director of the

Administrative Office of the United States Courts, and until such writing is received by the Director. Upon receipt by the Director of such writing, any rights to survivorship benefits for the survivors of such judicial official shall terminate, and all amounts credited to the individual account of such judicial official under section 376(e) [subsec. (e) of this section], together with interest at 3 percent per annum, compounded on December 31 of each year to such date of revocation, shall be returned to that judicial official in a lump-sum payment.

"(2) Any judicial official who makes a revocation under paragraph (1) of this subsection and who thereafter becomes eligible to make an election under section 376(b) of title 28, United States Code [subsec. (b) of this section], may make such election only if such judicial official redeposits, to the credit of the Judicial Survivors' Annuities Fund, the full amount of the lump-sum payment made to such judicial official under paragraph (1) of this subsection, together with interest at 3 percent per annum, compounded on December 31 of each year from the date of such revocation until the date upon which that amount is so redeposited.

"(3) Any judicial official who fails to revoke an election in accordance with paragraph (1) of this subsection shall be deemed to have irrevocably waived the right to make that revocation."

Section 7 of Pub.L. 94–554 provided: "That, at any time within one hundred and eighty days after the date upon which this Act becomes effective [see Effective and Applicability Provisions of 1976 Amendments note under this section] any judicial official who has, prior to that date, already participated in the judicial survivors annuity program created by the Act of August 3, 1956 (70 Stat. 1021) [which enacted this section] as amended, shall be entitled to revoke his or her earlier election to participate in that program and thereby completely withdraw from participation in the judicial survivors' annuities program created by this Act: *Provided*, That (a) any such revocation may be effected only by means of a writing filed with the Director of the Administrative Office of the United States Courts, (b) any such writing shall be deemed to have become effective no sooner than the date upon which that writing is received by the Director, (c) upon receipt of such a writing by the Director, any and all rights to survivorship benefits for such judicial official's survivors shall terminate, and all amounts credited to such judicial official's individual account, together with interest at 3 percent per annum, compounded on December 31 of each year to that date of revocation, shall thereafter be returned to that judicial official in a lump-sum refund payment, and (d) any judicial official who effects such a revocation and who subsequently again becomes eligible and elects to join the judicial survivors annuities program created by this Act under the provisions of section 376 of title 28, United States Code [this section] as amended by this Act, shall be permitted to do so only upon the redeposit of the full amount of the refund obtained under this section plus interest at 3 percent per annum, compounded on December 31 of each year from the date of the revocation until the date upon which that amount is redeposited. Any judicial official who fails to effect a revocation in accordance with the right conferred by this section within one hundred and eighty days after the date upon which this Act becomes effective shall be deemed to have irrevocably waived the right to that revocation."

Survivors' Annuities for Incumbents

Section 3(b) of Pub.L. 100–659 provided that: "In the case of a bankruptcy judge or magistrate who elects an annuity under section 2(c) [set out as a note under section 377 of this title], only service for which an annuity under subsection (b) or (c) and subsection (g) of section 377 of title 28, United States Code, as added by section 2 of this Act [section 377(b) or (c) and (g) of this title], is calculated under section 2(c) may be used in the computation of an annuity under section 376 of title 28, United States Code, as amended by subsection (a) of this section."

§ 377. Retirement of bankruptcy judges and magistrate judges

(a) Retirement based on years of service.—A bankruptcy judge or magistrate judge to whom this section applies and who retires from office after attaining the age of 65 years and serving at least 14 years, whether continuously or otherwise, as such bankruptcy judge or magistrate judge shall, subject to subsection (f), be entitled to receive, during the remainder of the judge's or magistrate judge's lifetime, an annuity equal to the salary being received at the time the judge or magistrate judge leaves office.

(b) Retirement upon failure of reappointment.— A bankruptcy judge or magistrate judge to whom this section applies, who is not reappointed following the expiration of the term of office of such judge or magistrate judge, and who retires upon the completion of the term shall, subject to subsection (f), be entitled to receive, upon attaining the age of 65 years and during the remainder of such bankruptcy judge's or magistrate judge's lifetime, an annuity equal to that portion of the salary being received at the time the judge or magistrate judge leaves office which the aggregate number of years of service, not to exceed 14, bears to 14, if—

(1) such judge or magistrate judge has served at least 1 full term as a bankruptcy judge or magistrate judge, and

(2) not earlier than 9 months before the date on which the term of office of such judge or magistrate judge expires, and not later than 6 months before such date, such judge or magistrate judge notified the appointing authority in writing that such judge or magistrate judge was willing to accept reappointment to the position in which such judge or magistrate judge was serving.

For purposes of this subsection, in the case of a bankruptcy judge, the written notice required by paragraph (2) shall be given to the chief judge of the circuit in which such bankruptcy judge is serving and, in the case of a magistrate judge, such notice shall be given to the chief judge of the district court in which the magistrate judge is serving.

(c) Service of at least 8 years.—A bankruptcy judge or magistrate judge to whom this section ap-

plies and who retires after serving at least 8 years, whether continuously or otherwise, as such a bankruptcy judge or magistrate judge shall, subject to subsection (f), be entitled to receive, upon attaining the age of 65 years and during the remainder of the judge's or magistrate judge's lifetime, an annuity equal to that portion of the salary being received at the time the judge or magistrate judge leaves office which the aggregate number of years of service, not to exceed 14, bears to 14. Such annuity shall be reduced by ⅙ of 1 percent for each full month such bankruptcy judge or magistrate judge was under the age of 65 at the time the judge or magistrate judge left office, except that such reduction shall not exceed 20 percent.

(d) **Retirement for disability.**—A bankruptcy judge or magistrate judge to whom this section applies, who has served at least 5 years, whether continuously or otherwise, as such a bankruptcy judge or magistrate judge, and who retires or is removed from office upon the sole ground of mental or physical disability shall, subject to subsection (f), be entitled to receive, during the remainder of the judge's or magistrate judge's lifetime, an annuity equal to 40 percent of the salary being received at the time of retirement or removal or, in the case of a judge or magistrate judge who has served for at least 10 years, an amount equal to that proportion of the salary being received at the time of retirement or removal which the aggregate number of years of service, not to exceed 14, bears to 14.

(e) **Cost-of-living adjustments.**—A bankruptcy judge or magistrate judge who is entitled to an annuity under this section is also entitled to a cost-of-living adjustment in such annuity, calculated and payable in the same manner as adjustments under section 8340(b) of title 5, except that any such annuity, as increased under this subsection, may not exceed the salary then payable for the position from which the judge or magistrate judge retired or was removed.

(f) **Election; annuity in lieu of other annuities.**—A bankruptcy judge or magistrate judge shall be entitled to an annuity under this section if the judge or magistrate judge elects an annuity under this section by notifying the Director of the Administrative Office of the United States Courts. A bankruptcy judge or magistrate judge who elects to receive an annuity under this section shall not be entitled to receive [1]

(1) any annuity to which such judge or magistrate judge would otherwise have been entitled under subchapter III of chapter 83, or under chapter 84 (except for subchapters III and VII), of title 5, for service performed as such a judge or magistrate judge or otherwise;

(2) an annuity or salary in senior status or retirement under section 371 or 372 of this title;

(3) retired pay under section 7447 of the Internal Revenue Code of 1986; or

(4) retired pay under section 7296 of title 38.

(g) **Calculation of service.**—(1) For purposes of calculating an annuity under this section—

(A) full-time service as a bankruptcy judge or magistrate judge to whom this section applies may be credited; and

(B) each month of service shall be credited as one-twelfth of a year, and the fractional part of any month shall not be credited.

(2)(A) In the case of an individual who is a bankruptcy judge to whom this section applies and who retires under this section or who is removed from office under subsection (d) upon the sole ground of mental or physical disability, any service of that individual as a United States magistrate judge to whom this section applies, and any service of that individual as a full-time judicial officer who performed the duties of a magistrate judge and a bankruptcy judge at the same time, shall be included for purposes of calculating years of service under subsection (a), (b), (c), or (d), as the case may be.

(B) In the case of an individual who is a magistrate judge to whom this section applies and who retires under this section or who is removed from office under subsection (d) upon the sole ground of mental or physical disability, any service of that individual as a bankruptcy judge to whom this section applies, and any service of that individual as a full-time judicial officer who performed the duties of magistrate judge and a bankruptcy judge at the same time, shall be included for purposes of calculating years of service under subsection (a), (b), (c), or (d), as the case may be.

(h) **Covered positions and service.**—This section applies to—

(1) any bankruptcy judge appointed under—

(A) section 152 of this title;

(B) section 34 of the Bankruptcy Act before the repeal of that Act by section 401 of the Act of November 6, 1978 (Public Law 95–598; 92 Stat. 2682); or

(C) section 404 of the Act of November 6, 1978 (Public Law 95–598; 92 Stat. 2549); and

(2) any United States magistrate judge appointed under section 631 of this title,

only with respect to service on or after October 1, 1979, as such a bankruptcy judge or magistrate judge.

(i) **Payments pursuant to court order.**—(1) Payments under this section which would otherwise be made to a bankruptcy judge or magistrate judge based upon his or her service shall be paid (in whole or in part) by the Director of the Administrative

Office of the United States Courts to another person if and to the extent expressly provided for in the terms of any court decree of divorce, annulment, or legal separation, or the terms of any court order or court-approved property settlement agreement incident to any court decree of divorce, annulment, or legal separation. Any payment under this paragraph to a person bars recovery by any other person.

(2) Paragraph (1) shall apply only to payments made by the Director of the Administrative Office of the United States Courts after the date of receipt by the Director of written notice of such decree, order, or agreement, and such additional information as the Director may prescribe.

(3) As used in this subsection, the term "court" means any court of any State, the District of Columbia, the Commonwealth of Puerto Rico, Guam, the Northern Mariana Islands, or the Virgin Islands, and any Indian tribal court or courts of Indian offense.

(j) Deductions, contributions, and deposits.—

(1) Deductions.—Beginning with the next pay period after the Director of the Administrative Office of the United States Courts receives a notice under subsection (f) that a bankruptcy judge or magistrate judge has elected an annuity under this section, the Director shall deduct and withhold 1 percent of the salary of such bankruptcy judge or magistrate judge. Amounts shall be so deducted and withheld in a manner determined by the Director. Amounts deducted and withheld under this subsection shall be deposited in the Treasury of the United States to the credit of the Judicial Officers' Retirement Fund. Deductions under this subsection from the salary of a bankruptcy judge or magistrate judge shall terminate upon the retirement of the bankruptcy judge or magistrate judge or upon completing 14 years of service for which contributions under this section have been made, whether continuously or otherwise, as calculated under subsection (g), whichever occurs first.

(2) Consent to deductions; discharge of claims.—Each bankruptcy judge or magistrate judge who makes an election under subsection (f) shall be deemed to consent and agree to the deductions from salary which are made under paragraph (1). Payment of such salary less such deductions (and any deductions made under section 376 of this title) is a full and complete discharge and acquittance of all claims and demands for all services rendered by such bankruptcy judge or magistrate judge during the period covered by such payment, except the right to those benefits to which the bankruptcy judge or magistrate judge is entitled under this section (and section 376).

(k) Deposits for prior service.—Each bankruptcy judge or magistrate judge who makes an election

under subsection (f) may deposit, for service performed before such election for which contributions may be made under this section, an amount equal to 1 percent of the salary received for that service. Credit for any period covered by that service may not be allowed for purposes of an annuity under this section until a deposit under this subsection has been made for that period.

(*l*) Individual retirement records.—The amounts deducted and withheld under subsection (j), and the amounts deposited under subsection (k), shall be credited to individual accounts in the name of each bankruptcy judge or magistrate judge from whom such amounts are received, for credit to the Judicial Officers' Retirement Fund.

(m) Annuities affected in certain cases.—

(1) Practicing law after retirement.—

(A) Forfeiture of annuity.—Subject to subparagraph (B), any bankruptcy judge or magistrate judge who retires under this section and who thereafter practices law shall forfeit all rights to an annuity under this section for all periods beginning on or after the first day on which he or she so practices law.

(B) Forfeiture not to apply where individual elects to freeze amount of annuity.—(i) If a bankruptcy judge or magistrate judge makes an election to practice law after retirement under this section—

(I) subparagraph (A) shall not apply to such bankruptcy judge or magistrate judge beginning on the date such election takes effect, and

(II) the annuity payable under this section to such bankruptcy judge or magistrate judge, for periods beginning on or after the date such election takes effect, shall be equal to the annuity to which such bankruptcy judge or magistrate judge is entitled on the day before such effective date.

(ii) An election under clause (i)—

(I) may be made by a bankruptcy judge or magistrate judge eligible for retirement under this section, and

(II) shall be filed with the Director of the Administrative Office of the United States Courts.

Such an election, once it takes effect, shall be irrevocable.

(iii) Any election under this subparagraph shall take effect on the first day of the first month following the month in which the election is made.

(2) Recall not permitted.—Any bankruptcy judge or magistrate judge who retires under this section and who thereafter practices law shall not

be eligible for recall under section 155(b), 375, or 636(h) of this title.

(3) Accepting other employment.—Any bankruptcy judge or magistrate judge who retires under this section and thereafter accepts compensation for civil office or employment under the United States Government (other than for the performance of functions as a bankruptcy judge or magistrate judge under section 155(b), 375, or 636(h) of this title) shall forfeit all rights to an annuity under this section for the period for which such compensation is received. For purposes of this paragraph, the term "compensation" includes retired pay or salary received in retired status.

(n) Lump-sum payments.—

(1) **Eligibility.**—(A) Subject to paragraph (2), an individual who serves as a bankruptcy judge or magistrate judge and—

(i) who leaves office and is not reappointed as a bankruptcy judge or magistrate judge for at least 31 consecutive days;

(ii) who files an application with the Administrative Office of the United States Courts for payment of the lump-sum credit;

(iii) is not serving as a bankruptcy judge or magistrate judge at the time of filing of the application; and

(iv) will not become eligible to receive an annuity under this section within 31 days after filing the application;

is entitled to be paid the lump-sum credit. Payment of the lump-sum credit voids all rights to an annuity under this section based on the service on which the lump-sum credit is based, until that individual resumes office as a bankruptcy judge or magistrate judge.

(B) Lump-sum benefits authorized by subparagraphs (C), (D), and (E) of this paragraph shall be paid to the person or persons surviving the bankruptcy judge or magistrate judge and alive on the date title to the payment arises, in the order of precedence set forth in subsection (o) of section 376 of this title, and in accordance with the last two sentences of that subsection. For purposes of the preceding sentence, the term "judicial official" as used in subsection (o) of section 376 shall be deemed to mean "bankruptcy judge or magistrate judge".

(C) If a bankruptcy judge or magistrate judge dies before receiving an annuity under this section, the lump-sum credit shall be paid.

(D) If all annuity rights under this section based on the service of a deceased bankruptcy judge or magistrate judge terminate before the total annuity paid equals the lump-sum credit, the difference shall be paid.

(E) If a bankruptcy judge or magistrate judge who is receiving an annuity under this section dies, annuity accrued and unpaid shall be paid.

(F) Annuity accrued and unpaid on the termination, except by death, of the annuity of a bankruptcy judge or magistrate judge shall be paid to that individual.

(G) Subject to paragraph (2), a bankruptcy judge or magistrate judge who forfeits rights to an annuity under subsection (m)(3) before the total annuity paid equals the lump-sum credit, shall be entitled to be paid the difference if the bankruptcy judge or magistrate judge files an application with the Administrative Office of the United States Courts for payment of that difference. A payment under this subparagraph voids all rights to an annuity on which the payment is based.

(2) **Spouses and former spouses.**—(A) Payment of the lump-sum credit under paragraph (1)(A) or a payment under paragraph (1)(G)—

(i) may be made only if any current spouse and any former spouse of the bankruptcy judge or magistrate judge are notified of the bankruptcy judge's or magistrate judge's application; and

(ii) shall be subject to the terms of a court decree of divorce, annulment, or legal separation or any court or court approved property settlement agreement incident to such decree, if—

(I) the decree, order, or agreement expressly relates to any portion of the lump-sum credit or other payment involved; and

(II) payment of the lump-sum credit or other payment would extinguish entitlement of the bankruptcy judge's or magistrate judge's spouse or former spouse to any portion of an annuity under subsection (i).

(B) Notification of a spouse or former spouse under this paragraph shall be made in accordance with such requirements as the Director of the Administrative Office of the United States Courts shall by regulation prescribe. The Director may provide under such regulations that subparagraph (A)(i) may be waived with respect to a spouse or former spouse if the bankruptcy judge or magistrate judge establishes to the satisfaction of the Director that the whereabouts of such spouse or former spouse cannot be determined.

(C) The Director shall prescribe regulations under which this paragraph shall be applied in any case in which the Director receives two or more orders or decrees described in subparagraph (A).

(3) **Definition.**—For purposes of this subsection, the term "lump-sum credit" means the unrefunded amount consisting of—

(A) retirement deductions made under this section from the salary of a bankruptcy judge or magistrate judge;

(B) amounts deposited under subsection (k) by a bankruptcy judge or magistrate judge covering earlier service; and

(C) interest on the deductions and deposits which, for any calendar year, shall be equal to the overall average yield to the Judicial Officers' Retirement Fund during the preceding fiscal year from all obligations purchased by the Secretary of the Treasury during such fiscal year under subsection (*o*);

but does not include interest—

(i) if the service covered thereby aggregates 1 year or less; or

(ii) for the fractional part of a month in the total service.

(*o*) Judicial Officers' Retirement Fund.—

(1) Establishment.—There is established in the Treasury a fund which shall be known as the "Judicial Officers' Retirement Fund". The Fund is appropriated for the payment of annuities, refunds, and other payments under this section.

(2) Investment of Fund.—The Secretary of the Treasury shall invest, in interest bearing securities of the United States, such currently available portions of the Judicial Officers' Retirement Fund as are not immediately required for payments from the Fund. The income derived from these investments constitutes a part of the Fund.

(3) Unfunded liability.—**(A)** There are authorized to be appropriated to the Judicial Officers' Retirement Fund amounts required to reduce to zero the unfunded liability of the Fund.

(B) For purposes of subparagraph (A), the term "unfunded liability" means the estimated excess, determined on an annual basis in accordance with the provisions of section 9503 of title 31, of the present value of all benefits payable from the Judicial Officers' Retirement Fund over the sum of—

(i) the present value of deductions to be withheld under this section from the future basic pay of bankruptcy judges and magistrate judges; plus

(ii) the balance in the Fund as of the date the unfunded liability is determined.

In making any determination under this subparagraph, the Comptroller General shall use the applicable information contained in the reports filed pursuant to section 9503 of title 31, with respect to the retirement annuities provided for in this section.

(C) There are authorized to be appropriated such sums as may be necessary to carry out this paragraph.

(Added Pub.L. 100–659, § 2(a), Nov. 15, 1988, 102 Stat. 3910, and amended Pub.L. 101–650, Title III, §§ 321, 325(b)(3),

Dec. 1, 1990, 104 Stat. 5117, 5121; Pub.L. 102–40, Title IV, § 402(d)(2), May 7, 1991, 105 Stat. 239.)

1 So in original. Probably should be "receive—"

HISTORICAL AND STATUTORY NOTES

References in Text

Section 7447 of the Internal Revenue Code of 1986, referred to in subsec. (f)(3), is classified to section 7447 of Title 26, Internal Revenue Code.

Section 34 of the Bankruptcy Act, referred to in subsec. (h)(1)(B), was classified to section 62 of former Title 11, Bankruptcy, and was omitted in the enactment of revised Title 11 by Section 101 of Pub.L. 95–598, Nov. 6, 1978, 92 Stat. 2549 the Bankruptcy Act was repealed effective Oct. 1, 1979, by Sections 401(a), 402(a) of Pub.L. 95–598.

Section 404 of the Act of November 6, 1978 (Pub.L. 95–598), referred to in subsec. (h)(1)(C), and formerly set out as a note preceding section 151 of this title, was repealed by Pub.L. 98–353, Title I, § 114, July 10, 1984, 98 Stat. 343.

Effective and Applicability Provisions

1988 Acts

Section 9 of Pub.L. 100–659 provided that:

"**(a) In general.**—Subject to subsection (b), this Act and the amendments made by this Act [enacting this section and section 8440a of Title 5, Government Organization and Employees, amending sections 155, 375, 376, 604, 631, and 636 of this title and sections 8334 and 8402 of Title 5 and enacting provisions set out as notes under this section and sections 1 and 376 of this title] shall take effect on the date of enactment of this Act [Nov. 15, 1988] and shall apply to bankruptcy judges and magistrates who retire on or after the date of the enactment of this Act.

"**(b) Exception for judges and magistrates retiring on or after July 31, 1987.**—A bankruptcy judge or magistrate who left office on or after July 31, 1987, and before the date of the enactment of this Act [Nov. 15, 1988] may elect to receive an annuity, or to participate in the Judicial Survivors' Annuity System, under the amendments made by this Act if such bankruptcy judge or magistrate, within 60 days after so leaving office, accepted office or employment with the United States Government or a State government or was eligible at the time he or she left office for an immediate annuity under title 5, United States Code. Any election under this subsection shall not be valid unless it is made within 6 months after the date of the enactment of this act [Nov. 15, 1988] and under the same conditions as other persons who may make elections under the amendments made by this Act, except that any such person who makes an election under this subsection shall not receive a lump-sum credit under section 8342 or 8424 of title 5, United States Code [section 8342 or 8424 of Title 5], for prior service and shall not be required to make contributions for prior years of creditable service."

Change of Name

"United States magistrate judge" substituted for "United States magistrate" in text pursuant to section 321 of Pub.L. 101–650, set out as a note under 28 U.S.C.A. § 631.

United States magistrate appointed under section 631 of this title to be known as United States magistrate judge after Dec. 1, 1990, with any reference to United States magistrate or magistrate in this title, in any other Federal

statute, etc., deemed a reference to United States magistrate judge appointed under section 631 of this title, see section 321 of Pub.L. 101–650, set out as a note under section 631 of this title.

Qualified Magistrate Judges

Pub.L. 107–116, Title V, § 515, Jan. 10, 2002, 115 Stat. 2220, provided that:

"**(a)** In this section the term 'qualified magistrate judge' means any person who—

"**(1)** retired as a magistrate judge before November 15, 1988; and

"**(2)** On the date of filing an election under subsection (b)—

"**(A)** is serving as a recalled magistrate judge on a full-time basis under section 636(h) of title 28, United States Code [28 U.S.C.A. § 636(h)]; and

"**(B)** has completed at least 5 years of full-time recall service.

"**(b)** The director of the administrative office of the United States courts may accept the election of a qualified magistrate judge to—

"**(1)** receive an annuity under section 377 of title 28, United States Code [this section]; and

"**(2)** come within the purview of section 376 of such title [28 U.S.C.A. § 376].

"**(c)** Full–time recall service performed by a qualified magistrate judge shall be credited for service in calculating an annuity elected under this section.

"**(d)** The Director of the Administrative Office of the United States Courts may promulgate regulations to carry out this section."

Report to Congress on Financial Operation of Retirement Annuity Program

Pub.L. 100–659, § 8, Nov. 15, 1988, 102 Stat. 3920, provided that: "The Director of the Administrative Office of the United States Courts shall, not later than 5 years after the date of the enactment of this Act [Nov. 15, 1988], submit a report to the Congress on the financial operation of the retirement annuity program established under this Act and the amendments made by this Act [see Effective and Applicability Provisions of 1988 Amendments note set out under this section]. The report shall, in particular, include a discussion of the deductions from salary and deposits made for contributions to the annuity program and the need for continuing the deductions at the level established under the amendments made by this Act."

[For termination, effective May 15, 2000, of reporting provisions of Pub.L. 100–659, § 8, set out above, see Pub.L. 104–66, § 3003, as amended, set out as a note under 31 U.S.C.A. § 1113, and the 7th item on page 12 of House Document No. 103–7.]

Retirement Annuities for Incumbent Bankruptcy Judges and Magistrates

Section 2(c) of Pub.L. 100–659 provided that:

"**(1) Retirement annuity under Title 5 and section 377 of Title 28.**—A bankruptcy judge or United States magistrate in active service on the effective date of this Act [Nov. 15, 1988] shall, subject to paragraph (2), be entitled, in lieu of the annuity otherwise provided under the amendments made by this section [enacting this section], to—

"**(A)** an annuity under subchapter III of chapter 83, or under chapter 84, of Title 5, United States Code [section 8331 et seq. or section 8401 et seq. of Title 5, Government Organization and Employees], as the case may be, for creditable service before the date on which service would begin to be credited for purposes of subparagraph (B), and

"**(B)** an annuity calculated under subsection (b) or (c) and subsection (g) of section 377 of title 28, United States Code, as added by this section [subsecs. (b) or (c) and (g) of this section], for any service as a full-time bankruptcy judge or magistrate on or after October 1, 1979 (as specified in the election pursuant to paragraph (2)) for which deductions and deposits are made under subsections (j) and (k) of such section 377 [subsecs. (j) and (k) of this section], as applicable, without regard to the minimum number of years of service as such a bankruptcy judge or magistrate, except that—

"**(i)** in the case of a judge or a magistrate who retires with less than 8 years of service, the annuity under subsection (c) of section 377 of title 28, United States Code [subsec. (c) of this section], shall be equal to that proportion of the salary being received at the time the judge or magistrate leaves office which the years of service bears to 14, subject to a reduction in accordance with subsection (c) of such section 377 if the bankruptcy judge or magistrate is under age 65 at the time he or she leaves office, and

"**(ii)** the aggregate amount of the annuity initially payable on retirement under this subsection may not exceed the rate of pay for the bankruptcy judge or magistrate which is in effect on the day before the retirement becomes effective.

"**(2) Filing of notice of election.**—A bankruptcy judge or magistrate shall be entitled to an annuity under this subsection only if the judge or magistrate files a notice of that election with the Director of the Administrative Office of the United States Courts specifying the date on which service would begin to be credited under section 377 of title 28, United States Code [this section], in lieu of chapter 83 or chapter 84 of title 5, United States Code [section 8331 et seq. or 8401 et seq. of Title 5].

"**(3) Lump-sum credit under Title 5.**—A bankruptcy judge or magistrate who makes an election under paragraph (2) shall be entitled to a lump-sum credit under section 8342 or 8424 of title 5, United States Code [section 8342 or 8424 of Title 5], as the case may be, for any service which is covered under section 377 of title 28, United States Code [this section], as added by this section, pursuant to that election, and with respect to which any contributions were made by the judge or magistrate under the applicable provisions of title 5, United States Code.

"**(4) Recall.**—With respect to any bankruptcy judge or magistrate receiving an annuity under this subsection who is recalled to serve under section 375 of title 28, United States Code [section 375 of this title]—

"**(A)** the amount of compensation which such recalled judge or magistrate receives under subsection (c) of such section shall be calculated on the basis of the annuity received under this subsection; and

"**(B)** such recalled judge or magistrate may serve as a reemployed annuitant to the extent permitted by

subsection (e) of section 375 of such title [section 375(e) of this title].

Section 377(m)(3) of title 28, United States Code, as added by subsection (a) of this section [subsec. (m)(3) of this section], shall not apply with respect to service as a reemployed annuitant described in subparagraph (B)."

CHAPTER 19—DISTRIBUTION OF REPORTS AND DIGESTS

§ 411. Supreme Court reports; printing, binding, and distribution

(a) The decisions of the Supreme Court of the United States shall be printed, bound, and distributed in the preliminary prints and bound volumes of the United States Reports as soon as practicable after rendition, to be charged to the proper appropriation for the judiciary. The number and distribution of the copies shall be under the control of the Joint Committee on Printing.

(b) Reports printed prior to June 12, 1926, shall not be furnished the Secretary of the Army, the Secretary of the Navy, or the Secretary of the Air Force.

(c) The Public Printer, or other printer designated by the Supreme Court of the United States, upon request, shall furnish to the Superintendent of Documents the reports required to be distributed under the provisions of this section.

(June 25, 1948, c. 646, 62 Stat. 904; May 24, 1949, c. 139, § 68, 63 Stat. 99; Oct. 31, 1951, c. 655, § 41, 65 Stat. 725; July 10, 1952, c. 632, § 4, 66 Stat. 540.)

§ 412. Sale of Supreme Court reports

The Public Printer, or other printer designated by the Supreme Court of the United States shall print such additional bound volumes and preliminary prints of such reports as may be required for sale to the public. Such additional copies shall be sold by the Superintendent of Documents, as provided by law.

(June 25, 1948, c. 646, 62 Stat. 906; July 10, 1952, c. 632, § 5, 66 Stat. 541.)

§ 413. Publications; distribution to courts

Distribution of publications to Federal courts in accordance with the provisions of this chapter shall not be made to any place where such court is held in a building not owned or controlled by the United States

unless such publications are committed to the custody of an officer of the United States at such building.

The Attorney General and the Director in the procurement of law books, books of reference or periodicals may exchange or sell similar items and apply the allowance or proceeds to payment in whole or in part of the cost of the items procured.

(June 25, 1948, c. 646, 62 Stat. 906; May 24, 1949, c. 139, § 69, 63 Stat. 100; July 10, 1952, c. 632, § 6, 66 Stat. 541.)

§ 414. Transmittal of books to successors

All government publications and law books furnished to justices, judges, clerks of courts, and United States attorneys of the United States and its territories and possessions, and other officers of the United States or an agency thereof shall be transmitted to their successors in office. All permanent or bound books and publications furnished under this chapter except those books furnished to the Library of Congress for international exchange shall remain the property of the United States and shall be marked plainly, "The Property of the United States".

(June 25, 1948, c. 646, 62 Stat. 906; Oct. 18, 1962, Pub.L. 87–845, § 7, 76A Stat. 699.)

HISTORICAL AND STATUTORY NOTES

Effective and Applicability Provisions

1962 Acts

Amendment by Pub.L. 87–845 effective Jan. 2, 1963, see section 25 of Pub.L. 87–845, set out as a note under Section 14 of Title 18, Crimes and Criminal Procedure.

[§ 415. Repealed. Pub.L. 97–164, Title I, § 113, Apr. 2, 1982, 96 Stat. 29]

HISTORICAL AND STATUTORY NOTES

Section, Acts June 25, 1948, c. 646, 62 Stat. 906; May 24, 1949, c. 139, § 70, 63 Stat. 100, provided for the distribution of copies of the decisions of the Court of Claims. See section 174(b) of this title.

Effective Date of Repeal

Repeal effective Oct. 1, 1982, see section 402 of Pub.L. 97–164, set out as a note under section 171 of this title.

CHAPTER 21—GENERAL PROVISIONS APPLICABLE TO COURTS AND JUDGES

[1] So in original. Does not conform to section catchline.

HISTORICAL AND STATUTORY NOTES
Change of Name
"United States magistrate judge" substituted for "United States magistrate" in item 455 pursuant to section 321 of Pub.L. 101–650, set out as a note under 28 U.S.C.A. § 631.

§ 451. Definitions

As used in this title:

The term "court of the United States" includes the Supreme Court of the United States, courts of appeals, district courts constituted by chapter 5 of this title, including the Court of International Trade and any court created by Act of Congress the judges of which are entitled to hold office during good behavior.

The terms "district court" and "district court of the United States" mean the courts constituted by chapter 5 of this title.

The term "judge of the United States" includes judges of the courts of appeals, district courts, Court of International Trade and any court created by Act of Congress, the judges of which are entitled to hold office during good behavior.

The term "justice of the United States" includes the Chief Justice of the United States and the associate justices of the Supreme Court.

The term "district" and "judicial district" mean the districts enumerated in Chapter 5 of this title.

The term "department" means one of the executive departments enumerated in section 1 of Title 5, unless the context shows that such term was intended to describe the executive, legislative, or judicial branches of the government.

The term "agency" includes any department, independent establishment, commission, administration, authority, board or bureau of the United States or any corporation in which the United States has a proprietary interest, unless the context shows that such term was intended to be used in a more limited sense.

(June 25, 1948, c. 646, 62 Stat. 907; Mar. 18, 1959, Pub.L. 86–3, § 10, 73 Stat. 9; Sept. 12, 1966, Pub.L. 89–571, § 3, 80 Stat. 764; Nov. 6, 1978, Pub.L. 95–598, Title II, § 213, 92 Stat. 2661; Oct. 10, 1980, Pub.L. 96–417, Title V, § 501(10), 94 Stat. 1742; Apr. 2, 1982, Pub.L. 97–164, Title I, § 114, 96 Stat. 29.)

HISTORICAL AND STATUTORY NOTES
References in Text
Section 1 of Title 5, referred to in text, is section 1 of former Title 5. Executive Departments and Government Officers and Employees, the provisions of which are covered by section 101 of Title 5, Government Organization and Employees.

Codifications
The paragraphs of this section defining the term "court of the United States" and the term "judge of the United States" were amended by Pub.L. 95–598, Title II, § 213, Nov. 6, 1978, 92 Stat. 2668, effective June 28, 1984, pursuant to Pub.L. 95–598, Title IV, § 402(b), Nov. 6, 1978, 92 Stat. 2682, as amended by Pub.L. 98–249, § 1(a), Mar. 31, 1984, 98 Stat. 116; Pub.L. 98–271, § 1(a), Apr. 30, 1984, 98 Stat. 163; Pub.L. 98–299, § 1(a), May 25, 1984, 98 Stat. 214; Pub.L. 98–325, § 1(a), June 20, 1984, 98 Stat. 268, set out as a note preceding section 101 of Title 11, Bankruptcy, to read as follows:

The term "court of the United States" includes the Supreme Court of the United States, courts of appeals, district courts constituted by chapter 5 of this title, including the Court of International Trade and any court created by Act of Congress the judges of which are entitled to hold office during good behavior, and bankruptcy courts, the judges of which are entitled to hold office for a term of 14 years.

The term "judge of the United States" includes judges of the courts of appeals, district courts, Court of International Trade and any court created by Act of Congress, the judges of which are entitled to hold office during good behavior, and judge of the bankruptcy courts, the judges of which are entitled to hold office for a term of 14 years.

Section 402(b) of Pub.L. 95–598 was amended by section 113 of Pub.L. 98–353, Title I, July 10, 1984, 98 Stat. 343, by substituting "shall not be effective" for "shall take effect on June 28, 1984", thereby eliminating the amendment by section 213 of Pub.L. 95–598, effective June 27, 1984, pursuant to section 122(c) of Pub.L. 98–353, set out as an Effective and Applicability Provisions note under section 151 of this title.

Section 121(a) of Pub.L. 98–353 directed that section 402(b) of Pub.L. 95–598 be amended by substituting "the date of enactment of the Bankruptcy Amendments and Federal Judgeship Act of 1984 [i.e. July 10, 1984]" for "June 28, 1984". This amendment was not executed in view of the prior amendment to section 402(b) of Pub.L. 95–598 by section 113 of Pub.L. 98–353.

Effective and Applicability Provisions

1982 Acts

Amendment by Pub.L. 97–164 effective Oct. 1, 1982, see section 402 of Pub.L. 97–164, set out as a note under section 171 of this title.

1980 Acts

Amendment by Pub.L. 96–417 effective on Nov. 1, 1980 and applicable with respect to civil actions pending on or commenced on or after such date, see section 701(a) of Pub.L. 96–417, as amended, set out as a note under section 251 of this title.

1959 Acts

Section 10 of Pub.L. 86–3 provided in part that the amendment of this section shall be effective upon the admission of the State of Hawaii into the Union. Admission of Hawaii into the Union was accomplished Aug. 21, 1959 upon issuance of Proc. No. 3309, Aug. 21, 1959, 25 F.R. 6868, 73 Stat. c74, as required by sections 1 and 7(c) of Pub.L. 86–3, Mar. 18, 1959, 73 Stat. 4, set out as notes preceding Section 491 of Title 48, Territories and Insular Possessions.

"Circuit Court of Appeals;" "Senior Circuit Judge," Etc. Defined

Section 32 of Act June 25, 1948, as amended by Act May 24, 1949, c. 139, § 127, 63 Stat. 107, provided that:

"**(a)** All laws of the United States in force on September 1, 1948, in which reference is made to a 'circuit court of appeals'; 'senior circuit judge'; 'senior district judge'; 'presiding judge'; 'chief justice,' except when reference to the Chief Justice of the United States is intended; or 'justice', except when used with respect to a justice of the Supreme Court of the United States in his capacity as such or as a circuit justice, are hereby amended by substituting 'court of appeals' for 'circuit court of appeals'; 'chief judge of the circuit' for 'senior circuit judge'; 'chief judge of the district court' for 'senior district judge'; 'chief judge' for 'presiding judge'; 'chief judge' for 'chief justice', except when reference to the Chief Justice of the United States is intended; and 'judge' for 'justice', except when the latter term is used with respect to a justice of the Supreme Court of the United States in his capacity as such or as a circuit justice.

"**(b)** All laws of the United States in force on September 1, 1948, in which reference is made to the Supreme Court of the District of Columbia or to the District Court of the United States for the District of Columbia are amended by substituting 'United States District Court for the District of Columbia' for such designations.

"**(c)** All laws of the United States in force on September 1, 1948, in which reference is made to the 'Conference of Senior Circuit Judges', or to the 'Judicial Conference of Senior Circuit Judges' are amended by substituting 'Judicial Conference of the United States' for such designations.

"**(d)** This section shall not be construed to amend historical references to courts or judicial offices which have no present or future application to such courts or offices."

Judges of the United States

Section 2(a) of Act June 25, 1948, c. 646, 62 Stat. 985, amended Sept. 3, 1954, c. 1263, § 51(a), 68 Stat. 1245, provided that: "(a) The Chief Justices of the United States Court of Appeals for the District of Columbia, the District Court of the United States for the District of Columbia, and the Court of Claims [now United States Court of Federal Claims], and the presiding judge of the Court of Customs and Patent Appeals [now United States Court of Appeals for the Federal Circuit], in office on the effective date of this Act shall be the chief judges of their respective courts. The Chief Justice of the United States Court of Appeals for the District of Columbia and the Associate Justices thereof, the Chief Justice of the District Court of the United States for the District of Columbia (formerly named the Supreme Court of the District of Columbia) and the Associate Justices thereof, the Chief Justice of the Court of Claims [now United States Court of Federal Claims], and the presiding judge of the Court of Customs and Patent Appeals [now United States Court of Appeals for the Federal Circuit], in office on the effective date of this Act, shall be judges of the United States within the meaning of Section 451 of Title 28, Judiciary and Judicial Procedure, of the United States Code, set out in Section 1 of this Act. The Chief Justice of the United States Court of Appeals for the District of Columbia and the Associate Justices thereof, in office on the effective date of this Act, shall be circuit judges of the District of Columbia Circuit and vested with all the rights, powers, and duties thereof, and the said Chief Justice of the United States Court of Appeals for the District of Columbia shall be Chief Judge of said Circuit. The Chief Justice of the District Court of the United States for the District of Columbia (formerly named the Supreme Court of the District of Columbia) and the Associate Justices thereof, in office on the effective date of this Act, shall be district judges for the District of Columbia and vested with all the rights, powers, and duties thereof."

Section 51(b) of Act Sept. 3, 1954, provided that this amendment should take effect as of Sept. 1, 1948.

§ 452. Courts always open; powers unrestricted by expiration of sessions

All courts of the United States shall be deemed always open for the purpose of filing proper papers, issuing and returning process, and making motions and orders.

The continued existence or expiration of a session of a court in no way affects the power of the court to do any act or take any proceeding.

(June 25, 1948, c. 646, 62 Stat. 907; Oct. 16, 1963, Pub.L. 88–139, § 2, 77 Stat. 248.)

§ 453. Oaths of justices and judges

Each justice or judge of the United States shall take the following oath or affirmation before performing the duties of his office: "I, _____ _____, do solemnly swear (or affirm) that I will administer justice without respect to persons, and do equal right to the poor and to the rich, and that I will faithfully and impartially discharge and perform all the duties incumbent upon me as _____ under the Constitution and laws of the United States. So help me God."

(June 25, 1948, c. 646, 62 Stat. 907; Dec. 1, 1990, Pub.L. 101–650, Title IV, § 404, 104 Stat. 5124.)

HISTORICAL AND STATUTORY NOTES
Effective and Applicability Provisions
1990 Acts
 Amendment by section 404 of Pub.L. 101–650 effective 90 days after Dec. 1, 1990, see section 407 of Pub.L. 101–650, set out as a note under section 332 of this title.

§ 454. Practice of law by justices and judges

Any justice or judge appointed under the authority of the United States who engages in the practice of law is guilty of a high misdemeanor.

(June 25, 1948, c. 646, 62 Stat. 908.)

§ 455. Disqualification of justice, judge, or magistrate judge

(a) Any justice, judge, or magistrate judge of the United States shall disqualify himself in any proceeding in which his impartiality might reasonably be questioned.

(b) He shall also disqualify himself in the following circumstances:

(1) Where he has a personal bias or prejudice concerning a party, or personal knowledge of disputed evidentiary facts concerning the proceeding;

(2) Where in private practice he served as lawyer in the matter in controversy, or a lawyer with whom he previously practiced law served during such association as a lawyer concerning the matter, or the judge or such lawyer has been a material witness concerning it;

(3) Where he has served in governmental employment and in such capacity participated as counsel, adviser or material witness concerning the proceeding or expressed an opinion concerning the merits of the particular case in controversy;

(4) He knows that he, individually or as a fiduciary, or his spouse or minor child residing in his household, has a financial interest in the subject matter in controversy or in a party to the proceeding, or any other interest that could be substantially affected by the outcome of the proceeding;

(5) He or his spouse, or a person within the third degree of relationship to either of them, or the spouse of such a person:

(i) Is a party to the proceeding, or an officer, director, or trustee of a party;

(ii) Is acting as a lawyer in the proceeding;

(iii) Is known by the judge to have an interest that could be substantially affected by the outcome of the proceeding;

(iv) Is to the judge's knowledge likely to be a material witness in the proceeding.

(c) A judge should inform himself about his personal and fiduciary financial interests, and make a reasonable effort to inform himself about the personal financial interests of his spouse and minor children residing in his household.

(d) For the purposes of this section the following words or phrases shall have the meaning indicated:

(1) "proceeding" includes pretrial, trial, appellate review, or other stages of litigation;

(2) the degree of relationship is calculated according to the civil law system;

(3) "fiduciary" includes such relationships as executor, administrator, trustee, and guardian;

(4) "financial interest" means ownership of a legal or equitable interest, however small, or a relationship as director, adviser, or other active participant in the affairs of a party, except that:

(i) Ownership in a mutual or common investment fund that holds securities is not a "financial interest" in such securities unless the judge participates in the management of the fund;

(ii) An office in an educational, religious, charitable, fraternal, or civic organization is not a "financial interest" in securities held by the organization;

(iii) The proprietary interest of a policyholder in a mutual insurance company, of a depositor in a mutual savings association, or a similar proprietary interest, is a "financial interest" in the organization only if the outcome of the proceeding could substantially affect the value of the interest;

(iv) Ownership of government securities is a "financial interest" in the issuer only if the outcome of the proceeding could substantially affect the value of the securities.

(e) No justice, judge, or magistrate judge shall accept from the parties to the proceeding a waiver of any ground for disqualification enumerated in subsection (b). Where the ground for disqualification arises only under subsection (a), waiver may be accepted provided it is preceded by a full disclosure on the record of the basis for disqualification.

(f) Notwithstanding the preceding provisions of this section, if any justice, judge, magistrate judge, or bankruptcy judge to whom a matter has been assigned would be disqualified, after substantial judicial time has been devoted to the matter, because of the appearance or discovery, after the matter was assigned to him or her, that he or she individually or as a fiduciary, or his or her spouse or minor child residing in his or her household, has a financial interest in a party (other than an interest that could be substantially affected by the outcome), disqualification is not required if the justice, judge, magistrate judge, bankruptcy judge, spouse or minor child, as the case may be, divests himself or herself of the interest that provides the grounds for the disqualification.

(June 25, 1948, c. 646, 62 Stat. 908; Dec. 5, 1974, Pub.L. 93–512, § 1, 88 Stat. 1609; Nov. 6, 1978, Pub.L. 95–598, Title II, § 214(a), (b), 92 Stat. 2661; Nov. 19, 1988, Pub.L. 100–702, Title X, § 1007, 102 Stat. 4667; Dec. 1, 1990, Pub.L. 101–650, Title III, § 321, 104 Stat. 5117.)

HISTORICAL AND STATUTORY NOTES

Change of Name

"United States magistrate judge" substituted for "United States magistrate" in text pursuant to section 321 of Pub.L. 101–650, set out as a note under 28 U.S.C.A. § 631.

Effective and Applicability Provisions

1978 Acts

Amendment by Pub.L. 95–598 effective Oct. 1, 1979, see section 402(c) of Pub.L. 95–598, set out as a note preceding section 101 of Title 11, Bankruptcy. For procedures relating to bankruptcy matters during transition period, see note preceding section 151 of this title.

1974 Acts

Section 3 of Pub.L. 93–512 provided that: "This Act [amending this section] shall not apply to the trial of any proceeding commenced prior to the date of this Act [Dec. 5, 1974], nor to appellate review of any proceeding which was fully submitted to the reviewing court prior to the date of this Act."

§ 456. Traveling expenses of justices and judges; official duty stations

(a) The Director of the Administrative Office of the United States Courts shall pay each justice or judge of the United States, and each retired justice or judge recalled or designated and assigned to active duty, while attending court or transacting official business at a place other than his official duty station for any continuous period of less than thirty calendar days (1) all necessary transportation expenses certified by the justice or judge; and (2) payments for subsistence expenses at rates or in amounts which the Director establishes, in accordance with regulations which the Director shall prescribe with the approval of the Judicial Conference of the United States and after considering the rates or amounts set by the Administrator of General Services and the President pursuant to section 5702 of title 5. The Director of the Administrative Office of the United States Courts shall also pay each justice or judge of the United States, and each retired justice or judge recalled or designated and assigned to active duty, while attending court or transacting official business under an assignment authorized under chapter 13 of this title which exceeds in duration a continuous period of thirty calendar days, all necessary transportation expenses and actual and necessary expenses of subsistence actually incurred, notwithstanding the provisions of section 5702 of title 5, in accordance with regulations which the Director shall prescribe with the approval of the Judicial Conference of the United States.

(b) The official duty station of the Chief Justice of the United States, the Justices of the Supreme Court of the United States, and the judges of the United States Court of Appeals for the District of Columbia Circuit, the United States Court of Appeals for the Federal Circuit, and the United States District Court for the District of Columbia shall be the District of Columbia.

(c) The official duty station of the judges of the United States Court of International Trade shall be New York City.

(d) The official duty station of each district judge shall be that place where a district court holds regular sessions at or near which the judge performs a substantial portion of his judicial work, which is nearest the place where he maintains his actual abode in which he customarily lives.

(e) The official duty station of a circuit judge shall be that place where a circuit or district court holds regular sessions at or near which the judge performs a substantial portion of his judicial work, or that place where the Director provides chambers to the judge where he performs a substantial portion of his judicial work, which is nearest the place where he maintains his actual abode in which he customarily lives.

(f) The official duty station of a retired judge shall be established in accordance with section 374 of this title.

(g) Each circuit or district judge whose official duty station is not fixed expressly by this section shall notify the Director of the Administrative Office of the United States Courts in writing of his actual abode and official duty station upon his appointment and from time to time thereafter as his official duty station may change.

(June 25, 1948, c. 646, 62 Stat. 908; Aug. 8, 1953, c. 376, 67 Stat. 488; Aug. 7, 1959, Pub.L. 86–138, 73 Stat. 285; Nov. 6, 1978, Pub.L. 95–598, Title II, § 215, 92 Stat. 2661; Oct. 10, 1980, Pub.L. 96–417, Title V, § 501(11), 94 Stat. 1742; Apr. 2, 1982, Pub.L. 97–164, Title I, § 115(a) (1), 96 Stat. 30; Jan. 2, 1986, Pub.L. 99–234, Title I, § 107(d), 99 Stat. 1759.)

HISTORICAL AND STATUTORY NOTES

Codifications

The amendment by Pub.L. 95–598 in 1978 to be effective Apr. 1, 1984, was never actually executed to text in view of the later amendment of this section by Pub.L. 97–164, eff. Oct. 1, 1982, which completely revised this section both as it would exist just prior to Oct. 1, 1982, and as it would become effective Apr. 1, 1984. See 1978 and 1982 Amendments notes under this section.

Effective and Applicability Provisions

1986 Acts

Amendment by Pub.L. 99–234 effective on the effective date of regulations to be promulgated not later than 150 days after Jan. 2, 1986, or 180 days after Jan. 2, 1986, whichever occurs first, see section 301(a) of Pub.L. 99–234, set out as a

note under section 5701 of Title 5, Government Organization and Employees.

1982 Acts

Amendment by Pub.L. 97–164 effective Oct. 1, 1982, see section 402 of Pub.L. 97–164, set out as a note under section 171 of this title.

1980 Acts

Amendment by Pub.L. 96–417 effective on Nov. 1, 1980 and applicable with respect to civil actions pending on or commenced on or after such date, see section 701(a) of Pub.L. 96–417, as amended, set out as a note under section 251 of this title.

Promulgation of Regulations by Director

Director to promulgate regulations effectuating increases in reimbursement for expenses, see section 6 of Pub.L. 87–139, Aug. 14, 1961, 75 Stat. 340, set out as a note under section 604 of this title.

Report on Transportation Needs

Pub.L. 99–550, § 3, Oct. 27, 1986, 100 Stat. 3070, provided that: "Within one year after the date of enactment of this Act [Oct. 27, 1986], the Director of the Administrative Office of the United States Courts shall prepare, in consultation with the Marshal of the Supreme Court of the United States, the Clerk of the United States Court of Military Appeals [now United States Court of Appeals for the Armed Forces] and the Court Administrator of the United States Tax Court, and transmit to the Congress, appropriate recommendations concerning the transportation needs of the judicial branch and of courts established pursuant to Article I of the Constitution [U.S.C.A. Const. Art. I]."

§ 457. Records; obsolete papers

The records of district courts and of courts of appeals shall be kept at one or more of the places where court is held. Such places shall be designated by the respective courts except when otherwise directed by the judicial council of the circuit.

Papers of any court established by Act of Congress which have become obsolete and are no longer necessary or useful, may be disposed of with the approval of the court concerned in the manner provided by sections 366–380 of Title 44 and in accordance with the rules of the Judicial Conference of the United States. (June 25, 1948, c. 646, 62 Stat. 908; Nov. 6, 1978, Pub.L. 95–598, Title II, § 216, 92 Stat. 2661.)

HISTORICAL AND STATUTORY NOTES

References in Text

Sections 366–380 of Title 44, referred to in text, were repealed and the provisions thereof reenacted as chapter 33 (Section 3301 et seq.) of Title 44, Public Printing and Documents, by Pub.L. 90–620, Oct. 22, 1968, 82 Stat. 1238.

Codifications

The first paragraph of this section was amended by Pub.L. 95–598, Title II, § 216, Nov. 6, 1978, 92 Stat. 261, effective June 28, 1984, pursuant to Pub.L. 95–598, Title IV, § 402(b), Nov. 6, 1978, 92 Stat. 2682, as amended by Pub.L. 98–249, § 1(a), Mar. 31, 1984, 98 Stat. 116; Pub.L. 98–271, § 1(a),

Apr. 30, 1984, 98 Stat. 163; Pub.L. 98–299, § 1(a), May 25, 1984, 98 Stat. 214; Pub.L. 98–325, § 1(a), June 20, 1984, 98 Stat. 268, set out as an Effective and Applicability Provisions note preceding section 101 of Title 11, Bankruptcy by substituting "The records of bankruptcy courts, of district courts, and of courts of appeals" for "The records of district courts and of courts of appeals".

Section 402(b) of Pub.L. 95–598 was amended by section 113 of Pub.L. 98–353, Title I, July 10, 1984, 98 Stat. 343, by substituting "shall not be effective" for "shall take effect on June 28, 1984", thereby eliminating the amendment by section 216 of Pub.L. 95–598, effective June 27, 1984, pursuant to section 122(c) of Pub.L. 98–353, set out as an Effective and Applicability Provisions note under section 151 of this title.

Section 121(a) of Pub.L. 98–353 directed that section 402(b) of Pub.L. 95–598 be amended by substituting "the date of enactment of the Bankruptcy Amendments and Federal Judgeship Act of 1984 [i.e. July 10, 1984]" for "June 28, 1984". This amendment was not executed in view of the prior amendment to section 402(b) of Pub.L. 95–598 by section 113 of Pub.L. 98–353.

§ 458. Relative of justice or judge ineligible to appointment

(a)(1) No person shall be appointed to or employed in any office or duty in any court who is related by affinity or consanguinity within the degree of first cousin to any justice or judge of such court.

(2) With respect to the appointment of a judge of a court exercising judicial power under article III of the United States Constitution [U.S.C.A. Const. Art. III] (other than the Supreme Court), subsection (b) shall apply in lieu of this subsection.

(b)(1) In this subsection, the term—

 (A) "same court" means—

 (i) in the case of a district court, the court of a single judicial district; and

 (ii) in the case of a court of appeals, the court of appeals of a single circuit; and

 (B) "member"—

 (i) means an active judge or a judge retired in senior status under section 371(b); and

 (ii) shall not include a retired judge, except as described under clause (i).

(2) No person may be appointed to the position of judge of a court exercising judicial power under article III of the United States Constitution [U.S.C.A. Const. Art. III] (other than the Supreme Court) who is related by affinity or consanguinity within the degree of first cousin to any judge who is a member of the same court. (June 25, 1948, c. 646, 62 Stat. 908; Oct. 27, 1998, Pub.L. 105–300, § 1(a), 112 Stat. 2836.)

HISTORICAL AND STATUTORY NOTES

Effective and Applicability Provisions

1998 Acts

Section 1(b) of Pub.L. 105–300 provided that: This Act [amending this section] shall take effect on the date of enactment of this Act [Oct. 27, 1998] and shall apply only to any individual whose nomination is submitted to the Senate on or after such date."

§ 459. Administration of oaths and acknowledgments

Each justice or judge of the United States may administer oaths and affirmations and take acknowledgments.

(June 25, 1948, c. 646, 62 Stat. 908.)

§ 460. Application to other courts

(a) Sections 452 through 459 and section 462 of this chapter shall also apply to the United States Court of Federal Claims, to each court created by Act of Congress in a territory which is invested with any jurisdiction of a district court of the United States, and to the judges thereof.

(b) The official duty station of each judge referred to in subsection (a) which is not otherwise established by law shall be that place where the court holds regular sessions at or near which the judge performs a substantial portion of his judicial work, which is nearest the place where he maintains his actual abode in which he customarily lives.

(June 25, 1948, c. 646, 62 Stat. 908; Oct. 31, 1951, c. 655, § 43(a), 65 Stat. 725; July 7, 1958, Pub.L. 85–508, § 12(e), 72 Stat. 348; Nov. 6, 1978, Pub.L. 95–598, Title II, § 217(a), 92 Stat. 2661; Apr. 2, 1982, Pub.L. 97–164, Title I, § 115(b)(1), 96 Stat. 31; Oct. 29, 1992, Pub.L. 102–572, Title IX, § 902(b)(1), 106 Stat. 4516.)

HISTORICAL AND STATUTORY NOTES

Effective and Applicability Provisions

1992 Acts

Amendment by Pub.L. 102–572 effective Oct. 29, 1992, see section 911 of Pub.L. 102–572, set out as a note under section 171 of this title.

1982 Acts

Amendment by Pub.L. 97–164 effective Oct. 1, 1982, see section 402 of Pub.L. 97–164, set out as a note under section 171 of this title.

1978 Acts

Amendment by Pub.L. 95–598 effective Nov. 6, 1978, see section 402(d) of Pub.L. 95–598, set out as a note preceding section 101 of Title 11, Bankruptcy.

1958 Acts

Amendment by Pub.L. 85–508 effective Jan. 3, 1959 upon admission of Alaska into the Union pursuant to Proc. No. 3269, Jan. 3, 1959, 24 F.R. 81, 73 Stat. c16, as required by section 1 and 8(c) of Pub.L. 85–508, see notes set out under section 81A of this title and preceding section 21 of Title 48, Territories and Insular Possessions.

Change of Name

References to United States Claims Court deemed to refer to United States Court of Federal Claims and references to Claims Court deemed to refer to Court of Federal Claims, see section 902(b) of Pub.L. 102–572, set out as a note under section 171 of Title 28, Judiciary and Judicial Procedure.

§ 461. Adjustments in certain salaries

(a)(1) Subject to paragraph (2), effective at the beginning of the first applicable pay period commencing on or after the first day of the month in which an adjustment takes effect under section 5303 of title 5 in the rates of pay under the General Schedule (except as provided in subsection (b)), each salary rate which is subject to adjustment under this section shall be adjusted by an amount, rounded to the nearest multiple of $100 (or if midway between multiples of $100, to the next higher multiple of $100) equal to the percentage of such salary rate which corresponds to the most recent percentage change in the ECI (relative to the date described in the next sentence), as determined under section 704(a)(1) of the Ethics Reform Act of 1989. The appropriate date under this sentence is the first day of the fiscal year in which such adjustment in the rates of pay under the General Schedule takes effect.

(2) In no event shall the percentage adjustment taking effect under paragraph (1) in any calendar year (before rounding), in any salary rate, exceed the percentage adjustment taking effect in such calendar year under section 5303 of title 5 in the rates of pay under the General Schedule.

(b) Subsection (a) shall not apply to the extent it would reduce the salary of any individual whose compensation may not, under section 1 of article III of the Constitution of the United States, be diminished during such individual's continuance in office.

(Added Pub.L. 94–82, Title II, § 205(a)(1), Aug. 9, 1975, 89 Stat. 422, and amended Pub.L. 101–194, Title VII, § 704(a)(2)(A), Nov. 30, 1989, 103 Stat. 1769; Pub.L. 101–509, Title V, § 529 [Title I, § 101(b)(4)(J)], Nov. 5, 1990, 104 Stat. 1427, 1440; Pub.L. 103–356, Title I, § 101(4), Oct. 13, 1994, 108 Stat. 3411.)

HISTORICAL AND STATUTORY NOTES

References in Text

The General Schedule, referred to in subsec. (a), is set out under section 5332 of Title 5, Government Organization and Employees.

Section 704(a)(1) of the Ethics Reform Act of 1989, referred to in subsec. (a), is section 704(a)(1) of Pub.L. 101–194, which is set out as a note under section 5318 of Title 5, Government Organization and Employees.

Effective and Applicability Provisions

1994 Acts

Amendment to this section by section 101(4) of Pub.L. 103–356 effective Dec. 31, 1994, see section 101 of Pub.L. 103–356 set out as a note under section 31 of Title 2, The Congress.

1990 Acts

Amendment to this section (together with any notes enacted or amended hereunder) by the Federal Employees Pay Comparability Act of 1990, as incorporated in section 529 [Title III, § 305] of Pub.L. 101–509, to take effect on May 4, 1991, except that the Office of Personnel Management may establish an earlier effective date, but not earlier than Feb. 3, 1991, for any such provisions with respect to which the Office determines an earlier effective date to be appropriate, see Ex. Ord. No. 12748, Feb. 1, 1991, 56 F.R. 4521, set out as a note under section 5301 of Title 5, Government Organization and Employees.

Amendment by Pub.L. 101–509 effective on such date as the President shall determine, but not earlier than 90 days, and not later than 180 days, after Nov. 5, 1990, see section 529 [Title III, § 305] of Pub.L. 101–509, set out as a note under section 5301 of Title 5, Government Organization and Employees.

1989 Acts

Amendment to this section by section 704(a)(2)(A) of Pub.L. 101–194 to take effect Jan. 1, 1991, see section 704(b) of Pub.L. 101–194, set out as a note under section 5318 of Title 5, Government Organization and Employees.

Increase in Salaries

2006—Ex. Ord. No. 13393, Dec. 22, 2005, 70 F.R. 76655, set out as a note under 5 U.S.C.A. § 5332, adjusted the rates of basic pay or salaries for certain Judicial offices and positions, effective on the first day of the first applicable pay period beginning on or after Jan. 1, 2006. See Schedule 7—Judicial Salaries, of that Executive Order, set out in a note under 5 U.S.C.A. § 5332 and also set out in a note under 28 U.S.C.A. § 5.

Salary Adjustments for Justices and Judges

Pub.L. 109–115, Div. A, Title IV, § 405, Nov. 30, 2005, 119 Stat. 2470, provided that: "Pursuant to section 140 of Public Law 97–92 [Pub.L. 97–92, Title IV, § 140, Dec. 15, 1981, 95 Stat. 1200, as amended, which is set out as a note under this section], and from funds appropriated in this Act, Justices and judges of the United States are authorized during fiscal year 2006, to receive a salary adjustment in accordance with 28 U.S.C. 461 [this section]".

Pub.L. 108–491, § 1, Dec. 23, 2004, 118 Stat. 3973, provided that: "Pursuant to section 140 of Public Law 97–92 [Pub.L. 97–92, Title IV, § 140, Dec. 15, 1981, 95 Stat. 1200, as amended, which is set out as a note under this section], Justices and judges of the United States are authorized during fiscal year 2005 to receive a salary adjustment in accordance with section 461 of title 28, United States Code [this section]."

Pub.L. 108–447, Div. B, Title III, § 306, Dec. 8, 2004, 118 Stat. 2895, provided that: "Pursuant to section 140 of Public Law 97–92 [Pub.L. 97–92, Title IV, § 140, Dec. 15, 1981, 95 Stat. 1200, as amended, which is set out as a note under this section], and from funds appropriated in this Act [Departments of Commerce, Justice, and State, the Judiciary, and Related Agencies Appropriations Act, 2005, Pub.L. 108–447, Div. B, Dec. 8, 2004, 118 Stat. 2853; see Tables for classification], Justices and judges of the United States are authorized during fiscal year 2005, to receive a salary adjustment in accordance with 28 U.S.C. 461 [this section]."

Pub.L. 108–167, § 1, Dec. 6, 2003, 117 Stat. 2031, provided that: "Pursuant to section 140 of Public Law 97–92 [Pub.L.

97–92, Title IV, § 140, Dec. 15, 1981, 95 Stat. 1200, as amended, which is set out as a note under this section], Justices and judges of the United States are authorized during fiscal year 2004 to receive a salary adjustment in accordance with section 461 of title 28, United States Code [this section]."

Pub.L. 108–6, § 1, Feb. 13, 2003, 117 Stat. 10, provided that: "Pursuant to section 140 of Public Law 97–92 [Pub.L. 97–92, § 140, Dec. 15, 1981, 95 Stat. 1200, as amended, which is set out as a note under this section], Justices and judges of the United States are authorized during fiscal year 2003 to receive a salary adjustment in accordance with section 461 of title 28, United States Code [this section]."

Pub.L. 107–77, Title III, § 305, Nov. 28, 2001, 115 Stat. 783, provided in part that: "Pursuant to section 140 of Public Law 97–92 [set out as a note under this section], Justices and judges of the United States are authorized during fiscal year 2002, to receive a salary adjustment in accordance with 28 U.S.C. 461."

Pub.L. 106–553, § 1(a)(2) [Title III, § 309], Dec. 21, 2000, 114 Stat. 2762, 2762A–89, provided that: "Pursuant to section 140 of Public Law 97–92 [set out below], Justices and judges of the United States are authorized during fiscal year 2001, to receive a salary adjustment in accordance with 28 U.S.C. 461 [this section], only if for the purposes of each provision of law amended by section 704(a)(2) of the Ethics Reform Act of 1989 (5 U.S.C. 5318 note), adjustments under section 5303 of title 5, United States Code, shall take effect in fiscal year 2001."

Pub.L. 106–113, Div. B, § 1000(a)(1) [Title III, § 304], Nov. 29, 1999, 113 Stat. 1535, 1501A–36, provided in part that: "Pursuant to section 140 of Public Law 97–92 [set out as a note under this section], Justices and judges of the United States are authorized during fiscal year 2000, to receive a salary adjustment in accordance with 28 U.S.C. 461."

Pub.L. 105–119, Title III, § 306, Nov. 26, 1997, 111 Stat. 2493, provided that: "Pursuant to section 140 of Public Law 97–92 [set out as a note under this section], justices and judges of the United States are authorized during fiscal year 1998, to receive a salary adjustment in accordance with 28 U.S.C. 461 [this section]."

Pub.L. 102–395, Title III, § 304, Oct. 6, 1992, 106 Stat. 1859, provided that: "Pursuant to section 140 of Public Law 97–92 [set out as a note under this section], Justices and judges of the United States are authorized during fiscal year 1993, to receive a salary adjustment in accordance with 28 U.S.C. 461 [this section]."

Pub.L. 102–140, Title III, § 305, Oct. 28, 1991, 105 Stat. 810, provided that: "Pursuant to section 140 of Public Law 97–92 [set out as a note under this section], Justices and judges of the United States are authorized during fiscal year 1992, to receive a salary adjustment in accordance with 28 U.S.C. 461 [this section]."

Pub.L. 101–520, Title III, § 321, Nov. 5, 1990, 104 Stat. 2285, provided that: "Pursuant to section 140 of Public Law 97–92 [set out as a note under this section], Justices and judges of the United States are authorized during calendar year 1991 to receive a salary adjustment in accordance with 28 U.S.C. section 461 [this section]."

For provisions that, effective the first day of the first applicable pay period that begins on or after January 1, 1991, the rate of basic pay for the Chief Justice of the United States, an associate justice of the Supreme Court of the United States, a judge of a United States circuit court, a judge of a district court of the United States, and a judge of the United States Court of International Trade shall be increased in the amount of 25 percent of their respective rates (as last in effect before the increase), rounded to the nearest multiple of $100 (or, if midway between multiples of $100, to the next higher multiple of $100), and related provisions, see Pub.L. 101–194, Title VII, § 703, Nov. 30, 1989, 103 Stat. 1768, set out as a note under section 5318 of Title 5, Government Organization and Employees.

For provisions authorizing, for purposes of section 140 of Pub.L. 97–92 (set out as a note under this section), appropriate salary increases for Federal judges and Justices of the Supreme Court, to be determined, effective for pay periods beginning on or after Nov. 30, 1989, as if the provisions of section 620(b) of Pub.L. 100–440 (5 U.S.C. 5305 note) and section 619(b) of Pub.L. 101–136 (5 U.S.C. 5303 note) had never been enacted, together with related provisions, see section 702 of Pub.L. 101–194, set out as a note under section 5303 of Title 5, Government Organization and Employees.

Pub.L. 100–202, § 101(a) [Title IV, § 406], Dec. 22, 1987, 101 Stat. 1329, 1329–26, provided that: "Pursuant to section 140 of Public Law 97–92 [set out as a note under this section], during fiscal year 1988, justices and judges of the United States shall receive the same percentage increase in salary accorded to employees paid under the General Schedule (pursuant to 5 U.S.C. 5305)."

Pub.L. 99–500, Title I, § 101(b) [Title IV, § 406], Oct. 18, 1986, 100 Stat. 1783–39, 1783–64; Pub.L. 99–591, Title I, § 101(b), [Title IV, § 406], Oct. 30, 1986, 100 Stat. 3341–39, 3341–64, provided that: "Pursuant to section 140 of Public Law 97–92 [set out as a note under this section], during fiscal year 1987, justices and judges of the United States shall receive the same percentage increase in salary accorded to employees paid under the General Schedule (pursuant to 5 U.S.C. 5305) [5 U.S.C.A. § 5305]."

Pub.L. 99–88, Title I, § 100, Aug. 15, 1985, 99 Stat. 310, provided in part that: "Effective on the first day of the first applicable pay period commencing on or after January 1, 1985, each rate of pay subject to adjustment by section 461 of title 28, United States Code [this section], shall be increased by an amount, rounded to the nearest multiple of $100 (or if midway between multiples of $100, to the next higher multiple of $100), equal to the overall percentage of the adjustment taking effect under section 5305 of title 5, United States Code [section 5305 of Title 5, Government Organization and Employees], in the rates of pay under the General Schedule during fiscal year 1985."

Pub.L. 98–369, Div.B., Title II, § 2207, July 18, 1984, 98 Stat. 1060, provided that: "Effective on the first day of the first applicable pay period commencing on or after January 1, 1984, each rate of pay subject to adjustment by section 461 of title 28, United States Code [this section], shall be increased by an amount, rounded to the nearest multiple of $100 (or if midway between multiples of $100, to the next higher multiple of $100), equal to the overall percentage of the adjustment taking effect under section 5305 of title 5, United States Code [section 5305 of Title 5, Government

Organization of Employees], in the rates of pay under the General Schedule during fiscal year 1984."

Pub.L. 95–66, § 1(3), July 11, 1977, 91 Stat. 270, set out as a note under section 5318 of Title 5, Government Organization and Employees, provided that the first adjustment which, but for the enactment of Pub.L. 95–66, would have been made in the salary and rate of pay of justices, judges, commissioners, and referees under this section after July 11, 1977, would not take effect.

Salary Rate Limitations or Use of Funds

1982—Limitation on the use of funds appropriated or authority made available for the period Oct. 1, 1982, through Sept. 30, 1983, by any Act to pay the salary or pay of any individual in an office or position in the legislative, executive, or judicial branch, or in the government of the District of Columbia, at a rate equal to or greater than Level V of the Executive Schedule, see section 306(a), (b), and (d) of S.2939, Ninety-seventh Congress, 2nd Session, as reported Sept. 22, 1982, which was incorporated by reference in Pub.L. 97–276, § 101(e), Oct. 2, 1982, 96 Stat. 1189, to be effective as if enacted into law, and which is set out as a note under section 5318 of Title 5, Government Organization and Employees.

1981—Limitation on use of funds appropriated for the fiscal year ending Sept. 30, 1982, by any Act to pay the salary or pay of any individual in the legislative, executive, or judicial branch in a position equal or above Level V of the Executive Schedule, see section 305(a), (b), and (d) of H.R. 4120, as reported July 9, 1981, which was incorporated by reference in Pub.L. 97–92, § 101(g), Dec. 15, 1981, 95 Stat. 1190, to be effective as if enacted into law, and section 141 of Pub.L. 97–92, set out as notes under section 5318 of Title 5, Government Organization and Employees.

1980—Limitations on use of funds for fiscal year ending Sept. 30, 1981, appropriated by any Act to pay the salary or pay of any individual in legislative, executive, or judicial branch in position equal to or above level V of the Executive Schedule, see section 101(c) of Pub.L. 96–536, as amended, set out as a note under section 5318 of Title 5.

1979—Applicability to funds appropriated by any Act for fiscal year ending Sept. 30, 1980, of limitation of section 304 of Pub.L. 95–391 on use of funds to pay the salary or pay of any individual in legislative, executive, or judicial branch in position equal to or above level V of the Executive Schedule, see section 101 of Pub.L. 96–86, set out as a note under section 5318 of Title 5.

1978—Limitations on use of funds for fiscal year ending Sept. 30, 1979, appropriated by any Act to pay the salary or pay of any individual in legislative, executive, or judicial branch in position equal or above level V of the Executive Schedule, see section 304 of Pub.L. 95–391 and section 613 of Pub.L. 95–429, set out as a note under section 5318 of Title 5.

Specific Congressional Authorization Required for Salary Increases for Federal Judges and Justices of the Supreme Court

Pub.L. 97–92, § 140, Dec. 15, 1981, 95 Stat. 1200, as amended Pub.L. 107–77, Title VI, § 625, Nov. 28, 2001, 115 Stat. 803, provided that: "Notwithstanding any other provision of law or of this joint resolution [Pub.L. 97–92], none of the funds appropriated by this joint resolution or by any other Act shall be obligated or expended to increase, after the date of enactment of this joint resolution [Dec. 15, 1981],

any salary of any Federal judge or Justice of the Supreme Court, except as may be specifically authorized by Act of Congress hereafter enacted: *Provided,* That nothing in this limitation shall be construed to reduce any salary which may be in effect at the time of enactment of this joint resolution [Dec. 15, 1981] nor shall this limitation be construed in any manner to reduce the salary of any Federal judge or of any Justice of the Supreme Court. This section [this note] shall apply to fiscal year 1981 and each fiscal year thereafter."

§ 462. Court accommodations

(a) Sessions of courts of the United States (except the Supreme Court) shall be held only at places where the Director of the Administrative Office of the United States Courts provides accommodations, or where suitable accommodations are furnished without cost to the judicial branch.

(b) The Director of the Administrative Office of the United States Courts shall provide accommodations, including chambers and courtrooms, only at places where regular sessions of court are authorized by law to be held, but only if the judicial council of the appropriate circuit has approved the accommodations as necessary.

(c) The limitations and restrictions contained in subsection (b) of this section shall not prevent the Director from furnishing chambers to circuit judges at places within the circuit other than where regular sessions of court are authorized by law to be held, when the judicial council of the circuit approves.

(d) The Director of the Administrative Office of the United States Courts shall provide permanent accommodations for the United States Court of Appeals for the Federal Circuit and for the United States Court of Federal Claims only at the District of Columbia. However, each such court may hold regular and special sessions at other places utilizing the accommodations which the Director provides to other courts.

(e) The Director of the Administrative Office of the United States Courts shall provide accommodations for probation officers, pretrial service officers, and Federal Public Defender Organizations at such places as may be approved by the judicial council of the appropriate circuit.

(f) Upon the request of the Director, the Administrator of General Services is authorized and directed to provide the accommodations the Director requests, and to close accommodations which the Director recommends for closure with the approval of the Judicial Conference of the United States.

(Added Pub.L. 97–164, Title I, § 115(c)(1), Apr. 2, 1982, 96 Stat. 31, and amended Pub.L. 100–702, Title X, § 1015, Nov. 19, 1988, 102 Stat. 4669; Pub.L. 102–572, Title IX, § 902(b)(1), Oct. 29, 1992, 106 Stat. 4516.)

HISTORICAL AND STATUTORY NOTES

Effective and Applicability Provisions

1992 Acts

Amendment by Pub.L. 102–572 effective Oct. 29, 1992, see section 911 of Pub.L. 102–572, set out as a note under section 171 of this title.

1982 Acts

Section effective Oct. 1, 1982, see section 402 of Pub.L. 97–164, set out as a note under section 171 of this title.

Change of Name

References to United States Claims Court deemed to refer to United States Court of Federal Claims and references to Claims Court deemed to refer to Court of Federal Claims, see section 902(b) of Pub.L. 102–572, set out as a note under section 171 of Title 28, Judiciary and Judicial Procedure.

§ 463. Expenses of litigation

Whenever a Chief Justice, justice, judge, officer, or employee of any United States court is sued in his official capacity, or is otherwise required to defend acts taken or omissions made in his official capacity, and the services of an attorney for the Government are not reasonably available pursuant to chapter 31 of this title, the Director of the Administrative Office of the United States Courts may pay the costs of his defense. The Director shall prescribe regulations for such payments subject to the approval of the Judicial Conference of the United States.

(Added Pub.L. 97–164, Title I, § 116(a), Apr. 2, 1982, 96 Stat. 32.)

HISTORICAL AND STATUTORY NOTES

Effective and Applicability Provisions

1982 Acts

Section effective Oct. 1, 1982, see section 402 of Pub.L. 97–164, set out as a note under section 171 of this title.

PART II—DEPARTMENT OF JUSTICE

CHAPTER 43—UNITED STATES MAGISTRATE JUDGES

HISTORICAL AND STATUTORY NOTES

Change of Name

"United States magistrate judge" substituted for "United States magistrate" in the chapter heading pursuant to section 321 of Pub.L. 101–650, set out as a note under 28 U.S.C.A. § 631.

§ 631. Appointment and tenure

(a) The judges of each United States district court and the district courts of the Virgin Islands, Guam, and the Northern Mariana Islands shall appoint United States magistrate judges in such numbers and to serve at such locations within the judicial districts as the Judicial Conference may determine under this chapter. In the case of a magistrate judge appointed by the district court of the Virgin Islands, Guam, or the Northern Mariana Islands, this chapter shall apply as though the court appointing such a magistrate judge were a United States district court. Where there is more than one judge of a district court, the appointment, whether an original appointment or a reappointment, shall be by the concurrence of a majority of all the judges of such district court, and when there is no such concurrence, then by the chief judge. Where the conference deems it desirable, a magistrate judge may be designated to serve in one or more districts adjoining the district for which he is appointed. Such a designation shall be made by the concurrence of a majority of the judges of each of the district courts involved and shall specify the duties to be performed by the magistrate judge in the adjoining district or districts.

(b) No individual may be appointed or reappointed to serve as a magistrate judge under this chapter unless:

(1) He has been for at least five years a member in good standing of the bar of the highest court of a State, the District of Columbia, the Commonwealth of Puerto Rico, the Territory of Guam, the Commonwealth of the Northern Mariana Islands, or the Virgin Islands of the United States, except that an individual who does not meet the bar membership requirements of this paragraph may be appointed and serve as a part-time magistrate judge if the appointing court or courts and the conference find that no qualified individual who is a member of the bar is available to serve at a specific location;

(2) He is determined by the appointing district court or courts to be competent to perform the duties of the office;

(3) In the case of an individual appointed to serve in a national park, he resides within the exterior boundaries of that park, or at some place reasonably adjacent thereto;

(4) He is not related by blood or marriage to a judge of the appointing court or courts at the time of his initial appointment; and

(5) He is selected pursuant to standards and procedures promulgated by the Judicial Conference of the United States. Such standards and procedures shall contain provision for public notice of all vacancies in magistrate judge positions and for the establishment by the district courts of merit selection panels, composed of residents of the individual judicial districts, to assist the courts in identifying and recommending persons who are best qualified to fill such positions.

(c) A magistrate judge may hold no other civil or military office or employment under the United States: *Provided, however,* That, with the approval of the conference, a part-time referee in bankruptcy or a clerk or deputy clerk of a court of the United States may be appointed and serve as a part-time United States magistrate judge, but the conference shall fix the aggregate amount of compensation to be received for performing the duties of part-time magistrate judge and part-time referee in bankruptcy, clerk or deputy clerk: *And provided further,* That retired officers and retired enlisted personnel of the Regular and Reserve components of the Army, Navy, Air Force, Marine Corps, and Coast Guard, members of

the Reserve components of the Army, Navy, Air Force, Marine Corps, and Coast Guard, and members of the Army National Guard of the United States, the Air National Guard of the United States, and the Naval Militia and of the National Guard of a State, territory, or the District of Columbia, except the National Guard disbursing officers who are on a full-time salary basis, may be appointed and serve as United States magistrate judges.

(d) Except as otherwise provided in sections 375 and 636(h) of this title, no individual may serve under this chapter after having attained the age of seventy years: *Provided, however,* That upon a majority vote of all the judges of the appointing court or courts, which is taken upon the magistrate judge's attaining age seventy and upon each subsequent anniversary thereof, a magistrate judge who has attained the age of seventy years may continue to serve and may be reappointed under this chapter.

(e) The appointment of any individual as a full-time magistrate judge shall be for a term of eight years, and the appointment of any individuals as a part-time magistrate judge shall be for a term of four years, except that the term of a full-time or part-time magistrate judge appointed under subsection (k) shall expire upon—

(1) the expiration of the absent magistrate judge's term,

(2) the reinstatement of the absent magistrate judge in regular service in office as a magistrate judge,

(3) the failure of the absent magistrate judge to make timely application under subsection (j) of this section for reinstatement in regular service in office as a magistrate judge after discharge or release from military service,

(4) the death or resignation of the absent magistrate judge, or

(5) the removal from office of the absent magistrate judge pursuant to subsection (i) of this section,

whichever may first occur.

(f) Upon the expiration of his term, a magistrate judge may, by a majority vote of the judges of the appointing district court or courts and with the approval of the judicial council of the circuit, continue to perform the duties of his office until his successor is appointed, or for 180 days after the date of the expiration of the magistrate judge's term, whichever is earlier.

(g) Each individual appointed as a magistrate judge under this section shall take the oath or affirmation prescribed by section 453 of this title before performing the duties of his office.

(h) Each appointment made by a judge or judges of a district court shall be entered of record in such court, and notice of such appointment shall be given at once by the clerk of that court to the Director.

(i) Removal of a magistrate judge during the term for which he is appointed shall be only for incompetency, misconduct, neglect of duty, or physical or mental disability, but a magistrate judge's office shall be terminated if the conference determines that the services performed by his office are no longer needed. Removal shall be by the judges of the district court for the judicial district in which the magistrate judge serves; where there is more than one judge of a district court, removal shall not occur unless a majority of all the judges of such court concur in the order of removal; and when there is a tie vote of the judges of the district court on the question of the removal or retention in office of a magistrate judge, then removal shall be only by a concurrence of a majority of all the judges of the council. In the case of a magistrate judge appointed under the third sentence of subsection (a) of this section, removal shall not occur unless a majority of all the judges of the appointing district courts concur in the order of removal; and where there is a tie vote on the question of the removal or retention in office of a magistrate judge, then removal shall be only by a concurrence of a majority of all the judges of the council or councils. Before any order or removal shall be entered, a full specification of the charges shall be furnished to the magistrate judge, and he shall be accorded by the judge or judges of the removing court, courts, council, or councils an opportunity to be heard on the charges.

(j) Upon the grant by the appropriate district court or courts of a leave of absence to a magistrate judge entitled to such relief under chapter 43 of title 38, such court or courts may proceed to appoint, in the manner specified in subsection (a) of this section, another magistrate judge, qualified for appointment and service under subsections (b), (c), and (d) of this section, who shall serve for the period specified in subsection (e) of this section.

(k) A United States magistrate judge appointed under this chapter shall be exempt from the provisions of subchapter I of chapter 63 of title 5.
(June 25, 1948, c. 646, 62 Stat. 915; May 24, 1949, c. 139, § 73, 63 Stat. 100; July 9, 1952, c. 609, § 1, 66 Stat. 509; July 25, 1956, c. 722, 70 Stat. 642; Oct. 17, 1968, Pub.L. 90–578, Title I, § 101, 82 Stat. 1108; Oct. 17, 1976, Pub.L. 94–520, § 2, 90 Stat. 2458; Nov. 6, 1978, Pub.L. 95–598, Title II, § 231, 92 Stat. 2665; Oct. 10, 1979, Pub.L. 96–82, § 3(a)–(d), 93 Stat. 644, 645; Aug. 6, 1982, Pub.L. 97–230, 96 Stat. 255; Nov. 14, 1986, Pub.L. 99–651, Title II, § 201(a)(1), 100 Stat. 3646; Nov. 15, 1988, Pub.L. 100–659, § 5, 102 Stat. 3918; Nov. 19, 1988, Pub.L. 100–702, Title X, § 1003(a)(2), 102 Stat. 4665; June 30, 1989, Pub.L. 101–45, Title II, § 104, 103 Stat. 122; Dec. 1, 1990, Pub.L. 101–650, Title III, §§ 308(b), 321, 104 Stat. 5112, 5117; Oct. 13, 1994, Pub.L.

103–353, § 2(c), 108 Stat. 3169; Nov. 13, 2000, Pub.L. 106–518, Title II, § 201, 114 Stat. 2412.)

HISTORICAL AND STATUTORY NOTES

References in Text

Subsections (j) and (k) of this section, referred to in subsec. (e), probably mean subsecs. (j) and (k) prior to amendment by Pub.L. 103–353, § 2(c)(1), (2), Oct. 13, 1994, 108 Stat. 3169, which redesignated subsec. (k) as (j) and struck out former subsec. (j).

Codifications

Subsec. (c) of this section was amended by Pub.L. 95–598, Title II, § 231, Nov. 6, 1978, 92 Stat. 2665, effective June 28, 1984, pursuant to Pub.L. 95–598, Title IV, § 402(b), Nov. 6, 1978, 92 Stat. 2682, as amended by Pub.L. 98–249, § 1(a), Mar. 31, 1984, 98 Stat. 116; Pub.L. 98–271, § 1(a), Apr. 30, 1984, 98 Stat. 163; Pub.L. 98–299, § 1(a), May 25, 1984, 98 Stat. 214; Pub.L. 98–325, § 1(a), June 20, 1984, 98 Stat. 268, set out as an Effective Date note preceding section 101 of Title 11, Bankruptcy, by striking out "a part-time referee in bankruptcy or" following "of the conference," and "part-time referee in bankruptcy," following "magistrate and".

Section 402(b) of Pub.L. 95–598 was amended by section 113 of Pub.L. 98–353, Title I, July 10, 1984, 98 Stat. 343, by substituting "shall not be effective" for "shall take effect on June 28, 1984," thereby eliminating the amendment by section 231 of Pub.L. 95–598, effective June 27, 1984, pursuant to section 122(c) of Pub.L. 98–353, set out as an Effective Date note under section 151 of this title.

Section 121(a) of Pub.L. 98–353 directed that section 402(b) of Pub.L. 95–598 be amended by substituting "the date of enactment of the Bankruptcy Amendments and Federal Judgeship Act of 1984 [i.e. July 10, 1984]" for "June 28, 1984". This amendment was not executed in view of the prior amendment to section 402(b) of Pub.L. 95–598 by section 113 of Pub.L. 98–353.

Effective and Applicability Provisions

1994 Acts

Amendment by section 2(c) of Pub.L. 103–353 effective with respect to reemployments initiated on or after the first day after the 60–day period beginning on Oct. 13, 1994, except as otherwise provided, see section 8 of Pub.L. 103–353, set out as a note under section 4301 of Title 38, Veterans' Benefits.

1988 Acts

Amendment by Pub.L. 100–659 effective Nov. 15, 1988, and applicable to bankruptcy judges and magistrates who retire on or after Nov. 15, 1988, with exception for judges and magistrates retiring on or after July 31, 1987, see section 9 of Pub.L. 100–659, set out as an Effective Date note under section 377 of this title.

1986 Acts

Amendment by Pub.L. 99–651 effective Jan. 1, 1987, see section 203 of Pub.L. 99–651, set out as a note under section 155 of this title.

1979 Acts

Section 3(g) of Pub.L. 96–82 provided that: "The amendment made by subsection (c) of this section [enacting subsec. (b)(5) of this section] shall not take effect until 30 days after the meeting of the Judicial Conference of the United States next following the effective date of this Act [Oct. 10, 1979]." [The meeting of the Judicial Conference took place on Mar. 5 and 6, 1980.]

1968 Acts

Section 403 of Pub.L. 90–578 provided that: "Except as otherwise provided by sections 401 and 402 of this title [set out as Appointment of Magistrate and Applicable Law notes under this section], this Act [which amended this chapter and sections 202, 3006A, 3041, 3043, 3045, 3060, 3102, 3116, 3184, 3191, 3195, 3401, 3402, 3569, and 3771 of Title 18, Crimes and Criminal Procedure, and enacted provisions set out as notes under this section] shall take effect on the date of its enactment [Oct. 17, 1968]."

Change of Name

Section 321 of Pub.L. 101–650 provided that: "After the enactment of this Act [Dec. 1, 1990], each United States magistrate appointed under section 631 of title 28, United States Code [this section], shall be known as a United States magistrate judge, and any reference to any United States magistrate or magistrate that is contained in title 28, United States Code [this title], in any other Federal statute, or in any regulation of any department or agency of the United States in the executive branch that was issued before the enactment of this Act [Dec. 1, 1990], shall be deemed to refer to a United States magistrate judge appointed under section 631 of title 28, United States Code [this section]."

Transfer of Functions

For transfer of authorities, functions, personnel, and assets of the Coast Guard, including the authorities and functions of the Secretary of Transportation relating thereto, to the Department of Homeland Security, and for treatment of related references, see 6 U.S.C.A. §§ 468(b), 551(d), 552(d) and 557, and the Department of Homeland Security Reorganization Plan of November 25, 2002, as modified, set out as a note under 6 U.S.C.A. § 542.

Severability of Provisions

Section 501 of Pub.L. 90–578 provided that: "If any provision of this Act [which amended this chapter and sections 202, 3006A, 3041, 3043, 3045, 3060, 3102, 3116, 3184, 3191, 3195, 3401, 3402, 3569, and 3771 of Title 18, Crimes and Criminal Procedure, and enacted provisions set out as notes under this section] or the application thereof to any person or circumstances is held invalid, the validity of the remainder of the Act [such sections] and of its application to other persons and circumstances shall not be affected."

Short Title

1979 Amendments

Section 1 of Pub.L. 96–82 provided: "That this Act [amending this section, sections 604, 633, 634, 635, 636, and 1915 of this title, and section 3401 of Title 18, Crimes and Criminal Procedure, and enacting provisions set out as notes under this section] may be cited as the 'Federal Magistrate Act of 1979'."

1968 Acts

Section 1 of Pub.L. 90–578 provided: "That this Act [which amended this chapter and sections 202, 3006A, 3041, 3043, 3045, 3060, 3102, 3116, 3184, 3191, 3195, 3401, 3402, 3569, and 3771 of Title 18, Crimes and Criminal Procedure, and enact-

ed provisions set out as notes under this section] may be cited as the 'Federal Magistrates Act'."

Applicable Law

Section 402 of Pub.L. 90–578 provided that:

"(a) All provisions of law relating to the powers, duties, jurisdiction, functions, service, compensation, and facilities of United States commissioners, as such provisions existed on the day preceding the date of enactment of this Act [Oct. 17, 1968], shall continue in effect in each judicial district until but not on or after (1) the date on which the first United States magistrate [now United States magistrate judge] assumes office within such judicial district pursuant to section 631 of chapter 43, title 28, United States Code, as amended by this Act [this section], or (2) the third anniversary of the date of enactment of this Act [Oct. 17, 1968], whichever date is earlier.

"(b) On and after the date on which the first United States magistrate assumes office within any judicial district pursuant to section 631 of chapter 43, title 28, United States Code, as amended by this Act [this section], or the third anniversary of the date of enactment of this Act [Oct. 17, 1968], whichever date is earlier—

"(1) the provisions of chapter 43, title 28, United States Code, as amended by this Act [this chapter], shall be effective within such judicial district except as otherwise specifically provided by section 401(b) of this title [set out as Appointment of Magistrates note under this section]; and

"(2) within such judicial district every reference to a United States commissioner contained in any previously enacted statute of the United States (other than sections 8331(1)(E), 8332(i), 8701(a)(7), and 8901(1)(G) of title 5), any previously promulgated rule of any court of the United States, or any previously promulgated regulation of any executive department or agency of the United States, shall be deemed to be a reference to a United States magistrate duly appointed under section 631 of chapter 43, title 28, United States Code, as amended by this Act [this section].

"(c) The administrative powers and duties of the Director of the Administrative Office of the United States Courts with respect to United States commissioners under the provisions of chapter 41, title 28, United States Code, as such provisions existed on the day preceding the date of enactment of this Act [Oct. 17, 1968], shall continue in effect until no United States commissioner remains in service."

Appointment of Magistrates

Section 401 of Pub.L. 90–578 provided that:

"(a) No individual may serve as a United States commissioner within any judicial district after the date on which a United States magistrate assumes office in such judicial district.

"(b) An individual serving as a United States commissioner within any judicial district on the date of enactment of this Act [Oct. 17, 1968] who is a member in good standing of the bar of the highest court of any State may be appointed to the office of United States magistrate for an initial term, and may be reappointed to such office for successive terms, notwithstanding his failure to meet the bar membership qualification imposed by section 631(b)(1) of chapter 43, title 28, United States Code [subsec. (b)(1) of this section]: *Provided, however,* That any appointment or reappointment of

such an individual must be by unanimous vote of all the judges of the appointing district court or courts."

Authorization of Appropriations

Section 10 of Pub.L. 96–82 provided that: "Such sums as may be necessary to carry out the purposes of this Act [see Short Title of 1979 Amendments note under this section] are hereby authorized to be appropriated for expenditure on or after October 1, 1979."

Due Consideration by Merit Selection Panels of Women, Blacks, Hispanics, and Other Minorities

Section 3(e) of Pub.L. 96–82 provided that: "The merit selection panels established under section 631(b)(5) of title 28, United States Code [subsec. (b)(5) of this section], in recommending persons to the district court, shall give due consideration to all qualified individuals, especially such groups as women, blacks, Hispanics, and other minorities."

Judicial Conference Study of the Future of the Magistrate System

Section 9 of Pub.L. 96–82 provided for a study by the Judicial Conference of the United States to begin within 90 days after the effective date of Pub.L. 96–82, which was approved Oct. 10, 1979, and to be completed and made available to Congress within 24 months thereafter respecting the future of the magistrate system.

Jurisdictional Limitation of Commissioner Holding Office on July 9, 1952

Section 2 of Act July 9, 1952, provided that: "The jurisdiction of the United States commissioner holding office as commissioner of the Great Smoky Mountains National Park on the date of enactment of this Act [July 9, 1952] shall be limited to the portion of the park situated in North Carolina."

Magistrates Serving Prior to Promulgation of Magistrate Selection Standards and Procedures by Judicial Conference; Reappointment; Certification as Qualified

Section 3(f) of Pub.L. 96–82 provided that: "Magistrates serving prior to the promulgation of magistrate selection standards and procedures by the Judicial Conference of the United States may only exercise the jurisdiction conferred under the amendment made by section 2 of this Act [enacting section 636(c) of this title] after having been reappointed under such standards and procedures or after having been certified as qualified to exercise such jurisdiction by the judicial council of the circuit in which the magistrate serves."

Special Commissioner for Grand Canyon National Park; Appointment; Jurisdiction; Compensation

Pub.L. 86–258, Sept. 14, 1959, 73 Stat. 546, provided: "That the United States District Court for the District of Arizona shall appoint a special commissioner for the Grand Canyon National Park, Arizona. The commissioner shall hold office for four years, unless sooner removed by the district court, and he shall be subject to the general laws and requirements applicable to United States commissioners.

"Sec. 2. The jurisdiction of the commissioner in adjudicating cases brought before him shall be limited to the trial, and sentencing upon conviction, of persons charged with the commission of those misdemeanors classified as petty offenses (18 U.S.C. 1) [section 1 of Title 18, Crimes and

Criminal Procedure] relating to the violation of Federal laws or regulations applicable within the park: *Provided,* That any person charged with a petty offense may elect to be tried in the district court of the United States; and the commissioner shall apprise the defendant of his right to make such election, but shall not proceed to try the case unless the defendant, after being so apprised, signs a written consent to be tried before the commissioner. The exercise of additional functions by the commissioner shall be consistent with and be carried out in accordance with the authority, laws, and regulations of general application to United States commissioners. The rules of procedure set forth in title 18, section 3402, of the United States Code [section 3402 of Title 18], shall be followed in the handling of cases by such commissioner. The probation laws shall be applicable to persons tried by the commissioner and he shall have power to grant probation.

"Sec. 3. The commissioner shall receive an annual salary to be fixed by the district court with the approval of the Judicial Conference of the United States and shall account for all fees, fines, and costs collected by him as public moneys. He shall reside within the boundary of the park or at some place reasonably adjacent thereto designated by the Secretary of the Interior with the approval of the district court."

§ 632. Character of service

(a) Full-time United States magistrate judges may not engage in the practice of law, and may not engage in any other business, occupation, or employment inconsistent with the expeditious, proper, and impartial performance of their duties as judicial officers.

(b) Part-time United States magistrate judges shall render such service as judicial officers as is required by law. While so serving they may engage in the practice of law, but may not serve as counsel in any criminal action in any court of the United States, nor act in any capacity that is, under such regulations as the conference may establish, inconsistent with the proper discharge of their office. Within such restrictions, they may engage in any other business, occupation, or employment which is not inconsistent with the expeditious, proper, and impartial performance of their duties as judicial officers.

(June 25, 1948, c. 646, 62 Stat. 916; Oct. 17, 1968, Pub.L. 90–578, Title I, § 101, 82 Stat. 1110; Pub.L. 101–650, Title III, § 321, Dec. 1 1990, 104 Stat. 5117.)

HISTORICAL AND STATUTORY NOTES

Effective and Applicability Provisions

1968 Acts

Amendment by Pub.L. 90–578 effective Oct. 17, 1968, except when a later effective date is applicable, which is the earlier of date when implementation of amendment by appointment of magistrates and assumption of office takes place or third anniversary of enactment of Pub.L. 90–578 on Oct. 17, 1968, see section 403 of Pub.L. 90–578, set out as a note under section 631 of this title.

Change of Name

"United States magistrate judge" substituted for "United States magistrate" in text pursuant to section 321 of Pub.L. 101–650, set out as a note under 28 U.S.C.A. § 631.

§ 633. Determination of number, locations, and salaries of magistrate judges

(a) Surveys by the Director.—

(1) The Director shall, within one year immediately following the date of the enactment of the Federal Magistrates Act, make a careful survey of conditions in judicial districts to determine (A) the number of appointments of full-time magistrates and part-time magistrates required to be made under this chapter to provide for the expeditious and effective administration of justice, (B) the locations at which such officers shall serve, and (C) their respective salaries under section 634 of this title. Thereafter, the Director shall, from time to time, make such surveys, general or local, as the conference shall deem expedient.

(2) In the course of any survey, the Director shall take into account local conditions in each judicial district, including the areas and the populations to be served, the transportation and communications facilities available, the amount and distribution of business of the type expected to arise before officers appointed under this chapter (including such matters as may be assigned under section 636(b) of this chapter), and any other material factors. The Director shall give consideration to suggestions from any interested parties, including district judges, United States magistrate judges or officers appointed under this chapter, United States attorneys, bar associations, and other parties having relevant experience or information.

(3) The surveys shall be made with a view toward creating and maintaining a system of full-time United States magistrate judges. However, should the Director find, as a result of any such surveys, areas in which the employment of a full-time magistrate judge would not be feasible or desirable, he shall recommend the appointment of part-time United States magistrate judges in such numbers and at such locations as may be required to permit prompt and efficient issuance of process and to permit individuals charged with criminal offenses against the United States to be brought before a judicial officer of the United States promptly after arrest.

(b) Determination by the conference.—Upon the completion of the initial surveys required by subsection (a) of this section, the Director shall report to the district courts, the councils, and the conference his recommendations concerning the number of full-time magistrates and part-time magistrates, their respective locations, and the amount of their respective salaries under section 634 of this title. The district

courts shall advise their respective councils, stating their recommendations and the reasons therefor; the councils shall advise the conference, stating their recommendations and the reasons therefor, and shall also report to the conference the recommendations of the district courts. The conference shall determine, in the light of the recommendations of the Director, the district courts, and the councils, the number of full-time United States magistrates and part-time United States magistrates, the locations at which they shall serve, and their respective salaries. Such determinations shall take effect in each judicial district at such time as the district court for such judicial district shall determine, but in no event later than one year after they are promulgated.

(c) **Changes in number, locations, and salaries.**— Except as otherwise provided in this chapter, the conference may, from time to time, in the light of the recommendations of the Director, the district courts, and the councils, change the number, locations, and salaries of full-time and part-time magistrate judges, as the expeditious administration of justice may require.

(June 25, 1948, c. 646, 62 Stat. 916; Aug. 13, 1954, c. 728, § 1(a), (b), 68 Stat. 703, 704; Sept. 2, 1957, Pub.L. 85–276, §§ 1, 2, 71 Stat. 600; Oct. 17, 1968, Pub.L. 90–578, Title I, § 101, 82 Stat. 1111; Oct. 10, 1979, Pub.L. 96–82, § 4, 93 Stat. 645; Nov. 14, 1986, Pub.L. 99–651, Title II, § 202(d), 100 Stat. 3648; Dec. 1, 1990, Pub.L. 101–650, Title III, § 321, 104 Stat. 5117.)

HISTORICAL AND STATUTORY NOTES

References in Text

Date of the enactment of the Federal Magistrates Act, referred to in subsec. (a)(1), means Oct. 17, 1968, the date of enactment of Pub.L. 90–578.

Effective and Applicability Provisions

1986 Acts

Amendment by Pub.L. 99–651 effective Jan. 1, 1987, see section 203 of Pub.L. 99–651, set out as a note under section 155 of this title.

1968 Acts

Amendment by Pub.L. 90–578 effective Oct. 17, 1968, except when a later effective date is applicable, which is the earlier of date when implementation of amendment by appointment of magistrates and assumption of office takes place or third anniversary of enactment of Pub.L. 90–578 on Oct. 17, 1968, see section 403 of Pub.L. 90–578, set out as a note under section 631 of this title.

Change of Name

"United States magistrate judge" substituted for "United States magistrate" in the section headings, and subsecs. (a)(2), (a)(3), and (c) pursuant to section 321 of Pub.L. 101–650, set out as a note under 28 U.S.C.A. § 631. Previously, United States commissioners, referred to in text, were replaced by United States magistrates pursuant to Pub.L. 90–578, Oct. 17, 1968, 82 Stat. 1118. See chapter 43 of Title 28, 28 U.S.C.A. § 631 et seq.

United States magistrate appointed under section 631 of this title to be known as United States magistrate judge after Dec. 1, 1990, with any reference to United States magistrate or magistrate in this title, in any other Federal statute, etc., deemed a reference to United States magistrate judge appointed under section 631 of this title, see section 321 of Pub.L. 101–650, set out as a note under section 631 of this title.

§ 634. Compensation

(a) Officers appointed under this chapter shall receive, as full compensation for their services, salaries to be fixed by the conference pursuant to section 633, at rates for full-time United States magistrate judges up to an annual rate equal to 92 percent of the salary of a judge of the district court of the United States, as determined pursuant to section 135, and at rates for part-time magistrate judges of not less than an annual salary of $100, nor more than one-half the maximum salary payable to a full-time magistrate judge. In fixing the amount of salary to be paid to any officer appointed under this chapter, consideration shall be given to the average number and the nature of matters that have arisen during the immediately preceding period of five years, and that may be expected thereafter to arise, over which such officer would have jurisdiction and to such other factors as may be material. Disbursement of salaries shall be made by or pursuant to the order of the Director.

(b) Except as provided by section 8344, title 5, relating to reductions of the salaries of reemployed annuitants under subchapter III of chapter 83 of such title and unless the office has been terminated as provided in this chapter, the salary of a full-time United States magistrate judge shall not be reduced, during the term in which he is serving, below the salary fixed for him at the beginning of that term.

(c) All United States magistrate judges, effective upon their taking the oath or affirmation of office, and all necessary legal, clerical, and secretarial assistants employed in the offices of full-time United States magistrate judges shall be deemed to be officers and employees in the judicial branch of the United States Government within the meaning of subchapter III (relating to civil service retirement) of chapter 83, chapter 87 (relating to Federal employees' group life insurance), and chapter 89 (relating to Federal employees' health benefits program) of title 5. Part-time magistrate judges shall not be excluded from coverage under these chapters solely for lack of a prearranged regular tour of duty. A legal assistant appointed under this section shall be exempt from the provisions of subchapter I of chapter 63 of title 5, unless specifically included by the appointing judge or by local rule of court.

(June 25, 1948, c. 646, 62 Stat. 917; Oct. 17, 1968, Pub.L. 90–578, Title I, § 101, 82 Stat. 1112; Sept. 21, 1972, Pub.L.

92–428, 86 Stat. 721; Oct. 17, 1976, Pub.L. 94–520, § 1, 90 Stat. 2458; Nov. 6, 1978, Pub.L. 95–598, Title II, § 232, 92 Stat. 2665; Oct. 10, 1979, Pub.L. 96–82, § 8(b), 93 Stat. 647; July 10, 1984, Pub.L. 98–353, Title I, § 108(a), Title II, § 210, 98 Stat. 342, 351; Dec. 22, 1987, Pub.L. 100–202, § 101(a) [Title IV, § 408 (b)], 101 Stat. 1329, 1329–27; Nov. 19, 1988, Pub.L. 100–702, Title X, § 1003(a)(4), 102 Stat. 4665; Dec. 1, 1990, Pub.L. 101–650, Title III, § 321, 104 Stat. 5117.)

HISTORICAL AND STATUTORY NOTES

Codifications

Subsec. (a) of this section was amended by Pub.L. 95–598, Title II, § 232, Nov. 6, 1978, 92 Stat. 2665, effective June 28, 1984, pursuant to Pub.L. 95–598, Title IV, § 402(b), Nov. 6, 1978, 92 Stat. 2682, as amended by Pub.L. 98–249, § 1(a), Mar. 31, 1984, 98 Stat. 116; Pub.L. 98–271, § 1(a), Apr. 30, 1984, 98 Stat. 163; Pub.L. 98–299, § 1(a), May 25, 1984, 98 Stat. 214; Pub.L. 98–325, § 1(a), June 20, 1984, 98 Stat. 268, set out as an Effective Date note preceding section 101 of Title 11, Bankruptcy, to read as follows:

"(a) Officers appointed under this chapter shall receive as full compensation for their services salaries to be fixed by the conference pursuant to section 633 of this title, at rates not to exceed $48,500 per annum, subject to adjustment in accordance with section 225 of the Federal Salary Act of 1967 and section 461 of this title, except that the salary of a part-time United States magistrate shall not be less than $100 nor more than one-half the maximum salary payable to a full-time magistrate. In fixing the amount of salary to be paid to any officer appointed under this chapter, consideration shall be given to the average number and the nature of matters that have arisen during the immediately preceding period of five years, and that may be expected thereafter to arise, over which such officer would have jurisdiction and to such other factors as may be material. Disbursement of salaries shall be made by or pursuant to the order of the Director."

Section 402(b) of Pub.L. 95–598 was amended by section 113 of Pub.L. 98–353, Title I, July 10, 1984, 98 Stat. 343, by substituting "shall not be effective" for "shall take effect on June 28, 1984", thereby eliminating the amendment by section 232 of Pub.L. 95–598, effective June 27, 1984, pursuant to section 122(c) of Pub.L. 98–353, set out as an Effective Date note under section 151 of this title.

Section 121(a) of Pub.L. 98–353 directed that section 402(b) of Pub.L. 95–598 be amended by substituting "the date of enactment of the Bankruptcy Amendments and Federal Judgeship Act of 1984 [i.e. July 10, 1984] " for "June 28, 1984". This amendment was not executed in view of the prior amendment to section 402(b) of Pub.L. 95–598 by section 113 of Pub.L. 98–353.

Effective and Applicability Provisions

1987 Acts

Amendment by section 101(a) [Title IV, § 408(b)] of Pub.L. 100–202 (amending subsec. (a) of this section) effective Oct. 1, 1988, and any salary affected by its provisions to be adjusted at the beginning of the first applicable pay period commencing on or after such date, see section 101(a) [Title IV, § 408(d)] of Pub.L. 100–202, set out as a note under section 153 of this title.

1984 Acts

Amendment by section 108(a) of Pub.L. 98–353 effective July 10, 1984, see section 122(a) of Pub.L. 98–353, set out as a note under section 151 of this title.

1968 Acts

Amendment by Pub.L. 90–578 effective Oct. 17, 1968, except when a later effective date is applicable, which is the earlier of date when implementation of amendment by appointment of magistrates and assumption of office takes place or third anniversary of enactment of Pub.L. 90–578 on Oct. 17, 1968, see section 403 of Pub.L. 90–578, set out as a note under section 631 of this title.

Change of Name

"United States magistrate judge" substituted for "United States magistrate" in text pursuant to section 321 of Pub.L. 101–650, set out as a note under 28 U.S.C.A. § 631.

Continuation of Maximum Rates of Salary of Full-Time and Part-Time United States Magistrates in Effect on June 27, 1984

Section 108(b) of Pub.L. 98–353 provided that: "The maximum rates for salary of full-time and part-time United States magistrates in effect on June 27, 1984, shall remain in effect until changed as a result of a determination made under section 634(a) of title 28, United States Code [subsec. (a) of this section], as amended by this Act."

[Section 108(b) of Pub.L. 98–353 effective June 27, 1984, see section 122(c) of Pub.L. 98–353, set out as an Effective and Applicability Provisions note under section 151 of this title.]

Salary Increases of 1987

Maximum salaries of U.S. magistrates (full-time) and U.S. magistrates (part-time) increased respectively to $72,500 and $36,200 per annum, on recommendation of the President of the United States, see note set out under section 358 of Title 2, The Congress.

§ 635. Expenses

(a) Full-time United States magistrate judges serving under this chapter shall be allowed their actual and necessary expenses incurred in the performance of their duties, including the compensation of such legal assistants as the Judicial Conference, on the basis of the recommendations of the judicial councils of the circuits, considers necessary, and the compensation of necessary clerical and secretarial assistance. Such expenses and compensation shall be determined and paid by the Director under such regulations as the Director shall prescribe with the approval of the conference. The Administrator of General Services shall provide such magistrate judges with necessary courtrooms, office space, furniture and facilities within United States courthouses or office buildings owned or occupied by departments or agencies of the United States, or should suitable courtroom and office space not be available within any such courthouse or office building, the Administrator of General Services, at the request of the Director, shall procure and pay for suitable courtroom and office space, furniture and facilities for such magistrate judge in another build-

ing, but only if such request has been approved as necessary by the judicial council of the appropriate circuit.

(b) Under such regulations as the Director shall prescribe with the approval of the conference, the Director shall reimburse part-time magistrate judges for actual expenses necessarily incurred by them in the performance of their duties under this chapter. Such reimbursement may be made, at rates not exceeding those prescribed by such regulations, for expenses incurred by such part-time magistrate judges for clerical and secretarial assistance, stationery, telephone and other communications services, travel, and such other expenses as may be determined to be necessary for the proper performance of the duties of such officers: *Provided, however,* That no reimbursement shall be made for all or any portion of the expense incurred by such part-time magistrate judges for the procurement of office space.

(June 25, 1948, c. 646, 62 Stat. 917; Oct. 17, 1968, Pub.L. 90–578, Title I, § 101, 82 Stat. 1112; Oct. 10, 1979, Pub.L. 96–82, § 8(a), 93 Stat. 646; Dec. 1, 1990, Pub.L. 101–650, title III, § 321, 104 Stat. 5117.)

HISTORICAL AND STATUTORY NOTES

Effective and Applicability Provisions

1968 Acts

Amendment by Pub.L. 90–578 effective Oct. 17, 1968, except when a later effective date is applicable, which is the earlier of date when implementation of amendment by appointment of magistrates and assumption of office takes place or third anniversary of enactment of Pub.L. 90–578 on Oct. 17, 1968, see section 403 of Pub.L. 90–578, set out as a note under section 631 of this title.

Change of Name

"United States magistrate judge" substituted for "United States magistrate" in text pursuant to section 321 of Pub.L. 101–650, set out as a note under 28 U.S.C.A. § 631.

§ 636. Jurisdiction, powers, and temporary assignment

(a) Each United States magistrate judge serving under this chapter shall have within the district in which sessions are held by the court that appointed the magistrate judge, at other places where that court may function, and elsewhere as authorized by law—

(1) all powers and duties conferred or imposed upon United States commissioners by law or by the Rules of Criminal Procedure for the United States District Courts;

(2) the power to administer oaths and affirmations, issue orders pursuant to section 3142 of title 18 concerning release or detention of persons pending trial, and take acknowledgements, affidavits, and depositions;

(3) the power to conduct trials under section 3401, title 18, United States Code, in conformity with and subject to the limitations of that section;

(4) the power to enter a sentence for a petty offense; and

(5) the power to enter a sentence for a class A misdemeanor in a case in which the parties have consented.

(b)(1) Notwithstanding any provision of law to the contrary—

(A) a judge may designate a magistrate judge to hear and determine any pretrial matter pending before the court, except a motion for injunctive relief, for judgment on the pleadings, for summary judgment, to dismiss or quash an indictment or information made by the defendant, to suppress evidence in a criminal case, to dismiss or to permit maintenance of a class action, to dismiss for failure to state a claim upon which relief can be granted, and to involuntarily dismiss an action. A judge of the court may reconsider any pretrial matter under this subparagraph (A) where it has been shown that the magistrate judge's order is clearly erroneous or contrary to law.

(B) a judge may also designate a magistrate judge to conduct hearings, including evidentiary hearings, and to submit to a judge of the court proposed findings of fact and recommendations for the disposition, by a judge of the court, of any motion excepted in subparagraph (A), of applications for posttrial[1] relief made by individuals convicted of criminal offenses and of prisoner petitions challenging conditions of confinement.

(C) the magistrate judge shall file his proposed findings and recommendations under subparagraph (B) with the court and a copy shall forthwith be mailed to all parties.

Within ten days after being served with a copy, any party may serve and file written objections to such proposed findings and recommendations as provided by rules of court. A judge of the court shall make a de novo determination of those portions of the report or specified proposed findings or recommendations to which objection is made. A judge of the court may accept, reject, or modify, in whole or in part, the findings or recommendations made by the magistrate judge. The judge may also receive further evidence or recommit the matter to the magistrate judge with instructions.

(2) A judge may designate a magistrate judge to serve as a special master pursuant to the applicable provisions of this title and the Federal Rules of Civil Procedure for the United States district courts. A judge may designate a magistrate judge to serve as a special master in any civil case, upon consent of the

parties, without regard to the provisions of rule 53(b) of the Federal Rules of Civil Procedure for the United States district courts.

(3) A magistrate judge may be assigned such additional duties as are not inconsistent with the Constitution and laws of the United States.

(4) Each district court shall establish rules pursuant to which the magistrate judges shall discharge their duties.

(c) Notwithstanding any provision of law to the contrary—

(1) Upon the consent of the parties, a full-time United States magistrate judge or a part-time United States magistrate judge who serves as a full-time judicial officer may conduct any or all proceedings in a jury or nonjury civil matter and order the entry of judgment in the case, when specially designated to exercise such jurisdiction by the district court or courts he serves. Upon the consent of the parties, pursuant to their specific written request, any other part-time magistrate judge may exercise such jurisdiction, if such magistrate judge meets the bar membership requirements set forth in section 631(b)(1) and the chief judge of the district court certifies that a full-time magistrate judge is not reasonably available in accordance with guidelines established by the judicial council of the circuit. When there is more than one judge of a district court, designation under this paragraph shall be by the concurrence of a majority of all the judges of such district court, and when there is no such concurrence, then by the chief judge.

(2) If a magistrate judge is designated to exercise civil jurisdiction under paragraph (1) of this subsection, the clerk of court shall, at the time the action is filed, notify the parties of the availability of a magistrate judge to exercise such jurisdiction. The decision of the parties shall be communicated to the clerk of court. Thereafter, either the district court judge or the magistrate judge may again advise the parties of the availability of the magistrate judge, but in so doing, shall also advise the parties that they are free to withhold consent without adverse substantive consequences. Rules of court for the reference of civil matters to magistrate judges shall include procedures to protect the voluntariness of the parties' consent.

(3) Upon entry of judgment in any case referred under paragraph (1) of this subsection, an aggrieved party may appeal directly to the appropriate United States court of appeals from the judgment of the magistrate judge in the same manner as an appeal from any other judgment of a district court. The consent of the parties allows a magistrate judge designated to exercise civil jurisdiction under paragraph (1) of this subsection to direct the entry of a judgment of the district court in accordance with the Federal Rules of Civil Procedure. Nothing in this paragraph shall be construed as a limitation of any party's right to seek review by the Supreme Court of the United States.

(4) The court may, for good cause shown on its own motion, or under extraordinary circumstances shown by any party, vacate a reference of a civil matter to a magistrate judge under this subsection.

(5) The magistrate judge shall, subject to guidelines of the Judicial Conference, determine whether the record taken pursuant to this section shall be taken by electronic sound recording, by a court reporter, or by other means.

(d) The practice and procedure for the trial of cases before officers serving under this chapter shall conform to rules promulgated by the Supreme Court pursuant to section 2072 of this title.

(e) **Contempt authority.—**

(1) **In general.—**A United States magistrate judge serving under this chapter shall have within the territorial jurisdiction prescribed by the appointment of such magistrate judge the power to exercise contempt authority as set forth in this subsection.

(2) **Summary criminal contempt authority.—**A magistrate judge shall have the power to punish summarily by fine or imprisonment, or both, such contempt of the authority of such magistrate judge constituting misbehavior of any person in the magistrate judge's presence so as to obstruct the administration of justice. The order of contempt shall be issued under the Federal Rules of Criminal Procedure.

(3) **Additional criminal contempt authority in civil consent and misdemeanor cases.—**In any case in which a United States magistrate judge presides with the consent of the parties under subsection (c) of this section, and in any misdemeanor case proceeding before a magistrate judge under section 3401 of title 18, the magistrate judge shall have the power to punish, by fine or imprisonment, or both, criminal contempt constituting disobedience or resistance to the magistrate judge's lawful writ, process, order, rule, decree, or command. Disposition of such contempt shall be conducted upon notice and hearing under the Federal Rules of Criminal Procedure.

(4) **Civil contempt authority in civil consent and misdemeanor cases.—**In any case in which a United States magistrate judge presides with the consent of the parties under subsection (c) of this section, and in any misdemeanor case proceeding before a magistrate judge under section 3401 of title 18, the magistrate judge may exercise the civil

contempt authority of the district court. This paragraph shall not be construed to limit the authority of a magistrate judge to order sanctions under any other statute, the Federal Rules of Civil Procedure, or the Federal Rules of Criminal Procedure.

(5) Criminal contempt penalties.—The sentence imposed by a magistrate judge for any criminal contempt provided for in paragraphs (2) and (3) shall not exceed the penalties for a Class C misdemeanor as set forth in sections 3581(b)(8) and 3571(b)(6) of title 18.

(6) Certification of other contempts to the district court.—Upon the commission of any such act—

(A) in any case in which a United States magistrate judge presides with the consent of the parties under subsection (c) of this section, or in any misdemeanor case proceeding before a magistrate judge under section 3401 of title 18, that may, in the opinion of the magistrate judge, constitute a serious criminal contempt punishable by penalties exceeding those set forth in paragraph (5) of this subsection, or

(B) in any other case or proceeding under subsection (a) or (b) of this section, or any other statute, where—

(i) the act committed in the magistrate judge's presence may, in the opinion of the magistrate judge, constitute a serious criminal contempt punishable by penalties exceeding those set forth in paragraph (5) of this subsection,

(ii) the act that constitutes a criminal contempt occurs outside the presence of the magistrate judge, or

(iii) the act constitutes a civil contempt,

the magistrate judge shall forthwith certify the facts to a district judge and may serve or cause to be served, upon any person whose behavior is brought into question under this paragraph, an order requiring such person to appear before a district judge upon a day certain to show cause why that person should not be adjudged in contempt by reason of the facts so certified. The district judge shall thereupon hear the evidence as to the act or conduct complained of and, if it is such as to warrant punishment, punish such person in the same manner and to the same extent as for a contempt committed before a district judge.

(7) Appeals of magistrate judge contempt orders.—The appeal of an order of contempt under this subsection shall be made to the court of appeals in cases proceeding under subsection (c) of this section. The appeal of any other order of contempt issued under this section shall be made to the district court.

(f) In an emergency and upon the concurrence of the chief judges of the districts involved, a United States magistrate judge may be temporarily assigned to perform any of the duties specified in subsection (a), (b), or (c) of this section in a judicial district other than the judicial district for which he has been appointed. No magistrate judge shall perform any of such duties in a district to which he has been temporarily assigned until an order has been issued by the chief judge of such district specifying (1) the emergency by reason of which he has been transferred, (2) the duration of his assignment, and (3) the duties which he is authorized to perform. A magistrate judge so assigned shall not be entitled to additional compensation but shall be reimbursed for actual and necessary expenses incurred in the performance of his duties in accordance with section 635.

(g) A United States magistrate judge may perform the verification function required by section 4107 of title 18, United States Code. A magistrate judge may be assigned by a judge of any United States district court to perform the verification required by section 4108 and the appointment of counsel authorized by section 4109 of title 18, United States Code, and may perform such functions beyond the territorial limits of the United States. A magistrate judge assigned such functions shall have no authority to perform any other function within the territory of a foreign country.

(h) A United States magistrate judge who has retired may, upon the consent of the chief judge of the district involved, be recalled to serve as a magistrate judge in any judicial district by the judicial council of the circuit within which such district is located. Upon recall, a magistrate judge may receive a salary for such service in accordance with regulations promulgated by the Judicial Conference, subject to the restrictions on the payment of an annuity set forth in section 377 of this title or in subchapter III of chapter 83, and chapter 84, of title 5 which are applicable to such magistrate judge. The requirements set forth in subsections (a), (b)(3), and (d) of section 631, and paragraph (1) of subsection (b) of such section to the extent such paragraph requires membership of the bar of the location in which an individual is to serve as a magistrate judge, shall not apply to the recall of a retired magistrate judge under this subsection or section 375 of this title. Any other requirement set forth in section 631(b) shall apply to the recall of a retired magistrate judge under this subsection or section 375 of this title unless such retired magistrate judge met such requirement upon appointment or reappointment as a magistrate judge under section 361.

(June 25, 1948, c. 646, 62 Stat. 917; Oct. 17, 1968, Pub.L. 90–578, Title I, § 101, 82 Stat. 1113; Mar. 1, 1972, Pub.L. 92–239, §§ 1, 2, 86 Stat. 47; Oct. 21, 1976, Pub.L. 94–577, § 1, 90 Stat. 2729; Oct. 28, 1977, Pub.L. 95–144, § 2, 91 Stat.

1220; Oct. 10, 1979, Pub.L. 96–82, § 2, 93 Stat. 643; Oct. 12, 1984, Pub.L. 98–473, Title II, § 208, 98 Stat. 1986; Nov. 8, 1984, Pub.L. 98–620, Title IV, § 402(29)(B), 98 Stat. 3359; Nov. 14, 1986, Pub.L. 99–651, Title II, § 201(a)(2), 100 Stat. 3647; Nov. 15, 1988, Pub.L. 100–659, § 4(c), 102 Stat. 3918; Nov. 18, 1988, Pub.L. 100–690, Title VII, § 7322, 102 Stat. 4467; Nov. 19, 1988, Pub.L. 100–702, Title IV, § 404(b)(1), Title X, § 1014, 102 Stat. 4651, 4669; Dec. 1, 1990, Pub.L. 101–650, Title III, §§ 308(a), 321, 104 Stat. 5112, 5117; Oct. 19, 1996, Pub.L. 104–317, Title II, §§ 201, 202(b), 207, 110 Stat. 3848, 3849, 3851; Nov. 13, 2000, Pub.L. 106–518, Title II, §§ 202, 203(b), 114 Stat. 2412, 2414; Nov. 2, 2002, Pub.L. 107–273, Div. B, Title III, § 3002(b), 116 Stat. 1805; Sept. 9, 2005, Pub.L. 109–63, § 2(d), 119 Stat. 1995.)

¹ So in original. Probably should be "post-trial".

HISTORICAL AND STATUTORY NOTES

References in Text

The Rules of Criminal Procedure for the United States District Courts, referred to in subsec. (a)(1), are classified to Title 18, Crimes and Criminal Procedure.

The Federal Rules of Civil Procedure for the United States district courts, referred to in subsec. (b)(2) and (c)(3), are classified to this title.

Effective and Applicability Provisions

1988 Acts

Amendment by section 404(b)(1) of Pub.L. 100–702 effective Dec. 1, 1988, see section 407 of Pub.L. 100–702, set out as a note under section 2071 of this title.

Amendment to this section by Pub.L. 100–659 to take effect on Nov. 15, 1988, and shall apply to bankruptcy judges and magistrates who retire on or after Nov. 15, 1988, with special election provisions for bankruptcy judges, etc., who left office on or after July 31, 1987, and before Nov. 15, 1988, see section 9 of Pub.L. 100–659, set out as a note under section 377 of this title.

1986 Acts

Amendment by Pub.L. 99–651 effective Jan. 1, 1987, see section 203 of Pub.L. 99–651, set out as a note under section 155 of this title.

1984 Acts

Amendment by Pub.L. 98–620 not to apply to cases pending on Nov. 8, 1984, see section 403 of Pub.L. 98–620, set out as a note under section 1657 of this title.

1968 Acts

Amendment by Pub.L. 90–578 effective Oct. 17, 1968, except when a later effective date is applicable, which is the earlier of date when implementation of amendment by appointment of magistrates and assumption of office takes place or third anniversary of enactment of Pub.L. 90–578 on Oct. 17, 1968, see section 403 of Pub.L. 90–578, set out as a note under section 631 of this title.

Change of Name

"United States magistrate judge" substituted for "United States magistrate" in text pursuant to section 321 of Pub.L. 101–650, set out as a note under 28 U.S.C.A. § 631.

§ 637. Training

The Federal Judicial Center shall conduct periodic training programs and seminars for both full-time and part-time United States magistrate judges, including an introductory training program for new magistrate judges, to be held within one year after initial appointment.

(June 25, 1948, c. 646, 62 Stat. 917; Oct. 17, 1968, Pub.L. 90–578, Title I, § 101, 82 Stat. 1114; Dec. 1, 1990, Pub.L. 101–650, Title III, § 321, 104 Stat. 5117.)

HISTORICAL AND STATUTORY NOTES

Effective and Applicability Provisions

1968 Acts

Amendment by Pub.L. 90–578 effective Oct. 17, 1968, except when a later effective date is applicable, which is the earlier of date when implementation of amendment by appointment of magistrates and assumption of office takes place or third anniversary of enactment of Pub.L. 90–578 on Oct. 17, 1968, see section 403 of Pub.L. 90–578, set out as a note under section 631 of this title.

Change of Name

"United States magistrate judge" substituted for "United States magistrate" in text pursuant to section 321 of Pub.L. 101–650, set out as a note under 28 U.S.C.A. § 631.

§ 638. Dockets and forms; United States Code; seals

(a) The Director shall furnish to United States magistrate judges adequate docket books and forms prescribed by the Director. The Director shall also furnish to each such officer a copy of the current edition of the United States Code.

(b) All property furnished to any such officer shall remain the property of the United States and, upon the termination of his term of office, shall be transmitted to his successor in office or otherwise disposed of as the Director orders.

(c) The Director shall furnish to each United States magistrate judge appointed under this chapter an official impression seal in a form prescribed by the conference. Each such officer shall affix his seal to every jurat or certificate of his official acts without fee.

(June 25, 1948, c. 646, 62 Stat. 917; Oct. 17, 1968, Pub.L. 90–578, Title I, § 101, 82 Stat. 1114; Dec. 1, 1990, Pub.L. 101–650, Title III, § 321, 104 Stat. 5117.)

HISTORICAL AND STATUTORY NOTES

Effective and Applicability Provisions

1968 Acts

Amendment by Pub.L. 90–578 effective Oct. 17, 1968, except when a later effective date is applicable, which is the earlier of date when implementation of amendment by appointment of magistrates and assumption of office takes place or third anniversary of enactment of Pub.L. 90–578 on Oct. 17, 1968, see section 403 of Pub.L. 90–578, set out as a note under section 631 of this title.

Change of Name

"United States magistrate judge" substituted for "United States magistrate" in text pursuant to section 321 of Pub.L. 101–650, set out as a note under 28 U.S.C.A. § 631.

§ 639.　Definitions

As used in this chapter—

(1) "Conference" shall mean the Judicial Conference of the United States;

(2) "Council" shall mean the Judicial Council of the Circuit;

(3) "Director" shall mean the Director of the Administrative Office of the United States Courts;

(4) "Full-time magistrate judge" shall mean a full-time United States magistrate judge;

(5) "Part-time magistrate judge" shall mean a part-time United States magistrate judge; and

(6) "United States magistrate judge" and "magistrate judge" shall mean both full-time and part-time United States magistrate judges.

(June 25, 1948, c. 646, 62 Stat. 917; Oct. 17, 1968, Pub.L. 90–578, Title I, § 101, 82 Stat. 1114; Dec. 1, 1990, Pub.L. 101–650, Title III, § 321, 104 Stat. 5117.)

HISTORICAL AND STATUTORY NOTES

Effective and Applicability Provisions

1968 Acts

Amendment by Pub.L. 90–578 effective Oct. 17, 1968, except when a later effective date is applicable, which is the earlier of date when implementation of amendment by appointment of magistrates and assumption of office takes place or third anniversary of enactment of Pub.L. 90–578 on Oct. 17, 1968, see section 403 of Pub.L. 90–578, set out as a note under section 631 of this title.

Change of Name

"United States magistrate judge" substituted for "United States magistrate" in text pursuant to section 321 of Pub.L. 101–650, set out as a note under 28 U.S.C.A. § 631.

CHAPTER 44—ALTERNATIVE DISPUTE RESOLUTION

§ 651.　Authorization of alternative dispute resolution

(a) **Definition.**—For purposes of this chapter, an alternative dispute resolution process includes any process or procedure, other than an adjudication by a presiding judge, in which a neutral third party participates to assist in the resolution of issues in controversy, through processes such as early neutral evaluation, mediation, minitrial, and arbitration as provided in sections 654 through 658.

(b) **Authority.**—Each United States district court shall authorize, by local rule adopted under section 2071(a), the use of alternative dispute resolution processes in all civil actions, including adversary proceedings in bankruptcy, in accordance with this chapter, except that the use of arbitration may be authorized only as provided in section 654. Each United States district court shall devise and implement its own alternative dispute resolution program, by local rule adopted under section 2071(a), to encourage and promote the use of alternative dispute resolution in its district.

(c) **Existing alternative dispute resolution programs.**—In those courts where an alternative dispute resolution program is in place on the date of the enactment of the Alternative Dispute Resolution Act of 1998, the court shall examine the effectiveness of that program and adopt such improvements to the program as are consistent with the provisions and purposes of this chapter [28 U.S.C.A. § 651 et seq.].

(d) **Administration of alternative dispute resolution programs.**—Each United States district court shall designate an employee, or a judicial officer, who is knowledgeable in alternative dispute resolution practices and processes to implement, administer, oversee, and evaluate the court's alternative dispute resolution program. Such person may also be responsible for recruiting, screening, and training attorneys to serve as neutrals and arbitrators in the court's alternative dispute resolution program.

(e) **Title 9 not affected.**—This chapter [28 U.S.C.A. § 651 et seq.] shall not affect title 9, United States Code.

(f) **Program support.**—The Federal Judicial Center and the Administrative Office of the United States Courts are authorized to assist the district courts in the establishment and improvement of alternative dispute resolution programs by identifying particular practices employed in successful programs and providing additional assistance as needed and appropriate. (Added Pub.L. 100–702, Title IX, § 901(a), Nov. 19, 1988, 102 Stat. 4659, and amended Pub.L. 105–315, § 3, Oct. 30, 1998, 112 Stat. 2993.)

HISTORICAL AND STATUTORY NOTES

References in Text

The enactment of the Alternative Dispute Resolution Act of 1998, referred to in subsec. (c), is the enactment of Pub.L. 105–315, 112 Stat. 2993, which was approved Oct. 30, 1998.

Effective and Applicability Provisions

1988 Acts

Section 906 of Title IX of Pub.L. 100–702, as amended Pub.L. 103–192, § 1(a), Dec. 14, 1993, 107 Stat. 2292, which provided that, effective December 31, 1994, this chapter, as added by section 901 of Pub.L. 100–702, and the item relating to this chapter in the table of chapters at the beginning of part III of this title, were repealed, except that the provisions of this chapter were to continue to apply through final disposition of all actions in which referral to arbitration was made before the date of repeal, was itself repealed by Pub.L. 103–420, § 3(b), Oct. 25, 1994, 108 Stat. 4345.

Section 907 of Title IX of Pub.L. 100–702 provided that: "This title and the amendments made by this title [enacting this chapter, provisions set out as notes under this section and section 652 of this title] shall take effect 180 days after the date of enactment of this Act [Nov. 19, 1988]."

Findings and Declaration of Policy

Pub.L. 105–315, § 2, Oct. 30, 1998, 112 Stat. 2993, provided that:

"Congress finds that—

"(1) alternative dispute resolution, when supported by the bench and bar, and utilizing properly trained neutrals in a program adequately administered by the court, has the potential to provide a variety of benefits, including greater satisfaction of the parties, innovative methods of resolving disputes, and greater efficiency in achieving settlements;

"(2) certain forms of alternative dispute resolution, including mediation, early neutral evaluation, minitrials, and voluntary arbitration, may have potential to reduce the large backlog of cases now pending in some Federal courts throughout the United States, thereby allowing the courts to process their remaining cases more efficiently; and

"(3) the continued growth of Federal appellate court-annexed mediation programs suggests that this form of alternative dispute resolution can be equally effective in resolving disputes in the Federal trial courts; therefore, the district courts should consider including mediation in their local alternative dispute resolution programs."

Authorization of Appropriations

Pub.L. 105–315, § 11, Oct. 30, 1998, 112 Stat. 2998, provided that: "There are authorized to be appropriated for each fiscal year such sums as may be necessary to carry out chapter 44 of title 28, United States Code [28 U.S.C.A. § 651 et seq.], as amended by this Act [Alternative Dispute Resolution Act of 1998, Pub.L. 105–315, Oct. 30, 1998, 112 Stat. 2993, amending sections 651 to 658 of this title, amending a provision set out as a note under section 652 of this title, and enacting notes set out under this section]."

Section 905 of Title IX of Pub.L. 100–702, as amended Pub.L. 103–192, § 1(b), Dec. 14, 1993, 107 Stat. 2292; Pub.L. 103–420, § 3(a), Oct. 25, 1994, 108 Stat. 4345; Pub.L. 105–53, § 1, Oct. 6, 1997, 111 Stat. 1173, provided that: "There are authorized to be appropriated for each fiscal year to the judicial branch such sums as may be necessary to carry out the purposes of chapter 44 [this chapter], as added by section 901 of this Act. Funds appropriated under this section shall be allocated by the Administrative Office of the United States Courts to Federal judicial districts and the Federal Judicial Center. The funds so appropriated are authorized to remain available until expended."

Effect on Judicial Rulemaking Powers

Section 904 of Title IX of Pub.L. 100–702 provided that: "Nothing in this title [enacting this chapter and provisions set out as notes under this section and section 652 of this title], or in chapter 44 [this chapter], as added by section 901 of this Act, is intended to abridge, modify, or enlarge the rule making powers of the Federal judiciary."

Model Procedures

Section 902 of Title IX of Pub.L. 100–702 provided that: "The Judicial Conference of the United States may develop model rules relating to procedures for arbitration under chapter 44 [this chapter], as added by section 901 of this Act. No model rule may supersede any provision of such chapter 44, this title [enacting this chapter and provisions set out as notes under this section and section 652 of this title], or any law of the United States."

Reports by Director of Administrative Office of United States Courts and by Federal Judicial Center

Pub.L. 100–702, Title IX, § 903, Nov. 19, 1988, 102 Stat. 4663, provided that:

"(a) Annual Report by Director of Administrative Office of the United States Courts.—The Director of the Administrative Office of the United States Courts shall include in the annual report of the activities of the Administrative Office required under section 604(a)(3) [section 604(a)(3) of this title], statistical information about the implementation of chapter 44 [this chapter], as added by section 901 of this Act."

"(b) Report by Federal Judicial Center.—Not later than 5 years after the date of enactment of this Act [Nov. 19, 1988], the Federal Judicial Center, in consultation with the Director of the Administrative Office of the United States Courts, shall submit to the Congress a report on the implementation of chapter 44 [this chapter], as added by section 901 of this Act, which shall include the following:

"(1) A description of the arbitration programs authorized by such chapter, as conceived and as implemented in the judicial districts in which such programs are authorized.

"(2) A determination of the level of satisfaction with the arbitration programs in those judicial districts by a sampling of court personnel, attorneys, and litigants whose cases have been referred to arbitration.

"(3) A summary of those program features that can be identified as being related to program acceptance both within and across judicial districts.

"(4) A description of the levels of satisfaction relative to the cost per hearing of each program.

"(5) Recommendations to the Congress on whether to terminate or continue chapter 44, or alternatively, to enact an arbitration provision in title 28, United States Code [this title], authorizing arbitration in all Federal district courts."

[For termination, effective May 15, 2000, of reporting provisions of this note, see Pub.L. 104–66, § 3003, as amended, set out as a note under 31 U.S.C.A. § 1113, and the 11th item on page 12 of House Document No. 103–7.]

Treatment of Expired Provisions

Pub.L. 103–192, § 2, Dec. 14, 1993, 107 Stat. 2292, provided that: "Chapter 44 of title 28, United States Code [this chapter], and the item relating to that chapter in the table of chapters at the beginning of part III of such title [analysis preceding section 601 of this title], shall be effective on or after the date of the enactment of this Act [Dec. 14, 1993] as if such chapter and item had not been repealed by section 906 of the Judicial Improvements and Access to Justice Act [section 906 of Pub.L. 100–702, set out as an Effective Date of Repeal note under this section] as such section was in effect on the day before the date of the enactment of this Act [Dec. 14, 1993]."

§ 652. Jurisdiction

(a) Consideration of alternative dispute resolution in appropriate cases.—Notwithstanding any provision of law to the contrary and except as provided in subsections (b) and (c), each district court shall, by local rule adopted under section 2071(a), require that litigants in all civil cases consider the use of an alternative dispute resolution process at an appropriate stage in the litigation. Each district court shall provide litigants in all civil cases with at least one alternative dispute resolution process, including, but not limited to, mediation, early neutral evaluation, minitrial, and arbitration as authorized in sections 654 through 658. Any district court that elects to require the use of alternative dispute resolution in certain cases may do so only with respect to mediation, early neutral evaluation, and, if the parties consent, arbitration.

(b) Actions exempted from consideration of alternative dispute resolution.—Each district court may exempt from the requirements of this section specific cases or categories of cases in which use of alternative dispute resolution would not be appropriate. In defining these exemptions, each district court shall consult with members of the bar, including the United States Attorney for that district.

(c) Authority of the Attorney General.—Nothing in this section shall alter or conflict with the authority of the Attorney General to conduct litigation on behalf of the United States, with the authority of any Federal agency authorized to conduct litigation in the United States courts, or with any delegation of litigation authority by the Attorney General.

(d) Confidentiality provisions.—Until such time as rules are adopted under chapter 131 of this title [28 U.S.C.A. § 2071 et seq.] providing for the confidentiality of alternative dispute resolution processes under this chapter [28 U.S.C.A. § 651 et seq.], each district court shall, by local rule adopted under section 2071(a), provide for the confidentiality of the alternative dispute resolution processes and to prohibit disclosure of confidential dispute resolution communications.

(Added Pub.L. 100–702, Title IX, § 901(a), Nov. 19, 1988, 102 Stat. 4659, and amended Pub.L. 105–315, § 4, Oct. 30, 1998, 112 Stat. 2994.)

HISTORICAL AND STATUTORY NOTES

Effective and Applicability Provisions

1988 Acts

Section 906 of Pub.L. 100–702, as amended, which provided that, effective Dec. 31, 1994, this section was repealed, with certain exceptions, was itself repealed by Pub.L. 103–420, § 3(b), Oct. 25, 1994, 108 Stat. 4345. See section 906 of Pub.L. 100–702, set out as a note under section 651 of this title.

Section effective 180 days after Nov. 19, 1988, see section 907 of Pub.L. 100–702, set out as a note under section 651 of this title.

Treatment of Expired Provisions

This section to continue to be effective on or after Dec. 14, 1993 as if it had not been repealed by section 906 of Pub.L. 100–702, as such section was in effect on the day before such date, see Treatment of Expired Provisions note set out under section 651 of this title.

Exception to Limitation on Money Damages

Section 901(c) of Pub.L. 100–702, which provided that notwithstanding this section a district court listed in section 658 of this title whose local rule on Nov. 19, 1988 provided for a limitation on money damages with respect to cases referred to arbitration of not more than $150,000 may continue to apply the higher limitation, was repealed by Pub.L. 105–315, § 12(a), Oct. 30, 1998, 112 Stat. 2998.

§ 653. Neutrals

(a) Panel of neutrals.—Each district court that authorizes the use of alternative dispute resolution processes shall adopt appropriate processes for making neutrals available for use by the parties for each category of process offered. Each district court shall promulgate its own procedures and criteria for the selection of neutrals on its panels.

(b) Qualifications and training.—Each person serving as a neutral in an alternative dispute resolution process should be qualified and trained to serve as a neutral in the appropriate alternative dispute resolution process. For this purpose, the district court may use, among others, magistrate judges who have been trained to serve as neutrals in alternative dispute resolution processes, professional neutrals from the private sector, and persons who have been trained to serve as neutrals in alternative dispute resolution processes. Until such time as rules are adopted under chapter 131 of this title [28 U.S.C.A. § 2071 et seq.] relating to the disqualification of neutrals, each district court shall issue rules under section 2071(a) relating to the disqualification of neutrals (including, where appropriate, disqualification under section 455 of this title, other applicable law, and professional responsibility standards).

(Added Pub.L. 100–702, Title IX, § 901(a), Nov. 19, 1988, 102 Stat. 4660, and amended Pub.L. 105–315, § 5, Oct. 30, 1998, 112 Stat. 2995.)

HISTORICAL AND STATUTORY NOTES

Effective and Applicability Provisions

1988 Acts

Section 906 of Pub.L. 100–702, as amended, which provided that, effective Dec. 31, 1994, this section was repealed, with certain exceptions, was itself repealed by Pub.L. 103–420, § 3(b), Oct. 25, 1994, 108 Stat. 4345. See section 906 of Pub.L. 100–702, set out as a note under section 651 of this title.

Section effective 180 days after Nov. 19, 1988, see section 907 of Pub.L. 100–702, set out as a note under section 651 of this title.

Treatment of Expired Provisions

This section to continue to be effective on or after Dec. 14, 1993 as if it had not been repealed by section 906 of Pub.L. 100–702 as such section was in effect on the day before such date, see Treatment of Expired Provisions note set out under section 651 of this title.

§ 654. Arbitration

(a) Referral of actions to arbitration.—Notwithstanding any provision of law to the contrary and except as provided in subsections (a), (b), and (c) of section 652 and subsection (d) of this section, a district court may allow the referral to arbitration of any civil action (including any adversary proceeding in bankruptcy) pending before it when the parties consent, except that referral to arbitration may not be made where—

(1) the action is based on an alleged violation of a right secured by the Constitution of the United States;

(2) jurisdiction is based in whole or in part on section 1343 of this title; or

(3) the relief sought consists of money damages in an amount greater than $150,000.

(b) Safeguards in consent cases.—Until such time as rules are adopted under chapter 131 of this title relating to procedures described in this subsection, the district court shall, by local rule adopted under section 2071(a), establish procedures to ensure that any civil action in which arbitration by consent is allowed under subsection (a)—

(1) consent to arbitration is freely and knowingly obtained; and

(2) no party or attorney is prejudiced for refusing to participate in arbitration.

(c) Presumptions.—For purposes of subsection (a)(3), a district court may presume damages are not in excess of $150,000 unless counsel certifies that damages exceed such amount.

(d) Existing programs.—Nothing in this chapter is deemed to affect any program in which arbitration is conducted pursuant to section [1] title IX of the Judicial Improvements and Access to Justice Act (Public Law 100–702), as amended by section 1 of Public Law 105–53.

(Added Pub.L. 100–702, Title IX, § 901(a), Nov. 19, 1988, 102 Stat. 4660, and amended Pub.L. 105–315, § 6, Oct. 30, 1998, 112 Stat. 2995.)

[1] So in original. The word "section" probably should not appear.

HISTORICAL AND STATUTORY NOTES

References in Text

Title IX of the Judicial Improvements and Access to Justice Act, referred to in subsec. (d), is Pub.L. 100–702, Title IX, Nov. 19, 1988, 102 Stat. 4663. See Codifications note under this section.

Codifications

Section title IX of the Judicial Improvements and Access to Justice Act, referred to in subsec. (d), probably should read section 905 of title IX of the Judicial Improvements and Access to Justice Act, which is Pub.L. 100–702, Title IX, § 905, Nov. 19, 1988, 102 Stat. 4663, set out as a note under section 651 of this title.

Effective and Applicability Provisions

1988 Acts

Section 906 of Pub.L. 100–702, as amended, which provided that, effective Dec. 31, 1994, this section was repealed, with certain exceptions, was itself repealed by Pub.L. 103–420, § 3(b), Oct. 25, 1994, 108 Stat. 4345. See section 906 of Pub.L. 100–702, set out as a note under section 651 of this title.

Section effective 180 days after Nov. 19, 1988, see section 907 of Pub.L. 100–702, set out as a note under section 651 of this title.

Treatment of Expired Provisions

This section to continue to be effective on or after Dec. 14, 1993 as if it had not been repealed by section 906 of Pub.L. 100–702 as such section was in effect on the day before such date, see Treatment of Expired Provisions note set out under section 651 of this title.

§ 655. Arbitrators

(a) Powers of arbitrators.—An arbitrator to whom an action is referred under section 654 shall have the power, within the judicial district of the district court which referred the action to arbitration—

(1) to conduct arbitration hearings;

(2) to administer oaths and affirmations; and

(3) to make awards.

(b) Standards for certification.—Each district court that authorizes arbitration shall establish standards for the certification of arbitrators and shall certify arbitrators to perform services in accordance with such standards and this chapter. The standards shall include provisions requiring that any arbitrator—

(1) shall take the oath or affirmation described in section 453; and

(2) shall be subject to the disqualification rules under section 455.

(c) **Immunity.**—All individuals serving as arbitrators in an alternative dispute resolution program under this chapter are performing quasi-judicial functions and are entitled to the immunities and protections that the law accords to persons serving in such capacity.

(Added Pub.L. 100–702, Title IX, § 901(a), Nov. 19, 1988, 102 Stat. 4661, and amended Pub.L. 105–315, § 7, Oct. 30, 1998, 112 Stat. 2996.)

HISTORICAL AND STATUTORY NOTES

Effective and Applicability Provisions

1988 Acts

Section 906 of Pub.L. 100–702, as amended, which provided that, effective Dec. 31, 1994, this section was repealed, with certain exceptions, was itself repealed by Pub.L. 103–420, § 3(b), Oct. 25, 1994, 108 Stat. 4345. See section 906 of Pub.L. 100–702, set out as a note under section 651 of this title.

Section effective 180 days after Nov. 19, 1988, see section 907 of Pub.L. 100–702, set out as a note under section 651 of this title.

Treatment of Expired Provisions

This section to continue to be effective on or after Dec. 14, 1993 as if it had not been repealed by section 906 of Pub.L. 100–702 as such section was in effect on the day before such date, see Treatment of Expired Provisions note set out under section 651 of this title.

§ 656. Subpoenas

Rule 45 of the Federal Rules of Civil Procedure (relating to subpoenas) applies to subpoenas for the attendance of witnesses and the production of documentary evidence at an arbitration hearing under this chapter.

(Added Pub.L. 100–702, Title IX, § 901(a), Nov. 19, 1988, 102 Stat. 4662, and amended Pub.L. 105–315, § 8, Oct. 30, 1998, 112 Stat. 2996.)

HISTORICAL AND STATUTORY NOTES

Effective and Applicability Provisions

1988 Acts

Section 906 of Pub.L. 100–702, as amended, which provided that, effective Dec. 31, 1994, this section was repealed, with certain exceptions, was itself repealed by Pub.L. 103–420, § 3(b), Oct. 25, 1994, 108 Stat. 4345. See section 906 of Pub.L. 100–702, set out as a note under section 651 of this title.

Section effective 180 days after Nov. 19, 1988, see section 907 of Pub.L. 100–702, set out as a note under section 651 of this title.

Treatment of Expired Provisions

This section to continue to be effective on or after Dec. 14, 1993 as if it had not been repealed by section 906 of Pub.L.

100–702 as such section was in effect on the day before such date, see Treatment of Expired Provisions note set out under section 651 of this title.

§ 657. Arbitration award and judgment

(a) **Filing and effect of arbitration award.**—An arbitration award made by an arbitrator under this chapter, along with proof of service of such award on the other party by the prevailing party or by the plaintiff, shall be filed promptly after the arbitration hearing is concluded with the clerk of the district court that referred the case to arbitration. Such award shall be entered as the judgment of the court after the time has expired for requesting a trial de novo. The judgment so entered shall be subject to the same provisions of law and shall have the same force and effect as a judgment of the court in a civil action, except that the judgment shall not be subject to review in any other court by appeal or otherwise.

(b) **Sealing of arbitration award.**—The district court shall provide, by local rule adopted under section 2071(a), that the contents of any arbitration award made under this chapter shall not be made known to any judge who might be assigned to the case until the district court has entered final judgment in the action or the action has otherwise terminated.

(c) **Trial de novo of arbitration awards.**—

(1) **Time for filing demand.**—Within 30 days after the filing of an arbitration award with a district court under subsection (a), any party may file a written demand for a trial de novo in the district court.

(2) **Action restored to court docket.**—Upon a demand for a trial de novo, the action shall be restored to the docket of the court and treated for all purposes as if it had not been referred to arbitration.

(3) **Exclusion of evidence of arbitration.**—The court shall not admit at the trial de novo any evidence that there has been an arbitration proceeding, the nature or amount of any award, or any other matter concerning the conduct of the arbitration proceeding, unless—

(A) the evidence would otherwise be admissible in the court under the Federal Rules of Evidence; or

(B) the parties have otherwise stipulated.

(Added Pub.L. 100–702, Title IX, § 901(a), Nov. 19, 1988, 102 Stat. 4662, and amended Pub.L. 105–315, § 9, Oct. 30, 1998, 112 Stat. 2997.)

HISTORICAL AND STATUTORY NOTES

Effective and Applicability Provisions

1988 Acts

Section 906 of Pub.L. 100–702, as amended, which provided that, effective Dec. 31, 1994, this section was repealed, with

certain exceptions, was itself repealed by Pub.L. 103–420, § 3(b), Oct. 25, 1994, 108 Stat. 4345. See section 906 of Pub.L. 100–702, set out as a note under section 651 of this title.

Section effective 180 days after Nov. 19, 1988, see section 907 of Pub.L. 100–702, set out as a note under section 651 of this title.

Treatment of Expired Provisions

This section to continue to be effective on or after Dec. 14, 1993 as if it had not been repealed by section 906 of Pub.L. 100–702 as such section was in effect on the day before such date, see Treatment of Expired Provisions note set out under section 651 of this title.

§ 658. Compensation of arbitrators and neutrals

(a) **Compensation.**—The district court shall, subject to regulations approved by the Judicial Conference of the United States, establish the amount of compensation, if any, that each arbitrator or neutral shall receive for services rendered in each case under this chapter.

(b) **Transportation allowances.**—Under regulations prescribed by the Director of the Administrative Office of the United States Courts, a district court may reimburse arbitrators and other neutrals for actual transportation expenses necessarily incurred in the performance of duties under this chapter.

(Added Pub.L. 100–702, Title IX, § 901(a), Nov. 19, 1988, 102 Stat. 4662, and amended Pub.L. 105–315, § 10, Oct. 30, 1998, 112 Stat. 2997.)

HISTORICAL AND STATUTORY NOTES

Effective and Applicability Provisions

1988 Acts

Section 906 of Pub.L. 100–702, as amended, which provided that, effective Dec. 31, 1994, this section was repealed, with certain exceptions, was itself repealed by Pub.L. 103–420, § 3(b), Oct. 25, 1994, 108 Stat. 4345. See section 906 of Pub.L. 100–702, set out as a note under section 651 of this title.

Section effective 180 days after Nov. 19, 1988, see section 907 of Pub.L. 100–702, set out as a note under section 651 of this title.

Treatment of Expired Provisions

This section to continue to be effective on or after Dec. 14, 1993 as if it had not been repealed by section 906 of Pub.L. 100–702 as such section was in effect on the day before such date, see Treatment of Expired Provisions note set out under section 651 of this title.

PART IV—JURISDICTION AND VENUE

HISTORICAL AND STATUTORY NOTES

Codifications

The analysis of chapters comprising Part IV was amended by Pub.L. 95–598, Title II, § 241(b), Nov. 6, 1978, 92 Stat. 2671, effective June 28, 1984, pursuant to Pub.L. 95–598, Title IV, § 402(b), Nov. 6, 1978, 92 Stat. 2682, as amended by Pub.L. 98–249, § 1(a), Mar. 31, 1984, 98 Stat. 116; Pub.L. 98–271, § 1(a), Apr. 30, 1984, 98 Stat. 163; Pub.L. 98–299, § 1(a), May 25, 1984, 98 Stat. 214; Pub.L. 98–325, § 1(a), June 20, 1984, 98 Stat. 268, set out as an Effective Date note preceding section 101 of Title 11, Bankruptcy, by adding:

Section 402(b) of Pub.L. 95–598 was amended by section 113 of Pub.L. 98–353, Title I, July 10, 1984, 98 Stat. 343, by substituting "shall not be effective" for "shall take effect on June 28, 1984", thereby eliminating the amendment by section 241(b) of Pub.L. 95–598, effective June 27, 1984, pursuant to section 122(c) of Pub.L. 98–353, set out as an Effective and Applicability Provisions note under section 151 of this title.

Section 121(a) of Pub.L. 98–353 directed that section 402(b) of Pub.L. 95–598 be amended by substituting "the date of enactment of the Bankruptcy Amendments and Federal Judgeship Act of 1984 [i.e. July 10, 1984]" for "June 28, 1984". This amendment was not executed in view of the prior amendment to section 402(b) of Pub.L. 95–598 by section 113 of Pub.L. 98–353.

Change of Name

References to United States Claims Court deemed to refer to United States Court of Federal Claims and references to Claims Court deemed to refer to Court of Federal Claims, see section 902(b) of Pub.L. 102–572, set out as a note under section 171 of Title 28, Judiciary and Judicial Procedure.

CHAPTER 81—SUPREME COURT

HISTORICAL AND STATUTORY NOTES

Definitions of Courts and Judges

Section 32 of Act June 25, 1948, as amended by Act May 24, 1949, c. 139, § 127, 63 Stat. 107, provided:

"(a) All laws of the United States in force on September 1, 1948, in which reference is made to a 'circuit court of appeals'; 'senior circuit judge'; 'senior district judge'; 'presiding judge'; 'chief justice', except when reference to the Chief Justice of the United States is intended; or 'justice', except when used with respect to a justice of the Supreme Court of the United States in his capacity as such or as a circuit justice, are hereby amended by substituting 'court of appeals' for 'circuit court of appeals'; 'chief judge of the circuit' for 'senior circuit judge'; 'chief judge of the district court' for 'senior district judge'; 'chief judge' for 'presiding judge'; 'chief judge' for 'chief justice', except when reference to the Chief Justice of the United States is intended; and 'judge' for 'justice', except when the latter term is used with respect to a justice of the Supreme Court of the United States in his capacity as such or as a circuit justice.

"(b) All laws of the United States in force on September 1, 1948, in which reference is made to the Supreme Court of the District of Columbia or to the District Court of the United States for the District of Columbia are amended by substituting 'United States District Court for the District of Columbia' for such designations.

"(c) All laws of the United States in force on September 1, 1948, in which reference is made to the 'Conference of Senior Circuit Judges', or to the 'Judicial Conference of Senior Circuit Judges' are amended by substituting 'Judicial Conference of the United States' for such designations.

"(d) This section shall not be construed to amend historical references to courts or judicial offices which have no present or future application to such courts or offices."

§ 1251. Original jurisdiction

(a) The Supreme Court shall have original and exclusive jurisdiction of all controversies between two or more States.

(b) The Supreme Court shall have original but not exclusive jurisdiction of:

(1) All actions or proceedings to which ambassadors, other public ministers, consuls, or vice consuls of foreign states are parties;

(2) All controversies between the United States and a State;

(3) All actions or proceedings by a State against the citizens of another State or against aliens.

(June 25, 1948, c. 646, 62 Stat. 927; Sept. 30, 1978, Pub.L. 95–393, § 8(b), 92 Stat. 810.)

HISTORICAL AND STATUTORY NOTES

Effective and Applicability Provisions

1978 Acts

Amendment by Pub.L. 95–393 effective at the end of the 90-day period beginning on Sept. 30, 1978, see section 9 of Pub.L. 95–393, set out as a note under section 254a of Title 22, Foreign Relations and Intercourse.

Statutes Governing Writs of Error to Apply to Appeals

Act Jan. 31, 1928, c. 14, § 2, 45 Stat. 54, amended Apr. 26, 1928, c. 440, 45 Stat. 466; June 25, 1948, c. 646, § 23, 62 Stat. 990, provided that: "All Acts of Congress referring to writs of error shall be construed as amended to the extent necessary to substitute appeal for writ of error." See, also, notes preceding section 1 of this title.

[§ 1252. Repealed. Pub.L. 100–352, § 1, June 27, 1988, 102 Stat. 662]

HISTORICAL AND STATUTORY NOTES

Section, Acts June 25, 1948, c. 646, 62 Stat. 928; Oct. 31, 1951, c. 655, § 47, 65 Stat. 726; July 7, 1958, Pub.L. 85–508, § 12(e), (f), 72 Stat. 348; Mar. 18, 1959, Pub.L. 86–3, § 14(a), 73 Stat. 10, provided for direct appeals to Supreme Court from decisions invalidating Acts of Congress.

Effective Date of Repeal

Repeal of section effective ninety days after June 27, 1988, except that such repeal shall not apply to cases pending in the Supreme Court on such effective date or affect the right to review or the manner of reviewing the judgment or decree of a court which was entered before such effective date, see section 7 of Pub.L. 100–352, set out as a note under section 1254 of this title.

§ 1253. Direct appeals from decisions of three-judge courts

Except as otherwise provided by law, any party may appeal to the Supreme Court from an order granting or denying, after notice and hearing, an interlocutory or permanent injunction in any civil action, suit or proceeding required by any Act of Congress to be heard and determined by a district court of three judges.

(June 25, 1948, c. 646, 62 Stat. 928.)

§ 1254. Courts of appeals; certiorari; certified questions

Cases in the courts of appeals may be reviewed by the Supreme Court by the following methods:

(1) By writ of certiorari granted upon the petition of any party to any civil or criminal case, before or after rendition of judgment or decree;

(2) By certification at any time by a court of appeals of any question of law in any civil or criminal case as to which instructions are desired, and upon such certification the Supreme Court may give binding instructions or require the entire record to be sent up for decision of the entire matter in controversy.

(June 25, 1948, c. 646, 62 Stat. 928; June 27, 1988, Pub.L. 100–352, § 2(a), (b), 102 Stat. 662.)

HISTORICAL AND STATUTORY NOTES

Effective and Applicability Provisions

1988 Acts

Section 7 of Pub.L. 100–352 provided that: "The amendments made by this Act [amending this section by striking out 'appeal;' in heading and by striking out par. (2) and redesignating former par. (3) as (2), and amending sections 1257, 1258, 2101, 2104, and 2350 of this title, section 437h of Title 2, The Congress, section 136w of Title 7, Agriculture, section 1631e of Title 22, Foreign Relations and Intercourse, section 652 of Title 25, Indians, section 988 of Title 33, Navigation and Navigable Waters, section 1652 of Title 43, Public Lands, and sections 719, 743, and 1105 of Title 45, Railroads, and repealing sections 1252 and 2103 of this title] shall take effect ninety days after the date of the enactment of this Act [June 27, 1988], except that such amendments shall not apply to cases pending in the Supreme Court on the effective date of such amendments or affect the right to review or the manner of reviewing the judgment or decree of a court which was entered before such effective date."

[§§ 1255, 1256. Repealed. Pub.L. 97–164, Title I, § 123, Apr. 2, 1982, 96 Stat. 36]

HISTORICAL AND STATUTORY NOTES

Section 1255, Act June 25, 1948, c. 646, 62 Stat. 928, authorized the Supreme Court to review cases in the Court of Claims by writ of certiorari and by certification of questions of law.

Section 1256, Act June 25, 1948, c. 646, 62 Stat. 928, authorized the Supreme Court to review cases in the Court of Customs and Patent Appeals by writ of certiorari.

Effective Date of Repeal

Repeal effective Oct. 1, 1982, see section 402 of Pub.L. 97–164, set out as Effective and Applicability Provisions of 1982 Amendments note under section 171 of this title.

§ 1257. State courts; certiorari

(a) Final judgments or decrees rendered by the highest court of a State in which a decision could be had, may be reviewed by the Supreme Court by writ of certiorari where the validity of a treaty or statute of the United States is drawn in question or where the validity of a statute of any State is drawn in question on the ground of its being repugnant to the Constitution, treaties, or laws of the United States, or where any title, right, privilege, or immunity is specially set up or claimed under the Constitution or the treaties or

statutes of, or any commission held or authority exercised under, the United States.

(b) For the purposes of this section, the term "highest court of a State" includes the District of Columbia Court of Appeals.

(June 25, 1948, c. 646, 62 Stat. 929; July 29, 1970, Pub.L. 91–358, Title I, § 172(a)(1), 84 Stat. 590; June 27, 1988, Pub.L. 100–352, § 3, 102 Stat. 662.)

HISTORICAL AND STATUTORY NOTES

Effective and Applicability Provisions

1988 Acts

Amendment by section 3 of Pub.L. 100–352 effective ninety days after June 27, 1988, except that such amendment not to apply to cases pending in the Supreme Court on such effective date or affect the right to review or the manner of reviewing the judgment or decree of a court which was entered before such effective date, see section 7 of Pub.L. 100–352, set out as a note under section 1254 of this title.

1970 Acts

Section 199(a) of Title 1 of Pub.L. 91–358 provided that: "The effective date of this title (and the amendments made by this title) [which enacted sections 1363, 1451, and 2113 of this title, and amended this section and sections 292 and 1869 of this title, section 5102 of Title 5, Government Organization and Employees, and section 260a of Title 42, the Public Health and Welfare] shall be the first day of the seventh calendar month which begins after the date of the enactment of this Act [July 29, 1970]."

§ 1258. Supreme Court of Puerto Rico; certiorari

Final judgments or decrees rendered by the Supreme Court of the Commonwealth of Puerto Rico may be reviewed by the Supreme Court by writ of certiorari where the validity of a treaty or statute of the United States is drawn in question or where the validity of a statute of the Commonwealth of Puerto Rico is drawn in question on the ground of its being repugnant to the Constitution, treaties, or laws of the United States, or where any title, right, privilege, or immunity is specially set up or claimed under the Constitution or the treaties or statutes of, or any commission held or authority exercised under, the United States.

(Added Pub.L. 87–189, § 1, Aug. 30, 1961, 75 Stat. 417, and amended, Pub.L. 100–352, § 4, June 27, 1988, 102 Stat. 662.)

HISTORICAL AND STATUTORY NOTES

Effective and Applicability Provisions

1988 Acts

Amendment by section 4 of Pub.L. 100–352 effective ninety days after June 27, 1988, except that such amendment not to apply to cases pending in the Supreme Court on such effective date or affect the right to review or the manner of reviewing the judgment or decree of a court which was entered before such effective date, pursuant to section 7 of Pub.L. 100–352, set out as a note under section 1254 of this title.

§ 1259. Court of Appeals for the Armed Forces; certiorari

Decisions of the United States Court of Appeals for the Armed Forces may be reviewed by the Supreme Court by writ of certiorari in the following cases:

(1) Cases reviewed by the Court of Appeals for the Armed Forces under section 867(a)(1) of title 10.

(2) Cases certified to the Court of Appeals for the Armed Forces by the Judge Advocate General under section 867(a)(2) of title 10.

(3) Cases in which the Court of Appeals for the Armed Forces granted a petition for review under section 867(a)(3) of title 10.

(4) Cases, other than those described in paragraphs (1), (2), and (3) of this subsection, in which the Court of Appeals for the Armed Forces granted relief.

(Added Pub.L. 98–209, § 10(a)(1), Dec. 6, 1983, 97 Stat. 1405, and amended Pub.L. 101–189, Div. A, Title XIII, § 1304(b)(3), Nov. 29, 1989, 103 Stat. 1577; Pub.L. 103–337, Div. A, Title IX, § 924(d)(1)(C), (2)(A), Oct. 5, 1994, 108 Stat. 2832.)

HISTORICAL AND STATUTORY NOTES

Effective and Applicability Provisions

1983 Acts

Section effective on the first day of the eighth calendar month beginning after Dec. 6, 1983, see section 12(a)(1) of Pub.L 98–209, set out as a note under section 801 of Title 10, Armed Forces.

CHAPTER 83—COURTS OF APPEALS

HISTORICAL AND STATUTORY NOTES

Codifications

The table of sections for chapter 83 was amended by Pub.L. 95–598, Title II, § 236(b), Nov. 6, 1978, 92 Stat. 2667, effective June 28, 1984, pursuant to Pub.L. 95–598, Title IV, § 402(b), Nov. 6, 1978, 92 Stat. 2682, as amended by Pub.L. 98–249, § 1(a), Mar. 31, 1984, 98 Stat. 116; Pub.L. 98–271, § 1(a), Apr. 30, 1984, 98 Stat. 163; Pub.L. 98–299, § 1(a), May 25, 1984, 98 Stat. 214; Pub.L. 98–325, § 1(a), June 20,

1984, 98 Stat. 268, set out as an Effective and Applicability Provisions note preceding section 101 of Title 11, Bankruptcy, by adding:

"1293. Bankruptcy appeals.".

Section 402(b) of Pub.L. 95–598 was amended by section 113 of Pub.L. 98–353, Title I, July 10, 1984, 98 Stat. 343, by substituting "shall not be effective" for "shall take effect on June 28, 1984", thereby eliminating the amendment by section 236(a) of Pub.L. 95–598, effective June 27, 1984, pursuant to section 122(c) of Pub.L. 98–353, set out as an Effective and Applicability Provisions note under section 151 of this title.

Section 121(a) of Pub.L. 98–353 directed that section 402(b) of Pub.L. 95–598 be amended by substituting "the date of enactment of the Bankruptcy Amendments and Federal Judgeship Act of 1984 [i.e. July 10, 1984]" for "June 28, 1984". This amendment was not executed in view of the prior amendment to section 402(b) of Pub.L. 95–598 by section 113 of Pub.L. 98–353.

§ 1291. Final decisions of district courts

The courts of appeals (other than the United States Court of Appeals for the Federal Circuit) shall have jurisdiction of appeals from all final decisions of the district courts of the United States, the United States District Court for the District of the Canal Zone, the District Court of Guam, and the District Court of the Virgin Islands, except where a direct review may be had in the Supreme Court. The jurisdiction of the United States Court of Appeals for the Federal Circuit shall be limited to the jurisdiction described in sections 1292(c) and (d) and 1295 of this title.

(June 25, 1948, c. 646, 62 Stat. 929; Oct. 31, 1951, c. 655, § 48, 65 Stat. 726; July 7, 1958, Pub.L. 85–508, § 12(e), 72 Stat. 348; Apr. 2, 1982, Pub.L. 97–164, Title I, § 124, 96 Stat. 36.)

HISTORICAL AND STATUTORY NOTES

Effective and Applicability Provisions

1982 Acts

Amendment by Pub.L. 97–164 effective Oct. 1, 1982, see section 402 of Pub.L. 97–164, set out as a note under section 171 of this title.

1958 Acts

Amendment of section by Pub.L. 85–508 effective Jan. 3, 1959, upon admission of Alaska into the Union pursuant to Proc. No. 3269, Jan. 3, 1959, 24 F.R. 81, 73 Stat. c16, as required by sections 1 and 8(c) of Pub.L. 85–508, see notes set out under section 81A of this title and preceding section 21 of Title 48, Territories and Insular Possessions.

Termination of United States District Court for the District of the Canal Zone

For termination of the United States District Court for the District of the Canal Zone at end of the "transition period", being the 30–month period beginning Oct. 1, 1979, and ending midnight Mar. 31, 1982, see Paragraph 5 of Article XI of the Panama Canal Treaty of 1977 and sections 3831 and 3841 to 3843 of Title 22, Foreign Relations and Intercourse.

§ 1292. Interlocutory decisions

(a) Except as provided in subsections (c) and (d) of this section, the courts of appeals shall have jurisdiction of appeals from:

(1) Interlocutory orders of the district courts of the United States, the United States District Court for the District of the Canal Zone, the District Court of Guam, and the District Court of the Virgin Islands, or of the judges thereof, granting, continuing, modifying, refusing or dissolving injunctions, or refusing to dissolve or modify injunctions, except where a direct review may be had in the Supreme Court;

(2) Interlocutory orders appointing receivers, or refusing orders to wind up receiverships or to take steps to accomplish the purposes thereof, such as directing sales or other disposals of property;

(3) Interlocutory decrees of such district courts or the judges thereof determining the rights and liabilities of the parties to admiralty cases in which appeals from final decrees are allowed.

(b) When a district judge, in making in a civil action an order not otherwise appealable under this section, shall be of the opinion that such order involves a controlling question of law as to which there is substantial ground for difference of opinion and that an immediate appeal from the order may materially advance the ultimate termination of the litigation, he shall so state in writing in such order. The Court of Appeals which would have jurisdiction of an appeal of such action may thereupon, in its discretion, permit an appeal to be taken from such order, if application is made to it within ten days after the entry of the order: *Provided, however,* That application for an appeal hereunder shall not stay proceedings in the district court unless the district judge or the Court of Appeals or a judge thereof shall so order.

(c) The United States Court of Appeals for the Federal Circuit shall have exclusive jurisdiction—

(1) of an appeal from an interlocutory order or decree described in subsection (a) or (b) of this section in any case over which the court would have jurisdiction of an appeal under section 1295 of this title; and

(2) of an appeal from a judgment in a civil action for patent infringement which would otherwise be appealable to the United States Court of Appeals for the Federal Circuit and is final except for an accounting.

(d)(1) When the chief judge of the Court of International Trade issues an order under the provisions of section 256(b) of this title, or when any judge of the Court of International Trade, in issuing any other interlocutory order, includes in the order a statement

that a controlling question of law is involved with respect to which there is a substantial ground for difference of opinion and that an immediate appeal from that order may materially advance the ultimate termination of the litigation, the United States Court of Appeals for the Federal Circuit may, in its discretion, permit an appeal to be taken from such order, if application is made to that Court within ten days after the entry of such order.

(2) When the chief judge of the United States Court of Federal Claims issues an order under section 798(b) of this title, or when any judge of the United States Court of Federal Claims, in issuing an interlocutory order, includes in the order a statement that a controlling question of law is involved with respect to which there is a substantial ground for difference of opinion and that an immediate appeal from that order may materially advance the ultimate termination of the litigation, the United States Court of Appeals for the Federal Circuit may, in its discretion, permit an appeal to be taken from such order, if application is made to that Court within ten days after the entry of such order.

(3) Neither the application for nor the granting of an appeal under this subsection shall stay proceedings in the Court of International Trade or in the Court of Federal Claims, as the case may be, unless a stay is ordered by a judge of the Court of International Trade or of the Court of Federal Claims or by the United States Court of Appeals for the Federal Circuit or a judge of that court.

(4)(A) The United States Court of Appeals for the Federal Circuit shall have exclusive jurisdiction of an appeal from an interlocutory order of a district court of the United States, the District Court of Guam, the District Court of the Virgin Islands, or the District Court for the Northern Mariana Islands, granting or denying, in whole or in part, a motion to transfer an action to the United States Court of Federal Claims under section 1631 of this title.

(B) When a motion to transfer an action to the Court of Federal Claims is filed in a district court, no further proceedings shall be taken in the district court until 60 days after the court has ruled upon the motion. If an appeal is taken from the district court's grant or denial of the motion, proceedings shall be further stayed until the appeal has been decided by the Court of Appeals for the Federal Circuit. The stay of proceedings in the district court shall not bar the granting of preliminary or injunctive relief, where appropriate and where expedition is reasonably necessary. However, during the period in which proceedings are stayed as provided in this subparagraph, no transfer to the Court of Federal Claims pursuant to the motion shall be carried out.

(e) The Supreme Court may prescribe rules, in accordance with section 2072 of this title, to provide for an appeal of an interlocutory decision to the courts of appeals that is not otherwise provided for under subsection (a), (b), (c), or (d).

(June 25, 1948, c. 646, 62 Stat. 929; Oct. 31, 1951, c. 655, § 49, 65 Stat. 726; July 7, 1958, Pub.L. 85–508, § 12(e), 72 Stat. 348; Sept. 2, 1958, Pub.L. 85–919, 72 Stat. 1770; Apr. 2, 1982, Pub.L. 97–164, Title I, § 125, 96 Stat. 36; Nov. 8, 1984, Pub.L. 98–620, Title IV, § 412, 98 Stat. 3362; Nov. 19, 1988, Pub.L. 100–702, Title V, § 501, 102 Stat. 4652; Oct. 29, 1992, Pub.L. 102–572, Title I, § 101, Title IX, §§ 902(b), 906(c), 106 Stat. 4506, 4516, 4518.)

HISTORICAL AND STATUTORY NOTES

Effective and Applicability Provisions

1992 Acts

Amendment by sections 902(b) and 906(c) of Pub.L. 102–572 effective Oct. 29, 1992, see section 911 of Pub.L. 102–572, set out as a note under section 171 of this title.

Amendment by section 906(c) of Pub.L. 102–572 effective Oct. 29, 1992, see section 911 of Pub.L. 102–572, set out as a note under section 171 of Title 28, Judiciary and Judicial Procedure.

Amendment by section 101 of Pub.L. 102–572 effective Jan. 1, 1993, see section 1101(a) of Pub.L. 102–572, set out as a note under section 905 of Title 2, The Congress.

1988 Acts

Section 502 of Title V of Pub.L. 100–702 provided that: "The amendment made by section 501 [enacting subsec. (d)(4) of this section] shall apply to any action commenced in the district court on or after the date of enactment of this title [Nov. 19, 1988]."

1982 Acts

Amendment by Pub.L. 97–164 effective Oct. 1, 1982, see section 402 of Pub.L. 97–164, set out as a note under section 171 of this title.

1958 Acts

Amendment of section by Pub.L. 85–508 effective Jan. 3, 1959, upon admission of Alaska into the Union pursuant to Proc. No. 3269, Jan. 3, 1959, 24 F.R. 81, 73 Stat. c16, as required by Section 1 and 8(c) of Pub.L. 85–508, see notes set out under Section 81A of this title and preceding Section 21 of Title 48, Territories and Insular Possessions.

Change of Name

References to United States Claims Court deemed to refer to United States Court of Federal Claims and references to Claims Court deemed to refer to Court of Federal Claims, see section 902(b) of Pub.L. 102–572, set out as a note under section 171 of Title 28, Judiciary and Judicial Procedure.

Termination of United States District Court for the District of the Canal Zone

For termination of the United States District Court for the District of the Canal Zone at end of the "transition period", being the 30–month period beginning Oct. 1, 1979, and ending midnight Mar. 31, 1982, see Paragraph 5 of Article XI of the Panama Canal Treaty of 1977 and sections 3831 and 3841 to 3843 of Title 22, Foreign Relations and Intercourse.

[§ **1293.** Repealed. **Pub.L. 87–189, § 3, Aug. 30, 1961, 75 Stat. 417**]

HISTORICAL AND STATUTORY NOTES

Section, Acts June 25, 1948, c. 646, 62 Stat. 929; Mar. 18, 1959, Pub.L. 86–3, § 14(b), 73 Stat. 10, provided for appeal from supreme court of Puerto Rico to court of appeals for first circuit. See section 1258 of this title.

Codifications

A subsequent section 1293, as added by Pub.L. 95–598, Title II, § 236a, Nov. 6, 1978, 92 Stat. 2667, effective June 28, 1984, pursuant to Pub.L. 95–598, Title IV, § 402(b), Nov. 6, 1978, 92 Stat. 2682, as amended by Pub.L. 98–249, § 1(a), Mar. 31, 1984, 98 Stat. 116; Pub.L. 98–271, § 1(a), Apr. 30, 1984, 98 Stat. 163; Pub.L. 98–299, § 1(a), May 25, 1984, 98 Stat. 214; Pub.L. 98–325, § 1(a), June 20, 1984, 98 Stat. 268, set out as an Effective and Applicability Provisions note preceding section 101 of Title 11, Bankruptcy, read as follows:

§ 1293. Bankruptcy appeals

(a) The courts of appeals shall have jurisdiction of appeals from all final decisions of panels designated under section 160(a) of this title.

(b) Notwithstanding section 1482 of this title, a court of appeals shall have jurisdiction of an appeal from a final judgment, order, or decree of an appellate panel created under section 160 or a District court of the United States or from a final judgment, order, or decree of a bankruptcy court of the United States if the parties to such appeal agree to a direct appeal to the court of appeals.

Section 402(b) of Pub.L. 95–598 was amended by section 113 of Pub.L. 98–353, Title I, July 10, 1984, 98 Stat. 343, by substituting "shall not be effective" for "shall take effect on June 28, 1984", thereby eliminating the addition of subsequent section 1293 by section 236(a) of Pub.L. 95–598, effective June 27, 1984, pursuant to section 122(c) of Pub.L. 98–353, set out as an Effective and Applicability Provisions note under section 151 of this title.

Section 121(a) of Pub.L. 98–353 directed that section 402(b) of Pub.L. 95–598 be amended by substituting "the date of enactment of the Bankruptcy Amendments and Federal Judgeship Act of 1984 [i.e. July 10, 1984]" for "June 28, 1984". This amendment was not executed in view of the prior amendment to section 402(b) of Pub.L. 95–598 by section 113 of Pub.L. 98–353.

§ 1294. Circuits in which decisions reviewable

Except as provided in sections 1292(c), 1292(d), and 1295 of this title, appeals from reviewable decisions of the district and territorial courts shall be taken to the courts of appeals as follows:

(1) From a district court of the United States to the court of appeals for the circuit embracing the district;

(2) From the United States District Court for the District of the Canal Zone, to the Court of Appeals for the Fifth Circuit;

(3) From the District Court of the Virgin Islands, to the Court of Appeals for the Third Circuit;

(4) From the District Court of Guam, to the Court of Appeals for the Ninth Circuit.

(June 25, 1948, c. 646, 62 Stat. 930; Oct. 31, 1951, c. 655, § 50(a), 65 Stat. 727; July 7, 1958, Pub.L. 85–508, § 12(g), 72 Stat. 348; Mar. 18, 1959, Pub.L. 86–3, § 14(c), 73 Stat. 10; Aug. 30, 1961, Pub.L. 87–189, § 5, 75 Stat. 417; Nov. 6, 1978, Pub.L. 95–598, Title II, § 237, 92 Stat. 2667; Apr. 2, 1982, Pub.L. 97–164, Title I, § 126, 96 Stat. 37.)

HISTORICAL AND STATUTORY NOTES

Codifications

This section was amended by Pub.L. 95–598, Title II, § 237, Nov. 6, 1978, 92 Stat. 2667, effective June 28, 1984, pursuant to Pub.L. 95–598, Title IV, § 402(b), Nov. 6, 1978, 92 Stat. 2682, as amended by Pub.L. 98–249, § 1(a), Mar. 31, 1984, 98 Stat. 116; Pub.L. 98–271, § 1(a), Apr. 30, 1984, 98 Stat. 163; Pub.L. 98–299, § 1(a), May 25, 1984, 98 Stat. 214; Pub.L. 98–325, § 1(a), June 20, 1984, 98 Stat. 268, set out as an Effective and Applicability Provisions note preceding section 101 of Title II, Bankruptcy, to read as follows:

§ 1294. Circuits in which decisions reviewable

Except as provided in sections 1292(c), 1292(d), and 1295 of this title, appeals from reviewable decisions of the district, bankruptcy, and territorial courts shall be taken to the courts of appeals as follows:

(1) From a district court of the United States to the court of appeals for the circuit embracing the district;

(2) From the United States District Court for the District of the Canal Zone, to the Court of Appeals for the Fifth Circuit;

(3) From the District Court of the Virgin Islands, to the Court of Appeals for the Third Circuit;

(4) From the District Court of Guam, to the Court of Appeals for the Ninth Circuit;

(5) From a panel designated under section 160(a) of this title to the court of appeals for the circuit in which the panel was so designated;

(6) From a bankruptcy court of the United States to the court of appeals for the circuit embracing the district in which the bankruptcy court is located.

Section 402(b) of Pub.L. 95–598 was amended by section 113 of Pub.L. 98–353, Title I, July 10, 1984, 98 Stat. 343, by substituting "shall not be effective" for "shall take effect on June 28, 1984", thereby eliminating the amendment by section 237 of Pub.L. 95–598, effective June 27, 1984, pursuant to section 122(c) of Pub.L. 98–353, set out as an Effective and Applicability Provisions note under section 151 of this title.

Section 121(a) of Pub.L. 98–353 directed that section 402(b) of Pub.L. 95–598 be amended by substituting "the date of enactment of the Bankruptcy Amendments and Federal Judgeship Act of 1984 [i.e. July 10, 1984]" for "June 28, 1984". This amendment was not executed in view of the prior amendment to section 402(b) of Pub.L. 95–598 by section 113 of Pub.L. 98–353.

Effective and Applicability Provisions

1982 Acts

Amendment by Pub.L. 97–164 effective Oct. 1, 1982, see section 402 of Pub.L. 97–164, set out as a note under section 171 of this title.

1959 Acts

Amendment of section by Pub.L. 86–3 effective upon the admission of the State of Hawaii into the Union, see note set out under section 91 of this title. Admission of Hawaii into the Union was accomplished Aug. 21, 1959 upon issuance of Proc. No. 3309, Aug. 21, 1959, 25 F.R. 6868, 73 Stat. c74, as required by sections 1 and 7(c) of Pub.L. 86–3, Mar. 18, 1959, 73 Stat. 4, set out as notes preceding section 491 of Title 48, Territories and Insular Possessions.

1958 Acts

Amendment of section by Pub.L. 85–508 effective Jan. 3, 1959, upon admission of Alaska into the Union pursuant to Proc. No. 3269, Jan. 3, 1959, 24 F.R. 81, 73 Stat. c16, as required by sections 1 and 8(c) of Pub.L. 85–508, see notes set out under section 81A of this title and preceding section 21 of Title 48, Territories and Insular Possessions.

Termination of United States District Court for the District of the Canal Zone

For termination of the United States District Court for the District of the Canal Zone at end of the "transition period", being the 30–month period beginning Oct. 1, 1979, and ending midnight Mar. 31, 1982, see Paragraph 5 of Article XI of the Panama Canal Treaty of 1977 and sections 3831 and 3841 to 3843 of Title 22, Foreign Relations and Intercourse.

§ 1295. Jurisdiction of the United States Court of Appeals for the Federal Circuit

(a) The United States Court of Appeals for the Federal Circuit shall have exclusive jurisdiction—

(1) of an appeal from a final decision of a district court of the United States, the United States District Court for the District of the Canal Zone, the District Court of Guam, the District Court of the Virgin Islands, or the District Court for the Northern Mariana Islands, if the jurisdiction of that court was based, in whole or in part, on section 1338 of this title, except that a case involving a claim arising under any Act of Congress relating to copyrights, exclusive rights in mask works, or trademarks and no other claims under section 1338(a) shall be governed by sections 1291, 1292, and 1294 of this title;

(2) of an appeal from a final decision of a district court of the United States, the United States District Court for the District of the Canal Zone, the District Court of Guam, the District Court of the Virgin Islands, or the District Court for the Northern Mariana Islands, if the jurisdiction of that court was based, in whole or in part, on section 1346 of this title, except that jurisdiction of an appeal in a case brought in a district court under section 1346(a)(1), 1346(b), 1346(e), or 1346(f) of this title or under section 1346(a)(2) when the claim is founded upon an Act of Congress or a regulation of an executive department providing for internal revenue shall be governed by sections 1291, 1292, and 1294 of this title;

(3) of an appeal from a final decision of the United States Court of Federal Claims;

(4) of an appeal from a decision of—

(A) the Board of Patent Appeals and Interferences of the United States Patent and Trademark Office with respect to patent applications and interferences, at the instance of an applicant for a patent or any party to a patent interference, and any such appeal shall waive the right of such applicant or party to proceed under section 145 or 146 of title 35;

(B) the Under Secretary of Commerce for Intellectual Property and Director of the United States Patent and Trademark Office or the Trademark Trial and Appeal Board with respect to applications for registration of marks and other proceedings as provided in section 21 of the Trademark Act of 1946 (15 U.S.C. 1071); or

(C) a district court to which a case was directed pursuant to section 145, 146, or 154(b) of title 35;

(5) of an appeal from a final decision of the United States Court of International Trade;

(6) to review the final determinations of the United States International Trade Commission relating to unfair practices in import trade, made under section 337 of the Tariff Act of 1930 (19 U.S.C. 1337);

(7) to review, by appeal on questions of law only, findings of the Secretary of Commerce under U.S. note 6 to subchapter X of chapter 98 of the Harmonized Tariff Schedule of the United States (relating to importation of instruments or apparatus);

(8) of an appeal under section 71 of the Plant Variety Protection Act (7 U.S.C. 2461);

(9) of an appeal from a final order or final decision of the Merit Systems Protection Board, pursuant to sections 7703(b)(1) and 7703(d) of title 5;

(10) of an appeal from a final decision of an agency board of contract appeals pursuant to section 8(g)(1) of the Contract Disputes Act of 1978 (41 U.S.C. 607(g)(1));

(11) of an appeal under section 211 of the Economic Stabilization Act of 1970;

(12) of an appeal under section 5 of the Emergency Petroleum Allocation Act of 1973;

(13) of an appeal under section 506(c) of the Natural Gas Policy Act of 1978; and

(14) of an appeal under section 523 of the Energy Policy and Conservation Act.

(b) The head of any executive department or agency may, with the approval of the Attorney General, refer to the Court of Appeals for the Federal Circuit for judicial review any final decision rendered by a board of contract appeals pursuant to the terms of any contract with the United States awarded by that department or agency which the head of such depart-

ment or agency has concluded is not entitled to finality pursuant to the review standards specified in section 10(b) of the Contract Disputes Act of 1978 (41 U.S.C. 609(b)). The head of each executive department or agency shall make any referral under this section within one hundred and twenty days after the receipt of a copy of the final appeal decision.

(c) The Court of Appeals for the Federal Circuit shall review the matter referred in accordance with the standards specified in section 10(b) of the Contract Disputes Act of 1978. The court shall proceed with judicial review on the administrative record made before the board of contract appeals on matters so referred as in other cases pending in such court, shall determine the issue of finality of the appeal decision, and shall, if appropriate, render judgment thereon, or remand the matter to any administrative or executive body or official with such direction as it may deem proper and just.

(Added Pub.L. 97–164, Title I, § 127(a), Apr. 2, 1982, 96 Stat. 37, and amended Pub.L. 98–622, Title II, § 205(a), Nov. 8, 1984, 98 Stat. 3388; Pub.L. 100–418, Title I, § 1214(a)(3), Aug. 23, 1988, 102 Stat. 1156; Pub.L. 100–702, Title X, § 1020(a)(3), Nov. 19, 1988, 102 Stat. 4671; Pub.L. 102–572, Title I, § 102(c), Title IX, § 902(b)(1), Oct. 29, 1992, 106 Stat. 4507, 4516; Pub.L. 106–113, Div. B, § 1000(a)(9) [Title IV, §§ 4402(b)(2), 4732(b)(14)], Nov. 29, 1999, 113 Stat. 1536, 1501A–560, 1501A–584.)

HISTORICAL AND STATUTORY NOTES

References in Text

The Harmonized Tariff Schedule of the United States, referred to in subsec. (a)(7), is not carried in the Code. See Publication of Harmonized Tariff Schedule note set out under section 1202 of Title 19, Customs Duties.

Section 211 of the Economic Stabilization Act of 1970, referred to in subsec. (a)(11), is section 211 of Pub.L. 91–379, Title II, Aug. 15, 1970, as added Pub.L. 92–210, § 2, Dec. 22, 1971, 85 Stat. 743, as amended, which is set out as a note under TECA Rule 3, this title, and in codified form under section 1904 of Title 12, Banks and Banking.

Section 5 of the Emergency Petroleum Allocation Act of 1973, referred to in subsec. (a)(12), is section 5 of Pub.L. 93–159, Nov. 27, 1973, 87 Stat. 633, as amended, which was classified to section 754 of Title 15, Commerce and Trade, prior to the omission of such section pursuant to section 760g of Title 15.

Section 506(c) of the Natural Gas Policy Act of 1978, referred to in subsec. (a)(13), is section 506(c) of Pub.L. 95–621, Title V, Nov. 9, 1978, 92 Stat. 3404, which is classified to section 3416(c) of Title 15, Commerce and Trade.

Section 523 of the Energy Policy and Conservation Act, referred to in subsec. (a)(14), is section 523 of Pub.L. 94–163, Title V, Dec. 22, 1975, 89 Stat. 962, which is classified to section 6393 of Title 42, The Public Health and Welfare.

Effective and Applicability Provisions

1999 Acts

Amendment by Pub.L. 106–113 [§ 4732], effective 4 months after Nov. 29, 1999, see Pub.L. 106–113 [§ 4731], set out as a note under section 1 of Title 35.

Amendment by Pub.L. 106–113 [§ 4402], to take effect on the date that is six months after Nov. 29, 1999 and, except for a design patent application filed under chapter 16 of Title 35, to be applicable to any application filed on or after the date that is six months after Nov. 29, 1999, see Pub.L. 106–113 [§ 4405], set out as a note under section 154 of Title 35.

1992 Acts

Amendment by section 902(b)(1) of Pub.L. 102–572 effective Oct. 29, 1992, see section 911 of Pub.L. 102–572, set out as a note under section 171 of this title.

Amendment by Pub.L. 102–572 effective Jan. 1, 1993, see section 1101(a) of Pub.L. 102–572, set out as a note under section 905 of Title 2, The Congress.

1988 Acts

Amendment by Pub.L. 100–418 effective Jan. 1, 1989, and applicable with respect to articles entered on or after such date, see section 1217(b)(1) of Pub.L. 100–418, set out as an Effective and Applicability Provisions note under section 3001 of Title 19, Customs Duties.

1984 Acts

Amendment by Pub.L. 98–622 applicable to all United States patents granted before, on, or after Nov. 8, 1984, and to all applications for United States patents pending on or filed after that date, except as otherwise provided, see section 106 of Pub.L. 98–622, set out as a note under section 103 of Title 35, Patents.

Amendment by Pub.L. 98–622, effective three months after Nov. 8, 1984, see section 207 of Pub.L. 98–622, set out as a note under section 7 of Title 35, Patents.

1982 Acts

Section effective Oct. 1, 1982, see section 402 of Pub.L. 97–164, set out as a note under section 171 of this title.

Abolition of Temporary Emergency Court of Appeals

Section 102(d), (e) of Pub.L. 102–572 provided that:

"**(d) Abolition of Court.**—The Temporary Emergency Court of Appeals created by section 211(b) of the Economic Stabilization Act of 1970 [set out as a note under TECA Rule 3, this title] is abolished, effective 6 months after the date of the enactment of this Act [Oct. 29, 1992].

"**(e) Pending cases.**—(1) Any appeal which, before the effective date of abolition described in subsection (d), is pending in the Temporary Emergency Court of Appeals but has not been submitted to a panel of such court as of that date shall be assigned to the United States Court of Appeals for the Federal Circuit as though the appeal had originally been filed in that court.

"(2) Any case which, before the effective date of abolition described in subsection (d), has been submitted to a panel of the Temporary Emergency Court of Appeals and as to which the mandate has not been issued as of that date shall remain with that panel for all purposes and, notwithstanding the provisions of sections 291 and 292 of title 28, United States Code [sections 291 and 292 of this title], that panel shall be assigned to the United States Court of Appeals for the Federal Circuit for the purpose of deciding such case."

Termination of United States District Court for the District of the Canal Zone

For termination of the United States District Court for the District of the Canal Zone at end of the "transition period", being the 30–month period beginning Oct. 1, 1979, and ending midnight Mar. 31, 1982, see Paragraph 5 of Article XI of the Panama Canal Treaty of 1977 and sections 3831 and 3841 to 3843 of Title 22, Foreign Relations and Intercourse.

Transfer of Cases and Petitions Pending in Court of Claims and in Court of Customs and Patent Appeals on October 1, 1982

For provisions directing that any case pending before the Court of Claims on Oct. 1, 1982, in which a report on the merits has been filed by a commissioner, or in which there is pending a request for review, and upon which the court has not acted, and any matter pending before the United States Court of Customs and Patent Appeals on Oct. 1, 1982, be transferred to the United States Court of Appeals for the Federal Circuit, and that any petition for rehearing, reconsideration, alteration, modification, or other change in any decision of the United States Court of Claims or the United States Court of Customs and Patent Appeals rendered prior to Oct. 1, 1982, that has not been determined by either of those courts on that date, or that is filed after that date, be determined by the United States Court of Appeals for the Federal Circuit, see section 403(a)–(c) of Pub.L. 97–164, set out as a note under section 171 of this title.

§ 1296. Review of certain agency actions

(a) Jurisdiction.—Subject to the provisions of chapter 179, the United States Court of Appeals for the Federal Circuit shall have jurisdiction over a petition for review of a final decision under chapter 5 of title 3 of—

(1) an appropriate agency (as determined under section 454 of title 3);

(2) the Federal Labor Relations Authority made under part D of subchapter II of chapter 5 of title 3, notwithstanding section 7123 of title 5; or

(3) the Secretary of Labor or the Occupational Safety and Health Review Commission, made under part C of subchapter II of chapter 5 of title 3.

(b) Filing of petition.—Any petition for review under this section must be filed within 30 days after the date the petitioner receives notice of the final decision.

(Added Pub.L. 104–331, § 3(a)(1), Oct. 26, 1996, 110 Stat. 4069.)

HISTORICAL AND STATUTORY NOTES

Effective and Applicability Provisions

1996 Acts

Section 3(d) of Pub.L. 104–331 provided that: "The amendments made by this section [enacting this section, sections 1413, and 3901 to 3908 of this title, and amending sections 1346 and 2402 of this title] shall take effect on October 1, 1997."

Prior Provisions

A prior section 1296, Pub.L. 97–164, Title I, § 127(a), Apr. 2, 1982, 96 Stat. 39, relating to precedence of cases in the United States Court of Appeals for the Federal Circuit, was repealed by Pub.L. 98–620, Title IV, § 402(29)(C), Nov. 8, 1984, 98 Stat. 3359.

CHAPTER 85—DISTRICT COURTS; JURISDICTION

Sec.
1368. Counterclaims in unfair practices in international trade.
1369. Multiparty, multiforum jurisdiction.

HISTORICAL AND STATUTORY NOTES

Codifications

The table of sections for chapter 85 was amended by Pub.L. 95–598, Title II, § 238(b), Nov. 6, 1978, 92 Stat. 2668, effective June 28, 1984, pursuant to Pub.L. 95–598, Title IV, § 402(b), Nov. 6, 1978, 92 Stat. 2682, as amended by Pub.L. 98–249, § 1(a), Mar. 31, 1984, 98 Stat. 116; Pub.L. 98–271, § 1(a), Apr. 30, 1984, 98 Stat. 163; Pub.L. 98–299, § 1(a), May 25, 1984, 98 Stat. 214; Pub.L. 98–325, § 1(a), June 20, 1984, 98 Stat. 268, by substituting "1334. Bankruptcy appeals." for "1334. Bankruptcy matters and proceedings.".

Section 402(b) of Pub.L. 95–598 was amended by section 113 of Pub.L. 98–353, Title I, July 10, 1984, 98 Stat. 343, by substituting "shall not be effective" for "shall take effect on June 28, 1984", thereby eliminating the amendment by section 238(b) of Pub.L. 95–598, effective June 27, 1984, pursuant to section 122(c) of Pub.L. 98–353, set out as an Effective Date note under section 151 of this title.

Section 121(a) of Pub.L. 98–353 directed that section 402(b) of Pub.L. 95–598 be amended by substituting "the date of enactment of the Bankruptcy Amendments and Federal Judgeship Act of 1984 [i.e. July 10, 1984]" for "June 28, 1984". This amendment was not executed in view of the prior amendment to section 402(b) of Pub.L. 95–598 by section 113 of Pub.L. 98–353.

Effective and Applicability Provisions

2002 Acts

Amendments by section 11020(b) of Pub.L. 107–273 shall apply to a civil action if the accident giving rise to the cause of action occurred on or after the 90th day after Nov. 2, 2002, see section 11020(c) of Pub.L. 107–273, set out as a note under 28 U.S.C.A. § 1369.

§ 1330. Actions against foreign states

(a) The district courts shall have original jurisdiction without regard to amount in controversy of any nonjury civil action against a foreign state as defined in section 1603(a) of this title as to any claim for relief in personam with respect to which the foreign state is not entitled to immunity either under sections 1605–1607 of this title or under any applicable international agreement.

(b) Personal jurisdiction over a foreign state shall exist as to every claim for relief over which the district courts have jurisdiction under subsection (a) where service has been made under section 1608 of this title.

(c) For purposes of subsection (b), an appearance by a foreign state does not confer personal jurisdiction with respect to any claim for relief not arising out of any transaction or occurrence enumerated in sections 1605–1607 of this title.

(Added Pub.L. 94–583, § 2(a), Oct. 21, 1976, 90 Stat. 2891.)

HISTORICAL AND STATUTORY NOTES

Effective and Applicability Provisions

1976 Acts

Section effective 90 days after Oct. 21, 1976, see section 8 of Pub.L. 94–583, set out as a note under section 1602 of this title.

§ 1331. Federal question

The district courts shall have original jurisdiction of all civil actions arising under the Constitution, laws, or treaties of the United States.

(June 25, 1948, c. 646, 62 Stat. 930; July 25, 1958, Pub.L. 85–554, § 1, 72 Stat. 415; Oct. 21, 1976, Pub.L. 94–574, § 2, 90 Stat. 2721; Dec. 1, 1980, Pub.L. 96–486, § 2(a), 94 Stat. 2369.)

HISTORICAL AND STATUTORY NOTES

Effective and Applicability Provisions

1980 Acts

Section 4 of Pub.L. 96–486 provided: "This Act [amending this section and section 2072 of Title 15, Commerce and Trade, and enacting provisions set out as a note under section 1 of this title] shall apply to any civil action pending on the date of enactment of this Act [Dec. 1, 1980]."

1958 Acts

Section 3 of Pub.L. 85–554 provided that: "This Act [amending this section and sections 1332 and 1445 of this title] shall apply only in the case of actions commenced after the date of the enactment of this Act [July 25, 1958]."

§ 1332. Diversity of citizenship; amount in controversy; costs

(a) The district courts shall have original jurisdiction of all civil actions where the matter in controversy exceeds the sum or value of $75,000, exclusive of interest and costs, and is between—

 (1) citizens of different States;

 (2) citizens of a State and citizens or subjects of a foreign state;

 (3) citizens of different States and in which citizens or subjects of a foreign state are additional parties; and

 (4) a foreign state, defined in section 1603(a) of this title, as plaintiff and citizens of a State or of different States.

For the purposes of this section, section 1335, and section 1441, an alien admitted to the United States for permanent residence shall be deemed a citizen of the State in which such alien is domiciled.

(b) Except when express provision therefor is otherwise made in a statute of the United States, where the plaintiff who files the case originally in the Federal courts is finally adjudged to be entitled to recover less than the sum or value of $75,000, computed without regard to any setoff or counterclaim to which the defendant may be adjudged to be entitled, and

exclusive of interest and costs, the district court may deny costs to the plaintiff and, in addition, may impose costs on the plaintiff.

(c) For the purposes of this section and section 1441 of this title—

(1) a corporation shall be deemed to be a citizen of any State by which it has been incorporated and of the State where it has its principal place of business, except that in any direct action against the insurer of a policy or contract of liability insurance, whether incorporated or unincorporated, to which action the insured is not joined as a party-defendant, such insurer shall be deemed a citizen of the State of which the insured is a citizen, as well as of any State by which the insurer has been incorporated and of the State where it has its principal place of business; and

(2) the legal representative of the estate of a decedent shall be deemed to be a citizen only of the same State as the decedent, and the legal representative of an infant or incompetent shall be deemed to be a citizen only of the same State as the infant or incompetent.

(d)(1) In this subsection—

(A) the term "class" means all of the class members in a class action;

(B) the term "class action" means any civil action filed under rule 23 of the Federal Rules of Civil Procedure or similar State statute or rule of judicial procedure authorizing an action to be brought by 1 or more representative persons as a class action;

(C) the term "class certification order" means an order issued by a court approving the treatment of some or all aspects of a civil action as a class action; and

(D) the term "class members" means the persons (named or unnamed) who fall within the definition of the proposed or certified class in a class action.

(2) The district courts shall have original jurisdiction of any civil action in which the matter in controversy exceeds the sum or value of $5,000,000, exclusive of interest and costs, and is a class action in which—

(A) any member of a class of plaintiffs is a citizen of a State different from any defendant;

(B) any member of a class of plaintiffs is a foreign state or a citizen or subject of a foreign state and any defendant is a citizen of a State; or

(C) any member of a class of plaintiffs is a citizen of a State and any defendant is a foreign state or a citizen or subject of a foreign state.

(3) A district court may, in the interests of justice and looking at the totality of the circumstances, decline to exercise jurisdiction under paragraph (2) over a class action in which greater than one-third but less than two-thirds of the members of all proposed plaintiff classes in the aggregate and the primary defendants are citizens of the State in which the action was originally filed based on consideration of—

(A) whether the claims asserted involve matters of national or interstate interest;

(B) whether the claims asserted will be governed by laws of the State in which the action was originally filed or by the laws of other States;

(C) whether the class action has been pleaded in a manner that seeks to avoid Federal jurisdiction;

(D) whether the action was brought in a forum with a distinct nexus with the class members, the alleged harm, or the defendants;

(E) whether the number of citizens of the State in which the action was originally filed in all proposed plaintiff classes in the aggregate is substantially larger than the number of citizens from any other State, and the citizenship of the other members of the proposed class is dispersed among a substantial number of States; and

(F) whether, during the 3–year period preceding the filing of that class action, 1 or more other class actions asserting the same or similar claims on behalf of the same or other persons have been filed.

(4) A district court shall decline to exercise jurisdiction under paragraph (2)—

(A)(i) over a class action in which—

(I) greater than two-thirds of the members of all proposed plaintiff classes in the aggregate are citizens of the State in which the action was originally filed;

(II) at least 1 defendant is a defendant—

(aa) from whom significant relief is sought by members of the plaintiff class;

(bb) whose alleged conduct forms a significant basis for the claims asserted by the proposed plaintiff class; and

(cc) who is a citizen of the State in which the action was originally filed; and

(III) principal injuries resulting from the alleged conduct or any related conduct of each defendant were incurred in the State in which the action was originally filed; and

(ii) during the 3-year period preceding the filing of that class action, no other class action has been filed asserting the same or similar factual allegations against any of the defendants on behalf of the same or other persons; or

(B) two-thirds or more of the members of all proposed plaintiff classes in the aggregate, and the primary defendants, are citizens of the State in which the action was originally filed.

(5) Paragraphs (2) through (4) shall not apply to any class action in which—

 (A) the primary defendants are States, State officials, or other governmental entities against whom the district court may be foreclosed from ordering relief; or

 (B) the number of members of all proposed plaintiff classes in the aggregate is less than 100.

(6) In any class action, the claims of the individual class members shall be aggregated to determine whether the matter in controversy exceeds the sum or value of $5,000,000, exclusive of interest and costs.

(7) Citizenship of the members of the proposed plaintiff classes shall be determined for purposes of paragraphs (2) through (6) as of the date of filing of the complaint or amended complaint, or, if the case stated by the initial pleading is not subject to Federal jurisdiction, as of the date of service by plaintiffs of an amended pleading, motion, or other paper, indicating the existence of Federal jurisdiction.

(8) This subsection shall apply to any class action before or after the entry of a class certification order by the court with respect to that action.

(9) Paragraph (2) shall not apply to any class action that solely involves a claim—

 (A) concerning a covered security as defined under 16(f)(3) [1] of the Securities Act of 1933 (15 U.S.C. 78p(f)(3)) and section 28(f)(5)(E) of the Securities Exchange Act of 1934 (15 U.S.C. 78bb(f)(5)(E));

 (B) that relates to the internal affairs or governance of a corporation or other form of business enterprise and that arises under or by virtue of the laws of the State in which such corporation or business enterprise is incorporated or organized; or

 (C) that relates to the rights, duties (including fiduciary duties), and obligations relating to or created by or pursuant to any security (as defined under section 2(a)(1) of the Securities Act of 1933 (15 U.S.C. 77b(a)(1)) and the regulations issued thereunder).

(10) For purposes of this subsection and section 1453, an unincorporated association shall be deemed to be a citizen of the State where it has its principal place of business and the State under whose laws it is organized.

(11)(A) For purposes of this subsection and section 1453, a mass action shall be deemed to be a class action removable under paragraphs (2) through (10) if it otherwise meets the provisions of those paragraphs.

 (B)(i) As used in subparagraph (A), the term "mass action" means any civil action (except a civil action within the scope of section 1711(2)) in which monetary relief claims of 100 or more persons are proposed to be tried jointly on the ground that the plaintiffs' claims involve common questions of law or fact, except that jurisdiction shall exist only over those plaintiffs whose claims in a mass action satisfy the jurisdictional amount requirements under subsection (a).

 (ii) As used in subparagraph (A), the term "mass action" shall not include any civil action in which—

 (I) all of the claims in the action arise from an event or occurrence in the State in which the action was filed, and that allegedly resulted in injuries in that State or in States contiguous to that State;

 (II) the claims are joined upon motion of a defendant;

 (III) all of the claims in the action are asserted on behalf of the general public (and not on behalf of individual claimants or members of a purported class) pursuant to a State statute specifically authorizing such action; or

 (IV) the claims have been consolidated or coordinated solely for pretrial proceedings.

 (C)(i) Any action(s) removed to Federal court pursuant to this subsection shall not thereafter be transferred to any other court pursuant to section 1407, or the rules promulgated thereunder, unless a majority of the plaintiffs in the action request transfer pursuant to section 1407.

 (ii) This subparagraph will not apply—

 (I) to cases certified pursuant to rule 23 of the Federal Rules of Civil Procedure; or

 (II) if plaintiffs propose that the action proceed as a class action pursuant to rule 23 of the Federal Rules of Civil Procedure.

 (D) The limitations periods on any claims asserted in a mass action that is removed to Federal court pursuant to this subsection shall be deemed tolled during the period that the action is pending in Federal court.

(e) The word "States", as used in this section, includes the Territories, the District of Columbia, and the Commonwealth of Puerto Rico.

(June 25, 1948, c. 646, 62 Stat. 930; July 26, 1956, c. 740, 70 Stat. 658; July 25, 1958, Pub.L. 85–554, § 2, 72 Stat. 415; Aug. 14, 1964, Pub.L. 88–439, § 1, 78 Stat. 445; Oct. 21, 1976, Pub.L. 94–583, § 3, 90 Stat. 2891; Nov. 19, 1988, Pub.L. 100–702, Title II, §§ 201(a), 202(a), 203(a), 102 Stat. 4646; Oct. 19, 1996, Pub.L. 104–317, Title II, § 205(a), 110 Stat. 3850; Feb. 18, 2005, Pub.L. 109–2, § 4(a), 119 Stat. 9.)

[1] So in original. Reference to "16(f)(3)" probably should be preceded by "section".

HISTORICAL AND STATUTORY NOTES

References in Text

Rule 23 of the Federal Rules of Civil Procedure, referred to in subsec. (d)(1)(B) and (11)(C)(ii), is set out following the code sections of this title.

Section 16(f) of the Securities Act of 1933, referred to in subsec. (d)(9)(A), does not contain a par. (3). See Act May 27, 1933, c. 38, Title I, § 16(f), 48 Stat. 84, as amended, which is classified to 15 U.S.C.A. § 78p(f).

Section 28(f)(5)(E) of the Securities Exchange Act of 1934, referred to in subsec. (d)(9)(A), is May 27, 1933, c. 38, Title I, § 2(f)(5)(E), 48 Stat. 74, as amended, which is classified to 15 U.S.C.A. § 78bb(f)(5)(E).

Section 2(a)(1) of the Securities Act of 1933, referred to in subsec. (d)(9)(C), is May 27, 1933, c. 38, Title I, § 2(a)(1), 48 Stat. 74, as amended, which is classified to 15 U.S.C.A. § 77b(a)(1).

Effective and Applicability Provisions

2005 Acts

Pub.L. 109–2, § 9, Feb. 18, 2005, 119 Stat. 14, provided that: "The amendments made by this Act [the Class Action Fairness Act of 2005, which enacted this note and 28 U.S.C.A. §§ 1453 and 1711 to 1715, amended 28 U.S.C.A. §§ 1332, 1335, and 1603, and enacted provisions set out as notes under 28 U.S.C.A. §§ 1711, 2071, and 2074] shall apply to any civil action commenced on or after the date of enactment of this Act [Feb. 18, 2005]."

1996 Acts

Section 205(b) of Pub.L. 104–317 provided that: "The amendment made by this section [amending this section] shall take effect 90 days after the date of enactment of this Act [Oct. 19, 1996]."

1988 Acts

Section 201(b) of Title II of Pub.L. 100–702 provided that: "The amendments made by this section [amending amount in controversy in subsecs. (a) and (b) of this section] shall apply to any civil action commenced on or after the 180th day after the date of enactment of this title [Nov. 19, 1988]."

Section 202(b) of Title II of Pub.L. 100–702 provided that: "The amendment made by this section [amending subsec. (c) of this section] shall apply to any civil action commenced in or removed to a United States district court on or after the 180th day after the date of enactment of this title [Nov. 19, 1988]."

Section 203(b) of Title II of Pub.L. 100–702 provided that: "The amendment made by this section [amending subsec. (a) of this section by enacting citizenship of permanent resident alien provision] shall apply to claims in civil actions commenced in or removed to the United States district courts on or after the 180th day after the date of enactment of this title [Nov. 19, 1988]."

1976 Acts

Amendment by Pub.L. 94–583 effective 90 days after Oct. 21, 1976, see section 8 of Pub.L. 94–583, set out as a note under section 1602 of this title.

1964 Acts

Section 2 of Pub.L. 88–439 provided that: "The amendment made by this Act to section 1332(c), title 28, United States Code [subsec. (c) of this section], applies only to causes of action arising after the date of enactment of this Act [Aug. 14, 1964]."

1958 Acts

Amendment of section by Pub.L. 85–554 applicable only in the case of actions commenced after July 25, 1958, see

section 3 of Pub.L. 85–554, set out as a note under section 1331 of this title.

§ 1333. Admiralty, maritime and prize cases

The district courts shall have original jurisdiction, exclusive of the courts of the States, of:

(1) Any civil case of admiralty or maritime jurisdiction, saving to suitors in all cases all other remedies to which they are otherwise entitled.

(2) Any prize brought into the United States and all proceedings for the condemnation of property taken as prize.

(June 25, 1948, c. 646, 62 Stat. 931; May 24, 1949, c. 139, § 79, 63 Stat. 101.)

§ 1334. Bankruptcy cases and proceedings

(a) Except as provided in subsection (b) of this section, the district courts shall have original and exclusive jurisdiction of all cases under title 11.

(b) Except as provided in subsection (e)(2), and notwithstanding any Act of Congress that confers exclusive jurisdiction on a court or courts other than the district courts, the district courts shall have original but not exclusive jurisdiction of all civil proceedings arising under title 11, or arising in or related to cases under title 11.

(c)(1) Except with respect to a case under chapter 15 of title 11, nothing in this section prevents a district court in the interest of justice, or in the interest of comity with State courts or respect for State law, from abstaining from hearing a particular proceeding arising under title 11 or arising in or related to a case under title 11.

(2) Upon timely motion of a party in a proceeding based upon a State law claim or State law cause of action, related to a case under title 11 but not arising under title 11 or arising in a case under title 11, with respect to which an action could not have been commenced in a court of the United States absent jurisdiction under this section, the district court shall abstain from hearing such proceeding if an action is commenced, and can be timely adjudicated, in a State forum of appropriate jurisdiction.

(d) Any decision to abstain or not to abstain made under subsection (c) (other than a decision not to abstain in a proceeding described in subsection (c)(2)) is not reviewable by appeal or otherwise by the court of appeals under section 158(d), 1291, or 1292 of this title or by the Supreme Court of the United States under section 1254 of this title. Subsection (c) and this subsection shall not be construed to limit the applicability of the stay provided for by section 362 of title 11, United States Code, as such section applies to an action affecting the property of the estate in bankruptcy.

(e) The district court in which a case under title 11 is commenced or is pending shall have exclusive jurisdiction—

 (1) of all the property, wherever located, of the debtor as of the commencement of such case, and of property of the estate; and

 (2) over all claims or causes of action that involve construction of section 327 of title 11, United States Code, or rules relating to disclosure requirements under section 327.

(June 25, 1948, c. 646, 62 Stat. 931; Nov. 6, 1978, Pub.L. 95–598, Title II, § 238(a), 92 Stat. 2667; July 10, 1984, Pub.L. 98–353, Title I, § 101(a), 98 Stat. 333; Oct. 27, 1986, Pub.L. 99–554, Title I, § 144(e), 100 Stat. 3096; Dec. 1, 1990, Pub.L. 101–650, Title III, § 309(b), 104 Stat. 5113; Oct. 22, 1994, Pub.L. 103–394, Title I, § 104(b), 108 Stat. 4109; Apr. 20, 2005, Pub.L. 109–8, Title III, § 324(a), Title VIII, § 802(c)(2), Title XII, § 1219, 119 Stat. 98, 145, 195.)

HISTORICAL AND STATUTORY NOTES

References in Text

Chapter 15 of title 11, referred to in subsec. (c), is 11 U.S.C.A. § 1501 et seq.

Codifications

This section was amended by Pub.L. 95–598, Title II, § 238(a), Nov. 6, 1978, 92 Stat. 2668, effective June 28, 1984, pursuant to Pub.L. 95–598, Title IV, § 402(b), Nov. 6, 1978, 92 Stat. 2682, as amended by Pub.L. 98–249, § 1(a), Mar. 31, 1984, 98 Stat. 116; Pub.L. 98–271, § 1(a), Apr. 30, 1984, 98 Stat. 163; Pub.L. 98–299, § 1(a), May 25, 1984, 98 Stat. 214; Pub.L. 98–325, § 1(a), June 20, 1984, 98 Stat. 268, set out as an Effective and Applicability Provisions note preceding section 101 of Title 11, Bankruptcy, to read as follows:

"**§ 1334. Bankruptcy appeals**

"**(a)** The district courts for districts for which panels have not been ordered appointed under section 160 of this title shall have jurisdiction of appeals from all final judgments, orders, and decrees of bankruptcy courts.

"**(b)** The district courts for such districts shall have jurisdiction of appeals from interlocutory orders and decrees of bankruptcy courts, but only by leave of the district court to which the appeal is taken.

"**(c)** A district court may not refer an appeal under that section to a magistrate or to a special master."

Section 402(b) of Pub.L. 95–598 was amended by section 113 of Pub.L. 98–353 by substituting "shall not be effective" for "shall take effect on June 28, 1984", thereby eliminating the amendment by section 238(a) of Pub.L. 95–598, effective June 27, 1984, pursuant to section 122(c) of Pub.L. 98–353, set out as an Effective and Applicability Provisions note under 28 U.S.C.A. § 151.

Section 121(a) of Pub.L. 98–353 directed that section 402(b) of Pub.L. 95–598 be amended by substituting "the date of enactment of the Bankruptcy Amendments and Federal Judgeship Act of 1984 [i.e. July 10, 1984]" for "June 28, 1984". This amendment was not executed in view of the prior amendment to section 402(b) of Pub.L. 95–598 by section 113 of Pub.L. 98–353.

Effective and Applicability Provisions

2005 Acts

Pub.L. 109–8, Title III, § 324(b), Apr. 20, 2005, 119 Stat. 98, provided that: "This section [amending subsecs. (b) and (e) of this section] shall only apply to cases filed after the date of enactment of this Act [Apr. 20, 2005]."

Except as otherwise provided, amendments by Pub.L. 109–8 effective 180 days after April 20, 2005, and inapplicable with respect to cases commenced under Title 11 before the effective date, see Pub.L. 109–8, § 1501, set out as a note under 11 U.S.C.A. § 101.

1994 Acts

Amendment by Pub.L. 103–394 effective on Oct. 22, 1994, and not to apply with respect to cases commenced under Title 11 of the United States Code before Oct. 22, 1994, see section 702 of Pub.L. 103–394, set out as a note under section 101 of Title 11, Bankruptcy.

1986 Acts

Amendment by Pub.L. 99–554 effective 30 days after Oct. 27, 1986, except as otherwise provided for, see section 302(a) of Pub.L. 99–554, as amended, set out as a note under section 581 of this title.

1984 Acts

Amendment by Pub.L. 98–353, except for subsec. (c)(2), effective July 10, 1984, see section 122(a) of Pub.L. 98–353, set out as a note under section 151 of this title.

Subsec. (c)(2) not applicable with respect to cases under Title 11, Bankruptcy, that are pending on July 10, 1984, or to proceedings arising in or related to such cases, see section 122(b) of Pub.L. 98–353, set out as a note under section 151 of this title.

Separability of Provisions

If any provision of or amendment made by Pub.L. 103–394 or the application of such provision or amendment to any person or circumstance is held to be unconstitutional, the remaining provisions of and amendments made by Pub.L. 103–394 and the application of such provisions and amendments to any person or circumstance shall not be affected thereby, see section 701 of Pub.L. 103–394, set out as a note under section 101 of Title 11, Bankruptcy.

Jurisdiction Over and Transfer of Bankruptcy Cases and Proceedings

Section 115 of Pub.L. 98–353 provided that:

"**(a)** On the date of the enactment of this Act [July 10, 1984] the appropriate district court of the United States shall have jurisdiction of—

"**(1)** cases, and matters and proceedings in cases, under the Bankruptcy Act [former Title 11, Bankruptcy] that are pending immediately before such date in the bankruptcy courts continued by section 404(a) of the Act of November 6, 1978 (Public Law 95–598; 92 Stat. 2687) [Pub.L. 95–598, Title IV, § 404(a), Nov. 6, 1978, 92 Stat. 2683, formerly set out as a note preceding section 151 of this title], and

"**(2)** cases under title 11 of the United States Code [Title 11, Bankruptcy], and proceedings arising under title 11 of the United States Code or arising in or related to cases under title 11 of the United States Code, that are pending immediately before such date in the bankruptcy courts continued by section 404(a) of the Act of November 6, 1978 (Public Law 95–598; 92 Stat. 2687).

"(b) On the date of the enactment of this Act [July 10, 1984], there shall be transferred to the appropriate district court of the United States appeals from final judgments, orders, and decrees of the bankruptcy courts pending immediately before such date in the bankruptcy appellate panels appointed under section 405(c) of the Act of November 6, 1978 (Public Law 95–598; 92 Stat. 2685) [formerly set out as a note preceding section 1471 of this title]."

§ 1335. Interpleader

(a) The district courts shall have original jurisdiction of any civil action of interpleader or in the nature of interpleader filed by any person, firm, or corporation, association, or society having in his or its custody or possession money or property of the value of $500 or more, or having issued a note, bond, certificate, policy of insurance, or other instrument of value or amount of $500 or more, or providing for the delivery or payment or the loan of money or property of such amount or value, or being under any obligation written or unwritten to the amount of $500 or more, if

(1) Two or more adverse claimants, of diverse citizenship as defined in subsection (a) or (d) of section 1332 of this title, are claiming or may claim to be entitled to such money or property, or to any one or more of the benefits arising by virtue of any note, bond, certificate, policy or other instrument, or arising by virtue of any such obligation; and if (2) the plaintiff has deposited such money or property or has paid the amount of or the loan or other value of such instrument or the amount due under such obligation into the registry of the court, there to abide the judgment of the court, or has given bond payable to the clerk of the court in such amount and with such surety as the court or judge may deem proper, conditioned upon the compliance by the plaintiff with the future order or judgment of the court with respect to the subject matter of the controversy.

(b) Such an action may be entertained although the titles or claims of the conflicting claimants do not have a common origin, or are not identical, but are adverse to and independent of one another.
(June 25, 1948, c. 646, 62 Stat. 931; Feb. 18, 2005, Pub.L. 109–2, § 4(b)(1), 119 Stat. 12.)

HISTORICAL AND STATUTORY NOTES
Effective and Applicability Provisions
2005 Acts

Amendments by Class Action Fairness Act of 2005, Pub.L. 109–2, Feb. 18, 2005, 119 Stat. 4, applicable to any civil action commenced on or after Feb. 18, 2005, see Pub.L. 109–2, § 9, set out as a note under 28 U.S.C.A. § 1332.

§ 1336. Surface Transportation Board's orders

(a) Except as otherwise provided by Act of Congress, the district courts shall have jurisdiction of any civil action to enforce, in whole or in part, any order of the Surface Transportation Board, and to enjoin or suspend, in whole or in part, any order of the Surface Transportation Board for the payment of money or the collection of fines, penalties, and forfeitures.

(b) When a district court or the United States Court of Federal Claims refers a question or issue to the Surface Transportation Board for determination, the court which referred the question or issue shall have exclusive jurisdiction of a civil action to enforce, enjoin, set aside, annul, or suspend, in whole or in part, any order of the Surface Transportation Board arising out of such referral.

(c) Any action brought under subsection (b) of this section shall be filed within 90 days from the date that the order of the Surface Transportation Board becomes final.
(June 25, 1948, c. 646, 62 Stat. 931; Aug. 30, 1964, Pub.L. 88–513, § 1, 78 Stat. 695; Jan. 2, 1975, Pub.L. 93–584, § 1, 88 Stat. 1917; Apr. 2, 1982, Pub.L. 97–164, Title I, § 128, 96 Stat. 39; Oct. 29, 1992, Pub.L. 102–572, Title IX, § 902(b)(1), 106 Stat. 4516; Dec. 29, 1995, Pub.L. 104–88, Title III, § 305(a)(1), (2), 109 Stat. 944.)

HISTORICAL AND STATUTORY NOTES
Effective and Applicability Provisions
1995 Acts

Amendment by Pub.L. 104–88 effective Jan. 1, 1996, see section 2 of Pub.L. 104–88, set out as a note under section 701 of Title 49, Transportation.

1992 Acts

Amendment by Pub.L. 102–572 effective Oct. 29, 1992, see section 911 of Pub.L. 102–572, set out as a note under section 171 of this title.

1982 Acts

Amendment by Pub.L. 97–164 effective Oct. 1, 1982, see section 402 of Pub.L. 97–164, set out as a note under section 171 of this title.

1975 Acts

Amendment by Pub.L. 93–584 not applicable to actions commenced on or before the last day of the first month beginning after Jan. 2, 1975, and actions to enjoin or suspend orders of the Interstate Commerce Commission which are pending when this amendment becomes effective shall not be affected thereby, but shall proceed to final disposition under the law existing on the date they were commenced, see section 10 of Pub.L. 93–584, set out as a note under section 2321 of this title.

§ 1337. Commerce and antitrust regulations; amount in controversy, costs

(a) The district courts shall have original jurisdiction of any civil action or proceeding arising under any Act of Congress regulating commerce or protecting trade and commerce against restraints and monopolies: *Provided, however,* That the district courts shall have original jurisdiction of an action brought under section 11706 or 14706 of title 49, only if the matter in controversy for each receipt or bill of lading exceeds $10,000, exclusive of interest and costs.

(b) Except when express provision therefor is otherwise made in a statute of the United States, where a plaintiff who files the case under section 11706 or 14706 of title 49, originally in the Federal courts is finally adjudged to be entitled to recover less than the sum or value of $10,000, computed without regard to any setoff or counterclaim to which the defendant may be adjudged to be entitled, and exclusive of any interest and costs, the district court may deny costs to the plaintiff and, in addition, may impose costs on the plaintiff.

(c) The district courts shall not have jurisdiction under this section of any matter within the exclusive jurisdiction of the Court of International Trade under chapter 95 of this title.

(June 25, 1948, c. 646, 62 Stat. 931; Oct. 20, 1978, Pub.L. 95–486, § 9(a), 92 Stat. 1633; Oct. 10, 1980, Pub.L. 96–417, Title V, § 505, 94 Stat. 1743; Jan. 12, 1983, Pub.L. 97–449, § 5(f), 96 Stat. 2442; Dec. 29, 1995, Pub.L. 104–88, Title III, § 305(a)(3), 109 Stat. 944.)

HISTORICAL AND STATUTORY NOTES

Effective and Applicability Provisions

1995 Acts

Amendment by Pub.L. 104–88 effective Jan. 1, 1996, see section 2 of Pub.L. 104–88, set out as a note under section 701 of Title 49, Transportation.

1980 Acts

Amendment by Pub.L. 96–417 effective on Nov. 1, 1980 and applicable with respect to civil actions pending on or commenced on or after such date, see section 701(a) of Pub.L. 96–417, as amended, set out as a note under section 251 of this title.

§ 1338. Patents, plant variety protection, copyrights, mask works, designs, trademarks, and unfair competition

(a) The district courts shall have original jurisdiction of any civil action arising under any Act of Congress relating to patents, plant variety protection, copyrights and trademarks. Such jurisdiction shall be exclusive of the courts of the states in patent, plant variety protection and copyright cases.

(b) The district courts shall have original jurisdiction of any civil action asserting a claim of unfair competition when joined with a substantial and related claim under the copyright, patent, plant variety protection or trademark laws.

(c) Subsections (a) and (b) apply to exclusive rights in mask works under chapter 9 of title 17, and to exclusive rights in designs under chapter 13 of title 17, to the same extent as such subsections apply to copyrights.

(June 25, 1948, c. 646, 62 Stat. 931; Dec. 24, 1970, Pub.L. 91–577, Title III, § 143(b), 84 Stat. 1559; Nov. 19, 1988, Pub.L. 100–702, Title X, § 1020(a)(4), 102 Stat. 4671; Oct. 28, 1998, Pub.L. 105–304, Title V, § 503(b)(1), (2)(A), 112 Stat.

2917; Nov. 29, 1999, Pub.L. 106–113, Div. B, § 1000(a)(9) [Title III, § 3009(1)], 113 Stat. 1536, 1501A–551.)

HISTORICAL AND STATUTORY NOTES

Effective and Applicability Provisions

1998 Acts

Amendment by Pub.L. 105–304, effective Oct. 28, 1998, see section 505 of Pub.L. 105–304, set out as a note under section 1301 of Title 17, Copyrights.

1970 Acts

Amendment by Pub.L. 91–577 effective Dec. 24, 1970, see section 141 of Pub.L. 91–577, set out as a note under section 2321 of Title 7, Agriculture.

§ 1339. Postal matters

The district courts shall have original jurisdiction of any civil action arising under any Act of Congress relating to the postal service.

(June 25, 1948, c. 646, 62 Stat. 932.)

§ 1340. Internal revenue; customs duties

The district courts shall have original jurisdiction of any civil action arising under any Act of Congress providing for internal revenue, or revenue from imports or tonnage except matters within the jurisdiction of the Court of International Trade.

(June 25, 1948, c. 646, 62 Stat. 932; Oct. 10, 1980, Pub.L. 96–417, Title V, § 501(21), 94 Stat. 1742.)

HISTORICAL AND STATUTORY NOTES

Effective and Applicability Provisions

1980 Acts

Amendment by Pub.L. 96–417 effective on Nov. 1, 1980 and applicable with respect to civil actions pending on or commenced on or after such date, see section 701(a) of Pub.L. 96–417, as amended, set out as a note under section 251 of this title.

§ 1341. Taxes by States

The district courts shall not enjoin, suspend or restrain the assessment, levy or collection of any tax under State law where a plain, speedy and efficient remedy may be had in the courts of such State.

(June 25, 1948, c. 646, 62 Stat. 932.)

HISTORICAL AND STATUTORY NOTES

Short Title

1948 Acts

This section is commonly known as the Tax Injunction Act.

§ 1342. Rate orders of State agencies

The district courts shall not enjoin, suspend or restrain the operation of, or compliance with, any order affecting rates chargeable by a public utility and made by a State administrative agency or a rate-making body of a State political subdivision, where:

(1) Jurisdiction is based solely on diversity of citizenship or repugnance of the order to the Federal Constitution; and,

(2) The order does not interfere with interstate commerce; and,

(3) The order has been made after reasonable notice and hearing; and,

(4) A plain, speedy and efficient remedy may be had in the courts of such State.

(June 25, 1948, c. 646, 62 Stat. 932.)

§ 1343. Civil rights and elective franchise

(a) The district courts shall have original jurisdiction of any civil action authorized by law to be commenced by any person:

(1) To recover damages for injury to his person or property, or because of the deprivation of any right or privilege of a citizen of the United States, by any act done in furtherance of any conspiracy mentioned in section 1985 of Title 42;

(2) To recover damages from any person who fails to prevent or to aid in preventing any wrongs mentioned in section 1985 of Title 42 which he had knowledge were about to occur and power to prevent;

(3) To redress the deprivation, under color of any State law, statute, ordinance, regulation, custom or usage, of any right, privilege or immunity secured by the Constitution of the United States or by any Act of Congress providing for equal rights of citizens or of all persons within the jurisdiction of the United States;

(4) To recover damages or to secure equitable or other relief under any Act of Congress providing for the protection of civil rights, including the right to vote.

(b) For purposes of this section—

(1) the District of Columbia shall be considered to be a State; and

(2) any Act of Congress applicable exclusively to the District of Columbia shall be considered to be a statute of the District of Columbia.

(June 25, 1948, c. 646, 62 Stat. 932; Sept. 3, 1954, c. 1263, § 42, 68 Stat. 1241; Sept. 9, 1957, Pub.L. 85–315, Part III, § 121, 71 Stat. 637; Dec. 29, 1979, Pub.L. 96–170, § 2, 93 Stat. 1284.)

HISTORICAL AND STATUTORY NOTES

Effective and Applicability Provisions

1979 Acts

Section 3 of Pub.L. 96–170 provided that: "The amendments made by this Act [amending this section and section 1983 of Title 42, The Public Health and Welfare] shall apply with respect to any deprivation of rights, privileges, or immunities secured by the Constitution and laws occurring after the date of the enactment of this Act [Dec. 29, 1979]."

§ 1344. Election disputes

The district courts shall have original jurisdiction of any civil action to recover possession of any office, except that of elector of President or Vice President, United States Senator, Representative in or delegate to Congress, or member of a state legislature, authorized by law to be commenced, wherein it appears that the sole question touching the title to office arises out of denial of the right to vote, to any citizen offering to vote, on account of race, color or previous condition of servitude.

The jurisdiction under this section shall extend only so far as to determine the rights of the parties to office by reason of the denial of the right, guaranteed by the Constitution of the United States and secured by any law, to enforce the right of citizens of the United States to vote in all the States.

(June 25, 1948, c. 646, 62 Stat. 932.)

§ 1345. United States as plaintiff

Except as otherwise provided by Act of Congress, the district courts shall have original jurisdiction of all civil actions, suits or proceedings commenced by the United States, or by any agency or officer thereof expressly authorized to sue by Act of Congress.

(June 25, 1948, c. 646, 62 Stat. 933.)

§ 1346. United States as defendant

(a) The district courts shall have original jurisdiction, concurrent with the United States Court of Federal Claims, of:

(1) Any civil action against the United States for the recovery of any internal-revenue tax alleged to have been erroneously or illegally assessed or collected, or any penalty claimed to have been collected without authority or any sum alleged to have been excessive or in any manner wrongfully collected under the internal-revenue laws;

(2) Any other civil action or claim against the United States, not exceeding $10,000 in amount, founded either upon the Constitution, or any Act of Congress, or any regulation of an executive department, or upon any express or implied contract with the United States, or for liquidated or unliquidated damages in cases not sounding in tort, except that the district courts shall not have jurisdiction of any civil action or claim against the United States founded upon any express or implied contract with the United States or for liquidated or unliquidated damages in cases not sounding in tort which are subject to sections 8(g)(1) and 10(a)(1) of the Contract Disputes Act of 1978. For the purpose of this paragraph, an express or implied contract with the Army and Air Force Exchange Service, Navy Ex-

changes, Marine Corps Exchanges, Coast Guard Exchanges, or Exchange Councils of the National Aeronautics and Space Administration shall be considered an express or implied contract with the United States.

(b)(1) Subject to the provisions of chapter 171 of this title, the district courts, together with the United States District Court for the District of the Canal Zone and the District Court of the Virgin Islands, shall have exclusive jurisdiction of civil actions on claims against the United States, for money damages, accruing on and after January 1, 1945, for injury or loss of property, or personal injury or death caused by the negligent or wrongful act or omission of any employee of the Government while acting within the scope of his office or employment, under circumstances where the United States, if a private person, would be liable to the claimant in accordance with the law of the place where the act or omission occurred.

(2) No person convicted of a felony who is incarcerated while awaiting sentencing or while serving a sentence may bring a civil action against the United States or an agency, officer, or employee of the Government, for mental or emotional injury suffered while in custody without a prior showing of physical injury.

(c) The jurisdiction conferred by this section includes jurisdiction of any set-off, counterclaim, or other claim or demand whatever on the part of the United States against any plaintiff commencing an action under this section.

(d) The district courts shall not have jurisdiction under this section of any civil action or claim for a pension.

(e) The district courts shall have original jurisdiction of any civil action against the United States provided in section 6226, 6228(a), 7426, or 7428 (in the case of the United States district court for the District of Columbia) or section 7429 of the Internal Revenue Code of 1986.

(f) The district courts shall have exclusive original jurisdiction of civil actions under section 2409a to quiet title to an estate or interest in real property in which an interest is claimed by the United States.

(g) Subject to the provisions of chapter 179, the district courts of the United States shall have exclusive jurisdiction over any civil action commenced under section 453(2) of title 3, by a covered employee under chapter 5 of such title.
(June 25, 1948, c. 646, 62 Stat. 933; Apr. 25, 1949, c. 92, § 2(a), 63 Stat. 62; May 24, 1949, c. 139, § 80(a), (b), 63 Stat. 101; Oct. 31, 1951, c. 655, § 50(b), 65 Stat. 727; July 30, 1954, c. 648, § 1, 68 Stat. 589; July 7, 1958, Pub.L. 85–508, § 12(e), 72 Stat. 348; Aug. 30, 1964, Pub.L. 88–519, 78 Stat. 699; Nov. 2, 1966, Pub.L. 89–719, Title II, § 202(a), 80 Stat. 1148; July 23, 1970, Pub.L. 91–350, § 1(a), 84 Stat. 449; Oct. 25, 1972, Pub.L. 92–562, § 1, 86 Stat. 1176; Oct. 4, 1976,

Pub.L. 94–455, Title XII, § 1204(c) (1), Title XIII, § 1306(b) (7), 90 Stat. 1697, 1719; Nov. 1, 1978, Pub.L. 95–563, § 14(a), 92 Stat. 2389; Apr. 2, 1982, Pub.L. 97–164, Title I, § 129, 96 Stat. 39; Sept. 3, 1982, Pub.L. 97–248, Title IV, § 402(c) (17), 96 Stat. 669; Oct. 22, 1986, Pub.L. 99–514, § 2, 100 Stat. 2095; Oct. 29, 1992, Pub.L. 102–572, Title IX, § 902(b)(1), 106 Stat. 4516; Apr. 26, 1996, Pub.L. 104–134, Title I, § 101[(a)][Title VIII, § 806], 110 Stat. 1321–75; renumbered Title I May 2, 1996, Pub.L. 104–140, § 1(a), 110 Stat. 1327, and amended Oct. 26, 1996, Pub.L. 104–331, § 3(b)(1), 110 Stat. 4069.)

HISTORICAL AND STATUTORY NOTES

Senate Revision Amendment

The provisions of Title 28, U.S.C., section 932, which related to application of the Federal Rules of Civil Procedure, were originally set out in section 2676 of this revised title, but such section 2676 was eliminated by Senate amendment. See 80th Congress Senate Report No. 1559, amendment No. 61.

1949 Acts

This section corrects typographical errors in section 1346(a)(1) of Title 28, U.S.C., and in section 1346(b) of such title.

House Report No. 276, see 1949 U.S. Code Cong. Service, p. 1226.

Senate Report No. 303 and House Report No. 352, see 1949 U.S.Code Cong.Service, p. 1248.

1951 Acts

Senate Report No. 1020, see 1951 U.S. Code Cong. and Adm. Service, p. 2578.

1954 Acts

House Report No. 659 and Conference Report No. 2276, see 1954 U.S. Code Cong. and Adm. News, p. 2716.

1958 Acts

House Report No. 624, see 1958 U.S. Code Cong. and Adm. News, p. 2933.

1964 Acts

Senate Report No. 1390, see 1964 U.S. Code Cong. and Adm. News, p. 3254.

1966 Acts

Senate Report No. 1708, see 1966 U.S. Code Cong. and Adm. News, p. 3722.

1970 Acts

House Report No. 91–933, see 1970 U.S. Code Cong. and Adm. News, p. 3477.

1972 Acts

House Report No. 92–1559, see 1972 U.S. Code Cong. and Adm. News, p. 4547.

1976 Acts

House Report Nos. 94–658 and 94–1380, Senate Report No. 94–938(Parts I and II), and House Conference Report No. 94–1515, see 1976 U.S. Code Cong. and Adm. News, p. 2897.

1978 Acts

Senate Report No. 95–1118, see 1978 U.S. Code Cong. and Adm. News, p. 5235.

1982 Acts

Senate Report No. 97–275, see 1982 U.S. Code Cong. and Adm. News, p. 11.

Senate Report No. 97–494, House Conference Report No. 97–760 and Statements by Legislative Leaders, see 1982 U.S. Code Cong. and Adm. News, p. 781.

1996 Acts

House Report No. 104–820, see 1996 U.S. Code Cong. and Adm. News, p. 4348.

References in Text

The internal-revenue laws, referred to in subsec. (a)(1), are classified generally to Title 26, Internal Revenue Code.

Sections 8(g)(1) and 10(a)(1) of the Contract Disputes Act of 1978, referred to in subsec. (a)(2), are sections 8(g)(1) and 10(a)(1) of Pub.L. 95–563, Nov. 1, 1978, 92 Stat. 2387, 2388, which are classified to sections 607(g)(1) and 609(a)(1) of Title 41, Public Contracts.

Sections 6226, 6228(a), 7426, 7428, and 7429 of the Internal Revenue Code of 1986, referred to in subsec. (e), are classified to sections 6226, 6228(a), 7426, 7428, and 7429, respectively, of Title 26, Internal Revenue Code.

Effective and Applicability Provisions

1996 Acts

Amendment by Pub.L. 104–331 effective October 1, 1997, see section 3(d) of Pub.L. 104–331, set out as a note under section 1296 of this title.

1992 Acts

Amendment by Pub.L. 102–572 effective Oct. 29, 1992, see section 911 of Pub.L. 102–572, set out as a note under section 171 of this title.

1982 Acts

Amendment by Pub.L. 97–248 applicable to partnership taxable years beginning after Sept. 3, 1982, with provision for the applicability of the amendment to any partnership taxable year ending after Sept. 3, 1982, if the partnership, each partner, and each indirect partner requests such application and the Secretary of the Treasury or his delegate consents to such application, see section 407(a)(1) and (3) of Pub.L. 97–248, as amended, set out as a note under section 6221 of Title 26, Internal Revenue Code.

Amendment by Pub.L. 97–164 effective Oct. 1, 1982, see section 402 of Pub.L. 97–164, set out as a note under section 171 of this title.

1978 Acts

Amendment by Pub.L. 95–563 effective with respect to contracts entered into 120 days after Nov. 1, 1978 and, at the election of the contractor, with respect to any claim pending at such time before the contracting officer or initiated thereafter, see section 16 of Pub.L. 95–563, set out as a note under section 601 of Title 41, Public Contracts.

1970 Acts

Section 2 of Pub.L. 91–350 provided that:

"(a) In addition to granting jurisdiction over suits brought after the date of enactment of this Act [July 23, 1970], the provisions of this Act [amending this section and section 1491 of this title and section 724a of former Title 31, Money and Finance], shall also apply to claims and civil actions dismissed before or pending on the date of enactment of this Act if the claim or civil action is based upon a transaction,

omission, or breach that occurred not more than six years prior to the date of enactment of this Act [July 23, 1970].

"(b) The provisions of subsection (a) of this section shall apply notwithstanding a determination or judgment made prior to the date of enactment of this Act that the United States district courts or the United States Court of Claims [now United States Court of Federal Claims] did not have jurisdiction to entertain a suit on an express or implied contract with a nonappropriated fund instrumentality of the United States described in section 1 of this Act."

1966 Acts

Section 203 of Title II of Pub.L. 89–719 provided that: "The amendments made by this title [amending this section and sections 1402 and 2410 of this title] shall apply after the date of the enactment of this Act [Nov. 2, 1966]."

1958 Acts

Amendment of section by Pub.L. 85–508 effective Jan. 3, 1959, upon admission of Alaska into the Union pursuant to Proc. No. 3269, Jan. 3, 1959, 24 F.R. 81, 73 Stat. c16, as required by sections 1 and 8(c) of Pub.L. 85–508, see notes set out under section 81A of this title and preceding former section 21 of Title 48, Territories and Insular Possessions.

Transfer of Functions

For transfer of authorities, functions, personnel, and assets of the Coast Guard, including the authorities and functions of the Secretary of Transportation relating thereto, to the Department of Homeland Security, and for treatment of related references, see 6 U.S.C.A. §§ 468(b), 551(d), 552(d) and 557, and the Department of Homeland Security Reorganization Plan of November 25, 2002, as modified, set out as a note under 6 U.S.C.A. § 542.

Savings Clause for Act Oct. 31, 1951

Act June 4, 1956, c. 363, 70 Stat. 246, which was formerly set out as a note under this section, and which conferred jurisdiction on district courts of certain actions to recover pay of employees who had been dismissed, was repealed by Pub.L. 89–554, § 8(a), Sept. 6, 1966, 80 Stat. 658.

Severability of Provisions

If any provision of section 101[a] [Title VIII] of Pub.L. 104–134, an amendment made by such Title, or the application of such provision or amendment to any person or circumstance is held to be unconstitutional, the remainder of such Title, the amendments made by such Title, and the application of the provisions of such Title to any person or circumstance not affected thereby, see section 101[a] [Title VIII, § 810] of Pub.L. 104–134, set out as a note under section 3626 of Title 18, Crimes and Criminal Procedure.

Termination of United States District Court for the District of the Canal Zone

For termination of the United States District Court for the District of the Canal Zone at end of the "transition period", being the 30–month period beginning Oct. 1, 1979, and ending midnight Mar. 31, 1982, see Paragraph 5 of Article XI of the Panama Canal Treaty of 1977 and sections 3831 and 3841 to 3843 of Title 22, Foreign Relations and Intercourse.

§ 1347. Partition action where United States is joint tenant

The district courts shall have original jurisdiction of any civil action commenced by any tenant in common or joint tenant for the partition of lands where the United States is one of the tenants in common or joint tenants.

(June 25, 1948, c. 646, 62 Stat. 933.)

§ 1348. Banking association as party

The district courts shall have original jurisdiction of any civil action commenced by the United States, or by direction of any officer thereof, against any national banking association, any civil action to wind up the affairs of any such association, and any action by a banking association established in the district for which the court is held, under chapter 2 of Title 12, to enjoin the Comptroller of the Currency, or any receiver acting under his direction, as provided by such chapter.

All national banking associations shall, for the purposes of all other actions by or against them, be deemed citizens of the States in which they are respectively located.

(June 25, 1948, c. 646, 62 Stat. 933.)

HISTORICAL AND STATUTORY NOTES

Exception as to Transfer of Functions

Functions vested by any provision of law in the Comptroller of the Currency, referred to in this section, were not included in the transfer of functions of officers, agencies and employees of the Department of the Treasury to the Secretary of the Treasury, made by 1950 Reorg. Plan No. 26, § 1, eff. July 31, 1950, 15 F.R. 4935, 64 Stat. 1280, set out in Appendix 1 to Title 5, Government Organization and Employees. See section 321(c)(2) of Title 31 Money and Fiance.

§ 1349. Corporation organized under federal law as party

The district courts shall not have jurisdiction of any civil action by or against any corporation upon the ground that it was incorporated by or under an Act of Congress, unless the United States is the owner of more than one-half of its capital stock.

(June 25, 1948, c. 646, 62 Stat. 934.)

§ 1350. Alien's action for tort

The district courts shall have original jurisdiction of any civil action by an alien for a tort only, committed in violation of the law of nations or a treaty of the United States.

(June 25, 1948, c. 646, 62 Stat. 934.)

HISTORICAL AND STATUTORY NOTES

Torture Victim Protection

Pub.L. 102–256, Mar. 12, 1992, 106 Stat. 73, provided that:

"**Section 1. Short Title.**

"This Act may be cited as the 'Torture Victim Protection Act of 1991'.

"**Sec. 2. Establishment of civil action.**

"**(a) Liability.**—An individual who, under actual or apparent authority, or color of law, of any foreign nation—

"**(1)** subjects an individual to torture shall, in a civil action, be liable for damages to that individual; or

"**(2)** subjects an individual to extrajudicial killing shall, in a civil action, be liable for damages to the individual's legal representative, or to any person who may be a claimant in an action for wrongful death.

"**(b) Exhaustion of remedies.**—A court shall decline to hear a claim under this section if the claimant has not exhausted adequate and available remedies in the place in which the conduct giving rise to the claim occurred.

"**(c) Statute of limitations.**—No action shall be maintained under this section unless it is commenced within 10 years after the cause of action arose.

"**Sec. 3. Definitions.**

"**(a) Extrajudicial killing.**—For the purposes of this Act, the term 'extrajudicial killing' means a deliberated killing not authorized by a previous judgment pronounced by a regularly constituted court affording all the judicial guarantees which are recognized as indispensable by civilized peoples. Such term, however, does not include any such killing that, under international law, is lawfully carried out under the authority of a foreign nation.

"**(b) Torture.**—For the purposes of this Act—

"**(1)** the term 'torture' means any act, directed against an individual in the offender's custody or physical control, by which severe pain or suffering (other than pain or suffering arising only from or inherent in, or incidental to, lawful sanctions), whether physical or mental, is intentionally inflicted on that individual for such purposes as obtaining from that individual or a third person information or a confession, punishing that individual for an act that individual or a third person has committed or is suspected of having committed, intimidating or coercing that individual or a third person, or for any reason based on discrimination of any kind; and

"**(2)** mental pain or suffering refers to prolonged mental harm caused by or resulting from—

"**(A)** the intentional infliction or threatened infliction of severe physical pain or suffering;

"**(B)** the administration or application, or threatened administration or application, of mind altering substances or other procedures calculated to disrupt profoundly the senses or the personality;

"**(C)** the threat of imminent death; or

"**(D)** the threat that another individual will imminently be subjected to death, severe physical pain or suffering, or the administration or application of mind altering substances or other procedures calculated to disrupt profoundly the senses or personality."

§ 1351. Consuls, vice consuls, and members of a diplomatic mission as defendant

The district courts shall have original jurisdiction, exclusive of the courts of the States, of all civil actions and proceedings against—

(1) consuls or vice consuls of foreign states; or

(2) members of a mission or members of their families (as such terms are defined in section 2 of the Diplomatic Relations Act).

(June 25, 1948, c. 646, 62 Stat. 934; May 24, 1949, c. 139, § 80(c), 63 Stat. 101; Sept. 30, 1978, Pub.L. 95–393, § 8(a)(1), 92 Stat. 810.)

HISTORICAL AND STATUTORY NOTES

References in Text

Section 2 of the Diplomatic Relations Act, referred to in par. (2), is section 2 of Pub.L. 95–393, Sept. 30, 1978, 92 Stat. 808, which is classified to section 254a of Title 22, Foreign Relations and Intercourse.

Effective and Applicability Provisions

1978 Acts

Amendment by Pub.L. 95–393 effective at the end of the 90-day period beginning on Sept. 30, 1978, see section 9 of Pub.L. 95–393, set out as a note under section 254a of Title 22, Foreign Relations and Intercourse.

§ 1352. Bonds executed under federal law

The district courts shall have original jurisdiction, concurrent with State courts, of any action on a bond executed under any law of the United States, except matters within the jurisdiction of the Court of International Trade under section 1582 of this title.

(June 25, 1948, c. 646, 62 Stat. 934; Oct. 10, 1980, Pub.L. 96–417, Title V, § 506, 94 Stat. 1743.)

HISTORICAL AND STATUTORY NOTES

Effective and Applicability Provisions

1980 Acts

Amendment by Pub.L. 96–417 applicable with respect to civil actions commenced on or after the 90th day after Nov. 1, 1980, see section 701(c)(1)(B) of Pub.L. 96–417, as amended, set out as a note under section 251 of this title.

§ 1353. Indian allotments

The district courts shall have original jurisdiction of any civil action involving the right of any person, in whole or in part of Indian blood or descent, to any allotment of land under any Act of Congress or treaty.

The judgment in favor of any claimant to an allotment of land shall have the same effect, when properly certified to the Secretary of the Interior, as if such allotment had been allowed and approved by him; but this provision shall not apply to any lands held on or before December 21, 1911, by either of the Five Civilized Tribes, the Osage Nation of Indians, nor to any of the lands within the Quapaw Indian Agency.

(June 25, 1948, c. 646, 62 Stat. 934.)

§ 1354. Land grants from different states

The district courts shall have original jurisdiction of actions between citizens of the same state claiming lands under grants from different states.

(June 25, 1948, c. 646, 62 Stat. 934.)

§ 1355. Fine, penalty or forfeiture

(a) The district courts shall have original jurisdiction, exclusive of the courts of the States, of any action or proceeding for the recovery or enforcement of any fine, penalty, or forfeiture, pecuniary or otherwise, incurred under any Act of Congress, except matters within the jurisdiction of the Court of International Trade under section 1582 of this title.

(b)(1) A forfeiture action or proceeding may be brought in—

(A) the district court for the district in which any of the acts or omissions giving rise to the forfeiture occurred, or

(B) any other district where venue for the forfeiture action or proceeding is specifically provided for in section 1395 of this title or any other statute.

(2) Whenever property subject to forfeiture under the laws of the United States is located in a foreign country, or has been detained or seized pursuant to legal process or competent authority of a foreign government, an action or proceeding for forfeiture may be brought as provided in paragraph (1), or in the United States District court [1] for the District of Columbia.

(c) In any case in which a final order disposing of property in a civil forfeiture action or proceeding is appealed, removal of the property by the prevailing party shall not deprive the court of jurisdiction. Upon motion of the appealing party, the district court or the court of appeals shall issue any order necessary to preserve the right of the appealing party to the full value of the property at issue, including a stay of the judgment of the district court pending appeal or requiring the prevailing party to post an appeal bond.

(d) Any court with jurisdiction over a forfeiture action pursuant to subsection (b) may issue and cause to be served in any other district such process as may be required to bring before the court the property that is the subject of the forfeiture action.

(June 25, 1948, c. 646, 62 Stat. 934; Oct. 10, 1980, Pub.L. 96–417, Title V, § 507, 94 Stat. 1743; Oct. 28, 1992, Pub.L. 102–550, Title XV, § 1521, 106 Stat. 4062.)

[1] So in original. Probably should be capitalized.

HISTORICAL AND STATUTORY NOTES

Effective and Applicability Provisions

1992 Acts

Except as otherwise provided, amendment by Pub.L. 102–550 effective Oct. 28, 1992, see section 2 of Pub.L. 102–550, set out as a note under section 5301 of Title 42, The Public Health and Welfare.

1980 Acts

Amendment by Pub.L. 96–417 applicable with respect to civil actions commenced on or after the 90th day after Nov. 1,

1980, see section 701(c)(1)(B) of Pub.L. 96–417, as amended, set out as a note under section 251 of this title.

§ 1356. Seizures not within admiralty and maritime jurisdiction

The district courts shall have original jurisdiction, exclusive of the courts of the States, of any seizure under any law of the United States on land or upon waters not within admiralty and maritime jurisdiction, except matters within the jurisdiction of the Court of International Trade under section 1582 of this title. (June 25, 1948, c. 646, 62 Stat. 934; Oct. 10, 1980, Pub.L. 96–417, Title V, § 508, 94 Stat. 1743.)

HISTORICAL AND STATUTORY NOTES

Effective and Applicability Provisions

1980 Acts

Amendment by Pub.L. 96–417 applicable with respect to civil actions commenced on or after the 90th day after Nov. 1, 1980, see section 701(c)(1)(B) of Pub.L. 96–417, as amended, set out as a note under section 251 of this title.

§ 1357. Injuries under Federal laws

The district courts shall have original jurisdiction of any civil action commenced by any person to recover damages for any injury to his person or property on account of any act done by him, under any Act of Congress, for the protection or collection of any of the revenues, or to enforce the right of citizens of the United States to vote in any State. (June 25, 1948, c. 646, 62 Stat. 934.)

§ 1358. Eminent domain

The district courts shall have original jurisdiction of all proceedings to condemn real estate for the use of the United States or its departments or agencies. (June 25, 1948, c. 646, 62 Stat. 935.)

§ 1359. Parties collusively joined or made

A district court shall not have jurisdiction of a civil action in which any party, by assignment or otherwise, has been improperly or collusively made or joined to invoke the jurisdiction of such court. (June 25, 1948, c. 646, 62 Stat. 935.)

§ 1360. State civil jurisdiction in actions to which Indians are parties

(a) Each of the States listed in the following table shall have jurisdiction over civil causes of action between Indians or to which Indians are parties which arise in the areas of Indian country listed opposite the name of the State to the same extent that such State has jurisdiction over other civil causes of action, and those civil laws of such State that are of general application to private persons or private property shall have the same force and effect within such Indian country as they have elsewhere within the State:

State of	Indian country affected
Alaska	All Indian country within the State
California	All Indian country within the State
Minnesota	All Indian country within the State, except the Red Lake Reservation
Nebraska	All Indian country within the State
Oregon	All Indian country within the State, except the Warm Springs Reservation
Wisconsin	All Indian country within the State

(b) Nothing in this section shall authorize the alienation, encumbrance, or taxation of any real or personal property, including water rights, belonging to any Indian or any Indian tribe, band, or community that is held in trust by the United States or is subject to a restriction against alienation imposed by the United States; or shall authorize regulation of the use of such property in a manner inconsistent with any Federal treaty, agreement, or statute or with any regulation made pursuant thereto; or shall confer jurisdiction upon the State to adjudicate, in probate proceedings or otherwise, the ownership or right to possession of such property or any interest therein.

(c) Any tribal ordinance or custom heretofore or hereafter adopted by an Indian tribe, band, or community in the exercise of any authority which it may possess shall, if not inconsistent with any applicable civil law of the State, be given full force and effect in the determination of civil causes of action pursuant to this section. (Added Aug. 15, 1953, c. 505, § 4, 67 Stat. 589, and amended Aug. 24, 1954, c. 910, § 2, 68 Stat. 795; Aug. 8, 1958, Pub.L. 85–615, § 2, 72 Stat. 545; Nov. 6, 1978, Pub.L. 95–598, Title II, § 239, 92 Stat. 2668; July 10, 1984, Pub.L. 98–353, Title I, § 110, 98 Stat. 342.)

HISTORICAL AND STATUTORY NOTES

Codifications

Subsec. (a) of this section was amended by Pub.L. 95–598, Title II, § 239, Nov. 6, 1978, 92 Stat. 2668, effective June 28, 1984, pursuant to Pub.L. 95–598, Title IV, § 402(b), Nov. 6, 1978, 92 Stat. 2682, as amended by Pub.L. 98–249, § 1(a), Mar. 31, 1984, 98 Stat. 116; Pub.L. 98–271, § 1(a), Apr. 30, 1984, 98 Stat. 163; Pub.L. 98–299, § 1(a), May 25, 1984, 98 Stat. 214; Pub.L. 98–325, § 1(a), June 20, 1984, 98 Stat. 268, set out as an Effective and Applicability Provisions note preceding section 101 of Title 11, Bankruptcy, by substituting "Alaska All Indian country within the State" for "Alaska All Indian country within the Territory".

Section 402(b) of Pub.L. 95–598 was amended by section 113 of Pub.L. 98–353 by substituting "shall not be effective" for "shall take effect on June 28, 1984", thereby eliminating the amendment by section 239 of Pub.L. 95–598, effective June 27, 1984, pursuant to section 122(c) of Pub.L. 98–353, set out as an Effective and Applicability Provisions note under section 151 of this title.

Section 121(a) of Pub.L. 98–353 directed that section 402(b) of Pub.L. 95–598 be amended by substituting "the date of

enactment of the Bankruptcy Amendments and Federal Judgeship Act of 1984 [i.e. July 10, 1984]" for "June 28, 1984". This amendment was not executed in view of the prior amendment to section 402(b) of Pub.L. 95–598 by section 113 of Pub.L. 98–353.

Effective and Applicability Provisions

1984 Acts

Amendment by Pub.L. 98–353 effective July 10, 1984, see section 122(a) of Pub.L. 98–353, set out as a note under section 151 of this title.

Admission of Alaska as State

Admission of Alaska into the Union was accomplished Jan. 3, 1959 upon issuance of Proc. No. 3269, Jan. 3, 1959, 24 F.R. 81, 73 Stat. c16, as required by sections 1 and 8(c) of Pub.L. 85–508, July 7, 1958, 72 Stat. 339, set out as notes preceding former section 21 of Title 48, Territories and Insular Possessions.

Amendment of State Constitutions to Remove Legal Impediment; Effective Date

Section 6 of Act Aug. 15, 1953, provided that: "Notwithstanding the provisions of any Enabling Act for the admission of a State, the consent of the United States is hereby given to the people of any State to amend, where necessary, their State constitution or existing statutes, as the case may be, to remove any legal impediment to the assumption of civil and criminal jurisdiction in accordance with the provisions of this Act [adding section 1360 of this title and section 1162 of Title 18]: *Provided,* That the provisions of this Act shall not become effective with respect to such assumption of jurisdiction by any such State until the people thereof have appropriately amended their State constitution or statutes as the case may be."

Consent of United States to Other States to Assume Jurisdiction

Act Aug. 15, 1953, c. 505, § 7, 67 Stat. 590, which gave consent of the United States to any other State not having jurisdiction with respect to criminal offenses or civil causes of action, or with respect to both, as provided for in this section and section 1162 of Title 18, Crimes and Criminal Procedure, to assume jurisdiction at such time and in such manner as the people of the State shall, by legislative action, obligate and bind the State to assumption thereof, was repealed by section 403(b) of Pub.L. 90–284, Title IV, Apr. 11, 1968, 82 Stat. 79, such repeal not to affect any cession of jurisdiction made pursuant to such section prior to its repeal.

Retrocession by State of jurisdiction acquired by State pursuant to section 7 of Act Aug. 15, 1953, prior to its repeal, see section 1323 of Title 25, Indians.

§ 1361. Action to compel an officer of the United States to perform his duty

The district courts shall have original jurisdiction of any action in the nature of mandamus to compel an officer or employee of the United States or any agency thereof to perform a duty owed to the plaintiff.
(Added Pub.L. 87–748, § 1(a), Oct. 5, 1962, 76 Stat. 744.)

§ 1362. Indian tribes

The district courts shall have original jurisdiction of all civil actions, brought by any Indian tribe or band with a governing body duly recognized by the Secretary of the Interior, wherein the matter in controversy arises under the Constitution, laws, or treaties of the United States.
(Added Pub.L. 89–635, § 1, Oct. 10, 1966, 80 Stat. 880.)

§ 1363. Jurors' employment rights

The district courts shall have original jurisdiction of any civil action brought for the protection of jurors' employment under section 1875 of this title.
(Added Pub.L. 95–572, § 6(b)(1), Nov. 2, 1978, 92 Stat. 2457.)

HISTORICAL AND STATUTORY NOTES

Effective and Applicability Provisions

1978 Acts

Section 7 of Pub.L. 95–572 provided that:

"(a) Except as provided in subsection (b) of this section, the amendments made by this Act [enacting sections 1363 and 1875, renumbering as section 1364 prior section 1363, and amending sections 1863, 1865, 1866, 1869, and 1871 of this title] shall apply with respect to any grand or petit juror summoned for service or actually serving on or after the date of enactment of this Act [Nov. 2, 1978].

"(b) The amendment made by section 5 of this Act [to section 1871 of this title] shall apply with respect to any grand or petit juror serving on or after the sixtieth day following the date of enactment of this Act [Nov. 2, 1978]."

Prior Provisions

A prior section 1363 was renumbered 1366.

§ 1364. Direct actions against insurers of members of diplomatic missions and their families

(a) The district courts shall have original and exclusive jurisdiction, without regard to the amount in controversy, of any civil action commenced by any person against an insurer who by contract has insured an individual, who is, or was at the time of the tortious act or omission, a member of a mission (within the meaning of section 2(3) of the Diplomatic Relations Act (22 U.S.C. 254a(3))) or a member of the family of such a member of a mission, or an individual described in section 19 of the Convention on Privileges and Immunities of the United Nations of February 13, 1946, against liability for personal injury, death, or damage to property.

(b) Any direct action brought against an insurer under subsection (a) shall be tried without a jury, but shall not be subject to the defense that the insured is immune from suit, that the insured is an indispensable party, or in the absence of fraud or collusion, that the insured has violated a term of the contract, unless the contract was cancelled before the claim arose.

(Added Pub.L. 95–393, § 7(a), Sept. 30, 1978, 92 Stat. 809, and amended Pub.L. 97–241, Title II, § 203(b)(4), Aug. 24, 1982, 96 Stat. 291; Pub.L. 100–204, Title I, § 138(a), Dec. 22, 1987, 101 Stat. 1347.)

HISTORICAL AND STATUTORY NOTES

Codifications

Two other sections 1364 were renumbered sections 1365 and 1366 of this title.

Effective and Applicability Provisions

1987 Acts

Section 138(b) of Pub.L. 100–204 provided that: "The amendment made by subsection (a) [amending subsec. (a) of this section] shall apply to the first tortious act or omission occurring after the date of enactment of this Act [Dec. 22, 1987]."

1982 Acts

Amendment by Pub.L. 97–241 effective Oct. 1, 1982, see section 204 of Pub.L. 97–241, set out as a note under section 4301 of Title 22, Foreign Relations and Intercourse.

1978 Acts

Section effective at the end of the 90 day period beginning on Sept. 30, 1978, see section 9 of Pub.L. 95–393, set out as a note under section 254a of Title 22, Foreign Relations and Intercourse.

§ 1365. Senate actions

(a) The United States District Court for the District of Columbia shall have original jurisdiction, without regard to the amount in controversy, over any civil action brought by the Senate or any authorized committee or subcommittee of the Senate to enforce, to secure a declaratory judgment concerning the validity of, or to prevent a threatened refusal or failure to comply with, any subpena or order issued by the Senate or committee or subcommittee of the Senate to any entity acting or purporting to act under color or authority of State law or to any natural person to secure the production of documents or other materials of any kind or the answering of any deposition or interrogatory or to secure testimony or any combination thereof. This section shall not apply to an action to enforce, to secure a declaratory judgment concerning the validity of, or to prevent a threatened refusal to comply with, any subpena or order issued to an officer or employee of the executive branch of the Federal Government acting within his or her official capacity, except that this section shall apply if the refusal to comply is based on the assertion of a personal privilege or objection and is not based on a governmental privilege or objection the assertion of which has been authorized by the executive branch of the Federal Government.

(b) Upon application by the Senate or any authorized committee or subcommittee of the Senate, the district court shall issue an order to an entity or person refusing, or failing to comply with, or threatening to refuse or not to comply with, a subpena or

order of the Senate or committee or subcommittee of the Senate requiring such entity or person to comply forthwith. Any refusal or failure to obey a lawful order of the district court issued pursuant to this section may be held by such court to be a contempt thereof. A contempt proceeding shall be commenced by an order to show cause before the court why the entity or person refusing or failing to obey the court order should not be held in contempt of court. Such contempt proceeding shall be tried by the court and shall be summary in manner. The purpose of sanctions imposed as a result of such contempt proceeding shall be to compel obedience to the order of the court. Process in any such action or contempt proceeding may be served in any judicial district wherein the entity or party refusing, or failing to comply, or threatening to refuse or not to comply, resides, transacts business, or may be found, and subpenas for witnesses who are required to attend such proceeding may run into any other district. Nothing in this section shall confer upon such court jurisdiction to affect by injunction or otherwise the issuance or effect of any subpena or order of the Senate or any committee or subcommittee of the Senate or to review, modify, suspend, terminate, or set aside any such subpena or order. An action, contempt proceeding, or sanction brought or imposed pursuant to this section shall not abate upon adjournment sine die by the Senate at the end of a Congress if the Senate or the committee or subcommittee of the Senate which issued the subpena or order certifies to the court that it maintains its interest in securing the documents, answers, or testimony during such adjournment.

[(c) Repealed. Pub.L. 98–620, Title IV, § 402(29)(D), Nov. 8, 1984, 98 Stat. 3359]

(d) The Senate or any committee or subcommittee of the Senate commencing and prosecuting a civil action or contempt proceeding under this section may be represented in such action by such attorneys as the Senate may designate.

(e) A civil action commenced or prosecuted under this section, may not be authorized pursuant to the Standing Order of the Senate "authorizing suits by Senate Committees" (S. Jour. 572, May 28, 1928).

(f) For the purposes of this section the term "committee" includes standing, select, or special committees of the Senate established by law or resolution. (Added Pub.L. 95–521, Title VII, § 705(f)(1), Oct. 26, 1978, 92 Stat. 1879, § 1364, and amended Pub.L. 98–620, Title IV, § 402(29)(D), Nov. 8, 1984, 98 Stat. 3359; renumbered § 1365, Pub.L. 99–336, § 6(a)(1)(B), June 19, 1986, 100 Stat. 638; Pub.L. 104–292, § 4, Oct. 11, 1996, 110 Stat. 3460.)

HISTORICAL AND STATUTORY NOTES

Effective and Applicability Provisions

1984 Acts

Amendment by Pub.L. 98–620 not to apply to cases pending on Nov. 8, 1984, see section 403 of Pub.L. 98–620, set out as a note under section 1657 of this title.

1978 Acts

Section effective Jan. 3, 1979, see section 717 of Pub.L. 95–521, set out as a note under section 288 of Title 2, The Congress.

§ 1366. Construction of references to laws of the United States or Acts of Congress

For the purposes of this chapter, references to laws of the United States or Acts of Congress do not include laws applicable exclusively to the District of Columbia.

(Added Pub.L. 91–358, Title I, § 172(c)(1), July 29, 1970, 84 Stat. 590, § 1363; renumbered § 1364, Pub.L. 95–572, § 6(b)(1), Nov. 2, 1978, 92 Stat. 2456; renumbered § 1366, Pub.L. 99–336, § 6(a)(1)(C), June 19, 1986, 100 Stat. 639.)

HISTORICAL AND STATUTORY NOTES

Effective and Applicability Provisions

1970 Acts

Section effective first day of seventh calendar month which begins after July 29, 1970, see section 199(a) of Pub.L. 91–358, set out as a note under section 1257 of this title.

§ 1367. Supplemental jurisdiction

(a) Except as provided in subsections (b) and (c) or as expressly provided otherwise by Federal statute, in any civil action of which the district courts have original jurisdiction, the district courts shall have supplemental jurisdiction over all other claims that are so related to claims in the action within such original jurisdiction that they form part of the same case or controversy under Article III of the United States Constitution. Such supplemental jurisdiction shall include claims that involve the joinder or intervention of additional parties.

(b) In any civil action of which the district courts have original jurisdiction founded solely on section 1332 of this title, the district courts shall not have supplemental jurisdiction under subsection (a) over claims by plaintiffs against persons made parties under Rule 14, 19, 20, or 24 of the Federal Rules of Civil Procedure, or over claims by persons proposed to be joined as plaintiffs under Rule 19 of such rules, or seeking to intervene as plaintiffs under Rule 24 of such rules, when exercising supplemental jurisdiction over such claims would be inconsistent with the jurisdictional requirements of section 1332.

(c) The district courts may decline to exercise supplemental jurisdiction over a claim under subsection (a) if—

(1) the claim raises a novel or complex issue of State law,

(2) the claim substantially predominates over the claim or claims over which the district court has original jurisdiction,

(3) the district court has dismissed all claims over which it has original jurisdiction, or

(4) in exceptional circumstances, there are other compelling reasons for declining jurisdiction.

(d) The period of limitations for any claim asserted under subsection (a), and for any other claim in the same action that is voluntarily dismissed at the same time as or after the dismissal of the claim under subsection (a), shall be tolled while the claim is pending and for a period of 30 days after it is dismissed unless State law provides for a longer tolling period.

(e) As used in this section, the term "State" includes the District of Columbia, the Commonwealth of Puerto Rico, and any territory or possession of the United States.

(Added Pub.L. 101–650, Title III, § 310(a), Dec. 1, 1990, 104 Stat. 5113.)

HISTORICAL AND STATUTORY NOTES

References in Text

The Federal Rules of Civil Procedure, referred to in subsec. (b), are set out in this title.

Effective and Applicability Provisions

1990 Acts

Section 310(c) of Pub.L. 101–650 provided that: "The amendments made by this section [enacting this section] shall apply to civil actions commenced on or after the date of the enactment of this Act [Dec. 1, 1990]."

§ 1368. Counterclaims in unfair practices in international trade.

The district courts shall have original jurisdiction of any civil action based on a counterclaim raised pursuant to section 337(c) of the Tariff Act of 1930, to the extent that it arises out of the transaction or occurrence that is the subject matter of the opposing party's claim in the proceeding under section 337(a) of that Act.

(Added Pub.L. 103–465, Title III, § 321(b)(3)(A), Dec. 8, 1994, 108 Stat. 4946.)

HISTORICAL AND STATUTORY NOTES

References in Text

Section 337 of the Tariff Act of 1930, referred to in text, is section 337 of Act June 17, 1930, c. 497, Title III, 46 Stat. 703, which is classified to section 1337 of Title 19, Customs Duties.

Effective and Applicability Provisions

1994 Acts

Section applicable with respect to complaints filed under section 1337 of Title 19, Customs Duties, on or after the date on which the WTO Agreement enters into force with respect to the United States, Jan. 1, 1995, or in cases under section

1337 of Title 19 in which no complaint is filed, with respect to investigations initiated under such section on or after such date, see section 322 of Pub.L. 103–465, set out as a note under section 1337 of Title 19.

§ 1369. Multiparty, multiforum jurisdiction

(a) In general.—The district courts shall have original jurisdiction of any civil action involving minimal diversity between adverse parties that arises from a single accident, where at least 75 natural persons have died in the accident at a discrete location, if—

(1) a defendant resides in a State and a substantial part of the accident took place in another State or other location, regardless of whether that defendant is also a resident of the State where a substantial part of the accident took place;

(2) any two defendants reside in different States, regardless of whether such defendants are also residents of the same State or States; or

(3) substantial parts of the accident took place in different States.

(b) Limitation of jurisdiction of district courts.—The district court shall abstain from hearing any civil action described in subsection (a) in which—

(1) the substantial majority of all plaintiffs are citizens of a single State of which the primary defendants are also citizens; and

(2) the claims asserted will be governed primarily by the laws of that State.

(c) Special rules and definitions.—For purposes of this section—

(1) minimal diversity exists between adverse parties if any party is a citizen of a State and any adverse party is a citizen of another State, a citizen or subject of a foreign state, or a foreign state as defined in section 1603(a) of this title;

(2) a corporation is deemed to be a citizen of any State, and a citizen or subject of any foreign state, in which it is incorporated or has its principal place of business, and is deemed to be a resident of any

State in which it is incorporated or licensed to do business or is doing business;

(3) the term "injury" means—

(A) physical harm to a natural person; and

(B) physical damage to or destruction of tangible property, but only if physical harm described in subparagraph (A) exists;

(4) the term "accident" means a sudden accident, or a natural event culminating in an accident, that results in death incurred at a discrete location by at least 75 natural persons; and

(5) the term "State" includes the District of Columbia, the Commonwealth of Puerto Rico, and any territory or possession of the United States.

(d) Intervening parties.—In any action in a district court which is or could have been brought, in whole or in part, under this section, any person with a claim arising from the accident described in subsection (a) shall be permitted to intervene as a party plaintiff in the action, even if that person could not have brought an action in a district court as an original matter.

(e) Notification of judicial panel on multidistrict litigation.—A district court in which an action under this section is pending shall promptly notify the judicial panel on multidistrict litigation of the pendency of the action.

(Added Pub.L. 107–273, Div. C, Title I, § 11020(b)(1)(A), Nov. 2, 2002, 116 Stat. 1826.)

HISTORICAL AND STATUTORY NOTES

Effective and Applicability Provisions

2002 Acts

Pub.L. 107–273, Div. C, Title I, § 11020(c), Nov. 2, 2002, 116 Stat. 1829, provided that: "The amendments made by subsection (b) [enacting this section and 28 U.S.C.A. §§ 1697 and 1785 and amending 28 U.S.C.A. §§ 1391 and 1441] shall apply to a civil action if the accident giving rise to the cause of action occurred on or after the 90th day after the date of the enactment of this Act [Nov. 2, 2002]."

CHAPTER 87—DISTRICT COURTS; VENUE

HISTORICAL AND STATUTORY NOTES

Codifications

Amendment by Pub.L. 104–331, § 3(b)(2)(B), Oct. 26, 1996, 110 Stat. 4069, which directed the addition of item 1413 to the end of chapter 37 of this title, was executed by adding item 1413 to the end of this chapter, as the probable intent of Congress.

The table of sections for chapter 87 was amended by Pub.L. 95–598, Title II, § 240(b), Nov. 6, 1978, 92 Stat. 2668, effective June 28, 1984, pursuant to Pub.L. 95–598, Title IV, § 402(b), Nov. 6, 1978, 92 Stat. 2682, as amended by Pub.L. 98–249, § 1(a), Mar. 31, 1984, 98 Stat. 116; Pub.L. 98–271, § 1(a), Apr. 30, 1984, 98 Stat. 163; Pub.L. 98–299, § 1(a), May 25, 1984, 98 Stat. 214; Pub.L. 98–325, § 1(a), June 20, 1984, 98 Stat. 268, set out as an effective dates note preceding section 101 of Title 11, Bankruptcy, by adding "1408, Bankruptcy appeals."

Section 402(b) of Pub.L. 95–598 was amended by section 113 of Pub.L. 98–353, Title 1, July 10, 1984, 98 Stat. 343, by substituting "shall not be effective" for "shall take effect on June 28, 1984," thereby eliminating the amendment by section 240(b) of Pub.L. 95–598, effective June 27, 1984, pursuant to section 122(e) of Pub.L. 98–353, set out as an Effective Date, note under section 151 of this title.

Section 121(a) of Pub.L. 98–353 directed that section 402(b) of Pub.L. 95–598 be amended by substituting "the date of enactment of the Bankruptcy Amendments and Federal Judgeship Act of 1984 [i.e. July 10, 1984]" for "June 28, 1984". This amendment was not executed in view of the prior amendment to section 402(b) of Pub.L. 95–598 by section 113 of Pub.L. 98–353.

Effective and Termination Dates

Pub.L. 105–304, Title V, §§ 502(c)(3), 505, Oct. 28, 1998, 112 Stat. 2917, 2918, provided that effective Oct. 28, 1998 and remaining in effect until the end of the 2-year period beginning on Oct. 28, 1998, the item relating to section 1400 is amended by inserting ", mask works, and designs" after "Patents and copyrights".

§ 1391. Venue generally

(a) A civil action wherein jurisdiction is founded only on diversity of citizenship may, except as otherwise provided by law, be brought only in (1) a judicial district where any defendant resides, if all defendants reside in the same State, (2) a judicial district in which a substantial part of the events or omissions giving rise to the claim occurred, or a substantial part of property that is the subject of the action is situated, or (3) a judicial district in which any defendant is subject to personal jurisdiction at the time the action is commenced, if there is no district in which the action may otherwise be brought.

(b) A civil action wherein jurisdiction is not founded solely on diversity of citizenship may, except as otherwise provided by law, be brought only in (1) a judicial district where any defendant resides, if all defendants reside in the same State, (2) a judicial district in which a substantial part of the events or omissions giving rise to the claim occurred, or a substantial part of property that is the subject of the action is situated, or (3) a judicial district in which any defendant may be found, if there is no district in which the action may otherwise be brought.

(c) For purposes of venue under this chapter, a defendant that is a corporation shall be deemed to reside in any judicial district in which it is subject to personal jurisdiction at the time the action is commenced. In a State which has more than one judicial district and in which a defendant that is a corporation is subject to personal jurisdiction at the time an action is commenced, such corporation shall be deemed to reside in any district in that State within which its contacts would be sufficient to subject it to personal jurisdiction if that district were a separate State, and, if there is no such district, the corporation shall be deemed to reside in the district within which it has the most significant contacts.

(d) An alien may be sued in any district.

(e) A civil action in which a defendant is an officer or employee of the United States or any agency thereof acting in his official capacity or under color of legal authority, or an agency of the United States, or the United States, may, except as otherwise provided by law, be brought in any judicial district in which (1) a defendant in the action resides, (2) a substantial part of the events or omissions giving rise to the claim occurred, or a substantial part of property that is the subject of the action is situated, or (3) the plaintiff resides if no real property is involved in the action. Additional persons may be joined as parties to any such action in accordance with the Federal Rules of Civil Procedure and with such other venue requirements as would be applicable if the United States or one of its officers, employees, or agencies were not a party.

The summons and complaint in such an action shall be served as provided by the Federal Rules of Civil Procedure except that the delivery of the summons and complaint to the officer or agency as required by the rules may be made by certified mail beyond the territorial limits of the district in which the action is brought.

(f) A civil action against a foreign state as defined in section 1603(a) of this title may be brought—

(1) in any judicial district in which a substantial part of the events or omissions giving rise to the claim occurred, or a substantial part of property that is the subject of the action is situated;

(2) in any judicial district in which the vessel or cargo of a foreign state is situated, if the claim is asserted under section 1605(b) of this title;

(3) in any judicial district in which the agency or instrumentality is licensed to do business or is doing business, if the action is brought against an agency or instrumentality of a foreign state as defined in section 1603(b) of this title; or

(4) in the United States District Court for the District of Columbia if the action is brought against a foreign state or political subdivision thereof.

(g) A civil action in which jurisdiction of the district court is based upon section 1369 of this title may be brought in any district in which any defendant resides or in which a substantial part of the accident giving rise to the action took place.

(June 25, 1948, c. 646, 62 Stat. 935; Oct. 5, 1962, Pub.L. 87–748, § 2, 76 Stat. 744; Dec. 23, 1963, Pub.L. 88–234, 77 Stat. 473; Nov. 2, 1966, Pub.L. 89–714, §§ 1, 2, 80 Stat. 1111; Oct. 21, 1976, Pub.L. 94–574, § 3, 90 Stat. 2721; Oct. 21, 1976, Pub.L. 94–583, § 5, 90 Stat. 2897; Nov. 19, 1988, Pub.L. 100–702, Title X, § 1013(a), 102 Stat. 4669; Dec. 1, 1990, Pub.L. 101–650, Title III, § 311, 104 Stat. 5114; Dec. 9, 1991, Pub.L. 102–198, § 3, 105 Stat. 1623; Oct. 29, 1992, Pub.L. 102–572, Title V, § 504, 106 Stat. 4513; Oct. 3, 1995, Pub.L. 104–34, § 1, 109 Stat. 293; Nov. 2, 2002, Pub.L. 107–273, Div. C, Title I, § 11020(b)(2), 116 Stat. 1827.)

HISTORICAL AND STATUTORY NOTES

References in Text

The Federal Rules of Civil Procedure, referred to in subsec. (e), are set out in this title.

Effective and Applicability Provisions

2002 Acts

Amendments by section 11020(b) of Pub.L. 107–273 shall apply to a civil action if the accident giving rise to the cause of action occurred on or after the 90th day after Nov. 2, 2002, see section 11020(c) of Pub.L. 107–273, set out as a note under 28 U.S.C.A. § 1369.

1992 Acts

Amendment by Pub.L. 102–572 effective Jan. 1, 1993, see section 1101(a) of Pub.L. 102–572, set out as a note under section 905 of Title 2, The Congress.

1988 Acts

Section 1013(b) of Title X of Pub.L. 100–702 provided that: "The amendment made by this section [amending this section] takes effect 90 days after the date of enactment of this title [Nov. 19, 1988]."

1976 Acts

Amendment by Pub.L. 94–583 effective 90 days after Oct. 21, 1976, see section 8 of Pub.L. 94–583, set out as a note under section 1602 of this title.

§ 1392. Defendants or property in different districts in same State

Any civil action, of a local nature, involving property located in different districts in the same State, may be brought in any of such districts.

(June 25, 1948, c. 646, 62 Stat. 935; Oct. 1, 1996, Pub.L. 104–220, § 1, 110 Stat. 3023.)

[§ 1393. Repealed. Pub.L. 100–702, Title X, § 1001(a), Nov. 19, 1988, 102 Stat. 4664]

HISTORICAL AND STATUTORY NOTES

Section, Act June 25, 1948, c. 646, 62 Stat. 935, related to divisional venue in civil cases of a single defendant or defendants in different divisions.

Effective Date of Repeal

Section 1001(b) of Pub.L. 100–702 provided that "The amendments made by this section [repealing this section] take effect 90 days after the date of enactment of this Act [Nov. 19, 1988]."

§ 1394. Banking association's action against Comptroller of Currency

Any civil action by a national banking association to enjoin the Comptroller of the Currency, under the provisions of any Act of Congress relating to such associations, may be prosecuted in the judicial district where such association is located.

(June 25, 1948, c. 646, 62 Stat. 935.)

HISTORICAL AND STATUTORY NOTES

Exception as to Transfer of Functions

Functions vested by any provision of law in the Comptroller of the Currency, referred to in this section, were not included in the transfer of functions of officers, agencies and employees of the Department of the Treasury to the Secretary of the Treasury, made by Reorg. Plan No. 26 of 1950, § 1, eff. July 31, 1950, 15 F.R. 4935, 64 Stat. 1280. See section 321(c)(2) of Title 31, Money and Finance.

§ 1395. Fine, penalty or forfeiture

(a) A civil proceeding for the recovery of a pecuniary fine, penalty or forfeiture may be prosecuted in the district where it accrues or the defendant is found.

(b) A civil proceeding for the forfeiture of property may be prosecuted in any district where such property is found.

(c) A civil proceeding for the forfeiture of property seized outside any judicial district may be prosecuted in any district into which the property is brought.

(d) A proceeding in admiralty for the enforcement of fines, penalties and forfeitures against a vessel may be brought in any district in which the vessel is arrested.

(e) Any proceeding for the forfeiture of a vessel or cargo entering a port of entry closed by the President in pursuance of law, or of goods and chattels coming from a State or section declared by proclamation of the President to be in insurrection, or of any vessel or vehicle conveying persons or property to or from such State or section or belonging in whole or in part to a resident thereof, may be prosecuted in any district

into which the property is taken and in which the proceeding is instituted.

(June 25, 1948, c. 646, 62 Stat. 936.)

HISTORICAL AND STATUTORY NOTES

Senate Revision Amendment

While section 3745(c) of Title 26, U.S.C., Internal Revenue Code, is one of the sources of this section, it was eliminated from the schedule of repeals by Senate amendment. Therefore, such section 3745(c) remains in Title 26. See 80th Congress Senate Report No. 1559.

Said section 3745(c) was subsequently repealed by Act May 24, 1949, c. 139, § 142, 63 Stat. 110.

§ 1396. Internal revenue taxes

Any civil action for the collection of internal revenue taxes may be brought in the district where the liability for such tax accrues, in the district of the taxpayer's residence, or in the district where the return was filed.

(June 25, 1948, c. 646, 62 Stat. 936.)

HISTORICAL AND STATUTORY NOTES

Senate Revision Amendment

While section 3744 of Title 26, U.S.C., Internal Revenue Code [1939], is one of the sources of this section, it was eliminated from the schedule of repeals by Senate amendment. Therefore, it remains in Title 26 [I.R.C.1939]. See 80th Congress Senate Report No. 1559.

Said section 3744 was subsequently repealed by Act May 24, 1949, c. 139, § 142, 63 Stat. 110.

§ 1397. Interpleader

Any civil action of interpleader or in the nature of interpleader under section 1335 of this title may be brought in the judicial district in which one or more of the claimants reside.

(June 25, 1948, c. 646, 62 Stat. 936.)

§ 1398. Interstate Commerce Commission's orders

(a) Except as otherwise provided by law, a civil action brought under section 1336(a) of this title shall be brought only in a judicial district in which any of the parties bringing the action resides or has its principal office.

(b) A civil action to enforce, enjoin, set aside, annul, or suspend, in whole or in part, an order of the Interstate Commerce Commission made pursuant to the referral of a question or issue by a district court or by the United States Court of Federal Claims, shall be brought only in the court which referred the question or issue.

(June 25, 1948, c. 646, 62 Stat. 936; Aug. 30, 1964, Pub.L. 88–513, § 2, 78 Stat. 695; Jan. 2, 1975, Pub.L. 93–584, § 2, 88 Stat. 1917; Apr. 2, 1982, Pub.L. 97–164, Title I, § 130, 96 Stat. 39; Oct. 29, 1992, Pub.L. 102–572, Title IX, § 902(b)(1), 106 Stat. 4516.)

HISTORICAL AND STATUTORY NOTES

Effective and Applicability Provisions

1992 Acts

Amendment by Pub.L. 102–572 effective Oct. 29, 1992, see section 911 of Pub.L. 102–572, set out as a note under section 171 of this title.

1982 Acts

Amendment by Pub.L. 97–164 effective Oct. 1, 1982, see section 402 of Pub.L. 97–164, set out as a note under section 171 of this title.

1975 Acts

Amendment by Pub.L. 93–584 not applicable to actions commenced on or before the last day of the first month beginning after Jan. 2, 1975, and actions to enjoin or suspend orders of the Interstate Commerce Commission which are pending when this amendment becomes effective shall not be affected thereby, but shall proceed to final disposition under the law existing on the date they were commenced, see section 10 of Pub.L. 93–584, set out as a note under section 2321 of this title.

Abolition of Interstate Commerce Commission and Transfer of Functions

Interstate Commerce Commission abolished and functions of Commission transferred, except as otherwise provided in Pub.L. 104–88, to Surface Transportation Board effective Jan. 1, 1996, by sections 702 of Title 49, Transportation, and section 101 of Pub.L. 104–88, set out as a note under section 701 of title 49. References to Interstate Commerce Commission deemed to refer to Surface Transportation Board, a member or employee of the Board, or Secretary of Transportation, as appropriate, see section 205 of Pub.L. 104–88, set out as a note under section 701 of Title 49.

§ 1399. Partition action involving United States

Any civil action by any tenant in common or joint tenant for the partition of lands, where the United States is one of the tenants in common or joint tenants, may be brought only in the judicial district where such lands are located or, if located in different districts in the same State, in any of such districts.

(June 25, 1948, c. 646, 62 Stat. 936.)

§ 1400. Patents and copyrights, mask works, and designs

(a) Civil actions, suits, or proceedings arising under any Act of Congress relating to copyrights or exclusive rights in mask works or designs may be instituted in the district in which the defendant or his agent resides or may be found.

(b) Any civil action for patent infringement may be brought in the judicial district where the defendant resides, or where the defendant has committed acts of infringement and has a regular and established place of business.

(June 25, 1948, c. 646, 62 Stat. 936; Nov. 19, 1988, Pub.L. 100–702, Title X, § 1020(a)(5), 102 Stat. 4671; Oct. 28, 1998,

Pub.L. 105–304, Title V, § 503(c)(1), (2), 112 Stat. 2917; Aug. 5, 1999, Pub.L. 106–44, § 2(a), 113 Stat. 223.)

HISTORICAL AND STATUTORY NOTES

Senate Revision Amendment

Title 17 of the United States Code was enacted into positive law by Act July 30, 1947, c. 391, 61 Stat. 652, and, in such enactment, section 35 of the prior title became section 111 of the new title, and all Acts from which sections of the prior title had been derived, were repealed. Therefore, this paragraph should read: "Based on Title 28, U.S.C., 1940 ed., § 109 (Mar. 3, 1911, c. 231, § 48, 36 Stat. 1100), and section 111 of Title 17, U.S.C., 1946 ed., Copyrights." By Senate amendment, section 111 of Title 17 U.S.C., is included in the schedule of repeals. See 80th Congress Senate Report No. 1559.

1988 Acts

House Report No. 100–889, see 1988 U.S. Code Cong. and Adm. News, p. 5982.

1998 Acts

House Conference Report No. 105–796 and Statement by President, see 1998 U.S. Code Cong. and Adm. News, p. 645.

Effective and Applicability Provisions

1998 Acts

Amendment by Pub.L. 105–304, effective Oct. 28, 1998, see section 505 of Pub.L. 105–304, set out as a note under section 1301 of Title 17, Copyrights.

§ 1401. Stockholder's derivative action

Any civil action by a stockholder on behalf of his corporation may be prosecuted in any judicial district where the corporation might have sued the same defendants.

(June 25, 1948, c. 646, 62 Stat. 936.)

§ 1402. United States as defendant

(a) Any civil action in a district court against the United States under subsection (a) of section 1346 of this title may be prosecuted only:

(1) Except as provided in paragraph (2), in the judicial district where the plaintiff resides;

(2) In the case of a civil action by a corporation under paragraph (1) of subsection (a) of section 1346, in the judicial district in which is located the principal place of business or principal office or agency of the corporation; or if it has no principal place of business or principal office or agency in any judicial district (A) in the judicial district in which is located the office to which was made the return of the tax in respect of which the claim is made, or (B) if no return was made, in the judicial district in which lies the District of Columbia. Notwithstanding the foregoing provisions of this paragraph a district court, for the convenience of the parties and witnesses, in the interest of justice, may transfer any such action to any other district or division.

(b) Any civil action on a tort claim against the United States under subsection (b) of section 1346 of this title may be prosecuted only in the judicial district where the plaintiff resides or wherein the act or omission complained of occurred.

(c) Any civil action against the United States under subsection (e) of section 1346 of this title may be prosecuted only in the judicial district where the property is situated at the time of levy, or if no levy is made, in the judicial district in which the event occurred which gave rise to the cause of action.

(d) Any civil action under section 2409a to quiet title to an estate or interest in real property in which an interest is claimed by the United States shall be brought in the district court of the district where the property is located or, if located in different districts, in any of such districts.

(June 25, 1948, c. 646, 62 Stat. 937; Sept. 2, 1958, Pub.L. 85–920, 72 Stat. 1770; Nov. 2, 1966, Pub.L. 89–719, Title II, § 202(b), 80 Stat. 1149; Oct. 25, 1972, Pub.L. 92–562, § 2, 86 Stat. 1176; Apr. 2, 1982, Pub.L. 97–164, Title I, § 131, 96 Stat. 39.)

HISTORICAL AND STATUTORY NOTES

Effective and Applicability Provisions

1982 Acts

Amendment by Pub.L. 97–164 effective Oct. 1, 1982, see section 402 of Pub.L. 97–164, set out as a note under section 171 of this title.

1966 Acts

Subsec. (c) of this section applicable after Nov. 2, 1966, see section 203 of Pub.L. 89–719, set out as a note under section 1346 of this title.

§ 1403. Eminent domain

Proceedings to condemn real estate for the use of the United States or its departments or agencies shall be brought in the district court of the district where the land is located or, if located in different districts in the same State, in any of such districts.

(June 25, 1948, c. 646, 62 Stat. 937.)

§ 1404. Change of venue

(a) For the convenience of parties and witnesses, in the interest of justice, a district court may transfer any civil action to any other district or division where it might have been brought.

(b) Upon motion, consent or stipulation of all parties, any action, suit or proceeding of a civil nature or any motion or hearing thereof, may be transferred, in the discretion of the court, from the division in which pending to any other division in the same district. Transfer of proceedings in rem brought by or on behalf of the United States may be transferred under this section without the consent of the United States where all other parties request transfer.

(c) A district court may order any civil action to be tried at any place within the division in which it is pending.

(d) As used in this section, the term "district court" includes the District Court of Guam, the District Court for the Northern Mariana Islands, and the District Court of the Virgin Islands, and the term "district" includes the territorial jurisdiction of each such court.

(June 25, 1948, c. 646, 62 Stat. 937; Oct. 18, 1962, Pub.L. 87–845, § 9, 76A Stat. 699; Oct. 19, 1996, Pub.L. 104–317, Title VI, § 610(a), 110 Stat. 3860.)

HISTORICAL AND STATUTORY NOTES

Effective and Applicability Provisions

1996 Acts

Section 610(c) of Pub.L. 104–317 provided that: " The amendments made by this section [amending this section and section 1406 of this title] apply to cases pending on the date of the enactment of this Act [Oct. 19, 1996] and to cases commenced on or after such date."

1962 Acts

Amendment of section by Pub.L. 87–845 effective Jan. 2, 1963, see section 25 of Pub.L. 87–845, set out as a note under section 14 of Title 18, Crimes and Criminal Procedure.

Termination of United States District Court for the District of the Canal Zone

For termination of the United States District Court for the District of the Canal Zone at end of the "transition period", being the 30–month period beginning Oct. 1, 1979, and ending midnight Mar. 31, 1982, see Paragraph 5 of Article XI of the Panama Canal Treaty of 1977 and sections 3831 and 3841 to 3843 of Title 22, Foreign Relations and Intercourse.

§ 1405. Creation or alteration of district or division

Actions or proceedings pending at the time of the creation of a new district or division or transfer of a county or territory from one division or district to another may be tried in the district or division as it existed at the institution of the action or proceeding, or in the district or division so created or to which the county or territory is so transferred as the parties shall agree or the court direct.

(June 25, 1948, c. 646, 62 Stat. 937.)

§ 1406. Cure or waiver of defects

(a) The district court of a district in which is filed a case laying venue in the wrong division or district shall dismiss, or if it be in the interest of justice, transfer such case to any district or division in which it could have been brought.

(b) Nothing in this chapter shall impair the jurisdiction of a district court of any matter involving a party who does not interpose timely and sufficient objection to the venue.

(c) As used in this section, the term "district court" includes the District Court of Guam, the District Court for the Northern Mariana Islands, and the District Court of the Virgin Islands, and the term "district" includes the territorial jurisdiction of each such court.

(June 25, 1948, c. 646, 62 Stat. 937; May 24, 1949, c. 139, § 81, 63 Stat. 101; Sept. 13, 1960, Pub.L. 86–770, § 1, 74 Stat. 912; Oct. 18, 1962, Pub.L. 87–845, § 10, 76A Stat. 699; Apr. 2, 1982, Pub.L. 97–164, Title I, § 132, 96 Stat. 39; Oct. 19, 1996, Pub.L. 104–317, Title VI, § 610(b), 110 Stat. 3860.)

HISTORICAL AND STATUTORY NOTES

Effective and Applicability Provisions

1996 Acts

Amendment by section 610(b) of Pub.L. 104–317 to apply to cases pending on Oct. 19, 1996, and to cases commenced on or after such date, see section 610(c) of Pub.L. 104–317, set out as a note under section 1404 of this title.

1982 Acts

Amendment by Pub.L. 97–164 effective Oct. 1, 1982, see section 402 of Pub.L. 97–164, set out as a note under section 171 of this title.

1962 Acts

Amendment of section by Pub.L. 87–845 effective Jan. 2, 1963, see section 25 of Pub.L. 87–845, set out as a note under section 14 of Title 18, Crimes and Criminal Procedure.

1960 Acts

Section 4 of Pub.L. 86–770 provided in part that: "The amendments made by sections 1 and 2 of this Act [adding subsec. (c) of this section and section 1506 of this title] shall apply to any case or proceeding pending on, or brought after, the date of enactment of this Act [Sept. 13, 1960] in the district courts or the Court of Claims."

Termination of United States District Court for the District of the Canal Zone

For termination of the United States District Court for the District of the Canal Zone at end of the "transition period", being the 30–month period beginning Oct. 1, 1979, and ending midnight Mar. 31, 1982, see Paragraph 5 of Article XI of the Panama Canal Treaty of 1977 and sections 3831 and 3841 to 3843 of Title 22, Foreign Relations and Intercourse.

§ 1407. Multidistrict litigation

(a) When civil actions involving one or more common questions of fact are pending in different districts, such actions may be transferred to any district for coordinated or consolidated pretrial proceedings. Such transfers shall be made by the judicial panel on multidistrict litigation authorized by this section upon its determination that transfers for such proceedings will be for the convenience of parties and witnesses and will promote the just and efficient conduct of such actions. Each action so transferred shall be remanded by the panel at or before the conclusion of such pretrial proceedings to the district from which it was transferred unless it shall have been previously terminated: *Provided, however,* That the panel may separate any claim, cross-claim, counter-claim, or third-

party claim and remand any of such claims before the remainder of the action is remanded.

(b) Such coordinated or consolidated pretrial proceedings shall be conducted by a judge or judges to whom such actions are assigned by the judicial panel on multidistrict litigation. For this purpose, upon request of the panel, a circuit judge or a district judge may be designated and assigned temporarily for service in the transferee district by the Chief Justice of the United States or the chief judge of the circuit, as may be required, in accordance with the provisions of chapter 13 of this title. With the consent of the transferee district court, such actions may be assigned by the panel to a judge or judges of such district. The judge or judges to whom such actions are assigned, the members of the judicial panel on multidistrict litigation, and other circuit and district judges designated when needed by the panel may exercise the powers of a district judge in any district for the purpose of conducting pretrial depositions in such coordinated or consolidated pretrial proceedings.

(c) Proceedings for the transfer of an action under this section may be initiated by—

(i) the judicial panel on multidistrict litigation upon its own initiative, or

(ii) motion filed with the panel by a party in any action in which transfer for coordinated or consolidated pretrial proceedings under this section may be appropriate. A copy of such motion shall be filed in the district court in which the moving party's action is pending.

The panel shall give notice to the parties in all actions in which transfers for coordinated or consolidated pretrial proceedings are contemplated, and such notice shall specify the time and place of any hearing to determine whether such transfer shall be made. Orders of the panel to set a hearing and other orders of the panel issued prior to the order either directing or denying transfer shall be filed in the office of the clerk of the district court in which a transfer hearing is to be or has been held. The panel's order of transfer shall be based upon a record of such hearing at which material evidence may be offered by any party to an action pending in any district that would be affected by the proceedings under this section, and shall be supported by findings of fact and conclusions of law based upon such record. Orders of transfer and such other orders as the panel may make thereafter shall be filed in the office of the clerk of the district court of the transferee district and shall be effective when thus filed. The clerk of the transferee district court shall forthwith transmit a certified copy of the panel's order to transfer to the clerk of the district court from which the action is being transferred. An order denying transfer shall be filed in each district wherein there is a case pending in which the motion for transfer has been made.

(d) The judicial panel on multidistrict litigation shall consist of seven circuit and district judges designated from time to time by the Chief Justice of the United States, no two of whom shall be from the same circuit. The concurrence of four members shall be necessary to any action by the panel.

(e) No proceedings for review of any order of the panel may be permitted except by extraordinary writ pursuant to the provisions of title 28, section 1651, United States Code. Petitions for an extraordinary writ to review an order of the panel to set a transfer hearing and other orders of the panel issued prior to the order either directing or denying transfer shall be filed only in the court of appeals having jurisdiction over the district in which a hearing is to be or has been held. Petitions for an extraordinary writ to review an order to transfer or orders subsequent to transfer shall be filed only in the court of appeals having jurisdiction over the transferee district. There shall be no appeal or review of an order of the panel denying a motion to transfer for consolidated or coordinated proceedings.

(f) The panel may prescribe rules for the conduct of its business not inconsistent with Acts of Congress and the Federal Rules of Civil Procedure.

(g) Nothing in this section shall apply to any action in which the United States is a complainant arising under the antitrust laws. "Antitrust laws" as used herein include those acts referred to in the Act of October 15, 1914, as amended (38 Stat. 730; 15 U.S.C. 12), and also include the Act of June 19, 1936 (49 Stat. 1526; 15 U.S.C. 13, 13a, and 13b) and the Act of September 26, 1914, as added March 21, 1938 (52 Stat. 116, 117; 15 U.S.C. 56); but shall not include section 4A of the Act of October 15, 1914, as added July 7, 1955 (69 Stat. 282; 15 U.S.C. 15a).

(h) Notwithstanding the provisions of section 1404 or subsection (f) of this section, the judicial panel on multidistrict litigation may consolidate and transfer with or without the consent of the parties, for both pretrial purposes and for trial, any action brought under section 4C of the Clayton Act.

(Added Pub.L. 90–296, § 1, Apr. 29, 1968, 82 Stat. 109, and amended Pub.L. 94–435, Title III, § 303, Sept. 30, 1976, 90 Stat. 1396.)

HISTORICAL AND STATUTORY NOTES

References in Text

The Federal Rules of Civil Procedure, referred to in subsec. (f), are set out in this title.

Section 4C of the Clayton Act, referred to in subsec. (h), is section 4C of Act Oct. 15, 1914, c. 323, as added by Pub.L. 94–435, Title III, § 301, Sept. 30, 1976, 90 Stat. 1394, which is classified to section 15c of Title 15, Commerce and Trade.

§ 1408. Venue of cases under title 11

Except as provided in section 1410 of this title, a case under title 11 may be commenced in the district court for the district—

(1) in which the domicile, residence, principal place of business in the United States, or principal assets in the United States, of the person or entity that is the subject of such case have been located for the one hundred and eighty days immediately preceding such commencement, or for a longer portion of such one-hundred-and-eighty-day period than the domicile, residence, or principal place of business, in the United States, or principal assets in the United States, of such person were located in any other district; or

(2) in which there is pending a case under title 11 concerning such person's affiliate, general partner, or partnership.

(Added Pub.L. 98–353, Title I, § 102(a), July 10, 1984, 98 Stat. 334.)

HISTORICAL AND STATUTORY NOTES

Effective and Applicability Provisions

1984 Acts

Section effective July 10, 1984, see section 122(a) of Pub.L. 98–353, set out as a note under section 151 of this title.

Prior Provisions

A prior section 1408, added by Pub.L. 95–598, Title II, § 240(a), Nov. 6, 1978, 92 Stat. 2668, which related to bankruptcy appeals, did not become effective pursuant to section 402(b) of Pub.L. 95–598, as amended, set out as an Effective and Applicability Provisions note preceding section 101 of Title 11, Bankruptcy.

§ 1409. Venue of proceedings arising under title 11 or arising in or related to cases under title 11

(a) Except as otherwise provided in subsections (b) and (d), a proceeding arising under title 11 or arising in or related to a case under title 11 may be commenced in the district court in which such case is pending.

(b) Except as provided in subsection (d) of this section, a trustee in a case under title 11 may commence a proceeding arising in or related to such case to recover a money judgment of or property worth less than $1,100 [1] or a consumer debt of less than $16,425 [1], or a debt (excluding a consumer debt) against a noninsider of less than $10,950 [1], only in the district court for the district in which the defendant resides.

(c) Except as provided in subsection (b) of this section, a trustee in a case under title 11 may commence a proceeding arising in or related to such case as statutory successor to the debtor or creditors under section 541 or 544(b) of title 11 in the district court for the district where the State or Federal court sits in which, under applicable nonbankruptcy venue provisions, the debtor or creditors, as the case may be, may have commenced an action on which such proceeding is based if the case under title 11 had not been commenced.

(d) A trustee may commence a proceeding arising under title 11 or arising in or related to a case under title 11 based on a claim arising after the commencement of such case from the operation of the business of the debtor only in the district court for the district where a State or Federal court sits in which, under applicable nonbankruptcy venue provisions, an action on such claim may have been brought.

(e) A proceeding arising under title 11 or arising in or related to a case under title 11, based on a claim arising after the commencement of such case from the operation of the business of the debtor, may be commenced against the representative of the estate in such case in the district court for the district where the State or Federal court sits in which the party commencing such proceeding may, under applicable nonbankruptcy venue provisions, have brought an action on such claim, or in the district court in which such case is pending.

(Added Pub.L. 98–353, Title I, § 102(a), July 10, 1984, 98 Stat. 334, and amended Pub.L. 109–8, Title IV, § 410, Apr. 20, 2005, 119 Stat. 106.)

[1] Dollar amount as adjusted by the Judicial Conference of the United States. See Adjustment of Dollar Amounts notes set out under this section and 11 U.S.C.A. § 104.

HISTORICAL AND STATUTORY NOTES

Effective and Applicability Provisions

2007 Acts

Increase of dollar amounts by Judicial Conference of the United States by notice published Feb. 14, 2007, 72 F.R. 7082 effective April 1, 2007, and increase not applicable to cases commenced before the effective date of the adjustments, i.e., April 1, 2007. See Adjustment of Dollar Amounts notes under 11 U.S.C.A. § 104 and this section.

2005 Acts

Except as otherwise provided, amendments by Pub.L. 109–8 effective 180 days after April 20, 2005, and inapplicable with respect to cases commenced under Title 11 before the effective date, see Pub.L. 109–8, § 1501, set out as a note under 11 U.S.C.A. § 101.

1984 Acts

Section effective July 10, 1984, see section 122(a) of Pub.L. 98–353, set out as a note under section 151 of this title.

Adjustment of Dollar Amounts

For adjustment of dollar amounts specified in subsec. (b) of this section by the Judicial Conference of the United States, effective Apr. 1, 2007, see note set out under 11 U.S.C.A. § 104.

By notice published Feb. 14, 2007, 72 F.R. 7082, the Judicial Conference of the United States adjusted the dollar

amounts in provisions specified in subsec. (b) of this section, effective Apr. 1, 2007, as follows:

Adjusted $1,000 to $1,100.

Adjusted $15,000 to $16,425.

Adjusted $10,000 to $10,950.

§ 1410. Venue of cases ancillary to foreign proceedings

A case under chapter 15 of title 11 may be commenced in the district court of the United States for the district—

(1) in which the debtor has its principal place of business or principal assets in the United States;

(2) if the debtor does not have a place of business or assets in the United States, in which there is pending against the debtor an action or proceeding in a Federal or State court; or

(3) in a case other than those specified in paragraph (1) or (2), in which venue will be consistent with the interests of justice and the convenience of the parties, having regard to the relief sought by the foreign representative.

(Added Pub.L. 98–353, Title I, § 102(a), July 10, 1984, 98 Stat. 335, and amended Pub.L. 109–8, Title VIII, § 802(c)(4), Apr. 20, 2005, 119 Stat. 146.)

HISTORICAL AND STATUTORY NOTES

References in Text

Chapter 15 of title 11, referred to in text, is 11 U.S.C.A. § 1501 et seq.

Effective and Applicability Provisions

2005 Acts

Except as otherwise provided, amendments by Pub.L. 109–8 effective 180 days after April 20, 2005, and inapplicable with respect to cases commenced under Title 11 before the effective date, see Pub.L. 109–8, § 1501, set out as a note under 11 U.S.C.A. § 101.

1984 Acts

Section effective July 10, 1984, see section 122(a) of Pub.L. 98–353, set out as a note under section 151 of this title.

§ 1411. Jury trials

(a) Except as provided in subsection (b) of this section, this chapter and title 11 do not affect any right to trial by jury that an individual has under applicable nonbankruptcy law with regard to a personal injury or wrongful death tort claim.

(b) The district court may order the issues arising under section 303 of title 11 to be tried without a jury.

(Added Pub.L. 98–353, Title I, § 102(a), July 10, 1984, 98 Stat. 335.)

HISTORICAL AND STATUTORY NOTES

Effective and Applicability Provisions

1984 Acts

Section, except subsec. (a), effective July 10, 1984, see section 122(a) of Pub.L. 98–353, set out as a note under section 151 of this title.

Subsec. (a) not applicable with respect to cases under Title 11, Bankruptcy, that are pending on July 10, 1984, or to proceedings arising in or related to such cases, see section 122(b) of Pub.L. 98–353, set out as a note under section 151 of this title.

§ 1412. Change of venue

A district court may transfer a case or proceeding under title 11 to a district court for another district, in the interest of justice or for the convenience of the parties.

(Added Pub.L. 98–353, Title I, § 102(a), July 10, 1984, 98 Stat. 335.)

HISTORICAL AND STATUTORY NOTES

Effective and Applicability Provisions

1984 Acts

Section effective July 10, 1984, see section 122(a) of Pub.L. 98–353, set out as a note under section 151 of this title.

§ 1413. Venue of cases under chapter 5 of title 3

Notwithstanding the preceding provisions of this chapter, a civil action under section 1346(g) may be brought in the United States district court for the district in which the employee is employed or in the United States District Court for the District of Columbia.

(Added Pub.L. 104–331, § 3(b)(2)(A), Oct. 26, 1996, 110 Stat. 4069.)

HISTORICAL AND STATUTORY NOTES

Codifications

Amendment by Pub.L. 104–331, § 3(b)(2)(A), which directed the addition of this section to the end of chapter 37 of this title, was executed by adding this section to the end of this chapter, as the probable intent of Congress.

Effective and Applicability Provisions

1996 Acts

Amendment by Pub.L. 104–331, § 3(b)(2)(B), effective October 1, 1997, see section 3(d) of Pub.L. 104–331, set out as a note under section 1296 of this title.

CHAPTER 89—DISTRICT COURTS; REMOVAL OF CASES FROM STATE COURTS

¹ So in original. Does not conform to section catchline.

§ 1441. Actions removable generally

(a) Except as otherwise expressly provided by Act of Congress, any civil action brought in a State court of which the district courts of the United States have original jurisdiction, may be removed by the defendant or the defendants, to the district court of the United States for the district and division embracing the place where such action is pending. For purposes of removal under this chapter, the citizenship of defendants sued under fictitious names shall be disregarded.

(b) Any civil action of which the district courts have original jurisdiction founded on a claim or right arising under the Constitution, treaties or laws of the United States shall be removable without regard to the citizenship or residence of the parties. Any other such action shall be removable only if none of the parties in interest properly joined and served as defendants is a citizen of the State in which such action is brought.

(c) Whenever a separate and independent claim or cause of action within the jurisdiction conferred by section 1331 of this title is joined with one or more otherwise non-removable claims or causes of action, the entire case may be removed and the district court may determine all issues therein, or, in its discretion, may remand all matters in which State law predominates.

(d) Any civil action brought in a State court against a foreign state as defined in section 1603(a) of this title may be removed by the foreign state to the district court of the United States for the district and division embracing the place where such action is pending. Upon removal the action shall be tried by the court without jury. Where removal is based upon this subsection, the time limitations of section 1446(b) of this chapter may be enlarged at any time for cause shown.

(e)(1) Notwithstanding the provisions of subsection (b) of this section, a defendant in a civil action in a State court may remove the action to the district court of the United States for the district and division embracing the place where the action is pending if—

(A) the action could have been brought in a United States district court under section 1369 of this title; or

(B) the defendant is a party to an action which is or could have been brought, in whole or in part, under section 1369 in a United States district court and arises from the same accident as the action in State court, even if the action to be removed could not have been brought in a district court as an original matter.

The removal of an action under this subsection shall be made in accordance with section 1446 of this title, except that a notice of removal may also be filed before trial of the action in State court within 30 days after the date on which the defendant first becomes a party to an action under section 1369 in a United States district court that arises from the same accident as the action in State court, or at a later time with leave of the district court.

(2) Whenever an action is removed under this subsection and the district court to which it is removed or transferred under section 1407(j) has made a liability determination requiring further proceedings as to damages, the district court shall remand the action to the State court from which it had been removed for the determination of damages, unless the court finds that, for the convenience of parties and witnesses and in the interest of justice, the action should be retained for the determination of damages.

(3) Any remand under paragraph (2) shall not be effective until 60 days after the district court has issued an order determining liability and has certified its intention to remand the removed action for the determination of damages. An appeal with respect to the liability determination of the district court may be taken during that 60–day period to the court of appeals with appellate jurisdiction over the district court. In the event a party files such an appeal, the remand shall not be effective until the appeal has been finally disposed of. Once the remand has become effective, the liability determination shall not be subject to further review by appeal or otherwise.

(4) Any decision under this subsection concerning remand for the determination of damages shall not be reviewable by appeal or otherwise.

(5) An action removed under this subsection shall be deemed to be an action under section 1369 and an action in which jurisdiction is based on section 1369 of this title for purposes of this section and sections 1407, 1697, and 1785 of this title.

(6) Nothing in this subsection shall restrict the authority of the district court to transfer or dismiss an action on the ground of inconvenient forum.

(f) The court to which a civil action is removed under this section is not precluded from hearing and

determining any claim in such civil action because the State court from which such civil action is removed did not have jurisdiction over that claim.

(June 25, 1948, c. 646, 62 Stat. 937; Oct. 21, 1976, Pub.L. 94–583, § 6, 90 Stat. 2898; June 19, 1986, Pub.L. 99–336, § 3(a), 100 Stat. 637; Nov. 19, 1988, Pub.L. 100–702, Title X, § 1016(a), 102 Stat. 4669; Dec. 1, 1990, Pub.L. 101–650, Title III, § 312, 104 Stat. 5114; Dec. 9, 1991, Pub.L. 102–198, § 4, 105 Stat. 1623; Nov. 2, 2002, Pub.L. 107–273, Div. C, Title I, § 11020(b)(3), 116 Stat. 1827.)

HISTORICAL AND STATUTORY NOTES

References in Text

Section 1407(j) of Title 28, referred to in subsec. (e)(2), does not exist.

Effective and Applicability Provisions

2002 Acts

Amendments by section 11020(b) of Pub.L. 107–273 shall apply to a civil action if the accident giving rise to the cause of action occurred on or after the 90th day after Nov. 2, 2002, see section 11020(c) of Pub.L. 107–273, set out as a note under 28 U.S.C.A. § 1369.

1986 Acts

Section 3(b) of Pub.L. 99–336 provided that: "The amendment made by this section [amending this section] shall apply with respect to claims in civil actions commenced in State courts on or after the date of the enactment of this section [June 19, 1986]."

1976 Acts

Amendment by Pub.L. 94–583 effective 90 days after Oct. 21, 1976, see section 8 of Pub.L. 94–583, set out as a note under section 1602 of this title.

§ 1442. Federal officers or agencies sued or prosecuted

(a) A civil action or criminal prosecution commenced in a State court against any of the following may be removed by them to the district court of the United States for the district and division embracing the place wherein it is pending:

(1) The United States or any agency thereof or any officer (or any person acting under that officer) of the United States or of any agency thereof, sued in an official or individual capacity for any act under color of such office or on account of any right, title or authority claimed under any Act of Congress for the apprehension or punishment of criminals or the collection of the revenue.

(2) A property holder whose title is derived from any such officer, where such action or prosecution affects the validity of any law of the United States.

(3) Any officer of the courts of the United States, for any act under color of office or in the performance of his duties;

(4) Any officer of either House of Congress, for any act in the discharge of his official duty under an order of such House.

(b) A personal action commenced in any State court by an alien against any citizen of a State who is, or at the time the alleged action accrued was, a civil officer of the United States and is a nonresident of such State, wherein jurisdiction is obtained by the State court by personal service of process, may be removed by the defendant to the district court of the United States for the district and division in which the defendant was served with process.

(June 25, 1948, c. 646, 62 Stat. 938; Oct. 19, 1996, Pub.L. 104–317, Title II, § 206(a), 110 Stat. 3850.)

§ 1442a. Members of armed forces sued or prosecuted

A civil or criminal prosecution in a court of a State of the United States against a member of the armed forces of the United States on account of an act done under color of his office or status, or in respect to which he claims any right, title, or authority under a law of the United States respecting the armed forces thereof, or under the law of war, may at any time before the trial or final hearing thereof be removed for trial into the district court of the United States for the district where it is pending in the manner prescribed by law, and it shall thereupon be entered on the docket of the district court, which shall proceed as if the cause had been originally commenced therein and shall have full power to hear and determine the cause.

(Added Aug. 10, 1956, c. 1041, § 19(a), 70A Stat. 626.)

HISTORICAL AND STATUTORY NOTES

Codifications

Section was from the Uniform Code of Military Justice, Act May 5, 1950, c. 169, § 9, 64 Stat. 146, which was based on Article 117, Articles of War, Act June 4, 1920, c. 227, subch. II, § 1, 41 Stat. 811, as amended June 24, 1948, c. 625, Title II, § 242, 62 Stat. 642.

§ 1443. Civil rights cases

Any of the following civil actions or criminal prosecutions, commenced in a State court may be removed by the defendant to the district court of the United States for the district and division embracing the place wherein it is pending:

(1) Against any person who is denied or cannot enforce in the courts of such State a right under any law providing for the equal civil rights of citizens of the United States, or of all persons within the jurisdiction thereof;

(2) For any act under color of authority derived from any law providing for equal rights, or for refusing to do any act on the ground that it would be inconsistent with such law.

(June 25, 1948, c. 646, 62 Stat. 938.)

§ 1444. Foreclosure action against United States

Any action brought under section 2410 of this title against the United States in any State court may be removed by the United States to the district court of the United States for the district and division in which the action is pending.

(June 25, 1948, c. 646, 62 Stat. 938; May 24, 1949, c. 139, § 82, 63 Stat. 101.)

§ 1445. Nonremovable actions

(a) A civil action in any State court against a railroad or its receivers or trustees, arising under sections 1–4 and 5–10 of the Act of April 22, 1908 (45 U.S.C. 51–54, 55–60), may not be removed to any district court of the United States.

(b) A civil action in any State court against a carrier or its receivers or trustees to recover damages for delay, loss, or injury of shipments, arising under section 11706 or 14706 of title 49, may not be removed to any district court of the United States unless the matter in controversy exceeds $10,000, exclusive of interest and costs.

(c) A civil action in any State court arising under the workmen's compensation laws of such State may not be removed to any district court of the United States.

(d) A civil action in any State court arising under section 40302 of the Violence Against Women Act of 1994 may not be removed to any district court of the United States.

(June 25, 1948, c. 646, 62 Stat. 939; July 25, 1958, Pub.L. 85–554, § 5, 72 Stat. 415; Oct. 17, 1978, Pub.L. 95–473, § 2(a)(3)(A), 92 Stat. 1465; Oct. 20, 1978, Pub.L. 95–486, § 9(b), 92 Stat. 1634; Sept. 13, 1994, Pub.L. 103–322, Title IV, § 40302(e)(5), 108 Stat. 1942; Dec. 29, 1995, Pub.L. 104–88, Title III, § 305(b), 109 Stat. 944; Oct. 11, 1996, Pub.L. 104–287, § 3, 110 Stat. 3388.)

HISTORICAL AND STATUTORY NOTES

References in Text

The Act of April 22, 1908, referred to in subsec. (a), popularly referred to as the [second] Employers' Liability Act, is Act Apr. 22, 1908, c. 149, 35 Stat. 65, as amended, which is classified generally to chapter 2 (section 51 et seq.) of Title 45, Railroads. For complete classification of this Act to the Code, see Short Title note set out under section 51 of Title 45 and Tables.

Section 40302 of the Violence Against Women Act of 1994, referred to in subsec. (d), means section 40302 of Pub.L. 103–322, the Violent Crime Control and Law Enforcement Act of 1994 (Title IV of such Act is the Violence Against Women Act of 1994), which is classified to section 13981 of Title 42, The Public Health and Welfare.

Effective and Applicability Provisions

1996 Acts

Amendment by section 3 of Pub.L. 104–287 effective on July 5, 1994, see section 8(1) of Pub.L. 104–287, set out as a note under section 5303 of Title 49, Transportation.

1995 Acts

Amendment by Pub.L. 104–88 effective Jan. 1, 1996, see section 2 of Pub.L. 104–88, set out as a note under section 701 of Title 49, Transportation.

1958 Acts

Amendment of section by Pub.L. 85–554 applicable only in the case of actions commenced after July 25, 1958, see section 3 of Pub.L. 85–554, set out as a note under section 1331 of this title.

§ 1446. Procedure for removal

(a) A defendant or defendants desiring to remove any civil action or criminal prosecution from a State court shall file in the district court of the United States for the district and division within which such action is pending a notice of removal signed pursuant to Rule 11 of the Federal Rules of Civil Procedure and containing a short and plain statement of the grounds for removal, together with a copy of all process, pleadings, and orders served upon such defendant or defendants in such action.

(b) The notice of removal of a civil action or proceeding shall be filed within thirty days after the receipt by the defendant, through service or otherwise, of a copy of the initial pleading setting forth the claim for relief upon which such action or proceeding is based, or within thirty days after the service of summons upon the defendant if such initial pleading has then been filed in court and is not required to be served on the defendant, whichever period is shorter.

If the case stated by the initial pleading is not removable, a notice of removal may be filed within thirty days after receipt by the defendant, through service or otherwise, of a copy of an amended pleading, motion, order or other paper from which it may first be ascertained that the case is one which is or has become removable, except that a case may not be removed on the basis of jurisdiction conferred by section 1332 of this title more than 1 year after commencement of the action.

(c)(1) A notice of removal of a criminal prosecution shall be filed not later than thirty days after the arraignment in the State court, or at any time before trial, whichever is earlier, except that for good cause shown the United States district court may enter an order granting the defendant or defendants leave to file the notice at a later time.

(2) A notice of removal of a criminal prosecution shall include all grounds for such removal. A failure to state grounds which exist at the time of the filing of the notice shall constitute a waiver of such grounds, and a second notice may be filed only on grounds not existing at the time of the original notice. For good

cause shown, the United States district court may grant relief from the limitations of this paragraph.

(3) The filing of a notice of removal of a criminal prosecution shall not prevent the State court in which such prosecution is pending from proceeding further, except that a judgment of conviction shall not be entered unless the prosecution is first remanded.

(4) The United States district court in which such notice is filed shall examine the notice promptly. If it clearly appears on the face of the notice and any exhibits annexed thereto that removal should not be permitted, the court shall make an order for summary remand.

(5) If the United States district court does not order the summary remand of such prosecution, it shall order an evidentiary hearing to be held promptly and after such hearing shall make such disposition of the prosecution as justice shall require. If the United States district court determines that removal shall be permitted, it shall so notify the State court in which prosecution is pending, which shall proceed no further.

(d) Promptly after the filing of such notice of removal of a civil action the defendant or defendants shall give written notice thereof to all adverse parties and shall file a copy of the notice with the clerk of such State court, which shall effect the removal and the State court shall proceed no further unless and until the case is remanded.

(e) If the defendant or defendants are in actual custody on process issued by the State court, the district court shall issue its writ of habeas corpus, and the marshal shall thereupon take such defendant or defendants into his custody and deliver a copy of the writ to the clerk of such State court.

(f) With respect to any counterclaim removed to a district court pursuant to section 337(c) of the Tariff Act of 1930, the district court shall resolve such counterclaim in the same manner as an original complaint under the Federal Rules of Civil Procedure, except that the payment of a filing fee shall not be required in such cases and the counterclaim shall relate back to the date of the original complaint in the proceeding before the International Trade Commission under section 337 of that Act.

(June 25, 1948, c. 646, 62 Stat. 939; May 24, 1949, c. 139, § 83, 63 Stat. 101; Sept. 29, 1965, Pub.L. 89–215, 79 Stat. 887; July 30, 1977, Pub.L. 95–78, § 3, 91 Stat. 321; Nov. 19, 1988, Pub.L. 100–702, Title X, § 1016(b), 102 Stat. 4669; Dec. 9, 1991, Pub.L. 102–198, § 10(a), 105 Stat. 1626; Dec. 8, 1994, Pub.L. 103–465, Title III, § 321(b)(2), 108 Stat. 4946; Oct. 19, 1996, Pub.L. 104–317, Title VI, § 603, 110 Stat. 3857.)

HISTORICAL AND STATUTORY NOTES

References in Text

The Federal Rules of Civil Procedure, referred to in subsec. (a), are set out in this title.

Codifications

Section 10(a)(5)(A) of Pub.L. 102–198, which directed that subsec. (d) of this section be amended by substituting "removal" for "the removal", was executed by making such substitution at the first appearance of the term "the removal", as the probable intent of Congress.

1994 Acts

House Report No. 103–826 (Parts I and II) and Statement of Administrative Action, see 1994 U.S. Code Cong. and Adm. News, p. 3773.

Effective and Applicability Provisions

1994 Acts

Amendment by section 321(b)(2) of Pub.L. 103–465 applicable with respect to complaints filed under section 1337 of Title 19, Customs Duties, on or after the date on which the WTO Agreement enters into force with respect to the United States, Jan. 1, 1995, or in cases under section 1337 of Title 19 in which no complaint is filed, with respect to investigations initiated under such section on or after such date, see section 322 of Pub.L. 103–465, set out as a note under section 1337 of Title 19.

1977 Acts

Amendment by Pub.L. 95–78 effective Oct. 1, 1977, see section 4 of Pub.L. 95–78, set out as a note under section 3771 of Title 18, Crimes and Criminal Procedure.

§ 1447. Procedure after removal generally

(a) In any case removed from a State court, the district court may issue all necessary orders and process to bring before it all proper parties whether served by process issued by the State court or otherwise.

(b) It may require the removing party to file with its clerk copies of all records and proceedings in such State court or may cause the same to be brought before it by writ of certiorari issued to such State court.

(c) A motion to remand the case on the basis of any defect other than lack of subject matter jurisdiction must be made within 30 days after the filing of the notice of removal under section 1446(a). If at any time before final judgment it appears that the district court lacks subject matter jurisdiction, the case shall be remanded. An order remanding the case may require payment of just costs and any actual expenses, including attorney fees, incurred as a result of the removal. A certified copy of the order of remand shall be mailed by the clerk to the clerk of the State court. The State court may thereupon proceed with such case.

(d) An order remanding a case to the State court from which it was removed is not reviewable on appeal or otherwise, except that an order remanding a case to the State court from which it was removed pursuant to section 1443 of this title shall be reviewable by appeal or otherwise.

(e) If after removal the plaintiff seeks to join additional defendants whose joinder would destroy subject matter jurisdiction, the court may deny joinder, or permit joinder and remand the action to the State court.

(June 25, 1948, c. 646, 62 Stat. 939; May 24, 1949, c. 139, § 84, 63 Stat. 102; July 2, 1964, Pub.L. 88–352, Title IX, § 901, 78 Stat. 266; Nov. 19, 1988, Pub.L. 100–702, Title X, § 1016(c), 102 Stat. 4670; Dec. 9, 1991, Pub.L. 102–198, § 10(b), 105 Stat. 1626; Oct. 1, 1996, Pub.L. 104–219, § 1, 110 Stat. 3022.)

HISTORICAL AND STATUTORY NOTES
Exception to Subsection (d)

Section 3(c) of Act Aug. 4, 1947, c. 458, 61 Stat. 732, provided in part that the United States shall have the right to appeal from any order of remand entered in any case removed to a United States district court pursuant to the provisions of Act Apr. 12, 1926, c. 115, 44 Stat. 239. These Acts referred to herein relate to restrictions on land of the Five Civilized Tribes of Oklahoma and are set out as notes under section 355 of Title 25, Indians.

§ 1448. Process after removal

In all cases removed from any State court to any district court of the United States in which any one or more of the defendants has not been served with process or in which the service has not been perfected prior to removal, or in which process served proves to be defective, such process or service may be completed or new process issued in the same manner as in cases originally filed in such district court.

This section shall not deprive any defendant upon whom process is served after removal of his right to move to remand the case.

(June 25, 1948, c. 646, 62 Stat. 940.)

§ 1449. State court record supplied

Where a party is entitled to copies of the records and proceedings in any suit or prosecution in a State court, to be used in any district court of the United States, and the clerk of such State court, upon demand, and the payment or tender of the legal fees, fails to deliver certified copies, the district court may, on affidavit reciting such facts, direct such record to be supplied by affidavit or otherwise. Thereupon such proceedings, trial, and judgment may be had in such district court, and all such process awarded, as if certified copies had been filed in the district court.

(June 25, 1948, c. 646, 62 Stat. 940; May 24, 1949, c. 139, § 85, 63 Stat. 102.)

§ 1450. Attachment or sequestration; securities

Whenever any action is removed from a State court to a district court of the United States, any attachment or sequestration of the goods or estate of the defendant in such action in the State court shall hold the goods or estate to answer the final judgment or decree in the same manner as they would have been held to answer final judgment or decree had it been rendered by the State court.

All bonds, undertakings, or security given by either party in such action prior to its removal shall remain valid and effectual notwithstanding such removal.

All injunctions, orders, and other proceedings had in such action prior to its removal shall remain in full force and effect until dissolved or modified by the district court.

(June 25, 1948, c. 646, 62 Stat. 940.)

§ 1451. Definitions

For purposes of this chapter—

(1) The term "State court" includes the Superior Court of the District of Columbia.

(2) The term "State" includes the District of Columbia.

(Added Pub.L. 91–358, Title I, § 172(d)(1), July 29, 1970, 84 Stat. 591.)

HISTORICAL AND STATUTORY NOTES
Effective and Applicability Provisions
1970 Acts

Section effective the first day of the seventh calendar month which begins after July 29, 1970, see section 199(a) of Pub.L. 91–358, set out as a note under section 1257 of this title.

§ 1452. Removal of claims related to bankruptcy cases

(a) A party may remove any claim or cause of action in a civil action other than a proceeding before the United States Tax Court or a civil action by a governmental unit to enforce such governmental unit's police or regulatory power, to the district court for the district where such civil action is pending, if such district court has jurisdiction of such claim or cause of action under section 1334 of this title.

(b) The court to which such claim or cause of action is removed may remand such claim or cause of action on any equitable ground. An order entered under this subsection remanding a claim or cause of action, or a decision to not remand, is not reviewable by appeal or otherwise by the court of appeals under section 158(d), 1291, or 1292 of this title or by the Supreme Court of the United States under section 1254 of this title.

(Added Pub.L. 98–353, Title I, § 103(a), July 10, 1984, 98 Stat. 335, and amended Pub.L. 101–650, Title III, § 309(c), Dec. 1, 1990, 104 Stat. 5113.)

HISTORICAL AND STATUTORY NOTES
Effective and Applicability Provisions
1984 Acts

Section effective July 10, 1984, see section 122(a) of Pub.L. 98–353, set out as a note under section 151 of this title.

§ 1453. Removal of class actions

(a) Definitions.—In this section, the terms "class", "class action", "class certification order", and "class member" shall have the meanings given such terms under section 1332(d)(1).

(b) In general.—A class action may be removed to a district court of the United States in accordance with section 1446 (except that the 1–year limitation under section 1446(b) shall not apply), without regard to whether any defendant is a citizen of the State in which the action is brought, except that such action may be removed by any defendant without the consent of all defendants.

(c) Review of remand orders.—

(1) **In general.**—Section 1447 shall apply to any removal of a case under this section, except that notwithstanding section 1447(d), a court of appeals may accept an appeal from an order of a district court granting or denying a motion to remand a class action to the State court from which it was removed if application is made to the court of appeals not less than 7 days after entry of the order.

(2) **Time period for judgment.**—If the court of appeals accepts an appeal under paragraph (1), the court shall complete all action on such appeal, including rendering judgment, not later than 60 days after the date on which such appeal was filed, unless an extension is granted under paragraph (3).

(3) **Extension of time period.**—The court of appeals may grant an extension of the 60–day period described in paragraph (2) if—

(A) all parties to the proceeding agree to such extension, for any period of time; or

(B) such extension is for good cause shown and in the interests of justice, for a period not to exceed 10 days.

(4) **Denial of appeal.**—If a final judgment on the appeal under paragraph (1) is not issued before the end of the period described in paragraph (2), including any extension under paragraph (3), the appeal shall be denied.

(d) Exception.—This section shall not apply to any class action that solely involves—

(1) a claim concerning a covered security as defined under section 16(f) (3) of the Securities Act of 1933 (15 U.S.C. 78p(f)(3)) and section 28(f)(5)(E) of the Securities Exchange Act of 1934 (15 U.S.C. 78bb(f)(5)(E));

(2) a claim that relates to the internal affairs or governance of a corporation or other form of business enterprise and arises under or by virtue of the laws of the State in which such corporation or business enterprise is incorporated or organized; or

(3) a claim that relates to the rights, duties (including fiduciary duties), and obligations relating to or created by or pursuant to any security (as defined under section 2(a)(1) of the Securities Act of 1933 (15 U.S.C. 77b(a)(1)) and the regulations issued thereunder).

(Added Pub.L. 109–2, § 5(a), Feb. 18, 2005, 119 Stat. 12.)

HISTORICAL AND STATUTORY NOTES

References in Text

Section 16(f)(3) of the Securities Act of 1933, referred to in subsec. (d)(1), is May 27, 1933, c. 38, Title I, § 16(f)(3), 48 Stat. 84, as amended, which is classified to 15 U.S.C.A. § 78p(f)(3).

Section 28(f)(5)(E) of the Securities Exchange Act of 1934, referred to in subsec. (d)(1), is May 27, 1933, c. 38, Title I, § 2(f)(5)(E), 48 Stat. 74, as amended, which is classified to 15 U.S.C.A. § 78bb(f)(5)(E).

Section 2(a)(1) of the Securities Act of 1933, referred to in subsec. (d)(3), is May 27, 1933, c. 38, Title I, § 2(a)(1), 48 Stat. 74, as amended, which is classified to 15 U.S.C.A. § 77b(a)(1).

Effective and Applicability Provisions

2005 Acts

Amendments by Class Action Fairness Act of 2005, Pub.L. 109–2, Feb. 18, 2005, 119 Stat. 4, applicable to any civil action commenced on or after Feb. 18, 2005, see Pub.L. 109–2, § 9, set out as a note under 28 U.S.C.A. § 1332.

[CHAPTER 90—DISTRICT COURTS AND BANKRUPTCY COURTS] [OMITTED]

HISTORICAL AND STATUTORY NOTES

Codifications

Chapter 90, consisting of sections 1471 to 1482, which was added by Pub.L.95–598, Title II, § 241(a), Nov. 6, 1978, 92 Stat. 2668, and which related to district courts and bankruptcy courts, did not become effective pursuant to section 402(b) of Pub.L. 95–598, as amended, set out as an Effective and Applicability Provisions note preceding section 101 of Title 11, Bankruptcy.

Transition to New Court System

Pub.L. 95–598, Title IV, § 409, Nov. 6, 1978, 92 Stat. 2687, as amended by Pub.L. 98–249, § 1(d), Mar. 31, 1984, 98 Stat. 116; Pub.L. 98–271, § 1(d), Apr. 30, 1984, 98 Stat. 163; Pub.L. 98–299, § 1(d), May 25, 1984, 98 Stat. 214; Pub.L. 98–325, § 1(d), June 20, 1984, 98 Stat. 268; Pub.L. 98–353, Title I, § 121(d), July 10, 1984, 98 Stat. 346, was repealed by Pub.L. 98–353, Title I, §§ 114, 122(a), July 10, 1984, 98 Stat. 343, 346, eff. July 10, 1984. The repealed section had provided for transfer to the new court system of 1) cases, and

matters and proceedings in cases, under the Bankruptcy Act [former Title 11] pending at the end of Sept. 30, 1983, in the courts of bankruptcy continued under section 404(a) of Pub.L. 95–598, with certain exceptions, and 2) cases and proceedings arising under or related to cases under Title 11 pending at the end of July 9, 1984, in the courts of bankruptcy continued under section 404(a) of Pub.L. 95–598, and directed that civil actions pending on July 9, 1984, over which a bankruptcy court had jurisdiction on July 9, 1984, not abate, that actions not finally determined before Apr. 1, 1985, be removed to a bankruptcy court under this chapter, and that all law books, publications, etc., furnished bankruptcy judges as of July 9, 1984, be transferred to the United States bankruptcy courts under the supervision of the Director of the Administrative Office of the United States Courts.

[§§ 1471 to 1482. Omitted]

CHAPTER 91—UNITED STATES COURT OF FEDERAL CLAIMS

§ 1491. Claims against United States generally; actions involving Tennessee Valley Authority

(a)(1) The United States Court of Federal Claims shall have jurisdiction to render judgment upon any claim against the United States founded either upon the Constitution, or any Act of Congress or any regulation of an executive department, or upon any express or implied contract with the United States, or for liquidated or unliquidated damages in cases not sounding in tort. For the purpose of this paragraph, an express or implied contract with the Army and Air Force Exchange Service, Navy Exchanges, Marine Corps Exchanges, Coast Guard Exchanges, or Exchange Councils of the National Aeronautics and Space Administration shall be considered an express or implied contract with the United States.

(2) To provide an entire remedy and to complete the relief afforded by the judgment, the court may, as an incident of and collateral to any such judgment, issue orders directing restoration to office or position, placement in appropriate duty or retirement status, and correction of applicable records, and such orders may be issued to any appropriate official of the United States. In any case within its jurisdiction, the court shall have the power to remand appropriate matters to any administrative or executive body or official with such direction as it may deem proper and just. The Court of Federal Claims shall have jurisdiction to render judgment upon any claim by or against, or dispute with, a contractor arising under section 10(a)(1) of the Contract Disputes Act of 1978, including a dispute concerning termination of a contract, rights in tangible or intangible property, compliance with cost accounting standards, and other nonmonetary disputes on which a decision of the contracting officer has been issued under section 6 of that Act.

(b)(1) Both the Unites [1] States Court of Federal Claims and the district courts of the United States shall have jurisdiction to render judgment on an action by an interested party objecting to a solicitation by a Federal agency for bids or proposals for a proposed contract or to a proposed award or the award of a contract or any alleged violation of statute or regulation in connection with a procurement or a proposed procurement. Both the United States Court of Federal Claims and the district courts of the United States shall have jurisdiction to entertain such an action without regard to whether suit is instituted before or after the contract is awarded.

(2) To afford relief in such an action, the courts may award any relief that the court considers proper, including declaratory and injunctive relief except that any monetary relief shall be limited to bid preparation and proposal costs.

(3) In exercising jurisdiction under this subsection, the courts shall give due regard to the interests of national defense and national security and the need for expeditious resolution of the action.

(4) In any action under this subsection, the courts shall review the agency's decision pursuant to the standards set forth in section 706 of title 5.

(c) Nothing herein shall be construed to give the United States Court of Federal Claims jurisdiction of any civil action within the exclusive jurisdiction of the Court of International Trade, or of any action against,

or founded on conduct of,¹ the Tennessee Valley Authority, or to amend or modify the provisions of the Tennessee Valley Authority Act of 1933 with respect to actions by or against the Authority.

(June 25, 1948, c. 646, 62 Stat. 940; July 28, 1953, c. 253, § 7, 67 Stat. 226; Sept. 3, 1954, c. 1263, § 44(a), (b), 68 Stat. 1241; July 23, 1970, Pub.L. 91–350, § 1(b), 84 Stat. 449; Aug. 29, 1972, Pub.L. 92–415, § 1, 86 Stat. 652; Nov. 1, 1978, Pub.L. 95–563, § 14(i), 92 Stat. 2391; Oct. 10, 1980, Pub.L. 96–417, Title V, § 509, 94 Stat. 1743; Apr. 2, 1982, Pub.L. 97–164, Title I, § 133(a), 96 Stat. 39; Oct. 29, 1992, Pub.L. 102–572, Title IX, §§ 902(a), 907(b)(1), 106 Stat. 4516, 4519; Oct. 19, 1996, Pub.L. 104–320, § 12(a), 110 Stat. 3874.)

1 So in original.

HISTORICAL AND STATUTORY NOTES

References in Text

The Contracts Disputes Act of 1978, referred to in subsec. (a)(2), is Pub.L. 95–563, Nov. 1, 1978, 92 Stat. 2383, which is classified principally to chapter 9 (section 601 et seq.) of Title 41, Public Contracts. Sections 6 and 10(a)(1) of such Act are classified to sections 605 and 609(a)(1), respectively, of Title 41. For complete classification of this Act to the Code, see Short Title note set out under section 601 of Title 41 and Tables.

The Tennessee Valley Authority Act of 1933, referred to in subsec. (c), is Act May 18, 1933, c. 32, 48 Stat. 58, as amended, which is classified generally to chapter 12A (section 831 et seq.) of Title 16, Conservation. For complete classification of this Act to the Code, see section 831 of Title 16 and Tables.

Effective and Applicability Provisions

1996 Acts

Section 12(b) of Pub.L. 104–320 provided that: "This section and the amendments made by this section [amending subsecs. (a)(3), (b), and (c) of this section] shall take effect on December 31, 1996 and shall apply to all actions filed on or after that date."

1992 Acts

Amendments by section 902(a) of Pub.L. 102–572 effective Oct. 29, 1992, see section 911 of Pub.L. 102–572, set out as a note under section 171 of this title.

Section 907(b)(2) of Pub.L. 102–572 provided that: "The amendment made by paragraph (1) [amending subsec. (a)(2) of this section] shall be effective with respect to all actions filed before, on, or after the date of the enactment of this Act [Oct. 29, 1992], except for those actions which, before such date of enactment, have been the subject of—

"(A) a final judgment of the United States Claims Court, if the time for appeal of that judgment has expired without an appeal having been filed, or

"(B) a final judgment of the Court of Appeals for the Federal Circuit."

1982 Acts

Amendment by Pub.L. 97–164 effective Oct. 1, 1982, see section 402 of Pub.L. 97–164, set out as a note under section 171 of this title.

1980 Acts

Amendment by Pub.L. 96–417 effective Nov. 1, 1980 and applicable with respect to civil actions pending on or com-menced on or after such date, see section 701(a) of Pub.L. 96–417, as amended, set out as a note under section 251 of this title.

1978 Acts

Amendment by Pub.L. 95–563 effective with respect to contracts entered into 120 days after Nov. 1, 1978, and, at the election of the contractor, with respect to any claim pending at such time before the contracting officer or initiated thereafter, see section 16 of Pub.L. 95–563, set out as a note under section 601 of Title 41, Public Contracts.

1972 Acts

Section 2 of Pub.L. 92–415 provided that: "This Act [amending this section] shall be applicable to all judicial proceedings pending on or instituted after the date of its enactment [Aug. 29, 1972]."

1970 Acts

Amendment by Pub.L. 91–350 applicable to claims and civil actions dismissed before or pending on July 23, 1970, if the claim or civil action was based upon a transaction, omission, or breach that occurred not more than six years prior to July 23, 1970, notwithstanding a determination or judgment made prior to July 23, 1970, that the United States district courts or the United States Court of Claims did not have jurisdiction to entertain a suit on an express or implied contract with a nonappropriated fund instrumentality of the United States, see section 2 of Pub.L. 91–350, set out as a note under section 1346 of this title.

Transfer of Functions

For transfer of authorities, functions, personnel, and assets of the Coast Guard, including the authorities and functions of the Secretary of Transportation relating thereto, to the Department of Homeland Security, and for treatment of related references, see 6 U.S.C.A. §§ 468(b), 551(d), 552(d) and 557, and the Department of Homeland Security Reorganization Plan of November 25, 2002, as modified, set out as a note under 6 U.S.C.A. § 542.

Sunset Provisions

Section 12(d) of Pub.L. 104–320 provided that: "The jurisdiction of the district courts of the United States over the actions described in section 1491(b)(1) of title 28, United States Code [subsec. (b)(1) of this section] (as amended by subsection (a) of this section) shall terminate on January 1, 2001 unless extended by Congress. The savings provisions in subsection (e) [section 12(e) of Pub.L. 104–320, set out as a note under this section] shall apply if the bid protest jurisdiction of the district courts of the United States terminates under this subsection [this note]."

Savings Provisions

Section 12(e) of Pub.L. 104–320 provided that:

"(1) **Orders.**—A termination under subsection (d) [section 12(d) of Pub.L. 104–320, set out as a note under this section] shall not terminate the effectiveness of orders that have been issued by a court in connection with an action within the jurisdiction of that court on or before December 31, 2000. Such orders shall continue in effect according to their terms until modified, terminated, superseded, set aside, or revoked by a court of competent jurisdiction or by operation of law.

"(2) **Proceedings and applications.**—(A) a [sic] termination under subsection (d) shall not affect the jurisdiction of

a court of the United States to continue with any proceeding that is pending before the court on December 31, 2000.

"(B) Orders may be issued in any such proceeding, appeals may be taken therefrom, and payments may be made pursuant to such orders, as if such termination had not occurred. An order issued in any such proceeding shall continue in effect until modified, terminated, superseded, set aside, or revoked by a court of competent jurisdiction or by operation of law.

"(C) Nothing in this paragraph prohibits the discontinuance or modification of any such proceeding under the same terms and conditions and to the same extent that proceeding could have been discontinued or modified absent such termination."

Study on Concurrent Jurisdiction

Section 12(c) of Pub.L. 104–320 provided that: "No earlier than 2 years after the effective date of this section [see section 12(b) of Pub.L. 104–320, set out as a note under this section], the United States General Accounting Office [now Government Accountability Office] shall undertake a study regarding the concurrent jurisdiction of the district courts of the United States and the Court of Federal Claims over bid protests to determine whether concurrent jurisdiction is necessary. Such a study shall be completed no later than December 31, 1999, and shall specifically consider the effect of any proposed change on the ability of small businesses to challenge violations of Federal procurement law."

§ 1492. Congressional reference cases

Any bill, except a bill for a pension, may be referred by either House of Congress to the chief judge of the United States Court of Federal Claims for a report in conformity with section 2509 of this title.

(June 25, 1948, c. 646, 62 Stat. 941; Oct. 15, 1966, Pub.L. 89–681, § 1, 80 Stat. 958; Apr. 2, 1982, Pub.L. 97–164, Title I, § 133(b), 96 Stat. 40; Oct. 29, 1992, Pub.L. 102–572, Title IX, § 902(a)(1), 106 Stat. 4516.)

HISTORICAL AND STATUTORY NOTES

Effective and Applicability Provisions

1992 Acts

Amendment by Title IX of Pub.L. 102–572 effective Oct. 29, 1992, see section 911 of Pub.L. 102–572, set out as a note under section 171 of this title.

1982 Acts

Amendment by Pub.L. 97–164 effective Oct. 1, 1982, see section 402 of Pub.L. 97–164, set out as a note under section 171 of this title.

[§ 1493. Repealed. July 28, 1953, c. 253, § 8, 67 Stat. 226]

HISTORICAL AND STATUTORY NOTES

Section, Act June 25, 1948, c. 646, 62 Stat. 941, authorized the Court of Claims to give legal advice to the heads of executive departments in matters referred to it by such heads, if the Court had jurisdiction over such matters.

§ 1494. Accounts of officers, agents or contractors

The United States Court of Federal Claims shall have jurisdiction to determine the amount, if any, due to or from the United States by reason of any unsettled account of any officer or agent of, or contractor with, the United States, or a guarantor, surety or personal representative of any such officer, agent or contractor, and to render judgment thereof,[1] where—

(1) claimant or the person he represents has applied to the proper department of the Government for settlement of the account;

(2) three years have elapsed from the date of such application without settlement; and

(3) no suit upon the same has been brought by the United States.

(June 25, 1948, c. 646, 62 Stat. 941; July 28, 1953, c. 253, § 9, 67 Stat. 226; Sept. 3, 1954, c. 1263, § 44(c), 68 Stat. 1242; Apr. 2, 1982, Pub.L. 97–164, Title I, § 133(c) (1), 96 Stat. 40; Oct. 29, 1992, Pub.L. 102–572, Title IX, § 902(a)(1), 106 Stat. 4516.)

[1] So in original. Probably should be "thereon".

HISTORICAL AND STATUTORY NOTES

Effective and Applicability Provisions

1992 Acts

Amendment by Title IX of Pub.L. 102–572 effective Oct. 29, 1992, see section 911 of Pub.L. 102–572, set out as a note under section 171 of this title.

1982 Acts

Amendment by Pub.L. 97–164 effective Oct. 1, 1982, see section 402 of Pub.L. 97–164, set out as a note under section 171 of this title.

§ 1495. Damages for unjust conviction and imprisonment; claim against United States

The United States Court of Federal Claims shall have jurisdiction to render judgment upon any claim for damages by any person unjustly convicted of an offense against the United States and imprisoned.

(June 25, 1948, c. 646, 62 Stat. 941; Apr. 2, 1982, Pub.L. 97–164, Title I, § 133(c) (1), 96 Stat. 40; Oct. 29, 1992, Pub.L. 102–572, Title IX, § 902(a)(1), 106 Stat. 4516.)

HISTORICAL AND STATUTORY NOTES

Effective and Applicability Provisions

1992 Acts

Amendment by Title IX of Pub.L. 102–572 effective Oct. 29, 1992, see section 911 of Pub.L. 102–572, set out as a note under section 171 of this title.

1982 Acts

Amendment by Pub.L. 97–164 effective Oct. 1, 1982, see section 402 of Pub.L. 97–164, set out as a note under section 171 of this title.

§ 1496. Disbursing officers' claims

The United States Court of Federal Claims shall have jurisdiction to render judgment upon any claim by a disbursing officer of the United States or by his administrator or executor for relief from responsibility for loss, in line of duty, of Government funds, vouchers, records or other papers in his charge.

(June 25, 1948, c. 646, 62 Stat. 941; Apr. 2, 1982, Pub.L. 97–164, Title I, § 133(c)(1), 96 Stat. 40; Oct. 29, 1992, Pub.L. 102–572, Title IX, § 902(a)(1), 106 Stat. 4516.)

HISTORICAL AND STATUTORY NOTES

Effective and Applicability Provisions

1992 Acts

Amendment by Title IX of Pub.L. 102–572 effective Oct. 29, 1992, see section 911 of Pub.L. 102–572, set out as a note under section 171 of this title.

1982 Acts

Amendment by Pub.L. 97–164 effective Oct. 1, 1982, see section 402 of Pub.L. 97–164, set out as a note under section 171 of this title.

§ 1497. Oyster growers' damages from dredging operations

The United States Court of Federal Claims shall have jurisdiction to render judgment upon any claim for damages to oyster growers on private or leased lands or bottoms arising from dredging operations or use of other machinery and equipment in making river and harbor improvements authorized by Act of Congress.

(June 25, 1948, c. 646, 62 Stat. 941; Apr. 2, 1982, Pub.L. 97–164, Title I, § 133(c), 96 Stat. 40; Oct. 29, 1992, Pub.L. 102–572, Title IX, § 902(a)(1), 106 Stat. 4516.)

HISTORICAL AND STATUTORY NOTES

Effective and Applicability Provisions

1992 Acts

Amendment by Title IX of Pub.L. 102–572 effective Oct. 29, 1992, see section 911 of Pub.L. 102–572, set out as a note under section 171 of this title.

1982 Acts

Amendment by Pub.L. 97–164 effective Oct. 1, 1982, see section 402 of Pub.L. 97–164, set out as a note under section 171 of this title.

§ 1498. Patent and copyright cases

(a) Whenever an invention described in and covered by a patent of the United States is used or manufactured by or for the United States without license of the owner thereof or lawful right to use or manufacture the same, the owner's remedy shall be by action against the United States in the United States Court of Federal Claims for the recovery of his reasonable and entire compensation for such use and manufacture. Reasonable and entire compensation shall include the owner's reasonable costs, including reasonable fees for expert witnesses and attorneys, in pursuing the action if the owner is an independent inventor, a nonprofit organization, or an entity that had no more than 500 employees at any time during the 5–year period preceding the use or manufacture of the patented invention by or for the United States. Nothwithstanding [1] the preceding sentences, unless the action has been pending for more than 10 years from the time of filing to the time that the owner applies for such costs and fees, reasonable and entire compensation shall not include such costs and fees if the court finds that the position of the United States was substantially justified or that special circumstances make an award unjust.

For the purposes of this section, the use or manufacture of an invention described in and covered by a patent of the United States by a contractor, a subcontractor, or any person, firm, or corporation for the Government and with the authorization or consent of the Government, shall be construed as use or manufacture for the United States.

The court shall not award compensation under this section if the claim is based on the use or manufacture by or for the United States of any article owned, leased, used by, or in the possession of the United States prior to July 1, 1918.

A Government employee shall have the right to bring suit against the Government under this section except where he was in a position to order, influence, or induce use of the invention by the Government. This section shall not confer a right of action on any patentee or any assignee of such patentee with respect to any invention discovered or invented by a person while in the employment or service of the United States, where the invention was related to the official functions of the employee, in cases in which such functions included research and development, or in the making of which Government time, materials or facilities were used.

(b) Hereafter, whenever the copyright in any work protected under the copyright laws of the United States shall be infringed by the United States, by a corporation owned or controlled by the United States, or by a contractor, subcontractor, or any person, firm, or corporation acting for the Government and with the authorization or consent of the Government, the exclusive action which may be brought for such infringement shall be an action by the copyright owner against the United States in the Court of Federal Claims for the recovery of his reasonable and entire compensation as damages for such infringement, including the minimum statutory damages as set forth in section 504(c) of title 17, United States Code: *Provided*, That a Government employee shall have a right of action against the Government under this subsection except where he was in a position to order, influence, or induce use of the copyrighted work by

the Government: *Provided, however,* That this sub-section shall not confer a right of action on any copyright owner or any assignee of such owner with respect to any copyrighted work prepared by a person while in the employment or service of the United States, where the copyrighted work was prepared as a part of the official functions of the employee, or in the preparation of which Government time, material, or facilities were used: *And provided further,* That be-fore such action against the United States has been instituted the appropriate corporation owned or con-trolled by the United States or the head of the appropriate department or agency of the Government, as the case may be, is authorized to enter into an agreement with the copyright owner in full settlement and compromise for the damages accruing to him by reason of such infringement and to settle the claim administratively out of available appropriations.

Except as otherwise provided by law, no recovery shall be had for any infringement of a copyright covered by this subsection committed more than three years prior to the filing of the complaint or counter-claim for infringement in the action, except that the period between the date of receipt of a written claim for compensation by the Department or agency of the Government or corporation owned or controlled by the United States, as the case may be, having authority to settle such claim and the date of mailing by the Government of a notice to the claimant that his claim has been denied shall not be counted as a part of the three years, unless suit is brought before the last-mentioned date.

(c) The provisions of this section shall not apply to any claim arising in a foreign country.

(d) Hereafter, whenever a plant variety protected by a certificate of plant variety protection under the laws of the United States shall be infringed by the United States, by a corporation owned or controlled by the United States, or by a contractor, subcontrac-tor, or any person, firm, or corporation acting for the Government, and with the authorization and consent of the Government, the exclusive remedy of the owner of such certificate shall be by action against the United States in the Court of Federal Claims for the recovery of his reasonable and entire compensation as damages for such infringement: *Provided,* That a Government employee shall have a right of action against the Government under this subsection except where he was in a position to order, influence, or induce use of the protected plant variety by the Government: *Provided, however,* That this subsection shall not confer a right of action on any certificate owner or any assignee of such owner with respect to any protected plant variety made by a person while in the employment or service of the United States, where such variety was prepared as a part of the official functions of the employee, or in the prepara-

tion of which Government time, material, or facilities were used: *And provided further,* That before such action against the United States has been instituted, the appropriate corporation owned or controlled by the United States or the head of the appropriate agency of the Government, as the case may be, is authorized to enter into an agreement with the certifi-cate owner in full settlement and compromise, for the damages accrued to him by reason of such infringe-ment and to settle the claim administratively out of available appropriations.

(e) Subsections (b) and (c) of this section apply to exclusive rights in mask works under chapter 9 of title 17, and to exclusive rights in designs under chapter 13 of title 17 [17 U.S.C.A. § 1301 et seq.], to the same extent as such subsections apply to copyrights.

(June 25, 1948, c. 646, 62 Stat. 941; May 24, 1949, c. 139, § 87, 63 Stat. 102; Oct. 31, 1951, c. 655, § 50(c), 65 Stat. 727; July 17, 1952, c. 930, 66 Stat. 757; Sept. 8, 1960, Pub.L. 86–726, §§ 1, 4, 74 Stat. 855, 856; Dec. 24, 1970, Pub.L. 91–577, Title III, § 143(d), 84 Stat. 1559; Oct. 19, 1976, Pub.L. 94–553, Title I, § 105(c), 90 Stat. 2599; Apr. 2, 1982, Pub.L. 97–164, Title I, § 133(d), 96 Stat. 40; Nov. 19, 1988, Pub.L. 100–702, Title X, § 1020(a)(6), 102 Stat. 4671; Oct. 29, 1992, Pub.L. 102–572, Title IX, § 902(a), 106 Stat. 4516; Oct. 19, 1996, Pub.L. 104–308, § 1(a), 110 Stat. 3814; Dec. 16, 1997, Pub.L. 105–147, § 3, 111 Stat. 2680; Oct. 28, 1998, Pub.L. 105–304, Title V, § 503(d), 112 Stat. 2917.)

1 So in original. Probably should be "Notwithstanding".

HISTORICAL AND STATUTORY NOTES

References in Text

Hereafter, referred to in subsec. (b), probably means the date of enactment of Pub. L. 86–726 [which, among other changes, added subsec. (b)], which was approved on Sept. 8, 1960.

The copyright laws of the United States, referred to in subsec. (b), are classified generally to Title 17, Copyrights.

The "hereafter" set out at the beginning of subsec. (d) probably means after Dec. 24, 1970, the date of enactment of Pub.L. 91–577 which added subsec. (d).

Effective and Applicability Provisions

1998 Acts

Amendment by Pub.L. 105–304, effective Oct. 28, 1998, see section 505 of Pub.L. 105–304, set out as a note under section 1301 of Title 17, Copyrights.

1996 Acts

Section 1(b) of Pub.L. 104–308 provided that: "The amend-ment made by subsection (a) [amending subsec. (a) of this section] shall apply to actions under section 1498(a) of title 28, United States Code [subsec. (a) of this section], that are pending on, or brought on or after, the date of the enactment of this Act [Oct. 19, 1996]."

1992 Acts

Amendments by Title IX of Pub.L. 102–572 effective Oct. 29, 1992, see section 911 of Pub.L. 102–572, set out as a note under section 171 of Title 28, Judiciary and Judiciary Proce-dure.

1982 Acts

Amendment by Pub.L. 97–164 effective Oct. 1, 1982, see section 402 of Pub.L. 97–164, set out as a note under section 171 of this title.

1976 Acts

Amendment by Pub.L. 94–553 effective Jan. 1, 1978, see section 102 of Pub.L. 94–553, set out as a note preceding section 101 of Title 17, Copyrights.

1970 Acts

Amendment by Pub.L. 91–577 effective Dec. 24, 1970, see section 141 of Pub.L. 91–577, set out as a note under section 2321 of Title 7, Agriculture.

Waiver of Immunity for Members of Congress

Section 2 of Pub.L. 86–726 provided that: "Nothing in this Act [amending this section and section 2386 of Title 10, Armed Forces] shall be construed to in any way waive any immunity provided for Members of Congress under article I of section 6 of the Constitution of the United States."

§ 1499. Liquidated damages withheld from contractors under chapter 37 of title 40

The United States Court of Federal Claims shall have jurisdiction to render judgment upon any claim for liquidated damages withheld from a contractor or subcontractor under section 3703 of title 40.

(June 25, 1948, c. 646, 62 Stat. 942; Aug. 13, 1962, Pub.L. 87–581, Title II, § 202(a), 76 Stat. 360; Apr. 2, 1982, Pub.L. 97–164, Title I, § 133(e) (1), (2) (A), 96 Stat. 40, 41; Dec. 1, 1990, Pub.L. 101–650, Title III, § 325(b)(7), 104 Stat. 5121; Oct. 29, 1992, Pub.L. 102–572, Title IX, § 902(a)(1), 106 Stat. 4516; Aug. 21, 2002, Pub.L. 107–217, § 3(g)(3), 116 Stat. 1299; Sept. 27, 2006, Pub.L. 109–284, § 4(2), 120 Stat. 1211.)

HISTORICAL AND STATUTORY NOTES

References in Text

Chapter 37 of Title 40, referred to in the section heading, is Contract Work Hours and Safety Standards, 40 U.S.C.A. § 3701 et seq.

Effective and Applicability Provisions

1992 Acts

Amendment by Title IX of Pub.L. 102–572 effective Oct. 29, 1992, see section 911 of Pub.L. 102–572, set out as a note under section 171 of Title 28, Judiciary and Judicial Procedure.

1982 Acts

Amendment by Pub.L. 97–164 effective Oct. 1, 1982, see section 402 of Pub.L. 97–164, set out as a note under section 171 of this title.

1962 Acts

Amendment of section by Pub.L. 87–581 effective 60 days after Aug. 13, 1962, but shall not affect contracts existing or thereafter entered into pursuant to invitations for bids outstanding on Aug. 13, 1962, see section 204 of Pub.L. 87–581, set out as a note under section 327 of former Title 40, Public Buildings, Property and Works.

Continued Jurisdiction Upon Claims Under Section 324 of Title 40

Pub.L. 87–581, Title II, § 202(a), Aug. 13, 1962, 76 Stat. 360 provided that: "The Court of Claims [now Court of Federal Claims] shall continue to have jurisdiction to render judgment upon any claim for a penalty withheld from a contractor or subcontractor under section 324 of title 40, United States Code [repealed], in connection with any contract subject to said section existing on the effective date of this Act [60 days after Aug. 13, 1962; see Pub.L. 87–581, Title II, § 204, Aug. 13, 1962, 76 Stat. 360, repealed Pub.L. 107–217, § 6(b), Aug. 21, 2002, 116 Stat. 1316], or thereafter entered into pursuant to invitations for bids that are outstanding at the time of the enactment of this Act [Aug. 13, 1962]."

§ 1500. Pendency of claims in other courts

The United States Court of Federal Claims shall not have jurisdiction of any claim for or in respect to which the plaintiff or his assignee has pending in any other court any suit or process against the United States or any person who, at the time when the cause of action alleged in such suit or process arose, was, in respect thereto, acting or professing to act, directly or indirectly under the authority of the United States.

(June 25, 1948, c. 646, 62 Stat. 942; Apr. 2, 1982, Pub.L. 97–164, Title I, § 133(e) (1), 96 Stat. 40; Oct. 29, 1992, Pub.L. 102–572, Title IX, § 902(a)(1), 106 Stat. 4516.)

HISTORICAL AND STATUTORY NOTES

Effective and Applicability Provisions

1992 Acts

Amendment by Title IX of Pub.L. 102–572 effective Oct. 29, 1992, see section 911 of Pub.L. 102–572 , set out as a note under section 171 of this title.

1982 Acts

Amendment by Pub.L. 97–164 effective Oct. 1, 1982, see section 402 of Pub.L. 97–164, set out as a note under section 171 of this title.

§ 1501. Pensions

The United States Court of Federal Claims shall not have jurisdiction of any claim for a pension.

(June 25, 1948, c. 646, 62 Stat. 942; Apr. 2, 1982, Pub.L. 97–164, Title I, § 133(e) (1), 96 Stat. 40; Oct. 29, 1992, Pub.L. 102–572, Title IX, § 902(a)(1), 106 Stat. 4516.)

HISTORICAL AND STATUTORY NOTES

Effective and Applicability Provisions

1992 Acts

Amendment by Title IX of Pub.L. 102–572 effective Oct. 29, 1992, see section 911 of Pub.L. 102–572, set out as a note under section 171 of this title.

1982 Acts

Amendment by Pub.L. 97–164 effective Oct. 1, 1982, see section 402 of Pub.L. 97–164, set out as a note under section 171 of this title.

§ 1502. Treaty cases

Except as otherwise provided by Act of Congress, the United States Court of Federal Claims shall not have jurisdiction of any claim against the United States growing out of or dependent upon any treaty entered into with foreign nations.

(June 25, 1948, c. 646, 62 Stat. 942; May 24, 1949, c. 139, § 88, 63 Stat. 102; Apr. 2, 1982, Pub.L. 97–164, Title I, § 133(e) (1), 96 Stat. 40; Oct. 29, 1992, Pub.L. 102–572, Title IX, § 902(a)(1), 106 Stat. 4516.)

HISTORICAL AND STATUTORY NOTES

Effective and Applicability Provisions

1992 Acts

Amendment by Title IX of Pub.L. 102–572 effective Oct. 29, 1992, see section 911 of Pub.L. 102–572, set out as a note under section 171 of this title.

1982 Acts

Amendment by Pub.L. 97–164 effective Oct. 1, 1982, see section 402 of Pub.L. 97–164, set out as a note under section 171 of this title.

§ 1503. Set-offs

The United States Court of Federal Claims shall have jurisdiction to render judgment upon any set-off or demand by the United States against any plaintiff in such court.

(June 25, 1948, c. 646, 62 Stat. 942; Apr. 2, 1982, Pub.L. 97–164, Title I, § 133(e) (1), 96 Stat. 40; Oct. 29, 1992, Pub.L. 102–572, Title IX, § 902(a)(1), 106 Stat. 4516.)

HISTORICAL AND STATUTORY NOTES

Effective and Applicability Provisions

1992 Acts

Amendment by Title IX of Pub.L. 102–572 effective Oct. 29, 1992, see section 911 of Pub.L. 102–572, set out as a note under section 171 of this title.

1982 Acts

Amendment by Pub.L. 97–164 effective Oct. 1, 1982, see section 402 of Pub.L. 97–164, set out as a note under section 171 of this title.

[§ 1504. Repealed. Pub.L. 97–164, Title I, § 133(f), Apr. 2, 1982, 96 Stat. 41]

HISTORICAL AND STATUTORY NOTES

Section, Act June 25, 1948, c. 646, 62 Stat. 942, directed that the Court of Claims [now Court of Federal Claims] have jurisdiction to review by appeal final judgments in the district courts in civil actions based on tort claims brought under section 1346(b) of this title if the notice of appeal filed in the district court had affixed to it a written consent on behalf of the appellees that the appeal be taken to the Court of Claims.

Effective Date of Repeal

Repeal effective Oct. 1, 1982, see section 402 of Pub.L. 97–164, set out as an Effective and Applicability Provisions of 1982 Amendments note under section 171 of this title.

§ 1505. Indian claims

The United States Court of Federal Claims shall have jurisdiction of any claim against the United States accruing after August 13, 1946, in favor of any tribe, band, or other identifiable group of American Indians residing within the territorial limits of the United States or Alaska whenever such claim is one arising under the Constitution, laws or treaties of the United States, or Executive orders of the President, or is one which otherwise would be cognizable in the Court of Federal Claims if the claimant were not an Indian tribe, band or group.

(Added May 24, 1949, c. 139, § 89(a), 63 Stat. 102, and amended Apr. 2, 1982, Pub.L. 97–164, Title I, § 133(g), 96 Stat. 41; Oct. 29, 1992, Pub.L. 102–572, Title IX, § 902(a), 106 Stat. 4516.)

HISTORICAL AND STATUTORY NOTES

Effective and Applicability Provisions

1992 Acts

Amendment by Title IX of Pub.L. 102–572 effective Oct. 29, 1992, see section 911 of Pub.L. 102–572, set out as a note under section 171 of this title.

1982 Acts

Amendment by Pub.L. 97–164 effective Oct. 1, 1982, see section 402 of Pub.L. 97–164, set out as a note under section 171 of this title.

[§ 1506. Repealed. Pub.L. 97–164, Title I, § 133(h), Apr. 2, 1982, 96 Stat. 41]

HISTORICAL AND STATUTORY NOTES

Section, added Pub.L. 86–770, § 2(a), Sept. 13, 1960, 74 Stat. 912, provided that if a case within the exclusive jurisdiction of the district courts was filed in the Court of Claims [now Court of Federal Claims], the Court of Claims, if it were in the interest of justice, had to transfer such case to any district court in which it could have been brought at the time such case was filed, where the case would proceed as if it had been filed in the district court on the date it was filed in the Court of Claims.

Effective Date of Repeal

Repeal effective Oct. 1, 1982, see section 402 of Pub.L. 97–164, set out as a note under section 171 of this title.

§ 1507. Jurisdiction for certain declaratory judgments

The United States Court of Federal Claims shall have jurisdiction to hear any suit for and issue a declaratory judgment under section 7428 of the Internal Revenue Code of 1986.

(Added Pub.L. 94–455, Title XIII, § 1306(b)(9)(A), Oct. 4, 1976, 90 Stat. 1720, and amended Pub.L. 97–164, Title I, § 133(i), Apr. 2, 1982, 96 Stat. 41; Pub.L. 99–514, § 2, Oct. 22, 1986, 100 Stat. 2095; Pub.L. 102–572, Title IX, § 902(a)(1), Oct. 29, 1992, 106 Stat. 4516.)

HISTORICAL AND STATUTORY NOTES

References in Text

Section 7428 of the Internal Revenue Code of 1986, referred to in text, is classified to section 7428 of Title 26, Internal Revenue Code.

Effective and Applicability Provisions

1992 Acts

Amendment by Title IX of Pub.L. 102–572 effective Oct. 29, 1992, see section 911 of Pub.L. 102–572, set out as a note under section 171 of this title.

1982 Acts

Amendment by Pub.L. 97–164 effective Oct. 1, 1982, see section 402 of Pub.L. 97–164, set out as a note under section 171 of this title.

1976 Acts

Section applicable with respect to pleadings filed with the United States Tax Court, the district court of the United States for the District of Columbia, or the United States Court of Claims more than 6 months after Oct. 4, 1976, but only with respect to determinations (or requests for determinations) made after Jan. 1, 1976, see section 1306(c) of Pub.L. 94–455, set out as a note under section 7428 of Title 26, Internal Revenue Code.

§ 1508. Jurisdiction for certain partnership proceedings

The Court of Federal Claims shall have jurisdiction to hear and to render judgment upon any petition under section 6226 or 6228(a) of the Internal Revenue Code of 1986.

(Added Pub.L. 97–248, Title IV, § 402(c)(18)(A), Sept. 3, 1982, 96 Stat. 669, and amended Pub.L. 99–514, § 2, Oct. 22, 1986, 100 Stat. 2095; Pub.L. 102–572, Title IX, § 902(a)(2), Oct. 29, 1992, 106 Stat. 4516.)

HISTORICAL AND STATUTORY NOTES

References in Text

Sections 6226 and 6228(a) of the Internal Revenue Code of 1986, referred to in text, are classified to sections 6226 and 6228(a) of Title 26, Internal Revenue Code.

Effective and Applicability Provisions

1992 Acts

Amendment by Title IX of Pub.L. 102–572 effective Oct. 29, 1992, see section 911 of Pub.L. 102–572, set out as a note under section 171 of this title.

1982 Acts

Section applicable to partnership taxable years beginning after Sept. 3, 1982, with provision for the applicability of this section to any partnership taxable year ending after Sept. 3, 1982, if the partnership, each partner, and each indirect partner requests such application and the Secretary of the Treasury or his delegate consents to such application, see section 407(a)(1) and (3) of Pub.L. 97–248, set out as a note under section 6221 of Title 26, Internal Revenue Code.

§ 1509. No jurisdiction in cases involving refunds of tax shelter promoter and understatement penalties

The United States Court of Federal Claims shall not have jurisdiction to hear any action or proceeding for any refund or credit of any penalty imposed under section 6700 of the Internal Revenue Code of 1986 (relating to penalty for promoting abusive tax shelters, etc.) or section 6701 of such Code (relating to penalties for aiding and abetting understatement of tax liability).

(Added Pub.L. 98–369, Div. A, Title VII, § 714(g)(2), July 18, 1984, 98 Stat. 962, and amended Pub.L. 99–514, § 2, Oct. 22, 1986, 100 Stat. 2095; Pub.L. 102–572, Title IX, § 902(a)(1), Oct. 29, 1992, 106 Stat. 4516.)

HISTORICAL AND STATUTORY NOTES

References in Text

Sections 6700 and 6701 of the Internal Revenue Code of 1986, referred to in text, are classified to sections 6700 and 6701, respectively, of Title 26, Internal Revenue Code.

Effective and Applicability Provisions

1992 Acts

Amendment by Title IX of Pub.L. 102–572 effective Oct. 29, 1992, see section 911 of Pub.L. 102–572, set out as a note under section 171 of this title.

1984 Acts

Section 714(g)(4) of Pub.L. 98–369 provided that: "The amendments made by this subsection [enacting this section and amending section 7422 of Title 26, Internal Revenue Code] shall apply to any claim for refund or credit filed after the date of the enactment of this Act [July 18, 1984]."

[CHAPTER 93—REPEALED]

[§§ 1541 to 1546. Repealed. Pub.L. 97–164, Title I, § 134, Apr. 2, 1982, 96 Stat. 41]

HISTORICAL AND STATUTORY NOTES

Section 1541, Acts June 25, 1948, c. 646, 62 Stat. 942; June 2, 1970, Pub.L. 91–271, Title I, § 102, 84 Stat. 274; July 26, 1979, Pub.L. 96–39, Title X, § 1001(b)(4)(A), 93 Stat. 305; Oct. 10, 1980, Pub.L. 96–417, Title IV, § 401(a), Title V, § 501(23), (24), 94 Stat. 1740, 1742, gave the Court of Cus-

toms and Patent Appeals exclusive jurisdiction of appeals from all final decisions of the Court of International Trade and from interlocutory orders of the Court of International Trade granting, continuing, modifying, refusing, or dissolving injunctions, or refusing to dissolve or modify injunctions, and with discretion to entertain appeals from certain orders of the Court of International Trade. See section 1295(a)(5) of this title.

Section 1542, Acts June 25, 1948, c. 646, 62 Stat. 942; May 24, 1949, c. 139, § 89(b), 63 Stat. 102, gave the Court of Customs and Patent Appeals jurisdiction of appeals from

decisions of the Board of Appeals and the Board of Interference Examiners of the Patent Office as to patent applications and interferences, at the instance of an applicant for a patent or any party to a patent interference, with such appeal by an applicant to waive his right to proceed under section 63 of Title 35, and the Commissioner of Patents as to trade-mark applications and proceedings as provided in section 1071 of Title 15. See section 1295(a) (4) of this title.

Section 1543, Acts June 25, 1948, c. 646, 62 Stat. 943; Oct. 10, 1980, Pub.L. 96–417, Title IV, § 401(b) (1), 94 Stat. 1740, gave the Court of Customs and Patent Appeals jurisdiction to review final determinations of the United States International Trade Commission made under section 337 of the Tariff Act of 1930 relating to unfair trade practices in import trade. See section 1295(a) (6) of this title.

Section 1544, added Pub.L. 89–651, § 8(c) (1), Oct. 14, 1966, 80 Stat. 901, gave the Court of Customs and Patent Appeals jurisdiction to review, by appeal on questions of law only, findings of the Secretary of Commerce under headnote 6 to schedule 8, part 4, of the Tariff Schedules of the United States (relating to importation of instruments or apparatus). See section 1295(a) (7) of this title.

Section 1545, added Pub.L. 91–577, Title III, § 143(a), Dec. 24, 1970, 84 Stat. 1558, gave the Court of Customs and Patent Appeals nonexclusive jurisdiction of appeals under section 71 of the Plant Variety Protection Act, classified to section 2461 of Title 7, Agriculture. See section 1295(a) (8) of this title.

Section 1546, added Pub.L. 96–417, Title IV, § 402(a), Oct. 10, 1980, 94 Stat. 1740, gave the Court of Customs and Patent Appeals all of the powers in law and in equity of, or conferred by statute upon, a court of appeals of the United States.

Effective Date of Repeal

Repeal effective Oct. 1, 1982, see section 402 of Pub.L. 97–164, set out as a note under section 171 of this title.

CHAPTER 95—COURT OF INTERNATIONAL TRADE

HISTORICAL AND STATUTORY NOTES

Prior Provisions

A prior Chapter 95—Customs Court, comprising sections 1581 and 1582, was omitted from the Code upon the general revision of this chapter by Pub.L. 96–417, Title II, § 201, Oct. 10, 1980, 94 Stat. 1728.

§ 1581. Civil actions against the United States and agencies and officers thereof

(a) The Court of International Trade shall have exclusive jurisdiction of any civil action commenced to contest the denial of a protest, in whole or in part, under section 515 of the Tariff Act of 1930.

(b) The Court of International Trade shall have exclusive jurisdiction of any civil action commenced under section 516 of the Tariff Act of 1930.

(c) The Court of International Trade shall have exclusive jurisdiction of any civil action commenced under section 516A of the Tariff Act of 1930.

(d) The Court of International Trade shall have exclusive jurisdiction of any civil action commenced to review—

(1) any final determination of the Secretary of Labor under section 223 of the Trade Act of 1974 with respect to the eligibility of workers for adjustment assistance under such Act;

(2) any final determination of the Secretary of Commerce under section 251 of the Trade Act of 1974 with respect to the eligibility of a firm for adjustment assistance under such Act; and

(3) any final determination of the Secretary of Commerce under section 271 of the Trade Act of 1974 with respect to the eligibility of a community for adjustment assistance under such Act.

(e) The Court of International Trade shall have exclusive jurisdiction of any civil action commenced to review any final determination of the Secretary of the Treasury under section 305(b)(1) of the Trade Agreements Act of 1979.

(f) The Court of International Trade shall have exclusive jurisdiction of any civil action involving an application for an order directing the administering authority or the International Trade Commission to make confidential information available under section 777(c)(2) of the Tariff Act of 1930.

(g) The Court of International Trade shall have exclusive jurisdiction of any civil action commenced to review—

(1) any decision of the Secretary of the Treasury to deny a customs broker's license under section 641(b)(2) or (3) of the Tariff Act of 1930, or to deny a customs broker's permit under section 641(c)(1) of such Act, or to revoke a license or permit under section 641(b)(5) or (c)(2) of such Act;

(2) any decision of the Secretary of the Treasury to revoke or suspend a customs broker's license or permit, or impose a monetary penalty in lieu thereof, under section 641(d)(2)(B) of the Tariff Act of 1930; and

(3) any decision or order of the Customs Service to deny, suspend, or revoke accreditation of a private laboratory under section 499(b) of the Tariff Act of 1930.

(h) The Court of International Trade shall have exclusive jurisdiction of any civil action commenced to review, prior to the importation of the goods involved, a ruling issued by the Secretary of the Treasury, or a refusal to issue or change such a ruling, relating to classification, valuation, rate of duty, marking, restricted merchandise, entry requirements, drawbacks, vessel repairs, or similar matters, but only if the party commencing the civil action demonstrates to the court that he would be irreparably harmed unless given an opportunity to obtain judicial review prior to such importation.

(i) In addition to the jurisdiction conferred upon the Court of International Trade by subsections (a)–(h) of this section and subject to the exception set forth in subsection (j) of this section, the Court of International Trade shall have exclusive jurisdiction of any civil action commenced against the United States, its agencies, or its officers, that arises out of any law of the United States providing for—

 (1) revenue from imports or tonnage;

 (2) tariffs, duties, fees, or other taxes on the importation of merchandise for reasons other than the raising of revenue;

 (3) embargoes or other quantitative restrictions on the importation of merchandise for reasons other than the protection of the public health or safety; or

 (4) administration and enforcement with respect to the matters referred to in paragraphs (1)–(3) of this subsection and subsections (a)–(h) of this section.

This subsection shall not confer jurisdiction over an antidumping or countervailing duty determination which is reviewable either by the Court of International Trade under section 516A(a) of the Tariff Act of 1930 or by a binational panel under article 1904 of the North American Free Trade Agreement or the United States–Canada Free–Trade Agreement and section 516A(g) of the Tariff Act of 1930.

(j) The Court of International Trade shall not have jurisdiction of any civil action arising under section 305 of the Tariff Act of 1930.

(Added Pub.L. 96–417, Title II, § 201, Oct. 10, 1980, 94 Stat. 1728, and amended Pub.L. 98–573, Title II, § 212(b)(1), Oct. 30, 1984, 98 Stat. 2983; Pub.L. 99–514, Title XVIII, § 1891(1), Oct. 22, 1986, 100 Stat. 2926; Pub.L. 100–449, Title IV, § 402(a), Sept. 28, 1988, 102 Stat. 1883; Pub.L. 103–182, Title IV, § 414(a)(1), Title VI, § 684(a)(1), Dec. 8, 1993, 107 Stat. 2147, 2219.)

Termination of Amendments

For provisions directing that, except for transition provisions relating to proceedings regarding protective orders and undertakings, and binational panel and extraordinary challenge committee reviews, the amendment to this section by Title IV of Pub.L. 103–182 shall cease to have effect with respect to any country on the date on which such country ceases to be a NAFTA country, see 19 U.S.C.A. § 3451.

Termination of United States–Canada Free–Trade Agreement

For provisions directing that the amendments made by Pub.L. 100–449, which amended this section, shall cease to have effect on the date on which the United States–Canada Free–Trade Agreement ceases to be in force, see section 501(c) of Pub.L. 100–449, set out in the note under 19 U.S.C.A. § 2112.

Articles 1906 and 2106 of the Agreement authorize either the United States or Canada to terminate the Agreement on 6–month notice if, at the end of the 7–year period following the date of the entry into effect of the Agreement, no agreement has been entered into between the United States and Canada on a substitute system of antidumping and countervailing duties.

HISTORICAL AND STATUTORY NOTES

References in Text

Sections 515 and 516 of the Tariff Act of 1930, referred to in subsecs. (a) and (b), respectively, are classified, respectively, to sections 1515 and 1516 of Title 19, Customs Duties.

The Trade Act of 1974, referred to in subsec. (d)(1) to (3), is Pub.L. 93–618, Jan. 3, 1975, 88 Stat.1978, as amended, which is classified principally to chapter 12 (section 2101 et seq.) of Title 19. Sections 223, 251, and 271 of the Trade Act of 1974 are classified to sections 2273, 2341, and 2371, respectively, of Title 19. For complete classification of this Act to the Code, see References in Text note set out under section 2101 of Title 19 and Tables.

Section 305(b)(1) of the Trade Agreements Act of 1979, referred to in subsec. (e), is classified to section 2515(b)(1) of Title 19, Customs Duties.

Sections 777(c)(2), 641(b), (c), (d), and 305 of the Tariff Act of 1930, referred to in subsecs. (f), (g), and (j), are classified to sections 1677f(c)(2), 1641, (b), (c), (d), and 1305, respectively, of Title 19, Customs Duties.

Section 499(b) of the Tariff Act of 1930, referred to in subsec. (g)(3), is classified to section 1499(b) of Title 19, Customs Duties.

Section 516A of the Tariff Act of 1930, referred to in subsec. (i), is classified to section 1516a of Title 19.

The United States–Canada Free–Trade Agreement, referred to in subsec. (i), was entered into on Jan. 2, 1988. The Agreement is not set out in the Code.

Effective and Applicability Provisions

1993 Acts

Amendment by section 414 of Pub.L. 103–182 effective on the date the North American Free Trade Agreement enters into force with respect to the United States [Jan. 1, 1994], but not to apply to any final determination described in section 1516a(a)(1)(B) or (2)(B)(i), (ii), or (iii) of Title 19, Customs Duties, notice of which is published in the Federal Register before such date, or to a determination described in section 1516a(a)(2)(B)(vi) of Title 19 notice of which is received by the Government of Canada or Mexico before such date, or to any binational panel review under the United States-Canada Free-Trade Agreement, or to any extraordinary challenge arising out of any such review that was commenced before such date, see section 416 of Pub.L. 103–182, set out as a note under section 3431 of Title 19.

Amendment by section 684(a)(1) of Pub.L. 103–182 effective Dec. 8, 1993, see section 692 of Pub.L. 103–182, set out as a note under section 58c of Title 19, Customs Duties.

1988 Acts

Amendment by Pub.L. 100–449 effective on the date the United States–Canada Free–Trade Agreement enters into force, (Jan. 1, 1989), and to cease to have effect on the date the Agreement ceases to be in force, see section 501(a), (c) of Pub.L. 100–449, set out in a note under section 2112 of Title 19, Customs Duties. [A Presidential Memorandum on the Canada–United States Free–Trade Agreement, dated Dec. 31, 1988, directing the Secretary of State to exchange notes with the Government of Canada to provide for the entry into force of the Agreement on Jan. 1, 1989, is set out in 24 Weekly Compilation of Presidential Documents 1688, Jan. 2, 1989.]

1984 Acts

Amendment by Pub.L. 98–573 to take effect on the close of the 180th day after Oct. 30, 1984, see section 214(d) of Pub.L. 98–573, set out as a note under section 1304 of Title 19, Customs Duties.

1980 Acts

Section effective on Nov. 1, 1980, and applicable with respect to civil actions pending on or commenced on or after such date, see section 701(a) of Pub.L. 96–417, as amended, set out as a note under section 251 of this title.

Subsecs. (d) and (g) to (i) of this section applicable with respect to civil actions commenced on or after Nov. 1, 1980, see section 701(b)(1)(A) of Pub.L. 96–417, as amended, set out as a note under section 251 of this title.

Transfer of Functions

For transfer of the functions, personnel, assets, and liabilities of the United States Customs Service of the Department of the Treasury, including the functions of the Secretary of the Treasury relating thereto, to the Secretary of Homeland Security, and for treatment of related references, see 6 U.S.C.A. §§ 203(1), 551(d), 552(d) and 557, and the Department of Homeland Security Reorganization Plan of November 25, 2002, as modified, set out as a note under 6 U.S.C.A. § 542.

Prior Provisions

A prior section 1581, Act June 25, 1948, c. 646, 62 Stat. 943, related to powers of the Customs Court generally and was omitted in the general revision of this chapter by Pub.L. 96–417. See section 1585 of this title.

Application of Amendments Relating to Accreditation of Private Laboratories

Section 684(b) of Pub.L. 103–182 provided that: "For purposes of applying the amendments made by subsection (a) [amending subsec. (g) of this section, and sections 2631, 2636, 2640 and 2642 of this title], any decision or order of the Customs Service denying, suspending, or revoking the accreditation of a private laboratory on or after the date of the enactment of this Act [Dec. 8, 1993] and before regulations to implement section 499(b) of the Tariff Act of 1930 [section 1499(b) of Title 19, Customs Duties] are issued shall be treated as having been denied, suspended, or revoked under such section 499(b)."

Prior History of Court

The United States Customs Court, the predecessor of the Court of International Trade, was omitted in the general revision of this chapter by Pub.L. 96–417.

The predecessor of the United States Customs Court was the Board of General Appraisers which was created by the Customs Administrative Act of June 10, 1890. The Board was under the administrative supervision of the Secretary of the Treasury.

From 1890 to 1926, the Board of General Appraisers had jurisdiction over all protests from decisions of the collectors of customs and appeals for reappraisement under sections 13 and 14 of the Customs Administrative Act of June 10, 1890, c. 407, 26 Stat. 136.

The Customs Court was established by Act May 28, 1926, c. 411, §§ 1, 2, 44 Stat. 669, sections 405a and 405b of Title 19, Customs Duties, and said act transferred to it all the jurisdiction and powers of the former Board of General Appraisers. The Tariff Act of June 1930, c. 497, Title IV, § 518, 46 Stat. 737, section 1518 of Title 19, continued the Customs Court as constituted on June 17, 1930 with, however, several important changes.

§ 1582. Civil actions commenced by the United States

The Court of International Trade shall have exclusive jurisdiction of any civil action which arises out of an import transaction and which is commenced by the United States—

(1) to recover a civil penalty under section 592, 593A, 641(b)(6), 641(d)(2)(A), 704(i)(2), or 734(i)(2) of the Tariff Act of 1930;

(2) to recover upon a bond relating to the importation of merchandise required by the laws of the United States or by the Secretary of the Treasury; or

(3) to recover customs duties.

(Added Pub.L. 96–417, Title II, § 201, Oct. 10, 1980, 94 Stat. 1729, and amended Pub.L. 98–573, Title II, § 212(b)(2), Oct. 30, 1984, 98 Stat. 2983; Pub.L. 99–514, Title XVIII, § 1891(2), Oct. 22, 1986, 100 Stat. 2926; Pub.L. 103–182, Title VI, § 684(c), Dec. 8, 1993, 107 Stat. 2219.)

HISTORICAL AND STATUTORY NOTES

References in Text

Sections 592, 593A, 641(b)(2), 641(d)(2)(A), 704(i)(2), and 734(i)(2) of the Tariff Act of 1930, referred to in par. (1), are classified to sections 1592, 1593a, 1641(b)(6), 1641(d)(2)(A), 1671c(i)(2), and 1673c(i)(2) of Title 19, Customs Duties.

Effective and Applicability Provisions

1993 Acts

Amendment by section 684(c) of Pub.L. 103–182 effective Dec. 8, 1993, see section 692 of Pub.L. 103–182, set out as a note under section 58c of Title 19, Customs Duties.

1984 Acts

Amendment by Pub.L. 98–573 to take effect on the close of the 180th day after Oct. 30, 1984, see section 214(d) of Pub.L. 98–573, set out as a note under section 1304 of Title 19, Customs Duties.

1980 Acts

Section applicable with respect to civil actions commenced on or after the 90th day after Nov. 1, 1980, see section 701(c)(1)(A) of Pub.L. 96–417, as amended, set out as a note under section 251 of this title.

Prior Provisions

A prior section 1582, Acts June 25, 1948, c. 646, 62 Stat. 943; June 2, 1970, Pub.L. 91–271, Title I, § 110, 84 Stat. 278; July 26, 1979, Pub.L. 96–39, Title X, § 1001(b)(4)(B), 93 Stat. 305, related to the jurisdiction of the Customs Court and was omitted in the general revision of this chapter by Pub.L. 96–417.

§ 1583. Counterclaims, cross-claims, and third-party actions

In any civil action in the Court of International Trade, the court shall have exclusive jurisdiction to render judgment upon any counterclaim, cross-claim, or third-party action of any party, if (1) such claim or action involves the imported merchandise that is the subject matter of such civil action, or (2) such claim or action is to recover upon a bond or customs duties relating to such merchandise.

(Added Pub.L. 96–417, Title II, § 201, Oct. 10, 1980, 94 Stat. 1729.)

HISTORICAL AND STATUTORY NOTES

Effective and Applicability Provisions

1980 Acts

Section applicable with respect to civil actions commenced on or after Nov. 1, 1980, see section 701(b)(1)(A) of Pub.L. 96–417, as amended, set out as a note under section 251 of this title.

Prior Provisions

A prior section 1583, Act June 25, 1948, c. 646, 62 Stat. 943, related to certain cases of exclusive jurisdiction of the Customs Court and was repealed by Pub.L. 91–271, Title I, § 111, June 2, 1970, 84 Stat. 278.

§ 1584. Civil actions under the North American Free Trade Agreement or the United States–Canada Free–Trade Agreement

The United States Court of International Trade shall have exclusive jurisdiction of any civil action which arises under section 777(f) of the Tariff Act of 1930 and is commenced by the United States to enforce administrative sanctions levied for violation of a protective order or an undertaking.

(Added Pub.L. 100–449, Title IV, § 402(d)(1), Sept. 28, 1988, 102 Stat. 1884, and amended Pub.L. 103–182, Title IV, § 414(a)(2), Dec. 8, 1993, 107 Stat. 2147.)

Termination of Amendments

For provisions directing that, except for transition provisions relating to proceedings regarding protective orders and undertakings, and binational panel and extraordinary challenge committee reviews, the amendment to this section by Title IV of Pub.L. 103–182 shall cease to have effect with respect to any country on the date on which such country ceases to be a NAFTA country, see 19 U.S.C.A. § 3451.

Termination of United States–Canada Free–Trade Agreement

For provisions directing that the amendments made by Pub.L. 100–449, which enacted this section, shall cease to have effect on the date on which the United States–Canada Free–Trade Agreement ceases to be in force, see section 501(c) of Pub.L. 100–449, set out in the note under 19 U.S.C.A. § 2112.

Articles 1906 and 2106 of the Agreement authorize either the United States or Canada to terminate the Agreement on 6–month notice if, at the end of the 7–year period following the date of the entry into effect of the Agreement, no agreement has been entered into between the United States and Canada on a substitute system of antidumping and countervailing duties.

HISTORICAL AND STATUTORY NOTES

References in Text

Section 777(f) of the Tariff Act of 1930, referred to in text, is classified to section 1677f(f) of Title 19, Customs Duties.

Effective and Applicability Provisions

1993 Acts

Amendment by section 414 of Pub.L. 103–182 effective on the date the North American Free Trade Agreement enters into force with respect to the United States [Jan. 1, 1994], but not to apply to any final determination described in section 1516a(a)(1)(B) or (2)(B)(i), (ii), or (iii) of Title 19, Customs Duties, notice of which is published in the Federal Register before such date, or to a determination described in section 1516a(a)(2)(B)(vi) of Title 19 notice of which is received by the Government of Canada or Mexico before such date, or to any binational panel review under the United States-Canada Free-Trade Agreement, or to any extraordi-

nary challenge arising out of any such review that was commenced before such date, see section 416 of Pub.L. 103–182, set out as a note under section 3431 of Title 19.

1988 Acts

Section effective on the date the United States–Canada Free–Trade Agreement enters into force (Jan. 1, 1989), and to cease to have effect on the date the Agreement ceases to be in force, see section 501(a), (c), of Pub.L. 100–449, set out in a note under section 2112 of Title 19, Customs Duties. [A Presidential Memorandum on the Canada–United States Free–Trade Agreement, dated Dec. 31, 1988, directing the Secretary of State to exchange notes with the Government of Canada to provide for the entry into force of the Agreement on Jan. 1, 1989, is set out in 24 Weekly Compilation of Presidential Documents 1688, Jan. 2, 1989.]

Prior Provisions

A prior section 1584, added Pub.L. 96–417, Title II, § 201, Oct. 10, 1980, 94 Stat. 1729, which provided that if a civil action within the exclusive jurisdiction of the Court of International Trade were commenced in a district court of the United States, the district court, in the interest of justice, would transfer such civil action to the Court of International Trade, where such action proceeded as if it had been commenced in the Court of International Trade in the first instance, and that if a civil action within the exclusive jurisdiction of a district court, a court of appeals, or the Court of Customs and Patent Appeals were commenced in the Court of International Trade, the Court of International Trade, in the interest of justice, would transfer such civil action to the appropriate district court or court of appeals or to the Court of Customs and Patent Appeals where such action proceeded as if it had been commenced in such court in the first instance, was repealed by Pub.L. 97–164, Title I, § 135, Apr. 2, 1982, 96 Stat. 41, eff. Oct. 1, 1982.

§ 1585. Powers in law and equity

The Court of International Trade shall possess all the powers in law and equity of, or as conferred by statute upon, a district court of the United States.

(Added Pub.L. 96–417, Title II, § 201, Oct. 10, 1980, 94 Stat. 1730.)

CHAPTER 97—JURISDICTIONAL IMMUNITIES OF FOREIGN STATES

§ 1602. Findings and declaration of purpose

The Congress finds that the determination by United States courts of the claims of foreign states to immunity from the jurisdiction of such courts would serve the interests of justice and would protect the rights of both foreign states and litigants in United States courts. Under international law, states are not immune from the jurisdiction of foreign courts insofar as their commercial activities are concerned, and their commercial property may be levied upon for the satisfaction of judgments rendered against them in connection with their commercial activities. Claims of foreign states to immunity should henceforth be decided by courts of the United States and of the States in conformity with the principles set forth in this chapter.

(Added Pub.L. 94–583, § 4(a), Oct. 21, 1976, 90 Stat. 2892.)

HISTORICAL AND STATUTORY NOTES

Effective and Applicability Provisions

1976 Acts

Section 8 of Pub.L. 94–583 provided that: "This Act [enacting this chapter and section 1330 of this title, amending sections 1332, 1391, and 1441 of this title, and enacting provisions set out as notes under this section] shall take effect ninety days after the date of its enactment [Oct. 21, 1976]."

Separability of Provisions

Section 7 of Pub.L. 94–583 provided that: "If any provision of this Act [enacting this chapter and section 1330 of this title, amending sections 1332, 1391, and 1441 of this title, and enacting provisions set out as notes under this section and section 1 of this title] or the application thereof to any foreign state is held invalid, the invalidity does not affect other provisions or applications of the Act which can be given effect without the invalid provision or application, and to this end the provisions of this Act are severable."

Short Title

1976 Acts

Authorization to cite Pub.L. 94–583, which enacted this chapter, as the "Foreign Sovereign Immunities Act of 1976", see section 1 of Pub.L. 94–583, set out as a note under section 1 of this title.

§ 1603. Definitions

For purposes of this chapter—

(a) A "foreign state", except as used in section 1608 of this title, includes a political subdivision of a foreign state or an agency or instrumentality of a foreign state as defined in subsection (b).

(b) An "agency or instrumentality of a foreign state" means any entity—

(1) which is a separate legal person, corporate or otherwise, and

(2) which is an organ of a foreign state or political subdivision thereof, or a majority of whose shares or other ownership interest is owned by a foreign state or political subdivision thereof, and

(3) which is neither a citizen of a State of the United States as defined in section 1332(c) and (e) of this title, nor created under the laws of any third country.

(c) The "United States" includes all territory and waters, continental or insular, subject to the jurisdiction of the United States.

(d) A "commercial activity" means either a regular course of commercial conduct or a particular commercial transaction or act. The commercial character of an activity shall be determined by reference to the nature of the course of conduct or particular transaction or act, rather than by reference to its purpose.

(e) A "commercial activity carried on in the United States by a foreign state" means commercial activity carried on by such state and having substantial contact with the United States.

(Added Pub.L. 94–583, § 4(a), Oct. 21, 1976, 90 Stat. 2892, and amended Pub.L. 109–2, § 4(b)(2), Feb. 18, 2005, 119 Stat. 12.)

HISTORICAL AND STATUTORY NOTES

Effective and Applicability Provisions

2005 Acts

Amendments by Class Action Fairness Act of 2005, Pub.L. 109–2, Feb. 18, 2005, 119 Stat. 4, applicable to any civil action commenced on or after Feb. 18, 2005, see Pub.L. 109–2, § 9, set out as a note under 28 U.S.C.A. § 1332.

1976 Acts

Section effective 90 days after Oct. 21, 1976, see section 8 of Pub.L. 94–583, set out as a note under section 1602 of this title.

§ 1604. Immunity of a foreign state from jurisdiction

Subject to existing international agreements to which the United States is a party at the time of enactment of this Act a foreign state shall be immune from the jurisdiction of the courts of the United States and of the States except as provided in sections 1605 to 1607 of this chapter.

(Added Pub.L. 94–583, § 4(a), Oct. 21, 1976, 90 Stat. 2892.)

HISTORICAL AND STATUTORY NOTES

References in Text

The time of enactment of this Act, referred to in text, probably means the time of enactment of Pub.L. 94–583, which was approved on Oct. 21, 1976.

Effective and Applicability Provisions

1976 Acts

Section effective 90 days after Oct. 21, 1976, see section 8 of Pub.L. 94–583, set out as a note under section 1602 of this title.

§ 1605. General exceptions to the jurisdictional immunity of a foreign state

(a) A foreign state shall not be immune from the jurisdiction of courts of the United States or of the States in any case—

(1) in which the foreign state has waived its immunity either explicitly or by implication, notwithstanding any withdrawal of the waiver which the foreign state may purport to effect except in accordance with the terms of the waiver;

(2) in which the action is based upon a commercial activity carried on in the United States by the foreign state; or upon an act performed in the United States in connection with a commercial activity of the foreign state elsewhere; or upon an act outside the territory of the United States in connection with a commercial activity of the foreign state elsewhere and that act causes a direct effect in the United States;

(3) in which rights in property taken in violation of international law are in issue and that property or any property exchanged for such property is present in the United States in connection with a commercial activity carried on in the United States by the foreign state; or that property or any property exchanged for such property is owned or operated by an agency or instrumentality of the foreign state and that agency or instrumentality is engaged in a commercial activity in the United States;

(4) in which rights in property in the United States acquired by succession or gift or rights in immovable property situated in the United States are in issue;

(5) not otherwise encompassed in paragraph (2) above, in which money damages are sought against a foreign state for personal injury or death, or damage to or loss of property, occurring in the United States and caused by the tortious act or omission of that foreign state or of any official or employee of that foreign state while acting within the scope of his office or employment; except this paragraph shall not apply to—

(A) any claim based upon the exercise or performance or the failure to exercise or perform a discretionary function regardless of whether the discretion be abused, or

(B) any claim arising out of malicious prosecution, abuse of process, libel, slander, misrepresentation, deceit, or interference with contract rights;

(6) in which the action is brought, either to enforce an agreement made by the foreign state with or for the benefit of a private party to submit to arbitration all or any differences which have arisen or which may arise between the parties with respect to a defined legal relationship, whether contractual or not, concerning a subject matter capable of settlement by arbitration under the laws of the United States, or to confirm an award made pursuant to such an agreement to arbitrate, if (A) the arbitration takes place or is intended to take place in the United States, (B) the agreement or award is or may be governed by a treaty or other international agreement in force for the United States calling for the recognition and enforcement of arbitral awards, (C) the underlying claim, save for the agreement to arbitrate, could have been brought in a United States court under this section or section 1607, or (D) paragraph (1) of this subsection is otherwise applicable; or

(7) not otherwise covered by paragraph (2), in which money damages are sought against a foreign state for personal injury or death that was caused by an act of torture, extrajudicial killing, aircraft sabotage, hostage taking, or the provision of material support or resources (as defined in section 2339A of title 18) for such an act if such act or provision of material support is engaged in by an official, employee, or agent of such foreign state while acting within the scope of his or her office, employment, or agency, except that the court shall decline to hear a claim under this paragraph—

(A) if the foreign state was not designated as a state sponsor of terrorism under section 6(j) of the Export Administration Act of 1979 (50 U.S.C. App. 2405(j)) or section 620A of the Foreign Assistance Act of 1961 (22 U.S.C. 2371) at the time the act occurred, unless later so designated as a result of such act or the act is related to Case Number 1:00CV03110(EGS) in the United States District Court for the District of Columbia; and

(B) even if the foreign state is or was so designated, if—

(i) the act occurred in the foreign state against which the claim has been brought and the claimant has not afforded the foreign state a reasonable opportunity to arbitrate the claim in accordance with accepted international rules of arbitration; or

(ii) neither the claimant nor the victim was a national of the United States (as that term is defined in section 101(a)(22) of the Immigration and Nationality Act) when the act upon which the claim is based occurred.

(b) A foreign state shall not be immune from the jurisdiction of the courts of the United States in any case in which a suit in admiralty is brought to enforce a maritime lien against a vessel or cargo of the foreign state, which maritime lien is based upon a commercial activity of the foreign state: *Provided, That—*

(1) notice of the suit is given by delivery of a copy of the summons and of the complaint to the person, or his agent, having possession of the vessel or cargo against which the maritime lien is asserted; and if the vessel or cargo is arrested pursuant to process obtained on behalf of the party bringing the suit, the service of process of arrest shall be deemed to constitute valid delivery of such notice, but the party bringing the suit shall be liable for any damages sustained by the foreign state as a result of the arrest if the party bringing the suit had actual or constructive knowledge that the vessel or cargo of a foreign state was involved; and

(2) notice to the foreign state of the commencement of suit as provided in section 1608 of this title is initiated within ten days either of the delivery of notice as provided in paragraph (1) of this subsection or, in the case of a party who was unaware that the vessel or cargo of a foreign state was involved, of the date such party determined the existence of the foreign state's interest.

(c) Whenever notice is delivered under subsection (b)(1), the suit to enforce a maritime lien shall thereafter proceed and shall be heard and determined according to the principles of law and rules of practice of suits in rem whenever it appears that, had the vessel been privately owned and possessed, a suit in rem might have been maintained. A decree against the foreign state may include costs of the suit and, if the decree is for a money judgment, interest as ordered by the court, except that the court may not award judgment against the foreign state in an amount greater than the value of the vessel or cargo upon which the maritime lien arose. Such value shall be determined as of the time notice is served under subsection (b)(1). Decrees shall be subject to appeal and revision as provided in other cases of admiralty and maritime jurisdiction. Nothing shall preclude the plaintiff in any proper case from seeking relief in personam in the same action brought to enforce a maritime lien as provided in this section.

(d) A foreign state shall not be immune from the jurisdiction of the courts of the United States in any action brought to foreclose a preferred mortgage, as defined in section 31301 of title 46. Such action shall be brought, heard, and determined in accordance with the provisions of chapter 313 of title 46 and in accordance with the principles of law and rules of practice of suits in rem, whenever it appears that had the vessel been privately owned and possessed a suit in rem might have been maintained.

(e) For purposes of paragraph (7) of subsection (a)—

(1) the terms "torture" and "extrajudicial killing" have the meaning given those terms in section 3 of the Torture Victim Protection Act of 1991;

(2) the term "hostage taking" has the meaning given that term in Article 1 of the International Convention Against the Taking of Hostages; and

(3) the term "aircraft sabotage" has the meaning given that term in Article 1 of the Convention for the Suppression of Unlawful Acts Against the Safety of Civil Aviation.

(f) No action shall be maintained under subsection (a)(7) unless the action is commenced not later than 10 years after the date on which the cause of action arose. All principles of equitable tolling, including the period during which the foreign state was immune from suit, shall apply in calculating this limitation period.

(g) Limitation on discovery.—

(1) In general.—(A) Subject to paragraph (2), if an action is filed that would otherwise be barred by section 1604, but for subsection (a)(7), the court, upon request of the Attorney General, shall stay any request, demand, or order for discovery on the United States that the Attorney General certifies would significantly interfere with a criminal investigation or prosecution, or a national security operation, related to the incident that gave rise to the cause of action, until such time as the Attorney General advises the court that such request, demand, or order will no longer so interfere.

(B) A stay under this paragraph shall be in effect during the 12–month period beginning on the date on which the court issues the order to stay discovery. The court shall renew the order to stay discovery for additional 12–month periods upon motion by the United States if the Attorney General certifies that discovery would significantly interfere with a criminal investigation or prosecution, or a national security operation, related to the incident that gave rise to the cause of action.

(2) Sunset.—(A) Subject to subparagraph (B), no stay shall be granted or continued in effect under paragraph (1) after the date that is 10 years after the date on which the incident that gave rise to the cause of action occurred.

(B) After the period referred to in subparagraph (A), the court, upon request of the Attorney General, may stay any request, demand, or order for discovery on the United States that the court finds a substantial likelihood would—

(i) create a serious threat of death or serious bodily injury to any person;

(ii) adversely affect the ability of the United States to work in cooperation with foreign and international law enforcement agencies in investigating violations of United States law; or

(iii) obstruct the criminal case related to the incident that gave rise to the cause of action or undermine the potential for a conviction in such case.

(3) Evaluation of evidence.—The court's evaluation of any request for a stay under this subsection filed by the Attorney General shall be conducted ex parte and in camera.

(4) Bar on motions to dismiss.—A stay of discovery under this subsection shall constitute a bar to the granting of a motion to dismiss under rules 12(b)(6) and 56 of the Federal Rules of Civil Procedure.

(5) Construction.—Nothing in this subsection shall prevent the United States from seeking protective orders or asserting privileges ordinarily available to the United States.

(Added Pub.L. 94–583, § 4(a), Oct. 21, 1976, 90 Stat. 2892, and amended Pub.L. 100–640, § 1, Nov. 9, 1988, 102 Stat. 3333; Pub.L. 100–669, § 2, Nov. 16, 1988, 102 Stat. 3969; Pub.L. 101–650, Title III, § 325(b)(8), Dec. 1, 1990, 104 Stat. 5121; Pub.L. 104–132, Title II, § 221(a), Apr. 24, 1996, 110 Stat. 1241; Pub.L. 105–11, Apr. 25, 1997, 111 Stat. 22; Pub.L. 107–77, Title VI, § 626(c), Nov. 28, 2001, 115 Stat. 803; Pub.L. 107–117, Div. B, Ch. 2, § 208, Jan. 10, 2002, 115 Stat. 2299; Pub.L. 109–304, § 17(f)(2), Oct. 6, 2006, 120 Stat. 1708.)

HISTORICAL AND STATUTORY NOTES

References in Text

Section 101(a)(22) of the Immigration and Nationality Act, referred to in subsec. (a)(7)(B)(ii), is classified to section 1101(a)(22) of Title 8, Aliens and Nationality.

Chapter 313 of Title 46, referred to in subsec. (d), is Commercial Instruments and Maritime Liens, 46 U.S.C.A. § 31301 et seq.

Section 3 of the Torture Victim Protection Act of 1991, referred to in subsec. (e)(1), is section 3 of Pub.L. 102–256, Mar. 12, 1992, 106 Stat. 73, set out in a note under section 1350 of this title.

Effective and Applicability Provisions

1997 Acts

Section 1 of Pub.L. 105–11 provided in part that the amendment of subsec. (a)(7)(B)(ii) by Pub.L. 105–11 is effective with respect to any cause of action arising before, on, or after April 25, 1997.

1996 Acts

Section 221(c) of Pub.L. 104–132 provided that: "The amendments made by this subtitle [amending this section and section 1610 of this title] shall apply to any cause of action arising before, on, or after the date of the enactment of this Act [Apr. 24, 1996]."

1988 Acts

Section 3 of Pub.L. 100–640 provided that: "The amendments made by this Act [amending this section and section 1610 of this title] shall apply to actions commenced on or after the date of the enactment of this Act [Nov. 9, 1988]."

1976 Acts

Section effective 90 days after Oct. 21, 1976, see section 8 of Pub.L. 94–583, set out as a note under section 1602 of this title.

Civil Liability for Acts of State Sponsored Terrorism

Pub.L. 104–208, Div. A, Title I, § 101(c) [Title V, § 589], Sept. 30, 1996, 110 Stat. 3009–172, provided that:

"**(a)** An official, employee, or agent of a foreign state designated as a state sponsor of terrorism designated under section 6(j) of the Export Administration Act of 1979 [section 2405(j) of the Appendix to Title 50, War and National Defense] while acting within the scope of his or her office, employment, or agency shall be liable to a United States national or the national's legal representative for personal injury or death caused by acts of that official, employee, or agent for which the courts of the United States may maintain jurisdiction under section 1605(a)(7) of title 28, United States Code [subsec. (a)(7) of this section] for money damages which may include economic damages, solatium, pain, and suffering, and punitive damages if the acts were among those described in section 1605(a)(7) [subsec. (a)(7) of this section].

"**(b)** Provisions related to statute of limitations and limitations on discovery that would apply to an action brought under 28 U.S.C. 1605(f) and (g) [subsecs. (f) and (g) of this section] shall also apply to actions brought under this section. No action shall be maintained under this action [SIC] if an official, employee, or agent of the United States, while acting within the scope of his or her office, employment, or agency would not be liable for such acts if carried out within the United States."

§ 1606. Extent of liability

As to any claim for relief with respect to which a foreign state is not entitled to immunity under section 1605 or 1607 of this chapter, the foreign state shall be liable in the same manner and to the same extent as a private individual under like circumstances; but a foreign state except for an agency or instrumentality thereof shall not be liable for punitive damages; if, however, in any case wherein death was caused, the law of the place where the action or omission occurred provides, or has been construed to provide, for damages only punitive in nature, the foreign state shall be liable for actual or compensatory damages measured by the pecuniary injuries resulting from such death which were incurred by the persons for whose benefit the action was brought.

(Added Pub.L. 94–583, § 4(a), Oct. 21, 1976, 90 Stat. 2894, and amended Pub.L. 105–277, Div. A, § 101(h) [Title I, § 117(b)], Oct. 21, 1998, 112 Stat. 2681–491; Pub.L. 106–386, Div. C, § 2002(f)(2), Oct. 28, 2000, 114 Stat. 1543; Pub.L. 107–297, Title II, § 201(c)(3), Nov. 26, 2002, 116 Stat. 2337.)

HISTORICAL AND STATUTORY NOTES

Effective and Applicability Provisions

1998 Acts

Amendment by section 117(b) of Pub.L. 105–277 to apply to any claim for which a foreign state is not immune under section 1605(a)(7) of this title arising before, on, or after Oct. 21, 1998, see Pub.L. 105–277, Div. A, § 101(h) [Title I, § 117(c)], set out as a note under section 1610 of this title.

1976 Acts

Section effective 90 days after Oct. 21, 1976, see section 8 of Pub.L. 94–583, set out as a note under section 1602 of this title.

Waiver of Exception to Immunity from Attachment or Execution

Provisions formerly authorizing the President to waive the requirements of section 117(b) of Pub.L. 105–277 [Div. A, § 101(h), Title I], (which amended this section) in the interest of national security, set out in Pub.L. 105–277, Div. A, § 101(h) [Title I, § 117(d)], Oct. 21, 1998, 112 Stat. 2681–491, which formerly appeared as a note under section 1610 of this title, were repealed by Pub.L. 106–386, Div. C, § 2002(f)(2), Oct. 28, 2000, 114 Stat. 1543.

§ 1607. Counterclaims

In any action brought by a foreign state, or in which a foreign state intervenes, in a court of the United States or of a State, the foreign state shall not be accorded immunity with respect to any counterclaim—

(a) for which a foreign state would not be entitled to immunity under section 1605 of this chapter had such claim been brought in a separate action against the foreign state; or

(b) arising out of the transaction or occurrence that is the subject matter of the claim of the foreign state; or

(c) to the extent that the counterclaim does not seek relief exceeding in amount or differing in kind from that sought by the foreign state.

(Added Pub.L. 94–583, § 4(a), Oct. 21, 1976, 90 Stat. 2894.)

HISTORICAL AND STATUTORY NOTES

Effective and Applicability Provisions

1976 Acts

Section effective 90 days after Oct. 21, 1976, see section 8 of Pub.L. 94–583, set out as a note under section 1602 of this title.

§ 1608. Service; time to answer; default

(a) Service in the courts of the United States and of the States shall be made upon a foreign state or political subdivision of a foreign state:

(1) by delivery of a copy of the summons and complaint in accordance with any special arrangement for service between the plaintiff and the foreign state or political subdivision; or

(2) if no special arrangement exists, by delivery of a copy of the summons and complaint in accordance with an applicable international convention on service of judicial documents; or

(3) if service cannot be made under paragraphs (1) or (2), by sending a copy of the summons and complaint and a notice of suit, together with a translation of each into the official language of the foreign state, by any form of mail requiring a signed receipt, to be addressed and dispatched by the clerk of the court to the head of the ministry of foreign affairs of the foreign state concerned, or

(4) if service cannot be made within 30 days under paragraph (3), by sending two copies of the summons and complaint and a notice of suit, together with a translation of each into the official language of the foreign state, by any form of mail requiring a signed receipt, to be addressed and dispatched by the clerk of the court to the Secretary of State in Washington, District of Columbia, to the attention of the Director of Special Consular Services—and the Secretary shall transmit one copy of the papers through diplomatic channels to the foreign state and shall send to the clerk of the court a certified copy of the diplomatic note indicating when the papers were transmitted.

As used in this subsection, a "notice of suit" shall mean a notice addressed to a foreign state and in a form prescribed by the Secretary of State by regulation.

(b) Service in the courts of the United States and of the States shall be made upon an agency or instrumentality of a foreign state:

(1) by delivery of a copy of the summons and complaint in accordance with any special arrangement for service between the plaintiff and the agency or instrumentality; or

(2) if no special arrangement exists, by delivery of a copy of the summons and complaint either to an officer, a managing or general agent, or to any other agent authorized by appointment or by law to receive service of process in the United States; or in accordance with an applicable international convention on service of judicial documents; or

(3) if service cannot be made under paragraphs (1) or (2), and if reasonably calculated to give actual notice, by delivery of a copy of the summons and complaint, together with a translation of each into the official language of the foreign state—

(A) as directed by an authority of the foreign state or political subdivision in response to a letter rogatory or request or

(B) by any form of mail requiring a signed receipt, to be addressed and dispatched by the clerk of the court to the agency or instrumentality to be served, or

(C) as directed by order of the court consistent with the law of the place where service is to be made.

(c) Service shall be deemed to have been made—

(1) in the case of service under subsection (a)(4), as of the date of transmittal indicated in the certified copy of the diplomatic note; and

(2) in any other case under this section, as of the date of receipt indicated in the certification, signed and returned postal receipt, or other proof of service applicable to the method of service employed.

(d) In any action brought in a court of the United States or of a State, a foreign state, a political subdivision thereof, or an agency or instrumentality of a foreign state shall serve an answer or other responsive pleading to the complaint within sixty days after service has been made under this section.

(e) No judgment by default shall be entered by a court of the United States or of a State against a foreign state, a political subdivision thereof, or an agency or instrumentality of a foreign state, unless the claimant establishes his claim or right to relief by evidence satisfactory to the court. A copy of any such default judgment shall be sent to the foreign state or political subdivision in the manner prescribed for service in this section.

(Added Pub.L. 94–583, § 4(a), Oct. 21, 1976, 90 Stat. 2894.)

HISTORICAL AND STATUTORY NOTES

Effective and Applicability Provisions

1976 Acts

Section effective 90 days after Oct. 21, 1976, see section 8 of Pub.L. 94–583, set out as a note under section 1602 of this title.

§ 1609. Immunity from attachment and execution of property of a foreign state

Subject to existing international agreements to which the United States is a party at the time of enactment of this Act the property in the United States of a foreign state shall be immune from attachment arrest and execution except as provided in sections 1610 and 1611 of this chapter.

(Added Pub.L. 94–583, § 4(a), Oct. 21, 1976, 90 Stat. 2895.)

HISTORICAL AND STATUTORY NOTES

References in Text

The time of enactment of this Act, referred to in text, probably means the time of enactment of Pub.L. 94–583, which was approved on Oct. 21, 1976.

Effective and Applicability Provisions

1976 Acts

Section effective 90 days after Oct. 21, 1976, see section 8 of Pub.L. 94–583, set out as a note under section 1602 of this title.

§ 1610. Exceptions to the immunity from attachment or execution

(a) The property in the United States of a foreign state, as defined in section 1603(a) of this chapter, used for a commercial activity in the United States, shall not be immune from attachment in aid of execution, or from execution, upon a judgment entered by a court of the United States or of a State after the effective date of this Act, if—

(1) the foreign state has waived its immunity from attachment in aid of execution or from execution either explicitly or by implication, notwithstanding any withdrawal of the waiver the foreign state may purport to effect except in accordance with the terms of the waiver, or

(2) the property is or was used for the commercial activity upon which the claim is based, or

(3) the execution relates to a judgment establishing rights in property which has been taken in violation of international law or which has been exchanged for property taken in violation of international law, or

(4) the execution relates to a judgment establishing rights in property—

(A) which is acquired by succession or gift, or

(B) which is immovable and situated in the United States: *Provided,* That such property is not used for purposes of maintaining a diplomatic or consular mission or the residence of the Chief of such mission, or

(5) the property consists of any contractual obligation or any proceeds from such a contractual obligation to indemnify or hold harmless the foreign state or its employees under a policy of automobile or other liability or casualty insurance covering the claim which merged into the judgment, or

(6) the judgment is based on an order confirming an arbitral award rendered against the foreign state, provided that attachment in aid of execution, or execution, would not be inconsistent with any provision in the arbitral agreement, or

(7) the judgment relates to a claim for which the foreign state is not immune under section 1605(a)(7), regardless of whether the property is or was involved with the act upon which the claim is based.

(b) In addition to subsection (a), any property in the United States of an agency or instrumentality of a foreign state engaged in commercial activity in the United States shall not be immune from attachment in aid of execution, or from execution, upon a judgment entered by a court of the United States or of a State after the effective date of this Act, if—

(1) the agency or instrumentality has waived its immunity from attachment in aid of execution or from execution either explicitly or implicitly, notwithstanding any withdrawal of the waiver the agency or instrumentality may purport to effect except in accordance with the terms of the waiver, or

(2) the judgment relates to a claim for which the agency or instrumentality is not immune by virtue of section 1605(a) (2), (3), (5), or (7), or 1605(b) of this chapter, regardless of whether the property is or was involved in the act upon which the claim is based.

(c) No attachment or execution referred to in subsections (a) and (b) of this section shall be permitted until the court has ordered such attachment and execution after having determined that a reasonable period of time has elapsed following the entry of judgment and the giving of any notice required under section 1608(e) of this chapter.

(d) The property of a foreign state, as defined in section 1603(a) of this chapter, used for a commercial activity in the United States, shall not be immune from attachment prior to the entry of judgment in any action brought in a court of the United States or of a State, or prior to the elapse of the period of time provided in subsection (c) of this section, if—

(1) the foreign state has explicitly waived its immunity from attachment prior to judgment, notwithstanding any withdrawal of the waiver the foreign state may purport to effect except in accordance with the terms of the waiver, and

(2) the purpose of the attachment is to secure satisfaction of a judgment that has been or may ultimately be entered against the foreign state, and not to obtain jurisdiction.

(e) The vessels of a foreign state shall not be immune from arrest in rem, interlocutory sale, and execution in actions brought to foreclose a preferred mortgage as provided in section 1605(d).

(f)(1)(A) Notwithstanding any other provision of law, including but not limited to section 208(f) of the Foreign Missions Act (22 U.S.C. 4308(f)), and except as provided in subparagraph (B), any property with respect to which financial transactions are prohibited or regulated pursuant to section 5(b) of the Trading with the Enemy Act (50 U.S.C. App. 5(b)), section 620(a) of the Foreign Assistance Act of 1961 (22 U.S.C. 2370(a)), sections 202 and 203 of the International Emergency Economic Powers Act (50 U.S.C. 1701–1702), or any other proclamation, order, regulation, or license issued pursuant thereto, shall be subject to execution or attachment in aid of execution of any judgment relating to a claim for which a foreign state (including any agency or instrumentality or such state) claiming such property is not immune under section 1605(a)(7).

(B) Subparagraph (A) shall not apply if, at the time the property is expropriated or seized by the foreign state, the property has been held in title by a natural person or, if held in trust, has been held for the benefit of a natural person or persons.

(2)(A) At the request of any party in whose favor a judgment has been issued with respect to a claim for which the foreign state is not immune under section 1605(a)(7), the Secretary of the Treasury and the Secretary of State should make every effort to fully, promptly, and effectively assist any judgment creditor or any court that has issued any such judgment in identifying, locating, and executing against the property of that foreign state or any agency or instrumentality of such state.

(B) In providing such assistance, the Secretaries—

(i) may provide such information to the court under seal; and

(ii) should make every effort to provide the information in a manner sufficient to allow the court to direct the United States Marshall's office to promptly and effectively execute against that property.

(3) Waiver.—The President may waive any provision of paragraph (1) in the interest of national security.

(Added Pub.L. 94–583, § 4(a), Oct. 21, 1976, 90 Stat. 2896, and amended Pub.L. 100–640, § 2, Nov. 9, 1988, 102 Stat. 3333; Pub.L. 100–669, § 3, Nov. 16, 1988, 102 Stat. 3969; Pub.L. 101–650, Title III, § 325(b)(9), Dec. 1, 1990, 104 Stat. 5121; Pub.L. 104–132, Title II, § 221(b), Apr. 24, 1996, 110 Stat. 1243; Pub.L. 105–277, Div. A, § 101(h) [Title I, § 117(a)], Oct. 21, 1998, 112 Stat. 2681–491; Pub.L. 106–386, Div. C, § 2002(g)(1), Oct. 28, 2000, 114 Stat. 1543; Pub.L. 107–297, Title II, § 201(c)(3), Nov. 26, 2002, 116 Stat. 2337.)

HISTORICAL AND STATUTORY NOTES

References in Text

The effective date of this Act, referred to in subsecs. (a) and (b), is 90 days after Oct. 21, 1976, see section 8 of Pub.L. 94–583, set out as an Effective and Applicability Provisions note under section 1602 of this title.

Effective and Applicability Provisions

1998 Acts

Pub.L. 105–277, § 101(h) [Title I, § 117(c)], provided that: "The amendments made by subsections (a) and (b) [amending this section and section 1606 of this title] shall apply to any claim for which a foreign state is not immune under section 1605(a)(7) of title 28, United States Code, arising before, on, or after the date of enactment of this Act [Oct. 21, 1998]."

1996 Acts

Amendment by Pub.L. 104–132 to apply to any cause of action arising before, on, or after Apr. 24, 1996, see section 221(c) of Pub.L. 104–132, set out as a note under section 1605 of this title.

1988 Acts

Amendment to this section by section 2 of Pub.L. 100–640, enacting subsec. (e) of this section, to apply to actions commenced on or after Nov. 9, 1988, see section 3 of Pub.L. 100–640, set out as a note under section 1605 of this title.

1976 Acts

Section effective 90 days after Oct. 21, 1976, see section 8 of Pub.L. 94–583, set out as a note under section 1602 of this title.

Treatment of Terrorist Assets

Pub.L. 107–297, Title II, § 201(a), (b), (d), Nov. 26, 2002, 116 Stat. 2337, provided that:

"**(a) In general.**—Notwithstanding any other provision of law, and except as provided in subsection (b) [of this note], in every case in which a person has obtained a judgment against a terrorist party on a claim based upon an act of terrorism, or for which a terrorist party is not immune under section 1605(a)(7) of title 28, United States Code, the blocked assets of that terrorist party (including the blocked assets of any agency or instrumentality of that terrorist party) shall be subject to execution or attachment in aid of execution in order to satisfy such judgment to the extent of any compensatory damages for which such terrorist party has been adjudged liable.

"**(b) Presidential waiver.**—

"**(1) In general.**—Subject to paragraph (2), upon determining on an asset-by-asset basis that a waiver is necessary in the national security interest, the President may waive the requirements of subsection (a) [of this note] in connection with (and prior to the enforcement of) any judicial order directing attachment in aid of execution or execution against any property subject to the Vienna Convention on Diplomatic Relations or the Vienna Convention on Consular Relations.

"**(2) Exception.**—A waiver under this subsection shall not apply to—

"**(A)** property subject to the Vienna Convention on Diplomatic Relations or the Vienna Convention on Consular Relations that has been used by the United States for any nondiplomatic purpose (including use as rental property), or the proceeds of such use; or

"**(B)** the proceeds of any sale or transfer for value to a third party of any asset subject to the Vienna Convention on Diplomatic Relations or the Vienna Convention on Consular Relations."

"**(d) Definitions.**—In this section [this note] the following definitions shall apply:

"**(1) Act of terrorism.**—The term 'act of terrorism' means—

"**(A)** any act or event certified under section 102(1) [Pub.L. 107–297, Title I, § 102(1), Nov. 26, 2002, 116 Stat. 2323, which is set out in a note under 15 U.S.C.A. § 6701]; or

"**(B)** to the extent not covered by subparagraph (A), any terrorist activity (as defined in section 212(a)(3)(B)(iii) of the Immigration and Nationality Act (8 U.S.C. 1182(a)(3)(B)(iii))).

"**(2) Blocked asset.**—The term 'blocked asset' means—

"**(A)** any asset seized or frozen by the United States under section 5(b) of the Trading With the Enemy Act (50 U.S.C. App. 5(b)) or under sections 202 and 203 of

the International Emergency Economic Powers Act (50 U.S.C. 1701; 1702); and

"**(B)** Does not include property that—

"**(i)** is subject to a license issued by the United States Government for final payment, transfer, or disposition by or to a person subject to the jurisdiction of the United States in connection with a transaction for which the issuance of such license has been specifically required by statute other than the International Emergency Economic Powers Act (50 U.S.C. 1701 et seq.) or the United Nations Participation Act of 1945 (22 U.S.C. 287 et seq.); or

"**(ii)** in the case of property subject to the Vienna Convention on Diplomatic Relations or the Vienna Convention on Consular Relations, or that enjoys equivalent privileges and immunities under the law of the United States, is being used exclusively for diplomatic or consular purposes.

"**(3) Certain property.**—The term 'property subject to the Vienna Convention on Diplomatic Relations or the Vienna Convention on Consular Relations' and the term 'asset subject to the Vienna Convention on Diplomatic Relations or the Vienna Convention on Consular Relations' mean any property or asset, respectively, the attachment in aid of execution or execution of which would result in a violation of an obligation of the United States under the Vienna Convention on Diplomatic Relations or the Vienna Convention on Consular Relations, as the case may be.

"**(4) Terrorist party.**—The term 'terrorist party' means a terrorist, a terrorist organization (as defined in section 212(a)(3)(B)(vi) of the Immigration and Nationality Act (8 U.S.C. 1182(a)(3)(B)(vi))), or a foreign state designated as a state sponsor of terrorism under section 6(j) of the Export Administration Act of 1979 (50 U.S.C. App. 2405(j)) or section 620A of the Foreign Assistance Act of 1961 (22 U.S.C. 2371)."

Waiver of Exception to Immunity from Attachment or Execution

Pub.L. 105–277, Div. A, § 101(h) [Title I, § 117(d)], Oct. 21, 1998, 112 Stat. 2681–491, which had provided authority for the President to waive the requirements of section 117 of Pub.L. 105–277 [amending this section and section 1606 of this title and enacting provisions set out as notes under this section] in the interest of national security, was repealed by Pub.L. 106–386, Div. C, § 2002(g)(2), Oct. 28, 2000, 114 Stat. 1543; Pub.L. 107–297, Title II, § 201(c)(3), Nov. 26, 2002, 116 Stat. 2337.

§ 1611. Certain types of property immune from execution

(a) Notwithstanding the provisions of section 1610 of this chapter, the property of those organizations designated by the President as being entitled to enjoy the privileges, exemptions, and immunities provided by the International Organizations Immunities Act shall not be subject to attachment or any other judicial process impeding the disbursement of funds to, or on the order of, a foreign state as the result of an action brought in the courts of the United States or of the States.

(b) Notwithstanding the provisions of section 1610 of this chapter, the property of a foreign state shall be immune from attachment and from execution, if—

(1) the property is that of a foreign central bank or monetary authority held for its own account, unless such bank or authority, or its parent foreign government, has explicitly waived its immunity from attachment in aid of execution, or from execution, notwithstanding any withdrawal of the waiver which the bank, authority or government may purport to effect except in accordance with the terms of the waiver; or

(2) the property is, or is intended to be, used in connection with a military activity and

(A) is of a military character, or

(B) is under the control of a military authority or defense agency.

(c) Notwithstanding the provisions of section 1610 of this chapter, the property of a foreign state shall be immune from attachment and from execution in an action brought under section 302 of the Cuban Liberty and Democratic Solidarity (LIBERTAD) Act of 1996 to the extent that the property is a facility or installation used by an accredited diplomatic mission for official purposes.

(Added Pub.L. 94–583, § 4(a), Oct. 21, 1976, 90 Stat. 2897, and amended Pub.L. 104–114, Title III, § 302(e), Mar. 12, 1996, 110 Stat. 818.)

HISTORICAL AND STATUTORY NOTES

References in Text

The International Organizations Immunities Act, referred to in subsec. (a), is Act Dec. 29, 1945, c. 652, Title I, 59 Stat. 669, as amended, which is classified principally to section 288 et seq. of Title 22, Foreign Relations and Intercourse. For complete classification of this Act to the Code, see Short Title note set out under section 288 of Title 22 and Tables.

Section 302 of the Cuban Liberty and Democratic Solidarity (LIBERTAD) Act of 1996, referred to in subsec. (c), is Pub.L. 104–114, Title III, § 302, Mar. 12, 1996, 110 Stat. 815, which is classified to section 6082 of Title 22, Foreign Relations and Intercourse.

Effective and Applicability Provisions

1996 Acts

Amendment by section 302(e) of Pub.L. 104–114 effective Aug. 1, 1996, except as otherwise provided, see section 6085 of Title 22, Foreign Relations and Intercourse.

1976 Acts

Section effective 90 days after Oct. 21, 1976, see section 8 of Pub.L. 94–583, set out as a note under section 1602 of this title.

CHAPTER 99—GENERAL PROVISIONS

§ 1631. Transfer to cure want of jurisdiction

Whenever a civil action is filed in a court as defined in section 610 of this title or an appeal, including a petition for review of administrative action, is noticed for or filed with such a court and that court finds that there is a want of jurisdiction, the court shall, if it is in the interest of justice, transfer such action or appeal to any other such court in which the action or appeal could have been brought at the time it was filed or noticed, and the action or appeal shall proceed as if it had been filed in or noticed for the court to which it is transferred on the date upon which it was actually filed in or noticed for the court from which it is transferred.

(Added Pub.L. 97–164, Title III, § 301(a), Apr. 2, 1982, 96 Stat. 55.)

HISTORICAL AND STATUTORY NOTES

Effective and Applicability Provisions

1982 Acts

Section effective Oct. 1, 1982, see section 402 of Pub.L. 97–164, set out as a note under section 171 of this title.

PART V—PROCEDURE

CHAPTER 111—GENERAL PROVISIONS

§ 1651. Writs

(a) The Supreme Court and all courts established by Act of Congress may issue all writs necessary or appropriate in aid of their respective jurisdictions and agreeable to the usages and principles of law.

(b) An alternative writ or rule nisi may be issued by a justice or judge of a court which has jurisdiction. (June 25, 1948, c. 646, 62 Stat. 944; May 24, 1949, c. 139, § 90, 63 Stat. 102.)

HISTORICAL AND STATUTORY NOTES

Writ of Error

Act Jan. 31, 1928, c. 14, § 2, 45 Stat. 54, as amended Apr. 26, 1928, c. 440, 45 Stat. 466; June 25, 1948, c. 646, § 23, 62 Stat. 990, provided that: "All Acts of Congress referring to writs of error shall be construed as amended to the extent necessary to substitute appeal for writ of error."

§ 1652. State laws as rules of decision

The laws of the several states, except where the Constitution or treaties of the United States or Acts of Congress otherwise require or provide, shall be regarded as rules of decision in civil actions in the courts of the United States, in cases where they apply. (June 25, 1948, c. 646, 62 Stat. 944.)

§ 1653. Amendment of pleadings to show jurisdiction

Defective allegations of jurisdiction may be amended, upon terms, in the trial or appellate courts. (June 25, 1948, c. 646, 62 Stat. 944.)

§ 1654. Appearance personally or by counsel

In all courts of the United States the parties may plead and conduct their own cases personally or by counsel as, by the rules of such courts, respectively, are permitted to manage and conduct causes therein. (June 25, 1948, c. 646, 62 Stat. 944; May 24, 1949, c. 139, § 91, 63 Stat. 103.)

§ 1655. Lien enforcement; absent defendants

In an action in a district court to enforce any lien upon or claim to, or to remove any incumbrance or lien or cloud upon the title to, real or personal property within the district, where any defendant cannot be served within the State, or does not voluntarily appear, the court may order the absent defendant to appear or plead by a day certain.

Such order shall be served on the absent defendant personally if practicable, wherever found, and also upon the person or persons in possession or charge of such property, if any. Where personal service is not practicable, the order shall be published as the court may direct, not less than once a week for six consecutive weeks.

If an absent defendant does not appear or plead within the time allowed, the court may proceed as if the absent defendant had been served with process within the State, but any adjudication shall, as regards the absent defendant without appearance, affect only the property which is the subject of the action. When a part of the property is within another district, but within the same state, such action may be brought in either district.

Any defendant not so personally notified may, at any time within one year after final judgment, enter

his appearance, and thereupon the court shall set aside the judgment and permit such defendant to plead on payment of such costs as the court deems just.

(June 25, 1948, c. 646, 62 Stat. 944.)

§ 1656. Creation of new district or division or transfer of territory; lien enforcement

The creation of a new district or division or the transfer of any territory to another district or division shall not affect or divest any lien theretofore acquired in a district court upon property within such district, division or territory.

To enforce such lien, the clerk of the court in which the same is acquired, upon the request and at the cost of the party desiring the same, shall make a certified copy of the record thereof, which, when filed in the proper court of the district or division in which such property is situated after such creation or transfer shall be evidence in all courts and places equally with the original thereof; and, thereafter like proceedings shall be had thereon, and with the same effect, as though the case or proceeding had been originally instituted in such court.

(June 25, 1948, c. 646, 62 Stat. 944; Nov. 6, 1978, Pub.L. 95–598, Title II, § 242, 92 Stat. 2671.)

HISTORICAL AND STATUTORY NOTES

Codifications

This section, was amended by Pub.L. 95–598, Title II, § 242, Nov. 6, 1978, 92 Stat. 2671, effective June 28, 1984, pursuant to Pub.L. 95–598, Title IV, § 402(b), Nov. 6, 1978, 92 Stat. 2682, as amended by Pub.L. 98–249, § 1(a), Mar. 31, 1984, 98 Stat. 116; Pub.L. 98–271, § 1(a), Apr. 30, 1984, 98 Stat. 163; Pub.L. 98–299, § 1(a), May 25, 1984, 98 Stat. 214; Pub.L. 98–325, § 1(a), June 20, 1984, 98 Stat. 268, set out as an Effective and Applicability Provisions note preceding section 101 of Title 11, Bankruptcy, by inserting "or in a bankruptcy court" following "a district court".

Section 402(b) of Pub.L. 95–598 was amended by section 113 of Pub.L. 98–353, Title I, July 10, 1984, 98 Stat. 343, by substituting "shall not be effective" for "shall take effect on June 28, 1984", thereby eliminating the amendment by section 242 of Pub.L. 95–598, effective June 27, 1984, pursuant to section 122(c) of Pub.L. 98–353, set out as an Effective and Applicability Provisions note under section 151 of this title.

Section 121(a) of Pub.L. 98–353 directed that section 402(b) of Pub.L. 95–598 be amended by substituting "the date of enactment of the Bankruptcy Amendments and Federal Judgeship Act of 1984 [i.e. July 10, 1984]" for "June 28, 1984". This amendment was not executed in view of the prior amendment to section 402(b) of Pub.L. 95–598 by section 113 of Pub.L. 98–353.

§ 1657. Priority of civil actions

(a) Notwithstanding any other provision of law, each court of the United States shall determine the order in which civil actions are heard and determined, except that the court shall expedite the consideration of any action brought under chapter 153 or section 1826 of this title, any action for temporary or preliminary injunctive relief, or any other action if good cause therefor is shown. For purposes of this subsection, "good cause" is shown if a right under the Constitution of the United States or a Federal Statute (including rights under section 552 of title 5) would be maintained in a factual context that indicates that a request for expedited consideration has merit.

(b) The Judicial Conference of the United States may modify the rules adopted by the courts to determine the order in which civil actions are heard and determined, in order to establish consistency among the judicial circuits.

(Added Pub.L. 98–620, Title IV, § 401(a), Nov. 8, 1984, 98 Stat. 3356.)

HISTORICAL AND STATUTORY NOTES

Codifications

Pub.L. 101–647, Title XXV, § 2527(b), Nov. 29, 1990, 104 Stat. 4877, purported to amend section 1657 of Title 18, Crimes and Criminal Procedure, by inserting "section 11, 12, or 13 of the Federal Deposit Insurance Act" after "consideration of any action brought under", which amendment could not be executed to the text of section 1657 of Title 18. Such amendment was probably intended to amend this section.

Effective and Applicability Provisions

1984 Acts

Section 403 of Pub.L. 98–620 provided that: "The amendments made by this subtitle [subtitle A of Title IV of Pub.L. 98–620, enacting this section, amending sections 596, 636, 1364, 2284, and 2349 of this title, sections 437g, 437h and 687 of Title 2, The Congress, section 552 of Title 5, Government Organization and Employees, sections 8, 136d, 136h, 136n, 136w, 194, 1366, 1600 and 1601 of Title 7, Agriculture, section 1464 of Title 12, Banks and Banking, sections 18a, 21, 45, 57a–1, 78k–1, 687a, 687c, 719h, 1415, 2003 and 2622 of Title 15, Commerce and Trade, sections 1463a, 1910, 3117, and 3168 of Title 16, Conservation, sections 1964 and 1966 of Title 18, Crimes and Criminal Procedure, sections 346a and 348 of Title 21, Food and Drugs, section 618 of Title 22, Foreign Relations and Intercourse, section 640d–3 of Title 25, Indians, sections 3310, 6110, 6363, 7609, 9010 and 9011 of Title 26, Internal Revenue Code, sections 110, 160, 660 and 1303 of Title 29, Labor, section 816 of Title 30, Mineral Lands and Mining, section 2022 of Title 38, Veterans' Benefits, section 3628 of Title 39, Postal Service, sections 300j–9, 504, 6508 and 8514 of Title 42, The Public Health and Welfare, sections 1062, 1349, 1652 and 2011 of Title 43, Public Lands, sections 355, 745, 1018 and 1205 of Title 45, Railroads, section 402 of Title 47, Telegraphs, Telephones, and Radiotelegraphs, section 2305 of Title 49 Appendix, Transportation, section 792a of Title 50, War and National Defense, sections 462 and 1984 of the Appendix to Title 50, repealing sections 1296 and 2647 of this title, section 28 of Title 15, Commerce and Trade, and section 3614 of Title 42, The Public Health and Welfare, and amending provisions set out as a note under section 2304 of Title 10, Armed Forces] shall not apply to cases pending on the date of the enactment of this subtitle [Nov. 8, 1984]."

§ 1658. Time limitations on the commencement of civil actions arising under Acts of Congress

(a) Except as otherwise provided by law, a civil action arising under an Act of Congress enacted after the date of the enactment of this section may not be commenced later than 4 years after the cause of action accrues.

(b) Notwithstanding subsection (a), a private right of action that involves a claim of fraud, deceit, manipulation, or contrivance in contravention of a regulatory requirement concerning the securities laws, as defined in section 3(a)(47) of the Securities Exchange Act of 1934 (15 U.S.C. 78c(a)(47)), may be brought not later than the earlier of—

(1) 2 years after the discovery of the facts constituting the violation; or

(2) 5 years after such violation.

(Added Pub.L. 101–650, Title III, § 313(a), Dec. 1, 1990, 104 Stat. 5114, and amended Pub.L. 107–204, Title VIII, § 804(a), July 30, 2002, 116 Stat. 801.)

HISTORICAL AND STATUTORY NOTES

References in Text

The date of the enactment of this section, referred to in text, is the date of enactment of this section by section 313(a) of Pub.L. 101–650, which was approved Dec. 1, 1990.

Effective and Applicability Provisions

2002 Acts

Pub.L. 107–204, Title VIII, § 804(b), July 30, 2002, 116 Stat. 801, provided that: "The limitations period provided by section 1658(b) of title 28, United States Code [subsec. (b) of this section], as added by this section [section 804 of Pub.L. 107–204, which amended this section], shall apply to all proceedings addressed by this section that are commenced on or after the date of enactment of this Act [July 30, 2002]."

1990 Acts

Section 313(c) of Pub.L. 101–650 provided that: "The amendments made by this section [enacting this section] shall apply with respect to causes of action accruing on or after the date of the enactment of this Act [Dec. 1, 1990]."

No Creation of Actions

Pub.L. 107–204, Title VIII, § 804(c), July 30, 2002, 116 Stat. 801, provided that: "Nothing in this section [Pub.L. 107–204, Title VIII, § 804, July 30, 2002, 116 Stat. 801, which amended this section and enacted provisions set out as a note under this section] shall create a new, private right of action."

§ 1659. Stay of certain actions pending disposition of related proceedings before the United States International Trade Commission

(a) Stay.—In a civil action involving parties that are also parties to a proceeding before the United States International Trade Commission under section 337 of the Tariff Act of 1930, at the request of a party to the civil action that is also a respondent in the proceeding before the Commission, the district court shall stay, until the determination of the Commission becomes final, proceedings in the civil action with respect to any claim that involves the same issues involved in the proceeding before the Commission, but only if such request is made within—

(1) 30 days after the party is named as a respondent in the proceeding before the Commission, or

(2) 30 days after the district court action is filed, whichever is later.

(b) Use of Commission record.—Notwithstanding section 337(n)(1) of the Tariff Act of 1930, after dissolution of a stay under subsection (a), the record of the proceeding before the United States International Trade Commission shall be transmitted to the district court and shall be admissible in the civil action, subject to such protective order as the district court determines necessary, to the extent permitted under the Federal Rules of Evidence and the Federal Rules of Civil Procedure.

(Added Pub.L. 103–465, Title III, § 321(b)(1)(A), Dec. 8, 1994, 108 Stat. 4945.)

HISTORICAL AND STATUTORY NOTES

References in Text

Section 337 of the Tariff Act of 1930, referred to in text, is section 337 of Act June 17, 1930, c. 497, Title III, 46 Stat. 703, which is classified to section 1337 of Title 19, Customs Duties.

Effective and Applicability Provisions

1994 Acts

Section applicable with respect to complaints filed under section 1337 of Title 19, Customs Duties, on or after the date on which the WTO Agreement enters into force with respect to the United States, Jan. 1, 1995, or in cases under section 1337 of Title 19 in which no complaint is filed, with respect to investigations initiated under such section on or after such date, see section 322 of Pub.L. 103–465, set out as a note under section 1337 of Title 19.

CHAPTER 113—PROCESS

§ 1691. Seal and teste of process

All writs and process issuing from a court of the United States shall be under the seal of the court and signed by the clerk thereof.

(June 25, 1948, c. 646, 62 Stat. 945.)

HISTORICAL AND STATUTORY NOTES

Immunity from Seizure under Judicial Process of Cultural Objects Imported for Temporary Exhibition or Display

Presidential determination of cultural significance of objects and exhibition or display thereof in the national interest, see section 2459 of Title 22, Foreign Relations and Intercourse.

§ 1692. Process and orders affecting property in different districts

In proceedings in a district court where a receiver is appointed for property, real, personal, or mixed, situated in different districts, process may issue and be executed in any such district as if the property lay wholly within one district, but orders affecting the property shall be entered of record in each of such districts.

(June 25, 1948, c. 646, 62 Stat. 945.)

§ 1693. Place of arrest in civil action

Except as otherwise provided by Act of Congress, no person shall be arrested in one district for trial in another in any civil action in a district court.

(June 25, 1948, c. 646, 62 Stat. 945.)

§ 1694. Patent infringement action

In a patent infringement action commenced in a district where the defendant is not a resident but has a regular and established place of business, service of process, summons or subpoena upon such defendant may be made upon his agent or agents conducting such business.

(June 25, 1948, c. 646, 62 Stat. 945.)

§ 1695. Stockholder's derivative action

Process in a stockholder's action in behalf of his corporation may be served upon such corporation in any district where it is organized or licensed to do business or is doing business.

(June 25, 1948, c. 646, 62 Stat. 945.)

§ 1696. Service in foreign and international litigation

(a) The district court of the district in which a person resides or is found may order service upon him of any document issued in connection with a proceeding in a foreign or international tribunal. The order may be made pursuant to a letter rogatory issued, or request made, by a foreign or international tribunal or upon application of any interested person and shall direct the manner of service. Service pursuant to this subsection does not, of itself, require the recognition or enforcement in the United States of a judgment, decree, or order rendered by a foreign or international tribunal.

(b) This section does not preclude service of such a document without an order of court.

(Added Pub.L. 88–619, § 4(a), Oct. 3, 1964, 78 Stat. 995.)

HISTORICAL AND STATUTORY NOTES

Treaties and Conventions; Service Abroad of Judicial and Extrajudicial Documents in Civil or Commercial Matters; Observance On and After Feb. 10, 1969, by United States and Citizens and Persons Subject to Jurisdiction of United States

For text of Convention, see provisions set out as a note under Rule 4, Federal Rules of Civil Procedure, 28 U.S.C.A.

§ 1697. Service in multiparty, multiforum actions

When the jurisdiction of the district court is based in whole or in part upon section 1369 of this title, process, other than subpoenas, may be served at any place within the United States, or anywhere outside the United States if otherwise permitted by law.

(Added Pub.L. 107–273, Div. C, Title I, § 11020(b)(4)(A)(i), Nov. 2, 2002, 116 Stat. 1828.)

HISTORICAL AND STATUTORY NOTES

Effective and Applicability Provisions

2002 Acts

Amendments by section 11020(b) of Pub.L. 107–273 shall apply to a civil action if the accident giving rise to the cause of action occurred on or after the 90th day after Nov. 2, 2002, see section 11020(c) of Pub.L. 107–273, set out as a note under 28 U.S.C.A. § 1369.

CHAPTER 114—CLASS ACTIONS

§ 1711. Definitions

In this chapter:

(1) **Class.**—The term "class" means all of the class members in a class action.

(2) **Class action.**—The term "class action" means any civil action filed in a district court of the United States under rule 23 of the Federal Rules of Civil Procedure or any civil action that is removed to a district court of the United States that was originally filed under a State statute or rule of judicial procedure authorizing an action to be brought by 1 or more representatives as a class action.

(3) **Class counsel.**—The term "class counsel" means the persons who serve as the attorneys for the class members in a proposed or certified class action.

(4) **Class members.**—The term "class members" means the persons (named or unnamed) who fall within the definition of the proposed or certified class in a class action.

(5) **Plaintiff class action.**—The term "plaintiff class action" means a class action in which class members are plaintiffs.

(6) **Proposed settlement.**—The term "proposed settlement" means an agreement regarding a class action that is subject to court approval and that, if approved, would be binding on some or all class members.

(Added Pub.L. 109–2, § 3(a), Feb. 18, 2005, 119 Stat. 5.)

HISTORICAL AND STATUTORY NOTES

References in Text

Rule 23 of the Federal Rules of Civil Procedure, referred to in par. (2), is set out following the code sections of this title.

Effective and Applicability Provisions

2005 Acts

Enactment of this section by Class Action Fairness Act of 2005, Pub.L. 109–2, Feb. 18, 2005, 119 Stat. 4, applicable to any civil action commenced on or after Feb. 18, 2005, see Pub.L. 109–2, § 9, set out as a note under 28 U.S.C.A. § 1332.

Findings and Purposes

Pub.L. 109–2, § 2, Feb. 18, 2005, 119 Stat. 4, provided that:

"(a) **Findings.**—Congress finds the following:

"(1) Class action lawsuits are an important and valuable part of the legal system when they permit the fair and efficient resolution of legitimate claims of numerous parties by allowing the claims to be aggregated into a single action against a defendant that has allegedly caused harm.

"(2) Over the past decade, there have been abuses of the class action device that have—

"(A) harmed class members with legitimate claims and defendants that have acted responsibly;

"(B) adversely affected interstate commerce; and

"(C) undermined public respect for our judicial system.

"(3) Class members often receive little or no benefit from class actions, and are sometimes harmed, such as where—

"(A) counsel are awarded large fees, while leaving class members with coupons or other awards of little or no value;

"(B) unjustified awards are made to certain plaintiffs at the expense of other class members; and

"(C) confusing notices are published that prevent class members from being able to fully understand and effectively exercise their rights.

"(4) Abuses in class actions undermine the National judicial system, the free flow of interstate commerce, and the concept of diversity jurisdiction as intended by the framers of the United States constitution, in that State and local courts are—

"(A) keeping cases of national importance out of Federal court;

"(B) sometimes acting in ways that demonstrate bias against out-of-State defendants; and

"(C) making judgments that impose their view of the law on other States and bind the rights of the residents of those States.

"(b) **Purposes.**—The purposes of this Act [the Class Action Fairness Act of 2005, which enacted this note, this chapter, and 28 U.S.C.A. § 1453, amended 28 U.S.C.A. §§ 1332, 1335, and 1603, and enacted provisions set out as notes under 28 U.S.C.A. §§ 1332, 2071, and 2074] are to—

"(1) assure fair and prompt recoveries for class members with legitimate claims;

"(2) restore the intent of the framers of the United States Constitution by providing for Federal court consideration of interstate cases of national importance under diversity jurisdiction; and

"(3) benefit society by encouraging innovation and lowering consumer prices."

[Enactment of this note by Class Action Fairness Act of 2005, Pub.L. 109–2, Feb. 18, 2005, 119 Stat. 4, applicable to any civil action commenced on or after Feb. 18, 2005, see Pub.L. 109–2, § 9, set out as a note under 28 U.S.C.A. § 1332.]

§ 1712. Coupon settlements

(a) **Contingent fees in coupon settlements.**—If a proposed settlement in a class action provides for a recovery of coupons to a class member, the portion of any attorney's fee award to class counsel that is attributable to the award of the coupons shall be based on the value to class members of the coupons that are redeemed.

(b) **Other attorney's fee awards in coupon settlements.—**

(1) **In general.**—If a proposed settlement in a class action provides for a recovery of coupons to class members, and a portion of the recovery of the coupons is not used to determine the attorney's fee

to be paid to class counsel, any attorney's fee award shall be based upon the amount of time class counsel reasonably expended working on the action.

(2) Court approval.—Any attorney's fee under this subsection shall be subject to approval by the court and shall include an appropriate attorney's fee, if any, for obtaining equitable relief, including an injunction, if applicable. Nothing in this subsection shall be construed to prohibit application of a lodestar with a multiplier method of determining attorney's fees.

(c) Attorney's fee awards calculated on a mixed basis in coupon settlements.—If a proposed settlement in a class action provides for an award of coupons to class members and also provides for equitable relief, including injunctive relief—

(1) that portion of the attorney's fee to be paid to class counsel that is based upon a portion of the recovery of the coupons shall be calculated in accordance with subsection (a); and

(2) that portion of the attorney's fee to be paid to class counsel that is not based upon a portion of the recovery of the coupons shall be calculated in accordance with subsection (b).

(d) Settlement valuation expertise.—In a class action involving the awarding of coupons, the court may, in its discretion upon the motion of a party, receive expert testimony from a witness qualified to provide information on the actual value to the class members of the coupons that are redeemed.

(e) Judicial scrutiny of coupon settlements.—In a proposed settlement under which class members would be awarded coupons, the court may approve the proposed settlement only after a hearing to determine whether, and making a written finding that, the settlement is fair, reasonable, and adequate for class members. The court, in its discretion, may also require that a proposed settlement agreement provide for the distribution of a portion of the value of unclaimed coupons to 1 or more charitable or governmental organizations, as agreed to by the parties. The distribution and redemption of any proceeds under this subsection shall not be used to calculate attorneys' fees under this section.

(Added Pub.L. 109–2, § 3(a), Feb. 18, 2005, 119 Stat. 6.)

HISTORICAL AND STATUTORY NOTES

Effective and Applicability Provisions

2005 Acts

Enactment of this section by Class Action Fairness Act of 2005, Pub.L. 109–2, Feb. 18, 2005, 119 Stat. 4, applicable to any civil action commenced on or after Feb. 18, 2005, see Pub.L. 109–2, § 9, set out as a note under 28 U.S.C.A. § 1332.

§ 1713. Protection against loss by class members

The court may approve a proposed settlement under which any class member is obligated to pay sums to class counsel that would result in a net loss to the class member only if the court makes a written finding that nonmonetary benefits to the class member substantially outweigh the monetary loss.

(Added Pub.L. 109–2, § 3(a), Feb. 18, 2005, 119 Stat. 7.)

HISTORICAL AND STATUTORY NOTES

Effective and Applicability Provisions

2005 Acts

Enactment of this section by Class Action Fairness Act of 2005, Pub.L. 109–2, Feb. 18, 2005, 119 Stat. 4, applicable to any civil action commenced on or after Feb. 18, 2005, see Pub.L. 109–2, § 9, set out as a note under 28 U.S.C.A. § 1332.

§ 1714. Protection against discrimination based on geographic location

The court may not approve a proposed settlement that provides for the payment of greater sums to some class members than to others solely on the basis that the class members to whom the greater sums are to be paid are located in closer geographic proximity to the court.

(Added Pub.L. 109–2, § 3(a), Feb. 18, 2005, 119 Stat. 7.)

HISTORICAL AND STATUTORY NOTES

Effective and Applicability Provisions

2005 Acts

Enactment of this section by Class Action Fairness Act of 2005, Pub.L. 109–2, Feb. 18, 2005, 119 Stat. 4, applicable to any civil action commenced on or after Feb. 18, 2005, see Pub.L. 109–2, § 9, set out as a note under 28 U.S.C.A. § 1332.

§ 1715. Notifications to appropriate Federal and State officials

(a) Definitions.—

(1) Appropriate Federal official.—In this section, the term "appropriate Federal official" means—

(A) the Attorney General of the United States; or

(B) in any case in which the defendant is a Federal depository institution, a State depository institution, a depository institution holding company, a foreign bank, or a nondepository institution subsidiary of the foregoing (as such terms are defined in section 3 of the Federal Deposit Insurance Act (12 U.S.C. 1813)), the person who has the primary Federal regulatory or supervisory responsibility with respect to the defendant, if some or all of the matters alleged in the class action are subject to regulation or supervision by that person.

(2) Appropriate State official.—In this section, the term "appropriate State official" means the person in the State who has the primary regulatory or supervisory responsibility with respect to the defendant, or who licenses or otherwise authorizes the defendant to conduct business in the State, if some or all of the matters alleged in the class action are subject to regulation by that person. If there is no primary regulator, supervisor, or licensing authority, or the matters alleged in the class action are not subject to regulation or supervision by that person, then the appropriate State official shall be the State attorney general.

(b) In general.—Not later than 10 days after a proposed settlement of a class action is filed in court, each defendant that is participating in the proposed settlement shall serve upon the appropriate State official of each State in which a class member resides and the appropriate Federal official, a notice of the proposed settlement consisting of—

(1) a copy of the complaint and any materials filed with the complaint and any amended complaints (except such materials shall not be required to be served if such materials are made electronically available through the Internet and such service includes notice of how to electronically access such material);

(2) notice of any scheduled judicial hearing in the class action;

(3) any proposed or final notification to class members of—

(A)(i) the members' rights to request exclusion from the class action; or

(ii) if no right to request exclusion exists, a statement that no such right exists; and

(B) a proposed settlement of a class action;

(4) any proposed or final class action settlement;

(5) any settlement or other agreement contemporaneously made between class counsel and counsel for the defendants;

(6) any final judgment or notice of dismissal;

(7)(A) if feasible, the names of class members who reside in each State and the estimated proportionate share of the claims of such members to the entire settlement to that State's appropriate State official; or

(B) if the provision of information under subparagraph (A) is not feasible, a reasonable estimate of the number of class members residing in each State and the estimated proportionate share of the claims of such members to the entire settlement; and

(8) any written judicial opinion relating to the materials described under subparagraphs (3) through (6).

(c) Depository institutions notification.—

(1) Federal and other depository institutions.—In any case in which the defendant is a Federal depository institution, a depository institution holding company, a foreign bank, or a non-depository institution subsidiary of the foregoing, the notice requirements of this section are satisfied by serving the notice required under subsection (b) upon the person who has the primary Federal regulatory or supervisory responsibility with respect to the defendant, if some or all of the matters alleged in the class action are subject to regulation or supervision by that person.

(2) State depository institutions.—In any case in which the defendant is a State depository institution (as that term is defined in section 3 of the Federal Deposit Insurance Act (12 U.S.C. 1813)), the notice requirements of this section are satisfied by serving the notice required under subsection (b) upon the State bank supervisor (as that term is defined in section 3 of the Federal Deposit Insurance Act (12 U.S.C. 1813)) of the State in which the defendant is incorporated or chartered, if some or all of the matters alleged in the class action are subject to regulation or supervision by that person, and upon the appropriate Federal official.

(d) Final approval.—An order giving final approval of a proposed settlement may not be issued earlier than 90 days after the later of the dates on which the appropriate Federal official and the appropriate State official are served with the notice required under subsection (b).

(e) Noncompliance if notice not provided.—

(1) In general.—A class member may refuse to comply with and may choose not to be bound by a settlement agreement or consent decree in a class action if the class member demonstrates that the notice required under subsection (b) has not been provided.

(2) Limitation.—A class member may not refuse to comply with or to be bound by a settlement agreement or consent decree under paragraph (1) if the notice required under subsection (b) was directed to the appropriate Federal official and to either the State attorney general or the person that has primary regulatory, supervisory, or licensing authority over the defendant.

(3) Application of rights.—The rights created by this subsection shall apply only to class members or any person acting on a class member's behalf, and shall not be construed to limit any other rights affecting a class member's participation in the settlement.

(f) Rule of construction.—Nothing in this section shall be construed to expand the authority of, or

impose any obligations, duties, or responsibilities upon, Federal or State officials.

(Added Pub.L. 109–2, § 3(a), Feb. 18, 2005, 119 Stat. 7.)

HISTORICAL AND STATUTORY NOTES

References in Text

Section 3 of the Federal Deposit Insurance Act, referred to in subsecs. (a)(1)(B) and (c)(2), is Act Sept. 21, 1950, c. 967, § 2[3], 64 Stat. 873, as amended, which is classified to 12 U.S.C.A. § 1813. A Federal depository institution is defined in 12 U.S.C.A. § 1813(c)(4); a State depository institution, in 12 U.S.C.A. § 1813(c)(5); a depository institution holding company, in 12 U.S.C.A. § 1813(w)(1); a foreign bank, in 12 U.S.C.A. § 1813(s)(1); and State bank supervisor, in 12 U.S.C.A. § 1813(r)(1).

Effective and Applicability Provisions

2005 Acts

Enactment of this section by Class Action Fairness Act of 2005, Pub.L. 109–2, Feb. 18, 2005, 119 Stat. 4, applicable to any civil action commenced on or after Feb. 18, 2005, see Pub.L. 109–2, § 9, set out as a note under 28 U.S.C.A. § 1332.

CHAPTER 115—EVIDENCE; DOCUMENTARY

§ 1731. Handwriting

The admitted or proved handwriting of any person shall be admissible, for purposes of comparison, to determine genuineness of other handwriting attributed to such person.

(June 25, 1948, c. 646, 62 Stat. 945.)

§ 1732. Record made in regular course of business; photographic copies

If any business, institution, member of a profession or calling, or any department or agency of government, in the regular course of business or activity has kept or recorded any memorandum, writing, entry, print, representation or combination thereof, of any act, transaction, occurrence, or event, and in the regular course of business has caused any or all of the same to be recorded, copied, or reproduced by any photographic, photostatic, microfilm, micro-card, miniature photographic, or other process which accurately reproduces or forms a durable medium for so reproducing the original, the original may be destroyed in the regular course of business unless its preservation is required by law. Such reproduction, when satisfactorily identified, is as admissible in evidence as the original itself in any judicial or administrative proceeding whether the original is in existence or not and an enlargement or facsimile of such reproduction is likewise admissible in evidence if the original reproduction is in existence and available for inspection under direction of court. The introduction of a reproduced record, enlargement, or facsimile does not preclude admission of the original. This subsection[1] shall not be construed to exclude from evidence any document or copy thereof which is otherwise admissible under the rules of evidence.

(June 25, 1948, c. 646, 62 Stat. 945; Aug. 28, 1951, c. 351, §§ 1, 3, 65 Stat. 205, 206; Aug. 30, 1961, Pub.L. 87–183, 75 Stat. 413; Jan. 2, 1975, Pub.L. 93–595, § 2(b), 88 Stat. 1949.)

1 Probably should be read as "section". Section formerly was subsec. (b) of this section.

§ 1733. Government records and papers; copies

(a) Books or records of account or minutes of proceedings of any department or agency of the United States shall be admissible to prove the act, transaction or occurrence as a memorandum of which the same were made or kept.

(b) Properly authenticated copies or transcripts of any books, records, papers or documents of any department or agency of the United States shall be admitted in evidence equally with the originals thereof.

(c) This section does not apply to cases, actions, and proceedings to which the Federal Rules of Evidence apply.

(June 25, 1948, c. 646, 62 Stat. 946; Jan. 2, 1975, Pub.L. 93–595, § 2(c), 88 Stat. 1949.)

HISTORICAL AND STATUTORY NOTES

References in Text

The Federal Rules of Evidence, referred to in subsec. (c), are set out in this title.

§ 1734. Court record lost or destroyed, generally

(a) A lost or destroyed record of any proceeding in any court of the United States may be supplied on application of any interested party not at fault, by substituting a copy certified by the clerk of any court in which an authentic copy is lodged.

(b) Where a certified copy is not available, any interested person not at fault may file in such court a verified application for an order establishing the lost or destroyed record.

Every other interested person shall be served personally with a copy of the application and with notice of hearing on a day stated, not less than sixty days after service. Service may be made on any nonresident of the district anywhere within the jurisdiction of the United States or in any foreign country.

Proof of service in a foreign country shall be certified by a minister or consul of the United States in such country, under his official seal.

If, after the hearing, the court is satisfied that the statements contained in the application are true, it shall enter an order reciting the substance and effect of the lost or destroyed record. Such order, subject to intervening rights of third persons, shall have the same effect as the original record.

(June 25, 1948, c. 646, 62 Stat. 946.)

§ 1735. Court record lost or destroyed where United States interested

(a) When the record of any case or matter in any court of the United States to which the United States is a party, is lost or destroyed, a certified copy of any official paper of a United States attorney, United States marshal or clerk or other certifying or recording officer of any such court, made pursuant to law, on file in any department or agency of the United States and relating to such case or matter, shall, on being filed in the court to which it relates, have the same effect as an original paper filed in such court. If the copy so filed discloses the date and amount of a judgment or decree and the names of the parties thereto, the court may enforce the judgment or decree as though the original record had not been lost or destroyed.

(b) Whenever the United States is interested in any lost or destroyed records or files of a court of the United States, the clerk of such court and the United States attorney for the district shall take the steps necessary to restore such records or files, under the direction of the judges of such court.

(June 25, 1948, c. 646, 62 Stat. 946.)

§ 1736. Congressional Journals

Extracts from the Journals of the Senate and the House of Representatives, and from the Executive Journal of the Senate when the injunction of secrecy is removed, certified by the Secretary of the Senate or the Clerk of the House of Representatives shall be received in evidence with the same effect as the originals would have.

(June 25, 1948, c. 646, 62 Stat. 947.)

HISTORICAL AND STATUTORY NOTES

Transfer of Functions

Any reference in any provision of law enacted before Jan. 4, 1995, to a function, duty, or authority of the Clerk of the House of Representatives treated as referring, with respect to that function, duty, or authority, to the officer of the House of Representatives exercising that function, duty, or authority, as determined by the Committee on House Oversight of the House of Representatives, see section 2(1) of Pub.L. 104–14, set out as a note preceding section 21 of Title 2, The Congress.

§ 1737. Copy of officer's bond

Any person to whose custody the bond of any officer of the United States has been committed shall, on proper request and payment of the fee allowed by any Act of Congress, furnish certified copies thereof, which shall be prima facie evidence in any court of the execution, filing and contents of the bond.

(June 25, 1948, c. 646, 62 Stat. 947.)

§ 1738. State and Territorial statutes and judicial proceedings; full faith and credit

The Acts of the legislature of any State, Territory, or Possession of the United States, or copies thereof, shall be authenticated by affixing the seal of such State, Territory or Possession thereto.

The records and judicial proceedings of any court of any such State, Territory or Possession, or copies thereof, shall be proved or admitted in other courts within the United States and its Territories and Possessions by the attestation of the clerk and seal of the court annexed, if a seal exists, together with a certificate of a judge of the court that the said attestation is in proper form.

Such Acts, records and judicial proceedings or copies thereof, so authenticated, shall have the same full faith and credit in every court within the United States and its Territories and Possessions as they have by law or usage in the courts of such State, Territory or Possession from which they are taken.

(June 25, 1948, c. 646, 62 Stat. 947.)

§ 1738A. Full faith and credit given to child custody determinations

(a) The appropriate authorities of every State shall enforce according to its terms, and shall not modify except as provided in subsections (f), (g), and (h) of this section, any custody determination or visitation determination made consistently with the provisions of this section by a court of another State.

(b) As used in this section, the term—

(1) "child" means a person under the age of eighteen;

(2) "contestant" means a person, including a parent or grandparent, who claims a right to custody or visitation of a child;

(3) "custody determination" means a judgment, decree, or other order of a court providing for the custody of a child, and includes permanent and temporary orders, and initial orders and modifications;

(4) "home State" means the State in which, immediately preceding the time involved, the child lived with his parents, a parent, or a person acting as parent, for at least six consecutive months, and in the case of a child less than six months old, the State in which the child lived from birth with any of such persons. Periods of temporary absence of any of such persons are counted as part of the six-month or other period;

(5) "modification" and "modify" refer to a custody or visitation determination which modifies, replaces, supersedes, or otherwise is made subsequent to, a prior custody or visitation determination concerning the same child, whether made by the same court or not;

(6) "person acting as a parent" means a person, other than a parent, who has physical custody of a child and who has either been awarded custody by a court or claims a right to custody;

(7) "physical custody" means actual possession and control of a child;

(8) "State" means a State of the United States, the District of Columbia, the Commonwealth of Puerto Rico, or a territory or possession of the United States; and

(9) "visitation determination" means a judgment, decree, or other order of a court providing for the visitation of a child and includes permanent and temporary orders and initial orders and modifications.

(c) A child custody or visitation determination made by a court of a State is consistent with the provisions of this section only if—

(1) such court has jurisdiction under the law of such State; and

(2) one of the following conditions is met:

(A) such State (i) is the home State of the child on the date of the commencement of the proceeding, or (ii) had been the child's home State within six months before the date of the commencement of the proceeding and the child is absent from such State because of his removal or retention by a contestant or for other reasons, and a contestant continues to live in such State;

(B) (i) it appears that no other State would have jurisdiction under subparagraph (A), and (ii) it is in the best interest of the child that a court of such State assume jurisdiction because (I) the child and his parents, or the child and at least one contestant, have a significant connection with such State other than mere physical presence in such State, and (II) there is available in such State substantial evidence concerning the child's present or future care, protection, training, and personal relationships;

(C) the child is physically present in such State and (i) the child has been abandoned, or (ii) it is necessary in an emergency to protect the child because the child, a sibling, or parent of the child has been subjected to or threatened with mistreatment or abuse;

(D) (i) it appears that no other State would have jurisdiction under subparagraph (A), (B), (C), or (E), or another State has declined to exercise jurisdiction on the ground that the State whose jurisdiction is in issue is the more appropriate forum to determine the custody or visitation of the child, and (ii) it is in the best interest of the child that such court assume jurisdiction; or

(E) the court has continuing jurisdiction pursuant to subsection (d) of this section.

(d) The jurisdiction of a court of a State which has made a child custody or visitation determination consistently with the provisions of this section continues as long as the requirement of subsection (c)(1) of this section continues to be met and such State remains the residence of the child or of any contestant.

(e) Before a child custody or visitation determination is made, reasonable notice and opportunity to be heard shall be given to the contestants, any parent whose parental rights have not been previously terminated and any person who has physical custody of a child.

(f) A court of a State may modify a determination of the custody of the same child made by a court of another State, if—

(1) it has jurisdiction to make such a child custody determination; and

(2) the court of the other State no longer has jurisdiction, or it has declined to exercise such jurisdiction to modify such determination.

(g) A court of a State shall not exercise jurisdiction in any proceeding for a custody or visitation determination commenced during the pendency of a proceeding in a court of another State where such court of that other State is exercising jurisdiction consistently with the provisions of this section to make a custody or visitation determination.

(h) A court of a State may not modify a visitation determination made by a court of another State unless the court of the other State no longer has jurisdiction to modify such determination or has declined to exercise jurisdiction to modify such determination.

(Added Pub.L. 96–611, § 8(a), Dec. 28, 1980, 94 Stat. 3569, and amended Pub.L. 105–374, § 1, Nov. 12, 1998, 112 Stat. 3383; Pub.L. 106–386, Div. B, Title III, § 1303(d), Oct. 28, 2000, 114 Stat. 1512.)

HISTORICAL AND STATUTORY NOTES

Report on Effects of Parental Kidnapping Laws in Domestic Violence Cases

Pub.L. 106–386, Div. B, Title III, § 1303(a) to (c), Oct. 28, 2000, 114 Stat. 1512, provided that:

"**(a) In general.**—The Attorney General shall—

"(1) conduct a study of Federal and State laws relating to child custody, including custody provisions in protection orders, the Uniform Child Custody Jurisdiction and Enforcement Act adopted by the National Conference of Commissioners on Uniform State Laws in July 1997, the Parental Kidnaping Prevention Act of 1980 [Pub.L. 96–611, Dec. 28, 1980, 94 Stat. 3568] and the amendments made by that Act, and the effect of those laws on child custody cases in which domestic violence is a factor; and

"(2) submit to Congress a report describing the results of that study, including the effects of implementing or applying model State laws, and the recommendations of the Attorney General to reduce the incidence or pattern of violence against women or of sexual assault of the child.

"**(b) Sufficiency of defenses.**—In carrying out subsection (a) with respect to the Parental Kidnaping Prevention Act of 1980 [Pub.L. 96–611, Dec. 28, 1980, 94 Stat. 3568] and the amendments made by that Act [see Tables for classification], the Attorney General shall examine the sufficiency of defenses to parental abduction charges available in cases involving domestic violence, and the burdens and risks encountered by victims of domestic violence arising from jurisdictional requirements of that Act and the amendments made by that Act.

"**(c) Authorization of appropriations.**—There is authorized to be appropriated to carry out this section $200,000 for fiscal year 2001."

Congressional Findings and Declaration of Purpose

Section 7 of Pub.L. 96–611 provided that:

"**(a)** The Congress finds that—

"(1) there is a large and growing number of cases annually involving disputes between persons claiming rights of custody and visitation of children under the laws, and in the courts, of different States, the District of Columbia, the Commonwealth of Puerto Rico, and the territories and possessions of the United States;

"(2) the laws and practices by which the courts of those jurisdictions determine their jurisdiction to decide such disputes, and the effect to be given the decisions of such disputes by the courts of other jurisdictions, are often inconsistent and conflicting;

"(3) those characteristics of the law and practice in such cases, along with the limits imposed by a Federal system on the authority of each such jurisdiction to conduct investigations and take other actions outside its own boundaries, contribute to a tendency of parties involved in such disputes to frequently resort to the seizure, restraint, concealment, and interstate transportation of children, the disregard of court orders, excessive relitigation of cases, obtaining of conflicting orders by the courts of various jurisdictions, and interstate travel and communication that is so expensive and time consuming as to disrupt their occupations and commercial activities; and

"(4) among the results of those conditions and activities are the failure of the courts of such jurisdictions to give full faith and credit to the judicial proceedings of the other jurisdictions, the deprivation of rights of liberty and property without due process of law, burdens on commerce among such jurisdictions and with foreign nations, and harm to the welfare of children and their parents and other custodians.

"**(b)** For those reasons it is necessary to establish a national system for locating parents and children who travel from one such jurisdiction to another and are concealed in connection with such disputes, and to establish national standards under which the courts of such jurisdictions will determine their jurisdiction to decide such disputes and the effect to be given by each such jurisdiction to such decisions by the courts of other such jurisdictions.

"**(c)** The general purposes of sections 6 to 10 of this Act [enacting this section and sections 654(17) and 663 of Title 42, The Public Health and Welfare, amending section 655(a) of Title 42, and enacting provisions set out as notes under this section and sections 663 and 1305 of Title 42 and 1073 of Title 18, Crimes and Criminal Procedure] are to—

"(1) promote cooperation between State courts to the end that a determination of custody and visitation is rendered in the State which can best decide the case in the interest of the child;

"(2) promote and expand the exchange of information and other forms of mutual assistance between States which are concerned with the same child;

"(3) facilitate the enforcement of custody and visitation decrees of sister States;

"(4) discourage continuing interstate controversies over child custody in the interest of greater stability of home environment and of secure family relationships for the child;

"(5) avoid jurisdictional competition and conflict between State courts in matters of child custody and visitation which have in the past resulted in the shifting of children from State to State with harmful effects on their well-being; and

"(6) deter interstate abductions and other unilateral removals of children undertaken to obtain custody and visitation awards."

State Court Proceedings for Custody Determinations; Priority Treatment; Fees, Costs, and Other Expenses

Section 8(c) of Pub.L. 96–611 provided that: "In furtherance of the purposes of section 1738A of title 28, United States Code [this section], as added by subsection (a) of this section, State courts are encouraged to—

"(1) afford priority to proceedings for custody determinations; and

"(2) award to the person entitled to custody or visitation pursuant to a custody determination which is consistent with the provisions of such section 1738A [this section], necessary travel expenses, attorneys' fees, costs of private investigations, witness fees or expenses, and other expenses incurred in connection with such custody determination in any case in which—

"(A) a contestant has, without the consent of the person entitled to custody or visitation pursuant to a custody determination which is consistent with the provisions of such section 1738A [this section], (i) wrongfully removed the child from the physical custody of such person, or (ii) wrongfully retained the child after a visit or other temporary relinquishment of physical custody; or

"(B) the court determines it is appropriate."

§ 1738B. Full faith and credit for child support orders

(a) General rule.—The appropriate authorities of each State—

(1) shall enforce according to its terms a child support order made consistently with this section by a court of another State; and

(2) shall not seek or make a modification of such an order except in accordance with subsections (e), (f), and (i).

(b) Definitions.—In this section:

"child" means—

(A) a person under 18 years of age; and

(B) a person 18 or more years of age with respect to whom a child support order has been issued pursuant to the laws of a State.

"child's State" means the State in which a child resides.

"child's home State" means the State in which a child lived with a parent or a person acting as parent for at least 6 consecutive months immediately preceding the time of filing of a petition or comparable pleading for support and, if a child is less than 6 months old, the State in which the child lived from birth with any of them. A period of temporary absence of any of them is counted as part of the 6–month period.

"child support" means a payment of money, continuing support, or arrearages or the provision of a benefit (including payment of health insurance, child care, and educational expenses) for the support of a child.

"child support order"—

(A) means a judgment, decree, or order of a court requiring the payment of child support in periodic amounts or in a lump sum; and

(B) includes—

(i) a permanent or temporary order; and

(ii) an initial order or a modification of an order.

"contestant" means—

(A) a person (including a parent) who—

(i) claims a right to receive child support;

(ii) is a party to a proceeding that may result in the issuance of a child support order; or

(iii) is under a child support order; and

(B) a State or political subdivision of a State to which the right to obtain child support has been assigned.

"court" means a court or administrative agency of a State that is authorized by State law to establish the amount of child support payable by a contestant or make a modification of a child support order.

"modification" means a change in a child support order that affects the amount, scope, or duration of the order and modifies, replaces, supersedes, or otherwise is made subsequent to the child support order.

"State" means a State of the United States, the District of Columbia, the Commonwealth of Puerto Rico, the territories and possessions of the United States, and Indian country (as defined in section 1151 of title 18).

(c) Requirements of child support orders.—A child support order made by a court of a State is made consistently with this section if—

(1) a court that makes the order, pursuant to the laws of the State in which the court is located and subsections (e), (f), and (g)—

(A) has subject matter jurisdiction to hear the matter and enter such an order; and

(B) has personal jurisdiction over the contestants; and

(2) reasonable notice and opportunity to be heard is given to the contestants.

(d) Continuing jurisdiction.—A court of a State that has made a child support order consistently with this section has continuing, exclusive jurisdiction over the order if the State is the child's State or the residence of any individual contestant unless the court of another State, acting in accordance with subsections (e) and (f), has made a modification of the order.

(e) Authority to modify orders.—A court of a State may modify a child support order issued by a court of another State if—

(1) the court has jurisdiction to make such a child support order pursuant to subsection (i); and

(2)(A) the court of the other State no longer has continuing, exclusive jurisdiction of the child support order because that State no longer is the child's State or the residence of any individual contestant; or

(B) each individual contestant has filed written consent with the State of continuing, exclusive jurisdiction for a court of another State to modify the order and assume continuing, exclusive jurisdiction over the order.

(f) Recognition of child support orders.—If 1 or more child support orders have been issued with regard to an obligor and a child, a court shall apply the following rules in determining which order to recognize for purposes of continuing, exclusive jurisdiction and enforcement:

(1) If only 1 court has issued a child support order, the order of that court must be recognized.

(2) If 2 or more courts have issued child support orders for the same obligor and child, and only 1 of the courts would have continuing, exclusive jurisdiction under this section, the order of that court must be recognized.

(3) If 2 or more courts have issued child support orders for the same obligor and child, and more than 1 of the courts would have continuing, exclusive jurisdiction under this section, an order issued by a court in the current home State of the child must be recognized, but if an order has not been issued in the current home State of the child, the order most recently issued must be recognized.

(4) If 2 or more courts have issued child support orders for the same obligor and child, and none of the courts would have continuing, exclusive jurisdiction under this section, a court having jurisdiction over the parties shall issue a child support order, which must be recognized.

(5) The court that has issued an order recognized under this subsection is the court having continuing, exclusive jurisdiction under subsection (d).

(g) Enforcement of modified orders.—A court of a State that no longer has continuing, exclusive jurisdiction of a child support order may enforce the order with respect to nonmodifiable obligations and unsatisfied obligations that accrued before the date on which a modification of the order is made under subsections (e) and (f).

(h) Choice of law.—

(1) **In general.**—In a proceeding to establish, modify, or enforce a child support order, the forum State's law shall apply except as provided in paragraphs (2) and (3).

(2) **Law of State of issuance of order.**—In interpreting a child support order including the duration of current payments and other obligations of support, a court shall apply the law of the State of the court that issued the order.

(3) **Period of limitation.**—In an action to enforce arrears under a child support order, a court shall apply the statute of limitation of the forum State or the State of the court that issued the order, whichever statute provides the longer period of limitation.

(i) Registration for modification.—If there is no individual contestant or child residing in the issuing State, the party or support enforcement agency seeking to modify, or to modify and enforce, a child support order issued in another State shall register that order in a State with jurisdiction over the nonmovant for the purpose of modification.

(Added Pub.L. 103–383, § 3(a), Oct. 22, 1994, 108 Stat. 4064, and amended Pub.L. 104–193, Title III, § 322, Aug. 22, 1996, 110 Stat. 2221; Pub.L. 105–33, Title V, § 5554, Aug. 5, 1997, 111 Stat. 636.)

HISTORICAL AND STATUTORY NOTES

Effective and Applicability Provisions

1997 Acts

Amendments by Pub.L. 105–33 made by sections 5531 to 5556 to take effect as if included in the enactment of Title III of the Personal Responsibility and Work Opportunity Reconciliation Act of 1996 (Pub.L. 104–193, Aug. 22, 1996, 110 Stat. 2105), except for amendments made by section 5532(b)(2) (amending section 608(a)(3)(A) of Title 42, The Public Health and Welfare), see section 5557 of Pub.L. 105–33, set out as a note under section 608 of Title 42, The Public Health and Welfare.

1996 Acts

For effective date of Title III of Pub.L. 104–193, see section 395(a) to (c) of Pub.L. 104–193, set out as a note under section 654 of Title 42, The Public Health and Welfare.

Congressional Findings and Declaration of Purpose

Section 2 of Pub.L. 103–383 provided that:

"**(a) Findings.**—The Congress finds that—

"(1) there is a large and growing number of child support cases annually involving disputes between parents who reside in different States;

"(2) the laws by which the courts of different jurisdictions determine their authority to establish child support orders are not uniform;

"(3) those laws, along with the limits imposed by the Federal system on the authority of each State to take certain actions outside its own boundaries—

"(A) encourage noncustodial parents to relocate outside the States where their children and the custodial parents reside to avoid the jurisdiction of the courts of

such States, resulting in an increase in the amount of interstate travel and communication required to establish and collect on child support orders and a burden on custodial parents that is expensive, time consuming, and disruptive of occupations and commercial activity;

"(B) contribute to the pressing problem of relatively low levels of child support payments in interstate cases and to inequities in child support payments levels that are based solely on the noncustodial parent's choice of residence;

"(C) encourage a disregard of court orders resulting in massive arrearages nationwide;

"(D) allow noncustodial parents to avoid the payment of regularly scheduled child support payments for extensive periods of time, resulting in substantial hardship for the children for whom support is due and for their custodians; and

"(E) lead to the excessive relitigation of cases and to the establishment of conflicting orders by the courts of various jurisdictions, resulting in confusion, waste of judicial resources, disrespect for the courts, and a diminution of public confidence in the rule of law; and

"(4) among the results of the conditions described in this subsection are—

"(A) the failure of the courts of the States to give full faith and credit to the judicial proceedings of the other States;

"(B) the deprivation of rights of liberty and property without due process of law;

"(C) burdens on commerce among the States; and

"(D) harm to the welfare of children and their parents and other custodians.

"(b) Statement of policy.—In view of the findings made in subsection (a), it is necessary to establish national standards under which the courts of the various States shall determine their jurisdiction to issue a child support order and the effect to be given by each State to child support orders issued by the courts of other States.

"(c) Purposes.—The purposes of this Act [enacting this section and a provision set out as a note under section 1 of this title] are—

"(1) to facilitate the enforcement of child support orders among the States;

"(2) to discourage continuing interstate controversies over child support in the interest of greater financial stability and secure family relationships for the child; and

"(3) to avoid jurisdictional competition and conflict among State courts in the establishment of child support orders."

§ 1738C. Certain acts, records, and proceedings and the effect thereof

No State, territory, or possession of the United States, or Indian tribe, shall be required to give effect to any public act, record, or judicial proceeding of any other State, territory, possession, or tribe respecting a relationship between persons of the same sex that is treated as a marriage under the laws of such other State, territory, possession, or tribe, or a right or claim arising from such relationship.

(Added Pub.L. 104–199, § 2(a), Sept. 21, 1996, 110 Stat. 2419.)

§ 1739. State and Territorial nonjudicial records; full faith and credit

All nonjudicial records or books kept in any public office of any State, Territory, or Possession of the United States, or copies thereof, shall be proved or admitted in any court or office in any other State, Territory, or Possession by the attestation of the custodian of such records or books, and the seal of his office annexed, if there be a seal, together with a certificate of a judge of a court of record of the county, parish, or district in which such office may be kept, or of the Governor, or secretary of state, the chancellor or keeper of the great seal, of the State, Territory, or Possession that the said attestation is in due form and by the proper officers.

If the certificate is given by a judge, it shall be further authenticated by the clerk or prothonotary of the court, who shall certify, under his hand and the seal of his office, that such judge is duly commissioned and qualified; or, if given by such Governor, secretary, chancellor, or keeper of the great seal, it shall be under the great seal of the State, Territory, or Possession in which it is made.

Such records or books, or copies thereof, so authenticated, shall have the same full faith and credit in every court and office within the United States and its Territories and Possessions as they have by law or usage in the courts or offices of the State, Territory, or Possession from which they are taken.

(June 25, 1948, c. 646, 62 Stat. 947.)

§ 1740. Copies of consular papers

Copies of all official documents and papers in the office of any consul or vice consul of the United States, and of all official entries in the books or records of any such office, authenticated by the consul or vice consul, shall be admissible equally with the originals.

(June 25, 1948, c. 646, 62 Stat. 947.)

§ 1741. Foreign official documents

An official record or document of a foreign country may be evidenced by a copy, summary, or excerpt authenticated as provided in the Federal Rules of Civil Procedure.

(June 25, 1948, c. 646, 62 Stat. 948; May 24, 1949, c. 139, § 92(b), 63 Stat. 103; Oct. 3, 1964, Pub.L. 88–619, § 5(a), 78 Stat. 996.)

HISTORICAL AND STATUTORY NOTES

Treaties and Conventions; Taking of Evidence Abroad in Civil or Commercial Matters; Observance On and After Oct. 7, 1972, by United States and Citizens and Persons Subject to Jurisdiction of United States

For text of Convention, see provisions set out as a note under section 1781 of this title.

[§ 1742. Repealed. Pub.L. 88–619, § 6(a), Oct. 3, 1964, 78 Stat. 996]

HISTORICAL AND STATUTORY NOTES

Section, Act June 25, 1948, c. 646, 62 Stat. 948, related to authentication and certification of copies of documents relating to land titles, by persons having custody of such of any foreign government or its agents, certification by an American minister or consul that they be true copies of the originals, the recording of such copies in the office of the General Counsel for the Department of the Treasury, and to the evidentiary value of such copies.

§ 1743. Demand on postmaster

The certificate of the Postmaster General or the Government Accountability Office of the mailing to a postmaster of a statement of his account and that payment of the balance stated has not been received shall be sufficient evidence of a demand notwithstanding any allowances or credits subsequently made. A copy of such statement shall be attached to the certificate.

(June 25, 1948, c. 646, 62 Stat. 948; July 7, 2004, Pub.L. 108–271, § 8(b), 118 Stat. 814.)

HISTORICAL AND STATUTORY NOTES

Change of Name

"Government Accountability Office" substituted for "General Accounting Office" in text on authority of Pub.L. 108–271, § 8(b), cited in the credit to this section and set out as a note under 31 U.S.C.A. § 702, which provided that any reference to the General Accounting Office in any law, rule, regulation, certificate, directive, instruction, or other official paper in force on July 17, 2004, to refer and apply to the Government Accountability Office.

Transfer of Functions

The office of Postmaster General of the Post Office Department was abolished and all functions, powers, and duties of the Postmaster General were transferred to the United States Postal Service by Pub.L. 91–375, § 4(a), Aug. 12, 1970, 84 Stat. 773, set out as a note under section 201 of Title 39, Postal Service.

§ 1744. Copies of United States Patent and Trademark Office documents, generally

Copies of letters patent or of any records, books, papers, or drawings belonging to the United States Patent and Trademark Office and relating to patents, authenticated under the seal of the United States Patent and Trademark Office and certified by the Under Secretary of Commerce for Intellectual Property and Director of the United States Patent and Trademark Office, or by another officer of the United States Patent and Trademark Office authorized to do so by the Director, shall be admissible in evidence with the same effect as the originals.

Any person making application and paying the required fee may obtain such certified copies.

(June 25, 1948, c. 646, 62 Stat. 948; May 24, 1949, c. 139, § 92(c), 63 Stat. 103; Nov. 29, 1999, Pub.L. 106–113, Div. B, § 1000(a)(9) [Title IV, § 4732(b)(15)(B), (C)], 113 Stat. 1536, 1501A–584.)

HISTORICAL AND STATUTORY NOTES

Effective and Applicability Provisions

1999 Acts

Amendment by Pub.L. 106–113 [§ 4732], effective 4 months after Nov. 29, 1999, see Pub.L. 106–113 [§ 4731], set out as a note under section 1 of Title 35.

Change of Name

Patent Office and Commissioner of Patents redesignated Patent and Trademark Office and Commissioner of Patents and Trademarks, respectively, by section 3 of Pub.L. 93–596, Jan. 2, 1975, 88 Stat. 1949, set out as a note under section 1 of Title 35, Patents.

Transfer of Functions

The functions of all officers of the Department of Commerce and all functions of all agencies and employees of such Department, were, with a few exceptions, transferred to the Secretary of Commerce, with power vested in him to authorize their performance or the performance of any of his functions by any of such officers, agencies, and employees, by 1950 Reorg. Plan No. 5, §§ 1, 2, eff. May 24, 1950, 15 F.R. 3174, 64 Stat. 1263, set out in Appendix 1 to Title 5, Government Organization and Employees. The Patent Office [now Patent and Trademark Office], referred to in this section, is an agency of the Department of Commerce, and the Commissioner of Patents [now Commissioner of Patents and Trademarks], referred to in this section, is an officer of such Department.

§ 1745. Copies of foreign patent documents

Copies of the specifications and drawings of foreign letters patent, or applications for foreign letters patent, and copies of excerpts of the official journals and other official publications of foreign patent offices belonging to the United States Patent and Trademark Office, certified in the manner provided by section 1744 of this title are prima facie evidence of their contents and of the dates indicated on their face.

(June 25, 1948, c. 646, 62 Stat. 948, § 1746; renumbered § 1745 and amended May 24, 1949, c. 139, § 92(d), (e), 63 Stat. 103; Oct. 3, 1964, Pub.L. 88–619, § 7(a), 78 Stat. 996; Nov. 29, 1999, Pub.L. 106–113, Div. B, § 1000(a)(9) [Title IV, § 4732(b)(16)], 113 Stat. 1536, 1501A–585.)

HISTORICAL AND STATUTORY NOTES

Effective and Applicability Provisions

1999 Acts

Amendment by Pub.L. 106–113 [§ 4732], effective 4 months after Nov. 29, 1999, see Pub.L. 106–113 [§ 4731], set out as a note under section 1 of Title 35.

Change of Name

Patent Office redesignated Patent and Trademark Office by section 3 of Pub.L. 93–596, Jan. 2, 1975, 88 Stat. 1949, set out as a note under section 1 of Title 35, Patents.

Prior Provisions

A prior section 1745, Act June 25, 1948, c. 646, 62 Stat. 948, related to printed copies of patent specifications and drawings, prior to repeal by Act May 24, 1949, c. 139, § 92(d), 63 Stat. 103.

§ 1746. Unsworn declarations under penalty of perjury

Wherever, under any law of the United States or under any rule, regulation, order, or requirement made pursuant to law, any matter is required or permitted to be supported, evidenced, established, or proved by the sworn declaration, verification, certificate, statement, oath, or affidavit, in writing of the person making the same (other than a deposition, or an oath of office, or an oath required to be taken before a specified official other than a notary public), such matter may, with like force and effect, be supported, evidenced, established, or proved by the unsworn declaration, certificate, verification, or statement, in writing of such person which is subscribed by

him, as true under penalty of perjury, and dated, in substantially the following form:

(1) If executed without the United States: "I declare (or certify, verify, or state) under penalty of perjury under the laws of the United States of America that the foregoing is true and correct. Executed on (date).

(Signature)".

(2) If executed within the United States, its territories, possessions, or commonwealths: "I declare (or certify, verify, or state) under penalty of perjury that the foregoing is true and correct. Executed on (date).

(Signature)".

(Added Pub.L. 94–550, § 1(a), Oct. 18, 1976, 90 Stat. 2534.)

HISTORICAL AND STATUTORY NOTES

Prior Provisions

A prior section 1746 was renumbered section 1745 of this title by Act May 24, 1949.

CHAPTER 117—EVIDENCE; DEPOSITIONS

HISTORICAL AND STATUTORY NOTES

Deposition in Admiralty Cases

Prior to the general unification of civil and admiralty procedure and the rescission of the Admiralty Rules on July 1, 1966, Revised Statutes, §§ 863 to 865, as amended, which related to depositions de bene esse, when and how taken, notice, mode of taking, and transmission to court, provided as follows:

"Sec. 863. The testimony of any witness may be taken in any civil cause depending in a district court by deposition de bene esse, when the witness lives at a greater distance from the place of trial than one hundred miles, or is bound on a voyage to sea, or is about to go out of the United States, or out of the district in which the case is to be tried, and to a greater distance than one hundred miles from the place of trial, before the time of trial, or when he is ancient and infirm. The deposition may be taken before any judge of any court of the United States, or any clerk of a district court, or any chancellor, justice, or judge of a supreme or superior court, mayor or chief magistrate of a city, judge of a county court or court of common pleas of any of the United States, or any notary public, not being of counsel or attorney to either of the parties, nor interested in the event of the cause. Reasonable notice must first be given in writing by the party or his attorney proposing to take such deposition, to the opposite party or his attorney of record, as either may be nearest, which notice shall state the name of the witness

and the time and place of the taking of his deposition; and in all cases in rem, the person having the agency or possession of the property at the time of seizure shall be deemed the adverse party, until a claim shall have been put in; and whenever, by reason of the absence from the district and want of an attorney of record or other reason, the giving of the notice herein required shall be impracticable, it shall be lawful to take such depositions as there shall be urgent necessity for taking, upon such notice as any judge authorized to hold courts in such district shall think reasonable and direct. Any person may be compelled to appear and depose as provided by this section, in the same manner as witnesses may be compelled to appear and testify in court.

"Sec. 864. Every person deposing as provided in the preceding section [R.S. § 863] shall be cautioned and sworn to testify the whole truth, and carefully examined.

"His testimony shall be reduced to writing or typewriting by the officer taking the deposition, or by some person under his personal supervision, or by the deponent himself in the officer's presence, and by no other person, and shall, after it has been reduced to writing or typewriting, be subscribed by the deponent. [As amended May 23, 1900, c. 541, 31 Stat. 182.]

"Sec. 865. Every deposition taken under the two preceding sections [R.S. §§ 863, 864] shall be retained by the magistrate taking it, until he delivers it with his own hand into the court for which it is taken; or it shall, together with a certificate of the reasons as aforesaid of taking it and of the notice, if any, given to the adverse party, be by him sealed up and directed to such court, and remain under his seal until opened in court. But unless it appears to the satisfaction of the court that the witness is then dead, or gone out of the United States, or to a greater distance than one hundred miles from the place where the court is sitting, or that, by reason of age, sickness, bodily infirmity, or imprisonment, he

is unable to travel and appear at court, such deposition shall not be used in the cause."

R.S. §§ 863 to 865, as amended, quoted above, were applicable to admiralty proceedings only. Proceedings in bankruptcy and copyright are governed by Rule 26 et seq. of Federal Rules of Civil Procedure. See also Rules of Bankruptcy Procedure set out in Title 11, Bankruptcy.

§ 1781. Transmittal of letter rogatory or request

(a) The Department of State has power, directly, or through suitable channels—

(1) to receive a letter rogatory issued, or request made, by a foreign or international tribunal, to transmit it to the tribunal, officer, or agency in the United States to whom it is addressed, and to receive and return it after execution; and

(2) to receive a letter rogatory issued, or request made, by a tribunal in the United States, to transmit it to the foreign or international tribunal, officer, or agency to whom it is addressed, and to receive and return it after execution.

(b) This section does not preclude—

(1) the transmittal of a letter rogatory or request directly from a foreign or international tribunal to the tribunal, officer, or agency in the United States to whom it is addressed and its return in the same manner; or

(2) the transmittal of a letter rogatory or request directly from a tribunal in the United States to the foreign or international tribunal, officer, or agency to whom it is addressed and its return in the same manner.

(June 25, 1948, c. 646, 62 Stat. 949; Oct. 3, 1964, Pub.L. 88–619, § 8(a), 78 Stat. 996.)

TREATIES AND CONVENTIONS
CONVENTION ON THE TAKING OF EVIDENCE ABROAD IN CIVIL OR COMMERCIAL MATTERS

The States signatory to the present Convention,

Desiring to facilitate the transmission and execution of Letters of Request and to further the accommodation of the different methods which they use for this purpose.

Desiring to improve mutual judicial co-operation in civil or commercial matters.

Have resolved to conclude a Convention to this effect and have agreed upon the following provisions—

*　*　*　*　*　*　*

CHAPTER I—LETTERS OF REQUEST
Article 1

In civil or commercial matters a judicial authority of a Contracting State may, in accordance with the provisions of the law of that State, request the competent authority of another Contracting State, by means of a Letter of Request, to obtain evidence, or to perform some other judicial act.

A Letter shall not be used to obtain evidence which is not intended for use in judicial proceedings, commenced or contemplated.

The expression "other judicial act" does not cover the service of judicial documents or the issuance of any process by which judgments or orders are executed or enforced, or orders for provisional or protective measures.

Article 2

A Contracting State shall designate a Central Authority which will undertake to receive Letters of Request coming from a judicial authority of another Contracting State and to transmit them to the authority competent to execute them. Each State shall organize the Central Authority in accordance with its own law.

Letters shall be sent to the Central Authority of the State of execution without being transmitted through any other authority of that State.

Article 3

A Letter of Request shall specify—

(a) the authority requesting its execution and the authority requested to execute it, if known to the requesting authority;

(b) the names and addresses of the parties to the proceedings and their representatives, if any;

(c) the nature of the proceedings for which the evidence is required, giving all necessary information in regard thereto;

(d) the evidence to be obtained or other judicial act to be performed.

Where appropriate, the Letter shall specify, inter alia—

(e) the names and addresses of the persons to be examined;

(f) the questions to be put to the persons to be examined or a statement of the subject-matter about which they are to be examined;

(g) the documents or other property, real or personal, to be inspected;

(h) any requirement that the evidence is to be given on oath or affirmation, and any special form to be used;

(i) any special method or procedure to be followed under Article 9.

A Letter may also mention any information necessary for the application of Article 11.

No legalization or other like formality may be required.

Article 4

A Letter of Request shall be in the language of the authority requested to execute it or be accompanied by a translation into that language.

Nevertheless, a Contracting State shall accept a Letter in either English or French, or a translation into one of these languages, unless it has made the reservation authorized by Article 33.

A Contracting State which has more than one official language and cannot, for reasons of internal law, accept

Letters in one of these languages for the whole of its territory, shall, by declaration, specify the language in which the Letter or translation thereof shall be expressed for execution in the specified parts of its territory. In case of failure to comply with this declaration, without justifiable excuse, the costs of translation into the required language shall be borne by the State of origin.

A Contracting State may, by declaration, specify the language or languages other than those referred to in the preceding paragraphs, in which a Letter may be sent to its Central Authority.

Any translation accompanying a Letter shall be certified as correct, either by a diplomatic officer or consular agent or by a sworn translator or by any other person so authorized in either State.

Article 5

If the Central Authority considers that the request does not comply with the provisions of the present Convention, it shall promptly inform the authority of the State of origin which transmitted the Letter of Request, specifying the objections to the Letter.

Article 6

If the authority to whom a Letter of Request has been transmitted is not competent to execute it, the Letter shall be sent forthwith to the authority in the same State which is competent to execute it in accordance with the provisions of its own law.

Article 7

The requesting authority shall, if it so desires, be informed of the time when, and the place where, the proceedings will take place, in order that the parties concerned, and their representatives, if any, may be present. This information shall be sent directly to the parties or their representatives when the authority of the State of origin so requests.

Article 8

A Contracting State may declare that members of the judicial personnel of the requesting authority of another Contracting State may be present at the execution of a Letter of Request. Prior authorization by the competent authority designated by the declaring State may be required.

Article 9

The judicial authority which executes a Letter of Request shall apply its own law as to the methods and procedures to be followed.

However, it will follow a request of the requesting authority that a special method or procedure be followed, unless this is incompatible with the internal law of the State of execution or is impossible of performance by reason of its internal practice and procedure or by reason of practical difficulties.

A Letter of Request shall be executed expeditiously.

Article 10

In executing a Letter of Request the requested authority shall apply the appropriate measures of compulsion in the instances and to the same extent as are provided by its internal law for the execution of orders issued by the authori-

ties of its own country or of requests made by parties in internal proceedings.

Article 11

In the execution of a Letter of Request the person concerned may refuse to give evidence in so far as he has a privilege or duty to refuse to give the evidence—

(a) under the law of the State of execution; or

(b) under the law of the State of origin, and the privilege or duty has been specified in the Letter, or, at the instance of the requested authority, has been otherwise confirmed to that authority by the requesting authority.

A Contracting State may declare that, in addition, it will respect privileges and duties existing under the law of States other than the State of origin and the State of execution, to the extent specified in that declaration.

Article 12

The execution of a Letter of Request may be refused only to the extent that—

(a) in the State of execution the execution of the Letter does not fall within the functions of the judiciary; or

(b) the State addressed considers that its sovereignty or security would be prejudiced thereby.

Execution may not be refused solely on the ground that under its internal law the State of execution claims exclusive jurisdiction over the subject-matter of the action or that its internal law would not admit a right of action on it.

Article 13

The documents establishing the execution of the Letter of Request shall be sent by the requested authority to the requesting authority by the same channel which was used by the latter.

In every instance where the Letter is not executed in whole or in part, the requesting authority shall be informed immediately through the same channel and advised of the reasons.

Article 14

The execution of the Letter of Request shall not give rise to any reimbursement of taxes or costs of any nature.

Nevertheless, the State of execution has the right to require the State of origin to reimburse the fees paid to experts and interpreters and the costs occasioned by the use of a special procedure requested by the State of origin under Article 9, paragraph 2.

The requested authority whose law obliges the parties themselves to secure evidence, and which is not able itself to execute the Letter, may, after having obtained the consent of the requesting authority, appoint a suitable person to do so. When seeking this consent the requested authority shall indicate the approximate costs which would result from this procedure. If the requesting authority gives its consent it shall reimburse any costs incurred; without such consent the requesting authority shall not be liable for the costs.

CHAPTER II—TAKING OF EVIDENCE BY DIPLOMATIC OFFICERS, CONSULAR AGENTS AND COMMISSIONERS

Article 15

In a civil or commercial matter, a diplomatic officer or consular agent of a Contracting State may, in the territory of another Contracting State and within the area where he exercises his functions, take the evidence without compulsion of nationals of a State which he represents in aid of proceedings commenced in the courts of a State which he represents.

A Contracting State may declare that evidence may be taken by a diplomatic officer or consular agent only if permission to that effect is given upon application made by him or on his behalf to the appropriate authority designated by the declaring State.

Article 16

A diplomatic officer or consular agent of a Contracting State may, in the territory of another Contracting State and within the area where he exercises his functions, also take the evidence, without compulsion, of nationals of the State in which he exercises his functions or of a third State, in aid of proceedings commenced in the courts of a State which he represents, if—

(a) a competent authority designated by the State in which he exercises his functions has given its permission either generally or in the particular case, and

(b) he complies with the conditions which the competent authority has specified in the permission.

A Contracting State may declare that evidence may be taken under this Article without its prior permission.

Article 17

In a civil or commercial matter, a person duly appointed as a commissioner for the purpose may, without compulsion, take evidence in the territory of a Contracting State in aid of proceedings commenced in the courts of another Contracting State if—

(a) a competent authority designated by the State where the evidence is to be taken has given its permission either generally or in the particular case; and

(b) he complies with the conditions which the competent authority has specified in the permission.

A Contracting State may declare that evidence may be taken under this Article without its prior permission.

Article 18

A Contracting State may declare that a diplomatic officer, consular agent or commissioner authorized to take evidence under Articles 15, 16 or 17, may apply to the competent authority designated by the declaring State for appropriate assistance to obtain the evidence by compulsion. The declaration may contain such conditions as the declaring State may see fit to impose.

If the authority grants the application it shall apply any measures of compulsion which are appropriate and are prescribed by its law for use in internal proceedings.

Article 19

The competent authority, in giving the permission referred to in Articles 15, 16 or 17, or in granting the application referred to in Article 18, may lay down such conditions as it deems fit, *inter alia*, as to the time and place of the taking of the evidence. Similarly it may require that it be given reasonable advance notice of the time, date and place of the taking of the evidence; in such a case a representative of the authority shall be entitled to be present at the taking of the evidence.

Article 20

In the taking of evidence under any Article of this Chapter persons concerned may be legally represented.

Article 21

Where a diplomatic officer, consular agent or commissioner is authorized under Articles 15, 16 or 17 to take evidence—

(a) he may take all kinds of evidence which are not incompatible with the law of the State where the evidence is taken or contrary to any permission granted pursuant to the above Articles, and shall have power within such limits to administer an oath or take an affirmation;

(b) a request to a person to appear or to give evidence shall, unless the recipient is a national of the State where the action is pending, be drawn up in the language of the place where the evidence is taken or be accompanied by a translation into such language;

(c) the request shall inform the person that he may be legally represented and, in any State that has not filed a declaration under Article 18, shall also inform him that he is not compelled to appear or to give evidence;

(d) the evidence may be taken in the manner provided by the law applicable to the court in which the action is pending provided that such manner is not forbidden by the law of the State where the evidence is taken;

(e) a person requested to give evidence may invoke the privileges and duties to refuse to give the evidence contained in Article 11.

Article 22

The fact that an attempt to take evidence under the procedure laid down in this Chapter has failed, owing to the refusal of a person to give evidence, shall not prevent an application being subsequently made to take the evidence in accordance with Chapter I.

CHAPTER III—GENERAL CLAUSES

Article 23

A Contracting State may at the time of signature, ratification or accession, declare that it will not execute Letters of Request issued for the purpose of obtaining pretrial discovery of documents as known in Common Law countries.

Article 24

A Contracting State may designate other authorities in addition to the Central Authority and shall determine the extent of their competence. However, Letters of Request may in all cases be sent to the Central Authority.

Federal States shall be free to designate more than one Central Authority.

Article 25

A Contracting State which has more than one legal system may designate the authorities of one of such systems, which shall have exclusive competence to execute Letters of Request pursuant to this Convention.

Article 26

A Contracting State, if required to do so because of constitutional limitations, may request the reimbursement by the State of origin of fees and costs, in connection with the execution of Letters of Request, for the service of process necessary to compel the appearance of a person to give evidence, the costs of attendance of such persons, and the cost of any transcript of the evidence.

Where a State has made a request pursuant to the above paragraph, any other Contracting State may request from that State the reimbursement of similar fees and costs.

Article 27

The provisions of the present Convention shall not prevent a Contracting State from—

(a) declaring that Letters of Request may be transmitted to its judicial authorities through channels other than those provided for in Article 2;

(b) permitting, by internal law or practice, any act provided for in this Convention to be performed upon less restrictive conditions;

(c) permitting, by internal law or practice, methods of taking evidence other than those provided for in this Convention.

Article 28

The present Convention shall not prevent an agreement between any two or more Contracting States to derogate from—

(a) the provisions of Article 2 with respect to methods of transmitting Letters of Request;

(b) the provisions of Article 4 with respect to the languages which may be used;

(c) the provisions of Article 8 with respect to the presence of judicial personnel at the execution of Letters;

(d) the provisions of Article 11 with respect to the privileges and duties of witnesses to refuse to give evidence;

(e) the provisions of Article 13 with respect to the methods of returning executed Letters to the requesting authority;

(f) the provisions of Article 14 with respect to fees and costs;

(g) the provisions of Chapter II.

Article 29

Between Parties to the present Convention who are also Parties to one or both of the Conventions on Civil Procedure signed at the Hague on the 17th of July 1905 [99 British Foreign and State Papers 990] and the 1st of March 1954 [286 UNTS 265], this Convention shall replace Articles 8–16 of the earlier Conventions.

Article 30

The present Convention shall not affect the application of Article 23 of the Convention of 1905, or of Article 24 of the Convention of 1954.

Article 31

Supplementary Agreements between Parties to the Conventions of 1905 and 1954 shall be considered as equally applicable to the present Convention unless the Parties have otherwise agreed.

Article 32

Without prejudice to the provisions of Articles 29 and 31, the present Convention shall not derogate from conventions containing provisions on the matters covered by this Convention to which the Contracting States are, or shall become Parties.

Article 33

A State may, at the time of signature, ratification or accession exclude, in whole or in part, the application of the provisions of paragraph 2 of Article 4 and of Chapter II. No other reservation shall be permitted.

Each Contracting State may at any time withdraw a reservation it has made; the reservation shall cease to have effect on the sixtieth day after notification of the withdrawal.

When a State has made a reservation, any other State affected thereby may apply the same rule against the reserving State.

Article 34

A State may at any time withdraw or modify a declaration.

Article 35

A Contracting State shall, at the time of the deposit of its instrument of ratification or accession, or at a later date, inform the Ministry of Foreign Affairs of the Netherlands of the designation of authorities, pursuant to Articles 2, 8, 24 and 25.

A Contracting State shall likewise inform the Ministry, where appropriate, of the following—

(a) the designation of the authorities to whom notice must be given, whose permission may be required, and whose assistance may be invoked in the taking of evidence by diplomatic officers and consular agents, pursuant to Articles 15, 16 and 18 respectively;

(b) the designation of the authorities whose permission may be required in the taking of evidence by commissioners pursuant to Article 17 and of those who may grant the assistance provided for in Article 18;

(c) declarations pursuant to Articles 4, 8, 11, 15, 16, 17, 18, 23 and 27;

(d) any withdrawal or modification of the above designations and declarations;

(e) the withdrawal of any reservation.

Article 36

Any difficulties which may arise between Contracting States in connection with the operation of this Convention shall be settled through diplomatic channels.

Complete Annotation Materials, see Title 28 U.S.C.A.

Article 37

The present Convention shall be open for signature by the States represented at the Eleventh Session of the Hague Conference on Private International Law.

It shall be ratified, and the instruments of ratification shall be deposited with the Ministry of Foreign Affairs of the Netherlands.

Article 38

The present Convention shall enter into force on the sixtieth day after the deposit of the third instrument of ratification referred to in the second paragraph of Article 37.

The Convention shall enter into force for each signatory State which ratifies subsequently on the sixtieth day after the deposit of its instrument of ratification.

Article 39

Any State not represented at the Eleventh Session of the Hague Conference on Private International Law which is a Member of this Conference or of the United Nations or of a specialized agency of that Organization, or a Party to the Statute of the International Court of Justice may accede to the present Convention after it has entered into force in accordance with the first paragraph of Article 38.

The instrument of accession shall be deposited with the Ministry of Foreign Affairs of the Netherlands.

The Convention shall enter into force for a State acceding to it on the sixtieth day after the deposit of its instrument of accession.

The accession will have effect only as regards the relations between the acceding State and such Contracting States as will have declared their acceptance of the accession. Such declaration shall be deposited at the Ministry of Foreign Affairs of the Netherlands; this Ministry shall forward, through diplomatic channels, a certified copy to each of the Contracting States.

The Convention will enter into force as between the acceding State and the State that has declared its acceptance of the accession on the sixtieth day after the deposit of the declaration of acceptance.

Article 40

Any State may, at the time of signature, ratification or accession, declare that the present Convention shall extend to all the territories for the international relations of which it is responsible, or to one or more of them. Such a declaration shall take effect on the date of entry into force of the Convention for the State concerned.

At any time thereafter, such extensions shall be notified to the Ministry of Foreign Affairs of the Netherlands.

The Convention shall enter into force for the territories mentioned in such an extension on the sixtieth day after the notification indicated in the preceding paragraph.

Article 41

The present Convention shall remain in force for five years from the date of its entry into force in accordance with the first paragraph of Article 38, even for States which have ratified it or acceded to it subsequently.

If there has been no denunciation, it shall be renewed tacitly every five years.

Any denunciation shall be notified to the Ministry of Foreign Affairs of the Netherlands at least six months before the end of the five year period.

It may be limited to certain of the territories to which the Convention applies.

The denunciation shall have effect only as regards the State which has notified it. The Convention shall remain in force for the other Contracting States.

Article 42

The Ministry of Foreign Affairs of the Netherlands shall give notice to the States referred to in Article 37, and to the States which have acceded in accordance with Article 39, of the following—

(a) the signatures and ratifications referred to in Article 37;

(b) the date on which the present Convention enters into force in accordance with the first paragraph of Article 38;

(c) the accessions referred to in Article 39 and the dates on which they take effect;

(d) the extensions referred to in Article 40 and the dates on which they take effect;

(e) the designations, reservations and declarations referred to in Articles 33 and 35;

(f) the denunciations referred to in the third paragraph of Article 41.

IN WITNESS WHEREOF the undersigned, being duly authorized thereto, have signed the present Convention.

DONE at The Hague, on the 18th day of March 1970, in the English and French languages, both texts being equally authentic, in a single copy which shall be deposited in the archives of the Government of the Netherlands, and of which a certified copy shall be sent, through the diplomatic channel, to each of the States represented at the Eleventh Session of the Hague Conference on Private International Law. [Signatures omitted.]

Convention on the taking of evidence abroad in civil or commercial matters. Done at The Hague March 18, 1970; entered into force for the United States October 7, 1972. TIAS 7444; 23 UST 2555

Annotations to the Convention

"Report of the U.S. Delegation on the Evidence Convention", 8 Int'l Legal Materials 804 (1969).

Amram, "Explanatory Report on the Convention on the Taking of Evidence Abroad in Civil and Commercial Matters—Message from the President of the United States", Sen.Exec. A, 92nd Cong., 2d Sess. (Feb. 1, 1972).

Edwards, "Taking of Evidence Abroad in Civil or Commercial Matters", 18 Int'l and Comp.L.Q. 646 (1969).

Amram, "U.S. Ratification of the Hague Convention on the Taking of Evidence Abroad" 67 Am.J. Int'l L. (1973).

Model for Letters of Request Recommended for Use in Applying the Hague Convention of 18 March 1970 on the Taking of Evidence Abroad in Civil or Commercial Matters

Request for International Judicial Assistance Pursuant to the Hague Convention of 18 March 1970 on the Taking of Evidence in Civil or Commercial Matters

N.B. Under the first paragraph of article 4, the Letter of Request shall be in the language of the authority requested to execute it or be accompanied by a translation into that language. However, the provisions of the second and third paragraphs may permit use of other languages.

In order to avoid confusion, please spell out the name of the month in each date.

I. *(Items to be included in all Letters of Request.)*

 1. Sender _____*(identity and address)*_____

 2. Central Authority of the Requested State _____*(identity and address)*_____

 3. Person to whom the executed request is to be returned _____*(identity and address)*_____

II. *(Items to be included in all Letters of Request.)*

 4. In conformity with article 3 of the Convention, the undersigned applicant has the honour to submit the following request:

 5. a. Requesting judicial authority (article 3, a) _____*(identity and address)*_____

 b. To the competent authority of (article 3, a) _____*(the requested State)*_____

 6. Names and addresses of the parties and their representatives (article 3, b)

 a. Plaintiff

 b. Defendant

 c. Other parties

 7. Nature and purpose of the proceedings and summary of the facts (article 3, c)

 8. Evidence to be obtained or other judicial act to be performed (article 3, d)

III. *(Items to be completed where applicable.)*

 9. Identity and address of any person to be examined (article 3, e)

10. Questions to be put to the persons to be examined or statement of the subject-matter about which they are to be examined (article 3, f)

_____(or see attached list)_____

11. Documents or other property to be inspected (article 3, g)

_____(specify whether it is to be produced, copied, valued, etc.)_____

12. Any requirement that the evidence be given on oath or affirmation and any special form to be used (article 3, h)

_____(In the event that the evidence cannot be taken in the manner requested, specify whether it is to be taken in such manner as provided by local law for the formal taking of evidence.)_____

13. Special methods or procedure to be followed (articles 3, i and 9)

14. Request for notification of the time and place for the execution of the Request and identity and address of any person to be notified (article 7)

15. Request for attendance or participation of judicial personnel of the requesting authority at the execution of the letter of Request

16. Specification of privilege or duty to refuse to give evidence under the law of the State of origin (article 11, b)

17. The fees and costs incurred which are reimbursable under the second paragraph of article 14 or under article 26 of the Convention will be borne by

_____(identity and address)_____

IV. *(Items to be included in all Letters of Request.)*

18. Date of request

19. Signature and seal of the requesting authority

TREATIES AND CONVENTIONS
INTER–AMERICAN CONVENTION ON LETTERS ROGATORY

The Governments of the Member States of the Organization of American States, desirous of concluding a convention on letters rogatory, have agreed as follows:

I. USE OF TERMS
Article 1

For the purposes of this Convention the terms "exhortos" and "cartas rogatorias" are synonymous in the Spanish text. The terms "letters rogatory", "commissions rogatoires", and "cartas rogatórias" used in the English, French and Portu-

guese texts, respectively, cover both "exhortos" and "cartas rogatorias".

II. SCOPE OF THE CONVENTION
Article 2

This Convention shall apply to letters rogatory, issued in conjunction with proceedings in civil and commercial matters held before the appropriate judicial or other adjudicatory authority of one of the States Parties to this Convention, that have as their purpose:

a. The performance of procedural acts of a merely formal nature, such as service of process, summonses or subpoenas abroad;

b. The taking of evidence and the obtaining of information abroad, unless a reservation is made in this respect.

Article 3

This Convention shall not apply to letters rogatory relating to procedural acts other than those specified in the preceding article; and in particular it shall not apply to acts involving measures of compulsion.

III. TRANSMISSION OF LETTERS ROGATORY
Article 4

Letters rogatory may be transmitted to the authority to which they are addressed by the interested parties, through judicial channels, diplomatic or consular agents, or the Central Authority of the State of origin or of the State of destination, as the case may be.

Each State Party shall inform the General Secretariat of the Organization of American States of the Central Authority competent to receive and distribute letters rogatory.

IV. REQUIREMENTS FOR EXECUTION
Article 5

Letters rogatory shall be executed in the States Parties provided they meet the following requirements:

a. The letter rogatory is legalized, except as provided for in Articles 6 and 7 of this Convention. The letter rogatory shall be presumed to be duly legalized in the State of origin when legalized by the competent consular or diplomatic agent;

b. The letter rogatory and the appended documentation are duly translated into the official language of the State of destination.

Article 6

Whenever letters rogatory are transmitted through consular or diplomatic channels or through the Central Authority, legalization shall not be required.

Article 7

Courts in border areas of the States Parties may directly execute the letters rogatory contemplated in this Convention and such letters shall not require legalization.

Article 8

Letters rogatory shall be accompanied by the following documents to be delivered to the person on whom process, summons or subpoena is being served:

a. An authenticated copy of the complaint with its supporting documents, and of other exhibits or rulings that serve as the basis for the measure requested;

b. Written information identifying the judicial or other adjudicatory authority issuing the letter, indicating the time-limits allowed the person affected to act upon the request, and warning of the consequences of failure to do so;

c. Where appropriate, information on the existence and address of the court-appointed defense counsel or of competent legal-aid societies in the State of origin.

Article 9

Execution of letters rogatory shall not imply ultimate recognition of the jurisdiction of the judicial or other adjudicatory authority issuing the letter rogatory or a commitment to recognize the validity of the judgment it may render or to execute it.

V. EXECUTION
Article 10

Letters rogatory shall be executed in accordance with the laws and procedural rules of the State of destination.

At the request of the judicial or other adjudicatory authority issuing the letter rogatory, the authority of the State of destination may execute the letter through a special procedure, or accept the observance of additional formalities in performing the act requested, provided this procedure or the observance of those formalities is not contrary to the law of the State of destination.

Article 11

The authority of the State of destination shall have jurisdiction to determine any issue arising as a result of the execution of the measure requested in the letter rogatory.

Should such authority find that it lacks jurisdiction to execute the letter rogatory, it shall ex officio forward the documents and antecedents of the case to the authority of the State which has jurisdiction.

Article 12

The costs and other expenses involved in the processing and execution of letters rogatory shall be borne by the interested parties.

The State of destination may, in its discretion, execute a letter rogatory that does not indicate the person to be held responsible for costs and other expenses when incurred. The identity of the person empowered to represent the applicant for legal purposes may be indicated in the letter rogatory or in the documents relating to its execution.

The effects of a declaration in forma pauperis shall be regulated by the law of the State of destination.

Article 13

Consular or diplomatic agents of the States Parties to this Convention may perform the acts referred to in Article 2 in the State in which they are accredited, provided the performance of such acts is not contrary to the laws of that State. In so doing, they shall not perform any acts involving measures of compulsion.

VI. GENERAL PROVISIONS

Article 14

States Parties belonging to economic integration systems may agree directly between themselves upon special methods and procedures more expeditious than those provided for in this Convention. These agreements may be extended to include other States in the manner in which the parties may agree.

Article 15

This Convention shall not limit any provisions regarding letters rogatory in bilateral or multilateral agreements that may have been signed or may be signed in the future by the States Parties or preclude the continuation of more favorable practices in this regard that may be followed by these States.

Article 16

The States Parties to this Convention may declare that its provisions cover the execution of letters rogatory in criminal, labor, and "contentious-administrative" cases, as well as in arbitrations and other matters within the jurisdiction of special courts. Such declarations shall be transmitted to the General Secretariat of the Organization of American States.

Article 17

The State of destination may refuse to execute a letter rogatory that is manifestly contrary to its public policy ("ordre public").

Article 18

The States Parties shall inform the General Secretariat of the Organization of American States of the requirements stipulated in their laws for the legalization and the translation of letters rogatory.

VII. FINAL PROVISIONS

Article 19

This Convention shall be open for signature by the Member States of the Organization of American States.

Article 20

This Convention is subject to ratification. The instruments of ratification shall be deposited with the General Secretariat of the Organization of American States.

Article 21

This Convention shall remain open for accession by any other State. The instrument of accession shall be deposited with the General Secretariat of the Organization of American States.

Article 22

This Convention shall enter into force on the thirtieth day following the date of deposit of the second instrument of ratification.

For each State ratifying or acceding to the Convention after the deposit of the second instrument of ratification, the Convention shall enter into force on the thirtieth day after deposit by such State of its instrument of ratification or accession.

Article 23

If a State Party has two or more territorial units in which different systems of law apply in relation to the matters dealt with in this Convention, it may, at the time of signature, ratification or accession, declare that this Convention shall extend to all its territorial units or only to one or more of them.

Such declaration may be modified by subsequent declarations, which shall expressly indicate the territorial unit or units to which the Convention applies. Such subsequent declarations shall be transmitted to the General Secretariat of the Organization of American States, and shall become effective thirty days after the date of their receipt.

Article 24

This Convention shall remain in force indefinitely, but any of the States Parties may denounce it. The instrument of denunciation shall be deposited with the General Secretariat of the Organization of American States. After one year from the date of deposit of the instrument of denunciation, the Convention shall no longer be in effect for the denouncing State, but shall remain in effect for the other States Parties.

Article 25

The original instrument of this Convention, the English, French, Portuguese and Spanish texts of which are equally authentic, shall be deposited with the General Secretariat of the Organization of American States. The Secretariat shall notify the Member States of the Organization of American States and the States that have acceded to the Convention of the signatures, deposits of instruments of ratification, accession, and denunciation as well as of reservations, if any. It shall also transmit the information mentioned in the second paragraph of Article 4 and in Article 18 and the declarations referred to in Articles 16 and 23 of this Convention.

IN WITNESS WHEREOF the undersigned Plenipotentiaries, being duly authorized thereto by their respective Governments, have signed this Convention.

DONE AT PANAMA CITY, Republic of Panama, this thirtieth day of January one thousand nine hundred and seventy-five.

[Signatures omitted]

Inter-American Convention on Letters Rogatory.

Done at Panama January 30, 1975; entered into force for the United States August 27, 1988.

ADDITIONAL PROTOCOL TO THE INTER-AMERICAN CONVENTION ON LETTERS ROGATORY

The Governments of the Member States of the Organization of American States, desirous of strengthening and facilitating international cooperation in judicial procedures as provided for in the Inter-American Convention on Letters Rogatory done in Panama on January 30, 1975, have agreed as follows:

I. SCOPE OF PROTOCOL

Article 1

This Protocol shall apply only to those procedural acts set forth in Article 2(a) of the Inter–American Convention on Letters Rogatory, hereinafter referred to as "the Convention". For the purposes of this Protocol, such acts shall be understood to mean procedural acts (pleadings, motions, orders, and subpoenas) that are served and requests for information that are made by a judicial or other adjudicatory authority of a State Party to a judicial or administrative authority of another State Party and are transmitted by a letter rogatory from the Central Authority of the State of origin to the Central Authority of the State of destination.

II. CENTRAL AUTHORITY

Article 2

Each State Party shall designate a central authority that shall perform the functions assigned to it in the Convention and in this Protocol. At the time of deposit of their instruments of ratification or accession to this Protocol, the States Parties shall communicate the designations to the General Secretariat of the Organization of American States, which shall distribute to the States Parties to the Convention a list containing the designations received. The Central Authority designated by a State Party in accordance with Article 4 of the Convention may be changed at any time. The State Party shall inform the above-mentioned Secretariat of such change as promptly as possible.

III. PREPARATION OF LETTERS ROGATORY

Article 3

Letters rogatory shall be prepared on forms that are printed in the four official languages of the Organization of American States or in the languages of the State of origin and of the State of destination and conform to Form A contained in the Annex to this Protocol.

Letters rogatory shall be accompanied by the following:

a. Copy of the complaint or pleading that initiated the action in which the letter rogatory was issued, as well as a translation thereof into the language of the State of destination;

b. Untranslated copy of the documents attached to the complaint or pleading;

c. Untranslated copy of any rulings ordering issuance of the letter rogatory;

d. Form conforming to Form B annexed to this Protocol and containing essential information for the person to be served or the authority to receive the documents; and

e. Certificate conforming to Form C annexed to this Protocol on which the Central Authority of the State of destination shall attest to execution or non-execution of the letter rogatory.

The copies shall be regarded as authenticated for the purposes of Article 8(a) of the Convention if they bear the seal of the judicial or other adjudicatory authority that issued the letter rogatory.

A copy of the letter rogatory together with Form B and the copies referred to in items a, b, and c of this Article shall be delivered to the person notified or to the authority to which the request is addressed. One of the copies of the letter rogatory and the documents attached to it shall remain in the possession of the State of destination; the untranslated original, the certificate of execution and the documents attached to them shall be returned to the Central Authority of the State of origin through appropriate channels.

If a State Party has more than one official language, it shall, at the time of signature, ratification or accession to this Protocol, declare which language or languages shall be considered official for the purposes of the Convention and of this Protocol. If a State Party comprises territorial units that have different official languages, it shall, at the time of signature, ratification or accession to this Protocol, declare which language or languages in each territorial unit shall be considered official for the purposes of the Convention and of this Protocol. The General Secretariat of the Organization of American States shall distribute to the States Parties to this Protocol the information contained in such declarations.

IV. TRANSMISSION AND PROCESSING OF LETTERS ROGATORY

Article 4

Upon receipt of a letter rogatory from the Central Authority in another State Party, the Central Authority in the State of destination shall transmit the letter rogatory to the appropriate judicial or administrative authority for processing in accordance with the applicable local law.

Upon execution of the letter rogatory, the judicial or administrative authority or authorities that processed it shall attest to the execution thereof in the manner prescribed in their local law, and shall transmit it with the relevant documents to the Central Authority. The Central Authority of the State Party of destination shall certify execution of the letter rogatory to the Central Authority of the State Party of origin on a form conforming to Form C of the Annex, which shall not require legalization. In addition, the Central Authority of the State of destination shall return the letter rogatory and attached documents to the Central Authority of the State of origin for delivery to the judicial or other adjudicatory authority that issued it.

V. COSTS AND EXPENSES

Article 5

The processing of letters rogatory by the Central Authority of the State Party of destination and its judicial or administrative authorities shall be free of charge. However, this State Party may seek payment by parties requesting execution of letters rogatory for those services which, in accordance with its local law, are required to be paid for directly by those parties.

The party requesting the execution of a letter rogatory shall, at its election, either select and indicate in the letter rogatory the person who is responsible in the State of destination for the cost of such services or, alternatively, shall attach to the letter rogatory a check for the fixed amount that is specified in Article 6 of this Protocol for its processing by the State of destination and will cover the cost of such services or a document proving that such amount has been transferred by some other means to the Central Authority of the State of destination.

The fact that the cost of such services ultimately exceeds the fixed amount shall not delay or prevent the processing or execution of the letter rogatory by the Central Authority or the judicial or administrative authorities of the State of destination. Should the cost exceed that amount, the Central Authority of the State of destination may, when returning the executed letter rogatory, seek payment of the outstanding amount due from the party requesting execution of the letter rogatory.

Article 6

At the time of deposit of its instrument of ratification or accession to this Protocol with the General Secretariat of the Organization of American States, each State Party shall attach a schedule of the services and the costs and other expenses that, in accordance with its local law, shall be paid directly by the party requesting execution of the letter rogatory. In addition, each State Party shall specify in the above-mentioned schedule the single amount which it considers will reasonably cover the cost of such services, regardless of the number or nature thereof. This amount shall be paid when the person requesting execution of the letter rogatory has not designated a person responsible for the payment of such services in the State of destination but has decided to pay for them directly in the manner provided for in Article 5 of this Protocol.

The General Secretariat of the Organization of American States shall distribute the information received to the States Parties to this Protocol. A State Party may at any time notify the General Secretariat of the Organization of American States of changes in the above-mentioned schedules, which shall be communicated by the General Secretariat to the other States Parties to this Protocol.

Article 7

States Parties may declare in the schedules mentioned in the foregoing articles that, provided there is reciprocity, they will not charge parties requesting execution of letters rogatory for the services necessary for executing them, or will accept in complete satisfaction of the cost of such services either the single fixed amount specified in Article 6 or another specified amount.

Article 8

This Protocol shall be open for signature and subject to ratification or accession by those Member States of the Organization of American States that have signed, ratified, or acceded to the Inter–American Convention on Letters Rogatory signed in Panama on January 30, 1975.

This Protocol shall remain open for accession by any other State that accedes or has acceded to the Inter–American Convention on Letters Rogatory, under the conditions set forth in this article.

The instruments of ratification and accession shall be deposited with the General Secretariat of the Organization of American States.

Article 9

This Protocol shall enter into force on the thirtieth day following the date on which two States Parties to the Convention have deposited their instruments of ratification or accession to this Protocol.

For each State ratifying or acceding to the Protocol after its entry into force, the Protocol shall enter into force on the thirtieth day following deposit by such State of its instrument of ratification or accession, provided that such State is a Party to the Convention.

Article 10

If a State Party has two or more territorial units in which different systems of law apply in relation to matters dealt with in this Protocol, it may, at the time of signature, ratification or accession, declare that this Protocol shall extend to all its territorial units or only to one or more of them.

Such declaration may be modified by subsequent declarations that shall expressly indicate the territorial unit or units to which this Protocol applies. Such subsequent declarations shall be transmitted to the General Secretariat of the Organization of American States, and shall become effective thirty days after the date of their receipt.

Article 11

This Protocol shall remain in force indefinitely, but any of the States Parties may denounce it. The instrument of denunciation shall be deposited with the General Secretariat of the Organization of American States. After one year from the date of deposit of the instrument of denunciation, the Protocol shall no longer be in effect for the denouncing State, but shall remain in effect for the other States Parties.

Article 12

The original instrument of this Protocol and its Annex (Forms A, B and C), the English, French, Portuguese and Spanish texts of which are equally authentic, shall be deposited with the General Secretariat of the Organization of American States, which will forward an authenticated copy of the text to the Secretariat of the United Nations for registration and publication in accordance with Article 102 of its Charter. The General Secretariat of the Organization of American States shall notify the Member States of that Organization and the States that have acceded to the Protocol of the signatures, deposits of instruments of ratification, accession and denunciation, as well as of reservations, if any. It shall also transmit to them the information mentioned in Article 2, the last paragraph of Article 3, and Article 6 and the declarations referred to in Article 10 of this Protocol.

IN WITNESS WHEREOF the undersigned Plenipotentiaries, being duly authorized thereto by their respective Governments, have signed this Protocol.

DONE AT MONTEVIDEO, Republic of Uruguay, this eighth day of May, one thousand nine hundred and seventy-nine.

[Signatures omitted]

ANNEX TO THE ADDITIONAL PROTOCOL
TO THE INTER–AMERICAN CONVENTION ON LETTERS ROGATORY
FORM A

LETTER ROGATORY 1

1	2
REQUESTING JUDICIAL OR OTHER ADJUDICATORY AUTHORITY Name Address	CASE: DOCKET No.:

3	4
CENTRAL AUTHORITY OF THE STATE OF ORIGIN Name Address	CENTRAL AUTHORITY OF THE STATE OF DESTINATION Name Address

5	6
REQUESTING PARTY Name Address	COUNSEL TO THE REQUESTING PARTY Name Address

PERSON DESIGNATED TO ACT IN CONNECTION WITH THE LETTER ROGATORY

Name

Is this person responsible for
costs and expenses?
YES ☐ NO ☐

Address

*If not, check in the amount of
_____ is attached
*Or proof of payment is attached

The Central Authority signing this letter rogatory has the honor to transmit to you in triplicate the documents listed below and, in conformity with the Protocol to the Inter–American Convention on Letters Rogatory:

* A. Requests their prompt service on:

The undersigned authority requests that service be carried out in the following manner:

* (1). In accordance with the special procedure or additional formalities that are described below, as provided for in the second paragraph of Article 10 of the above-mentioned Convention; or

* (2). By service personally on the identified addressee or, in the case of a legal entity, on its authorized agent; or

* (3). If the person or the authorized agent of the entity to be served is not found, service shall be made in accordance with the law of the State of destination.

* B. Requests the delivery of the documents listed below to the following judicial or administrative authority:

Authority _____

* C. Requests the Central Authority of the State of destination to return to the Central Authority of the State of origin one copy of the documents listed below and attached to this letter rogatory, and an executed Certificate on the attached Form C.

Done at _____ this _____ date of _____, 19____.

Signature and stamp of the judicial or other adjudicatory authority of the State of origin	Signature and stamp of the Central Authority of the State of origin

Title or other identification of each document to be delivered:

(Attach additional pages, if necessary.)

1 Complete the original and two copies of this form; if A(1) is applicable, attach the original and two copies of the translation of this item in the language of the State of destination.

* Delete if inapplicable.

ANNEX TO THE ADDITIONAL PROTOCOL
TO THE INTER–AMERICAN CONVENTION ON LETTERS ROGATORY

FORM B

ESSENTIAL INFORMATION FOR THE ADDRESSEE 1

To (Name and address of the person being served)_____

You are hereby informed that (Brief statement of nature of service) _____

A copy of the letter rogatory that gives rise to the service or delivery of these documents is attached to this document. This copy also contains essential information for you. Also attached are copies of the complaint or pleading initiating the action in which the letter rogatory was issued, of the documents attached to the complaint or pleading, and of any rulings that ordered the issuance of the letter rogatory.

ADDITIONAL INFORMATION

I*

FOR SERVICE

A. The document being served on you (original or copy) concerns the following:

B. The remedies sought or the amount in dispute is as follows:

C. By this service, you are requested:

D. * In case of service on you as a defendant you can answer the complaint before the judicial or other adjudicatory authority specified in Form A, Box 1 (State place, date and hour):

* You are being summoned to appear as: _____

* If some other action is being requested of the person served, please describe: _____

E. If you fail to comply, the consequences might be: _____

F. You are hereby informed that a defense counsel appointed by the Court or the following legal aid societies are available to you at the place where the proceeding is pending.
Name: _____

Address: _____

The documents listed in Part III are being furnished to you so that you may better understand and defend your interests.

II *

FOR INFORMATION FROM JUDICIAL OR ADMINISTRATIVE AUTHORITY

To: _____

(Name and address of the judicial or administrative authority)

You are respectfully requested to furnish the undersigned authority with the following information:

The documents listed in Part III are being furnished to you to facilitate your reply.

III

LIST OF ATTACHED DOCUMENTS

(Attach additional pages if necessary.)

Done at _____ this _____ day of _____, 19___

_____ _____

Signature and stamp of the Signature and stamp of
judicial or other adjudicatory the Central Authority
authority of the State of origin of the State of Origin

1 Complete the original and two copies of this form in the language of the State of origin and two copies in the language of the State of destination.
* Delete if inapplicable.

ANNEX TO THE ADDITIONAL PROTOCOL
TO THE INTER–AMERICAN CONVENTION ON LETTERS ROGATORY

FORM C

CERTIFICATE OF EXECUTION[1]

To: _____

(Name and address of judicial or other adjudicatory authority that issued the letter rogatory)

In conformity with the Additional Protocol to the Inter–American Convention on Letters Rogatory, signed at Montevideo on May 8, 1979, and in accordance with the attached original letter rogatory, the undersigned Central Authority has the honor to certify the following:

*A. That one copy of the documents attached to this Certificate has been served or delivered as follows:

Date: _____

At (Address) _____

By one of the following methods authorized by the Convention.

*(1) In accordance with the special procedure or additional formalities that are described below, as provided for in the second paragraph of Article 10 of the above-mentioned Convention, or

*(2) By service personally on the identified addressee or, in the case of a legal entity, on its authorized agent, or

*(3) If the person or the authorized agent of the entity to be served was not found, in accordance with the law of the State of destination: (Specify method used)

*B. That the documents referred to in the letter rogatory have been delivered to:

Identity of person _____

Relationship to the addressee _____
 (family, business or other)

*C. That the documents attached to the Certificate have not been served or delivered for the following reason(s):

*D. In conformity with the Protocol, the party requesting execution of the letter rogatory is requested to pay the outstanding balance of costs in the amount indicated in the attached statement.

Done at _____ the _____ day of _____ 19__

Signature and stamp of Central Authority of the State of destination

Where appropriate, attach originals or copies
of any additional documents proving service
or delivery, and identify them.
1 Complete the original and one copy in the language of the State of destination.
* Delete if inapplicable.

Additional Protocol to the Inter–American Convention on Letters Rogatory, with Annex. Done at Montevideo May 8, 1979; entered into force for the United States August 27, 1988.

§ 1782. Assistance to foreign and international tribunals and to litigants before such tribunals

(a) The district court of the district in which a person resides or is found may order him to give his

testimony or statement or to produce a document or other thing for use in a proceeding in a foreign or international tribunal, including criminal investigations conducted before formal accusation. The order may be made pursuant to a letter rogatory issued, or request made, by a foreign or international tribunal or upon the application of any interested person and may direct that the testimony or statement be given, or the document or other thing be produced, before a person appointed by the court. By virtue of his appointment, the person appointed has power to administer any necessary oath and take the testimony or statement. The order may prescribe the practice and procedure, which may be in whole or part the practice and procedure of the foreign country or the international tribunal, for taking the testimony or statement or producing the document or other thing. To the extent that the order does not prescribe otherwise, the testimony or statement shall be taken, and the document or other thing produced, in accordance with the Federal Rules of Civil Procedure.

A person may not be compelled to give his testimony or statement or to produce a document or other thing in violation of any legally applicable privilege.

(b) This chapter does not preclude a person within the United States from voluntarily giving his testimony or statement, or producing a document or other thing, for use in a proceeding in a foreign or international tribunal before any person and in any manner acceptable to him.

(June 25, 1948, c. 646, 62 Stat. 949; May 24, 1949, c. 139, § 93, 63 Stat. 103; Oct. 3, 1964, Pub.L. 88–619, § 9(a), 78 Stat. 997; Feb. 10, 1996, Pub.L. 104–106, Div. A, Title XIII, § 1342(b), 110 Stat. 486.)

HISTORICAL AND STATUTORY NOTES
References in Text

The Federal Rules of Civil Procedure, referred to in subsec. (a), are set out in this title.

§ 1783.　Subpoena of person in foreign country

(a) A court of the United States may order the issuance of a subpoena requiring the appearance as a witness before it, or before a person or body designated by it, of a national or resident of the United States who is in a foreign country, or requiring the production of a specified document or other thing by him, if the court finds that particular testimony or the production of the document or other thing by him is necessary in the interest of justice, and, in other than a criminal action or proceeding, if the court finds, in addition, that it is not possible to obtain his testimony in admissible form without his personal appearance or to obtain the production of the document or other thing in any other manner.

(b) The subpoena shall designate the time and place for the appearance or for the production of the document or other thing. Service of the subpoena and any order to show cause, rule, judgment, or decree authorized by this section or by section 1784 of this title shall be effected in accordance with the provisions of the Federal Rules of Civil Procedure relating to service of process on a person in a foreign country. The person serving the subpoena shall tender to the person to whom the subpoena is addressed his estimated necessary travel and attendance expenses, the amount of which shall be determined by the court and stated in the order directing the issuance of the subpoena.

(June 25, 1948, c. 646, 62 Stat. 949; Oct. 3, 1964, Pub.L. 88–619, § 10(a), 78 Stat. 997.)

HISTORICAL AND STATUTORY NOTES
References in Text

The Federal Rules of Civil Procedure, referred to in subsec. (b), are set out in this title.

§ 1784.　Contempt

(a) The court of the United States which has issued a subpoena served in a foreign country may order the person who has failed to appear or who has failed to produce a document or other thing as directed therein to show cause before it at a designated time why he should not be punished for contempt.

(b) The court, in the order to show cause, may direct that any of the person's property within the United States be levied upon or seized, in the manner provided by law or court rules governing levy or seizure under execution, and held to satisfy any judgment that may be rendered against him pursuant to subsection (d) of this section if adequate security, in such amount as the court may direct in the order, be given for any damage that he might suffer should he not be found in contempt. Security under this subsection may not be required of the United States.

(c) A copy of the order to show cause shall be served on the person in accordance with section 1783(b) of this title.

(d) On the return day of the order to show cause or any later day to which the hearing may be continued, proof shall be taken. If the person is found in contempt, the court, notwithstanding any limitation upon its power generally to punish for contempt, may fine him not more than $100,000 and direct that the fine and costs of the proceedings be satisfied by a sale of the property levied upon or seized, conducted upon the notice required and in the manner provided for sales upon execution.

(June 25, 1948, c. 646, 62 Stat. 949; Oct. 3, 1964, Pub.L. 88–619, § 11, 78 Stat. 998.)

§ 1785.　Subpoenas in multiparty, multiforum actions

When the jurisdiction of the district court is based in whole or in part upon section 1369 of this title, a

subpoena for attendance at a hearing or trial may, if authorized by the court upon motion for good cause shown, and upon such terms and conditions as the court may impose, be served at any place within the United States, or anywhere outside the United States if otherwise permitted by law.

(Added Pub.L. 107–273, Div. C, Title I, § 11020(b)(4)(B)(i), Nov. 2, 2002, 116 Stat. 1828.)

HISTORICAL AND STATUTORY NOTES
Effective and Applicability Provisions
2002 Acts

Amendments by section 11020(b) of Pub.L. 107–273 shall apply to a civil action if the accident giving rise to the cause of action occurred on or after the 90th day after Nov. 2, 2002, see section 11020(c) of Pub.L. 107–273, set out as a note under 28 U.S.C.A. § 1369.

Prior Provisions

A prior section 1785, Act June 25, 1948, c. 646, 62 Stat. 950, relating to the privilege against self-incrimination on examination under letters rogatory (see section 1782(a) of this title), was repealed by Pub.L. 88–619, § 12(a), Oct. 3, 1964, 78 Stat. 998.

CHAPTER 119—EVIDENCE; WITNESSES

§ 1821. Per diem and mileage generally; subsistence

(a)(1) Except as otherwise provided by law, a witness in attendance at any court of the United States, or before a United States Magistrate Judge, or before any person authorized to take his deposition pursuant to any rule or order of a court of the United States, shall be paid the fees and allowances provided by this section.

(2) As used in this section, the term "court of the United States" includes, in addition to the courts listed in section 451 of this title, any court created by Act of Congress in a territory which is invested with any jurisdiction of a district court of the United States.

(b) A witness shall be paid an attendance fee of $40 per day for each day's attendance. A witness shall also be paid the attendance fee for the time necessarily occupied in going to and returning from the place of attendance at the beginning and end of such attendance or at any time during such attendance.

(c)(1) A witness who travels by common carrier shall be paid for the actual expenses of travel on the basis of the means of transportation reasonably utilized and the distance necessarily traveled to and from such witness's residence by the shortest practical route in going to and returning from the place of attendance. Such a witness shall utilize a common carrier at the most economical rate reasonably avail-

able. A receipt or other evidence of actual cost shall be furnished.

(2) A travel allowance equal to the mileage allowance which the Administrator of General Services has prescribed, pursuant to section 5704 of title 5, for official travel of employees of the Federal Government shall be paid to each witness who travels by privately owned vehicle. Computation of mileage under this paragraph shall be made on the basis of a uniformed table of distances adopted by the Administrator of General Services.

(3) Toll charges for toll roads, bridges, tunnels, and ferries, taxicab fares between places of lodging and carrier terminals, and parking fees (upon presentation of a valid parking receipt), shall be paid in full to a witness incurring such expenses.

(4) All normal travel expenses within and outside the judicial district shall be taxable as costs pursuant to section 1920 of this title.

(d)(1) A subsistence allowance shall be paid to a witness when an overnight stay is required at the place of attendance because such place is so far removed from the residence of such witness as to prohibit return thereto from day to day.

(2) A subsistence allowance for a witness shall be paid in an amount not to exceed the maximum per diem allowance prescribed by the Administrator of General Services, pursuant to section 5702(a) of title 5, for official travel in the area of attendance by employees of the Federal Government.

(3) A subsistence allowance for a witness attending in an area designated by the Administrator of General Services as a high-cost area shall be paid in an amount not to exceed the maximum actual subsistence allowance prescribed by the Administrator, pursuant to section 5702(c)(B) of title 5, for official travel in such area by employees of the Federal Government.

(4) When a witness is detained pursuant to section 3144 of title 18 for want of security for his appearance, he shall be entitled for each day of detention when not

in attendance at court, in addition to his subsistence, to the daily attendance fee provided by subsection (b) of this section.

(e) An alien who has been paroled into the United States for prosecution, pursuant to section 212(d)(5) of the Immigration and Nationality Act (8 U.S.C. 1182(d)(5)), or an alien who either has admitted belonging to a class of aliens who are deportable or has been determined pursuant to section 240 of such Act (8 U.S.C. 1252(b)[1]) to be deportable, shall be ineligible to receive the fees or allowances provided by this section.

(f) Any witness who is incarcerated at the time that his or her testimony is given (except for a witness to whom the provisions of section 3144 of title 18 apply) may not receive fees or allowances under this section, regardless of whether such a witness is incarcerated at the time he or she makes a claim for fees or allowances under this section.

(June 25, 1948, c. 646, 62 Stat. 950; May 10, 1949, c. 96, 63 Stat. 65; May 24, 1949, c. 139, § 94, 63 Stat. 103; Oct. 31, 1951, c. 655, § 51(a), 65 Stat. 727; Sept. 3, 1954, c. 1263, § 45, 68 Stat. 1242; Aug. 1, 1956, c. 826, 70 Stat. 798; Mar. 27, 1968, Pub.L. 90–274, § 102(b), 82 Stat. 62; Oct. 27, 1978, Pub.L. 95–535, § 1, 92 Stat. 2033; Dec. 1, 1990, Pub.L. 101–650, Title III, §§ 314(a), 321, 104 Stat. 5115, 5117; Oct. 14, 1992, Pub.L. 102–417, § 2(a)–(c), 106 Stat. 2138; Sept. 30, 1996, Pub.L. 104–208, Div. C, Title III, § 308(g)(5)(E), 110 Stat. 3009–623.)

[1] So in original. Reference in parenthesis should probably be "(8 U.S.C. 1229a)".

HISTORICAL AND STATUTORY NOTES

References in Text

Clause (B) of section 5702(c) of title 5, referred to in subsec. (d)(3), was redesignated clause (2) by Pub.L. 96–54, § 2(a)(36), Aug. 14, 1979, 93 Stat. 383. Thereafter subsec. (c) of section 5702 of Title 5, which related to conditions under which an employee could be reimbursed for actual and necessary expenses of official travel when the maximum per diem allowance was less than these expenses, was struck out in its entirety, and subsec. (e) of that section was redesignated as subsec. (c) thereof, by Pub.L. 99–234, Title I, § 102, Jan. 2, 1986, 99 Stat. 1756. Both amendments were made without any conforming amendments to this section.

Effective and Applicability Provisions

1996 Acts

Amendment by section 308(g)(5)(E) of Div. C of Pub.L. 104–208, effective, with certain exceptions and subject to certain transitional rules, on the first day of the first month beginning more than 180 days after Sept. 30, 1996, see section 309 of Pub.L. 104–208, set out as a note under section 1101 of Title, Aliens and Nationality.

1992 Acts

Section 2(d) of Pub.L. 102–417 provided that: "The amendments made by this section [amending this section] shall be effective on and after the date of the enactment of this act [Oct. 14, 1992] and shall apply to any witness who testified before such date and has not received any fee or allowance

under section 1821 of title 28, United States Code [this section], relating to such testimony."

1978 Acts

Section 2 of Pub.L. 95–535 provided that: "The amendments made by this Act [amending this section] shall take effect on October 1, 1978, or on the date of enactment [Oct. 27, 1978], whichever occurs later."

1968 Acts

Amendment by Pub.L. 90–274 effective 270 days after Mar. 27, 1968, except as to cases in which an indictment has been returned or a petit jury empaneled prior to such effective date, see section 104 of Pub.L. 90–274, set out as a note under section 1861 of this title.

Change of Name

"United States magistrate judge" substituted for "United States magistrate" in text pursuant to section 321 of Pub.L. 101–650, set out as a note under 28 U.S.C.A. § 631.

Severability of Provisions

If any provision of Division C of Pub.L. 104–208 or the application of such provision to any person or circumstances is held to be unconstitutional, the remainder of Division C of Pub.L. 104–208 and the application of the provisions of Division C of Pub.L. 104–208 to any person or circumstance not to be affected thereby, see section 1(e) of Pub.L. 104–208, set out as a note under section 1101 of Title 8, Aliens and Nationality.

Payment of Fact Witness Fee to Incarcerated Person Prohibited

Pub.L. 102–395, Title I, § 108, Oct. 6, 1992, 106 Stat. 1841, provided that: "Notwithstanding 28 U.S.C. 1821 [this section], no funds appropriated to the Department of Justice in fiscal year 1993 or any prior fiscal year, or any other funds available from the Treasury of the United States, shall be obligated or expended to pay a fact witness fee to a person who is incarcerated testifying as a fact witness in a court of the United States, as defined in 28 U.S.C. 1821(a)(2) [subsec. (a)(2) of this section]."

Similar provisions were contained in the following prior appropriations Acts:

Pub.L. 102–140, Title I, § 110, Oct. 28, 1991, 105 Stat. 795.

Pub.L. 102–27, Title II, § 102, Apr. 10, 1991, 105 Stat. 136.

§ 1822. Competency of interested persons; share of penalties payable

Any person interested in a share of any fine, penalty or forfeiture incurred under any Act of Congress, may be examined as a witness in any proceeding for the recovery of such fine, penalty or forfeiture by any party thereto. Such examination shall not deprive the witness of his share.

(June 25, 1948, c. 646, 62 Stat. 950.)

[§ 1823. Repealed. Pub.L. 91–563, § 5(a), Dec. 19, 1970, 84 Stat. 1478]

HISTORICAL AND STATUTORY NOTES

Section, Acts June 25, 1948, c. 646, 62 Stat. 950; May 24, 1949, c. 139, § 95, 63 Stat. 103; Oct. 5, 1949, c. 601, 63 Stat.

704; July 7, 1952, c. 581, 66 Stat. 439; July 28, 1955, c. 424, § 3, 69 Stat. 394, related to payment of witness fees to officers and employees of the United States, and is now covered by sections 5515, 5537, 5751, and 6322 of Title 5, Government Organization and Employees.

§ 1824. Mileage fees under summons as both witness and juror

No constructive or double mileage fees shall be allowed by reason of any person being summoned both as a witness and a juror.

(June 25, 1948, c. 646, 62 Stat. 951.)

§ 1825. Payment of fees

(a) In any case in which the United States or an officer or agency of the United States is a party, the United States marshal for the district shall pay all fees of witnesses on the certificate of the United States attorney or assistant United States attorney, and in the proceedings before a United States magistrate judge, on the certificate of such magistrate judge, except that any fees of defense witnesses, other than experts, appearing pursuant to subpoenas issued upon approval of the court, shall be paid by the United States marshal for the district—

(1) on the certificate of a Federal public defender or assistant Federal public defender, in a criminal case in which the defendant is represented by such Federal public defender or assistant Federal public defender, and

(2) on the certificate of the clerk of the court upon the affidavit of such witnesses' attendance given by other counsel appointed pursuant to section 3006A of title 18, in a criminal case in which a defendant is represented by such other counsel.

(b) In proceedings in forma pauperis for a writ of habeas corpus, and in proceedings in forma pauperis under section 2255 of this title, the United States marshal for the district shall pay, on the certificate of the district judge, all fees of witnesses for the party authorized to proceed in forma pauperis, except that any fees of witnesses for such party, other than experts, appearing pursuant to subpoenas issued upon approval of the court, shall be paid by the United States marshal for the district—

(1) on the certificate of a Federal public defender or assistant Federal public defender, in any such proceedings in which a party is represented by such Federal public defender or assistant Federal public defender, and

(2) on the certificate of the clerk of the court upon the affidavit of such witnesses' attendance given by other counsel appointed pursuant to section 3006A of title 18, in any such proceedings in which a party is represented by such other counsel.

(c) Fees and mileage need not be tendered to a witness upon service of a subpoena issued on behalf of the United States or an officer or agency of the United States, upon service of a subpoena issued on behalf of a defendant represented by a Federal public defender, assistant Federal public defender, or other attorney appointed pursuant to section 3006A of title 18, or upon service of a subpoena issued on behalf of a party authorized to proceed in forma pauperis, if the payment of such fees and mileage is to be made by the United States marshal under this section.

(June 25, 1948, c. 646, 62 Stat. 951; Sept. 2, 1965, Pub.L. 89–162, 79 Stat. 618; Nov. 14, 1986, Pub.L. 99–651, Title I, § 104, 100 Stat. 3645; Dec. 1, 1990, Pub.L. 101–650, Title III, § 321, 104 Stat. 5117.)

HISTORICAL AND STATUTORY NOTES

Effective and Applicability Provisions

1986 Acts

Amendment to this section by section 104 of Pub.L. 99–651 to take effect one hundred and twenty days after Nov. 14, 1986, see section 105 of Pub.L. 99–651, set out as a note under section 3006A of Title 18, Crimes and Criminal Procedure.

Change of Name

"United States magistrate judge" substituted for "United States magistrate" in text pursuant to section 321 of Pub.L. 101–650, set out as a note under 28 U.S.C.A. § 631.

§ 1826. Recalcitrant witnesses

(a) Whenever a witness in any proceeding before or ancillary to any court or grand jury of the United States refuses without just cause shown to comply with an order of the court to testify or provide other information, including any book, paper, document, record, recording or other material, the court, upon such refusal, or when such refusal is duly brought to its attention, may summarily order his confinement at a suitable place until such time as the witness is willing to give such testimony or provide such information. No period of such confinement shall exceed the life of—

(1) the court proceeding, or

(2) the term of the grand jury, including extensions,

before which such refusal to comply with the court order occurred, but in no event shall such confinement exceed eighteen months.

(b) No person confined pursuant to subsection (a) of this section shall be admitted to bail pending the determination of an appeal taken by him from the order for his confinement if it appears that the appeal is frivolous or taken for delay. Any appeal from an order of confinement under this section shall be disposed of as soon as practicable, but not later than thirty days from the filing of such appeal.

(c) Whoever escapes or attempts to escape from the custody of any facility or from any place in which or to which he is confined pursuant to this section or section 4243 of title 18, or whoever rescues or attempts to rescue or instigates, aids, or assists the escape or attempt to escape of such a person, shall be subject to imprisonment for not more than three years, or a fine of not more than $10,000, or both. (Added Pub.L. 91–452, Title III, § 301(a), Oct. 15, 1970, 84 Stat. 932, and amended Pub.L. 98–473, Title II, § 1013, Oct. 12, 1984, 98 Stat. 2142.)

§ 1827. Interpreters in courts of the United States

(a) The Director of the Administrative Office of the United States Courts shall establish a program to facilitate the use of certified and otherwise qualified interpreters in judicial proceedings instituted by the United States.

(b)(1) The Director shall prescribe, determine, and certify the qualifications of persons who may serve as certified interpreters, when the Director considers certification of interpreters to be merited, for the hearing impaired (whether or not also speech impaired) and persons who speak only or primarily a language other than the English language, in judicial proceedings instituted by the United States. The Director may certify interpreters for any language if the Director determines that there is a need for certified interpreters in that language. Upon the request of the Judicial Conference of the United States for certified interpreters in a language, the Director shall certify interpreters in that language. Upon such a request from the judicial council of a circuit and the approval of the Judicial Conference, the Director shall certify interpreters for that circuit in the language requested. The judicial council of a circuit shall identify and evaluate the needs of the districts within a circuit. The Director shall certify interpreters based on the results of criterion-referenced performance examinations. The Director shall issue regulations to carry out this paragraph within 1 year after the date of the enactment of the Judicial Improvements and Access to Justice Act.

(2) Only in a case in which no certified interpreter is reasonably available as provided in subsection (d) of this section, including a case in which certification of interpreters is not provided under paragraph (1) in a particular language, may the services of otherwise qualified interpreters be used. The Director shall provide guidelines to the courts for the selection of otherwise qualified interpreters, in order to ensure that the highest standards of accuracy are maintained in all judicial proceedings subject to the provisions of this chapter.

(3) The Director shall maintain a current master list of all certified interpreters and otherwise qualified

interpreters and shall report periodically on the use and performance of both certified and otherwise qualified interpreters in judicial proceedings instituted by the United States and on the languages for which interpreters have been certified. The Director shall prescribe, subject to periodic review, a schedule of reasonable fees for services rendered by interpreters, certified or otherwise, used in proceedings instituted by the United States, and in doing so shall consider the prevailing rate of compensation for comparable service in other governmental entities.

(c)(1) Each United States district court shall maintain on file in the office of the clerk, and each United States attorney shall maintain on file, a list of all persons who have been certified as interpreters by the Director in accordance with subsection (b) of this section. The clerk shall make the list of certified interpreters for judicial proceeding available upon request.

(2) The clerk of the court, or other court employee designated by the chief judge, shall be responsible for securing the services of certified interpreters and otherwise qualified interpreters required for proceedings initiated by the United States, except that the United States attorney is responsible for securing the services of such interpreters for governmental witnesses.

(d)(1) The presiding judicial officer, with the assistance of the Director of the Administrative Office of the United States Courts, shall utilize the services of the most available certified interpreter, or when no certified interpreter is reasonably available, as determined by the presiding judicial officer, the services of an otherwise qualified interpreter, in judicial proceedings instituted by the United States, if the presiding judicial officer determines on such officer's own motion or on the motion of a party that such party (including a defendant in a criminal case), or a witness who may present testimony in such judicial proceedings—

(A) speaks only or primarily a language other than the English language; or

(B) suffers from a hearing impairment (whether or not suffering also from a speech impairment)

so as to inhibit such party's comprehension of the proceedings or communication with counsel or the presiding judicial officer, or so as to inhibit such witness' comprehension of questions and the presentation of such testimony.

(2) Upon the motion of a party, the presiding judicial officer shall determine whether to require the electronic sound recording of a judicial proceeding in which an interpreter is used under this section. In making this determination, the presiding judicial officer shall consider, among other things, the qualifica-

tions of the interpreter and prior experience in interpretation of court proceedings; whether the language to be interpreted is not one of the languages for which the Director has certified interpreters, and the complexity or length of the proceeding. In a grand jury proceeding, upon the motion of the accused, the presiding judicial officer shall require the electronic sound recording of the portion of the proceeding in which an interpreter is used.

(e)(1) If any interpreter is unable to communicate effectively with the presiding judicial officer, the United States attorney, a party (including a defendant in a criminal case), or a witness, the presiding judicial officer shall dismiss such interpreter and obtain the services of another interpreter in accordance with this section.

(2) In any judicial proceedings instituted by the United States, if the presiding judicial officer does not appoint an interpreter under subsection (d) of this section, an individual requiring the services of an interpreter may seek assistance of the clerk of court or the Director of the Administrative Office of the United States Courts in obtaining the assistance of a certified interpreter.

(f)(1) Any individual other than a witness who is entitled to interpretation under subsection (d) of this section may waive such interpretation in whole or in part. Such a waiver shall be effective only if approved by the presiding judicial officer and made expressly by such individual on the record after opportunity to consult with counsel and after the presiding judicial officer has explained to such individual, utilizing the services of the most available certified interpreter, or when no certified interpreter is reasonably available, as determined by the presiding judicial officer, the services of an otherwise competent interpreter, the nature and effect of the waiver.

(2) An individual who waives under paragraph (1) of this subsection the right to an interpreter may utilize the services of a noncertified interpreter of such individual's choice whose fees, expenses, and costs shall be paid in the manner provided for the payment of such fees, expenses, and costs of an interpreter appointed under subsection (d) of this section.

(g)(1) There are authorized to be appropriated to the Federal judiciary, and to be paid by the Director of the Administrative Office of the United States Courts, such sums as may be necessary to establish a program to facilitate the use of certified and otherwise qualified interpreters, and otherwise fulfill the provisions of this section and the Judicial Improvements and Access to Justice Act, except as provided in paragraph (3).

(2) Implementation of the provisions of this section is contingent upon the availability of appropriated funds to carry out the purposes of this section.

(3) Such salaries, fees, expenses, and costs that are incurred with respect to Government witnesses (including for grand jury proceedings) shall, unless direction is made under paragraph (4), be paid by the Attorney General from sums appropriated to the Department of Justice.

(4) Upon the request of any person in any action for which interpreting services established pursuant to subsection (d) are not otherwise provided, the clerk of the court, or other court employee designated by the chief judge, upon the request of the presiding judicial officer, shall, where possible, make such services available to that person on a cost-reimbursable basis, but the judicial officer may also require the prepayment of the estimated expenses of providing such services.

(5) If the Director of the Administrative Office of the United States Courts finds it necessary to develop and administer criterion-referenced performance examinations for purposes of certification, or other examinations for the selection of otherwise qualified interpreters, the Director may prescribe for each examination a uniform fee for applicants to take such examination. In determining the rate of the fee for each examination, the Director shall consider the fees charged by other organizations for examinations that are similar in scope or nature. Notwithstanding section 3302(b) of title 31, the Director is authorized to provide in any contract or agreement for the development or administration of examinations and the collection of fees that the contractor may retain all or a portion of the fees in payment for the services. Notwithstanding paragraph (6) of this subsection, all fees collected after the effective date of this paragraph and not retained by a contractor shall be deposited in the fund established under section 1931 of this title and shall remain available until expended.

(6) Any moneys collected under this subsection may be used to reimburse the appropriations obligated and disbursed in payment for such services.

(h) The presiding judicial officer shall approve the compensation and expenses payable to interpreters, pursuant to the schedule of fees prescribed by the Director under subsection (b)(3).

(i) The term "presiding judicial officer" as used in this section refers to any judge of a United States district court, including a bankruptcy judge, a United States magistrate judge, and in the case of grand jury proceedings conducted under the auspices of the United States attorney, a United States attorney.

(j) The term "judicial proceedings instituted by the United States" as used in this section refers to all proceedings, whether criminal or civil, including pretrial and grand jury proceedings (as well as proceedings upon a petition for a writ of habeas corpus initiated in the name of the United States by a relator)

conducted in, or pursuant to the lawful authority and jurisdiction of a United States district court. The term "United States district court" as used in this subsection includes any court which is created by an Act of Congress in a territory and is invested with any jurisdiction of a district court established by chapter 5 of this title.

(k) The interpretation provided by certified or otherwise qualified interpreters pursuant to this section shall be in the simultaneous mode for any party to a judicial proceeding instituted by the United States and in the consecutive mode for witnesses, except that the presiding judicial officer, sua sponte or on the motion of a party, may authorize a simultaneous, or consecutive interpretation when such officer determines after a hearing on the record that such interpretation will aid in the efficient administration of justice. The presiding judicial officer, on such officer's motion or on the motion of a party, may order that special interpretation services as authorized in section 1828 of this title be provided if such officer determines that the provision of such services will aid in the efficient administration of justice.

(*l*) Notwithstanding any other provision of this section or section 1828, the presiding judicial officer may appoint a certified or otherwise qualified sign language interpreter to provide services to a party, witness, or other participant in a judicial proceeding, whether or not the proceeding is instituted by the United States, if the presiding judicial officer determines, on such officer's own motion or on the motion of a party or other participant in the proceeding, that such individual suffers from a hearing impairment. The presiding judicial officer shall, subject to the availability of appropriated funds, approve the compensation and expenses payable to sign language interpreters appointed under this section in accordance with the schedule of fees prescribed by the Director under subsection (b)(3) of this section.

(Added Pub.L. 95–539, § 2(a), Oct. 28, 1978, 92 Stat. 2040, and amended Pub.L. 100–702, Title VII, §§ 702–710, Nov. 19, 1988, 102 Stat. 4654–4657; Pub.L. 101–650, Title III, § 321, Dec. 1, 1990, 104 Stat. 5117; Pub.L. 104–317, Title III, § 306, Title IV, § 402(a), Oct. 19, 1996, 110 Stat. 3852, 3854.)

HISTORICAL AND STATUTORY NOTES

References in Text

The date of the enactment of the Judicial Improvements and Access to Justice Act, referred to in subsec. (b)(1), is the date of enactment of Pub.L. 100–702, which was approved Nov. 19, 1988.

The Judicial Improvements and Access to Justice Act, referred to in subsec. (g)(1), is Pub.L. 100–702, Nov. 19, 1988, 102 Stat. 4642. For complete classification of this Act to the Code, see Short Title note set out under section 1 of this title and Tables.

The effective date of this paragraph, referred to in subsec. (g)(5), probably means the date of enactment of Pub.L. 104–317, which was approved Oct. 19, 1996.

Effective and Applicability Provisions

1988 Acts

Section 712 of Title VII of Pub.L. 100–702 provided that: "This title [amending subsecs. (a) to (e) and (g) to (k) of this section and enacting provisions set out as notes under this section and section 1 of this title] shall become effective upon the date of enactment [Nov. 19, 1988]."

1978 Acts

Section effective 90 days after Oct. 28, 1978, see section 10(b) of Pub.L. 95–539, set out as a note under section 602 of this title.

Change of Name

"United States magistrate judge" substituted for "United States magistrate" in text pursuant to section 321 of Pub.L. 101–650, set out as a note under 28 U.S.C.A. § 631.

Short Title

1978 Acts

For Short title of Pub.L. 95–539 as "Court Interpreters Act", see section 1 of Pub.L. 95–539, set out as a note under section 1 of this title.

Impact on Existing Programs

Section 711 of Title VII of Pub.L. 100–702 provided that: "Nothing in this title [amending subsecs. (a) to (e) and (g) to (k) of this section and enacting provisions set out as notes under this section and section 1 of this title] shall be construed to terminate or diminish existing programs for the certification of interpreters."

Payment for Contractual Services

Section 402(b) of Pub.L. 104–317 provided that: "Notwithstanding sections 3302(b), 1341, and 1517 of title 31, United States Code [sections 3302(b), 1341, and 1517 of Title 31, Money and Finance], the Director of the Administrative Office of the United States Courts may include in any contract for the development or administration of examinations for interpreters (including such a contract entered into before the date of the enactment of this Act [Oct. 19, 1996]) a provision which permits the contractor to collect and retain fees in payment for contractual services in accordance with section 1827(g)(5) of title 28, United States Code [subsec. (g)(5) of this section]."

§ 1828. Special interpretation services

(a) The Director of the Administrative Office of the United States Courts shall establish a program for the provision of special interpretation services in criminal actions and in civil actions initiated by the United States (including petitions for writs of habeas corpus initiated in the name of the United States by relators) in a United States district court. The program shall provide a capacity for simultaneous interpretation services in multidefendant criminal actions and multidefendant civil actions.

(b) Upon the request of any person in any action for which special interpretation services established

pursuant to subsection (a) are not otherwise provided, the Director, with the approval of the presiding judicial officer, may make such services available to the person requesting the services on a reimbursable basis at rates established in conformity with section 9701 of title 31, but the Director may require the prepayment of the estimated expenses of providing the services by the person requesting them.

(c) Except as otherwise provided in this subsection, the expenses incident to providing services under subsection (a) of this section shall be paid by the Director from sums appropriated to the Federal judiciary. A presiding judicial officer, in such officer's discretion, may order that all or part of the expenses shall be apportioned between or among the parties or shall be taxed as costs in a civil action, and any moneys collected as a result of such order may be used to reimburse the appropriations obligated and disbursed in payment for such services.

(d) Appropriations available to the Director shall be available to provide services in accordance with subsection (b) of this section, and moneys collected by the Director under that subsection may be used to reimburse the appropriations charged for such services. A presiding judicial officer, in such officer's discretion, may order that all or part of the expenses shall be apportioned between or among the parties or shall be taxed as costs in the action.

(Added Pub.L. 95–539, § 2(a), Oct. 28, 1978, 92 Stat. 2042, and amended Pub.L. 97–258, § 3(g), Sept. 13, 1982, 96 Stat. 1065.)

HISTORICAL AND STATUTORY NOTES

Effective and Applicability Provisions

1978 Acts

Section effective 90 days after Oct. 28, 1978, see section 10(b) of Pub.L. 95–539, set out as a note under section 602 of this title.

CHAPTER 121—JURIES; TRIAL BY JURY

§ 1861. Declaration of policy

It is the policy of the United States that all litigants in Federal courts entitled to trial by jury shall have the right to grand and petit juries selected at random from a fair cross section of the community in the district or division wherein the court convenes. It is further the policy of the United States that all citizens shall have the opportunity to be considered for service on grand and petit juries in the district courts of the United States, and shall have an obligation to serve as jurors when summoned for that purpose.

(June 25, 1948, c. 646, 62 Stat. 951; Sept. 9, 1957, Pub.L. 85–315, Part V, § 152, 71 Stat. 638; Mar. 27, 1968, Pub.L. 90–274, § 101, 82 Stat. 54.)

HISTORICAL AND STATUTORY NOTES

Effective and Applicability Provisions

1968 Acts

Section 104 of Pub.L. 90–274 provided that: "This Act [amending this section and sections 1821, 1862–1869, and 1871 of this title, repealing section 867 of Title 48, Territories and Insular Possessions, and enacting provisions set out as notes under this section] shall become effective two hundred and seventy days after the date of enactment [Mar. 27, 1968]: *Provided,* That this Act shall not apply in any case in which an indictment has been returned or petit jury empaneled prior to such effective date."

Short Title

1978 Acts

Pub.L. 95–572, § 1, Nov. 2, 1978, 92 Stat. 2453, provided that: "This Act [which enacted sections 1363 and 1875 of this title, renumbered as section 1364 prior section 1363 of this title, amended sections 1863, 1865, 1866, 1869, and 1871 of this title, and enacted provisions set out as a note under section 1363 of this title] may be cited as the 'Jury System Improvements Act of 1978'."

1968 Acts

Section 1 of Pub.L. 90–274 provided: "That this Act [amending this section and sections 1821, 1862–1869, and 1871 of this title, repealing section 867 of Title 48, Territories and Insular Possessions, and enacting material set out as notes under this section] may be cited as the 'Jury Selection and Service Act of 1968'."

§ 1862. Discrimination prohibited

No citizen shall be excluded from service as a grand or petit juror in the district courts of the United States or in the Court of International Trade on

account of race, color, religion, sex, national origin, or economic status.

(June 25, 1948, c. 646, 62 Stat. 952; Mar. 27, 1968, Pub.L. 90–274, § 101, 82 Stat. 54; Oct. 10, 1980, Pub.L. 96–417, Title III, § 302(c), 94 Stat. 1739.)

HISTORICAL AND STATUTORY NOTES

Effective and Applicability Provisions

1980 Acts

Amendment by Pub.L. 96–417 effective on Nov. 1, 1980 and applicable with respect to civil actions pending on or commenced on or after such date, see section 701(a) of Pub.L. 96–417, as amended, set out as a note under section 251 of this title.

1968 Acts

Amendment by Pub.L. 90–274 effective 270 days after Mar. 27, 1968, except as to cases in which an indictment has been returned or a petit jury empaneled prior to such effective date, see section 104 of Pub.L. 90–274, set out as a note under section 1861 of this title.

§ 1863. Plan for random jury selection

(a) Each United States district court shall devise and place into operation a written plan for random selection of grand and petit jurors that shall be designed to achieve the objectives of sections 1861 and 1862 of this title, and that shall otherwise comply with the provisions of this title. The plan shall be placed into operation after approval by a reviewing panel consisting of the members of the judicial council of the circuit and either the chief judge of the district whose plan is being reviewed or such other active district judge of that district as the chief judge of the district may designate. The panel shall examine the plan to ascertain that it complies with the provisions of this title. If the reviewing panel finds that the plan does not comply, the panel shall state the particulars in which the plan fails to comply and direct the district court to present within a reasonable time an alternative plan remedying the defect or defects. Separate plans may be adopted for each division or combination of divisions within a judicial district. The district court may modify a plan at any time and it shall modify the plan when so directed by the reviewing panel. The district court shall promptly notify the panel, the Administrative Office of the United States Courts, and the Attorney General of the United States, of the initial adoption and future modifications of the plan by filing copies therewith. Modifications of the plan made at the instance of the district court shall become effective after approval by the panel. Each district court shall submit a report on the jury selection process within its jurisdiction to the Administrative Office of the United States Courts in such form and at such times as the Judicial Conference of the United States may specify. The Judicial Conference of the United States may, from time to time, adopt rules and regulations governing the provisions

and the operation of the plans formulated under this title.

(b) Among other things, such plan shall—

(1) either establish a jury commission, or authorize the clerk of the court, to manage the jury selection process. If the plan establishes a jury commission, the district court shall appoint one citizen to serve with the clerk of the court as the jury commission: *Provided, however,* That the plan for the District of Columbia may establish a jury commission consisting of three citizens. The citizen jury commissioner shall not belong to the same political party as the clerk serving with him. The clerk or the jury commission, as the case may be, shall act under the supervision and control of the chief judge of the district court or such other judge of the district court as the plan may provide. Each jury commissioner shall, during his tenure in office, reside in the judicial district or division for which he is appointed. Each citizen jury commissioner shall receive compensation to be fixed by the district court plan at a rate not to exceed $50 per day for each day necessarily employed in the performance of his duties, plus reimbursement for travel, subsistence, and other necessary expenses incurred by him in the performance of such duties. The Judicial Conference of the United States may establish standards for allowance of travel, subsistence, and other necessary expenses incurred by jury commissioners.

(2) specify whether the names of prospective jurors shall be selected from the voter registration lists or the lists of actual voters of the political subdivisions within the district or division. The plan shall prescribe some other source or sources of names in addition to voter lists where necessary to foster the policy and protect the rights secured by sections 1861 and 1862 of this title. The plan for the District of Columbia may require the names of prospective jurors to be selected from the city directory rather than from voter lists. The plans for the districts of Puerto Rico and the Canal Zone may prescribe some other source or sources of names of prospective jurors in lieu of voter lists, the use of which shall be consistent with the policies declared and rights secured by sections 1861 and 1862 of this title. The plan for the district of Massachusetts may require the names of prospective jurors to be selected from the resident list provided for in chapter 234A, Massachusetts General Laws, or comparable authority, rather than from voter lists.

(3) specify detailed procedures to be followed by the jury commission or clerk in selecting names from the sources specified in paragraph (2) of this subsection. These procedures shall be designed to ensure the random selection of a fair cross section

of the persons residing in the community in the district or division wherein the court convenes. They shall ensure that names of persons residing in each of the counties, parishes, or similar political subdivisions within the judicial district or division are placed in a master jury wheel; and shall ensure that each county, parish, or similar political subdivision within the district or division is substantially proportionally represented in the master jury wheel for that judicial district, division, or combination of divisions. For the purposes of determining proportional representation in the master jury wheel, either the number of actual voters at the last general election in each county, parish, or similar political subdivision, or the number of registered voters if registration of voters is uniformly required throughout the district or division, may be used.

(4) provide for a master jury wheel (or a device similar in purpose and function) into which the names of those randomly selected shall be placed. The plan shall fix a minimum number of names to be placed initially in the master jury wheel, which shall be at least one-half of 1 per centum of the total number of persons on the lists used as a source of names for the district or division; but if this number of names is believed to be cumbersome and unnecessary, the plan may fix a smaller number of names to be placed in the master wheel, but in no event less than one thousand. The chief judge of the district court, or such other district court judge as the plan may provide, may order additional names to be placed in the master jury wheel from time to time as necessary. The plan shall provide for periodic emptying and refilling of the master jury wheel at specified times, the interval for which shall not exceed four years.

(5)(A) except as provided in subparagraph (B), specify those groups of persons or occupational classes whose members shall, on individual request therefor, be excused from jury service. Such groups or classes shall be excused only if the district court finds, and the plan states, that jury service by such class or group would entail undue hardship or extreme inconvenience to the members thereof, and excuse of members thereof would not be inconsistent with sections 1861 and 1862 of this title.

(B) specify that volunteer safety personnel, upon individual request, shall be excused from jury service. For purposes of this subparagraph, the term "volunteer safety personnel" means individuals serving a public agency (as defined in section 1203(6) of title I of the Omnibus Crime Control and Safe Streets Act of 1968) in an official capacity, without compensation, as firefighters or members of a rescue squad or ambulance crew.

(6) specify that the following persons are barred from jury service on the ground that they are exempt: (A) members in active service in the Armed Forces of the United States; (B) members of the fire or police departments of any State, the District of Columbia, any territory or possession of the United States, or any subdivision of a State, the District of Columbia, or such territory or possession; (C) public officers in the executive, legislative, or judicial branches of the Government of the United States, or of any State, the District of Columbia, any territory or possession of the United States, or any subdivision of a State, the District of Columbia, or such territory or possession, who are actively engaged in the performance of official duties.

(7) fix the time when the names drawn from the qualified jury wheel shall be disclosed to parties and to the public. If the plan permits these names to be made public, it may nevertheless permit the chief judge of the district court, or such other district court judge as the plan may provide, to keep these names confidential in any case where the interests of justice so require.

(8) specify the procedures to be followed by the clerk or jury commission in assigning persons whose names have been drawn from the qualified jury wheel to grand and petit jury panels.

(c) The initial plan shall be devised by each district court and transmitted to the reviewing panel specified in subsection (a) of this section within one hundred and twenty days of the date of enactment of the Jury Selection and Service Act of 1968. The panel shall approve or direct the modification of each plan so submitted within sixty days thereafter. Each plan or modification made at the direction of the panel shall become effective after approval at such time thereafter as the panel directs, in no event to exceed ninety days from the date of approval. Modifications made at the instance of the district court under subsection (a) of this section shall be effective at such time thereafter as the panel directs, in no event to exceed ninety days from the date of modification.

(d) State, local, and Federal officials having custody, possession, or control of voter registration lists, lists of actual voters, or other appropriate records shall make such lists and records available to the jury commission or clerks for inspection, reproduction, and copying at all reasonable times as the commission or clerk may deem necessary and proper for the performance of duties under this title. The district courts shall have jurisdiction upon application by the Attorney General of the United States to compel compliance with this subsection by appropriate process.

(June 25, 1948, c. 646, 62 Stat. 952; Mar. 27, 1968, Pub.L. 90–274, § 101, 82 Stat. 54; Apr. 6, 1972, Pub.L. 92–269, § 2, 86 Stat. 117; Nov. 2, 1978, Pub.L. 95–572, § 2(a), 92 Stat.

2453; Nov. 19, 1988, Pub.L. 100–702, Title VIII, § 802(b), (c), 102 Stat. 4657, 4658; Oct. 29, 1992, Pub.L. 102–572, Title IV, § 401, 106 Stat. 4511.)

HISTORICAL AND STATUTORY NOTES

References in Text

Section 1203(6) of title I of the Omnibus Crime Control and Safe Streets Act of 1968, referred to in subsec. (b)(5)(B), is section 1203(6) of Pub.L. 90–351, Title I, as added Pub.L. 96–157, § 2, Dec. 27, 1979, 93 Stat. 1220, which is classified to section 3796b(6) of Title 42, The Public Health and Welfare.

The date of enactment of the Jury Selection and Service Act of 1968, referred to in subsec. (c), is the date of enactment of Pub.L. 90–274, which was approved on Mar. 27, 1968.

Effective and Applicability Provisions

1992 Acts

Amendment by Pub.L. 102–572 effective Jan. 1, 1993, see section 1101(a) of Pub.L. 102–572, set out as a note under section 905 of Title 2, The Congress.

1978 Acts

Amendment by Pub.L. 95–572 applicable with respect to any grand or petit juror summoned for service or actually serving on or after Nov. 2, 1978, see section 7(a) of Pub.L. 95–572, set out as a note under section 1363 of this title.

1968 Acts

Amendment by Pub.L. 90–274 effective 270 days after Mar. 27, 1968, except as to cases in which an indictment has been returned or a petit jury empaneled prior to such effective date, see section 104 of Pub.L. 90–274, set out as a note under section 1861 of this title.

Refilling of Master Jury Wheel Not Later Than September 1, 1973; Refilling of Qualified Jury Wheel Not Later Than October 1, 1973; Retroactive Effect

Sections 3 and 4 of Pub.L. 92–269 provided that:

"Sec. 3. (a) Each judicial district and each division or combination of divisions within a judicial district, for which a separate plan for random selection of jurors has been adopted pursuant to section 1863 of title 28, United States Code [this section], other than the District of Columbia and the districts of Puerto Rico and the Canal Zone, shall not later than September 1, 1973, refill its master jury wheel with names obtained from the voter registration lists for, or the lists of actual voters in, the 1972 general election.

"(b) The District of Columbia and the judicial districts of Puerto Rico and the Canal Zone shall not later than September 1, 1973, refill their master jury wheels from sources which include the names of persons eighteen years of age or older.

"(c) The qualified jury wheel in each judicial district, and in each division or combination of divisions in a judicial district for which a separate plan for random selection of jurors has been adopted, shall be refilled from the master jury wheel not later than October 1, 1973.

"Sec. 4. (a) Nothing in this Act [amending this section and section 1865 of this title] shall affect the composition of any master jury wheel or qualified jury wheel prior to the date on which it is first refilled in compliance with the terms of section 3.

"(b) Nothing in this Act shall affect the composition or preclude the service of any jury empaneled on or before the date on which the qualified jury wheel from which the jurors' names were drawn is refilled in compliance with the provisions of section 3."

§ 1864. Drawing of names from the master jury wheel; completion of juror qualification form

(a) From time to time as directed by the district court, the clerk or a district judge shall publicly draw at random from the master jury wheel the names of as many persons as may be required for jury service. The clerk or jury commission may, upon order of the court, prepare an alphabetical list of the names drawn from the master jury wheel. Any list so prepared shall not be disclosed to any person except pursuant to the district court plan or pursuant to section 1867 or 1868 of this title. The clerk or jury commission shall mail to every person whose name is drawn from the master wheel a juror qualification form accompanied by instructions to fill out and return the form, duly signed and sworn, to the clerk or jury commission by mail within ten days. If the person is unable to fill out the form, another shall do it for him, and shall indicate that he has done so and the reason therefor. In any case in which it appears that there is an omission, ambiguity, or error in a form, the clerk or jury commission shall return the form with instructions to the person to make such additions or corrections as may be necessary and to return the form to the clerk or jury commission within ten days. Any person who fails to return a completed juror qualification form as instructed may be summoned by the clerk or jury commission forthwith to appear before the clerk or jury commission to fill out a juror qualification form. A person summoned to appear because of failure to return a juror qualification form as instructed who personally appears and executes a juror qualification form before the clerk or jury commission may, at the discretion of the district court, except where his prior failure to execute and mail such form was willful, be entitled to receive for such appearance the same fees and travel allowances paid to jurors under section 1871 of this title. At the time of his appearance for jury service, any person may be required to fill out another juror qualification form in the presence of the jury commission or the clerk or the court, at which time, in such cases as it appears warranted, the person may be questioned, but only with regard to his responses to questions contained on the form. Any information thus acquired by the clerk or jury commission may be noted on the juror qualification form and transmitted to the chief judge or such district court judge as the plan may provide.

(b) Any person summoned pursuant to subsection (a) of this section who fails to appear as directed shall be ordered by the district court forthwith to appear

and show cause for his failure to comply with the summons. Any person who fails to appear pursuant to such order or who fails to show good cause for noncompliance with the summons may be fined not more than $100 or imprisoned not more than three days, or both. Any person who willfully misrepresents a material fact on a juror qualification form for the purpose of avoiding or securing service as a juror may be fined not more than $100 or imprisoned not more than three days, or both.

(June 25, 1948, c. 646, 62 Stat. 952; Mar. 27, 1968, Pub.L. 90–274, § 101, 82 Stat. 57; Nov. 19, 1988, Pub.L. 100–702, Title VIII, § 803(a), 102 Stat. 4658.)

HISTORICAL AND STATUTORY NOTES

Effective and Applicability Provisions

1968 Acts

Amendment by Pub.L. 90–274 effective 270 days after Mar. 27, 1968, except as to cases in which an indictment has been returned or a petit jury empaneled prior to such effective date, see section 104 of Pub.L. 90–274, set out as a note under section 1861 of this title.

§ 1865. Qualifications for jury service

(a) The chief judge of the district court, or such other district court judge as the plan may provide, on his initiative or upon recommendation of the clerk or jury commission, or the clerk under supervision of the court if the court's jury selection plan so authorizes, shall determine solely on the basis of information provided on the juror qualification form and other competent evidence whether a person is unqualified for, or exempt, or to be excused from jury service. The clerk shall enter such determination in the space provided on the juror qualification form and in any alphabetical list of names drawn from the master jury wheel. If a person did not appear in response to a summons, such fact shall be noted on said list.

(b) In making such determination the chief judge of the district court, or such other district court judge as the plan may provide, or the clerk if the court's jury selection plan so provides, shall deem any person qualified to serve on grand and petit juries in the district court unless he—

(1) is not a citizen of the United States eighteen years old who has resided for a period of one year within the judicial district;

(2) is unable to read, write, and understand the English language with a degree of proficiency sufficient to fill out satisfactorily the juror qualification form;

(3) is unable to speak the English language;

(4) is incapable, by reason of mental or physical infirmity, to render satisfactory jury service; or

(5) has a charge pending against him for the commission of, or has been convicted in a State or Federal court of record of, a crime punishable by imprisonment for more than one year and his civil rights have not been restored.

(June 25, 1948, c. 646, 62 Stat. 952; Mar. 27, 1968, Pub.L. 90–274, § 101, 82 Stat. 58; Apr. 6, 1972, Pub.L. 92–269, § 1, 86 Stat. 117; Nov. 2, 1978, Pub.L. 95–572, § 3(a), 92 Stat. 2453; Nov. 19, 1988, Pub.L. 100–702, Title VIII, § 803(b), 102 Stat. 4658; Nov. 13, 2000, Pub.L. 106–518, Title III, § 305, 114 Stat. 2418.)

HISTORICAL AND STATUTORY NOTES

Effective and Applicability Provisions

1978 Acts

Amendment by Pub.L. 95–572 applicable with respect to any grand or petit juror summoned for service or actually serving on or after Nov. 2, 1978, see section 7(a) of Pub.L. 95–572, set out as a note under section 1363 of this title.

1968 Acts

Amendment by Pub.L. 90–274 effective 270 days after Mar. 27, 1968, except as to cases in which an indictment has been returned or a petit jury empaneled prior to such effective date, see section 104 of Pub.L. 90–274, set out as a note under section 1861 of this title.

§ 1866. Selection and summoning of jury panels

(a) The jury commission, or in the absence thereof the clerk, shall maintain a qualified jury wheel and shall place in such wheel names of all persons drawn from the master jury wheel who are determined to be qualified as jurors and not exempt or excused pursuant to the district court plan. From time to time, the jury commission or the clerk shall publicly draw at random from the qualified jury wheel such number of names of persons as may be required for assignment to grand and petit jury panels. The jury commission or the clerk shall prepare a separate list of names of persons assigned to each grand and petit jury panel.

(b) When the court orders a grand or petit jury to be drawn, the clerk or jury commission or their duly designated deputies shall issue summonses for the required number of jurors.

Each person drawn for jury service may be served personally, or by registered, certified, or first-class mail addressed to such person at his usual residence or business address.

If such service is made personally, the summons shall be delivered by the clerk or the jury commission or their duly designated deputies to the marshal who shall make such service.

If such service is made by mail, the summons may be served by the marshal or by the clerk, the jury commission or their duly designated deputies, who shall make affidavit of service and shall attach thereto any receipt from the addressee for a registered or certified summons.

(c) Except as provided in section 1865 of this title or in any jury selection plan provision adopted pursuant to paragraph (5) or (6) of section 1863(b) of this title, no person or class of persons shall be disqualified, excluded, excused, or exempt from service as jurors: *Provided,* That any person summoned for jury service may be (1) excused by the court, or by the clerk under supervision of the court if the court's jury selection plan so authorizes, upon a showing of undue hardship or extreme inconvenience, for such period as the court deems necessary, at the conclusion of which such person either shall be summoned again for jury service under subsections (b) and (c) of this section or, if the court's jury selection plan so provides, the name of such person shall be reinserted into the qualified jury wheel for selection pursuant to subsection (a) of this section, or (2) excluded by the court on the ground that such person may be unable to render impartial jury service or that his service as a juror would be likely to disrupt the proceedings, or (3) excluded upon peremptory challenge as provided by law, or (4) excluded pursuant to the procedure specified by law upon a challenge by any party for good cause shown, or (5) excluded upon determination by the court that his service as a juror would be likely to threaten the secrecy of the proceedings, or otherwise adversely affect the integrity of jury deliberations. No person shall be excluded under clause (5) of this subsection unless the judge, in open court, determines that such is warranted and that exclusion of the person will not be inconsistent with sections 1861 and 1862 of this title. The number of persons excluded under clause (5) of this subsection shall not exceed one per centum of the number of persons who return executed jury qualification forms during the period, specified in the plan, between two consecutive fillings of the master jury wheel. The names of persons excluded under clause (5) of this subsection, together with detailed explanations for the exclusions, shall be forwarded immediately to the judicial council of the circuit, which shall have the power to make any appropriate order, prospective or retroactive, to redress any misapplication of clause (5) of this subsection, but otherwise exclusions effectuated under such clause shall not be subject to challenge under the provisions of this title. Any person excluded from a particular jury under clause (2), (3), or (4) of this subsection shall be eligible to sit on another jury if the basis for his initial exclusion would not be relevant to his ability to serve on such other jury.

(d) Whenever a person is disqualified, excused, exempt, or excluded from jury service, the jury commission or clerk shall note in the space provided on his juror qualification form or on the juror's card drawn from the qualified jury wheel the specific reason therefor.

(e) In any two-year period, no person shall be required to (1) serve or attend court for prospective service as a petit juror for a total of more than thirty days, except when necessary to complete service in a particular case, or (2) serve on more than one grand jury, or (3) serve as both a grand and petit juror.

(f) When there is an unanticipated shortage of available petit jurors drawn from the qualified jury wheel, the court may require the marshal to summon a sufficient number of petit jurors selected at random from the voter registration lists, lists of actual voters, or other lists specified in the plan, in a manner ordered by the court consistent with sections 1861 and 1862 of this title.

(g) Any person summoned for jury service who fails to appear as directed shall be ordered by the district court to appear forthwith and show cause for his failure to comply with the summons. Any person who fails to show good cause for noncompliance with a summons may be fined not more than $100 or imprisoned not more than three days, or both.

(June 25, 1948, c. 646, 62 Stat. 952; May 24, 1949, c. 139, § 96, 63 Stat. 103; Mar. 27, 1968, Pub.L. 90–274, § 101, 82 Stat. 58; Dec. 11, 1970, Pub.L. 91–543, 84 Stat. 1408; Nov. 2, 1978, Pub.L. 95–572, § 2(b), 92 Stat. 2453; Jan. 12, 1983, Pub.L. 97–463, § 2, 96 Stat. 2531; Nov. 19, 1988, Pub.L. 100–702, Title VIII, § 801, 102 Stat. 4657.)

HISTORICAL AND STATUTORY NOTES

Effective and Applicability Provisions

1978 Acts

Amendment by Pub.L. 95–572 applicable with respect to any grand or petit juror summoned for service or actually serving on or after Nov. 2, 1978, see section 7(a) of Pub.L. 95–572, set out as a note under section 1363 of this title.

1968 Acts

Amendment by Pub.L. 90–274 effective 270 days after Mar. 27, 1968, except as to cases in which an indictment has been returned or a petit jury empaneled prior to such effective date, see section 104 of Pub.L. 90–274, set out as a note under section 1861 of this title.

§ 1867. Challenging compliance with selection procedures

(a) In criminal cases, before the voir dire examination begins, or within seven days after the defendant discovered or could have discovered, by the exercise of diligence, the grounds therefor, whichever is earlier, the defendant may move to dismiss the indictment or stay the proceedings against him on the ground of substantial failure to comply with the provisions of this title in selecting the grand or petit jury.

(b) In criminal cases, before the voir dire examination begins, or within seven days after the Attorney General of the United States discovered or could have discovered, by the exercise of diligence, the grounds therefor, whichever is earlier, the Attorney General may move to dismiss the indictment or stay the pro-

ceedings on the ground of substantial failure to comply with the provisions of this title in selecting the grand or petit jury.

(c) In civil cases, before the voir dire examination begins, or within seven days after the party discovered or could have discovered, by the exercise of diligence, the grounds therefor, whichever is earlier, any party may move to stay the proceedings on the ground of substantial failure to comply with the provisions of this title in selecting the petit jury.

(d) Upon motion filed under subsection (a), (b), or (c) of this section, containing a sworn statement of facts which, if true, would constitute a substantial failure to comply with the provisions of this title, the moving party shall be entitled to present in support of such motion the testimony of the jury commission or clerk, if available, any relevant records and papers not public or otherwise available used by the jury commissioner or clerk, and any other relevant evidence. If the court determines that there has been a substantial failure to comply with the provisions of this title in selecting the grand jury, the court shall stay the proceedings pending the selection of a grand jury in conformity with this title or dismiss the indictment, whichever is appropriate. If the court determines that there has been a substantial failure to comply with the provisions of this title in selecting the petit jury, the court shall stay the proceedings pending the selection of a petit jury in conformity with this title.

(e) The procedures prescribed by this section shall be the exclusive means by which a person accused of a Federal crime, the Attorney General of the United States or a party in a civil case may challenge any jury on the ground that such jury was not selected in conformity with the provisions of this title. Nothing in this section shall preclude any person or the United States from pursuing any other remedy, civil or criminal, which may be available for the vindication or enforcement of any law prohibiting discrimination on account of race, color, religion, sex, national origin or economic status in the selection of persons for service on grand or petit juries.

(f) The contents of records or papers used by the jury commission or clerk in connection with the jury selection process shall not be disclosed, except pursuant to the district court plan or as may be necessary in the preparation or presentation of a motion under subsection (a), (b), or (c) of this section, until after the master jury wheel has been emptied and refilled pursuant to section 1863(b)(4) of this title and all persons selected to serve as jurors before the master wheel was emptied have completed such service. The parties in a case shall be allowed to inspect, reproduce, and copy such records or papers at all reasonable times during the preparation and pendency of such a motion. Any person who discloses the contents

of any record or paper in violation of this subsection may be fined not more than $1,000 or imprisoned not more than one year, or both.

(June 25, 1948, c. 646, 62 Stat. 953; Sept. 2, 1957, Pub.L. 85–259, 71 Stat. 583; Mar. 27, 1968, Pub.L. 90–274, § 101, 82 Stat. 59.)

HISTORICAL AND STATUTORY NOTES
Effective and Applicability Provisions
1968 Acts

Amendment by Pub.L. 90–274 effective 270 days after Mar. 27, 1968, except as to cases in which an indictment has been returned or a petit jury empaneled prior to such effective date, see section 104 of Pub.L. 90–274, set out as a note under section 1861 of this title.

§ 1868. Maintenance and inspection of records

After the master jury wheel is emptied and refilled pursuant to section 1863(b)(4) of this title, and after all persons selected to serve as jurors before the master wheel was emptied have completed such service, all records and papers compiled and maintained by the jury commission or clerk before the master wheel was emptied shall be preserved in the custody of the clerk for four years or for such longer period as may be ordered by a court, and shall be available for public inspection for the purpose of determining the validity of the selection of any jury.

(June 25, 1948, c. 646, 62 Stat. 953; Mar. 27, 1968, Pub.L. 90–274, § 101, 82 Stat. 60.)

HISTORICAL AND STATUTORY NOTES
Effective and Applicability Provisions
1968 Acts

Amendment by Pub.L. 90–274 effective 270 days after Mar. 27, 1968, except as to cases in which an indictment has been returned or a petit jury empaneled prior to such effective date, see section 104 of Pub.L. 90–274, set out as a note under section 1861 of this title.

§ 1869. Definitions

For purposes of this chapter—

(a) "clerk" and "clerk of the court" shall mean the clerk of the district court of the United States, any authorized deputy clerk, and any other person authorized by the court to assist the clerk in the performance of functions under this chapter;

(b) "chief judge" shall mean the chief judge of any district court of the United States;

(c) "voter registration lists" shall mean the official records maintained by State or local election officials of persons registered to vote in either the most recent State or the most recent Federal general election, or, in the case of a State or political subdivision thereof that does not require registration as a prerequisite to voting, other official lists of persons qualified to vote in such election. The term shall also include the list of eligible voters main-

tained by any Federal examiner pursuant to the Voting Rights Act of 1965 where the names on such list have not been included on the official registration lists or other official lists maintained by the appropriate State or local officials. With respect to the districts of Guam and the Virgin Islands, "voter registration lists" shall mean the official records maintained by territorial election officials of persons registered to vote in the most recent territorial general election;

(d) "lists of actual voters" shall mean the official lists of persons actually voting in either the most recent State or the most recent Federal general election;

(e) "division" shall mean: (1) one or more statutory divisions of a judicial district; or (2) in statutory divisions that contain more than one place of holding court, or in judicial districts where there are no statutory divisions, such counties, parishes, or similar political subdivisions surrounding the places where court is held as the district court plan shall determine: *Provided*, That each county, parish, or similar political subdivision shall be included in some such division;

(f) "district court of the United States", "district court", and "court" shall mean any district court established by chapter 5 of this title, and any court which is created by Act of Congress in a territory and is invested with any jurisdiction of a district court established by chapter 5 of this title;

(g) "jury wheel" shall include any device or system similar in purpose or function, such as a properly programed electronic data processing system or device;

(h) "juror qualification form" shall mean a form prescribed by the Administrative Office of the United States Courts and approved by the Judicial Conference of the United States, which shall elicit the name, address, age, race, occupation, education, length of residence within the judicial district, distance from residence to place of holding court, prior jury service, and citizenship of a potential juror, and whether he should be excused or exempted from jury service, has any physical or mental infirmity impairing his capacity to serve as juror, is able to read, write, speak, and understand the English language, has pending against him any charge for the commission of a State or Federal criminal offense punishable by imprisonment for more than one year, or has been convicted in any State or Federal court of record of a crime punishable by imprisonment for more than one year and has not had his civil rights restored. The form shall request, but not require, any other information not inconsistent with the provisions of this title and required by the district court plan in the interests of the sound administration of justice. The form shall also elicit the sworn statement that his responses are true to the best of his knowledge. Notarization shall not be required. The form shall contain words clearly informing the person that the furnishing of any information with respect to his religion, national origin, or economic status is not a prerequisite to his qualification for jury service, that such information need not be furnished if the person finds it objectionable to do so, and that information concerning race is required solely to enforce nondiscrimination in jury selection and has no bearing on an individual's qualification for jury service.

(i) "public officer" shall mean a person who is either elected to public office or who is directly appointed by a person elected to public office;

(j) "undue hardship or extreme inconvenience", as a basis for excuse from immediate jury service under section 1866(c) (1) of this chapter, shall mean great distance, either in miles or traveltime, from the place of holding court, grave illness in the family or any other emergency which outweighs in immediacy and urgency the obligation to serve as a juror when summoned, or any other factor which the court determines to constitute an undue hardship or to create an extreme inconvenience to the juror; and in addition, in situations where it is anticipated that a trial or grand jury proceeding may require more than thirty days of service, the court may consider, as a further basis for temporary excuse, severe economic hardship to an employer which would result from the absence of a key employee during the period of such service;

(k) "publicly draw", as referred to in sections 1864 and 1866 of this chapter, shall mean a drawing which is conducted within the district after reasonable public notice and which is open to the public at large under the supervision of the clerk or jury commission, except that when a drawing is made by means of electronic data processing, "publicly draw" shall mean a drawing which is conducted at a data processing center located in or out of the district, after reasonable public notice given in the district for which juror names are being drawn, and which is open to the public at large under such supervision of the clerk or jury commission as the Judicial Conference of the United States shall by regulation require; and

(*l*) "jury summons" shall mean a summons issued by a clerk of court, jury commission, or their duly designated deputies, containing either a preprinted or stamped seal of court, and containing the name of the issuing clerk imprinted in preprinted, type, or facsimile manner on the summons or the envelopes transmitting the summons.

(June 25, 1948, c. 646, 62 Stat. 953; Oct. 16, 1963, Pub.L. 88–139, § 2, 77 Stat. 248; Mar. 27, 1968, Pub.L. 90–274, § 101, 82 Stat. 61; July 29, 1970, Pub.L. 91–358, Title I, § 172(b), 84 Stat. 590; Sept. 29, 1972, Pub.L. 92–437, § 1, 86 Stat. 740; Nov. 2, 1978, Pub.L. 95–572, §§ 3(b), (4), 92 Stat. 2453; Nov. 6, 1978, Pub.L. 95–598, Title II, § 243, 92 Stat. 2671; Nov. 14, 1986, Pub.L. 99–650, § 3, 100 Stat. 3641; Nov. 19, 1988, Pub.L. 100–702, Title VIII, §§ 802(a), 804, 102 Stat. 4657, 4658.)

HISTORICAL AND STATUTORY NOTES

References in Text

The Voting Rights Act of 1965, referred to in subsec. (c), is Pub.L. 89–110, Aug. 6, 1965, 79 Stat. 437, as amended, which is classified generally to subchapters I–A (Section 1973 et seq.), I–B (Section 1973aa et seq.), and I–C (Section 1973bb et seq.) of chapter 20 of Title 42, The Public Health and Welfare. For complete classification of this Act to the Code, see Short Title note set out under section 1973 of Title 42 and Tables.

Codifications

Subsec. (f) of this section was amended by Pub.L. 95–598, Title II, § 243, Nov. 6, 1978, 92 Stat. 2671, effective June 28, 1984, pursuant to Pub.L. 95–598, Title IV, § 402(b), Nov. 6, 1978, 92 Stat. 2682, as amended by Pub.L. 98–249, § 1(a), Mar. 31, 1984, 98 Stat. 116; Pub.L. 98–271, § 1(a), Apr. 30, 1984, 98 Stat. 163; Pub.L. 98–299, § 1(a), May 25, 1984, 98 Stat. 214; Pub.L. 98–325, § 1(a), June 20, 1984, 98 Stat. 268, set out as an Effective and Applicability Provisions note preceding section 101 of Title 11, Bankruptcy, by inserting "chapter 6 of title 28, United States Code," following "chapter 5 of title 28, United States Code,".

Section 402(b) of Pub.L. 95–598 was amended by section 113 of Pub.L. 98–353, Title I, July 10, 1984, 98 Stat. 343, by substituting "shall not be effective" for "shall take effect on June 28, 1984", thereby eliminating the amendment by section 243 of Pub.L. 95–598, effective June 27, 1984, pursuant to section 122(c) of Pub.L. 98–353, set out as an Effective and Applicability Provisions note under section 151 of this title.

Section 121(a) of Pub.L. 98–353 directed that section 402(b) of Pub.L. 95–598 be amended by substituting "the date of enactment of the Bankruptcy Amendments and Federal Judgeship Act of 1984 [i.e. July 10, 1984]" for "June 28, 1984". This amendment was not executed in view of the prior amendment to section 402(b) of Pub.L. 95–598 by section 113 of Pub.L. 98–353.

Effective and Applicability Provisions

1986 Acts

Section 4(a) of Pub.L. 99–650 provided in part that: "The provisions of this Act [amending this section] shall take effect 180 days after the date of enactment of this Act [Nov. 14, 1986]".

1978 Acts

Amendment by Pub.L. 95–572 applicable with respect to any grand or petit juror summoned for service or actually serving on or after Nov. 2, 1978, see section 7(a) of Pub.L. 95–572, set out as a note under section 1363 of this title.

1972 Acts

Section 2 of Pub.L. 92–437 provided that: "This Act [amending subsec. (h) of this section] shall take effect on the sixtieth day after the date of its enactment [Sept. 29, 1972]".

1970 Acts

Amendment by Pub.L. 91–358 effective the first day of the seventh calendar month which begins after July 29, 1970, see section 199(a) of Pub.L. 91–358, set out as a note under section 1257 of this title.

1968 Acts

Amendment by Pub.L. 90–274 effective 270 days after Mar. 27, 1968, except as to cases in which an indictment has been returned or a petit jury empaneled prior to such effective date, see section 104 of Pub.L. 90–274, set out as a note under section 1861 of this title.

Termination of United States District Court for the District of the Canal Zone

For termination of the United States District Court for the District of the Canal Zone at end of the "transition period", being the 30–month period beginning Oct. 1, 1979, and ending midnight Mar. 31, 1982, see Paragraph 5 of Article XI of the Panama Canal Treaty of 1977 and sections 3831 and 3841 to 3843 of Title 22, Foreign Relations and Intercourse.

§ 1870. Challenges

In civil cases, each party shall be entitled to three peremptory challenges. Several defendants or several plaintiffs may be considered as a single party for the purposes of making challenges, or the court may allow additional peremptory challenges and permit them to be exercised separately or jointly.

All challenges for cause or favor, whether to the array or panel or to individual jurors, shall be determined by the court.

(June 25, 1948, c. 646, 62 Stat. 953; Sept. 16, 1959, Pub.L. 86–282, 73 Stat. 565.)

§ 1871. Fees

(a) Grand and petit jurors in district courts appearing pursuant to this chapter shall be paid the fees and allowances provided by this section. The requisite fees and allowances shall be disbursed on the certificate of the clerk of court in accordance with the procedure established by the Director of the Administrative Office of the United States Courts. Attendance fees for extended service under subsection (b) of this section shall be certified by the clerk only upon the order of a district judge.

(b)(1) A juror shall be paid an attendance fee of $40 per day for actual attendance at the place of trial or hearing. A juror shall also be paid the attendance fee for the time necessarily occupied in going to and returning from such place at the beginning and end of such service or at any time during such service.

(2) A petit juror required to attend more than thirty days in hearing one case may be paid, in the discretion of the trial judge, an additional fee, not exceeding $10 more than the attendance fee, for each

day in excess of thirty days on which he is required to hear such case.

(3) A grand juror required to attend more than forty-five days of actual service may be paid, in the discretion of the district judge in charge of the particular grand jury, an additional fee, not exceeding $10 more than the attendance fee, for each day in excess of forty-five days of actual service.

(4) A grand or petit juror required to attend more than ten days of actual service may be paid, in the discretion of the judge, the appropriate fees at the end of the first ten days and at the end of every ten days of service thereafter.

(5) Certification of additional attendance fees may be ordered by the judge to be made effective commencing on the first day of extended service, without reference to the date of such certification.

(c)(1) A travel allowance not to exceed the maximum rate per mile that the Director of the Administrative Office of the United States Courts has prescribed pursuant to section 604(a)(7) of this title for payment to supporting court personnel in travel status using privately owned automobiles shall be paid to each juror, regardless of the mode of transportation actually employed. The prescribed rate shall be paid for the distance necessarily traveled to and from a juror's residence by the shortest practical route in going to and returning from the place of service. Actual mileage in full at the prescribed rate is payable at the beginning and at the end of a juror's term of service.

(2) The Director shall promulgate rules regulating interim travel allowances to jurors. Distances traveled to and from court should coincide with the shortest practical route.

(3) Toll charges for toll roads, bridges, tunnels, and ferries shall be paid in full to the juror incurring such charges. In the discretion of the court, reasonable parking fees may be paid to the juror incurring such fees upon presentation of a valid parking receipt. Parking fees shall not be included in any tabulation of mileage cost allowances.

(4) Any juror who travels to district court pursuant to summons in an area outside of the contiguous forty-eight States of the United States shall be paid the travel expenses provided under this section, or actual reasonable transportation expenses subject to the discretion of the district judge or clerk of court as circumstances indicate, exercising due regard for the mode of transportation, the availability of alternative modes, and the shortest practical route between residence and court.

(5) A grand juror who travels to district court pursuant to a summons may be paid the travel expenses provided under this section or, under guide-

lines established by the Judicial Conference, the actual reasonable costs of travel by aircraft when travel by other means is not feasible and when certified by the chief judge of the district court in which the grand juror serves.

(d)(1) A subsistence allowance covering meals and lodging of jurors shall be established from time to time by the Director of the Administrative Office of the United States Courts pursuant to section 604(a)(7) of this title, except that such allowance shall not exceed the allowance for supporting court personnel in travel status in the same geographical area. Claims for such allowance shall not require itemization.

(2) A subsistence allowance shall be paid to a juror when an overnight stay is required at the place of holding court, and for the time necessarily spent in traveling to and from the place of attendance if an overnight stay is required.

(3) A subsistence allowance for jurors serving in district courts outside of the contiguous forty-eight States of the United States shall be allowed at a rate not to exceed that per diem allowance which is paid to supporting court personnel in travel status in those areas where the Director of the Administrative Office of the United States Courts has prescribed an increased per diem fee pursuant to section 604(a)(7) of this title.

(e) During any period in which a jury is ordered to be kept together and not to separate, the actual cost of subsistence shall be paid upon the order of the court in lieu of the subsistence allowances payable under subsection (d) of this section. Such allowance for the jurors ordered to be kept separate or sequestered shall include the cost of meals, lodging, and other expenditures ordered in the discretion of the court for their convenience and comfort.

(f) A juror who must necessarily use public transportation in traveling to and from court, the full cost of which is not met by the transportation expenses allowable under subsection (c) of this section on account of the short distance traveled in miles, may be paid, in the discretion of the court, the actual reasonable expense of such public transportation, pursuant to the methods of payment provided by this section. Jurors who are required to remain at the court beyond the normal business closing hour for deliberation or for any other reason may be transported to their homes, or to temporary lodgings where such lodgings are ordered by the court, in a manner directed by the clerk and paid from funds authorized under this section.

(g) The Director of the Administrative Office of the United States Courts shall promulgate such regulations as may be necessary to carry out his authority under this section.

(June 25, 1948, c. 646, 62 Stat. 953; May 24, 1949, c. 139, § 97, 63 Stat. 103; July 14, 1949, c. 333, 63 Stat. 411; Sept. 7, 1957, Pub.L. 85–299, 71 Stat. 618; Sept. 2, 1965, Pub.L. 89–165, 79 Stat. 645; Mar. 27, 1968, Pub.L. 90–274, § 102(a), 82 Stat. 62; Nov. 2, 1978, Pub.L. 95–572, § 5, 92 Stat. 2454; Dec. 1, 1990, Pub.L. 101–650, Title III, § 314(b), 104 Stat. 5115; Oct. 29, 1992, Pub.L. 102–572, Title IV, § 402, 106 Stat. 4511.)

HISTORICAL AND STATUTORY NOTES

Effective and Applicability Provisions

1992 Acts
Amendment by Pub.L. 102–572 effective Jan. 1, 1993, see section 1101(a) of Pub.L. 102–572, set out as a note under section 905 of Title 2, The Congress.

1978 Acts
Amendment by Pub.L. 95–572 applicable with respect to any grand or petit juror serving on or after the sixtieth day following Nov. 2, 1978, see section 7(b) of Pub.L. 95–572, set out as a note under section 1363 of this title.

1968 Acts
Amendment by Pub.L. 90–274 effective 270 days after Mar. 27, 1968, except as to cases in which an indictment has been returned or a petit jury empaneled prior to such effective date, see section 104 of Pub.L. 90–274, set out as a note under section 1861 of this title.

Refreshment of Jurors
Pub.L. 101–162, Title IV, Nov. 21, 1989, 103 Stat. 1012, provided in part: "That for fiscal year 1990 and hereafter, funds appropriated under this heading [Courts of Appeals, District Courts and Other Judicial Services and Fees of Jurors and Commissioners] shall be available for refreshment of jurors."

§ 1872. Issues of fact in Supreme Court
In all original actions at law in the Supreme Court against citizens of the United States, issues of fact shall be tried by a jury.

(June 25, 1948, c. 646, 62 Stat. 953.)

§ 1873. Admiralty and maritime cases
In any case of admiralty and maritime jurisdiction relating to any matter of contract or tort arising upon or concerning any vessel of twenty tons or upward, enrolled and licensed for the coasting trade, and employed in the business of commerce and navigation between places in different states upon the lakes and navigable waters connecting said lakes, the trial of all issues of fact shall be by jury if either party demands it.

(June 25, 1948, c. 646, 62 Stat. 953.)

§ 1874. Actions on bonds and specialties
In all actions to recover the forfeiture annexed to any articles of agreement, covenant, bond, or other specialty, wherein the forfeiture, breach, or nonperformance appears by default or confession of the defendant, the court shall render judgment for the plaintiff for such amount as is due. If the sum is

uncertain, it shall, upon request of either party, be assessed by a jury.

(June 25, 1948, c. 646, 62 Stat. 953.)

§ 1875. Protection of jurors' employment
(a) No employer shall discharge, threaten to discharge, intimidate, or coerce any permanent employee by reason of such employee's jury service, or the attendance or scheduled attendance in connection with such service, in any court of the United States.

(b) Any employer who violates the provisions of this section—

(1) shall be liable for damages for any loss of wages or other benefits suffered by an employee by reason of such violation;

(2) may be enjoined from further violations of this section and ordered to provide other appropriate relief, including but not limited to the reinstatement of any employee discharged by reason of his jury service; and

(3) shall be subject to a civil penalty of not more than $1,000 for each violation as to each employee.

(c) Any individual who is reinstated to a position of employment in accordance with the provisions of this section shall be considered as having been on furlough or leave of absence during his period of jury service, shall be reinstated to his position of employment without loss of seniority, and shall be entitled to participate in insurance or other benefits offered by the employer pursuant to established rules and practices relating to employees on furlough or leave of absence in effect with the employer at the time such individual entered upon jury service.

(d)(1) An individual claiming that his employer has violated the provisions of this section may make application to the district court for the district in which such employer maintains a place of business and the court shall, upon finding probable merit in such claim, appoint counsel to represent such individual in any action in the district court necessary to the resolution of such claim. Such counsel shall be compensated and necessary expenses repaid to the extent provided by section 3006A of title 18, United States Code.

(2) In any action or proceeding under this section, the court may award a prevailing employee who brings such action by retained counsel a reasonable attorney's fee as part of the costs. The court may tax a defendant employer, as costs payable to the court, the attorney fees and expenses incurred on behalf of a prevailing employee, where such costs were expended by the court pursuant to paragraph (1) of this subsection. The court may award a prevailing employer a reasonable attorney's fee as part of the costs only if the court finds that the action is frivolous, vexatious, or brought in bad faith.

(Added Pub.L. 95–572, § 6(a) (1), Nov. 2, 1978, 92 Stat. 2456, and amended Pub.L. 97–463, § 1, Jan. 12, 1983, 96 Stat. 2531.)

HISTORICAL AND STATUTORY NOTES

Effective and Applicability Provisions

1978 Acts

Section applicable with respect to any grand or petit juror summoned for service or actually serving on or after Nov. 2, 1978, see section 7(a) of Pub.L. 95–572, set out as a note under section 1363 of this title.

§ 1876.　Trial by jury in the Court of International Trade

(a) In any civil action in the Court of International Trade which is to be tried before a jury, the jury shall be selected in accordance with the provisions of this chapter and under the procedures set forth in the jury selection plan of the district court for the judicial district in which the case is to be tried.

(b) Whenever the Court of International Trade conducts a jury trial—

(1) the clerk of the district court for the judicial district in which the Court of International Trade is sitting, or an authorized deputy clerk, shall act as clerk of the Court of International Trade for the purposes of selecting and summoning the jury;

(2) the qualifications for jurors shall be the same as those established by section 1865(b) of this title for jurors in the district courts of the United States;

(3) each party shall be entitled to challenge jurors in accordance with section 1870 of this title; and

(4) jurors shall be compensated in accordance with section 1871 of this title.

(Added Pub.L. 96–417, Title III, § 302(a), Oct. 10, 1980, 94 Stat. 1739.)

HISTORICAL AND STATUTORY NOTES

Effective and Applicability Provisions

1980 Acts

Section applicable with respect to civil actions commenced on or after Nov. 1, 1980, see section 701(b) (1) (C) of Pub.L. 96–417, as amended, set out as a note under section 251 of this title.

§ 1877.　Protection of jurors

(a) Subject to the provisions of this section and title 5 of the United States Code, subchapter 1 of chapter 81, title 5, United States Code, applies to a Federal grand or petit juror, except that entitlement to disability compensation payments does not commence until the day after the date of termination of service as a juror.

(b) In administering this section with respect to a juror covered by this section—

(1) a juror is deemed to receive monthly pay at the minimum rate for grade GS–2 of the General Schedule unless his actual pay as a Government employee while serving on court leave is higher, in which case monthly pay is determined in accordance with section 8114 of title 5, United States Code, and

(2) performance of duty as a juror includes that time when a juror is (A) in attendance at court pursuant to a summons, (B) in deliberation, (C) sequestered by order of a judge, or (D) at a site, by order of the court, for the taking of a view.

(Added Pub.L. 97–463, § 3(1), Jan. 12, 1983, 96 Stat. 2531.)

HISTORICAL AND STATUTORY NOTES

References in Text

The General Schedule, referred to in subsec. (b)(1), is set out under 5 U.S.C.A. § 5332.

§ 1878.　Optional use of a one-step summoning and qualification procedure

(a) At the option of each district court, jurors may be summoned and qualified in a single procedure, if the court's jury selection plan so authorizes, in lieu of the two separate procedures otherwise provided for by this chapter. Courts shall ensure that a one-step summoning and qualification procedure conducted under this section does not violate the policies and objectives set forth in sections 1861 and 1862 of this title.

(b) Jury selection conducted under this section shall be subject to challenge under section 1867 of this title for substantial failure to comply with the provisions of this title in selecting the jury. However, no challenge under section 1867 of this title shall lie solely on the basis that a jury was selected in accordance with a one-step summoning and qualification procedure authorized by this section.

(Added Pub.L. 100–702, Title VIII, § 805(a), Nov. 19, 1988, 102 Stat. 4658, and amended Pub.L. 102–572, Title IV, § 403(a), Oct. 29, 1992, 106 Stat. 4512.)

HISTORICAL AND STATUTORY NOTES

Effective and Applicability Provisions

1992 Acts

Amendment by Pub.L. 102–572 effective Jan. 1, 1993, see section 1101(a) of Pub.L. 102–572, set out as a note under section 905 of Title 2, The Congress.

Savings Provisions

Section 403(c) of Pub.L. 102–572 provided that: "For courts participating in the experiment authorized under section 1878 of title 28, United States Code [this section] (as in effect before the effective date of this section [see Effective and Applicability Provisions of 1992 Amendments note set out under this section]), the amendment made by subsection (a) of this section [amending this section] shall be effective on and after January 1, 1992."

CHAPTER 123—FEES AND COSTS

HISTORICAL AND STATUTORY NOTES

Change of Name

"United States magistrate judge" substituted for "United States magistrate" in text pursuant to section 321 of Pub.L. 101–650, set out as a note under 28 U.S.C.A. § 631. Previously, United States commissioners, referred to in text, were replaced by United States magistrates pursuant to Pub.L. 90–578, Oct. 17, 1968, 82 Stat. 1118. See chapter 43 of Title 28, 28 U.S.C.A. § 631 et seq.

§ 1911. Supreme Court

The Supreme Court may fix the fees to be charged by its clerk.

The fees of the clerk, cost of serving process, and other necessary disbursements incidental to any case before the court, may be taxed against the litigants as the court directs.

(June 25, 1948, c. 646, 62 Stat. 954.)

§ 1912. Damages and costs on affirmance

Where a judgment is affirmed by the Supreme Court or a court of appeals, the court in its discretion may adjudge to the prevailing party just damages for his delay, and single or double costs.

(June 25, 1948, c. 646, 62 Stat. 954.)

§ 1913. Courts of appeals

The fees and costs to be charged and collected in each court of appeals shall be prescribed from time to time by the Judicial Conference of the United States. Such fees and costs shall be reasonable and uniform in all the circuits.

(June 25, 1948, c. 646, 62 Stat. 954.)

JUDICIAL CONFERENCE SCHEDULE OF FEES

Court of Appeals Miscellaneous Fee Schedule

(Issued in accordance with 28 U.S.C. § 1913)

(Effective 01/01/2007)

The following are fees to be charged for services provided by the courts of appeals. No fees are to be charged for services rendered on behalf of the United States, with the exception of those specifically prescribed in items 2, 4 and 5. No fees under this schedule shall be charged to federal agencies or programs which are funded from judiciary appropriations, including, but not limited to, agencies, organizations, and individuals providing services authorized by the Criminal Justice Act, 18 U.S.C. § 3006A, and Bankruptcy Administrator programs.

(1) For docketing a case on appeal or review, or docketing any other proceeding, $450. A separate fee shall be paid by each party filing a notice of appeal in the district court, but parties filing a joint notice of appeal in the district court are required to pay only one fee. A docketing fee shall not be charged for the docketing of an application for the allowance of an interlocutory appeal under 28 U.S.C. § 1292(b), unless the appeal is allowed. A docketing fee shall not be charged for the docketing of a direct bankruptcy appeal or a direct bankruptcy cross appeal when the fee has been collected by the bankruptcy court in accordance with Item 15 or Item 21 of the Bankruptcy Court Miscellaneous Fee Schedule.

(2) For every search of the records of the court and certifying the results thereof, $26. This fee shall apply to services rendered on behalf of the United States if the information requested is available through electronic access.

(3) For certifying any document or paper, whether the certification is made directly on the document, or by separate instrument, $9.

(4) For reproducing any record or paper, 50 cents per page. This fee shall apply to paper copies made from either: (1) original documents; or (2) microfiche or microfilm reproductions of the original records. This fee shall apply to services rendered on behalf of the United States if the record or paper requested is available through electronic access.

(5) For reproduction of recordings of proceedings, regardless of the medium, $26, including the cost of materials. This fee shall apply to services rendered on behalf of the United States if the reproduction of the recording is available electronically.

(6) For reproduction of the record in any appeal in which the requirement of an appendix is dispensed with by any

court of appeals pursuant to Rule 30(f), F.R.A.P., a flat fee of $71.

(7) For each microfiche or microfilm copy of any court record, where available, $5.

(8) For retrieval of a record from a Federal Records Center, National Archives, or other storage location removed from the place of business of the court, $45.

(9) For a check paid into the court which is returned for lack of funds, $45.

(10) Fees to be charged and collected for copies of opinions shall be fixed, from time to time, by each court, commensurate with the cost of printing.

(11) The court may charge and collect fees commensurate with the cost of providing copies of the local rules of court. The court may also distribute copies of the local rules without charge.

(12) The clerk shall assess a charge for the handling of registry funds deposited with the court, to be assessed from interest earnings and in accordance with the detailed fee schedule issued by the Director of the Administrative Office of the United States Courts.

(13) Upon the filing of any separate or joint notice of appeal or application for appeal from the Bankruptcy Appellate Panel, or notice of the allowance of an appeal from the Bankruptcy Appellate Panel, or of a writ of certiorari, $5 shall be paid by the appellant or petitioner.

(14) The court may charge and collect a fee of $200 per remote location for counsel's requested use of videoconferencing equipment in connection with each oral argument.

(15) For original admission of attorneys to practice, $150 each, including a certificate of admission. For a duplicate certificate of admission or certificate of good standing, $15.

ELECTRONIC PUBLIC ACCESS FEE SCHEDULE (eff. 9/20/06)

As directed by Congress, the Judicial Conference has determined that the following fees are necessary to reimburse expenses incurred by the judiciary in providing electronic public access to court records. These fees shall apply to the United States unless otherwise stated. No fees under this schedule shall be charged to federal agencies or programs which are funded from judiciary appropriations, including, but not limited to, agencies, organizations, and individuals providing services authorized by the Criminal Justice Act, 18 U.S.C. § 3006A, and bankruptcy administrator programs.

I. For electronic access to court data via dial-up service: 60 cents per minute. For electronic access to court data via a federal judiciary Internet site: eight cents per page, with the total for any document, docket sheet, or case-specific report not to exceed the fee for thirty pages–provided however that transcripts of federal court proceedings shall not be subject to the thirty-page fee limit. Attorneys of record and parties in a case (including *pro se* litigants) receive one free electronic copy of all documents filed electronically, if receipt is required by law or directed by the filer. No fee is owed under this provision until an account holder accrues charges of more than $10 in a calendar year. Consistent with Judicial Conference policy, courts may, upon a showing of cause, exempt indigents, bankruptcy case trustees, individual researchers associated with educational institutions, courts, section 501(c)(3) not-for-profit organizations and pro bono

ADR neutrals from payment of these fees. Courts must find that parties from the classes of persons or entities listed above seeking exemption have demonstrated that an exemption is necessary in order to avoid unreasonable burdens and to promote public access to information. Any user granted an exemption agrees not to sell for profit the data obtained as a result. Any transfer of data obtained as the result of a fee exemption is prohibited unless expressly authorized by the court. Exemptions may be granted for a definite period of time and may be revoked at the discretion of the court granting the exemption.

II. For printing copies of any record or document accessed electronically at a public terminal in the courthouse: ten cents per page. This fee shall apply to services rendered on behalf of the United States if the record requested is remotely available through electronic access.

III. For every search of court records conducted by the PACER Service Center, $26 per name or item searched.

IV. For the PACER Service Center to reproduce on paper any record pertaining to a PACER account, if this information is remotely available through electronic access, 50 cents per page.

V. For a check paid to the PACER Service Center which is returned for lack of funds, $45.

JUDICIAL CONFERENCE POLICY NOTES

Courts should not exempt local, state or federal government agencies, members of the media, attorneys or others not members of one of the groups listed above. Exemptions should be granted as the exception, not the rule. A court may not use this exemption language to exempt all users. An exemption applies only to access related to the case or purpose for which it was given. The prohibition on transfer of information received without fee is not intended to bar a quote or reference to information received as a result of a fee exemption in a scholarly or other similar work.

The electronic public access fee applies to electronic court data viewed remotely from the public records of individual cases in the court, including filed documents and the docket sheet. Electronic court data may be viewed free at public terminals at the courthouse and courts may provide other local court information at no cost. Examples of information that can be provided at no cost include: local rules, court forms, news items, court calendars, opinions, and other information–such as court hours, court location, telephone listings–determined locally to benefit the public and the court.

Miscellaneous Fee Schedules
Registry Fund Fees

Effective June 12, 1989, a fee will be assessed for handling funds deposited in noncriminal proceedings with the court and held in interest bearing accounts or instruments pursuant to 28 U.S.C. § 2041 and Federal Rules of Civil Procedure rule 67. For new accounts, i.e., investments made on or after June 12, 1989, the fee will be equal to the first 45 days income earned on the deposit. Each subsequent deposit of new principal in the same case or proceeding will be subject to the fee. Reinvestment of prior deposits will not be subject to the fee. For existing accounts, i.e., investments held by the court prior to June 12, 1989, a fee will be assessed equal to the first 45 days of income earned beginning 30 days after June 12, 1989. Subsequent deposits of new principal in the

same account will be subject to the fee. Subsequent reinvestment of existing deposits will not be subject to the fee.

The fee will apply only once to each sum deposited regardless of the length of time deposits are held and will not exceed income actually earned on the account.

The fee does not apply in the District Courts of Guam, Northern Mariana Islands, the Virgin Islands, the United States Claims Court, or other courts whose fees are not set under 28 U.S.C. §§ 1913, 1914, and 1930.

Registry Fund Fees—Item 12
(55 F.R. 42867, October 24, 1990)

Effective December 1, 1990, the registry fee assessment provisions were revised and converted from a one-time charge equal to all income earned in the first 45 days of the investment to a charge of 10 percent of the income earned while funds are held in the court registry. Additionally, the fee was extended to any funds placed in the court's registry and invested regardless of the nature of the action underlying the deposit.

The new method will not be applied on investments in cases from which a fee has been exacted based on the prior method (interest earned in the first 45 days the funds were invested or the first 45 days following July 12, 1989). The new method will also not be applied in cases where the investment instrument has a maturity date greater than one year, but where a fee under the prior method applies but has not been deducted.

The fee does not apply in the District Courts of Guam, the Northern Mariana Islands, the Virgin Islands, the United States Claims Court, or any other federal court whose fees are not set under 28 U.S.C. §§ 1913, 1914, and 1930.

Registry Fund Fees—Item 12
(56 F.R. 56356, November 4, 1991)

Effective February 3, 1992, the registry fee assessment provisions are revised and converted from a charge equal to 10 percent of the income earned while funds are held in the court's registry to a variable rate based on the amount deposited with the court and, in certain cases, the length of time funds are held in the court's registry.

The revised fee will be a fee of 10 percent of the total income received during each income period from investments of less than $100,000,000 of registry funds in income-bearing accounts. On investments exceeding $100,000,000 the 10 percent fee shall be reduced by one percent for each increment of $50,000,000 over the initial $100,000,000. For those deposits where funds are placed in the registry by court order for a time certain, for example, by the terms of an adjudicated trust, the fee will be further reduced. This further reduction will amount to 2.5 percent for each five-year interval or part thereof. The total minimum fee to be charged will be no less than two percent of the income on investments.

The following table sets out the fee schedule promulgated by this notice:

REGISTRY—SCHEDULE OF FEES
[% of income earned]

Amount of deposit *	0–5 yrs.	>5–10 yrs.	>10–15 yrs.	>15 yrs.
less than 100M	10	7.5	5.0	2.5
100M–<150M	9	6.5	4.0	2.0
150M–<200M	8	5.5	3.0	2.0

Amount of deposit *	0–5 yrs.	>5–10 yrs.	>10–15 yrs.	>15 yrs.
200M–<250M	7	4.5	2.0	2.0
250M–<300M	6	3.5	2.0	2.0
300M–<350M	5	2.5	2.0	2.0
350M–<400M	4	2.0	2.0	2.0
400M–<450M	3	2.0	2.0	2.0
over 450M	2	2.0	2.0	2.0

* Except where otherwise authorized by the Director, each deposit into any account is treated separately in determining the fee.

The new fee applies to all earnings applied to investments on and after the effective date of this change, except for earnings on investments in cases being administered under the provisions of the May 11, 1989 notice [54 FR 20407], i.e., to which the fee equal to the first 45 days income is applicable.

The fee, as modified herein, will continue to apply to any case where the court has authorized the investment of funds placed in its custody or held by it in trust in its registry regardless of the nature of the underlying action.

The fee does not apply in the District Court of Guam, the Northern Mariana Islands, the Virgin Islands, the United States Claims Court, or any other Federal court whose fees are not set under 28 U.S.C. §§ 1913, 1914, and 1930.

HISTORICAL AND STATUTORY NOTES

Appeals Filed in Courts of Appeals

Pub.L. 109–171, Title X, § 10001(b), Feb. 8, 2006, 120 Stat. 183, provided that: "The $250 fee for docketing a case on appeal or review, or docketing any other proceeding, in a court of appeals, as prescribed by the Judicial Conference, effective as of January 1, 2005, under section 1913 of title 28, United States Code [this section], shall be increased to $450."

[This note effective 60 days after Feb. 8, 2006, see Pub.L. 109–171, § 10001(d), set out as a note under 28 U.S.C.A. § 1914]

Court Fees for Electronic Access to Information

Pub.L. 102–140, Title III, § 303, Oct. 28, 1991, 105 Stat. 810, as amended Pub.L. 104–317, Title IV, § 403(b), Oct. 19, 1996, 110 Stat. 3854; Pub.L. 107–347, Title II, § 205(e), Dec. 17, 2002, 116 Stat. 2915, provided that:

"(a) The Judicial Conference may, only to the extent necessary, prescribe reasonable fees, pursuant to sections 1913, 1914, 1926, 1930, and 1932 of title 28, United States Code [this section and sections 1914, 1926, 1930, and 1932 of this title], for collection by the courts under those sections for access to information available through automatic data processing equipment. These fees may distinguish between classes of persons, and shall provide for exempting persons or classes of persons from the fees, in order to avoid unreasonable burdens and to promote public access to such information. The Director of the Administrative Office of the United States Courts, under the direction of the Judicial Conference of the United States, shall prescribe a schedule of reasonable fees for electronic access to information which the Director is required to maintain and make available to the public.

"(b) The Judicial Conference and the Director shall transmit each schedule of fees prescribed under paragraph (a) to the Congress at least 30 days before the schedule becomes effective. All fees hereafter collected by the Judiciary under paragraph (a) as a charge for services rendered shall be

deposited as offsetting collections to the Judiciary Automation Fund pursuant to 28 U.S.C. 612(c)(1)(A) [section 612(c)(1)(A) of this title] to reimburse expenses incurred in providing these services."

[Amendment by Pub.L. 107–347, § 205, effective 120 days after Dec. 17, 2002, see section 402(a) of Pub.L. 107–347, set out as a note under 44 U.S.C.A. § 3601.]

Similar provisions were contained in the following prior appropriation Act:

 Pub.L. 101–515, Title IV, § 404, Nov. 5, 1990, 104 Stat. 2132.

§ 1914. District court; filing and miscellaneous fees; rules of court

(a) The clerk of each district court shall require the parties instituting any civil action, suit or proceeding in such court, whether by original process, removal or otherwise, to pay a filing fee of $350, except that on application for a writ of habeas corpus the filing fee shall be $5.

(b) The clerk shall collect from the parties such additional fees only as are prescribed by the Judicial Conference of the United States.

(c) Each district court by rule or standing order may require advance payment of fees.

(June 25, 1948, c. 646, 62 Stat. 954; Nov. 6, 1978, Pub.L. 95–598, Title II, § 244, 92 Stat. 2671; June 19, 1986, Pub.L. 99–336, § 4(a), 100 Stat. 637; Oct. 18, 1986, Pub.L. 99–500, Title I, § 101(b) [Title IV, § 407(a)], 100 Stat. 1783–39, 1783–64, and Oct. 30, 1986, Pub.L. 99–591, Title I, § 101(b) [Title IV, § 407(a)], 100 Stat. 3341–39, 3341–64; Oct. 19, 1996, Pub.L. 104–317, Title IV, § 401(a), 110 Stat. 3853; Pub.L. 108–447, Div. B, Title III, § 307(a), Dec. 8, 2004, 118 Stat. 2895; Feb. 8, 2006, Pub.L. 109–171, Title X, § 10001(a), 120 Stat. 183.)

JUDICIAL CONFERENCE SCHEDULE OF FEES

District Court Miscellaneous Fee Schedule

[The Judicial Conference of the United States, at its session on March 7–9, 1979, set forth the schedule of fees to be charged in the United States district courts pursuant to this section. That new schedule became effective on October 1, 1979. At its March 1987 meeting, the Judicial Conference amended the schedule of fees to be effective May 1, 1987. Amendments to this revision of the schedule of fees were adopted at the September, 1988 and March, 1990 meetings of the Judicial Conference. At its 1991 meeting, the Judicial Conference amended its schedule of fees to be effective Feb. 3, 1992. At its March 1991 meeting, the Judicial Conference amended its schedule of fees to be effective Oct. 19, 1992, with later implementation. At its March, 1993 meeting, the Judicial Conference amended its schedule of fees to be effective May 6, 1993. At its September, 1993 meeting, the Judicial Conference amended its schedule of fees to be effective October 1, 1993. At its 1994 meeting, the Judicial Conference amended its schedule of fees to be effective January 1, 1995. At its March 15, 1995 meeting, the Judicial Conference amended its schedule of fees to be effective April 18, 1995, and at its 1996 meetings it adopted amendments to be effective April 1, 1996 and December 18, 1996. At its

1997 meeting, the Judicial Conference amended its schedule of fees to be effective January 1, 1998. At its 1999 meeting, the Judicial Conference amended its schedule of fees to be effective October 1, 1999. The Judicial Conference subsequently adopted amendments to its fee schedule effective February 1, 2001. At its March 2001 meeting, the Judicial Conference amended its schedule of fees to be effective July 1, 2001. The Judicial Conference adopted amendments to its fee schedule effective November 1, 2003. The Judicial Conference at its March 16, 2004 meeting adopted amendments to its fee schedule to be effective June 1, 2004.]

[The Administrative Office of the United States Courts provided for Registry Fund Fees effective June 12, 1989.]

Following are fees to be charged for services provided by the district courts. No fees are to be charged for services rendered on behalf of the United States, with the exception of those specifically prescribed in items 2, 4 and 5. No fees under this schedule shall be charged to federal agencies or programs which are funded from judiciary appropriations, including, but not limited to, agencies, organizations, and individuals providing services authorized by the Criminal Justice Act, 18 U.S.C. § 3006A, and Bankruptcy Administrator programs.

(1) For filing or indexing any document not in a case or proceeding for which a filing fee has been paid, $39.

(2) For every search of the records of the district court conducted by the clerk of the district court or a deputy clerk, $26 per name or item searched. This fee shall apply to services rendered on behalf of the United States if the information requested is available through electronic access.

(3) For certification of any document or paper, whether the certification is made directly on the document or by separate instrument, $9. For exemplification of any document or paper, twice the amount of the fee for certification.

(4) For reproducing any record or paper, $.50 per page. This fee shall apply to paper copies made from either: (1) original documents; or (2) microfiche or microfilm reproductions of the original records. This fee shall apply to services rendered on behalf of the United States if the record or paper requested is available through electronic access.

(5) For reproduction of recordings of proceedings, regardless of the medium, $26, including the cost of materials. This fee shall apply to services rendered on behalf of the United States, if the reproduction of the recording is available electronically.

(6) For each microfiche sheet of film or microfilm jacket copy of any court record, where available, $5.

(7) For retrieval of a record from a Federal Records Center, National Archives, or other storage location removed from the place of business of the court, $45.

(8) For a check paid into the court which is returned for lack of funds, $45.

(9) For an appeal to a district judge from a judgment of conviction by a magistrate in a misdemeanor case, $32.

(10) For original admission of attorneys to practice, $150 each, including a certificate of admission. For a duplicate certificate of admission or certificate of good standing, $15.

(11) The court may charge and collect fees commensurate with the cost of providing copies of the local rules of court. The court may also distribute copies of the local rules without charge.

(12) The clerk shall assess a charge for the handling of registry funds deposited with the court, to be assessed from interest earnings and in accordance with the detailed fee schedule issued by the Director of the Administrative Office of the United States Courts.

(13) For filing an action brought under Title III of the Cuban Liberty and Democratic Solidarity (LIBERTAD) Act of 1996, P.L. 104–114, 110 Stat. 785 (1996), $5,431. (This fee is in addition to the filing fee prescribed in 28 U.S.C. § 1914(a) for instituting any civil action other than a writ of habeas corpus.)

ELECTRONIC PUBLIC ACCESS FEE SCHEDULE (eff. 9/20/06)

As directed by Congress, the Judicial Conference has determined that the following fees are necessary to reimburse expenses incurred by the judiciary in providing electronic public access to court records. These fees shall apply to the United States unless otherwise stated. No fees under this schedule shall be charged to federal agencies or programs which are funded from judiciary appropriations, including, but not limited to, agencies, organizations, and individuals providing services authorized by the Criminal Justice Act, 18 U.S.C. § 3006A, and bankruptcy administrator programs.

I. For electronic access to court data via dial-up service: 60 cents per minute. For electronic access to court data via a federal judiciary Internet site: eight cents per page, with the total for any document, docket sheet, or case-specific report not to exceed the fee for thirty pages–provided however that transcripts of federal court proceedings shall not be subject to the thirty-page fee limit. Attorneys of record and parties in a case (including *pro se* litigants) receive one free electronic copy of all documents filed electronically, if receipt is required by law or directed by the filer. No fee is owed under this provision until an account holder accrues charges of more than $10 in a calendar year. Consistent with Judicial Conference policy, courts may, upon a showing of cause, exempt indigents, bankruptcy case trustees, individual researchers associated with educational institutions, courts, section 501(c)(3) not-for-profit organizations and pro bono ADR neutrals from payment of these fees. Courts must find that parties from the classes of persons or entities listed above seeking exemption have demonstrated that an exemption is necessary in order to avoid unreasonable burdens and to promote public access to information. Any user granted an exemption agrees not to sell for profit the data obtained as a result. Any transfer of data obtained as the result of a fee exemption is prohibited unless expressly authorized by the court. Exemptions may be granted for a definite period of time and may be revoked at the discretion of the court granting the exemption.

II. For printing copies of any record or document accessed electronically at a public terminal in the courthouse: ten cents per page. This fee shall apply to services rendered on behalf of the United States if the record requested is remotely available through electronic access.

III. For every search of court records conducted by the PACER Service Center, $26 per name or item searched.

IV. For the PACER Service Center to reproduce on paper any record pertaining to a PACER account, if this information is remotely available through electronic access, 50 cents per page.

V. For a check paid to the PACER Service Center which is returned for lack of funds, $45.

JUDICIAL CONFERENCE POLICY NOTES

Courts should not exempt local, state or federal government agencies, members of the media, attorneys or others not members of one of the groups listed above. Exemptions should be granted as the exception, not the rule. A court may not use this exemption language to exempt all users. An exemption applies only to access related to the case or purpose for which it was given. The prohibition on transfer of information received without fee is not intended to bar a quote or reference to information received as a result of a fee exemption in a scholarly or other similar work.

The electronic public access fee applies to electronic court data viewed remotely from the public records of individual cases in the court, including filed documents and the docket sheet. Electronic court data may be viewed free at public terminals at the courthouse and courts may provide other local court information at no cost. Examples of information that can be provided at no cost include: local rules, court forms, news items, court calendars, opinions, and other information–such as court hours, court location, telephone listings–determined locally to benefit the public and the court.

Registry Fund Fees—Item 13
(54 F.R 20407, May 11, 1989)

Effective June 12, 1989, a fee will be assessed for handling funds deposited in noncriminal proceedings with the court and held in interest bearing accounts or instruments pursuant to 28 U.S.C. § 2041 and Federal Rules of Civil Procedure rule 67. For new accounts, i.e, investments made on or after June 12, 1989, the fee will be equal to the first 45 days income earned on the deposit. Each subsequent deposit of new principal in the same case or proceeding will be subject to the fee. Reinvestment of prior deposits will not be subject to the fee. For existing accounts, i.e., investments held by the court prior to June 12, 1989, a fee will be assessed equal to the first 45 days of income earned beginning 30 days after June 12, 1989. Subsequent deposits of new principal in the same account will be subject to the fee. Subsequent reinvestment of existing deposits will not be subject to the fee.

The fee will apply only once to each sum deposited regardless of the length of time deposits are held and will not exceed income actually earned on the account.

The fee does not apply in the District Courts of Guam, Northern Mariana Islands, the Virgin Islands, the United States Claims Court, or other courts whose fees are not set under 28 U.S.C. § 1914.

Registry Fund Fees—Item 13
(55 F.R. 42867, October 24, 1990)

Effective December 1, 1990, the registry fee assessment provisions were revised and converted from a one-time charge equal to all income earned in the first 45 days of the investment to a charge of 10 percent of the income earned while funds are held in the court registry. Additionally, the fee was extended to any funds placed in the court's registry and invested regardless of the nature of the action underlying the deposit.

The new method will not be applied on investments in cases from which a fee has been exacted based on the prior method (interest earned in the first 45 days the funds were invested or the first 45 days following July 12, 1989). The

new method will also not be applied in cases where the investment instrument has a maturity date greater than one year, but where a fee under the prior method applies but has not been deducted.

The fee does not apply in the District Courts of Guam, the Northern Mariana Islands, the Virgin Islands, the United States Claims Court, or any other federal court whose fees are not set under 28 U.S.C. §§ 1913, 1914, and 1930.

Registry Fund Fees—Item 13
(56 F.R. 56356, November 4, 1991)

Effective February 3, 1992, the registry fee assessment provisions are revised and converted from a charge equal to 10 percent of the income earned while funds are held in the court's registry to a variable rate based on the amount deposited with the court and, in certain cases, the length of time funds are held in the court's registry.

The revised fee will be a fee of 10 percent of the total income received during each income period from investments of less than $100,000,000 of registry funds in income-bearing accounts. On investments exceeding $100,000,000 the 10 percent fee shall be reduced by one percent for each increment of $50,000,000 over the initial $100,000,000. For those deposits where funds are placed in the registry by court order for a time certain, for example, by the terms of an adjudicated trust, the fee will be further reduced. This further reduction will amount to 2.5 percent for each five-year interval or part thereof. The total minimum fee to be charged will be no less than two percent of the income on investments.

The following table sets out the fee schedule promulgated by this notice:

REGISTRY—SCHEDULE OF FEES

[% of income earned]

Amount of deposit *	0–5 yrs.	>5–10 yrs.	>10–15 yrs.	>15 yrs.
less than 100M	10	7.5	5.0	2.5
100M–<150M	9	6.5	4.0	2.0
150M–<200M	8	5.5	3.0	2.0
200M–<250M	7	4.5	2.0	2.0
250M–<300M	6	3.5	2.0	2.0
300M–<350M	5	2.5	2.0	2.0
350M–<400M	4	2.0	2.0	2.0
400M–<450M	3	2.0	2.0	2.0
over 450M	2	2.0	2.0	2.0

* Except where otherwise authorized by the Director, each deposit into any account is treated separately in determining the fee.

The new fee applies to all earnings applied to investments on and after the effective date of this change, except for earnings on investments in cases being administered under the provisions of the May 11, 1989 notice [54 FR 20407], i.e., to which the fee equal to the first 45 days income is applicable.

The fee, as modified herein, will continue to apply to any case where the court has authorized the investment of funds placed in its custody or held by it in trust in its registry regardless of the nature of the underlying action.

The fee does not apply in the District Court of Guam, the Northern Mariana Islands, the Virgin Islands, the United States Claims Court, or any other Federal court whose fees are not set under 28 U.S.C. §§ 1913, 1914, and 1930.

HISTORICAL AND STATUTORY NOTES

Codifications

Pub.L. 99–591 is a corrected version of Pub.L. 99–500.

Effective and Applicability Provisions

2006 Acts

Pub.L. 109–171, Title X, § 10001(d), Feb. 8, 2006, 120 Stat. 184, provided that: "This section and the amendment made by this section [amending this section and enacting provisions set out as notes under 28 U.S.C.A. §§ 1913 and 1931] shall take effect 60 days after the date of the enactment of this Act [Feb. 8, 2006]."

2004 Acts

Pub.L. 108–447, Div. B, Title III, § 307(c), Dec. 8, 2004, 118 Stat. 2895, provided that: "This section [amending subsec. (a) of this section and subsecs. (a) and (b) of 28 U.S.C.A. § 1931] shall take effect 60 days after the date of the enactment of this Act [Dec. 8, 2004]."

1996 Acts

Section 401(c) of Pub.L. 104–317 provided that: "This section [amending this section and section 1931 of this title] shall take effect 60 days after the date of the enactment of this Act [Oct. 19, 1996]."

1986 Acts

Section 4(c) of Pub.L. 99–336 provided that: "The amendments made by this section [amending this section and provisions of the District of Columbia Code not classified to this Code] shall apply with respect to any civil action, suit, or proceeding instituted on or after the date of the enactment of this Act [June 19, 1986]."

1978 Acts

Amendment by Pub.L. 95–598 effective Oct. 1, 1979, see section 402(c) of Pub.L. 95–598, set out as a note preceding section 101 of Title 11, Bankruptcy.

Court Fees for Electronic Access to Information

Judicial Conference to prescribe reasonable fees for collection by courts under this section for access to information available through automatic data processing equipment and fees to be deposited in Judiciary Automation Fund, see section 303 of Pub.L. 102–140, set out as a note under section 1913 of this title.

§ 1915. Proceedings in forma pauperis

(a)(1) Subject to subsection (b), any court of the United States may authorize the commencement, prosecution or defense of any suit, action or proceeding, civil or criminal, or appeal therein, without prepayment of fees or security therefor, by a person who submits an affidavit that includes a statement of all assets such prisoner possesses that the person is unable to pay such fees or give security therefor. Such affidavit shall state the nature of the action, defense or appeal and affiant's belief that the person is entitled to redress.

(2) A prisoner seeking to bring a civil action or appeal a judgment in a civil action or proceeding without prepayment of fees or security therefor, in addition to filing the affidavit filed under paragraph

(1), shall submit a certified copy of the trust fund account statement (or institutional equivalent) for the prisoner for the 6–month period immediately preceding the filing of the complaint or notice of appeal, obtained from the appropriate official of each prison at which the prisoner is or was confined.

(3) An appeal may not be taken in forma pauperis if the trial court certifies in writing that it is not taken in good faith.

(b)(1) Notwithstanding subsection (a), if a prisoner brings a civil action or files an appeal in forma pauperis, the prisoner shall be required to pay the full amount of a filing fee. The court shall assess and, when funds exist, collect, as a partial payment of any court fees required by law, an initial partial filing fee of 20 percent of the greater of—

(A) the average monthly deposits to the prisoner's account; or

(B) the average monthly balance in the prisoner's account for the 6–month period immediately preceding the filing of the complaint or notice of appeal.

(2) After payment of the initial partial filing fee, the prisoner shall be required to make monthly payments of 20 percent of the preceding month's income credited to the prisoner's account. The agency having custody of the prisoner shall forward payments from the prisoner's account to the clerk of the court each time the amount in the account exceeds $10 until the filing fees are paid.

(3) In no event shall the filing fee collected exceed the amount of fees permitted by statute for the commencement of a civil action or an appeal of a civil action or criminal judgment.

(4) In no event shall a prisoner be prohibited from bringing a civil action or appealing a civil or criminal judgment for the reason that the prisoner has no assets and no means by which to pay the initial partial filing fee.

(c) Upon the filing of an affidavit in accordance with subsections (a) and (b) and the prepayment of any partial filing fee as may be required under subsection (b), the court may direct payment by the United States of the expenses of (1) printing the record on appeal in any civil or criminal case, if such printing is required by the appellate court; (2) preparing a transcript of proceedings before a United States magistrate judge in any civil or criminal case, if such transcript is required by the district court, in the case of proceedings conducted under section 636(b) of this title or under section 3401(b) of title 18, United States Code; and (3) printing the record on appeal if such printing is required by the appellate court, in the case of proceedings conducted pursuant to section 636(c) of this title. Such expenses shall be paid when author-

ized by the Director of the Administrative Office of the United States Courts.

(d) The officers of the court shall issue and serve all process, and perform all duties in such cases. Witnesses shall attend as in other cases, and the same remedies shall be available as are provided for by law in other cases.

(e)(1) The court may request an attorney to represent any person unable to afford counsel.

(2) Notwithstanding any filing fee, or any portion thereof, that may have been paid, the court shall dismiss the case at any time if the court determines that—

(A) the allegation of poverty is untrue; or

(B) the action or appeal—

(i) is frivolous or malicious;

(ii) fails to state a claim on which relief may be granted; or

(iii) seeks monetary relief against a defendant who is immune from such relief.

(f)(1) Judgment may be rendered for costs at the conclusion of the suit or action as in other proceedings, but the United States shall not be liable for any of the costs thus incurred. If the United States has paid the cost of a stenographic transcript or printed record for the prevailing party, the same shall be taxed in favor of the United States.

(2)(A) If the judgment against a prisoner includes the payment of costs under this subsection, the prisoner shall be required to pay the full amount of the costs ordered.

(B) The prisoner shall be required to make payments for costs under this subsection in the same manner as is provided for filing fees under subsection (a)(2).

(C) In no event shall the costs collected exceed the amount of the costs ordered by the court.

(g) In no event shall a prisoner bring a civil action or appeal a judgment in a civil action or proceeding under this section if the prisoner has, on 3 or more prior occasions, while incarcerated or detained in any facility, brought an action or appeal in a court of the United States that was dismissed on the grounds that it is frivolous, malicious, or fails to state a claim upon which relief may be granted, unless the prisoner is under imminent danger of serious physical injury.

(h) As used in this section, the term "prisoner" means any person incarcerated or detained in any facility who is accused of, convicted of, sentenced for, or adjudicated delinquent for, violations of criminal law or the terms and conditions of parole, probation, pretrial release, or diversionary program.

(June 25, 1948, c. 646, 62 Stat. 954; May 24, 1949, c. 139, § 98, 63 Stat. 104; Oct. 31, 1951, c. 655, § 51(b), (c), 65 Stat.

727; Sept. 21, 1959, Pub.L. 86–320, 73 Stat. 590; Oct. 10, 1979, Pub.L. 96–82, § 6, 93 Stat. 645; Dec. 1, 1990, Pub.L. 101–650, Title III, § 321, 104 Stat. 5117; Apr. 26, 1996, Pub.L. 104–134, Title I, § 101[(a)] [Title VIII, § 804(a), (c) to (e)], 110 Stat. 1321–73, 1321–74, 1321–75; renumbered Title I May 2, 1996, Pub.L. 104–140, § 1(a), 110 Stat. 1327.)

HISTORICAL AND STATUTORY NOTES

Change of Name

"United States magistrate judge" substituted for "United States magistrate" in text pursuant to section 321 of Pub.L. 101–650, set out as a note under 28 U.S.C.A. § 631.

Severability of Provisions

If any provision of section 101[a] [Title VIII] of Pub.L. 104–134, an amendment made by such Title, or the application of such provision or amendment to any person or circumstance is held to be unconstitutional, the remainder of such Title, the amendments made by such Title, and the application of the provisions of such Title to any person or circumstance not affected thereby, see section 101[a] [Title VIII, § 810] of Pub.L. 104–134, set out as a note under section 3626 of Title 18, Crimes and Criminal Procedure.

§ 1915A.　Screening

(a) Screening.—The court shall review, before docketing, if feasible or, in any event, as soon as practicable after docketing, a complaint in a civil action in which a prisoner seeks redress from a governmental entity or officer or employee of a governmental entity.

(b) Grounds for dismissal.—On review, the court shall identify cognizable claims or dismiss the complaint, or any portion of the complaint, if the complaint—

(1) is frivolous, malicious, or fails to state a claim upon which relief may be granted; or

(2) seeks monetary relief from a defendant who is immune from such relief.

(c) Definition.—As used in this section, the term "prisoner" means any person incarcerated or detained in any facility who is accused of, convicted of, sentenced for, or adjudicated delinquent for, violations of criminal law or the terms and conditions of parole, probation, pretrial release, or diversionary program. (Added Pub.L. 104–134, Title I, § 101[(a)][Title VIII, § 805(a)], Apr. 26, 1996, 110 Stat. 1321–75; renumbered Title I Pub.L. 104–140, § 1(a), May 2, 1996, 110 Stat. 1327.)

HISTORICAL AND STATUTORY NOTES

Severability of Provisions

If any provision of section 101[a] [Title VIII] of Pub.L. 104–134, an amendment made by such Title, or the application of such provision or amendment to any person or circumstance is held to be unconstitutional, the remainder of such Title, the amendments made by such Title, and the application of the provisions of such Title to any person or circumstance not affected thereby, see section 101[a] [Title VIII, § 810] of Pub.L. 104–134, set out as a note under section 3626 of Title 18, Crimes and Criminal Procedure.

§ 1916.　Seamen's suits

In all courts of the United States, seamen may institute and prosecute suits and appeals in their own names and for their own benefit for wages or salvage or the enforcement of laws enacted for their health or safety without prepaying fees or costs or furnishing security therefor.
(June 25, 1948, c. 646, 62 Stat. 955.)

§ 1917.　District courts; fee on filing notice of or petition for appeal

Upon the filing of any separate or joint notice of appeal or application for appeal or upon the receipt of any order allowing, or notice of the allowance of, an appeal or of a writ of certiorari $5 shall be paid to the clerk of the district court, by the appellant or petitioner.
(June 25, 1948, c. 646, 62 Stat. 955.)

§ 1918.　District courts; fines, forfeitures and criminal proceedings

(a) Costs shall be included in any judgment, order, or decree rendered against any person for the violation of an Act of Congress in which a civil fine or forfeiture of property is provided for.

(b) Whenever any conviction for any offense not capital is obtained in a district court, the court may order that the defendant pay the costs of prosecution.
(June 25, 1948, c. 646, 62 Stat. 955.)

§ 1919.　Dismissal for lack of jurisdiction

Whenever any action or suit is dismissed in any district court, the Court of International Trade, or the Court of Federal Claims for want of jurisdiction, such court may order the payment of just costs.
(June 25, 1948, c. 646, 62 Stat. 955; Oct. 10, 1980, Pub.L. 96–417, Title V, § 510, 94 Stat. 1743; Oct. 29, 1992, Pub.L. 102–572, Title IX, § 908(a), (b)(1), 106 Stat. 4519.)

HISTORICAL AND STATUTORY NOTES

Effective and Applicability Provisions

1992 Acts

Amendment by Title IX of Pub.L. 102–572 effective Oct. 29, 1992, see section 911 of Pub.L. 102–572, set out as a note under section 171 of this title.

1980 Acts

Amendment by Pub.L. 96–417 applicable with respect to civil actions commenced on or after Nov. 1, 1980, see section 701(b)(1)(E) of Pub.L. 96–417, as amended, set out as a note under section 251 of this title.

§ 1920.　Taxation of costs

A judge or clerk of any court of the United States may tax as costs the following:

(1) Fees of the clerk and marshal;

(2) Fees of the court reporter for all or any part of the stenographic transcript necessarily obtained for use in the case;

(3) Fees and disbursements for printing and witnesses;

(4) Fees for exemplification and copies of papers necessarily obtained for use in the case;

(5) Docket fees under section 1923 of this title;

(6) Compensation of court appointed experts, compensation of interpreters, and salaries, fees, expenses, and costs of special interpretation services under section 1828 of this title.

A bill of costs shall be filed in the case and, upon allowance, included in the judgment or decree.

(June 25, 1948, c. 646, 62 Stat. 955; Oct. 28, 1978, Pub.L. 95–539, § 7, 92 Stat. 2044.)

HISTORICAL AND STATUTORY NOTES

Effective and Applicability Provisions

1978 Acts

Amendment by Pub.L. 95–539 effective Oct. 28, 1978, see section 10(a) of Pub.L. 95–539, set out as a note under section 602 of this title.

§ 1921. United States marshal's fees

(a)(1) The United States marshals or deputy marshals shall routinely collect, and a court may tax as costs, fees for the following:

(A) Serving a writ of possession, partition, execution, attachment in rem, or libel in admiralty, warrant, attachment, summons, complaints, or any other writ, order or process in any case or proceeding.

(B) Serving a subpoena or summons for a witness or appraiser.

(C) Forwarding any writ, order, or process to another judicial district for service.

(D) The preparation of any notice of sale, proclamation in admiralty, or other public notice or bill of sale.

(E) The keeping of attached property (including boats, vessels, or other property attached or libeled), actual expenses incurred, such as storage, moving, boat hire, or other special transportation, watchmen's or keepers' fees, insurance, and an hourly rate, including overtime, for each deputy marshal required for special services, such as guarding, inventorying, and moving.

(F) Copies of writs or other papers furnished at the request of any party.

(G) Necessary travel in serving or endeavoring to serve any process, writ, or order, except in the District of Columbia, with mileage to be computed from the place where service is returnable to the place of service or endeavor.

(H) Overtime expenses incurred by deputy marshals in the course of serving or executing civil process.

(2) The marshals shall collect, in advance, a deposit to cover the initial expenses for special services required under paragraph (1)(E), and periodically thereafter such amounts as may be necessary to pay such expenses until the litigation is concluded. This paragraph applies to all private litigants, including seamen proceeding pursuant to section 1916 of this title.

(3) For purposes of paragraph (1)(G), if two or more services or endeavors, or if an endeavor and a service, are made in behalf of the same party in the same case on the same trip, mileage shall be computed to the place of service or endeavor which is most remote from the place where service is returnable, adding thereto any additional mileage traveled in serving or endeavoring to serve in behalf of the party. If two or more writs of any kind, required to be served in behalf of the same party on the same person in the same case or proceeding, may be served at the same time, mileage on only one such writ shall be collected.

(b) The Attorney General shall from time to time prescribe by regulation the fees to be taxed and collected under subsection (a). Such fees shall, to the extent practicable, reflect the actual and reasonable cost of the service provided.

(c)(1) The United States Marshals Service shall collect a commission of 3 percent of the first $1,000 collected and 1½ percent on the excess of any sum over $1,000, for seizing or levying on property (including seizures in admiralty), disposing of such property by sale, setoff, or otherwise, and receiving and paying over money, except that the amount of commission shall be within the range set by the Attorney General. if [1] the property is not disposed of by marshal's sale, the commission shall be in such amount, within the range set by the Attorney General, as may be allowed by the court. In any case in which the vessel or other property is sold by a public auctioneer, or by some party other than a marshal or deputy marshal, the commission authorized under this subsection shall be reduced by the amount paid to such auctioneer or other party. This subsection applies to any judicially ordered sale or execution sale, without regard to whether the judicial order of sale constitutes a seizure or levy within the meaning of State law. This subsection shall not apply to any seizure, forfeiture, sale, or other disposition of property pursuant to the applicable provisions of law amended by the Comprehensive Forfeiture Act of 1984 (98 Stat. 2040).

(2) The Attorney General shall prescribe from time to time regulations which establish a minimum and maximum amount for the commission collected under paragraph (1).

(d) The United States marshals may require a deposit to cover the fees and expenses prescribed under this section.

(e) Notwithstanding section 3302 of title 31, the United States Marshals Service is authorized, to the extent provided in advance in appropriations Acts—

 (1) to credit to such Service's appropriation all fees, commissions, and expenses collected by such Service for—

 (A) the service of civil process, including complaints, summonses, subpoenas, and similar process; and

 (B) seizures, levies, and sales associated with judicial orders of execution; and

 (2) to use such credited amounts for the purpose of carrying out such activities.

(June 25, 1948, c. 646, 62 Stat. 955; Sept. 9, 1950, c. 937, 64 Stat. 824; Aug. 31, 1962, Pub.L. 87–621, § 1, 76 Stat. 417; Nov. 10, 1986, Pub.L. 99–646, § 39(a), 100 Stat. 3600; Nov. 18, 1988, Pub.L. 100–690, Title VII, § 7608(c), 102 Stat. 4515; Nov. 29, 1990, Pub.L. 101–647, Title XII, § 1212, 104 Stat. 4833.)

¹ So in original. Probably should be capitalized.

HISTORICAL AND STATUTORY NOTES

References in Text

The Comprehensive Forfeiture Act of 1984, referred to in subsec. (c)(1), is chapter III (sections 301 to 322) of Title II of Pub.L. 98–473, Oct. 12, 1984, 98 Stat. 2040, as amended. For complete classification of this Act to the Code, see Short Title of 1984 Amendments note set out under section 1961 of Title 18, Crimes and Criminal Procedure, and Tables.

Effective and Applicability Provisions

1986 Acts

Section 39(b) of Pub.L. 99–646 provided that: "The amendments made by this section [amending this section] shall take effect 30 days after the date of enactment of this Act [Nov. 10, 1986]."

1962 Acts

Section 3 of Pub.L. 87–621 provided that: "This Act [amending this section] shall become effective ninety days after enactment [Aug. 31, 1962]."

Collection and Disposition of Fees and Expenses for Services

Pub.L. 101–162, Title II, Nov. 21, 1989, 103 Stat. 997, provided in part: "That notwithstanding the provisions of title 31 U.S.C. 3302 [section 3302 of Title 31, Money and Finance], for fiscal year 1990 and hereafter the Director of the United States Marshals Service may collect fees and expenses for the services authorized by 28 U.S.C. 1921 as amended by Public Law 100–690 [this section], and credit such fees to this appropriation to be used for salaries and other expenses incurred in providing these services."

§ 1922. Witness fees before United States magistrate judges

The fees of more than four witnesses shall not be taxed against the United States, in the examination of any criminal case before a United States magistrate judge, unless their materiality and importance are first approved and certified to by the United States attorney for the district in which the examination is had.

(June 25, 1948, c. 646, 62 Stat. 956; Oct. 17, 1968, Pub.L. 90–578, Title IV, § 402(b)(2), 82 Stat. 1118; Dec. 1, 1990, Pub.L. 101–650, Title III, § 321, 104 Stat. 5117.)

HISTORICAL AND STATUTORY NOTES

Change of Name

"United States magistrate judge" substituted for "United States magistrate" in text pursuant to section 321 of Pub.L. 101–650, set out as a note under 28 U.S.C.A. § 631. Previously, United States commissioners, referred to in text, were replaced by United States magistrates pursuant to Pub.L. 90–578, Oct. 17, 1968, 82 Stat. 1118. See chapter 43 of Title 28, 28 U.S.C.A. § 631 et seq.

§ 1923. Docket fees and costs of briefs

(a) Attorney's and proctor's docket fees in courts of the United States may be taxed as costs as follows:

$20 on trial or final hearing (including a default judgment whether entered by the court or by the clerk) in civil, criminal, or admiralty cases, except that in cases of admiralty and maritime jurisdiction where the libellant recovers less than $50 the proctor's docket fee shall be $10;

$20 in admiralty appeals involving not over $1,000;

$50 in admiralty appeals involving not over $5,000;

$100 in admiralty appeals involving more than $5,000;

$5 on discontinuance of a civil action;

$5 on motion for judgment and other proceedings on recognizances;

$2.50 for each deposition admitted in evidence.

(b) The docket fees of United States attorneys and United States trustees shall be paid to the clerk of court and by him paid into the Treasury.

(c) In admiralty appeals the court may allow as costs for printing the briefs of the successful party not more than:

$25 where the amount involved is not over $1,000;

$50 where the amount involved is not over $5,000;

$75 where the amount involved is over $5,000.

(June 25, 1948, c. 646, 62 Stat. 956; June 18, 1954, c. 304, 68 Stat. 253; Nov. 6, 1978, Pub.L. 95–598, Title II, § 245, 92 Stat. 2671.)

HISTORICAL AND STATUTORY NOTES

Codifications

Section 408(c) of Pub.L. 95–598, Nov. 6, 1978, 92 Stat. 2687, as amended by Pub.L. 98–166, Title II, § 200, Nov. 28,

1983, 97 Stat. 1081; Pub.L. 98–353, Title III, § 323, July 10, 1984, 98 Stat. 358; Pub.L. 99–429, Sept. 30, 1986, 100 Stat. 985; Pub.L. 99–500, § 101(b) [title II, § 200], Oct. 18, 1986, 100 Stat. 1783–39, 1783–45, and Pub.L. 99–591, § 101(b) [Title II, § 200], Oct. 30, 1986, 100 Stat. 3341–39, 3341–45; Pub.L. 99–554, Title III, § 307(a), Oct. 27, 1986, 100 Stat. 3125, which provided for the deletion of any references to United States Trustees in this title at a prospective date, was repealed by Pub.L. 99–554, Title III, § 307(b), Oct. 27, 1986, 100 Stat. 3125.

[For effective date of repeal, see section 302 of Pub.L. 99–554, set out as a note under section 581 of Title 28.]

Effective and Applicability Provisions

1978 Acts

Amendment by Pub.L. 95–598 effective Oct. 1, 1979, see section 402(c) of Pub.L. 95–598, set out as a note preceding section 101 of Title 11, Bankruptcy.

§ 1924. Verification of bill of costs

Before any bill of costs is taxed, the party claiming any item of cost or disbursement shall attach thereto an affidavit, made by himself or by his duly authorized attorney or agent having knowledge of the facts, that such item is correct and has been necessarily incurred in the case and that the services for which fees have been charged were actually and necessarily performed.

(June 25, 1948, c. 646, 62 Stat. 957.)

§ 1925. Admiralty and maritime cases

Except as otherwise provided by Act of Congress, the allowance and taxation of costs in admiralty and maritime cases shall be prescribed by rules promulgated by the Supreme Court.

(June 25, 1948, c. 646, 62 Stat. 957.)

§ 1926. Court of Federal Claims

(a) The Judicial Conference of the United States shall prescribe from time to time the fees and costs to be charged and collected in the United States Court of Federal Claims.

(b) The court and its officers shall collect only such fees and costs as the Judicial Conference prescribes. The court may require advance payment of fees by rule.

(June 25, 1948, c. 646, 62 Stat. 957; Apr. 2, 1982, Pub.L. 97–164, Title I, § 139(p)(1), 96 Stat. 44; Oct. 29, 1992, Pub.L. 102–572, Title IX, § 902(b), 106 Stat. 4516.)

JUDICIAL CONFERENCE SCHEDULE OF FEES

United States Court of Federal Claims Fee Schedule

[The Federal Courts Improvement Act of 1982 [Pub.L. 97–164, Apr. 2, 1982, 96 Stat. 25] added a new Sec. 1926 to Title 28, United States Code [this section], authorizing the Judicial Conference to prescribe from time to time the fees and costs to be charged and collected in the United States Claims Court [now Court of Federal Claims]. A fee schedule

was approved, effective October 1, 1982. At its March 1987 meeting, the Judicial Conference amended the schedule of fees to be effective May 1, 1987. Amendments to this revision of the schedule of fees were adopted at the September, 1988 and March, 1990 meetings of the Judicial Conference. The Judicial Conference amended the schedule of fees at its September, 1992 meeting to be effective Nov. 15, 1992. The Judicial Conference amended the schedule of fees at its March 15, 1995 meeting to be effective April 18, 1995. The Judicial Conference amended the schedule of fees at its 1996 meeting to be effective April 15, 1996. The Judicial Conference amended the schedule of fees at its 1999 meeting to be effective October 1, 1999. The Judicial Conference subsequently adopted amendments to its fee schedule effective February 1, 2001. The Judicial Conference amended the schedule of fees at its March 2001 meeting to be effective July 1, 2001 The Judicial Conference adopted amendments to its fee schedule effective November 1, 2003. The Judicial Conference at its March 16, 2004 meeting adopted amendments to its fee schedule to be effective June 1, 2004.]

Following are fees to be charged for services provided by the United States Court of Federal Claims. No fees are to be charged for services rendered on behalf of the United States, with the exception of those specifically prescribed in items 2 and 8. No fees under this schedule shall be charged to federal agencies or programs which are funded from judiciary appropriations, including, but not limited to, agencies, organizations, and individuals providing services authorized by the Criminal Justice Act, 18 U.S.C. § 3006A, and Bankruptcy Administrator programs.

(1) For filing a civil action or proceeding, $250.

(2) For reproducing any record or paper, $.50 per page. This fee shall apply to paper copies made from either: (a) original documents; or (b) microfiche or microfilm reproduction of the original records. This fee shall apply to services rendered on behalf of the United States if the record or paper requested is available through electronic access.

(3) For certification of any document or paper, whether the certification is made directly on the document or by separate instrument, $9. For exemplification of any document or paper, twice the amount of the charge for certification.

(4) For admission of attorneys to practice, $150 each, including a certificate of admission. For a duplicate certificate of admission or certificate of good standing, $15.

(5) For receipt of a monthly listing of court orders and opinions, $19 per year.

(6) The court may charge and collect fees commensurate with the cost of providing copies of the local rules of court. The court may also distribute copies of the local rules without charge.

(7) For a check paid into the court which is returned for lack of funds, $45.

(8) For every search of the records of the Court of Federal Claims conducted by the clerk of the court or a deputy clerk, $26 per name or item searched. This fee shall apply to services rendered on behalf of the United States if the information requested is available through electronic access.

ELECTRONIC PUBLIC ACCESS FEE SCHEDULE (eff. 9/20/06)

As directed by Congress, the Judicial Conference has determined that the following fees are necessary to reim-

burse expenses incurred by the judiciary in providing electronic public access to court records. These fees shall apply to the United States unless otherwise stated. No fees under this schedule shall be charged to federal agencies or programs which are funded from judiciary appropriations, including, but not limited to, agencies, organizations, and individuals providing services authorized by the Criminal Justice Act, 18 U.S.C. § 3006A, and bankruptcy administrator programs.

I. For electronic access to court data via dial-up service: 60 cents per minute. For electronic access to court data via a federal judiciary Internet site: eight cents per page, with the total for any document, docket sheet, or case-specific report not to exceed the fee for thirty pages–provided however that transcripts of federal court proceedings shall not be subject to the thirty-page fee limit. Attorneys of record and parties in a case (including *pro se* litigants) receive one free electronic copy of all documents filed electronically, if receipt is required by law or directed by the filer. No fee is owed under this provision until an account holder accrues charges of more than $10 in a calendar year. Consistent with Judicial Conference policy, courts may, upon a showing of cause, exempt indigents, bankruptcy case trustees, individual researchers associated with educational institutions, courts, section 501(c)(3) not-for-profit organizations and pro bono ADR neutrals from payment of these fees. Courts must find that parties from the classes of persons or entities listed above seeking exemption have demonstrated that an exemption is necessary in order to avoid unreasonable burdens and to promote public access to information. Any user granted an exemption agrees not to sell for profit the data obtained as a result. Any transfer of data obtained as the result of a fee exemption is prohibited unless expressly authorized by the court. Exemptions may be granted for a definite period of time and may be revoked at the discretion of the court granting the exemption.

II. For printing copies of any record or document accessed electronically at a public terminal in the courthouse: ten cents per page. This fee shall apply to services rendered on behalf of the United States if the record requested is remotely available through electronic access.

III. For every search of court records conducted by the PACER Service Center, $26 per name or item searched.

IV. For the PACER Service Center to reproduce on paper any record pertaining to a PACER account, if this information is remotely available through electronic access, 50 cents per page.

V. For a check paid to the PACER Service Center which is returned for lack of funds, $45.

JUDICIAL CONFERENCE POLICY NOTES

Courts should not exempt local, state or federal government agencies, members of the media, attorneys or others not members of one of the groups listed above. Exemptions should be granted as the exception, not the rule. A court may not use this exemption language to exempt all users. An exemption applies only to access related to the case or purpose for which it was given. The prohibition on transfer of information received without fee is not intended to bar a quote or reference to information received as a result of a fee exemption in a scholarly or other similar work.

The electronic public access fee applies to electronic court data viewed remotely from the public records of individual cases in the court, including filed documents and the docket sheet. Electronic court data may be viewed free at public terminals at the courthouse and courts may provide other local court information at no cost. Examples of information that can be provided at no cost include: local rules, court forms, news items, court calendars, opinions, and other information–such as court hours, court location, telephone listings–determined locally to benefit the public and the court.

HISTORICAL AND STATUTORY NOTES
Effective and Applicability Provisions

1992 Acts

Amendment by Pub.L. 102–572 effective Oct. 29, 1992, see section 911 of Pub.L. 102–572, set out as a note under section 171 of this title.

1982 Acts

Amendment by Pub.L. 97–164 effective Oct. 1, 1982, see section 402 of Pub.L. 97–164, set out as a note under section 171 of this title.

Court Fees for Electronic Access to Information

Judicial Conference to prescribe reasonable fees for collection by courts under this section for access to information available through automatic data processing equipment and fees to be deposited in Judiciary Automation Fund, see section 303 of Pub.L. 102–140, set out as a note under section 1913 of this title.

§ 1927. Counsel's liability for excessive costs

Any attorney or other person admitted to conduct cases in any court of the United States or any Territory thereof who so multiplies the proceedings in any case unreasonably and vexatiously may be required by the court to satisfy personally the excess costs, expenses, and attorneys' fees reasonably incurred because of such conduct.

(June 25, 1948, c. 646, 62 Stat. 957; Sept. 12, 1980, Pub.L. 96–349, § 3, 94 Stat. 1156.)

§ 1928. Patent infringement action; disclaimer not filed

Whenever a judgment is rendered for the plaintiff in any patent infringement action involving a part of a patent and it appears that the patentee, in his specifications, claimed to be, but was not, the original and first inventor or discoverer of any material or substantial part of the thing patented, no costs shall be included in such judgment, unless the proper disclaimer has been filed in the United States Patent and Trademark Office prior to the commencement of the action.

(June 25, 1948, c. 646, 62 Stat. 957; Nov. 29, 1999, Pub.L. 106–113, Div. B, § 1000(a)(9) [Title IV, § 4732(b)(17)], 113 Stat. 1536, 1501A–585.)

HISTORICAL AND STATUTORY NOTES
Effective and Applicability Provisions

1999 Acts

Amendment by Pub.L. 106–113 [§ 4732], effective 4 months after Nov. 29, 1999, see Pub.L. 106–113 [§ 4731], set out as a note under section 1 of Title 35.

Change of Name

Patent Office redesignated Patent and Trademark Office by section 3 of Pub.L. 93–596, Jan. 2, 1975, 88 Stat. 1949, set out as a note under section 1 of Title 35, Patents.

§ 1929. Extraordinary expenses not expressly authorized

Where the ministerial officers of the United States incur extraordinary expense in executing Acts of Congress, the payment of which is not specifically provided for, the Attorney General may allow the payment thereof.

(June 25, 1948, c. 646, 62 Stat. 957.)

§ 1930. Bankruptcy fees

(a) The parties commencing a case under title 11 shall pay to the clerk of the district court or the clerk of the bankruptcy court, if one has been certified pursuant to section 156(b) of this title, the following filing fees:

(1) For a case commenced under—

(A) chapter 7 of title 11, $245, and

(B) chapter 13 of title 11, $235.

(2) For a case commenced under chapter 9 of title 11, equal to the fee specified in paragraph (3) for filing a case under chapter 11 of title 11. The amount by which the fee payable under this paragraph exceeds $300 shall be deposited in the fund established under section 1931 of this title.

(3) For a case commenced under chapter 11 of title 11 that does not concern a railroad, as defined in section 101 of title 11, $1,000.

(4) For a case commenced under chapter 11 of title 11 concerning a railroad, as so defined, $1,000.

(5) For a case commenced under chapter 12 of title 11, $200.

(6) In addition to the filing fee paid to the clerk, a quarterly fee shall be paid to the United States trustee, for deposit in the Treasury, in each case under chapter 11 of title 11 for each quarter (including any fraction thereof) until the case is converted or dismissed, whichever occurs first. The fee shall be $250 for each quarter in which disbursements total less than $15,000; $500 for each quarter in which disbursements total $15,000 or more but less than $75,000; $750 for each quarter in which disbursements total $75,000 or more but less than $150,000; $1,250 for each quarter in which disbursements total $150,000 or more but less than $225,000; $1,500 for each quarter in which disbursements total $225,000 or more but less than $300,000; $3,750 for each quarter in which disbursements total $300,000 or more but less than $1,000,000;

$5,000 for each quarter in which disbursements total $1,000,000 or more but less than $2,000,000; $7,500 for each quarter in which disbursements total $2,000,000 or more but less than $3,000,000; $8,000 for each quarter in which disbursements total $3,000,000 or more but less than $5,000,000; $10,000 for each quarter in which disbursements total $5,000,000 or more. The fee shall be payable on the last day of the calendar month following the calendar quarter for which the fee is owed.

(7) In districts that are not part of a United States trustee region as defined in section 581 of this title, the Judicial Conference of the United States may require the debtor in a case under chapter 11 of title 11 to pay fees equal to those imposed by paragraph (6) of this subsection. Such fees shall be deposited as offsetting receipts to the fund established under section 1931 of this title and shall remain available until expended.

An individual commencing a voluntary case or a joint case under title 11 may pay such fee in installments. For converting, on request of the debtor, a case under chapter 7, or 13 of title 11, to a case under chapter 11 of title 11, the debtor shall pay to the clerk of the district court or the clerk of the bankruptcy court, if one has been certified pursuant to section 156(b) of this title, a fee of the amount equal to the difference between the fee specified in paragraph (3) and the fee specified in paragraph (1).

(b) The Judicial Conference of the United States may prescribe additional fees in cases under title 11 of the same kind as the Judicial Conference prescribes under section 1914(b) of this title.

(c) Upon the filing of any separate or joint notice of appeal or application for appeal or upon the receipt of any order allowing, or notice of the allowance of, an appeal or a writ of certiorari $5 shall be paid to the clerk of the court, by the appellant or petitioner.

(d) Whenever any case or proceeding is dismissed in any bankruptcy court for want of jurisdiction, such court may order the payment of just costs.

(e) The clerk of the court may collect only the fees prescribed under this section.

(f)(1) Under the procedures prescribed by the Judicial Conference of the United States, the district court or the bankruptcy court may waive the filing fee in a case under chapter 7 of title 11 for an individual if the court determines that such individual has income less than 150 percent of the income official poverty line (as defined by the Office of Management and Budget, and revised annually in accordance with section 673(2) of the Omnibus Budget Reconciliation Act of 1981) applicable to a family of the size involved and is unable to pay that fee in installments. For purposes of this paragraph, the term "filing fee" means

the filing fee required by subsection (a), or any other fee prescribed by the Judicial Conference under subsections (b) and (c) that is payable to the clerk upon the commencement of a case under chapter 7.

(2) The district court or the bankruptcy court may waive for such debtors other fees prescribed under subsections (b) and (c).

(3) This subsection does not restrict the district court or the bankruptcy court from waiving, in accordance with Judicial Conference policy, fees prescribed under this section for other debtors and creditors. (Added Pub.L. 95–598, Title II, § 246(a), Nov. 6, 1978, 92 Stat. 2671, and amended Pub.L. 98–353, Title I, § 111(a), (b), July 10, 1984, 98 Stat. 342; Pub.L. 99–500, Title I, § 101(b) [Title IV, § 407(b)], Oct. 18, 1986, 100 Stat. 1783–64; Pub.L. 99–554, Title I, §§ 117, 144(f), Oct. 27, 1986, 100 Stat. 3095, 3097; Pub.L. 99–591, Title I, § 101(b) [Title IV, § 407(b)], Oct. 30, 1986, 100 Stat. 3341–64; Pub.L. 101–162, Title IV, § 406(a), Nov. 21, 1989, 103 Stat. 1016; Pub.L. 102–140, Title I, § 111(a), Oct. 28, 1991, 105 Stat. 795; Pub.L. 103–121, Title I, § 111(a)(1), (b)(1), Oct. 27, 1993, 107 Stat. 1164; Pub.L. 104–91, Title I, § 101(a), Jan. 6, 1996, 110 Stat. 11; Pub.L. 104–99, Title II, § 211, Jan. 26, 1996, 110 Stat. 37; Pub.L. 104–208, Div. A, Title I, § 101(a) [Title I, § 109(a)], Sept. 30, 1996, 110 Stat. 3009–18; Pub.L. 106–113, Div. B, § 1000(a)(1) [Title I, § 113], Nov. 29, 1999, 113 Stat. 1535, 1501A–20; Pub.L. 106–518, Title I, §§ 103 to 105, Nov. 13, 2000, 114 Stat. 2411; Pub.L. 109–8, Title III, § 325(a), Title IV, § 418, Apr. 20, 2005, 119 Stat. 98, 108; Pub.L. 109–13, Div. A, Title VI, § 6058(a), May 11, 2005, 119 Stat. 297; Pub.L. 109–171, Title X, § 10101(a), Feb. 8, 2006, 120 Stat. 184.)

JUDICIAL CONFERENCE SCHEDULE OF FEES

Bankruptcy Court Miscellaneous Fee Schedule

(Issued in accordance with 28 U.S.C. § 1930(b))

(Effective 01/01/2007)

[The Judicial Conference of the United States at its session on March 7–9, 1979, set forth the schedule of fees to be charged in bankruptcy courts pursuant to this section. That schedule became effective on October 1, 1979. At its sessions in March and September 1980, March, 1981, March, 1987, and March and September, 1988, the Judicial Conference amended the schedule of fees. The Administrative Office of the United States Courts provided for Registry Fund Fees effective June 12, 1989. At its September, 1989 meeting, the Judicial Conference again amended the schedule of fees, such amendments effective pursuant to 1989 Judicial Conference Statement. The schedule of fees was again amended by the Judicial Conference at its March, 1990 and September, 1990 meetings. At its 1991 meeting, the Judicial Conference amended the schedule of fees to be effective Feb. 3, 1992. At its March 1991 meeting the Judicial Conference adopted Item 23 to be effective Oct. 19, 1992, with later implementation. At its September, 1992 meeting the Judicial Conference amended Item 8 to be effective Dec. 1, 1992. At its March, 1993 meeting the Judicial Conference amended its fee schedule effective May 6, 1993. At its September, 1993 meeting the Judicial Conference amended its fee schedule to be effective November 8, 1993. At its 1994 meeting, the Judicial Conference amended

its fee schedule to be effective January 1, 1995. At its September, 1995 meeting the Judicial Conference amended its fee schedule to be effective November 9, 1995, and at its 1996 meetings it adopted amendments to be effective April 1, 1996 and October 28, 1996. At its 1997 meeting the Judicial Conference amended its fee schedule to be effective January 1, 1998. At its 1999 meeting the Judicial Conference amended its fee schedule to be effective October 1, 1999. The Judicial Conference subsequently adopted amendments to its fee schedule effective February 1, 2001. At its March 2001 meeting the Judicial Conference amended its fee schedule to be effective July 1, 2001. The Judicial Conference adopted amendments to its fee schedule effective January 1, 2002; and effective November 1, 2003. The Judicial Conference at its March 16, 2004 meeting adopted amendments to its fee schedule to be effective June 1, 2004. The Judicial Conference adopted amendments to its fee schedule effective January 1, 2005; and effective September 20, 2005; and effective October 17, 2005; and effective January 1, 2007.]

Following are fees to be charged for services provided by the bankruptcy courts. No fees are to be charged for services rendered on behalf of the United States, with the exception of those specifically prescribed in items 1, 3, and 5, or to bankruptcy administrators appointed under Public Law No. 99–554, § 302(d)(3)(I). No fees under this schedule shall be charged to federal agencies or programs which are funded from judiciary appropriations, including, but not limited to, agencies, organizations, and individuals providing services authorized by the Criminal Justice Act, 18 U.S.C. § 3006A.

(1) For reproducing any record or paper, $.50 per page. This fee shall apply to paper copies made from either: (1) original documents; or (2) microfiche or microfilm reproductions of the original records. This fee shall apply to services rendered on behalf of the United States if the record or paper requested is available through electronic access.

(2) For certification of any document or paper, whether the certification is made directly on the document or by separate instrument, $9. For exemplification of any document or paper, twice the amount of the charge for certification.

(3) For reproduction of recordings of proceedings, regardless of the medium, $26, including the cost of materials. This fee shall apply to services rendered on behalf of the United States, if the reproduction of the recording is available electronically.

(4) For amendments to a debtor's schedules of creditors, lists of creditors, matrix, or mailing lists, $26 for each amendment, provided the bankruptcy judge may, for good cause, waive the charge in any case. No fee is required when the nature of the amendment is to change the address of a creditor or an attorney for a creditor listed on the schedules or to add the name and address of an attorney for a listed creditor.

(5) For every search of the records of the bankruptcy court conducted by the clerk of the bankruptcy court or a deputy clerk, $26 per name or item searched. This fee shall apply to services rendered on behalf of the United States if the information requested is available through electronic access.

(6) For filing a complaint, $250. If the United States, other than a United States trustee acting as a trustee in a case under Title 11, or a debtor is the plaintiff, no fee is required. If a trustee or debtor in possession is the plaintiff,

the fee should be payable only from the estate and to the extent there is any estate realized. If a child support creditor or its representative is the plaintiff, and if such plaintiff files the form required by § 304(g) of the Bankruptcy Reform Act of 1994, no fee is required.

(7) For filing or indexing any document not in a case or proceeding for which a filing fee has been paid, $39.

(8) In all cases filed under title 11, the clerk shall collect from the debtor or the petitioner a miscellaneous administrative fee of $39. This fee may be paid in installments in the same manner that the filing fee may be paid in installments, consistent with the procedure set forth in Federal Rule of Bankruptcy Procedure 1006.

(9) Upon the filing of a petition under Chapter 7 of the Bankruptcy Code, the petitioner shall pay $15 to the clerk of the court for payment to trustees serving in cases as provided in 11 U.S.C. § 330(b)(2). An application to pay the fee in installments may be filed in the manner set forth in Federal Rule of Bankruptcy Procedure 1006(b).

(10) Upon the filing of a motion to convert a case to Chapter 7 of the Bankruptcy Code, the movant shall pay $15 to the clerk of court for payment to trustees serving in cases as provided in 11 U.S.C. § 330(b)(2). Upon the filing of a notice of conversion pursuant to Section 1208(a) or Section 1307(a) of the Code, $15 shall be paid to the clerk of the court for payment to trustees serving in cases as provided in 11 U.S.C. § 330(b)(2). If the trustee serving in the case before the conversion is the movant, the fee shall be payable only from the estate that exists prior to conversion. For filing a motion to convert or a notice of conversion, a fee shall be charged in the amount of the difference between the current filing fee for the chapter under which the case was originally commenced and the current filing fee for the chapter to which the case is requested to be converted. If the filing fee for the chapter to which the case is requested to be converted is less than the fee paid at the commencement of the case, no refund shall be provided. A fee shall not be assessed under this item for converting a Chapter 7 or 13 case to a Chapter 11 case as the fee for these actions is collected pursuant to statute under 28 U.S.C. § 1930(a).

(11) For filing a motion to reopen a Bankruptcy Code case, a fee shall be collected in the same amount as the filing fee prescribed by 28 U.S.C. § 1930(a) for commencing a new case on the date of reopening. The reopening fee should be charged when a case is closed without a discharge being entered. If the motion to reopen is made for a Chapter 7 case, an additional fee of $15 shall be paid to the clerk of the court for payment to trustees serving in cases as provided in 11 U.S.C. § 330(b)(2). For filing a motion to reopen a Chapter 15 case, a fee shall be charged in the same amount as the filing fee required under Item 16 of this schedule for commencing a new case on the date of reopening. The reopening fee will not be charged if the reopening is necessary: (1) to permit a party to file a complaint to obtain a determination under Rule 4007(b), or, (2) when a creditor is violating the terms of the discharge under 11 U.S.C. § 524. The court may waive this fee under appropriate circumstances or may defer payment of the fee from trustees pending discovery of additional assets. If payment is deferred, the fee shall be waived if no additional assets are discovered.

(12) For each microfiche sheet of film or microfilm jacket copy of any court record, where available, $5.

(13) For retrieval of a record from a Federal Records Center, National Archives, or other storage location removed from the place of business of the court, $45.

(14) For a check paid into the court which is returned for lack of funds, $45.

(15) For docketing a proceeding on appeal or review from a final judgment of a bankruptcy judge pursuant to 28 U.S.C. § 158(a) and (b), $250. A separate fee shall be paid by each party filing a notice of appeal in the bankruptcy court, but parties filing a joint notice of appeal in the bankruptcy court are required to pay only one fee. If a trustee or debtor in possession is the appellant, the fee should be payable only from the estate and to the extent there is any estate realized. Upon notice from the court of appeals that a direct appeal from the bankruptcy court has been authorized, the appellant shall pay an additional $200.

(16) For filing a Chapter 15 proceeding, the fee shall be the same amount as the fee for a case commenced under Chapter 11 of Title 11 as required by 28 U.S.C. § 1930(a)(3).

(17) The court may charge and collect fees commensurate with the cost of providing copies of the local rules of court. The court may also distribute copies of the local rules without charge.

(18) The clerk shall assess a charge for the handling of registry funds deposited with the court, to be assessed from interest earnings and in accordance with the detailed fee schedule issued by the Director of the Administrative Office of the United States Courts.

(19) When a joint case filed under § 302 of Title 11 is divided into two separate cases at the request of the debtor(s), a fee shall be charged equal to the current filing fee for the chapter under which the joint case was commenced. If the motion to divide the case is made for a Chapter 7 case, an additional fee of $15 shall be paid to the clerk of the court for payment to trustees serving in cases as provided in 11 U.S.C. § 330(b)(2).

(20) For filing a motion to terminate, annul, modify, or condition the automatic stay provided under § 362(a) of Title 11, a motion to compel abandonment of property of the estate pursuant to Rule 6007(b) of the Federal Rules of Bankruptcy Procedure, or a motion to withdraw the reference of a case or proceeding under 28 U.S.C. § 157(d), $150. No fee is required for a motion for relief from the co-debtor stay or for a stipulation for court approval of an agreement for relief from a stay. If a child support creditor or its representative is the movant, and if such movant files the form required by § 304(g) of the Bankruptcy Reform Act of 1994, no fee is required.

(21) For docketing a cross appeal from a bankruptcy court determination, $250. If a trustee or debtor in possession is the appellant, the fee should be payable only from the estate and to the extent there is any estate realized. Upon notice from the court of appeals that a direct cross from the bankruptcy court has been authorized, the cross appellant shall pay an additional $200.

ELECTRONIC PUBLIC ACCESS FEE SCHEDULE (eff. 9/20/06)

As directed by Congress, the Judicial Conference has determined that the following fees are necessary to reimburse expenses incurred by the judiciary in providing electronic public access to court records. These fees shall apply

to the United States unless otherwise stated. No fees under this schedule shall be charged to federal agencies or programs which are funded from judiciary appropriations, including, but not limited to, agencies, organizations, and individuals providing services authorized by the Criminal Justice Act, 18 U.S.C. § 3006A, and bankruptcy administrator programs.

I. For electronic access to court data via dial-up service: 60 cents per minute. For electronic access to court data via a federal judiciary Internet site: eight cents per page, with the total for any document, docket sheet, or case-specific report not to exceed the fee for thirty pages–provided however that transcripts of federal court proceedings shall not be subject to the thirty-page fee limit. Attorneys of record and parties in a case (including *pro se* litigants) receive one free electronic copy of all documents filed electronically, if receipt is required by law or directed by the filer. No fee is owed under this provision until an account holder accrues charges of more than $10 in a calendar year. Consistent with Judicial Conference policy, courts may, upon a showing of cause, exempt indigents, bankruptcy case trustees, individual researchers associated with educational institutions, courts, section 501(c)(3) not-for-profit organizations and pro bono ADR neutrals from payment of these fees. Courts must find that parties from the classes of persons or entities listed above seeking exemption have demonstrated that an exemption is necessary in order to avoid unreasonable burdens and to promote public access to information. Any user granted an exemption agrees not to sell for profit the data obtained as a result. Any transfer of data obtained as the result of a fee exemption is prohibited unless expressly authorized by the court. Exemptions may be granted for a definite period of time and may be revoked at the discretion of the court granting the exemption.

II. For printing copies of any record or document accessed electronically at a public terminal in the courthouse: ten cents per page. This fee shall apply to services rendered on behalf of the United States if the record requested is remotely available through electronic access.

III. For every search of court records conducted by the PACER Service Center, $26 per name or item searched.

IV. For the PACER Service Center to reproduce on paper any record pertaining to a PACER account, if this information is remotely available through electronic access, 50 cents per page.

V. For a check paid to the PACER Service Center which is returned for lack of funds, $45.

JUDICIAL CONFERENCE POLICY NOTES

Courts should not exempt local, state or federal government agencies, members of the media, attorneys or others not members of one of the groups listed above. Exemptions should be granted as the exception, not the rule. A court may not use this exemption language to exempt all users. An exemption applies only to access related to the case or purpose for which it was given. The prohibition on transfer of information received without fee is not intended to bar a quote or reference to information received as a result of a fee exemption in a scholarly or other similar work.

The electronic public access fee applies to electronic court data viewed remotely from the public records of individual cases in the court, including filed documents and the docket sheet. Electronic court data may be viewed free at public terminals at the courthouse and courts may provide other local court information at no cost. Examples of information that can be provided at no cost include: local rules, court forms, news items, court calendars, opinions, and other information–such as court hours, court location, telephone listings–determined locally to benefit the public and the court.

STATEMENT RESPECTING 1988 AMENDMENTS FROM ADMINISTRATIVE OFFICE OF UNITED STATES COURTS

The Director of the Administrative Office of the United States Courts in a memorandum to the Chief Judges of the United States Courts of Appeals, United States District Courts, and United States Bankruptcy Courts, dated April 19, 1988, provided in part that: "The amendment establishing a fee for filing a petition ancillary to a foreign proceeding under § 304 of the Bankruptcy Code will become effective May 1, 1988. The amendment expanding the exemption for services rendered 'to the United States' to include services rendered to bankruptcy administrators simply expresses a policy which has been in effect since the creation of the bankruptcy administrator program by Congress in the Bankruptcy Judges, United States Trustees and Family Farmer Bankruptcy Act of 1986. [Pub.L. No. 99–554, § 302(d)(3)(I).]"

Statement from 1989 Meeting of Judicial Conference

The Judicial Conference, at the September 20, 1989 meeting, provided in part that Item 21 takes effect on December 21, 1989. The Conference further provided that: "The remaining fees, Items 20 and 22, take effect on January 11, 1990, pending approval of the Appropriations Committees."

Registry Fund Fees—Item 19
(54 FR 20407, May 11, 1989)

Effective June 12, 1989, a fee will be assessed for handling funds deposited in noncriminal proceedings with the court and held in interest bearing accounts or instruments pursuant to 28 U.S.C. § 2041 and Federal Rules of Civil Procedure rule 67. For new accounts, i.e., investments made on or after June 12, 1989, the fee will be equal to the first 45 days income earned on the deposit. Each subsequent deposit of new principal in the same case or proceeding will be subject to the fee. Reinvestment of prior deposits will not be subject to the fee. For existing accounts, i.e., investments held by the court prior to June 12, 1989, a fee will be assessed equal to the first 45 days of income earned beginning 30 days after June 12, 1989. Subsequent deposits of new principal in the same account will be subject to the fee. Subsequent reinvestment of existing deposits will not be subject to the fee.

The fee will apply only once to each sum deposited regardless of the length of time deposits are held and will not exceed income actually earned on the account.

The fee does not apply in the District Courts of Guam, Northern Mariana Islands, the Virgin Islands, the United States Claims Court, or other courts whose fees are not set under 28 U.S.C. § 1930.

Registry Fund Fees—Item 19
(55 F.R. 42867, October 24, 1990)

Effective December 1, 1990, the registry fee assessment provisions were revised and converted from a one-time charge equal to all income earned in the first 45 days of the investment to a charge of 10 percent of the income earned

while funds are held in the court registry. Additionally, the fee was extended to any funds placed in the court's registry and invested regardless of the nature of the action underlying the deposit.

The new method will not be applied on investments in cases from which a fee has been exacted based on the prior method (interest earned in the first 45 days the funds were invested or the first 45 days following July 12, 1989). The new method will also not be applied in cases where the investment instrument has a maturity date greater than one year, but where a fee under the prior method applies but has not been deducted.

The fee does not apply in the District Courts of Guam, the Northern Mariana Islands, the Virgin Islands, the United States Claims Court, or any other federal court whose fees are not set under 28 U.S.C. §§ 1913, 1914, and 1930.

Registry Fund Fees—Item 19
(56 F.R. 56356, November 4, 1991)

Effective February 3, 1992, the registry fee assessment provisions are revised and converted from a charge equal to 10 percent of the income earned while funds are held in the court's registry to a variable rate based on the amount deposited with the court and, in certain cases, the length of time funds are held in the court's registry.

The revised fee will be a fee of 10 percent of the total income received during each income period from investments of less than $100,000,000 of registry funds in income-bearing accounts. On investments exceeding $100,000,000 the 10 percent fee shall be reduced by one percent for each increment of $50,000,000 over the initial $100,000,000. For those deposits where funds are placed in the registry by court order for a time certain, for example, by the terms of an adjudicated trust, the fee will be further reduced. This further reduction will amount to 2.5 percent for each five-year interval or part thereof. The total minimum fee to be charged will be no less than two percent of the income on investments.

The following table sets out the fee schedule promulgated by this notice:

REGISTRY—SCHEDULE OF FEES
[% of income earned]

Amount of deposit *	0–5 yrs.	>5–10 yrs.	>10–15 yrs.	>15 yrs.
less than 100M	10	7.5	5.0	2.5
100M–<150M	9	6.5	4.0	2.0
150M–<200M	8	5.5	3.0	2.0
200M–<250M	7	4.5	2.0	2.0
250M–<300M	6	3.5	2.0	2.0
300M–<350M	5	2.5	2.0	2.0
350M–<400M	4	2.0	2.0	2.0
400M–<450M	3	2.0	2.0	2.0
over 450M	2	2.0	2.0	2.0

* Except where otherwise authorized by the Director, each deposit into any account is treated separately in determining the fee.

The new fee applies to all earnings applied to investments on and after the effective date of this change, except for earnings on investments in cases being administered under the provisions of the May 11, 1989 notice [54 FR 20407], i.e., to which the fee equal to the first 45 days income is applicable.

The fee, as modified herein, will continue to apply to any case where the court has authorized the investment of funds placed in its custody or held by it in trust in its registry regardless of the nature of the underlying action.

The fee does not apply in the District Court of Guam, the Northern Mariana Islands, the Virgin Islands, the United States Claims Court, or any other Federal court whose fees are not set under 28 U.S.C. §§ 1913, 1914, and 1930.

HISTORICAL AND STATUTORY NOTES
References in Text

Chapter 7, 11, 12, or 13 of title 11, referred to in text, is 11 U.S.C.A. § 701 et seq., 11 U.S.C.A. § 1101 et seq., 11 U.S.C.A. § 1201 et seq., or 11 U.S.C.A. § 1301 et seq., respectively.

Section 673(2) of the Omnibus Budget Reconciliation Act of 1981, referred to in subsec. (f)(1), is Pub.L. 97–35, Title VI, § 673(2), Aug. 13, 1981, as added Pub.L. 105–285, Title II, § 201, Oct. 27, 1998, 112 Stat. 2729, which is classified to 42 U.S.C.A. § 9902(2).

Codifications

Pub.L. 99–591 is a corrected version of Pub.L. 99–500.

The Chapter 11 filing fee will not change from its current amount of $1,000. It appears that Congress intended to increase chapter 11 filing fees from $1,000 to $2,750. However, there is a drafting error in the language of the Deficit Reduction Act of 2005 which references the incorrect statutory subsection [Pub.L. 109–171, Title X, § 10101(a)(2), Feb. 8, 2006, 120 Stat. 184]. Thus, the chapter 11 fee, at this time, is unaltered. See 2006 Amendments note set out under this section.

Section 101(a) of Pub.L. 104–91, as amended by section 211 of Pub.L. 104–99, provided in part that section 111(a) of the General Provisions for the Department of Justice in Title I of the Departments of Commerce, Justice, and State, the Judiciary, and Related Agencies Appropriations Act, 1996 (H.R. 2076) as passed by the House of Representatives on Dec. 6, 1995, was enacted into permanent law. Such section 111(a) of H.R. 2076 amended subsec. (a)(6) of this section. See 1996 Amendments note set out under this section.

Effective and Applicability Provisions
2006 Acts

Pub.L. 109–171, Title X, § 10101(c), Feb. 8, 2006, 120 Stat. 184, provided that: "This section and the amendments made by this section [amending this section and enacting provisions set out as a note under 28 U.S.C.A. § 1931] shall take effect 60 days after the date of the enactment of this Act [Feb. 8, 2006]."

2005 Acts

Amendment by Pub.L. 109–13, § 6058(a), amending Pub.L. 109–8, § 325, which amended this section, effective immediately after the enactment of the Bankruptcy Abuse Prevention and Consumer Protection Act of 2005 [Pub.L. 109–8, Apr. 20, 2005, 119 Stat. 23], see Pub.L. 109–13, § 6058(b), set out as a note under 28 U.S.C.A. § 589a.

Except as otherwise provided, amendments by Pub.L. 109–8 effective 180 days after April 20, 2005, and inapplicable with respect to cases commenced under Title 11 before the effective date, see Pub.L. 109–8, § 1501, set out as a note under 11 U.S.C.A. § 101.

1999 Acts

Amendment by Pub.L. 106–113, [§ 113], effective 30 days after Nov. 29, 1999, see Pub.L. 106–113, [§ 113], set out as a note under section 589a of this title.

1993 Acts

Section 111(a) of Pub.L. 103–121 provided in part that amendment by section 111(a)(1) of Pub.L. 103–121, amending subsec. (a)(1) of this section, is effective 30 days after Oct. 27, 1993.

Section 111(b) of Pub.L. 103–121 provided in part that amendment by section 111(b)(1) of Pub.L. 103–121, amending subsec. (a)(3) of this section, is effective 30 days after Oct. 27, 1993.

1991 Acts

Amendment by Pub.L. 102–140 effective 60 days after the date of the enactment of Pub.L. 102–140, which was approved Oct. 28, 1991, see section 111(a) of Pub.L. 102–140, set out as a note under section 589a of this title.

1986 Acts

Amendment by Pub.L. 99–554 effective 30 days after Oct. 27, 1986, except as otherwise provided for, see section 302(a) of Pub.L. 99–554, set out as a note under section 581 of this title.

Amendment by Pub.L. 99–554, § 117(4), not to become effective in or with respect to certain specified judicial districts until, or apply to cases while pending in such district before, the expiration of the 270-day period beginning 30 days after Oct. 27, 1986, or of the 30-day period beginning on the date the Attorney General certifies under section 303 of Pub.L. 99–554 the region specified in a paragraph of section 581(a) of Title 28, as amended by section 111(a) of Pub.L. 99–554, that includes such district, whichever occurs first, see section 302(d)(1) of Pub.L. 99–554, set out as a note under section 581 of this title.

Amendment by Pub.L. 99–554, § 117(4), not to become effective in or with respect to certain specified judicial districts until, or apply to cases while pending in such district before, the expiration of the 2-year period beginning 30 days after Oct. 27, 1986, or of the 30-day period beginning on the date the Attorney General certifies under section 303 of Pub.L. 99–554 the region specified in a paragraph of section 581(a) of Title 28, as amended by section 111(a) of Pub.L. 99–554, that includes such district, whichever occurs first, see section 302(d)(2) of Pub.L. 99–554, set out as a note under section 581 of this title.

Amendment by Pub.L. 99–554, § 117(4), not to become effective in or with respect to judicial districts established for the States of Alabama and North Carolina until, or apply to cases while pending in such district before, such district elects to be included in a bankruptcy region established in section 581(a) of Title 28, as amended by section 111(a) of Pub.L. 99–554, or Oct. 1, 2002, whichever occurs first, and, except as otherwise provided for, with respect to cases under chapters 7, 11, 12, and 13 of Title 11 commenced before 30 days after Oct. 27, 1986, and pending in a judicial district in the States of Alabama or North Carolina before any election made under section 302(d)(3)(A) of Pub.L. 99–554 by such district becomes effective or Oct. 1, 2002, whichever occurs first, amendments by Pub.L. 99–554 not to apply until Oct. 1, 2003, or the expiration of the 1-year period beginning on the date such election becomes effective, whichever occurs first, and further, in any judicial district in Alabama or North

Carolina not making the election described in section 302(d)(3)(A) of Pub.L. 99–554, any person appointed under regulations issued by the Judicial Conference to administer estates in cases under Title 11 authorized to establish, etc., a panel of private trustees, and to supervise cases and trustees in cases under chapters 7, 11, 12, and 13 of Title 11, until amendments by sections 201 to 231 of Pub.L. 99–554 effective in such district, see section 302(d)(3)(A) to (F), (H), (I) of Pub.L. 99–554, set out as a note under section 581 of this title.

Deposit in the general receipts of the Treasury of funds collected as a result of the amendments made by section 117 of Pub.L. 99–554 in a judicial district in the States of Alabama or North Carolina under section 1930(a) of Title 28 before the date the amendments made by sections 201 to 231 of Pub.L. 99–554 take effect in such districts, and notwithstanding section 589a of Title 28, see section 302(d)(3)(G) of Pub.L. 99–554, set out as a note under section 581 of this title.

Amendment by Pub.L. 99–554, § 117(4), except as otherwise provided, with respect to cases under chapters 7, 11, 12, and 13 of Title 11 commenced before 30 days after Oct. 27, 1986, and pending in a judicial district referred to in section 581(a) of Title 28, as amended by section 111(a) of Pub.L. 99–554, for which a United States trustee is not authorized before 30 days after Oct. 27, 1986 to be appointed, not applicable until the expiration of the 3-year period beginning on Oct. 27, 1986, or of the 1-year period beginning on the date the Attorney General certifies under section 303 of Pub.L. 99–554 the region specified in a paragraph of such section 581(a) that includes, such district, whichever occurs first, see section 302(e)(1), (2) of Pub.L. 99–554, set out as a note under section 581 of this title.

Rule of construction regarding fees for cases under Title 11 for any conduct or period occurring before section 1930(a)(6) of Title 28 becomes effective in the district in which such case is pending, see section 302(e)(3) of Pub.L. 99–554, set out as a note under section 581 of this title.

1984 Acts

Amendment by Pub.L. 98–353 effective July 10, 1984, see section 122(a) of Pub.L. 98–353, set out as a note under section 151 of this title.

1979 Acts

Section effective Oct. 1, 1979, see section 402(c) of Pub.L. 95–598, set out as a note preceding section 101 of Title 11, Bankruptcy.

Use of Increased Receipts

Pub.L. 109–8, Title III, § 325(e), Apr. 20, 2005, 119 Stat. 99, which pertained to the use of increased receipts from fees under subsec. (a) of this section, was omitted in the general amendment of Pub.L. 109–8, § 325, by Pub.L. 109–13, Div. A, Title VI, § 6058(a), May 11, 2005, 119 Stat. 297. Such amendment by Pub.L. 109–13, § 6058(a), effective immediately after the enactment of the Bankruptcy Abuse Prevention and Consumer Protection Act of 2005 [Pub.L. 109–8, Apr. 20, 2005, 119 Stat. 23], see Pub.L. 109–13, § 6058(b), set out as a note under 28 U.S.C.A. § 589a.

[Except as otherwise provided, amendments by Pub.L. 109–8 effective 180 days after April 20, 2005, and inapplicable with respect to cases commenced under Title 11 before the

effective date, see Pub.L. 109–8, § 1501, set out as a note under 11 U.S.C.A. § 101.]

Effective and Applicability Provisions of 1989 Amendments; Miscellaneous Fees

Section 406(a) of Pub.L. 101–162 provided in part that: "Pursuant to section 1930(b) of title 28 [subsec. (b) of this section] the Judicial Conference of the United States shall prescribe a fee of $60 on motions seeking relief from the automatic stay under 11 U.S.C. section 362(b) [section 362(b) of Title 11, Bankruptcy] and motions to compel abandonment of property of the estate. The fees established pursuant to the preceding two sentences shall take effect 30 days after the enactment of this Act [Nov. 21, 1989]."

Accrual and Payment of Quarterly Fees in Chapter 11 Cases After Jan. 27, 1996; Confirmation Status of Plans

Section 101(a) of Pub.L. 104–91, as amended Pub.L. 104–99, Title II, § 211, Jan. 26, 1996, 110 Stat. 37; Pub.L. 104–208, Div. A, Title I, § 101(a) [Title I, § 109(d)], Sept. 30, 1996, 110 Stat. 3009–19, provided, in part: "That, notwithstanding any other provision of law, the fees under 28 U.S.C. 1930(a)(6) [subsec. (a)(6) of this section] shall accrue and be payable from and after January 27, 1996, in all cases (including, without limitation, any cases pending as of that date), regardless of confirmation status of their plans."

Collection and Disposition of Fees in Bankruptcy Cases

Section 404(a) of Pub. L. 101–162 provided that: "For fiscal year 1990 and hereafter, such fees as shall be collected for the preparation and mailing of notices in bankruptcy cases as prescribed by the Judicial Conference of the United States pursuant to 28 U.S.C. 1930(b) [subsec. (b) of this section] shall be deposited to the 'Courts of Appeals, District Courts, and Other Judicial Services, Salaries and Expenses' appropriation to be used for salaries and other expenses incurred in providing these services."

Court Fees for Electronic Access to Information

Judicial Conference to prescribe reasonable fees for collection by courts under this section for access to information available through automatic data processing equipment and fees to be deposited in Judiciary Automation Fund, see section 303 of Pub.L. 102–140, set out as a note under section 1913 of this title.

Issuance of Notices to Creditors and Other Interested Parties

Section 403 of Pub.L. 101–162 provided that: "Notwithstanding any other provision of law, for fiscal year 1990 and hereafter, (a) The Administrative Office of the United States Courts, or any other agency or instrumentality of the United States, is prohibited from restricting solely to staff of the Clerks of the United States Bankruptcy Courts the issuance of notices to creditors and other interested parties. (b) The Administrative Office shall permit and encourage the preparation and mailing of such notices to be performed by or at the expense of the debtors, trustees or such other interested parties as the Court may direct and approve. (c) The Director of the Administrative Office of the United States Courts shall make appropriate provisions for the use of and accounting for any postage required pursuant to such directives."

Report on Bankruptcy Fees

Section 111(d) of Pub.L. 103–121 provided that:

"**(1) Report required.**—Not later than March 31, 1998, the Judicial Conference of the United States shall submit to the Committees on the Judiciary of the House of Representatives and the Senate, a report relating to the bankruptcy fee system and the impact of such system on various participants in bankruptcy cases.

"**(2) Contents of report.**—Such report shall include—

"**(A)(i)** an estimate of the costs and benefits that would result from waiving bankruptcy fees payable by debtors who are individuals, and

"**(ii)** recommendations regarding various revenue sources to offset the net cost of waiving such fees; and

"**(B)(i)** an evaluation of the effects that would result in cases under chapters 11 and 13 of title 11, United States Code [sections 1101 et seq. and 1301 et seq., respectively, of Title 11, Bankruptcy], from using a graduated bankruptcy fee system based on assets, liabilities, or both of the debtor, and

"**(ii)** recommendations regarding various methods to implement such a graduated bankruptcy fee system.

"**(3) Waiver of fees in selected districts.**—For purposes of carrying out paragraphs (1) and (2), the Judicial Conference of the United States shall carry out in not more than six judicial districts, throughout the 3–year period beginning on October 1, 1994, a program under which fees payable under section 1930 of title 28, United States Code [this section], may be waived in cases under chapter 7 of title 11, United States Code [section 701 et seq. of Title 11], for debtors who are individuals unable to pay such fees in installments.

"**(4) Study of graduated fee system.**—For purposes of carrying out paragraphs (1) and (2), the Judicial Conference of the United States shall carry out, in not fewer than six judicial districts, a study to estimate the results that would occur in cases under chapters 11 and 13 of title 11, United States Code [sections 1101 et seq. and 1301 et seq., respectively, of Title 11], if filing fees payable under section 1930 of title 28, United States Code [this section], were paid on a graduated scale based on assets, liabilities, or both of the debtor."

§ 1931. Disposition of filing fees

(a) Of the amounts paid to the clerk of court as a fee under section 1914(a) or as part of a judgment for costs under section 2412(a)(2) of this title, $190 shall be deposited into a special fund of the Treasury to be available to offset funds appropriated for the operation and maintenance of the courts of the United States.

(b) If the court authorizes a fee under section 1914(a) or an amount included in a judgment for costs under section 2412(a)(2) of this title of less than $250, the entire fee or amount, up to $190, shall be deposited into the special fund provided in this section. (Added Pub.L. 99–500, Title I, § 101(b) [Title IV, § 407(c)], Oct. 18, 1986, 100 Stat. 1783–64, and Pub.L. 99–591, Title I, § 101(b) [Title IV, § 407(c)], Oct. 30, 1986, 100 Stat. 3341–64, and amended Pub.L. 101–162, Title IV, § 406(d), Nov. 21, 1989, 103 Stat. 1016; Pub.L. 102–572, Title III, § 301(b), Oct.

29, 1992, 106 Stat. 4511; Pub.L. 104–317, Title IV, § 401(b), Oct. 19, 1996, 110 Stat. 3853; Pub.L. 108–447, Div. B, Title III, § 307(b), Dec. 8, 2004, 118 Stat. 2895.)

HISTORICAL AND STATUTORY NOTES

Codifications

Pub.L. 99–591 is a corrected version of Pub.L. 99–500.

Effective and Applicability Provisions

2004 Acts

Amendments by Pub.L. 108–447, Div. B, § 307(b), shall take effect 60 days after December 8, 2004, see Pub.L. 108–447, Div. B, § 307(c), set out as a note under 28 U.S.C.A. § 1914.

1996 Acts

Amendment by section 401(b) of Pub.L. 104–317 effective 60 days after Oct. 19, 1996, see section 401(c) of Pub.L. 104–317, set out as a note under section 1914 of this title.

1992 Acts

Amendment by Pub.L. 102–572 effective Jan. 1, 1993, see section 1101(a) of Pub.L. 102–572, set out as a note under section 905 of Title 2, The Congress.

Expenditure Limitation

Pub.L. 109–171, Title X, § 10001(c), Feb. 8, 2006, 120 Stat. 183, provided that: "Incremental amounts collected by reason of the enactment of this section [Pub.L. 109–171, Title X, § 10001, Feb. 8, 2006, 120 Stat. 183, which amended 28 U.S.C.A. § 1914 and enacted this note and provisions set out as notes under 28 U.S.C.A. §§ 1913 and 1914] shall be deposited in a special fund in the Treasury to be established after the enactment of this Act [Feb. 8, 2006]. Such amounts shall be available for the purposes specified in section 1931(a) of title 28, United States Code [subsec. (a) of this section], but only to the extent specifically appropriated by an Act of Congress enacted after the enactment of this Act [Feb. 8, 2006]."

[This note effective 60 days after Feb. 8, 2006, see Pub.L. 109–171, § 10001(d), set out as a note under 28 U.S.C.A. § 1914]

Pub.L. 109–171, Title X, § 10101(b), Feb. 8, 2006, 120 Stat. 184, provided that: "Incremental amounts collected by reason of the amendments made by subsection (a) [amending 28 U.S.C.A. § 1930] shall be deposited in a special fund in the Treasury to be established after the enactment of this Act [Feb. 8, 2006]. Such amounts shall be available for the purposes specified in section 1931(a) of title 28, United States Code [subsec. (a) of this section], but only to the extent specifically appropriated by an Act of Congress enacted after the enactment of this Act [Feb. 8, 2006]."

[This note effective 60 days after Feb. 8, 2006, see Pub.L. 109–171, § 10101(c), set out as a note under 28 U.S.C.A. § 1930]

Disposition of Miscellaneous Fees

Pub.L. 106–518, Title I, § 102, Nov. 13, 2000, 114 Stat. 2411, provided that: "For fiscal year 2001 and each fiscal year thereafter, any portion of miscellaneous fees collected as prescribed by the Judicial Conference of the United States under sections 1913 [this section], 1914(b), 1926(a), 1930(b), and 1932 of title 28, United States Code, exceeding the amount of such fees in effect on September 30, 2000, shall be

deposited into the special fund of the Treasury established under section 1931 of title 28, United States Code [this section]."

Collection and Deposit of Miscellaneous Bankruptcy Fees

Section 406(b) of Pub.L. 101–162, as amended Pub.L. 103–121, Title I, § 111(a)(3), (b)(4), Oct. 27, 1993, 107 Stat. 1164; Pub.L. 106–113, Div. B, § 1000(a)(1) [Title I, § 113], Nov. 29, 1999, 113 Stat. 1535, 1501A–20; Pub.L. 106–518, Title II, § 209(a), Nov. 13, 2000, 114 Stat. 2415; Pub.L. 109–8, Title III, § 325(c), Apr. 20, 2005, 119 Stat. 99; Pub.L. 109–13, Div. A, Title VI, § 6058(a), May 11, 2005, 119 Stat. 297, provided that: "All fees as shall be hereafter collected for any service not of a kind described in any of the items enumerated as items 1 through 7 and as items 9 through 18, as in effect on November 21, 1989, of the bankruptcy miscellaneous fee schedule prescribed by the Judicial Conference of the United States under section 1930(b) of title 28, United States Code [28 U.S.C.A. § 1930(b)], 28.87 percent of the fees collected under section 1930(a)(1)(A) of that title [28 U.S.C.A. § 1930(a)(1)(A)], 35.00 percent of the fees collected under section 1930(a)(1)(B) of that title [28 U.S.C.A. § 1930(a)(1)(B)], and 25 percent of the fees collected under section 1930(a)(3) of that title [28 U.S.C.A. § 1930(a)(3)] shall be deposited as offsetting receipts to the fund established under section 1931 of that title [this section] and shall remain available to the Judiciary until expended to reimburse any appropriation for the amount paid out of such appropriation for expenses of the Courts of Appeals, District Courts, and other Judicial Services and the Administrative Office of the United States Courts. The Judicial Conference shall report to the Committees on Appropriations of the House of Representatives and the Senate on a quarterly basis beginning on the first day of each fiscal year regarding the sums deposited in said fund."

[Amendment by Pub.L. 109–13, § 6058(a), to Pub.L. 109–8, § 325(c), which amended this note, effective immediately after the enactment of the Bankruptcy Abuse Prevention and Consumer Protection Act of 2005 [Pub.L. 109–8, Apr. 20, 2005, 119 Stat. 23], see Pub.L. 109–13, § 6058(b), set out as a note under 28 U.S.C.A. § 589a.]

[Amendment of this note by Pub.L. 109–8, § 325(c), effective during 2–year period beginning on Apr. 20, 2005, see Pub.L. 109–8, § 325(d), set out as a note under 28 U.S.C.A. § 589a.]

[For termination, effective May 15, 2000, of provisions relating to a quarterly report to the Committees on Appropriations of the House of Representatives and the Senate in section 406(b) of Pub.L. 101–162, as amended, set out as a note above, see Pub.L. 104–66, § 3003, as amended, set out as a note under 31 U.S.C.A. § 1113 and page 12 of House Document No. 103–7.]

[Amendment of this note by Pub.L. 106–113, [§ 113], effective 30 days after Nov. 29, 1999, see Pub.L. 106–113, [§ 113], set out as a note under section 589a of this title.]

[Pub.L. 106–518, Title II, § 209(b), Nov. 13,, 2000, 114 Stat. 2415, provided that: "The amendment made by subsection (a) [amending this note] shall not apply with respect to fees collected before the date of enactment of this Act [Nov. 13, 2000]."

[Section 111(a) of Pub.L. 103–121 provided in part that amendment of this note by section 111(a)(3) of Pub.L. 103–121 is effective 30 days after Oct. 27, 1993.]

[Section 111(b) of Pub.L. 103–121 provided in part that amendment of this note by section 111(b)(4) of Pub.L. 103–121 is effective 30 days after Oct. 27, 1993.]

Disposition of Fees

Section 404 of Pub.L. 104–317 provided that:

"(a) **Disposition of attorney admission fees.**—For each fee collected for admission of an attorney to practice, as prescribed by the Judicial Conference of the United States pursuant to section 1914 of title 28, United States Code [section 1914 of this title], $30 of that portion of the fee exceeding $20 shall be deposited into the special fund of the Treasury established under section 1931 of title 28, United States Code [this section]. Any portion exceeding $5 of the fee for a duplicate certificate of admission or certificate of good standing, as prescribed by the Judicial Conference of the United States pursuant to section 1914 of title 28, United States Code [section 1914 of this title], shall be deposited into the special fund of the Treasury established under section 1931 of title 28, United States Code [this section].

"(b) **Disposition of bankruptcy complaint filing fees.**—For each fee collected for filing an adversary complaint in a bankruptcy proceeding, as established in Item 6 of the Bankruptcy Court Miscellaneous Fee Schedule prescribed by the Judicial Conference of the United States [set out under section 1930 of this title] pursuant to section 1930(b) of title 28, United States Code [section 1930(b) of this title], the portion of the fee exceeding $120 shall be deposited into the special fund of the Treasury established under section 1931 of title 28, United States Code [this section].

"(c) **Effective date.**—This section shall take effect 60 days after the date of the enactment of this Act [Oct. 19, 1996]."

§ 1932.[1] Judicial Panel on Multidistrict Litigation

The Judicial Conference of the United States shall prescribe from time to time the fees and costs to be charged and collected by the Judicial Panel on Multidistrict Litigation.

(Added Pub.L. 104–317, Title IV, § 403(a)(1), Oct. 19, 1996, 110 Stat. 3854.)

[1] Another section 1932 is set out post.

JUDICIAL CONFERENCE SCHEDULE OF FEES

Judicial Panel on Multidistrict Litigation Fee Schedule

[The Judicial Conference of the United States issued pursuant to this section the schedule of the fees to be charged and collected by the Judicial Panel on Multidistrict Litigation effective October 1, 1999. The Judicial Conference at its March 2001 meeting adopted amendments to its fee schedule to be effective July 1, 2001. The Judicial Conference adopted amendments to its fee schedule effective January 1, 2002; and effective November 1, 2003. The Judicial Conference at its March 16, 2004 meeting adopted amendments to its fee schedule to be effective June 1, 2004.]

Following are fees to be charged for services provided by the Judicial Panel on Multidistrict Litigation. No fees are to be charged for services rendered on behalf of the United States, with the exception of those specifically prescribed in items 1 and 3. No fees under this schedule shall be charged to federal agencies or programs which are funded from judiciary appropriations, including, but not limited to, agencies, organizations, and individuals providing services authorized by the Criminal Justice Act, 18 U.S.C. § 3006A.

(1) For every search of the records of the court conducted by the clerk of the court or a deputy clerk, $26 per name or item searched. This fee shall apply to services rendered on behalf of the United States if the information requested is available through electronic access.

(2) For certification of any document or paper, whether the certification is made directly on the document or by separate instrument, $9.

(3) For reproducing any record or paper, $.50 per page. This fee shall apply to paper copies made from either: (1) original documents; or (2) microfiche or microfilm reproductions of the original records. This fee shall apply to services rendered on behalf of the United States if the record or paper requested is available through electronic access.

(4) For retrieval of a record from a Federal Records Center, National Archives, or other storage location removed from the place of business of the court, $45.

(5) For a check paid into the Panel which is returned for lack of funds, $45.

ELECTRONIC PUBLIC ACCESS FEE SCHEDULE (eff. 9/20/06)

As directed by Congress, the Judicial Conference has determined that the following fees are necessary to reimburse expenses incurred by the judiciary in providing electronic public access to court records. These fees shall apply to the United States unless otherwise stated. No fees under this schedule shall be charged to federal agencies or programs which are funded from judiciary appropriations, including, but not limited to, agencies, organizations, and individuals providing services authorized by the Criminal Justice Act, 18 U.S.C. § 3006A, and bankruptcy administrator programs.

I. For electronic access to court data via dial-up service: 60 cents per minute. For electronic access to court data via a federal judiciary Internet site: eight cents per page, with the total for any document, docket sheet, or case-specific report not to exceed the fee for thirty pages–provided however that transcripts of federal court proceedings shall not be subject to the thirty-page fee limit. Attorneys of record and parties in a case (including *pro se* litigants) receive one free electronic copy of all documents filed electronically, if receipt is required by law or directed by the filer. No fee is owed under this provision until an account holder accrues charges of more than $10 in a calendar year. Consistent with Judicial Conference policy, courts may, upon a showing of cause, exempt indigents, bankruptcy case trustees, individual researchers associated with educational institutions, courts, section 501(c)(3) not-for-profit organizations and pro bono ADR neutrals from payment of these fees. Courts must find that parties from the classes of persons or entities listed above seeking exemption have demonstrated that an exemption is necessary in order to avoid unreasonable burdens and to promote public access to information. Any user granted an

exemption agrees not to sell for profit the data obtained as a result. Any transfer of data obtained as the result of a fee exemption is prohibited unless expressly authorized by the court. Exemptions may be granted for a definite period of time and may be revoked at the discretion of the court granting the exemption.

II. For printing copies of any record or document accessed electronically at a public terminal in the courthouse: ten cents per page. This fee shall apply to services rendered on behalf of the United States if the record requested is remotely available through electronic access.

III. For every search of court records conducted by the PACER Service Center, $26 per name or item searched.

IV. For the PACER Service Center to reproduce on paper any record pertaining to a PACER account, if this information is remotely available through electronic access, 50 cents per page.

V. For a check paid to the PACER Service Center which is returned for lack of funds, $45.

JUDICIAL CONFERENCE POLICY NOTES

Courts should not exempt local, state or federal government agencies, members of the media, attorneys or others not members of one of the groups listed above. Exemptions should be granted as the exception, not the rule. A court may not use this exemption language to exempt all users. An exemption applies only to access related to the case or purpose for which it was given. The prohibition on transfer of information received without fee is not intended to bar a quote or reference to information received as a result of a fee exemption in a scholarly or other similar work.

The electronic public access fee applies to electronic court data viewed remotely from the public records of individual cases in the court, including filed documents and the docket sheet. Electronic court data may be viewed free at public terminals at the courthouse and courts may provide other local court information at no cost. Examples of information that can be provided at no cost include: local rules, court forms, news items, court calendars, opinions, and other information–such as court hours, court location, telephone listings–determined locally to benefit the public and the court.

§ 1932.[1] Revocation of earned release credit

In any civil action brought by an adult convicted of a crime and confined in a Federal correctional facility, the court may order the revocation of such earned good time credit under section 3624(b) of title 18, United States Code, that has not yet vested, if, on its own motion or the motion of any party, the court finds that—

(1) the claim was filed for a malicious purpose;

(2) the claim was filed solely to harass the party against which it was filed; or

(3) the claimant testifies falsely or otherwise knowingly presents false evidence or information to the court.

(Added Pub.L. 104–134, Title I, § 101[(a)][Title VIII, § 809(a)], Apr. 26, 1996, 110 Stat. 1321–76; renumbered Title I Pub.L. 104–140, § 1(a), May 2, 1996, 110 Stat. 1327.)

1 Another section 1932 is set out ante.

HISTORICAL AND STATUTORY NOTES

Severability of Provisions

If any provision of section 101[a] [Title VIII] of Pub.L. 104–134, an amendment made by such Title, or the application of such provision or amendment to any person or circumstance is held to be unconstitutional, the remainder of such Title, the amendments made by such Title, the application of the provisions of such Title to any person or circumstance not affected thereby, see section 101[a] [Title VIII, § 810] of Pub.L. 104–134, set out as a note under section 3626 of Title 18, Crimes and Criminal Procedure.

CHAPTER 125—PENDING ACTIONS AND JUDGMENTS

§ 1961. Interest

(a) Interest shall be allowed on any money judgment in a civil case recovered in a district court. Execution therefor may be levied by the marshal, in any case where, by the law of the State in which such court is held, execution may be levied for interest on judgments recovered in the courts of the State. Such interest shall be calculated from the date of the entry of the judgment, at a rate equal to the weekly average 1–year constant maturity Treasury yield, as published by the Board of Governors of the Federal Reserve System, for the calendar week preceding.[1] the date of the judgment. The Director of the Administrative Office of the United States Courts shall distribute notice of that rate and any changes in it to all Federal judges.

(b) Interest shall be computed daily to the date of payment except as provided in section 2516(b) of this title and section 1304(b) of title 31, and shall be compounded annually.

(c)(1) This section shall not apply in any judgment of any court with respect to any internal revenue tax case. Interest shall be allowed in such cases at the underpayment rate or overpayment rate (whichever is appropriate) established under section 6621 of the Internal Revenue Code of 1986.

(2) Except as otherwise provided in paragraph (1) of this subsection, interest shall be allowed on all final

judgments against the United States in the United States Court of Appeals for the Federal circuit,[2] at the rate provided in subsection (a) and as provided in subsection (b).

(3) Interest shall be allowed, computed, and paid on judgments of the United States Court of Federal Claims only as provided in paragraph (1) of this subsection or in any other provision of law.

(4) This section shall not be construed to affect the interest on any judgment of any court not specified in this section.

(June 25, 1948, c. 646, 62 Stat. 957; Apr. 2, 1982, Pub.L. 97–164, Title III, § 302(a), 96 Stat. 55; Sept. 13, 1982, Pub.L. 97–258, § 2(m) (1), 96 Stat. 1062; Jan. 12, 1983, Pub.L. 97–452, § 2(d)(1), 96 Stat. 2478; Oct. 22, 1986, Pub.L. 99–514, § 2, Title XV, § 1511(c)(17), 100 Stat. 2095, 2745; Oct. 29, 1992, Pub.L. 102–572, Title IX, § 902(b)(1), 106 Stat. 4516; Dec. 21, 2000, Pub.L. 106–554, § 1(a)(7) [Title III, § 307(d)(1)], 114 Stat. 2763, 2763A–636.)

[1] So in original. The period probably should not appear.
[2] So in original. Probably should be "Circuit,".

HISTORICAL AND STATUTORY NOTES

References in Text

Section 6621 of the Internal Revenue Code of 1986, referred to in subsec. (c)(1), is section 6621 of Title 26, Internal Revenue Code.

Codifications

Amendment of subsec. (b) by Pub.L. 97–452, substituting "section 1304(b) of title 31" for "section 1302 of the Act of July 27, 1956 (31 U.S.C. 724a)" was executed without reference to the intervening amendment by Pub.L. 97–258, as the probable intent of Congress.

Effective and Applicability Provisions

1992 Acts

Amendment by Pub.L. 102–572 effective Oct. 29, 1992, see section 911 of Pub.L. 102–572, set out as a note under section 171 of this title.

1986 Acts

Amendment by section 1511(c)(17) of Pub.L. 99–514 applicable for purposes of determining interest for periods after Dec. 31, 1986, see section 1511(d) of Pub.L. 99–514, set out as a note under section 47 of Title 26, Internal Revenue Code.

1982 Acts

Section 2(m) of Pub.L. 97–258 provided in part that the amendment to subsec. (b) would be effective on Oct. 1, 1982.

Amendment by Pub.L. 97–164 effective Oct. 1, 1982, see section 402 of Pub.L. 97–164, set out as a note under section 171 of this title.

Calculation of Interest

The method of calculation of interest on money judgments in civil cases recovered in district courts changed as of December 21, 2000, the date of enactment of Pub.L. 106–554, § 1(a)(7) [Title III, § 307(d)(1)] which amended subsec. (a) of this section. It was formerly calculated at a rate equal to the coupon issue yield equivalent (as determined by the Secretary of the Treasury) of the average accepted auction price

for the last auction of fifty-two week United States Treasury bills (for past rates, see Table set out below). It is now calculated at a rate equal to the weekly average 1-year constant maturity Treasury yield, as published by the Board of Governors of the Federal Reserve System. For information regarding weekly releases, see *www.federalreserve.gov*.

52–WEEK T–BILL RATE TABLE OF CHANGES

Date of Auction	Equivalent Coupon Issue Yield
12/11/74	7.07%
01/08/75	6.80%
02/05/75	5.61%
03/05/75	5.99%
04/02/75	6.92%
04/30/75	6.84%
05/28/75	6.17%
06/24/75	6.72%
07/24/75	7.27%
08/20/75	7.89%
09/17/75	7.90%
10/18/75	7.07%
11/13/75	6.40%
12/10/75	6.88%
01/07/76	5.92%
02/04/76	5.92%
03/03/76	6.29%
03/31/76	6.13%
04/29/76	5.98%
05/26/76	6.72%
06/23/76	6.47%
07/21/76	6.25%
08/19/76	5.97%
09/15/76	5.89%
10/13/76	5.41%
11/09/76	5.49%
12/08/76	4.95%
01/05/77	4.97%
02/02/77	5.65%
03/02/77	5.52%
03/30/77	5.44%
04/27/77	5.45%
05/25/77	5.71%
06/22/77	5.72%
07/20/77	5.98%
08/17/77	6.49%
09/14/77	6.55%
10/12/77	7.07%
11/09/77	6.98%
12/07/77	6.99%
01/04/78	6.99%
02/01/78	7.29%
03/01/78	7.34%
03/29/78	7.36%
04/26/78	7.58%
05/24/78	7.97%
06/21/78	8.27%
07/19/78	8.43%
08/16/78	8.50%
09/13/78	8.59%
10/12/78	8.90%
11/08/78	10.17%
12/06/78	10.17%
01/03/79	10.51%

Date of Auction	Equivalent Coupon Issue Yield	Date of Auction	Equivalent Coupon Issue Yield
01/31/79	10.21%	11/01/83	9.86%
02/28/79	10.40%	11/23/83	9.93%
04/04/79	10.09%	12/22/83	10.10%
04/25/79	10.10%	01/19/84	9.87%
05/23/79	10.01%	02/16/84	10.11%
06/20/79	9.63%	03/15/84	10.60%
07/18/79	9.70%	04/12/84	10.81%
08/15/79	10.05%	05/15/84	11.74%
09/12/79	10.88%	06/07/84	12.08%
10/10/79	12.83%	07/10/84	12.17%
11/07/79	13.18%	08/02/84	11.93%
12/05/79	11.98%	08/30/84	11.98%
01/02/80	12.25%	09/27/84	11.36%
01/30/80	12.45%	10/25/84	10.33%
02/27/80	15.28%	11/27/84	9.50%
03/26/80	16.46%	12/20/84	9.08%
04/23/80	11.45%	01/17/85	9.09%
05/21/80	9.02%	02/14/85	9.17%
06/18/80	8.08%	03/14/85	10.08%
07/16/80	8.25%	04/11/85	9.15%
08/13/80	9.75%	05/14/85	8.57%
09/10/80	10.93%	06/06/85	7.70%
10/08/80	13.33%	07/09/85	7.60%
10/30/80	13.67%	08/01/85	8.18%
11/26/80	14.97%	08/29/85	7.91%
12/23/80	13.49%	09/26/85	7.87%
01/22/81	14.68%	10/24/85	8.08%
02/19/81	14.39%	11/26/85	7.87%
03/19/81	12.76%	12/19/85	7.57%
04/16/81	14.63%	01/16/86	7.85%
05/14/81	16.70%	02/13/86	7.71%
06/11/81	14.82%	03/13/86	7.06%
07/09/81	15.57%	04/10/86	6.31%
08/07/81	16.60%	05/13/86	6.56%
09/03/81	17.26%	06/05/86	7.03%
10/01/81	16.55%	07/08/86	6.35%
10/29/81	14.84%	07/31/86	6.18%
11/25/81	11.58%	08/28/86	5.63%
12/23/81	14.02%	09/25/86	5.79%
01/21/82	14.92%	10/23/86	5.75%
02/18/82	14.87%	11/20/86	5.77%
03/18/82	14.03%	12/23/86	5.93%
04/15/82	14.30%	01/15/87	5.75%
05/13/82	13.64%	02/12/87	6.09%
06/10/82	13.61%	03/12/87	6.04%
07/08/82	13.79%	04/09/87	6.30%
08/05/82	12.41%	05/12/87	7.02%
09/02/82	11.32%	06/04/87	7.00%
09/30/82	10.41%	07/02/87	6.64%
10/28/82	9.29%	08/04/87	6.98%
11/24/82	9.07%	09/01/87	7.22%
12/23/82	8.75%	09/30/87	7.88%
01/20/83	8.65%	10/22/87	6.90%
02/17/83	8.99%	11/19/87	6.93%
03/17/83	9.16%	12/17/87	7.22%
04/14/83	8.98%	01/14/88	7.14%
05/12/83	8.72%	02/11/88	6.59%
06/09/83	9.59%	03/10/88	6.71%
07/07/83	10.25%	04/07/88	7.01%
08/09/83	10.74%	05/05/88	7.20%
09/01/83	10.58%	06/02/88	7.59%
09/29/83	9.98%	06/30/88	7.54%
		07/28/88	7.95%
		08/25/88	8.32%

Complete Annotation Materials, see Title 28 U.S.C.A.

Date of Auction	Equivalent Coupon Issue Yield	Date of Auction	Equivalent Coupon Issue Yield
09/22/88	8.04%	06/24/93	3.54%
10/20/88	8.15%	07/22/93	3.58%
11/17/88	8.55%	08/19/93	3.43%
12/15/88	9.20%	09/16/93	3.40%
01/12/89	9.16%	10/14/93	3.38%
02/15/89	9.32%	11/16/93	3.57%
03/09/89	9.43%	12/09/93	3.61%
04/06/89	9.31%	01/06/94	3.67%
05/04/89	9.15%	02/03/94	3.74%
06/01/89	8.85%	03/03/94	4.22%
06/29/89	8.16%	03/31/94	4.51%
07/27/89	7.75%	04/28/94	5.02%
08/24/89	8.27%	5/26/94	5.28%
09/21/89	8.19%	6/23/94	5.31%
10/19/89	7.90%	7/21/94	5.49%
11/16/89	7.69%	8/18/94	5.67%
12/14/89	7.66%	9/15/94	5.69%
01/11/90	7.74%	10/13/94	6.06%
02/13/90	7.97%	11/10/94	6.482%
03/08/90	8.36%	12/08/94	7.22%
04/05/90	8.32%	1/5/95	7.34%
05/03/90	8.70%	2/2/95	7.03%
05/31/90	8.24%	3/2/95	6.57%
06/28/90	8.09%	3/30/95	6.41%
07/26/90	7.88%	4/27/95	6.28%
08/23/90	7.95%	5/25/95	5.88%
09/20/90	7.78%	6/22/95	5.53%
10/26/90	7.51%	7/20/95	5.70%
11/15/90	7.28%	8/17/95	5.89%
12/13/90	7.02%	9/14/95	5.52%
01/10/91	6.62%	10/12/95	5.62%
02/12/91	6.21%	11/15/95	5.45%
03/07/91	6.46%	12/7/95	5.35%
04/04/91	6.26%	1/4/96	5.16%
05/02/91	6.07%	2/1/96	4.89%
05/30/91	6.09%	2/29/96	5.25%
06/27/91	6.39%	4/2/96	5.46%
07/25/91	6.26%	4/25/96	5.60%
08/22/91	5.68%	5/23/96	5.62%
09/19/91	5.57%	6/20/96	5.89%
10/17/91	5.42%	7/18/96	5.81%
11/14/91	4.98%	8/15/96	5.67%
12/12/91	4.41%	9/12/96	5.90%
01/09/92	4.02%	10/10/96	5.64%
02/06/92	4.21%	11/7/96	5.49%
03/05/92	4.58%	12/5/96	5.45%
04/02/92	4.55%	1/2/97	5.61%
04/30/92	4.40%	1/30/97	5.64%
05/28/92	4.26%	2/27/97	5.67%
06/25/92	4.11%	3/26/97	6.00%
07/23/92	3.51%	4/24/97	6.06%
08/20/92	3.41%	5/22/97	5.88%
09/17/92	3.13%	6/19/97	5.65%
10/15/92	3.24%	7/17/97	5.56%
11/17/92	3.76%	8/14/97	5.58%
12/10/92	3.72%	9/11/97	5.60%
01/07/93	3.67%	10/9/97	5.49%
02/04/93	3.45%	11/6/97	5.42%
03/04/93	3.21%	12/4/97	5.468%
04/06/93	3.37%	1/6/98	5.341%
04/30/93	3.25%	1/29/98	5.232%
05/27/93	3.54%	2/26/98	5.407%
		3/26/98	5.391%
		4/23/98	5.407%

Complete Annotation Materials, see Title 28 U.S.C.A.

Date of Auction	Equivalent Coupon Issue Yield
5/21/98	5.434%
6/18/98	5.413%
7/16/98	5.375%
8/18/98	5.271%
9/15/98	4.730%
10/13/98	4.242%
11/9/98	4.616%
12/8/98	4.513%
1/5/99	4.545%
2/2/99	4.584%
3/2/99	4.918%
3/30/99	4.732%
4/27/99	4.727%
5/25/99	4.879%
6/22/99	5.163%
7/20/99	4.966%
8/17/99	5.224%
9/14/99	5.285%
10/13/99	5.411%
11/9/99	5.471%
12/7/99	5.670%
1/4/00	5.997%
2/1/00	6.287%
2/29/00	6.197%
5/31/00	6.375%
8/29/00	6.241%
11/28/00	6.052%

§ 1962.　Lien

Every judgment rendered by a district court within a State shall be a lien on the property located in such State in the same manner, to the same extent and under the same conditions as a judgment of a court of general jurisdiction in such State, and shall cease to be a lien in the same manner and time. This section does not apply to judgments entered in favor of the United States. Whenever the law of any State requires a judgment of a State court to be registered, recorded, docketed or indexed, or any other act to be done, in a particular manner, or in a certain office or county or parish before such lien attaches, such requirements shall apply only if the law of such State authorizes the judgment of a court of the United States to be registered, recorded, docketed, indexed or otherwise conformed to rules and requirements relating to judgments of the courts of the State.

(June 25, 1948, c. 646, 62 Stat. 958; Nov. 29, 1990, Pub.L. 101–647, Title XXXVI, § 3627, 104 Stat. 4965.)

HISTORICAL AND STATUTORY NOTES

Effective and Applicability Provisions

1990 Acts

Amendment by section 3627 of Pub.L. 101–647 effective 180 days after Nov. 29, 1990, see section 3631 of Pub.L. 101–647, set out as a note under section 3001 of this title.

§ 1963.　Registration of judgments for enforcement in other districts

A judgment in an action for the recovery of money or property entered in any court of appeals, district court, bankruptcy court, or in the Court of International Trade may be registered by filing a certified copy of the judgment in any other district or, with respect to the Court of International Trade, in any judicial district, when the judgment has become final by appeal or expiration of the time for appeal or when ordered by the court that entered the judgment for good cause shown. Such a judgment entered in favor of the United States may be so registered any time after judgment is entered. A judgment so registered shall have the same effect as a judgment of the district court of the district where registered and may be enforced in like manner.

A certified copy of the satisfaction of any judgment in whole or in part may be registered in like manner in any district in which the judgment is a lien.

The procedure prescribed under this section is in addition to other procedures provided by law for the enforcement of judgments.

(June 25, 1948, c. 646, 62 Stat. 958; Aug. 23, 1954, c. 837, 68 Stat. 772; July 7, 1958, Pub.L. 85–508, § 12(o), 72 Stat. 349; Nov. 19, 1988, Pub.L. 100–702, Title X, § 1002(a), (b)(1), 102 Stat. 4664; Nov. 29, 1990, Pub.L. 101–647, Title XXXVI, § 3628, 104 Stat. 4965; Oct. 19, 1996, Pub.L. 104–317, Title II, § 203(a), 110 Stat. 3849.)

HISTORICAL AND STATUTORY NOTES

Effective and Applicability Provisions

1990 Acts

Amendment by section 3628 of Pub.L. 101–647 effective 180 days after Nov. 29, 1990, see section 3631 of Pub.L. 101–647, set out as a note under section 3001 of this title.

1988 Acts

Section 1002(c) of Title X of Pub.L. 100–702 provided that: "The amendments made by this section [amending this section and repealing section 1963A of this title] take effect 90 days after the date of enactment of this title [Nov. 19, 1988]."

1958 Acts

Amendment by Pub.L. 85–508 as effective Jan. 3, 1959, upon admission of Alaska into the Union pursuant to Proc. No. 3269, Jan. 3, 1959, 24 F.R. 81, as required by sections 1 and 8(c) of Pub.L. 85–508, see notes set out under section 81A of this title and preceding section 21 of Title 48, Territories and Insular Possessions.

[§ 1963A.　Repealed. Pub.L. 100–702, Title X, § 1002(b)(2), Nov. 19, 1988, 102 Stat. 4664]

HISTORICAL AND STATUTORY NOTES

Section, added Pub.L. 96–417, Title V, § 511(a), Oct. 10, 1980, 94 Stat. 1743, provided for registration of judgments of the Court of International Trade. See section 1963 of this title.

Section repealed 90 days after Nov. 19, 1988, see section 1002(c) of Pub.L. 100–702, set out as a note under section 1963 of this title.

§ 1964. Constructive notice of pending actions

Where the law of a State requires a notice of an action concerning real property pending in a court of the State to be registered, recorded, docketed, or indexed in a particular manner, or in a certain office or county or parish in order to give constructive notice of the action as it relates to the real property, and such law authorizes a notice of an action concerning real property pending in a United States district court to be registered, recorded, docketed, or indexed in the same manner, or in the same place, those requirements of the State law must be complied with in order to give constructive notice of such an action pending in a United States district court as it relates to real property in such State.

(Added Pub.L. 85–689, § 1(a), Aug. 20, 1958, 72 Stat. 683.)

HISTORICAL AND STATUTORY NOTES
Effective and Applicability Provisions

1958 Acts

Section 2 of Pub.L. 85–689 provided that: "The amendments made by this Act [adding this section] shall only be effective with respect to actions commenced in United States district courts more than one hundred and eighty days after the date of enactment of this Act [Aug. 20, 1958]."

CHAPTER 127—EXECUTIONS AND JUDICIAL SALES

Sec.
2001. Sale of realty generally.
2002. Notice of sale of realty.
2003. Marshal's incapacity after levy on or sale of realty.
2004. Sale of personalty generally.
2005. Appraisal of goods taken on execution.
2006. Execution against revenue officer.
2007. Imprisonment for debt.

§ 2001. Sale of realty generally

(a) Any realty or interest therein sold under any order or decree of any court of the United States shall be sold as a whole or in separate parcels at public sale at the courthouse of the county, parish, or city in which the greater part of the property is located, or upon the premises or some parcel thereof located therein, as the court directs. Such sale shall be upon such terms and conditions as the court directs.

Property in the possession of a receiver or receivers appointed by one or more district courts shall be sold at public sale in the district wherein any such receiver was first appointed, at the courthouse of the county, parish, or city situated therein in which the greater part of the property in such district is located, or on the premises or some parcel thereof located in such county, parish, or city, as such court directs, unless the court orders the sale of the property or one or more parcels thereof in one or more ancillary districts.

(b) After a hearing, of which notice to all interested parties shall be given by publication or otherwise as the court directs, the court may order the sale of such realty or interest or any part thereof at private sale for cash or other consideration and upon such terms and conditions as the court approves, if it finds that the best interests of the estate will be conserved thereby. Before confirmation of any private sale, the court shall appoint three disinterested persons to appraise such property or different groups of three appraisers each to appraise properties of different classes or situated in different localities. No private sale shall be confirmed at a price less than two-thirds of the appraised value. Before confirmation of any private sale, the terms thereof shall be published in such newspaper or newspapers of general circulation as the court directs at least ten days before confirmation. The private sale shall not be confirmed if a bona fide offer is made, under conditions prescribed by the court, which guarantees at least a 10 per centum increase over the price offered in the private sale.

(c) This section shall not apply to sales and proceedings under Title 11 or by receivers or conservators of banks appointed by the Comptroller of the Currency.

(June 25, 1948, c. 646, 62 Stat. 958; May 24, 1949, c. 139, § 99, 63 Stat. 104.)

§ 2002. Notice of sale of realty

A public sale of realty or interest therein under any order, judgment or decree of any court of the United States shall not be made without notice published once a week for at least four weeks prior to the sale in at least one newspaper regularly issued and of general circulation in the county, state, or judicial district of the United States wherein the realty is situated.

If such realty is situated in more than one county, state, district or circuit, such notice shall be published in one or more of the counties, states, or districts wherein it is situated, as the court directs. The notice shall be substantially in such form and contain such description of the property by reference or otherwise as the court approves. The court may direct that the publication be made in other newspapers.

This section shall not apply to sales and proceedings under Title 11 or by receivers or conservators of banks appointed by the Comptroller of the Currency.

(June 25, 1948, c. 646, 62 Stat. 959; May 24, 1949, c. 139, § 100, 63 Stat. 104.)

§ 2003.　Marshal's incapacity after levy on or sale of realty

Whenever a United States marshal dies, is removed from office, or the term of his commission expires, after levying on realty or any interest therein under a writ of execution issued by a court of the United States, and before sale or other final disposition thereof, like process shall issue to the succeeding marshal and the same proceedings shall be had as if such contingency had not occurred.

Whenever any such contingency arises after a marshal has sold any realty or interest therein and before a deed is executed, the court may, on application by the purchaser, or the plaintiff in whose action the sale was made, setting forth the facts of the case and the reason why the title was not perfected by such marshal, order the succeeding marshal to perfect the title and execute a deed to the purchaser, upon payment of the purchase money and unpaid costs.

(June 25, 1948, c. 646, 62 Stat. 959; May 24, 1949, c. 139, § 101, 63 Stat. 104.)

§ 2004.　Sale of personalty generally

Any personalty sold under any order or decree of any court of the United States shall be sold in accordance with section 2001 of this title, unless the court orders otherwise.

This section shall not apply to sales and proceedings under Title 11 or by receivers or conservators of banks appointed by the Comptroller of the Currency.

(June 25, 1948, c. 646, 62 Stat. 959.)

§ 2005.　Appraisal of goods taken on execution

Whenever State law requires that goods taken on execution be appraised before sale, goods taken under execution issued from a court of the United States shall be appraised in like manner.

The United States marshal shall summon the appraisers in the same manner as the sheriff is required to summon appraisers under State law.

If the appraisers fail to attend and perform their required duties, the marshal may sell the goods without an appraisal. Appraisers attending and performing their duties, shall receive the fees allowed for appraisals under State law.

(June 25, 1948, c. 646, 62 Stat. 959.)

§ 2006.　Execution against revenue officer

Execution shall not issue against a collector or other revenue officer on a final judgment in any proceeding against him for any of his acts, or for the recovery of any money exacted by or paid to him and subsequent-

ly paid into the Treasury, in performing his official duties, if the court certifies that:

(1) probable cause existed; or

(2) the officer acted under the directions of the Secretary of the Treasury, the Director, Bureau of Alcohol, Tobacco, Firearms, and Explosives, Department of Justice, or other proper Government officer.

When such certificate has been issued, the amount of the judgment shall be paid out of the proper appropriation by the Treasury.

(June 25, 1948, c. 646, 62 Stat. 960; Nov. 25, 2002, Pub.L. 107–296, Title XI, § 1112(*l*), 116 Stat. 2277.)

HISTORICAL AND STATUTORY NOTES

Effective and Applicability Provisions

2002 Acts

Amendment to this section by Pub.L. 107–296 effective 60 days after Nov. 25, 2002, see Pub.L. 107–296, § 4, set out as a note under 6 U.S.C.A. § 101.

§ 2007.　Imprisonment for debt

(a) A person shall not be imprisoned for debt on a writ of execution or other process issued from a court of the United States in any State wherein imprisonment for debt has been abolished. All modifications, conditions, and restrictions upon such imprisonment provided by State law shall apply to any writ of execution or process issued from a court of the United States in accordance with the procedure applicable in such State.

(b) Any person arrested or imprisoned in any State on a writ of execution or other process issued from any court of the United States in a civil action shall have the same jail privileges and be governed by the same regulations as persons confined in like cases on process issued from the courts of such State. The same requirements governing discharge as are applicable in such State shall apply. Any proceedings for discharge shall be conducted before a United States magistrate judge for the judicial district wherein the defendant is held.

(June 25, 1948, c. 646, 62 Stat. 960; Oct. 17, 1968, Pub.L. 90–578, Title IV, § 402(b)(2), 82 Stat. 1118; Dec. 1, 1990, Pub.L. 101–650, Title III, § 321, 104 Stat. 5117.)

HISTORICAL AND STATUTORY NOTES

Change of Name

"United States magistrate judge" substituted for "United States magistrate" in text pursuant to section 321 of Pub.L. 101–650, set out as a note under 28 U.S.C.A. § 631. Previously, United States commissioners, referred to in text, were replaced by United States magistrates pursuant to Pub.L. 90–578, Oct. 17, 1968, 82 Stat. 1118. See chapter 43 of Title 28, 28 U.S.C.A. § 631 et seq.

CHAPTER 129—MONEYS PAID INTO COURT

§ 2041. Deposit of moneys in pending or adjudicated cases

All moneys paid into any court of the United States, or received by the officers thereof, in any case pending or adjudicated in such court, shall be forthwith deposited with the Treasurer of the United States or a designated depositary, in the name and to the credit of such court.

This section shall not prevent the delivery of any such money to the rightful owners upon security, according to agreement of parties, under the direction of the court.

(June 25, 1948, c. 646, 62 Stat. 960; Sept. 13, 1982, Pub.L. 97–258, § 2(g) (4) (C), 96 Stat. 1061.)

HISTORICAL AND STATUTORY NOTES

Registry Administration Account

Pub.L. 100–459, Title IV, Oct. 1, 1988, 102 Stat. 2211, provided in part: "That any funds hereafter collected by the Judiciary as a charge for services rendered in administering accounts kept in a court's registry shall be deposited into a separate account entitled 'Registry Administration Account' in the Treasury of the United States. Such funds shall remain available to the Judiciary until expended to reimburse any appropriation for the amount paid out of such appropriation for expenses of the Courts of Appeals, District Courts and Other Judicial Services and the Administrative Office of the United States Courts."

§ 2042. Withdrawal

No money deposited under section 2041 of this title shall be withdrawn except by order of court.

In every case in which the right to withdraw money deposited in court under section 2041 has been adjudicated or is not in dispute and such money has remained so deposited for at least five years unclaimed by the person entitled thereto, such court shall cause such money to be deposited in the Treasury in the name and to the credit of the United States. Any claimant entitled to any such money may, on petition to the court and upon notice to the United States attorney and full proof of the right thereto, obtain an order directing payment to him.

(June 25, 1948, c. 646, 62 Stat. 960; Sept. 13, 1982, Pub.L. 97–258, § 2(g) (4) (D), 96 Stat. 1061.)

§ 2043. Deposit of other moneys

Except for public moneys deposited under section 2041 of this title, each clerk of the United States courts shall deposit public moneys that the clerk collects into a checking account in the Treasury, subject to disbursement by the clerk. At the end of each accounting period, the earned part of public moneys accruing to the United States shall be deposited in the Treasury to the credit of the appropriate receipt accounts.

(Added Pub.L. 97–258, § 2(g) (4) (E), Sept. 13, 1982, 96 Stat. 1061.)

§ 2044. Payment of fine with bond money

On motion of the United States attorney, the court shall order any money belonging to and deposited by or on behalf of the defendant with the court for the purposes of a criminal appearance bail bond (trial or appeal) to be held and paid over to the United States attorney to be applied to the payment of any assessment, fine, restitution, or penalty imposed upon the defendant. The court shall not release any money deposited for bond purposes after a plea or a verdict of the defendant's guilt has been entered and before sentencing except upon a showing that an assessment, fine, restitution or penalty cannot be imposed for the offense the defendant committed or that the defendant would suffer an undue hardship. This section shall not apply to any third party surety.

(Added Pub.L. 101–647, Title XXXVI, § 3629(a), Nov. 29, 1990, 104 Stat. 4966.)

HISTORICAL AND STATUTORY NOTES

Effective and Applicability Provisions

1990 Acts

Section to take effect 180 days after Nov. 29, 1990, see section 3631 of Pub.L. 101–647, set out as a note under section 3001 of this title.

CHAPTER 131—RULES OF COURTS

§ 2071. Rule-making power generally

(a) The Supreme Court and all courts established by Act of Congress may from time to time prescribe

rules for the conduct of their business. Such rules shall be consistent with Acts of Congress and rules of practice and procedure prescribed under section 2072 of this title.

(b) Any rule prescribed by a court, other than the Supreme Court, under subsection (a) shall be prescribed only after giving appropriate public notice and an opportunity for comment. Such rule shall take effect upon the date specified by the prescribing court and shall have such effect on pending proceedings as the prescribing court may order.

(c)(1) A rule of a district court prescribed under subsection (a) shall remain in effect unless modified or abrogated by the judicial council of the relevant circuit.

(2) Any other rule prescribed by a court other than the Supreme Court under subsection (a) shall remain in effect unless modified or abrogated by the Judicial Conference.

(d) Copies of rules prescribed under subsection (a) by a district court shall be furnished to the judicial council, and copies of all rules prescribed by a court other than the Supreme Court under subsection (a) shall be furnished to the Director of the Administrative Office of the United States Courts and made available to the public.

(e) If the prescribing court determines that there is an immediate need for a rule, such court may proceed under this section without public notice and opportunity for comment, but such court shall promptly thereafter afford such notice and opportunity for comment.

(f) No rule may be prescribed by a district court other than under this section.

(June 25, 1948, c. 646, 62 Stat. 961; May 24, 1949, c. 139, § 102, 63 Stat. 104; Nov. 19, 1988, Pub.L. 100–702, Title IV, § 403(a)(1), 102 Stat. 4650.)

HISTORICAL AND STATUTORY NOTES

Senate Revision Amendment

By Senate amendment, all provisions relating to the Tax Court were eliminated. Therefore, section 1111 of Title 26, U.S.C., Internal Revenue Code, was not one of the sources of this section as finally enacted. However, no change in the text of this section was necessary. See 80th Congress Senate Report No. 1559.

1949 Acts

This amendment clarifies section 2071 of Title 28, U.S.C., by giving express recognition to the power of the Supreme Court to prescribe its own rules and by giving a better description of its procedural rules.

1988 Acts

House Report No. 100–889, see 1988 U.S. Code Cong. and Adm. News, p. 5982.

Effective and Applicability Provisions

1988 Acts

Section 407 of Title IV of Pub.L. 100–702 provided that: "This title [enacting sections 332(d)(4), 604(a)(19) [redesignated (a)(20)], 2071(b)–(f), and 2072–2074 of this title; amending sections 331, 332(d)(1), 372(c)(11), 636(d), 2071(a) [formerly designated 2071], and 2077(b) of this title and sections 460n–8 of Title 16, Conservation and 3402 of Title 18, Crimes and Criminal Procedure; redesignating as 604(a)(23) former section 604(a)(18) of this title; repealing former section 2072 and section 2076 of this title and sections 3771 and 3772 of Title 18; and enacting provisions set out as notes under this section] shall take effect on December 1, 1988."

1983 Acts

Pub.L. 97–462, § 4, Jan. 12, 1983, 96 Stat. 2530, provided: "The amendments made by this Act [which amended Rule 4 of the Federal Rules of Civil Procedure, added Form 18–A, Appendix of Forms, enacted provisions set out as notes under this section, and amended section 951 of Title 18, Crimes and Criminal Procedure] shall take effect 45 days after the enactment of this Act [Jan. 12, 1983]."

Savings Provisions

Section 406 of Title IV of Pub.L. 100–702 provided that: "The rules prescribed in accordance with law before the effective date of this title [Dec. 1, 1988] and in effect on the date of such effective date [Dec. 1, 1988] shall remain in force until changed pursuant to the law as amended by this title [see Effective and Applicability Provisions of 1988 Amendments note under this section]."

Short Title

1983 Acts

Pub.L. 97–462, § 1, Jan. 12, 1983, 96 Stat. 2527, provided: "That this Act [which amended Rule 4 of the Federal Rules of Civil Procedure, enacted Form 18–A, Appendix of Forms, enacted provisions set out as notes under this section, and amended section 951 of Title 18, Crimes and Criminal Procedure] may be cited as the 'Federal Rules of Civil Procedure Amendments Act of 1982'."

Rulemaking Authority of Supreme Court and Judicial Conference

Pub.L. 109–2, § 8, Feb. 18, 2005, 119 Stat. 14, provided that: "Nothing in this Act [the Class Action Fairness Act of 2005, which enacted this note and 28 U.S.C.A. §§ 1453 and 1711 to 1715, amended 28 U.S.C.A. §§ 1332, 1335, and 1603, and enacted provisions set out as notes under 28 U.S.C.A. §§ 1332, 1711, and 2074] shall restrict in any way the authority of the Judicial Conference and the Supreme Court to propose and prescribe general rules of practice and procedure under chapter 131 of title 28, United States Code [this chapter]."

[Enactment of this note by Class Action Fairness Act of 2005, Pub.L. 109–2, Feb. 18, 2005, 119 Stat. 4, applicable to any civil action commenced on or after Feb. 18, 2005, see Pub.L. 109–2, § 9, set out as a note under 28 U.S.C.A. § 1332.]

Admiralty Rules

The Rules of Practice in Admiralty and Maritime Cases, promulgated by the Supreme Court on Dec. 20, 1920, effective Mar. 7, 1921, as revised, amended, and supplemented, were rescinded, effective July 1, 1966, in accordance with the general unification of civil and admiralty procedure which became effective July 1, 1966. Provision for certain distinc-

tively maritime remedies were preserved however in the Supplemental Rules for Certain Admiralty and Maritime Claims, Rules A to F, Federal Rules of Civil Procedure.

Tax Court Rulemaking Not Affected

Section 405 of Title IV of Pub.L. 100–702 provided that: "The amendments made by this title [see Effective and Applicability Provisions of 1988 Amendments note set out under this section] shall not affect the authority of the Tax Court to prescribe rules under section 7453 of the Internal Revenue Code of 1986 [section 7453 of Title 26, Internal Revenue Code]."

§ 2072. Rules of procedure and evidence; power to prescribe

(a) The Supreme Court shall have the power to prescribe general rules of practice and procedure and rules of evidence for cases in the United States district courts (including proceedings before magistrate judges thereof) and courts of appeals.

(b) Such rules shall not abridge, enlarge or modify any substantive right. All laws in conflict with such rules shall be of no further force or effect after such rules have taken effect.

(c) Such rules may define when a ruling of a district court is final for the purposes of appeal under section 1291 of this title.

(Added Pub.L. 100–702, Title IV, § 401(a), Nov. 19, 1988, 102 Stat. 4648, and amended Pub.L. 101–650, Title III, §§ 315, 321, Dec. 1, 1990, 104 Stat. 5115, 5117.)

HISTORICAL AND STATUTORY NOTES

Effective and Applicability Provisions

1988 Acts

Section effective Dec. 1, 1988, see section 407 of Pub.L. 100–702, set out as a note under section 2071 of this title.

Change of Name

"United States magistrate judge" substituted for "United States magistrate" in text pursuant to section 321 of Pub.L. 101–650, set out as a note under 28 U.S.C.A. § 631.

Prior Provisions

A prior section 2072, Acts June 25, 1948, c. 646, 62 Stat. 961; May 24, 1949, c. 139, § 103, 63 Stat. 104; July 18, 1949, c. 343, § 2, 63 Stat. 446; May 10, 1950, c. 174, § 2, 64 Stat. 158; July 7, 1958, Pub.L. 85–508, § 12(m), 72 Stat. 348; Nov. 6, 1966, Pub.L. 89–773, § 1, 80 Stat. 1323, which authorized the Supreme Court to prescribe rules of civil procedure, was repealed by Pub.L. 100–702, Title IV, §§ 401(a), 407, Nov. 19, 1988, 102 Stat. 4648, 4652, effective Dec. 1, 1988.

Admiralty Rules

The Rules of Practice in Admiralty and Maritime Cases, promulgated by the Supreme Court on Dec. 20, 1920, effective Mar. 7, 1921, as revised, amended, and supplemented, were rescinded, effective July 1, 1966, in accordance with the general unification of civil and admiralty procedure which became effective July 1, 1966. Provision for certain distinctively maritime remedies were preserved however, in the Supplemental Rules for Certain Admiralty and Maritime

Claims, Rules A to F, Federal Rules of Civil Procedure, this title.

Applicability to Virgin Islands

Rules of civil procedure promulgated under this section as applicable to the District Court of the Virgin Islands, see section 1614 of Title 48, Territories and Insular Possessions.

§ 2073. Rules of procedure and evidence; method of prescribing

(a)(1) The Judicial Conference shall prescribe and publish the procedures for the consideration of proposed rules under this section.

(2) The Judicial Conference may authorize the appointment of committees to assist the Conference by recommending rules to be prescribed under sections 2072 and 2075 of this title. Each such committee shall consist of members of the bench and the professional bar, and trial and appellate judges.

(b) The Judicial Conference shall authorize the appointment of a standing committee on rules of practice, procedure, and evidence under subsection (a) of this section. Such standing committee shall review each recommendation of any other committees so appointed and recommend to the Judicial Conference rules of practice, procedure, and evidence and such changes in rules proposed by a committee appointed under subsection (a)(2) of this section as may be necessary to maintain consistency and otherwise promote the interest of justice.

(c)(1) Each meeting for the transaction of business under this chapter by any committee appointed under this section shall be open to the public, except when the committee so meeting, in open session and with a majority present, determines that it is in the public interest that all or part of the remainder of the meeting on that day shall be closed to the public, and states the reason for so closing the meeting. Minutes of each meeting for the transaction of business under this chapter shall be maintained by the committee and made available to the public, except that any portion of such minutes, relating to a closed meeting and made available to the public, may contain such deletions as may be necessary to avoid frustrating the purposes of closing the meeting.

(2) Any meeting for the transaction of business under this chapter, by a committee appointed under this section, shall be preceded by sufficient notice to enable all interested persons to attend.

(d) In making a recommendation under this section or under section 2072 or 2075, the body making that recommendation shall provide a proposed rule, an explanatory note on the rule, and a written report explaining the body's action, including any minority or other separate views.

(e) Failure to comply with this section does not invalidate a rule prescribed under section 2072 or 2075 of this title.

(Added Pub.L. 100–702, Title IV, § 401(a), Nov. 19, 1988, 102 Stat. 4649, and amended Pub.L. 103–394, Title I, § 104(e), Oct. 22, 1994, 108 Stat. 4110.)

HISTORICAL AND STATUTORY NOTES

Effective and Applicability Provisions

1994 Acts

Amendment by Pub.L. 103–394 effective on Oct. 22, 1994, and not to apply with respect to cases commenced under Title 11 of the United States Code before Oct. 22, 1994, see section 702 of Pub.L. 103–394, set out as a note under section 101 of Title 11, Bankruptcy.

1988 Acts

Section effective Dec. 1, 1988, see section 407 of Pub.L. 100–702, set out as a note under section 2071 of this title.

Separability of Provisions

If any provision of or amendment made by Pub.L. 103–394 or the application of such provision or amendment to any person or circumstance is held to be unconstitutional, the remaining provisions of and amendments made by Pub.L. 103–394 and the application of such provisions and amendments to any person or circumstance shall not be affected thereby, see section 701 of Pub.L. 103–394, set out as a note under section 101 of Title 11, Bankruptcy.

Prior Provisions

A prior section 2073, Acts June 25, 1948, c. 646, 62 Stat. 961; May 24, 1949, c. 139, § 104, 63 Stat. 104; May 10, 1950, c. 174, § 3, 64 Stat. 158, which empowered the Supreme Court to prescribe, by general rules, the practice and procedure in admiralty and maritime cases in the district courts, was repealed by Pub.L. 89–773, § 2, Nov. 6, 1966, 80 Stat. 1323, which provided in part that the repeal of section 2073 should not operate to invalidate or repeal rules adopted under the authority of such section prior to the enactment of Pub.L. 89–773, which rules should remain in effect until superseded by rules prescribed under the authority of former section 2072 of this title as amended by Pub.L. 89–773. See sections 2071 to 2074 of this title.

More Complete Information Regarding Assets of the Estate

Pub.L. 109–8, Title IV, § 419, Apr. 20, 2005, 119 Stat. 109, provided that:

"**(a) In general.—**

"**(1) Disclosure.**—The Judicial Conference of the United States, in accordance with section 2075 of title 28 of the United States Code and after consideration of the views of the Director of the Executive Office for United States Trustees, shall propose amended Federal Rules of Bankruptcy Procedure and in accordance with rule 9009 of the Federal Rules of Bankruptcy Procedure [set out in Title 11] shall prescribe official bankruptcy forms directing debtors under chapter 11 of title 11 of United States Code [11 U.S.C.A. § 1101 et seq.], to disclose the information described in paragraph (2) by filing and serving periodic financial and other reports designed to provide such information.

"**(2) Information.**—The information referred to in paragraph (1) is the value, operations, and profitability of any closely held corporation, partnership, or of any other entity in which the debtor holds a substantial or controlling interest.

"**(b) Purpose.**—The purpose of the rules and reports under subsection (a) [of this note] shall be to assist parties in interest taking steps to ensure that the debtor's interest in any entity referred to in subsection (a)(2) [of this note] is used for the payment of allowed claims against debtor."

[Except as otherwise provided, amendments by Pub.L. 109–8 effective 180 days after April 20, 2005, and inapplicable with respect to cases commenced under Title 11 before the effective date, see Pub.L. 109–8, § 1501, set out as a note under 11 U.S.C.A. § 101.]

Standard Form Disclosure Statement and Plan

Pub.L. 109–8, Title IV, § 433, Apr. 20, 2005, 119 Stat. 110, provided that: "Within a reasonable period of time after the date of enactment of this Act [Apr. 20,. 2005], the Judicial Conference of the United States shall prescribe in accordance with rule 9009 of the Federal Rules of Bankruptcy Procedure [set out in Title 11] official standard form disclosure statements and plans of reorganization for small business debtors (as defined in section 101 of title 11, United States Code, as amended by this Act), designed to achieve a practical balance between—

"**(1)** the reasonable needs of the courts, the United States trustee, creditors, and other parties in interest for reasonably complete information; and

"**(2)** economy and simplicity for debtors."

[Except as otherwise provided, amendments by Pub.L. 109–8 effective 180 days after April 20, 2005, and inapplicable with respect to cases commenced under Title 11 before the effective date, see Pub.L. 109–8, § 1501, set out as a note under 11 U.S.C.A. § 101.]

Uniform Reporting Rules and Forms for Small Business Cases

Pub.L. 109–8, Title IV, § 435, Apr. 20, 2005, 119 Stat. 111, provided that:

"**(a) Proposal of rules and forms.**—The Judicial Conference of the United States shall propose in accordance with section 2073 of title 28 of the United States Code [this section] amended Federal Rules of Bankruptcy Procedure, and shall prescribe in accordance with rule 9009 of the Federal Rules of Bankruptcy Procedure [set out in Title 11] official bankruptcy forms, directing small business debtors to file periodic financial and other reports containing information, including information relating to—

"**(1)** the debtor's profitability;

"**(2)** the debtor's cash receipts and disbursements; and

"**(3)** whether the debtor is timely filing tax returns and paying taxes and other administrative expenses when due.

"**(b) Purpose.**—The rules and forms proposed under subsection (a) [of this note] shall be designed to achieve a practical balance among—

"**(1)** the reasonable needs of the bankruptcy court, the United States trustee, creditors, and other parties in interest for reasonably complete information;

"**(2)** a small business debtor's interest that required reports be easy and inexpensive to complete; and

"**(3)** the interest of all parties that the required reports help such debtor to understand such debtor's financial condition and plan the such debtor's future."

[Except as otherwise provided, amendments by Pub.L. 109–8 effective 180 days after April 20, 2005, and inapplicable with respect to cases commenced under Title 11 before the effective date, see Pub.L. 109–8, § 1501, set out as a note under 11 U.S.C.A. § 101.]

§ 2074. Rules of procedure and evidence; submission to Congress; effective date

(a) The Supreme Court shall transmit to the Congress not later than May 1 of the year in which a rule prescribed under section 2072 is to become effective a copy of the proposed rule. Such rule shall take effect no earlier than December 1 of the year in which such rule is so transmitted unless otherwise provided by law. The Supreme Court may fix the extent such rule shall apply to proceedings then pending, except that the Supreme Court shall not require the application of such rule to further proceedings then pending to the extent that, in the opinion of the court in which such proceedings are pending, the application of such rule in such proceedings would not be feasible or would work injustice, in which event the former rule applies.

(b) Any such rule creating, abolishing, or modifying an evidentiary privilege shall have no force or effect unless approved by Act of Congress.

(Added Pub.L. 100–702, Title IV, § 401(a), Nov. 19, 1988, 102 Stat. 4649.)

HISTORICAL AND STATUTORY NOTES

Effective and Applicability Provisions

1988 Acts

Section effective Dec. 1, 1988, see section 407 of Pub.L. 100–702, set out as a note under section 2071 of this title.

Prior Provisions

A prior section 2074, Act July 27, 1954, c. 583, § 1, 68 Stat. 567, which empowered the Supreme Court to prescribe rules for review of decisions of the Tax Court of the United States, was repealed by Pub.L. 89–773, § 2, Nov. 6, 1966, 80 Stat. 1323, which provided in part that the repeal of section 2074 of this title should not operate to invalidate or repeal rules adopted under the authority of such section prior to the enactment of Pub.L. 89–773, which rules should remain in effect until superseded by rules prescribed under the authority of former section 2072 of this title as amended by Pub.L. 89–773. See sections 2071 to 2074 of this title.

Amendments to Civil Rules Proposed March 27, 2003

Pub.L. 109–2, § 7, Feb. 18, 2005, 119 Stat. 13, provided that: "Notwithstanding any other provision of law, the amendments to rule 23 of the Federal Rules of Civil Procedure, which are set forth in the order entered by the Supreme Court of the United States on March 27, 2003, shall take effect on the date of enactment of this Act [Feb. 18, 2005] or on December 1, 2003 (as specified in that order), whichever occurs first."

[Enactment of this note by Class Action Fairness Act of 2005, Pub.L. 109–2, Feb. 18, 2005, 119 Stat. 4, applicable to any civil action commenced on or after Feb. 18, 2005, see Pub.L. 109–2, § 9, set out as a note under 28 U.S.C.A. § 1332.]

Amendments to Criminal Rules Proposed April 29, 2002

Pub.L. 107–273, Div. C, Title I, § 11019(a), Nov. 2, 2002, 116 Stat. 1825, provided that: "The proposed amendments to the Federal Rules of Criminal Procedure that are embraced by an order entered by the Supreme Court of the United States on April 29, 2002, shall take effect on December 1, 2002, as otherwise provided by law, but with the amendments made in subsection (b) [amending Rule 16 of the Federal Rules of Criminal Procedure]."

Amendments to Criminal Rules Proposed April 29, 1994

Pub.L. 103–322, Title XXIII, § 230101, Sept. 13, 1994, 108 Stat. 2077, provided that:

"**(a) Modification of proposed amendments.**—The proposed amendments to the Federal Rules of Criminal Procedure which are embraced by an order entered by the Supreme Court of the United States on April 29, 1994, shall take effect on December 1, 1994, as otherwise provided by law, but with the following amendments:

"**(b) In general.**—Rule 32 of the Federal Rules of Criminal Procedure is amended by—

"**(1)** striking 'and' following the semicolon in subdivision (c)(3)(C);

"**(2)** striking the period at the end of subdivision (c)(3)(D) and inserting '; and';

"**(3)** inserting after subdivision (c)(3)(D) the following:

" '**(E)** if sentence is to be imposed for a crime of violence or sexual abuse, address the victim personally if the victim is present at the sentencing hearing and determine if the victim wishes to make a statement or present any information in relation to the sentence.';

"**(4)** in subdivision (c)(3)(D), striking 'equivalent opportunity' and inserting in lieu thereof 'opportunity equivalent to that of the defendant's counsel';

"**(5)** in the last sentence of subdivision (c)(4), striking 'and (D)' and inserting '(D), and (E)';

"**(6)** in the last sentence of subdivision (c)(4), inserting 'the victim,' before 'or the attorney for the Government.'; and

"**(7)** adding at the end the following:

" '**(f) Definitions.**—For purposes of this rule—

" '**(1)** "victim" means any individual against whom an offense has been committed for which a sentence is to be imposed, but the right of allocution under subdivision (c)(3)(E) may be exercised instead by—

" '**(A)** a parent or legal guardian if the victim is below the age of eighteen years or incompetent; or

" '**(B)** one or more family members or relatives designated by the court if the victim is deceased or incapacitated;

if such person or persons are present at the sentencing hearing, regardless of whether the victim is present; and

" '**(2)** "crime of violence or sexual abuse" means a crime that involved the use or attempted or threatened use of physical force against the person or property of another,

or a crime under chapter 109A of title 18, United States Code.'

"(c) Effective date.—The amendments made by subsection (b) [amending Rule 32 of the Federal Rules of Criminal Procedure] shall become effective on December 1, 1994."

Amendments to Civil Rules Proposed April 30, 1991

Pub.L. 102–198, § 11, Dec. 9, 1991, 105 Stat. 1626, provided that:

"(a) Technical amendment.—Rule 15(c)(3) of the Federal Rules of Civil Procedure for the United States Courts, as transmitted to the Congress by the Supreme Court pursuant to section 2074 of title 28, United States Code [this section], to become effective on December 1, 1991, is amended by striking 'Rule 4(m)' and inserting 'Rule 4(j)'.

"(b) Amendment to Forms.—Form 1–A, Notice of Lawsuit and Request for Waiver of Service of Summons, and Form 1–B, Waiver of Service of Summons, included in the transmittal by the Supreme Court described in subsection (a), shall not be effective and Form 18–A, Notice and Acknowledgment for Service by Mail, abrogated by the Supreme Court in such transmittal, effective December 1, 1991, shall continue in effect on or after that date."

Amendments to Civil Rules Proposed April 28, 1982

Pub.L. 97–462, § 5, Jan. 12, 1983, 96 Stat. 2530, provided: "The amendments to the Federal Rules of Civil Procedure [Rule 4], the effective date [Aug. 1, 1982] of which was delayed [to Oct. 1, 1983] by the Act [Pub.L. 97–227] entitled 'An Act to delay the effective date of proposed amendments to rule 4 of the Federal Rules of Civil Procedure', [proposed by the Supreme Court of the United States and transmitted to the Congress by the Chief Justice on Apr. 28, 1982], approved August 2, 1982 (96 Stat. 246), shall not take effect."

Pub.L. 97–227, Aug. 2, 1982, 96 Stat. 246, provided: "That notwithstanding the provisions of section 2072 of title 28, United States Code, [section 2072 of this title] the amendments to rule 4 of the Federal Rules of Civil Procedure as proposed by the Supreme Court of the United States and transmitted to the Congress by the Chief Justice on April 28, 1982, shall take effect on October 1, 1983, unless previously approved, disapproved, or modified by Act of Congress.

"Sec. 2. This Act shall be effective as of August 1, 1982, but shall not apply to the service of process that takes place between August 1, 1982, and the date of enactment of this Act [Aug. 2, 1982]."

Amendments to Criminal Rules and Rules of Evidence Proposed April 30, 1979; Postponement of Effective Date

Pub.L. 96–42, July 31, 1979, 93 Stat. 326, provided: "That notwithstanding any provision of section 3771 or 3772 of title 18, United States Code [section 3771 or 3772 of Title 18, Crimes and Criminal Procedure] or of section 2072, 2075, or 2076 of title 28 of the United States Code [sections 2072, 2075 and 2076 of this title] to the contrary—

"(1) the amendments proposed by the United States Supreme Court and transmitted by the Chief Justice on April 30, 1979, to the Federal Rules of Criminal Procedure affecting rules 11(e)(6), 17(h), 32(f), and 44(c), and adding new rules 26.2 and 32.1, and the amendment so proposed and transmitted to the Federal Rules of Evidence affecting rule 410, shall not take effect until December 1, 1980, or until and

then only to the extent approved by Act of Congress, whichever is earlier; and

"(2) the amendment proposed by the United States Supreme Court and transmitted by the Chief Justice on April 30, 1979, affecting rule 40 of the Federal Rules of Criminal Procedure shall take effect on August 1, 1979, with the following amendments:

"(A) In the matter designated as paragraph (1) of subdivision (d), strike out 'in accordance with Rule 32.1(a).'

"(B) In the matter designated as paragraph (2) of subdivision (d), strike out 'in accordance with Rule 32.1(a)(1)'."

Approval and Effective Date of Amendments Proposed November 20, 1972 and December 18, 1972

Pub.L. 93–595, § 3, Jan. 2, 1975, 88 Stat. 1949, provided that: "The Congress expressly approves the amendments to the Federal Rules of Civil Procedure [Rules 30(c), 32(c), 43 and 44.1] and the amendments to the Federal Rules of Criminal Procedure [Rules 26, 26.1 and 28], which are embraced by the orders entered by the Supreme Court of the United States on November 20, 1972, and December 18, 1972, and such amendments shall take effect on the one hundred and eightieth day beginning after the date of the enactment of this Act [Jan. 2, 1975]."

Approval and Effective Date of Rules Governing Section 2254 Cases and Section 2255 Proceedings for United States District Courts

Pub.L. 94–426, § 1, Sept. 28, 1976, 90 Stat. 1334, provided: "That the rules governing section 2254 cases in the United States district courts and the rules governing section 2255 proceedings for the United States district courts, as proposed by the United States Supreme Court, which were delayed by the Act entitled 'An Act to delay the effective date of certain proposed amendments to the Federal Rules of Criminal Procedure and certain other rules promulgated by the United States Supreme Court' (Public Law 94–349), are approved with the amendments set forth in section 2 of this Act and shall take effect as so amended, with respect to petitions under section 2254 and motions under section 2255 of title 28 of the United States Code [sections 2254 and 2255 of this title] filed on or after February 1, 1977."

Amendments to Rules of Evidence Proposed on April 29, 1994

Pub.L. 103–322, Title IV, § 40141, Sept. 13, 1994, 108 Stat. 1918, provided that:

"(a) Modification of proposed amendment.—The proposed amendments to the Federal Rules of Evidence that are embraced by an order entered by the Supreme Court of the United States on April 29, 1994, shall take effect on December 1, 1994, as otherwise provided by law, but with the amendment made by subsection (b).

"(b) Rule.—Rule 412 of the Federal Rules of Evidence is amended to read as follows:

" **'Rule 412. Sex Offense Cases; Relevance of Alleged Victim's Past Sexual Behavior or Alleged Sexual Predisposition**

" **'(a) Evidence generally inadmissible.**—The following evidence is not admissible in any civil or criminal proceeding involving alleged sexual misconduct except as provided in subdivisions (b) and (c):

" '(1) Evidence offered to prove that any alleged victim engaged in her sexual behavior.

" '(2) Evidence offered to prove any alleged victim's sexual predisposition.

" '(b) **Exceptions.—**

" '(1) In a criminal case, the following evidence is admissible, if otherwise admissible under these rules:

" '(A) evidence of specific instances of sexual behavior by the alleged victim offered to prove that a person other than the accused was the source of semen, injury or other physical evidence;

" '(B) evidence of specific instances of sexual behavior by the alleged victim with respect to the person accused of the sexual misconduct offered by the accused to prove consent or by the prosecution; and

" '(C) evidence the exclusion of which would violate the constitutional rights of the defendant.

" '(2) In a civil case, evidence offered to prove the sexual behavior or sexual predisposition of any alleged victim is admissible if it is otherwise admissible under these rules and its probative value substantially outweighs the danger of harm to any victim and of unfair prejudice to any party. Evidence of an alleged victim's reputation is admissible only if it has been placed in controversy by the alleged victim.

" '(c) **Procedure to determine admissibility.—**

" '(1) A party intending to offer evidence under subdivision (b) must—

" '(A) file a written motion at least 14 days before trial specifically describing the evidence and stating the purpose for which it is offered unless the court, for good cause requires a different time for filing or permits filing during trial; and

" '(B) serve the motion on all parties and notify the alleged victim or, when appropriate, the alleged victim's guardian or representative.

" '(2) Before admitting evidence under this rule the court must conduct a hearing in camera and afford the victim and parties a right to attend and be heard. The motion, related papers, and the record of the hearing must be sealed and remain under seal unless the court orders otherwise.

"(c) **Technical amendment.—**The table of contents for the Federal Rules of Evidence is amended by amending the item relating to rule 412 to read as follows:

" '**412. Sex Offense Cases; Relevance of Alleged Victim's Past Sexual Behavior or Alleged Sexual Predisposition:**

" '(a) Evidence generally inadmissible.

" '(b) Exceptions.

" '(c) Procedure to determine admissibility.' "

Congressional Approval Requirement for Proposed Rules of Evidence for United States Courts and Amendments to Federal Rules of Civil Procedure and Criminal Procedure; Suspension of Effectiveness of Such Rules

Pub.L. 93–12, Mar. 30, 1973, 87 Stat. 9, provided: "That notwithstanding any other provisions of law, the Rules of Evidence for United States Courts and Magistrates, the Amendments to the Federal Rules of Civil Procedure, and the Amendments to the Federal Rules of Criminal Procedure, which are embraced by the orders entered by the Supreme Court of the United States on Monday, November 20, 1972, and Monday, December 18, 1972, shall have no force or effect except to the extent, and with such amendments, as they may be expressly approved by Act of Congress."

Postponement of Effective Date of Proposed Rules and Forms Governing Proceedings Under Sections 2254 and 2255 of this Title

Pub.L. 94–349, § 2, July 8, 1976, 90 Stat. 822, provided: "That, notwithstanding the provisions of section 2072 of title 28 of the United States Code [section 2072 of this title], the rules and forms governing section 2254 [section 2254 of this title] cases in the United States district courts and the rules and forms governing section 2255 [section 2255 of this title] proceedings in the United States district courts which are embraced by the order entered by the United States Supreme Court on April 26, 1976, and which were transmitted to the Congress on or about April 26, 1976, shall not take effect until thirty days after the adjournment sine die of the 94th Congress, or until and to the extent approved by Act of Congress, whichever is earlier."

§ 2075. Bankruptcy rules

The Supreme Court shall have the power to prescribe by general rules, the forms of process, writs, pleadings, and motions, and the practice and procedure in cases under title 11.

Such rules shall not abridge, enlarge, or modify any substantive right.

The Supreme Court shall transmit to Congress not later than May 1 of the year in which a rule prescribed under this section is to become effective a copy of the proposed rule. The rule shall take effect no earlier than December 1 of the year in which it is transmitted to Congress unless otherwise provided by law.

The bankruptcy rules promulgated under this section shall prescribe a form for the statement required under section 707(b)(2)(C) of title 11 and may provide general rules on the content of such statement.

(Added Pub.L. 88–623, § 1, Oct. 3, 1964, 78 Stat. 1001, and amended Pub.L. 95–598, Title II, § 247, Nov. 6, 1978, 92 Stat. 2672; Pub.L. 103–394, Title I, § 104(f), Oct. 22, 1994, 108 Stat. 4110; Pub.L. 109–8, Title XII, § 1232, Apr. 20, 2005, 119 Stat. 202.)

HISTORICAL AND STATUTORY NOTES

Effective and Applicability Provisions

2005 Acts

Except as otherwise provided, amendments by Pub.L. 109–8 effective 180 days after April 20, 2005, and inapplicable with respect to cases commenced under Title 11 before the effective date, see Pub.L. 109–8, § 1501, set out as a note under 11 U.S.C.A. § 101.

1994 Acts

Amendment by Pub.L. 103–394 effective on Oct. 22, 1994, and not to apply with respect to cases commenced under Title 11 of the United States Code before Oct. 22, 1994, see

section 702 of Pub.L. 103–394, set out as a note under section 101 of Title 11, Bankruptcy.

1978 Acts

Amendment by Pub.L. 95–598 effective Nov. 6, 1978, see section 402(d) of Pub.L. 95–598, set out as a note preceding section 101 of Title 11, Bankruptcy.

Separability of Provisions

If any provision of or amendment made by Pub.L. 103–394 or the application of such provision or amendment to any person or circumstance is held to be unconstitutional, the remaining provisions of and amendments made by Pub.L. 103–394 and the application of such provisions and amendments to any person or circumstance shall not be affected thereby, see section 701 of Pub.L. 103–394, set out as a note under section 101 of Title 11, Bankruptcy.

Additional Rulemaking Power

Pub.L. 95–598, Title IV, § 410, Nov. 6, 1978, 92 Stat. 2687, provided that: "The Supreme Court may issue such additional rules of procedure, consistent with Acts of Congress, as may be necessary for the orderly transfer of functions and records and the orderly transition to the new bankruptcy court system created by this Act [see Tables for complete classification of Pub.L. 95–598]."

Applicability of Rules to Cases Under Title 11

Pub.L. 95–598, Title IV, § 405(d), Nov. 6, 1978, 92 Stat. 2685, provided that: "The rules prescribed under section 2075 of title 28 of the United States Code and in effect on September 30, 1979, shall apply to cases under title 11, to the extent not inconsistent with the amendments made by this Act, or with this Act [see Tables for complete classification of Pub.L. 95–598], until such rules are repealed or superseded by rules prescribed and effective under such section, as amended by section 248 of this Act."

Rules Promulgated by Supreme Court

Pub.L. 98–353, Title III, § 320, July 10, 1984, 98 Stat. 357, provided that: "The Supreme Court shall prescribe general rules implementing the practice and procedure to be followed under section 707(b) of title 11, United States Code [section 707(b) of Title 11, Bankruptcy]. Section 2075 of title 28, United States Code [this section], shall apply with respect to the general rules prescribed under this section."

[§ 2076. Repealed. Pub.L. 100–702, Title IV, § 401(c), Nov. 19, 1988, 102 Stat. 4650]

HISTORICAL AND STATUTORY NOTES

Section, added Pub.L. 93–595, § 2(a)(1), Jan. 2, 1975, 88 Stat. 1948, and amended Pub.L. 94–149, § 2, Dec. 12, 1975, 89 Stat. 806, related to Federal Rules of Evidence prescribed by the Supreme Court and amendment thereof. See sections 2072 to 2074 of this title.

Effective Date of Repeal

Section repealed effective Dec. 1, 1988, see section 407 of Pub.L. 100–702, set out as a note under section 2071 of this title.

§ 2077. Publication of rules; advisory committees

(a) The rules for the conduct of the business of each court of appeals, including the operating procedures of such court, shall be published. Each court of appeals shall print or cause to be printed necessary copies of the rules. The Judicial Conference shall prescribe the fees for sales of copies under section 1913 of this title, but the Judicial Conference may provide for free distribution of copies to members of the bar of each court and to other interested persons.

(b) Each court, except the Supreme Court, that is authorized to prescribe rules of the conduct of such court's business under section 2071 of this title shall appoint an advisory committee for the study of the rules of practice and internal operating procedures of such court and, in the case of an advisory committee appointed by a court of appeals, of the rules of the judicial council of the circuit. The advisory committee shall make recommendations to the court concerning such rules and procedures. Members of the committee shall serve without compensation, but the Director may pay travel and transportation expenses in accordance with section 5703 of title 5.

(Added Pub.L. 97–164, Title II, § 208(a), Apr. 2, 1982, 96 Stat. 54, and amended Pub.L. 100–702, Title IV, § 401(b), Nov. 19, 1988, 102 Stat. 4650; Pub.L. 101–650, Title IV, § 406, Dec. 1, 1990, 104 Stat. 5124.)

HISTORICAL AND STATUTORY NOTES

Effective and Applicability Provisions

1990 Acts

Amendment by section 406 of Pub.L. 101–650 effective 90 days after Dec. 1, 1990, see section 407 of Pub.L. 101–650, set out as a note under section 332 of this title.

1988 Acts

Amendment by Pub.L. 100–702 effective Dec. 1, 1988, see section 407 of Pub.L. 100–702, set out as a note under section 2071 of this title.

1982 Acts

Section effective Oct. 1, 1982, see section 402 of Pub.L. 97–164, set out as a note under section 171 of this title.

CHAPTER 133—REVIEW—MISCELLANEOUS PROVISIONS

§ 2101. Supreme Court; time for appeal or certiorari; docketing; stay

(a) A direct appeal to the Supreme Court from any decision under section 1253 of this title, holding unconstitutional in whole or in part, any Act of Congress, shall be taken within thirty days after the entry of the interlocutory or final order, judgment or decree. The record shall be made up and the case docketed within sixty days from the time such appeal is taken under rules prescribed by the Supreme Court.

(b) Any other direct appeal to the Supreme Court which is authorized by law, from a decision of a district court in any civil action, suit or proceeding, shall be taken within thirty days from the judgment, order or decree, appealed from, if interlocutory, and within sixty days if final.

(c) Any other appeal or any writ of certiorari intended to bring any judgment or decree in a civil action, suit or proceeding before the Supreme Court for review shall be taken or applied for within ninety days after the entry of such judgment or decree. A justice of the Supreme Court, for good cause shown, may extend the time for applying for a writ of certiorari for a period not exceeding sixty days.

(d) The time for appeal or application for a writ of certiorari to review the judgment of a State court in a criminal case shall be as prescribed by rules of the Supreme Court.

(e) An application to the Supreme Court for a writ of certiorari to review a case before judgment has been rendered in the court of appeals may be made at any time before judgment.

(f) In any case in which the final judgment or decree of any court is subject to review by the Supreme Court on writ of certiorari, the execution and enforcement of such judgment or decree may be stayed for a reasonable time to enable the party aggrieved to obtain a writ of certiorari from the Supreme Court. The stay may be granted by a judge of the court rendering the judgment or decree or by a justice of the Supreme Court, and may be conditioned on the giving of security, approved by such judge or justice, that if the aggrieved party fails to make application for such writ within the period allotted therefor, or fails to obtain an order granting his application, or fails to make his plea good in the Supreme Court, he shall answer for all damages and costs which the other party may sustain by reason of the stay.

(g) The time for application for a writ of certiorari to review a decision of the United States Court of Appeals for the Armed Forces shall be as prescribed by rules of the Supreme Court.

(June 25, 1948, c. 646, 62 Stat. 961; May 24, 1949, c. 139, § 106, 63 Stat. 104; Dec. 6, 1983, Pub.L. 98–209, § 10(b), 97 Stat. 1406; June 27, 1988, Pub.L. 100–352, § 5(b), 102 Stat. 663; Oct. 5, 1994, Pub.L. 103–337, Div. A, Title IX, § 924(d)(1)(C), 108 Stat. 2832.)

HISTORICAL AND STATUTORY NOTES

Effective and Applicability Provisions

1988 Acts

Amendment by section 5(b) of Pub.L. 100–352, which substituted "section 1253" for "sections 1252, 1253 and 2282" in subsec. (a), effective ninety days after June 27, 1988, except that such amendment not to apply to cases pending in the Supreme Court on such effective date or affect the right to review or the manner of reviewing the judgment or decree of a court which was entered before such effective date, see section 7 of Pub.L. 100–352, set out as a note under section 1254 of this title.

1983 Acts

Amendment by Pub.L. 98–209 effective on the first day of the eighth calendar month beginning after Dec. 6, 1983, see section 12(a)(1) of Pub.L. 98–209, set out as a note under section 801 of Title 10, Armed Forces.

§ 2102. Priority of criminal case on appeal from State court

Criminal cases on review from State courts shall have priority, on the docket of the Supreme Court, over all cases except cases to which the United States is a party and such other cases as the court may decide to be of public importance.

(June 25, 1948, c. 646, 62 Stat. 962.)

[§ 2103. Repealed. Pub.L. 100–352, § 5(c), June 27, 1988, 102 Stat. 663]

HISTORICAL AND STATUTORY NOTES

Section, Acts June 25, 1948, c. 646, 62 Stat. 962; Sept. 19, 1962, Pub.L. 87–669, § 1, 76 Stat. 556, provided that appeal from State court or from a United States court of appeals improvidently taken be regarded as petition for writ of certiorari.

Effective Date of Repeal

Repeal of section effective ninety days after June 27, 1988, except that such repeal not to apply to cases pending in the Supreme Court on such effective date or affect the right to review or the manner of reviewing the judgment or decree of a court which was entered before such effective date, see section 7 of Pub.L. 100–352, set out as a note under section 1254 of this title.

§ 2104. Reviews of State court decisions

A review by the Supreme Court of a judgment or decree of a State court shall be conducted in the same manner and under the same regulations, and shall have the same effect, as if the judgment or decree reviewed had been rendered in a court of the United States.

(June 25, 1948, c. 646, 62 Stat. 962; June 27, 1988, Pub.L. 100–352, § 5(d)(1), 102 Stat. 663.)

HISTORICAL AND STATUTORY NOTES
Effective and Applicability Provisions
1988 Acts

Amendment by section 5(d)(1) of Pub.L. 100–352 effective ninety days after June 27, 1988, except that such amendment not to apply to cases pending in the Supreme Court on such effective date or affect the right to review or the manner of reviewing the judgment or decree of a court which was entered before such effective date, see section 7 of Pub.L. 100–352, set out as a note under section 1254 of this title.

§ 2105. Scope of review; abatement

There shall be no reversal in the Supreme Court or a court of appeals for error in ruling upon matters in abatement which do not involve jurisdiction.

(June 25, 1948, c. 646, 62 Stat. 963.)

§ 2106. Determination

The Supreme Court or any other court of appellate jurisdiction may affirm, modify, vacate, set aside or reverse any judgment, decree, or order of a court lawfully brought before it for review, and may remand the cause and direct the entry of such appropriate judgment, decree, or order, or require such further proceedings to be had as may be just under the circumstances.

(June 25, 1948, c. 646, 62 Stat. 963.)

§ 2107. Time for appeal to court of appeals

(a) Except as otherwise provided in this section, no appeal shall bring any judgment, order or decree in an action, suit or proceeding of a civil nature before a court of appeals for review unless notice of appeal is filed, within thirty days after the entry of such judgment, order or decree.

(b) In any such action, suit or proceeding in which the United States or an officer or agency thereof is a party, the time as to all parties shall be sixty days from such entry.

(c) The district court may, upon motion filed not later than 30 days after the expiration of the time otherwise set for bringing appeal, extend the time for appeal upon a showing of excusable neglect or good cause. In addition, if the district court finds—

(1) that a party entitled to notice of the entry of a judgment or order did not receive such notice from the clerk or any party within 21 days of its entry, and

(2) that no party would be prejudiced,

the district court may, upon motion filed within 180 days after entry of the judgment or order or within 7 days after receipt of such notice, whichever is earlier, reopen the time for appeal for a period of 14 days from the date of entry of the order reopening the time for appeal.

(d) This section shall not apply to bankruptcy matters or other proceedings under Title 11.

(June 25, 1948, c. 646, 62 Stat. 963; May 24, 1949, c. 139, §§ 107, 108, 63 Stat. 104; Nov. 6, 1978, Pub.L. 95–598, Title II, § 248, 92 Stat. 2672; Dec. 9, 1991, Pub.L. 102–198, § 12, 105 Stat. 1627.)

HISTORICAL AND STATUTORY NOTES
Senate Revision Amendment

By Senate amendment, all provisions relating to the Tax Court were eliminated. Therefore, section 1142 of Title 26, U.S.C., Internal Revenue Code, was not one of the sources of this section as finally enacted. However, no change in the text of this section was necessary. See 80th Congress Senate Report No. 1559.

1949 Acts

This amendment to section 2107 of Title 28, U.S.C., restores the former 15-day limitation of time within which to appeal from an interlocutory order in admiralty.

This amendment eliminates as surplusage the words "in any such action, suit or proceeding," from the fourth paragraph of section 2107 of Title 28, U.S.C., and corrects a typographical error in the same paragraph.

1991 Acts

House Report No. 102–322, see 1991 U.S. Code Cong. and Adm. News, p. 1303.

Codifications

This section was amended by Pub.L. 95–598, Title II, § 248, Nov. 6, 1978, 92 Stat. 2672, effective June 28, 1984, pursuant to Pub.L. 95–598, Title IV, § 402(b), Nov. 6, 1978, 92 Stat. 2682, as amended by Pub.L. 98–249, § 1(a), Mar. 31, 1984, 98 Stat. 116; Pub.L. 98–271, § 1(a), Apr. 30, 1984, 98 Stat. 163; Pub.L. 98–299, § 1(a), May 25, 1984, 98 Stat. 214; Pub.L. 98–325, § 1(a), June 20, 1984, 98 Stat. 268 [set out as an Effective and Applicability Provisions note preceding section 101 of Title 11, Bankruptcy], by adding "or the bankruptcy court" following "district court" and by striking out the final paragraph relating to nonapplicability to bankruptcy matters or other proceedings under Title 11.

Section 402(b) of Pub.L. 95–598 was amended by section 113 of Pub.L. 98–353, Title I, July 10, 1984, 98 Stat. 343, by substituting "shall not be effective" for "shall take effect on June 28, 1984", thereby eliminating the amendment by section 248 of Pub.L. 95–598, effective June 27, 1984, pursuant to section 122(c) of Pub.L. 98–353, set out as an Effective Date note under section 151 of this title.

Section 121(a) of Pub.L. 98–353 directed that section 402(b) of Pub.L. 95–598 be amended by substituting "the date of enactment of the Bankruptcy Amendments and Federal Judgeship Act of 1984 [i.e. July 10, 1984]" for "June 28,

1984". This amendment was not executed in view of the prior amendment to section 402(b) of Pub.L. 95–598 by section 113 of Pub.L. 98–353.

§ 2108.　Proof of amount in controversy

Where the power of any court of appeals to review a case depends upon the amount or value in controversy, such amount or value, if not otherwise satisfactorily disclosed upon the record, may be shown and ascertained by the oath of a party to the case or by other competent evidence.

(June 25, 1948, c. 646, 62 Stat. 963.)

§ 2109.　Quorum of Supreme Court justices absent

If a case brought to the Supreme Court by direct appeal from a district court cannot be heard and determined because of the absence of a quorum of qualified justices, the Chief Justice of the United States may order it remitted to the court of appeals for the circuit including the district in which the case arose, to be heard and determined by that court either sitting in banc or specially constituted and composed of the three circuit judges senior in commission who are able to sit, as such order may direct. The decision of such court shall be final and conclusive. In the event of the disqualification or disability of one or more of such circuit judges, such court shall be filled as provided in chapter 15 of this title.

In any other case brought to the Supreme Court for review, which cannot be heard and determined because of the absence of a quorum of qualified justices, if a majority of the qualified justices shall be of opinion that the case cannot be heard and determined at the next ensuing term, the court shall enter its order affirming the judgment of the court from which the case was brought for review with the same effect as upon affirmance by an equally divided court.

(June 25, 1948, c. 646, 62 Stat. 963.)

[§ 2110.　Repealed. Pub.L. 97–164, Title I, § 136, Apr. 2, 1982, 96 Stat. 41]

HISTORICAL AND STATUTORY NOTES

Section, Act June 25, 1948, c. 646, 62 Stat. 964; May 24, 1949, c. 139, § 109, 63 Stat. 105, provided that appeals to the Court of Claims in tort claims cases, as provided in section 1504 of this title, be taken within 90 days after the entry of the final judgment of the district court.

Effective Date of Repeal

Repeal effective Oct. 1, 1982, see section 402 of Pub.L. 97–164, set out as a note under section 171 of this title.

§ 2111.　Harmless error

On the hearing of any appeal or writ of certiorari in any case, the court shall give judgment after an examination of the record without regard to errors or defects which do not affect the substantial rights of the parties.

(Added May 24, 1949, c. 139, § 110, 63 Stat. 105.)

§ 2112.　Record on review and enforcement of agency orders

(a) The rules prescribed under the authority of section 2072 of this title may provide for the time and manner of filing and the contents of the record in all proceedings instituted in the courts of appeals to enjoin, set aside, suspend, modify, or otherwise review or enforce orders of administrative agencies, boards, commissions, and officers. Such rules may authorize the agency, board, commission, or officer to file in the court a certified list of the materials comprising the record and retain and hold for the court all such materials and transmit the same or any part thereof to the court, when and as required by it, at any time prior to the final determination of the proceeding, and such filing of such certified list of the materials comprising the record and such subsequent transmittal of any such materials when and as required shall be deemed full compliance with any provision of law requiring the filing of the record in the court. The record in such proceedings shall be certified and filed in or held for and transmitted to the court of appeals by the agency, board, commission, or officer concerned within the time and in the manner prescribed by such rules. If proceedings are instituted in two or more courts of appeals with respect to the same order, the following shall apply:

(1) If within ten days after issuance of the order the agency, board, commission, or officer concerned receives, from the persons instituting the proceedings, the petition for review with respect to proceedings in at least two courts of appeals, the agency, board, commission, or officer shall proceed in accordance with paragraph (3) of this subsection. If within ten days after the issuance of the order the agency, board, commission, or officer concerned receives, from the persons instituting the proceedings, the petition for review with respect to proceedings in only one court of appeals, the agency, board, commission, or officer shall file the record in that court notwithstanding the institution in any other court of appeals of proceedings for review of that order. In all other cases in which proceedings have been instituted in two or more courts of appeals with respect to the same order, the agency, board, commission, or officer concerned shall file the record in the court in which proceedings with respect to the order were first instituted.

(2) For purposes of paragraph (1) of this subsection, a copy of the petition or other pleading which institutes proceedings in a court of appeals and which is stamped by the court with the date of filing shall constitute the petition for review. Each agen-

cy, board, commission, or officer, as the case may be, shall designate by rule the office and the officer who must receive petitions for review under paragraph (1).

(3) If an agency, board, commission, or officer receives two or more petitions for review of an order in accordance with the first sentence of paragraph (1) of this subsection, the agency, board, commission, or officer shall, promptly after the expiration of the ten-day period specified in that sentence, so notify the judicial panel on multidistrict litigation authorized by section 1407 of this title, in such form as that panel shall prescribe. The judicial panel on multidistrict litigation shall, by means of random selection, designate one court of appeals, from among the courts of appeals in which petitions for review have been filed and received within the ten-day period specified in the first sentence of paragraph (1), in which the record is to be filed, and shall issue an order consolidating the petitions for review in that court of appeals. The judicial panel on multidistrict litigation shall, after providing notice to the public and an opportunity for the submission of comments, prescribe rules with respect to the consolidation of proceedings under this paragraph. The agency, board, commission, or officer concerned shall file the record in the court of appeals designated pursuant to this paragraph.

(4) Any court of appeals in which proceedings with respect to an order of an agency, board, commission, or officer have been instituted may, to the extent authorized by law, stay the effective date of the order. Any such stay may thereafter be modified, revoked, or extended by a court of appeals designated pursuant to paragraph (3) with respect to that order or by any other court of appeals to which the proceedings are transferred.

(5) All courts in which proceedings are instituted with respect to the same order, other than the court in which the record is filed pursuant to this subsection, shall transfer those proceedings to the court in which the record is so filed. For the convenience of the parties in the interest of justice, the court in which the record is filed may thereafter transfer all the proceedings with respect to that order to any other court of appeals.

(b) The record to be filed in the court of appeals in such a proceeding shall consist of the order sought to be reviewed or enforced, the findings or report upon which it is based, and the pleadings, evidence, and proceedings before the agency, board, commission, or officer concerned, or such portions thereof (1) as the rules prescribed under the authority of section 2072 of this title may require to be included therein, or (2) as the agency, board, commission, or officer concerned, the petitioner for review or respondent in enforce-

ment, as the case may be, and any intervenor in the court proceeding by written stipulation filed with the agency, board, commission, or officer concerned or in the court in any such proceeding may consistently with the rules prescribed under the authority of section 2072 of this title designate to be included therein, or (3) as the court upon motion of a party or, after a prehearing conference, upon its own motion may by order in any such proceeding designate to be included therein. Such a stipulation or order may provide in an appropriate case that no record need be filed in the court of appeals. If, however, the correctness of a finding of fact by the agency, board, commission, or officer is in question all of the evidence before the agency, board, commission, or officer shall be included in the record except such as the agency, board, commission, or officer concerned, the petitioner for review or respondent in enforcement, as the case may be, and any intervenor in the court proceeding by written stipulation filed with the agency, board, commission, or officer concerned or in the court agree to omit as wholly immaterial to the questioned finding. If there is omitted from the record any portion of the proceedings before the agency, board, commission, or officer which the court subsequently determines to be proper for it to consider to enable it to review or enforce the order in question the court may direct that such additional portion of the proceedings be filed as a supplement to the record. The agency, board, commission, or officer concerned may, at its option and without regard to the foregoing provisions of this subsection, and if so requested by the petitioner for review or respondent in enforcement shall, file in the court the entire record of the proceedings before it without abbreviation.

(c) The agency, board, commission, or officer concerned may transmit to the court of appeals the original papers comprising the whole or any part of the record or any supplemental record, otherwise true copies of such papers certified by an authorized officer or deputy of the agency, board, commission, or officer concerned shall be transmitted. Any original papers thus transmitted to the court of appeals shall be returned to the agency, board, commission, or officer concerned upon the final determination of the review or enforcement proceeding. Pending such final determination any such papers may be returned by the court temporarily to the custody of the agency, board, commission, or officer concerned if needed for the transaction of the public business. Certified copies of any papers included in the record or any supplemental record may also be returned to the agency, board, commission, or officer concerned upon the final determination of review or enforcement proceedings.

(d) The provisions of this section are not applicable to proceedings to review decisions of the Tax Court of the United States or to proceedings to review or

enforce those orders of administrative agencies, boards, commissions, or officers which are by law reviewable or enforceable by the district courts.

(Added Pub.L. 85–791, § 2, Aug. 28, 1958, 72 Stat. 941, and amended Pub.L. 89–773, § 5(a), (b), Nov. 6, 1966, 80 Stat. 1323; Pub.L. 100–236, § 1, Jan. 8, 1988, 101 Stat. 1731.)

HISTORICAL AND STATUTORY NOTES

Effective and Applicability Provisions

1988 Acts

Section 3 of Pub.L. 100–236 provided that: "The amendments made by this Act [amending subsec. (a) of this section and section 1369(b) of Title 33, Navigation and Navigable Waters] take effect 180 days after the date of the enactment of this Act [Jan. 8, 1988], except that the judicial panel on multidistrict litigation may issue rules pursuant to subsection (a)(3) of section 2112 of title 28, United States Code (as added by section 1) [subsec. (a)(3) of this section], on or after such date of enactment."

Savings Provisions

Section 5(c) of Pub.L. 89–773 provided that: "The amendments of section 2112 of title 28 of the United States Code

[this section] made by this Act shall not operate to invalidate or repeal rules adopted under the authority of that section prior to the enactment of this Act [Nov. 6, 1966], which rules shall remain in effect until superseded by rules prescribed under the authority of section 2072 of title 28 of the United States Code [section 2072 of this title] as amended by this Act."

§ 2113. Definition

For purposes of this chapter, the terms "State court", "State courts", and "highest court of a State" include the District of Columbia Court of Appeals.

(Added Pub.L. 91–358, Title I, § 172(a)(2)(A), July 29, 1970, 84 Stat. 590.)

HISTORICAL AND STATUTORY NOTES

Effective and Applicability Provisions

1970 Acts

Section effective the first day of the seventh calendar month which begins after July 29, 1970, see section 199(a) of Pub.L. 91–358, set out as a note under section 1257 of this title.

PART VI—PARTICULAR PROCEEDINGS

* [Chapters 157, 158, 167, 169, 173, 175 and 178 have been omitted.—Ed.]

1 So in original. The period probably should not appear.

HISTORICAL AND STATUTORY NOTES

Effective and Applicability Provisions

1996 Acts

Amendment of analysis by section 3(e) of Pub.L. 104–331, effective Oct. 1, 1997, see section 3(d) of Pub.L. 104–331, set out as a note under section 1296 of this title.

CHAPTER 151—DECLARATORY JUDGMENTS

Sec.
2201. Creation of remedy.
2202. Further relief.

§ 2201. Creation of remedy

(a) In a case of actual controversy within its jurisdiction, except with respect to Federal taxes other than actions brought under section 7428 of the Internal Revenue Code of 1986, a proceeding under section 505 or 1146 of title 11, or in any civil action involving an antidumping or countervailing duty proceeding regarding a class or kind of merchandise of a free trade area country (as defined in section 516A(f)(10) of the Tariff Act of 1930), as determined by the administering authority, any court of the United States, upon the filing of an appropriate pleading, may declare the rights and other legal relations of any interested party seeking such declaration, whether or not further relief is or could be sought. Any such declaration shall have the force and effect of a final judgment or decree and shall be reviewable as such.

(b) For limitations on actions brought with respect to drug patents see section 505 or 512 of the Federal Food, Drug, and Cosmetic Act.

(June 25, 1948, c. 646, 62 Stat. 964; May 24, 1949, c. 139, § 111, 63 Stat. 105; Aug. 28, 1954, c. 1033, 68 Stat. 890; July 7, 1958, Pub.L. 85–508, § 12(p), 72 Stat. 349; Oct. 4, 1976, Pub.L. 94–455, Title XIII, § 1306(b)(8), 90 Stat. 1719; Nov. 6, 1978, Pub.L. 95–598, Title II, § 249, 92 Stat. 2672; Sept. 24, 1984, Pub.L. 98–417, Title I, § 106, 98 Stat. 1597; Sept. 28, 1988, Pub.L. 100–449, Title IV, § 402(c), 102 Stat. 1884; Nov. 16, 1988, Pub.L. 100–670, Title I, § 107(b), 102 Stat. 3984; Dec. 8, 1993, Pub.L. 103–182, Title IV, § 414(b), 107 Stat. 2147.)

Termination of Amendments

For provisions directing that, except for transition provisions relating to proceedings regarding protective orders and undertakings, and binational panel and extraordinary challenge committee reviews, the amendment to this section by Title IV of Pub.L. 103–182 shall cease to have effect with respect to any country on the date on which such country ceases to be a NAFTA country, see 19 U.S.C.A. § 3451.

For provisions directing that the amendments made by Pub.L. 100–449, which amended this section, shall cease to have effect on the date on which the United States-Canada Free-Trade Agreement ceases to be in force, see section 501(c) of Pub.L. 100–449, set out in the note under 19 U.S.C.A. § 2112.

Articles 1906 and 2106 of the Agreement authorize either the United States or Canada to terminate the Agreement on 6-month notice if, at the end of the 7-year period following the date of the entry into effect of the Agreement, no agreement has been entered into between the United States and Canada on a substitute system of antidumping and countervailing duties.

HISTORICAL AND STATUTORY NOTES

References in Text

Section 7428 of the Internal Revenue Code of 1986, referred to in subsec. (a), is classified to section 7428 of Title 26, Internal Revenue Code.

Section 516A(f)(10) of the Tariff Act of 1930, referred to in subsec. (a), is classified to section 1516a(f)(10) of Title 19, Customs Duties.

Sections 505 and 512 of the Federal Food, Drug, and Cosmetic Act, referred to in subsec. (b), are classified to sections 355 and 360b, respectively, of Title 21, Food and Drugs.

Effective and Applicability Provisions

1993 Acts

Amendment of this section by section 414 of Pub.L. 103–182 to take effect on the date the North American Free Trade Agreement enters into force with respect to the United States, but not to apply to any final determination described in section 1516a(a)(1)(B) or (2)(B)(i), (ii), or (iii) of Title 19, Customs Duties, notice of which is published in the Federal Register before such date, or to a determination described in section 1516a(a)(2)(B)(vi) of Title 19 notice of which is received by the Government of Canada or Mexico before such date, or to any binational panel review under the United States-Canada Free-Trade Agreement, or to any extraordinary challenge arising out of any such review that was commenced before such date, see section 416 of Pub.L. 103–182, set out as a note under section 3431 of Title 19.

1988 Acts

Amendment by Pub.L. 100–449 effective on the date the United States-Canada Free-Trade Agreement enters into force (Jan. 1, 1989), and to cease to have effect on the date the Agreement ceases to be in force, see section 501(a), (c) of Pub.L. 100–449, set out in a note under section 2112 of Title 19, Customs Duties. [A Presidential Memorandum on the Canada-United States Free-Trade Agreement, dated Dec. 31, 1988, directing the Secretary of State to exchange notes with the Government of Canada to provide for the entry into force of the Agreement on Jan. 1, 1989, is set out in 24 Weekly Compilation of Presidential Documents 1688, Jan. 2, 1989.]

1978 Acts

Amendment by Pub.L. 95–598 effective Oct. 1, 1979, see section 402(c) of Pub.L. 95–598, set out as a note preceding section 101 of Title 11, Bankruptcy.

1976 Acts

Amendment by Pub.L. 94–455 applicable with respect to pleadings filed with the United States Tax Court, the District Court of the United States for the District of Columbia, or the United States Court of Claims more than 6 months after Oct. 4, 1976, but only with respect to determinations (or requests for determinations) made after Jan. 1, 1976, see section 1306(c) of Pub.L. 94–455, set out as a note under section 7428 of Title 26, Internal Revenue Code.

1958 Acts

Amendment by Pub.L. 85–508 effective Jan. 3, 1959, upon admission of Alaska into the Union pursuant to Proc. No. 3269, Jan. 3, 1959, 24 F.R. 81, 73 Stat. c. 16, as required by sections 1 and 8(c) of Pub.L. 85–508, see notes set out under section 81A of this title and preceding section 21 of Title 48, Territories and Insular Possessions.

Amount in Controversy

Jurisdictional amount increased from $3,000 to $50,000 in diversity of citizenship cases, see section 1332 of this title.

§ 2202. Further relief

Further necessary or proper relief based on a declaratory judgment or decree may be granted, after reasonable notice and hearing, against any adverse party whose rights have been determined by such judgment.

(June 25, 1948, c. 646, 62 Stat. 964.)

CHAPTER 153—HABEAS CORPUS

HISTORICAL AND STATUTORY NOTES

Codifications

The table of sections for chapter 153 was amended by Pub.L. 95–598, Title II, § 250(b), Nov. 6, 1978, 92 Stat. 2672, effective June 28, 1984, pursuant to Pub.L. 95–598, Title IV, § 402(b), Nov. 6, 1978, 92 Stat. 2682, as amended by Pub.L. 98–249, § 1(a), Mar. 31, 1984, 98 Stat. 116; Pub.L. 98–271, § 1(a), Apr. 30, 1984, 98 Stat. 163; Pub.L. 98–299, § 1(a), May 25, 1984, 98 Stat. 214; Pub.L. 98–325, § 1(a), June 20, 1984, 98 Stat. 268, set out as an Effective and Applicability Provisions note preceding section 101 of Title 11, Bankruptcy, by adding:

"2256. Habeas corpus from bankruptcy courts.".

Section 402(b) of Pub.L. 95–598 was amended by section 113 of Pub.L. 98–353, Title I, July 10, 1984, 98 Stat. 343, by substituting "shall not be effective" for "shall take effect on June 28, 1984", thereby eliminating the amendment by section 250(b) of Pub.L. 95–598, effective June 27, 1984, pursuant to section 122(c) of Pub.L. 98–353, set out as an Effective and Applicability Provisions note under section 151 of this title.

Section 121(a) of Pub.L. 98–353 directed that section 402(b) of Pub.L. 95–598 be amended by substituting "the date of enactment of the Bankruptcy Amendments and Federal Judgeship Act of 1984 [i.e. July 10, 1984]" for "June 28, 1984". This amendment was not executed in view of the prior amendment to section 402(b) of Pub.L. 95–598 by section 113 of Pub.L. 98–353.

§ 2241. Power to grant writ

(a) Writs of habeas corpus may be granted by the Supreme Court, any justice thereof, the district courts

and any circuit judge within their respective jurisdictions. The order of a circuit judge shall be entered in the records of the district court of the district wherein the restraint complained of is had.

(b) The Supreme Court, any justice thereof, and any circuit judge may decline to entertain an application for a writ of habeas corpus and may transfer the application for hearing and determination to the district court having jurisdiction to entertain it.

(c) The writ of habeas corpus shall not extend to a prisoner unless—

(1) He is in custody under or by color of the authority of the United States or is committed for trial before some court thereof; or

(2) He is in custody for an act done or omitted in pursuance of an Act of Congress, or an order, process, judgment or decree of a court or judge of the United States; or

(3) He is in custody in violation of the Constitution or laws or treaties of the United States; or

(4) He, being a citizen of a foreign state and domiciled therein is in custody for an act done or omitted under any alleged right, title, authority, privilege, protection, or exemption claimed under the commission, order or sanction of any foreign state, or under color thereof, the validity and effect of which depend upon the law of nations; or

(5) It is necessary to bring him into court to testify or for trial.

(d) Where an application for a writ of habeas corpus is made by a person in custody under the judgment and sentence of a State court of a State which contains two or more Federal judicial districts, the application may be filed in the district court for the district wherein such person is in custody or in the district court for the district within which the State court was held which convicted and sentenced him and each of such district courts shall have concurrent jurisdiction to entertain the application. The district court for the district wherein such an application is filed in the exercise of its discretion and in furtherance of justice may transfer the application to the other district court for hearing and determination.

(e)(1) No court, justice, or judge shall have jurisdiction to hear or consider an application for a writ of habeas corpus filed by or on behalf of an alien detained by the United States who has been determined by the United States to have been properly detained as an enemy combatant or is awaiting such determination.

(2) Except as provided in paragraphs (2) and (3) of section 1005(e) of the Detainee Treatment Act of 2005 (10 U.S.C. 801 note), no court, justice, or judge shall have jurisdiction to hear or consider any other action against the United States or its agents relating to any aspect of the detention, transfer, treatment, trial, or conditions of confinement of an alien who is or was detained by the United States and has been determined by the United States to have been properly detained as an enemy combatant or is awaiting such determination.

(June 25, 1948, c. 646, 62 Stat. 964; May 24, 1949, c. 139, § 112, 63 Stat. 105; Sept. 19, 1966, Pub.L. 89–590, 80 Stat. 811; Dec. 30, 2005, Pub.L. 109–148, Div. A, Title X, § 1005(e)(1), 119 Stat. 2742; Jan. 6, 2006, Pub.L. 109–163, Title XIV, § 1405(e)(1), 119 Stat. 3477; Oct. 17, 2006, Pub.L. 109–366, § 7(a), 120 Stat. 2635.)

HISTORICAL AND STATUTORY NOTES

References in Text

Section 1005(e) of the Detainee Treatment Act of 2005, referred to in subsec. (e)(2), probably means Pub.L. 109–148, Div. A, Title X, § 1005, Dec. 30, 2005, 119 Stat. 2740, which is set out in a note under 10 U.S.C.A. § 801 note. Pub.L. 109–163, Div. A, Title XIV, Jan. 6, 2006, 119 Stat. 3474, also enacted a "Detainee Treatment Act of 2005", see Short Title note under 42 U.S.C.A. § 2000dd and Tables, but that Act contains no section 1005(e).

Effective and Applicability Provisions

2006 Acts

Pub.L. 109–366, § 7(b), Oct. 17, 2006, 120 Stat. 2635, provided that: "The amendment made by subsection (a) [amending this section] shall take effect on the date of the enactment of this Act [Oct. 17, 2006], and shall apply to all cases, without exception, pending on or after the date of the enactment of this Act which relate to any aspect of the detention, transfer, treatment, trial, or conditions of detention of an alien detained by the United States since September 11, 2001."

Treaty Obligations not Establishing Grounds for Certain Claims

Pub.L. 109–366, § 5, Oct. 17, 2006, 120 Stat. 2631, provided that:

"**(a) In general.**—No person may invoke the Geneva Conventions or any protocols thereto in any habeas corpus or other civil action or proceeding to which the United States, or a current or former officer, employee, member of the Armed Forces, or other agent of the United States is a party as a source of rights in any court of the United States or its States or territories.

"**(b) Geneva conventions defined.**—In this section, the term 'Geneva Conventions' means—

"(1) the Convention for the Amelioration of the Condition of the Wounded and Sick in Armed Forces in the Field, done at Geneva August 12, 1949 (6 UST 3114);

"(2) the Convention for the Amelioration of the Condition of the Wounded, Sick, and Shipwrecked Members of the Armed Forces at Sea, done at Geneva August 12, 1949 (6 UST 3217);

"(3) the Convention Relative to the Treatment of Prisoners of War, done at Geneva August 12, 1949 (6 UST 3316); and

"(4) the Convention Relative to the Protection of Civilian Persons in Time of War, done at Geneva August 12, 1949 (6 UST 3516)."

§ 2242. Application

Application for a writ of habeas corpus shall be in writing signed and verified by the person for whose relief it is intended or by someone acting in his behalf.

It shall allege the facts concerning the applicant's commitment or detention, the name of the person who has custody over him and by virtue of what claim or authority, if known.

It may be amended or supplemented as provided in the rules of procedure applicable to civil actions.

If addressed to the Supreme Court, a justice thereof or a circuit judge it shall state the reasons for not making application to the district court of the district in which the applicant is held.

(June 25, 1948, c. 646, 62 Stat. 965.)

§ 2243. Issuance of writ; return; hearing; decision

A court, justice or judge entertaining an application for a writ of habeas corpus shall forthwith award the writ or issue an order directing the respondent to show cause why the writ should not be granted, unless it appears from the application that the applicant or person detained is not entitled thereto.

The writ, or order to show cause shall be directed to the person having custody of the person detained. It shall be returned within three days unless for good cause additional time, not exceeding twenty days, is allowed.

The person to whom the writ or order is directed shall make a return certifying the true cause of the detention.

When the writ or order is returned a day shall be set for hearing, not more than five days after the return unless for good cause additional time is allowed.

Unless the application for the writ and the return present only issues of law the person to whom the writ is directed shall be required to produce at the hearing the body of the person detained.

The applicant or the person detained may, under oath, deny any of the facts set forth in the return or allege any other material facts.

The return and all suggestions made against it may be amended, by leave of court, before or after being filed.

The court shall summarily hear and determine the facts, and dispose of the matter as law and justice require.

(June 25, 1948, c. 646, 62 Stat. 965.)

§ 2244. Finality of determination

(a) No circuit or district judge shall be required to entertain an application for a writ of habeas corpus to inquire into the detention of a person pursuant to a judgment of a court of the United States if it appears that the legality of such detention has been determined by a judge or court of the United States on a prior application for a writ of habeas corpus, except as provided in section 2255.

(b)(1) A claim presented in a second or successive habeas corpus application under section 2254 that was presented in a prior application shall be dismissed.

(2) A claim presented in a second or successive habeas corpus application under section 2254 that was not presented in a prior application shall be dismissed unless—

(A) the applicant shows that the claim relies on a new rule of constitutional law, made retroactive to cases on collateral review by the Supreme Court, that was previously unavailable; or

(B)(i) the factual predicate for the claim could not have been discovered previously through the exercise of due diligence; and

(ii) the facts underlying the claim, if proven and viewed in light of the evidence as a whole, would be sufficient to establish by clear and convincing evidence that, but for constitutional error, no reasonable factfinder would have found the applicant guilty of the underlying offense.

(3)(A) Before a second or successive application permitted by this section is filed in the district court, the applicant shall move in the appropriate court of appeals for an order authorizing the district court to consider the application.

(B) A motion in the court of appeals for an order authorizing the district court to consider a second or successive application shall be determined by a three-judge panel of the court of appeals.

(C) The court of appeals may authorize the filing of a second or successive application only if it determines that the application makes a prima facie showing that the application satisfies the requirements of this subsection.

(D) The court of appeals shall grant or deny the authorization to file a second or successive application not later than 30 days after the filing of the motion.

(E) The grant or denial of an authorization by a court of appeals to file a second or successive application shall not be appealable and shall not be the subject of a petition for rehearing or for a writ of certiorari.

(4) A district court shall dismiss any claim presented in a second or successive application that the court of appeals has authorized to be filed unless the appli-

cant shows that the claim satisfies the requirements of this section.

(c) In a habeas corpus proceeding brought in behalf of a person in custody pursuant to the judgment of a State court, a prior judgment of the Supreme Court of the United States on an appeal or review by a writ of certiorari at the instance of the prisoner of the decision of such State court, shall be conclusive as to all issues of fact or law with respect to an asserted denial of a Federal right which constitutes ground for discharge in a habeas corpus proceeding, actually adjudicated by the Supreme Court therein, unless the applicant for the writ of habeas corpus shall plead and the court shall find the existence of a material and controlling fact which did not appear in the record of the proceeding in the Supreme Court and the court shall further find that the applicant for the writ of habeas corpus could not have caused such fact to appear in such record by the exercise of reasonable diligence.

(d)(1) A 1-year period of limitation shall apply to an application for a writ of habeas corpus by a person in custody pursuant to the judgment of a State court. The limitation period shall run from the latest of—

(A) the date on which the judgment became final by the conclusion of direct review or the expiration of the time for seeking such review;

(B) the date on which the impediment to filing an application created by State action in violation of the Constitution or laws of the United States is removed, if the applicant was prevented from filing by such State action;

(C) the date on which the constitutional right asserted was initially recognized by the Supreme Court, if the right has been newly recognized by the Supreme Court and made retroactively applicable to cases on collateral review; or

(D) the date on which the factual predicate of the claim or claims presented could have been discovered through the exercise of due diligence.

(2) The time during which a properly filed application for State post-conviction or other collateral review with respect to the pertinent judgment or claim is pending shall not be counted toward any period of limitation under this subsection.

(June 25, 1948, c. 646, 62 Stat. 965; Nov. 2, 1966, Pub.L. 89–711, § 1, 80 Stat. 1104; Apr. 24, 1996, Pub.L. 104–132, Title I, §§ 101, 106, 110 Stat. 1217, 1220.)

§ 2245. Certificate of trial judge admissible in evidence

On the hearing of an application for a writ of habeas corpus to inquire into the legality of the detention of a person pursuant to a judgment the certificate of the judge who presided at the trial resulting in the judgment, setting forth the facts occurring at the trial, shall be admissible in evidence. Copies of the certifi-

cate shall be filed with the court in which the application is pending and in the court in which the trial took place.

(June 25, 1948, c. 646, 62 Stat. 966.)

§ 2246. Evidence; depositions; affidavits

On application for a writ of habeas corpus, evidence may be taken orally or by deposition, or, in the discretion of the judge, by affidavit. If affidavits are admitted any party shall have the right to propound written interrogatories to the affiants, or to file answering affidavits.

(June 25, 1948, c. 646, 62 Stat. 966.)

§ 2247. Documentary evidence

On application for a writ of habeas corpus documentary evidence, transcripts of proceedings upon arraignment, plea and sentence and a transcript of the oral testimony introduced on any previous similar application by or in behalf of the same petitioner, shall be admissible in evidence.

(June 25, 1948, c. 646, 62 Stat. 966.)

§ 2248. Return or answer; conclusiveness

The allegations of a return to the writ of habeas corpus or of an answer to an order to show cause in a habeas corpus proceeding, if not traversed, shall be accepted as true except to the extent that the judge finds from the evidence that they are not true.

(June 25, 1948, c. 646, 62 Stat. 966.)

§ 2249. Certified copies of indictment, plea and judgment; duty of respondent

On application for a writ of habeas corpus to inquire into the detention of any person pursuant to a judgment of a court of the United States, the respondent shall promptly file with the court certified copies of the indictment, plea of petitioner and the judgment, or such of them as may be material to the questions raised, if the petitioner fails to attach them to his petition, and same shall be attached to the return to the writ, or to the answer to the order to show cause.

(June 25, 1948, c. 646, 62 Stat. 966.)

§ 2250. Indigent petitioner entitled to documents without cost

If on any application for a writ of habeas corpus an order has been made permitting the petitioner to prosecute the application in forma pauperis, the clerk of any court of the United States shall furnish to the petitioner without cost certified copies of such documents or parts of the record on file in his office as may be required by order of the judge before whom the application is pending.

(June 25, 1948, c. 646, 62 Stat. 966.)

Complete Annotation Materials, see Title 28 U.S.C.A.

§ 2251. Stay of State court proceedings

(a) In general.—

(1) Pending matters.—A justice or judge of the United States before whom a habeas corpus proceeding is pending, may, before final judgment or after final judgment of discharge, or pending appeal, stay any proceeding against the person detained in any State court or by or under the authority of any State for any matter involved in the habeas corpus proceeding.

(2) Matter not pending.—For purposes of this section, a habeas corpus proceeding is not pending until the application is filed.

(3) Application for appointment of counsel.— If a State prisoner sentenced to death applies for appointment of counsel pursuant to section 3599(a)(2) of title 18 in a court that would have jurisdiction to entertain a habeas corpus application regarding that sentence, that court may stay execution of the sentence of death, but such stay shall terminate not later than 90 days after counsel is appointed or the application for appointment of counsel is withdrawn or denied.

(b) No further proceedings.—After the granting of such a stay, any such proceeding in any State court or by or under the authority of any State shall be void. If no stay is granted, any such proceeding shall be as valid as if no habeas corpus proceedings or appeal were pending.

(June 25, 1948, c. 646, 62 Stat. 966; Mar. 9, 2006, Pub.L. 109–177, Title V, § 507(f), 120 Stat. 251.)

HISTORICAL AND STATUTORY NOTES

Application to Pending Cases

Pub.L. 109–177, Title V, § 507(d), Mar. 9, 2006, 120 Stat. 251, provided that:

"(1) **In general.**—This section and the amendments made by this section [enacting 28 U.S.C.A. § 2265, amending 28 U.S.C.A. §§ 2251, 2261, and 2266, and repealing 28 U.S.C.A. § 2265] shall apply to cases pending on or after the date of enactment of this Act [Mar. 9, 2006].

"(2) **Time limits.**—In a case pending on the date of enactment of this Act [Mar. 9, 2006], if the amendments made by this section [enacting 28 U.S.C.A. § 2265, amending 28 U.S.C.A. §§ 2251, 2261, and 2266, and repealing 28 U.S.C.A. § 2265] establish a time limit for taking certain action, the period of which began on the date of an event that occurred prior to the date of enactment of this Act [Mar. 9, 2006], the period of such time limit shall instead begin on the date of enactment of this Act [Mar. 9, 2006]."

§ 2252. Notice

Prior to the hearing of a habeas corpus proceeding in behalf of a person in custody of State officers or by virtue of State laws notice shall be served on the attorney general or other appropriate officer of such

State as the justice or judge at the time of issuing the writ shall direct.

(June 25, 1948, c. 646, 62 Stat. 967.)

§ 2253. Appeal

(a) In a habeas corpus proceeding or a proceeding under section 2255 before a district judge, the final order shall be subject to review, on appeal, by the court of appeals for the circuit in which the proceeding is held.

(b) There shall be no right of appeal from a final order in a proceeding to test the validity of a warrant to remove to another district or place for commitment or trial a person charged with a criminal offense against the United States, or to test the validity of such person's detention pending removal proceedings.

(c)(1) Unless a circuit justice or judge issues a certificate of appealability, an appeal may not be taken to the court of appeals from—

(A) the final order in a habeas corpus proceeding in which the detention complained of arises out of process issued by a State court; or

(B) the final order in a proceeding under section 2255.

(2) A certificate of appealability may issue under paragraph (1) only if the applicant has made a substantial showing of the denial of a constitutional right.

(3) The certificate of appealability under paragraph (1) shall indicate which specific issue or issues satisfy the showing required by paragraph (2).

(June 25, 1948, c. 646, 62 Stat. 967; May 24, 1949, c. 139, § 113, 63 Stat. 105; Oct. 31, 1951, c. 655, § 52, 65 Stat. 727; Apr. 24, 1996, Pub.L. 104–132, Title I, § 102, 110 Stat. 1217.)

§ 2254. State custody; remedies in Federal courts

(a) The Supreme Court, a Justice thereof, a circuit judge, or a district court shall entertain an application for a writ of habeas corpus in behalf of a person in custody pursuant to the judgment of a State court only on the ground that he is in custody in violation of the Constitution or laws or treaties of the United States.

(b)(1) An application for a writ of habeas corpus on behalf of a person in custody pursuant to the judgment of a State court shall not be granted unless it appears that—

(A) the applicant has exhausted the remedies available in the courts of the State; or

(B)(i) there is an absence of available State corrective process; or

(ii) circumstances exist that render such process ineffective to protect the rights of the applicant.

(2) An application for a writ of habeas corpus may be denied on the merits, notwithstanding the failure of

the applicant to exhaust the remedies available in the courts of the State.

(3) A State shall not be deemed to have waived the exhaustion requirement or be estopped from reliance upon the requirement unless the State, through counsel, expressly waives the requirement.

(c) An applicant shall not be deemed to have exhausted the remedies available in the courts of the State, within the meaning of this section, if he has the right under the law of the State to raise, by any available procedure, the question presented.

(d) An application for a writ of habeas corpus on behalf of a person in custody pursuant to the judgment of a State court shall not be granted with respect to any claim that was adjudicated on the merits in State court proceedings unless the adjudication of the claim—

(1) resulted in a decision that was contrary to, or involved an unreasonable application of, clearly established Federal law, as determined by the Supreme Court of the United States; or

(2) resulted in a decision that was based on an unreasonable determination of the facts in light of the evidence presented in the State court proceeding.

(e)(1) In a proceeding instituted by an application for a writ of habeas corpus by a person in custody pursuant to the judgment of a State court, a determination of a factual issue made by a State court shall be presumed to be correct. The applicant shall have the burden of rebutting the presumption of correctness by clear and convincing evidence.

(2) If the applicant has failed to develop the factual basis of a claim in State court proceedings, the court shall not hold an evidentiary hearing on the claim unless the applicant shows that—

(A) the claim relies on—

(i) a new rule of constitutional law, made retroactive to cases on collateral review by the Supreme Court, that was previously unavailable; or

(ii) a factual predicate that could not have been previously discovered through the exercise of due diligence; and

(B) the facts underlying the claim would be sufficient to establish by clear and convincing evidence that but for constitutional error, no reasonable factfinder would have found the applicant guilty of the underlying offense.

(f) If the applicant challenges the sufficiency of the evidence adduced in such State court proceeding to support the State court's determination of a factual issue made therein, the applicant, if able, shall produce that part of the record pertinent to a determination of the sufficiency of the evidence to support such determination. If the applicant, because of indigency

or other reason is unable to produce such part of the record, then the State shall produce such part of the record and the Federal court shall direct the State to do so by order directed to an appropriate State official. If the State cannot provide such pertinent part of the record, then the court shall determine under the existing facts and circumstances what weight shall be given to the State court's factual determination.

(g) A copy of the official records of the State court, duly certified by the clerk of such court to be a true and correct copy of a finding, judicial opinion, or other reliable written indicia showing such a factual determination by the State court shall be admissible in the Federal court proceeding.

(h) Except as provided in section 408 of the Controlled Substances Act, in all proceedings brought under this section, and any subsequent proceedings on review, the court may appoint counsel for an applicant who is or becomes financially unable to afford counsel, except as provided by a rule promulgated by the Supreme Court pursuant to statutory authority. Appointment of counsel under this section shall be governed by section 3006A of title 18.

(i) The ineffectiveness or incompetence of counsel during Federal or State collateral post-conviction proceedings shall not be a ground for relief in a proceeding arising under section 2254.

(June 25, 1948, c. 646, 62 Stat. 967; Nov. 2, 1966, Pub.L. 89–711, § 2, 80 Stat. 1105; Apr. 24, 1996, Pub.L. 104–132, Title I, § 104, 110 Stat. 1218.)

HISTORICAL AND STATUTORY NOTES

Senate Revision Amendments

Senate amendment to this section, Senate Report No. 1559, amendment No. 47, has three declared purposes, set forth as follows:

"The first is to eliminate from the prohibition of the section applications in behalf of prisoners in custody under authority of a State officer but whose custody has not been directed by the judgment of a State court. If the section were applied to applications by persons detained solely under authority of a State officer it would unduly hamper Federal courts in the protection of Federal officers prosecuted for acts committed in the course of official duty.

"The second purpose is to eliminate, as a ground of Federal jurisdiction to review by habeas corpus judgments of State courts, the proposition that the State court has denied a prisoner a 'fair adjudication of the legality of his detention under the Constitution and laws of the United States.' The Judicial Conference believes that this would be an undesirable ground for Federal jurisdiction in addition to exhaustion of State remedies or lack of adequate remedy in the State courts because it would permit proceedings in the Federal court on this ground before the petitioner had exhausted his State remedies. This ground would, of course, always be open to a petitioner to assert in the Federal court after he had exhausted his State remedies or if he had no adequate State remedy.

"The third purpose is to substitute detailed and specific language for the phrase 'no adequate remedy available.' That phrase is not sufficiently specific and precise, and its meaning should, therefore, be spelled out in more detail in the section as is done by the amendment."

1966 Acts

Senate Report No. 1797, see 1966 U.S. Code Cong. and Adm. News, p. 3663.

References in Text

Section 408 of the Controlled Substances Act, referred to in subsec. (h), is classified to section 848 of Title 21, Food and Drugs.

Approval and Effective Date of Rules Governing Section 2254 Cases and Section 2255 Proceedings for United States District Courts

Pub.L. 94–426, § 1, Sept. 28, 1976, 90 Stat. 1334, provided: "That the rules governing section 2254 cases in the United States district courts and the rules governing section 2255 proceedings for the United States district courts, as proposed by the United States Supreme Court, which were delayed by the Act entitled 'An Act to delay the effective date of certain proposed amendments to the Federal Rules of Criminal Procedure and certain other rules promulgated by the United States Supreme Court' (Public Law 94–349), are approved with the amendments set forth in section 2 of this Act and shall take effect as so amended, with respect to petitions under section 2254 and motions under section 2255 of title 28 of the United States Code filed on or after February 1, 1977."

Postponement of Effective Date of Proposed Rules Governing Proceedings Under Sections 2254 and 2255 of this Title

Rules and forms governing proceedings under sections 2254 and 2255 of this title proposed by Supreme Court order of Apr. 26, 1976, effective 30 days after adjournment sine die of 94th Congress, or until and to the extent approved by Act of Congress, whichever is earlier, see section 2 of Pub.L. 94–349, set out as a note under section 2074 of this title.

§ 2255. Federal custody; remedies on motion attacking sentence

A prisoner in custody under sentence of a court established by Act of Congress claiming the right to be released upon the ground that the sentence was imposed in violation of the Constitution or laws of the United States, or that the court was without jurisdiction to impose such sentence, or that the sentence was in excess of the maximum authorized by law, or is otherwise subject to collateral attack, may move the court which imposed the sentence to vacate, set aside or correct the sentence.

Unless the motion and the files and records of the case conclusively show that the prisoner is entitled to no relief, the court shall cause notice thereof to be served upon the United States attorney, grant a prompt hearing thereon, determine the issues and make findings of fact and conclusions of law with respect thereto. If the court finds that the judgment was rendered without jurisdiction, or that the sentence imposed was not authorized by law or otherwise open to collateral attack, or that there has been such a denial or infringement of the constitutional rights of the prisoner as to render the judgment vulnerable to collateral attack, the court shall vacate and set the judgment aside and shall discharge the prisoner or resentence him or grant a new trial or correct the sentence as may appear appropriate.

A court may entertain and determine such motion without requiring the production of the prisoner at the hearing.

An appeal may be taken to the court of appeals from the order entered on the motion as from a final judgment on application for a writ of habeas corpus.

An application for a writ of habeas corpus in behalf of a prisoner who is authorized to apply for relief by motion pursuant to this section, shall not be entertained if it appears that the applicant has failed to apply for relief, by motion, to the court which sentenced him, or that such court has denied him relief, unless it also appears that the remedy by motion is inadequate or ineffective to test the legality of his detention.

A 1-year period of limitation shall apply to a motion under this section. The limitation period shall run from the latest of—

(1) the date on which the judgment of conviction becomes final;

(2) the date on which the impediment to making a motion created by governmental action in violation of the Constitution or laws of the United States is removed, if the movant was prevented from making a motion by such governmental action;

(3) the date on which the right asserted was initially recognized by the Supreme Court, if that right has been newly recognized by the Supreme Court and made retroactively applicable to cases on collateral review; or

(4) the date on which the facts supporting the claim or claims presented could have been discovered through the exercise of due diligence.

Except as provided in section 408 of the Controlled Substances Act, in all proceedings brought under this section, and any subsequent proceedings on review, the court may appoint counsel, except as provided by a rule promulgated by the Supreme Court pursuant to statutory authority. Appointment of counsel under this section shall be governed by section 3006A of title 18.

A second or successive motion must be certified as provided in section 2244 by a panel of the appropriate court of appeals to contain—

(1) newly discovered evidence that, if proven and viewed in light of the evidence as a whole, would be sufficient to establish by clear and convincing evidence that no reasonable factfinder would have found the movant guilty of the offense; or

(2) a new rule of constitutional law, made retroactive to cases on collateral review by the Supreme Court, that was previously unavailable.

(June 25, 1948, c. 646, 62 Stat. 967; May 24, 1949, c. 139, § 114, 63 Stat. 105; Apr. 24, 1996, Pub.L. 104–132, Title I, § 105, 110 Stat. 1220.)

HISTORICAL AND STATUTORY NOTES

References in Text

Section 408 of the Controlled Substances Act, referred to in text, is classified to section 848 of Title 21, Food and Drugs.

Approval and Effective Date of Rules Governing Section 2254 Cases and Section 2255 Proceedings For United States District Courts

Pub.L. 94–426, § 1, Sept. 28, 1976, 90 Stat. 1334, provided: "That the rules governing section 2254 cases in the United States district courts and the rules governing section 2255 proceedings for the United States district courts, as proposed by the United States Supreme Court, which were delayed by the Act entitled 'An Act to delay the effective date of certain proposed amendments to the Federal Rules of Criminal Procedure and certain other rules promulgated by the United States Supreme Court' (Public Law 94–349), are approved with the amendments set forth in section 2 of this Act and shall take effect as so amended, with respect to petitions under section 2254 and motions [sections 2254 and 2255 of this title] under section 2255 of title 28 of the United States Code filed on or after February 1, 1977."

Postponement of Effective Date of Proposed Rules and Forms Governing Proceedings Under Sections 2254 and 2255 of this Title

Rules and forms governing proceedings under this section and section 2254 of this title proposed by Supreme Court order of Apr. 26, 1976, effective 30 days after adjournment sine die of 94th Congress, or until and to the extent approved by Act of Congress, whichever is earlier, see section 2 of Pub.L. 94–349, set out as a note under section 2074 of this title.

[§ 2256. Omitted]

HISTORICAL AND STATUTORY NOTES

Codifications

This section as added by Pub. L. 95–598, Title II, § 250(a), Nov. 6, 1978, 92 Stat. 2672, effective June 28, 1984, pursuant to Pub. L. 95–598, Title IV, § 402(b), Nov. 6, 1978, 92 Stat. 2682, as amended by Pub. L. 98–249, § 1(a), Mar. 31, 1984, 98 Stat. 116; Pub. L. 98–271, § 1(a), Apr. 30, 1984, 98 Stat. 163; Pub. L. 98–299, § 1(a), May 25, 1984, 98 Stat. 214; Pub. L. 98–325, § 1(a), June 20, 1984, 98 Stat. 268 [set out as an Effective and Applicability Provisions note preceding section 101 of Title 11, Bankruptcy], read as follows:

§ 2256. Habeas corpus from bankruptcy courts

A bankruptcy court may issue a writ of habeas corpus—

(1) when appropriate to bring a person before the court—

(A) for examination;

(B) to testify; or

(C) to perform a duty imposed on such person under this title; or

(2) ordering the release of a debtor in a case under title 11 in custody under the judgment of a Federal or State court if—

(A) such debtor was arrested or imprisoned on process in any civil action;

(B) such process was issued for the collection of a debt—

(i) dischargeable under title 11; or

(ii) that is or will be provided for in a plan under chapter 11 or 13 of title 11; and

(C) before the issuance of such writ, notice and a hearing have been afforded the adverse party of such debtor in custody to contest the issuance of such writ.

Section 402(b) of Pub. L. 95–598 was amended by section 113 of Pub. L. 98–353 Title I, July 10, 1984, 98 Stat. 343, by substituting "shall not be effective" for "shall take effect on June 28, 1984", thereby eliminating the amendment by section 250(a) of Pub. L. 95–598, effective June 27, 1984, pursuant to section 122(c) of Pub. L. 98–353, set out as an Effective and Applicability Provisions note under section 151 of this title.

Section 121(a) of Pub. L. 98–353 directed that section 402(b) of Pub. L. 95–598 be amended by substituting "the date of enactment of the Bankruptcy Amendments and Federal Judgeship Act of 1984 [i.e. July 10, 1984]" for "June 28 1984". This amendment was not executed in view of the prior amendment to section 402(b) of Pub. L. 95–598 by section 113 of Pub. L. 98–353.

Prior Provisions

A prior section 2256, added Pub. L. 95–144, § 3, Oct. 28, 1977, 91 Stat. 1220, which related to jurisdiction of proceedings relating to transferred offenders, was transferred to section 3244 of Title 18, Crimes and Criminal Procedure, by Pub. L. 95–598, Title III, § 314(j), Nov. 6, 1978, 92 Stat. 2677.

CHAPTER 154—SPECIAL HABEAS CORPUS PROCEDURES IN CAPITAL CASES

Complete Annotation Materials, see Title 28 U.S.C.A.

§ 2261. Prisoners in State custody subject to capital sentence; appointment of counsel; requirement of rule of court or statute; procedures for appointment

(a) This chapter shall apply to cases arising under section 2254 brought by prisoners in State custody who are subject to a capital sentence. It shall apply only if the provisions of subsections (b) and (c) are satisfied.

(b) Counsel.—This chapter is applicable if—

(1) the Attorney General of the United States certifies that a State has established a mechanism for providing counsel in postconviction proceedings as provided in section 2265; and

(2) counsel was appointed pursuant to that mechanism, petitioner validly waived counsel, petitioner retained counsel, or petitioner was found not to be indigent.

(c) Any mechanism for the appointment, compensation, and reimbursement of counsel as provided in subsection (b) must offer counsel to all State prisoners under capital sentence and must provide for the entry of an order by a court of record—

(1) appointing one or more counsels to represent the prisoner upon a finding that the prisoner is indigent and accepted the offer or is unable competently to decide whether to accept or reject the offer;

(2) finding, after a hearing if necessary, that the prisoner rejected the offer of counsel and made the decision with an understanding of its legal consequences; or

(3) denying the appointment of counsel upon a finding that the prisoner is not indigent.

(d) No counsel appointed pursuant to subsections (b) and (c) to represent a State prisoner under capital sentence shall have previously represented the prisoner at trial in the case for which the appointment is made unless the prisoner and counsel expressly request continued representation.

(e) The ineffectiveness or incompetence of counsel during State or Federal post-conviction proceedings in a capital case shall not be a ground for relief in a proceeding arising under section 2254. This limitation shall not preclude the appointment of different counsel, on the court's own motion or at the request of the prisoner, at any phase of State or Federal post-conviction proceedings on the basis of the ineffectiveness or incompetence of counsel in such proceedings. (Added Pub.L. 104–132, Title I, § 107(a), Apr. 24, 1996, 110 Stat. 1221, and amended Pub.L. 109–177, Title V, § 507(a), (b), Mar. 9, 2006, 120 Stat. 250.)

HISTORICAL AND STATUTORY NOTES

Effective and Applicability Provisions

1996 Acts

Section 107(c) of Pub.L. 104–132 provided that: "Chapter 154 of title 28, United States Code (as added by subsection (a)) [this chapter] shall apply to cases pending on or after the date of enactment of this Act [Apr. 24, 1996]."

§ 2262. Mandatory stay of execution; duration; limits on stays of execution; successive petitions

(a) Upon the entry in the appropriate State court of record of an order under section 2261(c), a warrant or order setting an execution date for a State prisoner shall be stayed upon application to any court that would have jurisdiction over any proceedings filed under section 2254. The application shall recite that the State has invoked the post-conviction review procedures of this chapter and that the scheduled execution is subject to stay.

(b) A stay of execution granted pursuant to subsection (a) shall expire if—

(1) a State prisoner fails to file a habeas corpus application under section 2254 within the time required in section 2263;

(2) before a court of competent jurisdiction, in the presence of counsel, unless the prisoner has competently and knowingly waived such counsel, and after having been advised of the consequences, a State prisoner under capital sentence waives the right to pursue habeas corpus review under section 2254; or

(3) a State prisoner files a habeas corpus petition under section 2254 within the time required by section 2263 and fails to make a substantial showing of the denial of a Federal right or is denied relief in the district court or at any subsequent stage of review.

(c) If one of the conditions in subsection (b) has occurred, no Federal court thereafter shall have the authority to enter a stay of execution in the case, unless the court of appeals approves the filing of a second or successive application under section 2244(b). (Added Pub.L. 104–132, Title I, § 107(a), Apr. 24, 1996, 110 Stat. 1222.)

HISTORICAL AND STATUTORY NOTES

Effective and Applicability Provisions

1996 Acts

Section applicable to cases pending on or after Apr. 24, 1996, see section 107(c) of Pub.L. 104–132, set out as a note under section 2261 of this title.

§ 2263. Filing of habeas corpus application; time requirements; tolling rules

(a) Any application under this chapter for habeas corpus relief under section 2254 must be filed in the appropriate district court not later than 180 days after final State court affirmance of the conviction and sentence on direct review or the expiration of the time for seeking such review.

(b) The time requirements established by subsection (a) shall be tolled—

(1) from the date that a petition for certiorari is filed in the Supreme Court until the date of final disposition of the petition if a State prisoner files the petition to secure review by the Supreme Court of the affirmance of a capital sentence on direct review by the court of last resort of the State or other final State court decision on direct review;

(2) from the date on which the first petition for post-conviction review or other collateral relief is filed until the final State court disposition of such petition; and

(3) during an additional period not to exceed 30 days, if—

(A) a motion for an extension of time is filed in the Federal district court that would have jurisdiction over the case upon the filing of a habeas corpus application under section 2254; and

(B) a showing of good cause is made for the failure to file the habeas corpus application within the time period established by this section.

(Added Pub.L. 104–132, Title I, § 107(a), Apr. 24, 1996, 110 Stat. 1223.)

HISTORICAL AND STATUTORY NOTES

Effective and Applicability Provisions

1996 Acts

Section applicable to cases pending on or after Apr. 24, 1996, see section 107(c) of Pub.L. 104–132, set out as a note under section 2261 of this title.

§ 2264. Scope of Federal review; district court adjudications

(a) Whenever a State prisoner under capital sentence files a petition for habeas corpus relief to which this chapter applies, the district court shall only consider a claim or claims that have been raised and decided on the merits in the State courts, unless the failure to raise the claim properly is—

(1) the result of State action in violation of the Constitution or laws of the United States;

(2) the result of the Supreme Court's recognition of a new Federal right that is made retroactively applicable; or

(3) based on a factual predicate that could not have been discovered through the exercise of due diligence in time to present the claim for State or Federal post-conviction review.

(b) Following review subject to subsections (a), (d), and (e) of section 2254, the court shall rule on the claims properly before it.

(Added Pub.L. 104–132, Title I, § 107(a), Apr. 24, 1996, 110 Stat. 1223.)

HISTORICAL AND STATUTORY NOTES

Effective and Applicability Provisions

1996 Acts

Section applicable to cases pending on or after Apr. 24, 1996, see section 107(c) of Pub.L. 104–132, set out as a note under section 2261 of this title.

§ 2265. Certification and judicial review

(a) **Certification.—**

(1) **In general.—**If requested by an appropriate State official, the Attorney General of the United States shall determine—

(A) whether the State has established a mechanism for the appointment, compensation, and payment of reasonable litigation expenses of competent counsel in State postconviction proceedings brought by indigent prisoners who have been sentenced to death;

(B) the date on which the mechanism described in subparagraph (A) was established; and

(C) whether the State provides standards of competency for the appointment of counsel in proceedings described in subparagraph (A).

(2) **Effective date.—**The date the mechanism described in paragraph (1)(A) was established shall be the effective date of the certification under this subsection.

(3) **Only express requirements.—**There are no requirements for certification or for application of this chapter other than those expressly stated in this chapter.

(b) **Regulations.—**The Attorney General shall promulgate regulations to implement the certification procedure under subsection (a).

(c) **Review of certification.—**

(1) **In general.—**The determination by the Attorney General regarding whether to certify a State under this section is subject to review exclusively as provided under chapter 158 of this title.

(2) **Venue.—**The Court of Appeals for the District of Columbia Circuit shall have exclusive jurisdiction over matters under paragraph (1), subject to

review by the Supreme Court under section 2350 of this title.

(3) Standard of review.—The determination by the Attorney General regarding whether to certify a State under this section shall be subject to de novo review.

(Added Pub.L. 109–177, Title V, § 507(c)(1), Mar. 9, 2006, 120 Stat. 250.)

HISTORICAL AND STATUTORY NOTES

References in Text

Chapter 158 of this title, referred to in subsec. (c)(1), is Orders of Federal Agencies; Review, 28 U.S.C.A. § 2341 et seq.

Prior Provisions

A prior section 2265, added Pub.L. 104–132, Title I, § 107(a), Apr. 24, 1996, 110 Stat. 1223, relating to application to State unitary review procedure, was repealed by Pub.L. 109–177, Title V, § 507(c)(1), Mar. 9, 2006, 120 Stat. 250.

§ 2266. Limitation periods for determining applications and motions

(a) The adjudication of any application under section 2254 that is subject to this chapter, and the adjudication of any motion under section 2255 by a person under sentence of death, shall be given priority by the district court and by the court of appeals over all noncapital matters.

(b)(1)(A) A district court shall render a final determination and enter a final judgment on any application for a writ of habeas corpus brought under this chapter in a capital case not later than 450 days after the date on which the application is filed, or 60 days after the date on which the case is submitted for decision, whichever is earlier.

(B) A district court shall afford the parties at least 120 days in which to complete all actions, including the preparation of all pleadings and briefs, and if necessary, a hearing, prior to the submission of the case for decision.

(C)(i) A district court may delay for not more than one additional 30–day period beyond the period specified in subparagraph (A), the rendering of a determination of an application for a writ of habeas corpus if the court issues a written order making a finding, and stating the reasons for the finding, that the ends of justice that would be served by allowing the delay outweigh the best interests of the public and the applicant in a speedy disposition of the application.

(ii) The factors, among others, that a court shall consider in determining whether a delay in the disposition of an application is warranted are as follows:

(I) Whether the failure to allow the delay would be likely to result in a miscarriage of justice.

(II) Whether the case is so unusual or so complex, due to the number of defendants, the nature of the prosecution, or the existence of novel questions of fact or law, that it is unreasonable to expect adequate briefing within the time limitations established by subparagraph (A).

(III) Whether the failure to allow a delay in a case that, taken as a whole, is not so unusual or so complex as described in subclause (II), but would otherwise deny the applicant reasonable time to obtain counsel, would unreasonably deny the applicant or the government continuity of counsel, or would deny counsel for the applicant or the government the reasonable time necessary for effective preparation, taking into account the exercise of due diligence.

(iii) No delay in disposition shall be permissible because of general congestion of the court's calendar.

(iv) The court shall transmit a copy of any order issued under clause (i) to the Director of the Administrative Office of the United States Courts for inclusion in the report under paragraph (5).

(2) The time limitations under paragraph (1) shall apply to—

(A) an initial application for a writ of habeas corpus;

(B) any second or successive application for a writ of habeas corpus; and

(C) any redetermination of an application for a writ of habeas corpus following a remand by the court of appeals or the Supreme Court for further proceedings, in which case the limitation period shall run from the date the remand is ordered.

(3)(A) The time limitations under this section shall not be construed to entitle an applicant to a stay of execution, to which the applicant would otherwise not be entitled, for the purpose of litigating any application or appeal.

(B) No amendment to an application for a writ of habeas corpus under this chapter shall be permitted after the filing of the answer to the application, except on the grounds specified in section 2244(b).

(4)(A) The failure of a court to meet or comply with a time limitation under this section shall not be a ground for granting relief from a judgment of conviction or sentence.

(B) The State may enforce a time limitation under this section by petitioning for a writ of mandamus to the court of appeals. The court of appeals shall act on the petition for a writ of mandamus not later than 30 days after the filing of the petition.

(5)(A) The Administrative Office of the United States Courts shall submit to Congress an annual

report on the compliance by the district courts with the time limitations under this section.

(B) The report described in subparagraph (A) shall include copies of the orders submitted by the district courts under paragraph (1)(B)(iv).

(c)(1)(A) A court of appeals shall hear and render a final determination of any appeal of an order granting or denying, in whole or in part, an application brought under this chapter in a capital case not later than 120 days after the date on which the reply brief is filed, or if no reply brief is filed, not later than 120 days after the date on which the answering brief is filed.

(B)(i) A court of appeals shall decide whether to grant a petition for rehearing or other request for rehearing en banc not later than 30 days after the date on which the petition for rehearing is filed unless a responsive pleading is required, in which case the court shall decide whether to grant the petition not later than 30 days after the date on which the responsive pleading is filed.

(ii) If a petition for rehearing or rehearing en banc is granted, the court of appeals shall hear and render a final determination of the appeal not later than 120 days after the date on which the order granting rehearing or rehearing en banc is entered.

(2) The time limitations under paragraph (1) shall apply to—

(A) an initial application for a writ of habeas corpus;

(B) any second or successive application for a writ of habeas corpus; and

(C) any redetermination of an application for a writ of habeas corpus or related appeal following a remand by the court of appeals en banc or the Supreme Court for further proceedings, in which case the limitation period shall run from the date the remand is ordered.

(3) The time limitations under this section shall not be construed to entitle an applicant to a stay of execution, to which the applicant would otherwise not be entitled, for the purpose of litigating any application or appeal.

(4)(A) The failure of a court to meet or comply with a time limitation under this section shall not be a ground for granting relief from a judgment of conviction or sentence.

(B) The State may enforce a time limitation under this section by applying for a writ of mandamus to the Supreme Court.

(5) The Administrative Office of the United States Courts shall submit to Congress an annual report on the compliance by the courts of appeals with the time limitations under this section.

(Added Pub.L. 104–132, Title I, § 107(a), Apr. 24, 1996, 110 Stat. 1224, and amended Pub.L. 109–177, Title V, § 507(e), Mar. 9, 2006, 120 Stat. 251.)

HISTORICAL AND STATUTORY NOTES

Effective and Applicability Provisions

1996 Acts

Section applicable to cases pending on or after Apr. 24, 1996, see section 107(c) of Pub.L. 104–132, set out as a note under section 2261 of this title.

CHAPTER 155—INJUNCTIONS; THREE–JUDGE COURTS

[§ 2281. Repealed. Pub.L. 94–381, § 1, Aug. 12, 1976, 90 Stat. 1119]

HISTORICAL AND STATUTORY NOTES

Section, Act June 25, 1948, c. 646, 62 Stat. 968, provided that an interlocutory or permanent injunction restraining the enforcement, operation or execution of a State statute on grounds of unconstitutionality should not be granted unless the application has been heard and determined by a three-judge district court.

Effective Date of Repeal

Repeal by Pub.L. 94–381 not applicable to any action commenced on or before Aug. 12, 1976, see section 7 of Pub.L. 94–381, set out as an Effective and Applicability Provisions of 1976 Amendments note under section 2284 of this title.

[§ 2282. Repealed. Pub.L. 94–381, § 2, Aug. 12, 1976, 90 Stat. 1119]

HISTORICAL AND STATUTORY NOTES

Section, Act June 25, 1948, c. 646, 62 Stat. 968, provided that an interlocutory or permanent injunction restraining the enforcement, operation or execution of any Act of Congress on grounds of unconstitutionality should not be granted unless the application therefor has been heard and determined by a three-judge district court.

Effective Date of Repeal

Repeal by Pub.L. 94–381 not applicable to any action commenced on or before Aug. 12, 1976, see section 7 of Pub.L. 94–381, set out as an Effective and Applicability Provisions of 1976 Amendments note under section 2284 of this title.

§ 2283. Stay of State court proceedings

A court of the United States may not grant an injunction to stay proceedings in a State court except as expressly authorized by Act of Congress, or where necessary in aid of its jurisdiction, or to protect or effectuate its judgments.

(June 25, 1948, c. 646, 62 Stat. 968.)

§ 2284. Three-judge court; when required; composition; procedure

(a) A district court of three judges shall be convened when otherwise required by Act of Congress, or when an action is filed challenging the constitutionality of the apportionment of congressional districts or the apportionment of any statewide legislative body.

(b) In any action required to be heard and determined by a district court of three judges under subsection (a) of this section, the composition and procedure of the court shall be as follows:

(1) Upon the filing of a request for three judges, the judge to whom the request is presented shall, unless he determines that three judges are not required, immediately notify the chief judge of the circuit, who shall designate two other judges, at least one of whom shall be a circuit judge. The judges so designated, and the judge to whom the request was presented, shall serve as members of the court to hear and determine the action or proceeding.

(2) If the action is against a State, or officer or agency thereof, at least five days' notice of hearing of the action shall be given by registered or certified mail to the Governor and attorney general of the State.

(3) A single judge may conduct all proceedings except the trial, and enter all orders permitted by the rules of civil procedure except as provided in this subsection. He may grant a temporary restraining order on a specific finding, based on evidence submitted, that specified irreparable damage will result if the order is not granted, which order, unless previously revoked by the district judge, shall remain in force only until the hearing and determination by the district court of three judges of an application for a preliminary injunction. A single judge shall not appoint a master, or order a reference, or hear and determine any application for a preliminary or permanent injunction or motion to vacate such an injunction, or enter judgment on the merits. Any action of a single judge may be reviewed by the full court at any time before final judgment.

(June 25, 1948, c. 646, 62 Stat. 968; June 11, 1960, Pub.L. 86–507, § 1(19), 74 Stat. 201; Aug. 12, 1976, Pub.L. 94–381, § 3, 90 Stat. 1119; Nov. 8, 1984, Pub.L. 98–620, Title IV, § 402(29)(E), 98 Stat. 3359.)

HISTORICAL AND STATUTORY NOTES

References in Text

The rules of civil procedure, referred to in subsec. (b)(3), are classified generally to this title.

Effective and Applicability Provisions

1984 Acts

Amendment by Pub.L. 98–620 not to apply to cases pending on Nov. 8, 1984, see section 403 of Pub.L. 98–620, set out as a note under section 1657 of this title.

1976 Acts

Section 7 of Pub.L. 94–381 provided that: "This Act [amending this section and section 2403 of this title and repealing sections 2281 and 2282 of this title] shall not apply to any action commenced on or before the date of enactment [Aug. 12, 1976]."

CHAPTER 159—INTERPLEADER

§ 2361. Process and procedure

In any civil action of interpleader or in the nature of interpleader under section 1335 of this title, a district court may issue its process for all claimants and enter its order restraining them from instituting or prosecuting any proceeding in any State or United States court affecting the property, instrument or obligation involved in the interpleader action until further order of the court. Such process and order shall be returnable at such time as the court or judge thereof directs, and shall be addressed to and served by the United States marshals for the respective districts where the claimants reside or may be found.

Such district court shall hear and determine the case, and may discharge the plaintiff from further liability, make the injunction permanent, and make all appropriate orders to enforce its judgment.

(June 25, 1948, c. 646, 62 Stat. 970; May 24, 1949, c. 139, § 117, 63 Stat. 105.)

CHAPTER 161—UNITED STATES AS PARTY GENERALLY

§ 2401. Time for commencing action against United States

(a) Except as provided by the Contract Disputes Act of 1978, every civil action commenced against the United States shall be barred unless the complaint is filed within six years after the right of action first accrues. The action of any person under legal disability or beyond the seas at the time the claim accrues may be commenced within three years after the disability ceases.

(b) A tort claim against the United States shall be forever barred unless it is presented in writing to the appropriate Federal agency within two years after such claim accrues or unless action is begun within six months after the date of mailing, by certified or registered mail, of notice of final denial of the claim by the agency to which it was presented.

(June 25, 1948, c. 646, 62 Stat. 971; Apr. 25, 1949, c. 92, § 1, 63 Stat. 62; Sept. 8, 1959, Pub.L. 86–238, § 1(3), 73 Stat. 472; July 18, 1966, Pub.L. 89–506, § 7, 80 Stat. 307; Nov. 1, 1978, Pub.L. 95–563, § 14(b), 92 Stat. 2389.)

HISTORICAL AND STATUTORY NOTES

Senate Revision Amendment

Subsection (b) amended in the Senate to insert the 1 year limitation on the bringing of tort actions and to include the limitation upon the time in which tort claims not exceeding $1000 must be presented to the appropriate Federal agencies for administrative disposition. 80th Congress Senate Report No. 1559, Amendment No. 48.

1949 Acts

House Report No. 276, see 1949 U.S. Code Cong. Service, p. 1226.

1959 Acts

Senate Report No. 797, see 1959 U.S. Code Cong. and Adm. News, p. 2272.

1966 Acts

Senate Report No. 1327, see 1966 U.S. Code Cong. and Adm. News, p. 2515.

1978 Acts

Senate Report No. 95–1118, see 1978 U.S. Code Cong. and Adm. News, p. 5235.

References in Text

The Contract Disputes Act of 1978, referred to in subsec. (a), is Pub.L. 95–563, Nov. 1, 1978, 92 Stat. 2383, as amended, which is classified principally to chapter 9 (section 601 et seq.) of Title 41, Public Contracts. For complete classification of this Act to the Code, see Short Title note set out under section 601 of Title 41 and Tables.

Effective and Applicability Provisions

1978 Acts

Amendment by Pub.L. 95–563 effective with respect to contracts entered into 120 days after Nov. 1, 1978 and, at the election of the contractor, with respect to any claim pending at such time before the contracting officer or initiated thereafter, see section 16 of Pub.L. 95–563, set out as a note under section 601 of Title 41, Public Contracts.

1966 Acts

Amendment by Pub.L. 89–506 applicable to claims accruing six months or more after July 18, 1966, see section 10 of Pub.L. 89–506, set out as a note under section 2672 of this title.

§ 2402. Jury trial in actions against United States

Subject to chapter 179 of this title, any action against the United States under section 1346 shall be tried by the court without a jury, except that any action against the United States under section 1346(a)(1) shall, at the request of either party to such action, be tried by the court with a jury.

(June 25, 1948, c. 646, 62 Stat. 971; July 30, 1954, c. 648, § 2(a), 68 Stat. 589; Oct. 26, 1996, Pub.L. 104–331, § 3(b)(3), 110 Stat. 4069.)

HISTORICAL AND STATUTORY NOTES

Effective and Applicability Provisions

1996 Acts

Amendment by section 3(b)(3) of Pub.L. 104–331, effective Oct. 1, 1997, see section 3(d) of Pub.L. 104–331, set out as a note under section 1296 of this title.

§ 2403. Intervention by United States or a State; constitutional question

(a) In any action, suit or proceeding in a court of the United States to which the United States or any

agency, officer or employee thereof is not a party, wherein the constitutionality of any Act of Congress affecting the public interest is drawn in question, the court shall certify such fact to the Attorney General, and shall permit the United States to intervene for presentation of evidence, if evidence is otherwise admissible in the case, and for argument on the question of constitutionality. The United States shall, subject to the applicable provisions of law, have all the rights of a party and be subject to all liabilities of a party as to court costs to the extent necessary for a proper presentation of the facts and law relating to the question of constitutionality.

(b) In any action, suit, or proceeding in a court of the United States to which a State or any agency, officer, or employee thereof is not a party, wherein the constitutionality of any statute of that State affecting the public interest is drawn in question, the court shall certify such fact to the attorney general of the State, and shall permit the State to intervene for presentation of evidence, if evidence is otherwise admissible in the case, and for argument on the question of constitutionality. The State shall, subject to the applicable provisions of law, have all the rights of a party and be subject to all liabilities of a party as to court costs to the extent necessary for a proper presentation of the facts and law relating to the question of constitutionality.

(June 25, 1948, c. 646, 62 Stat. 971; Aug. 12, 1976, Pub.L. 94–381, § 5, 90 Stat. 1120.)

HISTORICAL AND STATUTORY NOTES

Effective and Applicability Provisions

1976 Acts

Amendment by Pub.L. 94–381 not applicable to any action commenced on or before Aug. 12, 1976, see section 7 of Pub.L. 94–381, set out as a note under section 2284 of this title.

§ 2404.　Death of defendant in damage action

A civil action for damages commenced by or on behalf of the United States or in which it is interested shall not abate on the death of a defendant but shall survive and be enforceable against his estate as well as against surviving defendants.

(June 25, 1948, c. 646, 62 Stat. 971.)

§ 2405.　Garnishment

In any action or suit commenced by the United States against a corporation for the recovery of money upon a bill, note, or other security, the debtors of the corporation may be summoned as garnishees. Any person so summoned shall appear in open court and depose in writing to the amount of his indebtedness to the corporation at the time of the service of the summons and at the time of making the deposition, and judgment may be entered in favor of the United States for the sum admitted by the garnishee to be

due the corporation as if it had been due the United States. A judgment shall not be entered against any garnishee until after judgment has been rendered against the corporation, nor until the sum in which the garnishee is indebted is actually due.

When any garnishee deposes in open court that he is not and was not at the time of the service of the summons indebted to the corporation, an issue may be tendered by the United States upon such deposition. If, upon the trial of that issue, a verdict is rendered against the garnishee, judgment shall be entered in favor of the United States, pursuant to such verdict, with costs.

Any garnishee who fails to appear at the term to which he is summoned shall be subject to attachment for contempt.

(June 25, 1948, c. 646, 62 Stat. 971.)

§ 2406.　Credits in actions by United States; prior disallowance

In an action by the United States against an individual, evidence supporting the defendant's claim for a credit shall not be admitted unless he first proves that such claim has been disallowed, in whole or in part, by the Government Accountability Office, or that he has, at the time of the trial, obtained possession of vouchers not previously procurable and has been prevented from presenting such claim to the Government Accountability Office by absence from the United States or unavoidable accident.

(June 25, 1948, c. 646, 62 Stat. 972; July 7, 2004, Pub.L. 108–271, § 8(b), 118 Stat. 814.)

HISTORICAL AND STATUTORY NOTES

Change of Name

"Government Accountability Office" substituted for "General Accounting Office" in text on authority of Pub.L. 108–271, § 8(b), cited in the credit to this section and set out as a note under 31 U.S.C.A. § 702, which provided that any reference to the General Accounting Office in any law, rule, regulation, certificate, directive, instruction, or other official paper in force on July 17, 2004, to refer and apply to the Government Accountability Office.

§ 2407.　Delinquents for public money; judgment at return term; continuance

In an action by the United States against any person accountable for public money who fails to pay into the Treasury the sum reported due the United States, upon the adjustment of his account the court shall grant judgment upon motion unless a continuance is granted as specified in this section.

A continuance may be granted if the defendant, in open court and in the presence of the United States attorney, states under oath that he is equitably entitled to credits which have been disallowed by the Government Accountability Office prior to the com-

mencement of the action, specifying each particular claim so rejected, and stating that he cannot safely come to trial.

A continuance may also be granted if such an action is commenced on a bond or other sealed instrument and the court requires the original instrument to be produced.

(June 25, 1948, c. 646, 62 Stat. 972; Pub.L. 108–271, § 8(b), July 7, 2004, 118 Stat. 814.)

HISTORICAL AND STATUTORY NOTES

Change of Name

"Government Accountability Office" substituted for "General Accounting Office" in text on authority of Pub.L. 108–271, § 8(b), cited in the credit to this section and set out as a note under 31 U.S.C.A. § 702, which provided that any reference to the General Accounting Office in any law, rule, regulation, certificate, directive, instruction, or other official paper in force on July 17, 2004, to refer and apply to the Government Accountability Office.

§ 2408. Security not required of United States

Security for damages or costs shall not be required of the United States, any department or agency thereof or any party acting under the direction of any such department or agency on the issuance of process or the institution or prosecution of any proceeding.

Costs taxable, under other Acts of Congress, against the United States or any such department, agency or party shall be paid out of the contingent fund of the department or agency which directed the proceedings to be instituted.

(June 25, 1948, c. 646, 62 Stat. 972.)

§ 2409. Partition actions involving United States

Any civil action by any tenant in common or joint tenant owning an undivided interest in lands, where the United States is one of such tenants in common or joint tenants, against the United States alone or against the United States and any other of such owners, shall proceed, and be determined, in the same manner as would a similar action between private persons.

Whenever in such action the court orders a sale of the property or any part thereof the Attorney General may bid for the same in behalf of the United States. If the United States is the purchaser, the amount of the purchase money shall be paid from the Treasury upon a warrant drawn by the Secretary of the Treasury on the requisition of the Attorney General.

(June 25, 1948, c. 646, 62 Stat. 972.)

§ 2409a. Real property quiet title actions

(a) The United States may be named as a party defendant in a civil action under this section to adjudicate a disputed title to real property in which the United States claims an interest, other than a security interest or water rights. This section does not apply to trust or restricted Indian lands, nor does it apply to or affect actions which may be or could have been brought under sections 1346, 1347, 1491, or 2410 of this title, sections 7424, 7425, or 7426 of the Internal Revenue Code of 1986, as amended (26 U.S.C. 7424, 7425, and 7426), or section 208 of the Act of July 10, 1952 (43 U.S.C. 666).

(b) The United States shall not be disturbed in possession or control of any real property involved in any action under this section pending a final judgment or decree, the conclusion of any appeal therefrom, and sixty days; and if the final determination shall be adverse to the United States, the United States nevertheless may retain such possession or control of the real property or of any part thereof as it may elect, upon payment to the person determined to be entitled thereto of an amount which upon such election the district court in the same action shall determine to be just compensation for such possession or control.

(c) No preliminary injunction shall issue in any action brought under this section.

(d) The complaint shall set forth with particularity the nature of the right, title, or interest which the plaintiff claims in the real property, the circumstances under which it was acquired, and the right, title, or interest claimed by the United States.

(e) If the United States disclaims all interest in the real property or interest therein adverse to the plaintiff at any time prior to the actual commencement of the trial, which disclaimer is confirmed by order of the court, the jurisdiction of the district court shall cease unless it has jurisdiction of the civil action or suit on ground other than and independent of the authority conferred by section 1346(f) of this title.

(f) A civil action against the United States under this section shall be tried by the court without a jury.

(g) Any civil action under this section, except for an action brought by a State, shall be barred unless it is commenced within twelve years of the date upon which it accrued. Such action shall be deemed to have accrued on the date the plaintiff or his predecessor in interest knew or should have known of the claim of the United States.

(h) No civil action may be maintained under this section by a State with respect to defense facilities (including land) of the United States so long as the lands at issue are being used or required by the United States for national defense purposes as determined by the head of the Federal agency with jurisdiction over the lands involved, if it is determined that the State action was brought more than twelve years after the State knew or should have known of the claims of the United States. Upon cessation of such use or requirement, the State may dispute title to

such lands pursuant to the provisions of this section. The decision of the head of the Federal agency is not subject to judicial review.

(i) Any civil action brought by a State under this section with respect to lands, other than tide or submerged lands, on which the United States or its lessee or right-of-way or easement grantee has made substantial improvements or substantial investments or on which the United States has conducted substantial activities pursuant to a management plan such as range improvement, timber harvest, tree planting, mineral activities, farming, wildlife habitat improvement, or other similar activities, shall be barred unless the action is commenced within twelve years after the date the State received notice of the Federal claims to the lands.

(j) If a final determination in an action brought by a State under this section involving submerged or tide lands on which the United States or its lessee or right-of-way or easement grantee has made substantial improvements or substantial investments is adverse to the United States and it is determined that the State's action was brought more than twelve years after the State received notice of the Federal claim to the lands, the State shall take title to the lands subject to any existing lease, easement, or right-of-way. Any compensation due with respect to such lease, easement, or right-of-way shall be determined under existing law.

(k) Notice for the purposes of the accrual of an action brought by a State under this section shall be—

(1) by public communications with respect to the claimed lands which are sufficiently specific as to be reasonably calculated to put the claimant on notice of the Federal claim to the lands, or

(2) by the use, occupancy, or improvement of the claimed lands which, in the circumstances, is open and notorious.

(*l*) For purposes of this section, the term "tide or submerged lands" means "lands beneath navigable waters" as defined in section 2 of the Submerged Lands Act (43 U.S.C. 1301).

(m) Not less than one hundred and eighty days before bringing any action under this section, a State shall notify the head of the Federal agency with jurisdiction over the lands in question of the State's intention to file suit, the basis therefor, and a description of the lands included in the suit.

(n) Nothing in this section shall be construed to permit suits against the United States based upon adverse possession.

(Added Pub.L. 92–562, § 3(a), Oct. 25, 1972, 86 Stat. 1176, and amended Pub.L. 99–514, § 2, Oct. 22, 1986, 100 Stat. 2095; Pub.L. 99–598, Nov. 4, 1986, 100 Stat. 3351.)

HISTORICAL AND STATUTORY NOTES
References in Text
Section 208 of the Act July 10, 1952, referred to in subsec. (a), is section 208 (a) to (d) of Act July 10, 1952, c. 651, 66 Stat. 560. Section 208 (a) to (c) is classified to section 666 of Title 43, Public Lands. Section 208(d) is not classified to the Code.

§ 2410. Actions affecting property on which United States has lien

(a) Under the conditions prescribed in this section and section 1444 of this title for the protection of the United States, the United States may be named a party in any civil action or suit in any district court, or in any State court having jurisdiction of the subject matter—

(1) to quiet title to,

(2) to foreclose a mortgage or other lien upon,

(3) to partition,

(4) to condemn, or

(5) of interpleader or in the nature of interpleader with respect to,

real or personal property on which the United States has or claims a mortgage or other lien.

(b) The complaint or pleading shall set forth with particularity the nature of the interest or lien of the United States. In actions or suits involving liens arising under the internal revenue laws, the complaint or pleading shall include the name and address of the taxpayer whose liability created the lien and, if a notice of the tax lien was filed, the identity of the internal revenue office which filed the notice, and the date and place such notice of lien was filed. In actions in the State courts service upon the United States shall be made by serving the process of the court with a copy of the complaint upon the United States attorney for the district in which the action is brought or upon an assistant United States attorney or clerical employee designated by the United States attorney in writing filed with the clerk of the court in which the action is brought and by sending copies of the process and complaint, by registered mail, or by certified mail, to the Attorney General of the United States at Washington, District of Columbia. In such actions the United States may appear and answer, plead or demur within sixty days after such service or such further time as the court may allow.

(c) A judgment or decree in such action or suit shall have the same effect respecting the discharge of the property from the mortgage or other lien held by the United States as may be provided with respect to such matters by the local law of the place where the court is situated. However, an action to foreclose a mortgage or other lien, naming the United States as a party under this section, must seek judicial sale. A

sale to satisfy a lien inferior to one of the United States shall be made subject to and without disturbing the lien of the United States, unless the United States consents that the property may be sold free of its lien and the proceeds divided as the parties may be entitled. Where a sale of real estate is made to satisfy a lien prior to that of the United States, the United States shall have one year from the date of sale within which to redeem, except that with respect to a lien arising under the internal revenue laws the period shall be 120 days or the period allowable for redemption under State law, whichever is longer, and in any case in which, under the provisions of section 505 of the Housing Act of 1950, as amended (12 U.S.C. 1701k), and subsection (d) of section 3720 of title 38 of the United States Code, the right to redeem does not arise, there shall be no right of redemption. In any case where the debt owing the United States is due, the United States may ask, by way of affirmative relief, for the foreclosure of its own lien and where property is sold to satisfy a first lien held by the United States, the United States may bid at the sale such sum, not exceeding the amount of its claim with expenses of sale, as may be directed by the head (or his delegate) of the department or agency of the United States which has charge of the administration of the laws in respect to which the claim of the United States arises. In any case where the United States is a bidder at the judicial sale, it may credit the amount determined to be due it against the amount it bids at such sales.

(d) In any case in which the United States redeems real property under this section or section 7425 of the Internal Revenue Code of 1986, the amount to be paid for such property shall be the sum of—

(1) the actual amount paid by the purchaser at such sale (which, in the case of a purchaser who is the holder of the lien being foreclosed, shall include the amount of the obligation secured by such lien to the extent satisfied by reason of such sale),

(2) interest on the amount paid (as determined under paragraph (1)) at 6 percent per annum from the date of such sale, and

(3) the amount (if any) equal to the excess of (A) the expenses necessarily incurred in connection with such property, over (B) the income from such property plus (to the extent such property is used by the purchaser) a reasonable rental value of such property.

(e) Whenever any person has a lien upon any real or personal property, duly recorded in the jurisdiction in which the property is located, and a junior lien, other than a tax lien, in favor of the United States attaches to such property, such person may make a written request to the officer charged with the administration of the laws in respect of which the lien of the United States arises, to have the same extinguished. If after appropriate investigation, it appears to such officer that the proceeds from the sale of the property would be insufficient to wholly or partly satisfy the lien of the United States, or that the claim of the United States has been satisfied or by lapse of time or otherwise has become unenforceable, such officer may issue a certificate releasing the property from such lien.

(June 25, 1948, c. 646, 62 Stat. 972; May 24, 1949, c. 139, § 119, 63 Stat. 105; July 7, 1958, Pub.L. 85–508, § 12(h), 72 Stat. 348; June 11, 1960, Pub.L. 86–507, § 1(20), 74 Stat. 201; Nov. 2, 1966, Pub.L. 89–719, Title II, § 201, 80 Stat. 1147; Oct. 22, 1986, Pub.L. 99–514, § 2, 100 Stat. 2095; Nov. 29, 1990, Pub.L. 101–647, Title XXXVI, § 3630, 104 Stat. 4966; Aug. 6, 1991, Pub.L. 102–83, § 5(c)(2), 105 Stat. 406; Oct. 19, 1996, Pub.L. 104–316, Title I, § 114, 110 Stat. 3834.)

HISTORICAL AND STATUTORY NOTES

References in Text

The internal revenue laws, referred to in subsec. (b), are classified generally to Title 26, Internal Revenue Code.

Section 7425 of the Internal Revenue Code of 1986, referred to in subsec. (d), is classified to section 7425 of Title 26, Internal Revenue Code.

Effective and Applicability Provisions

1996 Acts

Amendment by Pub.L. 104–316 effective Oct. 19, 1996, see section 101(e) of Pub.L. 104–316, set out as a note under section 130c of Title 2, The Congress.

1990 Acts

Amendment by section 3630 of Pub.L. 101–647 effective 180 days after Nov. 29, 1990, see section 3631 of Pub.L. 101–647, set out as a note under section 3001 of this title.

1966 Acts

Amendment of section by Pub.L. 89–719 applicable after Nov. 2, 1966, see section 203 of Pub.L. 89–719, set out as a note under section 1346 of this title.

1958 Acts

Amendment of section by Pub.L. 85–508 effective Jan. 3, 1959, upon admission of Alaska into the Union pursuant to Proc. No. 3269, Jan. 3, 1959, 24 F.R. 81, 73 Stat. c16, as required by sections 1 and 8(c) of Pub.L. 85–508, see notes set out under section 81A of this title and preceding section 21 of Title 48, Territories and Insular Possessions.

§ 2411.　Interest

In any judgment of any court rendered (whether against the United States, a collector or deputy collector of internal revenue, a former collector or deputy collector, or the personal representative in case of death) for any overpayment in respect of any internal-revenue tax, interest shall be allowed at the overpayment rate established under section 6621 of the Internal Revenue Code of 1986 upon the amount of the overpayment, from the date of the payment or collection thereof to a date preceding the date of the refund check by not more than thirty days, such date to be

determined by the Commissioner of Internal Revenue. The Commissioner is authorized to tender by check payment of any such judgment, with interest as herein provided, at any time after such judgment becomes final, whether or not a claim for such payment has been duly filed, and such tender shall stop the running of interest, whether or not such refund check is accepted by the judgment creditor.

(June 25, 1948, c. 646, 62 Stat. 973; May 24, 1949, c. 139, § 120, 63 Stat. 106; Jan. 3, 1975, Pub.L. 93–625, § 7(a)(2), 88 Stat. 2115; Apr. 2, 1982, Pub.L. 97–164, Title III, § 302(b), 96 Stat. 56; Oct. 22, 1986, Pub.L. 99–514, § 2, Title XV, § 1511(c)(18), 100 Stat. 2095, 2746.)

HISTORICAL AND STATUTORY NOTES

References in Text

Section 6621 of the Internal Revenue Code of 1986, referred to in text, is classified to section 6621 of Title 26, Internal Revenue Code.

Effective and Applicability Provisions

1986 Acts

Amendment by section 1511(c)(18) of Pub.L. 99–514 applicable for purposes of determining interest for periods after Dec. 31, 1986, see section 1511(d) of Pub.L. 99–514, set out as a note under section 47 of Title 26, Internal Revenue Code.

1982 Acts

Amendment by Pub.L. 97–164 effective Oct. 1, 1982, see section 402 of Pub.L. 97–164, set out as a note under section 171 of this title.

1975 Acts

Amendment by Pub.L. 93–625 effective July 1, 1975, and applicable to amounts outstanding on such date or arising thereafter, see section 7(e) of Pub.L. 93–625, set out as a note under section 6621 of Title 26, Internal Revenue Code.

§ 2412. Costs and fees

(a)(1) Except as otherwise specifically provided by statute, a judgment for costs, as enumerated in section 1920 of this title, but not including the fees and expenses of attorneys, may be awarded to the prevailing party in any civil action brought by or against the United States or any agency or any official of the United States acting in his or her official capacity in any court having jurisdiction of such action. A judgment for costs when taxed against the United States shall, in an amount established by statute, court rule, or order, be limited to reimbursing in whole or in part the prevailing party for the costs incurred by such party in the litigation.

(2) A judgment for costs, when awarded in favor of the United States in an action brought by the United States, may include an amount equal to the filing fee prescribed under section 1914(a) of this title. The preceding sentence shall not be construed as requiring the United States to pay any filing fee.

(b) Unless expressly prohibited by statute, a court may award reasonable fees and expenses of attorneys, in addition to the costs which may be awarded pursuant to subsection (a), to the prevailing party in any civil action brought by or against the United States or any agency or any official of the United States acting in his or her official capacity in any court having jurisdiction of such action. The United States shall be liable for such fees and expenses to the same extent that any other party would be liable under the common law or under the terms of any statute which specifically provides for such an award.

(c)(1) Any judgment against the United States or any agency and any official of the United States acting in his or her official capacity for costs pursuant to subsection (a) shall be paid as provided in sections 2414 and 2517 of this title and shall be in addition to any relief provided in the judgment.

(2) Any judgment against the United States or any agency and any official of the United States acting in his or her official capacity for fees and expenses of attorneys pursuant to subsection (b) shall be paid as provided in sections 2414 and 2517 of this title, except that if the basis for the award is a finding that the United States acted in bad faith, then the award shall be paid by any agency found to have acted in bad faith and shall be in addition to any relief provided in the judgment.

(d)(1)(A) Except as otherwise specifically provided by statute, a court shall award to a prevailing party other than the United States fees and other expenses, in addition to any costs awarded pursuant to subsection (a), incurred by that party in any civil action (other than cases sounding in tort), including proceedings for judicial review of agency action, brought by or against the United States in any court having jurisdiction of that action, unless the court finds that the position of the United States was substantially justified or that special circumstances make an award unjust.

(B) A party seeking an award of fees and other expenses shall, within thirty days of final judgment in the action, submit to the court an application for fees and other expenses which shows that the party is a prevailing party and is eligible to receive an award under this subsection, and the amount sought, including an itemized statement from any attorney or expert witness representing or appearing in behalf of the party stating the actual time expended and the rate at which fees and other expenses were computed. The party shall also allege that the position of the United States was not substantially justified. Whether or not the position of the United States was substantially justified shall be determined on the basis of the record (including the record with respect to the action or failure to act by the agency upon which the civil action is based) which is made in the civil action for which fees and other expenses are sought.

(C) The court, in its discretion, may reduce the amount to be awarded pursuant to this subsection, or deny an award, to the extent that the prevailing party during the course of the proceedings engaged in conduct which unduly and unreasonably protracted the final resolution of the matter in controversy.

(D) If, in a civil action brought by the United States or a proceeding for judicial review of an adversary adjudication described in section 504(a)(4) of title 5, the demand by the United States is substantially in excess of the judgment finally obtained by the United States and is unreasonable when compared with such judgment, under the facts and circumstances of the case, the court shall award to the party the fees and other expenses related to defending against the excessive demand, unless the party has committed a willful violation of law or otherwise acted in bad faith, or special circumstances make an award unjust. Fees and expenses awarded under this subparagraph shall be paid only as a consequence of appropriations provided in advance.

(2) For the purposes of this subsection—

(A) "fees and other expenses" includes the reasonable expenses of expert witnesses, the reasonable cost of any study, analysis, engineering report, test, or project which is found by the court to be necessary for the preparation of the party's case, and reasonable attorney fees (The amount of fees awarded under this subsection shall be based upon prevailing market rates for the kind and quality of the services furnished, except that (i) no expert witness shall be compensated at a rate in excess of the highest rate of compensation for expert witnesses paid by the United States; and (ii) attorney fees shall not be awarded in excess of $125 per hour unless the court determines that an increase in the cost of living or a special factor, such as the limited availability of qualified attorneys for the proceedings involved, justifies a higher fee.);

(B) "party" means (i) an individual whose net worth did not exceed $2,000,000 at the time the civil action was filed, or (ii) any owner of an unincorporated business, or any partnership, corporation, association, unit of local government, or organization, the net worth of which did not exceed $7,000,000 at the time the civil action was filed, and which had not more than 500 employees at the time the civil action was filed; except that an organization described in section 501(c)(3) of the Internal Revenue Code of 1986 (26 U.S.C. 501(c)(3)) exempt from taxation under section 501(a) of such Code, or a cooperative association as defined in section 15(a) of the Agricultural Marketing Act (12 U.S.C. 1141j(a)), may be a party regardless of the net worth of such organization or cooperative association or for purposes of

subsection (d)(1)(D), a small entity as defined in section 601 of Title 5;

(C) "United States" includes any agency and any official of the United States acting in his or her official capacity;

(D) "position of the United States" means, in addition to the position taken by the United States in the civil action, the action or failure to act by the agency upon which the civil action is based; except that fees and expenses may not be awarded to a party for any portion of the litigation in which the party has unreasonably protracted the proceedings;

(E) "civil action brought by or against the United States" includes an appeal by a party, other than the United States, from a decision of a contracting officer rendered pursuant to a disputes clause in a contract with the Government or pursuant to the Contract Disputes Act of 1978;

(F) "court" includes the United States Court of Federal Claims and the United States Court of Appeals for Veterans Claims;

(G) "final judgment" means a judgment that is final and not appealable, and includes an order of settlement;

(H) "prevailing party", in the case of eminent domain proceedings, means a party who obtains a final judgment (other than by settlement), exclusive of interest, the amount of which is at least as close to the highest valuation of the property involved that is attested to at trial on behalf of the property owner as it is to the highest valuation of the property involved that is attested to at trial on behalf of the Government; and

(I) "demand" means the express demand of the United States which led to the adversary adjudication, but shall not include a recitation of the maximum statutory penalty (i) in the complaint, or (ii) elsewhere when accompanied by an express demand for a lesser amount.

(3) In awarding fees and other expenses under this subsection to a prevailing party in any action for judicial review of an adversary adjudication, as defined in subsection (b)(1)(C) of section 504 of title 5, United States Code, or an adversary adjudication subject to the Contract Disputes Act of 1978, the court shall include in that award fees and other expenses to the same extent authorized in subsection (a) of such section, unless the court finds that during such adversary adjudication the position of the United States was substantially justified, or that special circumstances make an award unjust.

(4) Fees and other expenses awarded under this subsection to a party shall be paid by any agency over which the party prevails from any funds made available to the agency by appropriation or otherwise.

(e) The provisions of this section shall not apply to any costs, fees, and other expenses in connection with any proceeding to which section 7430 of the Internal Revenue Code of 1986 applies (determined without regard to subsections (b) and (f) of such section). Nothing in the preceding sentence shall prevent the awarding under subsection (a) of section 2412 of title 28, United States Code, of costs enumerated in section 1920 of such title (as in effect on October 1, 1981).

(f) If the United States appeals an award of costs or fees and other expenses made against the United States under this section and the award is affirmed in whole or in part, interest shall be paid on the amount of the award as affirmed. Such interest shall be computed at the rate determined under section 1961(a) of this title, and shall run from the date of the award through the day before the date of the mandate of affirmance.

(June 25, 1948, c. 646, 62 Stat. 973; July 18, 1966, Pub.L. 89–507, § 1, 80 Stat. 308; Oct. 21, 1980, Pub. L. 96–481, Title II, § 204(a), (c), 94 Stat. 2327, 2329; Sept. 3, 1982, Pub. L. 97–248, Title II, § 292(c), 96 Stat. 574; Aug. 5, 1985, Pub. L. 99–80, §§ 2, 6(a), (b)(2), 99 Stat. 184, 186; Oct. 22, 1986, Pub.L. 99–514, § 2, 100 Stat. 2095; Oct. 29, 1992, Pub.L. 102–572, Title III, § 301(a), Title V, §§ 502(b), 506(a), Title IX, § 902(b)(1), 106 Stat. 4511–4513, 4516; Dec. 21, 1995, Pub.L. 104–66, Title I, § 1091(b), 109 Stat. 722; Mar. 29, 1996, Pub.L. 104–121, Title II, § 232, 110 Stat. 863; Pub.L. 105–368, Title V, § 512(b)(1)(B), Nov. 11, 1998, 112 Stat. 3342.)

HISTORICAL AND STATUTORY NOTES

References in Text

The Contract Disputes Act of 1978, referred to in subsec. (d)(2)(E), (3), is Pub. L. 95–563, Nov. 1, 1978, 92 Stat. 2383, as amended, which is classified principally to chapter 9 (section 601 et seq.) of Title 41, Public Contracts. For complete classification of this Act to the Code, see Short Title note set out under section 601 of Title 41 and Tables.

Section 7430 of the Internal Revenue Code of 1986, referred to in subsec. (e), is classified to section 7430 of Title 26, Internal Revenue Code.

Effective and Applicability Provisions

1998 Acts

Amendment by Pub.L. 105–368 effective on the first day of the first month beginning more than 90 days after Nov. 11, 1998, see section 513 of Pub.L. 105–368, set out as a note under section 7251 of Title 38.

1996 Acts

Amendment by Pub.L. 104–121 applicable to civil actions and adversary adjudications commenced on or after March 29, 1996, see section 233 of Pub.L. 104–121, set out as a note under section 504 of Title 5, Government Organization and Employees.

1992 Acts

Section 506(b) of Pub.L. 102–572 provided that: "The amendment made by subsection (a) [amending subsec. (d)(2)(F) of this section] shall apply to any case pending before the United States Court of Veterans Appeals on the date of the enactment of this Act [Oct. 29, 1992], to any appeal filed in that court on or after such date, and to any appeal from that court that is pending on such date in the United States Court of Appeals for the Federal Circuit."

Section 506(d) of Pub.L. 102–572 provided that: "This section, and the amendment made by this section [amending subsec. (d)(2)(F) of this section and enacting provisions set out as notes under this section], shall take effect on the date of the enactment of this Act [Oct. 29, 1992]."

Amendment by section 902(b)(1) of Pub.L. 102–572 effective Oct. 29, 1992, see section 911 of Pub.L. 102–572, set out as a note under section 171 of this title.

Amendments by sections 301(a) and 502(b) of Pub.L. 102–572 effective Jan. 1, 1993, see section 1101(a) of Pub.L. 102–572, set out as a note under section 905 of Title 2, The Congress.

1985 Acts

Amendment by Pub. L. 99–80 applicable to cases pending on or commenced on or after Aug. 5, 1985, but with provision for additional applicability to certain prior cases and to prior board of contracts appeals cases, see section 7 of Pub. L. 99–80, set out as a note under section 504 of Title 5, Government Organization and Employees.

1982 Acts

Amendment by Pub.L. 97–248 applicable to civil actions or proceedings commenced after Feb. 28, 1983, see section 292(e)(1) of Pub.L. 97–248, as amended, set out as a note under section 7430 of Title 26, Internal Revenue Code.

1980 Acts

Amendment by section 204(a) of Pub.L. 96–481 to take effect on Oct. 1, 1981, and applicable to any adversary adjudication, as defined in section 504(b)(1)(C) of Title 5, and to civil actions and adversary adjudications described in this section, which are pending on, or commenced on or after, Oct. 1, 1981, see section 208 of Pub.L. 96–481, as amended, set out as a note under section 504 of Title 5, Government Organization and Employees.

Section 204(c) of Pub.L. 96–481 which provided in part that effective Oct. 1, 1984, subsec. (d) of this section is repealed, except that the provisions of subsec. (d) shall continue to apply through final disposition of any adversary adjudication initiated before the date of repeal, was repealed by Pub.L. 99–80, § 6(b)(2), Aug. 5, 1985, 99 Stat. 186.

1966 Acts

Section 3 of Pub.L. 89–507 provided that: "These amendments [to this section and section 2520 of this title] shall apply only to judgments entered in actions filed subsequent to the date of enactment of this Act [July 18, 1966]. These amendments [to this section and section 2520 of this title] shall not authorize the reopening or modification of judgments entered prior to the enactment of this Act [July 18, 1966]."

Fees Awarded to Non-attorney Practitioners

Pub.L. 107–330, Title IV, § 403, Dec. 6, 2002, 116 Stat. 2833, provided that: "The authority of the United States Court of Appeals for Veterans Claims to award reasonable fees and expenses of attorneys under section 2412(d) of title 28, United States Code [Subsec. (d) of this section], shall include authority to award fees and expenses, in an amount determined appropriate by the United States Court of Ap-

peals for Veterans Claims, of individuals admitted to practice before the Court as non-attorney practitioners under subsection (b) or (c) of Rule 46 of the Rules of Practice and Procedure of the United States Court of Appeals for Veterans Claims."

Savings Provisions

Section 206 of Pub.L. 96–481, as amended by Pub.L. 99–80, § 3, Aug. 5, 1985, 99 Stat. 186, provided that:

"(a) Except as provided in subsection (b), nothing in section 2412(d) of title 28, United States Code, as added by section 204(a) of this title [subsec. (d) of this section], alters, modifies, repeals, invalidates, or supersedes any other provision of Federal law which authorizes an award of such fees and other expenses to any party other than the United States that prevails in any civil action brought by or against the United States.

"(b) Section 206(b) of the Social Security Act (42 U.S.C. 406(b)(1)) [section 406(b) of Title 42, The Public Health and Welfare] shall not prevent an award of fees and other expenses under section 2412(d) of title 28, United States Code [subsec. (d) of this section]. Section 206(b)(2) of the Social Security Act [section 406(b)(2) of Title 42] shall not apply with respect to any such award but only if, where the claimant's attorney receives fees for the same work under both section 206(b) of that Act [section 406(b) of Title 42] and section 2412(d) of title 28, United States Code [subsec. (d) of this section], the claimant's attorney refunds to the claimant the amount of the smaller fee."

Congressional Findings and Purposes

For Congressional findings and purposes relating to 1980 amendment of this section, see section 202 of Pub.L. 96–481, set out as a note under section 504 of Title 5, Government Organization and Employees.

Fee Agreements

Section 506(c) of Pub.L. 102–572 provided that: "Section 5904(d) of title 38, United States Code [section 5904(d) of Title 38, Veterans' Benefits], shall not prevent an award of fees and other expenses under section 2412(d) of title 28, United States Code [subsec. (d) of this section]. Section 5904(d) of title 38, United States Code, shall not apply with respect to any such award but only if, where the claimant's attorney receives fees for the same work under both section 5904 of title 38, United States Code, and section 2412(d) of title 28, United States Code, the claimant's attorney refunds to the claimant the amount of the smaller fee."

Nonliability of Judicial Officers for Costs

Pub.L. 104–317, Title III, § 309(a), Oct. 19, 1996, 110 Stat. 3853, provided that: "Notwithstanding any other provision of law, no judicial officer shall be held liable for any costs, including attorney's fees, in any action brought against such officer for an act or omission taken in such officer's judicial capacity, unless such action was clearly in excess of such officer's jurisdiction."

Revival of Previously Repealed Provisions

For revival of subsec. (d) of this section effective on or after Aug. 5, 1985, as if it had not been repealed by section 204(c) of Pub.L. 96–481, and repeal of section 204(c) of Pub.L. 96–481, see section 6 of Pub.L. 99–80, set out as a note under section 504 of Title 5, Government Organization and Employees.

§ 2413. Executions in favor of United States

A writ of execution on a judgment obtained for the use of the United States in any court thereof shall be issued from and made returnable to the court which rendered the judgment, but may be executed in any other State, in any Territory, or in the District of Columbia.

(June 25, 1948, c. 646, 62 Stat. 974.)

§ 2414. Payment of judgments and compromise settlements

Except as provided by the Contract Disputes Act of 1978, payment of final judgments rendered by a district court or the Court of International Trade against the United States shall be made on settlements by the Secretary of the Treasury. Payment of final judgments rendered by a State or foreign court or tribunal against the United States, or against its agencies or officials upon obligations or liabilities of the United States, shall be made on settlements by the Secretary of the Treasury after certification by the Attorney General that it is in the interest of the United States to pay the same.

Whenever the Attorney General determines that no appeal shall be taken from a judgment or that no further review will be sought from a decision affirming the same, he shall so certify and the judgment shall be deemed final.

Except as otherwise provided by law, compromise settlements of claims referred to the Attorney General for defense of imminent litigation or suits against the United States, or against its agencies or officials upon obligations or liabilities of the United States, made by the Attorney General or any person authorized by him, shall be settled and paid in a manner similar to judgments in like causes and appropriations or funds available for the payment of such judgments are hereby made available for the payment of such compromise settlements.

(June 25, 1948, c. 646, 62 Stat. 974; Aug. 30, 1961, Pub.L. 87–187, § 1, 75 Stat. 415; Nov. 1, 1978, Pub.L. 95–563, § 14(d), 92 Stat. 2390; Oct. 10, 1980, Pub.L. 96–417, Title V, § 512, 94 Stat. 1744; Oct. 19, 1996, Pub.L. 104–316, Title II, § 202(k), 110 Stat. 3843.)

HISTORICAL AND STATUTORY NOTES

References in Text

The Contract Disputes Act of 1978, referred to in first paragraph, is Pub.L. 95–563, Nov. 1, 1978, 92 Stat. 2383, as amended, which is classified principally to chapter 9 (section 601 et seq.) of Title 41, Public Contracts. For complete classification of this Act to the Code, see Short Title note set out under section 601 of Title 41 and Tables.

Effective and Applicability Provisions

1980 Acts

Amendment by Pub.L. 96–417 effective on Nov. 1, 1980, and applicable with respect to civil actions pending on or commenced on or after such date, see section 701(a) of Pub.L. 96–417, as amended, set out as a note under section 251 of this title.

1978 Acts

Amendment by Pub.L. 95–563 effective with respect to contracts entered into 120 days after Nov. 1, 1978, and, at the election of the contractor, with respect to any claim pending at such time before the contracting officer or initiated thereafter, see section 16 of Pub.L. 95–563, set out as a note under section 601 of Title 41, Public Contracts.

Transfer of Functions

Effective June 30, 1996, the functions of the Comptroller General under this section to be transferred to the Director of the Office of Management and Budget, contingent upon the additional transfer to the Office of Management and Budget of such personnel, budget authority, records, and property of the General Accounting Office relating to such functions as the Comptroller General and the Director jointly determine to be necessary, see section 211 of Pub.L. 104–53, set out as a note under section 501 of Title 31, Money and Finance.

§ 2415. Time for commencing actions brought by the United States

(a) Subject to the provisions of section 2416 of this title, and except as otherwise provided by Congress, every action for money damages brought by the United States or an officer or agency thereof which is founded upon any contract express or implied in law or fact, shall be barred unless the complaint is filed within six years after the right of action accrues or within one year after final decisions have been rendered in applicable administrative proceedings required by contract or by law, whichever is later: *Provided*, That in the event of later partial payment or written acknowledgment of debt, the right of action shall be deemed to accrue again at the time of each such payment or acknowledgment: *Provided further*, That an action for money damages brought by the United States for or on behalf of a recognized tribe, band or group of American Indians shall not be barred unless the complaint is filed more than six years and ninety days after the right of action accrued: *Provided further*, That an action for money damages which accrued on the date of enactment of this Act in accordance with subsection (g) brought by the United States for or on behalf of a recognized tribe, band, or group of American Indians, or on behalf of an individual Indian whose land is held in trust or restricted status, shall not be barred unless the complaint is filed sixty days after the date of publication of the list required by section 4(c) of the Indian Claims Limitation Act of 1982: *Provided*, That, for those claims that are on either of the two lists published pursuant to the Indian Claims Limitation

Act of 1982, any right of action shall be barred unless the complaint is filed within (1) one year after the Secretary of the Interior has published in the Federal Register a notice rejecting such claim or (2) three years after the date the Secretary of the Interior has submitted legislation or legislative report to Congress to resolve such claim or more than two years after a final decision has been rendered in applicable administrative proceedings required by contract or by law, whichever is later.

(b) Subject to the provisions of section 2416 of this title, and except as otherwise provided by Congress, every action for money damages brought by the United States or an officer or agency thereof which is founded upon a tort shall be barred unless the complaint is filed within three years after the right of action first accrues: *Provided*, That an action to recover damages resulting from a trespass on lands of the United States; an action to recover damages resulting from fire to such lands; an action to recover for diversion of money paid under a grant program; and an action for conversion of property of the United States may be brought within six years after the right of action accrues, except that such actions for or on behalf of a recognized tribe, band or group of American Indians, including actions relating to allotted trust or restricted Indian lands, may be brought within six years and ninety days after the right of action accrues, except that such actions for or on behalf of a recognized tribe, band, or group of American Indians, including actions relating to allotted trust or restricted Indian lands, or on behalf of an individual Indian whose land is held in trust or restricted status which accrued on the date of enactment of this Act in accordance with subsection (g) may be brought on or before sixty days after the date of the publication of the list required by section 4(c) of the Indian Claims Limitation Act of 1982: *Provided*, That, for those claims that are on either of the two lists published pursuant to the Indian Claims Limitation Act of 1982, any right of action shall be barred unless the complaint is filed within (1) one year after the Secretary of the Interior has published in the Federal Register a notice rejecting such claim or (2) three years after the Secretary of the Interior has submitted legislation or legislative report to Congress to resolve such claim.

(c) Nothing herein shall be deemed to limit the time for bringing an action to establish the title to, or right of possession of, real or personal property.

(d) Subject to the provisions of section 2416 of this title and except as otherwise provided by Congress, every action for the recovery of money erroneously paid to or on behalf of any civilian employee of any agency of the United States or to or on behalf of any member or dependent of any member of the uniformed services of the United States, incident to the

employment or services of such employee or member, shall be barred unless the complaint is filed within six years after the right of action accrues: *Provided,* That in the event of later partial payment or written acknowledgment of debt, the right of action shall be deemed to accrue again at the time of each such payment or acknowledgment.

(e) In the event that any action to which this section applies is timely brought and is thereafter dismissed without prejudice, the action may be recommenced within one year after such dismissal, regardless of whether the action would otherwise then be barred by this section. In any action so recommenced the defendant shall not be barred from interposing any claim which would not have been barred in the original action.

(f) The provisions of this section shall not prevent the assertion, in an action against the United States or an officer or agency thereof, of any claim of the United States or an officer or agency thereof against an opposing party, a co-party, or a third party that arises out of the transaction or occurrence that is the subject matter of the opposing party's claim. A claim of the United States or an officer or agency thereof that does not arise out of the transaction or occurrence that is the subject matter of the opposing party's claim may, if time-barred, be asserted only by way of offset and may be allowed in an amount not to exceed the amount of the opposing party's recovery.

(g) Any right of action subject to the provisions of this section which accrued prior to the date of enactment of this Act shall, for purposes of this section, be deemed to have accrued on the date of enactment of this Act.

(h) Nothing in this Act shall apply to actions brought under the Internal Revenue Code or incidental to the collection of taxes imposed by the United States.

(i) The provisions of this section shall not prevent the United States or an officer or agency thereof from collecting any claim of the United States by means of administrative offset, in accordance with section 3716 of title 31.

(Added Pub.L. 89–505, § 1, July 18, 1966, 80 Stat. 304, and amended Pub.L. 92–353, July 18, 1972, 86 Stat. 499; Pub.L. 92–485, Oct. 13, 1972, 86 Stat. 803; Pub.L. 95–64, July 11, 1977, 91 Stat. 268; Pub.L. 95–103, Aug. 15, 1977, 91 Stat. 842; Pub.L. 96–217, § 1, Mar. 27, 1980, 94 Stat. 126; Pub.L. 97–365, § 9, Oct. 25, 1982, 96 Stat. 1754; Pub.L. 97–394, Title I, § 2, Dec. 30, 1982, 96 Stat. 1976; Pub.L. 97–452, § 2(d)(2), Jan. 12, 1983, 96 Stat. 2478; Pub.L. 98–250, § 4(a), Apr. 3, 1984, 98 Stat. 118.)

HISTORICAL AND STATUTORY NOTES

References in Text

The date of enactment of this Act, referred to in subsecs. (a), (b), and (g), means the date of enactment of Pub.L. 89–505, which was approved on July 18, 1966.

The Indian Claims Limitation Act of 1982, referred to in subsecs. (a) and (b), is Pub.L. 97–394, Title I, §§ 2–6, Dec. 30, 1982, 96 Stat. 1976–1978, which amended this section and enacted provisions set out as notes under this section. For complete classification of this Act to the Code, see Short Title of 1982 Amendments note set out under this section and Tables.

This Act, referred to in subsec. (h), means Pub.L. 89–505, July 18, 1966, 80 Stat. 304, which enacted this section and section 2416 of this title. For complete classification of this Act to the Code see Tables.

Short Title

1982 Amendments

Section 1 of Pub.L. 97–394, as amended by Pub.L. 98–250, § 4(b), Apr. 3, 1984, 98 Stat. 119, provided that: "Sections 2 through 6 of this Act [sections 2–6 of Pub.L. 97–394, which amended this section and enacted provisions set out as a note under this section] may be cited as the 'Indian Claims Limitation Act of 1982'."

Legislative Proposals Respecting Appropriateness of Resolution By Litigation of Unresolved Indian Claims

Section 2 of Pub.L. 96–217 provided that: "Not later than June 30, 1981, the Secretary of the Interior, after consultation with the Attorney General, shall submit to the Congress legislative proposals to resolve those Indian claims subject to the amendments made by the first section of this Act [amending this section] that the Secretary of the Interior or the Attorney General believes are not appropriate to resolve by litigation."

Publication of List of Indian Claims; Additional Claims; Time to Commence Action; Rejection of Claims; Claims Resolved By Legislation

Sections 3 to 6 of Pub.L. 97–394 provided that:

"Sec. 3. (a) Within ninety days after the enactment of this Act [Dec. 30, 1982], the Secretary of the Interior (hereinafter referred to as the 'Secretary') shall publish in the Federal Register a list of all claims accruing to any tribe, band or group of Indians or individual Indian on or before July 18, 1966, which have at any time been identified by or submitted to the Secretary under the 'Statute of Limitation Project' undertaken by the Department of the Interior and which, but for the provisions of this Act [sections 2–6 of Pub.L. 97–394; see Short Title of 1982 Amendments note set out under this section] would be barred by the provisions of section 2415 of title 28, United States Code [this section]: *Provided,* That the Secretary shall have the discretion to exclude from such list any matter which was erroneously identified as a claim and which has no legal merit whatsoever.

"(b) Such list shall group the claims on a reservation-by-reservation, tribe-by-tribe, or State-by-State basis, as appropriate, and shall state the nature and geographic location of each claim and only such other additional information as may be needed to identify specifically such claims.

"(c) Within thirty days after the publication of this list, the Secretary shall provide a copy of the Indian Claims Limitation Act of 1982 [sections 2–6 of Pub.L. 97–394; see short title of 1982 Amendments note under this section] and a copy of the Federal Register containing this list, or such

parts as may be pertinent, to each Indian tribe, band or group whose rights or the rights of whose members could be affected by the provisions of section 2415 of title 28, United States Code [this section].

"**Sec. 4.** (a) Any tribe, band or group of Indians or any individual Indian shall have one hundred and eighty days after the date of the publication in the Federal Register of the list provided for in section 3 of this Act [section 3 of Pub.L. 97–394] to submit to the Secretary any additional specific claim or claims which such tribe, band or group of Indians or individual Indian believes may be affected by section 2415 of title 28, United States Code [this section], and desires to have considered for litigation or legislation by the United States.

"**(b)** Any such claim submitted to the Secretary shall be accompanied by a statement identifying the nature of the claim, the date when the right of action allegedly accrued, the names of the potential plaintiffs and defendants, if known, and such other information needed to identify and evaluate such claim.

"**(c)** Not more than thirty days after the expiration of the one hundred and eighty day period provided for in subsection (a) of this section, the Secretary shall publish in the Federal Register a list containing the additional claims submitted during such period: *Provided,* That the Secretary shall have the discretion to exclude from such list any matter which has not been sufficiently identified as a claim.

"**Sec. 5.** (a) Any right of action shall be barred sixty days after the date of the publication of the list required by section 4(c) of this Act [section 4(c) of Pub.L. 97–394] for those pre-1966 claims which, but for the provisions of this Act [sections 2–6 of Pub.L. 97–394; see Short Title of 1982 Amendments note set out under this section] would have been barred by section 2415 of title 28, United States Code [this section], unless such claims are included on either of the lists required by section 3 or 4(c) of this Act [section 3 or 4(c) of Pub.L. 97–394].

"**(b)** If the Secretary decides to reject for litigation any of the claims or groups or categories of claims contained on either of the lists required by section 3 or 4(c) of this Act [section 3 or 4(c) of Pub.L. 97–394], he shall send a report to the appropriate tribe, band, or group of Indians, whose rights or the rights of whose members could be affected by such rejection, advising them of his decision. The report shall identify the nature and geographic location of each rejected claim and the name of the potential plaintiffs and defendants if they are known or can be reasonably ascertained and shall, briefly, state the reasons why such claim or claims were rejected for litigation. Where the Secretary knows or can reasonably ascertain the identity of any of the potential individual Indian plaintiffs and their present addresses, he shall provide them with written notice of such rejection. Upon the request of any Indian claimant, the Secretary shall, without undue delay, provide to such claimant any nonprivileged research materials or evidence gathered by the United States in the documentation of such claim.

"**(c)** The Secretary, as soon as possible, after providing the report required by subsection (b) of this section, shall publish a notice in the Federal Register identifying the claims covered in such report. With respect to any claim covered by such report, any right of action shall be barred unless the complaint is filed within one year after the date of publication in the Federal Register.

"**Sec. 6.** (a) If the Secretary determines that any claim or claims contained in either of the lists as provided in sections 3 or 4(c) of this Act [sections 3 or 4(c) of Pub.L. 97–394] is not appropriate for litigation, but determines that such claims may be appropriately resolved by legislation, he shall submit to the Congress legislation to resolve such claims or shall submit to Congress a report setting out options for legislative resolution of such claims.

"**(b)** Any right of action on claims covered by such legislation or report shall be barred unless the complaint is filed within 3 years after the date of submission of such legislation or legislative report to Congress."

[For termination of reporting provisions pertaining to proposed legislation to resolve Indian claims, effective May 15, 2000, see Pub.L. 104–66, § 3003, as amended, set out as a note under 31 U.S.C.A. § 1113, and the last item on page 113 of House Document No. 103–7.]

§ 2416. Time for commencing actions brought by the United States—Exclusions

For the purpose of computing the limitations periods established in section 2415, there shall be excluded all periods during which—

 (a) the defendant or the res is outside the United States, its territories and possessions, the District of Columbia, or the Commonwealth of Puerto Rico; or

 (b) the defendant is exempt from legal process because of infancy, mental incompetence, diplomatic immunity, or for any other reason; or

 (c) facts material to the right of action are not known and reasonably could not be known by an official of the United States charged with the responsibility to act in the circumstances; or

 (d) the United States is in a state of war declared pursuant to article I, section 8, of the Constitution of the United States.

(Added Pub.L. 89–505, § 1, July 18, 1966, 80 Stat. 305.)

CHAPTER 163—FINES, PENALTIES AND FORFEITURES

Sec.
2467.　Enforcement of foreign judgment.

§ 2461.　Mode of recovery

(a) Whenever a civil fine, penalty or pecuniary forfeiture is prescribed for the violation of an Act of Congress without specifying the mode of recovery or enforcement thereof, it may be recovered in a civil action.

(b) Unless otherwise provided by Act of Congress, whenever a forfeiture of property is prescribed as a penalty for violation of an Act of Congress and the seizure takes place on the high seas or on navigable waters within the admiralty and maritime jurisdiction of the United States, such forfeiture may be enforced by libel in admiralty but in cases of seizures on land the forfeiture may be enforced by a proceeding by libel which shall conform as near as may be to proceedings in admiralty.

(c) If a person is charged in a criminal case with a violation of an Act of Congress for which the civil or criminal forfeiture of property is authorized, the Government may include notice of the forfeiture in the indictment or information pursuant to the Federal Rules of Criminal Procedure. If the defendant is convicted of the offense giving rise to the forfeiture, the court shall order the forfeiture of the property as part of the sentence in the criminal case pursuant to to the Federal Rules of Criminal Procedure and section 3554 of title 18, United States Code. The procedures in section 413 of the Controlled Substances Act (21 U.S.C. 853) apply to all stages of a criminal forfeiture proceeding, except that subsection (d) of such section applies only in cases in which the defendant is convicted of a violation of such Act.

(June 25, 1948, c. 646, 62 Stat. 974; Apr. 25, 2000, Pub.L. 106–185, § 16, 114 Stat. 221; Mar. 9, 2006, Pub.L. 109–177, Title IV, § 410, 120 Stat. 246.)

HISTORICAL AND STATUTORY NOTES

References in Text

The Federal Rules of Criminal Procedure, referred to in subsec. (c), are set out in Title 18, Rules of Criminal Procedure, Fed.Rules Cr.Proc., Rule 1 et seq., 18 U.S.C.A.

Section 413 of the Controlled Substances Act, referred to in subsec. (c), is Pub.L. 91–513, Title II, § 413, as added Pub.L. 98–473, Title II, § 303, Oct. 12, 1984, 98 Stat. 2044, as amended, which is classified to 21 U.S.C.A. § 853. The Controlled Substances Act (CSA), is title II of Pub.L. 91–513, Oct. 27, 1970, 84 Stat. 1242, as amended, which is classified principally to subchapter I of chapter 13, of Title 21, 21 U.S.C.A. § 801 et seq. For complete classification of Title II to the Code, see Short Title note set out under 21 U.S.C.A. § 801 and Tables.

Effective and Applicability Provisions

2000 Acts

Amendments by Pub.L. 106–185, applicable to any forfeiture proceeding commenced on or after the date that is 120 days after April 25, 2000, see section 21 of Pub.L. 106–185, set out as a note under section 1324 of Title 8.

Federal Civil Penalties Inflation Adjustment

Pub.L. 101–410, Oct. 5, 1990, 104 Stat. 890, as amended Pub.L. 104–134, Title III, § 31001(s)(1), Apr. 26, 1996, 110 Stat. 1321–373; Pub.L. 105–362, Title XIII, § 1301(a), Nov. 10, 1998, 112 Stat. 3293, provided that:

"SHORT TITLE

"**Section 1.** This Act may be cited as the 'Federal Civil Penalties Inflation Adjustment Act of 1990'.

"FINDINGS AND PURPOSE

"**Sec. 2.** **(a) Findings.**—The Congress finds that—

"**(1)** the power of Federal agencies to impose civil monetary penalties for violations of Federal law and regulations plays an important role in deterring violations and furthering the policy goals embodied in such laws and regulations;

"**(2)** the impact of many civil monetary penalties has been and is diminished due to the effect of inflation;

"**(3)** by reducing the impact of civil monetary penalties, inflation has weakened the deterrent effect of such penalties; and

"**(4)** the Federal Government does not maintain comprehensive, detailed accounting of the efforts of Federal agencies to assess and collect civil monetary penalties.

"**(b) Purpose.**—The purpose of this Act is to establish a mechanism that shall—

"**(1)** allow for regular adjustment for inflation of civil monetary penalties;

"**(2)** maintain the deterrent effect of civil monetary penalties and promote compliance with the law; and

"**(3)** improve the collection by the Federal Government of civil monetary penalties.

"DEFINITIONS

"**Sec. 3.** For purposes of this Act, the term—

"**(1)** 'agency' means an Executive agency as defined under section 105 of title 5, United States Code [5 U.S.C.A. § 105], and includes the United States Postal Service;

"**(2)** 'civil monetary penalty' means any penalty, fine, or other sanction that—

"**(A)(i)** is for a specific monetary amount as provided by Federal law; or

"**(ii)** has a maximum amount provided for by Federal law; and

"**(B)** is assessed or enforced by an agency pursuant to Federal law; and

"**(C)** is assessed or enforced pursuant to an administrative proceeding or a civil action in the Federal courts; and

"**(3)** 'Consumer Price Index' means the Consumer Price Index for all-urban consumers published by the Department of Labor.

"CIVIL MONETARY PENALTY INFLATION ADJUSTMENT REPORTS

"**Sec. 4.** The head of each agency shall, not later than 180 days after the date of enactment of the Debt Collection Improvement Act of 1996 [Apr. 26, 1996], and at least once every 4 years thereafter—

"**(1)** by regulation adjust each civil monetary penalty provided by law within the jurisdiction of the Federal agency, except for any penalty (including any addition to tax and additional amount) under the Internal Revenue Code of 1986 [26 U.S.C.A. § 1 et seq.], the Tariff Act of 1930 [19 U.S.C.A. § 1202 et seq.], the Occupational Safety and Health Act of 1970 [29 U.S.C.A. § 651 et seq.], or the Social Security Act [42 U.S.C.A. § 301 et seq.], by the inflation adjustment described under section 5 of this Act; and

"**(2)** publish each such regulation in the Federal Register.

"COST-OF-LIVING ADJUSTMENTS OF CIVIL MONETARY PENALTIES

"**Sec. 5. (a) Adjustment.**—The inflation adjustment under section 4 shall be determined by increasing the maximum civil monetary penalty or the range of minimum and maximum civil monetary penalties, as applicable, for each civil monetary penalty by the cost-of-living adjustment. Any increase determined under this subsection shall be rounded to the nearest—

"**(1)** multiple of $10 in the case of penalties less than or equal to $100;

"**(2)** multiple of $100 in the case of penalties greater than $100 but less than or equal to $1,000;

"**(3)** multiple of $1,000 in the case of penalties greater than $1,000 but less than or equal to $10,000;

"**(4)** multiple of $5,000 in the case of penalties greater than $10,000 but less than or equal to $100,000;

"**(5)** multiple of $10,000 in the case of penalties greater than $100,000 but less than or equal to $200,000; and

"**(6)** multiple of $25,000 in the case of penalties greater than $200,000.

"**(b) Definition.**—For purposes of subsection (a), the term 'cost-of-living adjustment' means the percentage (if any) for each civil monetary penalty by which—

"**(1)** the Consumer Price Index for the month of June of the calendar year preceding the adjustment, exceeds

"**(2)** the Consumer Price Index for the month of June of the calendar year in which the amount of such civil monetary penalty was last set or adjusted pursuant to law.

"ANNUAL REPORT

"**Sec. 6.** Any increase under this Act in a civil monetary penalty shall apply only to violations which occur after the date the increase takes effect."

[Former Sec. 6 repealed by Pub.L. 105–362, Title XIII, § 1301(a)(1), Nov. 10, 1998, 112 Stat. 3293.]

"**Sec. 7. [Redesignated as Sec. 6.** Pub.L. 105–362, Title XIII, § 1301(a)(2), Nov. 10, 1998, 112 Stat. 3293.]

[Pub.L. 104–134, Title III, § 31001(s)(2), Apr. 26, 1996, 110 Stat. 1321–373, provided that: "The first adjustment of a civil monetary penalty made pursuant to the amendment made by paragraph (1) [amending Pub.L. 101–410, set out as a note under this section] may not exceed 10 percent of such penalty."]

[Any reference in any provision of law enacted before Jan. 4, 1995, to the Committee on Government Operations of the House of Representatives treated as referring to the Committee on Government Reform and Oversight of the House of Representatives, except that any reference in any provision of law enacted before Jan. 4, 1995, to the Committee on Government Operations of the House of Representatives treated as referring to the Committee on the Budget of the House of Representatives in the case of a provision of law relating to the establishment, extension, and enforcement of special controls over the Federal budget, see section 1(a)(6) and (c)(2) of Pub.L. 104–14, set out as a note preceding section 21 of Title 2, The Congress.]

Memorandum of President of the United States, May 3, 1991, 56 F.R. 21911, delegated to Director of Office of Management and Budget responsibility of President for submitting reports on civil monetary penalties to Committee on Governmental Affairs of the Senate and Committee on Government Operations of the House of Representatives and to Congress as required by sections 4 and 6 of the Federal Civil Penalties Inflation Adjustment Act of 1990, Pub.L. 101–410, set out as a note under this section.

§ 2462. Time for commencing proceedings

Except as otherwise provided by Act of Congress, an action, suit or proceeding for the enforcement of any civil fine, penalty, or forfeiture, pecuniary or otherwise, shall not be entertained unless commenced within five years from the date when the claim first accrued if, within the same period, the offender or the property is found within the United States in order that proper service may be made thereon.

(June 25, 1948, c. 646, 62 Stat. 974.)

§ 2463. Property taken under revenue law not repleviable

All property taken or detained under any revenue law of the United States shall not be repleviable, but shall be deemed to be in the custody of the law and subject only to the orders and decrees of the courts of the United States having jurisdiction thereof.

(June 25, 1948, c. 646, 62 Stat. 974.)

§ 2464. Security; special bond

(a) Except in cases of seizures for forfeiture under any law of the United States, whenever a warrant of arrest or other process in rem is issued in any admiralty case, the United States marshal shall stay the execution of such process, or discharge the property arrested if the process has been levied, on receiving from the respondent or claimant of the property a bond or stipulation in double the amount claimed by the libellant, with sufficient surety, to be approved by the judge of the district court where the case is pending, or, in his absence, by the collector of the port, conditioned to answer the decree of the court in such case. Such bond or stipulation shall be returned

to the court, and judgment or decree thereon, against both the principal and sureties, may be secured at the time of rendering the decree in the original case. The owner of any vessel may deliver to the marshal a bond or stipulation, with sufficient surety, to be approved by the judge of the district court, conditioned to answer the decree of such court in all or any cases that are brought thereafter in such court against the vessel. Thereupon the execution of all such process against such vessel shall be stayed so long as the amount secured by such bond or stipulation is at least double the aggregate amount claimed by libellants in such suits which are begun and pending against such vessel. Similar judgments or decrees and remedies may be had on such bond or stipulation as if a special bond or stipulation had been filed in each of such suits.

(b) The court may make necessary orders to carry this section into effect, particularly in giving proper notice of any such suit. Such bond or stipulation shall be indorsed by the clerk with a minute of the suits wherein process is so stayed. Further security may be required by the court at any time.

(c) If a special bond or stipulation in the particular case is given under this section, the liability as to said case on the general bond or stipulation shall cease. The parties may stipulate the amount of the bond or stipulation for the release of a vessel or other property to be not more than the amount claimed in the libel, with interest, plus an allowance for libellant's costs. In the event of the inability or refusal of the parties to so stipulate, the court shall fix the amount, but if not so fixed then a bond shall be required in the amount prescribed in this section.

(June 25, 1948, c. 646, 62 Stat. 974.)

HISTORICAL AND STATUTORY NOTES

Transfer of Functions

All offices of Collector of Customs, Comptroller of Customs, Surveyor of Customs, and Appraiser of Merchandise in the Bureau of Customs of the Department of the Treasury to which appointments were required to be made by the President with the advice and consent of the Senate were ordered abolished, with such offices to be terminated not later than December 31, 1966, by 1965 Reorg. Plan No. 1, eff. May 25, 1965, 30 F.R. 7035, 79 Stat. 1317, set out in Appendix 1 to Title 5, Government Organization and Employees. All functions of the offices eliminated were already vested in the Secretary of the Treasury by 1950 Reorg. Plan No. 26, eff. July 31, 1950, 15 F.R. 4935, 64 Stat. 1280, set out in Appendix 1 to Title 5.

§ 2465. Return of property to claimant; liability for wrongful seizure; attorney fees, costs, and interest

(a) Upon the entry of a judgment for the claimant in any proceeding to condemn or forfeit property seized or arrested under any provision of Federal law—

(1) such property shall be returned forthwith to the claimant or his agent; and

(2) if it appears that there was reasonable cause for the seizure or arrest, the court shall cause a proper certificate thereof to be entered and, in such case, neither the person who made the seizure or arrest nor the prosecutor shall be liable to suit or judgment on account of such suit or prosecution, nor shall the claimant be entitled to costs, except as provided in subsection (b).

(b)(1) Except as provided in paragraph (2), in any civil proceeding to forfeit property under any provision of Federal law in which the claimant substantially prevails, the United States shall be liable for—

(A) reasonable attorney fees and other litigation costs reasonably incurred by the claimant;

(B) post-judgment interest, as set forth in section 1961 of this title; and

(C) in cases involving currency, other negotiable instruments, or the proceeds of an interlocutory sale—

(i) interest actually paid to the United States from the date of seizure or arrest of the property that resulted from the investment of the property in an interest-bearing account or instrument; and

(ii) an imputed amount of interest that such currency, instruments, or proceeds would have earned at the rate applicable to the 30–day Treasury Bill, for any period during which no interest was paid (not including any period when the property reasonably was in use as evidence in an official proceeding or in conducting scientific tests for the purpose of collecting evidence), commencing 15 days after the property was seized by a Federal law enforcement agency, or was turned over to a Federal law enforcement agency by a State or local law enforcement agency.

(2)(A) The United States shall not be required to disgorge the value of any intangible benefits nor make any other payments to the claimant not specifically authorized by this subsection.

(B) The provisions of paragraph (1) shall not apply if the claimant is convicted of a crime for which the interest of the claimant in the property was subject to forfeiture under a Federal criminal forfeiture law.

(C) If there are multiple claims to the same property, the United States shall not be liable for costs and attorneys fees associated with any such claim if the United States—

(i) promptly recognizes such claim;

(ii) promptly returns the interest of the claimant in the property to the claimant, if the proper-

ty can be divided without difficulty and there are no competing claims to that portion of the property;

(iii) does not cause the claimant to incur additional, reasonable costs or fees; and

(iv) prevails in obtaining forfeiture with respect to one or more of the other claims.

(D) If the court enters judgment in part for the claimant and in part for the Government, the court shall reduce the award of costs and attorney fees accordingly.

(June 25, 1948, c. 646, 62 Stat. 975; Apr. 25, 2000, Pub.L. 106–185, § 4(a), 114 Stat. 211.)

HISTORICAL AND STATUTORY NOTES
Effective and Applicability Provisions

2000 Acts

Amendments by Pub.L. 106–185, applicable to any forfeiture proceeding commenced on or after the date that is 120 days after April 25, 2000, see section 21 of Pub.L. 106–185, set out as a note under section 1324 of Title 8.

§ 2466. Fugitive disentitlement

(a) A judicial officer may disallow a person from using the resources of the courts of the United States in furtherance of a claim in any related civil forfeiture action or a claim in third party proceedings in any related criminal forfeiture action upon a finding that such person—

(1) after notice or knowledge of the fact that a warrant or process has been issued for his apprehension, in order to avoid criminal prosecution—

(A) purposely leaves the jurisdiction of the United States;

(B) declines to enter or reenter the United States to submit to its jurisdiction; or

(C) otherwise evades the jurisdiction of the court in which a criminal case is pending against the person; and

(2) is not confined or held in custody in any other jurisdiction for commission of criminal conduct in that jurisdiction.

(b) Subsection (a) may be applied to a claim filed by a corporation if any majority shareholder, or individual filing the claim on behalf of the corporation is a person to whom subsection (a) applies.

(Added Pub.L. 106–185, § 14(a), Apr. 25, 2000, 114 Stat. 219, and amended Pub.L. 107–56, Title III, § 322, Oct. 26, 2001, 115 Stat. 315; Pub.L. 109–162, Title XI, § 1171(c), Jan. 5, 2006, 119 Stat. 3123; Pub.L. 109–177, Title IV, § 406(a)(1), Mar. 9, 2006, 120 Stat. 244.)

HISTORICAL AND STATUTORY NOTES
Codifications

Pub.L. 109–177, § 406(a)(1), which directed the amendment of directory language of Pub.L. 107–56, § 322, was incapable of execution due to prior identical amendment by

Pub.L. 109–162, 1171(c). See 2006 Amendments notes under this section.

Effective and Applicability Provisions

2006 Acts

Pub.L. 109–162, Title XI, § 1172(c), Jan. 5, 2006, 119 Stat. 3123, provided in part that the amendment of the directory language of Pub.L. 107–56, § 322 was "effective on the date of enactment of that section [Oct. 26, 2001]".

2000 Acts

Pub.L. 106–185, § 14(c), Apr. 25, 2000, 114 Stat. 219, provided that: "The amendments made by this section [adding this section] shall apply to any case pending on or after the date of the enactment of this Act [Apr. 25, 2000]."

4–Year Congressional Review; Expedited Consideration

Effective on and after the first day of fiscal year 2005, amendments by Title III (§§ 301 to 377) of Pub.L. 107–56 shall terminate if Congress enacts a joint resolution, and such resolution shall be given expedited consideration, see Pub.L. 107–56, Title III, § 303, Oct. 26, 2001, 115 Stat. 298, set out as a note under 31 U.S.C.A. § 5311.

§ 2467. Enforcement of foreign judgment

(a) Definitions.—In this section—

(1) the term "foreign nation" means a country that has become a party to the United Nations Convention Against Illicit Traffic in Narcotic Drugs and Psychotropic Substances (referred to in this section as the "United Nations Convention") or a foreign jurisdiction with which the United States has a treaty or other formal international agreement in effect providing for mutual forfeiture assistance; and

(2) the term "forfeiture or confiscation judgment" means a final order of a foreign nation compelling a person or entity—

(A) to pay a sum of money representing the proceeds of an offense described in Article 3, Paragraph 1, of the United Nations Convention, any violation of foreign law that would constitute a violation or an offense for which property could be forfeited under Federal law if the offense were committed in the United States, or any foreign offense described in section 1956(c)(7)(B) of title 18, or property the value of which corresponds to such proceeds; or

(B) to forfeit property involved in or traceable to the commission of such offense.

(b) Review by attorney general.—

(1) In general.—A foreign nation seeking to have a forfeiture or confiscation judgment registered and enforced by a district court of the United States under this section shall first submit a request to the Attorney General or the designee of the Attorney General, which request shall include—

(A) a summary of the facts of the case and a description of the proceedings that resulted in the forfeiture or confiscation judgment;

(B) certified [1] copy of the forfeiture or confiscation judgment;

(C) an affidavit or sworn declaration establishing that the foreign nation took steps, in accordance with the principles of due process, to give notice of the proceedings to all persons with an interest in the property in sufficient time to enable such persons to defend against the charges and that the judgment rendered is in force and is not subject to appeal; and

(D) such additional information and evidence as may be required by the Attorney General or the designee of the Attorney General.

(2) Certification of request.—The Attorney General or the designee of the Attorney General shall determine whether, in the interest of justice, to certify the request, and such decision shall be final and not subject to either judicial review or review under subchapter II of chapter 5, or chapter 7, of title 5 (commonly known as the "Administrative Procedure Act").

(c) Jurisdiction and venue.—

(1) In general.—If the Attorney General or the designee of the Attorney General certifies a request under subsection (b), the United States may file an application on behalf of a foreign nation in district court of the United States seeking to enforce the foreign forfeiture or confiscation judgment as if the judgment had been entered by a court in the United States.

(2) Proceedings.—In a proceeding filed under paragraph (1)—

(A) the United States shall be the applicant and the defendant or another person or entity affected by the forfeiture or confiscation judgment shall be the respondent;

(B) venue shall lie in the district court for the District of Columbia or in any other district in which the defendant or the property that may be the basis for satisfaction of a judgment under this section may be found; and

(C) the district court shall have personal jurisdiction over a defendant residing outside of the United States if the defendant is served with process in accordance with rule 4 of the Federal Rules of Civil Procedure.

(d) Entry and enforcement of judgment.—

(1) In general.—The district court shall enter such orders as may be necessary to enforce the judgment on behalf of the foreign nation unless the court finds that—

(A) the judgment was rendered under a system that provides tribunals or procedures incompatible with the requirements of due process of law;

(B) the foreign court lacked personal jurisdiction over the defendant;

(C) the foreign court lacked jurisdiction over the subject matter;

(D) the foreign nation did not take steps, in accordance with the principles of due process, to give notice of the proceedings to a person with an interest in the property of the proceedings [2] in sufficient time to enable him or her to defend; or

(E) the judgment was obtained by fraud.

(2) Process.—Process to enforce a judgment under this section shall be in accordance with rule 69(a) of the Federal Rules of Civil Procedure.

(3) Preservation of property.—

(A) In general.—To preserve the availability of property subject to a foreign forfeiture or confiscation judgment, the Government may apply for, and the court may issue, a restraining order pursuant to section 983(j) of title 18, at any time before or after an application is filed pursuant to subsection (c)(1) of this section.

(B) Evidence.—The court, in issuing a restraining order under subparagraph (A)—

(i) may rely on information set forth in an affidavit describing the nature of the proceeding or investigation underway in the foreign country, and setting forth a reasonable basis to believe that the property to be restrained will be named in a judgment of forfeiture at the conclusion of such proceeding; or

(ii) may register and enforce a restraining order that has been issued by a court of competent jurisdiction in the foreign country and certified by the Attorney General pursuant to subsection (b)(2).

(C) Limit on grounds for objection.—No person may object to a restraining order under subparagraph (A) on any ground that is the subject of parallel litigation involving the same property that is pending in a foreign court.

(e) Finality of foreign findings.—In entering orders to enforce the judgment, the court shall be bound by the findings of fact to the extent that they are stated in the foreign forfeiture or confiscation judgment.

(f) Currency conversion.—The rate of exchange in effect at the time the suit to enforce is filed by the foreign nation shall be used in calculating the amount stated in any forfeiture or confiscation judgment requiring the payment of a sum of money submitted for registration.

(Added Pub.L. 106–185, § 15(a), Apr. 25, 2000, 114 Stat. 219, and amended Pub.L. 107–56, Title III, § 323, Oct. 26, 2001, 115 Stat. 315.)

1 So in original. Probably should be preceded by "a".

2 So in original. The phrase "of the proceedings" probably should not appear.

HISTORICAL AND STATUTORY NOTES

References in Text

Rule 4 of the Federal Rules of Civil Procedure, referred to in subsec. (c)(2)(C), is set out in this title.

Effective and Applicability Provisions

2000 Acts

Enactment by Pub.L. 106–185, applicable to any forfeiture proceeding commenced on or after the date that is 120 days after April 25, 2000, see section 21 of Pub.L. 106–185, set out as a note under section 1324 of Title 8.

4–Year Congressional Review; Expedited Consideration

Effective on and after the first day of fiscal year 2005, amendments by Title III (§§ 301 to 377) of Pub.L. 107–56 shall terminate if Congress enacts a joint resolution to that effect; such resolution shall be given expedited consideration, see Pub.L. 107–56, Title III, § 303, Oct. 26, 2001, 115 Stat. 298, set out as a note under 31 U.S.C.A. § 5311.

CHAPTER 165—UNITED STATES COURT OF FEDERAL CLAIMS PROCEDURE

1 So in original. Does not conform to section catchline.

§ 2501. Time for filing suit

Every claim of which the United States Court of Federal Claims has jurisdiction shall be barred unless the petition thereon is filed within six years after such claim first accrues.

Every claim under section 1497 of this title shall be barred unless the petition thereon is filed within two years after the termination of the river and harbor improvements operations on which the claim is based.

A petition on the claim of a person under legal disability or beyond the seas at the time the claim accrues may be filed within three years after the disability ceases.

A suit for the fees of an officer of the United States shall not be filed until his account for such fees has been finally acted upon, unless the Government Accountability Office fails to act within six months after receiving the account.

(June 25, 1948, c. 646, 62 Stat. 976; Sept. 3, 1954, c. 1263, § 52, 68 Stat. 1246; Apr. 2, 1982, Pub.L. 97–164, Title I, § 139(a), 96 Stat. 42; Oct. 29, 1992, Pub.L. 102–572, Title IX, § 902(a)(1), 106 Stat. 4516; July 7, 2004, Pub.L. 108–271, § 8(b), 118 Stat. 814.)

HISTORICAL AND STATUTORY NOTES

Effective and Applicability Provisions

1992 Acts

Amendment by Title IX of Pub.L. 102–572 effective Oct. 29, 1992, see section 911 of Pub.L. 102–572, set out as a note under section 171 of Title 28, Judiciary and Judicial Procedure.

1982 Acts

Amendment by Pub.L. 97–164 effective Oct. 1, 1982, see section 402 of Pub.L. 97–164, set out as a note under section 171 of this title.

Change of Name

"Government Accountability Office" substituted for "General Accounting Office" in text on authority of Pub.L. 108–271, § 8(b), cited in the credit to this section and set out as a note under 31 U.S.C.A. § 702, which provided that any reference to the General Accounting Office in any law, rule, regulation, certificate, directive, instruction, or other official paper in force on July 17, 2004, to refer and apply to the Government Accountability Office.

§ 2502. Aliens' privilege to sue

(a) Citizens or subjects of any foreign government which accords to citizens of the United States the right to prosecute claims against their government in its courts may sue the United States in the United States Court of Federal Claims if the subject matter of the suit is otherwise within such court's jurisdiction.

(b) See section 7422(f) of the Internal Revenue Code of 1986 for exception with respect to suits involving internal revenue taxes.

(June 25, 1948, c. 646, 62 Stat. 976; Nov. 2, 1966, Pub.L. 89–713, § 3(b), 80 Stat. 1108; Apr. 2, 1982, Pub.L. 97–164, Title I, § 139(a), 96 Stat. 42; Oct. 22, 1986, Pub.L. 99–514, § 2, 100 Stat. 2095; Oct. 29, 1992, Pub.L. 102–572, Title IX, § 902(a)(1), 106 Stat. 4516.)

HISTORICAL AND STATUTORY NOTES

References in Text

Section 7422(f) of the Internal Revenue Code of 1986, referred to in subsec. (b), is classified to section 7422(f) of Title 26, Internal Revenue Code.

Effective and Applicability Provisions

1992 Acts

Amendment by Title IX of Pub.L. 102–572 effective Oct. 29, 1992, see section 911 of Pub.L. 102–572, set out as a note under section 171 of Title 28, Judiciary and Judicial Procedure.

1982 Acts

Amendment by Pub.L. 97–164 effective Oct. 1, 1982, see section 402 of Pub.L. 97–164, set out as a note under section 171 of this title.

1966 Acts

Amendment by Pub.L. 89–713, which added subsec. (b) to this section, applicable to suits brought against officers, employees, or personal representatives instituted 90 days or more after Nov. 2, 1966, see section 3(d) of Pub.L. 89–713, set out as a note under section 7422 of Title 26, Internal Revenue Code.

§ 2503. Proceedings generally

(a) Parties to any suit in the United States Court of Federal Claims may appear before a judge of that court in person or by attorney, produce evidence, and examine witnesses.

(b) The proceedings of the Court of Federal Claims shall be in accordance with such rules of practice and procedure (other than the rules of evidence) as the Court of Federal Claims may prescribe and in accordance with the Federal Rules of Evidence.

(c) The judges of the Court of Federal Claims shall fix times for trials, administer oaths or affirmations, examine witnesses, receive evidence, and enter dispositive judgments. Hearings shall, if convenient, be held in the counties where the witnesses reside.

(d) For the purpose of construing sections 1821, 1915, 1920, and 1927 of this title, the United States Court of Federal Claims shall be deemed to be a court of the United States.

(June 25, 1948, c. 646, 62 Stat. 976; Sept. 3, 1954, c. 1263, § 53, 68 Stat. 1246; Apr. 2, 1982, Pub.L. 97–164, Title I, § 139(b)(1), 96 Stat. 42; Oct. 29, 1992, Pub.L. 102–572, Title IX, §§ 902(a), 909, 106 Stat. 4516, 4519.)

HISTORICAL AND STATUTORY NOTES

References in Text

The Federal Rules of Evidence, referred to in subsec. (b), are set out in this title.

Effective and Applicability Provisions

1992 Acts

Amendment by Title IX of Pub.L. 102–572 effective Oct. 29, 1992, see section 911 of Pub.L. 102–572, set out as a note under section 171 of Title 28, Judiciary and Judicial Procedure.

1982 Acts

Amendment by Pub.L. 97–164 effective Oct. 1, 1982, see section 402 of Pub.L. 97–164, set out as a note under section 171 of this title.

§ 2504. Plaintiff's testimony

The United States Court of Federal Claims may, at the instance of the Attorney General, order any plaintiff to appear, upon reasonable notice, before any judge of the court and be examined on oath as to all matters pertaining to his claim. Such examination shall be reduced to writing by the judge, and shall be returned to and filed in the court, and may, at the discretion of the attorneys for the United States, be read and used as evidence on the trial. If any plaintiff, after such order is made and due and reasonable notice thereof is given to him, fails to appear, or refuses to testify or answer fully as to all material matters within his knowledge, the court may order that the case shall not be tried until he fully complies with such order.

(June 25, 1948, c. 646, 62 Stat. 976; Apr. 2, 1982, Pub.L. 97–164, Title I, § 139(c), 96 Stat. 42; Oct. 29, 1992, Pub.L. 102–572, Title IX, § 902(a)(1), 106 Stat. 4516.)

HISTORICAL AND STATUTORY NOTES

Effective and Applicability Provisions

1992 Acts

Amendment by Title IX of Pub.L. 102–572 effective Oct. 29, 1992, see section 911 of Pub.L. 102–572, set out as a note under section 171 of Title 28, Judiciary and Judicial Procedure.

1982 Acts

Amendment by Pub.L. 97–164 effective Oct. 1, 1982, see section 402 of Pub.L. 97–164, set out as a note under section 171 of this title.

§ 2505. Trial before judges

Any judge of the United States Court of Federal Claims may sit at any place within the United States to take evidence and enter judgment.

(June 25, 1948, c. 646, 62 Stat. 976; Sept. 3, 1954, c. 1263, § 54(a), (b), 68 Stat. 1246; Apr. 2, 1982, Pub.L. 97–164, Title I, § 139(d), 96 Stat. 42; Oct. 29, 1992, Pub.L. 102–572, Title IX, § 902(a)(1), 106 Stat. 4516.)

HISTORICAL AND STATUTORY NOTES

Effective and Applicability Provisions

1992 Acts

Amendment by Title IX of Pub.L. 102–572 effective Oct. 29, 1992, see section 911 of Pub.L. 102–572, set out as a note under section 171 of Title 28, Judiciary and Judicial Procedure.

1982 Acts

Amendment by Pub.L. 97–164 effective Oct. 1, 1982, see section 402 of Pub.L. 97–164, set out as a note under section 171 of this title.

§ 2506. Interest of witness

A witness in a suit in the United States Court of Federal Claims shall not be exempt or disqualified because he is a party to or interested in such suit. (June 25, 1948, c. 646, 62 Stat. 977; Apr. 2, 1982, Pub.L. 97–164, Title I, § 139(e), 96 Stat. 42; Oct. 29, 1992, Pub.L. 102–572, Title IX, § 902(a)(1), 106 Stat. 4516.)

HISTORICAL AND STATUTORY NOTES
Effective and Applicability Provisions
1992 Acts

Amendment by Title IX of Pub.L. 102–572 effective Oct. 29, 1992, see section 911 of Pub.L. 102–572, set out as a note under section 171 of Title 28, Judiciary and Judicial Procedure.

1982 Acts

Amendment by Pub.L. 97–164 effective Oct. 1, 1982, see section 402 of Pub.L. 97–164, set out as a note under section 171 of this title.

§ 2507. Calls and discovery

(a) The United States Court of Federal Claims may call upon any department or agency of the United States or upon any party for any information or papers, not privileged, for purposes of discovery or for use as evidence. The head of any department or agency may refuse to comply with a call issued pursuant to this subsection when, in his opinion, compliance will be injurious to the public interest.

(b) Without limitation on account of anything contained in subsection (a) of this section, the court may, in accordance with its rules, provide additional means for the discovery of any relevant facts, books, papers, documents or tangible things, not privileged.

(c) The Court of Federal Claims may use all recorded and printed reports made by the committees of the Senate or House of Representatives. (June 25, 1948, c. 646, 62 Stat. 977; Sept. 3, 1954, c. 1263, § 55(a)–(c), 68 Stat. 1247; Apr. 2, 1982, Pub.L. 97–164, Title I, § 139(f), 96 Stat. 42; Oct. 29, 1992, Pub.L. 102–572, Title IX, § 902(a), 106 Stat. 4516.)

HISTORICAL AND STATUTORY NOTES
Effective and Applicability Provisions
1992 Acts

Amendment by Title IX of Pub.L. 102–572 effective Oct. 29, 1992, see section 911 of Pub.L. 102–572, set out as a note under section 171 of Title 28, Judiciary and Judicial Procedure.

1982 Acts

Amendment by Pub.L. 97–164 effective Oct. 1, 1982, see section 402 of Pub.L. 97–164, set out as a note under section 171 of this title.

§ 2508. Counterclaim or set-off; registration of judgment

Upon the trial of any suit in the United States Court of Federal Claims in which any setoff, counterclaim, claim for damages, or other demand is set up on the part of the United States against any plaintiff making claim against the United States in said court, the court shall hear and determine such claim or demand both for and against the United States and plaintiff.

If upon the whole case it finds that the plaintiff is indebted to the United States it shall render judgment to that effect, and such judgment shall be final and reviewable.

The transcript of such judgment, filed in the clerk's office of any district court, shall be entered upon the records and shall be enforceable as other judgments. (June 25, 1948, c. 646, 62 Stat. 977; July 28, 1953, c. 253, § 10, 67 Stat. 227; Sept. 3, 1954, c. 1263, § 47(a), 68 Stat. 1243; Apr. 2, 1982, Pub.L. 97–164, Title I, § 139(g), 96 Stat. 42; Oct. 29, 1992, Pub.L. 102–572, Title IX, § 902(a)(1), 106 Stat. 4516.)

HISTORICAL AND STATUTORY NOTES
Effective and Applicability Provisions
1992 Acts

Amendment by Title IX of Pub.L. 102–572 effective Oct. 29, 1992, see section 911 of Pub.L. 102–572, set out as a note under section 171 of Title 28, Judiciary and Judicial Procedure.

1982 Acts

Amendment by Pub.L. 97–164 effective Oct. 1, 1982, see section 402 of Pub.L. 97–164, set out as a note under section 171 of this title.

§ 2509. Congressional reference cases

(a) Whenever a bill, except a bill for a pension, is referred by either House of Congress to the chief judge of the United States Court of Federal Claims pursuant to section 1492 of this title, the chief judge shall designate a judge as hearing officer for the case and a panel of three judges of the court to serve as a reviewing body. One member of the review panel shall be designated as presiding officer of the panel.

(b) Proceedings in a congressional reference case shall be under rules and regulations prescribed for the purpose by the chief judge who is hereby authorized and directed to require the application of the pertinent rules of practice of the Court of Federal Claims insofar as feasible. Each hearing officer and each review panel shall have authority to do and perform any acts which may be necessary or proper for the efficient performance of their duties, including the power of subpena and the power to administer oaths and affirmations. None of the rules, rulings, findings, or conclusions authorized by this section shall be subject to judicial review.

(c) The hearing officer to whom a congressional reference case is assigned by the chief judge shall proceed in accordance with the applicable rules to

determine the facts, including facts relating to delay or laches, facts bearing upon the question whether the bar of any statute of limitation should be removed, or facts claimed to excuse the claimant for not having resorted to any established legal remedy. He shall append to his findings of fact conclusions sufficient to inform Congress whether the demand is a legal or equitable claim or a gratuity, and the amount, if any, legally or equitably due from the United States to the claimant.

(d) The findings and conclusions of the hearing officer shall be submitted by him, together with the record in the case, to the review panel for review by it pursuant to such rules as may be provided for the purpose, which shall include provision for submitting the report of the hearing officer to the parties for consideration, exception, and argument before the panel. The panel, by majority vote, shall adopt or modify the findings or the conclusions of the hearing officer.

(e) The panel shall submit its report to the chief judge for transmission to the appropriate House of Congress.

(f) Any act or failure to act or other conduct by a party, a witness, or an attorney which would call for the imposition of sanctions under the rules of practice of the Court of Federal Claims shall be noted by the panel or the hearing officer at the time of occurrence thereof and upon failure of the delinquent or offending party, witness, or attorney to make prompt compliance with the order of the panel or the hearing officer a full statement of the circumstances shall be incorporated in the report of the panel.

(g) The Court of Federal Claims is hereby authorized and directed, under such regulations as it may prescribe, to provide the facilities and services of the office of the clerk of the court for the filing, processing, hearing, and dispatch of congressional reference cases and to include within its annual appropriations the costs thereof and other costs of administration, including (but without limitation to the items herein listed) the salaries and traveling expenses of the judges serving as hearing officers and panel members, mailing and service of process, necessary physical facilities, equipment, and supplies, and personnel (including secretaries and law clerks).

(June 25, 1948, c. 646, 62 Stat. 977; Oct. 15, 1966, Pub.L. 89–681, § 2, 80 Stat. 958; Apr. 2, 1982, Pub.L. 97–164, Title I, § 139(h), 96 Stat. 42; Oct. 29, 1992, Pub.L. 102–572, Title IX, § 902(a), 106 Stat. 4516.)

HISTORICAL AND STATUTORY NOTES

Effective and Applicability Provisions

1992 Acts

Amendment by Title IX of Pub.L. 102–572 effective Oct. 29, 1992, see section 911 of Pub.L. 102–572, set out as a note

under section 171 of Title 28, Judiciary and Judicial Procedure.

1982 Acts

Amendment by Pub.L. 97–164 effective Oct. 1, 1982, see section 402 of Pub.L. 97–164, set out as a note under section 171 of this title.

Termination of Reporting Requirements

For termination of reporting provisions of this section, effective May 15, 2000, see Pub.L. 104–66, § 3003, as amended, set out as a note under 31 U.S.C.A. § 1113, and page 13 of House Document No. 103–7.

§ 2510. Referral of cases by Comptroller General

(a) The Comptroller General may transmit to the United States Court of Federal Claims for trial and adjudication any claim or matter of which the Court of Federal Claims might take jurisdiction on the voluntary action of the claimant, together with all vouchers, papers, documents, and proofs pertaining thereto.

(b) The Court of Federal Claims shall proceed with the claims or matters so referred as in other cases pending in such Court and shall render judgment thereon.

(June 25, 1948, c. 646, 62 Stat. 977; July 28, 1953, c. 253, § 11, 67 Stat. 227; Sept. 3, 1954, c. 1263, § 47(b), 68 Stat. 1243; Nov. 1, 1978, Pub.L. 95–563, § 14(h)(1), (2)(A), 92 Stat. 2390; Apr. 2, 1982, Pub.L. 97–164, Title I, § 139(i)(1), 96 Stat. 43; Oct. 29, 1992, Pub.L. 102–572, Title IX, § 902(a), 106 Stat. 4516.)

HISTORICAL AND STATUTORY NOTES

Effective and Applicability Provisions

1992 Acts

Amendment by Title IX of Pub.L. 102–572 effective Oct. 29, 1992, see section 911 of Pub.L. 102–572, set out as a note under section 171 of Title 28, Judiciary and Judicial Procedure.

1982 Acts

Amendment by Pub.L. 97–164 effective Oct. 1, 1982, see section 402 of Pub.L. 97–164, set out as a note under section 171 of this title.

1978 Acts

Amendment by Pub.L. 95–563 effective with respect to contracts entered into 120 days after Nov. 1, 1978, and, at the election of the contractor, with respect to any claim pending at such time before the contracting officer or initiated thereafter, see section 16 of Pub.L. 95–563, set out as a note under section 601 of Title 41, Public Contracts.

§ 2511. Accounts of officers, agents or contractors

Notice of suit under section 1494 of this title shall be given to the Attorney General, to the Comptroller General, and to the head of the department requested to settle the account in question.

The judgment of the United States Court of Federal Claims in such suit shall be conclusive upon the

parties, and payment of the amount found due shall discharge the obligation.

The transcript of such judgment, filed in the clerk's office of any district court, shall be entered upon the records, and shall be enforceable as other judgments. (June 25, 1948, c. 646, 62 Stat. 977; July 28, 1953, c. 253, § 12, 67 Stat. 227; Apr. 2, 1982, Pub.L. 97–164, Title I, § 139(j), 96 Stat. 43; Oct. 29, 1992, Pub.L. 102–572, Title IX, § 902(a)(1), 106 Stat. 4516.)

HISTORICAL AND STATUTORY NOTES

Effective and Applicability Provisions

1992 Acts

Amendment by Title IX of Pub. L. 102–572 effective Oct. 29, 1992, see section 911 of Pub.L. 102–572, set out as a note under section 171 of Title 28, Judiciary and Judicial Procedure.

1982 Acts

Amendment by Pub.L. 97–164 effective Oct. 1, 1982, see section 402 of Pub.L. 97–164, set out as a note under section 171 of this title.

Termination of Reporting Requirements

For termination of reporting provisions of subsec. (i) of this section, effective May 15, 2000, see Pub.L. 104–66, § 3003, as amended, set out as a note under 31 U.S.C.A. § 1113, and the 1st provision on page 14 of House Document No. 103–7.

§ 2512. Disbursing officers; relief

Whenever the United States Court of Federal Claims finds that any loss by a disbursing officer of the United States was without his fault or negligence, it shall render a judgment setting forth the amount thereof, and the Government Accountability Office shall allow the officer such amount as a credit in the settlement of his accounts.
(June 25, 1948, c. 646, 62 Stat. 978; Apr. 2, 1982, Pub.L. 97–164, Title I, § 139(j)(2), 96 Stat. 43; Oct. 29, 1992, Pub.L. 102–572, Title IX, § 902(a)(1), 106 Stat. 4516; Pub.L. 108–271, § 8(b), July 7, 2004, 118 Stat. 814.)

HISTORICAL AND STATUTORY NOTES

Effective and Applicability Provisions

1992 Acts

Amendment by Title IX of Pub.L. 102–572 effective Oct. 29, 1992, see section 911 of Pub.L. 102–572, set out as a note under section 171 of Title 28, Judiciary and Judicial Procedure.

1982 Acts

Amendment by Pub.L. 97–164 effective Oct. 1, 1982, see section 402 of Pub.L. 97–164, set out as a note under section 171 of this title.

Change of Name

"Government Accountability Office" substituted for "General Accounting Office" in text on authority of Pub.L. 108–271, § 8(b), cited in the credit to this section and set out as a note under 31 U.S.C.A. § 702, which provided that any reference to the General Accounting Office in any law, rule, regulation, certificate, directive, instruction, or other official paper in force on July 17, 2004, to refer and apply to the Government Accountability Office.

§ 2513. Unjust conviction and imprisonment

(a) Any person suing under section 1495 of this title must allege and prove that:

(1) His conviction has been reversed or set aside on the ground that he is not guilty of the offense of which he was convicted, or on new trial or rehearing he was found not guilty of such offense, as appears from the record or certificate of the court setting aside or reversing such conviction, or that he has been pardoned upon the stated ground of innocence and unjust conviction and

(2) He did not commit any of the acts charged or his acts, deeds, or omissions in connection with such charge constituted no offense against the United States, or any State, Territory or the District of Columbia, and he did not by misconduct or neglect cause or bring about his own prosecution.

(b) Proof of the requisite facts shall be by a certificate of the court or pardon wherein such facts are alleged to appear, and other evidence thereof shall not be received.

(c) No pardon or certified copy of a pardon shall be considered by the United States Court of Federal Claims unless it contains recitals that the pardon was granted after applicant had exhausted all recourse to the courts and that the time for any court to exercise its jurisdiction had expired.

(d) The Court may permit the plaintiff to prosecute such action in forma pauperis.

(e) The amount of damages awarded shall not exceed $100,000 for each 12–month period of incarceration for any plaintiff who was unjustly sentenced to death and $50,000 for each 12–month period of incarceration for any other plaintiff.
(June 25, 1948, c. 646, 62 Stat. 978; Sept. 3, 1954, c. 1263, § 56, 68 Stat. 1247; Apr. 2, 1982, Pub.L. 97–164, Title I, § 139(j)(2), 96 Stat. 43; Oct. 29, 1992, Pub.L. 102–572, Title IX, § 902(a)(1), 106 Stat. 4516; Oct. 30, 2004, Pub.L. 108–405, Title IV, § 431, 118 Stat. 2293.)

HISTORICAL AND STATUTORY NOTES

Effective and Applicability Provisions

1992 Acts

Amendment by Title IX of Pub.L. 102–572 effective Oct. 29, 1992, see section 911 of Pub.L. 102–572, set out as a note under section 171 of Title 28, Judiciary and Judicial Procedure.

1982 Acts

Amendment by Pub.L. 97–164 effective Oct. 1, 1982, see section 402 of Pub.L. 97–164, set out as a note under section 171 of this title.

§ 2514. Forfeiture of fraudulent claims

A claim against the United States shall be forfeited to the United States by any person who corruptly practices or attempts to practice any fraud against the United States in the proof, statement, establishment, or allowance thereof.

In such cases the United States Court of Federal Claims shall specifically find such fraud or attempt and render judgment of forfeiture.

(June 25, 1948, c. 646, 62 Stat. 978; Apr. 2, 1982, Pub.L. 97–164, Title I, § 139(j)(2), 96 Stat. 43; Oct. 29, 1992, Pub.L. 102–572, Title IX, § 902(a)(1), 106 Stat. 4516.)

HISTORICAL AND STATUTORY NOTES

Effective and Applicability Provisions

1992 Acts

Amendment by Title IX of Pub.L. 102–572 effective Oct. 29, 1992, see section 911 of Pub.L. 102–572, set out as a note under section 171 of Title 28, Judiciary and Judicial Procedure.

1982 Acts

Amendment by Pub.L. 97–164 effective Oct. 1, 1982, see section 402 of Pub.L. 97–164, set out as a note under section 171 of this title.

§ 2515. New trial; stay of judgment

(a) The United States Court of Federal Claims may grant a plaintiff a new trial on any ground established by rules of common law or equity applicable as between private parties.

(b) Such court, at any time while any suit is pending before it, or after proceedings for review have been instituted, or within two years after the final disposition of the suit, may grant the United States a new trial and stay the payment of any judgment upon satisfactory evidence, cumulative or otherwise, that any fraud, wrong, or injustice has been done the United States.

(June 25, 1948, c. 646, 62 Stat. 978; Apr. 2, 1982, Pub.L. 97–164, Title I, § 139(j)(2), 96 Stat. 43; Oct. 29, 1992, Pub.L. 102–572, Title IX, § 902(a)(1), 106 Stat. 4516.)

HISTORICAL AND STATUTORY NOTES

Effective and Applicability Provisions

1992 Acts

Amendment by Title IX of Pub.L. 102–572 effective Oct. 29, 1992, see section 911 of Pub.L. 102–572, set out as a note under section 171 of Title 28, Judiciary and Judicial Procedure.

1982 Acts

Amendment by Pub.L. 97–164 effective Oct. 1, 1982, see section 402 of Pub.L. 97–164, set out as a note under section 171 of this title.

§ 2516. Interest on claims and judgments

(a) Interest on a claim against the United States shall be allowed in a judgment of the United States Court of Federal Claims only under a contract or Act of Congress expressly providing for payment thereof.

(b) Interest on a judgment against the United States affirmed by the Supreme Court after review on petition of the United States is paid at a rate equal to the weekly average 1–year constant maturity Treasury yield, as published by the Board of Governors of the Federal Reserve System, for the calendar week preceding the date of the judgment.

(June 25, 1948, c. 646, 62 Stat. 978; Sept. 3, 1954, c. 1263, § 57, 68 Stat. 1248; Apr. 2, 1982, Pub.L. 97–164, Title I, § 139(j)(2), Title III, § 302(d), 96 Stat. 43, 56; Sept. 13, 1982, Pub.L. 97–258, § 2(g)(5), (m)(3), 96 Stat. 1061, 1062; Oct. 29, 1992, Pub.L. 102–572, Title IX, § 902(a)(1), 106 Stat. 4516; Dec. 21, 2000, Pub.L. 106–554, § 1(a)(7) [Title III, § 307(d)(2)], 114 Stat. 2763, 2763A–636.)

HISTORICAL AND STATUTORY NOTES

Effective and Applicability Provisions

1992 Acts

Amendment by Title IX of Pub.L. 102–572 effective Oct. 29, 1992, see section 911 of Pub.L. 102–572, set out as a note under section 171 of Title 28, Judiciary and Judicial Procedure.

1982 Acts

Section 2(g)(5) of Pub.L. 97–258 provided in part that the amendment made to subsec. (b) would become effective on Oct. 1, 1982.

Amendment by Pub.L. 97–164 effective Oct. 1, 1982, see section 402 of Pub.L. 97–164, set out as a note under section 171 of this title.

Repeals

Section 302(d) of Pub.L. 97–164, set out in the credit of this section, was repealed by Pub.L. 97–258, § 2(m)(3), Sept. 13, 1982, 96 Stat. 1062, effective Oct. 1, 1982.

§ 2517. Payment of judgments

(a) Except as provided by the Contract Disputes Act of 1978, every final judgment rendered by the United States Court of Federal Claims against the United States shall be paid out of any general appropriation therefor, on presentation to the Secretary of the Treasury of a certification of the judgment by the clerk and chief judge of the court.

(b) Payment of any such judgment and of interest thereon shall be a full discharge to the United States of all claims and demands arising out of the matters involved in the case or controversy, unless the judgment is designated a partial judgment, in which event only the matters described therein shall be discharged.

(June 25, 1948, c. 646, 62 Stat. 979; Nov. 1, 1978, Pub.L. 95–563, § 14(e), (f), 92 Stat. 2390; Apr. 2, 1982, Pub.L. 97–164, Title I, § 139(k), 96 Stat. 43; Oct. 29, 1992, Pub.L. 102–572, Title IX, § 902(a)(1), 106 Stat. 4516; Oct. 19, 1996, Pub.L. 104–316, Title II, § 202(*l*), 110 Stat. 3843.)

HISTORICAL AND STATUTORY NOTES

References in Text

The Contract Disputes Act of 1978, referred to in subsec. (a), is Pub.L. 95–563, Nov. 1, 1978, 92 Stat. 2383, as amended, which is classified principally to chapter 9 (section 601 et seq.) of Title 41, Public Contracts. For complete classification of this Act to the Code, see Short Title note set out under section 601 of Title 41 and Tables.

Effective and Applicability Provisions

1992 Acts

Amendment by Title IX of Pub.L. 102–572 effective Oct. 29, 1992, see section 911 of Pub.L. 102–572, set out as a note under section 171 of Title 28, Judiciary and Judicial Procedure.

1982 Acts

Amendment by Pub.L. 97–164 effective Oct. 1, 1982, see section 402 of Pub.L. 97–164, set out as a note under section 171 of this title.

1978 Acts

Amendment by Pub.L. 95–563 effective with respect to contracts entered into 120 days after Nov. 1, 1978, and, at the election of the contractor, with respect to any claim pending at such time before the contracting officer or initiated thereafter, see section 16 of Pub.L. 95–563, set out as a note under section 601 of Title 41, Public Contracts.

Transfer of Functions

Effective June 30, 1996, the functions of the Comptroller General under this section to be transferred to the Director of the Office of Management and Budget, contingent upon the additional transfer to the Office of Management and Budget of such personnel, budget authority, records, and property of the General Accounting Office relating to such functions as the Comptroller General and the Director jointly determine to be necessary, see section 211 of Pub.L. 104–53, set out as a note under section 501 of Title 31, Money and Finance.

[§ 2518. Repealed. Pub.L. 97–164, Title I, § 139(*l*), Apr. 2, 1982, 96 Stat. 43]

HISTORICAL AND STATUTORY NOTES

Section, Act June 25, 1948, c. 646, 62 Stat. 979, directed the Secretary of the Treasury to certify to Congress for appropriation only such judgments of the Court of Claims as were not to be reviewed or were entered upon the mandate of the Supreme Court.

Effective Date of Repeal

Repeal effective Oct. 1, 1982, see section 402 of Pub.L. 97–164, set out as an Effective Date of 1982 Amendment note under section 171 of this title.

§ 2519. Conclusiveness of judgment

A final judgment of the United States Court of Federal Claims against any plaintiff shall forever bar any further claim, suit, or demand against the United States arising out of the matters involved in the case or controversy.

(June 25, 1948, c. 646, 62 Stat. 979; Apr. 2, 1982, Pub.L. 97–164, Title I, § 139(m), 96 Stat. 43; Oct. 29, 1992, Pub.L. 102–572, Title IX, § 902(a)(1), 106 Stat. 4516.)

HISTORICAL AND STATUTORY NOTES

Effective and Applicability Provisions

1992 Acts

Amendment by Title IX of Pub.L. 102–572 effective Oct. 29, 1992, see section 911 of Pub.L. 102–572, set out as a note under section 171 of Title 28, Judiciary and Judicial Procedure.

1982 Acts

Amendment by Pub.L. 97–164 effective Oct. 1, 1982, see section 402 of Pub.L. 97–164, set out as a note under section 171 of this title.

[§ 2520. Repealed. Pub.L. 106–518, Title II, § 207, Nov. 13, 2000, 114 Stat. 2414]

HISTORICAL AND STATUTORY NOTES

Section, Act June 25, 1948, c. 646, 62 Stat. 979; Sept. 3, 1954, c. 1263, § 58, 68 Stat. 1248; July 18, 1966, Pub.L. 89–507, § 2, 80 Stat. 308; Apr. 2, 1982, Pub.L. 97–164, Title I, § 139(n) (1)–(3), 96 Stat. 43, 44; Nov. 19, 1988, Pub.L. 100–702, Title X, § 1012(a)(1), 102 Stat. 4668; Oct. 29, 1992, Pub.L. 102–572, Title IX, § 902(a)(1), 106 Stat. 4516 related to fees for the filing of any petition.

Effective and Applicability Provisions

1988 Acts

Section 1012(a)(2) of Title X of Pub.L. 100–702 provided that: "The amendment made by this subsection [amending this section] shall take effect 30 days after the date of enactment of this title [Nov. 19, 1988]."

§ 2521. Subpoenas and incidental powers

(a) Subpoenas requiring the attendance of parties or witnesses and subpoenas requiring the production of books, papers, documents or tangible things by any party or witness having custody or control thereof, may be issued for purposes of discovery or for use of the things produced as evidence in accordance with the rules and orders of the court. Such subpoenas shall be issued and served and compliance therewith shall be compelled as provided in the rules and orders of the court.

(b) The United States Court of Federal Claims shall have power to punish by fine or imprisonment, at its discretion, such contempt of its authority as—

(1) misbehavior of any person in its presence or so near thereto as to obstruct the administration of justice;

(2) misbehavior of any of its officers in their official transactions; or

(3) disobedience or resistance to its lawful writ, process, order, rule, decree, or command.

(c) The United States Court of Federal Claims shall have such assistance in the carrying out of its lawful writ, process, order, rule, decree, or command as is available to a court of the United States. The United States marshal for any district in which the Court of Federal Claims is sitting shall, when requested by the chief judge of the Court of Federal Claims, attend any session of the Court of Federal Claims in such district.

(Added Sept. 3, 1954, c. 1263, § 59(a), 68 Stat. 1248, and amended Oct. 29, 1992, Pub.L. 102–572, Title IX, § 910(a), 106 Stat. 4519.)

HISTORICAL AND STATUTORY NOTES

Effective and Applicability Provisions

1992 Acts

Amendment by Title IX of Pub.L. 102–572 effective Oct. 29, 1992, see section 911 of Pub.L. 102–572, set out as a note under section 171 of Title 28, Judiciary and Judicial Procedure.

§ 2522. Notice of appeal

Review of a decision of the United States Court of Federal Claims shall be obtained by filing a notice of appeal with the clerk of the Court of Federal Claims within the time and in the manner prescribed for appeals to United States courts of appeals from the United States district courts.

(Added Pub.L. 97–164, Title I, § 139(q)(1), Apr. 2, 1982, 96 Stat. 44, and amended Pub.L. 102–572, Title IX, § 902(a), Oct. 29, 1992, 106 Stat. 4516.)

HISTORICAL AND STATUTORY NOTES

Effective and Applicability Provisions

1992 Acts

Amendment by Title IX of Pub.L. 102–572 effective Oct. 29, 1992, see section 911 of Pub.L. 102–572, set out as a note under section 171 of Title 28, Judiciary and Judicial Procedure.

1982 Acts

Section effective Oct. 1, 1982, see section 402 of Pub.L. 97–164, set out as a note under section 171 of this title.

CHAPTER 171—TORT CLAIMS PROCEDURE

§ 2671. Definitions

As used in this chapter and sections 1346(b) and 2401(b) of this title, the term "Federal agency" includes the executive departments, the judicial and legislative branches, the military departments, independent establishments of the United States, and corporations primarily acting as instrumentalities or agencies of the United States, but does not include any contractor with the United States.

"Employee of the government" includes (1) officers or employees of any federal agency, members of the military or naval forces of the United States, members of the National Guard while engaged in training or duty under section 115, 316, 502, 503, 504, or 505 of title 32, and persons acting on behalf of a federal agency in an official capacity, temporarily or permanently in the service of the United States, whether with or without compensation, and (2) any officer or employee of a Federal public defender organization, except when such officer or employee performs professional services in the course of providing representation under section 3006A of title 18.

"Acting within the scope of his office or employment", in the case of a member of the military or naval forces of the United States or a member of the National Guard as defined in section 101(3) of title 32, means acting in line of duty.

(June 25, 1948, c. 646, 62 Stat. 982; May 24, 1949, c. 139, § 124, 63 Stat. 106; July 18, 1966, Pub.L. 89–506, § 8, 80 Stat. 307; Dec. 29, 1981, Pub.L. 97–124, § 1, 95 Stat. 1666; Nov. 18, 1988, Pub.L. 100–694, § 3, 102 Stat. 4564; Oct. 30, 2000, Pub.L. 106–398, § 1 [Div. A, Title VI, § 665(b)], 114 Stat. 1654, 1654A–169; Nov. 13, 2000, Pub.L. 106–518, Title IV, § 401, 114 Stat. 2421.)

HISTORICAL AND STATUTORY NOTES

Effective and Applicability Provisions

2000 Acts

Pub.L. 106–398, § 1 [Div. A, Title VI, § 665(c)(2)], Oct. 30, 2000, 114 Stat. 1654, 1654A–169, provided that: "The amendment made by subsection (b) [amending this section] shall apply with respect to acts and omissions occurring before, on, or after the date of the enactment of this Act [Oct. 30, 2000]."

1988 Acts

Amendment by Pub.L 100–694 effective Nov. 18, 1988, and applicable to all claims, civil actions, and proceedings pending on, or filed on or after, Nov. 18, 1988, see section 8 of Pub.L. 100–694, set out as a note under section 2679 of this title.

1981 Acts

Amendment by Pub.L. 97–124 applicable only with respect to claims arising on or after Dec. 29, 1981, see section 4 of Pub.L. 97–124, set out as a note under section 1089 of Title 10, Armed Forces.

1966 Acts

Amendment of section by Pub.L. 89–506 applicable to claims accruing six months or more after July 18, 1966, see section 10 of Pub.L. 89–506, set out as a note under section 2672 of this title.

Severability of Provisions

Section 7 of Pub.L. 100–694 provided that: "If any provision of this Act or the amendments made by this Act [enacting section 831c–2 of Title 16, Conservation, amending sections 2671, 2674, and 2679 of this title, and enacting provisions set out as notes under sections 1, 2671, and 2679 of this title] or the application of the provision to any person or circumstance is held invalid, the remainder of this Act and such amendments and the application of the provision to any other person or circumstance shall not be affected by that invalidation."

Law Enforcement Officer Acting Within Scope of Office or Employment

Pub.L. 105–277, § 101(h) [Title VI, § 627], 112 Stat. 2681–519, as amended Pub.L. 106–58, Title VI, § 623, Sept. 29, 1999, 113 Stat. 471, provided that:

"(a) **Definitions.**—In this section—

"(1) the term 'crime of violence' has the meaning given that term in section 16 of title 18, United States Code; and

"(2) the term 'law enforcement officer' means any employee described in subparagraph (A), (B), or (C) of section 8401(17) of title 5, United States Code; and any special in the Diplomatic Security Service of the Department of State.

"(b) **Rules of construction.**—Effective on the date of enactment of this Act [Oct. 21, 1998] and thereafter, and notwithstanding any other provision of law, for purposes of chapter 171 of title 28, United States Code, or any other provision of law relating to tort liability, a law enforcement officer shall be construed to be acting within the scope of his or her office or employment, if the officer takes reasonable action, including the use of force, to—

"(1) protect an individual in the presence of the officer from a crime of violence;

"(2) provide immediate assistance to an individual who has suffered or who is threatened with bodily harm; or

"(3) prevent the escape of any individual who the officer reasonably believes to have committed in the presence of the officer a crime of violence."

Congressional Findings and Purposes

Section 2 of Pub.L. 100–694 provided that:

"(a) **Findings.**—the Congress finds and declares the following:

"(1) For more than 40 years the Federal Tort Claims Act [28 U.S.C.A. §§ 1346(b), 2671 et seq.] has been the legal mechanism for compensating persons injured by negligent or wrongful acts of Federal employees committed within the scope of their employment.

"(2) The United States, through the Federal Tort Claims Act, is responsible to injured persons for the common law torts of its employees in the same manner in which the common law historically has recognized the responsibility of an employer for torts committed by its employees within the scope of their employment.

"(3) Because Federal employees for many years have been protected from personal common law tort liability by a broad based immunity, the Federal Tort Claims Act has served as the sole means for compensating persons injured by the tortious conduct of Federal employees.

"(4) Recent judicial decisions, and particularly the decision of the United States Supreme Court in Westfall v. Erwin [1988, 108 S.Ct. 580], have seriously eroded the common law tort immunity previously available to Federal employees.

"(5) This erosion of immunity of Federal employees from common law tort liability has created an immediate crisis involving the prospect of personal liability and the threat of protracted personal tort litigation for the entire Federal workforce.

"(6) The prospect of such liability will seriously undermine the morale and well being of Federal employees, impede the ability of agencies to carry out their missions, and diminish the vitality of the Federal Tort Claims Act as the proper remedy for Federal employee torts.

"(7) In its opinion in Westfall v. Erwin [1988, 108 S.Ct. 580], the Supreme Court indicated that the Congress is in the best position to determine the extent to which Federal employees should be personally liable for common law torts, and that legislative consideration of this matter would be useful.

"(b) **Purpose.**—It is the purpose of this Act [enacting section 831c–2 of Title 16, Conservation, amending sections 2671, 2674, and 2679 of this title, and enacting provisions set out as notes under sections 1, 2671, and 2679 of this title] to protect Federal employees from personal liability for common law torts committed within the scope of their employment, while providing persons injured by the common law torts of Federal employees with an appropriate remedy against the United States."

§ 2672. Administrative adjustment of claims

The head of each Federal agency or his designee, in accordance with regulations prescribed by the Attorney General, may consider, ascertain, adjust, determine, compromise, and settle any claim for money damages against the United States for injury or loss of property or personal injury or death caused by the negligent or wrongful act or omission of any employee of the agency while acting within the scope of his office or employment, under circumstances where the United States, if a private person, would be liable to the claimant in accordance with the law of the place where the act or omission occurred: *Provided,* That any award, compromise, or settlement in excess of $25,000 shall be effected only with the prior written approval of the Attorney General or his designee. Notwithstanding the proviso contained in the preceding sentence, any award, compromise, or settlement may be effected without the prior written approval of the Attorney General or his or her designee, to the extent that the Attorney General delegates to the head of the agency the authority to make such award, compromise, or settlement. Such delegations may not exceed the authority delegated by the Attorney General to the United States attorneys to settle claims for money damages against the United States. Each

Federal agency may use arbitration, or other alternative means of dispute resolution under the provisions of subchapter IV of chapter 5 of title 5, to settle any tort claim against the United States, to the extent of the agency's authority to award, compromise, or settle such claim without the prior written approval of the Attorney General or his or her designee.

Subject to the provisions of this title relating to civil actions on tort claims against the United States, any such award, compromise, settlement, or determination shall be final and conclusive on all officers of the Government, except when procured by means of fraud.

Any award, compromise, or settlement in an amount of $2,500 or less made pursuant to this section shall be paid by the head of the Federal agency concerned out of appropriations available to that agency. Payment of any award, compromise, or settlement in an amount in excess of $2,500 made pursuant to this section or made by the Attorney General in any amount pursuant to section 2677 of this title shall be paid in a manner similar to judgments and compromises in like causes and appropriations or funds available for the payment of such judgments and compromises are hereby made available for the payment of awards, compromises, or settlements under this chapter.

The acceptance by the claimant of any such award, compromise, or settlement shall be final and conclusive on the claimant, and shall constitute a complete release of any claim against the United States and against the employee of the government whose act or omission gave rise to the claim, by reason of the same subject matter.

(June 25, 1948, c. 646, 62 Stat. 983; Apr. 25, 1949, c. 92, § 2(b), 63 Stat. 62; May 24, 1949, c. 139, § 125, 63 Stat. 106; Sept. 23, 1950, c. 1010, § 9, 64 Stat. 987; Sept. 8, 1959, Pub.L. 86–238, § 1(1), 73 Stat. 471; July 18, 1966, Pub.L. 89–506, §§ 1, 9(a), 80 Stat. 306, 308; Nov. 15, 1990, Pub.L. 101–552, § 8(a), 104 Stat. 2746.)

HISTORICAL AND STATUTORY NOTES

Effective and Applicability Provisions

1990 Acts

The termination of amendments by Pub.L. 101–552 and authority to use dispute resolution proceedings on Oct. 1, 1995, provided by section 11 of Pub.L. 101–552, set out as a note under section 571 of Title 5, Government Organization and Employees, was repealed by section 9 of Pub.L. 104–320.

1966 Acts

Section 10 of Pub.L. 89–506 provided that: "This Act [amending this section and sections 2401(b), 2671, 2675, 2677, 2678, and 2679(b) of this title, section 724a of former Title 31, Money and Finance, and section 4116(a) of Title 38, Veteran's Benefits (see Section 7316 of Title 38)] shall apply to claims accruing six months or more after the date of its enactment [July 18, 1966]."

Laws Unaffected

Section 424(b) of Act Aug. 2, 1946, c. 753, Title IV, 60 Stat. 847, provided that: "Nothing contained herein shall be deemed to repeal any provision of law authorizing any Federal agency to consider, ascertain, adjust, settle, determine, or pay any claim on account of damage to or loss of property or on account of personal injury or death, in cases in which such damage, loss, injury, or death was not caused by any negligent or wrongful act or omission of an employee of the Government while acting within the scope of his office or employment, or any other claim not cognizable under part 2 of this title."

§ 2673. Reports to Congress

The head of each federal agency shall report annually to Congress all claims paid by it under section 2672 of this title, stating the name of each claimant, the amount claimed, the amount awarded, and a brief description of the claim.

(June 25, 1948, c. 646, 62 Stat. 983.)

Repeal

Section 1(1) of Pub.L. 89–348, Nov. 8, 1965, 79 Stat. 1310, repealed the requirement that an annual report to Congress be made of the administrative adjustment of tort claims of $2,500 or less, stating the name of each claimant, the amount claimed, the amount awarded, and a brief description of the claim.

§ 2674. Liability of United States

The United States shall be liable, respecting the provisions of this title relating to tort claims, in the same manner and to the same extent as a private individual under like circumstances, but shall not be liable for interest prior to judgment or for punitive damages.

If, however, in any case wherein death was caused, the law of the place where the act or omission complained of occurred provides, or has been construed to provide, for damages only punitive in nature, the United States shall be liable for actual or compensatory damages, measured by the pecuniary injuries resulting from such death to the persons respectively, for whose benefit the action was brought, in lieu thereof.

With respect to any claim under this chapter, the United States shall be entitled to assert any defense based upon judicial or legislative immunity which otherwise would have been available to the employee of the United States whose act or omission gave rise to the claim, as well as any other defenses to which the United States is entitled.

With respect to any claim to which this section applies, the Tennessee Valley Authority shall be entitled to assert any defense which otherwise would have been available to the employee based upon judicial or legislative immunity, which otherwise would have been

available to the employee of the Tennessee Valley Authority whose act or omission gave rise to the claim as well as any other defenses to which the Tennessee Valley Authority is entitled under this chapter.

(June 25, 1948, c. 646, 62 Stat. 983; Nov. 18, 1988, Pub.L. 100–694, §§ 4, 9(c), 102 Stat. 4564, 4567.)

HISTORICAL AND STATUTORY NOTES

Effective and Applicability Provisions

1988 Acts

Amendment by Pub.L. 100–694 effective Nov. 18, 1988, and applicable to all claims, civil actions, and proceedings pending on, or filed on or after, Nov. 18, 1988, see section 8 of Pub.L. 100–694 set out as a note under section 2679 of this title.

§ 2675. Disposition by federal agency as prerequisite; evidence

(a) An action shall not be instituted upon a claim against the United States for money damages for injury or loss of property or personal injury or death caused by the negligent or wrongful act or omission of any employee of the Government while acting within the scope of his office or employment, unless the claimant shall have first presented the claim to the appropriate Federal agency and his claim shall have been finally denied by the agency in writing and sent by certified or registered mail. The failure of an agency to make final disposition of a claim within six months after it is filed shall, at the option of the claimant any time thereafter, be deemed a final denial of the claim for purposes of this section. The provisions of this subsection shall not apply to such claims as may be asserted under the Federal Rules of Civil Procedure by third party complaint, cross-claim, or counterclaim.

(b) Action under this section shall not be instituted for any sum in excess of the amount of the claim presented to the federal agency, except where the increased amount is based upon newly discovered evidence not reasonably discoverable at the time of presenting the claim to the federal agency, or upon allegation and proof of intervening facts, relating to the amount of the claim.

(c) Disposition of any claim by the Attorney General or other head of a federal agency shall not be competent evidence of liability or amount of damages.

(June 25, 1948, c. 646, 62 Stat. 983; May 24, 1949, c. 139, § 126, 63 Stat. 107; July 18, 1966, Pub.L. 89–506, § 2, 80 Stat. 306.)

HISTORICAL AND STATUTORY NOTES

References in Text

The Federal Rules of Civil Procedure, referred to in subsec. (a), are set out in the Appendix to this title.

Effective and Applicability Provisions

1966 Acts

Amendment of section by Pub.L. 89–506 applicable to claims accruing six months or more after July 18, 1966, see section 10 of Pub.L. 89–506, set out as a note under section 2672 of this title.

§ 2676. Judgment as bar

The judgment in an action under section 1346(b) of this title shall constitute a complete bar to any action by the claimant, by reason of the same subject matter, against the employee of the government whose act or omission gave rise to the claim.

(June 25, 1948, c. 646, 62 Stat. 984.)

§ 2677. Compromise

The Attorney General or his designee may arbitrate, compromise, or settle any claim cognizable under section 1346(b) of this title, after the commencement of an action thereon.

(June 25, 1948, c. 646, 62 Stat. 984; July 18, 1966, Pub.L. 89–506, § 3, 80 Stat. 307.)

HISTORICAL AND STATUTORY NOTES

Effective and Applicability Provisions

1966 Acts

Amendment of section by Pub.L. 89–506 applicable to claims accruing six months or more after July 18, 1966, see section 10 of Pub.L. 89–506, set out as a note under section 2672 of this title.

§ 2678. Attorney fees; penalty

No attorney shall charge, demand, receive, or collect for services rendered, fees in excess of 25 per centum of any judgment rendered pursuant to section 1346(b) of this title or any settlement made pursuant to section 2677 of this title, or in excess of 20 per centum of any award, compromise, or settlement made pursuant to section 2672 of this title.

Any attorney who charges, demands, receives, or collects for services rendered in connection with such claim any amount in excess of that allowed under this section, if recovery be had, shall be fined not more than $2,000 or imprisoned not more than one year, or both.

(June 25, 1948, c. 646, 62 Stat. 984; July 18, 1966, Pub.L. 89–506, § 4, 80 Stat. 307.)

HISTORICAL AND STATUTORY NOTES

Effective and Applicability Provisions

1966 Acts

Amendment of section by Pub.L. 89–506 applicable to claims accruing six months or more after July 18, 1966, see section 10 of Pub.L. 89–506, set out as a note under section 2672 of this title.

§ 2679. Exclusiveness of remedy

(a) The authority of any federal agency to sue and be sued in its own name shall not be construed to authorize suits against such federal agency on claims

which are cognizable under section 1346(b) of this title, and the remedies provided by this title in such cases shall be exclusive.

(b)(1) The remedy against the United States provided by sections 1346(b) and 2672 of this title for injury or loss of property, or personal injury or death arising or resulting from the negligent or wrongful act or omission of any employee of the Government while acting within the scope of his office or employment is exclusive of any other civil action or proceeding for money damages by reason of the same subject matter against the employee whose act or omission gave rise to the claim or against the estate of such employee. Any other civil action or proceeding for money damages arising out of or relating to the same subject matter against the employee or the employee's estate is precluded without regard to when the act or omission occurred.

(2) Paragraph (1) does not extend or apply to a civil action against an employee of the Government—

 (A) which is brought for a violation of the Constitution of the United States, or

 (B) which is brought for a violation of a statute of the United States under which such action against an individual is otherwise authorized.

(c) The Attorney General shall defend any civil action or proceeding brought in any court against any employee of the Government or his estate for any such damage or injury. The employee against whom such civil action or proceeding is brought shall deliver within such time after date of service or knowledge of service as determined by the Attorney General, all process served upon him or an attested true copy thereof to his immediate superior or to whomever was designated by the head of his department to receive such papers and such person shall promptly furnish copies of the pleadings and process therein to the United States attorney for the district embracing the place wherein the proceeding is brought, to the Attorney General, and to the head of his employing Federal agency.

(d)(1) Upon certification by the Attorney General that the defendant employee was acting within the scope of his office or employment at the time of the incident out of which the claim arose, any civil action or proceeding commenced upon such claim in a United States district court shall be deemed an action against the United States under the provisions of this title and all references thereto, and the United States shall be substituted as the party defendant.

(2) Upon certification by the Attorney General that the defendant employee was acting within the scope of his office or employment at the time of the incident out of which the claim arose, any civil action or proceeding commenced upon such claim in a State court shall be removed without bond at any time before trial by the Attorney General to the district court of the United States for the district and division embracing the place in which the action or proceeding is pending. Such action or proceeding shall be deemed to be an action or proceeding brought against the United States under the provisions of this title and all references thereto, and the United States shall be substituted as the party defendant. This certification of the Attorney General shall conclusively establish scope of office or employment for purposes of removal.

(3) In the event that the Attorney General has refused to certify scope of office or employment under this section, the employee may at any time before trial petition the court to find and certify that the employee was acting within the scope of his office or employment. Upon such certification by the court, such action or proceeding shall be deemed to be an action or proceeding brought against the United States under the provisions of this title and all references thereto, and the United States shall be substituted as the party defendant. A copy of the petition shall be served upon the United States in accordance with the provisions of Rule 4(d)(4) of the Federal Rules of Civil Procedure. In the event the petition is filed in a civil action or proceeding pending in a State court, the action or proceeding may be removed without bond by the Attorney General to the district court of the United States for the district and division embracing the place in which it is pending. If, in considering the petition, the district court determines that the employee was not acting within the scope of his office or employment, the action or proceeding shall be remanded to the State court.

(4) Upon certification, any action or proceeding subject to paragraph (1), (2), or (3) shall proceed in the same manner as any action against the United States filed pursuant to section 1346(b) of this title and shall be subject to the limitations and exceptions applicable to those actions.

(5) Whenever an action or proceeding in which the United States is substituted as the party defendant under this subsection is dismissed for failure first to present a claim pursuant to section 2675(a) of this title, such a claim shall be deemed to be timely presented under section 2401(b) of this title if—

 (A) the claim would have been timely had it been filed on the date the underlying civil action was commenced, and

 (B) the claim is presented to the appropriate Federal agency within 60 days after dismissal of the civil action.

(e) The Attorney General may compromise or settle any claim asserted in such civil action or proceeding in the manner provided in section 2677, and with the same effect.

(June 25, 1948, c. 646, 62 Stat. 984; Sept. 21, 1961, Pub.L. 87–258, § 1, 75 Stat. 539; July 18, 1966, Pub.L. 89–506, § 5(a), 80 Stat. 307; Nov. 18, 1988, Pub.L. 100–694, §§ 5, 6, 102 Stat. 4564.)

HISTORICAL AND STATUTORY NOTES

References in Text

The Federal Rules of Civil Procedures referred to in subsec. (d)(3), are set out in this title.

Effective and Applicability Provisions

1988 Acts

Section 8 of Pub.L. 100–694 provided that:

"**(a) General rule.**—This Act and the amendments made by this Act [enacting section 831c–2 of Title 16, Conservation; amending sections 2671, 2674, and 2679(b), (d) of this title, and enacting provisions set out as notes under this section and sections 1 and 2671 of this title] shall take effect on the date of the enactment of this Act [Nov. 18, 1988].

"**(b) Applicability to proceedings.**—The amendments made by this Act [amending sections 2671, 2674, and 2679 of this title] shall apply to all claims, civil actions, and proceedings pending on, or filed on or after, the date of the enactment of this Act [Nov. 18, 1988].

"**(c) Pending State proceedings.**—With respect to any civil action or proceeding pending in a State court to which the amendments made by this Act apply, and as to which the period for removal under section 2679(d) of title 28, United States Code [subsec. (d) of this section] (as amended by section 6 of this Act), has expired, the Attorney General shall have 60 days after the date of the enactment of this Act [Nov. 18, 1988] during which to seek removal under such section 2679(d) [subsec. (d) of this section].

"**(d) Claims accruing before enactment.**—With respect to any civil action or proceeding to which the amendments made by this Act apply in which the claim accrued before the date of the enactment of this Act [Nov. 18, 1988], the period during which the claim shall be deemed to be timely presented under section 2679(d)(5) of title 28, United States Code [subsec. (d)(5) of this section] (as amended by section 6 of this Act) shall be that period within which the claim could have been timely filed under applicable State law, but in no event shall such period exceed two years from the date of the enactment of this Act [Nov. 18, 1988]."

1966 Acts

Amendment of section by Pub.L. 89–506 applicable to claims accruing six months or more after July 18, 1966, see section 10 of Pub.L. 89–506, set out as a note under section 2672 of this title.

1961 Acts

Section 2 of Pub.L. 87–258 provided that: "The amendments made by this Act [adding subsecs. (b)–(e) of this section] shall be deemed to be in effect six months after the enactment hereof [Sept. 21, 1961] but any rights or liabilities then existing shall not be affected."

§ 2680. Exceptions

The provisions of this chapter and section 1346(b) of this title shall not apply to—

(a) Any claim based upon an act or omission of an employee of the Government, exercising due care, in the execution of a statute or regulation, whether or not such statute or regulation be valid, or based upon the exercise or performance or the failure to exercise or perform a discretionary function or duty on the part of a federal agency or an employee of the Government, whether or not the discretion involved be abused.

(b) Any claim arising out of the loss, miscarriage, or negligent transmission of letters or postal matter.

(c) Any claim arising in respect of the assessment or collection of any tax or customs duty, or the detention of any goods, merchandise, or other property by any officer of customs or excise or any other law enforcement officer, except that the provisions of this chapter and section 1346(b) of this title apply to any claim based on injury or loss of goods, merchandise, or other property, while in the possession of any officer of customs or excise or any other law enforcement officer, if—

(1) the property was seized for the purpose of forfeiture under any provision of Federal law providing for the forfeiture of property other than as a sentence imposed upon conviction of a criminal offense;

(2) the interest of the claimant was not forfeited;

(3) the interest of the claimant was not remitted or mitigated (if the property was subject to forfeiture); and

(4) the claimant was not convicted of a crime for which the interest of the claimant in the property was subject to forfeiture under a Federal criminal forfeiture law..[1]

(d) Any claim for which a remedy is provided by chapter 309 or 311 of title 46 relating to claims or suits in admiralty against the United States.

(e) Any claim arising out of an act or omission of any employee of the Government in administering the provisions of sections 1–31 of Title 50, Appendix.

(f) Any claim for damages caused by the imposition or establishment of a quarantine by the United States.

[(g) Repealed. Sept. 26, 1950, c. 1049, § 13(5), 64 Stat. 1043.]

(h) Any claim arising out of assault, battery, false imprisonment, false arrest, malicious prosecution, abuse of process, libel, slander, misrepresentation, deceit, or interference with contract rights: *Provided,* That, with regard to acts or omissions of investigative or law enforcement officers of the United States Government, the provisions of this chapter and section 1346(b) of this title shall apply to any claim arising, on or after the date of the enactment of this proviso, out of assault, battery,

false imprisonment, false arrest, abuse of process, or malicious prosecution. For the purpose of this subsection, "investigative or law enforcement officer" means any officer of the United States who is empowered by law to execute searches, to seize evidence, or to make arrests for violations of Federal law.

(i) Any claim for damages caused by the fiscal operations of the Treasury or by the regulation of the monetary system.

(j) Any claim arising out of the combatant activities of the military or naval forces, or the Coast Guard, during time of war.

(k) Any claim arising in a foreign country.

(*l***)** Any claim arising from the activities of the Tennessee Valley Authority.

(m) Any claim arising from the activities of the Panama Canal Company.

(n) Any claim arising from the activities of a Federal land bank, a Federal intermediate credit bank, or a bank for cooperatives.

(June 25, 1948, c. 646, 62 Stat. 984; July 16, 1949, c. 340, 63 Stat. 444; Sept. 26, 1950, c. 1049, §§ 2(a)(2), 13(5), 64 Stat. 1038, 1043; Aug. 18, 1959, Pub.L. 86–168, Title II, § 202(b), 73 Stat. 389; Mar. 16, 1974, Pub.L. 93–253, § 2, 88 Stat. 50; Apr. 25, 2000, Pub.L. 106–185, § 3(a), 114 Stat. 211; Oct. 6, 2006, Pub.L. 109–304, § 17(f)(4), 120 Stat. 1708.)

1 So in original. Second period probably should not appear.

HISTORICAL AND STATUTORY NOTES

References in Text

Chapter 309 or 311 of title 46, referred to in subsec. (d), are Suits in Admiralty Against the United States, 46 U.S.C.A. § 30901 et seq., and Commercial Instruments and Maritime Liens, 46 U.S.C.A. § 31101 et seq.

Sections 1–31 of Title 50, Appendix, referred to in subsec. (e), was in the original source of this section (section 943 [of Title 28, which was section 421] of Act Aug. 2, 1946) a reference to the Trading with the Enemy Act, as amended. The Trading with the Enemy Act is now comprised of sections 1 to 43, which are classified to sections 1 to 6, 7 to 39, and 41 to 44 of Title 50, Appendix, War and National Defense.

Date of the enactment of this proviso, referred to in subsec. (h), means Mar. 16, 1974, the date on which Pub.L. 93–253, enacting the proviso, was approved.

Panama Canal Company, referred to in subsec. (m), deemed to refer to Panama Canal Commission, see section 3602(b)(5) of Title 22, Foreign Relations and Intercourse.

Effective and Applicability Provisions

2000 Acts

Amendments by Pub.L. 106–185, applicable to any forfeiture proceeding commenced on or after the date that is 120 days after April 25, 2000, see section 21 of Pub.L. 106–185, set out as a note under section 1324 of Title 8.

1959 Acts

Amendment by Pub.L. 86–168 effective Jan. 1, 1960, pursuant to section 203(c) of Pub.L. 86–168.

1950 Acts

Section 14 of Act Sept. 26, 1950, provided that the repeal of subsec. (g) and amendment of subsec. (m) of this section by such Act shall take effect upon the effective date of the transfer to the Panama Canal Company, pursuant to the provisions of section 256 of the Canal Zone Code, as added by section 10 of such Act, of the Panama Canal together with the facilities and appurtenances related thereto.

Transfer of Functions

The Coast Guard was transferred to the Department of Transportation and all functions, powers, and duties, relating to the Coast Guard, of the Secretary of the Treasury and of all other offices and officers of the Department of the Treasury were transferred to the Secretary of Transportation by Pub.L. 89–670, § 6(b)(1), Oct. 15, 1966, 80 Stat. 938. Section 6(b)(2) of Pub.L. 89–670, however, provided that notwithstanding such transfer of functions, the Coast Guard shall operate as part of the Navy in time of war or when the President directs as provided in section 3 of Title 14, Coast Guard. See section 108 of Title 49, Transportation.

For transfer of certain functions relating to claims and litigation, insofar as they pertain to the Air Force, from the Secretary of the Army to the Secretary of the Air Force, see Secretary of Defense Transfer Order No. 34 [§ 1a(2)(4)], eff. July 1, 1949.

Applicability of Subsec. (j)

Section 1(a)(32) of Joint Res. July 3, 1952, c. 570, 66 Stat. 333, as amended by Joint Res. Mar. 31, 1953, c. 13, § 1, 67 Stat. 18 and Joint Res. June 30, 1953, c. 172, 67 Stat. 132, provided that subsec. (j) of this section should continue in force until six months after the termination of the national emergency proclaimed by the President on Dec. 16, 1950, by 1950 Proc. No. 2914, 15 F.R. 9029, set out as a note preceding section 1 of the Appendix to Title 50, War and National Defense, or such earlier date or dates as may be provided for by Congress, but in no event beyond Aug. 1, 1953. Section 7 of Joint Res. July 3, 1952, provided that it should become effective June 16, 1952.

Section 6 of Joint Res. July 3, 1952, c. 570, § 6, 66 Stat. 334, repealed Joint Res. Apr. 14, 1952, c. 204, 66 Stat. 54 as amended by Joint Res. May 28, 1952, c. 339, 66 Stat. 96; Joint Res. June 14, 1952, c. 437, 66 Stat. 137; Joint Res. June 30, 1952, c. 526, 66 Stat. 296, which continued provisions of subsection (j) of this section (see note above) until July 3, 1952. This repeal was made effective June 16, 1952, by section 7 of Joint Res. July 3, 1952.

Northern Mariana Islands as Foreign Country With Respect to Claims Accruing No More than Two Years Prior to Oct. 19, 1982

Pub.L. 97–357, Title II, § 204, Oct. 19, 1982, 96 Stat. 1708, provided: "That the Northern Mariana Islands shall not be considered a foreign country for purposes of subsection (k) of section 2680 of Title 28, United States Code [subsec. (k) of this section], with respect to claims which accrued no more than two years prior to the effective date of this Act [Oct. 19, 1982]."

Termination of National Emergency

Declaration of national emergency in effect on Sept. 14, 1976, was terminated two years from that date by Section 1601 of Title 50, War and National Defense.

CHAPTER 176—FEDERAL DEBT COLLECTION PROCEDURE

SUBCHAPTER A—DEFINITIONS AND GENERAL PROVISIONS

§ 3001. Applicability of chapter

(a) In general.—Except as provided in subsection (b), the[1] chapter provides the exclusive civil procedures for the United States—

(1) to recover a judgment on a debt; or

(2) to obtain, before judgment on a claim for a debt, a remedy in connection with such claim.

(b) Limitation.—To the extent that another Federal law specifies procedures for recovering on a claim or a judgment for a debt arising under such law, those procedures shall apply to such claim or judgment to the extent those procedures are inconsistent with this chapter.

(c) Amounts owing other than debts.—This chapter shall not apply with respect to an amount owing that is not a debt or to a claim for an amount owing that is not a debt.

(Added Pub.L. 101–647, Title XXXVI, § 3611, Nov. 29, 1990, 104 Stat. 4933.)

[1] So in original. Probably should be "this".

HISTORICAL AND STATUTORY NOTES

Effective and Applicability Provisions

1990 Acts

Section 3631 of Title XXXVI of Pub.L. 101–647 provided that:

"**(a)** Except as provided in subsection (b), this Act and the amendments made by this Act [Pub.L. 101–647, Title XXXVI, Nov. 29, 1990, 104 Stat. 4933, popularly known as the Federal Debt Collection Procedures Act of 1990. For distribution of this Act to the Code, see Short Title note set out under section 1 of this title and Tables] shall take effect 180 days after the date of the enactment of this Act [Nov. 29, 1990].

"**(b)(1)** The amendments made by title I of this Act [probably means subtitle A of Title XXXVI of Pub.L. 101–647, which enacted this chapter] shall apply with respect to actions pending on the effective date of this Act [180 days after Nov. 29, 1990] in any court on—

"**(A)** a claim for a debt; or

"**(B)** a judgment for a debt.

"**(2)** All notices, writs, orders, and judgments in effect in such actions shall continue in effect until superseded or modified in an action under chapter 176 of title 28 of the United States Code, as added by title I of this Act [this chapter].

"**(3)** For purposes of this subsection—

"**(A)** the term 'court' means a Federal, State, or local court, and

"**(B)** the term 'debt' has the meaning given such term in section and 3002(3) of such chapter [probably means section 3002(3) of this title]."

§ 3002. Definitions

As used in this chapter:

(1) "Counsel for the United States" means—

(A) a United States attorney, an assistant United States attorney designated to act on behalf of the United States attorney, or an attorney with the United States Department of Justice or with a Federal agency who has litigation authority; and

(B) any private attorney authorized by contract made in accordance with section 3718 of title 31 to conduct litigation for collection of debts on behalf of the United States.

(2) "Court" means any court created by the Congress of the United States, excluding the United States Tax Court.

(3) "Debt" means—

(A) an amount that is owing to the United States on account of a direct loan, or loan insured or guaranteed, by the United States; or

(B) an amount that is owing to the United States on account of a fee, duty, lease, rent, service, sale of real or personal property, overpayment, fine, assessment, penalty, restitution, damages, interest, tax, bail bond forfeiture, reimbursement, recovery of a cost incurred by the United States, or other source of indebtedness to the United States, but that is not owing under the terms of a contract originally entered into by only persons other than the United States;

and includes any amount owing to the United States for the benefit of an Indian tribe or individual Indian, but excludes any amount to which the United States is entitled under section 3011(a).

(4) "Debtor" means a person who is liable for a debt or against whom there is a claim for a debt.

(5) "Disposable earnings" means that part of earnings remaining after all deductions required by law have been withheld.

(6) "Earnings" means compensation paid or payable for personal services, whether denominated as wages, salary, commission, bonus, or otherwise, and includes periodic payments pursuant to a pension or retirement program.

(7) "Garnishee" means a person (other than the debtor) who has, or is reasonably thought to have, possession, custody, or control of any property in which the debtor has a substantial nonexempt interest, including any obligation due the debtor or to become due the debtor, and against whom a garnishment under section 3104 or 3205 is issued by a court.

(8) "Judgment" means a judgment, order, or decree entered in favor of the United States in a court and arising from a civil or criminal proceeding regarding a debt.

(9) "Nonexempt disposable earnings" means 25 percent of disposable earnings, subject to section 303 of the Consumer Credit Protection Act.

(10) "Person" includes a natural person (including an individual Indian), a corporation, a partnership, an unincorporated association, a trust, or an estate, or any other public or private entity, including a State or local government or an Indian tribe.

(11) "Prejudgment remedy" means the remedy of attachment, receivership, garnishment, or sequestration authorized by this chapter to be granted before judgment on the merits of a claim for a debt.

(12) "Property" includes any present or future interest, whether legal or equitable, in real, personal (including choses in action), or mixed property, tangible or intangible, vested or contingent, wherever located and however held (including community property and property held in trust (including spendthrift and pension trusts)), but excludes—

(A) property held in trust by the United States for the benefit of an Indian tribe or individual Indian; and

(B) Indian lands subject to restrictions against alienation imposed by the United States.

(13) "Security agreement" means an agreement that creates or provides for a lien.

(14) "State" means any of the several States, the District of Columbia, the Commonwealth of Puerto Rico, the Commonwealth of the Northern Marianas, or any territory or possession of the United States.

(15) "United States" means—

(A) a Federal corporation;

(B) an agency, department, commission, board, or other entity of the United States; or

(C) an instrumentality of the United States.

(16) "United States marshal" means a United States marshal, a deputy marshal, or an official of the United States Marshals Service designated under section 564.

(Added Pub.L. 101–647, Title XXXVI, § 3611, Nov. 29, 1990, 104 Stat. 4933.)

HISTORICAL AND STATUTORY NOTES

References in Text

Section 303 of the Consumer Credit Protection Act, referred to in par. (9), is classified to section 1673 of Title 15, Commerce and Trade.

Effective and Applicability Provisions

1990 Acts

Section to take effect 180 days after Nov. 29, 1990, except as otherwise provided, see section 3631 of Pub.L. 101–647, set out as a note under section 3001 of this title.

§ 3003. Rules of construction

(a) Terms.—For purposes of this chapter—

(1) the terms "includes" and "including" are not limiting;

(2) the term "or" is not exclusive; and

(3) the singular includes the plural.

(b) Effect on rights of the United States.—This chapter shall not be construed to curtail or limit the right of the United States under any other Federal law or any State law—

(1) to collect taxes or to collect any other amount collectible in the same manner as a tax;

(2) to collect any fine, penalty, assessment, restitution, or forfeiture arising in a criminal case;

(3) to appoint or seek the appointment of a receiver; or

(4) to enforce a security agreement.

(c) Effect on other laws.—This chapter shall not be construed to supersede or modify the operation of—

 (1) title 11;

 (2) admiralty law;

 (3) section 3713 of title 31;

 (4) section 303 of the Consumer Credit Protection Act (15 U.S.C. 1673);

 (5) a statute of limitation applicable to a criminal proceeding;

 (6) the common law or statutory rights to set-off or recoupment;

 (7) any Federal law authorizing, or any inherent authority of a court to provide, injunctive relief;

 (8) the authority of a court—

 (A) to impose a sanction under the Federal Rules of Civil Procedure;

 (B) to appoint a receiver to effectuate its order; or

 (C) to exercise the power of contempt under any Federal law;

 (9) any law authorizing the United States to obtain partition, or to recover possession, of property in which the United States holds title; or

 (10) any provision of any other chapter of this title, except to the extent such provision is inconsistent with this chapter.

(d) Preemption.—This chapter shall preempt State law to the extent such law is inconsistent with a provision of this chapter.

(e) Effect on rights of the United States under foreign and international law.—This chapter shall not be construed to curtail or limit the rights of the United States under foreign law, under a treaty or an international agreement, or otherwise under international law.

(f) Applicability of Federal Rules of Civil Procedure.—Except as provided otherwise in this chapter, the Federal Rules of Civil Procedure shall apply with respect to actions and proceedings under this chapter. (Added Pub.L. 101–647, Title XXXVI, § 3611, Nov. 29, 1990, 104 Stat. 4935.)

HISTORICAL AND STATUTORY NOTES

References in Text

The Federal Rules of Civil Procedure, referred to in subsecs. (c)(8)(A) and (f), are set out in this title.

Effective and Applicability Provisions

1990 Acts

Section to take effect 180 days after Nov. 29, 1990, except as otherwise provided, see section 3631 of Pub.L. 101–647, set out as a note under section 3001 of this title.

§ 3004. Service of process; enforcement; notice

(a) Manner of service.—A complaint, notice, writ, or other process required to be served in an action or proceeding under this chapter shall be served in accordance with the Federal Rules of Civil Procedure unless otherwise provided in this chapter.

(b) Nationwide enforcement.—(1) Except as provided in paragraph (2)—

 (A) any writ, order, judgment, or other process, including a summons and complaint, filed under this chapter may be served in any State; and

 (B) such writ, order, or judgment may be enforced by the court issuing the writ, order, or process, regardless of where the person is served with the writ, order, or process.

(2) If the debtor so requests, within 20 days after receiving the notice described in section 3101(d) or 3202(b), the action or proceeding in which the writ, order, or judgment was issued shall be transferred to the district court for the district in which the debtor resides.

(c) Notice and other process.—At such time as counsel for the United States considers appropriate, but not later than the time a prejudgment or postjudgment remedy is put into effect under this chapter, counsel for the United States shall exercise reasonable diligence to serve on the debtor and any person who the United States believes, after exercising due diligence, has possession, custody, or control of the property, a copy of the application for such remedy, the order granting such remedy, and the notice required by section 3101(d) or 3202(b). (Added Pub.L. 101–647, Title XXXVI, § 3611, Nov. 29, 1990, 104 Stat. 4936.)

HISTORICAL AND STATUTORY NOTES

References in Text

The Federal Rules of Civil Procedure, referred to in subsec. (a), are set out in this title.

Effective and Applicability Provisions

1990 Acts

Section to take effect 180 days after Nov. 29, 1990, except as otherwise provided, see section 3631 of Pub.L. 101–647, set out as a note under section 3001 of this title.

§ 3005. Application of chapter to judgments

This chapter shall not apply with respect to a judgment on a debt if such judgment is entered more than 10 years before the effective date of this chapter. (Added Pub.L. 101–647, Title XXXVI, § 3611, Nov. 29, 1990, 104 Stat. 4936.)

HISTORICAL AND STATUTORY NOTES

References in Text

For effective date of this chapter, referred to in text, see section 3631 of Pub.L. 101–647, set out as an Effective Date note under section 3001 of this title.

Effective and Applicability Provisions

1990 Acts

Section to take effect 180 days after Nov. 29, 1990, except as otherwise provided, see section 3631 of Pub.L. 101–647, set out as a note under section 3001 of this title.

§ 3006. Affidavit requirements

Any affidavit required of the United States by this chapter may be made on information and belief, if reliable and reasonably necessary, establishing with particularity, to the court's satisfaction, facts supporting the claim of the United States.

(Added Pub.L. 101–647, Title XXXVI, § 3611, Nov. 29, 1990, 104 Stat. 4936.)

HISTORICAL AND STATUTORY NOTES

Effective and Applicability Provisions

1990 Acts

Section to take effect 180 days after Nov. 29, 1990, except as otherwise provided, see section 3631 of Pub.L. 101–647, set out as a note under section 3001 of this title.

§ 3007. Perishable personal property

(a) **Authority to sell.**—If at any time during any action or proceeding under this chapter the court determines on its own initiative or upon motion of any party, that any seized or detained personal property is likely to perish, waste, or be destroyed, or otherwise substantially depreciate in value during the pendency of the proceeding, the court shall order a commercially reasonable sale of such property.

(b) **Deposit of sale proceeds.**—Within 5 days after such sale, the proceeds shall be deposited with the clerk of the court, accompanied by a statement in writing and signed by the United States marshal, to be filed in the action or proceeding, stating the time and place of sale, the name of the purchaser, the amount received, and an itemized account of expenses.

(c) **Presumption.**—For purposes of liability on the part of the United States, there shall be a presumption that the price paid at a sale under subsection (a) is the fair market value of the property or portion.

(Added Pub.L. 101–647, Title XXXVI, § 3611, Nov. 29, 1990, 104 Stat. 4937.)

HISTORICAL AND STATUTORY NOTES

Effective and Applicability Provisions

1990 Acts

Section to take effect 180 days after Nov. 29, 1990, except as otherwise provided, see section 3631 of Pub.L. 101–647, set out as a note under section 3001 of this title.

§ 3008. Proceedings before United States magistrate judges

A district court of the United States may assign its duties in proceedings under this chapter to a United States magistrate judge to the extent not inconsistent with the Constitution and laws of the United States.

(Added Pub.L. 101–647, Title XXXVI, § 3611, Nov. 29, 1990, 104 Stat. 4937, and amended Pub.L. 101–650, Title III, § 321, Dec. 1, 1990, 104 Stat. 5117.)

HISTORICAL AND STATUTORY NOTES

Effective and Applicability Provisions

1990 Acts

Section to take effect 180 days after Nov. 29, 1990, except as otherwise provided, see section 3631 of Pub.L. 101–647, set out as a note under section 3001 of this title.

Change of Name

"United States magistrate judges" substituted for "United States magistrates" in the catchline and "United States magistrate judge" substituted for "United States magistrate" in text pursuant to section 321 of Pub.L. 101–650, set out as a note under 28 U.S.C.A. § 631.

§ 3009. United States marshals' authority to designate keeper

Whenever a United States marshal is authorized to seize property pursuant to this chapter, the United States marshal may designate another person or Federal agency to hold for safekeeping such property seized.

(Added Pub.L. 101–647, Title XXXVI, § 3611, Nov. 29, 1990, 104 Stat. 4937.)

HISTORICAL AND STATUTORY NOTES

Effective and Applicability Provisions

1990 Acts

Section to take effect 180 days after Nov. 29, 1990, except as otherwise provided, see section 3631 of Pub.L. 101–647, set out as a note under section 3001 of this title.

§ 3010. Co-owned property

(a) **Limitation.**—The remedies available to the United States under this chapter may be enforced against property which is co-owned by a debtor and any other person only to the extent allowed by the law of the State where the property is located. This section shall not be construed to limit any right or interest of a debtor or co-owner in a retirement system for Federal military or civilian personnel established by the United States or any agency thereof or in a qualified retirement arrangement.

(b) **Definitions.**—For purposes of subsection (a)—

(1) the term "retirement system for Federal military or civilian personnel" means a pension or annuity system for Federal military or civilian personnel of more than one agency, or for some or all of such personnel of a single agency, established by statute

or by regulation pursuant to statutory authority; and

(2) the term "qualified retirement arrangement" means a plan qualified under section 401(a), 403(a), or 409 of the Internal Revenue Code of 1986 or a plan that is subject to the requirements of section 205 of the Employee Retirement Income Security Act of 1974.

(Added Pub.L. 101–647, Title XXXVI, § 3611, Nov. 29, 1990, 104 Stat. 4937.)

HISTORICAL AND STATUTORY NOTES

References in Text

Sections 401(a), 403(a) and 409 of the Internal Revenue Code of 1986, referred to in subsec. (b)(2), are set out in sections 401(a), 403(a) and 409, respectively, of Title 26, Internal Revenue Code.

Section 205 of the Employee Retirement Income Security Act of 1974, referred to in subsec. (b)(2), is classified to section 1055 of Title 29, Labor.

Effective and Applicability Provisions

1990 Acts

Section to take effect 180 days after Nov. 29, 1990, except as otherwise provided, see section 3631 of Pub.L. 101–647, set out as a note under section 3001 of this title.

§ 3011. Assessment of surcharge on a debt

(a) **Surcharge authorized.**—In an action or proceeding under subchapter B or C, and subject to subsection (b), the United States is entitled to recover a surcharge of 10 percent of the amount of the debt in connection with the recovery of the debt, to cover the cost of processing and handling the litigation and enforcement under this chapter of the claim for such debt.

(b) **Limitation.**—Subsection (a) shall not apply if—

(1) the United States receives an attorney's fee in connection with the enforcement of the claim; or

(2) the law pursuant to which the action on the claim is based provides any other amount to cover such costs.

(Added Pub.L. 101–647, Title XXXVI, § 3611, Nov. 29, 1990, 104 Stat. 4937.)

HISTORICAL AND STATUTORY NOTES

Effective and Applicability Provisions

1990 Acts

Section to take effect 180 days after Nov. 29, 1990, except as otherwise provided, see section 3631 of Pub.L. 101–647, set out as a note under section 3001 of this title.

§ 3012. Joinder of additional defendant

The United States or the debtor may join as an additional defendant in an action or proceeding under this chapter any person reasonably believed to owe money (including money owed on account of a require-

ment to provide goods or services pursuant to a loan or loan guarantee extended under Federal law) to the debtor arising out of the transaction or occurrence giving rise to a debt.

(Added Pub.L. 101–647, Title XXXVI, § 3611, Nov. 29, 1990, 104 Stat. 4938.)

HISTORICAL AND STATUTORY NOTES

Effective and Applicability Provisions

1990 Acts

Section to take effect 180 days after Nov. 29, 1990, except as otherwise provided, see section 3631 of Pub.L. 101–647, set out as a note under section 3001 of this title.

§ 3013. Modification or protective order; supervision of enforcement

The court may at any time on its own initiative or the motion of any interested person, and after such notice as it may require, make an order denying, limiting, conditioning, regulating, extending, or modifying the use of any enforcement procedure under this chapter.

(Added Pub.L. 101–647, Title XXXVI, § 3611, Nov. 29, 1990, 104 Stat. 4938.)

HISTORICAL AND STATUTORY NOTES

Effective and Applicability Provisions

1990 Acts

Section to take effect 180 days after Nov. 29, 1990, except as otherwise provided, see section 3631 of Pub.L. 101–647, set out as a note under section 3001 of this title.

§ 3014. Exempt property

(a) **Election to exempt property.**—An individual debtor may, in an action or proceeding under this chapter, elect to exempt property listed in either paragraph (1) or, in the alternative, paragraph (2). If such action or proceeding is against debtors who are husband and wife, one debtor may not elect to exempt property listed in paragraph (1) and the other debtor elect to exempt property listed in paragraph (2). If the debtors cannot agree on the alternative to be elected, they shall be deemed to elect paragraph (1). Such property is either—

(1) property that is specified in section 522(d) of title 11, as amended from time to time; or

(2)(A) any property that is exempt under Federal law, other than paragraph (1), or State or local law that is applicable on the date of the filing of the application for a remedy under this chapter at the place in which the debtor's domicile has been located for the 180 days immediately preceding the date of the filing of such application, or for a longer portion of such 180–day period than in any other place; and

(B) any interest in property in which the debtor had, immediately before the filing of such applica-

tion, an interest as a tenant by the entirety or joint tenant, or an interest in a community estate, to the extent that such interest is exempt from process under applicable nonbankruptcy law.

(b) Effect on assertion and manner of determination.—

(1) Statement.—A court may order the debtor to file a statement with regard to any claimed exemption. A copy of such statement shall be served on counsel for the United States. Such statement shall be under oath and shall describe each item of property for which exemption is claimed, the value and the basis for such valuation, and the nature of the debtor's ownership interest.

(2) Hearing.—The United States or the debtor, by application to the court in which an action or proceeding under this chapter is pending, may request a hearing on the applicability of any exemption claimed by the debtor. The court shall determine the extent (if any) to which the exemption applies. Unless it is reasonably evident that the exemption applies, the debtor shall bear the burden of persuasion.

(3) Stay of disposition.—Assertion of an exemption shall prevent the United States from selling or otherwise disposing of the property for which such exemption is claimed until the court determines whether the debtor has a substantial nonexempt interest in such property. The United States may not take possession of, dispose of, sell, or otherwise interfere with the debtor's normal use and enjoyment of an interest in property the United States knows or has reason to know is exempt.

(c) Debtors in joint cases.—Subject to the limitation in subsection (a), this section shall apply separately with respect to each debtor in a joint case.
(Added Pub.L. 101–647, Title XXXVI, § 3611, Nov. 29, 1990, 104 Stat. 4938.)

HISTORICAL AND STATUTORY NOTES
Effective and Applicability Provisions
1990 Acts
Section to take effect 180 days after Nov. 29, 1990, except as otherwise provided, see section 3631 of Pub.L. 101–647, set out as a note under section 3001 of this title.

§ 3015. Discovery as to debtor's financial condition

(a) In general.—Except as provided in subsection (b), in an action or proceeding under subchapter B or C, the United States may have discovery regarding the financial condition of the debtor in the manner in which discovery is authorized by the Federal Rules of Civil Procedure in an action on a claim for a debt.

(b) Limitation.—Subsection (a) shall not apply with respect to an action or proceeding under sub-

chapter B unless there is a reasonable likelihood that the debt involved exceeds $50,000.
(Added Pub.L. 101–647, Title XXXVI, § 3611, Nov. 29, 1990, 104 Stat. 4939.)

HISTORICAL AND STATUTORY NOTES
References in Text
The Federal Rules of Civil Procedure, referred to in subsec. (a), are set out in this title.

Effective and Applicability Provisions
1990 Acts
Section to take effect 180 days after Nov. 29, 1990, except as otherwise provided, see section 3631 of Pub.L. 101–647, set out as a note under section 3001 of this title.

SUBCHAPTER B—PREJUDGMENT REMEDIES

§ 3101. Prejudgment remedies

(a) Application.—(1) The United States may, in a proceeding in conjunction with the complaint or at any time after the filing of a civil action on a claim for a debt, make application under oath to a court to issue any prejudgment remedy.

(2) Such application shall be filed with the court and shall set forth the factual and legal basis for each prejudgment remedy sought.

(3) Such application shall—

(A) state that the debtor against whom the prejudgment remedy is sought shall be afforded an opportunity for a hearing; and

(B) set forth with particularity that all statutory requirements under this chapter for the issuance of the prejudgment remedy sought have been satisfied.

(b) Grounds.—Subject to section 3102, 3103, 3104, or 3105, a prejudgment remedy may be granted by any court if the United States shows reasonable cause to believe that—

(1) the debtor—

(A) is about to leave the jurisdiction of the United States with the effect of hindering, delaying, or defrauding the United States in its effort to recover a debt;

(B) has or is about to assign, dispose, remove, conceal, ill treat, waste, or destroy property with the effect of hindering, delaying, or defrauding the United States;

(C) has or is about to convert the debtor's property into money, securities, or evidence of

debt in a manner prejudicial to the United States with the effect of hindering, delaying, or defrauding the United States; or

(D) has evaded service of process by concealing himself or has temporarily withdrawn from the jurisdiction of the United States with the effect of hindering, delaying, or defrauding the United States; or

(2) a prejudgment remedy is required to obtain jurisdiction within the United States and the prejudgment remedy sought will result in obtaining such jurisdiction.

(c) Affidavit.—(1) The application under subsection (a) shall include an affidavit establishing with particularity to the court's satisfaction facts supporting the probable validity of the claim for a debt and the right of the United States to recover what is demanded in the application.

(2) The affidavit shall state—

(A) specifically the amount of the debt claimed by the United States and any interest or costs attributable to such debt;

(B) one or more of the grounds specified in subsection (b); and

(C) the requirements of section 3102(b), 3103(a), 3104(a), or 3105(b), as the case may be.

(3) No bond is required of the United States.

(d) Notice and hearing.—(1) On filing an application by the United States as provided in this section, the counsel for the United States shall prepare, and the clerk shall issue, a notice for service on the debtor against whom the prejudgment remedy is sought and on any other person whom the United States reasonably believes, after exercising due diligence, has possession, custody, or control of property affected by such remedy. Three copies of the notice shall be served on each such person. The form and content of such notice shall be approved jointly by a majority of the chief judges of the Federal districts in the State in which the court is located and shall be in substantially the following form:

"NOTICE

"You are hereby notified that this [property] is being taken by the United States Government ('the Government'), which says that [name of debtor] owes it a debt of $ [amount] for [reason for debt] and has filed a lawsuit to collect this debt. The Government says it must take this property at this time because [recite the pertinent ground or grounds from section 3101(b)]. The Government wants to make sure [name of debtor] will pay if the court determines that this money is owed.

"In addition, you are hereby notified that there are exemptions under the law which may protect some of this property from being taken by the Government if [name of debtor] can show that the exemptions apply. Below is a summary of the major exemptions which apply in most situations in the State of [State where property is located]:

"[A statement summarizing in plain and understandable English the election available with respect to such State under section 3014 and the types of property that may be exempted under each of the alternatives specified in paragraphs (1) and (2) of section 3014(a), and a statement that different property may be so exempted with respect to the State in which the debtor resides.]

"If you are [name of debtor] and you disagree with the reason the Government gives for taking your property now, or if you think you do not owe the money to the Government that it says you do, or if you think the property the Government is taking qualifies under one of the above exemptions, you have a right to ask the court to return your property to you.

"If you want a hearing, you must promptly notify the court. You must make your request in writing, and either mail it or deliver it in person to the clerk of the court at [address]. If you wish, you may use this notice to request the hearing by checking the box below and mailing this notice to the court clerk. You must also send a copy of your request to the Government at [address], so the Government will know you want a hearing. The hearing will take place within 5 days after the clerk receives your request, if you ask for it to take place that quickly, or as soon after that as possible.

"At the hearing you may explain to the judge why you think you do not owe the money to the Government, why you disagree with the reason the Government says it must take your property at this time, or why you believe the property the Government has taken is exempt or belongs to someone else. You may make any or all of these explanations as you see fit.

"If you think you live outside the Federal judicial district in which the court is located, you may request, not later than 20 days after you receive this notice, that this proceeding to take your property be transferred by the court to the Federal judicial district in which you reside. You must make your request in writing, and either mail it or deliver it in person to the clerk of the court at [address]. You must also send a copy of your request to the Government at [address], so the Government will know you want the proceeding to be transferred.

"Be sure to keep a copy of this notice for your own records. If you have any questions about your rights or about this procedure, you should contact a lawyer, an office of public legal assistance, or the clerk of the

court. The clerk is not permitted to give legal advice, but can refer you to other sources of information."

(2) By requesting, at any time before judgment on the claim for a debt, the court to hold a hearing, the debtor may move to quash the order granting such remedy. The court shall hold a hearing on such motion as soon as practicable, or, if requested by the debtor, within 5 days after receiving the request for a hearing or as soon thereafter as possible. The issues at such hearing shall be limited to—

(A) the probable validity of the claim for the debt for which such remedy was granted and of any defense or claim of exemption asserted by such person;

(B) compliance with any statutory requirement for the issuance of the prejudgment remedy granted;

(C) the existence of any ground set forth in subsection (b); and

(D) the inadequacy of alternative remedies (if any) to protect the interests of the United States.

(e) **Issuance of writ.**—On the court's determination that the requirements of subsections (a), (b), and (c) have been met, the court shall issue all process sufficient to put into effect the prejudgment remedy sought.

(Added Pub.L. 101–647, Title XXXVI, § 3611, Nov. 29, 1990, 104 Stat. 4939.)

HISTORICAL AND STATUTORY NOTES

Effective and Applicability Provisions

1990 Acts

Section to take effect 180 days after Nov. 29, 1990, except as otherwise provided, see section 3631 of Pub.L. 101–647, set out as a note under section 3001 of this title.

§ 3102. Attachment

(a) **Property subject to attachment.**—(1) Any property in the possession, custody, or control of the debtor and in which the debtor has a substantial nonexempt interest, except earnings, may be attached pursuant to a writ of attachment in an action or proceeding against a debtor on a claim for a debt and may be held as security to satisfy such judgment, and interest and costs, as the United States may recover on such claim.

(2) The value of property attached shall not exceed the amount by which the sum of the amount of the debt claimed by the United States and the amount of interest and costs reasonably likely to be assessed against the debtor by the court exceeds the aggregate value of the nonexempt interest of the debtor in any—

(A) property securing the debt; and

(B) property garnished or in receivership, or income sequestered, under this subchapter.

(b) **Availability of attachment.**—If the requirements of section 3101 are satisfied, a court shall issue a writ authorizing the United States to attach property in which the debtor has a substantial nonexempt interest, as security for such judgment (and interest and costs) as the United States may recover on a claim for a debt—

(1) in an action on a contract, express or implied, against the debtor for payment of money, only if the United States shows reasonable cause to believe that—

(A) the contract is not fully secured by real or personal property; or

(B) the value of the original security is substantially diminished, without any act of the United States or the person to whom the security was given, below the amount of the debt;

(2) in an action against the debtor for damages in tort;

(3) if the debtor resides outside the jurisdiction of the United States; or

(4) in an action to recover a fine, penalty, or tax.

(c) **Issuance of writ; contents.**—(1) Subject to subsections (a) and (b), a writ of attachment shall be issued by the court directing the United States marshal of the district where property described in subsection (a) is located to attach the property.

(2) Several writs of attachment may be issued at the same time, or in succession, and sent to different judicial districts until sufficient property is attached.

(3) The writ of attachment shall contain—

(A) the date of the issuance of the writ;

(B) the identity of the court, the docket number of the action, and the identity of the cause of action;

(C) the name and last known address of the debtor;

(D) the amount to be secured by the attachment; and

(E) a reasonable description of the property to be attached.

(d) **Levy of attachment.**—(1) The United States marshal receiving the writ shall proceed without delay to levy upon the property specified for attachment if found within the district. The marshal may not sell property unless ordered by the court.

(2) In performing the levy, the United States marshal may enter any property owned, occupied, or controlled by the debtor, except that the marshal may not enter a residence or other building unless the writ expressly authorizes the marshal to do so or upon specific order of the court.

(3) Levy on real property is made by entering the property and posting the writ and notice of levy in a conspicuous place upon the property.

(4) Levy on personal property is made by taking possession of it. Levy on personal property not easily taken into possession or which cannot be taken into possession without great inconvenience or expense may be made by affixing a copy of the writ and notice of levy on it or in a conspicuous place in the vicinity of it describing in the notice of levy the property by quantity and with sufficient detail to identify the property levied on.

(5) The United States marshal shall file a copy of the notice of levy in the same manner as provided for judgments in section 3201(a)(1). The United States marshal shall serve a copy of the writ and notice of levy on—

(A) the debtor against whom the writ is issued; and

(B) the person who has possession of the property subject to the writ;

in the same manner that a summons is served in a civil action and make the return thereof.

(e) Return of writ; duties of marshal; further return.—(1) A United States marshal executing a writ of attachment shall return the writ with the marshal's action endorsed thereon or attached thereto and signed by the marshal, to the court from which it was issued, within 5 days after the date of the levy.

(2) The return shall describe the property attached with sufficient certainty to identify it and shall state the location where it was attached, the date and time it was attached, and the disposition made of the property. If no property was attached, the return shall so state.

(3) If the property levied on is claimed, replevied under subsection (j)(2), or sold under section 3007 after the return, the United States marshal shall immediately make a further return to the clerk of the court showing the disposition of the property.

(4) If personal property is replevied, the United States marshal shall deliver the replevin bond to the clerk of the court to be filed in the action.

(f) Levy of attachment as lien on property; satisfaction of lien.—(1) A levy on property under a writ of attachment under this section creates a lien in favor of the United States on the property or, in the case of perishable property sold under section 3007, on the proceeds of the sale.

(2) Such lien shall be ranked ahead of any other security interests perfected after the later of the time of levy and the time a copy of the notice of levy is filed under subsection (d)(5).

(3) Such lien shall arise from the time of levy and shall continue until a judgment in the action is obtained or denied, or the action is otherwise dismissed. The death of the debtor whose property is attached does not terminate the attachment lien. Upon issuance of a judgment in the action and registration under this chapter, the judgment lien so created relates back to the time of levy.

(g) Reduction or dissolution of attachment.—(1) If an excessive or unreasonable attachment is made, the debtor may submit a motion to the court for a reduction of the amount of the attachment or its dissolution. Notice of such motion shall be served on the United States.

(2) The court shall order a part of the property to be released, if after a hearing the court finds that the amount of the attachment is excessive or unreasonable or if the attachment is for an amount larger than the sum of the liquidated or ascertainable amount of the debt and the amount of interest and costs likely to be taxed.

(3) The court shall dissolve the attachment if the amount of the debt is unliquidated and unascertainable by calculation.

(4) If any property claimed to be exempt is levied on, the debtor may, at any time after such levy, request that the court vacate such levy. If it appears to the court that the property so levied upon is exempt, the court shall order the levy vacated and the property returned to the debtor.

(h) Replevin of attached property by debtor; bond.—If attached property is not sold before judgment, the debtor may replevy such property or any part thereof by giving a bond approved by counsel for the United States or the court and payable to the United States in double the reasonable value of the property to be replevied or double the value of the claim, whichever is less.

(i) Preservation of personal property under attachment.—If personal property in custody of the United States marshal under a writ of attachment is not replevied, claimed, or sold, the court may make such order for its preservation or use as appears to be in the interest of the parties.

(j) Judgment and disposition of attached property.—

(1) **Judgment for the United States.**—On entry of judgment for the United States, the court shall order the proceeds of personal property sold pursuant to section 3007 to be applied to the satisfaction of the judgment, and shall order the sale of any remaining personal property and any real property levied on to the extent necessary to satisfy the judgment.

(2) Judgment for the United States when personal property replevied.—With respect to personal property under attachment that is replevied, the judgment which may be entered shall be against the debtor against whom the writ of attachment is issued and also against the sureties on the debtor's replevin bond for the value of the property.

(3) Restoration of property and exoneration of replevin bond.—If the attachment is vacated or if the judgment on the claim for the debt is for the person against whom the writ attachment is issued, the court shall order the property, or proceeds of perishable property sold under section 3007, restored to the debtor and shall exonerate any replevin bond.

(Added Pub.L. 101–647, Title XXXVI, § 3611, Nov. 29, 1990, 104 Stat. 4942.)

HISTORICAL AND STATUTORY NOTES

Effective and Applicability Provisions

1990 Acts

Section to take effect 180 days after Nov. 29, 1990, except as otherwise provided, see section 3631 of Pub.L. 101–647, set out as a note under section 3001 of this title.

§ 3103. Receivership

(a) Appointment of a receiver.—If the requirements of section 3101 are satisfied, a court may appoint a receiver for property in which the debtor has a substantial nonexempt interest if the United States shows reasonable cause to believe that there is a substantial danger that the property will be removed from the jurisdiction of the court, lost, concealed, materially injured or damaged, or mismanaged.

(b) Powers of receiver.—(1) The appointing court may authorize a receiver—

(A) to take possession of real and personal property and sue for, collect, and sell obligations upon such conditions and for such purposes as the court shall direct; and

(B) to administer, collect, improve, lease, repair or sell pursuant to section 3007 such real and personal property as the court shall direct.

A receiver appointed to manage residential or commercial property shall have demonstrable expertise in the management of these types of property.

(2) Unless expressly authorized by order of the court, a receiver shall have no power to employ attorneys, accountants, appraisers, auctioneers, or other professional persons.

(c) Duration of receivership.—A receivership shall not continue past the entry of judgment, or the conclusion of an appeal of such judgment, unless the court orders it continued under section 3203(e) or unless the court otherwise directs its continuation.

(d) Accounts; requirement to report.—A receiver shall keep written accounts itemizing receipts and expenditures, describing the property and naming the depository of receivership funds. The receiver's accounts shall be open to inspection by any person having an apparent interest in the property. The receiver shall file reports at regular intervals as directed by the court and shall serve the debtor and the United States with a copy thereof.

(e) Modification of powers; removal.—On motion of the receiver or on its own initiative, the court which appointed the receiver may remove the receiver or modify the receiver's powers at any time.

(f) Priority.—If more than one court appoints a receiver for particular property, the receiver first qualifying under law shall be entitled to take possession, control, or custody of the property.

(g) Compensation of receivers.—(1) A receiver is entitled to such commissions, not exceeding 5 percent of the sums received and disbursed by him, as the court allows unless the court otherwise directs.

(2) If, at the termination of a receivership, there are no funds in the hands of a receiver, the court may fix the compensation of the receiver in accordance with the services rendered and may direct the party who moved for the appointment of the receiver to pay such compensation in addition to the necessary expenditures incurred by the receiver which remain unpaid.

(3) At the termination of a receivership, the receiver shall file a final accounting of the receipts and disbursements and apply for compensation setting forth the amount sought and the services rendered by the receiver.

(Added Pub.L. 101–647, Title XXXVI, § 3611, Nov. 29, 1990, 104 Stat. 4944.)

HISTORICAL AND STATUTORY NOTES

Effective and Applicability Provisions

1990 Acts

Section to take effect 180 days after Nov. 29, 1990, except as otherwise provided, see section 3631 of Pub.L. 101–647, set out as a note under section 3001 of this title.

§ 3104. Garnishment

(a) In general.—If the requirements of section 3101 are satisfied, a court may issue a writ of garnishment against property (excluding earnings) in which the debtor has a substantial nonexempt interest and which is in the possession, custody, or control of a person other than the debtor in order to satisfy a claim for a debt. Co-owned property shall be subject to garnishment to the same extent as co-owned property is subject to garnishment under the law of the State in which such property is located. A court may issue simultaneous separate writs of garnishment to several garnishees. A writ of garnishment issued

under this subsection shall be continuing and shall terminate only as provided in section 3205(c)(10).

(b) Writ.—(1) Subsections (b)(2) and (c) of section 3205 shall apply with respect to garnishment under this section, except that for purposes of this section—

(A) earnings of the debtor shall not be subject to garnishment; and

(B) a reference in such subsections to a judgment debtor shall be deemed to be a reference to a debtor.

(2) The United States shall include in its application for a writ of garnishment—

(A) the amount of the claim asserted by the United States for a debt; and

(B) the date the writ is issued.

(c) Limitation.—The value of property garnished shall not exceed the amount by which the sum of the amount of the debt claimed by the United States and the amount of interest and costs reasonably likely to be assessed against the debtor by the court exceeds the aggregate value of the nonexempt interest of the debtor in any—

(1) property securing the debt; and

(2) property attached or in receivership, or income sequestered, under this subchapter.

(Added Pub.L. 101–647, Title XXXVI, § 3611, Nov. 29, 1990, 104 Stat. 4945.)

HISTORICAL AND STATUTORY NOTES

Effective and Applicability Provisions

1990 Acts

Section to take effect 180 days after Nov. 29, 1990, except as otherwise provided, see section 3631 of Pub.L. 101–647, set out as a note under section 3001 of this title.

§ 3105. Sequestration

(a) Property subject to sequestration.—(1) Any income from property in which the debtor has a substantial nonexempt interest may be sequestered pursuant to a writ of sequestration in an action or proceeding against a debtor on a claim for a debt and may be held as security to satisfy such judgment, and interest and costs, as the United States may recover on such claim.

(2) The amount of income sequestered shall not exceed the amount by which the sum of the amount of the debt claimed by the United States and the amount of interest and costs reasonably likely to be assessed against the debtor by the court exceeds the aggregate value of the nonexempt interest of the debtor in any—

(A) property securing the debt; and

(B) property attached, garnished, or in receivership under this subchapter.

(b) Availability of sequestration.—If the requirements of section 3101 are satisfied, a court shall issue a writ authorizing the United States to sequester income from property in which the debtor has a substantial nonexempt interest, as security for such judgment (and interest and costs) as the United States may recover on a claim for a debt—

(1) in an action on a contract, express or implied, against the debtor for payment of money, only if the United States shows reasonable cause to believe that—

(A) the contract is not fully secured by real or personal property; or

(B) the value of the original security is substantially diminished, without any act of the United States or the person to whom the security was given, below the amount of the debt;

(2) in an action against the debtor for damages in tort;

(3) if the debtor resides outside the jurisdiction of the United States; or

(4) in an action to recover a fine, penalty, or tax.

(c) Issuance of writ; contents.—(1) Subject to subsections (a) and (b), a writ of sequestration shall be issued by the court directing the United States marshal of the district where income described in subsection (a) is located to sequester the income.

(2) Several writs of sequestration may be issued at the same time, or in succession, and sent to different judicial districts until sufficient income is sequestered.

(3) The writ of sequestration shall contain—

(A) the date of the issuance of the writ;

(B) the identity of the court, the docket number of the action, and the identity of the cause of action;

(C) the name and last known address of the debtor;

(D) the amount to be secured by the sequestration; and

(E) a reasonable description of the income to be sequestered.

(d) Execution of writ.—(1) The United States marshal receiving the writ shall proceed without delay to execute the writ.

(2) The United States marshal shall file a copy of the notice of sequestration in the same manner as provided for judgments in section 3201(a)(1). The United States marshal shall serve a copy of the writ and notice of sequestration on—

(A) the debtor against whom the writ is issued; and

(B) the person who has possession of the income subject to the writ;

in the same manner that a summons is served in a civil action and make the return thereof.

(e) Deposit of sequestered income.—A person who has possession of the income subject to a writ of sequestration shall deposit such income with the clerk of the court, accompanied by a statement in writing stating the person's name, the name of the debtor, the amount of such income, the property from which such income is produced, and the period during which such income is produced.

(f) Return of writ; duties of marshal; further return.—(1) A United States marshal executing a writ of sequestration shall return the writ with the marshal's action endorsed thereon or attached thereto and signed by the marshal, to the court from which it was issued, within 5 days after the date of the execution.

(2) The return shall describe the income sequestered with sufficient certainty to identify it and shall state the location where it was sequestered, and the date and time it was sequestered. If no income was sequestered, the return shall so state.

(3) If sequestered income is claimed after the return, the United States marshal shall immediately make a further return to the clerk of the court showing the disposition of the income.

(g) Reduction or dissolution of sequestration.—(1) If an excessive or unreasonable sequestration is made, the debtor may submit a motion to the court for a reduction of the amount of the sequestration or its dissolution. Notice of such motion shall be served on the United States.

(2) The court shall order a part of the income to be released, if after a hearing the court finds that the amount of the sequestration is excessive or unreasonable or if the sequestration is for an amount larger than the sum of the liquidated or ascertainable amount of the debt and the amount of interest and costs likely to be taxed.

(3) The court shall dissolve the sequestration if the amount of the debt is unliquidated and unascertainable by calculation.

(h) Preservation of income under sequester.—If personal property in custody of the United States marshal under a writ of sequestration is not claimed, the court may make such order for its preservation or use as appears to be in the interest of the parties.

(i) Judgment and disposition of sequestered income.—

(1) **Judgment for the United States.**—On entry of judgment for the United States, the court shall order the sequestered income to be applied to the satisfaction of the judgment.

(2) **Restoration of income.**—If the sequestration is vacated or if the judgment on the claim for the debt is for the person against whom the writ of sequestration is issued, the court shall order the income restored to the debtor.

(Added Pub.L. 101–647, Title XXXVI, § 3611, Nov. 29, 1990, 104 Stat. 4946.)

HISTORICAL AND STATUTORY NOTES

Effective and Applicability Provisions

Section to take effect 180 days after Nov. 29, 1990, except as otherwise provided, see section 3631 of Pub.L. 101–647, set out as a note under section 3001 of this title.

SUBCHAPTER C—POSTJUDGMENT REMEDIES

§ 3201. Judgment liens

(a) Creation.—A judgment in a civil action shall create a lien on all real property of a judgment debtor on filing a certified copy of the abstract of the judgment in the manner in which a notice of tax lien would be filed under paragraphs (1) and (2) of section 6323(f) of the Internal Revenue Code of 1986. A lien created under this paragraph is for the amount necessary to satisfy the judgment, including costs and interest.

(b) Priority of lien.—A lien created under subsection (a) shall have priority over any other lien or encumbrance which is perfected later in time.

(c) Duration of lien; renewal.—(1) Except as provided in paragraph (2), a lien created under subsection (a) is effective, unless satisfied, for a period of 20 years.

(2) Such lien may be renewed for one additional period of 20 years upon filing a notice of renewal in the same manner as the judgment is filed and shall relate back to the date the judgment is filed if—

(A) the notice of renewal is filed before the expiration of the 20–year period to prevent the expiration of the lien; and

(B) the court approves the renewal of such lien under this paragraph.

(d) Release of judgment lien.—A judgment lien shall be released on the filing of a satisfaction of judgment or release of lien in the same manner as the judgment is filed to obtain the lien.

(e) Effect of lien on eligibility for Federal grants, loans or programs.—A debtor who has a

judgment lien against the debtor's property for a debt to the United States shall not be eligible to receive any grant or loan which is made, insured, guaranteed, or financed directly or indirectly by the United States or to receive funds directly from the Federal Government in any program, except funds to which the debtor is entitled as beneficiary, until the judgment is paid in full or otherwise satisfied. The agency of the United States that is responsible for such grants and loans may promulgate regulations to allow for waiver of this restriction on eligibility for such grants, loans, and funds.

(f) Sale of property subject to judgment lien.—(1) On proper application to a court, the court may order the United States to sell, in accordance with sections 2001 and 2002, any real property subject to a judgment lien in effect under this section.

(2) This subsection shall not preclude the United States from using an execution sale pursuant to section 3203(g) to sell real property subject to a judgment lien.

(Added Pub.L. 101–647, Title XXXVI, § 3611, Nov. 29, 1990, 104 Stat. 4948.)

HISTORICAL AND STATUTORY NOTES

References in Text

Section 6323(f) of the Internal Revenue Code of 1986, referred to in subsec. (a), is classified to section 6323(f) of Title 26, Internal Revenue Code.

Effective and Applicability Provisions

1990 Acts

Section to take effect 180 days after Nov. 29, 1990, except as otherwise provided, see section 3631 of Pub.L. 101–647, set out as a note under section 3001 of this title.

§ 3202. Enforcement of judgments

(a) Enforcement remedies.—A judgment may be enforced by any of the remedies set forth in this subchapter. A court may issue other writs pursuant to section 1651 of title 28, United States Code, as necessary to support such remedies, subject to rule 81(b) of the Federal Rules of Civil Procedure.

(b) Notice.—On the commencement by the United States of an action or proceeding under this subchapter to obtain a remedy, the counsel for the United States shall prepare, and clerk of the court shall issue, a notice in substantially the following form:

"NOTICE

"You are hereby notified that this [property] is being taken by the United States Government, which has a court judgment in [case docket number and jurisdiction of court] of $[amount] for [reason of debt].

"In addition, you are hereby notified that there are exemptions under the law which may protect some of this property from being taken by the United States Government if [name of judgment debtor] can show

that the exemptions apply. Below is a summary of the major exemptions which apply in most situations in the State of [State where property is located]:

"[A statement summarizing in plain and understandable English the election available with respect to such State under section 3014 and the types of property that may be exempted under each of the alternatives specified in paragraphs (1) and (2) of section 3014(a) and a statement that different property may be so exempted with respect to the State in which the debtor resides.]

"If you are [name of judgment debtor], you have a right to ask the court to return your property to you if you think the property the Government is taking qualifies under one of the above exemptions [For a default judgment:] or if you think you do not owe the money to the United States Government that it says you do.

"If you want a hearing, you must notify the court within 20 days after you receive this notice. You must make your request in writing, and either mail it or deliver it in person to the clerk of the court at [address]. If you wish, you may use this notice to request the hearing by checking the box below and mailing this notice to the court clerk. You must also send a copy of your request to the Government at [address], so the Government will know you want a hearing. The hearing will take place within 5 days after the clerk receives your request, if you ask for it to take place that quickly, or as soon after that as possible.

"At the hearing you may explain to the judge why you believe the property the Government has taken is exempt [For a default judgment:] or why you think you do not owe the money to the Government. [For a writ of execution:] If you do not request a hearing within 20 days of receiving this notice, your [property] may be sold at public auction and the payment used toward the money you owe the Government.

"If you think you live outside the Federal judicial district in which the court is located, you may request, not later than 20 days after your[1] receive this notice, that this proceeding to take your property be transferred by the court to the Federal judicial district in which you reside. You must make your request in writing, and either mail it or deliver it in person to the clerk of the court at [address]. You must also send a copy of your request to the Government at [address], so the Government will know you want the proceeding to be transferred.

"Be sure to keep a copy of this notice for your own records. If you have any questions about your rights or about this procedure, you should contact a lawyer, an office of public legal assistance, or the clerk of the

court. The clerk is not permitted to give legal advice, but can refer you to other sources of information."

(c) Service.—A copy of the notice and a copy of the application for granting a remedy under this subchapter shall be served by counsel for the United States on the judgment debtor against whom such remedy is sought and on each person whom the United States, after diligent inquiry, has reasonable cause to believe has an interest in property to which the remedy is directed.

(d) Hearing.—By requesting, within 20 days after receiving the notice described in section 3202(b), the court to hold a hearing, the judgment debtor may move to quash the order granting such remedy. The court that issued such order shall hold a hearing on such motion as soon as practicable, or, if so requested by the judgment debtor, within 5 days after receiving the request or as soon thereafter as possible. The issues at such hearing shall be limited—

 (1) to the probable validity of any claim of exemption by the judgment debtor;

 (2) to compliance with any statutory requirement for the issuance of the postjudgment remedy granted; and

 (3) if the judgment is by default and only to the extent that the Constitution or another law of the United States provides a right to a hearing on the issue, to—

 (A) the probable validity of the claim for the debt which is merged in the judgment; and

 (B) the existence of good cause for setting aside such judgment.

This subparagraph shall not be construed to afford the judgment debtor the right to more than one such hearing except to the extent that the Constitution or another law of the United States provides a right to more than one such hearing.

(e) Sale of property.—The property of a judgment debtor which is subject to sale to satisfy the judgment may be sold by judicial sale, pursuant to sections 2001, 2002, and 2004 or by execution sale pursuant to section 3203(g). If a hearing is requested pursuant to subsection (d), property with respect to which the request relates shall not be sold before such hearing. (Added Pub.L. 101–647, Title XXXVI, § 3611, Nov. 29, 1990, 104 Stat. 4949.)

1 So in original. Probably should be "you".

HISTORICAL AND STATUTORY NOTES

Effective and Applicability Provisions

1990 Acts

Section to take effect 180 days after Nov. 29, 1990, except as otherwise provided, see section 3631 of Pub.L. 101–647, set out as a note under section 3001 of this title.

§ 3203. Execution

(a) Property subject to execution.—All property in which the judgment debtor has a substantial nonexempt interest shall be subject to levy pursuant to a writ of execution. The debtor's earnings shall not be subject to execution while in the possession, custody, or control of the debtor's employer. Co-owned property shall be subject to execution to the extent such property is subject to execution under the law of the State in which it is located.

(b) Creation of execution lien.—A lien shall be created in favor of the United States on all property levied on under a writ of execution and shall date from the time of the levy. Such lien shall have priority over all subsequent liens and shall be for the aggregate amount of the judgment, costs, and interest. The execution lien on any real property as to which the United States has a judgment lien shall relate back to the judgment lien date.

(c) Writ of execution.—

 (1) Issuance.—On written application of counsel for the United States, the court may issue a writ of execution. Multiple writs may issue simultaneously, and successive writs may issue before the return date of a writ previously issued.

 (2) Form of writ.—

 (A) General contents.—A writ of execution shall specify the date that the judgment is entered, the court in which it is entered, the amount of the judgment if for money, the amount of the costs, the amount of interest due, the sum due as of the date the writ is issued, the rate of postjudgment interest, the name of the judgment debtor, and the judgment debtor's last known address.

 (B) Additional contents.—(i) Except as provided in clauses (ii) and (iii), the writ shall direct the United States marshal to satisfy the judgment by levying on and selling property in which the judgment debtor has a substantial nonexempt interest, but not to exceed property reasonably equivalent in value to the aggregate amount of the judgment, costs, and interest.

 (ii) A writ of execution issued on a judgment for the delivery to the United States of the possession of personal property, or for the delivery of the possession of real property, shall particularly describe the property, and shall require the marshal to deliver the possession of the property to the United States.

 (iii) A writ of execution on a judgment for the recovery of personal property or its value shall direct the marshal, in case a delivery of the specific property cannot be had, to levy and collect such value out of any property in which the

judgment debtor has a substantial nonexempt interest.

(d) Levy of execution.—

(1) In general.—Levy on property pursuant to a writ of execution issued under this section shall be made in the same manner as levy on property is made pursuant to a writ of attachment issued under section 3102(d).

(2) Death of judgment debtor.—The death of the judgment debtor after a writ of execution is issued stays the execution proceedings, but any lien acquired by levy of the writ shall be recognized and enforced by the court for the district in which the estate of the deceased is located. The execution lien may be enforced—

 (A) against the executor, administrator, or personal representative of the estate of the deceased; or

 (B) if there be none, against the deceased's property coming to the heirs or devisees or at their option against cash in their possession, but only to the extent of the value of the property coming to them.

(3) Records of United States marshal.—(A) A United States marshal receiving a writ of execution shall endorse thereon the exact hour and date of receipt.

(B) The United States marshal shall make a written record of every levy, specify the property on which levy is made, the date on which levy is made, and the marshal's costs, expenses, and fees.

(C) The United States marshal shall make a written return to the court on each writ of execution stating concisely what is done pursuant to the writ and shall deliver a copy to counsel for the United States who requests the writ. The writ shall be returned not more than—

 (i) 90 days after the date of issuance if levy is not made; or

 (ii) 10 days after the date of sale of property on which levy is made.

(e) Appointment of receiver.—Pending the levy of execution, the court may appoint a receiver to manage property described in such writ if there is a substantial danger that the property will be removed from the jurisdiction of the court, lost, materially injured or damaged, or mismanaged.

(f) Replevy; redemption.—

(1) Before execution sale.—(A) Before execution sale, the United States marshal may return property[1] to the judgment debtor any personal property taken in execution, on—

 (i) satisfaction of the judgment, interest, and costs, and any costs incurred in connection with scheduling the sale; or

 (ii) receipt from the judgment debtor of a bond—

 (I) payable to the United States, with 2 or more good and sufficient sureties to be approved by the marshal, conditioned on the delivery of the property to the marshal at the time and place named in the bond to be sold under subsection (g); or

 (II) for the payment to the marshal of a fair value thereof which shall be stated in the bond.

(B) A judgment debtor who sells or disposes of property replevied under subparagraph (A) shall pay the United States marshal the stipulated value of such property.

(C) If the judgment debtor fails to deliver such property to the United States marshal pursuant to the terms of the delivery described in subparagraph (A)(ii)(I) and fails to pay the United States marshal the stipulated value of such property, the United States marshal shall endorse the bond "forfeited" and return it to the court from which the writ of execution issued. If the judgment is not fully satisfied, the court shall issue a writ of execution against the judgment debtor and the sureties on the bond for the amount due, not exceeding the stipulated value of the property, on which execution no delivery bond shall be taken, which instruction shall be endorsed on the writ.

(2) After execution sale.—The judgment debtor shall not be entitled to redeem the property after the execution sale.

(g) Execution sale.—

(1) General procedures.—An execution sale under this section shall be conducted in a commercially reasonable manner—

 (A) Sale of real property.—

 (i) In general.—(I) Except as provided in clause (ii), real property, or any interest therein, shall be sold, after the expiration of the 90–day period beginning on the date of levy under subsection (d), for cash at public auction at the courthouse of the county, parish, or city in which the greater part of the property is located or on the premises or some parcel thereof.

 (II) The court may order the sale of any real property after the expiration of the 30–day period beginning on the date of levy under subsection (d) if the court determines that such property is likely to perish, waste, be destroyed, or otherwise substantially depreciate in value during the 90–day period beginning on the date of levy.

 (III) The time and place of sale of real property, or any interest therein, under execution shall be advertised by the United States mar-

shal, by publication of notice, once a week for at least 3 weeks prior to the sale, in at least one newspaper of general circulation in the county or parish where the property is located. The first publication shall appear not less than 25 days preceding the day of sale. The notice shall contain a statement of the authority by which the sale is to be made, the time of levy, the time and place of sale, and a brief description of the property to be sold, sufficient to identify the property (such as a street address for urban property and the survey identification and location for rural property), but it shall not be necessary for the notice to contain field notes. Such property shall be open for inspection and appraisal, subject to the judgment debtor's reasonable objections, for a reasonable period before the day of sale.

(IV) The United States marshal shall serve written notice of public sale by personal delivery, or certified or registered mail, to each person whom the marshal has reasonable cause to believe, after a title search is conducted by the United States, has an interest in property under execution, including lienholders, co-owners, and tenants, at least 25 days before the day of sale, to the last known address of each such person.

(ii) **Sale of city lots.**—If the real property consists of several lots, tracts, or parcels in a city or town, each lot, tract, or parcel shall be offered for sale separately, unless not susceptible to separate sale because of the character of improvements.

(iii) **Sale of rural property.**—If the real property is not located in a city or town, the judgment debtor may—

(I) divide the property into lots of not less than 50 acres or in such greater or lesser amounts as ordered by the court;

(II) furnish a survey of such prepared by a registered surveyor; and

(III) designate the order in which those lots shall be sold.

When a sufficient number of lots are sold to satisfy the amount of the execution and costs of sale, the marshal shall stop the sale.

(B) **Sale of personal property.**—(i) Personal property levied on shall be offered for sale on the premises where it is located at the time of levy, at the courthouse of the county, parish or city wherein it is located, or at another location if ordered by the court. Personal property susceptible of being exhibited shall not be sold unless it is present and subject to the view of those attending the sale unless—

(I) the property consists of shares of stock in corporations;

(II) by reason of the nature of the property, it is impractical to exhibit it; or

(III) the debtor's interest in the property does not include the right to the exclusive possession.

(ii)(I) Except as provided in subclause (II), personal property, or any interest therein, shall be sold after the expiration of the 30–day period beginning on the date of levy under subsection (d).

(II) The court may order the sale of any personal property before the expiration of such 30–day period if the court determines that such property is likely to perish, waste, be destroyed, or otherwise substantially depreciate in value during such 30–day period.

(iii) Notice of the time and place of the sale of personal property shall be given by the United States marshal by posting notice thereof for not less than 10 days successively immediately before the day of sale at the courthouse of any county, parish, or city, and at the place where the sale is to be made.

(iv) The United States marshal shall serve written notice of public sale by personal delivery, or registered or certified mail at their last known addresses, on the judgment debtor and other persons who the marshal has reasonable cause to believe, after diligent inquiry, have a substantial interest in the property.

(2) **Postponement of sale.**—The United States marshal may postpone an execution sale from time to time by continuing the required posting or publication of notice until the date to which the sale is postponed, and appending, at the foot of each such notice of a current copy of the following:

"The above sale is postponed until the _____ day of _____, 19____, at ____ o'clock ____.M., _____, United States Marshal for the District of _____, by _____, Deputy, dated _____."

(3) **Sale procedures.**—

(A) **Bidding requirements.**—A bidder at an execution sale of property, may be required by the United States marshal to make a cash deposit of as much as 20 percent of the sale price proposed before the bid is accepted.

(B) **Resale of property.**—If the terms of the sale are not complied with by the successful bidder, the United States marshal shall proceed to sell the property again on the same day if there is sufficient time. If there is insufficient time, the marshal shall schedule and notice a subsequent sale of the property as provided in paragraphs (1) and (2).

(4) Rights and liabilities of purchasers.—

 (A) Transfer of title after sale.—

 (i) If property is sold under this subsection and the successful bidder complies with the terms of the sale, the United States marshal shall execute and deliver all documents necessary to transfer to the successful bidder, without warranty, all the rights, titles, interests, and claims of the judgment debtor in the property.

 (ii) If the successful bidder dies before execution and delivery of the documents needed to transfer ownership, the United States marshal shall execute and deliver them to the successful bidder's estate. Such delivery to the estate shall have the same effect as if accomplished during the lifetime of the purchaser.

 (B) Purchaser considered innocent purchaser without notice.—The purchaser of property sold under execution shall be deemed to be an innocent purchaser without notice if the purchaser would have been considered an innocent purchaser without notice had the sale been made voluntarily and in person by the judgment debtor.

 (C) Liability of successful bidder who fails to comply.—A successful bidder at an execution sale who fails to comply with the terms of the sale shall forfeit to the United States the cash deposit or, at the election of the United States, shall be liable to the United States, on a subsequent sale of the property, for all net losses incurred by the United States as a result of such failure.

(h) Disposition of proceeds; further levy.—

 (1) Distribution of sale proceeds.—(A) The United States marshal shall first deliver to the judgment debtor such amounts to which the judgment debtor is entitled from the sale of partially exempt property.

 (B) The United States marshal shall next deduct from the proceeds of an execution sale of property an amount equal to the reasonable expenses incurred in making the levy of execution and in keeping and maintaining the property.

 (C) Except as provided in subparagraph (D), the United States marshal shall deliver the balance of the proceeds to the counsel for the United States as soon as practicable.

 (D) If more proceeds are received from the execution sale than is necessary to satisfy the executions held by the United States marshal, the marshal shall pay the surplus to the judgment debtor.

 (2) Further levy if execution not satisfied.—If the proceeds of the execution sale of the property levied on are insufficient to satisfy the execution, the United States marshal shall proceed on the same writ of execution to levy other property of the judgment debtor.

(Added Pub.L. 101–647, Title XXXVI, § 3611, Nov. 29, 1990, 104 Stat. 4950.)

1 So in original. The word "property" probably should not appear.

<div align="center">

HISTORICAL AND STATUTORY NOTES

</div>

Effective and Applicability Provisions

1990 Acts

 Section to take effect 180 days after Nov. 29, 1990, except as otherwise provided, see section 3631 of Pub.L. 101–647, set out as a note under section 3001 of this title.

§ 3204. Installment payment order

 (a) Authority to issue order.—Subject to subsection (c), if it is shown that the judgment debtor—

 (1) is receiving or will receive substantial nonexempt disposable earnings from self employment that are not subject to garnishment; or

 (2) is diverting or concealing substantial earnings from any source, or property received in lieu of earnings;

then upon motion of the United States and notice to the judgment debtor, the court may, if appropriate, order that the judgment debtor make specified installment payments to the United States. Notice of the motion shall be served on the judgment debtor in the same manner as a summons or by registered or certified mail, return receipt requested. In fixing the amount of the payments, the court shall take into consideration after a hearing, the income, resources, and reasonable requirements of the judgment debtor and the judgment debtor's dependents, any other payments to be made in satisfaction of judgments against the judgment debtor, and the amount due on the judgment in favor of the United States.

 (b) Modification of order.—On motion of the United States or the judgment debtor, and upon a showing that the judgment debtor's financial circumstances have changed or that assets not previously disclosed by the judgment debtor have been discovered, the court may modify the amount of payments, alter their frequency, or require full payment.

 (c) Limitation.—(1) An order may not be issued under subsection (a), and if so issued shall have no force or effect, against a judgment debtor with respect to whom there is in effect a writ of garnishment of earnings issued under this chapter and based on the same debt.

 (2) An order may not be issued under subsection (a) with respect to any earnings of the debtor except nonexempt disposable earnings.

(Added Pub.L. 101–647, Title XXXVI, § 3611, Nov. 29, 1990, 104 Stat. 4955.)

HISTORICAL AND STATUTORY NOTES

Effective and Applicability Provisions

1990 Acts

Section to take effect 180 days after Nov. 29, 1990, except as otherwise provided, see section 3631 of Pub.L. 101–647, set out as a note under section 3001 of this title.

§ 3205. Garnishment

(a) In general.—A court may issue a writ of garnishment against property (including nonexempt disposable earnings) in which the debtor has a substantial nonexempt interest and which is in the possession, custody, or control of a person other than the debtor, in order to satisfy the judgment against the debtor. Co-owned property shall be subject to garnishment to the same extent as co-owned property is subject to garnishment under the law of the State in which such property is located. A court may issue simultaneous separate writs of garnishment to several garnishees. A writ of garnishment issued under this subsection shall be continuing and shall terminate only as provided in subsection (c)(10).

(b) Writ.—

(1) **General requirements.**—The United States shall include in its application for a writ of garnishment—

(A) the judgment debtor's name, social security number (if known), and last known address;

(B) the nature and amount of the debt owed and the facts that not less than 30 days has elapsed since demand on the debtor for payment of the debt was made and the judgment debtor has not paid the amount due; and

(C) that the garnishee is believed to have possession of property (including nonexempt disposable earnings) in which the debtor has a substantial nonexempt interest.

(2) **Proper garnishee for particular property.**—

(A) If the property consists of a right to or share in the stock of an association or corporation, or interests or profits therein, for which a certificate of stock or other negotiable instrument is not outstanding, the corporation, or the president or treasurer of the association shall be the garnishee.

(B) If the property consists of an interest in a partnership interest, any partner other than the debtor shall be the garnishee on behalf of the partnership.

(C) If the property or a debt is evidenced by a negotiable instrument for the payment of money, a negotiable document of title or a certificate of stock of an association or corporation, the instrument, document, or certificate shall be treated as property capable of delivery and the person holding it shall be the garnishee, except that—

(i) subject to clause (ii), in the case of a security which is transferable in the manner set forth in State law, the entity that carries on its books an account in the name of the debtor in which is reflected such security shall be the garnishee; and

(ii) notwithstanding clause (i), the pledgee shall be the garnishee if such security is pledged.

(c) Procedures applicable to writ.—

(1) **Court determination.**—If the court determines that the requirements of this section are satisfied, the court shall issue an appropriate writ of garnishment.

(2) **Form of writ.**—The writ shall state—

(A) The nature and amount of the debt, and any cost and interest owed with respect to the debt.

(B) The name and address of the garnishee.

(C) The name and address of counsel for the United States.

(D) The last known address of the judgment debtor.

(E) That the garnishee shall answer the writ within 10 days of service of the writ.

(F) That the garnishee shall withhold and retain any property in which the debtor has a substantial nonexempt interest and for which the garnishee is or may become indebted to the judgment debtor pending further order of the court.

(3) **Service of writ.**—The United States shall serve the garnishee and the judgment debtor with a copy of the writ of garnishment and shall certify to the court that this service was made. The writ shall be accompanied by—

(A) an instruction explaining the requirement that the garnishee submit a written answer to the writ; and

(B) instructions to the judgment debtor for objecting to the answer of the garnishee and for obtaining a hearing on the objections.

(4) **Answer of the garnishee.**—In its written answer to the writ of garnishment, the garnishee shall state under oath—

(A) whether the garnishee has custody, control or possession of such property;

(B) a description of such property and the value of such interest;

(C) a description of any previous garnishments to which such property is subject and the extent to which any remaining property is not exempt; and

(D) the amount of the debt the garnishee anticipates owing to the judgment debtor in the future and whether the period for payment will be weekly or another specified period.

The garnishee shall file the original answer with the court issuing the writ and serve a copy on the debtor and counsel for the United States.

(5) Objections to answer.—Within 20 days after receipt of the answer, the judgment debtor or the United States may file a written objection to the answer and request a hearing. The party objecting shall state the grounds for the objection and bear the burden of proving such grounds. A copy of the objection and request for a hearing shall be served on the garnishee and all other parties. The court shall hold a hearing within 10 days after the date the request is received by the court, or as soon thereafter as is practicable, and give notice of the hearing date to all the parties.

(6) Garnishee's failure to answer or pay.—If a garnishee fails to answer the writ of garnishment or to withhold property in accordance with the writ, the United States may petition the court for an order requiring the garnishee to appear before the court to answer the writ and to so withhold property before the appearance date. If the garnishee fails to appear, or appears and fails to show good cause why the garnishee failed to comply with the writ, the court shall enter judgment against the garnishee for the value of the judgment debtor's nonexempt interest in such property (including nonexempt disposable earnings). The court may award a reasonable attorney's fee to the United States and against the garnishee if the writ is not answered within the time specified therein and a petition requiring the garnishee to appear is filed as provided in this section.

(7) Disposition order.—After the garnishee files an answer and if no hearing is requested within the required time period, the court shall promptly enter an order directing the garnishee as to the disposition of the judgment debtor's nonexempt interest in such property. If a hearing is timely requested, the order shall be entered within 5 days after the hearing, or as soon thereafter as is practicable.

(8) Priorities.—Judicial orders and garnishments for the support of a person shall have priority over a writ of garnishment issued under this section. As to any other writ of garnishment or levy, a garnishment issued under this section shall have priority over writs which are issued later in time.

(9) Accounting.—**(A)** While a writ of garnishment is in effect under this section, the United States shall give an annual accounting on the garnishment to the judgment debtor and the garnishee.

(B) Within 10 days after the garnishment terminates, the United States shall give a cumulative written accounting to the judgment debtor and garnishee of all property it receives under a writ of garnishment. Within 10 days after such accounting is received, the judgment debtor or garnishee may file a written objection to the accounting and a request for hearing. The party objecting shall state grounds for the objection. The court shall hold a hearing on the objection within 10 days after the court receives the request for a hearing, or as soon thereafter as is practicable.

(10) Termination of garnishment.—A garnishment under this chapter is terminated only by—

(A) a court order quashing the writ of garnishment;

(B) exhaustion of property in the possesion,[1] custody, or control of the garnishee in which the debtor has a substantial nonexempt interest (including nonexempt disposable earnings), unless the garnishee reinstates or reemploys the judgment debtor within 90 days after the judgment debtor's dismissal or resignation; or

(C) satisfaction of the debt with respect to which the writ is issued.

(Added Pub.L. 101–647, Title XXXVI, § 3611, Nov. 29, 1990, 104 Stat. 4956.)

[1] So in original. Probably should be "possession,".

HISTORICAL AND STATUTORY NOTES

Effective and Applicability Provisions

1990 Acts

Section to take effect 180 days after Nov. 29, 1990, except as otherwise provided, see section 3631 of Pub.L. 101–647, set out as a note under section 3001 of this title.

§ 3206. Discharge

A person who pursuant to an execution or order issued under this chapter by a court pays or delivers to the United States, a United States marshal, or a receiver, money or other personal property in which a judgment debtor has or will have an interest, or so pays a debt such person owes the judgment debtor, is discharged from such debt to the judgment debtor to the extent of the payment or delivery.

(Added Pub.L. 101–647, Title XXXVI, § 3611, Nov. 29, 1990, 104 Stat. 4959.)

HISTORICAL AND STATUTORY NOTES

Effective and Applicability Provisions

1990 Acts

Section to take effect 180 days after Nov. 29, 1990, except as otherwise provided, see section 3631 of Pub.L. 101–647, set out as a note under section 3001 of this title.

SUBCHAPTER D—FRAUDULENT TRANSFERS INVOLVING DEBTS

§ 3301. Definitions

As used in this subchapter:

(1) "Affiliate" means—

(A) a person who directly or indirectly owns, controls, or holds with power to vote, 20 percent or more of the outstanding voting securities of the debtor, other than a person who holds the securities—

(i) as a fiduciary or agent without sole discretionary power to vote the securities; or

(ii) solely to secure a debt, if the person has not exercised the power to vote;

(B) a corporation 20 percent or more of whose outstanding voting securities are directly or indirectly owned, controlled, or held with power to vote, by the debtor or a person who directly or indirectly owns, controls, or holds with power to vote, 20 percent or more of the outstanding voting securities of the debtor, other than the person who holds securities—

(i) as a fiduciary or agent without sole power to vote the securities; or

(ii) solely to secure a debt, if the person has not in fact exercised the power to vote;

(C) a person whose business is operated by the debtor under a lease or other agreement, or a person substantially all of whose assets are controlled by the debtor; or

(D) a person who operates the debtor's business under a lease or other agreement or controls substantially all of the debtor's assets.

(2) "Asset" means property of a debtor, but does not include—

(A) property to the extent it is encumbered by a valid lien;

(B) property to the extent it is generally exempt under nonbankruptcy law; or

(C) an interest in real property held in tenancy by the entirety, or as part of a community estate, to extent such interest is not subject to process by the United States holding a claim against only one tenant or co-owner.

(3) "Claim" means a right to payment, whether or not the right is reduced to judgment, liquidated, unliquidated, fixed, contingent, matured, unmatured, disputed, undisputed, legal, equitable, secured, or unsecured.

(4) "Creditor" means a person who has a claim.

(5) "Insider" includes—

(A) if the debtor is an individual—

(i) a relative of the debtor or of a general partner of the debtor;

(ii) a partnership in which the debtor is a general partner;

(iii) a general partner in a partnership described in clause (ii); or

(iv) a corporation of which the debtor is a director, officer, or person in control;

(B) if the debtor is a corporation—

(i) a director of the debtor;

(ii) an officer of the debtor;

(iii) a person in control of the debtor;

(iv) a partnership in which the debtor is a general partner;

(v) a general partner in a partnership described in clause (iv); or

(vi) a relative of a general partner, director, officer, or person in control of the debtor;

(C) if the debtor is a partnership—

(i) a general partner in the debtor;

(ii) a relative of a general partner in, a general partner of, or a person in control of the debtor;

(iii) another partnership in which the debtor is a general partner;

(iv) a general partner in a partnership described in clause (iii); or

(v) a person in control of the debtor.[1]

(D) an affiliate, or an insider of an affiliate as if the affiliate were the debtor; and

(E) a managing agent of the debtor.

(4)[2] "Lien" means a charge against or an interest in property to secure payment of a debt and includes a security interest created by agreement, a judicial lien obtained by legal or equitable process or proceedings, a common law lien, or a statutory lien.

(5)[3] "Relative" means an individual related, by consanguinity or adoption, within the third degree as determined by the common law, a spouse, or an individual so related to a spouse within the third degree as so determined.

(6)[4] "Transfer" means every mode, direct or indirect, absolute or conditional, voluntary or involuntary, of disposing of or parting with an asset or an interest in an asset, and includes payment of money, release, lease, and creation of a lien or other encumbrance.

(7)[5] "Valid lien" means a lien that is effective against the holder of a judicial lien subsequently obtained in legal or equitable proceeding.

(Added Pub.L. 101–647, Title XXXVI, § 3611, Nov. 29, 1990, 104 Stat. 4959.)

[1] So in original. The period probably should be a semicolon.
[2] So in original. Probably should be "(6)".
[3] So in original. Probably should be "(7)".

4 So in original. Probably should be "(8)".
5 So in original. Probably should be "(9)".

HISTORICAL AND STATUTORY NOTES

Effective and Applicability Provisions

1990 Acts

Section to take effect 180 days after Nov. 29, 1990, except as otherwise provided, see section 3631 of Pub.L. 101–647, set out as a note under section 3001 of this title.

§ 3302. Insolvency

(a) **In general.**—Except as provided in subsection (c), a debtor is insolvent if the sum of the debtor's debts is greater than all of the debtor's assets at a fair valuation.

(b) **Presumption.**—A debtor who is generally not paying debts as they become due is presumed to be insolvent.

(c) **Calculation.**—A partnership is insolvent under subsection (a) if the sum of the partnership's debts is greater than the aggregate, at a fair valuation, of—

(1) all of the partnership's assets; and

(2) the sum of the excess of the value of each general partner's non-partnership assets over the partner's non-partnership debts.

(d) **Assets.**—For purposes of this section, assets do not include property that is transferred, concealed, or removed with intent to hinder, delay, or defraud creditors or that has been transferred in a manner making the transfer voidable under this subchapter.

(e) **Debts.**—For purposes of this section, debts do not include an obligation to the extent such obligation is secured by a valid lien on property of the debtor not included as an asset.

(Added Pub.L. 101–647, Title XXXVI, § 3611, Nov. 29, 1990, 104 Stat. 4961.)

HISTORICAL AND STATUTORY NOTES

Effective and Applicability Provisions

1990 Acts

Section to take effect 180 days after Nov. 29, 1990, except as otherwise provided, see section 3631 of Pub.L. 101–647, set out as a note under section 3001 of this title.

§ 3303. Value for transfer or obligation

(a) **Transaction.**—Value is given for a transfer or an obligation if, in exchange for the transfer or obligation, property is transferred or an antecedent debt is secured or satisfied, but value does not include an unperformed promise made otherwise than in the ordinary course of the promisor's business to furnish support to the debtor or another person.

(b) **Reasonably equivalent value.**—For the purposes of sections 3304 and 3307, a person gives a reasonably equivalent value if the person acquires an interest of the debtor in an asset pursuant to a

regularly conducted, noncollusive foreclosure sale or execution of a power of sale for the acquisition or disposition of such interest upon default under a mortgage, deed of trust, or security agreement.

(c) **Present value.**—A transfer is made for present value if the exchange between the debtor and the transferee is intended by them to be contemporaneous and is in fact substantially contemporaneous.

(Added Pub.L. 101–647, Title XXXVI, § 3611, Nov. 29, 1990, 104 Stat. 4961.)

HISTORICAL AND STATUTORY NOTES

Effective and Applicability Provisions

1990 Acts

Section to take effect 180 days after Nov. 29, 1990, except as otherwise provided, see section 3631 of Pub.L. 101–647, set out as a note under section 3001 of this title.

§ 3304. Transfer fraudulent as to a debt to the United States

(a) **Debt arising before transfer.**—Except as provided in section 3307, a transfer made or obligation incurred by a debtor is fraudulent as to a debt to the United States which arises before the transfer is made or the obligation is incurred if—

(1)(A) the debtor makes the transfer or incurs the obligation without receiving a reasonably equivalent value in exchange for the transfer or obligation; and

(B) the debtor is insolvent at that time or the debtor becomes insolvent as a result of the transfer or obligation; or

(2)(A) the transfer was made to an insider for an antecedent debt, the debtor was insolvent at the time; and

(B) the insider had reasonable cause to believe that the debtor was insolvent.

(b) **Transfers without regard to date of judgment.**—(1) Except as provided in section 3307, a transfer made or obligation incurred by a debtor is fraudulent as to a debt to the United States, whether such debt arises before or after the transfer is made or the obligation is incurred, if the debtor makes the transfer or incurs the obligation—

(A) with actual intent to hinder, delay, or defraud a creditor; or

(B) without receiving a reasonably equivalent value in exchange for the transfer or obligation if the debtor—

(i) was engaged or was about to engage in a business or a transaction for which the remaining assets of the debtor were unreasonably small in relation to the business or transaction; or

(ii) intended to incur, or believed or reasonably should have believed that he would incur,

debts beyond his ability to pay as they became due.

(2) In determining actual intent under paragraph (1), consideration may be given, among other factors, to whether—

(A) the transfer or obligation was to an insider;

(B) the debtor retained possession or control of the property transferred after the transfer;

(C) the transfer or obligation was disclosed or concealed;

(D) before the transfer was made or obligation was incurred, the debtor had been sued or threatened with suit;

(E) the transfer was of substantially all the debtor's assets;

(F) the debtor absconded;

(G) the debtor removed or concealed assets;

(H) the value of the consideration received by the debtor was reasonably equivalent to the value of the asset transferred or the amount of the obligation incurred;

(I) the debtor was insolvent or became insolvent shortly after the transfer was made or the obligation was incurred;

(J) the transfer occurred shortly before or shortly after a substantial debt was incurred; and

(K) the debtor transferred the essential assets of the business to a lienor who transferred the assets to an insider of the debtor.

(Added Pub.L. 101–647, Title XXXVI, § 3611, Nov. 29, 1990, 104 Stat. 4961.)

HISTORICAL AND STATUTORY NOTES

Effective and Applicability Provisions

1990 Acts

Section to take effect 180 days after Nov. 29, 1990, except as otherwise provided, see section 3631 of Pub.L. 101–647, set out as a note under section 3001 of this title.

§ 3305. When transfer is made or obligation is incurred

For the purposes of this subchapter:

(1) A transfer is made—

(A) with respect to an asset that is real property (other than a fixture, but including the interest of a seller or purchaser under a contract for the sale of the asset), when the transfer is so far perfected that a good-faith purchaser of the asset from the debtor against whom applicable law permits the transfer to be perfected cannot acquire an interest in the asset that is superior to the interest of the transferee; and

(B) with respect to an asset that is not real property or that is a fixture, when the transfer is so far perfected that a creditor on a simple contract cannot acquire, otherwise than under this subchapter, a judicial lien that is superior to the interest of the transferee.

(2) If applicable law permits the transfer to be perfected as approved in paragraph (1) and the transfer is not so perfected before the commencement of an action or proceeding for relief under this subchapter, the transfer is deemed made immediately before the commencement of the action or proceeding.

(3) If applicable law does not permit the transfer to be perfected as provided in paragraph (1), the transfer is made when it becomes effective between the debtor and the transferee.

(4) A transfer is not made until the debtor has acquired rights in the asset transferred.

(5) An obligation is incurred—

(A) if oral, when it becomes effective between the parties; or

(B) if evidenced by a writing executed by the obligor, when such writing is delivered to or for the benefit of the obligee.

(Added Pub.L. 101–647, Title XXXVI, § 3611, Nov. 29, 1990, 104 Stat. 4962.)

HISTORICAL AND STATUTORY NOTES

Effective and Applicability Provisions

1990 Acts

Section to take effect 180 days after Nov. 29, 1990, except as otherwise provided, see section 3631 of Pub.L. 101–647, set out as a note under section 3001 of this title.

§ 3306. Remedies of the United States

(a) In general.—In an action or proceeding under this subchapter for relief against a transfer or obligation, the United States, subject to section 3307 and to applicable principles of equity and in accordance with the Federal Rules of Civil Procedure, may obtain—

(1) avoidance of the transfer or obligation to the extent necessary to satisfy the debt to the United States;

(2) a remedy under this chapter against the asset transferred or other property of the transferee; or

(3) any other relief the circumstances may require.

(b) Limitation.—A claim for relief with respect to a fraudulent transfer or obligation under this subchapter is extinguished unless action is brought—

(1) under section 3304(b)(1)(A) within 6 years after the transfer was made or the obligation was incurred or, if later, within 2 years after the trans-

fer or obligation was or could reasonably have been discovered by the claimant;

 (2) under subsection (a)(1) or (b)(1)(B) of section 3304 within 6 years after the transfer was made or the obligation was incurred; or

 (3) under section 3304(a)(2) within 2 years after the transfer was made or the obligation was incurred.

(Added Pub.L. 101–647, Title XXXVI, § 3611, Nov. 29, 1990, 104 Stat. 4963.)

HISTORICAL AND STATUTORY NOTES

References in Text

 The Federal Rules of Civil Procedure, referred to in subsec. (a), are set out in this title.

Effective and Applicability Provisions

1990 Acts

 Section to take effect 180 days after Nov. 29, 1990, except as otherwise provided, see section 3631 of Pub.L. 101–647, set out as a note under section 3001 of this title.

§ 3307. Defenses, liability, and protection of transferee

 (a) Good faith transfer.—A transfer or obligation is not voidable under section 3304(b) with respect to a person who took in good faith and for a reasonably equivalent value or against any transferee or obligee subsequent to such person.

 (b) Limitation.—Except as provided in subsection (d), to the extent a transfer is voidable in an action or proceeding by the United States under section 3306(a)(1), the United States may recover judgment for the value of the asset transferred, but not to exceed the judgment on a debt. The judgment may be entered against—

 (1) the first transferee of the asset or the person for whose benefit the transfer was made; or

 (2) any subsequent transferee, other than a good faith transferee who took for value or any subsequent transferee of such good-faith transferee.

 (c) Value of asset.—For purposes of subsection (b), the value of the asset is the value of the asset at the time of the transfer, subject to adjustment as the equities may require.

 (d) Rights of good faith transferees and obligees.—Notwithstanding voidability of a transfer or an obligation under this subchapter, a good-faith transferee or obligee is entitled, to the extent of the value given the debtor for the transfer or obligation, to—

 (1) a lien on or a right to retain any interest in the asset transferred;

 (2) enforcement of any obligation incurred; or

 (3) a reduction in the amount of the liability on the judgment.

 (e) Exceptions.—A transfer is not voidable under section 3304(a) or section 3304(b)(2) if the transfer results from—

 (1) termination of a lease upon default by the debtor when the termination is pursuant to the lease and applicable law; or

 (2) enforcement of a security interest in compliance with article 9 of the Uniform Commercial Code or its equivalent in effect in the State where the property is located.

 (f) Limitation of voidability.—A transfer is not voidable under section 3304(a)(2)—

 (1) to the extent the insider gives new value to or for the benefit of the debtor after the transfer is made unless the new value is secured by a valid lien;

 (2) if made in the ordinary course of business or financial affairs of the debtor and the insider; or

 (3) if made pursuant to a good-faith effort to rehabilitate the debtor and the transfer secured both present value given for that purpose and an antecedent debt of the debtor.

(Added Pub.L. 101–647, Title XXXVI, § 3611, Nov. 29, 1990, 104 Stat. 4963.)

HISTORICAL AND STATUTORY NOTES

Effective and Applicability Provisions

1990 Acts

 Section to take effect 180 days after Nov. 29, 1990, except as otherwise provided, see section 3631 of Pub.L. 101–647, set out as a note under section 3001 of this title.

§ 3308. Supplementary provision

 Except as provided in this subchapter, the principles of law and equity, including the law merchant and the law relating to principal and agent, estoppel, laches, fraud, misrepresentation, duress, coercion, mistake, insolvency, or other validating or invalidating cause shall apply to actions and proceedings under this subchapter.

(Added Pub.L. 101–647, Title XXXVI, § 3611, Nov. 29, 1990, 104 Stat. 4964.)

HISTORICAL AND STATUTORY NOTES

Effective and Applicability Provisions

1990 Acts

 Section to take effect 180 days after Nov. 29, 1990, except as otherwise provided, see section 3631 of Pub.L. 101–647, set out as a note under section 3001 of this title.

CHAPTER 179—JUDICIAL REVIEW OF CERTAIN ACTIONS BY PRESIDENTIAL OFFICES

§ 3901. Civil actions

(a) **Parties.**—In an action under section 1346(g) of this title, the defendant shall be the employing office alleged to have committed the violation involved.

(b) **Jury trial.**—In an action described in subsection (a), any party may demand a jury trial where a jury trial would be available in an action against a private defendant under the relevant law made applicable by chapter 5 of title 3. In any case in which a violation of section 411 of title 3 is alleged, the court shall not inform the jury of the maximum amount of compensatory damages available under section 411(b)(1) or 411(b)(3) of title 3.

(Added Pub.L. 104–331, § 3(c), Oct. 26, 1996, 110 Stat. 4070.)

HISTORICAL AND STATUTORY NOTES
Effective and Applicability Provisions

1996 Acts

Enactment of this section by section 3(c) of Pub.L. 104–331, effective Oct. 1, 1997, see section 3(d) of Pub.L. 104–331, set out as a note under section 1296 of this title.

§ 3902. Judicial review of regulations

In any proceeding under section 1296 or 1346(g) of this title in which the application of a regulation issued under chapter 5 of title 3 is at issue, the court may review the validity of the regulation in accordance with the provisions of subparagraphs (A) through (D) of section 706(2) of title 5. If the court determines that the regulation is invalid, the court shall apply, to the extent necessary and appropriate, the most relevant substantive executive agency regulation promulgated to implement the statutory provisions with respect to which the invalid regulation was issued. Except as provided in this section, the validity of regulations issued under this chapter is not subject to judicial review.

(Added Pub.L. 104–331, § 3(c), Oct. 26, 1996, 110 Stat. 4070.)

HISTORICAL AND STATUTORY NOTES
Effective and Applicability Provisions

1996 Acts

Enactment of this section by section 3(c) of Pub.L. 104–331, effective Oct. 1, 1997, see section 3(d) of Pub.L. 104–331, set out as a note under section 1296 of this title.

§ 3903. Effect of failure to issue regulations

In any proceeding under section 1296 or 1346(g) of this title, if the President, the designee of the President, or the Federal Labor Relations Authority has not issued a regulation on a matter for which chapter 5 of title 3 requires a regulation to be issued, the court shall apply, to the extent necessary and appropriate, the most relevant substantive executive agency regulation promulgated to implement the statutory provision at issue in the proceeding.

(Added Pub.L. 104–331, § 3(c), Oct. 26, 1996, 110 Stat. 4070.)

HISTORICAL AND STATUTORY NOTES
Effective and Applicability Provisions

1996 Acts

Enactment of this section by section 3(c) of Pub.L. 104–331, effective Oct. 1, 1997, see section 3(d) of Pub.L. 104–331, set out as a note under section 1296 of this title.

§ 3904. Expedited review of certain appeals

(a) **In general.**—An appeal may be taken directly to the Supreme Court of the United States from any interlocutory or final judgment, decree, or order of a court upon the constitutionality of any provision of chapter 5 of title 3.

(b) **Jurisdiction.**—The Supreme Court shall, if it has not previously ruled on the question, accept jurisdiction over the appeal referred to in subsection (a), advance the appeal on the docket, and expedite the appeal to the greatest extent possible.

(Added Pub.L. 104–331, § 3(c), Oct. 26, 1996, 110 Stat. 4070.)

HISTORICAL AND STATUTORY NOTES
Effective and Applicability Provisions

1996 Acts

Enactment of this section by section 3(c) of Pub.L. 104–331, effective Oct. 1, 1997, see section 3(d) of Pub.L. 104–331, set out as a note under section 1296 of this title.

§ 3905. Attorney's fees and interest

(a) **Attorney's fees.**—If a covered employee, with respect to any claim under chapter 5 of title 3, or a qualified person with a disability, with respect to any claim under section 421 of title 3, is a prevailing party in any proceeding under section 1296 or section 1346(g), the court may award attorney's fees, expert fees, and any other costs as would be appropriate if awarded under section 706(k) of the Civil Rights Act of 1964.

(b) **Interest.**—In any proceeding under section 1296 or section 1346(g), the same interest to compen-

sate for delay in payment shall be made available as would be appropriate if awarded under section 717(d) of the Civil Rights Act of 1964.

(c) Punitive damages.—Except as otherwise provided in chapter 5 of title 3, no punitive damages may be awarded with respect to any claim under chapter 5 of title 3.

(Added Pub.L. 104–331, § 3(c), Oct. 26, 1996, 110 Stat. 4070.)

HISTORICAL AND STATUTORY NOTES

References in Text

The Civil Rights Act of 1964, referred to in subsecs. (a) and (b), is Pub.L. 88–352, July 2, 1964, 78 Stat. 252, as amended. Title VII of such Act is classified generally to subchapter VI (section 2000e et seq.) of chapter 21 of Title 42, The Public Health and Welfare. Sections 706 and 717 of such Act are classified to sections 2000e–5 and 2000e–16, respectively, of Title 42. For complete classification of this Act to the Code, see Short Title note set out under section 2000a of Title 42 and Tables.

Effective and Applicability Provisions

1996 Acts

Enactment of this section by section 3(c) of Pub.L. 104–331, effective Oct. 1, 1997, see section 3(d) of Pub.L. 104–331, set out as a note under section 1296 of this title.

§ 3906. Payments

A judgment, award, or compromise settlement against the United States under this chapter (including any interest and costs) shall be paid—

(1) under section 1304 of title 31, if it arises out of an action commenced in a district court of the United States (or any appeal therefrom); or

(2) out of amounts otherwise appropriated or available to the office involved, if it arises out of an appeal from an administrative proceeding under chapter 5 of title 3.

(Added Pub.L. 104–331, § 3(c), Oct. 26, 1996, 110 Stat. 4071.)

HISTORICAL AND STATUTORY NOTES

Effective and Applicability Provisions

1996 Acts

Enactment of this section by section 3(c) of Pub.L. 104–331, effective Oct. 1, 1997, see section 3(d) of Pub.L. 104–331, set out as a note under section 1296 of this title.

§ 3907. Other judicial review prohibited

Except as expressly authorized by this chapter and chapter 5 of title 3, the compliance or noncompliance with the provisions of chapter 5 of title 3, and any action taken pursuant to chapter 5 of title 3, shall not be subject to judicial review.

(Added Pub.L. 104–331, § 3(c), Oct. 26, 1996, 110 Stat. 4071.)

HISTORICAL AND STATUTORY NOTES

Effective and Applicability Provisions

1996 Acts

Enactment of this section by section 3(c) of Pub.L. 104–331, effective Oct. 1, 1997, see section 3(d) of Pub.L. 104–331, set out as a note under section 1296 of this title.

§ 3908. Definitions

For purposes of applying this chapter, the terms "employing office" and "covered employee" have the meanings given those terms in section 401 of title 3.

(Added Pub.L. 104–331, § 3(c), Oct. 26, 1996, 110 Stat. 4071.)

HISTORICAL AND STATUTORY NOTES

Effective and Applicability Provisions

1996 Acts

Enactment of this section by section 3(c) of Pub.L. 104–331, effective Oct. 1, 1997, see section 3(d) of Pub.L. 104–331, set out as a note under section 1296 of this title.

CHAPTER 180—ASSUMPTION OF CERTAIN CONTRACTUAL OBLIGATIONS

Sec.
4001. Assumption of contractual obligations related to transfers of rights in motion pictures.

§ 4001. Assumption of contractual obligations related to transfers of rights in motion pictures

(a) Assumption of obligations.—(1)In the case of a transfer of copyright ownership under United States law in a motion picture (as the terms "transfer of copyright ownership" and "motion picture" are defined in section 101 of title 17) that is produced subject to 1 or more collective bargaining agreements negotiated under the laws of the United States, if the transfer is executed on or after the effective date of this chapter and is not limited to public performance rights, the transfer instrument shall be deemed to incorporate the assumption agreements applicable to the copyright ownership being transferred that are required by the applicable collective bargaining agreement, and the transferee shall be subject to the obligations under each such assumption agreement to make residual payments and provide related notices, accruing after the effective date of the transfer and applicable to the exploitation of the rights transferred, and any remedies under each such assumption agreement for breach of those obligations, as those obligations and remedies are set forth in the applicable collective bargaining agreement, if—

(A) the transferee knows or has reason to know at the time of the transfer that such collective bargaining agreement was or will be applicable to the motion picture; or

(B) in the event of a court order confirming an arbitration award against the transferor under the collective bargaining agreement, the transferor does not have the financial ability to satisfy the award within 90 days after the order is issued.

(2) For purposes of paragraph (1)(A), "knows or has reason to know" means any of the following:

(A) Actual knowledge that the collective bargaining agreement was or will be applicable to the motion picture.

(B)(i) Constructive knowledge that the collective bargaining agreement was or will be applicable to the motion picture, arising from recordation of a document pertaining to copyright in the motion picture under section 205 of title 17 or from publication, at a site available to the public on-line that is operated by the relevant union, of information that identifies the motion picture as subject to a collective bargaining agreement with that union, if the site permits commercially reasonable verification of the date on which the information was available for access.

(ii) Clause (i) applies only if the transfer referred to in subsection (a)(1) occurs—

(I) after the motion picture is completed, or

(II) before the motion picture is completed and—

 (aa) within 18 months before the filing of an application for copyright registration for the motion picture under section 408 of title 17, or

 (bb) if no such application is filed, within 18 months before the first publication of the motion picture in the United States.

(C) Awareness of other facts and circumstances pertaining to a particular transfer from which it is apparent that the collective bargaining agreement was or will be applicable to the motion picture.

(b) Scope of exclusion of transfers of public performance rights.—For purposes of this section, the exclusion under subsection (a) of transfers of copyright ownership in a motion picture that are limited to public performance rights includes transfers to a terrestrial broadcast station, cable system, or programmer to the extent that the station, system, or programmer is functioning as an exhibitor of the motion picture, either by exhibiting the motion picture on its own network, system, service, or station, or by initiating the transmission of an exhibition that is carried on another network, system, service, or station. When a terrestrial broadcast station, cable system, or programmer, or other transferee, is also functioning otherwise as a distributor or as a producer of the motion picture, the public performance exclusion does not affect any obligations imposed on the transferee to the extent that it is engaging in such functions.

(c) Exclusion for grants of security interests.— Subsection (a) shall not apply to—

(1) a transfer of copyright ownership consisting solely of a mortgage, hypothecation, or other security interest; or

(2) a subsequent transfer of the copyright ownership secured by the security interest described in paragraph (1) by or under the authority of the secured party, including a transfer through the exercise of the secured party's rights or remedies as a secured party, or by a subsequent transferee.

The exclusion under this subsection shall not affect any rights or remedies under law or contract

(d) Deferral pending resolution of bona fide dispute.—A transferee on which obligations are imposed under subsection (a) by virtue of paragraph (1) of that subsection may elect to defer performance of such obligations that are subject to a bona fide dispute between a union and a prior transferor until that dispute is resolved, except that such deferral shall not stay accrual of any union claims due under an applicable collective bargaining agreement.

(e) Scope of obligations determined by private agreement.—Nothing in this section shall expand or diminish the rights, obligations, or remedies of any person under the collective bargaining agreements or assumption agreements referred to in this section.

(f) Failure to notify.—If the transferor under subsection (a) fails to notify the transferee under subsection (a) of applicable collective bargaining obligations before the execution of the transfer instrument, and subsection (a) is made applicable to the transferee solely by virtue of subsection (a)(1)(B), the transferor shall be liable to the transferee for any damages suffered by the transferee as a result of the failure to notify.

(g) Determination of disputes and claims.—Any dispute concerning the application of subsections (a) through (f) shall be determined by an action in United States district court, and the court in its discretion may allow the recovery of full costs by or against any party and may also award a reasonable attorney's fee to the prevailing party as part of the costs.

(h) Study.—The Comptroller General, in consultation with the Register of Copyrights, shall conduct a study of the conditions in the motion picture industry that gave rise to this section, and the impact of this section on the motion picture industry. The Comptroller General shall report the findings of the study to the Congress within 2 years after the effective date of this chapter.

(Added Pub.L. 105–304, Title IV, § 406(a), Oct. 28, 1998, 112 Stat. 2902.)

HISTORICAL AND STATUTORY NOTES

Effective and Applicability Provisions

1998 Acts

Amendments by Title IV of Pub.L. 105–304 effective Oct. 28, 1998, except as otherwise provided, see section 407 of Pub.L. 105–304, set out as a note under section 108 of Title 17, Copyrights.

APPENDIX A
SELECTED STATE PROVISIONS

INTRODUCTION

The following pages contain the text of several Uniform Acts relating to civil procedural laws. These Acts were drafted by the National Conference of Commissioners on Uniform State Laws and are recommended for adoption in all states.

These Acts have been variously adopted among the states. The legislative deliberations of numerous others have been greatly informed by the content of the Uniform provisions.

The Uniform Acts are attended by Official Comments prepared by the drafters. These comments are a valuable insight into the text and its underlying influences (much like the Advisory Committee Notes pertaining to the Federal Rules).

UNIFORM LAW COMMISSIONERS' MODEL CLASS ACTIONS [ACT] [RULE]

Historical Note

The Uniform Class Actions Act was approved by the National Conference of Commissioners on Uniform State Laws in 1976 and officially changed to a Model Act in 1987.

PREFATORY NOTE

A class action is an equitable concept which originated as an exception to the general rule in equity that all persons (however numerous) materially interested in the subject matter of a suit were to be made parties to it. The class suit was an invention of equity to allow a suit to proceed when the parties interested in the subject were so numerous that it would have been impracticable to join them without long delays and inconveniences which would obstruct the purposes of justice. Under these conditions representatives of a class conduct litigation on behalf of themselves and all others similarly situated and the judgment binds all members.

The first state statute on class suits was the 1849 Amendment to the Field Code of New York which attempted to codify the pre-existing equity law on representative suits. Two types of representative suits which could be maintained under the rules of equity were specially adopted as allowable under the Field Code. The first type of suit involved actions where the question was one of a common or general interest and one or more class members sued for the benefit of the entire class. The second type involved cases in which the parties were very numerous and it was impracticable to bring them all before the court. A common interest or right was present among the members and the representatives sought to establish or enforce this right in order to benefit all the members of the class in common and injure none. Other states have adopted statutes modeled on these concepts.

In 1938 the Supreme Court adopted the Federal Rules of Civil Procedure including Rule 23 which governed class actions for federal courts. Many states have adopted a version of this rule. The 1938 Rule 23 created three separate categories of class actions based on the substantive character of the right asserted by the class and the *res judicata* effect of the class action judgments on nonappearing members. The first category, the "true" class suit, requires a common or joint cause of action that exists for all parties and the issues determined in the suit are preclusive to all class members. The second type is the "hybrid" suit requiring each member to have an interest in a specific fund or property which is in controversy and the judgment binds the rights of the class with respect to the property involved. The third type, "spurious," requires that a common question of law or fact affect the several rights involved and a common relief must be sought. The decree in such actions had no binding effect on nonappearing members. Class actions of the latter sort were merely invitations to join.

In 1966 Federal Rule 23 was amended. The new Rule 23 is divided into five subsections dealing with different procedural requirements for bringing suit. After satisfying the four prerequisites of subsection (a), a class suit must fit in one of the three categories of subsection (b) which describe appropriate occasions for maintaining a class action: 23(b)(1) where difficulties would be likely to arise if separate actions were brought by class members; 23(b)(2) where the party opposing the class has improperly acted on grounds generally applicable to the class so as to create a need for injunctive relief; or 23(b)(3) where common questions predominate over any questions affecting only individual class members and a class action is superior to other adjudicatory methods. A judgment under the amended rule binds all those whom the court finds to be members of the class. Several states have a version of this rule for their class action statute.

Presently three types of class action statutes predominate in the United States; (1) the Field Code provision, (2) state statutes modeled on Rule 23 of the Federal Rules of Civil Procedure as it existed prior to July, 1966, and (3) statutes modeled on the new Federal Rule 23. Some states still do not have a class action statute. State rules based on the Field Code and the earlier Federal Rule pose distinct problems and disadvantages in maintaining class suits. Recent Supreme Court decisions have severely limited the availability of the present Rule 23 as a group remedy. In Zahn v. International Paper Co., 414 U.S. 291 (1973) the Court held that each of the class members in a diversity action under Rule 23 must satisfy the jurisdictional amount of more than $10,000 and any members who do not must be dismissed from the case. In Eisen v. Carlisle & Jacquelin, 417 U.S. 156 (1974) the Supreme Court interpreted Rule 23(b)(3) and (c)(2) to require personal notice of the action to all identifiable class members with service costs to be borne by the plaintiffs.

More classes with claims will be seeking redress in state courts because the federal courts have severely restricted the availability of class actions in their forum. Presently state statutes vary in their treatment of class actions. A strong need exists for states to adopt a uniform class action act. Many activities have impact on large numbers of persons often from several states. Adoption of a uniform act will assist states in handling multistate class actions, thereby reducing multiplicity of litigation and the chance of inconsistent judgments. The Act provides supervision of the adequacy of representation by the representative parties to insure that the interests of the class will be protected. Subsections to cover special problems of the class action are provided: notice techniques, discovery of the members of the class, effect of the judgment on the members of the class, methods of fashioning relief, and liability for costs and expenses.

This Act applies whenever an action involving a class is commenced. When a final order refusing to certify a class action is entered, the application of this Act will terminate. The scope of this Act is similar to that of F.R.C.P. 23 and does not cover derivative actions by shareholders or suits by unincorporated associations.

Within the limits of practicality, due process requires that all individuals be afforded a meaningful opportunity to be

heard, Boddie v. Connecticut, 401 U.S. 371 (1971). A class action is a procedure by which people with small claims or limited means can exercise their rights and thereby make our system of justice more responsive to their needs.

UNIFORM LAW COMMISSIONERS' MODEL CLASS ACTIONS [ACT] [RULE]

Section 1. [Commencement of a Class Action]

One or more members of a class may sue or be sued as representative parties on behalf of all in a class action if:

(1) the class is so numerous or so constituted that joinder of all members, whether or not otherwise required or permitted, is impracticable; and

(2) there is a question of law or fact common to the class.

COMMENT

This section sets forth the requirements that must be satisfied if a class action is to be brought. Section 2 authorizes the certification of a class action.

Section 2. [Certification of Class Action]

(a) Unless deferred by the court, as soon as practicable after the commencement of a class action the court shall hold a hearing and determine whether or not the action is to be maintained as a class action and by order certify or refuse to certify it as a class action.

(b) The court may certify an action as a class action, if it finds that (1) the requirements of Section 1 have been satisfied, (2) a class action should be permitted for the fair and efficient adjudication of the controversy, and (3) the representative parties fairly and adequately will protect the interests of the class.

(c) If appropriate, the court may (1) certify an action as a class action with respect to a particular claim or issue, (2) certify an action as a class action to obtain one or more forms of relief, equitable, declaratory, or monetary, or (3) divide a class into subclasses and treat each subclass as a class.

COMMENT

The standard established under 2(b)(2) is elaborated in Section 3(a) and that established under 2(b)(3) is elaborated in Section 3(b).

Section 3. [Criteria Considered]

(a) In determining whether the class action should be permitted for the fair and efficient adjudication of the controversy, as appropriately limited under Section 2(c), the court shall consider, and give appropriate weight to, the following and other relevant factors:

(1) whether a joint or common interest exists among members of the class;

(2) whether the prosecution of separate actions by or against individual members of the class would create a risk of inconsistent or varying adjudications with respect to individual members of the class that would establish incompatible standards of conduct for a party opposing the class;

(3) whether adjudications with respect to individual members of the class as a practical matter would be dispositive of the interests of other members not parties to the adjudication or substantially impair or impede their ability to protect their interests;

(4) whether a party opposing the class has acted or refused to act on grounds generally applicable to the class, thereby making final injunctive relief or corresponding declaratory relief appropriate with respect to the class as a whole;

(5) whether common questions of law or fact predominate over any questions affecting only individual members;

(6) whether other means of adjudicating the claims and defenses are impracticable or inefficient;

(7) whether a class action offers the most appropriate means of adjudicating the claims and defenses;

(8) whether members not representative parties have a substantial interest in individually controlling the prosecution or defense of separate actions;

(9) whether the class action involves a claim that is or has been the subject of a class action, a government action, or other proceeding;

(10) whether it is desirable to bring the class action in another forum;

(11) whether management of the class action poses unusual difficulties;

(12) whether any conflict of laws issues involved pose unusual difficulties; and

(13) whether the claims of individual class members are insufficient in the amounts or interests involved, in view of the complexities of the issues and the expenses of the litigation, to afford significant relief to the members of the class.

(b) In determining under Section 2(b) that the representative parties fairly and adequately will protect the interests of the class, the court must find that:

(1) the attorney for the representative parties will adequately represent the interests of the class;

(2) the representative parties do not have a conflict of interest in the maintenance of the class action; and

(3) the representative parties have or can acquire adequate financial resources, considering Section 17, to assure that the interests of the class will not be harmed.

COMMENT

The factors listed in Section 3(a)(1) to (13), possibly along with other factors, are to be considered by the court in determining whether to certify the action as a class action. The factors may be given different weight by the court.

After an action has been brought as a class action, if the court determines that there is pending in another court an action which encompasses the action pending both as to general class and claim, it may refuse under Subsection 3(a)(9) and (10) to certify the action against or on behalf of the class if it concludes that this forum is not the most appropriate one. The court in making this decision should consider the sequence of the suits, the residence of the members of the class, where the transaction or occurrence involved took place, where the relevant evidence is available, and other pertinent facts.

Section 4. [Order on Certification]

(a) The order of certification shall describe the class and state: (1) the relief sought, (2) whether the action is maintained with respect to particular claims or issues, and (3) whether subclasses have been created.

(b) The order certifying or refusing to certify a class action shall state the reasons for the court's ruling and its findings on the facts listed in Section 3(a).

(c) An order certifying or refusing to certify an action as a class action is appealable.

(d) Refusal of certification does not terminate the action, but does preclude it from being maintained as a class action.

COMMENT

If class certification is denied, subsection (d) presupposes the existence of rules of civil procedure which will allow the action to continue with the representative parties as properly joined parties.

Denial of certification and the allowance of a personal action under subsection (d) does not affect any possible intervention or joinder of class members who are not representative parties under the applicable state laws.

Section 5. [Amendment of Certification Order]

(a) The court may amend the certification order at any time before entry of judgment on the merits. The amendment may (1) establish subclasses, (2) eliminate from the class any class member who was included in the class as certified, (3) provide for an adjudication limited to certain claims or issues, (4) change the relief sought, or (5) make any other appropriate change in the order.

(b) If notice of certification has been given pursuant to Section 7, the court may order notice of the amendment of the certification order to be given in terms and to any members of the class the court directs.

(c) The reasons for the court's ruling shall be set forth in the amendment of the certification order.

(d) An order amending the certification order is appealable. An order denying the motion of a member of a defendant class, not a representative party, to amend the certification order is appealable if the court certifies it for immediate appeal.

COMMENT

An order amending an order of certification is an appealable order as is an order certifying or refusing to certify an action as a class action.

A member of a defendant class can attempt to get out of a class action by seeking an amendment of the order of certification. If a member of a defendant class seeks an amendment which would delete him or her from the class and the court refused to make such an order, an appeal can be taken if the court certifies it for appeal.

Under Section 5(b) the court may order notice given of an amendment if it deems it desirable in light of the nature of the amendments and the notice previously given.

Section 6. [Jurisdiction over Multi–State Classes (Reserved)]
COMMENT

The Section is reserved for provisions that may be added to govern jurisdiction of the person over class members who are non-residents or lack traditional minimum contacts with the state. See Phillips Petroleum Company v. Shutts, 472 U.S. 797, 86 L.Ed.2d 628 (1985), rendering obsolete the jurisdictional limitations of this Section as contained in the 1976 version.

Section 7. [Notice of Action]

(a) Following certification, the court by order, after hearing, shall direct the giving of notice to the class.

(b) The notice, based on the certification order and any amendment of the order, shall include:

(1) a general description of the action, including the relief sought, and the names and addresses of the representative parties;

(2) a statement of the right of a member of the class under Section 8 to be excluded from the action by filing an election to be excluded, in the manner specified, by a certain date;

(3) a description of possible financial consequences on the class;

(4) a general description of any counterclaim being asserted by or against the class, including the relief sought;

(5) a statement that the judgment, whether favorable or not, will bind all members of the class who are not excluded from the action;

(6) a statement that any member of the class may enter an appearance either personally or through counsel;

(7) an address to which inquiries may be directed; and

(8) other information the court deems appropriate.

(c) The order shall prescribe the manner of notification to be used and specify the members of the class to be notified. In determining the manner and form of the notice to be given, the court shall consider the interests of the class, the relief requested, the cost of notifying the members of the class, and the possible prejudice to members who do not receive notice.

(d) Each member of the class, not a representative party, whose potential monetary recovery or liability is estimated to exceed $100 shall be given personal or mailed notice if his identity and whereabouts can be ascertained by the exercise of reasonable diligence.

(e) For members of the class not given personal or mailed notice under subsection (d), the court shall provide, as a minimum, a means of notice reasonably calculated to apprise the members of the class of the pendency of the action. Techniques calculated to assure effective communication of information concerning commencement of the action shall be used. The techniques may include personal or mailed notice, notification by means of newspaper, television, radio, posting in public or other places, and distribution through trade, union, public interest, or other appropriate groups.

(f) The plaintiff shall advance the expense of notice under this section if there is no counterclaim asserted. If a counterclaim is asserted the expense of notice shall be allocated as the court orders in the interest of justice.

(g) The court may order that steps be taken to minimize the expense of notice.

COMMENT

The hearing required by subsection (a) can be combined with the hearing required by Section 2(a).

Personal mailed notice to all members of the class is not required by this Act. For consideration of the notice required by the U.S. Constitution, see Gant v. City of Lincoln, 225 N.W.2d 549 (Neb.1975), and Cartt v. Superior Court In and For County of Los Angeles, 50 Cal.App.3d 960, 124 Cal.Rptr. 376 (Ct.App.1975).

The notice to be given may vary as to the persons to be notified and the form of notice and, to some extent, the content. Subsection (c) indicates that the court must consider a number of factors in deciding what type of notice to give.

Subsection (g) allows the court to order a defendant who has a mailing list of class members to co-operate with the representative parties in notifying the class members. Use of a computer or enclosing notice in a regular mailing would be possibilities.

Section 8. [Exclusion]

(a) A member of a plaintiff class may elect to be excluded from the action unless (1) he is a representative party, (2) the certification order contains an affirmative finding under paragraph (1), (2), or (3) of Section 3(a), or (3) a counterclaim under Section 11 is pending against the member or his class or subclass.

(b) Any member of a plaintiff class entitled to be excluded under subsection (a) who files an election to be excluded, in the manner and in the time specified in the notice, is excluded from and not bound by the judgment in the class action.

(c) The elections shall be [docketed] [made a part of the record] in the action.

(d) A member of a defendant class may not elect to be excluded.

COMMENT

Under some circumstances members of a plaintiff class cannot elect to be excluded because they are indispensable parties. This would be determined by the court in ruling on certification considering the criteria of Section 3(a). Such situations might arise in actions comparable to those under Federal Rule 23(b)(1); see 3B, Moore's Federal Practice,

¶ 23.35. In most situations members of a plaintiff class will be permitted to elect to be excluded.

A class member aggrieved by an affirmative finding under Section 3(a)(1), (2) or (3) might seek relief through one of the extraordinary writs or through an interlocutory appeal if authorized by the state practice.

Section 9. [Conduct of Action]

(a) The court on motion of a party or its own motion may make or amend any appropriate order dealing with the conduct of the action including, but not limited to, the following: (1) determining the course of proceedings or prescribing measures to prevent undue repetition or complication in the presentation of evidence or argument; (2) requiring, for the protection of the members of the class or otherwise for the fair conduct of the action, that notice be given as the court directs, of (i) any step in the action, (ii) the proposed extent of the judgment, or (iii) the opportunity of members to signify whether they consider the representation fair and adequate, to enter an appearance and present claims or defenses, or otherwise participate in the action; (3) imposing conditions on the representative parties or on intervenors; (4) inviting the attorney general to participate with respect to the question of adequacy of class representation; (5) making any other order to assure that the class action proceeds only with adequate class representation; and (6) making any order to assure that the class action proceeds only with competent representation by the attorney for the class.

(b) A class member not a representative party may appear and be represented by separate counsel.

COMMENT

The rules governing civil procedure in the courts of the state normally will govern procedures in class actions. Section 9 covers certain matters which deserve special consideration. Section 9(a)(4) does not limit the power of the attorney general to participate in litigation under other applicable provisions.

Section 10. [Discovery by or against Class Members]

(a) Discovery under [applicable discovery rules] may be used only on order of the court against a member of the class who is not a representative party or who has not appeared. In deciding whether discovery should be allowed the court shall consider, among other relevant factors, the timing of the request, the subject matter to be covered, whether representatives of the class are seeking discovery on the subject to be covered, and whether the discovery will result in annoyance, oppression, or undue burden or expense for the member of the class.

(b) Discovery by or against representative parties or those appearing is governed by the rules dealing with discovery by or against a party to a civil action.

COMMENT

Under Section 10 members of the class not representative parties and not appearing are not treated as parties to the litigation for discovery purposes. Discovery can be obtained of these members only on order of court.

Discovery against representative parties may include the representative parties' fee arrangement with counsel. Disclosure of this arrangement is required under Section 17.

Section 11. [Counterclaims]

(a) A defendant in an action brought by a class may plead as a counterclaim any claim the court certifies as a class action against the plaintiff class. On leave of court, the defendant may plead as a counterclaim a claim against a member of the class or a claim the court certifies as a class action against a subclass.

(b) Any counterclaim in an action brought by a plaintiff class must be asserted before notice is given under Section 7.

(c) If a judgment for money is recovered against a party on behalf of a class, the court rendering judgment may stay distribution of any award or execution of any portion of a judgment allocated to a member of the class against whom the losing party has pending an action in or out of state for a judgment for money, and continue the stay so long as the losing party in the class action pursues the pending action with reasonable diligence.

(d) A defendant class may plead as a counterclaim any claim on behalf of the class that the court certifies as a class action against the plaintiff. The court may certify as a class action a counterclaim against the plaintiff on behalf of a subclass or permit a counterclaim by a member of the class. The court shall order that notice of the counterclaim by the class, subclass, or member of the class be given to the members of the class as the court directs, in the interest of justice.

(e) A member of a class or subclass asserting a counterclaim shall be treated as a member of a plaintiff class for the purpose of exclusion under Section 8.

(f) The court's refusal to allow, or the defendant's failure to plead, a claim as a counterclaim in a class action does not bar the defendant from asserting the claim in a subsequent action.

COMMENT

Nothing in this Act precludes a party opposing the class from bringing an action against a member of the class concurrently with the class action or in the future. Subsection (f) makes the ordinary rules concerning compulsory counterclaims inapplicable in a class action under this Act.

The expense of notification of actions involving counterclaims is to be determined as provided in Section 7(f).

Section 12. [Dismissal or Compromise]

(a) Unless certification has been refused under Section 2, a class action, without the approval of the court

after hearing, may not be (1) dismissed voluntarily, (2) dismissed involuntarily without an adjudication on the merits, or (3) compromised.

(b) If the court has certified the action under Section 2, notice of hearing on the proposed dismissal or compromise shall be given to all members of the class in a manner the court directs. If the court has not ruled on certification, notice of hearing on the proposed dismissal or compromise may be ordered by the court which shall specify the persons to be notified and the manner in which notice is to be given.

(c) Notice given under subsection (b) shall include a full disclosure of the reasons for the dismissal or compromise including, but not limited to, (1) any payments made or to be made in connection with the dismissal or compromise, (2) the anticipated effect of the dismissal or compromise on the class members, (3) any agreement made in connection with the dismissal or compromise, (4) a description and evaluation of alternatives considered by the representative parties and (5) an explanation of any other circumstances giving rise to the proposal. The notice also shall include a description of the procedure available for modification of the dismissal or compromise.

(d) On the hearing of the dismissal or compromise, the court may:

(1) as to the representative parties or a class certified under Section 2, permit dismissal with or without prejudice or approve the compromise;

(2) as to a class not certified; permit dismissal without prejudice;

(3) deny the dismissal;

(4) disapprove the compromise; or

(5) take other appropriate action for the protection of the class and in the interest of justice.

(e) The cost of notice given under subsection (b) shall be paid by the party seeking dismissal, or as agreed in case of a compromise, unless the court after hearing orders otherwise.

COMMENT

This section covers class actions brought under Section 1 until certification has been refused under Section 2, as well as class actions certified under Section 2.

Section 13. [Effect of Judgment on Class]

In a class action certified under Section 2 in which notice has been given under Section 7 or 12, a judgment as to the claim or particular claim or issue certified is binding, according to its terms, on any member of the class who has not filed an election of exclusion under Section 8. The judgment shall name or describe the members of the class who are bound by its terms.

COMMENT

Section 13 deals with the application of a class action judgment to the members of the class. This Act does not deal with the preclusive effect of a class action upon a member of the class who has requested exclusion. This is a matter which is governed by the normal rules of res judicata/preclusion.

Section 14. [Costs]

(a) Only the representative parties and those members of the class who have appeared individually are liable for costs assessed against a plaintiff class.

(b) The court shall apportion the liability for costs assessed against a defendant class.

(c) Expenses of notice advanced under Section 7 are taxable as costs in favor of the prevailing party.

COMMENT

Section 14 specifies the liability of class members when costs are assessed against the class and provides for assessment of the expenses of notification under Section 7.

The nature of other costs and assessments against parties in a class action is left to the law generally applicable in the state.

Section 15. [Relief Afforded]

(a) The court may award any form of relief consistent with the certification order to which the party in whose favor it is rendered is entitled including equitable, declaratory, monetary, or other relief to individual members of the class or the class in a lump sum or installments.

(b) Damages fixed by a minimum measure of recovery provided by any statute may not be recovered in a class action.

(c) If a class is awarded a judgment for money, the distribution shall be determined as follows:

(1) The parties shall list as expeditiously as possible all members of the class whose identity can be determined without expending a disproportionate share of the recovery.

(2) The reasonable expense of identification and distribution shall be paid, with the court's approval, from the funds to be distributed.

(3) The court may order steps taken to minimize the expense of identification.

(4) The court shall supervise, and may grant or stay the whole or any portion of, the execution of the judgment and the collection and distribution of funds to the members of the class as their interests warrant.

(5) The court shall determine what amount of the funds available for the payment of the judgment cannot be distributed to members of the class individually because they could not be identified or located or because they did not claim or prove the

right to money apportioned to them. The court after hearing shall distribute that amount, in whole or in part, to one or more states as unclaimed property or to the defendant.

(6) In determining the amount, if any, to be distributed to a state or to the defendant, the court shall consider the following criteria: (i) any unjust enrichment of the defendant; (ii) the willfulness or lack of willfulness on the part of the defendant; (iii) the impact on the defendant of the relief granted; (iv) the pendency of other claims against the defendant; (v) any criminal sanction imposed on the defendant; and (vi) the loss suffered by the plaintiff class.

(7) The court, in order to remedy or alleviate any harm done, may impose conditions on the defendant respecting the use of the money distributed to him.

(8) Any amount to be distributed to a state shall be distributed as unclaimed property to any state in which are located the last known addresses of the members of the class to whom distribution could not be made. If the last known addresses cannot be ascertained with reasonable diligence, the court may determine by other means what portion of the unidentified or unlocated members of the class were residents of a state. A state shall receive that portion of the distribution that its residents would have received had they been identified and located. Before entering an order distributing any part of the amount to a state, the court shall give written notice of its intention to make distribution to the attorney general of the state of the residence of any person given notice under Section 7 or 12 and shall afford the attorney general an opportunity to move for an order requiring payment to the state.

COMMENT

Subsection (c)(3) is similar to subsection 7(g) in its purpose and scope and should be construed similarly.

Subsection 15(c)(5) provides for the possibility of escheat of funds available for the payment of the judgment if the court, applying the relevant criteria, so orders. The escheat provision is similar to that found in the Model Escheat of Postal Savings System Accounts Act.

If the court decides that undistributed funds available for the payment of the judgment should be distributed to the defendant, the court under subsection 15(c)(7), "in order to remedy or alleviate any harm done, may impose conditions on the defendant respecting the use of the money distributed to him." For example, if the plaintiff class sued for damage done because of the discharge of pollutants by the defendant and the class won a money judgment, the court might distribute to the defendant funds undistributed to the plaintiff class on condition that the defendant use the funds to install pollution-control devices.

Section 16. [Attorney's Fees]

(a) Attorney's fees for representing a class are subject to control of the court.

(b) If under an applicable provision of law a defendant or defendant class is entitled to attorney's fees from a plaintiff class, only representative parties and those members of the class who have appeared individually are liable for those fees. If a plaintiff is entitled to attorney's fees from a defendant class, the court may apportion the fees among the members of the class.

(c) If a prevailing class recovers a judgment for money or other award that can be divided for the purpose, the court may order reasonable attorney's fees and litigation expenses of the class to be paid from the recovery.

(d) If the prevailing class is entitled to declaratory or equitable relief, the court may order the adverse party to pay to the class its reasonable attorney's fees and litigation expenses if permitted by law in similar cases not involving a class or the court finds that the judgment has vindicated an important public interest. However, if any monetary award is also recovered, the court may allow reasonable attorney's fees and litigation expenses only to the extent that a reasonable proportion of that award is insufficient to defray the fees and expenses.

(e) In determining the amount of attorney's fees for a prevailing class the court shall consider the following factors:

(1) the time and effort expended by the attorney in the litigation, including the nature, extent, and quality of the services rendered;

(2) results achieved and benefits conferred upon the class;

(3) the magnitude, complexity, and uniqueness of the litigation;

(4) the contingent nature of success;

(5) in cases awarding attorney's fees and litigation expenses under subsection (d) because of the vindication of an important public interest, the economic impact on the party against whom the award is made; and

(6) appropriate criteria in the [state's Code of Professional Responsibility].

COMMENT

Most of the factors listed in subsection (e) are taken from Lindy Bros. v. American Radiator & Standard Sanitary Corp., 487 F.2d 161 (3rd Cir.1973).

Section 17. [Arrangements for Attorney's Fees and Expenses]

(a) Before a hearing under Section 2(a) or at any other time the court directs, the representative parties and the attorney for the representative parties shall file with the court, jointly or separately: (1) a statement showing any amount paid or promised them by

any person for the services rendered or to be rendered in connection with the action or for the costs and expenses of the litigation and the source of all of the amounts; (2) a copy of any written agreement, or a summary of any oral agreement, between the representative parties and their attorney concerning financial arrangements or fees and (3) a copy of any written agreement, or a summary of any oral agreement, by the representative parties or the attorney to share these amounts with any person other than a member, regular associate, or an attorney regularly of counsel with his law firm. This statement shall be supplemented promptly if additional arrangements are made.

(b) Upon a determination that the costs and litigation expenses of the action cannot reasonably and fairly be defrayed by the representative parties or by other available sources, the court by order may authorize and control the solicitation and expenditure of voluntary contributions for this purpose from members of the class, advances by the attorneys or others, or both, subject to reimbursement from any recovery obtained for the class. The court may order any available funds so contributed or advanced to be applied to the payment of any costs taxed in favor of a party opposing the class.

COMMENT

Section 17 requires this information to be disclosed in order to assist the court in making determinations concerning (1) adequacy of representation by the representative parties and by the attorney for the class, (2) any possible collusion between the representative parties and the attorney for the class, and (3) any possible conflict of interests among the representative parties and the class members.

This section is grounded on the idea that representative parties are fiduciaries for the class and that class actions are unique and require treatment different from ordinary actions.

If the information available under this section shows that an action has been improvidently brought, action can then be taken under Section 9(a)(5) or (6).

Section 18. [Statute of Limitations]

The statute of limitations is tolled for all class members upon the commencement of an action asserting a class action. The statute of limitations resumes running against a member of a class:

(1) upon his filing an election of exclusion;

(2) upon entry of an order of certification, or of an amendment thereof, eliminating him from the class;

(3) except as to representative parties, upon entry of an order under Section 2 refusing to certify the action as a class action; and

(4) upon dismissal of the action without an adjudication on the merits.

COMMENT

Section 18 adopts the principles of American Pipe and Construction Co. v. Utah, 414 U.S. 538, 94 S.Ct. 756, 38 L.Ed.2d 713 (1974), which held that the commencement of a class action under Federal Rule 23 suspends the applicable statute of limitation to all members of the class pending a determination of class action status.

Section 19. [Short Title]

This [Act] [Rule] may be cited as the "Uniform Law Commissioners' Model Class Actions [Act] [Rule]."

COMMENT

With the deletion of the jurisdictional and reciprocal provisions of former Section 6, the need for uniformity is diminished, and the Act or Rule is therefore re-titled as "Model."

Section 20. [Repeal]

The following acts and parts of acts are repealed:

Section 21. [Time of Taking Effect]

This [Act] [Rule] shall take effect _____.

UNIFORM CERTIFICATION OF QUESTIONS OF LAW [ACT] [RULE] (1995)

PREFATORY NOTE

The Problem Addressed by The Uniform Act/Rule

Since the announcement in *Erie R. Co. v. Tompkins*, 304 U.S. 64 (1938) that federal courts in nonfederal matters would be required to follow state law rather than some general common law, the federal courts have often been faced with the difficult problem of ascertaining state law when there is no controlling state constitutional provision, state statute or definitive state appellate judicial decision on the matter. In such circumstances, the federal courts have been forced to guess what the state court might rule if the precise issue of law were presented to it. Such speculation invited divergent answers to unsettled questions of state law from the federal courts and worked to undermine the two major purposes of the *Erie* doctrine; that is, the "discouragement of forum-shopping and the avoidance of inequitable administration of the laws." *Hanna v. Plumer*, 380 U.S. 460, 468 (1965). Essentially the same problem confronts a state appellate court when it determines that the law of another State should control the resolution of a key issue of law in a case pending before it, but where there is no controlling constitutional provision, statute or appellate decision in that other State on that issue of law.

The federal courts sought to try to avoid the problem by developing an abstention doctrine whereby the federal courts refrained from acting while the litigants attempted to obtain from the state court a definitive statement of the state law. This proved to be quite unsatisfactory. *See* 1A *Moore's Federal Practice* ¶ 0.203.

The History of the Use of Certification

Dissatisfaction with the use of the abstention doctrine led to efforts to find an alternative solution to the problem that also served the interests of cooperative judicial federalism. As a result, federal courts confronting issues of unsettled state law began to explore ways by which such issues could be submitted to, and answered by, the appropriate state court.[1] This process, known as "certification," has worked well to the extent it has been used. Among the various jurisdictions that have attempted to utilize certification, however, there are substantial differences in the procedures developed to accomplish the certification process. Where the procedures for certification have been relatively simple, and the appropriate state court has cooperated by agreeing to answer the question, certification has proven to be a more rapid and orderly method for handling the problem than the use of the abstention doctrine by the federal courts.

Over 35 years ago, the United States Supreme Court urged the use of the certified question by the Court of Appeals for the 5th Circuit, *Clay v. Sun Insurance Office*, 363 U.S. 207, 212 (1960). Three years later, the 5th Circuit expressed its approval of certification in *Green v. American Tobacco Co.*, 325 F.2d 673 (5th Cir.1963). In *Lehman Brothers v. Schein*, 416 U.S. 386 (1974), the United States Supreme Court again endorsed the use of certification by the federal courts in cases involving doubt as to issues of state law. While the Court noted that it did not mean to suggest that certification was obligatory in such cases, it made clear its strong approval of the use of certification, stating: "It [certification] does, of course, in the long run save time, energy, and resources and helps build a cooperative judicial federalism." *Lehman Brothers*, 416 U.S. at 391 (footnote omitted).

When, prior to the 1991, federal district courts took it upon themselves to decide issues of unsettled state law, a majority of the federal Courts of Appeals gave deference to those decisions when reviewing such issues on appeal. This "rule of deference" was ended by the decision of the United States Supreme Court in *Salve Regina v. Russell*, ___ U.S. ___, 111 S.Ct. 1217 (1991). Holding that the federal Courts of Appeals are required to independently review such state law issues, the Court expressly rejected the notion upon which the "rule of deference" was based; that is, that federal District Courts were better able to "intuit" answers to unsettled questions of state law than the federal Courts of Appeals. *Salve Regina College*, ___ U.S. ___, 111 S.Ct. at 1225. Thus, the Court further encouraged the federal trial courts to use certification when confronted with issues of unsettled state law.

The federal District Courts and federal Courts of Appeals have been increasingly relying upon certification to ascertain uncertain state law. A 1994 American Judicature Society study of all federal circuit court appellate decisions published since 1990 showed the importance of the certification process to the federal circuit appellate courts.[2] For example, the study revealed that the federal Court of Appeals for the 11th Circuit granted 90% of the certification applications it received. By comparison, the federal Court of Appeals for the 10th Circuit, which granted the lowest percentage of such applications, nevertheless granted more than a third of the certification applications submitted to it (34%).

Need for Uniformity

Since the certification of a question of law involves more than one jurisdiction, the development of procedures for

[1] The certified question of law has a long history in the United States and the English-speaking world. The British Law Ascertainment Act of 1859 provided for certification of questions of law within the British Empire, while the Foreign Law Ascertainment Act of 1861 made provision for certification of questions to foreign states. 9 *Halsbury's Statutes of England* (2d ed.) 58206. Within the federal court system, the Courts of Appeals and the Court of Claims have by statute been permitted to certify questions to the United States Supreme Court pursuant to 28 U.S.C. Secs. 1254–1255. *See* Moore and Vestal, *Present and Potential Role of Certification in Federal Appellate Procedure*, 35 Va.L.Rev. 1 (1940). In addition, a great

number of states have provided for certified questions within their court systems. At least two state supreme courts have held that they need no express grant of jurisdiction to answer certified questions from the federal court. *Shebester v. Triple Crown Insurers*, 826 P.2d 603 (Okla.1992); *Scott v. Bank One Trust Co.*, 577 N.E.2d 1077 (Ohio 1991).

[2] J. Goldschmidt, "Results of A National Survey of Federal Judges and State Supreme Court Justices Regarding Certification of Questions of Law," American Judicature Society, (Nov. 1994).

certification raises important issues of sovereignty, comity, and efficiency in the relationships between individual States and between the state and federal courts.

As of 1994, 44 state supreme courts and the Court of Appeals for the District of Columbia were authorized by constitutional provision, statute or court rule to answer certified questions of law from other courts. Of these, 19 States and the District of Columbia adopted the earlier versions of the Uniform Certification of Question of Law Act or amended versions of them. Nevertheless, the certification process is not utilized as frequently as it could and should be. One of the main reasons for this is that there is still widespread lack of uniformity in the laws of the various jurisdictions which authorize their courts to send and answer certified questions of law to and from other courts. A leading commentator argues that inconsistency of statutory language among the States has significantly impeded the use of certification. [3]

The Uniform Act/Rule provides a relatively simple and efficient means by which federal courts and state appellate courts can efficiently obtain answers to questions of law from the highest court of the controlling State. [4] Where adopted, it would allow a federal court or state appellate court, having determined that the law of another State controls a controversy, to avoid guessing what that law is when there is no definitive answer in the law of the controlling State. In-

stead, the court would simply certify the question of law to the highest court of the controlling State.

A combined *Erie* and state conflicts problem can also be handled under the Uniform Act/Rule. For example, a federal court sitting in State A might decide that the *Erie* doctrine applies so it should look to the law of State A on a problem. The federal court might then decide that the court in State A, under its conflicts of law rules, would look to the law of State B for the solution of the legal problem. Under the Uniform Act/Rule, the federal court in State A can ask the court in State B to answer the unsettled issue of its law on the point.

It is reasonable to expect that the goal of encouraging courts to certify questions of law in appropriate cases will be advanced as judges and lawyers become more aware of and familiar with the certification process. To this end, uniformity of law in this area is highly desirable in that it is likely to result in the greater use of certification.

Adopted by Legislature or Court

The Conference has promulgated the Uniform Act/Rule for certified questions in a form which can be enacted by a legislature or adopted by a court as a rule. In some jurisdictions, action by the highest court will suffice with no legislative action required.

[3] Ira P. Robbins, *The Uniform Certification of Questions of Law Act: A Proposal for Reform*, 18 JOURNAL OF LEGISLATION 127, 183 (1992). *See also,* Ira P. Robbins, *Interstate Certification of Questions of Law: A Valuable Process in Need of Reform,* 76 JUDICATURE 125 (1992); John B. Corr & Ira P. Robbins, *Interjurisdictional Certification and Choice of Law,* 41 VANDERBILT LAW REVIEW 411 (1988).

[4] The inclusion of certain bracketed language in sections 1, 2, and 3 of the Uniform Act/Rule would also authorize the state appellate court

to certify questions of law to a tribal court or answer questions of law from a tribal court. In addition, bracketed language in Sections 2 and 3 would, if included in the Act or Rule, authorize certifications to, and answers to questions from, appropriate courts in the jurisdictions of Mexico and Canada.

UNIFORM CERTIFICATION OF QUESTIONS
OF LAW [ACT] [RULE] (1995)

SECTION 1. DEFINITION[S]

In this [Act] [Rule]:

(1) "State" means a State of the United States, the District of Columbia, the Commonwealth of Puerto Rico, or any territory or insular possession subject to the jurisdiction of the United States.

[(2) "Tribe" means a tribe, band, or village of native Americans which is recognized by federal law or formally acknowledged by a State.]

Comment

A section containing definitions was not part of the 1967 Act. The definition of "State" is consistent with that used in other Uniform Acts.

The section affords States the option of authorizing a state court to certify questions to a tribal court or answer questions from a tribal court. However, it does not purport to authorize tribal courts to certify or answer questions. Tribal law determines whether the tribal court may certify a question to a state court or answer a question from a state court. A Tribe can adopt this Act as enabling legislation by simply replacing references to "this State" with "this Tribe" and by substituting the name of its highest court for the "Supreme Court" in Sections 2 and 3.

The definition of "Tribe" is broad and is intended to include both Native American tribes in the technical sense of that term and other Native American governmental units that perform functions similar to a tribe. The option of limiting the definition of "tribes" to those listed in 25 C.F.R. Part 2 was rejected because that list does not include certain Native American governmental units that have existing court systems.

SECTION 2. POWER TO CERTIFY

The [Supreme Court] [or an intermediate appellate court] of this State, on the motion of a party to pending litigation or its own motion, may certify a question of law to the highest court of another State [or of a tribe] [or of Canada, a Canadian province or territory, Mexico, or a Mexican state] if:

(1) the pending litigation involves a question to be decided under the law of the other jurisdiction;

(2) the answer to the question may be determinative of an issue in the pending litigation; and

(3) the question is one for which an answer is not provided by a controlling appellate decision, constitutional provision, or statute of the other jurisdiction.

Comment

This section replaces Section 8 of the 1967 Act. This revision organizes the Act so that the Power to Certify is set forth prior to the Power to Answer which makes the order of the Act easier to follow. Although limiting the power to certify to the highest court of a State would reduce the number of courts that could certify and correspondingly reduce the number of certified questions, the bracketed language from the 1967 Act authorizing certification by intermediate appellate courts is retained. The receiving court has the discretion to accept or reject a certified question and can use this power to avoid being burdened by an excessive number of certified questions.

As noted in the Comment to Section 1, this section affords States the option of permitting certification of a question of tribal law to a tribal court having the power to answer such questions.

Also included as an option is the bracketed language in this section and in Section 3 permitting certification to and from Canada, a Canadian province or territory, Mexico or a Mexican state. Because the concept of certification to and from international tribunals and courts of other nations still presents numerous uncertainties, this section does not include such other tribunals and courts at this time. Obviously, the enacting State is free to include any other courts it may choose.

The provisions of Section 8 of the 1967 Act have been revised to make it clear that certification is appropriate only when there is no "controlling constitutional provisions, statute or appellate decision" in the receiving State. This language replaces the term "controlling precedents" as used in the 1967 Act.

The 1967 Act's standard that a question may be certified if it "may be determinative of the cause" was revised to require that it "may be determinative of an issue in the pending litigation." A stricter standard requiring that the question

958

"must be" or "is" determinative of the issue of the cause was rejected due to concerns that a "must be" or "is" standard would spawn satellite controversies over whether the question was properly certified in light of the ultimate outcome of the underlying litigation.

SECTION 3. POWER TO ANSWER

The [Supreme Court] of this State may answer a question of law certified to it by a court of the United States or by [an appellate] [the highest] court of another State [or of a tribe] [or of Canada, a Canadian province or territory, Mexico, or a Mexican state], if the answer may be determinative of an issue in pending litigation in the certifying court and there is no controlling appellate decision, constitutional provision, or statute of this State.

Comment

This section replaces Section 1 of the 1967 Act. Revisions were made to this section to make it consistent with the "Power to Certify" section. The existence of a controlling constitutional provision, statute or appellate decision in the receiving State is a barrier to answering a certified question.

This section has been revised to replace the previous list of federal courts with the term "a court of the United States." This is intended to permit a court in a State adopting the section to answer questions certified by any United States court including bankruptcy courts. Ultimately, the receiving court retains the power to accept or reject a certified question so that it can control its docket even though the number of courts from whom it may receive a certified question has been expanded.

In dealing with the phrase "[an appellate] [the highest] court of another State ..." appearing in this section, an adopting jurisdiction should select one or the other of the bracketed alternatives. This Act seeks to promote the widest possible use of the certification process in order to promote judicial economy and the proper application of a particular jurisdiction's law in a foreign forum. For this reason, it is suggested that the first alternative be adopted. The term "appellate court" here contemplates any appellate court that has the ability to issue an officially published opinion with precedential effect in a jurisdiction; the term would not include, for example, a general trial court that has appellate jurisdiction from a limited trial court but whose rulings are not officially reported as precedent.

In view of the discretion vested by the Act in the receiving court to accept or reject questions, a reciprocity requirement is not included in the Act. However, in determining whether to accept a certified question, the receiving court may consider among other factors, whether the highest appellate court of the State from which the certification order is issued has authority to answer a certified question of law from an appellate court of the receiving State under essentially similar provisions.

SECTION 4. POWER TO REFORMULATE QUESTION

The [Supreme Court] of this State may reformulate a question of law certified to it.

Comment

This section is new and authorizes the receiving court to "reformulate" the certified question. Requiring a question to be answered precisely as it is certified imposes a counterproductive rigidity that could decrease the utility of the answer received. Permitting the receiving court to amend the certified question freely may also adversely affect the utility of the answer and result in the issuance of an advisory opinion. The term "reformulate" is intended to connote a retention of the specific terms and concepts of the question while allowing some flexibility in restating the question in light of the justiciable controversy pending before the certifying court.

SECTION 5. CERTIFICATION ORDER; RECORD

The court certifying a question of law to the [Supreme Court] of this State shall issue a certification order and forward it to the [Supreme Court] of this State. Before responding to a certified question, the [Supreme Court] of this State may require the certifying court to deliver all or part of its record to the [Supreme Court] of this State.

Comment

This section replaces Section 4 of the 1967 Act. The title of the section has been amended to indicate that the section deals not only with the issuance of the order but also with the handling of the record. The first sentence is deliberately less specific so as to accommodate different procedures that may exist in the courts of the various States.

SECTION 6. CONTENTS OF CERTIFICATION ORDER

(a) A certification order must contain:

(1) the question of law to be answered;

(2) the facts relevant to the question, showing fully the nature of the controversy out of which the question arose;

(3) a statement acknowledging that the [Supreme Court] of this State, acting as the receiving court, may reformulate the question; and

(4) the names and addresses of counsel of record and parties appearing without counsel.

(b) If the parties cannot agree upon a statement of facts, the certifying court shall determine the relevant facts and state them as a part of its certification order.

Comment

This section replaces Section 3 of the 1967 Act. It makes three changes. First, it provides that the order must expressly permit the receiving court to reformulate the question certified to it. Second, the new section requires that the certification order state the names and addresses of counsel of record and of unrepresented parties. This is intended for the convenience of the receiving court. Third, it requires the parties to attempt to agree on a statement of facts to be included in the certification order and requires the certifying court to determine the relevant facts and state them if the parties cannot agree.

This section applies to certification orders being issued to an adopting jurisdiction. Under the second sentence of Section 8 of this Act, the contents required in a certification order being sent by an adopting jurisdiction to another jurisdiction are governed by the rules and statutes of that receiving forum.

SECTION 7. NOTICE; RESPONSE

The [Supreme Court] of this State, acting as a receiving court, shall notify the certifying court of acceptance or rejection of the question and, in accordance with notions of comity and fairness, respond to an accepted certified question as soon as practicable.

Comment

This section is new and is intended to promote communication between the receiving and certifying court and to urge the receiving court to afford priority to answering certified questions of law consistent with notions of comity and fairness. The receiving court, may, but is not obligated to, advise the certifying court of the reasons for a rejection.

SECTION 8. PROCEDURES

After the [Supreme Court] of this State has accepted a certified question, proceedings are governed by [the rules and statutes governing briefs, arguments, and other appellate procedures]. Procedures for certification from this State to a receiving court are those provided in the rules and statutes of the receiving forum.

Comment

This section replaces Sections 6 and 9 of the 1967 Act.

SECTION 9. OPINION

The [Supreme Court] of this State shall state in a written opinion the law answering the certified question and send a copy of the opinion to the certifying court, counsel of record, and parties appearing without counsel.

Comment

This section is substantively the same as Section 7 of the 1967 Act. The Act contemplates an officially published opinion which will have precedential effect in the receiving State.

SECTION 10. COST OF CERTIFICATION

Fees and costs are the same as in [civil appeals] docketed before the [Supreme Court] of this State and must be equally divided between the parties unless otherwise ordered by the certifying court.

Comment

This section is substantively unchanged from Section 5 of the 1967 Act.

SECTION 11. SEVERABILITY

If any provision of this [Act] [Rule] or its application to any person or circumstance is held invalid, the invalidity does not affect other provisions or applications of this [Act] [Rule] which can be given effect without the invalid provision or application, and to this end the provisions of this [Act] [Rule] are severable.

Comment

This section is substantively the same as Section 10 of the 1967 Act.

SECTION 12. UNIFORMITY OF APPLICATION AND CONSTRUCTION

This [Act] [Rule] shall be applied and construed to effectuate its general purpose to make uniform law with respect to the subject of the [Act] [Rule] among States [enacting] [adopting] it.

Comment

This section is substantively the same as Section 11 of the 1967 Act.

SECTION 13. SHORT TITLE

This [Act] [Rule] may be cited as the Uniform Certification of Questions of Law [Act] [Rule] (1995).

Comment

This section is substantively the same as Section 12 of the 1967 Act.

SECTION 14. EFFECTIVE DATE

This [Act] [Rule] takes effect on _____.

Comment

This section is substantively the same as Section 13 of the 1967 Act.

UNIFORM ENFORCEMENT OF FOREIGN JUDGMENTS ACT

1964 REVISED ACT

Historical Note

The Revised Uniform Enforcement of Foreign Judgments Act was approved by the National Conference of commissioners on Uniform State Laws, and the American Bar Association, in 1964. The original Act, as adopted in 1948, is not duplicated in this pamphlet.

PREFATORY NOTE

Court congestion is a problem common to all states. Overcrowded dockets, overworked judges and court officials, with attendant delays, inevitably tend to lower standards for the administration of justice. One of the things that contributes to calendar congestion is the Federal necessity of giving full faith and credit to the judgments of courts of other states. U.S. Const. art. IV, § 1. While there is no constitutional requirement that a debtor who has had a full due process trial in one state need be given a second full scale trial on the judgment in another state, this is the only course generally available to creditors. The usual practice requires that an action be commenced on the foreign judgment. The full procedural requirements apply to the second action.

In 1948 the National Conference of Commissioners on Uniform State Laws approved the original Uniform Enforcement of Foreign Judgments Act. This act was a distinct advance over the usual method. It provided a summary judgment procedure for actions on foreign judgments. Even this advance, however, fell far short of the method provided by Congress in 1948 for the inter-district enforcement of the judgments of the Federal District Courts. 28 U.S.C., § 1963. Further, widespread adoption by the states of some form of the Federal Rules of Civil Procedure which include regular summary judgment practice made special summary judgment acts superfluous.

This 1964 revision of the Uniform Enforcement of Foreign Judgments Act adopts the practice which, in substance, is used in Federal courts. It provides the enacting state with a speedy and economical method of doing that which it is required to do by the Constitution of the United States. It also relieves creditors and debtors of the additional cost and harassment of further litigation which would otherwise be incident to the enforcement of the foreign judgment. This act offers the states a chance to achieve uniformity in a field where uniformity is highly desirable. Its enactment by the states should forestall Federal legislation in this field.

UNIFORM ENFORCEMENT OF FOREIGN JUDGMENTS ACT

Be it enacted

§ 1. [Definition]

In this Act "foreign judgment" means any judgment, decree, or order of a court of the United States or of any other court which is entitled to full faith and credit in this state.

§ 2. [Filing and Status of Foreign Judgments]

A copy of any foreign judgment authenticated in accordance with the act of Congress or the statutes of this state may be filed in the office of the Clerk of any [District Court of any city or county] of this state. The Clerk shall treat the foreign judgment in the same manner as a judgment of the [District Court of any city or county] of this state. A judgment so filed has the same effect and is subject to the same procedures, defenses and proceedings for reopening, vacating, or staying as a judgment of a [District Court of any city or county] of this state and may be enforced or satisfied in like manner.

§ 3. [Notice of Filing]

(a) At the time of the filing of the foreign judgment, the judgment creditor or his lawyer shall make and file with the Clerk of Court an affidavit setting forth the name and last known post office address of the judgment debtor, and the judgment creditor.

(b) Promptly upon the filing of the foreign judgment and the affidavit, the Clerk shall mail notice of the filing of the foreign judgment to the judgment debtor at the address given and shall make a note of the mailing in the docket. The notice shall include the name and post office address of the judgment creditor and the judgment creditor's lawyer, if any, in this state. In addition, the judgment creditor may mail a notice of the filing of the judgment to the judgment debtor and may file proof of mailing with the Clerk. Lack of mailing notice of filing by the Clerk shall not affect the enforcement proceedings if proof of mailing by the judgment creditor has been filed.

[(c) No execution or other process for enforcement of a foreign judgment filed hereunder shall issue until [_____] days after the date the judgment is filed.]

§ 4. [Stay]

(a) If the judgment debtor shows the [District Court of any city or county] that an appeal from the foreign judgment is pending or will be taken, or that a stay of execution has been granted, the court shall stay enforcement of the foreign judgment until the appeal is concluded, the time for appeal expires, or the stay of execution expires or is vacated, upon proof that the judgment debtor has furnished the security for the satisfaction of the judgment required by the state in which it was rendered.

(b) If the judgment debtor shows the [District Court of any city or county] any ground upon which enforcement of a judgment of any [District Court of any city or county] of this state would be stayed, the court shall stay enforcement of the foreign judgment for an appropriate period, upon requiring the same security for satisfaction of the judgment which is required in this state.

§ 5. [Fees]

Any person filing a foreign judgment shall pay to the Clerk of Court _____ dollars. Fees for docketing, transcription or other enforcement proceedings shall be as provided for judgments of the [District Court of any city or county of this state].

§ 6. [Optional Procedure]

The right of a judgment creditor to bring an action to enforce his judgment instead of proceeding under this Act remains unimpaired.

§ 7. [Uniformity of Interpretation]

This Act shall be so interpreted and construed as to effectuate its general purpose to make uniform the law of those states which enact it.

§ 8. **[Short Title]**

This Act may be cited as the Uniform Enforcement of Foreign Judgments Act.

§ 9. **[Repeal]**

The following Acts and parts of Acts are repealed:

(1)

(2)

(3)

§ 10. **[Taking Effect]**

This Act takes effect on _____.

UNIFORM INTERSTATE AND INTERNATIONAL
PROCEDURE ACT

Historical Note

The Uniform Interstate and International Procedure Act was approved by the National Conference of Commissioners on Uniform State Laws, and the American Bar Association, in 1962. It supersedes the Uniform Foreign Depositions Act (1920), the Uniform Judicial Notice of Foreign Law Act (1936), and the Uniform Proof of Statutes Act (1920).

PREFATORY NOTE

Civil litigation with interstate and international aspects is becoming an increasingly important element of judicial business. In many cases it is necessary to perform a procedural act, either with or without assistance from local officials, in a sister state or a foreign country. Conversely, domestic courts are being requested with greater frequency to render assistance to out-of-state tribunals and litigants. Unfortunately, existing law is frequently difficult to ascertain, inadequate, and ill-adjusted to conditions prevailing outside the forum state. The American Bar Association, recognizing the need for reform, recommended shortly after the Second World War that the President establish a Commission to investigate, and suggest measures for the improvement of existing procedures. In 1952, the President approved this recommendation, and in 1958, the United States Congress enacted legislation to establish a Commission and Advisory Committee on International Rules of Judicial Procedure. Act of Sept. 2, 1958, 72 Stat. 1743. This Commission and its Advisory Committee, in co-operation with the Columbia Law School Project on International Procedure, has drafted several amendments to the Federal Rules of Civil and Criminal Procedure and Titles 18, 22 and 28 of the United States Code that are presently being considered for adoption.

The Uniform Interstate and International Procedure Act presents for adoption by the states a comprehensive code for use in state litigation with interstate or international incidents. It is designed to clarify, consolidate, and improve existing law, and supplants the Uniform Foreign Depositions Act, the Uniform Judicial Notice of Foreign Law Act, and the Uniform Proof of Statutes Act.

Article I, a modified version of the Uniform Extra–Territorial Process Act, which was before the Conference at its 1961 meeting, specifies authorized bases of personal jurisdiction over persons and entities that are not within the state at the time the action is commenced. Article II provides several alternative methods by which service may be effected outside the state. Article III is designed to facilitate the taking of depositions to obtain testimony, documents, and other tangible evidence outside the state for use in domestic litigation. Both Article II and Article III contain provisions for rendering assistance to tribunals and litigants outside the enacting state. Article IV resolves problems attendant upon the determination of the law of a governmental unit outside the forum state. Article V concerns proof of official records kept outside the state.

UNIFORM INTERSTATE AND INTERNATIONAL PROCEDURE ACT

Be it enacted

Article I

BASES OF PERSONAL JURISDICTION OVER PERSONS OUTSIDE THIS STATE

§ 1.01 [Definition of Person]

As used in this Article, "person" includes an individual, his executor, administrator, or other personal representative, or a corporation, partnership, association or any other legal or commercial entity, whether or not a citizen or domiciliary of this state and whether or not organized under the laws of this state.

COMMENT

The definition of "person" used in this section is derived in part from section 1–201(28) (30) of the 1958 official text of the Uniform Commercial Code. Certain modifications in the definition appearing in that act have been necessary in order to conform to the subject matter of this article. Including a personal representative in the definition of a person permits acquisition of jurisdiction when acts of a deceased or an incompetent provide the basis of jurisdiction under this article.

In some cases the law of a state may require service on one or more specific individuals in order for jurisdiction to be acquired over a person. See comment to section 2.03.

The definition of "person" applies only to article I. In articles II through VI the word "person" is used in its ordinary sense. In states defining the word "person," that definition will apply to articles II through VI.

§ 1.02 [Personal Jurisdiction Based upon Enduring Relationship]

A court may exercise personal jurisdiction over a person domiciled in, organized under the laws of, or

maintaining his or its principal place of business in, this state as to any [cause of action] [claim for relief].

COMMENT

Section 1.02 sets forth bases for the exercise by a state of personal jurisdiction over a person who is outside the state as to any cause of action or claim for relief. In the situations dealt with in section 1.02 the defendant's enduring relationship or continuing contact with the state justifies the exercise of a wide range of jurisdiction.

Both the state where an individual is domiciled and the state where he maintains his principal place of business are authorized to exercise personal jurisdiction over him in all situations. This is a somewhat broader range of jurisdiction that states have customarily sought to exercise over individuals who maintain their principal place of business in the state.

The state where a legal entity was organized as well as the state where it maintains its principal place of business are permitted to exercise personal jurisdiction over the entity in all situations. This may constitute an expansion of the jurisdiction customarily exercised over an unincorporated association which maintains its principal place of business in the state. See Magruder & Foster, Jurisdiction over Partnerships, 37 Harv.L.Rev. 793, 828 (1924); Restatement (Second), Conflicts § 86 (Tent.Draft No. 3, 1956); Restatement, Judgments § 24 (1942); cf. Isaacs, Amenability of Unions to Service of Process, 32 N.Y.S.Bar Bull. 24 (1960). No change is made in the rules stating which persons have to be served in order to acquire jurisdiction; thus, local law that all members of an unincorporated association must be joined and served or only named officers need be named and served remains unchanged. See, *e.g.*, N.Y.Gen.Assoc.Law § 13 (president or treasurer).

In view of the increased possibility of acquiring personal jurisdiction under section 1.03, it is unnecessary to subject a corporation to suit on any cause of action or claim for relief in the many states in which it may be "doing business." In this respect section 1.02 restricts somewhat the jurisdiction some states have purported to exercise over foreign corporations which do business in the state but do not there maintain their principal place of business. The phrase "principal place of business" used in section 1.02 appears in the recent amendment to the United States Code covering diversity jurisdiction. See 28 U.S.C. § 1332 (1952).

"Cause of action" is the phrase used in the statutes, rules and cases of some states and is based upon the common law and Field Code; "claim for relief" is used in the Federal Rules of Civil Procedure and the law of those states based upon those rules. For purposes of the Uniform Interstate and International Procedure Act, they have the same meaning. See Comment to section 1.03(b).

§ 1.03 [Personal Jurisdiction Based upon Conduct]

(a) A court may exercise personal jurisdiction over a person, who acts directly or by an agent, as to a [cause of action] [claim for relief] arising from the person's

(1) transacting any business in this state;

(2) contracting to supply services or things in this state;

(3) causing tortious injury by an act or omission in this state;

(4) causing tortious injury in this state by an act or omission outside this state if he regularly does or solicits business, or engages in any other persistent course of conduct, or derives substantial revenue from goods used or consumed or services rendered, in this state; [or]

(5) having an interest in, using, or possessing real property in this state [; or

(6) contracting to insure any person, property, or risk located within this state at the time of contracting].

(b) When jurisdiction over a person is based solely upon this section, only a [cause of action] [claim for relief] arising from acts enumerated in this section may be asserted against him.

COMMENT

Each of the subdivisions in subsection (a) will independently support jurisdiction. In some instances, a jurisdictional basis may be found under more than one subdivision. Thus, a defendant's liability may arise under subdivision (1) "transacting business" and either subdivision (3) "causing tortious injury by an act or omission in this state" or subdivision (4) "causing a tortious injury in this state by an act or omission outside this state." Each of the subdivisions will support a cause of action under any theory of law. For example, a claim arising from "transacting business" may sound in contract, tort, or quasi contract. See comment to section 1.03(b).

The question whether a statute of limitations should be tolled even though jurisdiction over the defendant can be acquired under this article is not treated in this act. Whether a statute is tolled under these circumstances will depend upon an interpretation of its provisions.

Section 1.03(a)(1) is derived from the Illinois Act. Ill.Stat. Ann. c. 110, § 17(1)(a). This provision should be given the same expansive interpretation that was intended by the draftsmen of the Illinois Act and has been given by the courts of that state. See, e.g., Berlemann v. Superior Distributing Co., 17 Ill.App.2d 522, 151 N.E.2d 116 (1958). See generally Jenner, Jr. & Tone, Historical and Practice Notes, Smith–Hurd Illinois Stat.Ann. c. 110, § 17 (1956), id. (1961 Supp.); Cleary & Seder, Extended Jurisdictional Bases for the Illinois Courts, 50 Nw.U.L.Rev. 599, 607–09 (1955). The "transaction of any business in a state" is employed as a jurisdictional basis by an ever increasing number of state statutes. Mich.Stat.Ann. §§ 27A.705, 27A.715, 27A.725, 27A.735; N.Y.C.P.L.R. § 302(a)(1) (effective Sept. 1, 1963); Tenn.Code Ann. § 20–220; cf. N.H.Rev.Stat.Ann. § 300:11; Wyo.Stat.Ann. § 17–44.

Section 1.03(a)(2) is derived from Mich.Stat.Ann. §§ 27A.705, 27A.715, 27A.725, 27A.735. Essentially similar provisions are Mont.R.Civ.Pr. 4B(1)(e); Wis.Stat.Ann. tit. 25, § 262.05. Broad statutes which base jurisdiction upon the entry into a contract "to be performed in whole or in part by either party in the state" are Minn.Stat.Ann. § 303.13; Vt. Stat.Ann. tit. 12, § 855; cf. N.C.Gen.Stat. § 55–145(1).

The North Carolina statute (§ 55–145(3)) bases jurisdiction upon "the production, manufacture, or distribution of goods by such corporation with the reasonable expectation that those goods are to be used or consumed in this State and are so used or consumed" This provision was held unconstitutional as applied to the facts of the case in Erlanger Mills v. Cohoes Fibre Mills, 239 F.2d 502 (4th Cir.1956) and in Putnam v. Triangle Publications, 245 N.C. 432, 96 S.E.2d 445 (1957). On the other hand, it was held constitutional in Shepard v. Rheem Mfg. Co., 249 N.C. 454, 106 S.E.2d 704 (1959).

The constitutionality of section 1.03(a)(2) is supported by WSAZ, Inc. v. Lyons, 254 F.2d 242 (6th Cir.1958); Berlemann v. Superior Distributing Co., 17 Ill.App.2d 522, 151 N.E.2d 116 (1958); Beck v. Spindler, 256 Minn. 543, 99 N.W.2d 670 (1959); S. Howes Co. v. W.P. Milling Co., 277 P.2d 655 (Okla.1954); cf. McGee v. International Life Ins. Co., 355 U.S. 220 (1957).

Section 1.03(a)(3) applies when the tortious act or omission occurs in the state even though the resulting injury occurs elsewhere. The state where the tortious act or omission occurs will often be the most appropriate location for the trial of the action. Nelson v. Miller, 11 Ill.2d 378, 143 N.E.2d 673 (1957); Smyth v. Twin State Improvement Corp., 116 Vt. 569, 80 A.2d 664 (1951). For a similar approach, see Wis. Stat.Ann. tit. 25, § 262.05(3).

Section 1.03(1)(3) may have a narrower range of application than statutes which base jurisdiction upon the "commission of a tortious act" within the state (see, e.g., Ill.Stat.Ann. c. 110, § 17(1)(b); Me.Rev.Stat.Ann. c. 112, § 21(I)(B); N.Y.C.P.L.R. § 302(a)(2) (effective Sept. 1, 1963); N.C.Gen. Stat. §§ 55–145(a)), or upon the commission of a tort "in whole or in part" in the state. See, e.g., Minn.Stat.Ann. § 303.13(3); Vt.Stat.Ann. tit. 12, § 855. Some of these statutes have been interpreted to cover acts or omissions outside the state. See discussion of section 1.03(a)(4) below.

Section 1.03(a)(4) authorizes the exercise of jurisdiction when the tortious act or omission takes place without the state but the injury occurs within the state and there is some other reasonable connection between the state and the defendant. For a similar approach, see Wis.Stat.Ann. tit. 25, § 262.05(4). The rule is more restrictive than the Illinois statutes, as interpreted in Gray v. American Radiator & Standard Sanitary Corp., 22 Ill.2d 432, 176 N.E.2d 761 (1961), and the Michigan statute (Mich.Stat.Ann. §§ 27A.705, 27A.715, 27A.725, 27A.735). A sufficient nexus exists if (a) the defendant regularly advertises his products or services in the state or (b) carries on some other continuous course of activity there or (c) derives substantial revenue from goods used or consumed or from services rendered in the state. It is not necessary that this activity amount to the doing of business.

It should be noted that the regular solicitation of business or the persistent course of conduct required by section 1.03(a)(4) need have no relationship to the act or failure to act that caused the injury. No distinctions are drawn between types of tort actions.

In sustaining the exercise of jurisdiction over a defendant who has caused injury in the state by means of a tortious act done outside the state, the courts have often emphasized that the defendant had contacts with the state that bore no relation to the particular tort. See, e.g., Green v. Robertshaw–Fulton Controls Co., 204 F.Supp. 117 (S.D.Ind.1962);

Sonnier v. Time, 172 F.Supp. 576 (W.D.La.1959); Becker v. General Motors, 167 F.Supp. 164 (D.Md.1958); Jenkins v. Dell Publishing Co., 130 F.Supp. 104 (W.D.Pa.1955); Gordon Armstrong Co. v. Superior Court, 160 Cal.App.2d 211, 325 P.2d 21 (1958); Adamek v. Michigan Door Co., 260 Minn. 54, 108 N.W.2d 607 (1961); Shepard v. Rheem Mfg. Co., 249 N.C. 454, 106 S.E.2d 704 (1959).

Section 1.03(a)(5) is similar to statutes found in several states. See, e.g., Ill.Stat.Ann. c. 110, § 17(1)(c); Me.Rev. Stat.Ann. c. 112, § 21(I)(C); N.Y.C.P.L.R. § 302(a)(3) (effective Sept. 1, 1963); Pa.Stat.Ann. c. 1, tit. 12, § 331. See Dubin v. City of Philadelphia, 34 Pa.D. & C. 61 (Phil.Cty.Ct.1938); cf. N.J.R. 4:4–4(i). See generally, Note, Ownership, Possession or Use of the Property as a Basis of In Personam Jurisdiction, 44 Iowa L.Rev. 374 (1959). The provision is confined to actions arising from the ownership of an interest in, use or possession of real property. Although the Michigan and Wisconsin statutes (Mich.Stat.Ann. §§ 27A.705, 27A.715, 27A.725, 27A.735 (1962); Wis.Stat.Ann. tit. 25, § 262.05(6)) include the ownership, use or possession of personal property as a basis of jurisdiction, this basis has been excluded because of the difficulties that might be posed in situations such as those involving stolen property, conditional sales and chattel mortgages.

Section 1.03(a)(6) is derived from the Illinois and Michigan statutes. Ill.Stat.Ann. c. 110, § 17(1)(d); Mich.Stat.Ann. § 27A.705(4). The provision is placed in brackets because many states have similar and more explicit provisions in their insurance law. It is appropriate to treat this matter, which affects the insurance practice within the state, as part of the state's regulatory scheme for this industry. The power of the states in this area has been widely recognized. See, e.g., McGee v. International Life Ins. Co., 355 U.S. 220 (1957).

Not proposed for adoption are other special provisions better considered in connection with the substantive area of the law to which they relate. For example, the Michigan statute provides as a jurisdictional basis "Acting as a director, manager, trustee, or other officer of any corporation incorporated under the laws of, or having its principal place of business within, the state of Michigan." Mich.Stat.Ann. § 27A.705(6). A provision of this sort is of substantial importance in connection with shareholder derivative suits. It would most appropriately be placed with other statutes directly relating to corporations.

Section 1.03(b) is derived from Ill.Stat.Ann. c. 110, § 17(3), cf. N.Y.C.P.L.R. § 302(b) (effective Sept. 1, 1963).

The concept of cause of action or claim for relief should be broadly construed to cover an entire transaction so that, when possible, the entire dispute may be settled in a single litigation. Subdivision (b) is designed to prevent assertion of independent claims unrelated to any activity described in subdivision (a) of section 1.03.

A defendant may appear and consent to unlimited jurisdiction if he prefers to litigate all aspects of a related dispute. In states having a compulsory counterclaim rule, it may be desirable to provide that the defendant need not plead a counterclaim if jurisdiction is acquired under section 1.03. Cf. Proposed Amendments and Notes to Federal Rule 13, Preliminary Draft of Proposed Amendments to Rules of Civil Procedure for the United States District Courts 18–19 (October, 1961).

§ 1.04 [Service Outside the State]

When the exercise of personal jurisdiction is authorized by this Article, service may be made outside this state.

COMMENT

Section 1.04 explicitly authorizes service of process outside the state when personal jurisdiction is based on this Article. See Uniform Interstate and International Procedure Act, Article II, infra.

§ 1.05 [Inconvenient Forum]

When the court finds that in the interest of substantial justice the action should be heard in another forum, the court may stay or dismiss the action in whole or in part on any conditions that may be just.

COMMENT

This provision is derived from Wis.Stat.Ann. tit. 25, § 262.19. The Wisconsin provision contains details on motion practice that are not appropriate for a uniform statute. Among the factors listed in the Wisconsin provision that may be relied upon under section 1.05 in determining whether a case should be heard in another jurisdiction are the following:

(a) amenability of the parties to personal jurisdiction in the state and in any alternative forum;

(b) convenience to the parties and witnesses of trial in the state and in any alternative forum;

(c) differences in conflict of law rules applicable in the state and in any alternative forum; or

(d) any other factors having substantial bearing upon the selection of a convenient, reasonable and fair place of trial. Possible conditions for granting the stay suggested in the Wisconsin provision are consent of the parties to suit in the alternative forum and waiver of reliance upon statutes of limitations. See generally, Foster, Jr. Revision Notes, Wis.Stat.Ann. tit. 25, § 262.19 (West, Supp.1962).

§ 1.06 [Other Bases of Jurisdiction Unaffected]

A court of this state may exercise jurisdiction on any other basis authorized by law.

COMMENT

This Article does not purport to cover the bases of jurisdiction in a comprehensive or exhaustive fashion. The traditional bases of physical presence and of implied or actual consent are continued by section 1.06. And so too are quasi in rem and in rem jurisdiction. Where residence is an accepted basis, the use of the word "domicile" in section 1.02 of this Article does not exclude residence as a basis. States that adopt the entire Act, including section 6.01, should omit this section.

Article II

SERVICE

§ 2.01 [Manner and Proof of Service]

(a) When the law of this state authorizes service outside this state, the service, when reasonably calculated to give actual notice, may be made:

(1) by personal delivery in the manner prescribed for service within this state;

(2) in the manner prescribed by the law of the place in which the service is made for service in that place in an action in any of its courts of general jurisdiction;

(3) by any form of mail addressed to the person to be served and requiring a signed receipt;

(4) as directed by the foreign authority in response to a letter rogatory; or

(5) as directed by the court.

(b) Proof of service outside this state may be made by affidavit of the individual who made the service or in the manner prescribed by the law of this state, the order pursuant to which the service is made, or the law of the place in which the service is made for proof of service in an action in any of its courts of general jurisdiction. When service is made by mail, proof of service shall include a receipt signed by the addressee or other evidence of personal delivery to the addressee satisfactory to the court.

COMMENT

Service beyond the territorial limits of the state may involve difficulties that cannot be obviated by existing provisions, especially when service is attempted in a foreign country. See generally Smit & Miller, International Co-Operation in Civil Litigation—A Report on Practices and Procedures Prevailing in the United States 40–48 (Milan 1961); Smit, International Aspects of Federal Civil Procedure, 61 Colum.L.Rev. 1031, 1040–43 (1961). Service within the borders of some countries, when attempted in connection with litigation pending elsewhere, may be considered a judicial, and therefore a "sovereign," act that is offensive to the policy or contrary to the law of these countries. See also Note, 49 Am.J. of Int'l L. 379 (1955). Further, the enforcement of a judgment in the country in which the service was made may be embarrassed or prevented if the service did not comport with the law of that country.

By authorizing a series of alternatives when extra-territorial service is permitted by the law of the forum, section 2.01 permits accommodation to the policies and procedures of sister states and foreign countries. To make clear that due process notions remain applicable when service is made outside the state, a proviso has been inserted requiring that the service be reasonably calculated to give actual notice. See Milliken v. Meyer, 311 U.S. 457 (1940).

Service by personal delivery, permitted by section 2.01(1), is the manner of service that is not only traditionally pre-

ferred, but also most likely to lead to actual notice. See, e.g., Ill.Rev.Stat. c. 110, § 16; Wash.Rev.Code § 4.28.180. Specific provision for this type of service is desirable since some states fail to authorize service by personal delivery outside the state. E.g., Ark.Stat. §§ 27–339, 27–340; Calif.Ins.Code § 1612; N.Y.Veh. & Tfc.L. § 253.

Section 2.01(2) permits extraterritorial service to be made in the manner prescribed by the law of the place in which the service is effected. Provision for this manner of service is desirable since a foreign country is less likely to object to a manner of service prescribed by its own law than to other manners of service and since a number of foreign countries recognize foreign judgments only if they are based on service made in accordance with their laws. See Jones, International Judicial Assistance: Procedural Chaos and a Program for Reform, 62 Yale L.J. 515, 537 (1953); Smit, supra at 1041–42; Inter–American Judicial Committee, Report on Uniformity of Legislation on International Cooperation in Judicial Procedures 20 (1952). The chances of avoiding foreign objections and of obtaining foreign recognition of the domestic judgment will ordinarily be enhanced even further if, as permitted by section 2.02, the service pursuant to section 2.01(2) is made by a person designated by a court or the law of the foreign country. Ibid. However, the flexible provisions of section 2.02 do not exclude the possibility that service pursuant to section 2.01(2) be effected by another person. Careful study of the law of the foreign country should, of course, precede recourse to any manner of service.

Section 2.01(3), permitting service by mail requiring a signed receipt, provides for an inexpensive and expeditious manner of service. Since service by this form of mail requires activity within a foreign country only by that country's own postal authorities, it is unlikely to be forbidden abroad. And since service by this form of mail is reasonably calculated to lead to actual notice, constitutional problems are also avoided. See McGee v. International Life Ins. Co., 355 U.S. 220 (1957). Several states provide for service by registered mail. See, e.g., Ariz.R.Civ.Pr. 4(e)(2)(a); Hawaii Rev.Laws §§ 230–31, 230–32; Minn.Stat.Ann. § 303.13; Ohio Rev.Code § 3105.07. To insure that the documents reach the person to be served, section 2.01(3) requires that the mail be addressed to the person to be served and that a form of mail requiring a signed receipt be used. Both ordinary registered and certified mail and registered and certified mail, return receipt requested, meet the requirements of section 2.01(3). Certified mail, however, can be used only within the United States, its possessions and territories, and the careful process server will ordinarily employ registered or certified mail, return receipt requested, since this type of mail provides the most certain and efficient method of obtaining a signed receipt. Subsection (b) of this section, requiring that proof of service made pursuant to section 2.01(3) shall include a receipt signed by the addressee or other satisfactory evidence of delivery, provides an additional safeguard to insure that the mail actually reaches the addressee.

Recourse to service under section 2.01(4) will generally be necessary only in the case of service in a foreign country. A letter rogatory is a customary method for service outside the state in many parts of the world. See In re Letters Rogatory Out of First Civil Court of City of Mexico, 261 Fed. 652 (S.D.N.Y.1919); 44 Colum.L.Rev. 72 (1944); Note, 58 Yale L.J. 1193 (1949). In some countries, service in aid of litigation pending elsewhere can be accomplished only upon request to the foreign court, which in turn directs the service to be made. See, Jones, supra at 537; Longley, Serving Process, Subpoena and Other Documents in a Foreign Country, Proc.A.B.A., Sec. of Int'l & Comp.L. 34, 35 (1959); Smit, supra at 1041–42. When an examination of the law of the place in which the service is to be made indicates that the manners of service provided for in the other subsections may be objectionable, it is advisable for counsel to resort to section 2.01(4).

Section 2.01(5) adds flexibility by permitting the court to tailor the manner of service to fit the necessities of the particular case.

Subsection (b) is intended to facilitate proof of service outside the state. In addition to the more traditional forms of return, proof of service in accordance with the law of the place of service is permitted. This is a desirable alternative because in many countries foreign process servers, unaccustomed to the form or requirement of service prevalent in this country, have on occasion been unwilling to execute an affidavit of service. See Jones, International Judicial Assistance: Procedural Chaos and a Program for Reform, 62 Yale L.J. 515, 537 (1953); Longley, supra at 34, 35. Proof of service as directed by order of the court is permitted as a corollary to the manner of service permitted by section 2.01(5). The second sentence in the subsection is designed to insure that there be proper proof of delivery when service is made by mail under subsection (a)(3). On the type of evidence of delivery that may be satisfactory to a court when a return receipt is unavailable, see Aero Associates, Inc. v. La Metropolitana, 183 F.Supp. 357 (S.D.N.Y.1960).

The definition of "person" in section 1.01 is not applicable to articles II through VI. See comment to section 1.01.

§ 2.02 [Individuals Eligible to Make Service]

Service outside this state may be made by an individual permitted to make service of process under the law of this state or under the law of the place in which the service is made or who is designated by a court of this state.

COMMENT

Section 2.02 is intended to provide the party attempting service outside the state with an extensive group of persons eligible to make the service. In a foreign country, this will increase the possibility that the plaintiff will be able to find a person who can proceed unimpeded; it also may improve the chances of recognition of the judgment in the country of service. Under many state statutes, service can only be made by designated state or federal officials or special appointees, who, because directly connected with another "sovereign," may be offensive to the foreign country. See, e.g., Wyo.R.Civ.Pr. 4(c)(3). In addition, existing Department of State regulations do not permit our foreign service officials to serve process except in some narrowly defined cases. 22 C.F.R. §§ 92.85, 92.86, 92.92 (1958). Furthermore, when service is to be made outside the state, whether in a sister state or in a foreign country, service by an official of the forum state is ordinarily cumbersome and expensive.

§ 2.03 [Individuals to Be Served: Special Cases]

When the law of this state requires that in order to effect service one or more designated individuals be served, service outside this state under this Article must be made upon the designated individual or individuals.

COMMENT

Section 2.03 makes clear that when the law of the enacting state requires service on an individual in addition to, or in lieu of, service on a particular party, that requirement must be satisfied when service is made under this Article. Frequently, a requirement of this nature is imposed when one of the parties is an infant, incompetent, or an association or business organization. E.g., Wis.Stat.Ann. § 262.06(2). If service is to be made in a foreign country, it would also be advisable, for purposes of enforcing the judgment in that country, to comply with the service requirements of the foreign country as well as with the requirements of this section.

§ 2.04 [Assistance to Tribunals and Litigants Outside this State]

(a) [A court] [The _____ court] of this state may order service upon any person who is domiciled or can be found within this state of any document issued in connection with a proceeding in a tribunal outside this state. The order may be made upon application of any interested person or in response to a letter rogatory issued by a tribunal outside this state and shall direct the manner of service.

(b) Service in connection with a proceeding in a tribunal outside this state may be made within this state without an order of court.

(c) Service under this section does not, of itself, require the recognition or enforcement of an order, judgment, or decree rendered outside this state.

COMMENT

Section 2.04(a) authorizes judicial assistance to litigants and tribunals in sister states and foreign countries in making service within the enacting state. The bracketed matter is designed to give the enacting state a choice between authorizing all of its courts to render assistance or restricting these functions to one or more designated courts. The term "tribunal" is intended to encompass any body with judicial functions. A request for assistance in a letter rogatory will generally emanate from outside the United States. Under the law of a fair number of foreign countries, service abroad must or may be made by a letter rogatory addressed to a tribunal in the country in which the service is to be made See 44 Colum.L.Rev. 72 (1944). Both federal and state courts have been reluctant to comply with a letter rogatory containing a request for local service. See In Re Letters Rogatory Out of First Civil Court of City of Mexico, 261 Fed. 652 (S.D.N.Y.1919); Matter of Romero, 56 Misc. 319, 107 N.Y.Supp. 621 (Sup.Ct.1907).

Section 2.04(b) re-affirms the existing freedom to make service within a state of the United States on behalf of litigation pending elsewhere as long as the particular manner employed does not constitute a disturbance of the peace or other violation of law. See McCusker, Some United States Practices in International Judicial Assistance, 37 Dep't of State Bull. 808 (1957).

Section 2.04(c), providing that service under section 2.04 does not, of itself, require the recognition of an adjudication of the requesting tribunal, is designed to eliminate the objection that this section could be read to require a judgment based on such service be given greater effect than a judgment based on service made without judicial assistance.

§ 2.05 [Other Provisions of Law Unaffected]

This Article does not repeal or modify any other law of this state permitting another procedure for service.

COMMENT

Section 2.05 preserves any method for effecting extraterritorial service under the statutes, court rules, or judicial decisions of the enacting state. Many enactments and court decisions interpreting state statutes authorize such service. E.g., Me.Rev.Stat.Ann. c. 22, § 70; Minn.Stat.Ann. § 303.13; Wis.Stat.Ann. § 262.06; Chapman v. Superior Court, 162 Cal.App.2d 421, 328 P.2d 23 (Dist.Ct.App.1958); Ewing v. Thompson, 233 N.C. 564, 65 S.E.2d 17 (1951); Rushing v. Bush, 260 S.W.2d 900 (Tex.Ct.Civ.App.1953). Also preserved are any existing provisions for rendering assistance to foreign tribunals and litigants. States that adopt the entire Act, including section 6.01 should omit this section.

Article III

TAKING DEPOSITIONS

§ 3.01 [When and How a Deposition May Be Taken Outside this State]

(a) A deposition to obtain testimony or documents or other things in an action pending in this state may be taken outside this state:

(1) On reasonable notice in writing to all parties, setting forth the time and place for taking the deposition, the name and address of each person to be examined, if known, and if not known, a general description sufficient to identify him or the particular class or group to which he belongs and the name or descriptive title of the person before whom the deposition will be taken. The deposition may be taken before a person authorized to administer oaths in the place in which the deposition is taken by the law thereof or by the law of this state or the United States.

(2) Before a person commissioned by the court. The person so commissioned has the power by virtue of his commission to administer any necessary oath.

(3) Pursuant to a letter rogatory issued by the court. A letter rogatory may be addressed "To the Appropriate Authority in [here name the state or country]."

(4) In any manner before any person, at any time or place, or upon any notice stipulated by the parties. A person designated by the stipulation has the power by virtue of his designation to administer any necessary oath.

(b) A commission or a letter rogatory shall be issued after notice and application to the court, and on terms that are just and appropriate. It is not requisite to the issuance of a commission or a letter rogatory that the taking of the deposition in any other manner is impracticable or inconvenient, and both a commission and a letter rogatory may be issued in proper cases. Evidence obtained in a foreign country in response to a letter rogatory need not be excluded merely for the reason that it is not a verbatim transcript or that the testimony was not taken under oath or for any similar departure from the requirements for depositions taken within this state.

(c) When no action is pending, a court of this state may authorize a deposition to be taken outside this state of any person regarding any matter that may be cognizable in any court of this state. The court may prescribe the manner in which and the terms upon which the deposition shall be taken.

COMMENT

Under section 3.01(a)(1) a deposition may be taken anywhere outside the state on notice to all parties. It eliminates the distinction found in some states between depositions in sister states and foreign countries. See Ind.Ann.Stat. §§ 2–1516, 2–1518. It is also designed to bring improvement to existing provisions that are deficient in that they restrict the group of persons before whom examinations may be taken. E.g., Fla.R.Civ.Pr. 1.23(a). A deposition may be taken before a person who has authority to administer an oath in the place in which the examination is to be taken under the law of (1) the state in which the action is pending, or (2) the United States, or (3) the place in which the examination is to be taken. For a similar provision, see Ill.Ann.Stat. c. 110, § 101.19–2; Ala.Code tit. 7, § 474(12). See also Ky.R.Civ.Pr. 28.02; Mo.R.Civ.Pr. 57.03. The need to accommodate the public policy of many foreign countries makes it desirable to permit as large a group of persons as possible to take examinations. For instance, in a country that is inclined to regard the taking of depositions by a foreign official in aid of litigation pending in a court of another country as an infringement upon its sovereignty, it will be expedient to notice depositions before officers of the country in which the examination is taken. See generally Symposium, Letters Rogatory (Grossman ed. 1956); Smit & Miller, International Co–Operation in Civil Litigation—A

Report on Practices and Procedures Prevailing in the United States 48–55, 58–62 (Milan 1961); Doyle, Taking Evidence by Deposition and Letter Rogatory and Obtaining Documents in Foreign Territory, Proc.A.B.A., Sec.Int'l & Comp.L. 37 (1959); Heilpern, Procuring Evidence Abroad, 14 Tul.L.Rev. 29 (1939); Jones, International Judicial Assistance; Procedural Chaos and a Program for Reform, 62 Yale L.J. 515, 526–29 (1953); Note, 96 U. of Pa.L.Rev. 241 (1947); Smit, International Aspects of Federal Civil Procedure, 61 Colum.L.Rev. 1031, 1956–58 (1961).

Subsection (a)(2) permits examination outside the state pursuant to a commission issued by the court, a method long-recognized in this country. Stein v. Bowman, 38 U.S. (13 Peters) 209 (1839); Stocking v. Sage, 1 Conn. 519 (1816); Stiff v. Nugent, 17 La. (5 Rob.) 217 (216) (1843). A commission is an official appointment to take a deposition and is distinguished from a deposition under section 3.01(a)(1) by the fact that the latter is taken before a person designated by a party. Provision for a deposition by commission is found in most states. E.g., Calif.Code Civ.Pr. § 2024; Conn. Gen.Stat. tit. 52, c. 899, § 52–154; Ind.Stat.Ann. §§ 2–1516, 2–1518; Mo.R.Civ.Pr. 57.02, 57.04, 57.05. As a general rule, the commission will appoint a state official, a person competent to take testimony under the law of the foreign country, one of the United States consular officials stationed in the foreign country or some other appropriate person. See, e.g., Mass.Gen.Laws c. 233, § 41. The commission envisioned in section 3.01(a)(2) may provide either for oral examination or written interrogatories and cross-interrogatories. This liberality seems preferable to a provision that limits testimony by commission to written interrogatories. E.g., Wis.Stat. Ann. § 326.26(1). See also Mass.Gen.Laws c. 233, § 42. Should the issuing authority be of the opinion that due to expense or possible harassment the examination should be restricted to written interrogatories, it can so order.

The commission may be used in any foreign country, but any person involved in the taking of a deposition by commission should evaluate the sanctions that may be applied by him by any foreign country in which the taking of the deposition may be forbidden by local law. Compulsory process to assist a commissioner is frequently not available in civil law countries. In some instances, the appointment of a judicial officer in the country of examination may obviate any reluctance to permit the execution of the commission or provide compulsory process.

Section 3.01(a)(3) permits the taking of depositions pursuant to a letter rogatory. It should be necessary to resort to this alternative only to obtain testimony in a foreign country. As a general rule, a letter rogatory is sent abroad through our diplomatic channels. Some countries insist that it proceed in this manner. See, e.g., United States v. Paraffin Wax, 2255 Bags, 23 F.R.D. 289 (E.D.N.Y.1959) (Switzerland). In countries that object to the taking of depositions pursuant to stipulation, on notice, or by commission in aid of American litigation, a letter rogatory represents the only available method for the taking of depositions. Furthermore, if the witness is unwilling to testify and the foreign country will not issue a compulsory process in aid of an American commission, it may provide a means to compel his examination. See generally, Symposium, Letters Rogatory (Grossman ed. 1956).

In spite of the value of this device, comparatively few states, other than those that have adopted Rule 28(b) of the

Federal Rules of Civil Procedure, have provided for the letter rogatory. Among the states that have no provision for a letter rogatory, several courts have found implied authority for the issuance of a letter. Cf. In re Martinelli, 219 Mass. 58, 106 N.E. 557 (1914); State ex rel. Everett v. Bourne, 21 Ore. 218, 27 Pac. 1048 (1891). Specific authorization, however, is advisable.

Section 3.01(a)(4) is derived from Rule 29 of the Federal Rules of Civil Procedure. It appears in one form or another in the court rules of most states. E.g., Fla.R.Civ.Pr. 1.23(a); N.J.R.Civ.Pr. 4:19. Section 3.01(a)(4) permits the parties to shape the form of the examination to fit their particular needs and to limit expenses. It is included in this article because litigants should be given as much freedom in determining the terms of a deposition outside the state as they have in the case of a domestic deposition.

Section 3.01(b) gives the court discretion to fix the terms upon which to issue a commission or a letter rogatory. It can prescribe the method by which the depositions will be taken, the order and length of the examinations, and such collateral matters as the allocation of expenses. It must be kept in mind, however, that the rules and procedures in force in the place of examination may limit the effectiveness of the domestic court's discretion.

Many courts, both federal and state, have held that a letter rogatory will not be issued unless it is shown to be impossible or impractical to obtain a deposition by commission or on notice or that neither a commission nor a letter rogatory will be issued if another method for procuring testimony is available. See, e.g., United States v. Matles, 154 F.Supp. 574 (E.D.N.Y.1957); La Greca v. Giaquinta, 129 N.Y.S.2d 505 (Sup.Ct.Kings Cty.1954); Ohlweiler v. Ohlweiler, 72 Pa.Super. 518 (1919). On occasion these restrictions are embodied in procedural codes. See e.g., Calif.Code Civ.Pr. §§ 2018, 2024. They seem unsound. Since a letter rogatory will probably be the least expensive method for taking testimony abroad, litigants may prefer it to a deposition on notice or by commission. In many cases, it may be difficult to prove that testimony cannot be secured by other means. A letter rogatory may also be preferred when a witness will be a recalcitrant or when the witness states that he is willing to testify voluntarily, but the contingency exists that he will change his mind at the last moment and the foreign court will not order compulsory process. Section 3.01(b) eliminates the hierarchy among the types of depositions and provides that in appropriate cases a court may issue both a commission and a letter rogatory, the latter to be executed should the former fail. See Hite v. Keene, 137 Wis. 625, 119 N.W. 303 (1909).

In executing a letter rogatory, the courts of other countries may be expected to follow their customary procedure for taking depositions. In many non common-law countries, the judge questions the witness, sometimes without first administering an oath, attorneys put any supplemental questions, either to the witness or through the judge, and the judge dictates a summary of the testimony, which the witness acknowledges as correct. See Jones, supra, at 530–32; Doyle, supra, at 39–41; Smit, supra, at 1058–59. The last sentence of section 3.01(b) provides, contrary to the implications of some authority, that evidence obtained under a letter rogatory executed in a foreign country that does not strictly comply with the requirements of the forum state need not be excluded on that account. See The Mandu, 11 F.Supp. 845

(E.D.N.Y.1935). The section is consistent with several other cases. Nelson v. United States, 17 Fed.Cas. 1340 (No. 10,116) (C.C.D.Pa.1816); Winthrop v. Union Ins. Co., 30 Fed.Cas. 376 (No. 17,901) (C.C.D.Pa.1807); In re Derinza, 229 Mass. 435, 118 N.E. 942 (1918); Kueling v. Leherman, 9 Phil. 160, 30 Leg.Int. 432 (Dist.Ct.1873). The specific reference to the lack of an oath or a verbatim transcript is intended to be illustrative. Whether or to what degree the value or weight of the evidence may be affected by the method of taking or recording the testimony is left for determination by the trial court according to the circumstances of the particular case. Thus, if the testimony is taken under circumstances indicating that it is entitled to little credence it may be rejected. See Rhodes v. Industrial Commission, 77 Utah 408, 296 Pac. 600 (1931). Or, if the testimony is taken in a manner contrary to the procedure of the executive court, the court in which the action is pending may, in its discretion, reject it.

Subsection (c) permits the taking of a deposition outside the state when no action is pending and evidence must be preserved or is needed to assist any person in framing a complaint or for any other reason deemed sufficient by the court. Cf. Ark.Stat.Ann. § 28–348; Fla.R.Civ.Pr. 1.22. Although most states provide for the perpetuation of testimony, several statutes and rules are not readily adaptable to depositions outside the states. E.g., Minn.R.Civ.Pr. 27.01; Mo. Ann.Stat. § 492.440.

The definition of "person" in section 1.01 is not applicable to articles II through VI. See comment to section 1.01.

§ 3.02 [Assistance to Tribunals and Litigants Outside this State]

(a) [A court] [The _____ court] of this state may order a person who is domiciled or is found within this state to give his testimony or statement or to produce documents or other things for use in a proceeding in a tribunal outside this state. The order may be made upon the application of any interested person or in response to a letter rogatory and may prescribe the practice and procedure, which may be wholly or in part the practice and procedure of the tribunal outside this state, for taking the testimony or statement or producing the documents or other things. To the extent that the order does not prescribe otherwise, the practice and procedure shall be in accordance with that of the court of this state issuing the order. The order may direct that the testimony or statement be given, or document or other thing produced, before a person appointed by the court. The person appointed shall have power to administer any necessary oath.

(b) A person within this state may voluntarily give his testimony or statement or produce documents or other things for use in a proceeding before a tribunal outside this state.

COMMENT

This section clarifies and liberalizes the procedure for rendering assistance to tribunals and litigants outside the state in obtaining oral and tangible evidence. By permitting adjustment in several respects to the practice and procedure

of the requesting tribunal, this section goes beyond the Uniform Foreign Depositions Act, adopted by the National Conference of Commissioners on Uniform State Laws in 1920, and other similar acts. E.g., Mass.Ann.Laws c. 233, § 45; Wis.Stat. § 326.24. See also N.Y.C.P.L.R. 3102(e) (effective Sept. 1, 1963). The bracketed matter is designed to give the enacting state a choice between authorizing all of its courts to render assistance or restricting these functions to one or more designated courts.

Judicial assistance may be sought not only to compel testimony, but also to require the production of documents and other tangible evidence. The court, however, retains complete discretion to frame an appropriate order. In exercising this power, the court may take into account the nature and attitudes of the requesting government and the character of the proceedings. In addition, the court may impose fees for counsel, attendance of witnesses, interpreters, and stenographic services.

The term "tribunal" is intended to encompass any body performing a judicial function. Thus, for example, a request emanating from an investigating magistrate in a foreign country should be honored. See LeLievre, Letters Rogatory 13 (Grossman ed. 1956).

The court has complete discretion to prescribe the procedure to be followed. The practice of the requesting court may be employed. If the court fails to prescribe the applicable procedure, the procedure of the court issuing the order applies. Any person designated by the court to take testimo-

ny, has by virtue of his appointment the power to administer any necessary oath. This is intended to overcome expressions of doubt on this point. See Jones, Letters Rogatory 85–86 (Grossman ed. 1961); Smit, International Aspects of Federal Civil Procedure, 61 Colum.L.Rev. 1031, 1057 (1961). The court may order the testimony taken before a person designated by the foreign tribunal.

Subsection (b) re-affirms the existing freedom of persons within the United States voluntarily to give testimony or produce evidence for use in proceedings or investigations elsewhere. The explicit re-affirmation is desirable in order to stress the large degree of freedom existing in this area.

§ 3.03　[Other Provisions of Law Unaffected]

This Act does not repeal or modify any other law of this state permitting another procedure for obtaining testimony, documents, or other things for use in this state or in a tribunal outside this state.

COMMENT

This section contains a savings clause similar to that embodied in section 2.05. It preserves all methods for obtaining testimony, documents, or other tangible evidence outside the state for use in the state and all methods for rendering assistance in obtaining such evidence for use in a tribunal outside the state. States that adopt the entire act, including section 6.01 should omit this section.

Article IV

DETERMINATION OF FOREIGN LAW

§ 4.01　[Notice]

A party who intends to raise an issue concerning the law of any jurisdiction or governmental unit thereof outside this state shall give notice in his pleadings or other reasonable written notice.

COMMENT

To avoid unfair surprise and to recognize that issues of sister state or foreign law are often even more elusive than the law of the forum, section 4.01 requires that notice of an intention to raise an issue of foreign law shall be given in writing, either in the pleadings or by other reasonable written notice at a later time. Cf. Cal.Code Civ.Pr. § 1875(4). It adopts the position taken in proposed Federal Rule of Civil Procedure 43A and it supersedes the requirement, which still has force in many states, that a court may not consider foreign law unless it has been pleaded. See Geller v. McCown, 64 Nev. 102, 177 P.2d 461, rehearing denied, 64 Nev. 106, 178 P.2d 380 (1947). This article applies to any jurisdiction or governmental unit having laws, regulations, or rules.

Although a pleading requirement may be justified as a notice device, pleading is neither the only nor always the most desirable method of giving notice of the presence of an issue of foreign law. The shift in focus in many modern procedural systems from the pleading stage to other phases of pre-trial was intended to eliminate much of the hypertechnicality of pleading and time-consuming and sterile motion

practice that may polish the pleadings, but rarely disposes of the case on the merits. A requirement that notice of intent to rely on foreign law be given in the pleading only perpetuates prior notions and invites dilatory motions and amendments.

Further, to force a party to set forth the substance of the foreign law at the pleading stage may be an onerous burden in view of the frequent lack of command over the operative facts at that embryonic stage. In some states, this is partially ameliorated by liberal provisions for amendment of pleadings and for hypothetical and alternative pleadings. Even so, no reason exists for requiring counsel to examine extensively the complexities of foreign law or, for that matter, to engender reliance on the part of his opponent, before it is apparent what law will control. If notice to court and adversary is the goal, there is ample opportunity prior to trial or, if necessary, at trial for informal notification of an intent to rely on foreign law.

Any reasonable written notice will suffice. Notice by one party is sufficient to permit the opponent to present materials on the law claimed to be applicable. See Wilson v. Dailey, 191 Md. 432, 62 A.2d 284 (1948). The court must exercise discretion in determining the proper timing of the notice in the light of the requirements of the case and fairness to the parties. The section does not attempt to prohibit the raising of an issue of foreign law after any particular point in the litigation. In exceptional situations,

the issues may not become apparent until during or even after the trial, and, in appropriate cases, the notice may be given at that time.

§ 4.02 [Materials to be Considered]

In determining the law of any jurisdiction or governmental unit thereof outside this state, the court may consider any relevant material or source, including testimony, whether or not submitted by a party or admissible under the rules of evidence.

COMMENT

As is done by modern judicial notice statutes, section 4.02 permits the court to consider any material relevant to the issues of foreign law without regard to the rules of admissibility and whether presented to the court for consideration by counsel or discovered through its own research. For a similar provision, see N.Y.C.P.L.R. 4511(d) (effective Sept. 1, 1963); Va.Code Ann. § 8–273; W.Va.Code Ann. § 5711; cf. Utah R.Civ.Pr. 44(f). The desirability of the practice seems obvious. Although foreign law has been characterized as a fact for purposes of proof, an issue of foreign law is little different from an issue of domestic law and the trial court should have the same freedom of investigation it possesses on an issue concerning the law of the forum. Further, if foreign law is to be determined by the court, as required by section 4.03, the rules of evidence, designed primarily to shield the jury from irrelevant or prejudicial matter, are no longer needed to restrict the court's scope of investigation. These rules have often prevented the court from examining relevant material that was inadmissible under one of the exclusionary rules.

Permitting the court to engage in its own research not only on domestic, but also on foreign law represents a step forward from prior practice. Several states already provide that foreign law is to be treated in the same manner as domestic law. E.g., Miss.Code Ann. § 1761; No.Car.Gen. Stat. § 8–4. See also Ark.Stat.Ann. § 28–109; Va.Code Ann. § 8–273; W.Va.Code Ann. § 5711. Frequently, the court will have at its disposal better foreign law materials than counsel has presented or will wish to re-examine material that has been presented either in partisan fashion or in insufficient detail. The fear that a court might surprise the litigants with a decision based on its own research seems more apparent than real. Should the court come upon material that diverges substantially from that presented by the parties, it should, at least in the normal case, inform them of the fruits of its research. However, an inflexible notice requirement seems undesirable. See Schlesinger, Comparative Law 142 (2d ed. 1959); Wyzanski, A Trial Judge's Freedom and Responsibility, 7 Rec. of N.Y. City Bar Ass'n 280, 294–95 (1952). In the event that the court cannot or does not wish to engage in its own research, it is free to insist on a complete presentation of the issues of foreign law by counsel.

§ 4.03 [Court Decision and Review]

The court, not jury, shall determine the law of any governmental unit outside this state. Its determination is subject to review on appeal as a ruling on a question of law.

COMMENT

Section 4.03 affirms what has been recognized for some time by the commentators and both state and federal courts: the jury is not the appropriate organ for determining issues of foreign law. See, e.g., Liechti v. Roche, 198 F.2d 174 (5th Cir.1952); Janson v. Swedish American Line, 185 F.2d 212, 216 (1st Cir.1950) (dictum); Consequa v. Willings, 6 Fed.Cas. No. 3,128 (C.C.D.Pa.1816); Seton v. Delaware Ins. Co., 21 Fed.Cas. No. 12,675 (C.C.D.Pa.1808); Ferguson v. Clifford, 137 N.H. 86, 98 (1858); Inge v. Murphy, 10 Ala. 885 (1846); De Sobry v. Laistre, 2 Har. & John. 191, 219 (Md.1807); 1 Greenleaf, Evidence § 486 (15th ed. 1892); Story, Conflict of Laws § 638 (8th ed. 1883). Twenty-six states, by adopting the Uniform Judicial Notice of Foreign Law Act, and eleven other states, by statute, have adopted the position proposed in this section. See 9A Uniform Laws Ann. 318, 329 (1957); 9 Wigmore, Evidence § 2558 (3d ed. 1940).

In keeping with the treatment of foreign law as an issue for the court, the trial court's determination is made subject to review on appeal in the same manner as any other question of law. See Liechti v. Roche, 198 F.2d 174 (5th Cir.1952). The nature of the issues involved and the historic functions of the reviewing court render appropriate the equating of foreign and domestic law. The same approach is taken in section 3 of the Uniform Judicial Notice of Foreign Law Act. See also Tex.R.Civ.Pr. 184a; Vt.Stat.Ann. tit. 12, § 1699.

§ 4.40 [Other Provisions of Law Unaffected]

This Article does not repeal or modify any other law of this state permitting another procedure for the determination of foreign law.

COMMENT

This section contains a savings clause similar to those embodied in sections 2.05 and 3.03. States that adopt the entire act, including section 6.01 should omit this section.

Article V

PROOF OF OFFICIAL RECORDS

§ 5.01 [Domestic Record]

An official record kept within the United States, or any state, district, commonwealth, territory, insular possession thereof, or the Panama Canal Zone, the Trust Territory of the Pacific Islands, or the Ryukyu Islands, or an entry therein, when admissible for any purpose, may be evidenced by an official publication thereof or by a copy attested by the officer having the legal custody of the record, or by his deputy, and accompanied by a certificate that the officer has the

custody. The certificate may be made by a judge of a court of record having jurisdiction in the governmental unit in which the record is kept, authenticated by the seal of the court, or by any public officer having a seal of office and having official duties in the governmental unit in which the record is kept, authenticated by the seal of his office.

COMMENT

With the exception of minor changes in wording, section 5.01, which relates to the authentication of official records kept in the United States, corresponds to Proposed Amended Rule 44(a) for the Federal Rules of Civil Procedure. Present Federal Rule 44(a) or its equivalent exists in many states. E.g., Alaska R.Civ.Pr. 44(a); Colo.R.Civ.Pr. 44(a). Section 5.01 provides a more accurate description of a "domestic" record than does the present Federal Rule. It is not necessary that the record be a United States official record for section 5.01 to apply. All that is necessary is that the original be in one of the places enumerated in this section. Thus, for example, a record of a government in exile that is situated in this country may qualify under this section as well as section 5.02. Cf. Panco de Espana v. Federal Reserve Bank, 114 F.2d 438 (2d Cir.1940).

§ 5.02 [Foreign Record]

A foreign official record, or an entry therein, when admissible for any purpose, may be evidenced by an official publication or copy thereof, attested by a person authorized to make the attestation, and accompanied by a final certification as to the genuineness of the signature and official position (1) of the attesting person, or (2) of any foreign official whose certificate of genuineness of signature and official position either (a) relates to the attestation or (b) is in a chain of certificates of genuineness of signature and official position relating to the attestation. A final certification may be made by a secretary of embassy or legation, consul general, consul, vice consul, or consular agent of the United States, or a diplomatic or consular official of the foreign country assigned or accredited to the United States. If reasonable opportunity has been given to all parties to investigate the authenticity and accuracy of the documents, the court may, for good cause shown, (1) admit an attested copy without final certification or (2) permit the foreign official record to be evidenced by an attested summary with or without a final certification.

COMMENT

Section 5.02 provides flexibility in the proof of foreign official records. Because the term "legal custody," the formulation commonly found in existing state legislation, is inapposite to records kept in foreign countries in which the concept frequently is unknown, it has been eliminated, and the required capacity of the attesting officer or person is described in functional terms. This will enable any person who is authorized by the law of the foreign country to prepare and attest a copy even though he may not be charged with responsibility for maintaining the records.

One of the difficulties with present certification requirements is that they usually require one person, a United States foreign service officer, to certify to the genuineness of the attesting person's signature, the lawful incumbency of the office he purports to hold, and his authority. See Smit & Miller, International Co–Operation in Civil Litigation—A Report on Practices and Procedures Prevailing in the United States 66 (Milan 1961); Smit, International Aspects of Federal Civil Procedure, 61 Colum.L.Rev. 1031, 1063 (1961). Section 5.02 eliminates the certification as to authority, because United States consular officers are ordinarily unable to determine the complex issues of foreign law that are involved in the question of authority. Section 5.02 also alleviates the difficulties encountered under the usual certification requirements by permitting use of the chain-certification method. Under the chain-certification method, the original attestation is accompanied by a certification by another local official whose certification is in turn followed by that of an official of higher rank. The process continues until an official is reached about whom the consular official knows enough to permit him to issue the ultimate certification. The section also permits the "final certification" to be prepared by any one of a number of designated United States foreign service officers or by any diplomatic or consular official of the foreign country who is assigned or accredited to the United States. It may be based on information on record at the consulate or any other information deemed reliable by the certifying officer.

To afford as much flexibility as possible, the person preparing the "final certification" may certify not only the last, but any certificate that appears in the chain. In some cases, the person preparing the final certification may have the required information in regard to the official position and the genuineness of the signature of some intermediate foreign certifying official rather than the preceding official. The person preparing the final certification is therefore permitted to issue a certification as to the attesting person or of any foreign official in the chain of certificates.

Although section 5.02 facilitates proof of foreign official records, it is recognized that in some situations compliance may nevertheless be difficult or even impossible. The difficulty may be due to the fact that there is no American consul in the country in question, to a lack of co-operation on the part of foreign officials, or to the peculiarities that presently exist or may arise in the future in the law or practice of any one or more than a hundred foreign countries and their states and political subdivisions. Therefore, section 5.02 provides the court with discretionary power to admit a document that is uncertified, although attested, or a summary of the record rather than a copy. See Report of the Committee on Comparative Civil Procedure and Practice, Proc.A.B.A., Sec. Int'l & Comp.L. 123, 130–31 (1952); Model Code of Evidence §§ 517, 519.

This provision represents a departure from the common law rule and many existing statutes, which require a literal copy of the record. See Russo v. Metropolitan Life Ins. Co., 125 Conn. 132, 3 A.2d 844 (1939). See also Schlesinger, Comparative Law 56, n. 1 (2d ed. 1959). Since the summary is prepared by a disinterested governmental official, there is still a high probability that the substance of the document has been set forth accurately. Further, some nations will issue only extracts or summaries of certain official records. See United States v. Grabina, 119 F.2d 863 (2d Cir.1941). To

insure that a party procures the best caliber of evidence available, a showing of good cause is required.

The requirement that reasonable opportunity be given to all parties to examine into the authenticity and accuracy of an attested but uncertified copy or a summary is designed as a procedural safeguard. If this opportunity has not been given, the document may not be admitted. What constitutes reasonable opportunity will be determined by the court on the basis of the posture of the litigation and the importance of the document. Moreover, the document may be inspected by the opponent, his counsel, and experts. The latter may include not only foreign law experts, but also experts on questioned documents, so that forgeries may be detected by chemical examination of paper and ink.

The definition of "person" in section 1.01 is not applicable to articles II through VI. See comment to section 1.01.

§ 5.03 [Alternative Method for Certain Domestic and Foreign Records]

The statutes, codes, written laws, executive acts, or legislative or judicial proceedings of any domestic or foreign jurisdiction or governmental unit thereof may also be evidenced by any publication proved to be commonly accepted as proof thereof in the tribunals having jurisdiction in that governmental unit.

COMMENT

Section 5.03 modifies the Uniform Proof of Statutes Act, adopted by the National Conference of Commissioners on Uniform State Laws and the American Bar Association in 1920. Its inclusion in article V is designed to provide an alternative method for proving the written law and the executive, legislative, and judicial acts of any jurisdiction. Accordingly, it supplements sections 5.01 and 5.02 of this article and affords a simplified method for proving certain classes of documents that generally are published and the contents of which are common knowledge. Cf. Calif.Code Civ.Pr. § 1918. Neither this section nor the Uniform Proof of Statutes Act is intended to apply to secondary material. See Birch v. Birch, 136 Cal.App.2d 615, 289 P.2d 53 (1955). The changes in wording from the Uniform Proof of Statutes Act were required to take into account the overall scheme of article V.

§ 5.04 [Lack of Record]

A written statement that after diligent search no record or entry of a specified tenor is found to exist in the records designated by the statement, authenticated as provided in this Article in the case of a domestic record, or complying with the requirements of this Article for a summary in the case of a record in a foreign country, is admissible as evidence that the records contain no such record or entry.

COMMENT

This section is similar in content to Federal Rule 44(b) and to provisions found in many states. E.g., Tex.Stat.Ann. Art. 4731a, § 5. It represents a modification of the common law literal copy rule. When the written statement relates to the lack of a domestic record, it must be authenticated in accordance with the requirements of section 5.01. When the statement relates to the lack of a record in a foreign country, the requirements in section 5.02 for a summary, including the giving of reasonable notice to the parties, must be satisfied. As in the case of the summary the high probability of accuracy when a foreign official certifies to the non-existence of a record in his files, makes section 5.04 a desirable modification of prior practice.

§ 5.05 [Other Proof]

The proof of official records or of entry or lack of entry therein may be made by any other method authorized by law.

COMMENT

Section 5.05 preserves any method for the proof of foreign official records authorized by statute, treaty, or the rules of evidence. Thus, it is open to a litigant to prove an official record by the testimony of a person who has examined the original. Cal.Code Civ.Pr. § 1907; Mich.Stat.Ann. § 27.865; Tex.Stat.Ann. Art. 3731a, § 6. In addition, it authorizes the use of methods authorized by various Consular Conventions between the United States and foreign countries. E.g., Article X, Consular Convention with Italy, May 8, 1878, T.S. No. 178 (Dep't State 1878), 20 Stat. 725. See Russo v. Metropolitan Life Ins. Co., 125 Conn. 132, 3 A.2d 844 (1939). States that adopt the entire act, including section 6.01 should omit this section.

Article VI

MISCELLANEOUS

§ 6.01 [Other Provisions of Law Unaffected]

Except as otherwise provided herein, this Act does not repeal or modify any law of this state

(a) authorizing the exercise of jurisdiction on any basis other than the bases specified in Article I of this Act;

(b) permitting a procedure for service or for obtaining testimony, documents, or other things for use in this state or in a tribunal outside this state other than the procedures prescribed in Article II and Article III of this Act; or

(c) authorizing the determination of foreign law or the proof of official records or any entry or lack of entry therein by any method other than the methods prescribed in Article V of this Act.

COMMENT

This section is a comprehensive savings clause that can be used in a state adopting the entire act in lieu of sections 1.06, 2.05, 3.03, 4.04 and 5.05. For additional material explaining

the necessity for this savings clause, see the comments to those sections.

§ 6.02 [Uniformity of Interpretation]

This Act shall be so interpreted and construed as to effectuate its general purposes to make uniform the laws of those states which enact it.

§ 6.03 [Severability]

If any provision of this Act or the application thereof to any person or circumstance is held invalid, the invalidity does not affect other provisions or applications of the Act which can be given effect without the invalid provision or application, and to this end the provisions of this Act are severable.

§ 6.04 [Short Title]

This Act may be cited as the Uniform Interstate and International Procedure Act.

§ 6.05 [Repeal]

The following acts and parts of acts are repealed:

(1)

(2)

(3)

§ 6.06 [Time of Taking Effect]

This Act shall take effect _____.

APPENDIX B

CONSTITUTION OF THE UNITED STATES

UNANNOTATED

PREAMBLE

PREAMBLE

WE THE PEOPLE of the United States, in Order to form a more perfect Union, establish Justice, insure domestic Tranquility, provide for the common defence, promote the general Welfare, and secure the Blessings of Liberty to ourselves and our Posterity, do ordain and establish this CONSTITUTION for the United States of America.

ARTICLE I

Section. 1. All legislative Powers herein granted shall be vested in a Congress of the United States, which shall consist of a Senate and House of Representatives.

Section. 2. The House of Representatives shall be composed of Members chosen every second Year by the People of the several States, and the Electors in each State shall have the Qualifications requisite for Electors of the most numerous Branch of the State Legislature.

No Person shall be a Representative who shall not have attained to the Age of twenty five Years, and been seven Years a Citizen of the United States, and who shall not, when elected, be an Inhabitant of that State in which he shall be chosen.

[Representatives and direct Taxes shall be apportioned among the several States which may be included within this Union, according to their respective Numbers, which shall be determined by adding to the whole Number of free Persons, including those bound to Service for a Term of Years, and excluding Indians not taxed, three fifths of all other Persons.][1] The actual Enumeration shall be made within three Years after the first Meeting of the Congress of the United States, and within every subsequent Term of ten Years, in such Manner as they shall by Law direct. The Number of Representatives shall not exceed one for every thirty Thousand, but each State shall have at Least one Representative; and until such enumeration shall be made, the State of New Hampshire shall be entitled to chuse three, Massachusetts eight, Rhode-Island and Providence Plantations one, Connecticut five, New-York six, New Jersey four, Pennsylvania eight, Delaware one, Maryland six, Virginia ten, North Carolina five, South Carolina five, and Georgia three.

When vacancies happen in the Representation from any State, the Executive Authority thereof shall issue Writs of Election to fill such Vacancies.

The House of Representatives shall chuse their Speaker and other Officers; and shall have the sole Power of Impeachment.

[1] The clause of this paragraph inclosed in brackets was amended, as to the mode of apportionment of representatives among the several states, by the Fourteenth Amendment, § 2, and as to taxes on incomes without apportionment, by the Sixteenth Amendment.

Section. 3. [The Senate of the United States shall be composed of two Senators from each State, chosen by the Legislature thereof, for six Years; and each Senator shall have one Vote.][1]

Immediately after they shall be assembled in Consequence of the first Election, they shall be divided as equally as may be into three Classes. The Seats of the Senators of the first Class shall be vacated at the Expiration of the second Year, of the second Class at the Expiration of the fourth Year, and of the third Class at the Expiration of the sixth Year, so that one third may be chosen every second Year; [and if Vacancies happen by Resignation, or otherwise, during the Recess of the Legislature of any State, the Executive thereof may make temporary Appointments

until the next Meeting of the Legislature, which shall then fill such Vacancies.] [2]

No Person shall be a Senator who shall not have attained to the Age of thirty Years, and been nine Years a Citizen of the United States, and who shall not, when elected, be an Inhabitant of that State for which he shall be chosen.

The Vice President of the United States shall be President of the Senate, but shall have no Vote, unless they be equally divided.

The Senate shall chuse their other Officers, and also a President pro tempore, in the Absence of the Vice President, or when he shall exercise the Office of President of the United States.

The Senate shall have the sole Power to try all Impeachments. When sitting for that Purpose, they shall be on Oath or Affirmation. When the President of the United States is tried, the Chief Justice shall preside: And no Person shall be convicted without the Concurrence of two thirds of the Members present.

Judgment in Cases of Impeachment shall not extend further than to removal from Office, and disqualification to hold and enjoy any Office of honor, Trust or Profit under the United States: but the Party convicted shall nevertheless be liable and subject to Indictment, Trial, Judgment and Punishment, according to Law.

[1] This paragraph, inclosed in brackets, was superseded by the Seventeenth Amendment.

[2] The clause of this paragraph inclosed in brackets was superseded by the Seventeenth Amendment.

Section. 4. The Times, Places and Manner of holding Elections for Senators and Representatives, shall be prescribed in each State by the Legislature thereof; but the Congress may at any time by Law make or alter such Regulations, except as to the Places of chusing Senators.

The Congress shall assemble at least once in every Year, and such Meeting shall be on the [first Monday in December],[1] unless they shall by Law appoint a different Day.

[1] The clause of this paragraph inclosed in brackets was superseded by the Twentieth Amendment.

Section. 5. Each House shall be the Judge of the Elections, Returns and Qualifications of its own Members, and a Majority of each shall constitute a Quorum to do Business; but a smaller Number may adjourn from day to day, and may be authorized to compel the Attendance of absent Members, in such Manner, and under such Penalties as each House may provide.

Each House may determine the Rules of its Proceedings, punish its Members for disorderly Behaviour, and, with the Concurrence of two thirds, expel a Member.

Each House shall keep a Journal of its Proceedings, and from time to time publish the same, excepting such Parts as may in their Judgment require Secrecy; and the Yeas and Nays of the Members of either House on any question shall, at the Desire of one fifth of those Present, be entered on the Journal.

Neither House, during the Session of Congress, shall, without the Consent of the other, adjourn for more than three days, nor to any other Place than that in which the two Houses shall be sitting.

Section. 6. The Senators and Representatives shall receive a Compensation for their Services, to be ascertained by Law, and paid out of the Treasury of the United States. They shall in all Cases, except Treason, Felony and Breach of the Peace, be privileged from Arrest during their Attendance at the Session of their respective Houses, and in going to and returning from the same; and for any Speech or Debate in either House, they shall not be questioned in any other Place.

No Senator or Representative shall, during the Time for which he was elected, be appointed to any civil Office under the Authority of the United States, which shall have been created, or the Emoluments whereof shall have been encreased during such time; and no Person holding any Office under the United States, shall be a Member of either House during his Continuance in Office.

Section. 7. All Bills for raising Revenue shall originate in the House of Representatives; but the Senate may propose or concur with Amendments as on other Bills.

Every Bill which shall have passed the House of Representatives and the Senate, shall, before it becomes a Law, be presented to the President of the United States; If he approve he shall sign it, but if not he shall return it, with his Objections to that House in which it shall have originated, who shall enter the Objections at large on their Journal, and proceed to reconsider it. If after such Reconsideration two thirds of that House shall agree to pass the Bill, it shall be sent, together with the Objections, to the other House, by which it shall likewise be reconsidered, and if approved by two thirds of that House, it shall become a Law. But in all such Cases the Votes of both Houses shall be determined by Yeas and Nays, and the Names of the Persons voting for and against the Bill shall be entered on the Journal of each House respectively. If any Bill shall not be returned by the President within ten Days (Sundays excepted) after it shall have been presented to him, the Same shall be a Law, in like Manner as if he had signed it, unless the Congress by their Adjournment prevent its Return, in which Case it shall not be a Law.

Every Order, Resolution, or Vote to which the Concurrence of the Senate and House of Representatives may be necessary (except on a question of Adjournment) shall be presented to the President of the United States; and before the Same shall take Effect, shall be approved by him, or being disapproved by him, shall be repassed by two thirds of the Senate and House of Representatives, according to the Rules and Limitations prescribed in the Case of a Bill.

Section. 8. The Congress shall have Power To lay and collect Taxes, Duties, Imposts and Excises, to pay the Debts and provide for the common Defence and general Welfare of the United States; but all Duties, Imposts and Excises shall be uniform throughout the United States;

To borrow Money on the credit of the United States;

To regulate Commerce with foreign Nations, and among the several States, and with the Indian Tribes;

To establish an uniform Rule of Naturalization, and uniform Laws on the subject of Bankruptcies throughout the United States;

To coin Money, regulate the Value thereof, and of foreign Coin, and fix the Standard of Weights and Measures;

To provide for the Punishment of counterfeiting the Securities and current Coin of the United States;

To establish Post Offices and post Roads;

To promote the Progress of Science and useful Arts, by securing for limited Times to Authors and Inventors the exclusive Right to their respective Writings and Discoveries;

To constitute Tribunals inferior to the supreme Court;

To define and punish Piracies and Felonies committed on the high Seas, and Offences against the Law of Nations;

To declare War, grant Letters of Marque and Reprisal, and make Rules concerning Captures on Land and Water;

To raise and support Armies, but no Appropriation of Money to that Use shall be for a longer Term than two Years;

To provide and maintain a Navy;

To make Rules for the Government and Regulation of the land and naval Forces;

To provide for calling forth the Militia to execute the Laws of the Union, suppress Insurrections and repel Invasions;

To provide for organizing, arming, and disciplining, the Militia, and for governing such Part of them as may be employed in the Service of the United States, reserving to the States respectively, the Appointment of the Officers, and the Authority of training the Militia according to the discipline prescribed by Congress;

To exercise exclusive Legislation in all Cases whatsoever, over such District (not exceeding ten Miles square) as may, by Cession of particular States, and the Acceptance of Congress, become the Seat of the Government of the United States, and to exercise like Authority over all Places purchased by the Consent of the Legislature of the State in which the Same shall be, for the Erection of Forts, Magazines, Arsenals, dock-Yards, and other needful Buildings;—And

To make all Laws which shall be necessary and proper for carrying into Execution the foregoing Powers, and all other Powers vested by this Constitution in the Government of the United States, or in any Department or Officer thereof.

Section. 9. The Migration or Importation of such Persons as any of the States now existing shall think proper to admit, shall not be prohibited by the Congress prior to the Year one thousand eight hundred and eight, but a Tax or duty may be imposed on such Importation, not exceeding ten dollars for each Person.

The Privilege of the Writ of Habeas Corpus shall not be suspended, unless when in Cases of Rebellion or Invasion the public Safety may require it.

No Bill of Attainder or ex post facto Law shall be passed.

No Capitation, or other direct, Tax shall be laid, unless in Proportion to the Census or Enumeration herein before directed to be taken.[1]

No Tax or Duty shall be laid on Articles exported from any State.

No Preference shall be given by any Regulation of Commerce or Revenue to the Ports of one State over those of another; nor shall Vessels bound to, or from, one State, be obliged to enter, clear, or pay Duties in another.

No Money shall be drawn from the Treasury, but in Consequence of Appropriations made by Law; and a regular Statement and Account of the Receipts and Expenditures of all public Money shall be published from time to time.

No Title of Nobility shall be granted by the United States: And no Person holding any Office of Profit or Trust under them, shall, without the Consent of the Congress, accept of any present, Emolument, Office, or Title, of any kind whatever, from any King, Prince, or foreign State.

[1] This paragraph has been affected by the Sixteenth Amendment.

Section. 10. No State shall enter into any Treaty, Alliance, or Confederation; grant Letters of Marque and Reprisal; coin Money; emit Bills of Credit; make

any Thing but gold and silver Coin a Tender in Payment of Debts; pass any Bill of Attainder, ex post facto Law, or Law impairing the Obligation of Contracts, or grant any Title of Nobility.

No State shall, without the Consent of the Congress, lay any Imposts or Duties on Imports or Exports, except what may be absolutely necessary for executing it's inspection Laws: and the net Produce of all Duties and Imposts, laid by any State on Imports or Exports, shall be for the Use of the Treasury of the United States; and all such Laws shall be subject to the Revision and Controul of the Congress.

No State shall, without the Consent of Congress, lay any Duty of Tonnage, keep Troops, or Ships of War in time of Peace, enter into any Agreement or Compact with another State, or with a foreign Power, or engage in War, unless actually invaded, or in such imminent Danger as will not admit of delay.

ARTICLE II

Section. 1. The executive Power shall be vested in a President of the United States of America. He shall hold his Office during the Term of four Years, and, together with the Vice President, chosen for the same Term, be elected, as follows:

Each State shall appoint, in such Manner as the Legislature thereof may direct, a Number of Electors, equal to the whole Number of Senators and Representatives to which the State may be entitled in the Congress: but no Senator or Representative, or Person holding an Office of Trust or Profit under the United States, shall be appointed an Elector.

[The Electors shall meet in their respective States, and vote by Ballot for two Persons, of whom one at least shall not be an Inhabitant of the same State with themselves. And they shall make a List of all the Persons voted for, and of the Number of Votes for each; which List they shall sign and certify, and transmit sealed to the Seat of the Government of the United States, directed to the President of the Senate. The President of the Senate shall, in the Presence of the Senate and House of Representatives, open all the Certificates, and the Votes shall then be counted. The Person having the greatest Number of Votes shall be the President, if such Number be a Majority of the whole Number of Electors appointed; and if there be more than one who have such Majority, and have an equal Number of Votes, then the House of Representatives shall immediately chuse by Ballot one of them for President; and if no Person have a Majority, then from the five highest on the List the said House shall in like Manner chuse the President. But in chusing the President, the Votes shall be taken by States, the Representation from each State having one Vote; A quorum for this Purpose shall consist of a Member or Members from two thirds of the States, and a Majority of all the States shall be necessary to a Choice. In every Case, after the Choice of the President, the Person having the greatest Number of Votes of the Electors shall be the Vice President. But if there should remain two or more who have equal Votes, the Senate shall chuse from them by Ballot the Vice President.] [1]

The Congress may determine the Time of chusing the Electors, and the Day on which they shall give their Votes; which Day shall be the same throughout the United States.

No Person except a natural born Citizen, or a Citizen of the United States, at the time of the Adoption of this Constitution, shall be eligible to the Office of President; neither shall any Person be eligible to that Office who shall not have attained to the Age of thirty five Years, and been fourteen Years a Resident within the United States.

In Case of the Removal of the President from Office, or of his Death, Resignation, or Inability to discharge the Powers and Duties of the said Office, the Same shall devolve on the Vice President, and the Congress may by Law provide for the Case of Removal, Death, Resignation or Inability, both of the President and Vice President, declaring what Officer shall then act as President, and such Officer shall act accordingly, until the Disability be removed, or a President shall be elected.

The President shall, at stated Times, receive for his Services, a Compensation, which shall neither be encreased nor diminished during the Period for which he shall have been elected, and he shall not receive within that Period any other Emolument from the United States, or any of them.

Before he enter on the Execution of his Office, he shall take the following Oath or Affirmation:—"I do solemnly swear (or affirm) that I will faithfully execute the Office of President of the United States, and will to the best of my Ability, preserve, protect and defend the Constitution of the United States."

1 This paragraph, inclosed in brackets, was superseded by the Twelfth Amendment, post.

Section. 2. The President shall be Commander in Chief of the Army and Navy of the United States, and of the Militia of the several States, when called into the actual Service of the United States; he may require the Opinion, in writing, of the principal Officer in each of the executive Departments, upon any Subject relating to the Duties of their respective Offices,

and he shall have Power to grant Reprieves and Pardons for Offences against the United States, except in Cases of Impeachment.

He shall have Power, by and with the Advice and Consent of the Senate, to make Treaties, provided two thirds of the Senators present concur; and he shall nominate, and by and with the Advice and Consent of the Senate, shall appoint Ambassadors, other public Ministers and Consuls, Judges of the supreme Court, and all other Officers of the United States, whose Appointments are not herein otherwise provided for, and which shall be established by Law: but the Congress may by Law vest the Appointment of such inferior Officers, as they think proper, in the President alone, in the Courts of Law, or in the Heads of Departments.

The President shall have Power to fill up all Vacancies that may happen during the Recess of the Senate, by granting Commissions which shall expire at the End of their next Session.

Section. 3. He shall from time to time give to the Congress Information of the State of the Union, and recommend to their Consideration such Measures as he shall judge necessary and expedient; he may, on extraordinary Occasions, convene both Houses, or either of them, and in Case of Disagreement between them, with Respect to the Time of Adjournment, he may adjourn them to such Time as he shall think proper; he shall receive Ambassadors and other public Ministers; he shall take Care that the Laws be faithfully executed, and shall Commission all the Officers of the United States.

Section. 4. The President, Vice President and all civil Officers of the United States, shall be removed from Office on Impeachment for, and Conviction of, Treason, Bribery, or other high Crimes and Misdemeanors.

ARTICLE III

Section. 1. The judicial Power of the United States, shall be vested in one supreme Court, and in such inferior Courts as the Congress may from time to time ordain and establish. The Judges, both of the supreme and inferior Courts, shall hold their Offices during good Behaviour, and shall, at stated Times, receive for their Services, a Compensation, which shall not be diminished during their Continuance in Office.

Section. 2. The judicial Power shall extend to all Cases, in Law and Equity, arising under this Constitution, the Laws of the United States, and Treaties made, or which shall be made, under their Authority;—to all Cases affecting Ambassadors, other public Ministers and Consuls;—to all Cases of admiralty and maritime Jurisdiction;—to Controversies to which the United States shall be a Party;—to Controversies between two or more States;—between a State and Citizens of another State;—between citizens of different States;—between Citizens of the same State claiming Lands under Grants of different States, and between a State, or the Citizens thereof, and foreign States, Citizens or Subjects.[1]

In all Cases affecting Ambassadors, other public Ministers and Consuls, and those in which a State shall be Party, the supreme Court shall have original Jurisdiction. In all the other Cases before mentioned, the supreme Court shall have appellate Jurisdiction, both as to Law and Fact, with such Exceptions, and under such Regulations as the Congress shall make.

The Trial of all Crimes, except in Cases of Impeachment, shall be by Jury; and such Trial shall be held in the State where the said Crimes shall have been committed; but when not committed within any State, the Trial shall be at such Place or Places as the Congress may by Law have directed.

[1] This section has been affected by the Eleventh Amendment.

Section. 3. Treason against the United States, shall consist only in levying War against them, or in adhering to their Enemies, giving them Aid and Comfort. No Person shall be convicted of Treason unless on the Testimony of two Witnesses to the same overt Act, or on Confession in open Court.

The Congress shall have Power to declare the Punishment of Treason, but no Attainder of Treason shall work Corruption of Blood, or Forfeiture except during the Life of the Person attainted.

ARTICLE IV

Section. 1. Full Faith and Credit shall be given in each State to the public Acts, Records, and judicial Proceedings of every other State. And the Congress may by general Laws prescribe the Manner in which such Acts, Records and Proceedings shall be proved, and the Effect thereof.

Section. 2. The Citizens of each State shall be entitled to all Privileges and Immunities of Citizens in the several States.

A Person charged in any State with Treason, Felony, or other Crime, who shall flee from Justice, and be

found in another State, shall on Demand of the executive Authority of the State from which he fled, be delivered up, to be removed to the State having Jurisdiction of the Crime.

No Person held to Service or Labour in one State, under the Laws thereof, escaping into another, shall, in Consequence of any Law or Regulation therein, be discharged from such Service or Labour, but shall be delivered up on Claim of the Party to whom such Service or Labour may be due.[1]

1 This clause was affected by the Thirteenth Amendment.

Section. 3. New States may be admitted by the Congress into this Union; but no new State shall be formed or erected within the Jurisdiction of any other State; nor any State be formed by the Junction of two or more States, or Parts of States, without the Consent of the Legislatures of the States concerned as well as of the Congress.

The Congress shall have Power to dispose of and make all needful Rules and Regulations respecting the Territory or other Property belonging to the United States; and nothing in this Constitution shall be so construed as to Prejudice any Claims of the United States, or of any particular State.

Section. 4. The United States shall guarantee to every State in this Union a Republican Form of Government, and shall protect each of them against Invasion; and on Application of the Legislature, or of the Executive (when the Legislature cannot be convened) against domestic Violence.

ARTICLE V

The Congress, whenever two thirds of both Houses shall deem it necessary, shall propose Amendments to this Constitution, or, on the Application of the Legislatures of two thirds of the several States, shall call a Convention for proposing Amendments, which, in either Case, shall be valid to all Intents and Purposes, as Part of this Constitution, when ratified by the Legislatures of three fourths of the several States, or by Conventions in three fourths thereof, as the one or the other Mode of Ratification may be proposed by the Congress; Provided that no Amendment which may be made prior to the Year One thousand eight hundred and eight shall in any Manner affect the first and fourth Clauses in the Ninth Section of the first Article; and that no State, without its Consent, shall be deprived of its equal Suffrage in the Senate.

ARTICLE VI

All Debts contracted and Engagements entered into, before the Adoption of this Constitution, shall be as valid against the United States under this Constitution, as under the Confederation.

This Constitution, and the Laws of the United States which shall be made in Pursuance thereof; and all Treaties made, or which shall be made, under the Authority of the United States, shall be the supreme Law of the Land; and the Judges in every State shall be bound thereby, any Thing in the Constitution or Laws of any State to the Contrary notwithstanding.

The Senators and Representatives before mentioned, and the Members of the several State Legislatures, and all executive and judicial Officers, both of the United States and of the several States, shall be bound by Oath or Affirmation, to support this Constitution; but no religious Test shall ever be required as a Qualification to any Office or public Trust under the United States.

ARTICLE VII

The Ratification of the Conventions of nine States, shall be sufficient for the Establishment of this Constitution between the States so ratifying the Same.

DONE in Convention by the Unanimous Consent of the States present the Seventeenth Day of September in the Year of Our Lord one thousand seven hundred and Eighty seven and of the Independence of the United States of America the Twelfth. IN WITNESS whereof We have hereunto subscribed our Names.

Go. WASHINGTON—*Presidt. and deputy from Virginia*

Attest WILLIAM JACKSON *Secretary*

New Hampshire
JOHN LANGDON NICHOLAS GILMAN
Massachusetts
NATHANIEL GORHAM RUFUS KING
Connecticut
WM. SAML. JOHNSON ROGER SHERMAN
New York

ALEXANDER HAMILTON

New Jersey

WIL: LIVINGSTON
DAVID BREARLEY.

WM. PATERSON.
JONA: DAYTON

Pennsylvania

B FRANKLIN
THOMAS MIFFLIN
ROBT MORRIS
GEO. CLYMER

THOS. FITZSIMONS
JARED INGERSOLL
JAMES WILSON
GOUV MORRIS

Delaware

GEO: READ
GUNNING BEDFORD jun
JOHN DICKINSON

RICHARD BASSETT
JACO: BROOM

Maryland

JAMES MCHENRY
DAN OF ST THOS. JENIFER

DANL CARROLL

Virginia

JOHN BLAIR—

JAMES MADISON JR.

North Carolina

WM. BLOUNT
RICHD. DOBBS SPAIGHT

HU WILLIAMSON

South Carolina

J. RUTLEDGE
CHARLES COTESWORTH PINCKNEY

CHARLES PINCKNEY
PIERCE BUTLER

Georgia

WILLIAM FEW

ABR BALDWIN

Articles in Addition to, and Amendment of, the Constitution of the United States of America, Proposed by Congress, and Ratified by the Legislatures of the Several States Pursuant to the Fifth Article of the Original Constitution

ARTICLE [I]

Congress shall make no law respecting an establishment of religion, or prohibiting the free exercise thereof; or abridging the freedom of speech, or of the press; or the right of the people peaceably to assemble, and to petition the Government for a redress of grievances.

ARTICLE [II]

A well regulated Militia, being necessary to the security of a free State, the right of the people to keep and bear Arms, shall not be infringed.

ARTICLE [III]

No Soldier shall, in time of peace be quartered in any house, without the consent of the Owner, nor in time of war, but in a manner to be prescribed by law.

ARTICLE [IV]

The right of the people to be secure in their persons, houses, papers, and effects, against unreasonable searches and seizures, shall not be violated, and no Warrants shall issue, but upon probable cause, supported by Oath or affirmation, and particularly describing the place to be searched, and the persons or things to be seized.

ARTICLE [V]

No person shall be held to answer for a capital, or otherwise infamous crime, unless on a presentment or indictment of a Grand Jury, except in cases arising in the land or naval forces, or in the Militia, when in actual service in time of War or public danger; nor shall any person be subject for the same offence to be twice put in jeopardy of life or limb; nor shall be compelled in any criminal case to be a witness against himself, nor be deprived of life, liberty, or property, without due process of law; nor shall private property be taken for public use, without just compensation.

ARTICLE [VI]

In all criminal prosecutions, the accused shall enjoy the right to a speedy and public trial, by an impartial jury of the State and district wherein the crime shall have been committed, which district shall have been previously ascertained by law, and to be informed of the nature and cause of the accusation; to be confronted with the witnesses against him; to have compulsory process for obtaining witnesses in his favor, and to have the Assistance of Counsel for his defence.

ARTICLE [VII]

In Suits at common law, where the value in controversy shall exceed twenty dollars, the right of trial by jury shall be preserved, and no fact tried by a jury, shall be otherwise reexamined in any Court of the United States, than according to the rules of the common law.

ARTICLE [VIII]

Excessive bail shall not be required, nor excessive fines imposed, nor cruel and unusual punishments inflicted.

ARTICLE [IX]

The enumeration in the Constitution, of certain rights, shall not be construed to deny or disparage others retained by the people.

ARTICLE [X]

The powers not delegated to the United States by the Constitution, nor prohibited by it to the States, are reserved to the States respectively, or to the people.

ARTICLE [XI]

The Judicial power of the United States shall not be construed to extend to any suit in law or equity, commenced or prosecuted against one of the United States by Citizens of another State, or by Citizens or Subjects of any Foreign State.

ARTICLE [XII]

The Electors shall meet in their respective states, and vote by ballot for President and Vice-President, one of whom, at least, shall not be an inhabitant of the same state with themselves; they shall name in their ballots the person voted for as President, and in distinct ballots the person voted for as Vice-President, and they shall make distinct lists of all persons voted for as President, and of all persons voted for as Vice-President, and of the number of votes for each, which lists they shall sign and certify, and transmit sealed to the seat of the government of the United States, directed to the President of the Senate;—The President of the Senate shall, in the presence of the Senate and House of Representatives, open all the certificates and the votes shall then be counted;—The person having the greatest number of votes for President, shall be the President, if such number be a majority of the whole number of Electors appointed; and if no person have such majority, then from the persons having the highest numbers not exceeding three on

the list of those voted for as President, the House of Representatives shall choose immediately, by ballot, the President. But in choosing the President, the votes shall be taken by states, the representation from each state having one vote; a quorum for this purpose shall consist of a member or members from two-thirds of the states, and a majority of all the states shall be necessary to a choice. And if the House of Representatives shall not choose a President whenever the right of choice shall devolve upon them, before the fourth day of March next following, then the Vice-President shall act as President, as in the case of the death or other constitutional disability of the Presi-

dent.—The person having the greatest number of votes as Vice-President, shall be the Vice-President, if such number be a majority of the whole number of Electors appointed, and if no person have a majority, then from the two highest numbers on the list, the Senate shall choose the Vice-President; a quorum for the purpose shall consist of two-thirds of the whole number of Senators, and a majority of the whole number shall be necessary to a choice. But no person constitutionally ineligible to the office of President shall be eligible to that of Vice-President of the United States.[1]

[1] This Amendment was affected by the Twentieth Amendment.

ARTICLE XIII

Section 1. Neither slavery nor involuntary servitude, except as a punishment for crime whereof the party shall have been duly convicted, shall exist within the United States, or any place subject to their jurisdiction.

Section 2. Congress shall have power to enforce this article by appropriate legislation.

ARTICLE XIV

Section 1. All persons born or naturalized in the United States, and subject to the jurisdiction thereof, are citizens of the United States and of the State wherein they reside. No State shall make or enforce any law which shall abridge the privileges or immunities of citizens of the United States; nor shall any State deprive any person of life, liberty, or property, without due process of law; nor deny to any person within its jurisdiction the equal protection of the laws.

Section 2. Representatives shall be apportioned among the several States according to their respective numbers, counting the whole number of persons in each State, excluding Indians not taxed. But when the right to vote at any election for the choice of electors for President and Vice President of the United States, Representatives in Congress, the Executive and Judicial officers of a State, or the members of the Legislature thereof, is denied to any of the male inhabitants of such State, being twenty-one years of age, and citizens of the United States, or in any way abridged, except for participation in rebellion, or other crime, the basis of representation therein shall be reduced in the proportion which the number of such male citizens shall bear to the whole number of male citizens twenty-one years of age in such State.

Section 3. No person shall be a Senator or Representative in Congress, or elector of President and Vice President, or hold any office, civil or military, under the United States, or under any State, who, having previously taken an oath, as a member of Congress, or as an officer of the United States, or as a member of any State legislature, or as an executive or judicial officer of any State, to support the Constitution of the United States, shall have engaged in insurrection or rebellion against the same, or given aid or comfort to the enemies thereof. But Congress may by a vote of two-thirds of each House, remove such disability.

Section 4. The validity of the public debt of the United States, authorized by law, including debts incurred for payment of pensions and bounties for services in suppressing insurrection or rebellion, shall not be questioned. But neither the United States nor any State shall assume or pay any debt or obligation incurred in aid of insurrection or rebellion against the United States, or any claim for the loss or emancipation of any slave; but all such debts, obligations and claims shall be held illegal and void.

Section 5. The Congress shall have power to enforce, by appropriate legislation, the provisions of this article.

ARTICLE XV

Section 1. The right of citizens of the United States to vote shall not be denied or abridged by the United States or by any State on account of race, color, or previous condition of servitude.

Section 2. The Congress shall have power to enforce this article by appropriate legislation.

ARTICLE XVI

The Congress shall have power to lay and collect taxes on incomes, from whatever source derived, without apportionment among the several States, and without regard to any census or enumeration.

ARTICLE [XVII]

The Senate of the United States shall be composed of two Senators from each state, elected by the people thereof, for six years; and each Senator shall have one vote. The electors in each State shall have the qualifications requisite for electors of the most numerous branch of the State legislatures.

When vacancies happen in the representation of any State in the Senate, the executive authority of such State shall issue writs of election to fill such vacancies: *Provided,* That the legislature of any State may empower the executive thereof to make temporary appointments until the people fill the vacancies by election as the legislature may direct.

This amendment shall not be so construed as to affect the election or term of any Senator chosen before it becomes valid as part of the Constitution.

ARTICLE [XVIII] [Repealed. See Article XXI]

Section 1. After one year from the ratification of this article the manufacture, sale, or transportation of intoxicating liquors within, the importation thereof into, or the exportation thereof from the United States and all territory subject to the jurisdiction thereof for beverage purposes is hereby prohibited.

Section 2. The Congress and the several States shall have concurrent power to enforce this article by appropriate legislation.

Section 3. This article shall be inoperative unless it shall have been ratified as an amendment to the Constitution by the legislatures of the several States, as provided in the Constitution, within seven years from the date of the submission hereof to the States by the Congress.

ARTICLE [XIX]

The right of citizens of the United States to vote shall not be denied or abridged by the United States or by any State on account of sex.

Congress shall have power to enforce this article by appropriate legislation.

ARTICLE [XX]

Section 1. The terms of the President and Vice President shall end at noon on the 20th day of January, and the terms of Senators and Representatives at noon on the 3d day of January, of the years in which such terms would have ended if this article had not been ratified; and the terms of their successors shall then begin.

Sec. 2. The Congress shall assemble at least once in every year, and such meeting shall begin at noon on the 3d day of January, unless they shall by law appoint a different day.

Sec. 3. If, at the time fixed for the beginning of the term of the President, the President elect shall have died, the Vice President elect shall become Presi-

dent. If a President shall not have been chosen before the time fixed for the beginning of his term, or if the President elect shall have failed to qualify, then the Vice President elect shall act as President until a President shall have qualified; and the Congress may by law provide for the case wherein neither a President elect nor a Vice President elect shall have qualified, declaring who shall then act as President, or the manner in which one who is to act shall be selected, and such person shall act accordingly until a President or Vice President shall have qualified.

Sec. 4. The Congress may by law provide for the case of the death of any of the persons from whom the House of Representatives may choose a President whenever the right of choice shall have devolved upon them, and for the case of the death of any of the persons from whom the Senate may choose a Vice President whenever the right of choice shall have devolved upon them.

Sec. 5. Sections 1 and 2 shall take effect on the 15th day of October following the ratification of this article.

Sec. 6. This article shall be inoperative unless it shall have been ratified as an amendment to the Constitution by the legislatures of three-fourths of the several States within seven years from the date of its submission.

ARTICLE [XXI]

Section 1. The eighteenth article of amendment to the Constitution of the United States is hereby repealed.

Sec. 2. The transportation or importation into any State, Territory, or possession of the United States for delivery or use therein of intoxicating liquors, in violation of the laws thereof, is hereby prohibited.

Sec. 3. This article shall be inoperative unless it shall have been ratified as an amendment to the Constitution by conventions in the several States, as provided in the Constitution, within seven years from the date of the submission hereof to the States by the Congress.

ARTICLE [XXII]

Section 1. No person shall be elected to the office of the President more than twice, and no person who has held the office of President, or acted as President, for more than two years of a term to which some other person was elected President shall be elected to the office of the President more than once. But this Article shall not apply to any person holding the office of President when this Article was proposed by the Congress, and shall not prevent any person who may be holding the office of President, or acting as President, during the term within which this Article becomes operative from holding the office of President or acting as President during the remainder of such term.

Sec. 2. This Article shall be inoperative unless it shall have been ratified as an amendment to the Constitution by the legislatures of three-fourths of the several States within seven years from the date of its submission to the States by the Congress.

ARTICLE [XXIII]

Section 1. The District constituting the seat of Government of the United States shall appoint in such manner as the Congress may direct:

A number of electors of President and Vice President equal to the whole number of Senators and Representatives in Congress to which the District would be entitled if it were a State, but in no event more than the least populous State; they shall be in addition to those appointed by the States, but they shall be considered, for the purposes of the election of President and Vice President, to be electors appointed by a State; and they shall meet in the District and perform such duties as provided by the twelfth article of amendment.

Sec. 2. The Congress shall have power to enforce this article by appropriate legislation.

ARTICLE [XXIV]

Section 1. The right of citizens of the United States to vote in any primary or other election for President or Vice President, for electors for President or Vice President, or for Senator or Representative in Congress, shall not be denied or abridged by the United States or any State by reason of failure to pay any poll tax or other tax.

Sec. 2. The Congress shall have power to enforce this article by appropriate legislation.

ARTICLE [XXV]

Section 1. In case of the removal of the President from office or of his death or resignation, the Vice President shall become President.

Sec. 2. Whenever there is a vacancy in the office of the Vice President, the President shall nominate a Vice President who shall take office upon confirmation by a majority vote of both Houses of Congress.

Sec. 3. Whenever the President transmits to the President pro tempore of the Senate and the Speaker of the House of Representatives his written declaration that he is unable to discharge the powers and duties of his office, and until he transmits to them a written declaration to the contrary, such powers and duties shall be discharged by the Vice President as Acting President.

Sec. 4. Whenever the Vice President and a majority of either the principal officers of the executive departments or of such other body as Congress may by law provide, transmit to the President pro tempore of the Senate and the Speaker of the House of Representatives their written declaration that the President is unable to discharge the powers and duties of his office, the Vice President shall immediately assume the powers and duties of the office as Acting President.

Thereafter, when the President transmits to the President pro tempore of the Senate and the Speaker of the House of Representatives his written declaration that no inability exists, he shall resume the powers and duties of his office unless the Vice President and a majority of either the principal officers of the executive department or of such other body as Congress may by law provide, transmit within four days to the President pro tempore of the Senate and the Speaker of the House of Representatives their written declaration that the President is unable to discharge the powers and duties of his office. Thereupon Congress shall decide the issue, assembling within forty-eight hours for that purpose if not in session. If the Congress, within twenty-one days after receipt of the latter written declaration, or, if Congress is not in session, within twenty-one days after Congress is required to assemble, determines by two-thirds vote of both Houses that the President is unable to discharge the powers and duties of his office, the Vice President shall continue to discharge the same as Acting President; otherwise, the President shall resume the powers and duties of his office.

ARTICLE [XXVI]

Section 1. The right of citizens of the United States, who are eighteen years of age or older, to vote shall not be denied or abridged by the United States or by any State on account of age.

Sec. 2. The Congress shall have power to enforce this article by appropriate legislation.

ARTICLE [XXVII]¹

1 "Article [XXVII]" editorially added. Originally read "Article the second".

No law, varying the compensation for the services of the Senators and Representatives, shall take effect, until an election of Representatives shall have intervened.

APPENDIX C

RULES OF EVIDENCE FOR UNITED STATES COURTS AND MAGISTRATES

ARTICLE I. GENERAL PROVISIONS

Rule 101. Scope

These rules govern proceedings in the courts of the United States and before the United States bankruptcy judges and United States magistrate judges, to the extent and with the exceptions stated in rule 1101.

(Pub.L. 93–595, § 1, Jan. 2, 1975, 88 Stat. 1929; Mar. 2, 1987, eff. Oct. 1, 1987; Apr. 25, 1988, eff. Nov. 1, 1988; Apr. 22, 1993, eff. Dec. 1, 1993.)

Rule 102. Purpose and Construction

These rules shall be construed to secure fairness in administration, elimination of unjustifiable expense and delay, and promotion of growth and development of the law of evidence to the end that the truth may be ascertained and proceedings justly determined.

(Pub.L. 93–595, § 1, Jan. 2, 1975, 88 Stat.1929.)

Rule 103. Rulings on Evidence

(a) Effect of Erroneous Ruling.—Error may not be predicated upon a ruling which admits or excludes evidence unless a substantial right of the party is affected, and

(1) Objection.—In case the ruling is one admitting evidence, a timely objection or motion to strike appears of record, stating the specific ground of objection, if the specific ground was not apparent from the context; or

(2) Offer of Proof.—In case the ruling is one excluding evidence, the substance of the evidence was made known to the court by offer or was apparent from the context within which questions were asked.

Once the court makes a definitive ruling on the record admitting or excluding evidence, either at or before trial, a party need not renew an objection or offer of proof to preserve a claim of error for appeal.

(b) Record of Offer and Ruling.—The court may add any other or further statement which shows the character of the evidence, the form in which it was offered, the objection made, and the ruling thereon. It may direct the making of an offer in question and answer form.

(c) Hearing of Jury.—In jury cases, proceedings shall be conducted, to the extent practicable, so as to prevent inadmissible evidence from being suggested to the jury by any means, such as making statements or offers of proof or asking questions in the hearing of the jury.

(d) Plain Error.—Nothing in this rule precludes taking notice of plain errors affecting substantial rights although they were not brought to the attention of the court.

(Pub.L. 93–595, § 1, Jan. 2, 1975, 88 Stat. 1929; Apr. 17, 2000, eff. Dec. 1, 2000.)

Rule 104. Preliminary Questions

(a) Questions of admissibility generally. Preliminary questions concerning the qualification of a person to be a witness, the existence of a privilege, or the admissibility of evidence shall be determined by the court, subject to the provisions of subdivision (b). In making its determination it is not bound by the rules of evidence except those with respect to privileges.

(b) Relevancy conditioned on fact. When the relevancy of evidence depends upon the fulfillment of a condition of fact, the court shall admit it upon, or subject to, the introduction of evidence sufficient to support a finding of the fulfillment of the condition.

(c) Hearing of jury. Hearings on the admissibility of confessions shall in all cases be conducted out of the hearing of the jury. Hearings on other preliminary matters shall be so conducted when the interests of justice require, or when an accused is a witness and so requests.

(d) Testimony by accused. The accused does not, by testifying upon a preliminary matter, become subject to cross-examination as to other issues in the case.

(e) Weight and credibility. This rule does not limit the right of a party to introduce before the jury evidence relevant to weight or credibility.

(Pub.L. 93–595, § 1, Jan. 2, 1975, 88 Stat.1930; Mar. 2, 1987, eff. Oct. 1, 1987.)

Rule 105. Limited Admissibility

When evidence which is admissible as to one party or for one purpose but not admissible as to another party or for another purpose is admitted, the court, upon request, shall restrict the evidence to its proper scope and instruct the jury accordingly.

(Pub.L. 93–595, § 1, Jan. 2, 1975, 88 Stat. 1930.)

Rule 106. Remainder of or Related Writings or Recorded Statements

When a writing or recorded statement or part thereof is introduced by a party, an adverse party may require the introduction at that time of any other part or any other writing or recorded statement which ought in fairness to be considered contemporaneously with it.

(Pub.L. 93–595, § 1, Jan. 2, 1975, 88 Stat. 1930; Mar. 2, 1987, eff. Oct. 1, 1987.)

ARTICLE II. JUDICIAL NOTICE

Rule 201. Judicial Notice of Adjudicative Facts

(a) Scope of rule. This rule governs only judicial notice of adjudicative facts.

(b) Kinds of facts. A judicially noticed fact must be one not subject to reasonable dispute in that it is either (1) generally known within the territorial jurisdiction of the trial court or (2) capable of accurate and ready determination by resort to sources whose accuracy cannot reasonably be questioned.

(c) When discretionary. A court may take judicial notice, whether requested or not.

(d) When mandatory. A court shall take judicial notice if requested by a party and supplied with the necessary information.

(e) Opportunity to be heard. A party is entitled upon timely request to an opportunity to be heard as to the propriety of taking judicial notice and the tenor of the matter noticed. In the absence of prior notification, the request may be made after judicial notice has been taken.

(f) Time of taking notice. Judicial notice may be taken at any stage of the proceeding.

(g) Instructing jury. In a civil action or proceeding, the court shall instruct the jury to accept as conclusive any fact judicially noticed. In a criminal case, the court shall instruct the jury that it may, but is not required to, accept as conclusive any fact judicially noticed.

(Pub.L. 93–595, § 1, Jan. 2, 1975, 88 Stat. 1930.)

ARTICLE III. PRESUMPTIONS IN CIVIL ACTIONS AND PROCEEDINGS

Rule 301. Presumptions in General in Civil Actions and Proceedings

In all civil actions and proceedings not otherwise provided for by Act of Congress or by these rules, a presumption imposes on the party against whom it is directed the burden of going forward with evidence to rebut or meet the presumption, but does not shift to such party the burden of proof in the sense of the risk of nonpersuasion, which remains throughout the trial upon the party on whom it was originally cast.

(Pub.L. 93–595, § 1, Jan. 2, 1975, 88 Stat. 1931.)

Rule 302. Applicability of State Law in Civil Actions and Proceedings

In civil actions and proceedings, the effect of a presumption respecting a fact which is an element of a claim or defense as to which State law supplies the rule of decision is determined in accordance with State law.

(Pub.L. 93–595, § 1, Jan. 2, 1975, 88 Stat. 1931.)

ARTICLE IV. RELEVANCY AND ITS LIMITS

Rule 401. Definition of "Relevant Evidence"

"Relevant evidence" means evidence having any tendency to make the existence of any fact that is of consequence to the determination of the action more probable or less probable than it would be without the evidence.

(Pub.L. 93–595, § 1, Jan. 2, 1975, 88 Stat.1931.)

Rule 402. Relevant Evidence Generally Admissible; Irrelevant Evidence Inadmissible

All relevant evidence is admissible, except as otherwise provided by the Constitution of the United States, by Act of Congress, by these rules, or by other rules prescribed by the Supreme Court pursuant to

statutory authority. Evidence which is not relevant is not admissible.

(Pub.L. 93–595, § 1, Jan. 2, 1975, 88 Stat. 1931.)

Rule 403. Exclusion of Relevant Evidence on Grounds of Prejudice, Confusion, or Waste of Time

Although relevant, evidence may be excluded if its probative value is substantially outweighed by the danger of unfair prejudice, confusion of the issues, or misleading the jury, or by considerations of undue delay, waste of time, or needless presentation of cumulative evidence.

(Pub.L. 93–595, § 1, Jan. 2, 1975, 88 Stat. 1932.)

Rule 404. Character Evidence Not Admissible To Prove Conduct; Exceptions; Other Crimes

(a) Character evidence generally.—Evidence of a person's character or a trait of character is not admissible for the purpose of proving action in conformity therewith on a particular occasion, except:

(1) **Character of accused.**—In a criminal case, evidence of a pertinent trait of character offered by an accused, or by the prosecution to rebut the same, or if evidence of a trait of character of the alleged victim of the crime is offered by an accused and admitted under Rule 404(a)(2), evidence of the same trait of character of the accused offered by the prosecution;

(2) **Character of alleged victim.**—In a criminal case, and subject to the limitations imposed by Rule 412, evidence of a pertinent trait of character of the alleged victim of the crime offered by an accused, or by the prosecution to rebut the same, or evidence of a character trait of peacefulness of the alleged victim offered by the prosecution in a homicide case to rebut evidence that the alleged victim was the first aggressor;

(3) **Character of witness.**—Evidence of the character of a witness, as provided in Rules 607, 608, and 609.

(b) Other Crimes, Wrongs, or Acts.—Evidence of other crimes, wrongs, or acts is not admissible to prove the character of a person in order to show action in conformity therewith. It may, however, be admissible for other purposes, such as proof of motive, opportunity, intent, preparation, plan, knowledge, identity, or absence of mistake or accident, provided that upon request by the accused, the prosecution in a criminal case shall provide reasonable notice in advance of trial, or during trial if the court excuses pretrial notice on good cause shown, of the general nature of any such evidence it intends to introduce at trial.

(Pub.L. 93–595, § 1, Jan. 2, 1975, 88 Stat.1932; Mar. 2, 1987, eff. Oct. 1, 1987; Apr. 30, 1991, eff. Dec. 1, 1991; Apr. 17, 2000, eff. Dec. 1, 2000; Apr. 12, 2006, eff. Dec. 1, 2006.)

Rule 405. Methods of Proving Character

(a) Reputation or opinion. In all cases in which evidence of character or a trait of character of a person is admissible, proof may be made by testimony as to reputation or by testimony in the form of an opinion. On cross-examination, inquiry is allowable into relevant specific instances of conduct.

(b) Specific instances of conduct. In cases in which character or a trait of character of a person is an essential element of a charge, claim, or defense, proof may also be made of specific instances of that person's conduct.

(Pub.L. 93–595, § 1, Jan. 2, 1975, 88 Stat. 1932; Mar. 2, 1987, eff. Oct. 1, 1987.)

Rule 406. Habit; Routine Practice

Evidence of the habit of a person or of the routine practice of an organization, whether corroborated or not and regardless of the presence of eyewitnesses, is relevant to prove that the conduct of the person or organization on a particular occasion was in conformity with the habit or routine practice.

(Pub.L. 93–595, § 1, Jan. 2, 1975, 88 Stat. 1932.)

Rule 407. Subsequent Remedial Measures

When, after an injury or harm allegedly caused by an event, measures are taken that, if taken previously, would have made the injury or harm less likely to occur, evidence of the subsequent measures is not admissible to prove negligence, culpable conduct, a defect in a product, a defect in a product's design, or a need for a warning or instruction. This rule does not require the exclusion of evidence of subsequent measures when offered for another purpose, such as proving ownership, control, or feasibility of precautionary measures, if controverted, or impeachment.

(Pub.L. 93–595, § 1, Jan. 2, 1975, 88 Stat. 1932; Apr. 11, 1997, eff. Dec. 1, 1997.)

Rule 408. Compromise and Offers to Compromise

(a) Prohibited uses.—Evidence of the following is not admissible on behalf of any party, when offered to prove liability for, invalidity of, or amount of a claim that was disputed as to validity or amount, or to impeach through a prior inconsistent statement or contradiction:

(1) furnishing or offering or promising to furnish—or accepting or offering or promising to accept—a valuable consideration in compromising or attempting to compromise the claim; and

(2) conduct or statements made in compromise negotiations regarding the claim, except when offered in a criminal case and the negotiations related to a claim by a public office or agency in the exercise of regulatory, investigative, or enforcement authority.

(b) Permitted uses.—This rule does not require exclusion if the evidence is offered for purposes not prohibited by subdivision (a). Examples of permissible purposes include proving a witness's bias or prejudice; negating a contention of undue delay; and proving an effort to obstruct a criminal investigation or prosecution.

(Pub.L. 93–595, § 1, Jan. 2, 1975, 88 Stat. 1933; Apr. 12, 2006, eff. Dec. 1, 2006.)

Rule 409. Payment of Medical and Similar Expenses

Evidence of furnishing or offering or promising to pay medical, hospital, or similar expenses occasioned by an injury is not admissible to prove liability for the injury.

(Pub.L. 93–595, § 1, Jan. 2, 1975, 88 Stat.1933.)

Rule 410. Inadmissibility of Pleas, Plea Discussions, and Related Statements

Except as otherwise provided in this rule, evidence of the following is not, in any civil or criminal proceeding, admissible against the defendant who made the plea or was a participant in the plea discussions:

(1) a plea of guilty which was later withdrawn;

(2) a plea of nolo contendere;

(3) any statement made in the course of any proceedings under Rule 11 of the Federal Rules of Criminal Procedure or comparable state procedure regarding either of the foregoing pleas; or

(4) any statement made in the course of plea discussions with an attorney for the prosecuting authority which do not result in a plea of guilty or which result in a plea of guilty later withdrawn.

However, such a statement is admissible (i) in any proceeding wherein another statement made in the course of the same plea or plea discussions has been introduced and the statement ought in fairness be considered contemporaneously with it, or (ii) in a criminal proceeding for perjury or false statement if the statement was made by the defendant under oath, on the record and in the presence of counsel.

(Pub.L. 93–595, § 1, Jan. 2, 1975, 88 Stat. 1933; Pub.L. 94–149, § 1(9), Dec. 12, 1975, 89 Stat. 805; Apr. 30, 1979, eff. Dec. 1, 1980.)

Rule 411. Liability Insurance

Evidence that a person was or was not insured against liability is not admissible upon the issue whether the person acted negligently or otherwise wrongfully. This rule does not require the exclusion of evidence of insurance against liability when offered for another purpose, such as proof of agency, ownership, or control, or bias or prejudice of a witness.

(Pub.L. 93–595, § 1, Jan. 2, 1975, 88 Stat.1933; Mar. 2, 1987, eff. Oct. 1, 1987.)

Rule 412. Sex Offense Cases; Relevance of Alleged Victim's Past Sexual Behavior or Alleged Sexual Predisposition

(a) Evidence generally inadmissible.—The following evidence is not admissible in any civil or criminal proceeding involving alleged sexual misconduct except as provided in subdivisions (b) and (c):

(1) Evidence offered to prove that any alleged victim engaged in other sexual behavior.

(2) Evidence offered to prove any alleged victim's sexual predisposition.

(b) Exceptions.—

(1) In a criminal case, the following evidence is admissible, if otherwise admissible under these rules:

(A) evidence of specific instances of sexual behavior by the alleged victim offered to prove that a person other than the accused was the source of semen, injury or other physical evidence;

(B) evidence of specific instances of sexual behavior by the alleged victim with respect to the person accused of the sexual misconduct offered by the accused to prove consent or by the prosecution; and

(C) evidence the exclusion of which would violate the constitutional rights of the defendant.

(2) In a civil case, evidence offered to prove the sexual behavior or sexual predisposition of any alleged victim is admissible if it is otherwise admissible under these rules and its probative value substantially outweighs the danger of harm to any victim and of unfair prejudice to any party. Evidence of an alleged victim's reputation is admissible only if it has been placed in controversy by the alleged victim.

(c) Procedure to determine admissibility.—

(1) A party intending to offer evidence under subdivision (b) must—

(A) file a written motion at least 14 days before trial specifically describing the evidence and stating the purpose for which it is offered unless the court, for good cause requires a different time for filing or permits filing during trial; and

(B) serve the motion on all parties and notify the alleged victim or, when appropriate, the alleged victim's guardian or representative.

Complete Annotation Materials, see Title 28 U.S.C.A.

(2) Before admitting evidence under this rule the court must conduct a hearing in camera and afford the victim and parties a right to attend and be heard. The motion, related papers, and the record of the hearing must be sealed and remain under seal unless the court orders otherwise.
(Added Pub.L. 95–540, § 2(a), Oct. 28, 1978, 92 Stat. 2046, and amended Pub.L. 100–690, Title VII, § 7046(a), Nov. 18, 1988, 102 Stat. 4400; Apr. 29, 1994, eff. Dec. 1, 1994; Pub.L. 103–322, Title IV, § 40141(b), Sept. 13, 1994, 108 Stat. 1919.)

Rule 413. Evidence of Similar Crimes in Sexual Assault Cases

(a) In a criminal case in which the defendant is accused of an offense of sexual assault, evidence of the defendant's commission of another offense or offenses of sexual assault is admissible, and may be considered for its bearing on any matter to which it is relevant.

(b) In a case in which the Government intends to offer evidence under this rule, the attorney for the Government shall disclose the evidence to the defendant, including statements of witnesses or a summary of the substance of any testimony that is expected to be offered, at least fifteen days before the scheduled date of trial or at such later time as the court may allow for good cause.

(c) This rule shall not be construed to limit the admission or consideration of evidence under any other rule.

(d) For purposes of this rule and Rule 415, "offense of sexual assault" means a crime under Federal law or the law of a State (as defined in section 513 of title 18, United States Code) that involved—

(1) any conduct proscribed by chapter 109A of title 18, United States Code;

(2) contact, without consent, between any part of the defendant's body or an object and the genitals or anus of another person;

(3) contact, without consent, between the genitals or anus of the defendant and any part of another person's body;

(4) deriving sexual pleasure or gratification from the infliction of death, bodily injury, or physical pain on another person; or

(5) an attempt or conspiracy to engage in conduct described in paragraphs (1)–(4).
(Added Pub.L. 103–322, Title XXXII, § 320935(a), Sept. 13, 1994, 108 Stat. 2136.)

Rule 414. Evidence of Similar Crimes in Child Molestation Cases

(a) In a criminal case in which the defendant is accused of an offense of child molestation, evidence of the defendant's commission of another offense or offenses of child molestation is admissible, and may be considered for its bearing on any matter to which it is relevant.

(b) In a case in which the Government intends to offer evidence under this rule, the attorney for the Government shall disclose the evidence to the defendant, including statements of witnesses or a summary of the substance of any testimony that is expected to be offered, at least fifteen days before the scheduled date of trial or at such later time as the court may allow for good cause.

(c) This rule shall not be construed to limit the admission or consideration of evidence under any other rule.

(d) For purposes of this rule and Rule 415, "child" means a person below the age of fourteen, and "offense of child molestation" means a crime under Federal law or the law of a State (as defined in section 513 of title 18, United States Code) that involved—

(1) any conduct proscribed by chapter 109A of title 18, United States Code, that was committed in relation to a child;

(2) any conduct proscribed by chapter 110 of title 18, United States Code;

(3) contact between any part of the defendant's body or an object and the genitals or anus of a child;

(4) contact between the genitals or anus of the defendant and any part of the body of a child;

(5) deriving sexual pleasure or gratification from the infliction of death, bodily injury, or physical pain on a child; or

(6) an attempt or conspiracy to engage in conduct described in paragraphs (1)–(5).
(Added Pub.L. 103–322, Title XXXII, § 320935(a), Sept. 13, 1994, 108 Stat. 2135.)

Rule 415. Evidence of Similar Acts in Civil Cases Concerning Sexual Assault or Child Molestation

(a) In a civil case in which a claim for damages or other relief is predicated on a party's alleged commission of conduct constituting an offense of sexual assault or child molestation, evidence of that party's commission of another offense or offenses of sexual assault or child molestation is admissible and may be considered as provided in Rule 413 and Rule 414 of these rules.

(b) A party who intends to offer evidence under this Rule shall disclose the evidence to the party against whom it will be offered, including statements of witnesses or a summary of the substance of any

testimony that is expected to be offered, at least fifteen days before the scheduled date of trial or at such later time as the court may allow for good cause.

(c) This rule shall not be construed to limit the admission or consideration of evidence under any other rule.

(Added Pub.L. 103–322, Title XXXII, § 320935(a), Sept. 13, 1994, 108 Stat. 2137.)

ARTICLE V. PRIVILEGES

Rule 501. General Rule

Except as otherwise required by the Constitution of the United States or provided by Act of Congress or in rules prescribed by the Supreme Court pursuant to statutory authority, the privilege of a witness, person, government, State, or political subdivision thereof shall be governed by the principles of the common law as they may be interpreted by the courts of the United States in the light of reason and experience. However, in civil actions and proceedings, with respect to an element of a claim or defense as to which State law supplies the rule of decision, the privilege of a witness, person, government, State, or political subdivision thereof shall be determined in accordance with State law.

(Pub.L. 93–595, § 1, Jan. 2, 1975, 88 Stat. 1933.)

ARTICLE VI. WITNESSES

Rule 601. General Rule of Competency

Every person is competent to be a witness except as otherwise provided in these rules. However, in civil actions and proceedings, with respect to an element of a claim or defense as to which State law supplies the rule of decision, the competency of a witness shall be determined in accordance with State law.

(Pub.L. 93–595, § 1, Jan. 2, 1975, 88 Stat.1934.)

Rule 602. Lack of Personal Knowledge

A witness may not testify to a matter unless evidence is introduced sufficient to support a finding that the witness has personal knowledge of the matter. Evidence to prove personal knowledge may, but need not, consist of the witness' own testimony. This rule is subject to the provisions of rule 703, relating to opinion testimony by expert witnesses.

(Pub.L. 93–595, § 1, Jan. 2, 1975, 88 Stat. 1934; Mar. 2, 1987, eff. Oct. 1, 1987; Apr. 25, 1988, eff. Nov. 1, 1988.)

Rule 603. Oath or Affirmation

Before testifying, every witness shall be required to declare that the witness will testify truthfully, by oath or affirmation administered in a form calculated to awaken the witness' conscience and impress the witness' mind with the duty to do so.

(Pub.L. 93–595, § 1, Jan. 2, 1975, 88 Stat. 1934; Mar. 2, 1987, eff. Oct. 1, 1987.)

Rule 604. Interpreters

An interpreter is subject to the provisions of these rules relating to qualification as an expert and the administration of an oath or affirmation to make a true translation.

(Pub.L. 93–595, § 1, Jan. 2, 1975, 88 Stat. 1934; Mar. 2, 1987, eff. Oct. 1, 1987.)

Rule 605. Competency of Judge as Witness

The judge presiding at the trial may not testify in that trial as a witness. No objection need be made in order to preserve the point.

(Pub.L. 93–595, § 1, Jan. 2, 1975, 88 Stat. 1934.)

Rule 606. Competency of Juror as Witness

(a) At the trial. A member of the jury may not testify as a witness before that jury in the trial of the case in which the juror is sitting. If the juror is called so to testify, the opposing party shall be afforded an opportunity to object out of the presence of the jury.

(b) Inquiry into validity of verdict or indictment. Upon an inquiry into the validity of a verdict or indictment, a juror may not testify as to any matter or statement occurring during the course of the jury's deliberations or to the effect of anything upon that or any other juror's mind or emotions as influencing the juror to assent to or dissent from the verdict or indictment or concerning the juror's mental processes in connection therewith. But a juror may testify about (1) whether extraneous prejudicial information was improperly brought to the jury's attention, (2) whether any outside influence was improperly brought to bear upon any juror, or (3) whether there was a mistake in entering the verdict onto the verdict form. A juror's affidavit or evidence of any statement by the juror may not be received on a matter about which the juror would be precluded from testifying.

(Pub.L. 93–595, § 1, Jan. 2, 1975, 88 Stat. 1934; Pub.L. 94–149, § 1(10), Dec. 12, 1975, 89 Stat. 805; Mar. 2, 1987, eff. Oct. 1, 1987; Apr. 12, 2006, eff. Dec. 1, 2006.)

Rule 607. Who May Impeach

The credibility of a witness may be attacked by any party, including the party calling the witness.

(Pub.L. 93–595, § 1, Jan. 2, 1975, 88 Stat.1934; Mar. 2, 1987, eff. Oct. 1, 1987.)

Rule 608. Evidence of Character and Conduct of Witness

(a) Opinion and reputation evidence of character. The credibility of a witness may be attacked or supported by evidence in the form of opinion or reputation, but subject to these limitations: (1) the evidence may refer only to character for truthfulness or untruthfulness, and (2) evidence of truthful character is admissible only after the character of the witness for truthfulness has been attacked by opinion or reputation evidence or otherwise.

(b) Specific instances of conduct. Specific instances of the conduct of a witness, for the purpose of attacking or supporting the witness' character for truthfulness, other than conviction of crime as provided in rule 609, may not be proved by extrinsic evidence. They may, however, in the discretion of the court, if probative of truthfulness or untruthfulness, be inquired into on cross-examination of the witness (1) concerning the witness' character for truthfulness or untruthfulness, or (2) concerning the character for truthfulness or untruthfulness of another witness as to which character the witness being cross-examined has testified.

The giving of testimony, whether by an accused or by any other witness, does not operate as a waiver of the accused's or the witness' privilege against self-incrimination when examined with respect to matters that relate only to character for truthfulness.

(Pub.L. 93–595, § 1, Jan. 2, 1975, 88 Stat.1935; Mar. 2, 1987, eff. Oct. 1, 1987; Apr. 25, 1988, eff. Nov. 1, 1988; Mar. 27, 2003, eff. Dec. 1, 2003.)

Rule 609. Impeachment by Evidence of Conviction of Crime

(a) General rule.—For the purpose of attacking the character for truthfulness of a witness,

(1) evidence that a witness other than an accused has been convicted of a crime shall be admitted, subject to Rule 403, if the crime was punishable by death or imprisonment in excess of one year under the law under which the witness was convicted, and evidence that an accused has been convicted of such a crime shall be admitted if the court determines that the probative value of admitting this evidence outweighs its prejudicial effect to the accused; and

(2) evidence that any witness has been convicted of a crime shall be admitted regardless of the punishment, if it readily can be determined that establishing the elements of the crime required

proof or admission of an act of dishonesty or false statement by the witness.

(b) Time limit. Evidence of a conviction under this rule is not admissible if a period of more than ten years has elapsed since the date of the conviction or of the release of the witness from the confinement imposed for that conviction, whichever is the later date, unless the court determines, in the interests of justice, that the probative value of the conviction supported by specific facts and circumstances substantially outweighs its prejudicial effect. However, evidence of a conviction more than 10 years old as calculated herein, is not admissible unless the proponent gives to the adverse party sufficient advance written notice of intent to use such evidence to provide the adverse party with a fair opportunity to contest the use of such evidence.

(c) Effect of pardon, annulment, or certificate of rehabilitation.—Evidence of a conviction is not admissible under this rule if (1) the conviction has been the subject of a pardon, annulment, certificate of rehabilitation, or other equivalent procedure based on a finding of the rehabilitation of the person convicted, and that person has not been convicted of a subsequent crime that was punishable by death or imprisonment in excess of one year, or (2) the conviction has been the subject of a pardon, annulment, or other equivalent procedure based on a finding of innocence.

(d) Juvenile adjudications. Evidence of juvenile adjudications is generally not admissible under this rule. The court may, however, in a criminal case allow evidence of a juvenile adjudication of a witness other than the accused if conviction of the offense would be admissible to attack the credibility of an adult and the court is satisfied that admission in evidence is necessary for a fair determination of the issue of guilt or innocence.

(e) Pendency of appeal. The pendency of an appeal therefrom does not render evidence of a conviction inadmissible. Evidence of the pendency of an appeal is admissible.

(Pub.L. 93–595, § 1, Jan. 2, 1975, 88 Stat.1935; Mar. 2, 1987, eff. Oct. 1, 1987; Jan. 26, 1990, eff. Dec. 1, 1990; Apr. 12, 2006, eff. Dec. 1, 2006.)

Rule 610. Religious Beliefs or Opinions

Evidence of the beliefs or opinions of a witness on matters of religion is not admissible for the purpose of showing that by reason of their nature the witness' credibility is impaired or enhanced.

(Pub.L. 93–595, § 1, Jan. 2, 1975, 88 Stat.1936; Mar. 2, 1987, eff. Oct. 1, 1987.)

Rule 611. Mode and Order of Interrogation and Presentation

(a) Control by court. The court shall exercise reasonable control over the mode and order of interro-

gating witnesses and presenting evidence so as to (1) make the interrogation and presentation effective for the ascertainment of the truth, (2) avoid needless consumption of time, and (3) protect witnesses from harassment or undue embarrassment.

(b) Scope of cross-examination. Cross-examination should be limited to the subject matter of the direct examination and matters affecting the credibility of the witness. The court may, in the exercise of discretion, permit inquiry into additional matters as if on direct examination.

(c) Leading questions. Leading questions should not be used on the direct examination of a witness except as may be necessary to develop the witness' testimony. Ordinarily leading questions should be permitted on cross-examination. When a party calls a hostile witness, an adverse party, or a witness identified with an adverse party, interrogation may be by leading questions.

(Pub.L. 93–595, § 1, Jan. 2, 1975, 88 Stat. 1936; Mar. 2, 1987, eff. Oct. 1, 1987.)

Rule 612. Writing Used to Refresh Memory

Except as otherwise provided in criminal proceedings by section 3500 of title 18, United States Code, if a witness uses a writing to refresh memory for the purpose of testifying, either—

(1) while testifying, or

(2) before testifying, if the court in its discretion determines it is necessary in the interests of justice,

an adverse party is entitled to have the writing produced at the hearing, to inspect it, to cross-examine the witness thereon, and to introduce in evidence those portions which relate to the testimony of the witness. If it is claimed that the writing contains matters not related to the subject matter of the testimony the court shall examine the writing in camera, excise any portions not so related, and order delivery of the remainder to the party entitled thereto. Any portion withheld over objections shall be preserved and made available to the appellate court in the event of an appeal. If a writing is not produced or delivered pursuant to order under this rule, the court shall make any order justice requires, except that in criminal cases when the prosecution elects not to comply, the order shall be one striking the testimony or, if the court in its discretion determines that the interests of justice so require, declaring a mistrial.

(Pub.L. 93–595, § 1, Jan. 2, 1975, 88 Stat. 1936; Mar. 2, 1987, eff. Oct. 1, 1987.)

Rule 613. Prior Statements of Witnesses

(a) Examining witness concerning prior statement. In examining a witness concerning a prior statement made by the witness, whether written or not, the statement need not be shown nor its contents disclosed to the witness at that time, but on request the same shall be shown or disclosed to opposing counsel.

(b) Extrinsic evidence of prior inconsistent statement of witness. Extrinsic evidence of a prior inconsistent statement by a witness is not admissible unless the witness is afforded an opportunity to explain or deny the same and the opposite party is afforded an opportunity to interrogate the witness thereon, or the interests of justice otherwise require. This provision does not apply to admissions of a party-opponent as defined in rule 801(d)(2).

(Pub.L. 93–595, § 1, Jan. 2, 1975, 88 Stat.1936; Mar. 2, 1987, eff. Oct. 1, 1987; Apr. 25, 1988, eff. Nov. 1, 1988.)

Rule 614. Calling and Interrogation of Witnesses by Court

(a) Calling by court. The court may, on its own motion or at the suggestion of a party, call witnesses, and all parties are entitled to cross-examine witnesses thus called.

(b) Interrogation by court. The court may interrogate witnesses, whether called by itself or by a party.

(c) Objections. Objections to the calling of witnesses by the court or to interrogation by it may be made at the time or at the next available opportunity when the jury is not present.

(Pub.L. 93–595, § 1, Jan. 2, 1975, 88 Stat.1937.)

Rule 615. Exclusion of Witnesses

At the request of a party the court shall order witnesses excluded so that they cannot hear the testimony of other witnesses, and it may make the order of its own motion. This rule does not authorize exclusion of (1) a party who is a natural person, or (2) an officer or employee of a party which is not a natural person designated as its representative by its attorney, or (3) a person whose presence is shown by a party to be essential to the presentation of the party's cause, or (4) a person authorized by statute to be present.

(Pub.L. 93–595, § 1, Jan. 2, 1975, 88 Stat.1937; Mar. 2, 1987, eff. Oct. 1, 1987; Apr. 25, 1988, eff. Nov. 1, 1988; Pub.L. 100–690, Nov. 18, 1988, Title VII, § 7075(a), 102 Stat. 4405; Apr. 24, 1998, eff. Dec. 1, 1998.)

Rules 616 to 700. Reserved for future legislation

ARTICLE VII. OPINIONS AND EXPERT TESTIMONY

Rule 701. Opinion Testimony by Lay Witnesses

If the witness is not testifying as an expert, the witness' testimony in the form of opinions or inferences is limited to those opinions or inferences which are (a) rationally based on the perception of the witness, (b) helpful to a clear understanding of the witness' testimony or the determination of a fact in issue, and (c) not based on scientific, technical, or other specialized knowledge within the scope of Rule 702.

(Pub.L. 93–595, § 1, Jan. 2, 1975, 88 Stat.1937; Mar. 2, 1987, eff. Oct. 1, 1987; Apr. 17, 2000, eff. Dec. 1, 2000.)

Rule 702. Testimony by Experts

If scientific, technical, or other specialized knowledge will assist the trier of fact to understand the evidence or to determine a fact in issue, a witness qualified as an expert by knowledge, skill, experience, training, or education, may testify thereto in the form of an opinion or otherwise, if (1) the testimony is based upon sufficient facts or data, (2) the testimony is the product of reliable principles and methods, and (3) the witness has applied the principles and methods reliably to the facts of the case.

(Pub.L. 93–595, § 1, Jan. 2, 1975, 88 Stat. 1937; Apr. 17, 2000, eff. Dec. 1, 2000.)

Rule 703. Bases of Opinion Testimony by Experts

The facts or data in the particular case upon which an expert bases an opinion or inference may be those perceived by or made known to the expert at or before the hearing. If of a type reasonably relied upon by experts in the particular field in forming opinions or inferences upon the subject, the facts or data need not be admissible in evidence in order for the opinion or inference to be admitted. Facts or data that are otherwise inadmissible shall not be disclosed to the jury by the proponent of the opinion or inference unless the court determines that their probative value in assisting the jury to evaluate the expert's opinion substantially outweighs their prejudicial effect.

(Pub.L. 93–595, § 1, Jan. 2, 1975, 88 Stat.1937; Mar. 2, 1987, eff. Oct. 1, 1987; Apr. 17, 2000, eff. Dec. 1, 2000.)

Rule 704. Opinion on Ultimate Issue

(a) Except as provided in subdivision (b), testimony in the form of an opinion or inference otherwise admissible is not objectionable because it embraces an ultimate issue to be decided by the trier of fact.

(b) No expert witness testifying with respect to the mental state or condition of a defendant in a criminal case may state an opinion or inference as to whether the defendant did or did not have the mental state or condition constituting an element of the crime charged or of a defense thereto. Such ultimate issues are matters for the trier of fact alone.

(Pub.L. 93–595, § 1, Jan. 2, 1975, 88 Stat. 1937; Pub.L. 98–473, Title IV, § 406, Oct. 12, 1984, 98 Stat. 2067.)

Rule 705. Disclosure of Facts or Data Underlying Expert Opinion

The expert may testify in terms of opinion or inference and give reasons therefor without first testifying to the underlying facts or data, unless the court requires otherwise. The expert may in any event be required to disclose the underlying facts or data on cross-examination.

(Pub.L. 93–595, § 1, Jan. 2, 1975, 88 Stat. 1938; Mar. 2, 1987, eff. Oct. 1, 1987; Apr. 22, 1993, eff. Dec. 1, 1993.)

Rule 706. Court Appointed Experts

(a) **Appointment.** The court may on its own motion or on the motion of any party enter an order to show cause why expert witnesses should not be appointed, and may request the parties to submit nominations. The court may appoint any expert witnesses agreed upon by the parties, and may appoint expert witnesses of its own selection. An expert witness shall not be appointed by the court unless the witness consents to act. A witness so appointed shall be informed of the witness' duties by the court in writing, a copy of which shall be filed with the clerk, or at a conference in which the parties shall have opportunity to participate. A witness so appointed shall advise the parties of the witness' findings, if any; the witness' deposition may be taken by any party; and the witness may be called to testify by the court or any party. The witness shall be subject to cross-examination by each party, including a party calling the witness.

(b) **Compensation.** Expert witnesses so appointed are entitled to reasonable compensation in whatever sum the court may allow. The compensation thus fixed is payable from funds which may be provided by law in criminal cases and civil actions and proceedings involving just compensation under the fifth amendment. In other civil actions and proceedings the compensation shall be paid by the parties in such proportion and at such time as the court directs, and thereafter charged in like manner as other costs.

(c) **Disclosure of appointment.** In the exercise of its discretion, the court may authorize disclosure to the jury of the fact that the court appointed the expert witness.

(d) Parties' experts of own selection. Nothing in this rule limits the parties in calling expert witnesses of their own selection.

(Pub.L. 93–595, § 1, Jan. 2, 1975, 88 Stat.1938; Mar. 2, 1987, eff. Oct. 1, 1987.)

ARTICLE VIII. HEARSAY

Rule 801. Definitions

The following definitions apply under this article:

(a) Statement. A "statement" is (1) an oral or written assertion or (2) nonverbal conduct of a person, if it is intended by the person as an assertion.

(b) Declarant. A "declarant" is a person who makes a statement.

(c) Hearsay. "Hearsay" is a statement, other than one made by the declarant while testifying at the trial or hearing, offered in evidence to prove the truth of the matter asserted.

(d) Statements which are not hearsay. A statement is not hearsay if—

(1) Prior statement by witness. The declarant testifies at the trial or hearing and is subject to cross-examination concerning the statement, and the statement is (A) inconsistent with the declarant's testimony, and was given under oath subject to the penalty of perjury at a trial, hearing, or other proceeding, or in a deposition, or (B) consistent with the declarant's testimony and is offered to rebut an express or implied charge against the declarant of recent fabrication or improper influence or motive, or (C) one of identification of a person made after perceiving the person; or

(2) Admission by party-opponent. The statement is offered against a party and is (A) the party's own statement, in either an individual or a representative capacity or (B) a statement of which the party has manifested an adoption or belief in its truth, or (C) a statement by a person authorized by the party to make a statement concerning the subject, or (D) a statement by the party's agent or servant concerning a matter within the scope of the agency or employment, made during the existence of the relationship, or (E) a statement by a coconspirator of a party during the course and in furtherance of the conspiracy. The contents of the statement shall be considered but are not alone sufficient to establish the declarant's authority under subdivision (C), the agency or employment relationship and scope thereof under subdivision (D), or the existence of the conspiracy and the participation therein of the declarant and the party against whom the statement is offered under subdivision (E).

(Pub.L. 93–595, § 1, Jan. 2, 1975, 88 Stat.1938; Pub.L. 94–113, § 1, Oct. 16, 1975, 89 Stat. 576; Mar. 2, 1987, eff. Oct. 1, 1987; Apr. 11, 1997, eff. Dec. 1, 1997.)

Rule 802. Hearsay Rule

Hearsay is not admissible except as provided by these rules or by other rules prescribed by the Supreme Court pursuant to statutory authority or by Act of Congress.

(Pub.L. 93–595, § 1, Jan. 2, 1975, 88 Stat. 1939.)

Rule 803. Hearsay Exceptions; Availability of Declarant Immaterial

The following are not excluded by the hearsay rule, even though the declarant is available as a witness:

(1) Present sense impression. A statement describing or explaining an event or condition made while the declarant was perceiving the event or condition, or immediately thereafter.

(2) Excited utterance. A statement relating to a startling event or condition made while the declarant was under the stress of excitement caused by the event or condition.

(3) Then existing mental, emotional, or physical condition. A statement of the declarant's then existing state of mind, emotion, sensation, or physical condition (such as intent, plan, motive, design, mental feeling, pain, and bodily health), but not including a statement of memory or belief to prove the fact remembered or believed unless it relates to the execution, revocation, identification, or terms of declarant's will.

(4) Statements for purposes of medical diagnosis or treatment. Statements made for purposes of medical diagnosis or treatment and describing medical history, or past or present symptoms, pain, or sensations, or the inception or general character of the cause or external source thereof insofar as reasonably pertinent to diagnosis or treatment.

(5) Recorded recollection. A memorandum or record concerning a matter about which a witness once had knowledge but now has insufficient recollection to enable the witness to testify fully and accurately, shown to have been made or adopted by the witness when the matter was fresh in the witness' memory and to reflect that knowledge correctly. If admitted, the memorandum or record may be read into evidence but may not itself be received as an exhibit unless offered by an adverse party.

(6) Records of Regularly Conducted Activity.—A memorandum, report, record, or data compilation, in any form, of acts, events, conditions, opin-

ions, or diagnoses, made at or near the time by, or from information transmitted by, a person with knowledge, if kept in the course of a regularly conducted business activity, and if it was the regular practice of that business activity to make the memorandum, report, record or data compilation, all as shown by the testimony of the custodian or other qualified witness, or by certification that complies with Rule 902(11), Rule 902(12), or a statute permitting certification, unless the source of information or the method or circumstances of preparation indicate lack of trustworthiness. The term "business" as used in this paragraph includes business, institution, association, profession, occupation, and calling of every kind, whether or not conducted for profit.

(7) Absence of entry in records kept in accordance with the provisions of paragraph (6). Evidence that a matter is not included in the memoranda reports, records, or data compilations, in any form, kept in accordance with the provisions of paragraph (6), to prove the nonoccurrence or nonexistence of the matter, if the matter was of a kind of which a memorandum, report, record, or data compilation was regularly made and preserved, unless the sources of information or other circumstances indicate lack of trustworthiness.

(8) Public records and reports. Records, reports, statements, or data compilations, in any form, of public offices or agencies, setting forth (A) the activities of the office or agency, or (B) matters observed pursuant to duty imposed by law as to which matters there was a duty to report, excluding, however, in criminal cases matters observed by police officers and other law enforcement personnel, or (C) in civil actions and proceedings and against the Government in criminal cases, factual findings resulting from an investigation made pursuant to authority granted by law, unless the sources of information or other circumstances indicate lack of trustworthiness.

(9) Records of vital statistics. Records or data compilations, in any form, of births, fetal deaths, deaths, or marriages, if the report thereof was made to a public office pursuant to requirements of law.

(10) Absence of public record or entry. To prove the absence of a record, report, statement, or data compilation, in any form, or the nonoccurrence or nonexistence of a matter of which a record, report, statement, or data compilation, in any form, was regularly made and preserved by a public office or agency, evidence in the form of a certification in accordance with rule 902, or testimony, that diligent search failed to disclose the record, report, statement, or data compilation, or entry.

(11) Records of religious organizations. Statements of births, marriages, divorces, deaths, legitimacy, ancestry, relationship by blood or marriage, or other similar facts of personal or family history, contained in a regularly kept record of a religious organization.

(12) Marriage, baptismal, and similar certificates. Statements of fact contained in a certificate that the maker performed a marriage or other ceremony or administered a sacrament, made by a clergyman, public official, or other person authorized by the rules or practices of a religious organization or by law to perform the act certified, and purporting to have been issued at the time of the act or within a reasonable time thereafter.

(13) Family records. Statements of fact concerning personal or family history contained in family Bibles, genealogies, charts, engravings on rings, inscriptions on family portraits, engravings on urns, crypts, or tombstones, or the like.

(14) Records of documents affecting an interest in property. The record of a document purporting to establish or affect an interest in property, as proof of the content of the original recorded document and its execution and delivery by each person by whom it purports to have been executed, if the record is a record of a public office and an applicable statute authorizes the recording of documents of that kind in that office.

(15) Statements in documents affecting an interest in property. A statement contained in a document purporting to establish or affect an interest in property if the matter stated was relevant to the purpose of the document, unless dealings with the property since the document was made have been inconsistent with the truth of the statement or the purport of the document.

(16) Statements in ancient documents. Statements in a document in existence twenty years or more the authenticity of which is established.

(17) Market reports, commercial publications. Market quotations, tabulations, lists, directories, or other published compilations, generally used and relied upon by the public or by persons in particular occupations.

(18) Learned treatises. To the extent called to the attention of an expert witness upon cross-examination or relied upon by the expert witness in direct examination, statements contained in published treatises, periodicals, or pamphlets on a subject of history, medicine, or other science or art, established as a reliable authority by the testimony or admission of the witness or by other expert testimony or by judicial notice. If admitted, the statements may be read into evidence but may not be received as exhibits.

(19) Reputation concerning personal or family history. Reputation among members of a person's family by blood, adoption, or marriage, or among a person's associates, or in the community, concerning a person's birth, adoption, marriage, divorce, death, legitimacy, relationship by blood, adoption, or marriage, ancestry, or other similar fact of personal or family history.

(20) Reputation concerning boundaries or general history. Reputation in a community, arising before the controversy, as to boundaries of or customs affecting lands in the community, and reputation as to events of general history important to the community or State or nation in which located.

(21) Reputation as to character. Reputation of a person's character among associates or in the community.

(22) Judgment of previous conviction. Evidence of a final judgment, entered after a trial or upon a plea of guilty (but not upon a plea of nolo contendere), adjudging a person guilty of a crime punishable by death or imprisonment in excess of one year, to prove any fact essential to sustain the judgment, but not including, when offered by the Government in a criminal prosecution for purposes other than impeachment, judgments against persons other than the accused. The pendency of an appeal may be shown but does not affect admissibility.

(23) Judgment as to personal, family, or general history, or boundaries. Judgments as proof of matters of personal, family or general history, or boundaries, essential to the judgment, if the same would be provable by evidence of reputation.

(24) [Transferred to Rule 807]

(Pub.L. 93–595, § 1, Jan. 2, 1975, 88 Stat. 1939; Pub.L. 94–149, § 1(11), Dec. 12, 1975, 89 Stat. 805; Mar. 2, 1987, eff. Oct. 1, 1987; Apr. 11, 1997, eff. Dec. 1, 1997; Apr. 17, 2000, eff. Dec. 1, 2000.)

Rule 804. Hearsay Exceptions; Declarant Unavailable

(a) Definition of unavailability. "Unavailability as a witness" includes situations in which the declarant—

(1) is exempted by ruling of the court on the ground of privilege from testifying concerning the subject matter of the declarant's statement; or

(2) persists in refusing to testify concerning the subject matter of the declarant's statement despite an order of the court to do so; or

(3) testifies to a lack of memory of the subject matter of the declarant's statement; or

(4) is unable to be present or to testify at the hearing because of death or then existing physical or mental illness or infirmity; or

(5) is absent from the hearing and the proponent of a statement has been unable to procure the declarant's attendance (or in the case of a hearsay exception under subdivision (b)(2), (3), or (4), the declarant's attendance or testimony) by process or other reasonable means.

A declarant is not unavailable as a witness if exemption, refusal, claim of lack of memory, inability, or absence is due to the procurement or wrongdoing of the proponent of a statement for the purpose of preventing the witness from attending or testifying.

(b) Hearsay exceptions. The following are not excluded by the hearsay rule if the declarant is unavailable as a witness:

(1) Former testimony. Testimony given as a witness at another hearing of the same or a different proceeding, or in a deposition taken in compliance with law in the course of the same or another proceeding, if the party against whom the testimony is now offered, or, in a civil action or proceeding, a predecessor in interest, had an opportunity and similar motive to develop the testimony by direct, cross, or redirect examination.

(2) Statement under belief of impending death. In a prosecution for homicide or in a civil action or proceeding, a statement made by a declarant while believing that the declarant's death was imminent, concerning the cause or circumstances of what the declarant believed to be impending death.

(3) Statement against interest. A statement which was at the time of its making so far contrary to the declarant's pecuniary or proprietary interest, or so far tended to subject the declarant to civil or criminal liability, or to render invalid a claim by the declarant against another, that a reasonable person in the declarant's position would not have made the statement unless believing it to be true. A statement tending to expose the declarant to criminal liability and offered to exculpate the accused is not admissible unless corroborating circumstances clearly indicate the trustworthiness of the statement.

(4) Statement of personal or family history. (A) A statement concerning the declarant's own birth, adoption, marriage, divorce, legitimacy, relationship by blood, adoption, or marriage, ancestry, or other similar fact of personal or family history, even though declarant had no means of acquiring personal knowledge of the matter stated; or (B) a statement concerning the foregoing matters, and death also, of another person, if the declarant was related to the other by blood, adoption, or marriage or was so intimately associated with the other's family as to be likely to have accurate information concerning the matter declared.

(5) [Transferred to Rule 807]

(6) **Forfeiture by wrongdoing.** A statement offered against a party that has engaged or acquiesced in wrongdoing that was intended to, and did, procure the unavailability of the declarant as a witness.

(Pub.L. 93–595, § 1, Jan. 2, 1975, 88 Stat. 1942; Pub.L. 94–149, § 1(12), (13), Dec. 12, 1975, 89 Stat. 806; Mar. 2, 1987, eff. Oct. 1, 1987; Pub.L. 100–690, Title VII, § 7075(b), Nov. 18, 1988, 102 Stat. 4405; Apr. 11, 1997, eff. Dec. 1, 1997.)

Rule 805. Hearsay Within Hearsay

Hearsay included within hearsay is not excluded under the hearsay rule if each part of the combined statements conforms with an exception to the hearsay rule provided in these rules.

(Pub.L. 93–595, § 1, Jan. 2, 1975, 88 Stat. 1943.)

Rule 806. Attacking and Supporting Credibility of Declarant

When a hearsay statement, or a statement defined in Rule 801(d)(2)(C), (D), or (E), has been admitted in evidence, the credibility of the declarant may be attacked, and if attacked may be supported, by any evidence which would be admissible for those purposes if declarant had testified as a witness. Evidence of a statement or conduct by the declarant at any time, inconsistent with the declarant's hearsay statement, is not subject to any requirement that the declarant may have been afforded an opportunity to deny or explain. If the party against whom a hearsay statement has been admitted calls the declarant as a witness, the party is entitled to examine the declarant on the statement as if under cross-examination.

(Pub.L. 93–595, § 1, Jan. 2, 1975, 88 Stat. 1943; Mar. 2, 1987, eff. Oct. 1, 1987; Apr. 11, 1997, eff. Dec. 1, 1997.)

Rule 807. Residual Exception

A statement not specifically covered by Rule 803 or 804 but having equivalent circumstantial guarantees of trustworthiness, is not excluded by the hearsay rule, if the court determines that (A) the statement is offered as evidence of a material fact; (B) the statement is more probative on the point for which it is offered than any other evidence which the proponent can procure through reasonable efforts; and (C) the general purposes of these rules and the interests of justice will best be served by admission of the statement into evidence. However, a statement may not be admitted under this exception unless the proponent of it makes known to the adverse party sufficiently in advance of the trial or hearing to provide the adverse party with a fair opportunity to prepare to meet it, the proponent's intention to offer the statement and the particulars of it, including the name and address of the declarant.

(Added Apr. 11, 1997, eff. Dec. 1, 1997.)

ARTICLE IX. AUTHENTICATION AND IDENTIFICATION

Rule 901. Requirement of Authentication or Identification

(a) General provision. The requirement of authentication or identification as a condition precedent to admissibility is satisfied by evidence sufficient to support a finding that the matter in question is what its proponent claims.

(b) Illustrations. By way of illustration only, and not by way of limitation, the following are examples of authentication or identification conforming with the requirements of this rule:

(1) **Testimony of witness with knowledge.** Testimony that a matter is what it is claimed to be.

(2) **Nonexpert opinion on handwriting.** Nonexpert opinion as to the genuineness of handwriting, based upon familiarity not acquired for purposes of the litigation.

(3) **Comparison by trier or expert witness.** Comparison by the trier of fact or by expert witnesses with specimens which have been authenticated.

(4) **Distinctive characteristics and the like.** Appearance, contents, substance, internal patterns, or other distinctive characteristics, taken in conjunction with circumstances.

(5) **Voice identification.** Identification of a voice, whether heard firsthand or through mechanical or electronic transmission or recording, by opinion based upon hearing the voice at any time under circumstances connecting it with the alleged speaker.

(6) **Telephone conversations.** Telephone conversations, by evidence that a call was made to the number assigned at the time by the telephone company to a particular person or business, if (A) in the case of a person, circumstances, including self-identification, show the person answering to be the one called, or (B) in the case of a business, the call was made to a place of business and the conversation related to business reasonably transacted over the telephone.

(7) **Public records or reports.** Evidence that a writing authorized by law to be recorded or filed and in fact recorded or filed in a public office, or a

purported public record, report, statement, or data compilation, in any form, is from the public office where items of this nature are kept.

(8) Ancient documents or data compilation. Evidence that a document or data compilation, in any form, (A) is in such condition as to create no suspicion concerning its authenticity, (B) was in a place where it, if authentic, would likely be, and (C) has been in existence 20 years or more at the time it is offered.

(9) Process or system. Evidence describing a process or system used to produce a result and showing that the process or system produces an accurate result.

(10) Methods provided by statute or rule. Any method of authentication or identification provided by Act of Congress or by other rules prescribed by the Supreme Court pursuant to statutory authority.

(Pub.L. 93–595, § 1, Jan. 2, 1975, 88 Stat.1943.)

Rule 902. Self-authentication

Extrinsic evidence of authenticity as a condition precedent to admissibility is not required with respect to the following:

(1) Domestic public documents under seal. A document bearing a seal purporting to be that of the United States, or of any State, district, Commonwealth, territory, or insular possession thereof, or the Panama Canal Zone, or the Trust Territory of the Pacific Islands, or of a political subdivision, department, officer, or agency thereof, and a signature purporting to be an attestation or execution.

(2) Domestic public documents not under seal. A document purporting to bear the signature in the official capacity of an officer or employee of any entity included in paragraph (1) hereof, having no seal, if a public officer having a seal and having official duties in the district or political subdivision of the officer or employee certifies under seal that the signer has the official capacity and that the signature is genuine.

(3) Foreign public documents. A document purporting to be executed or attested in an official capacity by a person authorized by the laws of a foreign country to make the execution or attestation, and accompanied by a final certification as to the genuineness of the signature and official position (A) of the executing or attesting person, or (B) of any foreign official whose certificate of genuineness of signature and official position relates to the execution or attestation or is in a chain of certificates of genuineness of signature and official position relating to the execution or attestation. A final certification may be made by a secretary of an embassy or legation, consul general, consul, vice

consul, or consular agent of the United States, or a diplomatic or consular official of the foreign country assigned or accredited to the United States. If reasonable opportunity has been given to all parties to investigate the authenticity and accuracy of official documents, the court may, for good cause shown, order that they be treated as presumptively authentic without final certification or permit them to be evidenced by an attested summary with or without final certification.

(4) Certified copies of public records. A copy of an official record or report or entry therein, or of a document authorized by law to be recorded or filed and actually recorded or filed in a public office, including data compilations in any form, certified as correct by the custodian or other person authorized to make the certification, by certificate complying with paragraph (1), (2), or (3) of this rule or complying with any Act of Congress or rule prescribed by the Supreme Court pursuant to statutory authority.

(5) Official publications. Books, pamphlets, or other publications purporting to be issued by public authority.

(6) Newspapers and periodicals. Printed materials purporting to be newspapers or periodicals.

(7) Trade inscriptions and the like. Inscriptions, signs, tags, or labels purporting to have been affixed in the course of business and indicating ownership, control, or origin.

(8) Acknowledged documents. Documents accompanied by a certificate of acknowledgment executed in the manner provided by law by a notary public or other officer authorized by law to take acknowledgments.

(9) Commercial paper and related documents. Commercial paper, signatures thereon, and documents relating thereto to the extent provided by general commercial law.

(10) Presumptions under Acts of Congress. Any signature, document, or other matter declared by Act of Congress to be presumptively or prima facie genuine or authentic.

(11) Certified Domestic Records of Regularly Conducted Activity.—The original or a duplicate of a domestic record of regularly conducted activity that would be admissible under Rule 803(6) if accompanied by a written declaration of its custodian or other qualified person, in a manner complying with any Act of Congress or rule prescribed by the Supreme Court pursuant to statutory authority, certifying that the record—

(A) was made at or near the time of the occurrence of the matters set forth by, or from information transmitted by, a person with knowledge of those matters;

(B) was kept in the course of the regularly conducted activity; and

(C) was made by the regularly conducted activity as a regular practice.

A party intending to offer a record into evidence under this paragraph must provide written notice of that intention to all adverse parties, and must make the record and declaration available for inspection sufficiently in advance of their offer into evidence to provide an adverse party with a fair opportunity to challenge them.

(12) Certified Foreign Records of Regularly Conducted Activity.—In a civil case, the original or a duplicate of a foreign record of regularly conducted activity that would be admissible under Rule 803(6) if accompanied by a written declaration by its custodian or other qualified person certifying that the record—

(A) was made at or near the time of the occurrence of the matters set forth by, or from information transmitted by, a person with knowledge of those matters;

(B) was kept in the course of the regularly conducted activity; and

(C) was made by the regularly conducted activity as a regular practice.

The declaration must be signed in a manner that, if falsely made, would subject the maker to criminal penalty under the laws of the country where the declaration is signed. A party intending to offer a record into evidence under this paragraph must provide written notice of that intention to all adverse parties, and must make the record and declaration available for inspection sufficiently in advance of their offer into evidence to provide an adverse party with a fair opportunity to challenge them.

(Pub.L. 93–595, § 1, Jan. 2, 1975, 88 Stat. 1944; Mar. 2, 1987, eff. Oct. 1, 1987; Apr. 25, 1988, eff. Nov. 1, 1988; Apr. 17, 2000, eff. Dec. 1, 2000.)

Rule 903. Subscribing Witness' Testimony Unnecessary

The testimony of a subscribing witness is not necessary to authenticate a writing unless required by the laws of the jurisdiction whose laws govern the validity of the writing.

(Pub.L. 93–595, § 1, Jan. 2, 1975, 88 Stat.1945.)

ARTICLE X. CONTENTS OF WRITINGS, RECORDINGS AND PHOTOGRAPHS

Rule 1001. Definitions

For purposes of this article the following definitions are applicable:

(1) Writings and recordings. "Writings" and "recordings" consist of letters, words, or numbers, or their equivalent, set down by handwriting, typewriting, printing, photostating, photographing, magnetic impulse, mechanical or electronic recording, or other form of data compilation.

(2) Photographs. "Photographs" include still photographs, X-ray films, video tapes, and motion pictures.

(3) Original. An "original" of a writing or recording is the writing or recording itself or any counterpart intended to have the same effect by a person executing or issuing it. An "original" of a photograph includes the negative or any print therefrom. If data are stored in a computer or similar device, any printout or other output readable by sight, shown to reflect the data accurately, is an "original".

(4) Duplicate. A "duplicate" is a counterpart produced by the same impression as the original, or from the same matrix, or by means of photography, including enlargements and miniatures, or by mechanical or electronic re-recording, or by chemical reproduction, or by other equivalent techniques which accurately reproduces the original.

(Pub.L. 93–595, § 1, Jan. 2, 1975, 88 Stat. 1945.)

Rule 1002. Requirement of Original

To prove the content of a writing, recording, or photograph, the original writing, recording, or photograph is required, except as otherwise provided in these rules or by Act of Congress.

(Pub.L. 93–595, § 1, Jan. 2, 1975, 88 Stat. 1946.)

Rule 1003. Admissibility of Duplicates

A duplicate is admissible to the same extent as an original unless (1) a genuine question is raised as to the authenticity of the original or (2) in the circumstances it would be unfair to admit the duplicate in lieu of the original.

(Pub.L. 93–595, § 1, Jan. 2, 1975, 88 Stat. 1946.)

Rule 1004. Admissibility of Other Evidence of Contents

The original is not required, and other evidence of the contents of a writing, recording, or photograph is admissible if—

(1) Originals lost or destroyed. All originals are lost or have been destroyed, unless the proponent lost or destroyed them in bad faith; or

(2) Original not obtainable. No original can be obtained by any available judicial process or procedure; or

(3) Original in possession of opponent. At a time when an original was under the control of the party against whom offered, that party was put on notice, by the pleadings or otherwise, that the contents would be a subject of proof at the hearing, and that party does not produce the original at the hearing; or

(4) Collateral matters. The writing, recording, or photograph is not closely related to a controlling issue.

(Pub.L. 93–595, § 1, Jan. 2, 1975, 88 Stat. 1946; Mar. 2, 1987, eff. Oct. 1, 1987.)

Rule 1005. Public Records

The contents of an official record, or of a document authorized to be recorded or filed and actually recorded or filed, including data compilations in any form, if otherwise admissible, may be proved by copy, certified as correct in accordance with rule 902 or testified to be correct by a witness who has compared it with the original. If a copy which complies with the foregoing cannot be obtained by the exercise of reasonable diligence, then other evidence of the contents may be given.

(Pub.L. 93–595, § 1, Jan. 2, 1975, 88 Stat. 1946.)

Rule 1006. Summaries

The contents of voluminous writings, recordings, or photographs which cannot conveniently be examined in court may be presented in the form of a chart, summary, or calculation. The originals, or duplicates, shall be made available for examination or copying, or both, by other parties at reasonable time and place. The court may order that they be produced in court.

(Pub.L. 93–595, § 1, Jan. 2, 1975, 88 Stat. 1946.)

Rule 1007. Testimony or Written Admission of Party

Contents of writings, recordings, or photographs may be proved by the testimony or deposition of the party against whom offered or by that party's written admission, without accounting for the nonproduction of the original.

(Pub.L. 93–595, § 1, Jan. 2, 1975, 88 Stat. 1947; Mar. 2, 1987, eff. Oct. 1, 1987.)

Rule 1008. Functions of Court and Jury

When the admissibility of other evidence of contents of writings, recordings, or photographs under these rules depends upon the fulfillment of a condition of fact, the question whether the condition has been fulfilled is ordinarily for the court to determine in accordance with the provisions of rule 104. However, when an issue is raised (a) whether the asserted writing ever existed, or (b) whether another writing, recording, or photograph produced at the trial is the original, or (c) whether other evidence of contents correctly reflects the contents, the issue is for the trier of fact to determine as in the case of other issues of fact.

(Pub.L. 93–595, § 1, Jan. 2, 1975, 88 Stat. 1947.)

ARTICLE XI. MISCELLANEOUS RULES

Rule 1101. Applicability of Rules

(a) Courts and judges. These rules apply to the United States district courts, the District Court of Guam, the District Court of the Virgin Islands, the District Court for the Northern Mariana Islands, the United States courts of appeals, the United States Claims Court, and to United States bankruptcy judges and United States magistrate judges, in the actions, cases, and proceedings and to the extent hereinafter set forth. The terms "judge" and "court" in these rules include United States bankruptcy judges and United States magistrate judges.

(b) Proceedings generally. These rules apply generally to civil actions and proceedings, including admiralty and maritime cases, to criminal cases and proceedings, to contempt proceedings except those in which the court may act summarily, and to proceedings and cases under title 11, United States Code.

(c) Rule of privilege. The rule with respect to privileges applies at all stages of all actions, cases, and proceedings.

(d) Rules inapplicable. The rules (other than with respect to privileges) do not apply in the following situations:

(1) Preliminary questions of fact. The determination of questions of fact preliminary to admissibility of evidence when the issue is to be determined by the court under rule 104.

(2) Grand jury. Proceedings before grand juries.

(3) Miscellaneous proceedings. Proceedings for extradition or rendition; preliminary examinations in criminal cases; sentencing, or granting or revoking probation; issuance of warrants for arrest, criminal summonses, and search warrants; and proceedings with respect to release on bail or otherwise.

(e) Rules applicable in part. In the following proceedings these rules apply to the extent that matters of evidence are not provided for in the statutes which govern procedure therein or in other rules prescribed by the Supreme Court pursuant to statutory authority: the trial of misdemeanors and other petty offenses before United States magistrate judges; review of agency actions when the facts are subject to trial de novo under section 706(2)(F) of title 5, United States Code; review of orders of the Secretary of Agriculture under section 2 of the Act entitled "An Act to authorize association of producers of agricultural products" approved February 18, 1922 (7 U.S.C. 292), and under sections 6 and 7(c) of the Perishable Agricultural Commodities Act, 1930 (7 U.S.C. 499f, 499g(c)); naturalization and revocation of naturalization under sections 310–318 of the Immigration and Nationality Act (8 U.S.C. 1421–1429); prize proceedings in admiralty under sections 7651–7681 of title 10, United States Code; review of orders of the Secretary of the Interior under section 2 of the Act entitled "An Act authorizing associations of producers of aquatic products" approved June 25, 1934 (15 U.S.C. 522); review of orders of petroleum control boards under section 5 of the Act entitled "An Act to regulate interstate and foreign commerce in petroleum and its products by prohibiting the shipment in such commerce of petroleum and its products produced in violation of State law, and for other purposes", approved February 22, 1935 (15 U.S.C. 715d); actions for fines, penalties, or forfeitures under part V of title IV of the Tariff Act of 1930 (19 U.S.C. 1581–1624), or under the Anti–Smuggling Act (19 U.S.C. 1701–1711); criminal libel for condemnation, exclusion of imports, or other proceedings under the Federal Food, Drug, and Cosmetic Act (21 U.S.C. 301–392); disputes between seamen under sections 4079, 4080, and 4081 of the Revised Statutes (22 U.S.C. 256–258); habeas corpus under sections 2241–2254 of title 28, United States Code; motions to vacate, set aside or correct sentence under section 2255 of title 28, United States Code; actions for penalties for refusal to transport destitute seamen under section 4578 of the Revised Statutes (46 U.S.C. 679); actions against the United States under the Act entitled "An Act authorizing suits against the United States in admiralty for damage caused by and salvage service rendered to public vessels belonging to the United States, and for other purposes", approved March 3, 1925 (46 U.S.C. 781–790), as implemented by section 7730 of title 10, United States Code.

(Pub.L. 93–595, § 1, Jan. 2, 1975, 88 Stat. 1947; Pub.L. 94–149, § 1(14), Dec. 12, 1975, 89 Stat. 806; Pub.L. 95–598, Title II, § 251, Nov. 6, 1978, 92 Stat. 2673; Pub.L. 97–164, Title I, § 142, Apr. 2, 1982, 96 Stat. 45; Mar. 2, 1987, eff. Oct. 1, 1987; Apr. 25, 1988, eff. Nov. 1, 1988; Pub.L. 100–690, Title VII, § 7075(c), Nov. 18, 1988, 102 Stat. 4405; Apr. 22, 1993, eff. Dec. 1, 1993.)

Rule 1102. Amendments

Amendments to the Federal Rules of Evidence may be made as provided in section 2072 of title 28 of the United States Code.

(Pub.L. 93–595, § 1, Jan. 2, 1975, 88 Stat.1948); Apr. 30, 1991, eff. Dec. 1, 1991.)

Rule 1103. Title

These rules may be known and cited as the Federal Rules of Evidence.

(Pub.L. 93–595, § 1, Jan. 2, 1975, 88 Stat.1948.)

Dynamic Business Law

THE ESSENTIALS

Dynamic Business Law

THE ESSENTIALS

Nancy Kubasek
Bowling Green State University

M. Neil Browne
Bowling Green State University

Daniel J. Herron
Miami University

Andrea Giampetro-Meyer
Loyola College

Linda Barkacs
University of San Diego

**McGraw-Hill
Irwin**

Boston Burr Ridge, IL Dubuque, IA New York San Francisco St. Louis
Bangkok Bogotá Caracas Kuala Lumpur Lisbon London Madrid Mexico City
Milan Montreal New Delhi Santiago Seoul Singapore Sydney Taipei Toronto

Library of Congress Cataloging-in-Publication Data

Dynamic business law: the essentials / Nancy Kubasek … [et al.].
 p. cm.
 Includes index.
 ISBN-13: 978-0-07-337768-1 (alk. paper)
 ISBN-10: 0-07-337768-6 (alk. paper)
 1. Business law—United States. I. Kubasek, Nancy.
KF390.B84D963 2010
346.7307—dc22

 2008043945

About the Authors

Nancy K. Kubasek received her JD from the University of Toledo College of Law in 1981 and her BA from the Bowling Green State University 1978. She joined the BGSU faculty in 1982 and became an associate professor in 1988 and a full professor in 1993.

During her tenure at Bowling Green State University, she has primarily taught courses in business law, legal environment of business, environmental law, health care law, and moral principles. She has published over 75 articles, primarily in law reviews and business journals. Most of her substantive articles focus on environmental questions, and she writes a quarterly column about environmental issues for the *Real Estate Law Journal.* She has helped get students involved in legal research, and a number of her articles are co-authored with students. She has also published a number of pedagogical articles in teaching journals, focusing primarily on the teaching of critical thinking and ethics.

She wrote the first environmental law text for undergraduate students, *Environmental Law,* and co-authored *The Legal Environment of Business: A Critical Thinking Approach.* She has written supplemental materials, such as study guides, test banks, and instructors' manuals.

Active in many professional organizations, she has served as president of the Academy of Legal Studies in Business, the national organization for professors of legal studies in colleges of business. She has also served as president of the Tri-State Academy of Legal Studies in Business, her regional professional association.

In her leisure time, she and her husband, Neil Browne, fish for halibut and salmon in Alaska, as well as large-mouth bass in Florida. In addition, they are regular participants in polka, waltz, zydeco, and Cajun dance festivals in Europe and the United States. For almost 30 years, they have been successful tournament blackjack players as well. Both are avid exercisers—lifting weights, doing yoga, and running almost every day.

M. Neil Browne is senior lecturer and research associate and a distinguished teaching professor emeritus at Bowling Green State University. He received his BA in history and economics at the University of Houston, his PhD in economics at the University of Texas, and his JD from the University of Toledo. He has been a professor at Bowling Green for more than four decades.

Professor Browne teaches courses in jurisprudence, ethical reasoning, critical thinking, and economics at both the undergraduate and graduate levels. He has received recognition as the Silver Medalist National Professor of the Year, the Ohio Professor of the Year, and Distinguished Teacher and Master Teacher at Bowling Green State University, as well as numerous research awards from his university and from professional organizations. His consulting activities with corporate, government, and educational institutions focus on improving the quality of critical thinking in those organizations. In addition, he serves as a Rule 26 expert with respect to the quality of the reasoning used by expert witnesses called by the party opponent in legal actions.

Professor Browne has published 20 books and over 130 professional journal articles in law journals, as well as economics, sociology, and higher education journals. His current research interests focus on the relationship between orthodox economic thinking and legal policy. In addition, he is in the midst of writing books about the power of questionable assumptions in economics, the usefulness of asking questions as a learning strategy, and the importance of critical thinking in environmental arguments.

Professor Browne tries to find time for a broad array of outside activities. He and his wife, Nancy Kubasek, fish for halibut and salmon in Alaska, as well as large-mouth bass in Florida, as frequently as possible. In addition, they are regular participants in polka, waltz, zydeco, and Cajun dance festivals in Europe and the United States. For almost 30 years, they have been successful tournament blackjack players as well. Both are avid exercisers—lifting weights, doing yoga, and running almost every day.

Daniel J. Herron is a professor of business legal studies at Miami University in Oxford, Ohio. He received his law degree from Case Western Reserve University School of Law in 1978 and is a member of the Ohio and federal bars. He has taught at Miami University, his alma mater, since 1992, having previously taught at the University of Wyoming, Western Carolina University, the University of North Carolina–Wilmington, and Bowling Green State University. He has been a member of the Academy of Legal Studies in Business for nearly 25 years and has served as its executive secretary since 1991. His research interests focus on law and ethics, employment law, and legal history.

He has been married for over 30 years to his wife Deborah, and they have two children, Elisabeth and Christopher, and daughter-in-law Amanda and one grandchild, Jack. Herron and his wife reside in Oxford, Ohio, with their two beagles Max and Missy.

Andrea Giampetro-Meyer is chair of the Law and Social Responsibility Department in the Sellinger School of Business and Management at Loyola College in Maryland. She received her BS in business administration from Bowling Green State University and her JD from the Marshall-Wythe School of Law at the College of William and Mary.

Professor Giampetro's research focuses primarily on legal responses to race and gender discrimination in employment. Her teaching interests are wide-ranging. She teaches at all levels of higher education, from courses designed especially for first-year college students to courses designed for high-level business executives. Professor Giampetro's preferred courses are the undergraduate legal environment of business course and the graduate ethics and corporate social responsibility course.

Professor Giampetro has earned both national and local awards for teaching, including the Charles M. Hewitt Teaching Award from the Academy of Legal Studies in Business and the Henry W. Rodgers III Distinguished Teacher of the Year Award from Loyola College. She has experience helping new teachers understand how to work toward teaching excellence. At Loyola College, she serves as a faculty mentor, especially to teachers struggling with how to encourage students to engage in high-level discussion in class. Professor Giampetro has also written several instructors' manuals for textbooks. In these manuals, she strives to provide practical information that gives teachers ideas about how to engage students in meaningful ways.

Professor Giampetro has also received the Holmes-Cardozo Award from the Academy of Legal Studies in Business in recognition of excellence in legal scholarship. She has published numerous articles, and they have appeared in leading journals. In keeping with Loyola College's Jesuit mission, her favorite articles pursue themes related to social justice, especially as it relates to eliminating discrimination and oppression.

Professor Linda L. Barkacs received her JD from the University of San Diego in 1993. She also has a BA in political science from San Diego State University and an AA in accounting from Irvine Valley College.

Upon graduating from law school and passing the California bar exam, Professor Barkacs became an associate at a downtown San Diego law firm. During that time, she was involved in a number of high-profile trials, including a sexual harassment case against the City of Oceanside that resulted in a $1.2 million verdict. In 1997, Professor Barkacs and her husband Craig (also a professor at USD) started their own law firm specializing in business and civil litigation (in both federal and state courts), employment law cases, and appeals. They were also involved in numerous mediations and arbitrations.

Professor Barkacs began teaching at USD in 1997 and went full-time in spring 2002. As an educator, she has designed and taught numerous courses on law, ethics, and negotiation. She teaches in USD's undergraduate and graduate programs, including the Master of Science in Executive Leadership (a Ken Blanchard program), the Master of Science in Global Leadership, and the Master of Science in Supply Chain Management. Professor Barkacs often teaches in USD's study-abroad classes and has traveled extensively throughout Europe, Asia, and South America.

Professor Barkacs has received numerous awards for her teaching at USD, including 2007 Professor of the Year, USD Senior Class (universitywide); and 2006–2007 Top Three Finalist, USD Outstanding Undergraduate Business Educator. She and her husband are principals in The Barkacs Group (www.tbgexecutivetraining.com), a consulting firm that provides negotiation, ethics, and team training for the private sector. Professor Barkacs has published numerous journal articles in the areas of law, ethics, and negotiation. She and her husband are co-authoring a book on negotiation. She has been the president, vice president, conference chair, and treasurer for the Pacific Southwest Academy of Legal Studies in Business (www.pswalsb.net).

Professor Barkacs currently spends her time teaching, publishing, consulting for The Barkacs Group, and doing volunteer work for various civic causes. She enjoys walking, weight-lifting, and spending her free time with her husband and their three cats, Crystal, Caspar, and Phoenix.

Preface

We wrote this book because our primary sense of who we are as professionals is that we are teachers. We play various roles in our careers, but we are especially dedicated to our students. We want them to listen, read, create, and evaluate more effectively as a result of their experience in a business law class. Above all, we want them to sense the importance and excitement of the law.

We tried to construct a book that contains the basics of business law but does not get bogged down in the kind of details that would be more appropriate in an upper-level law class.

It is our pedagogical features that provide the distinctive value of this book. Each feature stands by itself as an aid to the kind of learning we hope to encourage. Yet the features are also a cohesive unit, contributing both to the liberal education of the students who read it and to their skills as decision makers in a market economy.

Specifically, we provide what competing texts deliver, an examination of the basic questions, concepts, and legal rules of business law. Our text must address the power and authority of constitutions, statutes, case law, and treaties as sources of law. Together the various elements of what we call "the law" make up the foundation and structure of the market exchange process.

Decisions to trade and produce require trust—trust that consumers, firms, workers, financial institutions, and asset owners will do as they promise and that violations of such promises will be unacceptable in the marketplace. Without guarantees that promises will be kept, market exchanges would grind to a halt. Business law provides these guarantees and the boundaries within which certain promises can be made and enforced.

Market decisions are made in a context—a persistently changing context. The law, in turn, is dynamic in response. New technologies and business practices bring new disputes over rights and responsibilities in a business setting.

Future business leaders need knowledge of existing business law, as well as a set of skills permitting them to adjust efficiently and effectively to new legal issues as they arise over the course of their careers.

We are excited about the contents of our features and want to explain the function of each of them in preparing students for leadership positions in business.

A. Global Boxes

GLOBAL Context

Business Ethics and Italian Taxes

When Italian corporations file their tax returns, the tax authorities assume that the corporations are underestimating their profits by 30 to 70 percent. This assumption proves to be true, yet the Italian Revenue Service does not press charges. In fact, purposely understating profits is the accepted practice within Italy.

is usually much higher than the original estimation but still less than face value.

This negotiating process, while it may seem foreign to Americans, is a common business practice in Italy. In the early 1980s an American banker learned the difficult lesson that, for a firm doing business in a foreign country, local custom has a significant impact on ethical practice. The banker refused, on ethical grounds, to underestimate

This first feature highlights the emerging, interconnected market. Where relevant, the chapters contain Global Context boxes. Because so many market decisions are made in an international context, learners need to familiarize themselves with the likelihood that a particular legal principle essential to doing business in one country may not be appropriate in other countries. The Global Context boxes illustrate how unique the law in a certain country often is. After reading these "stories of difference," readers will certainly better understand the need to discover relevant law in all jurisdictions where their market decisions have legal implications.

We believe that students learn innumerable valuable lessons about American business law by contrasting the concepts of our business law system with those of our primary trading partners. We typically use Canada, Japan, China, Russia, Mexico, and the European Union for our comparisons because modern business managers will more likely be interacting with the law in those particular jurisdictions.

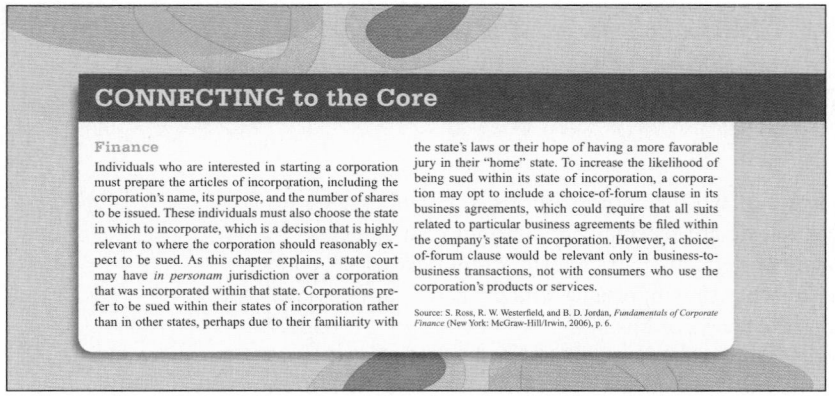

B. Connecting to the Core

The business curriculum, as experienced by students, can easily be seen as a collection of silos, with each silo, or academic department, walled off from the others with its own special language and issues. But successful business decisions start with recognition that decision makers should take advantage of the interrelatedness of the various subject areas.

To encourage the habit of seeing business decision making as connected and cohesive, most chapters contain a feature entitled "Connecting to the Core."

The purpose of that feature is to drive home the point that concepts from finance, accounting, marketing, management, and economics are closely linked to concepts and dilemmas in business law. The study of business law is best seen as a foundational component of the larger study of business administration.

C. Critical Thinking

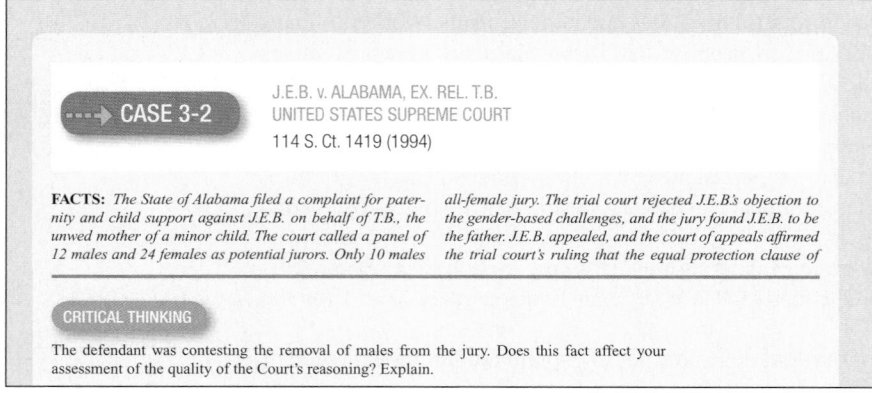

After each case in the book, we have provided critical thinking questions to highlight the need to think critically about the reasoning used by the court. In addition, we include in every chapter a Point/Counterpoint problem that encourages the reader to evaluate the conflicting reasoning surrounding a key issue in the chapter.

But we do much more than just ask a lot of critical thinking questions at particular locations throughout the chapters. We encourage the use of a step-by-step critical thinking approach that has been developed and used in classrooms in many countries. We do not just repeatedly urge students to "think critically." Instead, we describe for them what is meant by that phrase in the context of business law.

We include this step-by-step approach in Appendix 1A at the end of Chapter 1. Instructors who wish to emphasize critical thinking can use that appendix as a structured approach for learning how to evaluate legal reasoning.

D. Ethical Reasoning

Our book emphasizes consideration of all stakeholder interests in every market decision. Business ethics should never be an afterthought or something firms consider only because they think they must.

Instead, business ethics is what provides the social legitimacy for markets, what distinguishes markets from the life of the jungle. While market decisions are calculating and purposeful, they must at the same time reflect awareness that the good and the right provide social borders that elevate those decisions above simple greed and egoism.

Ethical discussion focuses on the basic observation that we are socially and globally interdependent as entrepreneurs, asset owners, workers, businesspeople, and consumers. Our inescapable contact with one another requires that our aspirations be defined, at least in part, by their impact on others.

Our text has several ethical reasoning possibilities in each chapter. But for the reader to make use of this emphasis requires a practical step-by-step approach. In other words, students need more than just a discussion about values or ethics.

They need to have some sense that the discussion is headed somewhere. They want to know, "How will my behavior be any more ethical after I have read the chapter and participated in the class discussions?" Our text answers their question.

Chapter 2 provides a clear explanation of our approach—an approach that students can use on a regular basis. The language and organization of our model of ethical reasoning leans implicitly on standard ethical theories. But it meets the challenge of a fast-paced business world. It pushes stakeholders to the forefront of market decisions, where they belong, and does so in a manner that is both powerful and doable without becoming tedious.

Business ethics serve as the guidelines we use to shape the world we wish to create. As such, they provide guidance for the kind of business behavior we want to reinforce. After each case discussion, we pause to think about the ethics of business law by asking a question derived from the practical approach to business ethics developed in Chapter 2.

The WPH Framework for Business Ethics

A useful set of ethical guidelines requires the recognition that managerial decisions must meet the following primary criteria (Exhibit 2-2):

- The decisions affect particular groups of stakeholders in the operations of the firm. The pertinent question is thus, *Whom* would this decision affect?
- The decisions are made in pursuit of a particular *purpose*. Business decisions are instruments toward an ethical end.
- The decisions must meet the standards of action-oriented business behavior. Managers need a doable set of guidelines for *How* to make ethical decisions.

CASE 3-2

J.E.B. v. ALABAMA, EX. REL. T.B.
UNITED STATES SUPREME COURT
114 S. Ct. 1419 (1994)

FACTS: The State of Alabama filed a complaint for paternity and child support against J.E.B. on behalf of T.B., the unwed mother of a minor child. The court called a panel of 12 males and 24 females as potential jurors. Only 10 males remained after three individuals were removed for cause. all-female jury. The trial court rejected J.E.B.'s objection to the gender-based challenges, and the jury found J.E.B. to be the father. J.E.B. appealed, and the court of appeals affirmed the trial court's ruling that the equal protection clause of the Fourteenth Amendment does not prohibit gender-based

CRITICAL THINKING

The defendant was contesting the removal of males from the jury. Does this fact affect your assessment of the quality of the Court's reasoning? Explain.

ETHICAL DECISION MAKING

Which ethical norm does the case decision serve?

E. E-Commerce Boxes

A central feature of modern business decisions is new technology, specifically the rapid spread of electronic commerce. This development has created new challenges and opportunities that were unforeseeable until very recently. By including boxes that call attention to these challenges, we think we can best convince students of the pervasive influence of this new, complicating aspect of business decisions.

E-COMMERCE and the Law

The Sliding-Scale Standard for Internet Transactions

Does a business that has Internet contact with a plaintiff in a different state satisfy the minimum-contacts standard?

A federal district court established the following "sliding-scale" standard in a 1997 case:*

[T]he likelihood that personal jurisdiction can be constitutionally exercised is directly proportionate to the nature and quality of commercial activity that an entity conducts over the Internet. This sliding scale is consistent with well developed personal jurisdiction principles.

At one end of the spectrum are situations where a defendant clearly does business over the Internet. If the defendant enters into contracts with residents of a foreign jurisdiction that involve the knowing and repeated transmission of computer files over the Internet, personal jurisdiction is proper.

At the opposite end are situations where a defendant has simply posted information on an Internet website which is accessible to users in foreign jurisdictions. A passive website that does little more than make information available to those who are interested in it is not grounds for the exercise of personal jurisdiction.

The middle ground is occupied by interactive websites where a user can exchange information with the host computer. In these cases, the exercise of jurisdiction is determined by examining the level of interactivity and commercial nature of the exchange of information that occurs on the website.

* Zippo Mfg. Co. v. Zippo Dot Com, Inc., 952 F. Supp. 1119 at 1124 (1997).

Walkthrough

We have designed our features around the things we do in our classes to encourage excitement about business law. We believe they provide Business Law Plus.

We also have a variety of supplementary material available for instructors, to aid in course development, and for students, to provide additional study.

Online Learning Center (www.mhhe.com/kubasekess)

With all of the possibilities that technology can offer, we've organized our Online Learning Center for ease of use for both instructor and student. Password-protected instructor materials can be found in the *Instructor Center*, including the Instructor's Manual, Testbank, PowerPoint presentation options, additional resources for classroom exercises, and notes on how to incorporate them all into the classroom. *You Be the Judge Online* (detailed below) is linked for accessibility and convenience. The *Student Center* offers opportunities for independent study, such as chapter quizzes and additional cases. Premium content includes narrated PowerPoint slides, iPod content, and streaming video.

Instructor's Manual
Written by our fellow co-author Andrea Giampetro-Meyer, this resource includes lecture notes, case briefs, answers to all questions in each chapter, assignment ideas, teaching assistance (emphasizing practical tips that new or part-time teachers can try right away), and suggested handouts.

Testbank
Prepared by Vonda Laughlin, of Carson-Newman College, our Testbank contains a variety of true/false, multiple-choice, and essay questions, as well as "scenario-based" questions, which are application-based and use a situation described in a narrative, with three to five multiple-choice test questions based on the situation.

Assurance of Learning Ready
Educational institutions are often focused on the notion of *assurance of learning,* an important element of many accreditation standards. *Dynamic Business Law: The Essentials* is designed specifically to support your assurance-of-learning initiatives with a simple, yet powerful, solution. We've aligned our Testbank questions with Bloom's taxonomy and AACSB guidelines, tagging each question according to its knowledge and skill areas.

Each Testbank question for *Dynamic Business Law: The Essentials* also maps to a specific chapter learning objective listed in the text. You can use our Testbank software, *EZ Test,* to easily query for learning objectives that directly relate to the learning objectives for your course. You can use the reporting features of EZ Test to aggregate student results in a similar fashion, making the collection and presentation of assurance-of-learning data quick and easy.

AACSB Standards
McGraw-Hill Companies is a proud corporate member of AACSB International. Understanding the importance and value of AACSB accreditation, the authors of *Dynamic Business Law: The Essentials* have sought to recognize the curricula guidelines detailed in the AACSB standards for business accreditation by connecting selected questions in the Testbank to the general knowledge and skill guidelines found in the AACSB standards.

The statements contained in *Dynamic Business Law: The Essentials* are provided only as a guide for the users of this text. The AACSB leaves content coverage and assessment clearly within the realm and control of the individual school, the mission of the school, and the faculty. The AACSB does charge schools with the obligation of doing assessment against their own content and learning goals. While *Dynamic Business Law: The Essentials* and the teaching package make no claim of any specific AACSB qualification or evaluation, we have, within the book, labeled selected questions according to the six general knowledge and skill areas. The labels or tags within *Dynamic Business Law: The Essentials* are as indicated. There are, of course, many more within the Testbank, the text, and the teaching package that may be used as a standard for your course.

EZ Test Online McGraw-Hill's EZ Test Online is a flexible and easy-to-use electronic testing program. The program allows instructors to create tests from book-specific items, accommodates a wide range of question types, and enables instructors to add their own questions. Multiple versions of the test can be created, and any test can be exported for use with course management systems such as WebCT, Blackboard, or any other course management system. EZ Test Online is accessible to busy instructors virtually anywhere via the Web, and the program eliminates the need for them to install test software. Utilizing EZ Test Online also allows instructors to create and deliver multiple-choice or true/false quiz questions using iQuiz for iPod. For more information about EZ Test Online, please see the Web site at www.eztestonline.com

PowerPoint Presentation Slides Developed by Jeff Penley at Catawba Valley Community College, two different sets of slides are available for instructors. The Basic set consists of an outline of each chapter. The Premium set expands on this outline to include hypotheticals and ethical dilemmas, allowing the instructor to incorporate application into the lecture.

Instructor Video DVD (ISBN: 0073262234)

The Instructor Video DVD contains clips from NBC and PBS that highlight current legal issues, with titles such as:

- Viacom Sues YouTube for Copyright Infringement (PBS)
- America's Number One Retailer, Wal-Mart, Faces the Biggest Civil Rights Case Ever against a U.S. Company (NBC)
- Courtroom or Circus? The Controversial Judge in Anna Nicole Smith's Courtroom Battle over Her Body Behaves Oddly (NBC)
- Government vs. Google (PBS)

Instructor notes located on the Web site give insight into how to incorporate related chapter segments into the classroom and offer questions to stimulate discussion.

You Be The Judge Online (www.mhhe.com/ybtj)

This interactive product includes 18 hypothetical business law cases. All the cases are based on real cases within our business law texts. Each case allows you to watch interviews of the plaintiff and defendant before the courtroom argument, see the courtroom proceedings, view relevant evidence, read other actual cases relating to the issues in the case, and then create your own ruling.

After your verdict is generated, view what an actual judge ruled (unscripted) in the case and then get the chance to defend or change your ruling. Topics include:

1. *Sexual harassment:* Did Sexy Prank Kill Promotion?
2. *Religious discrimination:* Dress Code Flips Burger Joint
3. *Fraud:* Blind Dates Go Bust
4. *Defamation:* Trashing the French Maid
5. *Partnership:* You Sunk My Partnership
6. *Warranty:* Who Is Distorting What?
7. *Verbal agreement:* Recording Studio Blues
8. *Liability:* Office Party Blame Game
9. *Property:* Subtracting the Addition
10. *Privacy/employment at will:* Fired for Whistling?
11. *Environmental law:* Digging Dogs Find Deadly Dirt
12. *Consumer law:* Misleading Menu Misery
13. *Tenant rights:* When the Lessee Leaves
14. *Consumer law:* The Not-So-Captive Audience
15. *Intellectual property:* Click Here, Get Sued
16. *Debt collection:* Overdue or Overdone?
17. *Intellectual property:* The Yoga Posture Puzzle
18. *Agency:* Duped by Duplication

Acknowledgments

This final component of the Preface contains a palpable tone of gratitude and humility. Any project the scope of *Dynamic Business Law: The Essentials* is a collective activity; the authors are but the visible component of a remarkably large joint effort. We want to thank several contributors by name, but there are doubtlessly many other students, colleagues, and friends who made essential contributions to these pages.

Our largest gratitude goes to the dozens of business law colleagues who saved us from many embarrassing errors, while tolerating our stubborn reluctance to adhere to certain of their suggestions. In addition, the book could not have been written without the competent and dedicated research assistance we received from Dan Tagliarina, Corinne Tagliarina, Lauren Biksacky, and Allison Smith.

We'd like to thank the following people for helping us with their comments and feedback on various stages of our manuscript:

Dan Bailey, *New River Community College*

Jay Ballantine, *University OF Colorado–Boulder*

Joyce Birdoff, *Nassau Community College*

Eli Bortman, *Babson College*

Rita Cain, *University of Missouri–Kansas City*

Peter Churchill, *Diablo Valley College*

Nancy Colden, *Northeast Wisconsin Technical College*

Joseph Flack, *Washtenaw Community College*

Jean Gohl-Noice, *Parkland College*

Bill Harwood, *Dutchess Community College*

Karen Holmes, *Hudson Valley Community College*

Michael Jalbert, *University of Akron*

Brian Keliher, *Grossmont College*

Edward Kissling, *Ocean County College*

Bree Langemo, *Sinclair Community College*

Russell Lott, *Northwest Mississippi Community College*

Richard Love, *Central Carolina Community College*

Alfonsina Minchella, *Roxbury Community College*

Christine Mooney, *Queensborough Community College*

Kelly Sayers, *Hudson Valley Community College*

Alexis Stokes, *Texas State University–San Marcos*

Scott Taylor, *Moberly Area Community College*

Cheryl Thomas, *Fayetteville Tech Community College*

Daphyne Thomas, *James Madison University*

Mary Torma, *Lorain County Community College*

Eric Yordy, *Northern Arizona University*

Mary Zarycki, *Hillsborough Community College–Brandon*

Finally, a book is but a raw, unsold manuscript until the skilled team at a publishing house starts to refine it. Our manuscript benefited immeasurably from the guidance of the multiple levels of skill provided to us by McGraw-Hill/Irwin. We respect and honor our Sponsoring Editor, Dana Woo; our Senior Development Editor, Christine Scheid; the book's Marketing Manager, Sarah Schuessler; and its Project Manager, Bruce Gin.

Brief Contents

Contents

Contents **xvii**

PART **4**

Negotiable Instruments and Banking

PART 5

Creditor's Rights and Bankruptcy

List of Cases

An Introduction to the Fundamentals of Dynamic Business Law

---→ **LEARNING OBJECTIVES**

After reading this chapter, you will be able to answer the following questions:

LO 1 What is business law?

LO 2 How does business law relate to business education?

LO 3 What are the purposes of law?

LO 4 What are alternative ways to classify the law?

LO 5 What are the sources of the law?

LO 6 What are the various schools of jurisprudence?

This book is for future business managers, especially those who wish to be leaders. An essential factor in preparing for that career is awareness of the legal issues arising in business. Businesses need to finance capital growth, purchase inputs, and hire and develop employees. In addition, they must sell to consumers, please owners, and comply with government rules. All these activities are full of potential legal conflicts.

Business law consists of the enforceable rules of conduct that govern commercial relationships. In other words, buyers and sellers interact in market exchanges within the rules that indicate the boundaries of legal business behavior. Constitutions, legislatures, regulatory bodies, and courts spell out what market participants may or may not legally do.

Understanding business law is necessary for future businesspeople because there simply is no market transaction that occurs outside legal guidelines. All contracts, employment decisions, and payments to a supplier are limited and protected by business law. Each of the six functional areas of business—management, production and transportation, marketing, research and development, accounting and finance, and human resource management—sits on a foundation of business law.

Law and Its Purposes

Many of us might like to impose rules on others, defining their rights and responsibilities. Few of us can do this as individuals, but a majority of citizens in a democracy can agree to establish rules for business behavior. They can permit certain authorities to make and enforce rules describing what behavior is permitted and encouraged in their community. These rules are what we refer to as the law, and they are enforceable in the courts of that community. Exhibit 1-1 provides a list of just a few of the numerous purposes fulfilled by the law.

Each purpose of the law is important, but taken as a unit, Exhibit 1-1 is a reminder of why we are very proud when we say we are a society of laws. The respect we give to the law as a source of authority is in part a recognition of the fact that in the absence of law, we would rely solely on the goodwill and dependability of one another. Most of us greatly prefer the law to that option.

Classification of the Law

There are many ways of thinking about the law. For example, we can divide law into *national* versus *international* law, *federal* versus *state* law, and *public* versus *private* law. Private law involves disputes between private individuals or groups. As an illustration, if a businessperson owns a computer equipment store and is delinquent in paying rent to the landlord, the dispute between them entails private law. Public law involves disputes between private individuals or groups and their government. For instance, if a computer store dumps waste behind its building in violation of local, state, or federal environmental regulations, the resulting dispute focuses on public law.

Another distinction among types of laws is civil law versus criminal law. Civil law involves the rights and responsibilities found in relationships between persons and between persons and their government. It also involves the remedies available when someone's rights are violated. One example of a civil law case involving a large business organization occurred in 1993. The

LO 1

business law
The enforceable rules of conduct that govern the actions of buyers and sellers in market exchanges.

LO 2

LO 3

law
Rules of conduct in any organized society that are enforced by the governing authority of the community.

private law
Law that involves suits between private individuals or groups.

LO 4

public law
Law that involves suits between private individuals or groups and their governments.

civil law
The body of laws that govern rights and responsibilities either between persons or between persons and their government.

Exhibit 1-1

Purposes of the Law

- Providing order such that one can depend on a promise or an expectation of obligations.
- Serving as an alternative to fighting.
- Facilitating a sense that change is possible, but only after a rational consideration of options.
- Encouraging social justice.
- Guaranteeing personal freedoms.
- Serving as a moral guide by indicating minimal expectations of citizens and organizations.

restaurant chain Jack-In-the-Box was ordered to pay damages after a two-year-old child died of food poisoning from *E. coli* and several other people became ill from eating the tainted meat.

In contrast to civil law, criminal law applies to situations in which someone commits an act against the public as a unit. These crimes are prosecuted not by individuals but by the state or federal government.

One example of a criminal law is the prohibition against insider trading on the stock exchange. Insider trading occurs when an individual uses insider, or secret, company information to increase her or his own finances or those of family or friends. For example, several years ago an IBM secretary allegedly told her husband, who told several other people, that the company was going to take over operations of Lotus Development. This information was spread among a number of individuals before it was publicly announced.

On the basis of this leak, 25 people bought stock that increased greatly in value following IBM's public announcement. The Securities and Exchange Commission filed charges against the 25 stock purchasers because they were creating an unfair trading environment for the public.

criminal law
A classification of law involving the rights and responsibilities an individual has with respect to the public as a whole.

Sources of Business Law

LO 5

How is law created, and where do we look to find the laws?

CONSTITUTIONS

The United States Constitution and the constitution of each state establish the fundamental principles and rules by which the United States and the individual states are governed. The term constitutional law refers to the general limits and powers of the federal and state governments as stated in their written constitutions. The U.S. Constitution is the supreme law of the land, the foundation for all laws in the United States. It is the primary authority when we are trying to identify the relationship between business organizations and government.

constitutional law
The general limits and powers of a government as interpreted from its written constitution.

STATUTES

Legislative actions, called *statutes,* are another important source of law. The assortment of rules and regulations put forth by legislatures is what we call statutory law. These legislative acts can be found in the United States Code when they are passed by Congress or in the various state codes when they are enacted by state legislatures. The codes are a collection of all the laws in one convenient location.

statutory law
The assortment of rules and regulations put forth by legislatures.

Because so much business activity occurs within the jurisdiction of state courts, business managers must be familiar with the local city and county ordinances that govern matters not covered by federal or state codes. These ordinances address important business considerations such as local taxes, environmental standards, zoning ordinances, and building codes.

For example, if you wish to open a Krispy Kreme franchise in Santa Fe, New Mexico, you must follow local guidelines regarding the area where you may build your store, the materials that you may use to build, and the state minimum wage that you must pay to employees making donuts. The regulations will be different if you wish to open your franchise in Toledo, Ohio, or Seattle, Washington.

While they are not a source of law in the same sense as constitutions and statutory law, model or uniform laws serve as a basis for some statutory law at the state level. Business activity is made more difficult when state laws vary. To prevent such problems, a group of legal scholars and lawyers formed the National Conference of Commissioners on Uniform State Laws (NCC). The NCC regularly urges states to enact model laws to provide greater uniformity of law. The response is entirely in the hands of the state legislatures. They can ignore a suggestion or adopt part or all of the proposed model law.

model laws
Laws created to account for the variability of laws among states. These laws serve to standardize the otherwise different interstate laws. Also called *model laws.*

The proposals of the NCC, while not laws themselves, have been adopted on more than 200 occasions by state legislatures. The NCC is an especially important influence on business law. Paired with the publications of the American Law Institute, the NCC became the source of the

Uniform Commercial Code (UCC). The UCC is a body of law so significant for business activities that it will be the focus of intensive study in several chapters of this text. The UCC laws include sales laws and other regulations affecting commerce, such as bank deposits and collections, title documents, and warranties. For example, these laws govern the different types of warranties that companies such as Microsoft, Sony, and Honda provide with their products.

CASES

Constitutions, legislatures, and administrative agencies encourage certain behavior and prevent other actions. But the boundaries of these laws are seldom self-explanatory. Consequently, law must be interpreted.

case law

The collection of legal interpretations made by judges. They are considered to be law unless otherwise revoked by a statutory law. Also known as *common law.*

Case law is the collection of legal interpretations made by judges. An alternative name for case law is common law. These interpretations are law unless they are revoked later by new statutory law.

Case law is especially significant for businesses because a modern business often operates in multiple legal jurisdictions. Because statutory laws are subject to interpretation, one court may have interpreted particular laws one way at one business location and a second court may interpret a similarly worded statute differently in a second business location.

Courts issue judicial decisions that often include interpretations of statutes and administrative regulations. These decisions contain the reasoning used by the courts to arrive at their decisions. The reasoning depends heavily on precedent, the use of past decisions to guide future decisions. An earlier decision in a similar fact pattern is a precedent that guides later decisions, thereby providing greater stability and predictability to the law.

precedent

A tool used by judges to make rulings on cases on the basis of key similarities to previous cases.

It is crucial that business managers pay attention to changes in the law and cases in which new precedents are set. These precedents must be taken into account when making future business decisions. For instance, courts sometimes make new rulings regarding the kinds of warnings companies should be required to provide to consumers about potential harm that could result from their products.

One example was a case filed against McDonald's. After a woman was severely burned by very hot coffee, the company was found negligent for failing to provide a warning label on its hot-beverage cups. Now many retailers of hot beverages provide warning labels on their beverage cups because of the precedent that was set by this case.

stare decisis

"Standing by the decision"; a principle stating that rulings made in higher courts are binding precedent for lower courts.

When courts rely on precedent, they are obeying stare decisis ("standing by their decision"). Following stare decisis creates greater predictability for both businesses and individuals that look to the courts for the rules on which they should rely when they engage in market exchanges. In accordance with stare decisis, rulings that are made in higher courts become binding precedent for lower courts. If an issue is brought before a state court, the court will ascertain whether the state supreme court has made a decision on a similar issue, which would have then set a binding precedent that the lower court would need to follow.

Even though this practice is meant to create a consistent and reliable justice system, different judges may view the facts of a case in different ways. In addition, courts are sometimes presented with a new issue and do not have a binding decision to follow. In such instances, they may look to decisions made in similar cases by nonbinding courts in other states or jurisdictions.

If a new issue comes before two state courts and there is no binding decision from the state supreme court, both state courts need to look for other rulings on similar cases. They are not bound by each other's decision, and so they might have different decisions on the same subject. The decisions in these lower courts can be appealed to the state appeals court however, and the appeals court's decision can be appealed to the state supreme court. If the state supreme court rules on the case, its decision is binding for the state but does not affect earlier decisions made by state courts. The state supreme court's decision affects only the decision being appealed and any future cases brought in the state on that particular subject.

One example of a case that has been used in accordance with stare decisis as a binding precedent is *Brown v. Board of Education,*[1] which abolished discriminatory policies for individuals

[1] 347 U.S. 483 (1954).

of different racial backgrounds. For instance, in *Regents of the University of California v. Bakke*,[2] the plaintiff, a white male, had applied to the University of California at Davis medical school two years in a row and been denied admittance. He alleged that the admissions process was discriminatory, because out of 100 slots, 16 were reserved for members of minority races.

The U.S. Supreme Court found that the school's admissions policy was not legal, referencing *Brown* and stating that the basic principle behind it and similar cases was that individuals could not be excluded on the basis of race or ethnicity. The Court wrote, "Preferring members of any one group for no reason other than race or ethnic origin is discrimination for its own sake."

Just as state statutes have been strongly influenced by the suggestions of the NCC, common law evolves with the assistance of a mechanism called Restatements of the Law. These Restatements are summaries of the common law rules in a particular area of the law that have been enacted by most states. The American Law Institute prepares these Restatements for contracts, agency, property, torts, and many other areas of law that affect business decisions. While the Restatements are not themselves a source of business law, judges frequently use them to guide their interpretations in a particular case.

In addition to the Restatements, many influences are at work in the minds of judges when they interpret constitutions, statutes, and regulations. For example, the values and social backgrounds of the judges function as lights and shadows, moving the judges toward particular legal decisions.

Restatements of the Law
Summaries of common law rules in a particular area of the law. Restatements do not carry the weight of law but can be used to guide interpretations of particular cases.

ADMINISTRATIVE LAW

Constitutions and statutes are never complete in the sense of covering all the detailed rules that affect government and business relations. The federal government, as well as state and local governments, has dozens of administrative agencies, whose task is to perform a particular government function. For example, the Environmental Protection Agency (EPA) has broad responsibilities to enforce federal statutes in the area of environmental protection.

Administrative law is the collection of rules and decisions made by all these administrative agencies. Just glance at Exhibit 1-2 to get a sense of the scope of a few of the major federal administrative agencies.

Businesses function within the rules established by agencies like these. For example, the Occupational Safety and Health Administration (OSHA) oversees health and workplace safety and makes sure that employees will be working in conditions that are not hazardous. One instance in which OSHA exercised its authority occurred in 1994, when OSHA settled a complaint with

administrative law
The collection of rules and decisions made by administrative agencies to fill in particular details missing from constitutions and statutes.

Exhibit 1-2
Major Federal Administrative Agencies

INDEPENDENT AGENCIES	EXECUTIVE AGENCIES
Commodity Futures Trading Commission (CFTC)	Federal Deposit Insurance Corporation (FDIC)
Consumer Product Safety Commission (CPSC)	Occupational Safety and Health Administration (OSHA)
Equal Employment Opportunity Commission (EEOC)	General Services Administration (GSA)
Federal Trade Commission (FTC)	National Aeronautics and Space Administration (NASA)
Federal Communications Commission (FCC)	Small Business Administration (SBA)
Interstate Commerce Commission (ICC)	International Development Cooperative Agency (IDCA)
National Labor Relations Board (NLRB)	National Science Foundation (NSF)
National Transportation Safety Board (NTSB)	Veterans Administration (VA)
Nuclear Regulatory Commission (NRC)	Office of Personnel Management (OPM)
Securities and Exchange Commission (SEC)	

[2] 438 U.S. 265 (1978).

United Parcel Service (UPS). The company was not providing adequate safety measures and equipment for workers who handled hazardous waste, and OSHA was responsible for making sure that UPS adapted its practices to follow federal safety guidelines.

TREATIES

A *treaty* is a binding agreement between two states or international organizations. Treaties may be called several things: international agreements, covenants, exchanges of letters, conventions, or protocols. In the United States, a treaty is generally negotiated by the executive branch. To be binding, it must then be approved by two-thirds of the Senate.

A treaty is similar to a contract in two important ways. Both treaties and contracts are attempts by parties to determine rights and obligations among themselves. In addition, when a party fails to obey a treaty or a contract, international law imposes liability on that party.

EXECUTIVE ORDERS

The president and state governors can issue directives requiring that officials in the executive branch perform their functions in a particular manner. The Code of Federal Regulations (CFR) contains all the executive orders created by the president. (The CFR is online at www.gpoaccess.gov/cfr/index.html.) Presidents claim the power to issue such orders on the basis of their Article II, Section 1, constitutional power to "take care that the laws be faithfully executed."

An illustration of an especially controversial executive order is Order 9066, issued by President Franklin Roosevelt during World War II. On the basis of this order, Japanese-Americans on the West Coast, as well as thousands of Italian-American and German-American families, were sent to internment camps for the duration of the war.

LO 6

SCHOOLS OF LEGAL INTERPRETATION

When legislators or courts make law, they do so guided by certain habits of mind and specific beliefs about human nature. These views guide them toward particular legal solutions and away from others. This section briefly describes several of the more common guides to legal interpretation.

Natural Law The term *natural law* refers to the idea that there are certain ethical laws and principles that are morally right and "above" the laws devised by humans. This concept suggests that individuals should have the freedom to disobey a law enacted by majorities of people if their individual conscience goes against the law and they believe the law is wrong. The idea that people have basic human rights, for example, is rooted in the concept of natural law.

For instance, Dow Chemical wants its suppliers to conform to U.S. environmental and labor laws, not just the local laws in the supplier's country, where regulations may not be as stringent. This reaction reflects the beliefs that people have a right to be treated fairly in their jobs and that they have a right as human beings to a clean environment.

legal positivism
A school of jurisprudence which holds that because society requires authority, a legal and authoritarian hierarchy should exist. When a law is made, therefore, obedience is expected because authority created it.

identification with the vulnerable
A school of jurisprudence which holds that society should be fair. Particular attention is therefore paid to the poor, the ill, and the elderly.

Legal Positivism Legal positivism is an interpretive guide that urges us, as its followers, to design our legal system on the basis of the belief that legitimate political authority deserves our obedience when it issues a rule. This idea stresses that society requires authority and the hierarchy that such authority demands. When a duly authorized branch of government issues a law, positivism would urge us to see our proper role as obedience. The law is then a set of appropriate commands.

This view sees law as something quite distinct from morality. Moral questions about the law should not interfere with our inclination to obey it. A judge with leanings in the direction of legal positivism, for example, might write that she is deciding to enforce the law in question but that her decision does not necessarily mean that she sees the law as the morally correct rule.

Identification with the Vulnerable Closely linked to pursuing legal change through natural law is pursuing change through identification with the vulnerable. Some members of our society

are able to take care of themselves in terms of most life situations. Others, especially the ill, children, the aged, the disabled, and the poor, require assistance to meet their fundamental needs of life, health, and education.

This guide to legal change is tied closely to the pursuit of fairness in our society. The metaphor of a level playing field is linked with some higher law or body of moral principles that connects all of us in the human community. We might look at a particular employment contract, for example, and react by observing that "it is just not fair." Our caring impulse as a human feels outrage at that legal arrangement. That outrage can be a stimulus for legal change. One example of identification with the vulnerable is minimum-wage laws. They reflect the beliefs that workers should receive a minimum hourly wage and that employers should not be allowed to pay them less.

Historical School: Tradition One of the most often used guidelines for shaping the law is tradition, or *custom,* which is also called the historical school. Stare decisis is rooted in this perspective. When we follow tradition, we attempt to link our future behavior to the behavior of those who faced similar problems in earlier historical periods. The logic of the approach is that we need not reinvent the wheel each time a legal problem arises. Past practice is assumed to have been the product of careful thought.

Legal Realism Legal realism is based on the idea that, when ruling on a case, judges need to consider more than just the law. This school of thought dictates that they also take factors such as social and economic conditions into consideration when making a judgment. Followers of legal realism argue that the law must not be the sole factor in deciding a case since legal guidelines were designed by humans and exist in an ever-changing society.

Judges who follow this school of thought are more likely to depart from past court decisions to account for the fact that our society is constantly shifting and evolving. Those who subscribe to legal realism also believe that the law can never be enforced with complete consistency. They argue that because judges are human, they will bring different methods of reasoning to very similar cases.

One example of a law that has been enacted to reflect changes in our society is the Family and Medical Leave Act (FMLA). This act mandates that businesses employing more than 50 people must provide their workers with up to 12 weeks' unpaid leave every year to take care of family-related affairs. This includes caring for ill parents, adopting a child, or having a child. The FMLA protects pregnant women who take time off work, as their employers must provide them with the same pay and the same or an equivalent job when they return to work. This act reflects the fact that more mothers are working outside the home and more women are returning to work soon after they have a child. The FMLA also protects new parents against some types of employer discrimination that might occur after they return.

Cost-Benefit Analysis From this perspective, we need to examine all the costs and benefits for alternative laws or decisions and place monetary values on those costs and benefits. If we possessed those calculations, we could use cost-benefit analysis as a guide to legal change, choosing the legal alternatives that maximized the ratio of benefits to costs. For instance, in a contract dispute someone using this approach would attempt to attach responsibility for the problem in such a way that total benefit is maximized in relation to costs.

This approach to legal change is tied closely to the pursuit of efficiency. If a law yields more benefits than costs, then we have saved resources. Those resources can, in turn, be used to provide us with more goods and services. Our economy is thus more efficient in the sense of producing more for less.

For example, regulations enacted by the EPA can affect costs and benefits in the national economy. Polluted land is an economic loss because it cannot be used for farming or recreation. Polluted water can be toxic for fish and cannot be used for drinking. Polluted air can cause health problems and result in higher health care costs. While EPA regulations may end up costing companies more initially in order to control pollutants, the cost of environmental cleanup, and the loss of productivity in the economy as a whole, may be greater than the resources companies expend to control pollution.

historical school
A school of jurisprudence that uses traditions as the model for future laws and behavior. Also called *tradition* or *custom.*

legal realism
A school of jurisprudence which holds that context must be considered as well as law. Context includes factors such as economic conditions and social conditions.

cost-benefit analysis
An economic school of jurisprudence in which all costs and benefits of a law are given monetary values. Those laws with the highest ratios of benefits to costs are then preferable to those with lower ratios.

Global and Comparative Law

Comparative and international law is extremely important for future business managers. Because of advances in technology and transportation, trade with other countries is far easier today than it was in past years. Now it is possible to make different components for the same product in various countries all over the world and then assemble them in another country. It is possible to operate an antique store in Poughkeepsie but sell to customers in Moscow or Taipei through a Web site.

As a result of this ease in trade, business managers must be familiar with global trade laws that regulate business practices among nations. For instance, the United States and other countries have entered into agreements such as the North American Free Trade Agreement (NAFTA) and the General Agreement on Tariffs and Trade (GATT). These agreements help establish the conditions of trade between countries.

It is also important that future business managers understand comparative law, comparing and studying the laws in different countries. Business managers need to be aware of various trade laws and restrictions in different countries so that they can act accordingly when they set out to do business in those countries. The European Union, for example, has laws that differ from ours in terms of regulating the taxes on Internet sales and the amount of pollution that can be released into the environment. Companies doing business in the EU must take these standards into account.

Another example of a company's conforming to different laws is the search engine company Google, which has agreed to restrict the content of searches performed on Google.cn, the Chinese version of the company's search engine. Google took this action to satisfy regulations set by the Chinese government, which did not want its citizens to have access to certain Web sites or pieces of information. To do business in China, Google had to conform to these standards. This loss of freedom of information or access to information was considered by some to be such an "evil" that they felt Google had violated its own mission statement to "do no evil."

Modern business managers must have an ongoing fascination with the law to function effectively. Business law tells business managers the basic rules of the business game. Play any game without having first studied the rules, and you will probably fail.

But, unlike an ordinary game, the business game has a rule book that is changing dynamically. In addition, increased globalization requires that business leaders be alert to legal differences among national jurisdictions.

Looking for more review material?

The Online Learning Center at **www.mhhe.com/kubasekess** contains this chapter's "Assignment on the Internet" and also a list of URLs for more information, entitled "On the Internet." Find both of them in the Student Center portion of the OLC, along with quizzes and other helpful materials.

Critical Thinking and Business Law

Success in the modern business firm requires the development of critical thinking skills—the ability to understand what someone is saying and then to apply a set of evaluative criteria to determine the worth of what was said. In other words, businesspeople need to be able to sort sense from nonsense by evaluating arguments about relevant business law.

A critical thinker is always asking, "Now does that make sense?" And there is no better context in which to develop critical thinking skills than in the study of the laws that affect business. Critical thinking skills learned in the study of business law will be easily transferred to the decisions of business stakeholders.

Legal reasoning is similar to other reasoning in some ways and different in others. When people, including lawyers and judges, reason, they do so for a purpose. Some problem or dilemma bothers them. The stimulus that gets them thinking is a *legal issue*. It is stated as a question because it is a call for action. It requires us to *do* something, to think about answers.

For instance, we may be interested in such issues as the following:

- When are union organizers permitted under the National Labor Relations Act to trespass on an employer's property?
- Do tobacco manufacturers have liability for the deaths of smokers?
- Must a business fulfill a contract when the contract is made with an unlicensed contractor in a state requiring that all contractors be licensed?

Each of these questions has several potential answers. Which answer best accomplishes a particular business objective? Which answers are consistent with the law? Here is where critical thinking is essential to business success. Some answers can get the decision maker into trouble; others will advance the intended purpose. Each answer is called a *conclusion*.

Business firms often come into contact with such conclusions in the form of laws or court decisions. Business managers are therefore both consumers of and contributors to these legal conclusions. As businesspeople learn about and react to decisions or conclusions made by courts, they have two primary methods of response:

1. Memorizing and understanding the conclusions or rules of law as a guide for future business decisions.
2. Making judgments about the quality of the conclusions.

This book encourages you to do both. There are many forms of critical thinking, but they all share one characteristic: They focus on the quality of someone's reasoning. Critical thinking is active; it challenges each of us to form judgments about the quality of the link between a set of reasons and the conclusion supposedly derived from them. In particular, we will be focusing on the link between a court's reasons and its conclusions.

Our reactions to legal arguments shape our efforts to either support the status quo in the legal environment of business or offer support for particular changes.

The following structure for critical thinking is a thoroughly tested method used by successful market decision makers. Every time you read a case, try to follow this pattern of careful thinking.

1. Find the facts.
 Facts: Here we are looking for the most basic building blocks in a legal decision or argument. These building blocks, or facts, provide the environment or context in which the legal issue is to be resolved. Certain events occurred; certain actions were or were not taken; particular persons behaved or failed to behave in specific ways. All of these and many more possibilities together make up the intricate setting for the playing out of the issue in question. We always wonder, What happened in this case?

2. Look for the issue.
 Issue: In almost any legal conflict, finding and expressing the issue is an important step in forming our reaction. The issue is the question that caused the lawyers and their clients to enter

critical thinking skills
The ability to understand the structure and worth of an argument by evaluating the facts, issue, reasons, and conclusion of that argument.

the legal system. Usually, there are several reasonable perspectives concerning the correct way to word the issue in dispute. Don't let the possibility of *multiple* useful ways to word the issue cause you any confusion. The legal issue is certainly not just anything that we say it is.

3. Identify the judge's reasons and conclusion.

 Reasons and conclusion: Judges do not form legal conclusions on the basis of whim. They have support for their decisions. That support consists of their reasons. When we ask someone *why* a judge formed a particular conclusion, we are showing our respect for reasons as the proper basis for any assertion. We want a world rich with opinions so that we can have a broad field of choice. But we should agree with only those legal opinions that have convincing reasons supporting the conclusion. Asking "Why?" is our way of saying, "I want to believe you, but you have an obligation to help me by sharing the reasons for your conclusion."

4. Locate in the decision the rules of law that govern the judge's reasoning.

 Rules of law: Judges cannot offer just any reasoning that they please. They must always look back over their shoulders at the laws and previous court decisions that together provide an anchor for current and future decisions. What makes legal reasoning so complex is that statutes and legal findings are never *crystal* clear. They may seem very clear, but judges and businesspeople have room for interpretive flexibility in their reasoning.

5. Apply critical thinking to the reasoning.

 Evaluation of the reasoning: A judge's reasoning, once it has been laid before us by following the steps discussed here, is a message that we may either accept or reject. One of the most exciting things about our legal system is its potential for change. Critical thinking in the legal context consists of examining the legal opinion in search of potential problems in the reasoning.

critical thinking in the legal context
Examining a legal opinion to search for potential problems in the reasoning.

Here is a small sample of some especially useful critical thinking guidelines for business managers to apply when thinking about business law:

- *Look for potential ambiguity in the reasoning.* The term *ambiguity* refers to a lack of clarity in a word or phrase in the reasoning. Many words have multiple meanings; until the intended meaning is discovered, we cannot tell whether we wish to agree or disagree with the reasoning.

- *Ask whether the analogies used in the decision are strong.* When judges follow particular precedents, they are saying that the key similarities between the facts in the precedent and those in the case at hand are so similar that it makes sense to apply the same rule of law in both. Are there key differences in the factual situations that raise questions about the quality of that analogy?

- *Check the quality of the judge's use of evidence in his or her reasoning.* Is the evidence used by the judge to support the opinion both abundant enough and reliable enough that we should agree with the reasoning?

- *Think about the extent to which important missing information prevents you from being totally confident about the judge's reasoning.* Is there important missing information that you would need to have before making up your mind?

- *Consider the possibility of rival causes.* When the judge claims that one action caused another, think about whether some alternative cause may have been responsible.

Business Ethics and White-Collar Crime

---→ **CASE OPENER**

Untenable Trading

In late 1997, John Freeman, employed at Goldman Sachs & Co., Inc., began misappropriating nonpublic information concerning impending mergers and acquisitions. Rather than using that information to make trades himself, Freeman began disclosing the insider information to James Cooper and Benton Erskine, with the understanding and agreement that they would share a portion of their trading profits with him.

During the course of the scheme, Cooper received Freeman's permission to tip other individuals who might be able to assist them. Freeman knew of two people to whom Cooper gave the tips. Cooper, however, also tipped certain individuals without Freeman's knowledge or consent, including Chad Conner, a stockbroker. Cooper began regularly tipping Conner, who, in turn, tipped numerous other brokerage clients.

In the early fall of 1998, Freeman left Goldman Sachs to work part-time for Credit Suisse First Boston (CSFB), another investment bank. While Freeman continued to misappropriate information from CSFB, Conner and his clients believed the information they were now receiving was not as profitable as it had been in the past. Conner told Cooper that one of his clients was willing to pay the "New York source" $100,000 to return to Goldman Sachs. Cooper communicated this offer to Freeman.

Prior to receiving this offer, Freeman had been apprehended by the FBI and had agreed to assist the agency. On February 23, 2000, Conner and Cooper participated in a three-way telephone and online conversation with an FBI agent posing as Freeman. During this telephone conversation, Conner reiterated his offer to pay Freeman $100,000 to return to Goldman Sachs. The agent posing as Freeman asked Conner to personally deliver $5,000 to Atlantic City, and Conner agreed. On March 4, 2000, FBI agents arrested Conner in Atlantic City and seized an envelope containing $5,000. Conner was subsequently charged with commercial bribery and 81 counts of insider trading.[1]

1. Do you believe Conner did anything illegal? Anything unethical?
2. If a person has inside information and does not trade on it himself but passes it on to another who uses it to trade, is the person who passed on the information guilty of insider trading?

[1] *United States v. Geibel*, 369 F.3d 682 (2004).

After reading this chapter, you will be able to answer the following questions:

LO 1 What are business ethics and the social responsibility of business?

LO 2 How are business law and business ethics related?

LO 3 How can we use the WPH framework to make ethical business decisions?

LO 4 What are the basic elements of a crime?

LO 5 What is white-collar crime?

LO 6 Who can be held responsible when a corporate crime is committed?

LO 7 What are the basic steps of a criminal proceeding?

LO 8 What laws attempt to prevent white-collar crime?

This chapter provides assistance for thinking systematically about issues of right and wrong in business conduct and recognizing when wrongful conduct has become criminal. The discussion begins with an explanation of key terms like *business ethics* and *social responsibility*. Then, because it is helpful to have a useful approach to ethical decision making, the chapter presents a practical method by which future business managers can think more carefully about the ethical dilemmas they will face during their careers. Next, the chapter introduces the elements of a crime and explains some common crimes that occur in the business context. After discussing how liability can be imposed on corporations and corporate executives, the chapter sets forth the steps of criminal procedure. The chapter concludes by discussing some of the laws used to fight business crime.

As the Case Opener illustrates, unethical behavior and crime can come in many forms and affect large numbers of people. Also, crimes can quickly expand in terms of the number of people involved. It is important to note that Freeman, Cooper, Conner, and everyone Conner told made large sums of money at the expense of other investors. Although a crime might seem like a victimless one at first, crime always has a victim, even if the victim is not readily identifiable.

Business Ethics and Social Responsibility

LO 1

ethics
The study and practice of decisions about what is good or right.

business ethics
The use of ethics and ethical principles to solve business dilemmas.

ethical dilemma
A question about how one should behave that requires one to reflect about the advantages and disadvantages of the optional choices for various stakeholders.

Ethics is the study and practice of decisions about what is good, or right. Ethics guides us when we are wondering what we should be doing in a particular situation. Business ethics is an application of ethics to the special problems and opportunities experienced by businesspeople. An ethical dilemma is a problem about what a firm should do for which no clear, right decision is available. Reasonable people can expect to disagree about optimal solutions to ethical dilemmas.

For example, imagine yourself in the position of a business manager at Wells Fargo Bank. You know that providing bank accounts for customers has costs attached to it. You want to cover those costs by charging the customers the cost of their checking accounts. By doing so, you can preserve the bank's revenue for shareholders and employees of Wells Fargo. So far, the decision seems simple. But an ethical dilemma soon appears.

You learn from recent government reports that 12 million families cannot afford to have bank accounts when they are charged a fee to maintain one. You want to do the right thing in this situation. But what would that be? The study of business ethics can help you resolve this dilemma by suggesting approaches you can use that will show respect for others while maintaining a healthy business enterprise.

Making such decisions would be much easier if managers could focus only on the impact of decisions on the firm. If, for example, a firm had as its only objective the maximization of profits, the "right thing" to do would be the option that had the largest positive impact on the firm's profits.

But businesses operate in a community. Communities have expectations for behavior of individuals, groups, and businesses. Different communities have different expectations of businesses. Trying to identify those expectations and deciding whether to fulfill them complicate business ethics. The community often expects firms to do much more than just provide a useful good or service at a reasonable price. For example, a community may expect firms to resist paying bribes, even when the payment of such fees is an ordinary cost of doing business in certain global settings.

The social responsibility of business consists of the expectations the community imposes on firms doing business within its borders. These expectations must be honored to a certain extent, even when a firm wishes to ignore them, because firms are always subject to the implicit threat that legislation will impose social obligations on them. So, if the community expects businesses to obey certain standards of fairness even when the standards interfere with profit maximization, firms that choose to ignore that expectation do so at their peril.

social responsibility of business
The expectations that a community places on the actions of firms inside that community's borders.

Business Law and Business Ethics

Before business managers consider the social responsibilities of firms in their communities, they need to gather all the relevant facts. Experienced managers know that assembling the facts is just the beginning of a thoughtful business decision. Next, it makes sense to ask, *Is it legal to go forward with this decision?*

The legality of the decision is the minimal standard that must be met. But the existence of that minimum standard is essential for the development of business ethics. To make this point, let's take a look at the growing practice of bribery in the absence of legal standards. In some countries businesses must pay bribes to receive legitimate supplies. Though the businessperson may be morally opposed to paying the bribes, the supplies are necessary to stay in business and there may be no other means of obtaining them.

Thus, foreign companies face an ethical dilemma: They must decide whether to pay bribes or find alternative sources of supplies. For instance, when McDonald's opened its doors in Moscow, it made arrangements to receive its supplies from foreign providers. These arrangements ensured that the franchise did not have to engage in questionable business practices.

The definition of business ethics refers to *standards* of business conduct. *It does not result in a set of correct decisions.* Business ethics can improve business decisions by serving as a reminder to not simply choose the first business option that comes to mind or the one that enriches the firm in the short run. But business ethics can never produce a list of correct business decisions that all ethical businesses will make.

Well-managed firms try to provide ethical leadership by establishing a code of ethics for the firm. For example, Exhibit 2-1 presents General Motors' statement about the importance of business ethics to GM. Notice, however, that this corporate code can never do more than provide guidance. The complications associated with managerial decisions do not permit any ethical guide to provide definitive lists of right and wrong decisions.

At the same time that business ethics guides decisions within firms, ethics helps guide the law. Law and business ethics serve as an interactive system—informing and assessing each other. For example, our ethical inclination to encourage trust, dependability, and efficiency in market exchanges shapes many of our business laws. The principles of contract law, for instance, facilitate market exchanges and trade because the parties to an exchange can count on the enforceability of agreements. Legal rules that govern the exchange have been shaped in large part by our sense of commercial ethics.

Business Ethics and Italian Taxes

When Italian corporations file their tax returns, the tax authorities assume that the corporations are underestimating their profits by 30 to 70 percent. This assumption proves to be true, yet the Italian Revenue Service does not press charges. In fact, purposely understating profits is the accepted practice within Italy.

Knowing the faulty nature of the tax return, the Revenue Service sends an "invitation to discuss" about six months after a corporation has filed. The parties agree on a meeting date. At the meeting the corporation's executives do not attend. Instead, they send a *commercialista* whose "function exists for the primary purpose of negotiating corporation tax payments."

Several rounds of bargaining take place between the *commercialista* and the tax authorities. On the basis of the corporation's taxes the previous year and the estimation of the current return, the two parties agree on a payment that is usually much higher than the original estimation but still less than face value.

This negotiating process, while it may seem foreign to Americans, is a common business practice in Italy. In the early 1980s an American banker learned the difficult lesson that, for a firm doing business in a foreign country, local custom has a significant impact on ethical practice. The banker refused, on ethical grounds, to underestimate profits on the tax return. The Italian Revenue Service suggested several times that he hire a *commercialista* and resubmit his tax return.

The American banker refused all such suggestions. Finally, the Revenue Service sent the American a notice that demanded payments 15 times larger than what he owed. The banker immediately arranged an appointment to express his outrage. When he arrived at the meeting, the Italian tax authorities were pleased to see him and said, "Now we can begin our negotiations."

WPH approach (to ethical decision making)
A set of ethical guidelines that urges us to consider whom an action affects, the purpose of the action, and how we view its morality (whether by utilitarian ethics, deontology, etc).

ethical guideline
A simple tool to help determine whether an action is moral.

Of course, different ethical understandings prevail in different countries. Thus, ethical conceptions shape business law and business relationships uniquely in each country. Increasingly, business leaders require sensitivity to the differences in legal guidelines in the various countries in which they operate. These differences are based on somewhat different understandings of ethical behavior among businesspeople in diverse countries.

As we mentioned above, business ethics does not yield one "correct" decision. So how are business managers to chart their way through the ethical decision-making process? One source of assistance consists of the general theories and schools of thought about ethics. Each ethical system provides a method for resolving ethical dilemmas by examining duties, consequences, or virtues.

In the interest of providing future business managers with a practical approach to business ethics *that they can use,* we suggest a three-step process: the WPH approach. This approach provides future business managers with some ethical guidelines, or practical steps, that serve as a dependable stimulus to ethical reasoning in a business context. Appendix 2A provides the theoretical basis for the WPH approach used in this book.

Exhibit 2-1

General Motors' Code of Business Conduct

The foundation for all conduct by GM and its employees is one of our core values:
Integrity. Integrity is essential to achieving our vision of becoming the world leader in transportation products and services, earning the enthusiasm of our customers, working together as a team, innovating, and continuously improving. We call this Winning With Integrity.

These Guidelines are designed to help GM and its employees understand and meet fundamental obligations that are vital to our success. Some of those obligations are legal duties. They are established by the laws, regulations, and court rulings applicable to our business. Other obligations result from policies GM establishes to make sure our actions align with our core values and cultural priorities. Compliance with both types of obligation—our legal duties and our internal policies—is vital to our goal of winning with integrity.

Employees who violate these guidelines may be subject to disciplinary action which, in the judgment of management, is appropriate to the nature of the violation and which may include termination of employment. Employees may also be subject to civil and criminal penalties if the law has been violated.

These guidelines state the conduct obligations of GM employees, directors, and others to whom they apply. Neither the guidelines nor an employee's observance of these constitute an employment contract or change the terms of the contract relationship between GM and any of its employees.

The WPH Framework for Business Ethics

A useful set of ethical guidelines requires the recognition that managerial decisions must meet the following primary criteria (Exhibit 2-2):

- The decisions affect particular groups of stakeholders in the operations of the firm. The pertinent question is thus, *Whom* would this decision affect?
- The decisions are made in pursuit of a particular *purpose.* Business decisions are instruments toward an ethical end.
- The decisions must meet the standards of action-oriented business behavior. Managers need a doable set of guidelines for *How* to make ethical decisions.

WHO ARE THE RELEVANT STAKEHOLDERS?

The stakeholders of a firm are the many groups of people affected by the firm's decisions. Any given managerial decision affects, in varying degrees, the following stakeholders:

1. Owners or shareholders.
2. Employees.
3. Customers.
4. Management.
5. The general community where the firm operates.
6. Future generations.

Managers should make sure they consider all relevant stakeholders when they engage in ethical reasoning.

stakeholders
The groups of people affected by a firm's decisions.

WHAT ARE THE ULTIMATE *PURPOSES* OF THE DECISION?

When we think about the ultimate reason or purpose that we make decisions in a business firm, we turn to the basic unit of business ethics—values. Values are positive abstractions that capture our sense of what is good or desirable. They are *ideas* that underlie conversations about business ethics. We derive our ethics from the interplay of values. Values represent our understanding of the purposes we will fulfill by making particular decisions.

values
Positive abstractions that capture our sense of what is good and desirable.

For example, we value honesty. We want to live in communities where the trust we associate with honesty prevails in our negotiations with one another. Business depends on the maintenance of a high degree of trust. No contract can protect us completely against every possible contingency. So we need some element of trust in one another when we buy and sell.

If we think about the definition of values for a moment, we realize two things. First, a huge number of values pull and push our decisions. Second, to state that a value is important in a particular situation is to start a conversation about what is meant by that particular value.

To help make WPH useful to you as a manager, Exhibit 2-3 outlines an efficient way to apply this second step in the WPH framework. The exhibit identifies four of the most important values influencing business ethics and presents alternative meanings for each. This table should not only help clarify the importance of values in your own mind but also enable you to question others who claim to be acting ethically.

For instance, a manager might be deciding whether to fire an employee whose performance is less than impressive. In making the decision, the manager explores alternative visions of key values such as justice and efficiency and then makes choices about which action to take. Values and their alternative meanings are often the foundation for different ethical decisions.

Exhibit 2-2

The WPH Process of Ethical Decision Making

1. **W—WHO (Stakeholders):**
 Customers
 Owners or investors
 Management
 Employees
 Community
 Future generations
2. **P—PURPOSE (Values):**
 Freedom
 Security
 Justice
 Efficiency
3. **H—HOW (Guidelines):**
 Public disclosure
 Universalization
 Golden Rule

Exhibit 2-3

Primary Values and
Business Ethics

VALUE	ALTERNATIVE MEANINGS
Freedom	1. To act without restriction from rules imposed by others.
	2. To possess the capacity or resources to act as one wishes.
	3. To escape the cares and demands of this world entirely.
Security	1. To possess a large-enough supply of goods and services to meet basic needs.
	2. To be safe from those wishing to interfere with your property rights.
	3. To achieve the psychological condition of self-confidence to such an extent that risks are welcome.
Justice	1. To receive the products of your labor.
	2. To treat all humans identically, regardless of race, class, gender, age, and sexual preference.
	3. To provide resources in proportion to need.
	4. To possess anything that someone else is willing to grant you.
Efficiency	1. To maximize the amount of wealth in society.
	2. To get the most from a particular output.
	3. To minimize costs.

HOW DO WE MAKE ETHICAL DECISIONS?

Making ethical decisions has always been one of our most confusing *and* important human challenges. In the process of meeting this challenge, we have discovered a few general, ethical guidelines to assist us. An *ethical guideline* provides one path to ethical conduct. Notice that all three ethical guidelines below reflect a central principle of business ethics: consideration of stakeholders.

The Golden Rule The idea that we should interact with other people in a manner consistent with the way we would like them to interact with us has deep historical roots. Both Confucius and Aristotle suggested versions of that identical guideline. One scholar has identified six ways the Golden Rule can be interpreted:

1. Do to others as you want them to gratify you.
2. Be considerate of others' feelings as you want them to be considerate of yours.
3. Treat others as persons of rational dignity like you.
4. Extend brotherly or sisterly love to others, as you would want them to do to you.
5. Treat others according to moral insight, as you would have others treat you.
6. Do to others as God wants you to do to them.

Regardless of the version of the Golden Rule we use, this guideline urges us to be aware that other people—their rights and needs—matter. The focus on others that is the foundation of the Golden Rule is also clearly reflected in a second ethical guideline: the public disclosure test.

Public Disclosure Test One way to think of the public disclosure test is to view it as a ray of sunlight that makes our actions visible, rather than obscured. The public disclosure test is sometimes called the "television test," for it requires us to imagine that our actions are being broadcast on national television. The premise behind this general guideline is that ethics is hard work, labor that we might resist if we did not have frequent reminders that we live in a community. Given our role as a member of a community, our self-concept is tied, at least in part, to how that community perceives us.

Universalization Test A third general guideline shares with the other two a focus on the "other"—the stakeholders whom our actions affect. Before we act, the universalization test asks us to consider what the world would be like were our decision copied by everyone else. Applying the universalization test causes us to wonder aloud: "Is what I am about to do the kind of action that, *were others to follow my example,* makes the world a better place for me and those I love?"

In summary, business managers can apply the WPH approach to most ethical dilemmas. The WPH framework provides a practical process suited to the frequently complex ethical dilemmas that business managers must address quickly in today's society.

White-Collar Crime

ELEMENTS OF A CRIME

LO 4

The purpose of criminal law is to punish an offender for causing harm to public health, safety, or morals. In a criminal proceeding, the *government* files the charges against the defendant. Thus, the government is always a party to a criminal action. Government involvement distinguishes criminal trials from civil proceedings. For civil actions, an individual person or corporation can file a suit. The difference exists because in a criminal trial society is seen as the victim, whereas in a civil trial there is an individual victim or victims.

Criminal laws usually define criminal behavior and set guidelines for punishment. To punish an individual for criminal behavior, the government must demonstrate the two elements of a crime:

1. Wrongful behavior, that is, *actus reus* (guilty act).
2. Wrongful state of mind, also known as *mens rea* (guilty mind).

The government thus must show that a defendant committed a prohibited act with a wrongful intent.

To prove the first element, *actus reus* (guilty act), the government must establish the nonmental elements of the crime. That is, the government must demonstrate that a prohibited act or a prohibited consequence resulted because of the behavior of the defendant.

To prove the second element, *mens rea* (guilty state of mind), the government must prove that the defendant acted with purpose, knowledge, recklessness, or negligence, depending on which of these states of mind is required by the law defining the relevant offense. The defendant's type of wrongful state of mind helps determine the seriousness of the punishment for the crime.

A defendant can *purposefully* commit a crime by engaging in a specific wrongful behavior to bring about a specific wrongful result. A defendant can *knowingly* commit a wrongful act if the person knows the act is wrongful or believes that the act is wrongful yet does nothing to confirm or disconfirm this belief. A defendant is *reckless* if a criminal act occurs when the individual consciously ignores substantial risk. Finally, a defendant is *negligent* if he or she does not meet a standard of care that the reasonable person would use in the context that led to the criminal act.

In certain cases, liability may be assessed even without establishing the guilty-mind criterion discussed above. Only certain crimes, typically violations of regulatory statutes, allow punishment to be assessed without having to prove guilty mind. When liability is assessed without the guilty-mind criterion, it is known as **liability without fault, or strict liability.** Liability without fault involves actions that, regardless of the care taken, are deemed illegal to engage in; such acts are specifically prohibited regardless of state of mind. Liability without fault would apply, for example, if a business were to sell cigarettes or alcohol to a minor. Although the business might not have intended to sell cigarettes or alcohol to a minor (thus lacking a guilty mind), the statutory violation still allows liability to be imposed.

CLASSIFICATION OF CRIMES

Crimes are divided into categories based on the seriousness of the offense. Today, the categories used are felonies, misdemeanors, and petty crimes. Felonies include serious crimes, such as murder, that are punishable by imprisonment for more than one year in a penitentiary or death. Misdemeanors are less serious crimes punishable by fines and/or imprisonment for less than

actus reus

Latin for "guilty act"; a wrongful behavior that is associated with the physical act of a declared crime.

mens rea

Latin for "guilty mind"; the mental state accompanying a wrongful behavior.

liability without fault

A legal term that imposes responsibility for damages regardless of the existence of negligence. Also called *strict liability.*

felony

A serious crime, such as murder, rape, or robbery, that is punishable by imprisonment for more than one year or death.

misdemeanor

A crime that is less serious than a felony and is punishable by a fine and/or imprisonment for less than one year.

one year. **Petty offenses,** such as violating a building code, are minor misdemeanors and are usually punishable by a jail sentence of less than six months or a small fine. The statute defining the crime usually establishes whether the crime is a felony, misdemeanor, or petty offense. Crimes may also be federal or state, depending on whether they are created by the state or federal legislature.

SPECIFIC WHITE-COLLAR CRIMES

Originally, white-collar crimes were distinguished from other crimes because of the social status of the offender. The more modern approach is to define **white-collar crime** as a variety of nonviolent illegal acts against society that occur most frequently in the business context. Clearly, the crimes described in the Case Opener fall under this broad definition of white-collar crime.

Mail fraud, bribery, embezzlement, and computer crimes are examples of offenses typically classified as white-collar crimes. These crimes occur more frequently than you might think. According to some estimates, one in three American households is the victim of white-collar crime every year.

The consequences of white-collar crimes are far-reaching. First, the cost of white-collar crimes can be tremendous. It is estimated that fraud in the health care industry alone costs society over $100 billion each year. Second, in cases where company employees commit the crime, many companies fail to report the crime to avoid publicity. Third, white-collar crimes can be costly to the environment. For example, improper disposal of chemicals, such as dumping chemicals in a stream, has long-term repercussions for marine life, the surrounding ecosystem, and any humans who may come in contact with the contaminated water source.

Of course, the amount of money collected in fines from corporate executives engaged in criminal activity has not been insignificant either. For example, in 1999, the government won over $490 million in fines, judgments, and settlements from health care fraud cases alone. Fines, however, are only one way that those found guilty of fraud and other white-collar crimes might be punished.

There are at least four alternative ways to punish white-collar criminals. First, confinement has been mandated for certain types of white-collar crimes. As the prevalence of white-collar crime has increased, so too has the number of white-collar offenders who are in jail. Second, white-collar criminals may be ordered to do community service, such as giving speeches about business crime. For instance, junk-bond king Michael Milliken was compelled to give speeches about corporate crime after he was convicted of insider trading. Third, judges may disqualify the individual from employment. For instance, the judge may prohibit the offender from engaging in an occupation where the same or a similar criminal act could occur again. Fourth, the offender can be placed under house arrest. Individuals must wear a sensor so that the government can monitor whether they have left their houses.

Bribery One of the better-known white-collar crimes is bribery. **Bribery** is the offering, giving, soliciting, or receiving of money or any object of value for the purpose of influencing the judgment or conduct of a person in a position of trust. *Bribery of a public official* is a statutory offense under federal law. The purpose of this law against bribery is to maintain the integrity of the government. This statute also covers bribes offered to witnesses in exchange for testimony. Perhaps one of the most publicized recent examples of bribery was the 2002 Winter Olympics bribery scandal in Salt Lake City, Utah. The Salt Lake City Olympics Bid Committee allegedly gave International Olympic Committee members between $4 million and $7 million in cash and other benefits. These benefits included college tuition assistance payments, shopping trips for bathroom fixtures and doorknobs, and trips to the Super Bowl.

To demonstrate bribery under this statute, the government must show three elements: (1) Something of value was offered, given, or promised to (2) a federal public official with (3) intent to influence that person's judgment or conduct. The "thing of value" element has been construed very liberally; actual commercial value is not necessary. For instance, had the Salt Lake City Olympics Bid Committee given a member of the International Olympic Committee shares of stock in a new Silicon Valley start-up called BellyUp.com but the shares turned out to be worthless because the start-up was never established, this act may constitute bribery even though the stock

is commercially worthless. Ultimately, the Department of Justice was unable to prove any of the 15 charges of bribery that it had filed against two members of the Salt Lake City Olympics Bid Committee. Several members of the committee resigned however. As a result of investigations into the matter, 10 members of the International Olympics Committee were fired and another 10 were sanctioned.

Additionally, the definition of "public official" is also expansive. The statute defines *public officials* as members of Congress, government officers and employees, and anyone "acting for or on behalf of" the federal government "in any official function, under or by authority of" a federal government department or agency. For example, individuals who work for private corporations that have some degree of responsibility for carrying out federal programs or policies are considered public officials. The Case Nugget provides an interesting twist on the crime of bribery.

CASE Nugget

A Question of Bribery?

United States of America, Plaintiff-Appellee, v. Sonya Evette Singleton, Defendant-Appellant
Circuit Court of Appeals for the Tenth Circuit

165 F.3d 1297 (1999)

Often, when two defendants are charged with a crime, a prosecutor might offer to give one defendant leniency in exchange for truthful testimony against the other. Are such prosecutor plea deals really bribes and thus violative of federal bribery law, which prohibits the exchange of anything of value for testimony? The Tenth Circuit did not think so in this case.

Sonya Singleton was charged with money laundering and conspiring to distribute cocaine. Her co-conspirator, Napoleon Douglas, entered into a plea agreement with the prosecuting attorney under which he agreed to testify truthfully. In exchange, the prosecuting attorney promised leniency; the government would not prosecute him for related offenses, and the attorney would advise the sentencing court of Douglas's cooperation. Singleton argued that such an agreement violated the "anti-gratuity" statute, U.S.C. § 201(c)(2). The district court allowed Douglas's testimony and convicted Singleton. A panel of the Tenth Circuit Court reversed the conviction, arguing that the attorney's promise for leniency did violate federal bribery law. The full circuit voted to rehear the case.

On rehearing, the court reinstated the defendant's conviction, noting that to hold otherwise would "deprive the sovereign of a recognized or established prerogative, title, or interest." The court held that from the common law, we have a long-standing practice sanctioning the testimony of accomplices against their confederates in exchange for leniency, and this long-standing practice created a vested sovereign prerogative in the government. In light of the long-standing practice of leniency for testimony, the court had to presume that if Congress had intended to overturn this ingrained aspect of American legal culture, it would have done so in clear, unmistakable, and unarguable language.

Another type of bribery is *commercial bribery,* which includes a bribe in exchange for new information or payoffs. For example, suppose Comdac Computers is looking for a company that manufactures a certain type of computer part. Jane Devlon owns such a company and realizes that if Comdac gets the computer parts from her, she will potentially make a lot of money. When Comdac sends its contractor to the Devlon factory, Devlon offers the contractor $500,000 in exchange for the contractor's promise that Comdac will buy all such parts from only her factory for the next year. Alternatively, she might offer the contractor $5,000 to disclose the

dollar amounts of the competing bids so that she can offer a better bid to earn the contract. This chapter's Case Opener also involves commercial bribery. Conner's offer of money to Freeman to return to his old job, so that he could provide better tips, is a commercial bribe.

One final type of bribery is the *bribery of foreign officials.* The purpose of the Foreign Corrupt Practices Act (FCPA) is to combat such bribery. The FCPA prohibits payments to foreign officials to corruptly influence an official act or decision or to influence a foreign government. You might think of the FCPA as an extension of the law to prevent bribery of a public official. The FCPA allows the government to prosecute those who bribe foreign officials.

But Congress does not pass laws affecting foreign affairs in a vacuum. Laws governing white-collar crime, like all laws, are dynamic, and one source of change in these laws is international law. Multinational organizations in which the United States is a member often pressure the United States to alter American law so that it conforms to certain international standards. Thus, for example, Congress amended the FCPA in 1998 to conform to the antibribery convention adopted by the Organization for Economic Cooperation and Development (OECD). The amendments broaden the scope of actions covered by the FCPA and the definition of a public official. As of this writing, it is expected that 30 OECD countries—such as Japan, South Korea, and Brazil—will adopt similar antibribery statutes. Before the amendment, U.S. companies complained that antibribery laws disadvantaged them because many European and Asian competitors were not subject to similar laws. Between May 1994 and April 1998, bribes were allegedly used to influence the outcomes of 239 international contract competitions.

Extortion Often confused with bribery, but completely different, is the crime of extortion. Extortion, otherwise known as *blackmail,* is the making of threats for the purpose of obtaining money or property. Whereas bribery is offering someone something to obtain a desired result, extortion involves the threat of doing something if the target of the extortion does not relinquish money or a specific piece of property. For example, if Conner in the Case Opener threatened to tell the government about Freeman's actions if he did not return to Goldman Sachs, then Conner would have committed extortion. Conner's actions would have been extortion because he would have issued a threat (to tell the government about Freeman's insider trading) for the purpose of obtaining money (to get Freeman to behave in a way that would enable Conner to make more money by receiving the more profitable tips from Goldman Sachs).

Fraud Criminal fraud encompasses a variety of means by which an individual intentionally uses some sort of misrepresentation to gain an advantage over another person. Fraud generally requires the following three elements: (1) a material false representation made with intent to deceive *(scienter),* (2) a victim's reasonable reliance on the false representation, and (3) damages. Both the federal and the state governments have passed a number of statutes codifying specific types of fraudulent schemes. These schemes to defraud include a multitude of frauds, such as credit card fraud, insurance fraud, and securities fraud. Exhibit 2-4 summarizes the fraudulent acts that might occur in the corporate setting, many of which are discussed below.

In June 2000, the FBI achieved its largest *securities fraud* crackdown in history when it arrested a group of Mafia leaders for a series of scams that cost investors an estimated $25 million. Government officials claimed that the Mob bought large stakes in small companies and then bribed and coerced brokers to promote the stocks to other investors at inflated prices.

The Enron scandal also involves securities fraud, with Enron's top executives allegedly overstating its earnings to maintain high stock prices. Complex accounting methods were used to hide the corporation's debt. Enron's top executives and big investors sold their stocks, while encouraging employees to continue buying company stocks. With the drastic decline in the company's stock value, many Enron employees lost much of their 401(k) investments.

Another specific type of securities fraud involved in the Enron case, as well as in this chapter's Case Opener, is insider trading. Illegal insider trading is generally a person's buying or selling of a security, in breach of a fiduciary duty or other relationship of trust and confidence, while in possession of material, nonpublic information about the security. Insider-trading violations may also include "tipping" such information, securities trading by the person "tipped," and securities trading by those who misappropriate such information.[2] Enron's big investors and top executives knew the stock prices were

extortion
A criminal offense in which a person obtains money, property, and/or services from another by wrongfully threatening or inflicting harm to his or her person, property, or reputation. Also called *blackmail.*

fraud
An intentional deception that causes harm to another.

insider trading
Illegal buying or selling of a corporation's stock or other securities by corporate insiders such as officers and directors, in breach of a fiduciary duty or other relationship of trust and confidence, while in possession of material, nonpublic information about the security.

[2] U.S. Securities and Exchange Commission, www.sec.gov/answers/insider.htm.

Exhibit 2-4

Selected Types of
Fraudulent Crimes

1. *Forgery:* The fraudulent making or altering of any writing in a way that changes the legal rights and liabilities of another.

2. *Defalcation:* The misappropriation of trust funds or money held in a fiduciary capacity.

3. *False entries:* The making of an entry into the books of a bank or corporation that is designed to represent the existence of funds that do not exist.

4. *False token:* A false document or sign of existence used to perpetrate a fraud, such as making counterfeit money.

5. *False pretense:* A designed misrepresentation of existing facts or conditions by which a person obtains another's money or goods, such as the writing of a worthless check.

6. *Fraudulent concealment:* The suppression of a material fact that a person is legally bound to disclose.

7. *Mail fraud:* The use of mails to defraud the public.

8. *Health care fraud:* Any fraudulent act committed in the provision of health care products or services.

9. *Telemarketing fraud:* Any scheme, including cramming and slamming, using the telephone to commit a fraudulent act.

10. *Ponzi scheme:* An investment swindle in which high profits are promised from fictitious sources and early investors are paid off with funds raised from later ones.

11. *Check kiting:* Drawing checks on an account in one bank and depositing them in an account in a second bank when neither account has sufficient funds to cover the amounts drawn. Just before the checks are returned for payment to the first bank, the kiter covers them by depositing checks drawn on the account in the second bank. Due to the delay created by the collection of funds by one bank from the other, known as the "float" time, an artificial balance is created.

12. *Pretexting:* Using fraudulent means to obtain information about someone's phone use.

overinflated due to the overstated earnings. They then used their knowledge, which was not public knowledge, to decide to sell off their stock before the price lowered drastically, thus engaging in insider trading. How might insider trading violate each of the ethical norms we have previously discussed?

Another example of insider trading involves Qwest Communications, a Denver-based local phone provider in 14 western and midwestern states. Qwest has been under investigation over the past few years for various white-collar crimes, including insider training. Robin Szeliga, Qwest's former chief financial officer, is the highest-ranking official at Qwest to admit wrongdoing in the scandal. She admits to selling 10,000 shares of Qwest stock in 2001 for a net profit of $125,000. Szeliga knew some of Qwest's business units would not meet their targets. She also knew Qwest had illegally used nonrecurring revenue to try to meet its goals. Because the information Robin acted on was not public, and because she gained substantially by acting on the private information, Szeliga recently pleaded guilty to a single count of insider trading.

Stock-option backdating is yet another type of securities fraud that the SEC has been increasingly cracking down on. Backdating occurs when an employee falsifies documents to make it appear as if the company had granted options on certain dates, but the dates are selected after the fact by looking backward for dates on which the stock price was low, thereby falsely inflating the net profits of the company. In 2007, Myron F. Olesnyckyj, the former general counsel of Monster Worldwide, Inc., pleaded guilty to securities fraud for participating in a multiyear scheme with other Monster executives to secretly backdate stock options granted to thousands of Monster officers, directors, and employees, including himself. By backdating and improperly accounting for options, Monster granted undisclosed compensation to its employees, failed to recognize compensation expenses, and overstated its net income by $340 million from 1997 through 2005. Olesnyckyj personally made $381,000 from the scheme, which he agreed to forfeit.

An additional type of fraud is false pretense. **False pretense** is the illegal obtainment of property belonging to another through materially false representation of an existing fact, with knowledge of the falsity of the representation and with the intent to defraud. For example, Jim goes door-to-door selling vacuum cleaners at an amazing discount. To obtain the discount, the

false pretense
Materially false representation of an existing fact, with knowledge of the falsity of the representation and with the intent to defraud.

customers must pay immediately, and the vacuum cleaner will be delivered in three to five business days. However, Jim possesses no vacuum cleaners and does not plan on delivering any. Jim has committed the crime of false pretense, as he illegally obtained another's property (the money he received as payment) by making a false representation (telling the "customers" they would be receiving a vacuum) with the knowledge of the falsity (he knew there were no vacuum cleaners) and the intent to defraud (he did not plan on delivering any vacuum cleaners).

forgery

A criminal falsification by imitating, impersonating, or altering a real document with the intent to deceive or defraud.

Forgery, the fraudulent making or altering of any writing in a way that changes the legal rights and liabilities of another, is another type of fraud. If you sign your colleague's name to the back of a check made out to your colleague, you have committed forgery.

One of the most frequently prosecuted frauds is *mail fraud,* which is the use of mails to defraud the public. The Mail Fraud Act of 1990 makes mail fraud a federal crime. To prove mail fraud, the government must demonstrate two elements: (1) an intent to defraud and (2) the use of or causing the use of mails to further the fraudulent scheme. Case 2-1 demonstrates the consideration of these two elements.

 CASE 2-1

UNITED STATES OF AMERICA v. GERSON COHEN
COURT OF APPEALS FOR THE THIRD CIRCUIT
171 F.3d 796 (1999)

FACTS: *Gerson Cohen, a meat salesperson for Butler Foods, made illegal cash payments to supermarkets' meat managers in an attempt to persuade them to buy their meat from Butler Foods. If the customer bought at least 10,000 pounds of meat per week, the cash payments usually amounted to one penny per pound of meat purchased. After a customer made the minimum purchase, Larry Lipoff, part-owner of Butler Foods, would give the cash payment to the salespeople, who then gave the cash to the customer. Over a period of three years, Cohen made payments totaling $111,548.21 to managers for Thriftway Food Stores. Invoices for the orders were sent through the mail but not by the defendant, although he knew the invoices would be mailed. The district court convicted Cohen on 25 counts of mail fraud, in violation of 18 U.S.C. § 1341. Cohen appealed his conviction.*

ISSUE: Does a person commit mail fraud if he does not personally place the documents in question in the mail?

REASONING: The court determined that a person commits mail fraud when the person knows that the use of the mail ordinarily follows his action. Here, defendant Cohen knew that the company's policy was to mail invoices to customers. Butler employees testified that it was standard business practice to send and receive invoice information from customers in the mail. These invoices were essential to supplying the illegal cash payments.

DECISION AND REMEDY: The conviction was affirmed. A person can commit mail fraud even if he is not the person who places the documents in the mail.

SIGNIFICANCE OF THE CASE: This case shows what prosecutors must prove in a mail fraud case. This theory is important to prosecutors, so it is important for them to know how to use the theory effectively.

CRITICAL THINKING

Are you persuaded that Thriftway was using the mails to perpetuate a fraudulent scheme? Why or why not?

ETHICAL DECISION MAKING

Return to the WPH process of ethical decision making. Whom does this decision affect? In other words, who are the stakeholders in this decision?

Congress amended the mail fraud statute in 1994 to include commercial carriers and courier services as substitutes for the U.S. mail. In other words, using FedEx or UPS to further a fraudulent scheme can be prosecuted as mail fraud. Similarly, the wire fraud statute attempts to prevent the use of wire, radio, or television transmissions to defraud the public.

Other types of fraud include health care fraud, telemarketing fraud, and bankruptcy fraud. The Department of Justice recently named *health care fraud* its top priority after violent crime. An example of health care fraud is the submission of false claims to insurance plans such as Medicare or Medicaid. Additionally, some doctors prescribe unneeded equipment to patients and then receive kickbacks from the manufacturers of the equipment.

Telemarketing fraud has also gained much attention recently. The National Fraud Information Center reported that telephone cramming was the top telemarketing fraud of 1998. *Cramming* is a scheme in which companies bill consumers for optional services that the consumers did not order. Another frequent telemarketing scheme is *slamming,* in which consumers are tricked into changing their phone service to another carrier without their consent.

The elderly, who have been more susceptible to telemarketing fraud, are often the specific targets of telemarketing schemes. Thus, the Department of Justice and the FBI have been collaborating on various undercover operations, such as Operation Senior Sentinel, to investigate and prosecute fraudulent telemarketers.

Another type of fraud involves bankruptcies. In 2004, more than 1.6 million bankruptcy filings occurred. An individual can file for bankruptcy to be relieved of oppressive debt. Yet claims need to be carefully reviewed to prevent *bankruptcy fraud.* For example, an individual might hide some assets so that they will not be considered during the proceedings. Conversely, a creditor (a party to whom another owes money) might file a false claim against a debtor (the party who owes money to a creditor). Thus, bankruptcy fraud can occur on the part of the debtor or the creditor. The U.S. Department of Justice estimates that 10 percent of all bankruptcy petitions contain some elements of fraud. However, between the year 2000 and the year 2005, only a few more than 1,000 defendants faced bankruptcy fraud charges.

Expect the number of defendants facing bankruptcy fraud to be on the rise with the culmination of the Justice Department's Operation Truth or Consequences. In October 2006, the Justice Department created an Internet hotline for the public to report suspected bankruptcy fraud to the U.S. Trustee Program. This hotline is just one aspect of the Department of Justice's revitalized commitment to combating bankruptcy fraud and protecting the integrity of the bankruptcy system.

Sometimes fraud cases can be very complex and involve multiple types of fraud. For example, in one case, a Beverly Hills lawyer was recently convicted of three counts of mail fraud, seven counts of wire fraud, and five counts of lying to a court hearing. In an elaborate fraudulent scheme, the lawyer had purchased a yacht for $1.9 million, sold it to two other partners to drive up its insurance value, and then had a company he owned repurchase the yacht and insure it for $3.5 million. Finally, he and his partners sunk the yacht and tried to collect the insurance.

A fraudulent crime that has recently come into the public eye is pretexting. *Pretexting* can be defined as using or causing others to use false pretenses, fraudulent statements, fraudulent or stolen documents, or other misrepresentations, including posing as an account holder or employee of a telecommunications carrier, to obtain telephone records of another. Pretexting entered the national lexicon in 2006 when news broke that the investigators Hewlett-Packard's board of directors had hired to locate the source of several leaks to the media were engaging in this practice. Under the federal Telephone Records and Privacy Protection Act of 2006, anyone convicted of employing fraudulent tactics to persuade phone companies to hand over confidential data about a customer's calling habits can be sent to prison for up to 10 years. Some states also have statutes outlawing pretexting.

Both individuals and businesses can be victims of fraud. To minimize the chances that your firm will be a victim of fraud, review Exhibit 2-5, "Fraud Prevention Tips," very carefully.

Embezzlement Joe is Kathleen's attorney. Kathleen gave Joe $5,000 to put in escrow, an account where Joe will have access to the money, although the money is not his to use as he pleases. Suppose Joe takes some of that money out of the account and uses it to gamble, and he "fixes" the records to cover up the fact that he has used some of the money for his personal use. He has committed the crime of embezzlement, the wrongful conversion of another's property by one who is

embezzlement
A wrongful conversion of another's funds or property by one who is lawfully in possession of those funds or that property.

Exhibit 2-5

Fraud Prevention
Tips

Red Flags Suggesting Possible Fraud

When you are looking at a brochure offering an investment opportunity that seems almost too good to be true, it may indeed not be as good as it seems, especially if it contains these red flags of fraud:

- *No independent proof of profitability:* The brochure provides the investment strategy but includes no details that can be verified, such as names and addresses of specific companies in which it invests.
- *Control by a single person.*
- *No audited financial statements and no evidence of internal controls.*
- *Unusually high rates of return:* Rates of return are significantly higher than those for other funds with a similar investment strategy.
- *New investors' reliance primarily on existing investors in deciding to invest.*

False "Assurances" That an Investment Opportunity Is Not Fraudulent

- *Long-time existence of investment opportunity:* A Ponzi scheme can operate for a long time. As long as the company keeps getting new investors, it can continue to use the new investors to pay off the few who insist on collecting their returns. Many investors may be content to accumulate paper profits, especially if there is a financial incentive for reinvestment of profits. For example, the Financial Advisory Fund had been in business for almost 20 years before its fraudulent foundation was uncovered.
- *A list of names and addresses of satisfied investors you can contact:* All such schemes will have some satisfied investors who have received payments from the new investment money.
- *Membership in the Better Business Bureau:* Any company can pay to join. If most of the investors have not attempted to withdraw their funds and the company is still getting new investments, there will be no disgruntled investors to complain to the BBB.
- *A report of profitability from Dun & Bradstreet:* Dun & Bradstreet does not do an independent financial audit of a company's profits. As stated on its Web site, Dun & Bradstreet simply provides the information regarding profits that it receives from companies.
- *Acceptance of money rolled over from IRAs:* There is no government check on the soundness of firms that roll over IRAs.
- *Bank references:* If a firm simply has a large amount of money in a checking account in a bank and has never sought a loan from the bank, the bank would have no reason to do any due diligence on the firm. Also, if the owner of the firm is personable and the account has never been overdrawn, the bank personnel may well give the firm a good reference.
- *Glossy brochures and television ads:* All you need for both is some money and the knowledge that many people may be overly impressed by a fancy brochure or ad campaign.

These tips come from Barry Minkow, who went from starting his own carpet cleaning business at the age of 16, to taking this multimillion-dollar company public at the age of 20, to facing a 23-year prison sentence and $26 million victim restitution payment at the age of 21 for massive fraud and theft perpetuated on behalf of his company, to now being a pastor and the cofounder of the Fraud Discovery Institute.

The fascinating story of how Barry Minkow, through fraudulent Ponzi schemes, check kiting, and theft, managed to build the multimillion-dollar ZZZZ Best Carpet Cleaning Company by the age of 20 is contained in his book, *Cleaning Up.* The book also provides insights into why some people may commit white-collar crimes, and it describes many of the long-running frauds Minkow has helped to uncover since deciding to use his understanding of the perpetuation of fraud to help uncover and prevent it.

GLOBAL Context

Embezzlement and Bribery in China

On March 8, 1982, in response to a concern about a rise in white-collar crimes, Chinese officials added a resolution entitled "Severely Punishing Criminals Who Do Great Damage to the Economy" to the Chinese Criminal Code. The provision targeted top-ranking officials by providing that any state functionaries who extort, accept bribes, or exploit their office would no longer receive the fixed-term punishment (usually 10 years) allocated for bribery and extortion. Instead, those officials found guilty of extortion and accepting bribes would be sentenced to life imprisonment or possibly put to death.

Bank fraud is another white-collar crime that may be punishable by death. In 2004, China executed four people, including employees of two of its Big Four state banks, for fraud totaling $15 million. Three of the cases involved China Construction Bank.

A former accounting officer at this bank worked with others to steal 20 million yuan ($2.4 million) from the bank using fake papers. He and an accomplice were executed, along with another Construction Bank employee who was found to have taken 20 million yuan from the bank in an unrelated case. Additionally, an official employed by the Bank of China was executed for cheating.

The precise number of people executed in China is not made available to the public. Estimates range from 5,000 to 10,000 a year, for crimes including murder, corruption, and on occasion even bottom-pinching. Most are executed by a single shot in the back of the head.

Such punishments may seem extreme, but the reaction of the Chinese to this increase in white-collar crime reflects the culture's unusually great concern for social harmony.

lawfully in possession of that property. Embezzlement is distinguished from larceny because the individual did not take the property from another; he was already in possession of the property.

Embezzlement usually occurs when an employee steals money. Thus, it is often employees in banks who commit the crime. However, as the recent embezzlement of $6.9 million from the American Cancer Society demonstrates, even nonprofit organizations are vulnerable to the crime of embezzlement. White-collar crimes such as embezzlement are a problem in many countries. For example, the Chinese government, which has been focusing on economic crimes, caught employees in two major Chinese banks altering deposit slips and bank orders to direct the money to personal accounts throughout China. Those employees received death sentences for embezzlement, as discussed in the Global Context box.

Computer Crimes The term computer crime refers broadly to any wrongful act that (1) is directed against computers, (2) uses computers to commit a crime, or (3) involves computers. Computer crime is not necessarily a new kind of crime but is, instead, a new way of committing traditional crimes. Consider fraud, a crime that has existed for centuries. Today, online auctions, such as eBay, are a common source of fraud in the United States. Indeed, some statistics suggest that, compared with nonelectronic methods, using computers is a more profitable method of committing crimes. According to federal officials, the average loss in a nonelectronic embezzlement is $23,500; in contrast, in a computer fraud case, the average loss is almost $500,000.[3]

Computer crimes are often difficult to prosecute, in large part because they are difficult to detect. A computer crime could be committed by an insider, such as an employee, or by an outsider, such as a hacker—a person who illegally accesses or enters another person's or a company's computer system to obtain information or to steal money. In addition, computer systems are quite open to attack. The American Society for Industrial Security has reported that the losses from computer crimes in a single year were more than $250 billion for U.S. companies. Furthermore, the attacks are frequent. The IRS alone detects 800 to 1,200 cases of computer system misuse annually.

computer crime
Crime committed using a computer.

hacker
A person who illegally accesses or enters another person's or a company's computer system to obtain information or to steal money.

[3] Charles Alexander, "The Wells Fargo Stick-Up," Time.com, www.time.com/time/magazine/article/0,9171,954673-3,00.html (accessed May 1, 2007).

25

Computer Use and Ethics

The use of computers to store and transfer important business information has resulted in a new set of ethical concerns. How private is the computer screen? Are companies allowed to collect information about their customers? Who owns the information customers give to e-businesses? E-commerce law is gradually adjusting to such questions. But, as the beginning of this chapter pointed out, knowing the law is just the first step in discovering the ethical business decision.

One case that considered questions related to e-commerce and privacy involved Toysmart.com and its privacy policy. In 2000, the Federal Trade Commission (FTC) filed a complaint against Toysmart.com, charging the online retailer with selling customer lists despite its earlier privacy statements that claimed its customers' personal data would never be shared with a third party. The customer lists were included as assets to be sold as part of the company's bankruptcy proceedings. The FTC issued a settlement with Toysmart.com allowing the lists to be sold as long as (1) the sale occurred before July 2001, (2) the lists would be sold to a family-oriented company, and (3) the buyer would agree to abide by the original Toysmart.com privacy policy. After the FTC imposed these restrictions, the end result was that customers' personal information was not sold.

The Toysmart.com case makes it clear that, for both ethical and legal reasons, companies that adopt a privacy policy need to think that policy through before announcing it to customers.

cyber terrorist
A hacker whose intention is the exploitation of a target computer or network to create a serious impact, such as the crippling of a communications network or the sabotage of a business or organization, which may have an impact on millions of citizens if the terrorist's attack is successful.

A **cyber terrorist** is a hacker whose intention is the exploitation of a target computer or network to create a serious impact, such as the crippling of a communications network or the sabotage of a business or organization. The activity of a cyber terrorist can have an impact on millions of citizens if the terrorist's attack is successful, particularly if it involved the computer systems of a major stock exchange, any bank, or any federal agency or government.

In an attempt to aid prosecutions of computer crimes, Congress passed the Counterfeit Access Device and Computer Fraud and Abuse Act of 1984 (also know as the Computer Fraud and Abuse Act, or CFAA). The act prohibits six broad categories of computer crimes:

1. Unauthorized use of or access to a computer to obtain classified military or foreign policy information with the intent to harm the United States or to benefit a foreign country.

2. Unauthorized use of a computer to collect financial or credit information protected under federal privacy law.

3. Unauthorized access to a federal computer and the use, modification, destruction, or disclosure of data it contains or the prevention of an authorized person's use of such data.

4. Alteration or modification of data in financial computers causing a loss of $1,000 or more.

5. Modification of data that impedes medical treatment to individuals.

6. Fraudulent transfer of computer passwords or other similar data that could aid unauthorized access that either (a) affects interstate commerce or (b) permits access to a government computer.

Computer crimes falling into the first category are felonies, whereas the others are misdemeanors.

The National Information Infrastructure Protection Act of 1996 amended the Computer Fraud and Abuse Act. One of the major changes to the CFAA is the substitution of the term *protected computers* for *federal interest computers* so that the statute now protects any computer attached to the Internet.

In a further attempt to aid prosecution of computer crimes, the U.S. Department of Justice formed the Computer Crime and Intellectual Property Section (CCIPS) in its Criminal Division. Attorneys in this division prosecute only federal computer crimes. They also coordinate their activities with numerous government entities, the private sector, scholars, and foreign representatives in an attempt to develop a global response to computer crime.

virus
A computer program that rearranges, damages, destroys, or replaces computer data.

Destruction of data is one of the most serious problems facing companies today. A **virus** is a computer program that rearranges, damages, destroys, or replaces computer data. Thus, if an employee or a hacker creates and releases a virus, a company can easily lose vital information.

The most economically destructive computer crime to date was the creation of the "love bug" virus. In May 2000, the virus spread rapidly throughout the world by e-mail. Once the e-mail was opened, it destroyed files on the user's computer, and then the virus sent itself to every address in that computer's e-mail address book. In the end, the virus caused over $10 billion in damages and halted computers in major companies and government agencies worldwide.

Companies can try to prevent the destruction of data by installing virus detection programs on their computers. However, the detection programs recognize only previously existing harmful files. As a result, if someone creates a new virus, the detection program is useless.

When an employee uses his or her computer in a manner not authorized by the employer, the employee has committed a crime. Employers, then, must clearly communicate with employees about authorized versus unauthorized behavior. For example, if an employee uses her work computer to run her own personal business on the side, her employer may argue that she is engaging in theft because she is not using her computer in an authorized manner. Thus, when you become a business manager, you will want to make sure that you explicitly list acceptable computer uses, along with the penalties associated with unauthorized use.

Corporate Criminal Liability

LO 6

An individual or a corporation can be charged with and convicted of a crime. However, there has been much debate over whether corporations should be held criminally responsible. Under the common law, a corporation could not be considered a criminal because it was not an actual person and thus did not have a "mind." Consequently, it could not meet the *mens rea* (guilty-mind) requirement for a crime. Slowly, however, courts began to impose liability on corporations for strict-liability offenses, those offenses that do not require state of mind. Next, courts imposed liability on corporations by imputing the state of mind of the employee to the corporation.

strict-liability offense
Offense for which no *mens rea* is required.

Currently, corporations can be held criminally accountable for almost any crime. However, they cannot be held liable for crimes that are punishable only by a prison sentence. In order for a corporation to be held criminally liable for the acts of an employee, the prosecutor must show that (1) the employee was acting within the scope of her or his employment; (2) the employee was acting with the purpose of benefiting the corporation; and (3) the act was imputed to the corporation.

In addition to corporations having criminal liability, corporate executives may also be personally liable for a business crime. The beneficiary of the crime is irrelevant, as corporate executives and officers can be found to be personally liable regardless of whether the crimes were committed for their personal benefit or for the benefit of the corporation.

Also, under the "responsible corporate officer" doctrine, a court may assess criminal liability on a corporate executive or officer even if he or she did not engage in, direct, or even know about a specific criminal violation. As Case 2-2 demonstrates, corporate executives sometimes have the responsibility and power to ensure the company's compliance with the law. If the executive fails to meet this responsibility, the executive can be held criminally liable.

Since *United States v. Park,* the general rule that corporate executives may be held accountable for the crimes arising from their failure to meet their responsibility has remained intact. The rule has, in fact, broadened so that now executives can be held criminally liable for offenses that we generally do not think of as crimes. For example, in *United States v. Iverson,*[4] a corporate officer of a waste treatment facility was convicted and sentenced for violating the Clean Water Act after he ordered employees to illegally dispose of wastewater. This case demonstrates that corporate executives can be sentenced not only for committing the common law crimes that we have traditionally understood to be criminal offenses but also for violating provisions of regulatory statutes that permit criminal sanctions. In such cases, vicarious liability, or liability imposed on one person for the acts of another, is assessed to the corporate executive. In fact, courts have held that employers are vicariously liable for the wrongful acts of their employees if the employer directed, partook in, or authorized the wrongful act.

vicarious liability
The liability or responsibility imposed on a person, a party, or an organization for damages caused by another; most commonly used in relation to employment, with the employer held vicariously liable for damages caused by its employees.

[4] 162 F.3d 1015 (1998).

UNITED STATES v. PARK
UNITED STATES SUPREME COURT
421 U.S. 658 (1975)

FACTS: *Defendant Park, the president of a national food-chain corporation, was charged, along with the corporation, with violating the Federal Food, Drug, and Cosmetic Act by allowing food in the warehouse to be exposed to rodent contamination. Park had conceded that his responsibility for the "entire operation" included warehouse sanitation, but he claimed that he had delegated the responsibility for sanitation to dependable subordinates. He admitted at trial that he had received a warning letter from the Food and Drug Administration regarding the unsanitary conditions at one of the company's warehouses. The trial court found the defendant guilty. The court of appeals reversed. The case was appealed to the U.S. Supreme Court.*

ISSUE: Can corporate executives be criminally liable for failing to ensure a company's compliance with the law?

REASONING: The Supreme Court has noted that the only way corporations can act is through their individual employees. The act in question, the Federal Food, Drug, and Cosmetic Act, requires stringent, affirmative actions on the part of corporate executives, but these standards are justified by the public interest in food safety. We expect executives such as Park to exercise appropriate authority and demonstrate supervisory responsibility. There is considerable evidence that Park had a duty to ensure sanitary conditions and that he violated that duty by failing to ensure that those to whom he delegated responsibility did their jobs. The Court said: "[T]he requirements of foresight and vigilance imposed on responsible corporate agents are beyond question, demanding, and perhaps onerous, but they are not more stringent than the public has a right to expect of those who voluntarily assume positions of authority in business enterprises whose services and products affect the health and well-being of the public that supports them."

DECISION AND REMEDY: The U.S. Supreme Court reversed the appellate court's reversal of the trial court's conviction, finding that corporate executives can be criminally liable for failing to ensure a company's compliance with the law.

SIGNIFICANCE OF THE CASE: This case signaled to corporate officials that they could no longer use ignorance as a defense, because a court will hold high-level corporate actors responsible for their company's failure to comply with the law, even if they were unaware of what was going on within their company.

CRITICAL THINKING

Given the rule laid down in this case, would there have been any evidence that the defendant could have presented that would have led to a different decision?

ETHICAL DECISION MAKING

Suppose you were in Park's position in this case. You allegedly allowed food in your warehouse to be exposed to rodent contamination. If you were guided by the public disclosure test, what would you decide to do?

LO 7

Criminal Procedure

Criminal procedure differs from civil procedure in several key ways. First, the government, referred to as the *prosecutor,* always brings the criminal case, whereas in a civil case, the party filing the case, the plaintiff, can be an individual, business, or government entity. Second, the outcome of each is different. In a criminal case, the objective is punishment, so the defendant may be fined or imprisoned; in a civil case, the objective is to remedy a wrong done to the plaintiff, so the defendant either will have to provide compensation to the plaintiff or may be subject to an equitable remedy such as an injunction or order for specific performance. Third, because the potential impact of losing a criminal case is so much more serious than the impact of losing a civil case, the Constitution provides a number of safeguards for the criminal defendant. These safeguards are set forth in Exhibit 2-6.

Exhibit 2-6

Constitutional Provisions That Safeguard Criminal Defendants' Rights

AMENDMENT	PROVISIONS
Fourth	• Protection from unreasonable search and seizure. • Restrictions on warrants.
Fifth	• Prohibition of double jeopardy. • Right not to incriminate oneself. • Right to due process.
Sixth	• Right to a speedy and public trial. • Right to a trial by an impartial jury of one's peers. • Right to be informed of the accusations against oneself. • Right to confront witnesses. • Right to have witnesses on one's side. • Right to counsel at various stages of the proceedings.
Eighth	• Freedom from excessive bail. • Freedom from excessive fines. • Freedom from cruel and unusual punishment.
Fourteenth	• Extension of the right to due process to all state matters. • Extension of most constitutional rights to defendants at the state level.

PRETRIAL PROCEDURE

Prior to an arrest, grand juries may conduct criminal investigatory proceedings or issue a grand jury subpoena for company records. Criminal proceedings generally begin when an individual is arrested for a crime. A law enforcement officer must perform the arrest. This officer is often a police officer but may also be an agent of another government agency, such as the Bureau of Alcohol, Tobacco and Firearms; the Federal Bureau of Investigation; or the Immigration and Naturalization Service.

A law enforcement officer should obtain an arrest warrant before an individual is taken into custody. Ordinarily, to obtain an arrest warrant, the law enforcement agent must demonstrate that there is probable cause, or a likelihood, that a suspect committed or is planning to commit a crime. A *magistrate,* the lowest-ranking judicial official, issues the arrest warrant. In certain circumstances, however, courts have recognized that law enforcement agents can arrest a suspect without a warrant if the officer believes there is probable cause but not enough time to obtain the warrant.

When law enforcement agents arrest individuals, the officers must inform the individuals of their Miranda rights. If they fail to do so, any information a defendant offers at the time of the arrest is not admissible at trial. To comply with the Supreme Court's requirements for protecting a citizen's rights, a law enforcement officer must inform the defendant of the following facts before questioning:

1. "You have the right to remain silent and refuse to answer any questions."
2. "Anything you say may be used against you in a court of law."
3. "You have the right to consult an attorney before speaking to the police and have an attorney present during any questioning now or in the future."
4. "If you cannot afford an attorney, one will be appointed for you before the questioning begins."
5. "If you do not have an attorney available, you have the right to remain silent until you have had an opportunity to consult with one."
6. "Now that I have advised you of your rights, are you willing to answer any questions without an attorney present?"

The Miranda rights are not absolute. In fact, the Supreme Court has several times created exceptions to the Miranda rights. For example, in *New York v. Quarles,*[5] the Court created a

arrest
The action in which the police, or a person acting under the law, seize, hold, or take an individual into custody.

probable cause
Any essential element and/or standard by which a lawful officer may make a valid arrest, conduct a personal or property search, or obtain a warrant.

Miranda rights
The rights that are read to an arrested individual by a law enforcement agent before the individual is questioned about the commission of a crime.

[5] 467 U.S. 649 (1984).

booking

After an individual is arrested, the procedure during which the name of the defendant and the alleged crime are recorded in the investigating agency's or police department's records.

first appearance

The initial appearance of an arrested individual before a judge who determines whether there was probable cause for the arrest. If the judge ascertains that probable cause did not exist, the individual is freed.

bail

A thing of value, such as a money bail bond or any other form of property, that is given to the court to temporarily allow a person's release from jail and to ensure his or her appearance in court.

information

A document prepared by the prosecutor and presented to the magistrate, demonstrating that there is enough evidence to charge the defendant and bring him or her to trial.

indictment

Finding by the grand jury that there is adequate evidence to charge the defendant and bring him or her to trial.

arraignment

The first appearance in court by the defendant, at which the defendant is advised of the pending charges, the right to counsel, and the right to trial by jury and he or she enters a plea to the charge.

nolo contendere

A plea in which the defendant does not admit guilt but agrees not to contest the charges.

petit jury

A group of 6 or 12 citizens who are summoned to and sworn by the court to hear evidence presented by both sides and render a verdict in a trial.

"public safety" exception to the Miranda rights. This exception allows statements to be used at trial, even if a person was not informed of his or her Miranda rights, if the need to protect the public is served by the admissibility of the statements in question.

After being arrested and read their Miranda rights, defendants are taken to the police station for **booking,** a procedure during which the name of the defendant and the alleged crime are recorded in the investigating agency's or police department's records. After the prosecutor files the complaint, the defendant makes the **first appearance,** which is the appearance before a magistrate who determines whether there was probable cause for the arrest. If the magistrate ascertains that probable cause did not exist, the individual is freed.

If the defendant committed a minor offense and pleads guilty, the magistrate sentences the individual. However, if the defendant claims innocence, the magistrate ensures that the defendant has a lawyer, or appoints one, if necessary, for an indigent defendant, and sets bail. **Bail** is the amount of money defendants pay to the court on release from custody as security that they will return for trial.

Next, the prosecutor has a choice: Should the case be prosecuted? The *Principles of Federal Prosecution,* established by the U.S. Department of Justice, suggest that at the federal level the decision to prosecute depends on two primary factors: (1) whether the evidence is sufficient to obtain a conviction and (2) whether prosecuting the case serves a federal interest. If the prosecutor decides not to go forward with the case, the defendant may still be liable for his or her actions in civil court.

If the prosecutor chooses to proceed with a criminal action, the prosecutor must demonstrate the likelihood that the defendant's actions and intent meet the elements of a crime by charging the defendant with a crime through an *information* or an *indictment.* For a misdemeanor, the prosecutor must present to the magistrate evidence sufficient to justify prosecution of the defendant. This is done through a written document called an **information,** a formal accusation stating the facts and specifying the violation of criminal law.

However, for a felony, the prosecutor must present a grand jury with evidence adequate to justify bringing the defendant to trial. If the grand jury agrees that the evidence is adequate, it issues an **indictment,** a written accusation of the crime allegedly committed by the defendant.

Note that the grand jury does not determine guilt. It is simply a group of citizens who consider evidence of criminal conduct presented by the prosecutor and then determine whether there is enough evidence to try the defendant for the crime.

In federal cases, a defendant accused of a felony has a constitutional right to a grand jury indictment. However, a felony prosecution may proceed by information if the defendant waives that right. For instance, in a high-profile case in which the defense attorney is trying to work out a deal with the prosecution, the defendant may ask that the case proceed by information. Federal misdemeanor cases may proceed by indictment or information.

If the criminal trial takes place in state court, the defendant may or may not have access to a grand jury. The U.S. Supreme Court has held that indictment by a grand jury is not a fundamental right, and thus states are not required to offer grand juries. About half the states still require that felony prosecutions be initiated by grand jury indictments; most of the rest use information as the method for commencing prosecution.

If the grand jury issues an indictment, the defendant appears in court to answer the indictment in a proceeding called the **arraignment.** At this time, the defendant enters a plea of guilty or not guilty. A defendant may also enter a plea of **nolo contendere,** whereby the defendant does not admit guilt but agrees not to contest the charges. The advantage of a nolo contendere plea over a guilty plea is that the former cannot be used against the defendant in a civil suit. If the defendant pleads not guilty, his case will be heard before a **petit jury,** which is a fact-finding jury.

At any time, the prosecutor and defendant can make a **plea bargain,** an agreement in which the prosecutor agrees to reduce charges, drop charges, or recommend a certain sentence if the defendant pleads guilty. Plea bargaining benefits both parties. The defendant gets a lesser sentence, and the prosecution saves time and resources by not trying the case. Businesspeople who commit crimes that affect business often engage in plea bargaining to avoid the publicity associated with a trial and the risk of a severe sentence.

TRIAL PROCEDURE

If the case goes to trial and the crime is a felony or a misdemeanor punishable by six months or more in prison, the defendant has a constitutional right to a jury trial. In most states, if the defendant waives the right to a jury trial, the judge will hear the case. When a judge is the fact finder in a case, the trial is called a bench trial.

In a criminal trial, the prosecutor has the burden of proof and the defendant does not have to prove anything. The burden of proof has two elements: the burden of production of evidence and the burden of persuasion. To meet the *burden of production of evidence,* the prosecution must produce any tangible evidence and testimony that prove the elements of the crime that the defendant allegedly committed. Along with producing evidence, the prosecution also has the *burden of persuasion:* The prosecutor must persuade the jury *beyond reasonable doubt* that the defendant committed the crime. The burden of proof, then, is higher in a criminal case than in a civil case, because in a civil case the burden of persuasion requires only that the claim be supported by a preponderance of the evidence.

The prosecution presents the government's case first, introducing evidence and examining witnesses to prove beyond a reasonable doubt that the defendant committed the crime. Once the prosecutions rests its case, it is the defendant's turn. The defendant either (1) can show, through examination of witnesses and introduction of evidence, that the prosecution did not meet its burden of proof or (2) can present an affirmative defense. An *affirmative defense* is a reason why the defendant, even though he or she did the physical acts alleged by the prosecution, should be excused from responsibility for those actions. Exhibit 2-7 lists some common affirmative defenses.

After the jury hears the case, it deliberates and tries to reach a verdict. A jury that is unable to reach a verdict is known as a "hung jury." If the jury finds the defendant not guilty, the accused is acquitted and released. If the jury returns a guilty verdict, the judge sets a date for sentencing.

POSTTRIAL PROCEDURE

If the petit jury returns a verdict of not guilty, the government cannot appeal the acquittal. However, if the verdict is guilty, the defendant may appeal the verdict by claiming that a prejudicial error of law occurred at the original trial. If there is no appeal, the defendant will be sentenced after the judge has received additional information relevant to sentencing. Figure 2-1 provides a review of the steps of a criminal procedure.

plea bargain
An agreement in which the prosecutor agrees to reduce charges, drop charges, or recommend a certain sentence if the defendant pleads guilty.

bench trial
A trial before a judge, with the judgment decided by the judge rather than a jury; occurs when the defendant has waived his or her right to a jury trial.

burden of proof
The duty of the plaintiff or prosecution to establish a claim or allegation by admissible evidence and to prove that the defendant committed all the essential elements of the crime to the jury's or court's satisfaction beyond any reasonable doubt, in order to convict the defendant.

Exhibit 2-7

Affirmative Defenses to Crimes

Infancy	A person who is not yet a legal adult may use this defense to defuse the guilty-mind requirement of a crime.
Mistake	The defendant says his or her honest and reasonable mistake negates the idea of a guilty mind.
Intoxication	The defendant says he or she took an intoxicant without awareness of its likely effect, mistook its identity, or took the intoxicant under force.
Insanity	The defendant had a severe mental illness that substantially impaired the defendant's capacity to understand and appreciate the moral wrongfulness of the act.
Duress	The defendant says he or she was forced to perform an act against his or her will.
Entrapment	The defendant would not have committed the crime or broken the law if not induced or tricked into doing so by law enforcement officers.
Necessity	The defendant was acting to prevent imminent harm, and there was no legal alternative to the action he or she took.
Justifiable use of force	Use of force was necessary to prevent imminent death or great bodily harm to the defendant or to another or to prevent the imminent commission of a forcible felony.

Figure 2-1

Steps in a Criminal
Procedure

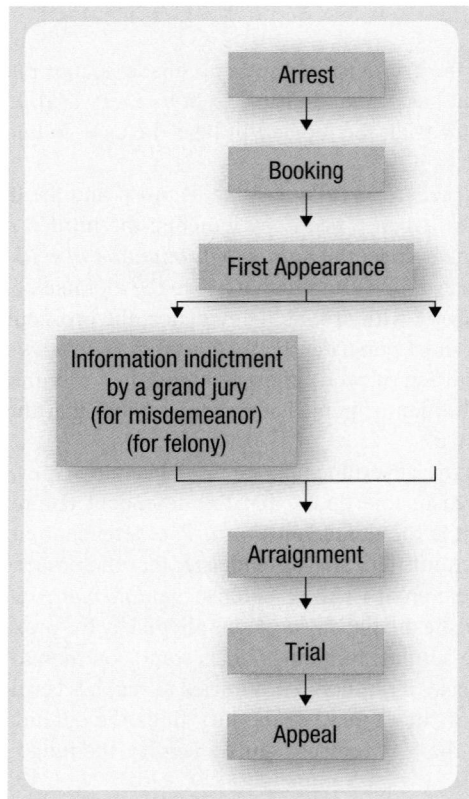

LO 8

Tools for Fighting Business Crime

While there are clearly a significant number of business-related crimes that can be committed, there are certain federal laws that help fight such crime. Three federal laws that have been somewhat successful in this battle are RICO, the False Claims Act, and the Sarbanes-Oxley Act of 2002. While these laws are currently extremely powerful white-collar-crime laws, RICO and the False Claims Act were created with different purposes in mind. Sarbanes-Oxley, however, was created to specifically combat white-collar crime.

RICO

Racketeer Influenced and Corrupt Organizations (RICO) Act
A U.S. law that provides extended penalties for criminal acts performed as part of an ongoing criminal organization.

One of the most important tools for fighting white-collar crime is Title IX of the Organized Crime Control Act of 1970: the **Racketeer Influenced and Corrupt Organizations (RICO) Act.** Although the statute was originally enacted to combat organized crime, in effect it prevents legitimate businesses from serving as covers for racketeering. This statute prohibits persons employed by or associated with an enterprise from engaging in a pattern of racketeering activity. Anyone whose business or property has been damaged by this pattern of racketeering activity can sue to recover treble damages and attorney fees in a civil action.

Demonstrating a claim under RICO requires proof of a pattern of racketeering. Courts have defined a pattern as more than one action. Thus, a one-time violator could not be prosecuted under RICO because there could be no pattern as yet. Some courts additionally have found that a pattern requires continued criminal activity over a "substantial" period of time. Although *pattern* is restricted to more than one act, racketeering has been defined broadly to include almost all criminal actions, such as acts of violence, fraud, bribery, securities fraud, and the provision of illegal goods and services. Therefore, RICO is an extremely effective tool in combating white-collar crimes.

In addition to being held civilly liable under RICO, a violator may also be subject to RICO's criminal penalties. A person found to have violated the act may be subject to a fine of up to $25,000 per violation, imprisonment for up to 20 years, or both.

THE FALSE CLAIMS ACT

Since 1986 private citizens have been using the False Claims Act to sue employers on behalf of the government for fraud against the government. For example, an employee in a health care facility might realize that his employer is submitting fraudulent claims to Medicare. The employee can bring a suit against the employer on behalf of the government for fraud against the government.

False Claims Act
An act that allows employees to sue employers on behalf of the federal government for fraud against the government. The employee retains a share of the recovery as a reward for his or her efforts.

If an employee realizes that her employer is committing fraud against the government, she must first notify the government of her intent to file the case on behalf of the government. If the government chooses to intervene and prosecute the case itself, with the help of the employee, the citizen would receive 25 percent of the amount recovered. If the government opts to not get involved, and the citizen continues with the case on behalf of the government, she receives 30 percent.

Certainly, an employee who brings a suit against his employer might be worried about retaliation, such as being fired or demoted. Thus, the act provides protection for those employees who use the law. If an employer is found guilty of retaliation, the employer may be forced to pay the employee twice the amount of back pay plus special damages.

The biggest reward thus far under the act was the approximately $51 million share that four whistle-blowers and their attorneys received for blowing the whistle on a Swiss drug company, Serono, for participating in a marketing scheme that resulted in physicians' illegally prescribing over $11.5 million worth of a drug that was paid for by Medicaid. The government settled the case against the company for $704 million. The reward in this case, however, was far above the norm. The Justice Department estimates that the median award in all the 425 cases settled between the act's inception and July 2001 was around $150,000. Between 1986 and the first quarter of 2006, the total amount of money recovered by the government was over $17 billion.

Despite the fact that some of these cases might not have been pursued had it not been for the False Claims Act, there are many people who are opposed to the act. Some argue that the whistle-blowers are receiving money that should belong to the taxpayers, while others say that the act prompts people to not report fraud right away but wait until the value of the case grows. Still others complain that the act results in frivolous lawsuits as employees try to find an "easy" way to make money.

Defenders of the False Claims Act point out that the act has led to some significant cases of fraud being reported that otherwise might have cost the government millions of dollars. They also point out that when an employee does report a fraudulent employer, it is going to be very difficult for that employee to get a job in that field in the future, and thus a significant incentive needs to be offered to get employees to report such fraud.

A number of False Claims Act cases have been filed against universities, including an interesting case filed in 2006 against Chapman University. In this case, three faculty members alleged that the institution for years encouraged early dismissals, resulting in many students' not getting the minimum classroom training required in several subjects. If the college had admitted that it had engaged in this practice, it would never have been accredited and thus never have received millions of dollars in federal grants and student aid, which the lawsuit claimed it took under false pretenses.[6] The case had not been resolved at the time this book went to press.

[6] Martin Van Der Werf, "Lawsuit U.: The Growing Reach of the False Claims Act Has Lawyers Fearing Trouble Everywhere," *Chronicle of Higher Education,* August 4, 2006, available at http://chronicle.com/weekly/v52/i48/48a02301.htm.

Income Taxation Accounting: The Impact of Disallowance Provisions of the IRS Code

In one of your tax or accounting courses, you probably learned about disallowance provisions of the IRS.* An important disallowance in the tax code is the one for payments considered to be in violation of public policy, such as bribes or fines. Initially the courts developed the principle that a payment that is in violation of public policy is not a necessary expense and therefore should not be deductible. While allowing deductions for fines or bribes might help a business's bottom line, it would clearly dilute the effect of any criminal penalty and would be, in effect, subsidizing a taxpayer's wrongdoing. So, when you think about it, you really learned about one of the tools for fighting white-collar crime in your tax or accounting class: the disallowance provision of the tax code that fights white-collar crime by not allowing criminals to deduct the amount they must pay for fines from their tax liability.

* William Hoffman, Jr., et al., *Individual Income Taxes 2006* (Thomson, 2006), pp. 6–11.

THE SARBANES-OXLEY ACT

Sarbanes-Oxley Act
An act that criminalizes specific nonaudit services when provided by a registered accounting firm to an audit client; also increases the punishment for a number of white-collar offenses. Also known as the *Public Company Accounting Reform and Investor Protection Act of 2002.*

Unlike RICO and the False Claims Act, the Sarbanes-Oxley Act of 2002 was intended to curb white-collar crime. Congress passed Sarbanes-Oxley largely in response to the business scandals of the early 2000s, such as Enron, WorldCom, and Global Crossing, as well as the accounting firm Arthur Andersen. While much of the act consists of new rules and regulations for accounting firms, part of the act specifically addresses the issue of white-collar crime.

Sarbanes-Oxley makes it illegal for registered public accounting firms to provide nonaudit services to an audit client. Section 201 of the act specifically names as illegal:

1. Bookkeeping or other services related to the accounting records or financial statements of the audit client.
2. Financial information systems design and implementation.
3. Appraisal or valuation services, fairness opinions, or contribution-in-kind reports.
4. Actuarial services.
5. Internal audit outsourcing services.
6. Management functions or human resources.
7. Broker or dealer, investment adviser, or investment banking services.
8. Legal services and expert services unrelated to the audit.
9. Any other service that the Board determines, by regulation, is impermissible.

In addition to criminalizing the activities listed above, Sarbanes-Oxley has amended the penalties associated with other white-collar crimes. Under Sarbanes-Oxley, it is now a felony to willfully fail to maintain proper records of audits and work papers for at least five years, and the punishment for not maintaining these records is up to 10 years' imprisonment. Also, the destruction of documents received updated punishments. The destruction of documents involved in a federal bankruptcy investigation is now a felony with possible sentences of up to 20 years' imprisonment. Similarly, the punishment for securities fraud has been increased to 25 years' imprisonment.

In addition, Sarbanes-Oxley has extended the statute of limitations regarding the discovery of fraud. The statute of limitations now extends to two years from the date of discovery of the fraud and five years from the criminal act. The old statute was one year from discovery and three from the act. Also, much like the False Claims Act, Sarbanes-Oxley has taken affirmative steps toward further protecting whistle-blowers.

 SUMMARY

Business Ethics and Social Responsibility	*Business ethics* is an application of ethics to the special problems and opportunities experienced by businesspeople.
	The *social responsibility of business* consists of the expectations that the community imposes on firms doing business with its citizens.
Business Law and Business Ethics	Business ethics builds on business law. The law both affects and is affected by evolving ethical patterns. But business law provides only a floor for business ethics, telling business leaders the minimally acceptable course of action.
The WPH Framework for Business Ethics	*Who are the relevant stakeholders?* This question determines which interests (consumers, employees, managers, owners) are being pushed and prodded.
	What are the ultimate purposes of the decision? This question determines which values (freedom, efficiency, security, and justice) are being upheld by the decision.
	How do we make ethical decisions? This question leads us to apply general ethical guidelines:

1. *Golden Rule:* Do unto others as you would have them do unto you.
2. *Public disclosure test:* If the public knew about this decision, how would you decide?
3. *Universalization test:* What would the world be like were your decision copied by everyone else?

White-Collar Crime	The elements of a crime are:

- *Actus reus:* Wrongful behavior (guilty act).
- *Mens rea:* Wrongful state of mind or intent (guilty mind).

Crimes are classified into three categories:

- *Felonies:* Serious crimes punishable by imprisonment for more than one year or death.
- *Misdemeanors:* Less serious crimes punishable by fines or imprisonment for less than one year.
- *Petty offenses:* Minor misdemeanors punishable by small fines or short jail sentences.

White-collar crimes include:

1. Bribery.
2. Extortion.
3. Fraud.
4. Embezzlement.
5. Computer crimes (destruction of computer data, unlawful appropriation of data or services).

Corporate Criminal Liability	Both corporations, as legal entities, and the corporate officers and managers can be held liable for crimes committed on behalf of the corporation.
Criminal Procedure	*Pretrial procedure:* The arrest, booking, first appearance, indictment, and arraignment.
	Trial procedure: Jury selection, trial with burden of proof on prosecution, jury deliberations, jury verdict, and (if guilty) sentencing hearing.
	Posttrial procedure: Appeal.
Tools for Fighting Business Crime	*RICO:* Prohibits persons employed by or associated with an enterprise from engaging in a pattern of racketeering activity. Anyone whose business or property has been damaged by this pattern of activity can sue under RICO to recover treble damages and attorney fees in a civil action.
	False Claims Act: Allows employees to sue employers on behalf of the federal government for fraud against the government. The employee retains a share of the recovery as a reward for his or her efforts.
	Sarbanes-Oxley Act: Criminalizes specific nonaudit services when provided by a registered accounting firm to an audit client; also increases the punishment for a number of white-collar offenses.

····▶ Point/Counterpoint

As you are considering this issue, you might want to think about statistics that would help you resolve it.

How Severely Should the Law Punish Individuals Convicted of White-Collar Crime?

LESS SEVERELY THAN VIOLENT CRIMINALS	MORE SEVERELY THAN VIOLENT CRIMINALS
Street crimes are different in kind from white-collar crimes. Whereas white-collar crime affects only individuals' property, street crime threatens individuals' lives and health. The law ought to recognize that protecting lives is more important than protecting property.	It is far from clear that white-collar crime has less serious consequences than street crime. For example, individuals who defraud the government in effect steal taxes paid by all members of society, whereas individuals in possession of small amounts of marijuana may never adversely affect other members of society.

Street crimes are different in kind from white-collar crimes. Whereas white-collar crime affects only individuals' property, street crime threatens individuals' lives and health. The law ought to recognize that protecting lives is more important than protecting property.

Moreover, white-collar crime tends to affect higher-income individuals, whereas street crime tends to affect lower-income individuals who lack the resources to protect themselves. Street crime disproportionately affects lower-income individuals who cannot afford the private security measures that higher-income individuals use to protect their persons and their property. The law ought to protect those who lack the power to protect themselves.

A third reason to punish white-collar crime less heavily than street crime is that white-collar criminals are more likely to engage in careful cost-benefit analysis when determining whether to commit white-collar crime. If the severity of the punishment, discounted by the chance they will get caught, is less than the expected payoff from the white-collar crime, rational individuals won't see the crime as a profitable enterprise. It seems less likely that street criminals engage in the same kind of careful cost-benefit analysis before deciding, for example, whether to use illegal drugs. Thus, the most effective punishment for undeterrable street crime is likely to be severe punishment that incapacitates the criminals so that they are unable to commit more street crime. White-collar crime, on the other hand, can effectively be curbed by setting the punishment just high enough to make the crime unprofitable.

It is far from clear that white-collar crime has less serious consequences than street crime. For example, individuals who defraud the government in effect steal taxes paid by all members of society, whereas individuals in possession of small amounts of marijuana may never adversely affect other members of society.

Indeed, white-collar crime affects all groups in society in both direct and indirect ways. Companies victimized by white-collar crime often must raise the prices of their goods to recoup the costs of the crime. Everyone in society feels the effects of the higher prices. Street crime, while by no means negligible, tends to affect smaller circles of people. Thus, to get the biggest bang for our buck, we should punish white-collar crime more heavily than street crime.

Another reason to punish white-collar crime more heavily than street crime focuses on the underlying causes of crime. Much street crime has its roots in other social problems. Often, individuals commit street crime because of the poor environments in which they were raised. Much white-collar crime, however, is committed by well-off individuals out of avarice. The law ought to dole out more severe punishments for crimes caused by individual responsibility, and society ought to use other mechanisms to address crime caused by aleatory factors.

····▶ Questions & Problems

1. How do business ethics and business law interact with each other?

2. How does the WPH approach to ethics respond to an ethical problem?

3. List and define the primary affirmative defenses used in criminal cases.

4. Explain the federal laws that are currently being used to try to fight white-collar crime.

5. Jarold Daniel Friedman worked as a temporary computer contractor for a pharmaceutical warehouse. The warehouse offered him a permanent position, but the warehouse required that he get a mumps vaccine, grown in chicken embryos, as a condition of his permanent employment. Friedman, a vegan, believed that the vaccination would violate his religious beliefs and declined to be vaccinated. As a result, the warehouse withdrew its offer of employment. Friedman claimed that the warehouse discriminated against him on the basis of religion. Do you agree with Friedman? Do employers have a duty to respect the beliefs of their employees? If so, what happens when that duty conflicts with employers' duty to provide a safe and healthy work environment? [*Friedman v. Southern California Permanente Medical Group,* 102 Cal. App. 4th 39 (2002).]

6. John Bigan owned a strip-mining operation in which he dug trenches to remove coal deposits. One of these trenches was nearly 20 feet deep and contained water about 10 feet deep. Bigan installed a pump in the trench to remove the water and asked Joseph Yania, the owner of another strip-mining operation, to help him start the pump. Bigan urged and taunted Yania, who could not swim, to jump from the edge of the trench into the water, where Bigan was working on the pump. Yania jumped and drowned. Yania's widow sued Bigan, alleging that he failed to rescue her husband. Do you think Bigan should have rescued Yania? Do you think the law should require that Bigan rescue Yania? Why or why not? What values are you employing in your argument? [*Yania v. Bigan,* 397 Pa. 316 (1959).]

7. Jennifer Erickson sued her employer, Bartell Drug Company, contending that its decision not to cover prescription contraceptives under its employee prescription drug plan constituted sex discrimination. Bartell argued that its decision was not sex discrimination because contraceptives were preventive, were voluntary, and did not treat an illness. With whom do you agree? Why? What values did you use to reach your conclusion? [*Erickson v. Bartell Drug Co.,* 141 F. Supp. 2d 1266 (2001).]

8. Entertainment Network, Inc. (ENI), a business that provided news, entertainment, and information via the Internet, sued government officials who prohibited the company from filming the execution of Oklahoma City bomber Timothy McVeigh and selling the footage of the execution online. The government officials argued that a Justice Department regulation prohibiting audio and visual recording devices at federal executions applied in the case at hand. ENI, however, argued that the regulation violated the company's First Amendment right to free speech.

How do you think the court should have ruled in this case? Do you think ENI might have altered its decision to broadcast the execution if it had applied the Golden Rule? [*Entm't Network, Inc. v. Lappin,* 134 F. Supp. 2d 1002 (2001).]

9. Kevin Gray, was found guilty of mail fraud. He had attempted to convince a businessman, Frank Patti, who was on trial for tax evasion and faced substantial jail time, that for $85,000 he would bribe the jury, thus avoiding the threat of jail for the businessman. A letter sent to Patti contained false material representations from the Gray. Patti's reliance on the information contained in the letter can be inferred from, among other things, the fact that he was prepared to call Patti at the pay phone at the time and location specified in the letter. Because the methods to be used by the Gray were hardly believable, Gray appealed his judgment on the ground that his fraudulent scheme was "so absurd" that a person of ordinary prudence would not have believed it, and therefore, his conduct fell outside the realm of conduct proscribed by the mail fraud statute. Should the appellate court overturn Gray's conviction? [*United States v. Gray,* 367 F. 3d 1263 (2004).]

10. Grand Central Partnership Social Services Corporation is a not-for-profit organization. The organization provides counseling, referrals, clothing, showers, and mail access for the homeless. Additionally, the organization implemented a program known as Pathways to Employment (PTE), designed to assist in the development of vocational skills. The program provided workshops covering topics such as interviewing skills and résumé writing. Participants in the PTE program were assigned to five areas: maintenance, food services, administration, outreach, and recycling. Each of these tasks related to the overall operation and goals of the center. Individuals participating in the PTE program were required to participate 40 hours per week and were paid between $40 and $60 per week. The plaintiffs, predominantly homeless and jobless individuals, alleged that the wages paid by Grand Central were below minimum wage and therefore unlawful. Grand Central argued that participants in the PTE program were trainees, not employees, and that the participants were learning valuable job readiness skills. Do you think that this is an appropriate distinction? What ethical issues should be considered? [*Archie v. Grand Central Partnership,* 997 F. Supp. 504 (1998).]

11. Robert Morris, a PhD student in computer science at Cornell University, designed a computer program known as a "worm" and released it onto the Internet. The worm spread and multiplied and eventually caused computers at various educational and military

institutions to crash. Morris argued that he released the worm to demonstrate to fellow graduate students the lack of security protecting computer networks. With what crime was he most likely charged? Was this prosecution successful? [*United States v. Robert Tappen Morris,* 928 F.2d 504 (1991).]

12. The Pasquantinos, while in New York, ordered liquor over the telephone from discount package stores in Maryland. They employed Hilts and others to drive the liquor over the Canadian border, without paying the required excise taxes. The drivers avoided paying taxes by hiding the liquor in their vehicles and failing to declare the goods to Canadian customs officials. During the time of the Pasquantinos' smuggling operation, between 1996 and 2000, Canada heavily taxed the importation of alcoholic beverages. The Pasquantinos and Hilts were indicted for charges of federal wire fraud. They contest no wire fraud existed because the federal government cannot enforce the revenue laws of Canada, and this therefore prevents the existence in the United States of a fraud charge. How did the Supreme Court rule? Should the Pasquantinos and Hilts be able to succeed in their legal argument? [*Pasquantino v. United States,* 125 S. Ct. 1766 (2005).]

13. Bernadette Sablan was fired from her job at the Bank of Hawaii for circumventing security procedures when retrieving files. One night after drinking at a bar with a friend, she entered an unlocked door at the bank. She went to her old workstation and logged on to the mainframe by using an old password. She contends that she simply accessed several files and logged out. The government argued that she changed and deleted several files. Regardless, her actions damaged several bank files. Sablan was charged with computer fraud. She argued that the government had to establish the *mens rea* element of the crime—that is, the government had to prove she intentionally tried to damage the files. The district court ruled that the intention element applied only to accessing the files. Sablan argued that the legislation in question was intended to apply only to those who intentionally damage computer data, and she appealed. How did the court of appeals rule? Why? [*United States v. Sablan,* 92 F.3d 865, 866 (9th Cir. 1996).]

Looking for more review material?

The Online Learning Center at **www.mhhe.com/kubasekess** contains this chapter's "Assignment on the Internet" and also a list of URLs for more information, entitled "On the Internet." Find both of them in the Student Center portion of the OLC, along with quizzes and other helpful materials.

Ethical Relativism and Situational Ethics

An ethical school of thought that may seem appealing on the surface is ethical relativism. Ethical relativism is a theory of ethics that denies the existence of objective moral standards. Rather, according to ethical relativism, individuals must evaluate actions on the basis of what they feel is best for themselves. Ethical relativism holds that when two individuals disagree over a question about morality, both individuals are correct because no objective standard exists to evaluate their actions. Instead, morality is relative, and thus no one can criticize another's behavior as immoral. Many people find ethical relativism attractive because it promotes tolerance.

Ethical relativism may appear attractive at first glance, but very few people are willing to accept the logical conclusions of this theory. For example, ethical relativism requires us to see murder as a moral action as long as the murderer believes that the action is best for himself or herself. Once a person accepts the appropriateness of criticizing behavior in some situations, the person has rejected ethical relativism and must develop a more complex ethical theory.

Situational ethics is a theory that at first appears similar to ethical relativism but is actually substantially different. Like ethical relativism, situational ethics requires that we evaluate the morality of an action by imagining ourselves in the position of the person facing the ethical dilemma. But unlike ethical relativism, situational ethics allows us to judge other people's actions. In other words, situational ethics holds that once we put ourselves in another person's shoes, we can evaluate whether that person's action was ethical.

While situational ethics provides a useful rule of thumb to use when thinking about the ethical decision-making process, it does not offer specific-enough criteria to be useful in many real-world situations. Once we imagine ourselves in the position of a person facing an ethical dilemma, situational ethics does not tell us *how* to evaluate that person's actions. An alternative school of ethical thought, however, provides a much more judgmental approach to ethical dilemmas.

Ethical relativism
The ethical theory that denies the existence of an ultimate ethical system. According to this theory, a decision must be determined ethical on the basis of its own context.

situational ethics
A branch of ethical relativism that urges us to envision ourselves in the shoes of others, yet allows us to judge the decisions of others.

Absolutism

Absolutism, or *ethical fundamentalism,* requires that individuals defer to a set of rules to guide them in the ethical decision-making process. Unlike ethical relativism and situational ethics, absolutism holds that whether an action is moral does not depend on the perspective of the person facing the ethical dilemma. Rather, whether an action is moral depends on whether the action conforms to the given set of ethical rules.

Of course, people disagree about which set of rules to follow. Why should we accept and act on any one absolutist set of rules? Absolutism cannot tell us, for example, why we ought to follow the doctrines set forth in the Koran and not Hindu doctrines.

Moreover, the unquestionable nature of the rules in most absolutist repositories seems overly inflexible when applied to different situations. For instance, "Thou shalt not kill" seems to be an absolute rule, but, in practice, killing in self-defense seems to be an acceptable exception to this rule.

absolutism
Any set of ethics that is based on rules. These rules are considered moral regardless of perspective or dilemma.

Consequentialism

In contrast to absolutism, consequentialism does not provide a rigid set of rules to follow regardless of the situation. Rather, as the word *consequentialism* suggests, this ethical approach "depends on the consequences." Consequentialism is a general approach to ethical dilemmas that requires that we inquire about the consequences to relevant people of our making a particular decision.

Utilitarianism is one form of consequentialism that business managers may find useful. Like many consequentialist theories of ethics, utilitarianism urges managers to take those actions

consequentialism
The ethical theory based on consequences. It states that in considering what action is ethical, the only thing that matters is its consequences.

utilitarianism
The ethical principle that urges individuals to act in a way that creates the most happiness for the largest number of people.

that provide the greatest pleasure after having subtracted the pain or harm associated with the action in question.

Utilitarianism has two main branches: act utilitarianism and rule utilitarianism. Act utilitarianism tells business managers to examine all the potential actions in each situation and choose the action that yields the greatest amount of pleasure over pain for all involved. For example, according to act utilitarianism, a business manager who deceives an employee may be acting morally if the act of deception maximizes pleasure over pain for everyone involved.

Rule utilitarians, on the other hand, see great potential for the abuse of act utilitarianism. Instead of advocating the maximization of pleasure over pain in each individual situation, rule utilitarianism holds that general rules that *on balance* produce the greatest amount of pleasure for all involved should be established and followed in each situation. Thus, even if the business manager's decision to deceive an employee maximizes pleasure over pain in a given situation, the act probably would not be consistent with rule utilitarianism because deception does not generally produce the greatest satisfaction.

Rule utilitarianism underlies many laws in the United States. For example, labor laws prohibit employers from hiring children to do manufacturing work, even though in some situations the transaction would maximize pleasure over pain.

One form of utilitarianism commonly applied by firms and government is cost-benefit analysis. When a business makes decisions based on cost-benefit analysis, it is comparing the pleasure and pain of its optional choices, as that pleasure and pain are measured in monetary terms.

As we have shown, consequentialism is not altogether helpful because of the extreme difficulty in making the required calculations about consequences. Another issue raises an important additional objection to consequentialist thinking: Where does the important social value of justice fit into consequentialist reasoning? Many business decisions could be beneficial in their consequences for a majority of the population, but is it fair to require that a few be harmed so that the majority can be improved? Consequentialism does not provide definite answers to these questions, but an alternative ethical theory does.

Deontology

Deontology is an alternative theoretical approach to consequentialism. When you see references to Kantian ethics, the analysis that follows the reference will be a discussion of the most famous of the deontological approaches to business ethics. Unlike a person espousing consequentialism, a person using a deontological approach will not see the relevance of making a list of harms and benefits that result from a particular decision. Instead, deontology consists of acting on the basis of the recognition that certain actions are right or wrong, regardless of their consequences. For example, a business leader might consider it wrong to terminate a person whose spouse has terminal cancer because a firm has an obligation to support its employees when they are vulnerable, *period*.

But how are business managers to decide whether an action is right or wrong? The German deontological philosopher Immanuel Kant proposed the categorical imperative to determine whether an action is right. According to the categorical imperative, an action is moral only if it would be consistent for everyone in society to act in the same way. Thus, for example, applying the categorical imperative would lead you to conclude that you should not cheat on a drug test, because if everyone acted in the same way, the drug test would be meaningless.

From the deontological viewpoint, the duties or obligations that we owe one another as humans are much more ethically significant than are measurements of the impacts of business decisions. For example, a person using a deontological theory of ethics may see any business behavior that violates our duty of trust as being wrong. To sell a car that one knows will probably not be usable after four years is, from this perspective, unethical. No set of positive consequences that might flow from the production decision can overcome the certainty of the deontological recognition that the sale is wrong.

Marginal glossary

act utilitarianism

States that the morally right action is the act producing the greatest amount of happiness for the greatest number of people. Act utilitarianism requires the individual to assess the context for each decision, as opposed to relying on general rules.

rule utilitarianism

A subset of utilitarianism that proposes a number of rules for determining generally what creates the most happiness.

cost-benefit analysis

An economic school of jurisprudence where all costs and benefits to a law are given monetary values. Those laws with the highest ratio of benefits to costs are then preferable to those with lesser ratios.

Kantian Ethics

A deontological theory of ethics based on the teachings of Immanuel Kant, which has as a fundamental belief the idea that a moral act is one that is based on a sense of duty. It is probably most well known for its principle of the categorical imperative, the idea that an action is moral only if it would be consistent for everyone in society to act in the same way.

deontology

The ethical theory that states that an action can be determined ethical regardless of its consequences.

categorical imperative

The principle that an act is ethical when we would wish for all people to act according to its dictates.

The duties that we owe others imply that human beings have fundamental rights based on the dignity of each individual. This principle of rights asserts that whether a business decision is ethical depends on how the decision affects the rights of all involved. This principle is foundational to Western culture: the Declaration of Independence, for example, asserts that everyone has the right to "life, liberty, and the pursuit of happiness."

But just as consequentialism is incredibly complicated, deontology is difficult to apply because people disagree about what duties we owe to one another and which duties are more important than others when they conflict. For example, imagine the dilemma of a scientist working for a tobacco firm who discovers that cigarettes are carcinogenic. She owes a duty of trust to her employer, but she also has a conflicting duty to the community to do no harm. Where would a business manager find a list of relevant duties under the deontological framework, and why should we accept and act on any particular list?

In addition, as with absolutism, the absolute nature of many deontological lists of duties and rights seems overly rigid when applied to a wide variety of contexts. For instance, saying that we owe a duty to respect human life sounds absolute. In application, however, we might be forced to harm one life to preserve other life. An alternative theory of ethics, called *virtue ethics,* avoids this rigidity problem by providing us with abstract goals to pursue continually.

> **principle of rights**
> The principle that judges the morality of a decision on the basis of how it affects the rights of all those involved.

Virtue Ethics

Virtue ethics is an ethical system in which the development of virtues, or positive character traits such as courage, justice, and truthfulness, is the basis for morality. A morally excellent (and thus good) person develops virtues and distinguishes them from vices, or negative character traits such as cowardice and vanity. This development of virtues occurs through practice. Virtues are the habits of mind that move us toward excellence, the good life, or human flourishing.

As a guide to business ethics, virtue ethics requires that managers act in such a way that they will increase their contributions to the good life. Virtue ethics tells them to follow the character traits that, upon introspective reflection, they see as consistent with virtue. Identifying the relevant virtues and vices requires reasoning about the kind of human behavior that moves us toward the good, successful, or happy life.

A difficulty with the application of virtue ethics is the lack of agreement about the meaning of "the good life." Without that agreement, we are not able to agree about what types of behavior are consistent with our achievement of that goal. Even so, virtue ethics is useful in reminding us that ethics is grounded in a sense of what it means to be virtuous—we need some moral beacon to call us toward a more morally excellent condition. An alternative theory of business ethics, the ethics of care, offers a clear conception of what is virtuous.

> **virtue ethics**
> The ethical system concerned with the development of character traits. This system proposes that a decision is ethical when it promotes positive character traits like honesty, courage, or fairness.

Ethics of Care

The ethics of care holds that the right course of action is the option most consistent with the building and maintaining of human relationships. Those who adhere to an ethic of care argue that traditional moral hierarchies ignore an important element of life: relationships. Care for the nurturing of our many relationships serves as a reminder of the importance of responsibility to others.

According to someone who adheres to an ethic of care, when one person cares for another person, the first person is acting morally. When other ethical theories emphasize different moral dimensions as a basis for resolving ethical dilemmas, they rarely consider the harm they might do to relationships; thus, from the perspective of the ethics of care, alternative theories of business ethics often encourage unethical behavior.

Ethics-of-care theorists argue that when one individual, the *caregiver,* meets the needs of one other person, the *cared-for* party, the caregiver is actually helping to meet the needs of all the

> **ethics of care**
> The ethical theory that places its emphasis on human interaction. According to this theory, what makes a decision ethical is how well it builds and promotes human relationships.

individuals who fall within the cared-for party's *web of care*. Thus, by specifically helping one other individual, the caregiver is assisting numerous people.

The strength of this theoretical approach is that it focuses on the basis of ethics in general: the significance of the interests of other people. The urging to care for relationships speaks to the fundamental basis of why we are concerned about ethics in the first place. Most of us do not need any encouragement to think about how a decision will affect us personally. But ethical reasoning requires that we weigh the impact of decisions on the larger community.

Let's examine how these ethical theories are applied in real-world firms. Exhibit 2A-1 is an abridged version of the Johnson & Johnson Credo, or statement of shared corporate values. General Robert Wood Johnson, who guided Johnson & Johnson from a small, family-owned business to a worldwide enterprise, believed the corporation had social responsibilities beyond the manufacturing and marketing of products. In 1943, he wrote and published the Johnson & Johnson Credo, a document outlining those responsibilities. Does the credo depend more on ethical relativism, situational ethics, absolutism, consequentialism, deontology, virtue ethics, or the ethics of care for its ethical vision?

Exhibit 2A-1 Johnson & Johnson's Credo

The Credo

We believe our first responsibility is to the doctors, nurses and patients, to mothers and fathers and all others who use our products and services. In meeting their needs everything we do must be of high quality. We must constantly strive to reduce our costs in order to maintain reasonable prices. Customers' orders must be serviced promptly and accurately. Our suppliers and distributors must have an opportunity to make a fair profit.

We are responsible to our employees, the men and women who work with us throughout the world. Everyone must be considered as an individual. We must respect their dignity and recognize their merit. They must have a sense of security in their jobs. Compensation must be fair and adequate, and working conditions clean, orderly and safe. We must be mindful of ways to help our employees fulfill their family responsibilities. Employees must feel free to make suggestions and complaints. There must be equal opportunity for employment, development and advancement for those qualified. We must provide competent management, and their actions must be just and ethical.

We are responsible to the communities in which we live and work and to the world community as well. We must be good citizens—support good works and charities and bear our fair share of taxes. We must encourage civic improvements and better health and education. We must maintain in good order the property we are privileged to use, protecting the environment and natural resources.

Our final responsibility is to our stockholders. Business must make a sound profit. We must experiment with new ideas. Research must be carried on, innovative programs developed and mistakes paid for. New equipment must be purchased, new facilities provided and new products launched. Reserves must be created to provide for adverse times. When we operate according to these principles, the stockholders should realize a fair return.

Used by permission Johnson & Johnson.

At a Glance

Theories of Business Ethics

Ethical approach	Description
Ethical relativism	Asserts that morality is relative.
Situational ethics	Requires that when we evaluate whether an action is ethical, we imagine ourselves in the position of the person facing an ethical dilemma.
Consequentialism	Considers the consequences (i.e., harms and benefits) of making a particular decision.
Deontology	Recognizes certain actions as right or wrong regardless of the consequences.
Virtue ethics	Encourages individuals to develop virtues (e.g., courage and truthfulness) that guide behavior.
Ethics of care	Holds that ethical behavior is determined by actions that care for and maintain human relationships.

The U.S. Legal System and Alternative Dispute Resolution

····▸ CASE OPENER

Questionable Jurisdiction over Caterpillar

James Lewis, a resident of Kentucky, sustained an injury while operating a Caterpillar bulldozer. He filed suit against Caterpillar, a company incorporated in Delaware but with its principal place of business in Illinois. Lewis also filed suit against the supplier of the bulldozer, Whayne Supply Company, whose principal place of business was Kentucky. Lewis filed his case in a Kentucky state court, alleging defective manufacture, negligence, failure to warn, and breach of warranty. Lewis and Whayne Supply Company agreed to settle out of court. Caterpillar then filed a motion to exercise its right of removal (its right to move the case from the state to the federal court system), arguing that the federal court had jurisdiction over the case because Caterpillar and Lewis were from different states. Lewis disagreed with Caterpillar's contention, claiming that because he had not completed his settlement with Whayne, the case still included a defendant (Whayne) from Lewis's state, Kentucky. Thus, Lewis argued, federal courts did not have jurisdiction over the case.

The court agreed with Caterpillar's argument and moved the case to a federal district court. Shortly thereafter, Lewis and Whayne finalized their settlement agreement, and the district court dismissed Whayne from the lawsuit. The federal district court granted Caterpillar a favorable judgment. Lewis, however, appealed the district court's decision, renewing his argument that the district court did not have jurisdiction over the case. The court of appeals agreed with Lewis, holding that because Whayne was a defendant in the case at the time that Caterpillar moved the case from state to federal court, the diversity of citizenship necessary to give the federal court jurisdiction over the case was absent. Thus, a state court should have resolved the dispute. Consequently, the appellate court vacated the district court's decision. Caterpillar then appealed to the U.S. Supreme Court.

1. What factors determine whether the state or federal court system hears a case?
2. If you were a businessperson with Caterpillar, why might you prefer a federal court to hear the dispute with Lewis rather than a state court?

After reading this chapter, you will be able to answer the following questions:

LO 1 What types of jurisdiction must a court have to render a binding decision in a case?

LO 2 What is venue?

LO 3 What are the threshold requirements that must be met before a court will hear a case?

LO 4 What are the steps in civil litigation?

LO 5 How are the various forms of alternative dispute resolution used by businesses today?

trial court
A court in which most civil or criminal cases start when they first enter the legal system. The parties present evidence and call witnesses to testify. Trial courts are referred to as courts of common pleas or county courts in state court systems and as district courts in the federal system. Also called *court of original jurisdiction* and *court of first instance.*

appellate court
A higher court, usually consisting of more than one judge, that reviews the decision and results of a lower court (either a trial court or a lower-level appellate court) when a losing party files for an appeal. Appellate courts do not hold trials but may request additional oral and written arguments from each party; they issue written decisions, which collectively constitute case law or the common law. Also called *court of appellate jurisdiction.*

question of law
An issue concerning the interpretation or application of a law.

question of fact
A question about an event or characteristic in the case.

As the Case Opener illustrates, when a dispute arises, parties in this country do not simply go "to court." They often must choose between federal and state court systems. This chapter examines these systems, as well as the trial procedures that apply in civil cases.

Jurisdiction

A useful way to understand jurisdiction is to think of it as referring to courts' power to hear cases and render decisions that bind the parties before them. A court must have several types of jurisdiction to decide any particular case.

ORIGINAL VERSUS APPELLATE JURISDICTION

Trial courts, or **courts of original jurisdiction,** have the power to hear and decide cases when they first enter the legal system. In these courts, the parties present evidence and call witnesses to testify. In most states, these courts are called *courts of common pleas* or *county courts.* In the federal system, these trial courts are called *federal district courts.*

Courts of appellate jurisdiction, or **appellate courts,** have the power to review previous judicial decisions to determine whether trial courts erred in their decisions. Appellate courts do not hold trials. Instead, appellate judges review transcripts of trial court proceedings and occasionally consider additional oral and written arguments from each party.

Appellate courts handle only questions of law, not questions of fact. A **question of law** is an issue concerning the interpretation or application of a law. In contrast, a **question of fact** is a question about an event or characteristic in the case. For example, whether a white student yelled racial slurs on a college campus is a question of fact. On the other hand, whether the First Amendment protects the student's right to utter racial slurs is a question of law.

Only judges can decide questions of law. Trial courts determine questions of fact. In a bench trial (a trial with no jury), the judge decides questions of fact; in a jury trial, the jury decides questions of fact. Appellate courts can, however, overrule trial courts' decisions on questions of fact, but only when the trial court's finding was clearly erroneous or when no trial evidence supports the trial court's finding.

CONNECTING to the Core

JURISDICTION OVER PERSONS AND PROPERTY

LO 1

In personam jurisdiction (literally, *jurisdiction over the person*) is a court's power to render a decision affecting the rights of the specific persons before the court. Generally, a court's power to exercise *in personam* jurisdiction extends only over a specific geographic region. In the state court system, a court's *in personam* jurisdiction usually extends to the state's borders. In the federal system, each court's jurisdiction extends across its geographic district.

A court acquires *in personam* jurisdiction over a person (the plaintiff) when she files a lawsuit with the court. The court acquires jurisdiction over the person the plaintiff is suing (the defendant) when it gives him a copy of the complaint and a summons. The complaint specifies the factual and legal basis for the lawsuit and the relief the plaintiff seeks. The summons is a court order that notifies the defendant of the lawsuit and explains how and when to respond to the complaint.

Service of process is the procedure by which courts present these documents to defendants. Traditionally, courts used personal service: An officer of the court handed the summons and complaint to the defendant. Recently, however, courts have employed other methods of service, including *residential service,* in which a court representative leaves the summons and complaint with a responsible adult at the defendant's home, and *service by certified* or *ordinary mail.*

If the defendant is a corporation, courts generally serve either the president of the corporation or an agent whom the corporation has appointed to receive service. Most states require that corporations appoint an agent for service when they incorporate. Corporations are subject to *in personam* jurisdiction in three locations: the state of their incorporation, the location of their main offices, and the geographic areas in which they conduct business.

Courts have *in personam* jurisdiction over persons only within a specific geographic region. In the past, a state court could not acquire *in personam* jurisdiction over out-of-state defendants unless it served the defendants within the court's home state. Thus, defendants who injured plaintiffs could evade legal action by leaving the state and remaining outside its borders.

To alleviate this problem, most states have enacted long-arm statutes that enable the court to serve defendants outside the state as long as the defendant has sufficient minimum contacts within the state. Each state has its own minimum-contact requirements, but most state statutes hold that acts like committing a tort or doing business in the state are sufficient to allow the state to serve a defendant. In the Caterpillar case, the company sold products in Kentucky, and its products caused an injury in the state. These two facts were sufficient minimum contacts to allow

in personam jurisdiction
The power of a court to require that a party (usually the defendant) or a witness come before the court. The court must have personal jurisdiction to enforce its judgments or orders against a party. *In personam* jurisdiction extends only to the state's borders in the state court system and across the court's geographic district in the federal system. Also called *personal jurisdiction* and *jurisdiction in personam.*

plaintiff
The person or party who initiates a lawsuit (also known as an action) before a court by filing a complaint with the clerk of the court against the defendant(s). Also known as *claimant* or *complainant.*

defendant
The person, party, or entity against whom a civil or criminal lawsuit is filed in a court of law.

complaint

A formal written document that begins a civil lawsuit; contains the plaintiff's list of allegations against the defendant, along with the damages the plaintiff seeks.

summons

A legal document issued by a court and addressed to a defendant that notifies him or her of the lawsuit and how and when to respond to the complaint. A summons may be used in both civil and criminal proceedings.

long-arm statute

A statute that enables a court to obtain jurisdiction against an out-of-state defendant as long as the defendant has sufficient minimum contacts within the state, such as committing a tort or doing business in the state.

in rem **jurisdiction**

The power of a court over the property or status of an out-of-state defendant located within the court's jurisdiction area.

quasi *in rem* **jurisdiction**

A type of jurisdiction exercised by a court over an out-of-state defendant's property that is within the jurisdictional boundaries of the court. It applies to personal suits against the defendant in which the property is not the source of the conflict but is sought as compensation by the plaintiff. Also called *attachment jurisdiction.*

subject-matter jurisdiction

The power of a court over the type of case presented to it.

the Kentucky court to serve Caterpillar, even though it was an out-of-state company. Contrast the facts in the Caterpillar case with those in the Case Nugget.

CASE Nugget

A Question of Minimum Contacts

Hagan v. Field
Court of Appeals of Texas, Fifth District, Dallas

2006 Tex. App. LEXIS 393

The plaintiff, a Texas resident, and the defendants, Colorado residents, were cat breeders who met at a cat show in Colorado. Subsequently, plaintiff sent two cats to the defendants in Colorado for breeding and sent a third cat to them to be sold. A dispute over the return of the two breeding cats arose, and plaintiff filed suit against the defendants in Texas. Defendants alleged that the Texas court lacked personal jurisdiction over them because they did not have minimum contacts with the state of Texas. The trial court disagreed, and the defendants appealed. The court of appeals reversed the decision of the trial court, finding that under the Texas long-arm statute, the Texas court could exercise jurisdiction over an out-of-state defendant only if (1) the defendant has purposefully established minimum contacts with the forum state, and (2) the exercise of jurisdiction comports with traditional notions of fair play and substantial justice.

In this case, the defendants were not residents of Texas and had no business in Texas. The only contact defendants had with Texas was a single trip they made to Texas to pick up two other cats, not related to the litigation, that they were going to take to a cat show. During that same visit, defendants took a cat unrelated to the lawsuit to see a Texas veterinarian, and plaintiff's husband assisted the defendants with a Web page for their business. These actions, even in combination with the defendants' sending the plaintiff a check for the proceeds from the breeding, were not found to constitute sufficient minimum contacts to give the Texas court jurisdiction. The defendants were not availing themselves of the benefits of the state of Texas, nor were their contacts sufficient to put them on notice that they could be subject to the court's jurisdiction.

If a defendant has property in a state, a plaintiff may file suit against the defendant's property instead of the owner. For example, suppose a Utah resident had not paid property taxes on a piece of land she owned in Idaho. Idaho courts have *in rem* **jurisdiction** (Latin for "jurisdiction over the thing") over the property. Thus, an Idaho state court has the power to seize the property and sell it to pay the property taxes in an *in rem* proceeding.

Courts can also gain **quasi** *in rem* **jurisdiction,** or *attachment jurisdiction,* over a defendant's property *unrelated* to the plaintiff's claim. For example, suppose Charlie, a Massachusetts resident, ran a red light while he was vacationing in California and collided with Jessica's car. Suppose further that Jessica suffered extensive injuries from the accident and successfully sued Charlie for $200,000 in a California state court. The California court can exercise quasi *in rem* jurisdiction over Charlie's California vacation home by seizing it, selling it, and transferring $200,000 to Jessica to satisfy her judgment against Charlie. If Charlie's vacation home is worth more than $200,000, however, the court must return the excess proceeds to Charlie.

SUBJECT-MATTER JURISDICTION

Subject-matter jurisdiction is a court's power to hear certain kinds of cases. Most industrialized countries have a single court system, with courts that have the power to hear both national law cases and local law cases. In contrast, the United States has both a state and a federal court

The Sliding-Scale Standard for Internet Transactions

Does a business that has Internet contact with a plaintiff in a different state satisfy the minimum-contacts standard?

A federal district court established the following "sliding-scale" standard in a 1997 case:*

> [T]he likelihood that personal jurisdiction can be constitutionally exercised is directly proportionate to the nature and quality of commercial activity that an entity conducts over the Internet. This sliding scale is consistent with well developed personal jurisdiction principles.

At one end of the spectrum are situations where a defendant clearly does business over the Internet. If the defendant enters into contracts with residents of a foreign jurisdiction that involve the knowing and repeated transmission of computer files over the Internet, personal jurisdiction is proper.

At the opposite end are situations where a defendant has simply posted information on an Internet Web site which is accessible to users in foreign jurisdictions. A passive Web site that does little more than make information available to those who are interested in it is not grounds for the exercise of personal jurisdiction.

The middle ground is occupied by interactive Web sites where a user can exchange information with the host computer. In these cases, the exercise of jurisdiction is determined by examining the level of interactivity and commercial nature of the exchange of information that occurs on the Web site.

* *Zippo Mfg. Co. v. Zippo Dot Com, Inc.,* 952 F. Supp. 1119 at 1124 (1997).

system. Subject-matter jurisdiction determines which court system may hear a particular case. Cases may fall under state jurisdiction, exclusive federal jurisdiction, or concurrent jurisdiction. Figure 3-1 illustrates the subject-matter-jurisdiction divisions.

Exclusive Federal Jurisdiction The federal court system has exclusive jurisdiction over very few cases: admiralty cases, bankruptcy cases, federal criminal prosecutions, lawsuits in which one state sues another state, and claims against the United States. Additionally, federal courts have exclusive jurisdiction over claims arising under federal statutes that specify exclusive federal jurisdiction.

State Jurisdiction The state court system has a broad range of jurisdiction; state courts have the power to hear all cases not within the exclusive jurisdiction of the federal court system. State courts also have exclusive jurisdiction over certain cases, such as cases concerning adoption and divorce. Most cases, therefore, fall under state court jurisdiction.

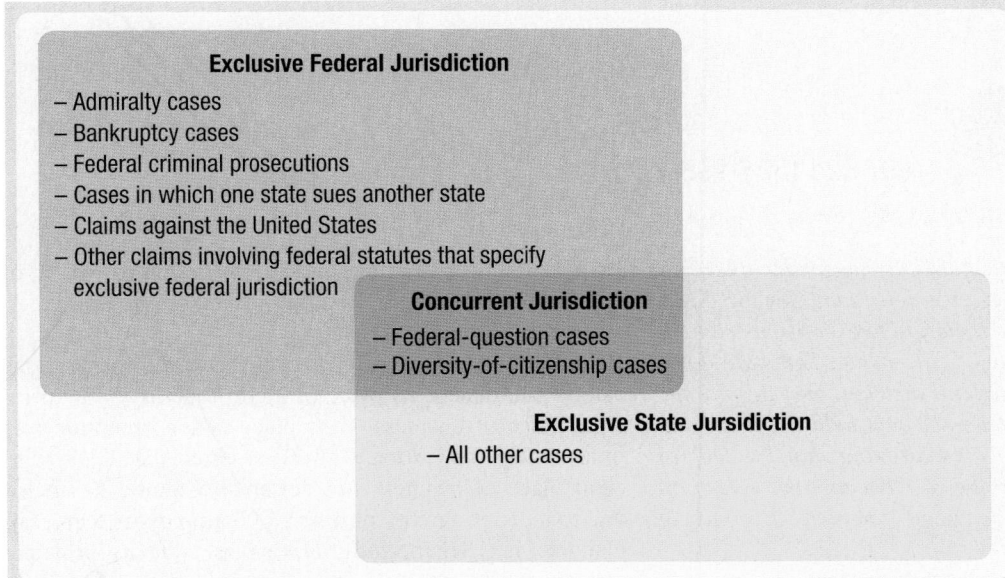

Figure 3-1

Subject-Matter-Jurisdiction Divisions

Exclusive Federal Jurisdiction
– Admiralty cases
– Bankruptcy cases
– Federal criminal prosecutions
– Cases in which one state sues another state
– Claims against the United States
– Other claims involving federal statutes that specify exclusive federal jurisdiction

Concurrent Jurisdiction
– Federal-question cases
– Diversity-of-citizenship cases

Exclusive State Jursidiction
– All other cases

The Caterpillar case fell under state court jurisdiction because its subject matter—product liability and negligence—did not place the case under the exclusive jurisdiction of the federal court system.

Concurrent Federal Jurisdiction Concurrent federal jurisdiction means that both state and federal courts have jurisdiction over a case. Concurrent jurisdiction covers two types of cases: federal-question and diversity-of-citizenship cases. *Federal-question* cases require an interpretation of the United States Constitution, a federal statute, or a federal treaty. For example, suppose a plaintiff alleges that a Florida campaign financing law violates his First Amendment free speech rights. Because this case raises a federal question, it falls under concurrent jurisdiction, and both state and federal courts have the power to hear it.

A *diversity-of-citizenship* case must satisfy two conditions: (1) the plaintiff(s) does (do) not reside in the same state as the defendant(s), and (2) the controversy concerns an amount in excess of $75,000. Courts use the location of a party's residence to determine whether diversity of citizenship exists. Most federal court cases are based on diversity of citizenship.

A business may reside in two states: the state of its incorporation and the state of its principal place of business. Thus, in the Case Opener, Caterpillar was a resident of Delaware, the state where it incorporated, and of Illinois, the state of its primary place of business.

It is important to note that diversity must be complete for a case to fall under concurrent jurisdiction. In the Caterpillar case, Lewis argued that diversity was not complete because both he and the supply company, the second defendant he originally sued, were residents of Kentucky. The appellate court agreed with his argument and overturned the district court's decision because the district court lacked subject-matter jurisdiction.

When a plaintiff files a case involving concurrent jurisdiction in state court, the defendant has a *right of removal.* This right entitles the defendant to transfer the case to federal court. Thus, either party to a case involving concurrent jurisdiction can put the case in the federal court system: The plaintiff can file the case in federal court initially; or if the case was initially filed in state court, the defendant can transfer the case to federal court by exercising her right of removal. In the Case Opener, Caterpillar exercised its right of removal, and the state trial court moved the case to a federal district court.

The issue of subject-matter jurisdiction often arises when the parties to a lawsuit disagree about whether to try the case in state or federal court, as Case 3-1 illustrates.

CASE 3-1

GAFFORD v. GENERAL ELECTRIC CO.
U. S. COURT OF APPEALS
997 F.2d 150 (1993)

FACTS: *Plaintiff Carol Gafford filed a gender discrimination suit in state court against defendant General Electric Co. The defendant filed a motion to exercise its right of removal based on diversity of citizenship. The state court transferred the case to a federal district court despite the plaintiff's objection. The federal court held the trial, and the plaintiff lost. She appealed, arguing that the federal court should not have tried the case because the defendant presented insufficient evidence of complete diversity of citizenship.*

ISSUE: Did the district court err in finding diversity of citizenship and hearing the case?

REASONING: The state of citizenship for corporations can be two places, its place of incorporation and its principal place of business. GE's place of incorporation was indisputably New York. Gafford asserted that GE's principal place of business was Jefferson County, Kentucky, due to its large facility of over 9,000 employees there. GE claimed that Schenectady, New York, was its principal

place of business because it kept basic corporate records and personnel records there, and GE submitted evidence to that effect. GE also produced evidence that facilities other than the one in Kentucky were larger and created more revenue. The court used the "total activity test," taking into account the type of business, the headquarters location, and the kinds and amounts of activity in other states:

> Where a corporation carries on its business in a number of states and no one state is clearly the state in which its business is principally conducted, the state in which the substantial part of its business is transacted and from which centralized general supervision of its business is exercised, is the state in which it has its principal place of business.

GE was not incorporated in Kentucky, nor was its principal place of business in Kentucky, which gave the case diversity of citizenship.

DECISION AND REMEDY: The court determined that the district court did not err in accepting the case for diversity of citizenship. The court affirmed the decision of the district court, in favor of General Electric Co.

SIGNIFICANCE OF THE CASE: This case shows the difficulties in determining corporate citizenship and affirms the necessity of examining each case on an individual basis to determine the principal place of business.

CRITICAL THINKING

Why did the court not find Kentucky to be GE's principal place of business, despite the fact that approximately 9,000 workers were employed there?

ETHICAL DECISION MAKING

The court in this instance may appear to be making a decision with no ethical content. However, ask, yourself: What stakeholders in GE would prefer that Kentucky be deemed the principal place of business for General Electric?

Venue

LO 2

Once a case is in the proper court system, venue determines which trial court in the system will hear the case. Venue is a matter of geographic location that each state's statutes determine. Usually, the trial court for the county where the defendant resides is the appropriate venue. If a case involves property, the trial court where the property is located is also an appropriate venue. Finally, if the focus of the case is a particular incident, the trial court where the dispute occurred is an appropriate venue. The plaintiff initially chooses from among the appropriate venues when she files the case.

If the location of the court where the plaintiff filed the case is an inconvenience to the defendant or if the defendant believes it will be difficult to select an unbiased jury in that venue, he may request that the judge move the case by filing a motion for a change of venue. The judge has the discretion to grant or deny the motion.

The Structure of the Court System

The U.S. legal system has two parallel court structures: a federal system and a state system. Once a plaintiff files a case in one of the systems, the case remains in that system throughout the appeals process. The only exception to this rule occurs when a party to a lawsuit appeals the decision of a state supreme court to the U.S. Supreme Court.

THE FEDERAL COURT SYSTEM

The federal court system derives its power from Article III, Section 2, of the U.S. Constitution and consists of three main levels: trial courts, intermediate appellate courts, and the court of last resort. Figure 3-2 illustrates this system.

venue
(1) The place where a hearing takes place. Its geographic location is determined by each state's statutes and based on where the parties live or where the event occurred or the alleged wrong was committed. (2) A legal doctrine relating to the selection of a court with subject-matter and personal jurisdiction that is the most appropriate geographic location for the resolution of the dispute.

Figure 3-2 The Federal Court System

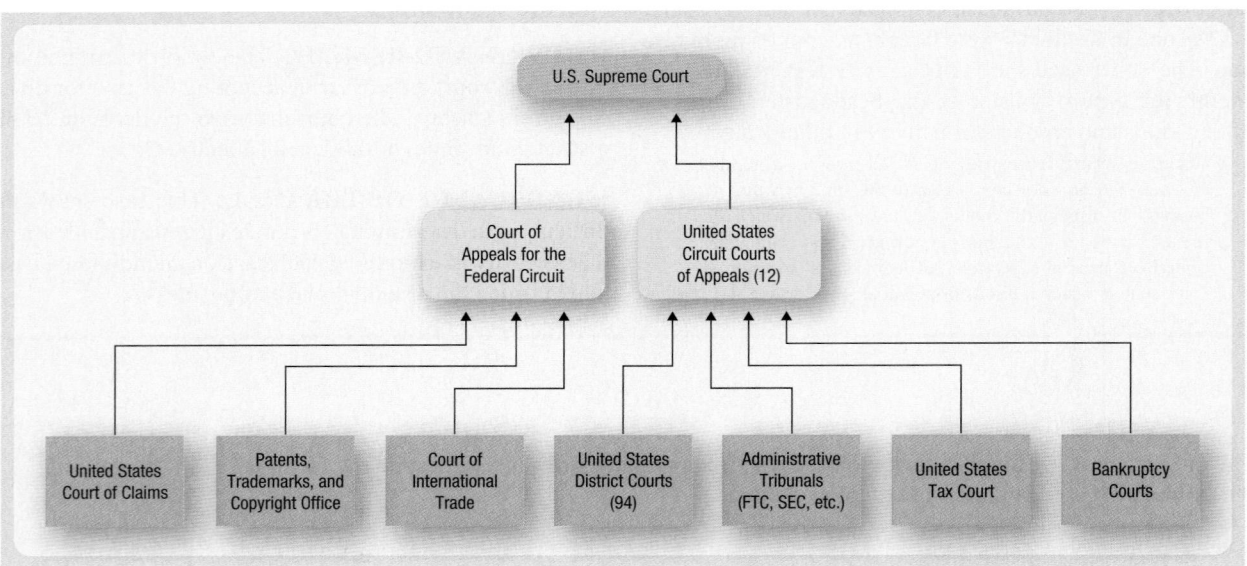

Federal Trial Courts In the federal court system, the trial courts, or courts of original jurisdiction, are U.S. district courts. The United States has 94 districts; each district has at least one trial court of general jurisdiction. Courts of general jurisdiction have the power to hear a wide range of cases and can grant almost any type of remedy. Almost every case in the federal system begins in one of these courts.

A small number of cases, however, do not begin in trial courts of general jurisdiction. For cases concerning certain subject matter, Congress has established special trial courts of limited jurisdiction. The types of cases heard by these special trial courts include bankruptcy cases, claims against the U.S. government, and copyright, patent, and trademark cases.

In an extremely limited number of cases, the U.S. Supreme Court functions as a trial court of limited jurisdiction. These cases include controversies between states and lawsuits against foreign ambassadors.

Intermediate Courts of Appeal The U.S. circuit courts of appeal make up the second level of courts in the federal system. The United States has 12 circuits, including a circuit for the District of Columbia. Each circuit court hears appeals from district courts in its geographic area. Additionally, a federal circuit court of appeals hears appeals from government administrative agencies. Figure 3-3 illustrates the geographic circuit divisions.

The Court of Last Resort The U.S. Supreme Court is the final appellate court in the federal system. Nine justices, who have lifetime appointments, make up the high court. Figure 3-4 identifies the nine justices on the U.S. Supreme Court in 2008.

The U.S. Supreme Court hears appeals of cases from the court of last resort in a state system. The Court will not, however, hear cases considering questions of pure state law. The Court also functions as a trial court on rare occasions. The structure and functioning of the U.S. Supreme Court system differ from those of similar courts in other countries, as the nearby Global Context box illustrates.

STATE COURT SYSTEMS

No uniform state court structure exists because each state has devised its own court system, but most states have a structure similar to the federal court system's structure.

Figure 3-3 The Circuits of the Federal Court System

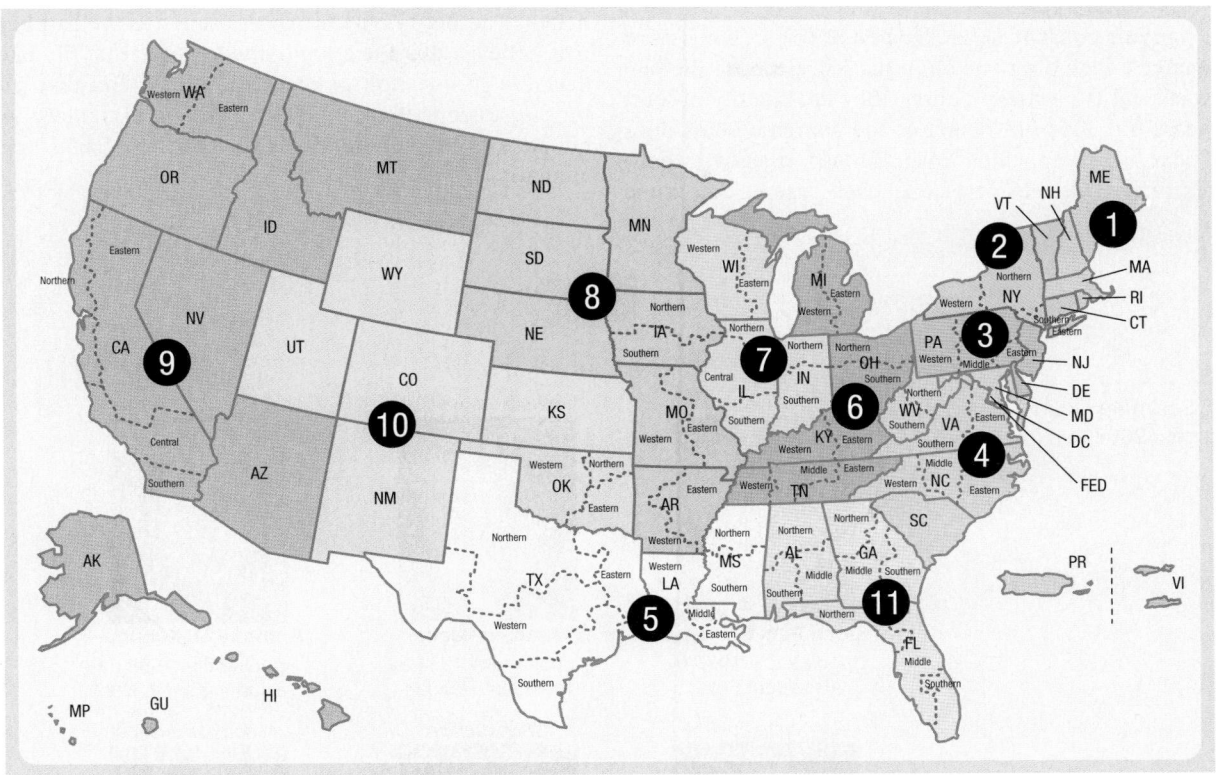

State Trial Courts In state court systems, most cases begin in a trial court of general jurisdiction. As in the federal system, state trial courts of general jurisdiction have the power to hear all cases over which the state court system has jurisdiction except those cases for which the state has established special trial courts of limited jurisdiction. Most states have a trial court of general jurisdiction in each county. The names of these courts vary by state, but most states refer to them as *courts of common pleas* or *county courts*. In some states, these courts have specialized divisions such as domestic relations and probate.

Most states also have trial courts of limited jurisdiction. Usually, these courts can grant only certain remedies. For example, small claims courts, a common type of court of limited jurisdiction in most states, may not grant damage awards larger than a specified amount. Other courts of limited jurisdiction have the power to hear only certain types of cases. For example, probate courts hear only cases about asset and obligation transfers after an individual's death.

Intermediate Courts of Appeal Intermediate courts of appeal, analogous to federal circuit courts of appeal, exist in approximately half the states. These courts usually have broad jurisdiction, hearing appeals from courts of general and limited jurisdictions, as well as from state administrative agencies. The names of these courts vary by state, but most states call them *courts of appeal* or *superior courts*.

Courts of Last Resort Appeals from the state intermediate courts of appeal lead cases to the state court of last resort. Most states call this court the *supreme court,* although some states refer to it as the *court of appeals.* Because approximately half of the states lack intermediate courts of appeal, appeals from trial courts in these states go directly to the state court of last resort.

The Supreme Court in Japan

The supreme court of Japan, located in Tokyo, consists of 15 justices, including one chief justice. Because the justices ascend from lower courts, they are usually at least 60 years old. The full bench of the supreme court does not hear every appealed case. Rather, a petit (small) bench of five justices first hears each case to determine whether to transfer the case to a hearing before the full bench. The petit court transfers a case to the full bench if it believes that the appellant can prove that the law or decision in question is unconstitutional. Because proving the unconstitutionality of a law is extremely difficult, the full bench generally hears fewer than 10 cases annually.

Figure 3-4

U.S. Supreme Court Justices, 2008

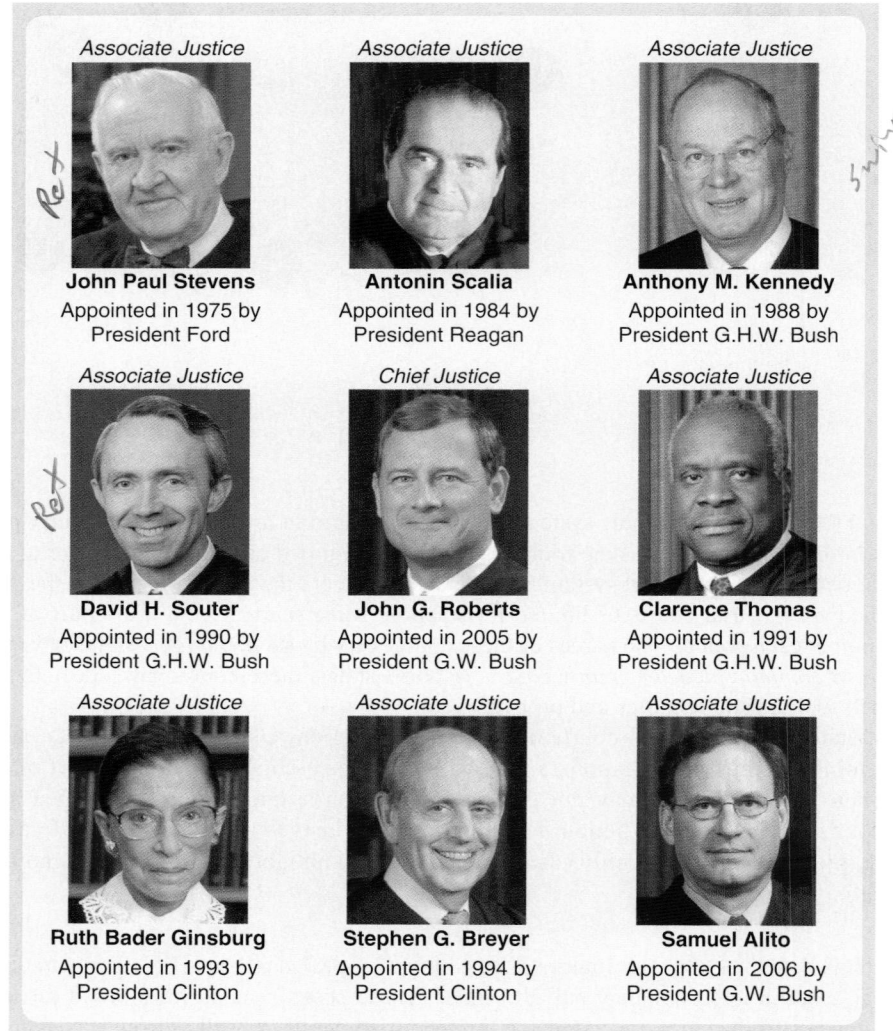

Associate Justice
John Paul Stevens
Appointed in 1975 by President Ford

Associate Justice
Antonin Scalia
Appointed in 1984 by President Reagan

Associate Justice
Anthony M. Kennedy
Appointed in 1988 by President G.H.W. Bush

Associate Justice
David H. Souter
Appointed in 1990 by President G.H.W. Bush

Chief Justice
John G. Roberts
Appointed in 2005 by President G.W. Bush

Associate Justice
Clarence Thomas
Appointed in 1991 by President G.H.W. Bush

Associate Justice
Ruth Bader Ginsburg
Appointed in 1993 by President Clinton

Associate Justice
Stephen G. Breyer
Appointed in 1994 by President Clinton

Associate Justice
Samuel Alito
Appointed in 2006 by President G.W. Bush

LO 3

Threshold Requirements

Before a case makes it to court, however, it must meet three *threshold requirements*. These requirements ensure that courts hear only cases that genuinely require adjudication. The three requirements are standing, case or controversy, and ripeness. (See Figure 3-5.)

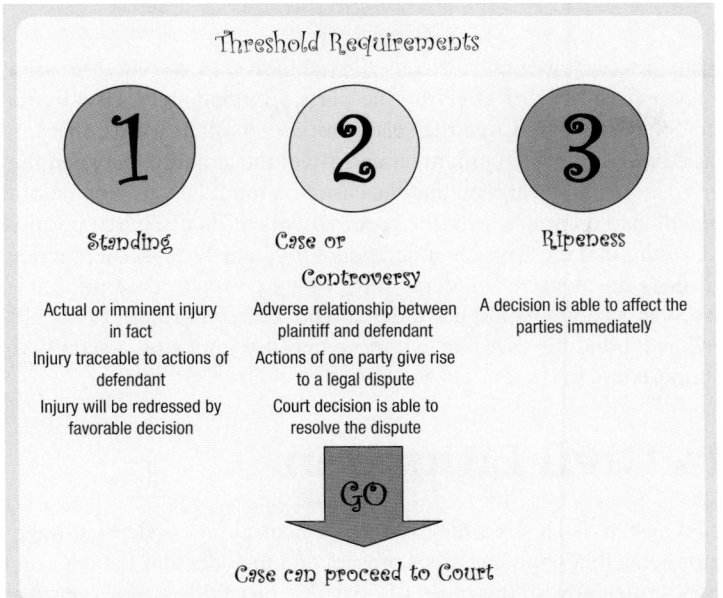

Figure 3-5

Threshold
Requirements

STANDING

A person who has the legal right to bring an action in court has standing (or *standing to sue*). For a person to have standing, the outcome of a case must personally affect him or her. Thus, if you hire a landscaper to mow your lawn every week and he fails to show up every other week, you have standing to sue your landscaper. But if your friend hired the landscaper, you lack the standing to sue on your friend's behalf because you do not have a personal stake in the outcome of the case.

The reason the American legal system requires this personal stake in the outcome is the belief that the plaintiff's personal stake stimulates her to present the best possible case. The requirements for standing, according to the 2000 U.S. Supreme Court case *Friends of the Earth v. Laidlaw Environmental Services,*[1] are (1) the plaintiff must have an injury in fact that is concrete and actual or imminent; (2) the injury must be fairly traceable to the challenged action of the defendant; and (3) it must be likely that the injury will be redressed by a favorable decision.[2] In applying those criteria to the Laidlaw case, the Supreme Court found that FOE members' testimony that they were afraid to fish and swim in a river they previously enjoyed satisfied the first two criteria. The Court held that although the FOE members would not directly receive money from a penalty against Laidlaw, they would benefit because the penalties would deter Laidlaw and other companies from polluting the river in the future.[3] The Court ruled in FOE's favor and assessed Laidlaw a $405,800 penalty payable to the U.S. Treasury.

CASE OR CONTROVERSY

The case-or-controversy (or *justifiable controversy*) requirement ensures that courts do not render advisory opinions. Three criteria are necessary for a case or controversy to exist. First, the relationship between the plaintiff and the defendant must be adverse. Second, actual or threatened actions of at least one of the parties must give rise to an actual legal dispute. Third, courts must have the ability to render a decision that will resolve the dispute. In other words, courts can give final judgments that solve existing problems; they cannot provide rulings about hypothetical situations.

[1] 120 S. Ct. 923 (2000).

[2] Ibid.

[3] Ibid.

standing
The legal right of a party or an individual to bring a lawsuit by demonstrating to the court sufficient connection to and harm from the law or action challenged (i.e., the plaintiff has to demonstrate that he or she is harmed or will be harmed). Otherwise, the court will dismiss the case, ruling that the plaintiff "lacks standing" to bring the suit.

case or controversy
A term used in the U.S. Constitution to describe the structure and requirements of conflicting claims of individuals that can be brought before a federal court for resolution. A case or controversy requires an actual dispute between parties over their legal rights that remains in conflict at the time the case is presented and that is a proper matter for judicial determination. Also referred to as *justifiable controversy.*

RIPENESS

ripeness

The readiness of a case for a decision to be made. The goal is to prevent premature litigation for a dispute that is insufficiently developed. A claim is not ripe for litigation if it rests on contingent future events that may not occur as anticipated or may not occur at all.

The case-or-controversy requirement is closely linked to the ripeness requirement. A case is *ripe* if a judge's decision is capable of affecting the parties immediately. Usually the issue of ripeness arises when one party claims that the case is moot—in other words, there is no point in the court's hearing the case because no judgment can affect the situation between the parties.

In the *Laidlaw* case, Laidlaw argued that the case was moot because by the time the case went to trial, the company had complied with the requirements of its discharge permits. The Supreme Court disagreed, ruling that the fact that a defendant voluntarily ceases a practice once litigation has commenced does not deprive a federal court of its power to determine the legality of the practice, because such a ruling would leave the defendant free to return to his old unlawful practices. Thus, the Court found the case was not moot because imposing a penalty on the defendant would have an important deterrent effect.[4]

LO 4

Steps in Civil Litigation

The U.S. litigation system is an adversary system: A neutral fact finder—a judge or jury—hears evidence and arguments that opposing sides present and then decides the case on the basis of the facts and law. Strict rules govern the types of evidence fact finders may consider. Theoretically, fact finders make informed and impartial rulings because each party has an incentive to find all relevant evidence and make the strongest possible arguments on behalf of her or his position.

Critics of the adversary system, however, point out several drawbacks: the time and expense each lawsuit requires, the damage a suit may cause to the litigating parties' relationship, and the unfair advantage to those with wealth and experience using the court system.

THE PRETRIAL STAGE

The *rules of civil procedure* govern civil case proceedings. The Federal Rules of Civil Procedure apply in all federal courts. Each state has its own set of rules, but most states' rules are very similar to the Federal Rules of Civil Procedure. In addition, each court usually has its own set of local court rules.

Informal Negotiations The initial attempt to resolve a business dispute is usually informal: a discussion or negotiation among the parties to try to find a solution. If the parties are unable to resolve their dispute, one party often seeks an attorney's advice. Together, the attorney and client may be able to resolve the dispute informally with the other party.

Pleadings The first formal stage of a lawsuit is the *pleading stage.* The plaintiff's attorney initiates a lawsuit by filing a *complaint* in the appropriate court. The complaint states the names of the parties to the action, the basis for the court's subject-matter jurisdiction, the facts on which the plaintiff bases her claim, and the relief the plaintiff seeks. The pleadings prevent surprises at trial; they allow attorneys to prepare arguments to counter the other side's claims. Exhibit 3-1 shows a typical complaint.

service of process

The procedure by which a court delivers a copy of the statement of claim or other legal documents, such as a summons, complaint, or subpoena, to the defendant.

default judgment

Judgment for the plaintiff that occurs when the defendant fails to respond to the complaint.

Service of Process To obtain *in personam* jurisdiction over a defendant and to satisfy due process, a court must notify the defendant of the pending lawsuit. Service of process occurs when a representative of the court serves (delivers) a copy of the complaint and a summons to the defendant.

The complaint explains the basis of the lawsuit to the defendant. The summons tells the defendant that if he or she does not respond to the lawsuit within a certain period of time, the plaintiff will receive a default judgment. A default judgment is a judgment in favor of the plaintiff that occurs when the defendant fails to answer the complaint and the plaintiff's complaint alleges facts that would support such a judgment.

[4] Ibid.

Exhibit 3-1

A Typical Complaint

THE COURT OF COMMON PLEAS
OF CLARK COUNTY, NEVADA

Bob Lyons and Sue Lyons, Plaintiffs

v.

Christine Collins, Defendant

COMPLAINT FOR NEGLIGENCE

Case No. _____

Now come the plaintiffs, Bob Lyons and Sue Lyons, and, for their complaint, allege as follows:

1. Plaintiffs, Bob Lyons and Sue Lyons, both of 825 Havercamp Street, are citizens of Clark County, in the state of Nevada, and defendant, Christine Collins, 947 Rainbow Ave., is a citizen of Clark County in the state of Nevada.

2. On May 1, 2001, the Defendant built a wooden hanging bridge across a stream that runs through the plaintiffs' property at 825 Havercamp Street.

3. Defendant negligently used ropes in the construction of the bridge that were not thick enough to sustain human traffic on the bridge.

4. At approximately 4:00 p.m., on May 20, 2001, the plaintiffs were attempting to carry a box of landscaping stones across the bridge when the ropes broke, and the bridge collapsed, causing plaintiffs to fall seven feet into the stream.

5. As a result of the fall, plaintiff, Bob Lyons, suffered a broken arm, a broken leg, and a skull fracture, incurring $160,000 in medical expenses.

6. As a result of the fall, plaintiff, Sue Lyons, suffered two broken cervical vertebrae, and a skull fracture, incurring $300,000 in medical expenses.

7. As a result of the fall, the landscaping stones, which had cost $1,200, were destroyed.

8. As a result of the foregoing injuries, plaintiff, Bob Lyons, was required to miss eight weeks of work, resulting in a loss of $2,400 in wages.

9. As a result of the foregoing injuries, plaintiff, Sue Lyons, was required to miss twelve weeks of work, resulting in a loss of $3,600 in wages.

WHEREFORE, Plaintiffs demand judgment in the amount of $467,200, plus costs of this action.

> Harlon Elliot
> Attorney for Plaintiff
> 824 Sahara Ave.
> Las Vegas, Nevada, 89117

JURY DEMAND

Plaintiff demands a trial by jury in this matter.

Defendant's Response The defendant responds to the complaint with an **answer**. In this document, the defendant denies, affirms, or claims no knowledge of the accuracy of the plaintiff's allegations.

answer
The response of the defendant to the plaintiff's complaint.

A defendant uses an *affirmative defense* when his or her answer admits that the facts contained in the complaint are accurate but also includes additional facts that justify the defendant's actions and provide a legally sound reason to deny relief to the plaintiff. For example, if a woman sued a man for battery because he punched her in the face, he might claim that he hit her only because she aimed a gun at him and threatened to shoot. His claim that he was acting in self-defense is an affirmative defense.

If the defendant plans to raise an affirmative defense, he must raise it in his answer to give the plaintiff adequate notice. If he fails to raise an affirmative defense in the answer, the judge will likely not allow him to raise it during the trial.

Exhibit 3-2

Defendant's Answer
and Counterclaim

THE COURT OF COMMON PLEAS OF CLARK COUNTY, NEVADA

Bob Lyons and Sue Lyons, Plaintiffs v. Christine Collins, Defendant
ANSWER AND COUNTERCLAIM FOR BREACH OF CONTRACT
Case No. _____

Now comes the defendant, Christine Collins, and answers the complaint of plaintiff herein as follows:

FIRST DEFENSE

1. Admits the allegations in paragraphs 1 and 2.
2. Denies the allegation in paragraph 3.
3. Is without knowledge as to the truth or falsity of the allegations contained in paragraphs 4, 5, 6, 7, 8, and 9.

SECOND DEFENSE

4. If the court believes the allegations contained in paragraph 3, which the defendant expressly denies, plaintiffs should still be denied recovery because they were informed prior to the construction of the bridge that there should be no more than one person on the bridge at one time, and that no individual weighing more than 200 pounds should be allowed to walk on the bridge.

COUNTERCLAIM

5. On April 15, the parties agreed that Defendant would build a wooden hanging bridge across a stream that runs through the defendants' property at 825 Havercamp Street, in exchange for which plaintiffs would pay defendant $2,000 upon completion of construction.
6. On May 1, 2001, the Defendant built the agreed upon ornament, wooden, hanging bridge across a stream that runs through the defendants' property at 825 Havercamp Street, but Plaintiffs failed to pay the agreed upon price for the bridge.
7. By their failure to pay, plaintiffs breached their contract and are liable to defendant for the contract price of $2,000.

WHEREFORE, defendant prays for a judgment dismissing the plaintiffs' complaint, and granting the defendant a judgment against plaintiff in the amount of $2,000 plus costs of this action.

Melissa Davenport
Attorney for Defendant
777 Decatur Ave.
Las Vegas, Nevada 89117

motion to dismiss
A request by the defendant that asks a judge or a court in a civil case to dismiss the case because even if all the allegations are true, the plaintiff is not entitled to any legal relief. Also called *demurrer.*

motion
An application by a party to a judge or a court in a civil case requesting an order in favor of the applicant.

counterclaim
A claim made by the defendant against the plaintiff that is filed along with the defendant's answer.

reply
A response by the plaintiff to the defendant's counterclaim.

Upon receiving the complaint, if the defendant believes that even though all the plaintiff's factual allegations are true, the law does not entitle the plaintiff to a favorable judgment, the defendant may file a motion to dismiss, or *demurrer.* (A motion is a request by a party for the court to do something; in this instance, the request is to dismiss the case.). In deciding whether to grant a motion to dismiss, a judge accepts the facts as stated by the plaintiff and rules on the legal issues in the case. Judges generally grant motions to dismiss only when it appears beyond a doubt that the plaintiff cannot prove any set of facts to justify granting the judgment she seeks.

If the defendant believes he has a claim against the plaintiff, he includes this counterclaim with the answer. As Exhibit 3-2 shows, the form of a counterclaim is identical to the form of a complaint. The defendant states the facts supporting his claim and asks for relief.

If the defendant files a counterclaim, the plaintiff generally files a reply. A reply is an answer to a counterclaim. In the reply, the plaintiff admits, denies, or claims a lack of knowledge as to the accuracy of the facts of the defendant's counterclaim. If the plaintiff plans to use an affirmative defense, she must raise it in the reply.

Pretrial Motions The early pleadings establish the legal and factual issues of the case. After the pleadings, the plaintiff or defendant may file a motion to conclude the case early, eliminate some claims, or gain some advantage. A party may move, or request, that the court do almost anything pertaining to the case. For example, if the plaintiff files a suit about the right to a piece of property, she may move that the court prohibit the current possessor of the land from selling it. Courts may grant or deny such motions at their discretion.

When a party files a motion with the court, the court sends a copy to the opposing attorney, who may respond to the motion, usually by requesting that the judge deny the motion. In many cases, the judge rules on the motion immediately. In other cases, the judge holds a hearing at which the attorneys for both sides argue how the judge should decide the motion.

Two primary pretrial motions are a motion for judgment on the pleadings and a motion for summary judgment. Once the parties file the pleadings, either party can file a **motion for judgment on the pleadings.** The motion is a request for the court to consider that all the facts in the pleadings are true and to apply the law to those facts. The court grants the motion if, after this process, it finds that the only reasonable decision is in favor of the moving party.

Either party can file a **motion for summary judgment** after the discovery process (described below). The motion asserts that no factual disputes exist and that if the judge applied the law to the undisputed facts, her only reasonable decision would be in favor of the moving party. The difference between this motion and a motion for judgment on the pleadings is that in a motion for summary judgment, the moving party may use affidavits (sworn statements from the parties or witnesses), relevant documents, and depositions or interrogatories (a party's sworn answers to written questions) to support his motion. The judge grants the motion if, after examining the evidence, she finds no factual disputes. If, however, she finds any factual issues about which the parties disagree, she denies the motion and sends the case to trial.

Discovery After filing the initial pleadings and motions, the parties gather information from each other through **discovery.** The discovery process enables the parties to learn about facts surrounding the case so that they are not surprised in the courtroom. Three common discovery tools are interrogatories, requests to produce documents, and depositions. ——

Interrogatories are written questions that one party sends to the other to answer under oath. Frequently, a *request to admit certain facts* accompanies interrogatories. Attorneys work with their clients to answer interrogatories and requested admissions of facts.

A **request to produce documents** (or other items) forces the opposing party to produce (turn over) certain information unless it is privileged or irrelevant to the case. Parties may request documents such as photographs, contracts, written estimates, medical records, tax forms, and other government documents. In tort cases, the defendant frequently asks the plaintiff to submit a mental- or physical-examination report.

Finally, the parties may obtain testimony from a witness before trial through a **deposition.** At a deposition, attorneys examine a witness under oath. A court reporter (stenographer) records every word the witness and attorneys speak. Both parties receive a copy of the testimony in document form. Depositions provide information and may also set up inconsistencies between a witness's testimony at the deposition and his testimony at trial. If a party discovers an inconsistency in the testimony of one of the other party's witnesses, she can bring the inconsistency to the fact finder's attention to diminish the witness's credibility. The parties may also use depositions when a witness is elderly, moving, or ill and thus may be unavailable at the time of the trial.

If a party does not comply with requests for discovery, the court may admit the facts the other party sought to discover. Attorneys who feel that certain material is outside the scope of the case often argue that the material is irrelevant to the case. If the court disagrees, however, the party must supply the requested information. Although these discovery tools are important in the United States, many countries do not have a discovery process.

Pretrial Conference A pretrial conference precedes the trial. A **pretrial conference** is an informal meeting of the judge with the attorneys representing the parties. During this conference, the parties try to narrow the legal and factual issues and possibly work out a settlement.

motion for judgment on the pleadings

In a civil case, a request made by either party, after pleadings have been entered, that asks a judge or a court to issue a judgment.

motion for summary judgment

In a civil case, a request made by either party that asks a judge or a court to promptly and expeditiously dispose of a case without a trial. Any evidence or information that would be admissible at trial under the rules of evidence, such as affidavits, interrogatories, depositions, and admissions, may be considered on a motion for summary judgment. A court may hold oral arguments or decide the motion on the basis of the parties' briefs and supporting documentation alone.

discovery

The pretrial phase in a lawsuit during which each party requests relevant documents and other evidence from the other side in an attempt to "discover" pertinent facts and avoid any surprises in the courtroom during the trial. Discovery tools include requests for admissions, interrogatories, depositions, requests for inspection, and document production requests.

interrogatories

A formal set of written questions that one party to a lawsuit asks the opposing party as part of the pretrial discovery process in order to clarify matters of evidence and help determine in advance what facts will be presented at any trial in the case. The questions must be answered in writing under oath or under penalty of perjury within a specified time. Also called *requests for further information.*

request to produce documents

In a lawsuit, the right of a party to examine and copy the opposing party's papers that are relevant to the case. A legal request may be made and the categories of the documents must be stated to allow the other party to know what documents he or she must produce.

deposition

A pretrial sworn and recorded testimony of a witness that is acquired out of court with no judge present.

pretrial conference

An informal meeting of the judge with the attorneys representing the parties before the actual trial begins.

voir dire

The process of questioning potential jurors to ensure that the jury will be made up of nonbiased individuals.

peremptory challenge

In a jury trial, the right of the plaintiff and the defendant in jury selection to reject, without stating a reason, a certain number of potential jurors who appear to have an unfavorable bias.

If the parties cannot reach a settlement, the attorneys and the judge discuss the administrative details of the trial: its length, witnesses, and any pretrial stipulations of fact or law to which the parties agree.

THE TRIAL

If a plaintiff seeks at least $20 in monetary damages, the Seventh Amendment to the U.S. Constitution entitles the parties to a jury trial. The plaintiff must, however, demand a jury trial in her or his complaint. Some types of trials require 12-person juries, but 6-person juries hear most civil cases. If the plaintiff seeks an equitable remedy (an injunction or other court order) or if the parties have waived their right to a jury, a judge serves as the fact finder in the case.

Trials have six stages: jury selection, opening statements, examination of witnesses, closing arguments, conference on jury instructions, and posttrial motions. The following sections describe these stages.

Jury Selection The jury selection process begins when the clerk of the courts randomly selects a number of potential jurors from the citizens within the court's jurisdiction. Once the potential jurors have reported for jury duty, the voir dire, or jury selection, process begins. The voir dire process selects the jurors who will decide the case, as well as two or three "alternate jurors" who will watch the trial and be available to replace any juror who, for some legitimate reason, must leave jury duty before the trial ends.

During voir dire, the judge and/or attorneys question potential jurors to determine whether they are able to render an unbiased opinion in the case. If a potential juror's response to a question indicates that she or he may be biased, either attorney may challenge, or ask the court to remove, that potential juror "for cause." For example, a lawyer could challenge for cause a potential juror who was a college roommate of the defendant. In most states, each party has a certain number of peremptory challenges. These peremptory challenges allow a party to challenge a certain number of potential jurors without giving a reason.

Peremptory challenges, however, may lead to abuse. For example, in the past, attorneys have used peremptory challenges to eliminate a certain class, ethnic group, or gender from the jury. In the 1986 case *Batson v. Kentucky*,[5] the U.S. Supreme Court ruled that race-based peremptory challenges in criminal cases violate the equal protection clause of the Fourteenth Amendment to the U.S. Constitution. (Chapter 5 discusses the amendments to the Constitution in more detail.) The Supreme Court later extended the ban on race-based challenges to civil cases. In Case 3-2, the U.S. Supreme Court addressed the issue of whether the equal protection clause covers gender-based challenges.

[5] 476 U.S. 79 (1986).

 CASE 3-2

J.E.B. v. ALABAMA, EX. REL. T.B.
UNITED STATES SUPREME COURT
114 S. Ct. 1419 (1994)

FACTS: *The State of Alabama filed a complaint for paternity and child support against J.E.B. on behalf of T.B., the unwed mother of a minor child. The court called a panel of 12 males and 24 females as potential jurors. Only 10 males remained after three individuals were removed for cause. The state used its peremptory challenges to remove nine male jurors and J.E.B. removed the tenth, resulting in an* *all-female jury. The trial court rejected J.E.B.'s objection to the gender-based challenges, and the jury found J.E.B. to be the father. J.E.B. appealed, and the court of appeals affirmed the trial court's ruling that the equal protection clause of the Fourteenth Amendment does not prohibit gender-based challenges. The Alabama Supreme Court declined to hear the appeal, and J.E.B. appealed to the U.S. Supreme Court.*

ISSUE Does the equal protection clause prohibit removing possible jurors during voir dire on the basis of their gender?

REASONING: Justice Blackmun delivered the opinion of the Court:

> Discrimination in jury selection, whether based on race or on gender, causes harm to the litigants, the community, and the individual jurors who are wrongfully excluded from participation in the judicial process. The litigants are harmed by the risk that the prejudice which motivated the discriminatory selection of the jury will infect the entire proceedings. The community is harmed by the State's participation in the perpetuation of invidious group stereotypes and the inevitable loss of confidence in our judicial system that state-sanctioned discrimination in the courtroom engenders.

As with race-based *Batson* claims, a party alleging gender discrimination must make a prima facie showing of intentional discrimination before the party exercising the challenge is required to explain the basis for the strike. When an explanation is required, it need not rise to the level of a "for cause" challenge; rather, it merely must be based on a juror characteristic other than gender and the proffered explanation may not be pretextual.

Equal opportunity to participate in the fair administration of justice is fundamental to our democratic system. It reaffirms the promise of equality under the law—that all citizens, regardless of race, ethnicity, or gender, have the chance to take part directly in our democracy. When persons are excluded from participation in our democratic processes solely because of race or gender, this promise of equality dims, and the integrity of our judicial system is jeopardized.

DECISION AND REMEDY: Yes, to remove a potential juror based solely on gender is a violation of the equal protection clause. The court of appeals decision was reversed, and the case was remanded in favor of J.E.B.

SIGNIFICANCE OF THE CASE: This case extended protection against being peremptorily removed from a jury on the basis of gender alone, thus putting gender protections on par with the protections for race and ethnicity. Although historically the extension of the Fourteenth Amendment's equal protection clause to gender has been used to protect women's equal rights, the court found that the clause was equally applicable when a man's equal rights were being violated.

CRITICAL THINKING

The defendant was contesting the removal of males from the jury. Does this fact affect your assessment of the quality of the Court's reasoning? Explain.

ETHICAL DECISION MAKING

Which ethical norm does the case decision serve?

The voir dire process has become more sophisticated over time. In cases involving significant amounts of money, rather than relying on their instinct or experience during jury selection, attorneys use professional jury selection services to identify demographic data to help select ideal jurors. Jury selection firms also provide additional services, including **mock trials,** in which mock jurors who are demographically similar to the real jurors hear the arguments and give feedback prior to the case, and **shadow juries,** in which shadow jurors sit in during the actual trial and deliberate at the end of each day to evaluate for the attorneys how each side is doing. Critics argue that jury selection services give an unfair advantage to one side when only one party can afford these services.

Opening Statements Once the attorneys have impaneled, or selected, a jury, the case begins with opening statements. Each party's attorney explains to the judge and jury what facts he or she intends to prove, the legal conclusions to which these facts lead, and how the fact finder should decide the case based on those facts.

The Examination of Witnesses and Presentation of Evidence Following opening statements, the plaintiff and defendant, in turn, present their cases-in-chief by examining witnesses and presenting evidence. The plaintiff has the burden of proving the case, meaning that if neither side presents a convincing case, the fact finder must rule in favor of the defendant. Thus, the plaintiff presents her case first.

mock trial
A contrived or imitation trial, with a jury created by the attorneys to assist them in preparing for the actual trial by enabling them to test theories, experiment with arguments, and try to predict the outcome of the real trial.

shadow jury
Jury selection firms set up imitation juries who sit in during the actual trial and deliberate at the end of each day to evaluate for the attorneys how each side is doing.

The procedure for each witness is the same. First, the plaintiff's attorney questions the witness in *direct examination.* The plaintiff's attorney asks the witness questions to elicit facts that support the plaintiff's case-in-chief. Questions must relate to matters about which the witness has direct knowledge. Attorneys cannot elicit "hearsay" from the witnesses. *Hearsay* is testimony about what a witness heard another person say. Hearsay is impermissible because the opposing attorney cannot question the person who made the original statement to determine the statement's veracity.

The federal rules of evidence also prohibit attorneys from asking leading questions. Leading questions are questions that imply a specific answer. For example, an attorney cannot ask a witness, "Did the defendant come to your office and ask you to purchase stock from him?" Instead, attorneys must ask questions such as, "When did you first encounter the defendant?"

After direct examination, opposing counsel may *cross-examine* the witness. Opposing counsel, however, may ask only questions related to the witness's direct examination. On cross-examination, attorneys can ask leading questions. Attorneys try to show inconsistencies in the witness's testimony, cast doubt on the claims of the plaintiff's case, and elicit information to support the defendant's case.

After cross-examination, the plaintiff's attorney may conduct a *redirect examination,* a series of questions aimed at repairing damage done by the cross-examination. At the judge's discretion, opposing counsel has an opportunity to *re-cross* the witness to question her testimony on redirect examination. The parties follow this procedure for each of the plaintiff's witnesses.

Immediately following the plaintiff's presentation of her case, the defendant may move for a **directed verdict.** This motion is a request for the court to direct a verdict for the defendant because even if the jury accepted all the evidence and testimony presented by the plaintiff as true, the jury would still have no legal basis for a decision in favor of the plaintiff. The federal court system refers to a motion for a directed verdict as a *motion for a judgment as a matter of law.* Courts rarely grant motions for a directed verdict because plaintiffs almost always present at least *some* evidence to support each element of the cause of action.

If the court denies the defendant's motion for a directed verdict, the defendant then presents his case. The parties question the defendant's witnesses in the same manner as they questioned the plaintiff's witnesses, except that the defendant's attorney conducts direct and redirect examination and the plaintiff's attorney conducts cross-examination and re-cross-examination.

Closing Arguments After the defendant's case, the attorneys present closing arguments. In closing arguments, each attorney summarizes evidence from the trial in a manner consistent with his or her client's case. The plaintiff's attorney presents her closing argument first, followed by the defendant's attorney, and the plaintiff has the option to present a rebuttal of the defendant's closing argument.

Jury Instructions In a jury trial, the judge "charges the jury" by instructing the jurors on how the law applies to the facts of the case. Both sides' attorneys submit statements to the judge explaining how they believe she should charge the jury. The judge's instructions are usually a combination of both sides' suggestions.

After the judge charges the jury, the jurors retire to the jury room to deliberate. Once they reach a decision, they return to the courtroom, where the judge reads their verdict and discharges them from their duty. Trial procedures in the United States are quite different from trial procedures in other countries, as the nearby Global Context box illustrates.

POSTTRIAL MOTIONS

Once the trial ends, the party who received the favorable verdict files a *motion for a judgment in accordance with the verdict.* Until the judge enters the judgment, the court has not issued a legally binding decision for the case.

The party who loses at trial has a number of available options. One option is to file a *motion for a judgment notwithstanding the verdict,* or *judgment non obstante verdicto,* asking the judge to issue a judgment contrary to the jury's verdict. To grant the motion, the judge must find that, when viewing the evidence in the light most favorable to the nonmoving party, a reasonable jury could not have found in favor of that party. In other words, as a matter of law, the judge must

directed verdict

A ruling by the judge, after the plaintiff has put forward his or her case but before any evidence is put forward by the defendant, in favor of the defendant because the plaintiff has failed to present the minimum amount of evidence necessary to establish his or her claim.

Trials in Japan

Civil procedure in Japan differs significantly from American civil procedure. The Japanese legal system has no juries and no distinct pretrial stage. Instead, a trial is a series of discrete meetings between the parties and the judge. At the first meeting, the parties identify the most critical and contested issues. They choose one and recess to gather evidence and marshal arguments on the issue.

At the next meeting, the judge rules on the chosen issue. If the judge decides against the plaintiff, the case is over. If the plaintiff wins, the process continues with the next issue. The process continues until the plaintiff loses an issue or until the judge decides all issues in the plaintiff's favor, resulting in a verdict for the plaintiff.

In addition, the discovery process in the Japanese court system is not as simple as it is in the United States. To obtain evidence, parties must convince the judge to order others to testify or produce documents. The judge can fine or jail parties who refuse to comply with such orders. Additionally, if a party does not comply with the judge's requests for discovery, the judge may admit the facts the other party sought to discover.

determine that the trial did not produce sufficient evidence to support the jury's verdict. This motion is similar to a motion for a directed verdict, except the parties cannot make this motion until *after* the jury issues a verdict. The federal court system refers to this motion as a *motion for judgment as a matter of law.*

The losing party can also file a *motion for a new trial.* Judges grant motions for a new trial only if they believe the jury's decision was clearly erroneous but they are not sure that the other side should necessarily have won the case. A judge often grants a motion for a new trial when the parties discover new evidence, when the judge made an erroneous ruling, or when misconduct during the trial may have prevented the jury from reaching a fair decision.

APPELLATE PROCEDURE

Either party may appeal the judge's decision on posttrial motions or on her or his final judgment. Sometimes, both parties appeal the same decision. For example, if a jury awarded the plaintiff $10,000 in damages, the plaintiff and the defendant may both appeal the amount of the judgment. Appellate courts, however, reverse only about 1 out of every 10 trial court decisions on appeal.

To be eligible for appeal, the losing party must argue that a *prejudicial error of law* occurred during the trial. A **prejudicial error** is a mistake so significant that it likely affected the outcome of the case. For example, a prejudicial error could occur if the judge improperly allowed hearsay evidence that enabled the plaintiff to prove an element of her case.

To appeal a case, the attorney for the appealing party (the appellant) files a notice of appeal with the clerk of the trial court within a prescribed time. The clerk then forwards the record of appeal to the appeals court. The record of appeal typically contains a number of items: the pleadings, a trial transcript, copies of the trial exhibits, copies of the judge's rulings on the parties' motions, the attorneys' arguments, jury instructions, the jury's verdict, posttrial motions, and the judgment order.

The appellant then files a **brief,** or written argument, with the court. Appellants file briefs to explain why the judgment in the lower court was erroneous and why the appeals court should reverse it. The attorney for the party who won in the lower court (the appellee) files an answering brief. The appellant may then file a reply brief in response to the appellee's brief. Generally, however, appellants do not file reply briefs.

The appeals court then usually allows the attorneys to present oral arguments before the court. The court considers these arguments, reviews the record of the case, and renders a decision.

There are four possible decisions an appellate court can render. The court can accept the lower court's judgment by **affirming** its decision. Alternatively, the appellate court may conclude that the lower court's decision was correct but the remedy was inappropriate, in which case it **modifies** the remedy. If the appellate court decides that the lower court was incorrect, it **reverses** the lower court's decision. Finally, if the appeals court thinks the lower court committed an error but does not know how that error affected the outcome of the case, it **remands** the case to the lower court for a new trial.

prejudicial error
An error of law that is so significant that it affects the outcome of the case.

brief
A written legal argument, which a party presents to a court, that explains why that party to the case should prevail. Also called *factum.*

affirm
An appellate court decision that accepts a lower court's judgment in a case that has been appealed.

modify
An appellate court decision that grants an alternative remedy in a case; rendered when the court finds that the decision of the lower court was correct but the remedy was not.

reverse
An appellate court decision that overturns the judgment of a lower court, concluding that the lower court was incorrect and its verdict cannot be allowed to stand.

remand
An appellate court decision that returns a case to the trial court for a new trial or for limited hearing on a specified subject matter; rendered when the court decides that an error was committed that may have affected the outcome of a case.

An appellate court usually has a bench with at least three judges. Appellate courts do not have juries; rather, the judges decide the case by majority vote. One of the judges who votes with the majority records the court's decision and its reasons in the *majority opinion.* These decisions have precedential value—that is, judges use these prior appellate court decisions to make decisions in future cases. Also, these decisions establish new guidelines in the law that all citizens must follow. If a judge agrees with the majority's decision but for different reasons, she may write a *concurring opinion,* stating the reasons she used to reach the majority's conclusion. Finally, judges disagreeing with the majority may write a *dissenting opinion,* giving their reasons for reaching a contrary conclusion. Attorneys arguing that a court should change the law frequently cite dissenting opinions from previous cases in their briefs. Likewise, appellate judges who change the law often cite dissenting opinions from past cases.

For most cases, only one appeal is available. In states with both an intermediate and a final court of appeals, a losing party may appeal from the intermediate appellate court to the state supreme court. In a limited number of cases, the losing party can appeal the decision of a state supreme court or a federal circuit court of appeals to the U.S. Supreme Court.

Appeal to the U.S. Supreme Court Every year thousands of individuals file appeals with the U.S. Supreme Court, but the Court hears, on average, only 80 to 90 cases each year. To file an appeal to the U.S. Supreme Court, a party files a petition asking the Court to issue a writ of certiorari, an order to the lower court to send to the Supreme Court the record of the case. The Court issues very few writs.

The justices review petitions and issue a writ only when at least four justices vote to hear the case (the *rule of four*). The court is most likely to issue a writ in four instances: (1) The case presents a substantial federal question that the Supreme Court has not yet addressed; (2) multiple circuit courts of appeal have decided the issue of the case in different ways; (3) a state court of last resort has ruled that a federal law is invalid or has upheld a state law that may violate federal law; or (4) a federal court has ruled that an act of Congress is unconstitutional. If the Supreme Court does not issue a writ of certiorari, the lower court's decision stands.

writ of certiorari

A Supreme Court order, issued after the Court decides to hear an appeal, mandating that the lower court send to the Supreme Court the record of the appealed case.

Alternative Dispute Resolution

alternative dispute resolution (ADR)

The resolution of legal problems through methods other than litigation.

Many firms find that using alternative dispute resolution (ADR) methods to resolve their legal problems offers many benefits. The term *ADR* refers to the resolution of legal disputes through methods other than litigation, such as negotiation, mediation, arbitration, summary jury trials, minitrials, neutral case evaluations, and private trials.

Why might a business prefer ADR to litigation? First, ADR methods are generally faster and cheaper. According to the National Arbitration Forum, the average time from filing a complaint to judgment through litigation is 25 months.[6] Because ADR is faster, it is usually cheaper. According to the American Intellectual Property Law Association, for cases valued in the $1 million to $25 million range, the average total cost of patent litigation for each party through the close of discovery is $1.9 million.[7] Through the end of trial, the average cost to each party is $3.5 million. Thus, if a party can resolve a dispute through alternative dispute resolution, this can save significant money.

Second, a business may wish to avoid the uncertainty associated with a jury decision; many forms of ADR give the participants more control over the resolution of the dispute. Specifically, the parties can select a neutral third party, frequently a person with expertise in the area of the dispute, to help facilitate resolution of the case. Third, a business may wish to avoid setting a precedent through a court decision. Fourth, a business may prefer ADR because it is confidential. Fifth, because many forms of ADR are less adversarial than litigation, ADR allows the parties to preserve a business relationship.

[6] National Arbitration Forum, *Business-to-Business Mediation/Arbitration vs. Litigation: What Courts, Statistics, & Public Perceptions Show about How Commercial Mediation and Commercial Arbitration Compare to the Litigation System,* January 2005, p. 3.

[7] AIPLA, *Report of the Economic Survey,* pp. 1-109–1-110.

Courts also generally support the use of ADR, which alleviates some of the pressure on the overwhelming court dockets. Congress has recognized the benefits of ADR methods through its enactment of the Alternative Dispute Resolution Act of 1998. This act requires that federal district courts have an ADR program along with a set of rules regarding the program. Additional evidence of congressional support for ADR comes from the passage of the Administrative Dispute Resolution Act, which mandates that federal agencies create internal ADR programs.

Primary Forms of ADR

NEGOTIATION

Many business managers make frequent use of negotiation, a bargaining process in which disputing parties interact informally, either with or without lawyers, to attempt to resolve their dispute. No neutral third party is involved. Thus, negotiation differs from other methods of dispute resolution because the parties maintain high levels of autonomy. Some courts require that parties negotiate before they bring their dispute to trial.

Before negotiation begins, each side must determine its goals for the negotiation. Moreover, each side must identify the information it is willing to give the other party. Because negotiation generally occurs in every case before a more formal dispute resolution method is chosen, negotiation is not necessarily considered an alternative to litigation.

negotiation
A bargaining process in which disputing parties interact informally to attempt to resolve their dispute.

MEDIATION

An extension of negotiation is mediation. In mediation, the disputing parties select a neutral party to help facilitate communication and suggest ways for the parties to solve their dispute. Therefore, the distinguishing feature of mediation is that the parties voluntarily select a neutral third party to help them work together to resolve the dispute. The neutral third party frequently has expertise in the area of the dispute.

Mediation begins when parties select a mediator. Each party then typically writes a mediation brief to explain why it should win. An important feature of mediation is that it allows multiple parties to participate in a dispute. The parties take turns explaining the dispute. One of the mediator's main goals is to help each party listen carefully to the opposing party's concerns. The mediator asks the parties to identify any additional concerns. The parties begin generating alternatives or solutions for the disputed points. The mediator helps the parties evaluate the alternatives by comparing the alternatives with the disputed points and interests identified earlier. Finally, the mediator assists the parties in agreeing to a solution.

The mediation concludes when the agreement between the parties is reached. The agreement is then usually put into the form of a contract and signed by the parties. The mediator may participate in the drafting of the contract. If one of the parties does not follow the agreement, that party can be sued for breach of contract. However, parties typically abide by the agreement because they helped to create it.

If mediation is not successful, the parties can turn to litigation or arbitration to resolve their dispute. However, nothing said during the mediation can be used in another dispute resolution method; the mediation process is confidential.

mediation
A type of intensive negotiation in which disputing parties select a neutral party to help facilitate communication and suggest ways for the parties to solve their dispute.

Advantages and Disadvantages of Mediation The primary advantage of mediation is that it helps the disputing parties preserve their relationships, which is especially attractive for businesses with a working relationship they would like to continue. A second advantage is the possibility of finding creative solutions. The goal of mediation is to find a compromise between the needs of various parties, rather than to find one party right and all the others wrong. A third advantage is the high level of autonomy mediation gives the participants. Instead of a neutral third party pronouncing a solution, the interested parties work together to create a solution, and this can make them more committed to following the agreement afterward.

These benefits can obviously be very worthwhile. However, we need to pay attention to the critics of the mediation process. One critique of mediation is that it creates an image of equal

parties working toward an equitable solution and thereby hides power imbalances that can lead to the party with greater power getting an agreement of greater benefit. A second critique is that some people who enter mediation have no intention of finding a solution but, instead, use mediation as a tactic to draw out the dispute.

Uses of Mediation Mediation is most commonly used in collective bargaining disputes, because it allows the workers to maintain a relationship with their employer while still having their needs addressed. Under the National Labor Relations Act (NLRA), a union must contact the Federal Mediation and Conciliation Services to attempt to mediate its demands before beginning a strike to achieve higher wages or better working hours.

Similarly, the Equal Employment Opportunity Commission (EEOC) encourages the mediation of employment discrimination claims. The EEOC has a mediation program that uses mediators employed by the EEOC, as well as external mediators trained in mediation and discrimination law. Mediation is also used extensively in environmental law, because environmental disputes are often best served by finding a compromise between the frequently multiple parties.

ARBITRATION

arbitration

A type of alternative dispute resolution wherein disputes are submitted for resolution to private nonofficial persons selected in a manner provided by law or the agreement of the parties.

One of the most frequently used methods of dispute resolution is arbitration, the resolution of a dispute by a neutral third party outside the judicial setting. Arbitration is frequently used in disagreements between employees and employers, and it is increasingly being used between consumers and businesses. Arbitration is often a voluntary process in that parties have a contractual agreement to arbitrate any disputes. This agreement may stipulate how the arbitrator will be selected and how the hearing will be administered.

Lawyers, professors, and other professionals typically serve as arbitrators. The general qualifications for being an arbitrator are honesty, impartiality, and subject-matter competence. Additionally, arbitrators are expected to follow the Arbitrator's Code of Ethics. Typically, parties choose arbitrators from the Federal Mediation and Conciliation Services (FMCS), a government agency, or the American Arbitration Association (AAA), a private, nonprofit organization.

The Arbitration Hearing The arbitration hearing is similar to a trial. Both parties present their case to a neutral third party; parties may represent themselves or use legal counsel. During this presentation, the parties may introduce witnesses and documentation, cross-examine the witnesses, and offer closing statements. The fact finder offers a legally binding decision. However, arbitration is also different from a trial in several ways. First, the arbitrator often takes a much more active role in an arbitration hearing than a judge takes in a trial, and the arbitrator can question witnesses. Second, no official written record of the hearing is kept in most arbitrations. Third, the rules of evidence applicable in a trial are typically relaxed in arbitration.

The Arbitrator's Award The arbitrator typically provides a decision within 30 days of the arbitration hearing. The arbitrator's decision is called an *award,* even if no monetary compensation is awarded. The arbitrator's decision differs from a judge's decision in several ways. The arbitrator does not have to state any findings of fact, conclusions of law, or reasons to support the award, and he or she is not as bound by precedent as a judge is. Also, because the arbitrator was hired to resolve a dispute between two parties, the arbitrator is more likely to make a compromise ruling instead of a win-lose ruling.

Unlike the case in most other forms of ADR, the arbitrator's decision is legally binding. In certain cases, a decision may be appealed to the district court. However, few of these cases are appealed. The courts give extreme deference to arbitrators' decisions.

The Federal Arbitration Act (FAA), the federal law enacted to encourage the use of arbitration, explicitly lists four grounds on which an arbitrator's award may be set aside: (1) The award was the result of corruption, fraud, or other undue means; (2) the arbitrator displayed bias or corruption; (3) the arbitrator refused to postpone the hearing despite sufficient cause, refused to hear relevant evidence, or otherwise misbehaved to prejudice the rights of one of the parties; (4) the arbitrator exceeded his or her authority or failed to use that authority to make a mutual, final, and

definite award. In a 2008 decision, the U.S. Supreme Court held that these grounds are the only grounds for appeal and that the parties in an arbitration proceeding do not have ability to give the courts additional grounds to set aside a decision.[8]

Consequently, in the United States, arbitration decisions are generally upheld. In fact, the Fifth Circuit recently held that "manifest disregard of the law and contrary to public policy are the only nonstatutory bases recognized by this circuit for the vacatur of an arbitration award."[9]

Advantages and Disadvantages of Arbitration Arbitration may be preferable to litigation for several reasons. First, arbitration is more efficient and less expensive. Second, parties have more control over the process of dispute resolution through arbitration. They choose the arbitrator and determine how formal the process will be. Third, the parties can choose someone to serve as the arbitrator who has expertise in the specific subject matter. Fourth, the arbitrator has greater flexibility in decision making than a judge has. Unlike judges, who are bound by precedent, arbitrators generally do not have to offer reasons for their decisions.

However, arbitration is not without its critics. First, arbitration panels are being used more frequently, resulting in a loss of some of the prior advantages of arbitration, such as efficiency and lower cost. Second, because appealing an arbitration award is so difficult, some scholars argue that injustice is more likely to occur. Third, some individuals are concerned that by agreeing to give up one's right to litigate, one may be losing important civil rights or giving up important potential remedies without really understanding which rights are being given up. Fourth, some scholars are afraid that if more and more employers and institutions turn to mandatory arbitration, it will become more like litigation. Fifth, some scholars are concerned about the privacy associated with arbitration. Companies and employers are able to "hide" their disputes through arbitration.

Binding Arbitration Clause Given the benefits associated with arbitration, parties may voluntarily submit their cases to arbitration. The primary method of securing arbitration is through a binding arbitration clause, a provision in a contract that mandates that all disputes arising under the contract must be settled by arbitration. The clause also typically states how the arbitrator will be selected. If parties have a binding arbitration agreement, the parties *must* resolve the dispute through arbitration. Both federal and state courts must uphold agreements to arbitrate. The Case Nugget on page 66 illustrates the courts' willingness to enforce binding arbitration agreements.

A constraint on binding arbitration clauses is that they must be drafted in such a way as to ensure that the courts do not see them as being unconscionable. An *unconscionable contract provision* has been defined as one in which the terms are "manifestly unfair or oppressive and are dictated by a dominant party."[10] The doctrine has been used most often to strike down binding arbitration clauses in consumer and employment contracts. Exhibit 3-3 offers tips on creating a binding arbitration clause.

binding arbitration clause
A contract provision mandating that all disputes arising under the contract must be settled by arbitration.

Other ADR Methods

MED-ARB

Med-arb is a dispute resolution process in which the parties agree to start out in mediation and, if the mediation is unsuccessful on one or more points, to move on to arbitration. In some cases, the same neutral third party may participate in both the mediation and the arbitration. Some critics argue that if parties know that the mediator may become the ultimate decision maker, they will be less likely to disclose information during the mediation stage. Others argue that having the same neutral mediator-arbitrator offers faster resolution because the third party is familiar with the facts of the case.[11]

med-arb
A type of dispute resolution process in which both parties agree to start out in mediation and, if unsuccessful, to move on to arbitration.

[8] *Hall Street Associates v. Mattell,* 2008 U.S. LEXIS 2911.

[9] *Kergosien et al. v. Ocean Energy, Inc.,* 390 F.3d 346 (5th Cir. 2004).

[10] *Farris v. County of Camden,* 61 F. Supp. 2d 307, 341 (D. N.J. 1999).

[11] See Gerald F. Phillips, *Same Neutral Med-Arb: What Does the Future Hold?,* Dispute Resolution Journal 60 (May-July 2005), p. 24

CASE Nugget

The Validity of Binding Arbitration Agreements

Preston v. Ferrer
United States Supreme Court

128 S. Ct. 978 (2008)

Under the FAA, is an administrative proceeding the same as a trial?

It has long been held that under the FAA, even if state statutes refer a state law controversy initially to a judicial forum, if the parties have agreed to submit that dispute to arbitration, the dispute must be arbitrated. Until 2008, however, the question existed of whether the same rule would apply when the state law directed that the first mode of resolution be an administrative proceeding rather than a court hearing. In this case, however, the U.S. Supreme Court ruled that for purposes of the FAA, an administrative proceeding was the equivalent of a judicial proceeding. In *Preston v. Ferrer*, the two had included a binding arbitration agreement in a contract for Preston to represent Ferrer. When Preston attempted to collect his fees, a question arose as to whether the matter had to be resolved by the California Labor Commission, which had jurisdiction over issues arising under the California Talent Agencies Act. The high court agreed with Ferrer that the dispute must be resolved through arbitration because the FAA preempted the state law. Even if a state law provides that an administrative forum has jurisdiction over a specific type of dispute, a binding arbitration agreement will supersede the forum declared by the state law.

Exhibit 3-3

Tips for Creating a Binding Arbitration Clause

Overall, make sure the clause treats both parties fairly.

1. Be clear and unmistakable about what you wish to arbitrate.
2. The arbitration clause must be bilateral.
3. State explicitly which party will pay the arbitrator's fees, and make sure that it will not cost the employee more to arbitrate than it would have cost to litigate. Specify how the arbitrator will be selected.
4. Spell out the costs associated with the arbitration.
5. Avoid limitations on the remedies available to the parties.
6. Consider other potential parties when determining where to hold the arbitration.

SUMMARY JURY TRIAL

summary jury trial
An abbreviated trial that leads to a nonbinding jury verdict.

A **summary jury trial** is an abbreviated trial that leads to a nonbinding jury verdict. Two advantages are inherent in this method of dispute resolution. First, it is quick; a summary jury trial lasts only a day. Second, because a jury offers a verdict, both parties get a chance to see how their case would fare before a jury of their peers. Each judge can set his or her own rules. The judge advises the jury on the law, and each party's lawyer presents an opening statement and a limited amount of evidence before the jury. The lawyers have limited time for their presentations, and witnesses do not usually testify. The jury reaches an advisory verdict, although the jury does not know that its verdict is nonbinding. The parties then enter into a settlement conference, where they decide either to accept the jury verdict, reject the verdict, or settle on some compromise. Approximately 95 percent of cases are settled at this time. However, if the case is not settled, it will go to a regular trial. At that trial, nothing from the summary jury trial is admissible as evidence.

MINITRIAL

A minitrial is similar to arbitration and mediation because it involves a neutral third party. However, despite the presence of a neutral third party, business representatives of the disputing corporations participate and have settlement authority. Lawyers for each side present their arguments before these executives and the neutral adviser, who then offers an opinion as to what the verdict would be if the case went to trial. The neutral adviser's opinion, like the jury's verdict in the summary jury trial, is not binding. Next, the corporate executives discuss settlement options. If they reach an agreement, they enter into a contract that reflects the terms of the settlement.

minitrial

A type of conflict resolution in which lawyers for each side present their arguments to a neutral adviser, who then offers an opinion as to what the verdict would be if the case went to trial. This decision is not binding.

EARLY NEUTRAL CASE EVALUATION

With *early neutral case evaluation,* the parties select a neutral third party and explain their respective positions to this neutral, who then evaluates the strengths and weaknesses of the case. The parties use this evaluation to reach a settlement. Eighteen federal district courts currently use early neutral case evaluation.[12]

PRIVATE TRIALS

Several states allow private trials, an ADR method in which a referee is selected and paid by the disputing parties to offer a legally binding judgment in a dispute. The referees do not have to have any specific training; however, because retired judges often serve as referees, this method is often referred to as "rent-a-judge." The cases are often heard privately to ensure confidentiality. The referee writes a report and files it with the trial judge, but a dissatisfied party reserves the right to request a new trial before a trial court judge. Private jury trials with experienced jury members are becoming more popular today as well. Private trials have been criticized because they seem to provide faster and cheaper justice for those who can afford the initial fee and because they "hide" the trial from the public eye.

private trial

An ADR method in which a referee is selected and paid by the disputing parties to offer a legally binding judgment in a dispute.

[12] Michael H. Diamant et al., *Strategies for Mediation, Arbitration, and Other Forms of Alternative Dispute Resolution,* SK074 ALI-ABA 205 (2005) [citing the CPR Institute for Dispute Resolution, www.cprador.org].

----> SUMMARY

Jurisdiction	*In personam jurisdiction* is the power of a court to render a decision affecting a person's legal rights.
	Subject-matter jurisdiction is the power of a court to render a decision in a particular type of case. The three forms of subject matter jurisdiction are state, exclusive federal, and concurrent.
Venue	*Venue* is the geographic location of the trial.
The Structure of the Court System	The U.S. has two parallel court structures: the state and federal systems. The federal structure has *district courts* (trial courts), *circuit courts of appeal,* and the *U.S. Supreme Court.* The state court structure varies by state but generally includes courts of common pleas (trial courts), state courts of appeal, and a state supreme court.
Threshold Requirements	*Standing:* For a party to have the legal right to file a case, the outcome of the case must personally affect that party.
	Case or controversy: There must be an issue before the court that a judicial decision is capable of resolving. Parties cannot ask the judge for an "advisory opinion."
	Ripeness: The case cannot be moot; it must be ready for a decision to be made.
Steps in Civil Litigation	The stages of a civil trial include pretrial, trial, posttrial, and appellate stages.
	Pretrial includes consultation with attorneys, pleadings, the discovery process, and the pretrial conference.
	The *trial* begins with jury selection, followed by opening statements, the plaintiff's case, the defendant's case, closing arguments, jury instructions, jury deliberations, the jury's verdict, and the judgment.

After the trial, parties may file *posttrial motions.*

The parties may then file *appeals* to the appropriate appellate court and, in some cases, to the U.S. Supreme Court.

Alternative Dispute Resolution *Alternative dispute resolution* is a way to settle problems without having to go to a costly and time-consuming trial.

Primary Forms of ADR The primary forms of ADR are *negotiation, mediation,* and *arbitration.*

Other ADR Methods Other methods of ADR include *med-arb, summary jury trials, minitrials, early neutral case evaluation,* and **private trials.**

⋯▸ Point/Counterpoint

Should Companies Be Allowed to Include Binding Arbitration Clauses in Consumer Contracts?

YES	NO
Arbitration is a much faster way to resolve a likely small dispute. Through the discovery process, a defendant could draw out a case for two to three years before the case would actually go to trial. Thus, the consumer benefits from the binding arbitration clause by forcing the defendant to resolve the dispute quickly.	Arbitration may require that the consumer pay more up-front costs to begin the dispute resolution process. For example, the consumer may have to pay for the costs of the arbitrator. To file a complaint, a consumer has to pay filing fees only, which cost around $150. To file a claim through the American Arbitration Association, a consumer has to pay between $500 and $1,000, and the consumer is required to advance the arbitrator's fees.
According to a recent study by Ernst & Young, 55 percent of consumer arbitrations were resolved in the consumer's favor.* Another study suggested that 93 percent of people who participated in arbitration thought that they were treated fairly.• Consumers receive fair and fast treatment through mandatory arbitration.	Many consumers are not likely to read all the fine print when applying for a credit card or purchasing a service. A consumer has no bargaining power to remove a mandatory arbitration clause from the contract; consequently, the consumer has no choice. It is unfair to force a consumer to submit a dispute to arbitration when she or he has no power to bargain regarding that aspect of the sales or service contract.
Consumers have a choice as to whether to purchase a good or service, and in some cases the purchase may include a requirement on how disputes will be resolved. If a consumer is opposed to a mandatory arbitration clause, the consumer can purchase the good or service from another provider.	Finally, because arbitration is secret, a company can "hide" its disputes from the general public. The public exposure associated with lawsuits encourages companies to better respond to and resolve disputes.
In conclusion, companies should be permitted to include binding arbitration clauses in their consumer contracts.	In conclusion, consumers are harmed more than helped by binding arbitration clauses in consumer contracts.

*Ernst & Young, "Outcomes of Arbitration: An Empirical Study of Consumer Lending Cases," www.adrforum.com/rcontrol/documents/ResearchStudiesAndStatistics/2005ErnstAndYoung.pdf.

•"Report to the Securities and Exchange Commission Regarding Arbitrator Conflict Disclosure Requirements in NASD and NYSE Securities Arbitrations," www.nyse.com/pdfs/arbconflict.pdf.

Questions & Problems

1. Explain the two types of jurisdiction that a court must have to hear a case and render a binding decision over the parties.

2. Explain the differences between trial courts and appellate courts.

3. Identify and define the alternative tools of discovery.

4. Explain the three threshold requirements a plaintiff must meet before he or she can file a lawsuit.

5. The citizens of each state elect state court judges. The president, on the other hand, appoints federal court judges for lifetime positions. Why might this difference lead to different rulings on similar cases? Which method—election or appointment—do you like better? Why? What are the advantages and disadvantages of each method?

6. Missouri was International Shoe Corporation's principal place of business, but the company employed between 11 and 13 salespersons in the state of Washington who exhibited samples and solicited orders for shoes from prospective buyers in Washington. The state of Washington assessed the company for contributions to a state unemployment fund. The state served the assessment on one of International Shoe Corporation's sales representatives in Washington and sent a copy by registered mail to the company's Missouri headquarters. International Shoe's representative challenged the assessment on numerous grounds, arguing that the state had not properly served the corporation. Is the corporation's defense valid? Why or why not? [*International Shoe Co. v. Washington,* 326 U.S. 310 (1945).]

7. The Robinsons, residents of New York, bought a new Audi car from Seaway Volkswagen Corp., a retailer incorporated in New York and with its principal place of business there. World-Wide Volkswagen, a company incorporated in New York and doing business in New York, New Jersey, and Connecticut, distributed the car to Seaway. Neither Seaway nor World-Wide did business in Oklahoma, and neither company shipped cars there. The Robinsons were driving through Oklahoma when another vehicle struck their Audi in the rear. The gas tank of the Audi exploded, injuring several members of the family. The Robinsons brought a product liability suit against the manufacturer, distributor, and retailer of the car in an Oklahoma state court. Seaway and World-Wide argued that the Oklahoma state court did not have *in personam* jurisdiction over them. After the state's trial court and supreme court held that the state did have *in personam* jurisdiction over Seaway

and World-Wide, they appealed to the U.S. Supreme Court. How do you think the Court decided in this case? Why? [*World-Wide Volkswagen Corp. v. Woodson,* 444 U.S. 286 (1980).]

8. Flanagan's, a New Jersey irrigation system installation company, ordered an irrigation pump from another New Jersey corporation, Aquarius, and paid a $3,500 down payment for the product. Watertronics, a Wisconsin corporation, manufactured the pump. Flanagan's had no direct contact with Watertronics other than a four-minute telephone conversation in which Flanagan's unsuccessfully attempted to get a better price on a pump. After receiving and installing the pump, Flanagan's was unhappy with its performance and so refused to pay the $34,000 balance due on the pump. Watertronics sued Flanagan's in Wisconsin state court. Flanagan's argued that the court could not exercise *in personam* jurisdiction over it. Do you think the Wisconsin state court had *in personam* jurisdiction over Flanagan's? Why or why not? [*Watertronics, Inc. v. Flanagan's Inc.,* 635 N.W.2d 27 (2001).]

9. Le Cabaret 481, Inc., an adult entertainment corporation, wanted to open a strip club in the city of Kingston. Kingston, however, passed an ordinance prohibiting adult businesses from operating within 300 feet of any church, school, nursery, public park, or residential property. Le Cabaret 481 filed a suit against the city, arguing that the ordinance left no feasible locations in the city for an adult business and thus violated the company's First Amendment right to free expression. The city, on the other hand, argued that Le Cabaret 481 did not present a ripe case to the court because the company had not applied for a building permit for its adult business. The company argued that it could not find a location for which it could apply for a permit. Do you think Le Cabaret 481 satisfied the ripeness requirement for its suit against the city? Why or why not? [*Le Cabaret 481, Inc. v. Municipality of Kingston,* 2005 U.S. Dist. LEXIS 706 (2005).]

10. Thirteen record labels filed a copyright violation suit against Hummer Winblad Venture Partners (Hummer), an owner of Napster, a peer-to-peer file-sharing network for online distribution of music. Hummer filed a counterclaim alleging antitrust violations against the record labels because they conspired to exclude independent music distributors like Napster from the online music distribution market. The record labels argued that Hummer lacked standing to make its counterclaims because Hummer, not Napster,

made the counterclaims and Hummer never competed directly with the record labels. Hummer, on the other hand, argued that it had standing because it financed Napster, a participant in the online music distribu-tion market. How do you think the court ruled in this case? Why? [*In re Napster Copyright Litig. v. Hummer Winblad Venture Partners,* 354 F. Supp. 2d 1113 (2005).]

Looking for more review material?

The Online Learning Center at **www.mhhe.com/kubasekess** contains this chapter's "Assignment on the Internet" and also a list of URLs for more information, entitled "On the Internet." Find both of them in the Student Center portion of the OLC, along with quizzes and other helpful materials.

Constitutional Law

⤍ CASE OPENER

**Regulations on Interstate Wine Sales:
A Violation of the Commerce Clause?**

Michigan and New York passed state statutes allowing in-state, but not out-of-state, wineries to sell wine directly to state residents. The statutes permitted out-of-state wine wholesalers, on the other hand, to sell to state residents. Thus, out-of-state wineries wishing to sell wine to Michigan and New York residents had to sell through a wholesaler. Because many small wineries produce insufficient quantities of wine to sell via wholesaler, however, the statutes effectively prohibited them from selling to Michigan and New York residents.

Michigan residents and an out-of-state winery challenged the statutes as violating the commerce clause of the U.S. Constitution. Michigan and New York argued that the Twenty-First Amendment protected the statutes. The Twenty-First Amendment states that "[t]he transportation or importation [of intoxicating liquors] into any state . . . for delivery or use therein, in violation of the laws thereof, is . . . prohibited." Moreover, the states argued that the statutes advanced legitimate public purposes: curbing wine sales to minors via the Internet, stemming tax evasion on wine sales, protecting public health and safety, and ensuring regulatory accountability.

The district court agreed with the states' argument, but on appeal, the appellate court ruled that the statutes violated the commerce clause. Michigan and New York then appealed the case to the U.S. Supreme Court.

1. Do you think the Michigan and New York statutes violate the commerce clause? Why?
2. Would your answer to the previous question change if the state statutes regulated the sale of corn instead of wine? Why?

After reading this chapter, you will be able to answer the following questions:

LO 1 What is federalism?

LO 2 What is the function of each branch of government, and how does each branch serve to check the others?

LO 3 What is the relationship between the supremacy clause and preemption?

LO 4 How does the commerce clause affect the power of both the state and federal governments to regulate?

LO 5 What is the difference between commercial and political speech, and why is that difference important?

LO 6 How do the rights guaranteed by the Bill of Rights affect business managers?

The U.S. Constitution sets forth the framework of our nation's government; it establishes a system of government that divides power between the federal government and the states. This system of government provides the focus for this chapter.

In this chapter we examine the constitutional provisions that affect business. Then we turn our focus to the primary source of the federal government's authority to regulate business: the commerce clause. We next examine the federal government's authority to tax and spend. Finally, in the last part of the chapter, we focus on how several amendments to the Constitution affect business.

LO 1

The U.S. Constitution

federalism

A system of government in which power is divided between a central authority and constituent political units.

The U.S. Constitution establishes a system of government based on the principle of federalism, according to which the authority to govern is divided between federal and state governments. According to the Tenth Amendment to the Constitution, all powers that the Constitution neither gives exclusively to the federal government nor takes from the states are reserved for the states. Because the federal government has only those powers granted to it by the Constitution, federal legislation that affects business must be based on an expressed constitutional grant of authority.

In addition to allocating authority between state and federal governments, the Constitution allocates the power of the federal government among the three branches of government. The first three articles of the Constitution establish three independent branches of the federal government: the legislative, executive, and judicial branches. The Constitution ensures that each branch maintains a separate sphere of power to prevent any one branch from obtaining undue power and monopolizing control of government.

The Constitution also establishes a system of *checks and balances*. Each branch's powers keep the other branches from dominating the government. For example, Congress, the legislative or lawmaking branch, has the power to enact legislation, but the president can veto a law that Congress passes. The legislature, however, can overturn a presidential veto with a two-thirds vote of the members of Congress. And if Congress passes a bill and the president signs it, the judiciary can strike it down as unconstitutional. Figure 4-1 illustrates the system of checks and balances in more detail.

CONNECTING to the Core

JUDICIAL REVIEW

Although the Constitution does not explicitly allow courts to review legislative and executive actions to determine whether they are constitutional, early common law established this process, known as **judicial review**. In the landmark 1803 U.S. Supreme Court case *Marbury v. Madison,* Chief Justice John Marshall wrote for the majority:

> [I]f a law be in opposition to the constitution; if both the law and the constitution apply to a particular case, so that the court must either decide that case [conforms] to the law, disregarding the constitution; or [conforms] to the constitution, disregarding the law; the court must determine which of these conflicting rules governs the case. This is of the very essence of judicial duty.

Judicial review also allows courts to review the constitutionality of lower courts' decisions.

judicial review
The power of a court to review legislative and executive actions, such as a law or an official act of a government employee or agent, to determine whether they are constitutional.

LO 2

Figure 4-1 The System of Checks and Balances

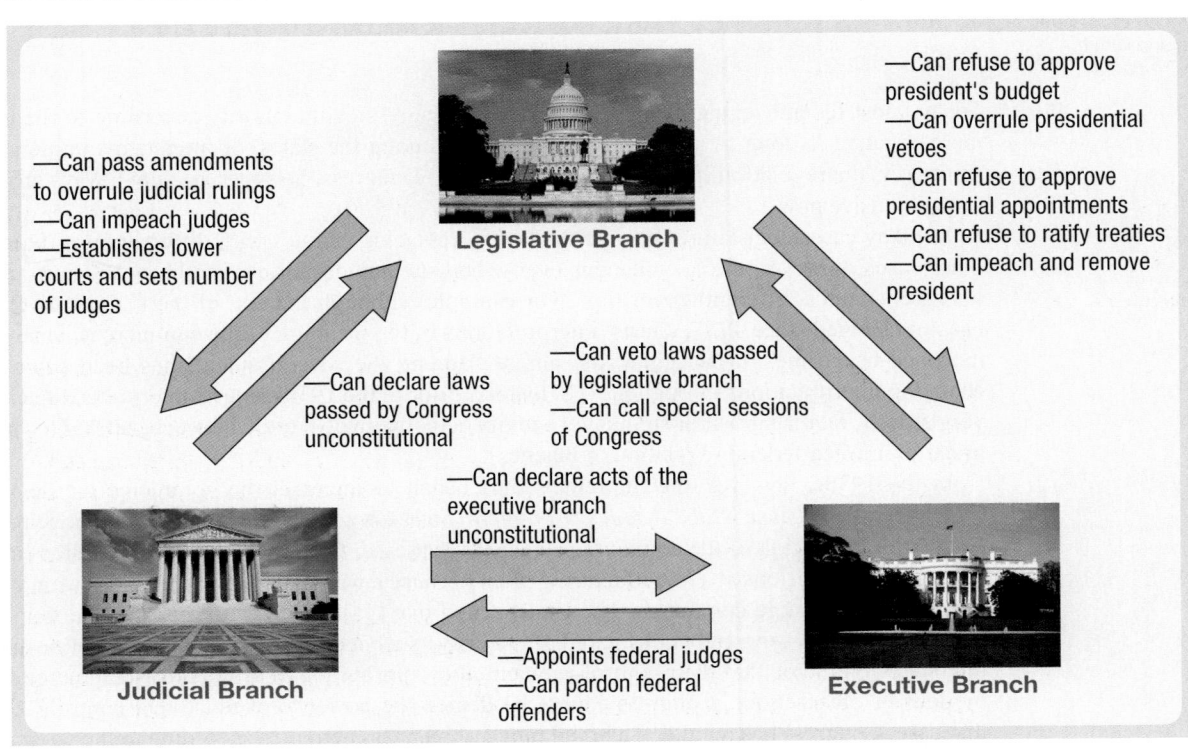

—Can pass amendments to overrule judicial rulings
—Can impeach judges
—Establishes lower courts and sets number of judges

Legislative Branch

—Can refuse to approve president's budget
—Can overrule presidential vetoes
—Can refuse to approve presidential appointments
—Can refuse to ratify treaties
—Can impeach and remove president

—Can declare laws passed by Congress unconstitutional

—Can veto laws passed by legislative branch
—Can call special sessions of Congress

—Can declare acts of the executive branch unconstitutional

Judicial Branch

—Appoints federal judges
—Can pardon federal offenders

Executive Branch

LO 3

The Supremacy Clause and Federal Preemption

supremacy clause

Article VI, Paragraph 2, of the U.S. Constitution, which states that the Constitution and all laws and treaties of the United States constitute the supreme law of the land. Thus, any state or local law that directly conflicts with the U.S. Constitution or federal laws or treaties is void.

The supremacy clause, located in Article VI of the Constitution, provides that the Constitution, laws, and treaties of the United States constitute the supreme law of the land, "any Thing in the Constitution or Laws of any State to the Contrary notwithstanding." Any state or local law that directly conflicts with the Constitution, federal laws, or treaties is void. Federal laws include rules passed by federal administrative agencies. For example, the Federal Aviation Administration has banned the use of cell phones on airplanes. If a Missouri law permitted cell phone usage on airplanes, it would be unconstitutional according to the supremacy clause.

In some areas, the state and federal governments have concurrent authority; that is, both governments have the power to regulate the same subject matter. In such cases, the states may regulate in the area as long as a person's compliance with the state regulation would not cause her or him to be in violation of a federal regulation. For example, Congress has established a number of environmental standards, but some states have passed even more protective standards.

federal preemption

A principle asserting the supremacy of federal legislation over state legislation when both pertain to the same subject matter.

Sometimes, however, in areas where the state and federal governments have concurrent authority, the federal government can decide to regulate that area exclusively. In such a situation, according to the doctrine of federal preemption, the state law is unconstitutional. To determine whether Congress intended to provide exclusive regulation, courts look to the language of the statute and transcripts of congressional hearings.

The Commerce Clause

commerce clause

Clause 3 of Article I, Section 8, of the U.S. Constitution, which authorizes and empowers Congress "To regulate Commerce with foreign Nations, and among the several States, and with the Indian Tribes."

The primary source of authority for federal regulation of business is the commerce clause, located in Article I, Section 8, of the Constitution. This clause states that the U.S. Congress has the power to "regulate Commerce with foreign Nations, and among the several States, and with the Indian Tribes." This allocation of authority simultaneously empowers the federal government and restricts the power of state governments.

THE COMMERCE CLAUSE AS A SOURCE OF AUTHORITY FOR THE FEDERAL GOVERNMENT

LO 4

Today, most federal regulations are exercises of congressional authority according to the commerce clause. As long as a law affects commerce among the states, or interstate commerce, in some way, the regulation is generally constitutional. Congress, however, has not always enjoyed such extensive power.

In many cases, legislatures change the law by replacing statutes with different ones. In many other cases, however, the law changes even when statutes do not change because courts often interpret statutes differently over time. For example, although the text of the commerce clause has not changed since 1787, courts' interpretations of the meaning of the commerce clause have morphed over time. In particular, the phrase "among the several states" has been subject to changing interpretations throughout U.S. history. Prior to the 1930s, courts interpreted the clause very strictly, requiring that the regulated activity actually involve trade between states. This interpretation limited federal regulation of business.

In the 1930s, however, the Supreme Court began to interpret the commerce clause more broadly. The 1937 case *NLRB v. Jones & Laughlin Steel Corp.* was a turning point in the Supreme Court's interpretation of the commerce clause. In that case, the Court ruled that Congress could regulate labor relations at a manufacturing plant because a work stoppage at the plant would seriously affect interstate commerce. The Court stated that "[a]lthough activities may be intrastate in character when separately considered, if they have such a close and substantial relationship to interstate commerce that their control is essential or appropriate to protect that commerce from burdens or obstructions, Congress cannot be denied the power to exercise that control." Since that case, Congress has regulated a broad range of business activities according to the commerce clause, through legislation such as the Federal Mine Safety and Health Act, which sets standards

for safety in coal mines; the Americans with Disabilities Act, which prohibits firms from discriminating against employees and potential employees who have disabilities; and the Consumer Protection Act, which criminalizes certain loan-sharking activities. Although businesses have challenged these statutes as being beyond the scope of congressional power, courts have upheld the statutes as valid exercises of congressional authority according to the commerce clause.

When the law changes, however, its movement is not always unidirectional. In fact, sometimes courts revert to standards and methods of interpretation that they rejected in the past. For example, the 1995 case *United States v. Lopez* marked a significant change in the nearly 60-year trend in the Supreme Court's interpretation of the commerce clause. In *Lopez,* the Court ruled that Congress had exceeded its commerce clause authority when it passed the Gun-Free School Zone Act, a law banning the possession of guns within 1,000 feet of any school. In its ruling, the Court said that Congress could not regulate in an area that had "nothing to do with commerce, or any sort of economic enterprise."

Case 4-1 illustrates how the Supreme Court applies the commerce clause to determine the constitutionality of statutes passed by Congress.

CASE 4-1

CHRISTY BRZONKALA v. ANTONIO J. MORRISON ET AL.
UNITED STATES SUPREME COURT
120 S. Ct. 1740 (2000)

FACTS: *Petitioner Christy Brzonkala and respondents Antonio Morrison and James Crawford were students at Virginia Polytechnic Institute (Virginia Tech). Brzonkala met the respondents at a campus party, where they allegedly assaulted and raped her; according to Brzonkala, Morrison subsequently made boasting, debasing, and vulgar remarks on campus about what he would do to women. Brzonkala claimed to be emotionally disturbed and depressed as a result. She was treated by a university psychiatrist, and soon after the rape she withdrew from the university.*

Brzonkala filed a complaint against the respondents under Virginia Tech's Sexual Assault Policy. Morrison was initially found guilty and suspended for two semesters, but his punishment was ultimately set aside.

Brzonkala then sued Morrison, Crawford, and Virginia Tech in federal court, alleging, among other claims, that Morrison's and Crawford's attack violated the Violence against Women Act. Morrison and Crawford moved to dismiss this complaint on the grounds that it failed to state a claim and that the act's (§ 13981's) civil remedy was unconstitutional.

The district court dismissed the complaint on grounds that Congress lacked authority to enact the section. The U.S. court of appeals affirmed the district court's conclusion.

ISSUE: Did Congress have the power under the commerce clause to enact the Violence against Women Act?

REASONING: Congress can regulate three broad categories of activities under its commerce powers. It can regulate the use of the channels of interstate commerce. It can regulate and protect the instrumentalities of interstate

commerce, or persons or things in interstate commerce, even though the threat may come only from intrastate activities. It can regulate those activities that substantially affect interstate commerce. The act is properly analyzed as a potential regulation of an activity that substantially affects commerce.

The most relevant precedent is *Lopez,* in which the Supreme Court held that the Gun-Free School Zones Act of 1990, which made it a federal crime to knowingly possess a firearm in a school zone, exceeded Congress's authority under the commerce clause. That statute was struck down because, first, by its terms it was unrelated to commerce, and whenever the courts have sustained federal regulation of intrastate activity based on the activity's substantial effects on interstate commerce, the activity in question has been some sort of economic endeavor.

Second, the statute had no express jurisdictional element to limit its reach to a discrete set of firearm possessions that additionally have an explicit connection with or effect on interstate commerce. Third, Congress had no findings about the effect of gun possession at school on interstate commerce. Fourth, the link between gun possession and a substantial effect on interstate commerce was attenuated. To uphold the law would have meant that there were no limits on what Congress could regulate.

Likewise, gender-motivated crimes of violence are not economic activity, and there was no jurisdictional element showing that the federal cause of action is in pursuance of Congress's power to regulate interstate commerce. There were some statistics showing the impact of gender-related

crime on victims and their families, but the Court had to decide whether these statistics demonstrate a substantial impact on interstate commerce, and the court did not believe they do. The Court found that the congressional finding relied on a method of reasoning the Court had already rejected as unworkable if any limit on congressional powers is to be maintained. It is not sufficient to find that gender-motivated violence affects interstate commerce "by deterring potential victims from traveling interstate, from engaging in employment in interstate business, and from transacting with business, and in places involved in interstate commerce; . . . by diminishing national productivity, increasing medical and other costs, and decreasing the supply of and the demand for interstate products."

Allowing such reasoning would give Congress the power to regulate almost any crime.

DECISION AND REMEDY: The Court affirmed the lower courts' decisions, holding that Congress may not regulate noneconomic, violent criminal conduct solely on the basis of that conduct's aggregate effect on interstate commerce.

SIGNIFICANCE OF THE CASE: The case clearly demonstrates an increasing willingness of the Court to limit congressional authority under the commerce clause. Note that the Court is not passing judgment on the quality of the law but is just saying that such a law would need to be passed by the state, not the federal, legislature.

CRITICAL THINKING

This case was a 5-4 decision. What reasoning do you think supported the dissent's opinion?

ETHICAL DECISION MAKING

Recall the WPH framework. What values led the majority to rule that Congress lacks authority to enact *§ 13981* of the Violence against Women Act? Do you think the values you listed are appropriate in this situation in spite of the individuals who are harmed by the decision?

THE COMMERCE CLAUSE AS A RESTRICTION ON STATE AUTHORITY

police power
Power retained by each state to pass laws that protect the health, safety, and welfare of its citizens.

dormant commerce clause
A restriction on states' authority that is implied in the commerce clause of the U.S. Constitution: The power given to Congress to enact legislation that affects interstate commerce in effect prohibits a state from passing legislation that improperly burdens interstate commerce.

The federal government's authority to regulate interstate commerce sometimes conflicts with the states' authority to regulate intrastate commerce. Courts have attempted to resolve this conflict by distinguishing between regulations of commerce and regulations under states' police power. Police power consists of the residual powers retained by each state to safeguard the health and welfare of its citizenry. Typical exercises of a state's police power include state criminal laws, building codes, zoning laws, sanitation standards for restaurants, and regulations for the practice of medicine.

Sometimes a state's use of its police power affects interstate commerce. If the purpose of a state law is to regulate interstate commerce or to discriminate against interstate commerce, the law is usually unconstitutional. Likewise, if a law substantially interferes with interstate commerce, it is generally unconstitutional. This restriction on states' authority to pass laws that substantially affect interstate commerce is called the dormant commerce clause.

Most cases are not so simple, however, and courts must balance the states' interest in protecting their citizens against the impact on interstate commerce. In balancing these competing interests, a court generally asks whether the state regulation is rationally related to a legitimate state end. If it is, the court then asks whether the regulatory burden imposed on interstate commerce is outweighed by the state's interest in enforcing the legislation. The court may also inquire whether there is a less drastic alternative available to attain the legitimate state purpose.

Although the supremacy clause establishes the sovereignty of federal law, courts generally presume that laws passed in accordance with states' police power are valid. For example, the city of Chicago passed an ordinance banning spray paint in the city as a means of reducing graffiti.

Paint manufacturers challenged the legislation as a violation of the dormant commerce clause, but the U.S. court of appeals upheld the legislation.

Case 4-2 illustrates an attempt to challenge a state regulation on the grounds that it places an undue burden on interstate commerce.

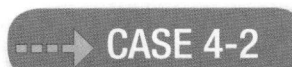

CASE 4-2

NATIONAL ELECTRICAL MANUFACTURERS ASSOCIATION v. WILLIAM H. SORRELL, ATTORNEY GENERAL OF THE STATE OF VERMONT, JOHN KASSEL, ET AL.
SECOND CIRCUIT COURT OF APPEALS

53 ERC 1385 (2001)

FACTS: *In 1998, the Vermont legislature enacted a statute that requires manufacturers of certain mercury-containing products (including thermostats, batteries, and lamps) to label their products and packaging to inform consumers that (1) the products contain mercury and (2), on disposal, should be recycled or disposed of as hazardous waste. The trade association of manufacturers of mercury-containing light bulbs (NEMA) brought action against state officials, seeking to have the law declared unconstitutional and asking for a preliminary injunction to prohibit enforcement of the law. The U.S. district court granted the preliminary injunction, and officials appealed.*

ISSUE: Does the state regulation violate the dormant commerce clause?

REASONING: There are two ways a law violates the "dormant" aspect of the commerce clause: by clearly discriminating against interstate commerce, or by imposing a burden on interstate commerce incommensurate with the local benefits secured.

The Supreme Court uses a balancing test to determine whether state statutes that incidentally burden interstate commerce violate the commerce clause. When a statute regulates evenhandedly to effectuate a legitimate local public interest, and its effects on interstate commerce are only incidental, it will be upheld unless the burden imposed on such commerce is clearly excessive in relation to the putative local benefits. If a legitimate local purpose is found, the extent of the burden that will be tolerated will depend on the nature of the local interest involved and on whether it could be promoted as well with a lesser impact on interstate activities.

To be struck down, the statute, at a minimum, must impose a burden on interstate commerce that is qualitatively or quantitatively different from that imposed on intrastate commerce. A regulation may disproportionately burden interstate commerce if it has the practical effect of requiring out-of-state commerce to be conducted at the regulating state's direction.

This law imposes the same labeling requirement on both in-state and out-of-state sellers and therefore does not disproportionately burden out-of-state sellers. As to the argument that the law subjects manufacturers to the possibility of multiple, inconsistent labeling requirements imposed by other states, there must be an actual conflict between the challenged regulation and regulations in place in other states before the court will put any weight on this argument, and no such conflict has been shown here. In fact, there is evidence that the Vermont statute is consistent with regimes under consideration by other states.

DECISION AND REMEDY: The state's labeling requirement did not violate the dormant commerce clause, so the state statute was upheld.

SIGNIFICANCE OF THE CASE: This case illustrates the type of analysis used by the court to determine whether a state statute's interference with interstate commerce is sufficient to justify striking down the statute.

CRITICAL THINKING

What different facts might have led the court to a different conclusion?

ETHICAL DECISION MAKING

Identify the primary stakeholders helped and hurt by the outcome of this case.

Taxing and Spending Powers of the Federal Government

No government can function without a source of revenue. Article I, Section 8, of the Constitution gives the federal government the "Power to lay and collect Taxes, Duties, Imports and Excises." The taxes laid by Congress, however, must be uniform across the states. In other words, the government cannot impose higher taxes on residents of one state than it imposes on those of another.

Although tax collection allows the government to provide essential services, the government can also use taxes for other purposes. For example, to encourage the development of certain industries and discourage the development of others, the government can provide tax credits for firms entering favored industries. As long as the "motive of Congress and the effect of its legislative action are to secure revenue for the benefit of the general government," the tax is constitutional. The fact that it also has a regulatory impact does not affect the constitutionality of the tax.

Article I, Section 8, also grants Congress spending power by authorizing it to "pay the Debts and provide for the common Defense and general Welfare of the United States." As with its power to tax, Congress can use its spending power to achieve social welfare objectives. For example, in *South Dakota v. Dole,* the Supreme Court upheld a federal statute that grants federal funds for state highways to only those states in which 21 is the legal drinking age.

Other Constitutional Restrictions on Government

THE PRIVILEGES AND IMMUNITIES CLAUSE

privileges and immunities clause
Clause in the U.S. Constitution requiring that a state grant citizens of other states the same legal benefits that it grants its own citizens.

Article IV, Section 2, of the Constitution states that "Citizens of each State shall be entitled to all Privileges and Immunities of Citizens in the several States." This provision, called the **privileges and immunities clause,** prohibits states from discriminating against citizens of other states when those nonresidents engage in ordinary and essential activities. These activities include buying and selling property, seeking employment, and using the court system. States may treat residents and nonresidents differently only when they have substantial reason for doing so.

For example, according to the privileges and immunities clause, a state cannot prohibit non-residents from opening restaurants in the state. States can, however, allow state universities to charge higher tuition to out-of-state students because residents pay taxes that fund state universities, while out-of-state students do not.

THE FULL FAITH AND CREDIT CLAUSE

full faith and credit clause
The clause of the U.S. Constitution (Article IV, Section 1) mandating that each state must recognize, respect, and enforce the public records, legislative acts, and judicial decisions of the other states.

Article IV, Section 1, of the Constitution contains the **full faith and credit clause.** This clause states, "Full Faith and Credit shall be given in each State to the public Acts, Records, and judicial Proceedings of every other State." This provision requires that courts in all states uphold contracts and public acts established in other states. For example, this clause protects wills, marriage and divorce decrees, and judgments in civil courts. Courts have held, however, that states do not have to give full faith and credit to laws that violate their "public policy." Thus, for example, although Massachusetts permits same-sex marriage, the full faith and credit clause does not require that other states recognize such marriages.

THE CONTRACT CLAUSE

Article I, Section 9, contains the contract clause, which states that government may not pass any "Law impairing the Obligation of Contract." In application, courts interpret this clause to mean that no law can be passed that will unreasonably interfere with existing contracts. For example, in the 1934 U.S. Supreme Court case *Home Building & Loan Association v. Blaisdell*, the Home Building & Loan Association challenged Minnesota's Mortgage Moratorium Act as a violation of the contract clause. The act, implemented temporarily during the Great Depression, authorized courts to extend the redemption periods of mortgages to delay foreclosures of mortgages on real estate. The Court ruled that the act's provisions were within the state's police power to protect its citizens and did not violate the contract clause. Although the act impaired contractual obligations between lenders and borrowers, the Court held that courts must balance even substantial contractual impairments against states' interest in protecting the welfare of their citizens.

contract clause
The clause in the U.S. Constitution that prohibits the government from unreasonably interfering with an existing contract.

The Amendments to the Constitution

The first 10 amendments to the U.S. Constitution, known as the Bill of Rights, substantially affect government regulation of business. These amendments prohibit the federal government from infringing on individual freedoms. Moreover, the Fourteenth Amendment extends most of the provisions in the Bill of Rights to the states, prohibiting state interference in citizens' exercise of their rights. Thus, the federal and state governments cannot deprive individuals of the freedoms protected by the Bill of Rights. Remember, however, that the amendments are only a limit on actions of the government. They do not limit the behavior of private employers, which is a common misunderstanding many citizens have.

Many other countries do not have constitutional provisions to protect citizens from the government. The Australian constitution, for example, creates the framework for government in Australia. In many of the countries that do have individual protections in their constitutions, these protections have emerged recently, as the Global Context box on Canada's constitution illustrates. Some other countries' constitutions provide rights that American citizens do not have. The constitution of Belarus, for example, guarantees citizens' right to health care.

Courts apply many amendments to corporations because corporations are treated, in most cases, as "artificial persons." The remainder of this chapter describes the amendments that most significantly affect the regulatory environment of business. Exhibit 4-1 summarizes the first ten amendments.

THE FIRST AMENDMENT

Freedom of Speech and Assembly The First Amendment guarantees freedom of speech, including gestures and other forms of expression, and of the press. It prohibits abridgment of the right to assemble peacefully and to petition the government for redress of grievances. Finally, it prohibits the government from aiding the establishment of religion and from interfering with the free exercise of religion.

Like other rights, First Amendment rights are not absolute. For example, a person does not have the right to yell "Fire!" in a crowded theater. Nor does the First Amendment protect false statements about another that are injurious to that person's reputation. Due to the difficulty of determining the boundaries of individual rights, courts hear a large number of First Amendment cases.

Political Speech. The First Amendment protections also apply to corporations. Courts do not, however, treat all corporate speech the same. Sometimes corporations engage in political speech; that is, they support political candidates or referenda. At one time, states restricted firms' political advertising because they feared that corporations, with their large assets, would drown out other voices. In the 1978 case *First National Bank of Boston v. Bellotti*, however, the U.S.

LO 5

political speech
Speech that is used to support political candidates or referenda. It is given a high level of protection by the First Amendment as compared to other types of speech.

Exhibit 4-1

Summary of the Bill
of Rights

LO 6

AMENDMENT	PROVISIONS
First	• Protects freedom of religion, press, speech, and peaceable assembly. • Ensures that citizens have the right to ask the government to redress grievances.
Second	• Finds that a well-regulated militia is necessary for security. • States that government cannot infringe on citizens' right to bear arms.
Third	• Provides that government cannot house soldiers in private residences during peacetime, or during war except for provisions in the law.
Fourth	• Protects citizens from unreasonable search and seizure. • Ensures that government issues warrants only with probable cause.
Fifth	• Ensures that government does not put citizens on trial except by the indictment of a grand jury. • Gives citizens the right not to testify against themselves. • Prevents government from trying citizens twice for the same crime. • Creates due process rights. • Provides that government cannot take private property for public use without just compensation.
Sixth	• Provides the right to a speedy public trial with an impartial jury, the right to know what criminal accusations a citizen faces, the right to have witnesses both against and for the accused, and the right to have an attorney.
Seventh	• States that in common lawsuits where the monetary value exceeds $20, citizens have the right to a trial by jury.
Eighth	• Provides that government will not set bail at excessive levels. • Prohibits government imposition of excessive fines. • Prohibits cruel and unusual punishment.
Ninth	• Provides that although the Bill of Rights names certain rights, such naming does not remove other rights retained by citizens.
Tenth	• Provides that powers that the Constitution does not give to the federal government are reserved for the states.

Supreme Court considered the constitutionality of a Massachusetts law that prohibited certain corporations from spending money to influence voters on issues that did not materially affect the corporation. The Court held that the law was unconstitutional, stating, "The concept that the government may restrict speech of some elements of our society in order to enhance the relative voice of others is wholly foreign to the First Amendment." The Court ruled that the First Amendment protects corporate political speech to the same extent as ordinary citizens' political speech.

commercial speech
Speech made by businesses about commercial matters, such as the sale of goods and services. It is protected by the First Amendment.

Commercial Speech. Not all corporate speech is political speech. Commercial speech is speech that conveys information related to the sale of goods and services. Courts analyze government restrictions on commercial speech according to a four-part test established in *Central Hudson Gas & Electric Corp. v. Public Service Commission of New York.* The *Central Hudson* test is illustrated in Figure 4-2.

In Case 4-3, the Supreme Court applied this test to several New York regulations.

BAD FROG BREWERY v. NEW YORK STATE LIQUOR AUTHORITY
U.S. COURT OF APPEALS FOR THE SECOND CIRCUIT
134 F. 3d 87 (1998)

FACTS: *Bad Frog, a Michigan corporation, manufactures and markets alcoholic beverages under its "Bad Frog" trademark. Each label prominently features an artist's rendering of a frog holding up its middle "finger." Versions of the label feature slogans such as "He just don't care," "An amphibian with an attitude," "Turning bad into good," and "The beer so good . . . it's bad."*

In May 1996, Bad Frog's New York distributor applied to the New York State Liquor Authority for brand-label approval and registration pursuant to Section 107-a(4)(a) of New York's Alcoholic Beverage Control Law. NYSLA denied the application in July. Explaining its rationale for the rejection, the authority found that the label "encourages combative behavior" and that the gesture and the slogan, "He just don't care," placed close to and in larger type than a warning concerning potential health problems, foster a defiance to the health warning on the label, entice underage drinkers, and invite the public not to heed conventional wisdom and to disobey standards of decorum.

In addition, the authority said that it considered that approval of this label means that the label could appear in grocery and convenience stores, with obvious exposure on the shelf to children of tender age, and that it is sensitive to the label's adverse effects on a youthful audience.

Bad Frog filed suit against the NYSLA in October 1996 and sought a preliminary injunction barring NYSLA from taking any steps to prohibit the sale of beer by Bad Frog under the controversial labels.

ISSUE: Is the picture of a frog "behaving badly" on a product label entitled to protection as commercial speech?

REASONING: In the words of the court:

> Bad Frog's label attempts to function, like a trademark, to identify the source of the product. Though the label communicates no information beyond the source of the product, the minimal information suffices to invoke the protections for commercial speech, articulated in the Central Hudson Case

Central Hudson sets forth the analytical framework for assessing governmental restrictions on commercial speech:

> [I]t at least must concern lawful activity and not be misleading. Next, we ask whether the asserted government interest is substantial. If both inquiries yield positive answers, we must determine whether the regulation directly advances the government interest asserted, and whether it is not more extensive than is necessary to serve that interest. The last two steps in the analysis have been considered, somewhat in tandem, to determine if there is a sufficient "'fit' between the [regulator's] ends and the means chosen to accomplish those ends." The burden to establish that

"reasonable fit" is on the governmental agency defending its regulation, though the fit need not satisfy a least-restrictive-means standard.

Applying the test, the labels concern lawful activity and not be misleading. The state claims two interests to support its asserted power to ban Bad Frog's labels: (i) the State's interest in "protecting children from vulgar and profane advertising," and (ii) the State's interest "in acting consistently to promote temperance, i.e., the moderate and responsible use of alcohol among those above the legal drinking age and abstention among those below the legal drinking age."

Both of the asserted interests are "substantial" because states have a compelling interest in protecting the physical and psychological well-being of minors, which includes shielding minors from the influence of literature that is not obscene by adult standards. The state also has a substantial interest in regulating alcohol consumption.

To meet the "direct advancement" requirement, a state must demonstrate that the law will directly restrict harms to that interest. In terms of protecting children from vulgarity, the restriction fails. Because of the wide range of vulgar displays throughout contemporary society, including comic books targeted directly at children, barring such displays from labels for alcoholic beverages cannot realistically be expected to reduce children's exposure to such displays to any significant degree. Attacking an almost insignificant part of a substantial problem is not sufficient.

As to the state interest in temperance, there was no evidence that viewing that gesture on a beer label will encourage disregard of health warnings or encourage underage drinking. Thus the law fails the third prong.

Finally, the law is more extensive than necessary to serve the asserted interest in insulating children from vulgarity. Less restrictive alternatives include restrictions on specific locations where children are more likely to view it, such as on billboards or on television advertising; restrictions on over-the-air-advertising; and segregation of the product in the store.

DECISION AND REMEDY: The court concluded that "the State's prohibition of the labels from use in all circumstances does not materially advance its asserted interests in insulating children from vulgarity or promoting temperance, and is not narrowly tailored to the interest concerning children." The court therefore reversed the lower court's denial of Bad Frog's request for injunctive relief with respect to the disapproval of its labels.

SIGNIFICANCE OF THE CASE: The case illustrates the application of the Central Hudson test.

CRITICAL THINKING

What law do you think would advance the state's articulated interests without running afoul of the First Amendment?

ETHICAL DECISION MAKING

Which stakeholders' interests are advanced by this ruling? Which ones are harmed?

Constitution Act of Canada

The United States is not alone in holding that its Constitution is the supreme law of the land. Section 52(1) of the Constitution Act of Canada, passed in 1982, states, "[T]he Constitution of Canada is the supreme law of Canada, and any law that is inconsistent with the provisions of the Constitution is, to the extent of the inconsistency, of no force or effect."

The Constitution Act established the Canadian Charter of Rights and Freedoms, which superseded the 1960 Canadian Bill of Rights. The previous Bill of Rights had applied only to the Canadian national government, not to the provincial governments. Like the Fourteenth Amendment of the U.S. Constitution, Section 32(1) of the Canadian Charter states that the charter applies to Canada's Parliament and national government and to the legislature and government of each province of Canada. Like the U.S. Bill of Rights, the Canadian Charter protects rights and fundamental freedoms, including freedom of conscience and religion, freedom of peaceful assembly and association, freedom from unreasonable searches and seizures, and the right to equal protection of the law. These rights and freedoms, however, are qualified. The charter states, in Section 1, "The Canadian Charter of Rights and Freedoms guarantees the rights and freedoms set out in the subject only to such reasonable limits prescribed by law as can be demonstrably justified in a free and democratic society." Of course, constitutional rights in the United States can be seen as being similarly limited by the courts' applying balancing tests in constitutional rights cases.

Figure 4-2

The *Central Hudson* Test for Commercial Speech

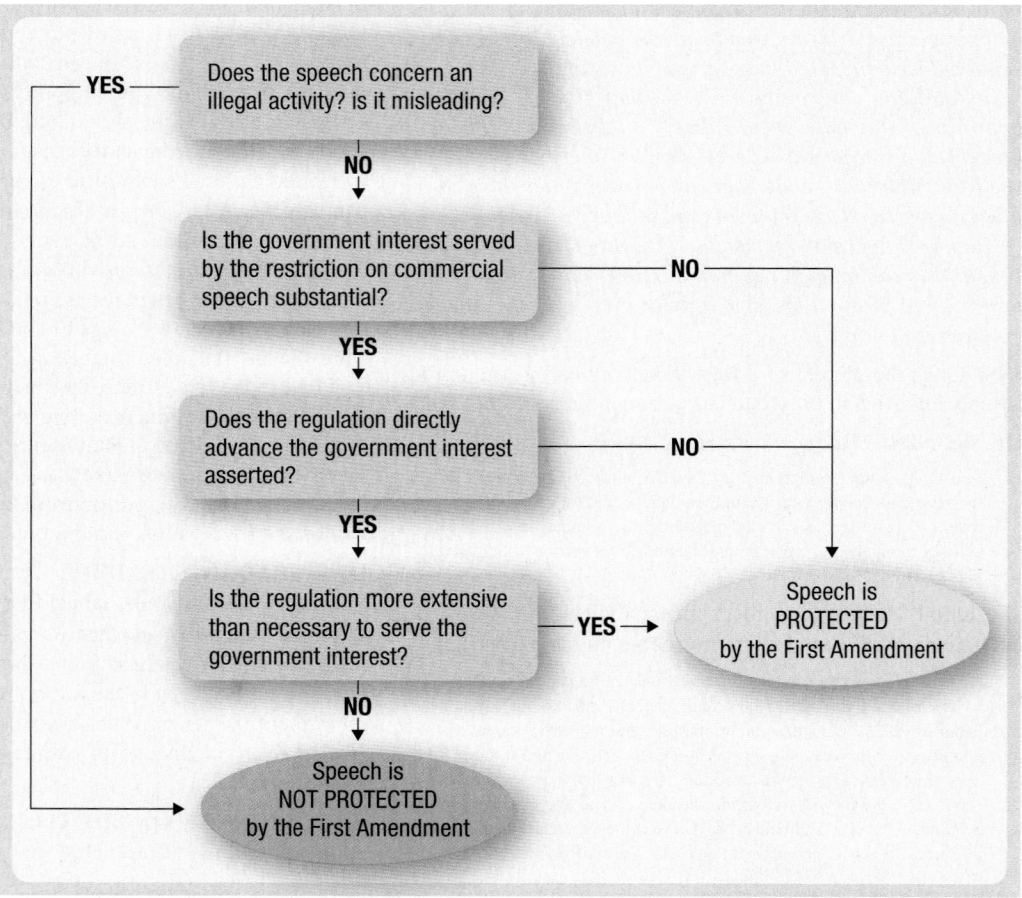

Unprotected Speech. The First Amendment right to free speech is not absolute. In the 1942 case *Chaplinsky v. New Hampshire,* the U.S. Supreme Court held:

> There are certain well-defined and narrowly limited classes of speech, the prevention and punishment of which have never been thought to raise any Constitutional problem. These include the lewd and obscene, the profane, the libelous, and the insulting or fighting words—those which by their very utterance inflict injury or tend to incite an immediate breach of the peace.

Free Speech in China

The Chinese constitution does not guarantee freedom of speech or assembly, nor does it recognize any form of natural rights or human rights. Instead, it recognizes citizens' rights, which are specifically enumerated in the Chinese constitution or laws. Not only does the Chinese constitution not provide protections for expressive activity, but numerous Chinese laws prohibit citizens from engaging in political acts directed against the regime—acts that are protected in the United States. For example, Article 25 of China's Publishing Control Act prohibits the publication of any material that opposes the basic rules of the constitution. Articles 7 and 12 of the Law on Assemblies, Processions, and Demonstrations prohibit assemblies, processions, and demonstrations that oppose these basic rules.

Thus, for example, the First Amendment does not protect defamation, or speech that harms the reputation of another. As you will learn in Chapter 6, moreover, courts may require that an individual who uses such speech compensate the person whose reputation was harmed by the speech.

The First Amendment does not protect obscenity, either, although in many cases courts find it difficult to determine whether particular speech constitutes obscenity. In the 1973 case *Miller v. California,* the U.S. Supreme Court established a three-part standard to determine whether speech is obscene:

1. Would the average person, applying contemporary community standards, find that the speech, taken as a whole, appeals to the prurient (marked by or arousing an immoderate or unwholesome interest or desire) interest?

2. Does the speech depict or describe, in a patently offensive way, sexual conduct specifically defined by law?

3. Does the speech, taken as a whole, lack serious literary, artistic, political, or scientific value?

If the answer to all three questions is yes, the First Amendment does not protect the speech in question. Can you identify any significant ambiguities in the *Miller* standard?

Fighting words are a third class of unprotected speech. In *Chaplinsky v. New Hampshire,* a man protesting the government called the city marshal a "damned racketeer" and a "damned Fascist." The city arrested him for violating a statute prohibiting the use of offensive, derisive, or annoying words toward another in a public place. The U.S. Supreme Court held: "The English language has a number of words and expressions which by general consent are 'fighting words' when said without a disarming smile. . . . Such words, as ordinary men know, are likely to cause a fight." The Court further held that "'damned racketeer' and 'damned Fascist' are epithets likely to provoke the average person to retaliation, and thereby cause a breach of the peace." Thus, the Court determined that the First Amendment did not protect the man's speech.

Many universities believe that "hate speech," or derogatory speech directed at members of another group, such as another race, satisfies the definition of fighting words. Thus, 60 percent of universities have banned verbal abuse and verbal harassment, and 28 percent of universities have banned advocacy of an offensive viewpoint. State and federal appellate courts have struck down many of these hate-speech codes, but no cases have reached the Supreme Court yet. The international community, however, is less protective of hate speech. For example, a United Nations declaration and a number of foreign laws state that hate speech is not a protected form of expression.

Freedom of Religion The First Amendment contains two provisions that protect citizens' freedom of religion. The **establishment clause** maintains that government "shall make no law respecting an establishment of religion." In the 1971 case *Lemon v. Kurtzman,* the U.S. Supreme Court codified the following three tests to determine whether a particular government statute violates the establishment clause:

1. Does the statute have a secular legislative purpose?

2. Does the statute's principal or primary effect either advance or inhibit religion?

3. Does the statute foster an excessive government entanglement with religion?

establishment clause
One of two provisions in the First Amendment of the U.S. Constitution that protect citizens' freedom of religion. It prohibits (1) the establishment of a national religion by Congress and (2) the preference of one religion over another or of religion over nonreligious philosophies in general.

To determine whether the statute fosters an excessive government entanglement with religion, courts examine the character and purposes of the institutions benefited, the nature of the aid that the government provides, and the resulting relationship between the government and the religious authority.

The free-exercise clause states that government cannot make a law "prohibiting the free exercise" of religion. Although government must remain neutral in matters of religion, determining whether a government action advances religion or merely allows free exercise of religion is often difficult. Likewise, determining whether a government action establishes religion or simply avoids interference with free exercise of religion is also difficult.

Issues concerning the establishment clause and the free-exercise clause often arise in workplace settings. In government workplaces, this conflict sometimes raises difficult issues. For example, in 1966, Tucker, an employee of the California Department of Education, insisted on signing office memos with his name and the letters "SOTLJC," an abbreviation for "Servant of the Lord Jesus Christ." In an attempt to avoid workplace disruptions and the appearance of government support for religion, Tucker's supervisor prohibited all displays of religious symbols in the workplace. The supervisor suspended Tucker for refusing to comply with the restrictions. When Tucker challenged the suspension on grounds that the rules interfered with his free exercise of religion, the appellate court agreed.

In private workplaces, issues related to free exercise of religion most often arise under Title VII, the federal law prohibiting employment discrimination. We discuss this important legislation in greater detail in Chapter 24.

THE FOURTH AMENDMENT

Freedom from Unreasonable Searches and Seizures The Fourth Amendment guarantees citizens the right to be "secure in their persons, their homes, and their personal property." Thus, it prohibits government from conducting unreasonable searches of individuals and seizing their property to use as evidence against them.

A search is unreasonable if the government official conducting the search does not first obtain a search warrant from a court. A search warrant is a court order that authorizes law enforcement agents to search for or seize items specifically described in the warrant. Government officials can obtain search warrants only if they can show *probable cause* to believe that the search will uncover specific evidence of criminal activity. In other words, the government officials must have a sufficient reason based on known facts to obtain a warrant.

The Supreme Court has ruled, however, that in certain circumstances, government officials do not need a search warrant. For example, when law enforcement officials believe it is likely that the items sought will be removed before they can obtain a warrant, they may conduct a search without a warrant. Law enforcement officials frequently conduct automobile searches without a warrant according to this rule.

In most other cases, though, law enforcement officials must obtain a warrant before conducting a search. For example, an Ohio law required that buyers of five or more beer kegs provide the beer distributor with the address of the party where the kegs would be consumed. Additionally, the law required that the buyers sign a form allowing police and liquor agents to enter their property without a warrant to search the premises to enforce state liquor laws. In 2001, a college professor challenged the law on grounds that it infringed on citizens' Fourth Amendment rights. Before the court decided the case, Ohio repealed the law.

In addition to protecting individuals and their homes, the Fourth Amendment also protects corporations and places of business. This protection generally applies in criminal cases, but Fourth Amendment issues also arise when government regulations authorize administrative agencies to conduct warrantless searches.

Although administrative searches usually require search warrants, courts have established an exception to this rule: If an industry has a long history of pervasive regulation, a warrantless search is not unreasonable. In such industries, administrative agencies can use warrantless searches to ensure that firms uphold regulations.

This *pervasive-regulation exception,* however, is not always easy to interpret. Courts have ruled that warrantless searches authorized by the Federal Mine Safety and Health Act are legal because the federal regulatory presence is comprehensive and well-defined. Thus, reasonable commercial-property owners ought to know that their property is subject to periodic inspections. A warrantless search based on the Occupational Safety and Health Act, however, may violate the Fourth Amendment because no significant legislation of working conditions existed before Congress passed that act in 1970. Hence, businesspeople covered by the law cannot reasonably anticipate warrantless searches.

CASE Nugget

How Does Technology Affect the Fourth Amendment?

United States v. Kyllo
United States Supreme Court (2001)

533 U.S. 27

Technological improvements have raised new issues in the application of the Fourth Amendment. New technologies have made eavesdropping and other covert activities easier. For example, in a 2001 U.S. Supreme Court case, police had information suggesting that Danny Kyllo grew marijuana in his home. Growing marijuana indoors requires heat lamps that use large amounts of electricity, and Kyllo had unusually high electric bills. The police used a thermal imager, an instrument that detects heat emissions, to provide them with the evidence necessary to obtain a warrant to physically search his house.

The Court addressed the issue of whether the use of thermal-imaging instruments on private property constituted a "search." Judges analyze cases by comparing them to past cases to see how other judges determined similar cases. Thus, in this case, the Court asked whether using thermal-imaging instruments is more like going through someone's garbage or more like using a high-powered telescope to look through someone's window. Previous Supreme Court cases held that the former behavior does not constitute a search but the latter scenario does constitute a search and therefore requires a warrant. The appellate court, examining the use of this technology for the first time, ruled that using thermal imaging was not a search prohibited by the Fourth Amendment without a warrant.

On appeal, however, the U.S. Supreme Court ruled that police use of thermal-imaging devices to detect heat patterns emanating from private homes constitutes a search that requires a warrant. The Court held, further, that the warrant requirement applies not only to the relatively crude thermal-imaging device but also to any "more sophisticated systems" that give the police knowledge that in the past would have required physical entry into the home. In explaining the Court's decision, Justice Scalia wrote that in the home, "all details are intimate details, because the entire area is held safe from prying government eyes." He added that the Court's precedents "draw a firm line at the entrance to one's house."

This case, however, is not necessarily the final word on the use of technology. The Court relied heavily on the fact that police used thermal imaging to see inside Kyllo's *home.* Thus, courts may in the future uphold thermal imaging of other locations.

THE FIFTH AMENDMENT

The Fifth Amendment protects individuals in several important ways. First, it protects against *self-incrimination,* meaning that in a criminal case, the defendant does not have to testify in court as a witness against himself or herself. The Fifth Amendment also protects against *double jeopardy.* Thus, government cannot try a person more than once for the same crime.

due process clause

A clause in the Fifth Amendment of the U.S. Constitution providing that the government cannot deprive an individual of life, liberty, or property without a fair and just hearing.

Due Process For businesspeople and corporations, the Fifth Amendment's due process clause provides extensive protection. This clause states that government cannot deprive a person of life, liberty, or property without *due process* of law.

The due process clause guarantees two types of due process: procedural and substantive. *Procedural due process* requires that the government use fair procedures when taking the life, liberty, or property of an individual or corporation. At a minimum, procedural due process entitles a person to notice of any legal action against her and to a hearing before an impartial tribunal. Originally, courts interpreted the due process clause as protecting an individual's right of procedural due process only in federal criminal proceedings. The subsequent passage of the Fourteenth Amendment extended the requirement of due process to criminal proceedings by state governments. Today, courts apply the due process clause to diverse situations, including the termination of welfare benefits, food stamps, or Social Security benefits; the suspension of a driver's license; the discharge of a public employee from his job; and the suspension of a student from school.

The procedures that government must follow when taking an individual's life, liberty, or property vary according to the nature of the taking. Generally, more procedures are necessary as the magnitude of potential deprivation increases.

Substantive due process refers to the basic fairness of laws that may deprive an individual of her life, liberty, or property. To satisfy the substantive due process requirement, government must have a proper purpose for enacting laws that restrict individuals' liberty or the use of their property. The standard for determining whether a law violates substantive due process depends on the nature of the potential deprivation. Laws affecting fundamental rights must bear a substantial relationship to a compelling government purpose. These fundamental rights generally include the rights protected in the Constitution: the right to vote, the right to travel freely from state to state, the right to privacy, and so on. Compelling state interests include, for example, public safety and national security.

Not all laws, however, affect fundamental rights. To show that a law that does not affect fundamental rights satisfies the substantive due process requirement, government must prove only that the law bears a rational relationship to a legitimate state interest. Courts uphold most government regulations according to this *rational-basis test.* For example, courts have upheld minimum-wage laws, rent control laws, banking regulations, environmental laws, and regulations prohibiting unfair trade practices according to the rational-basis test.

takings clause

A clause in the Fifth Amendment of the U.S. Constitution requiring that when government uses its power to take private property for public use, it must pay the owner just compensation, or fair market value, for the property. Also called *just-compensation clause.*

The Prohibition against Uncompensated Takings The Fifth Amendment provides that when government takes private property for public use, it must pay the owner *just compensation,* or fair market value, for her property. This provision is called the takings clause, and it applies to corporations. Several significant issues have arisen with respect to the takings clause. For example, what constitutes a "public use" for which government can take private property? This issue is explored in greater depth in Chapter 6.

The takings clause has prompted other issues as well. What happens, for instance, when a government regulation interferes so substantially with an individual's use of her property that it effectively "takes" her property? For example, environmental regulations often affect the way landowners can use their property. Under the case of *Lucas v. South Carolina Coastal Commission,* the Supreme Court held that if a regulation is so extensive that it leaves the property owner with no economically viable use of his land, the regulation constitutes a taking and the owner is entitled to compensation for the value of his property, even though the state did not seek to take title to his land.

The Privilege against Self-Incrimination Although most provisions of the Fifth Amendment apply to corporations, corporations do not enjoy the Fifth Amendment's protection against self-incrimination. Sole proprietors, however, are entitled to this protection. Thus, different businesses have different constitutional rights depending on their form of business organization.

For example, in the 1988 U.S. Supreme Court case *Braswell v. United States,* the Court distinguished between the rights of corporate-record custodians and sole proprietors. Braswell was both the operator and the sole shareholder of his business. When a grand jury issued a subpoena requiring that he produce corporate books and records, Braswell argued that the subpoena violated his Fifth Amendment privilege against self-incrimination. The Court denied Braswell's claim, writing that "subpoenaed business records are not privileged, and as a custodian for the records, the act of producing the records is in a representative capacity, not a personal one, so the records must be produced." The Court held that the subpoena would have violated Braswell's privilege against self-incrimination if his business had been a sole proprietorship.

THE NINTH AMENDMENT

The Right to Privacy The Ninth Amendment states, "The enumeration in the Constitution, of certain rights, shall not be construed to deny or disparage others retained by the people." Although this amendment does not expressly guarantee the right to privacy, courts have interpreted the Ninth Amendment, together with the First, Third, Fourth, and Fifth Amendments, as providing individuals with a right to privacy.

In the 1965 case *Griswold v. Connecticut,* the Supreme Court ruled that a Connecticut law prohibiting the use of contraceptives was unconstitutional because it violated individuals' right to privacy. Justice Douglas wrote:

> Specific guarantees in the Bill of Rights have penumbras [fringes]. . . . Various guarantees create zones of privacy. The right of association contained in the penumbra of the First Amendment is one. . . . The Third Amendment in its prohibition against the quartering of soldiers "in any house" in time of peace without the consent of the owner is another facet of that privacy. The Fourth Amendment explicitly affirms the "right of the people to be secure in their persons, houses, papers, and effects, against unreasonable searches and seizures." The Fifth Amendment in its Self-Incrimination Clause enables the citizen to create a zone of privacy which government may not force him to surrender to his detriment.

THE FOURTEENTH AMENDMENT *States*

Equal Protection The Fourteenth Amendment contains the **equal protection clause,** which prevents states from denying "the equal protection of the laws" to any citizen. This clause combats discrimination because it applies whenever government treats certain individuals differently than other similarly situated individuals, usually through a classification scheme.

As with the due process clause, to determine whether a law violates the equal protection clause, courts use different standards based on the nature of the rights the classification affects. Three different standards of scrutiny apply: strict scrutiny, intermediate scrutiny, and the rational-basis test.

If a law prevents individuals from exercising a fundamental right, or if the law's classification scheme involves suspect classifications, the action will be subject to **strict scrutiny.** *Suspect classifications* include classifications based on race, national origin, and citizenship. Courts uphold suspect classifications only if they are necessary to promote a compelling state interest. In cases involving suspect classifications, courts do not begin their analysis with a presumption that the classification is constitutional, so few laws pass the strict scrutiny standard.

equal protection clause
A clause in the Fourteenth Amendment of the U.S. Constitution that prevents states from denying "the equal protection of the laws" to any citizen. This clause implies that all citizens are created equal.

strict scrutiny
The most exacting standard of review used by the courts in determining the constitutionality of a statute; requires a compelling government interest and the least restrictive means of attaining that objective.

intermediate scrutiny
A standard of review under which a law must be necessary to achieve a substantial, or important, government interest and it must be narrowly tailored to that interest.

rational-basis test
The lowest standard of review; requires that a law be designed to protect a legitimate state interest and be rationally related to that interest.

For example, in the 1954 case *Brown v. Board of Education,* the U.S. Supreme Court ruled that the classification scheme used to racially segregate public schools violated the equal protection clause.

Several courts have held, however, that in some cases, remedying past discrimination against a group is a compelling state interest. Chapter 24 discusses this issue in greater detail.

If the law's classification scheme is based on gender or on the legitimacy of children, courts use intermediate scrutiny. According to this standard, the law is constitutional only if it is substantially related to an important government objective.

When a classification scheme involves other matters, courts apply a rational-basis test. According to this test, courts ask whether there is any justifiable reason to believe that the classification scheme advances a legitimate government interest. Because courts begin their analysis with a strong presumption that the government action is constitutional, almost all laws pass this test.

 SUMMARY

The U.S. Constitution	*Federalism:* The authority to govern is divided between two sovereigns, or supreme lawmakers: the federal government and the states.
	Separation of powers: The Constitution divides power among the legislative, executive, and judicial branches of government. The system of checks and balances allocates specific powers to each branch to keep the other branches from dominating government.
The Supremacy Clause and Federal Preemption	*Federal supremacy:* Any state or local law that directly conflicts with the U.S. Constitution or federal laws or treaties is void.
	Concurrent authority: Both state and federal governments have the power to regulate certain matters; generally, the federal government defers to the state.
	Federal preemption: The federal government uses this doctrine to strike down laws that do not directly conflict with a federal law but attempt to regulate an area within federal legislative jurisdiction.
The Commerce Clause	The *commerce clause* grants the federal government the authority to pass regulations that significantly affect interstate commerce. Today, this clause provides the basis for most federal government regulations.
	Police powers are the residual powers retained by states to pass laws to safeguard the health and welfare of their citizens.
	The *dormant commerce clause* prohibits states from passing laws that significantly interfere with interstate commerce.
Taxing and Spending Powers of the Federal Government	Congressional taxes must be uniform across all states. Congress can use taxes and spending for purposes other than generating revenue; e.g., it can use them to indirectly promote social goals.
Other Constitutional Restrictions on Government	The *privileges and immunities clause* prohibits states from discriminating against citizens of other states.
	The *full faith and credit clause* states that in civil matters, courts in all states must uphold rights established by legal documents.
	The *contract clause* states that Congress cannot pass laws that unreasonably interfere with existing contracts.
The Amendments to the Constitution	*First Amendment:*
	• Protects corporate speech in certain circumstances. It protects corporate political speech to the same extent that it protects individuals' political speech. The Central Hudson test determines whether the First Amendment protects particular corporate commercial speech.
	• Contains the *establishment clause,* which states that Congress may not make laws respecting an establishment of religion, and the *free-exercise clause,* which states that Congress may not make laws prohibiting the free exercise of religion.

Fourth Amendment:

- Protects both corporations and individuals from unreasonable government searches and seizures. Although administrative searches generally require a warrant, administrative agencies may inspect some industries without a warrant to ensure compliance with industry regulations.

Fifth Amendment:

- States that government cannot take an individual's life, liberty, or property without due process of law. There are two types of due process: *procedural due process,* which focuses on rules for enforcing laws and entitles individuals to notice of legal action against them, and *substantive due process,* which requires that government have a proper purpose for enacting laws that restrict individuals' liberty or the use of their property.

- States that if government takes private property for public use, it must compensate the owner. The extent to which some government regulations constitute takings, however, generates much litigation.

- Includes a privilege against self-incrimination, although the provision does not apply to corporations. Only individual citizens and sole proprietorships may exercise this right.

- Guarantees individuals equal protection under the law. Courts use three different standards of scrutiny in equal protection cases: (1) *strict scrutiny,* to analyze government actions that abridge fundamental rights or that include suspect classifications; (2) *intermediate scrutiny,* to analyze classifications based on gender or on legitimacy of children; (3) the *rational-basis test,* to analyze classifications involving other matters.

Ninth Amendment:

- Along with the First, Third, Fourth, and Fifth Amendments, this amendment provides individuals with a right to privacy.

Fourteenth Amendment:

- Applies the due-process clause to state governments and contains the equal protection clause, which prohibits states from denying the equal protection of the laws to any citizens.

 Point/Counterpoint

Is Judicial Review Consistent with Our System of Democracy?	
NO	YES
Our system of government is one of popular sovereignty: Voters have the liberty to make the laws under which they will live. As established in *Marbury v. Madison,* judicial review permits the Supreme Court to strike down laws passed by Congress—laws that ostensibly represent the will of a majority of Americans. The Supreme Court, however, is not politically accountable. By declaring a law unconstitutional, the Supreme Court makes it enormously difficult for voters to overturn that decision; only an amendment to the Constitution (requiring approval of two-thirds of Congress and three-quarters of the state legislatures) can override it. Judicial review stymies voters' liberty to govern themselves. Proponents of judicial review argue that it is necessary to protect the ideals in the Constitution. But the Constitution represents the values a majority of Americans held more than two centuries ago. The	Judicial review has an important role to play in ensuring that our democracy functions. Without the possibility of judicial review, elected representatives could pass laws to insulate themselves from political pressure. For example, Congress could pass a law making it a crime to criticize congresspersons. Such laws inhibit democracy from functioning well. The Supreme Court, insulated from political pressure, should exercise its power of judicial review to ensure participation and reinforce representation in the political process. Judicial review also allows the Supreme Court to transcend legislative preoccupation with immediate results and protect values at the center of our political system (e.g., protection of minority rights). Our system, moreover, has many countermajoritarian features. The Constitution established the Senate, in which Wyoming and California are on equal footing; and the electoral college, not a popular majority,

acts of the political branches of government, on the other hand, are more likely to accurately reflect the values of a majority of Americans today. Thus, to promote the values of a majority of Americans, the Supreme Court should refrain from judicial review.

Judicial review is especially problematic because the nine unelected justices of the Supreme Court are not likely to reflect the views of the nation as a whole. A vast majority of the justices throughout American history have been white, male, and wealthy. Thus, the values they promote when they strike down legislative acts are likely to differ from the values of a majority of Americans.

elects the president. Senate rules permit *filibustering,* allowing one senator to obstruct a proposed piece of legislation unless a supermajority of senators override the filibuster. In short, our system is *republican,* not majority rule. Judicial review is not inconsistent with this form of government.

Additionally, the Supreme Court has a high turnover rate. On average, a Supreme Court vacancy opens up every 22 months, so a one-term president can expect to fill two Supreme Court seats. This high turnover rate tends to ensure that the Court stays in step with the national pulse. And the political branches of government are not exactly the paradigms of deliberative democracy that high school textbooks make them out to be.

⟶ Questions & Problems

1. Explain how each branch of the government checks the power of the other branches.

2. How can both Sue and Sam be correct when Sue claims the commerce clause increases government's power and Sam claims the commerce clause reduces government's power?

3. What is the purpose of the contract clause?

4. How does the contract clause affect state regulation?

5. How does the First Amendment protection of corporate political speech differ from the protection of corporate commercial speech?

6. The state of Oklahoma required that all coal-burning power plants in the state purchase at least 10 percent of the coal they burned from Oklahoma coal mines. The state of Wyoming challenged the legislation. On what constitutional basis do you think Wyoming brought its action? Do you believe Wyoming's challenge was successful? Why or why not? [*Wyoming v. Oklahoma,* 502 U.S. 437 (1992).]

7. During a legal search of Alvin Smith's house, police discovered a large amount of child pornography. A subsequent police investigation revealed that Smith had taken 1,768 sexually explicit pictures of girls below the age of 18. The investigation also revealed that the children depicted in the pictures were Florida residents and that Smith, a Florida resident, took the pictures in his house. The paper on which the photographs were printed, however, came from Rochester, New York, and the photographs were processed by equipment made in California. The government prosecuted Smith for violating a federal statute prohibiting child pornography. Smith challenged his conviction on grounds that Congress overstepped its commerce clause authority because his production of child pornography did not involve or substantially

affect interstate commerce. Do you think the court agreed with Smith's argument? Why or why not? [*United States v. Smith,* 402 F.3d 1303 (2005).]

8. Deputy Catherine Hedges stopped Allan Hollowell for driving his truck 56 mph in a 35-mph zone. Hedges called for backup, and when other officers arrived, they discovered that Hollowell's license was suspended. The officers placed him under arrest, searched his person, and found marijuana and crack cocaine. Upon searching the truck, the officers discovered a set of scales, plastic bags, a laptop computer, and a large quantity of cocaine. The trial court found Hollowell guilty of two felonies and misdemeanors. Hollowell appealed, contending that the trial court erred by including the evidence police discovered searching his person and his truck. How do you think the supreme court of Indiana ruled in this case? [*Hollowell v. Indiana,* 753 N.E.2d. 612 (2001).]

9. An interstate trucking company filed suit against the state of Michigan, alleging that Michigan's $100 annual fee on trucks involved in intrastate commerce violates the dormant commerce clause. The trucking company argued that the fee discriminates against trucks involved in both intrastate and interstate commerce because they spend less time carrying cargo in Michigan than do trucks involved with solely intrastate commerce. The state argued that the fee is a valid exercise of its police power, intending to defray the costs of regulating the size and weight of trucks in Michigan. With whom do you think the U.S. Supreme Court sided in this case? Why? [*Am. Trucking Ass'ns v. Mich. PSC,* 125 S. Ct. 2419 (2005).]

10. The Federal Alcohol Administration Act prohibited beer labels from disclosing the alcohol content of the beer. Coors Brewing Company challenged the regulation. The government argued that it had a substantial

interest in preventing "strength wars" among beer producers. Moreover, the government argued, the act was narrowly tailored to further that interest. Apply the *Central Hudson* test to explain how you believe the U.S. Supreme Court ruled in this case. [*Rubin v. Coors Brewing Co.,* 115 S. Ct. 1585 (1995).]

11. Harris County arrested Carl Pruett for violating a law prohibiting bail-bond businesses from soliciting individuals with outstanding arrest warrants. The purpose of the law, according to the county, was to prevent individuals from fleeing the county when notified of their outstanding arrest warrants by bail-bonding companies. Pruett argued that the law was an unconstitutional restriction of his right to free speech. How do you think the court ruled in this case? Why? [*Harris County Bail Bond Bd. v. Pruett,* 2005 Tex. App. LEXIS 1912 (2005).]

12. The City of Toledo, Ohio, passed the Clean Indoor Air Ordinance, which required, among other provisions, that smoking was prohibited in bars and restaurants, except in separate smoking lounges that met very specific criteria. The lounge could not constitute more than 50 percent of the establishment's square footage into which the public is invited, must have a separate ventilation system, and cannot be located in an area where employees are required to work or be an area that the public must walk through to go to the restroom. An association of bar and restaurant owners challenged the law as a regulatory taking. The district court denied the claim and the association appealed. How do you think the appellate court ruled and why? [*D.A.R.E. Inc. v. City of Toledo,* 393 F.3d 692(2005).]

13. In April 1986 the FBI arrested Larry Dean Dusenbery in his home. After the FBI removed Dusenbery from the premises and placed him in custody, it obtained and executed a search warrant for his property. During the search, FBI agents seized drugs, drug paraphernalia, weapons, an automobile, and $21,939 in currency. Dusenbery pleaded guilty to a charge of possession with intent to distribute. The trial court sentenced him to 12 years in prison and a 6-year special parole. Two years later, the FBI began to administratively forfeit the seized possessions. This process required that the FBI send written notice of the forfeiture procedures to Dusenbery. The FBI, in accordance with this policy, sent letters to Dusenbery by certified mail to the federal corrections institution where he was incarcerated. The FBI sent identical letters to his home address and his mother's address. The FBI received no response, but nevertheless it proceeded with the forfeiture of his assets. Five years later, Dusenbery filed a motion requesting that the FBI return his property to him. He received a response from the United States government informing him that the FBI had returned all property not used in the drug business and had forfeited the rest of it. Dusenbery filed a civil suit claiming that the FBI denied his right of due process when it forfeited his property because he had never received the letter from the FBI. The district court ruled that the FBI had not violated his due process rights; the FBI satisfied his rights when it sent the notice. How do you think the appellate court ruled in this case? Why? [*Dusenbery v. United States,* 534 U.S. 161 (2002).]

14. In 1996 Congress passed the Telecommunications Act. This legislation addressed growing public concern that children could access, at least in part, sexually explicit programming through a phenomenon called "signal bleed." Signal bleed occurs when visual or audio portions of programs can be seen or heard despite cable providers' attempt to scramble the programs. The act required that cable providers fully scramble or otherwise fully block those channels or limit transmission to hours when children are unlikely to watch television. Most cable operators adopted the latter approach, broadcasting programs only during an eight-hour period at night. Playboy Entertainment Group, a firm that transmitted sexually explicit programming to cable television operators, filed suit against the federal government. The suit claimed that the Telecommunications Act violated the First Amendment, and it asked for an injunction prohibiting the act's enforcement. The district court ruled that the act imposed a content-based restriction on speech; the court concluded that although the government interests were compelling, the government could further those interests in a less restrictive way. How do you think the U.S. Supreme Court ruled in this case? Why? [*United States v. Playboy Entertainment Group,* 529 U.S. 803 (2000).]

Looking for more review material?

The Online Learning Center at **www.mhhe.com/kubasekess** contains this chapter's "Assignment on the Internet" and also a list of URLs for more information, entitled "On the Internet." Find both of them in the Student Center portion of the OLC, along with quizzes and other helpful materials.

Tort Law

---▶ **CASE OPENER**

Rubin v. U.S. News

Richard Rubin, chief executive of Republic Metals, a gold-refining company, agreed to be interviewed and photographed for a *U.S. News & World Report article.*[1] Rubin argued that he had been told the article was about the Peruvian value tax, a rebate given to those who export gold from Peru. However, when the article appeared in the magazine, it was titled "The Golden Age of Crime: Why International Drug Traffickers Are Invading the Global Gold Trade." The author of the article explained how the gold trade is used as a tool for money laundering, and Rubin, also pictured, was quoted as saying, "There's a dual economic system. There's on the books and there's off the books."

When Rubin discovered that the article was about money laundering, he brought suit against *U.S. News & World Report.* Rubin argued that the story implied he is or has been involved in money laundering through his gold-refining business and that this implication hurt his reputation. *U.S. News* issued a clarification stating that the purpose of the article was not to imply Rubin was involved in illegal activity.

1. Suppose you are Rubin. You are concerned that the article has damaged your gold-refining business. What do you do? Why?
2. Now suppose you are a manager at a company that does business with Rubin's refining company. You read the story in *U.S. News.* Does the story lead to any change in your business with Rubin? Why?

[1] See Susan R. Miller, "*U.S. News* Sued by Gold Trader," quoted in "Money Laundering Story," *Broward Daily Business Review,* May 25, 2000, p. A1; "News Magazine Sued," *National Law Journal,* June 12, 2000, p. B2.

---▶ **LEARNING OBJECTIVES**

After reading this chapter, you will be able to answer the following questions:

LO 1 How are torts classified?

LO 2 What are some of the most common intentional torts, and what are the elements needed to prove these torts?

As a future business manager, you will likely be involved in a situation where one party believes he or she has been injured by the actions of another party, in the same way Rubin believed he had been injured by the *U.S. News & World Report* article. Wrongs such as these are often referred to as *torts*. A **tort** is commonly defined as a wrong or injury to another, other than a breach of contract. In fact, *tort* is a French word meaning "wrong." This chapter first examines the goals of tort law and the three primary classifications of torts. Next, the chapter examines each of the categories of torts. It concludes by discussing damages that may be available in tort cases.

tort
A violation of another person's rights or a civil wrongdoing that does not arise out of a contract or statute; primary types are intentional, negligent, and strict-liability torts.

Introduction to Tort Law

Chapter 2 introduced criminal law and explained the punishment individuals may receive for committing crimes. Most of the actions that give rise to criminal prosecutions also provide the basis for a tort claim by the victim of the crime.

While the primary objectives of criminal law are to punish wrongdoers and preserve order in society, the primary objective of tort law is to provide compensation for injured parties. Tort law also contributes to maintaining order in society because it discourages private retaliation by injured persons and their friends. After all, we do not want to live in a community where vigilantes with tempers are roaming about righting some harm they believe has occurred to them.

A third objective of tort law is to give citizens a sense that they live in a just society. Our collective sense of right and wrong suggests that someone who creates harm should make things right by compensating those who were harmed. The recognition that one will have to pay for the personal injuries she or he causes may also serve to deter the commission of torts.

Although this chapter discusses torts as if they were the same everywhere, tort law is primarily state law, so states may have slightly different definitions of each tort. In describing torts, this chapter uses the definitions common in most states, noting the instances where there seems to be a significant difference in the way certain states define the tort.

Despite the public impression of a litigation explosion often conveyed by the media, tort litigation has been declining slightly since 1990.[2] The National Center for State Courts compiled statistics on tort filings in 15 states and found that from 1995 to 2004, there had been a general downward trend in the overall number of tort filings each year. In 2003, the last year for which detailed data are available, there were 198,377 tort filings in the 15 studied states.[3] However, even when the number of tort cases is not increasing, there are still enough cases filed each year that potential tort liability should concern a competent business manager.

[2] National Center for State Courts, www.ncsconline.org/D_Research/csp/2002_Files/2002_Tables_10-16.pdf (accessed September 9, 2005).

[3] *Examining the Work of State Courts, 2005: A National Perspective from the Court Statistics Project* (2006) p. 27. (The Court Statistics Project is a joint project of the National Center for State Courts, the State Justice Institute, and the Bureau of Justice Statistics of the Department of Justice.)

LO 1

intentional tort
A civil wrong resulting from an intentional act committed on the person, property, or economic interest of another. Intentional torts include assault, battery, conversion, false imprisonment, intentional infliction of emotional distress, trespass to land, and trespass to chattels.

negligent tort
A civil wrong that occurs when the defendant acts in a way that subjects other people to an unreasonable risk of harm (i.e., the defendant is careless, to someone else's detriment). Negligence claims are usually used to achieve compensation for accidents and injuries.

strict-liability tort
A civil wrong that occurs when the defendant takes an action that is inherently dangerous and cannot ever be undertaken safely, no matter what precautions the defendant takes. In such situations, a defendant is liable for the plaintiff's damages without any requirement that the plaintiff prove that the defendant was negligent.

LO 2

assault
A civil wrong that occurs when one person intentionally and voluntarily places another in fear or apprehension of an immediate, offensive physical harm. Assault does not require actual contact.

battery
A civil wrong that occurs when one person intentionally and voluntarily brings about a non-consented harmful or offensive contact with a person or something closely associated with him or her. Battery requires an actual contact.

Classification of Torts

Torts are most commonly classified as intentional, negligent, or strict-liability torts. Each category differs in terms of the elements needed to prove the tort, the available damages, the available defenses, and the degree of willfulness of the actor. Intentional torts occur when the defendant takes an action intending certain consequences will result or knowing certain consequences are likely to result. Negligent torts occur when the defendant acts in a way that subjects other people to an unreasonable risk of harm. In other words, the defendant is careless to someone else's detriment. Finally, strict-liability torts occur when the defendant takes an action that is inherently dangerous and cannot ever be undertaken safely, no matter what precautions the defendant takes. It is important to remember that when we discuss these classifications, we are referring to their use in the United States. The Chinese legal system, for example, narrowly defines the activities actionable under tort law.

Intentional Torts

Intentional torts are the most "willful" of torts. Intentional torts are predicated on the common element of intent. The intent at issue is not intent to harm but, rather, is intent to engage in a specific act, which ultimately results in an injury, physical or economic, to another. In fact, one does not need to establish a motive when proving liability in an intentional tort case. Moreover, in tort law it is assumed that people intend what could be considered the normal consequences of their actions. For example, were Rob to throw a rock toward a group of people, it would be assumed under the law that he intended to hit someone with the rock and that the person hit would be hurt, regardless of Rob's intention merely to scare the group of people.

As a general rule, each specific intentional tort has a set of elements that must be proved to establish the tort, along with specific defenses that can be raised against each tort. However, not all harms intentionally committed will fall neatly into an existing category of torts. Therefore, a general theory of intentional tort liability has been created to aid judges in their decision making. In Section 870 of the Restatement (Second) of Torts, the general theory is explained this way:

> One who intentionally causes injury to another is subject to liability to the other for that injury, if his conduct is generally culpable and not justifiable under the circumstances. This liability may be imposed although the actor's conduct does not come within a traditional category of tort liability.

Intentional torts are divided into the following three categories: (1) torts against persons, (2) torts against property, and (3) torts against economic interests. The following sections discuss a number of specific torts that fall into each category, along with the defenses for each.

INTENTIONAL TORTS AGAINST PERSONS

Torts against persons are intentional acts that harm an individual's physical or mental integrity. There are a significant number of these torts. Assault and battery are two of the most common. Imagine that after searching for a parking space for 20 minutes you finally pull into a spot. However, as soon as you turn off your car, a man who looks like Mike Tyson starts pounding on your car window. He angrily yells, "You took my spot! If you don't move your car now, I'm going to hit you so hard you won't remember what your car looks like!" The man has just assaulted you.

An assault occurs when one person places another in fear or apprehension of an immediate, offensive bodily contact. Therefore, in the above example, if you think the man is just joking and you start laughing, no assault has taken place because there is no fear or apprehension. Not only must you feel fear or apprehension, but that feeling must be reasonable under the circumstances.

An assault is often, but not always, followed by a battery, an intentional, unwanted, offensive bodily contact. Almost any unwanted, intentional contact constitutes a battery. Even contacts that are harmless, if unwanted, are batteries. And even if a touch is intended as a joke, if the reasonable person

would be offended, the contact is deemed "offensive."[4] To return to the example of the parking-space incident, if the man actually hit you, his action would constitute a battery. In contrast, if you both happened to be getting out of your respective cars at the same time and consequently bumped into each other, no battery would have occurred because there was no *intentional* bodily contact.

There are a limited number of defenses available to an action for a battery. A party charged with a battery may argue that the offended party consented to the contact. *Consent,* as a defense, mitigates the element of unwanted. A person cannot commit a battery if the contact was consented to and therefore wanted.

The most common defense to battery is *self-defense,* responding to the force of another with comparable force in order to defend oneself. In our parking-space example, if the man took a swing at you and you shoved him to try to keep him from hitting you, causing him to fall backward and hit his head on the street, he would not succeed in a case against you for battery because you could raise the defense of self-defense. To use this defense, you cannot use a greater level of force than is being used against you.

A third defense, *defense of others,* allows you to defend another by using the same degree of force that you could use to defend yourself. A final defense, *defense of property,* allows you to use reasonable force to defend your property from an intruder. The use of deadly force in defense of property is rarely, if ever, considered justified.

The tort alleged in this chapter's opening case was **defamation,** which is the intentional publication (communication to a third party) of a false statement harmful to an individual's reputation. In addition to the person who publishes a false statement, anyone who republishes, or in any manner repeats, a defamatory statement is also liable for defamation, even if he or she cites the original source of the defamation.

> **defamation**
> A false statement or an action that harms the reputation or character of an individual, business, product, group, government, or nation.

If the defamation is published in a permanent form, such as printed in a magazine or newspaper, it is known as *libel.* Television and radio broadcasts are also considered libel, since they are permanently recorded. In the case of libel, "general damages" are presumed. Thus, the victim would be entitled to compensation for the damages that are presumed to flow from defamation yet are hard to prove, such as the humiliation the victim would feel.

If the defamation is made orally, it is *slander.* In order to recover damages in a case of slander, the plaintiff must prove "special damages"; that is, the plaintiff must show specific monetary loss that resulted from the defamatory statements. While libel is contained in a permanent form, slander, by virtue of being spoken, is not. It is the lack of permanence that gives way to the special damages involved with slander. If the people who heard the slander do not act in a way to cause harm to the slandered person, there is no cause for compensation, which is one of the main goals of tort law.

One exception to the requirement of special damages occurs if the false statements constitute *slander per se.* Slander per se statements are considered to be so inherently harmful that general damages are presumed. The kinds of statements considered slander per se are claims that an individual (1) has a loathsome, communicable disease (traditionally venereal disease or leprosy); (2) has committed a crime for which imprisonment is a possibility; (3) is professionally incompetent; or (4), if a woman, has engaged in sexual misconduct.

If you say your boss is a tyrant or your roommate is a slob, are you in danger of being sued for defamation? You probably are not because such statements are not really statements of fact; rather, they are opinions, and subjective opinions that are not capable of being proved are generally not actionable.

One of the important elements of defamation is that the defamatory statement must be damaging to someone's reputation, as the Case Nugget illustrates. For example, when a convicted criminal serving three life sentences attempted to sue a journalist for alleged errors in an article detailing his criminal history, the journalist filed a motion to dismiss on grounds that the defendant was libel proof as a matter of law regarding claims about his criminal background. Upholding the dismissal, the court said the plaintiff's public reputation at the time the articles were published was so diminished with respect to a specific subject (his kidnapping and murder convictions) that he could not be further injured by allegedly false statements on that subject.[5]

[4] Restatement (Second) of Torts, sec. 19.

[5] *Thomas P. Lamb v. Tony Rizzo,* 391 F.3d 1133 (2004).

The increase in communication over the Internet has presented new questions for the law of defamation to answer. First, does a false statement made over this information network constitute defamation? Second, who can be held liable if defamation does exist?

The court first attempted to answer these issues in the case of *Cubby v. CompuServ.*[6] In that case, CompuServ was sued because of defamatory statements published on one of the forums available through its online information service. In holding that CompuServ could not be held liable, the court made an analogy between an online information service provider such as CompuServ and bookstores, saying, "CompuServ's CIS product is in essence an electronic, for profit library." The court went on to say that once CompuServ decides to carry a given publication such as a news forum, it has little or no editorial control over that forum. It would therefore be no more feasible for CompuServ to examine every publication it carries for defamatory material than it would be for libraries or booksellers to do so.

Since *Cubby* was decided, the Communications Decency Act of 1996 was passed. One section of this act gives immunity to providers of interactive computer services for liability they might otherwise incur on account of material disseminated by them but created by others.

A person who is accused of defamation can raise two defenses: truth and privilege. *Truth* is frequently considered to be an absolute defense. That is, one cannot be held liable for defamation, regardless of whether damages result, if the statement made was the truth. If I say Bill is a convicted felon, and he is, I have not committed defamation. Under ordinary circumstances, the fact that you *thought* a statement was true is not a defense. So if I honestly believe Bill is a convicted felon and I tell others he is, but he is not, then I have committed slander.

Privilege is an affirmative defense in a defamation action. An affirmative defense occurs when the defendant admits to the accusation but argues that there is a reason why he should not be held liable. A privilege is either absolute or conditional. When an absolute privilege exists, one cannot be sued for defamation for any false statements made, regardless of intent or knowledge of the falsity of the claim. Absolute privilege arises in only a limited number of circumstances. The speech and debate clause of the U.S. Constitution gives an absolute privilege to individuals speaking on the House and Senate floors during congressional debate. This privilege exists because the House wants to get to the truth of matters before it, and if people testifying before Congress had to fear they might be sued, they might be afraid to testify. Absolute privilege also arises during a judicial proceeding. Again, we do not want people to be afraid to testify in court, so we prohibit their being sued for whatever occurs within the courtroom. As the following Case Nugget illustrates, the concept of a judicial proceeding can extend beyond a traditional courtroom.

Conditional privilege is the second type. Under a conditional privilege, a party will not be held liable for defamation unless the false statement was made with actual malice. A statement is made with actual malice if it is made with *either* knowledge of its falsity or reckless disregard for its truth. Businesspersons should be most concerned about the conditional privilege that arises with respect to job recommendations. To encourage employers to give honest assessments of their former employees, this privilege protects an employer who makes a false statement about a former worker: The employer will not be held liable as long as the statement was made in good faith and was made only to those who had a legitimate interest in the information being communicated.

Another conditional privilege is the public figure privilege. Public figures are individuals who are in the public eye, typically politicians and entertainers. Because these individuals have a significant impact on our lives, we want to encourage free discussion about them, so we do not hold people liable for making false statements about them as long as the statements were not made with malice. This privilege does not seem to place an unfair burden on the public figure because such an individual can easily respond publicly to any false claims given that he or she is already in the public eye and has appropriate outlets available for giving his or her opinion.

There are those who believe a conditional privilege should apply when the defamatory statement is posted somewhere on the Internet. The reasoning behind application of the privilege in this context is that the person who has been defamed over the Internet can respond to the defamatory remarks in the same forum with minimal effort. Thus, there is less need for the stronger

absolute privilege
A special right, immunity, permission, or benefit given to certain individuals that allows them to make any statements about someone without being held liable for defamation for any false statement made, regardless of intent or knowledge of the falsity of the claim.

conditional privilege
A special right, immunity, permission, or benefit given to certain individuals that allows them to make any statements about someone without being held liable for defamation for any false statement made without actual malice.

actual malice
In defamation, either a person's knowledge that his or her statement or published material is false or the person's reckless disregard for whether it was false.

public figure privilege
A special right, immunity, or permission given to people that allows them to make any statements about public figures, typically politicians and entertainers, without being held liable for defamation for any false statement made without malice.

[6] 77b F. Supp. 135 (1991).

CASE Nugget

The Applicability of an Absolute Privilege

Hartman and Swinehart v. Keri

2008 Ind. LEXIS 265

On May 12, 2003, graduate students Virginia Hartman and Suzanne Swinehart filed formal complaints alleging sexual harassment by Dr. Gabe Keri, an assistant professor at Indiana University-Purdue University Fort Wayne (IPFW) from whom they had taken courses. IPFW charged Dr. Elaine Blakemore with the task of investigating the allegations; Dr. Blakemore submitted a report on June 30, 2003, that concluded Hartman and Swinehart's allegations were credible and commended their willingness to report the behavior. Furthermore, Blakemore suggested Keri be immediately removed from teaching positions. These findings and recommendations were further investigated by a three-person panel and Chancellor Wartell. Blakemore's report was supported and Keri was given a 100 percent research position with no use of his university office.

Keri appealed to the president of Purdue, who upheld the Chancellor's decision. In response, Keri filed suit against Hartman and Swinehart in the Allen Superior Court, claiming libel, slander, and malicious interference. Hartman and Swinehart moved for summary judgment, claiming their statements were protected by absolute privilege. This motion was denied. Hartman and Swinehart appealed.

In finding that the students' statements were entitled to absolute privilege, the judges explained that administrative proceedings that are quasi-judicial in nature are entitled to absolute protection. They applied the factors courts use to determine whether a proceeding is quasi-judicial in nature. These factors include whether the body has the power to: (1) exercise judgment and discretion; (2) hear and determine or to ascertain facts and make decisions; (3) make binding orders and judgments; (4) affect the personal or property rights of private persons; (5) examine witnesses and hear the litigation of issues on a hearing; or (6) enforce decisions or impose penalties.

legal protection we ordinarily give to private parties who are defamed. In addition, we want to encourage free expression and the exchange of ideas on the Internet. One way to do so is to allow people to openly respond to criticisms on the Internet. When people are overly concerned about making errors, free exchange is hindered. Relaxing defamation standards in regard to the Internet can encourage people to speak their minds freely. Thus far, however, no such privilege has been established. And when a person is found to have committed defamation on an online bulletin board or Web site, the damages can be significant. For example, a jury awarded $3 million to a university professor who sued a former student who had accused him of being a pedophile on a Web site she maintained.

INTENTIONAL TORTS AGAINST PROPERTY

Because businesses own property, anyone who manages a business should be concerned about torts against property. The most common torts a businessperson might be involved with are trespass to realty, nuisance, trespass to personalty, and conversion.

Trespass to Realty The tort of trespass to realty, also called *trespass to real property*, occurs when a person intentionally (1) enters the land of another without permission; (2) causes an object to be placed on the land of another without the landowner's permission; (3) stays on the

trespass to realty
A tort that occurs when someone goes on another's property without permission or places something on another's property without permission.

land of another when the owner tells him to depart; or (4) refuses to remove something he placed on the property that the landowner asked him to remove.

It is no defense for a person to argue that she thought she had a legal right to be on the property or she thought the land belonged to someone else. The intent refers to intentionally being on that particular piece of land. In a recent, unusual case heard in a small claims court in Westchester County, a plaintiff sued the defendant for trespass to realty when the defendant entered the plaintiff's property to serve the plaintiff with a reply affidavit for another legal action. The defendant had previously been barred from entering the plaintiff's property. The plaintiff argued that the defendant could not dictate how legal papers are served. The plaintiff sued for $3,000 in compensatory, nominal, and punitive damages. While the court ruled that the defendant committed trespass to realty, it awarded only nominal damages in the sum of $1.

Because guests are welcomed onto one's property, they are not considered trespassers. However, if a guest is asked to leave and he or she refuses, the person immediately becomes a trespasser and no longer maintains a right to be on the property in question. If charges were brought against such a person, that person could not raise the defense that he or she was a guest.

Also, when a trespasser is on someone's property, the trespasser is liable for damages she or he might cause to the property. Furthermore, under common law, a trespasser cannot hold an owner of property liable for damages the trespasser sustains while on the property. However, as of late, courts have been shifting away from this common law rule. Now, courts typically maintain that owners owe a reasonable duty to anyone who may end up on their property. The specifics of the duty vary by jurisdiction, as well as by the status of the parties. In some jurisdictions, it is possible, although rare, for owners to be liable for trespassers who were injured while trying to steal property from the owners.

private nuisance
A nuisance that affects only a single or very limited number of individuals.

Private Nuisance A private nuisance occurs when a person uses her property in an unreasonable manner that harms a neighbor's use or enjoyment of his property. Using one's property in a manner that caused the neighbor to be subjected to flooding, vibrations, excessive noise, or smoke could lead to a nuisance claim.

trespass to personal property
Temporary interference with another's use or enjoyment of his or her personal property.

Trespass to Personal Property A person commits trespass to personal property, also called *trespass to personalty,* by temporarily exerting control over another's personal property or interfering with the true owner's right to use the property. Under trespass to personal property, the trespasser is responsible for damages caused to the property, as well as for damages caused to the owner related to the trespasser's wrongful possession of the property. For example, if I take someone's bike from his garage and use it for a week, I have committed trespass to personalty. If I return the bike after it has a flat tire, I will have to compensate the owner for the cost of repairing the tire and any other expenses that resulted from my having the bike for a week. Also, if the bike was the only means the person had for getting to work, I would be responsible for the person's lost wages resulting from the missed work, because I took the person's means of transportation.

conversion
Permanent interference with another's use and enjoyment of his or her personal property.

Conversion Conversion occurs when a person permanently removes personal property from the owner's possession and control. When conversion occurs, the true owner can no longer regain the property. The owner usually recovers damages for the full value of the converted item, plus any additional damages that resulted from the loss.

It is not a defense to conversion for a person to argue that she believed she had a legal claim to the goods. For example, if Brittany accidentally takes Melvin's suitcase believing it to be hers and then loses it, she is still liable for conversion. Moreover, the possession of stolen goods also makes a person liable for conversion. Therefore, buying goods in good faith without knowledge of any impropriety also is not a defense to conversion. Even if a person bought the goods believing the purchase was legal, the person with the stolen goods is liable to the legal owner of the goods.

An illustration of conversion comes from a recent case heard in the Westchester County Supreme Court. An amateur race-car driver left her race car at a service station. While the car was in the possession of the service station, an employee of the station, with a known drinking problem, apparently drove the car, wrecked it, and totally destroyed it. The car could never be

returned in the condition it was in when brought to the station. The owner sued for conversion and recovered the value of the car in damages.

INTENTIONAL TORTS AGAINST ECONOMIC INTERESTS

All businesspersons should be familiar with the torts against economic interest. The five most common torts against economic interests, frequently referred to as "business torts," are disparagement, intentional interference with contract, unfair competition, misappropriation, and fraudulent misrepresentation. The first tort, disparagement, is similar to defamation, but it is a business's or product's reputation that has been tarnished.

The plaintiff in a disparagement case must prove that the defendant published a false statement of a material fact about the plaintiff's product or service that resulted in a loss of sales. When such statements are criticisms of the quality, honesty, or reputation of the business or product, the tort is sometimes called slander of quality (if spoken) or trade libel (if in printed form). If the statements relate to the ownership of the business property, the term slander of title is used.

Damages for disparaging are ordinarily based on a decrease in profits that can be linked to the publication of the false statement. An alternative, although less common, way to prove damages is to demonstrate that the plaintiff had been negotiating a contract with a third party but the third party lost interest shortly after the publication of the false statement. The profits the plaintiff would have made on the contract would be the damages.

Some interesting variations of the tort of disparagement have developed. For example, in 2007, California became the thirteenth state to recognize the tort of food disparagement, which critics call "veggie libel." Such laws provide ranchers and farmers with a cause of action when someone knowingly makes false, damaging statements about a food product. The California law was drafted in response to an incident during 2006 in which Taco Bell executives wrongly identified green onions grown at Boskovich Farms in Oxnard as the source of an *E. coli* outbreak that sickened 70 of the fast-food chain's customers.

A second tort against economic interests is the tort of intentional interference with contract. To successfully bring a claim of intentional interference with contract, the plaintiff must prove (1) a valid and enforceable contract between the two parties existed; (2) the defendant party knew of the existence of the contract and its terms; (3) the defendant intentionally undertook steps to cause one of the parties to breach the contract; and (4) the plaintiff was injured as a result of the breach.[7]

When a contract exists, clear liability is placed on third parties for inducing a party to the contract to breach the contract. However, when a prospective contract exists, a third party might be liable for inducing a party to pull out of the contract before it is formed. Because the essence of business involves competition, simply offering a better deal is not enough to create liability when a prospective contract exists. However, if a party uses illegal means to cause another party not to enter into a contract, the party who acted illegally is liable for interfering with contractual relations.[8]

The most common situation involving intentional interference with a contract in the business context occurs when one employer tries to lure an employee away from another employer. Liability in such a situation, however, is limited to the case where the employee has a contract for a set period of time and the prospective employer actually knows of the contract.

When a third party interferes with a contract, injured parties may recover damages for what was directly lost through the breached contract. They may also recover any losses suffered related to the breached contract, in addition to damages for emotional distress and harm to reputation.[9]

A third tort against economic interests, unfair competition, exists because of American views about the purpose of a business. Americans believe a business is intended to make a profit, and the law protects businesses acting on this profit motive. Therefore, when someone enters a business with the sole intent of driving another firm out of business, the law punishes this act as

disparagement
A business tort that occurs when a statement is intentionally used to defame a business product or service.

slander of quality
A business tort that occurs when false spoken statements criticize a business product or service and result in a loss of sales.

trade libel
A business tort that occurs when false printed statements criticize a business product or service and result in a loss of sales.

slander of title
A business tort that occurs when false published statements are related to the ownership of the business property.

food disparagement
A tort that provides ranchers and farmers with a cause of action when someone spreads false information about the safety of a food product.

intentional interference with contract
The tort that occurs when someone intentionally takes an action that will cause a person to breach a contract that she or he has with another.

unfair competition
The act of competing with another not to make a profit but for the sole purpose of driving that other out of business.

[7] Restatement (Second) of Torts, sec. 766.

[8] Restatement (Second) of Torts, sec. 766B.

[9] Restatement (Second) of Torts, sec. 774A.

unfair competition. For example, if there is only one jewelry store in town, Mark cannot come in and set up a store where he makes no profits, just to drive the other store out of business, so that an acquaintance of his can then move in and open up a legitimate jewelry store once the competition has been eliminated.

A fourth tort against economic interests is fraudulent misrepresentation, which occurs when one uses intentional deceit to facilitate personal gain. To establish that a fraudulent misrepresentation exists, a party must demonstrate all the following:

fraudulent misrepresentation
The tort that occurs when a misrepresentation is made with the intent to facilitate personal gain and with the knowledge that it is false.

1. A party knowingly, or with reckless disregard for the truth, misrepresented material facts and conditions.
2. The party intended to have other parties rely on the misrepresentations.
3. The injured party reasonably relied on the misrepresentations.
4. The injured party suffered damages because of a reliance on the misrepresentations.
5. A direct link exists between the injuries suffered and a reliance on the misrepresentations.[10]

As in the criminal act of fraud, in the civil act of fraudulent misrepresentation, a party materially misrepresents something and thereby causes another party to suffer damages. Typically, fraudulent misrepresentation applies only to the misrepresentation of material facts. However, when a party with expert knowledge regarding a specific matter states an opinion, any party reasonably relying on the statement, although it is an opinion and not fact, may recover damages under the tort of fraudulent misrepresentation.

Negligence

negligence
Behavior that creates an unreasonable risk of harm to others.

Negligence is behavior that creates an unreasonable risk of harm to others. Unlike intentional torts, which result from a person's willfully taking actions that are likely to cause injury, negligent torts involve the failure to exercise reasonable care to protect another's person or property.

Sometimes, however, harm occurs because an individual suffers an unfortunate accident, an incident that simply could not be avoided, even with reasonable care. For example, suppose Jonathan is driving on the highway when he suffers a stroke. Because of the stroke, he crashes into two other vehicles. He is not, however, liable for damages caused by the accident because he was not negligent. Yet if Jonathan had some type of warning that the stroke was going to occur, he might be liable for the accident.

LO 3

To win a negligence case, the plaintiff must prove four elements: (1) duty, (2) breach of duty, (3) causation, and (4) damages. (See Exhibit 5-1.) A plaintiff who cannot establish all four of these elements will be denied recovery.

DUTY

reasonable person standard
A measurement of the way members of society expect an individual to act in a given situation.

The plaintiff must first establish that the defendant owes a *duty* to the plaintiff. In some particular situations, the law specifies the duty of care one individual owes to another. In most cases, however, the courts use the reasonable person standard to determine the defendant's duty of care. The reasonable person standard is a measurement of the way members of society expect an individual to act in a given situation. To determine the defendant's duty of care, the judge or jury must determine

Exhibit 5-1

Elements of Negligence

To prove negligence, a plaintiff must demonstrate:

1. Duty
2. Breach of duty
3. Causation—actual and proximate
4. Damages

[10] Restatement (Second) of Torts, sec. 525.

the degree of care and skill that a reasonable person would exercise under similar circumstances. The judge or jury then uses this standard to evaluate the actions of the individual in the case.

When courts attempt to determine whether a reasonable person would have owed a duty to others, they consider four questions:

1. How likely was it that the harm would occur?
2. How serious was the potential harm?
3. How socially beneficial was the defendant's conduct that posed the risk of harm?
4. What costs would have been necessary to reduce the risk of harm?

In many situations, it is far from clear what a reasonable person would do. For example, if a reasonable person saw an infant drowning in a shallow swimming pool, what would she do? In most situations like this one, the law holds that individuals have no duty to rescue strangers from perilous situations.

In some cases, however, the courts hold that individuals have a duty to aid strangers in certain types of peril. For example, if Sam negligently hits Janice with his car and, as a result, Janice is lying in the street, Sam has a duty to remove her from that dangerous position. Similarly, employers have a special duty to protect their employees from dangerous situations.

The courts generally hold that landowners have a duty of care to protect individuals on their property. Similarly, businesses have a duty of care to customers who enter business property. It is important, therefore, for future business managers to be knowledgeable about this duty. Businesses should warn customers about risks they may encounter on business property. Some risks, however, are obvious, and businesses need not warn customers about them. For example, a business need not inform customers that they could get a paper cut from the pages of a book.

The courts generally hold that businesses have a duty of care to protect their customers against foreseeable risks about which the owner knew or reasonably should have known. For example, in *Haywood v. Baseline Construction Company,* a woman who tripped over lumber on the front porch of the House of Blues restaurant in Los Angeles sued for negligence. The business's attempt to warn customers by marking the lumber with yellow construction tape was insufficient to avoid the determination of negligence; the woman was awarded $91,366 in damages.

Professionals have more training than ordinary people. Thus, when professionals are serving in their professional capacity, courts generally hold that they have a higher duty of care to clients than does the ordinary person. A professional cannot defend against a negligence suit by claiming ignorance of generally accepted principles in her or his field of expertise. Clients who feel that they have suffered damages as a result of a professional's breach of her duty of care can bring a negligence case against her. These actions are frequently referred to as *malpractice cases.*

BREACH OF DUTY

Once the plaintiff has established that the defendant owes her a duty of care, she must prove that the defendant's conduct violated that duty. This violation is called a *breach of duty.* For example, the driver of an automobile owes the other passengers in his car a duty of care to obey traffic signs. If he fails to stop at a stop sign, he has violated his duty to follow traffic signs and has therefore breached his duty of care.

CAUSATION

Causation is the third element of a successful negligence claim, and it has two separate elements: actual cause and proximate cause. The plaintiff must prove both elements of causation to be able to recover damages.

The first element, **actual cause** (also known as *cause in fact*), is the determination that the defendant's breach of duty resulted directly in the plaintiff's injury. The courts commonly determine whether a breach of duty actually caused the plaintiff's injury by asking whether the plaintiff would have been injured if the defendant had fulfilled his or her duty. If the answer is no, then the actual cause of the plaintiff's injury was the defendant's breach. Actual cause is sometimes referred to as "but-for" causation because the plaintiff argues that the damages she suffered would not have occurred *but for* (except because of) the actions of the defendant.

actual cause
The determination that the defendant's breach of duty resulted directly in the plaintiff's injury.

E-COMMERCE and the Law

Negligence on the Internet

A commonly offered explanation for the increasing occurrence of violence is the increased violence portrayed in the media. Some plaintiffs try to hold owners of certain Web sites liable under negligence theories for violent acts committed by teenagers. For example, in *James v. Meow Media,* a 14-year-old boy took six guns to school and shot three of his classmates to death. The parents of the deceased classmates brought suit against several Internet Web sites and the creators and distributors of various video games. The parents argued that these defendants had a duty of ordinary care to the slain girls.

The courts have been consistent, however, in finding that it was not foreseeable that a boy who played certain video games and viewed certain Web sites would murder three of his classmates. In similar cases, courts have ruled that defendants (such as Web site owners, creators and distributors of video games, and directors and producers of movies) do not have a duty to protect a person from the criminal acts of a third party unless there is a special relationship that requires that the defendant act with that duty.

Although it appears that Web site owners, manufacturers, and producers will not be held liable, plaintiffs continue to bring suits against these groups of people. Can you think of an argument for why these groups of people might owe a duty of care to these plaintiffs?

proximate cause
The extent to which, as a matter of policy, a defendant may be held liable for the consequences of his or her actions. In the majority of states, proximate cause requires that the plaintiff and the plaintiff's damages were foreseeable at the time of the accident. In the minority of states, proximate cause exists if the defendant's actions led to the plaintiff's harm.

Proximate cause, sometimes referred to as *legal cause,* refers to the extent to which, as a matter of policy, a defendant may be held liable for the consequences of his actions. In most states, proximate cause is determined by foreseeability. Proximate cause is said to exist only when both the plaintiff and the plaintiff's damages were reasonably foreseeable at the time the defendant breached his duty to the plaintiff. Thus, if the defendant could not reasonably foresee the damages that the plaintiff suffered as a result of his action, the plaintiff's negligence claim will not be sustained because it lacks the element of proximate causation.

You must be able to foresee that either the plaintiff himself or herself or a person in the plaintiff's position would be hurt. If you are running a red light, it is foreseeable that a person will be crossing with the light. If you hit a person crossing with the light, we say the person hit was foreseeable. If it makes more sense, we could say "both a person in the plaintiff's position" and the "plaintiff's damages," but most people refer simply to "the plaintiff and the plaintiff's damages."

For example, if a defective tire on a vehicle blows out, it is foreseeable that the driver may lose control and hit a pedestrian. It is not foreseeable, however, that the pedestrian may be a scientist carrying a briefcase full of chemicals that may explode on impact, causing a third-floor window to shatter, injuring an accountant at his desk. In most states, the accountant would not succeed if he sued the tire manufacturer for negligence. The tire failure is not considered a proximate cause of the accountant's injury because the contents of the pedestrian's briefcase were highly unusual. The pedestrian, however, would be eligible to recover damages from the tire manufacturer because hitting a pedestrian is a foreseeable consequence of tire failure. Thus, the defect in the tire is a proximate cause of the pedestrian's injury.

Palsgraf v. Long Island Railroad Company is a well-known case in which the majority opinion set forth this majority rule of proximate cause as foreseeability. The dissent, however, set forth an alternative definition of proximate cause that is accepted today in a small minority of states. Courts following the minority definition do not distinguish actual cause from proximate cause. In these states, if the defendant's action constitutes an actual cause, it is also considered the proximate cause. Therefore, in these few states, both the pedestrian-scientist and the third-floor accountant would be able to recover damages from the tire manufacturer in the previous example.

DAMAGES

Damages are the final required element of a negligence action. The plaintiff must have sustained compensable injury as a result of the defendant's actions. Because the purpose of tort law is to compensate individuals who suffer injuries as a result of another's action or inaction, a person

102

Negligence in Germany

German law is concerned with the defendant's ability to foresee, understand, and avoid danger. Both mental and physical capabilities are taken into account. For example, the duty-of-care standard stipulates that "physical and mental disabilities or defects, panic, or confusion" exempt the defendant from being found negligent. Also, though the distinction is not recognized by a statute, the courts distinguish between conscious and unconscious negligence. *Conscious negligence* requires knowledge that the offense is about to occur and that it is an actual offense. *Unconscious negligence* occurs when the defendant is either unaware that the act constitutes an offense or unaware that the act is occurring at all. In such cases, the defendant is found not liable by reason of unconscious negligence.

cannot bring an action in negligence seeking only nominal damages. Rather, a person must seek **compensatory damages**, or damages intended to reimburse a plaintiff for her or his losses.

In typical negligence cases, courts rarely award **punitive damages**, or *exemplary damages,* which are imposed to punish the offender and deter others from committing similar offenses. Instead, courts usually award punitive damages in cases in which the offender has committed **gross negligence,** an action committed with extreme reckless disregard for the property of life of another person.

Plaintiff's Doctrines

The plaintiff has the burden of proving all four elements of a negligence case. Direct evidence of negligence by the defendant, however, is not always available. For example, there may have been no witnesses to the negligent conduct, and other evidence may have been destroyed. Therefore, two doctrines have been adopted by courts to aid plaintiffs in establishing negligence claims: *res ipsa loquitur* and negligence per se.

RES IPSA LOQUITUR

Res ipsa loquitur literally means "the thing speaks for itself." The plaintiff uses this doctrine to allow the judge or jury to infer that, more likely than not, the defendant's negligence was the cause of the plaintiff's harm, even though there is no direct evidence of the defendant's lack of due care. To establish *res ipsa loquitur* in most states, the plaintiff must demonstrate that:

1. The event was a kind that ordinarily does not occur in the absence of negligence.
2. Other responsible causes, including the conduct of third parties and the plaintiff, have been sufficiently eliminated.
3. The indicated negligence is within the scope of the defendant's duty to the plaintiff.

Proof of these three elements does not require a finding of negligence, however; it merely permits it. Once the plaintiff has demonstrated these three elements, the burden of proof shifts to the defendant, who must prove that he was not negligent to avoid liability.

One of the earliest uses of *res ipsa loquitur* was the case of *Escola v. Coca Cola.*[11] In that case, the plaintiff, a waitress, was injured when a bottle of Coca-Cola that she was removing from a case exploded in her hand. From the facts that (1) bottled soft drinks ordinarily do not spontaneously explode and (2) the bottles had been sitting in a case, undisturbed, in the restaurant for approximately 36 hours before the plaintiff simply removed the bottle from the case, the jury reasonably inferred that the defendant's negligence in the filling of the bottle resulted in its explosion. The plaintiff therefore recovered damages without direct proof of the defendant's negligence. Plaintiffs in numerous accident cases have subsequently used the doctrine where there

compensatory damages
Money awarded to a plaintiff as reimbursement for her or his losses; based on the amount of actual damage or harm to property, lost wages or profits, pain and suffering, medical expenses, disability, etc.

punitive damages
Compensation awarded to a plaintiff that goes beyond reimbursement for actual losses and is imposed to punish the defendant and deter such conduct in the future.

gross negligence
An action committed with extreme reckless disregard for the property or life of another person.

LO 4

res ipsa loquitur
A doctrine that allows the judge or jury to infer that, more likely than not, the defendant's negligence was the cause of the plaintiff's harm, even though there is no direct evidence of the defendant's lack of due care.

[11] 24 Cal. 2d 453, 150 P.2d 436 (1944).

CONNECTING to the core

has been no direct evidence of negligence. The defendant's best response to this doctrine is to demonstrate other possible causes of the accident. Case 5-1 illustrates the use of this doctrine.

CASE 5-1

JANET KAMBAT v. ST. FRANCIS HOSPITAL ET AL.
COURT OF APPEALS OF NEW YORK
89 N.Y.2D 489 (1997)

FACTS: *In August 1986, at St. Francis Hospital, Dr. Ralph Sperrazza performed an abdominal hysterectomy on Florence Fenzel. During the operation, 10 laparotomy pads were available for use. Dr. Sperrazza placed several of these pads inside Fenzel, next to the bowel. A few months following the operation, Fenzel began to complain of stomach pain. Approximately three months after the operation, x-rays of Fenzel's abdomen revealed a foreign object in her abdomen. A few days later, Dr. Robert Barone discovered that the foreign object partially or fully inside her bowel was an 18- by 18-inch laparotomy pad similar to the one used during Fenzel's hysterectomy. Barone removed the object. Fenzel's condition continued to worsen, and she died later that month due to infection-related illness.*

Fenzel's family sued the hospital for negligence in leaving the laparotomy pad inside Fenzel. During the trial, Fenzel's family produced evidence that the abdominal pads were available only in operating rooms, where patients could not access them. Three experts testified for Fenzel's family, arguing about the precise location of the pad inside the bowel. In contrast, the hospital argued that standard procedures were followed during the operation and all pads and medical instruments were counted after the operation. Furthermore, the hospital argued that laparotomy pads were left in places accessible to patients. Thus, the hospital claimed that the decedent had swallowed the pad.

The trial court refused to allow Fenzel's family to use res ipsa loquitur during the trial, and the jury ruled in favor of the hospital. The trial court argued that res ipsa loquitur was not applicable because lengthy and inconsistent expert testimony was not within the experience of a layperson. The appellate court agreed with the trial court's refusal to allow res ipsa loquitur. The plaintiffs appealed.

(continued)

ISSUE: *Should a plaintiff be allowed to use res ipsa loquitur in a malpractice case, or must there be expert testimony of causation in such cases?*

REASONING: *A plaintiff should be allowed to use res ipsa loquitur to allow the jury to infer negligence when the plaintiff has demonstrated three conditions.* First, the event must be of a kind that ordinarily does not occur in the absence of someone's negligence; second, it must be caused by an agency or instrumentality within the exclusive control of the defendant; and third, it must not have been due to any voluntary action or contribution on the part of the plaintiff.

The plaintiff need not conclusively eliminate all other possible causes. It is enough that the evidence supporting the three conditions affords a rational basis for concluding that "it is more likely than not" that the injury was caused by the defendant's negligence. In a case where the jury's common, everyday experience would allow the jury to make a rational conclusion regarding the likelihood of negligence leading to the kind of injury the plaintiff suffered, no expert testimony is required.

In this case, the plaintiffs' evidence that similar pads were used during the decedent's surgery, that the decedent was unconscious throughout the operation, that laparotomy pads are not accessible to patients, and that it would be anatomically impossible to swallow such a pad would be sufficient to allow a jury to conclude that the defendants must have negligently left the pad inside the decedent. The defendants' evidence that they used due care and that the decedent could have eaten the pad was not sufficient as a matter of law to prohibit the jury from inferring negligence on the part of the defendants.

DECISION AND REMEDY: The court reversed the appellate court's affirmance of the trial court's refusal to allow the jury to consider the plaintiff's argument based on *res ipsa loquitur,* and ordered a new trial at which *res ipsa loquitur* may be used.

SIGNIFICANCE OF THE CASE: *This case provides an illustration of the type of conditions that can lead a jury to infer negligence.*

CRITICAL THINKING

Can you think of any evidence that a defendant in such a case could have brought forth to convince the jury to not find the defendant negligent?

ETHICAL DECISION MAKING

Suppose you were a business manager for the hospital when this case was first brought to the hospital's attention. The plaintiff's attorney has contacted you, claiming that the doctor in this case was negligent. The attorney argues that the hospital should pay the plaintiff family in an attempt to compensate for the doctor's negligence. Suppose your actions are guided by the public disclosure test. What would your response to the plaintiff's attorney be?

NEGLIGENCE PER SE

Negligence per se (literally, "negligence in or of itself") is another doctrine that helps plaintiffs succeed in negligence cases. Negligence per se applies to cases in which the defendant has violated a statute enacted to prevent a certain type of harm from befalling a specific group to which the plaintiff belongs. If the defendant's violation causes the plaintiff to suffer from the type of harm that the statute intends to prevent, the violation is deemed negligence per se. The plaintiff does not have to show that a reasonable person would exercise a certain duty of care toward the plaintiff. Instead, the plaintiff can offer evidence of the defendant's violation of the statute to establish proof of the negligence.

For example, if Ohio passes a statute prohibiting the sale of alcohol to minors, and a minor runs a red light and kills two pedestrians while driving under the influence of alcohol sold to him illegally, the liquor store's violation of the statute prohibiting the sale of alcohol to minors establishes negligence per se on the part of the store. The families of the pedestrians do not need to establish that a reasonable person would have a duty not to sell alcohol to a minor. The Case Nugget provides another illustration of negligence per se.

negligence per se
A doctrine that allows a judge or jury to infer duty and breach of duty from the fact that a defendant violated a criminal statute that was designed to prevent the type of harm that the plaintiff incurred.

CASE Nugget

A Clear Illustration of Negligence per Se

O'Guin v. Bingham County
Superior Court of Idaho

122 P.3d 308 (Sup. Ct. Id., 2005)

Shaun and Alex O'Guin cut across a field on their way home from school and entered the back of a landfill that was not fenced off, despite a law that required it to be fenced. A portion of a wall of the landfill collapsed, killing the boys. The boys' parents sued the county that operated the landfill, alleging that failure to have the landfill properly fenced constituted negligence per se.

The court agreed, explaining that the following four elements of negligence per se had been met: (1) The statute or regulation clearly defines the required standard of conduct, (2) the statute or regulation must have been intended to prevent the type of harm the defendant's act or omission caused, (3) the plaintiff must be a member of the class of persons the statute or regulation was designed to protect, and (4) the violation must have been the proximate cause of death.

Defenses to Negligence

LO 5

The courts' doctrines of *res ipsa loquitur* and negligence per se help the plaintiff in a negligence case, but the courts permit certain defenses that relieve the defendant from liability even when the plaintiff has proved all four elements of negligence. Defendants can successfully rebut negligence claims with contributory negligence, comparative negligence, assumption of the risk, and other special negligence defenses.

CONTRIBUTORY NEGLIGENCE

contributory negligence
A defense to negligence whereby the defendant can escape all liability by proving that the plaintiff failed to act in a way that would protect him or her from an unreasonable risk of harm and that the plaintiff's negligent behavior contributed in some way to the plaintiff's accident.

last-clear-chance doctrine
A doctrine used by the plaintiff when the defendant establishes contributory negligence. If the plaintiff can establish that the defendant had the last opportunity to avoid the accident, the plaintiff may still recover, despite being contributorily negligent.

Contributory negligence, a defense once available in all states but replaced today in some states by the defense of comparative negligence (discussed in the next section), applies in cases in which both the defendant and the plaintiff were negligent. The defendant must prove that (1) the plaintiff's conduct fell below the standard of care needed to prevent unreasonable risk of harm and (2) the plaintiff's failure was a contributing cause of the plaintiff's injury. How can defendants use contributory negligence in a case? Some defense lawyers argue that if a plaintiff involved in a car accident failed to wear her seat belt, that failure constitutes contributory negligence because her action contributed to her injuries.

If the defendant successfully proves contributory negligence, no matter how slight the plaintiff's negligence, the plaintiff will be denied any recovery of damages. Because this defense seems unfair, many states have adopted the last-clear-chance doctrine. This doctrine allows the plaintiff to recover damages despite proof of contributory negligence as long as the defendant had a final clear opportunity to avoid the action that injured the plaintiff.

For example, suppose that Samantha and Nicole, in their cars, are facing each other while stopped at a red light. The light turns green, and Nicole starts to turn left at the intersection. Samantha sees Nicole start to turn, but she still continues to travel straight through the intersection and crashes into Nicole's car. Although Samantha had the right-of-way at the intersection, she could have avoided hitting Nicole's car by braking or swerving. Thus, according to the last-clear-chance doctrine, Nicole could recover damages.

COMPARATIVE NEGLIGENCE

Most states have replaced contributory negligence with comparative negligence, because the adoption of the last-clear-chance doctrine still left many situations in which an extremely careless defendant can cause a great deal of harm to a plaintiff who is barred from recovery due to minimal contributory negligence. There are two forms of comparative negligence: pure and modified. According to a pure comparative negligence defense, the court determines the percentage of fault of the defendant. The defendant is then liable for that percentage of the plaintiff's damages.

Courts calculate damages according to modified comparative negligence in the same manner, except that the defendant must be more than 50 percent at fault before the plaintiff can recover.

Twenty-eight states have adopted modified comparative negligence, thirteen have adopted pure comparative negligence, and nine have adopted contributory negligence. Every state has adopted one of these three defenses. Thus, the parties to a negligence suit cannot choose among them.

ASSUMPTION OF THE RISK

Another defense available to defendants facing negligence claims is called assumption of the risk. To use this defense successfully, a defendant must prove that the plaintiff voluntarily and unreasonably encountered the risk of the actual harm the defendant caused. In other words, the plaintiff willingly assumed as a risk the harm she suffered. There are two types of this defense. *Express assumption of the risk* occurs when the plaintiff expressly agrees (usually in a written contract) to assume the risk posed by the defendant's behavior. In contrast, *implied assumption of the risk* means that the plaintiff implicitly assumed a known risk.

The most difficult part of establishing this defense is showing that the plaintiff assumed the risk of the *actual* harm she suffered. A 1998 case against the Family Fitness Center illustrates an unsuccessful attempt to use assumption of the risk as a defense against a negligence claim.[12] In that case, the plaintiff was injured when a sauna bench on which he was lying collapsed beneath him at the defendant's facility. The trial court granted summary judgment in favor of the defendant on the basis of assumption of the risk. The plaintiff had signed a contract that included the following provision: "Buyer is aware that participation in a sport or physical exercise may result in accidents or injury, and Buyer assumes the risk connected with the participation in a sport or exercise and represents that Member is in good health and suffers from no physical impairment which would limit their use of FFC's facilities." The appellate court overturned the trial court's decision because the type of injury the plaintiff suffered was not the type of risk he had assumed. The court held that anyone signing a membership agreement could be deemed to have waived any hazard known to relate to the use of the health club facilities, such as the risk of a sprained ankle due to improper exercise or overexertion, a broken toe from a dropped weight, injuries due to malfunctioning exercise or sports equipment, or injuries from slipping in the locker room shower. No patron, however, could be charged with realistically appreciating the risk of injury from simply reclining on a sauna bench. Because the collapse of a sauna bench, when properly used, is not a "known risk," the court concluded that the plaintiff did not assume the risk of this incident as a matter of law.

SPECIAL DEFENSES TO NEGLIGENCE

Many states have additional ways to defend against a claim of negligence. For example, laws in some states hold that people in peril who receive voluntary aid from others cannot hold those offering aid liable for negligence. These laws, commonly called Good Samaritan statutes, attempt to encourage selfless and courageous behavior by removing the threat of liability.

The defendant in a negligence suit can also avoid liability by establishing a superseding cause. A *superseding cause* is an unforeseeable event that interrupts the causal chain between the defendant's breach of duty and the damages the plaintiff suffered. For example, suppose Jennifer is improperly storing ammonia in her garage when a meteor strikes her garage, spilling the ammonia into a stream nearby. Will, living downstream, drinks water from the stream and becomes dangerously ill. Because the meteor was unforeseeable, Jennifer is not liable for Will's

pure comparative negligence
A defense accepted in some states whereby the defendant is not liable for the percentage of harm that he or she can prove can be attributed to the plaintiff's own negligence.

modified comparative negligence
A defense accepted in some states whereby the defendant is not liable for the percentage of harm that he or she can prove can be attributed to the plaintiff's own negligence if the plaintiff's negligence is responsible for less than 50 percent of the harm; if the defendant establishes that the plaintiff's negligence caused more than 50 percent of the harm, the defendant has no liability.

assumption of the risk
A defense whereby the defendant must prove that the plaintiff voluntarily assumed the risk the defendant caused.

Good Samaritan statute
A statute that exempts from liability a person, such as a physician passerby, who voluntarily renders aid to an injured person but negligently, but not unreasonably negligently, causes injury while rendering the aid.

[12] *Leon v. Family Fitness Center, Inc.,* 61 Cal. App. 4th 1227 (1998).

injuries, even though she breached her duty of care to Will. Superseding causes allow the defendant to avoid liability because they are evidence that the defendant's breach of duty was not the proximate cause of the plaintiff's injuries. In other words, superseding causes disprove the causation element necessary to sustain a negligence claim.

LO 6

Strict Liability

strict liability

Liability in which responsibility for damages is imposed regardless of the existence of negligence. Also called *liability without fault*.

Strict liability is liability without fault. The law holds an individual liable without fault when the activity in which she engages satisfies three conditions: (1) It involves a risk of serious harm to people or property; (2) it is so inherently dangerous that it cannot ever be safely undertaken; and (3) it is not usually performed in the immediate community. Instead of banning such activities, the law allows people to engage in these activities but holds them liable for all resulting harm.

Inherently dangerous activities include dynamite blasting in a populated area and keeping animals that have not been domesticated. If an animal has shown a "vicious propensity," strict liability applies and the owner of the animal is responsible for any injuries suffered in an attack by the animal. If an individual keeps an animal that has not shown vicious propensity, he has a duty to warn and protect individuals who come into contact with the animal. Today, the theory of strict liability is used most commonly in cases where the plaintiff is claiming to have been injured by a product that was unreasonably dangerous.

Damages Available in Tort Cases

LO 7

There are three types of damages available in tort cases: compensatory, nominal, and punitive (see Exhibit 5-2). You will see this system of classifying damages again when we talk about damages in other contexts, such as in cases involving the breach of a contract.

COMPENSATORY DAMAGES

tortfeasor

A person who commits an intentional or through-negligence tort that causes a harm or loss for which a civil remedy may be sought.

As the primary objective of tort law is to compensate victims, the primary type of damages are *compensatory damages,* damages designed to compensate the victim for all the harm caused by the person who committed the tort, often referred to as the **tortfeasor**. While we seem to hear a lot about "runaway jury" awards, the overall median jury award for personal injury cases from 1998 to 2004 was $35,298. And that amount actually fell from $37,086 in 2003 to $35,000 in 2004.[13]

Compensatory damages are typically awarded for pain and suffering, costs of repairing damaged property, medical expenses, and lost wages. For example, suppose Rubin, in the Case Opener, could demonstrate that he and his company lost money because of the *U.S. News & World Report* article. He might be able to recover those losses from *U.S. News*. Surprisingly, attorney fees are

Exhibit 5-2

Types of Tort Damages

TYPE	PURPOSE	AMOUNT
Compensatory	To make the plaintiff whole again.	An amount equivalent to all losses caused by the tort, including compensation for pain and suffering, but not attorney fees.
Nominal	To recognize that the defendant committed a tort against the plaintiff.	A trivial amount, typically $1 to $5.
Punitive	To punish the defendant and deter future wrongdoers.	An amount based on two factors: the severity of the wrongful conduct and the wealth of the defendant.

[13] JVR news release, www.juryverdictresearch.com/Press_Room/Press_releases/Verdict_study/verdict_study41.html (accessed October 10, 2006).

not recoverable as compensatory damages, despite the fact that most plaintiffs could not bring an action against the tortfeasor without hiring an attorney. Because the plaintiffs in personal injury cases must usually pay their attorneys anywhere from one-third to one-half of their recovery, some argue that compensatory damages fail to meet the intended goal of properly compensating victims. Others point out that one of the ways plaintiffs can, in essence, recover their attorney fees is by increasing their pain and suffering damages enough to cover these expenses.

NOMINAL DAMAGES

Nominal damages are a small amount of money given to recognize that a defendant did indeed commit a tort in a case where there were no compensable damages suffered by the plaintiff. A plaintiff may receive nominal damages by simply failing to prove actual damages.

PUNITIVE DAMAGES

Punitive damages are awarded to punish the defendant. They are given only when the defendant's conduct is extremely outrageous. The purposes of punitive damages are both to punish the defendant and to deter him and others who are similarly situated from engaging in that kind of activity again. In awarding punitive damages, juries usually consider the egregiousness or willfulness of the tort and the wealth of the defendant. Obviously, the more wrongful the nature of the defendant's act, the greater the desire to send a message that such behavior will not be tolerated; and the greater the wealth of the defendant, the higher the damages must be to actually punish the defendant.

While the threat of large punitive damages is seen by many groups, including consumer advocates, as a good method for encouraging manufacturers to produce the safest possible products, others disagree. They believe that no threat beyond compensatory damages is required; and they argue that the main effect of punitive damages is to discourage innovation, because manufacturers will be afraid of the risk of producing a defective product, which could cost them millions in punitive damages.

Since the late 1970s, insurance companies and "tort reform" groups have been trying to limit the amount of punitive damages that can be assessed, using both the legislative process and the courts. The 1994 case of *Honda Motor Company v. Oberg*[14] provided tort reformers with their first judicial victory. In this case, the U.S. Supreme Court finally struck down a punitive-damage award as being a violation of due process. *Oberg,* however, was a limited victory because of two unique aspects of the case. First, the punitive damages were over 500 times the amount of the compensatory damages, which is extraordinarily rare. Second, the state law under which the damages were awarded was the only state law in the country that had no provision for judicial review of the amount of punitive-damage awards, and it was the denial of this safeguard that violated the due process clause. Because of its unusual facts, *Oberg* did not provide much guidance as to when punitive damages were so excessive as to violate due process.

A few years later, however, in *BMW v. Gore,*[15] the Supreme Court set forth a test that a number of commentators thought would substantially curb punitive-damage awards. The Court said three factors should be considered in determining whether an award was grossly excessive: "the degree of reprehensibility of the nondisclosure; the disparity between the harm or potential harm suffered by [the plaintiff] and his punitive damages award; and the difference between this remedy and the civil penalties authorized or imposed in comparable cases." However, a 1999 study found that the year after *BMW v. Gore,* punitive-damage awards across the country were not reduced any more frequently than they had been the year before the decision.[16]

Since *BMW v. Gore,* the Supreme Court has continued to encourage the courts to carefully scrutinize punitive-damage awards. In the 2001 case of *Cooper Industries, Inc. v. Leatherman Tool Group, Inc.,*[17] the high court ruled that appellate courts must review the trial court's decision on the constitutionality of an award *de novo,* meaning they should no longer give deference to the

nominal damages
Monetary damages awarded to a plaintiff in a very small amount, typically $1 to $5, to signify that the plaintiff has been wronged by the defendant even though the plaintiff suffered no compensable harm.

[14] 114 S. Ct. 2331 (1994).

[15] *BMW of North America v. Ira Gore, Jr.,* 116 S. Ct. 1589 (1995).

[16] James Dam, "Large Punitives Mostly Upheld, but $5B Award Overturned," *Lawyer's Weekly,* November 12, 2001, p. A1.

[17] 532 U.S. 424 (2001).

GLOBAL Context

Punitive Damages in Canada

Those who believe the U.S. tort system is in need of reform with respect to its treatment of punitive damages may look to their Canadian neighbors with envy. Punitive-damage awards in Canada are both rare and small.

A study in 1990 reported on punitive-damage awards in Ontario. The researchers found that the highest award was 50,000. *The majority of punitive-damage awards were less than 25,000;* the median award was approximately 20 percent of the compensatory-damage award in the particular case.

Following English common law, Canadian courts have traditionally restricted punitive damages to two situations: cases involving oppressive, arbitrary, or unconstitutional actions by government servants and cases in which the defendant's conduct was calculated to have made a profit in excess of compensatory damages. In 1989, the Canadian Supreme Court recognized that punitive damages could also be awarded for conduct deserving punishment because of its "harsh, vindictive, reprehensible, and malicious manner."

Two reasons seem to explain the differences in Canadian and American treatment of punitive damages. First, Canadians see something undignified about the flamboyant punitive-damage awards in the United States. Second, civil juries are much less common in Canada, and, in general, judges tend to be much more conservative than juries in making punitive-damage awards.

trial court's determination that the jury award was not unconstitutionally excessive and uphold it unless there was a clear abuse of discretion on the part of the trial court judge.

In the 2003 case *State Farm v. Campbell,*[18] the Supreme Court once again addressed the issue of how to properly determine punitive damages. The Campbells had won a jury verdict for $1 million in compensatory damages and $145 million in punitive damages after State Farm failed to settle what was clearly a valid claim. The high court ruled that punitive-damage awards should bear some relationship to the actual harm caused and should not focus on the wealth of the defendants. While refusing to draw a firm line as to what ratio of compensatories to punitives was acceptable, the Court did say that "in practice, few awards exceeding a single-digit ratio between punitive and compensatory damages, to a significant degree, will satisfy due process."[19] The Court also stated that damages should not focus on deterrence based on wealth or on actions unrelated to the case at hand. Case 5-2 demonstrates how the courts are applying these guidelines today.

[18] 123 S. Ct. 1513 (2003).
[19] Ibid., p. 1524.

 CASE 5-2

CLARK v. CHRYSLER CORPORATION
UNITED STATES COURT OF APPEALS FOR THE SIXTH CIRCUIT
2006 U.S. App. LEXIS 2435

FACTS: *Charles Clark was fatally injured in an automobile accident when he pulled into an intersection in front of an oncoming vehicle and collided with it. He was not wearing a seat belt and was consequently ejected from his vehicle. His wife sued Chrysler, claiming that its pickup truck was defectively and negligently designed.*

After a three-day trial, the jury rendered a unanimous verdict in favor of Mrs. Clark on claims of strict liability, negligence, and failure to warn. The jury found Chrysler *and Mr. Clark each 50 percent at fault, returning a verdict of $471,258.26 in compensatory damages and $3 million in punitive damages. The court entered a judgment against Chrysler for $3,235,629.13, reflecting 50 percent of the compensatory damages plus the $3 million punitive damages award. After a series of appeals, the last being an appeal of the trial court's motion to deny the defendant's motion to send the case back to the district court for a reduction of damages, the case finally landed at the circuit*

(continued)

court of appeals on the issue of whether the jury verdict was constitutionally excessive.

ISSUE: Should the plaintiff's $3 million punitive-damage award be struck down as constitutionally excessive when the amount of the compensatory damages is $471,258.26?

REASONING: Application of the *Gore* guideposts to this case renders the punitive-damage award excessive. According to *Gore,* five criteria are used to determine the reprehensibility of the defendant's conduct: (1) The harm caused was physical as opposed to economic; (2) the tortious conduct evinced an indifference to or a reckless disregard for the health or safety of others; (3) the target of the conduct had financial vulnerability; (4) the conduct involved repeated actions or was an isolated incident; and (5) the harm was the result of intentional malice, trickery, or deceit or mere accident. In this case, the physical harm suffered by Mr. Clark weighed strongly in favor of finding Chrysler's conduct reprehensible, but considering the four other factors leads to the conclusion that the factors as a whole show that Chrysler's conduct was not sufficiently reprehensible to warrant a $3 million punishment.

The second guidepost is the disparity between the actual or potential harm inflicted on the plaintiff and the punitive-damage award. Because the compensatory-damage award here is relatively small, a 1:1 ratio is inappropriate; but because of the lack of reprehensibility, a ratio higher than 2:1 would be unwarranted.

The third guidepost is the difference between the punitive-damage award and the civil or criminal penalties that could be imposed for comparable misconduct. Given *State Farm's* focus on civil penalties, a $3 million punitive-damage award is excessive in light of comparable civil penalties.

DECISION AND REMEDY: The damage award was excessive. Chrysler's motion was reversed and remanded, with instructions to enter a punitive-damage award in the amount of $471,258.26.

SIGNIFICANCE OF THE CASE: This case gives the courts a little more guidance as to when punitive damages may be considered excessive.

CRITICAL THINKING

Which of the criteria used by the judge seems ambiguous? How might that ambiguity have affected the outcome of the case?

ETHICAL DECISION MAKING

What values are guiding the judge's decision that the punitive-damage award was excessive? Do you think that the values promoted by the decision are appropriate for the situation? Why or why not?

SUMMARY

Introduction to Tort law	*Tort:* A civil wrong giving the injured party the right to bring a lawsuit against the wrongdoer to recover compensation for the injuries.
Classification of Torts	Torts are classified as intentional, negligent, and strict liability.
Intentional Torts	*Torts against persons* include assault, battery, and defamation.
	Torts against property include trespass to realty, private nuisance, trespass to personal property, and conversion.
	Torts against economic interest include disparagement, intentional interference with contract, unfair competition, misappropriation, and fraudulent misrepresentation.
Negligence	The plaintiff must prove four elements: duty, breach of duty, causation (actual and proximate), and damages.
Plaintiff's Doctrines	Doctrines used to establish negligence: • *Res ipsa loquitur* • Negligence per se

Defenses to Negligence	*Contributory negligence*
	Modified comparative negligence
	Pure comparative negligence
	Assumption of the risk
Strict Liability	Persons who engage in activities that are so inherently dangerous that no amount of due care can make them safe are strictly liable, regardless of the degree of care they used when undertaking the activity.
Damages Available in Tort Cases	*Compensatory damages,* to make the plaintiff whole again.
	Punitive damages, to punish the defendant and deter future wrongdoers.
	Nominal damages, to recognize that the defendant committed a tort against the plaintiff.

 Point/Counterpoint

Should Punitive Damages Be More Strictly Limited?

YES	NO

Excessive punitive damages are fundamentally unfair.

Punitive damages are not a normal part of the tort system. Tort law is supposed to be a way to compensate victims. Punitive damages are almost quasi-criminal in nature; they are designed to punish the defendant. And they reward a plaintiff with, in some cases, riches far beyond what any reasonable person would see as compensation. Tort cases, with the possibility of huge punitive-damage awards, have turned into nothing but litigation lotteries, which have nothing to do with the purposes of our tort system.

The possibility of a huge punitive-damage award causes people to bring all sorts of loony lawsuits in hopes of striking it rich. If punitive damages were more reasonable, you would not see people, for example, suing the phone company for publishing false information about a physician that led to a botched liposuction or suing NBC for millions because a *Fear Factor* episode that involved eating rats made a viewer "dizzy and lightheaded and caused him to vomit and run into a doorway."

Besides, unfair punitive-damage awards can ruin a defendant's good name and, in some cases, run target companies out of business. We must bring fairness back to our tort system by limiting punitive damages. Sure, damage awards have fallen since the *BMW* and *State Farm* cases, but they were so exorbitant that they could hardly have gone any higher! Besides, the fact that they have fallen does not mean that they have fallen to reasonable levels.

We need more stringent standards for punitive damages to bring predictability, efficiency, and fairness to our civil justice system. We must all work together for these necessary changes.

The BMW standard for excessive punitive damages strikes a fair balance, protecting the interests of both consumers and firms.

In the 20 years prior to the *BMW* case, courts handed down a number of huge punitive-damage awards, some even exceeding $100 million. However, in the years since the *BMW* case, we have seen that the court's three-pronged test has resulted in punitive-damage awards being much lower, generally staying below a 9-to-1 ratio of punitive to compensatory damages. They now appear to be much more reasonable and to fulfill their necessary function. If we examine the top 10 jury verdicts of 2005, the awards are significantly lower than those of 2004 and previous years. There is no longer any need to further limit punitive damages, as they are now reasonably related to the harm the defendant has caused and they are still large enough to deter behavior.

Punitive damages, in their current manifestation, fulfill two important functions. First, they represent an important way for a significantly harmed plaintiff to recover costs and attorney fees. Without the possibility of large punitive-damage awards, the plaintiff may not actually be compensated for his or her losses because so much of the recovery goes to the attorneys and costs of litigation.

Second, punitive damages perform a necessary deterrence function. If corporations no longer have to fear punitive-damage awards that will hurt them, they will lose some of their motivation to produce safe products and behave as responsible citizens.

With the *BMW* rule, as clarified by *State Farm,* we now have a system in which punitive damages can serve their intended purpose without posing an unreasonable risk to potential defendants.

1. Distinguish the three types of damages available in tort cases.

2. Explain why some people see punitive damages as a necessary aspect of our tort system, while others want to restrict their availability.

3. List five intentional torts, and explain the elements needed to prove each.

4. List and define the elements that are necessary to prove a case of negligence.

5. Explain the differences between contributory and comparative negligence.

6. Explain the relationship between negligence per se and *res ipsa loquitur.*

7. At 7:30 p.m. on February 3, 1995, Mary Ann Eckstein was driving her vehicle along a windy, unlit stretch of road. Ahead of her, Joan Sandow had parked her car on the left side of the street to distribute materials into the mailboxes on the right. Sandow was wearing dark clothes and a black raincoat. Eckstein was driving down the roadway using her high beams and slowed down when she saw Sandow's car on the side of the road. Eckstein then felt her car hit something and stopped to investigate. After she exited the car, she saw Sandow in the road. Sandow filed a negligence claim against Eckstein, seeking compensatory damages. Eckstein responded to the suit by alleging contributory negligence. The plaintiff responded by arguing that motorists have an added duty of care for pedestrians. The trial court found for Sandow. How do you think the appellate court found? What is the basis for your decision? [*Sandow v. Eckstein,* 67 Conn. App. 243 (2001).]

8. David Burton smoked Camel cigarettes for 43 years, and, in 1993, he developed serious circulatory problems in his legs. His doctor informed him that smoking was causing his circulatory problems. Two other doctors confirmed his doctor's diagnosis and recommended vascular bypass surgery, which Burton underwent unsuccessfully. After the operation, Burton had both of his legs amputated below the knee. Burton brought suit against the R. J. Reynolds Tobacco Company, alleging that the company negligently failed to warn him of the health hazards caused by smoking. R. J. Reynolds argued that it did not have a duty to warn Burton of the hazards that smoking posed to his health. What do you think? Should R. J. Reynolds be found negligent? Why? [*Burton v. R. J. Reynolds Tobacco Co.,* 397 F.3d 906 (2005).]

9. Paula Baddeaux was riding in a pickup truck with her fiancé Dave Zeringue. The rear tire on Zeringue's pickup truck blew out, and the poor road conditions resulted in the truck's flipping over. Both Baddeaux and Zeringue were seriously injured. They filed suit against the Department of Transportation and Development (DOTD), and a trial judge found the DOTD 75 percent responsible for the accident. Baddeaux was awarded $308,825.85. The DOTD appealed the trial judge's decision, arguing that Baddeaux's overweight condition contributed to the costliness of her recovery. Baddeaux had a history of weight problems, and at the time of the accident she weighed over 200 pounds. She sustained serious knee injuries, and in failing to follow her doctor's recommendation to lose weight, Baddeaux made the knee injuries difficult and costly to treat. Do you think this was sufficient to warrant comparative negligence? Why or why not? [*Baddeaux v. State of Louisiana Department of Transportation and Development,* 690 So. 2d 203 (1997).]

10. Thomas Gottier was a regular patron at his local Denny's restaurant, typically spending long hours drinking coffee or tea and reading. On the day in question, Gottier became impatient with the service he was receiving. Gottier searched for a manager to convey his complaint. Unable to locate a manager, Gottier saw his waiter (Bruner) and approached him. Witnesses report that Gottier approached Bruner in a rude manner, instructing him to get out of his way. When Bruner did not comply, Gottier pushed him and "kind of slapped" him in the face. Bruner responded by striking Gottier across the head with a coffee pot, causing lacerations. Gottier sued Bruner and Denny's for negligence and battery. Bruner defended his actions by claiming self-defense. Explain why you do or do not believe this defense will be successful. [*Gottier v. Denny's Restaurant,* 2001 Cal. App. LEXIS 2880.]

11. Erica Aponte, age seven, attended Thanksgiving dinner at the home of Michael and Deborah Castor, her aunt and uncle. Following dinner, Erica, accompanied by her cousin, went outside and crawled under/through an electric wire fence that enclosed Castor's horse paddock area. Erica was subsequently kicked in the face by Castor's horse, sustaining injury. Teresa Aponte, Erica's mother, filed suit against Castor, seeking damages for Erica's injuries. Castor filed a motion for summary judgment, arguing that because Erica did not have permission to leave the house or enter the paddock area, and did so without her parents' or Castor's knowledge, Erica was a trespasser and, therefore, he should not be held liable for her injuries. Aponte responded that Erica was a social

guest, not a trespasser; Castor should have warned Aponte regarding the dangerous nature of the horse; and genuine issues of material fact existed that would preclude the granting of summary judgment. The trial court granted summary judgment. Aponte appealed. How did the court rule on appeal? Why? [*Aponte v. Castor,* 155 Ohio App. 3d 553 (2003).]

12. Mathis entered into a contract with Pacific Cornetta under which he undertook to solicit orders for Pacific Cornetta's products from retailers in return for a 5 percent commission. This contract was terminable at will by either party. The next year, Mathis entered into a one-year contract with John Evans under which Evans agreed to serve as his subagent and to solicit orders for the various products Mathis handled, including those of Pacific Cornetta, in return for a commission of 1 percent on net sales. This agreement specified that either party could terminate it only on written notice of six months. A few months after Mathis's arrangement with Evans commenced, Pacific Cornetta began to criticize Mathis to Evans and initiated efforts to persuade Evans to break his contract with Mathis. Evans ultimately entered into a contract with Pacific Cornetta to act as its sales representative, and the following day Evans terminated his contract with Mathis without having given him the required notice. Two days later, Pacific Cornetta terminated its contract with Mathis. Mathis then filed an action against Pacific Cornetta for tortious interference with contractual relations. Was Mathis successful in his suit? Why? [*Mathis v. Liu,* 276 F.3d 1027 (2002).]

Real and Intellectual Property

---> **CASE OPENER**

Economic Redevelopment in Poletown

General Motors wished to expand its facility but was unable to acquire the land it needed, so it approached the Detroit Economic Development Corporation (DEDC) with a request that the DEDC use its power of eminent domain to acquire a large parcel of land on which members of the plaintiff organization, Poletown Neighborhood Council, resided and had small businesses. Once the DEDC had acquired the land, it would be conveyed to General Motors for its plant expansion. The justification for the use of eminent domain in the case would be that the acquisition and transfer of the property would create jobs for the economically depressed area.

The plaintiffs, who did not want their community destroyed, sued the city and the development council on the grounds that they were attempting to abuse their power of eminent domain to take private property for a private use.

1. Can business managers ask the city to buy real property for them when the owners do not wish to sell it?
2. What would determine whether the government can legally take the property for a corporation?

---> **LEARNING OBJECTIVES**

After reading this chapter, you will be able to answer the following questions:

LO 1 How are the topics of real and intellectual property related?

LO 2 How does real property law balance private and public rights?

LO 3 What are the interests in real property that one can hold?

LO 4 How does intellectual property law balance private and public rights?

LO 5 What are the similarities and differences among the methods for protecting various types of intellectual property?

Most Americans cherish the right to own property. For most Americans, this means the right to own real property, such as a house. Increasingly, Americans also cherish the right to own "intellectual property," the fruits of the mind, such as a manuscript for a novel. In this chapter we examine the nature of both real and intellectual property. The chapter starts by exploring how the two areas of law are related. Then, for both real and intellectual property, the chapter considers what interests individuals can hold in property and how both real and intellectual property laws balance private and public rights. The Case Opener considers a real property issue. By the end of the chapter, you will see that disputes like the General Motors–Poletown dispute can arise not only when the property in question is land but also when it is the fruits of an individual's mind.

LO 1

The Nature of Real and Intellectual Property

real property
Land and everything permanently attached to it.

intellectual property
Intangible property that is the product of one's mind and not one's hands.

Real property, commonly referred to as *realty,* is land and everything permanently attached to it. The type of ownership interest a person has in a piece of property determines his or her rights to the property. **Intellectual property** consists of the fruits of one's mind. The laws of intellectual property protect property that is primarily the result of mental creativity rather than physical effort. When we are thinking about property rights of any kind, it is important to remember that society, through laws, decides what rights individuals and communities have with regard to property.

One metaphor often used with regard to property is that of a bundle of sticks. Each stick represents a distinct right an individual can have with regard to property. The rights to possess property, use it, give it away, or take it away are all sticks. With regard to both real and intellectual property, one of the most important rights is the right to exclude others. For example, with regard to real property, an individual can put a fence around the land and ask others to stay off the land. For intellectual property, an individual can accomplish the same thing with a trademark or patent—the holder can put a virtual fence around the idea trademarked or patented and ask others to refrain from using the property.

With regard to real property, some other important sticks are the rights to sell, lease, or mortgage land and the right to allow someone limited access. The public also has important sticks, such as the right to take land, regulate it, and/or tax it. In the next section, the various types of interests a person may have in real property are described in detail. These interests may be conveyed or transferred under legal guidelines for property rights. Most transfers of property are voluntary. However, for the benefit of the public, and to protect public health, safety, and welfare, the government may require involuntary transfers of property.

LO 2

Real Property

There are a number of different types of interests in land, ranging from temporary to permanent to future. The duration of one's ownership interest and the power one has over using the land depend on the type of *estate* one is said to hold. The section below on interests in real property describes the various estates in detail. First, though, this chapter explores the landowner's rights that pertain to areas beyond the surface of the land itself.

EXTENT OF OWNERSHIP

When a person owns land, she or he owns more than just the surface. The airspace above the land, extending to the atmosphere, is also part of the legal concept of real property. Rights to airspace generally do not generate much controversy, but occasionally disputes arise that involve aircraft flying "too low" over individuals' property. Alternatively, a tree's branches may hang over into the airspace of the property next door, and the owner of that airspace may want to cut the overhanging branches.

In dense, commercial urban areas, airspace may actually be an asset. Owners of two commercial buildings might want to build an overhead walkway joining their buildings across a parking lot that you own. They will have to pay you handsomely for the right to build in your airspace.

In addition to having airspace rights, the owner of real property also has *water rights,* the legal ability to use water flowing across or underneath the property. However, these rights are somewhat restricted; one cannot deprive the landowners downstream from the use of the water by diverting the water elsewhere.

Finally, ownership of real property extends to *mineral rights;* these rights involve the land below the surface. The landowner has the legal ability to dig or mine the materials from the earth, and he may sell or give these rights to another person. Ownership of these *subsurface rights* includes the right to enter onto the property to remove the underground materials.

All these additional rights are illustrated in Figure 6-1.

INTERESTS IN REAL PROPERTY

Various interests in land are discussed below and summarized in Exhibit 6-1.

Fee Simple Absolute With regard to estates in land, a fee simple absolute is the most complete estate a person may have. Exclusive rights to ownership and possession of the land belong to the person who has a fee simple absolute. It is this type of estate to which most people refer when they speak of "buying" a house or piece of land. A fee-simple-absolute interest is passed to the owner's heirs when the owner of such an estate dies.

LO 3

fee simple absolute
An ownership interest in which the holder has exclusive rights to ownership and possession of the land; the most comprehensive type of estate.

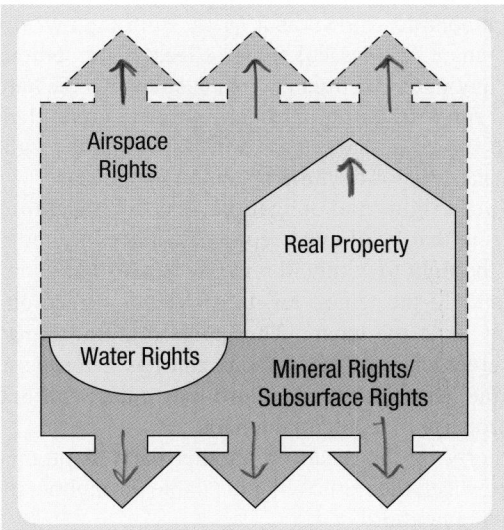

Figure 6-1

Extent of Rights

Exhibit 6-1

Possessory Estates in Land

INTEREST	EXTENT OF RIGHTS
Leasehold estate	Right to possess property for an agreed-on period of time.
Life estate	Right to possess property until death, subject to restriction against waste.
Conditional estate	Right that is comparable to a fee simple absolute except that interest will terminate on the happening or nonhappening of a specified condition.
Fee simple absolute	Right to possess property for life and pass it to heirs on death; the most encompassing interest.

conditional estate

An ownership interest in which the holder has the same interest as that in a fee simple absolute except that this interest is subject to a condition.

Conditional Estate The owner of a conditional estate possesses the same interest as the owner of a fee simple absolute except that this interest is subject to a condition: Should a certain required event fail to occur, or should a specific prohibited event occur, the interest will be terminated. For example, Todd may be given property rights to a Victorian house on the condition that he is to preserve it in its original form. If he violates this condition by turning the house into a piano showroom or a beer hall, the house either will revert to the original owner or will be transferred in accordance with the terms of the deed (the *deed* is the instrument used to convey real property).

life estate

An ownership interest in which the holder has the right to possess the property until her or his death.

Life Estate A life estate is granted for the lifetime of an individual; the right to possess the property terminates at the individual's death. On the death of the holder of the life estate, the property will go to another party as designated by the original grantor. Thus, this future owner has an interest in seeing that the life tenant does not *waste* the property; in other words, the life holder is not allowed to neglect or abuse the property in such a way that the property value is diminished. Should the life tenant fail to make necessary repairs, or should he or she use the property in ways damaging to its future value, the future holder could bring legal action against the holder of the life estate to recover damages for waste.

future interest

A person's present right to property ownership and possession in the future.

Future Interest A future interest is a person's present right to property ownership and possession in the future. Such an interest usually exists in conjunction with a life estate or a conditional estate. For example, Joe owns a life estate in Oak Hills Apartments, and on his death the property will pass to Sarah with fee-simple-absolute rights. Sarah, in this case, holds a future interest in Oak Hills Apartments, and if Joe allows the buildings to deteriorate from neglect, Sarah may sue Joe to enjoin him from engaging in waste of the property.

leasehold

A possessory interest, but not an ownership interest, transferred by contract.

Leasehold Estate The interest of a leasehold differs from the interests previously described in that the holder of such an estate has a possessory interest but not an ownership interest. This interest is transferred by a contract known as a *lease*. Both the owner of the property (the lessor, or landlord) and the tenant (the lessee) sign the lease. The contract generally specifies the property to be leased, the amount of the rent payments and when they are due, the duration of the leasehold, and any special rights or duties of either party. A leasehold gives the lessee, or tenant, exclusive rights to the use and possession of the land, including the right to exclude the property owner under most circumstances, for the term specified by the lease.

The tenant's and landlord's rights and obligations may vary according to the lease, but some states have statutes requiring that landlords keep the property in good condition for the tenant's use and giving the tenant the right to withhold rent payments should the landlord fail to maintain the premises. However, should the tenant fail to make the agreed-on payments without such grounds, the landlord may evict the tenant. The landlord is not allowed to enter the property, except when there is an emergency or when the tenant has given permission to enter to make repairs. Near the end of the leasehold, the landlord may enter with notice to the tenant for the purpose of showing the property to a potential tenant.

Subleasing of the property by the tenant to another party is permissible unless specifically prohibited by the lease. However, the initial tenant is liable throughout the entire term of the lease for payment of the rent to the landlord.

easement

An irrevocable right to use some part of another's land for a specific purpose without taking anything from it.

profit

The right to go onto someone's land and take part of the land or a product of it away from the land.

Nonpossessory Estates While most people think of interests in land as being possessory in nature, some estates do not include the right to possess the property. Such interests include easements, profits, and licenses. Easements and profits are similar in that they are neither ownership nor possessory interests and they are subject to similar rules, but they are not exactly the same. An easement is an irrevocable right to use some part of another's land for a specific purpose without taking anything from it. A profit is the right to go onto someone's land and take part of the land or a product of it away from the land. For example, if Bill has the right to drive his car across Jenny's property to get to his property, he has an easement; but if he has the right to go onto her property and remove the topsoil he needs from it for his landscaping business, he has a profit. Easements or profits can be transferred in multiple ways: by express agreement, inheritance, necessity, implication, or prescription. If the land that benefits from the easement or profit is sold, the nonpossessory interest goes with the property. Thus, if Bill sold his land to

Property Interests in Vietnam

In the United States, we take for granted the right to go out and purchase a piece of property if we have the money to do so. Property is not so freely available and transferable in all nations. Vietnam's new constitution, written in 1992, provides guidelines for the allocation, transfer, and sale of private property. However, the constitution still asserts that the people, or the state, own all the land. Thus, if individuals or private enterprises want to use land, they must pay tax on it as a form of rent. Those who agree to pay the tax on the land are granted a "use of right," which entitles them to extended use. The use of right also gives the renter the freedom to transfer the property. Technically, the property is not being transferred but, rather, the right to use the property.

Transference of property can occur only with the approval of a state official. The official ensures that the new owner intends to use the land for the original, state-approved purpose. Moreover, the new owner can never be given a longer term of right or more extensive rights over the land than the original owner had. Finally, the state official determines the price at which the property will be transferred. The government has specified certain prices depending on how the land is used. Considering the involvement of the state in such property transactions, the extent to which the Vietnamese enjoy private property rights is limited.

Sonny, Sonny would also receive the easement across Jenny's property. Similarly, if Jenny sold her property, the new owner would have the burden of Bill's easement as long as it had been properly recorded. Of course, just as easements and profits can be created, they can also be terminated, with the most common method of termination being by agreement. The easement holder may simply deed the easement back to the property owner. If the easement arose by necessity and the necessity no longer exists, the easement would terminate.

A **license** is a right to use another's property that is both temporary and revocable. For example, when a person purchases a theater ticket, he or she has the right to a specific use of the property for a limited time, subject to good behavior. No property interest goes to the license holder.

license
A revocable right to temporarily use another's property.

PROPERTY TRANSFER

The owner's ability to transfer real property is part of the value of property. Any or all of the owner's property may generally be transferred to anyone for any price or no price, as the owner desires.

However, to effectuate such a transfer, the owner must follow certain legal procedures. These procedures are *execution, delivery, acceptance,* and *recording* (see Figure 6-2), the last of which is required to protect the recipient of the property. Such a transfer is presumed to be the conveyance of a fee simple absolute, unless the contrary is stated.

Figure 6-2

Steps in a Voluntary Transfer

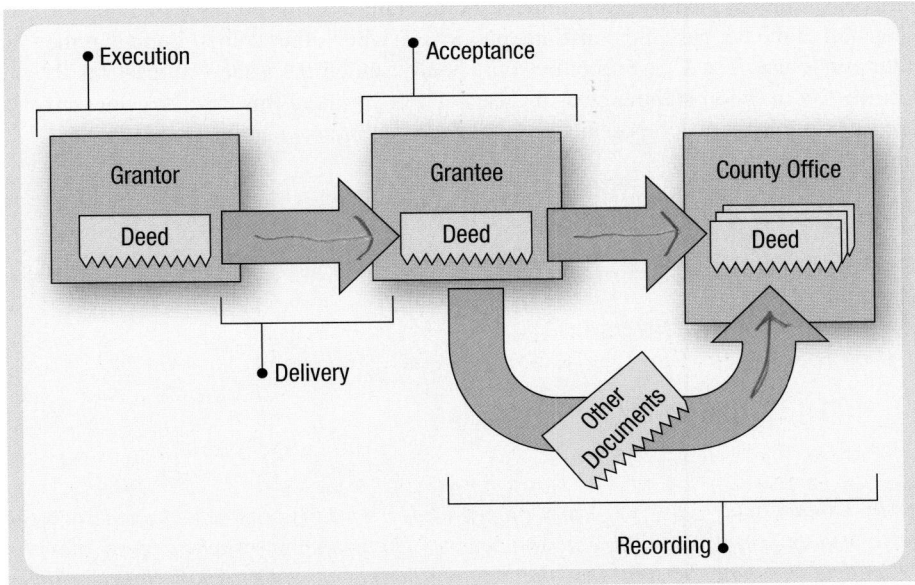

119

adverse possession

An involuntary property transfer in which a person acquires ownership of property by treating a piece of real property as his or her own, without protest or permission from the owner.

The transfer of the owner's interest in real property is not always voluntary. Transfer of property may also take place without the owner's knowledge and even, in some cases, against his or her will, by either adverse possession or condemnation. In **adverse possession** a person takes ownership of property by treating a piece of real property as his or her own, without protest or permission from the owner. Most states have established statutes determining a length of time after which such a possessor receives the ownership interest in the property. The exact lengths of time vary from state to state, but adverse possession must be *actual* (the person lives on or uses the land as an owner would), *open* (not secretive), and *notorious* (without the owner's permission). In some states, the adverse possessor must have performed certain acts such as the payment of real estate taxes. In other states, such possession must have taken place "under color of title"; in other words, the adverse possessor was operating under the assumption that he or she actually held the title to the land.

condemnation

The legal process by which a transfer of property is made against the protest of the property owner.

Condemnation is the legal process by which a transfer of property is made against the protest of the property owner. As you will remember from Chapter 4's discussion of the takings clause of the Fifth Amendment, the government has a constitutional right to take private property for the use of the public provided it pays the owner fair compensation. This right may be exercised at any government level, and sometimes it is exercised on behalf of a private company operating to benefit the public. For example, in the Case Opener about *Poletown,* a private business argued that the creation of new jobs was essential to the economic future of the area, and reducing unemployment through job creation took precedence over the residents' individual property rights.

When the government decides to exercise its power of eminent domain, it will first make an offer to purchase the property for what it believes is the fair market value. If the owner either does not want to sell or feels the price is too low, the government will initiate a condemnation proceeding and the court will determine whether the government body bringing the action has a valid claim that the taking is for a legitimate public purpose. If the court determines that, in fact, the taking of the property will benefit the public interest, the court will then determine the fair market value of the property. This price will be paid to the owner, and the property will be transferred to the government.

It is sometimes difficult to determine whether the exercise of eminent domain is actually for the public's benefit when the property will be conveyed by the government to another private individual. In the *Poletown* case, we see that a private corporation will clearly benefit from the government's taking of the property of the residents of the Poletown community. Could this benefit be described as being for a public use? Since the 1980s, businesses increasingly have been appealing to cities to use their power of eminent domain to assist the businesses in acquiring land that the owners have not wanted to sell. As this transference of property from one private individual to another is for the alleged public use of economic development, an increasing number of state supreme courts began to address the issue of whether economic development was a public use under the constraints of the Fifth Amendment. Some state supreme courts found that job creation and expansion of the tax base did constitute public use, while other courts found that they did not constitute public use. The U.S. Supreme Court finally settled the issue—at least for the present time—in the 5-4 decision summarized in Case 6-1. As you read this case, ask yourself whether there are any significant differences between the facts in *Poletown* and those in Case 6-1.

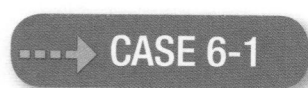 **CASE 6-1**

KELO v. CITY OF NEW LONDON
UNITED STATES SUPREME COURT
126 S. Ct. 326 (2005)

FACTS: *New London, a city in Connecticut, used its eminent domain authority to seize private property to sell to private developers. The city said developing the land would create jobs and increase tax revenues. Kelo Susette* *and others whose property was seized sued New London in state court. The property owners argued that the city violated the Fifth Amendment's takings clause, which guarantees that the government will not take private property*

for public use without just compensation. Specifically, the property owners argued that taking private property to sell to private developers was not public use. The Connecticut Supreme Court ruled for New London.

ISSUE: Does a city violate the Fifth Amendment's takings clause if the city takes private property and sells it for private development, with the hopes the development will help the city's bad economy?

REASONING:

- The city's taking of private property to sell for private development qualified as a "public use" within the meaning of the takings clause.

- The city was not taking the land simply to benefit a certain group of private individuals but was following an economic development plan. Such justifications should be given deference.

- The takings here qualified as "public use" despite the fact that the land was not going to be used by the public.

- The Fifth Amendment did not require "literal" public use, the majority said, but the "broader and more natural interpretation of public use as 'public purpose.'"

O'Connor's dissent:

- An unelected (therefore voter-unaccountable) private nonprofit corporation was the primary beneficiary of the government taking.

- "Any property may now be taken for the benefit of another private party, but the fallout from this decision will not be random. The beneficiaries are likely to be those citizens with disproportionate influence and power in the political process, including large corporations and development firms."

- The decision eliminates "any distinction between private and public use of property—and thereby effectively delete[s] the words 'for public use' from the Takings Clause of the Fifth Amendment."

DECISION AND REMEDY: The city has not violated the Fifth Amendment. Affirmed, for New London.

SIGNIFICANCE OF THE CASE: The U.S. Supreme Court expanded significantly what constitutes "public use." Many people believe the Supreme Court went too far—they agree with Justice O'Connor's opinion.

CRITICAL THINKING

When you examine the reasoning in both the majority and dissenting opinions, you can see that a significant conflict between the opinions exists because of the ambiguity of a key term. Identify this term, and explain how its interpretation affects the reasoning. How do you think the courts should define the term?

ETHICAL DECISION MAKING

Who are the primary stakeholders involved in this case? How are they affected by the ruling? What are the implications of this ruling in terms of the distinction between public and private property? Further, this case highlights an important value conflict. Can you explain how certain values would lead one to support the majority opinion, whereas different values would lead one to support the dissenting opinion? How might holding a different value determine how one predicts the implications of this ruling?

Whereas the *Kelo* and *Poletown* cases involve government attempts to take property from individuals to sell to companies, sometimes governments seek to take the property of one company for use by another company. For instance, in June 2000, Costco, a large retail chain, wanted to expand its warehouse in Lancaster, California. Afraid of losing the large store, which threatened to move if it could not expand, the city considered using its eminent domain powers to acquire an adjacent 99 Cents Only store so that Costco could obtain the property. This example demonstrates that even businesses may be at risk of losing their property to larger, more powerful businesses.

The response to the *Kelo* decision was widespread. President Bush issued an executive order limiting the taking of private property by the federal government to "situations in which the taking is for public use, with just compensation, and for the purpose of benefiting the general

Economics: Eminent Domain and Market Forces

Markets depend on voluntary transactions to allocate resources efficiently. Individuals are willing to buy goods as long as they get more benefit out of the goods than the price they pay for them. Similarly, individuals are willing to sell goods as long as the price they receive is higher than the benefit they would get from keeping the goods. Thus, voluntary transactions benefit the buyer and seller because they are both better off after making the exchange.

Economists call the difference between the price a buyer was willing to pay for a good and the price she actually pays for it her *consumer surplus.* Similarly, the difference between the price at which a seller was willing to sell a good and the price at which he actually sold it is his *producer surplus.* Consumer surplus and producer surplus are measures of *how much better off* market transactions make people. As long as individuals make transactions voluntarily, they enjoy a producer or consumer surplus.

Government's eminent domain power, however, distorts market forces by allowing *involuntary* transfers of property, as long as the government uses the property for "public benefit." If the government forces a private-property owner to sell her property, we know she is worse off as a result of the transaction. (After all, if the transaction makes her better off, she would have voluntarily agreed to sell her property.) Hence, her producer surplus is *negative.* If the taking is to yield a *net* public benefit, it must produce public benefits large enough to offset her negative producer surplus.

But when government uses its eminent domain power to transfer private property from one individual to another, it distorts the market in another way, too. When a business receives property to use for economic development from the government for less than it would have had to pay the owner, it is effectively receiving a subsidy from the government. *Subsidies* are government payments to producers. When government subsidizes some firms' land purchases, those firms can produce their products at a lower cost and earn higher economic profits than firms that did not receive the government subsidy.

Economics can't tell government whether it should exercise its eminent domain power to take private property from one individual and give it to another. Economics can, however, tell government about the costs that result when it distorts market forces.

public, and not merely for the purpose of advancing the economic interest of private parties to be given ownership or use of the property taken." During the year and a half after *Kelo,* 30 state legislatures enacted statutes limiting the use of eminent domain. Additionally, in 2006, nine states passed ballot measures restricting the definition of public use for purposes of eminent domain. Thus, it appears that the ultimate impact of the *Kelo* decision will be the opposite of what that decision held; by statute, a much more restrictive definition of public use will govern government takings. The case is also important because it shows how constitutional issues directly affect areas of the law, such as property law.

Intellectual Property

Intellectual property, property that comes from creativity, also carries a bundle of sticks, both for the creator of the property and for the community. The creators of intellectual property often want to keep the property to themselves. For example, creators of copyrighted work (creative work in a fixed form) do not want others to copy that work without permission.

At times, intellectual property is more complicated than real property. For example, copyright often impacts freedom of speech. If a songwriter creates a song, others may think they have the "right" to express themselves through this song, but a copyright may prevent this expression. Thus, copyright law and freedom of speech sometimes clash. Legislators and courts play an important role in responding to potential conflicts. They also balance the rights of innovators who create intellectual property with the interests of the community, especially interests in competition and freedom of expression. Courts and legislators decide what "sticks" to set aside for

creators of intellectual property. They also decide what is left for the public, including artists and other businesses. The following sections describe specific types of intellectual property.

TRADEMARKS

A trademark is a distinctive mark, word, design, picture, or arrangement that is used by a producer in conjunction with a product and tends to cause consumers to identify the product with the producer. Even the shape of a product or package may be a trademark if it is nonfunctional.

Even though the description of a trademark is very broad, there has still been substantial litigation over precisely what features can and cannot serve as a trademark. In one case, discussed in the Case Nugget, the U.S. Supreme Court grappled with the issue of whether a color can be a trademark.

LO 5

trademark
A distinctive mark, word, design, picture, or arrangement that is used by a producer in conjunction with a product and tends to cause consumers to identify the product with the producer.

CASE Nugget

Color as a Trademark?

Qualitex Co. v. Jacobson Products Co.
United States Supreme Court

514 U.S. 159 (1995)

For years, the plaintiff, Qualitex Co., had colored the dry-cleaning press pads it manufactured a special shade of green-gold. When Jacobson Products, a competitor, started coloring its pads the same shade of green-gold, Qualitex sued Jacobson Products for trademark infringement. The defendant challenged the legitimacy of the trademark, arguing that color alone should not quality for registration as a trademark.

The district court found in favor of the plaintiff, but the Ninth Circuit reversed, holding that color alone could not be registered as a trademark. The plaintiff appealed to the U.S. Supreme Court.

In writing for the majority that a color could constitute a trademark, Justice Breyer said that both the language of the Lanham Act and the basic underlying principles of trademark law would seem to include color within the universe of things that could qualify as a trademark. He noted that the broad language used to describe trademarks included "any word, name, symbol, or device, or any combination thereof." Human beings might use as a "symbol" or "device" almost anything at all that is capable of carrying meaning. Justice Breyer noted that a particular shape (of a Coca-Cola bottle), a particular sound (of NBC's three chimes), and even a particular scent (of plumeria blossoms on sewing thread) could be trademarked, and he reasoned that if a shape, a sound, and a fragrance can act as symbols, it made sense that so could a color.

He also noted that a color, if unusual enough in the context, could in fact come to identify goods with their source, just as descriptive words on a product could. The Court concluded that the green-gold color acts as a symbol that has developed secondary meaning (i.e., customers identified the green-gold color as Qualitex's) and identifies the press pads' source. The high court therefore reversed the decision in favor of the plaintiff.

A trademark used *intrastate* is protected under state common law. To be protected in *interstate* use, the trademark must be registered with the U.S. Patent Office under the Lanham Act of 1947. If a mark is registered, the holder of the mark may recover damages from an infringer who uses it to pass off goods as being those of the mark owner. The owner may also obtain an injunction prohibiting the infringer from using the mark. (Only the latter remedy is available for an unregistered mark.) Once the mark is registered, the registration must be renewed between the fifth and sixth

CONNECTING to the Core

Marketing: The Benefits of Trademarks

As you may have learned in your marketing class, trademarks arguably benefit both consumers and companies. A registered brand name, design, or picture provides consumers with a familiar symbol by which they can identify desirable products. Were companies permitted to copy images or names from other brands, consumers would likely be confused about which brand they were actually purchasing; consequently, they might purchase products that they were previously dissatisfied with or had no intention to purchase.

Trademarks benefit companies by building brand equity, in the sense that certain trademarks convey value that does not relate to a product's functionality. In other words, consumers might be willing to pay more for a particular brand even though there may be alternative products of comparable quality. For example, consumers are often willing to pay higher prices for Duracell batteries, Bose entertainment systems, and Microsoft software even though identically functional products are available at a lower price. Hence, trademarks benefit consumers by distinguishing products that they are purchasing, and they also allow companies to reap the benefits of brand equity—the higher prices that consumers are willing to pay for a particular brand.

Source: R. Kerin, S. Hartley, E. Berkowitz, and W. Rudelius, *Marketing* (New York: McGraw-Hill/Irwin, 2006), pp. 300–301.

years. After that initial renewal, the mark holder must renew the registration every 10 years. (If the mark was initially registered before 1990, however, renewal is necessary only every 20 years.)

To register a mark with the Patent Office, one must submit a drawing of the mark and indicate when it was first used in interstate commerce and how it is used. The Patent Office conducts an investigation to verify those facts and will register a trademark as long as it is not generic, descriptive, immoral, deceptive, the name of a person whose permission has not been obtained, or substantially similar to another's trademark.

Case 6-2 demonstrates a typical analysis used in a trademark infringement suit.

 CASE 6-2

TOYS "R" US, INC. v. CANARSIE KIDDIE SHOP, INC.
DISTRICT COURT OF THE EASTERN DISTRICT OF NEW YORK
559 F. Supp. 1189 (1983)

FACTS: *In 1961, plaintiff Toys "R" Us, Inc., obtained a trademark for "Toys 'R' Us" and aggressively advertised its products, children's toys and clothing, in stores across the country. In the late 1970s, defendant Canarsie Kiddie Shop opened two clothing shops called "Kids 'r' Us" within 2 miles of a Toys "R" Us shop. The defendant never tried to register its name. Toys "R" Us sued for trademark infringement in federal district court.*

ISSUE: Does "Kids 'r' Us" infringe on the mark "Toys 'R' Us"?

REASONING: To determine the likelihood of confusion associated with the defendant's mark, the court considered these factors:

- *Strength of the senior user's mark:* A mark can fall into one of four general categories, which, in order of ascending strength, are (1) generic (is entitled to no protection); (2) descriptive (has a secondary meaning and informs public about uses of product); (3) suggestive (suggests qualities of product but requires imagination); and (4) arbitrary or fanciful (does not describe the qualities of the product). The plaintiff's mark has a strong secondary meaning as a source of children's products, so the court determines the mark has medium strength. But it falls short of the arbitrary or fanciful protection.

- *Degree of similarity between the two marks:* The key question is, Do consumers have the impression that purchasing from the junior user is purchasing from

the senior user? Both parties use the phrase "R Us." However, the plaintiff uses an inverted capitalized "R," while the defendant uses a noninverted lower-case "r." The plaintiff uses "Toys" while the defendant uses "Kids." The plaintiff's letter is usually multicolored.

- *Proximity of the products:* Both the plaintiff and the defendant sell children's clothing and are direct competitors.
- *The likelihood that plaintiff will "bridge the gap":* First, the senior user will expand sales efforts to compete with the junior user. Second, consumers will assume that both parties are related companies.
- *Evidence of actual confusion:* When there is proof that consumers are actually confused by the use of the name, the senior user has a stronger case.
- *Junior user's good faith:* The owner of Kids 'r' Us asserted that he did not recall whether he was aware of the plaintiff's mark. The court does not believe him and

concludes that the defendant adopted the "Kids 'r' Us" mark with knowledge of the plaintiff's mark.

- *Quality of the junior user's product:* The Court is much more concerned about the possible violation if the quality of the clothing is poor because such clothing would then reflect poorly on the senior user.
- *Sophistication of the purchasers:* Because children's clothing is not a major expenditure, customers will not exercise the same degree of care in evaluating the clothes.
- *Junior user's goodwill:* The junior user did not expend a lot of money advertising and promoting its own name. Thus, the defendant doesn't have a strong equitable interest in retaining its name.

DECISION AND REMEDY: Judgment for the plaintiff. The defendant's use of its mark creates the likelihood of confusion and constitutes trademark infringement.

SIGNIFICANCE OF THE CASE: This case clarifies the factors to consider in a trademark infringement case.

CRITICAL THINKING

How does this case depend to a large extent on the definitions of a few particular terms? How good are the definitions used? What standard are you using to determine whether the definitions are good?

ETHICAL DECISION MAKING

If you were the owner of Canarsie Kiddie Shop, Inc., how would your decision to refer to your store as "Kids 'r' Us" change if you were to act in accordance with the Golden Rule? What values are in conflict when considering the decisions of the owner of Canarsie Kiddie Shop, Inc., and of one who follows the Golden Rule?

The term **trade dress** refers to the overall appearance and image of a product. Trade dress is entitled to the same protection as a trademark. The main focus of a case of trade-dress infringement is usually on whether there is likely to be consumer confusion. For example, in a recent case,[1] Tour 18, Ltd., a golf course, copied golf holes from famous golf courses without permission of the course owners. In copying a hole from one the most famous courses in the country, Harbour Town Hole 19, Tour 18 even copied the Harbour Town lighthouse, which is the distinctive feature of that hole. In its advertising, Tour 18 prominently featured pictures of this hole, including the lighthouse. The operator of the Harbour Town course sued Tour 18 for trade-dress infringement. The court found that there was infringement and made Tour 18 remove the lighthouse and disclaim in its advertising any affiliation with the owner of the Harbour Town course.

trade dress
The overall appearance and image of a product.

COPYRIGHTS

Copyrights protect the *expression* of creative ideas. That is, they do not protect the ideas themselves but protect only the fixed form that expresses the ideas. Copyrights protect a diverse range of creative works, such as books, periodicals, musical compositions, plays, motion pictures,

copyright
The protection of the expression of a creative work; i.e., protection of the fixed form that expresses the ideas.

[1] *Pebble Beach Co. v. Tour 18, Ltd.,* 942 F. Supp. 1513.

sound recordings, lectures, works of art, and computer programs. Titles and short phrases may not be copyrighted.

There are three criteria for a work to be copyrightable. First, it must be *fixed,* which means set out in a tangible medium of expression. Second, it must be *original.* Third, it must be *creative.* A copyright automatically arises under common law when the idea is expressed in tangible form. However, if the work is freely distributed without notice of copyright, the work falls into the public domain. A copyrighted work that is reproduced with the appropriate notice affixed is protected for the life of its creator plus 70 years.

Under the common law of copyright, an infringer may be enjoined only from reproducing a copyrighted work. For the creator to be able to not only seek an injunction but also recover damages arising from the infringement, the copyrighted work must be registered. One may register a

E-COMMERCE and the Law

Domain Names and Trade Names

If you have a very strong trademark, what better domain name to have than that trademark? Unfortunately, the same trademark may be owned by two companies selling noncompeting goods, yet there can be only one user of any single domain name. For example, "apple" is a trademark owned by both a computer company and the company that produces the Beatles' records. Both cannot establish a site identified as apple.com.

Domain names are important because they are the addresses by which people and businesses are located on the Web. A domain name is made up of a series of domains separated by periods. Most Web sites have two domains. The first-level domain, the one that the address ends with, generally identifies the type of site. For example, if it is a government site, the domain name will end in *gov;* an educational site, in *edu;* a network site, in *net;* an organization site, in *org;* and a business site, in *com.* These top-level domain names are the same worldwide.

The second-level domain is usually the name of whoever maintains the site. For a college, for example, it would be an abbreviation of the college name, such as *bgsu.* Businesses generally want to use their firm name or some other trademark associated with their product, because that name will obviously make it easiest for their customers to find them.

So how does a firm go about securing a domain name that reflects its trademark? Network Solutions, Inc. (NSI), which is funded by the National Science Foundation, is responsible for registering domain names. This entity acts on behalf of the Internet Network Information Center, which handles the daily administration of the domain name system in the United States.

Initially, a person applied to the NSI to use a specific domain name, and as long as no one else held that name,

registration was granted. Since 1995, however, the NSI has been a little more careful in handing out names. Anyone seeking to register a domain name must now state in the application that the name will not infringe on anyone else's intellectual property rights and that the registrant intends to use the name on a regular basis on the Internet.

A party may lose registration of a name by not using it for more than 90 days. Or the domain name may be canceled if the registrant lied on the registration application. If you have a registered trademark and you find that a party is using your trademark as a domain name and that party does not also have ownership of that mark, you may give written notice to the NSI; under its domain dispute policy, it will most likely put the name "on hold," meaning that no one can use the name. Of course, if that party had registered its domain name before you obtained the trademark, there is probably nothing you can do. The party will be entitled to retain the domain name.

Some firms have tried to get the domain name they desire by going to another country. That alternative is certainly a possibility. However, many countries require that your firm be incorporated within their borders before you can gain the right to the domain name there. An additional problem is that trademark law relating to domain names is even more unclear abroad.

For the new entrepreneur, the best advice is to try to simultaneously apply for federal trademark protection and register the domain name. And for those not yet on the Web, the sooner you get your domain name, the more likely you are to get the name you want. If you feel that your mark is being violated by another's domain name, you may want to sue the party for infringement, because the unauthorized use of another's trademark in a domain name has been found to be illegal. But you may be in for quite a fight because this is a new area of the law.

work by filing a form with the Register of Copyright and providing two copies of the copyrighted material to the Library of Congress. Whenever the work is reproduced, the appropriate notice of copyright *should* accompany it, although such notice is no longer required by law. Printed works, for example, should be published with the word *copyright* and the symbol © or the abbreviation *copr.,* followed by the first date of publication and the name of the copyright owner. Once the work is registered, as long as it is always accompanied by the notice of copyright when reproduced, the holder of the copyright has the additional right to sue an infringer for damages caused by the infringer's use of the copyrighted material and to recover any profits made by the infringer on the copyrighted material.

It is not always easy to determine whether a copyright has been infringed, even when two works are similar. After all, if we are talking about creative works, such as photographs of a famous scene, two people might independently take a very similar picture at completely different times and without even knowing of each other's work. Case 6-3 illustrates the court's reasoning in a successful copyright infringement case.

CASE 6-3

TY INC. v. GMA ACCESSORIES INC.
U.S. COURT OF APPEALS SEVENTH CIRCUIT
45 U.S.P.Q. 1519 (1998)

FACTS: *Ty began selling Beanie Babies. GMA started selling bean-bag stuffed animals three years later. Ty sought an injunction under the Copyright Act to stop the sale of GMA's "Preston the Pig" and "Louie the Cow." Ty argued that these animals violated its copyrights for "Squealer" (a pig) and "Daisy" (a cow).*

ISSUE: Did GMA violate Ty's copyright by copying Ty's Beanie Babies?

REASONING: The court asks: Did the alleged copier have access to the work he or she potentially copied? Did he or she actually copy the work? Access (and copying) may be inferred when the two works are so similar and unlike anything in the public domain that it is likely the second user copied the first. This inference can be rebutted by disproving access or showing independent creation. Looking at pictures of the two cows compels an inference of copying. If GMA must have had access to Ty's cow, it must have had access to the pig, too. GMA's pig is strikingly similar to Ty's pig but not to anything in the public domain (e.g., a real pig). The only evidence GMA presented was an affidavit by the designer, who swears she never looked at Squealer. However, the actual bean-bag animal looks more like Ty's design than the designer's drawing.

DECISION AND REMEDY: GMA engaged in copyright infringement. Ty was therefore granted an injunction.

SIGNIFICANCE OF THE CASE: The court made it clear that there are circumstances in which the act of copying can be inferred.

CRITICAL THINKING

What type of information could the defendant, GMA, have submitted in the previous case that might have kept the court from issuing the injunction?

ETHICAL DECISION MAKING

As an executive at GMA, how would you have responded to this case if your actions were guided by the Golden Rule? What values would be important in making your decision?

fair-use doctrine
The lawful use of a limited, noncommercial portion of another's work for purposes of criticism, comment, news reporting, teaching, scholarship, or research.

The **fair-use doctrine** provides that a portion of a copyrighted work may be reproduced for purposes of "criticism, comment, news reporting, teaching (including multiple copies for classroom use), scholarships, and research." In determining whether the fair-use doctrine provides a valid defense to a claim of copyright infringement, Section 107 of the Copyright Act requires that the court weigh the following four factors: the purpose and character of the use, the nature of the copyrighted work, the amount and substantiality of the portion used in relation to the copyrighted work as a whole, and the effect of the use on the potential market for or value of the copyrighted work. The following Case Nugget provides an example of the fair use doctrine.

CASE Nugget

A Question of Fair Use

Mattel, Inc. v. Walking Mountain Productions and Tom Forsythe
Ninth Circuit Court of Appeals

353 F.3d 792

Tom Forsythe was a photographer who took a series of photographs attempting to critique the objectification of women associated with Barbie and to attack the conventional beauty myth and the societal acceptance of women as objects, as embodied by Barbie dolls, which he believes that product is the most enduring of those products that feed on the insecurities of our beauty and perfection-obsessed consumer culture. He claimed that his art attempted to convey this serious message with an element of humor.

His photographs turn the glamorous, perfect image of Barbie on its head by displaying carefully positioned, nude, and sometimes frazzled looking Barbies in often ridiculous and apparently dangerous situations. For example, he shows Barbie about to be destroyed or harmed by domestic life in the form of kitchen appliances, yet continues displaying her well-known smile, disturbingly oblivious to her predicament. As portrayed in some of Forsythe's photographs, the appliances are substantial and overwhelming, while Barbie appears defenseless.

Forsythe promoted the sale of his photographs through a postcard depicting his work, a business card, and a Web site. He earned just a little over $3,000 from the photographs.

Mattel sued Forsythe for violating their copyright on Barbie. The trial court granted summary judgment to Forsythe, and Mattel appealed. In reviewing the lower court's decision, the court of appeals applied the four factors discussed above to find that the use of the Barbie image was protected by the fair use doctrine. Applying the first factor, the nature and character of the use, the court found the photographs were transformative works attempting to convey a message through the use of parody, and not primarily commercial in nature, a finding that weighs in favor of fair use. The second factor, the creative nature of the copyrighted work, works in Mattel's favor, but this factor is not as important as the others. Regarding the amount of the original work taken, the court analogized between the use of photographs of Barbie in a different setting the previously approved copying of a basic melody and adding elements that transform the work, and therefore this factor works in favor of the photographer. Finally, in terms of actual market harm, because of the parodic nature of the photographs, it is highly unlikely that it will substitute for products in Mattel's markets or the markets of Mattel's licensees. In light of the application of these four factors, the court of appeals affirmed the district court's granting of summary judgment to Forsythe and his photography company.

PATENTS

A patent protects a product, process, invention, or machine or a plant produced by asexual repro-
duction. For this protection to be granted, three criteria must be satisfied. First, the object of the
patent must be *novel,* or new. No one else must have previously made or published the plans for
this object. Second, the object must be *useful,* unless it is a design. It must provide some utility
to society. Third, the object must be *nonobvious.* The invention must not be one that a person of
ordinary skill in the trade could have easily discovered. When a patent is issued for an object, it
gives its holder the exclusive right to produce, sell, and use the object of the patent for 20 years
from the date of application. The holder of the patent may *license,* or allow others to manufacture
and sell, the patented object. In most cases, patents are licensed in exchange for the payment of
royalties, a sum of money paid for each use of the patented process.

The only restriction on the patent holder is that he or she may not use the patent for an illegal
purpose. The two most common illegal purposes are tying arrangements and cross licensing.
A tying arrangement occurs when the holder issues a license to use the patented object *only* if
the licensee agrees to buy some nonpatented product from the holder. Cross-licensing occurs
when two patent holders license each other to use their patents *only* on the condition that neither
licenses anyone else to use his or her patent without the other's consent. Both of these activities
are unlawful because they tend to reduce competition.

To obtain a patent, one generally contacts an attorney licensed to practice before the U.S. Pat-
ent Office. The attorney does a *patent search* to make sure that no other similar patent exists. If
none exist, the attorney fills out a patent application and files it with the Patent Office. The Patent
Office evaluates the application, and if the object meets the criteria already described, a patent
is issued within approximately two years. While two years may seem like a long time, it is short
compared to the six years it typically takes to secure a patent in Japan.

Once the patent is issued, the holder may bring a patent infringement suit in a federal court
against anyone who uses, sells, or manufactures the patented invention without the permission of
the patent holder. A successful action may result in an injunction prohibiting further use of the
patented item by the infringer and also an award of damages. Sometimes, however, the result of
the case is that the holder loses the patent. This loss would occur if the infringer is able to prove
that the Patent Office should not have issued the patent in the first place.

TRADE SECRETS

A trade secret is a process, product, method of operation, or compilation of information that
gives a businessperson an advantage over his or her competitors. Inventions and designs may
also be considered trade secrets. A trade secret is protected by the common law from unlawful
appropriation by competitors as long as it is kept secret and consists of elements not generally
known in the trade.

Competitors may discover a "secret" by any lawful means, such as by doing reverse engineer-
ing or by going on public tours of plants and observing the use of trade secrets. Lawful discovery
of a secret means there is no longer a trade secret to be protected.

If a competitor acquires a trade secret by unlawful means, the originator of the secret can
take legal action. To enjoin such a competitor from continuing the use of a trade secret and/or to
recover damages caused by the use of the secret, a plaintiff must prove that a trade secret actually
existed, that the defendant acquired it through unlawful means, and that the defendant used the
trade secret without the plaintiff's permission.

A common dilemma facing an inventor is whether to protect an invention through patent or
trade-secret law. If the inventor successfully patents the invention and defends the patent, the
inventor has a guaranteed exclusive monopoly on the use of the invention for 20 years, a substan-
tial period of time. The problem is that once this period is over, the patented good goes into the
public domain and everyone has access to it. There is also the risk that the patent may be success-
fully challenged and the protection lost prematurely.

Trade-secret law, on the other hand, could protect the invention in perpetuity. The problem is
that once someone discovers the secret lawfully, the protection is lost.

patent
Protection that grants
the holder the exclusive
right to produce, sell
and use the object of the
patent for 20 years; can
be obtained for a prod-
uct, process, invention,
or machine or a plant
produced by asexual
reproduction.

tying arrangement
An illegal agreement in
which the sale of one
product is tied to the
sale of another.

cross-licensing
An illegal contractual
arrangement in which
two or more parties
license each other to
use their specified intel-
lectual property *only* on
the condition that neither
licenses anyone else to
use the property without
the other's consent.

trade secret
A process, product,
method of opera-
tion, or compilation of
information that gives
a businessperson an
advantage over his or
her competitors.

SUMMARY

The Nature of Real And Intellectual Property

Real property is land and anything permanently affixed to the land.

Intellectual property is property that is primarily the result of mental creativity rather than physical effort.

Real Property

Fee simple absolute: Right to possess for life and devise to heirs on death; the most encompassing interest.

Conditional estate: Right that is comparable to a fee simple absolute except that the interest will terminate on the happening or nonhappening of a specified condition.

Leasehold estate: Right to possess property for an agreed-on period of time.

Easement: Irrevocable right to use a portion of someone else's land for a specified purpose.

License: Right to temporarily use another's property.

Intellectual Property

A *trademark* is a distinctive mark, word, design, picture, or arrangement that is used by a producer in conjunction with a product and tends to cause the consumer to identify the product with the producer. Trademarks used in interstate commerce can be protected under the Lanham Act.

A *copyright* protects the fixed form of the *expression* of an original, creative idea. The most common defense to an allegation of copyright infringement is the *fair-use doctrine,* which provides that a portion of a copyrighted work may be reproduced for purposes of "criticism, comment, news reporting, teaching (including multiple copies for classroom use), scholarships, and research."

A *patent* protects a product, process, invention, machine, or plant produced by asexual reproduction that meets the criteria of being novel, useful, and nonobvious. Obtaining a patent under the Lanham Act allows the holder to license the use of his or her patented idea for royalties as long as the holder does not enter into a tying arrangement or engage in cross-licensing.

Point/Counterpoint

The process of applying for a patent and keeping a patent can be difficult and costly. As you know, an alternative to patenting an invention is to protect it through trade-secret law.

Should Inventors Avoid the Hassles of Patent Protection and Protect Their Inventions through Trade-Secret Law?	
YES	NO
Inventors should choose to protect their inventions through trade-secret law. Trade-secret protection does not require registration with government agencies. Unlike patent protection, whereby the owner of the patent has exclusive rights to produce, sell, and use the object of the patent only for a limited time, trade-secret protection offers the owner of the trade secret exclusive rights indefinitely. For example, the unique process by which Coca-Cola makes its soft drink has been protected as a trade secret for over 100 years. This approach has prevented competitors from duplicating Coca-Cola's product. A patent holder also risks the chance of losing the patent if a challenger is able to show that the patent should not have been issued. Because trade-secret protection is not limited by registration requirements, inventors should use trade-secret law to protect their products.	Inventors should not choose to protect their inventions through trade-secret law. Protection through trade-secret law is risky. It is the responsibility of the owner of the trade secret to take precautionary measures to maintain the privacy of the trade secret. With technological advances, the chance of competitors' using legal methods such as reverse engineering to discover the trade secret is likely. An owner of a patent may bring a patent infringement suit if the patent has been used without permission. If a trade secret is discovered through lawful means, it is no longer a secret and the owner cannot bring actions against those using the product or process. Through patent protection the owner can decide whether to license the patent and can earn a profit from those who choose to use the product. The risks associated with trade-secret protection are too great to make it a desirable choice.

1. Explain the bundle-of-sticks idea as it relates to real property.

2. Explain the five possessory interests in land.

3. Explain the bundle-of-sticks idea as it relates to intellectual property.

4. How are trademarks and patents different?

5. Explain copyright infringement.

6. Willard W. Smith had owned a salvage yard since 1980. In 1984, the county enacted a zoning ordinance requiring a permit for salvage yards. Because the operation of Smith's yard predated the 1984 ordinance, he was not subjected to the permit requirement. A relevant regulation stated, "Any salvage yard which was licensed prior to June 12, 1988, may continue to be operated and maintained in accordance with the statutes and regulations in effect at the time the yard was initially licensed." In 1992, Smith sold the yard to Poole. Poole continued to use the property as a salvage yard. The use and operation of the property did not change. After Poole failed to apply for a permit, the circuit court found that the previous lawful, nonconforming use of the property was terminated when Smith sold the land to Poole. Poole appealed the court's decision. Do you think he was successful? Why or why not? [*Poole v. Berkeley County Planning Com'n,* 488 S.E.2d 349 (1997).]

7. Miller Brewing produced a reduced-calorie beer called "Miller Lite," which it began selling in the 1970s and spent millions of dollars advertising. In 1980, Falstaff Brewing Corporation started marketing a reduced-calorie beer called "Falstaff Lite." Miller filed an action seeking an injunction against Falstaff to prevent it from using the term *Lite.* What was the outcome of the case? [*Miller Brewing Co. v. Falstaff Brewing Corporation,* 655 F.2d 5 (1987).]

8. CMM brought suit against Ocean Coast Properties alleging federal copyright, trademark, and trade-dress infringement. CMM ran radio promotional contests entitled "Payroll Payoff" and "Paycheck Payoff." Both were registered as service marks in 1991. The radio station would announce a name, and if the person announced called the station, she or he was "on the payroll" until replaced by the next announced listener. The promotion was not original to CMM; rather, the idea for the promotion came from another station's promotion called "Working Women's Wednesday." After learning that the promotion was not original, another station, WPOR, began to run a promotion entitled "Payday Contest." Both WPOR and CMM used direct mail to advertise their promotions.

The brochures for the stations contained similar graphics and phrases. In arguing that the two promotions could create confusion, CMM testified that it had been contacted several times by listeners asking if its promotion was connected to WPOR's promotion. Do you think the court ruled in favor of CMM? [*CMM Cable Rep, Inc. v. Ocean Coast Properties Inc.,* 888 F. Supp. 192 (1995).]

9. Plaintiff Columbia Pictures Industries Inc. brought a copyright infringement action against Miramax Films Corp. The successful motion picture *Men in Black,* produced by Columbia Pictures, grossed over $250 million at the box office in 1997. In advertising the film, Columbia produced a copyrighted MIB poster and two copyrighted MIB trailers shown in theaters. The poster shows Will Smith and Tommy Lee Jones standing in front of the New York City skyline. They hold oversized weapons, and the copy reads "Protecting the Earth from the Scum of the Universe." The movie trailers use the same slogan and show a shadow of Smith and Jones superimposed over the letters *MIB.*

In 1998, Miramax Films Corporation produced the film *The Big One.* This was a documentary concerning corporate America's quest for profits at the expense of jobs and plant closings. Prior to the release, Miramax also produced posters and movie trailers. The posters featured Michael Moore, the writer and director of the film, standing in front of the New York City skyline with an oversized microphone. The copy reads "Protecting the Earth from the Scum of Corporate America." The slogan is used again in the movie trailer, and the trailer ends with a picture of Moore superimposed over the letters *TBO.*

The promotions for *The Big One* were pulled after Miramax received complaints from Columbia pictures. Columbia argued that Miramax used copyrighted material to generate profits for the film. Miramax contended that it was protected under the fair-use doctrine, and it argued that the films were not similar in nature. Whom do you think the court decided in favor of? Why? [*Columbia Pictures Industries Inc. v. Miramax Films Corp.,* 11 F. Supp. 1179 (57).]

10. The plaintiff, Lone Star Steakhouse, operates over 30 Lone Star Steakhouse & Saloon restaurants in the United States. The trademarks "Lone Star Café" and "Lone Star Steakhouse & Saloon" are owned by Lone Star Steakhouse. Clothing and accessories with the logo are sold in the restaurant. In 1991 the defendant, Alpha, opened a restaurant named "Lone Star Grill" in Arlington, Virginia. Alpha conducted extensive advertising in the Virginia and Washington, D.C., area.

The advertisements featured coupons with the words *Lone Star* and a five-pointed star similar to the one used by Lone Star Steakhouse. Lone Star Steakhouse operates four restaurants in Virginia and one restaurant in Washington, D.C. It testified that on several occasions customers presented coupons for Lone Star Grill. To prevent customer dissatisfaction, Lone Star Steakhouse would give customers free drinks, coupons, or meal discounts. Lone Star Steakhouse & Saloon brought a trademark infringement action against Lone Star Grill. How do you think the court decided, and why? [*Lone Star Steakhouse & Saloon v. Alpha of Virginia,* 43 F.3d 922 (1995).]

11. The Stop & Shop Supermarket and Big Y Foods are supermarkets offering the same services and competing for the same customers. In an advertisement introducing its new, easy-to-use scan saver cards, Stop & Shop Supermarket used the slogan "It's that Simple." The supermarket used the slogan in radio, television, and print advertisements. The service mark was licensed to the supermarket by plaintiff Fullerton, who owns the right to the service mark. After Stop & Shop started using the slogan, Big Y Foods began to use a similar slogan, "We Make Life Simple." Both service marks are always accompanied by the name of the store. Fullerton and Stop & Shop Supermarket brought an action alleging infringement of the service mark. Do you think that the court granted the injunction? Why or why not? [*The Stop & Shop Supermarket Company and Fullerton Corp. v. Big Y Foods Inc.,* 943 F. Supp. 120 (1996).]

12. Smith, a satirist and outspoken critic of Wal-Mart, created Web sites displaying designs and slogans that negatively parodied Wal-Mart's registered marks. These designs and slogans incorporated the word "Walocaust," a word Smith invented by combining the first three letters of Wal-Mart's name with the last six letters of the word "holocaust."

 Smith also sold novelty items printed with graphics that parodied the retailer's slogans on line, with the disclaimer that he was unaffiliated with the retailer. One design depicted a blue stylized bird modeled to resemble a Nazi eagle grasping a yellow smiley face in the same manner that a Nazi eagle is typically depicted grasping a swastika. Above the bird image, the word "WAL*OCAUST" was printed in a blue font comparable to that commonly used by Wal-Mart. The lower court found that Wal-Mart had failed to establish that a smiley face icon it used for advertising was distinctive enough to merit trademark protection, and that Smith's slogans and graphics were scathing parodies, and therefore did not violate any Wal-Mart trademarks nor cause dilution of their marks. Do you think the court of appeals upheld Smith's defense that it was engaged in parody, and that such parody precluded claims of trademark infringement and dilution? [*Smith v. Wal-Mart Stores, Inc.,* 475 F. Supp. 2d 1318, 2007 U.S. Dist. LEXIS 13335 (N.D. Ga., 2007).]

13. Superior Form Builders held a copyright for animal mannequins. The sculpted animal forms were used to mount animal skins. The owner of Superior Form Builders, Tommy Knight, considers the mannequins to be a form of artistic expression. The defendant, Dan Chase Taxidermy Supply Company, ordered four of Knight's mannequins from the Superior Form catalog. Chase, a competitor of Superior Form, ordered under a fictitious name. He used the mannequins to mount animal skins and made few changes to the forms. When Knight realized that Chase was using the Superior Form mannequins, he sued for copyright infringement. Chase argued that the copyright should never have been granted because the mannequins were useful and unoriginal. How do you think the court decided? [*Superior Form Builders, Inc v. Chase Taxidermy Supply Co.,* 74 F.3d 488 (4th Cir. 1996).]

14. GoTo.com's logo features a green circle surrounded by a yellow background, with the words *Go* and *To* printed in the circle. Disney Corp. started to use its logo, a green circle surrounded by a yellow background with the word *Go* printed inside, on its GoNetwork page. GoTo.com filed suit against Disney Corp., seeking an injunction. Do you think the court granted the injunction? What factors would it have considered in making its decision? [*GoTo.com, Inc. v. Walt Disney Corp.,* 202 F.3d 1199, 1207 (9th Cir. 2000).]

Looking for more review material?

The Online Learning Center at **www.mhhe.com/kubasekess** contains this chapter's "Assignment on the Internet" and also a list of URLs for more information, entitled "On the Internet." Find both of them in the Student Center portion of the OLC, along with quizzes and other helpful materials.

Introduction to Contracts and Agreement

---▶ CASE OPENER

The Problematic Promotion

Pepsi had a promotion whereby consumers were encouraged to collect "Pepsi points" by consuming Pepsi products. They could then redeem the points for merchandise. If they did not have quite enough points for the prize they wanted, they could buy the needed additional points for 10 cents each; however, at least 15 original Pepsi points had to accompany each order.

At the climax of an early commercial for the promotion, three young boys are sitting in front of a high school building, one reading his Pepsi Stuff catalog while the others drink Pepsi, all gazing in awe at an object rushing overhead as the military march in the background builds to a crescendo. A Harrier jet swings into view and lands by the side of the school building, next to a bicycle rack. Several students run for cover, and the velocity of the wind strips one hapless faculty member down to his underwear. While the faculty member is being deprived of his dignity, the voice-over announces: "Now the more Pepsi you drink, the more great stuff you're gonna get."

A teenager opens the cockpit of the fighter and can be seen, without a helmet, holding a Pepsi. He exclaims, "Sure beats the bus," and chortles. The military drumroll sounds a final time, as the following words appear: "Harrier Fighter 7,000,000 Pepsi Points." A few seconds later, the following appears in more stylized script: "Drink Pepsi—Get Stuff."

John Leonard decided to accept Pepsi's offer of the Harrier Fighter jet for 7 million Pepsi points. He quickly realized that it would be easier to raise the money to buy points than to collect the 7 million points. In early March 1996, he filled out an order form requesting the jet and submitted it to Pepsi, along with 15 Pepsi points and a check for $700,000.

In response, Pepsi sent him a letter saying, "The item that you have requested is not part of the Pepsi Stuff collection. It is not included in the catalogue or on the order form, and only catalogue merchandise can be redeemed under this program." John then sued for breach of contract.

1. Did Pepsi offer to sell the Harrier jet for 7 million points?
2. Did Leonard's submission of the order form constitute an acceptance?
3. Was the alleged contract in this case a bilateral or unilateral contract?

After reading this chapter, you will be able to answer the following questions:

LO 1 What is a contract?

LO 2 What are the sources of contract law?

LO 3 How can contracts be classified?

LO 4 What are the rules that guide the interpretation of contracts?

LO 5 What are the elements of a valid offer and valid acceptance?

LO 6 How does an offer terminate?

LO 1

contract

A promise or set of promises for the breach of which the law gives a remedy or the perfor-mance of which the law in some way recognizes a duty

agreement

One of the four elements necessary for a contract; consists of an offer made by one party, the offeror, and the acceptance of the offer by another party, the offeree.

offer

A key factor is the agreement element of a contract; consists of the terms and conditions set by one party, the offeror, and presented to another party, the offeree.

acceptance

A key factor in the agreement element of a contract; consists of the agreement of one party, the offeree, to the terms of the offer in the con-tract made by the other party, the offeror.

consideration

The bargained-for exchange; what each party gets in exchange for his or her promise under a contract.

The Definition of a Contract

This part of the text focuses on contracts. A **contract,** according to the Restatement (Second) of Contracts, is "a promise or set of promises for the breach of which the law gives a remedy or the performance of which the law in some way recognizes a duty."[1] Another, perhaps simpler, way to think of a contract is that it is a set of legally enforceable promises.

ELEMENTS OF A CONTRACT

A contract has four elements: the agreement, the consideration, contractual capacity, and a legal object. The **agreement** consists of an **offer** by one party, called the *offeror,* to enter into a con-tract, and an **acceptance** of the terms of the offer by the other party, called the *offeree.* The agree-ment is discussed in more detail in the latter part of this chapter.

The second element of a contract is the **consideration,** which is defined as the bargained-for exchange. Another way to think of the consideration is that it is what each party gets in exchange for his or her promise under the contract. Consideration is further discussed in Chapter 8.

The third element is **contractual capacity,** the legal ability to enter into a binding agreement. Most adults over the age of majority have the legal ability to enter into binding contracts, but Chapter 9 explains when people have either limited or no capacity to enter into these agreements. Persons who do not have the capacity to enter into legally binding contracts include those who are under the age of majority, intoxicated, or suffering from mental illness. Chapter 9 also dis-cusses the fourth element of a binding, legal contract, **legal object.** The contract cannot be either illegal or against public policy.

The elements of a contract, as well as defenses to its enforcement, are listed in Exhibit 7-1.

DEFENSES TO THE ENFORCEMENT OF A CONTRACT

Sometimes the parties may enter into what appears to be a legally binding and enforceable contract because all four elements of a contract are present, but one of the parties may have a defense to the contract's enforcement. Such defenses fall into two categories. The first, discussed in Chapter 10, is a **lack of genuine assent.** A contract is supposed to be entered into freely by both parties, but sometimes the offeror secures the acceptance of the agreement through improper means, such as fraud, duress, undue influence, or misrepresentation. In these situations, there really is no genuine

[1] Restatement (Second) of Contracts, sec. 1.

Exhibit 7-1

ELEMENTS OF A CONTRACT	DEFENSES TO A CONTRACT
Agreement	Lack of genuine assent
Consideration	Lack of proper form
Legal purpose	
Capacity	

A Valid Contract Has Four Elements, and No Defenses Can Be Raised against It

contractual capacity
The legal ability to enter into a binding agreement.

legal object
A purpose that does not violate a statute or public policy.

assent to the contract, and the offeree may be able to raise the lack of genuine assent as a defense to enforcement of the agreement.

The second defense, discussed in Chapter 11, is that the contract lacks the *proper form,* which typically means it lacks a writing. Certain contracts require a writing, and if there is none, the agreement will not be enforced. Chapter 12 discusses the performance and discharge of contracts, as well as remedies arising when a contract is breached.

Sources of Contract Law

LO 2

lack of genuine assent
A defense to the agreement of a contract in which the offeree claims that the offeror secured the agreement through improper means, such as duress, fraud, undue influence, or misrepresentation.

There are two primary sources of contract law: case law and the Uniform Commercial Code (UCC). A third source of law, which has become more important with increasing globalization, is the Convention on Contracts for International Sales of Goods (CISG). Chapters 7 through 12 of this book focus primarily on the law of contracts as established by the common law, and Chapters 14 and 15 focus on the law as established by the UCC and CSIG.

COMMON LAW

Today's law of contracts actually originated in judicial decisions in England, which were followed by the early courts in the United States. Since then, contract law has been modified by our legislatures and by rulings of our courts. The law of contracts is primarily common law, and so to find out what the law is, one could go to the Reporters and read the decisions, but an easier way to know the law would be to go to the Restatement (Second) of the Law of Contracts. Prominent legal scholars, recruited by the American Law Institute, organized the principles of the common law of contracts into the original *Restatement of the Law, Contracts.* The compilation has subsequently been revised and published as *Restatement of the Law Second, Contracts.*

The Restatement (Second) is not actually the law itself, although judges frequently cite it in cases because it is an authoritative statement of what the law is. As the common law of contracts evolved in the various states, not all states interpreted all aspects of the law in the same way, so while we can generalize about the law of contracts, one would of course always want to know exactly what the law at issue is in one's own state. In the Restatement (Second), the drafters often explain what the law about a particular matter is in the majority of states and then provide alternative approaches that other states have adopted.

UNIFORM COMMERCIAL CODE

Uniform Commercial Code (UCC)
A statutory source of contract law in the United States applicable to transactions involving the sale of goods. The UCC was created in 1952 and adopted by all 50 states, the District of Columbia, and the Virgin Islands; it may be modified by each state to reflect the wishes of the state legislature.

Having different laws governing contracts in different states did not make interstate commerce flow smoothly. To remedy some of the difficulties created by a patchwork of different laws governing commercial transactions, the National Conference of Commissioners on Uniform State Laws and the American Law Institute drafted a set of commercial laws that could be applicable to all states. This effort was called the Uniform Commercial Code (UCC). The UCC became law in each state that adopted it completely or partially as part of its state code. Thus, for example, if a firm enters into a contract governed by the Uniform Commercial Code in Ohio, it would be operating under the Ohio Uniform Commercial Code.

The part of the Uniform Commercial Code that is relevant to contracts is Article 2, which governs contracts for the sale (exchange for a price) of goods (tangible, movable objects). This part of the book will sometimes point out important differences between the UCC and the common law, but the UCC is discussed primarily in Chapters 13 and 14.

China

Compared to the United States, other countries have slightly different laws for different types of contracts. China, for example, not only has seven chapters of general provisions for contracts but also has chapters with special provisions for 15 different types of contracts. Some of the types of contracts for which special provisions have been drafted are contracts for sales, leases, loans, donations, construction projects, storage, and transportation.

Also relevant to contract law is Article 2A, which governs contracts for the lease of goods. For instance, if a person leased a car from a dealership, the lease contract would be governed by Article 2A. In contrast, if the person purchased a car from a dealership, the purchase contract would be governed by Article 2 of the UCC.

LO 3 · Classification of Contracts

Contracts are classified in a number of different ways. Different classifications are useful for different purposes, as the following discussion demonstrates.

BILATERAL VERSUS UNILATERAL CONTRACTS

All contracts can be classified as either bilateral or unilateral. Knowing whether a contract is bilateral or unilateral is important because that classification determines when the offeree is legally bound to perform. Whether a contract is bilateral or unilateral depends on what response the offeror (the party proposing the contract) expects from the offeree (the person agreeing to or accepting the contract).

bilateral contract
A promise exchanged for a promise.

If the offeror wants a promise from the offeree to form a binding contract, the contract is a **bilateral contract.** A bilateral contract is commonly defined as a promise in exchange for a promise. As soon as the promises are exchanged, a contract is formed and the parties' legal obligations arise. For example, when Shannon promises to pay Gary $1,000 in exchange for his promise to paint her car on July 1, they have a bilateral contract. If either party fails to perform, the other may sue for breach.

unilateral contract
A promise exchanged for an act.

In a **unilateral contract,** the offeror wants a performance to form the contract. The offeror wants the offeree to do something, not promise to do something. The most common unilateral offer is a reward. If Jim loses his dog, he may post a sign stating "$50 reward for the safe return of my Poodle, Frenchie." If Rita calls Jim and says, "Don't worry, I'll find your dog," she is not making a contract because the unilateral offer calls for an action, not a promise. Once she finds Frenchie and takes the dog to Jim, a contract is formed and Jim must pay.

Just as the offeree is under no obligation to actually do the act called for by the offeror, the offeror may revoke the offer at any time before performance. However, to prevent injustice, once an offeree begins performance, the offeror must hold the offer open for a reasonable time to allow the offeree to complete the performance.

In the Case Opener, the plaintiff would argue that Pepsi appeared to be making an offer for a unilateral contract. In its television commercial, Pepsi promised to provide a prize for a performance, the presentation of a set number of points. By submitting the requisite number of points, the plaintiff believed he was accepting a unilateral offer.

EXPRESS VERSUS IMPLIED CONTRACTS

express contract
A contract in which all the terms are clearly set forth in either written or spoken words.

implied contract
A contract that arises not from words of agreement but from the conduct of the parties.

Contracts are classified as express or implied, depending on how they are created. **Express contracts** have all their terms clearly set forth in either written or spoken words. The contract in the Case Opener was an express contract, as the terms were set forth in the ad and the catalog. **Implied contracts,** in contrast, arise not from words but from the conduct of the parties. For instance, when you have a dental emergency and your dentist pulls your severely infected tooth without prior negotiation about payment, or even any mention of payment, you have an implied contract for payment for his services.

As a general rule, three conditions must be met for the courts to find an implied, or as it is sometimes called, an *implied-in fact,* contract. First, the plaintiff provided some property or service to the defendant. Second, the plaintiff expected to be paid for such property or service and a reasonable person in the position of the defendant would have expected to pay for such property or services. Third, the defendant had an opportunity to reject the property or services but did not.

QUASI-CONTRACTS

Quasi-contracts are sometimes called *implied-in-law contracts,* but they are not actually contracts. Rather, to prevent one party from being unjustly enriched at the expense of another, the courts impose contractual obligations on one of the parties, as if that party had entered into a contract.

For example, assume Jones hears a noise out in his driveway. He looks out and sees a group of workers apparently getting ready to resurface his driveway. The doorbell rings, and he does not answer it. He goes down into his basement office and stays there until the workers have gone and he has a resurfaced driveway. When he receives a bill from the paving company, he refuses to pay on grounds that he did not ask to have the driveway done. In such a case, where Jones knew that the company was getting ready to bestow on him a benefit to which he was not entitled, the court will probably impose a quasi-contract, requiring that Jones pay the paving company the fair market value of the resurfacing. Imposing such a duty prevents Jones from being unjustly enriched at the expense of the paving company.

There are limits to the doctrine, however; specifically, the enrichment must be unjust. Sometimes a benefit may simply be conferred on you because of a mistake by the other party, and the courts will not make people pay for others' mistakes. In our example, had Jones been out of town when his driveway was repaved, he would have just gotten lucky. The courts are not going to make him pay for the pavers' mistake when he could have done nothing to prevent the benefit from being bestowed on him.

quasi-contract
A court-imposed contractual obligation to prevent unjust enrichment.

VALID, VOID, VOIDABLE, AND UNENFORCEABLE CONTRACTS

What everyone hopes to enter into, of course, is a valid contract. A valid contract is one that contains all the legal elements of a contract, as set forth in Exhibit 7-1. As a general rule, a valid contract is one that will be enforced. However, sometimes a contract may be valid yet unenforceable.

A valid contract may be unenforceable when there is some law that prohibits the courts from enforcing it. For example, the statute of frauds, discussed in Chapter 11, requires that certain contracts must be evidenced by a writing before they can be enforced. Similarly, the statute of limitations mandates that an action for breach of contract must be brought within a set period of time, thereby limiting the enforceability of the contract.

A void contract is, in effect, not a contract at all. Either its object is illegal or it has some defect that is so serious that it is not a contract. If you entered into a contract with an assassin to kill your business law professor, that would be a void contract because it is obviously illegal to carry out the terms of the agreement.

A contract is voidable if one or both of the parties have the ability to either withdraw from the contract or enforce it. If the parties discover that the contract is voidable after one or both have partially performed, and one party chooses to have the contract terminated, both parties must return anything they had already exchanged under the agreement so that they will be returned to the condition they were in at the time they entered into the agreement.

Certain types of errors in the formation of a contract lead to its being voidable. Typically, the person who can avoid the contract is the person whom the court is attempting to protect, or the party the court believes might be taken advantage of by the other party. For example, contracts by minors are usually voidable by the minor, as discussed in Chapter 9. Contracts entered into as a result of fraud, duress, or undue influence—a problem with the validity of the acceptance, as described in Chapter 10—may be avoided by the innocent party.

valid
A term applied to a contract that includes all four elements of a contract: agreement (offer and acceptance), consideration, contractual capacity, and legal object.

unenforceable
A term applied to a contract that, because of a law, cannot be enforced by the courts.

void
A term applied to a contract that is not valid because its object is illegal or it has some defect that is so serious that it is not a contract.

voidable
A term applied to a contract that one or both parties have the ability to either withdraw from or enforce.

EXECUTED VERSUS EXECUTORY CONTRACTS

Once all the terms of the contract have been fully performed, the contract is said to have been executed. As long as some of the duties under the contract have not yet been performed, the

executed
A term applied to a contract in which all of the terms have been fully performed.

executory
A term applied to a contract in which not all of the terms have been fully performed.

contract is considered executory. For example, if Randolph hires Carmine to paint his garage on Saturday for $800, with $200 paid as a down payment and the balance due on completion of the job, the contract becomes executory as soon as the agreement is reached. When the down payment has been made and the painting is halfway completed, the contract is still executory. Once the painting has been finished and the final payment made, the contract is an executed contract.

FORMAL VERSUS INFORMAL CONTRACTS

LO 4

formal contract
A contract that must have a special form or must be created in a specific manner.

Contracts may also be classified as formal or informal. Formal contracts are those that have a special form or must be created in a specific manner. The Restatement (Second) of Contracts identifies the following four types of formal contracts: (1) contracts under seal, (2) recognizances, (3) letters of credit, and (4) negotiable instruments.

contract under seal
A contract that has a seal certifying its legality. Such contracts require no consideration for them to be legal.

When people hear the term *formal contract,* what often comes to mind is a contract under seal. The term *under seal* comes from the days when a contract was literally sealed by a piece of soft wax into which an impression was made. Today, sealed contracts may still be literally sealed with wax or some other soft substance, but they are more likely to be simply identified with the word *seal* or the letters *L.S.* (an abbreviation for *locus sigilli,* which means "the place for the seal") at the end of the document. Preprinted contract forms with a seal printed on them can also be purchased today, and parties using such documents are presumed, without evidence to the contrary, to be adopting the seal for the contract.

recognizance
An obligation in which a party acknowledges in court that he or she will perform some specified act and/or pay a price on failure to do so.

States today do not require that contracts be under seal. However, 10 states still allow a contract without consideration to be enforced if it is under seal.

A recognizance arises when a party acknowledges in court that he or she will perform some specified act and/or pay a price on failure to do so. An example of a recognizance is a bond used as bail in a criminal case. The person agrees to return to court for trial or forfeit the bond.

letter of credit
A binding document that a buyer can request from a bank to guarantee that the payment for goods will be made to the seller.

A letter of credit is an agreement by the person or institution that issues the letter to pay a sum of money on receipt of an invoice and other documents. The Uniform Commercial Code governs letters of credit.

negotiable instrument
A written document signed by a person who makes an unconditional promise to pay a specific sum of money on demand or at a certain time to the holder of the instrument; an acceptable medium for exchanging value from one person to another.

A negotiable instrument is a written document signed by a person who makes an unconditional promise to pay a specific sum of money on demand or at a certain time to the holder of the instrument. The most common forms of negotiable instruments are checks, notes, drafts, and certificates of deposit. They are governed primarily by the UCC. (Negotiable instruments are discussed in greater detail in Chapters 15 and 16.)

informal contract
A contract that requires no formalities.

Any contract that is not a formal contract is an informal contract, also called a *simple contract.* Informal contracts may in fact be quite complex, but they are called "simple" because no formalities are required in making them.

The Agreement

The first element of a contract is the agreement. As noted earlier, this chapter focuses on contracts governed by common law, that is, contracts other than those for the sale of goods. Under the common law, the agreement begins when one party, the offeror, makes an offer to another party, the offeree.

LO 5

Elements of the Offer

An offer has three elements. Under the common law, these elements are intent, definite and certain terms, and communication to the offeree.

INTENT

intent
The intended purpose or goal of an action, especially in a contract.

The first element of the offer is intent. The offeror must manifest an intent to be bound by the offeree's acceptance. Contracts are interpreted using an objective standard, meaning that the courts are concerned with only the party's outward manifestations of his or her intent, not what is going on in that party's mind. The courts interpret the words and actions of the parties the way a reasonable person would interpret them.

Thus, if an individual is clearly joking or speaking out in anger, the reasonable person would not think that the individual seriously intended to make an offer and the courts would consequently not treat the words as an offer. If someone attempts to accept such an offer, the courts will not find that a contract has been made.

Sometimes an offeror may try to avoid a contract by later claiming that he was only joking when he made the offer, but the courts are not interested in one's hidden intent. As Case 7-1 demonstrates, if you joke too well, you may find yourself in an unwanted contract.

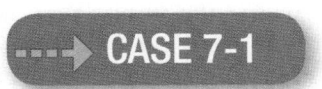

CASE 7-1

LUCY v. ZEHMER
SUPREME COURT OF APPEALS OF VIRGINIA
196 Va. 493, 84 S.E.2d 516 (1954)

FACTS: *Plaintiffs W. O. and J. C. Lucy had wanted to purchase Ferguson Farm from the Zehmers for at least eight years. One night, Lucy stopped by the establishment the Zehmers operated and said that he bet Zehmer wouldn't accept $50,00 for the place. Zehmer replied that he would, but he bet that Lucy would not pay $50,000 for it. Over the course of the evening, the parties drank whiskey and engaged in casual conversation, with the talk repeatedly returning to the sale of Ferguson Farm. Eventually Lucy got Zehmer to draw up a contract for the sale of the farm for $50,000.*

When Lucy later attempted to enforce the agreement, Zehmer refused to complete the sale, arguing that he had been drunk and that the agreement to sell the property had been made in jest. Lucy sued to enforce the agreement.

ISSUE: Had Lucy and Zehmer entered into a legally binding agreement?

REASONING: The mental assent of the parties is not a requirement for the formation of a contract. If the words or other acts of one of the parties have but one reasonable meaning, that party's undisclosed intention is immaterial unless the other party somehow knows that the party does not mean what his words and actions would clearly indicate to any reasonable observer.

In this case, not only did Lucy believe that Zehmer was serious when he drew up the contract, but there was no evidence to indicate that any action taken by Zehmer would have indicated that he was not serious. When Zehmer asked his wife to sign the writing that he drew up containing the terms of the sale, he whispered to her that he was joking, but whispered so quietly that Lucy could not and did not hear it. What happened appeared to be a good-faith offer and a good-faith acceptance, followed by the execution and apparent delivery of a written contract. Therefore, the parties would be held to their outward manifestations of entering into a binding agreement.

DECISION AND REMEDY: The parties had entered into a binding agreement, and the court enforced the agreement.

SIGNIFICANCE OF THE CASE: This case demonstrates that the courts look at the circumstances surrounding the alleged making of a contract and focus on the outward manifestations of a person's intent. It clearly sends the message that people need to be careful when joking about entering into a contract because a person who jokes too well might find herself or himself bound to an agreement that she or he did not really want to make.

CRITICAL THINKING

Why must a joke be visibly a joke to a reasonable observer for there to be no acceptance?

ETHICAL DECISION MAKING

What stakeholders are being protected by the reasoning that supports the rule the court applied in this case?

Preliminary Negotiations An invitation to negotiate or an expression of possible interest in an exchange is not an offer. For example, if Rachael asked Bill whether he would sell his car for $5,000, she is not making an offer; she is just inquiring about his potential willingness to sell. Likewise, when a firm or government entity requests bids for a construction project, the request is just an invitation for contractors to make offers. Thus the bids would be the offers.

Advertisements Another illustration of the offer to make an offer is the advertisement. If a custom furniture maker places an advertisement in the paper that reads, "Old-fashioned, hand-crafted cedar rocking chairs only $250 the first week in May," the store is merely inviting potential customers to come to the store and offer $250 for a rocker. Because no reasonable person would expect the store to be able to sell a rocking chair to every person who might see the ad, the court would interpret the intent of the store as being to invite readers to make an offer.

Under limited circumstances, however, an ad can be treated as an offer. If it appears from the wording of the ad that the store did in fact intend to make an offer, the courts will treat it as an offer. In general, when the ad specifies a limited quantity and provides a specific means by which the offer can be accepted, the courts will treat the ad as an offer, as demonstrated by the Case Nugget.

The plaintiff in the Case Opener tried to rely on the *Lefkowitz* case to argue that the Pepsi commercial was an offer because it was "clear, definite, explicit and left nothing to negotiation." After all, the commercial clearly stated that 7 million points earned a Harrier jet, and the catalog provided an additional means of buying the points for cash.

The court in that case, however, found that the commercial could not be regarded as sufficiently definite because it specifically reserved the details of the offer to a separate writing, the catalog. Also, the commercial itself made no mention of the steps a potential offeree would be required to take to accept the alleged offer of a Harrier jet.

The court further found that the only offer in this scenario was the plaintiff's letter of March 27, 1996, along with the order form and the appropriate number of Pepsi points. As Pepsi rejected this offer with its letter, there was no contract.

To prevent possible "bait-and-switch" advertising, some states have consumer protection laws requiring that advertisers state in their ads either that quantities of the item are limited to the first *X* number of people or that rain checks will be available if the item sells out.

CASE Nugget

When Is an Ad an Offer?

**Lefkowitz v. Great Minneapolis Surplus Store, Inc.
Supreme Court of Minnesota**

251 Minn.188, 86 N.W.2d 689 (1957)

In this case, the defendant had published a newspaper announcement stating: "Saturday 9 AM Sharp, 3 Brand New Fur Coats, Worth up to $1,000.00, First Come First Served $1 Each." Morris Lefkowitz arrived at the store, dollar in hand, but was informed that under the defendant's "house rules," the offer was open to ladies but not gentlemen. The court ruled that because the plaintiff had fulfilled all the terms of the advertisement and the advertisement was specific and left nothing open for negotiation, a contract had been formed.

From this case came the often-quoted exception to the rule that advertisements do not create any power of acceptance in potential offerees: an advertisement that is "clear, definite, and explicit, and leaves nothing open for negotiation." In that circumstance, "it constitutes an offer, acceptance of which will complete the contract."

Auctions Another situation in which what seems to be an offer may not be is the auction. When a person places a good with an auctioneer for sale by auction, is the seller making an offer or is the bidder? The answer depends on what kind of auction is taking place.

If nothing is stated to the contrary in the terms of the auction, an auction is presumed to be *with reserve*. In an auction with reserve, the seller is merely expressing an intent to receive offers. The auctioneer may withdraw the item from auction at any time before the auctioneer's hammer falls, signaling the acceptance of the bid. Similarly, at any time before the hammer falls, the bidder may also revoke the bid.

In an auction *without reserve,* the seller is treated as making an offer to accept the highest bid. Thus, the seller must accept the highest bid. Not surprisingly, very few auctions are without reserve.

DEFINITE AND CERTAIN TERMS

Under the common law, the terms of the offer must be definite and certain. In other words, all the material terms must be included. The *material terms* are those terms that allow a court to determine what the damages are in the event that one of the parties breaches the contract.

Sometimes an offer contains not the material term itself but a method for determining the term. For example, Guy's Sailboats is building Sara a sailboat, and the parties want to make it possible for her to pay one-third of the price of the boat in advance, one-third on delivery, and one-third in 12 monthly payments, with interest, beginning a month after delivery. Rather than stipulating an interest rate to be charged on the monthly payments, the contract might specify an external standard according to which the interest rate would be set through the course of the 12-month payment period.

The question of whether the terms of an alleged offer were adequate for the formation of a valid contract often arises in cases where one party believes that a contract had been formed and the other believes that there had been no contract because the terms of the alleged offer were not definite enough. That issue is the focus of Case 7-2.

 CASE 7-2

ANDRUS v. STATE, DEPARTMENT OF TRANSPORTATION,
AND CITY OF OLYMPIA
WASHINGTON STATE APPELLATE COURT
117 P.3d 1152 (Wash. App. 2005)

FACTS: *Scott Andrus applied for an at-will position as a building inspector with the city of Olympia. He received a call from Tom Hill, an engineering supervisor with the city. Hill stated, "You're our number one choice, and I'm offering you the job." Andrus responded "Great" and "Yes." Hill did not discuss the specifics of the job, so Andrus asked Hill to fax him those details. The city never sent such a fax or a written job offer and request for acceptance.*

On the same day that Andrus received the call from Hill, the city checked Andrus's employment references, including his current employer (the Washington Department of Transportation), which proved unsatisfactory. Hill called Andrus the next day, this time informing him that the city

had withdrawn the job offer because of further reference checks.

Andrus sued the city and the DOT, claiming wrongful discharge and arguing that the phone call from Hill was a valid offer for a contract of employment, which Andrus accepted immediately. He also alleged that the DOT was liable for defamation for providing a bad employment reference to the city. The superior court granted the city's request to dismiss his claims without a trial, and he appealed only the breach-of-contract claim against the city.

ISSUE: Did a valid contract exist between the city and Andrus?

(continued)

REASONING: In the words of the court:

An enforceable contract requires, among other things, an offer with *reasonably certain* terms. Restatement (Second) of Contracts § 33 (1979) ("The fact that one or more terms of a proposed bargain are left open or uncertain may show that a manifestation of intention is not intended to be understood as an offer or as an acceptance.") Hill's "job offer" contained no starting date, salary, or benefit information. Moreover, it was to be followed by a written offer and request for acceptance. Under these facts, the July 13 phone conversation did not form an employment contract.

DECISION AND REMEDY: A valid contract did not exist because of a lack of specific terms in the offer, and therefore the case was affirmed in favor of the city.

SIGNIFICANCE OF THE CASE: This case illustrates the importance of making sure that all the elements of the proposed contract appear in the offer.

CRITICAL THINKING

How could the original phone call from Hill have been considered an employment contract?

ETHICAL DECISION MAKING

How well would this decision hold up if we applied the public disclosure test to it?

COMMUNICATION TO THE OFFEREE

The offer must be communicated to the offeree or to the offeree's agent. Only the offeree to whom the offer was directed can accept the offer. If Bill overhears Sam offer to sell his car to Helen for $5,000, he cannot walk over and form a contract by accepting the offer. If he says to Sam, "I'll give you $5,000 for your car," he is not accepting the offer but, rather, is making a new offer.

LO 6

Termination of the Offer

At some point in time, offers terminate; when an offer terminates, it can no longer be accepted to form a binding contract. There are five ways to terminate an offer: revocation by the offeree, rejection by the offeree, death or incapacity of the offeror, destruction or subsequent illegality of the subject matter of the offer, and lapse of time or failure of other conditions stated in the offer.

REVOCATION BY THE OFFEROR

The offeror is said to be the "master of his offer" and, as such, can revoke it at any time, even if he says he will hold the offer open for a stated period of time. If Jim sends Carol a letter offering to mow her yard every week during the summer for the price of $20 per week as long as she responds to his offer within the next month, he can still change his mind and tell her at any time before she responds that he is no longer interested in working for her, thereby revoking his offer.

option contract

An agreement whereby the offeree gives the offeror a piece of consideration in exchange for the offeror's agreement to hold the offer open for the specified period of time.

If a person wishes to ensure that an offer will in fact be held open for a set period of time, the person may do so by entering into an option contract with the offeree. An **option contract** is an agreement whereby the offeree gives the offeror a piece of consideration in exchange for the offeror's agreement to hold the offer open for the specified period of time.

There is no requirement as to the value of the consideration. If the consideration is money, the parties may agree that if the offer is eventually accepted and a contract is formed, the consideration for the option contract will become part of the payment for the contract. This situation

frequently arises in contracts involving real estate. Jones may be considering opening a restaurant and would like to have the option of purchasing a lot owned by Smith, so he gives Smith $1,000 for a 30-day option to purchase the lot, with the provision that the $1,000 will be deducted from the purchase price if Jones purchases the property. In the event that Jones does not buy the property, Smith will keep the $1,000.

The UCC imposes an additional limitation on the offeror's ability to revoke the offer. A promise to hold an offer for the sale of a good open for a specified period cannot be revoked if it is made in writing and signed by a merchant.

As a general rule, the revocation of an offer is effective when it is received by the offeree. Because of this rule, if it is really important to the offeror to know that his offer has been revoked, he should personally deliver the revocation to the offeree.

REJECTION BY THE OFFEREE

The second means by which an offer can be terminated is rejection by the offeree. Regardless of how long the offer was stated to be open, once the offeree rejects it, it is terminated. In our earlier example, if Carol calls Jim and says that she is not interested in his working for her this summer or any summer because of the poor quality of the work he has done for her in the past but then calls him back an hour later to say that she has changed her mind and would like to hire him in accordance with his proposed terms, it is too late. There is no offer for her to accept because her rejection terminated the offer.

DEATH OR INCAPACITY OF THE OFFEROR

The offer terminates immediately if the offeror dies or loses the legal capacity to enter into the contract. This termination occurs even if the offeree does not know of the terminating event. The exception to this rule occurs when the parties had already entered into an option contract to hold the offer open for a set period of time. If an option contract exists, the administrator of the offeror's estate or the guardian of the offeror must hold the offer open until it expires in accordance with the option contract.

DESTRUCTION OR SUBSEQUENT ILLEGALITY OF THE SUBJECT MATTER

If the subject matter of the offer is destroyed or becomes illegal, the offer immediately terminates. For example, if Jamie offers Bill a job managing the riverboat casino he plans to open on January 1 but, before Bill accepts the offer, the state decides to no longer allow riverboat casinos to operate in the state, the offer of employment terminates.

LAPSE OF TIME OR FAILURE OF ANOTHER CONDITION SPECIFIED IN THE OFFER

As noted earlier, the offeror has the power to revoke the offer at any time, even if the offer states that it will be held open a set amount of time. But if the offer states that it will be held open for only a certain time, the offer will terminate when that time expires. In the absence of a time condition in the offer, the offer will expire after the lapse of a reasonable amount of time. What constitutes a reasonable amount of time varies, depending on the subject matter of the offer. For example, an offer by a retailer to purchase seasonal goods from a wholesaler would lapse before an offer to purchase goods that could be easily sold all year long.

Elements of the Acceptance

Once an offer has been made, the offeree has the power to accept that offer and form a contract. In examining the acceptance under the common law, the basic requirements for a valid acceptance parallel those for a valid offer. There should be a manifestation of intent to be bound by the acceptance to the contract, agreement to the definite and certain terms of the offer, and communication to the offeror.

MANIFESTATION OF INTENT TO BE BOUND TO THE CONTRACT

In general, there are two ways an offeree can manifest her or his intent to enter into the contract: by performance or by a return promise. The offeree must either do something or say something to form the contract.

Recall the distinction between a bilateral contract and a unilateral contract. If the offer is for a unilateral contract, the offeree can accept only by providing the requested performance. If Bill offered to pay $500 to anyone who returned his lost dog to him, Mary could accept the offer only by returning the dog. Bill did not want her promise, and if she called and promised to return the dog to him, that promise would have no legal effect because the only way to accept a unilateral offer is by performance.

With a bilateral contract, what the offeror wants to form the contract is not performance but, rather, a return promise. Sometimes, however, it is not clear whether the offeror wants performance or a return promise. In such a case, the offeree has the option of either performing or making a return promise.

Silence as a Form of Acceptance Silence, as a general rule, cannot be used to form a contract. For example, Lisa and Marie both work at a local diner where the manager is very flexible and lets the waitresses trade shifts. Marie calls Lisa and leaves her a voice-mail message saying, "I can't work my three night shifts this week. If you can cover them for me, I'll pay you an extra $40 on top of the money you'll receive from the boss for working my shifts. If I don't hear from you by 7 p.m. tomorrow, I'll assume we have a deal and you will work for me. Thanks so much!" If Lisa does not call back, no contract has been formed because silence under these circumstances would not constitute an acceptance,

The Restatement of Contracts, however, offers three circumstances under which silence can be an acceptance. First, the offeree receives the benefits of the offered services with reasonable opportunity to reject them and knowledge that some form of compensation is expected, yet the offeree remains silent. Second, the offeror tells the offeree that silence or inaction will constitute an acceptance, and the offeree, by remaining silent, *intends* to accept. Third, the parties, by their previous

Contracts in Japan

The Japanese tend to view contracts as ongoing relationships in which the parties work with each other to smooth out any problems that arise in performance of the contract. The Japanese tend to be suspicious of long, detailed contracts. They have a distinct preference for short, flexible contracts that leave a number of terms to be decided later.

When negotiating a contract with a Japanese businessperson, an American businessperson must recognize how the Japanese will interpret his attempts to include more details in the agreement. The American should think about which details are essential for inclusion.

course of dealing with each other, have established a pattern of behavior whereby it would be reasonable to assume that silence was intended to communicate acceptance. For example, a wholesaler and retailer have a long-standing relationship in which the wholesaler routinely ships a certain type of merchandise to the retailer, who rejects a shipment if it does not meet his needs. After such a pattern of behavior has been established, it is reasonable for the wholesaler to assume that when a shipment is not sent back, the retailer means to accept it.

ACCEPTANCE OF DEFINITE AND CERTAIN TERMS: THE MIRROR-IMAGE RULE

When a bilateral contract is being formed under the common law, the mirror-image rule applies to the acceptance. The mirror-image rule says that the terms of the acceptance must mirror the terms of the offer. If the terms of the acceptance do not mirror the terms of the offer, no contract is formed. Instead, the attempted acceptance is a counteroffer.

mirror-image rule The principle which holds that the terms of the acceptance must mirror the terms of the offer; if the terms of the acceptance do not mirror the terms of the offer, no contract is formed and the attempted acceptance is a counteroffer.

The mirror-image rule has caused a significant amount of trouble for businesses because often a buyer would make an offer on one form that contained not only the essential terms of the contract but also a number of additional, somewhat minor terms. Generally, the offer was on a standard form that had a place where the essential terms were written in. The seller would often return his standard form with its preprinted terms, along with the essential terms written in to match the terms of the offer. The problem was that because these preprinted forms did not match, there was legally no contract. If both parties performed their contracts, no problems arose; but the fact that there was no contract meant that on occasion one party could decide to simply not perform, leaving the other party with no remedy. Or, if the parties did perform, the buyer might perform according to the terms on the buyer's form and be sued for breach by the seller, who believed that the terms on the seller's form were the terms of the agreement.

To eliminate this problem of the "battle of the forms," UCC Section 2-207 significantly modified the mirror-image rule by providing that, as a general rule, an offeree may include in the acceptance terms that are additional to or different from the terms of the offer as long as (1) the offeror did not explicitly state in the offer that all terms of the offer must be accepted exactly as proposed; (2) the offeror does not promptly reject the new terms on receipt of the acceptance; and (3) the new terms do not materially change the terms of the original offer.

In the case of additional terms—terms related to issues not addressed in the original offer—if none of the foregoing conditions occur, a contract is formed and the terms of the agreement are those of the acceptance, as long as the parties are merchants. If the parties are not merchants, the additional terms are merely proposals for additions to the contract and must be accepted by the offeror.

If the terms of the acceptance are different from those in the offer, various states treat the terms differently. In most states, the terms are said to cancel each other out, and the courts then look to the UCC for neutral terms to insert into the contract.

COMMUNICATION TO THE OFFEROR

An offeror has the power to control the means by which the acceptance is communicated, and if the offeror specifies that only a certain means of communication will be accepted, then only that method of communication forms a valid offer. Suppose, for example, that Jennifer offers to paint Bill's car for $500 but says that he must accept the offer by telephone before midnight

on Thursday. If he sends her an e-mail Thursday morning accepting her offer, there is no valid contract. Even though e-mail might be a valid means of accepting a contract offer if no means is specified, when the offer is limited to a specific means of communicating the acceptance, only that means results in a valid contract. Thus Bill's attempted acceptance was simply a new offer.

If no means of communicating the acceptance is specified, any reasonable means is generally acceptable. Telephone, telegraph, mail, fax, and e-mail are all valid means of accepting an offer. If a person drafting an offer wishes acceptance to be only by a particular means, the offer must make it clear that only a certain means is allowed. As Case 7-3 illustrates, courts will carefully interpret provisions specifying the means of acceptance.

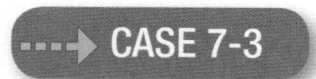

CASE 7-3

OSPREY L.L.C. v. KELLY-MOORE PAINT CO.
SUPREME COURT OF OKLAHOMA
984 P.2d 194, 1999 Okla. LEXIS 64

FACTS: *The plaintiff leased commercial premises to the defendant. The lease required that the defendant provide notice of its intent to renew the lease at least six months prior to the lease's expiration, and notice was to be given in writing and delivered personally or through registered first-class mail. The defendant attempted to extend the lease by faxing a renewal letter on the last day of the six-month notification period. Although fax records and telephone records confirmed that the fax was transmitted, the plaintiff denied receiving the fax.*

The plaintiff refused to renew the lease and demanded that the defendant vacate the premises at the end of the current lease term. The defendant refused to vacate the premises, so the plaintiff filed an action for forcible entry and detainer.

The trial court found that the faxed notice effectively renewed the lease, and the appeals court reversed. The supreme court granted certiorari.

ISSUE: In this case, was the fax of a notice of renewal on a lease sufficient communication when the lease contract specified that renewal must be delivered personally or by mail?

REASONING: The court noted that the issue of whether faxes can constitute sufficient notice of acceptance had been decided by a number of different courts with varying results. The majority had generally recognized that, despite the contention that there must be strict compliance with the notice terms of a lease option agreement, use of an alternative method does not render the notice defective if the substituted method performed the same function or served the same purpose as the authorized method.

The court in this case agreed with the reasoning of Kelley-Moore that language in a contract is given its plain and ordinary meaning, unless some technical term is used in a manner meant to convey a specific technical concept. The lease in this case specified that notice of acceptance "shall" be in writing and that delivery "may" be either in person or by certified or registered mail. Given the ordinary interpretation of *shall* as mandatory and *may* as permissive, the notice of acceptance of the lease at issue must be in writing, and that writing may be by the methods specified but may also be through other modes of transmission that would be just as effective.

The purpose of providing notice by personal delivery or registered mail is to ensure the delivery of the notice and to settle any dispute that might arise between the parties concerning whether the notice was received. A substituted method of notice that performs the same function and serves the same purpose as an authorized method of notice is not defective.

In this case, the contract provided that time was of the essence. The fax activity report and telephone company records confirm that the fax was transmitted successfully and that it was sent to Osprey's correct facsimile number on the last day of the deadline to extend the lease. The fax provided immediate written communication similar to personal delivery and, like a telegram, would be timely if it were properly transmitted before the expiration of the deadline to renew. Kelly-Moore's use of the fax served the same function and the same purpose as the two methods suggested by the lease, and it was transmitted before the expiration of the deadline to renew.

DECISION AND REMEDY: The court concluded that the faxed delivery of the written notice to renew the commercial lease was sufficient to exercise timely the renewal option of the lease given that this method of delivery fulfilled the same purpose as the permissive methods of delivery specified in the lease. The court therefore reversed in favor of the defendant.

(continued)

SIGNIFICANCE OF THE CASE: The case illustrates that sometimes, in interpreting a contract's specifications for means of acceptance, the court may be willing to look beyond the methods of delivery identified in the contract and instead focus on the intent of the parties in identifying potential means of communicating the acceptance.

CRITICAL THINKING

What line of reasoning might another court have followed to lead to a different outcome in this case?

ETHICAL DECISION MAKING

Consider Osprey's denial of receiving the fax in question from Kelly-Moore. If this denial does amount to a false claim, what is the motivation for the commission of this falsehood?

The Mailbox Rule Because not all acceptances are made in person, a rule needed to be developed to determine the point at which an acceptance made through the mail became effective. The courts settled on the mailbox rule, which provides that an acceptance is valid when it is placed in the mailbox, whereas a revocation is effective only when received by the offeree. Today, the mailbox rule has been expanded to apply to faxes in some jurisdictions, with courts holding that once the fax has been transmitted, the acceptance is effective.

mailbox rule
The principle which holds that an acceptance is valid when it is placed in the mailbox, whereas a revocation is effective only when received by the offeree. In some jurisdictions the mailbox rule has been expanded to faxes.

The Effect of an Acceptance after a Rejection As previously stated, if an acceptance is received after a rejection is received, the acceptance is not valid because the rejection terminated the offer. However, sometimes a rejection is dispatched, but before it is received, the acceptance is communicated to the offeror. In that case, a valid contract has been formed because the rejection is not effective until it is received. Suppose Brenda e-mails an offer to Harry, and he puts a rejection in the mail. Then, before the rejection is received, Harry calls Brenda and tells her he accepts. A valid contract has been formed, and the rejection will have no effect when it is received. However, if the telephone call had been made after Brenda had received the rejection, there would have been no contract.

E-COMMERCE and the Law

The Mailbox Rule and E-Commerce

The future of the mailbox rule is in question, at least as it applies to electronic acceptances. In the case of computer information transactions, such as acceptances via e-mail, the law is clear: Electronic acceptance is effective when received. For all other transactions, though, the law is unclear.

In a recent article, Valerie Watnick, a professor of business law at Baruch College, offered reasons why the mailbox rule should apply as a default rule in e-commerce cases in which the law is unclear. She offers justifications for her view:

1. The mailbox rule fosters certainty and helps courts avoid complex factual inquiries that are likely in electronic acceptance cases.

2. The mailbox rule is practical in that it supplies the date the contract was formed without sorting out circular communications.

3. Electronic communication is very much like mail, only faster. It is not instantaneous. Messages are broken into "packets" of information, which are sent along different routes to a final destination. Sometimes, it takes hours for a complete message to reach its final destination.

Watnick concludes: "[A] dispatch rule in electronic contracting will allow parties to freely contract through electronic means, without regard to whether both parties have knowledge of the existence of the contract at the moment of its formation." Do you agree with Watnick?

Source: Valerie Watnick, "The Electronic Formation of Contracts and the Common Law 'Mailbox Rule," *Baylor L. Rev.* 50 (2004), p. 175.

SUMMARY

The Definition of a Contract	Contracts at their simplest level are legally enforceable agreements. A *valid contract* is generally viewed as one that has the following elements: agreement, consideration, legal object, and parties with legal capacity.
Sources of Contract Law	There are two sources of contract law: the Uniform Commercial Code and state common law. The Uniform Commercial Code, in Article 2, governs contracts for the sale of goods. All other contracts are also governed by the UCC.
Classifications of Contracts	Contracts may be classified in a number of ways. Every contract is either unilateral or bilateral; express or implied; valid, voidable, or void; executed or executory; and formal or informal.
The Agreement	The *agreement* is the first element of a contract. It begins when one party, the offeror, makes an offer to another party, the offeree.
Elements of the Offer	A valid offer contains the manifestation of the offeror's intent to be bound to the definite and certain terms that are communicated to the offeree.
Termination of the Offer	An offer can be terminated by revocation by the offeror, rejection by the offeree, death or incapacity of the offeror, destruction or subsequent illegality of the subject matter of the offer, or lapse of time or failure of other conditions stated in the offer.
Elements of the Acceptance	An acceptance is valid when a manifestation of intent to be bound to the terms of the offer is communicated to the offeror by the offeree.

Point/Counterpoint

Recovery based on quasi-contract allows the court to impose liability on a party that did not enter into a contract; three conditions must exist: (1) A benefit was conferred on the defendant; (2) the defendant appreciated the benefit; and (3) because of the circumstances under which the defendant received the benefit, it would be unjust to allow the defendant to retain the benefit without compensating the party that conferred it.

Does the Third Prong of the Test for Imposition of Recovery in Quasi-Contract Unjustifiably Limit the Court's Ability to Impose Relief Where It Is Needed?	
YES	**NO**
Limiting the application of the doctrine to those circumstances in which the imposition of liability is required to prevent unjust enrichment is unfair.	

Looking at the case law, the "circumstances" that justify imposition of liability all focus on what the recipient of the benefit did. If he did not in some way acquiesce to the imposition of the benefit, no liability can be imposed. Such a limitation makes an artificial distinction based on the point in time at which the recipient discovers the conferral of the benefit. If there was some possible way for the recipient to have prevented the conferral, he has to pay; but if he had no way to prevent it, he does not have to pay. This distinction sounds fair enough at first glance, but it overlooks the fact that in either situation the recipient gets something he did not pay for and the other party conferred a benefit for no compensation. | The limitation is a necessary one, preventing those knowledgeable about the law from taking unfair advantage of those with less knowledge.

While it may seem unfair for someone to receive a benefit from another party when she did not give any value for that benefit, if she did not ask for the benefit and did not encourage the other party to provide it, there is no justification for making her pay for what is essentially the acting party's mistake. If we presume that neither party is acting with the intent of getting something undeserved, the recipient is still the most innocent party in the situation and, as such, should not be required to pay for the other party's mistake.

Further, while we say that one party is receiving a benefit, that recipient may be receiving a legal "benefit" that is of no value to her. It seems especially |

What if the benefit is really significant? What if ABC Construction builds a new garage for the Smiths, who were on vacation, instead of for their neighbors, who ordered the garage? Is it really fair for the Smiths to get that garage for free?

unfair to make someone pay for a "benefit" that she had no desire to obtain in the first place, even though many others may find that benefit highly desirable.

Questions & Problems

1. Explain why the first question a person should ask when getting ready to analyze a contract problem is, "Is this alleged contract a contract for the sale of a good?"

2. What is the difference between an offer for a unilateral contract and an offer for a bilateral contract? Why might that difference be important to understand?

3. What must a party prove to recover under the theory of quasi-contract?

4. What is the mirror-image rule?

5. What is the mailbox rule?

6. Anthony Maglica and Claire Halasz, as boyfriend and girlfriend, lived together, held themselves out as a married couple, and acted as companions toward each other. In fact, Claire changed her last name to "Maglica," even though the couple never married. Together, the couple worked in a business owned solely by Anthony, although Claire participated in a substantial part of the work. The company, Mag Instrument, was incorporated in 1974, and all shares went to Anthony. However, both Anthony and Claire were paid equal salaries. After the company began manufacturing flashlights, the company grew rapidly, now exceeding hundreds of millions of dollars in net worth. In 1992, Claire and Anthony separated, and subsequently Claire filed suit against Anthony for breach of contract and claimed damages under a theory of quasi-contract. No contract existed between Anthony and Claire. Does Claire have any remedy under a theory of quasi-contract? If so, what must she prove? [*Maglica v. Maglica,* 1998 Cal. App. LEXIS 750.]

7. Barry Pucello was injured in an automobile accident in 1979. One of Pucello's co-workers placed Pucello in contact with an attorney, Allen Feingold. Feingold called Pucello to recommend a doctor, and the next day Feingold and Pucello discussed the possibility of Feingold's representation. Although they did not discuss contingency-fee arrangements, Pucello gave Feingold some information about the accident. Immediately, Feingold began work on the case, inspecting the accident site, taking pictures, and obtaining a police report. Feingold also succeeded in obtaining an admission from the other driver. Less

than one month later, Feingold mailed Pucello a copy of his contingency-fee agreement, which provided for a 50-50 split in any remedy that might be obtained. Concerned by this high attorney fee, Pucello sought counsel from another attorney, who succeeded in obtaining recovery for Pucello for his injuries. Pucello also told Feingold to keep the pictures, reports, and admissions. Feingold, acknowledging that no express agreement existed with Pucello, argued that Pucello still benefited from his work, in that the other driver would be much more unlikely to alter his story after already admitting liability to Feingold. Does Feingold have a valid quasi-contract claim? Why or why not? [*Feingold v. Pucello,* 1995 Pa. Super. LEXIS 26.]

8. Frank Scheck offered to sell a piece of real estate to a specified prospective buyer, agreeing also to pay a broker, A. A. Marchiondo, a percentage of the sale price. Scheck fixed a six-day period during which the offer would be left open. However, Scheck changed his mind and sent a letter to Marchiondo in which Scheck said that he had revoked the offer. After Marchiondo's work in attempting to obtain the offeree's acceptance, Marchiondo received the letter on the morning of the sixth day, and later that day the offeree contacted Marchiondo and accepted the offer to purchase the real estate. Marchiondo claimed that Scheck could not terminate the offer, as a contract had been created, and that Scheck's failure to pay Marchiondo's commission constituted a breach of contract. The trial court dismissed Marchiondo's complaint, and Marchiondo appealed. Was Scheck's letter a proper termination of the offer? Why or why not? What was the appellate court's reasoning? [*Marchiondo v. Scheck,* 1967 N.M. LEXIS 2815.]

9. Marilyn Bouchard opened a restaurant called "Castle Garden Café" in Rhode Island in 2002, hiring Denise Raab. Bouchard and Raab began negotiating a transfer of real estate and ownership from Bouchard to Raab. Raab's attorney drafted a letter, outlining that the sale price of $180,000 would include the real estate, building, inventory, and equipment with equal monthly payments at a 5 percent interest rate to be paid over a period of 10 years. Neither party signed this document, and no other written documents were included

as part of the potential sale. The letter also provided that Raab would obtain a life insurance policy of $150,000. Thereafter, Raab obtained a life insurance policy for only $117,000, but she allowed the policy to lapse after three months. In 2003, Raab controlled the complete operation of the restaurant. Raab also occupied a garage on the premises as a temporary residence, making improvements valued at $20,800 to the garage and restaurant. Raab applied to have the liquor license transferred, as mentioned in the letter for transfer, but the city council never made a decision on the application, although Bouchard asked the city council to renew her own license. In 2004, Bouchard learned that real estate and personal property taxes were unpaid, along with the beverage and meal tax and corporate tax. Subsequently, Bouchard decided to close the restaurant, notifying Raab of the closure. Although the statute of frauds required that the alleged contract be in writing, the court held that Bouchard's admission that there was an oral agreement removed the application of the statute of frauds. Raab sued for specific performance of the contract. Were the terms of the agreement definite and certain enough to create an enforceable contract? Why or why not? [*Raab v. Bouchard,* 2005 R.I. Super. LEXIS 96.]

10. Hazelton Manufacturing is a wholesaler supplier of heating and cooling equipment, including boilers manufactured by H. B. Smith. In 2000, Hazelton received an unsolicited facsimile from Smith, quoting prices for three "Mills" boilers. Smith distributed the facsimile to a number of distributors, based on his understanding that the three boilers were needed for a construction project at Dartmouth High School. Although Smith would usually quote a "retail" price that distributors would later increase before resale, Smith indicated that the "net" price for all three boilers would not be discounted on sale to the distributor. Not realizing this refusal to discount, Hazelton considered the quoted price of $131,711 to be the retail price and reduced it to a "dealer" price of $88,200. Hazelton forwarded the dealer quotation, unsolicited, to numerous businesses, including I&R, as Hazelton believed these companies might be interested in the Dartmouth project. I&R considered Hazelton's quotation in its calculations for a subcontractor bid on the Dartmouth project. After I&R received the subcontractor bid, I&R contacted Hazelton to purchase the boilers at the quoted cost of $88,200. By this time, Hazelton recognized the error in the quotation and refused to sell the boilers to I&R. Subsequently, I&R purchased boilers from another company for $144,000 and sued Hazelton for the difference under a breach-of-contract theory. Was Hazelton's mistaken quotation an offer? Did I&R's contacting Hazelton to purchase the boilers for $88,200 constitute an acceptance? [*I&R Mech. Inc. v. Hazelton Mfg. Co,* 2004 Mass. App. LEXIS 1276.]

11. Sarah and Eddie Hogan wanted to sell 2.5 acres of land through their real estate agent, Darita Richardson. On December 10, 2001, Warren Kent offered to purchase the land for $52,500. An "Agreement to Buy or Sell" was created, which Kent signed right away. One term of the agreement was that the offer would expire on December 11, 2001, at 3 p.m., and it stated additionally, "Time is of the essence and all deadlines are final except where modifications, changes, or extensions are made in writing and signed by all parties." Although Richardson scheduled a meeting on December 11, 2001, at 2 p.m. with the Hogans, the Hogans failed to appear. However, the parties agreed to a two-day extension, lasting until December 13, 2001, at 3 p.m., and the extension was binding and irrevocable according to the "Addendum to Agreement to Purchase or Sell." The Hogans signed both documents at 9 a.m. on December 13, 2001. At about 11 a.m., Kent also signed the addendum. However, neither Kent's agent nor Richardson contacted the Hogans prior to 3 p.m. about Kent's acceptance. After 3 p.m., Richardson realized that the Hogans had not placed the date and time next to their signatures. When she met with the Hogans, they placed the date and the time as 4:48 p.m., informing Richardson that they, the Hogans, had changed their minds about the sale. Kent sued for specific performance of the contract. What effect, if any, did the failure to communicate the acceptance of the offer prior to 3 p.m. have in terms of whether a contract was formed? What do you think the appellate court's reasoning was? [*Kent v. Hogan,* 2004 La. App. LEXIS 2539.]

Looking for more review material?

The Online Learning Center at **www.mhhe.com/kubasekess** contains this chapter's "Assignment on the Internet" and also a list of URLs for more information, entitled "On the Internet." Find both of them in the Student Center portion of the OLC, along with quizzes and other helpful materials.

Consideration

Upper Deck—Contract Liability or Gift?

In 1988 the Upper Deck Company was a baseball card company with an idea for a better baseball card: one that had a hologram on it. By the 1990s Upper Deck was a major corporation whose value was at least a quarter of a billion dollars. In 1988, however, the outlook wasn't bright for Upper Deck, which lacked the funds for a $100,000 deposit it needed to buy some special paper by August 1. Without that deposit its contract with the major-league baseball players' association would have been jeopardized.

Upper Deck's corporate attorney, Anthony Passante, Jr., found the money. That evening, the directors of the company accepted the loan and, in gratitude, agreed that Passante should have 3 percent of the firm's stock. Passante never sought to collect the gift of stock, and later the company reneged on its promise. Passante sued for breach of oral contract.[1]

1. If you were on the jury, how would you decide the case? (The law of consideration will determine the outcome.) Was the offer of 3 percent of the firm's stock legal consideration for the loan? Or was it a mere gift?

2. Does Upper Deck have a moral obligation to give Passante the stock? If so, is this legally enforceable?

[1] *Passante v. McWilliam,* 53 Cal. App. 4th 1240 (1997).

After reading this chapter, you will be able to answer the following questions:

LO 1 What is promissory estoppel, and when can it be used?

LO 2 What is an illusory promise?

LO 3 How are the UCC rules regarding consideration different from the common law rules regarding consideration?

LO 4 What is the difference between a liquidated debt and an unliquidated debt?

LO 5 What is an accord and satisfaction?

What Is Consideration?

Consideration is required in every contract. It is what a person will receive in return for performing a contract obligation. Suppose, for example, that Dan agrees to purchase Mary's car for $1,000. Dan's payment of $1,000 is the consideration Mary will receive for her car. Mary's turning over ownership of the car to Dan is the consideration Dan will receive in exchange. In the business context, consideration is usually money. However, consideration can be anything, as long as it is the product of a bargained-for exchange. It consists of something of value given to another party in exchange for something else of value. The following are examples of consideration:

- A benefit to the promisor (e.g., a promise to stay in a job until a particular project is completed—this is a benefit to the employer).
- A detriment to the promisee (e.g., a promise to your football coach to refrain from riding your motorcycle during football season even though you love riding it).
- A promise to do something (e.g., a promise to cook dinner for your roommate for the next six months).
- A promise to refrain from doing something (e.g., a promise to stop drinking alcohol during exam week).

Rules of Consideration

As in any area of law, there are a number of rules governing consideration, as well as exceptions to the rules. The trick to understanding consideration is simply to understand the various rules and their exceptions. We explore these principles below.

LACK OF CONSIDERATION

LO 1

Rule: *For a promise to be enforced by the courts, there must be consideration.* A court will enforce one party's promise only if the other party promised something (an act, money, etc.) in exchange. For example, in a bilateral contract (a promise for a promise), the "consideration" for each promise is a return promise. Consider this example: Sue promises to pay Mike $2,000 for his car. Mike promises to sell Sue his car for $2,000. The exchange will be done tomorrow. There is an oral contract. Sue's promise to pay Mike $2,000 for the car is her consideration to Mike. Mike's promise to sell Sue the car for $2,000 is his consideration to Sue. There has been a mutual exchange of something of value—a promise to pay $2,000 and a promise to sell the car for $2,000.

In a unilateral contract (a promise for an act), one party's consideration is the promise and the other party's consideration is the act. Suppose your professor made the following statement in class: "If any student shows up at my house on Saturday and does the gardening, I will pay that student $100." You show up and do the gardening. The professor's consideration to you is the promise of the payment of $100 on completion of the gardening, and your consideration to the professor is the act of completing the gardening. Once again, there has been a mutual exchange of something of value. In Case 8-1, the court must decide whether continued employment is consideration for signing a noncompete agreement.

promissory estoppel
The legal enforcement of an otherwise unenforceable contract due to a party's detrimental reliance on the contract.

The exception to the rule requiring consideration is promissory estoppel. Promissory estoppel occurs when one party makes a promise knowing the other party will rely on it, the other party does rely on it, and the only way to avoid injustice is to enforce the promise. How does this work? Suppose that on graduation from college, Amanda receives a job offer across the country.

She gives up her apartment, cancels all her other job interviews, and moves all her possessions. After arriving, she rents a new apartment and shows up for work.

The only problem is that Amanda is told there is no job! May Amanda sue the employer? The answer in most states is yes, under the theory of promissory estoppel. She spent a lot of money in reliance on the job offer. She also moved across country. Amanda may be able to recover her reliance damages (i.e., money she spent in "reliance" on the job offer). Promissory estoppel is not awarded regularly, but in the right case it can provide a remedy where no other remedy exists.

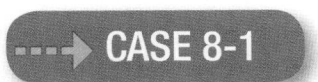

CASE 8-1

ANTHONY A. LABRIOLA v. POLLARD GROUP, INC.
SUPREME COURT OF WASHINGTON
152 Wn. 2d 828; 100 P.3d 791 (Sup. Ct. Wash. 2004)

FACTS: *Employer hired Employee to work as a salesperson. Under the employment agreement, Employer could terminate Employee without cause. Employee's compensation consisted of a base salary and commission from sales. The agreement also contained a restrictive covenant not to compete in the custom printing business for a period of three years after employment ended. The agreement had no geographic limitations. Nearly five years later, Employer requested and Employee executed a noncompete agreement requiring that Employee refrain from accepting employment with a competitor for a period of three years within 75 miles of Employer's business. Employee remained an "at-will" employee and received no additional benefits. A few months later, Employer announced a new commission sales compensation schedule. Employee determined that the new schedule would reduce his income by about 25 percent and sought employment for a similar position elsewhere. Employer discovered Employee's intention to seek employment with a competitor and terminated Employee. Employer sent a letter to the competitor interested in hiring Employee, stating its intent to enforce Employee's noncompete agreement. The competitor did not hire Employee. Employee remains unemployed despite actively seeking a position similar to the one he had held with Employer. Employee initiated suit against Employer, seeking a declaratory judgment that the noncompete agreement was null and void and that Employer tortiously interfered with Employee's business. The trial court ruled against Employee and upheld the agreement. The trial court also denied Employee's motion that the trial court modify the noncompete agreement's time restriction from three years to six months. Employee sought direct review of this court, which was granted.*

ISSUE: Is there consideration for the formation of a contract when an employee, already employed by the employer, executes a noncompete agreement but receives no new benefit?

REASONING: In the court's own words (abridged and slightly modified):

> Employee claims that the noncompete agreement fails for lack of consideration; in other words, a contract was not formed. Employer contends that the noncompete agreement is enforceable because future and continued employment and/or job training served as the Employer's consideration in exchange for Employee's execution of the noncompete agreement. The general rule in Washington is that consideration exists if the employee enters into a noncompete agreement when he or she is first hired. A noncompete agreement entered into after employment will be enforced if it is supported by independent consideration. Independent, additional consideration is required for the valid formation of a modification or subsequent agreement. There is no consideration when "one party is to perform some additional obligation while the other party is simply to perform that which he promised in the original contract." Independent consideration may include increased wages, a promotion, a fixed term of employment, and so on. Independent consideration involves new promises or obligations previously not required of the parties.

In the present case, Employer contends that continued employment served as consideration for the later noncompete agreement; however, Employee's noncompete agreement made no promises as to future employment and wages. Employer's president conceded that "no extra benefits or consideration or promises [were] made to [Employee] if he signed the noncompete."

Consideration is a bargained-for exchange of promises. A comparison of the status of the employer before and after the noncompete agreement confirms that the noncompete agreement was entered into without consideration. Employer did not incur additional duties or obligations from the noncompete agreement. Prior to execution of the noncompete agreement, Employee was an "at-will" employee. After Employee executed the noncompete agreement, he still remained an at-will employee terminable at Employer's pleasure. We hold that continued employment in this case did not serve as consideration by Employer in exchange for Employee's promise not to compete.

(continued)

DECISION AND REMEDY: The trial court's decision was reversed. The noncompete agreement lacked independent consideration and was not enforceable against the employee.

SIGNIFICANCE OF THE CASE: This case illustrates that for a contract to be binding, there must be consideration.

CRITICAL THINKING

What is the reasoning used by the court to support its decision? Are there any ambiguous words or phrases in that reasoning that you would want defined before you decided whether to agree with the court's ruling?

ETHICAL DECISION MAKING

Return to the WPH framework. Who are the stakeholders in this case? Is the decision of the employer consistent with how one would act when using the Golden Rule as one's guide?

ADEQUACY OF CONSIDERATION

Rule: *The court seldom considers adequacy of consideration.* What this rule means is that the court does not weigh whether you made a good bargain. Example: Donna purchases a stereo from Celia, a friend in her business law class. Donna pays $500 for the stereo but later realizes that the stereo is not worth $100. May Donna sue Celia? Typically, the answer is no. It is Donna's responsibility to do her research and determine what price she should pay. The court will not set aside the sale because she made a bad deal.

There is an exception to this rule. Suppose that you are on the verge of bankruptcy and your creditors are threatening legal action. You know that if you default on your mortgage, car payment, bank loans, credit card payments, and other bills, the court may order that your assets be sold to pay the creditors. Instead of risking this result, you decide to "sell" your assets. You sell your BMW to your best friend for $50 and your vacation house to your sister for $500. Now, asset-free, you declare bankruptcy, knowing that your creditors will be able to collect nothing. Is this permissible? The answer, of course, is no. In such a case, the court will look at "adequacy of consideration." If it appears that the "sale" of the assets was done to avoid payment to creditors, the court may set aside each sale and sell the assets to pay your creditors. In Case 8-2, the court had to consider whether $1 plus "love and affection" was adequate consideration for the transfer of property.

 CASE 8-2

THELMA AGNES SMITH v. DAVID PHILLIP RILEY
COURT OF APPEALS OF TENNESSEE, EASTERN
SECTION, AT KNOXVILLE
2002 Tenn. App. LEXIS 65 (2002)

FACTS: *Smith and Riley lived together out of wedlock for several years. They opened a joint checking account and, over time, both Smith and Riley deposited money into the account. In addition, Riley entered into a lease with Jerry Strickland and Wanda Strickland with respect to a residence owned by them. The lease was accompanied by an option to purchase. Almost four months later, Smith and Riley asked their attorney to prepare a bill of sale and an assignment. In the bill of sale, Riley transferred to Smith a one-half undivided interest in seven items of personal property. Riley also assigned to*

Smith a one-half undivided interest in the lease and option to purchase with the Stricklands; this interest included a right of survivorship in the one-half interest retained by Riley. The property Riley sold and assigned to Smith in the two agreements was stated in each to be "for and in consideration of the sum of One Dollar ($1.00) and other and good and valuable consideration, the sufficiency of which is hereby acknowledged." When the relationship ended, Smith filed suit against Riley in the trial court, seeking the dissolution of their "domestic partnership" and seeking to enforce the two written agreements with Riley regarding the sale and assignment of property to her. The trial court enforced the agreements and divided the parties' property. The defendant appealed, arguing that the agreements lacked consideration and were void as they were against public policy.

ISSUE: Is $1 plus love and affection adequate consideration for the two agreements between Smith and Riley?

REASONING: In the court's own words (abridged and slightly modified):

It is a well-settled principle of contract law that in order for a contract to be binding, it must, among other things, be supported by sufficient consideration. In expounding on the adequacy of consideration, the court has stated that it is not necessary that the benefit conferred or the detriment suffered by the promisee shall be equal to the responsibility assumed. Any consideration, however small, will support a promise. In the absence of fraud, the courts will not undertake to regulate the amount of the consideration. The parties are left to contract for themselves, taking for granted that the consideration is one valuable in the eyes of the law.

Quoting the United States Supreme Court, the court went on to state that "[a] stipulation in consideration of $1 is just as effectual and valuable a consideration as a larger sum stipulated for or paid." Indeed, the consideration of love and affection has been deemed sufficient to support a conveyance. Both the bill of sale and the assignment recite that they are undertaken "for and in consideration of the sum of One Dollar ($1.00) and other and good and valuable consideration, the sufficiency of which is hereby acknowledged." Facially, the documents are therefore supported by sufficient consideration, as clearly recognized by the Supreme Court. Moreover, Smith's "society and consortium"—a concept comparable to the love and affection—is further evidence of sufficient consideration to support these conveyances.

DECISION AND REMEDY: The judgment of the trial court was affirmed. The case was remanded for enforcement of the judgment and for collection of costs. Costs on appeal were taxed to the appellant, Riley.

SIGNIFICANCE OF THE CASE: This case demonstrates that courts will generally not consider the adequacy of consideration.

CRITICAL THINKING

What is the reasoning of the appellant in terms of why the consideration was not adequate to cause the contracts to be enforceable? What key rule of law did this reasoning overlook?

ETHICAL DECISION MAKING

What values are being advanced by the logic of the relevant rule of law in this case? In other words, what values prevent the rule of law from being that "consideration must be in an amount similar in value to the item or services being transferred in order for the contract to be enforceable"?

ILLUSORY PROMISE

LO 2

Rule: *An illusory promise is not consideration.* What is an illusory promise? Suppose Shawn offers to sell Molly his skis for $300. Molly responds, "I'll look at them in the morning, and if I like them, I'll pay you." At this point, Molly has not committed to doing anything. The law considers this an illusory promise—that is, it is not a promise at all. Moreover, an illusory promise is not consideration.

illusory promise
A situation in which a party appears to commit to something but really has not committed to anything. It is not a promise and thus not consideration.

PAST CONSIDERATION

Rule: *Past consideration is no consideration at all.* Consideration is an essential element of a contract. For a court to enforce a promise, both sides must offer consideration. Imagine that you

England has the same requirement for consideration as the United States and even shares the exception of promissory estoppel. However, England has an additional exception to the requirement for consideration: specialty contracts or deeds. In England, a *deed* is a document that creates a binding obligation between parties without consideration when certain formalities are honored.

These formalities include a written document signed by the person making it, a witness to the maker's signature, and delivery of the document to the other party with a statement or an accompanying act indicating the maker's intention to be bound by the deed. Deeds are used in England to create enforceable promises of gifts to charity. This exception to the requirement for consideration is also found in Canadian law.

have graduated from college and gotten a great job. After you have worked at the company for five years, your boss says to you, "Because you have done such a great job the last five years, I am going to give you 5 percent of the company stock." Six months later, you still have not received the stock. May you sue your boss to enforce the promise? The answer is no. For a promise to be enforceable, there must be bargaining and an exchange. In this example, there was no exchange. Work done in the past, by definition, has already been performed. As such, you have given nothing in exchange, and the court will not enforce the promise. You are at the mercy of your boss's goodwill to keep her promise. A promise cannot be based on consideration that was provided before the promise was made.

As you have probably guessed by now, there is an exception to this rule. Under the Restatement (Second) of Contracts (a persuasive, though not binding, authority), promises based on past consideration may be enforceable "to the extent necessary to avoid injustice." In some cases, if past consideration was given with expectation of future payment, the court may enforce the promise.

PREEXISTING DUTY

Rule: *A promise to do something that you are already obligated to do is not valid consideration.* There are actually two parts to this rule. First, *performance of a duty you are obligated to do under the law is not good consideration.* For example, a police officer is sworn to uphold the law. Part of that public duty involves catching suspected criminals. If someone offers a reward for the capture of a suspected criminal, the police officer may not collect the reward, as he or she was already obligated to apprehend the suspect. Second, *performance of an existing contractual duty is not good consideration.* Gene decides to have a pool built in his backyard. Under the existing contract, the pool is to be completed by June 1, just in time for summer. The pool contractor comes to Gene and explains that due to a shortage of workers, the completion date cannot be met; however, if Gene were to pay an extra $5,000, additional workers could be hired and the pool would be completed on time. Gene tells the contractor that he will pay the $5,000. On June 1, the pool is completed, and the contractor asks for the additional $5,000 payment. Is Gene legally obligated to pay? The answer is no. The pool contractor had a preexisting contractual duty to complete the pool by June 1. Gene is under no obligation to pay the additional money.

Exceptions to the Preexisting-Duty Rule There are exceptions to the preexisting duty rule:

- Unforeseen circumstances
- Additional work
- UCC—sale of goods

unforeseen circumstances
Events that a reasonable person would not be expected to anticipate.

If unforeseen circumstances cause a party to make a promise regarding an unfinished project, that promise is valid consideration. Let's once again consider the pool example. Suppose that Gene's pool contractor has been building pools in Gene's neighborhood for the last 20 years. During all that time, the contractor has never had any problem with rocks—until now.

While bulldozing the hole for the pool in Gene's backyard, the pool contractor hits solid rock. It is estimated that it will cost an additional $5,000 to clear the rock by using jackhammers and possibly even dynamite. The contractor explains that he is sorry, but unless Gene agrees to pay the additional money, he will not be able to finish the pool. Gene agrees to pay. When the pool is completed, the contractor asks for the additional $5,000. Will a court enforce this promise? The answer is yes. Even though the contractor is completing only what he was obligated to do under the contract, neither party knew of the solid rock. The contractor has given additional consideration (removal of the rock), and Gene will be held to his promise to pay the additional money.

If a party to a contract agrees to do additional work (i.e., more than she is obligated to do under the contract), the promise is valid consideration. Using the pool example, if the contractor asks Gene for an additional $10,000 but agrees to add a waterfall and a deck to the pool, the promise to do the additional work is consideration. If Gene agrees to pay the $10,000, that is his consideration. Both parties are now bound.

The rules and exceptions we have been discussing fall under the common law of contracts. The Uniform Commercial Code (UCC) has changed the common law in significant ways. Under Article 2 of the UCC (sale of goods), *an agreement modifying a contract needs no consideration to be binding.* This is an exception to the preexisting-duty rule. Under UCC Section 2-209:[2]

1. An agreement modifying a contract within this Article needs no consideration to be binding.
2. A signed agreement which excludes modification or rescission except by a signed writing cannot be otherwise modified or rescinded, but except as between merchants such a requirement on a form supplied by the merchant must be separately signed by the other party.

Gary is a manufacturer of blow dryers. He sends a purchase order for 10,000 white on/off switches to a switch manufacturer. Later, Gary telephones the switch manufacturer and changes his order to 5,000 white switches and 5,000 red switches. Under the UCC, no additional consideration is required for the modification of the agreement to be binding. Moreover, unless stated otherwise, such an agreement need not be in writing.

UNIFORM COMMERCIAL CODE: REQUIREMENT AND OUTPUT CONTRACTS

LO 3

Rule: *Under UCC Section 2-306, requirement and output contracts are permitted for the sale of goods.* A requirement contract is an agreement whereby the buyer agrees to purchase all of his goods from one seller. No quantity is stated in the contract. Under common law, such a contract would be void because the buyer has made no commitment and, therefore, there is no consideration. An output contract is an agreement whereby the seller guarantees to sell everything she produces to one buyer. Once again, no quantity is stated, and under common law, there is lack of consideration. Because such contracts are valued by merchants, under the UCC both requirement and output contracts are valid with the limitation that the output or requirement must be made in "good faith." The consideration, then, is that the party act in good faith. Neither party may take advantage of the other party either by requiring more than was expected when the deal was signed or by producing more than was expected when the deal was signed.

requirement contract
An agreement whereby the buyer agrees to purchase all of his or her goods from one seller and no quantity is stated in the contract; valid under the UCC but not under common law.

output contract
An agreement whereby the seller guarantees to sell everything he or she produces to one buyer and no quantity is stated; valid under the UCC but not under common law.

liquidated debt,
Debt for which there is no dispute between the parties about the fact that money is owed and the amount of money owed.

Partial Payment of a Debt

Partial payment of a debt may or may not be valid consideration, depending on whether the debt is liquidated or unliquidated. In a liquidated debt, there is no dispute about the fact that money is owed and the amount of money owed. Example: Natalie owes $3,000 on her credit card. She calls the credit card company and explains that she is a poor student and cannot afford to pay the entire $3,000. The credit card company agrees to accept $2,000 as payment in full. The following month,

[2] www.law.cornell.edu/ucc/2/article2.htm#s2-209.

CASE Nugget

Requirement Contracts

Mast Long Term Care v. Forest Hills Rest Home et al.
Court of Appeals of North Carolina

156 N.C. App. 556 (N.C. Ct. App. 2003)

Mast Long Term Care and Forest Hills Rest Home entered into an agreement whereby the rest home was to buy from Mast all the drugs needed for its patients that were not commonly stocked at the rest home. The rest home argued that the agreement was not a valid contract since it contained vague purchasing terms, obligating it to buy only those drugs not commonly stocked.

At the hearing, Forest Hills Rest Home argued that the vendor-pharmacist agreement between the parties lacked consideration. The agreement did not state any price terms with respect to the pharmaceuticals to be supplied. The court ruled that North Carolina law permitted requirement contracts and that the sale of drugs was governed by the North Carolina Uniform Commercial Code (UCC). Under the UCC, the omission of certain material terms did not invalidate the contract, because courts were permitted to read good-faith requirements into a contract. No definite amount needed to be stated in the agreement. Moreover, consideration need not consist of a promise to pay money for goods or services. Instead, it can take the shape of mutual promises to perform some act or to forbear from taking some action.

In this case, the consideration for the parties' agreement consisted of the plaintiff's promise to supply the defendant with certain pharmaceuticals and the defendant's counterpromise to stock the plaintiff's products at its pharmacy and sell them to its patients. Accordingly, the agreement does not fail for either lack of consideration or lack of specificity.

Natalie receives her new credit card statement showing that she owes the remaining $1,000. May the credit card company collect the additional $1,000? Yes! A creditor's promise to accept less than owed, when the debtor is already obligated to pay the full amount, is not binding.

The exception to the rule regarding liquidated debt occurs when the debtor offers different performance. Suppose Natalie offered the credit card company her car in full settlement of the $3,000 debt. If the credit card company accepts, regardless of the value of the car, the debt is paid in full and the credit card company may not sue Natalie for any additional money.

LO 4

LO 5

unliquidated debt
Debt for which the parties either dispute the fact that any money is owed or agree that some money is owed but dispute the amount.

In an **unliquidated debt,** the parties either dispute the fact that any money is owed or agree that some money is owed but dispute the amount. A dispute over an unliquidated debt may be settled for less than the full amount if the parties enter into an **accord and satisfaction.** For an accord and satisfaction to be enforceable, three requirements must be met:

1. The debt is unliquidated (i.e., the amount or existence of the debt is in dispute).

2. The creditor agrees to accept as full payment less than the creditor claims is owed.

3. The debtor pays the amount they have agree on.

accord and satisfaction
An arrangement between contracting parties whereby one of the parties substitutes a different performance for his or her original duty under the contract. The promise to perform the new duty is the *accord,* and the actual performance of that new duty is the *satisfaction.*

Under such circumstances, the debt is fully discharged. The *accord* is the new agreement to pay less than the creditor claims. The *satisfaction* is the payment, by the debtor, of the reduced amount. If the debtor fails to pay the new amount, the creditor may then sue for the full amount of the original debt. It pays to keep your word. In the Case Nugget, the court had to determine whether there was consideration in an accord and satisfaction.

One way that people sometimes attempt to create an accord and satisfaction is by sending a check to the creditor and writing "paid in full" on the check. Under common law, in many states this did create an accord and satisfaction, and if the creditor cashed the check, he or she was

CASE Nugget

Preexisting Duty Rule

Thomas v. CitiMortgage, Inc.
United States District Court for the Northern District of Illinois

2005 U.S. Dist. LEXIS 14641 (Dist. Ct. Ill. 2005)

In November 1979, Thomas assumed a previously existing mortgage, which CitiMortgage now holds. Under the terms of the mortgage, Thomas was required to make a monthly payment on the first day of each month. Beginning in April 1996, Thomas's payments on the mortgage became sporadic. On December 16, 1996, Thomas sent a letter to Lee Hilliard of CitiMortgage, stating that he had sent check 2279 to CitiMortgage on May 22, 1996, but that the check had apparently been lost. In the letter, Thomas also wrote:

> My primary concern is the effect on my credit rating and the fact that I have an application to refinace [sic] the mortgage which cannot be finalized, at great cost to me, unless this matter is resolved and my credit cleared up. I have enclosed a check in the amount of the monthly payment on condition that it be applied to tha [sic] May payment and that it will allow you to remove the negative material relative to my credit rating. I will put a stop payment on check # 2279, or if it has already been processed somehow, I can be given a credit at the closing of the new mortgage.

CitiMortgage never received or deposited check 2279, but it did cash the check enclosed with the December 16, 1996, letter and credited it to Thomas's account. At CitiMortgage as of 1996, mail was sorted in a central mail room. The persons processing checks lacked the authority either to accept conditions on payments or to change credit reports, as did Hilliard. In his breach-of-contract claim, Thomas asserted that he and CitiMortgage had entered an agreement whereby he would make a payment on his mortgage in exchange for CitiMortgage's agreement to "remove the negative material" from his credit rating. He further claimed that CitiMortgage accepted the contract when it cashed the check he enclosed with the December 16, 1996, letter. Whether Thomas's claim was considered an accord and satisfaction or a simple contract, he could not prevail unless he established that consideration supported the agreement.

Consideration can consist of a promise, an act, or a forebearance. Something one is already legally obligated to do, however, cannot constitute consideration. The *preexisting-duty rule* provides that where a party does what it is already legally obligated to do, there is no consideration because there has been no detriment. Thomas claimed that the payment he made with his December 16, 1996, letter constituted consideration for the agreement. As of December 16, 1996, however, Thomas was already two months in arrears on his mortgage payment. He had not made the payments due November 1, 1996, and December 1, 1996. Thus, he was already legally obligated—under the terms of the mortgage—to make the payment he enclosed with the December 16, 1996, letter. Accordingly, that payment could not be consideration for an additional agreement to "remove the negative material" from his credit rating.

bound to accept the lesser amount as payment in full. The UCC, however, has changed the scope of this rule. Under UCC Section 3-311, effective in 30 states, the rule remains in place but has two major exceptions.

First, in cases of business organizations, thousands of checks may be received each day. To protect themselves, businesses may notify their debtors that any offer to settle a claim for less than the amount owed must be sent to a particular address and/or person. If you check the terms printed on your credit card statement, you will likely find language directing you to send such payments to a different address and person than those to which regular payments are sent. This

CONNECTING to the Core

Finance

Students usually learn in their finance class that business owners and individuals must pay taxes on income. According to the IRS, whenever a bank or other creditor discharges a loan obligation by accepting a lower amount as full payment of the debt, the difference is income on which the borrower must pay taxes.

For example, if a small business owner borrows $100,000 from a bank but cannot repay the full $100,000, the bank might agree to accept only $80,000 as full payment of the debt. As mentioned in the text, the bank may be entitled to the unpaid $20,000 and could sue for the difference, as the bank received no additional consideration in exchange for its accepting the lower amount. But assuming the bank does not sue and fully intends to accept the $80,000 as full payment of the $100,000 loan, the business owner would then have an obligation to the IRS, namely, recognizing the unpaid $20,000 as taxable income. Because the business owner received $100,000 and repaid only $80,000 for the amount borrowed, the owner is financially in a better position, having $20,000 more than what he had prior to the loan transaction. Consequently, the IRS requires that the business owner report the $20,000 as income, on which he must pay taxes at the applicable rate.

Hence, although a bank may accept a lower amount as full payment of a liquidated debt, the owner would still have an obligation to the IRS to pay taxes on the difference between the amount initially owed to the bank and the amount repaid in full satisfaction of the debt.

safeguard protects businesses from inadvertently creating accord-and-satisfaction agreements. Below is an example:

> *Conditional Payments:* Any payment check or other form of payment that you send us for less than the full balance that is marked "paid in full" or contains a similar notation, or that you otherwise tender in full satisfaction of a disputed amount, must be sent to [address omitted]. We reserve all rights regarding these payments (e.g., if it is determined that there is no valid dispute or if any such check is received at any other address, we may accept the check and you will still owe any remaining balance).[3]

Second, if a business does inadvertently cash a "paid-in-full" check, the business has 90 days from the date it cashed that check to offer repayment in the same amount to the debtor. For example, if John owed $3,000 to his credit card company and he sent the company a $2,000 check marked "paid in full" and mailed to the correct address and person, the credit card company has 90 days to offer to repay John the $2,000. Once the offer has been made by the business, no accord and satisfaction exists.

[3] From Chase Visa statement.

 SUMMARY

What Is Consideration?	*Consideration* is something of value given in exchange for something else of value; it must be the product of a mutually bargained-for exchange.
Rules of Consideration	In order for a promise to be enforced by the courts, there must be *consideration*. A court will enforce one party's promise only if the other party promised something (an act, money, etc.) in exchange.
	Promissory estoppel occurs when one party makes a promise knowing the other party will rely on it, the other party does rely on it, and the only way to avoid injustice is to enforce the promise.
	The court seldom considers *adequacy of consideration*. What this means is that the court does not weigh whether you made a good bargain.
	An *illusory promise* is not consideration (i.e., it is not a promise at all).

Past consideration is generally no consideration at all. A promise cannot be based on consideration that was provided before the promise was made.

The *preexisting-duty rule* provides that when a party does what it is already legally obligated to do, there is no consideration because there has been no detriment.

A *requirement contract* is an agreement whereby the buyer agrees to purchase all his goods from one seller. No quantity is stated in the contract.

An *output contract* is an agreement whereby the seller guarantees to sell everything she produces to one buyer. Once again, no quantity is stated.

Partial Payment of a Debt

In a *liquidated debt,* there is no dispute about the fact that money is owed and the amount of money owed

In an *unliquidated debt,* the parties either dispute the fact that any money is owed or agree that some money is owed but dispute the amount.

For an *accord and satisfaction* to be enforceable, three requirements must be met: (1) The debt is unliquidated (i.e., the amount or existence of the debt is in dispute); (2) the creditor agrees to accept as full payment less than the creditor claims is owed; and (3) the debtor pays the amount they have agree on. The accord is the agreement, and the satisfaction is the payment of the reduced amount.

Point/Counterpoint

Should the Courts Require Consideration to Create a Binding Contract?

YES	NO
The rules of consideration have been established for many years, and precedent should be followed. Requiring consideration gives the court a way to distinguish binding promises from nonbinding promises. Without a requirement of consideration, there would be no way to distinguish between a promise made as a gift and a promise made as part of a contract. We have enough exceptions to the rule requiring consideration to make enforcement of the rule fair. For example, if a promise was made and there was expectation of economic benefit, some courts will permit enforcement of the promise under the moral-obligation exception. If we suddenly did not require consideration to create binding contracts, the courts would fill with civil cases of people trying to fulfill all kind of promises.	All promises should be enforced. There is no need to distinguish between binding promises and nonbinding promises if all promises are enforced. If a person makes a promise, the timing of the promise should not make a difference. For example, if Barbara's grandmother promises her $50,000 for "all you have done for me these last five years," why should Barbara be denied the $50,000 because it was based on acts she had done in the past (i.e., past consideration)? The right thing to do, both ethically and morally, would be to enforce this promise whether or not Barbara did the acts with expectation of payment. Under the current exception, if an act was done with expectation of payment, it meets the moral-obligation exception in some states. This exception rewards those who expect something when they do something good and punishes those who do the right thing with no expectation of reward.

Questions & Problems

1. List the four types of consideration described in the text.
2. What is required to prove promissory estoppel when consideration is missing?
3. Can $1 be adequate consideration? Why or why not?
4. List and describe the three exceptions to the preexisting-duty rule.

5. List the three elements of accord and satisfaction.

6. When Holloman applied for a job at Circuit City, she signed a "Dispute Resolution Agreement" (DRA) that stated: "This agreement requires you and Circuit City to arbitrate certain legal disputes related to your application for employment or employment with Circuit City." The job application then added, "Circuit City will consider your application only if this agreement is signed." Finally, the DRA stated, "I understand that my employment, compensation and terms and conditions of employment can be altered or terminated, with or without cause, and with or without notice, at any time, at the option of either Circuit City or myself." Holloman was hired, but she later quit and sued Circuit City, claiming she had been discriminated against and constructively discharged. Holloman argued that the arbitration agreement was illusory and not supported by consideration because of Circuit City's unilateral ability to terminate or modify the agreement. How should the court rule? Explain your reasoning. [*Holloman v. Circuit City Stores,* 162 Md. App. 332 (Md. Ct. App. 2005).]

7. On October 10, 2000, the Snoebergers transferred 2 acres of realty to their daughter and her husband, the Prendergasts. The only restriction in the deed, recorded the next day, was a denial of the right to maintain a mobile home or scrap yard on the property. The Prendergasts then began construction of a house on the site. On June 19, 2001, a "Memorandum" was executed by the four parties, notarized, and recorded. This memorandum stated, in pertinent part: "The parties agree the following described premises shall not be sold during the life of James Snoeberger and Barbara Snoeberger." On July 22, 2002, the Prendergasts filed a complaint asking the court to declare the memorandum unenforceable. They alleged that they wished to sell the house and property but the Snoebergers were trying to enforce the memorandum to prevent the sale. The question before the court was whether there was consideration to enforce the promise not to sell the premises. How should the court decide? Why? [*Prendergast et al. v James Snoeberger et al.,* 154 Ohio App. 3d 162 (Ohio Ct. App. 2003).]

8. On February 1, 2004, Zhang entered into a contract to buy former realtor Frank Sorichetti's Las Vegas home for $532,500. The contract listed a March closing date and a few household furnishings as part of the sale. On February 3, Sorichetti told Zhang that he was terminating the sale "to stay in the house a little longer" and that Nevada law allows the rescission of real property purchase agreements within three days of contracting. Sorichetti stated that he would sell the home, however, if Zhang paid more money. Zhang agreed. Another contract was drafted, reciting a new sales price, $578,000. This contract added to the included

household furnishings drapes that were not listed in the February 1 agreement, and it set an April, rather than March, closing date. The primary issue before the court was whether a real property purchase agreement is enforceable when it is executed by the buyer only because the seller would not perform under an earlier purchase agreement for a lesser price. Should the court enforce the second contract? Why or why not? [*Zhang v. The Eighth Judicial District Court of the State of Nevada,* 103 P.3d 20 (Sup. Ct. Nev. 2004).]

9. Drexel University sued to enforce a pledge agreement executed by Wirth less than two months before his death. The agreement stated that in consideration of the decedent's interest in education, and "intending to be legally bound," the decedent "irrevocably pledged and promised to pay" Drexel the sum of $150,000. The pledge agreement, which also was executed by representatives of Drexel, provided that the pledged sum "shall be used by" Drexel to create an endowed scholarship fund in the decedent's name, "per the terms of the attached Letter of Understanding." The letter of understanding, which also was executed by the decedent and representatives of Drexel, provided, inter alia, that the scholarship fund would become effective immediately on the transfer of the initial $50,000, which was to take place on or before December 31, 2000. The pledge agreement further stated, "I acknowledge that [Drexel's] promise to use the amount pledged by me shall constitute full and adequate consideration for this pledge." Was there consideration for the agreement? Explain your decision. [*Drexel University v. Wirth,* 14 A.D.3d 572 (Sup.Ct. N.Y. 2003).]

10. Five employees of American Electric Power Service Corp. (AEP) invented a new product. "In consideration of the sum of One Dollar (1.00), and of other good and valuable consideration paid to the undersigned Assignor," each employee signed an agreement giving AEP exclusive patent rights to the invention. Some of the employees sued, alleging that there was no contract because AEP never paid the one dollar. How do you think the court ruled? Explain your reasoning. [*Bennett et al. v. American Electric Power Service Corporation,* 2001 Ohio App. LEXIS 4357 (Ohio Ct. App. 2001).]

11. Between 1993 and 2002, defendant Apex Media Sales, Inc. (AMS), was plaintiff Adell Broadcasting's exclusive media representative for national religious and secular broadcast spot and program sales. Several months before the parties ended their relationship, Kevin Adell, the plaintiff's president, expressed dissatisfaction with the representation by AMS. He believed that the AMS sales staff was not selling available air time for full value and that AMS personnel, including its president, defendant Dennis Hart, were not available and responsive to the plaintiff's needs. AMS and Hart

were also dissatisfied with the relationship because the plaintiff owed them outstanding commission payments. On February 26, 2002, the parties amended their agreement in an attempt to save the relationship. The parties agreed that the plaintiff owed $568,461 in commissions but that AMS would consider an immediate payment of $370,000 as full satisfaction of all commissions owed through December 2001. The parties also agreed that the commission rate for AMS would decrease from 15 to 10 percent, that there would be a 30-day termination provision to end the business relationship, and that Adell Broadcasting would pay commissions to AMS on 30-day terms. The parties thereafter continued dealing with each other, but their problems did not abate. In April 2002, they severed the relationship. The plaintiff filed suit against AMS and Hart, alleging several causes of action. The defendants filed a countercomplaint seeking, among other things, rescission of the amended agreement. The plaintiff sought partial summary disposition on that claim, arguing that the defendants were barred from seeking rescission because they did not tender back the $370,000. On appeal, the court had to decide whether there was consideration for the amended agreement. How would you decide? Why? [*Adell Broadcasting Corp. et al. v. Apex Media Sales, Inc., et al.*, 708 N.W.2d 778 (2005).]

12. Arnone sued Deutsche Bank for a breach of oral contract after his termination from employment at the bank. Arnone claims that the bank refused to pay him a bonus for securing certain business for the bank, "despite the promises and assurances" of his supervisors that he had earned the bonus and that it would be paid to him in the amount of $825,000. Arnone led a formal presentation in September 1998 on behalf of the bank to bid for a potentially lucrative investment management appointment. By December 1998, the bank was awarded an account worth approximately $9 billion. In early December 1998, Arnone confirmed with his supervisor his expectation of a bonus of at least $800,000 based on the $9 billion in business brought into the bank. The bank ultimately was forced to forgo the account, due to no fault of Arnone. Arnone, however, maintains that the bank made a separate and distinct promise to pay him a bonus as if the business had been retained. He and his supervisors had several conversations regarding his bonus after the bank resigned from the account. According to Arnone, his supervisor said to him, "You know, Jerry, we're going to pay you as if the . . . business came in." Should the court enforce the supervisor's promise? Why or why not? [*Arnone v. Deutsche Bank et al.*, 2003 U.S. Dist. LEXIS 7941 (Dist. Ct. N.Y. 2003).]

13. In February 2000, CNS International Ministries, Inc., signed a contract with Eiman Brothers Roofing Systems. Under the contract, Eiman would provide CNS with a clay tile roof for one of its properties. Based on the size of the roof provided in CNS's plans, the total amount of the contract was $52,731. In May 2000, Eiman realized that the plan provided by CNS underestimated the roof's actual size, which required an additional 20 to 25 squares. Eiman, demanding a second contract, recalculated and rebid the project. In May 2000, CNS signed a contract modification proposal sent by Eiman, adding $23,000 in costs. With the work substantially complete, CNS noted problems in Eiman's performance and its alleged failure to deliver on assurances to correct those problems. Consequently, CNS ordered Eiman to stop working on the roof. Eiman then brought a breach-of-contract action. At the time of the alleged breach, CNS had paid a total of $29,000 on the contract. CNS claimed that the contract was unenforceable for lack of consideration, in that Eiman had a preexisting duty to CNS. Specifically, CNS argues that the May 2000 proposal called for Eiman to perform in exactly the same manner as that specified in the original contract. Did Eiman have a preexisting duty to CNS? Why or why not? [*Eiman Brothers Roofing Systems, Inc. v. CNS International Ministries, Inc.*, 158 S.W.3d 920 (2005).]

Looking for more review material?

The Online Learning Center at **www.mhhe.com/kubasekess** contains this chapter's "Assignment on the Internet" and also a list of URLs for more information, entitled "On the Internet." Find both of them in the Student Center portion of the OLC, along with quizzes and other helpful materials.

Capacity and Legality

----▶ **CASE OPENER**

A Wasted Education

Ten months before attaining the age of majority, the plaintiff paid for and received a course in elementary aviation from the defendant. Five months later, he purchased and received a limited commercial pilot's course from the defendant. Two months later, he entered into a contract with the defendant for an advanced course of instruction to become a transport pilot, but he withdrew from the course within the month and paid nothing. He reached the age of majority on July 20.

Six months after attaining the age of majority, he received a bill from the defendant for the balance due on his course. He visited the defendant's attorney and denied liability but said nothing about disaffirmance. He took no further action until a few days shy of a year from the day he attained the age of majority. At that time, he filed suit against the defendant, seeking to disaffirm his contracts for the aviation courses and seeking a return of the money he had paid for them on grounds that he had entered into the contracts as a minor and had the right to disaffirm them and recover what he had given up under the contracts. The defendant argued that the courses were necessaries and, as such, that the plaintiff was not entitled to disaffirm the contracts for them.[1]

1. Were the contracts for necessaries and, as such, not subject to being disaffirmed?
2. Even if the plaintiff had the right to disaffirm the contracts, was almost a year too long to wait to disaffirm them?

[1] *John P. Adamowski v. The Curtiss-Wright Flying Service, Inc.,* 300 Mass. 281; 15 N.E.2d 467; 1938 Mass. LEXIS 942.

----▶ **LEARNING OBJECTIVES**

After reading this chapter, you will be able to answer the following questions:

LO 1 When would a minor have only limited capacity to enter into a contract?

LO 2 How can a contract created when one is a minor be ratified after one is no longer a minor?

Capacity

This chapter examines the third and fourth elements of a contract. Capacity is the third element of a legally binding contract. A person who has legal capacity to contract is one who has the mental ability to understand his or her rights and obligations under a contract and therefore will presumably be able to understand how to comply with the terms of the agreement. *Incapacity,* or *incompetence,* as it is sometimes called, is some sort of mental or physical defect that prevents a natural person from being able to enter into a legally binding contract. Depending on the nature and extent of the defect, a person may have either no capacity, and therefore any attempted contract is void, or limited capacity, resulting in the ability to form only voidable contracts.

capacity
The legal ability to enter into a binding contract.

Historically, people with limited or no capacity included married women, minors, and insane persons. Through statutes, other categories were added for classes of people for whom guardians had been appointed, such as habitual drunkards, narcotic addicts, spendthrifts, the elderly, and convicts. Today, married women have been removed from the category of those lacking contractual capacity, although in a few states their capacity to enter into certain kinds of contracts is still limited. In this section of the chapter, we explain the current law limiting the capacity of some categories of persons to enter into legally binding agreements.

MINORS

LO 1

One of the oldest limitations on capacity is the ability of minors to enter into only voidable contracts. Today, in all but three states, a *minor* is someone under the age of 18.[2] In most states, however, a person is given full legal capacity to enter into contracts when he or she becomes emancipated before reaching the age of majority. *Emancipation* occurs when a minor's parents or legal guardians give up their right to exercise legal control over the minor, typically when the minor moves out of the parents' house and begins supporting himself or herself. Often the minor will petition the court for a declaration of emancipation. In most cases, when a minor marries, she or he is considered emancipated.

Disaffirmance of the Contract Because their contracts are voidable, minors have the right, until a reasonable time after reaching the age of majority, to disaffirm, or avoid, their contracts. There are no formalities required to disaffirm the contract; the minor need only manifest an intention to rescind the contract, either by words or by actions. However, the minor must avoid the entire contract; he or she cannot choose to disaffirm only a portion of it.

The obligations of the minor on disaffirmance vary from state to state. Traditionally, most states simply required that the minor notify the competent party of the intent to disaffirm and return to the competent party any consideration received under the contract that was still under the minor's control, regardless of the condition of the consideration. If the consideration has been destroyed or damaged, the minor returns whatever is left of it, and the other party has no recourse against the minor under most circumstances. For instance, if William, a minor, purchased a stereo

[2] In Alabama, Nebraska, and Wyoming, full capacity to contract does not arise until the person reaches the age of 19, which is the age of majority in those states. In Mississippi, the age of majority is still 21.

The Age of Majority in Great Britain

People in the United States take the idea of an "age of majority" for granted. The only debate seems to be over whether that age should be 18, 19, or 21. Yet in Great Britain there is no magical age at which a young person suddenly acquires the legal capacity to enter into a contract. British courts will not enforce contracts with immature minors. However, the determination of whether a person is too immature to enter into a contract is made on a case-by-case basis.

If a person under the age of 18 is considered by the courts to be able to look out for his or her own interests, the contract will be enforced. If not, the contract will be void. In determining whether the young person was mature enough to enter into the contract, a key factor is often the fairness of the agreement. The assumption is that if the agreement was one-sided and favored the adult, the young person probably lacked the maturity to enter into the contract.

receiver from Sound Systems, Inc., under a six-month contract and dropped it a week after he took it home, he could return it to the store in its broken condition and tell the owner that he wished to rescind the contract. He would be entitled to the return of his down payment and would owe no further obligations to the store.

Such a rule makes sense if you view minors as innocents in need of protection from competent adults who would otherwise take advantage of minors. However, the rule is not going to encourage competent parties to enter into contracts with minors, and some observers argue that it allows a knowledgeable and unethical minor to take advantage of a competent party. Consequently, a number of states have modified the duty of the minor on disaffirmance, holding that the minor has a duty of restitution that requires that she or he place the competent party back in the position that party was in at the time the contract was made.

Thus, continuing with the stereo receiver example, in some states William would have a duty of restoration that would require that he compensate the store owner for the difference between the value of the receiver in the condition it was in when given to William and its value in the condition it was in when returned. Case 9-1 illustrates the application of the majority rule for return of consideration on disaffirmance.

CASE 9-1

SWALBERG v. HANNEGAN
UTAH COURT OF APPEALS
883 P.2d 931 (Utah App. 1994)

FACTS: *The parties entered into a contract for the sale and purchase of an automobile. The minor's age was not discussed, and there was no allegation that the minor misrepresented his age. The minor made a down payment and promised to pay the remaining balance three months later. Thereafter, the minor disaffirmed the contract on the basis of his minority. The seller filed the complaint asking to have the contract enforced or to be put back into his precontractual state. The seller argued that the minor did not properly restore the automobile under Utah Code Ann. § 15-2-2 (1986) because it was returned in a condition that was worth substantially less than the* *purchase price. Utah Code Ann. § 15-2-2 (1986) states as follows:*

> A minor is bound not only for the reasonable value of necessities but also for his contracts, unless he disaffirms them before or within a reasonable time after he obtains his majority and restores to the other party all money or property received by him by virtue of said contracts and remaining within his control at any time after attaining his majority.

The trial court awarded a sum to the seller representing the remaining balance owed minus the value of the automobile when it was returned. The plaintiff appealed.

(continued)

ISSUE: Is a minor who disaffirms a contract required to restore the full value of the property received under the contract?

REASONING: The judge found that, from examining the plain and unambiguous language of the law, it is clear that disaffirmance requires only that the minor return the property he has in his possession in whatever condition it is in.

The court stated that in previous analogous cases the courts clearly pointed out that the purpose of the statute was to protect minors, and therefore any adult entering into a contract with a minor does so at her or his own risk because the law does not require that the minor return the adult to her or his precontract status.

DECISION AND REMEDY: The appellate court reversed the decision of the trial court, finding in favor of the minor and holding that a minor need not restore the contracting party to that party's precontract position in order to disaffirm a contract.

SIGNIFICANCE OF THE CASE: This case shows that the courts are willing to uphold a minor's right to avoid a contract even when the minor cannot return the consideration he or she received in its original condition.

CRITICAL THINKING

What facts about this case could you change that might have led the judge to a different conclusion?

ETHICAL DECISION MAKING

Does this case reflect a consideration of the interests of all the relevant stakeholders? What values do you think influenced the judge in deciding this case?

The disaffirmance must occur before or within a reasonable time of the minor's reaching the age of majority. What constitutes a reasonable time is determined on a case-by-case basis. For example, in the situation described in the Case Opener, the court found that it was not unreasonable for the defendant to disaffirm his contracts almost a year after attaining the age of majority.

In deciding to allow the disaffirmance, the court explained that the contracts were wholly executed and that there was no evidence that an earlier disaffirmance would have benefited the defendant or saved it from any harm. The court further noted that the plaintiff had made no use of his education in aviation, which had been of no apparent benefit to him. Under such circumstances, the court felt that a year was a reasonable time period within which to disaffirm a contract.

Exceptions to the Minor's Right to Disaffirm the Contract The minor's right to disaffirm is designed to protect the minor from competent parties that might otherwise take advantage of the minor. But there are certain situations in which, primarily for public policy reasons, either the courts or state legislatures have determined that the minor should not have the right to disaffirm the contract. As a general rule, most states will not allow a minor to disaffirm contracts for life insurance, health insurance, psychological counseling, the performance of duties related to stock and bond transfers and bank accounts, education loan contracts, child support contracts, marriage contracts, and contracts to enlist in the armed services.

Most of these exceptions apply in most, but not all, states. Another contractual issue on which the states disagree is the minor's misrepresentation of his or her age. While the majority rule is that misrepresentation does not affect a minor's right to disaffirm a contract, some states hold that when a minor who appears to be of the age of majority misrepresents his or her age and a competent party relies on that misrepresentation in good faith, the minor gives up the right to disaffirm the agreement. One justification for this rule is that any minor who is going to misrepresent his or her age does not need the protection that disaffirmance is designed to provide.

Other states have found a compromise between the two extreme positions either by requiring that the minor restore the competent party to that party's precontract position before allowing the

CONNECTING to the Core

Marketing

Although minors may lack the capacity to enter certain legally binding contracts, this lack of capacity has not deterred companies from heavily marketing their products to minors. Marketing experts understand very well the impact that sociocultural influences, such as family relationships, can have on consumer behavior. For instance, some research suggests that children develop strong brand preferences at age two, frequently maintaining these preferences for decades.

In response to such findings, some companies have been marketing products specifically for young children. Sony, for example, introduced "My First Sony" to children, hoping that this type of audio equipment would affect the children's purchasing decisions when they reached the age of majority. In addition, brand preferences in children may influence purchasing decisions of parents. According to one study, children under the age of 12 annually influence more than $300 billion in family purchases, and teenagers are responsible for influencing about $500 billion in family purchases, spending $175 million of their own money. On the basis of these large figures, perhaps it comes as little surprise that companies spend approximately $32 billion every year to reach preteens and teens, even if some of these children do not possess the capacity to make many of the purchases themselves.

Source: R. Kerin, S. Hartley, E. Berkowitz, and W. Rudelius, *Marketing* (New York: McGraw-Hill/Irwin, 2005), pp. 136–138. (citing "Get 'Em While They're Young," *Marketing News,* November 10, 1997, p. 2.)

disaffirmance or by allowing the minor to disaffirm but then giving the competent party the right to sue the minor in tort and recover damages for fraud.

Liability of Minors for Necessaries Contracts for necessaries are sometimes considered an exception to the rule that minors can disaffirm their contracts. Technically, a minor can disaffirm contracts for necessaries; however, the minor will be held liable for the reasonable value of the necessary. The purpose of this limitation is to ensure that minors are able to obtain the basic necessities of life when their parents will not provide them.

A *contract for a necessary* is a contract that supplies the minor with the basic necessities of life, generally thought of as food, clothing, shelter, and basic medical services. It is sometimes difficult, however, to determine whether something is in fact a necessary. Some courts define a necessary as what is needed for the minor to maintain his or her standard of living and financial and social status, but this can lead to a problem when an item that may be considered a necessary for a child of upper-income parents might be considered a luxury to a child of lower-income parents.

Whether an item is considered a necessary is also related to whether the minor's parents are willing to provide the item in question for the minor. For example, in a recent case, a minor chose to live independently, but her parents kept her bedroom open for her and were willing to have her return home any time. When she chose to return home after having fulfilled only two months of a year-long lease, the court found that the lease for the apartment was not a necessary because her parents had always been willing to provide a home for her.[3]

One of the issues raised in the Case Opener was whether the aviation classes constituted a necessary. The court found that, given the defendant's social class, it would be difficult to find that instruction in aviation was really a necessary. Although perhaps some forms of education might constitute a necessary under certain circumstances, the defendant's circumstances did not merit such a finding.

LO 2

Ratification Once a person reaches the age of majority, he or she may ratify, or legally affirm, contracts made as a minor. Once ratified, the contract is no longer voidable. Ratification may be either express or implied.

[3] *Kim Young v. Phillip Weaver,* 883 So. 2d 234 (Ala. Civ. App. 2003).

An *express ratification* occurs when, after reaching the age of majority, the person states, either orally or in writing, that he or she intends to be bound by the contract entered into as a minor. For example, when she is 17, Marcy enters into an agreement to purchase an automobile from Sam for 10 monthly payments of $1,000. After making the fifth payment, Marcy turns 18 and decides to move out of state. She e-mails Sam and tells him not to worry because even though she is moving, she still intends to make her monthly payments to purchase the car. She has expressly ratified the contract.

An *implied ratification* occurs when the former minor takes some action after reaching the age of majority that is consistent with an intent to ratify the contract. Going back to the previous example, if the day after she turns 18, Marcy enters into an agreement with Joe to sell him the car in six months, that action is obviously consistent with an intent to finish purchasing the car, so she has impliedly ratified the contract. Most courts find that continuing to act in accordance with the contract, such as continuing to make regular payments under a contract after reaching the age of majority, constitutes ratification. For example, if Marcy continued using the car and making payments on it for several months after reaching the age of majority, the courts would probably find that she had ratified the contract.

Parents' Liability for Their Children's Contracts, Necessaries, and Torts As a general rule, parents are not liable for the contracts entered into by their minor children. Because of this rule, merchants are often reluctant to enter into contracts with minors unless some competent person is willing to agree to cosign the contract. In that way, the competent person will be legally bound to perform the obligations undertaken by the minor if the minor no longer wishes to live up to the terms of the contract.

Parents do, however, have a legal duty to provide their children with the basic necessities of life, such as food, clothing, and shelter. Thus, they may be held liable in some states for the reasonable value of necessaries for which their children enter into contracts.

In most states, parents are not liable for the torts of their minor children; minors are liable for their own personal torts. In many states, however, parents may be liable in cases where a child causes harm because the parent failed to properly supervise the child, thereby subjecting others to an unreasonable risk of harm from the child.

MENTALLY INCAPACITATED PERSONS

Persons suffering from a mental illness or deficiency may have full, limited, or no legal capacity to enter into a binding contract, depending on the nature and extent of their mental deficiency. If a person suffers from mental problems yet still understands the nature of the contract and the obligations imposed by it, the person may enter into a binding, legal agreement. Suppose, for example, that Gina suffers from the delusion that she is a rock star. When an encyclopedia salesperson comes to her door, she buys a set of encyclopedias from him because she believes that it is important that she be knowledgeable to set a good example for her fans. As long as she understands that she is binding herself through a contract to make monthly payments for two years to pay for the encyclopedias, she is bound to the contract. If, after making a year of payments, she no longer suffers from her delusions and wishes to disaffirm the contract, she will not be able to do so because her delusions did not affect her understanding of what she was legally agreeing to do.

However, a person has only limited capacity to enter into a contract if he suffers from a mental illness or deficiency that prevents him from understanding the nature and obligations of the transaction he is entering into. If, in the above scenario, Gina's delusions prevented her from understanding that she was signing a contract, and she thought she was giving the salesperson her autograph when she signed the contract, the contract is voidable. She may disaffirm it at any time until a reasonable time after she no longer suffers from the mental deficiency. Once the mental deficiency has been removed, she may also choose to ratify the contract.

As with contracts of minors, a contract of a person suffering from a mental deficiency that is for necessaries can be enforced for the reasonable value of the necessary.

If a person's mental deficiencies have resulted in his being adjudicated insane and a guardian has been appointed for him, he has no capacity to enter into contracts and any contract he attempts to enter into is void. Guardians may be appointed not only for those who are adjudicated insane but also for those who are adjudicated habitual drunkards and those whose judgment has been impaired because of a condition such as Alzheimer's. In any case, although the person for whom the guardian has been appointed no longer has the legal capacity to enter into contracts, the guardian has the legal capacity to enter into contracts on that person's behalf.

INTOXICATED PERSONS

For purposes of determining capacity, intoxicated persons include those under the influence of alcohol or drugs. There is some variation among states in the treatment of the capacity of intoxicated persons to enter into contracts. As a general rule, most states follow the Restatement of Contracts, Section 16, which provides that contracts of an intoxicated person are voidable by the intoxicant if the other party had reason to know that because of the intoxicated person's condition, that person was unable to understand the nature and consequences of the transaction or is unable to act in a reasonable manner in relation to the transaction. If the intoxication merely causes someone to exercise poor judgment, the person's capacity to enter into a legally binding contract is not affected.

Likewise, if one party has no way of knowing that the other was intoxicated at the time the agreement was made, and the agreement is a fair one, it will be upheld by most courts. For example, Lisa e-mails Rob and offers to buy his antique car from him for $8,000. Rob has just broken up with his girlfriend and has been drinking nonstop all day. He gets the e-mail message and immediately responds in the affirmative. Lisa had no way of knowing Rob was intoxicated, and so they would have a valid contract in most states.

Once sober, the intoxicant has the ability to either ratify or disaffirm the contract. Because public policy does not favor intoxication, the courts tend to not be sympathetic to intoxicants and will fairly liberally interpret behavior that seems like ratification as ratifying the contract. If Jim became intoxicated at a bar one evening, and Randi took advantage of the situation by getting him to sign a contract to sell her his 2004 SUV for $8,000, any act Jim takes consistent with ratification after becoming sober will result in a binding contract. If Randi appears at his house the next morning with the cash, shows him the contract drafted on a napkin that he signed, and asks for the keys and the title, then by giving her the keys and saying, "I knew I shouldn't have drunk that much," Jim has entered into a binding contract.

If the contract is disaffirmed on the basis of intoxication, each party to the contract must return the other to the condition she or he was in at the time the contract was entered into. Also, as with contracts of other persons who have limited capacity, a contract of an intoxicated person for necessaries will be enforced for the reasonable value of the necessaries.

LO 3

Legality

To be enforceable, a contract must have a legal exchange as its subject and must be able to be performed legally. In the event of a contract with an illegal subject, it is the agreement or the bargain that is illegal, not the contract. By definition, contracts are legal. That is why when a contract is overturned due to being contrary to law, the contract is frequently declared void, as if it never existed, as opposed to being declared illegal. It is important to recognize, however, that contracts can be determined illegal even if they are not against a specific statute. When contracts are against generally accepted public policy, these agreements are determined to be **unenforceable,** and not void. No remedy is available for unenforceable agreements.

unenforceable
A term applied to a contract that, because of a law, cannot be enforced by the courts.

CONTRACTS THAT VIOLATE STATE OR FEDERAL STATUTES

As previously stated, certain agreements are illegal because either the subject or the performance of the agreement violates a state or federal statute. Given the various state and federal statutes,

there are a large number of possible ways in which contracts can violate a statute. Some of the more common ways are discussed below.

Agreements to Commit a Crime or Tort Contracts cannot be for an illegal subject or be carried out by illegal means. Therefore, any agreement to commit a crime or tort is illegal and unenforceable. However, should a legal contract be formed and then the subject of the contract becomes illegal under a new statute, the contract is considered to be discharged by law. For example, Jim agrees to work for Heather for one year as a poker dealer at her casino. After Jim and Heather enter into this employment agreement, the state government passes a law saying that poker may no longer be offered in casinos in the state. Because it would now be illegal for Jim to work as a dealer, the contract is discharged by law.

Licensing Statutes All 50 states have statutes requiring that people working in certain professions obtain a license before practicing their craft. For example, doctors of all varieties, plumbers, cosmetologists, lawyers, electricians, teachers, and stockbrokers are all required to obtain a license before practicing. While this list of professions is far from exhaustive, it demonstrates how widespread the licensing requirement can be in various states.

When licensing is required by law, people in certain fields must obtain a license before they can legally enter into an agreement to perform the restricted services. Frequently, such licenses can be obtained only after extensive schooling or training. The requirement of schooling and licensing demonstrates the concern society places on proper performance of duties in the designated professions.

In addition to indicating concern with proper performance, licensing statutes have two main purposes. The first is to give the government an avenue by which to regulate the specific industries. By requiring that professionals obtain a license, the government has some say over who can perform which jobs, as well as how many people can perform these jobs.

The second main purpose of licensing statutes is more closely related to the public interest. This second purpose is to protect the public's health, safety, and welfare. By imposing legal standards on a profession, the government is attempting to prevent people from being harmed due to substandard work. For example, surgery is a delicate, complicated process. It is not in the public's best interest to allow an unqualified person to perform surgery. Therefore, to limit the number of people who might be harmed during surgery, the government steps in and requires that surgeons, even after extensive schooling, obtain a license.

Given the different reasons for licensing various professionals, there are different outcomes when someone enters into an agreement with a person who is not lawfully licensed. The state in which the unlicensed person is practicing is also relevant because many licensing statutes occur at the state level and thus vary from state to state. For example, in some states, the statutes specify "no license, no contract." These states will not enforce any agreement with an unlicensed professional.

However, in a state that does not explicitly bar the enforcement of all contracts with unlicensed professionals, the courts typically examine the profession in question to determine why professionals in that field are required to be licensed. If the purpose of licensing is to provide government control over the profession, most states allow enforcement of the contract. Although the unlicensed professional is acting in violation of the law, there are no grave reasons that the contract should not be carried out. Nonetheless, because the professional is in violation of the law, he or she is usually required to pay a fine for working without the necessary license.

Conversely, if the licensing statute is intended to protect the public's health, safety, or welfare, the agreement is typically deemed illegal and unenforceable. Licensing statutes do not protect the public if people without the necessary licenses are allowed to practice the restricted professions. Returning to the example of surgeons, the public is made safer by the government's allowing only licensed professionals to perform surgery. Therefore, people cannot enter into a contract for professional service with unlicensed professionals when the law requires a license and the statute is intended to protect the public.

Usury Almost as widespread as licensing statutes, statutes prohibiting usury exist in nearly every state. **Usury** occurs when a party gives a loan at an interest rate exceeding the legal

usury
The lending of money at an exorbitant or unlawful rate of interest.

maximum. The legal maximum interest rate varies from state to state, but it is easy to determine the rate in any given state.

While usury statutes act as a ceiling in terms of setting a maximum possible rate, there are a few legal exceptions whereby loans may exceed the predetermined maximum. One exception relates to corporate loans. Most states with usury statutes allow corporations to lend and borrow at rates exceeding the maximum. The rationale behind the corporation exception is that if a business needs money to expand and is willing to pay the higher interest rate, the corporation should be afforded the opportunity to borrow. The converse is that if a corporation is willing to borrow at a high interest rate, parties should be allowed to lend at that rate for corporations only. The intent is to facilitate business transactions in order to keep the economy in a healthy state.

Another exception to usury statutes applies to smaller loans. Many states allow parties to make small loans at rates above the maximum to parties that cannot obtain a needed loan at the statutory maximum. The belief is that if people need money and the statutory maximum is not inducing people to lend, certain parties will make the necessary loans at a higher rate as long as the loan is "small," which is defined however the state chooses to define it. This exception is the principle that allows cash advancement institutions to operate.

In the event there is no exception allowing a usurious loan, the legal outcome varies by state. A minority of states declare all usurious loans void, which means the lending party is not entitled to recover either the interest or the principal. A larger number of states allow lenders to recover the principal amount they loaned, but these parties cannot collect any interest on the loan. In addition, a final group of states allow lenders to recover the principal as well as an amount of interest up to, but not exceeding, the statutory maximum. In essence, these states allow the lenders to recover all but the excess interest, as if the loan were given at the statutory maximum rate.

gambling

An agreement in which a party pays consideration (money placed during bets) for the chance, or opportunity, to obtain an amount of money or property.

Gambling As with licensing statutes, all states engage in at least some regulation of gambling. In this chapter, the term gambling refers to agreements in which parties pay consideration (money placed during bets) for the chance, or opportunity, to obtain an amount of money or property.

While gambling is still illegal in the vast majority of states, many states allow casino gambling. The states most notable for casino gambling are Nevada, New Jersey, and Louisiana. Some states allow certain other types of gambling, either intentionally or through legal loopholes. For example, given California's definition of gambling, betting on draw poker is legal. Some states make other exceptions, such as for horse tracks, casinos located on Native American reservations, or legal state-run lotteries.

Sabbath laws

Laws prohibiting the performance of certain activities on Sundays.

Sabbath Laws A large number of states still have what are known as *Sabbath, Sunday,* or *blue* laws on the books. Sabbath laws limit the types of business activities in which parties can legally engage on Sundays.

In most states with Sabbath law restrictions, these laws date back to colonial times. In fact, the term "blue law" is a reference to the blue paper on which New Haven, Connecticut, printed its Sabbath laws in 1781. New Haven's 1781 law prohibited shops from being opened, as well as prohibited all work, on the "Lord's day" (Sunday).

The activities restricted today by Sabbath laws vary from state to state. Most Sabbath laws pertain to the sale of alcoholic beverages. These laws tend to prohibit the sale of all alcohol or at least specific types either all day or at restricted times on Sundays. Some Sabbath laws go as far as to make it illegal to enter into any contractual relationship on a Sunday. However, an executed, or fully performed, contract created on a Sunday cannot be rescinded.

There are exceptions to Sabbath laws. Most states with Sabbath laws allow the performance of charity work on Sundays. In addition, Sabbath laws do not typically apply to contracts involving the obtaining of "necessities," typically defined as prescription medication, food, or anything else related to health or survival.

Regardless of how widespread Sabbath laws are, the vast majority of states do not enforce all, or at least some, of their Sabbath laws. In fact, some Sabbath laws have in the past been deemed unconstitutional according to the First Amendment. Nevertheless, if Sabbath laws are on the books, despite convention to the contrary, they can be applied, and some states do apply such

laws. As a businessperson, you should always find out whether Sabbath laws exist and, if they do, whether authorities enforce these laws.

AGREEMENTS THAT VIOLATE PUBLIC POLICY

Unlike agreements that are precluded by statute, some types of agreements are not illegal per se, as they are not in violation of any statute or legal code, but are unenforceable because courts have deemed them to be against commonly held public policy. Public policy involves both the government's concern for its citizens and the beliefs people hold regarding the proper subject of business transactions. The focus is "what is in society's best interest."

Contracts in Restraint of Trade It is a widely held belief in economics, as well as in America in general, that competition drives down prices, which is good for consumers. Accordingly, agreements that restrain trade are viewed as being harmful to consumers and thus against public policy. These restraints on trade are also known as *anticompetitive agreements.* Not only are anticompetitive agreements against public policy, but they also frequently violate antitrust laws.

There is an exception that allows specific types of restraints on trade. When a restraint on trade is reasonable, as determined by the courts, and the restraint is part of a subordinate, or ancillary, clause, the restraint is typically allowed. Such restraints are known as covenants not to compete, or *restrictive covenants.* Covenants not to compete tend to come in two varieties. The first involves noncompetition in the sale of an ongoing business, and the second involves noncompetition in employment, both of which are discussed below.

covenant not to compete
An agreement not to compete against a party for a set period of time within a designated geographic area.

The first category of permissible restraints on trade is covenants not to compete that involve the sale of an ongoing business. *Ongoing* refers to the status of the business being sold: The business is still running and will still run on its own; it is not being merged and is not closing down.

The public policy argument in favor of supporting restrictions with the sale of a business involves the fairness of the sale. Let us examine a hypothetical situation to see why this restraint on trade is allowed. Suppose you purchase a jewelry store from Ann Smith. Ann is a well-respected member of the community, and her business has been around for many years. The people in the community know the store, and they trust Ann to provide fair exchanges. As a well-informed businessperson, you know about Ann's reputation. In fact, her good reputation made the purchase more appealing.

Now suppose Ann turns around and opens another jewelry store a block away one month later. Ann's loyal customers are likely to go to her new store because they still trust her. In the meantime, Ann's good name is no longer associated with your store, and your business suffers accordingly. You entered into the sales agreement thinking you would benefit from Ann's good name, but in the end you overpaid for a business that lacks the benefit of Ann's name because Ann took her name with her when she went into competition with your store.

In the interest of self-proclaimed fairness, courts are willing to impose restrictions preventing Ann, or others in her position, from going into immediate competition with you, or others in your position. Public policy requests fairness in business transactions, and this fairness does not occur when people profit from a business transaction and then start a new business that destroys the business they just sold.

Consequently, the restraints to trade being discussed with the sale of an ongoing business involve the seller's ability to open up another business within a certain geographic location within a designated time period. As previously mentioned, to be enforceable, a covenant not to compete needs to be in a *subordinate* clause in the contract. If the covenant not to compete is a part of the main agreement, and therefore not subordinate, the agreement is typically considered unenforceable and void as it goes against public policy by providing unreasonable restraints to trade. The unreasonableness arises because when the covenant is an integral part of the contract, it cannot be objected to. In contrast, when the covenant is subordinate, the specific noncompetition clause can be removed and the agreement can go forward as planned. Case 9-2 illustrates the analysis of the court in a case involving a covenant not to compete signed in conjunction with the sale of a business.

The second category of permissible restraints on trade is covenants not to compete that involve employment contracts. The covenants in employment contracts are similar to those in

ALFRED W. GANN AND CONNIE A. GANN, HUSBAND
AND WIFE, PLAINTIFFS-APPELLEES, v. GERRY
MORRIS, DEFENDANT-APPELLANT
COURT OF APPEALS OF ARIZONA, DIVISION 2

122 Ariz. 517, 596 P.2d 43 (1979)

FACTS: *The defendant entered into an agreement to sell his silk-screening business or lettering shop to the plaintiffs. The agreement provided in part that the defendant would not enter into a silk-screening or lettering shop business within a geographic radius for a period of 10 years, would not compete in any manner whatsoever with the plaintiffs, and would refer all business contacts to the plaintiffs. The trial court found that the seller breached the contract by competing with the buyers and failing to refer all business under the terms of their contract. On appeal, the defendant argued that the contract, including the covenant not to compete, was unenforceable as a restraint of trade, which violated public policy.*

ISSUE: Is a covenant not to compete, signed in conjunction with the sale of a business, void as illegal because it violates the public policy against restraints of trade?

REASONING: In the court's own words (abridged and slightly modified):

> While covenants not to compete are partial restraints of trade, they are not illegal and can still be enforced where they are ancillary to contracts for employment or sale of a business and are reasonably limited as to time and territory. What is reasonable depends on the whole subject matter of the contract, the kind and character of the business, its location, the purpose to be accomplished by the restriction, and all the circumstances which show the intention of the parties. The rational for enforcing such

agreements in the case of a small business is that the owner had most likely developed a clientele and reputation in a specialized area, and part of what the buyer is purchasing is that good will generated by the business. If the original opens up in a nearby area, that good will may be diverted to the new business.

At the time of the sale in this case, one of the customers of the business had offices in Benson, Phoenix and San Manuel, an area extending beyond the 100-mile restriction in the agreement. Restrictions for 10 years or more have been upheld where it was determined that the covenant was reasonable under all the circumstances. Based on these facts, the scope of the covenant in this case is not unreasonable as broader than necessary to protect the interest of the buyers of a small silk screening business.

The appellate court found that the trial court's award of damages was "supported by invoices for sales made in violation of the agreement, and testimony of both buyer and seller as to average cost and profits per sale." The trial court simply awarded damages of the lost profits specifically established by the evidence.

DECISION AND REMEDY: The case was affirmed in favor of the plaintiffs in light of the reasonableness of the covenant not to compete.

SIGNIFICANCE OF THE CASE: The case illustrates how important the circumstances surrounding an agreement are when determining whether a covenant not to complete will be upheld.

CRITICAL THINKING

Provide an example of a piece of evidence that might have been provided by the defendant that would have indicated that the restraint was unreasonable.

ETHICAL DECISION MAKING

How well can the ethical stance of the judge be defended in this case, and what ethical guidelines can be used in the effort to do so?

sales contracts. However, with employment, the employee is agreeing not to compete with her boss, if she leaves, for a designated period of time within a designated geographic area.

These covenants in employment contracts are not unusual. In fact, many middle or upper-level managers enter into agreements not to compete with their employers. In such a covenant, the employee is agreeing not to work for competitors or to start his own competing business.

Covenants not to compete in employment contracts are legal in most states. However, to be legal, the covenant needs to protect a legitimate business interest. Furthermore, the covenant needs to be for a reasonable period of time and geographic area so that it does not unlawfully impinge on the employee's right to earn a living. The agreement must not be for a longer period of time or larger geographic region than is necessary to protect the employer's legitimate business interest.

Given the variations from state to state in other areas of the law, it should come as no surprise that the enforceability of covenants not to compete also varies from state to state. For example, California does not allow any covenants not to compete. On a different note, Texas requires that the employee gain a specific benefit from a contract, beyond employment, before its courts will enforce a covenant not to compete. The employee must be given, or gain, something even if the covenant not to compete is for a reasonable period of time and geographic region.

Unconscionable Contracts or Clauses When courts are asked to review contracts, fairness is not usually high on the courts' lists of things for which to look. Instead, courts typically assume that the contracting parties are intelligent, responsible adults. The belief is, barring proof of coercion, that parties enter into contracts because they want to do so. Nevertheless, there are times when agreements are so one-sided, or heavy-handed against one party, that the courts will not make the harmed, innocent person fulfill his or her contractual duties. These heavily one-sided agreements are known as **unconscionable** agreements. The term *unconscionable* refers to the fact that the agreement in question is so unfair that it is void of conscience.

Rules against unconscionable contracts exist in both the Restatement (Second) of Contracts and the Uniform Commercial Code. However, before the Restatement and the UCC existed, the common law would not enforce contracts the courts deemed to be too unfair, or unconscionable. Now UCC Section 2-302 states:

> (1) If the court as a matter of law finds the contract or any clause of the contract to have been unconscionable at the time it was made, the court may refuse to enforce the contract, or it may enforce the remainder of the contract without the clause, or it may so limit the application of any unconscionable clause as to avoid any unconscionable result; (2) When it is claimed or appears to the court that the contract or any clause thereof may be unconscionable, the parties shall be afforded a reasonable opportunity to present evidence as to its commercial setting, purpose, and effect to aid the court in making the determination.

Every state, with the exceptions of California and Louisiana, has incorporated the above UCC section into its state's UCC. Section 208 of the Restatement also incorporates the above section from the UCC.

There are two main types of unconscionable agreements, procedural and substantive. **Procedural unconscionability** relates to conditions that would impair one party's understanding of a contract, as well as to the integration of terms into a contract. Regarding impaired understanding of contractual terms, the factors can be anything from tiny, hard-to-read print on the back of an agreement to excessive use of legalese (unnecessarily technical legal language) or even the inability of a person to fully read over a contract and ask any questions before he or she was required to sign.

Most frequently, procedural unconscionability arises when one party presents the other with an adhesion contract. An **adhesion contract** is a contract created by a party to an agreement that is presented to the other party on a take-it-or-leave-it basis. That is, the contract is presented as complete and as the only chance the presented party (known as the *adhering party*) will have to enter into the agreement. While adhesion contracts are themselves legal, the presence of one does raise some potential problem indicators for courts. Given that adhesion contracts usually do not allow for debate regarding the agreement, courts tend to examine adhesion contracts to see if they can determine how voluntary the agreement really was.

Conversely, **substantive unconscionability** involves overly harsh or lopsided substance in an agreement. That is, if an agreement is terribly one-sided, it is probably invalid on the basis of substantive notions of fairness and fair dealing. Courts would find the following, for example, to be substantively unconscionable: high differences between cost and price in a sales agreement; agreements in which one party gains vastly more than the other; agreements in which one party is prevented from having any sort of equal benefit; agreements in which one party has little to

LO 4

unconscionable
A term applied to a contract in which one party has so much more bargaining power than the other party that the powerful party dictates the terms of the agreement and eliminates the other party's free will.

procedural unconscionability
Unconscionability that derives from the process of making a contract.

adhesion contract
A contract created by a party to an agreement that is presented to the other party on a take-it-or-leave-it basis. Such contracts are legal but are sometimes rescinded on the grounds of unconscionability and the absence of one party's free will to enter a contract.

substantive unconscionability
Unconscionability that derives from one-sided, unjust, or overly harsh substance in a contract.

no legal recourse, according to the agreement; and portions of an agreement that are completely unrelated to anything having to do with either party's business risk.

exculpatory clause

A statement in a contract that frees one party (usually the drafter of the agreement) from all liability arising out of performance of the contract; generally based on factors such as consumer ignorance or a great deal of unexplained fine print that serve to deprive the less powerful party of a meaningful choice.

Exculpatory Clauses An **exculpatory clause** is a statement releasing one of the parties to an agreement from all liability, regardless of who is at fault or what the injury suffered is. Because tort law attempts to return the wronged party to the state he or she was in before the wrong occurred, anything preventing this corrective mechanism is against public policy. It does not benefit society to allow some parties to get away with not having to pay for wrongs they commit simply because they state they will not be liable in various contracts. In fact, the patently unfair nature of an exculpatory clause is closely tied to the idea of unconscionable contracts.

Exculpatory clauses frequently show up in rental agreements for commercial or residential property. These clauses are often found to be against public policy. The reasoning is that sometimes people are injured while on property they are renting from another and sometimes the injuries are due to the carelessness, negligence, or other wrongdoings of the owner. Once again, it does not serve the public's interest to allow landlords, especially when it comes to residential property, to simply disavow all liabilities in advance. Were they allowed to do so, there would be nothing requiring that landlords fix problems in their rental units, including potentially lethal problems, such as faulty electric wiring or lead-based paint.

A basic test to determine whether an exculpatory clause is unenforceable is to see if the enforcing party engages in a business directly related to the public interest. Examples of such businesses include banks, transportation providers, and public utilities. Courts believe it is against the public interest to allow businesses engaging in work in the public's interest to not be held accountable to the public they are serving.

Another concern with large businesses that are serving the public interest is the unfair bargaining power they can possess in negotiating a contract. Given the power these businesses have, they could simply demand that all customers accept the exculpatory clause, thus escaping all possible liability. While the idea of these businesses' not being liable is bad, what is worse is that there would be no punitive financial motive for them to carefully conduct their business operations, or so the argument goes. As a result, the potential for increased accidents would be large. Obviously, it is not in the public's interest to have unsafe businesses that are not accountable to the public. Thus, these businesses cannot enforce exculpatory clauses.

Case 9-3 details a court's determination that an illegal exculpatory clause existed.

 CASE 9-3

ERIC LUCIER AND KAREN A. HALEY v. ANGELA AND JAMES WILLIAMS, CAMBRIDGE ASSOCIATES, LTD., AND AL VASYS
SUPERIOR COURT OF NEW JERSEY, APPELLATE DIVISION
841 A.2d 907 (2004)

FACTS: *Eric Lucier and Karen A. Haley, a young married couple, were first-time home buyers. They contracted with the Williams to purchase a single-family residence. Lucier and Haley engaged the services of Cambridge Associates, Ltd. (CAL), to perform a home inspection. Al Vasys had formed CAL and was its president. Lucier dealt directly with Vasys, and Vasys performed the inspection and issued the home inspection report on behalf of CAL.*

The home inspection agreement contained a provision limiting CAL's liability to "$500, or 50% of fees actually paid to CAL by Client, whichever sum is smaller." This provision,

and several others in the form agreement prepared by CAL, was followed by a line for placement of the client's initials. Lucier initialed this provision. The fee for the home inspection contract was $385, which Lucier paid to CAL.

Lucier claims that when he began to read the agreement, in Vasys' presence, he felt that some of the language was unfair and confusing. According to Lucier, Vasys stated that he would not change any provisions, it was a standard contract based on home inspections done in New Jersey, and Lucier would have to sign the agreement "as-is" or not at all. Vasys does not dispute this, but relies on Lucier's

signing the agreement and initialing the limitation-of-liability clause. Likewise, Lucier does not deny signing the contract or initialing that clause.

Lucier and Haley obtained title to the property from the Williams. Shortly after, they noticed leaks in the house. They engaged the services of a roofing contractor and found out the roof was defective. Lucier and Haley argue that Vasys should have observed and reported the problem to them. The cost of repair was about $8,000 to $10,000.

Lucier and Haley brought suit against the Williams, CAL, and Vasys, seeking damages to compensate them for the loss occasioned by the alleged defect. CAL and Vasys moved for partial summary judgment, seeking a declaration that the limit of their liability in the action, if any, was one-half the contract price, or $192.50. The motion for partial summary judgment was granted. Lucier and Haley then filed an appeal, seeking review of the partial summary judgment order.

ISSUE: Was the limitation of liability clause in the home inspection contract unconscionable?

REASONING: The courts find unconscionability to be "an amorphous concept obviously designed to establish a broad business ethic."

To avoid a contract on grounds of unconscionability, a court must first find that the contract is one of adhesion. Then it will examine "the subject matter of the contract, the parties' relative bargaining positions, the degree of economic compulsion motivating the 'adhering' party, and the public interests affected by the contract." In a situation where the potentially unconscionable provision limits a party's liability, the court pays particular attention to any inequality in the bargaining power and status of the parties, as well as the substance of the contract, keeping in mind the public policy against allowing parties to immunize themselves from liability for their own negligence, meaning that any limitation on such liability should be sufficient to provide a realistic incentive for the party to act diligently.

In the words of the court:

> Applying these principles to the home inspection contract before us, we find the limitation of liability provision unconscionable. We do not hesitate to hold it unenforceable for the following reasons: (1) the contract, prepared by the home inspector, is one of adhesion; (2) the par[...] a professional expert, have [...] and (3) the substance of the [...] and its fundamental purpose [...] is so nominal that it has the [...] all responsibility for the prof[...] the provision is contrary to ou[...] ing the purpose of a home ins[...] evaluation of a home's fitness [...] sionals to certain industry sta[...]

This is a classic contract o[...] tions leading up to its preparat[...] Lucier on a standardized pre-p[...] on a take-it-or-leave-it basis, w[...] any opportunity for him to negotiate or modify any of its terms.

The bargaining position between the parties was grossly disparate. Vasys has been in the home inspection business for twenty years. He has inspected thousands of homes. He has an engineering degree. He has served as an expert witness in construction matters. He holds various designations in the building and construction field. He advertises his company and holds it and himself out as possessing expertise in the home inspection field. Lucier and Haley, on the other hand, are unknowledgeable and unsophisticated in matters of home construction. They are consumers. They placed their trust in this expert. They had every reason to expect he would act with diligence and competence in inspecting the home they desired to purchase and discover and report major defects. The disparity in the positions of these parties is clear and substantial.

The foisting of a contract of this type in this setting on an inexperienced consumer clearly demonstrates a lack of fair dealing by the professional. The cost of homes in New Jersey is substantial.

The limitation of liability clause here is also against public policy. First, it allows the home inspector to circumvent the state's public policy of holding professional service providers to certain industry standards. Second, it contravenes the stated public policy of New Jersey regarding home inspectors.

With professional services, exculpation clauses are particularly disfavored. The very nature of a professional service is one in which the person receiving the service relies upon the expertise, training, knowledge and stature of the professional. Exculpation provisions are antithetical to such a relationship.

DECISION AND REMEDY: The contract was unconscionable, and therefore the court reversed the decision and remanded it back to the lower court for trial.

SIGNIFICANCE OF THE CASE: While courts do not frequently find contracts to be unenforceable due to unconscionability, this case provides a good illustration of when the court will find the doctrine applicable.

CRITICAL THINKING

From the facts you have about the case, does the judge seem to be making any assumptions without an adequate factual basis to support those assumptions?

ETHICAL DECISION MAKING

Examine the ethical nature of the parties to the case. Whose behavior was particularly blameworthy? Whose was praiseworthy? What facts from the case and what ethical guidelines support your characterizations?

While businesses closely linked to the public interest cannot enforce exculpatory clauses, not all exculpatory clauses are unlawful. To be able to enforce an exculpatory clause, the party seeking enforcement must be a private business or an individual and must *not* be important to the public interest. Such private businesses or individuals provide nonessential services and thus do not have the same bargaining power as the previously discussed groups, such as banks, utilities, and airlines. Given their lack of huge bargaining power, it is assumed that private businesses and individuals will enter on relatively equal terms and will voluntarily agree on or decline the final contract.

Examples of private businesses that can enforce exculpatory clauses include skiing facilities such as resorts or rental places, private gyms or health clubs, any business offering skydiving or bungee jumping, and amusement parks, to name a few. Because the services provided by all these businesses, as well as others in this category, are not something related to the public interest and not something in which people must engage, these parties are allowed to deny liability if the party with which they are contracting agrees to the exculpatory clause. Just because these parties *might* be able to enforce an exculpatory clause, however, does not mean the clause is always automatically enforceable.

LO 5 EFFECT OF ILLEGAL AGREEMENTS

Generally speaking, when an agreement is deemed illegal, courts will label the contract void. The reason most illegal agreements are void is that, in most cases, both parties are equally responsible for the illegal agreement. In the law, when both parties are equally responsible for an illegal agreement, as the parties are said to be *in pari delicto.*

in pari delicto
In equal fault.

When both parties are at fault, it does not make sense for the courts to attempt to salvage the agreement or reward either party. Therefore, most illegal agreements are void, meaning neither party can enforce the agreement and neither party is entitled to recovery.

However, it is not always the case that both parties are at fault. In the event that one party is not responsible for an illegal agreement or that there are special circumstances forgiving the illegality, it makes sense sometimes to allow one party to an illegal agreement to recover various damages.

The first exception to the general rule occurs when a member of a protected class is involved in an agreement that contradicts a statute intended to protect the specific class. In the event of such a contradiction, the member of the protected class is allowed to sue for performance. The reasoning is that if a statute is intended to protect a specific class, the statute should not be allowed to be used by people outside the class to harm those inside the class.

For example, a work agreement between a truck driver and his or her employer may specify that the driver gets paid for the number of hours worked. Yet certain statutes limit the number of hours truck drivers may drive in a given time period. If the truck driver accidentally drives more than the allowable hours, the driver has technically violated a statute. However, this violation does not allow the employer to refuse to pay the driver for the extra hours. Rather, the driver may sue the employer to enforce the work agreement.

The second exception to the voiding of illegal agreements occurs when there is a justifiable ignorance of facts. A *justifiable ignorance of facts* is one party's lack of knowledge regarding a provision of the agreement that would make it illegal. While ignorance of the law does not excuse illegal behavior, not knowing that the other party to a contract intended to fulfill the agreement through illegal means does function as an excuse.

When one of the parties is relatively innocent in the whole deal, the court may give back any consideration that party gave or may require an exchange for partial performance such that both parties can be returned to the positions they were in before they entered into the agreement. Conversely, if one party is completely innocent of any illegality and has completed his or her portion of the contract, then—depending on the reason the contract is considered illegal and depending on which state's laws are in question—the court might enforce the entire agreement.

A third exception to the general rule occurs when one of the parties withdraws from an illegal agreement. The key to any recovery is that the party must have withdrawn before any illegality

CASE Nugget

What Effect Does the Legality of a Contract Have on a Court Finding?

Biomedical Systems Corporation v. GE Marquette Medical Systems, Inc.
United States Court of Appeals for the Eighth Circuit

287 F.3d 707 (2002)

GE contracted with Biomedical to produce a new home uterine-activity monitor (HUAM) based on technology created by Biomedical. The GE-Biomedical contract required that GE obtain "510(k)" premarket notification clearance from the FDA. To receive 510(k) clearance, a manufacturer must give the FDA 90 days' notice that the manufacturer intends to "market a medical device (1) which is substantially equivalent to a device already approved by the FDA, and (2) which has the same intended use as the approved device."

Rather than seeking 510(k) approval, which would be granted or denied within 90 days, GE asked the FDA to reclassify GE's new HUAM from one class of regulated devices to another class of regulated devices. The reclassification process took three and a half years. Two and a half years after signing the contract, Biomedical sued GE in federal district court, alleging breach of contract and claiming $135 million in damages. The jury found for Biomedical and awarded $75 million in damages. On appeal, GE challenged the district court's ruling barring its illegality defense.

GE argued that it was entitled to judgment as a matter of law because the contract, which GE had drafted, required that GE illegally seek 510(k) approval for the new HUAM. The court disagreed, stating that the district court properly denied GE judgment as a matter of law on its illegality defense. The court claims that the contract unambiguously required that GE apply for 510(k) clearance and did not require that GE violate federal law. The court ultimately concluded, "Because the contract did not require illegal conduct on GE's part, we do not disturb the jury damage award."

occurred. If this is the case and if part or full performance has occurred, the party may recover value for whatever portion has been completed. However, if the party is involved in any way in the illegal activity, the party cannot recover at all.

Severable Contracts A severable contract, also known as a *divisible contract,* contains multiple parts that can each be performed separately. In addition, separate consideration is offered for each individual part. In essence, a severable contract is like numerous contracts in one. Conversely, an indivisible contract requires complete performance by both parties, even if it appears as though the contract contains multiple parts, similar to a severable contract.

With respect to illegality, severable contracts have a huge advantage over indivisible contracts: If a severable contract has both legal and illegal portions, the court has the option of declaring void only those sections of the agreement that are illegal. The court can then enforce the remaining, legal portions of the contract. Indivisible contracts must be enforced or rejected in their entirety. For a court to be able to enforce parts of a severable contract, the parts that are enforced must still represent the main purpose of the original agreement. If declaring parts of a contract void substantially alters the contract, the court is not likely to enforce the remaining portions of the agreement. Courts ultimately want to facilitate business transactions and enforce the legal wishes of parties, and severable contracts enable courts to do so.

severable contract
A contract that contains multiple parts that can each be performed separately.

indivisible contract
A contract that requires complete performance by both parties.

LO 6

SUMMARY

Capacity

Natural persons over the age of majority are presumed to have the full legal capacity to enter into binding, legal contracts.

A person has only limited capacity to enter into a legally binding contract if the person is:

- A minor.
- Suffering from a mental deficiency that prevents the person from understanding the nature and obligations of contracts.
- Intoxicated.

A person has no capacity to enter into a contract if the person:

- Has been adjudicated insane.
- Has been adjudicated a habitual drunkard.
- Has had a legal guardian appointed to enter into contracts on his or her behalf.

Legality

Contracts that do not have a legal object are not valid.

Contracts may lack a legal object because they violate a statute or violate public policy.

If the illegal portion of a contract can be severed from the legal portion, the courts may simply refuse to enforce the illegal parts and enforce the remaining legal parts.

Point/Counterpoint

Should the Law Bind Mentally Incompetent Individuals to Their Contracts?	
YES	NO

Holding mentally incompetent individuals to their contracts sharply increases the likelihood of fraud. If contract law bound such individuals to their contracts, unscrupulous sellers could legally encourage mentally incompetent individuals to enter into fraudulent contracts, and courts, bound to apply the law, would enforce those contracts. Hence, permitting mentally incompetent individuals to escape their contracts sends a message to opportunistic individuals that the law will not sanction their fraudulent practices.	The great majority of mentally incompetent individuals live with mentally competent relatives, friends, or guardians who watch out for their best interests. Compared to judges, these guardians are much more likely to be able to act in the best interests of the mentally incompetent.
In addition to discouraging fraud, contract laws that permit mentally incompetent individuals to void their contracts protect the most vulnerable members of society. The law binds mentally *competent* individuals to their contracts under the assumption that they are capable of looking out for their best interests. But mentally *incompetent* individuals lack the ability to protect their best interests. Critics call these types of laws paternalistic, but a major function of the law is to protect individuals such as the mentally incompetent who cannot protect themselves.	Moreover, this governmental regulation hurts mentally incompetent individuals more than it helps them. If mentally incompetent individuals can legally void their contracts, competent individuals will be less willing to enter into fair contracts with them. As a result, mentally incompetent individuals will have fewer opportunities to enter into contracts consistent with their best interests. Hence, although the purpose of allowing mentally incompetent individuals to escape their contracts is well meaning, the result is malicious to the very individuals the law intends to help.
Indeed, if the justification for contract law is rooted in our desire for individuals to be able to enter into mutually beneficial exchanges, allowing mentally incompetent	Proponents of allowing mentally incompetent individuals to void their contracts argue that doing so would discourage fraud. But their position encourages fraud against mentally competent individuals. If mentally incompetent individuals can escape their contracts, they have an incentive to enter risky contracts with mentally competent individuals.

individuals, who by definition cannot determine what is in their self-interest, to void their contracts is consistent with this justification.

Finally, proponents of binding mentally incompetent individuals to their contracts highlight courts' lack of institutional competence to determine mental competence. How can courts, they ask, reliably determine which individuals lack the mental competence to look out for their own interests?

Questions & Problems

1. How does the concept of the age of majority in Great Britain differ from that in the United States?

2. Explain the obligations of a minor who chooses to disaffirm a contract.

3. Go back to the discussion of contracts that cannot be disaffirmed by minors, and explain the policy reasons that support each of the exceptions. Can you make an argument for any additional kinds of contracts that should not be subject to disaffirmance by minors?

4. If all you know about a man is that his neighbors think he is crazy, you do not know whether a contract he entered into was valid, voidable, or void. Why not?

5. What factors determine whether a covenant not to compete is legal or illegal?

6. What is the relationship between contracts in restraint of trade and unconscionable contracts?

7. Hansen, a passenger on an America West flight, put a robotic head worth approximately $750,000 in the overhead compartment for storage during his flight. When he changed planes, he forgot to bring his robot head with him. By the time he realized what had happened, the plane with the robot head had already departed on another flight. Airline officials said they would retrieve it when the plane landed, and would ship it to him in San Francisco, but Hansen never received the head. He sued for damages for conversion and negligence. The airline was granted its motion for summary judgment on grounds that the loss was covered by a valid limitation of liability clause contained in the contract of passage, and that the airline had offered Hansen the opportunity to insure the head for a greater amount, but he had chosen not to. Do you think the award for summary judgment should have been upheld on appeal? Why or why not? [*Hanson v. American West Airlines,* F.Supp.2d, (2008 WL 926297, C.D., Calif., 2008).]

8. Sixteen-year-old Joseph Dodson bought a used pickup truck from Shrader's Auto for $4,900. Nine months later, the truck began malfunctioning, so Dodson took it to a mechanic, who informed Dodson that the truck might have a burnt valve. Dodson did not repair the truck but continued to drive it. A month later, the engine burned out and the truck would no longer run. Dodson disaffirmed the contract and returned the truck to Shrader's Auto, asking for a return of the purchase price. Shrader's Auto refused to return the purchase price to him and would not take possession of the truck. Dodson then left the truck in his front yard, where it was hit by an unknown driver. Dodson sued the owner of Shrader's Auto, seeking restitution of his purchase price. The trial court granted restitution of the purchase price to the plaintiff, and the defendants appealed. Why do you think the judgment of the trial court was either upheld or reversed on appeal? [*Dodson v. Shrader et al.,* 824 S.W.2d 545 (1992).]

9. Seigneur joined NFI, a health and fitness facility, to lose weight and become fit. She was in poor physical condition and had back problems that she discussed with NFI prior to signing a contract with the facility. The contract she ultimately signed contained a clause that said NFI was not responsible for injuries sustained during exercise. Seigneur claimed that she tore a muscle in her shoulder while doing a series of tests to evaluate her physical condition. The tear required surgery to be repaired, and her surgeon stated that he believed the injury was caused by her using an upper-torso weight machine during her fitness evaluation. She sued NFI for negligence. NFI filed a motion for summary judgment on the basis of the exculpatory clause. The trial court granted NFI's motion, and Seigneur appealed. Do you believe the appellate court upheld the motion for summary judgment? Why or why not? [*Seigneur v. National Fitness Institute, Inc.,* 752 A.2d 631 (Ct. App. Md. 2000).]

10. On July 16, 1997, Chicago Steel entered into a contract with ADT in which ADT agreed to design, sell, install, and/or maintain a fire alarm system and provide fire alarm monitoring and reporting services for Chicago Steel's plant at 6630 W. Wrightwood Avenue in Chicago. Under the terms of the contract, ADT was to maintain the fire alarm system and inspect it four times a year. Chicago Steel was to pay ADT $3,472 annually.

The contract stated that ADT was not an insurer and would be exempt from liability for damage to property, whether based on breach of contract, negligence, or strict liability. The contract also contained a limitation-of-damages clause limiting any liability on ADT's part to the greater of 10 percent of the annual service charge or $1,000. The contract, however, gave Chicago Steel the option to pay for an allocation of additional liability to ADT. The record reflects that Chicago Steel did not exercise that option.

On January 2, 1999, after the alarm system's installation, a fire occurred at the Wrightwood plant, causing substantial damage to property located there. The plaintiffs sued ADT, alleging that the failure of the alarm system and/or ADT's failure to maintain and monitor the system caused a delay in notification to the Chicago fire department and resulted in substantial property damage. Their complaint included four counts: (1) strict product liability, (2) breach of contract, (3) negligence, and (4) gross negligence.

ADT filed a motion to dismiss the plaintiffs' complaint, based in part on the exculpatory clause contained in its fire alarm installation and maintenance contract with Chicago Steel, which released ADT from future negligence, breach of contract, and strict-liability claims. The trial court granted the motion. On appeal, do you think the exculpatory clause was enforced by the appellate court? Why or why not? [*Chicago Steel Rule and Die Fabricators Company and Travelers Indemnity Company of Illinois v. ADT Security Systems, Inc., ADT Security Services, Inc.,* 327 Ill. App. 3d 642, 763 N.E.2d 839 (2002).]

Looking for more review material?

The Online Learning Center at **www.mhhe.com/kubasekess** contains this chapter's "Assignment on the Internet" and also a list of URLs for more information, entitled "On the Internet." Find both of them in the Student Center portion of the OLC, along with quizzes and other helpful materials.

Reality of Assent

----> CASE OPENER

A Disagreement over an Agreement

Patricia and Billy Welkener sought a divorce.[1] The two parties, having reached an agreement for the division of their property, appeared in court to recite into the record their agreement. In court, Patricia agreed, among other things, to receive $1,098.84 per month from Billy's retirement account.

At the conclusion of the hearing, the judge decreed the settlement to be final. Subsequently, Patricia asked the court to enter judgment that she receive 32.7 percent of Billy's retirement account, which is the percentage version of the amount she was previously awarded. Patricia argued that stating the award in terms of a percentage, rather than a specific amount, was important as this would allow her to share in any future increase in Billy's monthly retirement benefit.

Patricia further argued that when the agreement was announced in open court, she described the agreement in terms of dollars and cents as a means of describing the percentage she would be entitled to receive. She claimed that listing the amount in terms of a sum, as opposed to a percentage, was a mistake in the contract and, therefore, that the terms to which she agreed were not accurately reflected in the court's final decision.

1. Imagine you were the judge in this case. Do you think the agreement reached in court between the Welkeners accurately reflects what the parties intended?
2. Under which ethical system would Patricia Welkener be entitled to the change in terms? Why?

[1] *Welkener v. Welkener*, 71 S.W.3d 364 (2001).

----> LEARNING OBJECTIVES

After reading this chapter, you will be able to answer the following questions:

LO 1 Why is genuine assent important?

LO 2 What are the elements of mistake?

LO 1

The Importance of Genuine Assent

When two people talk to each other in the hope that an exchange will take place, all kinds of things can go wrong. Global business needs dependability. Just imagine what it would be like if "Yes" meant "Maybe"! Deals would be closed only to be reopened again and again. The costs of all purchases would soar. Businesses would be forced to charge extra to pay for all the extra time they had to spend to finally get to the point where "Yes" really meant "Yes."

To make business transactions smoother and more dependable, the law has developed rules about when "Yes" means "Yes." As Chapter 7 explained, you need an offer and an acceptance to form a contract. Sometimes, however, there is a problem with the acceptance. Certain problems with the acceptance, or the *yes,* may give rise to the claim that the acceptance was not really genuine and, therefore, that the resulting contract is not valid. In this chapter we are going to examine the problems that may arise with an acceptance that will make the resulting contract **voidable.** When a contact is voidable, it may be **rescinded,** or canceled.

voidable
A term applied to a contract that one or both parties have the ability to either withdraw from or enforce.

rescind
To cancel a contract.

The cancellation of a contract permits the person who canceled it to require the return of everything she gave the other party. At the same time, the person who rescinds the contract must herself return whatever she has received from the other party. A major theme of this chapter is that good business managers aim for genuine assent in their contracts. This chapter shows you how to achieve genuine assent. It explains the major obstacles to genuine assent: *mistake, misrepresentation, undue influence, duress,* and *unconscionability.* Knowing about these potential problems will help you to avoid them.

LO 2

Mistake

When people agree to buy or sell, they do so with a particular understanding about the nature of the good or service they are about to exchange. However, one or both parties may think they consented to exchange a particular thing only to find out later that no meeting of the minds had occurred. People may misunderstand either some fact about the deal or the value of what is being exchanged. We focus on misunderstandings about facts because they are the only issues that raise the potential of rescission in American courts.

European courts take a different approach to mistakes about *the value of performance* of a contract. In general, they agree with the reluctance of American courts to interfere with a contract just because the value of the item in question has changed since the agreement. The parties are assumed to have accepted the risk, when they made the contract, that the value might change later. However, European courts permit rescission of the contract for a mistake of value when the mistake involves more than 50 percent of the value at the time of the contract.

mistake
An erroneous belief about the facts of a contract at the time the contract is concluded. When a mistake occurs, legal assent is absent.

Legal assent is absent when a legal mistake occurs. The term *mistake* in contract law has a special meaning that deserves special attention because it is not quite the same as the ordinary use of the term. A **mistake** is an erroneous belief about the facts of a contract *at the time the contract is concluded.*

There is one more important aspect of the definition of mistake. Later in this chapter, when we discuss misrepresentation, our focus will be on incorrect beliefs about the facts of the contract caused by the other party's untrue statements. Mistakes in contract law do not result from the untrue statements of the other party to the contract.

Mistakes may be **unilateral,** the result of an error by *one* party about a material fact, that is, a fact that is important in the context of the particular contract. Alternatively, they may be **mutual,** shared by both parties to the agreement. This distinction is important in determining which contracts are voidable.

unilateral mistake
The result of an error by one party about a material fact, i.e., one that is important in the context of a particular contract.

mutual mistake
The result of an error by both parties about a material fact, i.e., one that is important in the context of a particular contract.

UNILATERAL MISTAKE

In general, a unilateral mistake does not void a contract. Courts are hesitant to interfere with a contract in a situation where one of the parties has a correct understanding of the material facts of the agreement. For instance, a widow seeking to rescind her and her husband's election to have his retirement benefits paid out over *his life* was not permitted to receive survivor's pension benefits. The court held that representatives of the retirement system had provided sufficient information to the plaintiff and her husband before they elected that particular form of payout.[2]

Sometimes, however, rescission is permitted for even unilateral mistakes. Because our economic well-being depends so heavily on reliable contracts, we want to be fully aware of the circumstances under which unilateral mistakes permit rescission. Any of the following conditions would permit a court to invalidate a contract on grounds of unilateral mistake:

1. One party made a mistake about a material fact and the other party either knew or had reason to know about the mistake.
2. The mistake was caused by a clerical error that did not result from gross negligence.
3. The mistake was so serious that the contract is unconscionable, that is, so unreasonable that it is outrageous.

These situations are rare, but it is important to be aware of them because any rescission can be costly in terms of time and lost opportunities.

Returning to the Welkeners in the Case Opener, suppose Patricia committed a unilateral mistake when she agreed to the terms of the division of property. What would she have to prove to demonstrate that a unilateral mistake was made such that the decision should be corrected? Did Patricia's supposed misunderstanding amount to a unilateral mistake?

MUTUAL MISTAKE

In cases where both parties to a contract are mistaken about either a current or a past material fact, either party can choose to rescind the contract. Rescinding such a contract is fair because any agreement between the parties was an illusion: An ambiguity in some key fact prevented the parties from being in actual agreement.

The famous story of the ship *Peerless*[3] has taught generations of students the importance of being very clear in defining material facts in any contract. The parties to the contract that led to the contract disagreement had agreed that the vessel *Peerless* would deliver the cotton they were exchanging. Unfortunately for them, there were two ships named *Peerless*. So when the deal was made, one party had one *Peerless* in mind while the other meant the second *Peerless*. The times the ships sailed were materially different, so the court rescinded the contract. *Warning:* Anticipate ambiguity in the material facts, and clarify them in advance to save yourself headaches later.

[2] *Ricks v. Missouri Local Government Employees Retirement System,* 1999 WL 663217 (MO. App. WD).
[3] *Raffles v. Wichelhaus,* 159 Eng. Rep. 375 (1864).

CASE Nugget

A Questionable Mistake

Mary W. Scott (Respondent-Appellant) v. Mid-Carolina Homes, Inc. (Appellant-Respondent) Court of Appeals of South Carolina

293 S.C. 191 (1987)

Mary Scott signed a contract to purchase a repossessed 1984 mobile home from Mid-Carolina Homes, Inc., for $5,644, to be paid in full before delivery. She gave the salesperson a check for $2,913.71 and agreed to pay the balance before the end of the month. Within the next week, the salesman called and told her he could not sell her the home because it had a bent frame, and the South Carolina Manufactured Housing Board would not permit him to sell a home with a bent frame. She offered to buy it as is and sign a waiver, but the salesman said that would not be legal. A few weeks later, Mid-Carolina sold the mobile home to another couple for $9,220. Scott sued and was awarded $3,600 actual damages and $6,400 punitive damages for breach of contract accompanied by a fraudulent act and $3,000.00 actual damages for violation of a state consumer protection law. The appeals court upheld the award.

On appeal, Mid-Carolina argued that it was entitled to rescind the contract because the salesperson was acting under a mistake of fact when he gave Scott the sales price. In upholding the award, the state supreme court explained that a contract may be rescinded for unilateral mistake only when the mistake has been induced by fraud, deceit, misrepresentation, concealment, or imposition of the party opposed to the rescission, without negligence on the part of the party claiming rescission, or when the mistake is accompanied by very strong and extraordinary circumstances that would make it a great wrong to enforce the agreement. Mid-Carolina had not demonstrated the presence of any of the circumstances that would justify a rescission. The salesperson was in the superior bargaining position to know the price, and the buyer's reliance on a salesperson's representation of the price was reasonable.

For a mutual mistake to interfere with legal consent, it must involve all the following:

1. A basic assumption about the subject matter of the contract.
2. A material effect on the agreement.
3. An adverse effect on a party that did not agree to bear the risk of mistake at the time of the agreement.

Courts will not void contracts for reason of mutual mistake if even one of the preceding attributes is missing.

For instance, to rise to the level of a basic assumption, the mistake would need to be about the existence, quality, or quantity of the items to be exchanged. To meet the second condition, the mistake must involve the essence of the agreement. A fact is material when it provides a basis for a person's agreeing to enter into the contract. The second element is not satisfied when the person attempting to avoid the contract simply claims that the item to be exchanged is not the one he had intended to exchange.

The third condition is necessary to protect those who bargain with someone who agreed, at the time of the agreement, to bear the risk of mistake but then later wishes to avoid that risk when the contract does not work out as well as he or she had planned. This situation might arise, for instance, if the adversely affected party had agreed in the contract to accept the items "as is" but later felt they were not worth the price paid. Case 10-1 offers you the opportunity to see the elements of mutual mistake analyzed in the sale of a business.

CASE 10-1

FACTS: *Wade Cook Financial Corporation purchased commercial property insurance from Caliber One Indemnity Company in 1998 that included $5,000,000 in earthquake coverage. In 1999, Cook renewed the policy, with the instructions to renew "under exactly the same terms" as the 1998 policy. Due to a clerical error, the earthquake coverage was changed to $500,000. Neither Cook nor Caliber One noticed this mistake. In 2000, Cook once again renewed the policy with terms identical to the 1999 policy. The $500,000 earthquake coverage mistake was replicated. On February 28, 2001, the Cook headquarters were damaged in an earthquake, and Cook filed a claim with Caliber One. At this time, Caliber One discovered the clerical error that had resulted in the reduction of the earthquake coverage, and it notified Cook that it would seek to be held only to the $500,000 limit. The federal district court granted summary judgment for Caliber One on the $500,000 limit, and Cook appealed, claiming the amount was a mutual mistake.*

ISSUE: Is the mutual-mistake doctrine applicable in this case even though both parties approved the contract containing the mistake?

REASONING: Both parties believed that they were renewing the contract under the original terms, including $5 million in earthquake coverage. Neither party was aware of the clerical error in 1999 or the reproduction of the error in 2000. According to *Washington Mutual Savings Bank v. Hedreen*, "Negligence in failing to observe that a writing does not express what has been assented to 'is not a bar to reformation of a contract when the reformation claim is based upon mutual . . . mistake." Therefore, simply because both parties had been negligent in catching the mistake does not mean that the mutual-mistake doctrine is not applicable in this case. Because the mistake was "relate[d] to a basic assumption on which both parties relied when making the contract" *(Denaxas v. Sandstone Court of Bellevue)*, the mutual-mistake doctrine is applicable in this case. Both parties believed that the contract was being renewed according to the original 1998 terms.

DECISION AND REMEDY: The decision of the district court was reversed, and the case was remanded to have the terms of the contract altered to fit the original terms of the 1998 contract.

SIGNIFICANCE OF THE CASE: This case demonstrates that a mutual mistake can occur even on a straightforward matter, such as the amount of insurance coverage, and that the parties should be held to their original joint assumption rather than the mistake included in the contract.

CRITICAL THINKING

What is fundamentally at issue in this dispute? That is, what basic question do the two sides disagree on? What evidence does each use to defend its position? Do you agree with the court's finding of which side's argument was superior? Why or why not? How might key pieces of evidence have been interpreted differently? Have they been considered in the most appropriate way? Should this change the outcome of the case?

ETHICAL DECISION MAKING

On the basis of the provided information, do your best to sketch the ethical considerations taken into account by each side in this dispute before to the lawsuit. Does your projection paint either side as approaching matters from the ethical high ground? What facts of the case led to your stance, and what ethical guidelines did you use to reach your conclusion? Did you find yourself making any assumptions about behaviors not justified in terms of available information? If so, what do you think caused you to make these assumptions? Why is this sort of phenomenon important to consider in thinking critically about the court's decision?

CONNECTING to the Core

LO 3

Misrepresentation

misrepresentation

An untruthful assertion by one of the parties about a material fact.

innocent misrepresentation

A false statement about a fact material to an agreement that the person who made the statement believed to be true.

scienter

Deliberately or knowingly.

negligent misrepresentation

A false statement of material fact made by a party who thinks it is true but who would have known the truth about the fact had he or she used reasonable care to discover or reveal it.

Misrepresentations are similar to mistakes. In both cases, at least one of the parties is in error about a fact material to the agreement. But a misrepresentation is an untruthful assertion by one of the parties about a material fact. One party said something that prevented the parties from having the mental agreement necessary for a legal contract. The parties only appeared to agree, so their contract lacked legal assent.

The courts are insistent that there must be a meeting of the minds for a valid contract. Thus, they might rescind a contract even though the person making the false assertion was entirely innocent of any intentional deception.

INNOCENT MISREPRESENTATION

An innocent misrepresentation is a false statement about a fact material to an agreement that the person who made the statement believed to be true. The person who made the false statement had no knowledge of the falsity of the claim. We say the person lacked scienter.

Innocent misrepresentations permit the party that was misled by the false statement to rescind the contract. However, because the party that made the false statement had no intent to mislead, the aggrieved party cannot sue for damages. The reasoning in such cases is similar to the arguments in a mutual-mistake case, as you might expect.

NEGLIGENT MISREPRESENTATION

In some contract negotiations, one party makes a statement of material fact that he thinks is true, but he is negligent in making the assertion. Such a negligent misrepresentation results when the party making the statement would have known the truth about the fact had he used reasonable care to discover or reveal it.

Even though there was no actual intent to deceive, the party making the false statement is treated in contract law as if the intent were present. If this standard seems unfair to you, remember that the courts find negligent misrepresentation only when the party making the false statement should have known the truth had she used the skills and competence required of a person in her position or profession. The impact of negligent misrepresentation is identical to that of fraudulent misrepresentations, discussed next.

FRAUDULENT MISREPRESENTATION

Any fraud on the part of a party to a contract provides a basis for rescission. The parties cannot be said to have assented when one of the parties was tricked into the "agreement" by a fraudulent misrepresentation. Thus, the agreement was not voluntary and can be rescinded on the grounds that there was no meeting of the minds.

Even in countries that are trying to encourage joint ventures and global commercial activity, such as the People's Republic of China, fraudulent claims can end the country's hospitality to agreements with outsiders.[4] In China, accusations of outsiders' fraudulent misrepresentation have resulted in heavy fines and even refusals to allow the fraudulent party to enter into any more agreements with Chinese firms. The point is that in most, if not all, cultures there is little judicial sympathy for those who consciously mislead others in commercial activities.

A **fraudulent misrepresentation** is a false representation of a material fact that is consciously false and is intended to mislead the other party. Fraudulent misrepresentation is **intentional misrepresentation**. Here scienter is clear. The party making the misrepresentation either knows or believes that the factual claim is false or knows that there is no basis for the assertion.

To understand the requirements for a finding of fraudulent misrepresentation, start with the two elements from the definition:

fraudulent misrepresentation
A false representation of a material fact that is consciously false and is intended to mislead the other party.

intentional misrepresentation
A false representation of a material fact made by a party who either knows or believes that the factual claim is false or knows that there is no basis for the assertion. Scienter is clear.

1. *A false statement about a past or existing fact that is material to the contract .*
2. *Intent to deceive.* Intent can be inferred from the particular circumstances.

Then add a third necessary element:

3. *Justifiable reliance on the false statement by the innocent party to the agreement.* Justifiable reliance is generally present unless the injured party knew, or should have known by the extravagance of the claim, that the false statement was indeed false. For example, a person could not justifiably rely on a claim by another that a hair on her head, while worth $1,000, was available for $10.

Finally, if damages are sought, the defrauded party must have been injured by the misrepresentation.

Each of these elements can become a source of debate in any attempt to rescind a contract on grounds of fraudulent misrepresentation. Thus, it is your responsibility as a person who will be involved with dozens of contracts in your business activities to know these elements. A rescinded contract is a time-consuming and expensive business opportunity that has gone wrong.

Pay careful attention to the facts in Case 10-2, and decide whether you believe the defendant committed fraud.

[4] Charles D. Paglee, "Contracts and Agreements in the People's Republic of China," www.qis.net/chinalaw/explan1.htm, updated March 6, 1998.

 CASE 10-2

MANDERVILLE v. PCG&S GROUP, INC.
COURT OF APPEAL OF CALIFORNIA,
FOURTH APPELLATE DISTRICT, DIVISION ONE
146 Cal. App. 4th 1486 (2007)

FACTS: *The plaintiff-buyers, the Mandervilles and the Rinears, were looking for a property they could purchase and subdivide so that they could build two homes. Through their agent, Fowler, they found a property in El Cajoh, California. The second MLS listing for the property stated, in part, "All Useable 2.62 Acres County States 1 Acre Min.*

Lot Size Could Be Split." The listing was placed by the sellers, through the defendant brokers, PCG&S Group, Inc. One of the brokers, Clark, placed the language in the listing after talking to a county representative, whose name and gender he could not recall.

The plaintiffs had seen the first MLS listing, which had been posted for 347 days, but did not inquire about the property at that time because it did not contain the language about splitting. Because this language was new, the plaintiffs asked their agent to confirm that the property could be split. The agent called one of the defendant brokers, who told her that the split had been approved by the county. Two days later, the plaintiffs made an offer on a California standard agreement form that included a statement that the buyer had the right to inspect and investigate the property and that the brokers did not guarantee the condition of the property. The form also contained the following paragraph: "All understandings between the parties are incorporated in this Agreement. Its terms are intended by the parties as a final, complete and exclusive expression of their Agreement with respect to its subject matter and may not be contradicted by evidence of any prior agreement or contemporaneous oral agreement."

During the escrow period, the plaintiffs received a disclosure package from the defendant that contained documents indicating that the property was the correct size for splitting but that it had a 24 zoning, which, under the county's master plan, meant the land was "impact-sensitive." After the close of escrow, the buyers hired a civil engineer to submit their request for permission to split the property. The engineer informed them that, in preparing the request, he had discovered that because of the property's designation as impact-sensitive, it could not be split.

The buyers then sued for intentional misrepresentation. The trial court granted summary judgment for the brokers on grounds that the buyers did not reasonably rely on the

misrepresentations because they had not diligently investigated the legal condition of the property and that their agreement contained a clause stating that all representations were incorporated into the agreement. The buyers appealed.

ISSUE: Should a lack of diligence and the existence of an exculpatory clause prohibit a buyer from raising a claim of intentional misrepresentation?

REASONING: Reliance exists when a defendant's misrepresentations are an immediate cause of his taking an action that altered his legal relations, and without which he would not have undertaken such an action. As a general rule, a plaintiff's negligence in failing to investigate a defendant's intentional misstatement is not sufficient to eliminate the possibility that a plaintiff's reliance on the statement was reasonable. The fact that a contract says a plaintiff has a right to investigate the condition of property that is the subject matter of the suit does not mean that he has a duty to do so. And any provision of a contract that would render a defendant not liable for fraud, that is, an exculpatory clause, would be void as a matter of public policy. Thus, the void exculpatory clause cannot render the plaintiff's reliance unreasonable as a matter of law. In this case it was indisputable that the brokers knew that the ability to split the property was questionable and that the ability to split the property might move a property that had sat on the market for a long period of time. Under the circumstances, the plaintiffs should have the opportunity to attempt to prove that they entered into the agreement because of the fraudulent misrepresentations of the defendants.

DECISION AND REMEDY: The summary judgment was reversed, and the plaintiffs will have the opportunity to prove the elements of fraudulent misrepresentation.

SIGNIFICANCE OF THE CASE: This case shows that misrepresentation is serious enough that courts will not let defendants hide behind an exculpatory clause.

CRITICAL THINKING

The issue this case focused on was one aspect of proving fraudulent misrepresentation: reasonable reliance. List the other elements the plaintiffs must prove, and use the available facts to show how they might prove misrepresentation.

ETHICAL DECISION MAKING

What stakeholders are most affected by the outcome of this case?

Let's now revisit each of the elements of fraudulent misrepresentation. While the elements may have seemed relatively straightforward when they were presented, they become more complicated in the context of actual disagreements among parties to a contract.

False Assertion of Fact For fraudulent misrepresentation to be the basis for a contract rescission, the statement of fact need not be an actual assertion. Either concealment or nondisclosure can

Consumer Contracts Law in Japan

In 1997, after studying the application of civil law in the country, the Japanese Social Policy Council, an advisory body to the prime minister, recognized that the environment surrounding consumers was growing more diversified and there was a significant gap between consumers and businesses in their access to information and knowledge as well as in their negotiating power. Because it cannot honestly be said that consumers and businesses are equal, as contracting parties are presumed to be under the country's Civil Code, the council developed a special Consumer Contracts Law. This legislation is considered to place consumers and businesses on a more equal footing in transactions.

Under the Consumer Contracts Law, if a business fails to provide a consumer with information or makes misrepresentations concerning basic or other important contractual matters that are necessary for the consumer to make a judgment about the contract, and if the consumer would not have entered into the contract had the information been provided or the misrepresentation not been made, the consumer may cancel the contract. This provision is applicable whenever a business, in trying to induce a consumer to enter into a contract, (1) fails to provide information about the contents of the contract, (2) fails to provide important information necessary for the consumer to make the decision to enter into the contract, or (3) makes misrepresentations. In many such cases, the consumer would not have been entitled to relief under the Civil Code because of its strict requirements for the application of fraud.

be treated as the equivalent of an actual assertion. **Concealment** involves the *active* hiding of the truth about a material fact, for example, removing 20,000 miles from the odometer on your car before selling it to me. **Nondisclosure** is different because it involves a failure to provide pertinent information about the projected contract. The courts have until recently been hesitant to use nondisclosure as a basis for rescinding a contract because it is a passive form of misleading conduct. Under ordinary situations associated with a legal bargain, it is not the obligation of one party to bring up any and all facts he or she might possess. Each individual is, to a large extent, treated as a responsible decision maker.

However, courts will now find nondisclosure as having the same legal effect as an actual false assertion under certain conditions:

1. *A relationship of trust exists between the parties to the contract.* In this situation the relationship provides a reasonable basis for one person's expectation that the other would never act to defraud him or her.

2. *There is failure to correct assertions of fact that are no longer true in light of events that have occurred since the initial consent to the terms of the agreement.* An illustration is my failing to inform you of the recent outbreak of rust on my "rust-free" car that you have agreed to purchase next month.

Nondisclosure is especially likely to provide the basis for rescission when one party has information about a basic assumption of the deal that is unavailable to the other party. As a result of this logic, sellers have a special duty to disclose because they know more about the structural makeup of the item being purchased.

Intent to Deceive Scienter is present when the party accused of making the fraudulent assertion believed that the assertion was false or made the claim without any regard for whether it was true or false. Alternatively, intent to deceive is present when the party making the false statement claims or implies that he or she has personal knowledge of the accuracy of the assertion. Any resulting assent is not legal because the injured party was not allowed to join the mind of the deceiving party. The party with scienter or intent to deceive wanted the contract to be fulfilled on the basis of a falsehood.

Justifiable Reliance on the False Assertion What responsibilities does the injured party have in instances where a false assertion was made by the other party? As we said earlier, the injured party has no justifiable claim of fraud when he or she relied on assertions that should have been obviously false. Anyone who pays for a house in reliance on the claim that it was "built before the founding of our country" cannot later try to rescind the contract on grounds of fraudulent misrepresentation.

In addition, parties to contracts cannot successfully claim they justifiably relied on a false assertion of fact when the error in the statement would have been clear to anyone who had inspected

concealment
The active hiding of the truth about a material fact.

nondisclosure
A failure to provide pertinent information about a projected contract.

the item being exchanged. However, even this duty to inspect is declining in modern contract law. Increasing responsibility is being placed on the person who made the erroneous assertion.

Before leaving this section about misrepresentation, consider what would have happened if Billy Welkener, in the Case Opener, had known he was going to receive a dramatic increase in his retirement benefits in a few years but failed to tell his then wife, Patricia? Would she be able to claim that the contract lacked assent because of Billy's misrepresentation? Although no evidence was presented to show that Billy knew of such an increase in benefits, it is important to consider all possible situations in determining whether a contract truly did contain assent.

LO 4

Undue Influence

undue influence
The situation in which one person has taken advantage of his or her dominant position in a relationship to unduly persuade the other person to the extent that the dominant person's persuasive efforts have interfered with the other person's ability to make his or her own decision.

When legal assent is present, both parties to the agreement are assumed to have made their own choices based on complete freedom to consent to or reject the terms of the bargain. However, many factors in our lives can work together to make our choices anything but free. Undue influence refers to those special relationships in which one person has taken advantage of his or her dominant position in the relationship to unduly persuade the other person. The persuasive efforts of the dominant person must have interfered with the ability of the other person to make his or her own decision. When people are bargaining with their attorney, doctor, guardian, relative, or anyone else in a relationship involving a high degree of trust, they can be persuaded by unusual pressures unique to that relationship.

CASE Nugget

A Case of Undue Influence

In re Cheryl E. Court of Appeals of California, Second Appellate District, Division Six

161 Cal. App. 3d 587 (1984)

At the time the plaintiff entered into an agreement to give her child up for adoption, she was 41 years old, had eight children, had never worked outside the home, had only a ninth-grade education, and had been receiving aid to dependent children. She had discussed the possibility of giving her baby up for adoption with a caseworker shortly before the child was born. She was evicted from her home the day before the child was born. The caseworker came to the hospital and told her she had to sign forms that would allow the baby, Cheryl, to receive medical care and be removed from the hospital. Shortly thereafter, an adoption worker (AW) met with the plaintiff in the parking lot of the Public Social Services Agency (PSSA) and told her that she could get her child back within a year if she changed her mind but if she did not sign the papers, the child might be given to her husband and his girlfriend. The AW told the plaintiff she did not need to read the document because it just contained everything they had discussed.

Several months later, the plaintiff met with the AW and her supervisor and told them she was ready to take her daughter back, but they told her she could no longer do that because the child had bonded with her foster preadoptive parents, with whom she had been living. The court found that the plaintiff had indeed relinquished her child as a result of fraud and undue influence. The appellate court agreed, finding that the following elements characterized the persuasion of the AW as sufficiently excessive to be indicative of undue influence: (1) discussion and consummation of the transaction in an unusual place, (2) insistent demand that the business be finished at once, (3) extreme emphasis on untoward consequences of delay, and (4) absence of third-party advisers to the subservient party.

Duress in Australia

Australia recognizes a special category of duress that is not set aside for special treatment in the United States: *duress of goods.* Duress of goods occurs whenever an illegitimate threat is made to hold on to goods unless a payment is made or an agreement is entered into. This situation can be contrasted to a situation in which someone legitimately holds on to goods when money is owed on them or the goods have been used as security for a loan.

Australia also recognizes *economic duress,* which is the unacceptable use of economic power to place the victim in a situation in which he or she has no practical alternative but to submit to the accompanying demand.

To prove economic duress, a plaintiff must establish that (1) pressure was used to procure his or her assent to

an agreement or to the payment of money, (2) the pressure was illegitimate in the circumstance, (3) the pressure in fact contributed to the person's assenting to the transaction, and (4) the person's assent to the transaction was reasonable in the circumstances.

Just as with economic duress in the United States, it is often unclear when pressure is illegitimate. A threat to do something unlawful is almost always undue pressure. A threat to use the civil legal process is usually considered lawful, unless the contemplated legal action would clearly be an abuse of process. "Driving a hard bargain" or refusing to do any more business with someone in the future is generally not regarded as economic duress, however.

The assent that results may not be legal consent. The courts may see the undue influence of the relationship as interfering with the free choice required for an enforceable contract. Whatever contracts result from undue influence can be voided.

Are all contracts among parties in situations where undue influence might arise thereby likely to be rescinded? Not necessarily. The courts look to the mental condition of the person who would ordinarily rely on the guidance of the dominant person. Courts look to the extent to which the dominant person used the persuasive powers of his or her dominance to "produce" the assent of the other person.

Factors that enter into the finding of undue influence are the following:

1. Was the dominant party rushing the other party to consent?
2. Did the dominant party gain undue enrichment from the agreement?
3. Was the nondominant party isolated from other advisers at the time of the agreement?
4. Is the contract unreasonable in the sense that the results of the exchange overwhelmingly benefit the dominant party?

The more of these factors present, the more likely a court is to rescind the contract on grounds of undue influence.

DURESS

Duress is a much more visible and active interference with free will than is undue influence. Duress is found when one party was forced into the agreement by the wrongful act of another.

The wrongful act may come in various forms. Any of the following would trigger a successful request for rescission on grounds of duress:

- One party threatens physical harm or extortion to gain consent to a contract.
- One party threatens to file a criminal lawsuit unless consent is given to the terms of the contract. (Threats to file a civil case against a party do not constitute duress unless the suit is frivolous.)
- One party threatens the other's economic interests (this is known as *economic duress*). For instance, Jim refuses to perform according to a contract unless Ellen either signs another contract with him or pays him a higher price than that specified in the original agreement.

duress
Any unlawful act or threat exercised on a person whereby the person is forced to enter into an agreement or to perform some other act against his or her will.

The injured party makes the case for duress by demonstrating that the threat left him or her no reasonable alternatives. The point is that the free will necessary for legal consent had been removed by the specifics of the threat.

Consider the extent to which the threat in Case 10-3 left the plaintiff no reasonable options other than signing the agreement.

FACTS: *In 1982, Ho Sung Kwon fabricated a modeling contest sponsored by Revlon in an attempt to develop a relationship with model Elizabeth Curran. Kwon, as the "supervisor" of the contest, accompanied Curran to Paris, where they were supposed to share a hotel room. Curran refused to stay in the single room with Kwon, and Kwon left the room. However, he had left his passport and $1,200 in cash in the room with Curran. The next morning, when Kwon discovered that his passport and money were missing, he reported the theft. Curran was stopped at the airport, where she was attempting to fly back to New York, and was arrested and held overnight. The French prosecutor set a trial date for two days later, and Curran sought the advice of both French and American counsel. Her father flew to Paris to give her support. Curran was acquitted of all charges. The next day, she signed a release that released Kwon and Revlon from any claims regarding the fabricated contest in return for a payment of $10,260. After Curran returned to the United States, she returned the payment to Kwon and disavowed the release. A year later she filed suit against Kwon and Revlon, alleging negligence, fraudulent misrepresentation, and false arrest. Kwon filed for summary judgment, citing the release Curran had signed. Curran claimed that she had signed the release under duress and that it was voidable. The district court awarded summary judgment to Kwon, and Curran appealed.*

ISSUE: Was Curran reasonable in feeling coerced into signing the release, which would render it voidable due to duress?

REASONING: In the words of Judge Ripple:

Curran makes no claim that she can meet the high standard of proof required under French law to prove the "violence" that

would justify vitiating the contract. Nor, assuming Illinois law did apply, do we believe that she could show the type of coercion contemplated by the governing Illinois cases . . . (defining duress as "a condition where one is induced by a wrongful act or threat of another to make a contract under circumstances which deprive him of the exercise of his free will, and it may be conceded that a contract executed under duress is voidable"). Put simply, she cannot, on this record, demonstrate that her execution of the release was not the product of her free will. As the district court noted, Curran had endured some difficult circumstances in the days before the execution of the release. Nevertheless, it is undisputed that, at the time she executed the document, she had been exonerated of any criminal charges under French law and had been assured that she was free to leave France. The claim that her freedom was contingent on her signing the release is simply not supported by the record. Indeed, she had rejected a settlement offer prior to the disposition of those charges. Moreover, at the time that she executed the release, she had the advice of both her French and American counsel and had familial support through the presence of her father. Under these circumstances, the record simply would not support a determination by the trier of fact that she executed the release under duress. She was not "bereft of the quality of mind essential to the making of a contract."

DECISION AND REMEDY: The court of appeals affirmed the decision of the district court that Curran's agreement to sign the release did not meet the standards of duress in France or in Illinois.

SIGNIFICANCE OF THE CASE: This case shows how strict the standards for duress are and how they can vary according to jurisdiction. Because duress typically requires strong evidence of coercion, a person cannot go back on an agreement because she changes her mind later.

CRITICAL THINKING

Why does Judge Ripple interpret the facts of this case as not logically leading to the plaintiff's being "bereft of the quality of mind essential to the making of a contract"? Are there any key assumptions in this reasoning process?

What models of psychological thought might lead to the conclusion that this situation would produce such a state in the plaintiff? Is Judge Ripple's stance adequately justified? Why or why not?

ETHICAL DECISION MAKING

The ethics of the individual parties directly involved in the relevant circumstances are questionable and interesting. Formulate an argument for whichever party you feel acted in a more ethically acceptable fashion, from the beginning of the provided information up to and including the original lawsuit. Justify your stance in terms of at least one ethical theory.

Defects in Assent in the Philippines

The law in the Philippines is somewhat unusual in the way it limits the time for rescinding a contract. In the Philippines, if consent is given through mistake, violence, intimidation, undue influence, or fraud, contracts are valid until they are annulled. The period within which to annul such a contract is four years. In cases of intimidation, violence, or undue influence, the time period is measured from the time the defect in the assent ceases. In cases of mistake or fraud, it is measured from the time of the discovery of the defect.

Unconscionability

LO 6

A final way to question the appropriateness of consent arises when one of the parties has so much more bargaining power than the other that he or she dictates the terms of the agreement. Such an agreement can be rescinded on grounds of **unconscionability.** The disproportionate amount of power possessed by one party to the contract has made a mockery of the idea of free will, a necessity for legal consent. The resulting contract is called an **adhesion contract.**

Although unconscionability has traditionally been limited to the sale of goods under the Uniform Commercial Code, many courts have not followed that tradition. When they see contracts written by one party and then presented to the other party with the threat to "take it or leave it," courts sometimes extend the idea of unconscionability beyond the sale of goods. Many recent cases on the unconscionability of contracts are based on binding arbitration agreements in employment contracts or in customer contracts, such as cell phone agreements or cable agreements.

In arguing for a switch from a dollar amount to a percentage, Patricia Welkener, in the Case Opener, claimed that the contract she entered into was unconscionable. Her argument was that the mistake of using an amount and not a percentage would preclude her award from ever increasing. As such, each month she would be cheated out of money to which she was entitled. As the months go by, the unfairness would be compounded, ultimately making the enforcement of the contract unconscionable. Do you think the court agreed with Patricia Welkener's logic?

unconscionability
Grounds for rescinding an unconscionable contract.

adhesion contract
A contract created by a party to an agreement that is presented to the other party on a take-it-or-leave-it basis.

···▶ SUMMARY

The Importance of Genuine Assent	If assent is not genuine, or legal, a contract may be voidable. For purposes of planning, it is important for people to understand the circumstances under which failure of assent may render their contracts voidable.
Mistake	*Mistakes* are erroneous beliefs about the material facts of a contract at the time the agreement is made. They may be either unilateral or mutual. Only under certain rare conditions are unilateral mistakes a basis for rescinding a contract. However, if both parties to a contract are mistaken about a material fact, either can opt to rescind the contract. In cases of mutual mistake, the agreement was not based on a meeting of the minds, a basic criterion for legal assent.
Misrepresentation	*Misrepresentation* is an intentional untruthful assertion by one of the parties about a material fact. An innocent misrepresentation occurs when the party making the false assertion believes it to be true. The misled party may rescind the contract. When a misrepresentation is fraudulent, any assent that is given is gained by deceit. The courts permit rescission for fraudulent misrepresentation. In addition to requiring false assertion and the intent to deceive, fraudulent misrepresentation also requires justifiable reliance on the assertion by the innocent party.
Undue Influence	*Undue influence* refers to the persuasive efforts of a dominant party who uses a special relationship with another party to interfere with that other's free choice of the terms of a contract. Any relationship in which one party has an unusual degree of trust in the other can trigger concern about undue influence in gaining the assent of the more dependent party.

Duress *Duress* occurs when one party threatens the other with a wrongful act unless assent is given. Such assent is not legal assent because coercion interferes with the threatened party's free will. For a court to rescind the agreement, the injured party must demonstrate that the duress left no reasonable alternatives to agreeing to the contract.

Unconscionability *Unconscionability* may be a basis for avoiding a contract if one party has so much relative bargaining power that he or she, in effect, dictates the terms of the contract. The resulting agreement is an adhesion contract.

----▶ Point/Counterpoint

The principles of legal assent are based on the belief that, in the main, each person can look out for himself or herself. Thus, parties are usually held to the agreements they make on the grounds that the terms were reached by decisions guided by the free wills of both parties. But we live in a world of rapid technological change, where chemicals, fibers, and services come in a blinding array of complexity, that could make decision making more difficult for some people.

Should Courts Provide More Protection from Agreements Based on Lack of Knowledge on the Part of the Buyer?	
YES	**NO**
Courts should protect buyers from assent that is based on ignorance. For an assent to be worthy of legal protection, the buyer must appreciate what he or she has agreed to purchase. Otherwise, contract law protects the strong from the weak. For assent to be a cornerstone of a fair legal framework, it must flow from something other than large-scale misunderstanding about the safety, composition, and longevity of what we purchase. Just go to any grocery store and ask yourself, "How much do I know about what I am about to assent to purchase?"	Existing contract law already contains adequate protection against severe cases of buyer confusion. Much of this chapter contains reasoning that buyers could use in certain instances to rescind an agreement. What is especially disturbing about the suggestion that courts should provide more protection for parties to a contract is the danger the suggestion poses for personal liberty and independence. What will happen to our incentive to learn and grow as individuals if we know that the local judge and jury are ready to protect us from our own failures to discover more about goods and services that we plan to purchase?

----▶ Questions & Problems

1. Explain the difference between a unilateral mistake and a mutual mistake.
2. Explain when a unilateral mistake can lead to a contract's being voidable.
3. Distinguish innocent misrepresentation from fraudulent misrepresentation.
4. Explain how nondisclosure can be treated as misrepresentation.
5. Explain the primary differences between duress and undue influence.
6. Olga Mestrovic, the wife of an internationally known sculptor and artist, died owning a number of his works of art. Her will directed that all the artwork be sold, with the proceeds split among the surviving family members. She also owned real estate that, likewise, was to be sold. The executor, 1st Source Bank, sold the real estate to Wilkins, along with specified pieces of personal property that were in the house, such as the refrigerator, stove, and French scones. When Wilkins took possession of the property, he complained to the bank that the property was a mess. The bank said it would either hire a rubbish removal service or allow Wilkins to clean it up and pay him for doing so.

In the process of cleaning up, Wilkins discovered eight drawings and one sculpture done by the artist.

Wilkins claimed that he owned these items under his agreement with the bank, but the bank sought to recover them. The probate court ruled that there was no contract for the sale of the works of art. What argument do you think Wilkins made on appeal? How do you think the court ruled? Why? [*Wilkins v. 1st Source Bank,* 548 N.E.2d 170 (Ind. Ct. App. 1990).]

7. A dealer in Seminole County, Florida, contacted Harley-Davidson to secure authorization to sell the dealership to PowerSports. Harley had questions about their business model to make sure it would meet the requirements Harley-Davidson had established for its dealers. Based on the answers provide by Power-Sports, the transfer of the dealership was approved. Shortly after approving the transfer, Harley-Davidson discovered that PowerSports had not intended to operate its dealership in accordance with the Harley business model which the firm required all dealerships to follow. Harley sued to rescind the transfer of the dealership on grounds that providing false answers to Harley-Davidson's queries during the negotiation of the transfer constituted misrepresentation. Harley also sought compensatory damages and punitive damages. The trial court held for PowerSports, and Harley-Davidson appealed. How do you think the appellate court resolved the appeal? Why? [*Harley-Davidson Motor Co. v. PowerSports, Inc.,* 319 F.3d 973 (7th Cir., 2003).]

8. In December 1992, Koontz entered into an agreement with Tatum & Denziger (T & D), an architectural firm, whereby the firm was to design a residence for Koontz at a price of 10 percent of the actual cost of construction. When the parties entered into the agreement, T & D estimated that the entire process, from design through final construction, should be able to be completed in less than 24 months. Koontz received the first plans in January 1993, sent them back for modification, and got the second set back on June 10, 1994. At that time, T & D estimated that the cost of construction would be $800,000. Koontz took bids for construction from three preselected contractors, and the bids he received ranged from $983,000 to $1,200,000. Koontz immediately terminated his contract with T & D and asked that all architectural fees paid through the date of the termination be returned. T & D offered to continue working on the project and suggested revisions to lower costs, but Koontz refused. He ultimately hired a different architect, who designed a house that Koontz constructed for $870,000.

After the house was completed in 1996, Koontz sued T & D for, among other claims, negligent misrepresentation, alleging that T & D negligently represented that the cost of the construction phase of the project would be significantly lower, that the design phase could be completed in a reasonable time, and that the architect's fees would be reasonable. T & D filed a motion for summary judgment, which was granted. What do you believe the outcome of Koontz's appeal was? Why? [*Koontz v. Thomas and Denzinger,* 1999 WL 31459 (S.C. App.).]

9. Audrey Vokes was a 51-year-old widow who wanted to become an "accomplished dancer." She was invited to attend a "dance party" at J. P. Davenports' School of Dancing, an Arthur Murray franchise. She subsequently signed up for dance classes, at which she received elaborate praise. Her instructor initially sold her eight half-hour dance lessons for $14.50 each, to be used one each month. Eventually, after being continually told that she had excellent potential and that she was developing into a beautiful dancer—when in fact she was not developing her dance ability and had no aptitude for dance—she ended up purchasing a total of 2,302 hours' worth of dance lessons for a total of $31,090.45. When it finally became clear to Vokes that she was not developing her dance skills, in part because she had trouble even hearing the musical beat, she sued Arthur Murray. What would be the basis of her argument? Her case was initially dismissed by the trial court. What do you think the result of her appeal was? [*Vokes v. Arthur Murray,* 212 So. 2d 906 (1968).]

10. Arnold Olson and his now deceased spouse deeded their property to their six children in perpetuity until they die. During a subsequent conversation with his son and daughter-in-law, held in the presence of two of the other children, he granted his son part of that property, which included the home and several buildings. He told the son and his wife that he would give him the part of the property with the buildings on it as long as they did not sell the property while he was alive, because he wanted to live in a trailer on the property. He then executed a second deed conveying the property, but he failed to include the life estate in this second deed.

The father lived in his trailer on the property for four years. Then the son told him that he would have to move because they were selling the property. The father and the other children sued to have the contract reformed on the grounds of mistake. The trial court agreed and reformed the contract to include the provision for the father's life estate. Why do you think the appellate court either affirmed or reversed the lower court's decision? [*Olson v. Olson,* 1998 WL 170111.]

11. The Winklers were interested in purchasing a home in the Valleyview Farms housing development. They contacted the developer, Galehouse, and selected a lot that cost $57,000. They asked the developer to show them plans for houses for which the construction

costs would range from $180,000 to $190,000, indicating that this was the price they would be willing to spend for construction only and wasn't to include the lot price. The developer gave them several books and plans to look at.

After the Winklers had several conversations with Galehouse, he drafted plans for a 2,261-square-foot house and gave the Winklers a quote of $198,000 for construction. The lot price was not included. After several months of adding options and upgrades to the plan, the cost rose to $242,000, excluding the lot. The parties then engaged in a couple of weeks of negotiations regarding the price of the construction and lot. Eventually they reached a compromise of a total price of $291,000 ($243,000 for the construction and $48,000 for the lot.)

Galehouse prepared a written contract to reflect the parties' agreement, but he forgot to include the lot price. The Winklers paid Galehouse $48,000, the lot price, as a deposit on the contract. When the construction was completed, and the Winklers were finalizing their loan from the bank, the parties discovered the drafting error. Galehouse sued to have the contract reformed to reflect the agreed-on price. Should the contract be reformed? Why or why not? [*Galehouse v. Winkler*, 1998 WL 312527.]

12. Plaintiff Stirlen was the chief financial officer for Supercuts. On numerous occasions, he informed Lipson, to whom he reported directly, and other corporate officers of various operating problems he felt contributed to the general decline in Supercuts' retail profits and of "accounting irregularities" he feared might be in violation of state and federal statutes and regulations. After Stirlen brought his concerns to the company's auditor, Lipson allegedly reprimanded him, accused him of being a "troublemaker," and

told him that if he did not reverse his position on the issues taken to the auditor he would no longer be considered a "member of the team." Stirlen was terminated the following month, and he subsequently filed suit for wrongful discharge. Supercuts' general counsel moved to compel arbitration under the compulsory arbitration provision of the employment contract between the parties.

The contract provided that all claims arising out of an individual's employment, including civil rights actions and tort claims, must be submitted to arbitration within one year of the date on which the dispute arose, or the employee waives his right to pursue the claim. Damages that could be awarded through arbitration were limited to "a money award not to exceed the amount of actual damages for breach of contract, less any proper offset for mitigation of such damages, and the parties shall not be entitled to any other remedy at law or in equity, including but not limited to other money damages, punitive damages, specific performance, and/or injunctive relief." In the event that an employee did submit a dispute to arbitration, the employee's employment would immediately cease, as would any claims he had to unpaid benefits, without any penalty to the company, pending the outcome of the arbitration.

The agreement did not totally prevent the use of the courts, however. It provided that the following need not be submitted to arbitration: "Any action initiated by the Company seeking specific performance or injunctive or other equitable relief in connection with any breach . . . of this Agreement."

The trial court found that this agreement was unconscionable. How do you believe the appellate court ruled on this case? Why? [*Stirlen v. Supercuts, Inc., et al.*, 51 Cal. App. 1519 (1997).]

Looking for more review material?

The Online Learning Center at **www.mhhe.com/kubasekess** contains this chapter's "Assignment on the Internet" and also a list of URLs for more information, entitled "On the Internet." Find both of them in the Student Center portion of the OLC, along with quizzes and other helpful materials.

Contracts in Writing and Third-Party Contracts

----▶ CASE OPENER

Fallout from a Forgettable Fight

On June 28, 1997, in Las Vegas, Nevada, heavyweight boxers Mike Tyson and Evander Holyfield met for what was to be a night to remember. During the third round of the fight, a desperate Tyson bit off a piece of Evander Holyfield's ear. The fight continued until moments later when Tyson bit Holyfield's other ear.[1] Tyson was disqualified, and numerous fans were unhappy with the outcome. Some fans were so outraged they decided to sue Tyson, the fight promoters, and the telecasters, seeking a refund.[2] The fans sued on the basis of, among other theories, a claim to being third-party beneficiaries to various contracts into which the defendants had entered.

1. Are the fans entitled to refunds based on a theory of third-party beneficiary rights? What type of beneficiaries would the fans have to be able to enforce contractual rights?

2. If you were one of the fight promoters, what sorts of contractual duties would you have to the viewers?

[1]CNN/SI, "Year in Review 1997," http://sportsillustrated.cnn.com/features/1997/yearinreview/topstories.
[2]*Castillo v. Tyson,* 268 A.D.2d 336 (2000).

----▶ LEARNING OBJECTIVES

After reading this chapter, you will be able to answer the following questions:

LO 1 What types of contracts fall within the Statute of Frauds?

LO 2 What are the requirements for a writing to satisfy the statute of frauds?

LO 3 What does the parol evidence rule do?

LO 4 What is the difference between an assignment and a delegation?

LO 5 What does it mean to say that the assignee stands in the shoes of the assignor?

LO 6 What is the difference between an intended and an incidental beneficiary?

LO 7 What is the difference between a creditor and a donee beneficiary?

Written contracts provide certain advantages oral contracts lack. Where disputes may arise regarding the specifics of the terms of an oral contract, such disputes are easier to settle when the contractual terms are solidified in writing. In addition, when parties to a contract write down their terms, the moment of writing allows both parties to reconsider their terms and ensure that the parties are advocating what they desire in the contract. In general, written contracts help business contracting flow more smoothly.

The idea of requiring that certain contracts be in writing comes from the English "Act for the Prevention of Frauds and Perjuries," passed in 1677. To prevent disputes over the existence of a contract, the act required that certain types of contracts, to be legally enforced, must be in writing and be signed by the party denying the existence of the contract. In the United States, the term *statute of frauds* is somewhat misleading, because there is no federal statute of frauds; rather, such legislation exists at the state level, with the exception of Louisiana. Maryland and New Mexico have statutes of frauds created by judicial decision rather than legislation. Interestingly, the English have repealed almost all their requirements for writing, while American states and courts are still expanding the requirements for what falls within the statute of frauds. The term *statute of frauds* is also misleading in another way: The statute of frauds does not relate to fraudulent contracts, nor does it address the issue of illegal contracts. Rather, the statute addresses the enforceability of contracts that fail to meet the requirements set forth in the statute. Furthermore, the statute serves to protect promisors from poorly considered oral contracts by requiring that certain contracts be in writing.

This chapter addresses some commonalities among the statutes of frauds of different states, while referring simply to the "statute of frauds" as if it were a unitary law. The chapter examines which contracts need to be in writing, as well as exceptions to the rule. Then the chapter examines the parol evidence rule, which discusses what types of oral evidence are admissible, and when, as related to contracts within the scope of the statute of frauds. The chapter concludes with a discussion of third party

Although a contract is typically an agreement between two parties, sometimes third parties have rights in the contract as well, either through assignments or as beneficiaries. The second half of this chapter focuses on how third parties gain rights to contracts.

Statute of Frauds

statute of frauds
State-level legislation that addresses the enforceability of contracts that fail to meet the requirements set forth in the statute; serves to protect promisors from poorly considered oral contracts by requiring that certain contracts be in writing.

LO 1

The statute of frauds has three main purposes. The first is to ease contractual negotiations by requiring sufficiently reliable evidence to prove the existence and specific terms of a contract. The second is to prevent unreliable oral evidence from interfering with a contractual relationship. Requiring a written contract prevents the admittance of oral evidence denying or substantially altering the contract. (This chapter discusses the admissibility, or lack thereof, of oral evidence later, in the section on the parol evidence rule.) The third is to prevent parties from entering into contracts with which they do not agree. The statute's requirements impose on parties the need to carefully consider the terms, agree to them, write them down, and sign the contract.

Contracts Falling within the Statute of Frauds

As previously stated, only specific types of contracts fall within the statute of frauds and thus are required to be evidenced in writing (see Figure 11-1). These types of contracts are (1) contracts whose terms prevent possible performance within one year, (2) promises made in consideration of marriage, (3) contracts for one party to pay the debt of another if the initial party fails to pay,

Figure 11-1

Contracts Falling
within the Statute
of Frauds

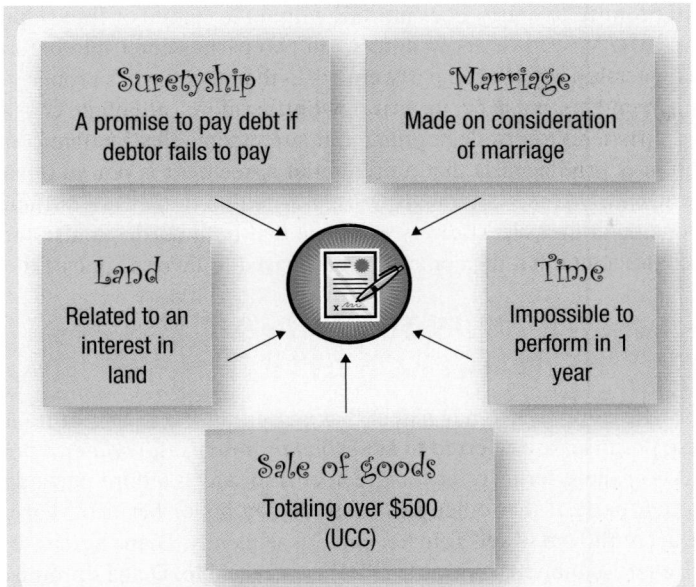

and (4) contracts related to an interest in land. Although required to be in writing under the Uniform Commercial Code (UCC), and not the statute of frauds, a related fifth category is contracts for the sale of goods totaling more than $500.[3]

CONTRACTS WHOSE TERMS PREVENT POSSIBLE PERFORMANCE WITHIN ONE YEAR

Contracts whose performance, based on the terms of the contract, could not possibly occur within one year fall within the statute of frauds and, therefore, must be in writing.[4] It is important to realize that the one-year period begins to run the day after the contract is created, *not* when the contract is scheduled to begin.

 The test for compliance with the one-year rule is not related to the likelihood of the completion of the contract within one year. Rather, the test considers the *possibility* of completing the contract within one year. For example, if Robert contracts with Elise for lifetime employment, they do not have to write and sign the agreement because it is possible for the contract to be completed within one year: Robert could die after two days of work. Moreover, Robert and Elise's contract, if oral, would be enforceable, as it is not within the statute of frauds. The possibility that a contract's terms could be performed within one year removes the contract from the statute's written requirements. Similarly, contracts for complex construction projects need not be in writing because, theoretically, they can be completed within one year if the crew works around the clock every day, even if the scenario is highly unlikely.

PROMISES MADE IN CONSIDERATION OF MARRIAGE

Agreements regarding marriage in which one party is gaining something other than a return on his or her promise to marry are within the statute of frauds and must be in writing.[5] In other words, when one party promises something to the other as part of an offer of marriage, the contract must be in writing to be enforceable.

 It is important to realize that mutual promises to marry do not fall within the statute of frauds. For example, if Ed and Jeanie promise each other they will get married, this agreement does not need to be in writing, as it does not fall within the statute.

[3] UCC § 2-201.

[4] Restatement (Second) of Contracts, sec. 130.

[5] Restatement (Second) of Contracts, sec. 124.

While a mutual promise to marry does not fall within the statute of frauds, prenuptial agreements do. A prenuptial agreement is an agreement two parties enter into before marriage that clearly states the ownership rights each party enjoys in the other party's property. To be enforceable, prenuptial agreements must be in writing. Furthermore, although consideration is not legally required, courts tend to privilege prenuptial agreements that involve consideration. The reason consideration is privileged is that a prenuptial agreement is not automatically enforceable just because it is in writing. Although writing is required, it is not sufficient to establish enforceability. Consideration at least offers evidence that both parties understand and agree to the terms of the contract and that the contract is not biased in favor of one of the parties.

CONTRACTS FOR ONE PARTY TO PAY THE DEBT OF ANOTHER IF THE INITIAL PARTY FAILS TO PAY

The contracts involving promises to pay a debt that are within the statute of frauds are of a very limited kind. These promises are referred to as *secondary promises, collateral promises,* or *suretyship promises.* All of these terms refer to agreements in which a third party agrees to pay the debt owed by another party if that other party fails to pay his or her debt. For example, Helen enters into a contract with Tom to sell Tom her car. Subsequently, Diana agrees to pay Tom's debt if he fails to pay Helen the money he owes her. To be enforceable, Diana's promise needs to be in writing because it is within the statute.

It is important to understand the distinction between primary and secondary obligations to know when the statute necessitates a written agreement. *Primary obligations* are debts entered into in an initial contract. Using our car-sale example, the primary obligation is Tom's promise to pay Helen for the car. Primary obligations are not within the statute of frauds and, therefore, need not be in writing to be enforceable.

Secondary obligations, however, are within the statute and need to be in writing. A *secondary obligation*, as explained above, arises when a party outside a primary agreement promises to fulfill one of the original party's (the primary debtor's) obligations if the original party (primary debtor) fails to fulfill his or her obligation.

A specific instance of a secondary obligation involves the administrator or executor of an estate. Administrators and executors of estates are responsible for paying the debts of an estate and then dividing the remaining wealth among the heirs. While an agreement to pay the estate's debts with the estate's funds need not be in writing, promises the administrator or executor makes to pay those debts personally are within the statute of frauds and must be in writing. Because the administrator or executor is paying with his or her own money, and not the estate's, the promises must be in writing to be enforceable—the administrator or executor has assumed a secondary obligation.

There is an exception as to when a promise to pay someone else's debt needs to be in writing: *the main-purpose rule.* If the main purpose for incurring a secondary obligation is to obtain a personal benefit, the promise does not fall within the statute and need not be in writing.[6] The assumption is that a party attempting to achieve a personal benefit will not back out of the agreement, and thus there is no need for a written record of the agreement. The court's job is to use the context surrounding the agreement to determine the third party's main purpose for entering the agreement.

CONTRACTS RELATED TO AN INTEREST IN LAND

Under the statute of frauds, land is considered real property, such as the land and soil itself, as well as anything attached to the land, such as trees or buildings. The statute is intended to prevent oral claims to the existence of a contract for the sale of land. That is, because the statute requires a writing as evidence of the contract, a claim to an oral contract for the sale of land is not enough to prove such a contract existed.

In addition to contracts for the sale of land, contracts transferring other interests in land are also within the statute of frauds. Mortgages and leases are within the statute of frauds because they are considered transfers of interest in land.

[6] Restatement (Second) of Contracts, sec. 116.

England and the Statute of Fraud

As stated in the text, England gave birth to the statute of frauds. While the United States, in addition to numerous other Western countries, has subsequently adopted versions of the 1677 English act, the English have gone in the opposite direction. Instead of expanding the powers and use of the 1677 act, the English have severely limited the number of cases falling within their statute of frauds.

Although formal complaints were levied against the English statute of frauds as early as 1937, no action was taken until 1953. In that year, the Law Reform Committee addressed numerous arguments that had been made in 1937 in favor of repeal of the statute of frauds. The 1953 committee recommended that Parliament repeal Section 4 of the 1677 act, the section that identified the specific types of contracts that must be in writing. The Law Reform Act of 1954 subsequently repealed Section 4, with one cautionary exception: The 1954 act still required that promises to pay for the debt of others be in writing. In other words, the only provision still active (requiring a writing) under the statute of frauds in the country that invented the statute is what we would call *suretyship* or *collateral* promise.

Determining exactly what constitutes an interest in land under the statute of frauds is difficult. While the sale of land and the transfer of mortgages and leases are within the statute, a number of things that seem as if they are interests in land do not fall within the statute. For example, promises to sell crops annually, agreements between parties for profit sharing from the sale of real property, and boundary disputes that have been settled through the use of land are not within the statute of frauds and, therefore, do not require evidence in writing. The Case Nugget presents a case related to land in which the parties disagreed as to whether a writing was needed.

CASE Nugget

What Is an "Interest in Land"?

Shelby's, Inc. v. Sierra Bravo, Inc.
Court of Appeals of Missouri, Southern District

68 S.W.3d 604 (2002)

Shelby's and Sierra entered into a written agreement in which Shelby's granted Sierra permission to use Shelby's land as disposal for waste and debris Sierra removed as part of the construction of a new highway. Shelby's claimed that the parties also entered into an oral contract for Sierra to construct a waterway and building pad on Shelby's property. Sierra never completed the construction and denied that an oral contract existed. Shelby's sued, and the jury found in its favor.

Sierra appealed on the basis that the oral agreement was within the statute of frauds and therefore unenforceable. Sierra saw the alleged oral agreement as involving a sale of an interest in land, which is within the statute of frauds. Therefore, the agreement, to be enforceable, would have had to be in writing.

The court firmly disagreed with Sierra's argument. The court stated:

> We agree with the well-reasoned argument of Respondent [Shelby's]. The contract in this case was not a "sale," much less a sale of an interest in lands. . . . Here, there was no transfer of ownership or title. The written agreement gave Appellant [Sierra] permission to deposit debris and soil on Respondent's land, not the right to do so. The oral contract was for the construction of a waterway and building pad and passed no interest in the land. . . . We decline to create a new category to which the statute of frauds applies, that of a contract for services for the deposit of dirt and soil on land. The trial court did not err in denying Appellant's motion for judgment notwithstanding the verdict. Appellant's point is denied and the judgment of the trial court is affirmed.

CONTRACTS FOR THE SALE OF GOODS TOTALING MORE THAN $500

Agreements in which the total price for a sale is $500 or more are required by the UCC, Section 2-201, to be recorded in a written contract or a memorandum. To satisfy this UCC requirement, the contract or memorandum need only state the quantity to be sold. Buyer, seller, price, and method of payment do not need to be included in the writing according to the UCC. Contractual terms beyond quantity may be written, but they need not be. In fact, terms other than quantity can be inexact or be left out of the writing as long as what is written does not contradict the parties' agreement. The contract will be enforceable for the stated quantity and not a unit more. Furthermore, for the contract to be enforceable against a party, the party against whom action is sought must have signed the written document.

In addition to sales contracts for $500 or more, there are other specific situations under the UCC for contracts that need to be in writing. These situations are contracts involving the sale of securities[7] and personal property[8] if the sale is greater than $5,000 in price.

FURTHER REQUIREMENTS SPECIFIC TO CERTAIN STATES

As discussed at the beginning of the chapter, the statute of frauds is actually state law. Consequently, certain states have various requirements not found in other states. While these requirements are not universal, it is important to note some of the distinctive elements of the statutes of frauds in a minority of the states.

Some states require a writing within the statute of frauds under what is called the *equal dignity rule*. Under the equal dignity rule, contracts that would normally fall under the statute and need a writing if negotiated by the principal must be in writing even if negotiated by an agent.

Within their statutes of frauds, a minority of states have special provisions related to promises to pay debt. One example pertains to a promise to pay a debt that has already been discharged because of bankruptcy. For such an agreement to be enforceable, it must be in writing to prevent the promisor from hiding behind the fact that the debt has been discharged. Another example involves a promise to pay a debt where collection of the debt is barred by a statute of limitations. As in the first example, if the agreement is not in writing, the promisor can easily prove that he or she does not need to pay. Therefore, the statutes of frauds in certain states require that both of these types of promises be in writing to be enforceable.

Exceptions to the Statute of Frauds

As with most legal rules, there are certain exceptions to which the statute of frauds does not apply, even though under normal circumstances it would. These exceptions are (1) admission, (2) partial performance, (3) promissory estoppel, and (4) although not under the statute of frauds, exceptions under the UCC.

ADMISSION

An admission is a statement made in court, under oath, or at some stage during a legal proceeding in which a party against whom charges have been brought admits that an oral contract existed, even though the contract was required to be in writing.[9] All states except Louisiana and California adhere to the admission exception. To the extent that the statute of frauds is intended to necessitate proper evidence of agreements, the admission exception is well reasoned. However, to the extent that the statute of frauds is intended to cause people to be cautious about clearly establishing the specifics of their agreements, the admission exception seems to unnecessarily punish honest parties while rewarding dishonest ones.

equal dignity rule
A rule requiring that contracts that would normally fall under the statute of frauds and need a writing if negotiated by the principal must be in writing even if negotiated by an agent.

admission
A statement made in court, under oath, or at some stage during a legal proceeding in which a party against whom charges have been brought admits that an oral contract existed, even though the contract was required to be in writing.

[7] UCC § 8-319.

[8] UCC § 81-206.

[9] Restatement (Second) of Contracts, sec. 133.

Similar to the statute of frauds, the UCC makes a comparable exception in cases where parties admit to the existence of an oral contract. However, unlike the statute of frauds, the UCC specifies that an oral contract required to be in writing but admitted to in court will be enforceable only for the quantity admitted.[10]

PARTIAL PERFORMANCE

Although the statute of frauds requires a writing for sales of interests in land, there is an exception based on the theory of partial performance. Under **partial performance,** if the buyer in an alleged contract for the sale of land has paid any portion of the sales price and either has begun to permanently improve the land or has taken possession of the land, the courts will consider the contract partially performed, and this partial performance will amount to proof of the contract.

Accordingly, partial performance can override the statute's requirement for a written agreement. The logic is that the actions of both parties demonstrate the existence of their agreement, so the agreement no longer needs to be in writing to be enforceable, even though a writing would otherwise be needed. Under similar sections of the UCC, a buyer or seller is responsible for an oral contract, which should have been in writing, to the extent that he or she accepts payment or delivery of the goods in question.[11]

partial performance
An exception to the statute of frauds in which the performance of portions of an unwritten agreement by one or both parties can constitute proof that an oral contract exists between the parties.

PROMISSORY ESTOPPEL

Under certain circumstances, when a party relies on an oral contract that is within the statute of frauds, and therefore should have been in writing, the reliance can create a situation in which the contract is enforceable. **Promissory estoppel** is the legal enforcement of an otherwise unenforceable contract due to a party's detrimental reliance on the contract.

For promissory estoppel to be in effect, the party's reliance must be to their own detriment. Furthermore, the reliance must have been reasonably foreseeable; that is, the party who did not rely on the contract should have known that the other party was going to rely on it.[12]

Suppose that, after accepting an offer on your current house, you enter into a contract to buy a house. However, the new house costs more than the sales price of your old house, and the person from whom you are buying knows about the sale of your old house and the difference in the prices. To pay for the price difference, you sell your collection of rare coins. Unfortunately, during this whole process, you forgot to create a written contract for the purchase of the new house. The other person now refuses to sell the house to you. You are now homeless and have sold off your only real assets. Because the other person reasonably should have known you were relying on the contract, and because you did so to your own detriment, under promissory estoppel you could win performance of the oral sales contract.

promissory estoppel
The legal enforcement of an otherwise unenforceable contract due to a party's detrimental reliance on the contract.

EXCEPTIONS UNDER THE UCC

In addition to the exceptions under the statute of frauds, exceptions also exist under the UCC as to when a contract ordinarily required to be in writing need not be in writing. For instance, under the UCC, oral contracts between merchants need not be in writing to be enforceable. Therefore, if one merchant agrees to sell goods to another, the contract is enforceable even if it is not in writing.

Likewise, oral contracts for customized goods are enforceable even if they would normally have to be in writing. The reasoning is that customized goods are not likely to be able to be sold to a general audience. Accordingly, if one party backs out of an oral arrangement for the sale of customized goods, the party that did not back out probably incurred unreasonable costs due to the negated contract. To prevent one party from bearing the cost of a canceled contract, the UCC allows oral agreements to be enforced when they are for customized goods.

[10] UCC § 2-201(3)(b).

[11] UCC § 2-201(3)(c).

[12] Restatement (Second) of Contracts, sec. 139.

CONNECTING to the Core

Management

As management classes stress, writing is an essential skill. One attribute of an effective business manager or lawyer is the ability to write well, and the more writing practice you have now, the more likely you are to be an effective writer in your professional career. Contracts under the statute of frauds are one example in which a business manager or lawyer is required to demonstrate her or his writing skills. But a business manager may engage frequently in other written communication, especially via e-mail, which tends to induce individuals to use a more relaxed, informal writing style, even though informalities via e-mail may not be appropriate in a professional setting.

Although this brief overview cannot provide an exhaustive list of writing principles, a few important principles you should keep in mind include knowing your purpose for the written communication, having a developed strategy for the writing (e.g., placing reasons in order from most important to least important, or least controversial to most controversial), avoiding ambiguity, using the active voice instead of the passive, and having a clear layout. These principles, if developed, will benefit you as a business manager, whether you draft a contract under the statute of frauds or merely engage regularly in written communications with a supervisor or client.

Source: K. Williams, *Management: A Practical Introduction* (New York: McGraw-Hill/Irwin, 2006), p. 507.

LO 2 Sufficiency of the Writing

Although there are no specific requirements for the form of a written contract under the statute of frauds, certain elements need to be present for a writing to constitute proper evidence of a written contract under the statute. It is worth mentioning that, in the absence of a single standard form, multiple documents can together evidence the existence of a written agreement under the statute.

Required elements in the writing include the identification of the parties to the contract, the subject of the agreement, the consideration if any is given, and any pertinent terms of the contract. Furthermore, the contract must be signed, but the signature does not need to be located at the end, which is the traditional location for a signature. In fact, the signature need not be the full signature; a mark, such as an initial, is permissible as long as the mark is placed with the intent that it function as a signature. While it is standard for both parties to sign the agreement, because the writing is being offered as proof of an agreement, only the party against whom action is sought needs to have signed the writing. If only one party signed, the agreement is enforceable against the signing party but not against the nonsigning party. The required elements can be contained in a memorandum, a written document, or a compilation of several written documents.

The requirements under the UCC for sales contracts vary slightly from those under the statute of frauds. The UCC does not require that the parties be named in the agreement. Rather, the UCC requires that the writing clearly state the quantity to be sold. Similar to the statute of frauds, the UCC allows a variety of written documents to constitute a writing. Some documents that count include faxes, e-mails, invoices, bills of lading, sales slips, checks, or any combination of these documents.

Also noteworthy is the fact that oral testimony can be elicited that establishes the existence of a writing that would meet the requirements under the statute of frauds. For example, testimony regarding an invoice for products sold, when the actual invoice is not produced, is enough in certain states to meet the requirements under the statute.

Case 11-1 demonstrates how judges go about determining what constitutes a writing and when a writing is sufficient under the statute of frauds.

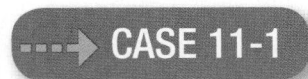

STEWART LAMLE v. MATTEL, INC.
U.S. COURT OF APPEALS FOR THE FEDERAL CIRCUIT
394 F.3d 1355 (2005)

FACTS: *Steward Lamle is the inventor of Farook, a board game. Lamle obtained two patents for Farook from the U.S. Patent and Trademark Office and negotiated with Mattel, Inc., regarding the licensing of Farook by Mattel. Early in the negotiations, Lamle signed Mattel's standard Product Disclosure Form, which contained the following provision:*

> *I understand that . . . no obligation is assumed by [Mattel] unless and until a formal written contract is agreed to and entered into, and then the obligation shall be only that which is expressed in the formal, written contract.*

The negotiations advanced, and a meeting was held on June 11 at which the parties discussed the terms of a licensing agreement. At the meeting, Mattel and Lamle agreed on many terms of the license, including a three-year term, the geographic scope, the schedule for payment, and the percentage royalty. Mattel asked Lamle to "draft a formal document memorializing 'the Deal'" and "promised [that] it would sign a formal, written contract before January 1, 1998."

Mattel employee Mike Bucher subsequently sent Lamle an e-mail entitled "Farook Deal" on June 26 that substantially repeated the terms agreed to at the June 11 meeting. The e-mail stated that the terms "have been agreed in principal [sic] by . . . Mattel subject to contract." The salutation "Best regards Mike Bucher" appears at the end of the email.

On October 8, Mattel notified Lamle of its decision not to go ahead with the production of Farook. Lamle filed action asserting, inter alia, a claim of breach of contract. The district court granted summary judgment in favor of Mattel on all claims. The court of appeals vacated that grant of summary judgment and remanded the case to the district court. The district court on remand again granted summary judgment in favor of Mattel on all claims. Lamle appealed again.

ISSUE: Does the e-mail from Mike Bucher constitute a writing that satisfies the statute of frauds?

REASONING: A writing that satisfies the statute of frauds must contain all the material terms of the contract (but not necessarily all the details of the contract) and be signed by the party being sued for enforcement. In his June 26 e-mail Bucher wrote that it "cover[ed] the basic points" and they had been agreed to by his superiors. The e-mail contained the license term, the geographic scope, the royalties, advance, and minimum amount to be paid. However, the contract did not contain several terms that Lamle claimed were agreed to in the oral contract. The materiality of the omitted terms was not clear, and a jury could reasonably decide either way.

California law allows typed names at the end of a telegram to serve as sufficient signatures under the statute of frauds. The court saw no significant difference between a typewritten name at the end of a telegram and a typed name at the end of an e-mail. Mattel did not dispute Bucher's agency authority to bind Mattel to an agreement; therefore, the signature at the end of the e-mail was sufficient under the statute of frauds. The other issues that Lamle must prove to win his case, that the parties intended to be bound by an oral contract on June 11 and that all of the material terms were covered in the e-mail, are issues of material fact for a jury to decide, which means that summary judgment is not appropriate.

DECISION AND REMEDY: The grant of summary judgment was vacated, and the case was remanded to the lower court.

SIGNIFICANCE OF THE CASE: This case demonstrates the broad standards that apply for a writing to be considered sufficient under the statute of frauds. Even a signed e-mail, if it contains the material terms, can be considered sufficient.

CRITICAL THINKING

What ambiguous term is going to be a key to the ultimate outcome of this case. Considering that ambiguity, what argument would you make as the plaintiff? What argument would you make as the defendant in the trial?

ETHICAL DECISION MAKING

What key stakeholders would be concerned about the ultimate outcome of this case?

Parol Evidence Rule

A problem arises with a written contract when a party asserts that the writing is in some way deficient. In order to smooth transactions by limiting the types of evidence admissible to address the written agreement, the courts rely heavily on the parol evidence rule. The parol evidence rule is a common law rule that specifically addresses the admissibility of oral evidence as it relates to written contracts. The parol evidence rule states that oral evidence of an agreement made prior to or contemporaneously with a written agreement is inadmissible when the parties intend to have the written agreement be the complete and final version of their agreement.[13] *Parol* in "parol evidence rule" means speech or words, specifically words outside the original writing.

The purpose of the parol evidence rule is to restrict evidence from being admitted that substantially contradicts the agreement in its written form. Therefore, evidence of prior agreements and negotiations, as well as of contemporaneous agreements and negotiations, is typically excluded under the parol evidence rule. A written agreement is assumed to be complete, and evidence contradicting this final agreement usually impedes business transactions, which is why the parol evidence rule exists.

However, when a court determines that the written agreement does *not* represent a complete and final version of the agreement, evidence may be admissible to further the court's understanding of the agreement. The admissible evidence is limited to additional elements, missing in the writing, that are consistent with the written agreement. These elements may be terms typically included in similar transactions that were left out of the specific writing, or they may be separate agreements in which consideration was offered.

A cautionary note is in order: "Parol evidence rule," on its face, is a misnomer. First and foremost, parol evidence applies to both parol (spoken words) and written speech. The parol evidence rule covers evidence extrinsic to the original writing and is not limited to spoken words. Second, the parol evidence rule is *not* a rule of evidence but, rather, relates to substantive legal issues, namely, what constitutes a legally binding agreement and how do we know what the agreement is. Third, the parol evidence rule is not a unitary concept or rule but an amalgamation of different rules and conditions.

Although the parol evidence rule applies to writings created at the same time as the written agreement, these writings tend to be treated differently than prior or contemporaneous oral agreements. That is, the writings are more readily admitted as part of the written agreement than is oral evidence regarding conditions or terms in the final agreement. The reasoning is that judges are allowed discretion in determining which documents constitute the final contract. As long as the contemporaneous written documents do not substantially contradict what is in the final writing, judges can deem these other writings to be part of the final written agreement. Consequently, the parol evidence rule does not usually exclude extrinsic written evidence.

Sometimes parties take the initiative and attempt to signal to judges that the written agreement is intended to be the final and complete statement of the agreement. A merger clause is a clause parties include in a written agreement within the statute of frauds that states that the written agreement accurately reflects the final, complete version of the agreement. Not all courts consider merger clauses to be conclusive proof of a contract. Nonetheless, where merger clauses are accepted, they greatly reduce the amount of guesswork courts must do in determining whether a written agreement was in fact intended to be the final statement of the agreement.

Exceptions to the Parol Evidence Rule

As with the statute of frauds, there are exceptions to the general applicability of the parol evidence rule. That is, there are situations where parol evidence, which is normally excluded, may be admissible in court. These exceptions pertain to (1) contracts that are subsequently modified,

[13] Restatement (Second) of Contracts, sec. 213.

(2) contracts conditioned on orally agreed-on terms, (3) contracts that are not final as they are part written and part oral, (4) contracts with ambiguous terms, (5) incomplete contracts, (6) contracts with obvious typographical errors, (7) voidable or void contracts, and (8) evidence of prior dealings or usage of trade.

CONTRACTS THAT HAVE BEEN SUBSEQUENTLY MODIFIED

Although parol evidence contradictory to the final terms is inadmissible, evidence regarding a contract's subsequent modification is admissible. To be admissible, the modification must have been made after the writing and the evidence must clearly indicate this later modification.

Despite the allowance of evidence to demonstrate modifications, not all evidence of modification is admissible. If the agreement is required to be in writing under the statute of frauds, oral modifications are unenforceable. However, oral evidence of a subsequent written agreement is admissible. In addition, if the contract's terms require that modification be in writing, oral modifications are inadmissible and unenforceable.[14]

CONTRACTS CONDITIONED ON ORALLY AGREED-ON TERMS

The parol evidence rule does not prevent parties from introducing evidence proving the written agreement was conditioned on terms agreed to orally. The reason the parol evidence rule does not apply is that the evidence being elicited does not substantially modify the written agreement. Rather, what is at issue with such evidence is the enforceability of the contract as written. No terms are altered, so the parol evidence rule does not apply.

When an entire contract is conditioned on something occurring first, that first thing is known as a **condition precedent**. Evidence of the existence of a condition precedent agreed to orally is admissible, as stated previously, because the contract is not modified by such evidence; rather, its enforceability is called into question. Since the statute of frauds is concerned primarily with the enforceability of agreements, it logically follows that the parol evidence rule does not apply to evidence of condition precedents.

condition precedent
In a contract, an event that must occur in order for a party's duty to arise.

NONFINALIZED, PARTIALLY WRITTEN AND PARTIALLY ORAL, CONTRACTS

When a contract consists of both written and oral elements, judges tend to treat the agreement as nonfinalized. Accordingly, the judge makes the assumption that the parties do not intend to have the written agreement represent the entire agreement. Therefore, oral evidence related to the contract is admissible because the written document is not the complete and final representation of the agreement.

CONTRACTS CONTAINING AMBIGUOUS TERMS

When a contract contains what the court deems to be ambiguous terms, the court is faced with a dilemma in interpretation. To attempt to reach the most accurate interpretation of the original agreement, the court allows evidence, even if it is oral, for the sole purpose of clarifying ambiguous terms. As with evidence regarding orally agreed-on condition precedents, evidence used to clarify ambiguity is believed not to modify the contract but, rather, to clarify it. Accordingly, oral evidence related to ambiguity is admissible *only* to clarify, and not to change, any of the contractual terms.

INCOMPLETE CONTRACTS

When a contract is fundamentally flawed because it is missing critical information, courts can allow parol evidence to provide the missing information. Typically, the missing information is related to essential terms of the contract. Parol evidence will be admitted to clarify the contract by filling in the missing parts while not modifying, in any substantial way, the written agreement.

[14] UCC § 2-209(2), (3).

Parol evidence is used to attempt to facilitate business transactions, as opposed to forcing the parties to enter into a new, complete agreement.

CONTRACTS WITH OBVIOUS TYPOGRAPHICAL ERRORS

Whenever a written agreement under the statute of frauds contains a serious, and obvious, typographical error, parol evidence is admissible to demonstrate that the typo was a typo, as well as to set forth the proper term. Allowing parol evidence to correct typos does not fundamentally alter the written agreement because the typo is not an accurate reflection of the parties' agreement. The agreement is not altered by correcting a typo; rather, the agreement is granted better clarity.

VOID OR VOIDABLE CONTRACTS

Certain conditions can make an otherwise valid contract void or voidable. (Refer to Chapter 7 for an in-depth discussion of what makes a contract void or voidable.) While the contract does not list these conditions, the courts allow parol evidence to demonstrate that the contract is void or voidable. As with the vast majority of the exceptions to the parol evidence rule, allowing evidence that proves a contract is void or voidable does not fundamentally alter the terms of the contract. Rather, the parol evidence would address the enforceability of the agreement, which is not the same as changing the terms of the agreement. Furthermore, evidence of a defense against a contract is admissible to prove a contract is void or avoidable.

EVIDENCE OF PRIOR DEALINGS OR USAGE OF TRADE

This final exception, although directly related to those already mentioned, actually falls under the UCC and not the statute of frauds. Regardless, this exception also allows otherwise inadmissible parol evidence for a specific reason.

According to the UCC, parol evidence is admissible for the sake of clarification if the evidence addresses prior dealings between the parties or usages of trade in the same business field as the parties are in.[15] Evidence related to past dealings can help clarify missing or ambiguous terms by examining how the parties had previously interacted. The assumption is that parties will continue to interact in a similar manner, because repeated interactions tend to indicate pleasant interactions between the parties. Therefore, if a term is missing or ambiguous, the courts rely on evidence of what was done between the parties in the past to attempt to gauge what was intended in the contract in question.

Similarly, when a contract is ambiguous or incomplete, the courts examine the standard practices in the business. Here, the courts are assuming that businesses intend to engage in standard transactions. Furthermore, the courts believe that common business practices might sometimes be overlooked and, therefore, not be included when these common practices accurately reflect the intentions of the parties involved. Once again, an exception to the applicability of the parol evidence rule is made to allow evidence to clarify a contract, as opposed to changing any material terms of the contract.

Integrated Contracts

integrated contract
A written contract intended to be the complete and final representation of the parties' agreement.

Integrated contracts are written contracts intended to be the complete and final representation of the parties' agreement. When the courts deem a contract integrated, unless one of the above exceptions applies, parol evidence is inadmissible. With partially integrated contracts, parol evidence is admissible to the extent it clarifies part of the contract or addresses the enforcement of the contract.[16] Therefore, the easiest test to determine the admissibility of parol evidence is to check whether the written contract, within the statute of frauds, is an integrated contract.

As was previously discussed, one way parties can indicate their desire to create an integrated contract is through the use of a merger clause. A merger clause explicitly states that the written contract is intended to be the complete and final version of the contract between the parties and

[15] UCC §§ 1-205 and 2-202.

[16] Restatement (Second) of Contracts, sec. 216.

that other possible agreements between the parties, besides the one in question, are not part of the final written agreement. In essence, a merger clause seeks to blend other agreements either into the final agreement or into something explicitly stated as being outside the final agreement. Most states will allow a merger clause to constitute the stated intent of the parties involved unless proof of a personal defense against the contract is offered by one of the parties. However, it is worth mentioning that some states consider merger clauses to be recommendations, but not necessarily binding on the parties involved.

Third-Party Rights to Contracts

As you read in Chapter 7, contracts involve agreements between two parties in which each party agrees to give something to or do something for the other party. Contracts are typically private agreements, in the sense that the focus of the contract is the two parties involved and no one else. Accordingly, parties not in *privity of contract* (i.e., parties other than the contracting parties) usually do not have rights to a contract. However, as frequently is the case in the law, there are exceptions to the general rule.

There are two main situations in which a third party gains rights to a contract to which she or he is not a party. In the first, one of the contracting parties transfers rights or duties to a third party. In the second, the third party is a direct beneficiary of a contract involving two other parties. The remainder of this chapter examines both of these situations.

Assignments and Delegations

Contracts typically involve an agreement between two parties in which each party agrees to do something for the other. That is, both parties are **obligors** (contractual parties who agreed to do something for each other) and **obligees** (contractual parties who agreed to receive something from each other). Consequently, contracts create a situation in which each party has a duty to perform the agreed-on action and a right to be the recipient of the other party's duty. These rights and duties can be transferred to *third parties*—parties not part of the original contract. The sections below discuss both the transferring of rights (assignment) and the transferring of duties (delegation) to third parties.

ASSIGNMENT

Assignment occurs when a party to a contract (an **assignor**) transfers her rights to a contract to a third party (an **assignee**). In other words, the assignor gives to the assignee the right to collect what was contractually agreed on in the original contract (see Figure 11-2). For example, Lisa agrees to sell her car to Luke for $8,000. Lisa then assigns her right to receive Luke's payment to Kelly. Kelly, who was not part of the original contract between Luke and Lisa, is an assignee and now has the right to receive payment from Luke for Lisa's car.

obligor
A contractual party who agreed to do something for the other party.

obligee
A contractual party who agreed to receive something from the other party.

LO 4

assignment
A contracting party's transfer of his or her rights to a contract to a third party.

assignor
In a contract, the party who transfers his or her rights to the contract to a third party (an assignee), giving the assignee the right to collect what was contractually agreed on in the original contract.

assignee
In a contract, the party who receives the rights of another party (an assignor) to collect what was contractually agreed on in the original contract.

Figure 11-2

Assignment of Rights

Duty to Perform

Obligee Assignor

Obligor

Assigns Right to Performance

Assignee

Performance Goes to Assignee

Assignment of Rights in China

Almost all developed market economies permit the free assignability of contract rights. Assignments are important because they play a crucial role in business financing. Banks and businesses make loans and pay debts through assignments. China, which has central planning rather than a free-market system, does not permit free assignment of contracts. Limited assignability is true of most centrally planned economies. When a contract is with the state, state approval by the proper authority must first be obtained, unless the contract allows for assignments. If the contract is with a private party, the assignor must get the obligor's approval before an assignment can be made. While not prevented, assignments are limited in China.

LO 5

When an assignor transfers her rights to an assignee, the assignor legally gives up all rights she previously had to collect on the contract.[17] Now the assignee may legally demand performance from the other party to the original contract. Returning to our example, once Lisa transfers her right to Kelly, Lisa can no longer require that Luke pay her for her car; however, Kelly can request that Luke pay her for Lisa's car.

The assignee essentially fills in for the assignor as the legal recipient of the contractual duties. As such, the assignee acquires the same rights the assignor had. The assignee is offered no additional protections. Moreover, the obligor (the other party to the contract, who owes a duty to the assignee) may raise any of the same defenses for nonperformance to the assignee as he would have been able to raise against the assignor. Thus, if Lisa failed to deliver her car to Luke, he can legally refuse to pay Kelly on the basis of Lisa's breach of contract. It does not matter that Kelly had no duty in the original contract; she is subject to the same defense Luke had against Lisa, and therefore Kelly would not be paid in this situation.

Although there is no legally required wording to be used or forms to be filled out for assignments to be valid, certain restrictions exist. First, although assignments may be given orally or in writing,[18] the UCC requires that assignments be in writing when the amount being assigned is greater than $5,000.[19] Furthermore, assignments covered by the statute of frauds also must be in writing. Because it is difficult to prove the existence of assignments given orally, it is usually suggested that assignments be in writing.

Second, an assignee must agree to accept the assigned rights. An assignee may decline an assignment if he has not legally agreed to the assignment and he declines in a timely fashion after learning about the assignment and its terms.[20] There is no protocol an assignee must follow to reject an assignment, but once the assignment is rejected, it is considered rejected from the time it was first offered. Third, in some situations contractual rights cannot be assigned.[21]

Rights That Cannot Be Assigned Exhibit 11-1 lists the four situations in which contractual rights cannot be assigned to a third party. We discuss each of them below.

First, the rights to a contract cannot be assigned when the contract is personal in nature. For a contract to be personal in nature, the obligor must have promised something specific to the person receiving it. Because the subject matter of the contract is personal, a third party cannot legally become the recipient. The one exception occurs when the only part of a contract left to be fulfilled is

Exhibit 11-1

Contractual Rights That Cannot Be Assigned

1. Rights that are personal in nature.
2. Rights that increase the obligor's risk or duties.
3. Rights whose assignment is prohibited by contract.
4. Rights whose assignment is prohibited by law or public policy.

[17] Restatement (Second) of Contracts, sec. 317.

[18] Restatement (Second) of Contracts, sec. 324.

[19] UCC § 1-206.

[20] Restatement (Second) of Contracts, sec. 327.

[21] Restatement (Second) of Contracts, sec. 317(2).

the payment,[22] because rights to payment can always be assigned. Case 11-2 demonstrates a situation in which a contractual duty cannot be assigned because the courts deemed it personal in nature.

[22] Restatement (Second) of Contracts, sec. 317 and 318.

CASE 11-2

TRAFFIC CONTROL SERVICES v. UNITED RENTALS NORTHWEST, INC.
SUPREME COURT OF NEVADA
87 P.3d 1054 (2004)

FACTS: *Phillip Burkhardt was a former United employee who took a job with NES. As a condition of employment with NES, he signed noncompetition and nondisclosure covenants. On June 30, 2002, United and NES entered into an asset purchase agreement. The purchase agreement was limited to certain assets and provided that "all contracts and agreements that are not listed as 'Assumed Contracts' are 'Excluded Assets.'" While the agreement listed other noncompetition covenants as assumed contracts, Burkhardt's noncompetition covenant was not on the list. The purchase agreement also stated that "none of the Assumed Contracts requiring a consent to assignment have been obtained prior to the Closing Date."*

A week before closure of the asset purchase, United requested or demanded that Burkhardt and a number of other employees sign new one-year noncompetition and nondisclosure covenants. Burkhardt refused.

On August 5, 2002, Burkhardt accepted employment with Traffic Control. United terminated Burkhardt's employment on August 8, 2002, after which he returned all his work-related items to company officials. NES and United filed a complaint alleging that Burkhardt obtained confidential information during his employment with them and subsequently used and disclosed NES/United confidential information, contacted United's clients, and attempted to solicit United's customers. The district court ultimately ruled in favor of United, enforcing the noncompetition covenant. Burkhardt appealed.

ISSUE: Are employee noncompetition covenants assignable?

REASONING: In the words of the court:

When an employee enters into a covenant not to compete with his employer, he may consider the character and personality of his employer to determine whether he is willing to be held to a contract that will restrain him from future competition with his employer, even after termination of employment. This does not mean, however, the employee is willing to suffer the same restriction with a stranger to the original obligation. Certainly, the sale of a business fundamentally alters the nature of an employment relationship.

Burkhardt testified, by way of deposition, to his concern about working for a company other than NES, especially United. In this, he covenanted specifically with NES not to compete with NES. At the hearing on the motion for a preliminary injunction, the district court agreed with Burkhardt the noncompetition covenant was personal in nature but concluded, because the covenant held value, it was assignable. Testimony also established United enjoyed a much greater volume of business in the trench shoring business than NES. Therefore, Burkhardt's obligation materially changed when the covenant was assigned. Burkhardt was thus "foreclosed from competing on any level with a much larger business entity."

DECISION AND REMEDY: Employee noncompetition agreements are of a personal nature and cannot be assigned without the express consent of an employee. The decision was reversed.

SIGNIFICANCE OF THE CASE: This case demonstrates why certain contracts are personal and therefore not automatically assignable.

CRITICAL THINKING

What evidence did the judge rely on in this case to make his decision? How would you judge the quality of this evidence?

ETHICAL DECISION MAKING

What ethical considerations do you think the judge relied on in making the decision in this case?

Second, rights cannot be assigned when the assignment would increase the risk or duties the obligor would face in fulfilling the original contract. For example, Ben agrees to replace the siding on Erin's two-bedroom ranch. Erin cannot assign her right to Ben's services to Chris, who lives in a three-story, five-bedroom house, because Ben's (the obligor's) duties would be greatly increased from the work required in the original contract with Erin to the work required in an agreement with Chris.

Third, rights cannot be assigned when the contract expressly forbids assignments. When parties include an *antiassignment clause* in their contract, the parties are attempting to limit their ability to assign their rights under the contract. However, the wording of the antiassignment clause is determinative regarding the effectiveness of the clause. That is, if worded improperly or ambiguously, the clause does not effectively limit assignments.

Most courts consider contractual prohibitions against assignments to be promises. Consequently, courts consider an assignment made despite an antiassignment clause to be effective, but the party who makes the assignment will still be liable for breaching the terms of the contract. Moreover, unless the clause is very specific in what it prohibits, the court will generally interpret the antiassignment clause as preventing delegation of duties, not assignment of rights.[23] A clause stating "All assignments are void under this contract" would be considered effective. In contrast, when a contract includes a clause explicitly permitting assignments, the parties may assign rights, even when assignments would normally be considered improper because of an increased duty, risk, or burden to the obligor.[24]

Even in the presence of an antiassignment clause, there are exceptions in which assignments can still be made. For instance, antiassignment clauses do not affect assignments made by operation of law. That is, if a law necessitates an assignment, such as in bankruptcy cases, the assignment is effective regardless of any contractual agreement to the contrary. Likewise, as previously stated, the right to assign monetary payments cannot be denied. Therefore, even when a contract has an antiassignment clause, either party may still assign his or her right to receive payment.[25] Part of the reason the law does not bar the right to receive payment is that businesses often transfer rights to payments in the regular course of business. Also, one's duty to pay is not affected when the party to whom one must make a payment changes. That is, no added burden is placed on the obligor when the recipient of a payment changes, requiring that payment be sent to a different party.

In addition, assignments for the right to receive damages for a breach of contract to sell goods or services are unaffected by antiassignment clauses.[26] Therefore, if one party breaches the contract, the other party can sue the breaching party and transfer the right to recovery to a third party.

Fourth, rights cannot be assigned when law or public policy forbids such assignments. Various state and federal statutes prohibit the assigning of specific rights. Even when no statute prohibits an assignment, if the assignment is determined to be against public policy, the assignment is deemed ineffective.

Except as outlined in this section, all other rights are presumed to be assignable. Once it has been established that an assignment is valid, notice should be given to the obligor regarding the assignment.

Notice of Assignment Although notice need not be given for a valid assignment, it is usually a good idea for the assignor or the assignee to notify the obligor of the assignment. Assignments are effective immediately, regardless of notice, but by providing notice the assignor can help avoid two serious complications with assignments.

[23] Restatement (Second) of Contracts, sec. 322(1), and UCC § 2-210(3).

[24] Restatement (Second) of Contracts, sec. 323(1).

[25] UCC § 9-318(4).

[26] UCC § 2-210(2).

The first complication involves the obligor's fulfilling of the contractual duty. Without notice of assignment, the obligor can discharge his contractual duties simply by fulfilling his duties to the assignor. Because fulfilling the contract discharges the obligor's duties, the act also constitutes a discharge of the assignee's claim on the assignor's right. However, after the obligor has been given notice, the obligor can discharge his contractual obligations only by fulfilling the contract for the assignee.

The second complication regarding a lack of notice involves the granting of multiple assignments of the same right. When an assignor assigns two or more parties the same right, confusion arises as to which party has the right to the contract. Most states use the **first-assignment-in-time rule,** which states that the first party granted the assignment is the party correctly entitled to the contractual right. By giving proper notice, a party can ensure that there is no confusion over when the assignment was made. Furthermore, a minority of states have adopted the **English rule,** which states that the first assignee to give notice of assignment to the obligor is the party with rights to the contract. Consequently, especially when living in a state using the English rule, parties are well advised to give notice of assignments to ensure they maintain their assigned rights.

The Restatement (Second) of Contracts states a view between the first-assignment-in-time rule and the English rule.[27] The Restatement grants legal right to the first assignee in most situations. However, if the first assignment is legally voidable or revocable by the assignor, subsequent assignments are considered evidence of the voiding or revocation of the first assignment. In such situations, the later assignee has legal right to the contract. Also, the later assignee is considered the legal owner of the contractual right if she offers something to the assignor as consideration and then obtains (1) performance by the obligor on his duty, (2) judgment requiring performance by the obligor, (3) a new contract with the obligor, or (4) evidence frequently used to signify a contractual right (e.g., a writing indicating a contractual obligation).

DELEGATION

A **delegation** occurs when a party to a contract (a **delegator**) transfers her duty to perform to a third party who is not part of the original contract (a **delegatee**). Whereas assignments transfer rights to a contract, delegations transfer duties. (See Figure 11-3.) Instead of the third party's

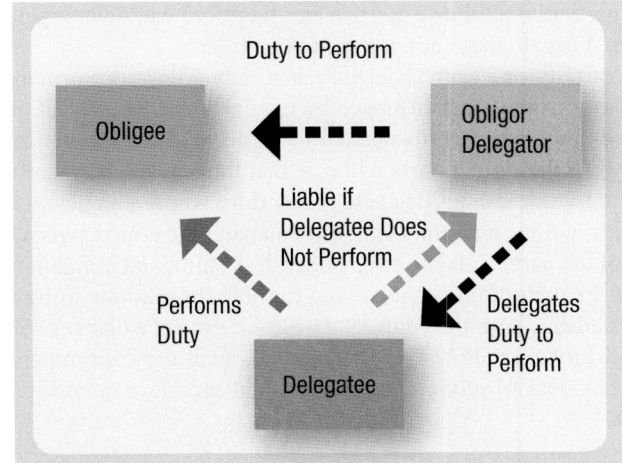

first-assignment-in-time rule
A rule that states that the first party granted the assignment is the party correctly entitled to the contractual right.

English rule
A rule that states that the first assignee to give notice of assignment to the obligor is the party with rights to the contract.

delegation
A contracting party's (a delegator's) transfer of his or her duty to perform to a third party who is not part of the original contract (a delegatee).

delegator
A party in a contract who transfers his or her duties to perform to a third party who is not a part of the original contract (a delegatee).

delegatee
A third party who is not part of the original contract but to whom duties to perform are transferred by one of the contracting parties (a delegator).

Figure 11-3

Assignment of Duties

Duty to Perform

Obligee

Obligor Delegator

Liable if Delegatee Does Not Perform

Performs Duty

Delegates Duty to Perform

Delegatee

[27] Sec. 342.

receiving something, as in an assignment, delegations require that the delegatee fulfill the delegator's contractual obligation to the obligee—the party to the contract to whom a duty is owed. For example, John contracts with Teresa to have her deliver machinery to his factory. Teresa then delegates her duty to Bill, who delivers the machinery to John.

One important distinction between assignments and delegations involves the rights of the transferring party—the assignor or the delegator. In assignments, after the assignment is made, the assignor has no right left to the original contract. Conversely, with delegations, the delegator is not relieved of his duty to perform by making a delegation. If the delegatee fails to fulfill the contract, the delegator is still liable to the obligee for fulfillment of the contract. In our example, if Bill fails to deliver the machinery to John, Teresa is liable to John for damages.

Duties That Cannot Be Delegated As with assignments, the starting assumption is that duties to a contract can be delegated. However, courts tend to examine delegations more closely than assignments. The reasoning is that an assignment usually does not affect the party to the contract who is not involved in the assignment (the obligor), whereas a delegation forces the party to the contract who is not involved in the delegation (the obligee) to receive performance of the contract from a party with whom the obligee did not directly contract.

Also, just as with assignments, in certain situations duties cannot be delegated to a third party (see Exhibit 11-2).[28] The first type of duty that cannot be delegated, mirroring assignments, is any duty of a personal nature. A duty is personal in nature when it requires the specific talents, skills, or expertise of the obligor. An interesting situation arises when the initial contract bears an implicit assumption that work will be performed by others. In such situations, if supervision is important to the task, the supervision could be considered to be a personal duty that the obligor may not delegate to others. For example, suppose you are planning to have a new building built and you contract with a well-respected construction manager. He will not build the building; the contract is for his management skills. His contractual duties would be considered personal and therefore cannot be delegated.

Delegation for personal duties is admissible where otherwise not allowed when there is an explicit or implicit contractual agreement to allow delegations. Usually, for a delegation of personal duties to be effective, the contract must state that delegations are permitted.

While personal duties typically cannot be delegated, any nonpersonal duties in a contract can be delegated. For example, the delivering of goods, mowing of one's lawn, paying of money, or painting of a house are all considered nonpersonal duties. These duties are nonpersonal because they do not require particular skill or expertise and therefore can be completed by most people. Accordingly, one can delegate these nonpersonal duties.

The second type of duty one cannot delegate is a duty whose performance by the delegatee would vary significantly from its performance by the delegator. To protect the obligee, who is a part of the original contract, when performance would differ substantially from that to which the obligee contractually has the right, courts will rule that the delegation is ineffective.

The third type of duty one cannot delegate is any duty whose delegation is prohibited by the contract. When parties include agreements not to delegate, the courts typically treat these inclusions as indications of the parties' desire to consider the contractual obligations as personal. Consequently, the courts frequently find otherwise-allowable delegations to be inappropriate when an agreement not to delegate is in the contract. However, even if a clause prohibiting delegations exists, the courts will probably allow delegations to occur if they are impersonal. For example, courts consider the payment of money impersonal, and therefore delegable, even if a contract prohibits delegations.

Exhibit 11-2

Duties That Cannot Be Delegated

1. Duties that are personal in nature.
2. Duties for which the delegatee's performance will vary significantly from the delegator's.
3. Duties in contracts that forbid delegations.

[28] Restatement (Second) of Contracts, sec. 318, and UCC § 2-210.

Management

Management classes teach that delegation is an important concept in a managerial environment. Although all forms of delegating need not take place in the context of a contract: *Delegation* in a general sense refers to one's authority and right to pass along certain responsibilities to another, such as a manager's delegating responsibility to an employee for the purpose of the employee's completing a particular task. The primary purpose of delegation in a business environment is efficiency, in the sense that tasks may be completed more quickly by delegatees (i.e., employees) while the delegators (i.e., managers) focus on supervising the quality of work of a larger number of delegatees.

Similar to delegation in a contractual context, delegation in a managerial context usually does not remove the manager's obligation to have the task completed if a delegatee fails to perform his or her task. Often, an employee's inadequate performance reflects poorly on the manager who delegated the task, even though the duty to perform was transferred to the employee. Therefore, whether delegation takes place in the context of a contract or a managerial environment, the delegator should be relatively active (compared to an assignor) to ensure that the delegatee is performing as expected, thereby increasing the likelihood of recognizing efficiency in either context.

Source: K. Williams, *Management: A Practical Introduction* (New York: McGraw-Hill/Irwin, 2006), p. 250.

Assignment of the Contract

Frequently, contracts contain ambiguous language that makes it unclear what is being assigned or delegated. Examples of ambiguous language are "I assign the contract" or "I assign all of my rights under the contract." When a court cannot clearly tell what the parties intended, the court usually considers the assignment to be both of rights and of duties. In other words, when ambiguous language is used, the court considers that the assignor has assigned his rights, as well as delegated any duties he had under the contract. (See Figure 11-4.) Doing so removes any right the assignor had to collect under the contract, but he is still liable to the obligee for any duties the delegatee, who is also the assignee, fails to perform.

Third-Party Beneficiary Contracts

We have thus far learned about one of the ways in which third parties may obtain rights to a contract: through assignments or delegations. We now move on to the other way, which is that the third party is an intended beneficiary of a third-party beneficiary contract. A third-party beneficiary contract

third-party beneficiary contract

A contract created when two parties enter into a contract agreement with the intended purpose of benefiting a third party.

Figure 11-4

Assignment of the Contract

217

is created when two parties enter into a contract with the intended end purpose of benefiting a third party. To be an intended third-party beneficiary, the third party does not need to be explicitly named in the contract, as long as the terms of the contract or events occurring after the creation of the contract make it clear who the intended recipient of the contractual benefits is.

LO 6 INTENDED BENEFICIARIES

Early in the common law, courts had difficulty when contracts were written to benefit third parties. The courts were not sure how to treat these contracts and usually deemed third parties to have no rights to contracts to which they were not in privity. Now, however, third parties who are intended beneficiaries have the right to enforce contracts. An **intended beneficiary** is a third party to a contract whom the contracting parties intended to benefit directly from their contract.

Intended beneficiaries may enforce their rights to a contract when both parties to the contract intended for the third party to benefit. In determining whether a third party is an intended beneficiary, courts ask if the contracting parties intended that the third party be the "direct," "primary," or "express" beneficiary of the contract.

The **promisor** in a third-party beneficiary contract is the party to the contract who made the promise that benefits the third party. The **promisee** is the party to the contract who owes something to the promisor in exchange for the promise made to the third-party beneficiary. For example, Amanda contracts with Alex to clean his house. In exchange, Alex will pay Amanda's credit card debt. The credit card company is the third-party beneficiary, as the contract is created to benefit the company. Alex is the promisor, for he made the promise to pay the third-party beneficiary. Amanda is the promisee because she owes a duty to the promisor, Alex.

In a third-party beneficiary contract, the intended beneficiary may sue the promisor to enforce the contract. Although the promisee typically owes something to the third-party beneficiary before the contract with the promisor exists, if the third party sues the promisee after the promisor does not fulfill his or her obligations, the promisee can then sue the promisor for breach of contract. Therefore, courts allow the third-party beneficiary to sue the promisor, thus eliminating the litigation that would ensue if the promisee sued the promisor. In our example, if Alex fails to pay the credit card company for Amanda's debt, the credit card company has the right to sue Alex, even though it is Amanda's debt.

Let us return to the Case Opener. The fans of the Tyson fight argued that they were third-party beneficiaries and therefore had rights under several contracts that were violated when Tyson was disqualified early in the fight. Boxing matches are widely viewed events, and one can argue that the fights are organized for the enjoyment of the fans. Does the idea of boxing matches' being organized for the fans make the fans the "direct," "primary," or "express" beneficiaries of contracts involved in the fight? In other words, are the fans of the Tyson fight intended beneficiaries to the contracts Tyson entered when agreeing to the fight? What else do we need to know before we can determine whether the fans have a legal right to a refund?

There are two types of intended beneficiaries: creditor beneficiaries and donee beneficiaries.

Creditor Beneficiaries A **creditor beneficiary** is a third party who benefits from a contract in which the promisor agrees to pay the promisee's debt. In our previous example, because Alex (the promisor) agreed to pay the debt of Amanda (the promisee), Amanda's credit card company is a creditor beneficiary.

Case 11-3 is a famous dispute in which the courts began to recognize the rights of third parties to sue promisors for performance.

Donee Beneficiaries The other type of intended beneficiaries is donee beneficiaries. **Donee beneficiaries** are third parties who benefit from a contract in which a promisor agrees to give a gift to the third party. The most common form of donee beneficiary contracts is life insurance policies. Someone (the promisee) pays premiums on a life insurance plan to have the insurer (the promisor) agree to pay a third party (the donee beneficiary) on the promisee's death.

intended beneficiary
A third party to a contract whom the contracting parties intended to benefit directly from their contact.

promisor
In a third-party beneficiary contract, the party to the contract who made the promise that benefits the third party.

promisee
In a third-party beneficiary contract, the party to the contract who owes something to the promisor in exchange for the promise made to the third party.

creditor beneficiary
A third party who benefits from a contract in which the promisor agrees to pay the promisee's debt.

donee beneficiary
A third party who benefits from a contract in which a promisor agrees to give a gift to the third party.

CASE 11-3

FACTS: *In November 1857, Holly, at the request of Fox, loaned him $300. Before loaning the money, Holly informed Fox that Holly owed Lawrence $300, due the next day. In consideration of the loan, at the time of the loan, Fox agreed to pay Lawrence for Holly the next day. Fox did not pay, and Lawrence sued him. Fox sought to dismiss the charges because there was no proof tending to show that Holly was indebted to Lawrence; Fox's agreement with Holly to pay Lawrence was void for want of consideration, and there was no privity between Lawrence and Fox. Fox's motion to dismiss was denied. The jury ultimately found in favor of Lawrence for the sum of the loan plus interest. Fox appealed and the judgment was affirmed. Fox then appealed again.*

ISSUE: Does Lawrence have the right to sue Fox, the promisor, for payment?

REASONING: There is a principle of law, found in English law as well as the law of many states, that if one person makes a promise to another for the purpose of benefiting a third party, that third person may "maintain an action upon it." Although many of the preceding cases in which this principle was applied were trust cases, nothing about the law requires that the case be a trust case. Fox's duty to pay Lawrence in return for the loan he received from Holly was a clear condition of the loan. The spoken promise is equal to a written promise in this case. Therefore, Lawrence should receive payment from Fox in the interest of justice, even if the law could be more narrowly interpreted.

DECISION AND REMEDY: The decision of the earlier court was affirmed. Fox was required to pay Lawrence as he had promised Holly.

SIGNIFICANCE OF THE CASE: This case was one of the earliest cases that upheld the rights of third parties to sue promisors to have agreements enforced.

CRITICAL THINKING

Form an opinion about the contemporary relevance of this ruling. Given the widespread and extremely significant changes in U.S. society and the world over the last 150 years, what is the justification for consideration of such an old case? How does this type of process aid our legal system? How might it detract from the reasonableness of modern deliberations?

ETHICAL DECISION MAKING

Consider the actions of Fox, both leading up to and through the course of the legal dispute. From an ethical standpoint, which stakeholders was Fox considering? What values was he attempting to uphold?

The fans in the Tyson case argued that they are intended beneficiaries. If the fans are correct, and we know Tyson did not have a debt to the fans, then they must be donee beneficiaries. Does an agreement to perform create a situation in which the audience members become the intended beneficiaries of the performance?

Vesting of Rights Although an intended beneficiary can enforce her rights to a contract, she cannot do so until her rights to the contract **vest,** that is, until the rights mature such that a party can legally act on the rights. Before a third party's rights have vested, the original contracting parties can make changes to the original contract without the permission of the third party. For example, third-party rights in a life insurance policy do not vest until the promisee's death. Consequently,

vest
To mature, as in the maturing of rights such that a party can legally act on the rights.

Jane (the promisee) can change the intended beneficiary of her life insurance policy from Mary to Peter. Jane does not need Mary's permission, and Mary cannot sue Jane, because Mary's rights have not vested.

Generally, one of three things must occur for a third party's right to a contract to vest.[29] First, under certain circumstances, third-party rights vest immediately. When rights vest immediately, the third party can enforce the contract at any time. These rights take effect instantaneously, even if the beneficiary does not know about the contract.

Second, rights may vest when the beneficiary decides to accept the rights to the contract. Sometimes the beneficiary must positively accept the rights, such as by notifying the contracting parties of acceptance. However, in the absence of an overt act of rejecting the rights to a contract, acceptance is assumed when the beneficiary becomes aware of the contract.

Third, rights may vest when the beneficiary changes his position because of reliance on the contractual rights. In other words, the beneficiary must take some action he would not have taken otherwise because he is expecting to benefit from the contract. For example, Vince is a third-party beneficiary to a contract. When he finds out about the contract, he decides to lease a new car because he is expecting to benefit from the contract. Obtaining the lease would cause his rights to the contract to vest because doing so demonstrates a change in position based on reliance on the contract.

If a contract specifies that the original contracting parties maintain the right to alter or rescind the contract, the vesting of the third party's rights does not preclude the promisor or the promisee from changing the original contract.

Many states hold that donee beneficiary rights vest before creditor beneficiary rights. The rationale is that even if the contract is altered when there is a creditor beneficiary, the creditor beneficiary still maintains her rights against the debtor (the promisee). Donee beneficiaries do not have the same rights as creditor beneficiaries, and thus many states allow their rights to vest more quickly than those of creditor beneficiaries.

LO 7

Creditor versus Donee Beneficiaries There are two main distinctions between creditor beneficiaries and donee beneficiaries (see Exhibit 11-3). The first distinction is based on the reason the third-party beneficiary contract was created. If the promise in the contract is intended to release a party from an obligation to a third party, such as the paying of one's debt, the contract involves a creditor beneficiary. Conversely, if the contract intends to grant a gift to a third party, the third party is a donee beneficiary.

The second distinction involves the conditions under which an intended beneficiary can enforce her rights under a contract. Creditor beneficiaries can enforce their rights under a contract whenever the contract is valid. Donee beneficiaries can enforce their rights to most contracts. However, some jurisdictions do not allow donee beneficiaries to enforce their contractual rights in all situations.

When a donee beneficiary can enforce his rights under a contract, he may do so only against the promisor. The reason the donee beneficiary cannot sue the promisee is that the promisee had

Exhibit 11-3

Creditor versus Donee Beneficiaries

CREDITOR BENEFICIARY	DONEE BENEFICIARY
Purpose of the Contract	
Contractual performance fulfills an obligation to a third party.	Contractual performance gives a gift to a third party.
Enforcement of Rights	
Beneficiary can enforce rights to a contract if the contract is valid and the rights have vested.	Beneficiary has limited ability to enforce contracts, depending on the jurisdiction.
Beneficiary can enforce rights against the promisor or the promisee.	Beneficiary can enforce rights against the promisor.

[29] Restatement (Second) of Contracts, sec. 311.

no duty to the donee beneficiary. In contrast, creditor beneficiaries can sue the promisor or the promisee for performance, as both parties owed a duty to the creditor beneficiary. However, if the creditor beneficiary wins a judgment against one party, she may not seek judgment against the other party. In addition, if a creditor beneficiary wins judgment against the promisee, the promisee may sue the promisor to recover under a theory of breach of contract.[30]

It is not always easy to determine when someone is a creditor or a donee beneficiary. Sometimes a contract is created for reasons that are intended both to be charitable and to pay a debt. Given the lack of clear distinction as to when someone is a creditor beneficiary and when he is a donee beneficiary, the Restatement (Second) of Contracts takes a different approach.[31] The Restatement focuses on the distinction between intended and incidental beneficiaries.

Creditor and donee beneficiaries are both intended beneficiaries, and according to the Restatement, intended beneficiaries have the right to enforce a contract. When it is clear that the contract was created for the benefit of a third party and that performance of the contractual duties will pay off the payee's debt or give a gift as the payee intended, the third party is an intended beneficiary.

INCIDENTAL BENEFICIARIES

Similar to intended beneficiaries, incidental beneficiaries are third-party beneficiaries to contracts. However, unlike the case with intended beneficiaries, the contracting parties do not *intend* to benefit incidental beneficiaries. An incidental beneficiary is one who unintentionally gains a benefit from a contract between other parties. (See Exhibit 11-4.) One significant difference between intended and incidental beneficiaries is that incidental beneficiaries cannot sue to enforce a contract. Incidental beneficiaries maintain no rights to enforce other people's contracts.

In determining whether a party is an incidental beneficiary, the courts take a reasonable person approach: They ask if a reasonable person in the position of the party in question would believe that the contracting parties intended to benefit him or her. If the reasonable person would believe that the contracting parties consciously intended to benefit him or her, the courts will consider the party an intended beneficiary. If the reasonable person would not find such intent, the third party is an incidental beneficiary.

As a thought experiment, consider the reasonable person test in the context of the Tyson dispute in the Case Opener. For the fans to be able to receive refunds, the reasonable person in the position of the fans would have to believe that Tyson intended to benefit him or her with Tyson's performance. Do the fans meet the reasonable person test?

The courts consider other elements besides the reasonable person approach when determining whether a party is an intended or incidental beneficiary. One factor the courts consider is whether performance of the contract is done directly to the third party. If nothing is explicitly done for or given to the third party, she or he cannot be an intentional beneficiary. The courts also examine the third-party's ability to control the specifics of performance of the contract. That is, if a third party has the ability to provide input regarding how the contractual duties are fulfilled, the third party is probably an intended beneficiary. For example, Dianne (the promisee) agrees to pay

incidental beneficiary
One who unintentionally gains a benefit from a contract between other parties.

INTENDED BENEFICIARIES	INCIDENTAL BENEFICIARIES
Contracting parties intended to benefit the third party with their contract.	Contracting parties did not intend to benefit the third party with their contract.
Beneficiary has the right to enforce the contract.	Beneficiary does not have the right to enforce the contract.
Beneficiary benefits from direct reception of contractual performance.	Beneficiary benefits from indirect circumstances created by contractual performance.

Exhibit 11-4

Intended versus Incidental Beneficiaries

[30] Restatement (Second) of Contracts, sec. 310.

[31] Restatement (Second) of Contracts, sec. 302.

Charles (the promisor) to paint Henry's (the third party's) house. Henry tells Charles what color he wants the house, as well as when Charles should be there to paint. Henry's ability to control how Charles paints the house demonstrates his status as an intended beneficiary. In addition, note that Charles renders performance directly to Henry, so the explicit-performance factor also indicates Henry's status as an intended beneficiary.

A third factor the courts examine in determining the type of third-party beneficiary is whether the contract directly states that the third party is the benefiting party. In our example, because Charles agreed in the contract to paint Henry's house, the contract lists Henry as the beneficiary. Consequently, Henry is an intended beneficiary. Although Henry meets all three additional tests (besides the reasonable person test), it is not necessary to meet all three. If a third party meets at least one of the last three tests, he is usually an intended beneficiary.

┉➤ SUMMARY

Statute of Frauds	The term *statute of frauds* refers to various state laws modeled after the 1677 English Act for the Prevention of Frauds and Perjuries. These state laws are intended to (1) ease contractual negotiations by requiring sufficient reliable evidence to prove the existence and specific terms of a contract, (2) prevent unreliable oral evidence from interfering with a contractual relationship, and (3) prevent parties from entering into contracts with which they do not agree.
Contracts Falling within the Statute of Frauds	1. Contracts whose terms prevent possible performance within one year. 2. Promises made in consideration of marriage. 3. Contracts for one party to pay the debt of another if the initial party fails to pay. 4. Contracts related to an interest in land. 5. Under the Uniform Commercial Code, contracts for the sale of goods totaling more than $500.
Exceptions to the Statute of Frauds	The exceptions include (1) admission, (2) partial performance, (3) promissory estoppel, and (4) various exceptions under the UCC.
Sufficiency of the Writing	A sufficient writing under the statute of frauds must clearly indicate (1) the parties to the contract, (2) the subject of the agreement, (3) the consideration given for the contract, (4) all relevant contractual terms, and (5) at least the signature of the party against whom action is brought. Under the UCC, a writing must clearly indicate (1) the quantity to be sold and (2) the signature of the party being sued. Under neither the statute of frauds nor the UCC must the writing be contained within one document.
Parol Evidence Rule	The *parol evidence rule* is a common law rule stating that oral evidence of an agreement made prior to or contemporaneously with a written agreement is inadmissible when the parties intend to have the written agreement be the complete and final version of their agreement.
Exceptions to the Parol Evidence Rule	1. Contracts that are subsequently modified. 2. Contracts conditioned on orally agreed-on terms. 3. Contracts that are not final as they are part written and part oral. 4. Contracts with ambiguous terms. 5. Incomplete contracts. 6. Contracts with obvious typographical errors. 7. Voidable or void contracts. 8. Evidence of prior dealings or usage of trade.
Integrated Contracts	*Integrated contracts* are written contracts, within the statute of frauds, intended to be the complete and final representation of the parties' agreement, thus precluding the admissibility of parol evidence other than in the exceptions listed above.
Third-Party Rights to Contracts	There are two main situations in which a third party gains rights to a contract to which she or he is not a party: (1) One of the contracting parties transfers rights or duties to the third party. (2) The third party is a direct beneficiary of a contract involving two other parties.

Assignments and Delegations

Contracts typically involve an agreement between two parties:

Obligor: Contractual party who owes a duty to the other party in privity of the contract.

Obligees: Contractual party who is owed a duty from the other party in privity of the contract.

An *assignment* is the transfer of rights under a contract to a third party.

Assignor: The party to a contract who transfers his or her rights to a third party.

Assignee: A party not in privity to a contract who is the recipient of a transfer of rights to a contract.

Contractual rights that cannot be assigned:

1. Rights that are personal in nature.
2. Rights that would increase the obligor's risks or duties.
3. Rights in a contract that expressly forbids assignment.

A *delegation* is the transfer of a duty under a contract to a third party.

Delegator: The party to a contract who transfers his or her duty to a third party.

Delegatee: A party not in privity to a contract who is the recipient of a transfer of a duty in a contract.

Contractual duties that cannot be assigned:

1. Duties that are personal in nature.
2. Duties whose performance by the delegatee would be substantially different from that which the obligee originally contracted.
3. Duties in a contract that expressly forbids delegation.

Assignment of the Contract

When ambiguous language is used, courts interpret the transfer to consist of an assignment of rights and a delegation of duties.

Third-Party Beneficiary Contracts

An *intended beneficiary* is a third party to a contract whom the contracting parties intended to benefit directly from their contract.

Promisor: A party to a contract who made the promise that benefits the third party.

Promisee: A party to a contract who owes something to the promisor in exchange for the promise made to the third-party beneficiary.

Creditor beneficiary: A third party who benefits from a contract in which the promisor agrees to pay the promisee's debt. *Donee beneficiary:* A third party who benefits from a contract in which a promisor agrees to give a gift to the third party.

Vest: The maturing of rights such that a party can legally act upon the rights

An *incidental beneficiary* is a third party who unintentionally gains a benefit from a contract between other parties. That is, it was never the conscious objective of the contracting parties to benefit the third party.

----> **Point/Counterpoint**

Does the United States Still Benefit from Having a Statute of Frauds?	
YES	NO
The statute of frauds provides great benefit to America. The rule serves as a social lubricant aiding business transactions. Because it requires that certain	The United States does not benefit from the statute of frauds, and the states should repeal the relevant sections of their laws.

types of contracts be in writing, we know that such a contract will either have enough evidence to prove its existence and terms or will be unenforceable. Since only certain contracts are required to be in writing, the rule does not preclude oral contracts, but it ensures that the most important contracts can be enacted without complications.

Another way in which the statute of frauds benefits America is by preventing unreliable evidence from being used in court. Human memories are notoriously weak and faulty, and it does not make sense to base important legal decisions on what someone says he or she remembers. Furthermore, people with a vested interest can change their testimony on the basis of changed circumstances in order to gain personally from the changed circumstances. However, with the requirement that certain contracts be in writing, the parties become bound to what they wrote and need not rely on faulty memory or biased testimony.

Finally, the act of writing gives people time to pause for reflection. No one benefits when parties hastily rush into an agreement they later regret. The problem of hasty agreements is lessened when the parties are required to take time to write out the terms of their agreement. Thoughtful reflection prevents parties from entering into contracts with which they do not agree, and this means fewer cases are brought due to one party's entering an unfair, or otherwise defective, agreement.

One of the greatest problems with the statute of frauds is that it acts as an impediment to contractual agreements. When parties agree, why should they be subjected to unnecessary formalities? The written requirements of the statute of frauds get in the way of business transactions more often than they help.

Furthermore, the required writing frequently imposes additional costs on the parties to an agreement. When even simple agreements (although this applies to the more technical ones as well), must be written, parties have to spend more time with the agreement. The time spent writing down an agreement in which neither party contests any of the terms is time *not* spent conducting other business. Frequently, the parties have to hire attorneys to write their contracts. The attorney fees impose additional costs on the parties to the agreement, helping to decrease whatever benefit might have been gained from the original agreement before the writing took place.

In addition, the statute of frauds provides unnecessary loopholes for unscrupulous people. Although most parties enter agreements in good faith, it is not uncommon for parties to seek a way out of contracts they cannot perform. The writing requirements are not always accurately fulfilled, and when this occurs, unethical parties can exploit minor technicalities to have a contract declared void. In the end, the innocent party is harmed by the writing requirement, and the unethical party escapes a bad situation with little to no harm. America is not served by a system that enables such behavior.

Questions & Problems

1. Explain how the requirements of the statute of frauds under the UCC are different from those under the common law.

2. List the kinds of contracts that require a writing under the statute of frauds.

3. Identify the exceptions to the parol evidence rule, and explain why some people might argue that the parol rule is not very effective.

4. Integrate the concept of assignments with the concept of delegations.

5. Why is it that incidental beneficiaries cannot enforce rights under a contract? Should they be able to enforce such rights?

6. Explain the difference between an assignor's liability and a delegator's liability after rights have been transferred to a third party.

7. Explain the desirability to business of allowing a transfer of rights or duties to third parties.

8. The McCartheys owned stock in a corporation that controlled the *Salt Lake City Tribune.* When that company merged with another company, as part of the deal, the McCartheys were told that they would have the right to repurchase the newspaper for five years after the merger. The detailed merger agreement did not mention the right to repurchase. When the company sold the newspaper to Newsmedia in five years, instead of allowing the McCartheys to repurchase the paper, the McCartheys sued for breach of contract. The trial court dismissed the claim on grounds that the statute of frauds barred enforcement of the oral agreement. How do you believe the appellate court ruled on the McCartheys' appeal? Why? [*MediaNews Group v. McCarthey,* 494 F.3d 1254 (10th Cir., 2007).]

9. The Laths were the owners of a farm that they wished to sell. Mrs. Mitchell considered purchasing the land but found that an ice house located across the road

was objectionable. Mitchell argued that the Laths orally agreed to remove the ice house in consideration of her promise to purchase the property, which she agreed to purchase for $8,400 in a written contract. After Mitchell moved into her new home and made several improvements to the land, the Laths never removed the ice house and expressly communicated their intention not to do so. Mitchell sued the Laths for breach of contract. What effect does the parol evidence rule have on the admissibility of the oral agreement to remove the ice house? Why this effect? [*Mitchill v. Lath,* 247 N.Y. 377 (1928).]

10. The defendant owed a large sum of money to numerous creditors. But the plaintiff was assigned all the debts and the right to receive repayment from the defendant, who owed $585,526. The plaintiff claimed that only $47,390 was still owed by the defendant, but the defendant claimed that he had not paid anything to the plaintiff as there had been no written agreement to channel payment to the plaintiff. Furthermore, the defendant claimed that the lack of a written agreement violated the statute of frauds. In response, the plaintiff claimed that the statute of frauds did not apply; the plaintiff invoked the exception of partial performance, as the money had already been transferred to the defendant. Which party's argument seems most convincing? Why? [*Net Connection v. GWBEH,* 2005 Va. Cir. LEXIS 35.]

11. R. E. Haase owned Whataburger franchise rights for the City of Longview, Texas. In 1992, Haase hired Joseph Glazer as a manager trainee; shortly thereafter, Haase promoted Glazer to supervisor for five of Haase's franchise restaurants. Glazer claimed that in 1994 Haase agreed to help Glazer establish a Whataburger franchise restaurant and that Glazer was to provide Haase with 2 percent of the net sales. Glazer claimed that this contract was evidenced by three letters from Haase to Whataburger and a cash-flow statement Glazer had prepared that indicated a 2 percent payment of net sales to Haase. By 1995, Glazer had not received a franchise, and he quit working for Haase. After Haase opened another franchise, Glazer sued for breach of contract, fraud, and fraudulent inducement. Does Glazer have an enforceable contract claim under the statute of frauds? Should the claim for fraud or fraudulent inducement have any bearing on whether the court should enforce Glazer's contract? [*Haase v. Glazer,* 62 S.W.3d 795 (TX 2001).]

12. Robert Reiss quit his job in Kansas and moved his family to Arkansas, where he began to work as a meat-cutter for Country Corner Food & Drug, Inc. Reiss's wife was pregnant at the time he began to work for Country Corner, so he discussed the provisions of family insurance with his employer, who allegedly agreed to provide insurance for all family members, including the baby. After Reiss's son was born, the child experienced health problems and spent some time in the hospital. After Reiss requested that his employer assume responsibility for the medical bills, Reiss was terminated. Reiss brought suit against Country Corner for breach of contract and compensation for medical expenses. Because the employment contract was never in writing, Country Corner claimed that the contract was unenforceable under the statute of frauds. In response, Reiss claimed that the statute of frauds did not apply because the employment was for an indefinite duration, and even if the statute of frauds applied, the exception of promissory estoppel should apply because Reiss relied to his detriment on his employer's promises. According to the court, which argument was most consistent with the principles of the statute of frauds? [*Country Corner Food & Drug, Inc. v. Reiss,* 1987 Ark. App. LEXIS 2586.]

13. California farmers and farming entities purchase water from Westlands Water District, which receives its water from the U.S. Bureau of Reclamation under a 1963 contract between Westlands and the bureau. In 1993, Westlands and other water districts sued the bureau for reducing their water supply. The farmers, though not parties to the 1963 contract, intervened as plaintiffs. After negotiations, all parties except the farmers stipulated to dismissal of the districts' complaint. The farmers pressed forward with, as relevant here, the claim that the United States had breached the contract. They contended they were third-party beneficiaries entitled to enforce the contract. The district court ultimately held that the farmers were neither contracting parties nor intended third-party beneficiaries of the contract. The Ninth Circuit affirmed. If you were on the Supreme Court, how would you rule on appeal? Justify your legal decision. [*Orff v. United States,* 125 S. Ct. 2606 (2005).]

14. The farmers are former customers of Ron Kaufman, the owner and operator of Southeast Implements, Inc., a Case International Harvester equipment dealership. Between 1996 and 1998, they agreed to purchase or lease various items of farm equipment from Southeast. In each instance, the farmers and Kaufman orally negotiated the terms of the purchases/leases, and Kaufman then prepared written purchase agreements for each transaction, assigning his rights thereunder to Case. Case, in turn, after approving the assignments and agreeing to finance the purchases/leases, paid Kaufman for the equipment and looked to the farmers, as debtors, for payment. The written purchase agreements, however, were prepared and assigned without the farmers' knowledge and did not reflect the terms of the oral contracts. Kaufman inflated the purchase/lease prices and forged the farmers' signatures, thereby obtaining thousands

of dollars in overpayments from Case. When Case became aware of Kaufman's fraud, it sent representatives to meet with the individual farmers. After verifying that the farmers were in possession of equipment covered by the forged purchase agreements, Case attempted to enforce the terms of the forged contracts. The farmers alleged that Case's assignment was improper because the rights assigned were not the ones to which the farmers agreed. The farmers filed suit against Case and Southeast. The court found in favor of Case, and the farmers appealed. Is Kaufman's assignment made to Case binding? What defenses might the farmers have against Case? [*Day v. Case Credit Corp.*, 427 F.3d 1148 (2005).]

15. CEI and NU were planning a multibillion-dollar merger. Among the terms and conditions of the underlying merger agreement, CEI agreed to purchase all of NU's outstanding shares for $3.6 billion—$1.2 billion over the prevailing market price. Shortly before the scheduled closing, CEI declared that NU had suffered a material adverse change that "dramatically lowered" NU's valuation, and CEI declined to proceed with the merger unless NU would agree to a lower share price. NU rejected the share price reduction, treated CEI's demand as an anticipatory repudiation and breach of the agreement, and declared that the merger was "effectively terminated." Both parties brought suit. The district court ruled that NU could sue on behalf of its shareholders for the $1.2 billion. The court reasoned that the merger agreement expressly designated NU's shareholders as intended third-party beneficiaries. Due to subsequent legal actions, both parties appealed. The appellate court then decided the issue of whether any NU shareholders were intended third-party beneficiaries. If you were on the court, how would you have ruled? Why? [*Consol. Edison, Inc. v. Northeast Utils.*, 426 F.3d 524 (2005).]

16. Debbie Esquivel rented a hotel room at the Baytown La Quinta. She asked the clerk where she could park a rented U-Haul moving van containing personal property and towing her car. A clerk told her to park on the street adjacent to the hotel and assured her the van would be safe "because of the security it [the hotel] provided." The next day, Esquivel's van and car were missing. Esquivel learned that Murray Guard provided security to the La Quinta in question. She sued Murray Guard, claiming she was an intended third-party beneficiary. The court granted Murray Guard's motion for summary judgment. Esquivel appealed. Does the contract between La Quinta and Murray Guard create intended third-party beneficiaries? Why? [*Esquivel v. Murray Guard, Inc.*, 992 S.W.2d 536 (1999).]

Looking for more review material?

The Online Learning Center at **www.mhhe.com/kubasekess** contains this chapter's "Assignment on the Internet" and also a list of URLs for more information, entitled "On the Internet." Find both of them in the Student Center portion of the OLC, along with quizzes and other helpful materials.

Discharge and Remedies

····▶ CASE OPENER

The Battle of the Pharmacies

Walgreen operated a pharmacy in a mall in Milwaukee, Wisconsin, owned by the Sara Creek Property Company. Under Walgreen's lease, Sara Creek promised not to rent space in the mall to anyone else who wanted to operate a pharmacy. Several years into the lease, Sara Creek informed Walgreen that it intended to buy out the anchor tenant in the mall and install a Phar-Mor discount store in its place. This store would include a pharmacy the same size as Walgreen's and would be within 200 feet of Walgreen's store. The Phar-Mor pharmacy would sell pharmaceuticals at a deeper discount than that of Walgreen. Walgreen was granted an injunction against the new lease by the Seventh Circuit Court of Appeals. Sara Creek appealed, claiming that monetary damages would be a more appropriate remedy and then the Phar-Mor pharmacy could be allowed to move in.[1]

1. Do you think monetary damages alone would be an adequate remedy for Walgreen?
2. What kind of remedy should the court grant Walgreen?

[1] *Walgreen Co. v. Sara Creek Property Co.,* U.S. Court of Appeals for the Seventh Circuit, 966 F.2d 273 (1992).

····▶ LEARNING OBJECTIVES

After reading this chapter, you will be able to answer the following questions:

LO 1 What are the primary methods for discharging a contract?

LO 2 What are the primary legal remedies available for a breach of contract?

LO 3 What are the primary equitable remedies available for a breach of contract?

Methods of Discharging a Contract

The previous five chapters focus primarily on how parties enter into a legally binding agreement. Once a party has entered into a binding agreement, how does the party terminate his or her obligation under the contract? That question is the focus of this chapter. When a party's obligations under a contract are terminated, they are said to be discharged. There are a number of ways by which a party's contractual obligations can be terminated, or discharged. The first, and the one most parties hope to secure from the other when they enter into an agreement, is performance. The others are the happening of a condition or its failure to occur, material breach by one or both parties, agreement of the parties, or operation of law. The chapter explains each of these methods.

CONDITIONS

conditional contract

A contract that becomes enforceable only on the happening or termination of a specified condition.

condition precedent

In a contract, an event that must occur in order for a party's duty to arise.

Under ordinary circumstances, a party's duty to perform the promise agreed to in a contract is absolute. Sometimes, however, a party's duty to perform may be affected by whether a certain condition occurs. Contracts containing conditions affecting the performance obligations of the parties are called conditional contracts. The conditions may be either implied by law or expressly inserted into the contract by the parties.

Discharge by Conditions Precedent, Subsequent, and Concurrent There are three types of conditions: condition precedent, condition subsequent, and concurrent conditions. A condition precedent is a particular event that must occur in order for a party's duty to arise. If the event does not occur, the party's duty to perform does not arise. Frequently, real estate contracts are conditioned on an event such as the buyer's being able to sell his current home by a certain date. If the home does not sell, the condition does not arise, and the parties have no duty to perform and are thus discharged from the contract.

Another common example of a contract containing a condition precedent is an insurance contract. If Bill purchases a life insurance contract, he is obligated to pay the monthly premiums specified in the contract, but the insurance company's obligation to perform arises only when he dies. His death is the condition that triggers the company's duty to pay his beneficiary. The key to this concept is that the condition must occur before a duty to perform arises.

condition subsequent

In a contract, a future event that terminates the obligations of the parties when it occurs.

A condition subsequent is a future event that terminates the obligations of the parties when it occurs. For example, John may enter into an agreement to lease an apartment for five years, conditioned on his not being called to active duty in the National Guard. If he is called to serve, his obligation to be bound by the lease is discharged.

concurrent conditions

In a contract, terms under which each party's performance is conditioned on the performance of the other; occur only when the parties are required to perform for each other simultaneously.

Concurrent conditions occur when each party's performance is conditioned on the performance of the other. They occur only when the parties are required to perform for each other simultaneously. For example, when a buyer is supposed to pay for goods on delivery, the buyer's duty to pay is impliedly conditioned on the seller's duty to deliver the goods, and the seller's duty to deliver the goods is impliedly conditioned on the buyer's duty to pay for the goods. The legal effect of a contract's being concurrently conditioned is that each party must offer to perform before being able to sue the other for nonperformance.

express condition

A condition specifically and explicitly stated in a contract and usually preceded by words such as *conditioned on, if, provided that, or when.*

Express and Implied Conditions Conditions in contracts are also described as being express or implied. Express conditions are explicitly stated in the contract and are usually preceded by words such as *conditioned on, if, provided that,* or *when.* For example, in a situation involving a potential sale of a house, the offer expressly required that the buyer make a deposit of $1,000 "on acceptance." The buyer wrote "accepted" on the offer and returned it but did not include the deposit. No deposit of money was ever made. The seller then canceled the transaction. Several weeks later, the buyer attempted to tender payment to the seller. The court found that under the terms of the contract, payment of the $1,000 was an express condition of acceptance and since the acceptance was incomplete, there was no contract.[2]

[2] *Smith v. Holmwood,* 231 Cal. App. 2d 549 (1965).

Implied conditions are those that are not explicitly stated but are inferred from the nature and language of the contract. For example, if a man enters into a contract with a builder to replace the windows in his house, there is an implied condition that the builder will be given access to the home so that she may fulfill her obligations under the contract.

DISCHARGE BY PERFORMANCE

In most situations, parties discharge their obligations by doing what they respectively agreed to do under the terms of the contract; this is called *discharge by performance.* Parties also discharge their duty by making an offer to perform and being ready, willing, and able to perform. This offer of performance is known as a tender. If a painter shows up at Sherry's house with his paint and ladders and is ready to start painting the garage, he has tendered performance. If Sherry refuses to let him start, the painter has now discharged his duties under the contract by his tender of performance and he may sue Sherry for material breach (discussed in detail later in this chapter).

Types of Performance There are two primary kinds of performance: complete performance and substantial performance. Performance may also be conditioned on the satisfaction of a party to the contract or of a third party.

Complete performance occurs when every aspect of the parties' duties under the contract is carried out perfectly. In many instances, complete performance is difficult, if not impossible, to attain, and courts today generally require only substantial performance.

Substantial performance occurs when the following conditions have been met: (1) completion of nearly all the terms of the agreement, (2) an honest effort to complete all the terms, and (3) no willful departure from the terms of the agreement. Substantial performance discharges the party's responsibilities under the contract, although the court may require that the party compensate the other party for any loss in value caused by the failure to meet all the standards set forth in the contract. For example, if a contract called for all bedrooms of a house to be painted blue but one was inadvertently painted green, the court may require that the contractor compensate the buyer with the amount that it will cost the buyer to have that room repainted. The difficulty of determining whether there has in fact been substantial performance is illustrated in the Case Nugget.

Performance Subject to Satisfaction of a Contracting Party Sometimes the performance of the contract is subject to the satisfaction of one of the contracting parties. In such a case, a party is not discharged from the contract until the other party is satisfied. Satisfaction is considered an express condition that must be met before the other party's obligation to pay for the performance arises.

Satisfaction may be judged according to either a subjective or an objective standard. When the judgment involved is a matter of personal taste, such as when a woman is having a dress custom made for her, the courts apply a subjective satisfaction standard. As long as the person, in good faith, is not satisfied, the other party is deemed to have not met the condition.

If the performance is related to a mechanical or utility standard, the objective satisfaction standard applies. Also, if the contract does not clearly specify that the satisfaction is to be personal, the objective standard applies. When an objective standard is used, the courts ask whether the reasonable person would be satisfied with the performance.

Sometimes a contract is conditioned on the satisfaction of a third party. Usually, such provisions arise in construction contracts specifying that before a buyer accepts a building, an architect must provide a certificate stating that the building was constructed according to the plans and specifications.

DISCHARGE BY MATERIAL BREACH

A *breach* occurs whenever a party fails to perform her obligations under the contract. If the breach is a minor one, it may entitle the nonbreaching party to damages but it does not discharge the nonbreaching party from the contract.

implied condition
A condition that is not specifically and explicitly stated but is inferred from the nature and language of the contract.

tender
An offer by a party in a contract to perform, along with being ready, willing, and able to perform, a duty outlined in that contract.

complete performance
Contract performance that occurs when all aspects of the parties' duties under the contract are carried out perfectly.

substantial performance
Contract performance that occurs when nearly all the terms of the agreement have been met, there has been an honest effort to complete all the terms, and there has been no willful departure from the terms of the agreement.

CASE Nugget

A Substantial or Insubstantial Performance?

Larry Pettit et al. v. Hampton and Beech, Inc., et al.
Court of Appeals of Connecticut

101 Conn. App. 502, 922 A.2d 300 (2007)

The plaintiffs contracted for construction of a new house with the defendant. They wanted their home to be a reverse image of the house depicted in the defendant's advertisement, and they also modified the plans by widening the kitchen and great room and extending the rear of the house. There were some delays in the construction. At the time of the issuance of the certificate of occupancy, which was one day after the closing date specified in the contract, the plaintiffs gave the defendants a punch card of items to be fixed, placed $20,000 of the purchase price in escrow, refused to set a new closing date, moved into a motel, and sued the defendant, claiming the defendant failed to substantially perform the contract.

The trial court found, pursuant to expert testimony, that reading and comprehending the blueprints provided by the plaintiffs were difficult for the framers and probably led to some of the shortcomings in the construction process. The court found that there were surface cracks in the concrete front porch because expansion joints were not installed and that the front steps, which were built to industry standards, had settled. The court further found that the porch could be repaired by resurfacing it and that the gap between the steps and the porch was a minor repair. The court awarded $3,238 to the plaintiffs to repair both problems.

There were cracks in the foundation, not uncommon after construction, which could be repaired for $700. Rather than following the blueprint requirement, the defendant used an alternate construction that provided better structural support and complied with the building code. The court awarded $105 to attach a joist to an existing one to add additional support, although this might not be necessary structurally. The court found that a beam needed to be installed under the kitchen and awarded $250 for the repair. Joint hangers were missing on the header and stringers of the stairway to the basement. Their omission was not a structural defect, and they easily could be installed at a cost of $75. Bridging and blocking were omitted or not nailed where ducts and pipes passed through joists, another nonstructural defect, and this could be remedied at a cost of $60. Settlement cracks in the walls, a common postconstruction phenomenon, could be repaired for $1,265. The court also awarded the plaintiffs $219.34 to replace a window over the garage.

The plaintiffs appealed on grounds that the proper standard for substantial performance was not applied and thus they were entitled to more damages. In affirming the lower court's judgment that the defendant had substantially performed, the appeals judge said that issuance of a certificate of occupancy may be evidence of substantial performance; it is not dispositive of the question. Other factors include the extent to which the injured party will be deprived of the benefit reasonably expected, the extent to which that party can be adequately compensated for the deficiency of performance, the extent to which the performing party will suffer forfeiture, the likelihood that the performing party will cure his failure in light of the circumstances and his reasonable assurances, and the extent of good faith and fair dealing on the part of the performing party. Applying the factors to the case, the ruling of the trial court judge was not clearly erroneous, and therefore his judgment was affirmed.

A **material breach,** however, discharges the nonbreaching party from his obligations under the contract. A material breach occurs when a party unjustifiably fails to substantially perform his obligations under the contract. It is often difficult to know when the court is going to determine that a breach is material. Case 12-1 demonstrates the analysis a court may use to determine whether a defendant's behavior constitutes material breach.

material breach

A substantial breach of a significant term or terms of a contract that excuses the nonbreaching party from further performance under the contract and gives the nonbreaching party the right to recover damages.

MILLER v. MILLS CONSTRUCTION, INC.
EIGHTH CIRCUIT COURT OF APPEALS
352 F.3d 1166 (8th Cir. 2003)

FACTS: *Mills Construction, Inc., contracted with the City of Brookings, South Dakota, to construct a series of buildings. One building required the erection of a steel clear span, so Mills subcontracted the erection of this building to Wilma Miller, who conducted business under the name Double Diamond Construction. Under their contract, Double Diamond agreed to supply the labor and equipment, while Mills agreed to obtain prefabricated steel from American Buildings Company (ABC) for the construction.*

When Double Diamond began construction of the building on April 15, the company recognized numerous problems with the materials supplied by ABC to Mills and notified Mills of the problems. Mills recommended that Double Diamond contact ABC directly, but when Double Diamond notified ABC, ABC did not resolve the problems with the materials. Therefore, Double Diamond discontinued construction on May 12, claiming that construction could not continue until ABC or Mills fixed the problems with the materials. Wilma Miller specified her concerns in a letter to ABC, Mills, and the City of Brookings, dated May 14, in which she also questioned the structural integrity of the building.

On May 15, an ABC representative visited the site, videotaped the building, and documented the alleged structural problems. However, the representative concluded that no problems existed with the structure, unless a tornado was to strike the building. Nevertheless, the building collapsed later that evening with winds estimated at 35 miles per hour.

Following the collapse, Double Diamond requested payment from Mills for the work completed prior to the collapse. When Mills did not pay the full amount for the work, Double Diamond filed suit for damages. Mills counterclaimed for breach of contract and negligence. The trial court found in favor of Double Diamond, concluding that Mills failed to provide appropriate materials for the construction. Mills appealed, claiming that the trial court did not specify that there had been a material breach.

ISSUE: Did the lower court find Mills's failure to supply appropriate materials to be a material breach of contract entitling Double Diamond to damages?

REASONING: The determination of whether a material breech has occurred does not turn on whether the term material has been used by the court. Rather, it is determined by whether the court has found that the essential purpose of the contract has not been fulfilled.

The district court found that Mills breached the contract by failing to provide the materials that were necessary for the essential purpose of the contract to be fulfilled, which was the construction of the arena by a specified date. Because Mills did not provide suitable building materials, Mills prevented proper construction of the building and made the structure vulnerable to collapse. Because of the sheer number of problems with the materials provided by Mills, and the fact that the plaintiff had notified Mills and ABC of the problem and gave them the chance to correct the defect, the district court found that it was impossible for Double Diamond to perform the contract.

From these facts, it is clear that an implied finding of material breach was implicit in the district court's finding that Mills breached the contract by failing to provide appropriate materials.

DECISION AND REMEDY: The lower court's decision was affirmed, in favor of the plaintiff, Miller (dba Double Diamond). Because the defendant materially breached the contract, Double Diamond was entitled to recover all the damage proximately caused by the breach, not to exceed the amount it would have gained by full performance.

SIGNIFICANCE OF THE CASE: This case illustrates the importance of the difference between a material breach and an immaterial breach.

CRITICAL THINKING

Can you think of any additional facts that, had they been present, might have changed the outcome of this case?

ETHICAL DECISION MAKING

Which stakeholders were affected by the actions of Mills that were examined in this case? Does the ruling protect values such as justice and fairness for the relevant parties? Why or why not?

In the Walgreen's dispute in the Case Opener, there was no question of whether the defendant had materially breached the contract. A key term of the 30-year lease between Walgreen's and the defendant was the exclusivity clause. Walgreen's would never have entered into the lease if it could not have been the only drugstore in the shopping center. To allow not just another discount drugstore in the shopping center but a deeper-discount drugstore that would open up right next door to Walgreen's was clearly a material breach of the agreement.

Anticipatory Repudiation Sometimes a contracting party may decide not to complete the contract before the actual time of performance. This situation often arises when market conditions change and one party realizes that it will not be profitable to carry out the terms of the contract. The breaching party may convey the anticipatory breach to the nonbreaching party either by making an express indication of her intent to no longer perform or by taking an action that would be inconsistent with her ability to carry out the contract when performance was due.

Once the contract has been anticipatorily repudiated, the nonbreaching party is discharged from his obligations under the contract. He is free to go ahead and sue for breach, as well as find another similar contract elsewhere. However, if the nonbreaching party wishes, he may decide to give the party who repudiated the opportunity to change her mind and still perform.

DISCHARGE BY MUTUAL AGREEMENT

Sometimes the parties to a contract agree to discharge each other from their obligations. They may do so through four primary means: discharge by mutual rescission, discharge by a substituted contract, discharge by accord and satisfaction, or discharge by novation.

Mutual Rescission Parties may agree that they simply wish to discharge each other from their mutual obligations and therefore may rescind or cancel the contract. For example, if James agreed to cater a graduation reception for Bill's son but it appears that the child is not going to graduate when planned, James could agree to no longer hold Bill responsible for paying him the agreed-on cost for the catering in exchange for Bill's agreement to no long expect James to cater the reception.

Substituted Contract Sometimes, instead of canceling the contract and terminating their relationship, the parties wish to substitute a new agreement in place of the original. The substituted contract immediately discharges the parties from their obligations under the old contract and replaces those obligations with the new obligations imposed by the substituted contract.

Accord and Satisfaction An accord and satisfaction is used when one of the parties wishes to substitute a different performance for his original duty under the contract. The promise to perform the new duty is called the *accord,* and the actual performance of that new duty is called the *satisfaction.* The party's duty under the contract is not discharged until the new duty is actually performed. Thus it is the satisfaction that discharges the party.

Management

As you may have learned in your management class, consensus is generally the goal when groups engage in some method of problem solving. Techniques for group problem solving include the use of interacting groups, nominal groups, and Delphi groups. *Interacting groups,* which are most commonly used, are groups in which the members deliberate, perhaps with much arguing and disagreement initially, until a consensus is reached. *Nominal groups* are those that involve no discussion at first, as group members are usually asked to write down as many ideas as possible and thereafter the ideas are written on a board and voted on by group members. *Delphi groups* involve the use of a diverse group of experts who anonymously complete questionnaires to produce ideas, and their combined judgments are evaluated to hopefully find a consensus of expert opinion.

While these methods may be useful in certain business environments, the goal of consensus is nevertheless just as critical in the context of contracts, particularly after a contract has been formed. For instance, if a party realizes he cannot perform the contract and cannot claim that the performance is impossible or impracticable, his only alternative to being sued by the other party is consensus, or mutual agreement, with the other party. If the nonperforming party is fortunate, the other party may agree to rescind the contract or create a substitute contract. The nonperforming party may choose to use the interacting-group problem-solving technique to hopefully reach a consensus.

Source: K. Williams, *Management: A Practical Introduction* (New York: McGraw-Hill/Irwin, 2006), pp. 221–223.

Novation Sometimes the parties to the agreement wish to replace one of the parties with a third party. This substitution of a party is called a **novation.** The original duties remain the same under the contract, but one party is discharged and the third party now takes that original party's place. All three parties must agree to the novation for it to be valid.

DISCHARGE BY OPERATION OF LAW

Sometimes a contract may be discharged not by anything the parties do but, rather, by operation of law. Alteration of the contract, bankruptcy, tolling of the statute of limitations, impossibility, commercial impracticability, and frustration of purpose are all situations in which a contract may be discharged by operation of law.

Alteration of the Contract The courts wish to uphold the sanctity of contracts. Therefore, if one of the parties materially alters a written contract without the knowledge of the other party, the courts have held that such alteration allows the innocent party to be discharged from the contract. For example, if a seller, without knowledge of the buyer, changes the price of the contract, the buyer can treat the contract as terminated.

Bankruptcy When a party files bankruptcy, the court allocates the assets of the bankrupt among the bankrupt's creditors and then issues the party a discharge in bankruptcy. Once the assets have been distributed, all the bankrupt's debts are discharged. (Bankruptcy is discussed in detail in Chapter 17.)

Tolling of the Statute of Limitations The tolling of the statute of limitations, that is, the expiration of the time allowed by the statute, does not technically discharge a party's obligations under the contract. However, once the statute of limitations has tolled, neither party can any longer sue the other for breach, so for all practical purposes the parties are no longer bound to perform.

Impossibility of Performance Sometimes an unforeseen event occurs that makes it physically or legally impossible for a party to carry out the terms of the contract. In such a situation, the parties

novation
In a contract, the substitution of a third party for one of the original parties; the duties remain the same under the contract, but one original party is discharged and the third party takes that original party's place.

233

will be discharged on grounds of impossibility of performance. Courts distinguish between *objective impossibility,* meaning it is in fact not possible to lawfully carry out one's contractual obligations, and *subjective impossibility,* meaning it would be very difficult to carry out the contract. Objective impossibility but not subjective impossibility discharges the parties' obligations under the contract.

For example, if farmer Gray has a contract with the Hunts Corporation to provide it with 100 bushels of tomatoes on August 30 and a flood wipes out Gray's crop, it is not physically impossible for him to comply with the agreement. He has to go out on the market and purchase 100 bushels of tomatoes to ship to the Hunts Corporation. It may be inconvenient, and perhaps subjectively impossible, but it is not objectively impossible.

In contrast, suppose farmer Jones owns a historic farmhouse built in 1827 and he agrees to sell it to Smith, but the night before the parties are to exchange money for the title, lightning strikes the farmhouse and it burns to the ground. It is now objectively impossible to comply with the terms of the contract, so the parties are discharged from their obligations. The historic farmhouse is not like tomatoes; the subject matter of the contract is forever destroyed and cannot be re-created.

There are three main situations in which the courts find objective impossibility. The first is *destruction of the subject matter,* as in the example of the historic farmhouse destroyed by fire. If we go back to the example of the tomatoes, note that we said the farmer still had to perform because it was still possible for him to obtain tomatoes elsewhere. To protect himself in the event that his crop was destroyed, farmer Gray could have drafted the contract to identify the subject matter as 100 bushels of tomatoes grown on the Smith family farm. In that case, if Smith's fields were flooded, it would be objectively impossible to comply with the contract because there would be no tomatoes from the Smith farm in existence.

The second situation of objective impossibility is the *death or incapacity of a party whose personal services are necessary* to fulfill the terms of the contract. For example, if a famous artist is commissioned to paint a portrait and the artist dies, the contract is discharged. The artist's style is unique, and there is no way for anyone to take over the artist's role.

The third situation is *subsequent illegality.* If the law changes after the contract was made, rendering the performance of the contract illegal, the contract is discharged. For example, Bill orders a case of a nutritional supplement from Osco Drugs and Supplements. Before his order can be filled, the nutritional supplement is banned because of recently discovered harmful side effects. The parties are now discharged from their duties because to sell the banned substance would be to violate the law.

Commercial Impracticability Commercial impracticability is seen by some as a response to a somewhat unfair harshness of the objective impossibility standard. Commercial impracticability is used when performance is still objectively possible but would be extraordinarily injurious or expensive to one party. Commercial impracticability arises when, because of an unforeseeable event, one party would incur unreasonable expense, injury, or loss if that party were forced to carry out the terms of the agreement.

According to the Restatement (Second) of Contracts, Section 261 (1981), discharge by reason of impracticability requires that the party claiming discharge prove the following three elements:

1. That an event occurred whose nonoccurrence was a basic assumption of the contract.
2. That continued performance is not commercially practicable.
3. That the party claiming discharge did not expressly or impliedly agree to performance in spite of impracticability that would otherwise justify his nonperformance.

It is sometimes difficult to know whether the potential harm to the party seeking to avoid the contract is sufficient to give rise to the use of commercial impracticability. The doctrine is most commonly used in situations where raw materials needed for manufacturing goods under the contract become extraordinarily expensive or difficult to obtain because of an embargo, war,

crop failure, or unexpected closure of a plant. Case 12-2 illustrates how the courts sometimes struggle to determine whether to apply the doctrine of commercial impracticability to discharge a contract.

·····➔ CASE 12-2

THRIFTY RENT-A-CAR SYSTEM v. SOUTH FLORIDA TRANSPORT
U.S. DISTRICT COURT FOR THE NORTHERN DISTRICT OF OKLAHOMA

2005 U.S. Dist. LEXIS 38489

FACTS: *The plaintiffs, Thrifty Rent-A-Car System and its affiliates DTG and Rental Car Finance Corp., allowed South Florida Transport (SFT), the defendant, to establish a Thrifty franchise. In 2003, they entered into four agreements, providing SFT the right to use Thrifty's trademark and business methods in exchange for payment to Thrifty of licensing and administrative fees and requiring SFT to maintain a fleet of automobiles for rent.*

In July 2004, SFT provided DTG with a check as payment, but it was returned for insufficient funds. SFT continued to make delinquent payments, and by August SFT owed Thrifty and DTG $1,134,819.40. Due to SFT's failure to make payments, Thrifty and DTG informed SFT that they were going to terminate the licensing agreements and repossess the vehicles, to which DTG had legal title. However, DTG agreed to postpone repossession due to predictions of severe weather and allowed SFT to continue renting vehicles until repossession was completed.

When DTG repossessed the vehicles, DTG noticed that numerous cars were missing, to which SFT notified DTG that it had sold 51 vehicles without authorization. By August 2005, SFT owed Thrifty and DTG $4,238,249.53. SFT claimed that several hurricanes rendered its business operations commercially impracticable. The plaintiffs filed a motion for summary judgment, seeking full reimbursement for the debts owed by SFT.

ISSUE: Under what circumstances will commercial impracticability excuse nonperformance of a contract?

REASONING IN THE WORDS OF THE COURT: The doctrine of commercial impracticability is typically invoked in cases involving the sale of goods.

Codified in section 2-615 of the Uniform Commercial Code (UCC), which has been adopted by the Oklahoma legislature, the doctrine of commercial impracticability provides a defense to a seller for a delay in delivery or nondelivery of promised goods if performance has been made impracticable by a contingency, the nonoccurrence of which is an assumption of the contract.

Commercial impracticability may excuse a party from performance of his obligations under a contract where performance has become commercially impracticable because of unforeseen supervening circumstances not within the contemplation of the parties at the time of contracting. UCC commentary provides that a party pleading commercial impracticability must demonstrate the "basic assumption" prong of the test also found in the impracticability of performance context, that is, that the nonoccurrence of the supervening event was a basic assumption of the parties at the time of contracting. A rise or a collapse in the market standing alone does not constitute a justification for failure to perform. A contract is deemed commercially impracticable when, due to unforeseen events, performance may only be obtained at "an excessive and unreasonable cost . . . or when all means of performance are commercially senseless." In applying the doctrine of commercial impracticability, the crucial question is "whether the cost of performance has in fact become so excessive and unreasonable that failure to excuse performance would result in grave injustice."

. . . The evidence strongly suggests that the nonoccurrence of hurricanes was not a basic assumption of the parties' agreements. Moreover, defendant provides no evidence to support a suggestion that the event of the hurricanes made the cost of performance of the terms of the agreements unduly burdensome, or even remotely more expensive. Finally, the Court observes, again, that SFT was behind on its payments to Thrifty and DTG before the arrival of the hurricanes in August 2004. No genuine issue

of material fact exists, and the Court holds that the defense of commercial impracticability is unavailable to defendant.

DECISION AND REMEDY: The plaintiffs' motion for summary judgment was granted.

SIGNIFICANCE OF THE CASE: This case illustrates how strictly courts look at the circumstances to determine whether to apply the doctrine of commercial impracticability.

CRITICAL THINKING

Especially given the increased rates of severe weather and natural disasters witnessed recently around the world, to what extent can parties entering into contracts reasonably be expected to plan for the effects of a rapidly changing global climate?

ETHICAL DECISION MAKING

What values do you think are furthered by the decision in this case? What values are being subordinated by this decision?

Frustration of Purpose Closely related to impracticability is frustration of purpose. Sometimes, when a contract is entered into, both parties recognize that the contract is intended to fulfill a particular purpose, and the happening of that purpose is said to be a basic assumption on which the contract is made. If, due to factors beyond the control of the parties, the event does not occur, and neither party had assumed the risk of the event's nonoccurrence, the contract may be discharged.

This doctrine arose from the so-called coronation cases in England. Numerous parties had contracted for rooms along the parade route for the king's coronation, but the king became ill and the coronation was canceled. The courts held that the parties' duties under the room contracts should be discharged and that any payments made in advance should be returned as the essential purposes of the contracts could no longer be fulfilled, through no fault of any of the parties.

Again, this doctrine is not frequently used. For example, if you contract for an organist to play at your daughter's wedding but the groom gets cold feet at the last moment and the wedding is canceled, you cannot use frustration of purpose to discharge the contract because the groom's changing his mind was a foreseeable event, even though it was unlikely.

Remedies

The fact that one party has breached a contract does not necessarily mean that the nonbreaching party will sue. A number of factors go into the decision of whether it makes sense to file suit. Some of those considerations are (1) the likelihood of success, (2) the desire or need to maintain an ongoing relationship with the potential defendant, (3) the possibility of getting a better or faster resolution through some form of alternative dispute resolution, and (4) the cost of litigation or some other form of ADR as compared to the value of the likely remedy.

The remedies the potential plaintiff will be thinking about can generally be classified as either *legal remedies* (also known as *money damages*) or *equitable remedies,* some form of court-ordered action. The distinction between legal and equitable remedies can be traced back to a time in our legal system's English roots when, instead of one unitary legal system, there were two separate courts, a court of law and a court of equity. When parties were seeking money damages, they went to the court of law; but when parties needed any remedy other than money damages, they went to the High Court of Chancery, which was a court of equity. When the United States was establishing its legal system, it combined both these types of powers in a unitary system. The reasons for this joinder are not known, but it seems likely that the primary reason was that the early colonists simply did not have the resources to support two separate systems. The courts did, however, still maintain the distinction between legal and equitable remedies. However, unlike

CASE Nugget

An Unforeseeable Event?

Liggett Restaurant Group, Inc. v. City of Pontiac
Michigan Court of Appeals

260 Mich. App. 127, 676 N.W.2d 633 (Mich. App. 2003)

Elias Brothers Restaurants, Inc., had a contract with the defendant, City of Pontiac Stadium Building Authority, to provide concessions at the Silverdome until 2000. The parties renegotiated the contract in 1990, and Elias Brothers agreed to pay additional consideration for the option to extend the contract until 2005 to coordinate with the end of the Detroit Lions' sublease. The additional consideration involved paying the city a higher percentage on profits from sales. This option was exercised on December 1, 1998, and the Detroit Lions prematurely discontinued playing in the Silverdome after the 2001 football season.

The plaintiff sought to use the frustration-of-purpose doctrine to discharge its obligations under the contract extension and therefore have returned to it the additional consideration it had paid under the extension. The plaintiff argued that the contract was made on the assumption that the Lions would play in the Silverdome until their lease ran out and thus that their early departure frustrated the purpose of the extension.

The court said the doctrine was inapplicable in this case. The court first set forth the conditions under which the doctrine applied: (1) The contract must be at least partially executory; (2) the frustrated party's purpose in making the contract must have been known to both parties when the contract was made; (3) this purpose must have been basically frustrated by an event not reasonably foreseeable at the time the contract was made, the occurrence of which was not due to the fault of the frustrated party and the risk of which was not assumed by him.

Then the court noted that the situation clearly did not meet the third criterion. Far from being an unforeseen event, the Lions' leaving prematurely was expressly addressed in the original contract by a paragraph specifying a reduction in the guaranteed minimum annual payment for each year in which the Lions did not play a minimum of eight games in the stadium.

judges in the old English courts, judges in the U.S. system have the power to award both legal and equitable remedies in the same case. This section discusses these various remedies.

LEGAL REMEDIES (MONETARY DAMAGES)

LO 2

Monetary damages are also referred to as *legal damages,* and they include compensatory, punitive, nominal, and liquidated damages. Whenever possible, courts award monetary damages rather than some form of equitable relief.

Compensatory Damages The most frequently awarded damages are compensatory damages, damages designed to put the plaintiff in the position he would have been in had the contract been fully performed. These damages are said to compensate the plaintiff for his loss of the benefit of the bargain. He can recover, however, only for those provable losses that were foreseeable at the time the contract was entered into. Sometimes, the plaintiff actually may have no losses. Suppose, for example, that Dr. Wilcox hires Jeremy to work exclusively as his research assistant during the fall semester, for a salary of $2,000 per month. If Wilcox breaches the contract and terminates Jeremy for no reason with two months left on the contract, and the only job Jeremy can get as a substitute pays only $500 per month, Jeremy is entitled to compensatory damages of $3,000. However, if Jeremy gets a new job that pays $2,500 per month, he is actually better off now, so he has no compensatory damages. Sometimes these damages are referred as *expectation damages* because they compensate a person for the benefit she or he expected to gain as a result of entering into the contract.

compensatory damages

Money awarded to a plaintiff as reimbursement for her or his losses; based on the amount of actual damage or harm to property, lost wages or profits, pain and suffering, medical expenses, disability, etc.

In addition to losing the benefit of the bargain, the plaintiff may suffer other losses caused directly by the breach. These losses may be compensated as *incidental damages*. For example, because Jeremy was unfairly terminated before his contractual term was over, he may have to spend money to find another job. His job search expenditures would be considered incidental damages.

Some kinds of contracts have special rules for determining their compensatory damages, namely, contracts for the sale of goods, contracts for the sale of land, and construction contracts. Each of these is discussed in a little more detail below.

Contracts for the sale of goods are governed today by the Uniform Commercial Code. If the seller breaches the contract, compensatory damages are generally calculated as the difference between the contract price and the market price on the day the goods were supposed to be delivered,[3] plus any incidental damages resulting from the breach. In other words, this measure of damages is the difference between what the buyer would have paid for the goods under the contract and what he or she is now going to have to pay to obtain the goods from another seller. Occasionally, however, the buyer may have no damages because the market price of the goods is lower than the parties had anticipated it would be at the date of delivery and so the buyer can now actually purchase the goods at a lower price than the contract price.

If the buyer breaches before accepting the goods, the seller would be able to resell the goods and recover as compensatory damages the difference between the price he sold the goods for and the contract price, plus any incidental expenses associated with the sale.[4] If the seller is unable to sell the goods to another buyer, as might be the case, for example, with shirts embroidered with a company's monogram, then the seller may be entitled to the contract price as damages. If the buyer breaches before the goods are even manufactured, the seller's damages would typically be based on the profits that would have been made from the sale.

In construction contracts, contracts whereby an owner enters into an agreement to have a building constructed, damages are calculated differently depending on who the breaching party is and what stage the construction is in when the breach occurs. If the contract is breached by the owner before the construction is begun, damages are simply lost profits, which are calculated by subtracting the projected costs of construction from the contract price. For example, if Cameron Construction Company anticipates building a warehouse for the Johnson Corporation and the contract price is $500,000 and the cost of raw materials and labor is $420,000, Cameron could recover $80,000 in lost profits if Johnson were to breach the contract before performance had begun.

If, however, Cameron Construction had already expended $20,000 on materials and labor on the job when the breach occurred, the company would be able to recover $100,000 in damages because the amount of damages when construction is in progress is measured by the lost profits plus any money already invested in the project. And if the breach by Johnson had occurred after construction was completed, then Cameron would be entitled to recover the entire contract price, plus interest from the time payment for the project was due.

If the construction company, or contractor, breaches the contract before or during the construction, the owner's damages are generally measured by the cost of hiring another company to complete the project, plus any incidental costs associated with obtaining a new contractor, as well as any costs arising from delays in the construction project. If the contractor completes the job but finishes after the date for completion, the owner is entitled to damages for the loss of the use of the building that she would have had if the contract had been completed in a timely manner.

consequential damages

In a contract, foreseeable damages that result from special facts and circumstances arising outside the contract itself. The damages must be within the contemplation of the parties at the time the breach occurs. Also called *special damages*.

Consequential Damages It should be apparent by now that contract law requires greater certainty in the proof of damages than does tort law. Damages are not recoverable for breach of contract unless they can be proved with a high degree of certainty. One type of damages in contract cases that is often especially difficult to prove is what are called consequential or special damages. Consequential damages are foreseeable damages that result from special facts and circumstances arising outside the contract itself. These damages must be within the contemplation of the parties at the time the breach occurs.

[3] UCC § § 2-708 and 2-713.

[4] UCC § § 2-706 and 2-710.

In the Case Nugget, the court distinguishes consequential damages from the damages that arise naturally from a breach of contract.

CASE Nugget

A Classic Case of Consequential Damages

Hadley v. Baxendale Court of Exchequer

156 Eng. Rep. 145 (1854)

The plaintiffs were millers whose mill was stopped when the crankshaft of the mill broke. They sent the shaft to Greenwich to be used as a model for a new crank. The plaintiffs' servant took the shaft to the defendant, a common carrier, and told the defendant's clerk that the mill was stopped and that the shaft must be sent immediately. At the time, however, most mills would have had extra crankshafts around somewhere, so without more being said, the clerk would not have known that the mill would not be soon back and running on a spare shaft. The clerk said the shaft would be delivered at Greenwich on the following day. The defendant's clerk was told that a special entry, if required, should be made to hasten the shaft's delivery. The delivery of the shaft at Greenwich was delayed by some neglect, and, consequently, the plaintiffs did not receive the new shaft for several days after they would otherwise have received it. During that time the mill was shut down, and the plaintiffs thereby lost the profits they would have received had the shaft been delivered on time. They sought to recover damages for lost profits during that time. The defendant argued that the lost profits were "too remote." The court decided for the plaintiffs and allowed the jury to consider the lost profits in awarding damages. The defendant appealed.

On appeal, the appellate judge set forth what has come to be the standard for consequential damages:

> Where two parties have made a contract which one of them has broken, the damages which the other party ought to receive in respect of such breach of contract should be such as may fairly and reasonably be considered either arising naturally, i.e., according to the usual course of things, from such breach of contract itself, or such as may reasonably be supposed to have been in the contemplation of both parties, at the time they made the contract, as the probable result of the breach of it. Now, if the special circumstances under which the contract was actually made were communicated by the plaintiffs to the defendants, and thus known to both parties, the damages resulting from the breach of such a contract, which they would reasonably contemplate, would be the amount of injury which would ordinarily follow from a breach of contract under these special circumstances so known and communicated. But, on the other hand, if these special circumstances were wholly unknown to the party breaking the contract, he, at the most, could only be supposed to have had in his contemplation the amount of injury which would arise generally, and in the great multitude of cases not affected by any special circumstances, from such a breach of contract. For, had the special circumstances been known, the parties might have specially provided for the breach of contract by special terms as to the damages in that case; and of this advantage it would be very unjust to deprive them.

In this case, the judge did not believe that the special circumstances had been communicated to the defendant. Thus it would have been unjust to hold the defendant liable for the damages, which he would not have contemplated as arising from the delayed delivery of a shaft.

Punitive Damages Just as in tort law, **punitive damages** in contract law are designed to punish the defendant and deter him and others from engaging in similar behavior in the future. Because

punitive damages
Compensation awarded to a plaintiff that goes beyond reimbursement for actual losses and is imposed to punish the defendant and deter such conduct in the future.

the primary objective of contract law, however, is to ensure that parties' expectations are met, punitive, or exemplary, damages are rarely awarded. Most jurisdictions award them only when the defendant has engaged in reprehensible conduct such as fraud. The primary factor in determining the amount of punitive damages is how much is necessary to "punish" the defendant; thus the amount depends on matters such as the wealth and income of the defendant.

Nominal Damages In a case where no actual damages resulted from the breach of contract, the court may award the plaintiff **nominal damages.** The award is typically for $1 or $5, but it serves to signify that the plaintiff has been wronged by the defendant.

nominal damages
Monetary damages awarded to a plaintiff in a very small amount, typically $1 to $5, to signify that the plaintiff has been wronged by the defendant even though the plaintiff suffered no compensable harm.

liquidated damages
Damages specified as a term of the contract, before a breach of contract occurs.

Liquidated Damages Typically, the court determines the amount of damages to which a non-breaching party is entitled. Sometimes, however, the parties recognize that if there is a breach of contract, it will probably be somewhat difficult for the court to determine exactly what the damages are. To prevent a difficult court battle, the parties specify in advance what the **liquidated damages** will be if there is a particular kind of breach. The parties specify these damages in what is called a *liquidated-,* or *stipulated-, damage clause* in the contract. The damages may be specified as either a fixed amount or a formula for determining how much money is due. Such clauses are frequently used in construction contracts when the buyer needs to know that the property is going to be available by a specific date so that she can make her plans for moving in. In such a case, the parties may estimate in advance what it will cost the buyer for storage and temporary housing if the property is not ready by the specified date. The courts generally enforce such clauses as long as they appear to bear a reasonable relationship to what the actual costs will be. If the amount specified is so unreasonable as to not bear any logical relationship to foreseeable costs, the courts declare the clause a penalty clause and do not enforce it. In Case 12-3, the court had to decide whether the clause at issue was an unenforceable penalty clause or a valid liquidated-damage clause.

CASE 12-3

S. BROOKE PURLL, INC., T/A PURLL CONSTRUCTION v.
PATRICK DARRELL VAILES
DISTRICT OF COLUMBIA COURT OF APPEALS
850 A.2d 1135 (2004)

FACTS: *The plaintiff hired the defendant to renovate his house and paid him a $5,000 initial payment under the construction contract but failed to do initial demolition work required under the contract. The contract contained a clause stating:*

> *The [owner] further agrees that if he shall cancel this Contract for any reason, whatsoever, then he shall pay to the contractor as fixed and liquidated damages, without proof of loss, the sum of money equal to Thirty Five Percent (35%) of the full contract price hereinabove stated. Furthermore, if it becomes necessary for the Contractor to file suit or take other legal action on this Contract because of a breach on the part of the party of the second part, the party of the second part agrees to pay reasonable attorney fees and court cost.*

The plaintiff sued the defendant contractor for return of his deposit, and the defendant counterclaimed for $36,102 and attorney fees, the amount that would be required under the liquidated-damage clause. *The trial court held that the plaintiff had breached the contract, but it found the liquidated-damage clause to be an unenforceable penalty clause and awarded the contractor $1,722. The defendant appealed.*

ISSUE: Was the clause imposing a payment of 35 percent of the contract value for breach by the owner a penalty clause or a valid liquidated-damage clause?

REASONING: Today, the trend is toward furthering freedom of contract through the enforcement of stipulated-damage provisions as long as they do not clearly disregard the principle of compensation. Such clauses simplify the resolution of a breach-of-contract dispute, as well as give the parties an opportunity to resolve the damage question without resorting to litigation, by setting the measure of

damages at the outset, before a breach even occurs. Such provisions are especially appropriate when the parties enter into a contract in which the damages to be ascertained are uncertain in amount and cannot be easily ascertained. Thus, the courts tend to uphold these clauses unless they are clearly unreasonable. The liquidated sum must simply bear a reasonable relation to the damages foreseeable at the time the contract was made. The burden of proof is on the breaching party to demonstrate that the damage clause is disproportionate to the foreseeable damages.

In this case, the plaintiff provided no such evidence. The full contract price was $103,148.71. The contractor testified without contradiction that two-thirds of the contract price represented materials and labor and one-third represented

his profit. The contractor explained that he consulted the Ames Construction Guide for the D.C. metropolitan area, which was customarily used in the industry for pricing construction jobs, in establishing his price. Thus, there was no evidence that the clause was unreasonable. The trial court had inappropriately struck the clause down because the contractor had failed to introduce evidence of his out-of-pocket expenses; such proof is not required to uphold a liquidated-damage clause.

DECISION AND REMEDY: The lower court's decision was reversed, in favor of the defendant contractor.

SIGNIFICANCE OF THE CASE: This case illustrates the preference for upholding liquidated-damage clauses.

CRITICAL THINKING

What evidence could the plaintiff have presented that might have changed the outcome of this case?

ETHICAL DECISION MAKING

The courts place the burden of proving the unreasonableness of a liquidated-damage clause on the breaching party. Which stakeholders benefit by this approach? Which stakeholders are disadvantaged by it?

Mitigation of Damages When a contract has been breached, the nonbreaching party is often angry at the breaching party and may wish to make the breaching party "pay through the nose." However, the courts do not allow a nonbreaching party to intentionally increase his damages. In fact, to recover damages in a breach-of-contract case, the plaintiff must demonstrate that he used reasonable efforts to minimize the damage resulting from the breach. This obligation is referred to as the *duty to mitigate one's damages.*

Thus, if you are the manager of a hotel, and a person who had booked 10 rooms for the week calls to cancel all the reservations, you have a duty to attempt to rent the rooms to minimize the damages. The mitigation must be reasonable, however, and no one is expected to settle for less than what was contemplated under the contract in order to mitigate the damages.

One area where interesting mitigation issues arise is cases in which an employee is wrongfully discharged and must seek new employment to mitigate her damages. If the employee does not seek alternative employment, the amount of lost wages recovered as damages will be reduced by the amount the employee reasonably could have earned in another job. If the employee does not find another job, the court must decide whether the employee could have found comparable alternative employment with reasonable effort. For example, in 1970, the California Supreme Court considered a classic case that involved an actress who was contracted to star in a musical motion picture that was to be filmed in the United States but was canceled prior to production. The court held that the requirement to mitigate damages did not require that the actress accept as an alternative a starring role in a western drama being filmed in Australia.[5]

[5] *Parker v. Twentieth Century-Fox Film Corp.,* 3 Cal. 3d 176, 474 P.2d 689 (1970).

Liquidated Damages in China

In the Contract Law of the People's Republic of China, Article 114 of Chapter 7, Liability for Breach of Contracts, provides for the equivalent of the liquidated-damage clause recognized under U.S. law. The first part of the Chinese law is almost identical to our law. It provides that the parties to a contract may agree that one party shall, when violating the contract, pay breach-of-contract damages of a certain amount in light of the breach or they may agree on the method of calculating compensation for losses resulting from the breach of contract.

However, the Chinese law has an interesting twist for circumstances in which the projected damages end up being different from what the actual damages are. If the agreed breach-of-contract damages are lower than the losses caused, any party may request that the people's court or an arbitration institution increase the amount; if the projected damages are excessively higher than the losses caused, any party may request that the people's court or an arbitration institution make an appropriate reduction.

LO 3

EQUITABLE REMEDIES

As noted earlier, equitable remedies grew out of the English court's authority to fashion remedies when the existing laws did not provide adequate ones. These remedies were typically unique solutions specifically crafted to the demands of the situation. Today, the most common equitable remedies include rescission and restitution, orders for specific performance, and injunctions.

As a carryover from the days of the English courts of law and equity, a party seeking equitable relief must meet five requirements. The party must prove that (1) there is no adequate legal remedy available; (2) irreparable harm to the plaintiff may result if the equitable remedy is not granted; (3) the contract is legally valid (except when seeking relief in quasi-contract); (4) the contract terms are clear and unambiguous; and (5) the plaintiff has "clean hands," that is, has not been deceitful or done anything in breach of the contract.

rescission
The termination of a contract.

restitution
The return of any property given up under a contract.

Rescission and Restitution Sometimes the parties simply want to be returned to their precontract status; they want to have the contract terminated and to have any transferred property returned to its original owner. That is, they want rescission and restitution. Rescission is the termination of the contract, and restitution is the return of any property given up under the contract.

Restitution and rescission are most frequently awarded in situations in which there is a lack of genuine assent (discussed in Chapter 10). When a party enters into a contract because of fraud, duress, undue influence, or a bilateral mistake, the contract is voidable and the party who wants out may seek to avoid the contract or, in other words, may seek rescission and restitution.

specific performance
An order of the court requiring that a non-breaching party fulfill the terms of the contract.

Specific Performance Specific performance is sometimes called *specific enforcement*. It is an order requiring that the breaching party fulfill the terms of the agreement. Courts are very reluctant to grant specific performance and will do so only when monetary damages simply are not adequate, typically because the subject matter of the contract is unique. If the subject matter of the contract is unique, then even if the nonbreaching party is given compensation, he cannot go elsewhere to buy the object from someone else, so this renders any kind of money damages inadequate. Primarily for historical reasons, every piece of real property is considered unique. Therefore, an order for specific performance would often be the appropriate remedy for the breach of a contract for the sale of a piece of real estate.

Under the UCC, orders for specific performance of a contract for the sale of goods may be awarded "where the goods are unique or in other proper circumstances."[6] While the other circumstances have not been delineated by the UCC, the case law reveals that a commonly accepted circumstance is one in which the good is scarce or is no longer being produced and therefore would be difficult to obtain on the open market.

injunction
A court order either forcing a party to do something or prohibiting a party from doing something.

Injunction An injunction is an order either forcing a person to do something or prohibiting a person from doing something. Most commonly, injunctions are prohibitions against actions. Such an injunction might be used, for example, as a remedy in a contract case involving a personal

[6]UCC § 2-716.

service. Mandy is a lounge singer, and she has a contract to perform at JZ's Lounge every week-end night from January through June. Two months into her contract she decides to go work for Bally's Lounge instead because Bally's will pay her twice as much money. There is no way to adequately calculate the damages that would arise from the singer's going over to the other club to perform, so money damages would not really be an adequate remedy. Instead, the owner of JZ's may obtain an injunction prohibiting Mandy from performing in any lounge until the end of June, when her term of performance under the contract will have been completed.

In the Walgreen's dispute in the Case Opener, the appellate court agreed with the trial court judge that it would be extremely difficult for the court to calculate how to adequately deter-mine the damages that Walgreen's would sustain if Sara Creek were allowed to simply vio-late the contract's exclusivity clause and lease space to another drugstore. The court would have had to determine how much business the new store would take from Walgreen's over the course of the next 10 years, and it felt that such a calculation would be almost impossible to figure. Hence, the court agreed that money damages would not be adequate and that an injunc-tion prohibiting the leasing of the space in violation of the exclusivity clause would be the only adequate remedy.

Sometimes, when a party is suing another for breach of contract, one of the parties is con-cerned that before the court has had a chance to decide the case, the other party will do some-thing to make it impossible for the concerned party to get the relief he would be entitled to. In such a situation, the concerned party may ask for a preliminary injunction to prohibit the other party from taking any action during the course of the lawsuit that would cause irreparable harm to any of the parties to the contract. For example, Jim agrees to sell Bob a very rare antique car for $15,000 but then says he is not going to comply with the terms of the agreement. Bob sues Jim for breach of contract, but before the case goes to trial, Bob finds out that Sara has told Jim that she is willing to pay him $20,000 for the car. Bob may seek a preliminary injunc-tion to prohibit Jim from selling the car to anyone else until the court decides whether Bob is entitled to an order for specific performance forcing Jim to sell the car to him. Thus the preliminary injunction fulfills the purpose of maintaining the status quo until the case can be finally decided.

Reformation Sometimes a written contract does not reflect the parties' actual agreement, or there may be inconsistencies in the contract, such as the price being listed as "$200,000 (twenty thousand dollars)." In such a case, the written document may be rewritten to reflect what the par-ties had agreed on.

Recovery Based on Quasi-Contract When an enforceable contract does not in fact exist, the court may grant a recovery based on quasi-contract; that is, the court may impose a contract-like obligation on a party to prevent an injustice from occurring. Recovery in quasi-contract is often sought when a party thought a valid contract existed and gave up something of value in rely-ing on the existence of a contract. To recover under a theory of quasi-contract, a plaintiff must prove that (1) the plaintiff conferred a benefit on the defendant; (2) the plaintiff had reasonably expected to be compensated for the benefit conferred on the defendant; (3) the defendant would be unjustly enriched from receiving the benefit without compensating the plaintiff for it.

 SUMMARY

Methods of Discharging a Contract	Contracts may be discharged in a number of different ways, including:
	• The happening of a condition subsequent or the nonhappening of a condition precedent.
	• Complete or substantial performance.
	• Material breach.
	• Mutual agreement.
	• Operation of law.

Remedies Courts may grant parties in a breach-of-contract action legal or equitable remedies. *Legal remedies,* or money damages, include:

- Compensatory damages.
- Nominal damages.
- Punitive damages.
- Liquidated damages.

Equitable remedies, which are granted only when legal remedies are inadequate, include:

- Restitution and rescission.
- Specific performance.
- Injunction.

 Point/Counterpoint

Should Nonbreaching Parties Be Required to Mitigate Damages?	
YES	NO
Courts' requiring nonbreaching parties to mitigate damages provides the most equitable solution when a contract is breached.	Courts' requiring nonbreaching parties to mitigate damages is unfair.

Courts' requiring nonbreaching parties to mitigate damages provides the most equitable solution when a contract is breached.

Although a nonbreaching party could understandably be frustrated with the breaching party, such a breach does not license the nonbreaching party to force the breaching party to provide full payment for the contract, especially when many costs could have been avoided. For example, if a city contracts with a company to construct a bridge across a river and the city later learns that the roads that would connect to the bridge would disrupt a nesting bald eagle, the company should not be permitted to still build the bridge and demand full payment. The city would then have to pay for a useless bridge, even though the company could have avoided the costs of building the bridge.

In this example and similar contexts, the breaching parties would have an incentive to do nothing and still demand payment, even though damages could have been reduced. For instance, if a person entered a two-year employment contract to work for a company but the company could not honor the contract, the nonbreaching party should not be entitled to sit at home for two years and still receive compensation. In other words, if nonbreaching parties were not required to mitigate damages—either by discontinuing performance, as in the bridge example, or by finding a reasonable replacement, such as a different job in the employment example—nonbreaching parties would run up the costs by completing performance under the contract or doing nothing. In the context of finding a reasonable alternative, nonbreaching parties would actually have an incentive to do nothing.

Courts' requiring nonbreaching parties to mitigate damages is unfair.

Contract law is designed to reward both parties for the agreement that they have reached. If one party is irresponsible and cannot perform as agreed, why should courts then punish the nonbreaching party by requiring him or her to mitigate damages? After all, the nonbreaching party likely made decisions subsequent to the contract on the assumption that the contract terms would be carried out, and mitigating damages introduces stress regarding those decisions.

For instance, if a hotel owner entered a contract with a person who agreed to rent 50 hotel rooms and a conference room for a weekend, the hotel owner would focus his time and energy on advertising for other weekends. To require the hotel owner, after learning that the person no longer wanted the rooms, to mitigate damages places stress on the owner that he would not have otherwise experienced. Instead of completely focusing on booking rooms for other weekends, the hotel owner must now take time away from advertising those rooms so that he can try to fill the 50 vacant rooms and conference room, even if he wants to sue for breach of contract.

In addition, requiring nonbreaching parties to mitigate damages encourages irresponsible behavior on the part of contracting parties. If a party knows she can breach a contract as long as she provides enough notice, she may be able to avoid most, if not all, liability. Returning to the hotel example, if the person who contracted to rent the 50 rooms notifies the hotel owner of the breach two months before the weekend she contracted for, the hotel owner could fill the rooms and the breaching party would likely not be liable for

Finally, mitigating damages promotes better relationships between contracting parties, making both parties more willing to contract again in the future.

any damages, even though the hotel owner incurred greater expense and spent additional time filling the rooms with other guests. "Mitigating damages," therefore, is just a fancy way of saying that the burden shifts back to the nonbreaching parties, rewarding the very people who should bear the costs of breaching contract.

Questions & Problems

1. Explain the difference between legal and equitable remedies.

2. Explain how the existence of conditions subsequent and precedent affects the discharge of a contract.

3. Explain the relationship between commercial impracticability and frustration of purpose.

4. When Barry Meyer asked Robyn Mitnick to marry him, he gave her an engagement ring that cost $19,500. Before the marriage, he asked her to sign a prenuptual agreement. She refused, and the engagement was broken. He asked her to return the ring, saying it was a gift conditioned on marriage. She refused, arguing that it was an unconditional gift. The trial court agreed, finding the engagement ring to be a conditional gift. Robin appealed. How do you think the court of appeals ruled, and why? [*Meyer v. Mitnick,* 244 Mich. App. 697 (2001 WL 171453, Ct. App., Mich., 2001).]

5. John Lawrence, a stockbroker, brought a suit against the Richman Group of Connecticut. He claimed that Richman violated a mutual-exclusivity agreement and failed to pay him the commission to which he was entitled. The district court granted a motion to dismiss the complaint because the contract on which both actions were based was illegal. The illegal contract, under federal securities law, was unenforceable and void. As a result, there could be no cause of action for breach of an illegal contract. Therefore, without an enforceable contract, there could be no claim for the breach of the implied covenant of good faith and fair dealing (on which the exclusivity agreement relied). Do you think the court, on appeal, upheld the dismissal? Why or why not? [*Lawrence v. The Richman Group Capital Corp.,* 358 F. Supp. 2d 29 (D. Conn. 2005).]

6. Posh Pooch Inc., which designs couture pet carriers and accessories, convinced the Italian corporation Nieri Argenti to manufacture various fine leather and related goods for Posh Pooch. Posh Pooch picked up some of the goods in Italy, but at least seven shipments were sent to its store in New York. At the bottom of 12 invoice forms sent to Posh Pooch from Nieri Argenti was a seven-line paragraph written in tiny type in Italian, under the heading "Condizioni Generali Di Vendita." The last sentence of this paragraph stated, "Per controversie e competente il Foro di Firenze," which translates as, "The courts of Florence have jurisdiction over disputes." Other than this paragraph, most of the invoice was either written in English or translated into English. There is no evidence that the parties otherwise discussed the forum for resolution of disputes.

Posh Pooch brought an action in New York against Nieri Argenti. At oral argument, the parties seemed to presume the existence of a contract between them for the sale of goods, but apparently they had not signed any written purchase contract. The parties did enter into two written confidentiality and nondisclosure agreements in 2003 that were written in English. Both agreements provided that New York law and international law would govern the construction of those agreements.

Nieri Argenti contends that the court should dismiss the action on the basis of the forum selection clause contained on the invoices sent to Posh Pooch. The court found that additional terms to a contract for the sale of goods "are to be construed as proposals for addition to the contract" and do not become part of the contract between merchants if they "materially alter it," unless both parties explicitly agree to the alteration. Do you believe the term in the contract requiring that the dispute be resolved in Italy should be enforced? Why or why not? [*Posh Pooch Inc. v. Nieri Argenti,* 2006 N.Y. Slip Op 50224U; 11 Misc. 3d 1055A (2006).]

7. Robert Ewalt was hired by Coos-Curry Electric Cooperative as its chief accountant in May 1999 and fired on August 26, 2002. He filed suit and claimed, among other things, that his discharge violated an employment contract between him and his employer. Ewalt signed an at-will employment provision that noted, in part, "I may resign or be terminated, with or without cause or notice, at any time."

The court interpreted Coos-Curry's "Policy Bulletin No. 41," which described enforcement of certain work rules by supervisors. The policy described a process of progressive discipline and included the statement that "violation of any of these rules will constitute just cause for disciplinary action up to and including discharge," along with a list of 22 different violations.

Ewalt argued that those guidelines created a contract under which his employment could be terminated only for just cause. The trial court rejected this argument, noting that he had signed an application that unambiguously stated that employment was at will. Nothing in the guidelines altered that preexisting employment relationship. Do you believe the appellate court upheld the trial court's decision? Why or why not? [*Ewalt v. Coos-Curry Electric Cooperative, Inc.,* 202 Ore. App. 257, 120 P.3d 1288 (2005).]

8. Andrew Finch, a stockbroker at Morgan Stanley Dean Witter & Co., assumed that his role in making Morgan Stanley the lead underwriter on the initial public offering (IPO) of Webmethods stock would allow him to allocate 75,000 shares of the stock to his clients. He prematurely acted on this belief by telling clients they could purchase the IPO shares through him. Several investors set up a vehicle at Morgan Stanley (Twin Fires) to purchase these funds through Finch.

Before the IPO of Webmethods was issued, Finch learned that his allotment was only 225 shares. Too embarrassed to tell his clients, Finch pretended that trading of the stock had been delayed. As the price of the stock shot up from $35 to $212 on the first day, the clients were celebrating—until they realized that they had never purchased as much stock as Finch led them to believe they had. The clients argued that an equitable remedy would be for Morgan Stanley to compensate them for the gains they would have made (nearly $12 million) had they purchased the stock as they had intended. Do you think the court ultimately agreed with the plaintiffs? Why or why not? If not, what remedy do you believe the plaintiffs would have been entitled to? [*Twin Fires Inv., LLC v. Morgan Stanley Dean Witter & Co.,* 445 Mass. 411, 837 N.E.2d 1121 (Mass. 2005).]

9. Williams owns two trucks that he uses to transport, under contract, frozen produce. Williams drives one truck himself and employs a driver to drive the other one. He provides the driver with a CB radio, cell phone, and expense money so that the driver can stay in communication with him. As a carrier, Williams is subject to the rules of the Department of Transportation for common carriers. One of these rules requires that all drivers be tested for drug use. Williams hired Hall as a driver but did not require that he take a drug test.

Williams had a contract with Mountaire Farms to pick up frozen-chicken produce from suppliers and deliver it to specific locations in New York and New Jersey. Williams assigned the delivery to Hall, who picked up the poultry but failed to deliver it because he was high on illegal drugs. Hall was arrested and the poultry recovered, but by the time it was recovered, the produce had spoiled, a loss valued at $33,373.63. Williams argued that he should be excused from liability under the contract on the grounds of commercial impracticability; the unforeseen drug use of his driver was an intervening circumstance beyond his control that prevented the fulfillment of the contract. Do you believe the doctrine of commercial impracticability is applicable in this case? Why or why not? [*Mountaire Farms, Inc. v. Williams,* Not Reported in A.2d, 2005 WL 1177569 (Del. Super. 2005).]

10. Shirley and Vince Ladner leased 10 acres of their land to J. D. Pigg, who used the land for his cattle farm. The Ladners and Pigg created a 10-year contract, providing that rent be paid annually on August 1. Pigg executed the lease with his first payment in cash in August 2000. On August 1, 2001, Mrs. Pigg attempted to mail the check for the second rent payment but placed the incorrect address on the envelope. Consequently, the check was returned to the Pigg residence, and Mrs. Pigg then properly forwarded the check to the Ladners. However, the Ladners did not receive the check until August 8, 2001, at which time they refused to accept payment and returned the check to Pigg. The Ladners claimed that the lease had been terminated by Pigg's failure to submit timely payment, as this failure constituted a material breach. Is Pigg's failure to tender payment on August 1 a material breach of the lease? Why or why not? [*Ladner v. Pigg,* 919 So. 2d 100 (Miss. App. 2005).]

11. NW agreed to sell real property in Tacoma to O'Connor & Associates. The purchase agreement was created, but an addendum provided that the sale was subject to NW's obtaining "plat approval" from the City of Tacoma. After NW encountered financial problems, NW was unsuccessful in its attempts to obtain plat approval from the city. Thereafter, NW asked O'Connor whether it would be interested in purchasing the property "as is," after which O'Connor could seek plat approval. O'Connor declined this offer, and subsequently NW sold the property to Tacoma Northpark. Concerned that O'Connor might sue, Tacoma filed an action to quiet title (an action to establish ownership) to the land; unsurprisingly, O'Connor filed a counterclaim against Tacoma and a cross-claim against NW. With regard to O'Connor's claim against NW for breach of contract, what is NW's best argument that it is not liable? How did the court decide?

[*Tacoma Northpark, LLC v. NW, LLC*, 96 P.3d 454 (Wash. App. 2004).]

12. Brad Gupta formed two companies, Ameriquest Holdings and Ananya Aviation, for which he purchased three airplanes that were in lease agreements with U.S. Airways and Continental Airlines. However, after the events of September 11, 2001, the two airlines did not renew their leases for the three planes now owned by Gupta. Consequently, Gupta could not continue his loan repayments, and U.S. Bancorp Equipment Finance foreclosed and sold the planes.

U.S. Bancorp sought to enforce the loan agreements for the millions of dollars still owed for Gupta's debt after the proceeds from the sale of the airplanes had been deducted. Gupta, however, argued that the events of September 11, 2001, resulted in immense losses to the airline industry and that performance of the loan agreements (i.e., repayment) was impossible. Did Gupta properly raise the defense of impossibility? What was the court's reasoning? [*U.S. Bancorp Equip. Fin., Inc. v. Ameriquest Holdings*, 2004 U.S. Dist. LEXIS 24709.]

Looking for more review material?

The Online Learning Center at **www.mhhe.com/kubasekess** contains this chapter's "Assignment on the Internet" and also a list of URLs for more information, entitled "On the Internet." Find both of them in the Student Center portion of the OLC, along with quizzes and other helpful materials.

Formation and Performance of Sales and Lease Contracts

---> **CASE OPENER**

Who Is Liable for Ears Falling Off: the Farmers, the Seed Company, or the Weather?

In the spring of 1981 Robert and William Peterson bought Migro Seed Company, Inc., corn seeds from John Sandall. Both Petersons were local farmers, and John Sandall, also a farmer, was Migro's area dealer. Migro produces hybrid seeds for sale, and the corn seeds bought by the Petersons were a "product of scientific genetic cross-breeding to produce a seed having desirable germination, growing, and production qualities."[1]

Around July 23, 1981, the Petersons discovered that nearly 70 percent of their corn, grown from the Migro seeds, had broken off at the ear level after a typical Nebraskan thunderstorm the evening before. However, corn growing from non-Migro seeds had not suffered such damage.

It turns out that silica in the sandy soil in this particular area of Nebraska had been absorbed by these plants, causing them to develop a brittle stalk and thus break at about the first ear-of-corn level. No other variety of corn seed had this problem. When John Sandall, the neighboring farmer and Migro dealer, sold the Petersons the 102 bags of seed, the literature accompanying the seed indicated that one of the Migro seed's attributes was "excellent stalk quality." When the crop was harvested, the Petersons harvested approximately 19½ bushels per acre of the Migro corn while averaging 113¾ bushels per acre of corn grown from seed provided by other seed companies. The Petersons brought a lawsuit for breach of contract.

1. Is the sale of seed a contract for the sale of goods when it was the resulting plant that may have been defective? Does this contract fall under UCC Article 2 or under common law?
2. Are the parties involved here merchants under the UCC and thus subject to a higher standard of care?

[1]See *Peterson v. North American Plant Breeders*, 218 Neb. 258, 354 N.W.2d 625 (1984).

After reading this chapter, you will be able to answer the following questions:

LO 1 What kinds of contracts fall under the UCC interpretations?

LO 2 What is a sales contract under the UCC?

LO 3 What is a merchant, and why is that designation significant?

LO 4 What is a lease contract?

LO 5 What is the CISG?

LO 6 What is the concept of title? How does it pass?

LO 7 What is risk of loss?

Businesses and organizations that purchase products need to be aware of which laws govern their purchases because the laws can differ. Three sources of laws that interpret sales contracts exist: state common law, the Uniform Commercial Code, and state statutory law. There is very little, if any, federal law that governs contracts for the buying and selling of items, and when such law does exist, it is highly specialized (e.g., the buying and selling of stock under laws created by the Securities and Exchange Commission).

This chapter introduces the Uniform Commercial Code. It explains the scope and significance of the UCC, discusses sections of the UCC that govern both sales and lease contracts, and reviews how these contracts are formed and executed.

The Uniform Commercial Code

THE SCOPE OF THE UCC

In some areas of law, federal statutes ensure that the same law applies in all the states. Federal statutes do not govern the formation of sales and lease contracts. Instead, each state passes its own laws to outline rules in this area. Consequently, laws vary from state to state. While all states (except Louisiana) follow the English common law, over 200 years of legal precedent that has developed in each separate state can create differences in contract interpretation and application. With the development of interstate commercial activities, these differences began to pose problems for parties from different states entering into a contract with each other. What was needed was some kind of uniform law for business transactions that all the states could adopt.

The Uniform Commercial Code (UCC) was created in 1952 and has been adopted by all 50 states, the District of Columbia, and the Virgin Islands. When a state adopts the UCC, that code becomes part of the law of that particular state; it becomes the commercial code for that state. The UCC is divided into sections known as *articles*. These articles cover a wide range of topics, from sales contracts to secured transactions (see Exhibit 13-1).

THE SIGNIFICANCE OF THE UCC

The UCC is significant because it clarifies sales law and makes this area of law more predictable to businesses that engage in transactions in more than one state. Essentially, the UCC facilitates commercial transactions.

Uniform Commercial Code (UCC)
A statutory source of contract law in the United States applicable to transactions involving the sale of goods. The UCC was created in 1952 and adopted by all 50 states, the District of Columbia, and the Virgin Islands; it may be modified by each state to reflect the wishes of the state legislature.

Exhibit 13-1

An Outline of the UCC

ARTICLE	TOPIC
1	General provisions
2	Sales
2(A)	Leases
3	Negotiable instruments
4	Bank deposits and collections
4(A)	Wire transfers
5	Letters of credit
6	Bulk transfers
7	Documents of title
8	Investment securities
9	Secured transactions

However, it is important to emphasize that the UCC does not pertain to all business transactions. Under UCC Article 2, the subject matter of this chapter, the UCC explains the creation and interpretation of sales contracts.

Articles 2 and 2(A) of the UCC

LO 1

Article 2 of the UCC governs sales contracts, while Article 2(A) governs lease contracts. Specifically, Article 2 focuses on contracts for the sale of goods; Article 2(A) focuses on contracts for the lease of goods. For the purpose of "selling something," the UCC divides all the items that can be bought and sold into three categories: goods, realty, and services (including intangible goods such as securities). Article 2 pertains only to the sale of goods. Nonetheless, Article 2 is not a comprehensive guide to sales contract formation.

When Article 2 is silent on an issue of sales contract formation or interpretation, the common law rules apply. Of course, if a state has passed statutory law regarding contracts, that law always supersedes the common law. Additionally, it is important to note that under the UCC the rules for transactions involving merchants differ from those for transactions involving regular buyers and sellers. Merchants will generally be held to a higher standard of care and behavior than nonmerchants. Every state except Louisiana[2] has adopted Article 2 of the UCC.

If you are not sure whether a contract falls under common law or under the UCC, the decision-tree in Exhibit 13-2 can help you make a determination. To use this rubric, consider the following definitions of many of its terms.

LO 2

sale
The passing of title from a seller to a buyer for a price.

goods
All physically existing things that are movable at the time of identification to the contract for sale.

ARTICLE 2 OF THE UCC

Sale Section 2-106(1) of the UCC states that a **sale** "consists of the passing of title from the seller to the buyer for a price." Thus, in the transaction involving the Petersons and Migro Seed Company, the sale consisted of the passing of title (right of ownership) of the seeds themselves from Migro to the Petersons for a price.

Goods Section 2-105 of the UCC defines **goods** as "all [tangible] things . . . which are movable at the time of identification to the contract for sale." Items are tangible if they exist physically. The issue in the Case Opener is whether the goods being bought are the seeds or the subsequent plants, which were defective. Note that Section 2-105 reads "at the time of identification to the

Exhibit 13-2

Common Law
or UCC?

1. Does the transaction involve a sale or lease (as opposed to, let's say, a gift)?
 If yes → go to question 2.
 If no → apply the appropriate area of common or statutory law.

2. Is the transaction for the sale or lease of a good?
 If yes → go to question 3.
 If no → apply common law.

3. If the contract is for the sale or lease of both goods and nongoods, which type of item is predominant in the contract?
 If goods → UCC Article 2 applies; go to question 4.
 If nongoods (real estate or services) → common law applies.

4. If this is a UCC Article 2 transaction, is either party a merchant?
 If yes → pay close attention to when the special rules on merchants apply.
 If no → then only "reasonable" care applies to the parties; no special or heightened duty of care applies to a party deemed to be a merchant.

[2] Louisiana's civil tradition is based on the Code Napoleon, or the French Civil Code.

contract." At the time that the contract was created by the Petersons, the items being sold were the seeds. Seeds are goods because they are tangible and can be moved. Some items are not goods under Article 2. For example, corporate stocks and copyrights are not tangible, so they are not goods. Real estate cannot be moved, so it is not a good. Yet items attached to real estate that are used for business activities are known as *trade fixtures* and are treated as goods under the UCC. Consider this Case Nugget.

Items taken from real estate may be treated as goods. Minerals, clay, and soil can all be treated as goods, with their sales contract governed by Article 2, if the owner takes these items out of the ground and then sells them to the buyer. Should the owner sell the buyer the right to come and remove the items, the contract would be governed not by the UCC but by common law for the sale of an interest in realty, in this case, an interest known as a "profit." Crops that are sold while still growing in the field are also considered goods, and their sales contracts are subject to UCC interpretation.

Mixed Goods and Services Contracts Sometimes, it is not easy to tell whether something is a good because a tangible item is tied to or mixed with something intangible, such as a service. For instance, if Migro had sold not just the seeds but also seminars on efficient crop management and crop rotation and if the Petersons had bought a "package deal" that included the seeds and the seminars, it would not have been as clear that the contract was for the sale of a good. A contract that combines a good with a service is a **mixed sale.** Article 2 applies to mixed sales if the goods are the predominant part of the transaction.

mixed sale
A contract that combines a good with a service.

CASE Nugget

The Difference between Realty and Personalty

J.K.S.P Restaurant v. County of Nassau
New York State Court of Appeals

513 N.Y.S.2d 716 (N.Y. App. Div. 1987)

A creditor foreclosed on a diner in Hampstead, New York. Furthermore, the county stepped into the case as well in order to secure past-due taxes. The diner was on a piece of property, but the diner itself was a prefabricated home that was placed on the real estate. When the creditor and county began foreclosure proceedings, they sought to take title to the land from the diner's owners. They argued that the diner itself was part of the realty as it had been affixed to the realty with the intention that it was a permanent fixture; moreover, they argued that its removal would materially alter the realty to which it was attached. The diner's owner claimed that the diner itself was a trade fixture not subject to the foreclosure (the original agreement listed only the "real property" as security for the debt).

The court surveyed a long line of legal precedents, both from New York and from other jurisdictions, in attempting to answer the question of whether the diner was a trade fixture or part of the realty. The court focused first on the issue of whether removing the diner would materially alter the real estate. The court held that the diner was indeed a trade fixture but then concluded that it could be a trade fixture as part of the realty (and thus subject to the foreclosure) or be a removable trade fixture and not subject to the foreclosure. In the end, the court ruled that two related questions needed answering: (1) Was the diner affixed to the realty in such a way as to indicate a permanent attachment? (2) Could the diner be moved without materially altering the realty? Since the record contained insufficient facts, the court sent the case back to the trial court for further review focusing on those two questions.

Marketing

While the determination of whether something is a "good" is useful for knowing whether Article 2 applies to a transaction, the term *good* may also be divided into several categories for marketing purposes. For instance, consumer goods are often classified in one of four categories: (1) convenience goods, (2) shopping goods, (3) specialty goods, and (4) unsought goods. *Convenience goods* (e.g., toothpaste, groceries, and hand soap) are generally inexpensive and are often promoted by differentiation in prices and widespread availability. *Shopping goods* (e.g.,

cameras, televisions, and clothing) are more expensive than most convenience goods, and marketing focuses largely on differentiating one company's goods from a competitor's. *Specialty goods* (e.g., Rolex watches, Lexus vehicles) are typically very expensive, involving marketing that emphasizes the uniqueness of the brand and status. *Unsought goods* (e.g., burial insurance, thesauri, etc.) are usually not heavily marketed, as demand and distribution are relatively low.

Source: R. Kerin, S. Hartley, E. Berkowitz, and W. Rudelius, *Marketing* (New York: McGraw-Hill/Irwin, 2005), pp. 264–265.

LO 3

merchant

A person who regularly sells goods as his or her business or trade or employs people to sell those goods is a merchant of those goods. Also, anyone who works for that person selling those goods is also a merchant. Plus, anyone who holds himself or herself out as a "merchant" or a "dealer" will be treated as a merchant under the UCC as well.

Merchants UCC Article 2 pertains to anyone buying and selling goods. However, the UCC distinguishes merchants from regular buyers and sellers; thus it contains provisions that either apply only to merchants or impose greater duties on merchants. The drafters of the UCC assumed that merchants have a greater ability to look out for themselves than do ordinary buyers and sellers. The following definition can be used to determine whether a seller or a buyer is a merchant under the UCC.

Think of questions about merchants as they relate to the transaction between the Petersons, Migro Seed Company, and John Sandall. Specifically, can any part of UCC Section 2-104(1) be used to argue that John Sandall is a merchant? What about the Petersons? Also, consider the possibility that if the Petersons are merchants, a court will assume that they need less protection than they would if they were nonmerchant buyers of the seeds. There is no question that Migro Seed Company is a merchant. However, if the Petersons sue John Sandall as well, is he a merchant and thus subject to a higher standard of care? If the Petersons are merchants, then as merchants in the business of farming, should they have known that their sandy soil, rich in silica, could pose a problem?

ARTICLE 2(A) OF THE UCC

lease

A transfer of the right to possession and use of goods for a term in return for consideration.

Every state except Louisiana has adopted Article 2 of the UCC. Article 2(A) covers contracts for the lease of goods. This section of the UCC is increasingly important, as consumers (both individuals and businesses) are more likely to lease goods today than ever before. Consumers lease cars, equipment, and machines. Article 2(A) does not cover leases related to real property.

LO 4

lessor

A person who transfers the right to possession and use of goods under a lease.

lessee

A person who acquires the right to possession and use of goods under a lease.

Leases UCC Section 2A-103(j) defines a lease as "a transfer of the right to possession and use of goods for a term in return for consideration." A lessor is "a person who transfers the right to possession and use of goods under a lease."[3] A lessee is "a person who acquires the right to possession and use of goods under a lease."[4] Thus, if you lease a car, the company that leases the car to you (the lessor) transfers the right of possession and use of the car to you (the lessee) in return for consideration (money). If, as part of the contract with Migro Seed Company, the Petersons had leased a machine that plows the fields and plants the seeds, the Petersons would have been lessees for that equipment rather than purchasers.

[3] UCC § 2A-103(p).

[4] UCC § 2A-103(o).

E-COMMERCE and the Law

The UCC and the Internet

The Uniform Commercial Code was designed to address the sale of tangible goods such as scooters, electric power tools, and jeans. Because the UCC was written long before the Internet and e-commerce boom, this legislation was not designed for transactions related to less tangible things, such as software and information. Not surprisingly, the UCC does not respond well to certain legal issues that arise in today's marketplace. For example, the UCC does not tell us the answers to these questions: What rules should govern computer software, which is likely to be licensed rather than sold as a good? What about downloadable software files? What rules should govern information providers like America Online (AOL), which provides a continuing service? What rules should govern the exchange of information, such as stock quotes? What rules cover travel reservations a person makes online?

The National Conference of Commissioners on Uniform State Laws (NCCUSL) has adopted the Uniform Commercial Information Transactions Act (UCITA), which answers the questions above and many more. This law promises to do for electronic contracting what the UCC did for transactions in physical goods: protect consumers by providing predictability, uniformity, and clear rules. As with the UCC, states will choose whether to adopt UCITA. In 2001, Virginia became the first state to enact UCITA, probably because major Internet-related companies (i.e., AOL, UUNET Technologies) are headquartered in northern Virginia.

Source: Robert Holleyman, "Updating Contract Law for the Digital Age," *USA Today* (magazine), March 1, 2000 (2000 WL 9014770); and Scott W. Burt, "Controversial New Rules for Computer Contracts," *Metropolitan Corporate Counsel* 8 (June 2000), col. 1.

How Sales and Lease Contracts Are Formed under the UCC

Earlier in this textbook, you studied the common law of contracts, from the rules for agreements to the remedies for breaches. Sales and lease contracts require the same components as general contracts, but some UCC provisions that govern contracts for the sale or lease of goods are not identical to the common law requirements you learned about in Part 2. This section highlights the most important provisions of the UCC with regard to the formation of sales and lease contracts.

FORMATION IN GENERAL

Contracts for the sale or lease of goods may be made in any manner sufficient to show agreement.[5] A court will uphold a contract for the sale or lease of goods as long as the parties intended to make a contract and there is a reasonably certain basis for giving an appropriate remedy.[6]

OFFER AND ACCEPTANCE

Offer Under the UCC, if certain contract terms are left open, it is acceptable to fill them in. Exhibit 13-3 indicates what generally happens under the UCC when certain terms of a contract

TERM LEFT OPEN	INTERPRETATION UNDER UCC
Price	A "reasonable price" is supplied at the time of delivery.
Payment	Payment is due at the time and place at which the buyer is to receive the goods.
Delivery	The place for delivery is the seller's place of business.
Time	The contract must be performed within a reasonable time.
Duration	The party that wants to terminate an ongoing contract must use good faith and give reasonable notification.
Quantity	Courts generally have no basis for determining a remedy.

Exhibit 13-3

The UCC and Open Terms

[5] UCC § § 2-204(1) and 2A-204(1).

[6] Ibid.

or lease are left open. The UCC also creates a new category of offers: the firm offer. Under UCC Section 2-205, offers made by merchants are considered **firm offers** if the offer (1) is made in writing and (2) gives assurances that it will be irrevocable for up to three months despite a lack of consideration for the irrevocability. If a firm offer is silent as to time, the UCC assumes a three-month irrevocability period. This contrasts sharply with the common law, under which an offer is revocable at any time prior to acceptance unless a period of irrevocability (also known as an *option*) is supported by some kind of consideration.

Acceptance　　Under the UCC, an acceptance may be made by any reasonable means of communication,[7] and it is effective when dispatched. It is important to note that the **mirror-image rule** that applies under common law does not apply under the UCC. Recall that the mirror-image rule states that an offeree's acceptance must be on the exact terms of the offer. If the acceptance includes additional terms, the acceptance becomes a counteroffer instead of an acceptance.

Under the UCC, additional terms are permitted in contracts for the sale or lease of goods. Under UCC Section 2-207(1), additional terms do not negate acceptance unless acceptance is made expressly conditional on assent to the additional terms.

CONSIDERATION

Sales and lease contracts require consideration. Under the common law, when a contract is modified, it must be supported by new consideration. The UCC eliminates that requirement for the modification of sales and lease contracts.[8] The UCC requires only that modifications be made in good faith.[9]

REQUIREMENTS UNDER THE STATUTE OF FRAUDS

Under common law, the statute of frauds requires that all material terms to a contract be in writing. Under the UCC, contracts for the sale of goods must be in writing if they are priced at $500 or more;[10] lease contracts that require payments of $1,000 or more must be in writing to be enforceable.[11] There is a significant difference between the statute of frauds and the UCC as to what constitutes a **writing** that satisfies the statute. Common law requires some kind of writing created or signed by the party who is contesting the enforceability of the contract.

This rule holds true under the UCC unless the parties are merchants. If two merchants have an oral agreement, a written memo from either party to the other is deemed to satisfy the statute of frauds, even if it is not acknowledged by the receiving party. If the memo is not objected to within 10 days of receipt, the oral agreement, memorialized by the memo, is binding.

UNCONSCIONABILITY

A contract or contract provision is *unconscionable* if it is so unfair that a court would be unreasonable if it enforced the contract. The UCC outlines actions a court can take if it discovers that a contract or lease provision or the contract or lease as a whole is unconscionable.[12] If a court finds that a contract or lease was unconscionable, in whole or in part, when it was made, the court either can refuse to enforce the contract or lease or can enforce the parts that are fair.

[7] UCC § § 2-206(1) and 2A-206(1).

[8] UCC § § 2-209(1) and 2A-208(1).

[9] UCC § 1-203.

[10] UCC § 2-201(1).

[11] UCC § 2A-201(1).

[12] UCC § § 2-302 and 2A-108.

firm offer

An offer made in writing and giving assurances that it will be irrevocable for not longer than three months despite a lack of consideration for the irrevocability.

mirror-image rule

The principle which holds that the terms of the acceptance must mirror the terms of the offer; if the terms of the acceptance do not mirror the terms of the offer, no contract is formed and the attempted acceptance is a counteroffer.

writing

A type of documentation that shows contractual intent and satisfies the statute of frauds requirement.

E-Start-Ups in Norway

Countries face different challenges with regard to e-start-ups. In Norway, e-businesses are starting up but not at the same rate as in other countries. E-start-ups from Norway have tended to incorporate outside the country.

One significant challenge e-start-ups face in Norway is that the country's stock market is not as advantageous as nearby stock markets, such as those in Stockholm and London. For example, it is difficult for a company to meet listing requirements for the Oslo Stock Exchange if the company has not yet generated profits. Norway recently relaxed the listing requirements but still requires a net-profit showing.

Another challenge is Norway's tax system. Although this country has one of the lowest corporate tax rates in Europe, certain tax liabilities are problematic for e-start-ups. For example, Norway taxes options to employees at a marginal tax rate of approximately 55 percent. Plus, the company pays a payroll tax of approximately 26 percent on the same benefit.

Finally, some of Norway's laws are not in line with the CISG. One important deviation relates to online agreements. While the CISG holds that an online agreement is binding when the seller has accepted the buyer's offer to buy, Norway's law states that agreement occurs when the buyer's acceptance has reached the knowledge of the seller. Norway is in the process of adopting CISG rules on the conclusion of agreements. By complying with the CISG, it is likely Norway will face fewer obstacles in promoting e-business.

Source: Oyvind Hovland, "Norway," *Corporate Finance*, April 1, 2000.

Contracts for the International Sale of Goods

THE SCOPE AND SIGNIFICANCE OF THE CISG

LO 5

By the 1970s, it became clear that, increasingly, businesses planned to conduct commercial transactions not only across state lines but also across country borders. In 1980, the United Nations Convention on Contracts for the International Sale of Goods (CISG) was offered as a treaty that countries could sign, indicating their willingness to allow this treaty to govern international business-to-business sales contracts.

The CISG is important because if a problem arises with an international sale and a party to the transaction initiates litigation, the UCC does not provide guidance in the litigation; instead, the CISG preempts the UCC. The CISG covers the same general topics as the UCC. For instance, the CISG covers offers, acceptances, and other contract topics. However, specific provisions of the CISG differ from the UCC. For example, the CISG requirements related to the statute of frauds are more lenient than those under the UCC. In particular, the CISG does not require that contracts be in writing.

United Nations Convention on Contracts for the International Sale of Goods (CISG)
The legal structure for international sales, including business-to-business sales contracts.

Title

Once the sales contract has been created and the parties are obligated to perform, the next issue to consider is the concept of title. *Title* means "ownership." The most important aspect of title is that a person must have title in order to pass title. In other words, you can't sell something that you don't own. Moreover, you can't give it away or use it as collateral for a loan. So what does it mean to have title?

THREE KINDS OF TITLE

There are three kinds of title: good title, void title, and voidable title. First, good title is title that is acquired from someone who already owns the goods free and clear. Next, void title is not true title. Someone who purchases stolen goods, knowingly or unknowingly, has void title. Finally, voidable title occurs in certain situations in which the contract between the original parties would be void but the goods have already been sold to a third party. The next few sections of the chapter discuss these types of title in detail.

good title
Title acquired from someone who already owns the goods free and clear.

void title
Not true title; e.g., the title held by someone who knowingly or unknowingly purchased stolen goods.

voidable title
Title that occurs in situations in which the contract between the original parties would be void but the goods have already been sold to a third party.

LO 6 **Acquiring Good Title**

The most obvious way of attaining good title is acquiring it from someone who has good title, that is, the person who owns it free and clear, without any qualifications. In contrast, someone who has come into possession of stolen goods never has good title and can never pass a good title. A person in possession of stolen goods has void title.

However, problems may arise when someone thinks he or she has good title but actually has void title. Consider Case 13-1, which concerns the sale of a stolen vehicle and whether a car dealership's title was voidable or void.

 CASE 13-1

ALFONSO CANDELA, APPELLANT, v. PORT MOTORS, INC., RESPONDENT, ET AL., DEFENDANT
SUPREME COURT OF NEW YORK, APPELLATE DIVISION, SECOND DEPARTMENT

208 A.D.2d 486; 617 N.Y.S.2d 49 (1994)

FACTS: *Candela purchased a car for approximately $19,000 from Port Motors, Inc. The police later seized the car, claiming that it may have been stolen. Candela brought suit against Port Motors for breach of warranty of title. Port's defense was that it indeed passed a good title to Candela. New York's Supreme Court, which is New York's trial court level, granted Port Motors' motion for summary judgment, agreeing with Port that the car dealer had voidable title. The case went up on appeal and considered the issue of whether good title can ever pass for stolen goods.*

ISSUE: Can a good-faith seller of stolen goods pass a voidable or even good title to a good-faith innocent buyer?

REASONING: In a word, no. Good faith and innocence have no bearing whatsoever on this matter. Someone who sells stolen goods, regardless of the degree of good faith, can never pass a voidable or good title to the buyer. The buyer has a void title, and therefore the rightful owner can reclaim the goods.

DECISION AND REMEDY: The Court of Appeals held that the only remedy is that, if the buyer did not receive a good title to the goods from the seller, the buyer could sue the seller for the money paid.

SIGNIFICANCE OF THE CASE: The significance of the decision is that if Port Motors purchased the vehicle from a thief, or from the successor to a thief, Port's title would be void and Port could not have conveyed good title to Candela.

CRITICAL THINKING

The appellate court reversed the trial court's decision, which had granted a summary judgment to Port. Candela is going to have the opportunity to have a court rule on whether Port Motors passed good title to him. What key facts will determine whether the title was void or voidable?

ETHICAL DECISION MAKING

Why would Port Motors, Inc., fight Candela in court? Shouldn't the car dealer want to make its customers happy? What ethical norm must be underlying Port Motors' behavior in contesting Candela's claim?

The key point to remember, which many people misunderstand, is that good faith is actually irrelevant when passing a void title. If a person has a void title (as in the best, and most frequent, example: a person has possession of stolen goods), then no matter how honorable the intentions of the seller are, that good-faith seller cannot pass anything to the buyer but another void title. The only exception to this is the entrustment situation, which is discussed later in the chapter.

VOIDABLE TITLE

When a seller transfers goods to a buyer, normally the buyer gets good title. However, the buyer gets only voidable title if any of the following apply:

- The buyer deceived the seller regarding his or her true identity.
- The buyer wrote a bad check for the goods.
- The buyer committed criminal fraud in securing the goods.
- The buyer and seller agreed that title would not pass until some later time.
- The buyer is a minor.

The first four of these situations that can create a voidable title are articulated in Section 2-403 of Article 2 of the UCC; the final one, the buyer is a minor, comes from common law. A seller who discovers any of these situations has the right to cancel the contract and reclaim the goods, even if they have already been delivered to the buyer. That is why the title is called *voidable.*

ENTRUSTMENT

If an owner *entrusts* the possession of goods to a merchant who deals in goods of that kind, the merchant can transfer all rights in the goods to a buyer in the ordinary course of business. One form of **entrustment** occurs when someone entrusts the possession of a good (e.g., a car) to a merchant and asks him to repair that good. Suppose the merchant fraudulently or accidentally sells the item as if it were part of his inventory.

entrustment
The transfer of goods to a merchant who ordinarily deals in that type of goods. If the merchant subsequently sells them to a good-faith third-party purchaser, the buyer acquires good title to the goods.

If the purchaser is a good-faith purchaser (i.e., did not know that the item belonged to someone else and paid a fair market value, not some unreasonable discounted value), then that purchaser gets a good title. The original owner's only recourse is to bring suit against the merchant. Again, the rationale behind this concept is the facilitation of commercial activity regarding good-faith purchasers in the marketplace.

TITLE VERSUS OTHER INTERESTS IN THE GOODS

The determination of who has good title does not always result in the expected and equitable solution to a problem. For example, suppose you purchased a couch at a furniture store. It is pretty safe to say that once you identify the couch and pay for it, you have "title" to it. Now suppose that when the store attempts to deliver the couch to your home, lightning hits the store's delivery truck and destroys the couch. Is the store legally obligated to replace the couch? Most of us would intuitively answer that it is. After all, you never took possession of the couch. However, as previously noted, *you* have title. Under pre-UCC law, this loss could have fallen on whoever had title at that time—and that person would be you. Under the UCC, if the store is a merchant, the risk of loss remains with the seller until the couch is actually delivered to you.

As a result of such dilemmas, the UCC breaks up the various issues traditionally correlated with title and treats them separately. Several different issues normally are thought of under the concept of title:

- *Ownership:* When does title actually transfer from the seller to the buyer, since the right to transfer ownership of the goods, whether through a subsequent sale or gift, is tied to title?

- *Encumbrance:* The right to encumber goods as collateral for a debt is dependent on who is holding title. When title passes is important because having title means that one can then sell or encumber the goods. In other words, having title means that one can pass title.

- *Loss:* In regard to the right to indemnification if the goods are damaged, when the risk of loss attaches is important. This is because, regardless of title passing, we need to know the seller's and buyer's responsibility to each other in the event that the goods are damaged or destroyed prior to the buyer's taking complete possession of the goods.

- *Insurable interest:* An *insurable interest* is the right to insure the goods against any risk exposure such as damage or destruction. When an insurable interest is created in the goods is important. Both the buyer and the seller can insure themselves for potential loss, in the event the goods are damaged or destroyed at some point in the transaction. A key point is identifying the earliest time in the transaction that the buyer can claim an insurable interest. The Case Nugget addresses that issue.

One very important point to note is that the parties are always free to create a contract that lays out and defines such issues as when title passes and when risk of loss passes. The UCC's rules are essentially the default rules for contracts that do not clearly spell out such provisions.

Let's look at each one of these issues within the context of the four kinds of sales contracts that Article 2 creates.

CASE Nugget

When Does Insurable Interest Arise?

National Compressor Corp. v. Carrow and McGee
Federal Circuit Court of Appeals

417 F.2d 97 (1969)

National Compressor bought a large compressor from Davis, who had bought the compressor from Carrow and McGee. Title to the compressor was not to pass to National Compressor until the compressor was removed from Carrow and McGee's property. Prior to the compressor's being moved (and title passing to National Compressor) a fire broke out at the site, destroying the compressor. National Compressor had already paid the $12,000 purchase price. The issue before the court was whether National Compressor had any kind of insurable interest since clearly title had not yet passed. The defendants claimed that National Compressor had no standing to bring the lawsuit as it had no "interest" in the property since title had yet to pass.

The court ruled otherwise, stating that National Compressor had an insurable and special interest in the good, thus giving it standing to sue. The court ruled:

> Where a third party so deals with goods *which have been identified to a contract* for sale as to cause actionable injury to a party to that contract (a) a right of action against the third party is in either party to the contract for sale who has title to or a security interest or a special property or an insurable interest in the goods; and if the goods have been destroyed or converted a right of action is also in the party who either bore the risk of loss under the contract for sale or has since the injury assumed that risk as against the other. . . .

The buyer obtains a special property and an insurable interest in goods by identification of existing goods as goods to which the contract refers even though the goods so identified are noncomforming and he has an option to return or reject them. Such identification can be made at any time and in any manner explicitly agreed to by the parties. In the absence of explicit agreement identification occurs (a) when the contract is made if it is for the sale of goods already existing and identified. [emphasis added]

Types of Sales Contracts

The UCC lays out essentially four broad factual scenarios for the sale of goods:

1. *Simple delivery contract:* A simple delivery contract occurs when the purchased goods are transferred to the buyer from the seller at either the time of the sale or some time later by the seller's delivery.

2. *Common-carrier delivery contract:* This type of contract occurs when the goods are delivered to the buyer via a common carrier, such as a trucking line.

3. *Goods-in-bailment contract:* This type of contract occurs when the purchased goods are in some kind of storage under the control of a third party, such as a warehouseman.

4. *Conditional sales contract:* A conditional sales contract occurs when the sale itself is contingent on approval, for example.

In the sections that follow, this chapter answers questions about ownership, encumbrance, loss, and insurable interest as they relate to these four types of sales contracts.

SIMPLE DELIVERY CONTRACT

With a **simple delivery contract,** the buyer and seller typically execute an agreement, and the buyer leaves with the goods. To most of us, it appears that title, risk of loss, and insurable interest all pass to the buyer at the moment the transaction is consummated and the buyer walks out with the goods. However, under the UCC, there are three distinct steps: (1) Title transfers to the buyer on the goods' being identified to the contract, that is, when the contract is executed; (2) risk of loss transfers to the buyer when the buyer takes possession; and (3) insurable interest is created in the buyer when the goods are identified to the contract, in other words, at the same time that title passes.

But what happens if the buyer comes back later to pick up the goods or arranges to have the seller, or an agent of the seller, deliver the goods at a later time? For the purposes of title and insurable interest, nothing really changes. The dilemma occurs with risk of loss.

Let's suppose a buyer and seller execute a contract in which the seller is going to deliver a refrigerator later in the day to the buyer. Through no fault of the seller, the refrigerator is damaged in a fire at the seller's store. Who has the risk of loss if neither party is at fault? In this case, the issue rests on the seller's status. If the seller is a merchant, as in this instance, the risk of loss remains with the seller until the goods are actually delivered to the buyer. If the seller is not a merchant, the risk of loss remains with the buyer under the rule of **tender of delivery.**

Simply put, tender of delivery is the moment the goods were available for the buyer to take. Consider this example: You purchase a dresser at a garage sale, but you want to go home and get your truck so that you can get it home easily. Unfortunately, a car hits the dresser and destroys it. You, the buyer, cannot get your money back because (1) the law does not consider the seller a merchant and (2) you could have taken the dresser with you when you bought it.

Note that the results are different if either party is at fault for the damage. In that case, the responsible person is liable under tort law for the damage caused. Case 13-2 considers who has the risk of loss between an innocent seller and an innocent buyer.

With a simple delivery contract whereby a seller transfers goods to a buyer without the middle-delivery common carrier, the various interests transfer as shown below. (*Note:* Even if the seller has its agent deliver the goods to the buyer, this is still a simple delivery.)

Simple delivery: seller → buyer

1. Title transfers on identification of the goods to the contract.

2. If the seller is a merchant, risk of loss transfers on delivery of the goods to the buyer; if the seller is not a merchant, risk of loss transfers when the goods are made available for the buyer to possess (tender of delivery).

3. The parties may buy insurance on their goods if they hold title or have any risk of loss or other economic interest.

simple delivery contract
Type of contract in which purchased goods are transferred to the buyer from the seller either at the time of the sale or sometime later by the seller's delivery.

tender of delivery
Requirement that the seller or lessor have and hold conforming goods at the disposal of the buyer or lessee and give the buyer or lessee reasonable notification to enable him or her to take delivery.

CASE 13-2

FACTS: *Emery's son had been making down payments on a Pacer Corvette sports car sold by an automobile dealership owned by Weed Chevrolet (Weed). Emery's son died prior to paying off and taking possession of the car. In the meantime, through no negligence or fault of the automobile dealership, the car was stolen from the dealership. Emery is suing to get back the monies paid and to cancel the contract. Weed is counterclaiming, stating that it is entitled to keep the down payments and also to recover damages in the amount of the difference between the purchase price of the Pacer and its market value on the date Emery sought to cancel the agreement. The trial court ruled in favor of Emery, and Weed appealed.*

ISSUE: In this case, who has the risk of loss (the loss of the value of the automobile)—Emery or the car dealership?

REASONING: The UCC is clear that in a simple delivery contract, when the seller is a merchant, risk of loss does not pass to the buyer until the goods are actually delivered and put into the buyer's possession. Even if the contract had been created and even if title passed when the goods were identified to the contract, risk of loss remains with the merchant. If the seller is a nonmerchant, the risk of loss would pass when the goods are available to the buyer to take possession; but that is not this situation. Of course, in this situation, the person ultimately liable is the thief.

DECISION AND REMEDY: The Court ruled that the risk of loss remained with the merchant seller and as such, the car dealership is liable for the loss of the car to the buyer.

SIGNIFICANCE OF THE CASE: Again, a common theme that we see here is the heightened standard of care imposed by the UCC on merchants. Practically speaking, however, why should the risk of loss transfer to the buyer before the buyer even has any control or possession over the goods? This ruling definitively answers that question by ruling that it should not.

CRITICAL THINKING

Is the court's decision consistent with your commonsense belief about whether risk of loss had passed? Explain how the court used the UCC to reach its conclusion.

ETHICAL DECISION MAKING

Which primary value does the court's decision show it prefers? Which primary value does Weed Chevrolet probably prefer?

COMMON-CARRIER DELIVERY CONTRACT

common-carrier delivery contract

A type of contract in which purchased goods are delivered to the buyer via an independent contractor, such as a trucking line.

If a buyer and seller execute a contract and the seller subsequently places the goods with a common carrier for delivery to the buyer, the parties have executed a **common-carrier delivery contract**. Note that a common carrier is an independent contractor and not an agent of the seller. What makes the common carrier an independent contractor, rather than an agent, is that the carrier controls the primary aspects of performance, such as how the goods are actually delivered.

The UCC names two kinds of delivery contracts in this category: origin, or shipment, contracts and destination contracts. *Shipment contracts* require that the seller ship the goods to the buyer via a common carrier. The seller is required to make proper shipping arrangements and deliver the goods into the common carrier's hands. Title passes to the buyer at the time and place of shipment.

Thus, the buyer bears the risk of loss while the goods are in transit. *Destination contracts* require that the seller deliver the goods to the destination stipulated in the sales contract. This may be the buyer's place of business or some other location. The seller bears the risk of loss until that time. Exhibit 13-4 identifies shipping terms that create the conditions of transit and delivery.

LO 7

With a shipment contract whereby a seller transfers goods to a buyer with delivery of the goods affected by a common carrier, the various interests transfer as follows:

Shipment contract: seller → common carrier → buyer

1. If the shipment contract is an origin contract (if the contract is vague or ambiguous, an origin contract will be presumed), the title passes to the buyer when the goods are turned over by the seller to the common carrier.

2. If the shipment contract is a destination contract, the title transfers from the seller to the buyer when the common carrier delivers the goods to the buyer.

3. The risk of loss in either situation—origin or destination contract—transfers from the seller to the buyer simultaneously with the title.

4. An insurable interest is created when the buyer and/or seller holds title or retains a risk of loss.

GOODS-IN-BAILMENT CONTRACT

A **goods-in-bailment contract** involves goods that are in some kind of storage (e.g., in a warehouse or on board a ship), so the seller cannot transfer physical possession of them. Instead, the seller has one of three documents indicating ownership of the goods: a negotiable document of title, a nonnegotiable document of title, or a contract or other instrument showing ownership that is not a negotiable or nonnegotiable document of title. If the seller has a negotiable document (i.e., a document containing the words "deliver to the order of [seller]"), then both title and risk of loss transfer from the seller to the buyer as soon as that negotiable instrument is endorsed over to the buyer. On the other hand, if the document is nonnegotiable (i.e., a document lacking the words "to the order of"), then the title passes with the instrument of title but the risk of loss does not pass to the buyer until the bailee (the custodian of the goods) is notified of the transfer or a reasonable time has elapsed since the transaction. Finally, if there is neither a negotiable or a nonnegotiable document of title, then the title passes at the time the sales contract is executed but the risk does not pass to the buyer until the bailee is notified of the transaction and acknowledges such notification.

goods-in-bailment contract
A type of contract in which the purchased goods are in some kind of storage under the control of a third party, such as a warehouseman.

With goods in bailment, the three interests—title, risk of loss, insurable interest—pass in the following way:

Seller → buyer, but the goods are elsewhere in some kind of storage and in a third party's possession and care.

1. Title passes from the seller to the buyer when the document of title (e.g., a warehouse receipt or a bill of lading) is actually endorsed or signed over to the buyer. If there is no document

Exhibit 13-4

TERM	EXPLANATION
FOB (free on board)	The selling price includes transportation costs, and the seller carries the risk of loss to either the place of shipment or the place of destination.
FAS (free alongside)	The seller, at seller's expense, delivers the goods alongside the ship before the risk passes to the buyer.
CIF or C&F (cost, insurance and freight; cost and freight)	The seller puts the goods in possession of a carrier before the risk passes to the buyer. Contracts are usually shipment contracts rather than destination contracts.
Delivery ex-ship (delivery from the carrying vessel)	Risk of loss passes to the buyer when the goods leave the ship.

Shipping Terms Specifying Requirements for Delivery

of title, then title passes when the goods are identified to the contract and the contract is executed.

2. Risk of loss passes to the buyer simultaneously with the document of title provided that the document of title is a negotiable one. If it is nonnegotiable, the risk does not pass until the bailee (the possessor or custodian of the goods) is notified or a reasonable time elapses. If there is no document of title, risk passes to the buyer on notification and acknowledgment by the bailee.

3. Insurable interest is created when either party has title, risk of loss, or some other economic interest attached to the goods (e.g., a creditor who secures a loan by taking the goods as collateral).

conditional sales contract

A type of contract in which the sale itself is contingent on approval; can be either a sale-on-approval contract or a sale-or-return contract.

sale-on-approval contract

A contract in which the seller allows the buyer to take possession of the goods before deciding whether to complete the contract by making the purchase.

sale-or-return contract

A contract in which the buyer and seller agree that the buyer may return the goods at a later time.

CONDITIONAL SALES CONTRACT

Conditional sales contracts are either sale-on-approval contracts or sale-or-return contracts. A contract is a sale-on-approval contract if the seller allows the buyer to take possession of the goods before deciding whether to complete the contract by making the purchase. Title and risk of loss remain with the seller until the buyer notifies the seller about the approval of the contract.

A sale-or-return contract occurs when the seller and buyer agree that the buyer may return the goods at a later time. Such contracts usually occur when the buyer is buying inventory to resell. For example, suppose the seller is a dress wholesaler and the buyer is a retailer who is purchasing the dresses to sell in her store. In their sale-or-return agreement, the insurable interest is created in the buyer once the goods are identified in the contract. Title and risk of loss depend on whether the goods are in bailment, delivered by common carrier, or delivered by the seller himself. Without an agreement to the contrary, if the buyer subsequently returns the dresses, she does so at her own expense and risk.

Risk of Loss during a Breach of Contract

WHEN THE SELLER IS IN BREACH

The failure to deliver goods is the most common way a sales contract is breached. If the seller does not provide the goods that were described in the contract, the buyer may either (1) accept the nonconforming goods as is or (2) reject the goods subject to the seller's curing the deficiency in the goods. The buyer may reject the goods if no cure is possible or the seller fails to cure the deficiency within a reasonable time. In all these instances, the risk of loss remains with the seller until either the buyer accepts the goods or the seller cures the deficiency and provides the buyer with conforming goods.

If a cure is not possible or if the seller has failed to cure the deficiency within a reasonable time, the buyer has the option to revoke the contract. (The remedies are discussed in subsequent chapters.) However, the UCC creates a disincentive for buyers who do so: If the risk of loss would have transferred to the buyer had there not been a breach, the risk transfers to the buyer to the extent of any insurance the buyer has. The loss reverts to the breaching seller only to the extent that the buyer's insurance does not cover it.

WHEN THE BUYER IS IN BREACH

Most buyer breaches occur when a buyer refuses to accept conforming goods from the seller and then the goods are subsequently lost or damaged. With an origin or shipment contract, the risk would have already transferred to the breaching buyer. However, if the contract is a destination contract, the risk remains with the seller. In order to encourage sellers to create origin contracts, the UCC requires that the risk of loss remain with the seller to the extent of the seller's insurance. If the seller does not have insurance or the loss exceeds the seller's insurance, the remainder transfers to the breaching buyer.

 SUMMARY

The Uniform Commercial Code	*Scope of the UCC:* The UCC is a uniform or model law that governs commercial transactions, from the sale of goods to secured transactions.
	Significance of the UCC: The UCC adds clarity and predictability to sales law.
Articles 2 and 2(A) of the UCC	*Article 2 (Sales)* covers contracts for the sale of goods.

- *Sale:* The passing of title from the seller to the buyer for a price.
- *Goods:* Tangible things that can be moved.
- *Mixed goods and services contracts:* Contracts that include both goods and services. Courts apply Article 2 if the goods are the predominant part of the transaction.
- *Merchants:* Buyers or sellers who (1) deal in goods of the kind, (2) by occupation, hold themselves out as having knowledge and skill unique to the practices or goods involved in the transaction, or (3) employ a merchant as a broker, agent, or other intermediary. Various provisions of the UCC distinguish merchants from ordinary buyers and sellers.

Article 2(A)(Leases) covers contracts for the lease of goods.

- *Leases:* Transfers of the right to possession and use of goods for a term in return for consideration.
- *Special kinds of leases:* Consumer leases and finance leases. The UCC outlines special rules and protections for each kind of lease.

How Sales and Lease Contracts Are Formed under the UCC	*Formation in general:* The UCC is more lenient than common law regarding contract formation. Courts look at the intent of the parties to a sales or lease contract.
	Offer and acceptance: Offers are valid even if terms are left open. The common law mirror-image rule does not apply to contracts for the sale or lease of goods. Courts look on a case-by-case basis to determine whether to allow additional terms.
	Consideration: When sales and lease contracts are modified, these modifications do not need to be supported by new consideration.
	Statute of frauds: Contracts for the sale of goods must be in writing if the goods are priced at $500 or more. Lease contracts that require payments of $1,000 or more must be in writing. Exceptions exist for:

- Specifically manufactured goods.
- Contracts that parties admit exist.
- Situations in which partial performance has occurred.

Unconscionability: Under the UCC, a court can refuse to enforce the parts of a contract or lease that are unfair or one-sided.

Contracts for the International Sale of Goods	*Scope of the CISG:* The CISG is a treaty countries can sign to govern international business-to-business sales contracts. Many major trading nations have signed the CISG.
	Significance of the CISG: The CISG is important because it, rather than the UCC, governs international sales contracts. The CISG provides clarity, predictability, and uniformity for businesses that operate in the global economy.
Title	There are three kinds of title: good title, void title, and voidable title.

- *Good title* is title that is acquired from someone who already owns the goods free and clear.
- *Void title* is not true title. Someone who purchases stolen goods has void title.
- *Voidable title* occurs in certain situations in which the contract between the original parties would be void but the goods have already been sold to a third party.

Acquiring Good Title	Article 2 of the Uniform Commercial Code covers issues related to acquiring good title.

- The most obvious way to attain *good title* is to acquire it from someone who has good title.
- Someone who has come into possession of stolen goods never has title and can pass only *void title.*
- A buyer gets *voidable title* if he or she has deceived the seller regarding his or her true identity, written a bad check for the goods, committed criminal fraud in securing the goods, or is a minor or if the buyer and seller agreed that title would not pass until some later time.

Third-party purchasers generally get good title.

If an owner *entrusts* the possession of goods to a merchant who deals in goods of that kind, the merchant can transfer all rights in the goods to a buyer in the ordinary course of business.

The UCC provides recourse for situations in which good title may not be enough for an equitable result. The UCC responds to issues related to the following:

- *Ownership* refers to transfer of title.
- *Encumbrance* refers to when goods may be used as collateral for a debt.
- *Loss* refers to who has the risk of loss, which matters when someone is seeking indemnification for damaged goods.
- *Insurable interest* refers to the right to insure goods against any risk exposure.

Types of Sales Contracts

A *simple delivery contract* is formed when the buyer and seller execute an agreement and the buyer leaves with the goods. *Title* transfers to the buyer when the contract is executed. *Risk of loss* transfers to the buyer when the buyer takes possession. *Insurable interest* is created in the buyer at the same time title passes.

A *common-carrier delivery contract* exists when a buyer and seller execute a contract and the seller subsequently places the goods with a common carrier. There are two types of common-carrier delivery contracts: origin, or shipment, contracts and destination contracts.

- In *shipment contracts,* title transfers to the buyer at the time and place of shipment. The buyer bears the risk of loss while the goods are in transit.
- In *destination contracts,* the seller bears the risk of loss until the seller delivers the goods to the destination stipulated in the sales contract.

A *goods-in-bailment contract* is one that identifies goods that are in some kind of storage. Rules regarding passage of title, risk of loss, and insurable interest vary depending on whether the seller has a negotiable document of title, a nonnegotiable document of title, or a contract showing ownership that is neither a negotiable nor nonnegotiable document of title.

A *conditional sales contract* includes sale-on-approval or sale-or-return contracts.

- In a *sale-on-approval contract,* title and risk of loss remain with the seller until the buyer notifies the seller about the approval of the contract.
- In a *sale-or-return contract,* the insurable interest is created in the buyer once the goods are identified in the contract. Title and risk of loss depend on whether the goods are in bailment, delivered by common carrier, or delivered by the seller.

Risk of Loss during a Breach of Contract

When the seller is in breach by failing to deliver goods, the buyer may either accept the nonconforming goods as is or reject the goods subject to the seller's curing the deficiencies in the goods. Risk of loss remains with the seller until the buyer accepts the goods or the deficiencies are corrected.

When the buyer is in breach because he or she has refused to accept conforming goods and then the goods are subsequently lost or damaged, who bears the risk of loss depends on the type of contract that exists between the buyer and the seller.

• • • ▶ Point/Counterpoint

If a merchant (bailee) is holding goods for someone for repair or storage and sells those goods to a good-faith purchaser, that good-faith purchaser gets good title and the previous owner may recover the loss only from the bailee by suing in the tort of conversion.

Is It Right That a Bailee Who Has Only Possession, Not Title, Can Pass a Good Title to a Purchaser?	
YES	NO
The primary purpose of the Uniform Commercial Code, in addition to attempting to "uniformize" manners and methods of commercial processes, is to facilitate and enable commercial activity.	The entrustment rule is an example of the Uniform Commercial Code's taking a principle to an illogical and inequitable conclusion.

To put it succinctly, purchasers should not have to look over their shoulders, so to speak, regarding every transaction for fear that the title may not be valid. The facilitation of commercial activity requires that a good-faith purchaser can rely on the sale to validate his or her title to the goods.

We see such a perspective in other areas of the Uniform Commercial Code. As we see in Article 9, on secured transactions, if a buyer in the ordinary course of business purchases an item that is encumbered, the purchaser gets title over the creditor.

This philosophy puts the greater goal of the Uniform Commercial Code ahead of any individualized inconvenience of losing title to goods in entrustment. The focus of the code is the facilitation of commerce, and therefore parties who put goods into entrustment must exercise due care in choosing a bailee.

There is no question that the focus of the Uniform Commercial Code is the facilitation of commerce, and the example (given by the opposing view) of the buyer in the ordinary course of business is valid except that it is misplaced. A merchant who has a voidable title can pass on a good title; a merchant who has a good title can obviously pass on a good title. But a merchant who has a void or bad title or no title at all cannot pass on a good title. This is a fundamental premise regarding the ability to pass title.

The entrustment rule is the exception to this title rule, and it is misplaced. First, common sense tells us that this situation occurs so infrequently as to negate the need for a special rule. Second, when it does occur, often the goods are unique or one of a kind and are not replaceable. Thus, the inequity in denying possession to the true owner of unique goods truly outweighs the need to facilitate commercial activity.

----▶ Questions & Problems

1. Explain what determines whether a contract is covered by the UCC.

2. How can good title be acquired?

3. What are the various types of sales contracts?

4. Thomas Helvey is suing the Wabash County Rural Electrical Company for breach of contract. The electric company caused 135-volt electricity to enter Helvey's home, damaging 110-volt appliances. Helvey brought suit claiming his contract with the electric company falls under UCC Article 2 for the sale of a good. Construct an argument for the plaintiff positing that electricity is a good. Why would this position be beneficial to the plaintiff? Next, construct an argument on behalf of the defendant positing that electricity is not a good under UCC Article 2. Which argument seems more persuasive to you? [*Helvey v. Wabash County REMC,* 278 N.E.2d 608 (1972).]

5. The plaintiff, Betty Epstein, visited a beauty parlor to get her hair dyed. In the dying process, the beautician used a prebleach solution manufactured by Clairol, Inc., and then a commercial dye manufactured by Sales Affiliate, Inc. The treatment went awry, and the plaintiff suffered severe hair loss, injuries to both hair and scalp, and some disfigurement. She sued the beauty salon, Clairol, and Sales Affiliate under Article 2 of the UCC. The defendants claimed that the contract was predominantly for services rather than for the sale of a good. How would you construct arguments supporting each side? What difference does it make whether the beauty treatment was a good or a service? [*Epstein v. Giannattasio,* 197 A.2d 342 (1963).]

6. An agricultural cooperative sued Carroll Nelson for breach of contract under UCC Article 2. Nelson was a Texas wheat farmer and had an oral contract with the cooperative for the purchase of his wheat. The cooperative had forwarded to Nelson a written confirmation of the agreement, but Nelson did not acknowledge or sign any confirmation. When the cooperative initiated the lawsuit, Nelson raised the statute of frauds as a defense. He claimed that because he was not a merchant, a signed memorandum with his signature of some sort was needed for the contract to be enforceable. The cooperative claimed that because Nelson was a merchant, the unobjected-to memorandum satisfied the statute of frauds for agreements between merchants. Is farmer Nelson a merchant? [*Nelson v. Co-operative Exchange,* 548 S.W.2d 352 (1977).]

7. Wisconsin Knife Works, having some unused manufacturing capacity, decided to try to manufacture spade bits for sale to its parent, Black & Decker, a large producer of tools, including drills. A spade bit is made out of a chunk of metal called a *spade bit blank,* and Wisconsin Knife Works had to find a source of supply for these blanks. National Metal Crafters was eager to supply the spade bit blanks. After some negotiating, Wisconsin Knife Works sent National Metal Crafters a series of purchase orders. On the back of each purchase order was printed "Acceptance of this Order, either by acknowledgement or performance, constitutes an unqualified agreement to the following." A list of "Conditions of Purchase" followed, of which the first was "No modification of this contract shall be binding upon Buyer [Wisconsin

Knife Works] unless made in writing and signed by Buyer's authorized representative. Buyer shall have the right to make changes in the Order by a notice, in writing, to Seller." The seller met the terms of the first two purchase orders from Wisconsin Knife Works. After the first two orders, National Metal Crafters was late with the deliveries. No delivery date had been specified on the purchase orders, but the delivery dates had been communicated orally between the two parties to the contract. Wisconsin Knife Works claimed that National Metal Crafters breached the contract. National Metal Crafters claimed that it had modified the dates for delivery and that Wisconsin had accepted these dates. What could constitute a binding modification after this contract was formed? [*Wisconsin Knife Works v. National Metal Crafters,* 781 F.2d 1280 (1986).]

8. Mitchell Aircraft Spares, Inc., has filed a lawsuit against European Aircraft Service (EAS) AG asserting claims for breach of contract and breach of warranty. Mitchell, an Illinois corporation, is a broker in the market for surplus aircraft parts. EAS is a Swedish corporation that buys parts from companies in Western Europe and the United States and sells these parts to a wide variety of purchasers. At issue is Mitchell's claim that it suffered damages in the amount of $120,000 because EAS sent it integrated drive generators with the wrong part numbers. In Mitchell's industry, specific part numbers are important. What law is likely to govern this dispute? Explain. [*Mitchell Aircraft Spares, Inc. v. European Aircraft Service AB,* 23 F. Supp. 2d 915 (1998).]

9. Mitchell Coach Manufacturing Company, Inc., produces motor homes and sells them to other retail dealers and directly to customers. Ronny Stephens was a customer. WW, Inc., bought and sold motor homes from Mitchell. Under their agreement, WW would pay Mitchell either a down payment on a motor home before the motor home was purchased or the entire amount due for the completed product. Also under the agreement, the title of the motor home remained with WW until Stephens paid in full. WW paid Mitchell a down payment of $10,000 for the construction of the motor home. Upon completion, the motor home was to be picked up by Stephens at Mitchell. WW paid the remaining balance to Mitchell, but the check was returned for lack of sufficient funds. Stephens, through a loan, had paid for the motor home in full, but WW had not paid Mitchell. Both Mitchell and Stephens claim title to the motor home. Who does title belong to? [*Mitchell Coach Manufacturing Company, Inc. v. Ronny Stephens,* 19 F. Supp. 2d 1277 (1998).]

10. Marilyn Thomas purchased an installed pool heater from Sunkissed. The pool heater was delivered to Marilyn's residence, but the delivery slip was signed by Nancy Thomas. Marilyn did not know of anyone by that name. She called Sunkissed to advise the company to move the heater. The neighborhood was not safe, and she was worried that the heater would be taken. The heater remained in her driveway for approximately four days. When Marilyn noticed that the heater was no longer in her driveway, she again contacted Sunkissed, but she was told "not to worry." Who was responsible for the loss of the heater? Did Sunkissed actually "deliver" the heater to Marilyn? How do you think the court decided? [*In re Marilyn Thomas,* 182 B.R. 347 (1995).]

11. In 1987, R. H. Love Gallery owned the title to a painting entitled *Marlton's Cove.* The gallery sold 50 percent of the painting to Altman Fine Arts, a New York art dealer, and 50 percent to Andre Lopoukhine, a Boston art dealer. In 1989, plaintiff Morgold, Inc., purchased Altman's 50 percent of the painting. Morgold and Lopoukhine decided to try to sell the painting. In 1990, Lopoukhine sold the painting to Mark Grossman. Lopoukhine did not pay Morgold the 50 percent due for the sale of the painting. Morgold argued that this lack of payment indicated that the title was never officially passed on to Grossman. Through an art dealer, Grossman sold the painting to Fred Keeler. In 1991, Morgold contacted Keeler and claimed to be the sole owner of the painting. Who do you believe owns title to the painting? [*Morgold, Inc. v. Keeler,* 891 F. Supp. 1361 (1995).]

12. MAN Roland agreed to sell Quantum Color Corporation a used press for $405,000. According to the contract, Quantum was supposed to pay $5,000 at the time of the contract, $265,000 at delivery, and the balance of $135,000 before the press was actually used. The first two payments were made, but MAN Roland did not receive the $135,000. MAN Roland alleged that Quantum had been using the press and, therefore, that Quantum was required to pay the balance. Quantum argued that MAN Roland breached the contract by delivering nonconforming goods. Part of the contract indicated that MAN Roland would provide standard equipment and installation, but MAN Roland did not install the equipment or provide Quantum with the standard equipment. How do you think the court settled this case? [*MAN Roland Inc. v. Quantum Color Corp.,* 57 F. Supp. 2d 576 (1999).]

13. Joseph Perna purchased a 1981 Oldsmobile at a traffic auction from Alfred Locascio. He was told that the New York City Parking Violations Bureau had seized the car. Perna subsequently sold the car to a co-worker, Elio Marino. Marino registered and insured the vehicle and also spent several hundred dollars on necessary repairs. While driving the vehicle, Marino's son was pulled over by the police

and arrested for driving a stolen vehicle. The charges were eventually dropped, but he spent the night in jail. Did Marino have title to the vehicle? How do you think the court resolved the conflict? [*Marino v. Perna,* 629 N.Y.S.2d 669 (1995).]

14. Mr. and Mrs. Kahr donated a bag of clothing to Goodwill. Unbeknownst to them, mixed in with the clothing was a bag of antique sterling-silver silverware valued in excess of $3,000. When the Kahrs realized what they had done, they immediately called Goodwill. However, Goodwill had sold the silverware for $15 to a purchaser. The Kahrs brought suit against the purchaser for the return of the silverware. Did they get it back because the silver was "lost property,"

or was this a classic entrustment case? [*Kahr v. Markland,* 543 N.E.2d 579 (1989).]

15. Lumber Sales, Inc., contracted to sell five train carloads of lumber to Brown under a destination contract. Lumber delivered four carloads, which Brown received and paid for. However, the fifth carload was delivered to a railroad siding about ½ mile from the buyer's place of business (the usual point of delivery). The buyer was notified of the delivery. However, before the buyer could secure the goods, they were stolen. Who bears the risk of loss, the buyer or the seller? Had delivery been affected even though the buyer had not taken possession of the goods? [*Lumber Sales, Inc. v. Brown,* 469 S.W. 888 (1971).]

Looking for more review material?

The Online Learning Center at **www.mhhe.com/kubasekess** contains this chapter's "Assignment on the Internet" and also a list of URLs for more information, entitled "On the Internet." Find both of them in the Student Center portion of the OLC, along with quizzes and other helpful materials.

Sales and Lease Contracts: Performance, Warranties, Remedies

----> CASE OPENER

Will the Sun Shine for Alpha Chi Omega?

Alpha Chi Omega, like all sororities, is steeped in tradition. The organization was founded in 1885 to help its members "seek the heights."[1] At the first appearance of the seven founders of Alpha Chi Omega, the women attached scarlet and olive streamers to their dresses. From that moment on, Alpha Chi Omega included particular colors as part of its traditions. Examples of these traditions include a choice of a particular flower (the red carnation), a stick pin that includes the colors scarlet and olive green, a coat of arms that includes the colors scarlet and olive green, and a variety of toasts and songs. For example, the song "We Believe" indicates that the sorority "believe[s] in sunshine [a]nd all the things it can do."[2]

In 1992, the Bowling Green State University (BGSU) chapter of Alpha Chi Omega faced a challenge to its traditions when it became involved in a dispute with a clothing company over the purchase of 168 imprinted sweaters and masks from Johnathan James Furlong for the sorority's Midnight Masquerade party, scheduled for October 24, 1992.

Through an oral contract, and a subsequent written description of the sweaters, the sorority agreed to buy the sweaters and masks from Furlong. The sorority gave him a $2,000 down payment and agreed to pay the remaining $1,612 balance when Furlong delivered the garments. Furlong had a two-year business relationship with the sorority, although he had never before interacted with the two sorority sisters who arranged for this particular deal, Emily Lieberman and Amy Altomondo.

Lieberman and Furlong agreed that the sweaters would include three colors, hunter green letters on top of maroon letters outlined in navy blue, and the masks would be hunter green. Furlong indicated that a third party would imprint the sweaters. Furlong also delivered to Lieberman a sample sweater with maroon letters so that she could see the color. Furlong confirmed with Lieberman by sending a two-page written description of the sweaters.

Furlong delivered the garments on October 23, 1992. On receipt of delivery, the sorority gave Furlong a check to pay off the balance of the purchase price. However, later that day, Lieberman inspected the garments and screamed in dismay when she discovered several unauthorized design changes. She asked the sorority's bank to stop payment on its check, and Altomondo called Furlong to tell him that

[1]Information for this case comes from www.alphachiomega.org. This site indicates that Alpha Chi Omega's open motto is "Together let us seek the heights." Information also comes from *Furlong v. Alpha Chi Omega Sorority,* 657 N.E.2d 866 (1993).

[2]Ibid.

the sweaters and masks did not meet Alpha Chi Omega's agreement and that the sorority was rejecting them.

In particular, Furlong had authorized the following changes to the garments without the knowledge or consent of Lieberman, Altomondo, or anyone in the sorority: On the sweaters, (1) the navy blue outline was eliminated, (2) each side was printed with two rather than three colors, (3) the maroon color was changed to red, and (4) the color scheme for the letters was changed from maroon and hunter green to navy blue; the masks were changed from hunter green to red. After rejecting the garments, Amy offered to return the sweaters and masks to Furlong, but Furlong said no.

Furlong believed that it was within his discretion to make these changes and that, due to time constraints, it would have been impossible for him to get approval from Lieberman or Altomondo prior to the printing. Furlong also believed that the sorority sisters should pay the remainder of the balance due and keep the sweaters and masks, but Alpha Chi Omega did not want the sweaters and masks and wanted its down payment back. At a minimum, Furlong wanted Alpha Chi Omega to compromise and pay a reduced price for the sweaters.

1. What are Alpha Chi Omega's obligations to Furlong? Should the sorority sisters compromise? Is the sorority too particular about the colors?

2. What are Furlong's obligations to Alpha Chi Omega? Should he reorder the sweaters and masks and get them right? Should he accept his loss and seek business elsewhere?

····▶ LEARNING OBJECTIVES

After reading this chapter, you will be able to answer the following questions:

LO 1 What is the difference between conforming and nonconforming goods?

LO 2 What is the perfect tender rule?

LO 3 What is the right to cure?

LO 4 What is commercial impracticability?

LO 5 What are the implied warranties of title, merchantability, and particular purpose?

LO 6 How are third parties affected by implied warranties?

LO 7 How can implied warranties be disclaimed?

LO 8 What is cover and resale?

LO 9 When are money damages available?

When individuals and/or organizations like Alpha Chi Omega enter into sales contracts or leases with others, they need to know their rights and obligations. Businesses such as Furlong's also need to know their rights and obligations so that they can engage in efficient business transactions. This chapter explains the performance obligations of sellers and buyers. In addition, it explains the performance obligations of lessors and lessees, which are similar to those

of buyers are sellers. The chapter explains the perfect tender rule and exceptions to this rule. It also explains the buyer's general obligation to inspect, pay for, and accept goods, and it discusses exceptions to this general obligation. Moreover, it further explains performance obligations under both express and implied warranties, breach of contract, and remedies available in the event of breach.

LO 1

The Basic Performance Obligation

The obligations of sellers/lessors and buyers/lessees are determined by (1) terms the parties outline in agreements, (2) custom, and (3) rules outlined by the Uniform Commercial Code (UCC). This chapter focuses on rules outlined by the UCC.

Under the UCC, sellers and lessors are *obligated to transfer and deliver conforming goods.* Buyers and lessees are *obligated to accept and pay for conforming goods in accordance with the contract.* Courts rely on UCC rules to clarify these obligations when the contract or lease the parties agreed to is unclear. In the Case Opener, Furlong is obligated to transfer and deliver conforming goods to Alpha Chi Omega. Alpha Chi Omega is obligated to accept and pay for conforming goods in accordance with the contract. What is a "conforming good" in the context of the dispute between Alpha Chi Omega and Furlong? Does the UCC obligate Alpha Chi Omega to accept and pay for the sweaters and masks? The question of what constitutes "conforming goods" is significant. This chapter addresses that topic after explaining how the idea of good faith places transactions in a particular context. What if there was an issue of mistake? Remember that at common law a unilateral mistake may still constitute a binding contract whereas a bilateral mistake will not. Issues of mistake often raise the corollary issue of unconscionability. Consider the Case Nugget.

CASE Nugget

Do Mistake and Unconscionability Affect the Enforceability of a Contract?

Donovan v. RRL Corporation
California Supreme Court

26 Cal. 4th 261 (2001)

The Donovans showed up at the defendant car dealership. After hearing the sales pitch, Mr. Donovan stated that he'd take the car at the price quoted in the newspaper, $25,995. The horrified salesman said that he could go as low as $37,995 but not $25,995. At that point, Donovan showed the salesman a copy of an ad that had been running in the local newspaper identifying the very same automobile for $25,995. The salesman responded that the advertisement had to be a mistake. Donovan said that he wanted the car at the $25,995 price. He subsequently brought an action in the municipal court in Orange County. The trial court found for RRL Corp. on mistake. However, the California court of appeals reversed, stating that all the material elements of a contract were clearly stated in the advertisement and that Donovan's acceptance of those terms constituted a good contract.

The California Supreme Court heard the case, reversing it on a combination of mistake and unconscionability. The supreme court found that a contract was indeed created but that the contract could be rescinded since the evidence showed that (1) the defendant's unilateral mistake was made in good faith; (2) the defendant did not bear the risk of the mistake; and, (3) the enforcement of a contract with an erroneous price would be unconscionable as a matter of law.

Nonconforming Goods in China and the CISG

The Uniform Commercial Code is not a model law that other countries have adopted. For example, China embraces the Convention on Contracts for the International Sale of Goods (CISG), not the UCC. Rules under the CISG differ from those under the UCC. Article 49(1) of the CISG allows *avoidance* (the term used for the buyer's refusing to accept nonconforming goods) only if there is substantial and foreseeable nonconformity of the goods. In other words, the CISG follows more closely the common law concept of substantial performance than it does the perfect tender rule.

Consider, for example, what would happen if an American company shipped nonconforming goods to another American company.* Under the UCC, the buyer could reject the nonconforming goods. If the American company shipped nonconforming goods to a Chinese buyer, the result would be different. It is likely a Chinese buyer would be permitted by the CISG to resort only to a remedy that included a reasonable price reduction for nonconforming goods. It is possible (but unlikely) that the Chinese buyer could pursue the issue of nonconforming goods as a criminal matter.

China is not the only country that does not apply the UCC. Hong Kong, Japan, and Indonesia are additional examples of Pacific Rim countries that do not apply UCC rules.

*Example from Jacques G. Boettcher, "The China Predicament," *Multinational Business Review* 9 (April 1, 2001).

GOOD FAITH

UCC Section 1-203 requires good faith in the performance and enforcement of every contract. *Good faith* means "honesty in fact." When the parties are merchants, the UCC imposes a higher standard. Between merchants, the UCC imposes not only honesty in fact but also reasonable commercial standards of fair dealing. This second requirement is often called commercial reasonableness. In the context of good faith, courts decide the specific obligations of sellers/lessors and buyers/lessees. The next few sections of the chapter discuss these specific obligations.

good faith
Honesty in fact.

commercial reasonableness
Reasonable commercial standards of fair dealing, required of merchants in addition to honesty in fact.

Specific Obligations of Sellers and Lessors

LO 2

THE PERFECT TENDER RULE

The UCC requires that sellers and lessors tender conforming goods to buyers and lessees. UCC Sections 2-503(1) and 2A-508(1) state that tender of delivery requires that the seller/lessor have and hold conforming goods at the disposal of the buyer/lessee and give the buyer/lessee reasonable notification to enable the buyer/lessee to take delivery. Conforming goods are goods that conform to contract specifications.

A common law rule known as the perfect tender rule required that the seller deliver goods in conformity with the terms of the contract, right down to the last detail. UCC Sections 2-601 and 2A-509 embrace the perfect tender rule. These sections indicate that if goods or tender of delivery fails *in any respect* to conform to the contract, the buyer/lessee has the right to accept the goods, reject the entire shipment, or accept part and reject part. Common law usually substitutes perfect tender with the doctrine of substantial performance. Substantial performance occurs when all the material elements of a contract are satisfied even if some nonmaterial requirements may not be satisfied. The perfect tender rule would not recognize the distinction between material and immaterial contractual requirements. See how the perfect tender rule is affected when good faith is an issue in the Case Nugget to follow.

tender of delivery
Requirement that the seller or lessor have and hold conforming goods at the disposal of the buyer or lessee and give the buyer or lessee reasonable notification to enable him or her to take delivery.

conforming goods
Goods that conform to contract specifications.

perfect tender rule
Requirement that the seller deliver the goods in conformity with the contract, down to the last detail.

CONNECTING to the Core

Marketing

Conforming goods are often customized purchases, similar to Alpha Chi Omega's request for customized sweaters and masks. To provide greater ease in consumers' purchasing customized products, many companies' Web sites are very interactive and personalized to enhance transactions between buyers and sellers. As you may have learned in your marketing course, these individualized systems are referred to as *choiceboards*. For example, Nike designed a choiceboard, the Nike iD Customized Product, which consumers can access on the Internet, that allows consumers to design, view, and purchase customized shoes and backpacks. Similarly, Dell's choiceboard allows consumers to build their own computers.

One of the primary benefits of companies' using choiceboards is that these companies can easily acquire information about consumers' preferences, permitting the companies to more easily fulfill consumers' specific needs. As a future business manager, you may want to consider the benefits of your company's using a choiceboard to market products, thereby allowing consumers to make customized purchases.

Source: R. Kerin, S. Hartley, E. Berkowitz, and W. Rudelius, *Marketing* (New York: McGraw-Hill/Irwin, 2005), pp. 560–561.

CASE Nugget

How Does Good Faith Affect Perfect Tender?

Y&N Furniture Inc. v. Nwabuoku
New York Court of Appeals

734 N.Y.S.2d 392 (2001)

The defendant, Nwabuoku, purchased $1,500 worth of furniture from the plaintiff, Y&N Furniture. Through an arrangement with the plaintiff, the defendant financed the purchase through a financing company named Beneficial. On receipt of the furniture, the defendant was to notify Beneficial that receipt was effected, and Beneficial would pay Y&N the $1,500 purchase price. Nwabuoku would then begin paying Beneficial the amount due plus interest according to their financing agreement.

Nwabuoku refused to acknowledge receipt to Beneficial and eventually rejected the goods, claiming that he did not want the furniture. The civil court of the City of New York found that Nwabuoku had rejected the goods, and the court cited the perfect tender rule as requiring "exact performance by the seller." Moreover, the court held that "rejection of goods must be within a reasonable time of their delivery or tender." The court indicated that Nwabuoku did indeed make a rightful rejection. However, the court noted that a rejection of goods must be based on some claim that the goods are in some way nonconforming. The defendant in this case had a disagreement over the terms of the financing (though the terms were clearly stated in the financing statements). The defendant made no claim of nonconforming goods. Thus, the court found that "in this case, too, we have a rejection that is not only 'wrongful,' but also in bad faith." A wrongful rejection is not necessarily in bad faith; the buyer may honestly believe that the goods fail to conform but may simply be mistaken. But a rejection that does not even purport to rest on an honest assessment of conformity of the goods has "the effect of destroying or injuring the right of the seller to receive the fruits of the contract."

Consider Case 14-1, which provides an illustration of a situation in which the UCC's version of the perfect tender rule was relevant when compared to the common law rule of material breach under the doctrine of substantial performance. As you read the case, think about Alpha Chi Omega's conflict over the sweaters and masks for the Midnight Masquerade party. Does this case give you a hint about whether the sun will shine for the sisters of Alpha Chi?

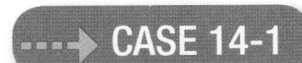 **CASE 14-1**

ALASKA PACIFIC TRADING CO. v.
EAGON FOREST PRODUCTS INC.
WASHINGTON APPELLATE DIVISION 1
933 P.2d 417 (1997)

FACTS: *Alaska Pacific Trading Company (ALPAC) and Eagon Forest Products, Inc., contracted to buy and sell raw logs. ALPAC and Eagon engaged in months of communications about a shipment of 15,000 cubic meters of logs from Argentina to Korea between the end of July and the end of August 1993. The delivery date passed without ALPAC shipping the logs. Eagon canceled the contract, alleging that ALPAC had breached the agreement by failing to deliver. ALPAC alleged that its failure to deliver was not a material breach and that the parties had modified the delivery date. Alternatively, ALPAC argued that Eagon breached the contract by failing to provide adequate assurances or repudiating the contract. The miscommunication between the parties occurred after the market for logs began to soften, making the contract less attractive to Eagon. ALPAC was reluctant to ship the goods because it was concerned that Eagon might not accept the shipment. However, Eagon never stated that it would not accept the cargo.*

ISSUE: The question for the court is whether to apply the common law doctrine of material breach or the UCC doctrine of perfect tender.

REASONING: In the court's own words:

> As a contract for the sale of goods, this contract is governed by the Uniform Commercial Code, Article II (UCC II) which replaced the common law of material breach, on which ALPAC relies, with the "perfect tender" rule. Under this rule, "If the goods or the tender of delivery fail in any respect to conform to the contract, the buyer may . . . reject the whole." . . . Both the plain language of the rule and the official comments clearly state that, if the tender of the goods differs from the terms of the contract in any way, the seller breaches the contract and the buyer is released from its duty to accept the goods.

DECISION AND REMEDY: The court applied the literal language of the UCC, holding that the perfect tender rule applied and that ALPAC's failure to deliver was a breach of contract.

SIGNIFICANCE OF THE CASE: Though difficult to measure at times, the perfect tender rule is a departure from the common law rule of substantial performance. Any deviation from the contract may indeed constitute a breach of the perfect tender rule, materiality notwithstanding.

Here, Eagon got lucky. The company got out of a contract that was unfavorable to it, given the softening market for logs. In what way did the judge simplify the case? Is it fair to say the judge oversimplified the case?

What ethical norm or value underlies the judge's decision? Explain.

 EXCEPTIONS TO THE PERFECT TENDER RULE

The perfect tender rule is not as inflexible as it appears. Although the rule itself demands perfection, both courts and UCC drafters have created exceptions that reduce the rule's rigidity. These exceptions limit the seller's obligation to deliver conforming goods and/or limit the buyer's power to reject goods that do not conform. The exceptions allow sellers/lessors and buyers/lessees to ask questions such as:

- What are the norms in the particular industry, and/or what past dealings have the parties had with one another?
- What does the parties' agreement say?
- Is it possible for the seller/lessor to cure or correct problems?
- What if the goods have been destroyed?
- What if nonconformity substantially impairs the value of goods?
- What if unforeseen circumstances make contract performance commercially impracticable?

Look again at these questions, and ask which might be relevant to Alpha Chi Omega's deal with Furlong. For example, we know Furlong had past dealings with Alpha Chi Omega. Had the sorority accepted and paid for nonconforming goods in the past? Could Furlong have corrected or "cured" the problems with the sweaters and masks? What would have happened if the sweaters and masks had met the agreement the parties outlined but then the goods were damaged in a flood? After reading the following subsections, determine whether these or any other exceptions might be relevant.

Norms in the Industry and Past Dealings between the Parties When the buyer alleges that goods failed to conform to contract specifications, the buyer does not automatically have the right to reject the goods. The UCC requires that courts consider norms in a particular trade. Sometimes, the norms for a particular trade do not permit a buyer to reject goods with minor flaws. UCC Section 1-205(2) defines usage of trade as any practice that members of an industry expect to be part of their dealings.

In addition to its requirement on usage of trade, the UCC requires that courts consider the ideas of course of dealing and course of performance. UCC 1-205(1) defines course of dealing as previous commercial transactions between the same parties. Under UCC 208(1), course of performance refers to the history of dealings between the parties in the particular contract at issue.

Exceptions Outlined in the Parties' Agreement Sometimes, language in the parties' agreement limits the rigidity of the perfect tender rule. For instance, parties may agree that the seller must have the opportunity to repair or replace nonconforming goods within a particular period of time. Alternatively, parties may agree with a level of performance that is less than perfect. They could indicate, by agreement, the expectation regarding performance.

The Seller's and Lessor's Right to Cure Under UCC Sections 2-508 and 2A-513, sellers and lessors have the right to cure or fix problems with nonconforming goods. In particular, sellers and lessors can repair, adjust, or replace defective or nonconforming goods as long as they give prompt notice of the intent to cure and go ahead and cure within the contract time for performance.

Destroyed Goods Under UCC Sections 2-613 and 2A-221, if goods are identified at the time the parties entered into a contract and the goods are destroyed through no fault of the parties before risk passes to the buyer or lessee, the parties are excused from performance. If the goods are only partially destroyed, the buyer can inspect the goods and decide whether to (1) treat the contract as void or (2) ask the seller for a reduction of the contract price and then accept the damaged goods.

Substantial Impairment Two sections of the UCC use the concept of substantial impairment to modify the perfect tender rule. The first applies when a buyer *revokes acceptance of goods*. UCC Section 2-608 indicates that a buyer who has accepted goods may later revoke the acceptance

usage of trade
Any practice that members of an industry expect to be part of their dealings.

course of dealing
Previous commercial transactions between the same parties.

course of performance
The history of dealings between the parties in the particular contract at issue.

LO 3

cure
A breaching party's right to provide conforming goods when nonconforming goods were initially delivered; subject to a reasonable time test.

substantial impairment
A concept, used to modify the perfect tender rule, whereby a buyer can revoke acceptance of goods and, with installment contracts, a buyer/lessee can reject an installment of a particular item only if the defects substantially impair the value of the goods.

only if the buyer can show that the defects substantially impair the value of the goods. The second applies when the buyer and seller have entered into an *installment contract*. UCC 2-612(2) and 2A-510(1) indicates that a buyer/lessee may reject an installment of a particular item only if the defects substantially impair the value of the goods and cannot be cured.

Commercial Impracticability UCC Sections 2-615(a) and 2A-405(a) state that a delay in delivery or nondelivery, in whole or in part, is not a breach in circumstances in which performance has been made impracticable because a contingency has occurred that was not contemplated when the parties reached an agreement. For example, this rule would be relevant if a change in government regulation that neither party contemplated forbids the import or export of a particular item the parties had agreed would be shipped. "WEATHER CONDITION"

LO 4

Specific Obligations of Buyers and Lessees

THE BASIC OBLIGATION: INSPECTION, PAYMENT, AND ACCEPTANCE

Under UCC Sections 2-301 and 2A-516(1), buyers and lessees are obligated to accept and pay for conforming goods in accordance with the contract. Before paying for and accepting the goods, buyers/lessees ordinarily inspect the goods to make sure they conform to the specifications in the parties' agreement.

EXCEPTIONS TO THE BASIC OBLIGATION

Buyers/lessees do not always end up accepting and paying for goods. Sometimes, on inspection, the buyer or lessee decides to reject the goods and refrain from paying for them. In this section, we take a look at exceptions to the buyer's/lessee's basic obligation. These exceptions allow sellers/lessors and buyers/lessees to ask questions such as:

- What forms of payment are allowed under the UCC?
- In what circumstances can a buyer reject goods?
- Is the buyer allowed to accept part but not all of the goods?
- In what circumstances can a buyer revoke acceptance of goods?
- How and when can a buyer reject nonconforming goods?
- Are installment contracts treated differently than other kinds of contracts?

Problems on Inspection If all goes well in a transaction over the sale or lease of goods, the buyer or lessee inspects the goods and then pays by any means the parties have agreed on, including payment by cash, check, or credit card. Unless the parties have agreed otherwise, the buyer or lessee typically inspects the goods before paying. Under UCC Sections 2-513(1) and 2A-515(1), the seller or lessor must provide an opportunity for inspection before enforcing payment.

The concept of reasonableness governs the inspection process. For example, inspection must take place at a reasonable time and place, in a reasonable way. Once the buyer or lessee inspects the goods, he or she decides whether to accept them. Sometimes, on inspection, the buyer or lessee decides not to accept the goods.

Problems with Acceptance When all goes well, UCC Sections 2-606(1) and 2A-515(1)(a) indicate that the buyer or lessee, after inspecting, signifies agreement to the seller or lessor that the goods are either (1) conforming or (2) acceptable even though they are nonconforming. UCC 2-602(1), 2-606(1), and 2A-515(1)(b) allow the seller or lessor to presume acceptance if the buyer or lessee fails to reject the goods within a reasonable period of time. UCC 2-601(c) and 2A-509(1) allow the buyer or lessee to make a partial acceptance when the goods are nonconforming and the seller or lessor has failed to cure the defects.

When goods are nonconforming, the buyer or lessee is allowed to revoke or withdraw acceptance of the goods. The previous section on specific obligations of sellers/lessors discussed this concept under the topic of substantial impairment. From the buyer's/lessee's perspective, the buyer or lessee may revoke acceptance if the nonconformity substantially impairs the value of the goods but only if he or she had a legitimate reason for the initial acceptance.

LO 5

Warranties

At common law, the obligations and responsibilities of the contractual parties are determined by the express terms of the contract. UCC contracts are the same but with a major addition: implied warranties. *Implied* means that the warranty or guarantee is automatically a part of the contract; the parties do not negotiate for it. At common law, the only implied warranty in a contract is the implied warranty of assignability. However, the UCC changes this part of contract law dramatically.

Let's look at the whole range of warranties in contract law. Warranties generally arise in conjunction with a sale or lease. They impose certain duties on the seller or lessor, and if the seller or lessor fails to live up to these duties, he or she may be sued for breach of warranty. There are three basic categories of warranties: warranties of title, express warranties, and implied warranties. Each is discussed in the following sections.

WARRANTIES OF TITLE

While no warranties automatically arise under the common law, the UCC assumes that the seller:

1. Has good and valid title to the goods.
2. Has the right to transfer title free and clear of any liens, judgments, or infringements of intellectual property rights of which the buyer does not have knowledge.

The UCC specifically permits buyers to recover from sellers who have breached these warranties of title. The only exceptions to title warranties occur if they are disclaimed or modified by specific language in the contract or if the seller is obviously unable to guarantee title, as would be the case, for instance, at a sheriff's sale of seized goods.

Clearly, if the buyer is aware of any problem with the transfer of goods, the buyer is indeed purchasing them at her own risk. Still, if the seller transfers goods to an unknowing buyer for which no good title passes or on which there are encumbrances or patent claims, the buyer may treat the contract as being in breach. Under such circumstances, the buyer may then avail herself of the remedies available under a breach situation.

EXPRESS WARRANTIES

Although the common law does not use the term *express warranties,* the concept and its application do exist in the common law. It seems only fair and equitable that promises made by a seller to induce a buyer to execute a sales contract should be enforceable. An express warranty is any description of a good's physical nature or its use, in either general or specific circumstances, that becomes part of the contract. To use common law language, an express warranty is a material term of the sale or lease contract.

Express warranties may be found in advertisements or brochures (e.g., "This electric saw comes with a lifetime guarantee"). Such a warranty may also be part of a written sales or lease contract; or it may be a salesperson's oral promise concerning the good, made while he is attempting to close the deal. A sample or model may also provide an express warranty. Generally speaking, if the buyer relies on representations, those representations become part of the contract in the form of express warranties.

IMPLIED WARRANTIES OF QUALITY

Implied warranties arise by operation of law under certain circumstances. Earlier, you read about the implied warranties of title that arise under the UCC. This section focuses on the three warranties of quality that arise under the UCC.

warranty

An assurance, either express or implied, by one party that the other party can rely on its representations of fact; in sales, a binding promise regarding a product in the event that the product does not meet the manufacturer's or seller's promises.

warranty of title

An assurance, inferred in every UCC sales transaction, that the seller has good and valid title to the goods and has the right to transfer title free and clear of any liens, judgments, or infringements of intellectual property rights of which the buyer does not have knowledge.

express warranty

Any description of a good's physical nature or its use, in either general or specific circumstances, that becomes part of a contract.

Implied Warranty of Merchantability Consider the following scenario: You purchase a toaster from a local discount store. When you use the toaster, all you get is either burnt toast or bread that is only slightly warm. You take the toaster back to the store and are met with this answer: "Well, we don't guarantee how well the toaster will work. After all, it does toast, either very, very lightly or very, very burnt." This answer, of course, is nonsense. There is a reasonable expectation of how a toaster will perform. That reasonable expectation is codified in the UCC *implied war-ranty of merchantability.*

To invoke this implied warranty, the buyer or lessee must have purchased or leased the good from a merchant. Thus, a dirt bike purchased at a bicycle shop is covered by the warranty of merchantability, but a bike that is bought from a neighbor is not, unless the neighbor is a bicycle merchant.

Under the UCC, the goods must be *merchantable,* meaning that they must:

1. Be able to pass without objection in the trade or market for similar goods.
2. In the case of fungible goods, be of fair average quality within the description.
3. Be fit for the ordinary purposes for which such goods are used.
4. Be produced, within the variations permitted by the agreement, with even kind, quality, and quantity in each unit and among all units involved.
5. Be adequately contained, packaged, and labeled as the agreement may require.
6. Conform to the promises or affirmations made on the container or label, if any.

The quintessential case defining and illustrating the implied warranty of merchantability is that of the Blue Ship Tearoom and Ms. Webster (see Case 14-2). The case concerned the merchantability of food.

implied warranty of merchantability

An assurance, inferred in every sale unless clearly disclaimed, that merchantable goods will conform to a reasonable performance expectation. The purchaser must have purchased or leased the good from a merchant.

PRISCILLA D. WEBSTER v. BLUE SHIP TEA ROOM, INC.
SUPREME JUDICIAL COURT OF MASSACHUSETTS
347 Mass. 421; 198 N.E.2d 309 (1964)

FACTS: *Priscilla Webster, a restaurant patron who ordered seafood chowder and choked on a fishbone, brought this case. She maintained that she would not have reasonably expected to find a bone in the chowder. As a result of the bone in the chowder, Webster suffered through several hospital procedures to remove the bone, at considerable cost and pain. At the trial, a jury found for Webster. The Blue Ship Tea Room, the defendant, appealed the case on the basis of the legal interpretation of the implied warranty of merchantability. The appellate decision has become a classic in American jurisprudential reasoning.*

ISSUE: Does a fishbone found in fish chowder render the chowder inedible, thereby breaching the implied warranty of merchantability?

REASONING: The court, in great detail, discussed the rich culinary history of New England seafood chowders. In going through the details of exactly how "good" chowder is made, the court praised the richness of thick, plump, delicious pieces of fish and shellfish. Completely ridding the chowder of any possibility of bones would require that the cook finely mince the seafood, depriving the dish of one of its hallmark characteristics. Further, the court argued that anyone eating good New England seafood chowder would know or should know that fishbones are indeed a possibility.

DECISION AND REMEDY: As lamentable as Webster's injuries were, the court found that the Blue Ship Tea Room had not breached its implied warranty of merchantability.

SIGNIFICANCE OF THE CASE: Common sense needs to apply in defining "merchantability." Clearly, a piece of bone in a hamburger is unreasonable and would violate the implied warranty. However, in cases where the buyer should expect a problem, such as a possible fishbone in a seafood dish, the buyer must be prepared to accept the situation.

(continued)

As with most legal decisions, the critical thinking activity that is most obvious is the need to reexamine the analogies used by the court in justifying its conclusion. The plaintiff wished the court to say that fish chowder was like what? What analogy did the defendant want the court to accept? Would the aptness of the analogy depend at all on the size of the bone in the fish chowder?

ETHICAL DECISION MAKING

The judge mainly used assumption of risk to rule against Webster, though she suffered an injury in fact. Should the restaurant have somehow compensated her? What would the WPH framework indicate should be done?

Implied Warranty of Fitness for a Particular Purpose Another important UCC implied warranty is the implied warranty of fitness for a particular purpose. This warranty comes about when a seller or lessor knows or has reason to know (1) why the buyer or lessee is purchasing or leasing the goods in question and (2) that the buyer or lessee is relying on him or her to make the selection. Under this warranty, a seller or lessor does not have to be a merchant.

An implied warranty of fitness for a particular purpose should not be confused with an express warranty. If the buyer walks into a store and the salesclerk says, "This saw will cut through metal," the seller has created an express warranty. However, if the buyer comes into the store and asks the salesclerk for a saw to cut through some copper tubing and the salesclerk refers the customer to a wall of different saws, it is reasonable for the buyer to assume that all the saws on the wall will satisfy the *particular purpose* that the buyer has indicated. Thus, an implied warranty of fitness for a particular purpose has been created.

implied warranty of fitness for a particular purpose

An assurance, inferred in any UCC sale, whereby when a seller or lessor knows or has reason to know (1) why the buyer or lessee is purchasing or leasing the goods in question and (2) that the buyer or lessee is relying on him or her to make the selection, the buyer or lessee has an enforceable warranty if such assurance is false.

Implied Warranty of Trade Usage The UCC, always diligent in its goal to facilitate the flow and ease of commercial activity, recognizes that a well-accepted course of dealing or trade usage may create implied warranties dependent on the circumstances. For example, if it is generally accepted in the trade that a certain product is always preassembled and shrink-wrapped, the failure of the seller to deliver the goods in that condition would be a breach of the implied warranty of trade usage.

implied warranty of trade usage

An assurance, inferred in the context of certain UCC sales, depending on the circumstances, that can be created through a well-accepted course of dealing or trade usage.

LO 6

Warranty Rights of Third Parties

The idea of a seller's being in breach of an implied warranty raises an entirely new issue: Is the seller liable to anyone other than the buyer? This question may initially sound peculiar. After all, the seller and the buyer are bound together by contract and if either breaches, then the breaching party is liable to the nonbreaching party.

However, consider this possible scenario: Jane buys a blender from a local store. Prior to using the blender, she lends it to her cousin Valerie to use at a party. While Valerie is blending drinks at the party, the blades fly off the blender and injure her. What obligation, if any, does the seller have to the injured Valerie? No contractual relationship exists between Valerie and the seller. However, it seems to be patently unfair to conclude that Valerie has no cause of action against the seller. The UCC recognizes this unfairness and clearly states that Valerie may indeed have a

cause of action based on breach of warranty against the seller. The states are given the following three choices regarding *third-party beneficiaries of warranties:*

1. Seller's warranties extend to the buyer's household members and guests.
2. Seller's warranties extend to any reasonable and foreseeable user.
3. Seller's warranties extend to anyone injured by the good.

Most states have adopted the second option.

Warranty Disclaimers and Waivers

LO 7

There really is no question as to whether an implied warranty may be disclaimed. The real question is *how* it is to be disclaimed. Generally speaking, if an implied warranty is to be disclaimed, the seller must do so in clear, unambiguous, conspicuous language. In order to disclaim the implied warranty of fitness for a particular purpose, the seller must disclaim the warranty in writing. The seller may disclaim the warranty of merchantability either orally or in writing; however, some states require that the term *merchantability* must be used in the disclaimer.

So, to avoid potential liability, a seller of corn for feed, for example, might decide to include in any sales contract for feed corn a clause that states, "No guarantees are made, either expressly or implied, that this feed corn has not been contaminated by mold or the toxin Fumonisin. Buyer is advised to test the corn to determine the presence of these potential contaminants." Of course, such a disclaimer might certainly have a negative impact on the sales of one's product.

The buyer may also waive both implied and express warranties. A buyer may waive these rights by (1) failing to examine goods for which an express warranty was created by a sample or model or (2) failing to comply with the seller's request to inspect the goods. Suppose, for example, that a printer requests that the buyer come into the shop to proof letterhead and envelopes. The buyer refuses, claiming that he is too busy, and tells the printer to go ahead and run the stationery. On receipt of the stationery, the buyer discovers that the numbers in the phone number are transposed, making the stationery useless. Unfortunately, the buyer has indeed waived his rights due to his failure to inspect.

A buyer may also waive her warranty rights under the contract by failing to comply with the statute of limitations. Under the UCC, the buyer or seller must bring a lawsuit on a breached contract within four years of when the breach occurred or when the nonbreaching party became aware of it. The buyer and seller are free to negotiate contractually a shorter time period (as long as it is not less than one year), but they are not free to negotiate a longer time period than the four years.

While the UCC remains the primary codification of both state and federal laws regarding sellers' warranties, there has also been specific legislation pertaining to this issue. The 1975 federal law known as the Magnuson-Moss Act requires that if a seller decides to issue a written warranty for a consumer good (the seller is not required to do so), the seller must indicate whether that warranty is a *full* warranty or a *limited* warranty. This applies to any consumer good sold for more than $10. If the written warranty is silent, it is presumed to be a full warranty, which means that if the good fails or is defective, the good or its defective part will be replaced. If replacement cannot be timely effected, the buyer has the right to a refund or a full replacement.

If the good is sold for more than $15, the written warranty must disclose a number of items of information—names and addresses of the warrantors, any limitations on the warranty, and the procedures required to activate the warranty remedies—all in readable and easily understood language, in other words, not in *legalese!*

The Goal of Contract Remedies

Of course, the laying out of these various contractual obligations gives rise to the question of what remedies are available if those obligations are breached. The obligations of sellers/lessors and buyers/lessees are determined by (1) terms the parties outline in agreements, (2) custom,

and (3) rules outlined by the Uniform Commercial Code, such as the various implied warranties described previously.

Remedies Available to Sellers and Lessors under the UCC

CANCEL THE CONTRACT

UCC Sections 2-703(f) and 2A-523(1)(a) allow a seller or lessor to cancel the contract if the buyer or lessee is in breach. The UCC requires sellers/lessors to notify buyers/lessees of the cancellation. Then the seller or lessor pursues remedies available under the UCC. Remember, these remedies give the seller/lessor the benefit of the bargain, and no more.

WITHHOLD DELIVERY

Sometimes a buyer breaches the contract or lease before the seller has delivered the goods. For instance, the buyer or lessee might fail to pay according to the terms of the agreement. UCC Sections 2-703(a) and 2A-523(1)(c) allow sellers or lessors to withhold delivery of goods when the buyer or lessee is in breach.

RESELL OR DISPOSE OF THE GOODS

Sellers or lessors are also allowed to resell or dispose of the goods when the buyer is in breach and the goods have not yet been delivered. The seller or lessor then holds the buyer or lessee liable for any loss. UCC Section 2-706 allows the seller to recover the difference between the resale price and contract price, plus incidental damages and minus expenses saved. Although buyers are liable for these damages, the seller gets to keep any profits it makes on the resale. UCC 2A-527(2) outlines a similar rule for lease agreements. The lessor is allowed to lease the goods to another party and recover unpaid lease payments and any deficiency between the lease payments due under the original lease contract and those due under the new contract. The lessor can also seek incidental damages.

SUE TO GET THE BENEFIT OF THE BARGAIN

In trying to give the seller or lessor the benefit of the bargain, and nothing more, courts often grant damages to recover the purchase price or lease payments due.

STOP DELIVERY

UCC Sections 2-705(1) and 2A-526(1) allow a seller or lessor to stop delivery of goods that are in transit. *In transit* means that the seller or lessor has delivered the goods to a carrier or bailee but the carrier or bailee has not yet turned them over to the buyer. Of course, the seller/lessor must give timely notice to the carrier/bailee so that the carrier/bailee is able to stop delivery. Also, the rules are different for insolvent and solvent buyers and lessees. If the buyer/lessee is insolvent, the carrier/bailee can stop delivery regardless of the quantity shipped. If the buyer/lessee is solvent, however, the carrier/bailee can stop delivery only if the quantity shipped is a large shipment (e.g., a carload or truckload).

RECLAIM THE GOODS

Under UCC Sections 2-709(1) and 2A-529(1), if the buyer or lessee has possession of the goods and is in breach, the seller or lessor can sue for the purchase price of the goods or for the lease payments due, plus incidental damages. In some circumstances, the UCC allows the seller or lessee to reclaim the goods. UCC 2-702(2) allows a seller to reclaim goods when the seller discovers the buyer is insolvent. UCC 2A-525(2) allows a lessor to reclaim goods when the lessee fails to make payments according to the lease terms.

Remedies Available to Buyers and Lessees under the UCC

CANCEL THE CONTRACT

Sometimes, sellers or lessors fail to deliver the goods or to deliver conforming goods and thus are in breach. UCC Sections 2-711(1) and 2A-508(1)(a) allow buyers and lessees to cancel the contract and then seek remedies that give them the benefit of the bargain. In Case 14-3, a buyer of heating coils canceled a contract with the seller because the coils did not work according to the buyer's specifications. The buyer subsequently sued for damages.

OBTAIN COVER

LO 8

Case 14-3 also explains the buyer's right to obtain cover. Under UCC Sections 2-712 and 2A-518, buyers and lessees are allowed to cover, or substitute, goods for those due under the sales or lease agreement.

cover
A buyer's right to substitute goods for those due under a sales or lease agreement when the seller provides nonconforming goods.

 As you read Case 14-3, notice that, in obtaining cover, the buyer must (1) demonstrate good faith in obtaining the substitute goods, (2) pay a reasonable amount for the substitute goods, (3) act without unreasonable delay in purchasing the substitute goods, and (4) purchase goods that are reasonable substitutes.

CASE 14-3

U.S.A. COIL & AIR, INC. v. HODESS BUILDING CO.
RHODE ISLAND SUPERIOR COURT

WL 66582 (R.I. Super. 1999)

FACTS: *U.S.A. Coil and Air, Inc. (USA), and Hodess Building Co. were involved in a legal dispute that arose after USA supplied cooling coils for an HVAC system, which was part of a "clean-room" project for Lockheed/Sanders. USA agreed to provide the needed coils to Hodess for $33,156. USA did provide the coils, but the coils failed to perform as specified.*

 USA subsequently sent Hodess replacement coils, but these, too, failed. USA believed the failure was related to Hodess's flawed system, not the coils. Hodess informed USA that it would replace the coils, using a different vendor to supply the coils.

 USA requested to have its coils returned, and Hodess agreed, as long as USA paid for shipping or sent someone to pick up the coils. Communication between the parties broke down. Hodess never paid the contract price of $33,156. USA (plaintiff) brought a breach-of-contract action to recover this amount. Hodess (defendant) counterclaimed for breach of contract and asked for its $83,374.95 in replacement costs.

ISSUE: Did Hodess have the right to cancel the contract and obtain replacement coils? If so, what is USA's

obligation? Is Hodess liable for the extra cost incurred by USA? Or is USA responsible for the purchase price of the original coils?

REASONING: In the court's own words:

If a buyer rightfully rejects a tender of goods in a contract such as this one, he is entitled to cancel the contract. UCC 2-711(1). Once the contract is cancelled, the buyer's obligation to pay the purchase price is discharged. UCC 2-106(3).

 USA does not dispute that both sets of coils it provided failed to conform to the performance specifications referenced in the contract purchase order . . . USA blames the system design for the failure. . . . [T]his court finds that the plaintiff breached the contract purchase order when it failed to provide coils which met the performance specifications. Thus, Hodess was excused from paying the purchase price.

 Moreover, with respect to USA's right to cure its breach, Hodess allowed USA the opportunity to do so. Hodess installed USA's replacement coils, carefully following USA's instructions and modifying the system at USA's suggestion. When the replacement coils failed, USA's attempts to cure the breach failed as well. . . . USA is not entitled to recover. . . .

 Hodess counterclaims, arguing breach of contract and seeking recovery of the replacement costs incurred due to the breach. Generally, "where a right of action for breach exists, compensatory damages will be given for the net amount of the

losses caused and gains prevented by the defendant's breach, in excess of savings made possible." The goal is to place the injured party in as good a position as he would have been if the contract had not been breached. . . . When a buyer justifiably revokes acceptance of goods, the measure of direct damages is the difference between the cost of cover and the contract price, less any expenses saved as a result of the seller's breach. UCC 2-711(1)(b). To cover, a buyer must "in good faith and without reasonable delay" make a "reasonable purchase or contract to purchase . . . goods in substitution for those due from the seller." UCC 2-712(1). Whether the buyer acted in good faith and in a reasonable manner is determined with reference to the conditions at the time and place the buyer attempted to cover. UCC 2-712 at comment 2. It is irrelevant that hindsight may later suggest a cheaper or more effective method. The burden of proof is on the seller of goods to prove that cover was not reasonably obtained.

DECISION AND REMEDY: The court stated: "Having found USA breached the contract, this court also concludes that USA is liable for the resulting damages incurred by Hodess. To replace the defective coils, Hodess incurred substantial expenses for engineering, supervision of, and replacement of the coils. Hodess documented its expenditures with receipts and project expense reports, demonstrating a total reasonable replacement cost of $83,734.95. USA did not present any evidence which would tend to dispute the reasonableness of cover costs. . . . Thus, using the damages formula enunciated in UCC 2-711(1)(b), Hodess is entitled to the replacement costs less the contract price [which was $33,156.00], or $50,578.95."

SIGNIFICANCE OF THE CASE: This decision shows a very formulaic, though commonsense, approach. Since USA breached and Hodess had to go out and cover, USA is responsible for any of Hodess's reasonable costs in excess of the original contract price.

CRITICAL THINKING

Hodess appears to have had an advantage in the case because it had better evidence. How so? How could USA have increased its chances of winning?

ETHICAL DECISION MAKING

Suppose Hodess later discovers that its system design was flawed and it was not really USA's fault that the coils did not work. Which ethical test or tests would encourage Hodess's executives to come forward with that information?

LO 9 SUE TO RECOVER DAMAGES

consequential damages

In a contract, foreseeable damages that result from special facts and circumstances arising outside the contract itself. The damages must be within the contemplation of the parties at the time the breach occurs. Also called *special damages*.

liquidated damages

Damages specified as a term of the contract, before a breach of contract occurs.

In Case 14-3, although Hodess was able to cover, it still incurred damages. Buyers such as Hodess, and lessees, are entitled to incidental and consequential damages. Consequential damages include damages for lost profits, as long as these damages are not too speculative. These monetary damages give the injured buyer or lessee the benefit of the bargain. There is also the availability of liquidated damages and even, under some situations, punitive damages.

Liquidated damages are damages identified *before* the breach occurs. The parties are free to negotiate, as part of the contract, a liquidated-damage clause in which the parties agree in advance what the damages will be for each party should a breach occur. Generally speaking, a court will enforce a liquidated-damage clause as long as it is not so far out of reasonable range as to be punitive in nature. Liquidated-damage clauses that are deemed to be punitive in nature are not enforceable.

The code provides for liquidated damages if the parties have not expressly negotiated a liquidated-damage clause. UCC Section 2-718 pertains to liquidated damages and allows the nonbreaching seller to claim against a breaching buyer 20 percent of the purchase price or $500, whichever is less, as liquidated damages.

Although the UCC does not mention the availability of punitive damages, other than in its voiding of liquidated damages that are punitive in nature, an issue that remains unsettled

is the awarding of punitive damages against a breaching party who intentionally or egregiously breaches the contract. You will remember from tort law that when a tort is committed either intentionally or recklessly, the court may infer legal malice and instruct a jury that it may consider the awarding of punitive damages in addition to compensatory damages. Although this concept is well settled in tort law, it has never been widely applied in contract law. Yet there are some who argue that it should be, especially to deter intentional breaches of contract.

RECOVER THE GOODS

UCC Sections 2-502 and 2A-522 allow buyers and lessees to recover the goods identified in the contract if the seller or lessor becomes insolvent within 10 days after receiving the first payment due under the agreement. Buyers or lessees are obligated to pay the remaining balance according to the terms of the agreement.

OBTAIN SPECIFIC PERFORMANCE

UCC Sections 2-716(1) and 2A-521(1) allow buyers and lessees to seek the remedy of specific performance when either (1) the goods are unique or (2) a remedy at law is inadequate. Specific performance usually requires that the seller or lessor deliver the particular goods identified in the contract.

specific performance
An order of the court requiring that a non-breaching party fulfill the terms of the contract.

REJECT NONCONFORMING GOODS

UCC Sections 2-601 and 2A-519 allow the buyer or lessee to reject nonconforming goods. The buyer or lessee may then obtain cover or cancel the contract.

REVOKE ACCEPTANCE OF NONCONFORMING GOODS

UCC Sections 2-608 and 2A-517 sometimes allow the buyer or lessee to revoke acceptance of nonconforming goods. For instance, in Case 14-3, Hodess rejected acceptance of the nonconforming coils USA provided. Hodess was allowed to reject acceptance because it had made a reasonable assumption that the nonconformity would be cured, but then the nonconformity was not cured within a reasonable amount of time.

ACCEPT THE NONCONFORMING GOODS AND SEEK DAMAGES

Under UCC Sections 2-607, 2-714, and 2A-519, buyers or lessees are allowed to accept nonconforming goods and then seek monetary damages to give them the benefit of the bargain. The buyer or lessee must give the seller or lessor reasonable notice of the defect.

Modifications or Limitations to the Remedies Otherwise Provided by the UCC

Parties to sales and lease contracts are allowed to modify or limit remedies. Under UCC Sections 2-719 and 2A-503, parties are allowed to create agreements that make it clear that the remedies outlined in the agreement are exclusive remedies. Courts uphold modifications or limitations to remedies unless the remedies fail in their essential purpose.

E-COMMERCE and the Law

Computer Contracts

Sometimes, computer purchasers are surprised to find out they are bound to agreements that were created when sellers included contracts in the box in which the computer was delivered. Some of these agreements limit the purchaser's remedies. For instance, in *Hill v. Gateway 2000,** Hill purchased a computer from Gateway 2000 by placing a telephone order. The computer arrived through the mail. Gateway had placed a contract in the computer's shipping box that indicated that the terms sent in the box were binding on the buyer unless the buyer returned the computer within 30 days. One of the terms in this contract was a provision that stated that any disputes between the parties would be resolved through arbitration. The order taker had not read any of the terms of the contract over the telephone when Hill placed the order. When the computer arrived, Hill did not read the contract. In an effort to avoid the arbitration clause, Hill asked the court to determine that Gateway 2000 could not limit buyers' remedies or avenues through which they seek remedies (i.e., through arbitration) by bundling hardware and legal documents. The court ruled that the contract was binding on the parties. The court stated, "A contract need not be read to be effective; people who accept take the risk that the unread terms may in retrospect prove unwelcome."†

*105 F.3d 1147 (1997).
†Ibid., p. 1148.

SUMMARY

The Basic Performance Obligation

Under the UCC, sellers and lessors are obligated *to transfer and deliver conforming goods.*

Buyers and lessees are obligated *to accept and pay for conforming goods in accordance with the contract.*

The UCC requires *good faith* in the performance and enforcement of every contract.

Specific Obligations of Sellers and Lessors

The *perfect tender rule* indicates that if goods or tender of delivery fail in any respect to conform to the contract, the buyer/lessee has the right to accept the goods, reject the entire shipment, or accept part and reject part.

Exceptions to the perfect tender rule allow sellers/lessors and buyers/lessees to consider:

- Norms in the industry and past dealings between the parties.
- Exceptions outlined in the parties' agreement.
- The seller's/lessor's right to cure.
- Excuse from performance when identified goods are destroyed through no fault of the parties.
- The concept of substantial impairment as it relates to revocation of acceptance and installment contracts.
- The concept of commercial impracticability.

Specific Obligations of Buyers and Lessees

If all goes well in a transaction over the sale or lease of goods, the buyer or lessee inspects the goods and then *pays* according to the agreement.

The seller or lessor must provide an opportunity for *inspection.*

- The concept of reasonableness governs the inspection process.
- After inspection, the buyer or lessee decides whether to accept the goods.

After inspecting, the buyer/lessee signifies *acceptance* or partial acceptance.

- Sellers or lessors sometimes presume acceptance.
- Partial acceptance is allowed in some circumstances.
- Buyers or lessees are allowed to revoke or withdraw acceptance of nonconforming goods.
- Buyers or lessees must issue reasonable notice if they decide to reject goods.

Cases in which a buyer decides to assert his or her right to reject nonconforming goods are often categorized under the heading "rescission or revocation of acceptance by buyer."

Warranties	A *warranty* is a promise on the part of the seller with respect to certain characteristics of the good.

Warranties of title:

- Passage of good title.
- Implied promise of no liens or judgments against title.
- Implied promise that title is not subject to any copyright, patent, or trademark infringement.

Express warranties:

- Description of the good's physical nature or its use.
- Either general or specific.
- Material term of the contract.
- Reliance of buyer on representations.

Implied warranties:

Implied warranty of merchantability: A warranty based on a reasonable expectation of performance of the purchased good. The good must:

- Pass without objection.
- Be of fair quality within the description.
- Be fit for ordinary uses.
- Have even quality.
- Be adequately packaged.
- Conform to promises made on the label.

Implied warranty of fitness: A warranty that arises when the seller knows the purpose for which the buyer is purchasing goods and the buyer relies on the seller's judgment.

Implied warranty of trade usage: A warranty that arises as a result of generally accepted trade practices.

Warranty Rights of Third Parties	The states have three choices regarding the warranty rights of third-party beneficiaries:

- Seller's warranties extend to the buyer's household members and guests.
- Seller's warranties extend to any reasonable and foreseeable user.
- Seller's warranties extend to anyone injured by the good.

Warranty Disclaimers and Waivers	Methods of waiving include:

- Seller does not make warranties in the first place (express warranty).
- Seller disclaims in clear, unambiguous, conspicuous language (implied warranty).
- Buyer fails or refuses to examine goods.
- Buyer fails to file suit within the time of the statute of limitations.

Magnuson-Moss Act: If a seller decides to issue a written warranty for a consumer good, the seller must indicate whether the warranty is full or limited.

The Goal of Contract Remedies	The goal of contract remedies is to give the parties the *benefit of the bargain they struck,* and nothing more.
Remedies Available to Sellers and Lessors under the UCC	When the buyer/lessee is in breach, the seller/lessor can:

- Cancel the contract.
- Withhold delivery.
- Sell or dispose of the goods.
- Sue to recover the purchase price, lease payments due, or some other measure of damages that gives the seller or lessor the benefit of the bargain.
- Stop delivery.
- Reclaim the goods.

Remedies Available to Buyers and Lessees under the UCC	When the seller/lessor is in breach, the buyer/lessee can:

- Cancel the contract.
- Obtain cover.

- Sue to recover damages.
- Recover the goods.
- Obtain specific performance.
- Reject nonconforming goods.
- Revoke acceptance of nonconforming goods.
- Accept the nonconforming goods and seek damages.

Modifications or Limitations to the Remedies Otherwise Provided by the UCC

Parties to sales and lease contracts are allowed to modify or limit remedies.

Courts uphold modifications or limitations to remedies unless the remedies fail in their essential purpose.

----▶ Point/Counterpoint

According to its critics, the application of the perfect tender rule can be a hypertechnical application of contractual obligations that really have no bearing on the substance of the contract but allow a party to escape contractual obligations on second thought.

Should the Perfect Tender Rule Be Ignored by the Courts and Replaced with the Common Law and CISG Concept of Substantial Performance?	
YES	NO
Common law really got it right through its cases holding that only material obligations must be complied with and immaterial ones are just that—immaterial and inconsequential. Common law has perfected, so to speak, the substantial-performance rule to a very workable conclusion. It gives the trier of fact flexibility in determining the impact of nonperformance in the overall scheme of the contractual relationship while keeping the focus on the intent of the parties and the ultimate injury or harmlessness of the noncompliance.	The underlying concept that is the foundation of contract law worldwide is the notion that the parties are free to negotiate the terms and conditions of their respective contracts. Nothing in the UCC prohibits the parties from negotiating a substantial-performance definition in the performance obligation of the contract.
Further, as we see more and more countries adopting the CISG, UCC concepts such as the perfect tender rule are out of sync with the rest of the commercial world. In the ever-accelerating venue of international transactions, uniformity is clearly the order of the day. We all need to be on the same page with contract interpretation.	However, by creating something other than the perfect tender rule, the courts send the message that the will of the parties may be frustrated if the noncompliance is somehow lessened to some level of immateriality. But who is better-suited to determine this immateriality: the parties or the courts? By including specific performance requirements in the contract, the parties indicate what is material and what is not material. This determination should be left undisturbed by the courts and common law.

----▶ Questions & Problems

1. What determines the obligations of sellers/lessors and buyers/lessees?

2. Explain what the good-faith and commercial reasonableness obligations are.

3. Explain what the perfect tender rule is and how it can be modified.

4. Amboy Closeouts, Inc., agreed to purchase 25,000 Christmas ornaments from Polar Trading, Inc.

Alcorn, president of Amboy, requested 14 cases of the ornaments as samples and agreed to purchase the samples if he was pleased with the quality. He received the samples and determined that they were in satisfactory condition, but the bill was never paid. Alcorn contacted Polar Trading to order more ornaments, but he was told that he needed to fax a copy of a deposit check in order to secure the shipment. Alcorn faxed a copy of the $2,000 deposit check to

Polar Trading, but he did not mail the check. Polar Trading sent a total of 352 ornaments to Alcorn. After receiving the shipment, Alcorn contacted Polar Trading and reported that many of the cases were defective. He had already sold some of the ornaments, but the rest were sent back. Polar Trading sold some of the returned ornaments but was unable to sell the complete shipment. Amboy argued that, under the UCC, it had the right to reject all the goods, accept all the goods, or partially accept and reject some of the goods. Further, Amboy argued that Polar Trading breached the contract by delivering defective goods and, therefore, no payment was due. How did the court decide? [*Polar Trading, Inc. v. Amboy Close-outs, Inc.,* 899 S.W.2d 577 (1995).]

5. Allied and Pulsar are both companies in the business of selling computer component parts. Allied ordered 50,000 computer chips from Pulsar and sold the chips to Apple. After inspecting the chips, Apple found 35,000 of them to be defective and returned the chips to Allied. Allied contacted Pulsar, and although the 30-day return period had expired, Pulsar agreed to take back the defective chips. Pulsar never replaced the chips, nor did it provide Allied with a refund for the 35,000 chips. Allied purchased other chips from an acceptable substitute and was able to refill Apple's request. Allied brought a suit against Pulsar, requesting a refund. Did Pulsar breach the contract? Did Pulsar cure the defective delivery? [*Allied Semi-Conductors International, Limited v. Pulsar Components International, Incorporated,* 907 F. Supp. 618 (1995).]

6. Wilbur Reed operated a small greenhouse in Montana. He ordered most of his plants from McCalif Grower Supplies. Reed often supplied local Kmart and Ernst stores with his products. During the holiday season, he agreed to provide them with poinsettia plants. Reed ordered the plants from McCalif, and McCalif had growers send the plants to Reed from Colorado. Reed's employee accepted the boxes at the airport and did not note any damages to the packaging. However, when the boxes were opened, the poinsettias appeared damaged. Reed contacted McCalif and notified it that the poinsettias were damaged as a result of poor packing. McCalif advised Reed to report the damages to the carrier, Delta Airlines. Delta paid Reed $924.66 in compensation. McCalif was not able to supply Reed with more poinsettias before the holiday season. As a result, Reed lost accounts to many of the stores. McCalif sued Reed for payment for the poinsettias, $3,223.56. Reed refused to pay and argued that McCalif had failed to deliver according to their contract. Whom did the court agree with? [*McCalif Grower Supplies, Inc. v. Wilbur Reed,* 900 P.2d 880 (1995).]

7. Rockland Industries agreed to purchase three containers of antimony oxide at $1.80 per pound from Manley-Regan Chemicals. Rockland produces drapes, and antimony oxide is used to fireproof the drapes. A representative from Manley-Regan, David Hess, worked with Conrad Ailstock, Rockland's purchasing agent. Hess informed Ailstock of a slight delay, but he assured Ailstock that the product, which was coming from China, was "on the water." Three months after the two companies had made the agreement, Hess contacted Ailstock to report that the product was not coming. According to Hess, Manley-Regan was considering legal claims against the Chinese supplier or the Chinese government. Rockland was forced to find another supplier, but the price was substantially higher. Rockland brought suit to recover the difference between Manley-Regan's quoted price and the price of the substitute antimony oxide. Is the commercial impracticability defense appropriate? Explain. [*Rockland Industries, Inc. v. Manley-Regan Chemicals Division,* 991 F. Supp. 468 (1998).]

8. Alamance Board of Education accepted a bid from Bobby Murray Chevrolet, a General Motors franchisee, to provide approximately 1,200 school bus chassis. After the agreement, the EPA enacted changes in allowed emission levels. The engines described in the bid were not in compliance with the more stringent standards. The school system purchased the chassis from another store and informed Murray that it intended to hold him liable for any excess in costs. The difference between the bid prices and the actual amounts totaled $150,152.94. Bobby Murray Chevrolet subsequently claimed that GM had breached its contract with Murray and that it became commercially impracticable to deliver the product. Will the concept of commercial impracticability excuse Bobby Murray Chevrolet's failure to perform? [*Alamance Board of Education v. Bobby Murray Chevrolet, Inc., v. General Motors Corporation,* 465 S.E.2d 306 (1996).]

9. David Cooper purchased a computer and software for his supermarket business. He was using a software program recommended and installed by the seller, Contemporary Computer Systems, Inc. The sales contract had a clause that stated that no refunds would be given after the 90-day warranty period. Cooper initially had problems with both the hardware and the software. Contemporary Computer Systems tried to remedy these problems. A pattern of problems and attempts to fix them went on for some time, far beyond the 90-day period expressly described in the contract. When Cooper had had enough, he decided to revoke the contract and demand his money back. Contemporary Computer Systems said the 90-day express clause in the

contract precludes this action. Who wins? [*David Cooper, Inc. v. Contemporary Computer Systems, Inc.,* 846 S.W.2d 777 (1993).]

10. Aubrey Reeves purchased a computer system for his business from Radio Shack Computer Center. Radio Shack is the local retailer for products sold by Tandy, its parent company. During negotiations, it became clear that Reeves needed software that Radio Shack could not provide. A Radio Shack salesperson referred Reeves to a software source book, let Reeves know he could choose compatible software from the source book, and informed him that Tandy does not support or service software from the source book. A disclaimer to this effect was in the source book. Reeves eventually purchased computers from Tandy, some software from Tandy, and more specialized software from a company called Lizcon. The Lizcon software did not meet Reeves's needs. Reeves subsequently sent a letter to Tandy, asking for rescission of the contract and damages. Can Reeves rescind? [*Aubrey's R.V. Center, Inc. v. Tandy Corporation,* 731 P.2d 1124 (1987).]

11. Landrum sold Gappelberg a big-screen television. The television had many defects, some of which Landrum and his service representatives fixed. Three weeks after the sale, the television stopped working altogether, and Gappelberg let Landrum know. Landrum promised to fix the television, but he did not. Gappelberg then requested return of consideration and asked the service representative to pick up the set but not to repair it because he would not accept it or a replacement. The question in the case was whether Gappelberg was allowed to prevent Landrum from curing the nonconforming television by his refusal to accept a replacement set. What did the court decide? Are you more sympathetic to Landrum or Gappelberg? [*Leitchfield Development Corp. v. Clark,* 757 S.W.2d 207 (1988).]

12. After living in their home for three years, Roger Nathaniel and Sharon Diamond sold the home to the plaintiffs, Marc Copland and Joan Lund. Nathaniel and Diamond hired a pest control company to inspect the home. The company reported that there was evidence of a previously treated infestation but that no evidence of active infestation was found. This report was provided to Copland and Lund prior to the sale of the home. The contract specified that the purchaser had inspected the premises and agreed to purchase it "as is." A year later, the plaintiffs discovered that levels of chlordane were present on the property. They also discovered that the home had been treated 10 years earlier for termites. At that time, chlordane was used to remove termites. Despite one toxicologist's report that the level of chlordane did not constitute a health concern, Copland and Lund spent $50,000 removing the contaminated soil from their property. They brought an action against the previous owners, Nathaniel and Diamond. How do you think the court decided? [*Copland v. Nathaniel,* 624 N.Y.S.2d 514 (1995).]

13. Mrs. Cipollone had been a lifetime smoker, starting back in the 1940s. She subsequently died in 1984 from lung cancer. Her husband brought suit against the cigarette companies of the Liggett Group and Philip Morris, citing breach of express warranty and fraud. Mr. Cipollone based these allegations on advertisements that the defendants ran on television, particularly during the *Arthur Godfrey Show.* At trial, the court did not permit the defendants to introduce evidence to show that Mrs. Cipollone did not rely on these advertising representations in deciding whether to continue smoking. Does the plaintiff have the burden to show that the express warranties were in fact relied on? Conversely, may the defense introduce evidence to show just the opposite? [*Cipollone v. Liggett Group Inc.,* 893 F.2d 541 (1992).]

14. A restaurant called "The Inn Between" entered into a contract to purchase a used restaurant computer system. The contract included installation and training from Remanco Metropolitan, Inc. The contract also required that Remanco keep the computer system in good operating order. The system was delivered and installed on March 29, 1995. The following day the computer malfunctioned and was down for three hours. Between March 30 and July 3, the restaurant contacted Remanco 48 times to report malfunctions. Though Remanco responded to each of the problems, the computer system continued to break down. Inn Between brought an action to revoke its acceptance of the computer system. It viewed the system as a nonconforming good. Remanco counterclaimed, seeking the unpaid price under the system maintenance agreement for non-return of the system. Which side gets the remedy it seeks? [*The Inn Between, Inc. v. Remanco Metropolitan, Inc.,* 662 N.Y.S.2d 1011 (1997).]

15. Charles Woods planned on opening a "Family Fun Center." The center would be an indoor recreational center with miniature golf, video games, and food services. Woods contacted Kenosha Associates to lease a building for the center. The lessor agreed to provide heat, ventilation, air-conditioning, bathrooms, and lighting for the building. After Woods signed the lease but before he was able to move into the building, Kenosha sent him a letter ending the agreement. Woods sued Kenosha for financial damages and lost profits he suffered as a result of the breach. The jury agreed with Woods and awarded

him $1,033,124.32 in damages. Kenosha Associates appealed the decision, arguing that the jury should not have been able to provide damages for loss of profits because this measure of damages was too speculative. Did the appellate court agree with the trial court's award of damages for lost profit? [*T & HW Enterprises v. Kenosha Associates,* 557 N.W.2d 480 (1996).]

Looking for more review material?

The Online Learning Center at **www.mhhe.com/kubasekess** contains this chapter's "Assignment on the Internet" and also a list of URLs for more information, entitled "On the Internet." Find both of them in the Student Center portion of the OLC, along with quizzes and other helpful materials.

Negotiable Instruments: Negotiability and Transferability

---▶ CASE OPENER

Oral Agreements and Negotiable Instruments

As a gambling facility, MGM Desert Inn Inc. regularly holds and executes negotiable instruments. During a period of two months, customer William E. Shack, Jr., entered MGM and delivered eight checks to the casino in exchange for markers. These checks, which totaled $93,400, were signed by Shack and dated at the time of transfer. When MGM sent Shack's checks to the bank for payment, they were dishonored because the funds in Shack's account were insufficient.

MGM filed an action in district court to obtain the $93,400. Shack contended that a casino host had told him that he had sufficient remaining casino credit to receive the markers. The district court judge ruled in favor of MGM, affirming its argument that the checks were negotiable instruments and stating that no evidence of an oral agreement between the casino and Shack was provided. The checks contained Shack's signature, on a specified date, and were to be payable on demand from Shack's bank to MGM. Shack was ordered to pay MGM $5,000 for attorney fees in addition to the $93,400 originally owed on the checks.[1]

1. If you were employed at MGM, what would you do to avoid future disputes with your patrons about the nature of payment agreements?

2. Assuming that Shack's claims about an oral agreement with MGM were true, would this affect your decision as to whether the checks' payments were currently due?

[1] *MGM Desert Inn, Inc., dba Desert Inn Hotel & Casino v. William E. Shack,* U.S. District Court, District of Nevada, 809 F. Supp. 783 (1993).

---▶ LEARNING OBJECTIVES

After reading this chapter, you will be able to answer the following questions:

LO 1 Why is there a need for negotiable instruments?

LO 2 What are the types of negotiable instruments recognized by the UCC?

LO 3 What are the requirements of negotiability?

Once a sales contract has been created and executed and the parties are aware of their respective obligations under the contract, the next phase is the *payment* by the buyer to the seller for the goods purchased. Payment is usually made in one of three ways: cash, credit arrangements (which are discussed in the chapter on secured transactions), or with a *substitute for cash.* It is this substitute for cash that is the focus of this chapter and the next one.

A substitute for cash, or a negotiable instrument, is a written document containing the signature of the creator who makes an unconditional promise or order to pay a sum certain in money at either a time certain or on demand. Negotiable instruments are executed on a daily basis in the form of checks, certificates of deposit, drafts, and promissory notes in exchange for goods, services, or business financing.

negotiable instrument
A written document signed by a person who makes an unconditional promise to pay a specific sum of money on demand or at a certain time to the holder of the instrument; an acceptable medium for exchanging value from one person to another.

The Need for Negotiable Instruments

LO 1

It is easy to figure out why using documents as payments greatly facilitates commercial transactions, especially in times when actual currency or cash is in short supply or when it is dangerous to transfer large amounts of currency or precious metals. These documents of payment are generically called *commercial paper,* and under Article 3 of the UCC they are specifically labeled *negotiable instruments.*

CONTRACTS AS COMMERCIAL PAPER

We have already discussed one common form of commercial paper: contracts. It does not matter whether the contract is a common law contract or a UCC Article 2 contract. Both kinds are examples of commercial paper. As such, through the process of assignment, these contracts may be circulated and transferred throughout the commercial world. Here is an illustration of assignment:

> Bob sells a bushel of apples to Betty; in exchange, Betty executes a contract to pay Bob $5 on demand. A few days later, Bob buys some oranges from Pat for $5. Instead of paying Pat the $5 in cash, Bob *assigns* Betty's obligation to pay Bob the $5 to Pat. When Pat demands the money from Betty, Betty will pay Pat the $5 and everyone will be square.

This illustration demonstrates the point that any contractual obligation, except for personal ones and nonassignable ones, may be transferred and thus is classified as commercial paper.

PROBLEMS WITH COMMERCIAL PAPER

Even though the illustration with Bob, Betty, and Pat is a simple one, it still contains a potential problem. Consider that fact pattern again, only this time assume that the apples Bob sold to Betty were all rotten. Betty did not know the apples' condition at the time because they looked and felt fine. It was only after cutting into them that the problem became apparent.

When Pat demands the $5 from Betty, Betty naturally is going to refuse, claiming that Bob had breached their original contract by delivering to her defective apples. Betty would be justified

and on legally safe ground to refuse to pay. Pat could do nothing against Betty and would have to go back and sue Bob. The commercial paper that Bob transferred to Pat was not acceptable. In other words, the whole reason for having the transferability of commercial paper as a substitute for currency is defeated under these circumstances.

LO 2

Types of Negotiable Instruments

Under Article 3, the UCC recognizes four specific types of negotiable instruments: notes and certificates of deposits, a highly specialized type of note; and drafts and checks, a highly specialized type of draft (UCC Section 3-104). A note is a promise by the *maker* of the note to pay a payee [UCC 3-103(a)(9)]. A draft is an order by a *drawer* to a drawee to pay a payee (in our example above, Bob could have drawn a draft ordering Betty to pay Pat $5, since Betty owed Bob $5) [UCC 3-103(a)(6)]. A note is a two-party instrument, whereas, by definition, a draft is a three-party instrument.

Notes and drafts can either be demand instruments or time instruments. With a demand instrument, the payee (or subsequent holder) can demand actual payment at any time. The UCC defines an instrument that is "payable on demand" as one that "(i) states that it is payable on demand or at sight, or otherwise indicates that it is payable at the will of the holder, or (ii) does not state any time of payment" [3-108(a)]. With a time instrument, payment can be made only at a specific time designated in the future. The UCC requires that an "instrument payable at a definite time" have a time easily determined from the document itself [3-108(b)].

Certificates of deposit and checks are specific illustrations of these distinctions. A certificate of deposit is a promise made by a bank to pay a payee a certain amount of money at a future time. The UCC defines a certificate of deposit as "an instrument containing an acknowledgment by a bank that a sum of money has been received by the bank and a promise by the bank to repay the sum of money. A certificate of deposit is a note of the bank" [3-104(j)]. Usually, a payee buys one of these instruments from a bank and then collects the principle plus a determined amount of interest in the future. However, because these instruments have a present value, even though they are not payable until some future time, the payee may transfer them or even sell them before the future date of payment.

A check is a specific draft, drawn by the owner of a checking account, ordering the bank to pay the payee from that drawer's account [UCC 3-104(f)]. A check is always a demand instrument and can never be a time instrument (postdating really does not affect the ability of the holder to cash the check before the post date). Types of checks include:

- *Cashier's check:* "[A] draft with respect to which the drawer and drawee are the same bank or branches of the same bank" [UCC 3-104(f)].
- *Traveler's check:* "[A]n instrument that (i) is payable on demand, (ii) is drawn on or payable at or through a bank, (iii) is designated by the term 'traveler's check' or by a substantially similar term, and (iv) requires, as a condition to payment, a countersignature by a person whose signature appears on the instrument" [UCC 3-104(i)].
- *Certified check:* "[A] check accepted by the bank on which it is drawn" [UCC 3-409(d)].

An Overview of the Law of Negotiable Instruments

For an instrument to be negotiable, specific requirements of *negotiability* must be met. However—and this is a very important concept that many people miss—if an instrument fails to qualify as a negotiable instrument, that does *not* mean that the instrument fails to be a perfectly good, perfectly enforceable contract. All it means is that the special rules regarding negotiable instruments do not apply. Once an instrument is a negotiable instrument, it has the potential of conferring on its possessor some special qualities. Let's go back to our example with Bob, Betty, and Pat. Use Figure 15-1 to follow the logic of the exchanges.

note
A promise by the maker of the note to pay the payee of the note.

draft
An instrument validating an order by a drawer to a drawee to pay a payee.

demand instrument
A type of draft that allows the payee to demand payment at any time from a holder.

time instrument
A type of draft that allows the payee to collect payment only at a specific time in the future.

certificate of deposit
A document whereby a bank promises to pay a payee a certain amount of money at a future time.

check
A special draft that orders a bank (the drawee) to pay a specified sum of money to the payee from the drawer's account.

Figure 15-1

Potential Complexity of Negotiable Instruments

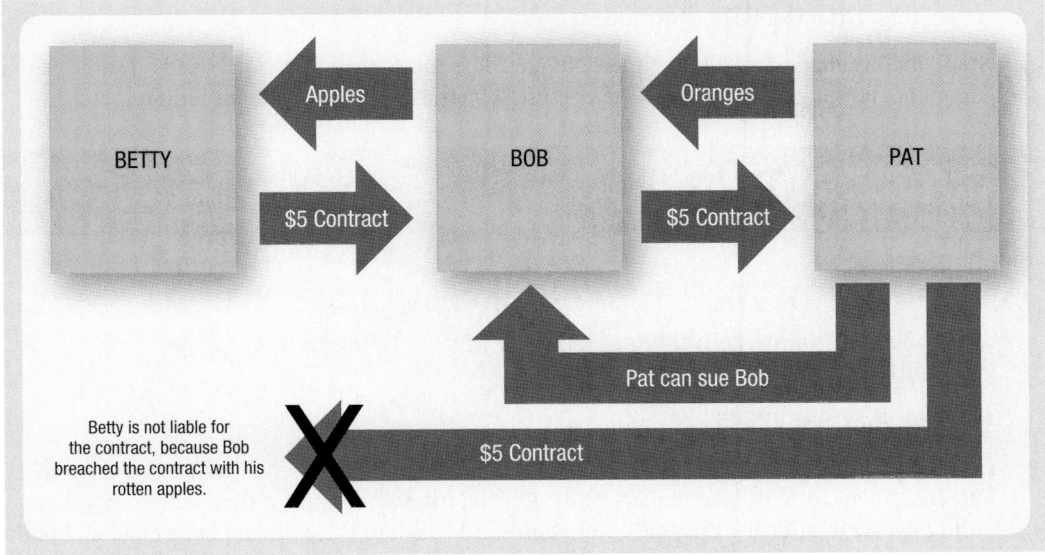

Betty buys apples from Bob for $5 and gives Bob a negotiable note promising to pay the $5 on demand. Bob then buys oranges from Pat for $5 and properly transfers (also known as *negotiates*) the $5 negotiable note to Pat. Pat presents the note to Betty for payment after Betty has found out that the apples she bought from Bob were all bad. Betty refuses to pay Pat the $5. Bob, that shady apple dealer, has disappeared. Pat sues Betty for the $5. Under the rules of negotiable instruments, Pat could very well prevail, and Betty, regardless of the awful apples she got from Bob, might just have to pay Pat.

That's an awful lot of information to jump in with right away, so we need to break down the steps. The following are the issues that have to be explored to understand this chain of events:

1. What constitutes a negotiable instrument?
2. How does one transfer a negotiable instrument?
3. What is the status of a holder of a negotiable instrument?
4. What happens when the person who created a negotiable instrument has a good defense for not honoring his or her paying on the instrument?

Clearly, when the contracts for such transactions are not in breach, everything works out fine. Potential problems, however, led to the evolution of the law surrounding negotiable commercial paper. The next section discusses the elements that make commercial paper a negotiable instrument. Remember that even when commercial paper does not meet the requirements for negotiability, it may still constitute an enforceable contract.

REQUIREMENTS FOR NEGOTIABILITY
LO 3

The UCC requires that for an instrument to be negotiable (do *not* equate *negotiable* with *enforceable*), the instrument must satisfy the six requirements in the following definition: A negotiable instrument is a written document that is signed by the maker or drawer with an unconditional promise or order to pay a sum certain in money on demand or at a time certain to the order of bearer [UCC 3-104(a)]. The six requirements are:

1. The instrument is a written document.
2. It is signed by the creator of the instrument.
3. The instrument has an unconditional promise or order to pay.

4. The amount to be paid is a sum certain in money.

5. Payment is to be made either on demand or at a fixed future time (a time *certain*).

6. The document must contain either the words of negotiability—"to the order of"—or words indicating that it is a bearer instrument.

Study the fascinating case in the Case Nugget. The courts made a ruling based on some of the requirements for negotiability. Does the contested instrument meet the other requirements?

CASE Nugget

Requirements for Negotiability

Andre Deeks, Plaintiff-Appellant, v. United States, Defendant-Appellee
U.S. Court of Appeals for the Federal Circuit

151 Fed. App. 936 (2005)

In 1792, Colonel Marinus Willett wrote a document, stating that in 1781 he had entered into an agreement with 60 members of the Oneida tribe. In return for their help in fighting during the Revolutionary War, the colonel promised each of the 60 members a blanket, but he later found himself unable to fulfill his commitment. In 2004, Andre Deeks filed suit against the U.S. government, claiming that he, as the possessor of Colonel Willett's note, was owed $3 million because the government had never paid its debt to the Oneida tribe. The trial court dismissed Deeks's case, stating that the case was time-barred and should have been filed by 1866. In addition, the trial court found that Deeks lacked standing to bring suit against the government because he had not shown that he had any relation to the Oneida tribe or that he had suffered any injury due to the breach of contract.

Deeks appealed, claiming that the document written by Colonel Willet was a "Bill of Credit in bearer form," which had transferred to him, the current possessor, the standing to sue for the document's enforcement. Deeks also accused the trial court of "nullifying laws governing negotiable instruments." The appeals court affirmed the decision of the trial court, again finding that the suit had been filed long after any applicable statute of limitations. Additionally, the appeals court "reject[ed] Deeks' contention that the Willett Document is a 'bill of credit' or some negotiable instrument, as the text reveals neither an intent that it be circulated as money . . . , nor an unconditional promise to pay a certain sum."

As you read through the following explanations pertaining to the requirements of negotiability, use Figure 15-2 as an example of the requirements as they apply to personal checks.

Written Document The written-document requirement is not as simple as it may appear. Clearly, the law does not permit an *oral* negotiable instrument. Telling someone that you unconditionally promise to pay her $50 next Tuesday does not create a negotiable instrument. However, under the right factual circumstances and when these words are provable, such a statement may be a binding, enforceable contract.

relative permanence
The quality of a negotiable instrument that ensures its longevity.

What makes the writing requirement a little complex is the mandate that the written document must have two characteristics: **relative permanence** and **movability.** Writing a negotiable instrument in the mud, for example, clearly lacks permanence; it will likely disappear as the mud dries. Thus, it is not a negotiable instrument. Likewise, the mud is something that one cannot move about in a commercially reasonable or expected manner. After all, one of the reasons for negotiable instruments is the ease with which they can be moved about.

movability
The quality of a negotiable instrument that ensures it is mobile and available.

Signature of the Maker or Drawer The UCC and cases interpreting the signature requirement are fairly liberal in interpreting what constitutes a signature. Anyone's affirmative mark, from a full-blown signature to an *X,* will suffice provided the party intended that the mark be placed

Figure 15-2

Requirements of Negotiability in a Check

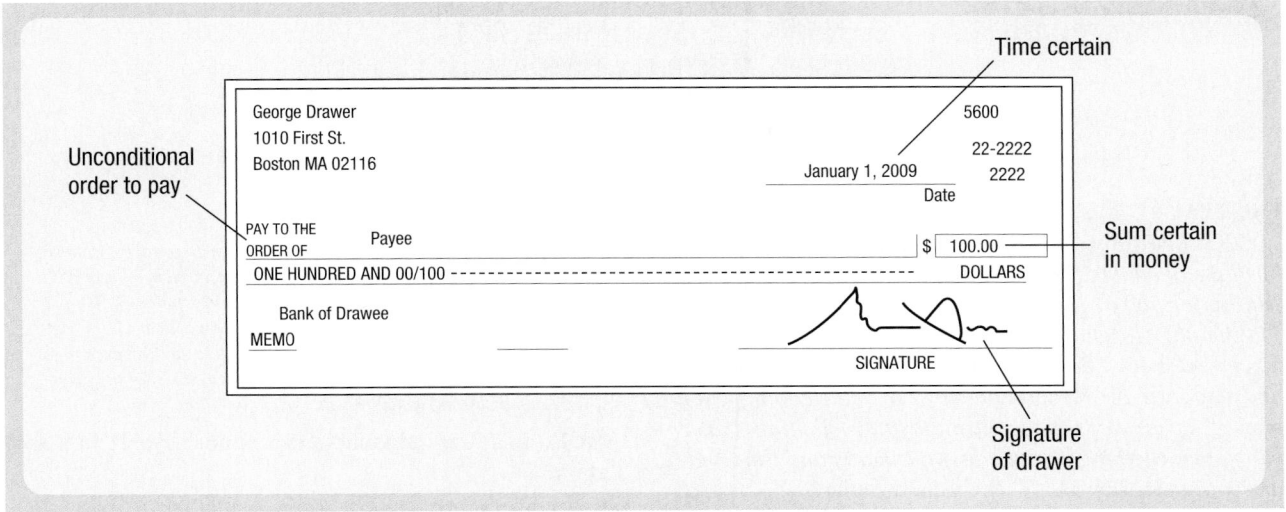

on the instrument and uses that mark to identify himself [UCC 1-201(39)]. The UCC specifies that a signature "may be made (i) manually or by means of a device or machine, and (ii) by the use of any name, including a trade or assumed name, or by a word, mark, or symbol executed or adopted by a person with present intention to authenticate a writing" [3-401(b)].

Likewise, the signature of a duly authorized agent also satisfies this requirement. An agent's signature on behalf of her principal binds the principal and satisfies the signature requirement [UCC 3-401(b)].

A handwritten negotiable instrument satisfies the signature requirement even when no formal signature is present. The handwritten statement "I, John Smith, promise to pay Roberta Alexander, or to bearer, the sum of $20 on Tuesday July 4, 2008" would satisfy the signature requirement because the handwriting affirms the maker's intent and, in that handwritten promise, the maker wrote his own name, John Smith.

Automated signatures, either by stamp or machine, satisfy the writing requirement as well. Even when the stamp or machine signature is fraudulently applied, such as by a person who had no authority to apply it, the signature may be valid if the maker or drawer intended that his or her name be affixed.

Unconditional Promise or Order to Pay The promise or order to pay must be specific and not implied. The language must be affirmative in nature [UCC 3-103(a)(9)]. For example, simply acknowledging a debt does not create language for payment; therefore, a common IOU is not a promise or an order to pay and thus cannot be a negotiable instrument.

The unconditional nature of the promise or order is often the controversial variable of this requirement of negotiability. Stated simply, the promise or order to pay cannot be contingent on something else's happening. An instrument stating "I promise to pay if the following occurs" is not a negotiable instrument. Remember: It may be a perfectly enforceable contract, but it fails to satisfy the terms of negotiability.

Sum Certain in Money Negotiable instruments must promise or order that payment be made in a national currency [UCC 3-104(a)]. For example, U.S. dollars, English pounds, euros, and Japanese yen all satisfy the currency requirement. Bushels of apples, gold, shares of stock, diamonds and rare gems, and the like, are not currencies. While promises to pay in apples or gold or stock may form a perfectly enforceable contract, the resulting instrument is not a negotiable instrument. An instrument promising payment in "German marks and rare French wine" would not be negotiable—even changing the *and* to an *or* would not salvage negotiability. Payment *must* be made in a currency. Case 15-1 establishes the idea that although the sum certain must be made in a currency, the specific type of currency is not relevant.

CASE 15-1

DIF BANK DEUTSCHE INVESTITIONS FINANZ GMBH v.
FLUORMATIC CORPORATION OF AMERICA
U.S. DISTRICT COURT, NORTHERN DISTRICT
OF ILLINOIS, EASTERN DIVISION
1991 U.S. Dist. LEXIS 520

FACTS: *DIF Bank is a company organized under the laws of the Federal Republic of Germany and is engaged in the business of banking. Fluormatic is a Delaware corporation with its principal place of business in Villa Park, Illinois. Multimatic Maschinen GmbH & Co. is a company organized under the laws of the Federal Republic of Germany and engaged in the manufacture of dry-cleaning equipment. Fluormatic is in the business of distributing and servicing dry-cleaning equipment. Multimatic and Fluormatic are both owned by Mr. H. F. Gustav Koetter.*

Between May 9, 1981, and July 11, 1986, Fluormatic regularly purchased dry-cleaning equipment from Multimatic. Fluormatic generally paid for the equipment either by promissory notes made payable to Multimatic in U.S. dollars or by endorsing drafts in deutsche marks drawn by Multimatic. Two promissory notes and six drafts are at controversy here. Multimatic received the notes and drafts from Fluormatic and discounted them to DIF Bank, which credited funds to Multimatic. DIF Bank presented the notes and drafts on their due dates, and payment was not made. DIF Bank gave Fluormatic notice of the dishonor, and the drafts were duly protested. DIF Bank brought a two-count complaint against Fluormatic for recovery on the instruments.

In the judge's words:

Fluormatic . . . argues that the drafts are not negotiable because they are not payable in a "sum certain" as required by paragraphs 3-104 and 3-106 of the Code. Ill. Rev. Stat. ch. 26, paras. 3-104 and 3-106 (1961). The drafts, while payable in German deutsche marks, do not specify an exchange rate. The failure to include an exchange rate, Fluormatic contends, requires the conclusion that the drafts are not payable in "a sum certain" as required under the Code.

ISSUE: Is a draft negotiable if it is not payable in a sum certain?

REASONING: Section 3-107(2) of the UCC provides:

(2) A promise or order to pay a sum stated in a foreign currency is for a *sum certain in money* and, unless a different medium of payment is specified in the instrument, may be satisfied by payment of that number of dollars which the stated foreign currency will purchase at the buying sight rate for that currency on the day on which the instrument is payable or, if payable on demand, on the day of demand. If such an instrument specifies a foreign currency as the medium of payment the instrument is payable in that currency. [emphasis added]

DECISION AND REMEDY: The judge overruled Fluormatic's objection, finding for the plaintiff.

SIGNIFICANCE OF THE CASE: By basing its decision on the clear intent of Section 3-107(2), the court is avoiding a possible obstruction to foreign trade.

CRITICAL THINKING

Why was the evidence provided by Fluormatic unacceptable? What conditions would the company have had to have met to be seen as acceptable to the court?

ETHICAL DECISION MAKING

Fluormatic's defense in this case was not strong. What values would have led the company to choose to settle the matter with DIF Bank rather than try the issue in court?

PAYABLE AT A TIME CERTAIN OR ON DEMAND A negotiable instrument must be payable on demand or at a specific time that can be computed from the instrument itself. Obviously, if the instrument states a specific date, the instrument has stated a time certain. If the instrument is dated and then states that "payment will be made 10 days after above date," the instrument is negotiable because the specific date can be calculated. A dated instrument stating that "payment

The End of the Float?

Consumers who rely on "float" (the time it takes for a check to go through the traditional check-clearing process) have a limited amount of time to enjoy the delayed payment afforded by the process. Businesses in many parts of the country are testing new technology that speeds up the check-clearing process. Soon, float might be an outdated tradition.

In Nevada, for instance, Nevada State Bank allows businesses that purchase a special service to scan checks, send them electronically, and get money for checks drawn on other banks much more quickly; the delay in check processing is cut by 40 percent. Other banks are testing similar products and services. In some states, businesses are substituting electronic images of checks for the checks themselves. Here's how the process works: (1) A customer gives a business a check in payment for a product or service, (2) the business scans the check and sends it to the bank providing the new check-clearing products and services, (3) the bank sends the image to the customer's bank, (4) the customer's bank prints a substitute check, and, quickly, (5) the customer's payment is deposited in the business's account at that business's bank.

It remains to be seen what kinds of litigation will emerge from this expedited process.

is to be made at some future time after the above date" is clearly nonnegotiable (though, again, it may be enforceable as a contract).

Likewise, an instrument that states that "payment will be made 10 days after delivery of the goods" but indicates nowhere in the instrument when delivery is to be made is not a negotiable instrument. (It might also be nonnegotiable if such a reference is construed to be a condition of payment as well.)

Demand instruments, such as checks, are payable as soon as they are issued. If an instrument is silent as to the time of payment, the UCC presumes that it is a demand instrument and thus it retains its negotiable status [3-108(a)].

Words of Negotiability Finally, for an instrument to be negotiable, the instrument must indicate that it was created for the purpose of being transferred. How can an instrument, or better yet its maker or drawer, indicate this purpose? It can do so by having the phrase "to the order of" near the payee's name. When a specific payee is named, this is known as an *order* instrument [UCC 3-109(b)]. For the maker or drawer to indicate that she anticipates the instrument she is creating will be circulated, she writes the phrase *to the order of* and then the name of the payee, or some variation of that wording. Examples of order negotiable-instrument language are "Pay to the order of Jim Smith" and "Pay to Jim Smith or his order."

LO 4

Negotiable instruments payable to whomever is bearing them are known as *bearer instruments* [UCC 3-109(a)]. Bearer instruments are treated like cash. Accordingly, one who comes into possession of a bearer instrument by any means, including theft, may claim the payment due on the instrument. Also, endorsing an order instrument, such as a check, converts the instrument into a bearer instrument that may be claimed by anyone in possession of it. Instruments payable to no one, to "X," or to "cash" are also considered bearer instruments.

The phrase *to the order of* is then necessary to create a negotiable instrument. Wordings such as "Pay to bearer," "Pay to Jim Smith or bearer," "Pay to cash," and "Pay to the order of cash [or bearer]" would all result in the paper's being negotiable.

Once the six elements of negotiability are satisfied, the instrument created is indeed negotiable.

Negotiation

One important characteristic of negotiable instruments is the ease associated with transferring the instrument to a third party. Once a negotiable instrument is created, it can be transferred to another party through negotiation. Negotiation is the transfer of possession to a third party who becomes the holder of the negotiable instrument (UCC Section 3-201). A party who possesses a negotiable instrument payable to the party or to the bearer of the instrument is a holder of the instrument [UCC 1-201(b)(21)].

When the rights to a negotiable instrument are transferred from one party to another, such a transfer is called a *negotiation*. It is important to understand that the rules of negotiation differ

negotiation (2)
(2) The transferring of the rights to a negotiable instrument from one party to another.

holder
A party in possession of a negotiable instrument.

European Union: Negotiable Instruments as Defined by the EEC

At the European Economic Council's Contractual Obligations Convention, the issue of how to characterize negotiable instruments was addressed. Definitions of negotiable instruments differ among member countries. Rather than creating one encompassing definition, however, the EEC decided to defer characterization of negotiable instruments to each country. In other words, each member country of the EEC decides what types of documents are to be considered negotiable instruments. While this decision may prevent problems arising from altering definitions, it could also cause problems in cross-border transactions.

To thwart such complications, the convention decided to define a general concept of negotiability. Therefore, if a transaction is defined as a negotiable instrument within a certain country, it must conform to certain general characteristics as defined by the EEC. These general characteristics are intended to dilute the complexities of cross-border transactions.

order instrument
An instrument payable to a specific, named payee.

bearer instrument
An instrument payable to cash or to whoever is in possession of the instrument.

slightly depending on whether the instrument is an order instrument (i.e., an instrument payable to a specific, named payee) or a bearer instrument (an instrument payable to cash or to whoever is in possession of the instrument) (UCC 3-109). Bearer paper requires only a delivery of the instrument to the holder by the payee. In contrast, order paper requires delivery *and* an endorsement.

DELIVERY

Delivery simply requires the physical handing of an instrument from the person who is entitled to it to the person who is intended to receive it. Thus, a bearer instrument that falls out a window, blown off someone's desk by the wind, and lands in someone else's hand has not been properly negotiated. This lucky person cannot legally demand payment of that instrument because she is not a proper holder. However, you could pass it on to someone who could legally collect on it.

Drawers must be careful when delivering an instrument because if the drawer is negligent in how he or she makes the delivery, the drawer may be liable for notes paid with forged or unauthorized endorsements. For example, if the drawer of a check mails the check to the wrong business, the drawer may be liable for the amount of the check when the wrong business cashes the check.

endorser
One who issues an endorsement.

endorsee
One who receives an endorsement.

allonge
Accompanying a negotiable instrument, a piece of paper that provides room for an endorsement if no room is available on the instrument itself.

blank endorsement
A payee's or last endorsee's signature on a negotiable instrument.

special endorsement
An endorser's signature accompanying the name of the endorsee.

ENDORSEMENT

Order paper must be *endorsed* as well as *delivered* to be negotiated. The person creating the endorsement is the endorser, and the person receiving the endorsement is the endorsee. Normally, there is a place on the negotiable instrument for endorsements (such as on the back of a check). If there is no room on the instrument or if all the room has been taken by previous endorsements, an allonge may be attached. An allonge is simply an additional piece of paper with the endorsements. It must be firmly attached (staples usually work; paper clips do not) [UCC 3-204(a)]. There are three kinds of endorsements that will affect the legal status of the negotiable instrument in different ways: unqualified, qualified, and restrictive endorsements.

Unqualified Endorsements: Blank and Special Endorsements There are two kinds of unqualified endorsements: blank and special. A blank endorsement is simply the payee's or last endorsee's signature, nothing else [UCC 3-205(b)]. The effect of this unqualified blank endorsement is that it turns an order paper into a bearer paper. An instrument with an unqualified blank endorsement may be negotiated by delivery only. A special endorsement consists of the signature of the endorser together with a named endorsee. An illustration would be "Pay to Jackie Jones" followed by the endorser's signature.

Note that in an endorsement, the words of negotiability, *to the order of,* are not needed. The instrument remains negotiable. However, adding those words keeps order paper as order paper and thus continues to require an endorsement and delivery for further negotiation.

Qualified Endorsements A qualified endorsement is one that includes the addition of the words *without recourse.* When negotiable instruments are passed from one party to another, the person transferring the instrument is guaranteeing certain aspects of the instrument by virtue of his or her signature.

NONCRIMINAL ENDORSEMENT PROBLEMS

In situations involving fraud or forgery, it should come as no surprise that problems with endorsements exist. These criminal endorsement issues are examined later in this chapter. However, even in situations not involving criminal offenses, endorsement problems may also arise. We consider these problems below.

Misspelled Name One problem with endorsements occurs when a negotiable instrument contains a misspelled name. In the event of a misspelled name, the holder may endorse the document with the misspelled name, the holder's actual name, or both. The typical practice is for the holder to endorse the instrument with the misspelled name followed by the holder's actual name, spelled properly.

Payable to a Legal Entity Another complication regarding endorsements involves instruments made payable to a legal entity. If the legal entity is an estate, organization, partnership, or the like, the instrument may be endorsed by any authorized representative of the entity. A variation of the same problem occurs when instruments are made payable to a public office. In such an event, the person holding the office may endorse the instrument. For example, when filing her local taxes, Sarah, not knowing whom to make her check payable to, filled in "pay to the order of County Tax Collector." Bill Deepockets, the county tax collector, may endorse the check, as he is the person currently holding the office listed on the check.

Alternative or Joint Payees A third endorsement problem arises when a negotiable instrument has been made payable to more than one person. Two possibilities arise when the instrument is payable to more than one person. The first possibility is that there are *alternative payees.* When the instrument reads "Pay to the order of Jones *or* Smith," the instrument contains alternative payees. In the event of alternative payees, the endorsement of any one of the listed payees is sufficient.

The second possibility is that there are *joint payees.* Joint payees exist when an instrument lists more than one person as a payee and the instrument is to be payable to *all* the listed payees, typically indicated by the word *and.* In the event of joint payees, the instrument would read, "Pay to the order of Smith *and* Jones." Instruments bearing joint payees require the endorsement of all listed payees before the instrument may be negotiated.

Courts have held that when an instrument is silent as to the issue of whether the listed payees are joint or alternative, the instrument is to be interpreted as containing alternative payees. That is, when an instrument does not specify whether the payees are joint or alternative, the endorsement of only one listed payee is required to negotiate the instrument.

Banking

So far, this chapter has explained what a negotiable instrument is, how a negotiable instrument is transferred, and some of the problems associated with negotiable instruments. The following sections discuss the negotiable instruments with which you are probably most familiar: checks. You have most likely written, cashed, and deposited checks; but, as you may have guessed, your relationship with the bank is more complicated than you originally thought.

When you open an account at a bank, you create a contractual relationship with the bank. This relationship is governed by Article 4 of the UCC. Within this relationship, both you, as the customer, and the bank have certain rights and duties. For example, you have the right to order a stop payment on a check for any or no reason. The corresponding duty of the bank is to follow this order.

As we explained earlier in this chapter, checks are considered negotiable instruments under Article 3 of the UCC. However, Article 4 of the UCC is also relevant; this section of the UCC governs the transfer of checks between banks. Thus, both Article 3 and Article 4 are relevant to this chapter.

Article 3 of the UCC outlines the requirements that negotiable instruments, including checks, must meet. Article 3 also establishes the rights and responsibilities pertaining to parties to negotiable instruments. Article 4 creates a framework controlling deposit and checking agreements between banks and customers. In addition, Article 4 directs the relationships between banks as checks are processed among different banks. Moreover, according to UCC Section 4-102(a), when conflicts arise between rules in Articles 3 and 4, Article 4 is to take precedent.

In 2003, Americans wrote approximately 70 billion checks. Clearly, checks are an enormous part of the bank-customer relationship. In fact, of all the negotiable instruments regulated by the UCC, checks are the most common type used. Thus, we begin our discussion of banking by taking a closer look at different types of checks. Then we examine the process of check collection: If the bank accepts a check, how is the money from one account actually transferred to another account? Next, we consider when a bank may charge a customer's account in the context of potential problems with checks, such as stale, postdated, and forged checks. Finally, we turn to an increasingly important element of the banking process: the electronic transfer of funds.

LO 5

drawer
The party that writes an order, or the person who writes a check.

drawee
The party that must obey an order. In the context of banking, the drawee is the bank that must pay the funds ordered by a customer's check.

payee
The party that receives the benefit of an order (check, etc.).

Checks

Although you have likely written a check, do you know what the actual characteristics of checks are? (The key terms and an illustration are provided in Exhibit 15-1 and Figure 15-3.) According to the UCC, a check is a special kind of draft. A *draft* is an instrument that is an order. Three parties are related to this order. First, a **drawer** is the party that gives the order. Second, a **drawee** is the party that must obey the order. For example, in Figure 15-3, the bank is the drawee. Finally, the **payee** is the party that receives the benefit of the order. Thus, when you write a check at the grocery store, you are the drawer ordering the drawee (your bank) to make a payment to the payee (the grocery store).

Exhibit 15-1

Key Terms for Checks

Draft	An instrument whereby one party orders a second party to pay an amount of money to the party listed on the instrument. A check is a draft in which the bank is the drawee.
Drawer	The party giving the order to pay on a draft.
Drawee	The party ordered to pay on a draft.
Payee	The party receiving the money from the draft.

Figure 15-3

A Check

A *check* is a special draft that orders the drawee, a bank, to pay a fixed amount of money on demand [UCC Section 3-104(f)]. The UCC defines a bank as "any business engaged in the business of banking" [4-105(1)]. Consequently, savings banks, savings and loans, credit unions, and trust companies are all considered banks. The drawer of a check writes the check and thus orders the bank to pay. The payee is the party to whom the check is written.

CASHIER'S CHECKS

A **cashier's check** is a check in which both the drawer and the drawee are the same bank [UCC 3-104(g)]. (See Figure 15-4 for an example.) The payee of the check is a specific person. In other words, the bank is drawing on itself and thus assumes the responsibility for paying the check to that specific person. Customers often purchase cashier's checks to give to creditors who want to be sure the funds represented by the check are available. Cashier's checks are useful because they are considered by many in the business community to be the near equivalent of cash.

TRAVELER'S CHECK

A **traveler's check** (see Figure 15-5) is an instrument that must (1) be payable on demand, (2) be drawn on or through a bank, (3) be designated by the phrase *traveler's check,* and (4) be countersigned by the person whose signature appears on the instrument [UCC 3-104(i)]. The drawer of a traveler's check is usually a large financial organization, such as American Express. The person who signs the traveler's check must sign it when she buys the checks; then, when she is ready to use the traveler's check to make some kind of payment, the same person must sign the traveler's check again, in the presence of the acceptor.

MONEY ORDERS

Money orders (see Figure 15-6), particularly personal money orders, are usually in the same form as personal checks and are considered checks under UCC Section 3-104. Both banks and nonbanks sell money orders. The money order states that a certain amount of money is to be paid to a particular person. The amount of money to be paid is usually already imprinted on the money order. The person purchasing the money signs the money order as the drawer and fills in the name of the person who is to receive the money.

CERTIFIED CHECKS

A **certified check** is a check that is accepted at the bank at which it is drawn [UCC 3-409(d)]. For example, suppose Hope writes a check to Jeremiah from her account at Citizens National

<div style="float:right">

LO 6

cashier's check
A check in which both drawer and drawee are the same bank.

traveler's check
An order that is payable on demand, is drawn on or through a bank, is designated by the phrase *traveler's check,* and requires a counter-signature by the person whose signature appears on the check.

certified check
A check that is accepted by the bank from which the funds are drawn.

Figure 15-4

A Cashier's Check

</div>

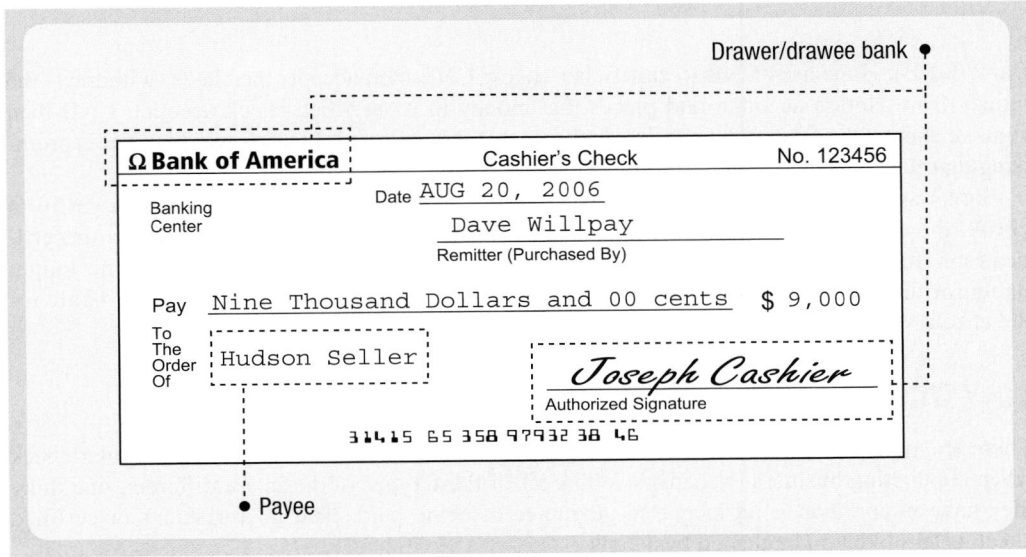

Figure 15-5

A Traveler's Check

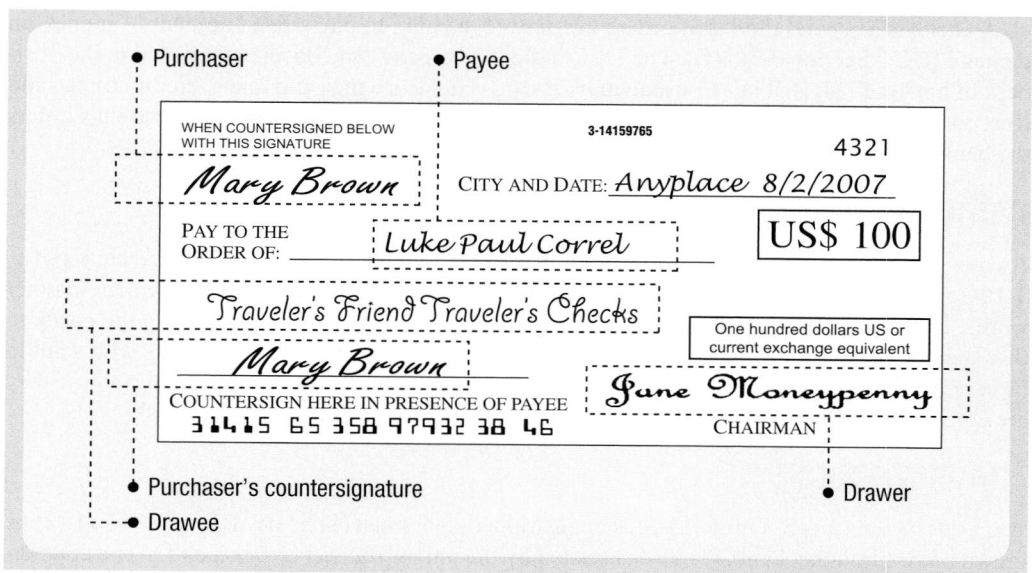

Figure 15-6

A Money Order

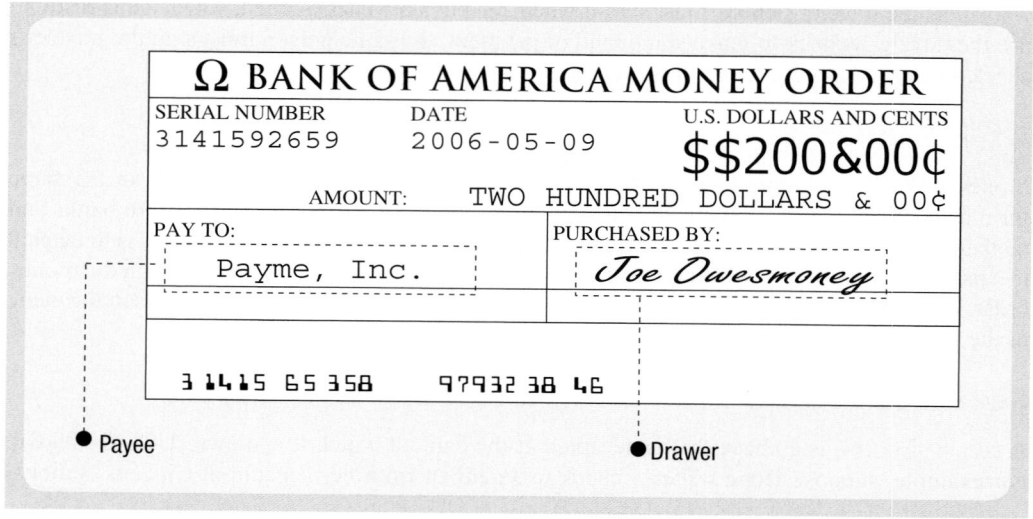

Bank (CNB). Hope asks CNB to certify her check. CNB then accepts the check, withdraws the money from Hope's account, and places that money in its certified-check account. CNB then signs or stamps the face of the check to indicate that it is certified. In other words, CNB is promising that funds are available to pay the check.

Banks are not required to certify checks [UCC 3-409(d)]. If a bank refuses to certify a check, the check is not considered dishonored; it merely lacks the extra protection of certification. However, once the bank does certify a check, the drawer of the check is no longer liable for the amount of the check [UCC 3-414(c)]. The bank has become primarily liable for the check.

WHY USE CASHIER'S OR CERTIFIED CHECKS?

There are a number of reasons to use a cashier's or certified check as opposed to a regular check when conducting business exchanges. While all of these types of drafts are different, one thing they have in common is an increased guarantee of being paid. That is, a cashier's or certified check is less likely to be denied by a bank.

Cashier's checks are a valuable business tool because the bank, and not the individual, is the drawer as well as the drawee. When a cashier's check is presented for payment, the bank, and not the individual, must pay for the cashier's check. The added guarantee of knowing that the bank is paying for the cashier's check makes the cashier's check a veritable guarantee to pay. One downside of the cashier's check is that it must be paid for in advance, including a small fee. However, because the cashier's check is paid for first, it can be purchased at any bank, regardless of whether one has an account at the bank.

Certified checks are useful in business because when a bank certifies a check, it essentially says that it cannot refuse liability on the check. A certified check is one the bank sets aside money for and agrees to pay when the certified check is presented. Despite the added guarantee, there are two main drawbacks to a certified check. The first is that a person must have an account at a specific bank to obtain a certified check. If the person does not have an account at the bank, he or she cannot obtain a certified check from that bank.

The second drawback is that banks do not have to certify checks. Banks may refuse to certify any check for any reason. Refusing to certify is not the same as dishonoring a check, but it does not provide the same guarantee that a certified check provides. While banks do not have to certify a check, they are not allowed to refuse to sell a cashier's check, as long as the payment is valid.

LOST, STOLEN, OR DESTROYED CASHIER'S OR CERTIFIED CHECKS

In the event a cashier's or certified check is lost, stolen, or destroyed, the UCC allows for recovery. According to UCC Section 3-312, the remitter (the party who purchased the check) or the payee may request a refund because the check was lost, stolen, or destroyed. With proper identification, the party should be able to obtain a full refund for the amount on the check.

The claim is enforceable when the claim is made; if it is a cashier's check, 90 days after the check was made; or if it is a certified check, 90 days after acceptance, whichever occurs last [UCC 3-312(b)(1)]. After the claim becomes enforceable, if no one presented the check for payment, a refund is issued and the bank is discharged of liability [UCC 3-312(b)(4)]. When a claim is made, the person making the claim warrants to the bank and any party who has an interest in the check that the check was really lost, stolen, or destroyed.

If the check was not lost, stolen, or destroyed, the holder barred from receiving payment on the check because of the claim may sue the person who made the claim for breach of warranty. A person filing a false claim is also subject to criminal penalties.

Accepting Deposits

LO 7

Charging a customer's account is only part of the bank-customer relationship; the bank must also credit a customer's account when the customer makes cash and check deposits to her account. This section considers the check collection process and examines several issues that focus on the availability of deposited money.

THE CHECK COLLECTION PROCESS

Suppose Jack Blackstone gives Molly Whetfield a check to pay her for her consulting services. When Molly deposits that check into her account, how does the money from Jack's account actually get transferred into Molly's account? This section considers the check collection process (see Figure 15-7) and examines several issues regarding deposits made to banks.

Check Collection within the Same Bank Sometimes the depositary bank is the same bank as the payor bank. When this is the case, the check is referred to as an "on-us item." For example, suppose Molly's and Jack's accounts are at the same bank. When Molly deposits Jack's check into her account, the check does not have to be sent to another bank because she and Jack share the same bank. Instead, the bank gives a "provisional" credit to Molly's account. If this bank does not

Figure 15-7

Illustration of the
Check Collection
Process

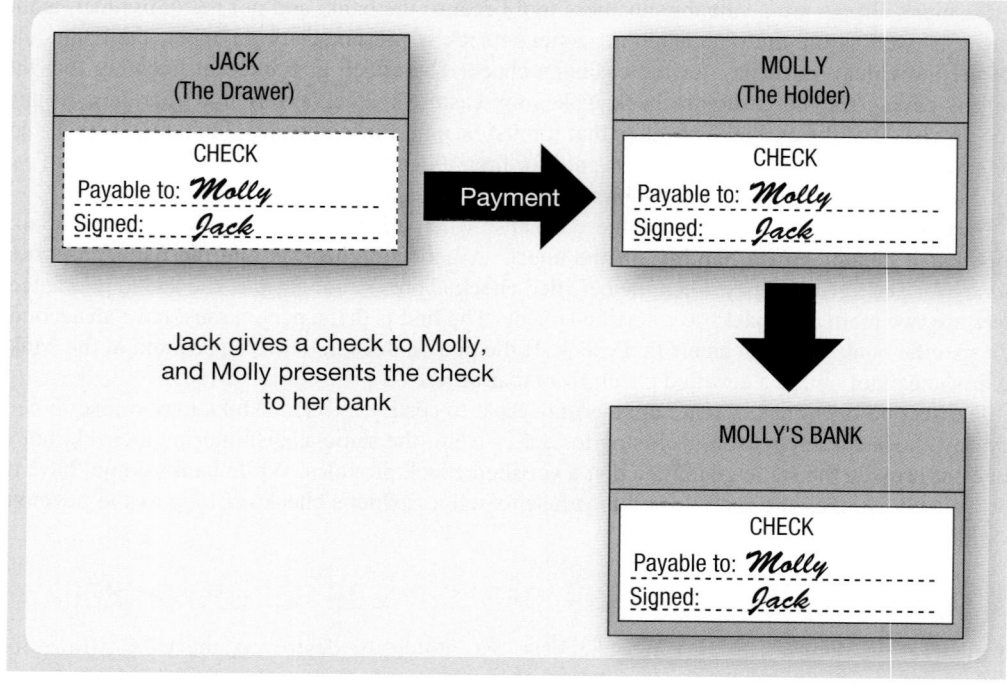

dishonor the check on the second day, the check is paid [UCC Section 4-215(e)(2)]. Finally, on
the third day, the provisional credit becomes an actual payment.

Check Collection between Different Banks Suppose that Jack and Molly have accounts at dif-
ferent banks. Molly's account is in Los Angeles, while Jack's account is in Miami. When Molly
deposits Jack's check at her bank in Los Angeles, her bank is the depositary bank. When a depos-
itary bank receives a check, it must present the check at the payor bank or send it through inter-
mediary banks to reach the payor bank. Once a bank receives a check, it must pass the check
on before midnight of the next day [UCC 4-202(b)]. When the check finally reaches the payor
bank, the payor bank must respond to the check by dishonoring it or becoming liable for the face
amount of the check (UCC 4-302).

The UCC allows banks to establish cutoff hours for making entries on their books. For exam-
ple, a bank may determine that 2 p.m. or later is the cutoff hour for handling checks (UCC 4-
108). If the bank receives a check after this deadline, the bank will defer posting this check to its
customer's account until the next day.

ELECTRONIC CHECK PRESENTMENT

In the past, checks were physically presented to each bank in the chain of collection. Now, checks
are transmitted electronically from bank to bank (UCC 4-110). Through electronic check pre-
sentment, a check can be processed on the day on which it is deposited. An item is encoded with
information that is transferred from one bank's computer to another bank's computer. The person
who enters the information into the computer (i.e., encodes the information) warrants that the
information is correct (UCC 4-209). Alternatively, the image of a check may be transmitted for
payment to other banks.

Substitute Checks To help facilitate electronic presentment, in 2004 Congress passed the *Check
Clearing for the 21st Century Act* (also known as *Check 21* or the *Check Truncation Act*). Check
21 allows banks to forgo sending original checks as part of the collection or return process and
instead send a truncated version. In place of the original paper check, a bank may send (1) a
substitute check or (2), by agreement, an electronic image of the check along with data from the
magnetic ink character recognition (MICR) line on the original check.

A substitute check is similar to the electronic image that may be sent in lieu of the original paper check. Check 21 defines a *substitute check* as a paper reproduction of the original check that conforms to the following requirements:

1. Contains a clear replication of the front and back of the original paper check.
2. Bears an MICR line with all the information on the original check's MICR line.
3. Conforms with generally applicable industry standards for paper stock, dimensions, and other general qualities.
4. Is suitable for automated processing in the same manner as the original paper check.

Check 21 provides the guidelines for the issuance and use of substitute checks. The act also allows the use of digital or paper substitutions for original paper checks.

AVAILABILITY SCHEDULE FOR DEPOSITED CHECKS

Once a check is considered deposited in a customer's account, when are the funds available to the customer? In the past, banks placed extended holds (e.g., 10 days) on deposited funds to ensure that the payor bank would not dishonor the check. If the check was from out of state, the bank might place a two-week hold on the check.

Because customers were frustrated with such extended holds on checks, Congress enacted the Expedited Funds Availability Act of 1987. This act created explicit timelines that mandate when banks must make deposited funds available to customers. If the risk of dishonor is low, the funds must be made available very quickly. For example, the first $100 of any amount deposited must be available to the depositor on the business day following the day of deposit [12 C.F.R. Section 229.10(a)–(c)]. The availability of the rest of the funds depends on whether the check is local, what the amount of the check is, and how the depositor wishes to withdraw the funds.

1. If the deposited check is drawn on a bank within the same Federal Reserve Bank area, the depositary bank must make the deposited funds available to the customer on the second business day following the deposit day [12 C.F.R. 229.10(b)].
2. If the deposited check is outside the same Federal Reserve Bank area, the depositary bank must make the funds available on the fifth business day following the day of deposit [12 C.F.R. 229.12(c)].

THE TRUTH-IN-SAVINGS ACT

In an effort to allow consumers to be better informed, Congress passed the Truth-in-Savings Act (TISA) in 1991. TISA requires that depositary institutions disclose, in great detail, the terms and conditions of their accounts. Depositary institutions include commercial banks, savings banks, credit unions, and savings and loan associations.

TISA requires that every bank inform its customers of a number of specific pieces of information relevant to the bank's accounts. This information is to be handed to the customer as a pamphlet, brochure, or handout before the customer opens a deposit account. The information that must be given to the customer includes:

1. The minimum balance required to open an account and to be paid interest.
2. The manner in which the balance of the account will be calculated.
3. The annual percentage yield of interest for the account.
4. The way interest on the account will be calculated.
5. Notification of any fees, charges, and penalties the account may be assessed and how they are calculated.
6. Notification of any limitations on withdrawals or deposits.

Furthermore, TISA and Regulation DD, which serves as the act's implementing regulation, require that banks pay interest based on the full balance of interest-bearing accounts daily. The requirement prevents banks from calculating interest on an account when the account is at its lowest balance.

When a Bank May Charge a Customer's Account

The following sections consider certain problems related to a bank's accepting and paying a customer's check.

WRONGFUL DISHONOR

When a customer opens a checking account, both the customer and the bank accept certain duties and rights. Generally, the customer assumes a duty to keep sufficient funds in her account to cover the checks written on her account. If the customer does not have enough funds to cover a check, the bank will dishonor the check, and the customer becomes liable for the amount of the check.

Similarly, under the *properly payable rule,* the bank has a duty to pay checks from the customer's account as long as the checks are "properly payable" [UCC 4-401(a)]. In other words, a check must be authorized by the drawer and must not violate agreement between the bank and the customer. Generally, for a check to be considered properly payable, it must:

1. Have the drawer's authorized signature on the check.
2. Be paid to a person entitled to enforce the check.
3. Not have been altered.
4. Not have been completed by addition of unauthorized terms if the check was incomplete.
5. Be paid on or after the date of the check.
6. Not be subject to a stop payment from the drawer.

If the bank wrongfully fails to pay a check—wrongfully dishonoring the check—the bank may be liable to the customer for damages. The UCC clearly states that banks can be held liable, but it does not cite a specific theory for recovery. Therefore, someone whose check was dishonored need prove only that the dishonoring was wrongful, and he or she will be entitled to recovery. Case 15-2 provides an example of the damages a customer may potentially recover from a bank for wrongful dishonor.

 CASE 15-2

THE TWIN CITY BANK v. KENNETH ISAACS
SUPREME COURT OF ARKANSAS
672 S.W.2d 651 (1984)

FACTS: *The Issacs discovered their checkbook was missing on Sunday, May 13, 1979. They promptly reported the loss to Twin City Bank the next day. They learned that two checks totaling $2,050 had been forged and charged to their account. When they reported the lost checkbook, their account balance was approximately $2,000.*

Because Mr. Issacs had been previously convicted of burglary, the bank thought he might be involved with the forgeries. Thus, the bank froze the Isaacses' account. However, the individual who forged the checks was discovered and convicted at the end of May 1979. The police notified the

bank that there was no evidence to connect the Issacs to the forgeries. Yet the bank continued to keep the account frozen. The Issacs filed suit for wrongful dishonor in June 1979. Their account was kept frozen for the next four years.

At trial, the jury awarded the Issacs $18,500 in compensatory damages and $45,000 in punitive damages. The bank appealed. The appellate judge noted:

On the issue of damages, the bank maintains there was insufficient evidence to support the $18,500 award for mental anguish, for loss of credit and loss of the bargain on a house, that the award of punitive damages should not have been given at all as there

was not only insufficient proof of actual damages but insufficient evidence of malice or intent to oppress on the part of the bank.

ISSUE: When is a bank that wrongfully dishonors the checks of an account holder liable for damages to the account holder?

REASONING: In the court's own words:

> The bank does not challenge the sufficiency of the evidence of its wrongful dishonor, but contends only that there was no evidence to support an award of damages. These arguments cannot be sustained.

The statute upon which this suit was based is Ark. Stat. Ann. § 85-4-402:

> Bank's liability to customer for wrongful dishonor — A payor bank is liable to its customer for damages proximately caused by the wrongful dishonor of an item.
>
> The jury was instructed that if they found the bank liable they were to fix the amount of money which would compensate the Isaacs "for any of the following elements of damage sustained which were proximately caused by the conduct of Twin City Bank: 1) Any amounts of money wrongfully held by the defendant and remaining unpaid 2) any mental anguish and embarrassment suffered by the plaintiffs 3) any financial losses sustained by the [Isaacs]."

Initially, there can be no serious question as to certain losses: the $2,000 wrongfully withheld by the bank for four years, and the value of two vehicles repossessed because the Isaacs did not have access to their funds, resulting in a loss of approximately $2,200. Additionally, after the account was frozen, the bank continued to charge the account a service charge and overdraft fees on checks written before the forgeries but presented after the account was frozen. . . .

Decisions upholding recovery for mental suffering under the code have found injury resulting from circumstances comparable to this case. In *North Shore Bank* v. *Palmer* for example, a $275 forged check was paid from Palmer's account. After the bank knew or should have known the check was forged, it charged Palmer with the $275 check and later wrongfully dishonored other checks. Part of the actual damages awarded was attributed to mental suffering for the "embarrassment and humiliation Palmer suffered from having been turned down for credit for the first time in his life." . . .

In this case, prior to the forgery incident the Isaacs' credit reputation with Twin City Bank was described by the bank as "impeccable" and the freezing of their funds had a traumatic effect on their lives. They obviously lost their credit standing with Twin City, and were unable to secure credit commercially at other institutions because of their status at Twin City. The Isaacs had to borrow from friends and family, and were left in a precarious position financially. They did not have use of their $2,000 for four years. The allegation relative to the loss of a house resulted from the dishonor of an earnest money check for a home they were planning to buy, ending prospects for the purchase at that time. . . . Finally, the Isaacs lost equities in two vehicles repossessed as a result of the withholding of their funds.

DECISION AND REMEDY: The court found that in addition to the losses mentioned above, there was sufficient evidence to sustain damages for mental suffering and loss of credit, as well as sufficient demonstration of some loss attributable to the inability to pursue the purchase of a home. The judge affirmed for the plaintiff.

SIGNIFICANCE OF THE CASE: A bank that wrongfully dishonors a check of an account holder is liable for (1) any amounts of money wrongfully held by the bank and remaining unpaid, (2) any mental anguish and embarrassment suffered by the account holder, and (3) any financial losses sustained by the account holder.

CRITICAL THINKING

The judge uses *North Shore Bank* to make analogies with the Isaacses' case. Do you think this analogy is effective?

ETHICAL DECISION MAKING

Return to the WPH framework. Suppose you are the bank manager who decided to keep a freeze on the Isaacses' funds for four years. If your actions are guided by the public disclosure test, would you have behaved differently?

STOP-PAYMENT ORDER

A customer can issue a **stop-payment order,** an order by a drawer that instructs the drawee bank not to pay a check that has been drawn on the customer's account (UCC 4-403). A customer issues a stop-payment order when he has issued a check that has not yet been accepted and he

stop-payment order
An order by a drawer that instructs the drawee bank not to pay an issued check.

wishes the check not to be accepted. If the bank pays a check in violation of a stop-payment order, the bank will incur liability for the damages suffered by the customer due to the stop payment [UCC 4-403(b)].

To be effective, the stop order must meet two requirements: (1) The customer must give the order in a reasonable time, and (2) the customer must describe the item with "reasonable certainty" [UCC 4-403(a)]. For example, the stop-payment order must be given promptly so that the bank has enough time to inform its tellers and other employees that they should not pay the check. Moreover, the UCC states that the stop-payment order must reach the bank by a certain cutoff time. Generally, the stop-payment order should list (1) the date of the check, (2) the name of the payee, (3) the amount of the check, (4) the number of the check, and (5) the checking account number.

POSTDATED CHECKS

Under previous versions of Articles 3 and 4 of the UCC, a check could not be charged to a customer's account until the date of the check. Thus, some customers attempted to hold off payment on a check by postdating the check and giving it to the payee. However, because banks generally use an automated system to process checks, checks are now frequently paid without regard to the date. If a bank pays a check before its date and thus depletes a customer's account, the bank could be liable to the customer for damages. Thus, some banks include certain clauses in their customer agreements that state they may pay checks regardless of the date.

The UCC presents a middle ground that protects a bank from liability while permitting customers to postdate checks. Section 4-401(c) states that customers can postdate checks but they must give the bank notice of the postdated check. Therefore, the bank can assume that it can pay all checks on presentment unless the bank has received notice. Most banks charge a processing fee for notice of a postdated check.

STALE CHECKS

stale check
A check that is not presented to a bank within six months of its date.

If a check is not presented to a bank within six months of its date, the check is considered a stale check. Banks are not required to honor stale checks.

FORGERIES AND ALTERATIONS

In 1999, attempted check fraud in the United States rose to approximately $2.2 billion, while merchants and banks suffered actual losses approximating $679 million through check fraud. Thus, banks are clearly concerned about the acceptance of altered or forged checks.

Checks Bearing Forged Signatures Under the properly payable rule, the bank may pay a check only if it is authorized by the customer. Who is liable if a bank cashes a check signed by an unauthorized person? In other words, what happens when someone forges a drawer's signature on a check?

The UCC has established that a forged signature has no legal effect as a signature of the drawer [3-403(a)]. Consequently, in most cases, if a bank pays a check when the drawer's signature has been forged, the bank will be liable for the amount of the check.

However, there are some exceptions to this rule. First, if the customer's negligence substantially contributed to a forged signature and the bank pays the check in good faith, the bank is not required to repay the customer [UCC 3-406(a)]. For example, if the customer is an employer who keeps a rubber stamp of his signature in an unlocked drawer, and an employee uses the signature stamp to create a check payable to herself, the customer has substantially contributed to the forged signature and will likely not be able to recover the amount of the check.

Another exception to the forgery liability rule is related to the customer's duty to examine his or her bank statement. Banks make a customer's statement available to the customer approximately once a month. This statement lists or includes all the checks that have been charged against the customer's account over the past month. A customer must examine her bank statement reasonably promptly for any forgeries or unauthorized payments. If the customer discovers a forgery or unauthorized payment, she must notify the bank promptly [UCC 4-406(c)]. Under the UCC, if the customer does not notify the bank of an unauthorized signature within 30 days after the statement was made available, she cannot hold the bank liable for the payment [4-406(d)]. See the Case Nugget, where this rule was applied.

CASE Nugget

Thirty Days to Report

Fernando Tatis v. U.S. Bancorp
U.S. Court of Appeals for the 6ᵗʰ Circuit

F.3d 672 (2007)

Plaintiff-appellant Fernando Tatis, a major-league baseball player, opened several banking accounts through US Bank. One of the accounts Tatis opened was a personal checking account about which he had received the terms and conditions before becoming the primary signatory for the account. When the account was initially established, Tatis asked that all bank statements be held in the bank's Professional Sports Division. The personal checks were then sent to Tatis's residence in Montreal, where an employee proceeded to take the checks and forge several of them between August and November 2001. Tatis later brought suit against the bank to recover his lost funds. The defendant contested Tatis's accusations and moved for summary judgment.

The district court granted the defendant's motion for summary judgment, and when Tatis moved for reconsideration with the district court, his motion was denied. Tatis then appealed the district court's decision to the Sixth Circuit of the U.S. Court of Appeals.

In the opinion written by Alan Sharp, the Sixth Circuit found that Tatis did not have the right to recover the funds from the bank. When the account was opened, Tatis was notified by the terms and conditions he received that he had only 30 days after the bank statements became available to report any unauthorized signatures or alterations. Although Tatis was not given the statements directly, they were made available to him and held at the location that he had requested.

By not reporting the first forgery that appeared on the first bank statement, Tatis lost rights to all subsequent funds that were taken. As a result of payments being made on the checks previously written by Tatis's employee, the bank could claim that Tatis had failed to report that the employee was not an authorized signatory on the account. Hence, even after Tatis noticed the forgeries, he was not able to recover any funds.

The duty to examine the bank statement is particularly important in cases where there have been multiple forgeries by the same forger, or "same wrongdoer." If a customer examines a statement and does not notify the bank of the first forgery within 30 days, the customer will be liable for future forgeries on the customer's account by the same wrongdoer.

Again, if the bank was negligent in paying the forged checks, the customer's liability for the checks may be diminished through comparative negligence [UCC 4-406(e)]. Regardless of the 30-day requirement for multiple forgeries or the care used in cashing a check, a customer must report a forgery within one year from the date the statement is available to the customer or he will lose the right to recover this money [UCC 4-406(f)].

Checks Bearing Forged Endorsements If a bank pays a check that has been fraudulently endorsed, who is responsible? In the same way that a drawer is not responsible for a check that bears the drawer's forged signature, the drawer is similarly not responsible for a check that has been fraudulently endorsed. Generally, when an endorsement has been forged, the first party to accept the forged instrument is ultimately liable for the loss because a forged endorsement does not legally transfer title [UCC 4-207(a)(2)]. However, the drawer again has a duty to examine her statement for fraudulent endorsements and then notify the bank. The drawer must report all forged endorsements within three years of receiving the returned forged items or her statement

containing the forged items. If the drawer does not report the forgery within three years, the bank is no longer liable for that customer's loss (UCC 4-111).

Altered Checks Remember, under the properly payable rule, a bank is to pay only those checks that are authorized. When a party makes an unauthorized change or alteration to a check, the check becomes unauthorized. The UCC defines alteration as a change (without consent) that modifies the obligation of a party to the instrument. Generally, if a bank pays a check that has been altered, the bank will be liable for the alteration.

alteration
An unauthorized change to an instrument that modifies the obligation of a party to the instrument.

A customer's substantial contribution to the alteration will limit the customer's ability to require that the bank credit his or her account. In other words, if the customer leaves large blank spaces open on the check and thus another party may easily alter the check, the customer will likely be liable for the altered amount of the check. Similarly, under the UCC, any drawer who leaves the dollar amount blank may not later protest paying whatever amount has been written on the check [UCC 4-401(d)(2)].

As in the case of forged signatures, the customer's duty to examine his bank statement also applies to looking for altered checks. Thus, if the customer does not discover the altered check or does not report the altered check within a reasonable time, the bank's liability for the altered check is reduced. Similarly, if both the customer and the bank are negligent in contributing to and paying an altered check, both parties will be responsible for a portion of the check.

Electronic Fund Transfers

CONSUMER FUND TRANSFERS

Consumer fund transactions are governed by the *Electronic Fund Transfer Act of 1978 (EFTA)*. This act sets out the rights and liabilities of the parties involved in electronic fund transfers (EFTs). Regulation E of the act allows the Federal Reserve Board to issue rules and regulations to enforce EFTA. The following transactions are considered consumer fund transactions: transactions in which a retail customer pays for an item with a debit card that allows the customer's bank account to be instantly charged, ATM transactions, and direct deposits of paychecks.

electronic fund transfer (EFT)
The transfer of funds by an electronic terminal, telephone, or computer.

Customer and Bank Rights and Responsibilities EFTA requires that merchants inform customers of their rights regarding EFTs. First, if a customer's ATM card is lost or stolen, the customer must notify the bank within two days. The customer is then liable for only the first $50 stolen. If the customer does not notify the bank, the customer will be held liable for up to $500 that is stolen. Second, the bank has a duty to provide a monthly statement that includes electronic fund transfers, and the customer has a duty to examine this bank statement for any unauthorized electronic fund transfers or errors. Third, the customer has a duty to notify the bank of any errors in the electronic transactions within 60 days of receiving the statement. Fourth, the bank is required to provide customers with receipts for electronic transactions. Fifth, the bank must notify the customer that preauthorized payments may be stopped; however, the customer must stop the payment by notifying the bank at any time up to three days before the preauthorized payment is

CONNECTING to the Core

Financial Accounting

Direct deposit is an attractive method for corporations to use in paying employees, as companies can control the timing of withdrawals from company bank accounts. In other words, every payroll day would show withdrawals from a company's bank account for each employee paid by direct deposit. The alternative to direct deposit is that companies would have to more closely monitor their company bank accounts after every payroll day, as some employees may take several days longer to cash or deposit their paychecks, and the amount within a company bank account would not necessarily reflect the amount remaining after each employee is paid.

However, direct deposit simplifies payroll procedures only for those employees who choose to be paid by direct deposit. What if certain employees still prefer to receive traditional paychecks? To further simplify payroll procedures, larger companies may choose to create special payroll accounts, from which these companies would issue regular checks or directly deposit funds in employees' accounts, depending on employees' preferences. Larger companies often prefer using payroll bank accounts because these companies can essentially use one check or one electronic transfer of funds from the regular company account to the payroll bank account, from which each employee would be paid. The separate payroll account allows a company to more easily reconcile transactions in a regular company account, because each payroll day shows up as one withdrawal from the regular account that is deposited into the payroll account.

K. Larson, J. Wild, and B. Chiappetta, *Principles of Financial Accounting* (New York: McGraw-Hill/Irwin, 2005), p. 446.

scheduled. While a customer may stop a preauthorized payment, a customer cannot order a stop payment on an EFT because such transfers occur instantaneously.

Unauthorized Transfers Under EFTA, an unauthorized electronic transfer is a federal felony punishable through criminal sanctions, such as a $10,000 fine or 10-year prison sentence. An electronic transfer is unauthorized if (1) it is initiated by a person who has no authority to transfer, (2) the customer receives no benefit from the transfer, and (3) the customer did not give his personal identification number to the unauthorized party.

When banks violate EFTA, consumers may recover actual and punitive damages, with the punitive damages totaling between $100 and $1,000. If the consumers are part of a class-action suit, the punitive damages are capped at $500,000 or 1 percent of the institution's net worth.

COMMERCIAL FUND TRANSFERS

Because EFTA did not cover all situations where funds may be electronically transferred, Article 4(A) of the UCC was issued to address commercial fund transfers. An important type of commercial fund transfer is a wire transfer. Funds are "wired" between two commercial parties. There are two major payment systems that coordinate wire payments: the Federal Reserve wire transfer network (Fedwire) and the New York Clearing House Interbank Payments Systems (CHIPS). These two systems account for the transfer of more than $1 trillion daily. This sum is substantially more than is transferred by any other means.

E-Money and Online Banking

With the rapid advancements in technology, the banking system is finding itself changing rapidly. Electronic payments, or e-payments, are becoming increasingly prevalent in daily life. Increasingly, bank transactions are being conducted electronically, marking a shift away from physical currency. In fact, it is possible for electronic forms of money to completely replace physical currency such as paper and coin money. Digital cash, money stored electronically on microchips, magnetic strips, or other computer media, would allow for the elimination of physical currency.

digital cash
Money stored electronically in place of physical currency.

311

e-money
Electronic money.

stored-value card
A plastic card that con-
tains data regarding
the value of the card,
thereby allowing EFTs to
be made.

Helping to lead the digital banking revolution are the various forms of e-money (electronic money). The most common example of e-money is stored-value cards. Stored-value cards are typically plastic cards that contain magnetic strips. The magnetic strips, similar to those on credit cards or ATM cards, contain data regarding the value of the card.

Related to the expansion of technology in banking is the increase in use of online banking. With online banking, banks allow customers to have electronic access to their accounts so that they can check their accounts, transfer money, order payments, pay bills, check their investments, and, through some banks, even trade stock. While services vary from bank to bank, many banks are offering at least some form of online banking to their customers.

ONLINE BANKING SERVICES

Although online banking services vary among banks, there are three services most banks with online banking offer: (1) bill consolidation and payment, (2) transfer of funds from one account to another, and (3) loan applications (an appearance at the bank to sign the loan is typically required to finalize the loan process). By offering these services, banks are able to cut down on their own costs as well as give customers greater control over their funds.

Despite the number of banking services offered online, not all banking services can be conducted over the Internet. For example, depositing and withdrawing funds are two services that cannot be conducted online.

REGULATORY COMPLIANCE

In the main, banks are in favor of the increased use of online banking. Part of the reason banks like online banking is that it helps reduce a bank's operating cost and thus increase its profits. One way online banking reduces cost is through paperless billing. By not having to send paper statements to their customers, banks save on paper, ink, envelopes, and postage. The bank posts all the information to the user's account online, and this does not cost the bank much at all.

Another reason banks are in favor of online banking is that it decreases what is known as "float" time. *Float time* is the period between the time a check is written and the time it is presented for final payment, during which a customer can still use his or her funds. As an electronic check does not have to physically transfer between banks, accounts can be credited or debited more quickly.

PRIVACY PROTECTION

Are e-money institutions the same as traditional financial institutions? Do the same laws apply? These two questions hold the key to the question: How secure are e-payments and e-money? The answer is, We do not know.

E-Money Payment Information Which laws apply to e-money is still mostly untested legal ground. That is, there is little clarity regarding which laws do apply to e-money. The Federal Reserve has explicitly stated that Regulation E, which regulates traditional electronic fund transfers, does not apply to e-money transactions. Nonetheless, laws regarding computer files, not directly related to banking, might apply to e-money, such as laws against unauthorized access of electronic files or communication. There are several such laws, but it is not clear whether they apply to e-money.

E-Money Issuer's Financial Records In 1978, Congress passed the Right to Financial Privacy Act [12 U.S.C. Section 3401 et seq.]. Under this act, financial institutions, such as banks, may not give a federal agency information regarding a person's finances without either that person's explicit consent or a warrant. The Right to Financial Privacy Act may apply to digital cash providers if the provider is considered a legal bank or credit provider that supplies customers with a card considered to be similar to a credit or debit card. However, given the lack of a physical location for digital cash providers, it is also possible that the Right to Financial Privacy Act does not apply, in which case digital cash providers may release a person's financial information freely to any federal agency.

Consumer Financial Data In an effort to further protect people's financial privacy, Congress passed the Financial Services Modernization Act, also known as the Gramm-Leach-Bliley Act [12 U.S.C. Sections 24a, 248b, 1820a, 1828b]. The act's purpose is to control how financial institutions handle customer information, thereby ultimately providing greater privacy protections to financial institution customers. Financial institutions are prohibited from disclosing personal information about their clients to third parties unless certain requirements set forth in the act are met. In addition, each financial institution is legally required to present customers with its privacy policies and practices.

----▶ SUMMARY

The Need for Negotiable Instruments	*Contracts as commercial paper:* any contractual obligations, except for personal ones and nonassignable ones, may be transferred and thus is a form of commercial paper. *Problems with commercial paper:* A breach of the contract invalidates the commercial paper.
Types of Negotiable Instruments	*Note:* A promise by the maker to pay a payee (e.g., a certificate of deposit). *Draft:* An order by the drawer to a drawee to pay a payee (e.g., a check). A note or draft can be either of the following: • *Demand instrument:* Payee can demand actual payment at any time. • *Time instrument:* Payment will be made only at a specific designated time.
An Overview of the Law of Negotiable Instruments	*Requirements for negotiability:* 1. Written document: • Relative permanence • Movability 2. Signature of the maker or drawer: • Affirmative mark • Duly authorized agent • Handwritten, even without signature • Automated signature 3. Unconditional order or promise to pay: • X Must be specific, not implied 4. Sum certain in money: • X Currency only, any currency acceptable 5. Payable at a time certain or on demand: • X Acceleration of payment • X Extension of payment 6. Words of negotiability: • X To the order of • X Order instrument *The significance of negotiability:* More than a two-party transaction.
Negotiation	*Delivery:* The physical handing over of a negotiable instrument. *Endorsements:* 1. Unqualified endorsements 2. Qualified endorsements
Banking	Article 3 of the UCC outlines the requirements that negotiable instruments, including checks, must meet, and it establishes the rights and responsibilities pertaining to parties to negotiable instruments. Article 4 creates a framework controlling deposit and checking agreements between banks and customers, and it directs the relationships between banks as checks are processed among different banks.

Checks

Draft: An instrument that is an order.

Drawer: The party that gives the order.

Drawee: The party that must obey the order.

Payee: The party that receives the benefit of the order.

Check: A special draft that orders the drawee, a bank, to pay a fixed amount of money on demand.

Cashier's check: A check in which both the drawer and the drawee are the same bank.

Traveler's check: An instrument that is payable on demand, is drawn on or through a bank, is designated by the phrase "traveler's check," and requires a countersignature by the person whose signature appears on the instrument.

Money order: An instrument stating that a certain amount of money is to be paid to a particular person.

Certified check: A check that is accepted at the bank at which it is drawn.

When a Bank May Charge a Customer's Account

Properly payable rule: A bank may pay an instrument only when it is authorized by the drawer and does not violate an agreement between the bank and the customer.

Wrongful dishonor: If a bank refuses to pay a properly payable check, the bank incurs liability.

Stop-payment order: A drawer orders the drawee bank to not pay a check that has been drawn on the drawer's account.

Postdated check: A customer can postdate a check but must give the bank notice of the post-dated check.

Stale check: A check is not presented to a bank within six months of its date.

Forgeries and alterations:

1. *Check bearing a forged signature:* Generally, the drawer is not liable for a forged check unless the drawer substantially contributed to the forgery.
2. *Check bearing a forged endorsement:* Neither the drawer nor the drawer's bank is liable for a forged endorsement.
3. *Altered check:* If an unauthorized change modifies the obligation of a party to the instrument, the drawer is generally not liable for the altered amount unless he or she negligently contributed to the alteration.

E-Money and Online Banking

Digital cash: Money is stored electronically on microchips, magnetic strips, or other computer media.

····▶ Point/Counterpoint

Should a Company Be Allowed to Require That Employees Receive Payment through Direct Deposit?	
YES	NO
A company should be allowed to require that employees receive payment through direct deposit because direct-deposit payment is the most efficient form of payment for both employers and employees.	A company should not be allowed to require that its employees receive payment through direct deposit. While direct deposit is a good option for employers to provide to employees, the choice of payment form should be left to the employees.
Direct deposit allows employers and employees security they would not have with mailed paychecks. Companies can keep track of employee payments more accurately when employees are paid through one payment method.	First, very few guidelines have been established regarding direct-deposit procedures. Employees would not necessarily be provided an in-depth statement discussing the details of each pay period. With direct deposit, employees have more difficulty ensuring that pay statements are accurate.
Through direct deposit, employers are assured that *all employees* are paid at the same time, on the	

same day. Neither employees nor employers need to be concerned with lost, stolen, delayed, or damaged paychecks.

Many people have already chosen the convenience of online banking for their other banking needs; adding direct deposit only simplifies their lives. In fact, studies show that the average worker spends between 8½ and 24 hours each year cashing and depositing their payroll checks.*

Direct deposit allows for a separate payroll account and more exact bookkeeping. The losses normally associated with stolen and doubled paychecks can be reinvested in the company, eventually allowing for potential salary/wage increases for all. Furthermore, a company saves a lot of money on paper costs alone by switching to direct deposit.

Many people willingly choose to directly deposit their paychecks. A company establishing a requirement of direct-deposit payment would only streamline and simplify the process for everyone involved.

Wage-based employees, for example, need to know exactly what they are paid per hour, for how many hours, so that the employees know whether they need to be paid overtime wages. Some direct-deposit statements list only the amount of money transferred to the employee's account.

Some employees simply prefer to literally hold and personally deposit a physical check. They also have a physical copy of their pay stub for paper records. The absence of a physical receipt creates "holes" in an individual's paper records. These holes can create problems when an individual gathers documents in preparation for tax season.

While companies can and should present to employees a list of the advantages of direct deposit, the ultimate decision should be left to the employees, because the employees are most heavily affected if their paychecks are not deposited properly.

* www.msmoney.com.

Questions & Problems

1. Explain the reason behind the need for negotiable instruments.

2. Are negotiable instruments more similar to money or contracts? Explain.

3. Identify and define each of the elements of negotiability.

4. Evaluate the following statement: "Order paper and bearer paper must be delivered to be negotiated."

5. Who are the three parties involved in the transfer of money through a check?

6. Explain the reason for the following policy: A customer has a duty to examine her or his bank statement.

7. Evaluate the following statement: "If a signature on a check is forged, the customer will never be responsible for the amount on the check."

8. Doseung Chung, the plaintiff, a horse player, was at Belmont Park Racetrack, which is owned by the defendant, New York Racing Association. While at the track, Chung was using a voucher to place bets on the races through an automated betting machine. After placing a bet, Chung took his betting ticket but forgot his voucher, which had thousands of dollars left on it. A few minutes later, he returned to the machine, but the voucher was gone. Chung put an electronic stop on the voucher, but the voucher had been cashed out about one minute after it was left in the machine. Chung subsequently sued the racetrack,

arguing that the track was negligent in not requiring proof of identity when patrons cash out their vouchers, which constitute negotiable instruments. How did the court rule? Why? [*Doseung Chung v. New York Racing Ass'n.,* 714 N.Y.S.2d 429 (2000).]

9. Bond issued a $300,000 note to Goss in 1988. The note was secured by a deed of land. Goss later entered into an agreement to purchase commercial property owned by RAM. In lieu of partial payment, Gaetani, general partner of RAM, accepted the $300,000 note. Supanich, a trustee for Goss, endorsed the note. The note endorsement read: "For value received, the undersigned hereby assigns and transfers all right, title and interest in and to within Note to Toney E. Gaetani, Sr." The endorsement did not contain the words *without recourse.* Bond paid no principal and only partial interest on the note. Gaetani brought an action against Goss, Supanich, and Bond. At issue was whether the endorsement language allowed Gaetani to recover directly against Goss. Despite the lack of the words *without recourse,* the trial court held that Gaetani could not recover from Goss. Do you think the court allowed Gaetani to recover from Goss on appeal? *Gaetani v. Goss-Golden,* 84 Cal. App. 4th 1118 (2000).]

10. Margaret Glodt died on February 26, 1996. Lisa S. Mac was appointed as administrator of her estate. James Glodt, Margaret's nephew, refused to turn over Margaret's checkbooks. Margaret had

checking accounts at two banks. Mac closed the accounts on November 27, 1996. She received statements from both banks around February 1997. She realized that most of the funds had been withdrawn from the accounts around the time of Margaret's death. Mac obtained copies of the checks and learned they were forgeries. James had forged the checks before Margaret's death, but the banks did not make payment until shortly after her death. Mac sued both of the banks. The banks claimed that Mac's action was precluded by the one-year time limit for a customer to discover and report a check with an unauthorized signature. How do you think the court decided? [*Mac v. Bank of America,* 76 Cal. App. 562 (1999).]

11. David Marx maintained a checking account with Whitney National Bank. Marx's January 1995 statement contained evidence of five forged checks totaling $2,373. Marx never reviewed the statement. He added his two children, Stanley Marx and Maxine Marx, to the account in April 1995. Stanley Marx reviewed the May 1995 bank statement and discovered 17 forged checks totaling almost $13,000. Five of these checks, totaling $10,000, appeared for the first time on the May statement. Joel Goodman, David Marx's grandson, was both the maker and the payee of the forged instruments. The Marxes admitted that Joel had access to his grandfather's checkbook whenever he visited David Marx. Marx filed suit against Whitney, asserting that it was obligated to restore the $10,000 to his checking account. Marx admitted that he was negligent for not looking at his January through April statements; he asked only for recovery of the forged checks identified in the May statement. Whitney claimed that Marx failed to exercise reasonable care in the handling of his account. Do you think the court found for Marx? Why or why not? [*Marx v. Whitney National Bank,* 713 So. 2d 1142 (1998).]

12. Two New Jersey casinos cashed checks totaling $143,000 drawn by Seigel, one of its patrons, on his cash management account at Merrill Lynch. Seigel placed a stop-payment order on the checks, but Merrill Lynch paid them by mistake. Merrill Lynch argued that it "stood in the shoes" of the casinos to whom valid and enforceable checks were given and therefore Seigel had not suffered any actual loss as a result of the payment of the check. The trial court granted summary judgment for Merrill Lynch. How do you think the case was decided on appeal? [*Seigel v. Merrill Lynch,* 745 A.2d 301 (2000).]

Looking for more review material?

The Online Learning Center at **www.mhhe.com/kubasekess** contains this chapter's "Assignment on the Internet" and also a list of URLs for more information, entitled "On the Internet." Find both of them in the Student Center portion of the OLC, along with quizzes and other helpful materials.

Holder in Due Course, Liability, and Defenses

Stolen Money Orders and Holder in Due Course Status

In December 1990, Stacy Anne Dillabough presented two American Express money orders in the amounts of $550 and $650 to Chuckie's Enterprise, Inc., a check-cashing business in Pennsylvania.[1] Later, in February 1991, Robert Lynn presented an American Express money order in the amount of $200 to Chuckie's. All money orders were endorsed, and the payees showed photo identification when presenting the money orders. Consequently, Chuckie's cashed the money orders and gave the appropriate amounts of money to Dillabough and Lynn.

When Chuckie's presented these money orders for payment at the American Express bank, American Express refused to honor the money orders because it discovered that the numbers on the money orders had been logged as stolen.[2] Another individual, Robert Triffin, purchased the American Express money orders from Chuckie's and took assignment of all of Chuckie's rights in the money orders. Triffin thus brought suit against American Express, along with Dillabough and Lynn.

At trial, American Express argued that the money orders were nonnegotiable and that the language on the back of each money order stated that American Express would not pay if the money order was stolen. Triffin argued that by purchasing the money orders from Chuckie's, he gained a special legal status, called *holder in due course* status, and, therefore, American Express's defense was not applicable to him.

1. Who do you think should bear the costs of the stolen money orders? In other words, should American Express be required to pay Triffin? Why or why not?

2. Suppose you are a business manager at Chuckie's. You learn that the court holds that American Express does not have to pay for the stolen money orders. Would you make any changes in your business? Would you be less likely to accept American Express money orders in the future?

[1]"Digests of Recent Opinions: Superior Court," *Pennsylvania Law Weekly,* February 19, 1996, p. 15.
[2]Michael A. Riccardi, "High Court to Decide Status of Money Orders; Is Amex Liable For Stolen Blank Papers?" *The Legal Intelligencer,* July 10, 1996, p. 1.

After reading this chapter, you will be able to answer the following questions:

LO 1 What is a holder in due course?

LO 2 What requirements must be met to obtain holder in due course status?

LO 3 What is the shelter principle?

LO 4 In what ways has the holder in due course doctrine been abused?

LO 5 What information is needed to determine signature liability?

LO 6 What is warranty liability?

LO 7 How does one avoid liability for negotiable instruments?

LO 1

Holder in Due Course Doctrine

Suppose you want to purchase computers for your office building. You contract with a computer seller, Data Corp., to buy 50 computers. As partial payment, you give Data Corp. a note for $30,000. Data Corp. negotiates the note to Data Corp.'s landlord, Morgan, for payment of rent.

Suppose Morgan meets all the requirements (which you will soon learn) to be a holder in due course. You discover your computers are damaged, and you claim that Data Corp. breached its contract with you. If Data Corp. still held the $30,000 note, you could refuse to honor the note and claim as a defense that Data Corp. breached the contract. However, remember that Data Corp. negotiated the note to Morgan. Since Morgan is a holder in due course, you must pay Morgan because a holder in due course has higher rights to a negotiated instrument. If Morgan were simply a holder, you could use the defense of breach of contract against Morgan.

REASON FOR HOLDER IN DUE COURSE STATUS

Do you think the elevated holder in due course status is fair? The purpose of holder in due course status is to protect a financial intermediary. In other words, someone who processes a payment should not be required to shoulder the transaction risks. Thus, the legal system offers greater legal protection to certain parties to encourage them to engage in financial transactions.

LO 2

Requirements for Holder in Due Course Status

holder in due course (HDC)
An individual who acquires a negotiable instrument in good faith.

To be considered a holder in due course (HDC), a party must meet four requirements regarding the taking of the instrument. These requirements are established in UCC Section 3-302:

1. The party must be a holder of a complete and authentic negotiable instrument.
2. The holder must take the instrument for value.
3. The holder must take the instrument in good faith.
4. The holder must take the instrument without notice of defects.

Meeting these requirements is very valuable as the Case Nugget demonstrates.

CASE Nugget

HDC Status to the Rescue

Watson Coatings, Inc. v. American Express Travel Services, Inc.
U.S. Court of Appeals for the 8th Circuit

436 F.3d 1036 (2006)

Christine Mayfield used to work for Watson Coatings, Inc., and part of her role there included that of company treasurer. During her time as treasurer, Mayfield wrote approximately 45 to 47 checks from Watson's account to American Express for personal debt totaling $745,969.39. With each check that was submitted, American Express credited Mayfield's personal account. After Mayfield was dismissed from Watson Coatings, the money she had taken was discovered and suit was filed against American Express for taking the money from Mayfield despite the checks' having been clearly labeled as belonging to Watson Coatings, Inc.

The district court granted American Express's motion for summary judgment, but Watson filed an appeal. In the opinion written by Judge Smith, the extent to which American Express can be considered a holder in due course of the checks written by Mayfield was considered. The judge explained that because a payee can be considered a holder in due course, American Express would qualify. However, the court also needed to decide whether holder in due course status would offer any protection to American Express.

The appeals court found that even though Watson had brought forth several common law claims against American Express, the fact that American Express is a holder in due course can serve as a defense. The checks had been accepted by American Express in good faith, making it the holder in due course of the documents. Thus, the court affirmed the district court's grant of summary judgment to American Express.

Case 16-1 examines the required elements of holder in due course status. We consider the required elements in closer detail after the case.

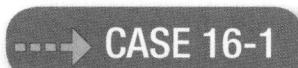 **CASE 16-1**

MICHAEL J. KANE, JR. v. GRACE KROLL
COURT OF APPEALS OF WISCONSIN
538 N.W.2d 605 (1995)

FACTS: *Michael Kane, Jr., sold Gerald Kroll, Jr., some cows. Gerald could not pay for the cows, so he arranged for his mother, Grace Kroll, to pay Kane. In exchange for her payment to Kane, Gerald planned to repay his mother with $6,100, the proceeds from his expected sale of a load of hay. Grace issued a personal check to Kane in the amount of $6,100. However, the next day, Gerald told his mother he would not be able to repay her because the sale of hay fell through. Thus, she stopped payment on the check to Kane. When Kane presented the check to the bank, the bank refused to pay.*

Kane filed suit against Grace to recover the $6,100. Grace argued that she had no legal obligation to repay Gerald's debt and thus no obligation to pay Kane. Kane argued that he was a holder in due course and was not subject to Grace's defense of failure of consideration. The trial court held that Kane was not a holder in due course because he did not prove he took the check in good faith and without notice of Grace's defenses. Kane appealed.

ISSUE: What are the requirements for a holder in due course?

REASONING: In the court's own words (abridged and slightly modified):

> The holder must take the instrument (1) for value; (2) in good faith; and (3) without notice that it is overdue or has been dishonored or of any defense against or claim to it on the part of any person. We examine each of these elements in turn.

First, a holder must take the instrument for value. A holder takes for value when he takes an instrument in payment for an antecedent claim against *any person*. In this case, Kane took the instrument from Grace in payment of Gerald's debt. . . .

Second, a holder must take the instrument in good faith, i.e., "honesty in fact in the conduct or transaction concerned." The holder's initial burden on the issues of notice and good faith is a slight one. As one commentator has noted:

> The burden of proof of the allegations in the Complaint rests upon the plaintiff. It is not necessary, however, that the plaintiff allege in the complaint that good faith was an integral part of the transaction at each stage. That is an affirmative defense which must be raised by the defendant, if at all.

In this case, Kane's affidavit supports his contention that he accepted the check in good faith for the payment of Gerald's antecedent debt. Moreover, none of the affidavits supplied by either party suggests evidence of bad faith on Kane's part. In the absence of such evidence, we conclude Kane took the check in good faith as a matter of law.

Finally, the last requirement to become a holder in due course is that the holder take the instrument without notice that it is overdue or has been dishonored or of any defense against it or claim to it on the part of any person. The knowledge of the defense for purposes of determining holder in due course status must exist at the time of issue. Therefore, we must examine whether Kane had knowledge of any defense at the time he took the check.

Because the requirement that a holder show that it did not have knowledge of a defense or claim to the instrument involves proof of a negative fact, the burden of proof is a slight one. In this case, the facts in Kane's affidavit suggest no knowledge of any claims or defenses, so the burden shifts to Grace to produce evidence that Kane had such knowledge. Grace argues that Kane was on notice that she had no preexisting obligation to pay her son's debt and that this constitutes knowledge of a defense.

DECISION AND REMEDY: The judge reversed and remanded the case. He decided that "Grace, like any drawer, had the power to stop payment on the check [and that stopping payment] does not constitute a defense that would prevent Kane from being a holder in due course. If it did, no holder would be a holder in due course because any drawer has the power to issue a stop payment order. . . . The fact that Gerald broke his promise to repay Grace the day after the check was issued does not affect Kane's status as a holder in due course. . . . Kane was a holder in due course."

SIGNIFICANCE OF THE CASE: The court spelled out the requirements for being a holder in due course.

CRITICAL THINKING

Are there ambiguities in the requirements one must meet to be a holder in due course? Did any ambiguity play a role in this decision?

ETHICAL DECISION MAKING

Think about the WPH process of ethical decision making. What is the ultimate purpose of the judge's decision that Kane was a holder in due course? In other words, what value was guiding the judge to conclude that Kane should receive holder in due course status?

BE A HOLDER OF A COMPLETE AND AUTHENTIC NEGOTIABLE INSTRUMENT

holder

A party in possession of a negotiable instrument.

Party Must Be a Holder First, as we mentioned earlier in the chapter, to be a holder in due course, a party taking the instrument must be a **holder**, a party who is in possession of an instrument that is payable to the party or to the bearer of the instrument [UCC Section 1-201(20)]. For example, if Adam Brewer possesses a check that states "Payable to Adam Brewer," Adam is a holder. However, suppose Adam asked his bank for a cashier's check to buy a boat from his

friend, Corey Baum. (See Figure 16-1.) Even though Adam possesses the cashier's check and his name appears on the check, he is not a holder of the check because it is payable to his friend. When Adam gives the cashier's check to his friend, Corey, the friend becomes the first holder of the cashier's check.

Similarly, if someone steals a check "Payable to Adam Brewer" and forges Adam's signature on the back of the check, this thief is not a holder of the check. (See Figure 16-2.) Because the check is payable to Adam Brewer and not the thief, the thief cannot be considered a holder, even if he forges Adam's name.

Instrument Must Be Negotiable Second, the instrument must be negotiable. A party cannot be a holder in due course of a nonnegotiable instrument. If an instrument lacks any of the requirements for negotiability as discussed in the previous chapter, the holder cannot be a holder in due course.

Instrument Must Be Complete and Authentic Third, the negotiable instrument must be complete and authentic [UCC 3-302(a)(1)]. When the instrument is issued or negotiated, the note must appear complete and authentic. What happens if the instrument is incomplete? For example, suppose that someone writing a check forgets to write the date on the check.

The UCC allows the holder to complete the check as long as the completion is consistent with the intent of the issuer (3-115). For example, suppose you write a check to a company to purchase some business supplies. Although you write the company's name, you forget to write the date. Under the UCC, the company may complete the instrument—in this instance, the check—by writing the date. However, if the person completes the instrument in a way that is inconsistent with the intent of the issuer, the instrument is considered materially altered.

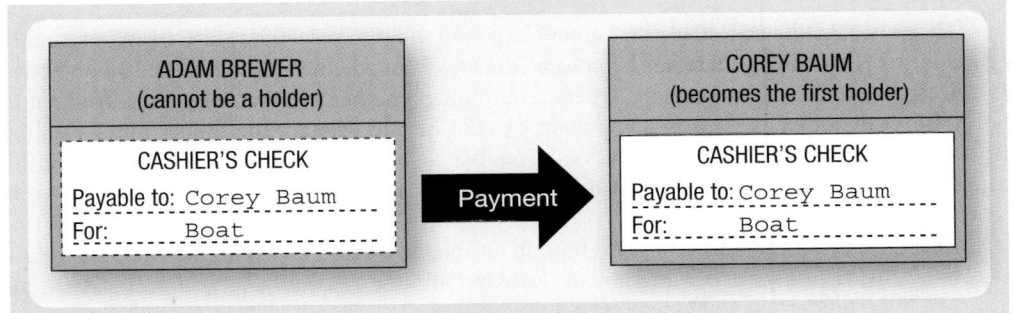

Figure 16-1

Illustration of the Relationship between Being a Payee and a Being a Holder

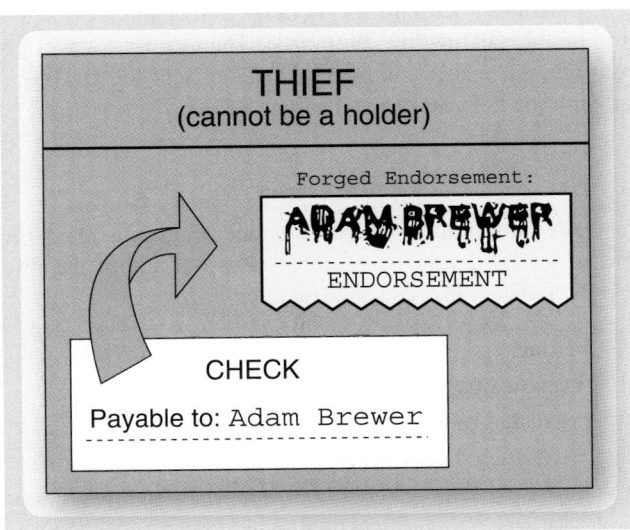

Figure 16-2

Illustration of a Failed Attempt to Become a Holder through Forgery

If an instrument has been clearly materially altered or is so irregular or incomplete that its authenticity is called into question, the UCC bars a person taking this flawed instrument from becoming a holder in due course [UCC 3-302(a)(1)].

TAKE INSTRUMENT FOR VALUE

The holder in due course must take the negotiable instrument "for value." In other areas of the law, taking something for value usually means taking something with consideration, a bargained-for promise. However, the for-value requirement is more stringent than consideration: The party must take the instrument in exchange for a promise that has already been performed. The UCC explicitly excludes from "value" any promises that have not yet been performed. In other words, the party must suffer an out-of-pocket loss (UCC 3-303). Why? If a party has not yet performed the promise, he or she has not completely committed financially to the transaction and thus should not receive special legal protection. Therefore, when a party receives a negotiable instrument as a gift or acquires it through mistake, the party will be a holder instead of an HDC.

A holder can take an instrument for value if the holder:

1. Performs the promise for which the instrument was issued.
2. Acquires a security interest or other lien in the instrument.
3. Takes the instrument for payment of a preceding claim.
4. Exchanges the instrument for another negotiable instrument.
5. Exchanges the instrument for an irrevocable obligation to a third party. [UCC 3-303(a)]

TAKE INSTRUMENT IN GOOD FAITH

The HDC must take the negotiable instrument in good faith [UCC 3-302(a)(2)(ii)]. What exactly is good faith? Historically, there has been some debate about whether *good faith* had an objective or subjective definition. For example, when determining whether a holder took an instrument in good faith in the objective sense, some courts would decide whether the holder purchased the instrument with a proper degree of caution through a usual and ordinary manner of conducting business. Looking at good faith in an objective sense means considering what the reasonable holder would have done.

However, other courts looked at good faith in a subjective sense by asking whether the holder acted honestly when taking the instrument. Looking at good faith in a subjective sense means considering the holder's actual behavior.

The UCC's definition of good faith is somewhere in the middle of the subjective and objective standards. The UCC defines good faith as "honesty in fact and the observance of reasonable commercial standards of fair dealing" [3-103(a)(4)]. Therefore, to act in good faith, a holder must not deviate from the reasonable commercial standards of fair dealing. The UCC drafters were most concerned with the fairness of the dealing.

TAKE INSTRUMENT WITHOUT NOTICE

Finally, a holder must take an instrument without notice of various claims to or defects of the negotiable instrument. If the holder has notice or is aware of any of the following defects, the holder cannot be an HDC [UCC3-302(a)]:

1. The instrument is overdue.
2. The instrument has been dishonored.
3. The instrument was issued as part of a series that is in default.
4. The instrument has been altered or contains an unauthorized signature.
5. There is a claim to the instrument. (These claims are described in Section 3-306.)
6. Another party has a defense or claim in recoupment to the instrument.

What Does It Mean to Have Notice? According to the UCC, a person has notice of a fact in any one of the following circumstances:

1. The person has actual knowledge of the fact.
2. The person receives notice or notification of it.
3. The facts and circumstances known to the person at the time in question give the person reason to know that the fact exists [UCC1-201(25)].

For example, suppose that Chuckie's, the check-cashing company in the Case Opener, received a letter from American Express that listed the numbers of the American Express money orders that had been stolen. As long as Chuckie's received this letter *before* it accidentally accepted the stolen money orders, Chuckie's would have notice of a defect and thus could not be a holder in due course. The UCC states that "to be effective, notice must be received at a time and in a manner that gives a reasonable opportunity to act on it" [3-302(f)].

Suppose that a person receives an instrument that has clearly been altered; however, the person taking the instrument does not inspect the instrument and thus does not notice the obvious alteration. As stated earlier, one of the requirements of becoming a holder in due course is that the holder accept a complete and authentic negotiable instrument [UCC 3-302(a)(1)]. Consequently, the question of a holder's awareness of such extreme irregularities does not matter; the very existence of such irregularities means that the holder cannot be a holder in due course.

If a person has notice of a defect before he or she gives value for the instrument but still gives value, the person will not be able to claim holder in due course status.

Overdue Instruments Suppose you accept a check from a business associate. Unfortunately, the check falls behind your desk and is lost for the next four months. If you try to negotiate this instrument to another party, that party will not be permitted to claim holder in due course status because the check is overdue. If a holder has notice that an instrument is overdue, the holder cannot claim holder in due course status. How does a holder know whether an instrument is overdue? Overdue status is dependent on the type of instrument. The UCC explains how two types of instruments—demand and time instruments—may be overdue (3-304).

Demand Instruments. A demand instrument, an instrument payable on demand, becomes overdue if it has been outstanding for an unreasonably long period of time after its date [UCC 3-304(a)(3)]. If the demand instrument is a check, the UCC states that the check is overdue 90 days after its date [3-304(a)(2)]. Thus, because your check has been outstanding for four months, it is overdue. The date on the check would give another party notice of its overdue status; thus, the party cannot claim HDC status.

demand instrument
A type of draft that allows the payee to demand payment at any time from a holder.

Time Instruments. A time instrument, an instrument payable at a definite time, becomes overdue at any time after the expressed due date on the instrument. Most of the rules regarding whether a time instrument is overdue depend on the payment structure of the instrument. For example, a time instrument may or may not be payable in installments. If the instrument requires that a party make payment in a lump sum rather than in installments, the instrument is overdue if the party does not make the lump-sum payment by the due date [UCC 3-304(b)(2)].

However, how does nonpayment of installments affect whether the instrument is overdue? Overdue status depends on whether a late payment applies to the principal or the interest on the instrument. If a party misses payment of an installment on the principal of an instrument, the instrument is overdue until this installment is paid [UCC 3-304(b)(1)]. However, if a party misses a payment of interest on this instrument, the instrument is not overdue [UCC 3-304(c)].

time instrument
A type of draft that allows the payee to collect payment only at a specific time in the future.

Why might a party have reason to know that an installment payment of principal was not made and thus the instrument is overdue? This information is usually included on a credit report. For example, if a bank is considering purchasing a consumer note from a retailer, the bank can determine whether all payments have been made on the note by looking at the consumer's credit report. If the credit report indicates that an installment had not been paid, the bank would have notice that the instrument was overdue.

dishonored
Refused; specifically, a payment that has been refused despite a holder's presenting an instrument in a timely and proper manner.

Dishonored Instruments If a holder is aware that an instrument he or she is taking has been dishonored, the holder cannot become an HDC. An instrument is dishonored when a party refuses

Exhibit 16-1

Defenses
and the Holder
in Due Course

A holder in due course is generally free from personal defenses but is subject to real defenses.
The holder in due course is *free* from the following personal defenses:

1. Lack or failure of consideration
2. Breach of contract
3. Fraud in the inducement in the underlying contract
4. Incapacity*
5. Illegality*
6. Duress*
7. Unauthorized completion or material alteration of the instrument
8. Unauthorized acquisition of the instrument

The HDC is *subject to* the following real defenses:

1. Fraud in the essence
2. Discharge of the party liable through bankruptcy
3. Forgery
4. Material alteration of a completed instrument
5. Infancy—when a party is below the legal age of consent

*Although an HDC cannot normally be submitted to the defenses of incapacity, illegality, or duress, these defenses do sometimes apply. If the incapacity, illegality, or duress was significant enough for a court to deem the original contract void, the HDC will be subject to that defense. Once incapacity (or illegality or duress) is present to the extent that the contract is void, the defense of incapacity (or illegality or duress) is a real defense. In other words, if the contract is void due to incapacity, illegality, or duress, a party can use that defense against an HDC.

to pay the instrument. For example, suppose you deposit a check from a customer into your company's account at a Wells Fargo bank. The customer has an account at Chase Manhattan. Wells Fargo credits your account and later presents the check for payment at Chase.

However, Chase refuses to pay because there are insufficient funds in your customer's account. Chase has dishonored the check and would likely stamp the phrase "insufficient funds" on your check. If you then tried to negotiate this check to another party, that party, seeing the words *insufficient funds,* would have notice that the check was dishonored.

However, if a party has no reason to know that a note has been dishonored, the party can become an HDC. Thus, if Chase did not stamp the phrase "insufficient funds" on the check, the new party would likely not have notice that the check was dishonored. Consequently, this new party could become an HDC.

Claims or Defenses If a party is aware of any claim or defense to an instrument, that party has notice and thus cannot become an HDC [UCC 3-302(a)(2)(v),(vi)]. However, if the party had no reason to know that various claims or defenses applied to an instrument even if the claims and defenses existed, the party would not be precluded from becoming an HDC.

Exhibit 16-1 provides a summary of the defenses that do and do not apply to the holder in due course.

LO 3 The Shelter Principle and HDC

shelter principle

The principle that when an item is transferred, the transferee acquires all the rights the transferor had to the item.

Generally, if an item is transferred from one person to another, the transferee acquires all the rights that the transferor had in the item. This idea is called the shelter principle [UCC Section 3-203(b)]. Therefore, following the shelter principle, even if a holder cannot attain holder in due course status, the holder can acquire the rights and privileges of an HDC *if* the item is being transferred *from* an HDC. Note that the instrument does not need to be transferred directly from an HDC for the recipient to have the rights of an HDC. Under the shelter principle, as long as the holder of an instrument can demonstrate that someone through the line of transfers had obtained the rights of an HDC, then all subsequent holders have the rights of an HDC.

Therefore, in the Case Opener, plaintiff Triffin received the American Express money orders from Chuckie's, a holder in due course. If Triffin did not qualify for HDC status on his own, he would have received the rights that Chuckie's, the transferor, had. In other words, Triffin is taking "shelter" in Chuckie's status as an HDC.

One exception to the shelter principle involves cases of fraud or other illegal activities. If a person engages in fraud or other illegal interference with an instrument, he or she may not become an HDC, even if obtaining the instrument later from an HDC.

The shelter principle may at first seem contrary to the idea of the HDC principle; however, the purpose of the shelter principle is to encourage the marketability of instruments. The greater protection offered to an HDC is very appealing; thus, allowing parties to achieve the rights of an HDC through the shelter principle encourages financial interactions.

Abuse of the Holder in Due Course Doctrine

LO 4

While HDC status offers great protection to financial intermediaries, the intermediaries might attempt to abuse this protection. For example, suppose you are starting a small business and a salesperson for a company called Office Supplies Made Easy comes to your new office and wants to sell you high-quality office supplies. You pay for the office supplies with a negotiable installment note on which you are supposed to pay three installments of $1,000. However, the next day, the Office Supplies Made Easy salesperson negotiates the note to a finance company.

When you receive your office supplies, you discover that the supplies are extremely low-quality and certainly not worth the $3,000 you agreed to pay. You call Office Supplies Made Easy, saying that you want to return the office supplies. However, an employee tells you that your installment note has been negotiated to the finance company, which became a holder in due course.

Consequently, the finance company calls your office every day because you have refused to pay for the low-quality supplies. You later discover that the finance company is in the practice of negotiating all notes from all salespersons of Office Supplies Made Easy. It appears to you that Office Supplies Made Easy and the finance company have some kind of arrangement so that the finance company can attain HDC status. Claims or defenses you have against Office Supplies Made Easy do not apply to the finance company.

When cases like this arise, judges look at the connection between the transferor and the transferee. If the companies are closely connected, as in the Office Supplies Made Easy example, some judges apply the salesperson's knowledge of your claims and defenses to the finance company. Consequently, this application prevents the finance company from achieving HDC status.

To ensure that companies cannot abuse the HDC status, the FTC created several rules in the 1970s that help to protect consumers against HDC abuse, as in the Office Supplies Made Easy example. The FTC rule requires that every consumer credit contract or any purchase money loan must contain the following statement in 10pt, boldface type:

> **ANY HOLDER OF THIS CONSUMER CREDIT CONTRACT IS SUBJECT TO ALL CLAIMS AND DEFENSES WHICH THE DEBTOR COULD ASSERT AGAINST THE SELLER OF GOODS OR SERVICES OBTAINED PURSUANT HERETO OR WITH THE PROCEEDS HEREOF. RECOVERY HEREUNDER BY THE DEBTOR SHALL NOT EXCEED AMOUNTS PAID BY THE DEBTOR HEREUNDER.**[3]

Consequently, no subsequent holder of the contract will have the rights of an HDC.

Liability

As you have seen, it is not always clear who should bear responsibility for the amount of a negotiable instrument. The following sections explain the various ways a party may be liable for a negotiable instrument. First, when a person signs a negotiable instrument, he or she is potentially

[3] FTC Holder in Due Course Regulations, 16 C.F.R. 433.2 (1978).

Negotiable Instruments in England and Similarities to the HDC Doctrine in the United States

In England, the doctrine of privity of contract declares that contracts are exclusive to those who created them. However, this doctrine often limits and complicates business transactions. The problems created by privity of contract in England can be countered by using a negotiable instrument. Unlike contracts, in England bills of exchange, promissory notes, and checks can be negotiated between parties.

Negotiable instruments are used in business, in England as in the United States, to facilitate business transactions. To ease the exchange and free flow of money in business transactions, businesses need to be able to transfer quickly money or other forms of payment. In the United States, companies can transfer their right to collect or their duty to perform under a contract. The English practice of privity prevents similar transfers. Accordingly, English businesses must be able to transfer money a different way in order to conduct regular business. It is the ease of transferability of negotiable instruments and the rights that come with a transferred negotiable instrument, as outlined in this chapter, that make negotiable instruments an ideal way for English businesses to avoid the problems created by the privity requirement.

signature liability
Liability attributed because of a party's signature on an instrument.

warranty liability
Liability attributed when the transfer of an instrument breaches a warranty associated with an instrument.

LO 5

primarily liable
Liable for paying the amount designated on an instrument when it is presented for payment.

maker
A person who has promised to pay a set sum to the holder of a promissory note or certificate of deposit.

acceptor
A person (drawee) who accepts and signs a draft to agree to pay the draft when it is presented.

secondarily liable
Liable for paying the amount designated on an instrument should the primarily liable party default.

endorser
One who issues an endorsement.

liable for the instrument. This type of liability is called signature liability. Second, in contrast, a party may be liable if the transfer of the instrument breaches a warranty associated with the instrument. This type of liability is called warranty liability. After we consider both signature and warranty liability, we examine the defenses to these types of liability. Finally, we investigate how liability for a negotiable instrument may be discharged.

Signature Liability

UCC Section 3-401(a) imposes liability if the party, or the party's agent, signs the instrument. If a party does not sign, the party cannot be held liable. Because the signature on an instrument leads to liability, it is important to know what counts as a signature. According to the UCC, a signature can be any name, word, mark, or symbol used by a party to authenticate a writing [3-401(b)]. Thus, if you wrote either your full name or an *X* with the intent to authenticate an instrument, either writing would constitute a signature.

PRIMARY LIABILITY OF MAKERS AND ACCEPTORS

A party who is primarily liable for an instrument must pay the stated amount on the instrument when it is presented for payment. This liability for the stated amount begins as soon as the instrument is issued. Moreover, the primarily liable party must pay without resorting to any other party. For example, suppose you own a business and write a check drawing on your funds in your business account at First National Bank. First National has primary liability for the check; it must pay the stated amount when the check is presented for payment.

The UCC establishes that certain parties—makers and acceptors—are primarily liable. First, a maker is a party who has promised to pay. For example, the maker of a promissory note is primarily liable for the amount of the note because that party has promised to pay the amount of the instrument. Moreover, UCC Section 3-412 states that a party who signs as an issuer of an instrument is liable for the amount of the instrument as soon as it is issued. For example, a bank that issues a cashier's check is primarily liable for the amount of the check as soon as the cashier's check is created (UCC 4-412).

Second, an acceptor, a drawee of a draft who accepts and signs the draft to agree to pay the draft when it is presented, is primarily liable [UCC 3-413(a)]. A party who accepts a draft by signing on the face of the draft is primarily liable (UCC 3-413). For example, when a bank accepts a check, it is primarily liable for the amount of the check (UCC 3-409).

SECONDARY LIABILITY OF DRAWERS AND ENDORSERS

A party who is secondarily liable for an instrument must pay the amount on the instrument if the primarily liable party defaults. Drawers and endorsers are secondarily liable parties. An endorser

E-COMMERCE and the Law

Signatures and the Internet

On June 30, 2000, the Electronic Signatures in Global and National Commerce Act (the *E-Sign Act*) became federal law. The E-Sign Act gives legal force to digital signatures and online contracts in financial, business, consumer, personal, and government contexts. For example, the act covers loan transactions made, insured, or guaranteed by the federal government. The act applies to "transferable records" and states that any instrument that is a loan relating to real property and that would be considered a note under Article 3 of the UCC is considered a transferable record. Thus, students can now electronically sign their student loans. Furthermore, citizens can file and digitally sign their tax returns.

What exactly is a digital signature? A *digital signature* is a personal identifier that can be broken into electronic code. In other words, the signer "stamps" a document with his or her "signature" by placing data unique to the signer on it. Currently, there are two types of digital signatures: biometric and key-based signatures. Biometric digital signatures stamp the document with unique physical characteristics such as a fingerprint. Key-based signatures use digital "keys." The signer has a public key and a private key. These keys scramble information so that only parties with appropriate keys may read the information. The signer can use the private key to sign documents.

David M. Nadler and Valerie M. Furman, "Landmark Electronic Signatures Legislation Becomes Effective," *Derivatives Litigation Reporter,* February 26, 2001.

is a party who signs an instrument to restrict payment of it, negotiate it, or incur liability [UCC 3-204(b)]. A **drawer** is a person who signs as a party ordering payment [UCC 3-103(a)(5)].

For example, if you write a check from your bank account that is payable to the electric company, you are the drawer of the check, the bank is the drawee, and the electric company is the holder of the check. The holder of the check (the electric company) presents the check to the drawee (the bank) for payment. **Presentment** is defined in the UCC as making a demand for the drawee to pay [3-501(a)]. The UCC creates specific rules that govern the time and manner of presentment.

Suppose the holder (the electric company) presented your check and the bank dishonored the check because of insufficient funds in your account. The UCC states that drawers of drafts are liable for an instrument only after it has been dishonored (3-414, 3-415). Thus, you (the drawer) are now liable for the check.

Three conditions must be met for a drawer or endorser to become liable. First, the holder of the instrument must present the instrument in a proper and timely fashion. Second, the instrument must be dishonored. Third, notice of the dishonor must be given to the drawer.

Presentment An instrument must be presented in a proper and timely manner. First, the instrument must be presented to the proper party. If the instrument is a note, the holder must present the note to the maker of the note. In contrast, if the instrument is a draft, the holder must present the instrument to the drawee. Thus, continuing our electric company example, the electric company must present the check to the bank (the drawee).

Second, the instrument must be presented to the proper party in a proper way. UCC Section 3-501(b) states that an instrument can be presented (1) by any commercially reasonable means, (2) through a clearinghouse procedure, or (3) at the place designated in the instrument.

Third, the instrument must be presented to the proper party in a timely manner. Thus, if the instrument is a note, the holder must present the note to the maker on the note's due date. If the instrument is a draft, such as a check, the holder must present the instrument within a *reasonable* time. The failure to present an instrument on time is the most common reason that improper presentment occurs, ultimately discharging unqualified endorsers from secondary liability.

Dishonor When a holder presents an instrument within a timely and proper manner but acceptance or payment is refused, the instrument has been *dishonored*. The instrument must be explicitly dishonored; a refusal to pay does not necessarily mean that the instrument has been dishonored. For example, suppose you are a holder of a check that is payable to your business. You present this check for payment, but the bank refuses to pay the check because you cannot present identification [UCC 3-501(b)(2)]. Likewise, a bank may refuse to pay on an instrument because the endorsement of the instrument is not proper. Again, this refusal to pay does not dishonor the

drawer
The party that writes an order, or the person who writes a check.

Presentment
The act of making a demand for the drawee to pay.

instrument. Remember, a secondarily liable party becomes liable *only* if a primarily liable party dishonors the instrument.

Notice of Dishonor The UCC provides a specific timeline in which notice of dishonor of an instrument must be given to a secondarily liable party (3-503). (The process of determining secondary liability is summarized in Exhibit 16-2.) If the party that dishonors an instrument is a collection bank, it must give notice before midnight of the next day [UCC 3-503(c)]. Other parties must give notice of the dishonor within 30 days of the day on which they receive notice of dishonor. This notice can be given in any commercially reasonable manner: oral, written, or electronic communication [UCC 3-503(b)]. The notice must identify the instrument in question and state that this instrument has been dishonored. If the word *dishonored* appears on the instrument, this writing is enough to constitute notice. As long as the holder gives notice to the secondarily liable parties about the dishonor of the instrument, the holder can sue the other parties.

If all three of these conditions are met, the holder can bring suit against a secondarily liable party. However, in most cases, while a secondarily liable party may have to pay a holder the amount of the instrument, the secondarily liable party can then seek recourse against the primarily liable party.

In the event an instrument contains more than one endorsement, each endorser is liable for the full amount to any subsequent endorser or to any holder. The secondary liability established through endorsement requires that an endorser pay anyone who endorses the instrument after him or her.

ACCOMMODATION PARTIES

Suppose that, after you graduate from college, you decide to start your own business. You need to borrow a significant amount of money from the bank, and you plan to create a promissory note. However, because you have never owned your own business and have little credit history, the bank is a little wary about whether you will be able to pay the note. Therefore, the bank decides to ask you to have a third party sign the note to ensure the bank will be paid. Consequently, your business law professor cosigns your note. This third party is called an **accommodation party**, a party who signs an instrument to provide credit for another party who has also signed the instrument [UCC 3-419(a)].

Accommodation parties may be primarily or secondarily liable for an instrument and can sign as makers, drawers, acceptors, or endorsers. However, accommodation parties more frequently sign as makers or endorsers. As a maker, an accommodation party has primary liability, but as an endorser, the party has secondary liability.

accommodation party
A party who signs an instrument to provide credit for another party who has also signed the instrument.

Exhibit 16-2

Summary of Process of Determining Secondary Liability

	NOTE	DRAFT
Holder must present instrument to?	Maker	Drawee
When should the instrument be presented?	On due date	Reasonable time; if a check, 30 days within date of check or 30 days within time of endorsement
If the instrument is presented and dishonored, who is usually now liable for the instrument?	Any endorser	Drawer or endorser
What are the requirements for an instrument to be officially dishonored so that a holder may then turn to secondarily liable parties?	1. Present to maker for payment 2. Maker dishonors 3. Holder gives notice of dishonor to secondarily liable parties (endorsers)	1. Present to drawee for payment 2. Drawee dishonors 3. Holder gives timely notice of dishonor to drawer or endorsers

Suppose you, in the example above, cannot pay your note, and your business professor, as an accommodation party, pays the note instead. This professor has a right of reimbursement to recover the money from you, the accommodated party [UCC 3-419(e)]. If, however, you, the accommodated party, pay the note when it is due, you cannot force the professor to contribute to the amount due on the loan.

UNAUTHORIZED SIGNATURES AND ENDORSEMENTS

As a general rule, if a signature to a negotiable instrument is unauthorized, the signature will not impose liability to the named party. This rule applies to two cases: forgery and unauthorized agents.

First, return to the accommodation party example above. Suppose you forged your business law professor's name to ensure that you would get your money to start your new business. If you could not pay on the note, your business law professor would not be forced to pay on the basis of the forged signature. Similarly, this rule applies to parties who forge the drawer's signature on a check. However, forgery in the employment context is treated differently, as we explain below in the section entitled "The Fictitious-Payee Rule."

Second, if an agent is not authorized to sign a negotiable instrument on behalf of a principal, the principal will generally not be liable for the instrument. Consequently, the agent would be personally liable for the instrument. However, if the principal decides to **ratify,** or approve of, the unauthorized agent's signature, the principal will then become liable for the instrument while the agent will escape personal liability [UCC 3-403(a)].

ratify
To approve an unauthorized agent's signature on an instrument.

How does a principal ratify an unauthorized signature? A principal could explicitly approve of the signature. For example, a Florida court held that a principal could not recover the amount of two checks he gave to his agent because the principal had ratified the signatures.[4] The agent, who was supposed to deposit two checks into the principal's account, forged the principal's signature and deposited the checks into the agent's account. The agent ultimately told the principal about the forged checks and the location of the money. The principal did nothing until the agent later ran away with the money, and the court ruled that the principal's inaction was the same as his approval of his signature.

Alternatively, if the principal accepts the benefits associated with this unauthorized signature, the principal in effect ratifies the signature by his or her conduct. For example, in *Rakestraw v. Rodriguez,*[5] a husband had forged his wife's signature in order to obtain a loan to start a grocery store. A few days later, the wife discovered the forgery, but she did nothing to correct it, and even participated in the business over the next few years. Part of running the business included sharing in the profits from the grocery store. When the business failed, the wife tried to avoid liability, claiming her husband forged her signature. The court ruled that her actions in sharing in profits and in helping run the business effectively ratified her signature.

This ratification of an unauthorized signature does not exclusively apply to the agent-principal relationship. Your business law professor could similarly choose to ratify your unauthorized signature of his name and thus would be liable for your promissory note.

However, these are some exceptions to the general rule that an unauthorized signature is not enforceable. Generally, the policy behind these exceptions is that courts want to place the burden on the parties who are in the best position to take a loss or take action to recover a loss. Moreover, particularly in regard to the last two rules that are discussed below (the imposter rule and the fictitious-payee rule), the court focuses on the intent of the party who is issuing the instrument.

Negligence In some cases, a party's negligence does not permit the party to escape liability for an unauthorized signature. If the party whose signature was forged behaved so negligently as to "substantially contribute to . . . the making of a forged signature," the party may be precluded from escaping liability (UCC 3-406).

For example, in *Thompson Maple Products v. Citizens National Bank,* Thompson[6] was a corporation that manufactured bowling pins from maple logs. Thompson would accept loads of logs

[4] *Fulka v. Florida Commercial Banks, Inc.,* 371 So. 2d 521 (Fla. Dist. Ct. App. 1979).

[5] 500 P.2d 1401 (Cal. 1972).

[6] 234 A.2d 32 (Pa. Super. Ct. 1967).

from timber owners. When a load arrived at the mill, a Thompson employee filled out a scaling slip that listed the name of the owner, along with the quantity and grade of the logs. Thompson office employees then used the slips to prepare checks for the owners of the logs. A Thompson employee, Emery Albers, took blank scaling slips and filled them out for fictitious loads of logs. The office employees, thinking the slips represented real loads of wood, then prepared checks for payment. Albers took the checks, forged the name of the owner of the logs, and cashed the checks or deposited them into his bank account at Citizens National Bank. The court ruled that Thompson "substantially contributed" to the forgeries because the blank scaling slips used to record loads of logs were easily accessible. In fact, office employees gave Albers two entire pads of these slips. Moreover, even though it was company policy for the slips to be initialed by authorized employees who were accepting the loads, Thompson office employees created checks even for slips that were not authorized. Thus, Thompson's negligence led to the conclusion that Thompson should be liable.

The Imposter Rule Suppose that Jamaar, a business manager, has been communicating through e-mail with Carlie, a potential employee. Jamaar has scheduled a meeting with Carlie. However, Samantha, without Carlie's knowledge, decides to impersonate Carlie at the interview. Samantha (as Carlie) tells Jamaar she will strongly consider signing an employment agreement if Jamaar will issue her a $200 check as a presigning bonus. Jamaar agrees and issues the check to Carlie that day. Samantha forges Carlie's name and deposits the check into her own account. Will Jamaar be liable for the amount of the check?

Jamaar's signature has not been forged; he clearly signed the check with intent to transfer money to Carlie. But he did not know that Carlie was actually Samantha. Is Samantha's signature considered a forgery? No. Under the UCC's imposter rule, if a maker or drawer issues a negotiable instrument to an imposter, the imposter's endorsement will be effective [UCC 3-404(a)]. The court considers the intent of the drawer or maker when issuing the instrument. Because Jamaar intended for Samantha (as Carlie) to have the instrument, her endorsement of the instrument is considered valid. Moreover, it is easier for Jamaar as maker or drawer to identify the true identity of Carlie than it would be for a later holder of the check to do so. Perhaps you are surprised by the imposter rule. The UCC, as stated, places an immense responsibility on Jamaar to ensure that he is not being duped. What values are in conflict here? Should Jamaar be forced to shoulder this responsibility?

The Fictitious-Payee Rule Suppose now that Jamaar, who has been authorized to write checks from the company account, draws bonus checks from the company account for five more potential employees. Unfortunately, Jamaar never actually interviewed these employees; thus, these people are not entitled to the bonuses. Jamaar takes these checks, which are made out to the fictitious potential employees, endorses the checks in their names, and deposits these checks into his personal bank account. These potential employees have no interest (i.e., no right to payment) in the checks and are thus called fictitious payees (UCC 3-404, 3-405). As with the endorsement in the imposter case, Jamaar's endorsement of the fictitious payees is not considered forgery [UCC 3-404(b)(2)]. Jamaar's company will be liable for the checks.

Why is the company liable? Courts view the company as being in a better position to bear the loss of the checks. The loss has occurred because Jamaar, a company employee, has acted wrongly. Although the company is liable for the amounts of the checks, the company can recover the money from Jamaar.

Warranty Liability

In the previous section, we explained how a party might be liable for an instrument on the basis of his or her signature on the instrument. In this section, we consider another type of liability: *warranty liability.* A party may be liable for an instrument because of a breach of warranty. There are two relevant types of warranties here: transfer warranties and presentment warranties.

imposter rule
A rule that holds that if one obtains a negotiable instrument by impersonating another and endorses it with the impersonated party's signature, the loss falls on the drawer of the instrument.

fictitious payee
Someone having no right to payment. The UCC fictitious-payee rule governs the liability of companies and their endorsed checks: Any check made out to a fictitious payee and endorsed must be honored and is not considered a forgery.

LO 6

Management

As the "Signature Liability" section has illustrated, employees of a company may engage in unethical behavior in their handling of checks. Therefore, employers have the important responsibility of hiring employees who will not engage in such questionable behavior. Selecting the best candidates for hire typically involves three methods. First, employers request that candidates provide background information by submitting applications, résumés, and references. Second, employers often interview prospective employees to obtain more information from the candidates and, at times, evaluate their responses to hypothetical situations. Third, employers may require that candidates take ability tests, job performance tests, personality tests, and drug tests. These three methods of the employee selection process are designed not only to help employers hire the best employees but also to ensure that employers do not hire candidates who have previously participated in unethical behavior for other employers. These methods do not guarantee that employees will behave ethically, particularly when handling checks, but this selection process might reduce the likelihood that an employer will hire a questionable employee.

Source: K. Williams, *Management: A Practical Introduction* (New York: McGraw-Hill/Irwin, 2006), pp. 286–289.

TRANSFER WARRANTY

A negotiable instrument can be transferred from one party to another. A party who transfers a negotiable instrument to another party in good faith for consideration creates **transfer warranties** regarding the instrument and the transfer itself [UCC 3-416(a)]. Transfer warranties always apply to the party to whom the instrument is transferred (the transferee).

transfer warranties
Warranties regarding a negotiable instrument and its transfer; created by a party who transfers the instrument.

When a party transfers an instrument for consideration, he or she warrants:

1. The transferor is entitled to enforce the negotiable instrument.
2. Signatures on the instrument are authentic and authorized.
3. The instrument has not been altered.
4. The instrument is not subject to a defense or claim in recoupment.
5. The transferor has no knowledge of insolvency proceedings against the maker, acceptor, or drawer of the instrument. [UCC 3-416(a)]

If the transfer is through endorsement, these warranties apply to any future holders. However, if the transfer does not occur through endorsement, the warranties apply only to the transferee.

These rules on whether the warranties apply to future holders or only to the immediate transferee are important because liability can be imposed for breach of warranty. If the warranties apply and there is a breach of one of the warranties, the parties can bring suit against the transferor, the warrantor, for damages suffered as a result of the breach [UCC 3-416(b)].

As soon as a transferee discovers that a breach of warranty has occurred, he or she can bring suit against the transferor. However, the transferee must give notice of the breach-of-warranty claim to the transferor within 30 days of discovering the breach [UCC 3-416(c)]. If the transferee does not give notice within 30 days of discovering the breach, the warranty will be discharged to some extent. If the transferred instrument is a check, the warranties cannot be disclaimed [UCC 3-416(c)].

While warranties on checks cannot be disclaimed, they can be disclaimed on other instruments. When parties agree to a disclaimer, an endorser can disclaim warranties by including in the endorsement the phrase *without warranties*. This endorsement is similar to the restrictive endorsement *without recourse,* which you learned about in the previous chapter. However, *without warranties* disclaims warranty liability, whereas *without recourse* disclaims contract liability.

PRESENTMENT WARRANTY

In the "Signature Liability" section, we discussed the requirements for a negotiable instrument to be properly presented for payment. Certain warranties are associated with the presentment of an instrument. Remember, presentment occurs when a party properly presents an instrument for acceptance and the party to whom it was presented accepts the instrument or pays it in good faith.

presentment warranty
A warranty covering the parties accepting an instrument for payment; created to ensure that the accepting or paying party is paying the proper party.

Why are presentment warranties needed? Parties who accept or pay instruments may worry that they are not paying the proper party. Thus, while transfer warranties apply to the transferee, presentment warranties cover parties who accept instruments for payment. Both the party presenting the instrument and any previous transferor of the instrument make presentment warranties. Therefore, if there is a breach of presentment warranty, the acceptor can recover damages from the presenting party or previous transferors. As with the notice rule for transfer warranties, a party must give notice of a breach of presentment warranty within 30 days.

There are two types of presentment warranties. These types depend on what kind of instrument is being presented to a certain kind of party. When a party presents an unaccepted draft to a drawee, the holder guarantees:

1. The warrantor of the instrument is entitled to enforce the instrument.
2. The instrument has not been altered.
3. The warrantor has no knowledge that the drawer's signature or the draft is unauthorized. [UCC 3-417(a)]

These warranties apply only to a drawee who pays or accepts a draft in good faith.

If the instrument is not an unaccepted draft presented to a drawee, only one presentment warranty applies. The party presenting the instrument guarantees that the warrantor is or was entitled to payment or authorized to obtain payment [UCC 3-417(d)(1)]. In other words, only warranty 1 listed above applies to presentments of instruments other than unaccepted drafts.

Case 16-2 considers whether a bank that cashed forged checks gives presentment and transfer warranties.

····▶ CASE 16-2

HALLIBURTON ENERGY SERVICES, INC. v.
FLEET NATIONAL BANK
U.S. DISTRICT COURT FOR THE SOUTHERN DISTRICT
OF TEXAS, HOUSTON DIVISION
334 F. Supp. 2d 930 (2004)

FACTS: *On March 20, 2000, Halliburton issued a check, drawn on a Citibank account, to Arthur Andersen for $215,000. The check was deposited in the U.S. mail. An unknown person stole the check from the mail and then altered the payee to "Paul A. Schumacher."*

On March 27, 2000, a person claiming to be Paul A. Schumacher opened a Fleet brokerage account from the bank's Internet site. The person posing as Paul A. Schumacher endorsed the altered check by signing the name "Paul A. Schumacher" on the back and presented it to Fleet, which honored it. Fleet then presented the check to Citibank, the drawee/payor bank. On March 30, 2000, Citibank charged Halliburton's checking account the sum of $215,000 because Citibank had paid the check in full.

On May 15, 2000, Arthur Andersen informed Halliburton it had not received the $215,000 check. A Halliburton employee working for Accounts Payable then contacted Citibank and learned that the check had been paid. On May 17, Halliburton requested the original check from Citibank. On receiving and examining the check, Halliburton saw that the payee's name had been altered and that the check had been endorsed by the fictitious payee, Paul A. Schumacher, "for deposit only."

On June 26, 2000, Citibank notified Fleet that Fleet had honored a fraudulently altered check and asked for prompt reimbursement of what Citibank deemed a wrongful payment. The request was denied. Citibank then assigned any claim it may have against Fleet to Halliburton. Halliburton sued, and filed for summary judgment.

ISSUE: When is a bank liable when it honors a check made out to a fictitious payee?

REASONING: In the court's own words:

> An impostor is "one who pretends to be someone else to deceive others, esp. to receive the benefits of a negotiable instrument," or "a person who practices deception under an assumed character, identity or name."

The impostor rule applies when a bank has honored a check made out to a fictitious payee. If the impostor's endorsement is effective, the collecting bank then becomes a "holder in due course." . . . Even a forger can effectively endorse an instrument. Unless the depository bank knew about the forgery, there is no breach of presentment warranty when the depository bank presents it to the drawee. Therefore, in such circumstances, the presenting bank is not liable for the drawer's or drawee's loss.

. . . The drawee may override the depository/collecting/presenting bank's affirmative defense only if the collecting bank failed "to exercise ordinary care in paying or taking the instrument and that failure contributed to loss resulting from the payment of the instrument." The "ordinary care" standard is just that: It does not mandate that a depository bank engage in peculiar vigilance. . . .

If the drawee bank can establish that the collecting bank failed to exercise ordinary care, the drawee may recover from the presenting bank "to the extent the failure to exercise ordinary care contributed to the loss."

DECISION AND REMEDY: The court found that "Halliburton has not presented evidence that Fleet was anything other than a holder in due course. In other words, Halliburton has not offered evidence of Fleet's bad faith, e.g., that Fleet's employees connived with the forger. Nor has Halliburton provided any evidence that Fleet had reason to believe the check had been fraudulently altered." The summary judgment motion was denied.

SIGNIFICANCE OF THE CASE: This case spells out when a bank that accepts a forged check provides warranties.

CRITICAL THINKING

The motion for summary judgment was denied because there was too much omitted information. As a judge, what information would you deem relevant that was missing from the case? Why is the missing information relevant to this case?

ETHICAL DECISION MAKING

Ethical reasoning requires consideration of all the relevant parties affected by the action on question. Who besides the BANK THAT HONORED THE CHECK AND Haliburton are affected by the issue in this set of facts?

Avoiding Liability for Negotiable Instruments

LO 7

If a party tries to enforce a negotiable instrument, a defendant can try to avoid liability in two ways. First, the defendant can try to claim a defense to liability. Second, the defendant can try to claim that the liability has been discharged.

DEFENSES TO LIABILITY

Earlier in the chapter, we listed defenses to liability that do or do not apply to a holder in due course. Here, we return to these defenses to liability. There are two categories of defenses: real defenses and personal defenses. **Real defenses,** also called universal defenses, apply to all parties. **Personal defenses** do not apply to holders in due course.

real defense
A liability defense that applies universally to all parties.

personal defense
A liability defense that is not applicable to holders in due course.

Real Defenses A party's right to enforce a negotiable instrument is subject to the following real defenses:

1. Infancy (being below the legal age of consent), to the extent that it makes a contract void.
2. Duress, to the extent that it makes a contract void.

3. Lack of legal capacity, to the extent that it makes a contract void.

4. Illegality of the transaction, to the extent that it makes a contract void.

5. Fraud in the factum.

6. Discharge through insolvency proceedings (bankruptcy).

7. Forgery.

8. Material alteration.

The first six defenses are stated explicitly in UCC Section 3-305. As we discussed earlier in this chapter, the UCC establishes forgery as a defense to liability because a party must have signed the instrument to be held liable. Finally, a material alteration of an instrument discharges a party of a liability [UCC 3-407(a)].

fraud in the factum
A liability defense available to a party who signs a negotiable instrument without knowing that it is a negotiable instrument.

Fraud in the Factum. When a party signs a negotiable instrument without knowing that it is, in fact, a negotiable instrument, the party can claim fraud in the factum (also called *fraud in the execution* and *fraud in the essence*) as a defense. For example, suppose Michael Jordan believes he is signing an autograph for a fan, but he is actually signing a promissory note. Because he did not intend to sign a negotiable instrument, he will not be held liable for the instrument.

Similarly, suppose you, a business manager, are negotiating with another company to purchase materials for your manufacturing business. After your negotiations, the company asks you to sign a document as a preorder for the materials. You hurriedly sign the document and leave. However, instead of signing a preorder, you have actually signed a note. Will you be held liable for this note? In this case, it depends on the extent to which the signing party had reason to know what he was signing.

For another illustration of these issues, see the Case Nugget.

CASE Nugget

Defense of Ignorance?

Laborer's Pension Fund v. A & C Envtl., Inc.
U.S. Court of Appeals for the 7ᵗʰ Circuit

301 F.3d 762 (2002)

A & C Environmental, Inc., is a corporation that transports and disposes of nonhazardous waste. In April 1999, A & C was asked to complete a job in Gary, Indiana, which prompted representatives from Laborer's Pension Fund to approach the company. Frattini of the fund asked Clark of A & C to sign a form that would guarantee the five individuals who would work in Gary, Indiana, the coverage of the local union. Clark was hesitant to sign the agreement because he feared that if someone within his company were covered under the union, the entire company would then be covered. It wasn't until after Frattini of the fund guaranteed Clark that the only employees of A & C who would be affected would be those working in Gary, Indiana, that the agreement was signed. When A & C did not pay dues for all of its employees, the fund brought suit for delinquent contributions.

The district court ruled against the fund as a result of the fraud-in-the-execution defense that was brought forth by A & C. The court decided that any reasonable juror would believe that Clark did not know that he was agreeing to pay the fund dues for each employee of A & C. The fund appealed to the U.S. Seventh Circuit Court of Appeals.

In the opinion written by Judge Ripple, the Seventh Circuit found that Clark may not have known what he was agreeing to. Unlike the district court, however, the appeals court found that Clark had a reasonable opportunity to review the document, which was written in English. Although Frattini of the fund had misrepresented the contents of the document to Clark, there was an opportunity to review the document that established dues for all employees of A & C. Thus, the court of appeals reversed the decision of the district court.

Although fraud in the factum is a real defense, courts have held that the signer's experience may determine whether the signer should have known what he or she was actually signing. Recall the situation with Jamaar in which he was solely responsible for ensuring the identity of the individual he was signing a check to. However, that level of responsibility is not required of Michael Jordan in this situation. Can you account for the difference in the two situations, pointing out the differing values and ethical norms?

As another example, consider *Schaeffer v. United Bank & Trust Co.*[7] United Bank sued Schaeffer to collect on a promissory note Schaeffer had signed as an accommodation maker. However, the Maryland court ultimately ruled that Schaeffer was not liable due to fraud in the factum. It turns out Schaeffer barely knew how to read, did not understand the document he was signing, and was lied to by the note's maker, who had told Schaeffer that Schaeffer's signature would serve as a character witness. The court ruled that United Bank was not a holder in due course and was subjected to Schaeffer's defense even if the bank were a holder in due course as the note was void due to fraud in the factum.

Material Alteration. The UCC defines a *material alteration* as "an unauthorized change in an instrument that purports to modify in any respect the obligation of a party, or an unauthorized addition of words or numbers or other change to an incomplete instrument relating to the obligation of a party" (3-407). Only unauthorized changes that affect the rights of the party are considered material alterations. Changes that typically fall under UCC Section 3-407 include changes to the parties to the instrument, the amount of the instrument, the date the instrument is due, and the applicable interest rate.

If the material alteration is fraudulent, the party whose rights have been affected by the change is completely discharged from the instrument [UCC 3-407(b)]. However, if the material alteration is not fraudulent, the instrument will be enforced only under the original terms.

Personal Defenses Personal defenses apply to holders, not holders in due course. Personal defenses can be divided into two categories. First, there are general defenses that can be asserted against the defendant on general contract theory. These defenses include:

1. Breach of contract or warranty.
2. Lack or failure of consideration.
3. Fraud in the inducement.
4. Illegality.
5. Mental incapacity.

Second, the UCC lists specific personal defenses created by provisions of Article 3. These defenses, summarized in Exhibit 16-3, include the following:

1. Defense of nonissuance, conditional issuance, or issuance for a special purpose [3-105(b)].
2. Defense of modification or nullification of an obligation by a separate agreement (3-117).
3. Defense of nondelivery of the instrument [3-105(b)].
4. Defense of unauthorized, nonfraudulent completion of an instrument (3-115).

DISCHARGE OF LIABILITY ON INSTRUMENTS

When a party's liability for a negotiable instrument is terminated, this party's liability has been discharged. In other words, the party is released from liability. Discharge can occur through a variety of ways. For example, as stated earlier, discharge of endorsers can occur if a party who has a right to enforce an instrument has materially altered the instrument. Keep in mind discharge is not effective against a holder in due course (UCC 3-601).

discharged
Released from liability for a negotiable instrument.

Discharge through Payment and Tender of Payment Earlier in this chapter, we discussed how a party becomes liable for an instrument by signing the instrument. If a party (or another party on the first party's behalf) who has signed an instrument has an obligation to pay and then pays the full amount due, all parties who are liable will be discharged (UCC 3-602).

[7] 360 A.2d 461 (Md. Ct. Spec. App. 1976).

Real (universal) defenses	Infancy (below the legal age of consent)*
	Duress*
	Lack of legal capacity*
	Illegality of the transaction*
	Fraud in the factum
	Discharge through insolvency proceedings
	Forgery
	Material alteration
Personal defenses	*Contract defenses:*
	Breach of contract or warranty
	Lack or failure of consideration
	Fraud in the inducement
	Illegality
	Mental incapacity
	Article 3 defenses:
	Nonissuance of an instrument
	Modification of an obligation by a separate agreement
	Nondelivery of the instrument
	Unauthorized, nonfraudulent completion of instrument

* To the extent that it makes a contract void.

For example, Stuart creates a note in which he promises to pay Vanessa $1,000. If Stuart pays the $1,000 on the due date, he will be discharged from liability on the note. However, if Stuart makes the payment on the note to John, knowing that John stole the note from Vanessa and is wrongfully possessing it, Stuart's obligation will not be discharged. Paying John does not discharge Stuart's liability because John, who stole the note, is not a holder and not entitled to the amount on the note [UCC 3-602(b)(2)].

Moreover, some parties' obligations on an instrument will be discharged if the obliged party tenders full payment on the due date but the holder of the instrument refuses to accept the money [UCC 3-603(b)]. If Stuart makes a proper tender of the full amount ($1,000) to Vanessa on the note's due date but she improperly refuses to accept the money, Stuart will still be liable for the $1,000 but will not have to pay interest on the amount. However, if any endorsers or accommodation parties are liable for Stuart's note, these parties' obligation will be discharged.

Discharge by Cancellation or Renunciation A party who is entitled to enforce an instrument may decide to cancel the instrument with or without consideration. Canceling the instrument discharges the obligation of a party who must pay the instrument (UCC 3-604). The party who decides to cancel the instrument may engage in an intentional voluntary act to cancel the instrument. For example, the party might write "Paid" on the instrument, intentionally destroy or mutilate the instrument, or give the instrument to the obliged party.

Alternatively, a party may renounce an instrument by promising not to sue to enforce the instrument. *Renunciation* occurs when a party agrees, in writing, not to sue the obliged party.

Discharge by Reacquisition *Reacquisition* occurs when a former holder of an instrument has the instrument transferred back to him or her by negotiation or other means. When reacquisition occurs, anyone who endorsed the instrument in between the initial acquisition and the

reacquisition by the holder has his or her endorsement canceled. When an endorsement is canceled, discharge occurs. The holder who reacquired the instrument can further negotiate the instrument, but the intermediate endorsers will not be held liable (UCC 3-207).

Discharge by Impairment of Recourse A right to recourse is the ability of a party to seek reimbursement. Typically, when a holder presents an instrument to an endorser, the endorser can seek recourse from prior endorsers, the maker, the drawer, or accommodating parties. However, if the holder has in some way impaired the endorser's ability to seek recourse from any of these parties, the endorser is not liable on the instrument [UCC 3-605(i)].

Discharge by Impairment of Collateral If a party posts collateral to ensure his performance of the negotiable instrument and the holder of the collateral impairs the value of the collateral, the party to the instrument is discharged from the instrument to the extent of the damage to the collateral [UCC 3-605(d)].

 SUMMARY

Holder in Due Course Doctrine	The HDC doctrine provides incentive for financial intermediaries to engage in transactions because they receive greater legal protection.
Requirements for Holder in Due Course Status	1. *Be a holder of a complete and authentic negotiable instrument.* 2. *Take the instrument for value:* The holder must suffer an out-of-pocket loss. 3. *Take the instrument in good faith:* The holder must take the instrument with "honesty in fact and the observance of reasonable commercial standards of fair dealing." 4. *Take the instrument without notice:* The holder must take the instrument without notice of the following defects: It is overdue, is dishonored, or is part of a series in default; it has been altered or has an unauthorized signature; or it is subject to claims or defenses.
The Shelter Principle and HDC	*Shelter principle:* If a holder cannot attain HDC status, the holder can acquire the rights and privileges of an HDC *if* the item is being transferred *from* an HDC.
Abuse of the Holder in Due Course Doctrine	*FTC rule:* Negotiation of consumer notes may not be subject to HDC status.
Liability	It is not always clear who should bear responsibility for the amount of a negotiable instrument. A party may be liable for a negotiable instrument if he or she signs the instrument or if the transfer of the instrument breaches a warranty associated with the instrument.
Signature Liability	A party can be held liable for an instrument only if the party has signed the instrument. *Primary liability of makers and acceptors:* They must pay the stated amount on the instrument when it is presented for payment. *Secondary liability of drawers and endorsers:* They must pay the amount on the instrument if the primarily liable party dishonors the instrument and the following three conditions are met: 1. Presentment 2. Dishonor 3. Notice of dishonor *Accommodation parties:* An accommodation party is one who signs an instrument to provide credit for another party who has also signed the instrument. *Unauthorized signature:* If a signature to a negotiable instrument is unauthorized, this unauthorized signature will not impose liability to the named party. 1. Negligence 2. Imposter rule 3. Fictitious-payee rule

Warranty Liability

Transfer warranty: When a party transfers an instrument to another party for consideration, the transferring party makes certain promises or warranties regarding the instrument and the transfer itself.

Presentment warranty: When a party properly presents an instrument for acceptance, that party makes certain promises regarding the instrument and the party who is entitled to payment.

Avoiding Liability for Negotiable Instruments

1. *Defenses to liability:* The arguments as to why a party should not be held liable for an instrument include:

 a. Real (universal) defenses
 b. Personal defenses

2. *Discharge of liability:* Release from liability can occur through:

 a. Discharge by payment or tender of payment.
 b. Discharge by cancellation or renunciation.
 c. Discharge by reacquisition.
 d. Discharge by impairment of recourse.
 e. Discharge by impairment of collateral.

 Point/Counterpoint

Should a Company Be Held Liable When an Employee's Work-Related Illegal Actions Include the Endorsement of Fraudulent Checks?	
YES	**NO**
A company should always be held liable for an employee's work-related illegal actions. The company hired the employee and put him in the position to commit an illegal action, so the company should be held responsible.	Companies should not be held liable for an employee's fraudulent checks. The employees, not the companies, should be held liable.
A company benefits from the work of each of its employees. If employees are profitable, company profits increase, the value of shareholder stock increases, and salaries increase; everyone benefits. Thus, because the company *benefits* when the employee is *profitable,* the company should also experience *losses* when the employee is *unprofitable* or *harmful.*	Every employee is an individual who controls his or her own actions. Though a company can try to monitor employee activities, if an employee wants to commit an illegal act, she will. Most companies hire smart, well-qualified people. Smart people can always find a way around even the best company security systems.
One of the factors in assigning liability for fraudulent checks is the ability of a party to bear the loss of the checks. A company is better equipped to bear a loss of funds than an individual. The losses occurred because of the actions of a specific *company* employee. Therefore, a company should shoulder the blame and pay for the losses from the fraudulent checks. After the company bears the losses of the checks, the company can then assess how to penalize the employee who endorsed the fraudulent checks.	Employees also need to feel the consequences of their own actions. If a corporation always takes the hit for an employee's poor decision, the employee cannot learn to change his behavior.
A company should be held liable for an employee's actions because the company has the ability to monitor employee activities and the company chose to use the employee to represent the company.	Companies should not be blamed for an employee's fraudulent checks because, sometimes, the bank responsible for paying out the fraudulent checks should be held responsible. Banks are companies as well, and as such, they should be aware of suspicious activities. When cashing large checks, the bank could easily require a verification code that would be known only by someone authorized to give checks.
	Employees make their own decisions and are not forced to act against the law. Therefore, the employees should be held personally accountable.

1. Explain the rationale for the following statement: "The purpose of holder in due course status is to encourage parties to engage in financial transactions."

2. What are the requirements of holder in due course status?

3. What is the distinction between primary liability and secondary liability for a signed negotiable instrument?

4. Evaluate the following statement: "A party can never be held liable for a negotiable instrument if he or she did not sign the check."

5. What are the similarities and differences between transfer and presentment warranties?

6. How are real defenses different from personal defenses to liability for a negotiable instrument?

7. L&M had a checking account with Wells Fargo Bank. Gentner performed consulting services for L&M, and L&M paid Gentner with a $60,000 check. Eleven days after issuing the check, L&M orally instructed Gentner to stop payment on the check. When Gentner presented the check to Wells Fargo for payment, the bank issued a cashier's check, payable to Gentner, for $60,000. Wells Fargo later placed a stop-payment order on the cashier's check, and when Gentner deposited the cashier's check at another bank, it was not honored. Gentner claimed that the original stop payment was never made by L&M and that Gentner was a holder in due course of the cashier's check. Wells Fargo argued that the holder in due course doctrine did not apply because Gentner purchased the cashier's check for payment to itself rather than the check's being purchased by another party for payment to Gentner. Gentner sued Wells Fargo for wrongful dishonor of a cashier's check. The trial court found for Gentner, determining that it was a holder in due course of the cashier's check. How do you think the case was decided on appeal? [*Gentner and Company, Inc. v. Wells Fargo Bank,* 76 Cal. App. 4th 1165 (1999).]

8. At the end of January 2001, while cleaning out his self-storage locker, Kim Griffith found a certificate of deposit purportedly issued by Mellon Bank, N.A., of Pittsburgh, Pennsylvania, on July 3, 1975, for the amount of $530,000 plus interest to be payable to bearer on August 4, 1975. The CD was in one of several books Griffith had purchased from an unnamed buyer. On its face, the certificate of deposit had not been marked paid. On August 15, 2002, more than a year after finding the certificate of deposit, Griffith presented it for payment in person at a Mellon Bank office in Pennsylvania. Mellon refused to honor the certificate of deposit, arguing that because the bearer certificate of deposit matured 27 years earlier, the certificate was questionable on its face and thus was not genuine. On the basis of Mellon's refusal to honor the certificate of deposit, Griffith filed suit against Mellon. Mellon argues that it has no records of the CD as not being paid and that, under Pennsylvania law, it falls to Griffith to prove nonpayment. Griffith argues that he is a holder in due course and is entitled to payment regardless of any possible defenses Mellon might raise. Is Griffith a holder in due course? Should he be able to collect on the CD? Why or why not? [*Griffith v. Mellon Bank, N.A.,* 328 F. Supp. 2d 536 (2004).]

9. Pershing & Co. discovered that five Royal Dutch certificates issued to Hilson & Co. were missing from its inventory. Pershing applied to its bank for replacements. The bank required that Pershing execute an "Affidavit for Lost Securities," stating that the certificates had been lost, stolen, or destroyed, and that it purchase an indemnity bond. Sixteen years later, Haber received four of the original missing stock certificates in a sealed envelope as a wedding present from his uncle. Haber's uncle did not take the certificates by endorsement and was not a holder in due course. Haber did not open the envelope until 1996. Haber sold the certificates, and the bank originally credited his account with $2.77 million. However, the bank later informed Haber that it was rescinding the sale, and it debited his account for the amount of the proceeds. Haber contended that it was a holder in due course of the certificates. Do you think Haber was a holder in due course of the stock certificates? Why or why not? [*Haber v. Fireman's Fund Insurance Surety Corp.,* 2000 U.S. Dist. LEXIS 9458 (2000).]

10. Joshua Herrera found a purse in a dumpster. He contacted the owner of the purse, and it was returned to its owner. After returning the purse, Herrera returned to the dumpster. He found a check written out to "cash." Herrera testified that he thought that meant that he "could get money for the check." He presented the check at a bank, and the bank teller instructed him to put his name on the payee line next to cash. Herrera added the words "to Joshua Herrera" to the payee line and endorsed the check. The trial court found Herrera guilty of forgery. On appeal Herrera argued that he did not alter the check because he did not change the legal efficacy of the check. Herrera claimed that the check was a bearer instrument and payable to anyone possessing the instrument. How do you think the court decided? [*State of New Mexico v. Joshua Herrera,* 2000 N.M. App. LEXIS 100 (2001).]

11. TUSRIF agreed to loan $200,000 to NCI for the development of a saw-milling enterprise in Russia. NCI was to repay the loan in 28 monthly installments. The parties prior to the signing of the note discussed the fee schedule. When TUSRIF sent the completed loan documents to NCI for signature, it mistakenly omitted the fee schedule page. Realizing its mistake, TUSRIF later attached two schedule pages to the note after it was signed. Because of the omission, NCI refused to make any payments on the note; instead, it claimed that the loan was not due until its maturity date. TUSRIF sued NCI for breach of the note. NCI claimed that its obligation under the note was discharged due to TUSRIF's material alteration of the note. Should the court accept NCI's defense? Why or why not? [*TUSRIF v. Neal & Company, Inc.,* 1998 U.S. Dist. LEXIS 13581 (1998).]

12. Olga Ensenat, an 88-year-old woman, had substantial investment accounts. Eventually her niece, Diana Flores, moved in to take care of Ensenat. While living with her, Flores withdrew on Ensenat's accounts, forged Ensenat's signature, and deposited the money into Flores's accounts. In the end Flores embezzled $157,386.30, all of which was deposited at Hancock Bank, where Flores had an account. Ensenat alleged that she did not herself withdraw or authorize any other person to withdraw retirement funds from her accounts. Ensenat sued Hancock Bank, claiming it was responsible because it allowed the checks to be paid or deposited without her endorsement, signature, or authorization. Did the court agree with Ensenat and find Hancock Bank liable for the deposited checks? Why or why not? [*Hancock Bank v. Ensenat,* 819 So. 2d 3 (2001).]

13. A thief stole checks from a customer of Decibel Credit Union. Over the next 40 days, the thief forged the signature on 14 of the stolen checks, stealing $2,350. All these checks were cashed at Pueblo Bank, where the thief had an account. On some days, the thief cashed two checks in one day. Pueblo Bank processed all 14 checks, and Decibel paid the checks. When Decibel's customer received his bank statement and learned that someone had been using his checks, he notified Decibel. Decibel demanded that Pueblo Bank reimburse it for the amounts of the stolen checks. Pueblo Bank declined. Decibel filed suit against Pueblo Bank. The trial court granted summary judgment for Decibel for the following reasons: (1) Decibel had given timely notice to Pueblo Bank as soon as the forgery was discovered by the customer; (2) by submitting the checks to Decibel for payment, Pueblo Bank triggered its responsibility for presentment and transfer warranties; and (3) because the warranties were triggered, Decibel was entitled to reimbursement. Pueblo Bank appealed. How did the judge rule on appeal? Who should be liable for the checks? [*Decibel Credit Union v. Pueblo Bank & Trust Company,* 996 P.2d 784 (2000).]

14. Michelle Campbell worked for Luiz Simmons as his secretary. After Campbell was hired, she formed an acquaintanceship with Simmons's outside bookkeeper, Denise Evans. Campbell began to forge Simmons's name to checks drawn on several of her employer's accounts. Because Evans was a participant in the scheme and because Simmons trusted his employees, Campbell's forgeries went undetected by Simmons for over two years. During this time, Michael Lennon sold Campbell his Chevrolet Blazer for $22,000. Campbell paid for the Blazer, in part, with a forged check from Simmons's account. Simmons and Lennon knew one another through a business relationship. Also, Lennon and Campbell were once romantically involved, during which time Campbell forged Lennon's name on credit card applications and accumulated $17,000 in credit card debt in Lennon's name. More than 15 months after the sale of the Chevrolet Blazer, Simmons discovered that Campbell, with the aid of Evans, had been embezzling funds from his accounts for over two years by forging his signature on checks. Simmons filed a complaint against Lennon to recover for the amount of the forged check he accepted as payment from Campbell. Simmons argued that Lennon should have known the check was a forgery because he knew Simmons, as well as had firsthand experience with Campbell's illegal actions. How did the court decide the case? Should Lennon have been more cautious in accepting a check from Campbell given their past interactions? [*Simmons v. Lennon,* 139 Md. App. 15 (2001).]

15. Cletus Onyekwere opened a checking account for his company, Weafri Well Services, with NatWest bank. Onyekwere and his wife were the only authorized signatories on the account. In January 1997, the bank received a letter requiring that Onyekwere's future statements be sent to an address in Nigeria. The bank claimed that this letter was suspicious, and it faxed a letter to Onyekwere to confirm the letter. Onyekwere never responded to the fax, and his address was never changed. Starting in February 1997, the Bank paid seven allegedly forged checks bearing what was believed to be Onyekwere's signature. The bank claimed that the forged signatures were not obvious; Onyekwere presented not admissible evidence that the employees should have discovered that the signature was forged. The last forged check, check 120, was returned for insufficient funds. The check and a statement were mailed to Onyekwere in early March. Onyekwere did not respond to the bank until the end of June. The bank tried to recover the amounts paid on

the seven checks, but no recovery was made. Onye-kwere sued the bank to recover the amounts debited from his company's account under the allegedly forged checks. Do you think the bank acted in accordance with reasonable commercial standards when paying the checks? What other information might help you make this decision? [*Weafri Well Services, Co. v. Fleet Bank,* 2000 U.S. Dist. LEXIS 14394 (2000).]

Looking for more review material?

The Online Learning Center at **www.mhhe.com/kubasekess** contains this chapter's "Assignment on the Internet" and also a list of URLs for more information, entitled "On the Internet." Find both of them in the Student Center portion of the OLC, along with quizzes and other helpful materials.

Secured Transactions, Creditors' Rights, and Bankruptcy

---▶ CASE OPENER

The Underpriced Boat

Alan H. Terris purchased a powerboat from OxBow Marina, Inc., an affiliate of General Motors. Terris planned to pay for the boat in installments and signed an agreement stating he would pay the total amount of the boat, $109,090.91, in 83 monthly payments of $673.93 and one final payment of $53,154.52. Under this agreement, General Motors Acceptance Corporation (GMAC) had the right to repossess the boat if he did not make his monthly payments.

Almost three years later, Terris was unable to make his monthly payments, and General Motors Acceptance Corporation repossessed the boat. After advertising the sale, GMAC sold the boat for $26,000. At the time of the sale, the amount that Terris owed GMAC for the boat was $65,350.42, so GMAC sought to recover the balance of $39,350.42 in court. However, Terris argued that the boat was sold for a price much lower than it was worth. He noted that the *N.A.D.A. Large Boat Appraisal Guide* indicated that the boat had a high book value of $53,010, an average book value of $43,470, and a low book value of $33,930, and that his boat was in good condition.[1]

1. If you were the judge deciding this case, would you grant GMAC the full $39,350.42 deficiency?
2. Suppose that you were the manager of GMAC. How could you ensure that you would receive full reimbursement for this boat and for every other item you repossess and sell?

[1] *General Motors Acceptance Corp v. Terris; Memorandum of Decision, Connecticut Law Tribune,* October 31, 1994, p. 1125.

---▶ LEARNING OBJECTIVES

After reading this chapter, you will be able to answer the following questions:

LO 1 What are the important definitions associated with secured transactions?

LO 2 How are secured interests created?

LO 3 How are secured interests perfected?

The agreement made between GMAC and Terris before Terris purchased the boat is a common component of business transactions. Such agreements are called secured transactions. A **secured transaction** is a transaction in which the payment of a debt is guaranteed by personal property owned by the debtor. In the Case Opener, Terris guaranteed that he would pay his debt (the debt he owes for the boat) by giving GMAC rights to the boat. In other words, he said, "If I don't pay you everything, you can take the boat from me."

Put yourself in the position of a creditor. If you were making a loan to someone, you would want to somehow ensure that the person repays you. If he does not repay you, you can take the secured property or asset to defray the damages associated with the individual's nonpayment. In contrast, a creditor that does not have a secured interest must file a lawsuit, obtain a judgment, and execute on the judgment to recover money for an unpaid debt.

Article 9 of the Uniform Commercial Code (UCC) governs secured transactions in personal property (as opposed to real property). Thus, throughout the chapter, we refer to Article 9 of the UCC. As of June 30, 2006, with some variation, all states had enacted Article 9. Thus, while the law governing secured transactions is state law, the states' enactment of Article 9 permits us to summarize across all states in discussing laws regarding secured transactions.

Important Definitions Associated with Secured Transactions

LO 1

It is important to understand the definitions of the terms used in secured transactions to understand how secured transactions are created. These definitions generally come from the UCC's definitions of the terms:

- A **secured interest** is an "interest in personal property or fixtures which secures payment or performance of an obligation" [UCC Section 1-201(37)]. Suppose Best Buy sells you a laptop on credit. Best Buy retains a secured interest in the laptop, which means that the store can repossess the laptop if you fail to make payments on it.
- A **secured party** is the party that holds the interest in the secured property. Thus, in the example above, Best Buy is the secured party. The secured party is also known as the *secured creditor.*
- A **debtor** is the party that has an obligation to the secured party, the person who owns the interest in the secured property. You, the laptop owner, are the debtor because you have an obligation to make payments.
- A **security agreement** is an agreement in which the debtor gives the secured interest to the secured party. Thus, when you made the agreement with Best Buy, you created a security agreement.
- **Collateral** is the property that is subject to the security interest. In the Best Buy example, the laptop is the collateral. Exhibit 17-1 lists different types of collateral under the UCC.

secured transaction
A transaction in which the payment of a debt is guaranteed by personal property owned by the debtor.

secured interest
An interest in personal property or fixtures that secures payment or performance to a creditor.

secured party
The party that holds the interest in a secured property.

debtor
A party that owes money to another party.

security agreement
An agreement in which the debtor gives the secured interest to the secured party.

collateral
The property that is subject to a secured interest.

343

Exhibit 17-1

Collateral under
the UCC

1. Goods (consumer goods, farm products, inventory, equipment, fixtures, and accessories)
2. Indispensable paper (documents of title, negotiable instruments, investment property, and chattel paper)
3. Intangibles (accounts, goodwill, literary rights)
4. Proceeds

LO 2

Creation of Secured Interests

How does a creditor become a secured party? To become a secured party, the creditor must gain a security interest in the collateral of the debtor. The secured party must take three steps to create the security interest:

1. The two parties create a security agreement and either (a) there is a record of the security agreement (usually a written agreement that describes the collateral and is signed by the debtor) or (b) the secured party is in possession of the collateral.
2. The secured party must give value to get the security agreement.
3. The debtor has a right in or to the collateral [UCC 9-203(b)].

Once these three criteria are met, the secured party's rights attach to the collateral. When **attachment** occurs, the creditor becomes the secured party who has a security interest in the collateral. Let's examine these criteria a little more closely.

attachment
The point at which a creditor becomes the secured party who has a security interest in the collateral.

WRITTEN AGREEMENT

The written agreement, often referred to as the *security agreement,* must be signed by the debtor. Moreover, the agreement must describe the collateral. The description of the collateral must be accurate and detailed enough for the description to reasonably identify the collateral. For example, in a description of a laptop that is serving as collateral, the serial number of the laptop might be listed in the written agreement. Let's go back to the GMAC case. The security agreement between Terris and GMAC/OxBow Marina, Inc., most likely included the following: (1) a statement that Terris is buying the boat on credit from GMAC/OxBow Marina; (2) a statement that GMAC/OxBow Marina is retaining a security interest in the boat; (3) a description of the boat, as well as its serial number; (4) the price of the boat, as well as the amount of the monthly payments due to GMAC/ OxBow; and (5) a description of the process of GMAC/OxBow's repossessing the boat.

It is important that the collateral be described clearly in the written agreement because the creditor could lose its rights to the collateral if the description is not clear.

VALUE

The secured party must give value. According to the UCC, *value* is consideration. Thus, in the Case Opener, the use of the boat was considered the value that GMAC gave to Terris. Alternatively, suppose you receive a loan from a company. The money is the value given by the company, the secured party.

DEBTOR RIGHTS IN THE COLLATERAL

The final criterion necessary for the attachment of the security interest is the debtor's rights in the collateral. Terris, the buyer of the boat, had a legal right to the boat (the collateral) after he signed his agreement.

purchase-money security interest (PMSI)
A security interest formed when a debtor uses borrowed money from the secured party to buy the collateral.

Purchase-Money Security Interest

Now that we have discussed the criteria necessary for the creation of a security interest, we briefly consider one specific type of security interest, the **purchase-money security interest (PMSI),** which is formed when a debtor uses borrowed money from the secured party to buy the collateral.

According to the UCC, a PMSI exists when a security interest is retained or taken by (1) the seller of the collateral to secure part or all of the purchase price or (2) a person who gives something of value to the debtor so that the debtor can gain rights to or use of the collateral (9-103). In our laptop example, you bought the laptop on credit from Best Buy. Best Buy extended credit to you for the entire purchase price of the laptop. In other words, Best Buy is lending you the money to buy the laptop. Because the laptop is the collateral, Best Buy has a PMSI.

Perfected Security Interest

Suppose that you borrow money from a bank and the bank has a secured interest in your wedding ring. You are supposed to make monthly payments to the bank, but you lose your job and suddenly cannot make the payments. When you fail to make these payments, you **default** on the loan. Because the bank has a secured interest in your ring, it can repossess your ring when you default on the loan.

But suppose you also borrowed money from another creditor, your boss, and you used your ring as collateral for that transaction. Your boss was unaware that you used the ring as collateral for your bank loan. Both your boss and your bank have an interest in your ring. Who gets the ring? The party that *perfects* its interest in the ring will have first claim to the ring.

When a party perfects its interest in collateral, it is legally protecting its claim to the collateral. **Perfection** is defined as the series of legal steps a secured party takes to protect its right in the collateral from other creditors who wish to have their debts returned through the same collateral. We consider below the various methods of perfection.

default
Failure to make payments on a loan.

perfection
The series of legal steps a secured party takes to protect its right in the collateral from the other creditors who wish to have their debt returned through the same collateral.

financing statement
A document that lists the names and addresses of all the parties involved in the transaction, a description of the collateral, and the signature of the debtor.

PERFECTION BY FILING

The most common way to perfect an interest is to file a financing statement with a state agency. According to the UCC, a **financing statement** should list the names and addresses of all the parties involved, a description of the collateral, and the signature of the debtor (UCC Section 9-502). First, the names and addresses of the statement are important elements because someone looking for the financing statement may wish to contact the secured party or the debtor. Second, the financing statement must be filed under the name of the debtor whether the debtor is an individual, a partnership, or a corporation. If the statement is filed under an incorrect name, the perfection is likely not effective. Third, the financing statement must include a description of the collateral. The purpose of including a description of the collateral is to inform other potential parties who might wish to lend money to the debtor. The description of the collateral may be replicated from the description of the collateral in the security agreement.

Once the financing statement is filed, the statement becomes public knowledge. Parties considering making a loan to another party are expected to reasonably look for notification of secured interests. Consequently, if you ask to borrow money from your boss, your boss should check with state agencies to ensure that you have not already used your ring as collateral. If your boss discovers that your bank has perfected its interest in your ring, your boss should not agree to loan you money with the ring as your collateral because the bank's perfection of the security interest means that the ring will go directly to the bank. Your boss would have a claim against the ring only as an unsecured creditor.

Place and Duration of Filing Suppose you need to file a financing statement. Where should you file? For how long is the filing effective? The place of filing depends on whether the debtor is an individual or a business. If the debtor is an individual, the secured party files the financing statement in the state in which the debtor resides. Alternatively, if the debtor is a registered business, the secured party files the financing statement in the state in which the business's certificate of organization was issued. If the debtor is an unregistered business, the secured party files the financing statement in the state where the chief executive office of the business is located. Finally, if the debtor is a foreign person or business, the secured party files the financing statement in Washington, D.C.

The actual place of filing changes from state to state. Sometimes the statements are filed with the secretary of state. Alternatively, the statements might be filed with the county clerk. Under the 1999 version of Article 9, each state must establish a central filing office.

Once you have filed the financing statement with the correct agency, for how long is the statement valid? Under the UCC, the statement is valid for five years (9-515). After the five years, the statement expires, and the security interest is not protected. However, within six months of the expiration date of the financing statement, the secured party can file a continuation statement, which is valid for another five years.

PERFECTION BY POSSESSION

pledge
The transfer of collateral to the secured party.

Sometimes a debtor gives a creditor the collateral to hold until the loan is paid off. For example, suppose that you borrow money from a bank and give the bank your diamond necklace to hold until you pay back the loan. The transfer of the collateral to the secured party is called a pledge. When the bank takes possession of the necklace, it has perfected its interest without filing a financing statement. Once you pay off the loan, the necklace is returned to you.

There are several advantages associated with perfection by possession. First, a secured party does not have to go through the hassle of filing a financing statement. In fact, the parties do not have to even create a written security agreement. Second, there is little chance that another party will loan money to the debtor relying on the collateral that another secured party possesses. Third, if the debtor defaults on the loan, the secured party already has possession of the collateral, so there is no hassle in trying to repossess.

It is often impractical to perfect possession because the debtor cannot benefit from the use of the collateral. For example, if you get a loan from a bank to purchase farm equipment, you likely need the farm equipment to produce crops that will enable you to make payments on the loan. As you read the Global Context box on secured transactions in Indonesia, think about the relationship between U.S. laws with respect to perfection by possession and Indonesian practices of security by possession.

instrument
A writing that serves as evidence of the right to payment of money.

Certain types of collateral *must* be perfected through possession. These types of collateral include instruments—writings that serve as evidence of rights to payment of money, such as certificates of deposit—and stocks and bonds.

AUTOMATIC PERFECTION

consumer good
A good used or bought for use primarily for personal, family, or household purposes.

If a retailer had to file a financing statement every time it sold on credit a laptop, a wide-screen television, or a washer and dryer, the retailer would do nothing but file statements. Moreover, it does not make sense for the retailer to possess the collateral. Thus, when a creditor sells a consumer good to a debtor on a credit basis or a creditor extends a loan to a debtor for the purchase of a consumer good, the security interest in the good perfects automatically. Under the UCC, a consumer good is a good used or bought for use primarily for personal, family, or household purposes [9-102(23)]. Thus, if an item is purchased for business use, the security interest would not perfect automatically; the secured party would have to file a financing statement.

PERFECTION OF MOVABLE COLLATERAL

When a debtor moves collateral to a different state, the creditor's security interest is usually good for four months in the new state before the creditor must refile. Failure to refile may cause that creditor to lose its priority against competing security interests.

PERFECTION OF SECURITY INTERESTS IN AUTOMOBILES AND BOATS

We have now discussed various methods of perfection: perfection by filing, perfection by possession, automatic possession, and perfection of movable collateral. Exhibit 17-2 provides a summary of the methods of perfection. None of these methods applies to perfection of automobiles and boats. Each state has created special laws that pertain to perfection of motor vehicles.

Secured Transactions in Indonesia

Rights governing secured transactions in Indonesia are subdivided into two categories. The first category includes security rights conferred by law. According to the Indonesian Civil Code, both movable and immovable assets belonging to the debtor constitute security. Thus, the creditors have equal preference over the debtor's assets unless otherwise specified in the contract.

The second category of security rights includes those created by private agreement. These include mortgages, pledges, and fiduciary transfers. Only mortgages and pledges are legally recognized for creating security interests over movable and immovable property. Mortgages govern immovable property, which is mostly land, while pledges act as security for tangible items, such as cars, and intangibles, such as patent rights. For a pledge to be legitimate, there must be physical transfer of the secured assets. The growing commercial market of Indonesia demanded a more flexible method of transfer for movable goods. In response to this need, fiduciary transfers have emerged. Fiduciary transfers require only a theoretical transfer of security rights, not a physical one as pledges do. Despite their commonality and popularity, these fiduciary transfers are not recognized in the Civil Code. This lack of recognition is in part explained by the novelty of this type of security.

Perfection by Filing

Chattel paper: Writing that indicates the debtor's monetary obligation as well as a secured interest

Documents of title: Papers that demonstrate the owner's possession of the goods (e.g., warehouse receipts)

Accounts: Rights to payments for goods sold or leased

General intangibles: Trademarks, copyrights, patents, etc.

Equipment: Goods purchased primarily for business use

Farm products: Products of livestock or crops

Inventory: Goods held for sale or lease

Fixtures: Goods that have become attached to real estate

Automatic Perfection

Purchase-money security interests in consumer goods

Perfection by Possession

Chattel paper
Documents of title
Instruments (stocks, bonds, checks, etc.)
Equipment

Perfection of Movable Collateral

Perfection typically good for four months after collateral moved to another state

Perfection of Security Interests in Automobiles and Boats

Notation of the interest on the certificate of title

Exhibit 17-2

Summary of the Different Methods of Perfection

Almost every state requires a certificate of title for any motor vehicle. Perfection of a security interest in a motor vehicle occurs when the secured party makes a notation of this interest on the certificate of title. Let's go back to the Case Opener again. By noting the secured interest on the title of Terris's boat, GMAC is automatically preventing Terris from using the boat as collateral for another loan.

The Scope of a Security Interest

LO 4

Generally, once a secured party perfects its interest in collateral, the perfection is effective until the collateral is sold, exchanged, or transferred. Our examination of security interests to this point has been concerned with property the debtor currently possesses. However, a security interest can also apply to personal property that is not yet in the debtor's possession.

AFTER-ACQUIRED PROPERTY

You borrow $60,000 from your bank to start an electronics store. However, you have recently graduated from college and have only your car, valued at $3,500, as collateral. The bank will take a security interest in your car, but it will also take a security interest in the materials that you will purchase to open your store. For example, you will need to create an inventory of televisions, computers, and stereos, which are after-acquired property, property acquired by the debtor after the security agreement is made. After-acquired property can be inventory, livestock, equipment, or almost any other kind of property. Under the UCC, a party may agree, through a clause in the security agreement, that the security interest will attach to after-acquired property. Whenever the debtor purchases new equipment or goods, the security interest is attached to the new good. Thus, whenever you buy a television to sell in your store, the bank's security interest in the television is attached.

PROCEEDS

When a debtor sells collateral, he or she receives proceeds, something that is exchanged for collateral. The secured party automatically has an interest in the proceeds. Why? If you use a good as collateral for a bank loan and then sell that good, the bank has nothing to secure its loan to you. Consequently, the security interest in the good also applies to the proceeds from the good.

Under the UCC, the secured party's interest in the proceeds lasts only 10 days after the debtor receives the proceeds. At that time, the secured party will typically need to file a new financing statement. The parties may also agree in the security agreement that there will be extended coverage of interest in the proceeds.

Termination of a Security Interest

Suppose that rather than defaulting on his loan payment, Terris paid GMAC the full amount for his boat as required under the agreement: $109,090.91. If a secured party has filed a financing statement and the debtor has repaid the secured party, the secured party must file a termination statement with the filing office. A termination statement is an amendment to a financing statement that states that the debtor has no obligation to the secured party [UCC Section 9-513(a)].

LO 5

Priority Disputes

We have spent much time discussing the perfection of a security interest. Why? Remember, perfection of an interest is supposed to serve as protection of the secured party's interest in collateral from other creditors. In this section, we consider various conflicts between creditors who claim interest in the same collateral. A conflict may arise with just a piece of property; however, priority disputes are most likely to arise when a debtor files for bankruptcy.

SECURED VERSUS UNSECURED CREDITORS

Generally, secured parties have priority over unsecured creditors. Thus, if two parties provide a loan based on the same collateral, the party with the secured interest will have priority in repossessing the collateral over the party with the unsecured interest. This priority to the collateral does not depend on the perfection of a secured interest. Rather, the priority depends on the *attachment* of the secured interest.

SECURED VERSUS SECURED CREDITORS

Who has priority to the collateral when both parties are secured creditors? If both parties are secured, the determination of priority for claim to collateral moves to considerations of time and perfection.

If there is a dispute between a perfected secured party and an unperfected secured party, the creditor with the perfected interest has priority over the unperfected interest. But what if the dispute is between two secured parties with perfected interests? The party that perfected its interest first will have priority in claim to the collateral (UCC 9-317). Finally, if neither party has perfected its security interest, the party that attached its security interest first will have first claim to the collateral.

PMSI Conflicts There is an exception to these priority rules. Generally, if a purchase-money security interest is involved, the perfected PMSI will almost always have priority over other claims to collateral. The rules regarding PMSIs depend on whether the collateral is inventory or noninventory.

First, if the PMSI is in inventory, the perfected PMSI has priority over a previously perfected non-PMSI if the following two conditions are met: (1) The PMSI party perfects its interest before or at the same time that the debtor receives his inventory, and (2) the PMSI party checks for previous secured interests and gives written notice to the holders of the PMSI [UCC 9-324(b)]. For example, General Electric Capital Commercial Automotive Inc. (GECC) entered into a security agreement with Spartan Motors, Ltd. GECC loaned Spartan over $1 million and secured this loan by attaching its rights to Spartan's entire inventory as collateral. GECC filed this agreement in the office of the Dutchess county clerk with the New York secretary of state. A few years later, Spartan signed another security agreement, but this time it was with General Motors Acceptance Corporation (GMAC). This agreement, however, was an agreement that involved a PMSI. GMAC loaned money to Spartan so that Spartan could purchase its inventory. Realizing that this was a PMSI, GMAC filed its agreement and notified GECC of its competing security interest.

The next year, Spartan filed a bankruptcy petition and went out of business. GMAC repossessed two BMWs that were purchased with the money it had loaned to Spartan and sold them in an auction for $194,500. GECC brought an action against GMAC on grounds that GECC's security interest had priority. In the end, the court found that because GMAC had a PMSI in inventory and notified GECC of the competing agreement, GMAC had priority to the profits from the sale of the BMWs.

SECURED PARTY VERSUS BUYER

If a debtor sells collateral in which a secured party has an interest, the security interest generally remains in effect. Suppose you obtain a loan from a bank and use your boat as collateral. You need more money, so you sell your boat. The bank's secured interest in the boat remains with the boat. If you default on the loan, the bank can seize the boat from the buyer. However, the UCC provides some exceptions to this general rule.

Buyers in the Ordinary Course of Business A buyer in the ordinary course of business is a person who routinely buys goods in good faith from a person who routinely sells these goods. Under the UCC, a buyer in the ordinary course of business can take the goods free of any security interest created by the seller of the good *even if* the security interest is perfected [9-320(a)]. What is the rationale for this rule? Asking buyers to determine whether a security interest in inventory exists is burdensome. Thus, the purpose of this rule is to encourage commerce. For example, if your company buys products from an electronics store in the ordinary course of business, you can take possession of these products free of any security interest created by the party who originally sold the products to the electronics store.

> **buyer in the ordinary course of business**
> A person who routinely buys goods in good faith from a person who routinely sells these goods.

Buyers of Consumer Goods Suppose you buy a digital camera for $800 on credit from Circuit City, an electronics store. Circuit City has a security agreement for a PMSI in the digital camera. (Remember, a PMSI in a consumer good perfects automatically.) However, you discover that you don't have enough money to pay for your rent. Consequently, you sell your digital camera to your neighbor, who is unaware of Circuit City's secured interest in the camera. Can Circuit City repossess the camera? Under the UCC, as long as the buyer is not aware of the security interest,

purchases the good for his or her personal use, and purchases the good before the secured party files a financial statement, the buyer obtains the good free of the security interest [9-320(b)]. Even though the secured party's interest perfects automatically, the secured party must have filed a financial statement to repossess a consumer good from another buyer.

Consider Case 17-1, in which the court considered the sale of consumer goods to a third party.

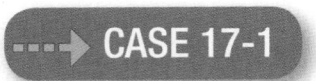 **CASE 17-1**

IN RE CHARLES T. LAU, DEBTOR
U.S. BANKRUPTCY COURT FOR THE NORTHERN DISTRICT
OF OHIO, WESTERN DIVISION
140 B.R. 172 (1992)

FACTS: *The defendant Charles Lau purchased a sofa, 45-inch television, sleeper sofa, loveseat, entertainment center, and gold chain, among other items, from Sears and charged them to his Sears account. Sears noted on the credit card receipt that it was taking a secured interest in the items purchased as a PMSI. Lau sometime later filed bankruptcy, prior to paying off the Sears card. Sears petitioned the bankruptcy court for permission to repossess the items charged on the Sears card. Lau claimed, and showed, that most of the items had been given to his girlfriend and her parents, who paid him for them.*

ISSUE: Sears claims that its PMSI supersedes the subsequent purchasers' claim. The legal question is, Who has the priority to the items: the seller who gave a PMSI or a subsequent purchaser.

REASONING: Clearly a filed PMSI would be "unbeatable" in this matter. Though Sears' PMSI automatically perfects with attachment, it has a superior claim to anyone else *except* a subsequent good-faith consumer purchaser. To protect against that one and only claim that can defeat a consumer PMSI, Sears would have had to file. It did not.

DECISION AND REMEDY: Since Sears did not file, its claim is subordinate to the subsequent purchasers. Therefore, Sears cannot repossess the items bought and paid for in good faith by the girlfriend or her parents.

SIGNIFICANCE OF THE CASE: While the UCC gives great deference to PMSIs, this case illustrates that benefits of doubt still lie with purchasers. Sears had the opportunity to file, but the prohibitive cost of perfection by filing makes that option unreasonable. Sears, or any seller of consumer goods, simply has to know that this is the risk of selling consumer goods on credit.

CRITICAL THINKING

What is the issue and conclusion in this case? What reasons do you think the judge used to support his argument? How convincing are you? What evidence would be needed for the judge to conclude in the opposite way?

ETHICAL DECISION MAKING

Return to the WPH process of ethical decision making. Suppose you are the manager of Sears. Before you decide to take this case to court, you have seemingly two options: (1) Prevent the discharge of Lau's debt to you in his bankruptcy hearing, or (2) repossess the items that Lau's girlfriend and her parents supposedly bought from him. Who would be affected by each of these decisions, and in what ways would they be affected?

Buyers of Chattel Paper and Instruments If a buyer purchases chattel paper, a writing that indicates both a monetary obligation and a security interest in a specific good, or an *instrument,* a writing that demonstrates a right to payment of money, in the ordinary course of business, the buyer can obtain the good free of any security interest. The buyer must typically be unaware of the security interest in the good. Why is there an exception for buyers of chattel paper and instruments? Both chattel paper and instruments are easily transferable. Consequently, the UCC provides that these forms of collateral can be sold to a buyer free of the secured party's interest.

Sometimes, the issue with a secured creditor is not the simple repossession of the collateral in question, but the collection of monies due on the collateral. In the following case nugget, the secured creditor repossessed collateral when the debtor filed bankruptcy. However, that property

chattel paper
A writing that indicates both a monetary obligation and a security interest in specific goods.

CASE Nugget

Rights of a Secured Party

In re Tower Air, Inc.
3rd Circuit Federal Court of Appeals

397 F.3d 191 (3d Cir. 2005)

In this case, the Third Circuit addressed the issue of whether a secured party may recover insurance proceeds for damage to collateral that had been repaired and returned to the lender.

Tower, an airline, borrowed $21 million from Finova to purchase of an aircraft and four aircraft engines. As part of the security agreement, Finova received a security interest in the aircraft and four engines (i.e., the collateral). Moreover, the security agreement provided that Tower would insure the collateral and that Finova would have a security interest in the insurance proceeds. The lender perfected its security interest in the planes, engines, and insurance.

In 1997, one of the engines was damaged. Using its own funds, Tower repaired the engine for $2.25 million (while $1.91 million was attributable to the accident). However, Tower did not submit an insurance claim.

Tower later filed for bankruptcy. All Tower's assets were to be liquidated to pay its debts through a Chapter 7 bankruptcy. However, because Finova had a secured interest, all collateral, including the repaired engine, was returned to the lender.

The bankruptcy trustee then discovered the insurance policy and filed a claim for $1.91 million. The insurance company settled the claim by paying approximately $950,000. However, Finova objected to the settlement and argued that it was entitled to the insurance proceeds pursuant to the security agreement. The bankruptcy court ruled that the insurance proceeds should be paid to Finova, and the district court agreed.

On appeal to the U.S. Court of Appeals for the Third Circuit, the trustee argued that Finova should not recover the insurance proceeds because it had already recovered the fully repaired engine. Thus, recovering both the insurance proceeds and the repaired engine would be unfair. The Third Circuit found that the plain language of the UCC stated that proceeds are "whatever is received upon the sale, exchange, collection or other disposition of collateral." Moreover, Section 9-306(a) states that "insurance payable by reason of loss or damage to the collateral is proceeds, except to the extent that it is payable to a person other than a party to the security agreement." Thus, under the plain language of the UCC, the insurance money was proceeds. The court ruled that Finova was permitted to recover the collateral and insurance money to the extent of the amount of the debt. Much of the collateral was damaged; thus, Finova was permitted to the full value of the insurance proceeds.

had been damaged and repaired by the debtor. The insurance policy covering the collateral had never paid on the damaged property. The secured creditor argued that it should also receive the insurance money as well as the property itself.

LO 6

Default

Generally, when a debtor fails to make payments on a loan or declares bankruptcy, the debtor has defaulted on the loan. However, the UCC does not define *default.* Consequently, each security agreement provides a specific definition of what is considered defaulting on the loan. Moreover, each agreement determines the procedures and consequences that occur in the event of default. Because the creditor is usually in a better bargaining position, the creditor usually determines the definition of default.

What are a secured party's remedies to recover its money when a debtor defaults on a loan? The secured party can (1) take possession of the collateral or (2) ignore its rights in the collateral and proceed to judgment. However, the party is not limited to just one of these remedies. If one method is unsuccessful, the party can attempt to pursue the other method. Note that these remedies are limited if the debtor has filed for bankruptcy.

TAKING POSSESSION OF THE COLLATERAL

If a debtor defaults on a loan, the secured party can take possession of the collateral (UCC 9-609). While the secured party may act without any court order to retain possession of the property, the secured party may not "breach the peace" in repossessing the property. Generally, if the secured party can repossess the collateral without using force or committing trespass, the action is not a breach of the peace. If the secured party is unable to repossess the property without breaching the peace, the party will file suit against the debtor to obtain a court order for the debtor to turn over the property.

Generally, the security agreement will state that if the debtor defaults on the loan, the debtor must turn over the collateral in a reasonable time and manner. If the debtor refuses to turn over the property, the secured party will typically hire a repossession company to obtain the collateral. Once the secured party has possession of the collateral, the party can choose to (1) dispose of the collateral or (2) retain the collateral.

Disposition of the Collateral Under the UCC, the secured party can sell, lease, or transfer the collateral in any commercially reasonable method (9-610). The secured party may sell the collateral in a private or public sale.

Once the collateral is sold, the proceeds must be paid in the following order: (1) paying the reasonable expenses of retaking and disposing of the collateral (including attorney fees), (2) satisfying the debt of the secured party, and (3) satisfying remaining holders of junior security interests [UCC 9-615(a)].

Retention of the Collateral Instead of disposing of the collateral, the secured party may choose to keep the collateral in full or partial satisfaction of the debt. However, the secured party must notify the debtor of this intent by sending written notice.

PROCEEDING TO JUDGMENT

Another remedy for a defaulted loan is the secured party's rejection of the right in the collateral and the party's filing of a suit against the debtor. The secured party can sue the debtor for the entire amount of the debt. Rather than taking the time to organize the sale of the collateral, the secured party may choose to file suit. In contrast, an unsecured creditor has just one option: to file suit and seek a judgment in the amount of the debt.

Bankruptcy and Reorganization

When an entity is unable to pay its debts, bankruptcy law provides various options for the entity to resolve these debts. Bankruptcy remedies are available to individuals, partnerships, and corporations.

Generally, a debtor is an entity that owes money to another entity. However, the term *debtor* is defined differently under each type of bankruptcy remedy; thus, an individual or company that is eligible for one type of bankruptcy might not be eligible for another type of bankruptcy.

The remainder of this chapter explains the various bankruptcy remedies available to debtors. We begin with a discussion of the goals of bankruptcy law and an overview of the Bankruptcy Code. Then we consider specific types of bankruptcy relief under the code.

The Bankruptcy Act and Its Goals

There are two general goals of bankruptcy laws. First, bankruptcy laws provide protection to creditors—entities to whom a debtor owes money. Bankruptcy laws ensure that creditors competing for a debtor's assets are treated equally and receive a fair share of the debtor's assets. Second, bankruptcy laws provide opportunities for debtors to gain a fresh financial start. In summary, bankruptcy law provides an organized method by which insolvent debtors—debtors who cannot pay their debts in a timely fashion—respond to their debts.

Bankruptcy law is federal law. Article I, Section 8, of the Constitution states: "The Congress shall have the power . . . To establish an uniform rule of naturalization and uniform laws on the subject of bankruptcies throughout the United States." Congress recently revised the Bankruptcy Code through the Bankruptcy Abuse Prevention and Consumer Protection Act of 2005 (BAPCPA). This revision includes the most comprehensive changes to bankruptcy law in over 25 years.

TITLE 11 OF THE UNITED STATES CODE

Title 11 of the United States Code (U.S.C.) contains the Bankruptcy Code, which is divided into chapters. Chapters 1, 3, and 5 provide the general definitions and provisions concerning bankruptcy case administration and debtors. These chapters apply to all types of bankruptcy relief. Chapters 7, 9, 11, 12, 13, and 15, briefly described in Exhibit 17-3, apply six specific types of bankruptcy relief.

Bankruptcy Proceedings

Most bankruptcy cases share a set of procedures, or certain actions that must be taken in every bankruptcy case. These actions are as follows:

1. All bankruptcy cases begin with a filing of petition for bankruptcy.
2. Once the petition is filed, the court grants an automatic stay for creditor actions against the debtor's estate. In other words, creditors' legal actions against the debtor must cease.

Specific Types of Relief Available

LO 7

Before a debtor files for one specific type of relief, the clerk of courts must give the debtor written notice of the other types of relief available. This requirement helps to ensure that the debtor has full information about the bankruptcy process.

creditor
An entity to which a debtor owes money.

insolvent debtor
A debtor who cannot pay debts in a timely fashion.

Bankruptcy Abuse Prevention and Consumer Protection Act of 2005 (BAPCPA)
A renovation in the system of bankruptcy enacted to address increased numbers of bankruptcy filings, significant losses associated with bankruptcy filings, loopholes and incentives that allowed for abuse, and the financial ability of debtors.

Exhibit 17-3

Types of Bankruptcy Relief by Chapter

Chapter 7	Sale of the debtor's assets by trustee and the distribution of money to creditors
Chapter 9	Adjustment of a municipality's debts
Chapter 11	Reorganization of the debtor's financial affairs under supervision of the bankruptcy court
Chapter 12	Reorganization of a family farmer's debts
Chapter 13	Reorganization of an individual's debts
Chapter 15	Recognition of insolvency proceedings pending in a foreign country and relief for foreign debtors

Under the Bankruptcy Abuse Prevention and Consumer Protection Act of 2005, an individual may not be considered a debtor under any chapter unless within 180 days prior to filing, he or she receives credit counseling from a nonprofit budget and credit counseling agency. If the individual does not fulfill the credit-counseling requirement, the bankruptcy court will dismiss the bankruptcy petition—even if the individual faces immediate home foreclosure or wage garnishment.

Moreover, the 2005 bankruptcy reforms attempt to prevent "repeat filers" from filing one bankruptcy claim after another. Under BAPCPA, if an individual was a debtor in a bankruptcy case that was dismissed within 180 days of the current case, the individual is generally not eligible to be a debtor under Chapters 7, 11, or 13. However, if the previous bankruptcy was completed rather than dismissed, the individual is generally permitted to file for bankruptcy again. If a party completes a Chapter 7 bankruptcy, the party is not permitted to seek a Chapter 7 bankruptcy again for eight years.

In the following sections we discuss the main types of relief available, including Chapter 7, 11, 12, and 13 bankruptcies.

CHAPTER 7: LIQUIDATION PROCEEDINGS

liquidation
The process in which a debtor turns over all assets to a trustee.

trustee
In bankruptcy proceedings, an individual who takes over administration of a debtor's estate.

The most familiar type of bankruptcy proceeding is liquidation, which is sometimes called *straight bankruptcy.* Liquidation occurs when a debtor turns over all assets to a trustee, an individual who takes over administration of the debtor's estate. Trustees are usually attorneys in private practice who specialize in bankruptcy law. Every Chapter 7 proceeding has a trustee who sells the nonexempt assets and distributes the proceeds of the sale among the creditors. Liquidation provides an organized method of selling the debtor's property to generate cash to pay creditors.

Who is defined as a debtor for liquidation purposes? Under Chapter 7 liquidation proceedings, individuals, partnerships, and corporations are considered debtors. Railroads, insurance companies, banks, savings and loan associations, industrial banks, credit unions, and health maintenance organizations are not eligible for Chapter 7 relief.

Petition Filing As is the case with most bankruptcies, liquidation begins when the petition is filed. Under Chapter 7, liquidation may be voluntary or involuntary; thus, a voluntary or involuntary petition is filed. The person filing the petition is also responsible for paying filing fees.

bankruptcy estate
The assets that are collected from a debtor who files for bankruptcy.

Voluntary Liquidation Petition. When the debtor decides to file for bankruptcy, he or she files a voluntary petition. The debtor must state that he or she understands the other types of bankruptcy relief available and chooses liquidation. Once the petition is filed, all the debtor's prepetition assets form the bankruptcy estate. Assets that the debtor gains after filing the petition are generally not part of the bankruptcy estate unless they fall under an exemption.

Involuntary Liquidation Petition. If a debtor isn't paying debts as they come due, creditors can attempt to force the debtor into bankruptcy by filing an involuntary petition under Chapter 7. By filing the petition, the creditors attempt to force the debtor to surrender his or her assets so that the proceeds from the sale of the assets may be distributed among the creditors. If the judge believes that creditors are using involuntary liquidation proceedings frivolously, the court may force the creditors to pay the attorney costs, fees of the debtor, and even punitive damages.

Not everyone can be forced into bankruptcy through Chapter 7. Farmers, ranchers, and nonprofit organizations are examples of debtors that cannot be forced into liquidation. Also, debtors that are ineligible to voluntarily file for Chapter 7 bankruptcy (railroads, insurance companies, banks, savings and loan associations, credit unions, and health maintenance organizations) are excluded from forced bankruptcy.

Dismissal of Petition A bankruptcy judge may dismiss a voluntary or involuntary bankruptcy petition. Under BAPCPA, a bankruptcy judge may dismiss a petition "for cause." One cause for dismissal is failure of the *means test.* If an individual's debt is primarily consumer debt and if the individual's income is above the median income in his or her state, the court may presume that the individual is abusing the bankruptcy provisions. However, the individual may continue with the petition under the presumption.

Automatic Stay Once a petition, voluntary or involuntary, is filed, the code provides for an automatic stay, or moratorium, for almost all creditor litigation against the debtor. During the stay, creditors cannot bring or continue legal action against the debtor or his property. For example, creditors cannot attempt to repossess property during bankruptcy proceedings. Moreover, if a creditor received a judgment against a debtor prior to the bankruptcy filing, the creditor may not enforce the judgment.

There are some exceptions to the stay. First, under BAPCPA, if the debtor was a debtor in a bankruptcy case that was dismissed within a year of the current bankruptcy case filing, the stay automatically terminates 30 days after the current filing. Second, legal actions to determine paternity or to collect child support or alimony payments are not subject to the stay. Third, the court may exclude secured creditors from the stay if they petition the court to show that they do not have "adequate protection" under the stay. If a creditor is aware of the stay and continues to engage in legal action against the debtor, the code provides that the debtor may recover damages, costs, attorney fees, and possibly even punitive damages.

> **automatic stay**
> After bankruptcy has been filed, a moratorium during which creditors cannot bring or continue action against the debtor or his or her property.

Order of Relief After a bankruptcy petition has been filed, the next step is for the court to determine whether an order of relief is granted. An order of relief means that bankruptcy relief is ordered; that is, the bankruptcy proceedings can continue. If the filing of the voluntary petition is proper, the petition automatically becomes an order of relief. Similarly, if a debtor does not object to an involuntary bankruptcy, the order of relief is automatic.

> **order of relief**
> An order stating that bankruptcy proceedings can continue.

Should the debtor challenge the involuntary petition for bankruptcy, a hearing will be held. At the hearing, the judge generally will grant the order of relief for involuntary bankruptcy if one of two conditions occurs:

1. The debtor isn't paying debts as they become due.
2. The custodian took possession of almost all the debtor's property within 120 days before filing the petition.

After the court enters the order of relief, a U.S. trustee, a government official appointed by the attorney general, selects an interim trustee. A *trustee* is the person responsible for collecting the debtor's available assets and liquidating the property into cash for the creditors. The interim trustee is responsible for organizing the creditors' meeting.

Creditors' Meeting Between 20 and 40 days after the order of relief has been granted, the interim trustee calls a creditors' meeting—a meeting of all the creditors listed in the Chapter 7 required schedule for liquidation. While the debtor and the interim trustee also attend this meeting, the bankruptcy judge does not attend.

> **creditors' meeting**
> A meeting of all the creditors listed in the Chapter 7 required schedule for liquidation.

If the debtor fails to appear at the meeting, the court may refuse to grant the bankruptcy. The principal purpose of the creditors' meeting is to enable the creditors and trustee to examine the debtor under oath regarding her financial affairs. The debtor's filing of the Chapter 7 required schedules does not necessarily provide enough information. Creditors want to know more about the way the debtor is handling her assets and property. Moreover, they want to ensure that the debtor is not concealing property. Not only does the trustee ask the debtor questions regarding her financial status, but the trustee also ensures that the debtor is aware of the other forms of bankruptcy relief as well as the consequences of filing for bankruptcy.

Another important purpose of the creditors' meeting is the election of a permanent trustee. The interim trustee might become the permanent trustee, or the creditors might elect a different one. The creditors elect the trustee because the trustee generally represents the creditors.

The Trustee The general duty of the trustee is to collect the debtor's available assets (i.e., the debtor's prefiling assets) and to liquidate the property to cash that will be distributed among the creditors. Thus, the trustee takes possession of the debtor's property and has it appraised. Moreover, the trustee examines the debtor's records and might even temporarily take over the debtor's business. If someone else holds the debtor's property, the trustee has the power to require that the person return that property. Next, the trustee separates the exempt property from the nonexempt property and sells the nonexempt property. In addition to selling the debtor's property, the trustee has a variety of powers that assist him in fulfilling his duties. First, the trustee has the power to

Exhibit 17-4

Federal Bankruptcy
Exemptions

1. Up to $15,000 for residence
2. Interest in a motor vehicle (not necessarily an automobile) up to $2,400
3. Interest, up to $400 for a particular item, in personal and household goods and furnishings, clothing, appliances, books, animals, crops, and musical instruments (aggregate total of all items limited to $8,000)
4. Interest in jewelry up to $1,000
5. $800 of any property the debtor chooses (functions as a "wild-card" exemption)
6. Tools of trade and professional books up to $1,500
7. Any unmatured life insurance contract owned by the debtor
8. Professionally prescribed health aids
9. Interest in any other property up to $800, plus any unused part of the homestead exemption up to $7,500
10. The right to receive certain personal injury awards up to $15,000
11. Retirement funds in an IRA or SEP

sue and be sued. He can initiate collection actions but must also defend against creditor actions. He has the right to assume or reject executory contracts. Moreover, he has the right to obtain credit. Finally, the trustee has the power to void certain liens against the debtor's property. For example, a debtor's ability to exempt property is hindered by any liens against such possessions. Consequently, the trustee is permitted to void these liens.

Exempt Property A debtor is not required to give up her nonexempt property. The trustee sorts the exempt property from the nonexempt property. The exemptions are stated in the Bankruptcy Code and are adjusted every three years based on the consumer price index.

There are federal exemptions as well as state exemptions. States, through legislation, can and have opted out of the federal exemptions to give debtors the option for state exemptions only. However, in some states, a debtor may choose whether to make state or federal exemptions; the debtor cannot make some state exemptions and some federal exemptions. Exhibit 17-4 lists the federal exemptions. In addition to having the exemptions in Exhibit 17-4, a debtor is entitled to 100 percent of Social Security benefits, veteran's benefits, and civil service retirement benefits. One exemption was recently added—retirement funds in an individual retirement account (IRA).

Why has Congress created such exemptions for property? Suppose that a debtor was forced to sell all his property through liquidation. Remember, one purpose of bankruptcy is to provide a debtor with a fresh start. If a debtor were forced to sell all his property, he would likely fall right back into debt again. Thus, the exemptions are for items considered necessary to earning a living.

Consider the dilemma regarding the retirement funds that are the focus of Case 17-2, which provides the Supreme Court's reasoning for why IRA funds are exempt.

 CASE 17-2

ROUSEY v. JACOWAY
UNITED STATES SUPREME COURT
544 U.S. 320 (2005)

FACTS: *The Rouseys worked for Northrup-Grumman. When they stopped working for Northrup-Grumman, the company required that the couple take a lump-sum distribution of their retirement accounts. The Rouseys placed these funds into two IRAs. Subsequent to these events, the Rouseys filed bankruptcy. The trustee claimed*

(continued)

that these IRAs were not exempt under the Bankruptcy Code. The bankruptcy and appeals courts agreed. The Rouseys appealed to the U.S. Supreme Court.

ISSUE: Do the individual IRA accounts satisfy two requirements under the Bankruptcy Code for exemption: (1) the right to receive the compensation due to a pension plan, annuity, profit-sharing plan, and the like; (2) the right to receive payment due to illness, disability, minimum retirement age of 59, and so on.

REASONING: The court found that the Rouseys' IRAs were the result of their pension plan from Northrup-Grumman and thus satisfied the first criterion. The second criterion was more problematic, as the trustee argued that the Rouseys could receive payments from their IRA at any time regardless of illness, disability, age, and so on. However, the Court ruled that since taking payments before the age of 59 invoked a substantial tax penalty, such a penalty in fact precluded the Rouseys from taking payment distribution "on demand." The Court found that the Rouseys' distribution of funds from their IRAs was in fact based on age. Thus the second criterion was satisfied.

DECISION AND REMEDY: The Supreme Court overruled the lower courts and held that the IRAs were exempt from the bankruptcy estate.

SIGNIFICANCE OF THE CASE: This decision put to rest one of the most compelling interests that employees have, protection of personal IRAs.

CRITICAL THINKING

One of the most controversial issues surrounding the judiciary is the notion of "judicial activism." "Judicial activism" is the claim that judges act outside of their role as judges and begin to legislate through judicial opinions. Critics argue that this role should be left to the legislatures, not the judiciary. Others argue that such interpretation is necessary to keep the law relevant and up-to-date. Do you believe that this case, coming from a relatively conservative Supreme Court, is an example of judicial activism?

ETHICAL DECISION MAKING

We can certainly understand the interests advanced by the decision made by the Court in this case. But what stakeholders are potentially harmed by this decision?

A debtor must file a list of the property that she or he claims is exempt. Under the Bankruptcy Code and the Bankruptcy Rules, creditors may file objections to the claimed exemptions. If a debtor improperly lists property as exempt and a creditor does not timely file an objection, the debtor will likely be permitted to claim the property as exempt.

Preferential Payments Because a major purpose of the Bankruptcy Code is to prevent debtors from making payments to one creditor and thus treating that creditor preferentially, the trustee has the power to recover preferential payments, or payments made by an insolvent debtor that give preferential treatment to one creditor over another. If the debtor made any payments within 90 days of the bankruptcy filing, the trustee can examine these payments as preferential payments. For a payment to be preferential, the trustee must show that the transfer gave the creditor more money than the creditor would have received through bankruptcy proceedings. Thus, other creditors are disadvantaged by the debtor's preferential payment.

preferential payment
A payment made by an insolvent debtor that gives preferential treatment to one creditor over another.

If the preferred creditor is an insider, such as a relative or partner, the trustee has the power to recover payments made within two years before the debtor's filing for bankruptcy. However, in such cases, the trustee must demonstrate the debtor's insolvency rather than assume insolvency. In contrast, the trustee may not recover preferential payments made for alimony or child support.

Fraudulent Transfers A trustee can recover preferential payments because these payments are not fair to creditors. Similarly, a trustee can void fraudulent transfers of property. These transfers can be actually or constructively fraudulent. An *actual fraudulent transfer* would be

fraudulent transfer
A transfer of property made with intent to defraud creditors or made for an amount significantly lower than the property's fair market value within two years of filing for bankruptcy.

made with intent to defraud creditors. Generally, there is no direct evidence of intent to defraud (e.g., an e-mail written by a debtor who states that he is transferring assets to hide them). To show *constructive* fraud, a trustee would establish intent through circumstantial evidence.

Similarly, if a debtor transfers property for an amount significantly lower than its fair market value, he or she may have engaged in a fraudulent transfer. Suppose that you are unable to pay your debts and are preparing to file for bankruptcy. You decide to sell your $50,000 boat to your business partner for $50. The trustee of your case could recover the boat if the sale occurred within two years of your filing for bankruptcy. Furthermore, you could be subject to criminal penalties for your attempt to hide your assets. By punishing debtors who attempt to hide their assets, the Bankruptcy Code provides protection for creditors.

Suppose that, instead of selling your boat to your business partner, you sold your boat to a creditor. Because you are making a payment to a creditor, the trustee would analyze this payment as a preferential payment (assessing how the other creditors would be harmed by this payment) rather than a fraudulent transfer (assessing the reasonableness of consideration for the transfer).

LO 8

Creditors' Claims Within 90 days of the creditors' meeting, all creditors (except secured creditors) must file a proof of claim with the bankruptcy court clerk to receive a portion of the debtor's estate. This proof of claim lists the creditor's name and address and the amount of the debt owed to the creditor. If the creditor fails to file such a claim, the creditor may not receive a portion of the debt. However, the fact that the claim was filed does not mean that the creditor will automatically receive a portion of the proceeds from the sale of the debtor's assets. The trustee must permit that the claim be allowed, and there are numerous defenses to creditors' claims.

When the trustee is sorting and examining the property, the trustee must determine whether a creditor has a secured interest in the debtor's property. If a secured interest exists, the creditor has first claim to the property. The debtor may decide to surrender the property to the creditor to satisfy the debt. Alternatively, the creditor may foreclose on the property and use the proceeds of the sale to reduce the debt owed to the creditor. However, the secured party is secured only to the value of the collateral.

All creditors do not have equal claims to the proceeds of the sale. Secured parties have priority over all unsecured parties in receiving portions of the proceeds of the liquidation. Thus, secured parties are paid first. The code establishes classes of priority claims. One class must be completely paid before anyone in another class receives any payment. If there are insufficient funds to fully pay all the creditors in one class, one class is paid proportionately and the lower classes get nothing. If a debtor improperly lists property as exempt and a creditor does not timely file an objection, the debtor will likely be permitted to claim the property as exempt.

The classes of priority claims among unsecured creditors are shown in Exhibit 17-5.

Exhibit 17-5

Classes of Priority Claims for Distribution

Class 1	Any unpaid domestic support obligations (alimony or child support)
Class 2	Court costs, trustee fees, attorney fees, and other administrative claims among expenses associated with the bankruptcy
Class 3	Unsecured claims in involuntary bankruptcy that arise through the debtor's ordinary business expenses from the date of filing the petition to the date of the appointment of the trustee
Class 4	Unsecured claims for unpaid wages, salaries, and commissions (up to $10,000 per individual) earned within 180 days of the filing of the petition
Class 5	Unsecured claims for contributions to employee retirement plans (up to $10,000 per employee)
Class 6	Unsecured claims by farmers and fishers (up to $4,000) against grain operators of grain storage facilities or fish storage or processing facilities
Class 7	Claims for deposits given to the debtor in connection with property or services never given
Class 8	Certain taxes and penalties due to government units
Class 9	Claims in bankruptcies related to federal depository institutions
Class 10	Unsecured claims for personal injuries and deaths caused by the debtor's operation of a motor vehicle while under the influence of alcohol or drugs

Discharge If a debtor has honestly dealt with her creditors during bankruptcy proceedings, the debtor is likely eligible for a discharge of her remaining debts. A discharge is a written federal court order signed by a bankruptcy judge stating that the debtor is immune from creditor actions to collect debts. When a debt is discharged, the debtor is essentially no longer responsible for the debt.

When is a discharge of debt appropriate? First, discharge of debt under Chapter 7 is available only to individuals, not partnerships or corporations. Second, discharge of debt is a privilege, not a right. A judge determines which debts are dischargeable. If the debtor has received a previous discharge of debt within eight years of the current filing for bankruptcy, the judge will likely refuse a new discharge of debt.

Exceptions to Discharge. Generally, most debts are discharged unless there are objections to the discharge or the debts are ineligible for discharge. If a major goal of bankruptcy law is to give debtors a fresh start, why are some debts nondischargeable? Some of the debts that are not dischargeable are debts to those who are in a weak bargaining position with the debtor. For example, child support and alimony payments are nondischargeable. Children and ex-spouses often depend on payments; consequently, the court will not permit the discharge of these debts. Exhibit 17-6 lists the debts that are nondischargeable as established by the Bankruptcy Code.

Revocation of Discharge. While a debt might be discharged, the discharge is not necessarily permanent. If the trustee or a creditor discovers that the debtor has acted fraudulently or dishonestly during the bankruptcy proceedings, the court may revoke the discharge within one year. The revocation of discharge allows the creditors to bring action against the debtor.

Reaffirmation of Debt A debtor may wish to repay a dischargeable debt. The debtor might owe money to a family member or a longtime business associate. To maintain a good relationship with these people, a debtor might choose to repay the debt instead of having the debt discharged. This repayment can occur through a reaffirmation agreement, an agreement in which the debtor agrees to pay the debt even though it could be discharged.

Unfortunately, creditors may attempt to pressure a debtor into reaffirming a debt. Congress was worried that debtors were unwisely surrendering their ability to discharge their debts by making reaffirmation agreements. Thus, Congress created the following extensive rules so that a decision for reaffirmation of debt cannot be an impulsive one:

1. The reaffirmation agreement must be made before the debt is discharged.
2. The debtor must be able to cancel the agreement, and the agreement must contain explicit information regarding the time frame in which the debtor may cancel the agreement.

discharge
A written federal court order signed by a bankruptcy judge stating that the debtor is immune from creditor actions to collect debt; i.e., a release from liability.

reaffirmation agreement
An agreement in which the debtor agrees to pay a debt even though it could have been discharged in bankruptcy.

Exhibit 17-6

Nondischargeable Debts under the Bankruptcy Code

1. Claims for back taxes or government fines within three years of filing for bankruptcy
2. Claims for liabilities against the debtor for his or her obtaining money or property under false pretenses, false representation, or fraud
3. Claims by creditors who weren't listed on the schedule and did not have notification of the bankruptcy proceedings
4. Claims based on fraud, embezzlement, and larceny by the debtor while she or he was acting in a fiduciary relationship
5. Alimony, child support, and some property settlements
6. Claims of willful or malicious conduct by the debtor that caused injury to another person or property
7. Specific student loans, unless payment of the loans imposes undue hardship on the debtor
8. Judgments against a debtor for claims resulting from the debtor's drinking and driving
9. Debts not discharged in previous bankruptcies
10. Claims for money borrowed to pay a tax to the United States that would be nondischargeable
11. Cash advances beyond $1,500 on a credit card

3. The agreement should contain a statement notifying the creditor that the law does not require the agreement.

4. The agreement must be filed with the bankruptcy court. Typically, the debtor's attorney files a form along with the agreement stating that the debtor is voluntarily entering the agreement and the agreement will not result in hardship to the debtor. Unless the attorney files this form, court approval for the agreement is needed.

CHAPTER 11: REORGANIZATIONS

The largest bankruptcy in U.S. history was the 2002 WorldCom bankruptcy filing. WorldCom had over $103 billion in assets at the time of filing. WorldCom filed under Chapter 11, which allows the creditors and debtor to create a plan to reorganize the debtor's financial affairs under the supervision of the bankruptcy court instead of liquidating the assets. Generally, the creditors and debtor agree that part of the debt will be discharged while the other part is or will be paid. Creditors generally agree to these plans because they believe that the value of the operating business is greater than the value of the business broken up and sold in pieces.

Who is eligible for Chapter 11 reorganization? Corporate debtors most frequently use Chapter 11 reorganization because they are permitted to remain in business. However, the debtor does not have to be a business entity to use reorganization; the debtor can be an individual unrelated to business. Stockbrokers, commodities brokers, banks, and savings and loan companies are not permitted to file under Chapter 11.

Most of the Chapter 11 reorganization procedures are similar to Chapter 7 liquidation procedures. Like liquidation, reorganization may be voluntary or involuntary. The reorganization process begins with the filing of the reorganization petition.

When the petition is filed, an automatic stay prohibits legal action against the debtor during the reorganization process. The debtor is required to file a list of creditors. Next, the order of relief is granted, and the court appoints a trustee, who appoints a creditors' committee of unsecured creditors. Because there may be hundreds of creditors, the creditors' committee is supposed to represent the interests of the range of creditors. The Bankruptcy Code contemplates seven creditors on the committee. The members of the creditors' committee have a fiduciary duty to the other creditors, and under BAPCPA, the creditors' committee must provide the other creditors with access to information.

Generally, the trustee is responsible for developing the reorganization plan to handle the creditors' claims. The *reorganization plan* is a contract between a debtor and his or her creditors. The goal of the plan is to rehabilitate the debtor while preserving the assets for the creditors. Reorganization plans usually state three things:

1. The classes of claims and interests in the debtor's property.

2. The treatment for each class of creditors.

3. A description of the means for execution of the agreement.

A debtor has an exclusive right to file a plan within the first 120 days of the case. If the debtor files a plan within this period, no one else may file a plan within the first 180 days after the debtor's filing. This period allows the debtor time to persuade the creditors to accept the plan. Once the plan has been developed, creditors must vote to accept the plan. For the plan to be accepted, two-thirds of the creditors of each class of creditors must vote to approve it. If the plan is approved, it will go before the court for confirmation. The court may decide to reject the plan if it is not in the best interests of the creditors. When the court confirms a plan, the debts not under the reorganization plan are discharged.

Collective Bargaining Agreements and Reorganization Through reorganization, a debtor can reject some contracts. In the early 1980s, legal scholars were concerned that debtors could use reorganization as a tool to avoid collective bargaining agreements. This issue became a serious concern when the Supreme Court held, in *National Labor Relations Board v. Bildisco & Bildisco,* that collective bargaining agreements are "executory contracts" and thus subject to rejection. In other words, a debtor was not required to engage in collective bargaining before rejecting part of the collective

bargaining agreement through reorganization. However, in the opinion, the judge stated that rejection is not permitted unless the reorganization procedures would benefit through the rejection.

After the Supreme Court decision was handed down in 1984, Congress amended the code to prevent debtors from misusing Chapter 11 to reject collective bargaining agreements. The amendments set forth procedures under which collective bargaining agreements can be rejected or modified.

CHAPTER 13: INDIVIDUAL REPAYMENT PLANS

Chapter 13, "Adjustments of Debts for Individuals," permits individuals to pay their debts to creditors in installment plans under the supervision of the court. Repayment plans may seem similar to reorganization. Any debtor who files under Chapter 13 could also have filed under Chapter 11. However, Chapter 13 repayment plans are usually simpler and less expensive. By statute, these plans last between 36 and 60 months.

Who is defined as a debtor for a Chapter 13 repayment plan? Only individuals are permitted to file under Chapter 13; partnerships and corporations are not eligible. Individuals must have a regular income and must owe less than $307,675 for fixed unsecured debts or $922,975 for fixed secured debts.

Filing the Petition As with the other forms of bankruptcy relief, the repayment process begins only when the debtor files the petition. However, repayment is distinct from other types of relief because repayment is voluntary only. A debtor cannot be forced into a repayment plan. In the petition, the debtor states that he is unable to pay his debts. The debtor might request an extension of time to pay the debts or ask that the total amount of debt be reduced.

Alternatively, the debtor might request a combination of those options. As in liquidation proceedings, the debtor commonly files various schedules listing the creditors as well as the debtor's assets. Furthermore, an automatic stay on litigation against the debtor is granted when the debtor files the petition. However, one of the benefits of Chapter 13 is that this stay applies to creditors' attempts to collect from co-debtors.

Creditors' Meeting and the Repayment Plan Proceedings After the debtor files the petition, the court calls a creditors' meeting. At this meeting, the debtor submits a plan of payment for her debts. This plan is not required to provide for the full payment of all claims. However, the plan must treat all same-class creditors equally, and the plan for repayment must not exceed a three-year period, unless the court approves otherwise.

Creditors do not vote to approve a Chapter 13 plan; if the court approves of the plan, the plan is accepted. The court holds a hearing to determine whether to confirm the plan. Unsecured creditors may object to the plan at the hearing. However, the court can overrule their objections if all the debtor's projected disposable income is used to make payments. If the court believes that the plan was created in good faith, the plan is accepted.

However, if the plan modifies a creditor's secured claim while proposing that the debtor keep the property securing the claim, the creditor may oppose the proposed plan. Court approval of an opposed plan that changes a secured claim is called a "cram down." Since BAPCPA, it has been harder for debtors to make changes to secured claims over the objections of creditors.

After the court approves the plan, the court appoints a trustee to carry out the repayment plan. Every Chapter 13 case has a trustee. The debtor makes monthly payments to the trustee based on his or her disposable income. The trustee then disburses payments to the creditors. Moreover, as payment for services, the trustee receives a percentage of the funds distributed to creditors.

Thirty days after the debtor files the plan, the debtor must begin making payments. The trustee must ensure that the debtor is making the payments. If the debtor fails to make payments, the court may decide to transfer the case to a liquidation bankruptcy or to refuse to grant the repayment plan.

Discharge of Debts under Repayment Proceedings After a debtor makes all payments under a repayment plan, the remaining debts are discharged. However, even if all payments are not made by the expiration of the plan, the court might discharge some of the debts if the debtor has experienced a severe hardship. Like liquidation, some debts, such as alimony and child support debts, are not dischargeable.

CHAPTER 12: FAMILY-FARMER PLANS

Chapter 12 provides for adjustment of the debts of family farmers. Chapter 12 was added to the code in the 1980s, in the midst of severe debt among large numbers of farmers. Many farmers had borrowed large amounts of money to increase their production; however, during that time there was a surplus of farm products. Consequently, many farmers faced serious financial problems. Congress addressed these problems with Chapter 12.

Not all farmers are eligible for Chapter 12 relief. A family farmer, under Chapter 12, must have regular annual income, and the farmer's gross income must be at least 50 percent farm-dependent. Moreover, 80 percent of the debt must be farm-related. Finally, the total debt must be under $1.5 million.

What are the family-farm relief proceedings? Congress modeled Chapter 12 after Chapter 13 relief. The procedure begins when the farmer files a Chapter 12 petition. Automatic stay is granted to protect the farmer from legal action. Within 90 days of the filing, the farmer must file a plan. A trustee is appointed to oversee the financial affairs and is permitted to sell unnecessary assets. The court holds a hearing to rule on the proposed plan. Unsecured creditors are entitled to at least liquidation value of the debt owed to them. Once the farmer fulfills his or her adjustment plan, the farmer will likely receive a discharge from his or her debts and retain possession of the farm.

 SUMMARY

Important Definitions Associated with Secured Transactions	*Secured interest:* An interest in personal property or fixtures that secures payment or performance of an obligation.
	Secured party: The person or party who holds the interest in the secured property.
	Debtor: The person or party who has an obligation to the secured party, the person who owns interest in the property.
	Security agreement: The agreement in which the debtor gives the secured interest to the secured party.
	Collateral: The property that is subject to the security interest.

Creation of Secured Interests

A security interest requires these three elements:

Written agreement: An agreement that describes the collateral and is signed by the debtor.
Value: An item of value given from the creditor to the debtor.
Debtor rights in the collateral: The rights of the debtor over the collateral.

Purchase-Money Security Interest

A *purchase-money security interest* is formed when a debtor uses borrowed money from the secured party to buy the collateral.

Perfected Security Interest

A *perfected security interest* is a security interest in which the creditor has legally protected his or her claim to the collateral. Methods of perfection include:

1. *Perfection by filing:* Perfection of an interest by filing a financing statement with a state agency.

 • *Place and duration of filing:* Generally, the financial statements for consumer goods must be filed with the county clerk, and the statement is valid for five years.

2. *Perfection by possession:* Perfection of an interest by holding the collateral of the debtor until the loan is paid off.

3. *Automatic perfection:* Perfection that automatically occurs when a retailer sells a consumer good.

4. *Perfection of movable collateral:* Perfection of an interest in collateral moved to another state by "reperfecting" the interest after four months.

5. *Perfection of security interests in automobiles and boats:* Perfection of an interest in an automobile or boat by noting the interest on the certificate of title.

The Scope of a Security Interest

After acquired property: A creditor has a security interest in property acquired by the debtor after the security agreement is made if a clause to this effect is included in the agreement.

Proceeds: A creditor automatically has rights to the proceeds from the sale of collateral for 10 days.

Termination of a Security Interest

Termination statement: An amendment to a financing statement stating that the debtor has no obligation to the secured party.

Priority Disputes

A *priority dispute* occurs when two corporations or individuals claim rights to the same collateral.

Secured versus unsecured: When an individual with a secured interest is disputing with an individual with an unsecured interest, the individual with the secured interest wins.

Secured versus secured: When two individuals with secured interests are disputing, the individual who perfected his or her interest first wins.

PMSI conflicts: If a party with a perfected purchase-money security interest disputes with another party, the PMSI party will almost always have a right to the collateral—regardless of when the agreement was perfected.

Secured party versus buyer: If a debtor sells his collateral, the creditor may dispute with the buyer over the collateral.

1. *Buyers in the ordinary course of business:* If a person buys the collateral in the ordinary course of business without realizing that it is collateral, she has a right to the good.
2. *Buyers of consumer goods:* As long as the consumer does not know that the product is secured, the buyer's new product is free of any security interest.
3. *Buyers of chattel paper and instruments:* If the buyer purchases chattel paper and instruments, he is free from any security interest.

Default

Default occurs when a debtor fails to pay back her or his loan. Remedies include:

1. *Taking possession of the collateral:* If a debtor defaults on a loan, the secured party can take possession of the collateral.
 - *Disposition of the collateral:* The creditor may sell, lease, or transfer the collateral.
 - *Retention of the collateral:* The creditor may choose to keep the collateral as payment of the debt.
2. *Proceeding to judgment:* A secured party may sue the debtor for the entire amount of the debt instead of dealing with the collateral.

Bankruptcy and Reorganization

A *debtor* is an entity that owes money to another entity. Bankruptcy law provides various options for debtors to resolve their debts. Bankruptcy remedies are available to individuals, partnerships, and corporations.

The Bankruptcy Act and Its Goals

Purpose:

1. To provide debtors with an opportunity to achieve a fresh financial start.
2. To offer protection to creditors.

Bankruptcy Proceedings

1. Every case begins with the filing of a petition for bankruptcy.
2. The court grants an automatic stay for creditor actions against the debtor's estate.
3. The court determines whether an order of relief should be granted.
4. The creditors meet with the debtor.
5. A payment plan is created and approved, usually by the creditors and the court.
6. Debts remaining after the plan is carried out are usually discharged.

Specific Types of Relief Available

Chapter 7: Sale of nonexempt assets and the distribution of money to the creditors.
Chapter 11: Reorganization of the debtor's financial affairs under supervision of the bankruptcy court.
Chapter 12: Adjustment of family farmers' debts.
Chapter 13: Adjustment of individuals' debts.

━━▶ Point/Counterpoint

Secured transactions give a creditor more security in ensuring that it will be repaid even if the debtor is unable to pay. As you learned in this chapter, when a debtor has both secured and unsecured creditors, the secured creditors will be paid first. Some scholars have argued that secured credit unfairly transfers risk to unsecured creditors.

Should Secured Credit Be Limited?	
YES	**NO**
Suppose an unsecured creditor extended a loan to a debtor. Years later, a secured creditor extends credit to the debtor and gains an interest in the debtor's property. The debtor's financial situation has changed since the unsecured loan. Because of the secured creditor's interest, the likelihood that the unsecured creditor will be paid in full is now lower. The unsecured creditor's only response is to increase its interest rate; however, the unsecured creditor does not necessarily know about the secured creditor's interest in the collateral. Consequently, when the debtor is unable to pay, the unsecured creditor may get nothing.	

Moreover, the availability of secured credit may force a debtor to encumber her assets to obtain credit. By limiting the availability of secured credit, both unsecured creditors and debtors will be treated more fairly. | Debtors and creditors are rational actors who have to make choices. An unsecured creditor makes a choice in extending credit to a debtor. The unsecured creditor makes money based on the interest it charges the debtor. Frequently, the interest rate on an unsecured loan is much higher than the interest rate on a secured loan. The unsecured creditor is compensated for the higher risk it may face.

Moreover, a debtor has a choice as to whether he wants to give the creditor an interest in his property. The debtor may choose a secured loan because of the lower interest rate. We should not restrict the debtor's choice.

Finally, many people who receive secured credit are economically disadvantaged. Limiting the availability of secured credit would harm these parties' ability to access credit. |

━━▶ Questions & Problems

1. What are the required elements of a security interest?

2. Describe the various ways in which secured interests are perfected.

3. How does bankruptcy law benefit debtors and creditors?

4. Under what circumstances would Chapter 11 be used rather than Chapter 7?

5. Maureen Mauro purchased a car from GMAC. GMAC was a secured party under the contract, and Mauro was responsible for making monthly payments. After Mauro defaulted in making her monthly payments, GMAC contacted Tri-City Auto Recovery to repossess the car. Tri-City employees Anthony and Edward Russo went to the Mauro home to tow the vehicle at 8:30 p.m. Mauro noticed that her headlights had been turned on and ran outside with an unloaded shotgun. She pointed the gun at Anthony Russo and told him to get out of the car. He stepped out of the car and attempted to grab the shotgun from Mauro. After calling the police, Mauro's husband also struggled with Anthony Russo. Edward Russo joined in the fight. The Mauros filed an action alleging that the repossession constituted a breach of peace. GMAC sought summary judgment dismissing the Mauros' claims for lack of merit. How do you think the court decided? [*Mauro v. GMAC,* 626 N.Y.S.2d 374 (1995).]

6. Both Purina Mills and Mountain Farm Credit Service (MFCS) claimed to be entitled to the proceeds from the sale of the debtor's cattle. Purina Mills argued that it held a first-priority, perfected security interest in the proceeds. Purina Mills supplied Grey Dawn Farms with feed on credit. Purina Mills obtained a security agreement and filed the financing statements necessary to perfect its security interest in the cattle. Grey Dawn Farms and MFCS had also entered into several security agreements. Though the cattle were offered

as collateral, MFCS never perfected its security interest. Grey Dawn Farms made plans to auction its cattle. After the auction, MFCS was paid in full. Purina Mills did not receive full compensation. Purina Mills subsequently demanded payment from MFCS. How do you think the court decided this case? [*Mountain Farm Credit Service v. Purina Mills, Inc.,* 459 S.E.2d 75 (1995).]

7. After Kelli Birrell defaulted on her car payments, Indiana Auto Sales & Repair paid an independent contractor $30 to repossess the car. The contractor's 15-year-old, unlicensed employee was directed to repossess the vehicle. During the repossession, the boy exceeded the speed limit and crashed into Birrell. She sustained serious personal injuries as a result of the collision. Birrell brought a lawsuit against Indiana Auto Sales & Repair for the injuries she sustained during the repossession. The trial court found in favor of Indiana Auto Sales & Repair. Birrell appealed the decision. Do you think the court of appeals affirmed or reversed the decision? Why or why not? [*Birrell v. Indiana Auto Sales & Repair,* 698 N.E.2d 6 (1998).]

8. Century Energy is a partnership in the business of producing oil and gas. Century received a loan from the First Interstate Bank of Commerce. A security agreement was executed, and two of Century's oil pumps, the F pump and the E pump, served as the collateral. First Interstate Bank perfected its security interest by filing the appropriate financial statements. Century subsequently developed a second business entity, Limited. Limited became indebted to New Oil, Inc., and the F pump was transferred to New Oil to satisfy the debt. First Interstate Bank became aware that New Oil claimed ownership of the F pump. New Oil notified First Interstate that it intended to sell the F pump. First Interstate brought an action to have the rights of the F pump determined. The trial court found that First Interstate Bank had a perfected security interest in the pumping unit that was superior to any interest of New Oil. New Oil appealed the decision. How do you think the court decided on appeal? [*New Oil, Inc. v. First Interstate Bank of Commerce,* 895 P.2d 871 (1995).]

9. James Koontz entered into an agreement with Chrysler to purchase a 1988 Plymouth Sundance. He was to make 60 monthly payments of $185.92. When Koontz defaulted on the loan, Chrysler notified him that the vehicle would be repossessed if the payments were not made. Koontz told Chrysler that he was planning on making up the payments, and he urged Chrysler not to repossess the car. Despite his urgings, Chrysler sent the M&M Agency to repossess the vehicle. When he heard the repossession in process, Koontz, who was in his underwear, ran outside and yelled,

"Don't take it!" Chrysler subsequently sold the vehicle and filed a complaint against Koontz to retrieve the balance of the loan. Koontz filed an affirmative defense and alleged that Chrysler had breached the peace when repossessing the car. The trial court ruled in favor of Chrysler. How do you think the court decided the case on appeal? [*Chrysler Credit Corp. v. Koontz,* 661 N.E.2d 1171 (1996).]

10. For-Med, Inc., and David Anderson executed a loan and security agreement in the amount of $79,924.89 with First Westside Bank. Anderson offered his 1978 Blue Bird motor home as collateral. After Anderson and For-Med defaulted on the loan, First Westside repossessed the motor home and sold it for $60,000. The motor home was very large, and First Westside claimed that it could not be left on its parking lot for show. Therefore, First Westside did not officially advertise that the motor vehicle was for sale. Rather, bids were solicited by word of mouth from financial institutions, dealers, and customers. A customer purchased the motor home, and after making $22,000 worth of repairs, he was able to sell the vehicle for only $58,000. First Westside sued For-Med and David Anderson to collect the difference between the loan and the sale price of the motor home. The court found in favor of First Westside. On appeal, For-Med and Anderson argued that the sale of the collateral was not commercially reasonable because First Westside failed to adequately advertise the motor home. Therefore, For-Med and Anderson believed that First Westside failed to obtain the best price under the circumstances. How do you think the court decided on appeal? Was the sale price of the collateral commercially unreasonable? [*First Westside Bank v. For-Med, Inc.,* 529 N.W.2d 66 (1995).]

11. Gergely, an obstetrician, performed an amniocentesis on Jordan Lee-Brenner's mother during her pregnancy. As a result of problems with the procedure, he was blinded in one eye. After his birth, and through his guardian, Lee-Brenner brought an action against Gergely, claiming that Gergely had misrepresented the need for amniocentesis and had performed it negligently. Lee-Brenner received an award for $780,282, which he failed to collect prior to Gergely's filing a Chapter 7 bankruptcy petition. Lee-Brenner moved to have the judgment set aside as a nondischargeable debt. The bankruptcy court dismissed his petition, so he appealed. On what grounds could he argue that the debt should not have been discharged? Do you think his argument was successful before the appellate court? [*In re Gergely,* 110 F.3d 1448 (9th Cir 1997).]

12. First Jersey Securities, Inc., filed a petition for Chapter 11 bankruptcy after the Securities and Exchange Commission (SEC) obtained a court order

against the firm to repay $75 million in illegal proceeds. On the same day that its petition was filed, First Jersey transferred $600,000 in assets to its attorneys, the law firm RSW, to pay for previous and future legal services. The trustee and SEC both challenged the transfer of the assets to the debtor's lawyers. The bankruptcy court and district court upheld the transfer. The trustee and SEC appealed. Why do you believe the circuit court either upheld or overturned the district court's ruling? [*In re First Jersey Securities, Inc.,* 180 F.3d 504 (3d Cir. 1999).]

13. On August 2, 2000, Sheldon B. Toibb filed a voluntary petition for relief under Chapter 7 of the Bankruptcy Code, disclosing assets that included stock in an electric power company. When he discovered that the stock had substantial value, he decided to avoid its liquidation by moving to convert his Chapter 7 case to one under Chapter 11's reorganization provisions. After the bankruptcy court granted his motion and he filed his reorganization plan, the court dismissed his petition, finding that he did not qualify for relief under Chapter 11 because he was not engaged in an ongoing business. The district court and the court of appeals affirmed. Why do you believe the U.S. Supreme Court reversed or affirmed the lower court's ruling? [*In re Sheldon Baruch Toibb, Petitioner,* 501 U.S. 157, 111 S. Ct. 2197.]

14. Debtors Bill Brandon Beard and Peggy Jane Beard came up with a plan that permitted them to remit payments directly to an unsecured creditor, without having to transfer the funds to that creditor through the bankruptcy trustee. The two lower courts recognized that by granting the debtors the right to make these direct remittances and thus to bypass the standing trustee, the debtors would thereby avoid having to pay certain statutory fees that the standing trustee would normally receive in the course of administering the Chapter 12 bankruptcy estate. The bankruptcy court approved the plan, as did the district court. The trustee appealed. Why should the appellate court affirm or overturn the lower court decision? [*In re Bill Brandon Beard and Peggy Jane Beard,* 45 F.3d 113 (6th Cir. 1985).]

Looking for more review material?

The Online Learning Center at **www.mhhe.com/kubasekess** contains this chapter's "Assignment on the Internet" and also a list of URLs for more information, entitled "On the Internet." Find both of them in the Student Center portion of the OLC, along with quizzes and other helpful materials.

Agency and Liability to Third Parties

····▶ **CASE OPENER**

National Farmers Union Insurance and an Independent Contractor

Elmer Oestman was an insurance agent for National Farmers Union Insurance Company. The company had a contract providing that the "local agent, acting solely as an independent contractor, is hereby authorized to solicit and submit written applications for insurance policies and other contracts of insurer strictly in accordance with the instructions and direction of insurer." The contract specifically stated that "[n]othing contained herein shall be construed as creating the relationship of employer and employee between the local agent and insurer." Oestman was commissioned through the insurer, filed his own taxes as a self-employed individual, set his own and his staff's working hours, had sole discretion in hiring and firing his staff, bore all expenses in selling insurance, and provided his own transportation and office equipment. When his employment was terminated, Oestman sued the insurance company, claiming a violation of the Age Discrimination in Employment Act of 1967.

1. On the basis of the agreement between Oestman and the insurance company, do you think Oestman is justified in filing a lawsuit against the insurance company for firing him? Why?
2. What rights does Oestman have as an independent contractor? How would these rights differ if he were an employee of the insurance company?

····▶ **LEARNING OBJECTIVES**

After reading this chapter, you will be able to answer the following questions:

LO 1 How is an agency relationship created?

LO 2 What are the different types of agency?

LO 3 What are the different types of agency relationships?

LO 4 What are the duties of the agent?

LO 5 What are the duties of the principal?

LO 6 What are the different types of authority of the agent?

LO 7 Do the principal and the agent have any contractual liability? How so?

LO 8 How can an agency relationship be terminated?

In the Case Opener, it is important to determine whether Oestman is an employee or an independent contractor of the insurance company because different legal obligations arise, depending on the nature of the relationship. One of the most important relationships in the business world is the *agency relationship,* in which the employee may be an agent of the employer, having the ability, among others, to bind that employer legally.

Agency relationships are crucial to running large businesses because the use of agents allows corporations to enter into contracts and therefore conduct business in multiple locations simultaneously. This chapter explores the nature and creation of the agency relationship, as well as the legal obligations that the parties take on when they form such a relationship.

Introduction to Agency Law

agency relationship
The association between one party and an agent who acts on behalf of that party.

agent
A party who has the authority to act on behalf of and bind another party.

principal
The party that an agent's authority can bind or act on behalf of.

agency
The fiduciary relationship that arises when one person consents to have another act on his behalf and subject to his control and the other consents to do so.

fiduciary
A person who has a duty to act primarily for another person's benefit.

Agency is generally defined as a relationship between a principal and an agent. In an **agency relationship,** the **agent** is authorized to act for and on behalf of the **principal,** who hires the agent to represent him or her. The Restatement of Agency defines **agency** as "the fiduciary relation that results from the manifestation of consent by one person to another that the other shall act in his behalf and subject to his control, and consent by the other so to act."[1] (A **fiduciary** is a person who has a duty to act primarily for another person's benefit. A lawyer, for example, is a fiduciary for his or her client. We discuss fiduciaries in depth later in this chapter.)

Agency law is primarily state law. Thus, while there are similarities among the laws governing agency relationships, they may vary somewhat from state to state. For example, at least 27 states have enacted statutes governing the behavior of sports agents. Twenty-three of those states impose civil penalties or damages on agents for violations of the athlete agent statutes. Twenty-four states (California and Florida, e.g.) have established criminal penalties for sports agents who violate the state statute. In contrast, only five states have criminalized statute violations by the athletes themselves.

Agency law is especially important for modern firms doing business in foreign countries. More and more companies are expanding their commercial ventures to overseas markets. While foreign countries offer fresh markets and eager consumers, American companies often run into legal difficulties in other countries. These difficulties may arise from a language barrier or simply a lack of knowledge about local laws. To avoid such problems, many companies hire agents familiar with local laws, customs, and customers to help them function smoothly in foreign markets.

LO 1

Creation of the Agency Relationship

Agency relationships are consensual relationships formed by informal oral agreements or formal written contracts. However, an agency relationship exists only when the principal takes action to ask another individual to act on behalf of the principal.

When can an agency relationship be created? First, an agency relationship can be created only for a lawful purpose in the same way that a contract cannot have an illegal purpose. Thus,

[1] Restatement (Second) of Agency, sec. 1(1). The Restatement is a valuable reference that is well respected in the legal profession. It is frequently cited by judges as well as attorneys and scholars in making legal arguments. The Restatement provides a summary of agency law.

Expressed agency	Formed by making a written or oral agreement
Implied authority	Formed by implication through the conduct of the parties
Agency by estoppel	Formed when a principal leads a third party to believe that another individual serves as his or her agent but the principal had made no agreement with the so-called agent
Agency by ratification	Exists when an individual misrepresents himself or herself as an agent for another party and the principal accepts or ratifies the unauthorized act

Exhibit 18-1

Creation of Agency
Relationships

LO 2

a principal could not hire an agent to kill someone on behalf of the principal.[2] Second, almost anyone can act as an agent. A contract made by an agent is viewed as a contract between the principal and a third party. Therefore, a person can serve as an agent regardless of age or competency.[3] However, if an individual does not have contractual capacity, the individual could not hire an agent to make contracts on his or her behalf. For example, because a contract entered into by a minor is voidable, most states do not allow minors to hire agents.

As long as these two criteria are met, agency relationships can be created based on any of the following four forms of authority:

1. By expressed agency or agency by agreement.
2. By implied authority.
3. By apparent agency or agency by estoppel.
4. By ratification.

The following sections discuss the types of agency formation, and Exhibit 18-1 presents a summary.

EXPRESSED AGENCY (AGENCY BY AGREEMENT)

When parties form an agency relationship by making a written or oral agreement, the agency is known as **expressed agency,** or **agency by agreement.** Expressed agency is the most common type of agency. As specified in the expressed agreement, the agent has the authority to contract on behalf of the principal. While a contract is not necessary, if an agency agreement is formed through a contract, the contract must meet all the elements of a contract discussed in Chapter 7. If a principal agrees to hire no other agent for a period of time or until a particular job is done, the principal and agent have entered into an exclusive agency contract.

One legal document that establishes agency relationships is a **power of attorney,** a document that gives an agent authority to sign legal documents on behalf of the principal. Power of attorney can be classified in several ways. First, a power of attorney can be general or specific. For example, with a general power of attorney, a principal gives an agent broad authority to sign legal documents on behalf of the principal. In contrast, with a specific power of attorney, a principal gives authority to an agent for only the specific areas or purposes listed in the agreement.

Powers of attorney are often given for business and health care purposes. In the health care instance, a principal gives power of attorney to an agent so that the agent can make decisions about the principal's medical care in case the principal cannot make those decisions. Given that a principal must have the ability to enter into contracts to enter into an agency relationship, a principal may not enact a power of attorney after becoming incompetent. Therefore, before incapacitation, a principal may create a durable power of attorney.

A **durable power of attorney** is a written document, created by a principal, expressing his or her wishes for an agent's authority not to be affected by the principal's subsequent incapacity. Alternatively, a durable power of attorney might become active only after a principal becomes incapacitated in any matter. Because the agreement is entered into before incapacitation, a durable power of attorney is legally binding after the principal becomes incapacitated.

expressed agency
An agency created in written or oral agreement. Also called *agency by agreement.*

power of attorney
A specific form of express authority, granting an agent specific powers.

durable power of attorney
A document that specifies that an agent's authority is intended to continue beyond the principal's incapacitation.

[2] Restatement (Second) of Agency, sec. 19.

[3] Restatement (Second) of Agency, sec. 21.

It is important to note a few additional points. First, the Restatement states, "[A]n agency relation exists only if there has been a manifestation by the principal to the agent that the agent may act on his account, and consent by the agent so to act."[4] Therefore, in addition to the above criteria, there needs to be agreement by the principal to have the person act as an agent and by the agent to act for the principal. As noted below, this agreement can be reached in several different ways.

Second, agency agreements usually do not need to be in writing. However, there are two important exceptions. First, agency agreements need to be in writing whenever an agreement is reached for an agent to enter into a contract that under the statute of frauds must be in writing. For example, Janet wants Phil to act as her agent. She grants him the power to enter into contracts. The statute of frauds, or, more specifically, the equal dignities rule, mandates that the type of contracts Phil is allowed to enter into must be in writing. Therefore, Phil's agreement with Janet must also be in writing. Also, whenever an agent is given power of attorney (discussed below), the agreement must be in writing.

Third, agents may perform their services gratuitously. A **gratuitous agent** is one who acts without consideration; that is, the agent is not paid for his or her services. Gratuitous agents function much like regular agents, with a few specific exceptions noted later in this chapter.

gratuitous agent
An agent who acts without being paid for his or her services.

AGENCY BY IMPLIED AUTHORITY

In some cases, an agency relationship is not created by an expressed agreement but, rather, is implied by the conduct of the parties. The circumstances of a situation determine the extent of an agent's ability to conduct business on behalf of the principal. However, the implied authority cannot conflict with any express authority.

APPARENT AGENCY (AGENCY BY ESTOPPEL)

Suppose a principal leads a third party to believe that another individual serves as his or her agent but the principal has made no agreement with the so-called agent. Does an agency relationship exist? Yes, because by his or her conduct, the principal has created **apparent agency,** or **agency by estoppel.** According to the principal's conduct, the agent has apparent authority to act; thus, the principal is estopped, or prevented, from denying that the individual is an agent.[5] When a third party relies on the principal's conduct and makes an agreement with an apparent agent, the principal must uphold any agreements made by the agent. If the principal attempts to deny an agency relationship existed, the third party must demonstrate that he or she reasonably believed, based on the principal's conduct, that an agency relationship existed. The court will consider the principal's conduct in determining whether an agency relationship existed.

apparent agency
An agency relationship created by operation of law when one party, by his actions, causes a third party to believe someone is his agent when that person actually has no authority. Also called *agency by estoppel.*

Suppose an executive of Emporium Carpet is interviewing a potential salesperson named Jose. In the course of the interview, the employer introduces Jose to some clients who are in the building. During the conversation, he says, "I cannot wait to have Jose in our firm. The sooner he works for us, the happier I will be." For some reason, Jose is not hired. But Jose happens to meet these clients later, and in the course of their conversations, the clients place an order with Jose, believing him to be an employee of Emporium Carpet. Emporium now has an obligation to fulfill the order because the third party reasonably believed Jose was an agent of Emporium.

The Case Nugget on the next page discusses the importance of apparent authority.

AGENCY BY RATIFICATION

Suppose Fred is driving home and sees a car with a "For Sale" sign in the window. He stops to look at the car because his friend wants to buy a used car. He's amazed at the price and quality of the car, so he tells the owner his friend wants to buy the car. The owner claims that another individual is coming to probably buy the car in an hour. So, to ensure that his friend gets this car, Fred signs a contract to purchase the car, but he notes on the contract that he is an agent of his friend. Because he is not an agent for his friend, the friend is not required to uphold the contract.

[4] Restatement (Second) of Agency, sec. 15.

[5] Restatement (Second) of Agency, sec. 8B.

CASE Nugget

Apparent Authority and Agency

Steven A. B. Hannington, Appellant, v. Trustees of the University of Pennsylvania and Dr. Mark Bernstein, Appellees
Superior Court of Pennsylvania

2002 Pa. Super. 314; 809 A.2d 406; 2002 Pa. Super. LEXIS 2873

Steven Hannington, a doctoral candidate at the University of Pennsylvania was expelled for outstanding tuition fees, which he claimed had been waived in exchange for organizing a two-day conference on behalf of the university's Energy Management and Policy Program. Hannington filed suit against the university for breach of contract, and the university countersued for the outstanding tuition, fees, and interest. Before the case went to trial, Hannington and the University negotiated a settlement through their attorneys. Hannington's attorney notified the court that an agreement had been reached, and he filed an "Order to Settle, End, and Discontinue." One month later, Hannington obtained new counsel and filed a motion to restore the case to the trial list, claiming that his previous attorney had exceeded the scope of his authority by settling the case without his express authority. Hannington's motion was denied by the trial court, and he appealed.

The appellate court affirmed the trial court's decision, citing the doctrine of apparent authority for three reasons. First, the university was innocent and free from fault. Second, Hannington's attorney notified the university in a letter that Hannington had approved of the attached settlement release. Third, the negotiations took place over a six-month period, during which Hannington "had clothed his lawyer with the authority to communicate with the University on his behalf. Therefore, it was reasonable for the University and its lawyer to believe that Appellant had expressly authorized the settlement agreement." The court ruled that, regardless of Hannington's claims regarding the conduct of his attorney, the settlement was enforceable. If Hannington's attorney had not exceeded the scope of his authority, the settlement would be enforceable on its own. If Hannington's attorney had exceeded the scope of his authority, the doctrine of apparent authority would be applicable, giving the university the right to rely on the representation of Hannington's attorney to enter into a binding contract.

However, if Fred's friend agrees to purchase the car, the friend has accepted him as the agent for the contract. Fred's friend is now bound by the contract, and Fred cannot be held liable for misrepresenting himself as the agent. This type of agency relationship is **agency by ratification.** As suggested in the example above, there are two requirements for agency by ratification:

agency by ratification An agency relationship that arises when an individual misrepresents himself or herself as an agent for another party and that party accepts the unauthorized act.

1. An individual must misrepresent himself or herself as an agent for another party.
2. The principal accepts or ratifies the unauthorized act.

For ratification to be effective, two additional requirements must be met:

1. The principal must have complete knowledge of all material facts regarding the contract.
2. The principal must ratify the entirety of the agent's act. (The principal cannot accept certain parts and reject other parts of the agent's act.)

Agency Relationships

LO 3

There are generally three types of business relationships to which agency laws are relevant: the principal-agent relationship, the employer-employee relationship, and the employer–independent contractor relationship. We discuss all three in the following sections and summarize them in Exhibit 18-2.

Exhibit 18-2

Types of Business
Relationships and
Their Significance
for Agency

RELATIONSHIP	HOW TO IDENTIFY	SIGNIFICANT FOR WHAT ISSUES?
Principal-agent	Parties have *agreed* that agent will have power to bind principal in contract.	Contract law
Employer-employee	Employer has right to *control* conduct of employees.	Tort law, tax law, wage law, discrimination law, copyright law
Employer–independent contractor	Employer has *no control* over details of conduct of independent contractor.	Tort law, tax law, wage law, discrimination law, copyright law

PRINCIPAL-AGENT RELATIONSHIP

The principal-agent relationship typically exists when an employer hires an employee to enter into contracts on behalf of the employer. This relationship is the most basic type of agency relationship. For example, suppose a salesclerk at Abercrombie & Fitch sells Amanda a shirt. The clerk is acting on behalf of the owner; consequently, any sales made by the salesclerk are binding on the owner of Abercrombie & Fitch. Similarly, think of all the advertisements seen on television in which a professional athlete speaks on behalf of a product. The athlete usually hires an agent to find and make agreements on behalf of the athlete to promote products.

EMPLOYER-EMPLOYEE RELATIONSHIP

Whenever an employer hires an employee to perform some sort of physical service, the parties have created an employer-employee relationship. The employee is subject to the control of the employer.[6] Generally, all employees are considered to be agents of the employer. Even employees not legally authorized to enter into contracts binding their employer, or to interact with third parties, are considered agents. While all employees are agents, the reverse is not true. That is, not all agents are employees.

EMPLOYER–INDEPENDENT CONTRACTOR RELATIONSHIP

independent contractor

A person who is hired to perform a task for another but who is not the other's employee.

Employers often hire independent contractors, persons who are not employees, to conduct certain tasks. The Restatement of Agency defines an independent contractor as "a person who contracts with another to do something for him but who is not controlled by the other nor subject to the other's right to control with respect to his physical conduct in the performance of the undertaking."[7] For example, building contractors, doctors, stockbrokers, and lawyers are independent contractors. Furthermore, building contractors, doctors, stockbrokers, and lawyers are agents, while not employees. However, not all independent contractors are agents. Independent contractors cannot enter into contracts on behalf of the principal unless authorized to do so by the principal.

Employee or Independent Contractor? The question of whether a worker is an employee or an independent contractor has important implications in terms of workers' compensation, workplace safety, and unemployment statutes. The employer-employee relationship is subject to the workers' compensation, workplace safety, employment discrimination, and unemployment statutes, while the employer–independent contractor relationship is not. Furthermore, as discussed later in this chapter, employers are generally liable in tort for the actions of their employees, while they are generally not liable for the actions of independent contractors.

When courts are deciding whether a worker is an employee or an independent contractor, perhaps the most important issue they consider is how much control the employer exerts over

[6] Restatement (Second) of Agency, sec. 2.

[7] Restatement (Second) of Agency, sec. 2.

Exhibit 18-3

Independent
Contractor or
Employee?

CRITERIA	EMPLOYEE	INDEPENDENT CONTRACTOR
Does the worker engage in a distinct occupation or an independently established business?	No	Yes
Is the work done under the employer's supervision, or does a specialist without supervision complete the work?	Employer supervision	Specialist without supervision
Does the employer supply the tools?	Yes	No
What skill is required for the occupation?	No specialized skill	Great degree of skill
What is the length of time for which the worker is employed?	Long time	Varies
Is the worker a regular part of the business of the employer?	Yes	No
How is the worker paid?	Regular payments according to time	When the job is completed

the agent.[8] If the employer has substantial control over day-to-day operations of the worker, the worker is generally considered an employee.

While the degree of control an employer maintains is the central factor courts look at in determining whether a person is an employee or an independent contractor, it is by no means the only factor examined. Exhibit 18-3 lists the additional criteria the court considers in deciding whether a worker is an employee or an independent contractor. These criteria were established in the Restatement of Agency.[9]

Duties of the Agent and the Principal

LO 4

An agency relationship is a fiduciary relationship of trust, confidence, and good faith. Thus, the formation of an agency relationship results in the creation of certain duties that the principal and agent owe each other. These duties are established in the agency agreement and are implied by the law. We discuss them in the following sections and present a summary in Exhibit 18-4.

PRINCIPAL'S DUTIES TO THE AGENT

LO 5

When a principal contractually agrees that another person can make agreements on his or her behalf, the principal owes certain duties to the agent. If these duties are not fulfilled, the principal has violated the agent's rights. Consequently, the agent can bring a suit against the principal. If

Exhibit 18-4

Summary of Duties
in an Agency
Relationship

PRINCIPAL TO AGENT	AGENT TO PRINCIPAL
Duty of compensation	Duty of loyalty
Duty of reimbursement and indemnification	Duty of performance
Duty of cooperation	Duty of notification
Duty to provide safe working conditions	Duty of obedience
	Duty of accounting

[8] Restatement (Second) of Agency, sec. 2(3).

[9] Restatement (Second) of Agency, sec. 220.

the agent is successful in bringing a suit against the principal, the agent is entitled to contract or tort remedies. Furthermore, if the principal has failed to meet duties owed to the agent, the agent can refuse to act on behalf of the principal until the failure is remedied.

duty to compensate
A principal's obligation to pay an agent for his or her services.

Duty of Compensation The principal has a duty to compensate the agent for services provided unless the parties have agreed that the agent will act gratuitously. The agency contract usually specifies the type and amount of compensation as well as the time at which the compensation will be given to the agent. Thus, if a person hires an attorney to represent her, she has a duty to pay that attorney, her agent. If there is no agreement on the amount the principal will compensate the agent, the courts suggest that compensation should be calculated according to the customary fee in the situation.[10]

duty of reimbursement and indemnification
A principal's obligation to reimburse an agent for any expenses or losses incurred by the agent on the principal's behalf.

Duty of Reimbursement and Indemnification The principal has a duty of reimbursement and indemnification to the agent. If an agent makes authorized expenditures in the course of working on behalf of the principal, the principal has a duty to reimburse the agent for the amount of money spent.[11] Thus, if an agent takes a trip on behalf of the principal, the principal must have authorized this trip if the agent is to be reimbursed by the principal.

Similarly, the principal has the duty to indemnify or reimburse the agent for any losses the agent incurs while working within the scope of authority on the principal's behalf.[12] For example, suppose an agent makes an agreement with a third party on behalf of the principal and the principal fails to uphold the agreement. The third party could sue the agent for damages because of the failure to uphold the agreement. The principal has a duty to indemnify the agent for the losses the third party regained.

duty of cooperation
A principal's obligation to assist an agent in the performance of the agent's duties and not to interfere with reasonable conduct of the agent.

Duty of Cooperation The principal also owes a duty of cooperation to the agent. Therefore, the principal must assist the agent in the performance of his or her duties. Furthermore, the principal can do nothing to interfere with the reasonable conduct of an agent. For example, suppose Suzy hired someone to sell her car for her. Suzy must be willing to let the agent show her car to interested buyers.

duty to provide safe working conditions
A principal's obligation to provide proper equipment, suitable premises, and a safe working environment in accordance with federal and state statutes.

Duty to Provide Safe Working Conditions The principal has a duty to provide safe working conditions for the agent. This includes equipment, premises, and other working conditions. If the principal is aware of unsafe working conditions, the principal has a duty to warn the agent of the potential danger and make the necessary repairs. Federal and state statutes, such as the Occupational Safety and Health Act (OSHA), set specific standards for the working environment. If an employer violates these standards, the employer may be subject to fines.

AGENT'S DUTIES TO THE PRINCIPAL

When an agent agrees to act on behalf of a principal, the agent is a *fiduciary,* a person in a position of trust and confidence, and as such owes certain duties to the principal. However, because the agent makes agreements on behalf of the principal, the agent is in a position to potentially harm the principal. If, for example, an agent makes numerous contracts the principal could not possibly carry out all at once, it is likely the third parties would sue the principal for not carrying out the agreements. If the agent breaches his or her fiduciary duties, the principal can sue the agent, and the principal may be entitled to a variety of contract and tort remedies beyond those stated in the contract.

duty of loyalty
An agent's obligation to act in the interest of the principal.

Duty of Loyalty Courts suggest that the duty of loyalty is perhaps the most important duty an agent owes to a principal. Because the agency relationship is a fiduciary relationship (i.e., a relationship of trust), the agent has a responsibility to act in the interest of the principal.[13] There are

[10] Restatement (Second) of Agency, sec. 443.

[11] Restatement (Second) of Agency, sec. 438.

[12] Restatement (Second) of Agency secs. 438 and 439.

[13] Restatement (Second) of Agency, sec. 401.

a number of ways the agent carries out her duty of loyalty to the principal, including avoiding conflicts of interest and protecting the principal's confidentiality.

An agent can in most situations represent and act on behalf of only one principal in an agreement. An agent usually cannot represent both the principal and a third party (who would then become another principal if represented by the same agent) in an agreement because there could be a conflict of interest. In addition, the agent has a duty to notify the principal of any offers from third parties.

For example, suppose Tony has hired a real estate agent to make land purchases for him. A third party notifies the real estate agent that some of her property will soon be going up for sale, and the third party wants to know whether Tony, the principal, would be interested in buying the property. The real estate agent cannot decide to buy that property for himself until (1) the agent has communicated the offer to Tony and (2) Tony has considered and rejected the offer.

The duty of loyalty also requires that the agent keep confidential any information about the principal during the course of agency, as well as after the agency relationship is terminated. The agent cannot disclose or misuse any information received during or after the agency relationship with the principal.

Duty of Notification Not only does the agent have to communicate offers from third parties, but the agent must also communicate any information the agent thinks could be important to the principal. This duty is known as the **duty of notification**.[14] For example, if a third party has made an agreement through an agent with a principal and the third party has failed to meet the agreement, the agent must notify the principal of this information in a timely manner. It is critical for an agent to inform the principal of all relevant information because the law typically assumes the principal is aware of all information revealed to the agent, regardless of whether the agent shares all this information with the principal. In Case 18-1 pay special attention to the duties of the agent to the principal.

duty of notification
An agent's obligation to inform the principal of the agent's actions on the principal's behalf and of all relevant information.

[14] Restatement (Second) of Agency, sec. 381.

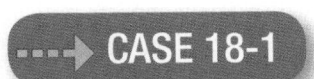

CASE 18-1

SIERRA PACIFIC INDUSTRIES v. JOSEPH H. CARTER
COURT OF APPEAL OF CALIFORNIA
104 Cal. App. 3d 579 (1980)

FACTS: *Joseph H. Carter, a licensed California real estate broker, was hired by Sierra Pacific Industries to sell a 10-acre parcel of land for an asking price of $85,000, of which Sierra Pacific would receive $80,000 and Carter $5,000. Carter showed the Willow Creek property to several prospective buyers; however, he eventually sold the property for $85,000 to his daughter and son-in-law, Debbie and David Benson, and retained the $5,000 commission without informing Sierra Pacific of his relationship to the buyers of the land. Sierra Pacific brought a claim of fraud against Carter. At trial, the jury ruled in favor of Carter; however, Sierra Pacific moved for a new trial, and the motion was granted. Carter appealed. The issue before the court was whether Carter had breached his duties to his principal, Sierra.*

ISSUE: What are the duties of an agent in an agency relationship?

REASONING: In the court's own words:

An agent bears a fiduciary relationship to his or her principal which requires, among other things, disclosure of all information in the agent's possession relevant to the subject matter of the agency. An agent may not compete with the principal, nor may he or she act as agent for another whose interests conflict with those of the principal.

In the context of an agreement to sell land on another's behalf, the general duties inherent in every agency become more specific. A real estate agent must refrain from dual representation in a sale transaction unless he or she obtains the consent of both principals after full disclosure. This means under most circumstances if the

agent is related to the buyer in a way which suggests a reasonable possibility the agent him or herself could indirectly be acquiring an interest in the subject property, the relationship is a "material fact" which must be disclosed.

There is no question Carter concealed information material to this transaction from his principal, Sierra Pacific. He claims he was exempted from the disclosure requirement, however, on the basis of a so-called "net listing." Under a net-listing agreement the seller agrees to take a fixed sum of money for his property and the broker is entitled to all additional sums as his commission. It is true under this type of arrangement a broker may not be obligated to disclose any relationship he has to the buyer.

DECISION AND REMEDY: The judge decided that the exception was not applicable to the facts of this case. He concluded that Carter owed a duty of disclosure to his principal, Sierra Pacific, and that the duty was breached. Apart from any actual and proximately caused loss on the price it received for its property, Sierra Pacific was entitled to recover the commission it paid to Carter. The judge found Carter liable to Sierra Pacific and affirmed the lower court's granting of a new trial.

SIGNIFICANCE OF THE CASE: When entering into agency relationships, all parties to the relationship need to understand their rights and duties. This case helps clarify those rights and duties.

CRITICAL THINKING

Why do you think the trial court jury concluded the opposite of the appellate judge's decision? Where does the jury's argument falter, according to the judge?

ETHICAL DECISION MAKING

The judge believed that Carter "concealed information material to this transaction from his principal, Sierra Pacific." What set of guidelines could Carter have followed in making a more ethical decision? What guidelines does the judge appear to be following in reaching his decision? Are the judge's guidelines ethically superior to those chosen by Carter? Why or why not?

duty of performance
An agent's obligation to perform the duties specified in the agency agreement and to do so with reasonable skill and care.

Duty of Performance The agent owes a *duty of performance* to the principal. This duty is twofold. First, the agent must perform the duties as specified in the agency agreement. For example, suppose an insurance agent contacts Bethany about purchasing a car insurance policy. Bethany agrees to purchase the policy, but for some reason the agent never obtains the policy for her. Bethany discovers the insurance agent's mistake when she gets into a car accident. The insurance agent did not meet the duty of performance. Consequently, Bethany could bring a claim against the insurance agent.

Second, the agent must perform the specified duties with reasonable skill and care. The agent is expected to provide the same standards of skill, care, and professionalism that the reasonable person in the same situation would provide. For example, when an attorney advertises that he is a specialist in a certain type of law, this lawyer will be held to the reasonable standard of care in that specialty of law.[15] A gratuitous agent cannot be found liable for a breach of contract for failure to perform because no contract exists between the principal and the agent. However, if a gratuitous agent begins to act as a regular agent, and the principal affirms the relationship, a duty to perform arises insofar as the agent has begun a specific task for the principal.

duty of obedience
An agent's obligation to follow the lawful instruction and direction of the principal.

Duty of Obedience Under the *duty of obedience,* the agent must follow the lawful instruction and direction of the principal.[16] Thus, if the agent makes an unauthorized agreement, the agent has failed to meet the duty of obedience. However, if the principal gives unlawful or unethical instructions, the agent is not required to behave in accordance with those instructions. For

[15] Restatement (Second) of Agency, sec. 379.

[16] Restatement (Second) of Agency, secs. 383 and 385.

Duties of the Agent in Australia

Agents in Australia and the United States share many of the same duties to the principal. Some of these shared duties are following the principal's instructions, exercising reasonable care and skill, and not divulging or concealing confidential information.

While similarities between the two countries exist, agents in Australia have a unique duty: When performing services, the agent is obligated to "act personally" on behalf of the principal. For example, suppose an agent is hired to sell apartments owned by the principal, and the agent then hires someone else to sell the apartments for him. According to the law in Australia, the agent cannot receive commission from the sale.

The basis for such a law is quite logical. The agent was hired to exercise personal skills, such as availability, in the absence of the principal. When no personal skill is demonstrated, the agent shall not be granted any compensation or reward. Specifying that duties must be performed personally may seem like an obvious and unnecessary stipulation, but this specificity is important in protecting the interests of the principal.

example, let's say a principal tells an agent to sell a basketball autographed by Michael Jordan; however, the agent knows that the principal forged the signature on the basketball. The agent is not required to obey the instructions of the principal.

Duty of Accounting Under the **duty of accounting,** the agent must keep an accurate account of the transactions of money and property made on behalf of the principal.[17] If the principal requests to see this accounting, the agent has a duty to provide the principal with the accounting. Part of the duty of accounting is the duty of the agent to keep separate accounts for the principal's funds and the agent's funds. The agent cannot allow the funds to "mix."

duty of accounting
An agent's obligation to keep an accurate account of the transactions of money and property made on behalf of the principal.

Rights and Remedies

PRINCIPAL'S RIGHTS AND REMEDIES AGAINST THE AGENT

Because the agency relationship generally *is* a contractual relationship, a principal has contract remedies available for breach of fiduciary duties. In addition, a principal may use tort remedies for an agent's misrepresentations, negligence, or other business failings that cause damage to the principal. Furthermore, when an agent breaches his or her fiduciary duties, the principal has the right to terminate the agency relationship. While numerous possible remedies are available to the principal, the three main remedies are constructive trust, avoidance, and indemnification.

Constructive Trust Agency relationships exist primarily for the benefit of the principal. Therefore, principals are the legal owners of anything an agent may come to possess through the employment or agency relationship. Accordingly, when an agent through deceit or other means retains profits or goods obtained through the employment or agency relationship, which by law belong to the principal, the agent has breached his or her fiduciary duties. For example, Joy is an agent of Sarah's selling real estate. Joy sells a piece of property for $2,000 more than Sarah anticipated. Joy then keeps the extra $2,000 and reports the sale at the price Sarah expected. By law the profits belong to Sarah, and Joy has breached her fiduciary duties by keeping the money.

Also, an agent may not use the agency relationship to obtain goods or property for himself when the principal desired to obtain the same goods or property. In an agency relationship, the principal always has right of first refusal. That is, before an agent may use the relationship for a personal acquisition, the principal has the opportunity to buy whatever goods or properties are in question. Returning to Sarah and Joy, if Joy were to buy a piece of land she knew Sarah wished to purchase, she again would have breached her fiduciary duties to Sarah.

When an agent illegally benefits from the agency relationship, the principal may enact a constructive trust on the profits, goods, or property in question. A **constructive trust** is an equitable trust

constructive trust
An equitable trust imposed on a person who wrongfully obtains or holds legal right to property he or she should not possess.

[17] Restatement (Second) of Agency, sec. 382.

imposed on a person who wrongfully obtains or holds legal right to property he or she should not possess. When a principal enacts a constructive trust, the court rules that the agent is merely holding the property or goods in trust for the principal, granting the principal legal right or possession.

Avoidance When an agency relationship exists through a contract and the agent breaches the agreement or his fiduciary duties, the principal may use her right of avoidance. *Avoidance* allows a principal to nullify any contract the agent negotiated. Which, if any, contracts are voided is at the discretion of the principal.

Indemnification Agents enter into contracts with third parties on behalf of the principal. If a third party believes that the agent is acting with actual or apparent authority, she may sue the principal for any breach of contract. However, when the breach was caused by the agent's negligence, the principal has a right to *indemnification*. That is, when sued by a third party, a principal may sue his agent to recover the amount assessed to the third party if the breach of contract is the agent's fault.

In addition to recovering for negligence, a principal can recover if an agent fails to follow the principal's instructions. Courts have had difficulty in determining when a principal gives limiting instructions and when he merely gives advice. Going against advice does not impose liability on an agent, but violating limiting instructions does. For a principal to avoid a potential lawsuit from a third party, he should notify the third party whenever a relationship with an agent ceases or limiting instructions are given.

AGENT'S RIGHTS AND REMEDIES AGAINST THE PRINCIPAL

While agency relationships are intended to benefit the principal, the agent is not without rights and remedies. Whenever a duty is imposed on the principal, a corresponding right exists for the agent. Agents have available tort and contract remedies, in addition to the right to demand an accounting.

Tort and Contract Remedies Agents, much like principals, have certain tort and contract remedies available for situations in which a principal violates an agency agreement. These remedies are the same as standard tort and contract remedies.

Demand for an Accounting When an agent feels she is not being properly compensated, especially when working on commission, the agent may *demand an accounting*. When an agent demands an accounting, she may withhold further performance of her duties until the principal supplies appropriate accounting data. For example, Hal is a used-car salesman working for Not a Lemon Car Dealers. When Hal receives his pay, he believes he has been shorted the appropriate amount he made on commission. Hal can request that Not a Lemon obtain an auditor to perform an audit and determine whether he was in fact paid the proper amount for his sales.

Specific Performance When a contract exists and a principal agrees to certain conditions but fails to perform, under contract remedies the agent may seek court assistance in forcing the principal to perform the contract as stipulated. However, when the agency relationship is not contractual or the contract is for personal services, an agent does not have the right to seek specific performance. In noncontractual relationships, an agent may recover for services rendered and/or future damages, but the agent may not force the principal to fulfill the specific contractual agreements or even to continue to employ the agent.

LO 6 Authority of the Agent: The Link to the Principal's Liability

Earlier in the chapter, we discussed how an agency relationship and its resulting authority could be created. That section introduced the important concepts of (1) expressed agency, or agency by agreement; (2) implied agency; and (3) apparent agency, or agency by estoppel.

Each of these avenues for creating agency includes a form of authority that attaches to that type of agency.

EXPRESS AUTHORITY

In an expressed agency relationship, the agent has **express authority,** which is often referred to as *actual authority.* The principal has explicitly instructed the agent to do something. Therefore, if the principal requests that her agent sell her house for $100,000, the agent has explicit authority to sell the house for that amount. Express authority is binding in the sense that it gives the agent the power to make transactions and agreements with third parties. Because an agent with express authority has specific goals he or she is to achieve, the agent is also granted the use of other means, beyond the expressed agreement, reasonably necessary to achieve the desired goal.[18]

When express authority is granted for an agent to enter into a contract legally required to be in writing, most states require that the grant of authority also be in writing. This requirement is known as the **equal dignity rule.** When an agency agreement fails to adhere to the equal dignity rule, the subsequent contracts are typically considered to be voidable by the principal. This rule is based on the statute of frauds.

There are two key exceptions to the equal dignity rule. The first pertains to executive officers. When an executive officer is conducting business in the usual course of her job, she need not obtain written approval from the corporation for every decision she makes. The second exception is rooted in common sense. The equal dignity rule does not apply to an agent when the agent is working in the direct presence of the principal.

IMPLIED AUTHORITY

In an implied agency relationship, the agent has **implied authority;** that is, the relationship is inferred from the conduct of the parties. Consequently, the authority of the agent is implied on the basis of words and actions of the principal to the agent.[19] An agent's implied authority is derived from an agent's express authority and consists of what is reasonably necessary for carrying out the agent's grant of express authority.

One way an agent may have implied authority is through custom. Therefore, it is important that third parties familiarize themselves with the trade. Furthermore, if an agent must make an agreement or transaction to carry out the transaction he or she has agreed to perform for the principal, we can generally infer the presence of the authority.

For example, suppose one agrees to serve as a manager for a store. The contract probably does not expressly give authority for every decision the manager might need to make. However, the manager has implied authority to make agreements and transactions that customarily go along with the manager's position.

Another example of implied authority revolves around anyone, such as a purchasing agent, who ordinarily is the person who everyone in the industry expects will make contracts for particular inputs. For someone to act as if the purchasing agent lacks authority to make such commitments on behalf of the firm would be to act contrary to the expected lines of authority.

APPARENT AUTHORITY AND ESTOPPEL

As you learned earlier in this chapter, apparent agency exists when a third party reasonably believes, on the basis of a *principal's* actions, that an agency relationship exists between the principal and another individual. Thus, if the third party reasonably believes that the agent has authority to represent the principal, the principal must uphold any agreements made with the agent, who has apparent authority.[20] The principal is prevented (estopped) from acting as if the agent had no such authority.

express authority
The authority of an agent that arises when the principal explicitly instructs the agent to do something. Also called *actual authority.*

equal dignity rule
A rule requiring that contracts that would normally fall under the statute of frauds and need a writing if negotiated by the principal must be in writing even if negotiated by an agent.

implied authority
The authority of an agent that arises by inference from the words and actions of the principal.

[18] Restatement (Second) of Agency, sec. 35.

[19] Restatement (Second) of Agency, sec. 33.

[20] Restatement (Second) of Agency, secs. 27 and 159.

LO 7

Contractual Liability of the Principal and Agent

In addition to identifying the type of authority an agent has, courts must identify a few other factors when making decisions about an agency relationship's liability to third parties. First, the court must determine the classification of the principal. Second, the court must decide whether the principal authorized the actions of the agent.

CLASSIFICATION OF THE PRINCIPAL

Classifications are made from the perspective of the third party. In other words, the extent of the third party's knowledge about the principal determines the classification of the principal.

What are potential ethical issues arising from questions about the authority of a particular agent? The law of agency places special weight on the viewpoint of the agency relationship from the perspective of the third party (neither the agent nor the principal). But who are the other stakeholders in a managerial decision who might be affected by the assignment of a particular form of authority?

disclosed principal

A principal whose identity is known to a third party. The third party is aware that the agent is making an agreement on behalf of the principal.

partially disclosed principal

A principal whose identity is not known by a third party, although the third party is aware that the agent is making an agreement on behalf of a principal. Also called *unidentified principal*.

undisclosed principal

A principal whose existence is not known by a third party. That is, the third party does not know an agent is acting on behalf of a principal.

When a principal is classified as a disclosed principal, the third party is aware that the agent is making an agreement on behalf of a principal and the third party also knows the identity of the principal. In contrast, if a third party is aware that an agent is making an agreement on behalf of a principal but the third party is unaware of the identity of the principal, the principal is classified as a partially disclosed principal or an unidentified principal. Finally, if a third party does not know an agent is acting on behalf of a principal, the principal is classified as an undisclosed principal. Remember, the classification of the principal is important because it is a significant factor in determining the liability of the principal.[21]

AUTHORIZED ACTS

When an agent acts within the scope of her authority on behalf of a disclosed or partially disclosed principal, the agent is not liable for the acts of the principal.[22] The principal is liable only if the agent has some kind of authority to act on the principal's behalf. With a disclosed principal, the agent is not liable because he or she is not a party to the transaction.

Yet if the principal is partially disclosed, the agent can be held liable herself because the courts generally treat the agent as a party to the contract. As a party to the contract, the agent may be found liable to the third party for contractual nonperformance.[23] Whether disclosed or partially disclosed, apart from any liability the agent might have, the principal is liable for the agreements made with the third party.

When the agent acts within her authority on behalf of an undisclosed principal, the law will likely hold the agent liable for the agreement. Remember, with an undisclosed principal, the third party is not aware of the existence of the principal. Thus, in the eyes of the third party, the agent is the only possible person who could be liable. Yet, if the agent is liable to the third party, then the undisclosed principal is liable to the agent. However, there are certain situations in which the agent is the only party liable for the contract. These situations are:

1. The contract expressly excludes the principal from the contract. In that the principal was not a party to the contract, he or she has no liability to the agent.

2. The agent enters into a contract that is a negotiable instrument. The Uniform Commercial Code (UCC) governs negotiable instruments and states that another party, that is, a principal, cannot be liable for a negotiable instrument if his name is not on the instrument or if the agent's signature does not indicate that the agreement was made in a representative capacity.[24]

[21] Restatement (Second) of Agency, sec. 4.

[22] Restatement (Second) of Agency, sec. 320.

[23] Restatement (Second) of Agency, sec. 321.

[24] UCC § 3-402(b)(2).

3. The third party enters into a contract with the agent that requires the performance of the agent. In this case, the third party may reject the performance of the principal. For example, if the agent is a photographer and she enters into a contract for her principal without disclosing this fact, the third party may reject the principal's attempt to fulfill the contract by taking the third party's picture.

4. If the principal or agent knows a third party would not enter into a contract with the principal if the principal's identity were disclosed, but the agent enters into a contract with the third party anyway, the agent will be the only party liable should the third party rescind the contract.

In situations in which a principal was undisclosed, a judgment for a third party against an agent, when the third party comes to know of the undisclosed principal's identity, releases the principal from liability.[25] Also, a judgment against a previously undisclosed principal frees the agent from liability.[26]

Exhibit 18-5 summarizes contractual liability to third parties for authorized acts of the agent.

UNAUTHORIZED ACTS

If an agent has no authority to act on behalf of a principal, but the agent still enters into a contract with a third party, the principal, regardless of the classification, is not bound to the contract unless the principal ratifies the agreement.

When the agent exceeds his authority to act on behalf of the principal, the agent will likely be personally liable to the third party. Yet, when the third party is aware that the agent does not represent the principal, the law does not hold the agent liable for the agreement. In almost all other cases in which the agent claims to have authority to contract on behalf of the principal, the law holds the agent liable to the third party. If an agent enters into a contract knowingly misrepresenting his alleged authority, the agent is liable to the third party in a tort action.

Agents who go beyond their authority when the principal is disclosed or partially disclosed are liable for a breach of implied warranty, not for a breach of contract. The agent cannot be found liable for breach of contract because the agent is never an intended party to the contract, even when exceeding his or her authority. The agent can breach the implied warranty intentionally, through a knowing misrepresentation, or unintentionally, through a good-faith mistake such as simply misjudging his or her authority. In either case, the agent is liable if the third party acted relying on the agent's alleged status.

Exhibit 18-6 summarizes the contractual liability of principals and agents to third parties for unauthorized acts of the agent.

Tort Liability and the Agency Relationship

If an agent commits a tort that injures a third party, the agent is personally liable for his or her actions, regardless of both the classification of the principal and the liability of the principal.[27] The principal may also be held liable for the agent's actions. This liability can arise from authorized or unauthorized acts. Furthermore, tortious liability of the principal can be established directly or indirectly. Finally, if an agent is an employee and the principal/employer controls the employee's behavior, the principal can be found liable. The next section introduces these methods of establishing tortious liability.

Exhibit 18-5

Contractual Liability to Third Parties for Authorized Agent Acts

CLASSIFICATION OF PRINCIPAL	AGENT LIABILITY?	PRINCIPAL LIABILITY?
Disclosed	No	Yes
Partially disclosed	Possibly	Yes
Undisclosed	Yes	Yes

Exhibit 18-6

Contractual Liability to Third Parties for Unauthorized Acts of the Agent

THIRD-PARTY BELIEF	AGENT LIABILITY?	PRINCIPAL LIABILITY?
Believes the agent has authority	Yes	No
Believes that the agent is mistaken about her authority	No	No

[25] Restatement (Second) of Agency, sec. 210.

[26] Restatement (Second) of Agency, sec. 337.

[27] Restatement (Second) of Agency, sec. 343.

PRINCIPAL'S TORTIOUS CONDUCT

The law holds a principal directly responsible for the tortious conduct of his agent under two conditions. First, if the principal directs the agent to commit a tort, the principal is liable for any damages caused by this tort. The principal is authorizing the agent's unlawful behavior; thus, the principal is held responsible.[28] Similarly, the principal is liable for an agent's tortious act if the principal, although not condoning the agent's conduct, ratifies the agent's actions knowing the agent acted improperly.[29]

Second, if the principal fails to provide proper instruments or tools or gives inadequate instructions to the agent concerning the necessity to employ competent agents, the law then holds the principal liable to a third party for negligence. Under this provision of liability, a principal is liable for his or her negligent hiring of an agent. Thus, a principal must use proper care in selecting an agent for a job. This doctrine of negligent hiring has been used when an agent commits a tort against a customer, who often argues that the principal is liable because he or she should have taken more care in hiring the agent.

respondeat superior

Latin for "let the superior speak"; the principle by which liability for harm caused by an agent/employee is held by the principal/employer.

vicarious liability

The liability or responsibility imposed on a person, a party, or an organization for damages caused by another; most commonly used in relation to employment, with the employer held vicariously liable for damages caused by its employees.

Respondeat Superior The doctrine of *respondeat superior* (a Latin phrase meaning "let the superior speak") is used in the context of the principal/employer–agent/employee relationship. The principal/employer holds **vicarious liability** (i.e., liability assigned without fault) for any harm caused by the agent/employee during the time the agent/employee is working for the principal. In other words, the principal/employer is liable, not because he or she was personally at fault but because he or she negligently hired an agent.

The rationale behind this doctrine is that employers should be held liable for employees who commit torts because the employer is furthering his or her business through the work of the employee. If the employer is benefiting by the work of the employee, the employer should also be responsible for the harms caused by the employee.

Therefore, when a third party is injured through the negligence of an employee during the course of the employee's work, the third party can sue either the employee or the employer.[30] To establish employer liability, the third party must establish that the wrongful act occurred within the scope of employment. The courts consider the following elements in determining whether an act has occurred within the course and scope of employment:[31]

1. Did the employer authorize the employee's act?
2. Did the act occur within the time and space limits of employment?
3. Was the act performed, at least in part, on behalf of the employer?
4. To what extent were the employer's interests advanced by the act?
5. To what extent were the private interests of the employee involved?
6. Did the employer provide the means (i.e., tools) by which the act occurred?
7. Did the employee use force that was not expected by the employer?
8. Did the employer know that the act would involve the commission of a serious crime?

For example, if an employee is a delivery driver and negligently injures a third party while making deliveries on behalf of the employer, both the employee and the employer will be held liable.

Now suppose that the delivery driver is using the company vehicle when he stops at a drive-through at a fast-food restaurant to get some coffee. Could the employer be liable to a third party for an accident involving the delivery driver? If an agent makes a substantial departure from the course of the employer's business, the employer is not liable.

Courts often refer to a substantial departure as a "frolic of his own." However, if the deviation from the employer's business is *not* substantial, the employer can still be held liable. In Case 18-2, the court considers the scope of the employment relationship.

[28] Restatement (Second) of Agency, sec. 212.

[29] Restatement (Second) of Agency, sec. 218.

[30] Restatement (Second) of Agency, secs. 216 and 219.

[31] Restatement (Second) of Agency, sec. 229.

CASE 18-2

IGLESIA CRISTIANA LA CASA DEL SENOR, INC., ETC. v. L.M.
COURT OF APPEAL OF FLORIDA, THIRD DISTRICT
783 So. 2d 353 (2001)

FACTS: *L.M. sued Ali Pacheco, the former pastor of Iglesia Cristiana la Casa del Senor, Inc. (the Church), as well as the Church, alleging that Pacheco had sexually assaulted her in July 1991 when she was a minor. The allegation of sexual assault formed the basis of L.M.'s claims against the Church based on respondeat superior. When the criminal act occurred, L.M. was 16 years old.*

Before the criminal act took place, Pacheco visited L.M.'s residence twice when L.M. had been left home alone. On another occasion, Pacheco visited L.M. at her school. L.M. told her mother about Pacheco's visit but did not advise anyone from the Church.

According to L.M., on July 8, 1991, Pacheco called her at work and invited her to lunch to discuss her parents' marital problems. L.M. accepted, and Pacheco picked her up from work. L.M. noticed a sandwich and soft drink in the car. Pacheco drove to a Marriott Hotel. L.M. testified that Pacheco led her to a room he had rented and told her not to worry because she would finally be cured. He then proceeded to sexually assault her. Pacheco testified that L.M. consented to having sex.

According to him, their meeting was prearranged. They had discussed the matter and had in fact been to the Marriot Hotel on the previous day intending to have sexual relations but had decided against it. Pacheco testified that he knew what he was doing was wrong, but he explained that it was a great temptation in his life.

The jury returned a verdict in L.M.'s favor, finding the Church liable for Pacheco's criminal act on the grounds of respondeat superior. The Church appealed.

ISSUE: Was Pacheco acting as an employee of the Church when he assaulted L.M.?

REASONING: The court stated that for the doctrine of *respondeat superior* to apply, Pacheco's employer could not be liable for the tortious or criminal acts of Pacheco "unless the acts were committed during the course of the employment and to further a purpose or interest, however excessive or misguided, of the employer. An employee's conduct is within the scope of his employment, when (1) the conduct is of the kind he was employed to perform, (2) the conduct occurs substantially within the time and space limits authorized or required by the work to be performed, and (3) the conduct is activated at least in part by a purpose to serve the master."

In the case of L.M., the sexual assault did not occur on Church property, and what Pacheco did was not the kind of behavior the Church hired Pacheco to perform. In addition, his act was not an expression of Pacheco's desire to serve the Church. Little counseling occurred on the day of the crime. The Church would have tried very hard to prevent his actions had it known of his plans.

DECISION AND REMEDY: The court reversed the trial court's judgment and entered judgment for the Church.

SIGNIFICANCE: *Respondeat superior* does not mean that the employer is responsible for whatever an employee might do while at work. This case spells out the requirements for such liability to be imposed on the principal.

CRITICAL THINKING

Assume that L.M.'s account of the crime is true. Examine the exception to the scope-of-employment criteria mentioned by the judge. How could the plaintiff make an argument, using that exception, that Pacheco's conduct was within the scope of his employment?

ETHICAL DECISION MAKING

The judge in this case outlines a doctrine for determining the liability of an employer for the actions of employees. What value preference is highlighted by that doctrine?

If the third party is able to establish employee negligence such that the employer is liable, the employer has the right to recover from the employee any damages he paid to the third party as a result of the employee's negligence. The right to recover damages is referred to as the *right of indemnification*. However, if the employee is innocent of negligence, the employer is also free of liability.

Intentional Torts and *Respondeat Superior* The agent is liable for any torts he or she commits. In the same way that the principal is responsible for the negligent acts of the employee under the doctrine of *respondeat superior,* the principal may be liable for any intentional torts of the employee. Furthermore, an employer may be responsible for any tortious acts of the employee if the employer knew or should have known that the employee had a tendency to commit a tortious act. Hence, a principal may be liable for negligent hiring if he or she fails to do a background check to learn about the tendencies of potential employees.

For example, the principal of an employee with a criminal background may be held liable for tortious acts committed by his or her hired agent, even though the employee may not recognize the wrongfulness of his act. Therefore, employers will most likely purchase liability insurance in case particular employees engage in tortious activities.

AGENT MISREPRESENTATION

If an agent misrepresents himself or herself to a third party, the principal may be tortiously liable for the agent's misrepresentation. Unlike tort liability, which is based on whether the agent/employee was acting in the scope of employment, *misrepresentation liability* depends on whether the principal authorized the agent's act. If the principal authorizes the agent to engage in an act and the agent misrepresents herself intentionally or unintentionally, the principal is always tortiously liable to someone who relied on the agent's misrepresentation.

If an agent has misrepresented herself, the third party has two options:

1. The third party can cancel the contract with the principal and be compensated for any money lost.
2. The third party can affirm the contract and sue the principal to recover damages.

PRINCIPAL'S LIABILITY AND THE INDEPENDENT CONTRACTOR

As we discussed earlier in this chapter, an independent contractor is not an employee of the individual who hires him or her to do work. The individual doing the hiring does not control the details of the independent contractor's performance. Consequently, an individual who hires an independent contractor cannot be held liable for the independent contractor's tortious actions under the doctrine of *respondeat superior.*

Suppose that while working on the outside of the building he is renovating, an independent contractor accidentally injures an innocent bystander when he drops a pile of bricks on the bystander. The owner of the building is not liable for the innocent bystander's injuries; the independent contractor is liable.[32]

If, however, the independent contractor engages in extremely hazardous activities, such as blasting operations, for the principal, the principal will be responsible for any damages by the independent contractor. Certain activities are held strictly liable because of their inherently dangerous nature. Thus, an employer cannot escape the strict liability associated with those hazardous activities simply by hiring an independent contractor to complete the activities. In addition, the employer cannot escape liability for an independent contractor's tort if the employer directs the contractor to commit the tort.

The Case Nugget demonstrates the role of tort principles in establishing the liability of those who employ independent contractors to engage in inherently dangerous activities.

[32] Restatement (Second) of Agency, sec. 250.

CASE Nugget

Liability When Hiring Independent Contractors

Larry S. Lawrence v. Bainbridge Apartments et al.
Court of Appeals of Missouri, Western District

957 S.W.2d 400 (1997)

In 1989, Smart Way Janitorial offered a bid to Larry Lawrence to wash the windows of Bainbridge Apartments. In May 1989, when Larry went to look at the apartments, he was told that Bainbridge wanted the windows washed from outside the building so that the residents would not be disturbed. The Bainbridge property consisted of six buildings: two seven-story buildings and four four-story buildings. Even though Lawrence could not create a safety line for washing the outside of the windows of the four-story buildings, the building manager insisted that Lawrence wash the windows from the outside. When Lawrence started washing the windows from the outside, he fell from one of the shorter buildings and suffered injuries. He brought a suit against Bainbridge Apartments, arguing that Bainbridge was negligent based on the "inherently dangerous–activity" exception to the doctrine that landowners are not vicariously liable for injuries caused by the negligence of an independent contractor or his employees.

The trial court ruled that because Lawrence had recovered workers' compensation benefits, the injury was not covered by the inherently dangerous–activity exception. The trial court granted summary judgment to Bainbridge; however, when Lawrence appealed, the decision was reversed and remanded because the court of appeals ruled that Lawrence was not a covered employee entitled to workers' compensation benefits.

The court argued that in establishing the rule of liability in this case, it would look to which party can best avoid the harm and manage the risk of loss of the inherently dangerous activity in question. An independent contractor who knows he will not be compensated by the landowner for his injuries has a strong incentive to take additional care and avoid neglect in performing his duties. This encourages him to demand additional safety measures and compensation before he agrees to undertake an inherently dangerous activity. The independent contractor is free to bargain and negotiate without restraint with the landowner. An independent contractor holds himself out as an expert who is uniquely qualified and skilled to bid for and perform the acts in question. As an expert, he is in a better position to understand the risks and costs involved in a particular job, and he may demand sufficient remuneration and safety measures to cover what he believes the attendant risks to be. In return for his bargained-for price, he accepts the allocation of the risk. The court held that an injured independent contractor, although uninsured, cannot recover under the inherently dangerous–activity exception.

Termination of the Agency Relationship

LO 8

There are multiple ways to end an agency relationship. The parties may act to terminate the relationship. Alternatively, some agencies terminate automatically by the lapse of time, fulfillment of purpose, or operation of law. If the agency relationship has ended, the agent no longer has authority to make agreements on behalf of the principal. However, the agent's apparent authority continues until the principal notifies third parties that the agency relationship has ended. What terminates the agency relationship?

actual notice

Notice of agency termination that is given by directly informing third parties, either orally or in writing.

constructive notice

Notice of agency termination that is usually given by publishing an announcement in a newspaper.

Notice of the termination of an agency relationship can be given in two general forms: actual or constructive. Actual notice of termination is given when third parties are directly informed, orally or in writing, that an agency agreement has terminated.[33] Actual notice must be given to third parties who have had business interactions with the agent. Also, when the agent's authority was granted in writing, actual notice must be given in writing. Parties not directly related to an agency agreement may receive constructive notice, which is how notice of the termination of an agency agreement is generally announced.[34] Constructive notice is most frequently delivered through publication in a generally circulating newspaper for the area where the agency agreement existed.

The issue of termination of the agency is especially important for global commerce. When parties are forming a contract of agency in a foreign jurisdiction, it is extremely important that the parties include the conditions of termination within the contract.

Termination of an agency relationship involving persons from separate jurisdictions often results in complicated legal battles over compensation and liability. For example, principals must be aware of local labor laws because these laws can create agents' compensation and pension rights that are unknown to the principal. Local legal counsel should be especially knowledgeable about the provisions surrounding termination of agency in the particular jurisdiction and be able to help managers avoid unnecessary legal battles.

For example, if a manager has business transactions in one of the European Union countries and wants to terminate an agency relationship, he or she would want to have access to knowledge about the intricacies of Chapter IV of the Agency Relationship Law, which focuses on termination. After the termination of an agency contract in the EU countries, the agent receives help from the law in collecting damages. A released agent receives compensation if the agent has brought the principal new customers from whom the principal continues to profit, if the agent is unable to otherwise recover costs incurred through the performance of the contract, or if the agent dies.

Under certain circumstances, however, the law in European Union countries prohibits the agent's receiving compensation. For instance, if the principal has terminated the contract due to the incapacity of the agent, the principal is not obligated to dispense compensation. Also, compensation is not payable if the agent terminates the contract or assigns rights and duties under the agency contract to another person.

TERMINATION BY ACTS OF PARTIES

The agency relationship can be terminated following certain acts. Several possibilities are discussed below.

Lapse of Time If an agency agreement specifies that the agency relationship will exist for a certain amount of time, the relationship will end when the amount of time expires.[35] For example, an agency agreement might state that the agency relationship will begin on September 1 and end on September 30. While the agent and principal can agree to continue the agency relationship through October, they will have to make a new agreement. The agent's express authority ends when the relationship ends; thus, it is the responsibility of the principal to notify third parties that the former agent no longer has the ability to act on the principal's behalf.

Fulfillment of Purpose Suppose a homeowner enters into an agreement with a real estate agent to sell his house. In other words, the very basis for the relationship is a function or purpose—the selling of a piece of real estate. Once the house is sold, the agent no longer has the authority to act on the seller's behalf. The agent has fulfilled the purpose of the agency relationship.[36]

Occurrence of a Specific Event An additional means of ending an agency relationship is the occurrence of a specific event. For example, John chooses Claire as an agent to move his bed to another location. Once the move has been made, the agency relationship would terminate.

[33] Restatement (Second) of Agency, sec. 136(2).

[34] Restatement (Second) of Agency, sec. 136(3).

[35] Restatement (Second) of Agency, sec. 105.

[36] Restatement (Second) of Agency, sec. 106.

Mutual Agreement by the Parties Remember, agency is a consensual agreement between two parties. Consequently, if the two parties mutually decide they do not wish to continue in the agency relationship, they can cancel the agreement and therefore terminate the agency relationship.

Revocation of Authority At any time, a principal can revoke an agent's authority.[37] Again, the basis of agency law is consensual agreement. If the principal does not want the agent to act on his behalf, the principal can revoke the agent's authority. However, the principal's revocation might constitute a breach of contract with the agent. Therefore, the principal could be liable for damages due to the breach of contract.[38] If the agent has somehow breached her fiduciary duty to the principal, the principal can revoke the agent's authority without being liable for damages to the agent.

Renunciation by the Agent In the same way that a principal terminates an agency relationship by revoking authority, the agent can terminate the agency relationship by renouncing the authority given to the agent. Again, the agent can be liable for breach of contract if the agency agreement has stated a specific amount of time the agency relationship is to exist.

Agency Coupled with an Interest An **agency coupled with an interest** is a special kind of agency relationship. Unlike regular agency agreements, an agency coupled with an interest is created for the agent's benefit, not for the principal's. Given that the agent is the one who benefits, an agency coupled with an interest is also known as *power given as security*. Because the agency arrangement is created to benefit the agent, the principal may not terminate the relationship. Rather, the agency relationship is terminated when an event occurs that discharges the principal's obligation.

agency coupled with an interest
An agency relationship that is created for the benefit of the agent, not the principal.

TERMINATION BY OPERATION OF LAW

Certain events lead to automatic termination of the agency relationship. These events may involve a situation in which the agent is unable to fulfill his task or one in which the principal does not desire to continue with the performance. In addition, automatic termination may occur when further pursuit of the agency relationship's objectives would be illegal. These events are discussed below.

Death If either the principal or the agent dies, the agency relationship is automatically terminated. Even if one party is unaware of the other party's death, the agency relationship no longer exists. Suppose an agent has authority to buy antiques on behalf of a principal. However, without the agent's knowing it, the principal dies, but the agent continues to purchase items on behalf of the principal. Those transactions are not binding on the principal's estate because as soon as the principal dies, the agent's authority to act is gone.

Insanity If a principal or agent becomes insane, the agency relationship is finished. Some states have modified this law so that unless the person has been adjudicated insane, the agency contract still exists.

Bankruptcy If the principal or agent files a bankruptcy petition, the agency relationship is generally no longer in existence. If the agent is filing for bankruptcy and the agent's credit is important to the agency relationship, the relationship will end. However, if the agent's financial history is not relevant to the agency relationship, the agency may continue. Insolvency, which is defined as the inability to pay debts or the condition of liabilities outweighing assets, does not necessarily result in the termination of the agency relationship.[39]

Changed Circumstances If there is an unusual change in circumstances that leads the agent to believe that the principal's instructions do not apply, the agency relationship terminates.[40] For

[37] Restatement (Second) of Agency, sec. 119.

[38] Restatement (Second) of Agency, sec. 118.

[39] Restatement (Second) of Agency, sec. 113.

[40] Restatement (Second) of Agency, sec. 109.

E-COMMERCE and the Law

Agents and Electronic Contracts in Singapore

Many legislatures have found it necessary to add or create certain laws in response to technology. Singapore, for instance, addressed the growing use of electronic contracts with new legislation in 1997. Because of the possibility of e-mail and electronic fraud, certain risks are associated with forming electronic contracts. The new legislation attempts to combat those risks and specifies the consequences of such fraud.

The fourth section of this legislation pertains to the formation of agency contracts. Agency contracts made electronically will be valid and enforceable if the principal or a principal's designated agent sent the contract. As for contracts made between third parties, certain circumstances must exist for the third party to make the assumption that the electronic record is that of the principal.

Either the third party follows a procedure of clarification previously agreed on by the principal or he or she sees the message originated from an agent who has been endorsed by the principal. Under either of these circumstances, the third party is legally allowed to assume that the electronic message originated with the principal.

If an agent in Singapore sends an electronic record not approved by the principal, the third party has the right to act as a result of that message. In the event such actions result in injuries or damages to the third party, the principal is responsible under law. The principal cannot claim that he or she was unaware of the agent's actions. While there may have been no actual awareness, Singapore does not recognize the lack of awareness as a defense.

Singapore's new legislation intends to protect third parties from the poor judgment of principals by creating this direct link between them. Making the principal answerable and liable to the third party increases the pressure to employ reliable agents.

example, suppose Smith contracts someone to act as her agent to sell a painting she found in her great-aunt's attic. Smith authorizes the agent to sell the painting for $5,000. However, in the course of showing the painting to several buyers, the agent learns the painting is a Van Gogh original. Thus, because the painting is worth much more than $5,000, the agent should infer that the principal does not want the original agency to continue.

Change in Law When a new law is passed subsequent to the formation of an agency agreement that makes the commission of the agency agreement illegal, the agency agreement is terminated. For example, Tyler hires Ryan to paint her house green. Then, after Ryan was hired, the city council passes a law making it illegal to paint one's house green. The new law automatically terminates the agency agreement.

Impossibility Suppose that while in the process of attempting to sell the painting in our earlier example, there is a fire in Smith's house and the painting is destroyed. Because it is impossible for the agent to sell the painting, it is impossible for the agency relationship to continue.[41]

Additionally, if the agent loses qualifications needed to perform duties for the principal, the agency relationship ends because of impossibility. For example, Jackson hires a lawyer to serve as his agent. However, the lawyer has unfortunately engaged in a series of illegal actions and is disbarred. Because the lawyer can no longer fulfill the functions Jackson has authorized him to perform, the agency relationship is terminated.

Disloyalty of Agent An agency agreement is terminated whenever the agent, unknown to the principal, acquires an interest against the principal's interest. The agency agreement is also terminated if the agent breaches the duty of loyalty he or she has to the principal.[42] For example, Mary is an attorney representing Lola in her suit against a pharmaceutical company. If the pharmaceutical company offers Mary a job and she accepts, the agency agreement would terminate because Mary has acquired an interest opposed to Lola's interests.

[41] Restatement (Second) of Agency, sec. 124.

[42] Restatement (Second) of Agency, sec. 112.

 SUMMARY

Introduction to Agency Law	*Agency:* The relationship between a principal and an agent. *Agent:* One authorized to act for and on behalf of a principal. *Principal:* One who hires an agent to represent him or her. *Fiduciary:* One with a duty to act primarily for another person's benefit.
Creation of the Agency Relationship	*Expressed agency:* Agency formed by making a written or oral agreement. *Power of attorney:* Document giving an agent authority to sign legal documents on behalf of the principal. *Durable power of attorney:* Power of attorney intended to continue to be effective, or to take effect, after the principal has become incapacitated. *Agency by implied authority:* Agency formed by implication through the conduct of the parties. *Agency by estoppel:* Agency formed when a principal leads a third party to believe that another individual serves as his or her agent but the principal has made no agreement with the so-called agent. *Agency by ratification:* Agency that exists when an individual misrepresents himself or herself as an agent for another party and the principal accepts or ratifies the unauthorized act.
Agency Relationships	An *agency relationship* is a fiduciary relationship (a relationship of trust) in which an agent acts on behalf of the principal. A *principal-agent relationship* exists when an employer hires an employee to enter into contracts on behalf of the employer. An *employer-employee relationship* exists when an employer hires an employee to perform some sort of physical service. An *employer–independent contractor relationship* exists when an employer hires a person other than an employees to conduct certain tasks.
Duties of the Agent and the Principal	*Principal:* • Duty of compensation • Duty of reimbursement and indemnification • Duty of cooperation • Duty of safe working conditions *Agent:* • Duty of loyalty • Duty of performance • Duty of notification • Duty of obedience • Duty of accounting
Rights and Remedies	*Principal:* • Constructive trust • Avoidance • Indemnification *Agent:* • Tort and contract remedies • Demand for an accounting • Specific performance
Authority of the Agent: The Link to the Principal's Liability	*Express authority:* The principal has explicitly instructed the agent to do something. *Implied authority:* The relationship is inferred from the conduct of the parties. *Apparent authority and estoppel:* Apparent agency exists when a third party reasonably believes on the basis of a principal's actions that an agency relationship exists between the principal and another individual.
Contractual Liability of the Principal and Agent	*Classification of the principal:* The principal must be classified as either disclosed, partially disclosed, or undisclosed.

Authorized acts: These are acts within the scope of the agent's authority.

Unauthorized acts: These are acts that go beyond the scope of the agent's authority.

Tort Liability and the Agency Relationship

Principal's tortious conduct: The law holds a principal directly responsible for his or her own tortious conduct under two conditions: (1) The principal directs the agent to commit a tortious act, and (2) the principal fails to provide proper instruments and tools or adequate instructions.

Agent misrepresentation: If an agent misrepresents himself or herself to a third party, the principal may be tortiously liable for the agent's misrepresentation

Respondeat superior: The principal/employer is liable not because he or she was personally at fault but because he or she negligently hired an agent.

Principal's Liability and the Independent Contractor

An individual who hires an independent contractor cannot be held liable for the independent contractor's tortious actions under the doctrine of *respondeat superior* unless the contractor engages in hazardous activities.

Termination of the Agency Relationship

Termination by acts of parties: This may occur by lapse of time, fulfillment of purpose, occurrence of a specific event, mutual agreement by the parties, revocation of authority, or renunciation by the agent.

Termination by operation of law: The agency relationship may be terminated automatically due to death, insanity, bankruptcy, changed circumstances, change in law, impossibility, or disloyalty of the agent.

 Point/Counterpoint

Should the Principal/Employer Be Indirectly Liable for the Actions of the Agent/Employee under the Doctrine of *Respondeat Superior?*	
YES	NO
The employer should be held responsible for the actions of the employee while the employee is working for the employer. The employer gains from the benefits of the employee's work. Hence, there is a certain symmetry in requiring that the employer also accept the fruits of the negative behavior of the employee. In short, the benefits the employer experiences from the employee are paid for in part by the risk the employer must assume for the possible negligence of that same employee. When a company hires an employee for a position for which he or she is not competent, the company should be punished for any harm the agent causes while acting in his or her hired position. The agent would not be in a position to cause harm had the company not negligently hired him or her in the first place. For example, if a pizza company hires a person with a marred driving record as a pizza delivery driver, the pizza company should be held accountable for any harm caused by that pizza driver while at work delivering pizza. Harm should be compensated, and the employer is usually in a much more secure financial position than is the employee to provide that compensation	The employer should not be held responsible for the actions of an employee while the employee is working for the employer. Employees make daily choices using basic human judgment. These employees are hired and trusted for their competence. If an employee makes a poor decision, he or she needs to be held individually responsible. Without a model of individual responsibility, individual workers need never fear the full consequences of their actions. The employees always know their parent companies will be forced to "take care of them" under the doctrine of *respondeat superior.* With the knowledge that their employers will be held somewhat accountable, employees do not necessarily exercise the same amount of caution as they would if they were held personally accountable for every decision they make. Consider the example of the pizza delivery driver. The delivery driver injures a third party while delivering pizzas for her company, perhaps because she accidentally drove through a red traffic signal. Though she was delivering a pizza for her employer, it is the pizza delivery driver, not the pizza company, who ran a red light and injured a pedestrian. Individuals should be held accountable for individual choices. The parent companies need to be held responsible only for decisions that the parent companies make directly.

Questions & Problems

1. Who can serve as an agent or a principal?

2. What are the similarities and differences between the types of agency relationships?

3. Why is it important to determine whether a worker is an independent contractor or an employee?

4. How is apparent agency, or agency by estoppel, different from expressed agency?

5. What are the different types of authority an agent might have, and why is it important to identify the type of an agent's authority?

6. When might a principal be liable for torts committed by an agent?

7. Explain how the doctrine of *respondeat superior* affects agency relationships.

8. Ward Manufacturing, Inc., decided to construct a casting facility on its property located in Blossburg, Pennsylvania. Ward entered into a written contract with Welliver-McGuire, Inc. Under the terms of the contract, Welliver agreed to indemnify Ward for any and all claims for bodily injury and property damage arising out of the performance of the work identified in the contract. Welliver assumed control, possession, and responsibility over the construction site throughout the project. Ward did, however, maintain an on-site representative to act as liaison and monitor the status of the project. Ward also had a safety representative on-site periodically to inspect the work site. Jonathon Olin worked as a carpenter for Welliver. Olin, while engaged in surveying activities on the Ward construction site, fell into an unbarricaded excavation pit allegedly covered with water and mud. As a result of the fall, Olin purportedly suffered severe injuries. Since the date of the accident, Olin has received total disability workers' compensation benefits from Welliver. Olin brought suit against Ward for negligence. Ward argued that Olin, through Welliver, was an independent contractor, and that Ward therefore was not liable to Olin for damages. Furthermore, Ward argued that Welliver, and not Ward, was in charge of the site. Ward then moved for summary judgment. Was Ward successful in its motion for summary judgment? Why? [*Olin v. George E. Logue, Inc.,* 119 F. Supp. 2d 464 (2000).]

9. John Ray Lawrence, an employee of H.W. Campbell Construction Company, was killed when his head was crushed in the "pinch point" area of a crane. Coastal Marine Services of Texas, Inc., owned the crane, and Campbell employees were using it on Coastal's property when the accident occurred. Campbell took custody of the crane and began continued occupation of Coastal's property. Campbell was an independent contractor of Coastal, and no written contract existed between the two companies. Coastal employees were not directing or supervising Campbell's work on the project, nor were they on the job site when the accident occurred. Lawrence's surviving family and estate sued Campbell and Coastal, alleging, among other things, negligence. During the trial Coastal asserted that the Lawrences had presented no evidence that Coastal retained the right to control Campbell's work, a prerequisite for finding Coastal liable under a premises liability theory. The trial court agreed and submitted an instruction precluding a finding of negligence based on the manner in which Coastal controlled the premises. The jury found no negligence on Coastal's part. At trial, in response to a series of hypothetical questions, Campbell employees testified that they would have complied with any instructions from Coastal about the movement of the crane if Coastal had given such instructions. On the basis of the Campbell employees' testimony, the court of appeals reversed the trial court's judgment, concluding that the testimony created a fact issue about Coastal's right to control the crane. Coastal appealed. What duties did Coastal owe Campbell as an independent contractor? How did the court rule on appeal? [*Coastal Marine Serv., Inc. v. Lawrence,* 988 S.W.2d 223 (1999).]

10. Land Transport employed Oscar Gonzalez to operate a Land Transport tractor-trailer rig. One day while working, Robert Nichols and Gonzalez were driving west on Route 9 toward Brewer, Maine. Gonzalez tried several times to pass Nichols in no-passing zones. Angered by Gonzalez's driving, Nichols made an obscene gesture to Gonzalez on two occasions. Thereafter, Gonzalez began to tailgate Nichols for several miles and continued to try to pass him. The two trucks then stopped at a traffic light. Nichols saw Gonzalez get out of his cab, and Nichols did the same. On approaching Gonzalez, Nichols attacked Gonzalez with a rubber-coated chain-linked cable. Nichols then grabbed Gonzalez, and they fell to the ground. During the scuffle, Gonzalez got up, brandished a knife, and stabbed Nichols. Nichols sued Gonzalez and Land Transport for the injuries he suffered. Land Transport moved for summary judgment. Was Land Transport successful with its motion for summary judgment? Why? [*Nichols v. Land Transport Corp.,* 103 F. Supp. 2d 25 (1999).]

11. Brian Olander became a State Farm insurance agent in 1981. In August 1996, Olander was charged with

murder after a violent altercation with a neighboring landowner. When Olander refused to take a leave of absence until the criminal charges were resolved, State Farm terminated his agency agreement and assigned other agents to serve the State Farm policyholders previously served by Olander's agency. In 1999, Olander brought suit against State Farm, alleging wrongful termination of the agency agreement. The district court granted State Farm's motion for summary judgment, concluding that Section III.A of the written State Farm Agent's Agreement unambiguously made the parties' contractual relationship terminable at will. On appeal, a divided panel of this court reversed. State Farm appealed. The issue on appeal may be quickly summarized. If the agreement was terminable at will by either party, then Olander has no wrongful termination claim, and his related claims were properly dismissed as well. Was the agency agreement one that could be terminated by either party? What duties did State Farm owe Olander when it terminated their agency agreement? [*Olander v. State Farm Mutual Automobile Ins. Co.,* 317 F.3d 807 (2003).]

12. Lisa was 19 years old and pregnant when she had to seek treatment at Memorial Hospital's emergency room. The initial examining physician ordered an ultrasound for Lisa. Bruce Wayne Tripoli, the ultrasound technician, administered the examination. A third party was not present during the ultrasound. Tripoli asked the plaintiff if she would like to know the sex of the baby. When she said yes, Tripoli falsely explained that to determine the sex he would have to scan "much further down." Then Tripoli inappropriately touched the plaintiff. Believing that contact in that private area was part of the examination, Lisa did not stop Tripoli. After describing Tripoli's behavior to her regular obstetrician, Lisa discovered that the behavior was not necessary and was inappropriate. Lisa then brought suit against Tripoli and the hospital, among others. The issue was whether Tripoli committed the sexual assault within the scope of his employment, thereby rendering the hospital "vicariously liable." For the type of liability the plaintiff was seeking, the employment situation must create a foreseeable risk that the employee might commit an offense. Was the hospital liable? [*Lisa M. v Henry Mayo Memorial Hospital* 907 P.2d 358 (Supreme Court of California 1995).]

13. In 1983, William and Carolyn Coldwell purchased an insurance premium that did not provide uninsured-motorist (UM) coverage. Mr. Coldwell was the only person named on the policy. Four years later, the insurance company offered UM coverage for the first time, at an additional premium. Mrs. Coldwell checked a box stating "I do not want [UM coverage] included in my policy" on her uninsured-motorist acceptance/rejection form, signed the form, and mailed it in. The insurance company removed UM coverage from the Coldwells' policy. In 1995, the Coldwells were in a major traffic accident with an uninsured motorist, who was faulted for the accident. The Coldwells eventually filed a complaint for a declaratory judgment on the issue of UM coverage with the insurance company, arguing that Mrs. Coldwell lacked the authority to enter into an agency relationship with the insurance company. How do you think the court decided? [*Coldwell v. Allstate Insurance Co.,* 1999 Ohio App. LEXIS 2758 (Ohio Ct. App. 1999).]

Looking for more review material?

The Online Learning Center at **www.mhhe.com/kubasekess** contains this chapter's "Assignment on the Internet" and also a list of URLs for more information, entitled "On the Internet." Find both of them in the Student Center portion of the OLC, along with quizzes and other helpful materials.

Forms of Business Organizations

---▶ CASE OPENER

The McDonald's Franchise Agreement

The McDonald's Corporation operates numerous fast-food restaurants worldwide, organizing many of them as franchises. One McDonald's franchise was sold to the Robertson family in 1971. The Robertsons operated their franchise restaurant in Jacksonville, Florida, for many years with few problems. The McDonald's Corporation later notified them, however, that the franchise had been violating part of the license agreement. After repeated incidents, McDonald's Corporation (the franchisor) demanded termination of the franchise.

1. Did McDonald's lawfully revoke the Robertsons' franchise?
2. What are some potential problems that a franchisor and a franchisee might experience in their relationship?

---▶ LEARNING OBJECTIVES

After reading this chapter, you will be able to answer the following questions:

LO 1 What are the major forms of business organizations?

LO 2 What are the advantages of each alternative form of business organization?

LO 3 What is the special significance of the operating agreement in a limited liability company?

LO 4 What are the differences among the different forms of business organizations?

LO 5 What are the specialized forms of business organizations?

If you are considering starting a business, the Internet can provide much information to help you decide which form of business you should create. This new format for acquiring information about which form of business is optimal should improve the quality of decisions about this crucial step in operating a business. For example, at Business Tools, http://smallbiz.findlaw.com/book, you can read more about sole proprietorships, partnerships, and corporations. Furthermore, using the Internet, you can learn about the laws that affect the forms of business within your specific state. For example, at Texas Business Forms, www.sos.state .tx.us/corp/forms.shtml, you can read about and actually retrieve the forms required to create various business types in Texas. Thus, the Internet can ease the difficulties associated with creating a business by increasing the information available to you about forms of business organizations.

Suppose that you get an idea to produce a novel product. You think that production of this new product could lead to enormous profits. But what is the best way to produce this product? Should you produce it yourself by creating your own business? Do you have enough money to create your own business? What are the legal ramifications for you if your business is not successful? What legal responsibilities do you have with respect to your business?

Maybe you share your idea for this new product with your best friend, who suggests that the two of you become partners in the production and sale of this product. What are the benefits associated with forming a partnership? What are the disadvantages? Are there other forms of businesses that you should consider?

Deciding what form of business to create is one of the most important decisions a business makes. The extent of liability, as well as the extent of the control the owner will have over the business, is dependent on the form of the business. However, the business world is not static, and businesses can, and do, change form over time. Accordingly, this chapter is relevant not only to new businesses but also to already existing businesses. The first section in this chapter introduces the major types of business organizations, describing how these forms are both created and ended. The second section considers several types of business organizations that are less well known but important nevertheless.

LO 1

Major Forms of Business Organizations

SOLE PROPRIETORSHIP

sole proprietorship
A business in which one person (sole proprietor) is in control of the management and profits.

sole proprietor
The single person at the head of a sole proprietorship.

If you decide to go into business on your own, you are creating a sole proprietorship, a business organization in which you, as the sole proprietor, are in sole control of the management and the profits. Thus, if you wanted to open a lawn-mowing business or a sewing shop, you would likely be creating a sole proprietorship. It is a naturally occurring form of business organization in the sense that if you started doing business without thinking about the form, you would be a sole proprietor.

Why might an entrepreneur choose to create a sole proprietorship over other business organizations? First, a sole proprietorship requires very few legal formalities. Thus, one advantage of the sole proprietorship is the ease of creating such a business. Second, a sole proprietor has complete control of the management of the business. Consequently, the sole proprietor has great freedom to hire employees, determine business hours, and expand or change the nature of the business. Finally, the sole proprietor keeps all the profits from the business. These profits are taxed as the personal income of the sole proprietor.

However, sole proprietorships have disadvantages, too. Suppose you are the sole proprietor of a restaurant in which someone is injured. This customer sues your business. You are personally liable for any losses or any obligations associated with the business. Consequently, if you accrue large debts because of your business, you might have to sell your home to cover those debts. Moreover, because the sole proprietorship is not considered a separate legal entity, you, as the

Exhibit 19-1

Advantages and Dis-
advantages of the
Sole Proprietorship

ADVANTAGES	DISADVANTAGES
1. Creation is easy. 2. Proprietor is in total control of management. 3. Proprietor keeps all profits.	1. Proprietor has personal liability for all losses. 2. Funding is limited to personal funds and loans.

owner and sole proprietor, can be personally sued. Sole proprietorships are terminated, however, when the sole proprietor dies.

Not only are you personally liable for any debts of the business, but the funding for your business is limited to your personal funds as well as loans you might be able to obtain. Thus, sole proprietorships often struggle in the initial stages of business because of large start-up costs in relation to the profits they make.

Sole proprietorships are by far the most popular form of business organization in the United States. Exhibit 19-1 summarizes their advantages and disadvantages.

An alternative form of business organization that retains many of the advantages of the sole proprietorship but that addresses the funding drawback in part is the partnership.

PARTNERSHIP

Suppose you and your best friend from college decide to create a business in which you plan to buy and sell used books and DVDs through the Internet. You both agree that you will share control of the Internet business and will split the profits equally. According to the Uniform Partnership Act, you have created a partnership, a voluntary association between two or more persons who co-own a business for profit. Except in a few cases, a partnership is not considered a separate legal entity and is dissolved when a partner dies. The Uniform Partnership Act (UPA) governs partnerships in most states in the absence of an express agreement.

What are the advantages associated with creating a partnership? First, the creation of a partnership is easy. The partners, each of whom is considered an agent of the partnership, are generally not required to create an official or even written agreement to create the partnership. Second, because the partnership is in most cases not considered a separate legal entity, the income from the business is taxed as individual income for each partner. Because the income is taxed as personal income, the partners can deduct the business losses.

While there are certain advantages to creating a partnership, there are also disadvantages associated with partnerships. Most importantly, the partners are personally liable for the debts of the partnership. For instance, suppose you are in a partnership with your best friend, who embezzles $50,000 through your partnership. Because of the partnership, you would likely be held personally liable for the debts of the partnership. In other words, you would likely be responsible for the $50,000. Exhibit 19-2 summarizes the advantages and disadvantages of partnerships.

partnership
A voluntary association between two or more people who co-own a business for profit.

Exhibit 19-2

Advantages
and Disadvantages
of Partnerships

ADVANTAGES	DISADVANTAGES
1. Creation is easy. 2. Income of business is personal income. 3. Business losses can be deducted from taxes.	1. Each partner has personal liability for all losses, including those of another partner (in most cases).

Although it is not listed in Exhibit 19-2, one advantage of a partnership is the ability to choose the people with whom you want to be partners. As the Case Nugget demonstrates, the courts recognize the right to choose one's partners as a basis for partnership law.

CASE Nugget

Do Partners Have a Duty to Remain Partners?

Colette Bohatch v. Butler & Binion
Supreme Court of Texas

977 S.W.2d 543

Colette Bohatch became an associate in the Washington, D.C., office of Butler & Binion in 1986. John McDonald and Richard Powers, both partners, were the only other attorneys in the office. After Bohatch was made a partner in February 1990, she became concerned that McDonald was overbilling Pennzoil, the main client of the office. Bohatch met with the law firm's managing partner, Louis Paine, to report her concern regarding McDonald's overbilling. In July 1990, McDonald met with Bohatch to report that Pennzoil was dissatisfied with her work.

The next day, Bohatch relayed her concern to Paine, as well as to two other members of the law firm's management committee. Paine led an investigation of Bohatch's complaint and discussed the billed hours with the in-house counsel at Pennzoil, who concluded that the bills were reasonable. In August 1990, Paine met with Bohatch, telling her that there was no basis for her claims against McDonald and that she should look for work elsewhere. The firm refused Bohatch a year-end partnership distribution for 1990. Finally, in August 1991, Bohatch was given until November to vacate her office. She filed suit in October 1991, and the firm voted to expel her from the partnership three days later.

At trial, the jury ruled that the firm breached the partnership agreement and its fiduciary duty and awarded Bohatch $57,000 for past lost wages, $250,000 for past mental anguish, $4,000,000 total in punitive damages (this amount was apportioned against several defendants), and attorney fees. Later, the trial court reduced the punitive damages to around $237,000. The court of appeals ruled that the firm's only duty to Bohatch was to not expel her in bad faith. When the court found no evidence that the firm fired Bohatch for self-gain, it ruled that Bohatch could not recover for breach of fiduciary duty. The case was appealed to the state supreme court.

The supreme court ruled that the firm did not owe Bohatch a duty to remain partners. While Bohatch presented a compelling argument that firms should not be permitted to expel partners who "whistle-blow" in good faith, the court could not ignore one basis of partnership law: a belief that partners should be allowed to choose their partners. The court found that forcing firms to keep whistle-blowing partners would cause partners to engage in business with people they could no longer trust, thereby undermining the viability of the partnership. Therefore, the supreme court affirmed the ruling of the court of appeals.

general partnership
A partnership in which the partners divide profits and management responsibility and share unlimited personal liability for the partnership's debts.

There are several types of partnerships: general partnerships, limited partnerships, and limited liability partnerships. A **general partnership** consists of an agreement that the partners will divide the profits (usually equally) and management responsibilities and share unlimited personal liability for the partnership's debts. Thus, in our Internet business example, you and your best friend would form a general partnership by agreeing to share the management responsibilities and profits as well as assuming unlimited personal liability.

Now imagine that your parents want to invest in your Internet business. Suppose that they want to share in the profits associated with the business but they do not want to share in the management responsibilities or assume personal liability for the debts of the partnership. Your parents can join your business as limited partners, and your partnership would become a limited partnership. A limited partnership (LP) is an agreement between at least one general partner and at least one limited partner. The *general* partners, you and your best friend, assume unlimited personal liability for the debts of the partnership. However, your parents, the *limited* partners, assume no liability for the partnership beyond the capital they have invested in the business. Moreover, the limited partners do not have any part in the management of the company. However, limited partners pay taxes on their share of the business profit.

If a limited partner dies, the limited partnership is usually unaffected. If a general partner dies, however, the limited partnership is usually dissolved.

The limited partnership must meet certain requirements that are not expected of general partnerships. First, the limited partnership must use the word *limited* in its title. Second, to create a limited partnership, the parties must file a certificate of partnership with a state office. If the certificate of partnership is incorrectly filed, or simply not filed at all, the courts will rule that a general partnership exists. Consequently, all parties will be held personally liable for all the debts of the partnership.

Now suppose that you are an attorney and a partner in a law firm with 30 other partners. Suppose further that one of your partners is sued because he was negligent in his duties as an attorney. This partner has unlimited liability because of professional malpractice. But will you and the other partners at the firm be held liable for this partner's malpractice?

If you and your fellow partners have created a limited liability partnership (LLP), a different form of partnership than the LP, all the partners assume liability for any partner's professional malpractice to the extent of the partnerships' assets. In other words, the limited liability partnership is different from other forms of partnerships because the partners' liability for professional malpractice is limited to the partnership. If one partner in an LLP is guilty of malpractice, the other partners' personal assets cannot be taken. Therefore, professionals who do business together commonly use the LLP. It is the extra protection awarded partners in an LLP that makes the LLP a *separate* form of partnership from a limited partnership. Limited partnerships are not the same as limited liability partnerships.

Limited liability partnerships are fairly new; in 1991, Texas was the first state to enact a statute permitting the creation of LLPs. Almost all states now have similar statutes. Like the limited partnership, the LLP has several special requirements. First, the business name must include the phrase *Limited Liability Partnership* or the abbreviation *LLP.* Second, the parties must file a form with the secretary of the state to create the LLP.

The LLP is not considered a separate legal entity. Each partner pays taxes on his or her share of the income of the business.

An alternative form of business organization, the corporation, separates business ownership from business control.

CORPORATION

When you hear the word *business,* you probably think about businesses such as Wal-Mart, Kmart, McDonald's, and Nike. Perhaps the most dominant form of business organization is the corporation, a legal entity formed by issuing stock to investors, who are the owners of the corporation. The investor-owners are called shareholders. These shareholders elect a board of directors, which is responsible for managing the business. The board of directors, in turn, hires officers to run the day-to-day business.

The corporation is considered a separate legal entity; thus, the corporation can be sued. None of the other forms of business we have discussed are considered separate legal entities. How does a corporation become a separate legal entity? It must be created according to state law.

What are the consequences of a corporation's status as a separate legal entity? First, while the corporation can be held liable, shareholders cannot be held personally liable for the debts of the corporation. Their liability is usually limited to the amount they have invested. Second, the corporation is not dissolved when the shareholders die. Third, the corporation must pay taxes on its profits. In addition, the shareholders must pay taxes on the dividends they receive from the corporation.

limited partnership (LP)
A partnership consisting of at least one general partner and at least one limited partner in which the general partners assume all liability for the partnership's debts and the limited partners assume no liability beyond their originally invested capital.

limited liability partnership (LLP)
A partnership in which all the partners assume liability for any partner's professional malpractice to the extent of the partnership's assets.

corporation
A legal entity formed by issuing stock to investors, who are the owners of the corporation.

shareholders
Investors in a corporation, who own the corporation.

CONNECTING to the Core

S corporation

A corporation that enjoys the tax status of a partnership.

One way that a corporation can avoid this double taxation is by forming an S corporation, a business organization formed under federal tax law that is considered a corporation yet is taxed like a partnership as long as it follows certain regulations. For example, the S corporation cannot have more than 75 shareholders. Any income of the corporation is taxed when it is distributed to the shareholders, who must report the income on their personal income tax forms. S corporations are always formed under federal law. S corporations cannot be formed under state law, whereas other forms of corporations are created under state law.

Exhibit 19-3 summarizes the advantages and disadvantages of the corporate form of business.

LIMITED LIABILITY COMPANY

limited liability company (LLC)

An unincorporated business that is taxed like a partnership, with the members paying personal income taxes, and has the limited liability of a corporation.

One of the newest forms of business organization in the United States is the limited liability company (LLC), an unincorporated form of business organization that many people see as combining the most advantageous features of partnerships and corporations. It combines the tax advantages and management flexibility of a partnership with the limited liability of a corporation.

This form of business organization was first recognized in the United States in 1977 in Wyoming and is now recognized in every state, although the rules regarding this new form did not evolve uniformly. As with other areas of law, the National Conference of Commissioners on Uniform State Laws recognized the desirability of bringing some uniformity to this area of law and drafted the Uniform Limited Liability Company Act (ULLCA) in 1995. In 2006, the commissioners revised the ULLCA. This act provides a model for states to follow, but it has not been uniformly adopted, so it is always necessary when establishing an LLC to check the exact requirement of the law for LLCs in the state in which you wish to create your company.

LO 2

Exhibit 19-3

Advantages and Disadvantages of Corporations

ADVANTAGES	DISADVANTAGES
1. Limited liability for shareholders	1. Corporate income taxed twice
2. Ease of raising capital by issuing stock	2. Formalities required in establishing and maintaining corporate form
3. Profits taxed as income to the shareholders, not the partners	

Key Reasons for the Rapid Acceptance of LLCs As previously mentioned, the LLC form offers its members the same limited liability for business debts offered by the corporate form. However, unlike the corporate form, it does not require that profits and losses be allocated in proportion to ownership interests. Also unlike corporations, LLCs are not required to hold an annual meeting and draft meeting minutes, so record keeping is simpler and more flexible. Unlike the case in limited partnerships, to obtain limited liability, the owner (referred to as a *member*) does not have to give up his or her right to participate in management of the LLC. In fact, an additional advantage of the LLC form is the flexibility it offers members in terms of alternative ways to structure its management.

The most frequently cited advantage of the LLC is that it is generally treated by the IRS like a partnership or sole proprietorship, with members reporting their share of the profits and losses of the LLC on their personal tax returns and no separate tax being assessed on the company itself, thereby allowing its members to avoid the double taxation that owners of a corporation pay. However, if an LLC's members prefer, they may elect to have the entity taxed like a corporation. In a situation where most of the profits are going to be reinvested in the business, this option allows the profits to be taxed at the lower corporate rate. So, while we think of the opportunity to avoid double taxation as a key benefit of the LLC, more important perhaps is the fact that the members have the choice of how they want to be taxed.

In our global environment, an increasingly important advantage of LLCs is that members need not be citizens or permanent residents of the United States. Other organizational forms, such as the subchapter S corporation, are available only when all the owners are U.S. citizens. Finally, as with a corporation, ordinary business expenses, such as salaries paid to owners, can be deducted from the profits of an LLC before the LLC's income is allocated to its owners for tax purposes.

Formation and Management of LLCs A limited liability company is formed by filing articles of organization in the state in which members want to establish their LLC. While precise requirements vary by state, typically the articles include the name of the business, which must include the words *Limited Liability Company* or the initials *LLC,* its principal business address, the name and address of a registered agent for service, the names of the owners, and information about how the company's management will be structured.

LLCs typically want to do business in states other than the state in which they are formed, and they usually need to register in every additional state in which they want to operate, a process typically referred to as *qualification.* Qualification simply entails filing a certificate of authority or a similar document and getting a business license in each additional state in which the business plans to operate. The LLC will usually be referred to as a *foreign company* in the additional states, and under most state statutes the LLC will be governed by the LLC rules of the state in which it was created, regardless of where it is transacting business.

For purposes of jurisdiction, however, an LLC is considered a citizen of every state in which its members reside. Remember that a party can be sued in federal court over a matter involving more than $75,000 when diversity of citizenship exists, that is, when no plaintiff and defendant are residents of the same state. For determining whether diversity exists, a corporation is considered a resident of both the state in which it is incorporated and the state in which it has its primary place of business. However, this rule does not apply to LLCs, as their citizenship is determined by the residences of their members. Consequently, if parties want to be more likely to be able to avail themselves of the federal courts, they may want to either limit their membership to individuals of only one or a few states or use a different form of business organization.

When members form an LLC, they typically draft an operating agreement, which is the foundational contract among the entity's owners. It spells out such matters as how the company is to be managed, how the profits and losses will be allocated, how interests may be transferred, and how and when the LLC may be dissolved. Any matter not covered in the operating agreement will be resolved in accordance with the state LLC statute; if a matter is not covered by the relevant statute, the principles of partnership law are generally followed.

While there is no requirement for an LLC to have a detailed, written operating agreement, to ensure the smooth functioning of the company, it is a good idea to have such an agreement. Failure to have a detailed, written agreement may result in a court's imposing standards on the company that may be very different from what the members had in mind when forming the company.

LO 3

It is very important, however, to make sure that everyone understands the terms of the operating agreement, because once the parties enter into such an agreement, the courts will enforce it.

One of the key issues to be determined in the operating agreement is how the company is to be managed. There are two options: member-managed and manager-managed. Under the ULLCA, unless the operating agreement specifies otherwise, LCCs are member-managed. In a *member-managed LLC,* all members participate in management, with decisions in the ordinary course of business activities made by a majority vote. The consent of all members, however, is required to sell, lease, exchange, or otherwise dispose of all, or substantially all, of the company's property; approve a merger or conversion to a different form; undertake any other act outside the ordinary course of the company's activities; and amend the operating agreement. The members in such an LLC all have the apparent and actual authority to enter into contracts on behalf of the LLC.

In a *manager-managed LLC,* the members select a group of managers to manage the affairs of the company. The managers may be selected from the members or may be nonmembers. The managers have the apparent and actual authority to enter into contracts on behalf of the LLC, while the members who are not managers do not have such authority. The managers owe the LLC and its members the same fiduciary duties as the officers and directors of a corporation owe to the corporation and its shareholders.

Dissolution of LLCs Under the ULLCA, an LLC dissolves on the happening of any event that the operating agreement specifies will cause dissolution, the consent of all the members, the passage of 90 consecutive days during which the company has no members, or the issuance of a court order for dissolution. Under the ULLCA and most state LLC statutes, a member's voluntary withdrawal from the LLC, referred to as *dissociation,* does not terminate the LLC.

LO 4

Exhibit 19-4 provides a comparison of the alternative forms of business organizations.

Exhibit 19-4

Comparison of Alternative Forms of Business Organizations

	SOLE PROPRIETORSHIP	GENERAL PARTNERSHIP	LIMITED PARTNERSHIP	CORPORATION	LIMITED LIABILITY COMPANY
Legal Position	Not a separate legal entity	Not a separate legal entity in most states	A separate legal entity	A separate legal entity	A separate legal entity for purposes of liability, but not always for taxes
Control Considerations	Sole proprietor has total control	Each partner is entitled to equal control	Each partner is entitled to equal control	Separation of ownership and control	Members control allocation of control
Liability	Sole proprietor has unlimited personal liability	Each partner has unlimited personal liability for partnership debts	Each partner has liability limited up to his or her capital contribution	Liability limited to loss of capital contribution	Liability limited to loss of capital contribution
Lifetime	Limited to life of proprietor	Limited by life of partners	Limited to life of general partners	Can have unlimited life	Operating agreement spells out the lifetime
Taxation	Profits are taxed directly as income to the sole proprietor	Profits are taxed as income for partners	Profits are taxed as income for partners	Profits are taxed as income to corporation and as income to the partners in the form of dividends	Operating agreement spells out whether profits will be taxed as a corporation or partnership
Transferability of Ownership Interest	Nontransferable	Nontransferable	Nontransferable	Generally unlimited transfer	Operating agreement spells out the transferability

Types of Business Organizations in China

Before one can understand business organizations in China, the concept of legal persons must be explained. This concept is at the root of all Chinese business law. The Civil Code of China defines *legal person* in the following way: "An organization which possesses civil legal capacity for civil acts and which, according to the law, independently enjoys civil rights and assumes civil obligations." The definition then describes two types of legal persons.

The first type is the *enterprise legal person*. An enterprise legal person is any enterprise that is privately, collectively, or state-owned. Before an organization is considered an enterprise, the local registrar must approve it. Approval depends on the satisfaction of four criteria: (1) existence of an outlined organizational structure, (2) an organizational title, (3) articles governing the structure, and (4) the necessary funds and property. A foreign-owned or foreign joint venture may also acquire enterprise legal person status by applying for approval and registration.

The second type of legal persons is *other legal persons.* These include government agencies, institutions, and associations. Government agencies need not apply for registration because they are given legal person status on their establishment. In certain situations, other institutions and associations are subject to approval and registration. The criteria they must meet before acquiring legal person status are identical to those for enterprises. In October 1998, the State Council specified which situations required registration for these institutions and associations.

Specialized Forms of Business Organizations

LO 5

In addition to the more traditional forms of business organizations mentioned above, the following specialized forms of business organizations have become increasingly important: cooperatives, joint stock companies, business trusts, syndicates, joint ventures, and franchises.

COOPERATIVE

A cooperative is an organization formed by individuals to market products. The cooperative is a business organization in which the members usually pool their resources together to gain some kind of advantage in the market. For instance, farmers might pool certain crops together to ensure that they get a high market price for their crops. Usually, members of the cooperative receive dividends in proportion to how many times per year they engage in business with the cooperative.

Cooperatives may be incorporated or unincorporated. Unincorporated cooperatives are treated like partnerships, meaning that the members share joint liability for the cooperative's actions. Members of incorporated cooperatives, on the other hand, enjoy limited liability just as do the shareholders of a corporation.

JOINT STOCK COMPANY

A joint stock company is a partnership agreement in which company members hold transferable shares while all the goods of the company are held in the names of the partners. Thus, the joint stock company is a mixture of a corporation and a partnership. As with the corporation, the members who hold shares of stock own the joint stock company. As with the partnership, the shareholders have personal liability, and in most cases the company is not a separate legal entity. The joint stock company is formed by agreement rather than statute.

BUSINESS TRUST

A business trust is a business organization governed by a group of trustees, who operate the trust for the beneficiaries. A written trust agreement establishes the duties and powers of the trustees and the interests of the beneficiaries.

As with a corporation, the trustees and beneficiaries enjoy limited liability, and in most states business trusts are taxed like corporations.

cooperative
An organization formed by individuals to market new products. Individuals in a cooperative pool their resources together to gain an advantage in the market.

joint stock company
A partnership agreement in which company members hold transferable shares while all the goods of the company are held in the names of the partners.

business trust
A business organization governed by a group of trustees, who operate the trust for beneficiaries.

trustee
A person who operates a trust for beneficiaries in a business trust.

beneficiary
A person who can expect to benefit from a relationship.

SYNDICATE

syndicate

An investment group that comes together for the explicit purpose of financing a specific large project.

An investment group that comes together for the explicit purpose of financing a specific large project is a syndicate. Syndicates are often used in the purchase of professional sports teams. The syndicate is quite useful in the sense that it can raise large amounts of money in a small amount of time. Syndicates are usually considered a type of joint venture, and thus they are almost always governed by partnership law.

JOINT VENTURE

joint venture

An association between two or more parties wherein the parties share profits and management responsibilities with respect to a specific project.

A joint venture is a relationship between two or more persons or corporations created for a specific business undertaking. This relationship may entail financing, producing, and selling goods, securities, and commodities. Participants in the joint venture usually share the profits and losses of the joint venture equally.

Joint ventures can be agreements between small businesses as well as agreements between very large businesses. For example, General Motors and Toyota have entered into a joint venture to create the Saturn line of cars. Generally, joint ventures are taxed like partnerships. In fact, from a legal standpoint, partnerships and joint ventures are virtually the same. Thus, courts frequently apply partnership law to joint ventures. Joint ventures differ from partnerships, however, because a joint venture is usually created for making and selling a single product while a partnership creates an ongoing full business. Once all the single products are sold, the joint venture is usually terminated. The members, however, can determine when the joint venture will end.

Despite the similarities, there are several minor differences between partnerships and joint ventures in the eyes of the law. First, if one of the members of a joint venture dies, the joint venture is not automatically terminated. Second, the members of a joint venture have less authority than general partners because members of a joint venture are not agents of the other members.

The parties who compose a joint venture usually share equal management of the task for which they have come together. They, however, can make an agreement to give one party greater management responsibilities. Furthermore, all the parties usually assume liability for the project. Each party can be held responsible for the liability of another party in the joint venture.

Like a partnership, a joint venture may be formed without drawing up a formal agreement. Case 19–1 illustrates how the courts determine whether a joint venture exists. What facts does

CASE 19-1

JUDY FITCHIE v. RICK YURKO
ILLINOIS COURT OF APPEALS
570 N.E.2d 892 (1991)

FACTS: *In February 1990, Rick Yurko purchased $100 worth of $1 scratch-off lottery tickets. Yurko had Phyllis Huisel, Judy Fitchie, and Frances Vincent help him scratch off his tickets. Yurko stated that if they helped him scratch off the tickets, they would be his partners and share in the winnings. Eventually, Judy uncovered a winning ticket that gave the owner a chance to compete for a $100,000 prize. Yurko stated that he would appear on television, and Phyllis, Judy, Frances, and Yurko agreed that Yurko would be their representative. Yurko wrote "F.J.P. Rick Yurko" on the back of the lottery ticket and said that they would be partners. The ticket was chosen for*
one of the spots on the television show. When Yurko appeared on the show, he won $100,000. However, Yurko claimed the $100,000 for himself. Phyllis, Judy, and Frances sued Yurko to recover their share of the award. The trial court ruled that Phyllis, Judy, and Frances were partners or joint venturers and thus entitled to shares of the $100,000. Yurko appealed.

ISSUE: Were Phyllis, Judy, Frances, and Yurko engaged in a joint venture?

REASONING: A joint venture is a partnership carried on for a single enterprise for profit. To determine whether a

(continued)

joint venture existed, the court examined the intent of the parties involved. The court considered four elements: an agreement to carry on an enterprise; a demonstration of intent to be joint venturers; a joint interest, such as each party's contribution of property, finances, effort, skill, or knowledge; and a provision for sharing of profits and losses. In this case, all four elements were satisfied. The parties agreed to carry on an enterprise when they agreed to scratch off the tickets together, and the parties agreed to be partners if they won any money. Each party contributed effort by scratching off the tickets. The parties also agreed to send Yurko as a representative on the television show and to share any money won by Yurko. The parties demonstrated intent to be joint venturers.

DECISION AND REMEDY: Phyllis, Judy, Frances, and Yurko were engaged in a joint venture. The trial court's ruling was affirmed.

SIGNIFICANCE OF THE CASE: This case demonstrates the importance of parties' intent when conducting business together. No formal agreement or written contract is required to form a joint venture, so parties may enter into a joint venture with relative ease. While joint ventures are easy to begin, this case also demonstrates that joint venturers must abide by the terms they create.

CRITICAL THINKING

When a court tries to determine intent, they must of necessity look at the behavior of the relevant parties. In this case, what kind of actions would have raised serious questions about whether the parties were indeed engaged in a joint venture?

ETHICAL DECISION MAKING

Place yourself in Yurko's position. What values would you promote in his situation? Consider the primary stakeholders in the situation. Are there ethical problems with Yurko's actions, or is he justified is claiming the winnings all to himself? Were the other involved parties acting in an ethically appropriate manner? Why or why not?

the judge rely on to determine whether a joint venture existed between Yurko and Huisel, Fitchie, and Vincent?

FRANCHISE

When you go into McDonald's to eat lunch, what type of business are you patronizing? You are likely eating at a franchise, a business that exists because of an arrangement between the franchisor, an owner of a trade name or trademark, and the franchisee, a person who sells goods or services under the trade name or trademark.

What are the advantages and disadvantages for the franchisor and the franchisee? Exhibits 19-5 and 19-6 summarize these advantages and disadvantages. First, the franchisee enjoys the franchisor's help in opening the franchise. Second, think about how many times you have driven through a strange town and felt relieved when you saw a Burger King. Even though you may have never been to that town before and did not know who controlled that particular business, you know Burger King. Before you walk into the restaurant, you know almost exactly what will be on the menu. Thus, on the one hand, the franchisee benefits from the franchisor's strong trade name or trademark. Moreover, the franchisee benefits from the franchisor's worldwide advertising of the trade name or trademark. The franchisor, on the other hand, does not take a large risk in creating the franchise, yet it can greatly benefit from the income it receives from the franchisee.

Generally, franchises fall into one of three categories. McDonald's and Burger King are examples of chain-style business operations. In a chain-style business operation, the franchise

franchise
A business arrangement between an owner of a trade name or trademark and a person who sells goods or services under the trade name or trademark.

franchisor
The owner of the trade name or trademark in a franchise.

franchisee
The seller of goods or services under a trade name or trademark in a franchise.

chain-style business operation
A type of franchise in which the franchise operates under the franchisor's business name and is required to follow the franchisor's standards and methods of business operation.

403

Exhibit 19-5

Advantages and Disadvantages to the Franchisee of Starting a Franchise

ADVANTAGES	DISADVANTAGES
1. Help from the franchisor in starting the franchise	1. Must meet the franchisor's standards or risk losing the franchise
2. Instant recognition due to the franchisor's strong trademark or trade name	2. Has little to no creative control over the business
3. Benefits from the franchisor's worldwide advertising	

Exhibit 19-6

Advantages and Disadvantages to the Franchisor of Starting a Franchise

ADVANTAGES	DISADVANTAGES
1. Low risk in starting a franchise	1. Has little control over the franchise
2. Increased income from franchises	2. Can become liable for the franchise if it exerts too much control

distributorship

A type of franchise in which the franchisor manufactures a product and licenses a dealer to sell the product in an exclusive territory.

manufacturing arrangement

A type of franchise in which the franchisor provides the franchisee with a formula or necessary ingredient to manufacture a product.

operates under the franchisor's business name and is required to follow the franchisor's standards and methods of business operation.

The second category of franchises is the distributorship. Distributorships are franchises in which the franchisor manufactures a product and licenses a dealer to sell the product in an exclusive territory. A car dealership is an example of a distributorship.

Finally, the third category of franchises is the manufacturing arrangement. In a manufacturing arrangement, the franchisor provides the franchisee with a formula or necessary ingredient to manufacture a product. The franchisee then manufactures the product and sells it according to the franchisor's standards.

Exhibit 19-7 describes the various types of franchises. Exhibit 19-8 provides a sense of just how important franchises are for the market economy.

Exhibit 19-7

Types of Franchises

FRANCHISE TYPE	DESCRIPTION
Chain-style business operation	Franchisor helps franchisee set up a business run under the franchisor's business name according to the franchisor's usual methods and standards.
Distributorship	Franchisor licenses franchisee to sell the franchisor's product in a specific area.
Manufacturing arrangement	Franchisor provides the franchisee with the technical knowledge needed to manufacture the franchisor's product.

Exhibit 19-8

The Top 10 Global Franchises, 2008

1. Subway
2. KFC
3. McDonalds.
4. Dunkin Donuts
5. Domino's Pizza LLC
6. Curves
7. RE/MAX Int'l. Inc.
8. Sonic Drive In
9. Pizza Hut
10. UPS Store

Source: Ranked by *Entrepreneur Magazine* on the basis of financial strength and stability, growth rate, and size of the system, www.entrepreneur.com/franzone/listings/fran500/0,5831,00.html.

Look at Case 19–2 to see how the supreme court of Arkansas determined whether a franchise agreement existed between Mary Kay Cosmetics and Janet Isbell.

CASE 19-2

MARY KAY, INC., A/K/A MARY KAY COSMETICS, INC.
v. JANET ISBELL
SUPREME COURT OF ARKANSAS
338 Ark. 556; 999 S.W.2d 669; 1999 Ark. LEXIS 443

FACTS: *In 1980, Janet Isbell signed an agreement to become a beauty consultant for Mary Kay. This agreement established that she would sell products to customers at home demonstration parties, but she was prohibited from selling the products in retail establishments. In 1981 and 1991, Isbell signed agreements to become a unit sales director. In addition to serving as a beauty consultant, Isbell recruited beauty consultants. In 1994, she rented a space in a shopping mall to serve as a training center. In April 1994, Mary Kay's legal coordinator contacted Isbell, stating that the store space was not to be used to sell Mary Kay products. According to the agreement, Isbell's office could not look like a Mary Kay store. In September 1995, the vice president of sales development notified Isbell that Mary Kay was terminating its agreements with Isbell. Isbell filed suit against Mary Kay, claiming that she was a franchise under the Arkansas Franchise Practices Act. She argued that Mary Kay violated the Franchise Practices Act by refusing to comply with the FPA provisions for termination of a franchise. The trial court granted summary judgment to Isbell, but it did not explain why Isbell's relationship with Mary Kay could be considered a franchise. The trial court ruled as a matter of law that Mary Kay's termination of Isbell had violated the act, and a jury awarded Isbell $110,583.33. Mary Kay appealed.*

ISSUE: Was Janet Isbell a franchisee of Mary Kay?

REASONING: Sections 4-72-203 and 4-72-202 (6) of the Arkansas Franchise Practices Act establish that the act applies only to a franchise that contemplates or requires the franchise to establish or maintain a place of business in the state. A place of business is defined as "a fixed geographical location at which the franchisee [1] displays for sale and sells the franchisor's goods or [2] offers for sale and sells the franchisor's services." In this case, there was no evidence that Isbell sold Mary Kay products from a fixed geographic location. Isbell was, in fact, prohibited from selling products from her office or center. Isbell was to sell products in customers' homes. Additionally, the agreements signed by Isbell make no mention of a fixed geographic location as a place of business. There was no evidence that Mary Kay contemplated that Isbell would maintain a place of a business in Arkansas.

DECISION AND REMEDY: The Arkansas Franchise Practices Act did not apply to Isbell because Isbell did not meet the definition of a franchise. The trial court's ruling was reversed, and the case was dismissed.

SIGNIFICANCE OF THE CASE: This case raises questions about legal protections for people like Janet Isbell who sell products for companies that, like Mary Kay, don't require the sellers to maintain a fixed place of business. If those sellers are not franchisees, what is their role? Independent contractors? Agents? Employees? What legal protections are offered to the sellers?

CRITICAL THINKING

What missing information would you call for when considering the facts of this case?

Would you interpret the Arkansas Franchise Practices Act and how it applies to the facts of the case differently than the judge did? Why or why not?

ETHICAL DECISION MAKING

Consider the WPH framework. What values was Isbell promoting? What values were in conflict? Was the court fair in assessing her actions in light of these values?

Franchise Law Because franchisors are usually larger than franchisees and have more resources, they often have the upper hand in franchise relationships. Federal and state laws, however, have been established to protect the franchisee in the franchise relationship.

A franchise is a contractual relationship between the franchisor and the franchisee. Thus, contract law, and the Uniform Commercial Code in particular, applies to the franchise relationship. If the terms of the contract are not met, either side can sue for breach of contract. For example, in *Ford Motor Co. v. Lyons,*[1] Lyons sued Ford for breach of its dealer franchise obligations. In the franchise agreement, Ford had agreed to send factory representatives to the dealership, as well as offer Lyons assistance with his business. However, Ford failed to perform its duties. Lyons sued, bringing forth evidence showing that Ford had intentionally failed to perform its contractual duties because one of the other dealership franchises was jealous of the dealership territory Ford had given to Lyons as part of the franchise agreement.

In addition, several laws that are more specific have been established to govern the franchise relationship. For example, the Federal Trade Commission has a franchise rule requiring that franchisors present prospective franchisees with the material facts necessary for the franchisee to make an informed decision about entering a franchise relationship. Moreover, the Automobile Dealers' Franchise Act of 1965 prohibits car dealership franchisors from terminating franchise relationships in bad faith. Thus, for example, DaimlerChrysler could not terminate its franchise relationship with a dealer because the dealer failed to meet impossible standards. Finally, the Petroleum Marketing Practices Act of 1979 outlines the reasons for which a franchisor may terminate a gas station franchise. Franchises must also be aware of federal antitrust laws. Antitrust laws prohibit specific forms of anticompetitive behavior and might be applicable to franchises.

Many states have adopted additional laws to protect franchisees. Fifteen states, for example, require that franchisors provide prospective franchisees with a host of information about the franchise relationship before the agreement can be signed. What ethical standards do you think these 15 states are promoting in their decision to mandate franchise protections?

franchise agreement
A contract whereby a company (the franchisor) grants permission (a license) to another entity (the franchisee) to use the franchisor's name, trademark, or copyright in the operation of a business and associated sale of goods in return for payment.

Creation of the Franchise In the franchise relationship, the parties make a franchise agreement regarding various factors: the payment to the franchisor, the location of the franchise, the restrictions the franchisee must follow, and the method of termination of the franchise.

First, the franchise agreement usually states that the franchisee is to pay a large sum to the franchisor for use of the trade name or trademark. Moreover, the agreement determines what percentage of the income from the sales of the goods will go to the franchisor.

Second, the agreement usually determines where the franchise will be located. If the franchise requires a building, the agreement specifies who will pay for buying or renting the building. Similarly, if the building must be constructed, the agreement states who is responsible for the costs of the construction of the building.

Third, the franchisor usually includes in the agreement certain business practices that are forbidden and other business standards that must be met. For example, the franchisor might require that the business meet specific levels of cleanliness. Moreover, the franchisor can set certain sales quotas as well as requirements for record keeping by the franchisee. The franchisor can require that the franchisee purchase certain supplies from the franchisor at a set price, but the franchisor cannot attempt to establish the price at which the franchisee must sell the goods.

The disagreement in the Case Opener arose because of these second and third factors in franchise agreements. First, McDonald's offered the Robertsons a new franchise, to be located a block from the existing franchise. McDonald's purchased the property, agreed to income guarantees, and planned to give the Robertsons the new franchise in exchange for the existing franchise, which McDonald's would thereafter close. Negotiations between McDonald's and the Robertsons, however, were unsuccessful; the Robertsons continually refused the offer. Second, because many McDonald's restaurants are owned by franchisees, McDonald's has established a "McDonald's System," which promotes business practices enhancing the quality of food and

[1] 405 N.W.2d 354 (Wis. Ct. App. 1987).

services at each restaurant. McDonald's also has quality, safety, and cleanliness (QSC) standards for each of its franchises. The Robertsons' franchise agreement stipulated that McDonald's could inspect the Robertsons' restaurant at any reasonable time.

Although the franchisor has the legal authority to ensure that the franchisee maintains the quality of goods and services associated with the franchise, the franchisor must be cautious. If it exercises too much authority in the day-to-day affairs of the business, the franchisor could be held liable for the torts of the franchisee's employees.

Termination of the Franchise The franchise agreement establishes how the franchise will be terminated. The franchise is usually established for a trial period, such as a year. If the franchisee does not meet the requirements established in the franchise agreement, the franchisor can terminate the franchise agreement, but the franchisor must give the franchisee sufficient notice of the termination. Furthermore, the termination usually must have cause. Much of the litigation associated with franchises regards wrongful termination of a franchise. The typical agreement gives the franchisor broad authority to terminate a franchise. In recent years, however, many states have been giving the franchisee greater termination protection.

The courts usually rely heavily on the written franchise agreement when determining whether a franchise was wrongfully terminated. Look at Case 19–3, which illustrates the importance of the written franchise agreement.

CASE 19-3

COUSINS SUBS SYSTEMS, INC.
v. MICHAEL R. MCKINNEY
U.S. DISTRICT COURT FOR THE EASTERN
DISTRICT OF WISCONSIN
59 F.Supp.2d 816 (1999)

FACTS: *Cousins Subs Systems entered into an agreement with Michael McKinney, a Minnesota businessman who owned a company that operated a chain of gas stations, for McKinney to operate several Cousins submarine sandwich shops. The sub shops were to be placed in the gas stations. In April 1998, McKinney became disillusioned with the agreement and terminated the agreement. McKinney claimed that Cousins guaranteed him annual sales at each of his franchises ranging from $250,000 to $500,000. Furthermore, McKinney argued that Cousins promised to provide advertising for the franchises. McKinney also claimed that Cousins guaranteed it would provide assistance in recruiting other franchises. McKinney alleges that he terminated the agreement because Cousins failed to uphold these promises. In June 1998, Cousins filed suit against McKinney for wrongfully terminating the agreement with Cousins. Later in 1998, McKinney filed a counterclaim against Cousins. Cousins filed a motion to dismiss the counterclaim.*

ISSUE: Did Cousins Subs Systems make misleading statements of material facts?

REASONING: McKinney alleges that Cousins violated the Minnesota statute prohibiting businesses from using false statements of material facts (or omissions of material facts) to sell franchises. McKinney claims that Cousins made false verbal statements of material facts; however, when an alleged verbal statement contradicts a written contract, the written contract carries more weight. In this case, the written contracts, signed by McKinney and Cousins and later entered as exhibits, contradict the verbal statements McKinney claims Cousins made. The contracts state that no promises were made regarding the profit McKinney would earn, that advertising was McKinney's responsibility, and that the contracts contained all terms, conditions, and promises made by Cousins.

DECISION AND REMEDY: As demonstrated by the contracts McKinney signed, Cousins did not make any misleading statements of material facts. The counterclaim was dismissed.

SIGNIFICANCE: It is unclear whether Cousins made the verbal promises alleged by McKinney. Regardless,

McKinney did sign contracts that contradicted the alleged verbal promises. This case demonstrates how important it is for businesspeople to read contracts thoroughly and to ensure that all terms, conditions, and promises are contained in those contracts.

CRITICAL THINKING

What are the primary facts of this case? How would you word the issue of the case in your own words?

The judge stated that the written terms of the contracts between Cousins and McKinney were inconsistent with any alleged oral agreements that they made. Do you agree that written contracts should overrule oral agreements in most instances? Why or why not?

ETHICAL DECISION MAKING

The court ruled in favor of Cousins. Who are the primary stakeholders affected by the court's ruling for Cousins?

The decisions of a court have implications for business ethics. While Chapter 2 distinguishes between what the law requires of a manager and what ethics requires, the relationship between the law and ethics is reciprocal. While ethical judgments lie behind various laws, it is also the case that law has impacts on business ethics. For example, in this case, the court's decision is reminding us that business ethics must pay attention to the various stakeholders who feel the impacts of any business agreement.

SUMMARY

Major Forms of Business Organizations

Sole proprietorship: The owner has total control and unlimited personal liability, and profits are taxed directly as income to the sole proprietor.

General partnership: For most purposes, the partnership is not a legal entity, and each partner has equal control and unlimited liability, with profits that are taxed as income for partners.

Limited partnership: Limited partnerships are similar to general partnerships, except that limited partners' liability is limited to the extent of their capital contributions.

Corporation: A corporation is a separate legal entity wherein the owners' liability is limited to the amount of their contributions and the profits are taxed as income to the corporation.

Limited liability company: A limited liability company combines the best tax and liability features of partnerships and corporations. In an LLC all members may participate in management of the business entity while enjoying a shield of limited liability for their personal assets.

Specialized Forms of Business Organizations

The specialized forms are cooperatives, joint stock companies, syndicates, business trusts, joint ventures, and franchises.

A *franchise* is a contractual relationship between the franchisor and the franchisee. Thus, contract law, and the Uniform Commercial Code in particular, applies to the franchise relationship. If the terms of the contract are not met, either side can sue for breach of contract.

·····➤ Point/Counterpoint

Should a New Restaurateur Open a New Location of a Restaurant Franchise Rather Than Become a Sole Proprietor?

YES	NO
A businessperson new to the restaurant business should open a restaurant as part of an existing franchise rather than begin an individual restaurant as a sole proprietor. A new restaurateur encounters substantial risks when opening a business as a sole proprietor. Sole proprietors have unlimited personal liability, meaning they are held solely accountable for the finances in their businesses. For example, a sole proprietor often needs to provide her house as collateral to obtain a small business loan. Additionally, a restaurant sole proprietor can be held personally liable for injury in her restaurant. This personal liability means the restaurant owner could be personally sued for employee or customer injury. One main advantage of becoming a franchisee is that the franchisee usually is not held solely liable for an injury. One primary concern should be that the businessperson is *new* to the restaurant business. The franchisee encounters limited financial risk. Additionally, a franchisor can fulfill the vital role of supervision and provide crucial guidance to a new businessperson. Because restaurant franchises are already successful, the new franchisee has a clear idea of business practices that have been proved successful by the franchisor. Further, most franchisors offer new franchisees a clear outline of forbidden practices that would endanger the new franchise as well as minimum standards (cleanliness, service) that will assist the new franchise. Sole proprietors must experience a "trial-and-error" time period as they learn which business practices should be implemented. The franchisor's assistance eliminates the trial-and-error period because the franchisee is informed of and warned not to repeat past errors.	A new restaurateur should open a new restaurant as a sole proprietor rather than a franchisee. A businessperson new to the restaurant business has greater potential for long-term success as a sole proprietor than as a franchisee. The main appeal of a franchise is less personal risk and liability at the start of the business. However, with careful research and expert advice, sole proprietors can obtain low-risk, longer-term loans that are unlikely to jeopardize their personal assets. Additionally, sole proprietors always hold the option of later adding a full business partner or a limited partner. Franchisees, however, usually do not retain that right after entering business with the franchisor. To decrease liability, sole proprietors can implement additional safety measures. One major disadvantage of opening a new franchise is that the new franchise must pay the franchisor a percentage of profits for the duration the new franchise exists. For a sole proprietor, after debts are repaid, all profits are kept in the business for improvements and personal income. Franchises are extremely restrictive in creativity. A sole proprietor is truly her own boss. A sole proprietor can change the "look" of her restaurant at any time. Sole proprietors can determine how many and which hours they would like to be in operation. Sole proprietors can also decide whether to hire a manager or manage their restaurants directly. Additionally, sole proprietors can decide how many and what kind of individuals they would like to employ at their restaurants. Franchisees often face restrictions and limitations regarding size, hours, management, and employment practices. Perhaps most important, a sole proprietor retains flexibility if the economy changes, which it frequently does. If need be, a sole proprietor can simply uproot the restaurant and move to a different location. Further, a sole proprietor can change her restaurant's menu and appearance if the customer constituency in her area changes.

·····➤ Questions & Problems

1. What is the distinction between a general partnership and a limited partnership?

2. Explain why a cooperative could not claim to be a syndicate.

3. Suppose you were asked to review and assess a franchise agreement. What responsibilities would you expect to be included in that agreement?

4. Heating & Air Specialists, Inc. (A/C), was interested in becoming a dealer of Lennox equipment and supplies. The parties signed a dealer agreement stating that either party could terminate the agreement with or without cause. A/C originally operated only one location but later became interested in expanding the franchise. A/C was given verbal authorization to sell Lennox equipment at a new location in Tulsa on a temporary basis. After A/C began to operate in Tulsa, other Lennox dealers in the area began to complain. Lennox subsequently decided to terminate A/C's franchise at the Tulsa location. Lennox testified that its decision to terminate the Tulsa franchise was a result of A/C's failure to keep its accounts current. After A/C continued to default on its payments, Lennox notified A/C that the entire franchise would be terminated. A/C filed suit against Lennox for unlawfully terminating the franchise. Lennox counterclaimed for the payments due. How do you think the court resolved this conflict? [*Heating & Air Specialists, Inc. v. Jones,* 180 F.3d 923 (1999).]

5. Lapinee Trade, Inc., entered into an oral agreement with Boon Rawd Brewery and began importing and distributing Singha beer in 1982. The beer was originally not well established in the American market, and Lapinee spent sufficient resources building a market for the beer. After successfully selling the beer in California, Lapinee obtained authorization from Boon Rawd to begin expanding into Arizona, Nevada, Washington, Texas, Minnesota, and Illinois. Though Boon Rawd and Lapinee originally enjoyed a good business relationship, the relationship began to deteriorate in the late 80s. In 1987, Boon Rawd terminated Lapinee as a distributor. No reasons for the termination were provided. Lapinee challenged the termination in the district court. The district court found that Boon Rawd had wrongfully terminated the distributorship agreement with Lapinee. The court held that it was the custom and practice in the beer industry to terminate distributorships only for a good cause. The court also stated, "Lapinee put great time and money into developing an American market for Singha beer and used its best efforts to build the market and sell Singha, and the distributorship was taken from it before it could reap any substantial benefit from its investment." Boon Rawd appealed the decision, stating that the termination was a result of Lapinee's failure to maintain clear business records. Do you think the court of appeals affirmed the earlier court's decision? Why or why not? [*Lapinee Trade v. Boon Rawd Brewery Account,* 91 F.3d 909 (1996).]

6. Clow gave birth to a baby at Riverside County Hospital in October 1967. Due to complications with the birth, as well as the malpractice of one of the attending resident medical students, Clow's son developed cerebral palsy. Clow sued the hospital for malpractice; the two parties settled out of court for $944,109. The hospital in turn sued Loma Linda University, whose medical school faculty provided teaching services to the hospital and whose medical students were residents at the hospital. The trial court jury found that the county hospital and the university were engaged in a joint venture and hence the university was liable for 50 percent of the settlement costs. Do you think the appellate court agreed with the trial court's finding? Why or why not? [*County of Riverside v. Loma Linda University,* 118 Cal. App. 3d 300 (1981).]

7. In 1975, Vylene, the operator of a restaurant franchise, and Naugles, the franchisor, entered into a 10-year franchise agreement. The agreement stated that Vylene would be given the opportunity to extend the franchise after expiration of the initial 10-year term "on terms and conditions to be negotiated." Vylene failed to make timely payments on its franchise fees and rent. At the end of the 10-year agreement, Naugles presented Vylene with a proposal to extend the franchise agreement. Vylene rejected the offer, believing that the conditions of the proposal would make it impossible to operate at a profit. Vylene continued to operate the business and used Naugles's federally registered trademarks. Naugles opened a new restaurant located fewer than 2 miles from Vylene's location. Naugles offered similar food options but at a much lower price. As a result of the new restaurant, Vylene's business deteriorated. Vylene subsequently filed an action against Naugles in bankruptcy court for relief based on Naugles's refusal to negotiate the extension offer. Naugles filed counterclaims for trademark violations, unfair competition, and misappropriation of trade secrets. The bankruptcy court held that Naugles had breached the franchise agreement and the covenant of good faith and fair dealing by opening a nearby competing franchise. The district court reversed the decision, finding that Naugles did not wrongfully terminate the franchise agreement. Vylene then brought the case to the court of appeals. How do you think the court decided? [*In re Vylene Enterprises, Inc.* 90 F.3d 1472 (1996).]

8. Shell Oil Company and AZ Services, Inc., entered into a five-year contractual relationship to establish a petroleum franchise. Under the agreement, AZ was required to use Shell's trademarks, brand name, service marks, and other Shell identifications. The agreement stated, "If Dealer fails to exercise the rights granted hereunder by failing . . . to maintain at Dealer's Station a representative amount of each grade of Shell branded motor fuel for resale to the public . . . Shell shall have grounds to terminate or not renew this Agreement." One year into the

relationship, AZ removed all Shell trademarks and identifications from the property, stopped selling Shell products, and began to sell the products of one of Shell's competitors. AZ's franchise agreement was immediately terminated, and Shell filed an action under the Petroleum Marketing Practices Act to force AZ to terminate the franchise and to vacate the service station. Do you think Shell was successful? Why or why not? [*Shell Oil Co. v. AZ Services, Inc.,* 990 F. Supp. 1406 (1997).]

9. Joe Orosco, an employee of Sun-Maid Growers, Inc., lost his arm in an industrial accident with a raisin elevator in 1991. Sun-Maid was one of four members of a marketing cooperative called the Sun-Diamond Corporation. According to the cooperative agreement, Sun-Diamond was authorized to provide certain management services to Sun-Maid. Orosco sued Sun-Maid and Sun-Diamond, arguing that both corporations were liable because they were involved in a joint venture to design, manufacture, construct, repair, maintain, install, and test the processing line on which Orosco lost his arm. Were the two corporations involved in a joint venture? What additional facts would you want to know before forming your answer? If they were involved in a joint venture, should Sun-Diamond be held liable for Orosco's injuries? Why or why not? [*Orosco v. Sun-Diamond Corp.,* 51 Cal. App. 4th 1659 (1997).]

10. Milburn Pierce was the sole proprietor of the Pierce Painting Company, a painting contracting company with two employees in addition to Pierce. Pierce bought workers' compensation insurance for his business through the Louisiana Workers' Compensation Corporation, but in the written agreement he chose to exclude himself from the policy's coverage. In August 2002, Pierce was working on a job for Tom Fullilove Construction Company when he fell off a roof. Pierce broke his left wrist and left femur and incurred more than $30,000 in medical bills for his treatment and therapy. Pierce filed a compensation claim in September 2002, and Fullilove paid his medical bills. In October 2002, Fullilove sued Pierce for reimbursement of the compensation payments. The Office of Workers' Compensation found for Fullilove. Pierce appealed, arguing that a Louisiana statute provided that a "sole proprietor with respect to such sole proprietorship may by written agreement elect not to be covered" under workers' compensation insurance. Thus, Pierce argued, he had elected not to be covered with respect to his sole proprietorship, a separate legal entity. But with respect to Tom Fullilove Construction Company, Pierce argued that he never elected not to be covered. How do you think the appellate court ruled? Why? [*Pierce v. Tom Fullilove Constr. Co.,* 892 So. 2d 757 (2005).]

11. "YOU AND I" was a thoroughbred racehorse owned by a syndicate composed of 40 equal ownership shares. The syndicate agreement stated that if an acceptable offer was made to purchase the horse from the syndicate, each syndicate member had a "first right to purchase" under which he could sell his interest in the horse or buy the interests of the other syndicate members who had elected to sell their interests in the horse. The syndicate agreement, however, required that if a syndicate member planned to exercise his first right to purchase, he had to notify the syndicate manager of his intent within 10 days of his receiving notification of the acceptable offer. In September 2003, Brereton Jones, a syndicate member and the syndicate manager, received an offer from Blooming Hills Farms to buy YOU AND I for $500,000. Jones sent a memo to all the syndicate members notifying them that Blooming Hills Farms had made the offer, that he believed the offer to be fair, and that he planned to sell his interest. Jones received word from 39 of the 40 syndicate members that they planned to sell their interest in YOU AND I. The following day, Never Tell Farm, a syndicate member, notified Jones that it planned to exercise its first right to purchase. Jones and Never Tell proceeded to negotiate over whether Never Tell would exercise its first right to purchase, and the 10-day window elapsed. When the negotiations fell through, Never Tell notified Jones of its intent to exercise its first right to purchase. Jones told Never Tell that it had not timely asserted its right and thus the horse had been sold to Blooming Hills Farms. Never Tell sued Jones, claiming that under the syndicate agreement it should have had the right to purchase the other syndicate members' interests in YOU AND I. With whom do you think the court sided in this case? Why? [*Never Tell Farm, LLC v. Airdrie Stud, Inc.,* 123 Fed. Appx. 194 (2005).]

12. Chic Miller operated a General Motors (GM) franchise car dealership. His written franchise agreement with GM stipulated that Miller had to maintain a floor-plan financing agreement with a lender to enable him to buy new cars from GM. Initially, Miller maintained a line of credit with a GM affiliate (GMAC), but he terminated the agreement because he felt that GMAC charged him an exorbitant interest rate. Miller was able to find another line of credit from Chase Manhattan Bank, but Chase withdrew its financing agreement with Miller after one year. Miller attempted to resume the agreement with GMAC, but GMAC refused. Miller alleged *ipse dixit* (an assertion without evidence) that GMAC discouraged other lenders from providing a line of credit to Miller. GM then notified Miller that it was terminating its franchise relationship with him because he failed to

satisfy the financing stipulation of the written franchise agreement. Two months after receiving this notice from GM, Miller attempted to sell his franchise to Kenneth Crowley, the owner of another car dealership. GM rejected this sale, alleging that Miller no longer had a franchise to sell because GM had terminated the franchise agreement two months earlier. Miller sued GM for failing to help his franchise obtain floor-plan financing and for rejecting the sale of his franchise to Crowley. How do you think the court ruled in this case? What requirements must GM meet to lawfully terminate a franchise? Did GM meet those requirements? [*Chic Miller's Chevrolet, Inc. v. GMC,* 352 F. Supp. 2d 251 (2005).]

13. Margaret Miller operated an H&R Block tax-preparation franchise for 15 years. She hired William Hehlen as an income tax return preparer for five years, from 1997 to 2001. Each year, Miller and Hehlen signed an employment agreement drawn up by H&R Block. The 2001 agreement was between Hehlen and "Margaret Miller, doing business as H&R Block," and included stipulations prohibiting Hehlen from reproducing confidential business information and from soliciting clients away from Miller's business. Hehlen maintained on his home computer a spreadsheet of customer names that he obtained from Miller. In April 2001, H&R Block terminated its franchise agreement with Miller, and Miller subsequently operated her business as a sole proprietorship under the name "MJM & Associates." Hehlen's employment with Miller ended after the 2001 tax season. In December 2001, Miller sent advertising postcards to clients referring to Hehlen as one of her associates. When Hehlen, who went to work for another H&R Block office, learned of the postcards, he began telephoning the customers whose names he had obtained from Miller. Miller learned of the calls in February 2002 and filed a cease-and-desist action against Hehlen, arguing that Hehlen was violating his employment contract with Miller. Hehlen argued that his employment contract was with Miller's H&R Block franchise, which ceased to exist after April 2001. Do you think Hehlen's employment contract was signed with Miller's franchise or with Miller's sole proprietorship? If you think Hehlen's contract was with Miller's franchise, should Miller have the right to enforce the contract provisions after H&R Block terminated her franchise agreement? Why or why not? [*Miller v. Hehlen,* 104 P.3d 193 (2005).]

14. Harvey Pierce was a work-release inmate from the local county jail who worked at an Arby's franchise restaurant owned by Dennis Rasmussen, Inc. (DRI). One day in June 1999, Pierce walked off the job without permission and crossed the street to wait for his former girlfriend, Robin Kerl, and her fiancé, David Jones, in the parking lot of the Wal-Mart store where both Kerl and Jones worked. When Kerl and Jones exited the store, Pierce shot both of them in the head, killing Jones and seriously injuring and permanently disabling Kerl. Pierce then shot himself and died immediately. Kerl and Jones's estate sued Arby's and DRI for negligent supervision, hiring, and retention, arguing that Arby's, the franchisor, was vicariously liable for the negligence of DRI, the franchisee. Do you think Arby's should be vicariously liable for the negligence of its franchisee? Why or why not? [*Kerl v. DRI and Arby's, Inc.,* 682 N.W.2d 328 (2004).]

Looking for more review material?

The Online Learning Center at **www.mhhe.com/kubasekess** contains this chapter's "Assignment on the Internet" and also a list of URLs for more information, entitled "On the Internet." Find both of them in the Student Center portion of the OLC, along with quizzes and other helpful materials.

Partnerships

Rockwell and a Potential Partnership

Seth Rockwell filed a motion against Eric Swenson to try to receive lost wages and reimbursement for expenses he had incurred while working as Swenson's employee. Swenson immediately moved for summary judgment because Rockwell was supposedly his partner, not his employee. If Rockwell was Swenson's partner, it was possible that he would not be able to retrieve lost funds.

The district court found that Rockwell was Swenson's employee and not his partner. Swenson appealed the decision, continuing to argue that Rockwell was a partner who had only the right to request an accounting of the corporation. Depending on the appellate court's decision, Rockwell would be awarded $41,580 in unpaid wages and $10,896.39 in nonreimbursed expenses. Additionally, a potential maritime lien would be imposed on Swenson.

1. Why would a potential partnership between Rockwell and Swenson have any influence on the outcome of this case?

2. What could Swenson have done to avoid this suit?

After reading this chapter, you will be able to answer the following questions:

LO 1 What is a partnership?

LO 2 What are the different ways in which a partnership can be formed?

LO 3 What are the rights of partners as they interact with each other?

LO 4 Are all members of a partnership liable for interactions with third parties?

LO 5 What are the steps involved in the termination of the partnership?

LO 6 How is a limited partnership formed?

LO 7 What are the rights and privileges of a limited partner as opposed to a general partner?

The Uniform Partnership Act (UPA) is the main statute governing partnership law. If there is no express partnership agreement, UPA establishes the rules for the partnership.

This chapter discusses the creation and operation of the partnership, how partnerships are terminated, and special types of partnerships. The chapter begins by considering the nature of the partnership relationship. Then it explains how a partnership is created and how partnerships function. Next, it discusses how a partnership is terminated. The chapter concludes with a look at special types of partnerships.

Nature of the Partnership

LO 1

partnership
A voluntary association between two or more people who co-own a business for profit.

What exactly is a partnership? According to UPA Section 6, a **partnership** is "an association of two or more persons to carry on as co-owners a business for profit." It is important that we analyze all four parts of this definition in order to determine its exact meaning and implications.

First, by "association," UPA means that the partnership is a voluntary and consensual relationship. Thus, no one could force someone else to enter into a partnership with him. Second, a partnership requires "two or more persons." UPA defines *persons* as "individuals, partnerships, corporations, and other associations." Therefore, almost any individual or group of people could serve as a partner, but these persons must have the legal capacity to be partners. For example, although minors can serve as partners, the resulting partnership agreement is voidable.

Third, in a partnership, the partners must "carry on as co-owners of a business for profit." Here *business* is defined as any trade, occupation, or profession. "Carrying on" a business refers to making several transactions. Finally, UPA requires that the partners be "co-owners" of the business, meaning the partners must share the profits or losses of the business as well as share in the management of the business.

Fourth, the final element of the definition of partnership is that it be "for profit," meaning that the partners must be intending to make some kind of profit from the business.

To summarize, a partnership has the following characteristics:

- *Voluntary* and *consensual* relationship.
- Between two or more *individuals, partnerships, corporations,* or other forms of business organization.
- Who engage in *numerous business transactions* over a period of time.
- Intending *to make a profit.*
- And *share* the *profits* and *management* of the business.

When parties dispute whether a partnership relationship exists, the courts will look for those factors in the case. The relationship between Rockwell and Swenson in the Case Opener did not constitute a partnership because it did not meet these criteria. The two men had never voluntarily or consensually entered into a partnership. There was no evidence that the profits or management duties were shared between the two men.

Probably the most important factor in determining whether a partnership exists is determining whether the profits from the business are shared. However, UPA has established several exceptions in which a sharing of profits does not constitute a partnership. For example, when an employer shares profits with an employee as payment for work, there is no partnership. Similarly, when a landlord accepts shares of profits for payment of rent, there is no

CONNECTING to the Core

Management: Partnerships—Will the Sum Be Greater?

Why would two individuals want to form a partnership agreement? Two separate parties may decide to form a partnership when they believe that the partnership will result in *synergy*, meaning that the combined efforts of both partners will likely be more profitable than the efforts of the individuals working separately. In other words, after accounting for all partnership-related expenses and taxes, the partnership would be earning more profit than a situation in which each individual engaged in a similar business without participating in a partnership. However, for future business managers, it is imperative to evaluate the likelihood that the "sum would be greater than the parts" when deciding whether to enter into a partnership agreement. Synergy is merely an ideal of partnership agreements, not a guaranteed outcome.

K. Williams, *Management: A Practical Introduction* (New York: McGraw-Hill/Irwin, 2006), p. 189.

partnership. If a party receives a share of profits for any of the following reasons, there is no partnership:

- Payment of a debt.
- Payment of an annuity to a widow or representative of a deceased partner.
- Payment from the sale of goodwill of a business or other property.
- Payment of interest on a loan.

Case 20-1 illustrates the court's analysis of whether a partnership relationship indeed exists.

 CASE 20-1

MAX NORMAN v. MONTGOMERY WHOLESALE LUMBER
COURT OF CIVIL APPEALS OF ALABAMA
678 So. 2d 1110; 1996 Ala. Civ. App. LEXIS 3

FACTS: *When Michael Norman failed to pay for lumber purchased from Montgomery Wholesale Lumber, Montgomery Lumber sued Michael Norman as a proprietor of Norman Builders. After Montgomery Lumber filed the complaint against Michael Norman, he filed a notice for bankruptcy. Montgomery Lumber then amended its complaint to add Max Norman, Michael's father, and Barbara Norman, Michael's wife, because they were part of the partnership, Norman Builders. Michael Norman, however, argued that he was the sole proprietor of Norman Builders. The trial court found that Norman Builders was a partnership consisting of Michael, Max, and Barbara. Max Norman appealed, arguing that the trial court erred in finding that Norman Builders was a partnership because each of the Normans testified that (1) there was no partnership, (2) there was no partnership agreement, and (3) neither Barbara nor Max shared in the profits, losses, or management of Norman Builders.*

ISSUE: Was Norman Builders a partnership?

REASONING: To determine whether a partnership existed, the court needed to determine how Max, Norman, and Barbara were related to the business. Did they share any joint property? Did they share the profits of the business? Did they share in the control and management of the business? In this case, Max, Michael, and Barbara all shared in the control and management of the business when negotiating contracts, building houses, paying debts, and signing contracts. In addition, Max and Barbara had company cellular telephones even though neither was an employee, and the company regularly deposited up to $2,000 in Barbara's savings account.

DECISION AND REMEDY: The evidence showed that Max, Michael, and Barbara were engaged in a partnership. The trial court's ruling was affirmed.

SIGNIFICANCE OF THE CASE: This case began because Michael Norman owed money to a supplier and went bankrupt. The supplier then sought the money from Max and Barbara, who did not think they were partners in

Michael's business. Because Max and Barbara fit the legal definition of a partner, Max and Barbara are now liable for the company's debts. This case should be a reminder of the protection offered by LLCs and LLPs, as well as the dangers of entering a partnership blindly.

CRITICAL THINKING

What evidence led the court to hold that Max Norman was a partner in the Norman Builders partnership?

ETHICAL DECISION MAKING

Notice that business ethics requires us to think beyond ourselves. Clearly Max Norman had good personal reason not to be labeled a partner. It would have cost a large sum of money to be included as a partner in Norman Builders. But ethics represents an appeal to our better selves. Use the universalization test to explain why one should not attempt to avoid partnership responsibilities.

Now that you know how the courts determine whether a partnership exists, what kind of legal status do partnerships have? Partnerships can be treated two different ways: as entities or as aggregates.

PARTNERSHIP AS A LEGAL ENTITY

legal entity
Any individual, proprietorship, partnership, corporation, association, or other organization that has, in the eyes of the law, the capacity to form an agreement, and the ability to assume an obligation, and to discharge an indebtedness.

In some respects, a partnership is treated as a *legal entity,* a person separate from the partnership. Thus, in some cases, the partnership has a life of its own.

First, a partnership is often considered a legal entity when it is sued or being sued. States determine when a partnership can or cannot be named in a suit. Second, under the doctrine of marshaling assets, assets are arranged in a certain order to pay for any outstanding debts. Partnership creditors have first priority in obtaining partnership assets, while individual personal creditors have first priority to the assets of the individual partners. Thus, the partnership assets are kept separate from the individual partners' assets.

Third, the title to property may be put in the partnership name. Therefore, the partnership may own property that individual partners do not hold. If the partners want to sell the partnership property to another party, all partners must participate in the transaction of the partnership property. Finally, every partner is considered to be an agent to the partnership, and every partner has a fiduciary relationship with the other partners.

PARTNERSHIP AS A LEGAL AGGREGATE

While in some cases the partnership is considered a separate legal entity, there are other cases in which the partnership is considered a legal aggregate of the partners. For instance, the debts of the partnership eventually become the debts of the individual partners. Furthermore, the partnership is not taxed as a separate being; instead, the partners pay taxes on the income generated through the partnership. Moreover, because the partnership ceases to exist when one of the partners dies (unless otherwise established by the partnership agreement), the partnership is considered an aggregate of the individual partners.

LO 2

Formation of the Partnership

While an explicit written agreement is not required to create a partnership, the partners are advised to create one. The written agreement ensures that the terms of the partnership will be upheld. For example, suppose that you and your partner orally agree that you will receive three-fourths of the profits because you are doing significantly more management tasks. However, when you distribute the funds, your partner sues you because you give him only one-fourth of

Forms of Partnerships in the ICT Sector in Developing Countries

In the information and communication technology (ICT) sector of developing countries, businesses are using partnerships between local and multinational companies to create a support structure for the ICT sector. Three forms of partnership are especially important: (1) industrial districts, (2) *keiretsus* (groups of businesses in which each individual business has a stake in the others), and (3) offshore partnerships.

Industrial districts are loosely structured collectives of small to medium-size firms located in a specific area. The firms are highly specialized in one or more phases of a production process. Industrial districts are coordinated through both personal relationships and marketlike mechanisms. One purpose of industrial districts is to pool local competencies.

Keiretsus bring foreign ICT companies into a partnership, and they serve as "hubs." Local ICT ventures serve the hubs. *Keiretsus* add the strength of a competent hub, but, over time, this strength could make it less likely that local firms will develop strength of their own.

Offshore partnerships combine the strengths of firms that operate in developing countries and firms that operate in countries that are foreign to the developing countries, for example, firms in the United States. Firms in developing countries use offshore partnerships to gain international exposure and technological competence. Foreign firms use offshore partnerships to gain (1) access to competent yet low-cost workers and (2) the opportunity to enter developing markets.

the profits. Without a written partnership agreement, the courts will have a difficult time ruling in your favor. A written agreement that creates a partnership is called the **articles of partnership.**

What kind of information do the articles of partnership usually include? First, the partners' names, as well as the name of the partnership, should be listed on the document. Second, the agreement should address the duration of the partnership. The agreement could include the date or event on which the partnership agreement would expire. Alternatively, the agreement could specify that the term of the partnership is indefinite. Third, the agreement should state the division of profits as well as losses. Fourth, the articles of partnership should establish the division of management duties. Fifth, the agreement should state exactly what capital contributions will be made by each partner. Creating articles of partnership can prevent legal problems by explicitly establishing the terms of the partnership agreement.

articles of partnership
The written agreement that creates a partnership.

PARTNERSHIP BY ESTOPPEL

In some cases, parties who are not named in partnership agreements can be considered partners. How? Suppose you create a partnership agreement with your best friend. When you interact with your first potential customer, you tell this customer that your parents are also partners in this business. On the basis of your parents' participation in the partnership, the customer decides to place an order to purchase certain goods from you. Your parents discover that you have reported that they are your partners, but they do not contact the customer to tell her that they are not your partners. When your business cannot afford to purchase these goods to sell them to the customer, the customer sues you as well as your parents. Because your parents were aware of the misrepresentation but did not correct it, they will be estopped from denying they are your partners. While they will not be able to claim the rights associated with being a partner (e.g., sharing the profits), in many states they could be held liable for the costs of the damages to the customer.

Most states recognize two situations in which a partnership by estoppel exists. First, as in the example above, if a third party is aware of a misrepresentation of partnership and consents to the misrepresentation, a partnership by estoppel is present. Second, if a nonpartner has represented himself or herself as a partner and a third party *reasonably relies* on this information to his or her detriment, the nonpartner can be held liable for the third party's damages.

Interactions between Partners

LO 3

The operation of the partnership encompasses two types of interactions: interactions between the partners and interactions between the partnership and third parties. The partners have certain rights and duties within each type of interaction.

DUTIES OF PARTNERS TO ONE ANOTHER

Most of the duties that partners hold to one another involve a duty to be loyal. They include the fiduciary duty to the other partners, the duty of obedience, and the duty of care.

Perhaps the most important duty of the partners is their fiduciary duty. They must, in good faith, work for the benefit of the partnership. They should not take any kind of action that will undermine the partnership. Consequently, the partners must not engage in any business that competes with the partnership.

Partners must disclose any material facts affecting the business. If a partner derives some kind of benefit from the partnership without the consent of the other partners, he or she must notify the partners of this benefit.

The second duty that the partners have to each other is the duty of obedience, to obey the partnership agreement. If they do not obey the agreement, they can be held liable for any losses that the partnership incurs.

The third duty the partners have is a duty of care to the other partners. Each partner must perform her management functions to the best of her abilities. If a partner makes an honest mistake in fulfilling her responsibilities to the partnership, she will not be held liable for the mistake.

RIGHTS OF THE PARTNERS IN THEIR INTERACTIONS WITH OTHER PARTNERS

According to the law, partners have certain rights regarding their interactions with other partners.

Right to Share in Management Unless otherwise stated in the partnership agreement, all partners have a right to participate equally in the management of the partnership. Even if one partner has an unusually large proportion of the management duties, each partner has one vote in determining how the partnership is managed. While most decisions are made by majority vote, some decisions require agreement by all partners. For instance, if the partners are voting on whether to change some element of the partnership agreement, all partners must agree with the change. Other types of decisions that require a unanimous vote include a decision to admit new partners or a decision to alter the nature of the firm's business.

Right to Share in Profits Each partner is entitled to a share of the profits of the partnership. How big is each partner's share? If the partnership agreement does not establish a certain division of profits, all partners will share the profits equally. Similarly, partners must share in the losses of the partnership. Thus, if there is no statement of how the losses will be divided among the partners, the losses will be divided in a proportion identical to the sharing of the profits.

Right to Compensation Unless otherwise agreed, no partner will receive compensation for his or her participation in the business. In other words, the partner will not receive a salary regardless of the amount of time and effort he or she devotes to the business. Of course, the partners may agree to create salaries for certain partners, but no partner enters the partnership relationship with a right to compensation for his or her business activities. If a partner dies during the term of the partnership, the surviving partner is, however, entitled to compensation for services in closing the business affairs.

Property Rights Partners have three property rights associated with the partnership: (1) the right to participate in the management of the business (discussed earlier), (2) the right to specific partnership property, and (3) the right to her partnership interest. Here, we examine the latter two property rights.

First, partners own the partnership property as *tenants in common,* which means that the partners own the property as a group. Any property that is brought into or acquired by the partnership is considered property of the partnership. If property is in the name of an individual partner but was purchased with partnership funds, the property is considered partnership property.

One way to determine whether specific property will be considered a partnership asset is to determine the relationship of the asset to the partnership. If the asset is closely related to the business of the partnership, it will likely be considered a partnership asset.

Each partner has the right to possess partnership property. However, a partner cannot use this property to pay a personal debt. Similarly, a partner cannot sell or use the property if the purpose is outside the partnership interest.

What happens to the partnership property if a partner dies? According to the **right of survivorship,** the rights in specific partnership property pass to the surviving partner(s). However, the surviving partners must account to the deceased partner's estate for the value of that partner's interest in the specific property.

Second, a partner has a right to an interest in the partnership. This interest, composed of a combination of the partner's share of the profits and a return of capital contributed by the partner, is part of the partner's personal property. If necessary, a partner can sell his or her interest in the partnership to a creditor. A partner's personal creditor cannot seize specific items of partnership property; however, the creditor can obtain a **charging order,** which entitles the creditor to the partner's profits. The charging order permits the partner to continue to act as a partner and engage in the partnership business; however, the creditor collects the partner's share of the profits.

Right to Inspect Books Each partner has the right to receive full information regarding partnership matters. This right corresponds to the fiduciary duty of the partners to disclose any information affecting the partnership. Thus, partners must have access to all partnership books and records and be allowed to make copies of these records. Unless otherwise agreed, the records must be kept at the principal business office.

Right to an Account An **accounting,** is a review and listing of all partnership assets and/or profit. The accounting typically lists the distribution of assets and profit to the partners. Each partner has a right to an accounting in four circumstances:

1. Whenever the partnership agreement provides for an account.
2. Whenever the copartners wrongfully exclude a partner from the partnership or from access to the books.
3. Whenever any partner fails to disclose a profit or benefit from the partnership, thus breaching his or her fiduciary duty.
4. Whenever circumstances render an account as "just and reasonable."

For example, in the Case Opener, Swenson argued that if Rockwell were a partner, he was not approaching the suit appropriately. If Rockwell were a partner and thought that Swenson was taking funds, Rockwell would have a partner's right to request an accounting to determine whether funds had been withheld.

Interactions between Partners and Third Parties

LO 4

Each partner can serve as an agent for the other partners as well as the partnership. Consequently, as long as a partner has authority to act, his act in performing business duties, as well as making agreements with third parties, is binding for the partnership. If the partner has authority to act and the partnership is bound by the act, each partner has unlimited personal liability for the obligation.

ACTUAL AUTHORITY OF THE PARTNERS

According to UPA, general agency principles establish that partners have the authority to bind a partnership in an agreement. Consequently, if a partner, following normal business procedures, establishes an agreement in which he or she binds the partnership to the agreement, both the partner and the partnership are liable for the obligation in the agreement.

right of survivorship
The right that specific partnership property will pass on to the surviving partner(s).

charging order
An order that entitles a creditor to collect a partner's profits.

accounting
A review and listing of all partnership assets and/or profit.

Suppose Brittany is a partner in a firm. While allegedly carrying on partnership business, she engages in a business transaction and binds the partnership to the agreement. Yet suppose Brittany really didn't have authority to bind the partnership to the agreement with the third party. In this case, both Brittany and the firm are liable for the obligation.

However, suppose that the third party is aware that Brittany does not have the authority to bind the partnership to the agreement. Since the party is aware that the authority is absent, Brittany will be held liable for the obligation but the partnership will not be held liable.

IMPLIED AUTHORITY OF THE PARTNERS

Because of the nature of the partnership, partners generally have greater implied authority than do typical agents. The implied authority of the partners is usually determined by the nature of the business. For instance, a partner typically has the implied authority to enter into agreements necessary to carry on partnership business. Thus, a partner has the authority to purchase goods that are necessary to perpetuate the business. However, a partner does not have implied authority to sell any property without the consent of all other partners.

LIABILITY TO THIRD PARTIES

jointly liable
A term applied to partners who share liability for the partnership's debts.

According to UPA, if a partnership is liable, each partner has unlimited personal liability. That is, all partners are jointly liable for the partnership's debts. Thus, if a party wants to bring a successful claim, the party must name all partners as defendants. Instead of naming every partner in a lawsuit, a party can simply name the partnership. If the party is successful at bringing his or her claim, each partner is liable for the judgment. If one partner pays the entire judgment, the other partners are required to indemnify, or reimburse, that partner.

joint and several liability
A type of liability in which a third party can choose to sue the partners separately or to sue all partners jointly in one action.

If a partner commits a tort or a breach of trust, all partners are jointly and severally liable. Joint and several liability means that a third party can choose to sue the partners separately or all partners jointly in one action. Suppose William sues your partnership, which has four partners. William might name one of the partners in the first action. If the partner is found liable, William can sue all three other partners separately. However, if in the first claim the court ruled that the partnership was not liable in any form, William cannot bring a successful claim against a second partner on the issue of the partner's liability.

If William brings a successful claim against a partner, he can collect the judgment only on the assets of one partner. The partner is required to reimburse the partnership for the damages it pays to William. Case 20-2 considers how partners in a partnership can be held liable for the negligence of one partner.

CASE 20-2

ERIC JOHNSON & LORI JOHNSON v. ST. THERESE MEDICAL CENTER
APPELLATE COURT OF ILLINOIS, SECOND DISTRICT
296 Ill. App. 3d 341; 694 N.E.2d 1088; 1998 Ill. App. LEXIS 301

FACTS: *In November 1990, Eric and Lori Johnson brought their 22-month-old daughter, Erica, to St. Therese Medical Center, where she was treated and released by Dr. Bruce Sands. Dr. Sands was a partner of Northern Illinois Emergency Physicians, Ltd. Drs. Richard Keller, Michael Oster, Thomas Braniff, Rodney Haenschen, and Phillip Gillespie were the other partners in the partnership. The Johnsons filed suit against Dr. Sands and the partnership. They argued that Dr. Sands negligently caused the death of Erica and* *that the partnership was liable because St. Therese acted on behalf of the partnership. A jury gave the Johnsons a $4 million award against Dr. Sands, St. Therese, and the partnership. Dr. Sands later filed for bankruptcy. In February 1997, the trial court judge ruled that the Johnsons could proceed against the general partners individually if they were partners at the time of the incident. Consequently, the plaintiffs started motions to withhold the wages of all the partners. Various court proceedings ensued in which various partners*

argued that they should not be held personally liable. In June 1997, the trial court ruled that the assets of Keller, Haenschen, and Braniff be turned over to the Johnsons.

ISSUE: Can a judgment against a partnership be enforced against the partners individually?

REASONING: Generally speaking, all partners are jointly and severally liable for everything chargeable to the partnership for the loss or injury of a third person due to any wrongful act or omission of any partner acting in the ordinary course of the business of the partnership. Additionally, a judgment against a partnership in its firm name does not bar an action to enforce the individual liability of any partner. The problem for the Johnsons comes when the court considers the *Cook* standard. In *Cook,* the court ruled that a judgment against a partnership in only the partnership's name did not provide notice to the individual partners that

the individual partners' assets were at risk, and therefore it did not allow recovery of the judgment from the individual partners. In this case, the Johnsons sued the partnership in the partnership's name—not the partners individually. Hence, the individual partners were not provided notice that their personal assets were at risk, and thus they were not provided due process.

DECISION AND REMEDY: The judgment in this case could not be enforced against the individual partners. The trial court's ruling was reversed.

SIGNIFICANCE OF THE CASE: This case demonstrates the importance of naming all relevant parties to a lawsuit. Had the Johnsons named the partnership *and* each individual partner as defendants in the original lawsuit, the Johnsons would likely have succeeded in collecting the judgment amount from the individual partners.

CRITICAL THINKING

The court seems to have relied heavily on a standard set in *Cook.* What information do you need to know about *Cook* to determine whether the court was drawing an apt or a faulty analogy?

ETHICAL DECISION MAKING

Suppose you were one of the partners in this case. If you were guided by duty ethics, would any of the details of the case described above be altered?

LIABILITY OF INCOMING PARTNERS

When a partnership adds another partner, the new partner assumes limited liability for any obligations that occurred before she was added. The new partner cannot be held personally liable for these obligations, but the capital that the new partner adds can be used to pay off these obligations. Clearly, because an incoming partner assumes limited liability, the dates of agreements, as well as the date that the new partner was added, are extremely important.

The Revised Uniform Partnership Act

The majority of the states have adopted a revised version of the Uniform Partnership Act that is typically referred to as the Revised Uniform Partnership Act (RUPA). Just as the original Uniform Partnership Act governs partnerships in the absence of an express agreement, RUPA is an updated version that has significantly changed several of the laws that relate to partnerships. Since being approved in 1996, RUPA has been adopted in roughly half of the states. Since the other half of the states have not yet adopted RUPA, it is wise to determine whether the state in which a partnership was formed operates under UPA or RUPA. Although RUPA generally serves to expand UPA, there is some disagreement between UPA and RUPA about the rules of partnership.

So far, we've discussed what a partnership is, how a partnership is formed, and how a partnership operates. In most cases, a partnership will not last forever. That is why we now turn our attention to how a partnership ends.

Silent Partnerships in Germany

The original intent behind silent partnerships was for two people to be able to engage in a partnership without having to inform the third party. Recently, both civil and common law countries have been moving away from this idea of total anonymity. For example, France permits the silent partner to choose whether he or she wishes to disclose the relationship. Germany, however, has held to the original intent of silent partnerships.

Under German law, a contract is formed between the silent partner (usually the financier) and the proprietor of the business. In exchange for his or her investment, the silent partner receives a designated share of the profits. Enlisting a silent partner does not require registration, and the company should continue to operate under the proprietor's name.

Because business is conducted under the proprietor's name and because the partnership remains a secret to the third party, the silent partner is not held personally liable for damages incurred in the course of business. This non-liability factor makes silent partnerships less widely used in Germany than other countries. Nevertheless, the non-liability allows for unique situations. For instance, a proprietor could enlist his or her child as a silent partner. The child would collect assets while remaining anonymous and ineligible for any liability claims. Nonliability guards the interests of the silent partner.

In Germany, the benefits swing in favor of the silent partner. While the proprietor transacts all the business and the third party remains unaware of the existence of the partnership relationship, the silent partner enjoys minimal responsibility and no risk of personal liability.

You may be initially surprised that the silent-partner arrangement is legal in Germany. But as a critical thinker you have a responsibility to rethink your reasoning. Can you create a list of reasons for why our own legal system should encourage silent partnerships?

Termination of the Partnership

Before the termination of any partnership can be considered to be complete, a partnership must experience what are referred to as the *dissolution stage* and the *winding-up stage.* The first of these stages, dissolution, is considered complete when any partner stops fulfilling the role of a partner to the business (by choice or default). The second stage, the winding-up stage, is completed by taking account of the assets of the partner who has left the partnership and redistributing them among the other partners. The rest of this section explains the steps that must occur within the dissolution and winding-up stages for the termination of the partnership to be considered complete.

DISSOLUTION OF THE BUSINESS

dissolution

The change in the relation of partners caused by any partner's ceasing to be associated with the carrying on of the partnership's business.

Section 29 of UPA defines **dissolution** as "the change in the relation of the partners caused by any partner's ceasing to be associated with the carrying on, as distinguished from the winding up"—the activity of completing unfinished partnership business, collecting and paying debts, collecting partnership assets, and taking inventory—"of the business." What might cause the dissolution of the partnership? The dissolution may occur by an act of the partners, an operation of the law, or an act of the court.

ACT OF PARTNERS The partnership is a voluntary and consensual relationship, so the partners have the power to dissolve the relationship at almost any time. There are many reasons why an act of the partners might lead to the dissolution of the partnership. First, the partners may simply agree that the partnership will terminate at a certain time. For example, suppose that Lisa and Jason, two partners in a college preparation business, are graduating from college. They are both planning to accept jobs at other firms; consequently, neither thinks that she or he will be able to continue the college preparation business. Perhaps, when their business was created, the partners might have agreed to dissolve the partnership when one of them graduated from college.

Alternatively, once partners reach a certain objective, they might agree to dissolve the partnership. As an illustration, consider a partnership to sell homes in a housing development. Once all of those homes are sold, the partners may agree to dissolve the partnership.

Let's return to the college preparation–business example. Suppose the original agreement was that the partnership would be terminated once either partner graduates from college. However, suppose the business is either a flop or an enormous success. The partners can then agree to dissolve the partnership early or extend the terms of the partnership after graduation.

What are the circumstances in which a partnership can be rightfully dissolved, meaning that the partnership dissolution did not violate the partnership agreement? We have established two of these circumstances above (dissolution after meeting an established objective and dissolution at the end of the term stated in the partnership agreement). The following are also circumstances in which the partnership can be rightfully terminated:

rightfully dissolved
A term applied to the dissolution of a partnership that does not violate its partnership agreement.

1. *A partner withdraws from the partnership at will.* (A *partnership at will* is an agreement that does not specify the objective or duration of the partnership.)

CASE Nugget

When Does a Partnership Dissolve?

**In re Leah Beth Woskob, Debtor; Alex Woskob; Helen Woskob; the Estate of Victor Woskob v. Leah Beth Woskob, Appellant
U.S. Court of Appeals for the Third Circuit**

305 F.3d 177 (2002)

In 1996, Leah Beth Woskob and Victor Woskob formed a partnership, the Legends Partnership, to construct, own, and operate the Legends, an apartment building. They were married at the time that the partnership was formed; however, they separated and filed for divorce the following year. During the divorce proceedings, Victor prevented Leah from receiving any of the partnership proceeds. Leah was granted a petition for special relief and awarded the exclusive right to manage and derive income from the partnership. Shortly thereafter, Victor filed for bankruptcy. Leah continued to file tax returns on behalf of the partnership, each of which listed Victor as a general partner. When Victor died in a car accident in 1999, Leah gave his estate notice that she was exercising her right to buy out Victor's interest in the partnership. Victor's estate sued, claiming that the partnership had been dissolved previously and requesting that someone be appointed to oversee the winding up of the partnership and a full accounting of the company's assets. When Leah filed for bankruptcy, the suits were moved to the bankruptcy court. The bankruptcy court ruled in favor of Leah, finding that the partnership had dissolved on Victor's death. Victor's estate appealed to the district court, which found that the partnership had dissolved two years before Victor's death, making Leah's attempt to buy out Victor's interest untimely. Leah appealed.

The task before the appeals court was to determine the timeliness of Leah's attempt to buy out Victor's interest in the partnership, which depended entirely on the date of the dissolution of the partnership. The court looked to the Uniform Partnership Act (UPA), which defined the dissolution of a partnership as "the change in the relation of the partners caused by any partner ceasing to be associated in the carrying on, as distinguished from the winding up, of the business." Victor's estate claimed that the dissolution of the partnership occurred at any one of three points, each at least 18 months prior to Victor's death. First, Victor excluded Leah from the partnership after they separated; second, Leah excluded Victor from the partnership after seeking special relief from the Court of Common Pleas; third, Victor filed for bankruptcy.

The appeals court found that the exclusions of Leah and Victor from the partnership were not, in and of themselves, grounds for automatic dissolution of the partnership. Rather, the exclusions could have provided a basis for dissolution, had either Leah or Victor sought judicial decree of the dissolution after the exclusions. In addition, bankruptcy in and of itself is not grounds for automatic dissolution of the partnership. If the nondebtor partner does not consent to continue the partnership with the debtor, bankruptcy may be grounds for dissolution. However, Leah continued to list Victor as a general partner on the tax returns she filed for the partnership, even after he filed for bankruptcy. Thus, the appeals court found that the partnership had not dissolved prior to Victor's death in 1999 and that Leah's attempt to buy out Victor's interest in the partnership was therefore timely.

Termination of Partnerships in Spain

In Spain, there are four specific situations in which full dissolution is permitted (*full dissolution* simply means that the partnership ends without litigation or a waiting period): (1) if a partner dies, (2) if a partner is declared insane and unfit to manage the business, (3) if a partner is declared bankrupt, (4) if a partner requests that the partnership be terminated.

In Spain there are other situations that call for provisional dissolution of the partnership. *Provisional dissolution* is followed by litigation to determine the legitimacy of the termination request. There are six situations of provisional, or partial, dissolution: (1) A partner fails to comply with provisions of the contract, (2) a partner unexplainably abandons the partnership and does not return on request,

(3) a partner fails to bring the capital he promised, (4) a partner is accused of fraud or mismanagement, (5) a partner exceeds the limits of her power, and (6) a partner uses capital belonging to the partnership in his own name.

In any of these circumstances, the partnership is temporarily dissolved pending the outcome of litigation. During partial dissolution, the accused is excluded from all managerial responsibilities and profits. He or she is also excluded from any liability to business conducted during this time.

The stage of provisional dissolution prevents those unfairly accused of certain behaviors from losing position in the partnership. The process, however, can be a tedious and lengthy one whether the partial dissolution is moved to complete termination or the partnership resumes.

2. *A partner withdraws in accordance with the partnership agreement.* The partnership agreement may establish specific reasons that a partner may withdraw.

3. *A partner is expelled from the partnership in accordance with the partnership agreement.* Suppose you are a partner in a law firm and you steal some type of property from the partnership. The partnership agreement will usually determine the cases in which a partner may be removed from the partnership, and theft is often one of the reasons for removal. Thus, your stealing would likely lead to your expulsion from the partnership.

If a partnership is rightfully dissolved, all partners can demand that the partnership be wound up and can participate in the winding up. Moreover, if the partners unanimously agree, they can continue the business using the partnership's name.

wrongful dissolution
A dissolution of a partnership in violation of its partnership agreement.

However, if a partner dissolves the partnership in violation of the partnership agreement, the partner can be held liable for **wrongful dissolution.** If a partner has wrongfully dissolved the partnership, that partner cannot require that the business be wound up. Furthermore, that partner can be held liable for damages to the remaining partners. The remaining partners can choose to continue the business under the partnership name or to wind up the business.

Operation of Law Several circumstances provided by law dissolve a partnership: if a partner dies, if a partner is adjudicated bankrupt, or if the partnership business engages in an activity that suddenly becomes illegal. For example, suppose Congress decides that cigarettes are illegal. If the partnership manufactures and sells cigarettes, the partnership would be automatically dissolved.

Act of the Court A partner may make application to the court to dissolve the partnership for several reasons. First, a partnership can be dissolved when a partner is adjudicated insane. Second, if it becomes impractical to carry out the business of the partnership (e.g., if the continuation of the partnership will result in lost profits only), the court will likely dissolve the partnership. Third, if a partner is incapable of carrying out his or her duties as established by the partnership agreement, the court can dissolve the partnership.

Fourth, the court can dissolve the partnership for other circumstances. For instance, suppose that the partners in the college preparation business begin bitterly disagreeing about how the business should be managed. The disagreement is contrary to the cooperation necessary for a partnership to exist. In this instance, the court can dissolve the partnership.

Exhibit 20-1 provides 13 reasons for dissolution of a partnership.

CONSEQUENCES OF DISSOLUTION

If a partner intends to dissolve or withdraw from the partnership, the partner must give the other partners notice of this intent. When the partnership is dissolved, the partner no longer has actual

✕ GLOBAL Context

Effects of Dissolution in Scotland

In many countries, a partner's ability to bind the partnership immediately ceases on the termination of the partnership. In Scotland, however, a partner may engage in business transactions in the name of the partnership for an unlimited time provided the transactions are necessary to wind up the affairs of the former relationship. The intention behind this law is to prepare for any instances in which a partnership wishes to terminate quickly but may have pending business.

The partners can go ahead and cease the relationship and then tie up any loose ends.

For example, a partnership waiting to collect profits from a certain venture can dissolve before the profits have been deposited. The Scottish law ensures that a bank is justified in accepting the signature of a partner wishing to deposit or withdraw money from a dissolved partnership's trust. The deposit and withdrawal are considered necessary in winding up the business of the partnership.

1. The term established in the partnership agreement expires.
2. The partnership meets its established objective.
3. A partner withdraws from the partnership at will.
4. A partner withdraws in accordance with the partnership agreement.
5. A partner is expelled from the partnership in accordance with the partnership agreement.
6. A partner dies.
7. A partner is adjudicated bankrupt.
8. The business of the partnership becomes illegal.
9. A partner is adjudicated insane.
10. A partner becomes incapable of performing the duties as established by the partnership agreement.
11. The business of the partnership can be carried on only at a loss of profits.
12. A disagreement between the partners is such that it undermines the nature of the partnership.
13. Other circumstances of the partnership necessitate the dissolution.

Exhibit 20-1

Reasons for Rightful Dissolution of the Partnership

authority to bind the partnership. However, if the partnership does not notify third parties of the dissolution, the partner can still have implied authority to bind the partnership. Suppose that Lisa, one of the partners in the college preparation business, intends to dissolve the partnership. However, Lisa has not yet notified Jason of her intent, and Jason makes an agreement to begin working with five new students to prepare them for college. Because Lisa has not yet given notice of her intent to dissolve, she is still liable for the agreement Jason has made.

To ensure that a dissolving partner does not create additional liability for a partnership, partnerships usually take active steps to notify third parties about dissolution. They often place a notice in the newspaper, for example. However, a partnership must provide direct verbal or written notice to any third party that has provided credit to the partnership.

Read the Global Context box on Scotland. What ethical behavior does the Scottish law encourage that might not be encouraged under American law?

After the dissolution of the partnership, the partners' next step is either winding up the business or continuing the partnership or business after the dissolution. We'll discuss winding up the business first.

WINDING UP THE BUSINESS

Once a partnership is liquidated, the partners begin the process of winding up, the activity of completing unfinished partnership business, collecting and paying debts, collecting partnership assets, and taking inventory. During the winding up, the partners must still fulfill their fiduciary duty to one another, in the sense that they must disclose all information about the partnership assets. However, during the winding-up process, the partners can now engage in business that competes with the partnership business.

winding up
The process of completing unfinished partnership business.

Who can demand that the winding-up process begin? As we stated earlier, if a partnership has been rightfully dissolved, any partner can demand that the winding-up stage begin. However, if a partner wrongfully dissolves a partnership, that partner has no right to demand a winding up. In Case 20-3, the court considered a demand for an accounting in the winding-up phase.

----→ **CASE 20-3**

ROBERT M. TAFOYA v. DEE S. PERKINS
COURT OF APPEALS OF COLORADO, DIVISION FOUR
932 P.2d 836; 1996 Colo. App. LEXIS 206; 20 BTR 1115

FACTS: *Robert Tafoya and Dee Perkins, brother and sister, entered into a partnership with Dee's husband, Eugene Perkins. The partnership involved the ownership and maintenance of an apartment complex. In 1979, the apartment complex was sold. The partnership took back a 10-year promissory note with a balloon payment due in 1989. Ten years later, when the balloon payment was due, Eugene Perkins purchased the apartments again at a foreclosure sale. In December 1989, Eugene Perkins issued a "Notice of Termination of Partnership" because of losses associated with the partnership. At the same time, Robert Tafoya ceased being associated with the partnership. In July 1990, Eugene Perkins died. The trial court ruled that Perkins's death, as well as Tafoya's separation from the partnership, was sufficient to dissolve the partnership. Dee Perkins continued to manage the property until January 1994, when she sold the property for a profit. Tafoya filed his complaint before the sale of the property, arguing that Perkins had breached her fiduciary duty. Tafoya requested an accounting of the partnership's assets. The trial court found no breach of fiduciary duty, yet it concluded that Tafoya was entitled to an accounting and awarded him a share of the proceeds from the apartment complex sale. Dee Perkins appealed, arguing that Tafoya's claim was barred by a statute of limitations.*

ISSUE: Is Tafoya's request for an accounting barred by a statute of limitations?

REASONING: In this case, regardless of the notice issued by Eugene Perkins, the partnership was dissolved when Tafoya ceased to be associated with the partnership. At the point that the partnership dissolved, the statute of limitations started to run. There is no clear statute of limitations for a request for an accounting. The court disagreed with Tafoya's claim that the applicable statute of limitations was six years because that statute of limitations applied to an action to recover an unliquidated, determinable amount of money due to Tafoya. In this case, the amount of money due him was not determinable from the partnership agreement or a simple computation. Rather, Tafoya was requesting an accounting to determine the amount of money due him. Thus, the applicable statute of limitations was a "catch-all" two-year period from the time of dissolution. Tafoya ceased to be associated with the partnership in 1989, thus dissolving the partnership, and did not file this action until 1994.

DECISION AND REMEDY: Tafoya's request for an accounting was barred by a statute of limitations, which had lapsed three years before Tafoya's request. The trial court's ruling was reversed.

SIGNIFICANCE OF THE CASE: Tafoya attempted to exercise a partner's basic right: the right to an accounting. However, Tafoya waited five years before attempting to determine whether the partnership owed him money. This case demonstrates exiting partners' responsibility to make timely requests for an accounting and to finish all partnership-related business quickly.

CRITICAL THINKING

How do you react to the evidence in this case? Does it strike you as being seriously incomplete? What additional information would you have liked to have had were you asked to decide this case?

ETHICAL DECISION MAKING

What were the primary values upheld by the court in its decision? If you were the judge reviewing the case, which values would motivate your decision?

CONNECTING to the Core

Accounting: Allocating Income among Partners

Most partnership agreements specify how profits will be divided among the partners. As you should remember from your accounting class, there are three common methods for dividing income or loss. First, a *stated ratio* basis provides each partner with a proportion of the total income or loss, based on agreement among the partners on the specific ratios. Second, the *capital balances* method divides income among the partners on the basis of individual capital contributions. Hence, if partner A contributes two-thirds of the total capital and partner B contributes the other one-third, partner A would receive two-thirds of the income and partner B would receive one-third of the total income. Third, the *services, capital, and stated ratio* method allocates income or loss on the basis of differences in service and capital contributions.

This third method of allocating income and loss provides salary allowances for differences in service contributions and interest allowances for differences in capital contributions while including a stated ratio for any remaining income or loss. For example, the partnership agreement for partner A and partner B might allocate salary allowances of $45,000 and $20,000, respectively, based on higher service levels for partner A. In addition, the partnership agreement might specify that each partner receive an interest allowance of 10 percent of each partner's beginning-year capital balance. Furthermore, any remaining income or loss would be divided equally between the partners. Assuming partner A had a beginning-year capital balance of $20,000 and partner B had $10,000, and assuming the partnership generated $100,000 net income, the accounting under the services, capital, and stated ratio method would be as follows: Partner A would receive $63,000 [$45,000 of salary allowance plus $2,000 interest allowance (10 percent of capital balance of $20,000) plus $16,000 (half the remaining balance)]; partner B would receive $37,000 [$20,000 of salary allowance plus $1,000 interest allowance (10 percent of capital balance of $10,000) plus $16,000 (half the remaining balance)]. However, as mentioned in this chapter, when the partnership agreement does not specify the allocation of income and losses, courts will generally divide profits and losses equally among the partners.

K. Larson, J. Wild, and B. Chiappetta, *Principles of Financial Accounting* (New York: McGraw-Hill/Irwin, 2005), pp. 471–473.

Once all the partnership assets have been gathered, the assets are distributed to the partners or any creditors that the partnership might have. If the partnership has been successful (i.e., has very little or no debt), the order of the distribution of assets is not too important. However, when the dissolved partnership has many creditors, the order of the distribution of the assets is immensely important. UPA establishes that when a partnership has debt, the distribution of liquidated assets must take the following order:

1. Payment to creditors of the partnership.
2. Payment of refunds or loans to partners for loans made to the firm.
3. Payment of partners for the capital they invested.
4. Payment of profits distributed to partners on the basis of the partnership agreement.

If the partners' liabilities for the partnership are greater than their liquidated assets, the partners are liable for the losses. Each partner must contribute his or her share of the losses to pay the creditors. If one partner is unable to contribute his or her share and another partner covers the first partner's unpaid share, the second partner has a right of contribution against the partner who did not pay.

CONTINUING THE PARTNERSHIP AFTER DISSOLUTION

After a partnership is dissolved, the remaining partners have several options. One option is to continue the partnership after dissolution. What happens to the noncontinuing partner? Regardless of why the partner is noncontinuing, this partner must receive his or her interest in the partnership. For example, if a noncontinuing partner holds 20 percent of the partnership in which the assets are valued at $10,000, this partner must receive $2,000 after dissolution.

CASE Nugget

What Duties Do Partners Owe after Dissolution?

Sanfurd G. Bluestein and Sylvia Krugman v. Robert Olden
U.S. District Court for the Southern District of New York

2004 U.S. Dist. LEXIS 3631

In 1978, Bluestein, Krugman, and Olden formed a partnership, the principal asset of which was a building located in New York City. For 26 years, Olden operated Olden Camera and Lens Company, Inc., in part of the building. Olden Camera itself had been in the building for more than 60 years. In 2001, the plaintiffs sent a letter to Olden to terminate the partnership in accordance with the terms of the partnership agreement. After the letter was sent, the partnership continued to operate in dissolution. The partners agreed to sell the building, but they could not agree on whom to sell to and how much to charge. Olden offered $9 million for the plaintiff's combined interest in the partnership, but he added that the plaintiffs must release any claims against him and his business, as well as any claims to profits from the partnership for 2002–2003. A competing offer from a third party contained no requirements and offered $15,400,000 for the building, but it provided for a reduction of the purchase price by $200,000 if Olden's business remained in the building.

The plaintiffs filed an order to show cause, requesting "1) the appointment of plaintiff Bluestein as Liquidating and/or Winding Up Partner of the general partnership; 2) a direction that Olden cooperate in the liquidation of the assets of the partnership; and 3) enjoining Olden from entering into any new leases or renewing any leases for space in the building." Because the partnership was terminated in accordance with the partnership agreement, the court ruled that Olden could not prevent maximization of the partnership's assets. Bluestein was appointed the liquidating partner and given sole authority to liquidate the partnership's assets and divide the proceeds after paying the partnership's debts. Olden was ordered to cooperate in the liquidation of the assets and enjoined from entering into or renewing any leases or agreements affecting the partnership's building in New York City. The court retained jurisdiction to ensure that the partners complied with its orders.

Perhaps the best way that partners can preserve a partnership business is through a *continuation agreement.* This agreement states that continuing partners can keep partnership property and carry on the partnership business, particularly in cases when a partner dies.

LO 6

Limited Partnerships

Chapter 19 introduced limited partnerships. Limited partnerships, also known as *special partnerships,* originated in Europe more than 500 years ago and have existed in the United States for nearly 200 years. Limited partnerships are attractive to potential investors because of the limited liability as well as the tax advantages associated with this form of business.

Recall that the limited partnership is an agreement between at least one general partner and at least one limited partner. The general partner has management responsibility for the partnership and assumes unlimited personal liability for the debts of the partnership. In contrast, the limited partner assumes no liability for the partnership beyond the capital he or she invested in the business.

Functioning as the equivalent of RUPA, the Revised Uniform Limited Partnership Act (RULPA) is the law governing limited partnerships. Like all law, RULPA is not static; it changes as lawmakers revise it to handle new issues that arise and to better achieve social goals. RULPA

limited partnership (LP)

A partnership consisting of at least one general partner and at least one limited partner in which the general partners assume all liability for the partnership's debts and the limited partners assume no liability beyond their originally invested capital.

E-COMMERCE and the Law

was originally drafted in 1976, revised in 1985, and revised again in 2001. About one-fourth of the states have adopted the 1976 version of RULPA, and about three-fourths have adopted the 1985 version. Only a handful of states have adopted the 2001 version. Louisiana is the only state not to have adopted any version of RULPA.

FORMATION OF THE LIMITED PARTNERSHIP

How is the limited partnership created? In contrast to the often-informal partnership agreements described earlier in the chapter, the formation of a limited partnership must follow very specific statutory requirements. The general and limited partners must sign a **certificate of limited partnership** and file this certificate with the secretary of state. If the partners do not correctly fill out or do not file this certificate, the partners will not receive limited liability.

certificate of limited partnership
A document signed on the formation of a limited partnership and filed with the secretary of state.

RIGHTS AND LIABILITIES OF THE LIMITED PARTNERS AND THE GENERAL PARTNERS

LO 7

Limited partners generally have all the rights given to partners in general partnerships, as discussed earlier. Thus, the limited partner (as well as the general partner) has the right to share in the profits of the business. Furthermore, the limited partner has the right to an account of the partnership. Moreover, if the general partner wants to add a partner to the partnership, the general partner must have the consent of all partners in the limited partnership. Finally, an additional right of limited partners is that they often recover their investment before general partners.

However, the limited partner has a few special rights under RULPA. For example, if a general partner fails to bring a suit on behalf of the limited partnership, the limited partner can bring the suit.

What about the duties and liabilities of the partnership? While there are not many distinctions between the rights of the general partner and those of the limited partner, there are numerous distinctions in the duties and liabilities of each partner.

For instance, the general partner has unlimited personal liability for the debts of the partnership. This broad liability is in contrast to the limited partner's limited liability, which is restricted to the amount of capital the partner has invested in the business. Thus, if you enter into a limited partnership by contributing $10,000 to the partnership, as a limited partner you cannot be held liable for more than $10,000.

A limited partner's limited personal liability depends on the partner's maintaining three conditions:

1. The limited partner has complied in good faith with the requirement that a certificate of limited partnership be filed.
2. The limited partner does not participate in the control of the business.
3. The limited partner's surname is not part of the partnership name.

If any of these conditions are violated, the limited partner surrenders his or her limited liability. For example, the general partner typically has exclusive control and management of the limited partnership. In contrast, the limited partner does not share in this control of the partnership. If the limited partner does share in the management of the company, the courts will likely rule that the partner has forfeited his or her limited liability. Exhibit 20-2 distinguishes several aspects of general partners and limited partners.

DISSOLUTION OF THE LIMITED PARTNERSHIP

Dissolution of the limited partnership is very similar to dissolution of the general partnership. The limited partner has no right or power to dissolve the partnership. While the death or bankruptcy of the limited partner rarely dissolves the partnership, the death of the general partner usually dissolves the partnership (unless the agreement specifies otherwise). According to RULPA, a limited partnership can be dissolved for the following reasons:

1. The expiration of the term established in the certificate of limited partnership.
2. The completion of the objective established in the certificate.
3. The unanimous written consent of all partners (limited and general).
4. The withdrawal of the general partner (unless the certificate establishes that other general partners will continue).
5. An act of the court.

If the limited partnership is dissolved, the limited partnership's assets are distributed in the same order as described earlier in this chapter (i.e., payment to third-party creditors, payment to partners who have loaned the partnership money, payment to the partners according to their investments in the partnership, and payment to the partners on the basis of their shares of the profits).

Exhibit 20-2

Comparison of General Partners and Limited Partners

	GENERAL PARTNER	LIMITED PARTNER
Control of business	Has *all* rights associated with controlling the business	Has *no* right to participate in the management and control of the business
Liability	Has unlimited personal liability for all partnership debts	Has liability limited to the amount of capital the partner has contributed to the business
Agency of partnership	Acts as an agent of the partnership	Is not an agent of the partnership

 SUMMARY

Nature of the Partnership	The Uniform Partnership Act defines a partnership as "an association of two or more persons to carry on as co-owners a business for profit." An essential element in a partnership is the sharing of profits from the partnership.
Formation of the Partnership	A partnership is created by the articles of partnership, which should include the names of each partner and the partnership, the duration of the partnership, the way profits will be divided, the division of management duties, and the contributions to be made by each partner.

Interactions between Partners

Each partner has specific duties, including:

- Duty to be loyal
- Duty of obedience
- Duty of care

Each partner has specific rights, including:

- Right to share in management
- Right to inspect books
- Right to compensation
- Rights to partnership property

Interactions between Partners and Third Parties	If a partnership has a liability, each partner has unlimited personal liability. All partners are jointly and severally liable for the commission of a tort by any partner. There is only implied liability when purchases are made to perpetuate the partnership's business.
The Revised Uniform Partnership Act	RUPA is a revised version of UPA, and its use varies from state to state.
Termination of the Partnership	Termination begins when a partnership dissolves. Once the partnership has been dissolved and the assets have been liquidated and distributed, the partnership has been terminated. *Dissolution* refers to the ceasing of a partnership. Acts of partners, the operation of the law, and acts of the court can serve to rightfully dissolve a partnership.

- *Consequences of dissolution:* A partner who wishes to dissolve or withdraw from the partnership must give notice of his intent. Third parties are usually contacted promptly about a dissolving partner to prevent the creation of additional liability for the partnership.

Winding up is the activity of completing unfinished partnership business, collecting and paying debts, collecting partnership assets, and taking inventory.

Limited Partnerships	The limited partnership involves an agreement between at least one general partner and at least one limited partner. This partnership permits investors to share in the profits of the partnership, yet it limits these limited partners' liability to the amount they invest in the business.

Point/Counterpoint

Should a Partnership Be Allowed to Expel a Partner on the Basis of Illegal Personal Conduct Unrelated to the Terms of the Partnership Agreement?	
YES	NO
A partnership should be able to expel a partner on the basis of illegal personal conduct even when the illegal conduct isn't specified in the partnership agreement.	If a partner participates in an illegal activity unrelated to the partnership agreement, the partnership should not be allowed to expel the individual on the basis of his or her involvement in the illegal activity.

It would be nearly impossible to create a partnership agreement that dictated every possible situation that would allow for dissolution of the partnership. Individuals are always expected to conduct themselves within the bounds of national, state, and local laws. Any illegal behavior should have implications for the partnership as an ongoing business enterprise.

A partner's personal behavior affects the entire partnership and associated business in many different ways. A partner's behavior outside the business atmosphere can damage the reputation of the company. For example, if one partner of a five-partner law firm is arrested for smoking marijuana, clients will associate this marijuana-smoking partner with the entire firm. Clients may first begin to question the single partner's priorities and ethical beliefs: If he participates in this illegal activity, in which other illegal activities does he partake? Does he keep faulty books? Will I be overcharged?

Next, clients (his clients and the other attorneys' clients) may begin to question the firm as a whole for allowing a man who partakes in illegal activities to remain a partner in the firm. Do all the attorneys participate in illegal activities?

While a partner may suffer personal legal consequences for his actions, the whole partnership suffers when one partner makes a poor personal choice. Therefore, the partnership should be able to decide the consequences.

The partners had the opportunity when formulating the partnership agreement to include a stipulation for the dissolution of the partnership if a partner engaged in illegal activity.

If the agreement does not specify the relevant illegal activities, an individual is not aware of the potential impact of her actions on her status as a partner. Had she known the possible consequences regarding her participation in the partnership, she might have acted differently. However, she cannot be expected to abide by restrictions that are not stated.

The logic behind dissolving the partnership on the basis of an unrelated activity is faulty. Is it logical to revoke an individual's driver's license because she looked at pornography in a state where such an activity is illegal? Additionally, an individual can make a poor personal choice and still be capable of performing her expected duties. A rule allowing partnerships to expel a partner on the basis of unrelated illegal activity could be easily abused. Partnerships that want to expel a partner for other reasons (inconvenience, additional profit, etc.) could easily say she participated in illegal activity and expel her from the partnership for that reason alone. A partner should not be expelled from a partnership because she participates in unrelated criminal activity. The partner already suffers personal legal consequences and should not experience additional penalties for an activity that has no impact on the partnership.

Questions & Problems

1. Explain each element of UPA's definition of a partnership.

2. Explain the need for partnership by estoppel.

3. What are the possible problems with any single list of the legal liabilities of a partner?

4. Paul Berkowitz is the minority shareholder of several related corporations and partnerships. He brought suit to force the appellants, Astro Moving and Storage Co., Inc., to produce certain books and records. Astro was currently in the process of voting to remove Berkowitz from his position as officer and director of the business entities. Berkowitz argued that his partner status gave him the right to inspect the books. According to Berkowitz, Astro had made an offer to buy him out, and he wanted to access the books to determine the true value of his shares. Do you think Berkowitz had a right to inspect the books? How do you think the court decided? [*Berkowitz v. Astro Moving and Storage Co., Inc.,* 658 N.Y.S. 2d 425 (1997).]

5. Ian M. Starr was a partner in the law firm Fordham & Starrett. After Starr's first year of employment, the firm's profits were divided evenly among all partners.

During his second year with the firm, Starr's relationship with the other partners began to deteriorate, and he quit the firm on the last day of the year. Listing several negative factors relevant to Starr's performance, the firm paid him less than half an equal share. Starr brought an action to recover amounts to which he claimed he was entitled according to the partnership agreement. He also claimed breach of fiduciary duty. Starr's former partners counterclaimed that Starr had violated his fiduciary duties to the partners and breached the partnership agreement. How do you think the court settled this conflict? [*Starr v. Fordham,* 648 N.E.2d 1261 (1995).]

6. The Vancouver Group is made up of five investors, Pietz, Wynne, Fordham, Indermuehle, and Smith. The group entered into a partnership with Robert Berry for the joint purchase of the Sundance Hotel and Casino. The group and Berry made an offer to purchase the hotel. Pietz agreed to supply $500,000 to the deal and post a $285,000 letter of credit. However, after receiving information that caused him to doubt Berry, Pietz withdrew his interests from the partnership. Berry threatened to sue Pietz for breach

of contract, fraud, and tortious breach of the covenant of good faith. Pietz and Berry settled, and Pietz subsequently sued the Vancouver Group for the cost of the settlement. The trial court rejected Pietz's claim of breach of fiduciary duty. He appealed the decision. How do you think the court decided? Was there a breach of fiduciary duty? [*Pietz v. Indermuehle,* 949 P.2d 449 (1998).]

7. Kevin Smith brought an action against Brown & Jones, his former law partnership. Smith alleged breach of the covenant of good faith and fair dealing and breach of fiduciary duty. According to the partnership agreement, Smith had the right to resign as long as he gave proper notice. The agreement also stated that a withdrawing partner would be compensated for work he or she had completed prior to withdrawing. Smith was compensated for only two-thirds of his contributions to the firm. He brought the suit to receive full compensation. How do you think the court decided? [*Smith v. Brown & Jones,* 633 N.Y.S.2d 436 (1995).]

8. Phillip Heller was a partner of the Pillsbury, Madison & Sutro law firm. The relationship between Heller and the firm was not strong, as Heller's work performance was unsatisfactory. He billed 1,000 hours fewer than he had estimated that he would produce, and he did not establish strong working relationships. Heller signed the partnership agreement in 1992. The agreement authorized the Executive Committee to expel partners. After Heller submitted a derogatory and lewd article entitled "Why I Fired My Secretary," the committee met and terminated Heller's partnership. Heller challenged the authority of the committee to expel him, regardless of whether he had signed the partnership agreement. Do you think the court agreed with him? Why or why not? [*Heller v. Pillsbury, Madison & Sutro,* 58 Cal. Rptr. 2d 336 (1996).]

9. Jones and Hardy entered into an oral partnership agreement. They planned to develop and lease certain areas of land. Together, they formed the Bloomington Knolls Association. Jones and Hardy began to experience financial problems, and they brought in a third partner, Jackson, to arrange for additional financing for the project. Jones subsequently dissolved the partnership and requested that he be given a portion of the land as his share of the partnership assets. Jackson and Hardy did not honor his request, and Jones never received any assets of the partnership. Jones moved for an accounting and winding up of partnership affairs and brought the case to court. The district court entered judgment against Hardy and Jackson, jointly and severally, for an amount representative of Jones's interest in the partnership. Jackson and Hardy appealed the district court's decision. How do you

think the court decided? [*MacKay v. Hardy,* 896 P.2d 626 (1995).]

10. Cider Mills, a limited partnership, was continued after the dissolution date for purposes of winding up. The partnership had entered into a contract for the sale of land three months prior to its dissolution date. The property was sold after the dissolution date. The parties disagreed as to the order in which payments would be made following the dissolution of the partnership. The limited partners argued that they should share in the profits from the sale. The court determined that the order of payment should be creditors, limited partners, general partners. Anthony Pappas, a limited partner, objected to the court's decision regarding the distribution of partnership assets. Do you think the court's decision was reversed on appeal? Why or why not. [*Pappas v. Arfaras,* 20 F. Supp. 2d 372 (1998).]

11. Richard H. Pettingell and Joseph A. Regan withdrew as partners from the Boston law firm of Morrison, Mahoney, & Miller. They brought an action to receive funds that they believed were due to them for voluntarily withdrawing from the firm. Pettingell and Regan left the partnership to establish a new, competing firm. The partnership agreement states that if a partner voluntarily withdraws from the firm and "engages in any activities which are in competition with the then-current activities of the firm, he shall forfeit all of the benefits" that would be received if the employee were to voluntarily withdraw. There was no evidence to indicate that the establishment of the new firm had seriously affected the original firm. Pettingell and Regan disagreed with the forfeiture provision of the partnership agreement. How do you think the court decided? [*Pettingell v. Morrison, Mahoney, & Miller,* 687 N.E.2d 1237 (1997).]

12. Mige Associates, a limited partnership, owned an apartment building. The building could have been developed into a housing cooperative. The projected profits for such a conversion were significant. The conversion required the signed agreement of one of Mige's general partners, Jon Meadow. Meadow's decision to sign the agreement was contingent on the promise that he receive more money from the deal than the other partners. After his request was denied, Meadow refused to sign the agreement. Two of the limited partners, Drucker and Schaffer, filed suit against Meadow. They claimed that he had breached his fiduciary responsibility to the general and limited partners of Mige Associates. The trial court found in favor of Meadow. How do you think the case was decided on appeal? Did the economic benefits of the conversion create a fiduciary obligation for Meadow to sign the agreement? [*Drucker v. Mige Associates,* 639 N.Y.S.2d 365 (1996).]

13. After the dissolution of a partnership formed to develop the Four Seasons Resort, TSA International Limited brought an action against Shimizu Corporation alleging breach of fiduciary duty. TSA had approached Shimizu in 1986 with plans for developing the hotel. The two companies formed a partnership, and they began to make plans for several golf and hotel developments. The loans TSA and Shimizu had taken out soon became delinquent. The partners met to negotiate the payment of the hotel and golf course loans. At the request of Shimizu, the agreements were drafted in Japanese. TSA subsequently filed a complaint asserting, among other things, breach of fiduciary duty. When reaching the agreements, Shimizu had discouraged TSA from hiring its own accountants or legal counsel because of "the long-term relationship of trust between Shimizu and TSA." TSA also alleged that Shimizu arranged the agreement so that substantial tax advantages would be obtained. The circuit court found in favor of Shimizu. How do you think the case was decided on appeal? Did Shimizu breach its fiduciary duty? [*TSA Intern. Ltd. v. Shimizu Corp.*, 990 P.2d 713 (1999).]

14. North Port Golf Associates (NPGA) is a limited partnership involved in real estate and golf course development. NPGA contacted the Palmer Course Design Company (PCDC) and the Arnold Palmer Golf Management Company (APGMC) to design and manage two championship golf courses. As part of the agreement, NPGA was prohibited from using Arnold Palmer's name to promote any other business. A disclaimer was placed on the official investment summary brochure of NPGA stating, "As described herein, golf course design and management services will be provided to the partnership by PCDC and APGMC, respectively. Neither of these companies, nor Arnold Palmer, is affiliated with the partnership or general partners." PCDC completed the design of the golf course, but APGMC terminated its contract after NPGA refused to pay. After the failure of the project, NPGA alleged that Arnold Palmer, APGMC, and PCDC were partners by estoppel and were partially responsible for the interests of the limited partnership. Do you think the court agreed with NPGA? Why or why not? [*Binkley v. Palmer*, 10 S.W.3d 166 (Mo. App. 1999).]

Looking for more review material?

The Online Learning Center at **www.mhhe.com/kubasekess** contains this chapter's "Assignment on the Internet" and also a list of URLs for more information, entitled "On the Internet." Find both of them in the Student Center portion of the OLC, along with quizzes and other helpful materials.

Corporations: Formation and Organization

----> **CASE OPENER**

The Formation of Goodyear Tire & Rubber Company

The Goodyear Tire & Rubber Company is the world's largest tire manufacturer, generating net sales of approximately $20 billion in 2007. Named after Charles Goodyear, the inventor of vulcanized rubber, Goodyear Tire incorporated in 1898, largely through the efforts of promoters and subscribers. As a corporation, Goodyear Tire is an "artificial person," a status with legal implications for both the corporation and its owners.

1. What are the legal implications of Goodyear's status as a corporation?
2. How do corporations form? What factors should be considered by a businessperson interested in forming a corporation?

----> **LEARNING OBJECTIVES**

After reading this chapter, you will be able to answer the following questions:

LO 1 What are the powers granted to corporations by the states?

LO 2 How are corporations formed?

LO 3 What is the role of a director, an officer, and a shareholder?

LO 4 What are the duties of directors, officers, and shareholders?

LO 5 In what ways can a director, officer, and shareholder be held liable?

LO 6 What are the rights of directors, officers, and shareholders?

LO 7 What are mergers and consolidations?

This chapter explains the steps necessary to establish a corporate entity. Although state law generally governs corporations and each state has its own corporate regulatory statutes, the Revised Model Business Corporation Act (RMBCA) is the basis of most state statutes. More than 25 states have adopted at least part of RMBCA.

In addition, the chapter describes the legal relationships among the many groups of individuals with various priorities and agendas within a corporation. Not surprisingly, these priorities and agendas often come into conflict. To ensure that individuals, corporations, and the public achieve fair outcomes to conflicts within corporations, statutory laws have been designed to delegate particular roles, duties, and rights to each group of individuals within corporations.

Characteristics of Corporations

How are corporations different from other forms of business organization?

LEGAL ENTITY

In American law, corporations are legal entities. In other words, corporations exist separately from their shareholders. Thus, corporations can sue or be sued by others.

RIGHTS AS A PERSON AND A CITIZEN

Courts consider corporations to be "legal persons." Thus, in most cases, corporations, like natural persons, have certain rights according to the Bill of Rights. Specifically, the Fifth and Fourteenth Amendments state that government cannot deprive any "person" of life, liberty, or property without due process. Courts have held that corporations are "persons" in this case and thus have a right to due process.

Furthermore, courts consider corporations to be persons with respect to the Fourth Amendment. Hence, the Fourth Amendment protects corporations from unreasonable searches and seizures. Finally, courts consider corporations to be persons that have free speech rights protected by the First Amendment.

CREATURE OF THE STATE

State incorporation statutes establish the requirements for corporate formation. Each individual corporation's charter creates a contract between that corporation and the state.

LIMITED LIABILITY

Because corporations are legal entities distinct from their shareholders, corporations are liable for corporate actions. Shareholders' liability, therefore, is limited to their investment in the corporation. For example, in 1977 Big O Tire Dealers sued Goodyear Tire & Rubber Company. Big O Tire accused Goodyear of copying its BIGFOOT trademark on new tires. The court agreed and awarded Big O Tire several million dollars in damages. The Goodyear corporation, and not individual Goodyear shareholders, paid the damages. Although payment of damages to Big O Tire may have reduced the dividends shareholders received, the court did not hold the shareholders individually liable for any portion of the award.

FREE TRANSFERABILITY OF CORPORATE SHARES

Generally, shareholders can freely transfer their corporate shares. For example, shareholders can sell their shares or give them to charity.

PERPETUAL EXISTENCE

The life of a corporation does not end when the lives of its owners end. If shareholders die, corporations do not dissolve. Similarly, if corporate directors or officers withdraw or

die, the corporation continues to exist. In some cases, the *articles of incorporation,* a document a corporation files with the state explaining its organization, may include a restriction on the duration of the corporation. Otherwise, in most states, corporations continue to exist indefinitely.

A small number of states, however, set a maximum length of existence for corporations. After the maximum duration expires, corporations must formally renew their corporate existence.

CENTRALIZED MANAGEMENT

Unless the articles of incorporation specify otherwise, shareholders do not participate in corporate management. Instead, shareholders elect a board of directors. The board, in turn, selects officers to manage the day-to-day business of the corporation.

CORPORATE TAXATION

Because corporations are separate legal entities, government taxes their income directly (S corporations are an exception; this chapter discusses them, and their tax advantages, in detail later). Corporations must pay federal and state taxes on their income.

Corporations, however, have control over their income. Corporations can distribute their income to shareholders in the form of dividends, although they do not receive tax deductions for distributing these dividends. When corporations distribute income to shareholders, the shareholders pay taxes on that income. Because the corporation pays income taxes and the shareholders are also paying taxes on their dividends, the dividends are subjected to double taxation, thus creating a disadvantage for corporations. Alternatively, corporations can keep profits, or retained earnings, to reinvest. Corporations' investment of retained earnings can lead to higher stock prices, thus benefiting shareholders when they sell their stock.

dividend
A distribution of corporate profits or income ordered by the directors and paid to the shareholders.

retained earnings
Profits that a corporation keeps.

LIABILITY FOR OFFICERS AND EMPLOYEES

Because the relationship between corporations and their directors, officers, and employees is an agency relationship, corporations are liable for torts and crimes committed by their agents during the scope of their employment. Courts refer to this liability as the doctrine of *respondeat superior* (Latin for "let the master answer"). Although in the past courts were reluctant to impose criminal liability on corporations, prosecutions today are much more common. Exhibit 21-1 presents a summary of nine characteristics of corporations.

Corporate Powers LO 1

Because corporations are creatures of the state, they have only those powers states grant them. States give powers to corporations through state incorporation statutes and through each corporation's articles of incorporation.

EXPRESS AND IMPLIED POWERS

State incorporation statutes typically grant the following express powers to corporations: the power to have perpetual existence, the power to sue and be sued in the corporation's name, the power to acquire property, the power to make contracts and borrow money, the power to lend money, the power to make charitable donations, and the power to establish rules for managing the corporation. Additionally, corporations may take whatever actions are necessary to execute these express powers. Thus,

Exhibit 21-1

Characteristics of Corporations

1. Separate legal entity
2. Status as "legal person" and "citizen"
3. Creature of the state
4. Limited liability of shareholders
5. Free transferability of corporate shares
6. Perpetual existence
7. Centralized management separate from owners
8. Unique taxation method
9. Corporate liability for torts and crimes of agents

corporations have implied powers. Generally, the statement of corporate purpose in each corporation's articles of incorporation gives each corporation its implied powers.

ULTRA VIRES ACT

If corporations act beyond their express and implied powers, the act is called an *ultra vires* (Latin for "beyond powers") act. Corporations commit *ultra vires* acts most frequently when they create contracts outside the scope of their powers.

Today, most state incorporation statutes permit businesses to incorporate for any lawful purpose, and thus most articles of corporation do not limit corporate powers. Hence, the doctrine of *ultra vires* is much less significant today than it was in the past because very few corporate acts qualify as *ultra vires.*

Historically, courts have ruled that *ultra vires* acts are null and void. More recently, however, courts have permitted corporations to use the *ultra vires* defense if neither party to the contract has performed the terms of the contract. Yet courts uphold *ultra vires* contracts if one of the parties has executed her or his part of the contract.

For example, suppose a timber corporation's articles of incorporation specified that the corporation's purpose was to harvest and sell timber. Suppose further that the directors of the corporation entered into an *ultra vires* contract with a machinery company to purchase machines to mine coal on the corporation's cleared land. As long as the machinery company has not delivered the machinery to the timber corporation, courts will hold the contract null and void. If, however, the machinery company has delivered the machinery to the timber corporation, courts will uphold the *ultra vires* contract and require that the timber corporation fulfill the terms of the contract. Can you see which party the court is trying to protect by upholding the *ultra vires* contract in this situation?

If a corporation commits an *ultra vires* act, RMBCA provides several remedies:

1. Shareholders may sue to prohibit the corporation from fulfilling the *ultra vires* contract.
2. The corporation or shareholders may sue corporate directors or officers for the damages caused by the *ultra vires* act.
3. The state attorney general can have the corporation dissolved or prevent the corporation from fulfilling the *ultra vires* contract.

Classification of Corporations

Corporations can be classified as public or private; profit or nonprofit; domestic, foreign, or alien; publicly or closely held; S corporations; or professional corporations.

PUBLIC OR PRIVATE

public corporation
A corporation that is created by government to help administer law.

private corporations
A corporation that is created by private persons and does not have government duties.

A **public corporation** is a corporation created by government to help administer law. Thus, public corporations often have specific government duties to fulfill. The Federal Deposit Insurance Corporation (FDIC) is an example of a public corporation. In contrast, private persons create **private corporations** for private purposes. Private corporations do not have government duties.

PROFIT OR NONPROFIT

for-profit corporation
A corporation whose objective is to make a profit.

nonprofit corporation
A corporation that operates for educational, charitable, social, religious, civic, or humanitarian purposes, rather than to earn a profit.

Most corporations are **for-profit corporations.** Thus, their objective is to operate for profit. Shareholders seeking to make a profit purchase the stock these corporations issue. This profit can take two forms. First, shareholders receive dividends from the corporation. Second, the market price of the stock can increase. Shareholders can then sell their stock at a higher price than the purchase price of the stock.

Nonprofit corporations may earn profits, but they do not distribute these profits to shareholders. In fact, nonprofit corporations do not have shareholders. More important, nonprofit corporations' objective is not to earn profit. They do not issue stock. Instead, nonprofit corporations provide services to their members (not shareholders). These corporations reinvest most of their profits in the business. Churches and charitable organizations are examples of nonprofit corporations.

DOMESTIC, FOREIGN, AND ALIEN CORPORATIONS

Every corporation is incorporated in a particular state. A corporation is a domestic corporation in the state in which it is incorporated. Many corporations, however, do business in more than one state. A corporation that does business in states other than the state in which it is incorporated must obtain a certificate of authority in each state in which it does business. A corporation is a foreign corporation in states in which it conducts business but is not incorporated. For example, the McDonald's Corporation is incorporated in Delaware but does business in all 50 states. Thus, McDonald's is a domestic corporation in Delaware and a foreign corporation in the other 49 states.

An alien corporation is a business incorporated in another country. Thus, if an American corporation wants to do business in Canada or Mexico, it is an alien corporation in those countries.

domestic corporation
A corporation in the state in which it is incorporated.

foreign corporation
A corporation in a state in which it conducts business but is not incorporated.

alien corporation
A business that is incorporated in a foreign country.

PUBLICLY HELD OR CLOSELY HELD

The stock of publicly held corporations is available to the public. Thus, if you want to invest in a corporation, you could purchase stock in a publicly held corporation. Most publicly held corporations have many shareholders, and managers of these corporations usually do not own large percentages of the corporation's stock. Shareholders wishing to sell their shares do not face many transfer restrictions.

In contrast, closely held corporations (also called *close, family,* or *privately held corporations*) generally do not offer stock to the general public. Shareholders are usually family members and friends who are often active in the business. Controlling shareholders typically manage closely held corporations. Because closely held corporations are often family businesses, they often maintain restrictions on the transfer of shares to prevent outsiders from obtaining control of the business. Although they account for only a small fraction of corporate assets and revenues, most U.S. corporations are closely held corporations.

publicly held corporation
A corporation whose stock is available to the public.

closely held corporation
A corporation that does not sell stock to the general public.

SUBCHAPTER S CORPORATION

S corporations are named after the subchapter of the Internal Revenue Code that provides for them. They are a particular type of closely held corporation. Government taxes S corporations differently from other corporations. Government taxes most corporations twice on their income: Corporations must pay income tax, and shareholders must pay taxes on dividends they receive. S corporations, however, enjoy the tax status of partnerships. Thus, shareholders of S corporations report their income from the corporation as personal income.

In addition to the avoidance of double taxation, S corporations offer two more important tax advantages. First, shareholders in an S corporation are allowed to deduct corporate losses from their personal income, ultimately lowering how much the shareholders have to pay in taxes. Second, depending on a shareholder's income, choosing to be an S corporation can result in the corporation's paying lower taxes.

To be classified as an S corporation, a corporation must meet certain requirements. First, it cannot have more than 100 shareholders. Second, only individuals, trusts, and (in certain circumstances) corporations can be shareholders (partnerships cannot be shareholders). Third, S corporations can issue only one class of shares, although not all shares must have identical voting rights. Fourth, all S corporations must be domestic corporations. Fifth, no shareholder of an S corporation can be a nonresident alien.

S corporation
A corporation that enjoys the tax status of a partnership.

PROFESSIONAL CORPORATION

If a group of dentists, doctors, or other professionals wants to practice as a corporation, all 50 states permit them to incorporate. Because of the nature of professional work, however, courts sometimes alter the liability associated with such corporations. For example, courts often impose personal liability on doctors in professional corporations for medical malpractice performed under their oversight.

Formation of the Corporation

The creation of a corporation involves two parts: general organizational activities and legal activities necessary for incorporation.

ORGANIZING AND PROMOTING THE CORPORATION

Two groups of important players are responsible for the organization of the corporation: promoters and subscribers.

promoter
A person who begins the corporate creation and organization process.

subscription agreement
An agreement between promoters (persons raising capital for a new corporation) and subscribers (investors), in which the subscribers agree to purchase stock in the new corporation.

subscriber
An investor who agrees to purchase stock in a new corporation.

Promoters Promoters begin the corporate creation and organization process by arranging for necessary capital, financing, and licenses. Promoters raise capital for the infant corporation by making subscription agreements with subscribers (investors) in which the subscribers agree to purchase stock in the new corporation.

Promoters have other organizational responsibilities besides making subscription agreements. For example, promoters prepare the corporation's incorporation papers. Promoters can also enter into contracts as needed to establish the new corporation. For example, promoters can purchase or lease buildings for the corporation. Frank Seiberling was the promoter who founded the Goodyear Tire & Rubber Company. In 1898, Seiberling purchased Goodyear's first plant in Akron, Ohio, with $3,500 borrowed from his brother-in-law. Seiberling also established Goodyear workers' hourly wages between 13 and 25 cents.

When problems with preincorporation contracts arise, courts generally hold promoters liable and rule that these contracts do not bind infant corporations. Courts usually hold that promoters are not agents of the infant corporation because promoters cannot serve as agents for a principal (the new corporation) that does not yet exist.

Once incorporated, however, corporations can accept or reject preincorporation agreements. However, even if a corporation accepts a preincorporation agreement, courts usually still hold promoters liable for the contract.

Subscribers Subscribers make offers to purchase stock in a corporation in the incorporation process. A subscriber becomes a shareholder once the corporation incorporates or accepts her purchase offer, whichever occurs first.

SELECTING A STATE FOR INCORPORATION

Next, an infant corporation must select a state in which to incorporate. Each state has different laws governing the incorporation process and different corporate tax rates. Other factors corporations consider when selecting a state for incorporation include the following:

• How much flexibility does the state grant to corporate management?
• What rights do state statutes give to shareholders?
• What restrictions does the state place on the distribution of dividends?
• Does the state offer any kind of protection against takeovers?

Although most corporations incorporate in the state in which they are located and do most of their business, more than half of all publicly held corporations, including more than half of the Fortune 500 companies, are incorporated in Delaware. Decades ago, Delaware law offered extremely low corporate tax rates and granted more extensive rights to management in the event of a takeover than did other states. Thus, in the 1940s and 1950s, many corporations changed their state of incorporation to Delaware. Since then, other states have made their corporate laws more attractive to corporations. Many corporations remain incorporated in Delaware, however, because Delaware courts are highly experienced in issues involving corporate law.

Closely held corporations and professional corporations, however, almost always incorporate in the state in which most of their stockholders live.

Although a corporation can incorporate in only one state, it can file a certificate of authority to do business in other states. Some states fine corporations that fail to obtain a certificate of

authority before conducting business in the state. Other states fine directors and officers of these corporations directly and hold them personally liable for contracts made in the state.

Once a corporation chooses a state for incorporation, it can begin the formal legal process of incorporation.

Legal Process of Incorporation

SELECTION OF CORPORATE NAME

All state incorporation statutes require that corporations indicate in the name of the corporation that the business is incorporated. Every corporation must attach *Corporation, Company, Limited,* or *Incorporated,* or an abbreviation of one of these terms, to the end of its business name. Additionally, every corporation must distinguish its name from the names of all other domestic or foreign corporations licensed to do business within the state. This requirement protects third parties from confusion about similar names. Once the corporation has chosen a name, this name is subject to the approval of the state.

INCORPORATORS

An **incorporator** is an individual who applies to the state for incorporation on behalf of a corporation. RMBCA requires only one incorporator to incorporate a business, although it permits more. Generally, incorporators' only duty is to sign the articles of incorporation.

incorporator
An individual who applies for incorporation on behalf of a corporation.

ARTICLES OF INCORPORATION

One of the most important elements of the corporate formation process is the **articles of incorporation,** a document providing basic information about the corporation. According to RMBCA, a corporation's articles of incorporation must include (1) the name of the corporation, (2) the address of the registered office, (3) the name of the registered agent (i.e., the specific person who receives legal documents on behalf of the corporation), and (4) the names and addresses of the incorporators.

The incorporators must execute and sign the articles of incorporation and file the document with the secretary of state, including the required filing fee, to legally form the corporation. Once the incorporators file the document, it governs the corporation. Next, the secretary of state usually issues a **certificate of incorporation,** a document certifying that the corporation is incorporated in the state and is authorized to conduct business.

articles of incorporation
A document that contains basic information about a corporation and is filed with the state.

certificate of incorporation
A document certifying that a corporation is incorporated in the state and is authorized to conduct business.

FIRST ORGANIZATIONAL MEETING

After the secretary of state issues the certificate of incorporation, the shareholders meet to elect the corporate board of directors, pass corporate bylaws, and carry out other corporate business. In some cases, however, shareholders name the board of directors before the first organizational meeting and list the board members in the articles of incorporation. In these situations, the directors usually run the meeting.

At the first organizational meeting, shareholders adopt a set of corporate **bylaws,** or rules and regulations that govern the corporation's internal management. The articles of incorporation determine who has the power to amend the corporate bylaws after the first organizational meeting: shareholders, directors, or both.

bylaws
Rules and regulations that govern a corporation's internal management.

Potential Problems with Formation of the Corporation

Most businesses incorporate to enjoy limited liability or the perpetual existence of the corporation. Shareholders enjoy these benefits, however, only if the promoters and incorporator formally and correctly incorporate the business. If the incorporator or promoters make an error or

Corporate Structure in Germany

German law establishes three tiers of corporate power. The board is the lowest tier, management makes up the second tier, and the supervisory board is the top tier. The supervisory board is similar to a board of directors in an American corporation. The supervisors must approve managers' actions, including appointments, distribution of profits, and actions that affect the corporation's capital. Without the consent of the supervisors, managers are nearly powerless.

Managers enjoy considerable power, however, when dealing with third parties. As representatives of the corporation, managers can act on their own discretion. Supervisors cannot limit managerial powers with respect to third parties. Because supervisors cede considerable control of the corporation to managers in these situations, supervisors have the power to appoint managers who they feel will be reliable.

Although the board makes up the lowest tier of corporate power, it exercises considerable influence. Shareholders elect the board, a group of at least three members that acts as a mediator between shareholders and management. Because both managers and supervisors understand the importance of shareholders' interests, they listen to the board's recommendations.

defective corporation

A corporation about which an error or omission was made during its incorporation process.

omission during the incorporation process, courts may rule that the organization is not a corporation. In this case, the organization is a *defective corporation.* Shareholders may be personally liable for a defective corporation's actions.

RESPONSES TO DEFECTIVE INCORPORATION

Suppose an incorporator incorrectly indicates the address of the corporate office in the articles of incorporation. Does the corporation still exist? Depending on the seriousness of the error, courts may disregard an error in the articles of incorporation by recognizing the corporation as a *de jure* or *de facto* corporation.

de jure corporation

Latin for "lawful corporation"; a corporation that has met the mandatory statutory provisions and thus received its certificate of incorporation.

De Jure Corporations A *de jure* corporation (literally, a "lawful corporation") has met the substantial elements of the incorporation process. A corporation that has received its certificate of incorporation has met the mandatory statutory provisions and is thus a *de jure* corporation. Courts usually hold that corporations that make minor errors in the incorporation process still enjoy *de jure* corporate status. Figure 21-1 illustrates the process for creating a *de jure* corporation.

Thus, even if the incorporator wrote the incorrect address of the corporate office in the articles of incorporation, courts would not revoke the corporation's limited liability. No party can question a *de jure* corporation's status as a corporate entity in court.

de facto corporation

Latin for "corporation in fact"; a corporation that has not substantially met the requirements of the state incorporation statutes.

De Facto Corporation Suppose, however, that the incorporator makes a more serious mistake or omission. For example, suppose the incorporator did not file the articles of incorporation with the secretary of state. In this case, courts may recognize the corporation as a *de facto* corporation (literally, a "corporation in fact"). A *de facto* corporation has not substantially met the requirements of the state incorporation statute, but courts recognize it as a corporation for most purposes to avoid

Figure 21-1

De Jure Corporation Formation

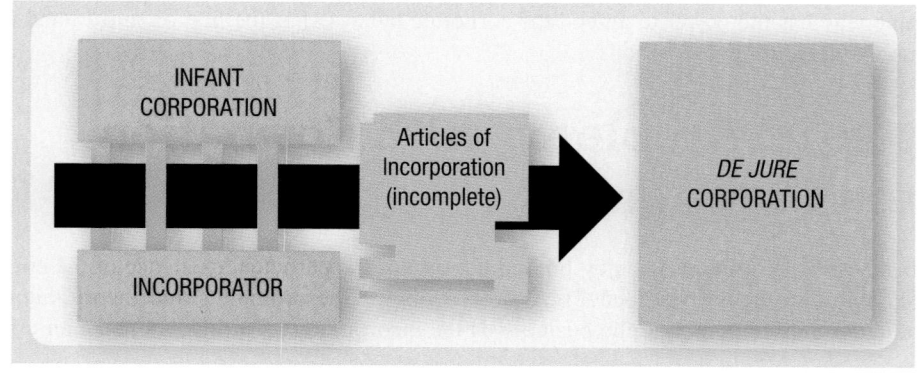

Figure 21-2

De Facto Corporation Recognition Process

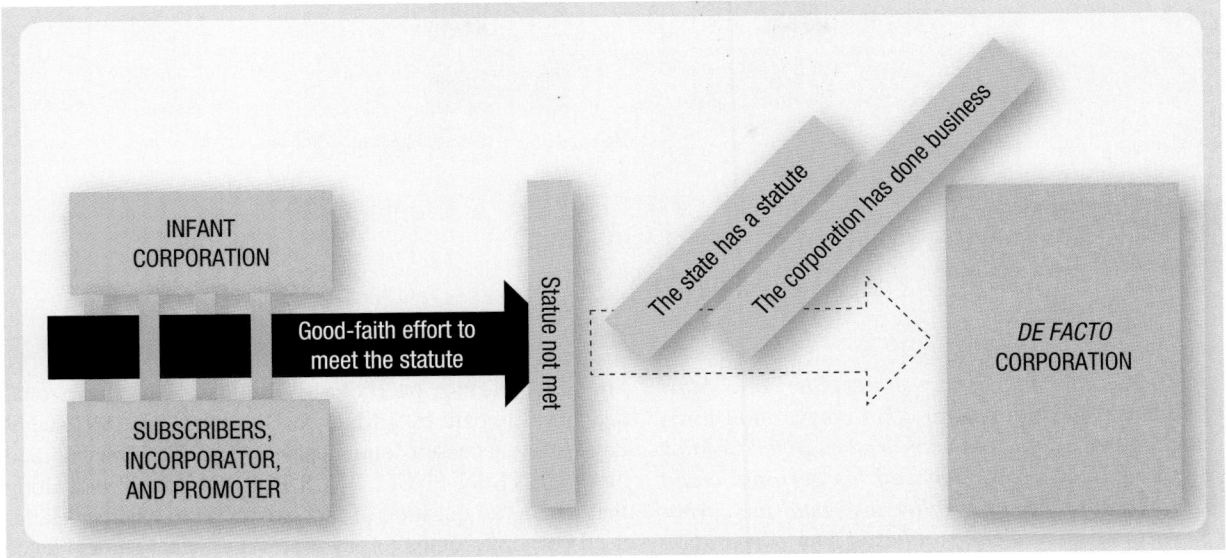

unfairness to third parties who believed it was properly incorporated. *De facto* corporations, regardless of whether the state has a general corporation statute, must meet the following requirements:

- The promoters, subscribers, and incorporator made a good-faith attempt to comply with the incorporation statute.
- The organization has already conducted business as a corporation.

The process for recognizing a corporation as a *de facto* corporation is depicted in Figure 21-2.
Only the state can challenge a *de facto* corporation's existence as a corporate entity.

Corporation by Estoppel Defective corporations cannot escape corporate entity status due to mistakes or omissions in their incorporation procedures. For example, suppose a corporation's articles of incorporation do not include the name of its registered agent. Suppose further that the corporation's directors, managers, and shareholders are unaware of the mistake. If the corporation conducts business with a third party who later sues for breach of contract, the corporation cannot claim that it is not a corporate entity to escape liability.

In such cases, courts hold that the corporation is a corporation by estoppel; thus, courts *estop* (prevent) the corporation from denying its corporate status. Although a court ruling of corporation by estoppel prevents the business from denying corporate status, it does not remedy the error or grant the organization corporate status for conducting future business.

If a corporation makes a significant error in the incorporation process and is not a *de jure* or *de facto* corporation, and corporation by estoppel does not apply to the situation, courts usually deny the organization corporate entity status. Thus, the organization does not enjoy limited shareholder liability.

corporation by estoppel
A defective corporation that has conducted business with a third party and therefore cannot deny its status as a corporation to escape liability.

Piercing the Corporate Veil In some cases, courts will deny limited liability to a corporation that would normally have *de jure* or *de facto* status because shareholders have used the corporation to engage in illegal or wrongful acts. Shareholders attempt to hide behind the "corporate veil" of limited liability to protect themselves from personal liability. In these cases, courts *pierce the corporate veil*, or impose personal liability on shareholders. Courts are likely to pierce the corporate veil when:

- A corporation lacked adequate capital when it initially formed.
- A corporation did not follow statutory mandates regarding corporate business.
- Shareholders' personal interests and corporate interests are commingled such that the corporation has no separate identity.
- Shareholders attempt to commit fraud through a corporation.

For example, corporations must keep corporate funds and records separate from shareholder funds and records. If a corporation does not carefully maintain these separate records, courts may pierce the corporate veil and impose personal liability on shareholders, as Case 21-1 illustrates.

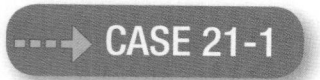

CASE 21-1

J-MART JEWELRY OUTLETS, INC. v. STANDARD DESIGN
COURT OF APPEALS OF GEORGIA
218 Ga. App. 459 (1995)

FACTS: *Jim Halter, the major shareholder of J-Mart Jewelry Outlets, Inc., and several other corporations, was aware that J-Mart was in financial trouble. Before J-Mart went out of business, Halter paid off his personal credit cards using corporate funds. Halter also paid the corporation $1 for a corporate car purchased with corporation funding. Four of J-Mart's creditors brought suit against Halter in an attempt to recover corporate funds. The trial court jury pierced the corporate veil to hold Halter personally responsible for the debts. Halter appealed the court's denial of his request for a directed verdict.*

ISSUE: Has the appellant used his position as the major shareholder of a corporation to disregard the legal separation between a shareholder and the corporation, thereby permitting a piercing of the corporate veil?

REASONING: The judge argued that for the veil to be pierced,

> [t]here must be evidence of abuse of the corporate form. Plaintiff must show that the defendant disregarded the separateness of legal entities by commingling on an interchangeable or joint basis or confusing the otherwise separate properties, records or control. . . .

Halter knew as early as late April but not later than June 1991 that J-Mart would have to cease operations as a result of its financial difficulties. There was direct evidence that the $6,902.87 balance on Halter's American Express personal account was paid by J-Mart on December 23, 1991, eight days before it ceased doing business. The check was marked "PAYMENT IN FULL: JIM'S PERSONAL[,]" indicating that a material question of fact existed as to whether Halter used corporate funds to pay a personal debt. The evidence also established that J-Mart, with knowledge that it would soon cease doing business, purchased a new Cadillac for Halter's use. It thereafter made three payments on the vehicle before transferring it to Halter for $1 and allowing him to assume the remaining payments, indicating the presence of further questions of material fact relative to a de facto unauthorized payment for Halter's personal benefit.

DECISION AND REMEDY: The court determined that "[i]n light of the evidence presented, the trial court properly denied the motion for a directed verdict upon the claim of Halter's personal liability for violation of the corporate form. . . . On appeal, we construe all the evidence most strongly in support of the verdict. . . . [T]he jury's verdict was proper and must stand."

SIGNIFICANCE OF THE CASE: This case illustrates the requirements that a plaintiff must meet to establish a basis for piercing the corporate veil and affirms the jury's role in judging material questions of fact in these cases.

CRITICAL THINKING

Given what you know of the facts of the case, is there any information Halter could have provided that would lead you to believe that he was not responsible for the debts? What would this information be?

ETHICAL DECISION MAKING

Describe the ethical conflict Halter was facing. For what purpose, or value, was he acting? Had Halter followed the Golden Rule, would he have chosen to act in the way he did? Given this information, what could have been done to convince Halter to refrain from using corporate funds to pay off his personal credit cards?

Corporate Financing

Corporations, like other businesses, need a source of funding. Corporations most commonly obtain financing by issuing and selling corporate securities: **debt securities** (bonds), which represent loans to a corporation, and **equity securities** (stocks), which represent ownership in a corporation.

debt securities
Securities that represent loans to a corporation.

equity securities
Securities that represent ownership in a corporation.

DEBT SECURITIES

Debt securities, or bonds, represent loans to a corporation from another party. Bonds are usually long-term loans on which the corporation promises to pay interest. Bonds frequently list a maturity date on which the corporation must repay the face amount of the loan. Before the maturity date, however, corporations usually pay bond holders fixed-dollar interest payments on a scheduled basis. Hence, bonds are sometimes called *fixed-income securities.*

EQUITY SECURITIES

Stocks and bonds are not identical. While bond owners have loaned money to a corporation, stock owners actually own part of a corporation. Thus, while bond owners have no voice in corporate management, stockholders have a voice in control of the corporation. Not all corporations issue bonds, but all corporations issue stock. Common stock and preferred stock are the two major types of stock.

Preferred Stock Owners of **preferred stock,** or *preferred shares,* enjoy preferences with respect to assets and dividends. Corporations often have several classes of preferred shares. Preferred stock shares many characteristics with bonds. For example, preferred stock owners usually receive a percentage of dividends associated with the face value of their preferred stock. Furthermore, corporations pay dividends to owners of preferred stock before they pay owners of common stock. Some corporations limit preferred stock owners' voting rights.

preferred stock
Stock that conveys preferences to its holders with respect to assets and dividends.

Common Stock Owners of **common stock,** or *common shares,* own a portion of a corporation but do not enjoy any preferences. A common stock owner is entitled to a portion of the corporation's dividends in proportion to the number of shares of common stock she owns. Common stock owners also have the right to vote in corporate elections. Each share is usually worth one vote in corporate elections. Thus, if you own 20,000 common shares of a corporation, you have 20,000 votes. In some cases, however, most notably the election of the board of directors, corporations use a method called *cumulative voting* to increase the influence of shareholders who own a small number of shares.

common stock
Corporate stock that does not convey any preferences to its holders.

Common stock owners have the lowest priority when a corporation distributes dividends. Creditors and preferred stock owners receive dividends first. Once a corporation pays these groups, however, common stock owners have a claim to the remainder of the corporate earnings.

Importance of Regulating Interactions among Directors, Officers, and Shareholders within a Corporation

The three major groups of individuals within a corporation are *directors, officers,* and *shareholders.* All three groups have different interests, and in many situations the interests of one group conflict with the interests of another. Statutory law provides rules to ensure that the directors, officers, and shareholders within a corporation work together to the benefit of all involved.

Although directors and officers play different roles within the corporation, they share the same goal. Both directors and officers attempt to ensure that their institution survives and that

they keep their jobs. Shareholders, on the other hand, have a different agenda. Their goal is to raise the value of the company's stock.

These different agendas can lead to conflict within corporations. If a corporation has an opportunity to make a decision that will raise the value of its stock quickly, shareholders will push the directors and officers to make this decision. However, if the directors and officers believe that the decision might jeopardize their jobs, they will resist the pressure of the shareholders. To resolve these conflicts, the law gives legal duties and rights to different groups within the corporation.

LO 3

Roles of Directors, Officers, and Shareholders

Before discussing the duties and rights of each position within the corporation, it is important to understand the specific roles that directors, officers, and shareholders play. The rights and duties of each group of individuals are dependent on these roles.

DIRECTORS' ROLES

Directors play a vital role within every corporation. When a corporation faces important decisions, the board of directors meets to decide what course of action the corporation will take.

Elections Typically, shareholders use a majority vote to elect directors. The only exception occurs during incorporation. Because there are no shareholders in the beginning, either the incorporators appoint board members or the corporate articles name the board members. This first board then serves until the first shareholder meeting, at which the shareholders elect a new board. The corporate articles or bylaws specify the number of corporate directors.

In the past, the minimum number of directors required was three, but today many states allow fewer. In fact, if a corporation has fewer than 50 shareholders, Section 7.32 of RMBCA allows companies to eliminate the board of directors altogether.

Interestingly, almost anyone can become a director. The legal requirements for director qualification are incredibly lax. In most states, directors are not even required to own stock in the corporation. In some cases, however, statutory law and corporate bylaws require not only ownership but also a minimum age.

Directors typically serve for one year, but most state statutes allow for longer terms if the terms of the various directors are staggered. These terms can be terminated and the directors can be removed from their positions *for cause*—for failing to perform a required duty. Directors who are removed for cause, however, can ask the courts to review the legality of the removal.

Meetings and Voting A minimum number of directors, or a quorum, must be present at each meeting of the board of directors for decisions made at the meeting to be valid. Quorum requirements are different in each state, but most states leave the decision up to the corporation itself. Because a quorum is required at each meeting, directors are notified whenever special meetings are called. Directors vote in person, and each director has one vote. While ordinary decisions require a majority vote, more important decisions sometimes require a two-thirds vote.

Directors as Managers Although directors meet to vote on major decisions about the corporation, they are also responsible for many day-to-day managerial activities of the company. The directors appoint, supervise, and remove corporate officers as they see fit, and they declare and pay corporate dividends to shareholders. They are also responsible for making financial decisions and authorizing corporate policy decisions. Some directors are also officers or employees of the corporation; these directors are known as *inside directors*. Directors who are not officers or employees of the corporation are called *outside directors*. Outside directors are further divided into two groups: *affiliated directors* and *unaffiliated directors*. Affiliated directors have business contacts with the corporation, while unaffiliated directors do not.

Because the day-to-day tasks of a corporation can be overwhelming for a small board of directors that has larger issues to address, directors often appoint an executive committee to handle day-to-day responsibilities.

OFFICERS' ROLES

Officers are executive managers whom the board of directors hires to run the organization. While directors are in charge of major policy decisions, officers run the day-to-day business of the corporation. Officers act as agents of the corporation, and thus the rules of agency apply to their work.

Qualifications required of officers are set forth in the corporate articles and bylaws of each corporation, but in most cases an individual may serve as both a director and an officer. Many corporations find it beneficial to include an officer on their board of directors so that the board can stay in touch with the day-to-day operations of the company.

SHAREHOLDERS' ROLES

Shareholders own the firm. As soon as an individual purchases the stock of a particular corporation, she becomes an owner of the corporation. While she is not legally recognized as an owner of corporate property, she has an *equitable,* or ownership, interest in the company. Shareholders are not directly responsible for the daily management of the corporation, but they elect the directors who are responsible for that management.

Power of Shareholders The articles of incorporation established within each corporation and general incorporation law in each state grant shareholders certain powers within the institution. Because shareholders must approve major corporate decisions, they are in a sense empowered to make major decisions for the corporation.

Their most influential power, however, is the power to elect and remove members of the board of directors. The board of directors is responsible for making crucial policy decisions for the corporation, and the shareholders have the power to decide who the directors will be.

Shareholders also have the power to propose ideas for the corporation. If a shareholder feels that he has a worthwhile idea for the company, he can include his proposal in the *proxy materials* sent out to the shareholders before their annual meeting. The Securities and Exchange Commission (SEC) has established that any shareholder who owns more than $1,000 worth of stock in the corporation can submit proposals to be included in proxy materials.

Meetings Typically, shareholders meet once a year, but in emergencies they can meet more often. The board of directors, shareholders who own at least 10 percent of the corporation's outstanding shares, and others authorized in the articles of incorporation may call a special shareholder meeting. Before each meeting, each shareholder receives notice of the time and place of the meeting. If the meeting is a special meeting, the purpose of the meeting is also included in the notice.

Like directors' meetings, shareholder meetings require a quorum. Generally, a quorum of shareholders exists when shareholders holding more than 50 percent of the outstanding shares are present. Once a quorum is present, a majority vote of the shares represented at the meeting is required to pass resolutions. Occasionally, however, articles of incorporation include supermajority provisions, which state that more than a majority is needed to pass major corporate proposals, such as corporate merger or dissolution.

Voting Like directors, each shareholder is entitled to one vote per share in most instances. Corporations practice unique voting processes, however, that alter the influence of each shareholder's votes. These voting processes are especially important for minority shareholders within a corporation. One voting process required in most states, called *cumulative voting,* ensures that minority shareholders have a voice in electing the board of directors.

The cumulative-voting process divides shareholders into majority and minority shareholders, and each group has a certain number of votes to cast in the election. The number of votes is determined by multiplying the number of shares the group owns by the number of open director

Exhibit 21-2

Roles of Direc-
tors, Officers, and
Shareholders

POSITION	ROLES
Directors	Vote on important corporate decisions. Appoint and supervise officers. Declare and pay corporate dividends. Manage the corporation.
Officers	Run the day-to-day business of the firm. Are agents of the corporation.
Shareholders	Elect a board of directors. Approve major decisions of the board.

positions. If a company is electing eight directors and the minority shareholders own 2,000 shares, the minority shareholders get 16,000 votes to cast in the election. If the majority share-holders in the same corporation own 8,000 shares, they get 64,000 votes.

Although it may seem that the minority shareholders have little influence in the election, the cumulative-voting process permits them to vote at least one director onto the board because they can cast all of their votes for one candidate. If the majority shareholders wish to elect all eight directors from their nominees, each nominee must receive more than 16,000 votes in order to beat the 16,000 votes of the minority nominee. However, because the majority shareholders have only 64,000 votes to cast in the election, they cannot cast more than 16,000 votes for eight candidates ($16,000 \times 8 = 128,000$). Thus, if the minority shareholders cast all of their 16,000 votes for one candidate, they guarantee that candidate's election.

Cumulative voting is more egalitarian than simple majority voting because it ensures that every voice within the corporation is heard. Cumulative voting, however, occurs only when the corporation's articles of incorporation provide for it.

Exhibit 21-2 summarizes the respective roles of directors, officers, and shareholders.

LO 4 Duties of Directors, Officers, and Shareholders

Because all individuals within a corporation depend on one another, the law requires that directors, officers, and shareholders perform certain duties within the business. In other words, individuals within the corporation have legal responsibilities to the corporation. These duties to the corporation are called *fiduciary duties*. Because individuals play different roles within the corporation, the fiduciary duties of individuals depend on whether they are directors, officers, or shareholders.

DUTIES OF DIRECTORS AND OFFICERS

Because the owners of the corporation, the shareholders, have little input in the day-to-day operations of the corporation, they trust the directors and officers to run the company to the best of their ability. Thus, directors and officers have duties to the shareholders and to the corporation. The two primary fiduciary duties of directors and officers are the duty of care and the duty of loyalty.

Duty of Care Directors and officers have a fiduciary *duty of care,* meaning that they must exercise *due care* when making decisions for the corporation. The phrase *due care* is ambiguous and various courts have interpreted it differently over time. In general, however, acting with due care requires that one exercise the care that an ordinary prudent person would exercise in the management of her own assets.

Because directors and officers have a duty to act in the best interest of the company, they must supervise, to a reasonable extent, employees who work for the corporation. They also have a duty to attend director and corporate business meetings. Most important, however, directors and officers have a fiduciary duty to make informed and reasonable business decisions.

When a B2B Company Cooks the Books

When a business student thinks about companies that "cook the books," it is not surprising that companies such as Enron, Tyco, and Adelphia come to mind. Issues related to the duty of care of officers and directors are expressed in questions such as, "Why did the officers and directors of the company fail to realize accountants were cooking company books? Were any officers or directors involved in the fraud?"

Students may have to revise their images of corrupt companies by adding business-to-business (B2B) e-commerce companies to their Enron-Tyco-Adelphia list. They may have to ask, "Why did the officers and directors of an *e-commerce business* fail to realize accountants were cooking company books? Were any officers or directors involved in the fraud?"

PurchasePro is one example of an e-commerce company that allegedly engaged in "overstating revenues, engaging in aggressive accounting practices and mismanaging corporate assets." Basically, the company manipulated its financial records to make it look far more successful than it really was. PurchasePro, which provided a business-to-business software company that gave companies access to an online marketplace, went bankrupt in September 2002.

Federal prosecutors charged company officers and directors with conspiracy, securities fraud, and obstruction of justice. Two senior officers, Jeffrey R. Anderson and Scott H. Miller, pleaded guilty to federal crimes in 2003. Their behavior was similar to that of officers of other, more well-known companies that have cooked the books—they had secret side deals with purchasers that gave the appearance of sales but the sales did not exist; they misrepresented the company's financial health, so investors could not make informed decisions; and, when news of alleged fraud surfaced, the officers used their energy to shred incriminating documents.

The directors and officers of Enron failed in their duty of care with regard to their shareholders by not acting in the best interest of the company. The directors and officers continued to urge employees to invest in the employee stock-sharing options, even though it appears that the directors and officers knew the stock was drastically overpriced. Furthermore, the directors and officers failed in their duty of care regarding oversight. The directors and officers either did not pay enough attention to see the collapse of the company's stock coming or purposely kept the information secret. Either way, the directors and officers at Enron breached their fiduciary duty of care and therefore are liable to their shareholders, many of whom were employees of Enron.

Directors and officers are expected to stay abreast of all important corporate matters. In other words, they must obtain information about business transactions, review contracts, read reports, and attend presentations. Because some directors are too busy to stay informed on every subject, RMBCA allows directors to make decisions on the basis of information gathered by other employees.

The decisions that corporate directors and officers make must not only be informed, however, but also be reasonable. If a director or officer is taken to court for breaching his duty of care by making an unreasonable decision, the court typically inquires whether the decision had any rational business purpose. In other words, the courts ask whether there was good reason to think that the decision *could* have helped the company.

Part of the duty of care a director or officer owes a corporation, as was previously stated, is to act in the corporation's best interest. Therefore, when the corporation is doing something the director or officer does not think is in its best interest, it is up to her to voice her dissent.

Duty of Loyalty Because directors and officers have great decision-making freedom, they have the power to make business decisions that will benefit themselves while harming the company. Thus, to protect shareholders, directors and officers have a fiduciary *duty of loyalty.* In other words, they have a fiduciary duty to put the corporation's interest above their own when making business decisions.

When directors or officers violate their duty of loyalty, they are self-dealing. There are two types of self-dealing in which a director or officer can engage. The first form of self-dealing, called *business self-dealing,* occurs when a director or officer makes decisions that benefit other companies with which he has a relationship. The second form of self-dealing, called *personal self-dealing,* occurs when a director or officer makes business decisions that benefit her personally. When Enron directors and officers advocated that employees buy more Enron stock so that

self-dealing
Any instance in which directors or officers make decisions that violate their corporate duty of loyalty.

the directors and officers would make more money, they engaged in self-dealing in breach of their fiduciary duty of loyalty.

In many situations, when a director or officer is self-dealing, he forces the corporation into unfair business deals. Directors and officers can also breach their fiduciary duty of loyalty, however, by *preventing* corporate opportunity. This breach usually happens when directors or officers own other companies that compete with their corporation without the consent of the board of directors or the shareholders. If a director or officer uses corporate assets to start another business, goes into the same line of business, or uses her position in the company to develop a new business that the company might have pursued, she is preventing corporate opportunity and can be held liable for violating her fiduciary duty of loyalty.

A director or officer convicted of breaching his duty of loyalty is required to cede to the corporation all the profits he earned as a result of the breach. The goal of the rule is to create incentives that discourage breaches of the duty of loyalty by taking from the director or officer all the profits that he made.

CASE Nugget

How Should Directors Handle Personal Interests That Conflict with Corporate Interests?

Patrick v. Allen

355 F. Supp. 2d 704 (2005)

RPO, a privately traded corporation, rented land to a private golf course of which several of RPO's directors were members. The directors charged the golf course enough rent to cover only the property taxes on the land. Patrick, a shareholder of RPO, brought a suit against the directors of RPO, alleging that RPO's directors breached their fiduciary duty of loyalty to the corporation by failing to maximize the value of the corporation for shareholders. The directors argued that they were exempt from liability under the business judgment rule. (The business judgment rule is covered in the section below entitled "Liabilities of Directors, Officers, and Shareholders.")

The U.S. District Court for the Southern District of New York ruled against the RPO's directors, holding:

> The business judgment rule will not protect a decision that was the product of fraud, self-dealing, or bad faith. Directors may benefit from the rule only if they possess a disinterested independence and do not stand in a dual relation which prevents a nonprejudicial exercise of judgment. It is black-letter, settled law that when a corporate director or officer has an interest in a decision, the business judgment rule does not apply. . . . A director is considered interested in a transaction if the director stands to receive a direct financial benefit from the transaction which is different from the benefit to shareholders generally. . . . The duty of loyalty requires a director to subordinate his own personal interests to the interest of the corporation.

The fiduciary duties of care and loyalty are rooted in ethics. Without these legal duties, directors and officers could pursue their own interests at the expense of others. Through these fiduciary duties, however, the law requires that directors and officers consider the interests of others. Think back to Chapter 2 and the different ethical guidelines used to make ethical decisions. Which ethical guideline is the legal system using when it delegates fiduciary duties?

Duty to Disclose Conflict of Interest Because there are many times when individual directors and officers may personally benefit from decisions made by the board of directors, the directors

and officers have a fiduciary duty to fully disclose conflicts of interest that arise in corporate transactions. Moreover, if the board of directors addresses an issue that might personally benefit a particular director, the director is required not only to disclose the self-interest but also to abstain from voting on that issue. Note that a decision can be made that will personally benefit one director or officer as long as (1) there is full disclosure of the interest and (2) the disinterested board members and/or disinterested shareholders approve the decision.

DUTIES OF SHAREHOLDERS

Although shareholders typically have few legal duties, in rare instances majority shareholders have fiduciary duties to the corporation and to minority shareholders. In some corporations, the majority shareholder owns such a significant portion of the corporation's stock that she essentially controls the firm. When the majority shareholder sells her shares, control of the company shifts to another individual. Thus, the majority shareholder in this situation has a fiduciary duty to act with care and loyalty when selling her shares.

As noted earlier, more than half of all U.S. publicly traded corporations are incorporated in Delaware. Thus, when Delaware courts rule on the duties of majority shareholders to minority shareholders, for example, the courts' rulings have a far-reaching impact. In Case 21-2, brought before the supreme court of Delaware, minority shareholders sued the majority shareholder within their corporation for violating its fiduciary duties.

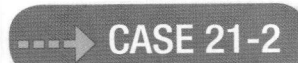 **CASE 21-2**

FRIEDA H. RABKIN v. PHILIP A. HUNT CHEMICAL CORP.
SUPREME COURT OF DELAWARE
498 A.2d 1099 (1985)

FACTS: *On March 1, 1983, Olin Corporation bought 63.4 percent of the outstanding shares of Hunt Chemical Corporation from Turner and Newall Industries, Inc., at $25 per share, which moved Olin into the position of majority shareholder. Before Turner and Newall Industries sold the shares to Olin, it insisted that Olin agree to pay $25 per share if Olin acquired the remaining Hunt stock within one year. On July 5, 1984, Hunt merged into Olin by buying out the remaining stock for $20 a share. The minority shareholders of Hunt then filed a suit against Olin that challenged the Olin-Hunt merger on the grounds that the price offered was grossly inadequate because Olin unfairly manipulated the timing of the merger to avoid the one-year commitment and that specific language in Olin's Schedule 13D, filed when it purchased the Hunt stock, constituted a price commitment by which Olin failed to abide, contrary to its fiduciary obligations to the minority shareholders. The trial judge dismissed the complaint on grounds that the only remedy legally available to the minority shareholders was an appraisal. The plaintiffs then sought and were denied leave to amend their complaints. They appealed.*

ISSUE: Did the alleged acts by Olin constitute unfair dealing that breached its fiduciary duty?

REASONING: The judge found that the allegations related to Olin's attitude toward the minority owners, together with the absence of any meaningful negotiations as to price, raised unanswered questions about the extent to which Olin fulfilled its duty of loyalty to Hunt. The court found strong-enough allegations concerning the possible avoidance of the one-year commitment to "support a claim of unfair dealing sufficient to defeat dismissal at this stage of the proceedings."

DECISION AND REMEDY: The decision was reversed because the judge found that the material facts were serious enough that a motion to dismiss should have been denied. At minimum, they constituted overreaching.

SIGNIFICANCE OF THE CASE: This case illustrates the kind of fact pattern that causes legal examination of a possible breach of fiduciary duty, and it establishes the court's reluctance to permit majority shareholders to abuse their power in relation to minority shareholders.

CRITICAL THINKING

What reasons does the court give for its conclusion? Are you persuaded by those reasons?

ETHICAL DECISION MAKING

Clearly, the court explicitly emphasizes a particular value in its ruling. What is this value? The court's vigorous emphasis of this particular value makes it difficult for the court to consider other values. Which value(s) does this ruling tend to ignore?

LO 5

Liabilities of Directors, Officers, and Shareholders

Because almost all individuals within a corporation have legal fiduciary duties to the corporation, almost all individuals within the firm can be held liable for harming the business by violating these duties. There are, however, certain instances in which directors, officers, and shareholders cannot be held liable for harming the business.

LIABILITY OF DIRECTORS AND OFFICERS

Directors and officers are held liable for many of the same actions because they have nearly identical fiduciary duties to the corporation. A shareholder can sue them if the shareholder feels that they have caused harm to the business by violating their fiduciary duties. Directors and officers can be held liable for the torts and crimes of their employees.

Liability for Torts and Crimes Although the corporations themselves are liable for the torts and crimes of their directors and officers, directors and officers can also be held personally responsible for their own torts and crimes. They can even be held personally responsible for the torts and crimes of other employees within the organization when they have failed to adequately supervise the employees' behavior.

According to the *responsible person doctrine,* a court may find a corporate officer criminally liable regardless of the extent to which the officer took part in the criminal activity. Even if the officer knew nothing about the criminal activity, the officer can still be held criminally liable if the court determines that a responsible person would have known about and could have prevented the illegal activity.

Corporate directors and officers may also be held liable for wrongful personal transactions involving company stock. Directors and officers who use inside information to trade the corporation's stock for a profit can be held liable for breaching their fiduciary duty to the shareholders from whom they purchase or to whom they sell the stock.

Business Judgment Rule Although directors and officers are expected to make decisions that are in the best interest of the corporation, they are not expected to make perfect decisions all the time. Many directors and officers make decisions that inadvertently harm the corporation. Although shareholders may want to hold their directors and officers liable for these decisions, the *business judgment rule* does not allow them to do so.

Under this rule, directors and officers are not liable for decisions that harm the corporation if they were acting in good faith at the time of the decision. In other words, if there was reason to believe that the decision was a good decision at the time, the directors and officers are not liable for the resulting harm.

Although the business judgment rule is not a statute, it is common law recognized by almost every court in the country. The rule is practical because it grants directors the freedom to work without constant fear of personal liability. The business judgment rule also encourages individuals to serve as directors by removing the threat of personal liability for inadvertent mistakes.

LIABILITY OF SHAREHOLDERS

The main liability that shareholders face is liability for the debts of the corporation. Because shareholders are the owners of the corporation, they are liable to the extent of their investment when the company loses money. There are rare instances, however, in which shareholders are personally liable.

For instance, in some cases, individuals sign stock subscription agreements before incorporation. Once an individual signs a stock subscription agreement, she is contractually obligated to purchase shares in the corporation. For par-value shares, or shares that have a fixed face value noted on the stock certificate, the shareholder must pay the corporation at least the par value of the stock. For no-par shares, or shares without a par value, the shareholder must pay the corporation the fair market value of the shares. The shareholder is personally liable for breach of contract if she does not buy shares.

Alternatively, a shareholder can be held personally responsible if he receives watered stock. Watered stock is stock issued to individuals below its fair market value. When watered stock is issued to a shareholder, the shareholder is individually liable for paying the difference between the price he paid for the shares and the stated corporate value of the shares.

par-value shares
Stock shares that have a fixed face value noted on the stock certificate.

no-par shares
Stock shares that do not have a par value.

watered stock
Stock that is issued to individuals below its fair market value.

Rights of Directors, Officers, and Shareholders

LO 6

Along with their specific roles and duties, directors, officers, and shareholders have specific rights within the corporation. Because shareholders are in a position of limited decision-making power, they have rights that allow them to participate within the corporation. Directors and officers also have specific rights that allow them to perform their duties within the corporation to the best of their abilities.

DIRECTORS' RIGHTS

The unique responsibilities of corporate directors call for unique rights. Directors have four major rights within a corporation: rights of compensation, participation, inspection, and indemnification.

All corporate directors have a *right to compensation* for their work, and different corporations grant compensation in different ways. Most directors hold other managerial positions within their companies and receive their compensation through those positions. Another common avenue for compensating directors is paying them nominal sums as honorariums for their contributions to the company.

Because directors are required to make informed business decisions, they have the *rights of participation and inspection.* In other words, they have the right to get involved in and understand every aspect of the business. A corporate director has the right to be notified of all meetings and has access to all books and records.

Finally, because directors are in positions of great legal vulnerability, they have the *right to indemnification.* That is, they have the right to reimbursement for any legal fees incurred in lawsuits against them.

OFFICERS' RIGHTS

Because corporate officers are technically employees of the corporation, their rights are defined by employment contracts drawn up by the board of directors or the incorporators. They are in a contractual relationship with the corporation and if they are removed from their positions in violation of the terms of the contract, the corporation may be liable for breach of contract.

Assigned Directors in Japan

A common corporate practice in Japan is for multiple corporations, banks, and companies to form hierarchical conglomerates known as *keiretsus*. There are two types of *keiretsus*. The first is a horizontal *keiretsu,* in which a powerful bank acts as the unifying agent under which several large corporations come together. With the exception of the bank, power is shared equally among the members. The second type is a vertical *keiretsu.* In contrast to horizontal *keiretsus,* vertical *keiretsus* are hierarchically ordered with an unequal distribution of power. Large corporations often control several hundred subordinate companies.

Power distribution within *keiretsus* plays a key role in determining the board of directors. Usually the main bank or parent corporation assigns its own executives to serve on the boards of the less powerful companies. The prosperity of these companies is important to the main banks and parent corporations. The assigned directors act as overseers, consultants, and mentors. They want to promote simultaneously the interests of the parent corporation and the growth of the subordinate ones. Thus, the subordinate companies do not view the assignment of directors as a sign of mistrust. To the Japanese the logic is patent: If the success of the *keiretsu* and the success of each company are reciprocal, all parties should work together to achieve the collective goal.

SHAREHOLDERS' RIGHTS

Although shareholders' most powerful right is the right to vote at shareholders' meetings, they also posses many other rights.

stock certificate
A document that serves as a stockholder's proof of ownership in a corporation.

Stock Certificates Some corporations issue stock certificates to shareholders as proof of ownership in the corporation. Each certificate includes the corporation's name and the number of shares represented by the certificate. An example of a stock certificate is shown in Figure 21-3. A shareholder's ownership in the corporation, however, does not depend on his possession of the physical stock certificate. For example, if the certificate is destroyed in a fire, the shareholder's ownership in the corporation is not destroyed.

Preemptive Rights Under common law, shareholders have *preemptive rights.* Preemptive rights give preference to shareholders to purchase shares of a new issue of stock. Each shareholder receives preference in proportion to the percentage of stock she already owns.

For example, suppose that a shareholder owns 1,500 shares in a corporation with 5,000 outstanding shares. She owns 30 percent of the corporation's outstanding stock. Now suppose that the corporation decides to issue an additional 10,000 shares. If the corporation does not grant

Figure 21-3

Example of a Stock Certificate

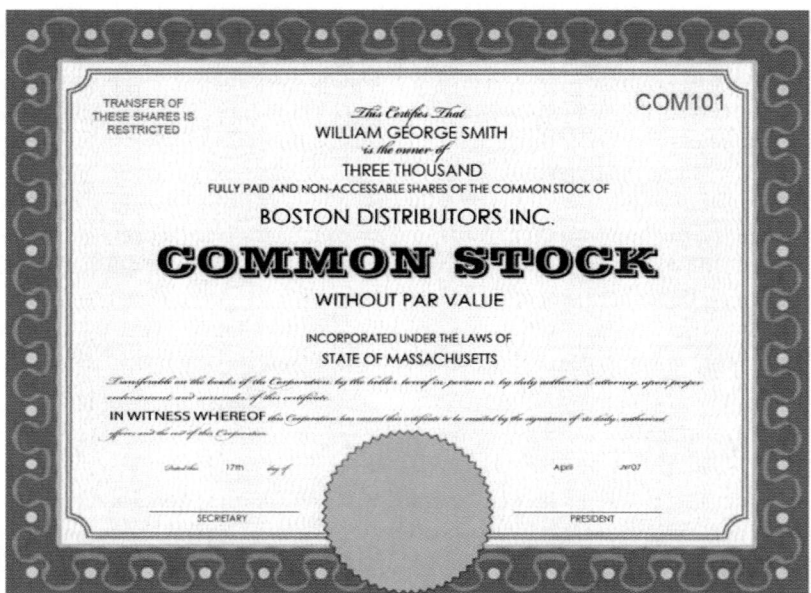

preemptive rights, her relative control of the corporation will fall because she now owns only 1,500 of the corporation's 15,000 outstanding shares, or 10 percent of its stock. In contrast, if the corporation does reserve preemptive rights, and the shareholder elects to purchase 3,000 shares of the newly issued stock, then she owns 4,500 shares of the corporation's 15,000 outstanding shares (30 percent). Thus, with preemptive rights, she can maintain her proportionate control of the corporation.

In most states, a corporation's bylaws can negate preemptive rights, so the corporation determines whether to grant preemptive rights. Preemptive rights are especially important for individuals who own stock in close corporations due to the relatively small number of issued shares. If a close corporation issues additional shares, an individual shareholder may lose proportional control over the firm if he does not buy newly issued shares. However, if preemptive rights exist within the corporation, all shareholders receive stock warrants, which they can redeem for a certain number of shares at a specified price within a given time period.

stock warrant
A type of security issued by a corporation (usually together with a bond or preferred stock) that gives the holder the right to purchase a certain amount of common stock at a stated price.

Dividends If directors fail to declare and distribute dividends, shareholders have the right to take legal action to force the directors to declare the dividends. In many cases, however, directors have good reason to hold dividends for a limited amount of time to finance major undertakings such as research or expansion. Thus, shareholders must show that the directors are acting unreasonably and abusing their discretion in withholding the dividend.

Inspection Rights All shareholders have the right to inspection under both statutory and common law. A shareholder can, moreover, appoint an agent to conduct the inspection on her behalf. To prevent abuse, however, this right has many limitations. Shareholders can inspect records and books only if they ask in advance and have a *proper purpose*. Many states have other statutory limitations to this right. For example, some states allow only shareholders with a minimum number of shares to inspect. Other states require that the shareholder own stock for a minimum amount of time before inspection. Additionally, corporations can deny shareholders' right to inspect confidential corporate information, such as trade secrets.

Share Transfer The law generally permits property owners to transfer their property to another person, and, in most cases, stock is considered transferable property. In closely held corporations, however, the transfer of stock is usually restricted so that shareholders can choose the corporation's other shareholders.

One method of restricting stock transferability is called the right of first refusal. If a corporation establishes this right in its bylaws, the corporation or its shareholders have the right to purchase any shares of stock offered for resale by a shareholder within a specified period of time.

right of first refusal
A method of restricting stock transferability whereby a corporation or its shareholders have the right to purchase any shares of stock offered for resale by a shareholder within a specified time frame.

Corporate Dissolution Shareholders have the right to petition the court to dissolve their corporation if they feel the company cannot continue to operate profitably. According to Section 14.30 of RMBCA, if a corporation engages in any of the following behaviors, shareholders have a legal right to initiate dissolution.

1. Directors are deadlocked in managerial decisions and harming the corporation.
2. Directors are acting in illegal, oppressive, or fraudulent ways.
3. Assets are being wasted or used improperly.
4. Shareholders are deadlocked and cannot elect directors.

Once dissolution has taken place and the corporation has settled its debts with its creditors, shareholders have a right to receive the remaining assets of the company in proportion to the number of shares they own.

Shareholder's Derivative Suit One of the shareholder's most important rights is the right to a derivative suit. If corporate directors fail to sue when the corporation has been harmed by an individual, another corporation, or a director, individual shareholders can file a shareholder's derivative suit on behalf of the corporation. In most jurisdictions, to be able to file a shareholder's derivative suit, a shareholder must have held stock at the time of the alleged wrongdoing.

shareholder's derivative suit
A lawsuit filed by a shareholder on behalf of the corporation.

Exhibit 21-3

Rights of Directors, Officers, and Shareholders

POSITION	RIGHT
Directors	Right to compensation
	Right to participation
	Right to inspection
	Right to indemnification
Officers	Rights determined in employment contract
Shareholders	Right to have stock certificates
	Preemptive rights
	Right to dividends
	Right to transfer shares
	Inspection rights
	Right to corporate dissolution
	Right to file a derivative suit
	Right to file a direct suit

shareholder's direct suit

A lawsuit filed by a shareholder against the corporation.

Before filing the suit, the shareholder must file a complaint with the board of directors. If nothing is done in response to the complaint, the shareholder can proceed with the suit. Enron shareholders brought shareholder's derivative suits against various directors and officers of Enron.

Derivative suits are important when shareholders believe that directors of the corporation are harming the corporation. It seems highly unlikely that directors will sue themselves for damages they cause in such cases. Thus, the shareholder's derivative suit is important for holding the directors accountable for their behavior. Because the shareholder files this suit on behalf of the corporation, all damages recovered are given to the corporation, not the individual shareholder.

Shareholder's Direct Suit In addition to their right to bring suit on behalf of the corporation, shareholders can also bring a direct suit against the corporation. In a shareholder's direct suit, the shareholder alleges that she has suffered damages caused by the corporation. For example, shareholders can bring a direct suit if the board of directors is improperly withholding dividends or if a shareholder is wrongly denied his right to inspect corporate records. If a court awards damages as a result of a shareholder's direct suit, the damages go to the shareholder personally.

Exhibit 21-3 summarizes the respective rights of directors, officers, and shareholders.

Introduction to Mergers and Consolidations

LO 7

Although many people believe that *mergers* and *consolidations* are synonymous, they are in fact two legally distinct procedures. Nevertheless, in both mergers and consolidations, corporations, shareholders, and creditors have the same rights and liabilities.

MERGERS

merger

A combination of two or more corporations in which only one of the corporations continues to exist.

A merger occurs when a legal contract combines two or more corporations and only one of the corporations continues to exist. A useful way to understand a merger is to think of one corporation absorbing another corporation (called an *absorbed corporation* or a *disappearing corporation*), yielding a single surviving corporation.

The surviving firm remains a single corporation, but it changes in several ways after the merger. First, its shareholders must amend its articles of incorporation according to the specific conditions of the merger. Second, the surviving corporation becomes liable for all debts and obligations of the absorbed corporation.

The surviving corporation also grows from the merger because it obtains the absorbed corporation's property and assets. Additionally, it acquires the absorbed corporation's rights, powers, and privileges.

CONSOLIDATIONS

consolidation

A combination of two or more corporations in which the combining corporations cease to exist and a new corporation is formed.

Like mergers, consolidations legally combine two or more corporations. In a consolidation, however, neither of the original corporations continues to exist legally. Rather, they form an entirely new corporation with its own legal status.

Because the new corporation has independent legal status, the articles of incorporation of the original companies are void. The shareholders of the new corporation create new articles of incorporation, called *articles of consolidation,* according to the details of the consolidation.

The consolidated firm assumes the liabilities, debts, and obligations of the original corporations. The new corporation also acquires the original corporations' property and assets. Finally, the consolidated corporation takes on the rights, privileges, and powers of the original companies.

Today, consolidations are very rare. As Section 11.01 of RMBCA reads, "In modern corporate practice consolidation transactions are obsolete since it is nearly always advantageous for one of the parties in the transaction to be the surviving corporation."

THE RIGHTS OF SHAREHOLDERS

When shareholders invest in corporations, they expect the board of directors to handle daily business issues. They also expect, however, to vote on exceptional matters, including mergers, consolidations, changes in partners, sales or leases of the corporation, and exchanges of assets. Because shareholders have a vested interest in the survival and prosperity of the corporation, these matters are of great significance to them. Thus, the merger and consolidation procedures require shareholder approval.

APPRAISAL RIGHTS

The law protects shareholders as a group from corporations, but it also protects individual shareholders from one another. Suppose that although an overwhelming majority of shareholders vote to approve a merger, a single shareholder dissents. In this situation, the law does not force the dissenting shareholder to become a shareholder in a corporation different from the one in which she originally invested. Thus, the law permits dissenting shareholders to exercise their appraisal rights. An **appraisal right** is a dissenting shareholder's right to have her shares appraised and to receive monetary compensation from the corporation for their value.

Strict procedures govern appraisal rights. Before a shareholder vote, dissenting shareholders must submit a notification of dissent. By conveying their disapproval before the vote, the dissenting shareholders may sway other shareholders to reconsider their decision. If, however, the shareholder vote approves the transaction, the dissenting shareholders must issue another statement demanding adequate compensation for their shares.

The corporation must then present the dissenting shareholders with a document stating the value of their shares. Shareholders and corporations often clash when determining the value of these shares. Generally, however, they use the value of the shares on the day before the shareholder vote. The language of the law is of little help; it ambiguously calls for the "fair value of shares" (RMBCA 13.01). If the dissenting shareholders and the corporation cannot reach an agreement, courts intervene to establish the shares' value.

Exhibit 21-4 summarizes the core concepts of corporation mergers.

Purchase of Stock

Besides engaging in mergers and consolidations, corporations can extend their operations by purchasing another corporation's stock. An acquiring corporation, or *aggressor,* can buy any or all of another corporation's voting shares. Through such a stock purchase, the purchasing corporation gains control of the selling corporation in a corporate *takeover.*

appraisal right
A dissenting shareholder's right to have his or her shares appraised and to receive monetary compensation from the corporation for their value.

takeover
The purchase of one corporation's stock by another corporation as a means of gaining control of the selling corporation.

Exhibit 21-4

Review of Mergers and Corporations

- A merger occurs when a legal contract combines two or more corporations and only one corporation continues to exist.
- A consolidation occurs when a legal contract combines two or more corporations and an entirely new corporation results.
- An appraisal right is a dissenting shareholder's right to have her or his shares appraised and to receive monetary compensation from the corporation for that value.

The Nature of Takeovers

hostile takeover

A takeover to which the management of the target corporation objects.

During the 1980s, not only did the number of corporate takeovers increase, but so too did the number of hostile takeovers. Hostile takeovers are takeovers to which the management of the target corporation objects. When a hostile takeover succeeds, the target corporation's management frequently compares the transition to a full-scale invasion characterized by layoffs and dramatic changes in company policy.

TYPES OF TAKEOVERS

tender offer

A type of takeover in which the aggressor corporation offers the target shareholders a price above their stock's current market value.

To initiate a stock purchase, the aggressor must appeal directly to the shareholders of the corporation it hopes to buy, known as the *target corporation.* The aggressor can offer several types of deals to the target shareholders. It can make a tender offer, in which it offers target shareholders a price above the current market value of the stock. Aggressors, however, often require that they receive a certain number of shares within a certain time frame.

Alternatively, the aggressor may make an exchange tender offer. In an exchange tender offer, the aggressor offers to exchange target shareholders' current stock for stock in the aggressor's corporation. The aggressor may also make a cash tender offer to the target shareholders in which it pays them cash for their stock.

exchange tender offer

A type of takeover in which the aggressor corporation offers to exchange the target shareholders' current stock for stock in the aggressor's corporation.

After acquiring a substantial number of the target corporation's shares, the aggressor initiates a proxy fight by fighting for control over target shareholders' proxies. Before an aggressor can gain control of the target corporation through proxies, it needs a key piece of information: a list of target shareholders. Although resistant target corporations often wish to conceal this information, federal securities law requires that target corporations assist aggressors in some ways. Thus, to avoid lengthy and expensive lawsuits, target corporations often provide a list of shareholders voluntarily.

cash tender offer

A type of takeover in which the aggressor corporation offers to pay the target shareholders cash for their stock.

Those seeking to acquire corporations have developed tactics to overcome the law's rules encouraging cooperation from target corporations. Because contacting each individual target shareholder is expensive, aggressors often try to win the favor of a few institutional investors that own a large block of shares. If an aggressor can obtain the proxies of these investors, it can win control of the target corporation.

RESPONSE TO TAKEOVERS

Once an aggressor has presented its offer to the target corporation's shareholders, the target corporation's board of directors must inform shareholders of all facts pertinent to shareholders' votes. After reviewing these material facts, the directors vote to accept or reject the offer and advise shareholders accordingly.

self-tender offer

A takeover-resistance strategy in which the target corporation offers to buy its shareholders' stock.

If the directors conclude that a takeover is not in the company's best interest, the company may employ many methods of resistance. One common method is a self-tender offer, in which the target corporation offers to buy its shareholders' stock. If the shareholders accept the offer, the target corporation maintains control of the business.

Alternatively, target corporations may defend themselves using leveraged buyouts. A leveraged buyout (LBO) occurs when a group within a corporation (usually management) buys all the outstanding corporate stock held by the public. Thus, the group gains control over corporate operations by "going private," or becoming a privately held corporation.

leveraged buyout (LBO)

A takeover-resistance strategy in which a group within the target corporation buys all the corporate stock held by the public, thereby turning the company into a privately held corporation.

LBOs are usually high-risk endeavors, however, because the target corporation must borrow money to purchase the outstanding stock. It may have to borrow money from an investment bank or issue corporate bonds.

In Case 21-3, the Georgia court of appeals considered the legality of a "golden parachute." A golden parachute is a clause in an executive's contract specifying that he/she will receive large benefits should the executive's employment be terminated. Management of the target firm in this case made an agreement with its top managers to win their cooperation in resisting a takeover.

ROYAL CROWN COMPANIES, INC. v. MCMAHON
COURT OF APPEALS OF GEORGIA

183 Ga. App. 543 (1987)

FACTS: *McMahon was the president of Arby's Inc., a subsidiary of Royal Crown Companies, Inc. It appeared that another corporation was positioning itself to buy Royal Crown. To reassure its top managers, Royal Crown enacted agreements stipulating that management would receive severance pay in the event of termination of employment or resignation after change of corporate control. McMahon resigned after the aggressor bought Royal Crown, but he did not receive his severance pay. He sued the corporation, and the trial court found in his favor. Royal Crown appealed.*

ISSUE: Is the golden-parachute contract a regular severance agreement, or is it unenforceable because it was made amid conflict of interest between management and the shareholders of Royal Crown?

REASONING: The judge argued that Royal Crown was trying to invalidate an enforceable severance agreement by claiming that the agreement was not enforceable because it was made in a context that was in conflict with the interests of the shareholders. The judge stated:

> Plaintiff was not a member of the board of directors which approved this agreement. Moreover, the agreement was offered

for the express purpose of protecting the shareholders by inducing the continued employment of plaintiff during a time of uncertainty when he might otherwise have been distracted by concerns for his own financial security to seek employment elsewhere.

Neither is the agreement void for failure of consideration. In the case at hand, plaintiff's employment was terminable at will and he was under no obligation to continue. The agreement was offered for the express purpose of inducing plaintiff to remain in his position during merger negotiations. Continued performance under a terminable-at-will contract furnishes sufficient consideration for the promise of additional severance pay.

DECISION AND REMEDY: The court affirmed the decision on behalf of McMahon and ordered enforcement of the severance agreement.

SIGNIFICANCE OF THE CASE: This case illustrates the trouble firms can get into when they are resisting a takeover. Royal Crown made an agreement to secure the loyalty of its top management, but when the time came to fulfill its part of the bargain, the company tried to argue that enforcement of such a contract would be unfair in light of the duties owed to shareholders.

CRITICAL THINKING

Is there any missing information you would ask for when considering the facts of this case? If you were to argue to reverse the trial court's decision, what reasons would you offer?

ETHICAL DECISION MAKING

Think about the WPH process of ethical decision making. What is the purpose of the court's decision? In other words, which value is upheld? What value is in conflict with the reasoning of the court?

Response to Termination

The "death" of a corporation occurs in two phases: *dissolution,* the legal termination of the corporation, and *liquidation,* the process by which the board of directors converts the corporation's assets into cash and distributes them among the corporation's creditors and shareholders.

DISSOLUTION

Dissolution may be voluntary or involuntary, depending on who initiates and compels the dissolution. *Voluntary dissolution* occurs when the directors or shareholders trigger the dissolution procedures. The directors can initiate the proposal and submit it to the shareholders for a vote, or the shareholders can begin dissolution procedures. Involuntary dissolution results when government or private parties successfully get a court order dissolving the corporation. Either way, for dissolution to be successful, shareholders must unanimously vote for the proposal.

Regardless of whether the directors or shareholders initiate dissolution, the corporation must follow specific procedures. First, the directors must file articles of dissolution with the secretary of state. These articles must include the company name, the date of dissolution, and the method of authorization of dissolution. Next, the directors must notify the shareholders. If shareholders or creditors have claims against the corporation, they must make them known within a stipulated time frame. Although the corporation establishes the time frame, the period must extend at least 120 days after the date of dissolution.

 SUMMARY

Characteristics of Corporations	*Legal entity.* *Rights as person and citizen.* *Creature of the state.* *Limited liability of shareholders.* *Unrestricted transferability of corporate shares.* *Perpetual existence.* *Centralized management.* *Corporate taxation.* *Liability for corporate agents.*
Corporate Powers	Corporations have both express and implied powers. An *ultra vires* act is a corporate action that is beyond the scope of the corporation's authority.
Classification of Corporations	*Public or private.* *For profit or nonprofit.* *Domestic, foreign, or alien.* *Publicly held or closely held.* *S corporations.* *Professional corporations.*
Formation of the Corporation	To create a corporation: • Promoters organize corporate formation. • Subscribers offer to purchase stock in the corporation during the formation process. • A state is selected for incorporation.
Legal Process of Incorporation	The legal requirements are: • Selecting the corporate name. • Drafting and filing the articles of incorporation. • Holding the first organizational meeting.
Potential Problems with Formation of the Corporation	Remedies for defective incorporation include: • *De jure* corporations. • *De facto* corporations. • Corporations by estoppel. • Piercing the corporate veil.

Corporate Financing	*Debt securities (bonds).*
	Equity securities (preferred stock and common stock).

Roles of Directors, Officers, and Shareholders

Directors:

- Minimum number required to attend the Board of Directors Meeting.
- Legally responsible for day-to-day managerial activities.

Officers:

- Run the day-to-day business of the organization.
- Act as agent of the corporation.

Shareholders:

- Approve major corporate decisions.
- Elect and Remove Members of Board of Directors.

Duties of Directors, Officers, and Shareholders

Directors and Officers:

- Duty of care.
- Duty of loyalty.
- Duty to disclose conflicts of interest.

Majority Shareholder:

- Duty of care and loyalty when selling shares.

Liabilities of Directors, Officers, and Shareholders

Directors and officers:

- Personally liable for their own torts and crimes.
- Liable for torts and crimes of others when there was inadequate supervision.

Shareholders:

- Liable for debts of the corporation to the extent of their investment.

Rights of Directors, Officers, and Shareholders

Directors:

- Compensation.
- Participation.
- Inspection.
- Indemnification.

Officers' rights are spelled out in their employment contract.

Shareholders:

- Right to vote at shareholders' meeting.
- Preemption.
- Inspection.
- Share transfer.
- Petition for dissolution.
- Direct and derivative suits against the corporation.

Introduction to Mergers and Consolidations

Merger: A legal contract whereby two or more corporations combine and only one of the corporations continues to exist.

Consolidation: A legal contract whereby two or more corporations combine and an entirely new corporation results.

Rights of shareholders: Shareholders vote only on exceptional matters regarding the corporation.

Appraisal right: An appraisal right is the shareholder's right to have her or his shares appraised and to receive monetary compensation for their value.

Purchase of Stock

An acquiring corporation can take control of another corporation by purchasing a substantial amount of its voting stock.

The Nature of Takeovers

A corporation can expand its size and operations by purchasing the stock of another firm.

A *hostile takeover* is a takeover to which the management of the target corporation objects.

Types of takeovers:

- Tender offers.
- Exchange offers.
- Cash tender offers.

Response to takeovers: Directors declare whether they accept or reject the offer. If they object to the offer, they can engage in methods of resistance.

Response to Termination

Dissolution is the legal death of a corporation.

 Point/Counterpoint

Should Corporations Be Allowed the Status of "Legal Personhood" and Be Given Full Protection under the Bill of Rights as Persons?

YES	NO
On May 10, 1886, in the case of *Santa Clara County v. The Southern Pacific Railroad Company,* the Supreme Court clearly decided that "other corporations" deserved "equal protection of the laws," specifically the Fourteenth Amendment.	The Bill of Rights, including the Fourteenth Amendment, was created at a time when corporations clearly existed in the United States. However, a stipulation to include corporations *as a separate entity* was not included in the Bill of Rights. Clearly, the creators of the Bill of Rights were aware that corporations existed at the time. The corporations were not mentioned as having rights *independent of the natural persons associated with the corporations,* so the Bill of Rights was not designed to protect corporations as "legal persons."
Several reasons support the position that corporations should be considered legal persons. A corporation is created by and is composed of natural persons. Actions on the corporation directly affect the natural persons associated with the corporation. The rights of the creators and shareholders cannot be violated, and violating the rights of the corporation indirectly violates the rights of the persons who created and are part of the corporation. Further, additional limitations should not be placed on a group of people simply because they have combined their efforts and formed a corporation.	Further, classifying corporations as legal persons and allowing them protection under the Bill of Rights, though advantageous for corporate interests, is harmful to human interests. For example, corporate money speaks much louder than one person's letter as a means of influencing politicians.
Logical limitations are in place to restrict corporations' existence as "persons." Corporations cannot become official citizens and cannot vote. Even though the political system affects the corporation, the natural citizens involved with the corporation are expected to vote with the corporation's best interest in mind.	If corporations are given rights as a natural person, the individuals making decisions behind the corporation are not held accountable to the larger world community. The corporation is punished for a poor decision rather than the individual who used poor judgment. When the corporation is punished rather than the individual who made the decision, the individual may not feel much, if any, of the consequences of his or her action.
Finally, corporations deserve the same rights as natural persons because a corporation fulfills the same obligations as natural persons as an entity separate from the natural persons associated with the corporation. For example, corporations pay government taxes on profits; the shareholders also pay taxes.	Lastly, corporations should not be considered legal persons and protected as such because corporations do not face the same restrictions as a natural person. A natural person's life must end; however, a corporation is allowed perpetual existence.
	Also, corporations do not face the same potential consequences as natural persons. A corporation cannot be sent to jail for its actions. A corporation cannot be rehabilitated and changed to become a profitable member of society if it breaks the law.

----➤ Questions & Problems

1. Name at least three characteristics that distin-guish corporations from other forms of business organization.

2. How is an *ultra vires* act related to a corporation's powers?

3. Compare and contrast common stock and preferred stock.

4. Explain the primary duties of officers and directors.

5. What is the business judgment rule?

6. The Metacon Gun Club operated an outdoor shoot-ing range adjacent to a river, a golf course, a riding stable, several private homes, and a state park. The Simsbury-Avon Preservation Society, a corporation composed of homeowners who live adjacent to the gun club, sued Metacon, alleging that the discharge of chromium, lead, lead shot, lead bullets, ammu-nition fragments, and ammunition wadding had contaminated the groundwater. The members of the society depended on water resources in the vicinity of the gun club. Metacon argued that the society was not a corporation at the time it filed the suit because the state returned its paperwork several days later due to a missing address. Thus, Metacon argued, the society was not a legal entity and did not have stand-ing to sue. How do you think the court ruled in this case? Why? [*Simsbury-Avon Pres. Soc'y, L.L.C. v. Metacon Gun Club, Inc.,* 2005 U.S. Dist. LEXIS 11699 (2005).]

7. Attorney Nicholas Kepple, the president of M&K Realty, drew up a contract for the sale of a parcel of land (Lot 5) from Howard Engelsen to M&K. To establish a purchase price for the sale, Engelsen had Lot 5 appraised. The appraisers based their appraisal of Lot 5 on several facts that Kepple and Engelsen learned were incorrect after they signed the contract. These facts included the total acreage of Lot 5 and whether Lot 5 could be divided into two separate lots without the need for a subdivision approval from the planning and zoning commissioner. After learning that these facts were in error, Kepple saw that the original purchase price was well below the market price for Lot 5, and he attempted to complete the sale for the original purchase price. Engelsen informed Kepple that he would not complete the sale of Lot 5 because M&K had never legally formed as a corporation under the state incorporation statutes and thus lacked the capacity to enter the contract in the first place. Do you think the court agreed with Engelsen's argument? Why or why not? [*BRJM LLC v. Output Systems, Inc., et al.,* 2005 Conn. Super. LEXIS 1699 (2005).]

8. Viola Scheutrum was killed when her car collided with a runaway horse on the highway. A police offi-cer at the scene noted that there were at least eight horses running free on the highway. The horses had escaped from the corral at the Sea Horse Ranch, Inc. The fence posts bordering the corral were old, weather-worn, bug-infested, and rotting. The horses had broken free from the corral on several previous occasions. Al Shipley, the president of Sea Horse Ranch, was aware of the inadequate condition of the fence. The state charged Sea Horse Ranch and Shipley with involuntary manslaughter. Do you think the court held the Sea Horse Ranch, as a corporation, and Shipley, its president, criminally liable? Why or why not? [*Sea Horse Ranch, Inc. v. Superior Court of San Mateo County,* 30 Cal. Rptr. 2d 681 (1994).]

9. Performance Nutrition, Inc. (PNI), developed, mar-keted, and sold nutritional supplements. In 1996, Kennedy Capital Management, a major stockholder of PNI, organized an election of the board of direc-tors to put in new management. Anthony Roth, a member of the board of directors, took over as the CEO of PNI. PNI faced financial difficulties, and Naturade, PNI's primary vendor, was interested in buying the company. Roth and officials at Naturade began negotiations, and Naturade assured Roth that a position would be created for him if the takeover was successful. According to the plan, PNI would file for bankruptcy, and Naturade would purchase its assets. Roth did not share the plan with any other shareholders or members of the board of directors. Although Naturade's offer was unreasonably low, Roth did not make any efforts to sell PNI's assets to any company other than Naturade. Before PNI filed for bankruptcy in 1997, Roth signed a letter of intent to sell PNI's assets to Naturade. Despite the obvious conflict of interest, Roth never included other PNI directors in the decision making. Do you think Roth breached his fiduciary duties to the company? Why or why not? [*In re Performance Nutrition, Inc.,* 239 B.R. 93 (1999).]

10. Rooney Enterprise, Inc., operates a cemetery. After receiving payments on pre-need and perpetual-care burial contracts, the corporation failed to make deposits into the appropriate accounts. Paul Rooney, the president of Rooney Enterprises, was criminally convicted for the corporation's failure to make the deposits. Rooney argued that the trial court erred in convicting him for the corporation's actions. No evidence was presented to suggest that Rooney's

duties included an accounting responsibility or direct corporate responsibility for withholding or depositing funds. How do you think the responsible person doctrine applies to this case? Was the

trial court correct in finding Rooney criminally responsible for the corporation's actions? Why or why not? [*Rooney v. Commonwealth of Virginia,* 500 S.E.2d 830 (1998).]

Looking for more review material?

The Online Learning Center at **www.mhhe.com/kubasekess** contains this chapter's "Assignment on the Internet" and also a list of URLs for more information, entitled "On the Internet." Find both of them in the Student Center portion of the OLC, along with quizzes and other helpful materials.

Securities Regulation

----▶ CASE OPENER

The Martha Stewart Case

On December 27, 2001, Martha Stewart's stockbroker, Peter Bacanovic, informed Stewart that two of his clients, Samuel Waksal, CEO of the biopharmaceutical company ImClone, and Waksal's daughter, had just sold all of their ImClone stock. Waksal secretly knew that the FDA was about to reject "Erbitux," a key cancer drug ImClone had developed. Stewart did not know about the impending FDA rejection of Erbitux, and information about Waksal's sale of ImClone's stock was not available to the public. After receiving the information about Waksal's transaction, Stewart instructed her broker to sell all of her shares of ImClone stock. The following day, the FDA announced its rejection of Erbitux, and ImClone's stock price plummeted 16 percent. Stewart's timely trade allowed her to avoid a $45,673 loss.

Eighteen months later, the Securities and Exchange Commission (SEC) filed charges against Stewart and her broker for illegal insider trading and securities fraud.[1]

1. Did Martha Stewart violate federal securities law? Why or why not?
2. Did Martha Stewart's broker violate securities law? Why or why not?

[1]www.sec.gov/news/press/2003-69.htm.

----▶ LEARNING OBJECTIVES

After reading this chapter, you will be able to answer the following questions:

LO 1 What is a security?

LO 2 What requirements are imposed by the Securities Act of 1933?

LO 3 How does the Securities Exchange Act of 1934 regulate the trading of securities?

LO 4 How are investment companies regulated?

LO 5 How do states regulate securities?

security

A financial instrument designated as a note, stock, or bond or any other instrument named in the Securities Act of 1933.

Companies frequently need to raise money to expand. One way they raise money is by issuing securities. For example, corporations issue corporate securities—stocks and bonds—to raise capital for corporate expansion.

However, a security is simply a piece of paper; it has no intrinsic value. Consequently, without securities regulations, corporations could easily commit fraud by issuing large numbers of securities and then refusing to repay them. Thus, the government heavily regulates securities issuance and trading.

Securities regulation is a relatively recent body of law. Before the Great Depression, government did not regulate securities, and fraudulent transactions occurred frequently. After the stock market crash in 1929, Congress passed several laws to regulate securities markets.

This chapter begins by defining *security*. It then examines federal securities regulations. Finally, the chapter briefly discusses state securities regulation.

What Is a Security?

Physically, a security is merely a piece of paper, as illustrated in Figure 21-3 of the previous chapter. But when investors buy securities, they are not buying a piece of paper. They are buying what the paper represents. The value of the security is based on what the paper represents.

Earlier, we loosely defined securities as stocks and bonds. To be more precise, securities include stocks, bonds, debentures, and warrants. Furthermore, certain items mentioned in securities acts, such as interests in oil and gas rights, are securities. In some cases, courts have even defined cosmetics, vacuum cleaners, and cemetery lots as securities. Finally, investment contracts, contracts in which individuals invest money with the expectation of making a profit, are securities. How can so many different things be securities?

The Securities Act of 1933 offers a complicated definition of *security*, and as a result, courts have struggled when determining whether a particular instrument is a security. In an effort to provide a framework for analysis, the U.S. Supreme Court stated in the 1985 case *Landreth Timber Co. v. Landreth* that courts should presumptively treat as a security any financial instrument designated as a note, stock, bond, or other instrument named in the 1933 act.

If the instrument in question does not have the characteristics of an instrument specifically named in the 1933 act, the courts apply a three-part test. In the classic 1946 case *SEC v. W. J. Howey Co.,*[2] the U.S. Supreme Court defined a security as an (1) investment in a common enterprise with the (2) reasonable expectation of profit gained (3) primarily or substantially from others' efforts. Anything that meets these three criteria is subject to security law. Case 22-1 illustrates how courts apply the *Howey* test.

[2] 328 U.S. 293, 66 S. Ct. 1100 (1946).

CASE 22-1

SECURITIES AND EXCHANGE COMMISSION v. LIFE PARTNERS, INC.
U.S. DISTRICT COURT FOR THE DISTRICT OF COLUMBIA
898 F. Supp. 14 (1995)

FACTS: *Life Partners, Inc. (LPI), facilitated the sale of life insurance policies of full-blown AIDS victims to investors at discount prices. While the life insurance policies are sold to investors, the insurance policy is in the name of LPI. When the policy holder dies, the investors recover the face value of the policy. This arrangement allegedly benefited both the* investors and the AIDS victims, who, when they sold their life insurance policies, received much needed money to cover their medical costs associated with their illness. The process of selling life insurance policies of terminally ill patients is known as a viatical settlement. The SEC argues that LPI was essentially creating securities by repackaging some of

the insurance policies. Consequently, the SEC brought suit against LPI for nonregistration under the 1933 act.

ISSUE: Are the products offered by the defendants investment contracts under Section 2(1) of the Securities Act?

REASONING IN THE WORDS OF THE COURT: An investment contract is a contract, transaction or scheme whereby a person invests his money [1] in a common enterprise and [2] is led to expect profits [3] solely from the efforts of the promoter or a third party. . . .

. . . The parties to the instant case do not contest that the buyers of viatical settlements are investing money. Therefore, the Court will concentrate on the three prongs of the *Howey* test. . . . Courts have identified three types of commonality in a quest to bring meaning and uniformity to this prong of the *Howey* test. The first is "horizontal commonality" which demands that the fortunes of two or more investors be joined in a pooling of interests. . . . The second type of commonality is "broad vertical" which considers whether the fortunes of investors are tied to the efforts of the promoter. . . . The final type of commonality is "strict vertical" which centers on whether fortunes of investors are tied to the fortunes of the promoter. . . . The Court need not decide which measure of commonality is appropriate because each type is present in the instant case

Horizontal commonality exists through LPI's sale of fractional interests in the death benefit due under a single policy. The fortunes of each investor are tied to that of the other investors in that policy, with proceeds to be divided on a *pro rata* basis as contemplated in *Revak* and *Wals.* . . . Both types of vertical commonality are also present in this case. The investors' fortunes are tied to those of the promoter since LPI takes title to the policies. From the perspective of both the insurance company and the insured, LPI is the new owner and beneficiary of the life insurance policies. Investors are dependent upon LPI to protect their interests, and their interests would be greatly affected by LPI's dissolution or insolvency. Such risks are sufficient to meet the test for vertical commonality.

1. Expectation of Profits

The Supreme Court has defined "expected profits" for purposes of securities law as an investor's anticipation of profits either through capital appreciation resulting from development of the initial investment, or participation in earnings resulting from use of investors' funds. . . . An instrument is likely to meet this prong of the *Howey* test when the purchaser's motivation is to receive a return on the investment rather than to use or consume the item. . . .

The undisputed evidence in this case indicates that investors in viatical settlements are concerned with gaining a return on their investment. "Rates of return on viatical settlements consistently out perform market rates by a wide margin."

2. Derived from the efforts of others.

It is clear from LPI's promotional materials that it offers diligence and expertise in discovering and evaluating the legal status of an insurance policy and the insured's medical condition before offering it for investment. After the investment is made, LPI offers continued services of a more ministerial nature: it periodically checks on whether the insured is alive; submits claims for death benefits to the insurance companies; accepts this payment; and computes and distributes *pro-rata* shares of benefits to investors. . . .

Defendants argue that the efforts of the promoter must continue after the investment for the instrument to qualify as an investment **contract.** This standard is satisfied here assuming *arguendo* that continued efforts after the investment are required. While the Court agrees with defendants that these post-investment activities are often ministerial in nature, two factors tip the balance in the SEC's favor. The first is the pre-investment work by LPI which is undeniably essential to the overall success of the investment. The efforts surrounding an investment should be considered in their entirety.[11] More importantly, defendants' post-investment efforts are critical since LPI, not the investor, has the contractual relationship with the insurance company. The investors are dependent on LPI because they lack any contractual rights *vis-a-vis* the insurance company and are strangers to both the insurance company and the other investors who bought interests in the same policy.

DECISION AND REMEDY: The court found that "LPI's basic policy is an investment contract that is subject to federal securities law." Accordingly, judgment was rendered for the plaintiff.

SIGNIFICANCE OF THE CASE: The case illustrates the application of the *Howey* doctrine and how it is used to identify securities.

CRITICAL THINKING

Why might the ambiguity in the definition of *security* be a problem in securities regulation?

ETHICAL DECISION MAKING

You probably have a good idea of the ethical theory you agree with most. Under that ethical theory, what is your opinion of the business of LPI?

Sweden's Securities Market

The Swedes divide securities into bonds and shares. Individuals invest in either the bond market or the stock market. Companies issue bonds to boost funds from sources outside their shareholders. Bondholders have a right to a fixed rate of interest regardless of whether the company earns a profit. Bondholders do not, however, have a right to take part in company decision making.

Companies issue shares to increase their equity capital. Unlike bond interest payments, shareholders' returns vary with the company's profits. Because shareholders' interests are closely tied to the success of the company, shareholders have a voice within the company. Generally, this voice comes in the form of a vote at general meetings.

Regulation of the stock and bond markets in Sweden is unique because Sweden has no equivalent of the SEC. Instead, banks themselves oversee the issuance of shares and bonds.

Securities Regulation

Two crucial acts regulate securities transactions. The Securities Act of 1933[3] regulates how companies issue corporate securities, while the Securities Exchange Act of 1934[4] oversees the purchase and sale of securities. Both attempt to provide greater stability to securities transactions. First, the acts mandate that investors have access to certain information when deciding whether to buy or sell securities. Second, the acts strive to curb fraudulent securities transactions.

THE SECURITIES AND EXCHANGE COMMISSION

The 1934 act created the Securities and Exchange Commission (SEC), an independent agency whose function is to administer federal securities laws. The SEC is headed by five individuals appointed by the president. These five individuals serve fixed five-year terms.

The SEC has a number of responsibilities. First, it is responsible for the enforcement of securities laws. Thus, in response to an allegation of violation of securities law, the SEC investigates and, if necessary, initiates an enforcement action against the violator. Enforcement actions often include penalties or injunctive remedies. If the violation is severe enough to warrant criminal prosecution, however, the Fraud Section of the Criminal Division Department of Justice will prosecute the alleged violator.

Second, the SEC interprets the securities acts and adopts rules to achieve the purposes of the acts. Thus, the SEC passes securities transaction regulations that have the force of law.

Third, the SEC regulates the activities of securities brokers, dealers, and advisers. All securities dealers and brokers must register with the SEC.

Fourth, the SEC regulates the trade of securities on securities exchanges. As you read about securities regulations in this chapter, remember that the SEC is responsible for their administration and enforcement. Exhibit 22-1 traces how the SEC's regulatory powers have evolved.

Other countries have bodies that serve functions similar to those of the SEC. In Singapore, for example, the government controls securities markets through the Securities Industry Council. The council is an advisory board to the minister of finance, who, on the basis of the council's advice, issues guidelines for exchanges, mergers, and trading.

LO 2 The Securities Act of 1933

Congress passed the Securities Act of 1933 in reaction to the mistrust of securities transactions before the Great Depression. Thus, a function of the act was to legitimize security transactions by requiring the registration of securities offered to the public. Through the

[3] 15 U.S.C. §§ 77a–77aa.
[4] 15 U.S.C. §§ 78a–78mm.

Exhibit 22-1

The Expansion
of SEC Powers
in the 1990s

Securities Enforcement Remedies and Penny Stock Reform Act of 1990

Permits the SEC to:

- Issue a cease-and-desist order against a violator of any federal securities law.
- Seek civil money penalties against any violators.
- Create rules to require that brokers and dealers provide information concerning prices and risk associated with the penny-stock market.

Market Reform Act of 1990

Allows the SEC to suspend securities trading if prices vary excessively in a short time period.

Securities Acts Amendments of 1990

Permit the SEC to seek punishment of violators of foreign securities laws.

National Securities Markets Improvement Act of 1996

Permits the SEC to exempt persons, securities, and transactions from securities regulations.

Sarbanes-Oxley Act of 2002

- Increases corporate disclosure requirements.
- Penalizes violators of securities laws more heavily.
- Holds corporate executives responsible for errors in corporate reports filed with the SEC.
- Requires earlier filing of financial and stock transaction reports.
- Creates and establishes SEC oversight over the Public Company Accounting Oversight Board to regulate public accounting firms.

registration process, investors have more information to make better-informed decisions about their securities purchases.

Section 5 of the 1933 act mandates that any corporation, partnership, association, or individual that offers the sale of securities to the public through the use of mails or through any facility of interstate commerce must register that security unless it qualifies for an exemption (discussed later in this section). Any issuer of securities must file a written registration statement and a prospectus with the SEC.

REGISTRATION STATEMENT

Although the SEC requires that different types of companies complete slightly different registration forms, the SEC requires certain elements from all companies. The registration statement generally contains (1) a description of the securities offered for sale, (2) an explanation of how proceeds from the sale of the securities will be used, (3) a description of the registrant's business and properties, (4) information about the management of the company, (5) a description of any pending lawsuits in which the registrant is involved, and (6) financial statements certified by an independent public accountant.

Caution: Although the SEC requires the registration of securities, the SEC does not "approve" these securities. In other words, the SEC does not make any judgment about the worth of securities; it simply enforces the requirement that issuers provide certain information to potential buyers.

PROSPECTUS

Along with filing a registration statement, issuers of securities must also file a prospectus with the SEC. A prospectus is a written document that contains most of the information that appears in the registration statement. The prospectus is different from the registration statement, however, because it is an advertising tool that issuers distribute to potential investors, who rely on the prospectus to help decide whether they should buy the securities.

The SEC requires, but cannot guarantee, the accuracy of facts stated in the registration statement and prospectus. If an issuer makes a false or misleading statement in a registration statement, the issuer can be subject to criminal or civil penalties. These penalties are discussed later in the chapter.

prospectus
A written document filed with the SEC that contains a description of a security and other financial information regarding the company offering the security; also distributed as an advertising tool to potential investors.

CONNECTING to the Core

Economics: Market Failure—Asymmetrical Information

Economics teaches that when certain conditions are met, markets allocate goods and services efficiently among individuals in society. When those necessary conditions are not present, the result is often what economists call a *market failure*—a failure of the market to produce efficient results.

For example, for markets to work well, buyers and sellers must have access to the same information about the goods being sold. Suppose you need to buy a used car, but you lack the ability to distinguish between dependable used cars and "lemons" (i.e., cars prone to breaking down). In contrast, your local used-car dealer knows exactly what is wrong with each car on his lot. Of course, he's probably not going to tell you the problems with the car you're thinking about buying; if he did, you might not buy it. So he tells you how great the car is, and you buy it. A week later, the car breaks down—you bought a lemon.

Economists call this problem *asymmetrical information*. It leads to a market failure because it results in

inefficient transactions that would not have taken place if both the buyer and the seller had access to the same information. You wouldn't have bought the car if you had known it was a lemon.

The asymmetrical information problem is present in unregulated securities markets. When investors purchase corporate securities, they lack knowledge about the securities' risks and potential rewards, whereas the companies issuing the securities know very well the risks and rewards the securities offer. In this situation, investors are unable to make efficient decisions about which securities to purchase, and the result is a market failure.

The Securities Act of 1933 attempts to remedy the asymmetrical information problem in the securities market. The act requires that all securities issuers disclose certain information to investors in the form of a prospectus. As a result, investors can appraise the value of the securities for themselves and make better investment choices.

George A. Akerlof, "The Market for 'Lemons': Quality Uncertainty and the Market Mechanism," *Quarterly Journal of Economics* 84 (1970) p. 488.

PERIODS OF THE FILING PROCESS

The filing process consists of three periods: prefiling, waiting, and posteffective.

Prefiling Period The prefiling period begins when an issuer starts to think about issuing securities, and it ends when the issuer files the registration statement and prospectus with the SEC. Before filing these documents, the issuer cannot make any offers to sell securities. The issuer can, however, negotiate with *underwriters,* investment banking firms that purchase securities from the issuing corporation with the intent to sell them to brokerage houses, which then sell them to the public.

Because they cannot offer to sell securities during the prefiling period, issuers, officers, directors, and underwriters usually try to avoid generating publicity about possibly issuing securities because the SEC may construe such publicity as an attempt to condition the market to generate interest in the securities. In fact, the SEC could consider speeches or press releases mentioning the potential issuance of securities to be an offer. The issuing firm is permitted, however, to publish a notice about the prospective offering, including the name of the issuer as well as a description of the potential securities, but the notice may not include the name of the underwriter.

red-herring prospectus

A prospectus with a warning written in red print at the top of the page telling investors that the registration has been filed with the SEC but not yet approved.

Waiting Period Once an issuer files a registration statement and prospectus, the waiting period begins. During this period, the SEC reviews the information filed by the issuing firm. Issuers must wait 20 days after the filing date to sell their securities. During the waiting period, issuers may make oral offers to sell the securities and may distribute a red-herring prospectus—a prospectus with a notice written in red print at the top of the page warning investors that the

registration has been filed with the SEC but not yet approved. Moreover, the issuer may publish a tombstone advertisement, a brief ad with a format similar to that of a tombstone.

Posteffective Period The posteffective period begins when the SEC declares the registration statement effective, and it ends when the issuer sells all securities offered or withdraws them from sale. During this time, investors may buy and sell the securities, but purchasers must receive a final prospectus, a version of the prospectus the buyer must receive at the point of sale. If an issuer does not send the purchaser a final prospectus, the issuer has violated the 1933 Securities Act.

tombstone advertisement
A print advertisement that announces a forth-coming sale of securities in a format similar to that of a tombstone.

SPECIAL REGISTRATION PROVISIONS

Amendments to the 1933 act stipulate more relaxed registration requirements for companies that have consistently satisfied applicable registration requirements. For example, *shelf registrations* permit certain qualified issuers to register securities that they will sell "off the shelf" on a delayed or continuous basis in the future. SEC Rule 415 requires that corporations using shelf registrations keep information in the original registration accurate and up to date.

EXEMPTIONS UNDER THE 1933 ACT

Although these complex registration requirements are standard for most securities, they do not apply to all securities in all situations. Some securities are exempt because of the nature of the securities themselves—*exempt securities*—and others are exempt when exchanged in certain ways—*exempt transactions.*

Exempt Securities The 1933 act provides that certain securities are exempt from the registration procedures described above. These securities are *unregistered unrestricted securities,* and they include:

1. Securities issued by governments, including municipal, state, and federal governments.
2. Securities issued by nonprofit issuers, such as religious institutions or charitable organizations.
3. Securities issued by financial institutions supervised by banking associations.
4. Securities issued as a result of corporation reorganization in which one security is exchanged for another security.
5. Stock dividends and stock splits.
6. Insurance and annuity contracts issued by insurance companies.
7. Securities issued by federally regulated carriers (i.e., railways).
8. Short-term notes with a maturity date that does not exceed nine months.
9. Securities sold before July 27, 1933.
10. An issuer's offer of up to $5 million in securities in a 12-month period.

Although the last exemption permits the issuer to avoid the complex requirements of full registration, Regulation A[5] nevertheless requires that the issuer file certain reports with the SEC. For example, the issuer must file a notice of issue and an offering circular and provide the offering circular to investors before sale of the securities. Even with these requirements, however, the registration process under Regulation A is much less burdensome than the full registration process. For example, Regulation A permits issuers to "test the waters" for interest in their securities before preparing the offering circular, selling any securities, or gaining the commitment of interested buyers.

Exempt Transactions If a security does not fall under one of the exempt categories described above, an issuer can nevertheless avoid registering the security by making certain exempt transactions. Such securities are *unregistered restricted securities.* Issuers might want to avoid

[5] 17 C.F.R. §§ 230.251–230.263.

the registration process because it can be costly, complicated, and time-consuming. Exempt transactions offer an opportunity to save time and money. Consequently, many issuers sell securities through exempt transactions.

Although these transactions are exempt from registration, issuers must still provide investors with information about the securities, such as annual reports and financial statements.

Exempt transactions include limited offers, intrastate issues, and resales of securities.

Limited Offers. Certain securities transactions known as *limited offers* are exempt from the registration process because they either involve small amounts of money or are offered only to sophisticated investors. The investors who participate in limited offers generally do not need the protection afforded by the registration process.

The SEC's Regulation D[6] enumerates three exemptions for limited offers (Rules 504, 505, and 506). Section 4(6) of the 1933 act contains an additional limited-offer exemption.

Private Placement Exemption (Rule 506) Issuers who make private offerings of securities are exempt from the registration process. These issuers, however, cannot advertise their private offerings to the general public. This exemption, usually referred to as the *private placement exemption,* allows firms to issue an unlimited number of securities to an unlimited number of accredited investors. Consequently, firms can easily raise large amounts of capital. Firms may not, however, issue to more than 35 unaccredited investors.

The SEC defines an accredited investor as:[7]

accredited investor
A private investor who is allowed to accept private securities offerings under certain specific guidelines set by the SEC.

1. Any natural person who has a net worth of at least $1 million.

2. Any natural person whose annual income has been at least $200,000 for the two previous years and expects to make at least $200,000 in the current year.

3. Any corporation or partnership with total assets in excess of $5 million.

4. Insiders of the issuers, such as executive officers or directors.

5. Registered investment companies, colleges and universities, banks, and insurance companies.

The SEC assumes that accredited investors are better able to evaluate the financial risk associated with buying securities. Consequently, government protection in the form of required registration is less imperative.

The SEC also requires that firms selling to unaccredited investors under Rule 506 believe that these investors have expertise regarding securities trading. The firms must believe that the investors, or their representatives, have reasonable ability to evaluate the financial risk associated with purchasing securities. If a firm privately offers any unaccredited investor the opportunity to purchase securities, all investors must receive the basic information contained in the registration statement (i.e., information about the issuing company and the securities). If no unaccredited investors are involved, however, the issuer does not have to disclose any information. While firms do not have to register these exempt securities with the SEC, they must notify the SEC of any sales made under the exemption.

The private placement exemption provides one of the easiest ways for firms to raise capital. Instead of making a public offering, firms can simply make a private offering to investors capable of ascertaining the risk associated with buying securities. The firms cannot, however, advertise the securities to the general public.

Rule 505 Rule 505 is very similar to Rule 506, but it has two important differences. First, according to Rule 505, a firm's private offerings may not exceed $5 million in a 12-month period, while under Rule 506, a firm may issue an unlimited number of securities. Second, according to Rule 506, if a firm issues securities to unaccredited investors, it must believe that they have the knowledge to evaluate the risk associated with the security. In contrast, under Rule 505, firms need not believe that investors have the reasonable ability to evaluate the risk of purchasing securities.

[6] www.law.uc.edu/CCL/33ActRls/regD.html.
[7] SEC Rule 501.

Rule 504 *Noninvestment firms*—firms that do not engage primarily in the buying and selling of securities—that offer no more than $1 million in securities over a 12-month period are exempt from registration. An unlimited number of both accredited and nonaccredited investors may purchase these securities; however, the firms must notify the SEC of their securities sales. Issuers need not disclose any information to investors.

Section 4(6) If a firm offers securities only to accredited investors for an amount less than $5 million, the issuer is exempt from registration. An unlimited number of accredited investors may participate in the transactions, but no unaccredited investors may buy these securities. Firms may not advertise these securities to the public. Issuers do not have to disclose any information to investors, but they must notify the SEC of any sales under this exemption. Moreover, investors who want to resell these securities must register them with the SEC.

Intrastate Issues. Under Section 3 of the 1933 act, any security offered or sold to a permanent resident of the single state where the issuer of the security resides and does business is exempt. Thus, local businesses can rely on local investors to raise an unlimited amount of capital without registration.

Courts and the SEC have interpreted this exemption very narrowly. Issuers must do at least 80 percent of their business within the state, receive at least 80 percent of their profits within the state, have at least 80 percent of their assets within the state, plan to use at least 80 percent of the profits within the state, and have their main offices in the state.

During the period of sale and at least nine months after the period of sale, buyers of these securities under the intrastate exemption may not resell them to nonresidents. Issuers must take precautions against interstate resales.

Resales. The 1933 Securities Act creates an exemption for "transactions by any person other than an issuer, underwriter, or dealer." Because another section of the act exempts dealers and brokers, only issuers and underwriters are not exempt from registering resales of securities.

Consequently, the average investor does not have to register securities when he or she wants to sell. If the investor acquired them through sales under Rule 505, Rule 506, or Section 4(6) (e.g., intrastate issues and limited offers), they are *restricted securities*. If an investor wants to resell a restricted security, she must register the securities unless she follows Rule 144 or Rule 144a.

> **restricted securities**
> Securities that have limited transferability and are usually issued in a private placement.

Rule 144 Under Rule 144, any person wanting to resell a restricted security is exempt from registration if certain criteria are met. First, the public must have access to adequate current information about the issuer. Second, the person selling the restricted security must have owned the security for at least two years. Third, the seller must sell the restricted securities in limited amounts in unsolicited broker transactions. Fourth, the seller must notify the SEC of the sale.

If a seller is not an affiliate of the issuer and has owned the securities for three years, he or she may sell the securities in unlimited amounts and is not subject to any of the criteria under Rule 144 for an exemption. An *affiliate* is a person who controls, is controlled by, or is in common control with the issuer. The 1933 act restricts sales by affiliates much more than sales by nonaffiliates. If an affiliate sells restricted or nonrestricted securities, he must meet all but one of the criteria to be exempt from registration. The affiliate does not need to hold a nonrestricted security for two years before reselling.

VIOLATIONS AND LIABILITY

If the SEC uncovers a potential violation of the 1933 act, it can (1) take administrative action, (2) take injunctive action, or (3) recommend criminal prosecution. If the SEC takes administrative action, it conducts a formal investigation of the potential violation by calling relevant witnesses to testify or produce evidence. If, through this investigation, the SEC uncovers evidence of a violation, the SEC may order an administrative proceeding before an administrative law judge, who can impose sanctions and even revoke a security's registration.

Usually the SEC takes injunctive action when it believes that a defendant is likely to continue to violate the law. Thus, the SEC may seek an injunction to prevent issuers from advertising securities by mail. In the Case Opener about Martha Stewart, the SEC sought an injunction prohibiting Stewart and her broker from violating securities laws and limiting her activities as an officer of a public company.

Finally, if the SEC recommends criminal action, the Department of Justice prosecutes criminal charges against the violators. Criminal penalties include a fine up to $10,000, imprisonment for up to five years, or both.

How might an issuing company violate the 1933 Securities Act? First, a company violates the act if it intentionally misleads investors by omitting or falsifying information on a registration statement or prospectus. Second, if a company is negligent in discovering a fraudulent statement, it can be liable. Third, an issuing company violates the act if it sells securities before the effective date of the registration statement.

Issuers charged with a violation of the 1933 act can raise several defenses. A company charged with the first or second violation described above may claim that the omitted or false statement was immaterial to the sale of the security. Similarly, if the issuer can prove that the plaintiff was aware of the omission or false statement when she bought the security, the defendant can avoid liability.

due diligence defense

A defense in which the defendant argues that he or she applied the appropriate degree of attention, care, and research expected of a party in a given situation and had reasonable grounds to believe that certain facts and statements were accurate and had no omission of material facts.

Any defendant except the issuer can assert the due diligence defense. This defense requires that the defendant demonstrate that she investigated the registration statement and had reasonable grounds to believe that the statement was accurate and had no omission of material facts.

If a defendant sold securities before the effective date of registration, however, she will almost certainly be liable because the 1933 act provides no defenses for this violation.

If an investor purchased securities and suffered damages as a result of an issuer's false or misleading statement, the investor is entitled to bring a civil suit to recover his losses. The burden of proof falls on the investor to demonstrate this incomplete or inaccurate disclosure of facts. Case 22-2 illustrates an investor's attempt to recover damages based on the omission of allegedly material facts from the prospectus and registration statement.

 CASE 22-2

STEVEN KLEIN, WARREN BRANDWINE v. GENERAL NUTRITION COMPANIES, INC.
U.S. COURT OF APPEALS FOR THE THIRD CIRCUIT
186 F.3d 338 (1999)

FACTS: *Steven Klein and Warren Brandwine purchased shares of General Nutrition Companies (GNC) common stock between February and May 1996. During this time period, GNC sold over 1.5 million shares in public offering, realizing proceeds of over $33 million. At the end of May 1996, GNC announced that its store sales would be 3 to 6 percent lower than the previous quarter. Consequently, the price of GNC stock fell from around $21.50 to $14. Klein and Brandwine asserted that GNC violated several securities regulations by failing to disclose material facts in its prospectus. They argued that GNC's failure to disclose this information led to an artificially inflated* stock price for the offering of securities. Consequently, Klein and Brandwine sued GNC under Sections 11 and 12(a)(2) of the Securities Act, which creates a private cause of action when a registration statement or prospectus omits a material fact that is required to make the other statements not misleading. The district court dismissed the case, and Klein and Brandwine appealed.*

ISSUE: Did the defendant's failure to disclose in the prospectus (1) a loss of third-party advertising support; (2) a worldwide shortage of deodorized distillate, a raw

material used to produce vitamin E; and (3) the fact that GNC's new store openings would siphon business from existing stores violate Sections 11and 12 of the Securities Act?

REASONING: For a fact's nondisclosure to violate the act, the fact must be material, meaning that "there is a substantial likelihood that a reasonable [investor] would consider it important in deciding how to [act],. . . taking into account such factors as the certainty of the information, its availability in the public domain, and the need for the information in light of cautionary statements being made."

Applying those factors, the nondisclosed information was immaterial. Regarding the loss of advertising support from third parties, the defendant simply had a concern that a decrease in sales by the third party might affect that party's ability to supply GNC with free advertising; a concern is not definite enough to require disclosure. Where an event is contingent or speculative in nature, it is difficult to ascertain whether the reasonable investor would have considered the omitted information significant at the time.

The free advertising was actually not suspended until a month after the public offering.

The worldwide vitamin E shortage did not need to be disclosed because it was public knowledge, and, furthermore, it was expected to be temporary. Federal securities laws do not require that a company state the obvious.

Finally, the failure of the prospectus to disclose that, at the time of the public offering, same-store sales were being adversely affected by the opening of new stores in close proximity to existing locations was not a violation because the prospectus adequately cautioned investors that GNC's expansion plans might not be achieved and might not be profitable.

DECISION AND REMEDY: The court held that "[a]ll of the alleged omissions are immaterial as a matter of law." The judgment was affirmed in favor of the defendant.

SIGNIFICANCE OF THE CASE: The case helps illustrate the kind of information that must be disclosed in a prospectus.

CRITICAL THINKING

This case was based on omitted information. An important skill in critical thinking is being able to determine whether omitted information is important. Klein and Brandwine felt that the omitted information was important, while the court did not. With whom do you agree, and why?

ETHICAL DECISION MAKING

What stakeholders benefited from the court's decision? Using your favorite ethical perspectives, do you think that these stakeholders deserved the benefits they derived from the court's decision? Why?

The Securities Exchange Act of 1934 LO 3

While the 1933 Securities Act regulates the issuance of securities, the 1934 Securities Exchange Act regulates the subsequent trading (resale) of securities, chiefly through the required registration of securities exchanges, brokers, dealers, and national securities associations. Moreover, the act requires that certain issuers file periodic reports with the SEC. The 1934 act also permits the SEC to monitor securities markets for fraud and market manipulation.

In one of the most closely watched business cases in years, the Supreme Court, in a 5-3 decision, protected those who are only secondary players in securities fraud, as long as the public did not rely on any explicit statements or actions by the secondary players. The case appears to limit the liability of accountants, lawyers, and others who may know about questionably fraudulent corporate behavior but can establish that they are not directly involved in it. The Case Nugget explains this case.

CASE Nugget

Aiders and Abettors Get a Free Pass from the Supreme Court

Stoneridge Inv. Partners, LLC v. Scientific-Atlanta, Inc.
United States Supreme Court

128 S. Ct. 761 (2008)

The facts in the case are fairly straightforward. At the request of Charter, which in mid-2000 was falling short of its cash-flow target, Scientific-Atlanta and Motorola agreed to increase their prices for the cable boxes they sold to Charter and to use the extra money to buy advertising on Charter's cable stations. The arrangement allowed Charter to treat the advertising purchases as current revenue while listing the money spent on cable boxes as a capital expense. By recording the advertising purchases as millions in extra revenue, Charter fooled its auditor into approving a financial statement that showed it met projected revenue and operating cash-flow numbers.

In rejecting the shareholders' claim against Scientific-Atlanta, the Court majority said that bankers, lawyers, and other third parties who did not directly mislead investors but worked with corporations that did cannot be sued by shareholders. The Court reasoned that the key test for liability is whether investors relied on an entity's actions or statements, and in this case investors had no knowledge of deceptive acts during the time in question. The Court noted that the primary punishment of such secondary offenders would come from criminal prosecutions and enforcement actions by the SEC.

Shareholder activists are concerned that this decision, in effect, offers less protection to shareholders in a variety of situations. Their concerns were strengthened when less than a week after the Stoneridge case, the high court turned down an appeal in a class action case in which several plaintiffs alleged that three investment banks, Credit Suisse, Merrill Lynch, and Barclays Bank, had aided and abetted Enron in the fraudulent practices that led to the giant corporation's filing bankruptcy. The plaintiffs were seeking up to $40 million in damages. The court of appeals in the case held that the shareholders could not sue the banks for fraud because the banks did not have primary liability for the matter under federal law

SECTION 10(B) AND RULE 10B-5

One of the most important sections of the 1934 act is Section 10(b), which prohibits the use of manipulative and deceptive devices to bypass SEC rules. Within this section, subsection 5 prohibits fraud associated with the purchase or sale of all securities. Thus, even though securities may be exempt from registration, they are still subject to Rule 10b-5:

> It shall be unlawful for any person, directly or indirectly, by use of any means or instrumentality of interstate commerce or of the mails, or of any facility of any national securities exchange,

a. to employ any device, scheme, or artifice to defraud,

b. to make any untrue statement of a material fact or to omit to state a material fact necessary in order to make the statements made, in light of circumstances under which they were made, not misleading, or

c. to engage in any act, practice, or course of business that operates or would operate as a fraud or deceit upon any person, in connection with the purchase or sale of any security.

Both Section 10(b) and Rule 10b-5 play an important role in preventing insider trading.

INSIDER TRADING

When a company employee or executive uses material inside information to make a profit, she or he is engaging in **insider trading**. Insider trading is illegal because it gives the violator an important advantage over the general public and shareholders.

Section 10(b) and Rule 10b-5 define *insiders* as corporate officers, directors, employees, lawyers, consultants, accountants, majority shareholders, or any other individuals who receive private information regarding the trading of securities.

A company employee or executive who has inside information may be liable depending on whether the information is material. If there is a material omission or misrepresentation during a securities transaction, the individual has violated Section 10(b) and Rule 10b-5. If the omission or misrepresentation is not material, however, the individual is not liable. Examples of material information include the following:

1. A change in the status of litigation against the company.
2. A change in dividends.
3. A contract for the sale of corporate assets or for the purchase of assets.
4. A new product, process, or discovery.
5. A significant change in the financial status of the company.

According to the SEC, an individual with material inside information should either refrain from using the information or disclose the information to the other parties involved in the transaction.[8] Case 22-3 is a classic example of how courts address insider trading.

insider trading
Illegal buying or selling of a corporation's stock or other securities by corporate insiders such as officers and directors, in breach of a fiduciary duty or other relationship of trust and confidence, while in possession of material, nonpublic information about the security.

[8] *Matter of Cady, Roberts & Co.,* 40 SEC 907 (1961).

CASE 22-3

SECURITIES AND EXCHANGE COMMISSION v. TEXAS GULF SULPHUR CO.
U.S. COURT OF APPEALS FOR THE SECOND CIRCUIT
401 F.2d 833 (1968)

FACTS: *In June 1963, Texas Gulf Sulphur (TGS) acquired the option to buy land in Timmons, Ontario. Preliminary drilling in November 1963 suggested that the land held great amounts of copper and zinc. This information was supposed to be kept secret; not even officers and executives at TGS were supposed to know about the results of the drilling. TGS acquired the land and resumed drilling in March 1964.*

From November 1963 to March 1964, certain directors, officers, and employees of TGS received "tips" and purchased TGS stock or options to buy shares at a fixed price. When drilling began in November 1963, these people had owned 1,135 shares of TGS stock and possessed no calls; thereafter they owned a total of 8,235 shares and possessed 12,300 calls.

In April 1964, when rumors of a major mineral find appeared in newspapers, TGS publicly claimed that the rumors had no factual basis; a few days later TSG confirmed that the strike was expected to yield many million tons of ore. Between the days that TGS claimed the rumors were false and later confirmed the rumors, two defendants, Clayton and Crawford, ordered a combined total of 500 shares of TGS stock. The SEC brought suit against TGS and 13 of its directors, officers, and employees for violation of Section 10(b) of the Exchange Act and SEC Rule 10(b)-5, seeking an injunction to prevent TGS from publishing misleading press releases and requesting rescission of TGS's purchases and stock options. The district court dismissed the charges against all defendants but Clayton and Crawford, and the SEC appealed.

ISSUE: Did the corporate employees possess inside information that should have precluded them from trading in the company's stock?

REASONING IN THE WORDS OF THE COURT: The essence of the Rule is that anyone who, trading for his own account in the securities of a corporation has "access, directly or indirectly, to information intended to be available

only for a corporate purpose and not for the personal bene-fit of anyone" may not take "advantage of such information knowing it is unavailable to those with whom he is deal-ing," i.e., the investing public. . . . Insiders, as directors or management officers are, of course, by this Rule, precluded from so unfairly dealing, but the Rule is also applicable to one possessing the information who may not be strictly termed an "insider" within the meaning of Sec. 16(b) of the Act. Thus, anyone in possession of material inside informa-tion must either disclose it to the investing public, or, if he is disabled from disclosing it in order to protect a corporate confidence, or he chooses not to do so, must abstain from trading in or recommending the securities concerned while such inside information remains undisclosed. So, it is here no justification for insider activity that disclosure was for-bidden by the legitimate corporate objective of acquiring options to purchase the land surrounding the exploration site; if the information was, as the SEC contends, material, its possessors should have kept out of the market until dis-closure was accomplished. . . .

The basic test of materiality * * * is whether a *reasonable* man would attach importance * * * in determining his choice of action in the transaction in question. . . . This, of course, encompasses any fact "* * * which in reasonable

and objective contemplation *might* affect the value of the corporation's stock or securities * * *." . . . Such a fact is a material fact and must be effectively disclosed to the invest-ing public prior to the commencement of insider trading in the corporation's securities. . . . disclosing the earnings and distributions of a company but also those facts which affect the probable future of the company and those which may affect the desire of investors to buy, sell, or hold the company's securities. . . .

Here . . . knowledge of the possibility . . . of the existence of a mine of the vast magnitude indicated by the remarkably rich drill core located rather close to the surface . . . might well have affected the price of TGS stock and would certainly have been an important fact to a reasonable, if speculative, investor in deciding whether he should buy, sell, or hold.

DECISION AND REMEDY: The court found that the "transactions in TGS stock or calls by individuals apprised of the drilling results were made in violation of Rule 10b-5." The judgment was reversed in favor of the plaintiff.

SIGNIFICANCE OF THE CASE: The case is signifi-cant because it clarifies the type of information a person may possess that qualifies him as an "inside trader" for purposes of the law.

CRITICAL THINKING

Again, omitted information is the concern of this case. Can you make a distinction between the omitted information here and that in Case 22-2?

ETHICAL DECISION MAKING

What values are being emphasized by the prohibition on insider trading?

THE PRIVATE SECURITIES LITIGATION REFORM ACT OF 1995

Although Rule 10b-5 was designed to encourage disclosure of accurate information, one of its unintended side effects was the deterrence of forecasts. Shareholders who purchased stock in corporations with high earning forecasts often brought suit against the corporations' directors if actual corporate earnings fell short of forecasted earnings, alleging that the directors violated Rule 10b-5 by disclosing misleading financial information.

Congress attempted to remedy this problematic side effect by passing the *Private Securities Litigation Reform Act of 1995 (PSLRA)*. Among other things, the act provides a "safe harbor" from liability for publicly held issuers who make financial forecasts as long as the forecasts are "accompanied by meaningful cautionary statements identifying important factors that could cause actual results to differ materially from those in the forward-looking statement."[9]

Innovative shareholders attempted to subvert the PSLRA by suing corporate directors in state courts. Congress responded to these efforts by passing the *Securities Litigation Uniform Stan-dards Act of 1998*. This act strictly limits shareholders' ability to bring class action suits against nationally traded corporations.

[9] 15 U.S.C. § 77z-2 (2005).

OUTSIDERS AND INSIDER TRADING

Not only may insiders be liable for omitting or misrepresenting material information, but certain "outsiders" may also be liable through two theories: *misappropriation theory* and the *tipper/tippee theory.* Consider whether Martha Stewart is liable under either theory.

Misappropriation Theory In addition to being a theory of tort (see Chapter 6), misappropriation can establish liability for insider trading. Misappropriation theory holds that if an individual wrongfully acquires (misappropriates) and uses inside information for trading for her personal gain, she is liable for insider trading. Because she wrongfully acquires inside information, she is essentially stealing information to use for her benefit.

Because it expands the SEC's power, application of misappropriation theory to insider trading has not gone uncontested. The Case Nugget describes the first case in which the SEC convinced the courts to apply misappropriation theory to Rule 10b-5.

misappropriation theory
A theory of insider trading that holds that if an individual wrongfully acquires (misappropriates) and uses inside information for trading for his or her personal gain, that person is liable for insider trading.

CASE Nugget

Using Misappropriation Theory to Establish a 10b-5 Violation

United States v. Carpenter
U.S. Court of Appeals for the Second Circuit

791 F.2d 1024 (1985)

In 1981, R. Foster Winans wrote the "Head on the Street" column for the *Wall Street Journal.* He was aware of the *Journal's* policy that all news material gained by employees in the course of their employment was confidential. However, Winans and Carpenter, a news clerk at the *Wall Street Journal,* participated in a scheme with stockbrokers Felis and Brant. Winans provided the brokers with securities-related information that was about to be printed in the "Head on the Street" column. Using this information, Felis and Brant would buy or sell the relevant securities. Carpenter was a messenger between Winans and the stockbrokers. The net profit on the use of the information for securities trading was $690,000. Felis's brokerage firm noticed a correlation between the "Head on the Street" column and the trading in Felis's account. Although Felis denied the connection, he began making plans to cover up the trading. Soon, the SEC began an investigation. Later, Winans and Carpenter revealed the entire scheme to the SEC. The SEC sued under Section 10(b) of the Securities Exchange Act of 1934, arguing that the securities information had been misappropriated. The district court found Winans and Felis guilty of misappropriation under 10(b), and Carpenter was convicted for aiding and abetting the commission of securities fraud. They appealed.

The appellate court held that the newspaper employees and broker, acting in concert, criminally violated the federal securities laws by misappropriating material, nonpublic information, in contravention of established policies of the newspapers, for their own profit in the purchase and sale of securities. This type of fraudulent act is the type of deceptive act that the securities laws are designed to protect against. It therefore falls under the broad prohibition of "any device, scheme, or artifice to defraud."

Over 10 years later, in *United States v. O'Hagan,*[10] the U.S. Supreme Court conclusively established that misappropriation theory is applicable to Rule 10b-5.

Tipper/Tippee Theory The tipper/tippee theory holds that any individual who acquires material inside information as a result of an insider's breach of duty has engaged in insider trading.

tipper/tippee theory
A theory of insider trading that holds that any individual (tippee) who acquires material inside information as a result of an insider's (tipper's) breach of duty has engaged in insider trading.

[10] 117 S. Ct. 2199 (1997).

tippee
An individual who receives confidential information from an insider.

tipper
An insider who gives inside information to someone.

This individual, one who has received a tip from an insider, is called a tippee. The insider who gives the inside tip is called the tipper.

Suppose that Jerry (the tipper) gives material inside information to Elaine (the tippee). Jerry is liable because he is passing on inside information. Furthermore, Elaine is liable if she makes trading decisions based on information that she should know is not public. Jerry is liable for any profits made by Elaine. Now suppose that Elaine passes the tip on to George. Elaine is now a tipper, and George is a tippee. Both Elaine and Jerry are liable for the profits made by George. George is liable for the profits of his transactions if he knew or should have known that the material information was not public.

SECTION 16(B)

statutory insiders
Certain large stockholders, executive officers, and directors who are deemed insiders by the Securities Exchange Act of 1934.

short-swing profits
Profits made from the sale of company stock within any six-month period by a statutory insider.

proxy
A writing signed by a shareholder that authorizes the individual named in the writing to exercise the shareholder's votes (corresponding to his or her shares of stock) at a shareholders' meeting.

proxy solicitation
The process of obtaining authority to vote on behalf of shareholders.

Under Section 16(a) of the 1934 act, certain large stockholders, executive officers, and directors are considered statutory insiders. All statutory insiders must file a report detailing their ownership and trading of the corporation's securities.

To prevent statutory insiders from using inside information for their personal gain, Section 16(b) of the 1934 act requires that statutory insiders return all short-swing profits, or profits made from the sale of company stock within any six-month period by a statutory insider, to the company. Even if the insider did not use the inside information to make the transaction, all short-swing profits belong to the corporation. Section 16(b) imposes strict liability on statutory insiders who earn short-swing profits. In other words, violators cannot use lack of intent or lack of knowledge as a defense. Certain transactions, however, such as bankruptcy proceedings, are exempt from Section 16(b).

PROXY SOLICITATIONS

A proxy is a writing signed by a shareholder that authorizes the individual named in the writing to exercise the shareholder's votes (corresponding to his shares of stock) at a shareholders' meeting. Corporate managers often contact shareholders to request that they give a certain manager authority to vote on their behalf in an upcoming meeting. This process of obtaining authority to vote on behalf of shareholders is called proxy solicitation. Because the proxy solicitation process is potentially susceptible to fraud, the SEC regulates the proxy solicitation process.

Section 14(a) states that an issuer making proxy solicitations must also furnish a written proxy statement to shareholders. This statement must disclose to the shareholder all facts pertinent to the voting that will occur in the meeting. See Exhibit 22-2 for an excerpt from an example of a proxy statement that explains the purpose of the statement.

Exhibit 22-2

Proxy Statement Opening

Proxy Statement Excerpt

General Electric Company
3135 Easton Turnpike
Fairfield, Connecticut 06828

This proxy statement is furnished in connection with the solicitation of proxies by General Electric Company on behalf of the Board of Directors for the 2007 Annual Meeting of Shareowners. Distribution of this proxy statement and a proxy form to shareowners is scheduled to begin on or about February 28, 2007.

You can ensure that your shares are voted at the meeting by submitting your instructions by telephone or by Internet, or by completing, signing, dating and returning the enclosed proxy form in the envelope provided. Submitting your instructions or proxy by any of these methods will not affect your right to attend the meeting and vote. A shareowner who gives a proxy may revoke it at any time before it is exercised by voting in person at the annual meeting, by delivering a subsequent proxy or by notifying the inspectors of election in writing of such revocation.

Source: General Electric, "Notice of 2007 Annual Meeting and Proxy Statement," www.ge.com/ar2006/pdf/ge_proxy2007.pdf.

VIOLATIONS OF THE 1934 ACT

The 1934 act authorizes both civil and criminal penalties. If an individual engages in insider trading, a violation of Section 10(b) or Rule 10b-5, she has committed a criminal offense punishable with a fine up to $1 million, a prison sentence up to 10 years, or both. If a defendant did not know of the rule she violated, she cannot be imprisoned. If a partnership or corporation engages in insider trading, it is subject to fines up to $2.5 million.

Both the SEC and private parties can bring civil actions against violators of the 1934 act. The SEC investigates alleged violations under the 1934 act. In the process of an investigation, the SEC can enter into consent orders with defendants or seek injunctions to stop certain actions by defendants.

Perhaps the most useful tool the SEC has for punishing those engaging in insider trading is the *Insider Trading Sanctions Act of 1984,* which permits the SEC to sue any individual who violates the 1934 act or who helps another person to engage in insider trading in violation of that act. If the SEC succeeds in demonstrating its claim, courts may assess a civil penalty up to triple the profits gained or losses avoided by the defendant.

Congress expanded the SEC's authority to punish violators of the 1934 act when it passed the *Insider Trading and Securities Fraud Enforcement Act of 1988.* This act subjects more individuals to civil liability for insider trading and grants the SEC power to award bounty payments (government rewards for acts beneficial to the public) to insider-trading whistle-blowers.

bounty payment
A government reward for an act that is beneficial to the public.

Private parties may also sue violators of the 1934 act. A private party may seek rescission of a contract to buy securities or may recover damages based on the violator's profits. If the court rules that an individual is liable for violations of the 1934 act, he can seek contribution from others, such as accountants or lawyers, who shared responsibility for the violation.

Regulation of Investment Companies

LO 4

In the past century, smaller investors have become important players in securities markets. Investment companies facilitate their involvement in securities markets by purchasing a large, diverse portfolio of securities and managing it on behalf of small investor-owners. However, because small investors often lack the resources and ability to adequately supervise investment companies, they can be subject to fraud and exploitation.

To prevent exploitation of small investors, Congress passed the *Investment Company Act of 1940,* providing for SEC regulation of investment companies. Congress later expanded the SEC's power to regulate investment companies under the *Investment Company Act Amendments of 1970* and the *National Securities Markets Improvement Act of 1996.*

The Investment Company Act defines an *investment company* as any entity (1) that is engaged primarily in the business of investing, reinvesting, or trading in securities or (2) that is engaged in such business and in which more than 40 percent of the company's assets are investment securities. The act excludes a number of institutions, however, including banks, insurance companies, savings and loans, and finance companies.

The act requires that all investment companies file a notification of registration with the SEC. Additionally, they must file annual reports with the SEC and hold all securities in the custody of a bank or member of the stock exchange. The act prohibits investment companies from purchasing securities on the margin (borrowing money to purchase securities), selling short (selling securities that the company does not yet own), or participating in joint trading accounts.

State Securities Laws

LO 5

Not only must issuers obey federal securities regulations, but they are also subject to state securities laws, often referred to as blue-sky laws. These laws regulate the offering and sale of purely intrastate securities. Hence, although certain securities are exempt from federal securities regulation, they may be subject to state securities laws.

blue-sky law
A law that regulates the offering and sale of purely intrastate securities.

E-COMMERCE and the Law

Marketing Securities on the Internet

Perhaps one of the most important and exciting developments in securities regulations is the explosion of the securities market on the Internet. The Web permits companies to sell securities in an online initial public offering (IPO), thereby avoiding the expensive filing requirements of a traditional IPO. For example, some Web sites allow customers to buy and sell securities online. This technology, however, presents a greater opportunity for fraud because anyone can create a Web site. Several cases of securities fraud have occurred simply because a company has offered "free stock" over the Internet. The SEC has issued cease-and-desist orders against companies that illegally offered free stock on their Web sites because they had not registered their stocks with the SEC.

Another type of online fraud, called "pumping and dumping," occurs when an owner of a particular stock tells other investors about the virtues of the stock, artificially increasing demand for the stock and pumping up its price, only to sell (dump) it for a quick profit. Unregulated message boards on the Internet permit pumping and dumping

on a fast and efficient basis. In response to the increasing use of this method of stock price manipulation, the SEC has pursued harsher and more frequent prosecution of individuals who engage in pumping and dumping online. The Web also provides potential investors with access to enormous amounts of information about securities. For example, the SEC maintains the Electronic Data Gathering, Analysis, and Retrieval (EDGAR) database to help investors access information about IPOs and other documents filed with the SEC. Visit www.sec.gov/edgar.shtml to learn more about EDGAR.

SEC regulations apply to online advertising and securities transactions. When a company delivers a paperless prospectus, it is subject to the following rules:

1. The company must provide timely and adequate notice of the delivery of information.

2. The company must use an easily accessible communication system, such as the Internet.

3. The company must create evidence of the delivery of information.

Many state securities laws serve functions similar to those of federal securities laws. For example, many states have laws requiring registration of securities issued within the state and requiring disclosure of certain information. Moreover, state laws regulate securities brokers and dealers. Although the purposes of state and federal securities regulations overlap, the specific regulations differ. Consequently, to encourage greater coordination between federal and state securities laws, most states have adopted the Uniform Securities Act.

 SUMMARY

What Is a Security?	As defined by the *Howey* test, a security is an investment in a common enterprise with the reasonable expectation of profit gained predominantly from others' efforts.
Securities Regulation	The Securities and Exchange Commission (SEC) was created in 1934 to enforce securities laws, interpret provisions of securities acts, and regulate the trade of securities as well as the activities of securities brokers, dealers, and advisers.
The Securities Act of 1933	A *registration statement* is a document containing a description of the securities offered for sale, an explanation of how proceeds from the sale will be used, a description of the registrant's business and properties, information about the management of the company, a description of any pending lawsuits, and certified financial statements

A *prospectus* is a written document that is similar to a registration statement and is used as a selling tool for potential investors

Periods of the filing process:

1. Prefiling period
2. Waiting period
3. Posteffective period

Unregistered unrestricted securities are exempt from the registration process. These include:

1. Securities issued by governments, including municipal, state, and federal governments.
2. Securities issued by nonprofit issuers, such as religious institutions or charitable organizations.
3. Securities issued by financial institutions supervised by banking associations.
4. Securities issued as a result of corporation reorganization in which one security is exchanged for another security.
5. Stock dividends and stock splits.
6. Insurance and annuity contracts issued by insurance companies.
7. Securities issued by federally regulated carriers (i.e., railways).
8. Short-term notes with a maturity date that does not exceed nine months.
9. Securities sold before July 27, 1933.
10. An issuer's offer of up to $5 million in securities in a 12-month period.

Certain kinds of transactions are exempt.
These include the following:

1. *Limited offers* involve small amounts of money or are offered only to sophisticated investors. There are four possible exemptions:
 a. *Private placement exemption:* Exempts private offerings of securities.
 b. *Rule 505:* States that private offerings may not exceed $5 million in a 12-month period and firms do not have to believe that investors have a reasonable ability to evaluate risk.
 c. *Rule 504:* Exempts noninvestment firms that offer no more than $1 million in securities in a 12-month period.
 d. *Section 4(6):* Exempts securities offered only to accredited investors for an amount less than $5 million.
2. *Intrastate issues* exempt local investors in local businesses.
3. *Resales* exempt transactions by any person other than an issuer, underwriter, or dealer.

Restricted securities are securities acquired under Rule 505, Rule 506, or Section 4(6) that must be registered for resale unless the investor follows Rule 144 or Rule 144(a).

Violations may result in:

1. Administrative action
2. Injunctive action
3. Criminal prosecution

The Securities Exchange Act of 1934

Section 10(b): Regulation that prohibits the use of manipulative and deceptive devices to bypass SEC rules.

Insider trading: Trading in which a company employee or executive uses material inside information to make a profit.

Misappropriation theory: Theory that an individual who wrongly acquires and uses inside information for profit is liable for insider trading.

Tipper/tippee theory: Theory that an individual who receives material inside information as a result of an insider's breach of duty is guilty of insider trading.

Statutory insiders: Certain stockholders, executive officers, and directors who must file a report detailing their ownership and trading of the corporation's securities.

Short-swing profits: Profits made from the sale of company stock within any six-month period by a statutory insider; by Section 16(b), these profits must be returned to the company.

Proxy: Document that authorizes an individual to vote a shareholder's share of stocks at a shareholders' meeting

Proxy solicitation: Process of obtaining the authority to vote on behalf of a shareholder.

Violations may result in:

1. Criminal penalties.
2. Civil penalties.
3. Suits against those involved in insider trading under the Insider Trading Sanctions Act of 1984.

Regulation of Investment Companies State securities laws serve functions similar to those of federal securities laws, and include blue-sky laws.

State Securities Laws *Blue-sky laws* regulate the offering and sale of securities within the state only.

Point/Counterpoint

Should the Government Decrease Regulation of Securities Markets?

YES	NO
The government currently overregulates securities markets.	The government currently underregulates securities markets.

The government currently overregulates securities markets.

Government regulation is inefficient and perpetually behind the times. For example, some securities do not provide investors with dividends or bond payments until several years after their issue date. The nature of these securities renders investors susceptible to fraud, yet they might not discover the fraud until several years later, at a point when the trail is cold and government is impotent to remedy the situation. In another infamous example, a 15-year-old in New Jersey used Internet chat rooms to "pump and dump" securities. He was able to make off with over $800,000 before the SEC discovered what he had done.

Left unregulated, securities markets will provide an efficient level of information and will punish those who commit securities fraud. Intelligent investors will refuse to purchase securities about which they have insufficient information and hence push companies that provide insufficient information out of the market. Alternatively, if companies themselves refuse to provide information about securities they issue, investors will demand information from other sources. This investor demand will encourage development of markets providing information about securities. Indeed, these information markets already exist in the form of publications (e.g., *The Wall Street Journal* and *The Financial Times)* and professional services (e.g., stockbrokers and financial advisers).

Moreover, as the chapter pointed out, the five leaders of the SEC are unelected. As a result, they are insulated from democratic pressure to regulate securities markets in a manner consistent with voters' goals. Thus, even if more government regulation were desirable in theory, in practice the SEC is ill-equipped to provide it.

The government currently underregulates securities markets.

A common and not unfounded perception of securities markets is that small investors frequently lose everything while big investors and insiders win big. Consider, for example, the corporate accounting scandals of the early 2000s. Insiders made off with millions of dollars, while many small investors lost their retirement savings. Unless the government does more to level the playing field, such scandals will continue to occur.

Markets produce efficient results only when certain conditions exist. As the Connecting to the Core box in this chapter pointed out, securities markets are plagued by asymmetrical information: Investors almost always know less about securities than do issuers. If left unremedied, asymmetrical information leaves investors susceptible to many forms of securities fraud.

Even if government is unable to catch every perpetrator of securities fraud, its ability to catch high-profile perpetrators and punish them heavily still serves as an effective deterrent to other potential violators. For example, the wide publicity of the Martha Stewart case, explained in the Case Opener, sent a strong message to investors that the SEC will punish outsiders who use even small pieces of inside information for personal gain.

Moreover, the unelected nature of SEC board members allows the president to appoint individuals with tremendous expertise. Perhaps Congress lacks the institutional competence to regulate complex securities markets efficiently, but experts who have spent their careers working with securities are more likely to be able to regulate effectively.

Government regulation of securities markets will never be perfect, but the appropriate comparison is not between government regulation and perfect regulation but between government regulation and available alternatives.

Questions & Problems

1. What was the stimulus for the creation of securities regulation? State the purposes of the two main federal securities laws.

2. What is the function of the SEC?

3. Explain the process of registering securities.

4. Why are certain securities transactions exempt from the registration process?

5. Why is it illegal to use inside information in making securities transactions?

6. How does the misappropriation theory apply to insider trading?

7. Alleging security fraud and breach of promissory notes under Section 10(b) of the federal Securities Exchange Act of 1934, plaintiff Dale LeBrun filed suit against the defendant, Kuswa. LeBrun was a vendor/supplier for Tomorrow Inc., a company that needed more capital to continue production of its products. LeBrun and his family and friends agreed to lend approximately $105,000 to Tomorrow Inc. For each of the six lenders, Kuswa drafted a document entitled "Agreement to Borrow Monies." The terms required that Kuswa repay the loan within 12 months and pay interest quarterly based on sales or pay 100 percent of the initial amount borrowed. The plaintiff continued to communicate with Kuswa through mail, but Kuswa did not make full payments on the loans within the specified year. The plaintiff argued that, under the Securities Exchange Act, the loans not repaid by the defendant were promissory notes that had matured a year ago. The defendant claimed that the promissory notes in question were not securities under the definition provided in the Securities Exchange Act and therefore no federal jurisdiction existed. How do you think the court decided? [*Lebrun v. Kuswa,* 24 F. Supp. 2d 641 (1998).]

8. Magma Power Company brought a suit against Dow Chemical Co. under Section 16(b) of the Securities Exchange Act of 1934. Dow owned at least 10 percent of Magma common stock and was the largest minority shareholder. In a 1995 merger, Magma became a wholly owned subsidiary of California Energy. The merger eliminated all minority shareholders, and the terms of the merger required that Magma compensate Dow for its prior minority interest. Instead of going forward with the compensation, Magma held that Dow, a statutory insider, had earned short-swing profits by trading in Magma stock. Dow's first transaction occurred on September 12, 1994. Dow sold 857,143 shares of Magma stock to Garantia Banking at the market price. Three weeks later, Dow reacquired the same amount of shares from

Garantia at the market price. More than six months later, Dow engaged in another trade. Magma argued that, on these last two occasions, Dow's transactions constituted a sale, and therefore Magma alleged that Dow earned short-swing profits. The district court denied Magma's motion and found in favor of Dow. How do you think the court decided on appeal? Why? [*Magma Power Company v. The Dow Chemical Company,* 136 F.3d 316 (2d Cir. 1998).]

9. Charles Zandford was a securities broker when he convinced William Wood to invest money with him that he would "conservatively" invest. The account would be for Wood and his daughter. Zandford sold shares of the Woods' mutual fund for his own benefit and wrote checks to himself from the Woods' account. Zandford generated the money in the Woods' account by selling securities. Zandford was convicted of 13 counts of wire fraud for the loss of $419,255 belonging to the Woods. The SEC subsequently filed a civil action against Zandford to prevent him from violating securities laws and to recover the gains Zandford had made on the Woods' account. Securities laws do not cover all types of fraud; rather, the laws cover only fraud that is sufficiently connected to a securities transaction. That is, the laws cover fraud that occurred "in the offer or sale of any securities." The district court granted summary judgment for the SEC. Zandford appealed the decision. Did the court of appeals affirm or reverse Zandford's civil conviction? Why? [*Securities and Exchange Commission v. Charles Zandford,* 238 F.3d 559 (2001).]

10. Edward Downe was hired by his close friend, Fred Sullivan, to serve as the director of Kidde, Inc. As a director of Kidde, Downe was kept informed of all financial developments. In the spring of 1987, rumors spread that Kidde was a target for takeover. Sullivan and his board of directors met with two companies, Hanson Trust PLC and Kohlberg Kravis Roberts, to discuss potential buyouts. On August 5, Sullivan announced that Kidde would accept the buyout offer of Hanson Trust PLC. As a result of the merger, Kidde stock increased from a price of $34 dollars in June to a price of $66 dollars on August 6. During the months prior to the merger, Downe and his close friend, Thomas Warde, purchased warrants to buy Kidde shares. For example, after speaking with Sullivan on June 28, Downe called Warde and the two invested over $500,000 in Kidde. Downe and Warde continued to add to their investments as Downe became more informed of the merger. The Securities and Exchange Commission filed a complaint against Warde and Downe, accusing them of insider trading,

a violation of Section 10(b) of the 1934 act. Warde and Downe insisted that their decisions to invest were based on "market savvy, rumor, and public information alone." The U.S. district court found Warde in violation of the Securities and Exchange Act of 1934. How do you think the court decided on appeal? [*SEC v. Warde,* 151 F.3d 42 (1998).]

11. Plaintiff Robert Taylor founded the Better Life Club. Membership cost $39 per year and included a subscription to his newsletter, discounts on seminars, and opportunities to participate in certain "wealth building projects." As a means of raising funds for advertising, Taylor developed the Advertising Club. Members paid money to the club and received a signed note from Taylor promising to repay double the original amount invested within 60 or 90 days. The SEC investigated Taylor and found him in violation of the registration provision of the Securities Act of 1933. Taylor did not register the notes because he did not believe that they qualified as securities. The SEC argued that the notes were investment contracts and therefore securities under the 1933 registration provision. Do you think Taylor's notes were securities under the 1933 act? Why or why not? [*SEC v. Better Life Club of America,* 995 F. Supp. 167 (1998).]

12. Atul Bhagat was an employee of Nvidia Corporation. Nvidia successfully competed for a multimillion-dollar contract to develop the X-Box video game console for Microsoft. Nvidia's CEO sent a companywide e-mail announcing that Nvidia had won the contract. The next morning, Nvidia's CEO sent several follow-up e-mails instructing Nvidia employees to keep the information about the contract confidential and prohibiting them from buying any Nvidia stock for several days. Later that morning, Bhagat purchased a large quantity of Nvidia stock. Four days later, after Nvidia publicly announced the contract with Microsoft, Bhagat sold his stock in the company for a substantial profit. When the SEC brought criminal charges against him for insider trading, Bhagat claimed he had not read the e-mails from Nvidia's CEO prior to making his purchases; thus, he had no insider information when he made his purchase. How do you think the court ruled? Why? [*United States v. Bhagat,* 2006 WL 288129 (2006).]

13. Vencor was a long-term health care provider that derived a large portion of its revenue from Medicare. When President Clinton proposed the Balanced Budget Act of 1997, many in the health care sector were alarmed because the act significantly changed aspects of Medicare. In July 1997, during the time the act was being considered, an internal Vencor memo detailed the act's potential impact on the company. However, the external communications made by Vencor were that earnings and returns would rise, causing some stock analysts to recommend Vencor as a "buy." Vencor did, in its literature, indicate that the effects of the budget act were unable to be assessed at that time and said that there was no guarantee that the act would not have an adverse effect. In October 1997, Vencor lowered its estimates of earnings due to analysis of the budget act, and Vencor's stock price fell from $42 5/8 to $30. Several investors filed a class action lawsuit against Vencor, alleging that Vencor made misleading and false statements about the company's position to raise its stock price. The investors alleged that Vencor had analyzed the budget act impact as early as April 1997 and also that Vencor's executive vice president had made statements in June 1997 acknowledging that the industry would fall on hard times because of cutbacks in Medicare. As well, between July and September 1997, Vencor executives divested themselves of $9.5 million in stock holdings. One executive of Vencor received more than $3 million in profits from his sales, which aroused curiosity in the financial media. The district court granted summary judgment for Vencor, and the court of appeals concluded that the investors had not stated a claim. However, the court of appeals agreed to a rehearing *en banc.* During the rehearing, Vencor maintained that its public statements about the budget act were not actionable because these statements were "soft information" protected by nondisclosure. The court of appeals was deeply divided in its decision. What reasons would the court give to overturn its decision? What reasons would the court give in support of its original decision? [*A. Carl Hedwig et al. v. Vencor, Inc., et al.,* 2001 U.S. App. LEXIS 11236, 2001 Fed. App. 0179P (2001).]

Looking for more review material?

The Online Learning Center at **www.mhhe.com/kubasekess** contains this chapter's "Assignment on the Internet" and also a list of URLs for more information, entitled "On the Internet." Find both of them in the Student Center portion of the OLC, along with quizzes and other helpful materials.

Administrative Law

---➤ **CASE OPENER**

Does the EPA Have an Obligation to Regulate Automobile Emissions?

On October 20, 1999, a group of 19 private organizations filed a rule-making petition asking the Environmental Protection Agency (EPA) to regulate "greenhouse gas emissions from new motor vehicles" under the Clean Air Act.[1] The petitioners cited the fact that 1998 was the "warmest year on record," that greenhouse gas emissions have significantly accelerated climate change, and that carbon dioxide is the most important man-made contribution to climate change. Fifteen months after the petition was filed, the EPA requested public comment on the issues. Then, on September 8, 2003, the EPA entered an order denying the rule-making petition, citing two reasons: (1) The Clean Air Act does not authorize the EPA to issue mandatory regulations to address global climate change; and (2) even if the agency had authority, it would be unwise to do so at this time. The case, *Massachusetts v. EPA*, eventually worked its way up to the U.S. Supreme Court, which had to decide whether the EPA was improperly failing to regulate carbon dioxide gas in automobile exhaust as a climate-changing pollutant.

1. What government entity is the final determiner of whether a particular type of rule will be issued by an agency?
2. Did the EPA err in not regulating greenhouse gases under the Clean Air Act?

[1]*Massachusetts v. EPA*, 549 U.S. 497 (2007).

---➤ **LEARNING OBJECTIVES**

After reading this chapter, you will be able to answer the following questions:

LO 1 What is administrative law?

LO 2 What is an administrative agency?

LO 3 How and why are administrative agencies created?

LO 4 What types of powers do administrative agencies have?

LO 5 What is the difference between an executive agency and an independent agency?

LO 6 What is the Administrative Procedures Act?

LO 7 How do formal, informal, and hybrid rule making differ from one another?

LO 8 What are the limits on agency power?

Introduction to Administrative Law

WHAT IS ADMINISTRATIVE LAW?

LO 1

administrative law
The collection of rules and decisions made by administrative agencies to fill in particular details missing from constitutions and statutes.

As a business owner or manager, you will need to be aware of regulations that affect your business. In addition to learning about laws passed by Congress, you will also need to know about rules passed by administrative agencies. Administrative law consists of the substantive and procedural rules created by administrative agencies (government bodies of the city, county, state, or federal government) involving applications, licenses, permits, available information, hearings, appeals, and decision making.

An administrative agency is generally defined as any body created by the legislative branch (e.g., Congress, a state legislature, or a city council) to carry out specific duties. Agencies have three types of power: *legislative, judicial, and executive.* They may make rules for an entire industry, adjudicate individual cases, and investigate corporate misconduct. Because legislative, judicial, and executive powers have traditionally been placed in separate branches of government by the Constitution, the role of administrative agencies has led some to refer to agencies as the unofficial "fourth branch of government." Although there is a semblance of truth to that characterization, administrative agencies are not in fact another branch, primarily because all their authority is simply delegated to them and they remain under the control of the three traditional branches of government.

LO 2

administrative agencies
Any government body created by the legislative branch (e.g., Congress, a state legislature, or a city council) to carry out specific duties.

Interstate Commerce Commission (ICC)
The first federal administrative agency; created to regulate the anticompetitive conduct of railroads.

The first federal administrative agency, the Interstate Commerce Commission (ICC), was created by Congress near the end of the 19th century. Congress felt that the anticompetitive conduct of railroads could best be controlled by a regulatory body. The ICC no longer exists as a separate agency,[2] but for over 100 years the ICC regulated passenger and freight transportation. Following the crash of the stock market and the Great Depression of the 1930s, Congress saw a need for additional agencies that could assist in guiding market decisions in the public interest. Since then, numerous agencies have been created whenever Congress believed there was an area that required more intense regulation than Congress could provide. In fact, after the Enron scandal there was talk that Congress might create a new agency to regulate the accounting industry. To date, no such agency has materialized.

LO 3

WHY AND HOW ARE AGENCIES CREATED?

When Congress sees a problem that it believes needs regulation, it may create an administrative agency to deal with that problem. The idea is that the agency can be staffed with people who have special expertise in the area the agency is regulating and therefore are capable of knowing what types of regulations are necessary to protect the citizens in that area. Agencies typically act more swiftly than Congress in creating and enacting new laws. Today, administrative agencies actually create more rules than Congress and the courts combined.

enabling legislation
A statute that specifies the name, functions, and specific powers of an administrative agency and grants the agency broad powers for the purpose of serving the public interest, convenience, and necessity.

Administrative agencies are created by Congress through passage of enabling legislation, which is a statute that specifies the name, functions, and specific powers of the administrative agency. Enabling statutes grant agencies broad powers for the purpose of serving the "public interest, convenience, and necessity." These broad powers include rule making, investigation, and adjudication.

[2] The functions of the ICC were transferred to the Transportation Department by Congress as part of a cost-saving measure.

LO 4

Rule Making Enabling statutes permit administrative agencies to issues rules that control individual and business behavior. These rules are, in effect, laws. If an individual or business fails to comply with agency rules, there are often civil, as well as criminal, penalties. Agencies may enact three types of rules: procedural, interpretive, and legislative.

Procedural rules are rules regarding the internal operations of an agency. *Interpretive rules* are rules that explain how the agency views the meaning of the statutes for which the agency has administrative responsibility. Finally, *legislative rules* are policy expressions that have the effect of law. The various rule-making processes are discussed later in this chapter.

Investigation Enabling statutes grant executive power to agencies to investigate potential violations of rules or statutes. Many times, companies cooperate with agencies and voluntarily furnish information. Other times, however, agencies must use their investigative powers, defined in their enabling legislation, to gather information. Such powers typically include the power to issue a subpoena (i.e., an order to appear at a particular time and place and provide testimony) and a subpoena *duces tecum* (i.e., an order to appear and bring specified documents).

Adjudication Enabling statutes delegate judicial power to agencies to settle or adjudicate individual disputes that an agency may have with businesses or individuals. After investigation, the agency holds an administrative hearing before an administrative law judge (ALJ). The ALJ will try to convince the parties to reach a settlement via a consent order, but the judge also has the authority to render a binding decision (order) after a hearing (administrative law matters are heard only by an ALJ, as there is no right to a jury trial in administrative agencies). An appeal to the full commission or the head of an agency may then be filed. That decision may be appealed to the circuit court of appeals. If there are no appeals, the ALJ's initial order becomes the final order. Decisions of ALJs are typically upheld.

Example of an Administrative Problem. The EPA administrator, using the congressional mandate under the Clean Air Act, sets forth rules governing the amount of certain hazardous air pollutants that may be emitted into the atmosphere. Using these standards, another branch of the EPA sends investigators to inspect a plant suspected of violating the act. If the inspector finds a violation and the EPA imposes a penalty, the plant operator will most likely contest the imposition of the fine, and a hearing will be held before an ALJ employed in another division of the EPA. If the matter is not settled at the hearing, the ALJ will preside over another hearing and render a binding order. That order may be appealed within the agency and finally to the federal court. The courts, however, typically defer to the expertise of the agency and the associated ALJ. In other words, most orders by an ALJ are upheld.

Types of Administrative Agencies

Agencies are classified as either executive or independent. The administrative head of an executive agency is appointed by the president with the advice and consent of the U.S. Senate. Executive-agency heads may be discharged by the president at any time, for any reason. When a new president is elected, he will typically place his appointees in charge of executive agencies. These agencies are generally located within the executive branch, under one of the cabinet-level departments. Hence, executive agencies are referred to as *cabinet-level agencies*. Examples of traditional executive agencies are the Federal Aviation Agency (FAA), located within the Department of Transportation, and the Food and Drug Administration (FDA), located within the Department of Health and Human Services.

Independent agencies are governed by a board of commissioners, one of whom is the chair. The president appoints the commissioners of independent agencies with the advice and consent of the Senate, but these commissioners serve fixed terms and cannot be removed except for cause. No more than a simple majority of an independent agency can be members of any single political party (e.g., if the board consists of seven members, no more than four may be from the same political party). Serving fixed terms is said to make the commissioners less accountable to the will of the executive (thus the term *independent* agency). These agencies are generally not

subpoena
An order to appear at a particular time and place and provide testimony.

subpoena *duces tecum*
An order to appear and bring specified documents.

administrative law judge (ALJ)
A judge who presides over an administrative hearing; may attempt to get the parties to settle but has the power to issue a binding decision.

consent order
A statement in which a company agrees to stop disputed behavior but does not admit that it broke the law.

order
A binding decision rendered by a judge.

executive agency
An agency that is typically located within the executive branch, under one of the cabinet-level departments. The agency head is appointed by the president with the advice and consent of the Senate.

independent agency
An agency that is typically not located within a government department. It is governed by a board of commissioners, who are appointed by the president with the advice and consent of the Senate.

Exhibit 23-1

Major Administrative
Agencies

INDEPENDENT AGENCIES	EXECUTIVE AGENCIES
Commodity Futures Trading Commission (CFTC)	Federal Deposit Insurance Corporation (FDIC)
Consumer Product Safety Commission (CPSC)	General Services Administration (GSA)
Equal Employment Opportunity Commission (EEOC)	International Development Corporation Agency (IDCA)
Federal Communications Commission (FCC)	National Aeronautics and Space Administration (NASA)
Federal Trade Commission (FTC)	National Science Foundation (NSF)
National Labor Relations Board (NLRB)	Occupational Safety and Health Administration (OSHA)
Nuclear Regulatory Commission (NRC)	Office of Personnel Management (OPM)
Securities and Exchange Commission (SEC)	Small Business Administration (SBA)
	Veterans Administration (VA)

LO 5

hybrid agencies
An agency that has
characteristics of both
executive and indepen-
dent agencies.

**Administrative Proce-
dures Act (APA)**
Federal legislation that
places limitations on
how agencies are run
and contains very spe-
cific guidelines on rule
making by agencies.

informal rule making
A type of rule making in
which an agency pub-
lishes a proposed rule
in the *Federal Register*,
considers public com-
ments, and then pub-
lishes the final rule.

located within any department. Examples of independent agencies are the Federal Trade Com-
mission (FTC), the Securities and Exchange Commission (SEC), and the Federal Communica-
tions Commission (FCC).

Another difference between these two types of agencies is the scope of their regulatory author-
ity. Executive agencies tend to have responsibility for making rules covering a broad spectrum of
industries and activities. Independent agencies, often called *commissions,* tend to have more narrow
authority over many facets of a particular industry, focusing on such activities as rate making and
licensing. Executive agencies have a tendency to focus more on *social* regulation, whereas indepen-
dent agencies are more often focused on what we refer to as *economic* regulation. Exhibit 23-1 lists
the major administrative agencies.

Some agencies do not fall clearly into one classification or the other. These agencies are typi-
cally referred to as hybrid agencies. Created as one type of agency, the body may share charac-
teristics of the other. The EPA, for example, was created as an independent agency, not located
within any department of the executive branch. Yet it is headed by a single administrator who
serves at the whim of the president. During the early 1990s, in fact, there were discussions of the
need to transform the EPA into a cabinet-level executive agency. (These initiatives did not get
beyond the discussion stage.) Another example is the "independent" Federal Energy Regulation
Commission (FERC), which has the typical structure of an independent agency yet is located
within the Department of Energy.

How Are Agencies Run?

LO 6

In 1946 Congress passed the Administrative Procedures Act (APA) as a major limitation on
how agencies are run. Prior to passage of APA, agencies could decide on their own how to make
rules, conduct investigations, and hold hearings and trials. Under APA, there are very specific
guidelines on rule making by agencies. The two most common types of rule making are *informal*
and *formal,* and there is a third type known as *hybrid.* Each is discussed below, along with a few
exemptions.

INFORMAL RULE MAKING

Federal Register
The government pub-
lication in which an
agency publishes each
proposed rule, along
with an explanation of
the legal authority for
issuing the rule and a
description of how the
public can participate in
the rule-making process,
and later publishes the
final rule.

The primary type of rule making used by administrative agencies is informal rule making, or
notice-and-comment rule making. Informal rule making applies in all situations in which the
agency's enabling legislation or other congressional directives do not require another form. An
agency initiates informal rule making by publishing the proposed rule in the *Federal Register*,
along with an explanation of the legal authority for issuing the rule and a description of how the

Exhibit 23-2

Steps in Informal
Rule Making

1	2	3	4	5
Agency drafts a rule in consultation with interested parties.	Proposed rule is published in the *Federal Register*.	Interested parties can file written comments about the draft within a 30-day period from its publication in the *Federal Register*.	Final draft of the rule is published in the *Federal Register* 30 days before it takes effect. A statement of the purpose of the rule and a cost–benefit analysis must accompany its publication.	Agency receives feedback from interested parties during the 30-day period and makes a determination whether the final draft should be rewritten. If not, it becomes law.

public can participate in the rule-making process. (The *Federal Register* can be accessed online at www.gpoaccess.gov/fr/index.html.)

After publication, opportunity is provided for all interested parties to submit written comments. The comments may contain data, arguments, or other information a person believes might influence the agency in its decision making. Although the agency is not required to hold hearings, it has the discretion to receive oral testimony if it wishes to do so. While the agency is not required to respond to all comments it receives, it is required to respond to comments that significantly concern the proposed rule. After considering the comments, the agency may alter the rule. It publishes the final rule, with a statement of its basis and purpose, in the *Federal Register*. This publication also includes the date on which the rule becomes effective, which must be at least 30 days after publication. Exhibit 23-2 summarizes the steps in the informal rule-making process.

Informal rule making is most often used because it is more efficient for the agency in terms of time and cost. No formal public hearing is required, and no formal record need be established. Some people believe that informal rule making is unfair because parties who are interested in the proposed rule have no idea what types of evidence the agency has received from other sources with respect to that rule. Thus, if the agency is relying on what one party might perceive as flawed or biased data, that party has no way to challenge that data.

FORMAL RULE MAKING

LO 7

The APA requires **formal rule making** when an enabling statute or other legislation requires that all regulations or rules be enacted by an agency as part of a formal hearing process that includes a complete transcript. This procedure is initiated in the same manner as is informal rule making, beginning with publication in the *Federal Register* of a notice of proposed rule making by the agency.

The second step in formal rule making is a public hearing at which witnesses give testimony on the pros and cons of the proposed rule and are subject to cross-examination. An official transcript of the hearing is kept. On the basis of information received at the hearing, the agency makes and publishes formal findings. On the basis of these findings, an agency may or may not promulgate a regulation. If a regulation is adopted, the final rule is published in the *Federal Register*. Because of the expense and time involved in obtaining a formal transcript and record, most enabling statutes do not require a formal rule-making procedure when promulgating regulations. If a statute is drafted in a manner that is at all ambiguous with respect to the type of rule making required, the court will *not* interpret the law as requiring formal rule making.

In the following case, the court must decide whether to require formal rule-making for substantive rules adopted by an agency.

formal rule making
A type of rule making that is used when legislation requires a formal hearing process with a complete transcript; consists of publication of the proposed rule in the *Federal register*, a public hearing, publication of formal findings, and publication of the final rule if adopted.

CASE Nugget

Do Substantive Rules Require Formal Procedure?

Alexis Perez v. John Ashcroft
U.S. District Court for the Northern District of Illinois, Eastern Division

236 F. Supp. 2d 899 (2002)

Perez, a native and citizen of Venezuela, had been a member of the Good Shepherd Church since November 1996. Beginning in December 1996 he had worked as that congregation's music director, a full-time paid position. Under the law, a limited number of visas are available to an immigrant who, among other things, seeks to enter the United States to work for an organization in a professional capacity in a religious vocation or occupation. The Immigration and Naturalization Service (INS) denied Perez's visa application on the basis of his lack of religious training. Perez argued that the INS adopted the requirement of religious training in violation of the Administrative Procedures Act (APA), because it is a substantive rule adopted without the use of notice and comment or other formal rule-making procedures. Perez argued that he met all of the requirements specified by the APA and INS regulations and, further, that the regulations contained no mention of a formal-religious-training requirement. INS countered that its imposition of the formal-training requirement—and its denial of Perez's visa request because he lacked that training—simply represented a reasonable interpretation of the regulations and that Perez's visa application was properly denied because he had no such training. There is no dispute that INS did not engage in any sort of formal rule-making process before adopting the requirement of formal religious training. The INS argued that the formal-training requirement was simply an interpretation of the regulations—more specifically, of the definition of "religious occupation"—and that therefore no formal rule making was necessary. The court disagreed.

All substantive rules adopted by an agency, that is, rules that create law, must be implemented through formal rule-making procedures.

HYBRID RULE MAKING

hybrid rule making
A type of rule making that combines features of formal and informal rule making; consists of publication in the *Federal Register,* a written-comment period, and an informal public hearing with restricted cross-examination.

After agencies began regularly making rules in accordance with the appropriate procedures, the flaws of each type of rule making became increasingly apparent. In response to these problems, a form of hybrid rule making became acceptable to the courts and legislature. Hybrid rule making is an attempt to combine the best features of both formal and informal rule making. The starting point, publication in the *Federal Register,* is the same. Publication is followed by the opportunity for submission of written comments, and then there is an informal public hearing with a more restricted opportunity for cross-examination than that in formal rule making. The publication of the final rule is done in the same manner as it is for other forms of rule making.

EXEMPTED RULE MAKING

interpretive rule
A rule that does not create any new rights or duties but is merely a detailed statement of the agency's interpretation of an existing law, including the actions a party is to take to be in compliance with the law.

The APA contains an exemption from rule making that allows an agency to decide whether public participation will be allowed. Exemptions include rule-making proceedings with regard to "military or foreign affairs" and "agency management or personnel." Exemptions are also granted for rule-making proceedings relating to "public property, loans, grants, benefits or contracts" of an agency. Military and foreign affairs often need speed and secrecy, which are incompatible with public notice and hearings. Other exemptions are becoming more difficult to justify in the eyes of the courts unless they meet one of the exemptions of the Freedom of Information Act (discussed later in this chapter).

Also exempted from the rule-making procedures are interpretive rules and general policy statements. An interpretive rule is a rule that does not create any new rights or duties but is

merely a detailed statement of the agency's interpretation of an existing law. Interpretive rules are generally very detailed, step-by-step statements of what actions a party is to take to be considered in compliance with an existing law. Case 23-1 demonstrates the courts' deference to reasonable agency interpretations of arguably unclear statutes.

CASE 23-1 NATIONAL CABLE & TELECOMMUNICATIONS ASSN. v. GULF POWER CO.
UNITED STATES SUPREME COURT
122 S. Ct. 782 (2002)

FACTS: *The Pole Attachments Act . . . requires the Federal Communications Commission (FCC) to set reasonable rates that can be charged by owners of utility poles, such as telephone and electric poles, for certain attachments to their poles. Under [the act] a "pole attachment" includes "any attachment by a cable television system or provider of telecommunications service" to a utility pole. Some pole-owning utilities challenged, in various Federal Courts of Appeals, an FCC order that interpreted the Act to cover attachments that provided commingled cable television and high-speed Internet services and to cover attachments by wireless telecommunications providers. . . . [T]he United States Court of Appeals for the Eleventh Circuit, in reversing the FCC on both points, held that (1) attachments for commingled services were not covered by either of the Act's two specific rate formulas . . . and (2) attachments for wireless communications were excluded from the Act by negative implication, where 224(a)(1) defined a "utility" as the owner of a pole that was used for wire communications.*

ISSUE: Is the FCC's interpretation of the Pole Attachments Act reasonable and entitled to deference by the federal courts?

REASONING: The Court stated, "The attachments at issue in this suit—ones which provide commingled cable

and Internet service and ones which provide wireless telecommunications—fall within the heartland of the Act." In the Court's reasoning:

> (1) The FCC's assertion of jurisdiction under the Act to regulate rates charged for attachments that provided commingled cable television and high-speed Internet access was reasonable and, therefore, entitled to deference, because the term "any attachment by a cable television system" in 224(a)(4) covered at least those attachments that provided cable television service.
>
> (2) The FCC's assertion of jurisdiction under the Act to regulate rates charged for attachments by wireless telecommunications providers was reasonable and, therefore, entitled to deference, because the term "any attachment by a . . . provider of telecommunications service" covered at least those that provided telecommunications . . .

The agency's decision, therefore, to assert jurisdiction over these attachments is reasonable and entitled to our deference.

DECISION AND REMEDY: On certiorari, the U.S. Supreme Court reversed and remanded.

SIGNIFICANCE OF THE CASE: This case demonstrates the deference of the courts to the interpretations of statutes by administrative agencies.

CRITICAL THINKING

Why is the concept of deference less helpful than it seems at first glance? In other words, does any habit of deference also have its limits?

ETHICAL DECISION MAKING

What values are advanced by a doctrine of deference in this case? What values are downplayed when courts uphold the doctrine of deference?

The following case demonstrates, once again, the deference federal courts give to agency interpretation of ambiguous statutes.

CASE Nugget

What Is the Authority of Agency Interpretation of Statutes?

Warner-Lambert Company v. United States
U.S. Court of Appeals for the Federal Circuit

425 F.3d 1381 (2005)

Warner-Lambert imports and sells lozenges in packages under the name "Halls Defense™ Vitamin C Supplement Drops." The drops are composed primarily of sugar and glucose syrup, which together constitute more than 95 percent of each drop. Vitamin C constitutes just under 2 percent of each drop, with the remaining small percentage consisting of citric acid, flavors, and color. The Customs Service reclassified imported vitamin C supplement drops from their previous duty-free status as medicaments to dutiable status as sugar confectionery. As a result, the drops were subject to a duty of 6.1 percent. Warner-Lambert sued in the Court of International Trade. On appeal, the Customs Service reclassification was upheld. In a six-page detailed letter ruling, Customs explained the reasons for its action, including that its prior classification of the drops was "based upon the belief that Vitamin C imparted therapeutic or prophylactic character to the merchandise" but that "additional research indicates that Vitamin C has not been shown in the U.S. to have substances which imbue it with therapeutic or prophylactic properties or uses." The Court of International Trade held that Customs justifiably concluded that although the merchandise "may possess medical properties, it is being marketed as much for its flavor as for its medicinal value. Thus, it cannot be said that this merchandise is suitable only for medical purposes." The drops are marketed to provide users with their requirement of vitamin C, not to prevent or cure disease.

If a statute is ambiguous and if the implementing agency's construction is reasonable, the federal courts must accept the agency's construction of the statute, even if the agency's reading differs from what the court believes is the best statutory interpretation.

policy statement
A general statement about the directions in which an agency intends to proceed with respect to its rule-making or enforcement activities; has no binding impact on anyone.

Policy statements are general statements about the directions in which an agency intends to proceed with respect to its rule-making or enforcement activities. Again, these statements have no binding impact on anyone; they do not directly affect anyone's legal rights or responsibilities.

A final exemption applies when public notice and comment procedures are "impracticable, unnecessary, or contrary to the public interest." This exemption is used most commonly either when the issue is so trivial that there would probably be very little, if any, public input or when the nature of the rule necessitates immediate action. Whenever an agency chooses to use this exception, it must make a "good-cause" finding and include in its publication of the final rule a statement explaining why there was no public participation in the process.

REGULATED NEGOTIATION

reg-neg
A type of rule making in which representatives of concerned interest groups and of the involved government agency participate in mediated bargaining sessions to reach an agreement, which is forwarded to the agency.

The exceedingly high number of challenges to regulations, as well as a growing belief that structured bargaining among competing interest groups might be the most efficient way to develop rules, has stimulated interest among a number of agencies in a relatively new form of rule making, often referred to as **reg-neg**. Each concerned interest group and the agency itself sends a representative to bargaining sessions led by a mediator. After the parties achieve a consensus, that agreement is forwarded to the agency.

The agency is then expected to publish the compromise as a proposed rule in the *Federal Register* and follow through with the appropriate rule-making procedures. The agency, however, is not bound to do so. If it does not agree with the proposal the group negotiated, the agency is free to try

to promulgate a completely different rule or a modification of the one obtained through the negotiation. The reasoning behind reg-neg is similar to that supporting the increased use of mediation. If the parties can sit down and try to work out a compromise solution together, that solution is much more likely to be accepted than one handed down by some authority. The parties who hammered out the agreement now have a stake in making it work because they helped to create it.

Admittedly, reg-neg is not possible in all situations. If there is an unmanageably large group of interests that would have to be represented, if any possible compromise would have to result from one group's backing away from a fundamental principle, or if two groups feel so antagonistic toward each other that they would be unable to rationally sit down and talk, reg-neg would probably not even be worth trying.

PROBLEMS ASSOCIATED WITH RULE MAKING

Agency employees are not subject to the same political pressures as legislators, but they are also not unbiased. Often the people with the necessary expertise to regulate specific areas come from the industry they are now going to be regulating. There is some concern that it will be difficult for regulators to ignore their past ties to industry and pass regulations that are in the public interest, especially when the regulations would increase costs to the industry or are opposed by the industry for other reasons. When people are discussing an agency in which they perceive this problem as existing, they often refer to the agency as being a "captured" agency. The counterargument is that those who have been deeply involved in an industry know it best.

Regulators must be sensitive to the role the economy plays in the public's willingness to accept or support certain regulations. When the economy is flourishing and unemployment is low, there is much greater acceptance of regulations. When unemployment is high, people are much more reluctant to accept regulations that they believe might cause some workers to lose their jobs and/or cause the prices of products to rise.

OTHER ADMINISTRATIVE ACTIVITIES

Agencies perform a variety of less well known but equally important tasks. These include advising, conducting research, issuing permits, and managing property. One of the most common situations in which individuals come into contact with agencies occurs when an agency advises businesses and individuals on whether the agency considers an activity legal or illegal. Agencies also conduct studies of industries and markets. For example, the FTC, OSHA, and FDA conduct studies to determine, respectively, the level of economic concentration, safety in the workplace, and safety of drugs. Also, agencies provide information to the general public on various matters through hotlines, publications, and seminars. Agencies also devote much of their time to issuing licenses or permits. The EPA, for example, helps protect the environment by requiring certain environmentally sound activities before granting permits. Local agencies are responsible for issuing liquor licenses and cabaret (dancing) permits to local bars and restaurants. Finally, agencies often are responsible for managing government property.

Case 23-2 illustrates limitations on a state agency's use of its powers to issue and, in this case, revoke the license of a real estate broker.

CASE 23-2

DEARBORN v. REAL ESTATE AGENCY
SUPREME COURT OF OREGON
53 P.3d 436 (Sup. Ct. Ore. 2002)

FACTS: *A 16-year-old male runaway was detained by police on drug charges. The youth reported that he had used drugs provided by the broker at the broker's apartment.* *The youth also reported that the broker had engaged in sexual acts while the youth was present and had shown the youth pictures of naked men. The police obtained a*

warrant and went into the broker's apartment. There they found the broker with a man, who told police that the broker had picked him up for the purpose of having sex with him and that the broker had obtained drugs for the man. The broker pleaded guilty to drug charges. The real estate commissioner revoked the broker's real estate license. . . . The Commissioner explained in his order that he was concerned that the broker would "indiscriminately seek sexual liaisons with strangers, who could be juveniles, and entice them with drugs." . . . The Commissioner also suggested that a broker who abuses cocaine and methamphetamine might convert money held in trust for clients to support his or her habit.

ISSUE: May an agency revoke a real estate broker's license on the basis of the broker's drug use and sexual liaisons that are unrelated to the broker's use of his position as a real estate licensee?

REASONING: In the court's own words:

> To be entitled to discipline a licensee, the Commissioner first must be able to show that one or more acts of a licensee violated one or more subsections of ORS 696.301 (1995). Whether this licensee—broker—has committed acts that violate those subsections is a question concerning the meaning and scope of those

subsections. Such an inquiry is a matter of statutory construction . . . we conclude . . . that the reference in subsection (31) to "any act or conduct . . . which constitutes or demonstrates bad faith, incompetence or untrustworthiness, or dishonest, fraudulent or improper dealing" is a reference to conduct that is substantially related to the broker's trustworthiness, competence, honesty, or good faith to engage in real estate activity. . . . As the Commissioner acknowledges in his order, however, there is "no evidence" that broker's criminal activities arose out of broker's "use of his position as a real estate licensee."

. . . [T]he Commissioner's right to discipline must arise out of something that a licensee *has done,* not out of something that a licensee *might do.* So far as this record discloses, none of broker's criminal acts had anything to do with his real estate activities. None involved clients, real estate, or money entrusted to broker. Without such a nexus, the Commissioner could not permissibly conclude that broker had violated ORS 696.301(26) (1995).

DECISION AND REMEDY: The court held that "the Commissioner erred in concluding that broker's drug possession convictions were 'substantially related' to broker's real estate activities."

SIGNIFICANCE OF THE CASE: This case demonstrates the limits on an agency's use of power.

CRITICAL THINKING

The court in this case is seeking a nexus between the criminal acts and the responsibilities of a real estate broker. What additional facts, had they existed, would have provided the link between the responsibilities of a real estate broker and the specific crimes in this case?

ETHICAL DECISION MAKING

What is the central value conflict in this case? What value was the real estate commissioner trying to uphold by his decision?

LO 8 Limitations on Agency Powers

There are four basic limits on agency power: political, statutory, judicial, and informational. The hope is that these limitations will keep the agencies and their thousands of employees from abusing their discretion.

POLITICAL LIMITATIONS

As discussed earlier in this chapter, the president appoints the administrative heads of all executive agencies with the advice and consent of the Senate. If the president is unhappy with the head of such an agency, that person may be fired at any time for any (or no) reason. As such, executive agencies are particularly accountable to the executive branch. Moreover, the political slant (liberal or conservative) of the agency is significantly influenced by the president.

Congress also has significant control over agencies, as the Senate must approve presidential nominees for them to become the administrative heads of agencies. Moreover, Congress has

control over the budgets of all agencies. If Congress decides that a particular agency is not performing as it wishes, that agency's budget may be cut or even defunded. Just prior to the Enron crisis, Congress, after being heavily lobbied by the accounting industry, threatened to defund the Securities and Exchange Commission (SEC). In effect, Congress did not like the SEC's proposal that stock options be charged as earnings. Arthur Levitt, then head of the SEC, heard the warning loud and clear and decided to walk away from his firmly held position. In later interviews, Levitt said it was his biggest regret as head of the SEC.[3]

STATUTORY LIMITATIONS

Congress has the power to create or dissolve an agency. If Congress is unhappy with an agency, it may amend the agency's enabling legislation and limit the agency's power. Moreover, in 1996 legislation was signed into law that gives Congress 60 days to review proposed agency rules. Congress may override those rules before they become effective. In addition, APA (passed by Congress in 1946) sets forth guidelines that all agencies must follow when engaged in rule making.

JUDICIAL LIMITATIONS

Any party (an individual or a business) that believes itself harmed by an administrative rule may challenge that rule in federal court once all administrative procedures are exhausted.[4] This is probably the biggest constraint on agency power. If a rule is subjected to judicial review, the court will consider the following:

1. *The facts of the case:* Courts typically defer to an agency's fact finding. The facts must be supported by **substantial evidence.**

2. *The agency's interpretation of the rule:* Once again, the courts typically defer to the expertise of the agency and uphold the agency's interpretation of the rule.

3. *The scope of the agency's authority:* Has the agency exceeded the authority granted it by its enabling legislation?

> **substantial evidence**
> A reviewing court reviews an agency's reasoning to determine whether it is "arbitrary" or "capricious," or whether it is supported by substantial **evidence.**[5]

While we typically think of judicial limitations as reining in overly zealous administrative regulators, the Case Opener illustrates that sometimes the judiciary is called on to restrict inaction by an agency. In *Massachusetts v. EPA,* the agency had resisted regulating greenhouse gases, arguing that carbon dioxide and similar gases are not pollutants under the Clean Air Act and, therefore, that the agency had no power to regulate them. When the high court reviewed the legislative mandate, however, it held that U.S. motor-vehicle emissions make a "meaningful contribution to greenhouse gas concentrations" and hence to global warming—and therefore the agency did have the authority to regulate such gases as air pollutants under the Clean Air Act. Nevertheless, as of 2008, a year after the Supreme Court's ruling, the EPA was still studying the matter and had not yet issued a regulation.

INFORMATIONAL LIMITATIONS

Agency power is limited by the Freedom of Information Act (FOIA), the Government in Sunshine Act, and the Privacy Act of 1974.

Freedom of Information Act The **Freedom of Information Act (FOIA),** passed in 1966, requires that federal agencies publish in the *Federal Register* places where the public can get information from the agencies. The act requires similar publication of proposed rules and policy statements. It requires that agencies make such items as staff manuals and interpretations of policies available for copying to individuals, on request. Finally, all federal government agencies must publish records electronically.

> **Freedom of Information Act (FOIA)**
> Federal legislation that mandates and facilitates public access to government information and records, including records about oneself. Sensitive information (e.g., on national security) is excluded.

[3] PBS video, *Bigger than Enron—How Greed and Politics Undercut America's Watchdogs,* 1999.

[4] In a few situations, a court may not review an agency action. These include situations involving politically sensitive issues and those in which the agency's enabling legislation prohibits judicial review.

[5] *SEC v. Chenery Corp.,* 318 U.S. 80, 89-93, 87 L. Ed. 626, 63 S. Ct. 454 (1943).

E-Government: Changing the Relationship between the Government and Citizens

According to the United Nations, *e-government,* which is defined as the delivery of government services through digital information technologies, including the Internet, is important because it reduces the cost of government while significantly improving the quality of services and citizen access. According to the latest UN report about this topic, e-government makes public administration more proactive, efficient, transparent, and service-oriented. Annual surveys by the UN have demonstrated significant progress of nations all around the world in e-government development, with the United States and Europe being among the leaders in this development.

The UN has characterized the development of e-government into the following stages:

Stage I—Emerging: A government's online presence is mainly comprised of a Web page and/or an official Web site; links to ministries or departments of education, health, social welfare, labor and finance may/may not exist. Much of the information is static and there is little interaction with citizens.

Stage II—Enhanced: Governments provide more information on public policy and governance. They have created links to archived information that is easily accessible to citizens, as, for instance, documents, forms, reports, laws and regulations, and newsletters.

Stage III—Interactive: Governments deliver online services such as downloadable forms for tax payments and applications for license renewals. In addition, the beginnings of an interactive portal or Web site with services to enhance the convenience of citizens are evident.

Stage IV—Transactional: Governments begin to transform themselves by introducing two-way interactions between "citizen and government." It includes options for paying taxes, applying for ID cards, birth certificates, passports and license renewals, as well as other similar G to C interactions, and allows the citizen to access these services online 24/7. All transactions are conducted online.

Stage V—Connected: Governments transform themselves into a connected entity that responds to the needs of its citizens by developing an integrated back office infrastructure. This is the most sophisticated level of online e-government initiatives and is characterized by:

1. Horizontal connections (among government agencies)
2. Vertical connections (central and local government agencies)
3. Infrastructure connections (interoperability issues)
4. Connections between governments and citizens
5. Connections among stakeholders (government, private sector, academic institutions, NGOs and civil society)

In addition, e-participation and citizen engagement are supported and encouraged by governments in the decision-making process.*

The most recent ranking of nations in terms of their progress toward development of effective e-government was as follows: (1) Sweden; (2) Denmark; (3) Norway; (4) United States; (5) Netherlands; (6) Republic of Korea; (7) Canada ; (8) Australia; (9) France; and (10) United Kingdom.[†] Sadly, the United States was at the top of the list in 2001, but because the Bush administration has failed to make a serious commitment to transforming the federal government through information technology and has failed to develop an overall e-government plan detailing where the government wants to go and how it wants to get there, other nations have made much more rapid progress in this area than has the United States.[‡]

*United Nations, "E-Government Survey 2008," http://unpan1.un.org/intradoc/groups/public/documents/UN/UNPAN028607.pdf.

[†] Ibid., p. 20.

[‡] Robert D. Atkinson (Progressive Policy Institute), "Unsatisfactory Progress: The Bush Administration's Performance on E-Government Initiatives," October 14, 2004, www.ppionline.org/ppi_ci.cfm?knlgAreaID=140&subsecID=290&content.ID=4252960.

Any individual or business may make a FOIA request to a federal government agency. Information may be obtained regarding how the agency gets and spends its money. Statistics and/or information collected by the agency on a given topic is also available. Perhaps most important, citizens are entitled to any records that the government has about them. For example, you could contact the Internal Revenue Service (IRS) and request all information that it has collected about you. FOIA does not apply to Congress, the federal courts, the executive staff of the White House, state or local governments, and private businesses. Exemptions to FOIA include, but are not limited to, national security, internal agency matters (e.g., personnel issues), criminal investigations, financial institutions, and an individual's private life.

Government in Sunshine Act The Government in Sunshine Act requires that agency business meetings be open to the public if the agency is headed by a collegiate body. A *collegiate body* consists of two or more persons, the majority of whom are appointed by the president with the advice and consent of the Senate. This open-meeting requirement applies only when a quorum is present. The law also requires that agencies keep records of closed meetings.

Privacy Act Under the Privacy Act of 1974, a federal agency may not disclose informa-tion about an individual to other agencies or organizations without that individual's written consent.

Federal and State Administrative Agencies

Currently more than 100 federal agencies are in operation, as well as countless state agencies. Often, when there is a federal agency, there are also comparable state agencies to which the fed-eral agency delegates much of its work. For example, the most important federal agency affecting environmental matters is the Environmental Protection Agency. Every state has a state environ-mental protection agency to which the federal EPA delegates primary authority for enforcing environmental protection laws. However, if at any time the state agency fails to enforce these laws, the federal EPA will step in to enforce them.

 SUMMARY

Introduction to Administrative Law	*Administrative law* consists of the substantive and procedural rules created by administrative agencies (government bodies of the city, county, state, or federal government) involving appli-cations, licenses, permits, available information, hearings, appeals, and decision making.
	An *administrative agency* is generally defined as any body created by the legislative branch (e.g., Congress, a state legislature, or a city council) to carry out specific duties.
	Administrative agencies are created by Congress through passage of *enabling legislation,* which is a statute that specifies the name, functions, and specific powers of the administrative agency. Enabling statutes grant agencies broad powers for the purpose of serving the "public interest, convenience, and necessity."
	Administrative law judge: An agency holds an administrative hearing before an ALJ. The ALJ may attempt to get the parties to settle but has the power to issue a binding decision.
Types of Administrative Agencies	*Executive agency:* The administrative head of an executive agency is appointed by the presi-dent with the advice and consent of the U.S. Senate. Executive-agency heads may be dis-charged by the president at any time, for any reason. Executive agencies are generally located within the executive branch, under one of the cabinet-level departments (and thus are referred to as *cabinet-level agencies*). Examples are the Federal Aviation Agency (FAA) and the Food and Drug Administration (FDA).
	Independent agency: Independent agencies are governed by a board of commissioners. The president appoints the commissioners with the advice and consent of the Senate. Commis-sioners serve fixed terms and cannot be removed except for cause. No more than a simple majority of an independent agency can be members of any single political party.
	Hybrid agency: Some agencies do not fall clearly into classification as an independent or an executive agency. These agencies are typically referred to as *hybrid agencies.* Created as one type of agency, the body may share characteristics of the other type. The EPA, for example, was created as an independent agency, not located within any department of the executive branch. Nevertheless, the head of the EPA is appointment by and serves at the pleasure of the President of the United States, which is characteristic of an executive agency.
How Are Agencies Run?	In 1946 Congress passed the *Administrative Procedures Act (APA)* as a major limitation on how agencies are run. Under APA, there are very specific guidelines on rule making by agencies.

- *X Informal rule making:* Under APA, the proposed rule is published in the *Federal Register,* and there is opportunity for public comment.
- *X Formal rule making:* Formal rule making requires that all rules be enacted by an agency as part of a formal hearing process that includes a complete transcript. It begins with a notice of proposed rule making by the agency in the *Federal Register.* Next, there is

a public hearing at which witnesses give testimony on the pros and cons of the proposed rule and are subject to cross-examination. The agency makes and publishes formal findings. If a regulation is adopted, the final rule is published in the *Federal Register*.

- *X Hybrid rule making:* Hybrid rule making is an attempt to combine the best features of formal and informal rule making. The starting point is publication in the *Federal Register,* followed by the opportunity for submission of written comments and then an informal public hearing with a more restricted opportunity for cross-examination than that in formal rule making.

- *X Exempted rule making:* APA contains an exemption from rule making that allows an agency to decide whether public participation will be allowed. Exemptions include rule-making proceedings with regard to "military or foreign affairs," "agency management or personnel," and "public property, loans, grants, benefits or contracts" of an agency.

Interpretive rules are rules that do not create any new rights or duties but are merely a detailed statement of the agency's interpretation of an existing law. They are generally very detailed, step-by-step statements of what actions a party is to take to be considered in compliance with an existing law.

In *reg-neg,* each concerned interest group and the agency itself sends a representative to bargaining sessions led by a mediator. If the parties achieve a consensus, that agreement is forwarded to the agency. The agency is then expected to publish the compromise as a proposed rule in the *Federal Register* and follow through with the appropriate rule-making procedures. If the agency does not agree with the proposal the group negotiated, the agency is free to try to promulgate a completely different rule or a modification of the one obtained through the negotiation.

Limitations on Agency Powers

There are four basic limits on agency power: political, statutory, judicial, and informational.

Freedom of Information Act: FOIA, passed in 1966, requires that federal agencies publish in the *Federal Register* places where the public can get information from the agencies. Any individual or business may make a FOIA request to a federal government agency. Information may be obtained regarding how the agency gets and spends its money; statistics and/or information collected by the agency on a given topic is available; and citizens are entitled to any records that the government has about them. Exemptions to FOIA include, but are not limited to, national security, internal agency matters (e.g., personnel issues), criminal investigations, financial institutions, and an individual's private life.

Government in Sunshine Act: This act requires that agency business meetings be open to the public if the agency is headed by a collegiate body (i.e., two or more persons, the majority of whom are appointed by the president with the advice and consent of the Senate). The law also requires that agencies keep records of closed meetings.

Privacy Act: Under the Privacy Act, a federal agency may not disclose information about an individual to other agencies or organizations without that individual's written consent.

Federal and State Administrative Agencies

Administrative agencies exist at both the state and federal level. For example, in many states, there is a state environmental protection agency that regulates in addition to the federal Environmental Protection Agency.

····▶ Point/Counterpoint

Do Agencies Have Too Much Power?	
YES	NO
The U.S. government is founded on separation of powers. That is why we have three branches of government: executive, legislative, and judicial. Giving administrative agencies all three powers—executive, legislative, and judicial—gives administrative agencies	Administrative agencies came into existence because Congress, as well as state and local governments, did not have the expertise, time, or resources to deal with specialized problems such as air pollution, securities regulation, and banking administration. Without

power to do anything they wish with virtually no oversight. Agencies hire people who formerly worked in industry. As such, these people often view regulation skeptically, yet these are the same people who run the agencies.

administrative agencies, these problems would not be addressed. An agency employs professionals with expertise and experience in the area the agency regulates. These people understand the industry and the ways in which it needs to be regulated.

Questions & Problems

1. How are federal agencies created?

2. Why are agencies created?

3. What are the three main powers given to agencies?

4. List the three categories of agencies.

5. Describe the adjudication process of agencies.

6. Describe the various types of rule making.

7. Greenwood, an OSHA inspector, was driving by a construction site and thought that perhaps the site was unsafe. He got out of his car and videotaped the site, causing the foreman to ask him to leave. Greenwood also took measurements at the site and ultimately filed a report for OSHA violations of construction rules. The company running the construction site was assessed $49,000 in fines for OSHA violations. The company petitioned the court for review of the decision, arguing that an inspection by OSHA without a warrant was a violation of the right to privacy under the Fourth Amendment. How do you think the court decided? Explain your reasoning. [*Lakeland Enterprises of Rhinelander, Inc. v. Chao,* 402 F.3d 739 (7th Cir. 2005).]

8. Invention Submission Corporation (ISC) brought a lawsuit under the Administrative Procedures Act (APA) against James Rogan in his official capacity as undersecretary of commerce for intellectual property and director of the U.S. Patent and Trademark Office (PTO). The PTO started an advertising campaign to warn inventors about invention promotion scams. After a reporter saw the PTO advertisement, he contacted the PTO about a testimonial given in the PTO advertisement. The reporter followed up with a story identifying ISC as the scam promoter. ISC contends that PTO's advertising campaign was both false and unauthorized, targeting ISC in order to penalize it and put it out of business. It argues that the Inventors' Rights Act of 1999 granted the PTO only limited authority to create a forum to publish complaints and responses to them and that the PTO's 2002 advertising campaign directed at ISC went beyond this stated authorization. Therefore, it asserts that the campaign was an illegal agency action and exceeded any statutory authority conferred on the PTO. Was the advertising campaign an illegal agency action? Should the court review PTO's actions? Why or why not? [*Invention Submission Corporation v. Rogan,* 357 F.3d 452 (4th Cir. 2004).]

9. Six conservation organizations filed a petition in Thurston County Superior Court asking that court to hold, pursuant to a provision in the Administrative Procedures Act (APA), that the Washington Forest Practices Board, the Washington Department of Ecology, and the Washington Department of Natural Resources (agencies) "failed to promulgate forest practice rules that advanced the environmental protection purposes and policies of the Forest Practices Act of 1974." The agencies countered by arguing that a formal petition for rule making must precede any petition for judicial review. Must an interest group exhaust administrative remedies before suing in a state or federal court? Why or why not? [*Northwest Ecosystem Alliance v. Washington Forest Practices Board,* 66 P.3d 614 (2003).]

10. Babington and other taxpayers sued both identified and unidentified employees of the Internal Revenue Service (IRS) for alleged violations of federal law. Under the appropriate statutes, a taxpayer who seeks redress because the IRS or its employees allegedly acted in violation of federal law must first file an administrative claim. A civil lawsuit in federal court is barred until such filing occurs. In the case of Babington and other taxpayers, all the administrative claims were to be sent "in writing to the Area Director, Attn: Compliance Technical Support Manager of the area in which the taxpayer currently resides." The taxpayers improperly sent their administrative claims to an agency office in Jacksonville, Florida, and not to the area director for compliance in Atlanta, Georgia. Have the taxpayers exhausted their administrative remedies? Assuming that an IRS employee (improperly) directed the taxpayers to send their administrative claim to the Jacksonville office, have the taxpayers exhausted their administrative remedies? Should the court assert jurisdiction and hear the claim? [*Babington et al. v. Everson et al.,* 2005 U.S. Dist. LEXIS 17571 (Fla. Dist. Ct. 2005).]

11. On January 21, 2003, Robbins filed an application for site plan approval to construct an asphalt plant within the town limits of Hillsborough. Robbins had entered into a contract to purchase the property prior to submitting his application for site plan review, and subsequently he purchased the property. At the time he filed his application, an asphalt plant was a permitted use in a general industrial (GI) district subject to a site plan review. The property on which the asphalt plant was to be constructed was zoned GI. In reliance on the zoning ordinance in effect at the time of his application, Robbins spent approximately $100,000 to engineer and submit a site plan to comply with the conditional-use requirements set forth in the ordinance and to prepare for the required public hearings before the Town of Hillsborough Board of Commissioners. Three public hearings were held. The board received evidence but reached no decision. At the close of the third hearing, the board scheduled a fourth hearing. Prior to the fourth hearing, the board amended the zoning ordinance to temporarily suspend review, consideration, and issuance of permits for manufacturing processes. Robbins's fourth hearing was canceled. Eventually, the suspension became a moratorium on permits until the end of the year. Robbins filed a complaint in Orange County Superior Court, alleging that he was entitled to rely on the language of the zoning ordinance in effect at the time he applied for the permit; that the board violated the law by failing to give notice of a public hearing or hold a public hearing prior to its decision to extend the moratorium; and that the defendant's decision to permanently prohibit asphalt plants was arbitrary and capricious. How should the court decide? Explain your answer. [*Robbins v. Town of Hillsborough*, 625 S.E.2d 813 (N.C. Ct. App. 2006).]

12. Tommy Robinson, a 60-year-old black male employee of the Food Safety and Inspection Service (FSIS), a division of the U.S. Department of Agriculture, alleged that the department discriminated against him on account of his age, sex, and race, in violation of Title VII of the Civil Rights Act of 1964, when it refused to promote him to the position of customer safety officer. The district court concluded that the complaint failed to state a claim for relief and dismissed it because Robinson failed to contact an equal employment opportunity (EEO) counselor and complain about the alleged discrimination. Federal sector employees, such as Robinson, who believe that they have been subject to discrimination, must initiate contact with an EEO counselor within 45 days of the effective date of the personnel action. An agency, however, "shall extend the 45-day time limit in paragraph (a)(1) of this section when the individual shows that . . . he or she did not know and reasonably should not have known that the discriminatory matter or personnel action occurred." In an attempt to get around the limitations bar, Robinson made two arguments: First, he said that he did not learn of the unlawful discrimination until November 15, 2001; and, second, he said that he did not learn that the person who obtained the position was white until sometime after he filed his grievance with the union on October 16, 2001. Robinson failed to make either argument to the district court. On appeal, he argued that the court of appeals should extend the 45-day time limit. How did the court of appeals rule? Why? [*Robinson v. Jojanns, Secretary of Agriculture*, 2005 U.S. App. LEXIS 19561 (11th Cir. Ct. App. 2005).]

13. Harvey is a producer and handler of organic blueberries and other crops, an organic inspector employed by USDA-accredited certifiers, and a consumer of organic foods. He alleged that multiple provisions of the National Organic Program Final Rule were inconsistent with the Organic Foods Production Act of 1990 (OFPA). OFPA is a law passed by Congress to set national standards for organic food. The rule is the secretary of agriculture's interpretation of that law, set forth as a regulation. Harvey alleged that the portions of the rule that permitted synthetic substances to be used in organic foods was inconsistent with the law as set forth in OFPA, which states that no synthetic ingredients may be added during processing or handling. Moreover, the rule allowed dairy animals classified as "organic" to be fed 80 percent organic food for 9 months prior to their sale, while the OFPA standard is 100 percent organic food for 12 months. Must agency interpretations of a statute be consistent with congressional intent? How should the court rule? [*Arthur Harvey v. Ann Veneman, Secretary of Agriculture*, 396 F.3d 28 (1st Cir.Ct. App. 2005).]

Looking for more review material?

The Online Learning Center at **www.mhhe.com/kubasekess** contains this chapter's "Assignment on the Internet" and also a list of URLs for more information, entitled "On the Internet." Find both of them in the Student Center portion of the OLC, along with quizzes and other helpful materials.

Employment and Discrimination Law

Brad Gets Fired from "So Clean!"

Brad has worked in the marketing department of "So Clean!" for the last five years. So Clean is a company that produces household cleaners. Brad is an excellent employee and was recently promoted. Shortly after his promotion, Brad decided to reveal publicly that he is a homosexual. His family and most of his co-workers have been very supportive.

Soon after his promotion and announcement that he is gay, Brad began having problems with his female boss, Jennifer. She began asking Brad questions about his personal life. At first it was small things, such as asking Brad if he was a smoker (he is, though only outside the workplace). Jennifer then began asking Brad very personal questions about his sexuality and told him she did not like weak men. The final straw for Brad occurred when Jennifer announced that she would "cure" his homosexuality and told him to come home with her that night after work or be fired. Jennifer was careful that there were never any witnesses around when she asked Brad personal questions or propositioned him.

Brad refused Jennifer's advances and was fired. He filed an administrative complaint with the Equal Employment Opportunity Commission (EEOC) alleging wrongful termination, retaliation, sexual harassment, and sexual discrimination. Jennifer's response was that she fired Brad because of "creative" differences about how to run the marketing department and because he is a smoker. Jennifer denied Brad's accusations about sexual discrimination and harassment.

1. Can an employer discriminate against an employee because he is gay?
2. What defenses does an employer have to a charge of discrimination?

After reading this chapter, you will be able to answer the following questions:

LO 1 What does it mean to be an at-will employee?

LO 2 What are the federal laws governing employment discrimination?

LO 1

When May an Employee Be Fired?

During the 18th and 19th centuries in the United States, employees had no protection in the workplace. An employee who was injured could be fired. In fact, an employer could fire a worker for no reason at all. This concept came to be known as *at-will employment*.[1] At-will employment applied in all states with no exceptions until 1959.[2]

Today, any employee who is not employed under a contract for a set duration or a collective bargaining agreement[3] is considered to be an at-will employee. This means that the employee may quit at any time for any reason or no reason at all, with no required notice to the employer.[4]

CASE Nugget

What Are the Limits to an At-Will Contract?

Brown v. Sabre, Inc.
Court of Appeals of Texas

173 S.W.3d 581 (Tx. Ct. App. 2005)

Brown was an employee of Sabre. After Sabre was sold to EDS, Brown and 4,000 other at-will employees had a choice of moving to EDS or quitting. Brown moved to EDS. In its handbook, the company reserved the right to alter, amend, modify, or terminate its policies at any time in its sole discretion. Under Sabre's vacation policy, vacation days were earned one year and taken the next year. Brown and others were told that EDS would honor this vacation policy, but then it changed the policy. Brown received pay for half his vacation days but lost the value of the other half of his vacation days. He sued for breach of contract.

The district court rejected Brown's claim, so he appealed. The appellate court affirmed the decision of the district court, holding that any modification of an employee's at-will employment status must be an express, rather than an implied, agreement and that it must be clear and specific. Statements in employee handbooks and policy manuals are general guidelines and do not create implied contracts. Given the disclaimer in the employee handbook, the employer had the right to amend, modify, or terminate the policy at any time.

[1] See *Toussaint v. Blue Cross & Blue Shield of Mich.,* 408 Mich. 579, 600, 292 N.W.2d 880, 885 (1980), for an extended discussion on the at-will rule.

[2] BambooWeb Dictionary, www.bambooweb.com/articles/a/t/At-Will_Employment.html. The first judicial exception to the at-will rule was created in *Peterman v. Intl. Bhd. of Teamsters, Chauffeurs, Warehousemen, and Helpers of Am., Local 396,* 174 Cal. App. 2d 184, 344 P.2d 44 (1959).

[3] Union employees are covered by collective bargaining agreements.

[4] Most employees do give an employer notice before leaving a job as a matter of professional courtesy. Such action, however, is not required under the law.

Exhibit 24-1

Federal Discrimina-
tion Laws

FEDERAL LEGISLATION	PURPOSE
Civil Rights Act of 1964 (CRA)—Title VII (as amended by the Civil Rights Act of 1991)	Protects employees against discrimination based on race, color, religion, national origin, and sex; also prohibits harassment based on the same protected categories.
Pregnancy Discrimination Act of 1987 (PDA)	Amends Title VII of the CRA, expanding the definition of sex discrimination to include discrimination based on pregnancy.
Age Discrimination in Employment Act of 1967 (ADEA)	Prohibits employers from refusing to hire, discharging, or discriminating in terms and conditions of employment on the basis of an employee's or applicant's being age 40 or older.
Americans with Disabilities Act (ADA)	Prohibits discrimination against employees and job applicants with disabilities.
Equal Pay Act of 1963	Prohibits an employer from paying workers of one gender less than the wages paid to employees of the opposite gender for work that requires equal skill, effort, and responsibility.

Similarly, an employer may fire the employee at any time, with no notice, for almost any reason. For example, your employer could decide he doesn't like the color of your shirt and fire you on the spot! The exception to the at-will rule is that an employer may not fire an employee for an illegal reason. What is an illegal reason? Broadly, any termination based on a violation of a state statute, a state constitution, a federal law, the U.S. Constitution, or a public policy is illegal. Exceptions to at-will employment have also been found through breaches of implied contracts with employees that were based on employee handbooks.[5]

Federal Employment Discrimination Laws Governing Employers

LO 2

Employees are protected in the workplace by a number of both federal and state laws. Federal laws apply to everyone in the United States. Federal law may be described as a "minimum" level of protection for all workers. State laws may give employees more, but not less, protection than federal laws. Exhibit 24-1 is an overview of some of the most important federal employment discrimination laws.

Civil Rights Act—Title VII

The Civil Rights Act (CRA) is divided into sections, called *titles*. Title VII of the Civil Rights Act of 1964 deals with discrimination in employment. It prohibits employers from hiring, firing, or otherwise discriminating in terms and conditions of employment, and it prohibits segregating employees in a manner that would affect their employment opportunities on the basis of their race, color, religion, sex, or national origin. There are two ways to prove discrimination under Title VII—disparate treatment and disparate impact.

Title VII of CRA applies to employers who have 15 or more employees for 20 consecutive weeks within one year and who are engaged in a business that affects commerce. The U.S. government, corporations owned by the government, agencies of the District of Columbia, Indian tribes, private clubs, unions, and employment agencies are also covered by Title VII of CRA.

Title VII of the Civil Rights Act of 1964 (CRA)
Federal law (amended by the Civil Rights Act of 1991) that protects employees against discrimination based on race, color, religion, national origin, and sex; also prohibits harassment based on the same protected categories.

[5] "Some challenges and exceptions to at-will employment include: breach of implied contracts through employee handbooks, public policy violations, reliance on an offer of employment, and intentional infliction of emotional distress" (Legal Database, www.legal-database.net/at-will.htm).

DISPARATE-TREATMENT DISCRIMINATION UNDER TITLE VII

disparate treatment
A form of intentional discrimination in which an employee is hired, fired, denied a promotion, or the like, based on membership in a protected class, this is a form of intentional discrimination.

In order to sue for **disparate treatment** under Title VII, the plaintiff must be a member of a protected class as listed in CRA. In other words, the employee must have been discriminated against on the basis of race, color, national origin, religion, or sex (i.e., gender). If the employee has been refused hire, fired, denied a promotion, or the like, based on membership in a protected class, this is a form of intentional discrimination and qualifies the employee to sue for disparate-treatment discrimination. Proving disparate-treatment discrimination in employment under Title VII is a three-step process:

1. Plaintiff (the employee) must demonstrate a prima facie case of discrimination.
2. Defendant (the employer) must articulate a legitimate, nondiscriminatory business reason for the action.
3. Plaintiff (the employee) must show that the reason given by the defendant (the employer) is a mere pretext.[6]

After all the evidence has been presented, the trier of fact (a jury in most cases)[7] must decide whether discrimination has occurred. The burden of proof in a civil case is preponderance of the evidence (i.e., more likely than not). If the jury finds in favor of the plaintiff-employee, damages must be assessed. Damages under Title VII of CRA include up to two years of back pay, compensatory damages, punitive damages (limited in some cases), attorney fees, court costs, court orders (including reinstatement), and remedial seniority. If the jury finds in favor of the defendant-employer, the plaintiff-employee receives nothing.

DISPARATE-IMPACT DISCRIMINATION UNDER TITLE VII

disparate impact
A form of discrimination that arises when an employer's policy or practice appears to apply to everyone equally but its actual effect is that it disproportionately limits employment opportunities for a protected class.

Disparate-impact cases are sometimes called *unintentional-discrimination cases.* While it is very difficult to prove disparate treatment, it is even more difficult to prove disparate impact. Disparate-impact cases arise when a plaintiff attempts to establish that while an employer's policy or practice appears to apply to everyone equally, its actual effect is that it disproportionately limits employment opportunities for a protected class.

The plaintiff proves a case based on disparate impact by first establishing statistically that the rule disproportionately restricts employment opportunities for a protected class. The burden of proof then shifts to the defendant, who can avoid liability by demonstrating that the practice or policy is a business necessity. The plaintiff, at this point, can still recover by proving that the "necessity" was promulgated as a pretext for discrimination.

The initial steps for proving a prima facie case of disparate impact were set forth in *Griggs v. Duke Power Co.*[8] In that case, the employer-defendant required that all applicants have a high school diploma and a successful score on a professionally recognized intelligence test for all jobs except laborer. The stated purpose of these criteria was to upgrade the quality of the workforce.

The plaintiff statistically demonstrated the discriminatory impact by showing that 34 percent of the white males in the state had high school diplomas, whereas only 12 percent of the black males did, and by introducing evidence from an EEOC study showing that 58 percent of the whites, compared to 6 percent of the blacks, had passed tests similar to the one given by the defendant. Because the defendant could not demonstrate any business-related justification for either employment policy, the plaintiff was successful. Requiring a high IQ or high school or college diploma may be necessary for some jobs but not for all jobs at Duke Power.

LO 3

sexual harassment
Unwelcome sexual advances, requests for sexual favors, and other verbal or physical conduct of a sexual nature that makes submission a condition of employment or a factor in employment decisions or that creates an intimidating, hostile, or offensive work environment. The two types are hostile environment and *quid pro quo.*

SEXUAL HARASSMENT UNDER TITLE VII

Harassment first developed in the context of discrimination based on sex, and it evolved to become applicable to other protected classes. The definition of **sexual harassment** stated in the Equal Employment Opportunity Commission (EEOC) guidelines and accepted by the U.S.

[6] *McDonnell Douglas v. Green,* 411 U.S. 792, 802 (1973).
[7] In a bench trial, the judge becomes the trier of fact as no jury is impaneled. A discrimination case could also be decided by a judge on motion for summary judgment.
[8] *Griggs v. Duke Power,* 401 U.S. 424 (1971).

Supreme Court is "unwelcome sexual advances, requests for sexual favors, and other verbal or physical conduct of a sexual nature" that implicitly or explicitly makes submission a term or condition of employment; makes employment decisions related to the individual dependent on submission to or rejection of such conduct; or has the purpose or effect of creating an intimidating, hostile, or offensive work environment. In the Case Opener, did the actions of Jennifer create a sexually hostile environment for Brad?

Two distinct forms of sexual harassment are recognized. The first, and generally easiest to prove, is *quid pro quo,* which occurs when a supervisor makes a sexual demand on someone and this demand is reasonably perceived as a term or condition of employment. The second form of sexual harassment involves the creation of a hostile work environment. Case 24-1 demonstrates the standard used by the U.S. Supreme Court to determine whether an employer's conduct has created a hostile work environment.

TERESA HARRIS v. FORKLIFT SYSTEMS, INC.
UNITED STATES SUPREME COURT
510 U.S.17, 114 S. Ct. 367 (1994)

FACTS: *During her tenure as a manager at defendant Forklift Systems, Inc., plaintiff Harris was repeatedly insulted by the defendant's president because of her gender and subjected to sexual innuendos. In front of other employees, the president frequently told Harris, "You're just a woman, what do you know?" He sometimes asked Harris and other female employees to remove coins from his pockets and made suggestive comments about their clothes. He suggested to Harris in front of others that they negotiate her salary at the Holiday Inn. When Harris complained, he said that he that would stop, but he continued behaving in the same manner, so Harris quit. She then filed an action against the defendant for creating an abusive work environment on the basis of her gender. The district court found in favor of the defendant, holding that some of the comments were offensive to the plaintiff but were not so serious as to severely affect Harris's psychological well-being or interfere with her work performance. The court of appeals affirmed. Plaintiff Harris appealed to the U.S. Supreme Court.*

ISSUE: Must an employee suffer serious psychological damage in order to pursue damages for a claim of sexual harassment?

REASONING: In the court's own words:

> As we made clear in *Meritor Savings Bank* v. *Vinson,* this language [of Title VII] "is not limited to 'economic' or 'tangible' discrimination. The phrase 'terms, conditions, or privileges of employment' evinces a congressional intent 'to strike at the entire spectrum of disparate treatment of men and women' in employment," which includes requiring people to work in

a discriminatorily hostile or abusive environment. When the workplace is permeated with "discriminatory intimidation, ridicule, and insult," that is "sufficiently severe or pervasive to alter the conditions of the victim's employment and create an abusive working environment."

This standard, which we reaffirm today, takes a middle path between making actionable any conduct that is merely offensive and requiring the conduct to cause a tangible psychological injury. As we pointed out in *Meritor,* "mere utterance of an . . . epithet which engenders offensive feelings in a employee," does not sufficiently affect conditions of employment to implicate Title VII. . . . Likewise, if the victim does not subjectively perceive the environment to be abusive, the conduct has not actually altered the conditions of the victim's employment, and there is no Title VII violation.

But Title VII comes into play before the harassing conduct leads to a nervous breakdown. A discriminatorily abusive work environment, even one that does not seriously affect employees' psychological well-being, can and often will detract from employees' job performance, discourage employees from remaining on the job, or keep them from advancing in their careers. Moreover, even without regard to these tangible effects, the very fact that the discriminatory conduct was so severe or pervasive that it created a work environment abusive to employees because of their race, gender, religion, or national origin offends Title VII's broad rule of workplace equality. The appalling conduct alleged in *Meritor,* and the reference in that case to environments "so heavily polluted with discrimination as to destroy completely the emotional and psychological stability of minority group workers," merely present some

especially egregious examples of harassment. They do not mark the boundary of what is actionable.

. . . Certainly Title VII bars conduct that would seriously affect a reasonable person's psychological well-being, but the statute is not limited to such conduct. So long as the environment would reasonably be perceived, and is perceived, as hostile or abusive, there is no need for it also to be psychologically injurious.

This is not, and by its nature cannot be, a mathematically precise test. But we can say that whether an environment is "hostile" or "abusive" can be determined only by looking at all the circumstances. These may include the frequency of the discriminatory conduct; its severity; whether it is physically threatening or humiliating, or a mere offensive utterance; and whether it unreasonably interferes with an employee's work performance. The effect on the employee's psychological well-being is, of course, relevant to determining whether the plaintiff actually found the environment abusive. But while psychological harm, like any other relevant factor, may be taken into account, no single factor is required.

DECISION AND REMEDY: The lower court's decision was reversed and remanded, in favor of the plaintiff.

SIGNIFICANCE: In this case, the Supreme Court for the first time held that harassment in and of itself is illegal and actionable, regardless of the amount of damage to the victim.

CRITICAL THINKING

Identify the Court's reasons for its finding. Do you think these reasons were sufficient to overturn the previous ruling? Why or why not?

ETHICAL DECISION MAKING

Imagine that the judge is operating under a duty-based system of ethics. What duty is she advocating in terms of employer–employee relationships? Would this ruling serve well as a universal standard?

Same-Sex Harassment—The Supreme Court Speaks Initially, same-sex harassment was not covered under CRA. By 1997, however, the courts were split on the issue. This issue was resolved in 1998 in *Oncale v. Sundowner Offshore Services, Inc.*[9] Oncale, a male, was forcibly subjected to sex-related, humiliating actions against him by other male employees. He was physically sexually assaulted and threatened with rape. He complained, to no avail, so he filed a lawsuit alleging discrimination based on sex. The district court granted a motion for summary judgment for the defendant employer, holding that a male had no cause of action under Title VII for harassment by male co-workers. The case was appealed to the U.S. Supreme Court, which concluded that sex discrimination consisting of same-sex sexual harassment is actionable under Title VII. The Court reversed the appellate court's order and remanded the case for further proceedings.

Harassment by Nonemployees under Title VII Employers may be held liable for harassment of their employees by nonemployees under very limited circumstances. If an employer knows that a customer repeatedly harasses an employee yet the employer does nothing to remedy the situation, the employer may be liable. For example, in *Lockhard v. Pizza Hut, Inc.,*[10] the franchise was held liable for the harassment of a waitress by two male customers because no steps had been taken to prevent the harassment.

HARASSMENT OF OTHER PROTECTED CLASSES UNDER TITLE VII

Hostile-environment issues have also been used in cases of discrimination based on religion and race. For example, in a 1986 case, *Snell v. Suffolk County,*[11] Hispanic and black corrections

[9] 523 U.S. 75, 118 S. Ct. 998 (1998).
[10] 162 F.3d 1062 (10th Cir. 1998).
[11] 782 F.2d 1094 (1986).

workers demonstrated that a hostile work environment existed by proving that they had been subjected to continuing verbal abuse and racial harassment by co-workers and that the county sheriff's department had done nothing to prevent the abuse. The white employees had continually used racial epithets and posted racially offensive materials on bulletin boards, such as a picture of a black man with a noose around his neck, cartoons favorably portraying the Ku Klux Klan, and a "black officers' study guide," consisting of children's puzzles. White officers once dressed a Hispanic inmate in a straw hat, sheet, and sign that said "spic." Such activities were found by the court to constitute a hostile work environment.

PREGNANCY DISCRIMINATION ACT OF 1987— AN AMENDMENT TO TITLE VII

In 1987, Title VII was amended by the Pregnancy Discrimination Act (PDA). This law expanded the definition of discrimination based on gender to include discrimination based on pregnancy. "Discrimination on the basis of pregnancy, childbirth or related medical conditions constitutes unlawful sex discrimination under Title VII."[12] Under the act, temporary disability caused by pregnancy must be treated the same as any other temporary disability.

DEFENSES TO CLAIMS UNDER TITLE VII

As a business owner or manager, how would you respond if one of your employees filed a lawsuit under Title VII? Are there any legal exceptions for discriminating against a protected class? The answer, surprising to many business owners and managers, is yes. The three most important defenses available to defendants in Title VII cases are the bona fide occupational qualification, merit, and seniority system defenses. These defenses are raised by the defendant after the plaintiff has established a prima facie case of discrimination based on either disparate treatment or disparate impact. They would obviously not be applicable to a claim based on harassment.

The Bona Fide Occupational Qualification Defense The bona fide occupational qualification (BFOQ) defense allows an employer to discriminate in hiring on the basis of sex, religion, or national origin (but not race or color) when doing so is necessary for the performance of the job. Necessity must be based on actual qualifications, not stereotypes about one group's abilities. For example, being a male cannot be a BFOQ for a job simply because it is a dirty job, although there may be a valid requirement that an applicant be able to lift a certain amount of weight if such lifting is a part of the job. Conversely, being a female may be a BFOQ for modeling female clothing. An employer would not be required or expected to hire a male for such a job. Employer arguments about inconvenience to the employer, such as having to provide two sets of restroom facilities, have not been persuasive in the courts. Nor have customer preferences to be served by a particular gender or nationality. The only exception to customer preference is sexual privacy (e.g., female restroom attendants in the women's restroom and male attendants in the men's room).[13]

The Merit Defense The merit defense is usually raised when hiring or promotion decisions are partially based on test scores. Professionally developed ability tests that are not designed, intended, or used to discriminate may be used. While these tests may have an adverse impact on a class, as long as they are manifestly related to job performance, they do not violate the act. Since 1978, the "Uniform Guidelines on Employee Selection Procedures" (UGESP) have guided government agencies charged with enforcing civil rights, and they provide guidance to employers and other interested persons about when ability tests are valid and job-related. Under these guidelines, tests must be validated in accordance with standards established by the American Psychological Association.

Three types of validation are acceptable: (1) *criterion-related validity*, which is the statistical relationship between test scores and objective criteria of job performance; (2) *content validity*, which

[12] EEOC, "Facts about Pregnancy Discrimination," www.eeoc.gov/facts/fs-preg.html.
[13] *In the Matter of the Accusation of the Department of Fair Employment and Housing v. San Luis Obispo Coastal Unified School District, Respondent;. Marlene Anne Mendes, Complainant,* Case No. E95-96 L-0725-00s, 98-14 (October 7, 1998). See www.dfeh.ca.gov/PrecedentialD/1998-14.html.

CONNECTING to the Core

isolates some skill used on the job and directly tests that skill; and (3) *construct validity,* wherein a psychological trait needed to perform the job is measured. A test that required a word processor to use a computer would be content-valid. A test of patience for a teacher would be construct-valid.

The Seniority System Defense A bona fide seniority system is a legal defense under Title VII. Even though a seniority system, in which employees are given preferential treatment based on their length of service, may perpetuate past discrimination, such systems are considered bona fide and are thus not illegal if (1) the system applies equally to all persons; (2) the seniority units follow industry practices; (3) the seniority system did not have its genesis in discrimination; and (4) the system is maintained free of any illegal discriminatory purpose.

REMEDIES UNDER TITLE VII

A plaintiff may seek both equitable and legal remedies for violations of Title VII. Courts have ordered parties to engage in diverse activities ranging from publicizing their commitment to minority hiring to establishing special training programs for minorities. A successful plaintiff may recover back pay for up to two years from the time of the discriminatory act.

A plaintiff who was not hired for a job because of a Title VII violation may also receive remedial seniority dating back to the time when the plaintiff was discriminated against; compensatory damages, including those for pain and suffering; and in some cases, punitive damages.

In cases based on discrimination other than race, however, punitive damages are capped at $300,000 for employers of more than 500 employees, $100,000 for firms with 101 to 200 employees, and $50,000 for firms with 100 or fewer employees. An employer will not be held vicariously liable for punitive damages as long as it made "good-faith efforts" to comply with federal law.

Attorney fees may be awarded to a successful plaintiff in Title VII cases. They are typically denied only when special circumstances would render the award unjust. If it is determined that the plaintiff's action was frivolous, unreasonable, or without foundation, the courts may award attorney fees to the prevailing defendant. For more information on Title VII, visit the EEOC Web site at www.eeoc.gov.

PROCEDURE FOR FILING A CLAIM UNDER TITLE VII

Filing a claim under Title VII is much more complicated than simply filing a lawsuit. Failure to follow the proper procedures within the strict time framework may result in a plaintiff's losing his or her right to file a lawsuit under Title VII.

The first step in initiating a Title VII action is the aggrieved party's filing of a charge with the state Equal Opportunity Commission or, if no such agency exists, the federal EEOC. A *charge* is a sworn statement that states the name of the charging party, the name(s) of the defendant(s), and the nature of the discriminatory act.

Within 10 days of receiving the charge, the EEOC must notify the alleged violator of the charge. Then the EEOC investigates the matter to determine whether there is "reasonable cause" to believe that a violation has occurred. If the EEOC does find such reasonable cause, it attempts to eliminate the discriminatory practice through conciliation, that is, by trying to negotiate a settlement between the two parties. If unsuccessful, the EEOC *may* file suit against the alleged discriminator in federal district court. Failure to file suit does not necessarily mean that the EEOC thinks the plaintiff does not have a valid claim; the EEOC may simply feel that the claim is not the type it wishes to use its limited resources on pursuing.

If the EEOC decides not to sue, it notifies the plaintiff of his or her right to file an action and issues the plaintiff a *right-to-sue letter,* which is not intended to be anything other than a statement that the plaintiff has followed the proper initial procedures and therefore may file a lawsuit. The plaintiff must have this letter in order to file a private action.

Age Discrimination in Employment Act of 1967

LO 4

The Age Discrimination in Employment Act of 1967 (ADEA) was enacted to prohibit employers from refusing to hire, discharging, or discriminating in terms and conditions of employment against employees or applicants age 40 or older. The language describing the prohibited conduct is virtually the same as that of Title VII, except that age is the prohibited basis for discrimination. ADEA applies to employers having 20 or more employees.

Americans with Disabilities Act

The goal of the Americans with Disabilities Act (ADA) is preventing employers from discriminating against employees and applicants with disabilities. ADA attempts to attain this objective by requiring that employers make reasonable accommodations to the known physical or mental disabilities of an otherwise-qualified person with a disability unless the necessary accommodation would impose an undue burden on the employer's business.

> When the ADA was before Congress, some members predicted a flood of lawsuits that would bankrupt or at least overburden business. . . . Studies have shown, however, that businesses have adapted to the ADA much more easily—and inexpensively—than the doomsayers predicted. . . . Law Professor Peter Blanck of the University of Iowa has studied business compliance with the ADA, including Sears Roebuck and many other large businesses, and found that compliance was often as easy as raising or lowering a desk, installing a ramp, or modifying a dress code. Another survey found that three-quarters of all changes cost less than $100. Moreover, the predicted flood of lawsuits proved to be imaginary. Almost 90 percent of the cases brought before the Equal Employment Opportunity Commission are thrown out. And only about 650 lawsuits were filed in the ADA's first five years—a small number compared to 6 million businesses, 666,000 public and private employers, and 80,000 units of state and local governments that must comply. The American Bar Association recently conducted a survey and learned that, of the cases that actually go to court, 98 percent are decided in favor of the defendants, usually businesses.[14]

ADA is enforced by the EEOC in the same way that Title VII is enforced. To bring a successful claim under ADA, the plaintiff must show that he or she meets all of the following:

- Had a disability.
- Was otherwise qualified for the job.
- Was excluded from the job solely because of that disability.

Age Discrimination in Employment Act of 1967 (ADEA)
Federal law that prohibits employers from refusing to hire, discharging, or discriminating in terms and conditions of employment on the basis of an employee's or applicant's being age 40 or older.

Americans with Disabilities Act (ADA)
Federal law that prohibits discrimination against employees and job applicants with disabilities.

[14] Center for an Accessible Society, "Disability Issues Information for Journalists," www.accessiblesociety.org/topics/ada.

Remedies for ADA violations are similar to those available under Title VII. A successful plaintiff may recover reinstatement, back pay, and injunctive relief. In cases of intentional discrimination, limited compensatory and punitive damages are also available. An employer who has repeatedly violated the act may be subject to fines of up to $100,000.

Discrimination Based on Sexual Orientation—Actionable?

There is currently no federal legislation that prohibits discrimination based on sexual orientation. However, state laws prohibiting such discrimination exist in 17 states.

What do these laws mean to Brad, the employee in our Case Opener? It depends on where Brad lives. If Brad lives in Texas and is fired for being gay, he has absolutely no legal rights and cannot sue his employer. Conversely, if Brad lives in California, he may sue Jennifer and So Clean, his employer, for discrimination based on sexual orientation. In California and a handful of other states, discriminating in terms of employment (i.e., failure to hire, firing, failure to promote) based on a person's sexual orientation is prohibited.

CASE Nugget

What Are the Elements of Sexual Orientation Discrimination?

Hope v. California Youth Authority
COURT OF APPEAL OF CALIFORNIA

134 Cal. App. 4th 577 (2005)

Hope got a job as a cook at a California Youth Authority (CYA) facility. Not long after he began working there, his supervisors starting calling him derogatory names based on his sexual orientation. Moreover, all cooks, including Hope, were entitled to have "wards" (those incarcerated at the facility) give them substantial assistance with their jobs, but Hope was stripped of his wards and forced to work alone. One of Hope's supervisors would take trash and throw it into the areas that Hope had just cleaned. When wards at the facility got physically dangerous toward Hope, he would fill out reports and turn them in to his supervisor. The supervisor would tear up the reports in front of the wards. Hope sued the CYA under California's Fair Employment and Housing Act (FEHA) for discrimination based on sexual orientation, retaliation, and harassment. A jury awarded Hope almost $2 million in damages. CYA appealed.

The appellate court concluded that substantial evidence supported the jury's determinations that Hope was subjected to harassment because of his sexual orientation, the harassment was sufficiently severe or pervasive, Hope's superiors either knew or should have known about the harassment and its cause, and Hope's supervisor did not take immediate and corrective action to stop the harassment.

May an Employer Discriminate against a Smoker?

In the Case Opener, Jennifer discovered that Brad was a smoker. Later, she fired him. One of Jennifer's given reasons for terminating Brad's employment was that he was a smoker. May Jennifer and So Clean legally fire an employee for smoking outside the workplace? The answer is, – "It depends!"

A recent trend has been for employers to consider a potential employee's lifestyle when deciding whether to hire that person. Employers argue that smokers have higher health care costs and miss more work, lowering productivity.

> The Centers for Disease Control and Prevention estimated that $75 billion is spent annually on medical expenses attributed to smoking. Businesses lose $82 billion in lost productivity from smokers. And smokers take about 6.5 more sick days a year than nonsmokers. About one in five Americans—or 46 million people—smoke.[15]

As a result, some companies either won't hire smokers or are threatening to fire current employees who will not or are unable to quit smoking. In 2005, Michigan-based Weyco, Inc., announced that it would terminate all workers who did not stop smoking.[16] Many states have passed laws preventing companies from engaging in such action.

> Michigan, with 1.9 million smokers and one of the highest cigarette taxes in the nation, has no "smoker's rights law" found in 29 other states, so there isn't much that employees can do. Weyco terminated four of its employees this month after they refused to submit to a smoking breath test in light of the company's new policy that bans tobacco use among its 200 employees during work and even when they are off the clock. "We are saying people can smoke if they choose to smoke. That's their choice," said Gary Climes, Weyco's chief financial officer. "But they just can't work for us."[17]

If Brad works in Michigan, Jennifer and So Clean may legally terminate him for smoking outside the workplace. Conversely, if Brad works in any of the 29 states with "smoker's rights laws," he could not be legally terminated for smoking outside the workplace. Finally, employers should be aware that giving breaks on health care plans to employees who are nonsmokers could be in violation of a "smoker's rights law."

Equal Pay Act of 1963

LO 5

While we generally think of Title VII as being the primary means of protecting women from discrimination, an earlier law actually was designed specifically to protect women from wage discrimination: the Equal Pay Act of 1963 (EPA). When EPA was passed, the average wages of women were less than 60 percent of those of men. The primary purpose of the law was to eliminate situations in which women, working alongside men or replacing men, would be paid lower wages for doing substantially the same job. EPA prohibits any employer from discriminating within any "establishment . . . between employees on the basis of sex by paying wages to employees in such establishment at a rate less than the rate at which he pays wages to employees of the opposite sex . . . for equal work on jobs the performance of which requires equal skill, effort, and responsibility, and which are performed under similar working conditions, except where payment is made pursuant to (i) a seniority system; (ii) a merit system; (iii) a system which measures earnings by quantity or quality of production; or (iv) differential based on any factor other than sex."[18]

Equal Pay Act of 1963 (EPA)
Federal law that prohibits an employer from paying workers of one gender less than the wages paid to employees of the opposite gender for work that requires equal skill, effort, and responsibility.

Additional Laws Governing the Employment Relationship

There are several major categories of state and federal laws that cover employee rights with regard to wages, benefits, and health and safety standards. Exhibit 24-2 lists significant state and federal legislation protecting employees.

FAIR LABOR STANDARDS ACT

The Fair Labor Standards Act (FLSA) requires that a minimum wage of a specified amount be paid to all employees in covered industries. The specified amount is periodically raised by Congress to compensate for increases in the cost of living caused by inflation. The most recent

Fair Labor Standards Act (FLSA)
Federal law that requires that a minimum wage of a specified amount be paid to all employees in covered industries; also mandates that employees who work more than 40 hours in a week be paid no less than 1½ times their regular wage for all hours beyond 40 worked in a given week.

[15] "Workers Fume as Firms Ban Smoking at Home," www.detnews.com/2005/business/0501/27/A01-71823.htm.
[16] Ibid.
[17] Ibid.
[18] 29 U.S.C. § 206(d)1.

Exhibit 24-2

Significant Laws
Governing the
Employment
Relationship

LAW	IMPACT
Wage and hour laws	Federal and state laws that impose minimum wage and hour requirements for employees
Family and Medical Leave Act (FMLA)	Federal act requiring that certain employers establish a policy that provides all eligible employees with up to 12 weeks of unpaid leave during any 12-month period for several family-related occurrences (e.g., birth of a child, care of sick spouse)
Unemployment compensation	State system, created by the Federal Unemployment Tax Act (FUTA), that provides unemployment compensation to qualified employees who lose their jobs
Workers' compensation laws	State laws that provide for financial compensation to employees or their dependents when a covered employee is injured on the job
Consolidated Omnibus Budget Reconciliation Act (COBRA)	Federal law that ensures that when employees lose their jobs or have their hours reduced to a level at which they would not be eligible to receive medical, dental, or optical benefits from their employer, the employees will be able to continue receiving benefits under the employers' policy for up to 18 months by paying the premiums for the policy
Employee Retirement Income Security Act (ERISA)	Federal law that sets minimum standards for most voluntarily established pension and health plans in private industry to provide protection for individuals in these plans. HIPAA and COBRA are amendments to ERISA
Occupational Safety and Health Act of 1970 (OSHA)	Federal law that established the Occupational Safety and Health Administration, the agency responsible for setting safety standards under the act, as well as enforcing the act through inspections and the levying of fines against violators

increase took effect on May 26, 2007, increasing from $5.15 to $5.85 per hour. By the summer of 2009, the federal minimum wage will be $7.25. This is the first increase in almost 10 years.

FLSA mandates that employees who work more than 40 hours in a week be paid no less than one and one half times their regular wage for all the hours beyond 40 that they work during a given week. Four categories of employees are excluded:

- Executives
- Administrative employees
- Professional employees
- Outside salespersons

FAMILY AND MEDICAL LEAVE ACT

Family and Medical Leave Act (FMLA)

Federal act requiring that employers provide all eligible employees with up to 12 weeks of leave during any 12-month period for several family-related occurrences (e.g., birth of a child, care of a sick spouse).

When the **Family and Medical Leave Act (FMLA)** went into effect in 1993, it was hailed by its supporters as a "breakthrough" in American law and feared by its opponents as an unwieldy encumbrance on business. FMLA covers all public employers, as well as private employers with 50 or more employees. It guarantees all eligible employees (those who have worked at least 25 hours a week for each of 12 months prior to the leave) up to 12 weeks of *unpaid* leave during any 12-month period for any of the following family-related occurrences:

- The birth of a child.
- The adoption of a child.
- The placement of a foster child in the employee's care.
- The care of a seriously ill spouse, parent, or child.
- A serious health condition that renders the employee unable to perform any of the essential functions of his or her job.

Parental Leave in the United Kingdom

Benefits are relative. Many in the United Kingdom compare their benefits to those of parents in France and feel they receive inadequate benefits; but in comparison to what parents in the United States receive, parents, especially mothers, in the United Kingdom are treated quite well. Women are entitled to 26 weeks off, regardless of how long they have worked for their employer. Statutory maternity pay (SMP) is paid for 36 weeks. For the first six weeks SMP is paid at 90 percent of average earnings, and for the remaining 30 weeks SMP is £108 a week or 90 percent of average weekly earnings if this is less.

Women can take another 26 weeks of additional maternity leave if they have completed 26 weeks' continuous service with their employer by the beginning of the fourteenth week before their expected week of childbirth. This leave is unpaid, but many employers provide some financial compensation during this period.

Fathers are entitled to two weeks' paid paternity leave that may be taken any time from the date of birth to eight weeks from the birth. Fathers get statutory paternity pay (SPP) of £108 a week or 90 percent of their average weekly earnings, whichever is less, for the two weeks.

UNEMPLOYMENT COMPENSATION

While FMLA in some cases helps employees retain their jobs, what happens if they lose their jobs? The Federal Unemployment Tax Act (FUTA),[19] passed in 1935, created a state system to provide unemployment compensation to qualified employees who lose their jobs. Under this law, employers pay taxes to the states, which deposit the money into the federal government's Unemployment Insurance Fund. Each state has an account from which it can access the money in the fund in accordance with the rules the state establishes for eligibility. States have different minimum standards for qualifying for unemployment compensation, although almost all states require that the applicant did not voluntarily quit or get fired for cause.

unemployment compensation
A state system, created by the Federal Unemployment Tax Act (FUTA), that provides unemployment compensation to qualified employees who lose their jobs.

WORKERS' COMPENSATION LAWS

Unlike many other laws affecting the employment relationship, workers' compensation legislation is purely state law. Our coverage of this topic must therefore be rather generalized. Prudent businesspeople will familiarize themselves with the workers' compensation statutes of the states within which their companies operate.

Workers' compensation laws ensure that covered workers who are injured on the job can receive financial compensation through an administrative procedure, rather than having to sue their employer. For administrative convenience, most states exclude certain types of businesses and small firms from coverage. Some states also allow businesses that have sufficient resources to be self-insured, rather than participating in the state program.

workers' compensation laws
State laws that provide for financial compensation to employees or their dependents when a covered employee is injured on the job.

CONSOLIDATED OMNIBUS BUDGET RECONCILIATION ACT OF 1985

The Consolidated Omnibus Budget Reconciliation Act (COBRA) ensures that employees who lose their jobs or have their hours reduced to a level at which they are no longer eligible to receive medical, dental, or optical benefits can pay to continue receiving benefits for themselves and their dependents under the employer's policy. The employee must pay the premiums for the policy, plus up to a 2 percent administration fee, to maintain the coverage for up to 18 months, or 29 months for a disabled worker. This is often quite expensive. An employee has 60 days after coverage would ordinarily terminate to decide whether to maintain the coverage.

This obligation does *not* arise under either of two conditions:

1. The employee is fired for gross misconduct.
2. The employer decides to eliminate benefits for all current employees.

Consolidated Omnibus Budget Reconciliation Act (COBRA)
Federal law that ensures that when employees lose their jobs or have their hours reduced to a level at which they would not be eligible to receive medical, dental, or optical benefits from their employer, the employees will be able to continue receiving benefits under the employer's policy for up to 18 months by paying the premiums for the policy.

[19] 26 U.S.C. § § 3301–3310.

EMPLOYEE RETIREMENT INCOME SECURITY ACT OF 1974

Employee Retirement Income Security Act (ERISA)
Federal law that sets minimum standards for most voluntarily established pension and health plans in private industry to provide protection for individuals in these plans.

The **Employee Retirement Income Security Act (ERISA)** is "a federal law that sets minimum standards for most voluntarily established pension and health plans in private industry to provide protection for individuals in these plans."[20] Under ERISA, employers must provide participants with all the following:

1. Plan information (i.e., features and funding).
2. Assurances of the fiduciary responsibility of those in charge of managing and controlling the plan assets.
3. A grievance and appeals process for participants to get benefits from their plans.
4. The right to sue for benefits and breaches of fiduciary duty.[21]

Employers are required to provide to employees, free of charge, a *summary plan description (SPD),* which provides information on how the plan operates, the benefits under the plan, how to apply for such benefits, when such benefits vest, and when benefits may be paid out.

OCCUPATIONAL SAFETY AND HEALTH ACT OF 1970

Occupational Safety and Health Act of 1970 (OSHA)
Federal law that established the Occupational Safety and Health Administration, the agency responsible for setting safety standards under the act and enforcing the act through inspections and the levying of fines against violators.

The federal government regulates workplace safety primarily through the **Occupational Safety and Health Act of 1970 (OSHA),** which requires that every employer "furnish to each of his employees . . . employment . . . free from recognized hazards that are likely to cause death or serious physical harm." The Occupational Safety and Health Administration (abbreviated OSHA, the same as the act) is the agency that is responsible for promulgating workplace safety standards, inspecting facilities to ensure compliance with the standards, and bringing enforcement actions against violators. In addition, OSHA undertakes educational programs for employers and employees.

LO 6

Employee Privacy in the Workplace

With the rapid expansion of technology, new issues related to workplace privacy have evolved. Technology has stimulated the growth of such issues in a number of ways. On the one hand, technology has given employers new ways to gather information about employees. On the other hand, new technologies have provided more temptations for employees to be "off the job" at work, thus creating a stimulus for more employer monitoring. For example, surveys have shown that 90 percent of employees with Internet access at work look at non-work-related Web sites at least once a day,[22] 90 percent receive non-work-related e-mail,[23] and 84 percent send non-work-related e-mail.[24] Given such statistics, it is understandable that employers would want to monitor what employees are doing when they are supposed to be on the job.

ELECTRONIC MONITORING AND COMMUNICATION

Omnibus Crime Control and Safe Streets Act of 1968
Federal statute banning employers from listening to the private telephone conversations of employees or disclosing the contents of these conversations. Employers may ban personal calls and monitor calls for compliance as long as they discontinue listening to any conversation once they determine it is personal.

Business owners need to understand the extent to which they can monitor employees' telephone conversations, read their e-mail, and listen to their voice mail. Questions related to such monitoring primarily involve the common law tort of invasion of privacy and two federal statutes: the Omnibus Crime Control and Safe Streets Act of 1968,[25] as amended by the Electronic Communications Privacy Act of 1986.[26]

Under the **Omnibus Crime Control and Safe Streets Act of 1968,** employers cannot listen to the private telephone conversations of employees or disclose the contents of these conversations. They may, however, ban personal calls and monitor calls for compliance as long as they discontinue listening to any conversation once they determine it is personal. Violators may be subject

[20] Department of Labor, Employee Retirement Income Security Act, www.dol.gov/dol/topic/health-plans/erisa.htm.
[21] Ibid.
[22] Dyland Loeb McClain, "I'll Be Right with You, Boss, as Soon as I Finish My Shopping," *New York Times,* January 10, 2001, p. G1.
[23] Ibid.
[24] Ibid.
[25] 18 U.S.C. § 2210 et seq.
[26] 18 U.S.C. §§ 2510–2521.

to fines of up to $10,000. Under the Electronic Communications Privacy Act of 1986 (ECPA), employee's privacy rights were extended to electronic forms of communication including e-mail and cellular phones. ECPA outlaws the intentional interception of electronic communications and the intentional disclosure or use of the information obtained through such interception.

<div style="float:right; width:30%;">
Electronic Communications Privacy Act of 1986 (ECPA)

Federal law that extended employees' privacy rights to electronic forms of communication including e-mail and cellular phones; outlaws the intentional interception of electronic communications and the intentional disclosure or use of the information obtained through such interception.
</div>

In recognition of the fact that employers may sometimes need to monitor employee conversations for the purpose of improving employee performance or protecting employees from harassing calls, ECPA includes a "business-extension exemption" that allows employers to monitor employee telephone conversations in the ordinary course of their employment. This exception is subject to the constraint that the employer cannot continue to listen to conversations after it becomes apparent that they are personal. Also, monitoring is allowed when employees give their prior consent.

The key question in cases involving employer monitoring and interception of employee communications via e-mail, telephone, or voice mail is whether the employee had a *reasonable expectation of privacy* with respect to the communication in question. Employers are in the strongest position if they have a clear policy establishing that there is no reasonable expectation of privacy. Employment law experts advise that having a clear employee privacy policy that employees sign will minimize the likelihood of being sued by employees for invasion of privacy. These policies should be spelled out in the employee handbook, as well as explained to employees. At a minimum, employer privacy policies should cover the following issues:

1. Employer monitoring of telephone conversations.
2. Employer surveillance policies.
3. Employee access to medical and personnel records.
4. Drug testing policies.
5. Lie detector policies.
6. Ownership of computers and all issues unique to the electronic workplace.

CASE Nugget

When Can Employees Be Forced to Take a Lie Detector Test?

Polkey v. Transtrecs Corp.
U.S. Court of Appeals for the Eleventh Circuit

404 F.3d 1264 (11th Cir. 2005)

Polkey was a supervisor in the mailroom at Pensacola Naval Air Station. The mailroom was run by a company called Transtrecs. After discovering that some mail had been tampered with, Polkey reported it to her supervisor. Transtrecs asked all six employees, including Polkey, to take a lie detector (i.e., polygraph) test. The employee most suspected was tested first, and the lie detector test indicated that he might have been the one who tampered with the mail. Polkey and the remaining employees then refused to take the lie detector test. Transtrecs fired Polkey. She sued for violation of the Employee Polygraph Protection Act (EPPA). The district court granted summary judgment for Polkey. Transtrecs appealed.

On appeal, the district court's judgment was affirmed. The court held that Transtrecs violated EPPA by requesting and even suggesting that the employees take a polygraph test. Transtrecs argued that it was exempt because of national security, but the appellate court said that this applies only to the government. Transtrecs was merely a contractor for the government. Transtrecs also argued that it was exempt because the polygraph was part of an ongoing investigation of Polkey and that she was under suspicion. For this exemption to apply, an employer must have an articulable basis in fact to indicate that the employee was involved in or responsible for an economic loss. Transtrecs could make no such showing. Polkey prevails.

Labor Laws and Unions

Many people would argue that the laws that improved workers' conditions most significantly were not any of those previously discussed but, rather, were the laws that gave employees the right to organize and bargain collectively over wages and terms and conditions of employment. During the Great Depression, workers were first given the right to organize, and since that time unionization rates have varied significantly. During the post-World War II period, over one-third of American workers were organized. Yet by 2005, only 12.5 percent of workers were unionized.[27]

Not all occupations are equally organized, with the main base of unions being in the industrial sector. Unions, however, are increasingly organizing professionals and those in the service industry. Today, nearly 4 in 10 government workers belong to a union, and protective service workers, a group that includes police and firefighters, had the highest unionization rate of all occupations during 2005: 37 percent.[28]

Labor-management relations in the United States today are governed by three major pieces of legislation:

collective bargaining
The process whereby workers organize collectively and bargain with employers regarding the workplace.

1. The Wagner Act of 1935.
2. The Taft-Hartley Act of 1947.
3. The Landrum-Griffin Act of 1959.

The Taft-Hartley Act amended the Wagner Act, and they are jointly referred to as the *National Labor Relations Act (NLRA)*.

Wagner Act
The first major piece of federal legislation adopted explicitly to encourage the formation of labor unions and provide for collective bargaining between employers and unions as a means of obtaining the peaceful settlement of labor disputes.

THE WAGNER ACT OF 1935

The first major piece of federal legislation adopted explicitly to encourage the formation of labor unions and provide for collective bargaining between employers and unions as a means of obtaining the peaceful settlement of labor disputes was the Wagner Act. Collective bargaining "consists of negotiations between an employer and a group of employees so as to determine the conditions of employment."[29]

The Wagner Act also created an administrative agency, the *National Labor Relations Board (NLRB)*, to interpret and enforce the NLRA. Finally, the act provides for judicial review in designated federal courts of appeal.

Taft-Hartley Act
Federal legislation designed to curtail some of the powers that unions had acquired under the Wagner Act; designates certain union actions as unfair. Also called *Labor-Management Relations Act.*

THE TAFT-HARTLEY ACT OF 1947

The 12 years between passage of the Wagner Act and that of the Taft-Hartley Act saw a huge growth in unionization, which resulted in an increase in workers' power. Public perception of this trend led to the passage of the Taft-Hartley Act, also known as the Labor-Management Relations Act, which was designed to curtail some of the powers the unions had acquired under the Wagner Act.

Landrum-Griffin Act
Federal legislation that primarily governs the internal operations of labor unions. It requires financial disclosures by unions, establishes penalties for financial abuses by union officials and includes "Labor's Bill of Rights" to protect employees from their own unions.

THE LANDRUM-GRIFFIN ACT OF 1959

The Landrum-Griffin Act primarily governs the internal operations of labor unions. This act, which was a response to evidence of certain undesirable internal labor union practices, requires certain financial disclosures by unions and establishes civil and criminal penalties for financial abuses by union officials. "Labor's Bill of Rights," contained in the act, protects employees from their own unions.

[27] Bureau of Labor Statistics, www.bls.gov/news.release/union2.nr0.htm.
[28] Ibid.
[29] Legal Information Institute, www.law.cornell.edu/topics/collective_bargaining.html.

THE NATIONAL LABOR RELATIONS BOARD

The **National Labor Relations Board (NLRB)** is the administrative agency that interprets and enforces the *National Labor Relations Act (NLRA)*. The NLRB's three primary functions are to:

1. Monitor the conduct of the employer and the union during an election to determine whether workers want to be represented by a union.
2. Prevent and remedy unfair labor practices by employers or unions.
3. Establish rules interpreting the act.

The NLRB has jurisdiction over all employees *except* those who work in federal, state, and local government and those covered by the Railway Labor Act (employees in the transportation industry); independent contractors; agricultural workers; household domestics; persons employed by a spouse or parent; and supervisors, managerial employees, and confidential employees.

National Labor Relations Board (NLRB)
An administrative agency created by the Wagner Act to interpret and enforce the National Labor Relations Act.

THE COLLECTIVE BARGAINING PROCESS

Once the union has been certified, union and management must begin to bargain in good faith about wages, hours, and other terms and conditions of work. Note that the NLRB can order only that the parties bargain in good faith; it cannot order them to reach an agreement with respect to any contract term.

Both the employer and the bargaining-unit representative are required by the NLRA to bargain collectively in good faith with respect to wages, hours, and other terms and conditions of employment

 SUMMARY

When May an Employee Be Fired?	*At-will employment* means that any employee who is not employed under a contract or a collective bargaining agreement may quit at any time for any reason or no reason at all, with no required notice to the employer. Moreover, the employer may fire the employee at any time, with no notice, for almost any reason.
Federal Employment Discrimination Laws Governing Employers	Federal law may be described as a "minimum" level of protection for all workers. State laws may give employees more, but not less, protection than federal laws. Some of the most important federal employment discrimination laws are: The Civil Rights Act of 1964 (CRA)- Title VII (as amended by the Civil Rights Act of 1991); Pregnancy Discrimination Act of 1987 (PDA); Age Discrimination in Employment Act of 1967 (ADEA); Americans with Disabilities Act; and Equal Pay Act of 1963.
Civil Rights Act— Title VII	Title VII of CRA (1964, as amended by the Civil Rights Act of 1991) protects employees against discrimination based on race, color, religion, national origin, and sex. It also prohibits harassment based on the same protected categories. Defenses to a charge of discrimination under Title VII include *merit, seniority system,* and *bona fide occupational qualification (BFOC).*

- *Disparate treatment:* If the employee has been hired, fired, denied a promotion, and so on, based on membership in a protected class under Title VII, this is a form of intentional discrimination and qualifies the employee to sue for disparate-treatment discrimination.
- *Disparate impact:* Disparate-impact cases arise when a plaintiff attempts to establish that while an employer's policy or practice appears to apply to everyone equally, its actual effect is that it disproportionately limits employment opportunities for a protected class.
- *Sexual harassment:* Sexual harassment includes unwelcome sexual advances, requests for sexual favors, and other verbal or physical conduct of a sexual nature that implicitly or explicitly makes submission a term or condition of employment; makes employment decisions related to the individual dependent on submission to or rejection of such conduct; or has the purpose or effect of creating an intimidating, hostile, or offensive work environment. Two recognized forms are *hostile environment* and *quid pro quo* harassment.

Pregnancy Discrimination Act of 1987: PDA amended Title VII of CRA, expanding the definition of sex discrimination to include discrimination based on pregnancy.

Equal Employment Opportunity Commission: The EEOC is the federal agency charged with overseeing Title VII of the Civil Rights Act. Administrative complaints must be filed with the EEOC (or an equivalent state agency) prior to filing a lawsuit for discrimination or harassment.

Age Discrimination in Employment Act of 1967

ADEA prohibits employers from refusing to hire, discharging, or discriminating in terms and conditions of employment on the basis of an employee's or applicant's being age 40 or older.

Americans with Disabilities Act

ADA prohibits discrimination against employees and job applicants with disabilities.

Discrimination Based on Sexual Orientation— Actionable?

There is currently no federal legislation that prohibits discrimination based on sexual orientation. What does exist are individual state laws that prohibit such discrimination. State laws prohibiting discrimination based on sexual orientation exist in seventeen states.

May an Employer Discriminate against a Smoker?

Some companies either won't hire smokers, or are threatening to fire current employees who will not or are unable to quit smoking. Many states have passed laws preventing companies from engaging in such action.

Equal Pay Act of 1963

EPA prohibits an employer from paying workers of one gender less than the wages paid to employees of the opposite gender for work that requires equal skill, effort, and responsibility.

Additional Laws Governing the Employment Relationship

Fair Labor Standards Act: Employers must follow federal minimum wage and hour laws. FLSA covers all employers engaged in interstate commerce or the production of goods for interstate commerce and requires that a "minimum wage" of a specified amount be paid to all employees in covered industries. The specified amount is periodically raised by Congress to compensate for increases in the cost of living caused by inflation. The current minimum wage is $5.85 per hour; by the summer of 2009, it will be $7.25.

Family and Medical Leave Act: The FMLA covers all public employers, as well as private employers with 50 or more employees. It guarantees all eligible employees (those who have worked at least 25 hours a week for each of 12 months prior to the leave) up to 12 weeks of unpaid leave during any 12-month period for any of the following family-related occurrences: the birth of a child; the adoption of a child; the placement of a foster child in the employee's care; the care of a seriously ill spouse, parent, or child; or a serious health condition that renders the employee unable to perform any of the essential functions of his or her job.

Unemployment compensation: The Federal Unemployment Tax Act (FUTA) created a state system that provides unemployment compensation to qualified employees who lose their jobs.

Workers' compensation laws: State laws that provide for financial compensation to employees or their dependents when a covered employee is injured on the job.

Consolidated Omnibus Budget Reconciliation Act: COBRA ensures that when employees lose their jobs or have their hours reduced to a level at which they would not be eligible to receive medical, dental, or optical benefits from their employer, the employees will be able to continue receiving benefits under the employer's policy for up to 18 months by paying the premiums for the policy.

Employee Retirement Income Security Act: ERISA sets minimum standards for most voluntarily established pension and health plans in private industry to provide protection for individuals in these plans

Occupational Safety and Health Act of 1970: The Occupational Safety and Health Administration is responsible for setting safety standards under OSHA, as well as enforcing the act through inspections and the levying of fines against violators.

Employee Privacy in the Workplace

Privacy issues are of increasing importance in the workplace. Privacy policies should cover matters such as employer surveillance policies, control of and access to medical and personnel records, drug testing, and e-mail policies.

Omnibus Crime Control and Safe Streets Act of 1968: Employers cannot listen to the private telephone conversations of employees or disclose the contents of these conversations. They may, however, ban personal calls and monitor calls for compliance as long as they discontinue listening to any conversation once they determine it is personal. Violators may be subject to fines of up to $10,000.

Electronic Communications Privacy Act of 1986: Under ECPA, employees' privacy rights were extended to electronic forms of communication including e-mail and cellular phones. ECPA outlaws the intentional interception of electronic communications and the intentional disclosure or use of the information obtained through such interception.

Labor Laws and Unions

Wagner Act of 1935: The Wagner Act was the first major piece of federal legislation adopted explicitly to encourage the formation of labor unions and provide for *collective bargaining* between employers and unions as a means of obtaining the peaceful settlement of labor disputes.

Collective bargaining: Collective bargaining consists of negotiations between an employer and a group of employees to determine the conditions of employment.

National Labor Relations Board: The Wagner Act created the NLRB, an administrative agency, to interpret and enforce the National Labor Relations Act (NLRA) and to provide for judicial review in designated federal courts of appeal.

Taft-Hartley Act of 1947: Also known as the *Labor-Management Relations Act,* the Taft-Hartley Act was designed to curtail some of the powers the unions had acquired under the Wagner Act. Just as the Wagner Act designated certain employer actions as unfair, the Taft-Hartley Act designated certain union actions as unfair.

Landrum-Griffin Act of 1959: The Landrum-Griffin Act primarily governs the internal operations of labor unions. It requires certain financial disclosures by unions and establishes civil and criminal penalties for financial abuses by union officials. "Labor's Bill of Rights," contained in the act, protects employees from their own unions.

▪▪▪▶ Point/Counterpoint

Should Employers Be Permitted to Fire Employees for Activities, Such as Smoking, That They Do Outside Working Hours?	
YES	**NO**
The Centers for Disease Control and Prevention estimated that $75 billion is spent annually on medical expenses attributed to smoking. Businesses lose $82 billion in lost productivity from smokers. Smokers take about 6.5 more sick days a year than nonsmokers.	Employers should have no say in what employees do outside the workplace. Forcing employees to take tests to reveal whether they are smokers is an invasion of the employees' privacy. Many employees are addicted to cigarettes and would unfairly lose badly needed employment if unable to quit smoking.

▪▪▪▶ Questions & Problems

1. Name five statutes that prohibit discrimination in employment.

2. Does Title VII apply to same-sex harassment?

3. What is the current amount of the federal minimum wage? When was the last time the federal minimum wage was increased?

4. What is required for an employee to be eligible for benefits under the Family and Medical Leave Act?

5. Whom does the Age Discrimination in Employment Act protect?

6. List the protected classes under the Civil Rights Act of 1964 (as amended in 1991).

7. Machinchick worked for PB Power for six years. He received excellent reviews. Two years after beginning work, he was promoted to vice president. Four years after his promotion, Machinchick got a new supervisor and the company adopted a new management approach. The new supervisor, Knowlton, stated his plan to "hand-pick employees whose mindset resides in the 21st Century." On April 7, 2002, Knowlton sent an e-mail in which he stated that he wanted to "strategically hire some younger engineers and designers." Two days later, Knowlton sent an e-mail to the Human Resources Department criticizing Machinchick's performance. A short time later, Machinchick, age 63, was fired. He was told to turn over his client base to Betz, age 42. Machinchick sued PB Power, alleging it had violated the Age Discrimination in Employment Act. The trial court granted a motion for summary judgment in favor of PB Power. Machinchick appealed. How should the appellate court decide? Has Machinchick shown enough evidence of age discrimination to warrant allowing the case to be heard by a jury? Explain your decision. [*Machinchick v. PB Power, Inc.,* 398 F.3d 345 (5th Cir. 2005).]

8. Safeway operates a bread-baking facility in Denver, Colorado. Safeway periodically holds company-sponsored outdoor barbecues for its employees, and it purchased a gas grill equipped with a 20-pound propane tank for the barbecues. To ensure that the grill had sufficient gas for the barbecues, Safeway purchased a 40-pound tank. The larger tanks have a warning label stating that they should not be used with a grill ordinarily equipped with a 20-pound tank. Safeway planned to hold an employee barbecue on July 17, 1998. The plant superintendent, Edward Boone, instructed the plant engineer, Jerry Lewis, to set up the grill for the barbecue. On being informed that the grill was not adequately cooking the meat, the plant manager, Jim Kirk, again summoned Lewis. Lewis and the day-shift maintenance foreman, Fred Lake, attempted to improve the flow of gas to the grill by checking the regulator and repositioning the tank. While Lewis and Lake were working on the grill, fuel escaped and a "ball of fire" erupted. Lewis suffered severe burns to his hand and Lake's facial hair was singed. After an investigation, an OSHA inspector issued a citation to Safeway. Safeway appealed the decision. Was this a workplace safety violation? Why or why not? [*Safeway, Inc. v. Occupational Safety & Health Rev. Comm.,* 382 F.3d 1189 (10th Cir. 2004).]

9. Jennifer Erickson was employed by Bartell Drug Company. Jennifer sued the company because its insurance plan failed to provide coverage for prescription contraceptives. She alleged that this was a form of sex discrimination under Title VII and a violation of the Pregnancy Discrimination Act (PDA). Her employer defended by arguing that its failure to provide coverage for prescription contraceptives did not violate Title VII or the PDA because contraceptives were voluntary, were preventive, and did not treat or prevent an illness or disease and because control of one's fertility was not pregnancy, childbirth, or a related medical condition under PDA. If you were the court, how would you decide? Is failure to provide insurance coverage of prescription contraceptives a form of sex discrimination? Or pregnancy discrimination? Both? Neither? Explain the reasons for your answer. [*Erickson v. Bartell Drug Co.,* 141 F. Supp. 2d 1266 (U.S. Dist. Ct., Wash., 2001).]

10. Patricia Corley and Joseph Smith were employed by the Detroit Board of Education to work in its adult education program. Corley was employed part-time as a counselor, and Smith was her supervisor. During the course of their employment, Corley and Smith became romantically involved in a relationship that lasted three or four years. The relationship ended when Smith started dating another employee, Barbara Finch. Corley alleged that after Smith and Finch became involved, Smith repeatedly threatened her with adverse employment action if she said or did anything that interfered with his relationship with Finch. Corley also alleged that Finch taunted, embarrassed, and humiliated her by causing her workstation to be moved and by engaging in "catty" conversations with others that were about her and intended to be overheard by her. According to Corley, the alleged harassment culminated when she was discharged at the conclusion of the 1995–1996 school year. Does Corley have a claim for sexual harassment? Explain your reasoning. [*Corley v. Detroit Bd. of Ed.,* 470 Mich. 274 (Mich. Sup. Ct. 2004).]

11. Antonucci worked as a dental assistant. She was stuck in the thumb with an instrument twice during a period of two months. Antonucci claimed that she feared for her health and safety. She quit her job and applied for unemployment compensation. Did Antonucci have "good cause" to quit her job? Should Antonucci be permitted to collect unemployment compensation? How do you think this matter was decided by the court? [*Antonucci v. State of Florida,* 793 So.2d 1116 (Fla. Dist. Ct. App. 2001).]

12. Cynthia Anderson worked for the city of Columbus, Georgia, answering telephone calls from citizens. Anderson knew that calls from citizens were recorded, but she was unaware that due to a glitch, the telephone system continued to record her statements through her headset after a call was terminated. Anderson made disparaging remarks about the city manager's office,

and her employment was terminated. Anderson sued the city, alleging that it had no right to record her private conversations with co-workers, which were unrelated to city business. Who should prevail? Why? [*Anderson v. City of Columbus, Georgia,* 2005 U.S. Dist. LEXIS 12612 (Ga. 2005).]

13. Barie Hamilton worked as a retail store manager for Bally of Switzerland. She claimed that she was sexually harassed by her female supervisor and that she was fired and given negative references because she filed a complaint about the supervisor's behavior. The employer claimed that Hamilton was fired because her store was losing money. Hamilton alleged that her supervisor's behavior included telling her that the supervisor was gay, inviting Hamilton for drinks after work, complimenting her appearance, and touching her breast on one occasion. Bally alleges that Hamilton was fired after a worldwide reorganization of the company. The question before the court is whether Hamilton has pled sufficient facts to constitute hostile-environment sexual harassment? What do you think the court decided? Why? [*Hamilton v. Bally of Switzerland,* 2005 U.S. Dist. LEXIS 9319 (S.D.N.Y., 2005).]

14. Following separate lawsuits by female prisoners in Michigan and by the Civil Rights Division of the U.S. Department of Justice, both of which alleged rampant sexual abuse of female prisoners in Michigan, the Michigan Department of Corrections (MDOC) barred males from working in certain positions at its female prisons. Specifically, the MDOC designated approximately 250 correctional officer and residential unit officer positions in housing units at female prisons as "female only." A group of MDOC employees, both males and females, sued the MDOC, alleging that the MDOC's plan violated Title VII of the Civil Rights Act of 1964. The issue before the court was whether gender was a bona fide occupational qualification for the positions in question. How do you think the court should rule? Why? [*Everson v. Michigan Dept. of Corrections,* 391 F.3d 737 (6th Cir. 2004).]

15. Anthony Romeo was an openly gay student at Seton Hall, a Catholic university. He claimed that he elected to attend Seton Hall in part because of its published antidiscrimination policy. In 2003, he applied to the Seton Hall University Department of Student Affairs for provisional recognition of a gay and lesbian student organization. Dr. Laura Wankel, vice president of student affairs at Seton Hall, responded to Romeo's application in a letter, stating in pertinent part: "I am informing you that your application for provisional recognition has been denied. No organization based solely upon sexual orientation may receive formal University recognition." Wankel went on to say that "the Division of Student Affairs remains prepared to work with gay and lesbian students to meet their needs. I am committed to working collaboratively with you and other students in fostering a positive, safe and caring community." Wankel then made a modest proposal giving the group some rights. The proposal, however, was not satisfactory to the students, and Romeo filed his complaint alleging violations of New Jersey's Law against Discrimination. He also cited Seton Hall's nondiscrimination policy: "No person may be denied employment or related benefits or admission to the University or to any of its programs or activities, either academic or nonacademic, curricular or extracurricular, because of race, color, religion, age, national origin, gender, sexual orientation, handicap and disability, or veteran's status." How should the court rule? May a Catholic university prevent recognition of a gay and lesbian student organization? Does the university's nondiscrimination policy make a difference? Why or why not? [*Romeo v. Seton Hall University,* 2005 N.J. Super. LEXIS 197 (N.J. Sup. Ct. 2005).]

Looking for more review material?

The Online Learning Center at **www.mhhe.com/kubasekess** contains this chapter's "Assignment on the Internet" and also a list of URLs for more information, entitled "On the Internet." Find both of them in the Student Center portion of the OLC, along with quizzes and other helpful materials.

Consumer Law

···▸ CASE OPENER

The Firestone Recall

On August 9, 2000, Bridgestone/Firestone Inc. announced a recall of 14.4 million tires, including all 15-inch Firestone ATX, ATX II, and 15-inch Wilderness AT tires used by Ford Motor Company on its popular SUVs. This announcement came 10 years after the first suit was filed against these companies for defective tires. Secrecy and protective orders within the courts kept this information hush-hush for 10 years until a local news station in Houston, Texas, got word in 1999 that Ford was replacing tires on Explorers in Saudi Arabia through what it called a "customer notification enhancement action." In response, the National Highway Traffic Safety Administration opened an investigation of the cases associated with these tires.[1]

In the original recall press release, Ford and Firestone claimed that they had each just been made aware of the safety problem and were consequently recalling the tires. However, some have argued that Ford and Firestone knew about the safety problems with the tires as much as 10 years earlier but did not inform the National Highway Traffic Safety Administration of the potential danger. Ford had been replacing tires not only in Saudi Arabia but also in Venezuela and Thailand.[2]

1. Suppose you were a member of Congress when this case emerged. What action would you take to ensure that situations such as this would not occur again?
2. Suppose you were the manager of Ford or Firestone. Would you have handled the situation differently, and if so, why?

[1]Terril Yue Jones, "Cause of Tire Failures Still a Matter of Dispute," *Los Angeles Times,* October 22, 2000, p. C1.
[2]Michael B. Bowden, "Firestone Tire Recall Could Have Broad Impact on Litigation," 2000 LWUSA 842 (2000).

···▸ LEARNING OBJECTIVES

After reading this chapter, you will be able to answer the following questions:

LO 1 What is the purpose of the Federal Trade Commission Act?

LO 2 How does the Federal Trade Commission determine what constitutes deceptive advertising?

LO 3 What is the purpose of labeling and packaging laws?

LO 4 What are the different acts that provide credit protection?

LO 5 What are the different laws that help ensure consumer health and safety?

Consumers buy products and services from sellers every day. In some instances, however, consumers do not have as much power in the transaction as the seller has. As we see in the Firestone case, the seller had more knowledge about the product, how it was made, and pricing strategies than did the consumers. Because Congress recognized the opportunities for sellers to take advantage of buyers in this way, it created laws that regulate transactions between consumers and sellers. A consumer law is a statute or administrative rule serving to protect consumer interests.

consumer law
A statute or administrative rule serving to protect consumer interests.

Various state and federal consumer laws protect consumers from unfair trade practices of sellers as well as unsafe products. Although the laws differ among the states, many of the state laws provide consumer protection exceeding that guaranteed by federal law. This chapter explores a range of consumer laws concerning deceptive advertising, product labeling, sales procedures, health and product safety, and consumer credit. First, however, it discusses a federal agency that is one of the most important creators and enforcers of consumer protection laws—the Federal Trade Commission.

The Federal Trade Commission

LO 1

Congress created the Federal Trade Commission (FTC) through the Federal Trade Commission Act of 1914.[3]

The FTC is an independent federal agency with five commissioners appointed by the president and confirmed by the Senate. Each commissioner serves a seven-year term. The president chooses one commissioner to serve as chair of the FTC.

How does the FTC meet its goal of protecting consumers? The FTC helps to protect consumers through two methods: (1) consumer education and (2) legal action. First, the FTC creates campaigns to educate consumers about laws that protect them. Second, the FTC educates businesses to help them comply voluntarily with consumer laws. For example, the FTC creates industry guides, interpretations of consumer laws, to encourage businesses to stop unlawful behavior. When businesses follow the FTC guidelines, they can cut potentially steep costs associated with violating consumer laws.

industry guides
Interpretations of consumer laws created by the FTC to encourage businesses to stop unlawful behavior.

HOW THE FTC BRINGS AN ACTION

The FTC receives a variety of complaints about businesses from consumer groups and individuals. When a consumer files a complaint with the FTC, he or she triggers a chain of events that could lead to an FTC action against the violator. The FTC typically begins a nonpublic investigation of the company.

If, after its investigation, the FTC believes that a company violated the law, the FTC sends a complaint to the alleged violator. At that time, the FTC may settle the complaint through a consent order with the company. A consent order is a statement in which the company agrees to

consent order
A statement in which a company agrees to stop disputed behavior but does not admit that it broke the law.

[3] 15 U.S.C. § § 41–58.

stop the disputed behavior but does not admit that it broke the law. Should the company violate the consent order, it will usually be forced to pay a fine.

If the company refuses to enter into a consent agreement, the FTC may then decide to issue a formal administrative complaint. The issuing of this complaint leads to a hearing before an administrative law judge. If the judge decides that the company has violated the law, the FTC issues a **cease-and-desist order,** requiring that the company stop the illegal behavior. However, the company may appeal this decision to the five commissioners. If the commissioners uphold the ruling, the company may appeal to the U.S. court of appeals and, finally, to the Supreme Court. If the courts uphold the FTC's decision, the company must follow the cease-and-desist order. If the company violates the order, the FTC can seek an injunction against the company or fine the company up to $10,000 per violation.

cease-and-desist order
An FTC order requiring that a company stop its illegal behavior.

TRADE REGULATION RULES

Bringing an action may be effective in protecting consumers from the activities of one company, but how can the FTC protect consumers if most companies within one industry are using the same unfair or deceptive practices? Bringing actions against all of these companies would be costly and time-consuming.

An alternative method of addressing these practices is through trade regulation rules. If the FTC finds that deception is pervasive in an industry, the FTC can recommend rule making. An administrative rule has the effect of law. Furthermore, the FTC can bring legal action against those who violate FTC rules.

LO 2

Deceptive Advertising

Section 5 of the Federal Trade Commission Act prohibits deceptive and unfair acts in commercial settings, including consumer purchases. This section of the chapter specifically analyzes **deceptive advertising,** the practice of advertising with claims that mislead or could mislead a reasonable consumer. **Puffing,** the use of generalities and clear exaggerations, is permissible.

The FTC decides whether an advertisement is deceptive on a case-by-case basis. Deceptive claims have three elements:[4] (1) a *material* misrepresentation, omission, or practice that is (2) *likely to mislead* a (3) *reasonable* consumer. When an advertised claim appears to be authentic but in fact is not, the advertising is deceptive. Moreover, if the advertisement is a **half-truth—** that is, the information presented is true but incomplete—the advertiser is deceiving the consumer. To combat deceptive advertisements and half-truths, the FTC requires **ad substantiation,** requiring that advertisers have a reasonable basis for the claims made in their advertisements. As Exhibit 25-1 points out, many have argued that "Made in the USA" labels are deceptive advertising.

An illustration of an FTC claim of deceptive advertising involved Body Wise International, Inc.'s "AG-Immune" dietary supplement. In 1995, Body Wise was prohibited from using false or unsubstantiated claims while advertising *any* of its products as part of its settlement with the FTC for using deceptive advertising to market a different dietary supplement. Body Wise then entered into a contract with Dr. Stoff to market AG-Immune. Stoff was paid royalties on every bottle of AG-Immune that Body Wise sold. However, no connection between Body Wise and Stoff was ever admitted in any of the advertisements for the product.

The FTC then alleged that Body Wise violated the 1995 order with its advertisements for AG-Immune. According to the FTC, Body Wise advertised that AG-Immune was able to "prevent or treat numerous diseases or conditions, including cancer, HIV/AIDS, heart disease, chronic fatigue syndrome, and asthma" and that scientific research supported the claims. Body Wise also allegedly claimed that AG-Immune improved the immune system's "ability to prevent or treat

deceptive advertising
The practice of advertising with claims that mislead or could mislead a reasonable consumer.

puffing
The use of generalities and clear exaggerations.

half-truth
Information that is true but is not complete.

ad substantiation
An FTC standard requiring that advertisers have a reasonable basis for the claims made in their ads.

[4] FTC, "Policy Statement on Deception," 1983.

Exhibit 25-1

"Made in the USA"
Labels and the FTC

Many companies boast that their products are "Made in the USA." But what exactly does it mean to be "Made in the USA"? The FTC is charged with setting forth standards to avoid deception and false advertising about products that are supposedly made in the USA.

In the past, the FTC stated that "Made in the USA" should not be used "unless all, or virtually all, of the components and labor are of U.S. origin." Thus, if a company assembled a product in the United States but shipped in some components from out of the country, the FTC would argue that "Made in the USA" should not be used.

The FTC's definition of the phrase was stricter than others' definitions. For example, NAFTA defines "Made in the USA" as a product for which at least 55 percent of the labor and components are from Canada, Mexico, or the United States. Customs draws the line at 50 percent.

In 1997, the FTC decided to continue enforcing the "all or virtually all" standard. Those with strong union ties had argued against any weaker definition, such as the 75 percent the FTC had been debating.

Source: Federal Trade Commission, FTC Consumer Report, "Complying with the Made in the USA Standard," www.ftc.gov/bcp/conline/pubs/buspubs/madeusa.shtm.

the aforementioned and many other diseases and conditions."[5] The FTC also argued that Stoff falsely claimed that the advertisements were supported by scientific data and that he was in a professional position to assess the efficacy of AG-Immune.

Body Wise and Stoff both agreed to settle with the FTC out of court. Both parties were responsible for paying hefty fines to the FTC for their deceptive advertisements. The main thrust of the FTC's argument was related to the fact that no scientific data existed to back Body Wise's claims regarding AG-Immune.

The existence of deceptive advertisements is not enough alone to prove damages for recovery when individual civil suits are filed. For example, in *Oliveira v. Amoco Oil Co.,*[6] a class action suit was brought against Amoco for deceptive advertisements. Amoco had made many claims over a seven-year period about the superiority of its premium gasoline. However, according to the plaintiffs, no scientific evidence supported Amoco's claims. The plaintiffs argued that the advertisements created a higher demand for Amoco gas, creating artificially high gas prices that hurt consumers regardless of specific reliance on the advertisements. The court rejected this argument, ruling that a "market theory" of causation is not enough to establish damages in an individual case. Moreover, reliance on the advertisements is a crucial element in establishing liability.

This case illustrates the importance of understanding specific consumer protection laws. Future business managers need to understand what kinds of advertising claims are permissible in our legal environment. To simplify this understanding for consumers and business owners, the FTC has classified certain types of deceptive or unfair advertising practices and created specific rules defining and prohibiting violations of these rules. The next section examines these classifications.

BAIT-AND-SWITCH ADVERTISING

When sellers advertise a low price for an item generally unavailable to the consumer and then push the consumer to buy a more expensive item, they are engaging in bait-and-switch advertising. The low advertised price "baits" the consumer. Then the salesperson "switches" the consumer to a higher-priced item. In 1968, the FTC prohibited bait-and-switch advertising.

According to the FTC's "Guides against Bait Advertising," a seller can engage in bait-and-switch advertising in several ways. For instance, the seller might advertise a low price but have too little of the advertised good in stock, or the seller might discourage employees from selling the advertised item. These bait-and-switch advertising techniques violate FTC rules.

bait-and-switch advertising
A deceptive practice in which a seller advertises a low-priced item, generally unavailable to the consumer, and then pushes the consumer to buy a more expensive item.

[5] Federal Trade Commission, "Body Wise International to Pay over $3.5 Million to Settle Federal and State Deceptive Advertising Charges for 'AG-Immune' Dietary Supplement," www.ftc.gov/opa/2005/01/bodywise.htm, January 18, 2005.
[6] 201 Ill. 2d 134 (2002).

CASE Nugget

Are "No Annual Fee" Offers Bait-and-Switch Advertising?

Paula E. Rossman, Individually and for All Others Similarly Situated, v. Fleet Bank (R.I.) National Association et al. U.S. Court of Appeals for the Third Circuit

280 F.3d 384 (2002)

In 1999, Paula Rossman received a credit card offer from Fleet Bank, advertising the "Fleet Platinum MasterCard" with a low annual percentage rate and no annual fee. A few months after Rossman's account was opened, Fleet imposed an annual fee. Fleet sent a letter to Rossman stating that a $35 annual fee would be charged to her account annually on the anniversary of her account's opening; however, a second letter notified Rossman that the annual fee would be charged to her account within months. Rossman sued Fleet, claiming that Fleet had violated the disclosure requirements of the Truth in Lending Act (TILA) and engaged in a bait-and-switch advertising scheme. The district court dismissed Rossman's TILA claim for failing to state a claim on which relief could be granted. Rossman appealed to the Third Circuit Court of Appeals.

The appeals court applied a two-part test to determine whether Fleet's statement that the card had no annual fee was lawful. "First, it must have disclosed all of the information required by the statute. And second, it must have been true—i.e., an accurate representation of the legal obligations of the parties at that time—when the relevant solicitation was mailed." Rossman claimed that Fleet was required to disclose all fees that were currently imposed, as well as any fees that may be imposed later. Rossman also claimed that Fleet's disclosure was misleading by suggesting that there would never be an annual fee. Additionally, Rossman claimed that Fleet engaged in a bait-and-switch scheme, using the "no-annual-fee" provision to lure consumers into a contract when Fleet had no intention of honoring that provision.

Fleet argued that it was not required to disclose any future fees that may be imposed, but only those that currently existed. Fleet also turned to a clause in the solicitation disclosure insert that stated it "reserve[d] the right to change the benefit features associated with your Card at any time." The court found that Fleet's disclosure, as placed and worded, did not adequately link itself to the no-annual-fee provision. Thus, if the annual fee was permitted to be changed within the first annual term of the agreement, the court found that the statement "no annual fee" was an inadequate disclosure.

Turning its attention to Rossman's claim that Fleet had engaged in a bait-and-switch advertising scheme, the court did not see Fleet's behavior as resembling the classic bait-and-switch design. Ordinarily, consumers are baited with certain terms, but the switch for less enticing products or terms is made before the consumer enters into an agreement or contract. Rather, the court found Fleet's behavior to be even more egregious because Fleet actually bound the consumer in a contract before making the switch to charging an annual fee. Thus, Fleet had violated the provisions of TILA. The appeals court reversed the district court's ruling and remanded for proceedings.

multiple-product order

A form of cease-and-desist order issued by the FTC that applies not only to a specified product but also to other products produced by the same firm.

FTC ACTIONS AGAINST DECEPTIVE ADVERTISING

If the FTC takes actions against a company and proves the advertising is deceptive, the FTC may issue a cease-and-desist order. To go a step beyond cease-and-desist orders, the FTC may also issue multiple-product orders. A **multiple-product order** is a form of cease-and-desist order issued by the FTC that applies not only to the product that was the subject of the action

CONNECTING to the Core

Economics

As you read in this chapter about the FTC's role in regulating advertising, think about how the FTC is fulfilling a government function discussed in your economics class: attempting to prevent one kind of market failure. Remember from your economics class that economists assume that markets exist in an almost perfect form. For a market to be perfect, certain conditions have to exist. When those conditions fail to exist, the government might act to correct the failure. For example, economists often assume that buyers must have perfect information about the products they are buying for the market to achieve optimal results. We recognize that sellers would often provide faulty information or conceal information if doing so would help them sell their products. Thus, the FTC, with its regulation of advertising, tries to prevent the problem of imperfect information, thereby improving the functioning of the market.

Source: David C. Colander, *Economics,* 6th ed. (New York: McGraw-Hill, 2006), pp. 432–434.

but also to other products produced by the same firm. Alternatively, the FTC may require that the company engage in corrective advertising (or *counteradvertising*), running advertisements in which the company explicitly states that the formerly advertised claims were untrue.

> **corrective advertising**
> Advertising in which the company explicitly states that formerly advertised claims were untrue. Also called *counteradvertising.*

The rationale for corrective advertising is that consumers who saw the previous ads will see the new ads; the new ads will then correct the deceptive advertising. In a commission decision regarding the deceptive advertising of Doan's Pills, Commissioner Sheila Anthony described the characteristics of a situation requiring corrective advertising:

> Requiring the dissemination of a truthful message to counteract beliefs created or reinforced by a respondent's deceptive message is an appropriate method of restoring the *status quo ante* and denying a respondent the ability to continue to profit from its deception. . . . Corrective advertising is an appropriate remedy if (1) the challenged ads have substantially created or reinforced a misbelief; and (2) the misbelief is likely to linger into the future.[7]

However, some companies—and even one of the commissioners of the FTC—argued that corrective advertising is a form of compelled speech and thus violates the First Amendment right to engage in free speech.

TELEMARKETING AND ELECTRONIC ADVERTISING

Consumer law, like all law, is dynamic, and technology is often a driving force of change in consumer law. Although technological developments provide consumers with a host of benefits, these developments are often prone to abuses not covered by existing consumer law. For example, telephones and fax machines facilitate fast and inexpensive communication around the world, but telemarketers can use these technologies to deceive consumers and invade their privacy. Hence, lawmakers have passed new laws to address these issues.

Two major acts regulate advertising by telephone and fax, the Telephone Consumer Protection Act of 1991 (TCPA) and the Telemarketing and Consumer Fraud and Abuse Prevention Act of 1994.[8] TCPA, which the Federal Communications Commission agency enforces, forbids phone solicitation using an automatic telephone dialing system or a prerecorded voice. TCPA also makes it illegal to transmit advertisements via fax unless the recipient agrees to the fax transmission. TCPA allows consumers to obtain a private right to legal action. In other words, the act gives consumers the right to recover for their losses. If a telemarketer violates TCPA, the consumer can recover either monetary losses or $500 per violation. However, if the telemarketer willfully violated the act, the court can decide to triple the amount owed to the consumer.

[7] FTC Press Release, "Doan's Pills Must Run Corrective Advertising: FTC Ads Claiming Doan's Is Superior in Treating Back Pain Were Unsubstantiated," May 27, 1999.
[8] 47 U.S.C. § 227.

Regulating the Psychological Aspects of Advertisements

The governments of Germany and Greece believe that consumers need protection from the potentially dangerous psychological effects of advertisements. Germany, in particular, has strict advertising regulations.

Specifically, ads that exert a "moral pressure" to purchase a product or service are outlawed in Germany. Urging the consumer to act out of gratitude, decency, or compassion might create this pressure. This regulation is applied stringently when there is no logical connection between the emotional appeal and the function of the product being promoted. For example, an advertisement that insinuated "good mothers" buy brand X peanut butter would be prohibited. Additionally, the German law prohibits marketers from using persons of authority to solicit business. For example, a marketer cannot ask the supervisor of a company to recommend a product to employees because the employees would feel obligated to purchase it.

The laws protecting consumers from the dangers of advertising in Greece vary from the German laws. If an ad "causes fear" by use of partially untrue statements, it is considered unlawful in Greece. In some instances, the use of *true* statements to evoke fear in the consumer is considered illegal.

Sometimes laws are ineffective in achieving their goals, however, so legislatures draft new laws to supplement existing law. Thus, even though the goals of consumer laws may not change, specific rules and provisions do. For example, despite the protection of TCPA, consumers still lost an estimated $40 billion in telemarketing fraud after the act went into effect.

To give consumers more protection against deceptive and abusive telemarketing practices, Congress enacted the Telemarketing and Consumer Fraud and Abuse Prevention Act of 1994.[9] Through this act, Congress asked the FTC to define "deceptive and abusive" telemarketing practices and required that the FTC create and enforce rules governing telemarketing that would prohibit such practices. Consequently, the FTC created the Telemarketing Sales Rule of 1995,[10] which requires that telemarketers (1) identify the call as a sales call; (2) identify the product name and seller; (3) tell the total cost of goods being sold; (4) notify the listener or reader of whether the sale is nonrefundable; and (5) remove the consumer's name from the potential contact list if the consumer so requests.

Moreover, the FTC established that certain telemarketing behaviors are abusive, such as using profane or obscene language toward a customer and calling to a person who has requested previously to be taken off the particular seller's calling list. Additionally, if the telemarketer calls a residence before 8 a.m. or after 9 p.m., the telemarketer is engaging in abusive behavior. If a telemarketer violates the rule, the FTC or the state attorney general may bring an action against the telemarketer. If the action is successful, the telemarketer can face fines up to $10,000 per violation.

While reviewing and amending the Telemarketing Sales Rule in 2002, the FTC created a "Do Not Call" registry. The FTC states that the purpose of the Do Not Call registry is to give consumers a choice regarding telemarketing calls. The registry makes it illegal for telemarketers to call any number that has been registered for more than 31 days. The registration lasts for five years, and it can be completed online through the FTC's Web site. Both the FTC and the Federal Communications Commission (FCC) are responsible for maintaining the list, with help from local state law enforcement officials.

The Global Context box discusses different restrictions placed on advertisements in other countries.

TOBACCO ADVERTISING

The tobacco industry's advertising is regulated through two acts: the Public Health Cigarette Smoking Act[11] of 1970 and the Smokeless Tobacco Health Education Act[12] of 1986. The Public

[9] 15 U.S.C. § § 6101–6108.
[10] 16 C.F.R. § 310.
[11] 15 U.S.C. § 1331.
[12] 15 U.S.C. § § 4401–4408.

Consumers on the Net

Every year, e-commerce becomes more and more popular. In 2006, 52 million individuals shopped online, and this was up from 35 million in 2005.* These consumers are likely to encounter some type of problem through e-commerce. Perhaps they will respond to an unsolicited e-mail claiming that the consumer can quickly earn big money. Or perhaps they will win their bid on an item through an Internet auction but will never receive the product.

Consumers can be defrauded on the Internet in numerous ways. The anonymity associated with Internet use makes it easier for sellers to engage in deceptive business practices. In 2002, the FTC received 51,000 complaints about online fraud and deception.

* Cap, Gemini, Ernst, & Young, "Global Online Retailing" (report), www.capemini.de/news/studien/ratking.html.

Health Cigarette Smoking Act prohibits radio and television cigarette advertisements, and the Smokeless Tobacco Act imposes the same restrictions for smokeless tobacco ads.

Labeling and Packaging Laws LO 3

When consumers examine a product to decide whether to buy it, the label often influences the decision to purchase. For example, many of us have purchased food because the label said the food was "low fat." Unfortunately, manufacturers can include or omit information on labels that misleads consumers.

Consequently, federal and state governments have passed laws that regulate product labeling. These laws generally require that the manufacturer provide accurate, understandable information on the label. Furthermore, if the product is potentially harmful, the manufacturer must make the consumer aware of the harm.

Several federal laws regulate product labeling. The Wool Products Labeling Act of 1939[13] requires accurate labeling of wool products. Similarly, the Fur Products Labeling Act of 1951[14] requires the accurate labeling of fur products. The Flammable Fabrics Act of 1953[15] makes it illegal to produce or distribute clothing "so highly flammable as to be dangerous when worn." The Fair Packaging and Labeling Act of 1966[16] requires that products carry labels that identify the product and provide specific information about the contents, such as the quantity of the contents and the size of a serving, if the number of servings is stated. Moreover, under this act, food product labels must show the nutritional content of the product. Similarly, the Nutrition Labeling and Education Act of 1990[17] requires that standard nutrition information (i.e., calories and fat) be provided on food labels. Additionally, this act defines the words *fresh* and *low fat*. In 1994, the FTC issued a statement saying that it would apply these label restrictions to food advertising to prevent deceptive advertising. Thus, not only do sellers need to be concerned about the use of *high, low,* and *light* on labels, but they are also required to use these words in particular ways in advertisements.

The goal of these laws is to provide consumers with specific information about product content. However, Congress has passed several laws that require information about the potential harms associated with a product. For example, the Federal Hazardous Substances Act of 1960 requires that all items containing dangerous substances carry warning labels.

Canada's cigarette labeling requirements are even more stringent than the U.S. requirements. In Canada, approximately 40 percent of cigarette packaging must be devoted to health warnings.[18] The Canadian Bureau of Tobacco Control, however, has proposed a new rule requiring that manufacturers dedicate 50 percent of cigarette packages to such warnings, which would include explicit pictures and images of mouth cancer or other severe diseases caused by cigarette use.[19]

[13] 15 U.S.C. § § 1331–1341.
[14] 15 U.S.C. § 69.
[15] 15 U.S.C. § 1191.
[16] 15 U.S.C. § 1451 et seq.
[17] 21 U.S.C. § 343-1.
[18] Tobacco Products Control Regulations, SOR/89-21.
[19] Action on Smoking and Health Press Release, "Majority of Canadians Want Larger Warnings on Cigarette Packages," October 2000.

Respecting Languages of the Consumer

U.S. consumers often purchase products that are labeled or give directions in various languages, such as Spanish and French. The United States does not require that other publications, such as billboards, restaurant menus, or television advertisements, be multilingual. However, such requirements do exist in France, Canada, and Quebec.

During the early 1970s, French consumers voiced concern about foreign imports. Most of those products were labeled in languages other than French, so it became difficult to read directions or determine the content and function of a product. The government responded by passing a law in 1975 that regulates the labels and advertising of imported goods. The law mandates that French and English have to be the languages used for product labels, instructions, and all forms of advertising.

Canada passed a similar decree concerning the use of the French language. The Consumer Packaging and Labeling Act of Canada requires that all goods be labeled in both French and English.

While France and Canada were legislating the inclusion of both languages, Quebec legislated the exclusion of English. The Charter of the French Language, drafted by the Quebec government, requires that all public signs and advertisements be solely in French. If a product is produced and sold in Quebec, its packaging and product instructions are also to be in French alone.

Sales

The FTC and other government agencies have the power to regulate sales. For example, the Federal Reserve Board of Governors has the power to govern credit provisions related to sales contracts through its Regulation Z.[20] The FTC has created rules that govern specific types of sales in which the consumer is in a more vulnerable position compared to a consumer who walks into a traditional retail setting. This section examines FTC regulation of three of these uncommonly vulnerable commercial settings: door-to-door, telephone, and mail-order sales.

DOOR-TO-DOOR SALES

Imagine that you hear a knock at your door, open it, and discover a salesperson for an Internet provider. The person who knocked knows that you have just purchased a computer and are interested in learning about the Internet. The salesperson explains the price of various programs by which you can become familiar with the Internet. You listen, but decide that you would like to get additional information from an alternative provider. However, the salesperson is extremely pushy; to get the salesperson out of your house, you decide to purchase one of his plans.

In most door-to-door sales, the consumer does not have a chance to compare products and services to find the best service for his or her money. In addition, many consumers find it difficult to escape a salesperson in their homes. It is much easier to walk out of a store. Because the consumer is in a particularly vulnerable position in a door-to-door sale, the FTC has created special rules for such sales.

The FTC created the Cooling-Off Rule, giving consumers three days to cancel purchases they make from salespeople who come to their homes. Moreover, the salesperson must notify the consumer, both verbally and in writing, that the sales transaction may be canceled. The FTC rule also requires that the consumer be notified in writing in the same language in which the oral negotiations were conducted, thereby preventing unscrupulous businesses from taking advantage of non-English speakers.

The following case provides an example of the kinds of pressures that the FTC is trying to offset: Consolidated Promotions offered consumers a free gift for setting up a meeting in their home to discuss Consolidated products. This in-home meeting was in fact a sales pitch for Consolidated's photography packages, which included film and discounted photo processing. These packages cost from $1,200 to $2,500. When Consolidated Promotions refused to cancel some of the consumers' contracts, the FTC approved a complaint and referred it to the Department of Justice. The FTC alleged that the company violated the Cooling-Off Rule by "1) failing to honor valid cancellation notices; 2) misrepresenting consumers' rights to cancel their contracts; and

[20] 12 C.F.R. § 226.

3) failing to inform each buyer orally of his or her right to cancel the order."[21] The FTC proposed that Consolidated Promotions enter into a consent decree whereby Consolidated would be required to send notice to all customers who bought a photography package after July 1, 1996, giving them an opportunity to cancel their contracts.

TELEPHONE AND MAIL-ORDER SALES

Most consumers have purchased at least one item from a catalog. Unfortunately, telephone and mail-order purchases trigger more complaints than do traditional retail or door-to-door sales. Suppose the office manager of a small accounting firm ordered five new chairs for the office through a catalog. The writing in the catalog indicated that the chairs would arrive within two weeks. The office manager called in the chair order, but six weeks later he had heard nothing from the company. What rights does he have in this situation?

The FTC originally addressed problems with mail-order sales through the 1975 Mail-Order Rule.[22] The Mail or Telephone Order Merchandise Rule of 1993 amended the 1975 Mail-Order Rule to extend protections to consumers who purchase goods over phone lines, including through computers and fax machines.

The 1993 rule established three key guidelines. First, sellers must ship items within the time promised. If they do not specify a time, the seller is limited to 30 days from receipt of the order. Second, if the seller cannot ship the item within the promised time, the seller must notify the customer in writing and offer an opportunity to cancel. Third, if a customer decides to cancel the order, the seller must refund the customer's money within a specified period of time.

Unsolicited Merchandise When a consumer goes to her mailbox only to discover that a company has sent her a book, must she pay for the book? Anyone who receives unsolicited merchandise may treat the item as a gift. The recipient may keep or dispose of the merchandise without any obligation to the sender. In accordance with the Postal Reorganization Act of 1970,[23] any unsolicited merchandise sent by mail is free to be used by the recipient as he or she sees fit with no obligation by the recipient to the sender.

FTC REGULATION OF SALES IN SPECIFIC INDUSTRIES

In certain industries, sellers have extensive opportunities to take advantage of customers. Thus, the FTC—and in some cases, Congress—creates special rules for certain sales practices specific to certain industries.

Used-Car Sales Consumers who purchase a used car often have very little information about the car's history. For instance, they do not know whether the car has been in an accident or whether there are any serious problems that are just not visible.

To protect used-car buyers, Congress passed the Odometer Act of 1973, which protects against odometer fraud in used-car sales. The FTC extended that act's protection through the 1984 Used Motor Vehicle Registration Rule.[24] Under this rule, a dealer must attach a buyer's guide label to any used car he or she is attempting to sell. The label must state that the car is being sold "as is." This label is a warning to the customer that the seller is not guaranteeing anything at all about the performance of the car. Furthermore, the label must include a suggestion that the buyer obtain an inspection for the used car before any decision to purchase.

Consumer protections against fraud in used-car sales vary widely from state to state. During the 1960s and 1970s there was widespread pressure to reform our legislative system to protect consumers from fraud; many states responded more favorably to that pressure than did others. All states enacted the Uniform Commercial Code (UCC), but in each case the UCC was enacted with significant variations. The difference between states was also heightened in that each state had unique nonuniform consumer protection statutes. Consequently, the consumer protection laws against used-car fraud (also known as "lemon laws") vary from state to state. Some states

[21] Federal Trade Commission Press Release, "FTC Settlement Protects Door-to-Door Sales Consumers," May 2, 2000.
[22] 16 C.F.R. § § 435.1–435.2.
[23] 16 C.F.R. § 256.
[24] 16 C.F.R. § § 455.1–455.5.

provide minimum protection, while others states, such as Minnesota, presume that one unsuccessful effort to repair a used car demonstrates nonrepairability. Minnesota's laws also extend statutory protection to potential buyers of returned vehicles by banning resale of automobiles returned because of major safety defects.[25]

Funeral Home Services Consumers who must purchase goods and services for a funeral and burial are often vulnerable for several reasons. The consumer is usually preoccupied with his or her loss of a relative or friend and is unlikely to "comparison shop." Additionally, grieving consumers can be more readily persuaded to purchase unnecessary, expensive items for this last tribute to their loved ones. To prevent funeral homes from taking advantage of these customers, the FTC created the 1984 Funeral Rule and revised it in 1994. The rule requires that those who operate funeral homes provide customers with itemized price information about funeral goods and services. Furthermore, funeral homes may not misrepresent legal or cemetery requirements or require that the customer buy certain funeral goods and services as a condition for receiving other funeral goods and services.

Real Estate Sales Because real estate purchases are probably one of the largest purchases a consumer will make, Congress passed several acts requiring that sellers disclose certain information about the property. First, the Interstate Land Sales Full Disclosure Act,[26] passed in 1968, requires disclosure of information to consumers so that they can make informed decisions about real estate purchases. Under this act, anyone planning to sell or lease 100 or more lots of unimproved land through a common promotional plan must file an initial statement of record with the Department of Housing and Urban Development's (HUD's) Office of Interstate Land Sales Registration. Before the developer can offer land for sale, HUD must approve the initial statement.

Congress provided more protection for people purchasing homes in the Real Estate Settlement Procedures Act of 1974[27] and its 1976 amendments. This act requires the disclosure of information regarding mortgage loans to the buyer. For example, the lender must give the buyer an estimate of the costs for finalizing the real estate purchase.

Online Sales With the ever-expanding reach of the Internet, there has been an increase in business-to-consumer (B2C) sales transactions. Anyone with an Internet connection can make purchases from his or her favorite stores, from Barnes & Noble to Macy's. Most existing consumer protection laws were developed to protect consumers in their interactions with businesses face-to-face. Hence, protecting consumers online requires new approaches. Although not a specific industry, the Internet facilitates such a huge volume of commerce that additional focused protective legislation is needed.

Despite the difficulty of prosecuting online fraud, the FTC has brought a number of enforcement actions against online businesses. The federal statutes already in existence prohibiting wire fraud apply to online transactions. In addition, several states have begun to amend statutes to explicitly protect online consumers.

LO 4 Credit Protection

The widespread use of credit to purchase goods and services means that consumer credit protection has become increasingly important. This section explores three key federal laws regulating the credit industry to protect consumers: the Truth-in-Lending Act, the Fair Credit Reporting Act, and the Fair Debt Collection Practices Act.

THE TRUTH IN LENDING ACT

One of the earliest, most significant statutes regulating credit is Title I of the Consumer Credit Protection Act (CCPA), referred to as the *Truth in Lending Act (TILA)*.[28] The purpose of the act is

[25] David A. Rice, "*Product Quality Laws and the Economics of Federalism,*" Boston University Law Review 65 (1985), p. 1.
[26] 15 U.S.C. § § 1701–1720.
[27] 12 U.S.C. § § 2601–2617.
[28] 15 U.S.C. § § 1601–1693r.

to require that sellers disclose the terms of the credit or loan to help consumers compare a variety of credit lines or loans. More important, consumers must be able to understand this disclosure of terms. TILA is administered, in part, by the Federal Reserve Board through the previously mentioned Regulation Z.

Suppose your business extends credit to customers. Are your credit lines through your business subject to TILA? First, TILA applies to consumer loans only. Second, TILA applies to those who lend money or arrange for credit through the ordinary course of business. Third, the credit or loan must be in the amount of $25,000 or less, unless the loan is secured by a mortgage on real estate. Fourth, the creditor must be making the loan to a natural person, not a legal entity. Fifth, the credit or loan must be subject to a finance charge or must have repayments of more than four installments.

All creditors subject to TILA must disclose the finance charge and the annual percentage rate of the credit or loan. This information must be disclosed in a meaningful way, which prevents creditors from burying the information in a large paragraph unrelated to the credit terms.

Consider the following example: In May 1999, a jury heard *Carlisle v. Whirlpool Financial National Bank.*[29] According to the case facts, Gulf Coast Electric's salespeople traveled door-to-door, selling satellite dishes through financing. The price of the satellite dish was $1,100. However, consumers could purchase this dish for approximately $200 in stores. The consumers argued that the salespeople hid the number of payments the buyers would have to pay, thereby violating TILA. The jury found in favor of the customers and awarded them $581 million.

Types of Loans under TILA TILA includes three categories of loans: open-end credit, closed-end credit, and credit card applications and solicitations. Each category has specific disclosure requirements. For example, an *open-end credit line* permits repeated transactions and assesses a finance charge on unpaid balances. A creditor of an open-end credit line is required to disclose information in periodic statements. In contrast, a *closed-end credit line* is one for a loan given for a specific amount of time. The creditor of a closed-end credit line must disclose the total amount financed and the number, amount, and due dates of payments. Finally, *credit card applications and solicitations* must include the APR, annual fees, and the grace period for paying without a finance charge.

Unauthorized Charges and Disputes TILA establishes certain consumer protection rules regarding unauthorized charges to credit cards. If your credit card is stolen and someone makes unauthorized purchases on your account, your liability for those charges cannot exceed $50 per card if prompt notification of the theft is made to the credit card company. If you notify the credit card company before unauthorized charges are made, you cannot be held liable for any of the charges. Similarly, if a credit card company sends you an unsolicited card in the mail and the card is stolen, you cannot be held liable for any of the charges.

TILA offers another protection to consumers who unknowingly purchase damaged goods using a credit card. If three requirements are met, consumers will not be obligated to pay for the good. First, the consumer must purchase the item near her home (i.e., the business is in the same state as the consumer's home or within 100 miles of the home). Second, the item must cost more than $50. Third, the consumer must make a good-faith effort to resolve the dispute, such as asking the store for a refund. If these requirements are met, the credit card company cannot bill the consumer for the damaged item.

Consumer Leasing Act In 1988, the Consumer Leasing Act (CLA)[30] amended TILA to provide greater protection for people leasing automobiles and other goods. CLA applies to those who lease goods as part of their regular business. For CLA to apply, the lease must be for a minimum of four months and the price must not exceed $25,000. Under CLA and its controlling regulation, Regulation M,[31] anyone leasing goods must disclose up front, in writing, all the material terms and conditions of the lease.

Equal Credit Opportunity Act In the 1970s, a woman old enough to have children would have had difficulty securing credit because creditors believed that married women with children would

[29] No. 97-068 (Cir. Ct., Hale Co., Ala).
[30] 15 U.S.C. § 1667–1667e.
[31] 12 C.F.R. Part 213.

be less likely to pay their debts. In response to this discrimination, Congress passed the Equal Credit Opportunity Act (ECOA)[32] as a 1974 amendment to TILA. This amendment makes it illegal for creditors to deny credit to individuals on the basis of race, religion, national origin, color, sex, marital status, or age. When determining the creditworthiness of a credit applicant, the creditor cannot use information about the applicant's marital status, nor can the creditor require that a spouse co-sign the application. Finally, the act prohibits creditors from denying credit on the basis of whether the applicant receives public assistance benefits.

Case Nugget

What Does the Law Require of a Loan Company?

Alvin Ricciardi, Appellant, v. Ameriquest Mortgage Company U.S. Court of Appeals for the Third Circuit

164 Fed. Appx. 221 (2006)

Alvin Ricciardi bought a home in May 2001, took out a home equity loan, and then applied for a loan to refinance the two mortgages through Ameriquest. Ricciardi closed the loan in September 2002, at which point he received the "Borrower's Acknowledgment of Final Loan Terms." The acknowledgment stated the terms of the loan that Ricciardi had originally requested, as well as the final terms of the loan. Ricciardi signed all the documents presented during the closing. Eight months later, Ricciardi filed suit against Ameriquest for violating the Equal Credit Opportunity Act, the Truth in Lending Act, and the Pennsylvania Unfair Trade Practices Act and Consumer Protection Law. The district court granted summary judgment regarding Ricciardi's ECOA claim, finding for Ameriquest. At a later nonjury trial, the court ruled in favor of Ameriquest on all counts of Ricciardi's claim as well as Ameriquest's counterclaim. Ricciardi appealed.

Ricciardi's appeal put forth three arguments. First, Ricciardi argued that the district court erred in granting summary judgment in favor of Ameriquest on his ECOA claim because Ameriquest failed to provide notice of its counteroffer before the closing of the loan. Second, Ricciardi argued that the district court erred in its adverse credibility finding. Third, Ricciardi argued that Ameriquest violated TILA by overcharging him for insurance and thereby gave him the right to rescind the loan. The appeals court rejected each of Ricciardi's arguments, affirming the ruling of the district court.

The appeals court addressed each of Ricciardi's arguments in turn. First, TILA requires that a creditor respond to an applicant within 30 days of receipt of a completed loan application. Ameriquest did respond to Ricciardi within 30 days. Contrary to Ricciardi's claim, Ameriquest was not required to respond in the form of a counteroffer. Additionally, there is no requirement that a counteroffer be received before the closing of the loan. Thus, Ricciardi's argument was without merit. Second, the appeals court found that the district court had not erred in its adverse credibility finding. Ricciardi contradicted himself numerous times on the record, in addition to committing fraud by misrepresenting his occupation and income on the loan application to Ameriquest. Third, the appeals court found that Ricciardi had not presented sufficient evidence to substantiate his claim that Ameriquest had overcharged him for insurance. In Pennsylvania, state-mandated insurance rates are published in the *Rate Manual*. The rates decrease if the property is being refinanced and was previously insured. Ricciardi failed to show that the property was previously insured; thus, the district court correctly found that there was no evidence that Ameriquest had overcharged Ricciardi.

[32] 15 U.S.C. § 1691–1691f.

THE FAIR CREDIT REPORTING ACT

If you own a credit card, you also have a credit report. If you apply for a new credit card or a loan, the creditor will check your credit history to make a judgment about your creditworthiness by examining a copy of your credit report. This report contains information about your financial transactions, such as payments on credit, debt collection, and other financial information the creditor needs to know about if entering a business transaction with you.

Because credit bureaus influence consumers' ability to make purchases and secure loans, Congress passed the Fair Credit Reporting Act (FCRA)[33] of 1970 to ensure accurate credit reporting. FCRA regulates the issuance of credit reports for limited business purposes, such as a determination of credit or insurance eligibility, employment, and licensing. If a credit bureau issues a consumer credit report for a reason not specified by FCRA, it may be held liable for damages and additional fines. Furthermore, anyone who uses a credit report for purposes other than those specified in the act may be held liable for damages.

In Case 25-1, a husband and wife sued banks that offered them preapproved credit cards but then rejected their applications. The couple argued that by rejecting the applications for the preapproved credit cards, the banks ultimately obtained their credit reports under false pretenses under FCRA.

[33] 15 U.S.C.§ 1681–1681t.

CASE 25-1

RICHARD D. KENNEDY AND SALLY S. KENNEDY v. CHASE MANHATTAN BANK, USA, N.A., ET AL.
U.S. COURT OF APPEALS FOR THE FIFTH CIRCUIT

369 F.3d 833 (2004)

FACTS: *Richard and Sally Kennedy received prequalified offers for credit card accounts from Chase Manhattan and Bank of America (BOA). On the basis of the representations made by the banks, the Kennedys believed they were preapproved for credit, and they accepted the offers by returning the applications. The banks, however, obtained consumer credit reports from Experian and Transunion and notified the Kennedys that, on the basis of the information in these reports, the banks would not open credit card accounts for the Kennedys. The Kennedys contended that the banks violated Section 1681q of the Fair Credit Reporting Act by obtaining information under the act under false pretenses. The banks filed for summary judgment, and the district court granted all the motions. The Kennedys appealed.*

ISSUE: After giving a "prequalified offer," may a bank obtain an individual's credit report to determine whether to extend credit?

REASONING: Section 1681q of the Fair Credit Reporting Act allows individuals to sue when banks obtain their credit information under false pretenses. To succeed in this case, the Kennedys needed to prove that the banks had an impermissible purpose in obtaining their credit reports. Section 1681q of the act allows banks to obtain consumer credit reports in connection with a credit transaction not initiated by the consumer if the transaction consists of a firm offer of credit or the consumer authorizes the report. In this case, the credit card offers sent to the Kennedys stated that the offered credit may not be extended if, after the Kennedys returned the applications, the banks obtained the Kennedys' credit reports and determined that the Kennedys did not meet the banks' standards for creditworthiness. The Kennedys signed the credit card offers, acknowledging notice that the banks would check their credit history and also authorizing the banks to access their credit information.

DECISION AND REMEDY: The credit card offers signed by the Kennedys showed that the banks did not obtain the Kennedys' credit information under false pretenses. The district court's ruling was affirmed, in favor of the defendants.

(continued)

SIGNIFICANCE OF THE CASE: This case shows that banks may send "prequalified" offers for credit cards without committing to extend credit to every customer. Banks are permitted to screen potential customers' credit history before deciding to extend credit—granted that those customers agree to the terms of the prequalified offer.

CRITICAL THINKING

Explain how rival causes affect this case. Considering the information available to you, what do you think is the most likely cause leading to the banks' obtaining the Kennedys' credit information?

ETHICAL DECISION MAKING

Who are the primary stakeholders affected by the facts in this case? How would it affect the quality of the decision making if judges were to simply forget about some of these stakeholders?

This case illustrates one application of the Fair Credit Reporting Act. FCRA establishes other duties for credit reporting. For example, a credit bureau cannot report obsolete information. (General credit information is considered obsolete after seven years.) However, a bankruptcy will be reported for 10 years. Also, any time a credit applicant is denied credit, the applicant has a right to the name and address of the credit bureau that reported the information. Finally, FCRA imposes a duty on the reporting agency to ensure that its information is as accurate as possible. Consequently, if a consumer reports an error in his or her credit report, the credit bureau is required to investigate the error and make the corrections in the report, if necessary.

THE FAIR DEBT COLLECTION PRACTICES ACT

Suppose a consumer owes $3,000 on his credit card and has not been able to make monthly payments for the past six months. The credit card company will likely refer the case to a collection agency, which will notify the consumer in an attempt to get him to pay the debt. The collection agency then may start calling the consumer regularly to discuss the debt. Next, the agency might start contacting the consumer's acquaintances, telling them about the debt in an effort to pressure the consumer into paying the debt.

This type of debt-collecting behavior is prohibited by the Fair Debt Collection Practices Act (FDCPA).[34] This act applies only to debt collectors who regularly attempt to collect debts on behalf of others. The following collection behaviors are expressly prohibited by FDCPA:

1. Contacting a debtor at work if the debtor's employer objects.
2. Contacting a debtor who has notified the collection agency that he or she wants no contact with the agency.
3. Contacting the debtor before 8 a.m. or after 9 p.m.
4. Contacting third parties about the debt (exceptions: contacting the debtor's parents, spouse, or financial adviser).
5. Using obscene or threatening language when communicating with the debtor.
6. Misrepresenting the collection agency as a lawyer or a police officer.

The act states that these restrictions apply to "debt collectors." Case 25-2 considers whether lawyers fall under the definition of *debt collector*.

[34] 15 U.S.C. § 1692.

CASE 25-2

GEORGE W. HEINTZ ET AL. v. DARLENE JENKINS
UNITED STATES SUPREME COURT
514 U.S. 291; 115 S. Ct. 1489 (1995)

FACTS: *Darlene Jenkins borrowed money from Gainer Bank to purchase a car. The loan required that Jenkins keep an insurance policy on the car. Jenkins had an insurance policy, but she let the insurance expire. The bank took out an insurance policy to cover the car. Next, Jenkins defaulted on her loan. Gainer Bank sued Jenkins to recover the money for the loan. George Heintz, a lawyer for the law firm representing Gainer Bank, sent a letter to Jenkins's lawyer. This letter indicated the amount Jenkins owed the bank, including $4,173 for the insurance. In response, Jenkins brought a Fair Debt Collection Practices Act suit against Heintz. She argued that Heintz was misrepresenting the amount Jenkins owed because the insurance policy was not only protecting her car against "loss or damage" but also against her failure to repay the bank's loan. The district court dismissed the suit, ruling that FDCPA does not apply to lawyers engaging in litigation. The court of appeals disagreed and reversed.*

ISSUE: Does the FDCPA apply to attorneys engaging in litigation?

REASONING: FDCPA defines a debt collector as a person "who regularly collects or attempts to collect, directly or indirectly, debts owed [to] . . . another." In an earlier version of FDCPA, attorneys were explicitly exempted from the definition of *debt collector*. Since then, Congress has revised FDCPA, repealing the exemption in its entirety. Congress did not enact a similar exemption for attorneys. Given Congress's actions, it seems that an attorney who regularly tries to obtain payment of debts through legal proceedings is a debt collector.

DECISION AND REMEDY: Attorneys may fall within FDCPA's definition of *debt collector* and are thus subject to the requirements of FDCPA. The appellate court's ruling was affirmed.

SIGNIFICANCE OF THE CASE: This case has significance for both debtors and those who attempt to collect debts. Firms may not hire attorneys to collect debts by means of unfair practices because attorneys are subject to the same standards as other debt collectors. Debtors can rest assured, knowing that all debt collectors will be held to the same standards of fairness.

CRITICAL THINKING

What ambiguity is central to this case? Do you agree with the way the Court interpreted the ambiguous word or phrase? Can you think of an alternative reasonable definition?

ETHICAL DECISION MAKING

Who are the primary stakeholders affected by the court's ruling? Does the Supreme Court have a stronger ethical obligation to protect the interests of some stakeholders over the interests of others? Explain.

This case illustrates only one example of an FDCPA violation. A debt holder could also be in violation of FDCPA if she did not send written notice to the debtor within five days of initial contact. This notice must include the amount of the debt as well as the name of the creditor. If a debt collector violates FDCPA, the collector is liable for actual damages, attorney fees, and other fines up to $1,000.

THE CREDIT CARD FRAUD ACT

Credit card fraud is a serious problem in the United States, costing consumers millions of dollars per year. Accordingly, Congress passed the Credit Card Fraud Act of 1984[35] to close existing loopholes in federal laws that allowed credit card fraud to be pervasive. The Credit Card Fraud Act states that it is unlawful to (1) possess an unauthorized credit card, (2) counterfeit or alter a credit card, (3) use the account number of another's credit card to perpetuate fraud, and (4) use a credit card obtained from a third party with his or her consent, even if the third party conspires to report the card as stolen. The act also increases the penalty for committing credit card fraud.

THE FAIR CREDIT BILLING ACT

Did your credit card company fail to extend your credit when it informed you that your credit would be extended? Were you ever charged for merchandise you did not purchase or receive? Were you ever charged twice for one purchase? If so, you have been the victim of a credit billing error. The Fair Credit Billing Act (FCBA) of 1986[36] was created to handle such billing errors, as well as many others.

FCBA, enforced by the FTC, creates procedures consumers are to follow in filing complaints when billing errors occur. FCBA also requires that the creditor explain to the consumer and FTC why the error occurred and promptly fix the error. When a complaint is filed, the creditor may not try to collect on the disputed amount or take any action against the consumer until the complaint is answered.

THE FAIR AND ACCURATE CREDIT TRANSACTIONS ACT

The Fair and Accurate Credit Transactions Act (FACTA) of 2003[37] was passed in response to the growing number of identity-theft cases. If someone thinks he is a victim of identity theft, he may contact the FTC, and an alert will be placed in his credit files. The credit files then serve as a national fraud alert system to better enable authorities to catch those who are stealing identities.

Several other requirements created by the act protect consumers. First, major credit reporting agencies are required to provide consumers with a free copy of their credit reports every 12 months. Second, receipts from credit card purchases are to list an abbreviated version of the card number to protect consumer accounts. Third, financial institutions must work with the FTC to "red-flag" suspicious transactions that might be a sign of identity theft. Fourth, assistance will be provided to victims of identity theft to help them rebuild their credit. Fifth, victims of identity theft may report fraud directly to creditors to protect their credit ratings.

LO 5 Consumer Health and Safety

The legislation and rules we have examined regulate the advertising, labeling, and sale of products. Now we turn to legislation regarding product safety. This legislation is directly related to the Firestone-Ford investigation. The purpose of such regulations is to ensure that companies like Firestone and Ford produce safe products for consumers who do not have all the information. The two main federal statutes that address product safety are the Federal Food, Drug, and Cosmetic Act and the Consumer Product Safety Act.

THE FEDERAL FOOD, DRUG, AND COSMETIC ACT

In 1906, Congress created the first federal legislation regulating food and drugs, the Pure Food and Drugs Act. Subsequently, Congress amended the Pure Food and Drugs Act when it created

[35] 18 U.S.C. § 1029(a)(1-4).
[36] 15 U.S.C. § 1601.
[37] Pub. L. No. 108–159, 117 Stat. 1952.

the Federal Food, Drug, and Cosmetic Act (FFDCA)[38] in 1938 to protect consumers against misbranded or adulterated food, drugs, medical devices, or cosmetics. The U.S. Food and Drug Administration (FDA), the agency responsible for administering FFDCA, creates standards to regulate food and drugs, thus protecting consumers. Specifically, the FDA must ensure that food, drugs, cosmetics, and medical devices meet specific safety standards.

Under FFDCA, the FDA must follow a set of procedures to determine whether a drug is safe to enter the market. Recently, the Supreme Court ruled on the issue of whether the FDA has the authority to regulate tobacco (see Case 25-3). According to the FDA, it (1) has authority to regulate drugs and (2) considers nicotine a drug.

[38] 21 U.S.C. § § 301–393.

CASE 25-3

FOOD AND DRUG ADMINISTRATION ET AL. v. BROWN & WILLIAMSON TOBACCO CORPORATION ET AL.
UNITED STATES SUPREME COURT
120 S. Ct. 1291 (2000)

FACTS: *Before 1995, the FDA consistently stated that it did not have the power to regulate tobacco. However, in 1995, the FDA established that nicotine is a "drug" and cigarettes and smokeless tobacco are "devices" for administering the drug. FFDCA grants the FDA authority to regulate drugs and devices. Consequently, in August 1996, the FDA issued a rule with restrictions on the sale, promotion, and labeling of tobacco products, directed at behaviors marketed to kids. A group of tobacco manufacturers, retailers, and advertisers filed suit against the FDA, arguing that it did not have authority to regulate tobacco products and that the advertising restrictions were not permissible under the Constitution. The district court ruled that FFDCA authorizes the FDA to regulate tobacco products and that the labeling requirements were permitted. The Fourth Circuit Court of Appeals reversed, finding Congress did not give the FDA jurisdiction to regulate tobacco products.*

ISSUE: Does the FDA have jurisdiction to regulate tobacco products?

REASONING: The majority (five justices) saw a fatal contradiction in the FDA's case. The FDA has jurisdiction to regulate products that are safe for their intended use. If the FDA has determined that nicotine and cigarettes are unsafe when used for their intended purposes, the FDA has a duty to ban those products—which has been explicitly prohibited by Congress. (Four dissenting justices believed that the FDA did have authority to regulate tobacco products because the FDA has authority to regulate articles intended to affect the structure or any function of the body.) Further, the majority looked to Congress's tobacco-specific legislation. Congress explicitly prohibits federal agencies from imposing health-related labeling requirements on tobacco products. (The dissenting justices believed that the majority overlooked the very purpose of FFDCA: to protect public health. Given the purpose of the statute, the FDA should be permitted to regulate tobacco products.)

DECISION AND REMEDY: The FDA does not have jurisdiction over tobacco products. The appellate court's ruling was affirmed.

SIGNIFICANCE OF THE CASE: The obvious significance of this case is that the FDA was not allowed to protect children from tobacco advertisements, but this case is also a good example of the conflict between the letter of the law and the purpose of the law. The majority of the justices based their ruling on the letter of the law: what Congress had previously said about the FDA's authority to regulate tobacco products, which led the majority to one conclusion. The minority of the justices based their dissent on the purpose of the law: the FDA's ability to protect the public's health, which led the minority to a different conclusion.

(continued)

CRITICAL THINKING

The first reason the majority offers for its conclusion that the FDA does not have authority to regulate tobacco is that the regulation of tobacco does not "fit" with the FDA's scheme for evaluating drugs. Consequently, the FDA would be forced to ban tobacco. What evidence does the court offer for this reason? Are you persuaded by the evidence?

ETHICAL DECISION MAKING

Consider both the majority and dissenting opinions. Who are the primary stakeholders affected by the decision that the FDA cannot regulate tobacco?

This case demonstrates the significant influence the FDA has over the lives and health of American citizens. It also illustrates the problems with some of its regulation devices. The Food and Drug Administration Modernization Act of 1997 amended FFDCA to help improve the regulation process, particularly for drugs and medical devices. For example, the 1997 act reauthorized a drug program that cut the time required for a drug review from 30 months to 15 months. The act also increased patient access to experimental drugs and accelerated the review of important new medications.

THE CONSUMER PRODUCT SAFETY ACT

In the Consumer Product Safety Act of 1972 Congress created and directed the Consumer Product Safety Commission (CPSC) to "protect the public against unreasonable risks of injuries and deaths associated with consumer products."[39]

The CPSC protects the public from injuries associated with consumer products in several ways. First, the CPSC issues and enforces mandatory standards regarding product safety. Similarly, the commission works with industries to develop voluntary product standards. If the CPSC cannot establish a standard that would adequately protect the public, it can ban consumer products from the market. In addition, the CPSC can administer existing product safety legislation. Examples of such legislation include the Child Protection and Toy Safety Act of 1969[40] and the Federal Hazardous Substance Act of 1960.[41]

Second, the CPSC can arrange for a recall of products. Although the CPSC has the authority to issue product recalls on its own, usually the CPSC works with companies that are voluntarily issuing recalls for dangerous products. For example, in August 2006, both Dell and Apple issued voluntary recalls, with the help of the CPSC, for lithium ion batteries sold in their laptops. Both companies received several separate complaints about their batteries overheating, and thus the CPSC aided the companies in the battery recall.

Third, the commission conducts research regarding potentially hazardous products. The National Highway Traffic Safety Administration (NHTSA) is similar to the CPSC in that it too conducts investigations about the safety of potentially hazardous products. The NHTSA, however, focuses primarily on motor vehicles. The NHTSA was the agency that investigated the Ford-Firestone case to determine exactly what was causing the tire blowouts in Ford Explorers.

Fourth, the CPSC educates consumers about product safety. One important way the CPSC offers this education is through the National Injury Information Clearinghouse.

This section examined two of the most significant laws governing the safety of consumer products. Exhibit 25-2 lists six additional consumer product safety laws.

[39] 15 U.S.C. § 2051.
[40] Amendments to 15 U.S.C. § § 1261, 1262, and 1274.
[41] 15 U.S.C. § § 1261–1277.

STATUTE	PURPOSE
Pure Food and Drugs Act of 1906 (amended by the Federal Food, Drug, and Cosmetic Act)	Forbids the adulteration and mislabeling of food and drugs
Meat Inspection Act of 1906 Wholesome Meat Act of 1967	Provides for meat inspection. Amended the Meat Inspection Act to promulgate standards for animal slaughter for meat
Flammable Fabrics Act of 1953	Prohibits the sale of highly flammable clothing
Child Protection and Toy Safety Act of 1969	Requires childproof devices and toy labeling
Toy Safety Act of 1984	Permits the Consumer Product Safety Commission to recall toys and other articles used by children
Drug-Price Competition and Patent-Term Restoration Act of 1984	Simplifies the Food and Drug Administration's process of approving generic drugs

Exhibit 25-2

Other Consumer Protection Laws

 SUMMARY

The Federal Trade Commission

How the FTC brings an action:

1. FTC conducts an investigation.
2. FTC sends a complaint to the violator.
3. FTC and the violator settle the complaint through a consent agreement.
4. If the company refuses to enter the consent agreement, the FTC may issue a formal administrative complaint, which leads to an administrative hearing.
5. If the company has violated the law, the FTC issues a cease-and-desist order.

If the company violates the order, the FTC can seek an injunction against the company or fine the company up to $10,000 per violation.

Deceptive Advertising

Bait-and-switch advertising: Advertising a low price to "bait" the consumer into the store only so that the salesperson can "switch" the consumer to another, higher-priced item

FTC actions against deceptive advertising:

- *Cease-and-desist actions:* Court orders requiring that firms stop their current advertising behavior.
- *Multiple-product orders:* Court orders requiring that firms stop current advertisements on numerous products, as opposed to one specified product.
- *Corrective advertising:* Advertising in which the company explicitly states that the formerly advertised claims were untrue.

Telemarketing and electronic advertising:

- *1991 Telephone Consumer Protection Act:* Telemarketers cannot use an automatic telephone dialing system or a prerecorded voice.
- *Telemarketing and Consumer Fraud and Abuse Prevention Act of 1994:* This act created certain requirements regarding when and how telemarketers may make calls.
- *Federal Do Not Call registry:* Telemarketers cannot call consumers who have voluntarily placed their phone numbers on the federal Do Not Call list.

Tobacco advertising: Cigarettes and smokeless-tobacco advertising is restricted.

Labeling and Packaging Laws

Federal and state governments have passed laws requiring that manufacturers provide accurate, understandable information on labels. Furthermore, if a product is potentially harmful, the manufacturer must make the consumer aware of the harm.

Sales

Door-to-door sales: The *Cooling-Off Rule* gives consumers three days to cancel purchases they make from salespeople who come to their homes.

Telephone and mail-order sales: The *Mail or Telephone Order Merchandise Rule of 1993* extends protections to those who purchase over the phone or by fax.

Unsolicited merchandise: Anyone receiving such merchandise may treat it as a gift.

FTC regulation of specific industries:

1. Used-car sales
2. Funeral home services
3. Real estate sales
4. Online sales

Credit Protection

The *Truth in Lending Act* requires that sellers disclose the terms of the credit or loan to facilitate the consumer's comparison of a variety of credit lines or loans.

The *Fair Credit Reporting Act* ensures accurate credit reporting.

The *Fair Debt Collection Practices Act* regulates the actions of debt collectors that regularly attempt to collect debts on behalf of others.

The *Credit Card Fraud Act* closes loopholes in federal laws to further punish people who commit credit card fraud.

The *Fair Credit Billing Act* seeks to rectify problems and abuses associated with credit billing errors.

The *Fair and Accurate Credit Transactions Act* takes affirmative actions to control and prosecute identity theft.

Consumer Health and Safety

The *Federal Food, Drug, and Cosmetic Act* protects consumers against misbranded or adulterated food, drugs, medical devices, and cosmetics.

The *Consumer Product Safety Act* created the Consumer Product Safety Commission (CPSC) to "protect the public against unreasonable risks of injuries and deaths associated with consumer products."

 Point/Counterpoint

Should Firms Be Prevented from Concealing Valuable Product Information from Consumers?	
YES	NO
Consumer protection legislation should protect consumers against sellers who wish to sell goods and services under cover of deception.	The best way to protect consumers is by placing responsibility on them to ask the right questions. They and only they know what they are seeking from a good or service. No regulatory agency understands why consumers are purchasing a particular product.
The great benefit of markets is that they satisfy consumers. But a consumer cannot be sovereign when he is asked to purchase a tainted version of the good he thought he was buying.	To try to protect consumers against any and all possible harm is to treat them as if they were infants, incapable of watching out for themselves.
When firms conceal information that they well know would affect the likelihood of a sale, they are encouraging a culture of mistrust. They are saying by their behavior that it is appropriate business behavior to deceive in the interest of encouraging an exchange.	A business firm should not be required to mention every attribute possessed by a product just to satisfy some utopian goal of full disclosure.

1. What is the goal of the FTC, and how does it achieve its goal? What are some pieces of legislation that enable the FTC to achieve its goal?

2. What are the elements of a deceptive advertisement, and how does the FTC prove an ad is deceptive?

3. What are the main provisions of the Truth in Lending Act, and how does it aid consumers?

4. Until 2002, the City of Bethlehem contractually retained the private law firm of Portnoff Law Associates, Ltd. (PLA) to collect payment for overdue water and sewer obligations. The city notified PLA of delinquent water and sewer assessments, and PLA then contacted homeowners in attempts to collect on those claims. On February 20, 2002, the city notified PLA of a delinquent water service obligation of Bridget and Michael Piper in the amount of $252.71. PLA sent numerous letters, some on its letterhead and some on the city's letterhead, as well as made a number of telephone calls to the Piper residence in an effort to secure payment of the delinquent water service fees. PLA has never disputed that the letters it sent to the Pipers failed to include the debt verification language required by Section 1692(g) of FDCPA. PLA has likewise never disputed that its letters did not state they were sent by a debt collector, the debt collector was attempting to collect a debt, and any information obtained by PLA would be used for that purpose, as required by Section 1692(e)(11) of FDCPA. Bridget Piper filed suit against PLA and two of its attorneys in the U.S. District Court for the Eastern District of Pennsylvania. The complaint alleged that PLA's attempts to collect payment of water and sewer bills owed to the city violated FDCPA. The complaint alleged that PLA violated this statute by failing to include statutory disclosures required for communications sent to consumers, by falsely representing or implying that the letters were from an attorney, and by collecting and attempting to collect fees not permitted by the agreement creating the debt or by law. Were the Pipers successful in their suit against PLA? Why? [*Piper v. Portnoff Law Assocs.,* 396 F.3d 227 (2005).]

5. On March 7, 2001, the U.S. District Court for the Eastern District of Virginia, after finding that H&R Block had willfully and maliciously engaged in a false and misleading advertising campaign aimed at preventing Liberty Tax Service and 13 of its franchisees from competing for customers, entered a permanent nationwide injunction against H&R Block requiring, among other things, that its advertisements "clearly and prominently" disclose whether an advertised product is actually a loan. On October 10, 2001, and January 10, 2002, Liberty filed two separate civil contempt motions alleging that H&R Block was in violation of the district court's injunction because its "Instant Money" advertisements used much smaller type and less apparent color print for the term *loan* than for terms such as *refund, check today,* and *instant money.* Liberty further alleged that H&R Block's advertisements failed to "clearly and prominently" disclose whether an advertised product was a loan because the loan disclosures contained therein were placed in areas that increased the likelihood they would go unnoticed and consequently unread. Liberty argued that the injunction's "clearly and prominently" language required that H&R Block's loan disclosures be presented in a manner that made them immediately noticeable to consumers. The district court ruled in favor of H&R Block because the reasonable person reading the H&R Block ads would be able to tell that the "Instant Money" campaign actually referred to loans taken out against an expected refund. Liberty appealed. Was Liberty successful on appeal? Why? [*JTH Tax, Inc. v. H&R Block E. Tax Servs.,* 359 F.3d 699 (2004).]

6. Brenda Laramore receives federal assistance pursuant to Section Eight of the United States Housing Act. "Section [Eight] is a federal program designed to assist the elderly, low income, and disabled pay rent for privately owned housing." The assistance generally comes in the form of a voucher the recipient can use to pay a portion of his or her rent. On October 21, 2002, Laramore telephoned Ritchie, the company responsible for managing the apartment in question, to request an application for a lease. The woman who took the call initially told Laramore the apartment was available to rent. After Laramore informed her she intended to use a Section 8 voucher to pay a portion of the rent, however, the woman told Laramore the apartment was not available to persons using Section 8 vouchers. On February 21, 2003, Laramore filed suit claiming that Ritchie violated ECOA by denying her a rental application because she receives public assistance. Ritchie moved to dismiss the complaint on the ground that a rental application is not a credit transaction under ECOA. The district court agreed with Ritchie and dismissed the suit. Laramore

appealed. Did Ritchie violate ECOA? Should ECOA apply to rental applications? [*Laramore v. Ritchie Realty Mgmt. Co.,* 397 F.3d 544 (2005).]

7. In August 1999, United Artists contracted with ABF, a company in the business of distributing advertisements by fax, to send a one-page advertisement for discount movie ticket packages. The following month, ABF transmitted the advertisement to about 90,000 fax machines in the Phoenix area. United Artists received $12,080 through the ad, and paid ABF $3,375 for its services. ESI is the only recipient that complained to United Artists about receiving the advertisement. After ESI received the faxed advertisement, it filed a complaint, alleging violation of the Telephone Consumer Protection Act (TCPA), which makes it unlawful for persons within the United States to, among other things, "use any telephone facsimile machine, computer, or other device to send an unsolicited advertisement to a telephone facsimile machine." ESI requested statutory damages of $500 per violation, with possible trebling (tripling) of those damages, and injunctive relief. ESI sought to represent a class consisting of "all persons and entities who received on a telephone facsimile machine" the particular advertisement sent by ABF for United Artists. United Artists objected to the class certification, arguing, among other things, that a class action suit could lead to liability against United Artists disproportionate to the harm caused. ESI offered to waive the statutory minimum recovery of $500 per violation and to reduce damages to $90 or, alternatively, to modify and reduce the number of the class. The trial court denied ESI's motion for certification of the class. ESI appealed the trial court's ruling. Should United Artists be required to pay for sending out its one-page fax? If you were on the court, how would you rule? Why? [*ESI Ergonomic Solutions, LLC v. UA Theatre Circuit, Inc.,* 50 P.3d 844 (2002).]

8. American Collections Enterprise, Inc. (ACEI), is a debt collector that contracted with Capital One in 2001 to provide debt collection services. Under the terms of the collection agreement, Capital One assigned delinquent accounts to ACEI for collection, and ACEI collected these debts on a contingent-fee basis. Pooja Goswami owed approximately $900 on her Capital One credit card and failed to pay. Capital One referred that debt to ACEI for collection on March 20, 2001, and ACEI pursued Goswami's delinquent account. It sent a collection notice letter to Goswami on December 7, 2001. A second form letter was sent on January 25, 2002, more than 180 days after the debt had been referred to ACEI. The second letter was sent to Goswami in an envelope that bore a half-inch-thick blue bar, across the entire envelope, containing the words "Priority Letter" in white. ACEI admitted that the markings on the envelope had been

developed to entice debtors to open the letter. The letter itself contained a second blue bar and "Priority Letter" marking as a header. After receiving the letter Goswami filed a complaint alleging violation of FDCPA, in particular 15 U.S.C. Sections 1692f(8) and 1692e(10). Goswami complained that the markings on the envelope violate Section 1692f(8), which prohibits any markings on debt collection letter envelopes besides the name and address of the sender and the addressee. She further complained that the contents of the letter were deceptive, in violation of Section 1692e(10). ACEI moved for summary judgment, arguing that neutral or benign expressions on an envelope, such as "priority letter," that in no way indicate it is a collection letter are not banned by FDCPA. The district court agreed, granted the defendant's summary judgment motion, and dismissed the case. Goswami appealed. Are the markings on the envelope and letter misleading and a violation of FDCPA? Why? [*Goswami v. Am. Collections Enter.,* 377 F.3d 488 (2004).]

9. Mary Grendahl's daughter Sarah became engaged to marry Lavon Phillips and moved in with him. Mary Grendahl became suspicious that Phillips was not telling the truth about his past. She did some preliminary investigation herself before she contacted Kevin Fitzgerald, a family friend who worked for McDowell, a private investigation agency. She asked Fitzgerald to do a "background check" on Phillips. Fitzgerald began his search by obtaining Phillips's Social Security number from a computer database and used it to request that Econ Control furnish a finder's report on Phillips. According to the president of Econ Control, a finder's report could be obtained without authorization of the person who was the subject of the report because the finder's report contained no information on credit history or creditworthiness, whereas a credit report requires authorization from the subject. Fitzgerald met with Mary Grendahl and gave her the results of his investigation, including the finder's report. Phillips brought suit against Mary Grendahl, McDowell Agency, and Econ Control, alleging, "Defendants willfully and maliciously obtained Plaintiff's credit report for impermissible and illegal purposes in violation of the Fair Credit Reporting Act." Phillips appended to his complaint a "Credit History" on himself, which, among other things, showed that Sherlock Information (the trade name of Econ Control) had requested a credit history on him. Phillips and the defendants filed cross-motions for summary judgment. The district court ruled in favor of the defendants, and Phillips appealed. Did the court find that Grendahl and the other defendants violated the Fair Credit Reporting Act through their investigation? Why? [*Phillips v. Grendahl,* 312 F.3d 357 (2002).]

10. Aroma Housewares Co. is a California corporation that distributes electric kitchen appliances. Aroma distributed between 30,000 and 40,000 juice extractors in the United States. The juicers employed a rapidly spinning metal grater, whose sharp teeth pulverized fruits and vegetables that were inserted through a plastic chute. Aroma began receiving consumer reports of failed juicers. Exploding juicers, the reports claimed, "[threw] with great violence pieces of the clear plastic cover and shreds of the razor-sharp separator screen as far as eight feet." One consumer called the juicer "an unsafe and dangerous machine which exploded in [his] face." A flying blade sliced the hand of another. And one injured woman was taken by ambulance to the hospital, where she stayed overnight, and she sustained permanent damage to her fingers, hand, and arm. In all, Aroma received complaints from 23 consumers. Aroma tested the juicers but was unable to replicate the malfunctions. It reported none of this to the Consumer Product Safety Commission. But some of the consumers did. Alerted to the problems, the commission asked the company to report what it knew about the dangers posed by its juicers. Aroma disclosed the consumer complaints, as well as the results of its own tests. A few months later, Aroma and the commission jointly announced that the juicers were being recalled. The United States subsequently sued Aroma, alleging that the company had violated the reporting requirements of the Consumer Product Safety Act. The district court granted partial summary judgment for the United States. Aroma appealed. Did Aroma violate CPSA? Should Aroma have reported the defective juicers even though it could not replicate the malfunctions? [*U.S. v. Mirama Enters.*, 387 F.3d 983 (2004).]

11. Seven plaintiffs brought suit against Boise Cascade for deceptive advertising. Boise Cascade produced a composite wood siding from 1960 to 1984. All seven of the plaintiffs live in homes covered in Boise Cascade's composite siding. Only two of the seven plaintiffs are original owners of their homes. The plaintiffs alleged that Boise Cascade's composite siding was defective and Boise Cascade deceptively advertised the composite siding. The complaint also claimed that Boise Cascade fraudulently and deceptively failed to disclose that its siding "performed poorly in the field," with a "high rate of failure," was sensitive to moisture, and required "highly particularized maintenance." None of the plaintiffs actually received any representations regarding the siding from Boise Cascade. The circuit court granted Boise Cascade summary judgment, finding that the claimed damages were not proximately caused by the alleged deceptive advertising as there was no evidence of reliance on the advertisements. The plaintiffs appealed. The appellate court reversed, holding that the circuit court erred by requiring privity, "some sort of direct contact between the plaintiffs and the representations made by Boise Cascade." According to the appellate court, consumers are afforded broad protection by prohibiting any deception or false promise. The appellate court further held that the circuit court erred in its conclusion that there was no proximate causation. The court held that reliance on deceptive advertisements can be proved by the fact that a market for a good existed. Boise Cascade appealed. How did the court ultimately rule on appeal? Why? [*Shannon v. Boise Cascade Corp.*, 208 Ill. 2d 517 (2004).]

12. Fairbanks Capital Corp. acquired 12,800 allegedly delinquent high-interest mortgages from Conti-Mortgage, including one owed by Chad and Frances Schlosser. Identifying itself as a debt collector, Fairbanks sent the Schlossers a letter asserting that their debt was in default. Fairbanks was mistaken; the Schlossers were not in default. The Schlossers tried to inform Fairbanks that they were not in default, and Fairbanks tried to foreclose. The foreclosure was eventually stopped. The Schlossers then filed suit claiming that Fairbanks's letter failed to notify them of their right to contest the debt, as required by the Fair Debt Collection Practices Act. The district court concluded that, because the debt was not actually in default when Fairbanks acquired it, Fairbanks was not a debt collector within the meaning of FDCPA. The court granted Fairbanks's motion to dismiss, and the Schlossers appealed. How did the court rule on appeal? Why? [*Schlosser v. Fairbanks Capital Corp.*, 323 F.3d 534 (2003).]

Looking for more review material?

The Online Learning Center at **www.mhhe.com/kubasekess** contains this chapter's "Assignment on the Internet" and also a list of URLs for more information, entitled "On the Internet." Find both of them in the Student Center portion of the OLC, along with quizzes and other helpful materials.

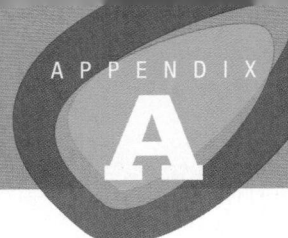
The Constitution of the United States of America

Preamble

We the People of the United States, in Order to form a more perfect Union, establish Justice, insure domestic Tranquility, provide for the common defense, promote the general Welfare, and secure the Blessings of Liberty to ourselves and our Posterity, do ordain and establish this Constitution for the United States of America.

Article I

Section 1 All legislative Powers herein granted shall be vested in a Congress of the United States, which shall consist of a Senate and House of Representatives.

Section 2 The House of Representatives shall be composed of Members chosen every second Year by the People of the several States, and the Electors in each State shall have the Qualifications requisite for Electors of the most numerous Branch of the State Legislature.

No Person shall be a Representative who shall not have attained to the age of twenty five Years, and been seven Years a Citizen of the United States, and who shall not, when elected, be an Inhabitant of that State in which he shall be chosen.

Representatives and direct Taxes shall be apportioned among the several States which may be included within this Union, according to their respective Numbers, which shall be determined by adding to the whole Number of free Persons, including those bound to Service for a Term of Years, and excluding Indians not taxed, three fifths of all other Persons.[1] The actual Enumeration shall be made within three Years after the first Meeting of the Congress of the United States, and within every subsequent Term of ten Years, in such Manner as they shall by Law direct. The Number of Representatives shall not exceed one for every thirty Thousand, but each State shall have at Least one Representative, and until such enumeration shall be made, the State of New Hampshire shall be entitled to choose three, Massachusetts eight, Rhode-Island and Providence Plantations one, Connecticut five, New York six, New Jersey four, Pennsylvania eight, Delaware one, Maryland six, Virginia ten, North Carolina five, South Carolina five, and Georgia three.

When vacancies happen in the Representation from any State, the Executive Authority thereof shall issue Writs of Election to fill such Vacancies.

The House of Representatives shall chuse their Speaker and other Officers; and shall have the sole Power of Impeachment.

Section 3 The Senate of the United States shall be composed of two Senators from each State, chosen by the Legislature thereof,[2] for six Years; and each Senator shall have one Vote.

Immediately after they shall be assembled in Consequence of the first Election, they shall be divided as equally as may be into three Classes. The Seats of the Senators of the first Class shall be vacated at the Expiration of the second Year, of the second Class at the Expiration of the fourth Year, and of the third Class at the Expiration of the sixth Year, so that one third may be chosen every second Year; and if Vacancies happen by Resignation, or otherwise, during the Recess of the Legislature of any State, the Executive thereof may make temporary Appointments until the next Meeting of the Legislature, which shall then fill such Vacancies.[3]

No Person shall be a Senator who shall not have attained to the Age of thirty Years, and been nine Years a Citizen of the United States, and who shall not, when elected, be an Inhabitant of that State for which he shall be chosen.

The Vice President of the United States shall be President of the Senate, but shall have no Vote, unless they be equally divided.

The Senate shall chuse their other Officers, and also a President pro tempore, in the Absence of the Vice President, or when he shall exercise the Office of President of the United States.

The Senate shall have the sole Power to try all Impeachments. When sitting for that Purpose, they shall be on Oath or Affirmation. When the President of the United States is tried, the Chief Justice shall preside: And no Person shall be convicted without the Concurrence of two thirds of the Members present.

[1] Changed by the Fourteenth Amendment.

[2] Changed by the Seventeenth Amendment.

[3] Changed by the Seventeenth Amendment.

Judgment in Cases of Impeachment shall not extend further than to removal from Office, and disqualification to hold and enjoy any Office of honor, Trust or Profit under the United States: but the Party convicted shall nevertheless be liable and subject to Indictment, Trial, Judgment and Punishment, according to Law.

Section 4 The Times, Places and Manner of holding Elections for Senators and Representatives, shall be prescribed in each State by the Legislature thereof; but the Congress may at any time by Law make or alter such Regulations, except as to the Places of chusing Senators.

The Congress shall assemble at least once in every Year, and such Meeting shall be on the first Monday in December, unless they shall by Law appoint a different Day.[4]

Section 5 Each House shall be the Judge of the Elections, Returns and Qualifications of its own Members, and a Majority of each shall constitute a Quorum to do Business; but a smaller Number may adjourn from day to day, and may be authorized to compel the Attendance of absent Members, in such Manner, and under such Penalties as each House may provide.

Each House may determine the Rules of its Proceedings, punish its Members for disorderly Behaviour, and with the Concurrence of two thirds, expel a Member.

Each House shall keep a Journal of its Proceedings, and from time to time publish the same, excepting such Parts as may in their Judgment require Secrecy; and the Yeas and Nays of the Members of either House on any question shall, at the Desire of one fifth of those Present, be entered on the Journal.

Neither House, during the Session of Congress, shall, without the Consent of the other, adjourn for more than three days, nor to any other Place than that in which the two Houses shall be sitting.

Section 6 The Senators and Representatives shall receive a Compensation for their Services, to be ascertained by Law, and paid out of the Treasury of the United States. They shall in all Cases, except Treason, Felony and Breach of the Peace, be privileged from Arrest during their Attendance at the Session of their respective Houses, and in going to and returning from the same; and for any Speech or Debate in either House, they shall not be questioned in any other Place.

No Senator or Representative shall, during the Time for which he was elected, be appointed to any civil Office under the Authority of the United States, which shall have been created, or the Emoluments whereof shall have been encreased during such time; and no Person holding any Office under the United States, shall be a Member of either House during his Continuance in Office.

Section 7 All Bills for raising Revenue shall originate in the House of Representatives; but the Senate may propose or concur with Amendments as on other Bills.

Every Bill which shall have passed the House of Representatives and the Senate, shall, before it becomes a Law, be presented to the President of the United States; If he approves he shall sign it, but if not he shall return it, with his Objections to that House in which it shall have originated, who shall enter the Objections at large on their Journal, and proceed to reconsider it. If after such Reconsideration two thirds of that House shall agree to pass the Bill, it shall be sent, together with the Objections, to the other House, by which it shall likewise be reconsidered, and if approved by two thirds of that House, it shall become a Law. But in all such Cases the Votes of both Houses shall be determined by Yeas and Nays, and the Names of the Persons voting for and against the Bill shall be entered on the Journal of each House respectively. If any Bill shall not be returned by the President within ten Days (Sundays excepted) after it shall have been presented to him, the Same shall be a Law, in like Manner as if he had signed it, unless the Congress by their Adjournment prevent its Return, in which Case it shall not be a Law.

Every Order, Resolution, or Vote to which the Concurrence of the Senate and House of Representatives may be necessary (except on a question of Adjournment) shall be presented to the President of the United States; and before the Same shall take Effect, shall be approved by him, or being disapproved by him, shall be repassed by two thirds of the Senate and House of Representatives, according to the Rules and Limitations prescribed in the Case of a Bill.

Section 8 The Congress shall have Power To lay and collect Taxes, Duties, Imposts and Excises, to pay the Debts and provide for the common Defence and general Welfare of the United States; but all Duties, Imposts and Excises shall be uniform throughout the United States.

To borrow Money on the credit of the United States;

To regulate Commerce with foreign Nations, and among the several States, and with the Indian Tribes;

To establish an uniform Rule of Naturalization, and uniform Laws on the subject of Bankruptcies throughout the United States;

To coin Money, regulate the Value thereof, and of foreign Coin, and fix the Standard of Weights and Measures;

To provide for the Punishment of counterfeiting the Securities and current Coin of the United States;

To establish Post Offices and post Roads;

To promote the Progress of Science and useful Arts, by securing for limited Times to Authors and Inventors the exclusive Right to their respective Writings and Discoveries;

To constitute Tribunals inferior to the supreme Court;

To define and punish Piracies and Felonies committed on the high Seas, and Offences against the Law of Nations;

To declare War, grant Letters of Marque and Reprisal, and make Rules concerning Captures on Land and Water;

[4] Changed by the Twentieth Amendment.

To raise and support Armies, but no Appropriation of Money to that Use shall be for a longer Term than two Years;

To provide and maintain a Navy;

To make Rules for the Government and Regulation of the land and naval Forces;

To provide for calling forth the Militia to execute the Laws of the Union, suppress Insurrections and repel Invasions;

To provide for organizing, arming, and disciplining, the Militia, and for governing such Part of them as may be employed in the Service of the United States, reserving to the States respectively, the Appointment of the Officers, and the Authority of training the Militia according to the discipline prescribed by Congress;

To exercise exclusive Legislation in all Cases whatsoever, over such District (not exceeding ten Miles square) as may, by Cession of particular States, and the Acceptance of Congress, become the Seat of the Government of the United States, and to exercise like Authority over all Places purchased by the Consent of the Legislature of the State in which the Same shall be, for the Erection of Forts, Magazines, Arsenals, dock-Yards, and other needful Buildings;—And

To make all Laws which shall be necessary and proper for carrying into Execution the foregoing Powers, and all other Powers vested by this Constitution in the Government of the United States, or in any Department or Officer thereof.

Section 9 The Migration or Importation of such Persons as any of the States now existing shall think proper to admit, shall not be prohibited by the Congress prior to the Year one thousand eight hundred and eight, but a Tax or duty may be imposed on such Importation, not exceeding ten dollars for each Person.

The Privilege of the Writ of Habeas Corpus shall not be suspended, unless when in Cases of Rebellion or Invasion the public Safety may require it.

No Bill of Attainder or ex post facto Law shall be passed.

No Capitation, or other direct, Tax shall be laid, unless in Proportion to the Census of Enumeration herein before directed to be taken.[5]

No Tax or Duty shall be laid on Articles exported from any State.

No Preference shall be given by any Regulation of Commerce or Revenue to the Ports of one State over those of another: nor shall Vessels bound to, or from, one State, be obliged to enter, clear, or pay Duties in another.

No Money shall be drawn from the Treasury, but in Consequence of Appropriations made by Law; and a regular Statement and Account of the Receipts and Expenditures of all public Money shall be published from time to time.

No Title of Nobility shall be granted by the United States: And no Person holding any Office of Profit or Trust under them, shall, without the Consent of the Congress, accept of any present, Emolument, Office, or Title, of any kind whatever, from any King, Prince, or foreign State.

Section 10 No State shall enter into any Treaty, Alliance, or Confederation; grant Letters of Marque and Reprisal; coin Money; emit Bills of Credit; make any Thing but gold and silver coin a Tender in Payment of Debts; pass any Bill of Attainder, ex post facto Law, or Law impairing the Obligation of Contracts, or grant any Title of Nobility.

No State shall, without the Consent of the Congress, lay any Imposts or Duties on Imports or Exports, except what may be absolutely necessary for executing its inspection Laws: and the net Produce of all Duties and Imposts, laid by any State on Imports or Exports, shall be for the Use of the Treasury of the United States; and all such Laws shall be subject to the Revision and Controul of the Congress.

No State shall, without the consent of Congress, lay any Duty of Tonnage, keep Troops, or Ships of War in time of Peace, enter into any Agreement or Compact with another State, or with a foreign Power, or engage in War, unless actually invaded, or in such imminent Danger as will not admit of delay.

Article II

Section 1 The executive Power shall be vested in a President of the United States of America. He shall hold his Office during the Term of four Years, and, together with the Vice President, chosen for the same Term, be elected, as follows

Each state shall appoint, in such Manner as the Legislature thereof may direct, a Number of Electors, equal to the whole Number of Senators and Representatives to which the State may be entitled in Congress: but no Senator or Representative, or Person holding an Office of Trust or Profit under the United States, shall be appointed an Elector.

The Electors shall meet in their respective States, and vote by Ballot for two Persons, of whom one at least shall not be an inhabitant of the same State with themselves. And they shall make a List of all the Persons voted for, and of the Number of Votes for each; which List they shall sign and certify, and transmit sealed to the Seat of the Government of the United States, directed to the President of the Senate. The President of the Senate shall, in the Presence of the Senate and House of Representatives, open all the Certificates, and the Votes shall then be counted. The Person having the greatest Number of Votes shall be the President, if such Number be a Majority of the whole Number of Electors appointed; and if there be more than one who have such Majority, and have an equal Number of Votes, then the House of Representatives shall immediately chuse by Ballot one of them for President; and if no

[5] Changed by the Sixteenth Amendment.

Person have a Majority, then from the five highest on the List the said House shall in like Manner chuse the President. But in chusing the President, the Votes shall be taken by States, the Representation from each State having one Vote; A quorum for this purpose shall consist of a Member or Members from two thirds of the States, and a Majority of all the States shall be necessary to a Choice. In every Case, after the Choice of the President, the Person having the greatest Number of Votes of the Electors shall be the Vice President. But if there should remain two or more who have equal Votes, the Senate shall chuse from them by Ballot the Vice President.[6]

The Congress may determine the Time of chusing the Electors, and the Day on which they shall give their Votes; which Day shall be the same throughout the United States.

No Person except a natural born Citizen, or a Citizen of the United States, at the time of the Adoption of this Constitution, shall be eligible to the Office of President; neither shall any Person be eligible to that Office who shall not have attained to the Age of thirty five Years, and been fourteen Years a Resident within the United States.

In Case of the Removal of the President from Office, or of his Death, Resignation, or Inability to discharge the Powers and Duties of the said Office, the Same shall devolve on the Vice President, and the Congress may by Law provide for the Case of Removal, Death, Resignation or Inability, both of the President and Vice President, declaring what Officer shall then act as President, and such Officer shall act accordingly, until the Disability be removed, or a President shall be elected.[7]

The President shall, at stated Times, receive for his Services, a Compensation, which shall neither be encreased nor diminished during the Period for which he shall have been elected, and he shall not receive within that Period any other Emolument from the United States, or any of them.

Before he enter on the Execution of his Office, he shall take the following Oath or Affirmation:—"I do solemnly swear (or affirm) that I will faithfully execute the Office of President of the United States, and will to the best of my Ability, preserve, protect, and defend the Constitution of the United States."

Section 2 The President shall be Commander in Chief of the Army and Navy of the United States, and of the Militia of the several States, when called into the actual Service of the United States; he may require the Opinion, in writing, of the principal Officer in each of the executive Departments, upon any Subject relating to the Duties of their respective Offices, and he shall have Power to grant Reprieves and Pardons for Offences against the United States, except in Cases of Impeachment.

He shall have Power, by and with the Advice and Consent of the Senate, to make Treaties, provided two thirds of the Senators present concur; and he shall nominate, and by and with the Advice and Consent of the Senate, shall appoint Ambassadors, other public Ministers and Consuls, Judges of the supreme Court, and all other Officers of the United States, whose Appointments are not herein otherwise provided for, and which shall be established by Law; but the Congress may by Law vest the Appointment of such inferior Officers, as they think proper, in the President alone, in the Courts of Law, or in the Heads of Departments.

The President shall have Power to fill up all Vacancies that may happen during the Recess of the Senate, by granting Commissions which shall expire at the End of their next Session.

Section 3 He shall from time to time give to the Congress Information of the State of the Union, and recommend to their Consideration such Measures as he shall judge necessary and expedient; he may, on extraordinary Occasions, convene both Houses, or either of them, and in Case of Disagreement between them, with Respect to the Time of Adjournment, he may adjourn them to such Time as he shall think proper; he shall receive Ambassadors and other public Ministers; he shall take Care that the Laws be faithfully executed, and shall Commission all the Officers of the United States.

Section 4 The President, Vice President and all civil Officers of the United States, shall be removed from Office on Impeachment for, and Conviction of, Treason, Bribery, or other high Crimes and Misdemeanors.

Article III

Section 1 The judicial Power of the United States, shall be vested in one supreme Court, and in such inferior Courts as the Congress may from time to time ordain and establish. The Judges, both of the supreme and inferior Courts, shall hold their Offices during good Behaviour, and shall, at stated Times, receive for their Services, a Compensation, which shall not be diminished during their Continuance in Office.

Section 2 The judicial Power shall extend to all Cases, in Law and Equity, arising under this Constitution, the Laws of the United States, and Treaties made, or which shall be made, under their Authority;—to all Cases affecting Ambassadors, other public Ministers and Consuls;—to all Cases of admiralty and maritime Jurisdiction;—to Controversies to which the United States shall be a party;—to Controversies between two or more States;—between a State and Citizens of another State;[8]—between Citizens of different States;—between Citizens of the same State claiming Lands under Grants of different States, and

[6] Changed by the Twelfth Amendment.
[7] Changed by the Twenty-fifth Amendment.

[8] Changed by the Eleventh Amendment.

between a State, or the Citizens thereof, and foreign States, Citizens or Subjects.

In all Cases affecting Ambassadors, other public Ministers and Consuls, and those in which a State shall be Party, the supreme Court shall have original Jurisdiction. In all the other Cases before mentioned, the supreme Court shall have appellate Jurisdiction, both as to Law and Fact, with such Exceptions, and under such Regulations as the Congress shall make.

The Trial of all Crimes, except in Cases of Impeachment, shall be by Jury: and such Trial shall be held in the State where the said Crimes shall have been committed; but when not committed within any State, the Trial shall be at such Place or Places as the Congress may by Law have directed.

Section 3 Treason against the United States, shall consist only in levying War against them, or in adhering to their Enemies, giving them Aid and Comfort. No Person shall be convicted of Treason unless on the Testimony of two Witnesses to the same overt Act, or on Confession in open Court.

The Congress shall have Power to declare the Punishment of Treason, but no Attainder of Treason shall work Corruption of Blood, or Forfeiture except during the Life of the Person attainted.

Article IV

Section 1 Full Faith and Credit shall be given in each State to the public Acts, Records, and judicial Proceedings of every other State. And the Congress may by general Laws prescribe the Manner in which such Acts, Records and Proceedings shall be proved, and the Effect thereof.

Section 2 The Citizens of each State shall be entitled to all Privileges and Immunities of Citizens in the several States.

A Person charged in any State with Treason, Felony, or other Crime, who shall flee from Justice, and be found in another State, shall on Demand of the executive Authority of the State from which he fled, be delivered up, to be removed to the State having Jurisdiction of the Crime.

No Person held to Service or Labour in one State, under the Laws thereof, escaping into another, shall, in Consequence of any Law or Regulation therein, be discharged from such Service or Labour, but shall be delivered up on Claim of the Party to whom such Service or Labour may be due.[9]

Section 3 New States may be admitted by the Congress into this Union; but no new State shall be formed or erected within the Jurisdiction of any other State; nor any State be formed by the Junction of two or more States, or Parts of States, without the Consent of the Legislatures of the States concerned as well as of the Congress.

[9] Changed by the Thirteenth Amendment.

The Congress shall have Power to dispose of and make all needful Rules and Regulations respecting the Territory or other Property belonging to the United States; and nothing in this Constitution shall be so construed as to Prejudice any Claims of the United States, or of any particular State.

Section 4 The United States shall guarantee to every State in this Union a Republican Form of Government, and shall protect each of them against Invasion; and on Application of the Legislature, or of the Executive (when the Legislature cannot be convened) against domestic Violence.

Article V

The Congress, whenever two thirds of both Houses shall deem it necessary, shall propose Amendments to this Constitution, or, on the Application of the Legislatures of two thirds of the several States, shall call a Convention for proposing Amendments, which, in either Case, shall be valid to all Intents and Purposes, as Part of this Constitution, when ratified by the legislatures of three fourths of the several States, or by Conventions in three fourths thereof, as the one or the other Mode of Ratification may be proposed by the Congress; Provided that no Amendment which may be made prior to the Year One thousand eight hundred and eight shall in any Manner affect the first and fourth Clauses in the Ninth Section of the first Article; and that no State, without its Consent, shall be deprived of its equal Suffrage in the Senate.

Article VI

All Debts contracted and Engagements entered into, before the Adoption of this Constitution, shall be as valid against the United States under this Constitution, as under the Confederation.

The Constitution, and the Laws of the United States which shall be made in Pursuance thereof; and all Treaties made, or which shall be made, under the Authority of the United States, shall be the supreme Law of the Land; and the Judges in every State shall be bound thereby, any Thing in the Constitution or Laws of any State to the Contrary notwithstanding.

The Senators and Representatives before mentioned, and the Members of the several State Legislatures, and all executive and judicial Officers, both of the United States and of the several States, shall be bound by Oath or Affirmation, to support this Constitution; but no religious Test shall ever be required as a Qualification to any Office or public Trust under the United States.

Article VII

The Ratification of the Conventions of nine States, shall be sufficient for the Establishment of this Constitution between the States so ratifying the Same.

Done in Convention by the Unanimous Consent of the States present the Seventeenth Day of September in the Year of our Lord one thousand seven hundred and eighty seven and of the Independance of the United States of America the Twelfth. In witness whereof We have hereunto subscribed our Names.

Amendments

[The first 10 amendments are known as the "Bill of Rights."]

Amendment I (Ratified 1791) Congress shall make no law respecting an establishment of religion, or prohibiting the free exercise thereof; or abridging the freedom of speech, or of the press; or the right of the people peaceably to assemble, and to petition the Government for a redress of grievances.

Amendment 2 (Ratified 1791) A well regulated Militia, being necessary to the security of a free State, the right of the people to keep and bear Arms, shall not be infringed.

Amendment 3 (Ratified 1791) No Soldier shall, in time of peace be quartered in any house, without the consent of the Owner, nor in time of war, but in a manner to be prescribed by law.

Amendment 4 (Ratified 1791) The right of the people to be secure in their persons, houses, papers, and effects, against unreasonable searches and seizures, shall not be violated, and no Warrants shall issue, but upon probable cause, supported by Oath or affirmation, and particularly describing the place to be searched, and the persons or things to be seized.

Amendment 5 (Ratified 1791) No person shall be held to answer for a capital, or otherwise infamous crime, unless on a presentment or indictment of a Grand Jury, except in cases arising in the land or naval forces, or in the Militia, when in actual service in time of War or public danger; nor shall any person be subject for the same offence to be twice put in jeopardy of life or limb; nor shall be compelled in any criminal case to be a witness against himself, nor be deprived of life, liberty, or property, without due process of law; nor shall private property be taken for public use, without just compensation.

Amendment 6 (Ratified 1791) In all criminal prosecutions, the accused shall enjoy the right to a speedy and public trial, by an impartial jury of the State and district wherein the crime shall have been committed, which district shall have been previously ascertained by law, and to be informed of the nature and cause of the accusation; to be confronted with the witnesses against him; to have

compulsory process for obtaining Witnesses in his favor, and to have assistance of counsel for his defence.

Amendment 7 (Ratified 1791) In Suits at common law, where the value in controversy shall exceed twenty dollars, the right of trial by jury shall be preserved, and no fact tried by a jury, shall be otherwise re-examined in any Court of the United States, than according to the rules of the common law.

Amendment 8 (Ratified 1791) Excessive bail shall not be required, nor excessive fines imposed, nor cruel and unusual punishments inflicted.

Amendment 9 (Ratified 1791) The enumeration in the Constitution, of certain rights, shall not be construed to deny or disparage others retained by the people.

Amendment 10 (Ratified 1791) The powers not delegated to the United States by the Constitution, nor prohibited by it to the States, are reserved to the States respectively, or to the people.

Amendment 11 (Ratified 1795) The Judicial power of the United States shall not be construed to extend to any suit in law or equity, commenced or prosecuted against one of the United States by Citizens of another State, or by Citizens or Subjects of any Foreign State.

Amendment 12 (Ratified 1804) The Electors shall meet in their respective states, and vote by ballot for President and Vice-President, one of whom, at least, shall not be an inhabitant of the same state with themselves; they shall name in their ballots the person voted for as President, and in distinct ballots the person voted for as Vice-President, and they shall make distinct lists of all persons voted for as President, and of all persons voted for as Vice-President, and of the number of votes for each, which lists they shall sign and certify, and transmit sealed to the seat of the government of the United States, directed to the President of the Senate;—The President of the Senate shall, in the presence of the Senate and House of Representatives, open all the certificates and the votes shall then be counted;—The person having the greatest number of votes for President, shall be the President, if such number be a majority of the whole number of Electors appointed; and if no person have such majority, then from the persons having the highest numbers not exceeding three on the list of those voted for as President, the House of Representatives shall choose immediately, by ballot, the President. But in choosing the President, the votes shall be taken by states, the representation from each state having one vote; a quorum for this purpose shall consist of a member or members from two-thirds of the states, and a majority of all the states shall be necessary to a choice. And if the House of Representatives shall

not choose a President whenever the right of choice shall devolve upon them, before the fourth day of March next following, then the Vice-President shall act as president, as in the case of the death or other constitutional disability of the President.[10]—The person having the greatest number of votes as Vice-President, shall be the Vice-President, if such number be a majority of the whole number of Electors appointed, and if no person have a majority, then from the two highest numbers on the list, the Senate shall choose the Vice-President; a quorum for the purpose shall consist of two-thirds of the whole number of Senators, and a majority of the whole number shall be necessary to a choice. But no person constitutionally ineligible to the office of President shall be eligible to that of Vice-President of the United States.

Amendment 13 (Ratified 1865) Section 1 Neither slavery nor involuntary servitude, except as a punishment for crime whereof the party shall have been duly convicted, shall exist within the United States, or any place subject to their jurisdiction.

Section 2 Congress shall have power to enforce this article by appropriate legislation.

Amendment 14 (Ratified 1868) Section 1 All persons born or naturalized in the United States, and subject to the jurisdiction thereof, are citizens of the United States and of the State wherein they reside. No State shall make or enforce any law which shall abridge the privileges or immunities of citizens of the United States; nor shall any State deprive any person of life, liberty, or property, without due process of law; nor deny to any person within its jurisdiction the equal protection of the laws.

Section 2 Representatives shall be apportioned among the several States according to their respective numbers, counting the whole number of persons in each State, excluding Indians not taxed. But when the right to vote at any election for the choice of electors for President and Vice President of the United States, Representatives in Congress, the Executive and Judicial officers of a State, or the members of the Legislature thereof, is denied to any of the male inhabitants of such State, being twenty-one[11] years of age, and citizens of the United States, or in any way abridged except for participation in rebellion, or other crime, the basis of representation therein shall be reduced in the proportion which the number of such male citizens shall bear to the whole number of male citizens twenty-one years of age in such State.

Section 3 No person shall be a Senator or Representative in Congress, or elector of President and Vice President, or hold any office, civil or military, under the United States, or under any State, who, having previously taken an oath, as a member of Congress, or as an officer of the United States, or as a member of any State legislature, or as an executive or judicial officer of any State, to support the Constitution of the United States, shall have engaged in insurrection or rebellion against the same, or given aid or comfort to the enemies thereof. But Congress may by a vote of two-thirds of each House, remove such disability.

Section 4 The validity of the public debt of the United States, authorized by law, including debts incurred for payment of pensions and bounties for services in suppressing insurrection or rebellion, shall not be questioned. But neither the United States nor any State shall assume or pay any debt or obligation incurred in aid of insurrection or rebellion against the United States, or any claim for the loss or emancipation of any slave; but all such debts, obligations and claims shall be held illegal and void.

Section 5 The Congress shall have power to enforce, by appropriate legislation, the provisions of this article.

Amendment 15 (Ratified 1870) Section 1 The right of citizens of the United States to vote shall not be denied or abridged by the United States or by any State on account of race, color, or previous condition of servitude.

Section 2 The Congress shall have power to enforce this article by appropriate legislation.

Amendment 16 (Ratified 1913) The Congress shall have power to lay and collect taxes on incomes, from whatever source derived, without apportionment among the several States, and without regard to any census or enumeration.

Amendment 17 (Ratified 1913) The Senate of the United States shall be composed of two Senators from each State, elected by the people thereof, for six years; and each Senator shall have one vote. The electors in each State shall have the qualifications requisite for electors of the most numerous branch of the State legislatures.

When vacancies happen in the representation of any State in the Senate, the executive authority of such State shall issue writs of election to fill such vacancies: *Provided,* That the legislature of any State may empower the executive thereof to make temporary appointments until the people fill the vacancies by election as the legislature may direct.

This amendment shall not be so construed as to affect the election or term of any Senator chosen before it becomes valid as part of the Constitution.

Amendment 18 (Ratified 1919; Repealed 1933) Section 1 After one year from the ratification of this article the manufacture, sale, or transportation of intoxicating liquors within, the importation thereof into, or the exportation thereof from the United States and all territory subject to the jurisdiction thereof for beverage purposes is hereby prohibited.

[10] Changed by the Twentieth Amendment.
[11] Changed by the Twenty-sixth Amendment.

Section 2 The Congress and the several States shall have concurrent power to enforce this article by appropriate legislation.

Section 3 This article shall be inoperative unless it shall have been ratified as an amendment to the Constitution by the legislatures of the several States, as provided in the Constitution, within seven years from the date of the submission hereof to the States by the Congress.[12]

Amendment 19 (Ratified 1920) The right of citizens of the United States to vote shall not be denied or abridged by the United States or by any State on account of sex.

Congress shall have power to enforce this article by appropriate legislation.

Amendment 20 (Ratified 1933) Section 1 The terms of the President and Vice President shall end at noon on the 20th day of January, and the terms of Senators and Representatives at noon on the 3d day of January, of the years in which such terms would have ended if this article had not been ratified; and the terms of their successors shall then begin.

Section 2 The Congress shall assemble at least once in every year, and such meeting shall begin at noon on the 3d day of January, unless they shall by law appoint a different day.

Section 3 If, at the time fixed for the beginning of the term of the President, the President elect shall have died, the Vice President elect shall become President. If a President shall not have been chosen before the time fixed for the beginning of his term, or if the President elect shall have failed to qualify, then the Vice President elect shall act as President until a President shall have qualified; and the Congress may by law provide for the case wherein neither a President elect nor a Vice President elect shall have qualified, declaring who shall then act as President, or the manner in which one who is to act shall be selected, and such person shall act accordingly until a President or Vice President shall have qualified.

Section 4 The Congress may by law provide for the case of the death of any of the persons from whom the House of Representatives may choose a President whenever the right of choice shall have devolved upon them, and for the case of the death of any of the persons from whom the Senate may choose a Vice President whenever the right of choice shall have devolved upon them.

Section 5 Sections 1 and 2 shall take effect on the 15th day of October following the ratification of this article.

Section 6 This article shall be inoperative unless it shall have been ratified as an amendment to the Constitution by the legislatures of three-fourths of the several States within seven years from the date of its submission.

Amendment 21 (Ratified 1933) Section 1 The eighteenth article of amendment to the Constitution of the United States is hereby repealed.

Section 2 The transportation or importation into any State, Territory, or possession of the United States for delivery or use therein of intoxicating liquors, in violation of the laws thereof, is hereby prohibited.

Section 3 This article shall be inoperative unless it shall have been ratified as an amendment to the Constitution by conventions in the several States, as provided in the Constitution, within seven years from the date of the submission hereof to the States by the Congress.

Amendment 22 (Ratified 1951) Section 1 No person shall be elected to the office of the President more than twice, and no person who has held the office of President, or acted as President, for more than two years of a term to which some other person was elected President shall be elected to the office of the President more than once. But this Article shall not apply to any person holding the office of President when this Article was proposed by the Congress, and shall not prevent any person who may be holding the office of President, or acting as President, during the term within which this Article becomes operative from holding the office of President or acting as President during the remainder of such term.

Section 2 This Article shall be inoperative unless it shall have been ratified as an amendment to the Constitution by the legislatures of three-fourths of the several States within seven years from the date of its submission to the States by the Congress.

Amendment 23 (Ratified 1961) Section 1 The District constituting the seat of Government of the United States shall appoint in such manner as the Congress may direct:

A number of electors of President and Vice President equal to the whole number of Senators and Representatives in Congress to which the District would be entitled if it were a State, but in no event more than the least populous State; they shall be in addition to those appointed by the States, but they shall be considered, for the purposes of the election of President and Vice President, to be electors appointed by a State; and they shall meet in the District and perform such duties as provided by the twelfth article of amendment.

Section 2 The Congress shall have power to enforce this article by appropriate legislation.

Amendment 24 (Ratified 1964) Section 1 The right of citizens of the United States to vote in any primary or other election for President or Vice President, for electors for President or Vice President, or for Senator or Representative in Congress, shall not be denied or abridged by the United States or any State by reason of failure to pay any poll tax or other tax.

[12] Repealed by the Twenty-first Amendment.

Section 2 The Congress shall have power to enforce this article by appropriate legislation.

Amendment 25 (Ratified 1967) Section 1 In case of the removal of the President from office or of his death or resignation, the Vice President shall become President.

Section 2 Whenever there is a vacancy in the office of the Vice President, the President shall nominate a Vice President who shall take office upon confirmation by a majority vote of both Houses of Congress.

Section 3 Whenever the President transmits to the President pro tempore of the Senate and the Speaker of the House of Representatives his written declaration that he is unable to discharge the powers and duties of his office, and until he transmits to them a written declaration to the contrary, such powers and duties shall be discharged by the Vice President as Acting President.

Section 4 Whenever the Vice President and a majority of either the principal officers of the executive departments or of such other body as Congress may by law provide, transmit to the President pro tempore of the Senate and the Speaker of the House of Representatives their written declaration that the President is unable to discharge the powers and duties of his office, the Vice President shall immediately assume the powers and duties of the office as Acting President.

Thereafter, when the President transmits to the President pro tempore of the Senate and the Speaker of the House of Representatives his written declaration that no inability exists, he shall resume the powers and duties of his office

unless the Vice President and a majority of either the principal officers of the executive department or of such other body as Congress may by law provide, transmit within four days to the President pro tempore of the Senate and the Speaker of the House of Representatives their written declaration that the President is unable to discharge the powers and duties of his office. Thereupon Congress shall decide the issue, assembling within forty-eight hours for that purpose if not in session. If the Congress, within twenty-one days after receipt of the latter written declaration, or, if Congress is not in session, within twenty-one days after Congress is required to assemble, determines by two-thirds vote of both Houses that the President is unable to discharge the powers and duties of his office, the Vice President shall continue to discharge the same as Acting President; otherwise, the President shall resume the powers and duties of his office.

Amendment 26 (Ratified 1971) Section 1 The right of citizens of the United States, who are eighteen years of age or older, to vote shall not be denied or abridged by the United States or by any State on account of age.

Section 2 The Congress shall have power to enforce this article by appropriate legislation.

Amendment 27 (Ratified 1992) No law, varying the compensation for the services of the Senators and Representatives, shall take effect, until an election of Representatives shall have intervened.

Uniform Commercial Code

Article 2–Sales

Part 1: Short Title, General Construction and Subject Matter

§ 2–101. Short Title. This Article shall be known and may be cited as Uniform Commercial Code—Sales.

§ 2–102. Scope; Certain Security and Other Transactions Excluded from This Article. Unless the context otherwise requires, this Article applies to transactions in goods; it does not apply to any transaction which although in the form of an unconditional contract to sell or present sale is intended to operate only as a security transaction nor does this Article impair or repeal any statute regulating sales to consumers, farmers or other specified classes of buyers.

§ 2–103. Definitions and Index of Definitions.

(1) In this Article unless the context otherwise requires
 (a) "Buyer" means a person who buys or contracts to buy goods.
 (b) "Good faith" in the case of a merchant means honesty in fact and the observance of reasonable commercial standards of fair dealing in the trade.
 (c) "Receipt" of goods means taking physical possession of them.
 (d) "Seller" means a person who sells or contracts to sell goods.
(2) Other definitions applying to this Article or to specified Parts thereof, and the sections in which they appear are:

(3) The following definitions in other Articles apply to this Article:

(4) In addition Article 1 contains general definitions and principles of construction and interpretation applicable throughout this Article.

As amended in 1994.
 See Appendix XI for material relating to changes made in text in 1994.

§ 2–104. Definitions: "Merchant"; "Between Merchants"; "Financing Agency".

(1) "Merchant" means a person who deals in goods of the kind or otherwise by his occupation holds himself out as having knowledge or skill peculiar to the practices or goods involved in the transaction or to whom such knowledge or skill may be attributed by his employment of an agent or broker or other intermediary who by his occupation holds himself out as having such knowledge or skill.

(2) "Financing agency" means a bank, finance company or other person who in the ordinary course of business makes advances against goods or documents of title or who by arrangement with either the seller or the buyer intervenes in ordinary course to make or collect payment due or claimed under the contract for sale, as by purchasing or paying the seller's draft or making advances against it or by merely taking it for collection whether or not documents of title accompany the draft. "Financing agency" includes also a bank or other person who similarly intervenes between persons who are in the position of seller and buyer in respect to the goods (Section 2–707).

(3) "Between merchants" means in any transaction with respect to which both parties are chargeable with the knowledge or skill of merchants.

§ 2–105. Definitions: "Transferability"; "Goods"; "Future" Goods; "Lot"; "Commercial Unit".

(1) "Goods" means all things (including specially manufactured goods) which are movable at the time of identification to the contract for sale other than the money in which the price is to be paid, investment securities (Article 8) and things in action. "Goods" also includes the unborn young of animals and growing crops and other identified things attached to realty as described in the section on goods to be severed from realty (Section 2–107).

(2) Goods must be both existing and identified before any interest in them can pass. Goods which are not both existing and identified are "future" goods. A purported present sale of future goods or of any interest therein operates as a contract to sell.

(3) There may be a sale of a part interest in existing identified goods.

(4) An undivided share in an identified bulk of fungible goods is sufficiently identified to be sold although the quantity of the bulk is not determined. Any agreed proportion of such a bulk or any quantity thereof agreed upon by number, weight or other measure may to the extent of the seller's interest in the bulk be sold to the buyer who then becomes an owner in common.

(5) "Lot" means a parcel or a single article which is the subject matter of a separate sale or delivery, whether or not it is sufficient to perform the contract.

(6) "Commercial unit" means such a unit of goods as by commercial usage is a single whole for purposes of sale and division of which materially impairs its character or value on the market or in use. A commercial unit may be a single article (as a machine) or a set of articles (as a suite of furniture or an assortment of sizes) or a quantity (as a bale, gross, or carload) or any other unit treated in use or in the relevant market as a single whole.

§ 2–106. Definitions: "Contract"; "Agreement"; "Contract for Sales"; "Sale"; "Present Sale"; "Conforming" to Contract; "Termination"; "Cancellation".

(1) In this Article unless the context otherwise requires "contract" and "agreement" are limited to those relating to the present or future sale of goods. "Contract for sale" includes both a present sale of goods and a contract to sell goods at a future time. A "sale" consists in the passing of title from the seller to the buyer for a price (Section 2–401). A "present sale" means a sale which is accomplished by the making of the contract.

(2) Goods or conduct including any part of a performance are "conforming" or conform to the contract when they are in accordance with the obligations under the contract.

(3) "Termination" occurs when either party pursuant to a power created by agreement or law puts an end to the contract otherwise than for its breach. On "termination" all obligations which are still executory on both sides are discharged but any right based on prior breach or performance survives.

(4) "Cancellation" occurs when either party puts an end to the contract for breach by the other and its effect is the same as that of "termination" except that the cancelling party also retains any remedy for breach of the whole contract or any unperformed balance.

§ 2–107. Goods to Be Severed from Realty: Recording.

(1) A contract for the sale of minerals or the like (including oil and gas) or a structure or its materials to be removed from realty is a contract for the sale of goods within this Article if they are to be severed by the seller but until severance a purported present sale thereof which is not effective as a transfer of an interest in land is effective only as a contract to sell.

(2) A contract for the sale apart from the land of growing crops or other things attached to realty and capable of severance without material harm thereto but not described in subsection (1) or of timber to be cut is a contract for the sale of goods within this Article whether the subject matter is to be severed by the buyer or by the seller even though it forms part of the realty at the time of contracting, and the parties can by identification effect a present sale before severance.

(3) The provisions of this section are subject to any third party rights provided by the law relating to realty records, and the contract for sale may be executed and recorded as a document transferring an interest in land and shall then constitute notice to third parties of the buyer's rights under the contract for sale. As amended in 1972.

Part 2: Form, Formation and Readjustment Of Contract

§ 2–201. Formal Requirements; Statute of Frauds.

(1) Except as otherwise provided in this section a contract for the sale of goods for the price of $500 or more is not enforceable by way of action or defense unless there is some writing sufficient to indicate that a contract for sale has been made between the parties and signed by the party against whom enforcement is sought or by his authorized agent or broker. A writing is not insufficient because it omits or incorrectly states a term agreed upon but the contract is not enforceable under this paragraph beyond the quantity of goods shown in such writing.

(2) Between merchants if within a reasonable time a writing in confirmation of the contract and sufficient against the sender is received and the party receiving it has reason to know its contents, it satisfies the requirements of subsection (1) against such party unless written notice of objection to its contents is given within 10 days after it is received.

(3) A contract which does not satisfy the requirements of subsection (1) but which is valid in other respects is enforceable

 (a) if the goods are to be specially manufactured for the buyer and are not suitable for sale to others in the ordinary course of the seller's business and the seller, before notice of repudiation is received and under circumstances which reasonably indicate that the goods are for the buyer, has made either a substantial beginning of their manufacture or commitments for their procurement; or

 (b) if the party against whom enforcement is sought admits in his pleading, testimony or otherwise in court that a contract for sale was made, but the contract is not enforceable under this provision beyond the quantity of goods admitted; or

 (c) with respect to goods for which payment has been made and accepted or which have been received and accepted (Section 2–606).

§ 2–202. Final Written Expression: Parol or Extrinsic Evidence.
Terms with respect to which the confirmatory memoranda of the parties agree or which are otherwise set forth in a writing intended by the parties as a final expression of their agreement with respect to such terms as are included therein may not be contradicted by evidence of any prior agreement or of a contemporaneous oral agreement but may be explained or supplemented

 (a) by course of dealing or usage of trade (Section 1–205) or by course of performance (Section 2–208); and

 (b) by evidence of consistent additional terms unless the court finds the writing to have been intended also as a complete and exclusive statement of the terms of the agreement.

§ 2–203. Seals Inoperative.
The affixing of a seal to a writing evidencing a contract for sale or an offer to buy or sell goods does not constitute the writing a sealed instrument and the law with respect to sealed instruments does not apply to such a contract or offer.

§ 2–204. Formation in General.

(1) A contract for sale of goods may be made in any manner sufficient to show agreement, including conduct by both parties which recognizes the existence of such a contract.

(2) An agreement sufficient to constitute a contract for sale may be found even though the moment of its making is undetermined.

(3) Even though one or more terms are left open a contract for sale does not fail for indefiniteness if the parties have intended to make a contract and there is a reasonably certain basis for giving an appropriate remedy.

§ 2–205. Firm Offers.
An offer by a merchant to buy or sell goods in a signed writing which by its terms gives assurance that it will be held open is not revocable, for lack of consideration, during the time stated or if no time is stated for a reasonable time, but in no event may such period of irrevocability exceed three months; but any such term of assurance on a form supplied by the offeree must be separately signed by the offeror.

§ 2–206. Offer and Acceptance in Formation of Contract.

(1) Unless otherwise unambiguously indicated by the language or circumstances

 (a) an offer to make a contract shall be construed as inviting acceptance in any manner and by any medium reasonable in the circumstances;

 (b) an order or other offer to buy goods for prompt or current shipment shall be construed as inviting acceptance either by a prompt promise to ship or by the prompt or current shipment of conforming or non-conforming goods, but such a shipment of non-conforming goods does not constitute an acceptance if the seller seasonably notifies the buyer that the shipment is offered only as an accommodation to the buyer.

(2) Where the beginning of a requested performance is a reasonable mode of acceptance an offeror who is not notified of acceptance within a reasonable time may treat the offer as having lapsed before acceptance.

§ 2–207. Additional Terms in Acceptance or Confirmation.

(1) A definite and seasonable expression of acceptance or a written confirmation which is sent within a reasonable time operates as an acceptance even though it states terms additional to or different from those offered or agreed upon, unless acceptance is expressly made conditional on assent to the additional or different terms.

(2) The additional terms are to be construed as proposals for addition to the contract. Between merchants such terms become part of the contract unless:

 (a) the offer expressly limits acceptance to the terms of the offer;

 (b) they materially alter it; or

 (c) notification of objection to them has already been given or is given within a reasonable time after notice of them is received.

(3) Conduct by both parties which recognizes the existence of a contract is sufficient to establish a contract for sale although the writings of the parties do not otherwise establish a contract. In such case the terms of the particular contract consist of those terms on which the writings of the parties agree, together with any supplementary terms incorporated under any other provisions of this Act.

§ 2–208. Course of Performance or Practical Construction.

(1) Where the contract for sale involves repeated occasions for performance by either party with knowledge of the nature of the performance and opportunity for objection to it by the other, any course of performance accepted or acquiesced in without objection shall be relevant to determine the meaning of the agreement.

(2) The express terms of the agreement and any such course of performance, as well as any course of dealing and usage of trade, shall be construed whenever reasonable as consistent with each other; but when such construction is unreasonable, express terms shall control course of performance and course of performance shall control both course of dealing and usage of trade (Section 1-205).

(3) Subject to the provisions of the next section on modification and waiver, such course of performance shall be relevant to show a waiver or modification of any term inconsistent with such course of performance.

§ 2–209. Modification, Rescission and Waiver.

(1) An agreement modifying a contract within this Article needs no consideration to be binding.

(2) A signed agreement which excludes modification or rescission except by a signed writing cannot be otherwise modified or rescinded, but except as between merchants such a requirement on a form supplied by the merchant must be separately signed by the other party.

(3) The requirements of the statute of frauds section of this Article (Section 2–201) must be satisfied if the contract as modified is within its provisions.

(4) Although an attempt at modification or rescission does not satisfy the requirements of subsection (2) or (3) it can operate as a waiver.

(5) A party who has made a waiver affecting an executory portion of the contract may retract the waiver by reasonable notification received by the other party that strict performance will be required of any term waived, unless the retraction would be unjust in view of a material change of position in reliance on the waiver.

§ 2–210. Delegation of Performance; Assignment of Rights.

(1) A party may perform his duty through a delegate unless otherwise agreed or unless the other party has a substantial interest in having his original promisor perform or control the acts required by the contract. No delegation of performance relieves the party delegating of any duty to perform or any liability for breach.

(2) Unless otherwise agreed all rights of either seller or buyer can be assigned except where the assignment would materially change the duty of the other party, or increase materially the burden or risk imposed on him by his contract, or impair materially his chance of obtaining return performance. A right to damages for breach of the whole contract or a right arising out of the assignor's due performance of his entire obligation can be assigned despite agreement otherwise.

(3) Unless the circumstances indicate the contrary a prohibition of assignment of "the contract" is to be construed as barring only the delegation to the assignee of the assignor's performance.

(4) An assignment of "the contract" or of "all my rights under the contract" or an assignment in similar general terms is an assignment of rights and unless the language or the circumstances (as in an assignment for security) indicate the contrary, it is a delegation of performance of the duties of the assignor and its acceptance by the assignee constitutes a promise by him to perform those duties. This promise is enforceable by either the assignor or the other party to the original contract.

(5) The other party may treat any assignment which delegates performance as creating reasonable grounds for insecurity and may without prejudice to his rights against the assignor demand assurances from the assignee (Section 2–609).

Part 3: General Obligation and Construction of Contract

§ 2–301. General Obligations of Parties. The obligation of the seller is to transfer and deliver and that of the buyer is to accept and pay in accordance with the contract.

§ 2–302. Unconscionable Contract or Clause.

(1) If the court as a matter of law finds the contract or any clause of the contract to have been unconscionable at the time it was made the court may refuse to enforce the contract, or it may enforce the remainder of the contract without the unconscionable clause, or it may so limit the application of any unconscionable clause as to avoid any unconscionable result.

(2) When it is claimed or appears to the court that the contract or any clause thereof may be unconscionable the parties shall be afforded a reasonable opportunity to present evidence as to its commercial setting, purpose and effect to aid the court in making the determination.

§ 2–303. Allocation or Division of Risks.
Where this Article allocates a risk or a burden as between the parties "unless otherwise agreed", the agreement may not only shift the allocation but may also divide the risk or burden.

§ 2–304. Price Payable in Money, Goods, Realty, or Otherwise.

(1) The price can be made payable in money or otherwise. If it is payable in whole or in part in goods each party is a seller of the goods which he is to transfer.

(2) Even though all or part of the price is payable in an interest in realty the transfer of the goods and the seller's obligations with reference to them are subject to this Article, but not the transfer of the interest in realty or the transferor's obligations in connection therewith.

§ 2–305. Open Price Term.

(1) The parties if they so intend can conclude a contract for sale even though the price is not settled. In such a case the price is a reasonable price at the time for delivery if
(a) nothing is said as to price; or
(b) the price is left to be agreed by the parties and they fail to agree; or
(c) the price is to be fixed in terms of some agreed market or other standard as set or recorded by a third person or agency and it is not so set or recorded.

(2) A price to be fixed by the seller or by the buyer means a price for him to fix in good faith.

(3) When a price left to be fixed otherwise than by agreement of the parties fails to be fixed through fault of one party the other may at his option treat the contract as cancelled or himself fix a reasonable price.

(4) Where, however, the parties intend not to be bound unless the price be fixed or agreed and it is not fixed or agreed there is no contract. In such a case the buyer must return any goods already received or if unable so to do must pay their reasonable value at the time of delivery and the seller must return any portion of the price paid on account.

§ 2–306. Output, Requirements and Exclusive Dealings.

(1) A term which measures the quantity by the output of the seller or the requirements of the buyer means such actual output or requirements as may occur in good faith, except that no quantity unreasonably disproportionate to any stated estimate or in the absence of a stated estimate to any normal or otherwise comparable prior output or requirements may be tendered or demanded.

(2) A lawful agreement by either the seller or the buyer for exclusive dealing in the kind of goods concerned imposes unless otherwise agreed an obligation by the seller to use best efforts to supply the goods and by the buyer to use best efforts to promote their sale.

§ 2–307. Delivery in Single Lot or Several Lots.
Unless otherwise agreed all goods called for by a contract for sale must be tendered in a single delivery and payment is due only on such tender but where the circumstances give either party the right to make or demand delivery in lots the price if it can be apportioned may be demanded for each lot.

§ 2–308. Absence of Specified Place for Delivery.
Unless otherwise agreed

(a) the place for delivery of goods is the seller's place of business or if he has none his residence; but
(b) in a contract for sale of identified goods which to the knowledge of the parties at the time of contracting are in some other place, that place is the place for their delivery; and
(c) documents of title may be delivered through customary banking channels.

§ 2–309. Absence of Specific Time Provisions; Notice of Termination.

(1) The time for shipment or delivery or any other action under a contract if not provided in this Article or agreed upon shall be a reasonable time.

(2) Where the contract provides for successive performances but is indefinite in duration it is valid for a reasonable time but unless otherwise agreed may be terminated at any time by either party.

(3) Termination of a contract by one party except on the happening of an agreed event requires that reasonable notification be received by the other party and an agreement dispensing with notification is invalid if its operation would be unconscionable.

§ 2–310. Open Time for Payment or Running of Credit; Authority to Ship Under Reservation.
Unless otherwise agreed

(a) payment is due at the time and place at which the buyer is to receive the goods even though the place of shipment is the place of delivery; and
(b) if the seller is authorized to send the goods he may ship them under reservation, and may tender the

documents of title, but the buyer may inspect the goods after their arrival before payment is due unless such inspection is inconsistent with the terms of the contract (Section 2–513); and

(c) if delivery is authorized and made by way of documents of title otherwise than by subsection (b) then payment is due at the time and place at which the buyer is to receive the documents regardless of where the goods are to be received; and

(d) where the seller is required or authorized to ship the goods on credit the credit period runs from the time of shipment but postdating the invoice or delaying its dispatch will correspondingly delay the starting of the credit period.

§ 2–311. Options and Cooperation Respecting Performance.

(1) An agreement for sale which is otherwise sufficiently definite (subsection (3) of Section 2–204) to be a contract is not made invalid by the fact that it leaves particulars of performance to be specified by one of the parties. Any such specification must be made in good faith and within limits set by commercial reasonableness.

(2) Unless otherwise agreed specifications relating to assortment of the goods are at the buyer's option and except as otherwise provided in subsections (1)(c) and (3) of Section 2–319 specifications or arrangements relating to shipment are at the seller's option.

(3) Where such specification would materially affect the other party's performance but is not seasonably made or where one party's cooperation is necessary to the agreed performance of the other but is not seasonably forthcoming, the other party in addition to all other remedies

(a) is excused for any resulting delay in his own performance; and

(b) may also either proceed to perform in any reasonable manner or after the time for a material part of his own performance treat the failure to specify or to cooperate as a breach by failure to deliver or accept the goods.

§ 2–312. Warranty of Title and Against Infringement; Buyer's Obligation Against Infringement.

(1) Subject to subsection (2) there is in a contract for sale a warranty by the seller that

(a) the title conveyed shall be good, and its transfer rightful; and

(b) the goods shall be delivered free from any security interest or other lien or encumbrance of which the buyer at the time of contracting has no knowledge.

(2) A warranty under subsection (1) will be excluded or modified only by specific language or by circumstances which give the buyer reason to know that the person selling does not claim title in himself or that he is purporting to sell only such right or title as he or a third person may have.

(3) Unless otherwise agreed a seller who is a merchant regularly dealing in goods of the kind warrants that the goods shall be delivered free of the rightful claim of any third person by way of infringement or the like but a buyer who furnishes specifications to the seller must hold the seller harmless against any such claim which arises out of compliance with the specifications.

§ 2–313. Express Warranties by Affirmation, Promise, Description, Sample.

(1) Express warranties by the seller are created as follows:

(a) Any affirmation of fact or promise made by the seller to the buyer which relates to the goods and becomes part of the basis of the bargain creates an express warranty that the goods shall conform to the affirmation or promise.

(b) Any description of the goods which is made part of the basis of the bargain creates an express warranty that the goods shall conform to the description.

(c) Any sample or model which is made part of the basis of the bargain creates an express warranty that the whole of the goods shall conform to the sample or model.

(2) It is not necessary to the creation of an express warranty that the seller use formal words such as "warrant" or "guarantee" or that he have a specific intention to make a warranty, but an affirmation merely of the value of the goods or a statement purporting to be merely the seller's opinion or commendation of the goods does not create a warranty.

§ 2–314. Implied Warranty: Merchantability; Usage of Trade.

(1) Unless excluded or modified (Section 2–316), a warranty that the goods shall be merchantable is implied in a contract for their sale if the seller is a merchant with respect to goods of that kind. Under this section the serving for value of food or drink to be consumed either on the premises or elsewhere is a sale.

(2) Goods to be merchantable must be at least such as

(a) pass without objection in the trade under the contract description; and

(b) in the case of fungible goods, are of fair average quality within the description; and

(c) are fit for the ordinary purposes for which such goods are used; and

(d) run, within the variations permitted by the agreement, of even kind, quality and quantity within each unit and among all units involved; and

(e) are adequately contained, packaged, and labeled as the agreement may require; and

(f) conform to the promise or affirmations of fact made on the container or label if any.

(3) Unless excluded or modified (Section 2–316) other implied warranties may arise from course of dealing or usage of trade.

§ 2–315. Implied Warranty: Fitness for Particular Purpose. Where the seller at the time of contracting has reason to know any particular purpose for which the goods are required and that the buyer is relying on the seller's skill or judgment to select or furnish suitable goods, there is unless excluded or modified under the next section an implied warranty that the goods shall be fit for such purpose.

§ 2–316. Exclusion or Modification of Warranties.

(1) Words or conduct relevant to the creation of an express warranty and words or conduct tending to negate or limit warranty shall be construed wherever reasonable as consistent with each other; but subject to the provisions of this Article on parol or extrinsic evidence (Section 2–202) negation or limitation is inoperative to the extent that such construction is unreasonable.

(2) Subject to subsection (3), to exclude or modify the implied warranty of merchantability or any part of it the language must mention merchantability and in case of a writing must be conspicuous, and to exclude or modify any implied warranty of fitness the exclusion must be by a writing and conspicuous. Language to exclude all implied warranties of fitness is sufficient if it states, for example, that "There are no warranties which extend beyond the description on the face hereof."

(3) Notwithstanding subsection (2)

(a) unless the circumstances indicate otherwise, all implied warranties are excluded by expressions like "as is", "with all faults" or other language which in common understanding calls the buyer's attention to the exclusion of warranties and makes plain that there is no implied warranty; and

(b) when the buyer before entering into the contract has examined the goods or the sample or model as fully as he desired or has refused to examine the goods there is no implied warranty with regard to defects which an examination ought in the circumstances to have revealed to him; and

(c) an implied warranty can also be excluded or modified by course of dealing or course of performance or usage of trade.

(4) Remedies for breach of warranty can be limited in accordance with the provisions of this Article on liquidation or limitation of damages and on contractual modification of remedy (Sections 2–718 and 2–719).

§ 2–317. Cumulation and Conflict of Warranties Express or Implied. Warranties whether express or implied shall be construed as consistent with each other and as cumulative, but if such construction is unreasonable the intention of the parties shall determine which warranty is dominant. In ascertaining that intention the following rules apply:

(a) Exact or technical specifications displace an inconsistent sample or model or general language of description.

(b) A sample from an existing bulk displaces inconsistent general language of description.

(c) Express warranties displace inconsistent implied warranties other than an implied warranty of fitness for a particular purpose.

§ 2–318. Third Party Beneficiaries of Warranties Express or Implied. Note: *If this Act is introduced in the Congress of the United States this section should be omitted. (States to select one alternative.)*

Alternative A
A seller's warranty whether express or implied extends to any natural person who is in the family or household of his buyer or who is a guest in his home if it is reasonable to expect that such person may use, consume or be affected by the goods and who is injured in person by breach of the warranty. A seller may not exclude or limit the operation of this section.

Alternative B
A seller's warranty whether express or implied extends to any natural person who may reasonably be expected to use, consume or be affected by the goods and who is injured in person by breach of the warranty. A seller may not exclude or limit the operation of this section.

Alternative C
A seller's warranty whether express or implied extends to any person who may reasonably be expected to use, consume or be affected by the goods and who is injured by breach of the warranty. A seller may not exclude or limit the operation of this section with respect to injury to the person of an individual to whom the warranty extends.
As amended in 1966.

§ 2–319. F.O.B. and F.A.S. Terms.

(1) Unless otherwise agreed the term F.O.B. (which means "free on board") at a named place, even though used only in connection with the stated price, is a delivery term under which

(a) when the term is F.O.B. the place of shipment, the seller must at that place ship the goods in the manner provided in this Article (Section 2–504) and bear the expense and risk of putting them into the possession of the carrier; or

(b) when the term is F.O.B. the place of destination, the seller must at his own expense and risk transport the goods to that place and there tender

delivery of them in the manner provided in this Article (Section 2–503);

(c) when under either (a) or (b) the term is also F.O.B. vessel, car or other vehicle, the seller must in addition at his own expense and risk load the goods on board. If the term is F.O.B. vessel the buyer must name the vessel and in an appropriate case the seller must comply with the provisions of this Article on the form of bill of lading (Section 2–323).

(2) Unless otherwise agreed the term F.A.S. vessel (which means "free alongside") at a named port, even though used only in connection with the stated price, is a delivery term under which the seller must

(a) at his own expense and risk deliver the goods alongside the vessel in the manner usual in that port or on a dock designated and provided by the buyer; and

(b) obtain and tender a receipt for the goods in exchange for which the carrier is under a duty to issue a bill of lading.

(3) Unless otherwise agreed in any case falling within subsection (1)(a) or (c) or subsection (2) the buyer must seasonably give any needed instructions for making delivery, including when the term is F.A.S. or F.O.B. the loading berth of the vessel and in an appropriate case its name and sailing date. The seller may treat the failure of needed instructions as a failure of cooperation under this Article (Section 2–311). He may also at his option move the goods in any reasonable manner preparatory to delivery or shipment.

(4) Under the term F.O.B. vessel or F.A.S. unless otherwise agreed the buyer must make payment against tender of the required documents and the seller may not tender nor the buyer demand delivery of the goods in substitution for the documents.

§ 2–320. C.I.F. and C. & F. Terms.

(1) The term C.I.F. means that the price includes in a lump sum the cost of the goods and the insurance and freight to the named destination. The term C. & F. or C.F. means that the price so includes cost and freight to the named destination.

(2) Unless otherwise agreed and even though used only in connection with the stated price and destination, the term C.I.F. destination or its equivalent requires the seller at his own expense and risk to

(a) put the goods into the possession of a carrier at the port for shipment and obtain a negotiable bill or bills of lading covering the entire transportation to the named destination; and

(b) load the goods and obtain a receipt from the carrier (which may be contained in the bill of lading) showing that the freight has been paid or provided for; and

(c) obtain a policy or certificate of insurance, including any war risk insurance, of a kind and on terms then current at the port of shipment in the usual amount, in the currency of the contract, shown to cover the same goods covered by the bill of lading and providing for payment of loss to the order of the buyer or for the account of whom it may concern; but the seller may add to the price the amount of the premium for any such war risk insurance; and

(d) prepare an invoice of the goods and procure any other documents required to effect shipment or to comply with the contract; and

(e) forward and tender with commercial promptness all the documents in due form and with any indorsement necessary to perfect the buyer's rights.

(3) Unless otherwise agreed the term C. & F. or its equivalent has the same effect and imposes upon the seller the same obligations and risks as a C.I.F. term except the obligation as to insurance.

(4) Under the term C.I.F. or C. & F. unless otherwise agreed the buyer must make payment against tender of the required documents and the seller may not tender nor the buyer demand delivery of the goods in substitution for the documents.

§ 2–321. C.I.F. or C. & F.: "Net Landed Weights"; "Payment on Arrival"; Warranty of Condition on Arrival. -

Under a contract containing a term C.I.F. or C. & F.

(1) Where the price is based on or is to be adjusted according to "net landed weights", "delivered weights", "out turn" quantity or quality or the like, unless otherwise agreed the seller must reasonably estimate the price. The payment due on tender of the documents called for by the contract is the amount so estimated, but after final adjustment of the price a settlement must be made with commercial promptness.

(2) An agreement described in subsection (1) or any warranty of quality or condition of the goods on arrival places upon the seller the risk of ordinary deterioration, shrinkage and the like in transportation but has no effect on the place or time of identification to the contract for sale or delivery or on the passing of the risk of loss.

(3) Unless otherwise agreed where the contract provides for payment on or after arrival of the goods the seller must before payment allow such preliminary inspection as is feasible; but if the goods are lost delivery of the documents and payment are due when the goods should have arrived.

§ 2–322. Delivery "Ex-Ship".

(1) Unless otherwise agreed a term for delivery of goods "ex-ship" (which means from the carrying vessel) or in

equivalent language is not restricted to a particular ship and requires delivery from a ship which has reached a place at the named port of destination where goods of the kind are usually discharged.

(2) Under such a term unless otherwise agreed

 (a) the seller must discharge all liens arising out of the carriage and furnish the buyer with a direction which puts the carrier under a duty to deliver the goods; and

 (b) the risk of loss does not pass to the buyer until the goods leave the ship's tackle or are otherwise properly unloaded.

§ 2–323. Form of Bill of Lading Required in Overseas Shipment; "Overseas".

(1) Where the contract contemplates overseas shipment and contains a term C.I.F. or C. & F. or F.O.B. vessel, the seller unless otherwise agreed must obtain a negotiable bill of lading stating that the goods have been loaded in board or, in the case of a term C.I.F. or C. & F., received for shipment.

(2) Where in a case within subsection (1) a bill of lading has been issued in a set of parts, unless otherwise agreed if the documents are not to be sent from abroad the buyer may demand tender of the full set; otherwise only one part of the bill of lading need be tendered. Even if the agreement expressly requires a full set

 (a) due tender of a single part is acceptable within the provisions of this Article on cure of improper delivery (subsection (1) of Section 2–508); and

 (b) even though the full set is demanded, if the documents are sent from abroad the person tendering an incomplete set may nevertheless require payment upon furnishing an indemnity which the buyer in good faith deems adequate.

(3) A shipment by water or by air or a contract contemplating such shipment is "overseas" insofar as by usage of trade or agreement it is subject to the commercial, financing or shipping practices characteristic of international deep water commerce.

§ 2–324. "No Arrival, No Sale" Term. Under a term "no arrival, no sale" or terms of like meaning, unless otherwise agreed,

 (a) the seller must properly ship conforming goods and if they arrive by any means he must tender them on arrival but he assumes no obligation that the goods will arrive unless he has caused the non-arrival; and

 (b) where without fault of the seller the goods are in part lost or have so deteriorated as no longer to conform to the contract or arrive after the contract time, the buyer may proceed as if there had been casualty to identified goods (Section 2–613).

§ 2–325. "Letter of Credit" Term; "Confirmed Credit".

(1) Failure of the buyer seasonably to furnish an agreed letter of credit is a breach of the contract for sale.

(2) The delivery to seller of a proper letter of credit suspends the buyer's obligation to pay. If the letter of credit is dishonored, the seller may on seasonable notification to the buyer require payment directly from him.

(3) Unless otherwise agreed the term "letter of credit" or "banker's credit" in a contract for sale means an irrevocable credit issued by a financing agency of good repute and, where the shipment is overseas, of good international repute. The term "confirmed credit" means that the credit must also carry the direct obligation of such an agency which does business in the seller's financial market.

§ 2–326. Sale on Approval and Sale or Return; Consignment Sales and Rights of Creditors.

(1) Unless otherwise agreed, if delivered goods may be returned by the buyer even though they conform to the contract, the transaction is

 (a) a "sale on approval" if the goods are delivered primarily for use, and

 (b) a "sale or return" if the goods are delivered primarily for resale.

(2) Except as provided in subsection (3), goods held on approval are not subject to the claims of the buyer's creditors until acceptance; goods held on sale or return are subject to such claims while in the buyer's possession.

(3) Where goods are delivered to a person for sale and such person maintains a place of business at which he deals in goods of the kind involved, under a name other than the name of the person making delivery, then with respect to claims of creditors of the person conducting the business the goods are deemed to be on sale or return. The provisions of this subsection are applicable even though an agreement purports to reserve title to the person making delivery until payment or resale or uses such words as "on consignment" or "on memorandum". However, this subsection is not applicable if the person making delivery

 (a) complies with an applicable law providing for a consignor's interest or the like to be evidenced by a sign, or

 (b) establishes that the person conducting the business is generally known by his creditors to be substantially engaged in selling the goods of others, or

 (c) complies with the filing provisions of the Article on Secured Transactions (Article 9).

(4) Any "or return" term of a contract for sale is to be treated as a separate contract for sale within the statute

of frauds section of this Article (Section 2–201) and as contradicting the sale aspect of the contract within the provisions of this Article on parol or extrinsic evidence (Section 2–202).

§ 2–327. Special Incidents of Sale on Approval and Sale or Return.

(1) Under a sale on approval unless otherwise agreed
 (a) although the goods are identified to the contract the risk of loss and the title do not pass to the buyer until acceptance; and
 (b) use of the goods consistent with the purpose of trial is not acceptance but failure seasonably to notify the seller of election to return the goods is acceptance, and if the goods conform to the contract acceptance of any part is acceptance of the whole; and
 (c) after due notification of election to return, the return is at the seller's risk and expense but a merchant buyer must follow any reasonable instructions.
(2) Under a sale or return unless otherwise agreed
 (a) the option to return extends to the whole or any commercial unit of the goods while in substantially their original condition, but must be exercised seasonably; and
 (b) the return is at the buyer's risk and expense.

§ 2–328. Sale by Auction.

(1) In a sale by auction if goods are put up in lots each lot is the subject of a separate sale.
(2) A sale by auction is complete when the auctioneer so announces by the fall of the hammer or in other customary manner. Where a bid is made while the hammer is falling in acceptance of a prior bid the auctioneer may in his discretion reopen the bidding or declare the goods sold under the bid on which the hammer was falling.
(3) Such a sale is with reserve unless the goods are in explicit terms put up without reserve. In an auction with reserve the auctioneer may withdraw the goods at any time until he announces completion of the sale. In an auction without reserve, after the auctioneer calls for bids on an article or lot, that article or lot cannot be withdrawn unless no bid is made within a reasonable time. In either case a bidder may retract his bid until the auctioneer's announcement of completion of the sale, but a bidder's retraction does not revive any previous bid.
(4) If the auctioneer knowingly receives a bid on the seller's behalf or the seller makes or procures such a bid, and notice has not been given that liberty for such bidding is reserved, the buyer may at his option avoid the sale or take the goods at the price of the last good faith bid prior to the completion of the sale. This subsection shall not apply to any bid at a forced sale.

Part 4: Title, Creditors and Good Faith Purchasers

§ 2–401. Passing of Title; Reservation for Security; Limited Application of This Section.
Each provision of this Article with regard to the rights, obligations and remedies of the seller, the buyer, purchasers or other third parties applies irrespective of title to the goods except where the provision refers to such title. Insofar as situations are not covered by the other provisions of this Article and matters concerning title become material the following rules apply:

(1) Title to goods cannot pass under a contract for sale prior to their identification to the contract (Section 2–501), and unless otherwise explicitly agreed the buyer acquires by their identification a special property as limited by this Act. Any retention or reservation by the seller of the title (property) in goods shipped or delivered to the buyer is limited in effect to a reservation of a security interest. Subject to these provisions and to the provisions of the Article on Secured Transactions (Article 9), title to goods passes from the seller to the buyer in any manner and on any conditions explicitly agreed on by the parties.
(2) Unless otherwise explicitly agreed title passes to the buyer at the time and place at which the seller completes his performance with reference to the physical delivery of the goods, despite any reservation of a security interest and even though a document of title is to be delivered at a different time or place; and in particular and despite any reservation of a security interest by the bill of lading
 (a) if the contract requires or authorizes the seller to send the goods to the buyer but does not require him to deliver them at destination, title passes to the buyer at the time and place of shipment; but
 (b) if the contract requires delivery at destination, title passes on tender there.
(3) Unless otherwise explicitly agreed where delivery is to be made without moving the goods,
 (a) if the seller is to deliver a document of title, title passes at the time when and the place where he delivers such documents; or
 (b) if the goods are at the time of contracting already identified and no documents are to be delivered, title passes at the time and place of contracting.
(4) A rejection or other refusal by the buyer to receive or retain the goods, whether or not justified, or a justified revocation of acceptance revests title to the goods in the seller. Such revesting occurs by operation of law and is not a "sale".

§ 2–402. Rights of Seller's Creditors Against Sold Goods.

(1) Except as provided in subsections (2) and (3), rights of unsecured creditors of the seller with respect to goods which have been identified to a contract for sale are

subject to the buyer's rights to recover the goods under this Article (Sections 2–502 and 2–716).

(2) A creditor of the seller may treat a sale or an identification of goods to a contract for sale as void if as against him a retention of possession by the seller is fraudulent under any rule of law of the state where the goods are situated, except that retention of possession in good faith and current course of trade by a merchant-seller for a commercially reasonable time after a sale or identification is not fraudulent.

(3) Nothing in this Article shall be deemed to impair the rights of creditors of the seller

 (a) under the provisions of the Article on Secured Transactions (Article 9); or

 (b) where identification to the contract or delivery is made not in current course of trade but in satisfaction of or as security for a pre-existing claim for money, security or the like and is made under circumstances which under any rule of law of the state where the goods are situated would apart from this Article constitute the transaction a fraudulent transfer or voidable preference.

§ 2–403. Power to Transfer; Good Faith Purchase of Goods; "Entrusting".

(1) A purchaser of goods acquires all title which his transferor had or had power to transfer except that a purchaser of a limited interest acquires rights only to the extent of the interest purchased. A person with voidable title has power to transfer a good title to a good faith purchaser for value. When goods have been delivered under a transaction of purchase the purchaser has such power even though

 (a) the transferor was deceived as to the identity of the purchaser, or

 (b) the delivery was in exchange for a check which is later dishonored, or

 (c) it was agreed that the transaction was to be a "cash sale", or

 (d) the delivery was procured through fraud punishable as larcenous under the criminal law.

(2) Any entrusting of possession of goods to a merchant who deals in goods of that kind gives him power to transfer all rights of the entruster to a buyer in ordinary course of business.

(3) "Entrusting" includes any delivery and any acquiescence in retention of possession regardless of any condition expressed between the parties to the delivery or acquiescence and regardless of whether the procurement of the entrusting or the possessor's disposition of the goods have been such as to be larcenous under the criminal law.

[*Publisher's Editorial Note: If a state adopts the repealer of Article 6—Bulk Transfers (Alternative A), subsec. (4) should read as follows:*]

(4) The rights of other purchasers of goods and of lien creditors are governed by the Articles on Secured Transactions (Article 9) and Documents of Title (Article 7).

[*Publisher's Editorial Note: If a state adopts Revised Article 6—Bulk Sales (Alternative B), subsec. (4) should read as follows:*]

(4) The rights of other purchasers of goods and of lien creditors are governed by the Articles on Secured Transactions (Article 9), Bulk Sales (Article 6) and Documents of Title (Article 7).

As amended in 1988.

 For material relating to the changes made in text in 1988, see section 3 of Alternative A (Repealer of Article 6—Bulk Transfers) and Conforming Amendment to Section 2–403 following end of Alternative B (Revised Article 6—Bulk Sales).

Part 5: Performance

§ 2–501. Insurable Interest in Goods; Manner of Identification of Goods.

(1) The buyer obtains a special property and an insurable interest in goods by identification of existing goods as goods to which the contract refers even though the goods so identified are non-conforming and he has an option to return or reject them. Such identification can be made at any time and in any manner explicitly agreed to by the parties. In the absence of explicit agreement identification occurs

 (a) when the contract is made if it is for the sale of goods already existing and identified;

 (b) if the contract is for the sale of future goods other than those described in paragraph (c), when goods are shipped, marked or otherwise designated by the seller as goods to which the contract refers;

 (c) when the crops are planted or otherwise become growing crops or the young are conceived if the contract is for the sale of unborn young to be born within twelve months after contracting or for the sale of crops to be harvested within twelve months or the next normal harvest season after contracting whichever is longer.

(2) The seller retains an insurable interest in goods so long as title to or any security interest in the goods remains in him and where the identification is by the seller alone he may until default or insolvency or notification to the buyer that the identification is final substitute other goods for those identified.

(3) Nothing in this section impairs any insurable interest recognized under any other statute or rule of law.

§ 2–502. Buyer's Right to Goods on Seller's Insolvency.

(1) Subject to subsection (2) and even though the goods have not been shipped a buyer who has paid a part or all of the price of goods in which he has a special property under the provisions of the immediately preceding section may on making and keeping good a tender of

any unpaid portion of their price recover them from the seller if the seller becomes insolvent within ten days after receipt of the first installment on their price.

(2) If the identification creating his special property has been made by the buyer he acquires the right to recover the goods only if they conform to the contract for sale.

§ 2–503. Manner of Seller's Tender of Delivery.

(1) Tender of delivery requires that the seller put and hold conforming goods at the buyer's disposition and give the buyer any notification reasonably necessary to enable him to take delivery. The manner, time and place for tender are determined by the agreement and this Article, and in particular

 (a) tender must be at a reasonable hour, and if it is of goods they must be kept available for the period reasonably necessary to enable the buyer to take possession; but

 (b) unless otherwise agreed the buyer must furnish facilities reasonably suited to the receipt of the goods.

(2) Where the case is within the next section respecting shipment tender requires that the seller comply with its provisions.

(3) Where the seller is required to deliver at a particular destination tender requires that he comply with subsection (1) and also in any appropriate case tender documents as described in subsections (4) and (5) of this section.

(4) Where goods are in the possession of a bailee and are to be delivered without being moved

 (a) tender requires that the seller either tender a negotiable document of title covering such goods or procure acknowledgment by the bailee of the buyer's right to possession of the goods; but

 (b) tender to the buyer of a non-negotiable document of title or of a written direction to the bailee to deliver is sufficient tender unless the buyer seasonably objects, and receipt by the bailee of notification of the buyer's rights fixes those rights as against the bailee and all third persons; but risk of loss of the goods and of any failure by the bailee to honor the non-negotiable document of title or to obey the direction remains on the seller until the buyer has had a reasonable time to present the document or direction, and a refusal by the bailee to honor the document or to obey the direction defeats the tender.

(5) Where the contract requires the seller to deliver documents

 (a) he must tender all such documents in correct form, except as provided in this Article with respect to bills of lading in a set (subsection (2) of Section 2–323); and

 (b) tender through customary banking channels is sufficient and dishonor of a draft accompanying the documents constitutes non-acceptance or rejection.

§ 2–504. Shipment by Seller.

Where the seller is required or authorized to send the goods to the buyer and the contract does not require him to deliver them at a particular destination, then unless otherwise agreed he must

 (a) put the goods in the possession of such a carrier and make such a contract for their transportation as may be reasonable having regard to the nature of the goods and other circumstances of the case; and

 (b) obtain and promptly deliver or tender in due form any document necessary to enable the buyer to obtain possession of the goods or otherwise required by the agreement or by usage of trade; and

 (c) promptly notify the buyer of the shipment.

Failure to notify the buyer under paragraph (c) or to make a proper contract under paragraph (a) is a ground for rejection only if material delay or loss ensues.

§ 2–505. Seller's Shipment Under Reservation.

(1) Where the seller has identified goods to the contract by or before shipment:

 (a) his procurement of a negotiable bill of lading to his own order or otherwise reserves in him a security interest in the goods. His procurement of the bill to the order of a financing agency or of the buyer indicates in addition only the seller's expectation of transferring that interest to the person named.

 (b) a non-negotiable bill of lading to himself or his nominee reserves possession of the goods as security but except in a case of conditional delivery (subsection (2) of Section 2–507) a non-negotiable bill of lading naming the buyer as consignee reserves no security interest even though the seller retains possession of the bill of lading.

(2) When shipment by the seller with reservation of a security interest is in violation of the contract for sale it constitutes an improper contract for transportation within the preceding section but impairs neither the rights given to the buyer by shipment and identification of the goods to the contract nor the seller's powers as a holder of a negotiable document.

§ 2–506. Rights of Financing Agency.

(1) A financing agency by paying or purchasing for value a draft which relates to a shipment of goods acquires to the extent of the payment or purchase and in addition to its own rights under the draft and any document of title securing it any rights of the shipper in the goods

including the right to stop delivery and the shipper's right to have the draft honored by the buyer.

(2) The right to reimbursement of a financing agency which has in good faith honored or purchased the draft under commitment to or authority from the buyer is not impaired by subsequent discovery of defects with reference to any relevant document which was apparently regular on its face.

§ 2–507. Effect of Seller's Tender; Delivery on Condition.

(1) Tender of delivery is a condition to the buyer's duty to accept the goods and, unless otherwise agreed, to his duty to pay for them. Tender entitles the seller to acceptance of the goods and to payment according to the contract.

(2) Where payment is due and demanded on the delivery to the buyer of goods or documents of title, his right as against the seller to retain or dispose of them is conditional upon his making the payment due.

§ 2–508. Cure by Seller of Improper Tender or Delivery; Replacement.

(1) Where any tender or delivery by the seller is rejected because non-conforming and the time for performance has not yet expired, the seller may seasonably notify the buyer of his intention to cure and may then within the contract time make a conforming delivery.

(2) Where the buyer rejects a non-conforming tender which the seller had reasonable grounds to believe would be acceptable with or without money allowance the seller may if he seasonably notifies the buyer have a further reasonable time to substitute a conforming tender.

§ 2–509. Risk of Loss in the Absence of Breach.

(1) Where the contract requires or authorizes the seller to ship the goods by carrier

(a) if it does not require him to deliver them at a particular destination, the risk of loss passes to the buyer when the goods are duly delivered to the carrier even though the shipment is under reservation (Section 2–505); but

(b) if it does require him to deliver them at a particular destination and the goods are there duly tendered while in the possession of the carrier, the risk of loss passes to the buyer when the goods are there duly so tendered as to enable the buyer to take delivery.

(2) Where the goods are held by a bailee to be delivered without being moved, the risk of loss passes to the buyer

(a) on his receipt of a negotiable document of title covering the goods; or

(b) on acknowledgment by the bailee of the buyer's right to possession of the goods; or

(c) after his receipt of a non-negotiable document of title or other written direction to deliver, as provided in subsection (4)(b) of Section 2–503.

(3) In any case not within subsection (1) or (2), the risk of loss passes to the buyer on his receipt of the goods if the seller is a merchant; otherwise the risk passes to the buyer on tender of delivery.

(4) The provisions of this section are subject to contrary agreement of the parties and to the provisions of this Article on sale on approval (Section 2–327) and on effect of breach on risk of loss (Section 2–510).

§ 2–510. Effect of Breach on Risk of Loss.

(1) Where a tender or delivery of goods so fails to conform to the contract as to give a right of rejection the risk of their loss remains on the seller until cure or acceptance.

(2) Where the buyer rightfully revokes acceptance he may to the extent of any deficiency in his effective insurance coverage treat the risk of loss as having rested on the seller from the beginning.

(3) Where the buyer as to conforming goods already identified to the contract for sale repudiates or is otherwise in breach before risk of their loss has passed to him, the seller may to the extent of any deficiency in his effective insurance coverage treat the risk of loss as resting on the buyer for a commercially reasonable time.

§ 2–511. Tender of Payment by Buyer; Payment by Check.

(1) Unless otherwise agreed tender of payment is a condition to the seller's duty to tender and complete any delivery.

(2) Tender of payment is sufficient when made by any means or in any manner current in the ordinary course of business unless the seller demands payment in legal tender and gives any extension of time reasonably necessary to procure it.

(3) Subject to the provisions of this Act on the effect of an instrument on an obligation (Section 3-310), payment by check is conditional and is defeated as between the parties by dishonor of the check on due presentment.

As amended in 1994.

See Appendix XI for material relating to changes made in text in 1994.

§ 2–512. Payment by Buyer Before Inspection. *1995 Amendments to text indicated by strikeout and underline*

(1) Where the contract requires payment before inspection non-conformity of the goods does not excuse the buyer from so making payment unless

(a) the non-conformity appears without inspection; or

(b) despite tender of the required documents the circumstances would justify injunction against honor under this Act (Section 5-109(b)).

(2) Payment pursuant to subsection (1) does not constitute an acceptance of goods or impair the buyer's right to inspect or any of his remedies.

As amended in 1995.

See Appendix XIV for material relating to changes made in text in 1995.

§ 2–513. Buyer's Right to Inspection of Goods.

(1) Unless otherwise agreed and subject to subsection (3), where goods are tendered or delivered or identified to the contract for sale, the buyer has a right before payment or acceptance to inspect them at any reasonable place and time and in any reasonable manner. When the seller is required or authorized to send the goods to the buyer, the inspection may be after their arrival.

(2) Expenses of inspection must be borne by the buyer but may be recovered from the seller if the goods do not conform and are rejected.

(3) Unless otherwise agreed and subject to the provisions of this Article on C.I.F. contracts (subsection (3) of Section 2–321), the buyer is not entitled to inspect the goods before payment of the price when the contract provides

(a) for delivery "C.O.D." or on other like terms; or

(b) for payment against documents of title, except where such payment is due only after the goods are to become available for inspection.

(4) A place or method of inspection fixed by the parties is presumed to be exclusive but unless otherwise expressly agreed it does not postpone identification or shift the place for delivery or for passing the risk of loss. If compliance becomes impossible, inspection shall be as provided in this section unless the place or method fixed was clearly intended as an indispensable condition failure of which avoids the contract.

§ 2–514. When Documents Deliverable on Acceptance; When on Payment.
Unless otherwise agreed documents against which a draft is drawn are to be delivered to the drawee on acceptance of the draft if it is payable more than three days after presentment; otherwise, only on payment.

§ 2–515. Preserving Evidence of Goods in Dispute.
In furtherance of the adjustment of any claim or dispute

(a) either party on reasonable notification to the other and for the purpose of ascertaining the facts and preserving evidence has the right to inspect, test and sample the goods including such of them as may be in the possession or control of the other; and

(b) the parties may agree to a third party inspection or survey to determine the conformity or condition of the goods and may agree that the findings shall be binding upon them in any subsequent litigation or adjustment.

Part 6: Breach, Repudiation and Excuse

§ 2–601. Buyer's Rights on Improper Delivery.
Subject to the provisions of this Article on breach in installment contracts (Section 2–612) and unless otherwise agreed under the sections on contractual limitations of remedy (Sections 2–718 and 2–719), if the goods or the tender of delivery fail in any respect to conform to the contract, the buyer may

(a) reject the whole; or

(b) accept the whole; or

(c) accept any commercial unit or units and reject the rest.

§ 2–602. Manner and Effect of Rightful Rejection.

(1) Rejection of goods must be within a reasonable time after their delivery or tender. It is ineffective unless the buyer seasonably notifies the seller.

(2) Subject to the provisions of the two following sections on rejected goods (Sections 2–603 and 2–604),

(a) after rejection any exercise of ownership by the buyer with respect to any commercial unit is wrongful as against the seller; and

(b) if the buyer has before rejection taken physical possession of goods in which he does not have a security interest under the provisions of this Article (subsection (3) of Section 2–711), he is under a duty after rejection to hold them with reasonable care at the seller's disposition for a time sufficient to permit the seller to remove them; but

(c) the buyer has no further obligations with regard to goods rightfully rejected.

(3) The seller's rights with respect to goods wrongfully rejected are governed by the provisions of this Article on Seller's remedies in general (Section 2–703).

§ 2–603. Merchant Buyer's Duties as to Rightfully Rejected Goods.

(1) Subject to any security interest in the buyer (subsection (3) of Section 2–711), when the seller has no agent or place of business at the market of rejection a merchant buyer is under a duty after rejection of goods in his possession or control to follow any reasonable instructions received from the seller with respect to the goods and in the absence of such instructions to make reasonable efforts to sell them for the seller's account if they are perishable or threaten to decline in value speedily. Instructions are not reasonable if on demand indemnity for expenses is not forthcoming.

(2) When the buyer sells goods under subsection (1), he is entitled to reimbursement from the seller or out of the proceeds for reasonable expenses of caring for and selling them, and if the expenses include no selling commission then to such commission as is usual in the trade or if there is none to a reasonable sum not exceeding ten per cent on the gross proceeds.

(3) In complying with this section the buyer is held only to good faith and good faith conduct hereunder is neither acceptance nor conversion nor the basis of an action for damages.

§ 2–604. Buyer's Options as to Salvage of Rightfully Rejected Goods.

Subject to the provisions of the immediately preceding section on perishables if the seller gives no instructions within a reasonable time after notification of rejection the buyer may store the rejected goods for the seller's account or reship them to him or resell them for the seller's account with reimbursement as provided in the preceding section. Such action is not acceptance or conversion.

§ 2–605. Waiver of Buyer's Objections by Failure to Particularize.

(1) The buyer's failure to state in connection with rejection a particular defect which is ascertainable by reasonable inspection precludes him from relying on the unstated defect to justify rejection or to establish breach

 (a) where the seller could have cured it if stated seasonably; or

 (b) between merchants when the seller has after rejection made a request in writing for a full and final written statement of all defects on which the buyer proposes to rely.

(2) Payment against documents made without reservation of rights precludes recovery of the payment for defects apparent on the face of the documents.

§ 2–606. What Constitutes Acceptance of Goods.

(1) Acceptance of goods occurs when the buyer

 (a) after a reasonable opportunity to inspect the goods signifies to the seller that the goods are conforming or that he will take or retain them in spite of their non-conformity; or

 (b) fails to make an effective rejection (subsection (1) of Section 2–602), but such acceptance does not occur until the buyer has had a reasonable opportunity to inspect them; or

 (c) does any act inconsistent with the seller's ownership; but if such act is wrongful as against the seller it is an acceptance only if ratified by him.

(2) Acceptance of a part of any commercial unit is acceptance of that entire unit.

§ 2–607. Effect of Acceptance; Notice of Breach; Burden of Establishing Breach After Acceptance; Notice of Claim or Litigation to Person Answerable Over.

(1) The buyer must pay at the contract rate for any goods accepted.

(2) Acceptance of goods by the buyer precludes rejection of the goods accepted and if made with knowledge of a non-conformity cannot be revoked because of it unless the acceptance was on the reasonable assumption that the non-conformity would be seasonably cured but acceptance does not of itself impair any other remedy provided by this Article for non-conformity.

(3) Where a tender has been accepted

 (a) the buyer must within a reasonable time after he discovers or should have discovered any breach notify the seller of breach or be barred from any remedy; and

 (b) if the claim is one for infringement or the like (subsection (3) of Section 2–312) and the buyer is sued as a result of such a breach he must so notify the seller within a reasonable time after he receives notice of the litigation or be barred from any remedy over for liability established by the litigation.

(4) The burden is on the buyer to establish any breach with respect to the goods accepted.

(5) Where the buyer is sued for breach of a warranty or other obligation for which his seller is answerable over

 (a) he may give his seller written notice of the litigation. If the notice states that the seller may come in and defend and that if the seller does not do so he will be bound in any action against him by his buyer by any determination of fact common to the two litigations, then unless the seller after seasonable receipt of the notice does come in and defend he is so bound.

 (b) if the claim is one for infringement or the like (subsection (3) of Section 2–312) the original seller may demand in writing that his buyer turn over to him control of the litigation including settlement or else be barred from any remedy over and if he also agrees to bear all expense and to satisfy any adverse judgment, then unless the buyer after seasonable receipt of the demand does turn over control the buyer is so barred.

(6) The provisions of subsections (3), (4) and (5) apply to any obligation of a buyer to hold the seller harmless against infringement or the like (subsection (3) of Section 2–312).

§ 2–608. Revocation of Acceptance in Whole or in Part.

(1) The buyer may revoke his acceptance of a lot or commercial unit whose non-conformity substantially impairs its value to him if he has accepted it

(a) on the reasonable assumption that its non-conformity would be cured and it has not been seasonably cured; or

(b) without discovery of such non-conformity if his acceptance was reasonably induced either by the difficulty of discovery before acceptance or by the seller's assurances.

(2) Revocation of acceptance must occur within a reasonable time after the buyer discovers or should have discovered the ground for it and before any substantial change in condition of the goods which is not caused by their own defects. It is not effective until the buyer notifies the seller of it.

(3) A buyer who so revokes has the same rights and duties with regard to the goods involved as if he had rejected them.

§ 2–609. Right to Adequate Assurance of Performance.

(1) A contract for sale imposes an obligation on each party that the other's expectation of receiving due performance will not be impaired. When reasonable grounds for insecurity arise with respect to the performance of either party the other may in writing demand adequate assurance of due performance and until he receives such assurance may if commercially reasonable suspend any performance for which he has not already received the agreed return.

(2) Between merchants the reasonableness of grounds for insecurity and the adequacy of any assurance offered shall be determined according to commercial standards.

(3) Acceptance of any improper delivery or payment does not prejudice the aggrieved party's right to demand adequate assurance of future performance.

(4) After receipt of a justified demand failure to provide within a reasonable time not exceeding thirty days such assurance of due performance as is adequate under the circumstances of the particular case is a repudiation of the contract.

§ 2–610. Anticipatory Repudiation. When either party repudiates the contract with respect to a performance not yet due the loss of which will substantially impair the value of the contract to the other, the aggrieved party may

(a) for a commercially reasonable time await performance by the repudiating party; or

(b) resort to any remedy for breach (Section 2–703 or Section 2–711), even though he has notified the repudiating party that he would await the latter's performance and has urged retraction; and

(c) in either case suspend his own performance or proceed in accordance with the provisions of this Article on the seller's right to identify goods to the contract notwithstanding breach or to salvage unfinished goods (Section 2–704).

§ 2–611. Retraction of Anticipatory Repudiation.

(1) Until the repudiating party's next performance is due he can retract his repudiation unless the aggrieved party has since the repudiation cancelled or materially changed his position or otherwise indicated that he considers the repudiation final.

(2) Retraction may be by any method which clearly indicates to the aggrieved party that the repudiating party intends to perform, but must include any assurance justifiably demanded under the provisions of this Article (Section 2–609).

(3) Retraction reinstates the repudiating party's rights under the contract with due excuse and allowance to the aggrieved party for any delay occasioned by the repudiation.

§ 2–612. "Installment Contract"; Breach.

(1) An "installment contract" is one which requires or authorizes the delivery of goods in separate lots to be separately accepted, even though the contract contains a clause "each delivery is a separate contract" or its equivalent.

(2) The buyer may reject any installment which is non-conforming if the non-conformity substantially impairs the value of that installment and cannot be cured or if the non-conformity is a defect in the required documents; but if the non-conformity does not fall within subsection (3) and the seller gives adequate assurance of its cure the buyer must accept that installment.

(3) Whenever non-conformity or default with respect to one or more installments substantially impairs the value of the whole contract there is a breach of the whole. But the aggrieved party reinstates the contract if he accepts a non-conforming installment without seasonably notifying of cancellation or if he brings an action with respect only to past installments or demands performance as to future installments.

§ 2–613. Casualty to Identified Goods. Where the contract requires for its performance goods identified when the contract is made, and the goods suffer casualty without fault of either party before the risk of loss passes to the buyer, or in a proper case under a "no arrival, no sale" term (Section 2–324) then

(a) if the loss is total the contract is avoided; and

(b) if the loss is partial or the goods have so deteriorated as no longer to conform to the contract the buyer may nevertheless demand inspection and at his option either treat the contract as avoided or accept the goods with due allowance from the contract price for the deterioration or the deficiency in quantity but without further right against the seller.

§ 2–614. Substituted Performance.

(1) Where without fault of either party the agreed berthing, loading, or unloading facilities fail or an agreed type of carrier becomes unavailable or the agreed manner of delivery otherwise becomes commercially impracticable but a commercially reasonable substitute is available, such substitute performance must be tendered and accepted.

(2) If the agreed means or manner of payment fails because of domestic or foreign governmental regulation, the seller may withhold or stop delivery unless the buyer provides a means or manner of payment which is commercially a substantial equivalent. If delivery has already been taken, payment by the means or in the manner provided by the regulation discharges the buyer's obligation unless the regulation is discriminatory, oppressive or predatory.

§ 2–615. Excuse by Failure of Presupposed Conditions.

Except so far as a seller may have assumed a greater obligation and subject to the preceding section on substituted performance:

(a) Delay in delivery or non-delivery in whole or in part by a seller who complies with paragraphs (b) and (c) is not a breach of his duty under a contract for sale if performance as agreed has been made impracticable by the occurrence of a contingency the non-occurrence of which was a basic assumption on which the contract was made or by compliance in good faith with any applicable foreign or domestic governmental regulation or order whether or not it later proves to be invalid.

(b) Where the causes mentioned in paragraph (a) affect only a part of the seller's capacity to perform, he must allocate production and deliveries among his customers but may at his option include regular customers not then under contract as well as his own requirements for further manufacture. He may so allocate in any manner which is fair and reasonable.

(c) The seller must notify the buyer seasonably that there will be delay or non-delivery and, when allocation is required under paragraph (b), of the estimated quota thus made available for the buyer.

§ 2–616. Procedure on Notice Claiming Excuse.

(1) Where the buyer receives notification of a material or indefinite delay or an allocation justified under the preceding section he may by written notification to the seller as to any delivery concerned, and where the prospective deficiency substantially impairs the value of the whole contract under the provisions of this Article relating to breach of installment contracts (Section 2–612), then also as to the whole,

(a) terminate and thereby discharge any unexecuted portion of the contract; or

(b) modify the contract by agreeing to take his available quota in substitution.

(2) If after receipt of such notification from the seller the buyer fails so to modify the contract within a reasonable time not exceeding thirty days the contract lapses with respect to any deliveries affected.

(3) The provisions of this section may not be negated by agreement except in so far as the seller has assumed a greater obligation under the preceding section.

Part 7: Remedies

§ 2–701. Remedies for Breach of Collateral Contracts Not Impaired. Remedies for breach of any obligation or promise collateral or ancillary to a contract for sale are not impaired by the provisions of this Article.

§ 2–702. Seller's Remedies on Discovery of Buyer's Insolvency.

(1) Where the seller discovers the buyer to be insolvent he may refuse delivery except for cash including payment for all goods theretofore delivered under the contract, and stop delivery under this Article (Section 2–705).

(2) Where the seller discovers that the buyer has received goods on credit while insolvent he may reclaim the goods upon demand made within ten days after the receipt, but if misrepresentation of solvency has been made to the particular seller in writing within three months before delivery the ten day limitation does not apply. Except as provided in this subsection the seller may not base a right to reclaim goods on the buyer's fraudulent or innocent misrepresentation of solvency or of intent to pay.

(3) The seller's right to reclaim under subsection (2) is subject to the rights of a buyer in ordinary course or other good faith purchaser under this Article (Section 2–403). Successful reclamation of goods excludes all other remedies with respect to them.
As amended in 1966.

§ 2–703. Seller's Remedies in General. Where the buyer wrongfully rejects or revokes acceptance of goods or fails to make a payment due on or before delivery or repudiates with respect to a part or the whole, then with respect to any goods directly affected and, if the breach is of the whole contract (Section 2–612), then also with respect to the whole undelivered balance, the aggrieved seller may

(a) withhold delivery of such goods;

(b) stop delivery by any bailee as hereafter provided (Section 2–705);

(c) proceed under the next section respecting goods still unidentified to the contract;

(d) resell and recover damages as hereafter provided (Section 2–706);

(e) recover damages for non-acceptance (Section 2–708) or in a proper case the price (Section 2–709);

(f) cancel.

§ 2–704. Seller's Right to Identify Goods to the Contract Notwithstanding Breach or to Salvage Unfinished Goods.

(1) An aggrieved seller under the preceding section may

(a) identify to the contract conforming goods not already identified if at the time he learned of the breach they are in his possession or control;

(b) treat as the subject of resale goods which have demonstrably been intended for the particular contract even though those goods are unfinished.

(2) Where the goods are unfinished an aggrieved seller may in the exercise of reasonable commercial judgment for the purposes of avoiding loss and of effective realization either complete the manufacture and wholly identify the goods to the contract or cease manufacture and resell for scrap or salvage value or proceed in any other reasonable manner.

§ 2–705. Seller's Stoppage of Delivery in Transit or Otherwise.

(1) The seller may stop delivery of goods in the possession of a carrier or other bailee when he discovers the buyer to be insolvent (Section 2–702) and may stop delivery of carload, truckload, planeload or larger shipments of express or freight when the buyer repudiates or fails to make a payment due before delivery or if for any other reason the seller has a right to withhold or reclaim the goods.

(2) As against such buyer the seller may stop delivery until

(a) receipt of the goods by the buyer; or

(b) acknowledgment to the buyer by any bailee of the goods except a carrier that the bailee holds the goods for the buyer; or

(c) such acknowledgment to the buyer by a carrier by reshipment or as warehouseman; or

(d) negotiation to the buyer of any negotiable document of title covering the goods.

(3) (a) To stop delivery the seller must so notify as to enable the bailee by reasonable diligence to prevent delivery of the goods.

(b) After such notification the bailee must hold and deliver the goods according to the directions of the seller but the seller is liable to the bailee for any ensuing charges or damages.

(c) If a negotiable document of title has been issued for goods the bailee is not obliged to obey a notification to stop until surrender of the document.

(d) A carrier who has issued a non-negotiable bill of lading is not obliged to obey a notification to stop received from a person other than the consignor.

§ 2–706. Seller's Resale Including Contract for Resale.

(1) Under the conditions stated in Section 2–703 on seller's remedies, the seller may resell the goods concerned or the undelivered balance thereof. Where the resale is made in good faith and in a commercially reasonable manner the seller may recover the difference between the resale price and the contract price together with any incidental damages allowed under the provisions of this Article (Section 2–710), but less expenses saved in consequence of the buyer's breach.

(2) Except as otherwise provided in subsection (3) or unless otherwise agreed resale may be at public or private sale including sale by way of one or more contracts to sell or of identification to an existing contract of the seller. Sale may be as a unit or in parcels and at any time and place and on any terms but every aspect of the sale including the method, manner, time, place and terms must be commercially reasonable. The resale must be reasonably identified as referring to the broken contract, but it is not necessary that the goods be in existence or that any or all of them have been identified to the contract before the breach.

(3) Where the resale is at private sale the seller must give the buyer reasonable notification of his intention to resell.

(4) Where the resale is at public sale

(a) only identified goods can be sold except where there is a recognized market for a public sale of futures in goods of the kind; and

(b) it must be made at a usual place or market for public sale if one is reasonably available and except in the case of goods which are perishable or threaten to decline in value speedily the seller must give the buyer reasonable notice of the time and place of the resale; and

(c) if the goods are not to be within the view of those attending the sale the notification of sale must state the place where the goods are located and provide for their reasonable inspection by prospective bidders; and

(d) the seller may buy.

(5) A purchaser who buys in good faith at a resale takes the goods free of any rights of the original buyer even though the seller fails to comply with one or more of the requirements of this section.

(6) The seller is not accountable to the buyer for any profit made on any resale. A person in the position of a seller (Section 2–707) or a buyer who has rightfully rejected or justifiably revoked acceptance must account for any excess over the amount of his security interest, as herein after defined (subsection (3) of Section 2–711).

§ 2–707. "Person in the Position of a Seller".

(1) A "person in the position of a seller" includes as against a principal an agent who has paid or become responsible for the price of goods on behalf of his principal or anyone who otherwise holds a security interest or other right in goods similar to that of a seller.

(2) A person in the position of a seller may as provided in this Article withhold or stop delivery (Section 2–705) and resell (Section 2–706) and recover incidental damages (Section 2–710).

§ 2–708. Seller's Damages for Non-acceptance or Repudiation.

(1) Subject to subsection (2) and to the provisions of this Article with respect to proof of market price (Section 2–723), the measure of damages for non-acceptance or repudiation by the buyer is the difference between the market price at the time and place for tender and the unpaid contract price together with any incidental damages provided in this Article (Section 2–710), but less expenses saved in consequence of the buyer's breach.

(2) If the measure of damages provided in subsection (1) is inadequate to put the seller in as good a position as performance would have done then the measure of damages is the profit (including reasonable overhead) which the seller would have made from full performance by the buyer, together with any incidental damages provided in this Article (Section 2–710), due allowance for costs reasonably incurred and due credit for payments or proceeds of resale.

§ 2–709. Action for the Price.

(1) When the buyer fails to pay the price as it becomes due the seller may recover, together with any incidental damages under the next section, the price

(a) of goods accepted or of conforming goods lost or damaged within a commercially reasonable time after risk of their loss has passed to the buyer; and

(b) of goods identified to the contract if the seller is unable after reasonable effort to resell them at a reasonable price or the circumstances reasonably indicate that such effort will be unavailing.

(2) Where the seller sues for the price he must hold for the buyer any goods which have been identified to the contract and are still in his control except that if resale becomes possible he may resell them at any time prior to the collection of the judgment. The net proceeds of any such resale must be credited to the buyer and payment of the judgment entitles him to any goods not resold.

(3) After the buyer has wrongfully rejected or revoked acceptance of the goods or has failed to make a payment due or has repudiated (Section 2–610), a seller who is held not entitled to the price under this section shall nevertheless be awarded damages for non-acceptance under the preceding section.

§ 2–710. Seller's Incidental Damages.
Incidental damages to an aggrieved seller include any commercially reasonable charges, expenses or commissions incurred in stopping delivery, in the transportation, care and custody of goods after the buyer's breach, in connection with return or resale of the goods or otherwise resulting from the breach.

§ 2–711. Buyer's Remedies in General; Buyer's Security Interest in Rejected Goods.

(1) Where the seller fails to make delivery or repudiates or the buyer rightfully rejects or justifiably revokes acceptance then with respect to any goods involved, and with respect to the whole if the breach goes to the whole contract (Section 2–612), the buyer may cancel and whether or not he has done so may in addition to recovering so much of the price as has been paid

(a) "cover" and have damages under the next section as to all the goods affected whether or not they have been identified to the contract; or

(b) recover damages for non-delivery as provided in this Article (Section 2–713).

(2) Where the seller fails to deliver or repudiates the buyer may also

(a) if the goods have been identified recover them as provided in this Article (Section 2–502); or

(b) in a proper case obtain specific performance or replevy the goods as provided in this Article (Section 2–716).

(3) On rightful rejection or justifiable revocation of acceptance a buyer has a security interest in goods in his possession or control for any payments made on their price and any expenses reasonably incurred in their inspection, receipt, transportation, care and custody and may hold such goods and resell them in like manner as an aggrieved seller (Section 2–706).

§ 2–712. "Cover"; Buyer's Procurement of Substitute Goods.

(1) After a breach within the preceding section the buyer may "cover" by making in good faith and without unreasonable delay any reasonable purchase of or contract to purchase goods in substitution for those due from the seller.

(2) The buyer may recover from the seller as damages the difference between the cost of cover and the contract price together with any incidental or consequential damages as hereinafter defined (Section 2–715), but less expenses saved in consequence of the seller's breach.

(3) Failure of the buyer to effect cover within this section does not bar him from any other remedy.

§ 2–713. Buyer's Damages for Non-delivery or Repudiation.

(1) Subject to the provisions of this Article with respect to proof of market price (Section 2–723), the measure of damages for non-delivery or repudiation by the seller is the difference between the market price at the time when the buyer learned of the breach and the contract price together with any incidental and consequential damages provided in this Article (Section 2–715), but less expenses saved in consequence of the seller's breach.

(2) Market price is to be determined as of the place for tender or, in cases of rejection after arrival or revocation of acceptance, as of the place of arrival.

§ 2–714. Buyer's Damages for Breach in Regard to Accepted Goods.

(1) Where the buyer has accepted goods and given notification (subsection (3) of Section 2–607) he may recover as damages for any non-conformity of tender the loss resulting in the ordinary course of events from the seller's breach as determined in any manner which is reasonable.

(2) The measure of damages for breach of warranty is the difference at the time and place of acceptance between the value of the goods accepted and the value they would have had if they had been as warranted, unless special circumstances show proximate damages of a different amount.

(3) In a proper case any incidental and consequential damages under the next section may also be recovered.

§ 2–715. Buyer's Incidental and Consequential Damages.

(1) Incidental damages resulting from the seller's breach include expenses reasonably incurred in inspection, receipt, transportation and care and custody of goods rightfully rejected, any commercially reasonable charges, expenses or commissions in connection with effecting cover and any other reasonable expense incident to the delay or other breach.

(2) Consequential damages resulting from the seller's breach include

 (a) any loss resulting from general or particular requirements and needs of which the seller at the time of contracting had reason to know and which could not reasonably be prevented by cover or otherwise; and

 (b) injury to person or property proximately resulting from any breach of warranty.

§ 2–716. Buyer's Right to Specific Performance or Replevin.

(1) Specific performance may be decreed where the goods are unique or in other proper circumstances.

(2) The decree for specific performance may include such terms and conditions as to payment of the price, damages, or other relief as the court may deem just.

(3) The buyer has a right of replevin for goods identified to the contract if after reasonable effort he is unable to effect cover for such goods or the circumstances reasonably indicate that such effort will be unavailing or if the goods have been shipped under reservation and satisfaction of the security interest in them has been made or tendered.

§ 2–717. Deduction of Damages from the Price.
The buyer on notifying the seller of his intention to do so may deduct all or any part of the damages resulting from any breach of the contract from any part of the price still due under the same contract.

§ 2–718. Liquidation or Limitation of Damages; Deposits.

(1) Damages for breach by either party may be liquidated in the agreement but only at an amount which is reasonable in the light of the anticipated or actual harm caused by the breach, the difficulties of proof of loss, and the inconvenience or nonfeasibility of otherwise obtaining an adequate remedy. A term fixing unreasonably large liquidated damages is void as a penalty.

(2) Where the seller justifiably withholds delivery of goods because of the buyer's breach, the buyer is entitled to restitution of any amount by which the sum of his payments exceeds

 (a) the amount to which the seller is entitled by virtue of terms liquidating the seller's damages in accordance with subsection (1), or

 (b) in the absence of such terms, twenty per cent of the value of the total performance for which the buyer is obligated under the contract or $500, whichever is smaller.

(3) The buyer's right to restitution under subsection (2) is subject to offset to the extent that the seller establishes

 (a) a right to recover damages under the provisions of this Article other than subsection (1), and

 (b) the amount or value of any benefits received by the buyer directly or indirectly by reason of the contract.

(4) Where a seller has received payment in goods their reasonable value or the proceeds of their resale shall be treated as payments for the purposes of subsection (2); but if the seller has notice of the buyer's breach before reselling goods received in part performance, his resale is subject to the conditions laid down in this Article on resale by an aggrieved seller (Section 2–706).

§ 2–719. Contractual Modification or Limitation of Remedy.

(1) Subject to the provisions of subsections (2) and (3) of this section and of the preceding section on liquidation and limitation of damages,

(a) the agreement may provide for remedies in addition to or in substitution for those provided in this Article and may limit or alter the measure of damages recoverable under this Article, as by limiting the buyer's remedies to return of the goods and repayment of the price or to repair and replacement of non-conforming goods or parts; and

(b) resort to a remedy as provided is optional unless the remedy is expressly agreed to be exclusive, in which case it is the sole remedy.

(2) Where circumstances cause an exclusive or limited remedy to fail of its essential purpose, remedy may be had as provided in this Act.

(3) Consequential damages may be limited or excluded unless the limitation or exclusion is unconscionable. Limitation of consequential damages for injury to the person in the case of consumer goods is prima facie unconscionable but limitation of damages where the loss is commercial is not.

§ 2–720. Effect of "Cancellation" or "Rescission" on Claims for Antecedent Breach. Unless the contrary intention clearly appears, expressions of "cancellation" or "rescission" of the contract or the like shall not be construed as a renunciation or discharge of any claim in damages for an antecedent breach.

§ 2–721. Remedies for Fraud. Remedies for material misrepresentation or fraud include all remedies available under this Article for non-fraudulent breach. Neither rescission or a claim for rescission of the contract for sale nor rejection or return of the goods shall bar or be deemed inconsistent with a claim for damages or other remedy.

§ 2–722. Who Can Sue Third Parties for Injury to Goods. Where a third party so deals with goods which have been identified to a contract for sale as to cause actionable injury to a party to that contract

(a) a right of action against the third party is in either party to the contract for sale who has title to or a security interest or a special property or an insurable interest in the goods; and if the goods have been destroyed or converted a right of action is also in the party who either bore the risk of loss under the contract for sale or has since the injury assumed that risk as against the other;

(b) if at the time of the injury the party plaintiff did not bear the risk of loss as against the other party to the contract for sale and there is no arrangement between them for disposition of the recovery, his suit or settlement is, subject to his own interest, as a fiduciary for the other party to the contract;

(c) either party may with the consent of the other sue for the benefit of whom it may concern.

§ 2–723. Proof of Market Price: Time and Place.

(1) If an action based on anticipatory repudiation comes to trial before the time for performance with respect to some or all of the goods, any damages based on market price (Section 2–708 or Section 2–713) shall be determined according to the price of such goods prevailing at the time when the aggrieved party learned of the repudiation.

(2) If evidence of a price prevailing at the times or places described in this Article is not readily available the price prevailing within any reasonable time before or after the time described or at any other place which in commercial judgment or under usage of trade would serve as a reasonable substitute for the one described may be used, making any proper allowance for the cost of transporting the goods to or from such other place.

(3) Evidence of a relevant price prevailing at a time or place other than the one described in this Article offered by one party is not admissible unless and until he has given the other party such notice as the court finds sufficient to prevent unfair surprise.

§ 2–724. Admissibility of Market Quotations. Whenever the prevailing price or value of any goods regularly bought and sold in any established commodity market is in issue, reports in official publications or trade journals or in newspapers or periodicals of general circulation published as the reports of such market shall be admissible in evidence. The circumstances of the preparation of such a report may be shown to affect its weight but not its admissibility.

§ 2–725. Statute of Limitations in Contracts for Sale.

(1) An action for breach of any contract for sale must be commenced within four years after the cause of action has accrued. By the original agreement the parties may reduce the period of limitation to not less than one year but may not extend it.

(2) A cause of action accrues when the breach occurs, regardless of the aggrieved party's lack of knowledge of the breach. A breach of warranty occurs when tender of delivery is made, except that where a warranty explicitly extends to future performance of the goods and discovery of the breach must await the time of such performance the cause of action accrues when the breach is or should have been discovered.

(3) Where an action commenced within the time limited by subsection (1) is so terminated as to leave available a remedy by another action for the same breach such other action may be commenced after the expiration of the time limited and within six months after the termination of the first action unless the termination resulted from voluntary discontinuance or from dismissal for failure or neglect to prosecute.

(4) This section does not alter the law on tolling of the statute of limitations nor does it apply to causes of action which have accrued before this Act becomes effective.

Article 2A: Leases

Part 1: General Provisions

§ 2A–101. Short Title. This Article shall be known and may be cited as the Uniform Commercial Code—Leases.

> *See Appendix VI [following Amendment 24 therein] for material relating to changes in the Official Comment to conform to the 1990 amendments to various sections of Article 2A.*

§ 2A–102. Scope. This Article applies to any transaction, regardless of form, that creates a lease.

§ 2A–103. Definitions and Index of Definitions.

(1) In this Article unless the context otherwise requires:

(a) "Buyer in ordinary course of business" means a person who in good faith and without knowledge that the sale to him [or her] is in violation of the ownership rights or security interest or leasehold interest of a third party in the goods buys in ordinary course from a person in the business of selling goods of that kind but does not include a pawnbroker. "Buying" may be for cash or by exchange of other property or on secured or unsecured credit and includes receiving goods or documents of title under a preexisting contract for sale but does not include a transfer in bulk or as security for or in total or partial satisfaction of a money debt.

(b) "Cancellation" occurs when either party puts an end to the lease contract for default by the other party.

(c) "Commercial unit" means such a unit of goods as by commercial usage is a single whole for purposes of lease and division of which materially impairs its character or value on the market or in use. A commercial unit may be a single article, as a machine, or a set of articles, as a suite of furniture or a line of machinery, or a quantity, as a gross or carload, or any other unit treated in use or in the relevant market as a single whole.

(d) "Conforming" goods or performance under a lease contract means goods or performance that are in accordance with the obligations under the lease contract.

(e) "Consumer lease" means a lease that a lessor regularly engaged in the business of leasing or selling makes to a lessee who is an individual and who takes under the lease primarily for a personal, family, or household purpose [if the total payments to be made under the lease contract, excluding payments for options to renew or buy, do not exceed $_____].

(f) "Fault" means wrongful act, omission, breach, or default.

(g) "Finance lease" means a lease with respect to which:

(i) the lessor does not select, manufacture, or supply the goods;

(ii) the lessor acquires the goods or the right to possession and use of the goods in connection with the lease; and

(iii) one of the following occurs:

(A) the lessee receives a copy of the contract by which the lessor acquired the goods or the right to possession and use of the goods before signing the lease contract;

(B) the lessee's approval of the contract by which the lessor acquired the goods or the right to possession and use of the goods is a condition to effectiveness of the lease contract;

(C) the lessee, before signing the lease contract, receives an accurate and complete statement designating the promises and warranties, and any disclaimers of warranties, limitations or modifications of remedies, or liquidated damages, including those of a third party, such as the manufacturer of the goods, provided to the lessor by the person supplying the goods in connection with or as part of the contract by which the lessor acquired the goods or the right to possession and use of the goods; or

(D) if the lease is not a consumer lease, the lessor, before the lessee signs the lease contract, informs the lessee in writing (a) of the identity of the person supplying the goods to the lessor, unless the lessee has selected that person and directed the lessor to acquire the goods or the right to possession and use of the goods from that person, (b) that the lessee is entitled under this Article to the promises and warranties, including those of any third party, provided to the lessor by the person supplying the goods in connection with or as part of the contract by which the lessor acquired the goods or the right to possession and use of the goods, and (c) that the lessee may communicate with the person supplying the goods to the lessor and receive an accurate and complete statement of those promises and warranties, including any disclaimers and limitations of them or of remedies.

(h) "Goods" means all things that are movable at the time of identification to the lease contract, or are fixtures (Section 2A–309), but the term does not include money, documents, instruments, accounts, chattel paper, general intangibles, or minerals or the like, including oil and gas, before extraction. The term also includes the unborn young of animals.

(i) "Installment lease contract" means a lease contract that authorizes or requires the delivery of goods in separate lots to be separately accepted, even though the lease contract contains a clause "each delivery is a separate lease" or its equivalent.

(j) "Lease" means a transfer of the right to possession and use of goods for a term in return for consideration, but a sale, including a sale on approval or a sale or return, or retention or creation of a security interest is not a lease. Unless the context clearly indicates otherwise, the term includes a sublease.

(k) "Lease agreement" means the bargain, with respect to the lease, of the lessor and the lessee in fact as found in their language or by implication from other circumstances including course of dealing or usage of trade or course of performance as provided in this Article. Unless the context clearly indicates otherwise, the term includes a sublease agreement.

(l) "Lease contract" means the total legal obligation that results from the lease agreement as affected by this Article and any other applicable rules of law. Unless the context clearly indicates otherwise, the term includes a sublease contract.

(m) "Leasehold interest" means the interest of the lessor or the lessee under a lease contract.

(n) "Lessee" means a person who acquires the right to possession and use of goods under a lease. Unless the context clearly indicates otherwise, the term includes a sublessee.

(o) "Lessee in ordinary course of business" means a person who in good faith and without knowledge that the lease to him [or her] is in violation of the ownership rights or security interest or leasehold interest of a third party in the goods, leases in ordinary course from a person in the business of selling or leasing goods of that kind but does not include a pawnbroker. "Leasing" may be for cash or by exchange of other property or on secured or unsecured credit and includes receiving goods or documents of title under a preexisting lease contract but does not include a transfer in bulk or as security for or in total or partial satisfaction of a money debt.

(p) "Lessor" means a person who transfers the right to possession and use of goods under a lease. Unless the context clearly indicates otherwise, the term includes a sublessor.

(q) "Lessor's residual interest" means the lessor's interest in the goods after expiration, termination, or cancellation of the lease contract.

(r) "Lien" means a charge against or interest in goods to secure payment of a debt or performance of an obligation, but the term does not include a security interest.

(s) "Lot" means a parcel or a single article that is the subject matter of a separate lease or delivery, whether or not it is sufficient to perform the lease contract.

(t) "Merchant lessee" means a lessee that is a merchant with respect to goods of the kind subject to the lease.

(u) "Present value" means the amount as of a date certain of one or more sums payable in the future, discounted to the date certain. The discount is determined by the interest rate specified by the parties if the rate was not manifestly unreasonable at the time the transaction was entered into; otherwise, the discount is determined by a commercially reasonable rate that takes into account the facts and circumstances of each case at the time the transaction was entered into.

(v) "Purchase" includes taking by sale, lease, mortgage, security interest, pledge, gift, or any other voluntary transaction creating an interest in goods.

(w) "Sublease" means a lease of goods the right to possession and use of which was acquired by the lessor as a lessee under an existing lease.

(x) "Supplier" means a person from whom a lessor buys or leases goods to be leased under a finance lease.

(y) "Supply contract" means a contract under which a lessor buys or leases goods to be leased.

(z) "Termination" occurs when either party pursuant to a power created by agreement or law puts an end to the lease contract otherwise than for default.

(2) Other definitions applying to this Article and the sections in which they appear are:

"Accessions"	Section 2A–310(1).
"Construction mortgage"	Section 2A–309(1) (d).
"Encumbrance"	Section 2A–309(1) (e).
"Fixtures"	Section 2A–309(1) (a).
"Fixture filing"	Section 2A–309(1) (b).
"Purchase money lease"	Section 2A–309(1) (c).

(3) The following definitions in other Articles apply to this Article:

"Account"	Section 9–106.
"Between merchants"	Section 2–104(3).
"Buyer"	Section 2–103(1) (a).
"Chattel paper"	Section 9–105(1) (b).
"Consumer goods"	Section 9–109(1).
"Document"	Section 9–105(1) (f).
"Entrusting"	Section 2–403(3).
"General intangibles"	Section 9–106.
"Good faith"	Section 2–103(1) (b).
"Instrument"	Section 9–105(1) (i).
"Merchant"	Section 2–104(1).
"Mortgage"	Section 9–105(1) (j).
"Pursuant to commitment"	Section 9–105(1) (k).
"Receipt"	Section 2–103(1) (c).
"Sale"	Section 2–106(1).
"Sale on approval"	Section 2–326.
"Sale or return"	Section 2–326.
"Seller"	Section 2–103(1) (d).

(4) In addition Article 1 contains general definitions and principles of construction and interpretation applicable throughout this Article.

As amended in 1990.

§ 2A–104. Leases Subject to Other Law.

(1) A lease, although subject to this Article, is also subject to any applicable:

 (a) certificate of title statute of this State: (list any certificate of title statutes covering automobiles, trailers, mobile homes, boats, farm tractors, and the like);

 (b) certificate of title statute of another jurisdiction (Section 2A–105); or

 (c) consumer protection statute of this State, or final consumer protection decision of a court of this State existing on the effective date of this Article.

(2) In case of conflict between this Article, other than Sections 2A–105, 2A–304(3), and 2A–305(3), and a statute or decision referred to in subsection (1), the statute or decision controls.

(3) Failure to comply with an applicable law has only the effect specified therein.

As amended in 1990.

§ 2A–105. Territorial Application of Article to Goods Covered by Certificate of Title.
Subject to the provisions of Sections 2A–304(3) and 2A–305(3), with respect to goods covered by a certificate of title issued under a statute of this State or of another jurisdiction, compliance and the effect of compliance or noncompliance with a certificate of title statute are governed by the law (including the conflict of laws rules) of the jurisdiction issuing the certificate until the earlier of (a) surrender of the certificate, or (b) four months after the goods are removed from that jurisdiction and thereafter until a new certificate of title is issued by another jurisdiction.

§ 2A–106. Limitation on Power of Parties to Consumer Lease to Choose Applicable Law and Judicial Forum.

(1) If the law chosen by the parties to a consumer lease is that of a jurisdiction other than a jurisdiction in which the lessee resides at the time the lease agreement becomes enforceable or within 30 days thereafter or in which the goods are to be used, the choice is not enforceable.

(2) If the judicial forum chosen by the parties to a consumer lease is a forum that would not otherwise have jurisdiction over the lessee, the choice is not enforceable.

§ 2A–107. Waiver or Renunciation of Claim or Right After Default.
Any claim or right arising out of an alleged default or breach of warranty may be discharged in whole or in part without consideration by a written waiver or renunciation signed and delivered by the aggrieved party.

§ 2A–108. Unconscionability.

(1) If the court as a matter of law finds a lease contract or any clause of a lease contract to have been unconscionable at the time it was made the court may refuse to enforce the lease contract, or it may enforce the remainder of the lease contract without the unconscionable clause, or it may so limit the application of any unconscionable clause as to avoid any unconscionable result.

(2) With respect to a consumer lease, if the court as a matter of law finds that a lease contract or any clause of a lease contract has been induced by unconscionable conduct or that unconscionable conduct has occurred in the collection of a claim arising from a lease contract, the court may grant appropriate relief.

(3) Before making a finding of unconscionability under subsection (1) or (2), the court, on its own motion or that of a party, shall afford the parties a reasonable opportunity to present evidence as to the setting, purpose, and effect of the lease contract or clause thereof, or of the conduct.

(4) In an action in which the lessee claims unconscionability with respect to a consumer lease:

 (a) If the court finds unconscionability under subsection (1) or (2), the court shall award reasonable attorney's fees to the lessee.

 (b) If the court does not find unconscionability and the lessee claiming unconscionability has brought or maintained an action he [or she] knew to be groundless, the court shall award reasonable attorney's fees to the party against whom the claim is made.

(c) In determining attorney's fees, the amount of the recovery on behalf of the claimant under subsections (1) and (2) is not controlling.

§ 2A–109. Option to Accelerate at Will.

(1) A term providing that one party or his [or her] successor in interest may accelerate payment or performance or require collateral or additional collateral "at will" or "when he [or she] deems himself [or herself] insecure" or in words of similar import must be construed to mean that he [or she] has power to do so only if he [or she] in good faith believes that the prospect of payment or performance is impaired.

(2) With respect to a consumer lease, the burden of establishing good faith under subsection (1) is on the party who exercised the power; otherwise the burden of establishing lack of good faith is on the party against whom the power has been exercised.

Part 2: Formation and Construction of Lease Contract

§ 2A–201. Statute of Frauds.

(1) A lease contract is not enforceable by way of action or defense unless:

(a) the total payments to be made under the lease contract, excluding payments for options to renew or buy, are less than $1,000; or

(b) there is a writing, signed by the party against whom enforcement is sought or by that party's authorized agent, sufficient to indicate that a lease contract has been made between the parties and to describe the goods leased and the lease term.

(2) Any description of leased goods or of the lease term is sufficient and satisfies subsection (1) (b), whether or not it is specific, if it reasonably identifies what is described.

(3) A writing is not insufficient because it omits or incorrectly states a term agreed upon, but the lease contract is not enforceable under subsection (1) (b) beyond the lease term and the quantity of goods shown in the writing.

(4) A lease contract that does not satisfy the requirements of subsection (1), but which is valid in other respects, is enforceable:

(a) if the goods are to be specially manufactured or obtained for the lessee and are not suitable for lease or sale to others in the ordinary course of the lessor's business, and the lessor, before notice of repudiation is received and under circumstances that reasonably indicate that the goods are for the lessee, has made either a substantial beginning of their manufacture or commitments for their procurement;

(b) if the party against whom enforcement is sought admits in that party's pleading, testimony or otherwise in court that a lease contract was made, but the lease contract is not enforceable under this provision beyond the quantity of goods admitted; or

(c) with respect to goods that have been received and accepted by the lessee.

(5) The lease term under a lease contract referred to in subsection (4) is:

(a) if there is a writing signed by the party against whom enforcement is sought or by that party's authorized agent specifying the lease term, the term so specified;

(b) if the party against whom enforcement is sought admits in that party's pleading, testimony, or otherwise in court a lease term, the term so admitted; or

(c) a reasonable lease term.

§ 2A–202. Final Written Expression: Parol or Extrinsic Evidence.

Terms with respect to which the confirmatory memoranda of the parties agree or which are otherwise set forth in a writing intended by the parties as a final expression of their agreement with respect to such terms as are included therein may not be contradicted by evidence of any prior agreement or of a contemporaneous oral agreement but may be explained or supplemented:

(a) by course of dealing or usage of trade or by course of performance; and

(b) by evidence of consistent additional terms unless the court finds the writing to have been intended also as a complete and exclusive statement of the terms of the agreement.

§ 2A–203. Seals Inoperative.

The affixing of a seal to a writing evidencing a lease contract or an offer to enter into a lease contract does not render the writing a sealed instrument and the law with respect to sealed instruments does not apply to the lease contract or offer.

§ 2A–204. Formation in General.

(1) A lease contract may be made in any manner sufficient to show agreement, including conduct by both parties which recognizes the existence of a lease contract.

(2) An agreement sufficient to constitute a lease contract may be found although the moment of its making is undetermined.

(3) Although one or more terms are left open, a lease contract does not fail for indefiniteness if the parties have intended to make a lease contract and there is a reasonably certain basis for giving an appropriate remedy.

§ 2A–205. Firm Offers.

An offer by a merchant to lease goods to or from another person in a signed writing that by its terms gives assurance it will be held open is not revocable, for lack of consideration, during the time stated or, if no time

is stated, for a reasonable time, but in no event may the period of irrevocability exceed 3 months. Any such term of assurance on a form supplied by the offeree must be separately signed by the offeror.

§ 2A–206. Offer and Acceptance in Formation of Lease Contract.

(1) Unless otherwise unambiguously indicated by the language or circumstances, an offer to make a lease contract must be construed as inviting acceptance in any manner and by any medium reasonable in the circumstances.

(2) If the beginning of a requested performance is a reasonable mode of acceptance, an offeror who is not notified of acceptance within a reasonable time may treat the offer as having lapsed before acceptance.

§ 2A–207. Course of Performance or Practical Construction.

(1) If a lease contract involves repeated occasions for performance by either party with knowledge of the nature of the performance and opportunity for objection to it by the other, any course of performance accepted or acquiesced in without objection is relevant to determine the meaning of the lease agreement.

(2) The express terms of a lease agreement and any course of performance, as well as any course of dealing and usage of trade, must be construed whenever reasonable as consistent with each other; but if that construction is unreasonable, express terms control course of performance, course of performance controls both course of dealing and usage of trade, and course of dealing controls usage of trade.

(3) Subject to the provisions of Section 2A–208 on modification and waiver, course of performance is relevant to show a waiver or modification of any term inconsistent with the course of performance.

§ 2A–208. Modification, Rescission and Waiver.

(1) An agreement modifying a lease contract needs no consideration to be binding.

(2) A signed lease agreement that excludes modification or rescission except by a signed writing may not be otherwise modified or rescinded, but, except as between merchants, such a requirement on a form supplied by a merchant must be separately signed by the other party.

(3) Although an attempt at modification or rescission does not satisfy the requirements of subsection (2), it may operate as a waiver.

(4) A party who has made a waiver affecting an executory portion of a lease contract may retract the waiver by reasonable notification received by the other party that strict performance will be required of any term waived, unless the retraction would be unjust in view of a material change of position in reliance on the waiver.

§ 2A–209. Lessee Under Finance Lease as Beneficiary of Supply Contract.

(1) The benefit of a supplier's promises to the lessor under the supply contract and of all warranties, whether express or implied, including those of any third party provided in connection with or as part of the supply contract, extends to the lessee to the extent of the lessee's leasehold interest under a finance lease related to the supply contract, but is subject to the terms of the warranty and of the supply contract and all defenses or claims arising therefrom.

(2) The extension of the benefit of a supplier's promises and of warranties to the lessee (Section 2A–209(1)) does not: (i) modify the rights and obligations of the parties to the supply contract, whether arising therefrom or otherwise, or (ii) impose any duty or liability under the supply contract on the lessee.

(3) Any modification or rescission of the supply contract by the supplier and the lessor is effective between the supplier and the lessee unless, before the modification or rescission, the supplier has received notice that the lessee has entered into a finance lease related to the supply contract. If the modification or rescission is effective between the supplier and the lessee, the lessor is deemed to have assumed, in addition to the obligations of the lessor to the lessee under the lease contract, promises of the supplier to the lessor and warranties that were so modified or rescinded as they existed and were available to the lessee before modification or rescission.

(4) In addition to the extension of the benefit of the supplier's promises and of warranties to the lessee under subsection (1), the lessee retains all rights that the lessee may have against the supplier which arise from an agreement between the lessee and the supplier or under other law.

As amended in 1990.

§ 2A–210. Express Warranties.

(1) Express warranties by the lessor are created as follows:

(a) Any affirmation of fact or promise made by the lessor to the lessee which relates to the goods and becomes part of the basis of the bargain creates an express warranty that the goods will conform to the affirmation or promise.

(b) Any description of the goods which is made part of the basis of the bargain creates an express warranty that the goods will conform to the description.

(c) Any sample or model that is made part of the basis of the bargain creates an express warranty that the whole of the goods will conform to the sample or model.

(2) It is not necessary to the creation of an express warranty that the lessor use formal words, such as "warrant" or

"guarantee," or that the lessor have a specific intention to make a warranty, but an affirmation merely of the value of the goods or a statement purporting to be merely the lessor's opinion or commendation of the goods does not create a warranty.

§ 2A–211. Warranties Against Interference and Against Infringement; Lessee's Obligation Against Infringement.

(1) There is in a lease contract a warranty that for the lease term no person holds a claim to or interest in the goods that arose from an act or omission of the lessor, other than a claim by way of infringement or the like, which will interfere with the lessee's enjoyment of its leasehold interest.

(2) Except in a finance lease there is in a lease contract by a lessor who is a merchant regularly dealing in goods of the kind a warranty that the goods are delivered free of the rightful claim of any person by way of infringement or the like.

(3) A lessee who furnishes specifications to a lessor or a supplier shall hold the lessor and the supplier harmless against any claim by way of infringement or the like that arises out of compliance with the specifications.

§ 2A–212. Implied Warranty of Merchantability.

(1) Except in a finance lease, a warranty that the goods will be merchantable is implied in a lease contract if the lessor is a merchant with respect to goods of that kind.

(2) Goods to be merchantable must be at least such as

 (a) pass without objection in the trade under the description in the lease agreement;

 (b) in the case of fungible goods, are of fair average quality within the description;

 (c) are fit for the ordinary purposes for which goods of that type are used;

 (d) run, within the variation permitted by the lease agreement, of even kind, quality, and quantity within each unit and among all units involved;

 (e) are adequately contained, packaged, and labeled as the lease agreement may require; and

 (f) conform to any promises or affirmations of fact made on the container or label.

(3) Other implied warranties may arise from course of dealing or usage of trade.

§ 2A–213. Implied Warranty of Fitness for Particular Purpose.
Except in a finance lease, if the lessor at the time the lease contract is made has reason to know of any particular purpose for which the goods are required and that the lessee is relying on the lessor's skill or judgment to select or furnish suitable goods, there is in the lease contract an implied warranty that the goods will be fit for that purpose.

§ 2A–214. Exclusion or Modification of Warranties.

(1) Words or conduct relevant to the creation of an express warranty and words or conduct tending to negate or limit a warranty must be construed wherever reasonable as consistent with each other; but, subject to the provisions of Section 2A–202 on parol or extrinsic evidence, negation or limitation is inoperative to the extent that the construction is unreasonable.

(2) Subject to subsection (3), to exclude or modify the implied warranty of merchantability or any part of it the language must mention "merchantability", be by a writing, and be conspicuous. Subject to sub-section (3), to exclude or modify any implied warranty of fitness the exclusion must be by a writing and be conspicuous. Language to exclude all implied warranties of fitness is sufficient if it is in writing, is conspicuous and states, for example, "There is no warranty that the goods will be fit for a particular purpose".

(3) Notwithstanding subsection (2), but subject to subsection (4),

 (a) unless the circumstances indicate otherwise, all implied warranties are excluded by expressions like "as is," or "with all faults," or by other language that in common understanding calls the lessee's attention to the exclusion of warranties and makes plain that there is no implied warranty, if in writing and conspicuous;

 (b) if the lessee before entering into the lease contract has examined the goods or the sample or model as fully as desired or has refused to examine the goods, there is no implied warranty with regard to defects that an examination ought in the circumstances to have revealed; and

 (c) an implied warranty may also be excluded or modified by course of dealing, course of performance, or usage of trade.

(4) To exclude or modify a warranty against interference or against infringement (Section 2A–211) or any part of it, the language must be specific, be by a writing, and be conspicuous, unless the circumstances, including course of performance, course of dealing, or usage of trade, give the lessee reason to know that the goods are being leased subject to a claim or interest of any person.

§ 2A–215. Cumulation and Conflict of Warranties Express or Implied.
Warranties, whether express or implied, must be construed as consistent with each other and as cumulative, but if that construction is unreasonable, the intention of the parties determines which warranty is dominant. In ascertaining that intention the following rules apply:

 (a) Exact or technical specifications displace an inconsistent sample or model or general language of description.

(b) A sample from an existing bulk displaces inconsistent general language of description.

(c) Express warranties displace inconsistent implied warranties other than an implied warranty of fitness for a particular purpose.

§ 2A–216. Third Party Beneficiaries of Express and Implied Warranties.

Alternative A

A warranty to or for the benefit of a lessee under this Article, whether express or implied, extends to any natural person who is in the family or household of the lessee or who is a guest in the lessee's home if it is reasonable to expect that such person may use, consume, or be affected by the goods and who is injured in person by breach of the warranty. This section does not displace principles of law and equity that extend a warranty to or for the benefit of a lessee to other persons. The operation of this section may not be excluded, modified, or limited, but an exclusion, modification, or limitation of the warranty, including any with respect to rights and remedies, effective against the lessee is also effective against any beneficiary designated under this section.

Alternative B

A warranty to or for the benefit of a lessee under this Article, whether express or implied, extends to any natural person who may reasonably be expected to use, consume, or be affected by the goods and who is injured in person by breach of the warranty. This section does not displace principles of law and equity that extend a warranty to or for the benefit of a lessee to other persons. The operation of this section may not be excluded, modified, or limited, but an exclusion, modification, or limitation of the warranty, including any with respect to rights and remedies, effective against the lessee is also effective against the beneficiary designated under this section.

Alternative C

A warranty to or for the benefit of a lessee under this Article, whether express or implied, extends to any person who may reasonably be expected to use, consume, or be affected by the goods and who is injured by breach of the warranty. The operation of this section may not be excluded, modified, or limited with respect to injury to the person of an individual to whom the warranty extends, but an exclusion, modification, or limitation of the warranty, including any with respect to rights and remedies, effective against the lessee is also effective against the beneficiary designated under this section.

§ 2A–217. Identification. Identification of goods as goods to which a lease contract refers may be made at any time and in any manner explicitly agreed to by the parties. In the absence of explicit agreement, identification occurs:

(a) when the lease contract is made if the lease contract is for a lease of goods that are existing and identified;

(b) when the goods are shipped, marked, or otherwise designated by the lessor as goods to which the lease contract refers, if the lease contract is for a lease of goods that are not existing and identified; or

(c) when the young are conceived, if the lease contract is for a lease of unborn young of animals.

§ 2A–218. Insurance and Proceeds.

(1) A lessee obtains an insurable interest when existing goods are identified to the lease contract even though the goods identified are nonconforming and the lessee has an option to reject them.

(2) If a lessee has an insurable interest only by reason of the lessor's identification of the goods, the lessor, until default or insolvency or notification to the lessee that identification is final, may substitute other goods for those identified.

(3) Notwithstanding a lessee's insurable interest under subsections (1) and (2), the lessor retains an insurable interest until an option to buy has been exercised by the lessee and risk of loss has passed to the lessee.

(4) Nothing in this section impairs any insurable interest recognized under any other statute or rule of law.

(5) The parties by agreement may determine that one or more parties have an obligation to obtain and pay for insurance covering the goods and by agreement may determine the beneficiary of the proceeds of the insurance.

§ 2A–219. Risk of Loss.

(1) Except in the case of a finance lease, risk of loss is retained by the lessor and does not pass to the lessee. In the case of a finance lease, risk of loss passes to the lessee.

(2) Subject to the provisions of this Article on the effect of default on risk of loss (Section 2A–220), if risk of loss is to pass to the lessee and the time of passage is not stated, the following rules apply:

(a) If the lease contract requires or authorizes the goods to be shipped by carrier

(i) and it does not require delivery at a particular destination, the risk of loss passes to the lessee when the goods are duly delivered to the carrier; but

(ii) if it does require delivery at a particular destination and the goods are there duly tendered while in the possession of the carrier, the risk of loss passes to the lessee when the goods are there duly so tendered as to enable the lessee to take delivery.

(b) If the goods are held by a bailee to be delivered without being moved, the risk of loss passes to the lessee on acknowledgment by the bailee of the lessee's right to possession of the goods.

(c) In any case not within subsection (a) or (b), the risk of loss passes to the lessee on the lessee's receipt of the goods if the lessor, or, in the case of a finance lease, the supplier, is a merchant; otherwise the risk passes to the lessee on tender of delivery.

§ 2A–220. Effect of Default on Risk of Loss.

(1) Where risk of loss is to pass to the lessee and the time of passage is not stated:
　(a) If a tender or delivery of goods so fails to conform to the lease contract as to give a right of rejection, the risk of their loss remains with the lessor, or, in the case of a finance lease, the supplier, until cure or acceptance.
　(b) If the lessee rightfully revokes acceptance, he [or she], to the extent of any deficiency in his [or her] effective insurance coverage, may treat the risk of loss as having remained with the lessor from the beginning.
(2) Whether or not risk of loss is to pass to the lessee, if the lessee as to conforming goods already identified to a lease contract repudiates or is otherwise in default under the lease contract, the lessor, or, in the case of a finance lease, the supplier, to the extent of any deficiency in his [or her] effective insurance coverage may treat the risk of loss as resting on the lessee for a commercially reasonable time.

§ 2A–221. Casualty to Identified Goods.
If a lease contract requires goods identified when the lease contract is made, and the goods suffer casualty without fault of the lessee, the lessor or the supplier before delivery, or the goods suffer casualty before risk of loss passes to the lessee pursuant to the lease agreement or Section 2A–219, then:

　(a) if the loss is total, the lease contract is avoided; and
　(b) if the loss is partial or the goods have so deteriorated as to no longer conform to the lease contract, the lessee may nevertheless demand inspection and at his [or her] option either treat the lease contract as avoided or, except in a finance lease that is not a consumer lease, accept the goods with due allowance from the rent payable for the balance of the lease term for the deterioration or the deficiency in quantity but without further right against the lessor.

Part 3: Effect of Lease Contract

§ 2A–301. Enforceability of Lease Contract.
Except as otherwise provided in this Article, a lease contract is effective and enforceable according to its terms between the parties, against purchasers of the goods and against creditors of the parties.

§ 2A–302. Title to and Possession of Goods.
Except as otherwise provided in this Article, each provision of this Article applies whether the lessor or a third party has title to the goods, and whether the lessor, the lessee, or a third party has possession of the goods, notwithstanding any statute or rule of law that possession or the absence of possession is fraudulent.

§ 2A–303. Alienability of Party's Interest Under Lease Contract or of Lessor's Residual Interest in Goods; Delegation of Performance; Transfer of Rights.

(1) As used in this section, "creation of a security interest" includes the sale of a lease contract that is subject to Article 9, Secured Transactions, by reason of Section 9–102(1) (b).
(2) Except as provided in subsections (3) and (4), a provision in a lease agreement which (i) prohibits the voluntary or involuntary transfer, including a transfer by sale, sublease, creation or enforcement of a security interest, or attachment, levy, or other judicial process, of an interest of a party under the lease contract or of the lessor's residual interest in the goods, or (ii) makes such a transfer an event of default, gives rise to the rights and remedies provided in subsection (5), but a transfer that is prohibited or is an event of default under the lease agreement is otherwise effective.
(3) A provision in a lease agreement which (i) prohibits the creation or enforcement of a security interest in an interest of a party under the lease contract or in the lessor's residual interest in the goods, or (ii) makes such a transfer an event of default, is not enforceable unless, and then only to the extent that, there is an actual transfer by the lessee of the lessee's right of possession or use of the goods in violation of the provision or an actual delegation of a material performance of either party to the lease contract in violation of the provision. Neither the granting nor the enforcement of a security interest in (i) the lessor's interest under the lease contract or (ii) the lessor's residual interest in the goods is a transfer that materially impairs the prospect of obtaining return performance by, materially changes the duty of, or materially increases the burden or risk imposed on, the lessee within the purview of subsection (5) unless, and then only to the extent that, there is an actual delegation of a material performance of the lessor.
(4) A provision in a lease agreement which (i) prohibits a transfer of a right to damages for default with respect to the whole lease contract or of a right to payment arising out of the transferor's due performance of the transferor's entire obligation, or (ii) makes such a transfer an event of default, is not enforceable, and such a transfer is not a transfer that materially impairs the prospect of obtaining return performance by, materially changes the duty of, or materially increases the burden or risk imposed on, the other party to the lease contract within the purview of subsection (5).

(5) Subject to subsections (3) and (4):

 (a) if a transfer is made which is made an event of default under a lease agreement, the party to the lease contract not making the transfer, unless that party waives the default or otherwise agrees, has the rights and remedies described in Section 2A–501(2);

 (b) if paragraph (a) is not applicable and if a transfer is made that (i) is prohibited under a lease agreement or (ii) materially impairs the prospect of obtaining return performance by, materially changes the duty of, or materially increases the burden or risk imposed on, the other party to the lease contract, unless the party not making the transfer agrees at any time to the transfer in the lease contract or otherwise, then, except as limited by contract, (i) the transferor is liable to the party not making the transfer for damages caused by the transfer to the extent that the damages could not reasonably be prevented by the party not making the transfer and (ii) a court having jurisdiction may grant other appropriate relief, including cancellation of the lease contract or an injunction against the transfer.

(6) A transfer of "the lease" or of "all my rights under the lease", or a transfer in similar general terms, is a transfer of rights and, unless the language or the circumstances, as in a transfer for security, indicate the contrary, the transfer is a delegation of duties by the transferor to the transferee. Acceptance by the transferee constitutes a promise by the transferee to perform those duties. The promise is enforceable by either the transferor or the other party to the lease contract.

(7) Unless otherwise agreed by the lessor and the lessee, a delegation of performance does not relieve the transferor as against the other party of any duty to perform or of any liability for default.

(8) In a consumer lease, to prohibit the transfer of an interest of a party under the lease contract or to make a transfer an event of default, the language must be specific, by a writing, and conspicuous.

As amended in 1990.

§ 2A–304. Subsequent Lease of Goods by Lessor.

(1) Subject to Section 2A–303, a subsequent lessee from a lessor of goods under an existing lease contract obtains, to the extent of the leasehold interest transferred, the leasehold interest in the goods that the lessor had or had power to transfer, and except as provided in subsection (2) and Section 2A–527(4), takes subject to the existing lease contract. A lessor with voidable title has power to transfer a good leasehold interest to a good faith subsequent lessee for value, but only to the extent set forth in the preceding sentence. If goods have been delivered under a transaction of purchase, the lessor has that power even though:

 (a) the lessor's transferor was deceived as to the identity of the lessor;

 (b) the delivery was in exchange for a check which is later dishonored;

 (c) it was agreed that the transaction was to be a "cash sale"; or

 (d) the delivery was procured through fraud punishable as larcenous under the criminal law.

(2) A subsequent lessee in the ordinary course of business from a lessor who is a merchant dealing in goods of that kind to whom the goods were entrusted by the existing lessee of that lessor before the interest of the subsequent lessee became enforceable against that lessor obtains, to the extent of the leasehold interest transferred, all of that lessor's and the existing lessee's rights to the goods, and takes free of the existing lease contract.

(3) A subsequent lessee from the lessor of goods that are subject to an existing lease contract and are covered by a certificate of title issued under a statute of this State or of another jurisdiction takes no greater rights than those provided both by this section and by the certificate of title statute.

As amended in 1990.

§ 2A–305. Sale or Sublease of Goods by Lessee.

(1) Subject to the provisions of Section 2A–303, a buyer or sublessee from the lessee of goods under an existing lease contract obtains, to the extent of the interest transferred, the leasehold interest in the goods that the lessee had or had power to transfer, and except as provided in subsection (2) and Section 2A–511(4), takes subject to the existing lease contract. A lessee with a voidable leasehold interest has power to transfer a good leasehold interest to a good faith buyer for value or a good faith sublessee for value, but only to the extent set forth in the preceding sentence. When goods have been delivered under a transaction of lease the lessee has that power even though:

 (a) the lessor was deceived as to the identity of the lessee;

 (b) the delivery was in exchange for a check which is later dishonored; or

 (c) the delivery was procured through fraud punishable as larcenous under the criminal law.

(2) A buyer in the ordinary course of business or a sublessee in the ordinary course of business from a lessee who is a merchant dealing in goods of that kind to whom the goods were entrusted by the lessor obtains, to the extent of the interest transferred, all of the lessor's and lessee's rights to the goods, and takes free of the existing lease contract.

(3) A buyer or sublessee from the lessee of goods that are subject to an existing lease contract and are covered by a certificate of title issued under a statute of this State or of another jurisdiction takes no greater rights than those provided both by this section and by the certificate of title statute.

§ 2A–306. Priority of Certain Liens Arising by Operation of Law.

If a person in the ordinary course of his [or her] business furnishes services or materials with respect to goods subject to a lease contract, a lien upon those goods in the possession of that person given by statute or rule of law for those materials or services takes priority over any interest of the lessor or lessee under the lease contract or this Article unless the lien is created by statute and the statute provides otherwise or unless the lien is created by rule of law and the rule of law provides otherwise.

§ 2A–307. Priority of Liens Arising by Attachment or Levy on, Security Interests in, and Other Claims to Goods.

(1) Except as otherwise provided in Section 2A–306, a creditor of a lessee takes subject to the lease contract.

(2) Except as otherwise provided in subsections (3) and (4) and in Sections 2A–306 and 2A–308, a creditor of a lessor takes subject to the lease contract unless:

 (a) the creditor holds a lien that attached to the goods before the lease contract became enforceable;

 (b) the creditor holds a security interest in the goods and the lessee did not give value and receive delivery of the goods without knowledge of the security interest; or

 (c) the creditor holds a security interest in the goods which was perfected (Section 9–303) before the lease contract became enforceable.

(3) A lessee in the ordinary course of business takes the leasehold interest free of a security interest in the goods created by the lessor even though the security interest is perfected (Section 9–303) and the lessee knows of its existence.

(4) A lessee other than a lessee in the ordinary course of business takes the leasehold interest free of a security interest to the extent that it secures future advances made after the secured party acquires knowledge of the lease or more than 45 days after the lease contract becomes enforceable, whichever first occurs, unless the future advances are made pursuant to a commitment entered into without knowledge of the lease and before the expiration of the 45-day period.

As amended in 1990.

§ 2A–308. Special Rights of Creditors.

(1) A creditor of a lessor in possession of goods subject to a lease contract may treat the lease contract as void if as against the creditor retention of possession by the lessor is fraudulent under any statute or rule of law, but retention of possession in good faith and current course of trade by the lessor for a commercially reasonable time after the lease contract becomes enforceable is not fraudulent.

(2) Nothing in this Article impairs the rights of creditors of a lessor if the lease contract (a) becomes enforceable, not in current course of trade but in satisfaction of or as security for a preexisting claim for money, security, or the like, and (b) is made under circumstances which under any statute or rule of law apart from this Article would constitute the transaction a fraudulent transfer or voidable preference.

(3) A creditor of a seller may treat a sale or an identification of goods to a contract for sale as void if as against the creditor retention of possession by the seller is fraudulent under any statute or rule of law, but retention of possession of the goods pursuant to a lease contract entered into by the seller as lessee and the buyer as lessor in connection with the sale or identification of the goods is not fraudulent if the buyer bought for value and in good faith.

§ 2A–309. Lessor's and Lessee's Rights When Goods Become Fixtures.

(1) In this section:

 (a) goods are "fixtures" when they become so related to particular real estate that an interest in them arises under real estate law;

 (b) a "fixture filing" is the filing, in the office where a mortgage on the real estate would be filed or recorded, of a financing statement covering goods that are or are to become fixtures and conforming to the requirements of Section 9–402(5);

 (c) a lease is a "purchase money lease" unless the lessee has possession or use of the goods or the right to possession or use of the goods before the lease agreement is enforceable;

 (d) a mortgage is a "construction mortgage" to the extent it secures an obligation incurred for the construction of an improvement on land including the acquisition cost of the land, if the recorded writing so indicates; and

 (e) "encumbrance" includes real estate mortgages and other liens on real estate and all other rights in real estate that are not ownership interests.

(2) Under this Article a lease may be of goods that are fixtures or may continue in goods that become fixtures, but no lease exists under this Article of ordinary building materials incorporated into an improvement on land.

(3) This Article does not prevent creation of a lease of fixtures pursuant to real estate law.

(4) The perfected interest of a lessor of fixtures has priority over a conflicting interest of an encumbrancer or owner of the real estate if:

 (a) the lease is a purchase money lease, the conflicting interest of the encumbrancer or owner arises before the goods become fixtures, the interest of the lessor is perfected by a fixture filing before the goods become fixtures or within ten days thereafter, and the lessee has an interest of record in the real estate or is in possession of the real estate; or

 (b) the interest of the lessor is perfected by a fixture filing before the interest of the encumbrancer or owner is of record, the lessor's interest has priority over any conflicting interest of a predecessor in title of the encumbrancer or owner, and the lessee has an interest of record in the real estate or is in possession of the real estate.

(5) The interest of a lessor of fixtures, whether or not perfected, has priority over the conflicting interest of an encumbrancer or owner of the real estate if:

 (a) the fixtures are readily removable factory or office machines, readily removable equipment that is not primarily used or leased for use in the operation of the real estate, or readily removable replacements of domestic appliances that are goods subject to a consumer lease, and before the goods become fixtures the lease contract is enforceable; or

 (b) the conflicting interest is a lien on the real estate obtained by legal or equitable proceedings after the lease contract is enforceable; or

 (c) the encumbrancer or owner has consented in writing to the lease or has disclaimed an interest in the goods as fixtures; or

 (d) the lessee has a right to remove the goods as against the encumbrancer or owner. If the lessee's right to remove terminates, the priority of the interest of the lessor continues for a reasonable time.

(6) Notwithstanding subsection (4) (a) but otherwise subject to subsections (4) and (5), the interest of a lessor of fixtures, including the lessor's residual interest, is subordinate to the conflicting interest of an encumbrancer of the real estate under a construction mortgage recorded before the goods become fixtures if the goods become fixtures before the completion of the construction. To the extent given to refinance a construction mortgage, the conflicting interest of an encumbrancer of the real estate under a mortgage has this priority to the same extent as the encumbrancer of the real estate under the construction mortgage.

(7) In cases not within the preceding subsections, priority between the interest of a lessor of fixtures, including the lessor's residual interest, and the conflicting interest of an encumbrancer or owner of the real estate who is not the lessee is determined by the priority rules governing conflicting interests in real estate.

(8) If the interest of a lessor of fixtures, including the lessor's residual interest, has priority over all conflicting interests of all owners and encumbrancers of the real estate, the lessor or the lessee may (i) on default, expiration, termination, or cancellation of the lease agreement but subject to the agreement and this Article, or (ii) if necessary to enforce other rights and remedies of the lessor or lessee under this Article, remove the goods from the real estate, free and clear of all conflicting interests of all owners and encumbrancers of the real estate, but the lessor or lessee must reimburse any encumbrancer or owner of the real estate who is not the lessee and who has not otherwise agreed for the cost of repair of any physical injury, but not for any diminution in value of the real estate caused by the absence of the goods removed or by any necessity of replacing them. A person entitled to reimbursement may refuse permission to remove until the party seeking removal gives adequate security for the performance of this obligation.

(9) Even though the lease agreement does not create a security interest, the interest of a lessor of fixtures, including the lessor's residual interest, is perfected by filing a financing statement as a fixture filing for leased goods that are or are to become fixtures in accordance with the relevant provisions of the Article on Secured Transactions (Article 9).

As amended in 1990.

§ 2A–310. Lessor's and Lessee's Rights When Goods Become Accessions.

(1) Goods are "accessions" when they are installed in or affixed to other goods.

(2) The interest of a lessor or a lessee under a lease contract entered into before the goods became accessions is superior to all interests in the whole except as stated in subsection (4).

(3) The interest of a lessor or a lessee under a lease contract entered into at the time or after the goods became accessions is superior to all subsequently acquired interests in the whole except as stated in subsection (4) but is subordinate to interests in the whole existing at the time the lease contract was made unless the holders of such interests in the whole have in writing consented to the lease or disclaimed an interest in the goods as part of the whole.

(4) The interest of a lessor or a lessee under a lease contract described in subsection (2) or (3) is subordinate to the interest of

 (a) a buyer in the ordinary course of business or a lessee in the ordinary course of business of any interest in the whole acquired after the goods became accessions; or

 (b) a creditor with a security interest in the whole perfected before the lease contract was made to the extent that the creditor makes subsequent advances without knowledge of the lease contract.

(5) When under subsections (2) or (3) and (4) a lessor or a lessee of accessions holds an interest that is superior to all interests in the whole, the lessor or the lessee may (a) on default, expiration, termination, or cancellation of the lease contract by the other party but subject to the provisions of the lease contract and this Article, or (b) if necessary to enforce his [or her] other rights and remedies under this Article, remove the goods from the whole, free and clear of all interests in the whole, but he [or she] must reimburse any holder of an interest in the whole who is not the lessee and who has not otherwise agreed for the cost of repair of any physical injury but not for any diminution in value of the whole caused by the absence of the goods removed or by any necessity for replacing them. A person entitled to reimbursement may refuse permission to remove until the party seeking removal gives adequate security for the performance of this obligation.

§ 2A–311. Priority Subject to Subordination. Nothing in this Article prevents subordination by agreement by any person entitled to priority.

As added in 1990.

Part 4: Performance of Lease Contract: Repudiated, Substituted and Excused

§ 2A–401. Insecurity: Adequate Assurance of Performance.

(1) A lease contract imposes an obligation on each party that the other's expectation of receiving due performance will not be impaired.

(2) If reasonable grounds for insecurity arise with respect to the performance of either party, the insecure party may demand in writing adequate assurance of due performance. Until the insecure party receives that assurance, if commercially reasonable the insecure party may suspend any performance for which he [or she] has not already received the agreed return.

(3) A repudiation of the lease contract occurs if assurance of due performance adequate under the circumstances of the particular case is not provided to the insecure party within a reasonable time, not to exceed 30 days after receipt of a demand by the other party.

(4) Between merchants, the reasonableness of grounds for insecurity and the adequacy of any assurance offered must be determined according to commercial standards.

(5) Acceptance of any nonconforming delivery or payment does not prejudice the aggrieved party's right to demand adequate assurance of future performance.

§ 2A–402. Anticipatory Repudiation. If either party repudiates a lease contract with respect to a performance not yet due under the lease contract, the loss of which performance will substantially impair the value of the lease contract to the other, the aggrieved party may:

(a) for a commercially reasonable time, await retraction of repudiation and performance by the repudiating party;

(b) make demand pursuant to Section 2A–401 and await assurance of future performance adequate under the circumstances of the particular case; or

(c) resort to any right or remedy upon default under the lease contract or this Article, even though the aggrieved party has notified the repudiating party that the aggrieved party would await the repudiating party's performance and assurance and has urged retraction. In addition, whether or not the aggrieved party is pursuing one of the foregoing remedies, the aggrieved party may suspend performance or, if the aggrieved party is the lessor, proceed in accordance with the provisions of this Article on the lessor's right to identify goods to the lease contract notwithstanding default or to salvage unfinished goods (Section 2A–524).

§ 2A–403. Retraction of Anticipatory Repudiation.

(1) Until the repudiating party's next performance is due, the repudiating party can retract the repudiation unless, since the repudiation, the aggrieved party has cancelled the lease contract or materially changed the aggrieved party's position or otherwise indicated that the aggrieved party considers the repudiation final.

(2) Retraction may be by any method that clearly indicates to the aggrieved party that the repudiating party intends to perform under the lease contract and includes any assurance demanded under Section 2A–401.

(3) Retraction reinstates a repudiating party's rights under a lease contract with due excuse and allowance to the aggrieved party for any delay occasioned by the repudiation.

§ 2A–404. Substituted Performance.

(1) If without fault of the lessee, the lessor and the supplier, the agreed berthing, loading, or unloading facilities fail or the agreed type of carrier becomes unavailable or the agreed manner of delivery otherwise becomes commercially impracticable, but a commercially reasonable substitute is available, the substitute performance must be tendered and accepted.

(2) If the agreed means or manner of payment fails because of domestic or foreign governmental regulation:

(a) the lessor may withhold or stop delivery or cause the supplier to withhold or stop delivery unless the lessee provides a means or manner of payment that is commercially a substantial equivalent; and

(b) if delivery has already been taken, payment by the means or in the manner provided by the regulation discharges the lessee's obligation unless the regulation is discriminatory, oppressive, or predatory.

§ **2A–405. Excused Performance.** Subject to Section 2A–404 on substituted performance, the following rules apply:

 (a) Delay in delivery or nondelivery in whole or in part by a lessor or a supplier who complies with paragraphs (b) and (c) is not a default under the lease contract if performance as agreed has been made impracticable by the occurrence of a contingency the nonoccurrence of which was a basic assumption on which the lease contract was made or by compliance in good faith with any applicable foreign or domestic governmental regulation or order, whether or not the regulation or order later proves to be invalid.

 (b) If the causes mentioned in paragraph (a) affect only part of the lessor's or the supplier's capacity to perform, he [or she] shall allocate production and deliveries among his [or her] customers but at his [or her] option may include regular customers not then under contract for sale or lease as well as his [or her] own requirements for further manufacture. He [or she] may so allocate in any manner that is fair and reasonable.

 (c) The lessor seasonably shall notify the lessee and in the case of a finance lease the supplier seasonably shall notify the lessor and the lessee, if known, that there will be delay or nondelivery and, if allocation is required under paragraph (b), of the estimated quota thus made available for the lessee.

§ 2A–406. Procedure on Excused Performance.

(1) If the lessee receives notification of a material or indefinite delay or an allocation justified under Section 2A–405, the lessee may by written notification to the lessor as to any goods involved, and with respect to all of the goods if under an installment lease contract the value of the whole lease contract is substantially impaired (Section 2A–510):

 (a) terminate the lease contract (Section 2A–505(2)); or

 (b) except in a finance lease that is not a consumer lease, modify the lease contract by accepting the available quota in substitution, with due allowance from the rent payable for the balance of the lease term for the deficiency but without further right against the lessor.

(2) If, after receipt of a notification from the lessor under Section 2A–405, the lessee fails so to modify the lease agreement within a reasonable time not exceeding 30 days, the lease contract lapses with respect to any deliveries affected.

§ 2A–407. Irrevocable Promises: Finance Leases.

(1) In the case of a finance lease that is not a consumer lease the lessee's promises under the lease contract become irrevocable and independent upon the lessee's acceptance of the goods.

(2) A promise that has become irrevocable and independent under subsection (1):

 (a) is effective and enforceable between the parties, and by or against third parties including assignees of the parties; and

 (b) is not subject to cancellation, termination, modification, repudiation, excuse, or substitution without the consent of the party to whom the promise runs.

(3) This section does not affect the validity under any other law of a covenant in any lease contract making the lessee's promises irrevocable and independent upon the lessee's acceptance of the goods.

As amended in 1990.

Part 5: Default

§ 2A–501. Default: Procedure.

(1) Whether the lessor or the lessee is in default under a lease contract is determined by the lease agreement and this Article.

(2) If the lessor or the lessee is in default under the lease contract, the party seeking enforcement has rights and remedies as provided in this Article and, except as limited by this Article, as provided in the lease agreement.

(3) If the lessor or the lessee is in default under the lease contract, the party seeking enforcement may reduce the party's claim to judgment, or otherwise enforce the lease contract by self-help or any available judicial procedure or nonjudicial procedure, including administrative proceeding, arbitration, or the like, in accordance with this Article.

(4) Except as otherwise provided in Section 1–106(1) or this Article or the lease agreement, the rights and remedies referred to in subsections (2) and (3) are cumulative.

(5) If the lease agreement covers both real property and goods, the party seeking enforcement may proceed under this Part as to the goods, or under other applicable law as to both the real property and the goods in accordance with that party's rights and remedies in respect of the real property, in which case this Part does not apply.

As amended in 1990.

§ **2A–502. Notice After Default.** Except as otherwise provided in this Article or the lease agreement, the lessor or

lessee in default under the lease contract is not entitled to notice of default or notice of enforcement from the other party to the lease agreement.

§ 2A–503. Modification or Impairment of Rights and Remedies.

(1) Except as otherwise provided in this Article, the lease agreement may include rights and remedies for default in addition to or in substitution for those provided in this Article and may limit or alter the measure of damages recoverable under this Article.

(2) Resort to a remedy provided under this Article or in the lease agreement is optional unless the remedy is expressly agreed to be exclusive. If circumstances cause an exclusive or limited remedy to fail of its essential purpose, or provision for an exclusive remedy is unconscionable, remedy may be had as provided in this Article.

(3) Consequential damages may be liquidated under Section 2A–504, or may otherwise be limited, altered, or excluded unless the limitation, alteration, or exclusion is unconscionable. Limitation, alteration, or exclusion of consequential damages for injury to the person in the case of consumer goods is prima facie unconscionable but limitation, alteration, or exclusion of damages where the loss is commercial is not prima facie unconscionable.

(4) Rights and remedies on default by the lessor or the lessee with respect to any obligation or promise collateral or ancillary to the lease contract are not impaired by this Article.

As amended in 1990.

§ 2A–504. Liquidation of Damages.

(1) Damages payable by either party for default, or any other act or omission, including indemnity for loss or diminution of anticipated tax benefits or loss or damage to lessor's residual interest, may be liquidated in the lease agreement but only at an amount or by a formula that is reasonable in light of the then anticipated harm caused by the default or other act or omission.

(2) If the lease agreement provides for liquidation of damages, and such provision does not comply with subsection (1), or such provision is an exclusive or limited remedy that circumstances cause to fail of its essential purpose, remedy may be had as provided in this Article.

(3) If the lessor justifiably withholds or stops delivery of goods because of the lessee's default or insolvency (Section 2A–525 or 2A–526), the lessee is entitled to restitution of any amount by which the sum of his [or her] payments exceeds:

 (a) the amount to which the lessor is entitled by virtue of terms liquidating the lessor's damages in accordance with subsection (1); or

 (b) in the absence of those terms, 20 percent of the then present value of the total rent the lessee was obligated to pay for the balance of the lease term, or, in the case of a consumer lease, the lesser of such amount or $500.

(4) A lessee's right to restitution under subsection (3) is subject to offset to the extent the lessor establishes:

 (a) a right to recover damages under the provisions of this Article other than subsection (1); and

 (b) the amount or value of any benefits received by the lessee directly or indirectly by reason of the lease contract.

§ 2A–505. Cancellation and Termination and Effect of Cancellation, Termination, Rescission, or Fraud on Rights and Remedies.

(1) On cancellation of the lease contract, all obligations that are still executory on both sides are discharged, but any right based on prior default or performance survives, and the cancelling party also retains any remedy for default of the whole lease contract or any unperformed balance.

(2) On termination of the lease contract, all obligations that are still executory on both sides are discharged but any right based on prior default or performance survives.

(3) Unless the contrary intention clearly appears, expressions of "cancellation," "rescission," or the like of the lease contract may not be construed as a renunciation or discharge of any claim in damages for an antecedent default.

(4) Rights and remedies for material misrepresentation or fraud include all rights and remedies available under this Article for default.

(5) Neither rescission nor a claim for rescission of the lease contract nor rejection or return of the goods may bar or be deemed inconsistent with a claim for damages or other right or remedy.

§ 2A–506. Statute of Limitations.

(1) An action for default under a lease contract, including breach of warranty or indemnity, must be commenced within 4 years after the cause of action accrued. By the original lease contract the parties may reduce the period of limitation to not less than one year.

(2) A cause of action for default accrues when the act or omission on which the default or breach of warranty is based is or should have been discovered by the aggrieved party, or when the default occurs, whichever is later. A cause of action for indemnity accrues when the act or omission on which the claim for indemnity is based is or should have been discovered by the indemnified party, whichever is later.

(3) If an action commenced within the time limited by subsection (1) is so terminated as to leave available a remedy by another action for the same default or breach of warranty or indemnity, the other action may be commenced after the expiration of the time limited and within 6 months after the termination of the first action unless the termination resulted from voluntary discontinuance or from dismissal for failure or neglect to prosecute.

(4) This section does not alter the law on tolling of the statute of limitations nor does it apply to causes of action that have accrued before this Article becomes effective.

§ 2A–507. Proof of Market Rent: Time and Place.

(1) Damages based on market rent (Section 2A–519 or 2A–528) are determined according to the rent for the use of the goods concerned for a lease term identical to the remaining lease term of the original lease agreement and prevailing at the times specified in Sections 2A–519 and 2A–528.

(2) If evidence of rent for the use of the goods concerned for a lease term identical to the remaining lease term of the original lease agreement and prevailing at the times or places described in this Article is not readily available, the rent prevailing within any reasonable time before or after the time described or at any other place or for a different lease term which in commercial judgment or under usage of trade would serve as a reasonable substitute for the one described may be used, making any proper allowance for the difference, including the cost of transporting the goods to or from the other place.

(3) Evidence of a relevant rent prevailing at a time or place or for a lease term other than the one described in this Article offered by one party is not admissible unless and until he [or she] has given the other party notice the court finds sufficient to prevent unfair surprise.

(4) If the prevailing rent or value of any goods regularly leased in any established market is in issue, reports in official publications or trade journals or in newspapers or periodicals of general circulation published as the reports of that market are admissible in evidence. The circumstances of the preparation of the report may be shown to affect its weight but not its admissibility.
As amended in 1990.

§ 2A–508. Lessee's Remedies.

(1) If a lessor fails to deliver the goods in conformity to the lease contract (Section 2A–509) or repudiates the lease contract (Section 2A–402), or a lessee rightfully rejects the goods (Section 2A–509) or justifiably revokes acceptance of the goods (Section 2A–517), then with respect to any goods involved, and with respect to all of the goods if under an installment lease contract the value of the whole lease contract is substantially impaired (Section 2A–510), the lessor is in default under the lease contract and the lessee may:
 (a) cancel the lease contract (Section 2A–505(1));
 (b) recover so much of the rent and security as has been paid and is just under the circumstances;
 (c) cover and recover damages as to all goods affected whether or not they have been identified to the lease contract (Sections 2A–518 and 2A–520), or recover damages for nondelivery (Sections 2A–519 and 2A–520);
 (d) exercise any other rights or pursue any other remedies provided in the lease contract.

(2) If a lessor fails to deliver the goods in conformity to the lease contract or repudiates the lease contract, the lessee may also:
 (a) if the goods have been identified, recover them (Section 2A–522); or
 (b) in a proper case, obtain specific performance or replevy the goods (Section 2A–521).

(3) If a lessor is otherwise in default under a lease contract, the lessee may exercise the rights and pursue the remedies provided in the lease contract, which may include a right to cancel the lease, and in Section 2A–519(3).

(4) If a lessor has breached a warranty, whether express or implied, the lessee may recover damages (Section 2A–519(4)).

(5) On rightful rejection or justifiable revocation of acceptance, a lessee has a security interest in goods in the lessee's possession or control for any rent and security that has been paid and any expenses reasonably incurred in their inspection, receipt, transportation, and care and custody and may hold those goods and dispose of them in good faith and in a commercially reasonable manner, subject to Section 2A–527(5).

(6) Subject to the provisions of Section 2A–407, a lessee, on notifying the lessor of the lessee's intention to do so, may deduct all or any part of the damages resulting from any default under the lease contract from any part of the rent still due under the same lease contract.
As amended in 1990.

§ 2A–509. Lessee's Rights on Improper Delivery; Rightful Rejection.

(1) Subject to the provisions of Section 2A–510 on default in installment lease contracts, if the goods or the tender or delivery fail in any respect to conform to the lease contract, the lessee may reject or accept the goods or accept any commercial unit or units and reject the rest of the goods.

(2) Rejection of goods is ineffective unless it is within a reasonable time after tender or delivery of the goods and the lessee seasonably notifies the lessor.

§ 2A–510. Installment Lease Contracts: Rejection and Default.

(1) Under an installment lease contract a lessee may reject any delivery that is nonconforming if the nonconformity substantially impairs the value of that delivery and cannot be cured or the nonconformity is a defect in the required documents; but if the nonconformity does not fall within subsection (2) and the lessor or the supplier gives adequate assurance of its cure, the lessee must accept that delivery.

(2) Whenever nonconformity or default with respect to one or more deliveries substantially impairs the value of the installment lease contract as a whole there is a default with respect to the whole. But, the aggrieved party reinstates the installment lease contract as a whole if the aggrieved party accepts a nonconforming delivery without seasonably notifying of cancellation or brings an action with respect only to past deliveries or demands performance as to future deliveries.

§ 2A–511. Merchant Lessee's Duties as to Rightfully Rejected Goods.

(1) Subject to any security interest of a lessee (Section 2A–508(5)), if a lessor or a supplier has no agent or place of business at the market of rejection, a merchant lessee, after rejection of goods in his [or her] possession or control, shall follow any reasonable instructions received from the lessor or the supplier with respect to the goods. In the absence of those instructions, a merchant lessee shall make reasonable efforts to sell, lease, or otherwise dispose of the goods for the lessor's account if they threaten to decline in value speedily. Instructions are not reasonable if on demand indemnity for expenses is not forthcoming.

(2) If a merchant lessee (subsection (1)) or any other lessee (Section 2A–512) disposes of goods, he [or she] is entitled to reimbursement either from the lessor or the supplier or out of the proceeds for reasonable expenses of caring for and disposing of the goods and, if the expenses include no disposition commission, to such commission as is usual in the trade, or if there is none, to a reasonable sum not exceeding 10 percent of the gross proceeds.

(3) In complying with this section or Section 2A–512, the lessee is held only to good faith. Good faith conduct hereunder is neither acceptance or conversion nor the basis of an action for damages.

(4) A purchaser who purchases in good faith from a lessee pursuant to this section or Section 2A–512 takes the goods free of any rights of the lessor and the supplier even though the lessee fails to comply with one or more of the requirements of this Article.

§ 2A–512. Lessee's Duties as to Rightfully Rejected Goods.

(1) Except as otherwise provided with respect to goods that threaten to decline in value speedily (Section 2A–511) and subject to any security interest of a lessee (Section 2A–508(5)):

 (a) the lessee, after rejection of goods in the lessee's possession, shall hold them with reasonable care at the lessor's or the supplier's disposition for a reasonable time after the lessee's seasonable notification of rejection;

 (b) if the lessor or the supplier gives no instructions within a reasonable time after notification of rejection, the lessee may store the rejected goods for the lessor's or the supplier's account or ship them to the lessor or the supplier or dispose of them for the lessor's or the supplier's account with reimbursement in the manner provided in Section 2A–511; but

 (c) the lessee has no further obligations with regard to goods rightfully rejected.

(2) Action by the lessee pursuant to subsection (1) is not acceptance or conversion.

§ 2A–513. Cure by Lessor of Improper Tender or Delivery; Replacement.

(1) If any tender or delivery by the lessor or the supplier is rejected because nonconforming and the time for performance has not yet expired, the lessor or the supplier may seasonably notify the lessee of the lessor's or the supplier's intention to cure and may then make a conforming delivery within the time provided in the lease contract.

(2) If the lessee rejects a nonconforming tender that the lessor or the supplier had reasonable grounds to believe would be acceptable with or without money allowance, the lessor or the supplier may have a further reasonable time to substitute a conforming tender if he [or she] seasonably notifies the lessee.

§ 2A–514. Waiver of Lessee's Objections.

(1) In rejecting goods, a lessee's failure to state a particular defect that is ascertainable by reasonable inspection precludes the lessee from relying on the defect to justify rejection or to establish default:

 (a) if, stated seasonably, the lessor or the supplier could have cured it (Section 2A–513); or

 (b) between merchants if the lessor or the supplier after rejection has made a request in writing for a full and final written statement of all defects on which the lessee proposes to rely.

(2) A lessee's failure to reserve rights when paying rent or other consideration against documents precludes recovery of the payment for defects apparent on the face of the documents.

§ 2A–515. Acceptance of Goods.

(1) Acceptance of goods occurs after the lessee has had a reasonable opportunity to inspect the goods and
 (a) the lessee signifies or acts with respect to the goods in a manner that signifies to the lessor or the supplier that the goods are conforming or that the lessee will take or retain them in spite of their nonconformity; or
 (b) the lessee fails to make an effective rejection of the goods (Section 2A–509(2)).

(2) Acceptance of a part of any commercial unit is acceptance of that entire unit.

§ 2A–516. Effect of Acceptance of Goods; Notice of Default; Burden of Establishing Default After Acceptance; Notice of Claim or Litigation to Person Answerable Over.

(1) A lessee must pay rent for any goods accepted in accordance with the lease contract, with due allowance for goods rightfully rejected or not delivered.

(2) A lessee's acceptance of goods precludes rejection of the goods accepted. In the case of a finance lease, if made with knowledge of a nonconformity, acceptance cannot be revoked because of it. In any other case, if made with knowledge of a nonconformity, acceptance cannot be revoked because of it unless the acceptance was on the reasonable assumption that the nonconformity would be seasonably cured. Acceptance does not of itself impair any other remedy provided by this Article or the lease agreement for nonconformity.

(3) If a tender has been accepted:
 (a) within a reasonable time after the lessee discovers or should have discovered any default, the lessee shall notify the lessor and the supplier, if any, or be barred from any remedy against the party not notified;
 (b) except in the case of a consumer lease, within a reasonable time after the lessee receives notice of litigation for infringement or the like (Section 2A–211) the lessee shall notify the lessor or be barred from any remedy over for liability established by the litigation; and
 (c) the burden is on the lessee to establish any default.

(4) If a lessee is sued for breach of a warranty or other obligation for which a lessor or a supplier is answerable over the following apply:
 (a) The lessee may give the lessor or the supplier, or both, written notice of the litigation. If the notice states that the person notified may come in and defend and that if the person notified does not do so that person will be bound in any action against that person by the lessee by any determination of fact common to the two litigations, then unless the person notified after seasonable receipt of the notice does come in and defend that person is so bound.
 (b) The lessor or the supplier may demand in writing that the lessee turn over control of the litigation including settlement if the claim is one for infringement or the like (Section 2A–211) or else be barred from any remedy over. If the demand states that the lessor or the supplier agrees to bear all expense and to satisfy any adverse judgment, then unless the lessee after seasonable receipt of the demand does turn over control the lessee is so barred.

(5) Subsections (3) and (4) apply to any obligation of a lessee to hold the lessor or the supplier harmless against infringement or the like (Section 2A–211).

As amended in 1990.

§ 2A–517. Revocation of Acceptance of Goods.

(1) A lessee may revoke acceptance of a lot or commercial unit whose nonconformity substantially impairs its value to the lessee if the lessee has accepted it:
 (a) except in the case of a finance lease, on the reasonable assumption that its nonconformity would be cured and it has not been seasonably cured; or
 (b) without discovery of the nonconformity if the lessee's acceptance was reasonably induced either by the lessor's assurances or, except in the case of a finance lease, by the difficulty of discovery before acceptance.

(2) Except in the case of a finance lease that is not a consumer lease, a lessee may revoke acceptance of a lot or commercial unit if the lessor defaults under the lease contract and the default substantially impairs the value of that lot or commercial unit to the lessee.

(3) If the lease agreement so provides, the lessee may revoke acceptance of a lot or commercial unit because of other defaults by the lessor.

(4) Revocation of acceptance must occur within a reasonable time after the lessee discovers or should have discovered the ground for it and before any substantial change in condition of the goods which is not caused by the nonconformity. Revocation is not effective until the lessee notifies the lessor.

(5) A lessee who so revokes has the same rights and duties with regard to the goods involved as if the lessee had rejected them.

As amended in 1990.

§ 2A–518. Cover; Substitute Goods.

(1) After a default by a lessor under the lease contract of the type described in Section 2A–508(1), or, if agreed, after other default by the lessor, the lessee may cover by making any purchase or lease of or contract to purchase or lease goods in substitution for those due from the lessor.

(2) Except as otherwise provided with respect to damages liquidated in the lease agreement (Section 2A–504)

or otherwise determined pursuant to agreement of the parties (Sections 1–102(3) and 2A–503), if a lessee's cover is by a lease agreement substantially similar to the original lease agreement and the new lease agreement is made in good faith and in a commercially reasonable manner, the lessee may recover from the lessor as damages (i) the present value, as of the date of the commencement of the term of the new lease agreement, of the rent under the new lease agreement applicable to that period of the new lease term which is comparable to the then remaining term of the original lease agreement minus the present value as of the same date of the total rent for the then remaining lease term of the original lease agreement, and (ii) any incidental or consequential damages, less expenses saved in consequence of the lessor's default.

(3) If a lessee's cover is by lease agreement that for any reason does not qualify for treatment under subsection (2), or is by purchase or otherwise, the lessee may recover from the lessor as if the lessee had elected not to cover and Section 2A–519 governs.

As amended in 1990.

§ 2A–519. Lessee's Damages for Nondelivery, Repudiation, Default, and Breach of Warranty in Regard to Accepted Goods.

(1) Except as otherwise provided with respect to damages liquidated in the lease agreement (Section 2A–504) or otherwise determined pursuant to agreement of the parties (Sections 1–102(3) and 2A–503), if a lessee elects not to cover or a lessee elects to cover and the cover is by lease agreement that for any reason does not qualify for treatment under Section 2A–518(2), or is by purchase or otherwise, the measure of damages for nondelivery or repudiation by the lessor or for rejection or revocation of acceptance by the lessee is the present value, as of the date of the default, of the then market rent minus the present value as of the same date of the original rent, computed for the remaining lease term of the original lease agreement, together with incidental and consequential damages, less expenses saved in consequence of the lessor's default.

(2) Market rent is to be determined as of the place for tender or, in cases of rejection after arrival or revocation of acceptance, as of the place of arrival.

(3) Except as otherwise agreed, if the lessee has accepted goods and given notification (Section 2A–516(3)), the measure of damages for nonconforming tender or delivery or other default by a lessor is the loss resulting in the ordinary course of events from the lessor's default as determined in any manner that is reasonable together with incidental and consequential damages, less expenses saved in consequence of the lessor's default.

(4) Except as otherwise agreed, the measure of damages for breach of warranty is the present value at the time and place of acceptance of the difference between the value of the use of the goods accepted and the value if they had been as warranted for the lease term, unless special circumstances show proximate damages of a different amount, together with incidental and consequential damages, less expenses saved in consequence of the lessor's default or breach of warranty.

As amended in 1990.

§ 2A–520. Lessee's Incidental and Consequential Damages.

(1) Incidental damages resulting from a lessor's default include expenses reasonably incurred in inspection, receipt, transportation, and care and custody of goods rightfully rejected or goods the acceptance of which is justifiably revoked, any commercially reasonable charges, expenses or commissions in connection with effecting cover, and any other reasonable expense incident to the default.

(2) Consequential damages resulting from a lessor's default include:

(a) any loss resulting from general or particular requirements and needs of which the lessor at the time of contracting had reason to know and which could not reasonably be prevented by cover or otherwise; and

(b) injury to person or property proximately resulting from any breach of warranty.

§ 2A–521. Lessee's Right to Specific Performance or Replevin.

(1) Specific performance may be decreed if the goods are unique or in other proper circumstances.

(2) A decree for specific performance may include any terms and conditions as to payment of the rent, damages, or other relief that the court deems just.

(3) A lessee has a right of replevin, detinue, sequestration, claim and delivery, or the like for goods identified to the lease contract if after reasonable effort the lessee is unable to effect cover for those goods or the circumstances reasonably indicate that the effort will be unavailing.

§ 2A–522. Lessee's Right to Goods on Lessor's Insolvency.

(1) Subject to subsection (2) and even though the goods have not been shipped, a lessee who has paid a part or all of the rent and security for goods identified to a lease contract (Section 2A–217) on making and keeping good a tender of any unpaid portion of the rent and security due under the lease contract may recover the goods identified from the lessor if the lessor becomes insolvent within 10 days after receipt of the first installment of rent and security.

(2) A lessee acquires the right to recover goods identified to a lease contract only if they conform to the lease contract.

§ 2A–523. Lessor's Remedies.

(1) If a lessee wrongfully rejects or revokes acceptance of goods or fails to make a payment when due or repudiates with respect to a part or the whole, then, with respect to any goods involved, and with respect to all of the goods if under an installment lease contract the value of the whole lease contract is substantially impaired (Section 2A–510), the lessee is in default under the lease contract and the lessor may:

(a) cancel the lease contract (Section 2A–505(1));

(b) proceed respecting goods not identified to the lease contract (Section 2A–524);

(c) withhold delivery of the goods and take possession of goods previously delivered (Section 2A–525);

(d) stop delivery of the goods by any bailee (Section 2A–526);

(e) dispose of the goods and recover damages (Section 2A–527), or retain the goods and recover damages (Section 2A–528), or in a proper case recover rent (Section 2A–529);

(f) exercise any other rights or pursue any other remedies provided in the lease contract.

(2) If a lessor does not fully exercise a right or obtain a remedy to which the lessor is entitled under subsection (1), the lessor may recover the loss resulting in the ordinary course of events from the lessee's default as determined in any reasonable manner, together with incidental damages, less expenses saved in consequence of the lessee's default.

(3) If a lessee is otherwise in default under a lease contract, the lessor may exercise the rights and pursue the remedies provided in the lease contract, which may include a right to cancel the lease. In addition, unless otherwise provided in the lease contract:

(a) if the default substantially impairs the value of the lease contract to the lessor, the lessor may exercise the rights and pursue the remedies provided in subsections (1) or (2); or

(b) if the default does not substantially impair the value of the lease contract to the lessor, the lessor may recover as provided in subsection (2).

As amended in 1990.

§ 2A–524. Lessor's Right to Identify Goods to Lease Contract.

(1) After default by the lessee under the lease contract of the type described in Section 2A–523(1) or 2A–523(3) (a) or, if agreed, after other default by the lessee, the lessor may:

(a) identify to the lease contract conforming goods not already identified if at the time the lessor learned of the default they were in the lessor's or the supplier's possession or control; and

(b) dispose of goods (Section 2A–527(1)) that demonstrably have been intended for the particular lease contract even though those goods are unfinished.

(2) If the goods are unfinished, in the exercise of reasonable commercial judgment for the purposes of avoiding loss and of effective realization, an aggrieved lessor or the supplier may either complete manufacture and wholly identify the goods to the lease contract or cease manufacture and lease, sell, or otherwise dispose of the goods for scrap or salvage value or proceed in any other reasonable manner.

As amended in 1990.

§ 2A–525. Lessor's Right to Possession of Goods.

(1) If a lessor discovers the lessee to be insolvent, the lessor may refuse to deliver the goods.

(2) After a default by the lessee under the lease contract of the type described in Section 2A–523(1) or 2A–523(3) (a) or, if agreed, after other default by the lessee, the lessor has the right to take possession of the goods. If the lease contract so provides, the lessor may require the lessee to assemble the goods and make them available to the lessor at a place to be designated by the lessor which is reasonably convenient to both parties. Without removal, the lessor may render unusable any goods employed in trade or business, and may dispose of goods on the lessee's premises (Section 2A–527).

(3) The lessor may proceed under subsection (2) without judicial process if it can be done without breach of the peace or the lessor may proceed by action.

As amended in 1990.

§ 2A–526. Lessor's Stoppage of Delivery in Transit or Otherwise.

(1) A lessor may stop delivery of goods in the possession of a carrier or other bailee if the lessor discovers the lessee to be insolvent and may stop delivery of carload, truckload, planeload, or larger shipments of express or freight if the lessee repudiates or fails to make a payment due before delivery, whether for rent, security or otherwise under the lease contract, or for any other reason the lessor has a right to withhold or take possession of the goods.

(2) In pursuing its remedies under subsection (1), the lessor may stop delivery until

(a) receipt of the goods by the lessee;

(b) acknowledgment to the lessee by any bailee of the goods, except a carrier, that the bailee holds the goods for the lessee; or

(c) such an acknowledgment to the lessee by a carrier via reshipment or as warehouseman.

(3) (a) To stop delivery, a lessor shall so notify as to enable the bailee by reasonable diligence to prevent delivery of the goods.

(b) After notification, the bailee shall hold and deliver the goods according to the directions of the lessor, but the lessor is liable to the bailee for any ensuing charges or damages.

(c) A carrier who has issued a nonnegotiable bill of lading is not obliged to obey a notification to stop received from a person other than the consignor.

§ 2A–527. Lessor's Rights to Dispose of Goods.

(1) After a default by a lessee under the lease contract of the type described in Section 2A–523(1) or 2A–523(3)(a) or after the lessor refuses to deliver or takes possession of goods (Section 2A–525 or 2A–526), or, if agreed, after other default by a lessee, the lessor may dispose of the goods concerned or the undelivered balance thereof by lease, sale, or otherwise.

(2) Except as otherwise provided with respect to damages liquidated in the lease agreement (Section 2A–504) or otherwise determined pursuant to agreement of the parties (Sections 1–102(3) and 2A–503), if the disposition is by lease agreement substantially similar to the original lease agreement and the new lease agreement is made in good faith and in a commercially reasonable manner, the lessor may recover from the lessee as damages (i) accrued and unpaid rent as of the date of the commencement of the term of the new lease agreement, (ii) the present value, as of the same date, of the total rent for the then remaining lease term of the original lease agreement minus the present value, as of the same date, of the rent under the new lease agreement applicable to that period of the new lease term which is comparable to the then remaining term of the original lease agreement, and (iii) any incidental damages allowed under Section 2A–530, less expenses saved in consequence of the lessee's default.

(3) If the lessor's disposition is by lease agreement that for any reason does not qualify for treatment under subsection (2), or is by sale or otherwise, the lessor may recover from the lessee as if the lessor had elected not to dispose of the goods and Section 2A–528 governs.

(4) A subsequent buyer or lessee who buys or leases from the lessor in good faith for value as a result of a disposition under this section takes the goods free of the original lease contract and any rights of the original lessee even though the lessor fails to comply with one or more of the requirements of this Article.

(5) The lessor is not accountable to the lessee for any profit made on any disposition. A lessee who has rightfully rejected or justifiably revoked acceptance shall account to the lessor for any excess over the amount of the lessee's security interest (Section 2A–508(5)).

As amended in 1990.

§ 2A–528. Lessor's Damages for Nonacceptance, Failure to Pay, Repudiation, or Other Default.

(1) Except as otherwise provided with respect to damages liquidated in the lease agreement (Section 2A–504) or otherwise determined pursuant to agreement of the parties (Sections 1–102(3) and 2A–503), if a lessor elects to retain the goods or a lessor elects to dispose of the goods and the disposition is by lease agreement that for any reason does not qualify for treatment under Section 2A–527(2), or is by sale or otherwise, the lessor may recover from the lessee as damages for a default of the type described in Section 2A–523(1) or 2A–523(3) (a), or, if agreed, for other default of the lessee, (i) accrued and unpaid rent as of the date of default if the lessee has never taken possession of the goods, or, if the lessee has taken possession of the goods, as of the date the lessor repossesses the goods or an earlier date on which the lessee makes a tender of the goods to the lessor, (ii) the present value as of the date determined under clause (i) of the total rent for the then remaining lease term of the original lease agreement minus the present value as of the same date of the market rent at the place where the goods are located computed for the same lease term, and (iii) any incidental damages allowed under Section 2A–530, less expenses saved in consequence of the lessee's default.

(2) If the measure of damages provided in subsection (1) is inadequate to put a lessor in as good a position as performance would have, the measure of damages is the present value of the profit, including reasonable overhead, the lessor would have made from full performance by the lessee, together with any incidental damages allowed under Section 2A–530, due allowance for costs reasonably incurred and due credit for payments or proceeds of disposition.

As amended in 1990.

§ 2A–529. Lessor's Action for the Rent.

(1) After default by the lessee under the lease contract of the type described in Section 2A–523(1) or 2A–523(3) (a) or, if agreed, after other default by the lessee, if the lessor complies with subsection (2), the lessor may recover from the lessee as damages:

(a) for goods accepted by the lessee and not repossessed by or tendered to the lessor, and for conforming goods lost or damaged within a commercially reasonable time after risk of loss passes to the lessee (Section 2A–219), (i) accrued and unpaid rent as of the date of entry of judgment in favor of

the lessor, (ii) the present value as of the same date of the rent for the then remaining lease term of the lease agreement, and (iii) any incidental damages allowed under Section 2A–530, less expenses saved in consequence of the lessee's default; and

(b) for goods identified to the lease contract if the lessor is unable after reasonable effort to dispose of them at a reasonable price or the circumstances reasonably indicate that effort will be unavailing, (i) accrued and unpaid rent as of the date of entry of judgment in favor of the lessor, (ii) the present value as of the same date of the rent for the then remaining lease term of the lease agreement, and (iii) any incidental damages allowed under Section 2A–530, less expenses saved in consequence of the lessee's default.

(2) Except as provided in subsection (3), the lessor shall hold for the lessee for the remaining lease term of the lease agreement any goods that have been identified to the lease contract and are in the lessor's control.

(3) The lessor may dispose of the goods at any time before collection of the judgment for damages obtained pursuant to subsection (1). If the disposition is before the end of the remaining lease term of the lease agreement, the lessor's recovery against the lessee for damages is governed by Section 2A–527 or Section 2A–528, and the lessor will cause an appropriate credit to be provided against a judgment for damages to the extent that the amount of the judgment exceeds the recovery available pursuant to Section 2A–527 or 2A–528.

(4) Payment of the judgment for damages obtained pursuant to subsection (1) entitles the lessee to the use and possession of the goods not then disposed of for the remaining lease term of and in accordance with the lease agreement.

(5) After default by the lessee under the lease contract of the type described in Section 2A–523(1) or Section 2A–523(3) (a) or, if agreed, after other default by the lessee, a lessor who is held not entitled to rent under this section must nevertheless be awarded damages for nonacceptance under Section 2A–527 or Section 2A–528.

As amended in 1990.

§ 2A–530. Lessor's Incidental Damages.
Incidental damages to an aggrieved lessor include any commercially reasonable charges, expenses, or commissions incurred in stopping delivery, in the transportation, care and custody of goods after the lessee's default, in connection with return or disposition of the goods, or otherwise resulting from the default.

§ 2A–531. Standing to Sue Third Parties for Injury to Goods.

(1) If a third party so deals with goods that have been identified to a lease contract as to cause actionable injury to a party to the lease contract (a) the lessor has a right of action against the third party, and (b) the lessee also has a right of action against the third party if the lessee:

 (i) has a security interest in the goods;

 (ii) has an insurable interest in the goods; or

 (iii) bears the risk of loss under the lease contract or has since the injury assumed that risk as against the lessor and the goods have been converted or destroyed.

(2) If at the time of the injury the party plaintiff did not bear the risk of loss as against the other party to the lease contract and there is no arrangement between them for disposition of the recovery, his [or her] suit or settlement, subject to his [or her] own interest, is as a fiduciary for the other party to the lease contract.

(3) Either party with the consent of the other may sue for the benefit of whom it may concern.

§ 2A–532. Lessor's Rights to Residual Interest.
In addition to any other recovery permitted by this Article or other law, the lessor may recover from the lessee an amount that will fully compensate the lessor for any loss of or damage to the lessor's residual interest in the goods caused by the default of the lessee.

As added in 1990.

Sarbanes-Oxley Act of 2002

Note: Only some sections are represented in this appendix. The full act can be found as a link on the text's Web site at www.mhhe.com/kubasekess.

Section 1. Short Title

(a) Short Title. This Act may be cited as the "Sarbanes-Oxley Act of 2002."

Title I—Public Company Accounting Oversight Board

Sec. 101. Establishment; administrative provisions.

Sec. 102. Registration with the Board.

Sec. 103. Auditing, quality control, and independence standards and rules.

Sec. 104. Inspections of registered public accounting firms.

Sec. 105. Investigations and disciplinary proceedings.

Sec. 106. Foreign public accounting firms.

Sec. 107. Commission oversight of the Board.

Sec. 108. Accounting standards.

Sec. 109. Funding.

Title II—Auditor Independence

Sec. 201. Services outside the scope of practice of auditors.

Sec. 202. Preapproval requirements.

Sec. 203. Audit partner rotation.

Sec. 204. Auditor reports to audit committees.

Sec. 205. Conforming amendments.

Sec. 206. Conflicts of interest.

Sec. 207. Study of mandatory rotation of registered public accounting firms.

Sec. 208. Commission authority.

Sec. 209. Considerations by appropriate State regulatory authorities.

Title II— Corporate Responsibility

Sec. 301. Public company audit committees.

Sec. 302. Corporate responsibility for financial reports.

Sec. 303. Improper influence on conduct of audits.

Sec. 304. Forfeiture of certain bonuses and profits.

Sec. 305. Officer and director bars and penalties.

Sec. 306. Insider trades during pension fund blackout periods.

Sec. 307. Rules of professional responsibility for attorneys.

Sec. 308. Fair funds for investors.

Title IV—Enhanced Financial Disclosures

Sec. 401. Disclosures in periodic reports.

Sec. 402. Enhanced conflict of interest provisions.

Sec. 403. Disclosures of transactions involving management and principal stockholders.

Sec. 404. Management assessment of internal controls.

Sec. 405. Exemption.

Sec. 406. Code of ethics for senior financial officers.

Sec. 407. Disclosure of audit committee financial expert.

Sec. 408. Enhanced review of periodic disclosures by issuers.

Sec. 409. Real time issuer disclosures.

Title V—Analyst Conflicts of Interest

Sec. 501. Treatment of securities analysts by registered securities associations and national securities exchanges.

Title VI—Commission Resources and Authority

Sec. 601. Authorization of appropriations.

Sec. 602. Appearance and practice before the Commission.

Sec. 603. Federal court authority to impose penny stock bars.

Sec. 604. Qualifications of associated persons of brokers and dealers.

Title VII—Studies and Reports

Sec. 701. GAO study and report regarding consolidation of public accounting firms.

Title VIII—Corporate and Criminal Fraud Accountability

Title IX—White-Collar Crime Penalty Enhancements

Title X—Corporate Tax Returns

Title XI—Corporate Fraud and Accountability

Sec. 302. Corporate Responsibility for Financial Reports.

(a) **Regulations Required.** The Commission shall, by rule, require, for each company filing periodic reports under section 13(a) or 15(d) of the Securities Exchange Act of 1934 (15 U.S.C. 78m, 78o(d)), that the principal executive officer or officers and the principal financial officer or officers, or persons performing similar functions, certify in each annual or quarterly report filed or submitted under either such section of such Act that—

(1) the signing officer has reviewed the report;

(2) based on the officer's knowledge, the report does not contain any untrue statement of a material fact or omit to state a material fact necessary in order to make the statements made, in light of the circumstances under which such statements were made, not misleading;

(3) based on such officer's knowledge, the financial statements, and other financial information included in the report, fairly present in all material respects the financial condition and results of operations of the issuer as of, and for, the periods presented in the report;

(4) the signing officers—

 (A) are responsible for establishing and maintaining internal controls;

 (B) have designed such internal controls to ensure that material information relating to the issuer and its consolidated subsidiaries is made known to such officers by others within those entities, particularly during the period in which the periodic reports are being prepared;

 (C) have evaluated the effectiveness of the issuer's internal controls as of a date within 90 days prior to the report; and

 (D) have presented in the report their conclusions about the effectiveness of their internal controls based on their evaluation as of that date;

(5) the signing officers have disclosed to the issuer's auditors and the audit committee of the board of directors (or persons fulfilling the equivalent function)—

 (A) all significant deficiencies in the design or operation of internal controls which could adversely affect the issuer's ability to record, process, summarize, and report financial data and have identified for the issuer's auditors any material weaknesses in internal controls; and

 (B) any fraud, whether or not material, that involves management or other employees who have a significant role in the issuer's internal controls; and

(6) the signing officers have indicated in the report whether or not there were significant changes in internal controls or in other factors that could significantly affect internal controls subsequent to the date of their evaluation, including any corrective actions with regard to significant deficiencies and material weaknesses.

(b) Foreign Reincorporations Have No Effect. Nothing in this section 302 shall be interpreted or applied in any way to allow any issuer to lessen the legal force of the statement required under this section 302, by an issuer having reincorporated or having engaged in any other transaction that resulted in the transfer of the corporate domicile or offices of the issuer from inside the United States to outside of the United States.

(c) Deadline. The rules required by subsection (a) shall be effective not later than 30 days after the date of enactment of this Act.

Sec. 306. Insider Trades during Pension Fund Blackout Periods.

(a) Prohibition of Insider Trading during Pension Fund Blackout Periods.

(1) IN GENERAL—Except to the extent otherwise provided by rule of the Commission pursuant to paragraph (3), it shall be unlawful for any director or executive officer of an issuer of any equity security (other than an exempted security), directly or indirectly, to purchase, sell, or otherwise acquire or transfer any equity security of the issuer (other than an exempted security) during any blackout period with respect to such equity security if such director or officer acquires such equity security in connection with his or her service or employment as a director or executive officer.

(2) REMEDY—

 (A) IN GENERAL—Any profit realized by a director or executive officer referred to in paragraph (1) from any purchase, sale, or other acquisition or transfer in violation of this subsection shall inure to and be recoverable by the issuer, irrespective of any intention on the part of such director or executive officer in entering into the transaction.

 (B) ACTIONS TO RECOVER PROFITS—An action to recover profits in accordance with this subsection may be instituted at law or in equity in any court of competent jurisdiction by the issuer, or by the owner of any security of the issuer in the name and in behalf of the issuer if the issuer fails or refuses to bring such action within 60 days after the date of request, or fails diligently to prosecute the action thereafter, except that no such suit shall be brought more than 2 years after the date on which such profit was realized.

(3) RULEMAKING AUTHORIZED—The Commission shall, in consultation with the Secretary of Labor, issue rules to clarify the application of this subsection and to prevent evasion thereof. Such rules shall provide for the application of the requirements of paragraph (1) with respect to entities treated as a single employer with respect to an issuer under section 414(b), (c), (m), or (o) of the Internal Revenue Code of 1986 to the extent necessary to clarify the application of such requirements and to prevent evasion thereof. Such rules may also provide for appropriate exceptions from the requirements of this subsection, including exceptions for purchases pursuant to an automatic dividend reinvestment program or purchases or sales made pursuant to an advance election.

(4) BLACKOUT PERIOD—For purposes of this subsection, the term "blackout period," with respect to the equity securities of any issuer—

 (A) means any period of more than 3 consecutive business days during which the ability of not fewer than 50 percent of the participants or beneficiaries under all individual account plans maintained by the issuer to purchase, sell, or otherwise acquire or transfer an interest in any equity of such issuer held in such an individual account plan is temporarily suspended by the issuer or by a fiduciary of the plan; and

 (B) does not include, under regulations which shall be prescribed by the Commission—

 (i) a regularly scheduled period in which the participants and beneficiaries may not purchase, sell, or otherwise acquire or transfer an interest in any equity of such issuer, if such period is—

 (I) incorporated into the individual account plan; and

 (II) timely disclosed to employees before becoming participants under the individual account plan or as a subsequent amendment to the plan; or

 (ii) any suspension described in subparagraph (A) that is imposed solely in connection with persons becoming participants or beneficiaries, or ceasing to be participants or beneficiaries, in an individual account plan by reason of a corporate merger, acquisition, divestiture, or similar transaction involving the plan or plan sponsor.

(5) INDIVIDUAL ACCOUNT PLAN—For purposes of this subsection, the term "individual account plan"

has the meaning provided in section 3(34) of the Employee Retirement Income Security Act of 1974 (29 U.S.C. 1002(34), except that such term shall not include a one-participant retirement plan (within the meaning of section 101(i)(8)(B) of such Act (29 U.S.C. 1021(i)(8)(B))).

(6) NOTICE TO DIRECTORS, EXECUTIVE OFFICERS, AND THE COMMISSION—In any case in which a director or executive officer is subject to the requirements of this subsection in connection with a blackout period (as defined in paragraph (4)) with respect to any equity securities, the issuer of such equity securities shall timely notify such director or officer and the Securities and Exchange Commission of such blackout period.

(b) Notice Requirements to Participants and Beneficiaries under ERISA.

(1) IN GENERAL—Section 101 of the Employee Retirement Income Security Act of 1974 (29 U.S.C. 1021) is amended by redesignating the second subsection (h) as subsection (j), and by inserting after the first subsection (h) the following new subsection:

(i) Notice of Blackout Periods to Participant or Beneficiary under Individual Account Plan.

"(1) DUTIES OF PLAN ADMINISTRATOR—In advance of the commencement of any blackout period with respect to an individual account plan, the plan administrator shall notify the plan participants and beneficiaries who are affected by such action in accordance with this subsection.

"(2) NOTICE REQUIREMENTS—

"(A) IN GENERAL—The notices described in paragraph (1) shall be written in a manner calculated to be understood by the average plan participant and shall include—

"(i) the reasons for the blackout period,

"(ii) an identification of the investments and other rights affected,

"(iii) the expected beginning date and length of the blackout period,

"(iv) in the case of investments affected, a statement that the participant or beneficiary should evaluate the appropriateness of their current investment decisions in light of their inability to direct or diversify assets credited to their accounts during the blackout period, and

"(v) such other matters as the Secretary may require by regulation.

"(B) NOTICE TO PARTICIPANTS AND BENEFICIARIES—Except as otherwise provided in this subsection, notices described in paragraph (1) shall be furnished to all participants and beneficiaries under the plan to whom the blackout period applies at least 30 days in advance of the blackout period.

"(C) EXCEPTION TO 30-DAY NOTICE REQUIREMENT—In any case in which—

"(i) a deferral of the blackout period would violate the requirements of subparagraph (A) or (B) of section 404(a)(1), and a fiduciary of the plan reasonably so determines in writing, or

"(ii) the inability to provide the 30-day advance notice is due to events that were unforeseeable or circumstances beyond the reasonable control of the plan administrator, and a fiduciary of the plan reasonably so determines in writing, subparagraph (B) shall not apply, and the notice shall be furnished to all participants and beneficiaries under the plan to whom the blackout period applies as soon as reasonably possible under the circumstances unless such a notice in advance of the termination of the blackout period is impracticable.

"(D) WRITTEN NOTICE—The notice required to be provided under this subsection shall be in writing, except that such notice may be in electronic or other form to the extent that such form is reasonably accessible to the recipient.

"(E) NOTICE TO ISSUERS OF EMPLOYER SECURITIES SUBJECT TO BLACKOUT PERIOD—In the case of any blackout period in connection with an individual account plan, the plan administrator shall provide timely notice of such blackout period to the issuer of any employer securities subject to such blackout period.

"(3) EXCEPTION FOR BLACKOUT PERIODS WITH LIMITED APPLICABILITY—In any case in which the blackout period applies only to 1 or more participants or beneficiaries in connection with a merger, acquisition, divestiture, or similar transaction involving the plan or plan sponsor and occurs solely in connection with becoming or ceasing to be a participant or beneficiary under the plan by reason of such merger, acquisition, divestiture, or transaction, the requirement of this subsection that the notice be provided to all participants and beneficiaries shall be treated as met if the notice required under paragraph (1) is provided to such participants or beneficiaries to whom the blackout period applies as soon as reasonably practicable.

"(4) CHANGES IN LENGTH OF BLACKOUT PERIOD—If, following the furnishing of the notice pursuant to this subsection, there is a change in the

beginning date or length of the blackout period (specified in such notice pursuant to paragraph (2)(A)(iii)), the administrator shall provide affected participants and beneficiaries notice of the change as soon as reasonably practicable. In relation to the extended blackout period, such notice shall meet the requirements of paragraph (2)(D) and shall specify any material change in the matters referred to in clauses (i) through (v) of paragraph (2)(A).

"(5) REGULATORY EXCEPTIONS—The Secretary may provide by regulation for additional exceptions to the requirements of this subsection which the Secretary determines are in the interests of participants and beneficiaries.

"(6) GUIDANCE AND MODEL NOTICES—The Secretary shall issue guidance and model notices which meet the requirements of this subsection.

"(7) BLACKOUT PERIOD—For purposes of this subsection—

 "(A) IN GENERAL—The term 'blackout period' means, in connection with an individual account plan, any period for which any ability of participants or beneficiaries under the plan, which is otherwise available under the terms of such plan, to direct or diversify assets credited to their accounts, to obtain loans from the plan, or to obtain distributions from the plan is temporarily suspended, limited, or restricted, if such suspension, limitation, or restriction is for any period of more than 3 consecutive business days.

 "(B) EXCLUSIONS—The term 'blackout period' does not include a suspension, limitation, or restriction—

 "(i) which occurs by reason of the application of the securities laws (as defined in section 3(a)(47) of the Securities Exchange Act of 1934),

 "(ii) which is a change to the plan which provides for a regularly scheduled suspension, limitation, or restriction which is disclosed to participants or beneficiaries through any summary of material modifications, any materials describing specific investment alternatives under the plan, or any changes thereto, or

 "(iii) which applies only to 1 or more individuals, each of whom is the participant, an alternate payee (as defined in section 206(d)(3)(K)), or any other beneficiary pursuant to a qualified domestic relations order (as defined in section 206(d)(3)(B)(i)).

"(8) INDIVIDUAL ACCOUNT PLAN—

 "(A) IN GENERAL—For purposes of this subsection, the term 'individual account plan' shall have the meaning provided such term in section 3(34), except that such term shall not include a one-participant retirement plan.

 "(B) ONE-PARTICIPANT RETIREMENT PLAN—For purposes of subparagraph (A), the term 'one-participant retirement plan' means a retirement plan that—

 "(i) on the first day of the plan year—

 "(I) covered only the employer (and the employer's spouse) and the employer owned the entire business (whether or not incorporated), or

 "(II) covered only one or more partners (and their spouses) in a business partnership (including partners in an S or C corporation (as defined in section 1361(a) of the Internal Revenue Code of 1986)),

 "(ii) meets the minimum coverage requirements of section 410(b) of the Internal Revenue Code of 1986 (as in effect on the date of the enactment of this paragraph) without being combined with any other plan of the business that covers the employees of the business,

 "(iii) does not provide benefits to anyone except the employer (and the employer's spouse) or the partners (and their spouses),

 "(iv) does not cover a business that is a member of an affiliated service group, a controlled group of corporations, or a group of businesses under common control, and

 "(v) does not cover a business that leases employees."

(2) ISSUANCE OF INITIAL GUIDANCE AND MODEL NOTICE—The Secretary of Labor shall issue initial guidance and a model notice pursuant to section 101(i)(6) of the Employee Retirement Income Security Act of 1974 (as added by this subsection) not later than January 1, 2003. Not later than 75 days after the date of the enactment of this Act, the Secretary shall promulgate interim final rules necessary to carry out the amendments made by this subsection.

(3) CIVIL PENALTIES FOR FAILURE TO PROVIDE NOTICE—Section 502 of such Act (29 U.S.C. 1132) is amended—

 (A) in subsection (a)(6), by striking "(5), or (6)" and inserting "(5), (6), or (7)";

 (B) by redesignating paragraph (7) of subsection (c) as paragraph (8); and

(C) by inserting after paragraph (6) of subsection (c) the following new paragraph:

"(7) The Secretary may assess a civil penalty against a plan administrator of up to $100 a day from the date of the plan administrator's failure or refusal to provide notice to participants and beneficiaries in accordance with section 101(i). For purposes of this paragraph, each violation with respect to any single participant or beneficiary shall be treated as a separate violation."

(3) PLAN AMENDMENTS—If any amendment made by this subsection requires an amendment to any plan, such plan amendment shall not be required to be made before the first plan year beginning on or after the effective date of this section, if—

(A) during the period after such amendment made by this subsection takes effect and before such first plan year, the plan is operated in good faith compliance with the requirements of such amendment made by this subsection, and

(B) such plan amendment applies retroactively to the period after such amendment made by this subsection takes effect and before such first plan year.

(C) EFFECTIVE DATE—The provisions of this section (including the amendments made thereby) shall take effect 180 days after the date of the enactment of this Act. Good faith compliance with the requirements of such provisions in advance of the issuance of applicable regulations thereunder shall be treated as compliance with such provisions.

Sec. 402. Enhanced Conflict of Interest Provisions.

(a) Prohibition on Personal Loans to Executives. Section 13 of the Securities Exchange Act of 1934 (15 U.S.C. 78m), as amended by this Act, is amended by adding at the end the following:

"(k) Prohibition on Personal Loans to Executives.

"(1) IN GENERAL—It shall be unlawful for any issuer (as defined in section 2 of the Sarbanes-Oxley Act of 2002), directly or indirectly, including through any subsidiary, to extend or maintain credit, to arrange for the extension of credit, or to renew an extension of credit, in the form of a personal loan to or for any director or executive officer (or equivalent thereof) of that issuer. An extension of credit maintained by the issuer on the date of enactment of this subsection shall not be subject to the provisions of this subsection, provided that there is no material modification to any term of any such extension of credit or any

renewal of any such extension of credit on or after that date of enactment.

"(2) LIMITATION—Paragraph (1) does not preclude any home improvement and manufactured home loans (as that term is defined in section 5 of the Home Owners' Loan Act (12 U.S.C. 1464)), consumer credit (as defined in section 103 of the Truth in Lending Act (15 U.S.C. 1602)), or any extension of credit under an open end credit plan (as defined in section 103 of the Truth in Lending Act (15 U.S.C. 1602)), or a charge card (as defined in section 127(c)(4)(e) of the Truth in Lending Act (15 U.S.C. 1637(c)(4)(e)), or any extension of credit by a broker or dealer registered under section 15 of this title to an employee of that broker or dealer to buy, trade, or carry securities, that is permitted under rules or regulations of the Board of Governors of the Federal Reserve System pursuant to section 7 of this title (other than an extension of credit that would be used to purchase the stock of that issuer), that is—

"(A) made or provided in the ordinary course of the consumer credit business of such issuer;

"(B) of a type that is generally made available by such issuer to the public; and

"(C) made by such issuer on market terms, or terms that are no more favorable than those offered by the issuer to the general public for such extensions of credit.

"(3) Rule of Construction for Certain Loans—Paragraph (1) does not apply to any loan made or maintained by an insured depository institution (as defined in section 3 of the Federal Deposit Insurance Act (12 U.S.C. 1813)), if the loan is subject to the insider lending restrictions of section 22(h) of the Federal Reserve Act (12 U.S.C. 375b)."

Sec. 403. Disclosures of Transactions Involving Management and Principal Stockholders.

(a) Amendment. Section 16 of the Securities Exchange Act of 1934 (15 U.S.C. 78p) is amended by striking the heading of such section and subsection (a) and inserting the following:

"Sec. 16. Directors, Officers, and Principal Stockholders.

"(a) Disclosures Required.

"(1) DIRECTORS, OFFICERS, AND PRINCIPAL STOCKHOLDERS REQUIRED TO FILE—Every person who is directly or indirectly the beneficial

owner of more than 10 percent of any class of any equity security (other than an exempted security) which is registered pursuant to section 12, or who is a director or an officer of the issuer of such security, shall file the statements required by this subsection with the Commission (and, if such security is registered on a national securities exchange, also with the exchange).

"(2) TIME OF FILING—The statements required by this subsection shall be filed—

"(A) at the time of the registration of such security on a national securities exchange or by the effective date of a registration statement filed pursuant to section 12(g);

"(B) within 10 days after he or she becomes such beneficial owner, director, or officer;

"(C) if there has been a change in such ownership, or if such person shall have purchased or sold a security-based swap agreement (as defined in section 206(b) of the Gramm-Leach-Bliley Act (15 U.S.C. 78c note)) involving such equity security, before the end of the second business day following the day on which the subject transaction has been executed, or at such other time as the Commission shall establish, by rule, in any case in which the Commission determines that such 2-day period is not feasible.

"(3) CONTENTS OF STATEMENTS—A statement filed—

"(A) under subparagraph (A) or (B) of paragraph (2) shall contain a statement of the amount of all equity securities of such issuer of which the filing person is the beneficial owner; and

"(B) under subparagraph (C) of such paragraph shall indicate ownership by the filing person at the date of filing, any such changes in such ownership, and such purchases and sales of the security-based swap agreements as have occurred since the most recent such filing under such subparagraph.

"(4) ELECTRONIC FILING AND AVAILABILITY—Beginning not later than 1 year after the date of enactment of the Sarbanes-Oxley Act of 2002—

"(A) a statement filed under subparagraph (C) of paragraph (2) shall be filed electronically;

"(B) the Commission shall provide each such statement on a publicly accessible Internet site not later than the end of the business day following that filing; and

"(C) the issuer (if the issuer maintains a corporate website) shall provide that statement on that corporate website, not later than the end of the business day following that filing."

(b) Effective Date. The amendment made by this section shall be effective 30 days after the date of the enactment of this Act.

Sec. 404. Management Assessment of Internal Controls.

(a) Rules Required. The Commission shall prescribe rules requiring each annual report required by section 13(a) or 15(d) of the Securities Exchange Act of 1934 (15 U.S.C. 78m or 78o(d)) to contain an internal control report, which shall—

(1) state the responsibility of management for establishing and maintaining an adequate internal control structure and procedures for financial reporting; and

(2) contain an assessment, as of the end of the most recent fiscal year of the issuer, of the effectiveness of the internal control structure and procedures of the issuer for financial reporting.

(b) Internal Control Evaluation and Reporting. With respect to the internal control assessment required by subsection (a), each registered public accounting firm that prepares or issues the audit report for the issuer shall attest to, and report on, the assessment made by the management of the issuer. An attestation made under this subsection shall be made in accordance with standards for attestation engagements issued or adopted by the Board. Any such attestation shall not be the subject of a separate engagement.

Sec. 802. Criminal Penalties for Altering Documents.

(a) In General. Chapter 73 of title 18, United States Code, is amended by adding at the end the following:

"Sec. 1519. Destruction, alteration, or falsification of records in Federal investigations and bankruptcy

"Whoever knowingly alters, destroys, mutilates, conceals, covers up, falsifies, or makes a false entry in any record, document, or tangible object with the intent to impede, obstruct, or influence the investigation or proper administration of any matter within the jurisdiction of any department or agency of the United States or any case filed under title 11, or in relation to or contemplation of any such matter or case, shall be fined under this title, imprisoned not more than 20 years, or both.

"Sec. 1520. Destruction of corporate audit records

"(a)

"(1) Any accountant who conducts an audit of an issuer of securities to which section 10A(a) of the Securities Exchange Act of 1934 (15 U.S.C. 78j-1(a)) applies, shall maintain all audit or review workpapers for a period of 5 years from the end of the fiscal period in which the audit or review was concluded.

"(2) The Securities and Exchange Commission shall promulgate, within 180 days, after adequate notice and an opportunity for comment, such rules and regulations, as are reasonably necessary, relating to the retention of relevant records such as workpapers, documents that form the basis of an audit or review, memoranda, correspondence, communications, other documents, and records (including electronic records) which are created, sent, or received in connection with an audit or review and contain conclusions, opinions, analyses, or financial data relating to such an audit or review, which is conducted by any accountant who conducts an audit of an issuer of securities to which section 10A(a) of the Securities Exchange Act of 1934 (15 U.S.C. 78j-1(a)) applies. The Commission may, from time to time, amend or supplement the rules and regulations that it is required to promulgate under this section, after adequate notice and an opportunity for comment, in order to ensure that such rules and regulations adequately comport with the purposes of this section.

"(b) Whoever knowingly and willfully violates subsection (a)(1), or any rule or regulation promulgated by the Securities and Exchange Commission under subsection (a)(2), shall be fined under this title, imprisoned not more than 10 years, or both.

"(c) Nothing in this section shall be deemed to diminish or relieve any person of any other duty or obligation imposed by Federal or State law or regulation to maintain, or refrain from destroying, any document."

Sec. 804. Statute of Limitations for Securities Fraud.

(a) In General. Section 1658 of title 28, United States Code, is amended—

(1) by inserting "(a)" before "Except"; and

(2) by adding at the end the following:

"(b) Notwithstanding subsection (a), a private right of action that involves a claim of fraud, deceit, manipulation, or contrivance in contravention of a regulatory requirement concerning the securities laws, as defined in section 3(a)(47) of the Securities Exchange Act of 1934 (15 U.S.C. 78c(a)(47)), may be brought not later than the earlier of—

"**(1)** 2 years after the discovery of the facts constituting the violation; or

"**(2)** 5 years after such violation."

(b) Effective Date. The limitations period provided by section 1658(b) of title 28, United States Code, as added by this section, shall apply to all proceedings addressed by this section that are commenced on or after the date of enactment of this Act.

(c) No Creation of Actions. Nothing in this section shall create a new, private right of action.

Sec. 806. Protection for Employees of Publicly Traded Companies Who Provide Evidence of Fraud.

(a) In General. Chapter 73 of title 18, United States Code, is amended by inserting after section 1514 the following:

"Sec. 1514A. Civil action to protect against retaliation in fraud cases

"**(a) Whistleblower Protection for Employees of Publicly Traded Companies.** No company with a class of securities registered under section 12 of the Securities Exchange Act of 1934 (15 U.S.C. 78l), or that is required to file reports under section 15(d) of the Securities Exchange Act of 1934 (15 U.S.C. 78o(d)), or any officer, employee, contractor, subcontractor, or agent of such company, may discharge, demote, suspend, threaten, harass, or in any other manner discriminate against an employee in the terms and conditions of employment because of any lawful act done by the employee—

"**(1)** to provide information, cause information to be provided, or otherwise assist in an investigation regarding any conduct which the employee reasonably believes constitutes a violation of section 1341, 1343, 1344, or 1348, any rule or regulation of the Securities and Exchange Commission, or any provision of Federal law relating to fraud against shareholders, when the information or assistance is provided to or the investigation is conducted by—

"**(A)** a Federal regulatory or law enforcement agency;

"**(B)** any Member of Congress or any committee of Congress; or

"**(C)** a person with supervisory authority over the employee (or such other person working for the employer who has the authority to investigate, discover, or terminate misconduct); or

"**(2)** to file, cause to be filed, testify, participate in, or otherwise assist in a proceeding filed or about to be filed (with any knowledge of the employer) relating to an alleged violation of section 1341, 1343, 1344, or 1348, any rule or regulation of the Securities and Exchange Commission, or any provision of Federal law relating to fraud against shareholders.

"(b) Enforcement Action.

"(1) IN GENERAL—A person who alleges discharge or other discrimination by any person in violation of subsection (a) may seek relief under subsection (c), by—

"(A) filing a complaint with the Secretary of Labor; or

"(B) if the Secretary has not issued a final decision within 180 days of the filing of the complaint and there is no showing that such delay is due to the bad faith of the claimant, bringing an action at law or equity for de novo review in the appropriate district court of the United States, which shall have jurisdiction over such an action without regard to the amount in controversy.

"(2) PROCEDURE—

"(A) IN GENERAL—An action under paragraph (1)(A) shall be governed under the rules and procedures set forth in section 42121(b) of title 49, United States Code.

"(B) EXCEPTION—Notification made under section 42121(b)(1) of title 49, United States Code, shall be made to the person named in the complaint and to the employer.

"(C) BURDENS OF PROOF—An action brought under paragraph (1)(B) shall be governed by the legal burdens of proof set forth in section 42121(b) of title 49, United States Code.

"(D) STATUTE OF LIMITATIONS—An action under paragraph (1) shall be commenced not later than 90 days after the date on which the violation occurs.

"(c) Remedies.

"(1) IN GENERAL—An employee prevailing in any action under subsection (b)(1) shall be entitled to all relief necessary to make the employee whole.

"(2) COMPENSATORY DAMAGES—Relief for any action under paragraph (1) shall include—

"(A) reinstatement with the same seniority status that the employee would have had, but for the discrimination;

"(B) the amount of back pay, with interest; and

"(C) compensation for any special damages sustained as a result of the discrimination, including litigation costs, expert witness fees, and reasonable attorney fees.

"(d) Rights Retained by Employee. Nothing in this section shall be deemed to diminish the rights, privileges, or remedies of any employee under any Federal or State law, or under any collective bargaining agreement."

(b) Clerical Amendment. The table of sections at the beginning of chapter 73 of title 18, United States Code, is amended by inserting after the item relating to section 1514 the following new item:

"1514A. Civil action to protect against retaliation in fraud cases."

Sec. 807. Criminal Penalties for Defrauding Shareholders of Publicly Traded Companies.

(a) In General. Chapter 63 of title 18, United States Code, is amended by adding at the end the following:

"Sec. 1348. Securities fraud

"Whoever knowingly executes, or attempts to execute, a scheme or artifice—

"(1) to defraud any person in connection with any security of an issuer with a class of securities registered under section 12 of the Securities Exchange Act of 1934 (15 U.S.C. 78l) or that is required to file reports under section 15(d) of the Securities Exchange Act of 1934 (15 U.S.C. 78o(d)); or

"(2) to obtain, by means of false or fraudulent pretenses, representations, or promises, any money or property in connection with the purchase or sale of any security of an issuer with a class of securities registered under section 12 of the Securities Exchange Act of 1934 (15 U.S.C. 78l) or that is required to file reports under section 15(d) of the Securities Exchange Act of 1934 (15 U.S.C. 78o(d));

shall be fined under this title, or imprisoned not more than 25 years, or both."

Sec. 906. Corporate Responsibility for Financial Reports.

(a) In General. Chapter 63 of title 18, United States Code, is amended by inserting after section 1349, as created by this Act, the following:

"Sec. 1350. Failure of corporate officers to certify financial reports

"(a) Certification of Periodic Financial Reports. Each periodic report containing financial statements filed by an issuer with the Securities Exchange Commission pursuant to section 13(a) or 15(d) of the Securities Exchange Act of 1934 (15 U.S.C. 78m(a) or 78o(d)) shall be accompanied by a written statement by the chief executive officer and chief financial officer (or equivalent thereof) of the issuer.

"(b) Content. The statement required under subsection (a) shall certify that the periodic report containing the

financial statements fully complies with the requirements of section 13(a) or 15(d) of the Securities Exchange Act pf 1934 (15 U.S.C. 78m or 78o(d)) and that information contained in the periodic report fairly presents, in all material respects, the financial condition and results of operations of the issuer.

"(c) Criminal Penalties. Whoever—

"(1) certifies any statement as set forth in subsections (a) and (b) of this section knowing that the periodic report accompanying the statement does not comport with all the requirements set forth in this section shall be fined not more than $1,000,000 or imprisoned not more than 10 years, or both; or

"(2) willfully certifies any statement as set forth in subsections (a) and (b) of this section knowing that the periodic report accompanying the statement does not comport with all the requirements set forth in this section shall be fined not more than $5,000,000, or imprisoned not more than 20 years, or both."

(b) Clerical Amendment. The table of sections at the beginning of chapter 63 of title 18, United States Code, is amended by adding at the end the following:

"1350. Failure of corporate officers to certify financial reports."

Glossary

A

absolute privilege A special right, immunity, permission, or benefit given to certain individuals that allows them to make any statements about someone without being held liable for defamation for any false statement made, regardless of intent or knowledge of the falsity of the claim.

acceptance A key factor in the agreement element of a contract; consists of the agreement of one party, the offeree, to the terms of the offer in the contract made by the other party, the offeror.

acceptor A person (drawee) who accepts and signs a draft to agree to pay the draft when it is presented.

accommodation party A party who signs an instrument to provide credit for another party who has also signed the instrument.

accord and satisfaction An arrangement between contracting parties whereby one of the parties substitutes a different performance for his or her original duty under the contract. The promise to perform the new duty is the *accord,* and the actual performance of that new duty is the *satisfaction.*

accounting A review and listing of all partnership assets and/or profit.

accredited investor A private investor who is allowed to accept private securities offerings under certain specific guidelines set by the SEC.

actual cause The determination that the defendant's breach of duty resulted directly in the plaintiff's injury.

actual malice In defamation, either a person's knowledge that his or her statement or published material is false or the person's reckless disregard for whether it was false.

actual notice Notice of agency termination that is given by directly informing third parties, either orally or in writing.

actus reus Latin for "guilty act"; a wrongful behavior that is associated with the physical act of a declared crime.

ad substantiation An FTC standard requiring that advertisers have a reasonable basis for the claims made in their ads.

adhesion contract A contract created by a party to an agreement that is presented to the other party on a take-it-or-leave-it basis. Such contracts are legal but are sometimes rescinded on the grounds of unconscionability and the absence of one party's free will to enter a contract.

administrative agency Any government body created by the legislative branch (e.g., Congress, a state legislature, or a city council) to carry out specific duties.

administrative law The collection of rules and decisions made by administrative agencies to fill in particular details missing from constitutions and statutes.

administrative law judge (ALJ) A judge who presides over an administrative hearing; may attempt to get the parties to settle but has the power to issue a binding decision.

Administrative Procedures Act (APA) Federal legislation that places limitations on how agencies are run and contains very specific guidelines on rule making by agencies.

admission A statement made in court, under oath, or at some stage during a legal proceeding in which a party against whom charges have been brought admits that an oral contract existed, even though the contract was required to be in writing.

adverse possession An involuntary property transfer in which a person acquires ownership of property by treating a piece of real property as his or her own, without protest or permission from the owner.

affirm An appellate court decision that accepts a lower court's judgment in a case that has been appealed.

after-acquired property Property acquired by a debtor after the security arrangement is made.

Age Discrimination in Employment Act of 1967 (ADEA) Federal law that prohibits employers from refusing to hire, discharging, or discriminating in terms and conditions of employment on the basis of an employee's or applicant's being age 40 or older.

agency The fiduciary relationship that arises when one person consents to have another act on his behalf and subject to his control and the other consents to do so.

agency by agreement See **expressed agency.**

agency by estoppel See **apparent agency.**

agency by ratification An agency relationship that arises when an individual misrepresents himself or herself as an agent for another party and that party accepts the unauthorized act.

agency coupled with an interest An agency relationship that is created for the benefit of the agent, not the principal.

agency relationship The association between one party and an agent who acts on behalf of that party.

agent A party who has the authority to act on behalf of and bind another party.

agreement One of the four elements necessary for a contract; consists of an offer made by one party, the offeror, and the acceptance of the offer by another party, the offeree.

alien corporation A business that is incorporated in a foreign country.

allonge Accompanying a negotiable instrument, a piece of paper that provides room for an endorsement if no room is available on the instrument itself.

alteration An unauthorized change to an instrument that modifies the obligation of a party to the instrument.

alternative dispute resolution (ADR) The resolution of legal problems through methods other than litigation.

Americans with Disabilities Act (ADA) Federal law that prohibits discrimination against employees and job applicants with disabilities.

answer The response of the defendant to the plaintiff's complaint.

apparent agency An agency relationship created by operation of law when one party, by his actions, causes a third party to believe someone is his agent when that person actually has no authority. Also called *agency by estoppel.*

appeal The act or fact of challenging the decision of a trial court after final judgment or other legal ruling by taking the matter to the appropriate appellate court, and in some cases to the U.S. Supreme Court, in an attempt to reverse the decision.

appellate court A higher court, usually consisting of more than one judge, that reviews the decision and results of a lower court (either a trial court or a lower-level appellate court) when a losing party files for an appeal. Appellate courts do not hold trials but may request additional oral and written arguments from each party; they issue written decisions, which collectively constitute case law or the common law. Also called *court of appellate jurisdiction.*

appraisal right A dissenting shareholder's right to have his or her shares appraised and to receive monetary compensation from the corporation for their value.

arbitration A type of alternative dispute resolution wherein disputes are submitted for resolution to private nonofficial persons selected in a manner provided by law or the agreement of the parties.

arraignment The first appearance in court by the defendant, at which the defendant is advised of the pending charges, the right to counsel, and the right to trial by jury and he or she enters a plea to the charge.

arrest The action in which the police, or a person acting under the law, seize, hold, or take an individual into custody.

articles of incorporation A document that contains basic information about a corporation and is filed with the state.

articles of partnership The written agreement that creates a partnership.

assault A civil wrong that occurs when one person intentionally and voluntarily places another in fear or apprehension of an immediate, offensive physical harm. Assault does not require actual contact.

assignee In a contract, the party who receives the rights of another party (an assignor) to collect what was contractually agreed on in the original contract.

assignment A contracting party's (an assignor's) transfer of his or her rights to a contract to a third party (an assignee).

assignor In a contract, the party who transfers his or her rights to the contract to a third party (an assignee), giving the assignee the right to collect what was contractually agreed on in the original contract.

assumption of the risk A defense whereby the defendant must prove that the plaintiff voluntarily assumed the risk the defendant caused.

attachment The point at which a creditor becomes the secured party who has a security interest in the collateral.

automatic stay After bankruptcy has been filed, a moratorium during which creditors cannot bring or continue action against the debtor or his or her property.

B

bail A thing of value, such as a money bail bond or any other form of property, that is given to the court to temporarily allow a person's release from jail and to ensure his or her appearance in court.

bait-and-switch advertising A deceptive practice in which a seller advertises a low-priced item, generally unavailable to the consumer, and then pushes the consumer to buy a more expensive item.

Bankruptcy Abuse Prevention and Consumer Protection Act of 2005 (BAPCPA) A renovation in the system of bankruptcy enacted to address increased numbers of bankruptcy filings, significant losses associated with bankruptcy filings, loopholes and incentives that allowed for abuse, and the financial ability of debtors.

bankruptcy estate The assets that are collected from a debtor who files for bankruptcy.

battery A civil wrong that occurs when one person intentionally and voluntarily brings about a nonconsented harmful or offensive contact with a person or something closely associated with him or her. Battery requires an actual contact.

bearer instrument An instrument payable to cash or to whoever is in possession of the instrument.

bench trial A trial before a judge, with the judgment decided by the judge rather than a jury; occurs when the defendant has waived his or her right to a jury trial.

beneficiary A person who can expect to benefit from a relationship.

bilateral contract A promise exchanged for a promise.

binding arbitration clause A contract provision mandating that all disputes arising under the contract must be settled by arbitration.

blank endorsement A payee's or last endorsee's signature on a negotiable instrument.

blank qualified endorsement An endorsement in which the name of the payee or beneficiary of the instrument is not mentioned, making it freely transferable on delivery, and the words *without recourse* limit the liability of the endorser.

blue-sky law A law that regulates the offering and sale of purely intrastate securities.

booking After an individual is arrested, the procedure during which the name of the defendant and the alleged crime are recorded in the investigating agency's or police department's records.

bounty payment A government reward for an act that is beneficial to the public.

bribery A corrupt and illegal activity in which a person offers, gives, solicits, or receives money, services, or anything of value in order to gain an illicit advantage.

brief A written legal argument, which a party presents to a court, that explains why that party to the case should prevail. Also called *factum.*

burden of proof The duty of the plaintiff or prosecution to establish a claim or allegation by admissible evidence and to prove that the defendant committed all the essential elements of

the crime to the jury's or court's satisfaction beyond any reasonable doubt, in order to convict the defendant.

business ethics The use of ethics and ethical principles to solve business dilemmas.

business law The enforceable rules of conduct that govern the actions of buyers and sellers in market exchanges.

business trust A business organization governed by a group of trustees, who operate the trust for beneficiaries.

buyer in the ordinary course of business A person who routinely buys goods in good faith from a person who routinely sells these goods.

bylaws Rules and regulations that govern a corporation's internal management.

C

capacity The legal ability to enter into a binding contract.

case law The collection of legal interpretations made by judges. They are considered to be law unless otherwise revoked by a statutory law. Also known as *common law.*

case or controversy A term used in the U.S. Constitution to describe the structure and requirements of conflicting claims of individuals that can be brought before a federal court for resolution. A case or controversy requires an actual dispute between parties over their legal rights that remains in conflict at the time the case is presented and that is a proper matter for judicial determination. Also referred to as *justifiable controversy.*

cash tender offer A type of takeover in which the aggressor corporation offers to pay the target shareholders cash for their stock.

cashier's check A check in which both drawer and drawee are the same bank.

cease-and-desist order An FTC order requiring that a company stop its illegal behavior.

certificate of deposit A document whereby a bank promises to pay a payee a certain amount of money at a future time.

certificate of incorporation A document certifying that a corporation is incorporated in the state and is authorized to conduct business.

certificate of limited partnership A document signed on the formation of a limited partnership and filed with the secretary of state.

certified check A check that is accepted by the bank from which the funds are drawn.

chain-style business operation A type of franchise in which the franchise operates under the franchisor's business name and is required to follow the franchisor's standards and methods of business operation.

charging order An order that entitles a creditor to collect a partner's profits.

chattel paper A writing that indicates both a monetary obligation and a security interest in specific goods.

check A special draft that orders a bank (the drawee) to pay a specified sum of money to the payee from the drawer's account.

circuit court of appeal A court that hears appeals from the district courts located within its circuit, as well as appeals from

decisions of federal administrative agencies. Also called *federal district court of appeal.*

civil law The body of laws that govern the rights and responsibilities either between persons or between persons and their government.

closely held corporation A corporation that does not sell stock to the general public.

collateral The property that is subject to a secured interest.

collective bargaining The process whereby workers organize collectively and bargain with employers regarding the workplace.

commerce clause Clause 3 of Article I, Section 8, of the U.S. Constitution, which authorizes and empowers Congress "To regulate Commerce with foreign Nations, and among the several States, and with the Indian Tribes."

commercial reasonableness Reasonable commercial standards of fair dealing, required of merchants in addition to honesty in fact.

commercial speech Speech made by businesses about commercial matters, such as the sale of goods and services. It is protected by the First Amendment.

common-carrier delivery contract A type of contract in which purchased goods are delivered to the buyer via an independent contractor, such as a trucking line.

common law See **case law.**

common stock Corporate stock that does not convey any preferences to its holders.

communication In a contract, an offer made to the offeree or the offeree's agent.

compensatory damages Money awarded to a plaintiff as reimbursement for her or his losses; based on the amount of actual damage or harm to property, lost wages or profits, pain and suffering, medical expenses, disability, etc.

complaint A formal written document that begins a civil lawsuit; contains the plaintiff's list of allegations against the defendant, along with the damages the plaintiff seeks.

complete performance Contract performance that occurs when all aspects of the parties' duties under the contract are carried out perfectly.

computer crime Crime committed using a computer.

concealment The active hiding of the truth about a material fact.

concurrent conditions In a contract, terms under which each party's performance is conditioned on the performance of the other; occur only when the parties are required to perform for each other simultaneously.

condemnation The legal process by which a transfer of property is made against the protest of the property owner.

condition precedent In a contract, an event that must occur in order for a party's duty to arise.

condition subsequent In a contract, a future event that terminates the obligations of the parties when it occurs.

conditional contract A contract that becomes enforceable only on the happening or termination of a specified condition.

conditional estate An ownership interest in which the holder has the same interest as that in a fee simple absolute except that this interest is subject to a condition.

conditional privilege A special right, immunity, permission, or benefit given to certain individuals that allows them to make any statements about someone without being held liable for defamation for any false statement made without actual malice.

conditional sales contract A type of contract in which the sale itself is contingent on approval; can be either a sale-on-approval contract or a sale-or-return contract.

conforming goods Goods that conform to contract specifications.

consent order A statement in which a company agrees to stop disputed behavior but does not admit that it broke the law.

consequential damages In a contract, foreseeable damages that result from special facts and circumstances arising outside the contract itself. The damages must be within the contemplation of the parties at the time the breach occurs. Also called *special damages.*

consideration The bargained-for exchange; what each party gets in exchange for his or her promise under a contract.

Consolidated Omnibus Budget Reconciliation Act (COBRA) Federal law that ensures that when employees lose their jobs or have their hours reduced to a level at which they would not be eligible to receive medical, dental, or optical benefits from their employer, the employees will be able to continue receiving benefits under the employer's policy for up to 18 months by paying the premiums for the policy.

consolidation The combination of two or more corporations in which the combining corporations cease to exist and a new corporation is formed.

constitutional law The general limits and powers of a government as interpreted from its written constitution.

constructive notice Notice of agency termination that is usually given by publishing an announcement in a newspaper.

constructive trust An equitable trust imposed on a person who wrongfully obtains or holds legal right to property he or she should not possess.

consumer good A good used or bought for use primarily for personal, family, or household purposes.

consumer law A statute or administrative rule serving to protect consumer interests.

contract A promise or set of promises for the breach of which the law gives a remedy or the performance of which the law in some way recognizes a duty.

contract clause The clause in the U.S. Constitution that prohibits the government from unreasonably interfering with an existing contract.

contract under seal A contract that has a seal certifying its legality. Such contracts require no consideration for them to be legal.

contractual capacity The legal ability to enter into a binding agreement.

contributory negligence A defense to negligence whereby the defendant can escape all liability by proving that the plaintiff failed to act in a way that would protect him or her from an unreasonable risk of harm and that the plaintiff's negligent behavior contributed in some way to the plaintiff's accident.

conversion Permanent interference with another's use and enjoyment of his or her personal property.

cooperative An organization formed by individuals to market new products. Individuals in a cooperative pool their resources together to gain an advantage in the market.

copyright The protection of the expression of a creative work; i.e., protection of the fixed form that expresses the ideas.

corporation A legal entity formed by issuing stock to investors, who are the owners of the corporation.

corporation by estoppel A defective corporation that has conducted business with a third party and therefore cannot deny its status as a corporation to escape liability.

corrective advertising Advertising in which the company explicitly states that formerly advertised claims were untrue. Also called *counteradvertising.*

cost-benefit analysis An economic school of jurisprudence in which all costs and benefits of a law are given monetary values. Those laws with the highest ratios of benefits to costs are then preferable to those with lower ratios.

counterclaim A claim made by the defendant against the plaintiff that is filed along with the defendant's answer.

course of dealing Previous commercial transactions between the same parties.

course of performance The history of dealings between the parties in the particular contract at issue.

court of appellate jurisdiction See **appellate court.**

court of original jurisdiction See **trial court.**

covenant not to compete An agreement not to compete against a party for a set period of time within a designated geographic area.

cover A buyer's right to substitute goods for those due under a sales or lease agreement when the seller provides nonconforming goods.

creditor An entity to which a debtor owes money.

creditor beneficiary A third party who benefits from a contract in which the promisor agrees to pay the promisee's debt.

creditors' meeting A meeting of all the creditors listed in the required schedule for liquidation.

criminal law A classification of law involving the rights and responsibilities an individual has with respect to the public as a whole.

critical thinking in the legal context Examining a legal opinion to search for potential problems in the reasoning.

critical thinking skills The ability to understand the structure and worth of an argument by evaluating the facts, issue, reasons, and conclusion of that argument.

cross-licensing An illegal contractual arrangement in which two or more parties license each other to use their specified intellectual property *only* on the condition that neither licenses anyone else to use the property without the other's consent.

cure A breaching party's right to provide conforming goods when nonconforming goods were initially delivered; subject to a reasonable time test.

cyber terrorist A hacker whose intention is the exploitation of a target computer or network to create a serious impact, such as the crippling of a communications network or the sabotage of a business or organization, which may have an impact on millions of citizens if the terrorist's attack is successful.

D

de facto **corporation** Latin for "corporation in fact"; a corporation that has not substantially met the requirements of the state incorporation statutes.

de jure **corporation** Latin for "lawful corporation"; a corporation that has met the mandatory statutory provisions and thus received its certificate of incorporation.

debt securities Securities that represent loans to a corporation.

debtor A party that owes money to another party.

deceptive advertising The practice of advertising with claims that mislead or could mislead a reasonable consumer.

defamation A false statement or an action that harms the reputation or character of an individual, business, product, group, government, or nation.

default Failure to make payments on a loan.

default judgment Judgment for the plaintiff that occurs when the defendant fails to respond to the complaint.

defective corporation A corporation about which an error or omission was made during its incorporation process.

defendant The person, party, or entity against whom a civil or criminal lawsuit is filed in a court of law.

delegatee A third party who is not part of the original contract but to whom duties to perform are transferred by one of the contracting parties (a delegator).

delegation A contracting party's (a delegator's) transfer of his or her duty to perform to a third party who is not part of the original contract (a delegatee).

delegator A party in a contract who transfers his or her duties to perform to a third party who is not a part of the original contract (a delegatee).

demand instrument A type of draft that allows the payee to demand payment at any time from a holder.

deposition A pretrial sworn and recorded testimony of a witness that is acquired out of court with no judge present.

digital cash Money stored electronically in place of physical currency.

directed verdict A ruling by the judge, after the plaintiff has put forward his or her case but before any evidence is put forward by the defendant, in favor of the defendant because the plaintiff has failed to present the minimum amount of evidence necessary to establish his or her claim.

discharge A written federal court order signed by a bankruptcy judge stating that the debtor is immune from creditor actions to collect debt; i.e., a release from liability.

discharged Released from liability for a negotiable instrument.

disclosed principal A principal whose identity is known to a third party. The third party is aware that the agent is making an agreement on behalf of the principal.

discovery The pretrial phase in a lawsuit during which each party requests relevant documents and other evidence from the other side in an attempt to "discover" pertinent facts and avoid any surprises in the courtroom during the trial. Discovery tools include requests for admissions, interrogatories, depositions, requests for inspection, and document production requests.

dishonored Refused; specifically, a payment that has been refused despite a holder's presenting an instrument in a timely and proper manner.

disparagement A business tort that occurs when a statement is intentionally used to defame a business product or service.

disparate impact A form of discrimination that arises when an employer's policy or practice appears to apply to everyone equally but its actual effect is that it disproportionately limits employment opportunities for a protected class.

disparate treatment A form of intentional discrimination in which an employee is hired, fired, denied a promotion, or the like, based on membership in a protected class.

dissolution The change in the relation of partners caused by any partner's ceasing to be associated with the carrying on of the partnership's business.

distributorship A type of franchise in which the franchisor manufactures a product and licenses a dealer to sell the product in an exclusive territory.

district court A trial court in the federal system.

dividend A distribution of corporate profits or income ordered by the directors and paid to the shareholders.

domestic corporation A corporation in the state in which it is incorporated.

donee beneficiary A third party who benefits from a contract in which a promisor agrees to give a gift to the third party.

dormant commerce clause A restriction on states' authority that is implied in the commerce clause of the U.S. Constitution: The power given to Congress to enact legislation that affects interstate commerce in effect prohibits a state from passing legislation that improperly burdens interstate commerce.

draft An instrument validating an order by a drawer to a drawee to pay a payee.

drawee The party that must obey an order. In the context of banking, the drawee is the bank that must pay the funds ordered by a customer's check.

drawer The party that writes an order, or the person who writes a check.

due diligence defense A defense in which the defendant argues that he or she applied the appropriate degree of attention, care, and research expected of a party in a given situation and had reasonable grounds to believe that certain facts and statements were accurate and had no omission of material facts.

due process clause A clause in the Fifth Amendment of the U.S. Constitution providing that the government cannot deprive an individual of life, liberty, or property without a fair and just hearing.

durable power of attorney A document that specifies that an agent's authority is intended to continue beyond the principal's incapacitation.

duress Any unlawful act or threat exercised on a person whereby the person is forced to enter into an agreement or to perform some other act against his or her will.

duty The standard of care a defendant must meet in order to not subject a person in the position of the plaintiff to an unreasonable risk of harm.

duty of accounting An agent's obligation to keep an accurate account of the transactions of money and property made on behalf of the principal.

duty of cooperation A principal's obligation to assist an agent in the performance of the agent's duties and not to interfere with reasonable conduct of the agent.

duty of loyalty An agent's obligation to act in the interest of the principal.

duty of notification An agent's obligation to inform the principal of the agent's actions on the principal's behalf and of all relevant information.

duty of obedience An agent's obligation to follow the lawful instruction and direction of the principal.

duty of performance An agent's obligation to perform the duties specified in the agency agreement and to do so with reasonable skill and care.

duty of reimbursement and indemnification A principal's obligation to reimburse an agent for any expenses or losses incurred by the agent on the principal's behalf.

duty to compensate A principal's obligation to pay an agent for his or her services.

duty to provide safe working conditions A principal's obligation to provide proper equipment, suitable premises, and a safe working environment in accordance with federal and state statutes.

E

easement An irrevocable right to use some part of another's land for a specific purpose without taking anything from it.

Electronic Communications Privacy Act of 1986 (ECPA) Federal law that extended employees' privacy rights to electronic forms of communication including e-mail and cellular phones; outlaws the intentional interception of electronic communications and the intentional disclosure or use of the information obtained through such interception.

electronic fund transfer (EFT) The transfer of funds by an electronic terminal, telephone, or computer.

embezzlement A wrongful conversion of another's funds or property by one who is lawfully in possession of those funds or that property.

e-money Electronic money.

Employee Retirement Income Security Act (ERISA) Federal law that sets minimum standards for most voluntarily established pension and health plans in private industry to provide protection for individuals in these plans.

enabling legislation A statute that specifies the name, functions, and specific powers of an administrative agency and grants the agency broad powers for the purpose of serving the "public interest, convenience, and necessity."

endorsee One who receives an endorsement.

endorsement for deposit or collection only The most common type of endorsement, providing that the instrument can only be deposited into an account.

endorser One who issues an endorsement.

English rule A rule that states that the first assignee to give notice of assignment to the obligor is the party with rights to the contract.

entrustment The transfer of goods to a merchant who ordinarily deals in that type of goods. If the merchant subsequently sells them to a good-faith third-party purchaser, the buyer acquires good title to the goods.

equal dignity rule A rule requiring that contracts that would normally fall under the statute of frauds and need a writing if negotiated by the principal must be in writing even if negotiated by an agent.

Equal Pay Act of 1963 (EPA) Federal law that prohibits an employer from paying workers of one gender less than the wages paid to employees of the opposite gender for work that requires equal skill, effort, and responsibility.

equal protection clause A clause in the Fourteenth Amendment of the U.S. Constitution that prevents states from denying "the equal protection of the laws" to any citizen. This clause implies that all citizens are created equal.

equity securities Securities that represent ownership in a corporation.

establishment clause One of two provisions in the First Amendment of the U.S. Constitution that protect citizens' freedom of religion. It prohibits (1) the establishment of a national religion by Congress and (2) the preference of one religion over another or of religion over nonreligious philosophies in general.

ethical dilemma A question about how one should behave that requires one to reflect about the advantages and disadvantages of the optional choices for various stakeholders.

ethical guideline A simple tool to help determine whether an action is moral.

ethics The study and practice of decisions about what is good or right.

exchange tender offer A type of takeover in which the aggressor corporation offers to exchange the target shareholders' current stock for stock in the aggressor's corporation.

exculpatory clause A statement in a contract that frees one party (usually the drafter of the agreement) from all liability arising out of performance of the contract; generally based on factors such as consumer ignorance or a great deal of unexplained fine print that serve to deprive the less powerful party of a meaningful choice.

executed A term applied to a contract in which all of the terms have been fully performed.

executive agency An agency that is typically located within the executive branch, under one of the cabinet-level departments. The agency head is appointed by the president with the advice and consent of the Senate.

executive order A directive that has the force of law but is issued by a governor or the president.

executory A term applied to a contract in which not all of the terms have been fully performed.

express authority The authority of an agent that arises when the principal explicitly instructs the agent to do something. Also called *actual authority.*

express condition A condition specifically and explicitly stated in a contract and usually preceded by words such as *conditioned on, if, provided that,* or *when.*

express contract A contract in which all the terms are clearly set forth in either written or spoken words.

express warranty Any description of a good's physical nature or its use, in either general or specific circumstances, that becomes part of a contract.

expressed agency An agency created in written or oral agreement. Also called *agency by agreement.*

extortion A criminal offense in which a person obtains money, property, and/or services from another by wrongfully threatening or inflicting harm to his or her person, property, or reputation. Also called *blackmail.*

F

Fair Labor Standards Act (FLSA) Federal law that requires that a minimum wage of a specified amount be paid to all employees in covered industries; also mandates that employees who work more than 40 hours in a week be paid no less than 1½ times their regular wage for all hours beyond 40 worked in a given week.

fair-use doctrine The lawful use of a limited, noncommercial portion of another's work for purposes of criticism, comment, news reporting, teaching, scholarship, or research.

False Claims Act An act that allows employees to sue employers on behalf of the federal government for fraud against the government. The employee retains a share of the recovery as a reward for his or her efforts.

false pretense Materially false representation of an existing fact, with knowledge of the falsity of the representation and with the intent to defraud.

Family and Medical Leave Act (FMLA) Federal act requiring that employers provide all eligible employees with up to 12 weeks of leave during any 12-month period for several family-related occurrences (e.g., birth of a child, care of a sick spouse).

federal preemption A principle asserting the supremacy of federal legislation over state legislation when both pertain to the same subject matter.

Federal Register The government publication in which an agency publishes each proposed rule, along with an explanation of the legal authority for issuing the rule and a description of how the public can participate in the rule-making process, and later publishes the final rule.

federalism A system of government in which power is divided between a central authority and constituent political units.

fee simple absolute An ownership interest in which the holder has exclusive rights to ownership and possession of the land; the most comprehensive type of estate.

felony A serious crime, such as murder, rape, or robbery, that is punishable by imprisonment for more than one year or death.

fictitious payee Someone having no right to payment. The UCC fictitious-payee rule governs the liability of companies and their endorsed checks: Any check made out to a fictitious payee and endorsed must be honored and is not considered a forgery.

fiduciary A person who has a duty to act primarily for another person's benefit.

financing statement A document that lists the names and addresses of all the parties involved in the transaction, a description of the collateral, and the signature of the debtor.

firm offer An offer made in writing and giving assurances that it will be irrevocable for not longer than three months despite a lack of consideration for the irrevocability.

first appearance The initial appearance of an arrested individual before a judge who determines whether there was probable cause for the arrest. If the judge ascertains that probable cause did not exist, the individual is freed.

first-assignment-in-time rule A rule that states that the first party granted the assignment is the party correctly entitled to the contractual right.

food disparagement A tort that provides ranchers and farmers with a cause of action when someone spreads false information about the safety of a food product.

for-profit corporation A corporation whose objective is to make a profit.

foreign corporation A corporation in a state in which it conducts business but is not incorporated.

forgery A criminal falsification by imitating, impersonating, or altering a real document with the intent to deceive or defraud.

formal contract A contract that must have a special form or must be created in a specific manner.

formal rule making A type of rule making that is used when legislation requires a formal hearing process with a complete transcript; consists of publication of the proposed rule in the *Federal Register,* a public hearing, publication of formal findings, and publication of the final rule if adopted.

franchise A business arrangement between an owner of a trade name or trademark and a person who sells goods or services under the trade name or trademark.

franchise agreement A contract whereby a company (the franchisor) grants permission (a license) to another entity (the franchisee) to use the franchisor's name, trademark, or copyright in the operation of a business and associated sale of goods in return for payment.

franchisee The seller of goods or services under a trade name or trademark in a franchise.

franchisor The owner of the trade name or trademark in a franchise.

fraud An intentional deception that causes harm to another.

fraud in the factum A liability defense available to a party who signs a negotiable instrument without knowing that it is a negotiable instrument.

fraudulent misrepresentation (1) The tort that occurs when a misrepresentation is made with the intent to facilitate personal

gain and with the knowledge that it is false. (2) In contracts, a false representation of a material fact that is consciously false and is intended to mislead the other party.

fraudulent transfer A transfer of property made with intent to defraud creditors or made for an amount significantly lower than the property's fair market value within two years of filing for bankruptcy.

free-exercise clause A clause in the First Amendment of the U.S. Constitution which states that government (state and federal) cannot make a law "prohibiting the free exercise" of religion. This clause is interpreted to include absolute freedom to believe and freedom to act that may face state restriction.

Freedom of Information Act (FOIA) Federal legislation that mandates and facilitates public access to government information and records, including records about oneself. Sensitive information (e.g., on national security) is excluded.

full faith and credit clause The clause of the U.S. Constitution (Article IV, Section 1) mandating that each state must recognize, respect, and enforce the public records, legislative acts, and judicial decisions of the other states.

future interest A person's present right to property ownership and possession in the future.

G

gambling An agreement in which a party pays consideration (money placed during bets) for the chance, or opportunity, to obtain an amount of money or property.

general partnership A partnership in which the partners divide profits and management responsibility and share unlimited personal liability for the partnership's debts.

good faith Honesty in fact.

Good Samaritan statute A statute that exempts from liability a person, such as a physician passerby, who voluntarily renders aid to an injured person but negligently, but not unreasonably negligently, causes injury while rendering the aid.

good title Title acquired from someone who already owns the goods free and clear.

goods All physically existing things that are movable at the time of identification to the contract for sale.

goods-in-bailment contract A type of contract in which the purchased goods are in some kind of storage under the control of a third party, such as a warehouseman.

gratuitous agent An agent who acts without being paid for his or her services.

gross negligence An action committed with extreme reckless disregard for the property or life of another person.

H

hacker A person who illegally accesses or enters another person's or a company's computer system to obtain information or to steal money.

half-truth Information that is true but is not complete.

historical school A school of jurisprudence that uses traditions as the model for future laws and behavior. Also called *tradition* or *custom.*

holder A party in possession of a negotiable instrument.

holder in due course (HDC) An individual who acquires a negotiable instrument in good faith.

hostile takeover A takeover to which the management of the target corporation objects.

hybrid agencies An agency that has characteristics of both executive and independent agencies.

hybrid rule making A type of rule making that combines features of formal and informal rule making; consists of publication in the *Federal Register,* a written-comment period, and an informal public hearing with restricted cross-examination.

I

identification with the vulnerable A school of jurisprudence which holds that society should be fair. Particular attention is therefore paid to the poor, the ill, and the elderly.

illusory promise A situation in which a party appears to commit to something but really has not committed to anything. It is not a promise and thus not consideration.

implied authority The authority of an agent that arises by inference from the words and actions of the principal.

implied condition A condition that is not specifically and explicitly stated but is inferred from the nature and language of the contract.

implied contract A contract that arises not from words of agreement but from the conduct of the parties.

implied warranty of fitness for a particular purpose An assurance, inferred in any UCC sale, whereby when a seller or lessor knows or has reason to know (1) why the buyer or lessee is purchasing or leasing the goods in question and (2) that the buyer or lessee is relying on him or her to make the selection, the buyer or lessee has an enforceable warranty if such assurance is false.

implied warranty of merchantability An assurance, inferred in every sale unless clearly disclaimed, that merchantable goods will conform to a reasonable performance expectation. The purchaser must have purchased or leased the good from a merchant.

implied warranty of trade usage An assurance, inferred in the context of certain UCC sales, depending on the circumstances, that can be created through a well-accepted course of dealing or trade usage.

imposter rule A rule that holds that if one obtains a negotiable instrument by impersonating another and endorses it with the impersonated party's signature, the loss falls on the drawer of the instrument.

in pari delicto In equal fault.

in personam **jurisdiction** The power of a court to require that a party (usually the defendant) or a witness come before the court. The court must have personal jurisdiction to enforce its judgments or orders against a party. *In personam* jurisdiction extends only to the state's borders in the state court system and across the court's geographic district in the federal system. Also called *personal jurisdiction* **and** *jurisdiction in personam.*

in rem **jurisdiction** The power of a court over the property or status of an out-of-state defendant located within the court's jurisdiction area.

incidental beneficiary One who unintentionally gains a benefit from a contract between other parties.

incorporator An individual who applies for incorporation on behalf of a corporation.

independent agency An agency that is typically not located within a government department. It is governed by a board of commissioners, who are appointed by the president with the advice and consent of the Senate.

independent contractor A person who is hired to perform a task for another but who is not the other's employee.

indictment Finding by the grand jury that there is adequate evidence to charge the defendant and bring him or her to trial.

indivisible contract A contract that requires complete performance by both parties.

industry guides Interpretations of consumer laws created by the FTC to encourage businesses to stop unlawful behavior.

informal contract A contract that requires no formalities.

informal rule making A type of rule making in which an agency publishes a proposed rule in the *Federal Register,* considers public comments, and then publishes the final rule.

information A document prepared by the prosecutor and presented to the magistrate, demonstrating that there is enough evidence to charge the defendant and bring him or her to trial.

injunction A court order either forcing a party to do something or prohibiting a party from doing something.

innocent misrepresentation A false statement about a fact material to an agreement that the person who made the statement believed to be true.

insider trading Illegal buying or selling of a corporation's stock or other securities by corporate insiders such as officers and directors, in breach of a fiduciary duty or other relationship of trust and confidence, while in possession of material, nonpublic information about the security.

insolvent debtor A debtor who cannot pay debts in a timely fashion.

instrument A writing that serves as evidence of the right to payment of money.

integrated contract A written contract intended to be the complete and final representation of the parties' agreement.

intellectual property Intangible property that is the product of one's mind and not one's hands.

intended beneficiary A third party to a contract whom the contracting parties intended to benefit directly from their contact.

intent The intended purpose or goal of an action, especially in a contract.

intentional interference with contract The tort that occurs when someone intentionally takes an action that will cause a person to breach a contract that she or he has with another.

intentional misrepresentation In a contract, a false representation of a material fact made by a party who either knows or believes that the factual claim is false or knows that there is no basis for the assertion. Scienter is clear.

intentional tort A civil wrong resulting from an intentional act committed on the person, property, or economic interest of another. Intentional torts include assault, battery, conversion, false imprisonment, intentional infliction of emotional distress, trespass to land, and trespass to chattels.

intermediate scrutiny A standard of review under which a law must be necessary to achieve a substantial, or important, government interest and it must be narrowly tailored to that interest.

interpretive rule A rule that does not create any new rights or duties but is merely a detailed statement of the agency's interpretation of an existing law, including the actions a party is to take to be in compliance with the law.

interrogatories A formal set of written questions that one party to a lawsuit asks the opposing party as part of the pretrial discovery process in order to clarify matters of evidence and help determine in advance what facts will be presented at any trial in the case. The questions must be answered in writing under oath or under penalty of perjury within a specified time. Also called *requests for further information.*

Interstate Commerce Commission (ICC) The first federal administrative agency; created to regulate the anticompetitive conduct of railroads.

J

joint and several liability A type of liability in which a third party can choose to sue the partners separately or to sue all partners jointly in one action.

joint stock company A partnership agreement in which company members hold transferable shares while all the goods of the company are held in the names of the partners.

joint venture An association between two or more parties wherein the parties share profits and management responsibilities with respect to a specific project.

jointly liable A term applied to partners who share liability for the partnership's debts.

judicial review The power of a court to review legislative and executive actions, such as a law or an official act of a government employee or agent to determine whether they are constitutional.

jurisdiction The power of a court to hear cases and render binding decisions.

L

lack of genuine assent A defense to the agreement of a contract in which the offeree claims that the offeror secured the agreement through improper means, such as duress, fraud, undue influence, or misrepresentation.

Landrum-Griffin Act Federal legislation that primarily governs the internal operations of labor unions. It requires financial disclosures by unions, establishes penalties for financial abuses by union officials and includes "Labor's Bill of Rights" to protect employees from their own unions.

last-clear-chance doctrine A doctrine used by the plaintiff when the defendant establishes contributory negligence. If the plaintiff can establish that the defendant had the last opportunity to avoid the accident, the plaintiff may still recover, despite being contributorily negligent.

law Rules of conduct in any organized society that are enforced by the governing authority of the community.

lease A transfer of the right to possession and use of goods for a term in return for consideration.

leasehold A possessory interest, but not an ownership interest, transferred by contract.

legal entity Any individual, proprietorship, partnership, corporation, association, or other organization that has, in the eyes of the law, the capacity to form an agreement, and the ability to assume an obligation and to discharge an indebtedness.

legal object A purpose that does not violate a statute or public policy.

legal positivism A school of jurisprudence which holds that because society requires authority, a legal and authoritarian hierarchy should exist. When a law is made, therefore, obedience is expected because authority created it.

legal realism A school of jurisprudence which holds that context must be considered as well as law. Context includes factors such as economic conditions and social conditions.

lessee A person who acquires the right to possession and use of goods under a lease.

lessor A person who transfers the right to possession and use of goods under a lease.

letter of credit A binding document that a buyer can request from a bank to guarantee that the payment for goods will be made to the seller.

leveraged buyout (LBO) A takeover-resistance strategy in which a group within the target corporation buys all the corporate stock held by the public, thereby turning the company into a privately held corporation.

liability without fault A legal term that imposes responsibility for damages regardless of the existence of negligence. Also called *strict liability.*

license A revocable right to temporarily use another's property.

life estate An ownership interest in which the holder has the right to possess the property until her or his death.

limited liability company (LLC) An unincorporated business that is taxed like a partnership, with the members paying personal income taxes, and has the limited liability of a corporation.

limited liability partnership (LLP) A partnership in which all the partners assume liability for any partner's professional malpractice to the extent of the partnership's assets.

limited partnership (LP) A partnership consisting of at least one general partner and at least one limited partner in which the general partners assume all liability for the partnership's debts and the limited partners assume no liability beyond their originally invested capital.

liquidated damages Damages specified as a term of the contract, before a breach of contract occurs.

liquidated debt Debt for which there is no dispute between the parties about the fact that money is owed and the amount of money owed.

liquidation The process in which a debtor turns over all assets to a trustee.

long-arm statute A statute that enables a court to obtain jurisdiction against an out-of-state defendant as long as the defendant has sufficient minimum contacts within the state, such as committing a tort or doing business in the state.

M

mailbox rule The principle which holds that an acceptance is valid when it is placed in the mailbox, whereas a revocation is effective only when received by the offeree. In some jurisdictions the mailbox rule has been expanded to faxes.

maker A person who has promised to pay a set sum to the holder of a promissory note or certificate of deposit.

manufacturing arrangement A type of franchise in which the franchisor provides the franchisee with a formula or necessary ingredient to manufacture a product.

material breach A substantial breach of a significant term or terms of a contract that excuses the nonbreaching party from further performance under the contract and gives the nonbreaching party the right to recover damages.

med-arb A type of dispute resolution process in which both parties agree to start out in mediation and, if unsuccessful, to move on to arbitration.

mediation A type of intensive negotiation in which disputing parties select a neutral party to help facilitate communication and suggest ways for the parties to solve their dispute.

members Owners of a limited liability company.

mens rea Latin for "guilty mind"; the mental state accompanying a wrongful behavior.

merchant A person who regularly sells goods as his or her business or trade or employs people to sell those goods is a merchant of those goods. Also, anyone who works for that person selling those goods is also a merchant. Plus, anyone who holds himself or herself out as a "merchant" or a "dealer" will be treated as a merchant under the as well.

merger A combination of two or more corporations in which only one of the corporations continues to exist.

merger clause A clause in a written agreement within the statute of frauds that states that the written agreement accurately reflects the final, complete version of the agreement.

minitrial A type of conflict resolution in which lawyers for each side present their arguments to a neutral adviser, who then offers an opinion as to what the verdict would be if the case went to trial. This decision is not binding.

Miranda rights The rights that are read to an arrested individual by a law enforcement agent before the individual is questioned about the commission of a crime.

mirror-image rule The principle which holds that the terms of the acceptance must mirror the terms of the offer; if the terms of the acceptance do not mirror the terms of the offer, no contract is formed and the attempted acceptance is a counteroffer.

misappropriation theory A theory of insider trading that holds that if an individual wrongfully acquires (misappropriates) and uses inside information for trading for his or her personal gain, that person is liable for insider trading.

misdemeanor A crime that is less serious than a felony and is punishable by a fine and/or imprisonment for less than one year.

misrepresentation An untruthful assertion by one of the parties about a material fact.

mistake An erroneous belief about the facts of a contract at the time the contract is concluded. When a mistake occurs, legal assent is absent.

mixed sale A contract that combines a good with a service.

mock trial A contrived or imitation trial, with a jury created by the attorneys to assist them in preparing for the actual trial by enabling them to test theories, experiment with arguments, and try to predict the outcome of the real trial.

model law See **uniform laws.**

modified comparative negligence A defense accepted in some states whereby the defendant is not liable for the percentage of harm that he or she can prove can be attributed to the plaintiff's own negligence if the plaintiff 's negligence is responsible for less than 50 percent of the harm; if the defendant establishes that the plaintiff's negligence caused more than 50 percent of the harm, the defendant has no liability.

modify An appellate court decision that grants an alternative remedy in a case; granted when the court finds that the decision of the lower court was correct but the remedy was not.

monetary damages Money claimed by or ordered paid to a party to compensate for injury or loss caused by the wrong of the opposite party.

money order A signed document indicating that funds are to be paid from the drawee to the drawer.

motion An application by a party to a judge or a court in a civil case requesting an order in favor of the applicant.

motion for judgment on the pleadings In a civil case, a request made by either party, after pleadings have been entered, that asks a judge or a court to issue a judgment.

motion for summary judgment In a civil case, a request made by either party that asks a judge or a court to promptly and expeditiously dispose of a case without a trial. Any evidence or information that would be admissible at trial under the rules of evidence, such as affidavits, interrogatories, depositions, and admissions, may be considered on a motion for summary judgment. A court may hold oral arguments or decide the motion on the basis of the parties' briefs and supporting documentation alone.

motion to dismiss A request by the defendant that asks a judge or a court in a civil case to dismiss the case because even if all the allegations are true, the plaintiff is not entitled to any legal relief. Also called *demurrer.*

movability The quality of a negotiable instrument that ensures it is mobile and available.

multiple-product order A form of cease-and-desist order issued by the FTC that applies not only to a specified product but also to other products produced by the same firm.

mutual mistake The result of an error by both parties about a material fact, i.e., one that is important in the context of a particular contract.

N

National Labor Relations Board (NLRB) An administrative agency created by the Wagner Act to interpret and enforce the National Labor Relations Act.

natural law A school of jurisprudence that recognizes the existence of higher law, or law that is morally superior to human laws.

negligence Behavior that creates an unreasonable risk of harm to others.

negligence per se A doctrine that allows a judge or jury to infer duty and breach of duty from the fact that a defendant violated a criminal statute that was designed to prevent the type of harm that the plaintiff incurred.

negligent misrepresentation A false statement of material fact made by a party who thinks it is true but who would have known the truth about the fact had he or she used reasonable care to discover or reveal it.

negligent tort A civil wrong that occurs when the defendant acts in a way that subjects other people to an unreasonable risk of harm (i.e., the defendant is careless, to someone else's detriment). Negligence claims are usually used to achieve compensation for accidents and injuries.

negotiable instrument A written document signed by a person who makes an unconditional promise to pay a specific sum of money on demand or at a certain time to the holder of the instrument; an acceptable medium for exchanging value from one person to another.

negotiation (1) A bargaining process in which disputing parties interact informally to attempt to resolve their dispute. (2) The transfer of the rights to a negotiable instrument from one party to another.

no-par shares Stock shares that do not have a par value.

nolo contendere A plea in which the defendant does not admit guilt but agrees not to contest the charges.

nominal damages Monetary damages awarded to a plaintiff in a very small amount, typically $1 to $5, to signify that the plaintiff has been wronged by the defendant even though the plaintiff suffered no compensable harm.

nondisclosure A failure to provide pertinent information about a projected contract.

nonprofit corporation A corporation that operates for educational, charitable, social, religious, civic, or humanitarian purposes, rather than to earn a profit.

note A promise by the maker of the note to pay the payee of the note.

notice-and-comment rule making See **informal rule making.**

novation In a contract, the substitution of a third party for one of the original parties; the duties remain the same under the contract, but one original party is discharged and the third party takes that original party's place.

O

obligee A contractual party who agreed to receive something from the other party.

obligor A contractual party who agreed to do something for the other party.

Occupational Safety and Health Act of 1970 (OSHA) Federal law that established the Occupational Safety and Health

Administration, the agency responsible for setting safety standards under the act and enforcing the act through inspections and the levying of fines against violators.

offer A key factor is the agreement element of a contract; consists of the terms and conditions set by one party, the offeror, and presented to another party, the offeree.

Omnibus Crime Control and Safe Streets Act of 1968
Federal statute banning employers from listening to the private telephone conversations of employees or disclosing the contents of these conversations. Employers may ban personal calls and monitor calls for compliance as long as they discontinue listening to any conversation once they determine it is personal.

option contract An agreement whereby the offeree gives the offeror a piece of consideration in exchange for the offeror's agreement to hold the offer open for the specified period of time.

order (1) An order to appear and bring specified documents. (2) A binding decision rendered by a judge.

order instrument An instrument payable to a specific, named payee.

order of relief An order stating that bankruptcy proceedings can continue.

output contract An agreement whereby the seller guarantees to sell everything he or she produces to one buyer and no quantity is stated; valid under the UCC but not under common law.

P

par-value shares Stock shares that have a fixed face value noted on the stock certificate.

parol evidence rule A common law rule that states that oral evidence of an agreement made prior to or contemporaneously with a written agreement is inadmissible when the parties intend to have the written agreement be the complete and final version of their agreement.

partial performance An exception to the statute of frauds in which the performance of portions of an unwritten agreement by one or both parties can constitute proof that an oral contract exists between the parties.

partially disclosed principal A principal whose identity is not known by a third party, although the third party is aware that the agent is making an agreement on behalf of a principal. Also called *unidentified principal*.

partnership A voluntary association between two or more people who co-own a business for profit.

past consideration Something given or done in the past by one party that later prompts a promise by another party. As such, nothing has been given in exchange, and the court will not enforce the promise.

patent Protection that grants the holder the exclusive right to produce, sell and use the object of the patent for 20 years; can be obtained for a product, process, invention, or machine or a plant produced by asexual reproduction.

payee The party that receives the benefit of an order (check, etc.).

peremptory challenge In a jury trial, the right of the plaintiff and the defendant in jury selection to reject, without stating a reason, a certain number of potential jurors who appear to have an unfavorable bias.

perfect tender rule Requirement that the seller deliver the goods in conformity with the contract, down to the last detail.

perfection The series of legal steps a secured party takes to protect its right in the collateral from the other creditors who wish to have their debt returned through the same collateral.

personal defense A liability defense that is not applicable to holders in due course.

personal property Any property that is not land or permanently affixed to the land.

petit jury A group of 6 to 12 citizens who are summoned to and sworn by the court to hear evidence presented by both sides and render a verdict in a trial.

petty offense A minor crime that is punishable by a small fine and/or imprisonment for less than six months in a jail.

plaintiff The person or party who initiates a lawsuit (also known as an action) before a court by filing a complaint with the clerk of the court against the defendant(s). Also known as *claimant* or *complainant*.

plea bargain An agreement in which the prosecutor agrees to reduce charges, drop charges, or recommend a certain sentence if the defendant pleads guilty.

pledge The transfer of collateral to the secured party.

police power Power retained by each state to pass laws that protect the health, safety, and welfare of its citizens.

policy statement A general statement about the directions in which an agency intends to proceed with respect to its rule-making or enforcement activities; has no binding impact on anyone.

political speech Speech that is used to support political candidates or referenda. It is given a high level of protection by the First Amendment as compared to other types of speech.

posteffective period In securities registration, the period that begins when the SEC declares the registration statement effective and ends when the issuer sells all securities offered or withdraws them from sale.

posttrial motion A request filed after a trial is over, by either party, to the trial court. A motion for new trial, a motion for judgment notwithstanding the verdict (JNOV), or a motion to amend or nullify the judgment are types of posttrial motions.

power of attorney A specific form of express authority, granting an agent specific powers.

precedent A tool used by judges to make rulings on cases on the basis of key similarities to previous cases.

preexisting duty A promise to do something that one is already obligated to do. It is not considered valid consideration.

preferential payment A payment made by an insolvent debtor that gives preferential treatment to one creditor over another.

preferred stock Stock that conveys preferences to its holders with respect to assets and dividends.

prefiling period In securities registration, the period that begins when an issuer starts to think about issuing securities and ends when the issuer files the registration statement and prospectus with the SEC.

Pregnancy Discrimination Act of 1987 (PDA) Federal law that amended Title VII of the Civil Rights Act of 1964, expanding the definition of sex discrimination to include discrimination based on pregnancy.

prejudicial error An error of law that is so significant that it affects the outcome of the case.

prenuptial agreement An agreement two parties enter into before marriage that clearly states the ownership rights each party enjoys in the other party's property. To be enforceable, the agreements must be in writing.

presentment The act of making a demand for the drawee to pay.

presentment warranty A warranty covering the parties accepting an instrument for payment; created to ensure that the accepting or paying party is paying the proper party.

pretrial An event that includes consultation with attorneys, pleadings, the discovery process, and the pretrial conference.

pretrial conference An informal meeting of the judge with the attorneys representing the parties before the actual trial begins.

prima facie Latin for "at first view"; term applied to evidence that is sufficient to raise a presumption that a wrong occurred.

primarily liable Liable for paying the amount designated on an instrument when it is presented for payment.

principal The party that an agent's authority can bind or act on behalf of.

principle of rights The principle that judges the morality of a decision on the basis of how it affects the rights of all those involved.

Privacy Act Federal law that mandates that a federal agency may not disclose information about an individual to other agencies or organizations without that individual's written consent.

private corporation A corporation that is created by private persons and does not have government duties.

private law Law that involves suits between private individuals or groups.

private nuisance A nuisance that affects only a single or very limited number of individuals.

private trial An ADR method in which a referee is selected and paid by the disputing parties to offer a legally binding judgment in a dispute.

privileges and immunities clause Clause in the U.S. Constitution requiring that a state grant citizens of other states the same legal benefits that it grants its own citizens.

probable cause Any essential element and/or standard by which a lawful officer may make a valid arrest, conduct a personal or property search, or obtain a warrant.

procedural due process The requirement that a government must use fair procedures before depriving a person of his or her life, liberty, or property.

procedural unconscionability Unconscionability that derives from the process of making a contract.

proceeds Something that is exchanged for a debtor's sold collateral.

profit The right to go onto someone's land and take part of the land or a product of it away from the land.

promisee In a third-party beneficiary contract, the party to the contract who owes something to the promisor in exchange for the promise made to the third party.

promisor In a third-party beneficiary contract, the party to the contract who made the promise that benefits the third party.

promissory estoppel The legal enforcement of an otherwise unenforceable contract due to a party's detrimental reliance on the contract.

promoter A person who begins the corporate creation and organization process.

prospectus A written document filed with the SEC that contains a description of a security and other financial information regarding the company offering the security; also distributed as an advertising tool to potential investors.

proximate cause The extent to which, as a matter of policy, a defendant may be held liable for the consequences of his or her actions. In the majority of states, proximate cause requires that the plaintiff and the plaintiff's damages were foreseeable at the time of the accident. In the minority of states, proximate cause exists if the defendant's actions led to the plaintiff's harm.

proxy A writing signed by a shareholder that authorizes the individual named in the writing to exercise the shareholder's votes (corresponding to his or her shares of stock) at a shareholders' meeting.

proxy solicitation The process of obtaining authority to vote on behalf of shareholders.

public corporation A corporation that is created by government to help administer law.

public figure privilege A special right, immunity, or permission given to people that allows them to make any statements about public figures, typically politicians and entertainers, without being held liable for defamation for any false statement made without malice.

public law Law that involves suits between private individuals or groups and their governments.

publicly held corporation A corporation whose stock is available to the public.

puffing The use of generalities and clear exaggerations.

punitive damages Compensation awarded to a plaintiff that goes beyond reimbursement for actual losses and is imposed to punish the defendant and deter such conduct in the future.

purchase-money security interest (PMSI) A security interest formed when a debtor uses borrowed money from the secured party to buy the collateral.

pure comparative negligence A defense accepted in some states whereby the defendant is not liable for the percentage of harm that he or she can prove can be attributed to the plaintiff's own negligence.

 Q

qualified endorsement An endorsement that does not bind the endorser to the negotiable instrument in the event that the creator does not honor that instrument.

quasi-contract A court-imposed contractual obligation to prevent unjust enrichment.

quasi *in rem* jurisdiction A type of jurisdiction exercised by a court over an out-of-state defendant's property that is within the jurisdictional boundaries of the court. It applies to personal suits against the defendant in which the property is not the source of the conflict but is sought as compensation by the plaintiff. Also called *attachment jurisdiction.*

question of fact A question about an event or characteristic in the case.

question of law An issue concerning the interpretation or application of a law.

R

Racketeer Influenced and Corrupt Organizations (RICO) Act A U.S. law that provides extended penalties for criminal acts performed as part of an ongoing criminal organization.

ratify To approve an unauthorized agent's signature on an instrument.

rational-basis test The lowest standard of review; requires that a law be designed to protect a legitimate state interest and be rationally related to that interest.

reaffirmation agreement An agreement in which the debtor agrees to pay a debt even though it could have been discharged in bankruptcy.

real defense A liability defense that applies universally to all parties.

real property Land and everything permanently attached to it.

reasonable person standard A measurement of the way members of society expect an individual to act in a given situation.

recognizance An obligation in which a party acknowledges in court that he or she will perform some specified act and/or pay a price on failure to do so.

red-herring prospectus A prospectus with a warning written in red print at the top of the page telling investors that the registration has been filed with the SEC but not yet approved.

reg-neg A type of rule making in which representatives of concerned interest groups and of the involved government agency participate in mediated bargaining sessions to reach an agreement, which is forwarded to the agency.

rejection Termination of a contract that occurs when an offeree does not accept the offer or terms of the contract.

relative permanence The quality of a negotiable instrument that ensures its longevity.

remand An appellate court decision that returns a case to the trial court for a new trial or for limited hearing on a specified subject matter; rendered when the court decides that an error was committed that may have affected the outcome of a case.

reply A response by the plaintiff to the defendant's counterclaim.

request to produce documents In a lawsuit, the right of a party to examine and copy the opposing party's papers that are relevant to the case. A legal request may be made and the categories of the documents must be stated to allow the other party to know what documents he or she must produce.

requirement contract An agreement whereby the buyer agrees to purchase all of his or her goods from one seller and no quantity is stated in the contract; valid under the UCC but not under common law.

res ipsa loquitur A doctrine that allows the judge or jury to infer that, more likely than not, the defendant's negligence was the cause of the plaintiff's harm, even though there is no direct evidence of the defendant's lack of due care.

rescind To cancel a contract.

rescission The termination of a contract.

respondeat superior Latin for "let the superior speak"; the principle by which liability for harm caused by an agent/employee is held by the principal/employer.

Restatements of the Law Summaries of common law rules in a particular area of the law. Restatements do not carry the weight of law but can be used to guide interpretations of particular cases.

restitution The return of any property given up under a contract.

restricted securities Securities that have limited transferability and are usually issued in a private placement.

retained earnings Profits that a corporation keeps.

reverse An appellate court decision that overturns the judgment of a lower court, concluding that the lower court was incorrect and its verdict cannot be allowed to stand.

revocation Termination of a contract that occurs when an offeror takes back the initial offer and annuls the opportunity for the offeree to accept the offer.

RICO Act See **Racketeer Influenced and Corrupt Organizations (RICO) Act.**

right of first refusal A method of restricting stock transferability whereby a corporation or its shareholders have the right to purchase any shares of stock offered for resale by a shareholder within a specified time frame.

right of survivorship The right that specific partnership property will pass on to the surviving partner(s).

rightfully dissolved A term applied to the dissolution of a partnership that does not violate its partnership agreement.

ripeness The readiness of a case for a decision to be made. The goal is to prevent premature litigation for a dispute that is insufficiently developed. A claim is not ripe for litigation if it rests on contingent future events that may not occur as anticipated or may not occur at all.

S

S corporation A corporation that enjoys the tax status of a partnership.

Sabbath laws Laws prohibiting the performance of certain activities on Sundays.

sale The passing of title from a seller to a buyer for a price.

sale-on-approval contract A contract in which the seller allows the buyer to take possession of the goods before deciding whether to complete the contract by making the purchase.

sale-or-return contract A contract in which the buyer and seller agree that the buyer may return the goods at a later time.

Sarbanes-Oxley Act An act that criminalizes specific non-audit services when provided by a registered accounting firm to an audit client; also increases the punishment for a number of white-collar offenses. Also known as the *Public Company Accounting Reform and Investor Protection Act of 2002.*

scienter Deliberately or knowingly.

search warrant A court order that authorizes law enforcement agents to search for or seize items specifically described in the warrant.

secondarily liable Liable for paying the amount designated on an instrument should the primarily liable party default.

secured interest An interest in personal property or fixtures that secures payment or performance to a creditor.

secured party The party that holds the interest in a secured property.

secured transaction A transaction in which the payment of a debt is guaranteed by personal property owned by the debtor.

security A financial instrument designated as a note, stock, or bond or any other instrument named in the Securities Act of 1933.

security agreement An agreement in which the debtor gives the secured interest to the secured party.

self-dealing Any instance in which directors or officers make decisions that violate their corporate duty of loyalty.

self-tender offer A takeover-resistance strategy in which the target corporation offers to buy its shareholders' stock.

service of process The procedure by which a court delivers a copy of the statement of claim or other legal documents, such as a summons, complaint, or subpoena, to the defendant.

severable contract A contract that contains multiple parts that can each be performed separately.

sexual harassment Unwelcome sexual advances, requests for sexual favors, and other verbal or physical conduct of a sexual nature that makes submission a condition of employment or a factor in employment decisions or that creates an intimidating, hostile, or offensive work environment. The two types are hostile environment and *quid pro quo.*

shadow jury Jury selection firms set up imitation juries who sit in during the actual trial and deliberate at the end of each day to evaluate for the attorneys how each side is doing.

shareholders Investors in a corporation, who own the corporation.

shareholder's derivative suit A lawsuit filed by a shareholder on behalf of the corporation.

shareholder's direct suit A lawsuit filed by a shareholder against the corporation.

shelter principle The principle that when an item is transferred, the transferee acquires all the rights the transferor had to the item.

short-swing profits Profits made from the sale of company stock within any six-month period by a statutory insider.

signature liability Liability attributed because of a party's signature on an instrument.

simple delivery contract Type of contract in which purchased goods are transferred to the buyer from the seller either at the time of the sale or sometime later by the seller's delivery.

slander of quality A business tort that occurs when false spoken statements criticize a business product or service and result in a loss of sales.

slander of title A business tort that occurs when false published statements are related to the ownership of the business property.

social responsibility of business The expectations that a community places on the actions of firms inside that community's borders.

sole proprietor The single person at the head of a sole proprietorship.

sole proprietorship A business in which one person (sole proprietor) is in control of the management and profits.

special damages See **consequential damages.**

special endorsement An endorser's signature accompanying the name of the endorsee.

special power of attorney A type of express authority that allows an agent to act on behalf of the principal only in regard to specifically outlined acts.

special qualified endorsement An endorser's signature accompanying the name of the endorsee.

specific performance An order of the court requiring that a nonbreaching party fulfill the terms of the contract.

stakeholders The groups of people affected by a firm's decisions.

stale check A check that is not presented to a bank within six months of its date.

standing The legal right of a party or an individual to bring a lawsuit by demonstrating to the court sufficient connection to and harm from the law or action challenged (i.e., the plaintiff has to demonstrate that he or she is harmed or will be harmed). Otherwise, the court will dismiss the case, ruling that the plaintiff "lacks standing" to bring the suit.

stare decisis "Standing by the decision"; a principle stating that rulings made in higher courts are binding precedent for lower courts.

statute of frauds State-level legislation that addresses the enforceability of contracts that fail to meet the requirements set forth in the statute; serves to protect promisors from poorly considered oral contracts by requiring that certain contracts be in writing.

statutory insiders Certain large stockholders, executive officers, and directors who are deemed insiders by the Securities Exchange Act of 1934.

statutory law The assortment of rules and regulations put forth by legislatures.

stock certificate A document that serves as a stockholder's proof of ownership in a corporation.

stock warrant A type of security issued by a corporation (usually together with a bond or preferred stock) that gives the holder the right to purchase a certain amount of common stock at a stated price.

stop-payment order An order by a drawer that instructs the drawee bank not to pay an issued check.

stored-value card A plastic card that contains data regarding the value of the card, thereby allowing EFTs to be made.

strict liability Liability in which responsibility for damages is imposed regardless of the existence of negligence. Also called *liability without fault.*

strict-liability offense Offense for which no *mens rea* is required.

strict-liability tort A civil wrong that occurs when the defendant takes an action that is inherently dangerous and cannot ever be undertaken safely, no matter what precautions the defendant takes. In such situations, a defendant is liable for the plaintiff's damages without any requirement that the plaintiff prove that the defendant was negligent.

strict scrutiny The most exacting standard of review used by the courts in determining the constitutionality of a statute; requires a compelling government interest and the least restrictive means of attaining that objective.

subject-matter jurisdiction The power of a court over the type of case presented to it.

subjective impossibility of performance In a contract, a situation in which it would be very difficult for a party to carry out his or her contractual obligations.

subpoena An order to appear at a particular time and place and provide testimony.

subpoena *duces tecum* An order to appear and bring specified documents.

subscriber An investor who agrees to purchase stock in a new corporation.

subscription agreement An agreement between promoters (persons raising capital for a new corporation) and subscribers (investors), in which the subscribers agree to purchase stock in the new corporation.

substantial evidence A reviewing court reviews an agency's reasoning to determine whether it is "arbitrary" or "capricious," or whether it is supported by substantial evidence.

substantial impairment A concept, used to modify the perfect tender rule, whereby a buyer can revoke acceptance of goods and, with installment contracts, a buyer/lessee can reject an installment of a particular item only if the defects substantially impair the value of the goods.

substantial performance Contract performance that occurs when nearly all the terms of the agreement have been met, there has been an honest effort to complete all the terms, and there has been no willful departure from the terms of the agreement.

substantive due process The requirement that laws depriving an individual of life, liberty, or property be fair and not arbitrary.

substantive unconscionability Unconscionability that derives from one-sided, unjust, or overly harsh substance in a contract.

summary jury trial An abbreviated trial that leads to a non-binding jury verdict.

summons A legal document issued by a court and addressed to a defendant that notifies him or her of the lawsuit and how and when to respond to the complaint. A summons may be used in both civil and criminal proceedings.

supremacy clause Article VI, Paragraph 2, of the U.S. Constitution, which states that the Constitution and all laws and treaties of the United States constitute the supreme law of the land.

Thus, any state or local law that directly conflicts with the U.S. Constitution or federal laws or treaties is void.

syndicate An investment group that comes together for the explicit purpose of financing a specific large project.

T

Taft-Hartley Act Federal legislation designed to curtail some of the powers that unions had acquired under the Wagner Act; designates certain union actions as unfair. Also called *Labor-Management Relations Act.*

takeover The purchase of one corporation's stock by another corporation as a means of gaining control of the selling corporation.

takings clause A clause in the Fifth Amendment of the U.S. Constitution requiring that when government uses its power to take private property for public use, it must pay the owner just compensation, or fair market value, for the property. Also called *just-compensation clause.*

tender An offer by a party in a contract to perform, along with being ready, willing, and able to perform, a duty outlined in that contract.

tender of delivery Requirement that the seller or lessor have and hold conforming goods at the disposal of the buyer or lessee and give the buyer or lessee reasonable notification to enable him or her to take delivery.

tender offer A type of takeover in which the aggressor corporation offers the target shareholders a price above their stock's current market value.

termination In a contract, the point at which an offer can no longer be accepted as part of a binding agreement or an offeree no longer has the power to form a legally binding contract by accepting the offer; can occur by revocation by the offeror, rejection by the offeree, death or incapacity of offeror, destruction or subsequent illegality of subject matter of the offer, or lapse of time or failure of other condition stated in the offer.

termination statement An amendment to a financing statement that states that the debtor has no obligation to the secured party.

third-party beneficiary A recipient of contractual benefits who is not one of the contracting parties; created when two parties enter into a contract with the intended purpose of benefiting a third party.

time instrument A type of draft that allows the payee to collect payment only at a specific time in the future.

tippee An individual who receives confidential information from an insider.

tipper An insider who gives inside information to someone.

tipper/tippee theory A theory of insider trading that holds that any individual (tippee) who acquires material inside information as a result of an insider's (tipper's) breach of duty has engaged in insider trading.

Title VII of the Civil Rights Act of 1964 (CRA) Federal law (amended by the Civil Rights Act of 1991) that protects employees against discrimination based on race, color, religion, national origin, and sex; also prohibits harassment based on the same protected categories.

tombstone advertisement A print advertisement that announces a forthcoming sale of securities in a format similar to that of a tombstone.

tort A violation of another person's rights or a civil wrongdoing that does not arise out of a contract or statute; primary types are intentional, negligent, and strict-liability torts.

tortfeasor A person who commits an intentional or through-negligence tort that causes a harm or loss for which a civil remedy may be sought.

trade dress The overall appearance and image of a product.

trade libel A business tort that occurs when false printed statements criticize a business product or service and result in a loss of sales.

trade secret A process, product, method of operation, or compilation of information that gives a businessperson an advantage over his or her competitors.

trademark A distinctive mark, word, design, picture, or arrangement that is used by a producer in conjunction with a product and tends to cause consumers to identify the product with the producer.

tradition See **historical school.**

transfer warranties Warranties regarding a negotiable instrument and its transfer; created by a party who transfers the instrument.

traveler's check An order that is payable on demand, is drawn on or through a bank, is designated by the phrase *traveler's check,* and requires a countersignature by the person whose signature appears on the check.

trespass to personal property Temporary interference with another's use or enjoyment of his or her personal property.

trespass to realty A tort that occurs when someone goes on another's property without permission or places something on another's property without permission.

trial An event in which parties to a dispute present evidence in court, before a judge or a jury, in order to achieve a resolution to their dispute.

trial court A court in which most civil or criminal cases start when they first enter the legal system. The parties present evidence and call witnesses to testify. Trial courts are referred to as courts of common pleas or county courts in state court systems and as district courts in the federal system. Also called *court of original jurisdiction* and *court of first instance.*

trustee (1) In bankruptcy proceedings, an individual who takes over administration of a debtor's estate. (2) A person who operates a trust for beneficiaries in a business trust.

tying arrangement Illegal agreement in which the sale of one product is tied to the sale of another.

U

unconscionability Grounds for rescinding an unconscionable contract.

unconscionable A term applied to a contract in which one party has so much more bargaining power than the other party that the powerful party dictates the terms of the agreement and eliminates the other party's free will.

undisclosed principal A principal whose existence is not known by a third party. That is, the third party does not know an agent is acting on behalf of a principal.

undue influence The situation in which one person has taken advantage of his or her dominant position in a relationship to unduly persuade the other person to the extent that the dominant person's persuasive efforts have interfered with the other person's ability to make his or her own decision.

unemployment compensation State system, created by the Federal Unemployment Tax Act (FUTA), that provides unemployment compensation to qualified employees who lose their jobs.

unenforceable A term applied to a contract that, because of a law, cannot be enforced by the courts.

unfair competition The act of competing with another not to make a profit but for the sole purpose of driving that other out of business.

unforeseen circumstances Events that a reasonable person would not be expected to anticipate.

unfortunate accident An incident that simply could not be avoided, even with reasonable care.

unidentified principal See *partially disclosed principal.*

Uniform Commercial Code (UCC) A statutory source of contract law in the United States applicable to transactions involving the sale of goods. The UCC was created in 1952 and adopted by all 50 states, the District of Columbia, and the Virgin Islands; it may be modified by each state to reflect the wishes of the state legislature.

uniform laws Laws created to account for the variability of laws among states. These laws serve to standardize the otherwise different interstate laws. Also called *model laws.*

unilateral contract A promise exchanged for an act.

unilateral mistake The result of an error by one party about a material fact, i.e., one that is important in the context of a particular contract.

United Nations Convention on Contracts for the International Sale of Goods (CISG) The legal structure for international sales, including business-to-business sales contracts.

universalization test The ethical guideline that urges us to consider, before we do an action, what the world would be like if everyone acted in this way.

unliquidated debt Debt for which the parties either dispute the fact that any money is owed or agree that some money is owed but dispute the amount.

unprotected speech Speech that is not protected by the First Amendment; includes hate speech, insulting or fighting words, defamation, and speech that harms the reputation of another.

usage of trade Any practice that members of an industry expect to be part of their dealings.

usury The lending of money at an exorbitant or unlawful rate of interest.

V

valid A term applied to a contract that includes all four elements of a contract: agreement (offer and acceptance), consideration, contractual capacity, and legal object.

values Positive abstractions that capture our sense of what is good and desirable.

venue (1) The place where a hearing takes place. Its geographic location is determined by each state's statutes and based on where the parties live or where the event occurred or the alleged wrong was committed. (2) A legal doctrine relating to the selection of a court with subject matter and personal jurisdiction that is the most appropriate geographic location for the resolution of the dispute.

vest To mature, as in the maturing of rights such that a party can legally act on the rights.

vicarious liability The liability or responsibility imposed on a person, a party, or an organization for damages caused by another; most commonly used in relation to employment, with the employer held vicariously liable for damages caused by its employees.

virus A computer program that rearranges, damages, destroys, or replaces computer data.

void A term applied to a contract that is not valid because its object is illegal or it has some defect that is so serious that it is not a contract.

void title Not true title; e.g., the title held by someone who knowingly or unknowingly purchased stolen goods.

voidable A term applied to a contract that one or both parties have the ability to either withdraw from or enforce.

voidable title Title that occurs in situations in which the contract between the original parties would be void but the goods have already been sold to a third party.

voir dire The process of questioning potential jurors to ensure that the jury will be made up of nonbiased individuals.

W

Wagner Act The first major piece of federal legislation adopted explicitly to encourage the formation of labor unions and provide for collective bargaining between employers and unions as a means of obtaining the peaceful settlement of labor disputes.

waiting period In securities registration, the period between the time an issuer files a registration statement and prospectus with the SEC requesting to offer a security and the time the offer is approved by the SEC, which is a minimum of 20 days.

warranty An assurance, either express or implied, by one party that the other party can rely on its representations of fact; in sales, a binding promise regarding a product in the event that the product does not meet the manufacturer's or seller's promises.

warranty liability Liability attributed when the transfer of an instrument breaches a warranty associated with an instrument.

warranty of title An assurance, inferred in every UCC sales transaction, that the seller has good and valid title to the goods and has the right to transfer title free and clear of any liens, judgments, or infringements of intellectual property rights of which the buyer does not have knowledge.

watered stock Stock that is issued to individuals below its fair market value.

white-collar crime A variety of nonviolent illegal acts against society that occur most frequently in the business context.

winding up The process of completing unfinished partnership business.

workers' compensation laws State laws that provide for financial compensation to employees or their dependents when a covered employee is injured on the job.

WPH approach (to ethical decision making) A set of ethical guidelines that urges us to consider whom an action affects, the purpose of the action, and how we view its morality (whether by utilitarian ethics, deontology, etc.).

writ of certiorari A Supreme Court order, issued after the Court decides to hear an appeal, mandating that the lower court send to the Supreme Court the record of the appealed case.

writing A type of documentation that shows contractual intent and satisfies the statute of frauds requirement.

wrongful dissolution A dissolution of a partnership in violation of its partnership agreement.

Name Index

Subject Index